Women and Gender in Medieval Europe

An Encyclopedia

WOMEN AND GENDER IN MEDIEVAL EUROPE

AN ENCYCLOPEDIA

Margaret Schaus

Editor

Routledge
Taylor & Francis Group
New York   London

Routledge is an imprint of the
Taylor & Francis Group, an informa business

Routledge
Taylor & Francis Group
270 Madison Avenue
New York, NY 10016

Routledge
Taylor & Francis Group
2 Park Square
Milton Park, Abingdon
Oxon OX14 4RN

© 2006 by Taylor & Francis Group, LLC
Routledge is an imprint of Taylor & Francis Group, an Informa business

Printed in the United States of America on acid-free paper
10 9 8 7 6 5 4 3 2 1

International Standard Book Number-10: 0-415-96944-1 (Hardcover)
International Standard Book Number-13: 978-0-415-96944-4 (Hardcover)

Visit the Taylor & Francis Web site at
http://www.taylorandfrancis.com

and the Routledge Web site at
http://www.routledge-ny.com

B&T   NBS/HE

CONTENTS

INTRODUCTION

Women and Gender in Medieval Europe: An Encyclopedia reflects the dramatic growth that has taken place in the study of medieval women and gender since the 1970s. Beginning then with essay collections and a handful of path-breaking journal articles, current research now yields a full scholarly palette ranging from monographs, editions of texts, and research articles to anthologies and introductions. This growth in scholarship has been matched by an increase in student interest and course offerings. Because much of the research in medieval women's and gender studies is published in journals and specialized volumes, it is time-consuming to access. *Women and Gender in Medieval Europe* serves as a much needed guide, making innovative scholarship available to a wider audience by explicating topics, providing interpretation, and selecting authoritative sources that will lead readers into the literature and research.

Scope

Women and Gender in Medieval Europe: An Encyclopedia addresses many areas of medieval women's activities, including female patronage of the arts and the church, female mysticism and devotional practices, women's medicine and understandings of the female body, and women's roles in politics and diplomacy. Gender issues are also of prime importance, and so masculinity is addressed in a variety of medieval contexts, ranging from chivalric tournaments to medieval views of St. Joseph. Identification and analysis of medieval gender roles provide an important context for understanding women's roles: a discussion of the norms and expectations for men provides the factual information needed to situate and compare the norms and expectations for women.

The entries in *Women and Gender in Medieval Europe* reflect the daily reality of medieval women from all walks of life. Such entries move beyond descriptions of individual women to address topics such as "Asceticism," "Clothing," "Procreation and Ideas of Conception," and "Social Status," providing a comprehensive understanding of medieval women's lives and experiences.

The individuals profiled in this reference work were chosen either for their historical significance or because they might represent groups of people, such as servants or the disabled. In the first category are such well-known figures as Geoffrey Chaucer, Joan of Arc, Christine de Pizan, and Matilda of Tuscany. In the second and smaller group are the mystic Gertrud of Ortenberg, the saintly servant Zita, and the nun artist Caterina Vigri. This two-tiered approach demonstrates the range of women's activities, unlike past scholarship that sometimes took account only of noble women.

Women and Gender in Medieval Europe takes Europe as its primary area from 450–1500 C. E., roughly the fall of the Roman Empire to the discovery of the Americas. Thus the entries dealing with Islamic topics treat conditions in Iberia or in Europe generally. The entries on Byzantine subjects are an exception geographically, but their inclusion is important both because of connections with Europe, like Theophano's impact as a Holy Roman empress, and for the comparisons between the two areas in terms of social practices.

This reference work takes a particular interest in historiography, in terms of the history of the field, documentary sources, and methodological approaches. Medieval women's history is treated at length. Entries cover many types of documents including household accounts, letters, and sister books (collective biographies of nuns). Groups of records are also included for the church, rural areas, and cities. For methodological approaches the volume gives detailed treatments to feminism and postmodernism as well as covering others approaches important to the study of the Middle Ages such as performance theory and queer theory. The aim is to help users develop a critical understanding of the historiography of medieval women and gender.

Authors

The authors of the entries are scholars and researchers in the field. In many cases the authors who contributed entries have published the definitive monograph on the subject in question, bringing their knowledge and analysis to the discussion. Such command of the material allowed authors to offer discussions that put the issues into perspective and help dispel mistaken assumptions, such as the idea that male practitioners did not give medical care to women.

How to Use This Book

Organization

The 563 entries in this volume are arranged in an easily accessible A to Z format, reflected in the alphabetical list of entries. A thematic list of entries has also been provided to assist the reader in easily locating relevant information.

Users may also consult the thorough, analytical index.

Entry Features

The entries range from 250 to over 4500 words in length. They are accompanied by selective bibliographies, which include both primary and secondary sources for further reading and research. Cross-references at the end of an entry direct the reader to related entries in the volume.

Overview Entries

Included are series of entries that together treat broad topics. Country overviews deal with women's status in a particular region: Burgundian Netherlands, Byzantium, Eastern Europe, England, Flanders, France, Northern, Frankish Lands, Germanic Lands, Iberia, Ireland, Italy, Occitania, Russia, Scandinavia, Scotland, and Wales. These entries are represented in the thematic list under "Countries, Realms, and Regions."

Literature overviews deal with representations of women in the following literatures: German, Hebrew, Iberian, Irish, Italian, Latin, Middle English, Occitan, Old English, Old French, and Old Norse. These entries appear in the thematic list under "Literature."

The "Literature" category also includes surveys of female writers in various languages (German, Italian, Latin Middle English, Old French, and Spanish) under articles beginning "Women Authors: German Texts," as well as coverage of broad literary topics, such as "Ballads," "Devotional Literature," and "Ovid: Medieval Reception of."

For law, there is a series of articles that treat learned and regional legal traditions including "Roman Law," "Barbarian Law Codes" and entries following "Law" for English, French, German, Islamic, and Jewish practices in regards to women and gender.

Thematic Coverage

In addition to the categories outlined above, the entries in *Women and Gender and Medieval Europe* address the following themes:

- Art, Architecture, and Archaeology: These entries include examinations of representations of women and gender in art, artistic production by women, and architectural structures such as monasteries and the home.
- Documentary Sources: Entries in this category provide coverage of documentation by and about women in a variety of sources including ownership marks on books, convent chronicles, and official records.

- Economy and Society: Cultural and social traditions and norms as they affected women, such as cosmetics, guilds, and inheritance, are treated by entries falling in this category.
- Education and Learning: These entries examine the types of education available to women as well as female literacy.
- Family and Kinship: The medieval status of, and attitudes toward, family members, including spouses, children, and the elderly, is explored in these entries. Articles in this category also look extensively at medieval marriage.
- Gender and Sexuality: These entries cover topics including abortion, concubinage, concepts of femininity and masculinity, and virginity, thus providing broad coverage of key gender contexts.
- Historiography: Scholarly methodologies and critical theories are considered in relation to the study of medieval women and gender.
- Medicine and Science: These entries explore medieval theory and practice, as well as topics in medieval gynecology.
- Music and Dance: The roles medieval women played as participants in and audiences of music and dance are explored.
- Persons: These entries include biographies of queens, noble women, authors, and saints, as well as notable medieval thinkers such as Christine de Pizan and Trota of Salerno.
- Politics: The actions of queens, empresses, and other women in authority are discussed in these entries, as are such political topics as the Crusades and diplomacy.
- Religion and Theology: In addition to biographical sketches of saints and holy women, these entries cover groups such as nuns, Beguines, and religious laywomen. They also analyze key religious topics, such as asceticism, the cult of Mary, and women's monasticism.

Appendices

Appendix I: Calendar of Female Saints lists the days for female saints observed each month. The calendar is intended to suggest the variety and number of holy women celebrated during the liturgical year.

Appendix II: Some Milestones in Medieval Women's History highlights key translations and scholarly works in the field of medieval women's studies.

Appendix III: Encyclopedia Cited References is a list of those works cited most frequently in the individual bibliographies found at the end of each entry.

Appendix IV: Web Resources for Medieval Women's and Gender Studies provides readers with a number of websites that present valuable scholarship on medieval women.

Margaret Schaus

Acknowledgments

A volume like this gives new meaning to the term "group effort." Contributors, advisors, student assistants, and publishers have all worked unstintingly. We are grateful to the authors for their interpretations, filled with insights and fascinating examples. From the beginning of this project we benefited from advice and articulate viewpoints generously offered by colleagues, including Judith Bennett, Joan Ferrante, Jo Ann McNamara, Monica Green, and Nancy Partner. Our subject advisors Lisa Bitel, Jane Burns, Amy Hollywood, and Pamela Sheingorn have been invaluable in determining topics to cover, persuading people to write, and contributing major entries in their respective areas. Student assistants at Haverford College have since 2003 maintained databases, recorded queries, and generally kept the project afloat. Our thanks go to Robin Dean, David Fask, Veronica Faust, Sarah Hendry, and Elizabeth Piastra. At Routledge, Kristen Holt and Marie-Claire Antoine have brought their considerable experience to the project. We thank all of the participants who have helped to build this work wherein medieval women's lives can be known.

Margaret Schaus
Thomas Izbicki
Susan Mosher Stuard

THE ROUTLEDGE ENCYCLOPEDIAS OF THE MIDDLE AGES

Formerly the Garland Encyclopedias of the Middle Ages, this comprehensive series began in 1993 with the publication of *Medieval Scandinavia*. A major enterprise in medieval scholarship, the series brings the expertise of scholars specializing in myriad aspects of the medieval world together in a reference source accessible to students and the general public as well as to historians and scholars in related fields. Each volume focuses on a geographical area or theme important to medieval studies and is edited by a specialist in that field, who has called upon a board of consulting editors to establish the article list and review the articles. Each article is contributed by a scholar and followed by a bibliography and cross-references to guide further research.

Routledge is proud to carry on the tradition established by the first volumes in this important series. As the series continues to grow, we hope that it will provide the most comprehensive and detailed view of the medieval world in all its aspects ever presented in encyclopedia form.

The present volume, *Women and Gender in Medieval Europe: An Encyclopedia,* edited by Margaret Schaus, is Volume 14 in the series.

CONTRIBUTORS

F. R. P. Akehurst
University of Minnesota

Barbara K. Altmann
University of Oregon

Katharina Altpeter-Jones
Duke University

Sahar Amer
University of North Carolina

Mark Angelos
Manchester College

Janice Archer
The Art Institute of Portland

Rowena E. Archer
Oxford University, U.K.

Elizabeth Archibald
University of Bristol, U.K.

Chara Armon
Independent Scholar

Dorsey Armstrong
Purdue University

Kathleen M. Ashley
University of Southern Maine

Denise Nowakowski Baker
University of North Carolina at Greensboro

Carroll Hilles Balot
Washington University in St. Louis

Sandra Bardsley
Moravian College

Teodolinda Barolini
Columbia University

Beth Allison Barr
Baylor University

Anne Clark Bartlett
DePaul University

Judith R. Baskin
University of Oregon

Elisheva Baumgarten
Bar-Ilan University, Israel

Alison Beach
The College of William and Mary

Cordelia Beattie
University of Edinburgh, Scotland

Brigitte Miriam Bedos-Rezak
New York University

Jeanette Beer
Purdue University

Susan Groag Bell
Stanford University

Constance H. Berman
University of Iowa

Jessalynn Bird
Oxford University, U.K., and Northwestern University

Lisa Bitel
University of Southern California

Alcuin Blamires
Goldsmiths College, University of London, U.K.

Virginia Blanton
University of Missouri–Kansas City

Elaine C. Block
Hunter College, City University of New York (emerita)

CONTRIBUTORS

Wim Blockmans
*Netherlands Institute for Advanced Study in
Humanities and Social Sciences, The Netherlands*

Renate Blumenfeld-Kosinski
University of Pittsburgh

Katrinette Bodarwé
Seminar fuer Mittlere und Neuere Geschichte, Germany

Constance B. Bouchard
The University of Akron

Susan Boynton
Columbia University

Sally M. Brasher
Shepherd University

Dorothy Ann Bray
McGill University

Phyllis R. Brown
Santa Clara University

Matilda Tomaryn Bruckner
Boston College

James A. Brundage
University of Kansas (emeritus)

Caroline Bruzelius
Duke University

William E. Burgwinkle
Cambridge University

E. Jane Burns
University of North Carolina

Kristin L. Burr
St. Joseph's University

Kim E. Butler
American University

Montserrat Cabré
Universidad de Cantabria, Spain

Nancy Caciola
University of California, San Diego

Esperança Camara
University of Saint Francis

Joanna Cannon
Courtauld Institute of Art

Mary Carruthers
New York University

Madeline H. Caviness
Tufts University

Valentina Cesco
Pennsylvania State University

Jane Chance
Rice University

Fredric L. Cheyette
Amherst College

Krijnie Ciggaar
University of Leiden, The Netherlands (emerita)

Katherine Clark
State University of New York, Brockport

Robert L. A. Clark
Kansas State University

Jeffrey Jerome Cohen
George Washington University

Olivia Remie Constable
University of Notre Dame

Rebecca W. Corrie
Bates College

Roisin Cossar
University of Manitoba, Canada

Andrée Courtemanche
Université Laval, Canada

Ann Crabb
James Madison University

Roger J. Crum
University of Dayton

Jo Ann Hoeppner Moran Cruz
Georgetown University

P. H. Cullum
University of Huddersfield, U.K.

Cynthia J. Cyrus
Vanderbilt University

Patricia Dailey
Columbia University

Roger Dalrymple
Oxford University, U.K.

Jean Dangler
Tulane University

David d'Avray
University College London, U.K.

Joyce de Vries
Auburn University

Theresia de Vroom
Loyola Marymount University

Elizabeth Valdez del Álamo
Montclair State University

Daisy Delogu
University of Chicago

Andrea Denny-Brown
University of California, Riverside

Marilynn R. Desmond
Binghamton University

Leah DeVun
Texas A&M University

Heath Dillard
Independent Scholar

Maria Dobozy
University of Utah

Eglal Doss-Quinby
Smith College

Anna Dronzek
University of Minnesota

Theresa Earenfight
Seattle University

Martha Easton
Bryn Mawr College

Bonnie Effros
Binghamton University

Donna Spivey Ellington
Gardner-Webb University

Dyan Elliott
Northwestern University

Marianne Elsakkers
Independent Scholar

Michael J. Enright
East Carolina University

Elizabeth Ewan
University of Guelph, Canada

Sharon Farmer
University of California, Santa Barbara

Hugh Feiss
Monastery of the Ascension, Idaho

Joan M. Ferrante
Columbia University

Sean L. Field
University of Vermont

Joanne Findon
Trent University

Laurie Finke
Kenyon College

David A. Flory
Purdue University

Deborah Fraioli
Simmons College

Emily C. Francomano
Georgetown University

A. Daniel Frankforter
Pennsylvania State University, Erie

Allen J. Frantzen
Loyola University

Katherine L. French
State University of New York, New Paltz

Carole Collier Frick
Southern Illinois University, Edwardsville

Yvonne Friedman
Bar-Ilan University, Israel

Rhoda Lange Friedrichs
Douglas College, Canada

CONTRIBUTORS

Amy M. Froide
Clark University

Alison L. Ganze
Valparaiso University

Kathleen Garay
McMaster University, Canada

Lynda Garland
University of New England, Australia

Philip Gavitt
Saint Louis University

P. J. P. Goldberg
University of York, U.K.

Cristina González
University of California, Davis

Michael E. Goodich
University of Haifa, Israel

Kristi Gourlay
University of Toronto

Monica H. Green
Arizona State University

Kate Greenspan
Skidmore College

Fiona J. Griffiths
New York University

Joan Tasker Grimbert
The Catholic University of America

Karen A. Grossweiner
University of Alaska, Fairbanks

Noah Guynn
University of California, Davis

Linda Guzzetti
Technische Universitat Berlin, Germany

Thomas Hahn
University of Rochester

Rosemary Drage Hale
Brock University, Canada

Dianne Hall
University of Melbourne, Australia

Wendy Harding
Université de Toulouse-Le Mirail, France

Ann T. Harrison
Michigan State University (emerita)

David Hay
University of Lethbridge, Canada

Sarah-Grace Heller
Ohio State University

Judith Herrin
King's College London, U.K.

Madonna J. Hettinger
The College of Wooster

Barbara Hill
Independent Scholar

Cynthia Ho
University of North Carolina

Amy Hollywood
University of Chicago

Carole Hough
University of Glasgow, Scotland

Jason M. Houston
University of Oklahoma

Martha Howell
Columbia University

David F. Hult
University of California, Berkeley

Lois L. Huneycutt
University of Missouri

Holly Hurlburt
Southern Illinois University, Carbondale

Ann M. Hutchinson
University of Toronto, Canada

Steinar Imsen
Norwegian University of Science and Technology

Thomas Izbicki
Johns Hopkins University

Katherine Ludwig Jansen
The Catholic University of America

Gerhard Jaritz
Central European University, Hungary

Madeleine Jeay
McMaster University, Canada

Jane E. Jeffrey
West Chester University of Pennsylvania

Jenny Jochens
Towson University (emerita)

E. D. Jones
University of Western Australia, Australia

Ruth Mazo Karras
University of Minnesota

Marie A. Kelleher
California State University, Long Beach

Henry Ansgar Kelly
University of California, Los Angeles

Theresa D. Kemp
University of Wisconsin, Eau Claire

Francis W. Kent
Monash University, Australia

Ann Kettle
University of St. Andrews, Scotland

Richard Keyser
Western Kentucky University

Beverly Mayne Kienzle
Harvard Divinity School

Catherine King
Open University, U.K.

Margaret L. King
Brooklyn College, City University of New York

Sharon Kinoshita
University of California, Santa Cruz

Julius Kirshner
University of Chicago (emeritus)

Ellen E. Kittell
University of Idaho

Gábor Klaniczay
Central European University, Hungary

Stacy Klein
Rutgers University

Anne L. Klinck
University of New Brunswick, Canada

Daniel T. Kline
University of Alaska, Anchorage

Lezlie Knox
Marquette University

Linda A. Koch
John Carroll University

Mia Korpiola
University of Helsinki, Finland

Desiree Koslin
Fashion Institute of Technology

Joëlle Koster
University of Rhode Island

Catherine Kovesi
The University of Melbourne, Australia

Maryanne Kowaleski
Fordham University

Roberta L. Krueger
Hamilton College

Thomas Kuehn
Clemson University

Irmeli S. Kuehnel
Independent Scholar

Norris J. Lacy
Pennsylvania State University

Carol Lansing
University of California, Santa Barbara

Lynn Marie Laufenberg
Sweet Briar College

Joanna L. Laynesmith
Independent Scholar

Becky R. Lee
York University, Canada

CONTRIBUTORS

Catherine Leglu
University of Bristol, U.K.

Elizabeth A. Lehfeldt
Cleveland State University

Maiju Lehmijoki-Gardner
Loyola College and University of Helsinki, Finland

Katherine J. Lewis
University of Huddersfield, U.K.

Erika Lauren Lindgren
University of Arizona

Amy Livingstone
Wittenberg University

Janet S. Loengard
Moravian College

Kimberly LoPrete
National University of Ireland, Ireland

William F. MacLehose
Alfred University

Elizabeth Makowski
Southwest Texas State University

Evyatar Marienberg
Tel Aviv University, Israel

Manuela Marín
Consejo Superior de Investigaciones Científicas (CSIC), Spain

Nancy Marino
Michigan State University

John Hilary Martin
Graduate Theological Union, California

Oscar Martin
Yale University

Therese Martin
University of Arizona

William P. Marvin
Colorado State University

Mavis Mate
University of Oregon

E. Ann Matter
University of Pennsylvania

Marie Anne Mayeski
Loyola Marymount University

Cristina Mazzoni
University of Vermont

June Hall McCash
Middle Tennessee State University (emerita)

Anne McClanan
Portland State University

Brian Patrick McGuire
Roskilde University, Denmark

Maud Burnett McInerney
Haverford College

Jo Ann McNamara
Hunter College, City University of New York (emerita)

Shannon McSheffrey
Concordia University, Canada

Carol M. Meale
University of Bristol, U.K.

Christine Meek
Trinity College, Ireland

Noël James Menuge
The Prince's Trust, U.K.

Gwenn Meredith
American University, Cairo, Egypt

Louise Mirrer
New York Historical Society

Scott B. Montgomery
University of Denver

Catherine M. Mooney
Weston Jesuit School of Theology

Leslie Zarker Morgan
Loyola College

Susan Signe Morrison
Southwest Texas State University

Joseph Morsel
Université Paris 1 Panthéon Sorbonne, France

Joan Mueller
Creighton University

Wolfgang Mueller
Fordham University

Carolyn Muessig
University of Bristol, U.K.

Anneke B. Mulder-Bakker
University of Leiden, The Netherlands

John H. Munro
University of Toronto, Canada

Saskia Murk-Jansen
Robinson College, Cambridge University

Jacqueline Murray
University of Guelph, Canada

María Narbona-Cárceles
Universidad de Navarra, Spain

Mary Natvig
Bowling Green State University

Derek Neal
Nipissing University, Canada

Carol Neel
Colorado College

Janet Nelson
King's College London, U.K.

Helen J. Nicholson
Cardiff University, Wales

Renée Nip
University of Groningen, The Netherlands

Margot McIlwain Nishimura
Rhode Island School of Design

Cordula Nolte
Universität Bremen, Germany

Marilyn Oliva
Fordham University

Judith Oliver
Colgate University

Lea T. Olsan
University of Louisiana at Monroe

Alexandra H. Olsen
University of Denver

Sherri Olson
University of Connecticut

Leah Otis-Cour
Université de Montpellier, France

Mark P. O'Tool
University of California, Santa Barbara

Monika C. Otter
Dartmouth College

Gale R. Owen-Crocker
University of Manchester, U.K.

William D. Paden
Northwestern University

Nira Pancer
University of Haifa, Israel

Thalia A. Pandiri
Smith College

Letizia Panizza
Royal Holloway, University of London, U.K.

John Carmi Parsons
University of Toronto, Canada

Nancy Partner
McGill University, Canada

Carol Braun Pasternack
University of California, Santa Barbara

Frederik Pedersen
University of Aberdeen, Scotland

Else Marie Wiberg Pedersen
Aarhus Universitet, Denmark

Bissera V. Pentcheva
Stanford University

Lisa Perfetti
Muhlenberg College

CONTRIBUTORS

Catherine Peyroux
New York University

Kim M. Phillips
University of Auckland, New Zealand

Lucy Pick
University of Chicago

Sara S. Poor
Princeton University

Karen Pratt
King's College, U.K.

Sara L. Preisig
Gonzaga University

Walter Prevenier
University of Gent

Darleen Pryds
Graduate Theological Union, Berkeley

F. Regina Psaki
University of Oregon

Helmut Puff
University of Michigan

Judy Quinn
Cambridge University, U.K.

Vivian Ramalingam
Independent Scholar

Adrian Randolph
Dartmouth College

Alisha Rankin
Harvard University

Ann Marie Rasmussen
Duke University

Sherry L. Reames
University of Wisconsin–Madison

Charles J. Reid, Jr.
University of St. Thomas

Thomas Renna
Saginaw Valley State University

Kathryn Reyerson
University of Minnesota

Rosalind Jaeger Reynolds
University of California, Berkeley

Geneviève Ribordy
St. Lawrence College, Canada

Amanda Richardson
University College Chichester, U.K.

Felicity Riddy
University of York, U.K.

Paula M. Rieder
University of Nebraska

Kathryn M. Ringrose
University of California, San Diego

Elizabeth Robertson
University of Colorado

J. Duncan Robertson
Augusta State University

Diana Robin
University of New Mexico

Joanne Maguire Robinson
University of North Carolina

Tova Rosen
Tel-Aviv University, Israel

Joel T. Rosenthal
State University of New York at Stony Brook

Miri Rubin
Queen Mary College, University of London, U.K.

Nina Rulon-Miller
Rowan University

Marianne Sághy
Central European University, Hungary

Claire L. Sahlin
Texas Women's University

Sarah Salih
University of East Anglia, U.K.

Eve Salisbury
Eastern Michigan University

Michelle M. Sauer
Minot State University

Francesca Canadé Sautman
Graduate Center, City University of New York

Helene Scheck
State University of New York at Albany

Wybren Scheepsma
Hogeschool Leiden, The Netherlands

Jane Tibbetts Schulenburg
University of Wisconsin–Madison

Marla Segol
Skidmore College

Dayle Seidenspinner-Núñez
University of Notre Dame

Miriam Shadis
Ohio University, Athens

Shulamith Shahar
Tel Aviv University, Israel (emeritus)

Pamela Sheingorn
Graduate Center, City University of New York

Karen Miriam Silen
University of California, Berkeley

Walter Simons
Dartmouth College

Katrin E. Sjursen
University of California, Santa Barbara

Patricia Skinner
University of Southampton, U.K.

Kathryn A. Smith
New York University

Susan L. Smith
University of California, San Diego

Susan Taylor Snyder
Benedictine College

Helen Solterer
Duke University

Janet T. Sorrentino
Washington College

Valerie Spear
The Australian National University, Australia

Claire Sponsler
University of Iowa

Peter Stabel
University of Antwerp, Belgium

Robin Chapman Stacey
University of Washington

Alan M. Stahl
Princeton University

Sarah Stanbury
College of the Holy Cross

Anne Rudloff Stanton
University of Missouri-Columbia

Robert Stanton
Boston College

Walter Stephens
Johns Hopkins University

Alexandra Sterling-Hellenbrand
Appalachian State University

Lorraine Kochanske Stock
University of Houston

Fiona Harris-Stoertz
Trent University, Canada

Steven Stofferahn
Indiana State University

Susan Mosher Stuard
Haverford College (emerita)

Almut Suerbaum
Oxford University, U.K.

Mary Suydam
Kenyon College

James Ross Sweeney
Pennsylvania State University

Victoria Sweet
University of California, San Francisco

Robert Sweetman
Institute for Christian Studies, Canada

Helen J. Swift
Magdalene College, Oxford University, U.K.

CONTRIBUTORS

Dana M. Symons
Simon Fraser University, Canada

Paul E. Szarmach
Medieval Academy of America

Alice-Mary Talbot
Dumbarton Oaks, Washington, D.C.

Andrew Taylor
University of Ottawa, Canada

Craig Taylor
University of York, U.K.

Jane Taylor
Collingwood College, University of Durham, U.K.

Isolde Thyrêt
Kent State University

Catherine Tkacz
Independent Scholar

Fiona Tolhurst
Alfred University

Laura Van Aert
University of Antwerp, Belgium

Elisabeth van Houts
Emmanuel College, Cambridge University

Sue Sheridan Walker
Northeastern Illinois University (emerita)

Martin W. Walsh
University of Michigan

Heather E. Ward
Independent Scholar

Andrew Wareham
King's College London, U.K.

Nancy Bradley Warren
Florida State University

Claire Waters
University of California, Davis

Nicholas Watson
Harvard University

Barbara F. Weissberger
University of Minnesota

Sarah Westphal-Wihl
Rice University

Merry E. Wiesner-Hanks
University of Wisconsin, Milwaukee

Ulrike Wiethaus
Wake Forest University

Rebecca Winer
Villanova University

Anne Winston-Allen
Southern Illinois University

Shelley Amiste Wolbrink
Drury University

Elliot R. Wolfson
New York University

Jeryldene M. Wood
University of Illinois

Shona Kelly Wray
University of Missouri

Ester Zago
University of Colorado at Boulder

Jan M. Ziolkowski
Harvard University

Amalia Zomeño
Consejo Superior de Investigaciones Científicas (CSIC), Spain

Patricia Zupan
Middlebury College

ALPHABETICAL LIST OF ENTRIES

THEMATIC LIST OF ENTRIES

Art, Architecture, and Archaeology

Archaeology
Architecture, Domestic
Architecture, Ecclesiastical
Architecture, Monastic
Art, Representations of Women in
Artists, Women
Body: Visual Representations of
Books of Hours
Burials and Tombs
Castles and Palaces
Caterina Vigri
Clothwork, Domestic
Devotional Art
Eroticism in Art
Gaze
Gender in Art
Grave Goods
Hagiography, Iconographic Aspects of
Icons, Byzantine
Jewelry
Marginalia, Manuscript
Mary, Virgin: in Art
Mikveh
Misericords
Nine Worthy Women
Nuns as Illuminators
Patronage, Artistic
Portrait Medals
Seals and Sigillography
Sheela Na Gigs
Space, Sacred: and Gender
Space, Secular: and Gender
Veronica's Veil

Countries, Realms, and Regions

Burgundian Netherlands
Byzantium
Eastern Europe
England
Flanders
France, Northern
Frankish Lands
Germanic Lands
Iberia
Ireland
Italy
Occitania
Russia
Scandinavia
Scotland
Wales

Documentary Sources

Book Ownership
Charters
Chronicles of the Northern Low Countries
Coinage
Conduct Literature
Genealogy
Hagiography
Household Accounts
Letter Writing
Miracles and Miracle Collections
Monastic Rules
Monastic Visitation
Mystics' Writings
Necrologies and Mortuary Rolls
Penitentials and Pastoral Manuals
Petitions
Proverbs, Riddles, and Gnomic Literature
Records, Ecclesiastical
Records, Rural
Records, Urban
Seals and Sigillography
Sermons and Preaching
Sister-Books and Other Convent Chronicles
Wills and Testaments

Economy and Society

Administration of Estates
Agriculture
Alewives and Brewing
Apprentices
Architecture, Domestic
Arms and Armor
Artisan Families, Women of
Breastfeeding and Wet-Nursing
Business
Captivity and Ransom
Chivalry
Cities and Towns
Clothing
Clothwork, Domestic
Consumption
Cosmetics
Death, Mourning, and Commemoration
Demography
Division of Labor
Domesticity
Dowry and Other Marriage Gifts
Economy
Feme Covert
Feme Sole
Fosterage
Gentry, Women of: England
Godparents
Gossip and Slander
Guild Members and Guilds
Heiresses
Heraldry
Home Manufacturing
Honor and Reputation
Household Accounts
Household Management
Hunting and Falconry
Inheritance
Investment and Credit
Ladies-in-Waiting
Landholding and Property Rights
Market and Tradeswomen
Mead-Giver
Merchant Families, Women of
Midwives
Migration and Mobility
Naming
Noble Women
Old Age
Peasants
Poverty
Prostitutes
Servants
Singlewomen
Slaves
Social Status
Textile Production for the Market
Tournaments
Violence
Wardship
Warfare
Work

Education and Learning

Aristotelian Concepts of Women and Gender
Audience, Women in the
Book Ownership
Books of Hours
Conduct Literature
Datini, Margherita
Devotional Literature
Dhuoda
Education, Beguine
Education, Lay
Education, Monastic
Exemplum
Fosterage
Humanism
Letter Writing
Literacy and Reading: Latin
Literacy and Reading: Vernacular
Mothers as Teachers
Nuns as Scribes
Proverbs, Riddles, and Gnomic Literature
Scholasticism
Sermons and Preaching
Universities

Family and Kinship

Adolescence
Betrothals
Chastity and Chaste Marriage
Children, Betrothal and Marriage of
Churching
Conjugal Debt
Divorce and Separation
Domestic Abuse
Family (Earlier Middle Ages)
Family (Later Middle Ages)
Genealogy
Girls and Boys

Godparents
Husbands and Husbandry
Infants and Infanticide
Kinship
Lying-In
Marriage Ceremonies
Marriage, Christian
Marriage and Concubinage in Scandinavia
Marriage, Impediments to
Marriage, Islamic: Iberia
Marriage, Jewish
Marriage Preaching
Pregnancy and Childbirth: Christian Women
Pregnancy and Childbirth: Jewish Women
Remarriage
Trousseau
Widows
Widows as Guardians

Gender and Sexuality

Abortion
Aristotelian Concepts of Women and Gender
Celibacy: Clerical and Priests' Concubines
Charivari
Chastity and Chaste Marriage
Concubines
Conjugal Debt
Contraception
Courtly Love
Courtship
Cross-Dressing
Cuckold
Defenses of Women
Eroticism in Art
Eroticism in Literature
Eunuchs
Femininity and Masculinity
Festivals of Misrule
Gender Ideologies
Gender in Art
Gender in History
Hermaphrodites
Illegitimacy
Impotence
Incest
Menstruation
Merchet and Leyrwite
Misogyny
Obscenity
Patriarchy and Patrilineage
Private and Public Spheres
Procreation and Ideas of Conception

Prostitutes
Rape and Raptus
Sexuality: Extramarital Sex
Sexuality: Female Same-Sex Relations
Sexuality: Male Same-Sex Relations
Sexuality, Regulation of
Sexuality: Sex in Marriage
Space, Sacred: and Gender
Space, Secular: and Gender
Virginity
Virile Women
Woman on Top

Historiography

Annales School of History
Cross-Cultural Approaches
Demography
Feminist Theories and Methodologies
Gender in History
History, Medieval Women's
Performance Theory
Postcolonial Theory
Postmodernism and Historiography
Power, Eileen
Prosopography
Psychoanalytic Theory
Queer Theory
Reader-Response Criticism
Renaissance, Historiography of
Women Medievalists in the Academy

Law

Barbarian Law Codes
Crime and Criminals
Feme Covert
Feme Sole
Law
Law, Canon
Law, Customary: French
Law, English Secular Courts of
Law, German
Law, Islamic: Iberia
Law, Jewish
Legal Agency
Marriage, Impediments to
Merchet and Leyrwite
Roman Law
Sumptuary Law
Wardship

Wergild
Witches

Literature

Amazons
Ancrene Wisse
Arthurian Literature
Audience, Women in the
Ballads
Beast Epic
Beatrice
Beauty
Belle Dame Sans Merci
Beowulf
Body in Literature and Religion
Constance
Criseyde
Danse Macabre des Femmes
Dawn Song (Alba)
Debate Literature
Defenses of Women
Devotional Literature
Drama
Epic, Italian
Epic, Old French
Epic, Spanish
Eroticism in Literature
Evangiles des Quenouilles
Exemplum
Fabliau
Floire and Blancheflor
Griselda
Guinevere
Hagiography
Isolde
Jacobus de Voragine's *Golden Legend*
Jewish Women: Latin and European Vernacular
    Literature
Katherine Group
Laughter
Literature, German
Literature, Hebrew
Literature, Iberian
Literature, Irish
Literature, Italian
Literature, Latin
Literature, Middle English
Literature, Occitan
Literature, Old English
Literature, Old French
Literature, Old Norse
Mary, Virgin: in Literature

Mélusine
Mermaids and Sirens
Minnesang
Misogyny
Muslim Women: Western Literature
Mythology, Medieval Reception of
Ovid, Medieval Reception of
Paston Letters
Pastourelle
Patronage, Literary
Performance in Lyric
Personifications Visualized as Women
Proverbs, Riddles, and Gnomic Literature
Réponse du Bestiaire d'Amour
Roman de Flamenca
Roman de la Rose and Its Reception
Roman de Silence
Romance, English
Romance, French
Romance, German
Romancero
Romances of Antiquity
Sentimental Romance
Skáldkonur
Supernatural Women
Translation
Trobairitz and Trobadors
Trouvères, Women
Unicorn
Valkyries
Voice, Female: in Literature
Wife of Bath
Wild Women
Woman's Song
Women Authors: German Texts
Women Authors: Italian Texts
Women Authors: Latin Texts
Women Authors: Middle English Texts
Women Authors: Old French Texts
Women Authors: Spanish Texts

Medicine and Science

Abortion
Breastfeeding and Wet-Nursing
Caesarean Section
Contraception
Cosmetics
Disabilities
Doctors and Healers
Gynecology
Hospitals
Infertility

Lepers
Lovesickness
Madness
Medicine
Menstruation
Midwives
Natural World
Plague
Secrets of Women
Trota of Salerno

Music and Dance

Dance
Mary, Virgin: in Music
Music, Women and
Nuns as Musicians
Performance in Lyric
Trobairitz and Troubadours
Trouvères, Women
Woman's Song

Persons

Adela of Blois
Adelheid
Aethelflaed
Aethelthryth of Ely
Agnes of Prague
Amalasuntha
Angela of Foligno
Anne of Beaujeu
Anne of Bohemia
Ava
Bake, Alijt
Beatrice of Nazareth
Beaufort, Margaret
Berenguela
Birgitta of Sweden
Blanche of Castile
Boccaccio, Giovanni
Bokenham, Osbern
Brigit
Brunhild and Fredegund
Castro, Inés de
Caterina Sforza
Caterina Vigri
Catherine of Genoa
Catherine of Siena
Cereta, Laura
Chaucer, Geoffrey
Chrétien de Troyes

Christina of Markyate
Christina the Astonishing
Christine de Pizan
Clare of Assisi
Clare of Montefalco
Clemence of Barking
Clotilda
Colette of Corbie
Compiuta Donzella
Constance of Sicily
Cornaro, Caterina
D'Este, Isabella and Beatrice
Dante Alighieri
Datini, Margherita
Dhuoda
Dolce of Worms
Dorothea of Montau
Douceline of Digne
Ebner, Margaretha
Edith
Eleanor of Aquitaine
Eleanor of Scotland
Elisabeth of Hungary
Elisabeth of Schönau
Ermengard
Fedele, Cassandra
Fina of San Gimignano
Frances of Rome
Gerson, Jean
Gertrude of Hackeborn
Gertrude of Nivelles
Gertrude of Ortenberg
Gertrude the Great
Godelieve of Gistel
Goscelin of St. Bertin
Gottfried von Strassburg
Guibert of Nogent's Mother
Hadewijch
Helena
Heloise
Herrad of Hohenbourg
Hild of Whitby
Hildegard of Bingen
Hrotsvit of Gandersheim
Humility of Faenza
Ida of Boulogne
Irene
Isabel I
Isabel of Aragon
Isabelle of France
Jacqueline of Bavaria
Jadwiga
Joan of Arc
Joan I
Julian of Norwich

Politics

Religion and Theology

A

ABBESSES

The title of abbess (Latin *abbatissa*) has been constructed as the feminine form of *abbas* (abbot/father) to correspond generally to the role of an abbot, the superior in spiritual and temporal matters of a community of monks. It represents the attempt to construct a female superior for a monastery of nuns with legal, ecclesiastical, and spiritual functions of leadership not usually granted to women. Therefore, the office of abbess does not merely exemplify the superior as mother of the community but as a kind of female father with paternal rights.

This concept did not arise with the earliest religious women's communities. The first leaders of female religious groups were called *mater monasterii, mater monacharum*, or, as by Augustine, *praeposita*. For the first time in 514, the title *abbess* appears in a sepulchral inscription for the superior Serena of an ancient monastery in Rome near the Basilica of St. Agnes *extra muros*. Bishop Caesarius of Arles was the first bishop to use the title abbess, in the rule which he wrote together with his sister Caesarea between approximately 512 and 534. Starting with an identification of the leading figure as *prior, senior*, or *mater*, he later uses the title *abbatissa* more and more, especially to indicate the formal independence of the leader from her bishop. In the following centuries the title came into general use by the popularization of the Benedictine Rule and its adaptation for women's monasteries. But, following the full establishment of the Benedictine Rule as the one and only monastic rule in Latin Europe during the tenth and eleventh centuries, the problem of abbesses' source of authority was never fully resolved in female communities. This was the reason why their jurisdictional rights and liturgical abilities were under constant discussion and why monastic rules had to be provided with explications of an abbess' authority (see, for example, Abelard, Letter 1: *Ad amicum suum consolatoria*, c. 54).

Abbesses are known as leaders of Benedictine monasteries, of houses of canonesses (*Stifte*) or Augustinian communities, and also of some of the later monastic congregations, such as Cistercians, Poor Clares, Fontevrists, and Birgittines. A lot of other women's communities never had their own abbesses, but continued to call their leaders *mater* or prioress. These terms referred to a merely temporary leadership, as was, for example, customary for the Dominicans, or the subordinated position of the nunnery, which was supervised by the abbot of a nearby cloister.

Election and Consecration

The office of an abbess is, in principle, elective. Commonly, the abbess was elected by all the nuns of a community, but in double monasteries or monasteries with added communities of canons, men were in some cases entitled to vote as well. The diocesan bishop had to preside over the election and confirm the elected candidate; in exempt houses he acted merely as a delegate of the pope. Women's monasteries that were part of a monastic congregation had to invite the minister general to preside over the election (as stated, for example, in the *bulla* of Pope Innocent IV for the Clares dating from 9 August 1253). The bishop or minister had the right to intervene if no candidate received the required number of votes and, in exceptional cases, could even select the successor. Although Gregory the Great tried to introduce an age limit and recommended that only virgins be elected, every honourable and fully valid member of the convent could become abbess, irrespective of age and social origin.

In reality, a great part of the better known abbesses descended from the noblest and more influential families. Often they were, therefore, invited from other monasteries or even enthroned as children as young as eleven or twelve years old, although the outside candidates had, nevertheless, to accept the way of life and rule of their new convent. This phenomenon of noble abbesses is interpreted differently. On the one hand, many founders of religious communities reserved the leadership for descendants of their own family at least for some generations, thus guaranteeing the further political and economic use of the land and wealth given to the monastery, as well as continuous commemoration (*memoria*) by prayers for the members of their family. Most foundation charters or royal confirmation charters granted the right of a free election of the abbess only if no suitable offspring of the founding family was available. But even that did not hinder kings or bishops from securing the office for their own candidates, especially kinswomen; even a letter of application is known from the eighth century. Thus, until the twelfth century, most abbesses seem to have been nominated by royal or noble families, and nunneries, therefore, must have been influenced to elect the already nominated candidates. On the other hand, it has been argued that the nunnery itself would have been disposed to elect the woman with the best political connections and noblest family background to secure its own interests. Furthermore, difficulties could arise from medieval society's notions of status and nobility; as when the abbess was less noble than other community members (see, for example, the problems in S. Croix, Poitiers, in 589). Formalised procedures of election are known predominantly from the high and late Middle Ages.

After the election, the abbess was usually consecrated by the bishop of the diocese according to the rites prescribed in the *Pontificale Romanum*, as well as in many monastic rituals. The ceremony took place during the Mass; as symbols of her office and a copy of the monastic rule were conferred on the new abbess. While some of the rites, for example the Romano-Germanic Pontifical, compiled c. 950, do not mention giving a *baculum* (a kind of pastoral staff) to the abbess, it seems to have been common for abbesses to use a staff as regalia. Further, it is unknown whether medieval abbesses were allowed to wear a ring as abbots and bishops did. In some communities the ceremony included the enthronement or the coronation of the abbess; on rare occasions she was even placed onto the altar (for example, in Herford, Germany).

From the eleventh century a division between abbess and community can be documented: some abbesses—especially of the more wealthy monasteries—had their own residences with chapels, separate incomes, and separate administration.

Internal Authority of the Abbess

The abbess exercised supreme domestic authority not only over the nuns of the community, but also over the canons or priests living there and the servants and all the families on the monastery's dependencies. In some areas, especially in Anglo-Saxon England and early medieval France, as well as later in the twelfth century at Fontevrault Abbey, double monasteries with joint communities of nuns and monks were led by abbesses. In accordance with the rule or the statutes of the particular order, the abbess could demand complete obedience from her nuns and ordain whatever was necessary for the maintenance of discipline in the community and the proper observance of the rule. Furthermore, she decided on the distribution of food and clothing and assigned the duties.

The abbess was responsible for the mundane welfare of the women whose care was entrusted to her and also for their eternal salvation, despite being incapable of performing the spiritual functions of the priesthood due to her gender. Therefore, she was only allowed to bless her nuns in the way a mother blessed her children, and, although she had to hear their daily confessions to impose discipline, she was deprived of the right to administer the sacrament of penance in the ninth century. Neither was the abbess allowed to preach publicly; she had to exhort her nuns in chapter to instruct them about the Christian faith and the interpretation of the Bible. It was difficult to draw a line between performing spiritual functions of the priesthood and fulfilling abbatial duties, so again and again during the Middle Ages canon law prohibited abbesses from overstepping their boundaries by blessing men or taking vows from their nuns or novices (as appears in the Capitularies of

Charlemagne and in Innocent III's warning in 1210 concerning the Cistercian abbesses of Burgos and Palencia in Spain).

External Duties of the Abbess

The abbess acted for her monastery in the secular world and also represented the outside world within the monastery. In strictly cloistered monasteries she was the only contact to the outside; otherwise she, together with the sister acting as gatekeeper, had to welcome and care for guests. Often their secular and spiritual duties forced abbesses into frequent contacts and even travels, as, for example, to visit their holdings or to represent their communities' interest before the secular and ecclesiastical rulers, although for less demanding tasks they could rely mostly on male officials, as, for example, a provost. However, throughout the Middle Ages, the discussion of an abbess' external authority was determined largely by her independence from clerical hierarchies and the question of enclosure, seen as necessary for women because of their inferior gender and their uncontrolled sexuality. Within the Carolingian reform, for example, the liberty of the abbess to leave her monastery was restricted by royal edicts. However, in the Anglo-Saxon era and in early medieval Saxony, as later in the more famous ladies' chapters (*Damenstifte*), the role of the abbess was less restricted and of great political importance, as exemplified by Mathild, abbess of Quedlinburg (+ 999), who represented King Otto III in Saxony.

(a) Powers Concerning Secular Jurisdiction

Abbesses were empowered to administer the temporal possessions of the monastery; therefore, they held seigniorial rights over fiefs, holdings, and serfs, and all secular rights in their domains. As sovereigns, abbesses began using seals in the twelfth century. Sporadically, they even had the privilege of coinage. In honour of their position they were entitled to *officia principalia,* such as a marshal or a chamberlain. Sometimes they were even entrusted with the administration of entire shires or counties (Sophie of Gandersheim, + 1039). In Germany the abbesses of Quedlinburg, Gandersheim, Lindau, Buchau, Regensburg, and other monasteries all belonged to the nobility of the Empire, and as such, they sat and voted in the Diet as members of the Rhenish bench. As an ecclesiastical sovereign, however, the abbess could only decide on issues of minor jurisdiction; for

questions of life and death, as well as war, she was dependent on her reeve.

(b) Ecclesiastical Jurisdiction

Although the office of abbess had no priestly functions and its own limitations were defined by canon law, in some exceptional cases abbesses whose monasteries were exempt were permitted to exercise a most extraordinary power approaching that of a bishop in terms of ecclesiastical jurisdiction.

In the diocese of Münster (Germany) most of the abbesses of the noble collegiate foundations were even called "archdeaconess," which further certified their quasi-episcopal jurisdiction and conferred on them an aspect of the bishop's ecclesiastical official duties. They were responsible for the religious and moral life of the population and the clerics. One of their duties was to guarantee people access to the sacraments and possibilities of penance. Furthermore, these abbesses had to organize the church services and the calendar of saints. Another part of this quasi-episcopal jurisdiction was the right to hold assemblies and to convoke synods, as well as to participate in them. The importance of Abbess Hild at the Synod of Whitby in 664 is the best-known example of such participation. Such abbesses gave canonical investiture to the holders of prebends, made visitations, held courts, regulated the activities of canons and priests, and reigned over the other monasteries in their region. They could even impose censures and excommunication. As archdeaconesses, abbesses were entrusted with the preservation of the Faith and the maintenance of ecclesiastical discipline. The spiritual care included the welfare of the poor, the establishment of hospitals, and the protection of Jews. Although some abbesses installed *capellani* as their agents or asked abbots in the vicinity for help, their authority to make decisions stayed unaffected until modern times.

Similar to such archdeaconesses, the abbess of the Cistercian monastery of Santa Maria la Real de las Huelgas was called "lawful *administratrix* in spirituals and temporals...of all the contents, churches, and hermitages of its filiation, of the villages and places under its jurisdiction, seigniory, and vassalage ... with plenary jurisdiction, privative, quasi-episcopal, *nullius diocesis.*" At a General Chapter of the Cistercians held in 1189, she was even made Abbess General of the Order for the Kingdom of Leon and Castile. Equal rights of jurisdiction have been exercised by the Cistercian abbess of Conversano in Italy and the abbesses of Fontrevault in France and Herford in Saxony.

Overall, despite their disputed position of office, abbesses were well known and quite successful rulers in the Middle Ages and an integral part of secular and ecclesiastical networks. However, there still remain comparative studies to be done, and in a lot of areas the knowledge about abbesses' rights and duties is based on assumptions. Even some relatively basic questions, such as under which circumstances a monastic community could install an abbess or which symbols were in use for the investiture, cannot yet be answered satisfactorily.

KATRINETTE BODARWÉ

References and Further Reading

Baucher, Joseph. "Abbesses." In *Dictionnaire de Droit Canonique, Vol. 1*, edited by Raoûl Naz. Paris: Letouzey & Ané, 1935 pp. 62–71.

Fürstenberg, Michael Freiherr von. *"Ordinaria loci" oder "Monstrum Westphaliae"? Zur kirchlichen Rechtsstellung der Äbtissin von Herford im europäischen Vergleich* (Studien und Quellen zur westfälischen Geschichte Bd.29). Paderborn: Bonifatius, 1995.

Lifshitz, Felice. "Is Mother Superior? Towards a History of Feminine Amtscharisma." In *Medieval Mothering* (Garland Reference Library of the Humanities 3), edited by John Carmi Parsons. New York, London: Garland Publishing, 1996, pp. 117–138.

Macy, Gary. "The Ordination of Women in the Early Middle Ages." *Theological Studies* 61, 3 (2000): 481–507.

Skinner, Mary S. "French Abbesses in Action: Structuring Carolingian and Cluniac Communities." *Magistra: A Journal of Women's Spirituality in History* 6, 1 (2000): 37–60.

Stafford, Pauline: "Powerful Women in the Early Middle Ages: Queens and Abbesses." In *The Medieval World*, edited by Peter Linehan and Janet L. Nelson. London: Routledge, 2001, pp. 398–415.

Van Engen, John. "Abbess: 'Mother and Teacher'." In *Voice of the Living Light: Hildegard of Bingen and Her World*, edited by Barbara Newman. Berkeley: University of California Press, 1998, pp. 30–51.

See also **Birgittine Order; Canonesses; Church; Cistercian Order; Double Monasteries; Fontevrault, Abbey and Order of; Hild of Whitby; Law, Canon; Monastic Rules; Monasticism and Nuns; Ordination of Women as Priests; Patronage, Ecclesiastical; Poor Clares Order; Sermons and Preaching**

ABORTION

Throughout the Middle Ages, members of the church hierarchy reminded Christians that abortion constituted a mortal sin and was worthy of eternal damnation. Reiterating precepts of ancient church councils, compilations of ecclesiastical (canon) law in the East and West instructed the faithful of the old patristic equation of abortion with manslaughter (*homicidium*) and imposed appropriate penances. In addition, early medieval books of penance spread the "biblical" distinction (from the Greco-Jewish *Septuagint*) between killings of unformed and formed fetuses, with only the latter amounting to actual rather than intended homicide. In trying to uncover medieval experiences of abortion, we depend on Christian sources consistently written by authors hostile to the practice. We will never know just how many medieval women resorted to abortion, the precise sex ratio (male versus female) of the victims, or how their number compared to the total of individuals using contraception or committing infanticide. All we can infer from the incessant admonitions in writing is that each form of birth control was common enough to worry medieval clerics. People seem to have accepted the notion that abortion entailed sin and warranted penance. At the same time, consequences other than spiritual peril remained unlikely as long as the decision to abort was backed by sufficient communal consent. Women were well advised to enlist the support of husbands and relatives prior to terminating a pregnancy. Abortions performed in the privacy of a home and shielded by family acquiescence were neither thoroughly investigated nor viewed as particularly "dishonorable."

In both the Eastern and the Western Churches the redemption of aborting sinners involved elements of "public" and "communal" justice, such as the initiation of the penitential process by way of anonymous denunciations or the performance of penance before everyone's eyes. It was only in the Latin West and not until the twelfth century, however, that abortion began to be treated as something more than a sin redeemable through fasting, shameful exposure, and pilgrimages. In formulating coherent and comprehensive doctrines for their newly established scholastic disciplines, academic jurists and theologians agreed that the penitential equation of abortion with homicide should extend to criminal prosecutions as well. In church courts, guilty clerics were to be barred or suspended from spiritual office. Before the secular judge, laypersons who had intentionally killed an "animated" (formed) human fetus would face execution for voluntary homicide. The killing of an unformed and not yet "human" fetus during the first forty to eighty days of gestation was regarded as attempted homicide.

By 1250, scholastic thinkers had created a sophisticated theory of criminal abortion. It was profoundly inspired by Christian standards and taught widely throughout the Latin West. Adoption of the new theory in actual court proceedings progressed at a much slower pace, allowing for local and procedural variations best understood as adjustments of ingrained assumptions about fertility as a family matter. Resistance to scholastic criminal norms was strongest in jurisdictions that relied on local and non-professional jurors, such as the German *Schöffenger-ichte* and the English common law courts. The *Ius commune* taught at the continental law schools seems to have encouraged greater rigidity, considering that the passing of the final sentence was left to professionally trained judges (*inquisitores*) instructed to act impartially and without regard for local interest groups. Yet, in line with jurors hesitant to monitor the reproductive behavior of their peers, *inquisitores* were held in check by highly restrictive procedural guidelines. In order to convict a defendant of criminal abortion, they had to find two eyewitnesses or obtain a full confession of guilt. Trials would not even begin unless a dead body had been recovered and there was proof of a concealed pregnancy.

There is disagreement among modern scholars as to the quality of medieval medical knowledge concerning abortions. Some have argued that midwives, contrary to the male establishment at the emerging faculties of medicine, possessed considerable expertise in contraceptive and abortive prescriptions. Sources leave no doubt that law courts regularly consulted women as sworn witnesses in matters pertaining to pregnancies and that scholastic teaching did not include midwifery in its curriculum. Still, only a limited amount of information about the abortive effect of herbal concoctions was passed on from antiquity. Academic physicians failed to distinguish clearly between reproductive and digestive organs and frequently offered the same medical advice for both. Proper dosage was of little concern. Below the university level, the creation of an organized body of information relating to "safe" abortions was hampered by the lack of a common language (Latin would have come closest) and the absence of a uniform nomenclature. Consequently, trust in the effectiveness of specific abortive treatments depended above all on individual perspective. Among those frightened by the prospect of an unwanted baby, reliance on "wise women" may have been strong. Meanwhile, the scholastic *Ius commune* punished with death the use of abortive potions, even if the fatal outcome was accidental and the fetus had not yet been animated.

Jurists considered tampering with medication as notoriously dangerous to mother and child. To deter unlicensed practitioners, they were prepared to eliminate important procedural safeguards. Abortions allegedly brought on by potions could be tried without eyewitnesses, the presence of a corpse, or prior concealment of pregnancy. Defendants could be subjected to torture at the judge's discretion. Specific cases of "dynamic" abortion (i.e., caused by herbal infusion) rarely appeared in late-medieval criminal courts. Allowing for condemnations on the basis of exceptionally weak judicial evidence, however, the charge facilitated the prosecution of a novel category of suspects: from the 1430s onward, accusations of witchcraft were routinely bolstered by allegations of dynamic abortion.

WOLFGANG MUELLER

References and Further Reading

Cohn, Samuel K. "Prosperity in the Countryside: The Price Women Paid." In *Women in the Streets: Essays on Sex and Power in Renaissance Italy*, edited by Samuel K. Cohn. Baltimore: Johns Hopkins University Press, 1996, pp. 137–165.

Hewson, M. Anthony. *Giles of Rome and the Medieval Theory of Conception: A Study of the 'De formatione corporis humani in utero.'* London: Athlone Press, 1975.

Hoffer, Peter, and N. Hull. *Murdering Mothers: Infanticide in England and New England 1558–1803*. New York: New York University Press, 1981.

Kieckhefer, Richard. "Avenging the Blood of Innocent Children: Anxiety Over Child Victims and the Origins of the European Witch Trials." In *The Devil, Heresy, and Witchcraft in the Middle Ages: Essays in Honor of Jeffrey B. Russell*, edited by Alberto Ferreiro. Leiden: Brill, 1998, pp. 91–109.

Langbein, John. *Torture and the Law of Proof: Europe and England in the Ancien Régime*. Chicago: University of Chicago Press, 1977.

Müller, Wolfgang P. *Die Abtreibung. Anfänge der Kriminalisierung 1140–1650*. Cologne, Weimar, and Vienna: Böhlau, 2000.

———. "Canon Law Versus Common Law. The Case of Abortion in Late Medieval England." In *Proceedings of the Tenth International Congress of Medieval Canon Law*, edited by Kenneth Pennington and Keith Kendall. Vatican City: Biblioteca Apostolica Vaticana, 2002, pp. 964–975.

Nardi, Enzo. *Procurato aborto nel mondo greco-latino*. Milan: Giuffrè, 1971.

Noonan, John. "An Almost Absolute Value in History." In *The Morality of Abortion: Legal and Historical Perspectives*, edited by John Noonan. Cambridge, MA: Harvard University Press, 1970, pp. 1–59.

Riddle, John. *Eve's Herbs: A History of Contraception and Abortion from the Ancient World to the Renaissance*. Cambridge, MA: Harvard University Press, 1997.

Troianos, Spiros. "The Embryo in Byzantine Canon Law." *Biopolitics* 3 (1991): 179–194.

See also **Contraception; Crime and Criminals; Gynecology; Infants and Infanticide; Inquisitions; Law, Canon; Midwives; Penitentials and Pastoral Manuals; Pregnancy and Childbirth: Christian Woman; Procreation and Ideas of Conception; Scholasticism; Single-women; Witches**

ADELA OF BLOIS

Conceived after her father's consecration as king of England, Adela (c. 1067–1137) was the youngest daughter of William the Conqueror and his wife Mathilda of Flanders, born almost certainly between November 1067 and May 1068. She became fully literate in Latin, as exemplified when she read aloud at a ceremony to translate relics, authenticated charters by writing her own name, and received praise for her literacy in the complex prose and verse works directed to her by leading literary figures of her generation. Most likely educated as a child alongside her professed sister, Cecilia, at Holy Trinity, the nunnery her parents founded in Caen, Adela, in turn, hired tutors to oversee the education of her children and promoted the use of written documents. When, as a wife and widow, she became a noted power broker, renowned for her wealth and the prudent generosity with which she distributed it, Adela could add literary patronage to the brides and bribes that served as the currency in the largely personalized politics of her day.

Betrothed in the early 1080s, Adela was married at Chartres, shortly after her fifteenth birthday (c. 1083 and certainly by 1085), to Stephen-Henry (b. c. 1044–1048), eldest son of count Thibaud III of Blois and Troyes, who was at least eighteen years her senior. Her dowry apparently consisted of moveable wealth rather than land, although her dower comprised castles, estates, and a forest across her husband's domains. Bearing one son, at the least, before her father-in-law's death (September 1089), the young countess secured her place in her new family; she eventually bore five sons and perhaps three daughters. When her husband became count of Blois, Chartres, and Meaux in his own right, she participated in all nonmilitary aspects of lordship, serving as a virtual co-count alongside him—the result of her high status, the age difference between the spouses, and the breadth of his domains. She was perfectly suited to serve as regent during Stephen's crusade ventures (1096–1099; 1101–1102) and after his death in the Holy Land (May 1102). Associating her sons in lordship as they came of age (William c. 1103 and Thibaud in 1107), she continued to rule as countess until she became a nun at Cluny's daughter house of Marcigny (April/May 1120).

As regent Adela earned a reputation for diplomacy, both for resolving vexed intermonastic disputes and in reconciling her brother, Henry I of England, with two exiled archbishops, Anselm of Canterbury (1105) and Thurstan of York (1120). She also generously supported Pope Paschal II during his 1107 tour of northern France and intervened with several prelates to ensure the election of her correspondent Baudri of Bourgueil as archbishop of Dol. Although her careful cultivation of the Capetian kings would not prevent warfare with Louis VI once he joined the coalition of princes intent on unseating Henry I as duke of Normandy (1111), Adela played a key role in the negotiations that led to a peace designed to last (1120) and served as the backdrop to her monastic retreat.

Personally devout—a saint's relics once cured her fevers, and she dedicated her youngest son to God—Adela supported a range of religious communities, from well-established Benedictine abbeys (e.g., St. Père in Chartres, St. Lomer in Blois, St. Ayoul in Provins, St. Germain in Auxerre, and multiple priories of Marmoutier) to newer foundations such as Tiron, the Cistercians, and the leper hospital in Chartres. She also worked with her most prominent bishop, Ivo of Chartres, to reform monasteries, from the nuns at Faremoutiers (her one notable intervention for a community of women) to houses of secular canons. Many of Adela's pious bequests had important economic and political benefits, as well as spiritual ones, and her cooperation with Ivo led to his support for her at critical political junctures, in spite of their occasional disputes. This lordly experience served her well during her last seventeen years at Marcigny, where Adela, most likely as prioress, served as a spiritual guide to her sisters, consolidated her community's lands and intervened in the counties she had left behind. Though she died on 8 March 1137, her memory was kept alive with anniversaries celebrated in churches across England and France and in the pursuits of the three sons who outlived her: count Thibaud IV of Blois (II of Troyes) (d. 1152), King Stephen of England (d. 1154), and Bishop Henry of Winchester (and abbot of Glastonbury) (d. 1172).

KIMBERLY LoPRETE

References and Further Reading

LoPrete, Kimberly A. "Adela of Blois and Ivo of Chartres: Piety, Politics, and the Peace in the Diocese of Chartres." *Anglo-Norman Studies* 14 (1991): 131–152.
———. "Adela of Blois as Mother and Countess." In *Medieval Mothering* (The New Middle Ages series, 3), edited by John Carmi Parsons and Bonnie Wheeler. New York & London: Garland, 1996, pp. 313–333.
———. "Adela of Blois: Familial Alliances and Female Lordship." In *Aristocratic Women in Medieval France*, edited by Theodore Evergates. Philadelphia: University of Pennsylvania Press, 1999, pp. 180–200.
———. "The Gender of Lordly Women: The Case of Adela of Blois." In *Studies on Medieval and Early Modern Women: Pawns or Players?*, edited by Christine Meek

and Catherine Lawless. Dublin: Four Courts Press, 2003, pp. 90–110.

Otter, Monika. "Baudri of Bourguiel, 'To Countess Adela.'" *Journal of Medieval Latin* 11 (2001): 60–141.

See also **Diplomacy and Reconciliation; France, Northern; Literacy and Reading: Latin; Monasticism and Nuns; Noble Women; Patronage, Ecclesiastical; Regents and Queen-Lieutenants**

ADELHEID

Adelheid (or Adelaide) (c. 932–999), daughter of the Burgundian king Rudolf II, had a great influence on European politics as queen of Italy and East Francia, and later as Roman empress. After the death of her father, she was educated at the court in Pavia, and in 947, she married King Lothar of Italy. When he died suddenly in 950, Adelheid became the center of the struggles for the Italian crown. At one point, she was captured but escaped to King Otto I of East Francia (later Germany), whom she married in 951. Being named *consors regni*, her influence is visible especially in Italian politics—one highlight was her coronation as empress in 962. After Otto's death in 973, Adelheid was the most influential advisor of her son Otto II, sometimes even his representative in Pavia. When he died suddenly in 983, she secured the succession of her young grandson Otto III with her daughter-in-law Theophano, the Byzantine princess. As advisor to her daughter Emma, queen of West Francia, Adelheid also influenced French politics. Dowries and inheritance enabled her to found and support several monasteries. She was especially attached to the reform movement of Cluny. After Otto III's coming of age, she retired to her favourite foundation in Selz until her death in 999. With the assistance of Cluny, a cult was established in remembrance of her ecclesiastical interests, and Adelheid was canonized in 1097. Adelheid as a person is well known through sources such as her biography, written by the monk Odilo of Cluny, as well as her correspondence and her personal memorial notes, which were preserved in the necrology of Merseburg. She was one of the most important political figures of her time, a *mater regnorum* (mother of several kingdoms).

KATRINETTE BODARWÉ

References and Further Reading

Corbet, Patrick, ed. *Adélaide de Bourgogne: genèse et représentations d'une sainteté impériale; actes du colloque international du Centre d'Études Médiévales, Auxerre 10 et 11 décembre 1999*. Dijon: Ed. de l'Univ. de Dijon, 2002.

Fößel, Amalie. *Die Königin im mittelalterlichen Reich: Herrschaftsausübung, Herrschaftsrechte, Handlungsspielräume*. Stuttgart: Thorbecke, 2000.

Gilsdorf, Sean, ed. *Queenship and Sanctity: The lives of Mathilda and the Epitaph of Adelheid*, translated by Sean Gilsdorf. Washington, D.C.: Catholic University of America Press, 2004.

Stafford, Pauline. "Powerful Women in the Early Middle Ages: Queens and Abbesses." In *The Medieval World*, edited by Peter Linehan and Janet L. Nelson. London: Routledge, 2001, pp. 398–415.

Weinfurter, Stephan. "Kaiserin Adelheid und das ottonische Kaisertum." *Frühmittelalterliche Studien* 33 (1999): 1–19.

See also **Cluniac Order; Hagiography; Ottonian Royal Women; Patronage, Ecclesiastical; Queens and Empresses: The West**

ADMINISTRATION OF ESTATES

For those women who were either born to land or married into landed families, there was the prospect of a life in great part taken up by estate management. The fact that on marriage the land was technically the property of husbands did not make much difference to the question of its management as far as women were concerned. A succession of medieval treatises assumed that women would be directly involved, either during their marriages or afterwards in widowhood. In her 1405 manual of advice for women, the Franco-Italian author Christine de Pizan stated that women needed to know how to administer estates because their husbands were so often absent. She insisted that such women needed to know all about the land, its value, revenues and expenditures, the rhythms of the year, all aspects of husbandry, and how to choose, supervise, and dismiss servants. Women needed a basic knowledge of the law and had to be able to defend the land in the courts or, if necessary, by military means.

How they learned these skills is not well recorded, since most education was informal. Much was undoubtedly taught by their mothers, husbands, and, as a last resort, by direct experience. As levels of lay literacy began to rise, landed women would certainly have learned to read. In his rules of estate management, written c. 1240 for the widowed countess of Lincoln, Robert Grosseteste clearly assumed that the countess could read, and, in the early fourteenth century, Francesco da Barberino declared that formal education was essential for any woman who was likely to inherit land. Responsibility for estates could fall to women at a very young age. Katherine Neville was but fifteen when her husband, John Mowbray, earl of Nottingham, went off to fight in France in

1415, and, during his unbroken absence between 1417 and 1422, it was she who was running the estates.

Under all circumstances, a woman's (or a man's) first resort was to turn to a council of advisers, but final administrative decisions rested with her or him. Recourse to the law was common, and, despite the absence of any legal status, it is clear that landed women did, in practice, pursue cases through the courts, especially if the land under threat was from their own patrimony. In 1420 Elizabeth Berkeley, countess of Warwick, appeared in person before the king's council to defend her claims to her Berkeley estates when they were challenged by a nephew. Between 1473 and 1476 Anne Neville, dowager duchess of Buckingham, had suits pending against twenty-three people, and Lady Margaret Beaufort brought twenty-eight suits for debt on the estates of her ward Edward, duke of Buckingham, in 1497–1498.

On many occasions, landed women faced the dangers of assault and attacks on property, and it is clear that de Pizan's advice on defense was not just theoretical. Elizabeth Berkeley complained that her nephew had put an armed force into the rectory house at her manor of Wotton-under-Edge and that his men had fired arrows and shouted obscenities at her.

It is among the archives of widows that historians have the best chance of observing female administration, for the widow not only had a legal status which made her fully legally responsible, rather than merely accountable to her husband, but she was also, in many cases, mistress of a considerable area. After 1215, a widow in England was entitled to both one-third of her husband's estates and to any jointure, land settled jointly in survivorship on a couple at the time of their marriage. These rights were not reduced by remarriage, and indeed successive widowhoods could increase land holdings substantially. Some of the best surviving administrative accounts of the period are for such women, one of the best sets being those of Elizabeth de Burgh, lady of Clare (d. 1360), who administered her lands alone for thirty-eight years. These show that women maintained the system of accounting common to all estates and that they could be extremely exacting and vigilant. The receivers-general, receivers, bailiffs, reeves, and many other lesser administrators were required to tender their annual accounts, and the system of taking valors (estimates of the likely annual revenues) was widely used by widows, doubtless driven by the experience they had gathered as wives. Incompetence or profligacy, such as that of Anne Talbot, the mother of Thomas Courtenay, Earl of Devon between 1422 and 1441, when the income from the comital estates appears to have dropped by one fifth, was rare. Unusual too was the disposal of land, such as that by Joan de Mohun in 1376 at the expense of the heirs. More common was the maintenance of high standards of administration and often some improvement, especially in reducing the burden of debt on estates. One of the best recorded widows of the later Middle Ages is Mahaut, countess of Artois and Burgundy, who was left in 1303 with three young children. Herself the heiress of Artois, she first had to fight off the claims of Robert, her nephew, before settling down to rule the territory, maintaining law and order through her officials, regularly checking her accounts, issuing charters to local towns to encourage trade, and distributing patronage to extend her networks of control. Wives and widows across Europe showed commitment to, and shared responsibility for, the administration of estates.

ROWENA E. ARCHER

References and Further Reading

Archer, Rowena E. "'How Ladies....Who Live on Their Manors Ought to Manage their Households and Estates': Women as Landholders and Administrators in the Later Middle Ages." In *Woman Is a Worthy Wight: Women in English Society, c. 1200–1500*, edited by P. J. P. Goldberg. Far Thrupp, England: Alan Sutton Publishing Ltd., 1992, pp. 149–181.

———. "The Estates and Finances of Margaret of Brotherton, c. 1320–1399." *Bulletin of the Institute of Historical Research* 60 (1987), 264–280.

de Pizan, Christine. *The Treasure of the City of Ladies, or the Book of the Three Virtues*, translated by Sarah Lawson. Harmondsworth: Penguin Publishing, 1985.

Henley, Walter de. *Walter of Henley's Husbandry and Other Treatises on Estate Management and Accounting* (1890). Oxford: Oxford University Press, 1971.

Ward, J. *English Noblewomen in the Later Middle Ages.* Harlow: Longman Publishing, 1992.

———. *Women in Medieval Europe, 1200–1500.* London: Pearson Education Limited, 2002.

See also **Beaufort, Margaret; Education, Lay; Heiresses; Household Accounts; Inheritance; Landholding and Property Rights; Law, English Secular Courts of; Literacy and Reading: Vernacular; Noble Women; Widows**

ADOLESCENCE

Did medieval young people experience a well-defined adolescence? The debate began in the 1960s when Philippe Ariès, a modern historian looking at family life throughout European history, argued that the concept of adolescence, as we understand it, only emerged in the eighteenth century. Subsequent scholars have found it necessary to distinguish between biological adolescence (the physiological transformation that takes place over the course of five or six years) and social adolescence (the extent to which a given society recognizes adolescence as a life stage distinct from childhood and full social adulthood). Since both anthropological and historical studies suggest that social adolescence, where it appears, is not universal in nature, but is instead to some degree situational, affected by factors such as wealth, vocation, social class, life experience, and culture, it seems likely that historians will never entirely agree about the presence or nature of adolescence in the Middle Ages.

Adolescence in the early Middle Ages (roughly 500 to 1050) has received relatively little attention from historians. Edward James argues that early medieval people had a theoretical conception of adolescence, based on ancient literature, but showed little awareness of it in their social practices or descriptions of individuals. Training for adult careers could begin well before puberty, and individuals often entered fully into adult roles around the age of fifteen. The age of majority—the legal age at which individuals could inherit property and act independently—varied among states, but usually was set in the mid-teens, again suggesting that social adolescence was not well defined.

Adolescence emerged as a more distinct life phase, for males at least, during the high and later Middle Ages (1050–1500). This can be attributed in part to the increasing complexity of society, including the widespread growth of cities, more centralized states, and literacy. Anthropologists find that more complex societies tend to have more prolonged adolescences. The growing complexity of society meant that young men had a wider range of career options than in the early Middle Ages. Training periods for careers such as knighthood and trades grew longer, and new institutions specializing in adolescent education, such as universities, emerged. Lawmakers in many regions raised the age of majority to the early twenties.

As the duration of adolescence changed, so did its image. Authors increasingly depicted adolescence as a time of license and irresponsibility, ideas found frequently in the Greek and Roman books being rediscovered at the time. Concerns about adolescent misbehavior and free choice encouraged monasteries to exclude children and adolescents until their midteens or twenties, and to supervise young people more carefully.

Although women shared in these changes to a degree, female adolescence was usually less distinct than that of men. Women had fewer new career or educational options, and their ages of majority rose less than men's during the high Middle Ages, often remaining in the mid-teens. Likewise, female monasteries were more likely to admit children and teenagers than were male monasteries. The extent to which women experienced a distinct social adolescence depended on region and social group. Where ages of marriage were higher, women appear to have enjoyed a more prolonged adolescence. In northwestern Europe, most women and men married in their mid-twenties. In Mediterranean regions, women married at younger ages, most often in their late teens or early twenties, and were more likely to be significantly younger than their husbands. This affected the career patterns of women. In England, girls often worked as servants during their adolescence, leaving home and experiencing a certain measure of freedom. In other parts of northwestern Europe, girls as well as boys might become apprentices, although there were always far fewer female apprentices. In Mediterranean regions such as Italy, unmarried girls did not usually undertake apprenticeship before marriage. Elite women, regardless of region, tended to marry younger than women in other social classes, because of the need for political alliances. Women in the highest ranks of English and French society often married at or before age twelve, the legal age of puberty for women. To a considerable degree, women entered an adult world at marriage and were expected to behave accordingly, although some allowances were made for very young brides—for example, consummation was delayed in some cases. Elite men also often married young, but their social adolescence did not end so abruptly, as they tended to continue their vocational training and wild behavior after marriage. James Schultz, examining elites in high medieval German romances, found little recognition of female adolescence. In general, even when social adolescence existed, females were not usually allowed the license given to their male peers.

FIONA HARRIS-STOERTZ

References and Further Reading

Ariès, Philippe. *Centuries of Childhood: A Social History of Family Life*, translated by R. Baldick. New York: Random House, 1962.

Chojnacki, Stanley. "Measuring Adulthood: Adolescence and Gender in Renaissance Venice." *Journal of Family History* 17 (1992): 371–395.

Eisenbichler, Konrad, ed. *The Premodern Teenager: Youth in Society, 1150–1650.* Toronto: Centre for Reformation and Renaissance Studies, 2002.

Goldberg, P. J. P. *Women, Work, and Life Cycle in a Medieval Economy: Women in York and Yorkshire c. 1300–1520.* Oxford: Clarendon Press, 1992.

Hanawalt, Barbara A. "Historical Descriptions and Prescriptions for Adolescence." *Journal of Family History* 17 (1992): 341–351.

Harris-Stoertz, Fiona. "Young Women in France and England, 1050–1300." *Journal of Women's History* 12 (2001): 22–46.

James, Edward. "Childhood and Youth in the Early Middle Ages." In *Youth in the Middle Ages*, edited by P. J. J. P. Goldberg and Felicity Riddy. York: York Medieval Press, 2004, pp. 11–23.

Levi, Giovanni, and Jean-Claude Schmitt, eds. *Ancient and Medieval Rites of Passage: A History of Young People in the West, Vol. I.* Cambridge and London: Belnap Press of Harvard University Press, 1997.

Lewis, Katherine J., Noël James Menuge, and Kim M. Phillips, eds. *Young Medieval Women.* New York: St. Martin's Press, 1999.

Phillips, Kim. *Medieval Maidens: Young Women and Gender in England, 1270–1540.* Manchester: Manchester University Press, 2003.

Schlegel, Alice, and Herbert Barry III. *Adolescence: An Anthropological Inquiry.* New York: The Free Press, 1991.

Schultz, James A. *The Knowledge of Childhood in the German Middle Ages, 1100–1350.* Philadelphia: University of Pennsylvania Press, 1995.

See also **Apprentices; Children, Betrothal and Marriage of; Demography; Education, Lay; Education, Monastic; Fosterage; Girls and Boys; Inheritance; Monastic Rules; Servants; Universities**

AETHELFLAED

Eldest daughter of Alfred the Great, sister of Edward the Elder, and aunt and fosterer of Aethelstan, Aethelflaed of Mercia (d. 918) led troops against the Vikings, built forts, endowed churches, issued charters, dealt with Irish-Norwegian pressures, and received the submission of the men of York. When her husband Aethelred died (911), she became the sole political and military authority in Mercia, working, as she and her husband had done earlier, in cooperation with Edward the Elder and recognizing his overlordship as King of Wessex. (In fact, given Aethelred's apparent illness and incapacity, Aethelflaed was de facto in power beginning c. 902.) This cooperation was ultimately successful in eliminating the Danish threat to Anglo-Saxon England and paved the way for the eventual unification of Mercia and Wessex.

The primary evidence for Aethelflaed's achievements occurs in the Anglo-Saxon Chronicle in versions B, C, and D. Versions B and C present a "Mercian Register" or an "Annals of Aethelflaed," perhaps based on a now-lost Latin source. This section violates the chronological order in B and C, and suddenly introduces a focus on Mercia. Aethelflaed is styled "Lady of the Mercians," which some scholars take as a semantic dodge for "queen," possibly reflecting uneasiness with queens (Alfred's wife Ealhswith never had the title) or downplaying royal aspirations in the face of Edward. The clumsy insertion of the Mercian Register in B and C compares with its smoother incorporation in D, where Aethelflaed's exploits are diminished and folded into the story of the House of Wessex.

PAUL E. SZARMACH

References and Further Reading

Bailey, Maggie. "Aelfwynn, Second Lady of the Mercians." In *Edward the Elder*, edited by N. J. Higham and D. H. Hill. London and New York: Routledge, 2001, pp. 112–127.

Keynes, Simon D. "Edward, King of the Anglo-Saxons." In *Edward the Elder*, edited by N. J. Higham and D. H. Hill. London and New York: Routledge, 2001, pp. 40–66.

Szarmach, Paul E. "Aethelfaed of Mercia: Mise en Page." In *Words and Works: Studies in Medieval English Language and Literature in Honour of Fred C. Robinson*, edited by Peter S. Baker and Nicholas Howe, Toronto, Buffalo, and London: University of Toronto Press, 1998, pp. 105–126.

Thompson, Victoria. *Dying and Death in Later Anglo-Saxon England.* Woodbridge: The Boydell Press, 2004.

Wainwright, F. T. "Aethelflaed, Lady of the Mercians." In *New Readings on Women in Old English Literature*, edited by Helen Damico and Alexandra Hennessey Olsen. Bloomington and Indianapolis: Indiana University Press, 1990, pp. 44–55. Originally published in *The Anglo-Saxons: Studies in Some Aspects of the History and Culture, Presented to Bruce Dickins*, edited by Peter Clemoes. London: Bowes and Bowes, 1959.

See also **History, Medieval Women's; Literature, Old English; Noble Women; Virile Women; Warfare**

AETHELTHRYTH OF ELY

Aethelthryth (c. 630–679, also known as Etheldreda or Audrey) founded an important monastery at Ely, Cambridgeshire in 672/673. Her life is witnessed by Stephen of Ripon in the *Life of Wilfrid* (written after 709) and Bede in *The Ecclesiastical History of the English People* (completed in 731). An East Anglian princess, Aethelthryth was related by marriage to Hild, abbess of Whitby, and to Aebbe, abbess of Coldingham. She first wed Tonberht, a man of the South Gyrwe, and later wed Ecgfrith, prince of Northumbria, and she is reputed to have retained her virginity in both marriages. The second alliance was formalized c. 660, and when Ecgfrith was crowned in 670, Aethelthryth became Queen of Northumbria.

Stephen of Ripon indicates that Aethelthryth held Bishop Wilfrid of York in high esteem and gave him land at Hexham on which to build a monastic church. Her spiritual devotion led the queen to divorce Ecgfrith, and in 671/672, she became a nun at Coldingham, under Ecgfrith's aunt. After a year, she returned to East Anglia and founded a monastic church on the Isle of Ely for both women and men.

Aethelthryth's asceticism is well documented by Bede, but little is known about her administration of the double house. At Aethelthryth's death in 679, her sister, Seaxburh, succeeded as abbess of Ely, and, in 695, she authorized the transfer of Aethelthryth's body from the cemetery into the church. Seaxburh found the corpse intact, which was understood to prove Aethelthryth's chastity within marriage. At this revelation, the community initiated a devotional cult, one that was interrupted by the Danish invasions but resumed c. 970 when Bishop Aethelwold of Winchester refounded Ely as a males-only institution.

Aethelwold's promotion of Aethelthryth as an icon of virginity is evident in the ornate representation of the abbess included in a sumptuous benedictional made for his personal use, as well as in the endowments he lavished upon the monastery in her honor. His gifts of patronage positioned Ely as the second wealthiest foundation at the Domesday inquest. The Anglo-Norman monks who took over the administration of the monastery embraced this important Saxon cult, and, during the twelfth century, they used the history of Aethelthryth's sovereignty to establish Ely as an episcopal see. The community's ability to promote their founder is manifested by twenty-five extant accounts of the saint's life (written in Latin, French, and English), records of significant pilgrim donations at Aethelthryth's shrine, church dedications throughout southern England, and over 100 surviving images of the saint in various media. These documents show that Aethelthryth was the most widely celebrated native female saint in late medieval England. Reverence for her continued after the Reformation, when her feast was included in the Book of Common Prayer.

VIRGINIA BLANTON

References and Further Reading

Bede. *Bede's Ecclesiastical History of the English People*, edited by Bertram Colgrave and R. A. B. Mynors. 1969. Reprint, Oxford: Clarendon Press, 1992.

Blanton-Whetsell, Virginia. "*Imagines Ætheldredae*: Mapping Hagiographic Representations of Abbatial Power and Religious Patronage." *Studies in Iconography* 23 (2002): 55–107.

Keynes, Simon. "Ely Abbey 672–1109." In *A History of Ely Cathedral*, edited by Peter Meadows and Nigel Ramsay. Woodbridge, Suffolk: Boydell, 2003, pp. 3–58.

Stephen of Ripon. *The Life of Bishop Wilfrid by Eddius Stephanus*, edited by Bertram Colgrave. 1927. Reprint, Cambridge: Cambridge University Press, 1985.

Wogan-Browne, Jocelyn. "Queens, Virgins and Mothers: Hagiographic Representations of the Abbess and Her Powers in Twelfth- and Thirteenth-Century Britain." In *Women and Sovereignty*, edited by Louise Olga Fradenburg. Edinburgh: Edinburgh University Press, 1992, pp. 14–35.

See also **Abbesses; Asceticism; Chastity and Chaste Marriage; England; Hild of Whitby; Monasticism and Nuns; Queens and Empresses: the West; Virginity**

AGNES OF PRAGUE

The Bohemian princess Agnes of Prague (1211–1282), joined Clare of Assisi in politicking for, and eventually securing, a Franciscan rule for women. The youngest of nine children, Agnes was born to King Přemysl Otakar I of Bohemia and Queen Constance of Hungary. Eager to expand his influence, Otakar engaged Agnes to Henry VII, son of Emperor Frederick II of Germany. Agnes began her formation as queen in Vienna, but Duke Leopold VI of Austria undermined Otakar's plans by arranging for his daughter, Margaret, to wed Henry instead.

In 1231, Frederick II sought Agnes's hand. In response, Agnes wrote to Pope Gregory IX and obtained permission to enter religious life. Enamored of the Franciscan ideal, Agnes built a hospital in Prague for the poor and sick in 1233, drawing upon her royal dowry, and established the Crosiers of the Red Star to administer the institution and care for its inmates. She also built a large monastery for women with a small convent attached for the Franciscan friars who would attend to their needs.

On June 11, 1234, Agnes entered the monastery that she had established, hoping to follow the example of Clare of Assisi. Clare wrote to Agnes, congratulating her on her choice. During the course of her life, Clare also wrote Agnes three other letters of advice and instruction. Unfortunately, Agnes's letters to Clare have been lost.

Agnes's greatest contribution was a series of privileges that she won from the papacy to secure the poverty of her monastery and a continued relationship with the Franciscan friars. These privileges paved the way for the papacy's 1253 approval of the Rule of St. Clare.

Agnes died in Prague on March 2, 1282.

JOAN MUELLER

References and Further Reading

Mueller, Joan. "Agnes of Prague and the Rule of St. Clare." *Studies in Spirituality* 13 (2003): 1–12.

———. *Clare's Letters to Agnes: Texts and Sources*. St. Bonaventure, N.Y.: The Franciscan Institute, 2001.

Soukupová, Helena. *The Convent of St. Agnes of Bohemia*. Prague: The National Gallery in Prague, 1993.

See also **Clare of Assisi; Monasticism and Nuns; Patronage, Ecclesiastical; Poor Clares Order; Poverty, Religious**

AGRICULTURE

Agriculture was central not only to the European economy of the Middle Ages but also to the daily and seasonal rhythms of the vast majority of medieval women and men. While peasant producers were directly involved in the cycles of intensive labor related to the land, noble and ecclesiastical landlords were dependent on the fruits of that agricultural labor to support their interests as warriors, clerics, and power brokers within the feudal and religious hierarchies. With approximately 90 percent of the population engaged in the production of food, the agricultural system of the Middle Ages (in many places called *manorialism,* as large landholders' estates were divided among different manors) created social as well as economic ties. The peasant family and village were the basic units of production within that system.

Peasant families did not own the land they worked; rather, they held, or had *tenure* of, the right of access to a number of acres in common fields distributed among the village as a whole. In exchange for this access to the land, they owed their manorial landlords three or four days of labor per week on the fields reserved for the lord (the *desmesne* lands) as well as a variety of extra services and dues at certain times in the agricultural calendar. Due to the seasonal nature of agricultural tasks and the costs of farm implements and the animals to pull them, much of the work on individual holdings and on the lord's demesne had to be done cooperatively by members of the community. Women's agricultural tasks typically included the maintenance of animals such as chickens, cows, and other animals whose byproducts could be taken to market. Women were also responsible for the extensive gardens that supplemented the family diet and served as seasonal cash crops for local markets. While men did most of the ploughing, women often participated in the harvest and were especially involved in the processing of the harvested grain.

Crops, equipment, and patterns of land usage varied across regions and from one period of economic development to the next. Nonetheless, some generalizations are useful. The predominance of grain production, legumous crops, viticulture, or pastoral farming in any given area was determined by climate and topography. Because cereal grains were a staple in the European diet, wheat, rye, barley, and oats were grown wherever the soil could be broken by the plough. The heavy, wheeled plough, pulled by a team of eight oxen, was the norm on the denser soils of northern Europe. In the later Middle Ages, an improved iron cutting edge that dug deeper into the soil and a moldboard that turned the soil to expose new nutrients made the plough more efficient and led to higher yields per acre. These improvements, along with the development of the horse collar, which allowed the team of oxen to be replaced by horses, helped to extend the arable land (or area under cultivation), as did the clearing of forests and drainage of swamps. With this extended arable area, many areas of western Europe were able to change from a two-field rotation of crops, with one field planted and one field lying fallow to rest and preserve its nutrients, to a system that allowed for one field to be used for a winter crop, such as wheat, one field for a spring crop, such as oats, and the third field to rest fallow. While this three-field crop rotation had the benefit of putting two-thirds of the arable land into production each year, it did not always guarantee a surplus crop, and peasant producers lived close to the margin of existence until the plague of the fourteenth century decimated the human population and made more land available to the survivors.

The marginal nature of grain harvests from year to year meant that most grain production could supply only local or regional markets. Legumes, such as peas and beans, were likewise grown for local markets. Viticulture, or the cultivation of vines, played a significant role in the distribution of agricultural land and tasks in regions of France, Burgundy, and parts of Italy, and it allowed production for a larger, long-distance market. In the later Middle Ages, more land was devoted to the raising of sheep for wool, especially in parts of England, Italy, and Spain, and this too allowed producers to be involved in long-distance markets.

Much of our knowledge of the intricate economic and social systems of agricultural production in the Middle Ages comes from records kept by the agents who managed the estates and held peasants to the terms of their contracts. Through these accounts we have learned that agricultural life was as socially complex as it was physically challenging.

MADONNA J. HETTINGER

References and Further Reading

Berman, Constance Hoffman. *Medieval Agriculture, the Southern French Countryside, and the Early Cistercians: A Study of 43 Monasteries.* Philadelphia: American Philosophical Society, 1986.

Coulton, G. G. *The Medieval Village.* Cambridge: Cambridge University Press, 1931.

Duby, Georges. *Rural Economy and Country Life in the Medieval West,* translated by Cynthia Postan. London: Arnold, 1968.

Hallam, H. E., ed. *The Agrarian History of England and Wales II: 1042–1350.* Cambridge: Cambridge University Press, 1988.

Hanawalt, Barbara H. *The Ties That Bound: Peasant Families in Medieval England.* New York: Oxford University Press, 1986.

Postan, M. M. *The Agrarian Life of the Middle Ages (Cambridge Economic History of Europe. Vol. I, 2nd ed.)* Cambridge: Cambridge University Press, 1966.

Power, Eileen. *Medieval People.* London: Methuen, 1924.

See also **Administration of Estates; Demography; Division of Labor; Household Management; Landholding and Property Rights; Migration and Mobility; Peasants; Plague; Records, Rural; Social Status; Work**

ALBA
See **Dawn Song (Alba)**

ALEWIVES AND BREWING

Ale was the common drink of people in northern Europe; it also played a prominent part in medieval culture. Safer to drink than water, the grain-based beverage provided an important part of people's daily nutritional requirement. Brewing was practised among the Celts, Scandinavians, and Germanic peoples from at least late antiquity. For most of the Middle Ages, brewing was dominated by women. Because of its importance, ale's production and sale became subject to extensive regulation; as a result, alewives (women who brewed and/or sold ale) are much more visible in the records than most other medieval female workers.

In England, the late-thirteenth-century assize of ale, enforced by local officials, regulated the price and quality of ale. Similar regulations existed in Scottish towns. Breakers of the assize were fined. In England, although not Scotland, these fines effectively became a licensing system, with all brewers paying fines; the resulting lists of names have allowed historians to trace brewing households in some English communities over many years. Some lists also exist for Welsh and Scottish towns. On the Continent, increasing regulation in northern European cities, as brewing became more urbanised and commercialised in the twelfth and thirteenth centuries, also made brewers more visible.

Brewing was a domestic skill expected of medieval women. Because ale spoiled quickly, many rural households alternated between brewing their own ale and selling any surplus, and purchasing it from neighbors. Brewing for sale was a part-time occupation, undertaken to supplement household income, although some women did brew full-time. In England, and probably elsewhere, demand for ale increased with rising living standards after the Black Death, providing more opportunities for women to earn a full- or part-time living from brewing, especially in the towns. Lists of citizens liable for brewing fees in some fifteenth-century German towns include large numbers of women. In England, there was an increase in the number of alehouses, where customers purchased ale and socialised. Women were also tavernkeepers in Germany, Denmark, and Poland.

Brewing offered women opportunities not found in many other trades. In England, a few women exercised office as aletasters. There is also some evidence of attempts to organise as a trade. However, the new opportunities may have mainly benefited married women. The number of single female brewers seems to have decreased during the fifteenth century, as commercial brewing increasingly became the preserve of married women who had the household and capital to undertake it. Single women in England mainly found employment in selling ale. In Scotland, in contrast, it was still common in 1500 for single women to set up as independent brewers.

The introduction of hopped beer, first produced in German towns in the thirteenth century and spreading through northern Europe in the fourteenth century, affected women's participation in brewing, although in different ways in different parts of Europe. Hopped beer lasted longer and could be made in larger quantities, but required greater capital outlay. Women were less able than men to invest, and the labor-intensive process was more difficult to balance with other domestic responsibilities. As a result, the more profitable beer brewing became dominated by men. In Europe, many women found employment working in the breweries. In England, hopped beer was introduced around 1400. Early English beer brewing was centered in London, where the number of female brewers declined over the fifteenth century, as women moved from brewing to retailing the new drink. Ale-brewing continued in much of the countryside, however, and in Scotland, it continued to dominate the brewing industry until well after 1500.

The effects of these economic changes on women have been debated. Some historians suggest that they had little effect, as women moved from low-status brewing in the eleventh to fourteenth centuries to low-status retailing in the fifteenth century. Others question whether the status of married brewers in the earlier period was as low as that of the later alewives and suggest that there was indeed some decline in women's status. Alewives were regarded in popular culture as swindlers and sexually promiscuous, and alehouses and taverns were commonly associated with licentiousness and disorder. There were increasing attempts in many countries in the late Middle Ages to regulate women's work in taverns, mainly because of their association with prostitution. On the other hand, there seems to have been little change in women's position in the brewing trade in the Low Countries until the seventeenth century, while in some European towns, the new opportunities provided by beer brewing benefited widows who took over breweries upon their husbands' deaths.

ELIZABETH EWAN

References and Further Reading

Bennett, Judith. *Ale, Beer and Brewsters in England: Women's Work in a Changing World, 1300–1600.* New York: Oxford University Press, 1996.

Howell, Martha C. *Women, Production, and Patriarchy in Late Medieval Cities.* Chicago: University of Chicago Press, 1986.

Martin, A. Lynn. *Alcohol, Sex, and Gender in Late Medieval and Early Modern Europe.* Houndmills: Palgrave, 2001.

Peters, Christine. *Women in Early Modern Britain, 1450–1640.* Houndmills: Palgrave Macmillan, 2004.

Uitz, Erika. *Women in the Medieval Town.* London: Barrie & Jenkins, 1990.

Unger, Richard. *Beer in the Middle Ages and the Renaissance.* Philadelphia: University of Pennsylvania Press, 2004.

See also **Business; Division of Labor; Honor and Reputation; Market and Tradeswomen**

ALMSGIVING AND CHARITY

Almsgiving and charity towards the poor, sick, and needy were enjoined upon all Christians, and by the later Middle Ages Christ was identified with the poor, so that giving alms to the poor was the same as giving them directly to Christ. This was based on the Biblical verse Matthew 25:41: "For I was hungry, and you gave me not to eat; I was thirsty, and you gave me not to drink. I was a stranger, and you took me not in; naked, and you covered me not; sick and in prison, and you did not visit me." These acts of charity were codified as the Seven Works of Mercy by the addition of the burial of the dead, based on the *Book of Tobit.* Women and children were also regarded as particularly vulnerable, and thus acts of charity could be gendered, as widows and orphans might be regarded as preferential recipients. While there is evidence that the early Church did see these last two groups as the major recipients of charity, with bishops being charged with their support, by the later Middle Ages they were less likely to be singled out, and women were more likely to be recipients because of their poverty than their gender or marital status.

Thomas Aquinas discussed almsgiving in his *Summa Theologica* (c. 1266–1273). He agreed on the need for almsgiving by all Christians but limited the extent to which dependents such as wives and servants could disburse the goods that belonged to the head of the household. This view was shared by other Italian writers, such as Bernardino of Siena (d. 1444), but may have been less of a concern in northern Europe, where wives may have been more economically independent.

There is disagreement among scholars as to how far there was increasing hostility towards the poor after the Black Death. There were concerns about the threat from able-bodied (male) laborers, but less so about the sick and needy of either sex. There is evidence for concern about the "shame-faced poor," that is, people of previously good economic and social standing who had fallen into poverty.

Practice

Almsgiving could either be organised within the household or directed through an institution such as a monastery or hospital. The female householder usually organised household giving, donating leftover food or outworn clothing to beggars at the kitchen door. Some women practised an extreme form of charity as devotion to Christ, where they gave away not only the waste and spare supplies, but large quantities of food and other goods belonging to the family. This could bring them into conflict with male family members, as it potentially threatened the economic stability of the family. This is found in the hagiographical accounts of several female saints, including Elisabeth of Hungary (d. 1231) and the servant Zita of Lucca (d. 1278) (although not always in eyewitness accounts). These suggest clerical support for female charity, and that the practice of charity was seen as particularly appropriate to women. Elisabeth founded a hospital at Marburg, where she tended the sick with her own hands, and gave away her money. Frances of Rome (d. 1440) also gave large quantities of food away, and begged alongside the poor. These women were probably trying to identify with the poor as well as help them. Some aristocratic and episcopal households had an almoner, a male official who was responsible for regular and formal support, often to a specific number of poor dependents, who might live in their own homes or within the household. Preference might be given to elderly or infirm former servants and tended to benefit males more than females, as male servants were more common (for example, Staindrop hospital in County Durham, founded in 1408 by Ralph, Earl of Westmorland, supported around a dozen poor gentlemen, grooms and yeomen, former servants of the earl). Charity and almsgiving are most easily seen in wills. Women usually only left wills as widows, and they were likely to distribute goods in kind, whereas men were more likely to distribute money, reflecting the resources available to them. Women were also more likely to distribute to a smaller circle, mainly of people known to them, whereas men were more likely to give to abstract collectivities and institutions. There is some evidence that women gave a higher proportion of their goods to charity, but this may be because the circumstances in which they were most likely to leave a will (as widows, and possibly without surviving children) encouraged the giving of alms. The nature of charity could be shaped by local circumstances, as in the giving of fuel by women in northern England in the later fourteenth and fifteenth centuries.

The main route by which almsgiving was directed via institutions was through monasteries and hospitals, and was performed by both men and women. However, women can also be found giving to other charitable purposes, such as prisons and the building of bridges and roads (such as the bridge at Puente la Reina in Spain, built to aid pilgrims on the road to Santiago de Compostela). This is traditionally ascribed to Queen Urraca of Leon-Castile but is probably older; however, the name (Queen's Bridge) indicates a female patron. Some Beguines also served the poor and sick in hospitals and leprosaria and distributed alms. In the later Middle Ages, guilds often took on the care of the needy, though there was often preference for their own members, which tended to benefit men more than women.

Monte delle doti (dowry investment funds) were established in Florence and a number of other northern Italian towns in the fifteenth century and provided a means by which poor fathers could invest towards dowries for their daughters. Guilds such as the Annunciation Guild of Rome also sometimes provided dowries for poor girls. In England, donations for poor girls' dowries can be found in wills, mainly of men, but were not institutionalised. Also to be found in Mediterranean Europe were houses for reformed prostitutes, such as the Casa de las Arrepentidas at Valencia, Spain, founded in 1345 by Na Soriana, a Dominican tertiary. These provided shelter for women who wished to leave prostitution. Civic authorities sometimes paid the dowries of such women.

The redemption of captives, that is, Christians who were in the hands of non-Christians (usually Muslims, for example, through seizure by North African pirates) was also a charitable activity from the later twelfth century, and a greater concern in Spain and Mediterranean Europe than in the north. It was mainly organised by the Mercedarian and Trinitarian orders, which dedicated a third of their incomes to this purpose. Redemption was mainly by the payment of ransom, but members of the orders sometimes offered themselves as substitutes for those they sought to redeem. Those who negotiated the release of captives were always men. The majority of those redeemed were male—primarily soldiers and sailors—but did include women and children.

P. H. CULLUM

References and Further Reading

Aquinas, Thomas. *Summa Theologica*. http://www.newadvent.org/summa/, 1920.

Boanas, Guy, and Roper, Lyndal. "Feminine Piety in Fifteenth-Century Rome: Santa Francesca Romana." In *Disciplines of Faith: Studies in Religion, Politics and Patriarchy*, edited by Jim Obelkevich, Lyndal Roper, and Raphael Samuel. London: Routledge and Kegan Paul Ltd, 1987, pp. 177–193.

Brodman, James William. *Charity and Welfare: Hospitals and the Poor in Medieval Catalonia*. Philadelphia: University of Pennsylvania Press, 1998.

Bynum, Caroline Walker. *Holy Feast and Holy Fast: The Religious Significance of Food to Medieval Women*. Berkeley and Los Angeles: University of California Press, 1987.

Cullum, P. H. "'*And Hir Name was Charite*:' Charitable Giving by and for Women in Late Medieval Yorkshire." In *Woman is a Worthy Wight: Women in English Society c. 1200–1500* (reprinted as *Women in Medieval English Society*), edited by P. J. P. Goldberg. Stroud, England: Sutton Publishing Ltd, 1992, pp. 182–211.

———. "Gendering Charity in Medieval Hagiography." In *Gender and Holiness: Men, Women and Saints in Late Medieval Europe*, edited by Samantha J. E. Riches and Sarah Salih. London: Routledge, 2002, pp. 135–151.

Farmer, Sharon. *Surviving Poverty in Medieval Paris: Gender, Ideology and the Daily Lives of the Poor*. Ithaca: Cornell University Press, 2002.

Henderson, John. *Piety and Charity in Late Medieval Florence*. Oxford: Clarendon Press, 1994.

Knowles, David, and R. Neville Hadcock. *Medieval Religious Houses: England and Wales*. Harlow: Longman, 1971.

Orme, Nicholas, and Margaret Webster. *The English Hospital, 1070–1570*. New Haven, Conn.: Yale University Press, 1995.

Otis, Leah Lydia. *Prostitution in Medieval Society: The History of an Urban Institution in Languedoc*. Chicago: University of Chicago Press, 1985.

Rawcliffe, Carol. *Medicine and Society in Later Medieval England*. Stroud, England: Sutton Publishing Ltd, 1995.

Rubin, Miri. *Charity and Community in Medieval Cambridge*. Cambridge: Cambridge University Press, 1987.

Taylor, Bruce. *Structures of Reform: the Mercedarian Order in the Spanish Golden Age*. Leiden and Boston: Brill, 2000.

See also **Beguines; Disabilities; Elisabeth of Hungary; Fasting and Food, Religious Aspects of; Hagiography; Hospitals; Lay Piety; Lepers; Patronage, Ecclesiastical; Poverty; Prostitutes; Wills; Zita and Other Servant Saints**

AMALASUNTHA

Amalasuntha (498–535) ruled Italy and the Ostrogoths as regent for a son and sole queen at the start of the Middle Ages. Theodoric, king of the Ostrogoths, occupied Italy and ruled it, with the approval of the eastern Roman emperor, until his death in 526. His throne passed to his ten-year-old grandson Athalaric. His daughter Amalasuntha, the boy's mother, governed as regent. She faced no serious challenge to her authority until 532, when a faction of Gothic nobles won control of the young king. She fought back by dispatching three of its leaders to distant posts, where she arranged their assassinations. Two years later Athalaric died, and Amalasuntha tried to stay in power by sharing the throne with the only surviving male in the royal line, her cousin Theodahad. She was initially protected by Theodahad's fear that an attack on her would invite reprisals from the Roman emperor in Constantinople. In 535, however, she was murdered. Relatives of the men she had assassinated were said to have killed her, but letters that passed between Theodahad and the emperor Justinian and Theodahad's wife and the empress Theodora (and the maneuvers of Justinian's ambassadors) suggest that Constantinople urged Theodahad to eliminate Amalasuntha. When Theodahad took the bait, he gave Justinian the excuse he sought to invade Italy, evict the Goths, and restore the Roman homeland to direct imperial control.

A. DANIEL FRANKFORTER

References and Further Reading

Aurelius Cassiodorus. *Variarum libri duodecim*. In *Patrologia Latina*, edited by Jacques-Paul Migne. LXIX:500-800. Paris, 1848. See also http://pld.chadwyck.co.uk/

Burns, Thomas S. *A History of the Ostrogoths*. Bloomington, IN: Indiana University Press, 1984.

Frankforter, A. Daniel. "Amalasuntha, Procopius, and a Woman's Place." *Journal of Women's History* 8(2) (1996): 41–57.

Mierow, Charles C., ed. and trans. *The Gothic History of Jordanes*. Princeton: Princeton University Press, 1915; Merchantville, NJ: Evolution Publishing, 2006.

Procopius of Caesarea. *History of the Wars* and *Secret History*, translated by Averil Cameron. New York: Twayne, 1967.

See also **Italy; Regents and Queen Lieutenants; Theodora**

AMAZONS

Mixing history, legend, and myth, Classical writers including Suetonius and Virgil described a tribe of fierce, bellicose women known as the Amazons. These representatives of female otherness inhabited the space just beyond the margins of the known landscape, variously located in areas of Anatolia, North Africa, and the Black Sea. In popular etymology, *Amazon* means "breastless," encouraging the erroneous notion that these women cut off one breast to practice archery more efficiently. The term more probably meant "those not breast-fed" or "moon women" from their devotion to Artemis, goddess of the hunt. Happily ignorant of cooking and sewing, activities that in ancient Greek culture typically gendered as "women's work," Amazons' chief pursuits were warfare, hunting, and training their female children to be warriors, reflecting their devotion to Ares, the god of war.

Wearing light armor and crescent-shaped shields, riding horses or chariots in lightning cavalry attacks, Amazons employed the bow and arrow, as well as the sword, javelin, or spear favored by male warriors. Targets of their empire-building assaults included the citadel of Athens. Celebrated male warriors with whom their various leaders reputedly engaged in battle, "Amazonomachy," included Achilles, who slew and loved Penthesilea, the Amazon mercenary fighting for Troy in the Trojan War; Hercules, who stole the "Girdle of Ares" worn by the Amazon queen Hippolyta; Theseus, whose siege of Hippolyta's Amazon kingdom and later marriage to either her or her sister Antiope provoked a counterattack on Athens; and Alexander the Great, who reputedly was seduced by the Amazon queen Thalestris during his Bactrian campaign in 329 BCE. These examples attest to the paradoxical fascination of the ancient Greeks with this otherwise abhorred female group who presented a distorted reflection of male-dominated Greek military society. Stories of these women carried over to medieval times and enjoyed wide popularity.

In the equally patriarchal culture of the European Middle Ages, female warriors inspired a similar attraction to and anxiety about the "power of women." Generally speaking, the downfall of mighty or authoritative biblical and historical male figures (Adam, Samson, Aristotle) was blamed on the women associated with them (Eve, Delilah, Phyllis). Because the Amazons' equestrian military culture paralleled the horse-dominated chivalric code of medieval knights, many medieval romances feature female characters either based on classical Amazons or representing fantasies about female knighthood. Twelfth- and thirteenth-century French "romances of antiquity" feature classical Amazons in romances adapted from epics: Penthesilea in the *Romance of Troie;* Camilla, Virgil's Amazon from the *Aeneid*, in the *Romance of Eneas*; and various Amazons in medieval romances about Alexander the Great. Giovanni Boccaccio's fourteenth-century Italian *Thesiad*, upon which English poet Geoffrey Chaucer later based his

Knight's Tale, depicts Theseus's war against the Amazons Hippolyta and Emelia. The *Romance of Silence* (c. 1250) portrays a spectacular cross-dressing female, Silence, who secretly impersonates a male knight to overcome a ban against female inheritance. Gyburc in Wolfram von Eschenbach's thirteenth-century German romance epic *Willehalm* dons armor and successfully defends the citadel of Orange in her husband's absence. Several works of the fifteenth-century author Christine de Pizan, especially the allegorical *Book of the City of Ladies*, which describes the building of a female citadel using stories about famous women as the foundation stones, included treatments of Amazons and other warrior women. De Pizan's 1429 *Poem of Joan of Arc* celebrates the military skills of her contemporary Joan of Arc, an authentic medieval female warrior.

Amazons were classified among the "marvels of the east," and popular late-medieval Spanish romances such as *Amadis of Gaul* and *Esplandian* responded with fantasies of gold and sexual fulfillment found on the Amazon queen Calafia's island, California. In response, early modern explorers named topographical features of the Americas, including the Amazon River and California, for Amazons.

LORRAINE KOCHANSKE STOCK

References and Further Reading

Kleinbaum, Abby Wettan. *The War Against the Amazons.* New York: McGraw-Hill, 1983.

Mayor, Adrienne, and Josiah Ober. "Amazons." In *Experience of War: An Anthology of Articles from MHQ, The Quarterly Journal of Military History*, edited by Robert Cowley. New York: Dell, 1992, pp. 12–23.

McLaughlin, Megan. "The Woman Warrior: Gender, Warfare, and Society in Medieval Europe." *Women's Studies* 17 (1990): 193–209.

Smith, Susan L. *The Power of Women: A Topos in Medieval Art and Literature*. Philadelphia: University of Pennsylvania Press, 1995.

Stock, Lorraine Kochanske. "'Arms and the (Wo)man' in Medieval Romance: The Gendered Arming of Female Warriors in the *Roman d'Eneas* and Heldris's *Roman de Silence*." *Arthuriana* 5 (1995): 56–83.

Tyrrell, William Blake. *Amazons: A Study in Athenian Mythmaking*. Baltimore: The Johns Hopkins University Press, 1984.

See also **Arms and Armor; Boccaccio, Giovanni; Chaucer, Geoffrey; Christine de Pizan; Joan of Arc; Roman de Silence; Romances of Antiquity; Virile Women; Warfare; Wolfram von Eschenbach; Woman on Top**

AMULETS
See **Magic and Charms**

ANCHORESSES

Anchoresses were female anchorites or recluses, that is, those who chose to be enclosed in a single room or rooms, often attached to or nearby a church, for the purposes of prayer and contemplation of God. The word *anchorite* comes from the Greek *anchoreta*, to withdraw from the world as did the Desert Fathers. Anchorholds usually had at least two windows: one into the church, through which the anchoress could witness and participate in the mass, and one through which she could communicate with the outside world. Sometimes anchorholds consisted of several rooms and a garden. At times several anchoresses lived in groups, and even sometimes with servants. Although, in the early Christian Church, anchorites were indistinguishable from hermits, by the twelfth century the word *anchorite* had the specific meaning of enclosure, and for the anchoress, who was not allowed to wander without supervision, that meant enclosure in an anchorhold in a town or city, usually at its center.

There were technically two kinds of anchoresses, *inclusa* and *reclusa*. *Inclusa* were those who wished to pursue a more ascetic and ecstatic contemplative life within the walls of a monastery. They had already proven themselves stable, dedicated contemplatives. Usually there was a rigorous three-year training period before such *incluses* were allowed to be enclosed. Most anchoresses, however, were not of this kind; rather, they were women, usually older women, who wished to pursue a contemplative life despite a lay history as wives, mothers, and landowners. Often their experiences as influential devout widows in their communities before enclosure were not markedly different from their experiences as anchoresses. Neither *incluses* nor *recluses* should be confused with mystics; although some might have had mystical visions, most anchoresses were unexceptional members of the religious community. Often they participated in the religious education of members of the community; at times they acted as counselors or spiritual advisors. Sometimes, if criticism of them has any truth to it, they were a little too involved in the community, entertaining visitors, teaching children, and even acting as local bankers.

Popularity of Anchoritism

Anchoritism grew in popularity around the time of the Fourth Lateran Council of 1215. This council declared the necessity of each individual to confess yearly and inspired the production of confession manuals for priests, guides to religious self-scrutiny for the layperson, and vernacular religious literature of many kinds. Furthermore, it helped kindle the desire of many laypeople for a more strictly regulated religious life both within the monasteries and outside of them. This period marks the proliferation of numerous forms of monasticism and mendicancy, as well as some institutions for women, such as beguinages. Institutions for women that responded to this new ascetic fervor, however, were limited, especially in England, and this may account for the notable rise of anchoritism among women in England. The anchoritic life for women was also more popular in continental Europe than usually noted, although it seems to have taken a slightly different form. In Europe, especially northern Europe, the anchorhold was viewed as a respectable place of retirement for older women, especially widows—those devout women who wished to focus their spirituality and become more actively engaged in their communities as religious leaders. In England, however, anchoresses seem to have been less actively involved in community life and more interested in retirement and seclusion. Although anchorholds in England were not far from city centers and some, like Julian of Norwich's cell, were right next to the marketplace, others, like the anchorhold associated with the readers of the *Ancrene Wisse,* were more removed from city life.

Enclosure

Anchoresses were not always officially enclosed, but when they were, they were enclosed in a ceremony that articulated their metaphorical commitment to be "dead to the world." In some enclosure rites, the anchoress was carried into the anchorhold in a coffin and then bricked in to the anchorhold while prayers from the Office of the Dead were said for her. Before entering an anchorhold, the postulant's credentials were carefully scrutinized, and afterwards her life was supervised—distantly by the bishop, and perhaps more locally by the parish priest or a spiritual advisor. The thirteenth-century Middle English religious guide for anchoresses, the *Ancrene Wisse,* tells us that the daily life of the anchoress consisted of a strict regime of prayers throughout the day and evening, manual labor in a garden if the anchorhold had a garden, and meetings with a spiritual advisor. The anchoress was discouraged from teaching, sewing, keeping animals (except a cat), gossiping with those outside the window of the anchorhold, and meeting with visitors, especially men, unless strictly supervised and attended by a servant, and only if absolutely necessary.

Social Status

Most anchoresses were anonymous. Records suggest that an anchoress was a prized member of a community, and they were often supported by small bequests from local lords; particularly famous anchoresses received bequests from the king. It was to one's spiritual well-being to contribute to the support of an anchoress, and indeed it was considered to be spiritually efficacious to have an anchoress in one's own town. Records also suggest that most anchoresses came from the upper and upper-middle classes, although there are some records that tell of a servant replacing an anchoress after her death. The anchoresses we know of suggest the wide range of education, motivations for entering an anchorhold, class, degree of political and ecclesiastical involvement, and temperament of those who pursued this form of religious life. One of the earliest English anchoresses we know of was Eve of Wilton (d. c. 1125), praised for her exceptional Latin literacy and known as a voracious reader. Loretta, Countess of Leicester, withdrew into an anchorhold in 1220 some time after her family fell out of favor with King John. The wealthy Katherine of Ledbury (b. 1272) gave up her lands some years after her husband's death and retired to an anchorhold supported by the revenues from that land. The most famous anchoress in England was the fourteenth-century Julian of Norwich, who entered an anchorhold after she had a series of mystical revelations. She acted as a leader in her community of nuns and even for those outside her spiritual community seeking spiritual advice. Margery Kempe tells of her visit to Julian's cell.

Anchoresses in northern continental Europe were particularly prominent and influential members of their communities. The widowed mother of Guibert of Nogent (c. 1055–c. 1125) chose to enter a cell she herself had commissioned and brought half of her family and her household with her. Living in her cell for at least forty years, she had dreams and visions, became known as a prophet, and grew to be highly influential locally. Yvette of Huy (1158–1228) entered an anchorhold after first withdrawing to a leper colony. From her cell she made predictions and commentaries that put pressure on the dean and canons of the town's main church, and she counseled wayward clerics, directing them to passages in the Bible. The prioress Juliana of Cornillon (1192–1258), who late in her life became an unofficial recluse, dedicated her life to developing a Feast of the Corpus Christi; although this was not realized in her lifetime, it came into being shortly after her death in 1264 through the influence of her confidante and student, the anchoress

Eve of St. Martin. Lame Margaret of Magdeburg's (c. 1210–1250) special role was to act as a teacher to visitors to her cell. While these five European anchoresses, described thoroughly by Mulder-Bakker, demonstrate the public influence an anchoress could have in a community, there are records of thousands more anchoresses about whom we know very little. Perhaps they, too, enjoyed such a prominent social and religious role, but it is also possible that they may have preferred anonymity. Nonetheless, while an anchoress herself may not have been publically active, her anchorhold would certainly have played a public role in the community.

ELIZABETH ROBERTSON

References and Further Reading

Clay, Rotha Mary. *Hermits and Anchorites of England.* London: Methuen, 1914. Reprint, Detroit: Singing Tree Press, 1968.

Mulder-Bakker, Anneke B. *Lives of the Anchoresses: The Rise of the Urban Recluse in Medieval Europe,* translated by Myra Heerspink Scholz. Philadelphia: University of Pennsylvania Press, 2005.

Warren, Ann. *Anchorites and Their Patrons in Medieval England.* Berkeley: University of California Press, 1985.

See also **Ancrene Wisse; Guibert of Nogent's Mother; Julian of Norwich; Margaret "the Cripple" of Magdeburg; Widows; Yvette of Huy**

ANCRENE WISSE

The anonymous thirteenth-century Middle English work known as the *Ancrene Wisse* is a religious guide for female recluses, as well as a lively and psychologically astute instance of early Middle English prose. The title of the work, the *Ancrene Wisse* or *Ancrene Riwle* (these are editorial rather than authorial titles), means guide or rule for anchoresses. Anchoresses were devout religious women who chose to be enclosed for life in a small room or rooms, usually attached to a church, and often at the center of a community, in order to devote themselves completely to contemplation of God. Anchoresses entered anchorholds either after first living in a convent or directly from secular life. The original work was written at the request of three sisters for a guide to the anchoritic life in the first quarter of the thirteenth century, at about the time of the Fourth Lateran Council (1215), which, in advocating confession for everyone once a year, inspired a flourishing output of vernacular religious texts written for lay audiences. It is not entirely clear in what language the original text was written; it appears in French, Latin, and English versions. Its original audience most probably read all three languages with varying degrees of proficiency. Since Latin education for religious women at this date was limited, it is plausible that the text was originally composed in English or French, and the localization of its early versions to the southeast Midlands, and possibly Herefordshire, far from the continent and the English centers where French predominated as the literary language of choice, suggests that it may well have been originally composed in English. Because of manuscript marginalia, some have localized it even more specifically to Wigmore Abbey, but that association is not definitive. Despite its very specific purposes and audience, the work was quickly disseminated; it was adapted for larger groups of anchoresses and nuns, and even for male monastics. The name of the author, undoubtedly male, is unknown. The author's citations and references to specific aspects of monastic rules associate him either with Augustinian canons or, as Bella Millett has recently argued, with the Dominicans. He may well have been a spiritual advisor of the three anchoresses. Recently, Anne Savage has argued that the women themselves helped shape the content of the work.

The form of English in which the text appears in the earliest manuscripts was called long ago by J.R.R. Tolkien the "AB" dialect, "A" referring to the language of the Corpus Christi 402 manuscript of the *Ancrene Wisse* and "B" to the language of Bodley 34, a group of religious texts known as the Katherine Group, which includes three saints' lives, a tract on virginity, and a homily on the guardianship of the soul, which may well have served as additional reading for either these anchoresses or larger groups of female religious. The AB dialect is of particular interest because it presents an unusually uniform grammar and orthography. This suggests a deliberate attempt by those writing in the AB dialect to codify their language and, furthermore, provides unprecedented information about the state of the language in post-conquest England. That the *Ancrene Wisse* and the Katherine Group were written in this sophisticated form of the language suggests that these works were being produced from a self-conscious literary center in Herefordshire. They stand as some of the few known major original works in production in England at this date. That many if not all of these texts are primarily for female readers suggests the crucial role women played as an audience of Middle English at a time when English was threatened by the presence of a conquering language, Norman French.

The *Ancrene Wisse* is indebted to Aelred of Rievaux's earlier letter to his sister on the reclusive life (c. 1160–1162), *On the Education of Recluses.* This work, written in Latin, shares with the *Ancrene Wisse* a general structure of an outer rule, with descriptions of daily anchoritic routines, and an inner rule, focused on spiritual refinement. Aelred's work ends with three spiritual meditations, on the past, present, and future. The meditation on the past is particularly compelling; in it Aelred proposes that the contemplative woman recreate Christ's life from birth to crucifixion as if she were present at these events. The meditation, with its wrenching evocation of Christ's suffering and dying designed to evoke compassion in the reader, is a fine example of the religious movement known as affective piety.

The *Ancrene Wisse* consists of an introduction and eight parts or distinctions. Like Aelred's letter, the work includes an outer rule concerning specifics of daily life and an inner rule concerning the spiritual life, but the *Ancrene Wisse*'s directions for the pursuit of daily life and its spiritual goals are at once more flexible and more detailed. The introduction specifies the work's status as a guide, rather than a rule, and presents itself as a flexible work offering general rather than mandatory guidance. The first part, "Devotions" (following M.D. Salu's titles for the distinctions), provides the anchoresses with a list of specific prayers to be said at particular times. Centering on the twin celebration of the Five Joys of Mary and the Eucharist, prayers of special meaning for female contemplatives (who were often urged to use Mary as their model and who were also encouraged to cultivate an incarnational theology), the directions include an unusual focus on the bodily performance of devotions. The next five sections of the work move from this outer rule to an "inner rule of the heart" and focus on the anchoress's discipline of her body as well as her mind. Part Two, "The Custody of the Senses," examines each sense in turn and urges the anchoress to protect all her senses from possible temptation, especially by identifying with the suffering of Christ in each of his senses. Part Three, "The Regulation of the Inward Feelings," especially focuses on the need to control anger, an emotion that may well have been rife in small groups of contemplatives. Part Four, "Temptations," rather surprisingly focuses on temptations to which the anchoress will almost inevitably succumb. Part Five, "Confession," demonstrates how the anchoress must confess such sins. The next chapter, "Penance," paves the way for the anchoress's romantic union with Christ, celebrated in the penultimate section, "Love." Rather than ending on the ascent of the anchoress to union with God, the author returns in Part Eight to the everyday world of the anchoress in a discussion of external rules. Emphasizing the metaphorical and literal meaning of her enclosure in the anchorhold, where she is meant to become dead to the world, it includes warnings against a range of worldly activities, such as keeping animals, weaving and embroidery, meeting visitors, running a school, and others—the surprising worldly dangers of living in an anchorhold where the anchoress is easily subject to the curiosity and demands of a stream of community passersby and spiritual seekers.

The *Ancrene Wisse* describes a seemingly harsh, extreme life, and its vision of a female contemplative in particular need of protection from sins of the flesh suggests the author's endorsement of the dominant ecclesiastical view of women as defined by their bodies. Nonetheless, the author shows deep respect for his readers and for the extraordinary emotional range available to them in the anchorhold. Unlike mystical writings, the work engages the pressures and goals of a demanding daily routine with psychological acumen and wit. Despite being confined to a very small space in uncomfortable conditions, the anchoress learns to transform physical discomfort and worldly distraction, even the most mundane of experiences and objects, into touchstones to the spiritual world. The work is a compelling account of an extraordinary form of religious life, but is also a superb example of the capacity of Early English prose to convey literary power.

ELIZABETH ROBERTSON

References and Further Reading

Aelred of Rievaulx (Aelredi Rievallensis). "De Institutione inclusarum." In *Opera Omnia*, edited by A. D. Hoste and C. H. Talbot. Turnholti, Belgium: Brepols, 1971.

———. "The Life of a Recluse." In *Treatises and the Pastoral Prayer* and *Works of Aelred of Rievaulx*, translated by Mary Paul McPherson. Kalamazoo, Mich.: Cistercian Publications, 1971.

Georgianna, Linda. *The Solitary Self: Individuality in the* Ancrene Wisse. Cambridge, Mass.: Harvard University Press, 1981.

Hasenfratz, Robert, ed. *The Ancrene Wisse*. Kalamazoo, Mich.: Medieval Institute Publications, 2000.

Millett, Bella. *Annotated Bibliographies of Old and Middle English Literature: II: Ancrene Wisse and the Katherine Group and the Wooing Group*. Cambridge: D. S. Brewer, 1996.

Robertson, Elizabeth. *Early English Devotional Prose and the Female Audience*. Nashville, Tennessee: University of Tennessee Press, 1990.

Savage, Anne, and Nicholas Watson. *Anchoritic Spirituality*. New York: Paulist Press, 1991.

Sitwell, Dom Gerard. *The Ancrene Riwle*, translated by M. B. Salu. South Bend, Ind.: Indiana University Press, 1955.

Wada, Yoko. *A Companion to the* Ancrene Wisse. Cambridge: D. S. Brewer, 2003.

See also **Anchoresses; Audiences, Women in the; Katherine Group; Spirituality, Christian**

ANGELA OF FOLIGNO

The Italian Franciscan laywoman Angela of Foligno (d. 1309) is known almost solely due to a dossier of texts referred to as the *Liber* ("Book"). Aside from a brief mention of her in Ubertino of Casale's *Arbor Vitae* in 1305, her name scarcely appears in medieval sources. The earliest manuscript of the *Liber* identifies her only as "L.," later elaborated as "Lella," the diminutive of "Angela," and then as "Angela." The *Liber* is divided into two parts: the *Memorial*, about three thousand lines long, and the slightly longer *Instructions*, which is a series of thirty-eight brief texts. This early version of the *Liber* was subsequently abbreviated into a shorter version that survives in a number of manuscripts and that some scholars have mistakenly thought to be the earlier version.

The *Memorial* purports to be Angela's own account of her spiritual journey, dictated to a Franciscan scribe identified in the text only as "Brother A." A relative and confessor of Angela, Brother A. says he encountered Angela screaming outside the Basilica of St. Francis during a pilgrimage to nearby Assisi. Fearing she might be possessed by an evil spirit, he compelled her to provide details of her experience so he could record it and consult a wise spiritual man. Converted from skeptic to devotee upon hearing the details of her ecstatic encounter with God, Brother A. then continued to record Angela's experiences over the next several years. His account interweaves Angela's extensive quotations, spoken in Umbrian and rendered by him into Latin, with his own comments about Angela. Internal evidence, including Brother A.'s frequent comments regarding the complex redactional process of the *Memorial*, show his considerable influence in shaping the text, despite his proclaimed intention of being a simple and faithful scribe.

The *Memorial* provides relatively little biographical information about Angela's life. She was born sometime in the thirteenth century, resided in Foligno, married an unnamed man, and had an unknown number of children whose names and genders are never given. At some point, Angela began to adopt a penitential lifestyle. She struggled to strip herself of her worldly attachments, which included enough property to suggest she was well-to-do. She prayed, successfully, for the deaths of her mother, husband, and children. Living then with an unnamed female companion, Angela followed the "rule of St. Francis" for the laity, which at this time probably included prescriptions regarding prayers, penance, and other pious practices. Angela was part of a lay movement that gradually became institutionalized as the Third Order of St. Francis, although she is not explicitly identified as belonging to the "Third Order"

until the late fourteenth century. A note appended to most manuscripts indicates that she died January 4, 1309.

Angela's spiritual experiences, which occupy most of the *Memorial*, include frequent visions and locutions. The penitent's journey to the cross takes her through spiraling experiences of desolation and consolation. Her growing awareness of her own sin and vileness causes her to suffer increasingly acute pains and torments. These are punctuated by experiences of ecstatic encounters with God. She swings dramatically between extreme doubt and absolute certainty until her experience of the cross finally plunges her so thoroughly into God that she experiences almost continual union.

Theological themes emphasized by Angela include the humanity of Christ, the Passion, the Trinity, and the Eucharist. Her insistence upon the priority of religious experience over learning, the ultimate ineffability of God, and the centrality of poverty and humility touch on points of bitter dispute among Franciscans of the time and suggest that she favored a stricter interpretation of the Franciscan rule.

The second part of the *Liber*, the *Instructions*, includes thirty-six "instructions," a brief notice about her death, and an epilogue. They were redacted by a variety of anonymous authors, perhaps including Brother A. Many of the texts were written only after Angela's death, some appearing for the first time only in later manuscripts. Their diverse ordering in the manuscript tradition suggests that no single authentic ordering ever existed. The texts, which vary in style and vocabulary, include Angela's own alleged accounts of mystical experiences and teachings, letters she wrote, and texts about her. Some instructions continue or elaborate themes found in the *Memorial*. Others introduce new material, including Angela's teaching about the Book of Life and the account given of her death.

The *Instructions* present Angela as the spiritual mother of a circle of devotees. These included male Franciscans, who probably wrote many or all of the texts and who are sometimes the subject or intended audience of the instructions. References to Angela's companion and other women and men in the *Liber* indicate that others also belonged to her circle.

CATHERINE M. MOONEY

References and Further Reading

Angela of Foligno and Brother A. *Il libro della Beata Angela da Foligno (Edizione critica)*, edited by Ludger Thier and Abele Calufetti. Grottaferrata (Rome): Collegii S. Bonaventurae ad Claras Aquas, 1985.

————. *Angela of Foligno: Complete Works*, translated by Paul Lachance. New York: Paulist Press, 1993.

Barone, Giulia, and Jacques Dalarun, eds. *Angèle de Foligno. Le dossier.* Rome: École française de Rome, 1999.

Dalarun, Jacques. "Angèle de Foligno a-t-elle existé?" In *Alla signorina: mélanges offerts à Noëlle de La Blanchardière*. Rome: École française de Rome, 1995, pp. 59–97.

Fusco, Roberto. *Amore e compassione. L'esperienza di Angela da Foligno.* Rome: Istituto Storico dei Cappuccini, 2001.

Mooney, Catherine M. "The Authorial Role of Brother A. in the Composition of Angela of Foligno's Revelations." In *Creative Women in Medieval and Early Modern Italy: A Religious and Artistic Renaissance*, edited by E. Ann Matter and John Coakley. Philadelphia: University of Pennsylvania Press, 1994, pp. 34–63.

See also **Asceticism; Autohagiography; Lay Piety; Laywomen, Religious; Mysticism and Mystics; Mystics' Writings; Theology.**

ANGLO-SAXON LITERATURE
See **Literature, Old English**

ANNALES SCHOOL OF HISTORY

The Annales School was a group of reform-minded French historians who published their work in a journal entitled *Annales d'Histoire Économique et Sociale*, founded at the University of Strasbourg in 1929. Medievalist Marc Bloch (1886–1944) joined with an early modern historian named Lucien Febvre (1878–1956) in an attempt to replace the highly compartmentalized writing that had characterized French historical study from the late nineteenth century onward. In 1946 the journal was renamed *Annales: Économies, Sociétés, Civilisations*. For the founders this marked a more coherent mission to create a new encompassing history—*histoire totale*—as they phrased it. According to their thinking, the discipline of history had reached a state of crisis by failing to account adequately for the disaster-ridden first half of the twentieth century. With a move to Paris in the late 1930s they became the sixth section of the *École des Hautes Études*, a centrally funded institute for study of the social sciences. This encouraged rapprochement with other social sciences (geography and economics in particular), and history became the dominant study among the social sciences in France, which was unparalleled in western countries.

Joined by Fernand Braudel (1902–1985), the Annales School advocated a comparative method rather than a search for the origins of the modern state system. Annales historians cast their histories over the long term—*la longue durée*—and favored study of the masses, mentalities, popular unrest, rise and decline in population, prices, and other features of society and economy that affected daily life. Annales School history was embraced by scholars from around the world, and certain works, like LeRoy Ladurie's study of a village in medieval France, *Montaillou* (1975), became best sellers.

It would seem that this analytic framework was adequate for including women and gender in history, but women were absent from the pages of most Annales history. Their lives and work were not part of the Annales emphasis on the masses, or on uprisings, or even, more remarkably, on population trends. This meant that the vision of *histoire totale* embraced by the school ignored half the population, a regrettable omission. The framework advocated by the school was appropriate for the study of women's daily lives and contributions to long-term change, but women were barely mentioned in the important texts of Bloch, Febvre, and Braudel.

Three initiatives begun in the 1970s changed that. The first, Ladurie's *Montaillou*, featured women's lives in a village of the Occitan that was investigated by the Inquisition for evidence of heretical leanings. The study provided anecdotal information on women's lives; indeed, the compelling persons whose stories turned the study into a best-seller were largely women. Second, Christiane Klapisch-Zuber, a member of the Annales, joined with the American historian David Herlihy to enter the data of the Florentine Catasto of 1427 into computers for analysis. This resulted in the vast *Tuscans and Their Families* (original French edition, 1978), the earliest comprehensive census data study in Western history. Women's lives and choices received significant attention, and gender became a category of analysis in this work. Klapisch-Zuber, who had become a *directeur d'etude*, followed this major study with numerous essays probing more deeply into women's lives and choices in late medieval and early Renaissance Florence. Third, Georges Duby and Michelle Perrot, who were associated with Annales scholars, produced a multivolume *Histoire des Femmes* covering ancient times to the present. This was the result of an international seminar that met beginning in 1980 in Paris under the leadership of Duby, Perrot, Klapisch-Zuber, and Pauline Schmitt Pantel. Contacts multiplied; Annales School historians collaborated with scholars from other European countries and the Americas who shared a similar vision. Among the cross-currents that came to influence the Annales was the study of gender and the new women's history.

More recently, *Clio: Histoire, Femmes et Sociétés* emerged in 1995 as a journal dedicated to women's history. As a project it reconsiders the question of female culture and attempts to integrate methodological and conceptual notions of gender into a relational history of women and men. The very name of the journal echoes *Annales: Économies, Sociétés, Civilisations*, and indeed its mission statement declares the intention of modeling itself on Annales (the school rather than the journal) in order to investigate women's history. *Clio* works to close the gap between contemporary French scholars' interest in women's history and the paradoxical lack of published scholarship on women in France. Klapisch-Zuber continues to play an important role in this project. For example, in "Guda et Claricia: Deux 'autoportraits' déminins du XIIe siècle," Klapisch-Zuber brings to light two female artists of the twelfth century who signed their names and left their silhouettes on their work. The project of women's history has become an important, if separate, project from Annales School history itself.

SUSAN MOSHER STUARD

References and Further Reading

Bloch, Marc. *Feudal Society*, translated by L. A. Manyon. Chicago: University of Chicago Press, 1962.

Braudel, Fernand. *The Mediterranean in the Age of Philip II*, translated by Sian Reynolds (from the second French edition). New York: Harper, 1976.

Burke, Peter. *The French Historical Revolution: The Annales School, 1929–1989*. Stanford, Calif.: Stanford University Press, 1990.

Duby, Georges, and Michelle Perrot. *History of Women in the West*. Cambridge, Mass.: Belknap Press of Harvard University Press, 1992–1994.

Fauré, Christine. "The Twilight of the Goddesses, or The Intellectual Crisis of French Feminism," translated by Lillian S. Robinson. *Signs, Journal of Women in Culture and Society* 7 (1981): 81–86.

Febvre, Lucien. *The Problem of Unbelief in the Sixteenth Century*, translated by Beatrice Gottlieb. Cambridge, Mass.: Harvard University Press, 1982.

Herlihy, David, and Christiane Klapisch-Zuber. *Tuscans and Their Families*. New Haven, Conn.: Yale University Press, 1985.

Klapisch-Zuber, Christiane. "Guda et Claricia: deux 'autoportraits' féminins du XII siècle." *Clio, histoire, femmes et sociétés* 19 (2004): 159–163.

———. *Women, Family, and Ritual in Renaissance Italy*, translated by Lydia Cochrane. Chicago: University of Chicago Press, 1985.

LeRoy Ladurie, Emmanuel. *Montaillou, Promised Land of Error*, translated by Barbara Bray. New York: Harper, 1979.

Stuard, Susan Mosher. "The Annales School and Feminist History." *Signs, Journal of Women in Culture and Society* 7 (1981): 135–143. Reprinted in *The Annales School, Critical Assessments*, edited by Stuart Clark. London and New York: Routledge, 1999.

Thébaud, Françoise, and Michelle Zancarini-Fournel. *Clio, Histoire, Femmes et Sociétés: naissance et histoire d'une revue*. http://clio.revues.org/document42.html (July 2005). Published in *Clio* 16 (2002).

See also **Feminist Theories and Methodologies; Gender in History; History, Medieval Women's**

ANNE OF BEAUJEU

Anne of Beaujeu (also known as Anne of France) (c. 1461–1522) was duchess of Bourbon and a steadying influence in French royal affairs. Louis XI of France (r. 1461–1483) and his second wife, Charlotte of Savoy, had three children who lived to adulthood: Anne, Jeanne, and Charles. Anne was married young to Pierre de Beaujeu, son of the duke of Bourbon. When Louis died in 1483, Anne—not her mother—was named guardian of her brother, Charles VIII (r. 1483–1498). Louis had curtailed the power of the nobles, and they tried to recoup their losses upon Charles' succession. The leader of the opposition was Louis of Orleans, husband of Anne's sister Jeanne and heir presumptive to the throne. The Beaujeus decreased resistance to their guardianship of the king by sacrificing some of Louis XI's more unpopular servants and reducing taxes. This allowed them to dominate the Estates General of 1484 and to defeat Orleans in the so-called Mad War of 1485. The Beaujeus increased French power in Brittany by marrying King Charles to Anne, the duke's heiress, kept peace with the papacy, and permitted Henry of Richmond (Henry VII) to challenge Richard III for the throne of England.

When Charles VIII took control of the government in 1491, the Beaujeus, who had become duke and duchess of Bourbon, retired to Pierre's estates, where "Madame la Grande" educated ladies of good birth. One factor in their withdrawal from government was disapproval of Charles' desire to claim the throne of Naples by force. Nonetheless, Anne governed during her brother's Italian campaign and later did the same for Louis XII (Orleans) during his wars. Anne left behind a book of lessons for her daughter Suzanne, balancing conventional values with sound political advice. Anne died in 1522, during the reign of Francis I, having outlived her siblings, husband, and daughter.

THOMAS IZBICKI

References and Further Reading

Anne of France. *Lessons for My Daughter*, translated by Sharon L. Jansen. Woodbridge, Suffolk, England: D. S. Brewer, 2004.

Jansen, Sharon L. *The Monstrous Regiment of Women: Female Rulers in Early Modern Europe*. New York: Palgrave Macmillan, 2002.

Pradel, Pierre. *Anne de France, 1461–1522*. Paris: Editions Publisud, 1986.

See also **Conduct Literature; Education, Lay; Mothers as Teachers; Noble Women; Regents and Queen-Lieutenants**

ANNE OF BOHEMIA

Anne of Bohemia (1366–1394), daughter of the Holy Roman Emperor Charles IV, married Richard II of England in 1381. Anne was initially scorned by some English contemporaries for her relative poverty and even her lack of beauty. In due course, however, she became immensely popular and was widely believed to have a calming influence on her erratic husband. Richard certainly loved her deeply. He demolished her palace at Sheen after her death.

As queen, Anne played a traditional role as merciful intercessor to the king, but the nature of her own interests is hard to determine. Her upbringing in Bohemia, home to a strong religious reform movement inspired by Jan Hus, and her advanced literacy gave her the reputation, shortly after her death, of having been a shield for English reformers (especially John Wycliffe) and their project to translate the Bible into English. On this basis, she was once claimed as one of the "nursing mothers of the Reformation," but her own religious leanings may have been highly orthodox. Chaucer associates her with Alceste, the Queen of the God of Love, who chastises Chaucer for writing the story of Criseyde's betrayal of Troilus and sets him to writing *The Legend of Good Women* as a penance.

The evidence suggests that Anne was pious, courageous, well educated, and politically astute. Her biography is largely limited to her public reputation, however, either as Richard's loyal queen (which she undoubtedly was), or Wycliffe's protector or Chaucer's censor, roles that may have been largely or entirely legendary.

ANDREW TAYLOR

References and Further Reading

Taylor, Andrew. "Anne of Bohemia and the Making of Chaucer." *Studies in the Age of Chaucer* 19 (1997): 95–119.

Thomas, Alfred. *Anne's Bohemia: Czech Literature and Society, 1310–1420.* Minneapolis: University of Minnesota Press, 1998.

Wallace, David J. "Anne of Bohemia, Queen of England and Chaucer's *Emperice.*" *Litteraria Pragensia: Studies in Literature and Culture* 5.9 (1995): 1–16.

See also **Chaucer, Geoffrey; England; Intercession; Patronage, Literary; Queens and Empresses: the West**

ANNE

Saint Anne was the apocryphal mother of the Virgin Mary and the focus of her own popular cult in the later Middle Ages. Not mentioned in the biblical account of Christ's lineage, Anne first appears in the apocryphal *Book of James* (second century), in which the birth and childhood of Mary are described.

In the early Middle Ages, Anne is a type of the sterile woman who conceives through divine intervention. With the rise of the cult of Mary, attention turned to Anne's role in Marian spirituality; debates over Mary's immaculate conception, which engaged theologians during the high Middle Ages, inevitably referred to Anne. Some believed Mary was conceived without sin by her parents' embrace before the Golden Gate of the Temple.

Another story about Anne that stimulated the imagination of writers and artists concerned her role as matriarchal founder of the Holy Kinship group. According to this narrative, Anne married three times—to Joachim, Cleophas, and Salome—each time producing a daughter named Mary. The three Marys then had sons who were Jesus and a number of his disciples. The story of the three marriages of Anne (the *trinubium*) was incorporated into the most influential legend of the later Middle Ages, Jacobus de Voragine's *Legenda aurea*, and by that route became a well-known part of biblical history for both laity and clergy. Consistently in medieval iconography, therefore, Saint Anne is represented as a holy mother. She is not only central to the lives of her daughter Mary and her grandson Jesus, but she is the founder of Jesus' matrilineal descent system, whose image was the Holy Kinship.

Theological controversies over the immaculate conception of Mary, as well as the circulation of narratives about the life of Anne and her large family, made her a popular saint in western Europe by the fourteenth century. Her feast was celebrated on July 26 in many places, and relics such as her veil at Apt or her head at Chartres stimulated pilgrimages to those shrines. Images of Saint Anne teaching the Virgin to read or sitting with both the Virgin and Christ on her lap (*Anna Selbdritt*) were common throughout Europe.

Like many medieval saints, Anne was also regarded as a saint to call on for help with specific problems of everyday life. Some of those problems were connected with her maternal and familial iconography; for example, she was regarded as one of the "marrying saints" who provided aid to married couples facing infertility. In many cases, however, prayers to Anne addressed situations unconnected to her place in the holy family. She was a patron of those in maritime vocations, a protector of those who faced the danger of voyages or storms. Elsewhere she was a patron of woodworkers, and she was often a saint to be invoked in time of plague. She was the name saint of many famous Annes, including Anne of Burgundy and Anne of Brittany. She was even adopted as the patron saint of Florence after an unpopular ruler was routed on Saint Anne's Day 1343.

The cult of Saint Anne was at its height in northern Europe around 1500, thanks to both ecclesiastical and bourgeois patronage. Numerous Lives of Anne circulated in the later fifteenth century with the support of humanist churchmen, including most notably Johannes Trithemius in his 1494 treatise, *Tractatis de Laudibus Sanctissimae Matris Annae*. Using these new texts about Anne, the ecclesiastical authorities promoted the foundation of shrines and confraternities dedicated to the saint in convent churches. There was also a significant increase in the production of paintings (often large altarpieces) with Anne and her family as subjects. In these paintings, Anne and her three daughters usually sit in a garden or enclosure with their children playing before them. The matrilineal message is emphasized since the husbands are absent or relegated to the back of the scene, peeping over the wall. Despite the matriarchal focus of Holy Kinship images, Anne and her husband Joachim could function in other sites as models for lay marriage. In their combination of piety and affluence, they represented the values of the urban middle class. By the early decades of the sixteenth century, however, the cult of Anne was under attack by reformers who denied the *trinubium* and wished to promote a male-centered Holy Family rather than the female-centered Holy Kinship. The Council of Trent (1545–1563) denigrated Saint Anne's role in sacred history with its consequent popular devotion, while art of the later sixteenth century shows Anne demoted from a powerful intercessory figure in her own right to the aged grandmother of Christ.

KATHLEEN M. ASHLEY

References and Further Reading

Ashley, Kathleen, and Pamela Sheingorn, eds. *Interpreting Cultural Symbols: Saint Anne in Late Medieval Society.* Athens, Ga.: University of Georgia Press, 1990.

Brandenbarg, Ton. "Saint Anne: A Holy Grandmother and Her Children." In *Sanctity and Motherhood: Essays on Holy Mothers in the Middle Ages*, edited by Anneke B. Muldur-Bakker. New York: Garland, 1995, pp. 31–65.

———. "St. Anne and Her Family: The Veneration of St. Anne in Connection with Concepts of Marriage and the Family in the Early Modern Period." In *Saints and She-Devils: Images of Women in the Fifteenth and Sixteenth Centuries*, edited by Lene Dresen-Coenders. London: Rubicon Press, 1987, pp. 101–127.

Nixon, Virginia. *Mary's Mother: Saint Anne in Late Medieval Europe.* University Park, Pa.: Pennsylvania State University Press, 2004.

See also **Hagiography; Holy Kinship; Immaculate Conception, Doctrine of; Mary, Virgin; Mary, Virgin: in Art**

APPRENTICES

Medieval industry was dominated by artisans, and women participated in artisan crafts, beginning their acquisition of skills as apprentices, as did men. However, overall, there were far fewer female apprentices than male in medieval Europe. Artisan industry was hierarchical, with at least three categories: apprentice or beginning employee, salaried employee or journeyman, and master, the head of a workshop. There is little, if any, evidence that women progressed to the top of this hierarchy. In a few trades, however, particularly in the region of Paris, women seem to have reached the status of master. Seven of the over one hundred guilds in Paris were led by women in the late thirteenth century. Women might also enjoy elevated status in a craft as the wives of guild masters. In other guilds across Europe, a woman could, at times, succeed to master status at the death of her husband. Overall, widows represented two to five percent of guild membership.

Female apprentices were recruited to those sectors of the medieval artisan industry in which women were most prominent: the food trades, encompassing occupations such as baker and brewster, and a host of occupations associated with the textile industries, including spinster, silk worker, gold thread spinner, and purse maker. Female guilds were concentrated in the luxury industry and export trade. Parisian female guilds focused on spinning silk and making decorative items, ribbons, head wear, and purses. Here women supervised the apprenticeship contracts of their workers. Women in Cologne had specialties in silk and in spinning of gold. In Rouen women were involved in guild activities and very likely trained and employed apprentices.

Geographically, the age of apprenticeship might differ, but the practical age of majority for women in the Middle Ages was twelve, and in Mediterranean Europe one finds contracts of apprenticeship binding women from approximately that age. For boys, fourteen was the age of majority. For both men and women, the legal age of majority followed the lead of Roman law at twenty-five.

Geographically, female apprentices might come from some distance to a large town to learn a trade. In general, boys and men came from farther afield and were recruited to a larger cross-section of trades than were girls and women. In terms of the length of apprenticeship, again, there is great variation. In Montpellier, the important distinction was not gender, but whether apprentices were of local or non-local origin, the latter dictating, in the case of both boys and girls, longer terms of apprenticeship. Then too, trades varied in the length of training required, and an apprentice's previous experience, most often unknown to the historian, might also affect the duration. Surviving apprenticeship contracts in Montpellier show women apprenticed two years for basket making and secondhand clothes marketing, while in tailoring, six years might be necessary, and in mercery work (ribbons, accessories, fabric adornments), eight years. There is one instance of a girl of twelve apprenticed ten years in the baking trade. Women generally did not apprentice themselves without the participation of a parent or relative, and the presence and authorization of a male relative were common. Boys of fourteen might apprentice themselves alone, but again, if they were foreigners, they usually had need of a sponsor or surety to vouch for them.

Apprenticeship arrangements included the length of time of indenture; the cost of training and/or the nature of support (whether in kind, in salary, or both) offered by the master; arrangements should the apprentice fall ill; the type of instruction offered; the requirements of the engagement, such as no departure before the end of the contractual term; and loyalty to the master. Contracts were binding and could carry penalties if breached. Generally, the structure of apprenticeship contracts was similar for men and women. Apprenticeship agreements survive for two English women from Yorkshire and Lincolnshire, to learn silkwork from the wives of London citizens. They were apprenticed to seven-year terms, with expectations of good behavior, loyalty to their masters, and stability in the household. In return, they were to receive instruction in their trade, discipline if necessary, food, clothing, and other necessities. In this case no payment was forthcoming, but there are instances where apprentices were paid. The apprenticeship contracts of southern Europe provide the same type of information regarding living conditions, arrangements in apprenticeship, recompense or the lack thereof for labor, and details on apprentice/master/mistress relations.

There is some suggestion that over time occupations such as the cloth industry became more male-dominated, with opportunities for women's participation diminished. In the late Middle Ages and early modern era, guild regulations were tightened as sworn corporations emerged. Future case studies can serve to pinpoint the specifics of women's experience in apprenticeship across a broad chronology and geography.

KATHRYN REYERSON

References and Further Reading

Bennett, Judith M., Elizabeth A. Clark, Jean F. O'Barr, and B. Anne Vilen, eds. *Sisters and Workers in the Middle Ages*. Chicago: The University of Chicago Press, 1989.
Epstein, Steven A. *Wage Labor and Guilds in Medieval Europe*. Chapel Hill and London: The University of North Carolina Press, 1991.
Hanawalt, Barbara A., ed. *The Evolution of Adolescence in Europe*. Special issue of *The Journal of Family History* 17 (1992).

See also **Alewives and Brewing; Artisan Families, Women of; Girls and Boys; Guild Members and Guilds; Textile Production for the Market; Widows; Work**

ARCHAEOLOGY

From the inception of archaeology as a professional discipline in late-nineteenth-century Europe, scholars frequently overlooked women as subjects of study and undervalued their roles in early societies. Despite the growing impact of second-wave feminism on academia as early as the 1960s, inequities in archaeology characterized by andocentric approaches were only redressed beginning in the mid-1980s. Reasons for the delay included the relative under-representation of women as professional archaeologists, the historic tendency to denigrate or underestimate women's creative, economic, and artistic contributions in prehistoric and more recent societies, and hesitation to embrace the concept of gender as a social construct rather than as an accurate reflection of biological sex. Now that most archaeologists have accepted gender as a legitimate category of research, greater attention is being paid not only to the changing aspects of women's labor, sexuality, and familial roles in various societies but also to related questions regarding the expression of masculinity, the nature and significance of homosexuality, and the constant evolution of gender-linked characteristics and activities.

Challenging Traditional Archaeology

On the whole, medieval archaeologists have been relatively slow to incorporate theory in comparison with their colleagues in anthropology and prehistoric archaeology, and thus the impact of gender approaches has been far less revolutionary. As opposed to the fields in which feminist scholars first sought to demonstrate the existence of matriarchal, or at least egalitarian, social hierarchies in hunter–gatherer communities, medieval archaeology has evolved more cautiously. Constrained by the written evidence of social mores for the period, gender archaeologists studying the medieval period have worked within the framework imposed by late pagan and early Christian descriptions of human activity in western Europe. Informed by gender methodology, however, they ask different questions of the evidence, and their discussions have stimulated long-overdue improvements in the excavation, conservation, display, and interpretation of medieval archaeological artifacts, monuments, and sites.

Early Middle Ages

In early medieval archaeology, the majority of studies traditionally focused on graves and cemeteries. Because burials often contained a large variety of artifacts in addition to skeletal remains, they were found with regularity in western Europe from the time of the Industrial Revolution, when the laying of rail lines, digging of ditches, and construction of new buildings occurred on an unprecedented scale. Before the advent of carbon 14 dating, the sites discovered with coinage and artifacts had the advantage of being more easily dated to specific chronological periods. Even those without coins might be classified and thus dated by their typological similarity to finds elsewhere. Although antiquaries and archaeologists initially used remains from early medieval cemeteries and churches to reinforce stereotypes of women as passive reflections of the status, wealth, and ethnic identity of their husbands or fathers, today these mortuary finds are being employed for very different objectives. Because sepulchers afforded families the opportunity to construct idealized portrayals of their deceased members, with gender identity comprising one facet of such images, grave remains represent an important source for understanding the contributions of women to kin and community.

Archaeologists have, therefore, used a combination of evidence from early medieval burial sites to challenge assumptions and create a more nuanced understanding of the division of labor, gender norms and expectations, and the gendering of space in the early Middle Ages. At the cemetery of Villey-St-Etienne in northern Gaul, for instance, despite the fact that grave #6 was enormous in size, the skeleton of a woman found inside it was accompanied by few grave goods; in this case, we may observe tension between the effort expended to bury her and the decision not to deposit the quantity and quality of artifacts usually found in a sepulcher of these dimensions. Although the interpretation of this site must remain uncertain since no written sources survive to document her identity or the circumstances in which she died, it has been proposed that she may have been a widow of high standing for whom grave goods were

no longer considered necessary or desirable. Rather than reading this grave as symptomatic of lack of recognition of the status of women in early medieval society, archaeologists are now open to seeing more subtle distinctions in the expression of status since the woman's possessions may have indeed been handed down to her heirs.

As more accurate techniques for the biological sexing of skeletons through osteological and DNA analysis have been developed, early medieval archaeologists and anthropologists have been able to reassess sepulchers in which the occupants were originally sexed by means of the artifacts with which they were buried rather than through methods independent of the archaeological context. Although only a limited number of graves have been discovered in which there were discrepancies between biological sex and gender (in other words, graves containing artifacts normally not associated with a particular sex), improved methodology has allowed scholars to present a more nuanced picture of the ways in which gender ideology affected burial. Moreover, as the chemical and biological study of human heredity and disease have grown increasingly sophisticated, specialists have also had the opportunity to explore nutrition, congenital illnesses and genetic traits, epidemics, and physical injuries, and the ways they comparatively affected the male and female members of early medieval populations.

While cemeteries have enabled archaeologists to study everything from early medieval social structure to production and trade, research on early medieval habitation, by contrast, is still in its relative infancy, and only in recent decades have there been more consistent efforts made to excavate exceptional examples of intact villages, for instance, in their entirety. While it is more difficult to ascribe activities at such sites to individuals of specific gender, since normally it is not possible to identify precisely who was engaged in the production of ceramics or the baking of bread, there have been fairly successful attempts to contextualize these occupations through comparison with paraphernalia found at contemporary furnished graves and written descriptions of such activities. As in the study of any society, however, it is clearly more useful to avoid establishing absolute gender associations with specific activities. Gender-linked roles were dynamic and repeatedly negotiated within specific communities; they therefore varied by region and period. Weaving and beer making, which were traditionally understood as women's work in the early Middle Ages, were both activities appropriated by men as the increasingly lucrative labor was professionalized by late medieval guilds across western Europe.

Central and Late Middle Ages

With respect to the central and late Middle Ages, mortuary archaeology has not had the same broad impact as it has for earlier periods, due in part to the difficulty of identifying graves from the era, since most lack archaeological artifacts. Moreover, the heavy reuse of late medieval Christian cemeteries in or near churches resulted in the frequent exportation of bones to ossuaries, charnel houses, or catacombs. Therefore, few sites remained undisturbed. Many former cemeteries were also subsequently occupied for other purposes, such as housing and manufacturing complexes, as city suburbs were more intensively occupied in the early modern period and later. Although there have certainly been exceptions, like intensive studies undertaken of leper cemeteries and church burials, late medieval mortuary archaeology has focused more on art historical studies of grave inscriptions and monuments than on the human remains they contained.

The majority of late medieval archaeological excavations have focused on the architectural remains of religious foundations, castles and fortresses, and production sites such as ports and royal and monastic workshops. In these analyses, theory has not found a significant voice, despite the fact that these locations afford important opportunities for the exploration of notions of gender. Although late medieval archaeology has often served as the handmaid of history rather than functioning as an independent discipline in such contexts, archaeologists since the 1990s have begun to ask questions about the divisions existing in or alternative uses of religious space, domestic households, feasting halls, and other features of elite ways of life. In conjunction with contemporary historical and literary evidence, these studies demonstrate that gender archaeology is a very useful tool by which to document and supplement the written record, since the field has great potential and may provide new insight into late medieval culture in ways previously unanticipated by specialists in the field.

BONNIE EFFROS

References and Further Reading

Conkey, Margaret W., and Janet D. Spector. "Archaeology and the Study of Gender." *Advances in Archaeological Method and Theory* 7 (1984): 1–38.

Effros, Bonnie. "Skeletal Sex and Gender in Merovingian Mortuary Archaeology." *Antiquity* 74 (2000): 632–639.

Gilchrist, Roberta. *Gender and Archaeology: Contesting the Past.* London: Routledge, 1999.

———. *Gender and Material Culture: The Archaeology of Religious Women.* London: Routledge, 1994.

Halsall, Guy. "Female Status and Power in Early Merovingian Central Austrasia: The Burial Evidence." *Early Medieval Europe* 5(1) (1996): 1–24.

Moore, Jenny, and Eleanor Scott, eds. *Individual People and Processes: Writing Gender and Sexuality into European Archaeology.* London: Leicester University Press, 1997.

Sørensen, Marie Louise Stig. *Gender Archaeology.* Cambridge: Polity Press, 2000.

Walde, D., and N. D. Willows, eds. *The Archaeology of Gender: Proceedings of the 22nd Chacmool Conference.* Calgary: University of Calgary Archaeological Association, 1991.

See also **Architecture, Domestic; Burials and Tombs; Death, Mourning, and Commemoration; Division of Labor; Gender Ideologies; Grave Goods; Lepers**

ARCHITECTURE, DOMESTIC

Gender was constituted notably in the context of architectural and settlement space, that is, both in the rooms which men and women frequented within buildings and in the layout of the wider settlement. In the medieval process of classifying female and male bodies, architectural segregation was fundamental for the social definition of values of masculinity and femininity, in monastic as well as in secular contexts. Such constructed values differed according to social status, so that the relationship of space and gender varied considerably across the settlement hierarchy, from hamlet or village to town or castle.

Like any other form of material culture, the architecture of segregation had many meanings that were also subject to change. The disposition of buildings and their interiors, different access and mobility, and materials and notions of permanence comprised gendered meaning and served as a stage for gendered performance. One sees the everyday experience of gender difference in the arena and architecture of domestic space.

Gendering Space

Investigation of access into buildings allows an objective identification of the degree of control and privacy, indicated by the relative position of a room within a structure. Such access analysis can show how social and gender relations within the household were architecturally arranged. Rooms reached immediately from the street may be seen as public space. They are unlikely to have been understood as private apartments, access to which was limited to selected members of the household. Such private spaces were located more deeply within the floor plan.

The relationship between gender and domestic buildings may be complicated by several issues, particularly the difficulty of distinguishing spaces that were specifically designed for, or used by, one sex rather than the other. Homes were often workplaces, and the same room might have been used for a variety of domestic and production purposes. Smaller houses had to be especially flexible in how their space was used. In the context of the medieval town, for instance, female and male routines surely coincided regularly. Moreover, the architecture of the urban home was a reflection of other kinds of status apart from gender. Class became more important in the design of the later medieval town houses. Accommodations for poorer urban dwellers—typical cottages containing no more than two rooms—offered no place for segregation; but overlapping spatial gender identities could be found even in the largest urban houses. The organization of domestic space into "safe," that is, female, and "dangerous," that is, male, zones may have been an influential ideal realized only in the wealthiest houses. The peasant home seems to have been a predominantly female domain for much of the year. Gender spheres there are likely to have been seasonal, with men in the house for greater periods during winter.

A larger number of existing or developing architectural and spatial subdivisions could lead to further and more explicit gendered distinctions. At least for urban England, an increase of gendered spatial differentiation may be assumed for the second half of the fifteenth century, when craft workshops became increasingly masculinized and mercantile households increasingly feminized. Detailed analysis, however, is often complicated by research problems with regard to dating and the chronology of change. In particular, the knowledge of the date of surviving buildings and how they were used and developed is often not sufficient to allow an easy correlation between changes in building type and short-term changes in social practice.

Upper-class women's accommodations were situated with an emphasis on privacy and comfort, embellished by warmth, rich colors, and soft textures. Technological inventions and developments influenced the gendered functionality of rooms. The adoption of the indoor chimney and fireplace, first in wealthier homes of the twelfth and thirteenth century, fostered the small room and increased the trend toward privacy. The bower (that is, a solar reserved for the lady of the house) became an essential part of domestic accommodation in castles. Moreover, such enhanced privacy affected intimacy and sexual mores.

The bodies of high-status women classified through gender also had to be hidden from strangers through architectural mechanisms of segregation and enclosure that included towers, private facilities for worship, exclusively female households, and physical boundaries such as walls, gardens, and other filtering systems like fences, gates, or staircases, which regulated access. The castle provides a good case for understanding the meaning of such gender segregation in the upper-class milieu. From the eleventh to the fifteenth century, the specific forms of the English castle developed and changed, until eventually the military and domestic functions were disjoined. The military role of the castle constituted its personification as a purely masculine domain. The female quarters were positioned in the segregated innermost and uppermost spaces of the castles, at the greatest distance from the main entrance. From their elevated and segregated position, women would have enjoyed substantial views of the castle interior while remaining out of view themselves. Increasing status seems to have been accompanied by greater segregation of the households for male and female members of the castle. The bias towards female segregation is obvious even where women appear to have been active in commissioning their quarters. This tendency represents an example of the way in which women were both active in interpreting material culture and complicit with it.

For English royal castles and palaces, it can also be shown that the queen's chambers were less permeable than those of the king from more "public" areas. The apartments of the queen were isolated from the ceremonial routes through the palace complexes. This segregation is evident not only in their siting, often close to gardens and courtyards, but also in the contemplative imagery within. While historical and architectural developments can be revealed that made their mark on kings' apartments, the general layout and position of queens' chambers appear to have remained constant. Changes in the function of the palace and the evolution of the household seem to have passed them by.

Issues of domestic architecture in the context of gendered performance were used metaphorically. Medieval medicine explained the physiology of the body through architectural metaphors, with the body's interior perceived as contained, domestic, and feminine. "Interior space, be it of the house or of the body, is a feminine place" (Henry de Mondeville, *Chirurgie*, Montpellier, 1306–1320).

The castle also became a metaphor for the female body, as a tabernacle protecting the precious virginity kept within. Architectural space was used to construct and reinforce a gendering of women's bodies that emphasized chastity and purity. The iconographic representation of chastity could be the tower, which had a central function in the martyrdom stories of the virgin saints, especially Saint Barbara, whose attribute it was.

GERHARD JARITZ

References and Further Reading

Dresbeck, LeRoy. "The Chimney and Social Change in Medieval England." *Albion* 3 (1971): 21–32.

Durning, Louise. "Woman on Top: Lady Margaret Beaufort's Buildings." In *Gender and Architecture*, edited by Louise Durning and Richard Wrigley. New York: Wiley, 1999, pp. 45–56.

Fairclough, Graham. "Meaningful Constructions: Spatial and Functional Analysis of Medieval Buildings." *Antiquity* 66 (1992): 348–366.

Gilchrist, Roberta. "Medieval Bodies in the Material World: Gender, Stigma and the Body." In *Framing Medieval Bodies*, edited by Sarah Kay and Miri Rubin. Manchester: Manchester University Press, 1994, pp. 43–61.

———. "Ambivalent Bodies: Gender and Medieval Archaeology." In *Invisible People and Processes: Writing Gender and Childhood into European Archaeology*, edited by Eleanor Scott and Jenny Moore. London: Leicester University Press, 1996, pp. 42–58.

———. *Gender and Archaeology: Contesting the Past.* London and New York: Routledge, 1999.

Grenville, Jane. "Houses and Households in Late Medieval England: An Archaeological Perspective." In *Medieval Women: Text and Contexts in Late Medieval Britain. Essays for Felicity Riddy*, edited by Jocelyn Wogan-Browne et al. Turnhout, Belgium: Brepols, 2000, pp. 309–328.

Rees Jones, Sarah. "Women's Influence on the Design of Urban Homes." In *Gendering the Master Narrative: Women and Power in the Middle Ages*, edited by Mary C. Erler and Maryanne Kowaleski. Ithaca, N.Y.: Cornell University Press, 2003, pp. 190–211.

Richardson, Amanda. "Gender and Space in English Royal Palaces c. 1160–c. 1547: A Study in Access Analysis and Imagery." *Medieval Archaeology* 47 (2003): 131–165.

See also **Castles and Palaces; Private and Public Spheres; Social Status; Space, Secular: and Gender**

ARCHITECTURE, ECCLESIASTICAL

Women have been centrally involved with the Christian religion from its earliest phases and played a prominent role in the events of the New Testament. Within several centuries of the founding of Christianity, however, the role of women in the church leadership and their physical location in religious space became marginalized, and they were progressively excluded from the hierarchy. However, evidence of gender separation within sacred space, although probable, is difficult to document before the sixth century in the east, and probably the seventh century in Rome.

In the Byzantine tradition, where churches were constructed with upper galleries, there is evidence that women were relegated to these spaces during liturgical services. In Roman architecture, generally basilican (that is to say, longitudinal as opposed to centralized) in plan, there are some indications that women occupied the north (left) aisle, sometimes separated from the nave by curtains suspended between the columns of the arcade. Mosaics occasionally suggest curtains as a form of separation between men and women in church interiors (at Sant'Apollinare Nuovo in Ravenna, for example). In some churches, the location of women was restricted to a small area of the church, sometimes at the west: this was the case, for example, in the twelfth century at Durham Cathedral in England, where women were not allowed beyond the westernmost piers of the nave.

The exclusion of women, or their separation from the main body of the church, is especially common in male monasticism, although important noble or royal female patrons were often allowed some access to the main sanctuary.

Rules and regulations on the separation of women religious from clergy and the lay congregation were particularly strict during periods of religious reform. The Gregorian reform of the eleventh century, and in particular the strictures of clerical celibacy, led to increased misogyny within the church and in literature produced by clerics. There is clear evidence of this in the context of women's monasticism, where strictures on enclosure became strikingly more rigid in the thirteenth century, especially in female branches of the new Mendicant orders; a particular example is the strict active enclosure of the Poor Clares (or Clarisses). This process culminated in the papal Bull *Pericoloso,* promulgated by Boniface VIII in 1300, in which strict enclosure was imposed upon all female communities of any order. There is evidence of opposition and resistance, as there was to be again with the renewed strictures imposed as a result of the Tridentine reform of the sixteenth century. In the sixteenth and seventeenth centuries, partly as a result of the early modern attempts at reform, Naples and Palermo developed particular types of raised choirs for nuns located above and behind the main altar, as well as high raised exterior loggias that gave a distant and protected view of the cities.

One important effect of the containment of women in reserved and enclosed sections of churches was their separation from the sacraments. This emerges quite clearly in the disposition of nuns' choirs, which were sometimes raised on balconies at the west end of the nave (for example, at Vadstena), from which they were further separated by a screen or a grill. Although the evidence of these arrangements is not always unambiguous, it is clear that in some examples the women religious would not have been able to see the elevation of the host at the altar. The examination of other surviving nunneries suggests that there was little, if any, visual participation in the Mass by choirs placed beside or behind the altar. The experience of the sacred thus seems to have become largely auditory rather than visual; this phenomenon has been associated with theories of the permeability (and lack of control) of the female body deriving from ancient philosophy and medicine.

There has been a long-standing association between the spaces allocated for women and the north side of the church. Representations of the Virgin Mary tend to locate her on the north (left) side of Christ (in scenes of the Coronation of the Virgin, or the Crucifixion, for example). This practice was confirmed not only in medieval parish practice (women seated on the north), but frequently also in burials.

Women have been notable patrons of ecclesiastical architecture and its decoration. Indeed, the role of women in founding churches and in pious works started in the earliest years of Christianity. In the Middle Ages, noble and royal women were conspicuous patrons of church decoration, as in the case of Queen Blanche of Castile, donor of the north transept rose window at Chartres Cathedral and the founder of the Cistercian convents of Maubuisson and Lys, both near Paris.

Perhaps one of the most important and striking periods of female patronage, however, is the late thirteenth and early fourteenth centuries in Europe in relation to the Mendicant orders (especially the Dominicans and Franciscans). Royal women played a pivotal role in the founding and building of churches and monasteries for both male and female communities of these orders, and they often requested burial for themselves and their families within the church. Striking examples are the nunneries of Pedralbes in Barcelona, Sta. Chiara in Naples, and Longchamp near Paris. The tie between royal women and the Franciscans was especially close.

A great many churches are dedicated to female saints, especially virgins and martyrs from the early Christian period (Saint Pudenziana, Saint Praessede, Saint Cecilia, Saint Restituta, Saint Catherine of Alexandria). But starting most conspicuously in the twelfth century and under the influence of Saint Bernard of Clairvaux, churches were increasingly dedicated to the Virgin Mary. The Virgin is also associated in particular with the main chapel on the central axis of large churches, and in the thirteenth century this developed into the phenomenon of lady chapels, especially frequent in Great Britain, where these became large and partially separate spaces behind the main altar, and sometimes, as at Ely, on the north side. Axial lady chapels can be seen at Salisbury and Wells cathedrals.

CAROLINE BRUZELIUS

References and Further Reading

Barber, C. "The Imperial Panels at San Vitale: A Reconsideration." *Byzantine and Modern Greek Studies* XIV (1990): 19–42.

Bruzelius, C. "Hearing Is Believing: Clarissan Architecture 1212–1340." *Gesta* XXXI (1992): 83–92. Reprinted in *Medieval Religion: New Approaches,* edited by C. Berman. Routledge, 2005, pp. 272–289.

———. "Nuns in Space: Strict Enclosure and the Architecture of the Clarisses in the Thirteenth Century." In *Clare of Assisi: A Medieval and Modern Woman,* edited by Ingrid Peterson. The Franciscan Institute, 1996, pp. 53–74.

———. "Queen Sancia of Mallorca and the Church of Sta. Chiara in Naples." *Memoirs of the American Academy in Rome* 40 (1995): 41–72.

Bynum, Caroline Walker. *Holy Feast and Holy Fast: The Significance of Food to Medieval Women.* Berkeley, Calif.: University of California Press, 1988.

de Benedictis, E. "The Senatorium and Matroneum in the Early Roman Church." *Rivista di Archeologia Cristiana* LVII (1965): 69–85.

Elliott, J., and C. Warr. *The Church of Santa Maria Donna Regina: Art, Iconography and Patronage in Fourteenth-Century Naples.* Burlington, Vt.: Ashgate Publishing, 2004.

Gilchrist, R. *Gender and Material Culture: The Archaeology of Religious Women.* London: Routledge, 1994.

Matthews, T. "An Early Roman Chancel Arrangement and Its Liturgical Uses." *Rivista di Archeologia Cristiana* XXXVIII (1965): 73–95.

Nichols, J. A., and L. T. Shank., eds. *Medieval Religious Women: Distant Echoes.* Kalamazoo, Mich.: Cistercian Publications, 1984.

Rosenwein, B. "Inaccessible Cloisters: Gregory of Tours and Episcopal Exemption." In *The World of Gregory the Great,* edited by K. Mitchell and I. Wood. Leiden: Brill, 2002, pp. 181–198.

Smith, J. "Women at the Tomb: Access to Relic Shrines in the Early Middle Ages." In *The World of Gregory the Great,* edited by K. Mitchell and I. Wood. Leiden: Brill, 2002, pp. 163–180.

See also **Architecture, Monastic; Blanche of Castile; Mary, Virgin; Misogyny; Monastic Enclosure; Monasticism and Nuns; Patronage, Artistic; Patronage, Ecclesiastical; Space, Sacred: and Gender**

ARCHITECTURE, MONASTIC

The architecture of monasticism, and especially that of major religious orders (Benedictines, Cistercians), is a rich and well-studied subject, but the buildings of women's communities received almost no attention until about 1990. The subject is therefore still in its infancy, in spite of a series of important and ground-breaking studies that took place in the fifteen or so years after 1990.

Sparse Evidence

There are still many difficulties, however: often the monasteries of women religious were especially vulnerable to the ravages of the Reformation, the Dissolution, and the ensuing religious wars. In France, the Revolution led to the almost complete obliteration of the monastic complexes of women. Greater evidence survives in Spain and Portugal, but here little historical or archaeological research has been undertaken and published. The best evidence for women's communities thus comes from those countries where there has been a continuous Catholic tradition and where women's monasticism has survived (Italy, Portugal, Spain). Yet (ironically) these structures, when still part of practicing communities, are difficult to study precisely because the rules of strict enclosure prohibit access to the internal spaces and often the archives, if they survive. As a rule, however, historical documentation of women's monasticism is either poor or entirely lacking. In the rare cases where monastic architecture does survive, it often does so in fragmentary form, as the economic conditions of nunneries, changes in the interpretation of the religious life, and, above all, the changes imposed by the regulations of the Council of Trent led to many modifications.

It should also be noted that in certain periods, and above all in the thirteenth century, women religious "inherited" or were given monastic complexes (often Benedictine) that had been designed and built for male communities; it is therefore sometimes difficult to differentiate the buildings of nuns from the (earlier) structures of male monasticism. This was particularly true of the monasteries established for the new female orders of the thirteenth century, such as those of the Poor Clares (or Clarisses), who were often installed in structures that were formerly occupied by Benedictine communities. Examples can be found at San Pietro in Vineis in Anagni, San Sebastiano outside Alatri, and San Silvestro and Santi Cosma e Damiano (San Cosimato) in Rome.

Archaeology has provided some of the most important evidence for early female communities, and here exceptional work has been done in Great Britain (Gilchrist, 1994). Other types of sources, such as the sixth-century rule written for a women's community by Caesarius of Arles, are important also. In all these instances, however, the student should recall that communities often underwent considerable change from one decade to another: choirs were moved, expanded, or contracted in relation to internal as well as external pressures. An excellent case in point is the location of the nuns' choir at Sta. Chiara in Assisi after c. 1260, which seems to have undergone numerous changes in location and character within the first decades of its existence.

There is one further consideration: monastic buildings were sometimes made of perishable materials, such as mud, cob, and wood. These types of structures can only be retrieved by archaeology, and then only at foundation level. The picture that we are now able to reconstruct of women's monasticism may, therefore, be biased in favor of those with more permanent, stone structures.

The Difficulties of Generalization

Under these circumstances, it is hazardous to generalize about monastic architecture for women. As numerous historians have noted, it is also true that women's houses tended to have greater economic difficulties than their male counterparts: the foundations were often smaller, and the nuns frequently depended upon male advisors or supervisors for the disposition and maintenance of their buildings, properties, and farms. Monasteries and their properties were also particularly vulnerable to attack or usurpation. Although women's monasteries were often initially established (in accordance with the Benedictine tradition) outside city walls, they were often moved to within cities or to suburban areas for greater protection. With few exceptions, it is only in the late twelfth and thirteenth centuries that we have evidence of monumental establishments founded by women for women, such as Pedralbes (Barcelona) and Sta. Chiara (Naples). This was the result of the development of a wave of spirituality and patronage among royal or noble women in particular, and it was particularly directed towards the Poor Clares.

As a result of these considerations, the architecture of women religious needs to be considered and studied with a different approach from that of male monasticism, as the creation of typologies and filiations is not often an effective tool for the study of women's houses. Rarely is there evidence of concern for a consistency of plan or layout within different orders of women's monasticism, nor did these institutions tend to have the organizational structures of general chapters or internal visitation that often existed among men's communities.

The evidence suggests that sometimes the architectural context was developed as much from domestic architecture as from an ecclesiastical tradition. This is especially true of urban communities, and it is a striking feature of some of the houses of the Beguines in the north. However, in other areas, such as parts of Umbria in Italy, the architectural structures of women's houses were closest to those of hermitages and anchoritic cells.

The anchoritic tradition is often evident in the modifications made to monastic churches converted to the use of a religious community of women. A good example of this phenomenon is the church of San Damiano outside Assisi, a small parish church modified for the use of women by the addition of a small choir beside the apse. Here, as in many structures for nuns, there may have been no direct view from the nun's choir of the altar, so that the liturgy was heard rather than seen by the female community. The separation of women from the altar and the resulting attenuation of their relationship to the Eucharist is one of the central features of monastic architecture for women, and this phenomenon may account for the high level of mysticism in many communities of religious women.

Enclosure

Although in the early medieval period there was considerable fluidity between male and female communities, or between monastic women and the lay public, the issue of enclosure soon became a central concept in the design of monastic spaces for women. Already in the sixth century, Caesarius of Arles mentioned that the nuns were prohibited from going into the church. The complexities of enclosure concerned the relationship of women religious not only to the lay public but also to the clergy, whose presence was essential for the administration of the sacraments. This was also the case in houses where there were communities of men and women, as at Fontevrault in the Anjou; here the women's community in the nave was distanced from the main altar by the choir of the male religious, and the separate spaces of the church were divided by metal grills. Elsewhere, the female community may have been separated by a wooden or masonry wall: Gilchrist (1994) proposed a reconstruction of St. Brigit's church in Kildare with a longitudinal wall between the male and female communities. This type of architecture is frequently found in the design of medieval hospitals, where men and women were also segregated from each other.

Women's monastic architecture was thus often modest and "domestic," in keeping with this tendency towards a less formalized architectural environment,

but on the other hand it tended towards greater rigidity in the internal divisions of space between the areas accessible to the clergy and public and those identified for the nuns. Here there are also difficulties in understanding the material, as the internal dispositions of nunneries have often been changed on many occasions, especially in relation to reform movements (including Boniface VIII's bull, *Pericoloso*, of 1300 and the Counter-Reformation); it is therefore often difficult, if not impossible, to reconstruct the original character of the internal divisions of the Middle Ages.

Women's Role

Another aspect of women's monasticism that merits far more study is the role of women themselves in designing and determining the spaces of the communities in which they lived as nuns or which they had founded, or both. There are scattered indications of women religious shaping the spaces for their communities; the most conspicuous example is perhaps St. Birgitta of Sweden, whose churches were designed to serve double communities of men and women, whose paths, however, were not to intersect. There developed as a result a series of churches made up of suspended choirs and altars for the nuns, those for the women facing east, and the choir of the male community facing west (Vadstena, Sweden). Elsewhere in Europe, a series of late thirteenth- and early fourteenth-century queens were instrumental in the foundation and design of a series of women's monasteries; perhaps the most famous of these is Queen Sancia of Mallorca in Naples, whose great double house of Sta. Chiara (which had both Clarissan and Franciscan communities) was designed on a scale unprecedented at the time. Here the devotion of the queen to the consecrated host led not only to the original dedication of the church to *Corpus Domini*, but also to the location of the nuns' choir directly behind the altar, so that the women would have a privileged view of the elevated and consecrated host. In the case of Queen Sancia, she was part of what has been described as a "feminine surge" towards the Franciscans in the late medieval period: queens and princesses everywhere in Europe, from Portugal to the British Isles, were avid patrons of the Poor Clares and Franciscans, and often retired to these houses when they became widows. Perhaps the earliest figure in this movement was St. Elisabeth of Hungary (Thuringia), who established a model for charitable and pious noblewomen and who was canonized soon after her death in 1231. Isabelle, younger sister of Louis IX of France, who entered the Clarissan monastery of Longchamp, was another important example for religious women.

Surviving examples of monasteries tend to be those of large-scale and lavishly funded houses. A certain number survive in Germany from the tenth century forward; some of these were prestigious noble or imperial foundations (for example, Essen, Gernrode) in which it would appear that the female community occupied the galleries over the aisles, or, in the case of Essen, the upper story of a *westwerk* modeled on the palatine chapel at Aachen. In Germany, Scandinavia, and eastern Europe it appears to have been quite standard for the nuns' choir to be placed in an upper gallery at the western end of the church (Konigsfelden).

In Italy and Spain, there appears to have been a greater preference for choirs at ground level, often placed adjacent to or behind the apse. These were often *ad hoc* arrangements or additions made when a monastery was converted for the use of religious women. In some cases, however, the location of the choir seems strikingly original: at San Pietro in Vineis, in Anagni, for example, a nuns' choir was installed above the south aisle by raising the aisle roof to the level of the roof over the nave; in this case, the small openings that had originally served as windows now became "listening holes" so that the community could hear the liturgy below. At the nunnery of San Sebastiano in Alatri, on the other hand, which had also previously been a Benedictine monastery, the choir was installed in an upper room to the west of the nave; there was some sort of opening (replaced in modern times by a door) in the upper wall between the two spaces. The choirs usually had a niche carved into the wall for the reserved host and were often adjacent to the dormitory. In the case of Anagni and Alatri, the degree of separation of the nuns' space from the church may suggest that the term "oratory" is more appropriate than "choir."

Austerity and Art

The form and scale of the other monastic buildings was usually in keeping with the simplicity and austerity of the church and choir. In simpler and poorer foundations, there was often no cloister, but simply a square court, sometimes with one covered walkway. Apart from the great royal and noble foundations of the late thirteenth and early fourteenth centuries, there is little evidence of the types of sophisticated plumbing and water-supply systems that were developed for male monasticism. The most secluded part of a nunnery was usually the dormitory, while the spaces in which contact was permitted with either the clergy (especially for confession) or lay visitors tended to be located near the entrance to the church or alongside the apse.

One important element of monastic architecture for women was its decoration. Choirs were often painted with narrative cycles of frescoes of considerable importance. At Sta. Chiara in Naples, for example, the artist Giotto was employed by the king and queen to execute a cycle of frescoes in the choir that depicted the Apocalypse, among other subjects (very little survives of this program). Elsewhere, choirs were decorated with narrative scenes of the lives of saints or cycles of the life and passion of Christ. These pictorial cycles would have been an important counterpart to the sound of the liturgy and also would have served as patterns for pious meditation.

As part of urban and population growth in the late thirteenth century, the focus of women's monastic life moved into the city, and the pattern of monastic vocation shifted from Benedictine to Mendicant. Whereas earlier monasticism for women had been supported by aristocratic patronage, the new types of houses were associated with lay and communal piety. Zarri noted in 1973 that in Bologna in 1250 the number of women's houses had grown from seven to thirty-six. This phenomenon was parallel with that of pious women (*pinzochere*) who lived lives of penitence, good works, and mystical experience in a domestic context without taking monastic vows. Women's communities often found far more sympathetic support among the Mendicant friars.

CAROLINE BRUZELIUS

References and Further Reading

Bond, James. "English Medieval Nunneries: Buildings, Precincts, and Estates." In *Women and Religion in Medieval England*, edited by Diana Wood. Oxford: Oxbow Books, 2003, pp. 46–90.

Bruzelius, C. "Hearing Is Believing: Clarissan Architecture 1212–1340." *Gesta* XXXI (1992): 83–92. Reprinted in *Medieval Religion: New Approaches*, edited by C. Berman. Routledge, 2005, pp. 272–289.

———. "Nuns in Space: Strict Enclosure and the Architecture of the Clarisses in the Thirteenth Century." In *Clare of Assisi: A Medieval and Modern Woman*, edited by Ingrid Peterson. The Franciscan Institute, 1996, pp. 53–74.

———. "Queen Sancia of Mallorca and the Church of Sta. Chiara in Naples." *Memoirs of the American Academy in Rome* 40 (1995): 41–72.

Bynum, Caroline Walker. *Holy Feast and Holy Fast: The Significance of Food to Medieval Women*. Berkeley, Calif.: University of California Press, 1988.

Elliott, J., and C. Warr. *The Church of Santa Maria Donna Regina: Art, Iconography and Patronage in Fourteenth-Century Naples*. Burlington, Vt.: Ashgate Publishing, 2004.

Gilchrist, R. *Gender and Material Culture: The Archaeology of Religious Women*. London: Routledge, 1994.

Zarri, G. "I monasteri femminili a Bologna tra il XIII e il XVII secolo." *Atti e memorie della Deputazione di storia patria per le province di Bologna*, n.s. 24 (1973): 133–224.

See also **Architecture, Ecclesiastical; Birgittine Order; Double Monasteries; Elisabeth of Hungary; Isabelle of France; Jouarre and Chelles; Matilda and the Monastery of Essen; Monastic Enclosure; Monasticism and Nuns; Patronage, Artistic; Patronage, Ecclesiastical; Poor Clares Order**

ARISTOTELIAN CONCEPTS OF WOMEN AND GENDER

Aristotle's views on women, like those of Freud in his later life, have provoked considerable resistance from modern scholars, and rightly so. The fourth-century BCE philosopher consistently emphasizes the inferiority of women in relation to men, and his views proved immensely influential from the thirteenth century onward in scholastic thought. True to his own fascination with creating categories to describe all things, Aristotle's views on women can be divided into two distinct types: women's physiology and women's political role. His views, and those of his adherents in the central and later Middle Ages, have as many modern critics (plus at least one medieval critic) as they had medieval adherents. Central to both his political and his biological observations of women are their subordination and inferiority to men.

In his discussion of a woman's role (here confined to the role of the wife) in the ancient Greek *polis* or city-state, Aristotle relegates women to the *oikos* or household rather than the public realm by noting emphatically that "the male is by nature superior and the female inferior, the one rules and the other is ruled" (Aristotle, *Politics*, 1254b10, tr. by B. Jowett, quoted in Lefkowitz and Fant, p. 38). He also notes that male rule over women is less absolute relative to men's control of slaves and children in the household. He describes the husband's power over his wife as "constitutional," which he notes would imply an equality of the two. However, he argues that true equality in the husband's rule over his wife is not possible precisely because of female inferiority, a sexual inequality that he labels as "permanent." Women are excluded from political or public power for the same reason. To emphasize this point, Aristotle cites the example of the city-state of Sparta, where women were involved in the political realm with (to his eyes) disastrous results.

Underlying his arguments denying women access to the public realm are Aristotle's attempts to naturalize and even biologize sexual difference. His natural philosophical books are most instructive and influential in this regard. In his *Generation of Animals*, Aristotle argues for a fundamental difference but also a complementarity between males and females of all species: "Now of course the female, *qua* female, is passive, and the male, *qua* male, is active" (GA 1.21, 729b14). Such universalizing statements allow him to argue that, in the reproductive process, the female supplies only unformed matter, which the male seed then transforms and shapes into a living being. For Aristotle, this line of argument reflects his larger interest, apparent in his physical and metaphysical works, in the connections between matter, as potentiality, and form, as actuality. Aristotle genders the distinction of matter and form in stating that the female is definable by an incapacity (here, to produce anything more than matter or blood) and is consequently a deformed male, requiring the formative warmth of male seed to complete the process of procreation (GA 1.20, 728a18; 2.3, 737a28). Aristotle also pathologizes parts of the female body and notes that menstrual blood has negative powers, particularly the ability to dull mirrors (Aristotle, *On Dreams*, 459b–460a).

Most of Aristotle's texts dealing with gender were unavailable to the Latin West for centuries, until their reintroduction during the intellectual ferment of the twelfth and thirteenth centuries, which witnessed a massive campaign of translation from Greek and Arabic sources. The New Aristotle, as modern scholars call the resurgence of his views in the West, quickly gained prominence in the early universities. Some of the earliest evidence of this renewal of Aristotelian natural philosophy, David of Dinant's notebooks, dating from the 1210s, incorporates the harshest elements of Aristotelian physiology: woman, like the child, is essentially an incomplete or even deformed man, and thus is the passive participant in reproduction (*Davidis de Dinanto Quaternulorum Fragmenta* (ed. Marian Kurdzialek, Studia Mediewisticzne 3 [Warsaw, 1963]), pp. 24 and 31). Despite opposition to some of his views, such as those on the eternity of the soul, thirteenth-century scholars actively continued and expanded upon the views of the Philosopher, as he became known. Albertus Magnus and many other scholastics attempted to reconcile Aristotle and the Christian heritage. Albertus argued that the female's imperfect state naturally desired perfection through union with the more perfect male (from *Quaestiones de Animalibus* 10.4, quoted in Cadden p. 160). In the 1270s, Giles of Rome emphatically sided with Aristotle in the debate over embryology, and denied "female sperm" or any active involvement by the female in conception and fetal development. This represented an assault on Galen's two-seed theory, in which both men and women provided seed at the moment of conception.

While Aristotelian views of women predominated from the thirteenth to the fifteenth centuries in western European thought, one famous voice resisted the Philosopher's claims of female inferiority. Christine de Pizan's *Book of the City of Ladies*, written in 1404–1405, criticizes many of the misogynist traditions her world had inherited, including those of Aristotle. First, de Pizan cites the contradictions between philosophers—and the contradictions between philosophy and theology—as evidence that his views should not be taken as "articles of faith." Later in the text, de Pizan affirms that the knowledge of such female notables as Minerva, Sappho, and Isis has benefited the world more than the thought of Aristotle (1.38.5).

Aristotelian views of gender are built around binary oppositions and complementarity: male and female, active and passive, strong and weak, public and private, shaper and shaped. Aristotle's natural philosophical views and methods influenced western European thought for much of the later Middle Ages, and were used by many to reaffirm the belief in women's inherently flawed nature.

WILLIAM F. MACLEHOSE

References and Further Reading

Allen, Prudence. *The Concept of Women: The Aristotelian Revolution 750 BC–AD 1250*. Toronto: University of Toronto Press, 1985.

Cadden, Joan. *Meanings of Sex Difference in the Middle Ages: Medicine, Science and Culture*. Cambridge: Cambridge University Press, 1993.

de Pizan, Christine. *The Book of the City of Ladies*, translated by Earl Jeffrey Richards. New York: Persea Books, 1982.

Hewson, M. Anthony. *Giles of Rome and the Medieval Theory of Conception: A Study of the* De formatione corporis humani in utero. London: Athlone Press, 1975.

Lefkowitz, Mary, and Maureen Fant. *Women's Life in Greece and Rome*, second edition. Baltimore: Johns Hopkins University Press, 1992.

Lemay, Helen. *Women's Secrets: A Translation of Pseudo-Albertus Magnus'* De secretis mulierum *with Commentaries*. Albany, N.Y.: State University of New York Press, 1992.

Maccagnolo, Enzo. "David of Dinant and the Beginnings of Aristotelianism in Paris." In *A History of Twelfth-Century Western Philosophy*, edited by Peter Dronke. Cambridge: Cambridge University Press, 1988, pp. 429–442.

Maclean, Ian. *The Renaissance Notion of Woman: A Study in the Fortunes of Scholasticism and Medical Science in European Intellectual life*. New York: Cambridge University Press, 1980.

See also **Christine de Pizan; Gender Ideologies; Misogyny; Private and Public Spheres; Procreation and Ideas of Conception; Scholasticism**

ARMS AND ARMOR

Arms and armor were deployed to construct, define, and signify gendered identities throughout the Middle Ages. Shield, sword, and spear were recognizable symbols of men and masculinity, just as spindle and distaff were symbols of women and femininity. Among the Germanic warriors of the early Middle Ages, the ceremonial bestowal of shield and spear ushered free boys into manhood. Peasant, monastic, and bourgeois conceptions of masculinity were never tied quite so closely to martial prowess, but aristocratic men continued to define themselves as *bellatores* ("those who make war") from the emergence of the knight in the eleventh century well into the early modern period. The twelfth-century chivalric poet and troubador Bertran de Born thus derided the manhood of those untrained in the use of lance and sword, while other knights shamed comrades into joining crusades by sending them presents of wool and distaffs. Scholastic authors such as Ptolemy of Lucca and Giles of Rome, together with secular and canon laws from regions as diverse as Lombard, Italy, high medieval Iceland, and late medieval France, attempted to enforce this gendered social order by explicitly forbidding women to bear arms or wear armor. Many cited Deuteronomy's prohibition (22:5) against crossdressing as precedent. Some legal collections made allowances for extraordinary circumstances, but the penalties prescribed were generally harsh—they ranged from fines and lesser outlawry up to execution (in the exceptionally politicized case of Jeanne d'Arc/Joan of Arc).

The normative prohibitions and binary symbolism of medieval arms and armor were not transparent reflections of social realities, however. Women operated the stonethrower that struck and killed Simon de Montfort the Elder, the leader of the Albigensian Crusade, at the siege of Toulouse in 1218, for example. While greater average upper-body strength may have given men a physical advantage when using certain close-combat weapons, modern archaeologists have now unearthed enough swords and spears from unmistakably female graves to show that men did not have a monopoly even on these. Women are known to have manufactured everything from bows and arrows to suits of mail, and some continued to use this equipment even as it grew heavier (and armor in particular became more common) in the high and later Middle Ages. In the twelfth and thirteenth centuries, knightly cavalry began to adopt the lance and great helm as opposed to the lighter spear and *spangenhelm*; chain armor not only grew to cover the lower arms and legs but also began to incorporate small plates designed to protect vital areas. In the late Middle Ages, both arms and armor grew heavier still, as full plate evolved out of chain/plate hybrids and the pike and halberd replaced the infantry spear. These changes do not appear to have had much effect on women, however—perhaps because few women were professional soldiers. Many women who took up arms did so in emergency situations such as sieges, where the use of unknightly weapons (bows, crossbows, rocks, etc.) was a necessity and hence more socially acceptable. Others, such as the Jeannes (d'Arc, de Montfort, and de Penthièvre) of the age of the Hundred Years War, proved themselves capable of using even the heaviest late-medieval equipment. Christine de Pizan, a contemporary and admirer of Jeanne d'Arc, advised all noble ladies to familiarize themselves with weapons and war in order to be capable of defending their families' interests militarily.

Armed women were also popular—if somewhat problematic—characters in medieval art and literature. To ancient legends of warrior goddesses and Amazons, medieval Europe added a host of memorable new figures, from Valkyries and Celtic queens to the women jousters of *The Ladies' Tournament*. But because the sword, spear, and arrow were common metaphors for masculinity and the phallus, conventional artists faced a daunting challenge: to sustain the gendered social hierarchy while satisfying their audience's taste for exoticism and transgression. Romances thus had difficulty portraying women as both armored and feminine, while illuminations of Jeanne d'Arc vacillated between girding her in armor and clothing her in a dress.

One popular method of deflating such gender tensions was satire. Hence, the marginalia in one medieval manuscript transformed the phallus into the very symbol of femininity by depicting women jousting not with lances but with distaffs. Other artists portrayed armed women as "forgetful of their true selves" (that is, honorary men). Some romances even attempted to gender the very armor itself by adorning the men's with more "masculine" apotropaic gems, while fashioning the women's in tighter and more revealing styles. Through these various strategies, artists worked to present transgression in a manner that buttressed rather than undermined social norms. Arms and armor thus provided one of the keystones for medieval constructions of gender.

DAVID HAY

References and Further Reading

Balzaretti, Ross. "'These Are the Things That Men Do, Not Women': The Social Regulation of Female Violence in Langobard Italy." In *Violence and Society in the Early Medieval West*, edited by Guy Halsall. Woodbridge, Suffolk, England: Boydell, 1998, pp. 175–192.

Blythe, James M. "Women in the Military: Scholastic Arguments and Medieval Images of Female Warriors." *History of Political Thought* 22(2) (2001): 242–269.

Clover, Carol J. "Maiden Warriors and Other Sons." *Journal of English and Germanic Philology* 85 (1986): 35–49.

de Pizan, Christine. *Treasure of the City of Ladies, or The Book of Three Virtues*, translated by Sarah Lawson. New York: Penguin, 1985.

Evans, Michael R. "'Unfit to Bear Arms': The Gendering of Arms and Armour in Accounts of Women on Crusade." In *Gendering the Crusades*, edited by Susan B. Edgington and Sarah Lambert. New York: Columbia University Press, 2002, pp. 45–58.

Hadley, D. M., and J. M. Moore. "'Death Makes the Man'? Burial Rite and the Construction of Masculinities in the Early Middle Ages." In *Masculinity in Medieval Europe*, edited by D. M. Hadley. London: Longman, 1999, pp. 21–38.

Karras, Ruth Mazo. *From Boys to Men: Formations of Masculinity in Late Medieval Europe*. Philadelphia: University of Pennsylania Press, 2003.

Nicholson, Helen, "Women on the Third Crusade," *Journal of Medieval History* 23(4) (1997): 335–349.

Orderic Vitalis, *Ecclesiastical History*, ed. and trans. Marjorie Chibnall, 6 vols. Oxford: Clarendon Press, 1969–1978.

Pulega, Andrea, ed. *Ludi e spettacoli nel Medioevo: I Tornei di Dame*. Cattedra di Filologia Romanza dell'Universita' degli Studi di Milano. Milan: Cisalpino Goliardica, 1975.

Solterer, H. "Figures of Female Militancy in Medieval France." *Signs* 16(3) (1991): 522–549.

Stock, L. K. "'Arms and the Woman' in Medieval Romance: the Gendered Arming of Female Warriors in the *Roman d'Eneas* and Heldris's *Roman de Silence*." *Arthuriana* 5 (1995): 56–83.

Von der Hagen, Friedrich Heinrich, ed. "Der vrouwen turnei." In *Gesamtabenteuer: Hundert altdeutsche Erzählungen*, 3 vols. 1850. Reprint, Darmstadt: Wissenschaftliche Buchgesellschaft, 1961, vol. 1, pp. 371–382.

See also **Amazons; Chivalry; Crusades and Crusading Literature; Tournaments; Valkyries; Violence; Warfare**

ART, REPRESENTATIONS OF WOMEN IN

Visual representations are highly charged in Jewish, Christian, and Muslim thought. Inherited from antiquity was the notion that the sculpted or painted image "stood for" the real person, whether a divinity, a ruler, or an ordinary person. Images might thus deserve special protection and respect. Or they might be broken in order to damage the referent (the subject). Or making them might be taboo, as expressed in the second commandment to Moses: "Thou shalt not make to thyself a graven thing, nor the likeness of any thing that is in heaven above, or in the earth beneath, nor of those things that are in the waters

Eyck, Jan van (c. 1390–1441). Eve and Musical Angels. Right panels from the Ghent Altarpiece (Altarpiece of the Mystic Lamb). Location: Cathedral of St. Bavo, Ghent, Belgium. Credit: Scala / Art Resource, NY.

Lim Limbourg Brothers (15th CE). June (Haymaking. In the background, the Palace and Sainte-Chapelle, Paris). Calendar miniature from the *Trés Riches Heures* du Duc de Berry. 1416. Ms.65, f.6v. Photo: R.G. Ojeda. Location: Musée Condé, Chantilly, France. Credit: Réunion des Musées Nationaux / Art Resource, NY.

under the earth," although it was never completely adhered to. Representational codes that assert the difference between art and reality distinguish the art of the period 450–1500 throughout Europe and the Mediterranean world from the art of pagan Greece and Rome or of the post-medieval period. Signs of transience, such as cast shadows and emotive expressions (except women's grief), were eschewed in the early period, and the radical physicality of anatomically correct bodies was not explored until the fifteenth century, and only in European art.

The situation was compounded by the notion that what we see impacts our very souls. In the Middle Ages it was thought that it might even have a physiological effect, such that if a pregnant woman looked at a malformed animal she would give birth to a freak; a thirteenth-century medical text called *The Secrets of Women* says that chimeras must not be painted on the bedroom walls for this reason. And ugly old women, as well as the mythical basilisk, could damage people with their gaze. Add to this one more element, gynophobia or anxiety about women's generative power and sexuality, and we can expect representations of women to be very heavily freighted. Whereas visual metaphors for phallic power are redolent, allusions to female genitalia are very rare except in the strange exhibiting

figures known as "sheela na gigs" that were sculpted on churches and castles.

Since medieval belief systems indicate anxiety about seeing, we can assume that visual representations were contemplated soberly and that their making and positioning was a deliberative matter. Much more was expected of such images than we currently associate with the visual arts, which we generally pursue in a personal way for aesthetic or entertainment value. On the other hand, it is widely recognized that even seemingly casual cultural production contributes to the ideological work of reinforcing societal norms, such as class systems or gender polarity, and medieval art was no exception to this, as Alexander has argued. The discussion that follows is informed by medieval concepts of vision and the modern concept of ideology. Examples are drawn from European art, though some readings are suggested that pursue the topic in Byzantium and Islam.

Woman as Deformity/Woman as Ideal Beauty

Aristotle's precepts that a girl baby is a failed male and that hybrids are unnatural exerted an influence throughout the Middle Ages on representations of women in art, as did Horace's mockery of a creature with the head of a lovely woman who "ends below in a black and ugly fish." By the thirteenth and fourteenth centuries, when freaks cavorted in the margins of manuscript pages and portals, mermaids and sirens were common among the deformities, especially in books made for male patrons. They warn of instability, and in some contexts hybrids had come to symbolize various aspects of sin. Thus it is puzzling that some Judaic illuminated manuscripts made in Germany in the fourteenth century show some biblical characters with birds' or beasts' heads. Mellinkoff has suggested that they are a subversive Christian artist's attempt to denigrate Jewish patrons. In one book, the "Birds' Head Haggadah" (available at the New York Public Library), only the women are depicted this way. Virtuous biblical women were appropriated as models for Christian queens; as Jordan has shown, Judith and Esther are treated as courteous heroines in the windows of the Sainte Chapelle (Palace Chapel) in Paris.

The Queen of Sheba was sometimes represented as black *and* beautiful (despite the Latin Bible's phrasing, "black *but* beautiful"), as in an enamel plaque made by Nicholas of Verdun for the pulpit of the Abbey Church of Königsfelden in Austria, in 1181. Yet she was viewed as a pagan temptress whose wiles had to be overcome by King Solomon. In fact, increased contact with darker-skinned people during the Crusades, whether Arabs or their African slaves, produced a reaction in the thirteenth century: for the first time, artists represented Europeans as white with pink cheeks (as opposed to shades of brown and pink), and this complexion was especially ascribed to beautiful women in art and literature. Thus, if she was seen as a prefiguration of *Ecclesia* (Church personified), the Queen of Sheba might be "pure" white.

The Problem of Nudity and the Female Body

Erotic nudes like the Venuses of antiquity disappeared almost completely from the artistic repertory in the Middle Ages, since they were pagan, seductive, and dangerous. Giles of Rome, an influential moralist whose treatises were used to raise the ruling class of the thirteenth century and later, described nude statues as hideous and liable to corrupt young men.

When a contemporary painter portrays some of the sensual beauty of Bathsheba as glimpsed by King David, he also follows the biblical story closely, emphasizing the dire consequences of this adulterous gaze. Eve was represented as the quintessential prototype of the nude female who entrapped a man and caused his downfall; she may mirror the serpent that tempts her if its head is represented as that of a woman. Even the sensual and vulnerable Eve on the wings of Van Eyck's great Ghent Altarpiece is associated with the painful outcome of her pregnancy, by means of the depiction above her of Cain killing Abel. In fact, being paraded naked in the street was represented in some municipal law books as a punishment for sexual sin (for men as well as women), so this naked Adam and Eve are also vested in shame.

Medical treatises generally avoided any naturalistic appearance of the body, presenting ideograms highly charged with strange notions such as that the female reproductive organs were those of a man turned inside; the invasive writing within the woman's body attests to the author's anxiety about the subject. Yet the body could be shown stripped for surgery, or for torture leading to sainthood, and representations of subjects like St. Agatha's and St. Catherine's mastectomies may have constituted a sado-erotic experience for the viewer.

Feminine Activities

The Genesis story was also used to reinforce notions of the gendered separation of work. A negative valence is created for manual work by virtue of the fact that it was a punishment. In the threefold class system envisaged by medieval writers, those who work are beneath those who fight and those who pray. Adam may be shown digging, and wearing an animal skin as if he is a herdsman, while Eve generally spins thread, and nurses a child. Comparable activities are being performed by women in the household of Potiphar in the sixth-century Byzantine *Vienna Genesis* manuscript. Weaving and sewing were domestic tasks assigned to women in the literature and art of antiquity and the Middle Ages. Modestly veiled female textile workers illustrate the Active Life on the north portal of Chartres Cathedral, facing nuns who embody the Contemplative Life. Their perfect containment in each building block of the arch gives them an aura of personification more than of individuality (*vita*, life, is feminine in Latin). They contrast with the fully clad but seductive prostitutes who actively cause the moral and fiscal downfall of the Prodigal Son in a window of the nave.

In the fourteenth century we hear that women who are too high-born to work at a loom might learn to read, and in fact there is evidence that French queens had large libraries of manuscripts in Latin and the vernacular and taught their children the alphabet. A popular model was provided by the image of Saint Anne teaching the Virgin Mary to read, as Sheingorn has shown. Yet the fact that these saintly prototypes are depicted standing, rather than comfortably seated, suggests that the function of female literacy was to read and chant from a prayer book, a reading that can be phonetic but not necessarily fully comprehended if the language is Latin. Individual book owners were often represented kneeling in prayer, as if they belonged to the class who pray even though married. The secular German law book known as the *Sachsenspiegel* or *Saxon Mirror* depicts a book among the property that passed down in the female line, along with the cloth-working tools, candle sticks, chests and mirrors, and the herds and flocks. Yet in the many other instances the illustrator wished to refer to this "women's stuff," s/he showed only the shears, or perhaps a goose, thus diminishing the housewife's domain and accomplishments; no woman in the law book is shown reading or holding a book.

There are other omissions in the representation of work. A pictorial cycle of monthly agricultural activities was inherited from Roman art and depicted in western Europe throughout the Middle Ages in many church portals, as well as in the calendar section of devotional books. Although the historical record indicates that peasant women worked in the fields, and love poetry is full of easily seduced shepherdesses, there are no representations of such women on calendar pages until the fifteenth century. And when they make an appearance, as in the *Très Riches Heures* of the Duke of Berry, the reader is invited to become a voyeur, spying on their bare ankles and shoulders as they labor. Whereas the high-born women on other pages (for example, April and May) are elaborately draped, the surfeit of rich cloth denoting the wealth of the patron, the peasant women are to be despised for their lack of decoration. The rhetoric of naturalism in all such pictures is suspect; the artist conjures a reality through topographic and botanical details that are calculated to persuade us of a social reality, when in fact they conjure a fantasy world. Even though records indicate that the rich (men as well as women) wore damasked and embroidered silks and velvets on special occasions, we know relatively little of real peasant attire. We do know that peasants experienced malnutrition, but skeletally thin peasant women would not have provided a feast for the eye of the lord of the castle. At the end of this calamitous century, marked by famine, war, and plague, the artist seems eager to show that all is well and prosperous under his patron's control. And well he might, because it was an old precept that bad rule led to such disasters.

Powerful Women

Women in the West were never accorded the secular authority of some Byzantine empresses, who ruled in their own right and are represented on their coinage bedecked in jewels and regalia. The good girl/bad girl polarity between the Virgin Mary and Eve carried over into secular representation in Europe and was accentuated toward the end of the Middle Ages.

Women might be placed on a pedestal in courtly love poetry (though we now realize that the standard metaphors often indicate that they were raped), but if they gained power over men they risked inverting the "natural" order that demanded a wife's obedience to her husband. Inversions such as Phyllis riding Aristotle, or a wife beating a man, were cautions against women's power, as Smith has shown.

Witchcraft in this era was seldom celebrated for its healing power (as it was originally), and became a pretext to accuse women, more than men, of poisoning or hexing their victims. The trials and burnings were seldom represented, but by 1500 prints showed nude female witches riding backwards on rams and enacting "Sabbath" rituals. Bad-girl images were elaborated in the illustrated *Danse Macabre des Femmes* (Dance of Death of Women), where females of all professions and classes are shown satirically at the moment of their death.

Yet Campbell has recognized that fourteenth-century scenes of love in the mural paintings of the Communal Palace of San Gimignano in Italy rise to a high level of human feeling and positive symbolism. And from the fifteenth century come several illustrated manuscripts that show the activities and influence of good lay women. Examples may be found in the works of Christine de Pizan, notably her *City of Ladies*, and in Giovanni Boccaccio's *De Claris Mulieribus* (*Concerning Famous Women*), presented in French translation as *Des Clercs et Nobles Femmes*. By drawing on diverse historical examples, Boccaccio also constructs a history of noble women, including artists and writers.

MADELINE H. CAVINESS

References and Further Reading

Alexander, Jonathan. "*Labeur* and *Paresse*: Ideological Representations of Medieval Peasant Labor." *The Art Bulletin* 72 (1990): 436–452.

Buettner, Brigitte. *Boccaccio's "Des Cleres Et Nobles Femmes": Systems of Signification in an Illuminated Manuscript.* College Art Association Monograph on the Fine Arts. Seattle: University of Washington Press, 1996.

Cameron, Averil, and A. Kuhrt. *Images of Women in Antiquity.* Detroit: Wayne State University Press, 1983.

Camille, Michael. *The Gothic Idol: Ideology and Image-Making in Medieval Art.* Cambridge New Art History and Criticism. New York: Cambridge University Press, 1989.

Campbell, C. Jean. *The Game of Courting, and the Art of the Commune of San Gimignano, 1290–1320.* Princeton: Princeton University Press, 1997.

Caviness, Madeline H. *Reframing Medieval Art: Difference, Margins, Boundaries.* Medford, Mass.: Tufts University Press, 2001 (http://Nils.lib.Tufts.edu/Caviness).

———. *Visualizing Women in the Middle Ages: Sight, Spectacle, and Scopic Economy.* The Middle Ages Series. Philadelphia: University of Pennsylvania Press, 2001.

Devisse, Jean. *The Image of the Black in Western Art, from the Early Christian Era to the "Age of Discovery": From the Demonic Threat to the Incarnation of Sainthood,* translated by William Granger Ryan. Cambridge, Mass.: Harvard University Press, 1976.

Grössinger, Christa. *Picturing Women in Late Medieval and Renaissance Art.* Manchester Medieval Studies. Manchester and New York: Manchester University Press, 1997.

Harrison, Ann Tukey, ed. *The Danse Macabre of Women: Ms. Fr. 995 of the Bibliothèque Nationale, with a Chapter by Sandra L. Hindman.* Kent, Ohio: Kent State University Press, 1994.

Jordan, Alyce A. "Material Girls: Judith, Esther, Narrative Modes and Models of Queenship in the Windows of the Ste.-Chapelle." *Word and Image* 15(4) (1999): 337–350.

Kalavresou, Yoli. *Byzantine Women and Their World,* Exhibition, Harvard University Museums, Cambridge. New York: Yale University Press, 2003.

Mellinkoff, Ruth. *Antisemitic Hate Signs in Hebrew Illuminated Manuscripts from Medieval Germany.* Jerusalem: Center for Jewish Art and The Hebrew University of Jerusalem, 1999.

Ruggles, D. Fairchild, ed. *Women, Patronage, and Self-Representation in Islamic Societies.* Albany: State University of New York Press, 2000.

Sheingorn, Pamela. "'The Wise Mother': The Image of St. Anne Teaching the Virgin Mary." *Gesta* 32 (1993): 69–80.

Smith, Susan L. *The Power of Women: A Topos in Medieval Art and Literature.* The Middle Ages Series. Philadelphia: University of Pennsylvania Press, 1995.

See also **Body, Visual Representations of; Book Ownership; Clothwork, Domestic; Courtly Love; Danse Macabre des Femmes; Empresses: Byzantium; Eroticism in Art; Eve; Gaze; Gender in Art; Hagiography; Literacy and Reading: Vernacular; Marginalia, Manuscript; Mary, Virgin: in Art; Mermaids and Sirens; Personifications Visualized as Women; Secrets of Women; Sheela Na Gigs; Witches; Woman on Top; Work**

ARTHURIAN LITERATURE

Casual readers of medieval Arthurian texts are likely to see the Arthurian world as a predominantly masculine domain. Camelot and the Round Table are a kind of "men's club," where the knights enjoy fellowship, celebrate their martial victories and sometimes confess their defeats, and accept new challenges such as the Grail quest. The Round Table is thus the locus of conventional Arthurian male bonding.

However, since knights may seek love as well as adventure, female characters also command their attention, as well as ours. A good many of the women are nameless servants or messengers, who often play crucial roles in the narrative despite their anonymity. Others are named and prominent, and they are arguably more varied in their roles and more complex in their presentation than are their male counterparts. Arthurian romances include women who are active and resourceful; some even function as knights and distinguish themselves on the battlefield. Others, the objects of knights' love or lust, influence events and behavior by inspiring men, by challenging them to undertake tasks or quests, and by either accepting or rejecting male blandishments. This statement leads us to what is traditionally, if misleadingly, called courtly love.

Arthurian Women and Courtly Love

The term "courtly love" is a nineteenth-century invention by medievalist Gaston Paris, who drew his conclusions from a single romance, *Lancelot, or The Knight of the Cart,* composed by French author Chrétien de Troyes in the 1170s. Paris saw courtly love as a social and amorous system in which the knight/lover (Lancelot in this instance) is subordinate to the whim of his lady (here, Guinevere). In fact, this romance offers a striking example of the woman's power to determine both the fate of the knight and the direction of the text. In one of the most famous scenes in medieval literature, Lancelot, given the opportunity to find the abducted queen more quickly if he will disgrace himself by riding in a cart used to transport criminals, accepts the invitation, hesitating only slightly before doing so. Later, Guinevere will object that his hesitation indicated less than absolute devotion to her, and he must make amends by repeatedly, upon her command, accepting disgrace unquestioningly.

This description of the intrigue of *Lancelot* emphasizes Guinevere's power and Lancelot's subservience, even as he plays a heroic and messianic role in other events. To some readers this presentation of the woman on a pedestal, exercising her authority at the knight's expense, has seemed to represent a literary empowerment of women. However, given Guinevere's imperious attitude, we might just as easily construe this text, and courtly love in general, as a representation of medieval misogyny masked as gallantry. It may thus be a case of exalting women for the wrong reasons and thereby undercutting the praise and presentation of female characters.

The major flaw in Gaston Paris's theory is his reliance on a single text that is hardly typical of Arthurian romance. Further examination of female roles leads us to a more useful, and double, conclusion. First, female roles are much more diverse and complex than Paris suggested; second, female characters are generally located at the intersection of two powerful cultural forces: traditional clerical misogyny and courtly idealism.

Diversity of Female Roles

It is hazardous to generalize about the function of women in Arthurian (or, more generally, medieval) literature: dealing with numerous texts from different cultures and centuries, we confront a full range of human motivations, behaviors, and emotions. The conventional view, of active men and passive but commanding females, is seriously oversimplified, and even Chrétien de Troyes's other romances give the lie to this stereotype. Enide, the heroine of his first romance (*Erec and Enide*, c. 1170), provokes, if only unintentionally, the central action of the romance, and she intervenes actively on several occasions to save her husband. In the following romance, Cligés, the eponymous hero, distinguishes himself in martial affairs, but it is the woman, Fénice, who makes decisions that determine the course of their love and ultimately of their lives.

The legend of Tristan and Iseut (Isolde) was originally distinct from the Arthurian legend but was soon grafted onto it, tenuously in the early French romances by Béroul and Thomas of England (both c. 1175), and then completely in the French prose *Tristan* (c. 1235), where Tristan becomes a knight of the Round Table. In these works Iseut shows herself to be, in many instances, an active and resourceful character, as responsible as Tristan for the decisions concerning the conduct of their illicit love, and more effective than he in saving them from detection. In Béroul, for example, she devises a clever and equivocal "true lie," an oath that enables her to confess her sin with Tristan while also swearing, truthfully if deceitfully, that she has never betrayed her husband.

Although Guinevere may be the most conspicuous example of the imperious woman, she is, if not passive, at least restricted in the range of her activity. Yet even her role is by no means consistent from work to work. In *Meraugis de Portlesguez*, a thirteenth-century French romance, Arthur and his knights debate the relative merits of two men to decide which one will have the woman they both love. Guinevere interrupts the discussion and takes command, rebuffing Arthur's effort to silence her. She orders the men out of the room and convenes a "court" in which only women make the decision. The roles of women in this romance are varied and complex: the young woman herself is not permitted to make her own choice, yet Guinevere has the power to expel Arthur from his own court and make decisions in his stead. On the other hand, the image of a commanding queen is attenuated by her contention that questions of love—though not matters of war or politics—are the domain of women.

One of the most complex female Arthurian characters is Morgan le Fay, a sorceress most often presented as Arthur's half-sister. She is frequently Arthur's ally, and when Arthur is mortally wounded, it is generally Morgan who transports him to Avalon to have his injuries tended. Yet she is also a jealous and vengeful woman with a particular dislike for Guinevere. In the French *Death of Arthur*, part of the huge Lancelot–Grail cycle (1215–1235), she attempts to turn Arthur against Lancelot and Guinevere by showing him images that Lancelot, previously her prisoner, painted to depict his affair with the queen. In the Middle English *Sir Gawain and the Green Knight* (c. 1400), Morgan is a withered hag whose hatred of Guinevere leads her to concoct the plot in which Gawain ostensibly risks losing his life.

Characterizations of other Arthurian women would further demonstrate their diversity—from nameless messengers to loyal wives to jealous shrews—but would also reveal that most of them are defined in terms of their relationship to males. A female character who stands out from others is Silence, a young woman whose name is also the title of a French romance by Heldris de Cornuälle (second half of the thirteenth century). Independent, capable, and successful, Silence lives her life as a man, first as a minstrel and then as a knight. Thus she too illustrates both the active and the admirable traits of some Arthurian women and also the fact that, once again, authors appear to reflect a patriarchal, if not explicitly misogynistic, culture by presenting women as accessory to males or, in the case of Silence, almost as a male surrogate. Interpretation of this romance is further complicated by the narrative criticism of male-line inheritance and the insertion of several openly antifeminist digressions. Moreover, Silence's success as a man in a man's world ends in her relatively traditional marriage.

Perceval's unnamed sister represents yet another category. In the French *Quest for the Holy Grail* (part of the Lancelot–Grail cycle), in Sir Thomas Malory's *Morte d'Arthur* (c. 1470), and elsewhere, she plays a crucial role in the Grail quest, despite the fact that women are expressly excluded from the enterprise. The explanation is surely that she does not fall into the same category as ladies at court but is instead a kind of female counterpart to Galahad: the two of them are symbolic representations of an ideal of moral perfection, an ideal attained by no other Arthurian characters.

With regard to most Arthurian women (Perceval's sister and Morgan being exceptions), convention appears to inscribe in the construction of female characters a deep ambiguity, less in their overt behavior than in the way readers may be led, whether by tradition, personal inclination, or textual strategies, to interpret them. One reader may take satisfaction in finding a good many females in Arthurian romance who are strong, capable women, able to either command men or, like Iseut, use intelligence to outwit them. Another reader may construe that same strength and resourcefulness as shrewishness, that intelligence as the deviousness and mendacity, the "feminine wiles," to which a woman must stoop in order to manipulate men and events. A few brief examples will suggest, however cursorily, the directions of contemporary approaches to the problem of "reading" Arthurian women.

Critical Approaches

We lack a full and systematic study of female agency in romance, though important contributions have been made in that direction. Maureen Fries, without focusing squarely on agency, provides a very straightforward and practical tool for categorizing female characters, dividing them, according to their intentions, into "female heroes," heroines, and counter-heroes. The unconventional term *female hero* refers to a character who escapes traditional definitions and is able to function heroically, as would her masculine counterpart. Thus, Fries's categories unavoidably continue to define females in terms of their relation to males and masculine societal roles. Nonetheless, establishment of these categories permits a reasonably clear delineation of roles, illustrating the diversity of female characters and the futility of conventional stereotypes.

Much recent feminist criticism of Arthurian (and more broadly, courtly) literature has gone beyond the straightforward categorizing of female characters and similarly beyond the tracking of overtly misogynistic treatments of women. Roberta L. Krueger, for example, studies the problem of women readers of romance. Adopting a triple perspective—women in particular texts, women as modern readers, and women as medieval audiences for romances—she suggests that the marginalization of women within romances corresponds to the marginalization of women historically, that is to say, their displacement from a subject position. She demonstrates as well the ways in which their displacement was the lot not only of female characters and most medieval women but also specifically of female patrons of romancers, such as Marie, the Countess of Champagne, who sponsored the *Knight of the Cart*, only to have Chrétien pass the completion of the project to another author. E. Jane Burns investigates the space in which we might read the "ambiguous status" of women—via their voices or their bodies—in medieval texts whose (generally) male authors appear to fill available space with prefabricated constructions of female characters.

Peggy McCracken, in *The Romance of Adultery*, studies questions of adultery and queenship, suggesting that the former offers a literary reflection of anxieties about real (historical) queens and about matters of legitimacy and succession. Paradoxically, the adultery of a romance queen (Guinevere or Iseut) may contribute to social stability, and it may be to the king's benefit to tolerate, if not approve, it: retribution would separate him from his favored knight and sow dissension in his court.

A good deal of the criticism concerning female characters in Arthurian literature serves not to solve or simplify their situation and role in romances but to problematize it and to demonstrate that the question is extraordinarily subtle and complex. Studies continue to identify the tensions underlying the construction of female characters, the product of an effort, by mostly male writers, to idealize women while promoting a masculine ethos within a culture in which misogyny was entrenched as doctrine and often as law.

NORRIS J. LACY

References and Further Reading

Bloch, Howard. *Medieval Misogyny and the Invention of Western Romantic Love*. Chicago: University of Chicago Press, 1991.

Burns, E. Jane. *Bodytalk: When Women Speak in Old French Literature*. Philadelphia: University of Pennsylvania Press, 1993.

———. *Courtly Love Undressed: Reading Through Clothes in Medieval French Culture*. Philadelphia: University of Pennsylvania Press, 2002.

Burns, E. Jane, and Roberta L. Krueger, eds. "Courtly Ideology and Woman's Place in Medieval French Literature." Special issue of *Romance Notes* 25.3 (1985).

Fenster, Thelma, ed. *Arthurian Women: A Casebook*. New York: Garland, 1996.

Ferrante, Joan. *Woman as Image in Medieval Literature from the Twelfth Century to Dante*. New York: Columbia University Press, 1975.

Gaunt, Simon. *Gender and Genre in Medieval French Literature*. Cambridge: Cambridge University Press, 1995.

Gravdal, Kathryn. *Ravishing Maidens: Writing Rape in Medieval French Literature and Law*. Philadelphia: University of Pennsylvania Press, 1991.

Kay, Sarah. *Courtly Contradictions: The Emergence of the Literary Object in the Twelfth Century*. Stanford: Stanford University Press, 2001.

Krueger, Roberta L. *Women Readers and the Ideology of Gender in Twelfth-Century Verse Romance*. Cambridge: Cambridge University Press, 1993.

Lejeune, Rita. "La Femme dans les littératures française et occitane du XIe au XIIe siècles." *Cahiers de Civilisation Médiévale* 20 (1977): 201–217.

McCracken, Peggy. *The Romance of Adultery: Queenship and Sexual Transgression in Old French Literature*. Philadelphia: University of Pennsylvania Press, 1998.

Partner, Nancy F. *Studying Medieval Women: Sex, Gender, Feminism*. Cambridge, Mass.: Medieval Academy of America, 1993.

See also **Audience, Women as; Chrétien de Troyes; Courtly Love; Courtship; Cross-Dressing; Femininity and Masculinity; Feminist Theories and Methodologies; Guinevere; Isolde; Literature, German; Literature, Middle English; Literature, Old French; Marie de France; Misogyny; Patriarchy and Patrilineage; Roman de Silence; Romance, English; Romance, French; Romance, German; Sexuality: Extramarital Sex; Supernatural Women**

ARTISAN FAMILIES, WOMEN OF

When at the end of the fourteenth century the founders' guild of York revised its ordinances, it provided that one Giles de Benoyne be allowed an additional apprentice "because he had no wife." Benoyne was presumably a widower, but his appeal illustrates a larger truth: a man in possession of a workshop must be married. The implication is that workshops regularly used the labour of wives, but also that a man was considered unfit to head a workshop unless he were (or at least had been) married. We may set this beside another observation. With the exception of building craftsmen, the place of work of the medieval artisan tended to coincide with his place of residence. This had two consequences: husbands did not go out to work and wives could work alongside their husbands whilst maintaining responsibility for those aspects of a household that were deemed women's work. It follows that, despite the optical illusion created by legal and administrative records that invariably identify workshops solely with the male "head," the medieval artisanal workshop was invariably associated with a married couple that constituted an essential partnership. Indeed, we are in danger of perceiving as real the medieval ideological notion that workshops were run by men and that women were merely ancillary; this is to ignore the evidence of widows running workshops and hence implicitly of wives being capable craftworkers in their own right.

Wives of artisans balanced two or three essentially complementary functions: they often assisted in the running of the workshop; they engaged in other economic activities; they managed households. The management of households involved day-to-day responsibility for the material welfare of husband, children, apprentices, and servants, particularly in terms of the provision of food, warmth, and clothing. Detailed letters of direction from the merchant Francesco Datini to his wife, Margherita, which mirror the voluminous instructions of the high bourgeois *Le Menagier de Paris*, indicate that high-status husbands were keen to maintain the notion that wives acted only on their *husbands'* authority. The same may have been true at this lower level of society, but this is not to deny such women considerable de facto autonomy. This is implicit in the English bourgeois normative text *How the Goodwife Taught her Daughter*, and also in the charitable provision made by bourgeois women of food, clothing, and fuel to the poor.

As our initial example implies, craft guilds, which were both devotional and economic in function, assumed that guild masters would normally be married. Given that, wives were understood to be associate members alongside their husbands, participating in guild feasts and aspects of the guild's devotional activities. These might include processions or even religious drama. (It is widely held that women were excluded from such drama, but this position tends to be rooted in surmise rather than evidence.) Equally, craft guilds sometimes made it explicit in their ordinances that women, including wives, were integral to the functioning of workshops. This is more conspicuous in some crafts, notably weaving, petty retailing, and candle making, than in others, though it is possible to find evidence of women in most occupations, even some that from a modern perspective would seem quite unexpected. In late-fourteenth-century Seville, for example, women were employed as masons and carpenters. We can also find examples of wives who followed occupations independently of their husbands. For example, a Florentine female weaver who took on two male apprentices in 1299 was married to a shoemaker. This example may be unusual, but the normative model of wives only working in their husbands' craft may mask more diverse social practice; it was commonplace for wives to pursue such supplementary trades as spinning or brewing as well as helping in the workshop or perhaps serving customers.

The capacity of wives to take an active role in workshop production, despite their general exclusion from apprenticeships and hence formally recognized routes to training, is beyond doubt. It is, for example, obliquely documented in wills, through evidence of husbands providing that apprentices remain with their widows or bequeathing them looms or other equipment. Similarly, widows sometimes left tools or even merchandise. Wives could and indeed must have learned hands-on from their husbands, if not previously as daughters or servants. It is apparent, however, that what may have appeared commonplace in late-fourteenth-century York was not necessarily true in other times and places. In northern Europe, at least from the later fifteenth century, we find craft guilds beginning to discriminate against women by restricting the ability of widows to maintain workshops or even, as with the weavers of Coventry in 1453 or Bristol in 1461, regulating against the participation of the wives of masters. This last was perhaps atypical, but is nevertheless symptomatic of a more conservative climate, which tended to see women as housewives and mothers rather than coworkers and business partners.

JEREMY GOLDBERG

References and Further Reading

Cohn, S. K., Jr. "Women and Work in Renaissance Italy." In *Gender and Society in Renaissance Italy*, edited by J. C. Brown and R. C. Davis. London: Longman, 1998, pp. 107–126.

Dillard, H. *Daughters of the Reconquest: Women in Castilian Town Society, 1100–1300*. Cambridge: Cambridge University Press, 1989.

Goldberg, P. J. P. *Women, Work and Life Cycle*. Oxford: Oxford University Press, 1992.

Hanawalt, B. A., ed. *Women and Work in Preindustrial Europe*. Bloomington, Ind.: Indiana University Press, 1986.

Herlihy, D. *Opera Muliebria: Women and Work in Medieval Europe*. New York: McGraw Hill, 1990.

Howell, M. C. *Women, Production, and Patriarchy in Late Medieval Cities*. Chicago: University of Chicago Press, 1986.

Kowaleski, M., and J. M. Bennett. "Crafts, Guilds, and Women." In *Sisters and Workers in the Middle Ages*, edited by J. M. Bennett, et al. Chicago: University of Chicago Press, 1989, pp.11–38.

See also **Alewives and Brewing; Apprentices; Business; Clothwork, Domestic; Feme Sole; Guild Members and Guilds; Household Management; Market and Tradeswomen; Textile Production for the Market; Widows; Work**

ARTISTS, WOMEN

The ability of women to undertake a professional artistic career in the medieval period was mediated by several key institutional and social factors. One institutional determinant was access to guild membership. Guild records document women working side by side with men in most professions, including the production of artisanal goods. However, women rarely constituted more than a small percentage of total workers, and they did not receive equal remuneration. Documentary evidence further suggests that professional prospects often depended upon familial ties, since many female artisans enrolled in guilds were the widows or daughters of men in the same professions. Although female guild enrollments could vary significantly by time and place, a general statistical increase correlates with the rise of urbanization throughout Europe in the period.

Determination of female authorship of cultural products is complicated by the fact that women typically produced small-scale, less prestigious objects ("crafts"), rather than the large-scale works produced by male sculptors, monumental painters, goldsmiths, and architects, which are privileged in the traditional canon of Western art history ("art"). Notwithstanding isolated examples of women working as sculptors and mural painters, such as the putative twelfth-century Spanish sculptress Sanccia Guidisalvi and the early fourteenth-century Castilian fresco painter Teresa Díaz, women were generally restricted to the professions of textile embroidery and manuscript illumination. Attributions are made further ambiguous by the medieval tradition of scribal humility and pre-Renaissance conceptions of authorship, with the result that few medieval artisans and painters signed their products. In addition, the workshop convention of a single prevailing style—that of the head male artisan—impedes the identification of works by female hands. For example, efforts to differentiate the illuminations of Bourgot from those of her father, the celebrated illuminator Jean Le Noir, in the Book of Hours they produced for Yolande de Flandres c. 1353 have proven unsuccessful. Lastly, the affixing of one or more signatures to a cultural product in itself does not clearly define authorship, since signatures could refer variously to patrons, authors, designers, scribes, or illuminators. There is considerable debate, for instance, regarding the precise role of the noted intellectual Christine de Pizan (1364–1431) in the design of the pictorial cycles for her books. Whether the learned twelfth-century German abbesses Hildegard of Bingen and Herrad of Hohenbourg contributed to the illuminations of the manuscript each authored (the *Scivias* of 1142–1152 and the *Hortus Deliciarum* of c. 1170, respectively) is similarly debated. The design input of the female teams that embroidered the images adorning two of the finest textiles of the period, the Bayeux Tapestry of c. 1070 and the Syon Cope of c. the late thirteenth century, is likewise unresolved.

Private Consumption of Art in Nunneries

The clearest evidence regarding female artistic authorship is not found in public professional contexts, but in the pictures produced for private consumption in convents. Among the oldest surviving self-portraits in Western art are those of the twelfth-century German nun Guda, who portrayed herself twice in illuminations for the c. 1154 Codex Sintram, which were produced in collaboration with the monk Sintram. The collaboration of Guda and Sintram represents a late example of male and female religious living in double monasteries and working together in scriptoria, which was common prior to the monastic reforms of the tenth and eleventh centuries. In the late medieval period, nuns cloistered in monasteries gained greater agency in managing both embroidered textiles and manuscript production and design. Although some goods were sold to the public to generate revenue for the nunnery (at times prompting guilds to regulate their competition), many were produced to serve the communal and private devotional needs of the nuns themselves. The term *Nonnenarbeiten* has derogatory implications in traditional art history, due to the fact that much "nuns' work" was technically naïve since access to the professional art world was especially limited for female religious. However, convents were often havens for learned women, including those of noble blood who served as abbesses, and young laywomen who received educations there. One particularly expressive self-portrait depicts the Bavarian laywoman Claricia, perhaps a student training in a scriptorium, swinging as the tail of the letter "Q" in a twelfth-century illuminated psalter.

Recent scholarship has explored the manner in which nuns developed a conceptually sophisticated visual vocabulary to complement their particular spiritual practices. Whether exploring unique interrelationships of word and image, devising liturgically based textual embellishments, or visualizing metaphors of bridal mysticism to figure the relationship between themselves and Christ, nuns used their authority to produce art that met their spiritual needs. Feminist art historians laud the identification of a uniquely gendered point of view in conventual art.

Poststructuralist art historians, with a complementary theoretical interest in deconstructing the multiple power structures informing historical phenomena, caution that this distinctive female devotional voice was mediated by corporate (that is, male-formulated) theology. For instance, in the case of the Poor Clare abbess, author, and painter Caterina Vigri in fifteenth-century Bologna, the metaphors of passionate maternity she visualized to serve the cloistered community of nuns functioned in concert with, and were ultimately subject to, institutionalized Franciscan theology of the Incarnation and Corpus Domini.

Although scant evidence pertains to female artists in non-Western areas, for example, Byzantium, Asia, and the Muslim world, limited documentation at present intimates similar institutional and social mediations (such as the correlation between patterns of professional access and urbanization, and access through paternal professional activity). Meanwhile, social historians persist in the archival investigations that will continue to produce more precise information regarding both Western and non-Western female cultural production in the medieval period.

KIM E. BUTLER

References and Further Reading

Carroll, Jane L., and Alison G. Stewart, eds. *Saints, Sinners, and Sisters: Gender and Northern Art in Medieval and Early Modern Europe.* Burlington, Vt.: Ashgate Publishing, 2003.

Chadwick, Whitney. *Women, Art, and Society.* 3rd ed. London and New York: Thames & Hudson Ltd., 2003.

Hamburger, Jeffrey F. *Nuns as Artists: The Visual Culture of a Medieval Convent.* Berkeley, Los Angeles, and London: University of California Press, 1997.

Harris Bluestone, Natalie, ed. *Double Vision: Perspectives on Gender and the Visual Arts.* Madison: Fairleigh Dickinson University Press; London and Cranbury, N.J.: Associated University Presses, 1995.

Mitchell, Linda E., ed. *Women in Medieval Western European Culture.* New York: Garland Publishing, 1999.

Parker, Roszika. *The Subversive Stitch: Embroidery and the Making of the Feminine.* London: Routledge, 1984.

Slatkin, Wendy. *Women Artists in History from Antiquity to the Present,* 4th ed. Upper Saddle River, N.J.: Prentice Hall, 2001.

Vigué, Jordi. *Great Women Masters of Art.* New York: Watson-Guptill Publications, 2003.

Weyl Carr, Annemarie. "Women as Artists in the Middle Ages: 'The Dark is Light Enough'." In *Dictionary of Women Artists,* edited by Delia Gaze. London and Chicago: Fitzroy Dearborn Publishers, 1997, pp. 3–21.

Wood, Jeryldene M. *Women, Art, and Spirituality: The Poor Clares of Early Modern Italy.* Cambridge and New York: Cambridge University Press, 1996.

See also **Artisan Families, Women of; Caterina Vigri; Christine de Pizan; Clothwork, Domestic; Devotional Art; Double Monasteries; Feminist Theories and**

ASCETICISM

The word *asceticism* comes from the Greek term for exercise or training. Rather than preparing for competitive games, however, the Christian ascetic disciplines her body in order to better serve God. Ascetic practice may take many forms: intensive prayer, vigils, fasting, flagellation, solitude, and sexual abstinence are among the most common. But whatever practice a person may embrace, the asceticism is informed by the same ideological underpinnings, centered on the notion that physical discipline serves the spiritual quest for God.

The Bible and the Eastern Church

There are a number of texts in the New Testament that support ascetic practice. Christ spoke about those who made themselves "eunuchs for the kingdom of heaven" (Matt. 19:11–12) in anticipation of the end of the world, a comment frequently interpreted as recommending chastity. But the ascetic strain in Christianity is especially indebted to the writings of St. Paul, who was influenced by the pagan philosophical tradition advocating disciplining the body so reason would prevail. Paul's neoplatonic perspective discerned an ongoing tension between body and soul. Hence Paul spoke of an ongoing war between his flesh and spirit that hampered his spiritual progress (Rom. 7.23; cf. Gal. 5.17). Like the ancients, who believed that marriage and sexual activity conflicted with the life of the mind, Paul encouraged sexual abstinence if possible, reasoning that sex and family life were distractions from service to God (1 Cor. 7.32).

There are a number of complex reasons why the ascetic lifestyle was especially appealing to women. Both classical philosophical and medical traditions associated man with ascendant spirit and woman with unruly flesh, an association seconded by the Pauline tradition. The author of the Epistle to the Ephesians further ordained that a husband should rule his wife as Christ rules the church, but love her as he would his own body (Eph. 5.22–30). This deprecation of the female body gave rise to the widespread conviction that a woman who subdued her body through different types of self-mortification achieved equivalence with men. Sexual abstinence in particular not only helped women overcome their biological inferiority, but also spared them the dangers of childbirth and the rule of a husband. Patristic writers perceived female ascetics as triumphing over the frailty of their sex, and often described such women in masculine terms. Since there are practically no female-authored writings remaining from this period, we do not know the extent to which women internalized such imagery. But it is certainly suggestive that one of the few exceptions, the Carthaginian martyr Perpetua (d. 203), recounted a dream in which she was transformed into a male gladiator before battling Satan.

Christian asceticism first became widespread in the east, where women figure prominently in a number of different venues. There are scriptural references to an order of widows—women who lived a life of sexual abstinence after their husbands' deaths and whose prayers were particularly valued by the Christian community (Acts 6.1; 1 Tim. 5.3–16). Consecrated virgins were a permanent fixture in the church from the second century. There are also scattered references to married couples who converted to absolute chastity, usually at the wife's behest, and pursued an ascetic lifestyle in their homes. Women were also among the early solitaries who withdrew to the Egyptian and Syrian desert to do penance.

Occasionally female ascetics became the center of controversy. For instance, a number of church authorities were outraged by the practice of syneisaktism—a domestic arrangement in which the growing number of clerics vowed to celibacy began to form domestic units with consecrated virgins (referred to as *syneisaktoi* in the East and *virgines subintroductae* in the West). This practice was seen as a test and proof of holiness. Although syneisaktism was condemned at the Council of Nicaea (325), it continued sporadically prior to the spread of female religious communities.

With the conversion of the Roman Empire in the fourth century, asceticism necessarily replaced martyrdom as the ultimate way of expressing devotion to God, and the number of ascetics grew. Treatises extolling the virtues of virginity proliferated, while women were actively recruited as consecrated virgins by patristic writers such as Ambrose (d. 397) and Jerome (d. 420). Jerome in particular attracted a learned circle of ascetically inclined Roman women of patrician birth.

Western Developments

In the Germanic successor states to Rome, female asceticism became increasingly channeled into monasticism. The women in question were generally of royal blood. With rare exceptions, such as the former Frankish queen Radegund (d. 587), the ascetic practices of these women were not particularly extreme, focusing on their rejection of court life.

The face of female asceticism changed over the course of the twelfth century, however, in terms of both personnel and degree of severity. With the flourishing of popular piety and the development of the penitential movement, female asceticism became more broadly based socially and numerically, but also more individualistic. Although monasticism remained an ideal, and the tradition of saintly princesses continued to flourish among the royal families of eastern Europe, female asceticism was to be particularly associated with the lay penitential movement and the burgeoning bourgeoisie. Some penitential communities, such as the Beguines of the Low Countries, arose spontaneously. But there were also lay affiliates to the Franciscans and Dominicans, known as members of the third order or tertiaries, who lived by a rule adapted for secular society. Many of the women attracted to this lifestyle either were or had been wives and mothers.

Ascetic Practices

The asceticism associated with some of the most visible of these laywomen was harsh, even by the standards of the desert solitaries. Women became particularly noted for their food asceticism: the Beguine Marie of Oignies (d. 1213) undertook marathon fasts, while Dominican tertiary Catherine of Siena (d. 1380) was said to exist on the consecrated host alone. Some women practiced startling acts of self-mortification: Marie of Oignies cut a huge piece of flesh from her side; Christina the Astonishing (d. 1224) was said to throw herself into ovens, submerge herself in cold streams, and hang herself from gallows; Dorothea of Montau (d. 1394) burned her nipples to negate pleasure while nursing. Moreover, holy women also welcomed externally wrought suffering: the holiness of Lydwine of Schiedam (d. 1433), for example, was manifested by the patience with which she endured the torments of her decomposing body; the revelation received by Julian of Norwich (d. after 1413) was in the course of an illness that she solicited as a favor from God many years before; despite the celebrated example of Francis of Assisi (d. 1226), the stigmata were almost exclusively visited upon women.

With few exceptions, women's asceticism was more extreme than parallel practices among men, but the reasons for this discrepancy are a source of scholarly

contention. Until recently, the prevailing view was that the women in question were suffering from internalized misogyny, hysteria, or both. Caroline Walker Bynum, however, has demonstrated the relationship between the intensely physical nature of female spirituality and the cult of the suffering Christ, a devotional orientation that coincided with the theological emphasis on the eucharist. Female asceticism and suffering was expressive of a deep identification with Christ's broken body. Rather than rejecting their bodies, these women could be regarded as sinking more deeply into their bodies, thereby representing Christ's humanity not only to themselves but to the Christian community at large. Because our perspective on these women is dependent on their male contemporaries, it is again impossible to know for certain the degree to which women themselves subscribed to this set of associations. Scholars such as André Vauchez and Dyan Elliott have drawn attention to the extent to which the male-authored hagiographies of female ascetics supported the church's larger theological program. Others, most notably Amy Hollywood, have argued that the preoccupation with the female body more accurately reflects the preoccupation of male authors rather than the spirituality of their female subjects.

The meaning of female asceticism, and the way it is expressed, changes greatly over time, yet there are certain elements that remain relatively static. From Christianity's earliest days, there has always been a large group of women who have chosen to express their piety in terms of ascetic abstention. Although we are unable to assess the spiritual gains, it is clear that asceticism brought with it some very tangible rewards. Ascetic chastity generally accorded women a degree of autonomy. Moreover, barred from positions of official authority in the church, women could distinguish themselves through ascetic practices, providing themselves with visibility, influence, and admiration not available to them through other means.

DYAN ELLIOTT

References and Further Reading

Bell, Rudolph. *Holy Anorexia*. Chicago: University of Chicago Press, 1985.
Brakke, David. *Athanasius and Asceticism*. Baltimore: The Johns Hopkins University Press, 1995.
Brown, Peter. *The Body and Society: Men, Women, and Sexual Renunciation in Early Christianity*. New York: Columbia University Press, 1988.
Bynum, Caroline Walker. *Fragmentation and Redemption: Essays on Gender and the Human Body in Medieval Religion*. New York: Zone Books, 1991.
———. *Holy Feast and Holy Fast: The Religious Significance of Food to Medieval Women*. Berkeley and Los Angeles: University of California Press, 1987.

Canon, Christopher. "Enclosure." In *The Cambridge Companion to Medieval Women's Writings*, edited by Carolyn Dinshaw and David Wallace. Cambridge: Cambridge University Press, 2003, pp. 109–123.

Castelli, Elizabeth. "'I Will Make Mary Male': Pieties of the Body and Gender Transformation of Christian Women in Late Antiquity." In *Body Guards: The Cultural Politics of Gender Ambiguity*, edited by Julia Epstein and Kristina Straub. New York: Routledge, 1991, pp. 29–49.

Clark, Elizabeth. "Ascetic Renunciation and Feminine Advancement: A Paradox of Late Ancient Christianity." In *Ascetic Piety and Women's Faith: Essays on Late Ancient Christianity*, edited by Elizabeth Clark. New York and Toronto: Edwin Mellen Press, 1986, pp. 175–208.

Cloke, Gillian. *This Female Man of God: Women and Spiritual Power in the Patristic Ages, A.D. 350–450*. London: Routledge, 1995.

Elliott, Dyan. *Proving Woman: Female Spirituality and Inquisitional Culture in the Later Middle Ages*. Princeton, N.J.: Princeton University Press, 2004.

———. "Woman: Flesh and Spirit." In *The Yale Guide to Medieval Holy Women*, edited by Alaistair Minnis and Rosalynn Voaden. New Haven, Conn.: Yale University Press, (forthcoming).

Elm, Susanna. *'Virgins of God': The Making of Asceticism in Late Antiquity*. Oxford: Clarendon Press, 1994.

Goodich, Michael. "The Contours of Female Piety in Later Medieval Hagiography." *Church History* 50 (1981): 20–32.

Hollywood, Amy. "Inside Out: Beatrice of Nazareth and Her Hagiographer." In *Gendered Voices: Medieval Saints and Their Interpreters*, edited by Catherine Mooney. Philadelphia: University of Pennsylvania Press, 1999, pp. 78–98.

Kieckhefer, Richard. *Unquiet Souls: Fourteenth-Century Saints and Their Religious Milieu*. Chicago: University of Chicago Press, 1984.

Klaniczay, Gábor. *Holy Rulers and Blessed Princesses: Dynastic Cults in Medieval Central Europe*, translated by Eva Pálmai. Cambridge: Cambridge University Press, 2002.

McNamara, Jo Ann. "The Need to Give: Suffering and Female Sanctity in the Middle Ages." In *Images of Sainthood in the Medieval Europe*, edited by Renate Blumenfeld-Kosinski and Timea Szell. Ithaca, N.Y.: Cornell University Press, 1991, pp. 199–221.

———. *A New Song: Celibate Women in the First Three Christian Centuries*. New York: Haworth Press, 1983.

Newman, Barbara. "Divine Power Made Perfect in Weakness: St. Hildegard on the Frail Sex." In *Medieval Religious Women*, Vol. 2, *Peaceweavers*, edited by John Nichols and Lillian Shank. Kalamazoo, Mich.: Cistercian Publications, 1987, pp. 103–122.

———. "Flaws in the Golden Bowl: Gender and Spiritual Formation in the Twelfth Century." In *From Virile Woman to WomanChrist: Studies in Medieval Religion and Literature*. Philadelphia: University of Pennsylvania Press, 1995, pp. 19–45.

Robertson, Elizabeth. "Medieval Medical Views of Women and Female Spirituality in the Ancrene Wisse and Julian of Norwich's Showings." In *Feminist Approaches to the Body in Medieval Literature*, edited by Linda Lomperis and Sarah Stanbury. Philadelphia: University of Pennsylvania Press, 1993, pp. 142–167.

Ruether, Rosemary. "Misogynism and Virginal Feminism in the Fathers of the Church." In *Religion and Sexism: Images of Woman in the Jewish and Christian Traditions*, edited by Rosemary Ruether. New York: Simon and Schuster, 1974, pp. 150–183.

Salisbury, Joyce. *Church Fathers, Independent Virgins*. London and New York: Verso Books, 1991.

Schulenburg, Jane Tibbetts. *Forgetful of Their Sex: Female Sanctity and Society ca. 500–1100*. Chicago: University of Chicago Press, 1998.

Vauchez, André. "Prosélytisme et action antihérétique en milieu feminin au XIIIe siècle: La Vie de Marie d'Oignies (d. 1213) par Jacques de Vitry." In *Propagande et contre-propagande religieuses*, edited by Jacques Marx. Brussels: Editions de l'Universitaire, 1987, pp. 95–110.

———. *Sainthood in the Later Middle Ages*, translated by Jean Birrell. Cambridge: Cambridge University Press, 1997.

Warren, Nancy. *Spiritual Economies: Female Monasticism in Later Medieval England*. Philadelphia: University of Pennsylvania Press, 2001.

Weinstein, Donald, and Rudolph Bell. *Saints and Society: The Two Worlds of Western Christendom, 1000–1700*. Chicago: University of Chicago Press, 1982.

See also **Anchoresses; Ancrene Wisse; Angela of Foligno; Beguines; Body in Literature and Religion; Bride of Christ: Imagery; Catherine of Genoa; Catherine of Siena; Celibacy, Clerical and Priests' Concubines; Chastity and Chaste Marriage; Christina the Astonishing; Christina of Markyate; Devotional Literature; Devotional Practices; Dorothea of Montau; Douceline of Digne; Elisabeth of Hungary; Eunuchs; Fasting and Food, Religious Aspects of; Gender Ideologies; Hagiography; Jerome, Influence of; Julian of Norwich; Laywomen, Religious; Margaret of Cortona; Marie of Oignies; Mary Magdalen; Mary the Egyptian; Monasticism and Nuns; Penitentials and Pastoral Manuals; Radegund; Sexuality: Regulation of; Tertiaries; Virginity; Virile Women; Vowesses; Widows**

AUDIENCE, WOMEN IN THE

It is not always easy to know whether women were readers, listeners, or spectators of a given medieval text. Factors that enable us to hypothesize a female audience include an author's appeal to a female patron, an overt declaration of writing for a female audience, records of manuscript ownership by women, content oriented towards women, and direct reference to women in the audience. These factors are not fully reliable, however. Studies of manuscript transmission show that many works reached readers not included among those explicitly addressed or envisioned by the author. We also know that women owned manuscripts that included works containing some of the most virulent misogyny. While the actual or even intended audience is often difficult to demonstrate, explicit addresses to women are sufficiently abundant to allow us a good understanding of the range of author–audience dynamics created for women when they were in the audience.

Underlying the relationship between the male author and his female readers was the belief—dominant among the clerical elite producing the majority of written texts in the medieval period—that because women were intellectually inferior, they tended to read superficially, at the literal rather than figurative or allegorical level. This attitude is exemplified in Chaucer's Wife of Bath, an "experiential" reader who picks and chooses elements of an authoritative tradition in order to justify her own desire to remarry. The belief in women's superficial reading is often manifested in the tone of condescension or paternalism towards female readers. It has been argued that didactic and conduct literature specifically written for women tended to use concrete imagery rather than abstractions and gave particular attention to engaging women's emotions and appealing to their personal experiences. Yet this attitude was by no means shared by all authors, and it is noteworthy that preachers might rely on the greater piety of women in their congregation to bring wayward husbands back to the path of virtue.

The great number of texts that address female readers testifies to the strong interest in women in the audience. Authors like Chrétien de Troyes dedicated their works to female patrons and claimed to have written their works at their request, flattering them in their prologues. Giovanni Boccaccio addressed his Decameron to "ladies in love," offering his stories as solace for the pains of love for which they had no other outlet because they were less free than men to engage in activities that would take them outside the home. Such overt declarations do not necessarily indicate an author's sincere intention to write for women or on their behalf. An author may use flattery as a tactic to discipline his female reader and encourage her to conform to standard gender ideology, as in much conduct literature. In the Decameron, the deferential stance of the narrator is replaced elsewhere in the work with a more salacious tone, as when he encourages any women readers who doubt his weightiness (seriousness) as a writer to "weigh" him. Such sexual innuendo, common in other narratives (and in drama, such as the French farce), suggests that women, even when apparently the privileged recipients of a work, could be used for the entertainment of a masculine audience, although it should be noted that women may well have been able to appreciate the humor of a narrator's banter or teasing.

Male authors were clearly concerned with how women would react to negative portrayals of female characters or other potentially offensive content. This anxiety is evident in the many "apologies" made to female readers, the sincerity of which is generally suspect. Chaucer apologizes for his representation of the faithless Criseyde by claiming he would more gladly have written about the faithfulness of Penelope. The narrator in the Roman de Silence closes the work by noting that the "good woman" ought not to be angry with his harsh portrayal of the romance's female protagonist, implying that any reader who objects is a "bad woman." Another pseudo-apology consists of blaming the author's source, as does Jean LeFèvre concerning his translation into French of the Lamentations of Matheolus. Authors also counter women's objections to their work by invoking the responsibility of the reader. Jean de Meun closes the Roman de la Rose by cautioning women to read properly and not to "defame" the great work or its author. Boccaccio tells any "prudish" or "self-righteous" ladies in his audience that his stories are blameless and that it is instead their dirty minds that are at fault. By the later Middle Ages, the ubiquitous dubious apology to women has itself become a topos exploited for humorous effect. Chaucer's Nun's Priest, in his tale of Chauntecleer the cock, facetiously bids the audience to pass over his blame of women because "Thise been the cokkes wordes, and nat myne."

While both flattery of female readers and apologies to them for offensive content are ultimately more in the service of men than of women, feminist scholars since the 1990s have investigated the extent to which women may actively have resisted the misogyny of the works they read. Given the paucity of written records of women's responses, assessing how women might have reacted to texts is a speculative endeavor relying on indirect evidence. Implicit in the author's apology, for example, is anxiety that his work will meet with resistance; the apology is an effort to forestall objections to his work. Another clue to women's resistant reading is the many inscribed female "readers" or respondents who challenge their male interlocutors. These challenges vary from the mocking put-downs of the passing knight's advances by the shepherdess of the pastourelle to the well-crafted replies of the women in the lyric (tenso or jeu-parti) to the more learned and rhetorically sophisticated response of the female respondent in Richard de Fournival's Bestiaire d'Amour. They also occur in the medieval Arab adab (collections of anecdotes, traditions, and etiquette). Female respondents offer contrary perspectives on love and courtship and critique the misogyny of the written tradition. The Wife of Bath famously hurled her husband's "Book of Wicked Wives" into the flames, thus dramatizing a woman's rejection of clerical antifeminism. Such resistant female readers in fiction were, of course, used most often to ironic effect; rarely should they be seen as straightforward advocates for women. Yet the recurrent use of such resistant figures suggests an awareness, even an anxiety, that women could resist the ideology of the authoritative tradition.

The arguments of fictional female readers also would later be used by the most famous female reader of the Middle Ages, Christine de Pizan, whose attacks on the *Romance of the Rose* have been foundational in our thinking about women's reception of medieval texts. Christine criticized Jean de Meun and other male authors not only for defaming women but for failing to consider the effect of this misogyny on women who read their works. Her allegorical *Book of the City of Ladies* (1405) opens with Christine reading the *Lamentations* of Matheolus and coming to detest herself and the entire feminine sex. Christine's self-loathing as a result of her reading is happily countered when Lady Reason appears before Christine and instructs her on the goodness of women through historical examples of exemplary women. Christine is also noteworthy in explicitly addressing her work to a female audience. Whereas male authors were particularly self-conscious in addressing women in the audience, female authors made surprisingly few such references. Marie de France dedicated her work to a male patron and nowhere addresses women in particular. While many known female authors wrote within a religious community, and thus can be said to have a primarily female audience, they also wrote for male spiritual advisers or benefactors and the audience addressed in their works was often gender neutral. Christine, however, consistently addresses women both in her *City of Ladies* and in *The Book of the Three Virtues*, which she wrote "for the instruction of women," hoping that it would be copied and read for years to come by women throughout the world.

LISA PERFETTI

References and Further Reading

Ashley, Kathleen, and Robert L. A. Clark, eds. *Medieval Conduct*. Minneapolis and London: University of Minnesota Press, 2001.

Bartlett, Anne Clark. *Male Authors, Female Readers: Representation and Subjectivity in Middle English Devotional Literature*. Ithaca and London: Cornell University Press, 1995.

Farmer, Sharon. "Persuasive Voices: Clerical Images of Medieval Wives." *Speculum* 61(3) (1986): 517–543.

Grisé, C. Annette. "Women's Devotional Reading in Late-Medieval England and the Gendered Reader." *Medium Aevum* 71(2) (2002): 209–225.

Krueger, Roberta. *Women Readers and the Ideology of Gender in Old French Verse Romance*. Cambridge: Cambridge University Press, 1993.

Mann, Jill. *Apologies to Women*. Cambridge: Cambridge University Press, 1990.

McDonald, Nicola F. "Chaucer's *Legend of Good Women*, Ladies at Court and the Female Reader." *Chaucer Review* 35(1) (2000): 22–42.

Pratt, Karen. "The Strains of Defense: The Many Voices in Jean LeFèvre's *Livre de Leesce*." In *Gender in Debate from the Early Middle Ages to the Renaissance*, edited by Thelma S. Fenster and Clare A. Lees. New York: Palgrave, 2002, pp. 113–133.

Robertson, Elizabeth. *Early English Devotional Prose and the Female Audience*. Knoxville: University of Tennessee Press, 1990.

Solterer, Helen. *The Master and Minerva: Disputing Women in French Medieval Culture*. Berkeley: University of California Press, 1995.

See also **Boccaccio, Giovanni; Chaucer, Geoffrey; Christine de Pizan; Debate Literature; Defenses of Women; Literacy and Reading: Latin; Literacy and Reading: Vernacular; Misogyny; Pastourelle; Patronage, Literary; Reader-Response Criticism; Résponse du Bestiaire d'Amour; Roman de la Rose and Its Reception; Roman de Silence; Wife of Bath**

AUGUSTINE, INFLUENCE OF

Augustine, who lived from 354 to 430, was born in the small town of Thagaste in Roman North Africa. He studied rhetoric in Carthage and, except for five years in Rome and Milan, where he taught rhetoric and converted to Christianity, spent most of his life in North Africa. He returned home from Italy in 388 and served as bishop of the city of Hippo from 395 until his death. Although he spent most of his life in a provincial backwater, Augustine had an enormous importance in the development of western Christian ideas about gender and sexuality; many have blamed him outright for the oppression of women in the Christian tradition. It is clear that Augustine, like most late antique Christian authors, was comfortable assuming that women were subordinate to men according to the order of creation, and, indeed, were created to bear children for men. In the Christian version of this scheme, male domination of women is a consequence of the original sin brought upon humans by the fall of Adam and Eve.

Relationships with Women

Augustine did have some intense and powerful relationships with women, especially his mother, Monica. Monica was a Christian, and it is her persistent attention to her son's spiritual life to which he attributes his ultimate conversion to Christianity after years of exploring more fashionable religious traditions like those of the Neoplatonists and the Manichees. Augustine's early dialogues portray her as a philosophical interlocutor, and it was with her, shortly before her death, that he had an experience of mystical union at the seaport of Ostia. The other important woman in Augustine's life was his companion, the mother of his son Adeodatus. She is often called his concubine, although Augustine never refers to her this way, and in his autobiographical *Confessions*, he describes his break with her as the painful price he needed to pay to marry into a good Christian family, something much desired by Monica. After this relationship, Augustine struggled with chastity but never did marry; rather, he adopted an ascetic life.

Unlike his contemporary Jerome, Augustine did not cultivate female companions, but he did have female correspondents, important Roman women who had taken refuge in North Africa after the sack of Rome by the Visigoths in 410. Augustine wrote to Proba about the nature of prayer and to Juliana about the decision of her daughter Demetrias to consecrate her virginity to God. His letters to other consecrated virgins and widows offered spiritual counsel on such topics as the death of family members, the vision of God in the next world, the equality of men and women in the Resurrection, heretics, and study. In letter 262, Augustine responds to Ecdicia's complaints about her husband's infidelity, that this is due in part to her one-sided decision to live a life of chaste asceticism against his will. Even though Augustine had a high view of sexual renunciation, and while he certainly did not approve of her husband's behavior, he tells Ecdicia that her marriage vows are holier than her quasi-monastic life. Augustine's letters 210 and 211 are addressed to the community of nuns in Hippo that had been led by his widowed sister. In letter 211 he offers a set of rules for the community; this is one (and some say the earliest) version of Augustine's monastic rule.

The Inferiority of Women

In spite of these relationships with women, Augustine believed they were inferior to men by reason of physicality, but he also taught a type of spiritual equality between men and women. Insofar as women participated in the category "human being," as this category was defined by men, they were spiritual equals of men. In a famous passage of *De trinitate*, Augustine tries to clarify how women are in God's image only when they are considered "humanity" along with males, but not as embodied female human beings:

The woman together with the man is the image of God, so that the whole substance is one image. But when she is assigned as a helpmate, which pertains to her alone, she is not the image of God; however, what pertains to man alone, he is the image of God just as fully and completely as he is joined with the woman into one. (*De trinitate* XII,7,10)

This is a restatement of 1 Corinthians 11:7, in which Paul says that men are forbidden to cover their heads because they are the reflection of God, but women must cover their heads since they are, rather, the reflection of the male. As feminist scholars have noted, this Pauline line seems to contradict Genesis 1:27–28, which states that male and female were both created in the image of God. But still, as Augustine's defenders have noted, in this limited sense, women and men are equally in the image of God, and equally able to be in the divine presence in the Resurrection. That means that women should be baptized and could be saved. But, even when women have the same rights to embodiment as men, they are still reminders of fallen human nature. Furthermore, in comparison to men, women are weak. Some women, like Saints Perpetua and Felicity, are still capable of heroic courage and fortitude in the face of martyrdom, but this is because famous female saints behaved *viriliter*—in a manly way.

Theoretical Perspectives

Some twentieth-century scholars of early Christianity have argued that it is to Augustine's credit that he insisted that women also participate in the category *homo*, and therefore in the image of God; even feminist scholars have made this argument. These sympathetic portraits conclude that the problem for Augustine is sexuality, not women, and that, for his culture, he was in fact rather positively disposed towards women since he considered women spiritual equals before God and treated the women he knew with respect. Of course, this explanation is not at all comforting to many feminist historians and theologians, some of whom have argued that Augustine's views on women were just a product of his negative attitude towards sexuality in general, influenced by his own experience. The tragedy, they say, is that these ideas of women's existential limits are enshrined in medieval theology and canon law and thus became the basis for Roman Catholic theology on those subjects. As early as 1977, Clark and Richardson showcased the obvious texts, prefacing Augustine's words with brief remarks highlighting how they affected later Christian doctrine. This has become the main modern critique of Augustine on gender: Augustine makes the body "the cornerstone of his theology" and is ultimately to blame for Christian sexual repression and misogyny altogether because of his pessimistic views of sexuality, politics, and human nature, ideas that eventually dominated in Western culture. Thus, it is not what Augustine meant but rather his legacy that really counts, since it is the source of Western Christian patriarchal anthropology. The most recent analysis of the issue brings to bear many pertinent facets of Augustine's culture, for example, the context of a slave society, to suggest important and still unexplored consequences of the relegation of women to the private sphere, including the history of the status and power of Christian women ascetics. The very fact that Ecdicia evoked such a reaction from Augustine suggests the tensions ascetic women were creating in fifth-century Christian society and looks ahead to the tensions that will be evident in medieval discussions of consecrated and enclosed women.

It is, then, not just the power of Augustine's writings but how well they fit into a late antique Christian anthropology that made such an impact on the Western Christian tradition. The irony of this is evident when the ever-changing Western Christian community has, from age to age, turned to see what Augustine, whose understanding of human nature has been thought to transcend the limits of his place and time, can explain about the humanity of women and the role of gender in human life.

E. ANN MATTER

References and Further Reading

Augustine of Hippo. *Confessions*, translated by Henry Chadwick. Oxford: Oxford University Press, 1998.
———, *Letters*, translated by Sister Wilfred Parsons. Fathers of the Church, vols. 12, 18, 20. New York: Fathers of the Church, 1951–1953.
Børresen, Kari Elisabeth. "In Defence of Augustine: How 'Femina' is 'homo.'" In *Collectanea Augustiniana. Festschrift für T. J. van Bavel*. Leuven: Leuven University Press, 1990, pp. 411–428.
Clark, Elizabeth, and Herbert Richardson. *Women and Religion: A Feminist Sourcebook of Christian Thought*. New York: Harper & Row, 1977.
Daly, Mary. *The Church and the Second Sex*. New York: Harper & Row, 1968.
Matter, E. Ann. "Augustine and Women." In *Augustine Through the Ages: An Encyclopedia*, edited by Allan Fitzgerald. Hamden, Conn.: Garland Publishing, 2000, pp. 887–892.
Miles, M. R. *Carnal Knowing: Female Nakedness and Religious Meaning in the Christian West*. Boston: Beacon Press, 1989.
Pagels, Elaine. *Adam, Eve, and the Serpent*. New York: Random House, 1988.
Power, Kim. *Veiled Desire: Augustine on Women*. New York: Continuum, 1996.
Ruether, Rosemary Radford. *Sexism and God-Talk: Toward a Feminist Theology*. Boston: Beacon Press, 1983.

See also **Chastity and Chaste Marriage; Eve; Gender Ideologies; Jerome, Influence of; Monastic Rules; Theology; Virile Women**

AUTOHAGIOGRAPHY

Autohagiography is an account of a holy person's life written or told by its subject, usually a woman. Although medieval autohagiographies are often called "spiritual autobiographies," they distinguish themselves from that capacious genre by their thematic, essentially ahistorical focus. Moreover, the authors often explicitly expressed their desire to convey a universal and spiritual, rather than a personal, truth. In the service of such truth, Julian of Norwich counseled the readers of her revelations, "for God's sake, ... for your own profit, ... leave off picturing the wretched worm ... to whom [the visions were] shown, and ... mightily, wisely, lovingly and meekly think of God, who, out of his courteous love and endless goodness would have this vision shown generally for the comfort of us all."

Autohagiographies rarely appear as texts unto themselves. Most often, autobiographical elements are contained within other forms: didactic treatises, letters, revelations, even poems; autobiography is an attribute of these works, not their purpose. Though they are indeed stories of lives told by their subject, autohagiographies reject the direct revelation of outward and inward experience that later became the identifying features of autobiographical writing. Many women's autohagiographies began as oral recitations: confessions to a priest, revelations to an abbess or a friend, sermons to fellow nuns, words uttered in ecstasy. Such texts were frequently taken down by others, copied, translated, retranslated, and finally incorporated into holy biographies. Magdalena of Freiburg's *Erklüarung des Vaterunsers*, a lengthy line-by-line meditation on the Pater Noster, appears in manuscript as a copy of jottings taken down swiftly, as the scribe strives to keep up with the mystic's outpourings. Elisabeth of Schönau dictated her visions to her brother, the monk Ekbert; Angela of Foligno's experiences and spiritual instructions were written, often in her voice, by her confessor, a friar to whom she had been supernaturally directed by St. Francis; Hildegard of Bingen chose as amanuensis Volmar, a monk with whom she felt special spiritual harmony, so that she could trust him to take down her words as she spoke them, correct her grammar, and read back the final version for her approval. In such cases, autohagiography served a public, myth-making purpose, not an individual one.

More closely related to traditional hagiography than to autobiography in the modern sense, autohagiography recounts natural and supernatural events with equal conviction, often advancing only the latter as explanation or justification for its subject's action. The genre shares with hagiography the intention to represent the life as exemplary rather than real, taking as its literary models earlier lives of the saints and martyrs, Bible stories and scripture-based narratives (like the popular devotional texts, *Meditations on the Life of Christ*), and religious allegories. Most significantly, autohagiography reconstructs the life of its subject to conform to cultural conceptions of holiness. Like the autobiographer, the autohagiographer arranges selected thoughts, feelings, and events into a coherent narrative, but, like the hagiographer, she (or he) reshapes those elements into conventional forms.

If autohagiography is not strictly autobiography, neither is it precisely hagiography, whose primary purposes are to honor the heroic deeds of the saints and to evoke admiration, imitation, and faith in readers and listeners. To write of oneself in the hagiographic mode, then, might be construed as an act of repellent self-regard, utterly at odds with hagiography's intentions. And indeed, autohagiographers, acutely aware of the problem, specifically denied writing for the purpose of honoring themselves or demonstrating their right to membership in the company of the saints. Rather, they wrote for the purpose of inspiring a feeling of shared human experience in their readers. In her introduction to *Le Sette Armi Spirituali*, Caterina of Bologna prays that "anyone who takes notice of this little work, made with divine assistance by me ... not attribute it to the vice of presumption, nor take any error from this little book, which I, the abovementioned little dog, have written in my own hand, solely for fear of the divine rebuke if I should be silent concerning what might be helpful to others."

This meant expressing a common identity, not an individual one, and expressing truths that existed beyond the realm of human sensibilities. To do so, autohagiographers sought to efface themselves in their text by using formulae of humility and submission. Margery Kempe, for example, is well known for her use of the phrase "this creature" to refer to herself throughout her *Book*; other writers referred to themselves as "a certain virgin," "a servant of God," "a poor little womanly figure," or even "a wretched worm." For similar reasons, autohagiographers often repressed historical detail, maintaining a deliberate silence about external particulars that might have distinguished them from their fellows, for identifiable events

and personalities were bound to obscure the spiritual truth they wished to convey. Caterina of Bologna's *Sette Armi Spirituali* is a case in point. In this two-part treatise she proposes her own personal trial, obedience, as the central problem of monastic life. In the first part she allegorically "arms" novices with the eponymous seven weapons, while in the second part she shows how the weapons are to be used in a disguised version of her own struggles with submission. The disguise consists of three elements characteristic of autohagiography: use of the third person; transformation of the personal into the general (for example, relatives offering to help her leave the convent become the devil trying to tempt "a certain virgin"); and rearrangement of accidental chronological order into spiritually significant order (the three visions chronicling her travails escalate in intensity, whereas the historical events which generated the visions occurred in a different, rather anticlimactic sequence).

Except when relating revelations, autohagiographers used few, if any, dates, nor did they regularly name people or places. They often omitted the parts of their lives that predated their conversion and disguised selected remaining incidents by arranging them, as Caterina did, to invoke the larger pattern of salvation history. They derived their devotional formulae from classical rhetoric, especially humility *topoi*, conventions of courtly submission, and apologies for failures of style or talent.

Autohagiography shares with other forms of medieval religious literature a concern for spiritual truth, orthodoxy, and authority. Expression of an individual's experience was expected to claim an authority greater than the writer's own (a Church Father, God, or a worthy pagan); to fit into a familiar pattern; and to illustrate a point of general applicability. Ostensibly personal elements also function conventionally within the genre, setting the scene for the central allegory, the battle between the World and the Spirit. The use of such conventions conferred legitimacy upon a genre in which women preached and taught, despite traditional prohibitions. Thus, for example, the scriptural dictum (I Cor. i.xxvii) that God has elected the weak to confound the strong (often cited in women's autohagiographies), cancelled, for many, St. Paul's ban on women's preaching and teaching. Catherine of Siena quoted the Lord as explaining, "I decided to send women, unknowing, weak and fragile by nature, but rich in my divine wisdom, to confound their [powerful men's] pride and rashness." Julian of Norwich addressed the issue even more directly: "God forbid that you should say or assume that I am a teacher, for I do not mean it so ... for I am a woman, ignorant, weak and frail.... But I know well what I am saying here, for I have it by the showing of him that is the sovereign teacher.... Just because I am a woman, should I therefore not tell you of the goodness of God, since I saw at the that same time that it is his will that it be known?" Women's authority to write, therefore, came not only from their visionary experience, from the mandate of God and the command of their confessor, but from the form in which they wrote. That is, they replaced traditional *auctores* not with experience but with genre.

The combination of intense religious fervor (the oft-noted "feminization" of late medieval piety), old-fashioned hagiographic models, such as those that glorify monastic virtues, and allegorical presentation of personal experience constitutes the particular feminine contribution to the art of autohagiography in the Middle Ages. But the visions, revelations, and admonitions in autohagiography also claimed authority, based upon events in their authors' own lives, for the composition of autohagiographies arose out of real, not fictive, experience. In accounts of their spiritual development almost all autohagiographers referred, however obliquely, to crucial events in their lives: the crises that precipitated their conversion, their loss of family, their rejection of marriage, their temptations. One of the most striking instances of autobiography recast as autohagiography appears in Angela of Foligno's *Liber de Verum Fidelium Experientia*. "It happened that my mother, who was a great impediment to me, died; and a short while later my husband and all my children died as well. And because, since the time I began to take the spiritual path, I had prayed to God that they would die, I felt great consolation...." Angela's intention here is to express an exemplary desire for God, not, as it might appear, callous selfishness. That family members constitute "impediments" to her spiritual development does not suggest that she does not love them or mourn their passing. But these are not the concerns of autohagiography. The spiritual message, to leave behind human attachments and devote oneself to God, erases the expression of personal feelings. Nevertheless, readers *are* meant to identify with Angela's loss in order that they may redirect their own unruly emotions into the more capacious channel of God's love and, like her, receive consolation.

KATE GREENSPAN

References and Further Reading

Atkinson, Clarissa. *Mystic and Pilgrim: The Book and the World of Margery Kempe*. Ithaca: Cornell University Press, 1983.

Bynum, Caroline Walker. *Holy Feast and Holy Fast*. Berkeley: University of California Press, 1987.

Curtius, Ernst R. *European Literature and the Latin Middle Ages*, translated by Willard R. Trask. Princeton: Princeton University Press, 1973.

Dronke, Peter. *Women Writers in the Middle Ages: A Critical Study of Texts from Perpetua (+203) to Marguérite Porete (+1310)*. Cambridge: Cambridge University Press, 1984.

Erskine, John A. "Margery Kempe and Her Models: The Role of the Authorial Voice." *Mystics Quarterly* 15 (1989): 75–85.

Gold, Penny Schine. *The Lady and the Virgin: Image, Attitude, and Experience in Twelfth-Century France*. Chicago and London: University of Chicago Press, 1985.

Greenspan, Kate. "Autohagiography and Medieval Women's Spiritual Autobiography." In *Gender and Text in the Middle Ages*, edited by Jane Chance. University of Florida Press, 1996, pp. 216–236.

Heffernan, Thomas J. *Sacred Biography: Saints and Their Biographers in the Middle Ages*. New York and Oxford: Oxford University Press, 1988.

Heilbrun, Carolyn G. *Writing a Woman's Life*. New York: Ballantine Books, 1988.

Hilary, Christine R. "The *Confessio* Tradition from Augustine to Chaucer." Dissertation, University of California–Berkeley, 1979.

Joensen, Leyvoy. "The Flesh Made Word: Allegory in the *Book of Margery Kempe*." In *Auto-Biographical Studies*: a/b 6(2) 1991, 169–182.

Johnson, Lynn Staley. "The Trope of the Scribe and the Question of Literary Authority in the Works of Julian of Norwich and Margery Kempe." *Speculum* 66 (1991): 820–838.

Kieckhefer, Richard. *Unquiet Souls: Fourteenth-Century Saints and Their Religious Milieu*. Chicago: University of Chicago Press, 1984.

Newman, Barbara. *Sister of Wisdom: St. Hildegard's Theology of the Feminine*. Berkeley: University of California Press, 1987.

Nichols, John, and Lillian T. Shank, eds. *Peaceweavers*. Medieval Religious Women 2. Kalamazoo, Mich.: Cistercian Publications, 1987.

O'Brien, Elmer. *Varieties of Mystic Experience*. New York and Toronto: Holt, Rinehart and Winston, 1964.

Pascal, Roy. *Design and Truth in Autobiography*. London: Routledge & Kegan Paul, 1960.

Petroff, Elizabeth Alvilda. *Medieval Women's Visionary Literature*. New York and Oxford: Oxford University Press, 1986.

Smith, Sidonie. *A Poetics of Women's Autobiography*. Bloomington, Ind.: Indiana University Press, 1987.

Thiébaux, Marcelle, trans. *The Writing of Medieval Women*. New York & London: Garland Publishing, 1987.

Weinstein, Donald, and Rudolph M. Bell. *Saints and Society: The Two Worlds of Western Christendom, 1000–1700*. Chicago: University of Chicago Press, 1982.

Weintraub, Karl. *The Value of the Individual: Self and Circumstance in Autobiography*. Chicago: University of Chicago Press, 1982.

Wilson, Katharina M., ed. *Medieval Women Writers*. Athens, Ga.: University of Georgia Press, 1984.

Wyschogrod, Edith. *Saints and Postmodernism: Revisioning Moral Philosophy*. Chicago: University of Chicago Press, 1990.

See also **Angela of Foligno; Audience, Women as; Bible, Women in; Bride of Christ: Imagery; Caterina Vigri; Devotional Literature; Feminist Theories and Methodologies; Hagiography; Hildegard of Bingen;**

Julian of Norwich; Kempe, Margery; Letter Writing; Mysticism and Mystics; Mystics' Writings; Sister-Books and Other Convent Chronicles

AVA

The last lines of a poem on the Last Judgement, transmitted in the twelfth century Vorau manuscript (Vorau Stiftsbibliothek, cod. 276), identify the author as a woman called Ava, the mother of two sons. It has been suggested that this Ava may be identical to a recluse whose death in 1127 is recorded in the annals of the monastery of Melk.

Her oeuvre consists of short religious poems. Two of these, the life of John the Baptist and an account of the life of Jesus, closely follow the gospel readings of the liturgical year and narrate events from the birth of John the Baptist to the resurrection. John is portrayed as the precursor of Christ; his birth marks the beginning of a new era in salvation history, and the epilogue recommends him as a powerful intercessor. The "Life of Jesus" concentrates on the events of Christ's life as recounted in the gospels, but it shows a marked predilection for dialogue scenes. In the miracle stories selected, women appear to play a prominent part, from the role of Mary at the wedding in Cana to the anointing of Jesus' feet, which is here attributed to Mary, the sister of Martha. The final section of the "Life of Jesus," a list of the seven gifts of the Holy Spirit, and two additional poems, the "Antichrist" and the "Last Judgement," complete the framework of salvation history that links all four poems.

While Ava addresses her audience in first-person plural forms, which highlight the effect of the narrated events for all Christians, she frequently refers to her work as a book, which may suggest that she was familiar with contemporary models of learned authorship.

ALMUT SUERBAUM

References and Further Reading

Ava, Ava's New Testament Narratives: When the Old Law Passed Away, trans. by James A. Rushing Jr. Kalamazoo, MI: Medieval Institute Publications, 2003.

Maurer, Friedrich, ed. *Die Dichtungen der Frau Ava.* Tübingen: Niemeyer, 1966.

See also **Literature, German; Theology; Women Authors: German Texts**

B

BAKE, ALIJT

Following a period during which she tried disparate forms of the spiritual life, Alijt Bake (1415–1455) chose, in 1440, the enclosed convent of canonesses at Galilea in Ghent. Galilea had only recently joined the Chapter of Windesheim, the monastic branch of the Devotio Moderna (Modern Devotion). Disappointed with the quality of the life of asceticism and virtue she encountered there, Bake was thrown into a deep spiritual crisis. But Christ Himself showed her the way in a vision on Ascension Day: she must remain at Galilea and from there bring about reforms of the monastic life.

Five years later Alijt Bake was elected prioress of Galilea, giving her the opportunity to put her plans for reform into action. Her own writings constitute the most important witness to this. Around 1446 the newly elected prioress wrote a number of treatises, which she intended to serve as testaments for her fellow sisters. The central theme of her teaching is most explicitly laid out in her treatise *De vier kruiswegen* (*The Four Ways of the Cross*), in which she argues for a radical emulation of the Suffering of Christ. Between 1451 and 1452 the prioress worked on a spiritual autobiography in two parts (of which the first part, the *Boeck der tribulatien* [*Book of Tribulations*], has been lost). In part two, *Mijn beghin ende voortganck* (*My Beginning and Progress*), she describes her spiritual path, a path that was certainly not without its trials. But in constant association with Christ, in visions and internal dialogues, she was able to shape her exceptional destiny.

Alijt Bake's last treatise carries the telling title *Brief uit de ballingschap* (*Letter from Exile*). In 1455, her life took a dramatic turn. By the authority of the administration of the Chapter of Windesheim, Bake was dismissed from her leadership position and banished. The *Letter* reveals that she had a serious clash of opinion with the administrators of Windesheim: Bake was a proponent of an interior life, based on a personal relationship with Christ. The Chapter of Windesheim held that women should limit themselves to external, visible forms of piety, such as obeying one's superiors or doing hard manual labor. At the same time, all nuns in the Windesheim monasteries were forbidden to write about their religious experiences. Alijt Bake died in 1455, at the age of 40.

WYBREN SCHEEPSMA

References and Further Reading

Bollmann, Anne. "'Being a Woman of My Own': Alijt Bake (1415–1455) as Reformer of the Inner Self." In *Seeing and Knowing: Women and Learning in Medieval Europe, 1200–1550*, edited by Anneke B. Mulder-Bakker. Turnhout: Brepols, 2004, pp. 67–96.

Dijk, Rudolf. Th. M. van. "De mystieke weg van Alijt Bake (1415–1455)." *Ons geestelijk erf* 66 (1992): 115–133.

Lievens, Robrecht. "Alijt Bake van Utrecht (1415–1455)." *Nederlands archief voor kerkgeschiedenis* 42 (1958): 127–151.

Ruh, Kurt. *Geschichte der abendländische Mystik*, vol. 4, *Die niederländische Mystik des 14. bis 16. Jahrhunderts*. München: C. H. Beck, 1999.

Scheepsma, Wybren. *Deemoed en devotie: De koorvrouwen van Windesheim en hun geschriften*. Amsterdam: Prometheus, 1997.

————. "Mysticism and Modern Devotion: Alijt Bakes (1415–1455) Lessons in the Mystical Way of Living." In *Spirituality Renewed: Studies on the Significant Representatives of the Modern Devotion*, edited by Hein Blommestijn, Charles Caspers, and Rijcklof Hofman. Leuven: Peeters, 2003, pp. 157–167.

————. *Medieval Religious Women in the Low Countries: The Modern Devotion, the Canonesses of Windesheim, and their Writings*, translated by David F. Johnson. Woodbridge, Suffolk, England: The Boydell Press, 2004.

————. "'Van die memorie der passien ons heren' van Alijt Bake." *Ons geestelijk erf* 68 (1994): 106–128.

————. "De trechter en de spin. Metaforen voor mystiek leiderschap van Alijt Bake." *Ons geestelijk erf* 69 (1995): 222–234.

Spaapen, B. "Middeleeuwse Passiemystiek, II. De vier kruiswegen van Alijt Bake." *Ons geestelijk erf* 40 (1966): 5–64.

————. "Middeleeuwse Passiemystiek, III. De autobiografie van Alijt Bake." *Ons geestelijk erf* 41 (1967): 209–301 and 321–350.

————. "Middeleeuwse Passiemystiek, IV. De brief uit de ballingschap." *Ons geestelijk erf* 41 (1967): 351–367.

————. "Middeleeuwse Passiemystiek, V. De kloosteronderrichtingen van Alijt Bake, 1 De weg van de ezel." *Ons geestelijk erf* 42 (1968): 5–32.

————. "De lessen van Palmzondag." *Ons geestelijk erf* 42 (1968): 225–261.

————. "De louteringsnacht van de actie." *Ons geestelijk erf* 42 (1968): 374–421.

————. "De weg der victorie." *Ons geestelijk erf* 43 (1969): 270–304.

See also **Asceticism; Canonesses; Modern Devotion; Devotional Literature; Flanders; Monasticism and Nuns; Mysticism and Mystics**

BALLADS

Most medieval ballads are narrative tales characterized by simple language and meter and episodic plots that emphasize dialogue and action. Usually sung or recited, they offered a compressed storyline driven by heightened emotional tension, fast-paced action, or spectacular events to audiences of both men and women ranging throughout the social scale, many of them already familiar with the stories being told. Some ballads were clearly part of memorial culture, while others have closer ties to literary works, suggesting a pattern of composition and dissemination involving both oral and literary traditions. Particularly in cases of oral transmission, ballads are notoriously difficult to date, and the extant medieval ballads were for the most part recorded in the fifteenth century or later, in many instances a long time after they were first enjoyed. The content of early ballads most often comes from medieval romance and epic, offering tales of heroic or royal figures and their adventures. Other common subjects included family life or love and relationships, often with an emphasis on courtship, seduction, rape, adultery, pregnancy, or star-crossed lovers. Though they occasionally come out on top, women are frequently involved in situations that emphasize their vulnerability, and violence is common—at times the woman perpetrates it, but usually she is the excuse or the target for violence. Though women may exert a fair degree of agency, it is often with dire consequences.

The action of many domestic ballads suggests a need to contain femininity and assert masculine power. The motif of the "walled-up wife," possibly of medieval origin, remains popular throughout the Balkans, with analogues in India. The variants involve the sacrifice of a woman who is immured alive or drowned in order to complete a building project that continually falls down or to fix a well that will not fill with water (Dundes 186–188, 190–192). Most often the woman is sacrificed by her husband or brothers, men who traditionally held power over medieval women's lives. Women are equally powerless in tales involving forced or prohibited marriages, as in the Hungarian ballad "Kate Kádár," thought by some scholars to originate in the late Middle Ages (Kadar 20). The ballad tells of how Martin Gyulai's mother forbade him to marry Kate Kádár because of her low social status. When Martin insists, his mother has Kate drowned, whereupon Martin drowns himself (Kadar 30–36). The mother's attempt to exercise power over her son is punished, but Kate's fate also points to the particular precariousness of the unmarried woman's position.

In the courtship story and its variations, women often play the role of love object, a figure of desirable sexuality to be obtained by men, with or without her consent. The woman may be in love with the hero, but equally a man may attempt to seduce or rape her when she refuses him. In medieval Castilian ballads, the rape of Muslim women serves as a way for Christian men to dominate Muslim men, and both Muslim and Jewish men talk and act submissively in response to the aggressive actions and language that define the masculinity of Christian men (Mirrer 49–50, 70–77). In many medieval Scandinavian ballads, the problem of rape is resolved by the death of the rapist (though in a few cases the woman marries him). Either the woman herself or her male relatives stab the man to death, or he is beheaded by the king or representatives of local justice (Jonsson et al. D145–93). These would seem to operate as cautionary tales—women were often warned not to go out where they could be seen by men, lest they be desired—that reveal the vulnerability of women in the medieval world.

In contrast, ballads involving outlaws or heroic figures focus, with very few exceptions, on male protagonists, paying little or no attention to women. In heroic ballads the hero surmounts impossible odds, and in most cases the focus is on fighting. Women, when present at all, serve as the motive for action (needing to be rescued or avenged) or as markers of status. Among the earliest English ballads are those of the outlaw Robin Hood. In these tales action centers on Robin's adventures, and Maid Marian is entirely absent from all but three ballads. Sometimes Robin defeats and kills those who set out to harm him, but more often he encounters and fights another man in the forest until the two become friends. Here, fighting serves as a way of bonding the two men in fellowship as they prove their worth by establishing themselves as equals. A figure like Marian would disrupt the focus on male interactions the ballads emphasize. In fact, "Robin Hood and Maid Marian," a late ballad and the only one to figure her prominently, places Marian in the position usually occupied by these male figures: disguised as a page, she wanders in search of Robin and ends up fighting him to a draw before they recognize one another. Other early modern ballads frequently featured cross-dressed women who succeeded in defying the strictures of society and parents to undertake adventures at sea or in war (Dugaw 31–42). But these were not the only ballads focused on women's lives in England during this period; cautionary antifeminist tales persisted in stories embellished from current events of women who were punished for crimes such as murdering their husbands or children.

DANA M. SYMONS

References and Further Reading

Bennett, Philip E., and Richard Firth Green, eds. *The Singer and the Scribe: European Ballad Traditions and European Ballad Cultures*. Amsterdam: Rodopi, 2004.

Child, Francis James. *The English and Scottish Popular Ballads*. 5 vols. New York: Dover Publications, 1965.

Dugaw, Dianne. *Warrior Women and Popular Balladry, 1650–1850*. Cambridge: Cambridge University Press, 1989.

Dundes, Alan. "The Ballad of 'The Walled-Up Wife.'" In *The Walled-Up Wife: A Casebook*, edited by Alan Dundes. Madison, Wis.: University of Wisconsin Press, 1996, pp. 185–204.

Jonsson, Bengt R., et al. *The Types of the Scandinavian Medieval Ballad: A Descriptive Catalogue*. Oslo: Universitetsforlaget, 1978.

Kadar, Marlene. "The Tragic Motif in the Ballad of 'Kata Kádár.'" *Hungarian Studies Review* 9(1) (1982): 19–38. [Includes a translation of the ballad.]

Knight, Stephen, and Thomas Olgren. *Robin Hood and Other Outlaw Tales*. 2nd ed. Kalamazoo, Mich.: Medieval Institute Publications, 2000.

Mirrer, Louise. *Women, Jews, & Muslims in the Texts of Reconquest Castile*. Ann Arbor, Mich.: University of Michigan Press, 1996.

See also **Audience, Women in the; Courtship; Crime and Criminals; Cross-Dressing; Domestic Abuse; Infants and Infanticide; Marriage, Impediments to; Misogyny; Rape and Raptus; Sexuality, Regulation of; Singlewomen; Violence**

BARBARIAN LAW CODES

The barbarian law codes are the written laws of the Germanic peoples who migrated to western Europe in late antiquity and the early medieval period. The barbarian laws, or *leges barbarorum*, were codified between the late fifth and ninth centuries CE. They were written in Latin, with the exception of the Old English laws. Many of the barbarian laws were part of the oral tradition before codification. The Germanic law codes were based on the principle of personality of law, which means that they applied to people of a certain group, not to people living in a certain area (territorial law).

The first Germanic tribes to settle in the former Roman Empire were the Visigoths (Spain), Ostrogoths (Italy), Burgundians (southeastern Gaul/France), and Franks (Gaul, Belgium, and Netherlands south of the Rhine). They were also the first to put their laws into writing. The *leges Visigothorum* (laws of the Visigoths) consist of a series of laws promulgated by Visigothic kings between the late fifth and early eighth centuries. The *Lex Romana Visigothorum* (LRV) or *Breviarium Alarici* (Alaric's Breviary) was issued by the Visigothic king Alaric II for his Roman subjects (506). It is a compendium of late Roman law, based chiefly on the *Codex Theodosianus* (438), a collection of fourth- and fifth-century imperial Roman law published by the Roman emperor Theodosius II. The LRV remained in use as a manual of Roman law throughout the Middle Ages. The compilations of Roman law issued by some Germanic kings are called *leges romanae*, 'Roman laws,' as opposed to the *leges barbarorum*.

The Burgundian law code, the *Lex Burgundionum* (also called *Liber Constitutionum* or *Lex Gundobada*), was devised in the early sixth century and influenced by Roman law. Its *lex romana* counterpart, the *Lex Romana Burgundionum*, contains Roman law for the Burgundian king's Gallo–Roman subjects and appeared in the same period. Also from the early sixth century is the Ostrogothic *Edictum Theoderici*, which was based primarily on Roman law and intended for both Ostrogoths and Romans. It was probably issued by king Theoderic the Great, but is often ascribed to the mid-fifth-century Visigothic king Theodoric II.

The laws of the Salian Franks, by far the most popular and influential Germanic codes, consist of the sixth-century *Pactus Legis Salicae* (PLS) and the eighth-century *Lex Salica* (LS). At least eighty manuscripts containing the various redactions of the PLS and LS have survived, including the ninth-century *Lex Salica Karolina* redactions. For dealings with their Roman subjects, the Frankish kings used the LRV. The term *Lex Salica* is also used to denote all the laws of the Salian Franks. The *Lex Ribuaria* (early seventh to eighth century) was based on various LS redactions and contains the laws of the Ripuarian Franks, a Frankish tribe from the vicinity of Cologne.

The earliest redaction of the laws of the Alamans (southwestern Germany, Alsace, Switzerland), the *Pactus Legis Alamannorum*, belongs to the early seventh century; the later redaction, the *Lex Alamannorum*, was compiled in the early eighth century. The *Lex Baiuvariorum*, the code of the Bavarians (southeastern Germany, Austria), was codified in the mid-eighth century. After the demise of the Ostrogothic kingdom in 554, the Lombards—also called Langobards—settled in northern and central Italy. Their laws, the *Leges Langobardorum*, were promulgated between 643 and 866; the oldest Lombard law is the *Edictum Rothari* (Rothari's Edict).

The latest barbarian codes written in Latin were compiled at the instigation of emperor Charlemagne for the four Germanic tribes living in the northernmost part of the Frankish empire (c. 802/803): the *Lex Frisionum, Lex Saxonum, Lex Thuringorum,* and *Lex-Francorum Chamavorum*. They contain the laws of the Frisians (Frisia, northern Netherlands), Saxons (northwestern Germany), Thuringians (central Germany), and Chamavian Franks (between Utrecht, Netherlands and Münster, Dutch-German border).

The Salic, Alamannic, Bavarian, and Lombard laws all contain ancient legal terms in the regional vernacular (called Malberg glosses in Salic law). The Anglo-Saxon law codes were the first Germanic codes issued in the vernacular. Æthelberht's code, two other Kentish codes, and Ine's West Saxon law code were written in Old English in the late sixth and seventh centuries; the other Anglo-Saxon laws, including the laws of the West Saxon king Alfred, are from the ninth century. Only one translation of Germanic law is known, an East Franconian translation of the LS (c. 830), of which only a fragment has survived.

Germanic law is mainly concerned with settling disputes in an agricultural society. Disputes involving private law (inheritance, property, livestock, etc.) and criminal law (theft, injuries, murder, rape, etc.) were settled by paying a compensatory sum of money to the injured party in order to avoid a feud. The accused is allowed to provide proof of his innocence or his statement with the aid of oath-helpers; sometimes proof by an ordeal (for example, boiling water) is demanded. Characteristic of Germanic law are the injury tariffs with their detailed fines for personal injuries. For instance, PLS 29.4 awards fifty *solidi* for cutting off a freeman's thumb—a quarter of the full *wergeld* (Old English *wergild*) for an adult male, and sexual harassment ("touching a woman's breast") must be compensated for with forty-five *solidi* (PLS 20.4). The compensation due for (fatal) injuries is linked to a person's *wergeld*, that is, the monetary value of a person's life. The amount of *wergeld* is related to a person's gender, age, and social status (free, half free, or slave). In Salic law the *wergeld* for a free woman who is capable of bearing children is six hundred *solidi*; for a woman in menopause or a young girl before menarche it is two hunderd *solidi* (PLS 24.8, 24.9, 41.15). Women were legally represented by male relatives or their husbands (*mundium*). However, a woman could inherit and own property that her husband was not allowed to dispose of without her consent. Usually her property consisted of her marriage endowment, that is, the bride-price (*pretium*) paid by her future husband, her father's wedding gifts, and the "morning gift" she received from her husband on the morning after their wedding.

MARIANNE ELSAKKERS

References and Further Reading

The standard editions of the Latin barbarian codes are published in the series *Monumenta Germaniae Historica* (MGH)*, Leges Nationum Germanicarum*, vols. 1, 2.1, 3.2, 4.1, 4.2, 5.1, and 5.2 (Hannover: Hahn, 1892–1969), and in the older *Monumenta Germaniae Historica, Leges,* vols. 4–5 (Hannover: Hahn, 1863–1889). (See also: http://www.dmgh.de)

Beck, Heinrich (ed.). *Reallexikon der Germanischen Altertumskunde (RGA)*. 2nd ed. Berlin: De Gruyter, 1968.

Bitel, Lisa M. *Women in Early Medieval Europe, 400–1100*. Cambridge: Cambridge University Press, 2002.

Christie, Neil. *The Lombards; the Ancient Longobards*. In *The Peoples of Europe*. Oxford: Blackwell, 1995.

Drew, Katherine Fischer. *Law and Society in Early Medieval Europe: Studies in Legal History*. London: Variorum Reprints, 1988.

———, ed. and trans. *The Burgundian Code: the Book of Constitutions or Law of Gundobad; Additional Enactments*. Philadelphia: University of Pennsylvania Press, 1949. Reprint, 1992.

———, ed. and trans. *The Lombard Laws*. Philadelphia: University of Pennsylvania Press, 1973.

———, ed. and trans. *The Laws of the Salian Franks*. Philadelphia: University of Pennsylvania Press, 1991.

Erler, A., E. Kaufmann, and W. Stammler (ed.). *Handwörterbuch zur Deutschen Rechtsgeschichte*, 5 vols. Berlin: Schmidt, 1971–1998.

Haenel, Gustav F. *Lex Romana Visigothorum*. Leipzig: Teubner, 1849. Reprint, Aalen: Scientia, 1962.

Klinck, Anne. "Anglo-Saxon women and the law." *Journal of Medieval History* 8 (1982): 107–121.

Liebermann, Felix (ed.). *Die Gesetze der Angelsachsen.* 3 vols. Halle am Saale: Niemeyer, 1903–1916.

Lutz, Liselotte (ed.). *Lexikon des Mittelalters,* 10 vols. München: Artemis Verlag, 1977–1999.

McKitterick, Rosamond. *The Carolingians and the Written Word.* Cambridge: Cambridge University Press, 1989.

Oliver, Lisi, ed. and trans. *The Beginnings of English Law.* Toronto: University of Toronto Press, 2002.

Reuter, Timothy. *Germany in the Early Middle Ages, c. 800–1056.* London: Longman, 1991.

Rivers, Theodore John, ed. and trans. *Laws of the Alamans and Bavarians.* Philadelphia: University of Pennsylvania Press, 1977.

———, ed. and trans. *Laws of the Salian and Ripuarian Franks.* New York: AMS Press, 1986.

Scott, S. P., ed. and trans. *The Visigothic Code (Forum Judicum).* Boston: The Boston Book Company, 1910. Reprint, Littleton, Colo.: Rothman & Co., 1980. (http://libro.uca.edu/vcode/visigoths.htm)

Temporini, Hildegard (ed.). *Aufstieg und Niedergang der Römische Welt: Geschichte und Kultur Roms im Spiegel der neueren Forschung.* Berlin: De Gruyter, 1972.

Wemple, Suzanne F. *Women in Frankish Society; Marriage and the Cloister 500 to 900.* Philadelphia: University of Pennsylvania Press, 1981.

Wolfram, Herwig. *History of the Goths,* translated by Thomas J. Dunlap. Revised edition. Berkeley, Calif.: University of California Press, 1990.

Wood, Ian N. *The Merovingian Kingdoms 450–751.* London: Longman, 1994.

Wormald, Patrick. *The Making of English Law: King Alfred to the Twelfth Century.* Vol. 1. *Legislation and its Limits.* Oxford: Blackwell, 1999.

See also **Crime and Criminals; Frankish Lands; Germanic Lands; Iberia; Italy; Legal Agency; Migration and Mobility; Social Status; Wergild**

BEAST EPIC

The medieval European beast epic, popular in the twelfth century, represented an allegorical genre that used animal figures to satirize the courtly values and mores of the aristocratic courts in France and the Germanic realm. The concepts of courtly love and romantic love played a major role in the themes of medieval narratives, and the animal epic arose as a vehicle of satire intended to cast the values of the aristocratic class in a humorous light. The beast epic has its roots in the fables of ancient Greece and Rome, and scholars have traced the earliest connections to Aesop's fables. Examples of beast epics written in Middle Latin include *Ecbasis captivi* (1140–1145) and *Isengrimus* (1148–1150). These two early works were written by Germanic priests and were intended to expose the corrupt lower clergy as well as the corrupt nobility. The earlier beast epics led to a specific form of twelfth-century fox and wolf verse narratives, and one of the most notable examples is the Old French *Roman de Renart* (between 1174 and 1205). It spawned several late medieval adaptations, created in the Dutch and Flemish region. These included the late-twelfth-century variants *Van den vos Renaerde* and *Reinaerts Historie*, as well as the verse epic *Reinke de vos.* In addition to the Dutch/Flemish works, an obscure Middle High German poet, Heinrich der Glichezare, produced a version of the fox epic, *Reinhart Fuchs* (c. 1189/1190).

The main themes in the medieval fox and wolf epics depict a series of confrontations between the fox and the wolf and his wife, the she-wolf Hersant, who are all masquerading as mock courtly figures. Hersant represents a courtly lady who is subsequently raped by the fox, who appears as a scoundrel and criminal. The ideals of courtly love, chivalry, honor, and justice are depicted in a satirical light, meant to ridicule the nobility's lack of morals, the justice system, and the Church.

Early research in the nineteenth century on beast epics in general and on the fox and wolf epics specifically concerned itself with studies of different manuscripts as sources for the literary material. Different versions of manuscripts were juxtaposed linguistically and thematically, and the comparative studies examined how Germanic versions related historically to the Middle Latin or Old French predecessors.

Subsequent scholarship in the first third of the twentieth century focused on comparing animal fabliaux in European countries and interpreting the techniques used in the different narratives for depicting human and societal foibles. For example, the Flemish/Dutch epics were compared thematically with the Old French *Roman de Renart.* Twelfth-century law and justice were examined in light of the legal processes in both France and Germanic Alsace, particularly in light of the rape trial of the fox. These studies illustrate an initial questioning of the sex roles depicted by the rapist fox, the cuckolded husband wolf, and the rape victim, Hersant.

From the late 1970s onward, the scholarship concentrated on specific themes in beast epics vis-à-vis fox and wolf tales, such as examining the individual characters in the narratives for their meaning. As an example, the figure of the lion king in the fox and wolf epics has been highlighted as the representation of either a corrupt or a weak secular leader. Scholars produced in-depth studies on the relationship between fox and wolf figures and how they relate to the female wolf figure from a sexual viewpoint.

In the 1990s, critical studies of the beast epic have centered on specific thematic interpretations of the events and characters. One examination looks at the entire legal system of justice and the application of law during the Germanic Staufer regime (in the twelfth-century Alsatian region) as depicted in the *Reinhart*

Fuchs epic. In particular, Hersant's rape trial is dissected in light of the legal context of twelfth-century Germanic Alsace. Historical legal sources are compared to the events and main characters in the trial proceedings to show how *Reinhart Fuchs,* in particular, represents a scathing satire of the system of justice in that era.

In 1997, the fox and wolf epic *Reinhart Fuchs* was reinterpreted using a gendered reading. The issues of courtly love, marriage, family, adultery, and rape became the focal points of this study, which casts a new light on how the main animal characters interact in gender roles. Future research calls for similar gendered reinterpretations of other beast epics like *Roman de Renart* and its European variants in the Flemish/Dutch region and Iberia.

IRMELI S. KUEHNEL

References and Further Reading

Baesecke, Georg. "Heinrich der Glichezare." In *Zeitschrift für Deutsche Philologie* 52 (1927): 1–22.

Best, Thomas W. *Reynard the Fox.* Boston: Twayne Publishers, 1983.

Bloch, R. Howard. *Medieval French Literature and Law.* Berkeley and Los Angeles: University of California Press, 1977.

Colledge, Eric. "Introduction." In *Reynard the Fox and Other Medieval Netherlands Secular Literature.* London: Sythoff Leyden/Heinemann, 1967, pp. 7–52.

Jauss, Hans Robert. *Untersuchungen zur mittelalterlichen Tierdichtung (Examinations of Medieval Animal Narratives).* Tübingen: Max Niemeyer Verlag, 1959.

Kuehnel, Irmeli S. *Reinhart Fuchs: A Gendered Reading.* Göppingen: Kümmerle Verlag, 1997.

Robertson, Sharon Short. "Those Beastly People: A Study of Human Beings in Animal Epics." In *Le Roman de Renard: On the Beast Epic,* edited by Adrian. Vaan den Hoven and Haijo Westra. Canadian Journal of Netherlandic Studies Special Issue, (1983): 63–68.

Terry, Patricia, ed. *Renard the Fox.* Berkeley and Los Angeles: University of California Press, 1992.

Wehrli, Max. "Vom Sinn des mittelalterlichen Tierepos." In *German Life and Letters.* N. S. 10 (1956/1957): 219–228.

Widmaier, Sigrid. *Das Recht im "Reinhart Fuchs."* Berlin: Walther de Gruyter, 1993.

See also **Chaucer, Geoffrey; Courtly Love; Crime and Criminals; Fabliau; Honor and Reputation; Law, Customary: French; Law, German; Literature, German; Literature, Old French; Obscenity; Rape and Raptus**

BEATRICE

Beatrice is a major figure in two works by Dante (1265–1321), the *Vita Nuova* and the *Divine Comedy.* She is cast as the inspiration for the love lyrics Dante cites in the *Vita Nuova,* and for the journey to a vision of God he undertakes in the *Comedy.* The name, meaning "one who blesses," may have been chosen for that reason or because it was the name of a woman Dante knew in Florence (Beatrice Portinari was identified by early commentators). In that name, Dante may also have been evoking several women important in Italian history: Beatrice, "duke" of Lorraine and countess of Tuscany, mother of Matilda of Tuscany, empress Beatrice, wife of Frederick I and mother of Henry VI, and particularly Beatrice of Savoy, mother of the four queens Dante mentions in Paradise VI, the youngest of them also a Beatrice, heir to Provence, and, as the wife of Charles of Anjou, queen of Sicily; among the several other Beatrices in the Savoy family were Beatrice dei Fieschi and the Beatrice who married Manfredi, son of Frederick II.

The Beatrice of the *Vita Nuova* dies in the middle of the story Dante constructs around his lyrics; the loss leads him to see a spiritual purpose in her life and his love. He leaves off the story of the *Vita Nuova* determined to find a more suitable mode to honor her, which he apparently finds in the *Comedy.* There she is the messenger of the Virgin Mary, sent from heaven to summon the classical poet Virgil to guide Dante on a journey through history, morality, and politics in Hell and Purgatory.

At the top of Purgatory, in the Earthly Paradise, Beatrice arrives to guide Dante the rest of the way to a vision of the Trinity. When she meets Dante she plays the role of a priest, confessing and absolving him. As she guides him through Paradise, she also teaches him theology, correcting him and major theologians along the way.

JOAN M. FERRANTE

References and Further Reading

Boccacio, Giovanni. *The Life of Dante,* translated by Vincenzo Llettino. New York and London: Garland Publishing, 1990.

Ferrante, Joan M. *Dante's Beatrice: Priest of an Androgynous God.* Binghamton, N.Y.: MRTS, 1992.

Harrison, Robert P. *The Body of Beatrice.* Baltimore: The Johns Hopkins University Press, 1988.

Holmes, Olivia. "Dante's Two Beloveds: Ethics as Erotic Choice." *Annali d'Italianistica* 19 (2001): 25–50.

Scott, John. "Dante's Admiral." *Italian Studies* 27 (1972): 28.

Singleton, Charles S. *Dante Studies 2: Journey to Beatrice.* Cambridge, Mass.: Harvard University Press, 1958.

See also **Dante Alighieri; Literature, Italian**

BEATRICE OF NAZARETH

Beatrice (c. 1200–1268) (also known as Beatrice of Tienen) was born at Tienen, near Leuven, the youngest of six children in a bourgeois family. She died in the Cistercian cloister of Nazareth, at Lier in the vicinity of Antwerp, where she had been prioress since 1237.

According to a Latin biography, *Vita Beatricis* (*The Life of Beatrice*), written after her death by an anonymous cleric, presumably around 1275, Beatrice received a thorough education. When she was seven, she was sent to live with a community of Beguines at Zoutleuven and was taught the liberal arts in a coeducational school for a year and later at the Cistercian monastery of Bloemendaal (or Florival). After she was allowed to make her profession as a nun in 1216, she continued her education at the Cistercian community of Rameia, where she studied manuscript production, especially of liturgical choir books. Thus fully educated, by the standards of her time, she, in 1218, helped found a new monastery, Maagdendaal, near her hometown. From 1221 she was back in Bloemendaal, where, in 1225, she was consecrated a virgin (the ritual taking place when a nun or a monk, after the novitiate, takes her or his monastic vows). Finally, in 1235, Bloemendaal sent her to help found a new daughter community, Nazareth, for which she copied choir books. Apart from being a copyist, Beatrice also functioned as teacher (*officio magistrali*), instructing in the "mysteries of the holy Scripture" (*VB* III, 230).

The biographer or hagiographer claims to have built his information on Beatrice's own vernacular diary-notes (*cedulae*), which she had kept secret until shortly before her death (*VB*, prologue). The fact that these notes (which seem to have been reflections on the Christological and Trinitarian mysteries rather than recollections of events in the community and society) are lost has given rise to much speculation. One likely theory is that these vernacular notes were disposed of around the year of 1275 in order to avoid accusations from inquisitors in a period when *mulieres religiosae* (religious women) were especially under suspicion from the church institution for their vernacular expositions on "the mysteries of Scripture which are scarcely accessible to experts in divine writings," according to Gilbert of Tournai.

Besides the diary notes, supplemented with information from those who had known Beatrice, the biographer incorporated his Latinized version of a vernacular treatise that Beatrice had also written: *De septem modis sancti amoris*. In 1926 Reypens succeeded in identifying a Middle Flemish manuscript as being her original, vernacular text: *Seven manieren van heiliger minnen* (*Seven Manners of Holy Love*), placed in a collection of sermons, *Limburgsche Sermonen*, from the fourteenth century. The vernacular treatise, the date of which we cannot determine, shows even more than the *vita* the depth of her

theology. It shifts focus from the Christological and Trinitarian mysteries of the *cedulae* to *Minne* (love), rendering a brief and clear description of the growth of a personal love of God in line with the love theology of Bernard of Clairvaux. Beatrice describes seven different *manieren* (ways, not grades) of loving God in the interaction of the soul's movements between purifying love (I), unselfishness of love (II), painful desire (III), infusion of love (IV), stormy or vehement (the term *orwoed*, a vehement storm or fire, that is also employed by Hadewijch and Ruusbroec) love (V), triumphant love (VI), and the desire for eternal love (VII).

There is a considerable difference between the hagiographer's version, where bodily elements are recurrently stressed, and Beatrice's own treatise, where the spiritual desire to be united with God is the focus. Whereas the *vita* is an *exemplum* depicting Beatrice as an exemplary, holy woman, Beatrice's own treatise is a systematic rendition of the lived faith of a contemplative woman. Her vernacular theology reflects the interrelation between self-knowledge and knowledge of God characteristic of Bernard's teaching, and she usually conveys her theology dialectically, which also applies to her thorough explication of the range and polarities of holy love. Propounding a theology of love, her focus is on the creation and recreation of the individual's godlikeness (Genesis 1:26–27) much more than on sin, and it is her conviction that she has been created by a loving God in his image and likeness. It should be noted that, whereas she follows tradition in her understanding of earthly life as an exile from the godlikeness for which humanity was created, Beatrice never refers to the biblical narrations on Adam and Eve. Perhaps because of her gender, both her theology and her understanding of humanity are formulated in the dialectic between God and humanity, not between man and woman.

ELSE MARIE WIBERG PEDERSEN

References and Further Reading

De Ganck, R. *The Life of Beatrice of Nazareth*. Kalamazoo, Mich.: Cistercian Publications, 1991.
———. *Beatrice of Nazareth in her Context*. Kalamazoo, Mich.: Cistercian Publications, 1991.
———. *Towards Unification with God: Beatrice of Nazareth in her Context, Part Three*. Kalamazoo, Mich.: Cistercian Publications, 1991.
Pedersen, E. M. W. "Image of God—Image of Mary—Image of Woman: On the Theology and Spirituality of Beatrice of Nazareth." *Cistercian Studies Quarterly* 29 (1994): 209–220.
———. "The In-Carnation of Beatrice of Nazareth's Theology." In *New Trends in Feminine Spirituality: The Holy Women of Liège and Their Impact*, edited by Juliette

Dor, Lesley Johnson, and Jocelyn Wogan-Browne. Brepols, 1999, pp. 61–79.

See also **Beguines; Cistercian Order; Education, Monastic; Flanders; Hadewijch; Monasticism and Nuns; Theology**

BEAUFORT, MARGARET

Margaret Beaufort (1443–1509) was descended from John of Gaunt, third son of Edward III of England, and his mistress (later third wife) Catherine Swynford. Beaufort was a key figure in the Tudor succession to the throne. Her father, John Beaufort, duke of Somerset, died in 1444, when his daughter was an infant. She was a ward of William de la Pole, Duke of Suffolk, who arranged her marriage to his son John. Upon the duke's death, the marriage was dissolved, and Margaret was married, on the initiative of King Henry VI, to his half-brother Edmund Tudor in 1453. Edmund died of the plague in 1456 while his young bride was pregnant with their son, Henry "Lord Richmond." Richmond was raised by others much of the time, but Margaret and her son remained close throughout their lives.

Margaret married Sir Henry Stafford in 1458, and through him she tried to promote the interests of her son during the reign of Edward IV. A marriage between Henry and Edward's oldest daughter, Elizabeth of York, was proposed as one means of reconciling Henry, a Lancastrian by descent through his mother, with the Yorkist king. Following Stafford's death in 1471, Margaret married Thomas Lord Stanley (d. 1504). With the death of Edward IV and the usurpation of the throne by Richard III in 1483, Margaret took an active role in conspiracies against the new king. At one time she was confined under her husband's care by Richard's command.

The victory of Henry of Richmond at Bosworth Field in 1485 was aided by the Stanleys. This promoted their interest, but Margaret attained even higher status as the mother of King Henry VII and the source of his claim to the throne. Henry also fulfilled her original intention by marrying Elizabeth of York. Margaret Beaufort took a vow of chastity and set herself up as *feme sole*, thus separating herself somewhat from Thomas Stanley, although he continued to visit her.

Lady Margaret became powerful in the land, collecting revenues and estates and pursuing legal claims to debts, even those owed her by servants; she also executed justice on her son's behalf, especially in Lincolnshire and the Midlands. Margaret Beaufort outlived her son by a few months, overseeing the execution of his will and the coronation of her grandson, Henry VIII. Margaret died in 1509 and was buried in Westminster Abbey with a tomb image executed by Pietro Torrigiano.

Apart from her assiduous promotion of the Tudor dynasty, Margaret Beaufort was a generous patron of piety and learning. She lived a devout but not overly austere life. Among her achievements was her own English translation, from a French version, of book four of *The Imitation of Christ*. She also commissioned a translation of the first three books from the Latin. These translations were published with Lady Margaret's patronage, as were other early printed books. Margaret Beaufort also supported the English universities, founding professorships of theology at Oxford and Cambridge. Guided by her confessor, John Fisher, she particularly enriched Cambridge University. She helped transform God's House into Christ's College. This was in part a memorial to Henry VI, a patron of that establishment, whom the Tudors tried to have canonized. Lady Margaret intended another foundation, turning St. John's Hospital into a college. This intention was not fulfilled until John Fisher secured papal support to protect the college from both royal and private claims on the Beaufort estate. These benefactions, combined with Margaret Beaufort's shrewd use of power, made her a formidable figure in early Tudor England.

THOMAS IZBICKI

References and Further Reading

Jones, Michael K., and Malcolm G. Underwood. *The King's Mother: Lady Margaret Beaufort, Countess of Richmond and Derby*. Cambridge: Cambridge University Press, 1992.

See also **Feme Sole; Noble Women; Patronage, Ecclesiastical; Universities; Wardship**

BEAUTY

Colour and light formed the foundations of medieval beauty. Clarity and vividness were associated with the divine but also with the things of this world, including human beauty. Ideals of male and female beauty were also dependent on age and social status.

From the twelfth century onwards, authors (including Chrétien de Troyes, Marie de France, Gottfried von Strassburg, and the authors of the Welsh *Mabinogion*) offer detailed accounts of female beauty. Matthew of Vendôme (c. 1175) and Geoffrey of Vinsauf (early thirteenth century) prescribe the chief elements: golden hair, curving dark eyebrows, gleaming white skin, rosy cheeks, delicate nose, sparkling grey or blue eyes, small red mouth, long white throat, sloping shoulders, long slender arms and fingers, small high breasts, a tiny waist, a rounded belly, long graceful legs, and dainty feet. Authors generally avoid describing female buttocks, hips, and genitals ("here the imagination speaks better than the tongue," says Geoffrey of Vinsauf), but visual representations of female nudes often show curving hips and hairless genitals. A slender silhouette is admired, though a rounded, thrust-forward belly is common in visual arts by the fourteenth century and is indicative not of pregnancy but of admiration for an S-bend posture. The female nude is not yet established as a dominant mode of representing the feminine ideal: nudity is reserved for Eve, personifications of *luxuria*, and the bodies of the saved and the damned. The beautiful female body is generally the clothed or "sartorial body," and poetic descriptions often linger over clothing and ornaments. Luminescence could thus be achieved through dress and jewels as well as complexion, while cosmetic procedures for plucking foreheads and eyebrows and obtaining white skin and teeth and blonde hair were described in medical texts, although condemned by moralizing authors. A handful of contemporary letters indicate that the slender ideal had appeal in life as well as in art. Although feminine beauty was heavily standardized, some room for variation was possible. The Virgin Mary, St. Katherine, Mary Magdalene, and courtly heroines occasionally have brown or auburn hair. The fourteenth-century Franciscan missionary Odoric of Pordenone describes the women of southern China as the most beautiful in the world, yet they can hardly have conformed to the poetic ideal.

Beautiful men were almost indistinguishable from women. Twelfth-century homoerotic poetry describes boys with wavy hair, ivory necks, sparkling eyes, blooming cheeks, lily-like flesh, perfect noses, red lips, and lovely teeth. Their beauty is said to fade as quickly as their youth. Other such works eschew androgyny in celebrating large penises. Examples of beautiful youths are found in non-homoerotic works too, including the *Mabinogion* and Gottfried's *Tristan*. Chrétien's lovers Cligés and Fenice "were both so fair that their beauty gave forth a ray which brightened the hall just like the sun," yet fifteen-year-old Cligés (with hair "like fine gold" and a face "like a freshly opened rose") is not entirely androgynous. "He has the wood as well as the bark," knowing about swordsmanship, archery, hawks, and dogs. By this metaphor, men had "the bark" of youth and beauty but also "the wood" of strength and valour, maturing to the handsomeness of middle age. This conforms with medieval models of the "ages of man" in which *adolescentia* was celebrated as a period of youthful beauty, energy, and romantic love, but middle age, with its peak of physical and mental strength, was the perfect age of man. Depictions of Christ in majesty represent a man in perfect age (solemn, kingly, bearded), where the Virgin Mary maintains the youthful maidenly state of woman's perfect age.

Texts as diverse as *The Song of Roland* and Norse sagas emphasize the size and strength of heroic men. Descriptions of actual kings sometimes mirror these themes. Einhard's description of Charlemagne highlights the Emperor's height, breadth, impressive bearing, and cheerful countenance. More than 600 years later, English, Italian, and French observers agreed that the English king Edward IV was "very princely to behold, of visage lovely, of body mighty, strongly and clean made." Just as men were allowed to go beyond the youthful ideal which limited the aesthetic appeal of women, so were they freed from the requirement of slenderness: both Charlemagne and Edward IV were excused their middle-aged corpulence.

In sum, the slim, white-skinned, small-breasted, radiantly luminous woman was by necessity also young, preferably virginal or pre-maternal, and of high social status. The ideal man was of equal nobility, yet could go beyond beauty to achieve a strength and stature to match his worldly authority.

KIM M. PHILLIPS

References and Further Reading

Boswell, John. *Christianity, Social Tolerance and Homosexuality: Gay People in Western Europe from the Beginning of the Christian Era to the Fourteenth Century*. Chicago: University of Chicago Press, 1980.

Burns, E. Jane. *Courtly Love Undressed: Reading Through Clothes in Medieval French Culture*. Philadelphia: University of Pennsylvania Press, 2002.

Chrétien de Troyes. *Arthurian Romances*, translated by D. D. R. Owen. London: Dent, 1987.

Eco, Umberto. *Art and Beauty in the Middle Ages*, translated by Hugh Bredin. New Haven, Conn.: Yale University Press, 1986.

Eco, Umberto, ed. *On Beauty: A History of a Western Idea*, translated by Alastair McEwen. London: Secker and Warburg, 2004.

Einhard. "The Life of Charlemagne." In *Two Lives of Charlemagne*, translated by Lewis Thorpe. Harmondsworth: Penguin, 1969.

Gantz, Jeffrey, trans. *The Mabinogion*. Harmondsworth: Penguin, 1976.

Geoffrey of Vinsauf. "The Poetria Nova." In *The Poetria Nova and its Sources in Early Rhetorical Doctrine*, edited and translated by Ernest Gallo. The Hague: Mouton, 1971.

Gottfried von Strassburg. *Tristan*, translated by A. T. Hatto. Harmondsworth: Penguin, 1960.

Heller, Sarah-Grace. "Light as Glamour: The Luminescent Ideal of Beauty in *The Romance of the Rose*." *Speculum* 76(4) (2001): 934–959.

Marie de France. *The Lais of Marie de France*, translated by Glyn S. Burgess and Keith Busby. Harmondsworth: Penguin, 1986.

Matthew of Vendôme. *The Art of Versification*, translated by Aubrey E. Galyon. Ames: Iowa State University Press, 1980.

Odoric of Pordenone. *The Travels of Friar Odoric*, translated by Henry Yule. Grand Rapids, Mich.: Eerdmans, 2002.

Owen, D. D. R., trans. *The Song of Roland*. Woodbridge, Suffolk, England: Boydell Press, 1990.

Phillips, Kim M. "Maidenhood as the Perfect Age of Woman's Life." In *Young Medieval Women*, edited by Katherine J. Lewis, Noël James Menuge, and Kim M. Phillips. New York: St Martin's Press, 1999, pp. 1–24.

Ross, Charles. *Edward IV*. New Haven, Conn.: Yale University Press, 1997.

Schultz, James A. "Bodies That Don't Matter: Heterosexuality Before Heterosexuality in Gottfried's *Tristan*." In *Sexualities in History: A Reader*, edited by Kim M. Phillips and Barry Reay. New York: Routledge, 2002, pp. 71–89.

Sekules, Veronica. "Women and Art in England in the Thirteenth and Fourteenth Centuries." In *Age of Chivalry: Art in Plantagenet England 1200–1400*, edited by Jonathan Alexander and Paul Binski. London: Royal Academy of Arts, in association with Weidenfeld and Nicolson, 1987, pp. 41–48.

Udry, Susan. "Robert de Blois and Geoffrey de la Tour Landry on Feminine Beauty: Two Late Medieval French Conduct Books for Women." *Essays in Medieval Studies: Proceedings of the Illinois Medieval Association* 19 (2002): 90–102.

See also **Art, Representations of Women in; Body, Visual Representations of; Clothing; Cosmetics; Courtly Love; Eroticism in Art; Eroticism in Literature; Femininity and Masculinity; Gender in Art; Portrait Medals**

BEGUINES

Beguines were lay women who lived a religious life alone or in communities but did not take solemn religious vows and were not considered nuns by the Catholic Church. Originating in the Low Countries (present-day Belgium and the Netherlands) around the year 1200, their movement spread to most parts of western Europe in the following decades. Although their way of life and activities were often a source of controversy, Beguine communities continued to exist in what is now Belgium and the Netherlands until very recently.

The Beguine movement had its roots in the religious and social changes that marked the high Middle Ages. While the Gregorian reform of the eleventh and early twelfth centuries attempted to strengthen church institutions and elevate the moral and spiritual authority of the priesthood, growing urbanization and the rise of a money economy generated new questions about Christian life in an evolving world, where attitudes toward wealth, poverty, and, more globally, traditional power structures seemed in need of revision. Lay people, now better educated and more literate, were interested in participating in these debates but found relatively few outlets within existing Church structures to do so. This was particularly true for women, who could not be ordained and whose work as nuns received scant recognition. The various heretical movements that developed in northwestern Europe in the High Middle Ages gave voice to such demands, yet they also testified to the growing intransigence of Church institutions in the face of dissent.

At the turn of the thirteenth century, a growing number of lay women in various towns of the Low Countries began to practice a new, informal religious lifestyle, either alone or with a few companions, within the confines of their family homes, at anchorholds, or at urban hospitals. Some of these women drew the attention of clerical admirers like James of Vitry and Thomas of Cantimpré, who regarded them as saintly role models and contributed an extensive hagiographical literature on the early Beguines. From these and other sources, we can identify four leading figures. Yvette (or Juetta) of Huy, an eighteen-year-old widowed mother of three, around 1181 began to devote her life to the care of lepers. Ten years later, she withdrew to an anchorhold, where she lived for thirty-six years until her death in 1228. Marie of Oignies, like Yvette, entered an arranged marriage at a young age (she was probably fourteen) but soon afterward agreed with her husband to lead a chaste life; from about 1191 onward she and her husband served lepers at the leprosarium of Willambroux, just outside Nivelles. Around 1207 Marie moved to Oignies, where until her death in 1213 she lived as a recluse close to the monastery of St. Nicolas, a house of regular canons. In Liège, a certain Odilia, also a widow, chose a life of chastity while remaining "in the world" around 1203; after her death in 1220, her son John continued her work by supporting other women who followed in her footsteps. The fourth inspirational leader was Jutta of Borgloon, an anchoress, who around 1200 guided Christina the Astonishing, Lutgard of Aywières, and possibly many others toward spiritual perfection. All of these women lived in the diocese of Liège, in the southeastern Low Countries, and were probably in touch with one another, but it is not at all certain that they coordinated their actions. The sources further suggest that, while these women were quite extraordinary because of their charisma, their visionary experiences, and (with the exception of Jutta) the support they received from influential clerics of the region, they were in fact only the most prominent among many women who around

1200 advocated the "semi-religious" life in the diocese of Liège and in other parts of the southern Low Countries but who have remained anonymous. It is therefore problematic and misleading to attribute the foundation of Beguine life to a single or even a few individuals.

By the 1230s these religious women (*mulieres religiosae*, as they were commonly called in contemporary Latin sources) began to organize themselves locally into more formal communities, "beguinages," acquiring common property and constructing their own chapels, houses for individual or communal life, and hospitals for the care of elderly Beguines and other women (the male counterparts of the Beguines, called "beghards," far less numerous than the women, were never affiliated with beguinages). These communities were often simple gatherings of up to a dozen or more women living in one or two houses, called Beguine "convents," whose members attended services in local parish churches. In the Low Countries (rarely elsewhere), Beguine communities could also take the form of "court beguinages" (*curtes beguinarum*), enclosed compounds of Beguine houses and convents, usually arranged around a central "Beguine" church, with hospitals and service buildings of all kinds close by. Such beguinages tended to be served by specially appointed priests who ministered to the Beguines in their own church but resided in homes just outside the compound. The latter type of Beguine community is first attested to in Aachen (1230), Cambrai (1233), Leuven and Ghent (1234), Namur (1235), and Valenciennes (1239). They became more numerous in the 1240s and 1250s, especially in the populous cities of Flanders and Brabant, where they constituted same-sex neighborhoods, some of which were quite large: Mechelen's beguinage of St. Catherine's probably housed about 1500 Beguines in the early sixteenth century. (In 1998, thirteen court beguinages that still survive in Flemish cities were placed on Unesco's "World Heritage List.") In the southern Low Countries alone, more than 300 Beguine communities of both types can be attested to before the mid-sixteenth century. The movement spread to the northern Low Countries; to northern France, including Paris; to the areas along the Rhine (with numerous communities in Cologne and Strasbourg) as far south as the Lake Constance region; to most of Germany, Switzerland, and parts of Bohemia; and even to the region of Marseilles in the south of France, where Douceline of Digne directed a small cluster of Beguine houses comparable to those of the Low Countries.

Members of Beguine communities made a vow of celibacy and obedience to the beguinage's rule and to its superior (the "mistress"), but usually not a vow of poverty: in fact, Beguines were expected to provide for themselves through work or income from their personal property, unless they were elderly or sickly. If a Beguine left the community (which she was allowed to do at any time), she could take her property with her, but would lose any investment she had made in the collective fund of the beguinage. Although Beguines did not adhere to the traditional monastic standard prescribing individual poverty, they quite clearly posited the ideal of a simple life that shunned material wealth and encouraged active charity to those in need, both within the Beguine community and in the larger urban world. The *Vitae* of such Beguines as Marie of Oignies, Ida of Nivelles, Ida of Leuven, and Margaret of Ypres (who all lived in the first half of the thirteenth century) often denounce the urban money economy and emphasize the virtue of manual labor and charitable works. Although some Beguines of a noble or urban upper-class background were quite wealthy, most of them, drawn from the lower strata of rural and urban society, earned only a modest living at the bottom ranks of the textile industry or as nurses and maids in hospitals and leprosaries.

Such concrete engagement with social problems should not obscure the fact that Beguines to a considerable degree withdrew from the world and often rejected conventional social roles for women. Many women joined a beguinage because they did not want to get married, or simply sought protection in an urban environment that was often dangerous for single women. They were also known to have helped women who wished to flee from an arranged or abusive marriage. Others, perhaps fewer in number, became Beguines because they did not have the kind of wealth or social status that would have gained them entry into traditional nunneries, or because they regarded themselves as poorly suited for life as a nun, which by the thirteenth century had become more strictly regulated. For those with a religious vocation, the rather informal Beguine existence allowed them to combine the active and contemplative life in new and creative ways. But whatever her reasons for joining may have been, the medieval Beguine devoted considerable time to daily prayer, both alone and in communal services, and to the exploration of a more profound religiosity through conversations with her peers.

Beguine spirituality was firmly centered on the contemplation of divine love. In its simplest form, it expressed itself in a devotion to the Eucharist, to Christ's Passion, and to the Virgin Mary. Juliana of Mont-Cornillon and Eve of St. Martin, respectively a Beguine and anchoress at Liège, instituted the feast of Corpus Christi in the 1240s; many Beguines expressed a particular desire to receive the Eucharist as often as possible, or gained miraculous sustenance from it throughout their ascetic life. Meditation on the Passion story and on Mary's role often led to the desire to follow in Christ's footsteps by experiencing His pain (for instance, Marie of Oignies and Elisabeth of Spalbeek were said to have displayed the Stigmata) or the Virgin Mary's Sorrows. In its more complex manifestations, Beguine reflection on the love of God inspired a mystical spirituality usually called "bridal mysticism" or "courtly mysticism." It was much inspired by twelfth-century monastic writings on the nuptial relationship between the soul and God as allegorized in the Song of Songs, and by the courtly love ideals of secular literature of the same period. Yet it often added other layers or themes: intricate contemplation of the mystery of the Trinity, the possibilities of deification, and, in a few cases, the supremacy of perfect love of God over other means of salvation. The "mystical" approach to knowing God necessarily became part of Beguine teaching, both orally and written, using vernacular languages rather than Latin. For that reason, the work of such early Beguines as Hadewijch and Mechthild of Magdeburg, to name only the better known authors, is often viewed as an important contribution to the rise of a "vernacular theology" in the thirteenth century.

The Beguines' penchant for mystical exploration of the divine drew skeptical and sometimes hostile reactions from different quarters. University-trained theologians tended to dismiss much of it as irrational or ill-advised, while Church officials had reservations about the Beguines' teaching activities, which sometimes resembled preaching (normally forbidden to women) or included the translation of Scripture into the vernacular, which always raised the possibility of heretical interpretation. The fact that some Beguines criticized immoral priests naturally antagonized members of the clergy.

The name *Beguine* demonstrates this suspicion. First given in its Latin form (*beggina* or *beguina*) in sources from around 1220, it was a pejorative term intended to cast doubts about Beguine orthodoxy. Although historians long thought that the word was derived from the Latin term *Albigenses*, used to describe the Cathar heretics of southern France (after the city of Albi, an important Cathar center), it is now firmly established that *beguina* is related to the Indo-European root *begg-*, which means "to mumble," to speak indistinctively, hence dishonestly. Critics of the movement frequently accused Beguines of false piety; their teachings were thus not to be trusted, and their claims to special knowledge of the divine dangerously misleading. Although Pope Honorius III had informally approved of their lifestyle in 1216, and papal letters of protection were sent out to various Beguine communities from 1233 onward, these doubts persisted. By the end of the thirteenth century, individual Beguines were sometimes formally accused of heresy. Large-scale persecution of Beguines began in earnest after the condemnation and execution of the French Beguine Marguerite Porete, the author of *The Mirror of Simple Souls*, in 1310, followed by several decrees against recalcitrant Beguines issued by the Council of Vienne in 1311–1312.

Because Beguine communities functioned largely independently from one another—each community observing its own rule—and no formal relations existed among them, they did not mount a concerted defense against the charges. A sharp industrial contraction that initiated the late medieval economic crisis around 1300 further undermined their position, because many Beguines employed in the manufacturing of textiles found themselves unemployed. In the end, their fate depended much upon their standing in the local community. In most parts of western Europe, Beguine communities were either suppressed or converted into houses of Franciscan or Dominican tertiaries. In the Low Countries, many small Beguine convents were closed, but the large court beguinages were maintained, albeit under closer scrutiny, by ecclesiastical and secular authorities. Although new waves of persecution did occur occasionally in later centuries, Beguine life persisted into the early modern era (the seventeenth century saw a great revival of Beguine communities in the southern Low Countries), and even into the modern period. By the end of the twentieth century, however, their numbers were significantly reduced. In the early twenty-first century, only a few quite elderly Beguines are left.

WALTER SIMONS

References and Further Reading

Dor, Juliette, Lesley Johnson, and Jocelyn Wogan-Browne, eds. *New Trends in Feminine Spirituality: The Holy Women of Liège and Their Impact.* Turnhout: Brepols, 1999.

Galloway, Penelope. "'Discreet and Devout Maidens': Women's Involvement in Beguine Communities in Northern France, 1200–1500." In *Medieval Women in Their Communities*, edited by Diane Watt, Toronto: Universty of Toronto Press, 1997, pp. 92–115.

Hollywood, Amy. *The Soul as Virgin Wife: Mechthild of Machdeburg, Marguerite Porete, and Meister Eckhart.* Notre Dame, Ind.: University of Notre Dame Press, 1995.

Lerner, Robert. *The Heresy of the Free Spirit in the Late Middle Ages.* Notre Dame, Ind.: University of Notre Dame Press, 1972.

Makowski, Elizabeth. *A Pernicious Sort of Woman: Quasi-Religious Women and Canon Lawyers in the Later Middle Ages.* Washington, D.C.: The Catholic University of America Press, 2005.

McDonnell, Ernst. *Beguines and Beghards in Medieval Culture, with Special Emphasis on the Belgian Scene.* New Brunswick, N.J.: Rutgers University Press, 1954.

McGinn, Bernard. *The Flowering of Mysticism: Men and Women in the New Mysticism (1200–1350).* Vol. 3 of *The Presence of God: A History of Western Christian Mysticism.* New York: Crossroad, 1998.

Mulder-Bakker, Anneke B. *Lives of the Anchoresses: The Rise of the Urban Recluse in Medieval Europe,* translated by Myra Meerspink Scholz. Philadelphia: University of Pennsylvania Press, 2005.

Murk-Jansen, Saskia. *Brides in the Desert: The Spirituality of the Beguines.* Maryknoll, N.Y.: Orbis Books, 1998.

Simons, Walter. *Cities of Ladies: Beguine Communities in the Medieval Low Countries, 1200–1565.* Philadelphia: University of Pennsylvania Press, 2001.

———. "'Staining the Speech of Things Divine': The Uses of Literacy in Medieval Beguine Communities." In *The Voice of Silence: Women's Literacy in a Men's Church,* edited by Thérèse de Hemptinne and María Eugenia Góngora. Turnhout: Brepols, 2004, pp. 85–110.

Wehrli-Johns, Martina, and Claudia Opitz, eds. *Fromme Frauen oder Ketzerinnen?: Leben und Verfolgung des Beginen im Mittelalter.* Freiburg: Herder, 1998.

Wilts, Hans. *Beginen im Bodenseeraum.* Sigmaringen: Jan Thorbecke Verlag, 1994.

See also **Bride of Christ: Imagery; Church; Douceline of Digne; Education, Beguine; Flanders; Hadewijch; Heretics and Heresies; Laywomen, Religious; Marguerite Porete; Monasticism and Nuns; Mysticism and Mystics; Tertiaries**

BELLE DAME SANS MERCI

The formidable Lady who refuses to accord her favour to any suitor originates in Alain Chartier's best-known and most popular poem, *La Belle Dame Sans Merci* (1424). Composed in eight hundred octosyllabic lines, it consists of a debate between the Lady and an aspirant Lover that is overheard by the poet-narrator. Chartier presents in a mixed tone that is part courtly, part satirical the Lady's rational skepticism as she cuts through the conventional courtly rhetoric of the Lover's appeals. Her position is radical: eloquent and spirited, she does not resemble the silent, idealized, female love-object of earlier lyric poetry; her stance as an independent woman is unprecedented.

The poem provoked a long series of literary responses and imitations, beginning with letters of outrage said to be written by ladies and men of the court, to which Chartier penned an apology, *L'Excusacion aux dames.* Both the poet and his female character are criticized for alleged defamation of women through the portrait of the heartless Lady. A subsequent cycle of fictional, poetic responses put the Lady on trial before a series of increasingly complex courts of law. The allegation of antifeminine sentiment incorporated the *Belle Dame* controversy into the larger *querelle des femmes*, the late-medieval literary debate about women. The case of the Lady is taken up in her favour by Martin Le Franc's *Le Champion des dames* (c. 1442); elsewhere, Chartier is recruited for the misogynists' cause.

The debate continued into the sixteenth century. An English translation, now believed to be by Richard Ros, appeared c. 1526.

HELEN J. SWIFT

References and Further Reading

Angelo, Gretchen. "A Most Uncourtly Lady: The Testimony of the *Belle Dame Sans Mercy.*" *Exemplaria* 15(1) (2003): 133–157.

Cayley, Emma J. *Debate and Dialogue: Alain Chartier in his Cultural Context.* Oxford University Press, forthcoming.

Chartier, Alain. *Alain Chartier and the Quarrel of the "Belle Dame Sans Mercy,"* edited and translated by Joan E. McRae. New York: Routledge, 2004.

Chartier, Alain, Baudet Herenc, and Achille Caulier. *Le Cycle de "La Belle Dame Sans Mercy,"* edited and translated by David F. Hult and Joan E. McRae. Paris: Champion, 2003.

Ros, Richard. "La *Belle Dame Sans Mercy.*" In *The Complete Works of Geoffrey Chaucer,* vol. 7 (supplement): *Chaucerian and Other Pieces,* edited by Walter W. Skeat. Oxford: Clarendon Press, 1897, pp. 299–326.

Solterer, Helen. *The Master and Minerva: Disputing Women in French Medieval Culture.* Berkeley: University of California Press, 1995, pp. 176–199.

Swift, Helen J. "Alain Chartier and the Death of Lyric Language." *Acta Neophilologica* 35(1–2) (2002): 57–65.

See also **Courtly Love; Debate Literature; Defenses of Women; Literature: Old French; Misogyny**

BEOWULF

Unlike most Old English literature, *Beowulf* presents a heroic world, set in fifth-century pagan Scandinavia; however, its manuscript, inscribed in the late tenth or early eleventh century, places it in a Christian intellectual context. About one-third of *Beowulf* narrates events concerning female characters, depicting powerful women who influence their society through speech and gesture, who through their marriages are meant to make peace between warring peoples, and who defend the rights of their sons, as well as women whose "masculine" violence needs to be tamed. Whether composed orally near the time of its setting or written at the time of the manuscript's creation, the fact that it does not show the serial monogamy and at least occasional polygyny practiced by high-status males in Anglo-Saxon England and other Germanic and Frankish regions suggests a fictive "conversion" of the heroic world to something more acceptable to the clerics who produced manuscripts.

Wealhtheow, wife to Hrothgar, the king of the Danes, exemplifies powers considered proper to noble women. Described as "wise in words," she is one of the major figures who evaluates Beowulf's claim that he will slay the marauding Grendel (lines 613–642). She contributes to order in the hall, as, "gold adorned," she carries the ceremonial drinking cup from king to older retainers, then younger, then guests. Wealhtheow argues against Hrothgar's desire to take Beowulf "as a son" after his victory over Grendel, asserting the rights of her own sons, and she herself negotiates with Beowulf by bestowing gifts (1168–1232). Hygd, wife to Hygelac, the king of Beowulf's people, the Geats, resembles her in demeanor and success in carrying out her queenly duties.

The limitations imposed by gender emerge in interspersed stories about problematic women and marriages. The marriage of Hildeburh, a Danish queen of the Frisians, dissolves in violence when the two peoples cannot keep peace in a single hall, and Beowulf predicts a similar bloody end for the planned marriage of Wealhtheow's daughter. While these stories indicate the frequent futility of "peaceweaver" marriages, "though the bride be good" (2031), other stories show inappropriately violent women. Hygd is contrasted with a "foreign queen" who "criminally" executed anyone who stared at her (1931–1940), until she married the "spear-bold" Offa and bore a son who was "helpfully . . . skillful in violence" (1949–1962), his proper violence confirming the gendering of her impropriety. Whether "mind-force" (*mod-þryðo*) is her name or a quality she wields (1931), her story suggests a desire to contain such force. In Grendel's mother, we see an *aglæcwif* (female fearsome assailant) who avenges her son's death, killing Hrothgar's favorite retainer. The poet depicts Beowulf's battle with her in sexual terms—an underwater cave, male and female bodies grappling, the male warrior's sword failing him, an ancient, "giantish" sword melting upon cutting off her head. Possibly a contest of the masculine against a more primal feminine or an enactment of the symbolic element of culture emerging from the semiotic (see Hala), the episode suggests the cultural vitality of the contest over violence, power, and gender; that God "grants victory" to the male warrior, rays of sun marking his blessing (1553–1556, 1570–1572), indicates the ecclesiastical bias of the manuscript culture.

CAROL BRAUN PASTERNACK

References and Further Reading

Damico, Helen. Beowulf's *Wealhtheow and the Valkyrie Tradition*. Madison, Wis.: University of Wisconsin Press, 1984.

Hala, James. "The Parturition of Poetry and the Birthing of Culture: The Ides Aglæcwif and Beowulf." *Exemplaria* 10(1) (1998): 29–50.

Ingham, Patricia Clare. "From Kinship to Kingship: Mourning, Gender, and Anglo-Saxon Community." In *Grief and Gender: 700–1700*, edited by Jennifer C. Vaught and Lynne Dickson Bruckner. New York: Palgrave-Macmillan, 2003.

Jack, George, ed. *Beowulf: A Student Edition*. Oxford: Clarendon Press, 1994, pp. 17–31.

Liuzza, R. M., trans. *Beowulf: A New Verse Translation*. Orchard Park, N.Y.: Broadview Literary Texts, 2000.

Olsen, Alexandra Hennessey. "Gender Roles." In *A Beowulf Handbook*, edited by Robert E. Bjork and John D. Niles. Lincoln, Neb.: University of Nebraska Press, 1997, pp. 311–324.

Overing, Gillian R. *Language, Sign, and Gender in* Beowulf. Carbondale, Ill.: Southern Illinois University Press, 1990.

Shippey, Tom. "Wicked Queens and Cousin Strategies in *Beowulf* and Elsewhere." *The Heroic Age* 5 (2001). http://www.mun.ca/mst/heroicage/issues/5/toc.html. (Accessed August 2005.)

See also **Diplomacy and Reconciliation; England; Femininity and Masculinity; Frankish Lands; Gender Ideologies; Kinship; Marriage, Christian; Literature, Old English; Literature, Old Norse; Mead-Giver; Noble Women; Paganism; Queens and Empresses: The West; Scandinavia; Violence; Virile Women**

BERENGUELA

Berenguela (1180–1246), princess of Castile and queen of León, was the eldest child of the Castilian king Alfonso VIII and his wife Leonor (Eleanor) Plantagenet. Castilian custom ordained that Berenguela would inherit the throne of Castile if none of her brothers survived. In 1198 Berenguela married her father's cousin Alfonso IX of León, in an effort to bring peace to the two kingdoms. Pope Innocent III forced the consanguineous couple to separate in 1203, but not before they had had five children: Leonor, Fernando, Berenguela, Constanza, and Alfonso. Berenguela returned to Castile; in 1214, she became the regent for her brother, Enrique I. Berenguela lost the regency, however, to the nobleman Álvaro de Lara, and civil war ensued. In 1217, Enrique was accidentally killed. Berenguela, declining the throne for herself, installed her son as King Fernando III; she ruled with him until her death. She arranged his marriages, and also the marriages and clerical careers of her other children and grandchildren, always promoting the interest of Castile. She arbitrated Fernando's peaceful accession to the throne of León, thus uniting the two kingdoms. Berenguela counseled her son regarding his crusades in al-Andalus, and ruled Castile-León in his absences. Berenguela was a powerful noble in her own right, possessing a number of territories and castles in Castile and León, and in the family tradition was a special patron of the Cistercian Order. She died in November 1246, and was buried, legend has it, in a plain tomb at the royal abbey of Las Huelgas in Burgos.

MIRIAM SHADIS

References and Further Reading

O'Callaghan, Joseph F. *A History of Medieval Spain.* Ithaca, N.Y.: Cornell University Press, 1975.
———, trans. *The Latin Chronicle of the Kings of Castile.* Tempe, Ariz.: Arizona Center for Medieval and Renaissance Studies, 2002.
Shadis, Miriam. "Berenguela of Castile's Political Motherhood: the Management of Sexuality, Marriage and Succession." In *Medieval Mothering,* edited by Bonnie Wheeler and John Carmi Parsons. New York: Garland, 1996, pp. 335–358.
———."Piety, Politics and Power: The Patronage of Leonor of England and Her Daughters Berenguela of León and Blanche of Castile." In *The Cultural Patronage of Medieval Women,* edited by June Hall McCash. Athens, Ga.: University of Georgia Press, 1996, pp. 202–227.

See also **Blanche of Castile; Cistercian Order; Iberia; Queens and Empresses: The West; Regents and Queen-Lieutenants; Succession**

BESTIAIRE D'AMOUR
See **Réponse du Bestiaire d'Amour**

BETROTHALS

Throughout the Middle Ages, creating a marriage was a long process that began with discussion between two families and ended with consummation. Betrothals represented the first official step of this process, as they concluded the marriage negotiations, announced the upcoming wedding, and ensured the realization of the alliance.

Early in the Middle Ages, betrothals existed in both the Roman and the Germanic traditions, albeit in two very different forms. In Roman law, a marriage was announced by the *sponsalia,* an engagement between the spouses. Often contracted many years before the wedding, this promise could be broken, and the betrothed could part before their union was formalized. The German version of the betrothal, the *desponsatio,* was much more binding. This first irrevocable step created a *matrimonium initiatum* (initiated marriage); during the ceremony, the bridegroom received authority over his future wife and, in return, delivered the bride price. The *traditio puellae* (transfer of the girl) followed later, as the woman was handed over to her husband and the marriage consummated. This Germanic two-step marriage was the dominant model throughout much of the early Middle Ages, with betrothals occupying a central place in the matrimonial process.

During the twelfth century, when the rules of marriage were becoming set in theology and canon law, Peter Lombard (c. 1100–1160) imposed the Roman *sponsalia* as the ecclesiastical form of the betrothals. These *verba de futuro* (words of the future) were simply the announcement of the marriage and could be dissolved as long as consummation had not taken place. Only the *verba de presenti* (words of the present) exchanged in church on the day of the wedding created a lasting marriage. In the eyes of the Church, betrothals were no longer essential and could be broken for serious motives such as a subsequent marriage, religious vows, dementia, prolonged delay, or fornication with one of the betrothed's relatives. While the Church recommended the adoption of its betrothal rites, such as a priestly blessing, these were no more necessary than the betrothals themselves.

Although canon law reduced the role of betrothals in favor of the wedding ceremony, medieval society continued to view them as an integral part of the creation of a valid union. Medieval documents rarely made the distinction between *verba de futuro* and *verba de presenti,* between a betrothal and a wedding. It appears that the two exchanges of consent were equally important steps of the matrimonial process, and that betrothals were as binding as a legal marriage.

The betrothals' importance is primarily linked to their role in the conclusion of the marriage negotiations. They concretely signaled that the talks had led to an agreement. During these negotiations—which were sometimes conducted in person and sometimes undertaken through representatives such as masters, lords, older family members, or, in the case of the aristocracy, embassies—families expressed their wishes and concerns regarding the alliance. With the betrothals, they expressed their satisfaction with the agreement and officially gave their son or daughter in marriage. On the day of the betrothals, the negotiations were sealed by a marriage contract that was signed by members of the two families and which dealt with all material and financial considerations and, in particular, with the crucial question of the dowry.

Considering the importance of the negotiations and of the marriage contract, the betrothals were very much a family affair. The parents' involvement varied with social class. Among the lower classes, the union was frequently the result of cooperation between parents and children; among the higher classes, families generally dictated the path to follow. At all levels, however, a good marriage was always supervised by parents, sometimes by masters and lords, and was based on economic and political considerations rather than on sentimental choices. Very often, the betrothed met for the first time on the day of their engagement, and their only role in the *consent* process was to acquiesce to their parents' decision.

Betrothals created a new alliance through an exchange of consents, officially between the future spouses but, in reality, between the families of the spouses. This event was surrounded by a number of rites, which varied socially and geographically. The betrothed pledged their truths (in old English, their *troth*, from which the word betrothal originates) through oral or written words, through exchanges of gifts, rings, or coins, which acted as tokens of the agreement, and through the joining of hands or the seal of a kiss. These various gestures symbolized the creation of a bond between them. In some areas, such as northern France, a Church ceremony accompanied the family celebrations; elsewhere, as in northern Italy, the procedure remained private, centered around the signature on a contract before a notary. Usually, a shared meal (a sumptuous feast among the nobility) accompanied betrothals. Whether private or public, these celebrations served to officially announce the agreement and the upcoming marriage.

Weeks, sometimes years, later, betrothals were followed by the wedding ceremony and by consummation, which concluded the marriage process. Much time could elapse between the two steps, especially if the betrothed were young, far apart, or in need of money for a dowry, qualifications for a trade, or land to support a family. When many years separated the two events, betrothals truly played their role: as a promise and pledge to marry, they ensured that the marriage agreement would be upheld. In a society where honor and the given word were of the utmost importance, betrothals were instrumental in ensuring that the wedding would take place. Although they were optional according to canon law, in reality a betrothal was an important event that could be revoked only exceptionally and with great difficulty. Most church courts would have rather imposed the completion of a marriage initiated by a public betrothal than applied canon law and allowed couples to renounce their word and break their promise. In the eyes of society, betrothals were a binding step in the marriage process, a proof that the marriage was on solid ground and approved by all, family and spouses alike.

GENEVIÈVE RIBORDY

References and Further Reading

Brundage, James A. *Sex, Law and Marriage in the Middle Ages.* Aldershot: Variorum, 1993.

Gaudemet, Jean. *Le mariage en Occident: Les mœurs et le droit.* Paris: Cerf, 1987.

Gottlieb, Beatrice. *The Family in the Western World from the Black Death to the Industrial Age.* Oxford: Oxford University Press, 1993.

Klapisch-Zuber, Christiane. *Women, Family and Ritual in Renaissance Italy.* Chicago: University of Chicago Press, 1985.

Ribordy, Geneviève. "Les fiançailles dans le rituel matrimonial de la noblesse française à la fin du Moyen Âge: tradition laïque ou création ecclésiastique?" *Revue historique* 303(4) (2001): 885–911.

Rousseau, C. M., and J. T. Rosenthal, eds. *Women, Marriage, and Family in Medieval Christendom. Essays in Memory of Michael M. Sheehan.* Kalamazoo, Mich.: Medieval Institute Publications, 1998.

See also **Children, Betrothal and Marriage of; Courtship; Dowry and Other Marriage Gifts; Family; Law, Canon; Marriage, Christian; Sexuality: Sex in Marriage; Weddings**

BIBLE, WOMEN IN

The Old Testament is foundational for both Jews and Christians, while the New Testament is the other key text for Christians. Within these Scriptures, women are participants in the covenant with God and often active in salvation history. The human person, whether male or female, has moral autonomy and accountability (for example, Adam and Eve; Ananias and Sapphira, Acts 5:1–11).

The soul, in relation to God, is often imaged as a woman and her beloved (for example, in the Song of Songs). The community in relation to God is likewise personified as female, both positively, as the faithful bride and fruitful spouse (for example, Isa. 9:1, Jer. 4:14, and Ezek. 16:8–14), and also negatively, as when the community acts idolatrously, as a prostitute or adulteress (Hos. 1–3). For Christians, these personifications culminate in the images of the Whore of Babylon as companion of the anti-Christ (Rev. 17), whose reign is brief, and the church (*Ecclesia,* a feminine noun) as the Bride of the Lamb, the reign of which is eternal (Rev. 21:9–14, 22:17).

The masculine generic is used throughout the Bible. Significantly, the biblical writers perceived it as inclusive. For instance, in the history of Susanna, the language of Psalm 118, one of the *Beatus vir* psalms ("Blessed is the man. . .") is used to praise the woman Susanna (Dan. 13:35); and the Mosaic law's punishment for perjury against one's "brother" and "neighbor" (Exod. 20:16, Deut. 5:20, 19:18–21) is applied to the perjurers against her (Dan. 13:61). In the New Testament, the Beatitudes are expressed in the masculine generic and are clearly universal. This generic use continues in church practice. For instance, in Byzantium, the two Sundays before Christmas celebrate the Holy Ancestors of Christ and the righteous of the Old Testament, both male and female.

A trait of Semitic narrative is spareness. Often persons are referred to by their roles rather than their names, particularly if they admirably fulfill that role, as do the Magi, or if they abysmally fail to do so, as does Potiphar's wife. Adele Reinhartz has shown that, compared to men, women are more frequently named in scripture. Although all priests are men, as are most prophets, judges, and rulers, Huldah and Anna are prophetesses, Deborah is a judge, and Sheba is ruled by a queen.

Mothers are involved in the education of their children in Scripture (Prov. 31, written by a queen; 4 Macc. 16:21–23, 18:12–14; Dan. 13:3). Though comments on schooling are rare, the education of a woman, Susanna, is emphasized (Dan. 13:3). Origen, Jerome, and Abelard drew on this passage to affirm that parents have a responsibility to educate their daughters as well as their sons. A medieval Jewish midrash presents Rebecca taking her sons to school.

Jesus emphasizes the spiritual equality of women. He converses with, heals, forgives, and teaches both men and women. As a result of Jesus' example, from the earliest days of Christianity women received the sacraments of baptism, anointing, and the Eucharist. Christ's parables and prophecies often include paired examples, and his example led to the balanced representation of the sexes in Christian preaching and art. A vivid example is the choir in the Minster in Ulm (1469–1474). Each half has carvings of several saints, male on the Gospel side and female, including twenty biblical women, on the Epistle side. A pastoral interest in providing each believer with a same-sex model at key points in life is seen in the medieval communion prayers, which cite the centurion and the woman with the ointment; in prayers for catechumens, which cite Abraham and Susanna, and in scriptures read during anointings, which cite the paralytic and Peter's mother-in-law.

A Christian innovation was to interpret biblical women, as well as men, as prefigurations of Christ. The Gospels, for example, present Susanna as a type of Christ by using her history as the narrative template for the Passion narratives. This new interpretation of women expressed the recognition that "women are equally capable with men of becoming holy" (the topic of a sermon by Clement of Alexandria). Other types of Christ include Jephthah's daughter, Judith, Esther, the widow of Zarephath, Jairus' daughter, the woman in the parable who finds the lost coin, and perhaps Mary Magdalene. At least once, the Jews interpreted Ruth as a type of the Messiah.

For the Jews Esther had considerable importance. Each year, as Christians read Esther's history during Lent, Jews read it during Purim. The antithesis of Esther is the daughter of Herodias, traditionally called Salome. Both Esther and Salome use their beauty to elicit a rash promise from a ruler, but Esther does so heroically at the risk of death in order to save the entire Jewish people from death, while Salome does so vindictively at no risk in order to put John the Baptist to death.

In the Eucharistic celebration, women's words are commemorated through the scripture readings and in hymns. In the East from the ninth century onwards, Martha's profession of faith (John 11:27) is focal in the prayer of the faithful recited before receiving communion. Miriam's song at the crossing of the Red Sea (Exod. 15:20–23) is sung at Vespers on Holy Saturday. Ephrem the Syrian and Jacob of Saruq praise her in hymns influential in the West (Hunt, par. 6).

Women's words are sung in both Gregorian and Byzantine chant. The words of Mary the Mother of God and of Elizabeth became independent prayers and hymns (Magnificat, Hail Mary). Annually, or even several times a year, the words of Martha of Bethany, the Samaritan woman, the Canaanite woman, and, from the Old Testament, Judith, Esther, Sarah, and Susanna are sung. The parable of the Ten Virgins (Matt. 25:1–13) became a liturgical play in Germany. Eastern hymnody often presents Eve, raised with Adam at Christ's Resurrection, as the herald of salvation; Eve is therefore sometimes designated "apostle."

Of key importance are the women present at Christ's tomb: Mary Magdalene, Joanna, Mary the mother of James, and Salome, the wife of Zebedee, and others. Several hymns focus on the angel's commission to these women to announce the Resurrection to the disciples, and Eastern church decoration frequently depicts their meeting with the angel at the tomb and Mary's encounter with the risen Christ. Gospel manuscripts and pilgrimage art also depict these events. The first liturgical drama in the West developed from the Easter dialogue between Mary Magdalene and the angel at the tomb. Legal texts cite these women to demonstrate the value of female witnesses.

For their roles in evangelizing, Mary Magdalene, Photina (lit. "enlightened woman," the woman at the well), Mariamne (the sister of Philip), and Junia (Rom. 16:7) are designated "Equal to the Apostles." The cycle of the Church year includes Sunday feasts named for the Samaritan woman (who was credited with evangelizing Carthage) and for the women at the tomb. Hymns by Romanos the Melode, Ephrem the Syrian, Kassia the nun, and others, as well as commentaries by Thomas Aquinas and others, praise these women.

The Byzantine East used the Septuagint, with Theodotion for the Book of Daniel. The biblical text for the medieval West was the Latin Vulgate. Significant losses affecting women in Scripture occurred when Luther redefined the biblical canon to imitate that of the Jews: Judith, Susanna, and the heroic mother of the Maccabees disappeared entirely, and Esther's Christ-like prayer was removed.

CATHERINE TKACZ

References and Further Reading

Hunt, Hannah M. "The Tears of the Sinful Woman: A Theology of Redemption in the Homilies of St. Ephraim and His Followers." *Hugoye: Journal of Syriac Studies* 1(2) (1998). http://syrcom.cua.edu/Hugoye/Vol1No2/HV1N2Hunt.html.

Menn, Esther M. "No Ordinary Lament: Relecture and Identity of the Distressed in Psalm 22." *Harvard Theological Review* 93(4) (2000): 301–341.

Ranft, Patricia. *Women and Spiritual Equality in Christian Tradition.* New York: St. Martin's Press, 1998.

Reinhartz, Adele. *"Why Ask My Name?": Anonymity and Identity in Biblical Narrative.* New York: Oxford University Press, 1998.

Tkacz, Catherine Brown. "Singing Women's Words as Sacramental Mimesis." *Recherches de Théologie et Philosophie Médiévales* 70(2) (2003): 275–328.

See also **Eve; Judith; Mary and Martha; Mary Magdalene; Mary, Virgin; Typology and Women**

BIRGITTA OF SWEDEN

Birgitta Birgersdotter (also known as Bridget) of Sweden (1302/1303–1373) was a prolific visionary writer, controversial moral reformer, founder of the Order of the Holy Savior (the Birgittine Order), and the only woman canonized in the fourteenth century. She was born into a powerful family in Uppland that was distantly related to the ruling Folkung dynasty. In 1316 Birgitta married Ulf Gudmarsson (d. c. 1344), who served as a judge in the province of Närke and a member of the king's council. During her marriage, she gave birth to eight children and oversaw a large estate. According to her hagiographers, she was a pious wife who encouraged her husband's spiritual progress, instructed her children in religious matters, cultivated ascetic practices, and cared for the poor and sick. Birgitta also served in the royal court as

an advisor to the Queen of Sweden, following the marriage in 1335 of King Magnus Eriksson to Blanche of Namur.

In the mid-1340s Birgitta was transformed from an aristocratic wife and mother to a visionary reformer and monastic founder. After undertaking a pilgrimage with her husband to Santiago de Compostela, and being widowed shortly thereafter, she reportedly heard a divine voice speaking to her from a bright cloud, calling her to become Christ's bride and channel of the Holy Spirit. For the remainder of her life, Birgitta transmitted over seven hundred visions, which she received in a trance-like state of ecstasy and presented as communications from God and other divine beings, including Christ, the Virgin Mary, and many saints. Four different clerics—Canon Mathias of Linköping, Prior Peter Olofsson of Alvastra, Master Peter Olofsson of Skänninge, and Alfonso Pecha of Jaén—served as scribes, translators, and editors of Birgitta's voluminous *Revelations*, which are filtered through uneven layers of editing. Although individual revelations sometimes correspond to specific political events and struggles in Birgitta's life, they generally proclaim God's imminent judgment on sinners and exhort corrupt political and ecclesiastical leaders to repent. They are characterized by vivid metaphors and corporeal imagery drawn from the Bible, nature, or domestic life; images of motherhood, clothing, and food are especially common.

After her husband's death, Birgitta resided periodically at the Cistercian monastery of Alvastra and participated in the life of the male religious community. She also traveled throughout Sweden, presenting messages harshly condemning the vices of Swedish aristocrats. Authenticated by an assembly of Swedish bishops, her early revelations circulated in written form and were also preached from the pulpit by priests. In 1346–1347 clerical supporters conveyed to an international audience her revelations proposing an end to the Hundred Years' War and exhorting the papacy in Avignon to return to Rome. During the latter half of the 1340s, Birgitta also received visions directing her to found a new religious order, dedicated to the Virgin Mary and intended primarily for women. The original house of the Birgittine Order was founded in Vadstena, and its first nuns and monks were officially consecrated in 1384.

In 1349 Birgitta moved permanently to Rome, in order to be present for the Jubilee Year of 1350, to seek approval for her monastic rule, and to work for the return of the papacy to the Eternal City. In Italy she adopted a quasi-monastic life along with her daughter Catherine (later venerated as a saint), traveled to shrines, and further established her reputation as a living conduit of divine revelation. Presented in her *Revelations* as God's chosen instrument and compared to the Hebrew prophets and the Virgin Mary, Birgitta offered advice to clerics and political leaders while recording messages about Christian practices, doctrines, and the spiritual conditions of the living and the dead. In 1372 Birgitta went on a pilgrimage to the Holy Land, where she received visions about the life of Christ, including an influential vision of the Nativity. Following her death on July 23, 1373, her remains were transported to Vadstena, Sweden, where her grave and the monastery she founded became a popular destination for pilgrimages and site of many purported miracles.

Pope Boniface IX canonized Birgitta of Sweden in 1391, and her canonization was reconfirmed by John XXIII in 1415 and Martin V in 1419. Her authority was debated during her lifetime and after her death, particularly at the Council of Constance, where Jean Gerson questioned the authenticity of her claims to divine inspiration, and at the Council of Basel, where theologians examined extracts from her *Revelations* for heresy. Despite the controversies, manuscripts and printed editions of Birgitta's *Revelations* circulated widely for well over three hundred years in Latin and many vernacular languages.

CLAIRE L. SAHLIN

References and Further Reading

Bridget of Sweden. *Birgitta of Sweden: Life and Selected Revelations*, edited by Marguerite Tjader Harris and translated by Albert Ryle Kezel. New York: Paulist Press, 1990.
——. *The Revelations of St. Birgitta of Sweden*, translated by Denis Searby. Introduction and notes by Bridget Morris. 4 vols. New York: Oxford University Press, 2005.
——. *Corpus Reuelacionum sancte Birgitte* (The Revelations of St. Bridget), edited by Sara Risberg. Riksarkivet. http://www.ra.se/ra/diplomatariet/crb/.
Morris, Bridget. *St. Birgitta of Sweden.* Woodbridge: The Boydell Press, 1999.
Morris, Bridget, and Veronica O'Mara, eds. *The Translation of the Works of St. Birgitta of Sweden into the Medieval European Vernaculars.* Turnhout: Brepols, 2000.
Sahlin, Claire L. *Birgitta of Sweden and the Voice of Prophecy.* Woodbridge: The Boydell Press, 2001.

See also **Birgittine Order; Bride of Christ: Imagery; Canonization of Saints; Gerson, Jean; Hagiography; Heretics and Heresy; Italy; Lay Piety; Mary, Virgin; Monastic Rules; Monasticism and Nuns; Noble Women; Pilgrims and Pilgrimage; Prophets; Scandinavia; Sermons and Preaching; Syon Abbey; Widows; Women Authors: Latin Texts**

BIRGITTINE ORDER

The Order of the Most Holy Savior (*Ordo Sanctissimi Salvatoris*), commonly known as the Birgittine Order, was founded by Birgitta of Sweden (1302/1303–1373), who claimed to receive its detailed monastic Rule (the *Regula Salvatoris*) through divine revelation. Birgitta established the Order in honor of the Virgin Mary and primarily for women, while envisioning that the Order would include a unified community of women and men under the authority of an abbess. According to her richly symbolic vision, sixty nuns and twelve brothers would represent the disciples of the early Christian community, while priests would signify the apostles and the abbess would correspond to the Virgin Mary. Possibly inspired by the double monastery at Fontevraud in France, Birgitta intended for the sisters and brothers to inhabit the same enclosure, although their quarters were to remain physically separate. The nuns were to be strictly enclosed and contemplative, responsible for singing and reading a liturgical office in honor of the Virgin Mary, the *Song of the Sisters* (*Cantus sororum*). Birgitta's series of revelations in praise of Mary's exalted role in salvation history, the *Word of the Angel* (*Sermo angelicus*), forms the basis of the office, which is interwoven with hymns composed by Peter Olofsson of Skänninge (d. 1378), Birgitta's confessor and close companion. Birgitta also ordained that the nuns wear a distinctive headdress, a white crown with five evenly spaced red spots symbolizing Christ's five wounds and crown of thorns. The ordained male members of the Order, under the guidance of their leader, known as the confessor general, were entrusted with preaching and administering the sacraments to the laity who visited the convent church as well as ministering to the spiritual needs of the sisters by serving the Eucharist, hearing confession, and providing religious instruction.

The mother house of the Birgittine Order was established on the shores of Lake Vättern in Vadstena, Sweden, at the royal estate donated in 1346 by King Magnus Eriksson and Queen Blanche of Namur. During Birgitta's lifetime, while she resided in Rome seeking approval for her monastic rule, a group of women and men congregated in Vadstena in anticipation of the Order's official establishment. Birgitta may have hoped to enter the Order herself, but she died before returning to Sweden. In 1370 and 1378 Popes Urban V and Urban VI approved Birgitta's monastic house in Vadstena, her Rule with modifications, and the monastic Order. Although it was not Birgitta's intention, her Order was instituted under the Augustinian monastic Rule with the Birgittine Rule subordinated to it.

In 1384 Vadstena Abbey was formally dedicated, and the first group of nuns, priests, and brothers was consecrated. Vadstena Abbey and its Gothic-style church, which Birgitta had designed and which housed her relics and those of her daughter Catherine, attracted throngs of pilgrims throughout the fifteenth century. Because of large donations, it became one of the most influential and wealthiest religious centers in late-medieval Scandinavia. The monastery held an extensive library of theological texts and sermon collections; approximately one-third of the manuscripts survive today. Its priests, whose sermons frequently quoted Birgitta's *Revelations*, became known for their prolific preaching, while the sisters were noted for their work as copyists and producers of ecclesiastical textiles.

The Birgittine Order quickly spread throughout Europe in the later Middle Ages, despite controversies in the fifteenth century concerning the right of monastic churches to grant certain indulgence privileges as well as the propriety of sisters and brothers living in one monastery under the authority of an abbess. Approximately twenty-five foundations were established by the end of the fifteenth century in Italy, Poland, Estonia, England, Denmark, Norway, Germany, Finland, and the Low Countries. Especially prominent among these monastic foundations was Syon Abbey in England, established at Twickenham by King Henry V in 1415 and still existing today, despite the Reformation, with an unbroken history. Recusant nuns from Syon Abbey went into exile in 1539 and again in 1559 until they returned to England in 1861. Like Vadstena, the abbey in Syon was known in the fifteenth century for its monastic library and preaching to pilgrims; its sisters were eager readers of vernacular religious texts.

During the reformations of the sixteenth century, many Birgittine monasteries were suppressed. The last brothers left Vadstena in 1550, and in 1595 the few remaining sisters took refuge with Birgittine nuns in Danzig, Poland, when Vadstena Abbey was closed. Today, the Birgittine Order exists in four different branches with houses not only throughout Europe, but also in Mexico, South America, India, the Philippines, the United States, Palestine, and Cuba.

CLAIRE L. SAHLIN

References and Further Reading

Bridget of Sweden. *Opera minora 1: Regula Saluatoris* (The Rule of the Savior), edited by Sten Eklund. Samlingar utgivna av Svenska fornskriftsällskapet, Ser. 2, vol. 8:1. Stockholm: Almqvist and Wiksell, 1975.

———. *The Word of the Angel*, translated by John E. Halborg. Toronto: Peregrina, 1996.

Cnattingius, Hans. *Studies in the Order of St. Bridget of Sweden: The Crisis in the 1420s.* Stockholm: Almqvist and Wiksell, 1963.

Morris, Bridget. *St. Birgitta of Sweden.* Woodbridge: The Boydell Press, 1999.

Nyberg, Tore. *Birgittinische Klostergründungen des Mittelalters.* Lund: C. W. K. Gleerup, 1965.

Zieman, Katherine. "Playing *Doctor*: St. Birgitta, Ritual Reading, and Ecclesiastical Authority." In *Voices in Dialogue: Reading Women in the Middle Ages*, edited by Linda Olson and Kathryn Kerby-Fulton. Notre Dame, Ind.: University of Notre Dame Press, 2005, pp. 307–334.

See also **Abbesses; Birgitta of Sweden; Double Monasteries; England; Fontevraud, Abbey and Order of; Literacy and Reading: Vernacular; Mary, Virgin; Monastic Enclosure; Monastic Rules; Monasticism and Nuns; Monasticism, Women's: Papal Policy; Scandinavia; Sermons and Preaching; Syon Abbey**

BLANCHE OF CASTILE

Blanche of Castile (1188–1252) was born to Alfonso VIII of Castile and Leonor of England and christened "Blanca." In 1200, Blanche was chosen by her maternal grandmother, Eleanor of Aquitaine, to marry Louis, the son of Philip Augustus of France. This arrangement resulted from a treaty between John of England (Blanche's uncle) and Philip Augustus. Blanche grew up with her young husband at the Parisian court. Her first child, born in 1205, died; ultimately Blanche had at least eleven children. Only Louis, Robert, Isabelle, Alphonse, and Charles survived to adulthood. Blanche also raised her nephew, the future Afonso III of Portugal. Although Blanche never returned to Castile, she corresponded with her family there, especially her sister, Berenguela of Castile.

In 1223, Blanche became queen of France when her husband succeeded to the throne as Louis VIII. Blanche's tenure as queen is obscure; she came into her own, however, after her husband's unexpected death in 1226. Louis's deathbed testament dictated that Blanche would be regent of the kingdom of France as well as guardian of their children. She immediately saw to the knighting and coronation of her young son Louis IX, and faced down the rebellious barons of France who opposed her regency. Although their discontent has often been ascribed to Blanche's gender and her origin as a Castilian, it was also likely that the barons opportunistically seized this unexpected weakness in the Capetian monarchy to advance their own interests. Over the next five years, Blanche secured her position by eliciting oaths of allegiance, handing out rewards, leading armies, razing and building castles (including the fortress still standing at Angers), and making treaties.

By 1234 she had pacified her most formidable opponent, Pierre Mauclerc, count of Brittany, and by 1235 had negotiated an important treaty with Henry III of England. Through personal negotiation she secured the allegiance of the young count of Champagne, Thibaud. This relationship inspired Thibaud's courtly love poetry addressed to the queen, and malicious gossip from other quarters. In 1231, conflict with the University of Paris provoked further lascivious doggerel about the queen. In her own time and since, Blanche's gender has attracted the attention of both her critics and her admirers: always in play is the idea that she somehow exceeded expectations of her sex.

Throughout her life, she worked to strengthen her son's power and authority. It is unclear when Blanche gave up her regency; historians assume it was in 1234, when Louis married Marguerite of Provence. Blanche's arrangement of Louis's marriage was part of a larger scheme to increase royal influence in the regions of Provence and Toulouse, a goal furthered by the marriages of Louis's brothers Alphonse and Charles to Jeanne of Toulouse and Beatrice of Provence, respectively.

Louis's assumption of full royal authority did not diminish Blanche's power: she worked closely and somewhat jealously with her son, overshadowing his wife Marguerite as queen of France. When, in 1248, Louis embarked on the Seventh Crusade, he named his mother as regent of France, despite her objections. Blanche, endowed with full royal powers, met this new challenge with the same determination, intelligence, and skill as before, raising money for the crusade, finishing many of Louis's projects, and stabilizing the government. It is noteworthy that, unlike her first regency, Blanche met with no opposition to her government in this period.

Deeply devout, Blanche taught her children (who included the future St. Louis and the Blessed Isabelle of France) to be profoundly pious. She worked closely with numerous churchmen, including popes, but she did not shy away from challenging the institutional church. Her conflict with the bishop of Beauvais epitomized several struggles in which Blanche successfully defended royal privilege against episcopal claims of jurisdiction.

Blanche of Castile was also an important patron, notably of the Cistercian Order, in the tradition of her natal family. Her foundations included the female abbeys of Notre-Dame la Royale (Maubuisson) and Notre-Dame du Lys. She also endowed the north transept window at Notre-Dame de Chartres. This window depicts the Virgin Mary enthroned with her son, surrounded by symbols of biblical, French, and Castilian power. It celebrates a major theme of Blanche's life, the power of a royal mother and her son.

Upon her deathbed, Blanche assumed the Cistercian habit; her body was buried at Maubuisson, and her heart at Notre-Dame du Lys. After her death in 1252, Blanche was widely mourned as a strong—even virile—ruler of France, and she is credited by historians with greatly strengthening the French monarchy and expanding the kingdom of France.

MIRIAM SHADIS

References and Further Reading

Berger, Élie. *Histoire de Blanche de Castille, reine de France.* Paris: Thorin et Fils, 1895.

Gronier-Prieur, Armande. *L'abbaye Notre Dame du Lys à Dammarie-les-Lys.* Verneuil-l'Etang, France: Amis des monuments et des sites de Seine-et-Marne, 1971.

Jordan, William Chester. *Louis IX and the Challenge of Crusade: A study in rulership.* Princeton: Princeton University Press, 1979.

Kinder, Terryl N. "Blanche of Castile and the Cistercians." *Commentarii Cistercienses* 27(3,4) (1976): 161–188.

Pernoud, Régine. *Blanche of Castile,* translated by Henry Noel. New York: Coward, McCann and Geoghegan, 1975.

Shadis, Miriam. "Blanche of Castile and Facinger's "Medieval Queenship": Reassessing the Argument." In *Capetian Women,* edited by Kathleen Nolan. New York: Palgrave Macmillan, 2003, pp. 137–161.

See also **Berenguela; Cistercian Order; Eleanor of Aquitaine; France, Northern; Isabelle of France; Queens and Empresses: The West; Regents and Queen-Lieutenants; Virile Women; Widows**

BLANCHEFLOR
See **Floire and Blancheflor**

BOCCACCIO, GIOVANNI

The model of the Italian prose tradition and preeminent Latin humanist Giovanni Boccaccio (1313, Tuscany?–1375, Certaldo [Florence]) is the most enigmatic of Italy's *Tre Corone* (Dante, Petrarch, and Boccaccio). Boccaccio's works span almost fifty years and numerous literary genres, from lyric poetry in the Italian vernacular to enormous encyclopedic works written in Latin. In the impressive variety of Boccaccio's literary tapestry few patterns stand out as boldly as his purported interest in portraying women. While it is remarkable that Boccaccio often writes to a female audience, the sheer multiplicity of voices that Boccaccio layers around his texts makes any conclusive statement of Boccaccio's attitude toward women difficult, if not impossible, to deduce.

The figure of Fiammetta personifies Boccaccio's ambiguous relationship to the literary conventions characterizing women in his time. In Boccaccio's earliest works, Fiammetta takes a role similar to Dante's Beatrice or Petrarch's Laura: she is the source of poetic inspiration and is more idealized than a real woman. However, because Fiammetta was always more corporeal and sexually charged than either Beatrice or Laura, her character reveals Boccaccio's tendency towards parody of existing literary conventions. Boccaccio's most interesting early work, *The Elegy of Lady Fiammetta*, demonstrates his ability to thematize and parody gender conventions while never programming explicit criticism in the text. Fiammetta gives voice to the objectified woman of the lyric tradition of Dante and Petrarch, although Boccaccio portrays her as more overwrought than psychologically complex. It is typical of Boccaccio's authorial self-seclusion that his Fiammetta is less his own invention than a female version of the iconic figure of the scorned lover present in the classical and medieval traditions. Boccaccio's questioning of gender categories written into the poet/lover relationship developed by Dante and Petrarch is couched in the conventions of the tradition itself.

In the *Decameron*, Boccaccio's best known and most complex work, Fiammetta becomes one of a chorus of characters who tell stories (one hundred in all) that obsessively return to discourses that highlight the role of women. Recent years have produced numerous fruitful readings of the *Decameron* in terms of feminist and gender studies. It is emblematic of the inherent flexibility in Boccaccio's text that the conclusions of these studies have determined the *Decameron* to be both a revolutionary proto-feminist text and overwhelmingly misogynistic. The "Proem," the "Introduction," and many of the stories of the *Decameron* indeed give women both autonomy and the ability to profit from their ingenuity. Other stories, and the "Introduction to the Fourth Day," fall into conventional misogyny. The final story of the *Decameron*, Griselda, has famously left generations of readers in a state of confusion about male and female gender roles and their relationship to human virtue. The most convincing readings of the *Decameron* view Boccaccio as undercutting all social conventions, including gender, political, ecclesiastical, and so on, as he playfully destabilizes his society's retreat into conventional thinking in the wake of the Black Death. Thus Boccaccio's questioning of gender falls into a broader project of experimentation with rhetoric and

genre. This reading also helps put Boccaccio's most troubling text, the vehemently misogynistic *Corbaccio*, into a credible literary context.

Although trying to tie Boccaccio down to one authorial stance on questions of gender is missing the point, it is important to note that Boccaccio wrote more about women than any of his contemporaries. Most of Boccaccio's early works have either a female protagonist or a strong female voice. In Boccaccio's later years (1355–1375) he produced mostly encyclopedic works in Latin, and one of these later works shows his continued interest in exploring questions of gender. His *Famous Women* follows the conventions of the classical biography of Plutarch and Suetonius and the humanist revival of that genre found in Petrarch and Boccaccio's own *Fates of Illustrious Men*. Boccaccio both imitates and subverts the generic conventions by not selecting the women to include in his catalogue based on classical or Christian virtues; rather, Boccaccio seems to qualify women's status on the same terms (political power, fame, or infamy) as classical biographies employed for men.

The balance of Boccaccio's literary works do not allow him to be classified as a proto-feminist, feminist, or misogynistic author. It is not that too little evidence exists to support a case. Instead, Boccaccio presents his reader with all possible perspectives so that she may arrive at her own decision. In this sense, Boccaccio does reveal himself to be a precociously modern writer. Boccaccio understood that his audience is gendered (and otherwise differentiated), and, as such, will necessarily play their own different games as readers.

JASON M. HOUSTON

References and Further Reading

Boccaccio, Giovanni. *The Decameron*, translated by Mark Musa and Peter Bondanella. New York: Mentor, 1982.
———. *The Elegy of Lady Fiammetta*, edited and translated by Mariangela Causa-Steindler and Thomas Mauch. Chicago: The University of Chicago Press, 1990.
———. *The Corbaccio, or the Labyrinth of Love*, translated and edited by A. Cassell. Binghamton, N.Y.: Medieval and Renaissance Texts and Studies, 1993.
———. *Tutte le opere di Giovanni Boccaccio*, edited by V. Branca. 10 vols. Milan: Mondadori, 1964–1994.
———. *Famous Women*, edited and translated by Virginia Brown. Cambridge, Mass.: Harvard University Press, 2001.
Barolini, Teodolina. "'Le parole son femmine e i fatti sono maschi.' Toward a Sexual Poetics of the *Decameron* (*Decameron II 10*)." *Studi sul Boccaccio* 21 (1993): 175–197.
Hollander, Robert. *Boccaccio's Two Venuses*. New York: New York University Press, 1977.

Marcus, Millicent. "Misogyny as Misreading: A Gloss on *Decameron* VIII, 7." *Stanford Italian Review* 4 (1984) 23–40.

Migiel, Marilyn. *A Rhetoric of the 'Decameron.'* Toronto: University of Toronto Press, 2003.

Psaki, F. Regina. "Women in the 'Decameron'." In *Approaches to Teaching Boccaccio's 'Decameron'*, edited by James H. McGregor. New York: The Modern Language Association of America, 2000, pp. 79–86.

Psaki, F. Regina, and C. Thomas Stillinger, eds. *Boccaccio and Feminist Criticism. Annali d'Italianistica* book series, forthcoming.

Smarr, Janet Levarie. *Boccaccio and Fiammetta: The Narrator as Lover.* Urbana, Ill.: University of Illinois Press, 1986.

See also **Beatrice; Constance; Dante Alighieri; Defenses of Women; Feminist Theories and Methodologies; Gender Ideologies; Griselda; Literature, Italian; Misogyny; Petrarch**

BODY IN LITERATURE AND RELIGION

Disassociating gender traits from the biological body has long proven to be impossible, for beliefs about the body dovetail with notions of masculinity and femininity. In the Middle Ages, the female body was often believed to be the inverted mirror image of its male counterpart: both sexes possessed the same physical characteristics, but men had sufficient vital heat to expel their genitals from within, whereas women's reproductive organs remained hidden from view. Because of this difference in heat, medical theory held that women's bodies were less perfect than those of men. The female body was associated with passivity, softness, and weakness, all traits justified by physical sexual differences. At the same time, the body also ensured that women had important functions in society both because of its reproductive capacity and its ability to represent concretely abstract concepts. A family's continuation relied on procreation, and marriages created political alliances between families.

The body's significance also derived from its representational potential, for images of the human form helped to establish social hierarchies. Just as Christ was the head of the church, tending members of the religious body of believers, spiritual leaders became the heads of their flocks, providing guidance. Similarly, the metaphor of the body defined relations between men and women: men served as the head, giving order to the (female) body, thereby reinforcing notions of male rationality and female emotionality.

In both literature and religion, representations of the female body could bolster conventional beliefs concerning gender roles. They could also challenge assumptions about what social position women were to occupy. Intentionally or not, these images could suggest that the interpretation of physical distinctions between the sexes depends on cultural factors. That is, the importance of male and female genital differences is not predetermined; historical circumstances influence the conception of appropriate behavior.

The Inspirational Body in Literature

Women's roles in literature mirror those of their nonfiction counterparts: female characters frequently wed and become (or ostensibly will become) mothers. The female figure is particularly notable, however, for its inspirational potential. In lyric poetry, the woman's body inspires desire, providing the foundation for the phenomenon that modern scholars have termed courtly love. Whether the narrator knows his beloved or falls in love with a faraway lady without ever having seen her, he presents himself as subservient to his lady. She thus theoretically holds him in her power, and his longing for her can cause great torment. Even when couched in spiritual terms, the narrator's desire is highly sensual. Nonetheless, gaining intimate knowledge of the lady's body proves challenging because she is traditionally of more noble social status and already married. The lady can show mercy to her suitor, but often she is haughty and maintains her distance, resulting in additional suffering in the name of love.

Often described in great detail from head to toe, the female body plays an equally inspirational role in the courtly romances first appearing in the twelfth century. Embodying the ideal physical appearance of the time, the lady motivates the knight wooing her to demonstrate his valor on the battlefield. Once he has established his superiority, he earns the right to claim the lady as his companion; she becomes his reward. The heroine's body thus serves as an object of admiration and pursuit, important for the chivalric feats that it occasions. The knight's body, too, merits attention, but for its prowess rather than its attractiveness. Happy endings depend on the pairing of the loveliest lady and the most accomplished knight. While the lady's beauty confirms that she has a noble moral character, her worth lies first and foremost in her body.

The Desiring Body in Literature

While the female body continued to play an inspirational role in literature throughout the Middle Ages, a more misogynistic depiction of women appeared with increasing frequency beginning in the thirteenth century. Authors highlight women's voracious sexual appetite, particularly in the *fabliaux*. The overwhelming desire to satisfy their bodily needs offers additional evidence of women's inability to master themselves and their bodies. Sexually desirous female characters are rarely faithful to one man, constantly seeking gratification outside the bounds of sanctioned relationships.

The Repugnant Body in Literature

The unseemly conduct of a lascivious woman could make her body repellent. Similarly, bodies that did not conform to medieval standards of beauty were considered repugnant. Owing to the correlation between physical appearance and moral character, bodies deemed ugly frequently heralded trouble in literature. Dwarves, for instance, may behave reprehensibly, striking other characters for no reason. Old women, too, often have a disruptive presence, displaying their ability to manipulate men or seeking to impede a hero's progress on quests.

The ugly female body takes on special importance in a number of late medieval English texts, including John Gower's *Confessio amantis*, Chaucer's "Wife of Bath's Tale," and the anonymous *Wedding of Sir Gawain and Dame Ragnelle*. In these tales, which adopt the folktale motif of the loathly lady and raise the issue of what women desire, an unappealing hag is transformed into a beautiful lady.

Literary Challenges to Convention

Literary works could also question assumptions concerning the female figure. Long before Christine de Pizan engaged in the fifteenth-century debate about female virtue or vice, multiple literary genres invited closer scrutiny of women's bodies. The inclusion of a female voice in works by either men or women could cast doubt upon the accuracy of gender stereotypes based on the body. Tales in which women cross-dress as men and successfully establish a male persona (such as the *Romance of Silence*), for example, imply that weakness and passivity are not inherently feminine traits. In these cases, the body serves as a site of performance, and the clothes influence spectators' perception of the body beneath them. Furthermore, accentuating the desirous female nature—which may involve false accusations of infidelity—draws attention to the fear that a seductive woman could cause men to lose control over their own flesh,

pointing to male desire or the inability of men to sexually satisfy a woman. The body could thus become a site of instability.

Works by female authors do not necessarily depict female characters in a flattering light, just as texts by men do not always portray women negatively. Nonetheless, certain female composers do focus on a woman's point of view. The unhappily married heroines in some of Marie de France's *lais*, which date to 1160–1170, bring to light the potential for jealous husbands to view the female body as a possession. In addition, they underscore the importance of maintaining virtue, highlighting the need for fidelity and silence in love. The *trobairitz*, writing in southern France in the late twelfth and the thirteenth centuries, echo the awareness of the perils of lost honor. Female narrators may acknowledge desire for the men who seek their love, yet reject a physical relationship out of concern for preserving their reputation. At times, they also uncover contradictions in the position of a lover claiming to place himself in his beloved's power when he in fact seeks equality. Calling attention to the female body and the importance of avoiding talk of lax morals, authors could point to the ways in which social codes shape the conception of female nature.

That texts raise questions, directly or indirectly, about the validity of stereotypes does not mean that they are feminist in today's terms. To the contrary, many authors refuting misogynistic portrayals of women underscore conventional traits, concentrating on devoted wives, daughters, and mothers. Similarly, threats that nontraditional heroines pose to hierarchies remain temporary. Eventually, these women reassume their expected place in society, often by marrying. Still, by implying that gender stereotypes stem from social norms rather than biology, their actions could provoke discussion and inspire the audience to reexamine notions about the female body and its role. In short, focusing on a woman's figure revealed the complex relationship between dominant ideologies and the body, gave the lie to strict binary oppositions differentiating men and women, and raised the possibility that the body was as much a product of culture as it was of nature.

The Body in Religion

The biblical image of the Word becoming flesh ensured that the body would be of particular interest to medieval religious writers. Church fathers had long struggled with the relationship between the body and the soul, at times manifesting contradictory stances in their work by simultaneously privileging and denigrating flesh. The human body was at once necessary and dangerous. It could serve as a medium for the soul and as a locus of learning; alternatively, its attachment to the material world could turn humankind away from focusing on salvation. Female flesh proved to be especially problematic. As in literary texts, the (inferior) female body often stands in counterpoint to the (superior) male mind. Women are frequently portrayed as weak, loquacious, and given to carnal and sensual pleasures, all traits suggestive of a lack of control over the inherently difficult body.

The Celibate Body

Yet women could be held up as models for their holiness. Until the late twelfth century, they attained this status chiefly by rising above their sex and becoming "like men." Doing so meant denying their sexuality; thus, virgins merited particular respect. Especially in hagiographic texts, their desire to avoid sexual relations permits them to engage in otherwise unacceptable behavior. Future female saints who cross-dress as men to ward off male sexual advances or prevent marriage act laudably. Those who do wed but refuse to consummate the marriage often even inspire their husbands to live piously. Married women with children, too, can gain spiritual authority in religious texts. Sacrificing their children for a higher purpose (as the Virgin Mary did) demonstrates a stronger commitment to God than to their family. Mothers who agree to their children's demise also prove their self-control and resistance to excessive emotionality. All of these women thus negate the body and become sexless.

The Maternal Body

During the twelfth century, religious language increasingly incorporated feminine imagery, focusing especially on the breasts and women's capacity to nurture. Drawing upon the belief that women possess an inherently loving body that can nourish and instruct, Bernard of Clairvaux (d. 1153) and the Cistercians in particular present abbots as mothers in their communities. Like mothers, they are to love and suckle those in their care. Twelfth-century authors also emphasize the image of Christ as a mother, a portrayal stretching back centuries to the Greek and Latin fathers. Because medieval medical theory held that mother's milk was processed blood, the interchangeability of the two fluids links Christ to mothers: just as a nursing mother feeds a child with her body, so Christ feeds his followers with his blood during the Eucharist.

The greater use of maternal imagery both reflected and reinforced the growing importance of the Virgin Mary. Mary's role as Christ's mother endowed her body with special significance: like that of other women in its reproductive capacity, it retained its purity even in bearing a child. Without original sin because she conceived immaculately, Mary was free of the pain of childbirth, as well. Virginity and motherhood converge in one exceptional body.

The rise of the veneration of Mary—seen as the "New Eve" and thus redeeming woman for her part in humankind's fall from grace—fostered the feminization of religious language. A greater emphasis on Christ's humanity during the twelfth century also contributed to the tendency. The depiction of men as mothers, however, remains symbolic; no writer suggests that possessing nurturing traits actually transforms men into women. Yet a more positive view of the female body had important implications for women, for whom the image was far more than allegorical. Those defending women against their critics could turn stereotypes of feminine weakness and carnality to their advantage. For instance, if Eve's creation from Adam's rib placed her in a subordinate position, having been fashioned from bone rather than earth also made her inherently more noble. Likewise, if her dependence on the bodily senses left her more prone to cede to the serpent's temptation, it also meant that she deserved less blame than Adam, whose rationality should have prevented him from succumbing.

The Bridal Body

Embracing the flesh in a spiritual context offered women a means of authority later in the Middle Ages. Beginning in the thirteenth century, communities of women—notably the nuns of Helfta and Beguines such as Hadewijch (early to mid-thirteenth century), Mechthild of Magdeburg (d. c. 1282/1297), and Marguerite Porete (d. 1310)—garnered attention for their visions in which God communicated directly with the mystic. Such visions conferred indubitable authority upon the woman, although giving voice to them could also lead to charges of heresy. Not infrequently, mystics employ erotic bridal imagery to describe their experiences. Desiring union with her beloved, the mystic can celebrate her body's capacity to join with her spouse. Instead of negating her flesh, she emphasizes her whole self; her body unites with Christ's body, and her will merges with God's.

Spirituality can thus permit women to honor the body; desire, however, is directed toward God rather than earthly pleasures. Paradoxically, the emphasis on physicality and sexuality may lead to the destruction of the body, subsumed by love.

The Suffering Body

Mystics of the late fourteenth and early fifteenth centuries, such as Margery Kempe and Julian of Norwich, often place special emphasis on the Passion. Christ's body and female flesh become linked in their common ability to suffer physically. In crucifixion visions, the visionary's body can stand in for that of Christ on the cross. Moreover, the blood from Christ's pierced side stands in parallel to the nourishing milk emanating from a mother's breast. In the case of ascetics, control over the flesh—manifested through fasting and other forms of physical deprivation—evokes Christ's physical afflictions. The Eucharist offered an especially potent symbol of Christ's physicality and humanity, uniting women's bodies and Christ. Many female visionaries display great devotion to the Eucharist, finding spiritual ecstasy in the physical act of taking communion.

Focusing on the female body could also provide a means for women to draw closer to Christ figuratively. Like the crucified Christ, whose death and resurrection offered salvation to the faithful, women, too, could sacrifice for others. Precisely because of their embodied state and capacity to suffer, women could serve as intercessors, using their tears, hunger, and prayers to replace the suffering of another. This role relies on the stereotype of woman as nurturer and mediator, qualities attributed to mothers. Nevertheless, it also places women in a position of influence, connecting them to God as they intercede for others.

KRISTIN L. BURR

References and Further Reading

Blamires, Alcuin. *The Case for Women in Medieval Culture.* Oxford: Clarendon Press, 1997.
Burns, E. Jane. *Bodytalk: When Women Speak in Old French Literature.* Philadelphia: University of Pennsylvania Press, 1993.
Bynum, Caroline Walker. *Holy Feast and Holy Fast: The Religious Significance of Food to Medieval Women.* Berkeley: University of California Press, 1988.
———. *Jesus as Mother: Studies in the Spirituality of the High Middle Ages.* Berkeley: University of California Press, 1982.
———. *The Resurrection of the Body in Western Christianity, 200–1336.* New York: Columbia University Press, 1995.
Cadden, Joan. *Meanings of Sex Differences in the Middle Ages.* Cambridge: Cambridge University Press, 1993.
Chance, Jane, ed. *Gender and Text in the Later Middle Ages.* Gainesville: University Press of Florida, 1996.
Colby, Alice M. *The Portrait in Twelfth-Century French Literature.* Geneva: Librairie Droz, 1965.
Ferrante, Joan. *Woman as Image in Medieval Literature.* New York: Columbia University Press, 1975.
Gold, Penny Schine. *The Lady and the Virgin.* Chicago: University of Chicago Press, 1985.
Kay, Sarah, and Miri Rubin, eds. *Framing Medieval Bodies.* Manchester and New York: Manchester University Press, 1994.
Lomperis, Linda, and Sarah Stanbury, eds. *Feminist Approaches to the Body in Medieval Literature.* Philadelphia: University of Pennsylvania Press, 1993.
Miles, Margaret R. *Fullness of Life: Historical Foundations for a New Asceticism.* Philadelphia: The Westminster Press, 1981.
Newman, Barbara. *From Virile Woman to WomanChrist: Studies in Medieval Religion and Literature.* Philadelphia: University of Pennsylvania Press, 1995.
Petroff, Elizabeth A. *Medieval Women's Visionary Literature.* New York: Oxford University Press, 1986.
Wiethaus, Ulrike. "Sexuality, Gender, and the Body in Late Medieval Women's Spirituality." *Journal of Feminist Studies in Religion* 7 (1991): 35–57.

See also **Asceticism; Beauty; Beguines; Body, Visual Representations of; Bride of Christ: Imagery; Christine de Pizan; Courtly Love; Cross-Dressing; Debate Literature; Defenses of Women; Fabliau; Fasting and Food, Religious Aspects of; Femininity and Masculinity; Gender Ideologies; Julian of Norwich; Kempe, Margery; Marie de France; Marie of Oignies; Marguerite Porete; Mechthild of Magdeburg; Procreation and Ideas of Conception; Romance of Silence; Romance, English; Sexuality: Extramarital Sex; Sexuality: Female Same-Sex Relations; Sexuality: Male Same-Sex Relations; Sexuality, Regulation of; Sexuality: Sex in Marriage; Trobairitz and Trobadors; Virginity; Virile Women**

BODY, VISUAL REPRESENTATIONS OF

The female body in the Christian, Jewish, and Muslim visual arts was almost always demurely covered. Ubiquitous dress for married women included long sleeves, robes that touched the ground, and a veil or wimple that covered the hair (also worn by Christian nuns). The naked female body demonstrated gynecological traits, stood as a figure for a nonphysical abstraction such as the soul, or invoked forbidden pagan goddess cults. It also narrated illicit sexual attraction, torment in hell, or the torture of saints. Unlike the nude male body, it never signified the microcosm, the zodiac, or even all humankind. A fundamental divide from ancient Greek and Roman as well as post-Renaissance western European art is that it very rarely conveyed the kind of sensuality or voluptuousness that we associate with "the nude."

Herr Bernger von Hornheim and his lady. Manesse-Lieder manuscript. (Cod. Pal. germ. 848, fol. 178, recto Location: University Library, Heidelberg, Germany. Credit: Foto Marburg / Art Resource, NY.

Nakedness conveyed no such comfort with sexual desires, an attitude strongly enforced by the Church fathers' reading of the temptation and fall in Genesis.

Yet clothing was often extremely sensuous in color, texture, and over-abundance, functioning at a symbolic level to embody both spiritual and courtly love and desire. Thus, visual representations of women's clothing cannot be taken as literal records of what real women wore, even though images must make some reference to conventions, social attitudes, and material wishes, and they are not contaminated by historicism. Indeed, they have much in common with modern fashion drawings and photographs that instill desire in women and play to their fantasies, yet also instruct them in feminine attire so that they will respect gender boundaries. Men's shorter hair and styles of dress functioned in the same way, but denote a wider range of activities and stations in life. A recent revival of interest in decorative men's clothing in our culture also brings us close to an appreciation of the rich and fashionable clothing seen on Christian men of the High Middle Ages, when princes and priests seem to have outshone ladies. Dressing was and is part of the performance of gender, class, and piety.

Depictions of Eve

In accordance with the biblical text of Genesis, Adam and Eve are represented completely nude before the fall. Eve's temptation of Adam to sin, by proferring him a forbidden apple from the Tree of Knowledge, was generally interpreted as sexual; St. Augustine and others speculated on the nonsexual means of reproduction available to humankind before the fall. In pictorial representations Eve often holds the apple close to her breast, and the couple invariably hides their genitals after the fall. She is closely associated with the serpent, which in the bronze doors of Hildesheim (1015) inserts itself between her legs. The horizontal pubescent figure of Eve from the Cathedral of Autun, showing a repentance that is appropriate to the portal where sinners petitioned for pardon, is nonetheless conflated with the serpent gliding on its belly through the garden as its punishment. By the thirteenth century Eve may be somewhat voluptuous, but her face is often mirrored in that of the serpent, into which she gazes with homosexual desire.

The Medical Body

Representations of birthing in sacred and secular narratives show the infant emerging from the folds of a long *chemise*, and women depicted as medical patients are also fully clothed, except in surgery or autopsy. Many writers disapproved of the latter, citing the case of Nero, who they said had his mother dissected to see where he came from, a scene often gruesomely depicted in manuscripts. Medical texts of all periods diagram the female body. One early-fifteenth-century colored outline drawing that is very traditional in its flat graphic rendering of the body inscribes sites of disease on a frontal nude with internal organs displayed, but a coiffed head renders the woman's pregnancy respectable since it is a sign of married status; her uterus is repeated above to demonstrate four fetal positions (London, Wellcome Museum, MS 49, fol. 38). Unlike the sheela na gigs treated elsewhere, the labia are seldom depicted.

The Taboo Body

From Early Christian times until about 1400, pagan statues were represented only in contexts of false-idol worship, including their attribution to Jewish and Muslim use in the High Middle Ages, as demonstrated by Camille. Even then, female idols were usually draped from the waist down. Idols of Venus, whose pagan nude statue still drew attention in Rome, made appearances in illuminated manuscripts of the *Miroir historiale* of Vincent of Beauvais and the *Roman de la Rose* of Guillaume de Lorris and Jean de Meung, but they are usually half-length or draped. A cult statue of Diana in Matthew Paris's chronicle of about 1245 has winged ankles like Eros, her head sprouts antlers and long ears, and her hands cover her breasts. She is evidently the impure counterpart of the devotional statues of the Virgin that so often appear on altars. Lot's wife was turned into a statue as a punishment; if she is represented naked she covers her pudenda, but the preferred form was an almost inhuman pillar of salt.

Formal Court Attire, Queen of Heaven and Earthly Empresses

In early Christian and Byzantine art it became conventional to dress the Mother of God in heavy imperial robes, with jeweled crown, earrings, and necklaces. This sumptuous attire resonates with the representations of living empresses, such as the famous frontal standing figure of Empress Theodora in the mid-sixth-century mosaics of the church of San Vitale in Ravenna. Figures that personified *Ecclesia* (Church) or *Sapientia* (Wisdom) were similarly represented throughout the Middle Ages, but with headdresses varied according to fashion. Some of the most splendid personifications of this kind are in the manuscripts of Hildegard of Bingen's works.

In the West, reigning queens are as elegantly dressed as their Byzantine counterparts but never as authoritative; in coronation scenes they adopt the humbly bowed head of the Virgin Mary enthroned beside Christ in heaven. Between the early thirteenth century and the late fourteenth, such figures are marked by a continuous proliferation of folds, eventually exhibiting linings of complimentary colors and an overabundance of cloth, as spectacular consumption.

The Narrow Line of Propriety in Dress

The *femme fatale*, whether a prostitute seducing the Prodigal Son, Potiphar's wife tempting Joseph, or even Judith visiting Holofernes' camp, was dressed to kill. Sculptors and painters quickly responded to the new texture of imported silks in the twelfth century, as Snyder has shown, and for a while clinging drapery revealed the thighs and breasts, even of good women. The good girl/bad girl distinction may be very subtle, but a tight girdle creates an hourglass figure for the prostitutes in the stained glass of Chartres of c. 1205. Hildegard of Bingen was criticized for dressing the nuns of Rupertsberg in flowing white silk, with diadems in their long, loose hair. The manuscript of her *Liber divinorum operum*, illuminated fifty years after her death, shows such slim-waisted creatures as God's Love (*caritas*) strengthened by wisdom, humility, and peace.

Generally, St. Paul's dictum that "Nature herself teaches you that while flowing locks disgrace a man, they are woman's glory. For her locks were given for covering" (I Corinthians 11:13–15) seems to have been taken to refer to virgins. Origen had castigated women for wearing cosmetics, and later churchmen ranted against their elaborate hairstyles and veils— which, however, evidently intrigued artists and patrons, especially in fashion-conscious secular fourteenth-century circles. The margins in women's books are full of elegant girls with netted hairdos, chaplets, and tightly fitted *chemises*. Sumptuary laws seem to have had little effect on representation and did not displace traditional color codes; for instance, although scarlet and purple were reserved for royalty (and cardinals), Mary Magdalene is recognizable by the red robes and luxury ointments of a prostitute.

Romantic and Spiritual Lovers

Few illustrations of romance literature did justice to the description of rich clothing, but an exceptional set of images accompanies the German poems in an early-fourteenth-century collection known as the Manesse Codex (Heidelberg, Universitätsbibliothek, cpg 848). The artists created a lyrical world of rose bowers, castles, and hills where lovers courted each other. Their layered colorful garments often had linings of *vair* (squirrel fur), denoting high birth (see illustration). On the other hand, just as women's "mystical" love of Christ is textualized in more carnal terms than romantic love, so too it is in devotional representations: In the late-thirteenth-century Rothschild Canticles, a fully clothed woman gazes longingly at the naked and wounded body of Christ, and a robed Christ addresses a naked female soul (*anima*).

Gender Bending

Cautionary texts inform us that cross-dressing was seldom approved of, unless a miracle provided a female saint like St. Uncumber, alias Wilgeforte, with a beard. Vernacular tales of women passing as men are seldom illustrated, but if so their long hair gives them away. Rulers and bishops are represented in garments only slightly shorter than women's, made of similarly rich and colorful fabrics. Yet their short hair and insignia of office (scepter, sword, or crosier) were exclusively masculine, preempting any suggestion that they appear effeminate.

MADELINE H. CAVINESS

References and Further Reading

Burns, E. Jane. *Courtly Love Undressed: Reading Through Clothes in Medieval French Culture.* Philadelphia: University of Pennsylvania Press, 2002.

Caviness, Madeline H. "Gender Symbolism and Text Image Relationships: Hildegard of Bingen's Scivias." In *Translation Theory and Practice in the Middle Ages*, edited by Jeanette Beer. Kalamazoo, Mich.: Medieval Institute Publications, 1997, pp. 71–111

———. "Hildegard as Designer to the Illustrations to Her Works." In *Hildegard of Bingen: The Context of Her Thought and Art*, edited by Charles Burnett and Peter Dronke. London: The Warburg Institute, 1998. Reprinted in Madeline H. Caviness. *Art in the Medieval West and its Audience.* Aldershot, England: Ashgate, 2001, pp. 29–42.

Derolez, A., and Peter Dronke, eds. *Hildegardis Bingensis Liber Divinorum Operum, Corpus Christianorum Continuatio Mediaevalis, 92.* Turnhout: Brepols, 1996.

Hamburger, Jeffrey F. *The Rothschild Canticles: Art and Mysticism in Flanders and the Rhineland Circa 1300.* New Haven, Conn.: Yale University Press, 1990.

Jones, Peter Murray. *Medieval Medical Miniatures.* Austin: University of Texas Press, 1985.

———. *Medieval Medicine in Illuminated Manuscripts.* London and Milan, Italy: The British Library; Centro Tibaldi, 1998.

Katzenellenbogen, Adolf. *Allegories of the Virtues and Vices in Medieval Art: From Early Christian Times to the Thirteenth Century*, translated by Alan J. P. Crick. Nendeln, Liechtenstein: Kraus Reprint, 1968.

Sekules, Veronica. *Medieval Art, Oxford History of Art.* Oxford: Oxford University Press, 2001.

Snyder, Janet. "Cloth from the Promised Land: Appropriated Islamic *Tiraz* in Twelfth-Century French Sculpture." In *Medieval Fabrications: Dress, Textiles, Clothwork, and Other Cultural Imaginings*, edited by E. Jane Burns. New York and Basingstoke: Palgrave Macmillan, 2004, pp. 147–164.

See also **Art, Representations of Women in; Body; Clothing; Cross-Dressing; Empresses: Byzantium; Eroticism in Art; Femininity and Masculinity; Gender Ideologies; Gender in Art; Personifications Visualized as Women; Queens and Empresses: The West; Sheela Na Gigs; Social Status; Sumptuary Law: Theodora**

BOKENHAM, OSBERN

An Augustinian friar at Clare Priory, Suffolk, Bokenham (c.1392/1393–after 1463) authored the only known Middle English collection of lives of female saints. Written between 1443 and 1447, the untitled legendary survives in a single manuscript, British Library Arundel 327. It contains the *vitae* of Saints Margaret of Antioch, Anne, Christine, Ursula and the eleven thousand virgins, Faith, Agnes, Dorothy, Mary Magdalene, Catherine of Alexandria, Cecilia, Agatha, Lucy, and Elizabeth of Hungary. Scholars have debated the meaning of the work's structure: Edwards proposes that a later compiler assembled the lives in no particular order; Delany holds that Bokenham modeled the legendary on Chaucer's *Legend of Good Women*; and Hilles argues that the legendary promotes motherhood and fertility in the interest of Yorkist monarchical ambitions.

In any case, the legendary is notable for Bokenham's detailed dedications to his patrons, prominent East Anglian women such as Katherine Denston, Isabelle Bourchier, Katherine Howard, and Elizabeth de Vere. The regional network of female patrons described by Bokenham corresponds to other evidence for a growing lay, largely female, audience for works of vernacular piety. The legendary's emphasis on feminine piety and fertility and Yorkist dynastic claims is extended in Bokenham's *Mappula Angliae* (1440s), a translation of portions of Ranulf Higden's *Polychronicon*. The same emphasis is found in two works widely attributed to Bokenham: a 1445 translation of portions of Claudian's *De consulatu Stilichonis* (*On the Consulship of Stilicho*) and an untitled genealogical poem, "A Dialogue Betwix a Secular Asking and a Frere Answeryng at the Grave of Dame Johan of Acres" (1456).

CARROLL HILLES BALOT

References and Further Reading

Bokenham, Osbern. *Legendys of Hooly Wummen by Osbern Bokenham*, edited by Mary S. Serjeantson. Early English Text Society O.S. 206. London: Oxford University Press, 1938.

Delany, Sheila. *Impolitic Bodies: Poetry, Saints, and Society in Fifteenth-Century England: The Work of Osbern Bokenham.* New York: Oxford University Press, 1998.

Edwards, A. S. G. "The Transmission and Audience of Osbern Bokenham's *Legendys of Hooly Wummen*." In *Late Medieval Religious Texts and Their Transmission. Essays in Honour of A. I. Doyle*, edited by A. J. Minnis. Cambridge: D. S. Brewer, 1994.

Hilles, Carroll. "Gender and Politics in Osbern Bokenham's Legendary." *New Medieval Literatures* 4 (2001): 189–212.

See also Anne; Audience, Women in the; Body, Visual Representations of; Catherine of Alexandria; Chastity and Chaste Marriage; Chaucer, Geoffrey; Devotional Literature; Elizabeth of Hungary; Hagiography; Jacobus de Voragine's *Golden Legend*; Lay Piety; Literacy and Reading: Vernacular; Literature, Middle English; Margaret of Antioch; Mary Magdalene; Noble Women; Patronage, Literary; Translation; Violence; Virgin Martyrs

BOOK OWNERSHIP

Up until the mid-fifteenth century, upon the invention of printing in the West, all "books" were manuscripts—that is, they were written by hand. Thus, any reference to a "book" or "books" in this article should be understood to mean a manuscript or manuscripts. Manuscripts made of animal skins called parchment, or its more luxurious and carefully prepared version known as vellum, could be rolls (of parchment), bound leaves, or pages. Most users and readers of books were men and women in religious institutions, either in colleges preparing men for the priesthood, monasteries, or convents. Most books in the early Middle Ages until the fourteenth century were written in Latin, and thus that language was a requirement for readers. Like priests and monks, nuns learned and read Latin. Benedictine monks and nuns following the Rule (formulated by the possibly mythical sixth-century siblings Benedict of Nursia and his sister Scholastica) were among the earliest such communities. Monasteries and convents owned all material objects, including books, in common, and hand-written books were so precious that in their libraries they were often chained to the desks where they could be read.

Private book ownership for individuals in this time was extremely expensive and unusual. Because only men could be priests, and nuns were cloistered in monasteries, individual women book-owners were very rare indeed. From known and accessible sources such as women's inventories, women's wills, dedications to women, and inscriptions in the books themselves, or from internal textual comments, certain statistics are clear. Thus research shows that approximately 150 individual women between the ninth and fifteenth centuries owned no more than one book each. But by the fifteenth century, a very small number of women owned what might be termed large collections, as for example Gabrielle de la Tour, who owned two hundred manuscripts in 1474. However, discovery of female book owners in this early period is complicated by the fact that many private possessions owned by women, or indeed acquired by women, were hidden in the accounts, wills, inventories, and libraries of their fathers, husbands, or brothers. Thus the actual number of female book-owners, and certainly the number of readers, was much larger than shown by figures such as those above that can definitely be ascribed to women. Moreover, the large area of central Europe reaching from Magdeburg east into the depth of Russia covered by laws known as the *Sachsenspiegel* (*Saxon Mirror*, promulgated in 1215 and summarizing customs of the previous three centuries) claimed that women should inherit religious books, as women were the customary readers of such books. In this part of Europe it was therefore considered unnecessary to bequeath such books to wives or daughters—it was the law.

Books of Piety

Indeed, most books during this period consisted of various religious texts, for example, sections of the Old and New Testaments, which comprise the Hebrew and Christian Bible. Sometimes only small sections of the Bible were prepared, such as "Psalters" (the whole or parts of the book of Psalms) in later medieval centuries, the *Golden Legend* (that is, apocryphal stories) supplemented biblical texts. Finally, most popular during the later Middle Ages was the "Book of Hours." Books of Hours varied and could be collections of prayers, biblical texts, or selections from the *Golden Legend* to be read at certain hours of the day. The most precious of these books were handsomely illustrated with gold leaf and exquisitely painted illustrations depicting the stories told within them. First and foremost of these stories were the lives of Christ and the Virgin Mary, with the expulsion of Adam and Eve from the Garden of Eden a close second. They often showed gory details of the martyrdom of innumerable saints. Occasionally, they exhibited the artist's or possibly the patron's or book-owner's sense of humor. For example, the Duke of Berry's *Belles Heures* (*Beautiful Hours*) tells the apocryphal story of St. Jerome's humiliation and depicts him with a long dark beard and tonsure in a bright blue woman's dress. In the later Middle Ages they were also often decorated with phenomena showing the artists' realistic understanding of nature, such as flowers, birds, insects, and animals, and calendar illustrations of the months of the year depicting seasonal labor of farm laborers, and aristocratic sports like deer and boar hunting and hawking.

Mothers as Teachers

While priests and preachers could improve their congregations' souls, it was considered especially important for women to be able to read, as they were expected to teach reading to their young children of both sexes, but particularly to their daughters, in order to instill the rudiments of the Christian religion in them. This concept was expressed in a letter to a woman friend by St. Jerome as early as 403, when he gave detailed instructions of how this was to be done: "Have a set of letters made for her of boxwood or of ivory and tell her their names. . . ." Jerome's principles were repeated throughout the medieval period by Christian moralists.

Most books available were used as teaching tools for mothers. Thus Blanche of Castile ordered a large Psalter, in the early thirteenth century, in order to teach her son, the future Louis IX of France, to read. The notorious queen of France, Isabeau of Bavaria, ordered a book of hours for teaching her daughter Jeanne in 1398 and a special alphabet Psalter and "A, b, c. de Psaumes" for her daughter Michelle in 1403. Isabeau also owned a copy of Christine de Pizan's *Enseignements moraux* (Moral Teachings), which had been written for Christine's own son and may have been used for the Dauphin, the Duke of Guienne, as it was presented to his mother, Queen Isabeau.

Women as Ambassadors of Culture

Book ownership was clearly the prerogative of the highest or wealthiest strata of society because it was very expensive, even though reimbursement to the scribe was minimal, as he would often be paid with room and board at the court or on the family estate. Because women of such high status were almost always married to achieve the political and economic projects of their male relatives, they were frequently forced into alliances across borders, bringing their books with them on marriage. For this reason it is difficult to consider women book-owners as members of specific nations or countries. As early as the eleventh century we know of Judith of Flanders, who first married Tostig, earl of Northumbria, and who, as his widow, later brought large English gospels illustrated in the English Winchester style to her second marriage to Welf of Bavaria. Other interesting examples are the fourteenth-century daughter of the Emperor Charles IV, Anne of Bohemia, who brought Czech and German gospels to England on her marriage to

Richard II, and Valentina Visconti, who brought a variety of Italian books to France on her marriage to Louis d'Orleans. The transfer of books from various European countries or nations across borders was often responsible for the transfer of artistic styles recognizable in the obvious changes in manuscript illuminations following the immigration of a book-owning bride. A good example of this is the collection of books that Anne of Bohemia brought from Prague in 1382 on her marriage to Richard II. Anne of Bohemia is also an important link in the late fourteenth century to the pre-Lutheran reforms, not only in religious thought but also its corollary, the need for vernacular biblical expression. The English reformer John Wycliffe used her arrival in London with her multi-language Bibles to promote his case against the bishops' insistence on Latin.

Secular Books and Books Translated into the Vernacular

Although books of piety as described in the previous section were predominant during most of the centuries under discussion, a variety of secular books also existed and were owned and surely read by women. These included chronicles, annals, romances, and instructions for planting, cooking, general deportment, and housekeeping. Chronicles and their cousins, "annals," were collections of histories, personal accounts, and anecdotes, usually anonymous, although in later centuries chroniclers were named. They were amusing to read and are often still used as historical source material despite their often fictive, or at least unsupported, information.

As book-owners and as readers, throughout the Middle Ages, women owned secular books written in the vernacular going back to the mid-thirteenth century. Eleanor of Provence, who married Henry III of England in 1236, owned a French copy of *The Roman of William the Conqueror*. A generation later, Eleanor of Castile, steeped in the tradition of her family's literary court and its vernacular translations of chronicles and law codes, continued with her interest in vernacular literature, Arthurian and Castilian romances, when she became the wife of the future Edward I of England in 1254. In c. 1233, when the future St. Louis, King Louis IX of France, commissioned a manuscript of the *Speculum Historiale* (*Mirror of History*) in Latin, his queen, Margaret of Provence, commissioned a concurrent vernacular French translation. Anne of Bohemia made a point of having her German books translated into English when she arrived in London to help her learn the language of her new realm. Her sister, Margaret, left Prague as a child bride to marry the king of Poland, with a Psalter in Latin, German, and Polish, having benefited from Anne's experience in England.

As early as 1170 Theodora Comnena ordered a translation of the *Song of Roland* into German when she established a literary court in Vienna with her husband Henry Jasomirgott. But by the end of the fourteenth century a number of women owned books of vernacular poetry by such diverse poets as the English Geoffrey Chaucer and the French Guillaume de Lorris, Eustache Dechamps, and Christine de Pizan. Chaucer, for example, wrote his *Legend of Good Women* in 1386 for the queen, Anne of Bohemia, because she had taken exception to his *Troilus and Criseyde* for painting women as disloyal. Like almost all poets of the later Middle Ages, Guillaume de Lorris and Christine de Pizan wrote allegorical poetry. Lorris's celebrated *Roman de la Rose* (*Romance of the Rose*) (c. 1230), an allegory about courtly love, was translated into Middle English during the lifetime of Chaucer, who died in 1400. In contrast, some of Christine de Pizan's poems extolled the delight of married love and the sadness of her widowhood.

Books Specifically Written for Women

A significant body of writing intended specifically for women (although it may also have been written with male readership in mind) was owned by women. These were writings suggesting the correct education and deportment for women. This type of literature comprises Vincent of Beauvais's treatise *De eruditione filiorum nobelium* (*On the Education and Instruction of Noble Children*), commissioned by the Queen of Louis IX of France, Margaret of Provence, between 1247 and 1249; Francesco da Barberino's *Regimento e costumi di donna* (*Rule and Customs for Ladies*), c. 1320; the Goodman of Paris (Le ménagier de Paris), whose 1393 *Traité de morale et d'économie* (*Treatise of Morals and Economy*) was a veritable housekeeping manual composed by this middle-aged man for his very young wife; and in 1405 Christine de Pizan's *Le Livre des trois Vertus* (*The Book of Three Virtues*).

Barberino, who had spent some time at the court in Provence, was intrigued by the customs of life that produced the literature of courtly love. The *Ménagier de Paris*, on the other hand, was specific and careful to give his child bride practical suggestions for every aspect of her married life and behavior. Thus he ensured that when she remarried after his death, she

would not reflect badly upon himself. His instructions detailed her employment and care of her servants (including when they were ill), the preservation of meats and fish, how to air sheets, and how to protect furs from moths. Presumably only one copy of his work existed—that owned by his young wife. Christine de Pizan's *Book of Three Virtues*, however, existed in innumerable manuscript copies in the collections of fifteenth-century women.

Finally, books describing and enumerating large numbers of heroic or exemplary women from the past and modeled on Plutarch's *Lives* were privately owned by an appreciable number of women. These books could act as inspiration to others. Well-known and significant examples of such books are Boccaccio's *De mulieribus claris* (*About Famous Women*) (1355, translated into French in 1401) and Christine de Pizan's *Le livre de la cité des dames* (1405) (*The Book of the City of Ladies*), in which she expressed her unique views.

SUSAN GROAG BELL

References and Further Reading

Bawcutt, Priscilla. "'My Bright Buke': Women and Their Books in Medieval and Renaissance Scotland." In *Medieval Women: Texts and Contexts in Late Medieval Britain. Essays for Felicity Riddy*, edited by Jocelyn Wogan-Browne, Rosalynn Voaden, Arlyn Diamond, Ann Hutchinson, and Carol M. Meale Johnson. Turnhout, Belgium: Brepols, 2000, pp. 17–34.

Bawcutt, Priscilla, and Bridget Henisch. "Scots Abroad in the Fifteenth Century: The Princesses Margaret, Isabella and Eleanor." In *Women in Scotland, c. 1100–1750*, edited by Elizabeth Ewan and Maureen M. Meikle. East Linton, UK: Tuckwell Press, 1999, pp. 45–55.

Bell, Susan Groag. "Medieval Women Book-Owners, Arbiters of Lay Piety and Ambassadors of Culture." *SIGNS: Journal of Women in Culture and Society* 7:4 (1982) 742–768.

Brown, Michelle P. "Female Book Ownership in England During the Ninth Century: The Evidence of the Prayerbooks." *Old English Newsletter* 28(3) (1995): A-57.

Cavanaugh, Susan. *A Study of Books Privately Owned in England, 1300–1450.* Philadelphia: University of Pennsylvania Press, 1980.

Caviness, Madeline H. "Anchoress, Abbess and Queen: Donors and Patrons or Intercessors and Matrons?" In *The Cultural Patronage of Medieval Women*, edited by June Hall McCash. Athens, Ga., and London: The University of Georgia Press, 1998, pp. 105–154.

Dutton, A. M. "Passing the Book: Testamentary Transmission of Religious Literature to and by Women in England." In *Women, the Book and the Godly: Selected Proceedings of the St. Hilda's Conference, 1993*, edited by L. Smith and J. H. M. Taylor. Woodbridge, UK: D. S. Brewer, 1995), pp. 41–54.

Friedman, John B. *Northern English Books, Owners and Makers in the Late Middle Ages.* Syracuse, N.Y.: Syracuse University Press, 1995.

Hanna, Ralph. "Some Norfolk Women and Their Books, c. 1390–1440." In *The Cultural Patronage of Medieval Women*, edited by June Hall McCash. Athens, Ga., and London: The University of Georgia Press, 1998, pp. 288–305.

Jambeck, Karen. "Patterns of Literary Patronage: England, 1200–c.1475." In *The Cultural Patronage of Medieval Women*, edited by June Hall McCash. Athens, Ga., and London: The University of Georgia Press, 1998, pp. 228–265.

Legaré, Anne-Marie. "Reassessing Women's Libraries in Late Medieval France: The Case of Jeanne de Laval." *Renaissance Studies* 10:2 (1996).

Meale, Carol. "'. . . All the bokes that I haue of latyn, englisch, and frensch': Laywomen and Their Books in Late Medieval England." In *Women and Literature in Britain, 1150–1500*, edited by Carol Meale. Cambridge: Cambridge University Press, 1993, pp. 128–158.

Parsons, John Carmi. "Of Queens, Courts, and Books: Reflections on the Literary Patronage of Thirteenth-Century Plantagenet Queens." In *The Cultural Patronage of Medieval Women*, edited by June Hall McCash. Athens, Ga., and London: The University of Georgia Press, 1998, pp. 175–201.

Penketh, Sandra. "Women and Books of Hours." In *Women and the Book: Assessing the Visual Evidence*, edited by L. Smith and J. H. M. Taylor. London and Toronto: University of Toronto Press, 1997, pp. 266–281.

See also **Books of Hours; Christine de Pizan; Conduct Literature; Defenses of Women; Education, Lay; Education, Monastic; Literacy and Reading: Latin; Literacy and Reading: Vernacular; Monasticism and Nuns; Mothers as Teachers; Patronage, Literary; Translation**

Master of Adelaide of Savoy (15th CE) and Master of Jean Rolin: January, the coronation of the queen and bean king. The book of hours of Adelaide of Savoy, duchess of Burgundy. French. Ms.76, fol.1R. 21.9x15 cm. Photo: R.G. Ojeda. Location: Musée Condé, Chantilly, France. Credit: Réunion des Musées Nationaux / Art Resource, NY.

BOOK PRODUCTION
See **Nuns as Scribes**

BOOKS OF HOURS

The book of hours was the principal prayer book of the late medieval laity, and the most commonly produced illuminated manuscript of the late Middle Ages and Renaissance. Although the majority of *horae* (the Latin plural for "hours," now used to signify a book of hours) were made in the bookshops of Paris, Rouen, Tours, Ghent, Bruges, and other cities in France and Flanders, where the genre enjoyed its greatest popularity, books of hours were produced in nearly every region of Europe, in printed editions as well as manuscripts. The central text of a book of hours is the Latin Hours, or Little Office, of the Virgin, a series of psalms, hymns, and other devotions, the majority excerpts from scripture, glorifying and invoking the aid of the Virgin Mary. An abbreviated version of the prayers in the breviary recited by the clergy during the celebration of the Divine Office, the text of the Hours of the Virgin is divided into eight sections, or hours, which correspond to the canonical hours—Matins, Lauds, Prime, Terce, Sext, None, Vespers, and Compline—the traditional times of the day established for clerical prayer. Books of hours may contain other offices, prayers, and devotional texts that give evidence of the religious preferences of their owners. Moreover, the vast majority of *horae*, even the modestly produced ones, seem to have been illustrated. The emergence of the book of hours is thus connected to some of the most significant developments in later medieval culture, including the growth of the Cult of the Virgin; lay aspiration to, and appropriation of, clerical forms of spirituality; the expansion of lay literacy and book ownership; the increase in public and private religious art; and the development of new forms of devotional imagery.

Origins, Development, Content, and Decoration

The practice of reciting the Hours of the Virgin originated in the monastic milieu and can be traced to at least the tenth century; the earliest manuscripts containing the Hours are dated a century later. In its original context, therefore, recitation of the Hours formed a part of the liturgical prayer regime of members of the religious orders and the clergy. The early medieval tradition of personal prayer books for private devotion is also relevant to the development of the book of hours. By c. 1200, the Hours of the Virgin had achieved broader popularity, and the clergy and lay nobility began to commission psalters—volumes of the book of Psalms, the principal private prayer book during this period—with the text of the Hours appended to them. The earliest independent books of hours date to the mid-thirteenth century, and from c. 1300, the popularity of the genre increased steadily, eclipsing, for the laity, that of the psalter-hours and, eventually, the psalter. The heyday of the book of hours was the fifteenth century, when the market for these manuscripts included all strata of the nobility as well as the middle classes.

The ideal devotional routine of the owner of a book of hours entailed reciting the Hours at seven different times of the day, in imitation of clerical practice: Matins and Lauds at night or upon rising, Prime at 6:00 AM, Terce at 9:00 AM, Sext at noon, None at 3:00 PM, Vespers in the early evening, and Compline before going to bed. The realities of lay life made this regime impractical, however, and many laypeople appear to have recited the Hours all at once, in the morning. Most examples are small-format, portable volumes that could easily be carried from the chamber to church or private chapel, the principal settings in which books of hours were used.

Unlike liturgical service books, whose contents were determined by Church mandate, the textual programs of books of hours could vary significantly according to the preferences and means of their patrons, as well as local custom: the only text required for a manuscript to be defined as a book of hours is the Hours of the Virgin itself. Nonetheless, certain texts occur in *horae* with enough regularity to be considered standard features of the genre. The majority of books of hours open with a calendar, which lists the major feasts and saints' days, graded (or ranked) by color to indicate their importance in the liturgical year, in the region, or to the book owner. The Penitential Psalms, a Litany of Saints, and the Office of the Dead occur in most examples, usually following the Hours of the Virgin. The texts of the Hours and Office of the Dead vary slightly according to the diocese or region for which the book was made: identifying a manuscript's "use" and the style of its illumination can aid in localizing and dating it. Memorials or suffrages (short prayers) of the saints are usually included, sometimes in the hour of Lauds. By the late fourteenth century, a series of gospel extracts was typically included following the calendar and preceding the Hours. The prayers "Obsecro te" ("I beseech you") and "O intemerata " ("O immaculate one"), petitions to the Virgin for her intercession written in the first person, also feature regularly. Books of hours frequently contain prayers and shorter offices devoted to a variety of sacred personages or entities. Among the most popular of these were the Hours of the Cross and the Holy Spirit; the "Salve sancta facies," the prayer to the holy face of Christ; and the "Stabat Mater," a rhymed prayer on the Virgin's grief at Jesus's sufferings.

Although books of hours are generally in Latin, vernacular languages played a role in the history of the genre. Many books of hours made in France include a calendar, rubrics, and popular prayers written in French. At the opposite end of the spectrum are North Netherlandish books of hours, which were almost always written in Dutch, the Latin text of the Hours having been translated into that vernacular language by the cleric Geert Grote (d. 1384) in the context of the religious reform movement known as the Devotio Moderna. Many books of hours produced in England before the late fourteenth century include significant amounts of devotional material written in Anglo-Norman French. Middle English texts occur primarily in later examples, including printed primers (as books of hours were also known in England).

Images were integral to books of hours. They marked important texts and served as foci and springboards for devout contemplation, structuring the book owner's experience of the devotions in her/his manuscript as well as mediating the reception of other texts, imagery, and rituals in the religious environment. In a typical example, a historiated initial or, more commonly, a miniature, opens each of the major text divisions. The standard cycle of images for the Hours of the Virgin was a series of Infancy subjects that emphasized the motherhood and queenship of the Virgin. Alternatively, the Hours were accompanied by a Passion cycle, an option popular with English and Dutch patrons. When illustrated, the calendar features imagery of the labors of the months and signs of the zodiac. Imagery of the saints embellished the suffrages or was included as full-page pictures. The Office of the Dead, whose recitation was believed to lessen the time spent by the deceased in Purgatory, was usually prefaced by an image of the

Last Judgment or a funeral service. While there were established traditions of illustration for nearly every important text in books of hours, many examples feature pictorial programs tailored to personalize the manuscripts for their owners. Books of Hours were also personalized through the inclusion of owner portraits, found most frequently at Matins of the Virgin and prefacing the "Obsecro te" and "O intemerata," which were usually illustrated with the Virgin and Child and Pietà, respectively. Owner portraits visualize both the practice of devout prayer and its goal: direct communication with the divine. At Matins in her book of hours of c. 1400, Margaret of Cleves, Duchess of Bavaria-Holland, kneels at a *prie-dieu* and wears prayer beads around her neck as she offers a petition, its words inscribed on a speech scroll, to the seated Virgin and Child. In the miniature illustrating the "Obsecro te" in her manuscript, produced in the third quarter of the fifteenth century, Amadée de Saluces, daughter and heiress of the marshall of Savoy, prays to the enthroned Virgin and Child, her illuminated book of hours open before her on a *prie-dieu*. The most lavishly decorated books of hours were embellished with elaborate frames or borders on every page or extensive programs of marginalia.

Ownership, Patronage, and Use

Although it achieved universal popularity, in its early history the book of hours appears to have been strongly connected to female ownership. The evidence of owner portraits and the incidence of prayers written in the feminine form suggest that the majority of extant thirteenth-century French, Franco-Flemish, and English *horae* were made for women. This does not mean that all of these manuscripts can be ascribed to female patronage, however: books of hours were frequently commissioned for women by their husbands, sometimes on the occasion of their marriage, or by their spiritual advisers. Several early-fourteenth-century English examples appear to have been commissioned by women or to have been the product of joint patronage. Around 1325, for instance, Hawisia de Bois, a member of a knightly family that had flourished in the English Midlands, commissioned a large, lavishly illustrated book of hours designed, in part, to facilitate pious commemoration of her distinguished ancestors, feudal associates, and neighbors. Our picture of manuscript patronage in the late fourteenth and early fifteenth centuries is dominated by the activities of the great royal and ducal bibliophiles, particularly Jean, Duc de Berry, who commissioned several books of hours famous for their exceptionally lavish, strongly personalized, and influential pictorial programs. The vast majority of fifteenth-century *horae* were produced for women and men of more modest means whose identities are largely unknown, and their book of hours may have been the only book they owned.

Although the book of hours was principally a vehicle of personal, private devotion, its uses spanned the private and public realms, and the practice of devout prayer using a book of hours had larger familial, communal, and social ramifications. As already noted, books of hours were used not only at home but also in the public context of the church, where they were contemplated and their prayers recited during the Mass or other services. A richly decorated book of hours was regarded as a sign of status and an important element of a fashionable self-presentation. Eustache Deschamps (d. 1406), court poet of the French king Charles V, satirized women's desire to own and display books of hours thus:

> A book of hours, too, must be mine,
> Where subtle workmanship will shine,
> Of gold and azure, rich and smart,
> Arranged and painted with great art,
> Covered with fine brocade of gold;
> And there must be, so as to hold
> The pages closed, two golden clasps.

The social obligation of pious remembrance and intercession on behalf of deceased family members and associates was achieved through recitation of the Office of the Dead and other texts in a book of hours. For the many book owners who recorded births, marriages, and deaths in the calendars of their volumes, *horae* served as archives of family history. As personalized devotional compendia, books of hours were frequently enriched by prayers or charms to be recited in a variety of situations, such as during childbirth or travel, for particular illnesses, or to guardian angels and patron saints, and these ancillary devotions reveal much about lay piety during the late Middle Ages. Moreover, as with psalters and psalter-hours before them, books of hours were the "first readers" of the late medieval laity. An important role of parents, and particularly mothers, was to teach their children to pray and to read using religious manuscripts; the programs of a few surviving *horae* were tailored to accommodate these pedagogical uses. The accounts of Isabeau of Bavaria, queen of Charles VI of France, reveal that she ordered a book of hours for her six-year-old daughter, Jeanne, in 1398. Around 1335, Isabel de Byron, wife of the Lancashire knight Robert de Neville of Hornby, commissioned a profusely illustrated book of hours whose pictorial program was adapted, in part, for the eyes of Isabel's young, unnamed daughter or granddaughter, portraits of whom occur on several folios of the manuscript. Books of hours were typically recited aloud, in a low voice, but their use has also been associated with the spread among the laity of the practice of silent reading. The pictures and texts in books of hours offered supernatural role models of piety, literacy, charity, compassion, obedience, humility, and fertility, and thereby inscribed in their owners socially sanctioned values and behaviors. The prayers in books of hours forged relationships not only between the individual devotee and the supernatural community, but also between the book owner and the "human community" of which she/he was a member.

KATHRYN A. SMITH

References and Further Reading

Backhouse, Janet. *Books of Hours*. London: The British Library, 1985.

Bell, Susan Groag. "Medieval Women Book Owners: Arbiters of Lay Piety and Ambassadors of Culture." Originally published in *Signs* 7(4) (1982), pp. 742–768. Reprinted in *Sisters and Workers in the Middle Ages*, edited by Judith M. Bennett, Elizabeth A. Clark, Jean F. O'Barr, B. Anne Vilen, and Sarah Westphal-Wihl. Chicago and London: The University of Chicago Press, 1989, pp. 312–332.

Bennett, Adelaide. "A Thirteenth-Century French Book of Hours for Marie." *The Journal of The Walters Art Gallery* 54 (1996): 21–50.

Brayer, Edith. *Lives d'Heures contenant des texts en français*. Centre National de la Recherche Scientifique, *Bulletin d'Information de l'Institut de Recherche et d'Histoire des Texts* 12 (1963): 31–102.

Caviness, Madeline H. "Patron or Matron? A Capetian Bride and a *Vade Mecum* for Her Marriage Bed." *Speculum* 68(2) (1993) 333–362.

De Hamel, Christopher. *A History of Illuminated Manuscripts*. Boston: David R. Godine, 1986, second, revised edition, London: Phaidon.

———. "Books of Hours: 'Imaging' the Word." In *The Bible as Book: The Manuscript Tradition*, edited by John L. Sharpe III and Kimberly van Kampen. London: The British Library Publications; and New Castle, Del.: Oak Knoll Press, 1998, pp. 137–143.

Delaissé, L. M. J. "The Importance of Books of Hours for the History of the Medieval Book." In *Gatherings in Honor of Dorothy E. Miner*, edited by Ursula E. McCracken, Lilian M. C. Randall, and Richard H. Randall, Jr. Baltimore: The Walters Art Gallery, 1974, pp. 203–225.

Donovan, Claire. *The De Brailes Hours: Shaping the Book of Hours in Thirteenth-Century Oxford*. Toronto and Buffalo: University of Toronto Press, 1991.

Drigsdahl, Erik. "New Tests for the Localization of the Hore Beate Marie Virginis." Center for Håndskriftstudier i Danmark. http://www.chd.dk/use/hv_chdtest.html (1997–2002).

Duffy, Eamon. *The Stripping of the Altars: Traditional Religion in England 1400–1580*. New Haven and London: Yale University Press, 1992.

Harthan, John. *Books of Hours and Their Owners*. London: Thames and Hudson, 1977.

Leroquais, Victor. *Les Livres d'Heures manuscrits de la Bibliothèque Nationale*. 2 vols. Paris: Protat Frères, 1927.

———. *Supplément aux Livres d'heures manuscrits de la Bibliothèque Nationale (acquisitions recent et donation Smith-Lesouëf)*. Mâcon: Protat Frères, 1943.

Muir, Bernard J. "The Early Insular Prayer Book Tradition and the Development of the Book of Hours." In *The Art of the Book: Its Place in Medieval Worship*, edited by Margaret M. Manion and Bernard J. Muir. Exeter: University of Exeter Press, 1998, pp. 9–19.

Naughton, Joan. "A Minimally-Intrusive Presence: Portraits in Illustrations for Prayers to the Virgin." In *Medieval Texts and Images: Studies of Manuscripts from the Middle Ages*, edited by Margaret M. Manion and Bernard J. Muir. Chur, Switzerland and New York: Harwood Academic Publishers, 1991, pp. 111–206.

Penketh, Sandra. "Women and Books of Hours." In *Women and the Book: Assessing the Visual Evidence*, edited by Jane H. M. Taylor and Lesley Smith. London: The British Library Publications; Toronto: University of Toronto Press, 1997, pp. 266–281.

Reinburg, Virginia. "Hearing Lay People's Prayer." In *Culture and Identity in Early Modern Europe (1500–1800): Essays in Honor of Natalie Zemon Davis*, edited by Barbara B. Diefendorf and Carla Hesse. Ann Arbor, Mich.: University of Michigan Press, 1993, pp. 19–39.

Saenger, Paul. "Books of Hours and the Reading Habits of the Late Middle Ages." In *The Culture of Print*, edited by Roger Chartier and translated by Lydia G. Cochrane. Princeton, N.J.: Princeton University Press, 1989, pp. 144–176.

Smith, Kathryn A. *Art, Identity and Devotion in Fourteenth-Century England: Three Women and Their Books of Hours*. London: The British Library Publications; Toronto: University of Toronto Press, 2003.

Wieck, Roger S. *Time Sanctified: The Book of Hours in Medieval Art and Life*. New York: George Braziller, Inc., in association with The Walters Art Gallery, Baltimore, 1988.

———. *Painted Prayers: The Book of Hours in Medieval and Renaissance Art*. George Braziller, Inc., in association with The Pierpont Morgan Library, New York, 1997.

The author wishes to acknowledge the assistance of Adelaide Bennett, Lucy Freeman Sandler, and Roger S. Wieck in preparing this entry.

See also **Art, Representations of Women in; Anne; Book Ownership; Modern Devotion; Devotional Art; Devotional Practices; Education, Lay; Hagiography; Lay Piety; Literacy and Reading: Latin; Literacy and Reading: Vernacular; Marginalia, Manuscript; Mary, Virgin; Mary, Virgin: in Art; Mothers as Teachers; Patronage, Artistic**

BOYS
See **Girls and Boys**

BREASTFEEDING AND WET-NURSING

The relationship between mothers and infants is universally complicated, especially in premodern, environmentally stressed societies. Most societies, with very few exceptions, have extolled maternal breastfeeding. This is true even when those women who could afford it sent their infants out to wet nurses. Before the widespread use of methods of artificial feeding, wet-nursing was critical to the survival of infants whose mothers died in childbirth or who were otherwise unable to feed them. Some historians of medieval society have seen in the apparent reluctance of women to breastfeed a reluctance to invest emotionally in an infant whose survival was precarious. Other historians have suggested that wealthy families who sent their children out to nurse did so as a matter of strategy, since lactation impedes fertility and wealthy women and their families wished to space births as close together as possible.

Attitudes towards maternal breastfeeding and wet-nursing in medieval Europe owed much to ancient medical literature by Soranus of Ephesus (fl. early second century CE) and Galen (129–c. 199 CE) as well as to Latin translations by Gerard of Cremona (d. 1187) of Arabic texts by Avicenna (d. 1037), and broad compendia such as those written by Bartholomeus Anglicus (fl. early thirteenth century). Although there were wide divergences of opinion among medical authorities, virtually all believed that in the first few days after birth the newborn should have nothing to eat, or if the infant seemed hungry, to feed it with goat's milk. Some commentators followed Soranus in suggesting that the mother's milk was unsuitable for the first three weeks; others followed Galen in allowing breast milk to be given after the third day. Thus medical opinion, both medieval and ancient, contributed to high infant mortality by denying infants the immunological benefits of colostrums (the easily digested breast milk produced in the first few days after birth).

Where ancient and medieval medicine did not necessarily accord a preference to breastfeeding or wet-nursing, Roman moralists in particular insisted on the importance of maternal breastfeeding and on avoiding wet nurses, who not only might disrupt the maternal bond but who also, via their milk, could pass on to the nursing child their defects of character. This did not completely exclude the possibility of using animal milk as a substitute for breastfeeding, but fears that children nursed on the milk of such animals would imbibe their animal natures made most experiments in this direction scattered and tentative. In the eyes of moralists, the human defects of wet nurses' characters were legion, ranging from their perceived rural coarseness, which could interfere with the child's proper speech development, to infanticide by overlaying (accidental suffocation in bed) and starvation. The most common accusation leveled against wet nurses was that they allowed children under their care to die but continued collecting payments. Stereotypes of wet nurses portrayed them as greedy and negligent peasant women, although areas that were highly urbanized often drew their wet nurses from within the urban population, especially in cities that were part of thriving trade networks that ensured a steady supply of slaves and servants.

Certain rural economies, especially in Mediterranean Europe, became known as places for the urban upper class as well as foundling hospitals to send their children. The wealthiest urban families might take in a wet nurse temporarily, but especially in periods of epidemic disease, they often sent their children into the countryside in the belief that rural air, especially in the mountains, had important health benefits for the child. Women who took up wet nursing as an occupation, at least in central Italy during the fourteenth and fifteenth centuries, were usually married, and their income served as a secondary rather than a primary household support. Medieval processions often included wet nurses as a corporate social group, with its own carnival songs praising the skill and efficiency with which they soothed children and changed their swaddling bands.

Both urban and rural wet nurses risked being caught up in an endless cycle of poverty as well as having to give up their own infants on either a temporary or a permanent basis. Wet nurses who worked for foundling hospitals often gave their own infant to the foundling hospital in order to be paid for providing milk to another of the hospital's charges. Hospital officials often accused wet nurses of defrauding the institution by surreptitiously arranging to have their own children returned to them and receiving payments from the hospital. Female infants who survived the institutional rigors of high mortality rates might receive a small dowry with which they eventually could marry and then take up wet nursing themselves.

Accusations of infanticide by overlaying were quite common, although in the cases where evidence is most abundant, patterns of mortality by age and gender suggest that many of these were cases of sudden infant death syndrome, since males under the age of fourteen months were the most vulnerable to "suffocation." Girls at wet nurse were more likely to suffer death by starvation. Certainly moralists and families alike found in the practices of both breastfeeding and wet-nursing yet another opportunity to project their anxieties concerning race, class, and gender onto a group of women who might be economically and socially marginal, but into whose hands parents entrusted the power of life and death over their progeny.

PHILIP GAVITT

References and Further Reading

Blaffer-Hrdy, Sarah. "Fitness Tradeoffs in the History and Evolution of Delegated Mothering with Special Reference to Wet-Nursing." *Ethology and Sociobiology* 13 (1992): 409–442.

Demaitre, Luke. "The Idea of Childhood and Child Care in Medical Writings of the Middle Ages." *Journal of Psychohistory* 4 (1977): 461–490.

Fildes, Valerie. *Breasts, Bottles, and Babies: A History of Infant Feeding.* Edinburgh: Edinburgh University Press, 1986.

———. *Wet Nursing: A History from Antiquity to the Present.* Oxford: Basil Blackwell, 1988.

Gavitt, Philip. *Charity and Children in Renaissance Florence: The Ospedale degli Innocenti, 1410–1536.* Ann Arbor: University of Michigan Press, 1990.

———. "Infant Death in Late Medieval Florence: the Smothering Hypothesis Reconsidered." In *Medieval Family Roles: A Book of Essays*, edited by Cathy Jorgensesn Itnyre. New York and London: Garland Publishing, 1996, pp. 137–153.

Haas, Louis. *The Renaissance Man and His Children: Childbirth and Early Childhood in Florence, 1300–1600.* New York: St. Martin's Press, 1998.

Klapisch-Zuber, Christiane. "Blood Parents and Milk Parents: Wet Nursing in Florence, 1300–1530." In *Women, Family, and Ritual in Renaissance Italy*, translated by Lydia Cochrane. Chicago and London: University of Chicago Press, 1985.

Otis, Leah L. "Municipal Wet Nurses in Fifteenth-Century Montpellier." In *Women and Work in Pre-Industrial Europe*, edited by Barbara Hanawalt. Bloomington, Ind.: Indiana University Press, 1986.

Origo, Iris. "The Domestic Enemy: Eastern Slaves in Tuscany in the Fourteenth and Fifteenth Centuries." *Speculum* 30 (1955): 321–366.

Ross, James Bruce. "The Middle-Class Child in Urban Italy, Fourteenth to Early Sixteenth Century." In *The History of Childhood*, edited by Lloyd de Mause. New York: The Psychohistory Press, 1974, pp. 183–228.

Shahar, Shulamith. "Infants, Infant Care, and Attitudes Towards Infancy in the Medieval Lives of Saints." *Journal of Psychohistory* 10 (1983): 281–309.

Trexler, Richard. "Infanticide in Florence: New Sources and First Results." *History of Childhood Quarterly* 1 (1973): 98–116.

Wickes, I. G. "A History of Infant Feeding." *Archives of Disease in Childhood* 28 (1953): 151–158, 232–240, 332–340, 416–422, 495–502.

See also **Contraception; Fosterage; Hospitals; Infants and Infanticide; Pregnancy and Childbirth**

BREWING

See **Alewives and Brewing**

BRIDE OF CHRIST: IMAGERY

Medieval bridal imagery is devotional and pedagogical rather than theological. It is found most frequently in what is generally termed "bridal," "affective," or "love" mysticism. Bridal imagery reached its peak of popularity in western Europe between the twelfth and fourteenth centuries, with much of its pervasiveness indebted to the reform-driven milieu of Cistercian monasticism. The imagery is more textual than artistic, and can be found in diverse religious genres, from poetry to sermons.

The ritual prototype for medieval bridal spirituality is found in the consecration liturgy for nuns as brides of Christ. It constitutes a variation of the *hieros gamos* (sacred marriage) symbolism found in other world religions. Christian doctrine assigned divinity to the bridegroom only, with the effect of reinforcing masculine gender privileges. Devotional practices, however, sometimes challenged such gender asymmetry by claiming "divine" status for the bride in her three interrelated manifestations as Ecclesia (Church), as the Virgin Mary, and as the human soul.

Bridal imagery is paradoxical and conflicted. It presents explicit erotic content, yet it also extols celibacy and pronounces the inherent sinfulness of sexual desire (concupiscence). From its scattered origins in Hebrew and Christian Scriptures (e.g., Song of Songs, Isaiah 54:4–7; Jeremiah 2:32; Revelation 19:7; Psalm 45:10–17), bridal imagery is circumscribed by its polar opposite, the prostitute (Hosea 1:2), underscoring the discriminatory double standard applied to female social and sexual roles, whether assigned to men or women.

The devotional use of bridal imagery emerged in the context of non-Christian Western social systems, which recognized a variety of marital and sexual contracts geared toward the maintenance of kinship systems and the economic and social survival of groups. Traditionally, a betrothal was negotiated between families rather than individuals, and could be contracted for children. Marriage was publicly recognized through the adult couple's initiation of sexual activities. Bridal spirituality thus evoked a strong erotic undercurrent and a host of contractual obligations and family alliances in an uneasy relationship with an increasingly restrictive Christian model.

Scholars generally credit the Cistercian reform movement with the revitalization and dissemination of bridal spirituality. Bridal metaphors appealed to an adult population of converts in that they could ease the radical transition from a secular to a religious lifestyle. It framed conversion as a betrothal and the contractual entry into a prestigious new spiritual "kin" with Christ as bridegroom and the human soul as chaste, that is, celibate bride. The psycho-spiritual aspects of bridal symbolism were articulated most prominently by the Cistercian abbot Bernard of Clairvaux (1090–1154), and further developed by contemporaries such as William of Saint-Thierry (1070/1090–1148). Vernacular adaptations flourished across Europe, as in the *St. Trudperter Hohelied* (c. 1150/1160) or in Middle English poetry devoted to the Virgin Mary.

Bernard's writings expound on all three manifestations of bridal imagery. The strand of images closest to biblical sources identifies *Ecclesia* as bride of Christ (cf. II Cor. 11:2; Rev. 19:6 ff). Medieval exegetes extended the bride-whore rhetoric to denounce Judaism, the opposite of Ecclesia, in the figure of *Synagoga*. Even an author valorizing the nuptial femininity of *Ecclesia*, such as the abbess Hildegard of Bingen (1098–1187), followed in the steps of Church Father St. Augustine (354–430), who declared that "A great and singular honor belongs to the bridegroom [Christ]: he found [*Ecclesia*] a harlot and made her a virgin" (*Sermo* I.8). Hildegard evoked Synagoga as wounded and maimed, as "pale from the head down to the navel and black from the navel to the feet, which were bloody. . . she had no eyes" (*Scivias* I.5).

Female mystics of the twelfth and thirteenth centuries developed audacious interpretations of the bride as a noble and strong woman transformed through love into full divinity, at times adapting courtly love metaphors as well. Prominent among them are the Beguine authors Mechthild of Magdeburg (c. 1212–1282) and Hadewijch (fl. middle of thirteenth century). Other women experienced visions of marrying Christ the bridegroom, including Gertrude the Great of Helfta (1256–1301/1302), Angela of Foligno (1248/1249–1309), and Catherine of Siena (1347–1380), who received stigmata in the form of a wedding band.

The third symbolic category identifies the Bride of Christ with Mary, Mother of God. As *Regina Coeli*, Queen of Heaven, she is coregent with Christ. The coronation of the Virgin Mary as Heavenly Bride and representative of Ecclesia is one of the most frequent artistic depictions of bridal imagery.

Further scholarly exploration of bridal imagery is needed in regard to apocalyptic themes, such as the marriage of the Lamb and the New Jerusalem (Rev. 19:7 ff), mutual influences of Christian and Jewish bridal language, especially in regard to interpretations of the Song of Songs, and the confluence of bridal mysticism with other mystical schools of thought.

ULRIKE WIETHAUS

References and Further Reading

Bynum, Caroline Walker. *Jesus as Mother: Studies in the Spirituality of the High Middle Ages*. Berkeley and Los Angeles, 1982.

Mechthild of Magdeburg. *The Flowing Light of the Godhead*, translated and introduced by Frank Tobin. New York: Paulist, 1998.

Neaman, Judith. "The Harlot Bride: From Biblical to Mystical Topos." In *On Pilgrimage*, edited by Margot H. King. Winnipeg: Peregrina Publishing, 1994.

Newman, Barbara. *Sister of Wisdom: St. Hildegard's Theology of the Feminine*. Berkeley and Los Angeles: University of California Press, 1987.

See also **Betrothals; Bible, Women in; Cistercian Order; Courtly Love; Devotional Literature; Eroticism in Literature; Femininity and Masculinity; Gender Ideologies; Hadewijch; Mary, Virgin; Mechthild of Magdeburg; Minnesang; Mysticism and Mystics; Sexuality: Extramarital Sex; Sexuality: Female Same-Sex Relations; Sexuality: Male Same-Sex Relations; Sexuality, Regulation of; Sexuality: Sex in Marriage; Song of Songs, Medieval Interpretation of; Soul; Typology and Women; Virginity**

BRIGIT

Brigit (c. 452–524/528) of Kildare was the founder and patron saint of the monastery of Kildare in the medieval Irish kingdom of Leinster. She is the earliest recognized female saint and abbess in Ireland. Her feast day is February 1. What is known of her rests entirely on legend and tradition, which has it that she was born in the mid-fifth century; that her father was a nobleman and her mother his slave; that she performed several miracles throughout her life; and that she was renowned for her charity and hospitality. Some have even seen her as a euhemerization (the result of the process of a human becoming worshipped as a god) of an Irish goddess of the same name, as she acquired several of the same attributes as the goddess, such as being the patron of poets, smiths, healers, and women in childbirth. She was revered as one of the leading saints of early medieval Ireland, together with Patrick and Columba. Her foundation at Kildare was a double house for both men and women, the only one recorded in Ireland, and an important episcopal seat in the medieval Irish Church. The abbess ruled as an equal to the bishop; one legend relates that Brigit was actually consecrated a bishop, but this cannot be proven in fact. Brigit is described in a seventh-century text as the abbess "whom all the abbesses of the Irish revere," and the office of abbess of Kildare remained the most prestigious position for an Irish female religious up until the twelfth century.

DOROTHY ANN BRAY

References and Further Reading

Connolly, Seán, trans. "Vita Prima Sanctae Brigitae." *Journal of the Royal Society of Antiquaries of Ireland* 119 (1989): 5–49.

Connolly, Seán, and J.-M. Picard, trans. "Cogitosus's *Life of St Brigit*." *Journal of the Royal Society of Antiquaries of Ireland* 117 (1987): 5–27.

Harrington, Christina. *Women in a Celtic Church: Ireland 450–1150*. Oxford: Oxford University Press, 2002.

Ó hAodha, Donncha, ed. and trans. *Bethu Brigte*. Dublin: Dublin Institute for Advanced Studies, 1978.

See also **Abbesses; Double Monasteries; Hagiography; Ireland; Monasticism and Nuns, Celtic**

BRUNHILD AND FREDEGUND

Brunhild (d. 613) and Fredegund (d. 596/597) are among the best known Merovingian queens. Both were heavily criticized by contemporary sources and became symbols of political perversity. Fredegund was a low-born servant who started her career as King Chilperic's mistress and ended as queen of Neustria. Although she is accused of ordering the assassination of Galswintha, Brunhild's sister, there is no evidence that she instigated the murder. After her husband's death, she functioned as regent for her surviving son, the future king Clothar II.

Unlike Fredegund, Brunhild was a Visigothic princess. She married Sigebert of Austrasia. As a royal widow, she became regent for her son and grandsons. She was a powerful queen and ruled Austrasia with little hindrance. In 613, abandoned by the Austrasian aristocracy, she was put to death by Clothar II. Brunhild and Fredegund were enemies, because each played a leading role in Merovingian dynastic conflicts.

Although different in their social origins and careers, these two queens can be considered archetypes of female power in a period when the notion of queenship had not yet crystallized. Lacking any institutionalized role, Merovingian queens were reliant on their husbands or sons, but alongside this dependence, they enjoyed a certain amount of sexual freedom and could participate in the cycle of violent feuds. Beyond their gendered weakness and reputations for evil, these two Merovingian queens exemplify the traditional political behavior which characterized the Merovingian elite.

NIRA PANCER

References and Further Reading

Gregory of Tours. *The History of the Franks*, edited and translated by Lewis Thorpe. Harmondsworth: Penguin, 1974.

Harrison, Dick. *The Age of Abbesses and Queens*. Sweden: Nordic Academic Press, 1998.

Nelson, Janet. "Queens as Jezebels: the Careers of Brunhild and Balthild in Merovingian History." In *Medieval Women*, edited by Derek Baker. Oxford: Basil Blackwell, 1985, pp. 31–77.

Pancer, Nira. *Sans peur et sans vergogne: De l'honneur et des femmes aux premiers temps mérovingiens*. Paris, Albin Michel, 2001.

Stafford, Pauline. *Queens, Concubines and Dowagers: The King's Wife in Early Middle Ages*. Athens, Ga.: University of Georgia Press, 1983.

Wood, Ian. *The Merovingian Kingdoms, 450–751*. London: Longman, 1994.

See also **Frankish Lands; Queens and Empresses: The West; Violence**

BURGUNDIAN NETHERLANDS

Dominating the economic, political, and cultural life of northwestern Europe in the late fourteenth and fifteenth centuries, the Burgundian Netherlands (1384–1556) comprised most of the modern-day Low Countries. This territory was under the control of the Burgundian dukes, a cadet branch of the French royal house. In contrast to the preceding period, the Burgundian era witnessed a general constriction in the political, social, and economic roles of women. The Burgundian dukes—Philip the Bold, John the Fearless, Philip the Good, and Charles the Bold—centralized their authority by expanding the bureaucracy, and women were no longer appointed to bureaucratic positions. What never disappeared was the capacity of women to hold princely office. Upon the death of her father, Charles, in 1477, Mary of Burgundy (1477–1482) became duchess; fifteen years later, her daughter, Margaret of Austria, was chosen governor of the region (1507–1530), in large part because the local populace preferred her to her father, Maximilian of Hapsburg. The region's preeminence in the later Middle Ages, however, owed more to its continuing vibrant and diverse economy than to political innovation. Industrialization and specialization, particularly in the manufacture of textiles, attained a degree of sophistication virtually unrivaled throughout late medieval Europe.

Women found employment at all levels of the economy and thus were able to maintain some degree of autonomy. They were not only peasants, fruit sellers, and innkeepers, but also fishers, tanners, and moneylenders. Above all, they combed, spun, wove and dyed wool, sheared, selvedged, and sold cloth. Such occupations were skilled, and travelers to the region, such as Luigi Guicciardini, remarked on the breadth and depth of literacy, in both French and Dutch, for women as well as men in the region. Access to the workplace, in conjunction with inheritance practices that generally privileged the spouse over progeny, enabled women to hold property (both movable and immovable) in their own name. These circumstances underlay the relatively large proportion of women identified as single in places such as Hulst (where they comprised one-quarter of all taxpayers in 1441), and in the fishing town of Blankenberghe, where, in the first quarter of the fifteenth century, single women made up almost twenty-three percent of the population.

Women were not generally considered to be under male legal guardianship. Although in most regions married men had become recognized as heads of households, single women could still make contracts, sue and be sued, testify, and stand surety. Because women tended to disappear into the conjugal unit, it has widely been assumed that, when they left the single state behind, they also relinquished rights—particularly property rights, which had been essential to their survival as autonomous single persons. Married women, however, retained interest not only in the property they brought to a marriage (dowries were uncommon), but also in that property which was acquired during the relationship. They often acted for the family in the absence of the male spouse and occasionally even when he was present. Throughout the later Middle Ages, women with their bastard children continued to constitute a legally and socially recognized, although somewhat disadvantaged, unit. Single women and their children, for example, made up a large proportion of the poor.

Marriage, albeit often in an unblessed form, remained the preferred state for both men and women. Even a notable portion of the clergy maintained quasi-marital households. Burgundian marriage practices were shaped by a number of circumstances. There is evidence that, before the Counter-Reformation, both men and women took pleasure in sex, both inside and—despite canonical teachings to the contrary—outside of marriage. This, combined with the twin pressures of economic constriction and family ambition, led to an uncoupling of marriage and sexual experience. While there is no doubt that some unions were based on passion and companionship, hard-headed concerns for economic and social status meant that many marriages were contracted on a less sentimental basis. Marriage opportunities came out of a matrix of propinquity, family networks and interests, class expectations, and economic concerns. Increasingly frequent abductions, both violent (rape) and voluntary (elopement), none-theless reflect widespread attempts, however, to thwart convention.

Women's experience in the Burgundian Netherlands must be viewed against a backdrop of increasing constriction, due not only to the crises of the fourteenth and fifteenth centuries, but also to increasing centralization of ducal government and the institutionalization of city offices. The imposition of French administrative procedures and Roman law valorized Parisian norms in both language and social practice. The infractions for which women were most often punished became increasingly those perceived as specific to a gendered female role: prostitution, neglect of house or of children, and quarrelling. This combination of economic, political, moral, and social constriction increasingly forced women out of the marketplace and into the increasingly dominant social unit, the household. Women began to find positions in trade and guilds closed off to them. In certain places, Beguines, for example, came to be prohibited from selling cloth. The refocusing of manufacture on cottage households effectively diminished women's autonomy, submerging and subordinating their economic activity within a domestic social unity now perceived as headed by a male householder.

ELLEN E. KITTELL

References and Further Reading

Blockmans, Wim, and Walter Prevenier. *The Promised Lands: The Low Countries Under Burgundian Rule, 1369–1530.* Philadelphia: University of Pennsylvania Press, 1999.

Danneel, Marianne. *Weduwen en wezen in het laat-middeleeuwse Gent.* Leuven: Garant, 1995.

Godding, Philippe. *Le droit privé dans les Pays-Bas méridionaux du 12e au 18e siècle.* Brussels: Palais des Académies, 1987.

Howell, Martha. *The Marriage Exchange: Property, Social Place, and Gender in Cities of the Low Countries, 1300–1550.* Chicago: University of Chicago Press, 1998.

———. *Women, Production, and Patriarchy in Late Medieval Cities.* Chicago: University of Chicago Press, 1986.

Kittell, Ellen, and Mary Suydam, eds. *The Texture of Society: Medieval Women in the Southern Low Countries.* New York: Palgrave Macmillan, 2004.

Prevenier, Walter, and Wim Blockmans. *The Burgundian Netherlands.* Cambridge: Cambridge University Press, 1986.

Simons, Walter. *Cities of Ladies: Beguine Communities in the Medieval Low Countries, 1200–1565.* Philadelphia: University of Pennsylvania Press, 2001.

See also **Beguines; Cities and Towns; Clothwork, Domestic; Education, Lay; Flanders; Hadewijch; Landholding and Property Rights; Market and Tradeswomen; Marriage, Christian; Mary of Burgundy; Rape and Raptus; Singlewomen; Textile Production for the Market; Work**

BURIALS AND TOMBS

Funerary monuments provide some of the most visible material documents of the status of medieval women. Guardians of family memory, women took an active part in the commemoration of the deceased, including the planning and design of tombs. Examples of female patronage and imagery survive from almost every major medieval society. Because tombs of the upper classes were more prominent, more protected, and more likely made of durable materials, their burials are more easily documented than others.

Christian Rome and the Frankish Lands

In contrast with pre-Christian culture, aristocratic women of Christian Rome were encouraged to take a public role in constructing monuments, including mausolea and chapels at saints' burial sites. Such funerary monuments were intended to reinforce group identity, whether of relatives, social group, or coreligionists. The empress regent Galla Placidia

Eleanor of Aquitaine. Wife of Henry II and mother of Richard I, the Lionhearted. Died 1204 in Fontevrault, France. Tombs of the Plantagenet Kings. 13th c. Location: Abbey, Fontevrault, France. Credit: Erich Lessing / Art Resource, NY.

(r. 425–437) constructed a mausoleum as part of the palace chapel in Ravenna. Renowned for its mosaics, the vaults are ornamented with starry skies and paradisal foliage. Family status is suggested by the Good Shepherd in imperial robes, and family origins by an image of Vincent of Saragossa. If Galla Placidia planned to be buried there, she did not achieve her purpose, for she died in Rome in 450 and her burial place is unknown.

The practise of burial *ad sanctos,* near the body of a saint, transformed cities during the early Middle Ages. Despite prohibitions against burials within city walls, religious communities sought to keep relics of their precious saints with them. The case of the saintly Queen Radegund (d. 587) documents the laments of the nuns who would not be able to tend her grave outside of Poitiers, since they were not allowed to leave their monastery. Eventually she was translated to a church within the city walls. As relics like hers were brought into urban churches, graveyards grew up surrounding church grounds. Well-to-do families established burial chapels within monasteries, a custom that endured past the Middle Ages. Individuals who could afford epitaphs or decorated tombs marked their resting places thus. Burial itself, like that of Radegund, could include embalming with herbs and spices in a linen shroud. Aristocrats were richly attired when buried, accompanied by weapons and luxury objects to indicate their status. On the other hand, Gertrude of Nivelles (d. 659), a member of the family that founded the Carolingian dynasty, requested to be buried in her old hair shirt and a linen veil left to her by a woman pilgrim. Such clothing attested to the abbess's humility, as well as to the sanctity of the donor.

Theodechilde (d. c. 662–667), abbess of the double monastery of Jouarre, was provided with an ornamental stone sarcophagus and an inscription celebrating her virtue. Using imagery traditional for women's monuments since early Christianity, the inscription describes her inviting the nuns to meet the bridegroom Christ as did the Wise Virgins (Matthew 25:1–13).

Iberia

Although tomb imagery was not always gender-specific, especially in the early Middle Ages, such themes were consistently associated with women. Sancha, wife of Fernán González, first Count of Castilla (d. c. 970), was buried in a late antique sarcophagus with a contemporary lid. Such reuse of older sarcophagi was frequent. To emphasize her status as wife, the portrait of a couple on her tomb was recarved with Sancha and Fernando's features. More individualized monuments developed from the late eleventh century onward. The sarcophagus of the Aragonese princess, Doña Sancha (d. 1096), was sculptured to depict her rank and expected salvation. Her soul appears as a nude child ascending to heaven, flanked by clergy and an image of Sancha herself enthroned with her sisters. They were eventually buried in the same sarcophagus at the convent she founded. On the back of the tomb are scenes of men in combat, which may refer to the Reconquest, but also to the struggle of virtue with vice.

The sarcophagus of Queen Blanca of Navarra, who died as a result of childbirth in 1156, is notable for its particularly rich expression of female experience. The queen is shown in her deathbed attended by angels who lift her soul, as if a newborn child, towards Christ on the lid above. On either side are male and female mourners, including her grief-stricken husband. It was in the Spanish kingdoms that tombs frequently depicted the death and burial of heroic or beloved figures with mourners lamenting their loss. Biblical imagery included the Visitation, the Adoration of the Magi, the Judgment of Solomon, the Massacre of the Innocents, Mary lamenting Jesus's crucifixion, and the Wise and Foolish Virgins. The woman's value as mother, intercessor, and protector of family interests is illustrated there. Blanca was interred in the Navarrese royal pantheon in Nájera, while her husband, Sancho (d. 1158), was laid to rest in Castilian Toledo. Their deceased infants were buried in Soria (Castilla); only one, Alfonso VIII, survived to maturity.

Queens and Empresses

As with Blanca, queens were not necessarily buried with their kings, but could exercise different prerogatives, depending upon circumstances and ambition. While ten Byzantine empresses from the fourth through the eleventh centuries shared their husbands' sarcophagi at the Church of the Holy Apostles in Constantinople, the same number had their own tombs. Several twelfth-century Crusader kings of Jerusalem found burial within the Church of the Holy Sepulcher, at the tomb of Jesus. Some Crusader queens (Morphia, d. before 1129, and her daughter Melisende, d. 1161) were interred in a corresponding situation, at the Church of Our Lady in Jehosaphat, where a cenotaph honored the Virgin Mary. It had

been assumed that many French queens were "excluded" from the royal resting place of Saint-Denis, but recent research indicates a separate reginal tradition there, as in England. Several, such as Adelaide of Maurienne (d. 1154), chose to be buried at monasteries they supported.

In other instances, women were the instigators in establishing and maintaining family monuments consolidating, at the same time, political claims. Fernando I (d. 1065), was persuaded by his queen, Sancha (d. 1067), to abandon his Castilian family's burial site in favor of her more prestigious royal pantheon in San Isidoro in León. Their granddaughter, Queen Urraca (d. 1126), commissioned frescoes for the crypt, including her grandparents kneeling at the Crucifixion. In contrast with the splendidly painted ceiling, the tombs themselves are undecorated. Around 1200, Eleanor of Aquitaine probably commissioned the innovative effigies of her second husband, Henry II of England (d. 1189), their son Richard I (d. 1199), and herself (d. 1204) at the convent of Fontevraud in the Aquitaine. These are among the earliest surviving life-size sculptured effigies. Although the kings are shown lying in state, Eleanor is alive and reading a book, a frequent attribute of aristocratic women.

Family and Territory

In the Low Countries and England between the thirteenth and fifteenth centuries, the tomb of kinship developed as a means to articulate familial identity and establish territorial hegemony. Typically, these monuments displayed an effigy of the occupant accompanied by members of the family, alive or deceased. Unlike Spanish examples, these figures do not participate in the funeral but are arranged on the tomb chest, in a hierarchy reflecting family history or relationships, identified by inscriptions, heraldic devices, or dress. The tomb of Queen Philippa of Hainault (d. 1369) exemplifies this genre. Consort of Edward III, she articulated English ambitions to claim the French throne and perhaps also to Hainault and Holland in the design of her tomb. Her most important male kin, all regents, appear at the head and foot of the tomb, with her children and their spouses along the sides. As these examples illustrate, funerary monuments consistently provided noble women an instrument by which to commemorate their role as procreators and promotors of family consciousness.

ELIZABETH VALDEZ DEL ÁLAMO

References and Further Reading

Brown, Peter. *The Cult of the Saints: Its Rise and Function in Latin Christianity*. Chicago: The University of Chicago Press, 1981.

Caldwell, Susan Havens. "Urraca of Zamora and San Isidoro in Leon: Fulfillment of a Legacy." *Woman's Art Journal* 7 (1986): 19–25.

Carrasco, Magdalena Elizabeth. "Spirituality in Context: The Romanesque Illustrated Life of St. Radegund of Poitiers." *The Art Bulletin* 72(3) (1990): 414–435.

Caviness, Madeline. "Anchoress, Abbess, and Queen: Donors and Patrons or Intercessors and Matron?" In *The Cultural Patronage of Medieval Women*, edited by June Hall McCash. Athens, Ga.: University of Georgia Press, 1996, pp. 105–154.

Effros, Bonnie. *Caring for Body and Soul: Burial and the Afterlife in the Merovingian Period*. University Park, Pa.: Pennsylvania State University Press, 2002.

Erlande-Brandenburg, Alain. *Le roi est mort: étude sur les funérailles, les séputures et les tombeaux des rois de France jusq'à la fin du XIIIe siècle*. Geneva: Droz, 1975.

Geary, Patrick J. *Phantoms of Remembrance: Memory and Oblivion at the End of the First Millennium*. Princeton, N.J.: Princeton University Press, 1994.

Mackie, Gillian. "New Light on the So-Called Saint Lawrence Panel at the Mausoleum of Galla Placidia, Ravenna." *Gesta* 29(1) (1990): 54–60.

Martin, Therese. "The Art of a Reigning Queen as Dynastic Propaganda in Twelfth-Century Spain." *Speculum* 80(4) (2005): 1134–1171.

———. "Queen as King: Patronage at the Romanesque Church of San Isidoro in León." Ph.D. dissertation, University of Pittsburgh, 2000.

Morganstern, Anne McGee. *Gothic Tombs of Kinship in France, the Low Countries, and England*. University Park, Pa.: The Pennsylvania State University Press, 2000.

Nolan, Kathleen. "The Queen's Body and Institutional Memory: The Tomb of Adelaide de Maurienne." In *Memory and the Medieval Tomb*, edited by Elizabeth Valdez del Alamo with Carol Stamatis Pendergast. Aldershot: Ashgate, 2000, pp. 249–267.

———. "The Queen's Choice: Eleanor of Aquitaine and the Tombs at Fontevraud." In *Eleanor of Aquitaine: Lord and Lady*, edited by Bonnie Wheeler and John Carmi Parsons. New York and Houndmills, England: Palgrave Macmillan, 2002, pp. 377–405.

Panofsky, Erwin. *Tomb Sculpture: Four Lectures on its Changing Aspects*. New York: Abrams, 1964. Reprint, 1992.

Parsons, John Carmi. "'Never was a body buried in England with such solemnity and honour': The Burials and Posthumous Commemorations of English Queens to 1500." In *Queens and Queenship in Medieval Europe*, edited by Anne Duggan. Woodbridge, England: Boydell and Brewer, 1997, pp. 317–337.

Ruiz Maldonado, Margarita. "La contraposición Superbia-Humilitas. El sepulcro de Doña Sancha y otras obras." *Goya* 146 (1978): 75–81.

Simon, David. "Doña Sancha Sarcophagus." In *The Art of Medieval Spain A.D. 500–1200*. New York: The Metropolitan Museum of Art/Abrams, 1993, pp. 229–232.

Valdez del Alamo, Elizabeth. "Lament for a Lost Queen: The Sarcophagus of Doña Blanca in Nájera." *The Art Bulletin* 78 (1996): 311–333. Reprinted in *Memory and the Medieval Tomb*, edited by Elizabeth Valdez del Alamo with Carol Stamatis Pendergast. Aldershot: Ashgate, 2000, pp. 43–79.

van Houts, Elizabeth. *Memory and Gender in Medieval Europe, 900–1200*. Toronto: University of Toronto Press, 1999.

Yasin, Anne Marie. "Funerary Monuments and Collective Identity: From Roman Family to Christian Community." *The Art Bulletin* 87(3) (2005): 433–457.

See also **Architecture, Ecclesiastical; Art, Representations of Women in; Bible, Women in; Book Ownership; Books of Hours; Death, Mourning and Commemoration; Devotional Art; Eleanor of Aquitaine; Family (Earlier Middle Ages); Family (Later Middle Ages); Gender in Art; Gertrude of Nivelles; Grave Goods; Hagiography; Jouarre and Chelles; Kinship; Mary, Virgin: in Art; Monasticism and Nuns; Noble Women; Patronage, Artistic; Patronage, Ecclesiastical; Queens and Empresses: the West; Radegund; Soul; Urraca**

BUSINESS

It is possible to trace women's participation in business in cities and towns, as lead investors in commercial and artisan industrial enterprises, as masters apprenticing assistants in some few guilds, and as real estate investors, among other occupations. Women were also household managers, procuresses of brothels, and simple market sellers, or shopkeepers. In rural areas women managed large estates in the absence of their men, and in the peasant context, peasant widows might succeed, as they did in medieval Provence, to the powers of *patria potestas*, the paternal authority enjoyed by their late husbands, as household heads.

In some instances husbands and wives worked together in the family enterprise. Certainly this was true in an agricultural context where men did major fieldwork, and women gardened and tended to household and child-rearing chores closer to the homestead. It was also the case in artisan industry and commerce that women might work with their husbands. At times wives had independent business careers. Margery Kempe ran brewing and wheat-milling establishments though her husband was a successful merchant in Lynne. Women owned their own shops in the wool industry in Barcelona in the early fourteenth century. Women of modest station sold foodstuffs, often fruits and vegetables, in urban market squares, setting up collapsible stands daily. Widows of artisans and merchants might direct businesses that they inherited from their late husbands. Noble heiresses and wives of nobles away on military or other matters ran large rural estates, and a few noble women, such as the twelfth-century vicountess Ermengard of Narbonne, directed lordships where political, economic, and legal responsibilities were intertwined. Although not as owners, abbesses administered their monasteries, managing economics and politics on a high level. On the other hand, there is some evidence that women inherited commercial tools and commercial spaces such as breweries; occupations could be passed down from one generation to the next.

The legal agency of women in business varied geographically across Europe. The married woman of northern Europe and Britain was legally a *feme coverte*, engaging in business only under the supervision and legal responsibility of her husband. On the other hand, the *feme sole* was empowered to engage in business on her own. In the German law of the *Sachsenpiegel (Saxon Mirror)*, husbands acted as guardians of their wives' goods, limiting business control. However, according to *Les Etablissements de Saint Louis (The Establishments of St. Louis)*, a married tradeswoman in northern France could defend herself legally in affairs involving her own business. In some Italian cities, such as Lucca, married women needed the consent of their husbands and close male relatives to sell or dispose of property. In southern France, Roman law allowed women to forgo legal protection, under the authority of the *Senatusconsultum Velleianum*, which theoretically prevented women from assuming legal engagements on behalf of others. This carved out greater legal agency for women, laying the foundation for their involvement in business. In Mediterranean Europe women invested in commercial partnerships, frequently as investors; they rarely functioned as traveling merchants.

Typically, women were most often present in the textile and food sectors of the medieval economy. In 1270 Etienne Boilieau noted five guilds in northern France related to the silk industry that were female-dominated. The Parisian Books of the Taille, tax records with seven levies extending over the period 1292–1313, reveal women in 172 occupations in 1292 and in 130 in 1313, about half the representation of men in both instances. Women were noted in money changing, jewelry production, mercery (ribbons, accessories, fabric adornments), in clothing production, as artists and scribes, as keepers of taverns, as peddlers, and others. Women of the Mediterranean world participated in similar activities. Genoese noblewomen directed the manufacture of gold thread. In the late Middle Ages, women of London enjoyed participation in the silk industry. In Ghent women served as moneychangers, lenders, innkeepers, and cloth wholesalers. Women were excluded from the notariate and from the law, and their participation in medicine was limited and officially prohibited in the later Middle Ages, as medicine became university-based in training,

though the presence of women in the care of the sick and in folk remedies persisted.

In all of these capacities, women would appear to be business "owners." While women's economic involvement in the Middle Ages was not a direct parallel of men's roles, women were well integrated into the local business community and conspicuous within the urban and rural economies of western Europe. Women found ways of operating independently and benefited from their extended networks of family and friends. More research would be useful in those areas of Europe in which the laws seem to limit business activities of women to determine whether practice followed the prescriptions of statute and law code.

KATHRYN REYERSON

References and Further Reading

Hanawalt, Barbara A., ed. *Women and Work in Preindustrial Europe*. Bloomington, Ind.: Indiana University Press, 1986.

Herlihy, David. *Opera Muliebria. Women and Work in Medieval Europe*. New York: McGraw-Hill, 1990.

See also **Abbesses; Administration of Estates; Alewives and Brewing; Apprentices; Artisan Families, Women of; Ermengard; Feme Coverte; Feme Sole; Investment and Credit; Kempe, Margery; Peasants; Widows; Work**

BYZANTIUM

Although Byzantine society was undeniably patriarchal, attitudes toward women were ambivalent. They were arguably a marginalised group, strictly controlled within a patriarchal framework, and if there was no seclusion *per se*, at least separation of the genders was ideologically considered a norm. In theory women, as the inferior sex, were supposed to be seldom seen and never heard in public. They were denied the power of giving instruction in church and debarred from all priestly functions. Nevertheless, the church acknowledged that women were spiritually equal to men, and there were many well-known female martyrs and saints, while the *Theotokos* (the 'Mother of God') was always a central figure in the devotion of both men and women and was seen as the mediator between humanity and Christ. The icon of the *Theotokos* holding the Christ child, known as the *Hodegetria*, was one of the holiest relics in Constantinople. While virginity was considered to be a primary virtue for both men and women, unless women entered the monastic life their major functions were expected to be marriage and the procreation of children. Motherhood was exalted in the cult of the *Theotokos* and infertility was thought to be a curse.

Gynaikonitis

It is increasingly clear, however, that women were not "secluded" in the Byzantine world, though, conventionally, they were supposed to lead quiet lives at home. The *gynaikonitis* (women's quarters), which was a feature of the palace and noble homes, was not an area to which women were restricted, but one where the women of the family could enjoy some privacy and pursue their normal occupations, such as spinning and weaving. It was generally staffed with eunuchs; males were not excluded, but those from outside the immediate family would not enter without invitation. "Respectable" women from the higher socio-economic class were clearly privileged enough to be able to stay at home and delegate activities outside the household to servants and retainers. The majority of the female population, however, which could include anything from housewives and small-scale retailers to prostitutes, maintained a ubiquitous presence on the streets of Constantinople as part of their daily routine. Some women had to work outside the house as a matter of course, and women generally would leave their homes to shop, attend church services, visit the baths or relatives, and participate in festivals and saints' days. We even know of girls and upper-class women ("women who had never before left the *gynaikonitis*") taking part in a spontaneous street riot, when the empress Zoe was threatened with tonsure and exile by her adopted nephew Michael V in April 1042:

> I myself saw many women, whom nobody till then had seen outside the women's quarters, appearing in public and shouting and beating their breasts and lamenting terribly at the empress's misfortune, but the rest were borne along like Maenads, and they formed no small band to oppose the offender. . . . (Michael Psellos, *Chronographia*, 5.26)

While the *gynaikonitis* in the palace certainly did not involve harem-like seclusion, on a number of occasions it was the site of conspiracy and intrigue: the murders of Nikephoros II Phokas and Romanos III Argyros were plotted there by their wives, and Theodora, wife of Justinian, was said to have hidden the heretic patriarch Anthimos in her quarters unsuspected for twelve years. While the story is certainly apocryphal, it conveys the popular perception of the size and secrecy, as well as the qualities of mystery and intrigue, seen as belonging to the imperial *gynaikonitis*.

In Byzantium, aristocratic women could be shopowners or supervise a workshop in the basement of their house, and women were deeply involved in retail trade and could be bakers, cooks, innkeepers, bath keepers, washerwomen, gynaecologists, midwives, dancers, prostitutes, weavers, matchmakers and sorcerers, or silk-workers. In the fourteenth century most of the sellers in the markets of Constantinople were women. Aristocratic women could be extremely wealthy in their own right: Danielis, a widow from Patras, in the ninth century, controlled "not a small part of the Peloponnese," and reportedly owned innumerable slaves, three thousand of whom were freed and settled in southern Italy. Such women were expected to take an active role in the maintenance of their household and supervision of family, servants, and property. Byzantine women had very important rights: a woman possessed her dowry, and daughters could inherit equally with their brothers in cases of intestate succession; widows were left as guardians of their children, and women appeared in court to present their own cases for property disputes and control of dowries.

Empresses

It has been widely accepted that there was segregation of men and women at court, at least before the period of the Komnenoi (1081–1185 CE), and that it was customary for men and women to be separated for ceremonial purposes such as receptions and banquets. Certainly the empress possessed her own court where she would preside over her own ceremonial sphere, consisting of the wives of officials of the state hierarchy. These women were granted court titles corresponding to those of their husbands, such as *magistrissai, patrikiai, protospathariai*, and *kandidatissai* (*magistrissai* were the wives of courtiers with the rank *magistros*, for example), and their public lives revolved around that of the empress. The need for an empress to oversee a court ceremonial sphere for women was generally accepted, and even validated Leo VI's third marriage to Eudokia Baiane in 900, which was technically illegal, because the women of the court needed an empress. Males and females at court shared the same space at least some of the time. In the time of Constantine VII Porphyrogennetos, the most eminent patrician woman (the *zoste patrikia*) ranked fourth in honour in the seating at imperial banquets, even if other women were notably absent from the guest lists for imperial banquets in the ninth and tenth centuries. Given a possible total of some two thousand male courtiers at the end of the ninth century, we have to postulate the existence of a proportionate number of "socially invisible" wives, who would have maintained a presence at specific imperial functions centred around the empress. The empress, when she travelled, could be accompanied by a vast retinue: Theodora, the wife of Justinian, was accompanied by no less than four thousand attendants when she visited the spa at Pythion, though her escort included some of the emperor's officials and not merely her own. It was even possible for an empress-consort to transcend gender boundaries, like Euphrosyne, the wife of Alexios III (1195–1203), who was considered by the historian Choniates to go to unacceptable extremes in holding her own court, at which not merely the wives of dignitaries, but all the dignitaries themselves had to pay her homage.

In the Byzantine empire, power was technically vested in the emperor. Nevertheless, a number of empresses played an important part in government and even took control of the empire when appropriate. Most commonly empresses came to power as regents for young sons, but not all regents were ready to step aside: Irene had her son Constantine VI blinded so that she could stay in power, and Eudokia Makrembolitissa was appointed as regent for her son Michael VII Doukas, even though he was technically of age. Co-ruling regents were officially acknowledged on coins, in acclamations, and in dating formulas, although generally (but not always) yielding precedence to the young emperor. Empresses could also, in exceptional circumstances, rule in their own right, though it was considered more normal that they should take the opportunity to choose a husband and make him emperor. Empresses also possessed power as consorts, but in these circumstances they were naturally bound by the wishes and temperaments of their husbands. The principle of collegiality, however, ensured that in certain cases they were seen almost as co-rulers. An empress interested in politics was able to interview ministers, clerics, and foreign ambassadors without reference to her husband, and correspond privately with world leaders. While the empress primarily presided in her own ceremonial sphere, she also could be present at court banquets, audiences, and the reception of envoys, as well as taking part in processions and in services in the city's churches; one of her main duties was the reception of the wives of foreign rulers and heads of state. Nor were empresses restricted to the capital: empress-consorts also accompanied their husbands on campaign.

Upon the death of an emperor without a nominated heir, the empress had the power to transfer the throne to a new incumbent, generally by marrying him. Zoe Porphyrogenneta, the heir to the throne in her own right, did so four times, legitimising the rule of three husbands and an adopted son. But widowed empress-consorts who had no blood tie with the dynasty were still able to determine the imperial succession, and it was usual but not necessary for the empress to marry this new candidate. Empresses ruled in the same way as emperors: they presided over the court, appointed officials, issued decrees, settled lawsuits, received ambassadors and heads of state, fulfilled the emperor's ceremonial role, and made decisions on matters of financial and foreign policy. They were, however, disadvantaged in not being able to lead an army.

Brides

In Byzantium, beauty was considered of great importance in young girls and a criterion for consideration as a bride even at an imperial level. Between 788 and 882, bride-shows were held five times to select a bride for the heir to the empire. Commissioners were sent out with a picture (*lavraton*) which portrayed an imperial ideal and had to compare the girls' faces to this ideal portrait, measure their height against an ideal measure, and check their feet against an ideal shoe size. The finalists were brought to the imperial palace where the heir to the throne would choose between them. In these bride-shows the background and family of the girls involved were not a primary consideration, and it is possible that this practice was instituted to avoid pressure from aristocratic families who wanted a daughter chosen as empress. Aristocratic Byzantine women were very aware of their family background, as is shown increasingly in their nomenclature, as they did not need to take the name of their husband or of their father. By the late twelfth century, women, like men, openly displayed all their family connections (such as Irene-Euphrosyne Komnene Doukaina Philanthropene Kantakouzene, an otherwise unknown nun who died c. 1202), and it was customary for empresses to retain their family name as empress.

Prostitution

Prostitution was endemic in the capital. Both Justinian and Michael IV established "homes" for women who wanted to escape from such a life, and Justinian instituted heavy penalties for those who entrapped young girls in prostitution. Nevertheless prostitutes could be encountered on the streets at all periods of Byzantine history, particularly in organised brothels, public baths, inns, and hippodromes, and took part in street festivals and riots. Theatrical performers such as circus artists and actresses were also expected to provide sexual services: Theodora, wife of the emperor Justinian, was a circus artist before her marriage. Prostitutes and mistresses were also a feature of life at court at most periods, and mistresses could be openly paraded as alternative empresses. Imperial mistresses would normally generate little more than lampoons in the street, but Constantine IX Monomachos' passion for his mistress, Skleraina, nearly led to a public riot and his deposition in March 1044 because the people feared for the safety of the elderly empress Zoe, whom they thought he intended to divorce or exile in favour of Skleraina.

Authors and Patrons

Women could play an important role as abbesses and nuns, and noble ladies founded monasteries and acted as patrons of literature. Female literacy was primarily confined to a reading knowledge of the Bible and certain saints' lives, but Byzantium did produce some exceptional female writers. One was the abbess Kassia, a poet and hymnographer of the ninth century who, in her nonliturgical poems, gives us unvarnished observations on friendship, beauty, women, good and bad fortune, the rich and the poor, and vices such as envy and stupidity. Another was the historian Anna Komnene, eldest daughter of the emperor Alexios I Komnenos, who had enjoyed an exceptional education and wrote a biography of her father, the *Alexiad*, in the first half of the twelfth century.

LYNDA GARLAND

References and Further Reading

Abrahamse, Dorothy de F. "Women's Monasticism in the Middle Byzantine Period: Problems and Prospects." *Byzantinische Forschungen* 9 (1985): 35–58.

Beauchamp, Joelle. *Le statut de la femme à Byzance (4e–7e siècle)*. 2 vols. Paris: de Boccard, 1990.

Garland, Lynda. "The Life and Ideology of Byzantine Women: A Further Note on Conventions of Behaviour and Social Reality as Reflected in Eleventh and Twelfth Century Historical Sources." *Byzantion* 58 (1988): 361–393.

———. *Byzantine Empresses*. London: Routledge, 1999.

Herrin, Judith. "In Search of Byzantine Women: Three Avenues of Approach." In *Images of Women in Antiquity*, edited by A. Cameron and A. Kuhrt. Detroit: Wayne State University Press, 1983, pp. 167–189.

———. "Women and the Faith in Icons in Early Christianity." In *Culture, Ideology and Politics. Essays for Eric Hobsbawn*, edited by R. Samuel and G. Stedman Jones. London: Routledge & Kegan Paul, 1983, pp. 56–83.

———. *Women in Purple*. Princeton, N.J.: Princeton University Press, 2001.

Hill, Barbara. "A Vindication of the Rights of Women to Power by Anna Komnene." *Byzantinische Forschungen* 23 (1996): 45–53.

Kazhdan, Alexander P. and Alice-Mary Talbot "Women and Iconoclasm." *Byzantinische Zeitschrift* 84/85 (1991/1992): 391–408.

Laiou, Angeliki E. "Observations on the Life and Ideology of Byzantine Women." *Byzantinische Forschungen* 9 (1985): 59–102.

———. *Gender, Society and Economic Life in Byzantium*. Aldershot: Variorum, 1992.

Nicol, Donald M. *The Byzantine Lady: Ten Portraits 1250–1500*. Cambridge: Cambridge University Press, 1994.

Ringrose, Kathleen M. "Living in the Shadows: Eunuchs and Gender in Byzantium." In *Third Sex, Third Gender: Beyond Sexual Dimorphism in Culture and History*, edited by G. Herdt. New York: Zone Books, 1994, pp. 85–110.

Talbot, Alice-Mary. "Blue-Stocking Nuns. Intellectual Life in the Convents of Late Byzantium." In *Okeanos: Essays Presented to Ihor Shevcenko on his 60th Birthday*, edited by C. Mango and O. Pritsak. Cambridge, Mass.: Ukrainian Research Institute, Harvard University, 1984, pp. 604–618.

———. *Holy Women of Byzantium: Ten Saints' Lives in English Translation*. Washington, D.C.: Dumbarton Oaks, 1996.

Topping, Eva C. "Women Hymnographers in Byzantium." *Diptycha* 3(1982/1983): 98–111.

Treadgold, Warren T. "The Bride-Shows of the Byzantine Emperors." *Byzantion* 49 (1979) 395–413.

See also **Empresses, Byzantine; Eunuchs; Icons, Byzantine; Irene; Komnene, Anna; Mary the Younger; Monasticism and Nuns, Byzantine; Ottonian Royal Women; Theodora**

C

CAESAREAN SECTION

The term *Caesarean birth* was not used before the Renaissance (François Rousset, the surgeon, originated it in his 1581 treatise on the operation), but the surgical extraction of fetuses had already been attested in ancient Rome. Pliny the Elder (23–79 CE), in his *Natural History*, connected surgical birth to the family name Caesar, and his remarks led to the mistaken assumption that Julius Caesar (d. 44 BCE) had been born that way.

The operation was almost exclusively performed *post mortem* in order to save the child of a woman who had died during the birth. This fact probably explains why ancient medical authorities did not mention the operation in their treatises. In the Middle Ages the first mentions of Caesarean births occur toward the end of the twelfth century. They do not come from medical texts but from decrees issued at various church councils. It appears that Odo of Sully, bishop of Paris from 1196 to 1208, was the first Church official to recommend that women who had died during childbirth should be cut open if the child was believed to still be alive. The Council of Canterbury (1236) made the same recommendation, adding that the mother's mouth should be held open during the procedure to supply the fetus with breath and that a midwife should have water at the ready for an emergency baptism. The problematic nature of making decisions at such a critical moment is dramatized by a decree of the Council of Trèves (1310), which states that, if the child dies right after the extraction (before being baptized), it will have to be buried in unconsecrated ground. If, however, it dies while still in the mother's womb, both of them can be buried in consecrated ground. In all these texts it is assumed that midwives perform Caesareans.

The first physician to mention Caesareans was Bernard of Gordon in his 1305 *Practica sive lilium medicinae* (*The practice or the lily of medicine*). Here he tells novice obstetricians of the possibility that a fetus may be kept alive after the mother's death in childbirth through the air in her arteries. If this happens, as quickly as possible the child should be extracted through an incision in the mother's abdomen, while her mouth and cervix are held open. Bernard must have received this advice from midwives, since no ancient textual tradition on Caesareans existed. While Bernard addressed male physicians, Guy de Chauliac, in his famous *Grande Chirurgie* (*Great Surgery*) of 1363, spoke to midwives in the context of Caesareans. His prescriptions for Caesareans are similar to Bernard's, except that he specifies the mother's left side for the incision.

Piero d'Argellata (d. 1423) was the first male physician to describe his own performance of a Caesarean in his *Chirurgia* (*Surgery*). He specified that he used a razor and made the incision along the mother's *linea alba*. It is not until Rousset in 1581 that we find a physician who claims that mothers survived a Caesarean. But Rousset's contemporaries doubted his accounts.

Images of Caesarean births can be found primarily in depictions of Julius Caesar's birth, especially in later manuscripts of the early-thirteenth-century

Birth of Julius Caesar. Julius Caesar is born by Caesarian section: a midwife lifts the mature-looking baby out of an incision in the mother's uterus. Shelfmark ID: Roy.16.G. VII. Folio No: 219. Min. Location: British Library, London, Great Britain. Credit: HIP / Art Resource, NY.

Faits des Romains (*Deeds of the Romans*) and some other accounts of Roman history, but for the most part not in the illustrations of medical texts. In some manuscripts of these Roman histories, a curved knife is shown as appropriate for the operation; the mother usually lies lifeless in a splendid bed, while attendants bathe the newborn. Interestingly, in the images dating from before 1400, midwives are shown as performing Caesareans, while later manuscripts show male physicians. This changeover corresponds to the indications in the medical texts where we find the first accounts of male participation in the operation in the fifteenth century. The professionalization of medicine and the exclusion of women from universities explain the growing absence of midwives from surgical births.

In addition to Julius Casear, other personages were believed to have been born by Caesareans. The twelfth-century German poet Eilhart claimed that Tristan had been born that way, and some German kings had the same legend attached to them. Especially striking are the late medieval images of Antichrist's birth by Caesarean, a tradition that cannot be found in any corresponding texts. The artists who chose to depict Antichrist's birth in this way probably wanted to highlight the unnaturalness of his birth and of his subsequent nefarious actions. But the Virgin Mary also performed Caesareans, as a number of miracle accounts attest. Today almost routine, Caesareans signaled a special destiny throughout the medieval period.

RENATE BLUMENFELD-KOSINSKI

References and Further Reading

Bernard of Gordon. *Practica sive lilium medicinae.* Lyon: Antoine Lambillon and Marinus Saracenus, 1491.

Blumenfeld-Kosinski, Renate. *Not of Woman Born: Representations of Caesarean Birth in Medieval and Renaissance Culture.* Ithaca, N.Y.: Cornell University Press, 1990.

Bullough, Vern. *The Development of Medicine as a Profession.* New York: Hafner, 1966.

Guy de Chauliac. *La grande chirurgie.* translated by E. Nicaise. Paris: Félix Alcan, 1890.

Laget, Mireille. *Naissances: L'accouchement avant l'âge de la clinique.* Paris: Seuil, 1982.

Pieto Argellata. *Chirurgia.* Venice: Octavianus Scotus, 1497.

Pliny. *Natural History.* with an English translation by H. Rackham. Cambridge, Mass.: Harvard University Press, 1942.

Pundel, J. *Histoire de l'opération césarienne.* Brussels: Presses Académiques Européennes, 1969.

Siraisi, Nancy C. *Medieval and Early Renaissance Medicine: An Introduction to Knowledge and Practice.* Chicago: University of Chicago Press, 1990.

Wyman, A. L. "The Female Practitioner of Surgery, 1400–1800." *Medical History* 28 (1984): 22–41.

Young, John H. *Caesarean Section: The History and the Development of the Operation from Earliest Times.* London: H. K. Lewis, 1944.

See also **Doctors and Healers; Gynecology; Infants and Infanticide; Midwives; Pregnancy and Childbirth**

CANONESSES

The term *canoness* first appears in the Latin West in the eighth century, although it had been used in the East to identify Christian women who held a special place in the life of the church—most likely as widows and virgins—from at least the fourth century. The origins of the term are obscure; perhaps it derived from the women's adherence to a rule, or canon, or perhaps it reflects their presence on the church's register, signaling their reliance on the church for material support. By the early Middle Ages, however, canonesses were generally recognized as women who had adopted the religious life and who lived in community, but yet differed from nuns in several important respects: they made no permanent vows, and thus could leave the community whenever they wished; they did not relinquish private property upon entering the community and even maintained separate residences and servants; they wore secular clothing rather than the black habit of Benedictine nuns; and they performed various public duties, largely freeing them from the requirement of claustration. Yet despite these differences, it is often difficult in practice to distinguish between nuns and canonesses during the early period, particularly given the tendency in the sources to refer to both as *sanctimoniales*.

With the reorganization of the Carolingian church in the eighth and early ninth centuries, attempts were made to impose order on the religious life and to subject all those who professed it to a recognized rule. Religious women were offered a choice, according to the late-eighth-century Council of Frankfurt, between the regular life in accordance with the Benedictine Rule and the canonical life. Some years later, at the Council of Aachen (816), the reformer Benedict of Aniane sought to bring the lives of canonesses more in line with monastic observance, requiring increased claustration, the veiling of canonesses, and limiting the women's contact with members of the opposite sex—even their priests. The rule for canonesses that resulted, the *Institutio Sanctimonialium*, comprised twenty-eight canons and combined selections from the writings of the Fathers with stipulations concerning the life of the community. However, the fact that the *Institutio* survives in only a few ninth-century copies suggests that it may not have been widely followed. Canonesses continued to maintain their distinctive way of life, as records from the period attest.

Communities of canonesses reached their apogee in Germany during the ninth and tenth centuries, when a series of new foundations with strong ties to the imperial court were established. The women of these communities, who came from noble families, maintained their power and prestige within the community and were active beyond its walls as well. Under the late-tenth-century rule of abbess Gerberga II, a niece of Otto I, the community at Gandersheim developed into an enormously powerful and independent house, with its own courts, the power to mint coins, a representative at the imperial assembly, and the right to direct protection from the pope. Gandersheim was also, like many houses of canonesses, a center of learning where daughters of the aristocracy could gain an education. The Latin writings of Hrotsvit of Gandersheim demonstrate her knowledge of a range of classical and medieval authors and reflect the richness of the community's library. Other communities, like Chelles, where Charlemagne's sister Gisela was abbess, were active in book production and included female scribes amongst their number.

By the middle of the eleventh century, reformers, concerned to rid the church of perceived corruption, once again turned their attention to houses of canonesses, denouncing the canonical way of life as degenerate. As with their criticism of unreformed or "secular" canons, these reformers focused on canonesses' ownership of private property, their rejection of a common dormitory, and their failure to live according to a recognized rule. Criticism of canonesses was renewed at the Second Lateran Council (1139) and, less than ten years later, at the Council of Rheims (1148). In response, many houses of canonesses adopted the Rule of Augustine and are known as "regular" rather than "secular" canonesses. As reform enthusiasm spread through the eleventh and twelfth centuries, many newly founded communities also adopted the Augustinian Rule, which, unlike the Benedictine Rule, included a version addressed specifically to women. In many cases, these reformed Augustinian houses maintained close ties with houses of canons, who as priests provided them with much-needed pastoral care. By the middle of the twelfth century, Augustinian houses were at the forefront of reform. However, canonesses in these communities were increasingly similar to nuns. Of the secular canonesses, with their traditions of independence and erudition, Jacques de Vitry scoffed in the early thirteenth century that they "prefer the nobility of the world to nobility of manners and religion."

FIONA J. GRIFFITHS

References and Further Reading

Crusius, Irene, ed. *Studien zum Kanonissenstift.* Göttingen: Vandenhoeck and Ruprecht, 2001.
Heinrich, Mary Pia. *The Canonesses and Education in the Early Middle Ages.* Washington, D.C.: Catholic University of America, 1924.
McNamara, Jo Ann Kay. *Sisters in Arms: Catholic Nuns through Two Millennia.* Cambridge, Mass.: Harvard University Press, 1996.
Parisse, Michel, "Les chanoinesses dans l'Empire germanique (IXe - XIe s.)." *Francia* 6 (1978):107–126.
Schaefer, K. H. *Die Kanonissenstifter im deutschen Mittelalter.* Stuttgart: F. Enke, 1907.
Wemple, Suzanne Fonay. *Women in Frankish Society: Marriage and the Cloister, 500 to 900.* Philadelphia: University of Pennsylvania Press, 1981.

See also **Abbesses; Education, Monastic; Herrad of Hohenburg; Hrotsvit of Gandersheim; Jouarre and Chelles; Monastic Enclosure; Monastic Rules; Monasticism and Nuns; Spiritual Care**

CANONIZATION OF SAINTS

To canonize someone is to put him or her on a list (canon) of those who are now in heaven. The Roman Catholic Church declares a person a saint to confirm that he or she is indeed among the blessed and can, therefore, be so venerated and can be asked to intercede before God. While the current process of canonization is under the authority of the pope, the procedure developed slowly in the Middle Ages. The process or cause involved both miracles and a holy way of life, since canonization acknowledges the saint's presence at the throne of God and affirms the saint's conduct on earth as worthy of imitation.

Martyrs and Confessors

For the first thousand years of Christianity there was no uniform method of making saints, or even a formal process. While St. Paul used the word *saint* simply to designate members of the Christian communities, the term quickly became associated with Christian martyrs, who were compared to Jesus, the first martyr. To die for the faith was deemed the ultimate sacrifice, which required no further evidence of the person's sanctity. Individual churches declared their heroes to be among the martyrs. By the third

Pinturicchio (1454–1513) Canonization of Saint Catherine of Siena: scenes from the life of Pope Pius II. Location: Duomo, Siena, Italy. Credit: Scala / Art Resource, NY.

century the Christian communities inscribed them in martyrologies. When the era of the persecutions ended in 313 with the Edict of Milan, the liturgical significance of the martyrs rapidly expanded. The literature which recorded and embellished their heroic deaths—in the Acts, Passions, and letters—became part of the communal worship, which included translations of the martyr's remains to a shrine or church.

After Constantine the new "martyr" was the "confessor," another kind of hero who suffered by combating heretics and schismatics. Chief among these were the doctors of the Church, such as Jerome, Ambrose, Basil, and Augustine. Another type of martyr was the ascetic who practiced heroic virtue in the desert or in a monastery. Some of these ascetics became saints not by any juridical pronouncement of the clergy, but simply by the "voice of the people." The name of the servant of God was often incorporated into the Mass, martyrologies, processions, pilgrimages, and prayers of petition. In the liturgy and sometimes in written Lives the saint's feast was celebrated on his or her "birthday," the day of death and entrance into heaven. Sanctity was largely local, although a few saints were known over wide areas. The reputation of some were disseminated by biographies, such as Athanasius' Life of Anthony and Sulpicius Severus' Life of Martin of Tours (d. c. 397). Saints' *vitae* became a literary genre, as the tales came to develop certain common characteristics, as would be expected, since the prototype "saint" was Christ. Hence certain aspects of a saint's career were taken from scripture.

In the fourth and fifth centuries the veneration of saints was closely tied to their tombs and to the miracles attributed to them after their deaths. This association of tomb and miracle accelerated with the conversion of the German peoples, who were particularly attracted to holy relics. The body of a saint was a *locus* of divine power. While the saint as an archetype of virtue was, to be sure, never forgotten, the servant of God's role as a powerful intercessor before the Almighty became paramount. The faithful appealed to the saint for military victories, good crops, protection from danger, and, above all, cures from physical ailments. Particularly influential in promoting the literary image of the saint as thaumaturge and intercessor was Pope Gregory the Great's (d. 604) biography of Saint Benedict of Nursia in his *Dialogues*.

Issues of Control

After the sixth century the role of the bishops over saints' cults increased, as they gained more control over the translations of saints' relics and the approval of new ones. The word *saint* was increasingly applied to those whose names appeared in the liturgical calendars. Monasteries in particular often promoted their own saints' cults, along with biographies that often made use of folklore. Carolingian councils attempted to impose some order on the proliferation of relics and translations. It was perhaps inevitable that the bishops of Rome would become more involved in the recognition of saints as the papacy grew in importance after the tenth century.

The first papal canonization occurred in Rome in 993, when Pope John XV proclaimed Bishop Ulric of Augsburg a saint. Gregory VII insisted on the exceptional sanctity of some previous pontiffs, and by the late twelfth century some popes claimed the right of the Roman Church to canonize and to translate the bodies of saints. As the causes of saints increased, so did the juridical basis of papal pronouncements. Innocent III explicitly related his power to make saints to his fullness of power. Prelates throughout Europe asked the Roman Church to canonize local servants of God. When, in 1234, the *Decretals* of Gregory IX made the right of canonization a papal reservation, episcopal canonization quickly disappeared.

Centralization

During the thirteenth century the papacy developed procedures to evaluate the proofs of a person's sanctity, which largely meant assessing the validity of miracles performed in the saint's name. The Curia often requested, moreover, a written *vita* to attest to the holy person's virtue. Thomas of Celano's *Life of Francis of Assisi* is a case in point. The request for canonization often came from religious communities—or even from an entire order—and civic authorities, both lay and ecclesiastic, as well as from bishops. The involvement of these groups was often necessary to obtain a favorable verdict from Rome, as the cost of pursuing a cause soared. The need for written evidence of the servant of God's virtues was not only for saints long deceased, but also for recent saints. The petitioner, who initiated the cause with the approval of the local bishop, appointed a postulator, who made a report on his investigation of the saint's life. The assessment of the miracles performed at the saint's tomb, or from a distance, involved numerous witnesses who testified on the servant of God's behalf. The *vitae* and legends (stories intended to be read aloud) of the saints were often compiled and distributed. An example is the famous *Golden Legend* (1260), compiled by the Dominican Jacobus of

Voragine. These accounts of the saints became increasingly important in papal canonizations. By the early fourteenth century the process of canonization was established, whereby the commission of inquiry made its report to a commission of three cardinals, who in turn made their recommendation to the holy see.

The canonization of saints in the High Middle Ages should be viewed not only as a juridical procedure, but as an integral part of social life. Christians looked upon saints as being living members of the Church, which included the heavenly and the earthly. Saints permeated every aspect of religious life, as intercessors, patrons, objects of pilgrimages and processions, models of behavior, and liturgical activities. The process of canonization gives the historian an insight into the changing patterns of spirituality, theology, and moral expectations.

THOMAS RENNA

References and Further Reading

Cunningham, Lawrence S. *The Meaning of Saints.* New York: Harper & Row, 1980.
———, *A Brief History of Saints.* Malden, Mass./Oxford, UK: Blackwell, 2005.
Dodds, Bill. *Your One-Stop Guide to How Saints Are Made.* Ann Arbor, MI: Servant, 2000.
Kemp, Eric W. *Canonization and Authority in the Western Church.* New York: AMS, 1980.
Menesto, Enrico. "The Apostolic Canonization Proceedings of Clare of Montefalco, 1318–1319." In *Women and Religion in Medieval and Renaissance Italy*, edited by Daniel Bornstein and Roberto Rusconi. Chicago: University of Chicago Press, 1996, pp. 104–129.
Vauchez, A. *Sainthood in the Later Middle Ages.* translated by Jean Birrell. Cambridge: Cambridge University Press, 1997.
Woodward, Kenneth L. *Making Saints: How the Catholic Church Determines Who Becomes a Saint, Who Doesn't, and Why.* New York: Simon and Schuster, 1996.

See also **Hagiography; Jacobus of Voragine's *Golden Legend*; Miracles and Miracle Collections; Relics and Reliquaries**

CAPTIVITY AND RANSOM

Rarely featured in chronicle accounts or *chansons de geste*, though sometimes found in miracle stories, most medieval captives were in fact women. Often spared along with children in siege capitulations, women could also be taken captive from civilian camps near battlefields.

It was seen as self-evident that captive women were raped. For most women, survival in captivity or the chance of being ransomed depended mainly on beauty and/or high rank. As women commanded lower ransoms than men, there was less incentive to keep female captives alive. Nonetheless, a captor might guard a beautiful or high-ranking captive and her virtue in hopes of upping her price. On the other hand, women's lower valuation facilitated their redemption from captivity.

Another survival mechanism was to marry into the opposing camp, frequently documented for female captives in Muslim sources. From both the Muslim and Christian perspective, a woman who fell into opposing hands faced a fate worse than death; women were expected to prefer death to sexual defilement. Jewish law differed in assuming that female captives were unable to remain sexually pure, thus allowing them to be reintegrated into their communities. Eastern Jewish marriage contracts contained clauses obligating a husband to redeem a captive wife.

Wives or daughters of important men could find themselves used as hostages in treaty agreements. This practice, prohibited in Spanish municipal law, is attested in the Latin East, where Baldwin II used his daughter as a hostage.

Even if ransomed, this by no means ended the tribulations of female captives. Reentry into their former societies was economically and socially difficult.

YVONNE FRIEDMAN

References and Further Reading

Blidstein, Gerald I. "The Personal Status of Apostate and Ransomed Women in Medieval Jewish Law" (Hebrew). *Shenaton Ha-Mishpat Ha-Ivri: Annual of the Institute for Research in Jewish Law* 3–4 (1976–1977): 35–116.

Friedman, Yvonne. "Captivity and Ransom: The Experience of Women." In *Gendering the Crusades*, edited by Susan B. Edgington and Sarah Lambert. Cardiff: University of Wales Press, 2001, pp. 121–139.

———. *Encounter between Enemies: Captivity and Ransom in the Latin Kingdom of Jerusalem*. Leiden: Brill, 2002, pp. 162–186.

Goitein, Salomon D. "Tyre-Tripoli-'Arqa Geniza Documents from the Beginning of the Crusade Period." *Jewish Quarterly Review* 66 (1975): 69–88.

Hitti, Philip K. *An Arab-Syrian Gentleman and Warrior in the Period of the Crusades: Memoirs of Usamah ibn-Munqidh*. New York: Columbia University Press, 1929.

Kulp-Hill, Kathleen. *Songs of Holy Mary of Alfonso X, The Wise: A Translation of the Cantigas de Santa Maria*. Tempe, Ariz.: Arizona Center for Medieval and Renaissance Studies, 2000. (Song 325) pp. 394–395.

Schmidt, Paul Gerhard. "*Peregrinatio periculosa*: Thomas von Froidmont über die Jerusalemfahrten seiner Schwester Margareta." In *Kontinuität und Wandel: Lateinische Poesie von Naevius bis Baudelaire Franco Munari zum 65. Geburstag*, edited by Ulrich Justus Stache, Wolfgang Maaz, and Fritz Wagner. Hildesheim: Weidmann, 1986, pp. 461–485.

See also **Rape and Raptus; Warfare**

CASTLES AND PALACES

Scholars of medieval castles and palaces have traditionally been silent on questions of gender and women. Palaces have acted as the backdrop to studies of court bureaucracy or constitutional history peopled almost entirely by "great men," while castles have been studied almost exclusively in terms of defense and warfare. From the early 1990s, however, analyses of domestic space in particular have put gender firmly on the historical agenda, and even where documentary sources are lacking, the complexity of interior patterns of access in high-status domestic architecture is recognized as having gendered significance. Yet European coverage remains patchy even where making women "visible" is concerned. For example, French high-status architecture has been subjected to meticulous scholarly analysis, but the apartments of French royal women have yet to receive detailed attention.

Although castles are now recognized as complex structures of which defense was just one facet, most people could confidently put forward a definition. "Palaces" are rather more problematic. Though the earliest surviving written reference in England dates to the late tenth century, and the concept was familiar in Europe from c. 800, only a tiny number of royal residences were referred to as such during the Middle Ages. Consequently, scholars have tended to reserve the term for the noncastle residences of the crown and higher nobility. Yet such distinctions were probably less clear-cut to contemporaries. Even the Tower of London, clearly a fortress, encompassed suites of well-appointed royal apartments. Compared with most castles, palaces generally did not emphasize defense. However, in regard to domestic space, the terms can be used interchangeably.

Late medieval palaces reemerged as a field of study in the early 1990s, and attention was paid to the involvement of royal women. In particular the influence of foreign-born queens consort on the development of English palatial architecture was hypothesized. To paraphrase O'Keeffe, such narratives reveal not *the* story of palaces, but *a* story of the construction of palaces, and although women were now included in that story there was little explicit discussion of gender. Parallel developments can be seen in castle studies. Valuable works have been, and still are, produced that include whole chapters on women as castellans and defenders. However, few explicitly address gender as part of the overall narrative, or acknowledge the role of architecture in its social construction. A significant proportion of female Irish castle-builders or owners, for example Rohesia de Verdun (d. 1247), seem to have flouted gender stereotypes generally, and it has been suggested that active involvement with castles might have influenced women's gender identities—a proposal that would repay further study.

The idea that architecture not only replicates but also constructs gender ideologies is not new. In the 1980s, high-status late Anglo-Saxon planning—notably the communal hall—was considered to be symptomatic of a relatively egalitarian social structure. That is, the comparatively unsegregated space of the hall both reflected and actively encouraged greater access to power for women and other less advantaged groups. This premise has since been disputed. Concomitantly the "retreat" from such communal spaces, represented by the establishment of separate households for noblemen and women by the early thirteenth century, has been read as evidence of a decline in women's status. However, the meaning of such segregation has now been problematized. Many interpretations center on contemporary ideas about the female body. The French surgeon Henri de Mondeville (1260–1320), for example, proposed that "interior space...is a feminine place; for the first dwelling-place of man is buried deep in the secret places of women" (Gilchrist). Scholars have recently correlated these ideas with the architecture of public and private space. More generally, women's association with the most "private" areas of castles and palaces is no longer equated solely with political and social marginalization. The household of Eleanor of Provence (d. 1291), for example, seems to have afforded her a unique power base during the factional struggles of the Lusignans, half-brothers of King Henry III, and her Savoyard relatives.

Detailed comparative studies of gendered spatial patterns in late medieval Europe might reveal much about similarities and differences in regional social organization. In continental Europe and in Scotland, kings' and queens' apartments were usually on different floors, the queen's traditionally above the king's as in King Charles V's (r. 1364–1380) Louvre, Paris, and the Emperor Charles IV's (r. 1346–1378) Karlstein Castle, near Prague. Yet when stacked lodgings briefly became popular in England at the end of the fifteenth century, the kings' rooms invariably occupied the higher floors. Through most of the Middle Ages, however, English royal apartments were generally on one level, as were those in the fourteenth-century palace of the Kings of Majorca at Perpignan near the French/Spanish border. Like many later royal residences, this was divided into kings' and queens' "sides," the queen closer to the great hall than the king—another rare pattern in English palaces and castles.

The great hall as a center of power, however symbolic, remains key to understanding gender dynamics. Here the ideal of separate gender domains organized according to a public/private divide is evident in the startling dearth of imagery depicting women in English halls throughout the later Middle Ages. Moreover from the mid-fourteenth century, as the meeting-places of chivalric brotherhoods, halls appear to have become equated with the martial ethic increasingly underlying the gender role of the male nobility. For example Edward the Black Prince (1330–1376) deliberately had his chambers built onto the impressive, ceremonial hall of Kennington Palace c. 1350. In contrast the apartments of his wife, Joan of Kent (1328–1385), were spatially distanced from it. Such a hypothesis calibrates other work. In particular the joint tombs fashionable from the third quarter of the fourteenth century—for example that of Richard II (r. 1377–1399) and Anne of Bohemia (d.1394)—have been seen as symbolizing women's increased political marginalization by replicating the growing emphasis on their intercessionary role. That is, the tombs embodied the joint responsibility for just rule underscored in the English coronation *ordo*, which stressed the queen's mercy and her role as mediator between her husband and the realm. But if fourteenth-century English halls were "male space," epitomised by the statues of kings commissioned for Westminster Hall by Richard II, this may not have been the case throughout Europe. The contemporary series of "kings" in the hall of the Palais de la Cité, Paris, included queens consort despite the exclusion of women from the succession under Salic Law.

Evidence from contemporary art, chronicles, and romances confirms that sexual segregation was practiced at formal occasions such as feasts and tournaments. Yet the picture was more complex in everyday life. Guests of both sexes would have been received in female households, as well as male officials and administrators, so that they were more sexually and socially mixed than those of their male counterparts. This is reflected in the types of imagery employed in the gendered domains of castles and palaces. In the chambers of medieval English kings, depictions of men far outweighed those of women, while in queens' rooms "mixed" imagery predominated—either depicting both sexes or neutral patterned motifs.

Many of the social patterns observed here continued into the early modern period. For example, sexual segregation was still practiced at formal occasions. During the 1503 wedding celebrations of Margaret Tudor (b. 1489) and James IV of Scotland at Holyrood, the king's and queen's parties dined in separate halls. Margaret's party remained socially and sexually diverse; noblewomen, including the ladies of her household, sat at one table, another accommodated noblemen, a third was occupied by gentlewomen, and a fourth by gentlemen.

A further aspect of gendered space in castles and palaces deserves highlighting. It was to Margaret's great chamber that James IV later went to dance. Although evidence is scant, such nuggets may indicate how queens' chambers were actually used through the Middle Ages. Certainly in 1302, Edward I and Margaret of France were sharing a bedchamber when fire broke out at Winchester Castle, and a 1238 attempt on Henry III's life at Woodstock was foiled because he was sharing a bed with Eleanor of Provence in her chamber—to the chagrin of the would-be assassin. Spatial segregation in medieval castles and palaces may have replicated ideas about gender difference and the social order, but the relative privacy of noblewomen's apartments clearly held resonance for both sexes.

AMANDA RICHARDSON

References and Further Reading

Coulson, Charles. *Castles in Medieval Society: Fortresses in England, France, and Ireland in the Central Middle Ages.* Oxford: Oxford University Press, 2003.

Dunbar, John G. *Scottish Royal Palaces: The Architecture of the Royal Residences during the Late Medieval and Early Renaissance Periods.* Edinburgh: Tuckwell Press, 1999.

Gilchrist, Roberta. "The Contested Garden: Gender, Space and Metaphor in the Medieval English Castle." In *Gender and Archaeology: Contesting the Past.* by Roberta Gilchrist. London: Routledge, 1999, pp. 109–145.

Howell, Margaret. *Eleanor of Provence: Queenship in Thirteenth-Century England.* Oxford: Blackwell, 1998.

James, T. B. *The Palaces of Medieval England c. 1050–1550.* London: Seaby, 1990.

Johnson, Matthew. *Behind the Castle Gate: From Medieval to Renaissance.* London: Routledge, 2002.

Meiron Jones, G. et al., eds, *The Seigneurial Residence in Western Europe AD c. 800–1600.* (BAR International Series 1088). Oxford: Archaeopress, 2002.

O'Keeffe, T. "Concepts of 'Castle' and the Construction of Identity in Medieval and Post-Medieval Ireland." *Irish Geography* 34 (1) (2001): 69–88.

Parsons, John C. "'Never was a body buried in England with such solemnity and honour': The Burials and Posthumous Commemorations of English Queens to 1500." In *Queens and Queenship in Medieval Europe,* edited by A. J. Duggan. Woodbridge, Suffolk: Boydell and Brewer, 1997, pp. 317–337.

Richardson, A. "Gender and Space in English Royal Palaces c. 1160–c. 1547: A Study in Access Analysis and Imagery." *Medieval Archaeology* 47 (2003): 131–165.

Steane, John M. *The Archaeology of Power: England and Northern Europe AD 800–1600.* Stroud: Tempus, 2001.

Tibbetts Schulenburg, J. "Female Sanctity: Public and Private Roles c. 500–1100." In *Women and Power in the Middle Ages,* edited by Mary Erler and Maryanne Kowaleski. Athens, Ga.: University of Georgia Press, 1988, pp. 102–125.

See also **Noble Women; Queens and Empresses: The West; Space, Sacred: and Gender; Space, Secular: and Gender; Warfare**

CASTRO, INÉS DE

Inés Pérez de Castro (d. 1355) was a daughter of the Galician nobleman, Pedro Fernández de Castro. In 1340, around the age of fifteen, she accompanied the Castilian Infanta Constanza to Portugal as a lady-in-waiting, when Constanza married the Portuguese heir, Pedro. The young Inés was notoriously beautiful, endowed with the nickname "Heron's neck," or *Colo de Garça.* Soon, a love affair began between Pedro and Inés, scandalizing the court and more seriously threatening Portuguese relations with Castile. King Afonso IV, Pedro's father, banished Inés, fearing her influence as well as the influence of her ambitious brothers. However, after Constanza died in 1345, having given birth to the eventual king Fernando, Pedro installed Inés in a household in Coimbra; eventually the couple had four children. With Inés's rise to power, her brothers gained influence at the Portuguese court, and anxiety increased as well concerning the legitimate succession to the throne. Alarmed, Afonso IV allowed his knights to assassinate Inés in 1355. Civil war ensued, with Pedro rebelling against his father, supported by Inés's brothers. Upon his succession in 1357, Pedro sought revenge against her murderers, and claimed that he and Inés had secretly been married. He erected a pair of elaborate marble tombs to memorialize her at the royal monastery of Alcobaça. Inés's sons lived to influence the Portuguese court, but Inés's story has been important historically mainly as the inspiration for many dramatic and poetic interpretations.

MIRIAM SHADIS

References and Further Reading

Jones, Haydn Tiago. *Historical and literary perspectives in the episode of Inês de Castro.* Ph.D. thesis, University of North Carolina, Chapel Hill, 1998.

Livermore, H.V. *History of Portugal.* Cambridge: Cambridge University Press, 1947.

See also **Iberia; Ladies-in-Waiting**

CATERINA SFORZA

Caterina Sforza (1462/1463–1509) is famous for her rule of the papal fiefs of Imola and Forlì in the Romanga region of Italy. An illegitimate daughter of the Duke of Milan, she married Girolamo Riario, nephew of Pope Sixtus IV, in 1477. When Riario was assassinated in 1488, Sforza seized control of his territories and proclaimed her triumph with a lewd gesture indicative of her political audacity (see Hairston). She then governed for twelve years as regent for her son. Considered a virago by her peers, Sforza constructed a ruling persona as loyal widow/mother and triumphant regent, and managed local and international conflicts through cunning diplomacy and strong defenses. Her performance as a powerful widow-regent was so successful that she was able to maintain lovers in her court, and even bore sons by Giacomo Feo and Giovanni di Pierfrancesco de' Medici (both possibly secret husbands). In 1500, Sforza personally fought Cesare Borgia's forces; nevertheless, she lost her territories. She spent her final years in Florence, where she concentrated on improving her family's status through the advancement of her sons' careers and management of their patrimony.

Throughout her life Sforza promoted her own fame and power through, among other things, cultural patronage. After her death, others exploited her history for diverse agendas including family glory and gender politics. Her legend was developed first by Niccolò Machiavelli and her descendants the Medici Grand Dukes of Tuscany, then by Italian nationalists beginning in the nineteenth century, and finally by twentieth and twenty-first century scholars of history and gender studies.

JOYCE DE VRIES

References and Further Reading

Breisach, Ernst. *Caterina Sforza: A Renaissance Virago.* Chicago: University of Chicago Press, 1967.

de Vries, Joyce. "Casting Her Widowhood: Contemporary and Posthumous Portraits of Caterina Sforza." In *Widowhood and Visual Culture in Early Modern Europe*, edited by Allison Levy. Hampshire: Ashgate Press, 2003, pp. 77–92.

Hairston, Julia L. "Skirting the Issue: Machiavelli's Caterina Sforza." *Renaissance Quarterly* 53 (3) (2000): 687–712.

Jansen, Sharon L. *The Monstrous Regiment of Women: Female Rulers in Early Modern Europe.* New York: Palgrave Macmillan, 2002.

Kelly, Joan. "Did Women Have a Renaissance?" In *Becoming Visible; Women in European History*, edited by Renate Bridenthal, Susan Mosher Stuard, Merry E. Wiesner. Second Edition. Boston: Houghton Mifflin, 1987, pp. 175–201. Reprinted in *Women, History, and Theory: The Essays of Joan Kelly*. Chicago: University of Chicago Press, 1984, pp. 19–50.

See also **Diplomacy and Reconciliation; Gender Ideologies; Illegitimacy; Italy; Noble Women; Patronage, Artistic; Regents and Queen-Lieutenants; Sexuality: Extramarital Sex; Virile Women; Warfare; Widows**

CATERINA VIGRI

Caterina Vigri (St. Catherine of Bologna) (c. 1413–1463) is an example of a fifteenth-century woman artist emerging from the cultural tradition of learned nuns. Versed in Latin, music, and painting, she was known for the mystical piety recorded in her spiritual writings, including *Le sette armi spirituali* (*The Seven Spiritual Weapons*). Vigri was born in Bologna and educated at court in Ferrara, where she entered the Convent of the Poor Clares in 1427. Elected abbess after moving to a new house established in Bologna in 1456, she composed spiritual tracts and painted images as acts of devotion and good works.

Vigri's surviving pictorial *oeuvre* is small (two independent paintings on panel and two on paper, an illumination and a number of decorated pages in her texts, and a painted wooden Christ Child) and is technically unsophisticated; however, her works are formally and conceptually complex in their intermingling of text and image. Furthermore, her art represents well the propensity of *Nonnenarbeiten* ("nuns' works") to address conventual spiritual practices in a unique way. Her biographer and fellow Clare, Suor Illuminata Bembo, recorded Caterina's particular love of painting images of the Divine Word represented by the swaddled Infant Christ. Although the pictorial emphasis on the Christ Child as subject reflects corporate (e.g., Franciscan) devotion to the cult of Corpus Domini and the Incarnation, it also figures the nuns' special identification with the passionate maternity of the Virgin Mary. As erotic metaphors are converted to ardent devotion toward Christ in Vigri's texts and images, so too the material richness typical of her works recasts early exposure to aristocratic wealth into a metaphor of spiritual splendor. Caterina Vigri died in Bologna in 1463. Her cult received papal authorization in 1524; she was beatified in 1592 and canonized in 1712.

KIM E. BUTLER

References and Further Reading

Chadwick, Whitney. *Women, Art, and Society.* 3rd ed. London and New York: Thames & Hudson Ltd., 2003, pp. 88–90.

Hamburger, Jeffrey F. *Nuns as Artists: The Visual Culture of a Medieval Convent.* Berkeley, Los Angeles, and London: University of California Press, 1997.

Wood, Jeryldene M. *Women, Art, and Spirituality: The Poor Clares of Early Modern Italy.* Cambridge and New York: Cambridge University Press, 1996.

———. "Vigri, Caterina [St. Catherine of Bologna]." In *Dictionary of Women Artists*, edited by Delia Gaze. London and Chicago: Fitzroy Dearborn Publishers, 1997. vol. II, pp. 1408–1410.

See also **Artists, Women; Devotional Art; Mysticism and Mystics; Nuns as Illuminators; Poor Clares Order**

CATHARS

Catharism was a Christian dualist movement that flourished in parts of western Europe, particularly southern France and northern Italy, between the twelfth and the fourteenth centuries. Among Cathars, belief varied widely from community to community but essentially this group taught the existence of two gods or principles, one good and the other evil. The good god, the God of the New Testament, had created the spiritual world, while the evil god, or Satan, identified by some Cathars with the god of the Old Testament, later created the physical world. All visible matter, including human bodies, was, therefore, tainted with sin. Human souls were genderless angels trapped in material bodies by Satan and doomed to be reborn in new, sinful bodies in every generation. Modern historians have debated whether the Cathars' rejection of the body, sex, and procreation as creations of Satan drew women to the sect or drove them away from it.

The Cathars taught that salvation lay only in a ritual called the *consolamentum*. This ritual, a sort of baptism by the laying on of hands, reunited the soul of the believer to the spirit paraclete. This process perfected the believer and made him or her incapable of sin and ensured entry into heaven upon physical death, thus releasing the believer from the cycle of reincarnation. Anything that the new perfect did before receiving the *consolamentum* did not affect salvation, and any sins committed after it showed that the ritual had been flawed in some way, and the subject could receive the ritual again. The perfects, those who had received the *consolamentum*, acted as the clergy of the sect through preaching and administering to the spiritual needs of believers who had not yet undergone the ritual. They also seem to have received at least a rudimentary theological education. Yet every perfect had to embrace an extremely ascetic life. Cathar perfects were not allowed to touch members of the opposite sex and even kept a rather strict diet that excluded all eggs, meat, and dairy products because they believed that eating any product of coitus would negate the *consolamentum* by proving that they had not been able to escape the teachings of Satan.

Because both men and women could become perfects, many twentieth-century historians argued that women were drawn to Catharism because of the promise of a sacerdotal role denied to them by the all-male Catholic priesthood. Peter Biller has challenged this notion by arguing that the Cathars' theological antagonism to sex and the body expressed a strong misogynistic tendency. Catharism denied the validity of marriage and, therefore, drove away women, particularly married women, because it insisted that they could not achieve salvation without renouncing their spouses and families. This interpretation of Cathar belief implied a conflict between Cathar doctrine and many women's social realities that women could only resolve by rejecting Catharism. Other historians, such as Anne Brenon, objected to such arguments because they were based primarily upon Catholic theological treatises and argued that in inquisitorial depositions very few women mentioned the Cathar doctrine of sex and the body as deterrents to involvement in the movement. Brenon believed that familial ties to Catharism influenced women's religious beliefs far more than personal concerns about doctrine and that, in fact, the importance of the family in the transmission of Cathar belief actually made women's roles as wives and mothers important to the movement in a functional sense, even if rejected by Cathar theology.

Undoubtedly, women who became perfects had the authority to preach, teach, and perform the *consolamentum*. Female believers, on the other hand, lived much as their Catholic neighbors did; they married and bore children and were subject to the same property rights and inheritance practices as other women. The practice of the *endura*, in which a believer could receive salvation through the *consolamentum* on his or her deathbed, meant that not all Cathar believers had to take up the extreme asceticism of the perfects. Cathar doctrine, therefore, most likely had little impact on the life of the average Cathar woman.

The persecutions of the thirteenth century, including the Albigensian Crusades (1208–1227) and the advent of the inquisition in 1232, forced most perfects into hiding, and their numbers steadily declined over the next century. During the very late period French Catharism began to exclude female perfects and became increasingly misogynistic. The last recorded French perfects, who were active in the first decades of the fourteenth century, performed the *consolamentum* on women only if the women were near death. They also reportedly taught that a woman had to be reborn as a man before she could achieve salvation. Late Italian perfects, on the other hand, continued to include women among their numbers.

Susan Taylor Snyder

References and Further Reading

Barber, Malcolm. "Women and Catharism." *Reading Medieval Studies* 3 (1977): 45–62.
———, *The Cathars: Dualist Heretics in Languedoc in the High Middle Ages.* New York: Longman, 2000.
Biller, Peter. "Cathars and Material Women." *Medieval Theology and the Natural Body*, edited by Peter Biller

and A. J. Minnis. Woodbridge: York Medieval Press, 1997, pp. 61–107.

Brenon, Anne. "The Voice of the Good Women: An Essay on the Pastoral and Sacerdotal Role of Women in the Cathar Church." *Women Preachers and Prophets Through Two Millenia of Christianity*, edited by Beverly Mayne Kienzle and Pamela J. Walker. Berkeley: University of California Press, 1998, pp. 114–133.

Lambert, Malcolm. *The Cathars*. Malden, Mass. Blackwell, 1998.

Lansing, Carol. *Power and Purity: Cathar Heresy in Medieval Italy*. Oxford: Oxford University Press, 1998.

Le Roy Ladurie, Emmanuel. *Montaillou: Cathars and Catholics in a French Village, 1294–1324*. translated by Barbara Bray. Harmondsworth: Penguin, 1990.

See also **Heretics and Heresy; Lay Piety; Lollards; Waldensians**

CATHERINE OF ALEXANDRIA

Catherine of Alexandria was the most popular female saint in medieval Europe, second only to the Virgin Mary, and deemed a powerful intercessor for her devotees. She is believed to have been martyred in the early fourth century, but the earliest references to her appear in the ninth century, and the first extant versions of her life date from the tenth. Thus it is highly unlikely that she was an historical person. The most influential version of the life of Saint Catherine was a Latin account known as the Vulgate, composed in the mid-eleventh century. It enjoyed a wide circulation even before being used by Jacobus of Voragine as the basis for his version of her life in the *Golden Legend*. Subsequently her Life was translated into many vernacular languages: English, Irish, Welsh, Anglo-Norman, Polish, Czech, Hungarian, French, German, and Spanish, often surviving in not just one, but several different versions. The Anglo-Norman Life of Catherine, written by Clemence of Barking, is one of the few medieval saints' lives known to have been written by a woman. Many churches and monasteries were dedicated to Catherine, as well as chapels and altars within churches, and she was a common guild patron. Representations of her life are also found in the form of wall paintings (e.g., Sporle church in Norfolk), stained glass (Erfurt Cathedral), altarpieces (the Getty altarpiece by the D'Arezzo brothers), manuscript illuminations (the *Très Belles Heures*), and embroidery (the Pienza Cope). In an attempt to kill her, the Emperor Maxentius had a torture device of spiked wheels created, but angels destroyed it. This gave rise to her iconographic emblem of the spiked wheel.

The starting point for the spread of the cult of Catherine in medieval Europe was her shrine at Mount Sinai, where, according to her Life, angels had carried her decapitated body. Her relics were discovered on the mountain at the end of the tenth century. With devotion chiefly from the Normans, relics of the saint were carried from Sinai to Europe to the monastery of the Holy Trinity in Rouen in the 1030s, where the cult spread more widely across western Europe. Therefore, Catherine's cult appeared sometime after the cults of other virgin martyrs such as Agatha, Agnes, and Cecilia had been established. Its great popularity partially rested on the ways in which her legend was based on an existing hagiographic type, but also presented a development of it, because the Life of Catherine provides the most detailed version of the basic virgin martyr pattern. Moreover, the life presents her as exceptional, even for a virgin martyr, particularly with respect to her status as a sovereign queen, and as a woman who received an explicitly academic education. This enabled her to defeat fifty philosophers whom Maxentius had brought in to try and convert her back to paganism. It was commonplace for virgin martyrs to describe themselves as the bride of Christ, but from the mid-thirteenth century onwards the Life of Catherine included a "prequel," which described her early life and mystical marriage to Christ. This became a standard part of her life during the fourteenth century and exists in two forms: a Continental version in which she weds the Christ child in a vision and an Anglo-Norman/English version in which she marries the adult Christ in an actual wedding ceremony.

These unique elements in her life can be related to the interest in her cult shown by particular groups. Her status as a queen probably accounts in part for her attraction to royal devotees such as the emperor Charles IV, Philip the Good Duke of Burgundy, and Richard III of England. Her education made her an appropriate patron for clerics and universities. In presenting her as the bride of Christ some fifteenth-century versions of her Life identify Catherine as a model of interiority and affective lay piety. Catherine's appeal was clearly wide ranging, encompassing people of all social backgrounds and of both sexes, but it appears that a particular connection was felt to exist between Catherine and women. Catherine's steadfast adherence to Christianity and virginity made her an obvious model for religious women. For example, the Catherine Group version of her Life was composed to provide inspiration for anchoresses. However, her appearance in conduct literature such as *The Book of the Chevalier of the Tour Landry* demonstrates that she was also presented as a model of demure femininity to lay women.

KATHERINE J. LEWIS

References and Further Reading

Beatie, Bruce A. "Saint Catherine of Alexandria: Traditional Themes and the Development of a Medieval Hagiographic German Narrative." *Speculum* 52 (1977): 785–800.

Jenkins, Jacqueline, and Katherine J. Lewis. *St Catherine of Alexandria: Texts and Contexts in Western Medieval Europe.* Turnhout: Brepols, 2003.

Lewis, Katherine J. *The Cult of St Catherine of Alexandria in Late Medieval England.* Woodbridge, Suffolk: The Boydell Press, 2000.

MacBain, William. "Five Old French Renderings of the 'Passio Sancte Caterine Virginis.'" In *Medieval Translators and their Craft*, edited by Jeanette Beer. Studies in Medieval Culture 25. Kalamazoo: Medieval Institute Publications, 1989, pp. 41–65.

Voragine, Jacob of, "The Life of St Catherine." In *The Golden Legend: Readings on the Saints II.* translated by William Granger Ryan. Princeton, N.J.: Princeton University Press, 1993, pp. 334–341.

Winstead, Karen A. "Capgrave's St. Catherine and the Perils of Gynecocracy." *Viator* 25 (1994): 361–376.

See also **Bride of Christ: Imagery; Clemence of Barking; Conduct Literature; Hagiography; Hagiography, Iconographic Aspects of; Jacobus of Voragine's *Golden Legend*; Katherine Group; Relics and Reliquaries; Virgin Martyrs**

CATHERINE OF GENOA

Born in Genoa to the aristocratic and ecclesiastically well-connected Fieschi family, Catherine (1447–1510) was refused entrance into a convent at age thirteen on account of her youth. In 1463, she was forced to marry Giuliano Adorno, an unfaithful and authoritarian nobleman who impoverished them and caused Catherine great suffering. Her mental anguish reached crisis proportions in 1473, when she was suddenly wounded by God's love and made acutely aware of her own wretchedness and God's mercy.

This life-changing experience shaped Catherine's spiritual teaching, ascetic practices, and charitable works. She believed God's love draws the creature to see its misery, to seek and suffer through the annihilation of its own will and humanity, until entirely absorbed in God. Similarly, in the fires of Purgatory God's burning love consumes sin until the soul becomes one with God. Catherine experienced visions and ecstasies, and was devoted to the Eucharist. Her extreme asceticism included wearing a hair shirt, swallowing filth to overcome her disgust, and prolonged prayer and fasting.

Her charitable activities for the poor and sick were renowned. After converting her husband, she lived celibately with him for about twenty years in the Hospital of Pammatone, which she directed from 1490 to 1496, performing heroically during several plagues. She inspired religious and charitable foundations, including the influential Oratory of Divine Love.

Catherine chose not to have a spiritual confessor for most of her life. She refuted a Dominican who contended her lay status made her less prepared to love God. Her large circle of disciples included priests, religious, and laity.

Catherine's life and teaching were recorded by disciples and a confessor (and not Catherine) in three Italian texts—her *Life*, the *Treatise on Purgatory*, and the *Spiritual Dialogue*. Their precise authorship is still debated.

Catherine died an excruciating death after a prolonged illness. She was canonized in 1737.

CATHERINE M. MOONEY

References and Further Reading

Bonzi, Umile. *S. Caterina Fiesch Adorno*, vol. 2. *Edizione critica dei manoscritti cateriniani.* [Torino]: Marietti, 1962.

Catherine of Genoa. (*Spiritual Dialogue*). *Purgation and Purgatory; The Spiritual Dialogue.* translated by Serge Hughes. New York: Paulist Press, 1979.

Life and Doctrine of Saint Catherine of Genoa. New York: Catholic Publication Society, 1874. Reprinted, *The Spiritual Doctrine of St. Catherine of Genoa.* Rockford, Ill.: Tan Books, 1989. Online, "Life and Doctrine of Saint Catherine" at http://www.ccel.org/ccel/catherine-q/life.toc.html

See also **Almsgiving and Charity; Asceticism; Chastity and Chaste Marriage; Confraternities; Devotional Practices; Lay Piety; Laywomen, Religious; Mystics' Writings**

CATHERINE OF SIENA

Although she only lived to the age of 33, Catherine di Giacomo di Benicasa (1347–1380) had a considerable impact on her city and the church. Catherine was born twenty-fourth of the twenty-five children of a Sienese wool dyer of comfortable means, and his wife. It is difficult to disentangle fact from legend in accounts of Catherine's youth. It is reasonably certain, however, that she was religious from her youth, refusing any chance to marry. Raymond of Capua, a prominent Dominican and her principal biographer, tells us that Catherine cut off her hair at age 15 to discourage suitors. At 18 she was granted a Dominican habit as one of the *mantellate* (penitent women wearing religious robes), and she lived a solitary life of prayer in her room. She only left it to attend services at San Domenico, the Dominican church in Siena. In 1368, she experienced a mystical marriage to Jesus, who then told her to serve the sick and impoverished.

Catherine's life of service bred legends. She practiced extreme austerities that did not keep her from doing nursing and caring for poor persons. Most famously, Catherine comforted Niccolò Toldo, a young man who had been condemned to death. Catherine soon was drawn into the politics of Siena, offering counsel and praying for the citizens. In the period from 1374 onward, Catherine began to travel outside Siena, trying to direct Christians away from feuding to the recovery of the Holy Land. This included a mission to Avignon on behalf of Florence that the Florentines promptly disowned in an effort to make a favorable peace with the pope. She also began sending letters to many persons, including a harsh rebuke of Florentine duplicity and advice to Pope Gregory XI that he should return the papacy from Avignon to Rome. Catherine's earnestness and love of truth occasionally blinded her to others' motives, but she never gave up her efforts to improve the state of church and Christendom. In this period (c. 1376), Catherine received the stigmata of Christ, but the marks were (at her request) invisible to others.

Catherine's final years were difficult. The Florentines once again used her as a diplomatic pawn in relations with the papacy. Irked by this, Catherine returned to Siena. Pope Gregory returned the papacy to Rome, but he died there in 1378 while preparing to return to Avignon. Gregory's death was followed by a schism that divided Christendom. Rival popes sat in Avignon and Rome. Catherine wrote letters urging acceptance of the Roman claimant, Urban VI, and he called her to Rome. Catherine's health collapsed, but she continued her life of prayer for a divided church. She dispatched Raymond of Capua to go to Avignon as an emissary for the ending of the Great Schism (1378–1418), but he did not risk the journey. Catherine remained in the Holy City, each day dragging her ailing body to St. Peter's for Mass. She died in Rome in 1380, and her body remained at the Dominican convent of Santa Maria sopra Minerva. Catherine was canonized by Pope Pius II, himself a Sienese, in 1461.

Catherine left a large corpus of letters. Recipients range from her mother, Mona Lapa, to the popes of her time. They include the mercenary leader John Hawkwood, the queen mother of Hungary, and a prostitute, to whom she wrote on the urging of the woman's brothers. These letters express both divine love and Catherine's love for God and neighbor. Her self-presentation is one of an apostle, living a life of self-sacrifice while serving others. Catherine's mystical teachings appear in the *Dialogue*, which dwells on God's love for humanity. (God is described as "mad" for love of the human race.) The *Dialogue* also reflects the author's concerns for the reform of the church. Nor was the welfare of individuals absent from the text. One of those closest to her thoughts was Raymond of Capua, who helped in the composition of the

text. Besides being Catherine's confessor and biographer, Raymond was active in ecclesiastical affairs. (As Master General of his order, he advanced reform of the friars' lives, launching the Observant movement of the fourteenth and fifteenth centuries.) Raymond's biography must be used carefully, because it presents Catherine as he wished her to be seen, de-emphasizing her active life, but it provides evidence from one of the persons closest to her life, which was indeed both active and contemplative.

THOMAS M. IZBICKI

References and Further Reading

Catherine of Siena. *The Dialogue*. translated by Suzanne Noffke. New York: Paulist Press, 1980.
———. *The Letters of Catherine of Siena*. translated by Suzanne Noffke. 2 vols. Tempe: Arizona Center for Medieval and Renaissance Studies, 2000.
Del Pozzo, Joan P. The Apotheosis of Niccolò Toldo: An Execution "Love Story": Appendix A Translation of Saint Catherine of Siena's Most Celebrated Letter. *MLN: Modern Language Notes* 110-1 (1995): 164–177.
Noffke, Suzanne. *Catherine of Siena: Vision Through a Distant Eye*. Collegeville, Minn.: Liturgical Press, 1996.
Scott, Karen. "'This is why I have put you among your neighbors': St. Bernard's and St. Catherine's Understanding of the Love of God and Neighbor." In *Atti del simposio internazionale cateriniano-bernardiniano, Siena, 17–20 aprile 1980*, edited by Domenico Maffei and Paolo Nardi. Siena: Accademia Senese degli Intronati, 1980. pp. 278–294.
———. "St. Catherine of Siena, 'Apostola.'" In *Church History* 61. 1 (March 1992): 34–46.
———. "Mystical Death, Bodily Death: Catherine of Siena and Raymond of Capua on the Mystic's Encounter with God." In *Gendered Voices: Medieval Saints and Their Interpreters*, edited by Catherine M. Mooney. Philadelphia: University of Pennsylvania Press, 1999. pp. 136–167.
———. "Catherine of Siena and Lay Sanctity in Fourteenth-Century Italy." In *Lay Sanctity, Medieval and Modern: A Search for Models*, edited by Ann W. Astell. South Bend, Ind.: University of Notre Dame Press, 2000, pp. 77–90.

See also **Asceticism; Bride of Christ: Imagery; Church; Dominican Order; Laywomen, Religious; Mysticism and Mystics; Spiritual Care; Tertiaries**

CELIBACY: CLERICAL AND PRIESTS' CONCUBINES

Beginning as early as the Council of Elvira in 306, church councils, especially those in the western portions of the Roman Empire, attempted to enforce celibacy for all clergy by legislating against both clerical marriage and concubinage. Laws that targeted concubinage, however, were difficult to enforce, especially during the early Middle Ages, when reformers were more likely to focus on the more troubling issue of clerical marriage. Even during the eleventh century, when Pope Gregory VII made clerical celibacy a core part of his reform legislation, clerical concubinage remained a widespread phenomenon.

By the High Middle Ages, however, reformers had largely put an end to the practice of clerical marriage, freeing them up to turn their attention to the related issue of clerical concubinage. In 1123, the First Lateran Council reiterated earlier prohibitions on clerical concubinage, and the canons of Lateran II (1139) further mandated that concubinous clerics be stripped of their benefices. Local councils and diocesan synods—often with the support of secular authorities—followed suit, advocating the suspension of concubinous clerics and excommunication of their concubines and declaring the offspring of such unions illegitimate.

Reform Efforts

Unfortunately for reformers, increasingly strict legislation against clerical concubinage in no way eradicated the practice. The presence of anticoncubinage legislation in the decrees of the Council of Trent (1545–1563) indicates that canonists and theologians continued to wrestle with the problem throughout the High and later Middle Ages. Part of the blame for the ineffectiveness of the new sanctions rests with the ecclesiastical courts, which tended to commute penalties against the clergy to fines, thereby blunting the impact of the intended reforms. Records of parish visitations further suggest that both concubines of clergy and their ecclesiastical partners were, in many cases, fully integrated into their communities. Parish records indicate that many concubines lived openly with their ordained partners, with the couple sometimes raising children together in the home they shared. Most parishioners reported incidences of clerical concubinage in a matter-of-fact manner, suggesting that clerical concubinage sparked no greater moral outrage than did the frequent incidence of fornication, reported in a similarly dispassionate tone.

There is no single pattern that defines all or even most relationships between clergy and their concubines in the Middle Ages; rather, these relationships varied as much as those between laypeople. Some couples remained together for only a short time, while others formed lasting unions in which the couple shared a home, children, and even grandchildren, and continued to do so even in the face of ecclesiastical censure. In many regions, these relationships were common knowledge among parishioners, who reported couples living together openly, and who

sometimes compared such couples to legitimate marriages. Some historians have suggested, however, that rural clergy were only open about their relationships because there was little possibility of hiding them within a small parish, where clergy were integrated into the life of the community; urban clergy seem not to have been as open about their relationships, and urban parishioners may have been less tolerant of clergy who kept concubines. Even in rural parishes, records attest to the fact that at least some clergymen tried to keep their relationships secret by discreetly maintaining their concubines, and sometimes their children, in towns or cities outside the parish.

Concubines

The concubines themselves seem to have been as varied as the relationships in which they took part. Historians have often assumed that concubines, whether of clergy or of laymen, were women on the margins of the social order for whom marriage was not an option. Parish records to a certain extent support this picture: many clerics' concubines were converts from Judaism or Islam, or women with few connections to the communities in which they lived. The majority of concubines, however, appear to have been ordinary women, fully integrated into the life of their communities, with strong family ties. Such women may have chosen a concubinage relationship over marriage for a number of reasons, including (but not limited to) unavailability of a husband, or impossibility of raising a dowry, or even marriage to a man from whom they were now separated. But the fact that many of these relationships persisted for years or even decades suggests that historians should not rule out genuine affection as a motivating factor for women who chose to become the concubines of clergymen.

A few clerics' concubines were ostracized within their own communities, as evidenced by the insulting language that some co-parishioners used when referring to them in the parish visitations. But negative portrayals of these women may well have been due to factors apart from their unorthodox relationships: many of the women singled out for insulting language were also accused by their neighbors of prostitution, pimping, or usury. It is certainly possible that such accusations themselves may have stemmed from parishioners' negative opinions of clerical concubines. Nevertheless, it is significant that instances in which parishioners characterized clerics' concubines so negatively are relatively rare, suggesting that, unlike canonists, ordinary laypeople did not view the status of cleric's concubine as automatic cause for censure.

Some historians, in fact, have gone so far as to propose that clerical concubinage offered women a degree of stability comparable to that enjoyed by married women. They argue that the concubine of a member of the clergy was in a special position since, unlike a layman's concubine, the cleric's concubine ran no risk of being displaced by a wife, and may have even enjoyed a portion of her partner's status within the community. But whereas a woman married in secret could eventually come forth to claim legitimate status as a wife, a clergyman's concubine could never harbor expectations of her position becoming legitimate. Centuries of legislation against clerical concubinage meant that, however well-accepted she might be within her community, a clerical concubine lacked status as such at law, and thus had no legal recourse if her partner repudiated her, either on his own initiative, or in response to orders from ecclesiastical superiors. In such cases, the women (and sometimes children) involved found themselves in untenable circumstances, as most clerics' concubines were economically dependent on their ordained partners. Sometimes a cleric who abandoned his concubine provided her with a dowry so she could make a good marriage, but such gestures were at the discretion of the individual clergyman, and parish records contain numerous stories of families and neighbors indignant at the desperate straits in which a concubine found herself after having been abandoned. Clearly there was a significant gap between, on the one hand, church authorities' insistence that concubinous clergy sever all ties with their "families," and, on the other hand, community expectations that a woman had a right to some measure of material support from her partner, even after separation.

To what extent, then, do the history of legislation against clerical concubinage and the historical experience of the concubines themselves correspond? The prescriptive sources tell a relatively linear tale of increasing restrictions against clerical "families," but descriptive sources like ecclesiastical court records and parish visitations paint a more complicated picture of relationships between clergy and their concubines. Although clerics' concubines had no official status in law, local records indicate that they were not necessarily marginalized within their communities. Furthermore, repeated legislation against clerical concubinage suggests the persistence of the practice, rather than its gradual disappearance. Although popes, councils, and synods had legislated against these unions since the earliest centuries, the concubines of clergymen remained a part of parish life throughout the Middle Ages, and beyond.

MARIE A. KELLEHER

References and Further Reading

Barstow, Anne Llewellyn. *Married Priests and the Reforming Papacy: The Eleventh-Century Debates*. New York and Toronto: E. Mellen Press, 1982.

Bornstein, Daniel. "Parish Priests in Late Medieval Cortona: The Urban and Rural Clergy," in *Quaderni di Storia Religiosa* 4 (1997): 165–193.

Brooke, Christopher N. L. "Gregorian Reform in Action: Clerical Marriage in England, 1050–1200." In *Change in Medieval Society: Europe North of the Alps, 1050–1500*, edited by Sylvia Thrupp. New York: Appleton-Century-Crofts, 1964, pp. 49–71.

Cochini, Christian. *Apostolic Origins of Priestly Celibacy*, trans. Nelly Marans. San Francisco: Ignatius Press, 1990.

Frassetto, Michael, ed. *Medieval Purity and Piety: Essays on Medieval Clerical Celibacy and Religious Reform*. New York and London: Garland, 1998.

Gaudemet, Jean. "Le célibat ecclésiastique: Le droit et la pratique du XIe au XIIIe s." *Zeitschrift der Savigny-Stiftung für Rechtsgeschichte, kanonistische Abteilung* 68 (1982), 1–31.

Haboucha, Reginetta. "Clerics, Their Wives, and Their Concubines in the 'Partidas' of Alfonso el Sabio," in *Homo Carnalis: The Carnal Aspect of Medieval Human Life*, edited by Helen Rodite Lemay. Binghamton, NY: SUNY Binghamton, 1990, pp. 85–104.

Kelleher, Marie A. "'Like Man and Wife': Clerics' Concubines in the Diocese of Barcelona." *Journal of Medieval History* 28 (2002): 349–360.

Lynch, John E. "Marriage and Celibacy of the Clergy: The Discipline of the Western Church, a Historico-Canonical Synopsis." *The Jurist* 32 (1972): Part I, 14–38; Part II, 189–212.

McNamara, Jo Ann. "Chaste Marriage and Clerical Celibacy." In *Sexual Practices and the Medieval Church*, edited by Vern L. Bullough and James Brundage. Buffalo, NY: Prometheus Books, 1982, pp. 22–33.

Rath, Brigitte. "'De sacramentis, concubinatu et ludo taxillorum...' Über ein böhmisches Visitationsprotokoll aus dem 14. Jahrhundert,' in *Von Menschen und ihren Zeichen. Sozialhistorische Untersuchungen zum Spätmittelalter und zur Neuzeit*, edited by Ingrid Matschinegg et al. Bielefeld: Verlag für Regionalgeschichte, 1990, pp. 41–59.

See also **Concubines; Illegitimacy; Law, Canon; Parishes; Records, Ecclesiastical; Sexuality: Extramarital Sex; Sexuality, Regulation of**

CELIBACY, LAY

See **Chastity and Chaste Marriage; Singlewomen**

CERETA, LAURA

One of the last great female humanist writers active in fifteenth-century Italy, Laura Cereta (born in Brescia, 1469–1499) was the first to put women's issues and her friendships with women front and center in her works. The daughter of a Brescian attorney, at the age of fifteen Cereta married a Venetian merchant, Pietro Serina, and was widowed a year later. Schooled in Latin and the classics by nuns, Cereta participated in humanist circles both in Brescia and the monastery at Chiari, where she may have first presented her comic dialogue "On the Death of an Ass" and read selections from her letterbook. Her letters, half of them to women, indicate how fully she saw herself as enmeshed in a historically constituted community of female intellectuals—a republic of women, *muliebris respublica,* as she portrayed the world she imagined (Robin 1997, p. 80). Containing eighty-two Latin epistles and her satirical dialogue, also in Latin, her collected *Epistolae* circulated widely, bringing her fame in her own lifetime, although the work did not appear in a printed edition until 1640, in Padua. Among her most passionately charged letters are those to her husband, revealing her struggle for power in the relationship and later her terrible grief at his death (Robin 1997, pp. 87–113). In a dispatch to the Brescian magistrate Luigi Dandolo she exposes the atrocities of war she witnessed with her own eyes when German troops invaded Rovereto and Calliano (Robin 1997, pp. 160–169). And in a pair of feminist manifestos, she dismisses the institutions of marriage and motherhood as traps to enslave women (to Pietro Zecchi, in Robin 1997, pp. 64–72). She also defends women's right to higher education, arguing that the female sex already has a brilliant history of poets, orators, scholars, and prophets (to Bibolo Semproni, in Robin 1997, pp. 72–80). Another diptych of philosophical letters, to the nun Deodata di Leno and a woman she calls "Europa solitaria," argues the case for and against Epicureanism. She asks, should the pleasures of the body be chosen at risk of abandoning one's duties as a citizen (Robin 1997, pp. 115–128)? Cereta's letters anticipate themes associated with the early feminism of the Enlightenment: namely, the representation of women as a collective and a community; the preoccupation with reconceptualizing gender; the privileging of the emotions in a genre assumed to be the exclusive domain of reason (humanist letters); the construction of housework as a barrier to women's intellectual aspirations; and the use of the salon and salon writing (for Cereta, the monastery and the letter) as a bridge for women into the public arena.

DIANA ROBIN

References and Further Reading

Cereta's letterbooks are extant in Rome (Vatican City, Biblioteca Apostolica Vaticana. Vat. Lat. 3176. Cart. 3. XVI in 73 fols. Contains eighty-three items); and Venice (Biblioteca Nazionale Marciana. Marc. Cod. Lat., XI.28 [4186] mbr. XV, 154 fols. Includes seventy-four items containing many lacunae.)

Cereta, Laura. *Laurae Ceretae Brixiensis Feminae Clarissimae Epistolae iam primum e MS in lucem productae,* edited by Jacopo Filippo Tomasini. Padua: Sebastiano Sardi, 1640.

———. *Collected Letters of a Renaissance Feminist,* translated and edited by Diana Robin. Chicago and London: University of Chicago Press, 1997.

King, Margaret L. and Albert Rabil, Jr. *Her Immaculate Hand: Selected Works By and About the Women Humanists of Quattrocento Italy.* Binghamton, NY: Medieval and Renaissance Texts, 1983.

Palma, M. "Cereto, Laura," in *Dizionario biografico degli italiani* 729–730.

Rabil, Albert Jr. *Laura Cereta: Quattrocento Humanist.* Binghamton, NY: Medieval and Renaissance Texts and Studies, 1981.

Robin, Diana. "Space, Woman, and Renaissance Discourse," in *Sex and Gender in Medieval and Renaissance Texts: The Latin Tradition,* edited by Barbara K. Gold, Paul Allen Miller, Charles Platter. Albany: State University of New York of New York Press, 1996, pp. 165–187.

———. "Humanism, Italy," pp. 153–157; "Laura Cereta," pp. 46–48; "The *Querelle des Femmes* in Renaissance Italy," pp. 270–273; "Learned Women," pp. 169–171, in the *Feminist Encyclopedia of Italian Literature,* edited by Rinaldina Russell, Westport, Conn: Greenwood Press, 1997b, pp. 153–157.

———. "Culture, Imperialism, and Humanist Criticism in the Italian City-States," in *The Cambridge History of Literary Criticism,* Volume 3: *The Renaissance. 1500–1700,* edited by Glyn P. Norton. Cambridge: Cambridge University Press, 1999, pp. 355–363.

———. "Cereta, Laura," in *Encyclopedia of the Renaissance.* Editor in Chief, Paul F. Grendler. New York: Charles Scribner's Sons, 1999, 1: 393–394.

———. "Humanism and Feminism in Laura Cereta's Public Letters," in *Women in Italian Renaissance Culture and Society,* edited by Letizia Panizza. Oxford: Legenda European Humanities Research Centre, University of Oxford, 2000, pp. 368–384.

———. "Laura Cereta: Biography, Latin Texts, Translations," in Laurie Churchill, ed., *Women Writing Latin,* Vol. 3. New York: Routledge, 2002, pp. 83–108.

See also **Defenses of Women; Fedele, Cassandra; Humanism; Italy; Letter Writing; Nogarola, Isotta; Renaissance, Historiography of; Sanuti, Nicolasa Castellani; Women Authors: Latin Texts**

CHARIVARI

From the French, charivari was a pervasive and popular ritual of shaming and humiliation, designed to single out, mock, punish and ultimately absorb deviant couples. The early versions of the ritual are found in the literature, iconography, and drama of the Middle Ages, but the charivari comes to us in full-blown form during the fifteenth and sixteenth centuries. The charivari is found across Europe and in various permutations. In English it is called "rough music," the

"Skimmington ride," or "the riding of the stang": in Italian, the *scampanate* and *mattinata*; in German it appears in various versions of the *haberfeld-treiben*, *thierjagen*, and *katzenmusik*.

Charivaris were characterized in general by noisy processions, attended by "rough music," cacophonies of banging pots, lampooning songs or rhymes, pounding marrow bones and whistles, animal bladders filled with rattling peas, shouts, and sometimes gunshots. The term *charivari*, was meant to mimic the noise made during the ritual. Charivaris frequently occurred at night (often on successive nights), and although they may have had various functions as censors of societal behavior outside the norm, they were largely associated with deviance in marriage, the most usual subjects being: the age difference between couples who were about to marry; the censure of premarital sex; the exposure of adultery and cuckoldry; the punishment for wife-beating; or the humiliation of the hen-pecked husband and/or the shrewish wife. They were also commonly used when a wedding deviated from expectation, for example, when a ritual "fee" in the form of either money, food, or drink to the guests was withheld.

Besides "rough music," the charivari might be composed of several other dramatic elements. These might include the parading and/or burning of effigies; the "production" of a mime or play upon a cart; imagined hunt; parodies of religious or legal rituals; the parading of men "armed" with household weapons such as pitchforks and coalrakes; and the display of horns. But the most important and pervasive aspect of the charivari involved the "riding" of the subject(s). This involved a mount of some sort, either a donkey or a horse, sometimes a cart, or a substitute horse; in England a "cowlstaff" or "stang" pole carried on men's shoulders. The riders might be the victims themselves, or there might be a proxy victim or an effigy; and riders might be presented as transvestite or unmasculine in nature. Sometimes victims were pelted with filth and might end up being ducked, sometimes with a "cucking stool," into a shallow pool of dirty water, a duck pond, or a ditch. Often a rider was made to face backwards, and sometimes ridings were seasonal, actually imbedded in local festivals, as opposed to the singling out of a particular couple. The ride of the victim(s) could range from comic to violent, resulting sometimes only in humiliation, other times in injury or even death.

THERESIA DE VROOM

References and Further Reading

Klapisch-Zuber, Christiane. *Women, Family and Ritual in Renaissance Italy*. Chicago: University of Chicago Press, 1985. See the chapter "The *Mattinata* in Medieval Italy," pp. 261–282.

Mathews, Grieco S. F., "The Body, Appearance, and Sexuality." In *A History of Women in the West: Resistance and Enlightenment Paradoxes*, edited by Natalie Zemon Davis and Arlette Farge. Cambridge, Mass.: Harvard University Press, 1993, pp. 46–84.

Vroom, Theresia de. "In the Context of 'Rough Music': The Representation of Unequal Couples in Some Medieval Plays." *European Medieval Drama* 2 (1998): 237–260.

See also **Honor and Reputation; Marriage, Christian; Sexuality: Extramarital Sex; Sexuality: Female Same Sex Relations; Sexuality: Male Same-Sex Relations; Sexuality, Regulation of; Sexuality: Sex in Marriage**

CHARMS
See **Magic and Charms**

CHARTERS

Charters are documents written in a standardized way certifying such legal acts as contracts, donations, or testaments, as well as juridical, royal, or papal instructions. From the downfall of the Roman administration until the sixth century, recording and keeping the former more temporary charters to testify a juridical act was of increasing importance in the Middle Ages. For its value it was vital to include all people related to the act in the written testament as well as to name as many witnesses as possible. Charters therefore are considered valuable sources because, contrary to normative texts, they describe authentic situations, and further unintentionally reveal information regarding social, political, and religious history. On the other hand, charters were subject to severe stylization. This resulted in the generous addition of invented details, where the common form required them; at the same time, uncommon features were left out.

Although limited in their ability to exercise and defend their rights, medieval women participated in these documented transactions as issuers, recipients, or subjects, but rarely as witnesses. Furthermore, noble women and abbesses had the privilege of certifying documents with their own seals from the twelfth century onward.

However, because of problematic and imbalanced textual traditions, charters of interest to ecclesiastical institutions are better preserved than, for example, charters of endowment or grants in marriage, which are known through formularies and example-collections. Nevertheless, considering the chances of survival, important differences in time and area and even between male and female religious communities must be noted. In Italy, for example, traditions of late antiquity resulted in early municipal documentation preserving private charters in great numbers.

Overall research on charters with regard to gender is still in its early stages. Herlihy (1962) undertook a quantitative analysis of the surviving early medieval private charters to gain an overview of the participation of women in donations to churches. Based on the results, he noted changes in women's general abilities to possess land. He, as well as Wemple (1981), who concentrated her study on charters from the monastery of Lorsch, tried to explain the fluctuations in their statistics of donations through changes in law of succession and family structures. However, new research found that these changing patterns of interaction were caused by declining interest in recording details: the more accepted the institution was, the less interest there was in documenting all persons participating in the transaction. The transactions of female donors especially got lost.

Unintended documented details about social life in private charters and testaments such as information about tenure structures and family organization, casual remarks about inheritance or purchase of holdings, as well as listings of owned or dedicated objects are rather more informative than quantitative studies. Donations can inform us about cults of saints, commemoration, and liturgical practices. However it is important to be aware of the formulaic and stylized elements in these documents.

Up to now, research regarding royal charters and women has focused on queens using their influence to intercede on behalf of protégées, and on situations in which queens issued charters themselves. Both situations concern women's political influence at royal courts.

As recipients female monasteries have also figured in studies interpreting the number and relevance of charters they received, and whether they could draft, copy, or archive them properly. Recent discussions have shown that religious women possessed fewer charters than their male counterparts, but whether that is due to lesser political relevance or a smaller chance of survival remains to be seen.

Overall the investigation of charters as sources, especially for women's history, is still in the process of development. There are still voluminous collections of private charters and even complete monastic archives, which are not edited or even catalogued, especially regarding late medieval documents, which deserve more attention. Basically, while using charters as sources, one has always to consider the special forms of these texts, as well as the individual interests, chances of survival, and context of transmission.

KATRINETTE BODARWÉ

References and Further Reading

Bodarwé, Katrinette. "Frühmittelalterliche Urkunden als frauengeschichtliche Quelle - Schenkerinnen und Zeuginnen in Fulda." In *Vielfalt der Geschichte: Lernen, Lehren und Erforschen vergangener Zeiten*, edited by Sabine Happ and Ulrich Nonn. Berlin: Wiss. Verl. Berlin, 2004, pp. 86–108.

———. "Gender and the Archive. The Preservation of Charters in Early Medieval Communities of Religious Women." In *Saints, Scholars and Politicians: Gender as a Tool in Medieval Studies: Festschrift in Honor of Anneke Mulder-Bakker*, edited by Mathilde van Dijk and René Nip. Turnhout: Brepols, 2005, pp. 109–130.

Broer, C. J. C. "Echtgenote, deelgenote, lotgenote: Over oorkonden als bron voor de vrouwengeschiedenis." In *Vrouw, familie en macht. Bronnen over vrouwen in de Middeleeuwen*, edited by Marco Mostert and others. Hilversum: Verloren, 1990, pp. 147–165.

Goetz, Hans-Werner. *Frauen im frühen Mittelalter: Frauenbild und Frauenleben im Frankenreich*. Weimar: Böhlau, 1995.

Gold, Penny S. "The Charters of le Ronceray d'Angers. Male/Female Interaction in Monastic Business." In *Medieval Women and the Sources of Medieval History*, edited by Joel T. Rosenthal. Athens: University of Georgia Press, 1990, pp. 122–132.

Hellmuth, Doris. *Frau und Besitz. Zum Handlungsspielraum von Frauen in Alamannien (700–940)*. Sigmaringen: Thorbecke, 1998.

Herlihy, David. "Land, Family and Women in Continental Europe (701–1200)." *Traditio* 18 (1962): 89–120

Signori, Gabrieli. *Vorsorgen - Vererben - Erinnern: kinder- und familienlose Erblasser in der städtischen Gesellschaft des Spätmittelalters*. Göttingen: Vandenhoeck & Ruprecht, 2001.

Skinner, Patricia. *Women in Medieval Italian Society, 500–1200*. Harlow: Longman, 2001.

Stieldorf, Andrea. *Rheinische Frauensiegel : zur rechtlichen und sozialen Stellung weltlicher Frauen im 13. und 14. Jahrhundert*. Cologne: Böhlau, 1999.

Wemple, Suzane Fonay. *Women in Frankish Society: Marriage and the Cloister (500 to 900)*. Philadelphia, Pa.: University of Pennsylvania Press, 1981.

See also **Administration of Estates; Monasticism and Nuns; Records, Ecclesiastical; Records, Rural; Records, Urban**

CHASTITY AND CHASTE MARRIAGE

Christianity has traditionally elevated chastity over marriage, a ranking supported by the New Testament. Although Christ's elliptical references to "eunuchs for the kingdom of heaven" (Matt. 19:11–12) have been interpreted as a recommendation for chastity, the real impetus came from St. Paul. His preference for chastity over marriage was largely pragmatic: the end of the world was at hand and, in this context, marriage and sexuality were dangerous distractions. Hence he urged individuals not yet married to remain so while those who "have wives be as if they had none" (1 Cor. 7:29).

Not supported yet.

His ambiguous instructions regarding the marriage of an anonymous virgin is also widely understood as endorsing total chastity in marriage, a phenomenon that came to be known as spiritual marriage (1 Cor. 7:36–38). Paul's apprehension of sexual activity was reinforced by the philosophical tradition which represented marriage as incompatible with the life of the mind. Already in the second century, however, zealous factions in the church began to ascribe a special meaning to the purity associated with chastity, especially virginity, as a realization of the angelic life that the elect would enjoy at the world's end (Matt. 22:30). The presence of groups of consecrated widows and virgins in the early church indicate that women were understandably drawn to a life of chastity. In addition to freeing women from the dangers of childbirth, a vow of chastity was widely perceived as enabling a woman to transcend her physical inferiority to achieve parity with men.

Spiritual Marriage

With the fourth-century conversion of the Roman Empire, ascetic fervor was on the rise and the virginal ideal began to make permanent inroads into the Christian ideology of marriage, lending theoretical ballast to spiritual marriage. Orthodox authorities such as Ambrose (d. 397) and Jerome (d. 420) extolled the merits of virginity and even claimed it was accorded extra merit in heaven, prompting an anti-ascetic backlash. In an effort to assert parity between marriage and virginity, Jovinian argued that Mary and Joseph went on to have children subsequent to the incarnation—a perfectly reasonable assumption in view of the scriptural references to Christ's brethren (Matt. 12:48; Luke 21:23). Jerome, however, countered with the assertion that both Mary and Joseph had consecrated their virginity to God and that their union remained unconsummated. Although Jerome regarded Joseph as Mary's guardian rather than husband, Augustine (d. 430) would uphold the spiritual marriage of Mary and Joseph as the ideal, asserting that its exceptional purity rendered it more perfect and more durable than its carnal counterpart. Augustine's argument was based on Roman matrimonial law, which emphasized consent over consummation in the formation of the contract. In the twelfth century, Augustine's consensual delineation of marriage would be upheld in the *Sentences* of Peter Lombard (c. 1140), and the union of Mary and Joseph enshrined at the center of Christian marriage.

Spiritual marriages existed well before they became the center of theological debate. In the second century, the *Sentences* of Sextus urged sexual abstention in marriage; the visionary Hermas was advised by his angelic guide to live with his wife as a sister; Clement of Alexandria also commended matrimonial chastity. Moreover, the apocryphal gospels, written sometime in the second and third centuries, represented spiritual marriage as a lively possibility in the ascetic circles of the Eastern church.

Spiritual marriage tends to follow two basic models. Either the couple would vow virginity on their wedding night, as eventually became exemplified in the fifth-century hagiographical representation of the marriage of Saints Cecilia and Valerian, or they would make a seasoned transition to chastity, usually after having children. In practice, spiritual marriage was something of a compromise formation, since it was often initiated by women who would have preferred a life of chastity, but were compelled to marry.

Women participating in spiritual marriages often enjoyed the relaxation of gender roles associated with female chastity, an effect that was already a bone of contention in the patristic period. Augustine wrote a very stern letter to the matron Ecdicia who, having convinced her husband to vow chastity, began to dress like a widow and assert financial autonomy. In keeping with his view of consensual marriage, Augustine argued the husband's rule was not impaired but actually strengthened by the suspension of sexual activity. But there were a number of contemporary examples that suggest the opposite. After nearly dying in childbirth, Melania the Younger (d. 438) finally convinced her husband, Pinian, to vow chastity and emerged as the dominant party of their union.

Separation of Spouses

As monasticism increasingly became an option, couples tended to pursue their vocation to chastity in separate religious communities. Such separations were favored by church authorities, who had gradually come to regard intramarital chastity with suspicion, not only for fear of sexual relapses but also for the potential disruption of normative gender roles. Even so, the phenomenon continued in a number of guises. In the Germanic successor states, many a queen was represented as either convincing her husband to vow chastity or unilaterally refusing to consummate the marriage. Bede claims that Queen Aethelthryth of Northumbria (d. 679) managed to preserve her chastity through not just one, but two marriages, before her exasperated second husband finally permitted her to take the veil. Chroniclers and hagiographers often put the topos of spiritual marriage to a somewhat cynical use: it was a convenient excuse for the repudiation of an infertile wife, as in the case of the Carolingian queen Ricardis (d. c. 895). It could also dignify an infertile union, as with the cult surrounding Empress Cunegund (d. 1033).

Even though spiritual marriage was usually undertaken voluntarily, it was temporarily wielded by the Western church as a disciplinary measure in its struggle to establish a celibate clergy. Authorities such as Pope Leo I (d. 461) forbade any husband ordained subsequent to marriage to abandon his wife, recommending cohabitation as brother and sister. There are a number of saintly bishops, such as Severus of Ravenna (d. c. 390), who allegedly succeeded in this transition. But conciliar evidence and the testimony of historians such as Gregory of Tours (d. 594) suggest that all too many of these clerical couples lapsed into marital relations. The church finally abandoned this strategy in the eleventh century when the Gregorian Reformers led an all-out attack on clerical marriage, reversing its previous position by forcing clerics to abandon their wives.

With the rise of popular piety in the High and later Middle Ages, spiritual marriage plays a visible role in a number of pious wives' struggle for autonomy. In keeping with the general democratization of sanctity in this period, moreover, spiritual marriage is not just attributed to a handful of elite saints, but becomes more broadly based socially. The fourteenth-century Provençal saints Elzear de Sabran and Dauphine de Puimichel, whose marriage of twenty-four years was never consummated, were members of the aristocracy. But women such as Mary of Oignies (d. 1213) and Margery Kempe (d. after 1438), who converted their husbands to chastity in the course of their marriages, were both members of the bourgeoisie.

Spiritual marriage as a practice was probably pioneered by pious women as a vehicle for greater freedom, but the concept was often manipulated for the opposite purpose. Augustine would argue that the transition to chastity increased the husband's authority; hagiographers could invoke the theme of spiritual marriage to conceal the repudiation of a wife; while it was deployed by the church to enforce clerical chastity. These many applications testify to the instability and ultimate malleability of any ideological construct.

DYAN ELLIOTT

References and Further Reading

Atkinson, Clarissa. "'Precious Balsam in a Fragile Glass': The Ideology of Virginity in the Later Middle Ages." *Journal of Family History* 8 (1983): 131–143.

Brown, Peter. *The Body and Society: Men, Women, and Sexual Renunciation in Early Christianity.* New York: Columbia University Press, 1988.

Bugge, John. *Virginitas: An Essay in the History of a Medieval Ideal.* The Hague: Martinus Nijhoff, 1975.

Castelli, Elizabeth. "Virginity and Its Meaning for Women's Sexuality in Early Christianity." *Journal of Feminist Studies in Religion* 2 (1986): 61–88.

Clark, Elizabeth. "John Chrysostom and the Subintroductae." *Church History* 46 (1977): 171–185.

De Gaiffier, Baudouin. "*Intactam sponsam relinquens* à propos la vie de S. Alexis." *Analecta Bollandiana* 65 (1947): 157–195.

Elliott, Dyan. *Spiritual Marriage: Sexual Abstinence in Medieval Wedlock.* Princeton, N.J.: Princeton University Press, 1993.

Elm, Susanna. *'Virgins of God': The Making of Asceticism in Late Antiquity.* Oxford: Clarendon Press, 1994.

Evans, Ruth. "Virginities." In *The Cambridge Companion to Medieval Women's Writing*, edited by Carolyn Dinshaw and David Wallace. Cambridge: Cambridge University Press, 2003, pp. 21–39.

Gold, Penny. "The Marriage of Mary and Joseph in the Twelfth-Century Theology of Marriage." In *Sexual Practices and the Medieval Church*, edited by Vern Bullough and James Brundage. Buffalo and New York: Pantheon, 1982, pp. 102–117, 249–251.

Labriolle, Pierre de. "Le 'mariage spirituel' dans l'antiquité chrétienne." *Revue historique* 137 (1921): 204–225.

McNamara, Jo Ann. "Chaste Marriage and Clerical Celibacy." In *Sexual Practices and the Medieval Church*, edited by Vern Bullough and James Brundage. Buffalo and New York: Pantheon, 1982, pp. 22–33, 231–235.

Salih, Sarah. *Versions of Virginity in Late Medieval England.* Woodbridge, Suffolk: D. S. Brewer, 2001.

Vauchez, André. *The Laity in the Middle Ages: Religious Beliefs and Devotional Practices*, edited by Daniel Bornstein. Trans. Margery Schneider. South Bend, Ind.: University of Notre Dame Press, 1993.

Wogan-Browne, Jocelyn. "Chaste Bodies: Frames and Experiences." In *Framing Medieval Bodies*, edited by Sarah Kay and Miri Rubin. Manchester and New York: Manchester University Press, 1994, pp. 24–42.

See also **Asceticism; Augustine, Influence of; Celibacy, Clerical and Priests' Concubines; Conjugal Debt; Gender Ideologies; Hagiography; Jerome, Influence of; Laywomen, Religious; Marriage, Christian; Sexuality: Regulation of; Virgin Martyrs; Virginity; Virile Women; Vowesses**

CHAUCER, GEOFFREY

Geoffrey Chaucer's father was a prominent London vintner and deputy to the king's butler, and as a boy Chaucer (c. 1340–1400) entered the royal household as a page to the Countess of Ulster, wife of Lionel, son of Edward III. He later served in a variety of civil service capacities for the king. Eventually made a knight, he was part of a rising class of "esquires en service" who earned the rank of knight by money and service rather than by blood and warfare. His position as inside and outside of the court marked Chaucer as a liminal figure, a position perhaps reflected in such characters as Pandarus in *Troilus and Criseyde*, a notorious go-between in the royal household, and certainly in his self-portrait in the *Canterbury Tales*, where he appears as one who is at once oblivious to his surroundings and unusually knowledgeable of all those around him. Described there as an elvish "popet," or doll, Chaucer's liminality might associate him with the feminine.

Chaucer traveled abroad frequently on the king's business, and during his trips to Italy in the 1370s was introduced to the poetry of Dante, Petrarch, and Boccaccio, all of whom, in combination with the great French writers of the day, such as Guillaume de Machaut, influenced his writing profoundly. A skilled diplomat—despite his association with numerous courtiers who came into conflict with Richard, some eventually executed—Chaucer managed to avoid condemnation even after the deposition of Richard II. He apparently suffered an initial setback in finances when Henry IV came to the throne, but his pension was reinstated by the new king, perhaps in response to his short poem, "A Complaint to His Purse," a lyric in which Chaucer describes his purse as a hard-hearted, fair lady who refuses to grant him favors. He was also associated with a group of so-called Lollard-knights, though Chaucer's relationship to Lollardy, a movement which would later become heretical, is unclear. Although Chaucer may well have written for the court, his primary sources of income derived from his services to the king's household, and he is buried in what later became poet's corner of Westminster Abbey, not for his poetry but for these services.

Chaucer and Women

Little is known about Chaucer's relationships to women. Probable compliments to Richard's wife, Anne of Bohemia, in the *Legend of Good Women* and in *Troilus and Criseyde*, suggest he was an admirer of Anne. He had close ties to the royal household since he was married to Phillippa Roet, sister of Katherine Swynford, long-time mistress, then third wife, of Richard II's uncle, John of Gaunt. Chaucer's early poem the *Book of The Duchess* was written in honor of Blanche of Lancaster, Gaunt's first wife, who died of the plague.

A tantalizing fragment of the Life Records (a collection of records concerning Chaucer's life as a courtier, diplomat, and civil servant from civil, ecclesiastical, and private sources) tells us that in 1380 Chaucer was released from the charge of *raptus* by Cecily Chaumpaigne. Almost nothing is known about Cecily, and the surviving documents concerning this *raptus* are difficult to interpret. The term *raptus* is ambiguous and can refer to forced coitus or abduction, often for the purposes of marriage. Christopher Cannon has argued that the term *raptus* in this case does refer to forced coitus. Whatever the meaning of the document, its implications for Chaucer's poetry are difficult to construe. Representations of rape do occur with some regularity in Chaucer's writing (for example, an attempted rape in "The Man of Law's Tale," a rape of a mother and daughter in "The Reeve's Tale," threat of rape in *Troilus and Criseyde*, and rape in the "Legend of Philomela") and Chaucer's understanding of rape is worth considering; indeed, Chaucer is one of the first to use the term *rape* in English, though the passage in which this word occurs in *Troilus and Criseyde* certainly refers to abduction without physical violation.

Writing in English

Chaucer is known as "the Father of English poetry," an attribution associating him with the establishment of a patriarchal English literary voice. Although his writing encompasses a variety of classes from the royal to the middle classes with a glance at laborers, his work is directed to the concerns and interests of the aristocracy, to whom he most likely read his work. He probably wrote initially in the language of literature of the court, French, and had some training in Latin. He is known above all, however, as the first to produce a large body of literature specifically written in English. His works include translations of Boethius and the *Romance of the Rose*, a number of short lyrics and several dream visions (*The Book of the Duchess*, *The House of Fame*, *The Parliament of Fowles*), the long narrative poem *Troilus and Criseyde*, the *Legend of Good Women*, and the *Canterbury Tales*, a collection of 29 poems, several of which are in the voices of women. Chaucer was well acquainted with the predominant courtly idiom, in which women are placed on a pedestal by a longing adulterous male lover, but his works suggest dislike of such motifs and many criticize courtly conventions, celebrating instead married love.

Portraits of Women

Chaucer was dubbed by Gavin Douglas as "womanis frend." Critics have debated whether or not his varied portraits of women are favorable to women. Carolyn

Dinshaw and Elaine Tuttle Hansen investigate Chaucer's complex and sensitive engagement with contemporary misogyny, articulated most clearly in the writings of the Church Fathers. His representations of women range from aristocratic courtly heroines to milkmaids, from contemporary figures including cloth merchants and prioresses to historical figures such as saints and classical heroines. His two most famous characters are Criseyde and the Wife of Bath. Chaucer bases much of his portrait of Criseyde on Boccaccio's *Il Filostrato*. Unlike Boccaccio, however, Chaucer resists condemning Criseyde as the quintessential faithless woman. In Jill Mann's view, Chaucer's unexpected play with gender roles, in which he allows Troilus to demonstrate feminine attributes, suggests Chaucer's sensitivity to the constructed nature of gender.

In the *Legend of Good Women*, fictionally occasioned by the God of Love's criticism of Chaucer for writing negative portraits of women, Chaucer contributes to the debate about women popular in continental literature and especially engaged by Christine de Pizan. He writes nine tales of classical women drawn from Ovid's *Heroides*. Chaucer's purposes in his defense of women are difficult to construe since the work is incomplete and since each female heroine is extolled for her passive victimization.

The female characters in the *Canterbury Tales* provoke controversial readings. The Wife of Bath is understood, on the one hand, as a skillful manipulator of Christian misogynistic discourse, perhaps a would-be cleric demonstrating her mastery of rhetoric despite her lack of formal education, and as a visionary rewriter of romance; on the other hand, she is seen as a wistful, aging woman who cannot envision herself as having an identity outside marriage and who in her tale inscribes male wish fulfillment. Constance, of the "Man of Law's Tale," is seen by some as a passive nothing subject to the whims of a Christian patriarchy, and by others as a skillful promulgator of Christianity and an effective agent despite apparent passivity. Griselda, heroine of the "Clerk's Tale," is particularly problematic, seen, on the one hand, as a passive victim of a brutal patriarchal economy whose passivity is so extreme that she allows her own children to be killed, and, on the other hand, as an exemplar of free will—by upholding a promise she makes to herself as much as to others she asserts her relative autonomy as a Christian subject. Despite the fact that major critical studies have presented thorough considerations of both positive and negative views of Chaucer, much work on Chaucer's historical relationships to women and on his representations of women still needs to be done.

ELIZABETH ROBERTSON

References and Further Reading

Benson, Larry et al. *The Riverside Chaucer*. Boston: Houghton Mifflin, 1987.
Cannon, Christopher. "*Raptus* in the Chaumpaigne Release and a Newly Discovered Document Concerning the Life of Geoffrey Chaucer." *Speculum* 68 (1993): 74–94.
Cox, Catherine. *Gender and Language in Chaucer*. Gainesville: University of Florida Press, 1997.
Crane, Susan. *Gender and Romance in Chaucer's Canterbury Tales*. Princeton, N.J.: Princeton University Press, 1991.
Dinshaw, Carolyn. *Chaucer's Sexual Poetics*. Madison, Wis.: University of Wisconsin Press, 1989.
Hansen, Elaine Tuttle. *Chaucer's Fictions of Gender*. Berkeley, Calif.: University of California Press, 1992.
Mann, Jill. *Feminizing Chaucer*. Cambridge, U.K.: D. S. Brewer, 1991, 2002.
———. *The Canterbury Tales*. New York: Penguin, 2005.
Martin, Priscilla. *Chaucer's Women: Nuns, Wives and Amazons*. Iowa City, Iowa: University of Iowa Press, 1990.
Patterson, Lee. *Chaucer and the Subject of History*. Madison, Wis.: University of Wisconsin Press, 1991.

See also **Constance; Courtly Love; Criseyde; Literacy and Reading, Vernacular; Literature, Middle English; Lollards; Patronage, Literary; Rape and Raptus; Wife of Bath**

CHELLES
See **Jouarre and Chelles**

CHILDBIRTH
See **Pregnancy and Childbirth: Christian Women; Pregnancy and Childbirth: Jewish Women**

CHILDREN
See **Children, Betrothal and Marriage of; Family (Earlier Middle Ages); Family (Later Middle Ages); Girls and Boys**

CHILDREN, BETROTHAL AND MARRIAGE OF

Medieval canonists and theologians distinguished promises to marry at a future time (betrothal) from promises to marry in the present (marriage), although this distinction was not as sharply etched in the minds of the laity. Formal betrothal contracts (*sponsalia*), with detailed specification of performance contingencies, were ordinarily concluded by high-status couples whose families and kinsmen were adroit at arranging socially and politically consequential marriages.

These acts of family diplomacy frequently affected very young children. The large majority of couples doubtlessly entered into informal, private agreements for future marriage or contracted marriages without the preliminary betrothal.

Under Roman civil and canon law, the minimum age for contracting marriage was twelve for girls and fourteen for boys, the ages roughly corresponding to the onset of puberty. The church followed Roman civil law in setting the minimum age for betrothal at the completion of seven years. A valid betrothal and marriage under civil and canon law was grounded in the freely given consent of the bride and groom. In southern Europe, it was customary for parents and kinsmen, with the assistance of professional match-makers, to arrange the marriage of a nubile girl—namely, choose a spouse, establish the dates of the betrothal and marriage, and settle the amount of her dowry. Unless the girl contested the betrothal, claiming that she was forced by her parents or kinsmen to accept the arranged marriage, her consent was presumed valid under civil and canon law.

While quantitative data on the ages at which couples were betrothed in the Middle Ages are not abundant, they can be estimated from ages at first marriage. In Italy women were married in their late teens to older men. The extreme case was fifteenth-century Florence, where the average age at first marriage for women was eighteen, and for men, thirty-one years. The available evidence suggests short intervals between betrothal and marriage, typically a year or less. In England after the Black Death, rural women tended to marry between their late teens and early twenties; urban women, in their twenties. In both cases husbands were three to four years older than their brides. English women were betrothed later than Italian women, while English men were betrothed earlier than their Italian counterparts.

Carolingian polyptychs, Norse sagas, saint's lives, chronicles, records of legal disputes, and family archives are among the primary sources testifying to the marriage of girls shortly after puberty. Chaucer's indefatigable Wife of Bath had married five times since the age of twelve. Likewise, at the age of twelve, Margaret of Beaufort was married to Edmund Tudor, and at age thirteen she became both a widow and the mother of the future King Henry VII. Royal and aristocratic families regularly secured alliances through the betrothal of children under twelve years of age. Isabelle of France was seven when her betrothal to King Richard II of England was arranged. The eleven betrothals and marriages celebrated by the Neville family between 1412 and 1436 included thirteen children under sixteen years, eight of whom had not yet reached twelve, and one of whom was only

six. Uncertainty hovered around the betrothals of docile young children, who, upon reaching marriageable age, were required to publicly affirm or disaffirm before a bishop or his court betrothals arranged on their behalf by parents and kinsmen. Consent transformed these betrothals into enforceable contracts.

An exceptional source for studying betrothals and marriages of young children is the *Decretals of Gregory IX* (1244). At the beginning of the title, "The Betrothal of the Prepubescent" (X 4. 2), Isidore of Seville (*Etym.* XI, 2) was cited as the source for the definition of pubescence, which he derived from pubis, named for the pudenda where the body's soft hair first appears. Puberty was not strictly determined by reaching the threshold ages, fourteen and twelve, but occurred when males could generate and females could become pregnant (X 4. 2. 3, *Puberes*). Making the physical capacity to engage in procreative sexual intercourse the defining feature of marriageable age made sense, given the difficulties in ascertaining someone's precise age in this period. In a dispute in which an older man "was betrothed to a certain girl in her cradle" and then married the girl's mother, Pope Alexander III (1159–1181) ruled that if the marriage of the man and the mother had been celebrated before the girl had reached the age of seven, they could remain joined in marriage, for betrothals "made in the cradle" were not enforceable (X 4. 2. 4, *Litteras tuae*). Another case concerned a girl just under the age of twelve whose parents married her off. Upon attaining the age of twelve, she sought dissolution of the marriage and permission to marry someone else, denying that she had consented to marriage with the man chosen by her parents or that she had had conjugal relations with him. Alexander decided that in cases in which the husband alleged under oath that he had had conjugal relations with his wife, as here, and she denied it, truth resided with the husband. In addition, he held that if a girl under, but nearing, the age of twelve years consented to her betrothal, it was binding insofar as it had been approved by her parents, blessed by a priest, and followed by sexual relations with the groom (X 4. 2. 6, *Continebatur*).

Disputed betrothals and marriages of young children not surprisingly entailed allegations of forced consent resulting in unions tantamount to bondage. Pope Urban III (1185–1187) adjudicated a Pisan case in which a twelve-year-old girl was betrothed to a boy aged nine or ten. She alleged that her parents had installed her against her will in the home of the boy's father; that she was forced to stay there for about a year until she eventually returned home; and that not withstanding her mother's threats, "she [did] not want to have the boy as a husband." The Archbishop of Pisa reported that the boy in fact had neither reached the age of fourteen nor had sexual relations with the girl. Urban instructed the archbishop to admonish the girl to wait for the boy to complete his fourteenth year. Should she decide not to wait, she was permitted to take another man as her husband (X 4. 2. 11, *Ex litteris*). These and other papal decretals sought to reconcile the requirement that children's consent to betrothal and marriage be freely given against children's natural obligation to obey the wishes of parents and kinsmen.

Few young children could, or would, resist the force of parental domination, as the determined twelve-year old in the Pisan case had done. Yet, it would be naïve to dismiss the practical relevance of the decretals on the grounds that more often than not a child's consent was a formality. If the papal decretals were far from definitive and unevenly translated into practice, they certainly established authoritative points of departure employed by jurists and judges in dealing with the perennial questions of consent and coercion attending child betrothals and marriages.

JULIUS KIRSHNER

References and Further Reading

Cavallar, Osvaldo and Julius Kirshner. "Making and Breaking Betrothal Contracts (*Sponsalia*) in Late Trecento Florence," in *'Panta rei': Studi dedicati a Manlio Bellomo*, edited by Orazio Condorelli. Rome: Il Cigno, 2004. Vol. 1, pp. 395–452.

Goldberg, P. J. P. "For Better or Worse: Marriage and Economic Opportunity for Women in Town and Country," in *Women in Medieval English Society*, edited by P. J. P. Goldberg Phoenix Mill, Stroud, Gloucestershire: Sutton Publishing, 1997, pp. 108–125.

Herlihy, David, and Christiane Klapisch-Zuber. *Tuscans and Their Families: A Study of the Florentine Catasto of 1427*. New Haven and London: Yale University Press, 1985.

Onclin, Willy. "L'âge requis pour le marriage dans le doctrine canonique médiévale," in *Proceedings of the Second International Congress of Medieval Canon Law*, edited by Stephan Kuttner and J. J. Ryan. Vatican City: Vatican Library, 1965, pp. 237–247.

Ribordy, Geneviève. *'Faire les nopces': Le mariage del noblesse française (1375–1475)*. Toronto: Pontifical Institute of Medieval Studies, 2004, pp. 76–82; *Women, Marriage, and Family in Medieval Christendom: Essays in Memory of Michael M. Sheehan*. Kalamazoo: Medieval Institute Publications, 1998.

Valsecchi, Chiara. "*Causa Matrimonialis est gravis et ardua. Consiliatores* e matrimonio fino al Concilio di Trento," in *Studi di storia del diritto II*. Milan: Giuffrè, 1999, pp. 407–580.

See also **Betrothals; Girls and Boys; Marriage, Christian**

CHIVALRY

An idealized set of behaviors for mounted warriors, and by extension for all noble men, developed in France into a more or less explicit set of expectations in the twelfth century, collectively called chivalry (both then and now—*chevalerie* in Old French). Chivalry is known especially through literary works, epics, and romances. Although modern writers sometimes speak of a "code" of chivalry, it is a mistake to do so, as that would imply a clear set of guidelines that everyone recognized, whether or not they followed them. In fact, the expectations of chivalry were inherently contradictory, which meant that it was impossible for one man to meet them all (even if he had wanted to). A major reason why chivalry failed to develop into a coherent set of rules is that it was an amalgam of a number of very different sorts of expectations.

Originally the word *chevalerie* simply meant battlefield virtues: being a good fighter, brave, and loyal to one's fellows. A warrior on horseback (mounted on a *cheval*, or horse) was a knight (*chevalier*) and should, it was assumed, practice chivalry. This is the meaning that chivalry has, for example, in the *Song of Roland*. Nobly born men from the twelfth century onward defined themselves militarily; and young nobles were trained to be knights, that is, mounted fighters. Among the wealthy, a young man would undergo a knighting ceremony to mark his coming of age, often including a tournament to show off his combat skills.

But this basic meaning of the term, implying a warrior, quickly combined with other meanings as well. Most significantly, chivalry increasingly became united with courtesy (*cortoisie*), a term simply meaning suitable behavior for someone at court. By the time that Chrétien de Troyes wrote his romances in the final decades of the twelfth century, "chivalry" was assumed to include *both* battlefield and courtly attributes. A noble courtier was someone well-educated, who knew how to dance elegantly, perhaps play a musical instrument, who kept himself clean and finely attired, and was always polite and gentle to ladies. In addition, courtliness contained within it many of the assumptions—ultimately derived from classical stoicism—of correct manly behavior as constituting self-control and a composed demeanor. Unsurprisingly, warrior violence and restrained good manners mingled uncomfortably.

This already uneasy mix was further complicated by attempts to Christianize chivalry. The "knight of Christ" was an old topos within Christian thought, meaning someone who fought on the side of God. Often the fighting was metaphorical; monks, for example, often referred to themselves as knights of Christ, fighting evil with their prayers. But both church leaders and knights themselves believed it possible for secular warriors also to be good Christians, by defending the poor and helpless or especially by fighting the infidel in the Holy Land. By the thirteenth century elaborate ceremonies began to be developed that stressed a young knight's simultaneous adoption of the attributes of a warrior and those of a devout Christian. A young man might spend the night in prayer before his formal knighting, and religious symbols were attached to his equipment; the sword, for example, was considered to represent the sign of the cross as the blade met the hilt.

In practice, of course, as everyone recognized, no one could at the same time be a ferocious fighter, a gentle wooer of ladies, and a deeply religious man. The inherent contradictions within any definition of chivalry were used as the starting point for many contemporary works of literature. Every author came up with his own definition, which seems to have been intended in part to refute the definitions of other authors. Many twelfth-century authors started their stories by saying that the deeds took place in ancient times, when men still understood chivalry, "unlike today." This false sense of nostalgia is rather ironic, given that the authors were writing when chivalry was brand new. Rather than simply glorifying chivalry, the authors critiqued many of its aspects, particularly its violence, and sought to indicate that not even the most glorious heroes of old could live up to chivalry's requirements. Indeed, the plots of many epics and romances turned on irreconcilable demands, such as those of love and honor, both of which were considered aspects of a chivalrous knight but which heroes, like Chretien's Erec, discovered they could not simultaneously follow. Only at the end of the Middle Ages, in the fourteenth and fifteenth centuries, did systematic treatises seek to set out clear definitions and guidelines on how a knight could meet them—and the multiplication of such treatises itself indicates that no single definition yet predominated.

CONSTANCE B. BOUCHARD

References and Further Reading

Bouchard, Constance Brittain. "*Strong of Body, Brave and Noble": Chivalry and Society in Medieval France*. Ithaca, N.Y.: Cornell University Press, 1998.
———. "*Every Valley Shall Be Exalted": The Discourse of Opposites in Twelfth-Century Thought*. Ithaca, N.Y.: Cornell University Press, 2003.
Chickering, Howell, and Thomas H. Seiler, eds. *The Study of Chivalry*. Kalamazoo, Mich.: Medieval Institute, 1988.
Flori, Jean. "La notion de chevalerie dans les chansons de geste du XIIe siècle: Étude historique de vocabulaire." *Le moyen âge* 81 (1975), 211–244, 407–445.
———. *L'essor de la chevalerie, XIe-XIIe siècles*. Geneva: Droz, 1986.
Jaeger, C. Stephen. *The Origins of Courtliness: Civilizing Trends and the Formation of Courtly Ideals, 939–1210*. Philadelphia: University of Pennsylvania Press, 1985.
Kaeuper, Richard W. *Chivalry and Violence in Medieval Europe*. Oxford: Oxford University Press, 1999.
Karras, Ruth Mazo. *From Boys to Men: Formations of Masculinity in Late Medieval Europe*. Philadelphia: University of Pennsylvania Press, 2003.
Keen, Maurice. *Chivalry*. New Haven: Yale University Press, 1984.
Painter, Sidney. *French Chivalry*. Baltimore: Johns Hopkins University Press, 1940.

See also **Courtly Love; Gender Ideologies; Tournaments; Warfare**

CHRÉTIEN DE TROYES

All we know about Chrétien de Troyes comes to us from his unusually abundant corpus. His extant works include five romances (c. 1165–1191), two lyric poems in the style of the troubadours, a translation of Ovid's *Philomela* (surviving only in the fourteenth-century *Ovide moralisé*), and possibly *Guillaume d'Angleterre*, a saint's life cast as a romance and signed by Chrétien (the attribution is disputed by scholars). The prologue to his second romance, *Cligès*, begins with an inventory of his works: *Erec et Enide* (the first Arthurian romance), translations of Ovid's treatises on love, two tales from the *Metamorphoses* (his tale of Pelops has been lost), and a story of "King Mark and Yseut the Blond," no longer extant but whose unexpected title tantalizingly evokes a version of the popular Tristan legend, which Chrétien continually reinvents in his romances. In *Le Chevalier de la Charrette* (The Knight of the Cart), commissioned by Marie de Champagne, Chrétien rewrites Arthurian history (as represented by Geoffrey of Monmouth and his French translator Wace), by introducing Lancelot as the queen's rescuer and lover. Their open-ended love story powers the enormous expansion of the *Prose Lancelot* at the heart of the thirteenth-century Vulgate Cycle and serves as the model for Gaston Paris's invention of "courtly love" in the nineteenth century, a term whose definition continues to cause passionate debate. Allusions to the *Charrette* in *Le Chevalier au lion* (The Knight of the Lion) suggest that Chrétien wrote both romances simultaneously, which may explain why a second author finished Lancelot's story, according to Chrétien's design, as Godefroi de Leigni claims in the epilogue. Chrétien's last romance, *Le Conte du graal* (The Story of the Grail), dedicated to Philip of Flanders, was left unfinished despite its unusual length (nine thousand plus verses rather than the usual seven thousand). Like the *Charrette*, it launched a powerful new story that generated countless retellings across the Middle Ages and into the modern era.

Chrétien's name and literary patrons locate him in the courtly culture of northern France. His works address an aristocratic public of ladies, knights, counts, and barons, connoisseurs able to appreciate his highly refined fictions, his art of finding in common matter—oral and written, Classical and vernacular, Breton and French—a point of departure for his own experiments in rewriting. Chrétien arranges stories into a "very beautiful *conjointure*" (joining), whose patterns woven into the narrative require us to discover the possible meanings they inscribe. Read out loud to a courtly audience, his romances invite the listeners to enjoy the apparent distance of Arthurian adventures, as well as their obvious, if indirect reflection of contemporary problems that undoubtedly engaged a twelfth-century public, as they continue to interest us: the balance of power among men, and between men and women, the relation between courtly values, especially love and prowess, the difficulty of deciphering truth in a world of appearances, the pitfalls and promise of language, the gray areas of life that mitigate against any easy solutions into black and white.

If women are by definition secondary in a world of romance centered on chivalric heroism, Chrétien has nevertheless invented a constellation of memorable female characters who play a variety of necessary roles that orient, support, and elucidate the heroes' quests. The title of his first romance fittingly gives equal billing to its male and female protagonists, as it puts into play the difficulties of integrating love and marriage, while maintaining an appropriate balance between public and private obligations, chivalry and love. Chrétien's romances show an unusual commitment to marital love but they by no means limit love's domain to the confines of social institutions; witness the extramarital liaisons of Fenice and Cligès, and Guenevere and Lancelot. Critics argue about the attitudes expressed toward these couples through narrators' voices and authorial architecture; what remains certain is Chrétien's focus on contradictory values and experiences, left unresolved in his romances through ambiguities and puzzles. Feminist critics suggest that Chrétien gives less and less place to heroines, but one might also argue that as each romance explores different issues, other roles for female characters emerge, including author-figures like Thessala and Lunete whose machinations move ahead the stories of Cligès and Yvain, the proliferation of ladies and damsels attracted by the erotic force field around Lancelot, or the mothers of Perceval, Gauvain, and Arthur, who assume enigmatic importance in the last romance, where the relationship between love and the (not yet holy) grail remains problematic.

MATILDA TOMARYN BRUCKNER

References and Further Reading

Bruckner, Matilda Tomaryn. "A Case for *mise en abyme*: Chrétien's *Chevalier de la Charrete*." In *Shaping Romance: Interpretation, Truth, and Closure in Twelfth-Century French Fictions*. Philadelphia, Pa.: University of Pennsylvania Press, 1993.

Burns, E. Jane. "Rewriting Men's Stories: Enide's Disruptive Mouths." In *Bodytalk: When Women Speak in Old French Literature*. Philadelphia, Pa.: University of Pennsylvania Press, 1993, pp. 151–202.

Chrétien de Troyes. *Yvain: The Knight of the Lion*. translated by Burton Raffel. New Haven and London: Yale University Press, 1987.

———. *Erec and Enide*. translated by Burton Raffel. New Haven and London: Yale University Press, 1997.

———. *Cligès*. translated by Burton Raffel. New Haven/London: Yale University Press, 1997.

———. *Lancelot: The Knight of the Cart*. translated by Burton Raffel. New Haven/London: Yale University Press, 1997.

———. *Perceval, The Story of the Grail*. translated by Burton Raffel. New Haven/London: Yale University Press, 1999.

Gaunt, Simon. "The Knight Meets his Match: Romance." In *Gender and Genre in Medieval French Literature*. Cambridge: Cambridge University Press, 1995, pp. 71–121.

Grimbert, Joan. "On Fenice's Vain Attempts to Revise a Romantic Archetype and Chrétien de Troyes's Fabled Hostility to the Tristan Legend." In *Reassessing the Heroine in Medieval French Literature*. edited by Kathy M. Krause. Gainesville: University Press of Florida, 2001, pp. 87–106.

Haidu, Peter. *Aesthetic Distance in Chrétien de Troyes: Irony and Comedy in* Cligès *and* Perceval. Geneva: Droz, 1968.

Hunt, Tony. *Chrétien de Troyes: Yvain*. Critical Guides to French Texts. London: Grant & Cutler, 1986.

Kelly, Douglas. *"Sens" and "Conjointure" in the "Chevalier de la charrette."* The Hague and Paris: Mouton, 1966.

Krueger, Roberta. *Women Readers and the Ideology of Gender in Old French Verse Romance*. Cambridge: Cambridge University Press, 1993.

Lacy, Norris. *The Craft of Chrétien de Troyes: An Essay on Narrative Art*. Leiden: Brill, 1980.

Lancelot and Guinevere: A Casebook. edited by Lori Walters. New York/London: Garland, 1996.

Maddox, Donald. *The Arthurian Romances of Chrétien de Troyes*. Cambridge: Cambridge University Press, 1991.

McCracken, Peggy. *The Romance of Adultery: Queenship and Sexual Transgression in Old French Literature*. Philadelphia, Pa.: University of Pennsylvania Press, 1998.

Pickens, Rupert. *The Welsh Knight: Paradoxicality in Chrétien's* Conte del Graal. Lexington, KY: French Forum, Publishers, 1977.

The Romances of Chrétien de Troyes: A Symposium. Edited by Douglas Kelly. Lexington, Ky.: French Forum Publishers, 1985.

Primary Sources

Chrétien de Troyes. *Romans, suivis des Chansons, avec, en appendice, Philomena*. La Pochothèque. Paris: La Librairie Générale Française, 1994.

CHRISTINA OF MARKYATE

Christina of Markyate (b. 1096–1098; d. 1155–1156), virtually unknown for centuries, has in the past fifty years emerged as a key figure in the history of female spirituality. She filled numerous roles that exercise the modern imagination: vowed virgin resisting forced marriage, resolute heroine fighting the cruel socialization of her family, spiritual friend and confidante of important churchmen, and leader of a major, well-supported female community at Markyate, near the monastery of St. Albans, Huntingdonshire. Most of what we know about Christina comes from the *Gesta Abbatum*, a chronicle of St. Alban's compiled in the 1250s; the *St. Albans Psalter*, a lavishly illuminated manuscript compiled during Christina's lifetime and commemorating her family and friends; and a vividly dramatic *Life* (c. 1140–1150) drawing on Christina's own reminiscences. Christina, *née* Theodora (she renamed herself Christina sometime after her religious calling), was born into the Anglo-Saxon nobility in Huntingdon. As a girl, she vowed in a parish church to remain a virgin for life. At sixteen, she fended off the sexual advances (caused by Satan, according to the *Life*) of Ranulf Flambard, the powerful bishop of Durham. Flambard subsequently arranged her marriage to Burthred, a young nobleman, with the approval of Christina's parents, who forced her to consent to the marriage, then tried to make her consummate it. The family then embarked on an extraordinary campaign of coercion, combining the temptations of aristocratic society (fine clothes, banquets, the chance to head a noble household), flattery, threats, and ugly sexualized violence worthy not just of hagiographical villains but of fairy tale menaces. Christina's mother, Beatrix, maddened by her daughter's adamantine refusals, declared that "she would not care who deflowered her daughter, provided that some way of deflowering her could be found." In successive lurid scenes in the *Life*, the parents encouraged Burthred to rape Christina, alternately thrust her into freezing water and burned her, and her mother tore out Christina's hair, beat her, and exhibited her at a banquet. (Parenthetically, it should be noted that decades later, Christina's family, who had fallen on hard times, sought out her protection, and that they were even singled out for prayers in the St. Alban's Psalter, which was altered for Christina's use.)

Christina initially obtained support from the local bishop, but bribed by her parents, the bishop ultimately ruled against her. Finally, she ran away and obtained sanctuary at the cell of Alfwen, a local hermit, where she lived for two years; for four further years, she stayed with the hermit Roger, in a cranny about fourteen inches wide. Burthred finally released her from her marriage vow, and she continued to reside at Markyate, where her holy solitude attracted many admirers and imitators. Geoffrey, abbot of St. Alban's, helped formalize her community at Markyate into a priory with Christina at its head, encouraged the writing of the *Life*, commissioned the magnificent psalter, and subsequently gave the priory extensive financial backing and much public favor. Geoffrey's close friendship with Christina and his support of Markyate priory caused great resentment in the St. Albans community: his frequent visits to Christina's cell at Markyate gave rise to many rumors about a sexual relationship, and the diverting of rents and agricultural income to Markyate and others of Christina's favorite charities was a source of great hostility among the monks. There is strong evidence that the *Life* remained unfinished, and its transmission was suppressed, because of lingering resentment towards Christina at St. Albans.

Christina's life contains many features crucial to the history of spirituality, sexuality, marriage, and mysticism. Her childhood vow of virginity—which she accompanied with the payment of a penny and which was confirmed by Sueno, a canon of Huntingdon—took the form of a wedding with Christ, and was formalized much later at St Albans, at Geoffrey's insistence. This vow—in canon law as in the hagiography—took precedence over her forced consent to marriage (although, if she had consummated it, the situation might have been different). In narrative form, thematic use of commonplaces, and personal psychology, the *Life* strongly resembles earlier virgin martyr stories. Christina's visions were highly personal: in her youth, they involved the support of Christ and the Virgin Mary for her virginity vow, and in later years they often took the form of predictions and intimate knowledge of others' thoughts. Relations with men loom large in her visionary life: she attracts, and is attracted by, the hermit Roger; she and an unnamed cleric struggle at length with mutual sexual attraction (sometimes in the form of lurid demonic visions); and her friendship with Geoffrey and other spiritual companions was full of intimacy and passion. This spiritual love, cast by the biographer in a language reminiscent of eroticism, was not the same as generalized *caritas*: personal and exclusive, it can perhaps be best described as a passion of the soul.

ROBERT STANTON

References and Further Reading

Fanous, Samuel and Henrietta Leyser, eds. *Christina of Markyate: A Twelfth-Century Holy Woman*. London and New York: Routledge, 2005.

Head, Thomas. "The Marriages of Christina of Markyate." *Viator* 21 (1990): 75–101.

Holdsworth, Christopher J. "Christina of Markyate." In *Medieval Women*, edited by Derek Baker. Oxford: Blackwell, 1978, pp. 185–204.

Karras, Ruth Mazo. "Friendship and Love in the Lives of Two Twelfth-Century English Saints." *Journal of Medieval History* 14 (1988): 305–320.

Koopmans, Rachel M. "The Conclusion of Christina of Markyate's *Vita*." *Journal of Ecclesiastical History* 51.4 (October 2000): 663–697.

Pächt, Otto; Dodwell, C.R.; and Francis Wormald, eds. *The St. Albans Psalter*. London: Warburg Institute, 1960.

"The St. Albans Psalter Website." University of Aberdeen. http://www.abdn.ac.uk/stalbanspsalter/english/index.shtml (August 2005).

Stanton, Robert. "Marriage, Socialization and Domestic Violence in the *Life of Christina of Markyate*." In *Domestic Violence in Medieval Texts*, edited by Eve Salisbury, Georgianna Donavin, and Merrall Llewellyn Price. Gainesville: University Press of Florida, 2002, pp. 242–271.

Talbot, C. H. *The Life of Christina of Markyate*. Oxford Medieval Texts. Oxford: Oxford University Press, 1959. Reprint Toronto and Buffalo: University of Toronto Press, 1987.

See also **Bride of Christ: Imagery; England; Hagiography; Monasticism and Nuns; Noble Women; Virginity**

CHRISTINA THE ASTONISHING

Christina the Astonishing was born in St. Trond, close to the Flemish-French language border, in what we now call Belgium. She achieved local notoriety during her lifetime (1150–1224), and a cult emerged after her death. She was mentioned by James of Vitry in his *Life of Marie d'Oignies* and became the subject of her own *Life* in 1232 at the hands of the Dominican Thomas of Cantimpré.

She grew up the youngest of three daughters of a burgher family. She and her sisters lived a religious life together even after their parents died. At some point she died, or seemed to, for at the wake, she revived and told of her soul's journey to purgatory, hell and then paradise, where she chose to return to her body so as to use her life's example to turn sinners toward a saving penitence. At first she fled human contact and so, suspected of demon possession, was jailed. After gaining her freedom, she took on a regime of spectacular public suffering. She was incarcerated a second time. After again gaining her freedom, she adopted a more moderate life pattern. Thereupon, she is recorded as living a mendicant life of begging, exercising a gift of prophesy, taking on a penitential regime on behalf of the souls of purgatory, and coming to a holy end marked by confirming signs and the solemn translation of her body.

Christina's *Life* is an odd piece of hagiography. It has been difficult for scholars to categorize it within the conventions of one or another hagiographical model. It has been suggested that she be viewed in terms of the type of the "fool for Christ," as a "somatic preacher" who uses her resurrected body, with its glorious qualities, to live purgatory as an object lesson for her onlookers, as a "demoniac saint" whose "madness" is the very condition for a certain agency. All of these types are extreme. Indeed, her hagiographer's use of hyperbole and spectacle allows her *Life* to function as a test case for theses about women and their religious experience, or alternatively about a male hagiographer's expectations about women and their religious worth and experience.

For all of that, however, it is doubtful whether Christina would have come to assume the place she has in discussions of medieval women and their religious experience had it not been for the success of Caroline Walker Bynum's use of Carol Gilligan and symbolic anthropology to identify the form of an intensely embodied feminine spirituality demonstrably distinct from contemporary male analogues. Her eye for and clever deployment of what might be termed "spiritual grotesques" (with which the *Life of Christina the Astonishing* is replete) has created a taste for medieval spiritual spectacle that has allowed this strange riddle of a medieval woman and her brief, idiosyncratic *Life* to assume an outsized place in the current scholarly consciousness of medieval women's spirituality and religious experience.

ROBERT SWEETMAN

References and Further Reading

Bynum, Caroline Walker. *Holy Feast and Holy Fast: The Religious Significance of Food to Medieval Women*. Berkeley and Los Angeles: University of California Press, 1987.

King, Margot H. "The Sacramental Witness of Christina *Mirabilis*: The Mystic Growth of a Fool for Christ's Sake." In *Peaceweavers: Medieval Religious Women*, edited by John A. Nichols and Lillian Thomas Shank. Kalamazoo: Cistercian Publications, 1987: 145–164.

Newman, Barbara. "Possessed by the Spirit: Devout Women, Demoniacs, and the Apostolic Life in the Thirteenth Century." *Speculum* 73 (1998): 733–770.

———. "Devout Women and Demoniacs in the World of Thomas of Cantimpré. *New Trends in Feminine Spirituality: The Holy Women of Liège and Their Impact*, edited by Juliette Dor, Lesley Johnson, and Jocelyn Wogan-Browne. Turnhout: Brepols, 1999, pp. 35–60.

Sweetman, Robert. "Christine of Saint-Trond's Preaching Apostolate: Thomas of Cantimpré's Hagiographical Method Revisited." *Vox Benedictina* 9 (1992): 67–97.

Thomas of Cantimpré. *Vita beatae Christinae mirabilis virginis*, edited by J. Pinius in *Acta Sanctorum* 32 (24 July, 5). Paris: Victor Palme, 1868. pp. 650–660.

Thomas of Cantimpre. *The Life of Christina Mirabilis.* Trans. Margot H. King. Toronto: Peregrina, 1995.

See also **Asceticism; Flanders; Hagiography; Laywomen, Religious; Lutgard of Aywières; Marie of Oignies; Prophets**

CHRISTINE DE PIZAN

Though born in Venice in 1364, Christine de Pizan carries the name of her father's birthplace, Pizzano. Her father, Tommaso da Pizzano, was recruited by the French king, Charles V, to be his court astrologer; as a consequence, Christine moved from Venice to Paris as a child in 1368. About 1379 she became the wife of Etienne de Castel, a notary and royal secretary, and by 1385 she was the mother of two sons and a daughter. When her husband died unexpectedly of the plague in 1389, she suddenly found herself a widow with three children and a widowed mother to provide for, her father having died just before her husband. These circumstances induced her to begin composing and circulating poetry early in the 1390s, both as a vehicle to express her grief at the loss of her husband and as a means of acquiring royal or ducal patronage in order to support her dependants. Her initial poems earned her significant attention, and

Christine de Pizan giving instructions. From the "Works of Christine de Pizan." France, 15th CE. Harl.4431. Fol. 261v. (detail). Location: British Library, London, Great Britain. Credit: HIP / Art Resource, NY.

over the next twenty-five years she produced a wide range of texts in prose, as well as verse for a number of patrons in a variety of genres. During this time she was also involved in the production of manuscripts of her works; her skillful use of the institutions of patronage and book production have led modern scholars to designate her the first professional woman of letters in European history. In 1418, the civil conflict between the Burgundians and Armagnacs forced Christine to withdraw from Paris to the safety of an abbey outside the city, perhaps to Poissy where her daughter was a nun. Removed from the court and scriptorium, her literary activity all but ceased, although she composed a final poem in 1429 to celebrate the triumph of Joan of Arc in lifting the siege of Orleans and having Charles VII crowned in Rheims. Since no more is heard from Christine de Pizan after the composition of this poem, she is generally thought to have died before witnessing Joan of Arc's trial and death in 1431.

Times

Christine lived during a tumultuous period in late medieval France, and she witnessed a considerable amount of war and social upheaval. The Hundred Years' War (1337–1451), a conflict between the French and English kings, led to intermittent battles and the siege of French cities by English armies throughout her lifetime. In addition, a dispute between two factions in the royal family, the Burgundians and the Armagnacs, erupted into open conflict in Paris from 1411 onward; it was this civil war that prompted Christine to leave Paris in 1418. In addition, both the monarchy and the papacy experienced crises in leadership. From 1368 until 1422, France was ruled by Charles VI, a king who experienced frequent bouts of madness, and from 1378, the Papal Schism resulted in the election of two competing popes. Throughout her writings, Christine frequently speaks of her personal trials, particularly her widowhood, but she addresses as well these military and political events that concerned France and shaped life in late medieval Paris.

Works

Christine de Pizan left a corpus of texts that would be considered remarkable for any medieval author, but is especially extraordinary for a woman writer whose gender placed her at a substantial disadvantage in terms of education and court culture. A survey of her major textual productions illustrates the range and pace of her literary activity. After gaining recognition for her lyrical compositions in the 1390s, she authored a verse epistle in 1399 (*The Letter of the God of Love*) that satirically criticizes the attitude towards women in the *Romance of the Rose*, a thirteenth-century allegory, and she proceeded to circulate three prose letters that offer a serious critique of the *Rose* as part of an epistolary debate on the merits of that poem (1401–1402). In 1400, she produced a mythological treatise, the *Letter of Othea to Hector*, a text composed in both prose and verse; in luxury manuscripts of her works, the *Othea* is a densely illustrated text that contributes as much to visual as to textual culture. She then wrote several texts that directly addressed French politics: a dream allegory, *The Path of Long Study* (1402–1403); a long verse narrative on universal history, the *The Transformations of Fortune* (1404); as well as a prose biography of her father's patron, Charles V, a book commissioned by the Duke of Burgundy (1404). When she came to write the *Book of the City of Ladies* in 1405, a prose allegory in defense of women, she focuses specifically on the gendered nature of history and culture, issues that had been ignored in the vision of universal history in *The Transformations of Fortune*. However, soon after producing the *City of Ladies,* she composed *The Book of the Three Virtues* (1405), a conduct book for women that endorsed the status quo rather than the visionary possibilities for women proposed by the *City of Ladies*. She also composed a political treatise organized as an autobiographical narrative, *Christine's Vision* (1405), as well as a treatise on political philosophy, the *Book of the Body Politic* (1404–1407); a book on the mechanics of warfare, the *Book of Deeds of Arms and of Chivalry* (1410), as well as a treatise on peace, *The Book of Peace* (1414). In addition, she wrote several debate poems and a significant number of devotional texts in prose. Her final text is the poem on Joan of Arc, the *Tale of Joan of Arc* (1429) previously mentioned.

The trajectory of Christine's literary career took her from poetry on personal topics into the composition of overtly political writings, including prose treatises; nonetheless, she continues to foreground herself as narrator of her texts throughout her literary career. While it is conventional for late-medieval poets to represent themselves as the speaker of their texts, Christine's gender calls attention to her authorial performance as a woman writer, not only when she writes about love or widowhood, but also when she attempts to use her writings to intervene in contemporary political crises. As a consequence, the corpus of her work offers a series of female voiced texts on the most serious political and social topics of her day, such as war, politics, and history, as well as on the status and conduct of women. Several of her texts were translated in the late medieval and early modern period (into English, Flemish, and Portuguese), and her writings survive in numerous manuscripts and early printed books. In addition, her writings on the *Romance of the Rose* are thought to have initiated the early modern debate on women known as the *querelle des femmes*.

MARILYNN R. DESMOND

References and Further Reading

Altmann, Barbara K. and Deborah L. McGrady. *Christine de Pizan: A Casebook*. New York: Routledge, 2003.

Christine de Pizan. *The Treasure of the City of Ladies or, The Book of the Three Virtues*. translated by Sarah Lawson. Harmondsworth: Penguin, 1985.

———. *The Writings of Christine de Pizan*. New York: Persea, 1993.

———. *The Selected Works of Christine de Pizan*. translated by Renate Blumenfeld-Kosinski and Kevin Brownlee. New York: Norton, 1997.

———. *The Book of the City of Ladies*. Trans. Rosalind Brown-Grant. London: Penguin, 1999.

Desmond, Marilynn. *Christine de Pizan and the Categories of Difference*. Minneapolis: University of Minnesota Press, 1998.

Willard, Charity Cannon. *Christine de Pizan: her Life and Works*. New York: Persea, 1984.

See also **Conduct Literature; Defenses of Women; Literature, Old French; Patronage, Literary; Roman de la Rose and Its Reception; Widows; Women Authors: Old French Texts**

CHRONICLES OF THE NORTHERN LOW COUNTRIES

The northern Low Countries fell almost entirely within the diocese of Utrecht, however without being a political and cultural entity. Most influential on Dutch historiography were several chronicles of the County of Holland and Zeeland. They had their origin in hagiography (from the tenth century) and were composed at the Abbey of Egmond, founded by Count Thierry II (d. 988), or at the court, where the focus shifted to the reigns of the counts. The history of the counts was interwoven with that of Utrecht and Gelre, Hainault and Brabant. Chronicles served to promote legitimation and identity and the main themes were politics, power, and war.

Incorporation into the Burgundian state in the fifteenth century meant a new impulse for historiography. Regarding women in the chronicles, the story about Countess Jacqueline of Bavaria, who was forced in 1433 to resign the county to Philip the Good of

Burgundy, was added, but essentially the tone did not change. Women played a minor role, although documentary sources prove that countesses were actively involved on behalf of husbands or children. Most information concerns dynastic relations, but women were mentioned only occasionally. In chronicles from the north, where central government was lacking, dynastic elements were absent, and so were women. The same can be said of town chronicles.

In monastic chronicles women were judged according to ecclesiastical interests. Abbesses, female founders, and benefactors figure in positive roles. The outstanding founders of the abbey of Berne, Folkold and Bescela, starting as an adulterous couple, ended like saints. However, Lady Reinwidis, benefactor and recluse of the abbey of Kloosterrade, caused a disturbance c. 1130 by surrounding herself with women. According to the chronicler, a woman on her own could not live without maids.

Chroniclers divided women into two categories according to status: on the one hand, wives and mothers, and, on the other hand, religious women. About 1000, Alpertus of Metz compared two sisters, Adela, wife of Balderic, and Abbess Liutgard. Adela talked too much, her dress reflected her debauchery and her face betrayed fickleness, but she taught her maids all kinds of textile arts and made the most sumptuous fabrics. Liutgard was wise, hospitable, visited the poor and benefited the church. Out of greed, Adela tried to poison her and destroy the nunnery. When chroniclers paid attention to women, they were presented as either extremely pious or as troublemakers. For instance, after her husband's death, Countess Petronilla (d. 1144) ruled the County of Holland and Zeeland for ten years, although her son had come of age. The chroniclers, nonetheless, picture her as a benefactor of the abbey of Egmond and founder of the nunnery of Rijnsburg.

Countess Aleida of Cleve (c. 1202) was described as a troublemaker, damaging the abbey of Egmond, despite the fact that she defended the county effectively against the Frisians. The chroniclers continue telling how, shortly after her husband's death in 1203, she married their only surviving child, Ada (d. 1223), to the Count of Loon (d. 1218), against her husband's intentions. The nobility rose in revolt because they did not want a foreign ruler tied to Aleida's apron-strings, and they were fearful that a woman always had a fickle mind. Ada's case, after Aleida's death, was very similar to that of Jacqueline of Bavaria. Her paternal uncle claimed the county, and successfully supported her adversaries. She died childless. The Herald of Bavaria (c. 1400) was the first to state that Ada rightfully inherited the county. He wrote this after Emperor Lewis III of Bavaria (d. 1347) invested his wife Margaret (d. 1354) with the county, when, in 1345, her brother, Count William IV, had died childless. Margaret and her son William, who first acted as her substitute, got caught in the faction struggle of the Cods and the Hooks. As a result, the chronicles tell, mother and child came to stand in opposition to one another. Like Ada before and Jacqueline after her, Margaret was defeated.

The chronicles of Melis Stoke (d. after 1314) and Willem the Procurator (d. 1335) also contain romantic stories, which might originate from troubadour songs and shed more light on women. For instance, there is the story of the Countess of Clermont who fell in love with Count Floris IV of Holland, who was killed in 1234 at a tournament in Corbie by her jealous husband. Or, the cunning Countess of Gelre, who persuaded her husband to marry their daughter Aleida to Count William I of Holland (d. 1222) and thus made peace between the counties. And, Countess Jeanne of Valois, who was very sad about the marriage of her daughter, because in her foresight she sensed trouble.

Historiographers of the sixteenth century and later did not focus on the role that a woman performed, but emphasized more and more her femininity.

RENÉE NIP

References and Further Reading

Augustus, L. and J. T. J. Jamar, ed. and tran. *Annales Rodenses. Kroniek van Kloosterrade*. Maastricht: Rijksarchief Limburg, 1995.

Bruch, H., Ed. *Chronographia Johannis de Beke*. Rijks Geschiedkundige Publicatiën, g.s. 143. The Hague: Martinus Nijhoff, 1973.

Bruch, H., Ed. *Johannes de Beke, Croniken van de Stichte van Utrecht ende van Hollant*. Rijks Geschiedkundige Publicatiën, g.s. 180. The Hague: Martinus Nijhoff, 1982.

Burgers, J. W. J. "Geschiedschrijving in Holland tot omstreeks 1300," *Jaarboek voor Middeleeuwse Geschiedenis* 3 (2000): 92–130.

Burgers, J. W. J., ed. *Rijmkroniek van Holland 366–1305 door een anonieme auteur en Melis Stoke*. Rijks Geschiedkundige Publicatiën, g.s. 251. The Hague: Instituut voor Nederlandse Geschiedenis, 2004 (www.inghist.nl).

Cordfunke, E. H. P. *Gravinnen van Holland. Huwelijk en huwelijkspolitiek van de graven uit het Hollandse huis*. Zutphen: Walburg Pers, 1987.

Gumbert-Hepp, Marijke ed. and tran. *Willem Procurator, Kroniek*. Hilversum: Verloren, 2001.

Hugenholtz, F. W. N. "Ada van Holland." In *Middeleeuwers over vrouwen*. Ed. R. E. V. Stuip and C. Vellekoop. Utrecht: H&S, 1985, vol. 1, pp. 12–26.

Janse, Antheun, ed. *Johan Huyssen van Kattendijke-kroniek*. Den Haag: Instituut voor Nederlandse Geschiedenis, 2005.

Narrative Historical Sources from the Medieval Low Countries. www.narrative-sources.be

Nip, Renée. "Conflicting Roles: Jacqueline of Bavaria (d. 1436), Countess and Wife." In *Saints, Scholars and Politicians*, edited by Mathilde van Dijk and Renée Nip. Turnhout: Brepols, 2005, pp. 189–207.

Oppermann, O., ed. *Fontes Egmundenses*. Utrecht: Kemink en Zoon N.V., 1933.

Rij, Hans van, ed. and tran. *Alpertus van Metz. Gebeurtenissen van deze tijd en Een fragment over bisschop Diederik I van Metz*. Amsterdam: Verloren, 1980.

Rij, H. van, ed. and tran. *Het stichtingskroniekje van de Abdij van Berne*. In *Egmond en Berne. Twee verhalende historische bronnen uit de middeleeuwen*. Den Haag: Brill, 1987.

Romein, Jan. *Geschiedenis van de Noord-Nederlandsche geschiedschrijving in de middeleeuwen*. Haarlem: Tjeenk Willink, 1932.

Stein, Robert. *Politiek en historiografie. Het ontstaansmilieu van Brabantse kronieken in de eerste helft van de vijftiende eeuw*. Leuven: Peeters, 1994.

Verbij-Schillings, Jeanne. *Beeldvorming in Holland. Heraut Beieren en de historiografie omstreeks 1400*. Amsterdam: Prometheus, 1995.

Vis, G. N. M. Marco Mostert, and P. J. Margy, ed. *Heiligenlevens, Annalen en Kronieken: Geschiedschrijving in middeleeuws Egmond*. Hilversum: Verloren, 1990.

See also **Burgundian Netherlands; Gender Ideologies; Jacqueline of Bavaria; Noble Women**

CHURCH

Even though Pentecost, the day the Holy Spirit descended upon the Apostles after the Ascension of Jesus (Acts 2), is traditionally considered the birthday of the Church, the development of an institutionalized form of Christianity took many years. The main reason for this delay is the fact that early Christians lived in vivid expectation of the *parousia*, the end-times marked by the second coming of Christ and, therefore, did not give much thought to establishing an institution. But as generations, and then centuries, passed, Christians increasingly shaped more overt forms of Christianity. Each group of Christians who met for worship was called an *ekklesia*, an assembly; as the connections between these groups grew stronger, the *ekklesia*, the Church, was seen as an ever-more structured hierarchy.

Early Church

By the second century, Christians were organized into geographical regions (called *dioceses*, a term taken from Roman imperial administration) each headed by a bishop. As the ecclesiastical hierarchy took shape, the nature of Christian leadership changed dramatically. In the earliest Christian communities, women had roles of *diakonia*, service to the community, usually interpreted as teaching and spreading the faith. We see evidence of this in the story of Mary and Martha, sisters of Bethany and leaders of a Christian community, in the Gospel of Luke, although it has been pointed out that the attention Luke gives to women leaders in the Christian community is muted by his concern for the appropriate secondary roles that women needed to take. The same ambivalence is found in the writings of the Apostle Paul; even though many scholars have pointed out Paul's undisputed role in the theology of male headship and women's subordination (1 Corinthians 7:3–4, 1 Corinthians 11:3–5), it is also the case that Paul argues for women's equality in a general way (Galatians 3:28) and mentions many women leaders. It has also been noted that Paul's distinctions of status in the community have at least as much to do with social rank as with gender. In general, one could say that the works of the New Testament canon, which were all written by the second decade of the second century show some hints of women's leadership roles (the stories of Mary and Martha, Mary Magdalene and Thecla), but also are clear about the reality of male authority. The New Testament writings that are most discriminatory with regard to gender are the so-called Pastoral Epistles (1 and 2 Timothy and Titus); they date from the early second century and model the "household code" of the late Roman Empire. In this world, men fill all the important Church offices. These writings had a great deal of authority in the Middle Ages because they were ascribed to Paul and were thought to be the incontrovertible teachings of the Apostles.

By the end of the second century, an increasingly exclusive male hierarchy was being established. The *Apostolic Tradition* of Hippolytus of Rome is very concerned with role distinctions, and draws a firm line between those church offices that require ordination by the laying on of hands and those that can be filled by appointment. Hippolytus names a great many church offices, including some that were held exclusively by women, such as the order of widows. He is careful to make clear, though, that widows do not have the same authority as (male) ministers consecrated by the laying on of hands, since they should be instituted by word only. The role of widows continued to be a troubling issue, as is clear from the *Didascalia Apostolorum*, a work purporting to be from the first century but probably written several centuries later. It refers to "good" and "bad" widows, and gives a number of counsels for keeping the latter under control. This work is very concerned with making clear categories of church offices, and forbids women from participating in ministries such as baptism, healing, and prayer. The *Didascalia* does recognize the office of deaconess (a clue that it is probably from the Eastern part of the Church) whose office was to minister particularly to other women. Although actual Christian life may not have been as tidy as the *Didascalia Apostolorum* wants to make it, it is noteworthy that this text limits women's charismatic and sacramental roles, while it does recognize the order of deaconesses, although under male clerical control.

Yet another early Christian text, the *Apostolic Constitutions*, a fourth-century document from Syria, weaves together sections from Hippolytus, the *Didascalia* and other early sources into a discussion of church hierarchy that places women firmly at the bottom. The first book of the *Apostolic Constitutions* combines a description of women's innate weakness with a warning about women's seductive power. This looks forward to an equation of women with carnality on the one hand and spiritual and intellectual weakness on the other, themes that become commonplace in later Latin Christianity. Indeed, the *Apostolic Constitutions* relates women's religious practices to paganism, emphasizing another accusation against women that will be seen throughout the Middle Ages. In some very important ways, then, the gender basis for church hierarchy had been established before the end of the classical period of the formulation of Christian doctrine. This gender-based hierarchy informed the thousand years of medieval Christianity and was not to change significantly before the twentieth century, when the ordination of women to ministerial positions equal to those of men became accepted in many Protestant denominations.

Once this pattern of male domination had been established, it was authorized by references to biblical verses of both the Old and the New Testament. The story of the Fall of Adam and Eve in Genesis 3 was especially important. In Genesis 3:17, Adam's curse is linked particularly to the fact that he listened to the voice of his wife; for this, he was condemned to work the earth for his living, and to die and return to the dust from which he came. This theme, that human hardships are primarily due to the weakness of women, is heard from Tertullian in the third century to the late fifteenth-century *Malleus Maleficarum (The Hammer of Witches)*. The Dominican author of this late medieval treatise explicitly retells the story of the third chapter of Genesis to explain why women are morally inferior to men: this is because the first woman was made from a bent rib, and so women are bent in a direction contrary (reversed order) to male human beings. The *Malleus* even gives an explanatory etymology for the word *femina*, the Latin word for woman; it comes, the text says, from *fe minus*, "less faith," because women are, by their very nature, weaker in faith than men.

Subordinate or Equal?

Such an understanding of Christian scripture was helped, no doubt, by the generally male-dominated societies of late antiquity and the Middle Ages. But one western theologian in particular, Augustine of Hippo, was fundamental in establishing a theological basis for the fundamental subordination of women to men. It has been noted that an important part of Augustine's theology was the idea that "man" was made in the image of God. But is this "man" to be understood as generic, encompassing all of humanity, male and female, or is "man" understood as specifically male? Augustine's answer to this is complicated. On the one hand, women must be in the image of God if they are capable of, even worthy of, salvation, since the central idea of the Incarnation of Jesus was that, by becoming human, Christ took on and made reparation for human sins. So, in this broad ontological way, Augustine says, women are in the image of God. Yet, in a more specific and incarnate way, with regard to the physical reality of women's bodies, women are not in the image of God in the way that men are. This argument, egalitarian in the most ontological sense and yet strictly hierarchical in the embodied reality of humans on earth, is another example of how the leadership roles available for women in the Church were severely limited by the fifth century, since women's spiritual inferiority could be understood as a reason to deny them the possibility of leadership in the Church. Women may have been thought to stand equally with men before God at the Last Judgment, but they certainly did not have equal access to the esoteric roles of spiritual and liturgical leadership here on earth.

Nevertheless, the possibility of salvation was an obvious catalyst for the religious devotion of many Christian women. In the second and third centuries, the period of the persecution of Christians by the powers of the Roman Empire, many women became famous as martyrs for the faith. Often these stories of exemplary women involve the refusal of marriage to a pagan king or official, followed by the glorious, if gory, death of the brave women. The classical version of this is the legend of Saint Catherine of Alexandria, who stood firm when tortured on the wheel, but was finally killed by beheading, after which angels took her head to Mount Sinai, where it is preserved today in the Monastery of Saint Catherine. Such women were praised for their lack of sexuality, the opposite attribute ascribed to their seductive first mother, Eve. In this way, women martyrs were thought to be *viriliter*, man-like. The primary example of this trick of a sex-change is the martyrdom of Saint Perpetua, who died in the Arena of Carthage in 203 when she was torn apart by a wild heifer. The *Passion* of Perpetua and her servant Felicity, said to have been written by Perpetua herself and redacted by another hand (some say Tertullian's), gives the most explicit example of how a woman is sanctified by becoming a man. Perpetua has a number of prophetic dreams in prison; in one, she enters into battle with a "foul Egyptian," that is, the devil. When Perpetua strips to prepare herself for battle, she finds that she has been turned into a man. This transformation does the trick; not only does Perpetua then prevail in battle, but she even throws the Egyptian down on the sand and treads on his head, an obvious reference to God's curse on the serpent in Genesis 3:15, when Adam is promised the power to tread on the serpent's head. The martyrdom texts in general, and the *Passion* of Perpetua in particular, make clear that women can shake off their weak and sinful nature, and become true leaders of the community, only by becoming male.

Monasticism

But where could a medieval Christian woman become male? Medieval women's lives were tightly controlled by their reproductive potential, as their divinely ordained life on earth was centered on the ability to bear children for men. But there was one earthly realm where women were equal to if separate from men, that is, the cloister. The institution of monasticism has a long and complex trajectory with regard to gender, beginning and ending in strict control by male ecclesiastics, with a moment of female empowerment in between. Women's monastic life was instituted by authors like the sixth-century Caesarius of Arles as a way of controlling the weak, sinful nature of women. But medieval monasticism, an institution that mediated much of the authority of the medieval church, turned out to be one place where women could actually exert some power. In the century after Caesarius, an abbess named Hilda ruled over a monastery of men and women at Whitby in northern England, and presided at a council where it was decided that the British church would follow the Roman rather than the Celtic liturgical calendar. By the twelfth century, there were such "double monasteries" of men and women on the Continent as well. In the cloister, the ancient stories of manly women saints were read in Chapter and at meals, and nuns were thus presented with a model of holiness, sternly celibate, stripped of weak feminine characteristics, that they could emulate.

We know that medieval abbesses did, in fact, take on many tasks that had been since the fourth century designated for men only, including preaching, reading the Gospel, and hearing confessions from the nuns of the community. In the twelfth century, Peter Abelard seemed to tacitly approve of some of these ministerial functions by women when he compared the office of abbess to that of deaconess in the early church. But there had been many restrictions put on women's ministry between the early deaconesses and the twelfth-century abbesses, and so it is not surprising that, in the early thirteenth century, Pope Innocent III made a point of forbidding "certain abbesses" in Spain the right to exercise any of these ministries. Innocent seems to have had in mind the well-connected community of Cistercian women at Las Huelgas, near Burgos, where the abbess had a good deal of worldly power as well as spiritual authority within her community. Whatever sense such power wielded by a monastic woman may have made in thirteenth-century Spain, the papal prohibition harked back to "apostolic" authority forbidding women to do such things; Innocent may have had in mind the patristic handbooks of ecclesiastical roles, or perhaps the New Testament as interpreted by Augustine, but he was clear about claiming this restriction to have been "apostolic." So once again, and now with a reference to ancient custom, women, were officially forbidden to take part in the roles of power and leadership of the Church. This prohibition became legal in yet another way when Innocent's letter on this case was quoted at length in the *Decretals* of Pope Gregory IX, under the heading "An abbess cannot bless monastics, hear confessions, and preach in public." The exclusion of women from the hierarchy of the Church, a concept that had become standard by the fourth century, was thus made into a legal definition in the thirteenth.

Brides of Christ

And yet, at the same time, there was another way in which the medieval church was marked by gender, the vision of the church as the Bride of Christ. Many scholars have commented on the irony of a male defined and identified institution portraying itself as a feminized, passive partner, but this image held great power in the Middle Ages. The Church as Bride was a biblical metaphor, found most explicitly at the end of the Apocalypse to John (21:9–10), where the Church, in the guise of the Heavenly Jerusalem, descends, bedecked as a bride, to her wedding with the Lamb. This image was joined in the medieval exegetical imagination to the passionate love between the Bride and the Bridegroom portrayed in the Song of Songs, a book of the Bible that was largely understood in medieval Christianity as the love song between Christ and the Church. This interpretation begins as early as Origen of Alexandria in the third century, and is powerfully recapitulated in the Song of Songs commentary of the fourth-century Cappadocian Gregory of Nyssa. But in the Latin Church, this powerful image comes into its own in the two great periods of medieval Latin exegesis, the ninth century (Haimo of Auxerre) and the twelfth century (Honorius Augustodunensis, Rupert of Deutz, and especially Bernard of Clairvaux). It is striking that some of the most profound religious thinkers of the medieval period were deeply involved in the image of the feminized church. Having removed women as much as possible from the life in the Church on earth, medieval male authors then turned around and made the Church into an idealized female figure, the protagonist of some heavily eroticized spirituality.

Given this irony, perhaps it is no surprise that this feminized image was not, actually, so popular among the strong women leaders of medieval Christianity. In fact, both Hildegard of Bingen in the twelfth century and Catherine of Siena in the fourteenth went out of their way to avoid referring to themselves as "Brides of Christ," or using the Song of Songs in any self-referential way, although their male confessors, spiritual directors, and biographers had no qualms about remembering them this way. This is one of the many ways in which medieval women's experience was mediated through a filter of male ecclesiastical control, a pattern that had many repercussions for the way some holy women are found in medieval hagiography. Other medieval women, in contrast, took this imagery and used it to their own empowerment. Clare of Assisi and Gertrude the Great, both head of women's communities in the thirteenth century, made the connection to the image of Bride a major reference point, encouraging their sister nuns to think of themselves this way. So did Hadewijch of Antwerp, a thirteenth-century Flemish Beguine. In some ways this seems very passive, yet there is also a way in which the imagery could be used subversively, in the very fact that the Bride was at once the human soul (the soul of a humble nun) and at the same time the church, the Heavenly Jerusalem, the Mother of us all.

Restricted Autonomy

The general pattern we observed in the early Church, that opportunities for women's autonomy and leadership in the Christian community diminished with every century, becoming more legalistically expressed

and more strictly enforced, has to be seen, in one way, as the increasing masculinization of the Church. In the later Middle Ages and early modern periods, this suspicion of women turned into hostility, as a concern about women's claims of sanctity led to persecution of women accused of "false sanctity," and, eventually, to the witch craze of the fifteenth, sixteenth, and seventeenth centuries, in which women in particular were targeted as enemies of the Church. Yet, this trend was accompanied and somewhat mitigated by an enduring romance with the image of the Church as inherently feminine. Perhaps medieval ecclesiastics (all male and celibate by definition) gained some spiritual solace from this ironic dichotomy, even as they continued to raise the barriers to women's full participation in the community. Medieval Church women (all celibate nuns by definition, and increasingly constricted by legislation about obedience and enclosure) were faced with a more difficult dilemma, but they could, for most of the Middle Ages, still gain some spiritual power from this imagery.

An analysis of the roles of women and gender in the Church, then, must take place on a number of levels. Institutional history shows a clear decline in the power of women from the second century to the fourth, and then a hardening of the prohibitions on women's leadership roles supported by claims to apostolic authority. By the High Middle Ages, this "eternal truth" of women's inferiority was inscribed in canon law. In the late Middle Ages and early modern period, it became part of a rationale for the persecution of women as witches. Increasing restrictions on women's societal roles mirrored all of this. And yet, the concomitant feminization of the church in theology, exegesis, and spiritual writings gave men and women both a way to identify with the spiritualized Church as especially beloved of God, the Bride of Christ.

E. ANN MATTER

References and Further Reading

Børresen, K. E. *Subordination and Equivalence: The Nature and Role of Woman in Augustine and Thomas Aquinas*, translated by C. H. Talbot. Washington, D.C.: The University Press of America, 1981.

Caesarius of Arles. *The Rule for Nuns*, translated by Maria Caritas McCarthy. Washington, D.C.: Catholic University Press, 1960.

Cardman, Francine. "Women, Ministry, and Church Order in Early Christianity," in Ross Shepard Kraemer and Mary Rose d'Angelo, *Women & Christian Origins*. New York: Oxford, 1999, pp. 300–329.

Castelli, Elizabeth A. "Paul on Women and Gender," in Ross Shepard Kraemer and Mary Rose d'Angelo, *Women & Christian Origins*. New York: Oxford, 1999, pp. 221–235.

Coakley, John. "Friars as Confidants of Holy Women in Medieval Dominican Hagiography," in *Images of Sainthood in Medieval Europe*, edited by Renate Blumenfeld-Kosinski and Timea Szell. Ithaca and London: Cornell University Press, 1991, pp. 222–246.

D'Angelo, Mary Rose. "Women Partners in the New Testament," *Journal of Feminist Studies in Religion* 6 (1990): 65–86.

————. "(Re) Presentations of Women in the Gospel of Matthew and Luke-Acts," in Ross Shepard Kraemer and Mary Rose d'Angelo, *Women & Christian Origins*. New York: Oxford, 1999, pp. 171–195.

Johnson, Penelope D. *Equal in Monastic Profession: Religious Women in Medieval France*. Chicago: University of Chicago Press, 1991.

Kramer, Heinrich. *Malleus Maleficarum*, translated by Montague Summers. London: The Pushkin Press, 1948, and widely anthologized, for example, in *Witchcraft in Europe, 400–1700: A Documentary History*, 2nd ed. edited by Alan Charles Kors and Edward Peters, revised by Edward Peters. Philadelphia: University of Pennsylvania Press, 2001.

MacDonald, Margaret Y. "Reading Real Women Through the Undisputed Letters of Paul," in Ross Shepard Kraemer and Mary Rose D'Angelo, *Women & Christian Origins*. New York: Oxford, 1999, pp. 199–220.

Matter, E. Ann. "Innocent III and the Keys to the Kingdom of Heaven," in *Women Priests: A Catholic Commentary on the Vatican Declaration*, edited by Leonard Swidler and Arlene Swidler. New York: Paulist Press, 1977, pp. 145–151.

————. "The Undebated Debate: Gender and the Image of God in Medieval Theology" for *Gender in Debate*, edited by Clare Lees and Thelma Fenster. New York: Palgrave, 2002, pp. 41–55.

McLaughlin, Mary Martin. "Abelard and the Dignity of Women: Twelfth-Century 'Feminism' in Theory and Practice," in *Pierre Abélard, Pierre le Vénérable*. Cluny: Abbaye de Cluny, 1972, pp. 288–334.

Perpetua of Carthage. *The Passion of Sts Perpetua and Felicitas*, translated by H. R. Musurillo, in *Medieval Women's Visionary Literature*, edited by Elizabeth Alvilda Petroff. New York: Oxford University Press, 1986, pp. 70–77.

Raming, Ida. *The Exclusion of Women from the Priesthood: Divine Law or Sex Discrimination?*, translated by N. R. Adams. Metuchen, N.J.: Scarecrow Press, 1976.

See also **Abbesses; Asceticism; Augustine, Influence of; Bride of Christ: Imagery; Catherine of Alexandria; Catherine of Siena; Clare of Assisi; Double Monasteries; Eve; Gertrude the Great; Hadewijch; Hild of Whitby; Hildegard of Bingen; Law, Canon; Mary and Martha; Monastic Enclosure; Monastic Rules; Monasticism and Nuns; Ordination of Women as Priests; Song of Songs, Medieval Interpretations of; Virgin Martyrs; Virile Women; Witches**

CHURCHING

Churching, *kirchgang* in German, was a ritual of purification performed for a woman on the occasion of her first visit to church after the birth of a baby. The French term, *les relevailles*, refers to the more social aspect of the ritual: the end of the mother's lying-in. Women from every level of society were churched, usually after every birth. Thus, churching was a common, though not universally practiced, custom throughout medieval Europe.

The origins of the ritual, however, are obscure. Many medieval references connect it with Leviticus 12:1–6, which forbids women from entering sacred space until they have completed a period of purification and presented an offering to the priest. The length of this period depended upon the sex of the child, either 40 days for a boy or 80 for a girl. Medieval practice certainly had some connection with these Mosaic proscriptions but was different enough that it ought not be considered simply a Christian adaptation of Jewish practice. In particular, canon law in the West never prohibited a woman from entering a church after giving birth, though it was a common and devout custom in many places and some clerics enforced the custom strictly. In addition, Christian mothers did not use ritual bathing (*mikveh*) as a part of their purification after childbirth, as did Jewish mothers. Finally, the length of time a mother was expected to refrain from entering a church varied according to local custom but was not determined by the sex of the baby. In both France and England evidence suggests that mothers waited about a month before returning to church.

Churching was also associated with the Feast of the Purification, which celebrated Mary's fulfillment of the Mosaic Law. The celebration included a procession with candles, hence the common name for the feast, Candlemas. This, perhaps, explains the fact that medieval women sometimes offered a candle at the time of their purification. In England, it was customary to bring a candle and other gifts as well, especially the child's christening cloth. In the later Middle Ages in both France and England, the candle was accompanied by or replaced with a monetary offering.

Early medieval evidence for the idea that women were considered impure after childbirth comes from the penitentials, which often closely follow Levitical proscriptions. An early ninth-century Frankish penitential mentions women coming to church for purification with a candle and an offering, and Carolingian chronicles mention the practice of women observing a period of purification after childbirth. The earliest liturgical evidence comes from the eleventh century. Liturgies of churching, as with other aspects of the rite, varied. Some German rites included the child, while French liturgies never did; French rites typically included a mass, other rites often did not. All of the liturgies included a blessing of the new mother, usually with holy water, as a rite of purification.

The meaning of churching was, however, complex and changed over time. In the early Middle Ages, restricting new mothers from entering a church was intended to protect sacred space from blood pollution. In the central Middle Ages, French bishops used the rite as a means of enforcing ecclesiastical legislation on marriage and clerical understanding of the marital debt, eventually transforming churching into a rite that honored marriage. In sermons, however, many French clerics continued to refer to the rite as purification from the pollutions of a bloody birth and the taint of lust experienced in the process of conception. In England, analysis of the liturgy suggests it was not only a rite of purification but also of transition and thanksgiving. The element of transition was marked by the mother's return to public life in the parish as well as to her husband's bed. Perhaps in acknowledgment of these, by the late Middle Ages the liturgical celebration was followed by a public celebration, which varied in character according to the social class of the mother. There are descriptions of elaborate feasts for English queens, more modest feasts among French bourgeoisie, and gatherings at taverns for poorer women. These occasions allowed families to demonstrate their social status and to declare the birth of a legitimate child. In contrast, Italian evidence, which has not yet been thoroughly studied, suggests that the ritual had little social importance and was not celebrated with feasting of any kind.

Outside England and France, research on medieval churching has been very limited. Further study of this ritual would add a great deal to our understanding of women in the Middle Ages.

PAULA M. RIEDER

References and Further Reading

Gibson, Gail McMurray. "Blessings from Sun and Moon: Churching as Women's Theater." In *Bodies and Disciplines: Intersections of Literature and History in Fifteenth-Century England*, edited by Barbara Hanawalt and David Wallace. Minneapolis: University of Minnesota Press, 1996, pp. 139–154.

Lee, Becky R. "The Purification of Women after Childbirth: A Window onto Medieval Perceptions of Women." *Florilegium* 14 (1995–1996): 43–55.

———. "Men's Recollections of a Women's Rite: Medieval English Men's Recollections Regarding the Rite of Purification of Women after Childbirth." *Gender and History* 14.2 (2002): 224–241.

Pierce, Joanne M. "'Green Women' and Blood Pollution: Some Medieval Rituals for the Churching of Women after Childbirth." *Studia Liturgica* 29 (1999): 191–215.

Rieder, Paula M. "Insecure Borders: Symbols of Clerical Privilege and Gender Ambiguity in the Liturgy of Churching." In *The Material Culture of Sex, Procreation, and Marriage in Premodern Europe*, edited by Anne L. McClanan and Karen Rosoff Encarnación. New York: Palgrave Press, 2002, pp. 93–113.

———. *On the Purification of Women: Churching in Northern France, 1100–1500*. New York: Palgrave Press, 2006.

See also **Conjugal Debt; Law, Canon; Lying-In; Mikveh; Pregnancy and Childbirth: Christian Women; Pregnancy and Childbirth: Jewish Women; Sexuality, Regulation of; Sexuality: Sex in Marriage**

CISTERCIAN ORDER

Among twelfth-century monastic reform groups who sought more austere religious lives, the Cistercians were the most popular. The traditional story told by Cistercians of the later twelfth century is that Cîteaux was founded in 1098 by Robert of Molesme. It was one of many groups that sought to reform Benedictine monastic life in imitation of the lives of the early Apostles and Desert Fathers. Robert soon returned to Molesme, itself a reform community of circa 1075, but some of his followers remained at Cîteaux. After difficult early years daughter-houses of Cîteaux began to be founded circa 1113. Among the first was Clairvaux, founded after the entrance into Cîteaux of Bernard of Fontaines, usually known as Bernard of Clairvaux, a convert to the religious life with earlier training in the urban schools, who would become the great early intellectual and spiritual leader of the Cistercians. Bernard was soon sent to found Clairvaux, where he remained as abbot until his death in 1153. Bernard's active preaching throughout Europe inspired many individuals to convert to the religious life at Clairvaux, among them the future Pope Eugenius III (1145–1153). Although there is no evidence that women were among those founding Cîteaux or Clairvaux, there were women at Molesme; and a daughter-house for them would be founded at Jully, not far from Clairvaux, in 1113. There female relatives of Bernard and his companions, including Bernard's sister Humbelina, became nuns. Bernard maintained close ties to Jully until the mid-1140s, when Eugenius III firmly attached those nuns to Molesme.

After the mid-twelfth century, bishops and popes seemed to have actively encouraged a move towards centralization in the practice of the religious life and monastic "umbrella-groups," the religious orders appeared. Such orders shared customs, internal dispute resolution, and visitation and were ruled by a head or governing body. In the Cistercian case this was the General Chapter, an annual, universal, mandatory assembly of all abbots held in mid-September at Cîteaux, where disputes were resolved and legislation aimed at unanimity of practice was adopted. Despite the fact that the Cistercian mother abbey at Cîteaux had been founded in 1098, the earliest written evidence for the Cistercian Order as an administrative entity comes from the 1150s. As more new reform houses sought affiliation with the Cistercians a written Charter of Charity was produced circa 1165. By the 1180s, many of the organizational issues for the regulation of such an order had been resolved, and an official version of the order's customary was produced around that time. By the end of the century papal exemption from local episcopal visitation led to the creation of filiation trees to organize visitation by leaders of the order. By 1215, the Cistercian Order had become the largest and most famous of the new religious orders, its rhetoric asserting its precocity in creating such an institution; and its prestige was confirmed when it was held up as the ideal by the Fourth Lateran Council, which enjoined all monastic communities to identify themselves with such a group.

In the early 1120s, Cîteaux's abbot, Stephen Harding, had founded a community of nuns at le Tart that developed its own congregation of daughter-houses. Cistercian nuns of Montreuil near Laon are reported circa 1150 by Herman of Tournai as working not at spinning and women's work but in the fields like the brothers of Clairvaux. Some reform communities seeking affiliation included both men and women, like the double-community at Obazine which, upon Cistercian affiliation in the 1160s, created a separate house for its women at nearby Coyroux. Savigniac houses of nuns were also attached to the Cistercian Order along with the rest of the Savigniacs in the 1160s. By 1189 the importance of women's houses among affiliated houses was such that the king of Castile wanted to create a congregation of women's houses, in imitation of those associated with le Tart, under the authority of his newly founded abbey of Cistercian nuns at las Huelgas near Burgos; the abbots refused, explaining that they had no authority to force existing houses of nuns in Spain to adhere to las Huelgas, but this does not mean there were no Cistercian nuns.

Contrary to received opinion, the huge religious and economic success of the Cistercians was not because of an overflowing of monks from the houses of Burgundy or because Cistercians created new religious communities on the frontiers of Europe. Cistercian numbers and wealth accumulated with the incorporation of independently founded houses each with recruits and endowment, the return to simplicity in liturgical practice, building, and lifestyle, by a rationalization of long-fragmented land and improvement of cultivation, intensive pastoralism and animal husbandry, tithe-exemptions, the introduction of lay-brothers and -sisters who worked on granges created out of land purchased from previous occupants, and the growth of demand in the twelfth-century economy, particularly for the meat and animal products that Cistercian practice encouraged because raising animals was less labor-intensive than cultivating fields.

The widespread affiliation of independently founded houses meant that the Cistercian Order numbered more than 500 men's houses by the end of the twelfth century. There were many twelfth-century women's houses, but the great surge of women's foundations was led by important secular women founders. In addition to such new foundations, the incorporation of many groups of religious women acting as sisters in hospitals in the first half of the thirteenth century meant that by the century's end the order's women's houses outnumbered those for men. Women's houses gradually lost possibilities for mutual support and local protection which had been associated with earlier visitation by abbesses or bishop-founders when in the mid-thirteenth century visitation of women's houses was placed under the authority of abbots of neighboring men's houses. The numbers of recruits and the assiduity with which thirteenth-century abbesses and their patrons created endowment and recruited novices meant that women's communities remained full to capacity at a time when men's were suffering a crisis of recruitment. As had the order's monks from an earlier date, communities of Cistercian nuns by the thirteenth century controlled large and productive tracts of land in many regions.

In the difficult years of the fifteenth century, particularly in areas hard hit by the Hundred Years' War, a number of houses of Cistercian women were suppressed (about twenty percent of those in what is today France), and their properties taken over by men's communities with the assent of the abbots of the General Chapter. The rest, along with most men's houses survived until the Reformation in England and the Empire, and elsewhere until the French Revolution. A series of reforms of the Cistercians in the early modern period led to the creation of the Strict Observance, a reform of the Cistercians revived in the nineteenth century. Its members today are the Trappists or Trappistines, but there also remain a few communities, primarily with roots in eastern Europe, of pre-Trappist Cistercians.

CONSTANCE H. BERMAN

References and Further Reading

Berman, Constance H. *Medieval Agriculture, the Southern French Countryside, and the Early Cistercians: A Study of Forty-Three Monasteries.* Philadelphia: American Philosophical Society, 1986.
———. "Cistercian nuns and the development of the order: the Abbey of Saint-Antoine-des-Champs outside Paris," in *The Joy of Learning and the Love of God:. Essays in*

Honor of Jean Leclercq, OSB, edited by E. Rozanne Elder. Kalamazoo, Mich.: Cistercian Publications. 1995, pp. 121–156.

———. "Abbeys for Cistercian Nuns in the Ecclesiastical Province of Sens: Foundation, Endowment and Economic Activities of the Earlier Foundations," *Revue Mabillon* 73 (1997): 83–113.

———. "Cistercian Women and Tithes," *Cîteaux* 49 (1998): 95–128.

———. "Were there Twelfth-Century Cistercian Nuns?" *Church History* 68 (1999): 824–864.

———. "Diversité et unanimité des cisterciens du XIIe siècle," *Unanimité et diversité cisterciennes*, edited by Nicole Bouter. Saint-Etienne: 2000, pp. 189–193.

———. *The Cistercian Evolution: The Invention of a Religious Order in Twelfth-Century Europe.* Philadelphia: University of Pennsylvania Press, 2000.

———. "The Labors of Hercules, the Cartulary, Church and Abbey for Nuns of La-Cour-Notre-Dame-de-Michery," *The Journal of Medieval History* 26 (2000): 33–70.

———. *Women and Monasticism in Medieval Europe: Sisters and Patrons of the Cistercian Reform.* Kalamazoo, Mich.: Published for TEAMS by Medieval Institute Publication, Western Michigan University, 2002.

Constable, Giles. *Medieval Monasticism: A Select Bibliography.* Toronto: University of Toronto Press, 1976.

———. *The Reformation of the Twelfth Century.* New York: Cambridge University Press, 1996.

Degler-Spengler, Brigitte. "The incorporation of Cistercian nuns into the order in the twelfth and thirteenth century," *Hidden Springs: Cistercian Monastic Women: Medieval Religious Women* 3:1, edited by John A. Nichols and Lillian Thomas Shank. Kalamazoo, Mich.: Cistercian Publications, 1995, pp. 85–134.

Lekai, Louis Julius. *The Cistercians: Ideals and Reality.* Kent, Ohio: Kent State University Press, 1977.

Leyser, Henrietta. *Hermits and the New Monasticism: A Study of Religious Communities in Western Europe, 1000–1150.* London: Macmillan, 1984.

Mahn, Jean Berthold. *L'ordre cistercien et son gouvernement, des origines au milieu du XIII siècle (1098–1265).* Paris: E. de Boccard, 1951.

Newman, Martha G. *The Boundaries of Charity: Cistercian Culture and Ecclesiastical Reform, 1098–1180.* Stanford, Calif.: Stanford University Press, 1996.

See also **Abbesses; Conversae and Conversi; Monastic Visitation; Monasticism and Nuns; Spiritual Care**

CITIES AND TOWNS

Cities and towns multiplied in Europe from the tenth century on, and immigration of men and women from rural areas caused urban populations to grow. Women, usually single, left the reassurance of rural social networks, including family, friends, and known contacts, for a new life in cities and towns. In the city they formed new communities, often with an occupational or spiritual focus. The urban economy offered more new occupational opportunities to women. As urban society became more complex, many social strata emerged. Urban mercantile women were part of an elite group, perhaps more confined to household management, as elaborated by the Ménagier de Paris in his advice to his young wife, or by Francesco Datini in letters to his wife, than working women of artisan or more modest strata. Prescriptive literature limiting the agency of elite urban women (Leon Battista Alberti) may not represent the norm.

Marriage was a matter of negotiation in medieval Europe. In most instances women needed a dowry to marry, leading in Italian towns to the establishment of dowry funds for girls. Cash, business investments, real property, or a combination thereof formed the basis of urban dowries. Testamentary legacies for poor girls to marry were common. Women's rights in inheritance varied according to the regional or local inheritance system. Daughters, having received dowries, were excluded from paternal inheritance in some towns of southern France and Italy.

The age of marriage varied from place to place across Europe. Women of the urban elite married earlier than artisan women and may, as a result of biology and fortune, have produced more children. In a city such as Genoa, men and women artisans married in their late twenties after they had established their careers. In Mediterranean towns where the marriage age of women of the urban elite was young, they often found themselves widowed, having married older men. In Florence the fate of the elite widow was not pleasant as she frequently remained in the control of her natal family, while her young children lived with their father's family. In general, though, widowed status was perhaps the most privileged for women of both urban and rural environments.

There is regional diversity across Europe in terms of the legal agency of women. Urban women used the court system in southern France, on their own behalf or as guardians of their children. They also appeared as witnesses in inquest proceedings in England, where women needed representation in court unless they were *femes soles*. In northern France, a married woman could defend herself in court in matters involving her own business. Sumptuary laws were passed throughout Europe in an attempt by authorities to control conspicuous consumption, for example, in the matter of silk fabrics. Sales and recognitions of debt denote the acquisition of silks by women, however, and last wills and testaments contain legacies of luxury garments to women who were not authorized by law to wear them. Urban women were punished for calumny and reprimanded for gossip and were guilty, at times, of sexual misconduct.

Women participated in many aspects of the urban economy as innkeepers, shopkeepers, domestic servants, peddlers, brewsters, tavernkeepers, wet-nurses, prostitutes, business, trade, and real estate investors, money lenders and borrowers, and even money changers in northern Europe, in a city such as Ghent. They appeared as heads of households in fiscal inventories for towns and cities. Women were generally excluded from university professions and from the notariate.

Throughout the Middle Ages women were denied a political role in urban government, though one does find noble women, such as the twelfth-century Vicountess Ermengard of Narbonne, occupying the position of lord in a town. The thirteenth-century countesses of Flanders, Jeanne and Margaret, ruled a principality where cities and towns were very important. Women did not attend political assemblies in most towns and had no participation on municipal councils. They were citizens of their towns but lacking in political enfranchisement. Women were not formally engaged in the urban militia or in the defense of urban fortifications, though their informal roles in siege crises must have been significant; some were skilled in combat as in Ghent.

Female religious, often from privileged families, filled urban monasteries. Women religious of orthodox inspiration might be cloistered, but not all religious women were so confined. In Italy, penitent women like Catherine of Siena frequently lived at home and were advised by local friars. In the case of Beguines of the Low Countries, they offered services to the sick, leaving the confines of their urban beguinages to do so. Lay women were also active in urban parishes and in urban philanthropy.

The old paradigm of a patriarchal society has been set aside in newer studies of urban women in favor of a situation in which they were able to function effectively in legal, social, and economic contexts. These findings need further testing across a diverse geography.

KATHRYN REYERSON

References and Further Reading

Farmer, Sharon. *Surviving Poverty in Medieval Paris. Gender, Ideology, and the Daily Lives of the Poor*. Ithaca and London: Cornell University Press, 2002.

Hanawalt, Barbara A., ed. *Women and Work in Preindustrial Europe*. Bloomington: Indiana University Press, 1986.

Nicholas, David. *The Domestic Life of a Medieval City: Women, Children, and the Family in Fourteenth-Century Ghent*. Lincoln and London: University of Nebraska Press, 1985.

See also **Artisan Families, Women of; Beguines; Conduct Literature; Datini, Margherita; Dowry and Other Marriage Gifts; Ermengard; Feme Sole; Gossip and Slander; Inheritance; Laywomen, Religious; Legal Agency; Marriage, Christian; Merchant Families, Women of; Monasticism and Nuns; Sumptuary Law; Warfare; Widows; Widows as Guardians; Work**

CLARE OF ASSISI

Clare of Assisi (1194–1253) was the daughter of Offreduccio di Favarone, an Assisi knight, and his wife, Ortolana. One of the earliest followers of St. Francis, Clare ran away from her noble palazzo and had her hair tonsured by Francis, making her unfit for marriage. When the knights of her family discovered her missing, they rode in force to the Benedictine church of San Paolo delle Abbadesse, where she had taken shelter. As Clare clung to the altar cloth in the abbey church, she removed her veil, showing her shaved head. Realizing her worthlessness as a bride, Offreduccio's knights left her to her fate.

Clare's sister Agnes also escaped to join her. Both Clare and Agnes were received by Francis and given the Monastery of San Damiano just outside Assisi. In the Church of San Damiano Francis had been given the command to "Go, repair my house, can't you see that it is falling into ruin." Clare spent the rest of her life in this monastery.

Clare's vision of religious life followed the theology of Francis best summarized in the scripture passage, "If you wish to be perfect, go, sell what you have and give the money to the poor, and you will have treasure in heaven. Then come follow me" (Matthew 19:21). Since religious life was considered to be the "life of perfection," those wishing to be perfect were given these instructions, according to the thinking of Francis, by Jesus himself. Anyone who wished to follow Jesus began by literally selling everything and giving it to the poor.

For Clare and Agnes, this meant that they needed to give their noble dowries to the poor rather than using them to endow their monastery. They wanted to rely totally on alms and on the resources of a few Franciscan brothers who begged for them.

Organizing a Monastic Life

In an effort to bring order to numerous expressions of religious enthusiasm at the time, the 1215 Fourth Lateran Council legislated that all religious houses needed to accept an approved rule. No doubt as a result of this, Francis demanded that Clare accept the title "abbess," possibly signaling an acceptance of the Benedictine Rule. Since the Franciscan Rule was not approved until 1223, the brothers were exempt from the Lateran decree by the will of the papacy, which realized their worth as preachers for the papal cause. Pope Honorius III, however, assigned the organization of the many communities of sisters in the central and northern Italian peninsula to Cardinal Ugolino Conti de Segni, who would later become Pope

Gregory IX. Ugolino fulfilled this task with considerable vigor, offering papal protection in return for the acceptance of the Benedictine Rule and his own constitutions.

Understanding that the core of her vocation was the following of the poor Christ by living without possessions, Clare accepted the demands of Ugolino, but not before she had secured a papal privilege that would protect the Franciscan nature of her life. This privilege, "the privilege of poverty," granted by Pope Gregory in 1228, was the right not to be forced to accept possessions. This meant that the sisters within the Monastery of San Damiano could remain completely dependent upon alms. In order to maintain this economy, it also meant that Franciscan brothers would need to live at the monastery to attend to the spiritual and temporal needs of the sisters.

While accepting the title of abbess, Clare defined her role as that of the servant of the San Damiano monastery. An example of silence, fasting, and prayer, Clare was remembered by her sisters primarily for her tenderness. She covered her sisters from the cold at night, washed the feet of the serving sisters, and did perhaps the most difficult job in the monastery, cleaning up after the sick sisters. Francis sent ill brothers to her, and the people of Assisi came to her with prayer petitions and with their sick children.

Advice to Agnes of Prague

In 1234, the Bohemian princess, Agnes of Prague, inspired by Clare's vision, began a Franciscan monastery for women. Over the course of her lifetime, Clare wrote four letters to Agnes. Masterpieces of Franciscan literature, these letters outline Clare's spirituality, her understanding of the Franciscan vocation, and, when read in context with other papal and royal correspondence, reveal the struggle of early Franciscan women to remain in poverty after Francis's death. Clare's first letter welcomes Agnes into the Franciscan life, describing her conversion as a "sacred business deal" with God by which she is destined, according to the Gospel, to gain "one-hundred fold." Comparing Agnes of Prague with her namesake, the ancient virgin-martyr Agnes of Rome, Clare congratulated the Bohemian princess on her choice of the Franciscan life over a life of courtly pomp.

Clare's second letter to Agnes supports the Bohemian princess's struggle to acquire the "privilege of poverty" for her own monastery. Her third letter congratulates Agnes on obtaining this privilege and instructs her concerning the fasting customs practiced at San Damiano. These fasting practices, of course, were directly related to the chosen poverty of the sisters who ate little in order to survive on alms. A fourth letter, written shortly before Clare's death, outlines Franciscan prayer as the meditation and contemplation of Christ at his birth, in his public life, on the cross, and risen in glory.

Rule of Saint Clare

Papal pressure to accept property continued under Pope Innocent IV. With the help of the politicking of Agnes of Prague and the genuine discontent among Franciscan sisters who were forced to profess the Benedictine Rule, Clare finally received papal approval of a Rule that she had written on her deathbed. Although much of this Rule is pieced together from the Rule of St. Francis and papal legislation, Clare placed an autobiographical chapter in the Rule in which she carefully described the poverty of her monastery as being without endowments and guaranteed income. This hard-won privilege, however, did not extend beyond San Damiano and a few other houses.

Clare died, surrounded by the sisters of San Damiano, on August 11, 1253. Two months later, the papacy initiated an inquiry into her sanctity. She was canonized by Pope Alexander IV on August 15, 1255.

JOAN MUELLER

References and Further Reading

Armstrong, Regis. *Clare of Assisi: Early Documents.* St. Bonaventure, N.Y.: The Franciscan Institute, 1993.
Bartoli, Marco. *Clare of Assisi.* Quincy, Ill.: Franciscan Press, 1993.
Gennaro, Clara. "Clare, Agnes, and Their Earliest Followers: From the Poor Ladies of San Damiano to the Poor Clares." *Women and Religion in Medieval and Renaissance Italy*, edited by Daniel Bornstein and Roberto Rusconi. Chicago: University of Chicago Press, 1996, pp. 39–55.
Mooney, Catherine M. "*Imitatio Christi* or *Imitatio Mariae*? Clare of Assisi and Her Interpreters." In *Gendered Voices: Medieval Saints and Their Interpreters*, edited by Catherine M. Mooney. Philadelphia: University of Pennsylvania Press, 1999, pp. 52–77.
Mueller, Joan. *Clare's Letters to Agnes: Texts and Sources.* St. Bonaventure, N.Y.: The Franciscan Institute, 2001.
———. "Poverty Legislation and Mutual Relations in the Early Franciscan Movement." *Collectanea Franciscana* 71 (2001): 389–419.
———. *Clare of Assisi: The Letters to Agnes.* Collegeville, Minn.: Liturgical Press, 2003.

See also **Agnes of Prague; Hagiography; Monastic Rules; Monasticism and Nuns; Poor Clares Order; Poverty, Religious**

CLARE OF MONTEFALCO

Clare (1268–1308) was the abbess of a monastery in Montefalco, Umbria, who was famous for her opposition to the heresy of the Free Spirit and for her penitential piety. Since she was associated with the Third Order of St. Francis before her monastery adopted the Augustinian Rule in 1290, her spiritual outlook always retained some Franciscan characteristics.

While growing up in Montefalco, Clare, from the age of six, visited her sister Giovanna at a hermitage nearby. This small community of women, common in Italy at the time, soon became a monastery, with Giovanna as the first abbess. With her passing in 1291, Clare, already well known for her pious devotion and ecstatic prayer, was elected in her stead. Some Franciscan members of the Free Spirit tried to win her over to their views. This sect did not believe in hell, and presumed they were exempt from the commandments because of their closeness to God. Like other contemporary women mystics Clare was considered a prophet, who possessed spiritual gifts and upheld Catholic orthodoxy. Clare was distinguished by her love of the poor, her emphasis on gratitude to God, and her ability to read minds. Her focus on Christ's passion is typical of attitudes of the time.

The extant sources reveal much about Clare's family, monastery, and the town of Montefalco. Her life is detailed in a biography (written c. 1309) by Berengar of Saint-Affrique and in a lengthy process of canonization of 1318–1319. These works emphasize her "miracle of the heart," a cross and other instruments of the Passion that were discovered inside her heart immediately after her death. (Her nuns, without permission, dissected her body.) For unknown reasons the process was interrupted and she was not declared a saint until 1881.

Clare's illustrious career tells us about the influence of women's communities in central Italy, c. 1300.

THOMAS RENNA

References and Further Reading

Berengario di Donadio. *Saint Clare of the Cross of Montefalco.* translated by M. J. O'Connell. Villanova, Pa.: Augustinian Press, 1999.

Menesto', Enrico. *Il processo di canonizzazione di Chiara da Montefalco.* Regione dell'Umbria–La Nuova Italia Editrice, Florence, 1984.

Park, Katherine. "Relics of a Fertile Heart: The 'Autopsy' of Clare of Montefalco." In *The Material Culture of Sex, Procreation, and Marriage in Premodern Europe,* edited by Anne L. McClanan and Karen Rosoff. Encarnación, New York: Palgrave, 2002, pp. 115–133.

See also **Abbesses; Canonization of Saints; Hagiography; Heretics and Heresies; Italy; Monasticism and Nuns; Prophets**

CLEMENCE OF BARKING

A signature at the end of a late twelfth-century Anglo-Norman verse life of St. Catherine of Alexandria, the virgin martyr, is all we have to identify the poet Clemence: "Jo ki sa vie ai translatee, / Par nun sui Clemence numee. / De Berkinge sui nunain. / Pur s'amur pris cest oevre en mein" (ll. 2689–2692: I who have translated [St. Catherine's] life, by name am called Clemence. I am a nun of Barking. For the love of her I undertook this work).

Barking Abbey, located just east of London, founded c. 670, had become by the twelfth century an important center for vernacular writing. Shortly before Clemence composed her life of St. Catherine, another nun there had written a verse translation of the life of St. Edward the Confessor by Aelred of Rievaulx. Other writings associated with the abbey include Guernes de Pont-Sainte-Maxence's life of Thomas Becket, patronized by abbess Marie, Thomas's sister; and Adgar's *Gracial,* a collection of miracles of the Virgin dedicated to another abbess, Henry II's natural daughter Maud. These references illustrate the political importance, and indeed the strong "feminist" tradition, of an institution where resident noblewomen encouraged the cultivation of vernacular letters, in accordance with their own cultural and spiritual needs.

Clemence's poem celebrates St. Catherine as the personification of the nun's vocation. Clemence translates faithfully her source, an eleventh-century Latin prose life known as the *Vulgata.* She adds moralizing digressions, and considerably amplifies a number of the saint's discourses, inflecting the legend toward the cult of the Virgin Mary. In these original passages, Clemence demonstrates her own, considerable literary skill and theological sophistication. Her understanding of the Incarnation, as Jocelyn Wogan-Browne has argued, reveals a familiarity with the thought of St. Anselm of Canterbury. Echoes of other vernacular verse lives—St. George, St. Lawrence, and St. Mary the Egyptian—and an apparent familiarity with Thomas's *Tristan* romance, place her in the center of the Anglo-Norman literary community, at a privileged moment in its history.

J. DUNCAN ROBERTSON

References and Further Reading

Batt, Catherine. "Clemence of Barking's Transformations of *courtoisie* in *La Vie de sainte Catherine d'Alexandrie,*" in Roger Ellis, ed., *Translation in the Middle Ages, New Comparison* 12 (1999): 102–133.

MacBain, William. *The Life of St. Catherine of Alexandria by Clemence of Barking,* Anglo-Norman Text Society 18. Oxford: Blackwell, 1964.

Robertson, Duncan. "Writing in the Textual Community: Clemence of Barking's Life of St. Catherine," *French Forum* 21 (1996): 5–28.

Wogan-Browne, Jocelyn. *Saints' Lives and Women's Literary Culture: Virginity and its Authorizations.* Oxford: Oxford University Press, 2001, pp. 227–245.

Wogan-Browne, Jocelyn and Glyn S. Burgess, *Virgin Lives and Holy Deaths: Two Exemplary Biographies for Anglo-Norman Women. The Life of St Catherine, The Life of St Lawrence.* London: Everyman, 1996.

See also **Hagiography; Literature, Old French; Virgin Martyrs; Women Authors: Old French Texts**

CLOTHING

Clothes and other adornments in the Middle Ages were highly charged indicators of wide-ranging cultural distinctions; their use and meaning, whether historically or in literary and visual representations of clothed bodies, extended far beyond the functions of practical cover or decorative adornment. From the historical Joan of Arc, whose cross-dressing as a warrior knight defied her interrogators' expectations of both class and gender, to the literary Griselda, whose banishment in a simple shift gave Christine de Pizan a forum for denouncing wife abuse, medieval clothing was used materially and symbolically to regulate social identities and to challenge them.

Regulatory and Ritual Clothing

In many instances, specific items of medieval dress provided a visual accounting of social classification and status. Garments were used to mark religious, military, and chivalric orders in the Middle Ages and to single out pilgrims, Jews, Muslims, heretics, lepers, prostitutes, the insane, and individuals condemned to death. Heraldic imagery recorded and displayed publicly the lineage of elite families. Saracens could not wear clothes that might allow them to be confused with Franks, and the devil was often represented in stripes for quick recognition. Complex robing and coronation rituals defined social relationships between royal, ecclesiastical, and warrior figures from Central Asia through Persia, the Byzantine Empire and the Middle East, to the medieval West. European liturgical vestments, endowed with official symbolism that maintained a hierarchy of rank and orders, were also deployed publicly in elaborate rituals of dressing and undressing priests. Clothing and bodily adornment for the dead held special symbolic significance. Even undergarments often served, in medieval literary texts, as key indicators of gendered social status.

Legal and Moral Restraints

Sumptuary laws, vernacular sermons, and didactic literary texts, which were marshaled to help regulate the consumption, display, and dispersal of clothing, also often expressed concern that individual items of dress had failed to perform an appointed regulatory function. Although sumptuary legislation varied widely among western European countries and municipalities, these laws attempted in general to regulate, seemingly with little effect, the extravagant use of costly fabrics and excessive yardage, focusing at times on the reputed excesses of women in particular, and at others, on making lesser nobles visually distinct from royalty or commoners distinct from the nobility.

However, the very materiality of clothing as a portable and highly valued commodity allowed it to circulate as currency, which could easily produce visual confusion among social ranks. English and French wills containing bequests of clothing provide important information about gift giving across status groups. Through the courtly culture of *largesse*, or generous giving, luxury garments circulated widely among members of both courtly and noncourtly worlds, as jongleurs and innkeepers were said to be compensated in rich clothes and furs, much as knights and other nobles were. Joan of Navarre's reputed exasperation at seeing hundreds of bourgeois women outfitted in silks and furs as if they were queens encapsulated the dilemma. If publicly displayed luxury clothing could fashion Joan into a French queen, it could also mint bourgeois queens in her image.

Demarcating and Defining Gender

Gender was also regulated through the monitoring of medieval clothing. Clerical authors typically expressed concern that excessive expenditure on women's costly attire would bring financial impoverishment to men, and that men's participation in donning lavish clothes would result in their own moral ruin. Even more important, however, was the fear often expressed in vernacular and Latin sermons that if men began to dress in the opulent style "of women," their extravagant clothing and adornment could obscure, rather than delineate, biological differences. Thus Saint Bernard exhorted knights not to wear the trinkets of women, to cut their effeminate long locks and discard their billowing tunics. And yet the possibility that changing clothing could alter or blur gender distinctions was explored at length in historical, pseudo-historical, hagiographic, and literary narratives of transvestite heroines. While female saints from Perpetua to Hildegund of Schönau cross-dressed as men, female protagonists, like the heroine in the *Romance of Silence*, disguised themselves as minstrels, knights, and warriors. Courtly lovers in the High Middle Ages sometimes profited from unisex garb to facilitate clandestine heterosexual liaisons. Whereas armor, the quintessential marker of chivalric masculinity, ironically provided the perfect cover for disguised females, loose-fitting unisex articles of courtly clothing were frequently bestowed upon men by female attendants in romance texts. Women who clothe men in this way, along with others like Queen Iseut, who elaborately dressed her disguised adulterous lover for the famous trial scene in the French *Romance of Tristan*, provided important alternatives to the traditional scenario of Pygmalion shaping and clothing Galatea.

Breaking the Rules

Ample evidence from the medieval period suggests that clothes could define their wearers socially both within and against established conventions. Conduct books, which record moral concerns about the production and consumption of fashionable clothes, also reveal that women's management of clothing and linens provided new opportunities for self-definition. Other sources show pious women using religious garb as a covert form of resistance against their husbands. Courtly literary texts feature female protagonists who deploy the clothing most often used to attire them as dolled-up beauties to starkly different effect. These heroines use clothes to create alternative systems of female passion, pleasure, and love service, signaling the lady's will, her command, her gift, and contract. Embroidery and clothwork, often used by literary courtly ladies in the making of love tokens, along with women's scarves or detachable sleeves given to knights to wear on their helmets in tournaments, can mark the lady's potentially substantial influence in shaping the course of the love scenario. Even the choice of a woman's dress to represent, allegorically, philosophical learning in Boethius's *Consolation of Philosophy* has been read as an image of feminine bodily difference that challenges, rather than underwrites, masculine wisdom. And surviving leather shoes from the Netherlands, decorated with embossed scenes from the Tristan story, show how that courtly narrative could be recast to reflect concerns with urban marriage.

Foreign Imports

At times, clerical denunciations of the excessive use of fabric and luxury garb also reveal an anxiety about foreignness. The costly silks, gems, and precious metals so often deprecated by moralists were not only imported; they originated from distant and unknown eastern cultures. And yet by the thirteenth century at least, eastern fabrics fashioned into western garments were used systematically in literary texts to signal ostensibly European identities. Literary courtly ladies, whose pure white skin and delicate facial features are typically augmented by extravagant attire, stand firmly at the cultural crossroads between Christian France and the Middle Eastern cities that give their names to the clothes these ladies wear: Phrygia, Damascus, Constantinople. Clerical and lay figures carved on French cathedral facades from the mid-twelfth century onward wear western-style garments decorated with Islamic detailing. European Church treasures in the High Middle Ages are filled with liturgical vestments and altar cloths fashioned from rich silks imported from Spain, Constantinople, and cities of the Levant. Many surviving Christian European alms purses, made of imported Islamic silks, are aptly if ironically termed "Saracen work."

Medieval garments also played an important role as holy relics: whether in the historical, extant chemise of King Louis IX held in the treasury of Notre Dame in Paris or the more elusive but widely known Virgin's *chemise* (shift) from Chartres Cathedral. As clothes no longer worn, these garments-turned-relics held special significance as bodily substitutes because of having touched the flesh of saints reputed to have possessed them.

E. JANE BURNS

References and Further Reading

Burns, E. Jane. *Courtly Love Undressed: Reading Through Clothes in Medieval French Culture*. Philadephia: University of Pennsylvania Press, 2002.
———, ed. *Medieval Fabrications: Dress, Textiles, Clothwork, and Other Cultural Imaginings*. New York: Palgrave Macmillan, 2004.
Crane, Susan. "Clothing and Gender Definition in Joan of Arc." *Journal of Medieval and Early Modern Studies* 26:2 (1996): 207–232.
———. *The Performance of Self: Ritual, Identity and Clothing During the Hundred Years War*. Philadelphia: University of Pennsylvania Press, 2002.
Crowfoot, Elizabeth, Frances Pritchard, and Kay Staniland. *Textiles and Clothing*. London: HMSO, 1992.
Gordon, Stewart, ed. *Robes and Honor: The Medieval World of Investiture*. New York: Palgrave Macmillan, 2001.

Hotchkiss, Valerie R. *Clothes Make the Man: Female Cross Dressing in Medieval Europe.* New York: Garland, 1996.

Pastoureau, Michel, ed. *Le Vêtement: histoire, archéologie et symbolique vestimentaires au Moyen Age.* Paris: Léopard d'Or, 1989.

Piponnier, Françoise and Perrine Mane. *Dress in the Middle Ages.* Trans. Caroline Beamish. New Haven: Yale University Press, 1997.

Snyder, Janet and Désirée Koslin, eds. *Encountering Medieval Textiles and Dress: Objects, Texts, Images.* New York: Palgrave Macmillan, 2003.

See also **Arms and Armor; Christine de Pizan; Clothing for Religious Women; Clothwork, Domestic; Conduct Literature; Courtly Love; Cross-Dressing; Gender Ideologies; Grave Goods; Griselda; Social Status; Sumptuary Law**

CLOTHING FOR RELIGIOUS WOMEN

Simple and inexpensive clothing for virtuous virgins was programmatic as the early Church developed. Uniformity of dress, however, and specificity as to color, cut, and accessories evolved only with the expansion of the reformed monastic orders from the twelfth century onwards. Patristic writers such as Tertullian (c. 160–225), Jerome (345–420) and John Chrysostom (c. 347–407) condemned female frivolity in dress and equated it with vice and lust. Undyed woolen cloth, preferably dark and made into body-concealing, generic garments, was prescribed for religious women during the early centuries, whereas the rules for later female orders enumerated colors and fabric types in detail. The Rule of Caesarius of Arles (c. 470–542), for instance, calls for simple clothing in natural white sheep's wool. By contrast, the rule of the Order of St. Savior established by Birgitta of Sweden (c. 1302–1373), is explicit as to items like the gray *wadmal* cloth to be used, the sleeves' length, and buttons made of wood.

Monastic garments were modeled on ideals of apostolic simplicity; and late antique shapes and names were retained. The dress of the medieval religious, now often termed "habit," consisted of a T-shaped *tunica* of wool, always worn with a belt. Underneath was a full-length, sleeved *camisia*, a shift made of wool, hemp, or linen. A woolen cloth rectangle with a hole for the head, the *scapular*, covered the tunic's front and back; its original use was for protection during manual work. During the divine service, and particularly among the contemplative orders, the *cuculla*, or choir cloak, was worn over the tunic. In medieval depictions, the *cuculla*'s sweeping dimensions and hanging sleeves are easily identified. Outside and in cold weather, a semicircular mantle, sometimes lined with fur, was worn over the tunic. As footwear, most of the religious orders used shoes. Only the more radical tertiaries wore sandals or went barefoot. Hose, sewn from bias-cut woolen cloth, was specified for some orders. Two sets of basic clothing were often provided to nuns for day-to-day and seasonal changes. Worn-out garments were passed on to the truly poor.

Religious women wore head veils and wimples covering throat and chest, just like most medieval secular females. Only unwed and royal women could show their hair. The veil was fastened by means of pins attached to a close-fitting bonnet, *coif*, or linen bands wrapped around the head, *vittae*. A nun-to-be, accepted as a postulant in a religious house, wore a white veil over the white linen under-veil. Prior to profession, she was tonsured with a short haircut; and, at the consecration ceremony, the bishop placed a black veil over the new nun's under-veil. This black veil would also be used for her burial. More than any other clothing item, the black veil was the nun's signifier.

Medieval religious orders may be divided by their founding rules. Dress styles and colors (black [B] and white [W] the most common) can be linked to this classification. Those obeying the fifth-century Rule of St. Benedict, considered the "First" order, were primarily contemplative orders and are therefore usually seen in *cucullae*. They are, in order of their founding: Benedictines (B); Cistercians (W); Gilbertines (W); Camaldolese (W); Vallombrosans (B); Carthusians (W); Olivetans (W), Humiliati (W); and Sylvestrines (B). The "Second" orders were governed by the Rule of St. Augustine, which allowed modifications to the tenets of obedience and poverty. These orders are less easily classified by their dress, to which changes were made over time. The tunic's color may be different from the scapular and mantle. This group includes: the Hospital orders, whose mantles often carried cross insignia; Premonstratensians (or Norbertines) (W); Trinitarians (W, with blue-red cross); Servites (B); Carmelites (B tunic, W mantle); Dominicans (W tunic, B mantle); and Birgittines (all gray). "Third" orders, obeying the Rule of St. Francis, incorporate several penitential groups as well as the Franciscan branches. Their various brown, gray, or light neutral dress colors evoke the shades of the coarse, unsorted sheep's wool made into cloth that was neither dyed nor fulled as well as finer wool fabrics. St. Clare's mantle survives today in her convent in Assisi, its lean cut and rough texture speaking eloquently of the adherence to the tenets of poverty.

The level of actual observance to the orders' clothing prescriptions is less easy to assess. Bishops visiting female houses often complained that the order's dress codes were ignored, either due to lack of funds or to the wish for sartorial display. Some nuns' testaments reveal that they owned secular garments in bright colors to give away. It seems clear that wealthy institutions could afford to follow the rule, and that some appear to have been lenient in the dress code's implementation, whereas poorer houses would have to make do with less than the rule's ideas of apostolic clothing and appearance.

DESIREE KOSLIN

References and Further Reading

Flury-Lemberg, Mechtild. *Textile Conservation and Research*. Bern: Abegg-Stiftung, 1988.

Hélyot, Pierre. *Histoire des Ordres Monastiques Religieux*. Paris: Nicolas Gosselin, 1714–1719.

Koslin, Désirée. *The Dress of Monastic and Religious Women as seen in the Art from the Early Middle Ages to the Reformation*. PhD dissertation, New York University, 1999.

McNamara, Jo Ann. *Sisters in Arms: Catholic Nuns Through Two Millennia*. Cambridge, Mass.: Harvard University Press, 1996.

Warr, Cordelia. "Religious Habits and Visual Propaganda. The Vision of the Blessed Reginald of Orléans," *Journal of Medieval History* 28 (2002): 43–72.

See also **Birgittine Order; Cistercian Order; Clare of Assisi; Clothing; Dominican Order; Gilbertine Order; Humiliati; Monastic Rules; Monastic Visitation; Monasticism and Nuns; Poor Clares Order; Premonstratensian Order; Tertiaries**

CLOTHWORK, DOMESTIC

Tradition associates the textile crafts with women. Clothmaking tools—spindle whorls, wool combs, shears, and weaving beaters—are characteristic female grave-goods in early medieval Europe. At that time, women wove wool or linen on a vertical loom, either the two-beam variety, or the warp-weighted loom which made use of weights made of clay or stone. Weaving remained an exclusively feminine occupation only until the introduction of mechanisation about the eleventh century. The horizontal loom, incorporating treadles operated by the feet, was, initially at least, a masculine tool. Its introduction coincided with increased urbanisation and facilitated professional manufacture of long lengths of cloth. Meanwhile the vertical loom, operated by women, survived in rural contexts, particularly in Scandinavia, or was diverted to specialist functions such as tapestry weaving. Women continued to weave narrow wares on small band looms and they braided belts and edgings on tablets throughout the Middle Ages. Female workers were particularly associated with products made from imported silk, playing a large part in the marketing as well as the manufacture of silk goods.

Spinning

Spinning, unlike weaving, remained in the feminine realm until modern times, even after the introduction of the spinning wheel sped up production; indeed, the term *spinster* is still applied solely to women. Since the proportion of time needed to prepare thread was much greater than that required to weave it into cloth, spinning must have been a constant, necessary occupation. Originally carried out with a distaff held in the left hand and a drop spindle rotated by the right, spinning could continue as a woman walked or watched a pot boil, and be set aside without damage as she attended to other tasks. When a woman is not engaged in spinning, the raw fibre is wound round the distaff, the spindle dangling from it by a length of spun thread.

Although spinning was associated with virtuous womanhood, and idleness at the distaff with sloth, satire suggests that men may have found the incessant spinning irritating and alienating—misericords at Malvern and Westminster show irate wives chasing husbands with raised distaff, while in the margin of fol. 60r of the Luttrell Psalter a woman brandishes her distaff to beat a man crouching abjectly at her feet. One of the earliest comic characters in English drama, Noah's wife in the Wakefield cycle of Mystery Plays, insists, as the Flood waters rise, that she cannot go into the ark as she has to finish her spinning.

Clothmaking

Until the Industrial Revolution, textile manufacture was intensely physical. Every thread in every item of clothing had passed between some woman's finger and thumb. Flax was kept moist during spinning with constant licks of saliva, loose rovings of wool were rolled down the thigh, and skeins were wound on the hands. Threads and cloth were measured against the human body. Clothworking was a communal feminine activity, and since, unlike production on modern machinery, it was not noisy, there was opportunity for talking, perhaps even singing. (The latter is recorded among early modern hand-fullers in Ireland who used the rhythm of the song to coordinate their work.) An Icelandic story tells of women's conversation at sewing. Weaving a large piece of cloth, such as a blanket or cloak, would be facilitated if two women worked together, passing the weft thread on a bobbin from one to the other. In the domestic sphere it was labour for mother to share with daughter. Great estates would employ whole workshops of women, to prepare the clothing and other textile necessities for the community. Illustrations in the Carolingian Utrecht Psalter and the English Eadwine Psalter show a group of women, talking animatedly, with a large hank of thread and a partially prepared loom.

The labour-intensive nature of cloth production made textiles precious. Their alteration and maintenance was an essential household task which largely fell to women—wives, daughters, female servants, and, in the monastic world, nuns. At the top of the social hierarchy, garments of the rich and royal, made of velvet and decorated with gold thread, were donated to churches where they were remade into vestments and other ecclesiastical cloths. In contrast the clothing of a male corpse found in a peat bog at Bernuthsfeld, Germany, radio-carbon dated to c. 660 A.D., included a tunic made up of a patchwork of forty-five pieces, an economical use of precious scraps of cloth. The employees of great households were regularly supplied with new clothing; used garments were given to social inferiors, sold, or recycled. Clothing was bequeathed. Enlarging garments for growing children, or adjusting them for new owners, were essential tasks at domestic and institutional levels. Women were occupied also with laundry, stain removal, repair work, and the constant renewing of garments and bed linen by cutting out worn parts and remaking the remainder, until the textile was reduced to rags. Even rags had their uses: in the ship-building industry at the Viking Age emporium of Haithabu (Hedeby, Germany), ships were tarred and caulked with torn up garments. Later, rags were used in papermaking, which first appeared in Europe in twelfth-century Italy, the technique imported from China, via Arabs. By the mid-fifteenth century, rag collection from industrial centres was a major occupation throughout Europe. Rags were taken to mills for sorting and pulping with water, a process that continued until the eighteenth century when a shortage of rags led to the substitution of vegetable fibres in paper production.

Clothmaking spanned the social scale. In the early medieval period, textile workers, even skilled ones, were sometimes slaves. Cloth manufacture for profit was evidently a respectable occupation for middle-class women (in the fourteenth century, Chaucer's Wife of Bath boasted of her expertise at weaving, combining this career with successive marriages). It was also a desirable skill for those of top status.

Charlemagne, King of the Franks and Holy Roman Emperor (742–814), had his daughters taught to spin. The burial of a high-ranking woman and her attendant, deposited in 834 at Oseberg, Norway, contained incomplete tablet weaving, a tapestry, looms, and equipment for winding thread. Royal women across western Europe created and patronised gold and silk embroidery of the highest standard, often for ecclesiastical use: Alpeide, sister of Holy Roman Emperor Charles the Bald, embroidered an inscription on a precious silk cushion for the head of Saint Remigius at the translation of that saint's relics in 852; Ælfflæd, wife of the English king Edward the Elder, commissioned in the early tenth century a stole and maniple, originally for the Bishop of Winchester but later given to the shrine of St. Cuthbert, now in Durham. Edith, who married the English king Edward the Confessor in 1045, exercised her personal skills and patronage to equip her husband more splendidly than any previous English king; his garments were decorated with gold embroidery, gemstones and pearls; his throne was covered with gold-embroidered textile and his floors with Spanish carpets.

However, illustrations in late medieval manuscripts of richly dressed ladies carrying out textile crafts should not be assumed to be an authentic representation of medieval life: their subject is often either biblical or classical. For example, the early fifteenth-century manuscript British Library Royal 16 G v (a French translation of Boccaccio's *De claris mulieribus*) has illuminations depicting Arachne, Gaia Caecilia and her ladies, Pamphila, daughter of Plates and Penelope, variously spinning, carding, and weaving according to the legends associated with them.

Embroidery

Decorative stitching on woven cloth—embroidery—is known from antiquity and examples from medieval Europe exist from the seventh century onward. Embroidery can be utilitarian—for example to personalize linen in communal laundry—or decorative in a simple way, concealing seams or edging a garment at the neckline, wrist, or hem. It can also be extremely elaborate and expensive, especially the prestigious gold and silk work that reached its apogee in the fourteenth and early fifteenth centuries. Embroidered motifs may be instructive, iconic, or symbolic, especially on ecclesiastical vestments and royal regalia. It is usually assumed that women carried out embroidery in medieval times and in fact the names of several early exponents are documented. The feminine aspect of embroidery has probably been exaggerated,

CLOTHWORK, DOMESTIC

however. The tradition that Mathilda, wife of William the Conqueror, was responsible, with the ladies of her court, for the Bayeux Tapestry (c. 1066–1087) has no authority, and indeed the Tapestry is clearly the product of professional workshops. Male embroiderers were employed in France by the eleventh century, and in the twelfth and thirteenth centuries when embroidery production was highly professionalized and well-documented, male workers were paid more than female.

Metaphors from Clothwork

The spinning of thread, and the cutting of it, occurs as a metaphor for life and death in many mythologies and religions and is often expressed in imagery of female cloth workers. Biblical use of the metaphor is reflected in the loom preparation scenes in Psalters, previously mentioned. Pagan female deities were imagined spinning and weaving: the Greek *Moirai* "Fates", three sisters, respectively spun the thread of human life, measured it out and cut it when the time came to die. Their Roman equivalents were the *Parcae* and the Scandinavian, the *Norns*. Northern mythology also included Valkyries, "choosers of the slain," female warriors who were depicted in the Icelandic poem *Darraðarljóð* as grisly weavers, with entrails for threads and severed heads as loom-weights.

Metaphorical use of woman as textile worker continued in Christian tradition. In apocryphal gospels, the young Virgin Mary was described as a skilled weaver and spinner. She was chosen to prepare the purple thread for weaving the veil of the temple, which would be severed at the crucifixion. Mary's spinning, therefore, is a metaphor for her part in Christ's incarnation. In medieval art she is often pictured with spinning, weaving, or knitting implements, familiar and domestic, but also reflecting both the apocryphal stories and the theological concept that Mary, by bearing Jesus Christ, clothed him in flesh. An illustration in a fourteenth-century pseudo-Bonaventure manuscript depicts Mary sewing, accompanied by two other women, one spinning, the other with scissors, thus offering a link between Christian theology and the pagan conception of woman creating and cutting cloth, which symbolises life itself.

GALE R. OWEN-CROCKER

Note: For References and Further Reading, see **Textile Production for the Market**

See also **Clothing; Clothing for Religious Women; Home Manufacturing; Household Management;** **Misericords; Sumptuary Law; Textile Production for the Market; Valkyries**

CLOTILDA

Clotilda, queen of the Franks (474–545), was the daughter of the Burgundian King Chilperic. Although most Burgundians professed Arianism, she was trained in the orthodox faith by her mother. After her parents' murder by her uncle King Gundobad in 490, she took refuge with her other uncle, King Godegisil, at Geneva. There, Clovis, the pagan king of the Franks, proposed marriage. She accepted his offer on the condition that her children would be baptized in the orthodox faith. According to Gregory of Tours, she played an important part in Clovis's conversion. After her husband's death, she retired to Tours, devoting her life to piety and charity. She died in 545 and was buried in the Church of the Apostles (St. Geneviève), which she built together with Clovis.

Although considered one of the most pious Merovingian queens, Clotilda's actions sometimes reflected a barbarian mentality. Her campaign for revenge against her parents' murderers corroborates the fact that she still obeyed a Germanic code of honor, far from the Christian ideal of *caritas* (divine love). Yet, beyond this paradoxical behavior, Clotilda certainly incarnates the traditional model of the holy royal missionary consort whose vocation was to bring her husband to Christianity. Her *vita*, based on Gregory of Tours's account, was written by Adson of Montier-en-Der between 956 and 960. It is interesting to note that in this later version, un-Christian Germanic behavior has been totally eradicated. From the tenth century onward, Clotilda was remembered as a dutiful Christian woman and a saintly queen.

NIRA PANCER

References and Further Reading

Gregory of Tours. *The History of the Franks*, edited and translated by Lewis Thorpe, Harmondsworth: Penguin, 1974.
Harrison, Dick. *The Age of Abbesses and Queens*. Sweden: Nordic Academic Press, 1998.
Scheibelreiter, Georg. "Clovis, le païen, Clotilde, la pieuse: À propos de la mentalité barbare," in *Clovis: Histoire et mémoire*, edited by Michel Rouche, 2 vols. Paris: Presses de l'Université de Paris-Sorbonne, 1997. t.1, pp. 348–367.
Stafford, Pauline. *Queens, Concubines and Dowagers: The King's Wife in Early Middle Ages*. Athens, Ga.: University of Georgia Press, 1983.
Wood, I. N. *The Merovingian Kingdoms, 450–751*, London: Longman, 1994, pp. 120–139.

See also **Conversion, Religious; Frankish Lands; Queens and Empresses: The West**

CLUNIAC ORDER

The monastery of Cluny, founded in Burgundy by the Duke of Aquitaine in 909–910, was one of a number of foundations of the Carolingian era that sought to return to the standards of Saint Benedict's sixth-century "Rule." Cluny's origins were rather humble, yet it was always considered a holy house, where the monks renounced the comforts of the world and practiced individual poverty. This meant that although the house itself might own a great deal, individual monks had nothing of their own. Their holiness was safeguarded by the duke's stipulation that no bishop or secular lord—including himself—should interfere in the monks' internal affairs, which were subject solely to the distant pope.

During the tenth century, it was a fairly common practice for a monastic house experiencing difficulties to be placed under the direction of a flourishing monastery. Then, once that house had been reformed, and when the abbot who had headed both houses died, the monks of each house would elect their own abbots. Cluny's own first abbot, Berno, also headed the monastery of Gigny, although after his death the two monasteries went their separate ways. Such houses as St. Bénigne of Dijon were reformed by Cluny in this way in the tenth century.

But in the eleventh century it became more common for a monastery given to Cluny to remain under the authority of Cluny's abbot. Such houses were known as priories, headed by a prior rather than an abbot. The monastery of Paray-le-Monial was the first important house to come permanently under Cluny's direction. Other Burgundian houses soon followed, including St. Marcel-lès-Chalon and La Charité.

In the later eleventh century, under Abbot Hugh (1049–1109), Cluny became the most influential monastery in western Europe, attracting gifts from kings as far away as Spain and grants of immunity from the pope. A number of Cluniac monks became bishops. Several monasteries, most notably Vézelay, came under Cluny's direction, although they kept their own abbots. The great church known as Cluny III was built, and it was the biggest church in Christendom until the end of the Middle Ages. An enormous church was needed because of the great flood of converts, comprised of boys offered to the monastery by their parents and mature adults who left the secular world to finish their lives in an aura of sanctity. The Duke of Burgundy, for example, became a monk at Cluny in 1078 after being wounded in battle.

Normally a married man could not leave his wife for the monastery, unless she too agreed to enter the church. The nunnery of Marcigny, some fifty kilometers from Cluny, was founded in 1054 for the wives and daughters of men who entered Cluny. The founders were the lords of Semur, the family of Abbot Hugh, and in the 1080s most of the secular members of the family followed their ecclesiastical relatives into Cluny and Marcigny.

The monastic life at Cluny at the end of the eleventh century was one of great display. The assumption was that to glorify God one needed the best in everything, including constant prayers and psalms, a beautifully designed and decorated church, and fine vestments. But another strand developed in eleventh-century thought, centered on the notion that God was best glorified through simplicity and poverty. Although Cluny and its monks could not be considered corrupt, by the twelfth century other groups of monks, especially the Cistercians, were often considered more holy and began to attract the bulk of gifts and converts.

The Cistercians had begun with the foundation of Cîteaux in 1098, a house originally scarcely distinguishable from a hermitage but which quickly attracted many young adult converts. Like the Cluniacs, they followed a version of the "Benedictine Rule," but with a much greater emphasis on simplicity and manual labor. By the middle of the twelfth century, the popularity of the Cistercians led to the foundation of numerous daughter-houses and to the creation of a true Order, in which the relationships between the different houses was spelled out and standards for everything from form of dress to the liturgy to the placement of churches was specified and enforced.

This kind of uniformity had no precedent at Cluny, where many houses had come under Cluny's direction and left again, and some (like St. Bénigne of Dijon and St. German of Auxerre), formerly under Cluny's direction, began to acquire their own priories. By the middle of the thirteenth century, however, by which time the number of Cluniac priories had expanded from a handful to dozens, there was a deliberate effort to establish some sort of uniformity, in part in imitation of the Cistercians, leading for the first time to a true Cluniac Order.

CONSTANCE B. BOUCHARD

References and Further Reading

Bouchard, Constance B. *Sword, Miter, and Cloister: Nobility and the Church in Burgundy, 980–1198.* Ithaca, N.Y.: Cornell University Press, 1987.

———. "Merovingian, Carolingian, and Cluniac Monasticism: Reform and Renewal in Burgundy." *Journal of Ecclesiastical History* 41 (1990), 365–388.

Hunt, Noreen. *Cluny Under Saint Hugh, 1049–1109.* London: Edward Arnold, 1969.

Iogna-Prat, Dominique. *Order and Exclusion: Cluny and Christendom Face Heresy, Judaism, and Islam (1000–1150).* translated by Graham Robert Edwards. Ithaca, N.Y.: Cornell University Press, 2002.

Richard, Jean, ed. *Le cartulaire de Marcigny-sur-Loire (1045–1044): Essais de reconstitution d'un manuscrit disparu.* Dijon: Bernigaud et Privat, 1957.

Rosenwein, Barbara H. *Rhinoceros Bound: Cluny in the Tenth Century.* Philadelphia: University of Pennsylvania Press, 1982.

———. *To Be the Neighbor of Saint Peter: The Social Meaning of Cluny's Property, 909–1049.* Ithaca, N.Y.: Cornell University Press, 1989.

Van Engen, John. "The 'Crisis of Cenobitism' Reconsidered: Benedictine Monasticism in the Years 1050–1150." *Speculum* 61 (1986), pp. 269–304.

Wischermann, Elsa Maria. *Marcigny-sur-Loire: Gründungs- und Frühgeschichte des ersten Cluniacenserinnen priorates (1055–1150).* Munich: W. Fink, 1986.

See also **Cistercian Order; Monasticism and Nuns**

COINAGE

The placing of a woman's name on medieval coinage was a declaration of her political rights and a recognition, at least by the officials of her mint, of her effective rule. As coins were the most widely disseminated government product, their message would have been available to people of all social groups, at least those with enough literacy to recognize the ruler's name on them. During the course of the Middle Ages, the names of about one hundred women appeared on the coinages of Europe, Byzantium, and the Islamic world; in most cases this recognition came as the culmination of a process of political, legal, and even military struggle.

The only group of medieval women who had an *ipso facto* right to mint were the abbesses of convents who received the privilege of "moneta" along with those to markets and tolls, usually in foundation charters issued by imperial rulers of the central Middle Ages. This right was exercised by nine German houses, most notably Eschwege, Gandersheim, Herford, and, especially, Quedlinburg (whose coinage continued well into the modern period). As was the case with other aspects of monastic rights throughout Europe, the control of coinage frequently became a source of conflict between the abbess and the lay advocate, who was theoretically her representative in secular matters. In the case of Eschwege, this conflict was resolved in a decree of Frederick Barbarossa of 1188 which confirmed that the abbess had the unquestioned right of setting the standards and images on the coinage and that the advocate's role was that of "amicable and competent service" to her. The dispute between the abbess of Quedlinburg and her lay advocate resulted in the appearance of the image of an armed knight next to a nun on one issue of the coinage; it was finally settled by a decree of Innocent III in 1207, which confirmed to the abbess and the chapter the sole right to the striking of coins.

Other women exercised a right to coinage as a result of their inheritance of other political powers, usually in the absence of a male heir. The ninth-century Byzantine empress Theodora appeared on both sides of her coinage during her sole rule, but had to give way in other periods to her sister Zoe's husband and adopted son. Another heiress who minted her own name was Empress Matilda of England, daughter of Henry I, whose coinage was issued during her twenty-year struggle for the throne with her cousin Stephen of Blois. Margaret of Hainault issued one of Europe's first high denomination coins in 1244 as successor to her father, Baldwin IX (the first Latin Emperor of Constantinople), and her older sister Johanna (who did not put her name on coins). When her political rights were challenged, Saint Louis restored to Margaret her lands and coinage until her death, at which time they were to be divided between her sons.

For an heiress, marriage did not always bring a loss of identity regarding coinage. Urraca of Castile may have ceded minting to her husband, Alfonso of Aragon, during their brief marriage, but for most of her reign, from 1109 to 1126, she put her name and image on her coinage and even granted minting rights to the monastery of Sahagún. Mary of Burgundy, daughter of Charles the Bold, kept her name on the coinage of many mints of the Low Countries in the fifteenth century even after her marriage to Maximilian of Austria.

Sometimes the question of the coinage rights of a married heiress was settled by compromise. Constance I of Sicily shared numismatic recognition with her husband, the emperor Henry VI, on the Sicilian coinage of the 1190s—her name appeared on the bronze coins, his on the gold, and both on the alloyed silver pennies. The best known numismatic couple is Isabella of Castile and Ferdinand of Aragon, each of whom brought a kingdom to their joined realm; their dual portrait appeared on the gold doubloons that were to have such a major history in the post-medieval world.

In most cases, however, a woman lost her inherited right to coinage along with her other political powers when she married. Mary of Anjou was typical of many heiresses in terms of recognition on the coinage; her name appeared only on the three years between the death in 1382 of her father, Louis I of Hungary, and her marriage to Sigismund of Luxembourg, whose name then was borne by the coins. The most famous medieval woman to issue coins was Eleanor of Aquitaine, whose issues in Aquitaine bear only her title of duchess and not her name; they were probably minted only after 1189, when her son Richard the Lionhearted became king of England.

As in many areas of medieval politics, the right to coinage was governed more by circumstance and power than by customary or statutory law. The appearance of women's names on coinage throughout the Middle Ages is testimony of the fact that many succeeded in establishing their rights, though often in the face of strong opposition.

ALAN M. STAHL

References and Further Reading

Brubaker, Leslie, and Helen Tobler. "The Gender of Money: Byzantine Empresses on Coins (324–802)." In *Gendering the Middle Ages*, edited by Pauline Stafford and Anneke B. Mulder-Bakker. Oxford, U.K.; Malden, Mass.: Blackwell, 2001, pp. 42–64.

Grierson, Philip. "Numismatics." In *Medieval Studies: An Introduction*, edited by James M. Powell. 2nd edition. Syracuse: Syracuse University Press, 1992, pp. 114–161.

Stahl, Alan M. "Coinage in the Name of Medieval Women." In *Medieval Women and the Sources of Medieval History*, edited by Joel Rosenthal. Athens, Ga.: University of Georgia Press, 1990, pp. 321–341.

See also **Abbesses; Constance of Sicily; Eleanor of Aquitaine; Isabel I; Matilda the Empress; Seals and Sigillography; Succession, Royal and Noble; Urraca**

COLETTE OF CORBIE

Colette (1381–1447) was born in the town of Corbie in Picardy, France, to Robert Boellet and Marguerite Moyon. Colette's extraordinary piety manifested itself during her youth; however, when her parents died and Dom Raoul de Roye, abbot of St. Pierre, became her guardian, he wanted her to marry. Eventually she convinced him to allow her to undertake life as a nun, and she was then enclosed as an anchoress. After a few years, she was released from her anchoritic vows. Accompanied by her confessor, Henri de la Baume, she gained an audience with Pope Benedict XIII, who authorized her to begin founding reformed houses for Franciscan nuns.

Colette's connection with Henri de la Baume, and this papal audience, mark her entry into the overlapping worlds of ecclesiastical and secular politics. Henri came from a family with strong ties to the house of Burgundy; Burgundian dukes and duchesses became important patrons for many of the foundations that Colette created during her lifetime. In turn, as the Burgundians struggled with their Armagnac rivals in France, and worked to assert their authority

in the Low Countries, they benefited from association with a woman who was already widely revered for sanctity in her lifetime.

Even Colette's powerful secular supporters, however, did not enable her to overcome the opposition of the Benedictine monks of St. Pierre to her founding a nunnery in Corbie. The monks were not alone in opposing Colette. When she turned her attention to reforming Franciscan friars, she faced substantial resistance. Also, within the Franciscan Order she had to deal with the attempts of the Observant Friars, particularly under the leadership of John of Capistrano, to assimilate her independent reforms.

Colette died March 6, 1447, in Ghent. In spite of her far-reaching reputation for sanctity in the fifteenth century, she was not beatified until 1740 and not canonized until May 24, 1807.

NANCY BRADLEY WARREN

References and Further Reading

Corblet, Jules. *Hagiographie du diocèse d'Amiens*, vol. 1. Paris: Dumoulin; Amiens: Prevost-Allo, 1868.

Lopez, Elisabeth. *Culture et sainteté: Colette de Corbie (1381–1447)*. Saint-Etienne: Publications de l'Université de Saint-Etienne, 1994.

———. *Histoire de Sainte Colette*. Paris: Desclée, 1998.

———. *Petite vie de Sainte Colette*. Paris: Desclée, 1998.

Warren, Nancy Bradley. *Women of God and Arms: Female Spirituality and Political Conflict, 1380–1600*. Philadelphia: University of Pennsylvania Press, 2005.

See also **Agnes of Prague; Clare of Assisi; Flanders; France, Northern; Monastic Rules; Poor Clares Order**

COMPIUTA DONZELLA

The poetic voice known as Compiuta Donzella (Accomplished Maiden), the earliest named female poet in Italian, is an historical enigma. Three sonnets are assigned to her, in only one (though major) manuscript collection of lyric poems, Vatican lat. 3793. Because the name *Compiuta*, while widely attested in the thirteenth century, is also a generic description, it has long been considered a pseudonym, and scholars have disagreed on whether this figure really existed as a female poet or was rather a literary pose by a male poet. Other thirteenth-century poets, such as Guittone d'Arezzo, Mastro Torrigiano, and (possibly) Chiaro Davanzati, praise the erudition and poetic talent of a figure who might be Compiuta Donzella; such references tend to support her historical existence. Indeed, based on historical and stylistic evidence, prominent Italianists such as Contini and Kleinhenz, have argued in favor of it.

Of the three sonnets attributed to her, two are particularly well-known. The first half of "A la stagion che 'l mondo foglia e flora" (In the season when the world leafs out and blooms) extols the beauty of spring, but the second half yokes the conventional nature-introduction to a contrastive lament over her imminent forced marriage. "Lascia vorria lo mondo, e Dio servire" (I would like to leave the world and serve God) can be read as a sequel to the first, although it can also stand alone: the poet finds the world wholly unsatisfactory and wishes to withdraw from it. The third poem is her reply in a debate poem on the subject of her own poetic prowess.

Regardless of her historical identity, the poems attributed to Compiuta Donzella are aesthetically accomplished and affectively vivid. They represent a dimension of women's experience and emotion that enriches the overwhelmingly masculine perspective of medieval Italian lyric poetry.

F. REGINA PSAKI

References and Further Reading

Contini, Gianfranco, ed. *Poeti del Duecento*, Vol. 1, part 1: *Testi arcaici, scuola siciliana, poesia cortese*. Rpt. Milan and Naples: Classici Ricciardi-Mondadori, 1995, pp. 433–438.

Kleinhenz, Christopher. "*Pulzelle e maritate*: Coming of Age, Rites of Passage, and the Question of Marriage in Some Early Italian Poets." In *Matrons and Marginal Women in Medieval Society*, edited by Robert R. Edwards and Vickie Ziegler. Woodbridge, Suffolk: Boydell Press, 1995, pp. 89–110.

See also **Literature, Italian; Women Authors: Italian Texts**

CONCUBINES

Concubinage is sometimes misconstrued as a forced liaison between a woman and man. However, illicit sexual relationships of concubinage during the European Middle Ages differed from those of biblical histories. The simple definition of the term *concubine* is usually confused with that of *mistress*, but until the seventeenth century, a *mistress* only referred to a married woman or older spinster, whereas during the medieval period, *concubine* meant a woman engaged in extramarital sexual relations. Evidence of concubines and concubinage appears throughout the ages; often concubines were grimly depicted as kept, immoral women. Yet, during the eleventh and twelfth centuries, particularly in the Anglo-Norman kingdom, women and men entered into sexual liaisons that boosted a family's political status without bringing legal or ecclesiastical condemnations upon themselves, any of their sexual partners, or their offspring.

Reasons for becoming a concubine varied over time and place. Some women of poor status became concubines of lords and even priests for survival. These relationships would see to their protection, and ensure that their basic needs of feeding and clothing, of paramount importance to women of the lower classes, were met. Widows without dowries or the means to support themselves might be tempted into concubinage, even against the will of families and the Church. Carol Lansing, Gene Brucker, and others concentrate on the occurrences of concubinage and the plight of lower-class women primarily in Italy and France during the periods between the thirteenth through the fifteenth centuries, while Margaret Rosenthal introduces an *Honest Courtesan* by the name of Veronica Franco (1546–1591), in her book of the same name. These are equally significant to the study of concubines; each instance needs separate consideration for an accurate portrayal of concubinage in the European Middle Ages.

Concubines of Clergy

A controversial issue relating to concubinage was that of women living with priests. These women, not legal wives, had children and, usually in all eyes except those of the Church, considered themselves bound to their men. This practice came under intense scrutiny by the Church when some very zealous arbiters of ecclesiastical practices took it upon themselves to sever these concubinal relationships regardless of the ages or families involved. One example is Gerald of Wales who, as archdeacon of Brecknock in the later twelfth century, entered the home of an aging priest who refused to give up his concubine. Gerald literally threw the man into the street. While this priest refused to accept his archdeacon's criticisms, the trend for blind acceptance of concubinal relationships was a divisive issue between the Church and the laity by the end of the twelfth century.

In analyzing this controversy, it is important to note that women and men did not always receive similar treatment from the Church. For example, certain sexual lapses in England might be ignored, whereas in France, Spain, or the Holy Roman Empire, the same behaviors would be condemned outright. For example by 1215, during the Fourth Lateran Council, Pope Innocent III spent much of the Council's time deciding where and how illegitimate sons of priests who wished to enter the Church could serve. This demonstrates a further instance of the sexual lapses of priests not remaining celibate. Though a great deal of effort was devoted to the sons of these relationships, little or no attention was paid to the fate of the women, pseudo-wives, or daughters produced by these relationships.

Interpretations of Concubinage

The manner in which or the reasons why medieval women became concubines, and subsequent interpretations of concubinage, have lacked fairness and in-depth examination. One particular weakness of appraisal involves the matter of the identity of those who recorded the events that give the closest accounts of medieval women. The sources tend to deny that concubines were legitimate members of society. The necessity of revising biased perspectives has done much to add women's experiences to the body of history, although the study of medieval women has limitations (for example, the study of women from the lower classes is limited due to the dearth of written records about them).

Thus concubinage in the Middle Ages is one critical vehicle by which women can be studied, rather than merely marginalized within society. Women, usually young girls, would be offered as concubines to ensure political stability; however, it can be suggested that women would voluntarily offer themselves to certain men for more personal advantage. On closer inspection of chronicled accounts, it appears that women and men frequently entered into sexual relationships that did not harm individuals or their offspring politically, socially, or ecclesiastically. As a result of their nobility, bastard children received political and social honors, high appointments within the Church, and knighthood, as did their "legitimate" counterparts.

Women such as Bertrade of Montfort, married to the French king Philip I, ran away with Fulk IV, count of Anjou (c. 1095). Church hierarchy considered her to be in a state of concubinage, as her divorce from Philip and subsequent marriage never received proper ecclesiastical recognition. Isabella of Vermandois, wife of Robert of Beaumont, left her husband and ran away with the earl of Warwick prior to her husband's death (c. 1114–1115), after which time she married the earl, to whom she bore several children. Her initial relationship with the earl of Warwick was considered to be one of voluntary concubinage, as there is no suggestion that the earl coerced Isabella into leaving her first husband. The infamous relationship between Heloise and her tutor/lover Abelard (c. 1122) reached the heights of scandal within the French Church even after Heloise succumbed to Abelard's entreaties first to marry him and then take holy

vows with reluctance. While Abelard suffered physical humiliation for his sexual liaison with Heloise, it can be argued that Heloise suffered emotionally at her enforced separation from Abelard, for whom, in her own words, she would rather be his "whore than his wife." The relationship between Eleanor of Aquitaine and Henry of Anjou (c. 1152) had no future until she voluntarily divorced her husband, Louis VII, King of France. This imbroglio exemplifies the actions of a woman who not only had the personal will, but the wealth and independence to divest herself of an unwanted marriage and, according to the Church, become an "illegitimate" wife of another. Queen Isabella, wife of Edward II (r. 1307–1327), had a concubinal relationship with Roger Mortimer, earl of Wigmore; eventually he lost his life, and she her power, through their political intrigues. In addition to Isabella, Alice Perrers, concubine of Edward III (r. 1327–1377), used her influence with the king to create political disturbances, but the king appeared to accede to her wishes in most instances. The same applied to Katherine Swynford, concubine and later third wife of John of Gaunt, third son of Edward III. She was influential with Gaunt through his first two marriages as his concubine, eventually becoming his wife.

Offspring of Concubines

In addition to these women are many who aligned themselves to Henry I of England (r. 1100–1135). Henry's illegitimate offspring numbered between twenty-four and twenty-six. Even without his two legitimate offspring, Henry fathered more children than any other English king. Unfortunately, the chroniclers omitted the names of most of the women who became his concubines, with only six names gleaned from contemporary documents, but these six women gave birth to fourteen of the more than twenty attributed to his concubinal relationships. Two of the most prolific women were Nesta, daughter of prince Rhys ap Tewdwr of South Wales, and Sybil Corbet, daughter of Robert Corbet, a minor Norman baron.

Nesta maintained successful relationships with two husbands and three lovers, not always discriminating between these liaisons. The result of these multiple relations was twelve, possibly thirteen children, all who survived infancy, with each one, sons and daughters, prospering in marriages, wealth, and conquest throughout the twelfth century and beyond. This amounted to active sexual and child-bearing years for Nesta between ages fifteen and forty-five, a thirty year period (c. 1090–1120). Sybil Corbet, on the other hand, had relations with only two men, Henry and her husband, Herbert fitz Herbert. Yet her relationship with these two men appeared as self-directed as Nesta's. She bore eight children, five to Henry and three to Herbert (c. 1105–1135). Sybil's husband replaced his father as Chamberlain, thereby giving her access to the royal circle, in constant contact with both the king and his respective wives. Her children received great honors, titles, and property; one illegitimate daughter was given in marriage to the king of Scotland. Neither Nesta nor Sybil suffered ecclesiastical or legal sanctions, nor did their husbands for accepting wives who engaged in concubinal relationships. Other women known to have illicit connections with Henry were Edith d'Oilly, wife of Robert constable of Oxford. Edith gave birth to two children from each man, gave to the Church, and established her children in successful political and social marriages. The Church willingly embraced Edith and her gifts, ignoring her concubinage to Henry in the face of her generosity.

Ansfride, Henry's first known concubine (c. 1084), bore three children to Henry, one while she was married to another man, and the other two during her widowhood. The Church accorded her full dignity "with a celebrated interment by the Abingdon brothers" in a "cloister before the host of the church" at Abingdon (c. 1118–1120). Grace de Tracy had one son with Henry I whose noble legacy extended to Grace's grandson, a king's knight, who was one of the men responsible for murdering Thomas Becket at Canterbury (1170). Henry's last known concubine was Isabella of Beaumont, youngest daughter of the previously mentioned Isabella of Vermandois, who had a daughter with Henry, his last known illegitimate child (c. 1128). This child was born after Henry's second marriage when he was sixty to Isabella's nineteen years. Isabella remained in high political favor as the wife of Gilbert de Clare and mother of the famous knight "Strongbow" who received honors under Henry II.

There appeared to be no negative effects for concubinage for these and many other women of this period nor for their respective husbands or children. Stories of the successful careers of their numerous children testify to this effect, though unfortunately the chroniclers, medieval men of the Church, failed to enumerate full accounts of the women. When they did record the lives of women in extramarital relationships, it was usually with the intent to condemn the sexual freedoms that had become common during this period. But not to be overlooked is the significant factor emphasizing the changes in concubinage by examining the legal situation of the children.

Legitimization of children varied over time. For example during early twelfth century England, Henry I merely recognized his illegitimate offspring in documents either giving them the "surname" fitz Roi, or fitz Henry, signifying his paternity. In some cases he would go further, as in the situation of Robert, later earl of Gloucester. Henry continually improved his recognition of this son by giving him the surname fitz Roi, then eventually calling him his most loved son. But this was only a favored filial position that never legitimized him in any statutes. It was not until later, during the High Middle Ages, that legitimization would take place. John of Gaunt legitimized his bastard children by his concubine (later third wife) Katherine Swynford long after the death of his second wife, but these children were still prevented from inheriting the throne of England. Yet from these descendents of Katherine Swynford and John of Gaunt the Tudor line emerged. By the sixteenth century, Henry VIII went through Parliamentary procedure to legitimize or bastardize his children, depending on his marital status.

By the later Middle Ages, the Church's message began to make an impression on the laity, leading to eventual changes in the sexual practices of Christendom. Gradually, concubinage and concubines were relegated to the backdrop of society, neither automatically enriching women's positions nor those of their illegitimate children.

GWENN MEREDITH

References and Further Reading

Bennett, Judith M. "Writing Fornication: Medieval Leyrwite and its Historians," in *Transactions of the Royal Historical Society* 13 (2003). 131–162.

Brucker, Gene. *Giovanni and Lusanna: Love and Marriage in Renaissance Florence*. Berkeley: University of California Press, 2004.

Brundage, James A. *Law, Sex, and Christian Society in Medieval Europe*. Chicago and London: The University of Chicago Press, 1987.

Lansing, Carol. *The Florentine Magnates: Lineage and Faction in a Medieval Commune*. Princeton: Princeton University Press, 1991.

———. "Concubines, Lovers, Prostitutes: Infamy and Female Identity in Medieval Bologna," in *Beyond Florence: The Contours of Medieval and Early Modern Italy*, edited by Paula Findlen, Michelle M. Fontaine, and Duane J. Osheim. Palo Alto, Calif.: Stanford University Press, 2003, pp. 85–100, 256–258.

McNamara, Jo Ann. "Women and Power Through the Family Revisited", in *Gendering the Master Narrative: Women and Power in the Middle Ages*, edited by Mary C. Erler and Maryanne Kowaleski. Ithaca, N.Y.: Cornell University Press, 2003, pp. 17–30.

Meredith, Gwenn. "Henry I's Concubines," in *Essays in Medieval Studies, Proceedings of the Illinois Medieval Association*, Vol. 19, edited by C. Stephen Jaeger and Allen J. Frantzen. Morgantown, W.V.: West Virginia University Press for the Illinois Medieval Association, 2002.

Rollo-Koster, Joëlle. "From Prostitutes to Brides of Christ: The Avignonese *Repenties* in the Late Middle Ages," in *Journal of Medieval and Early Modern Studies* 32, I (Winter 2002): 109–144.

Rosenthal, Margaret. *The Honest Courtesan*. Chicago: The University of Chicago Press, 1992.

See also Celibacy: Clerical and Priests' Concubines; Sexuality: Extramarital

CONDUCT LITERATURE

Literature imparting counsel about the conduct of life has a long history in Western culture. From antiquity, Greek poets and philosophers often offered advice on the household, the family, and social behavior within mythic, scientific, historical, or theoretical writings. Roman authors continued to impart instructions on marriage, the family, education, youth, adolescence, and old age, and moral, economic, and political life in a range of genres, including treatises, letters, and fables. Some works, such as those of Ovid, offered advice with a dose of irony. Although it is impossible to generalize about such a vast corpus, conduct-of-life books tended to advise restraint in self-governance, savvy management of emotions and passions, care of the soul as well as the body. Such didactic texts offer explicit or implicit views on sexuality and gender roles and, consequently, provide a rich field of investigation for historians of women and gender.

Didactic Works in Latin

Medieval moralists adapted many of the precepts devised in antiquity to Christian teachings and to the realities of contemporary social life. Classical authors continued to be copied in Latin and adapted throughout the Middle Ages. Numerous original works on social, moral, and spiritual life were also composed in Latin. One popular text, originating in the early Christian era, was the *Distichs of Cato*, a Latin collection of short rhyming couplets with moral sentences; it was widely used in schools throughout the Middle Ages, in Latin and vernacular editions. Christian morality, with its strictures on sexual behavior, frequently conflicted with pagan views, for example, with Ovid's cynical portrayal of love as predatory aggression disguised as artful seduction. The Bible, the lives of Saints, and the writings of the Church fathers became increasingly important sources for didactic literature. Beginning in the twelfth century, clerics began to translate and adapt classical authors into the vernacular and to compose original moral treatises in medieval Occitan, French, German, English, Italian, Spanish, and Portuguese.

Terminology and Genre

The genre of the "medieval conduct book" is difficult to pinpoint with precision. The terms *conduct books* (or *literature*) and *courtesy books* (or *literature*) are often used interchangeably in medieval scholarship to designate texts offering counsel to readers of either gender about social behavior. Some scholars distinguish between courtesy literature, which advises specifically about behavior and manners at court and in elite society (and tends to address men), and conduct literature, often addressed to women, which advises compliance within more confined spheres. Others employ "conduct literature" as a broad term encompassing many kinds of texts that attempt to systematize social behavior. Precepts about sociability and comportment are conveyed within a very broad array of medieval texts, some of which may be concerned primarily with practical, moral, and spiritual affairs. All such instructional texts fall within the broad domain of medieval didactic literature, which includes forms as diverse as rules for religious orders, treatises on table manners and carving, sermons, estates literature, exempla, bestiaries, fables, allegories and arts of love, dialogues, devotional manuals, mirrors for princes, and books on hunting, gardening, and housekeeping. This essay refers to selected key works and focuses on those addressed to women or written by women.

Early Didactic Literature

The earliest medieval books regulating conduct were composed for men and women in religious orders. The first books of lay instruction were written for royal and noble courts; princes and ladies were usually addressed in discrete sections or separate volumes. Pious precepts, moral teachings, and traditional views of social relations that upheld the feudal hierarchy tended to characterize the earliest vernacular works. As paper manuscripts replaced parchment, book production extended to the growing middle classes of artisans, merchants, and civil administrators for whom ownership of conduct books could be a means of social advancement. Later medieval books continue to espouse conservative views of family and marriage, but also often describe women's important contributions to household economies and their role as social agents.

Medieval Conduct Books for Women

A number of medieval conduct books are addressed in part or in their entirety to women, and a few were written by women authors. The eighth-century Frankish noblewoman Dhuoda wrote a Latin handbook for her son, William, who was separated from his mother as a boy. As she advises her son on piety and family honor, she reveals the strong role that literate women could play in shaping their children's education. Among the earliest lay works for women is the Occitan *Ensenhamen* of Garin lo Brun (late twelfth century), allegedly written at the behest of a high-born lady, which blends practical advice on dress with cautionary remarks on love. The *Livre des Manières* of Etienne de Fougères (late twelfth century), a poem about social estates or statuses, includes advice for clerks, knights, and serfs, as well as for all women, the fourth estate, who are categorized by their degree of virtue. St. Louis, King Louis IX, wrote a letter of instruction for his daughter, as well as one for his son; both espoused piety and religious duty, but Isabelle's sphere of action is more restricted than that of Philippe, destined to rule. The figure of a parent offering advice to a child or children remained popular as a frame for conduct books throughout the Middle Ages; it was often probably a fictional device.

Conduct books are generally considered to participate in the construction of social status and gender roles. In separate books for noblemen and ladies by the Catalan or Gascon poet Amanieu de Sescás (c. 1290s), both sexes are enjoined to practice "courtly" behavior. Yet some texts seem to encourage critical analysis of or even debate about that process. Robert de Blois's *Chastoiement des dames* (mid-thirteenth century), written as a companion to his *Enseignement des Princes*, was compiled within a courtly romance, *Beaudous*, in which a mother offers Robert's instructions to her sons. The mother's lessons include *Floris et Lyriopé,* a tale featuring a knight who cross-dresses to be near his beloved lady—a fascinating exemplum that calls into question the assimilation of sex and gender roles thought to be natural.

Another intriguing pair of works addressed to noblemen and noblewomen are the thirteenth-century German lyric poems *Der Winsbecke* and *Die Winsbeckin*, which are compiled together in the same lavish manuscript, the *Codex Manesse*. It has been noted by Rasmussen that the witty dialogue between mother and daughter in the *Winsbeckin* contrasts with the sermon-like speech of father to son in the *Winsbecke*, thus bringing a spirit of debate into the dissemination of moral advice.

Thirteenth and early fourteenth-century didactic works were often in verse; prose was the preferred form for later medieval treatises. One of the most substantial manuals for women is Francesco da Barberino's *Reggimento et costumi di donna* (1308–1320), composed of twenty lengthy sections that mix verse and prose. Written ostensibly for a Florentine lady who asks the author to offer advice to women, as he previously had to men, the book emphasizes the importance of virginity, patience, self-control, temperance, discernment, self-restraint, and a good reputation—all with the aim of creating a companionable wife, upon whose virtue a happy couple depends.

Works for Women after c. 1350

The earliest extant work of instruction for lay women in English, *What the Good Wife Taught Her Daughter* (mid-fourteenth century), promoted values associated with the developing urban mercantile class. Written in the voice of a mother imparting instructions to her daughter, the book advises girls to attend church regularly, work diligently, and comport themselves respectably within the confines of the home. Riddy has suggested that *Good Wife*'s author may have been a cleric who wrote not only for young women but also for adult women who supervised girls as servants and apprentices in urban bourgeois households.

As later medieval conduct books were transmitted in paper manuscripts and early printed editions, they reached audiences beyond their original intended readers. Geoffroy, Chevalier de la Tour Landry, a minor provincial knight from Anjou, wrote his book (1371–1372) for the instruction of his daughters, whom he described as "young and lacking reason" and whom he wished to protect against the kind of irresponsible men he had known in his youth. The author combines Biblical exempla of virtuous and wicked women with anecdotes from his personal experience to counsel his daughters about piety, chastity, modest demeanor and dress, sober comportment, and speech. His colorful tales sometimes portray crude behaviors, and the punishments meted out to women who transgress are often cruel. The Chevalier's occasionally ribald or grotesque tales, his insistence on female honor, his simultaneous espousal of conservative dress and acknowledgement of fashion's appeal, create an intriguing text that evidently appealed to new audiences. There are twenty-one extant French manuscripts, including paper copies, as well as English and German translations. Caxton published a Middle English version, *The Book of the*

Knight of the Tower, one of the earliest printed books. *Der Ritter vom Turm*, translated by Marquard vom Stein, is accompanied by woodprints portraying poignant, occasionally violent scenes of family life that are sometimes attributed to early Dürer.

In the *Ménagier de Paris* (c. 1385), an elderly husband offers advice to his young bride, an orphan whom he married at the age of fifteen. This vast compendium not only contains numerous moral exempla illustrating wifely obedience and chastity, including the tale of Griselda and the story of Prudence and Melibee. It also includes treatises on gardening and hawking and one of the earliest cookbooks, with hundreds of recipes. The Ménagier's book attests to woman's central role in the household and to the growing importance of books as instruments of domestic management and social advancement in urban bourgeois settings.

Christine de Pizan (c. 1364–1430) composed numerous works of moral instruction and political guidance for members of the courts of King Charles VI and the Dukes of Burgundy. She penned *Enseignements* [teachings] for her son and moral proverbs, both in verse. *Le Livre des Trois Vertus* (*The Book of Three Virtues*) was composed for young Margaret of Burgundy, who was only eleven when she married the dauphin, Louis de Guyenne. Christine's book is the first female-authored conduct book for lay women, and one of the first books to offer specific counsel to women of each social class (the princess, ladies at court, ladies on manors, religious women, wives of merchants and townspeople, poor women, and prostitutes). The book is sometimes compiled in manuscripts with the *Cité des Dames* (*City of Ladies*), Christine's eloquent defense of women against misogynistic slander, which offers numerous examples of virtuous women throughout history. Also known as the *Trésor de la Cité des Dames* (*Treasury of the City of Ladies*), the *Livre des Trois Vertus* was intended as a practical handbook to provide women with the moral instruction and social skills that would enable them to survive as honorable women within communities still pervaded by antifeminist prejudices. The *Cité des Dames* and *Trois Vertus* are key texts for the study of representations of female virtue and piety, women's authority and agency as well as women's complex social, moral, economic, social, and political roles. Christine's works were transmitted in lavishly illustrated manuscripts for elite readers, as well as in more modest paper manuscripts, and some were among the first printed books. Her precepts evidently reached a great number of readers; *Trois Vertus* was translated into Portuguese. It also inspired an instructional manual written in 1504 by Anne of Beaujeu, daughter of Louis XI, for her daughter,

Suzanne de Bourbon. Christine's didactic works can be seen as the continuation of a long classical and medieval tradition and as the bridge to the genre's continued popularity in the Renaissance.

Although conduct books and other forms of didactic literature were enormously popular throughout the Middle Ages, they have received until recently less attention from modern scholars than medieval epic and lyric poetry and verse and prose romance—genres with greater aesthetic appeal. The sociologist Norbert Elias argued that the "civilizing process" began in earnest with the publication of Renaissance courtesy texts, but medieval scholars have demonstrated that the process was well underway in medieval didactic literature. The French scholar Alain Montandon has embarked on a collaborative pan-European project to investigate the vast corpus of manuals of "savoir-faire," beginning with the Middle Ages, and there are numerous recent studies and editions of individual texts. Although their representations must be read as prescriptions of social ideals rather than as descriptions of social realities, medieval conduct books offer valuable insights into the construction of gender roles and into medieval views on masculinity, femininity, sexuality, and the family. Of evident value for social historians, these books have also attracted renewed attention from literary critics, who stress the complexities, ambiguities, and contradictions that subtend many of these apparently orthodox texts.

ROBERTA L. KRUEGER

References and Further Reading

Anne de France. *Les Enseignements d'Anne de France, Duchesse de Bourbonnais et d'Auvergne à sa fille Susanne de Bourbon*, edited by A. M. Chazaud. Moulins: C. Desrosiers, 1878. Repr. Marseilles: Lafitte, 1978.

Ashley, Kathleen A. and Robert L. A. Clark, eds. *Medieval Conduct*. Minneapolis: University of Minnesota Press, 2001.

Barberino, Francesco da. *Del Reggimento e Costumi di Donna*, edited by Guiseppe Sansone. Torino: Loescher/Chiantore, 1957. 2nd ed. Roma: Zauli, 1995.

Bornstein, Diane. *The Lady in the Tower: Medieval Courtesy Literature for Women*. Hamden, Conn.: The Shoestring Press, 1983.

Cato. *The Distichs of Cato: A Famous Medieval Textbook*. Ed. and trans. Wayland Johnson Chase. University of Wisconsin Studies in the Social Sciences and History 7. Madison: University of Wisconsin Press, 1922.

Christine de Pizan. *The Treasure of the City of Ladies or the Book of the Three Virtues*. translated by Sarah Lawson. New York: Penguin Books, 1985.

———. *Le Livre des Trois Vertus*, edited by Charity Cannon Willard and Eric Hicks. Paris: Champion, 1989.

De Gendt, Anne Marie. *L'Art d'Eduquer les nobles damoiselles: le 'Livre du chevalier de la Tour Landry.'* Paris: Champion, 2003.

Dhuoda. *Handbook for William: A Carolingian Woman's Counsel for Her Son*, edited by Carol Neel. Lincoln: University of Nebraska Press, 1991.

Elias, Norbert. *The Civilizing Process.* translated by Edmund Jephcott. New York: Urizen Books, 1978.

Etienne de Fougères. *Le Livre des manières*, edited by R. Anthony Lodge. Geneva: Droz, 1979.

Garin lo Brun. *L'Ensegnamen alla dama*, edited and translated by Laura Regina Bruno. Roma: Archivio Guido Izzi, 1996.

The Good Wife Taught Her Daughter. The Good Wyfe Wold a Pylgremage. The Thewis of Gud Women, edited by Tauno F. Mustanoja. Helsinki: Soumalaisen Kirjallisuuden Seuran, 1948.

Hentsch, Alice A. *De la littérature didactique du moyen âge s'adressant spécialement aux femmes.* Cahors: A Coueslant, 1903. Geneva: Slatkine Reprints, 1975.

Johnston, Mark. "Gender as Conduct in the Courtesy Guides for Aristocratic Boys and Girls of Amanieu de Sescás."*Essays in Medieval Studies* 20 (2003): 75–84.

Le Ménagier de Paris, edited by Georgina E. Brereton and Janet M. Ferrier. translated by Karin Ueltschi. Lettres Gothiques. Paris: Livre de poche, 1994.

Montandon, Alain. *Pour une histoire des traités de savoir-vivre en Europe.* Clermont-Ferrand: Association des publications de la Faculté des lettres et sciences humaines de Clermont-Ferrand, 1994.

———. *Bibliographie des traités de savoir-vivre en Europe du moyen âge à nos jours.* Vol. 1: *France-Angleterre-Allemagne*, edited by A. Montandon. Clermont-Ferrand: Association des Publications de la Faculté des Lettres et Sciences Humaines de Clermont-Ferrand, 1995.

Nicholls, Jonathan. *The Matter of Courtesy. Medieval Courtesy Books and the Gawain Poet.* Woodbridge: Suffolk: D. S. Brewer, 1985.

Rasmussen, Anne-Marie. "Fathers to Think Back Through: The Middle High German Mother-Daughter and Father-Son Advice Poems Known as *Die Winsbeckin* and *Der Winsbecke*." In Ashley and Clark, *Medieval Conduct*, pp. 106–134.

Riddy, Felicity. "Mother Knows Best: Reading Social Change in a Courtesy Text." *Speculum: A Journal of Medieval Studies* 71 (1996): 66–86.

Robert de Blois. *Robert de Blois: son œuvre didactique et narrative. Etude linguistique et littéraire suivie d'une édition critique avec commentaire et glossaire de 'L'Enseignement des Princes' et du 'Chastoiement des dames,'* edited by John Howard Fox. Paris: Nizet, 1950.

Roussel, Claude. "Le Legs de la Rose: modèles et préceptes de la sociabilité médiévale." In *Pour une histoire des traités de savoir-vivre en Europe*, edited by A. Montandon. Clermont-Ferrand: Association des Publications de la Faculté des Lettres et Sciences Humaines de Clermont-Ferrand, 1994, pp. 1–90.

La Tour Landry, Geoffrey de. *The Book of the Knight of the Tower.* Trans. William Caxton, edited by M.Y. Offord. New York: Oxford University Press, 1971.

———. *Le Livre du Chevalier de la Tour Landry pour l'Enseignement de ses filles*, edited by Anatole de Montaiglon. Paris: P. Jannet, 1854. Reprint Millwood, N.Y.: Krauss Reprint, 1982.

Winsbeckische Gedichte nebst Tirol und Fridebrant, edited by Albert Leitzmann. Revised by Ingo Reiffenstein. 3d ed. Altdeutsche Textbibliothek, vol. 9. Tübingen, Germany: Niemeyer, 1962.

See also **Anne of Beaujeu; Book Ownership; Christine de Pizan; Defenses of Women; Dhuoda; Education, Lay; Femininity and Masculinity; Gender Ideologies; Griselda; Misogyny; Mothers as Teachers; Ovid: Medieval Reception of; Social Status**

CONFESSORS AND SPIRITUAL ADVISORS
See **Spiritual Care**

CONFRATERNITIES

Confraternities (sometimes known as religious guilds or fraternities) were religious associations founded and administered by lay people with the support of local clergy, including bishops, priests, and members of the mendicant orders (Dominicans and Franciscans). They developed in cities and in the countryside across western Europe, and appeared as early as the tenth century in some places. As institutions, confraternities were flexible and long lasting; while much confraternity activity peaked in the thirteenth and fourteenth centuries, many survived the Catholic Reform movement of the sixteenth century, adapting to suit new social and religious realities. Confraternities ranged in size from small to very large; some were formed around individual parishes, while others drew members from across large cities.

Lay people in their confraternities furthered their own salvation by engaging in devotional, charitable, or penitential pious activities. Members of devotional confraternities frequently gathered to sing hymns, while charitable groups gave alms in the form of food, wine, and money to the poor, sick, and members of religious orders. Those who joined penitential confraternities often took part in rituals of self-flagellation as penance for sin. Despite their differences, all confraternities shared a few fundamental similarities: membership was voluntary, members' activities were determined by a set of written rules or statutes, and the governors of the associations were lay men. As well, all groups shared common activities, including regular religious services in which they prayed and listened to sermons together. In addition to their religious functions, confraternities throughout Europe also had social and political goals. Members saw themselves as kin and assisted each other during times of personal crisis, such as sickness or the death of a family member. The associations also played a role in the public life of their communities, including participation in attempts to pacify warring civic factions, and sponsorship of pageants designed to emphasize the confraternity's role within the community. The records left by confraternities are largely unpublished, and include membership or matriculation lists, statutes, records of property transfer, last wills or testaments, and minutes of meetings. These records provide valuable information about the complex nature of medieval religious culture.

Women played a role within many confraternities during the Middle Ages. They were usually eligible to join confraternities, especially those with a charitable and devotional focus. Confraternal statutes made provisions for them, noting, as in the 1262 statutes of the Congregation of the Virgin in the Italian city of Arezzo, that since there was no distinction between the souls of men and women before God, women could enter the company and engage in the same devotional activities as their male counterparts, thus sharing equally with men in the spiritual benefits of membership. Despite these inclusive statements, confraternal statutes also stipulated that men, not women, were eligible to serve as officials of the associations. This restriction reflected a broader limitation on women in medieval society: they were barred from active participation in the public realm. Confraternal offices were part of that realm, and thus were closed to women. Other restrictions on women's activities within confraternities reflected social consensus about their physical and emotional weakness. For instance, women who wished to join penitential companies that practiced self-flagellation needed permission from a male relative to do so. Once they became members, women were barred from flagellating themselves.

Scholarship on women in confraternities is in its infancy. Interest in the subject has arisen from the newly emerging field of confraternity studies as well as studies of medieval women's religiosity. As a result of this interest, scholars have examined confraternity records for examples of female members, with notable results. Examples of female participation in confraternities include the more than 1,700 women who joined the confraternity of the Misericordia Maggiore in the Italian city of Bergamo between the thirteenth and fourteenth centuries. As a result of these discoveries, scholars have debated the significance of women's membership in the associations. Some have argued that high levels of female participation in confraternities represented equally high levels of female influence in the associations. On the other hand, Giovanna Casagrande has posited a distinction between women's presence in confraternities and their real worth to the organizations. She argues that although women may have had their names recorded in confraternal matriculation lists, female members did not normally participate fully in the activities of the

institutions. She also argues that rather than presenting women with an opportunity to escape the confines of secular society, confraternities reflected the restrictions women encountered in the outside world. Related studies have shown that women's participation in confraternities waned over time, with highest participation in the thirteenth century, followed by falling levels of participation by the end of the fourteenth century.

But what did medieval women themselves think about confraternities? To find the answer, we examine sources such as testaments, which reveal that confraternities and religious guilds remained significant to women in the Middle Ages, even though female members occupied a lesser role within the associations as time passed. During the fourteenth century, women continued to name confraternities as recipients of their testamentary bequests. Female testators clearly believed that the institutions would provide them with spiritual assistance, even if they were unable to participate fully in the public life of confraternities. Recent work on religious guilds in late medieval England also suggests that the significance of women's participation in these groups should not be discounted. For instance, all-female guilds created to maintain the lights in parish churches were more informally constituted than those groups dominated by men, but both male and female guilds of this type took on similar responsibilities. Rather than lamenting women's lack of official influence in confraternities, then, scholars in the future may redefine participation, looking at ways in which women employed unofficial channels to work within confraternities. Another direction for future research might include a synthesis of women's roles in confraternities throughout western Europe. Studies to date have been confined to individual places. A broader study which synthesizes information from many locales could emphasize continuities as well as discontinuities in women's experience within these associations.

ROISIN COSSAR

References and Further Reading

Banker, James. *Death in the Community: Memorialization and Confraternities in an Italian Commune in the Late Middle Ages.* Athens, Ga.: University of Georgia Press, 1988.

Brolis, Maria Teresa. "A Thousand and More Women: the Register of Women for the Confraternity of Misericordia Maggiore in Bergamo, 1265–1339." *Catholic Historical Review.* 88, 2 (2002): pp. 230–246.

Casagrande, Giovanna. "Confraternities and Lay Female Religiosity in Late Medieval and Renaissance Umbria." In *The Politics of Ritual Kinship*, edited by Nicholas Terpstra. Cambridge: Cambridge University Press, 2000, pp. 48–66.

Cossar, Roisin. "'A Good Woman': Gender Roles and Female Religious Identity in Late Medieval Bergamo." *The Memoirs of the American Academy in Rome*. 46 (2001): 119–132.

Meersseman, Giles Gerard. *Ordo Fraternitatis: Confraternite e Pietà dei Laici nel Medioevo*. Rome: Herder Editrice, 1977.

Peters, Christine. *Patterns of Piety: Women, Gender and Religion in Late Medieval and Reformation England*. Cambridge: Cambridge University Press, 2003.

See also **Almsgiving and Charity; Devotional Practices; Lay Piety; Parishes; Records, Ecclesiastical; Rosary; Spirituality, Christian; Wills**

CONJUGAL DEBT

Conjugal debt was a doctrine of medieval theology, enforceable under canon law, that a married person possessed a tightly correlated set of rights and duties to claim sexual relations from his or her marital partner. The idea of the conjugal debt takes its origin in medieval reflection on the teaching of St. Paul that "the wife has not authority over her body, but the husband; the husband likewise has not authority over his body, but the wife. Do not deprive each other, except...by consent, for a time, that you may give yourself to prayer" (1 Corinthians 7: 4–5).

Patristic authors as early as St. Augustine (354–430) made the conjugal debt a feature of their theology when describing the obligation parties were under to satisfy the sexual demands of the other party. St. Augustine was inclined to stress the onerous nature of the conjugal debt, as in his letter to Ecdicia, a Roman noblewoman who, motivated by asceticism, had broken off sexual relations with her spouse. St. Augustine insisted that she was obliged to meet her husband's demands, but assured her that if she honored St. Paul's teaching it would count as a great good on her behalf before the heavenly court.

The canonistic writers of the High Middle Ages transformed this moral admonition into legally enforceable rights derived from the natural structure of marriage. The twelfth-century canonist Gratian (c. 1140) explored the limits of the Pauline verse that taught that married persons might only deprive one another of sexual relations through mutual consent and concluded that where both parties freely consented they might renounce their marital rights. Gratian's use of the language of rights to describe these steps would color subsequent ecclesiastical descriptions of marital relations until nearly our own day.

The canonists who followed in Gratian's steps built a large lattice-work of laws to protect the conjugal debt/right in the context of medieval life. The problem of the spouse who contracted leprosy tested the limits of these legal protections. Leprosy was one of the most feared diseases of the Middle Ages. Lepers, who had no hope of being cured, were ostracized and forced to move to the margins of medieval society. They were required to reside in leprosaria or in encampments on the edges of towns and villages. The uniform policy of the Middle Ages toward lepers was one of quarantine and isolation.

Marriage—and its accompanying conjugal debt—posed a great problem for this policy. Marriage, after all, was sacramental, unbreakable, and conferred inalienable and natural conjugal rights on both parties. The canonists resolved this seeming conflict in favor of the ill spouse. The healthy spouse might not be compelled to have sexual relations with the ill partner, but was still obligated to live close by and to tend to the ill partner's needs. The ill party, the canonists reasoned, had done nothing wrong, and so could not be deprived of her or his conjugal rights, now broadly understood to embrace material and moral assistance in the face of debilitating and deadly illness.

Feudal overlords were also expected to respect the conjugal rights of those subject to their authority. The canonists posed the question: Where a feudal lord demanded that a serf accompany him on military campaign and the serf's wife requested the conjugal debt, which obligation was to receive priority? The canonists sought out compromises that reflected the origin of the conjugal debt in natural law but that also did not entirely deprive the overlord of his rights within the feudal order. On the whole, the canonists were more sympathetic with the situation of the serf than one might have expected, recognizing that wives ordinarily had the greater claim except in emergencies, as when the lord was under direct attack by enemies and in danger of being defeated.

The use of rights language to describe the obligations parties owed one another was problematic in other contexts, however. Thus canonists were required to consider the question of the forcible consummation of marriage. At least a few canonists were willing to countenance the forceful use of "self-help" in situations where the other spouse was reluctant to go along, because of the rights that were at stake. The canonists here engaged in artificial and formalistic reasoning, grounding their conclusion on the formal equality that each party was understood to enjoy with respect to the conjugal debt.

The language of conjugal debts and conjugal rights has persisted to our own day. Within ecclesiastical law, one still finds regular references to rights within marriage. And the broader secular law, borrowing from canonistic sources, has made the language of conjugal debts and conjugal rights a feature of legal reasoning.

CHARLES J. REID, JR.

References and Further Reading

Elliott, Dyan. "Bernardino of Siena Versus the Marriage Debt." In *Desire and Discipline: Sex and Sexuality in the Premodern West*, edited by Jacqueline Murray and Konrad Eisenbichler. Toronto: University of Toronto Press, 1996, pp. 168–200.

Makowski, Elizabeth M. "The Conjugal Debt and Medieval Canon Law," *Journal of Medieval History* 3 (1977): 99–114.

Reid, Charles J. Jr., *Power Over the Body, Equality in the Family: Rights and Domestic Relations in Medieval Canon Law.* Grand Rapids, Mich.: Eerdmans, 2004.

See also **Law, Canon; Marriage, Christian; Sexuality, Regulation of; Sexuality: Sex in Marriage**

CONSTANCE

The Constance story is known to modern audiences primarily through Chaucer's "The Man of Law's Tale" in his *Canterbury Tales*, which has its sources in Nicholas Trivet's Anglo-Norman *Chronique* and Book II of John Gower's *Confessio Amantis*. All three versions tell how Constance (Custance), daughter of the Roman emperor, travels to marry the sultan of Syria, only to witness the slaughter of her bridegroom and the newly converted Syrian Christians at the hands of a conspiracy led by the sultan's mother. Constance is set adrift at sea for several years until she wrecks on the shore of Northumbria, where she is accused by a spurned suitor of murdering the wife of the constable who rescued her. Triumphantly acquitted through divine intervention, the beleaguered Constance marries the king of Northumbria and bears his son, but the king's jealous mother accuses her of birthing a changeling and again Constance is set adrift, this time with her child. After several more years Constance finds herself on the shores of Italy and returns to Rome, where she is eventually reunited with both father and husband.

The story participates in a constellation of folkloric motifs, including false accusations of unnatural or monstrous offspring, the heroine set adrift, and the mother-in-law as chief persecutor. It is generally thought to derive from two narrative groups common in folklore: the accused queen and the flight from an incestuous father. Elements from romance and hagiography are manifest in the Constance story as well. Its most widely recognized analog is the Middle English romance *Emare*; other analogs include the romances *Octavian* and *Valentine and Oursson*, and the Flemish play *Esmoreit*. There are also a number of parallels with Boccaccio's *Decameron* V, 2 and, possibly, II,7.

Most critics read Constance as a positive example of spiritual steadfastness, often in opposition to the Man of Law's materialism. There is less agreement among scholars as to whether Constance may be considered a figure of feminine strength or passivity. Recent studies have focused on the elision of the incest motif, particularly in Chaucer, whose narrator excoriates those who would speak of such abominations in the introduction to his tale.

ALISON L. GANZE

References and Further Reading

Archibald, Elizabeth. *Incest and the Medieval Imagination.* Oxford: Clarendon Press, 2001.

Black, Nancy B. *Medieval Narratives of Accused Queens.* Gainesville: University Press of Florida, 2003.

Bryan, W. F. and Germaine Dempster, eds. *Sources and Analogues of Chaucer's Canterbury Tales.* New York: Humanities Press, 1958.

Delaney, Sheila. *Writing Woman: Women Writers and Women in Literature Medieval to Modern.* New York: Schoken Books, 1983.

Manning, Stephen. "Chaucer's Constance: Pale and Passive." In *Chaucerian Problems and Perspectives: Essays Presented to Paul E. Beichner, C. S. C*, edited by Edward Vasta and Zacharias P. Thundy. South Bend, Ind.: University of Notre Dame Press, 1979, pp. 13–23.

Robertson, Elizabeth. "The 'Elvyssh' Power of Constance: Christian Feminism in Geoffrey Chaucer's The Man of Law's Tale." *Studies in the Age of Chaucer* 23 (2001): 143–180.

Schlauch, Margaret. *Chaucer's Constance and Accused Queens.* New York: New York University Press, 1927. Repr. AMS Press, 1973.

See also **Chaucer, Geoffrey; Hagiography; Incest; Romance: English**

CONSTANCE OF SICILY

Constance (1154–c.1198), queen of Sicily and Holy Roman Empress, was the daughter of King Roger II of Sicily, wife of the German emperor Henry VI, whom she married c. 1186, and mother of Emperor Frederick II, born in 1194. When her nephew William II died in 1189, Constance was left as the only legitimate heir to the kingdom of Sicily. However, her husband's ambition to add Sicily to his domains was temporarily blocked by Pope Clement III's approval of Roger's illegitimate grandson, Tancred Count of Lecce, as king. Constance thus found herself at the center of a scrappy war between her husband and her own kin, even being taken captive by Tancred. Although she was released without condition, her husband's unwillingness to come to a truce with Tancred when Constance was captured may have strained the marriage. When Henry finally prevailed, upon the death of Tancred without an effective heir in 1194, it seems he went to some trouble to minimise

Constance's effective power in Sicily. Nevertheless, she appears regularly making grants in her own name, and when Henry died in 1197, Constance ruled as regent for her young son Frederick until her own death in 1198. Dante placed her in the lowest sphere of heaven (*Paradiso*, Canto III) because she left the monastery to marry but remained a nun at heart.

PATRICIA SKINNER

References and Further Reading

Abulafia, David. *Frederick II: a Medieval Emperor.* London: Allen Lane, 1988.
Clementi, Dione. "Some Unnoticed Aspects of the Emperor Henry VI's Conquest of the Norman kingdom of Sicily," *Bulletin of the John Rylands Library* 36: (1953–1954), 328–359.
Fröhlich, W. "The Marriage of Henry VI and Constance of Sicily," *Anglo-Norman Studies*, 15: (1992), 99–116.
Matthew, Donald. *The Norman Kingdom of Sicily.* Cambridge: Cambridge University Press, 1992.

See also **Italy; Queens and Empresses: the West**

CONSUMPTION

The economic definition of *consumption* is the using up of goods and services, both necessities and luxuries, the definition of which varies with social class and income, and changes over time. In the medieval period, there was a sharp distinction in consumption that hinged on poverty or wealth. Rich courts and townspeople generally had available a higher level of goods, including artwork, spices, dyestuffs, and luxury clothing and ornament, whereas consumption for rural peasants consisted of the rudimentary basics of food, clothing, and shelter, and could vary dramatically between the occasional feast and famine. Early medieval practice and the mentality of the entire era (including the influence of mendicant ethical teachings about wealth) worked to contain material indulgence while still upholding the value of free economic competition. The moral issue of over-consumption in medieval Europe was a subject of societal concern, and excess was condemned by the Church and legislated against by both ecclesiastical law and secular government. Europeans believed that human consumption should be governed by the virtue of temperance. Christianity taught that gluttony and pride were two of the seven deadly sins (luxuria became a prominent sin by the fourteenth century).

Two events in medieval European history transformed the level at which people consumed: the material revolution of the twelfth century that flooded medieval Europe with newly available luxury goods, generating the first European sumptuary laws (Genoa, 1157), and the 1348 pandemic of plague that wiped out between one-third to one-half the population, ultimately revising the social order and redistributing the wealth.

Concern with consumption in Western civilization had existed since pre-Christian Greece, beginning in sixth-century BCE Sparta. Both Greek and Roman society passed legislation against public consumption that covered public display such as excesses in dining, the costumes of gladiators, numbers of flutists at social events, and even ostentatious furniture. Over-consumption was thought to bring disorder to society and even destabilize the established hierarchy. Tertullian was especially vocal among early Christian Church Fathers. Singling out women, he equated make-up and extravagant clothing with worldly sin, a diabolically inspired offense against God's creations. After Constantine's conversion of the Empire to Christianity in 325, ecclesiastical dicta concerning excesses of consumption (from the second Council of Nicaea in 787 to the Council of Constance in 1414–1418), were directed primarily at containing the sartorial display of clergy, however not the laity. Early Carolingian Europe saw little concern with consumption, due to a relative lack of luxury goods. However when the opportunity for indulgence did appear, regulations followed as well. Charlemagne's edict of 808 limited prices allowed for silks and fur.

As medieval European society stabilized, sumptuary laws were passed first in Italy, then France (1229), and Spain (1234). Legislation in the north followed with England (1316) and the lands of the Holy Roman Empire (1304–1350). It was in Italy, however, where the bulk of laws were enacted, over three hundred between 1157 and 1500. Public rites of passage such as weddings, baptisms, and funerals were especially targeted to control the splendor of guests' clothing, number of courses served, types of food and drink, numbers of gifts, and display of candles and silver plate. For funerals, emotional excesses such as wailing, the tearing of hair, or dramatically long pauses during services were banned. Excessive public display was considered a form of social "disorder" that could result in rowdy expressions of dissatisfaction with the government, which was to be avoided at all costs. Laws in northern Europe and in the southern Italic peninsula were issued largely by the edict of royal courts and, therefore, had a conservative agenda that sought to restrict any challenge to the ruling group. In northern Italy, however, the independent city-states (Florence, Venice, Siena, Genoa, and others), passed local legislation that tended to rein in the display of noble power, which allowed a new merchant elite to emerge.

Condemnations evolved from an emphasis on food and consumables to clothing and fashion by the later Middle Ages. Women's clothing, designed as displays of their familial wealth, became increasingly singled out for sumptuary regulation. Marie de Valois, wife of the French podestà in Florence in 1326, famously obtained permission for women there to wear formerly banned yellow and white silk braids in their hair, and in 1436, Christine Corner and other Venetian matrons successfully appealed to the pope to be able to sport "honorably" magnificent clothes. Fifteenth-century Florentine communal statutes concerning all kinds of consumption were collected under the telling rubric "De ornatu mulierum." In late medieval Europe, consumption rose to unprecedented heights among the rich. But laws passed to curb it only seemed to cause its proliferation. The ability to consume luxury goods demonstrated power, and even the Church began to change its attitude toward the ideal of poverty, wealth and consumption coming to be seen as the mark of honor and even an aid to salvation.

CAROLE COLLIER FRICK

References and Further Reading

Bynum, Caroline W. *Holy Feast and Holy Fast: The Religious Significance of Food to Medieval Women.* Berkeley: University of California Press, 1987.
Cipolla, Carlo M. "[The Economic Policies of Governments:] V: The Italian and Iberian Peninsulas," in Postan M. M. and H. J. Habbakuk eds. *The Cambridge Economic History of Europe.* vol. 3, *Economic Organisation and Policies in the Middle Ages,* edited by M. M. Postan, E. E. Rich, and Edward Miller. Cambridge: Cambridge University Press, 1963, pp. 397–429.
De Roover, Raymond. *San Bernardino of Siena and Sant'Antonino of Florence. The Two Great Economic Thinkers of the Middle Ages.* Boston, 1967.
Dyer, Christopher. "The Consumer and the Market in the Later Middle Ages," *Economic History Review* 43 (1989): 305–327.
Killerby, Catherine K. *Sumptuary Law in Italy 1200–1500.* Oxford: Oxford University Press, 2002.
Wood, Diana. *Medieval Economic Thought.* Cambridge: Cambridge University Press, 2002.

See also Clothing; Plague; Poverty, Religious; Sanuti, Nicolosa Castellani; Sumptuary Law

CONTRACEPTION

Contraception refers to methods or practices meant to allow heterosexual activity yet avoid production of offspring. The line between contraception (preventing conception from occurring in the first place) and abortion (the termination of a pregnancy that had already begun) was less clear-cut in the Middle Ages than it is now, largely because the *conceptus* was not really considered a fetus until it "quickened" or was "ensouled" (that is, until the woman perceived the movement of the fetus). Whether the methods and practices used to prevent pregnancy in the Middle Ages were fully effective is less important than evidence of the desire to separate the sex act from reproduction. Three criteria are therefore relevant to understanding medieval contraception: (1) whether there is evidence of the intent to prevent pregnancy and how it was viewed by religion and law; (2) what kinds of contraceptive knowledge were available; and (3) whether contraception was the concern of women only or also of men.

Islamic and Jewish Attitudes

The different religious traditions of medieval Europe had differing attitudes toward contraception and early abortion. In the Islamic world, contraception was permissible, and abortion was tolerated, though physicians were often more uncomfortable with the latter than were religious jurists. Because sexual relations between a male master and a female slave were considered licit (that is, in the eyes of the law they did not make the man adulterous vis-à-vis his wife or wives) yet produced other problems if she conceived (once she had borne him children she could not subsequently be sold), males often had reason to use contraception. Contraceptive methods might also be motivated, for both men and women, out of fear of the dangers of childbirth or to preserve the woman's beauty. *Coitus interruptus* (the man's withdrawal of his penis prior to ejaculation) was a favored method, though medical texts offer numerous chemical means of contraception. Woman-controlled methods (such as vaginal suppositories, which offered physical, as well as chemical, barriers to the man's semen) outnumber male-controlled methods by about four to one. Muslim jurists debated whether men or women could practice contraception without their partners' consent.

Among Jewish communities, use of a contraceptive sponge was permitted during lactation lest a new pregnancy rob the nursing child of its nourishment. There seems to have been no stigma attached to this practice, and it is referred to openly in rabbinical literature. *Coitus interruptus,* on the other hand, and other forms of "destruction of the seed" were prohibited.

Christian Attitudes

In Byzantium, Christian orthodox views equated abortion with murder, though some considered contraception more egregious because it killed many potential fetuses rather than just one. Among Latin Christians, views on contraception and abortion were primarily influenced by Saint Augustine of Hippo (d. 430), who had defined offspring as the second of three "goods of marriage" (the others being sexual fidelity and the sacrament that bound the husband and wife to God). Thus, any attempt to thwart the purpose of marriage was condemned. Canon law pronounced that it was more sinful for a man to impede conception when having intercourse with his wife than to engage in adultery with another woman.

In the early Middle Ages, religious writers spoke exclusively of "procuring poisons of sterility" (*venena sterilitatis procurare*), which has generally been interpreted as use of oral abortifacients; terminology for contraception *per se* is entirely absent from penitentials prior to the ninth century. In the early twelfth century, theologians and canon lawyers began to speak of "avoidance of offspring" (*vitatio prolis*), a more general concept that seems to have included such practices as *coitus interruptus* and anal intercourse.

Contraceptives

Contraceptives and abortifacients were never suppressed from early medieval Latin gynecological texts (which were derived largely from pagan Greek and Roman traditions), and some elements of Muslim attitudes and practices were adopted when Arabic medical writings were translated in the eleventh and twelfth centuries. The Benedictine monk Constantine the African (died before 1098–1099) did not translate a chapter on abortion from an Arabic text he was rendering into Latin, yet he openly supported the use of contraceptives on the belief that regular heterosexual activity was necessary for women's health, even if pregnancy should sometimes be avoided. This view was adopted by some other Latin medical writers, although, aside from Italian writers, it was rare for them to devote a separate chapter to the subject.

On Constantine's authority, the anonymous author of a twelfth-century Salernitan text, *On the Conditions of Women*, listed several contraceptive amulets—substances to be worn around the neck or carried in the hand to prevent pregnancy which, from our modern perspective, could not possibly have had anything more than a placebo effect. Nevertheless, a thesis proposed in the 1990s argued that medieval women had ample knowledge of chemically effective pharmaceutical agents to "provoke the menses" or "expel the fetus," thereby regularly maintaining control of their fertility. The flaw with this argument is that while certain herbal substances *could* be used to limit reproduction, not every attempt to provoke the menses was motivated by the desire to contracept, nor was every attempt to expel a fetus done because the child had been unwanted.

"Retained menses" (what we would call amenorrhea) was a major concern in medieval gynecology, and it was recognized that women could not conceive unless they were menstruating regularly. As the twelfth-century medical writer Trota of Salerno put it, emmenagogues (drugs or agents used to bring on or quicken menstruation) were "for provoking the menses because of whose retention the woman is *unable* to conceive." And "expelling the fetus" was a frequently necessary obstetrical intervention when the fetus had died *in utero* and did not emerge spontaneously. In other words, both practices could be motivated by pronatalistic concerns, not the desire to limit fertility.

Trota herself includes neither contraceptives nor abortifacients in her medical writings, and those medical authors who did so usually justified the inclusion on the grounds of preserving the woman's health. In fact, the widespread modern belief that medieval midwives were all experts in the knowledge of contracepting and aborting has never been documented. The belief may reflect an overly literal reading of the 1496 Dominican witch-hunters' manual, *The Hammer of Witches*, which made wild claims that "witch-midwives" regularly inhibited fertility. It is clear that magical practices were indeed associated with the placenta and other products of birth, and curses of sterility or impotence were common elements of witchcraft accusations. Yet midwives' contraceptive knowledge or practices are never mentioned by medical writers. Rather, it was more common for male writers to focus on prostitutes, whose low fertility was a commonplace, though even here they credited the nature of prostitution (for example, the belief that prostitutes did not experience pleasure in intercourse and therefore did not emit their own "seed") as much as prostitutes' own active contraceptive knowledge.

Whether women beyond those trained in the arts of prostitution were generally aware of contraceptive techniques is less clear. Beatrice de Planissoles, a suspected heretic in early fourteenth-century Montaillou (southern France), recounts how her male lover, a priest, brought to their trysts a contraceptive amulet which he had her wear when they made love; he was always sure to take it back from her when he left, lest she take another lover. Clearly, control over contraceptive knowledge in this situation lay with the man, who was concerned not only with avoiding pregnancy but also with controlling his partner's sexuality. *Coitus interruptus*, which Biller suggests may have been the main method of "avoiding offspring" from the thirteenth century, likewise gave the male partner control over contraception.

Christian medical writers became increasingly cautious about how they shared contraceptive knowledge toward the end of the Middle Ages. In Latin gynecological texts contraceptive instructions were sometimes put into cipher; in vernacular gynecological texts addressed to women they were deleted entirely. Even "legitimate" remedies to expel the dead fetus were hedged with warnings that they should not be shared with suspect women. Statements about "womanly arts" of limiting fertility suggest that there existed an "underground" female culture where contraceptive and abortifacient knowledge circulated freely. If so, historians have yet to find adequate evidence to prove it.

MONICA GREEN

References and Further Reading

Barratt, Alexandra, ed. *The Knowing of Woman's Kind in Childing: A Middle English Version of Material Derived from the 'Trotula' and Other Sources*. Medieval Women: Texts and Contexts, 4. Turnhout: Brepols, 2001.

Baumgarten, Elisheva. *Mothers and Children: Jewish Family Life in Medieval Europe*. Princeton, N.J.: Princeton University Press, 2004.

Biller, Peter. *The Measure of Multitude: Population in Medieval Thought*. Oxford: Oxford University Press, 2000.

Boswell, John E. *The Kindness of Strangers: The Abandonment of Children in Western Europe from Late Antiquity to the Renaissance*. New York: Pantheon Books, 1988.

Brundage, James A. *Law, Sex, and Christian Society in Medieval Europe*. Chicago: University of Chicago Press, 1987.

Elsakkers, Marianne. "Abortion, Poisoning, Magic, and Contraception in Eckhardt's *Pactus Legis Salicae*." *Amsterdamer Beiträge zur älteren Germanistik* 57 (2003): 233–267.

Fournier, Jacques. "Inquisition Records." In *Readings in Medieval History*. Volume II. *The Later Middle Ages*, edited by Patrick J. Geary. Peterborough: Broadview Press, 1999, 524–544. Includes the testimony of Beatrice de Planissoles.

Green, Monica H. "Constantinus Africanus and the Conflict Between Religion and Science." In *The Human Embryo: Aristotle and the Arabic and European Traditions*, edited by G. R. Dunstan. Exeter: Exeter University Press, 1990, pp. 47–69.

———. review of John Riddle, *Eve's Herbs: A History of Contraception and Abortion in the West* (Cambridge, Mass.: Harvard University Press, 1997). In *Bulletin of the History of Medicine* 73 (1999): 308–311.

———., ed. and trans. *The 'Trotula': A Medieval Compendium of Women's Medicine*. Philadelphia: University of Pennsylvania Press, 2001.

Green, Monica H. and Linne R. Mooney. "The *Sickness of Women*." In *Sex, Aging, and Death in a Medieval Medical Compendium: Trinity College Cambridge MS R.14.52, Its Text, Language, and Scribe*, edited by M. Teresa Tavormina. Medieval and Renaissance Texts and Studies. Tempe, Ariz.: Arizona State University Press, 2005.

McClanan, Anne. "'Weapons to Probe the Womb': The Material Culture of Abortion and Contraception in the Early Byzantine Period." In *The Material Culture of Sex, Procreation, and Marriage in Premodern Europe*, edited by Anne L. McClanan and Karen Rosoff Encarnación. New York: Palgrave, 2002, pp. 33–57.

Musallam, B. F. *Sex and Society in Islam: Birth Control Before the Nineteenth Century*. Cambridge: Cambridge University Press, 1983.

Noonan, John T. *Contraception: A History of Its Treatment by the Catholic Theologians and Canonists*. Enlarged edition. Cambridge, Mass.: Belknap Press of Harvard University Press, 1986.

Patlagean, Evelyne. "Birth Control in the Early Byzantine Empire." In *Biology of Man in History: Selections from the Annales, économies, sociétés, civilisations*. Baltimore: The Johns Hopkins University Press, 1975, pp. 1–22.

See also **Abortion; Breastfeeding and Wet-Nursing; Gynecology; Infertility; Menstruation; Penitentials and Pastoral Manuals; Pregnancy and Childbirth: Christian Women; Pregnancy and Childbirth: Jewish Women; Prostitutes; Secrets of Women; Sexuality; Sexuality: Extramarital Sex; Sexuality: Female Same-Sex Relations; Sexuality: Male Same-Sex Relations; Sexuality, Regulation of; Sexuality: Sex in Marriage; Trota of Salerno**

CONVERSAE AND CONVERSI

Conversae and *conversi* are associated with the new monasticism of the central Middle Ages (and up into the modern age). The term's meaning is not consistent. Only in the mid-twelfth century did it come to refer to a second-class religious, a female or male celibate laborer within the religious community. In the late eleventh century, *conversae/i* were those who entered a monastery *ad conversionem*, the "converted ones" who entered religious life from some other status. *Conversae* were often widows or, like *conversi*, had been married before. Sometimes their entire family entered the religious life. Such "converts" could also be secular priests or canonesses who converted to a life following a religious rule. In late-eleventh century documents from la Sauve Majeure near Bordeaux *conversi* were distinguished from child-oblates; many of its "converts" were knights converted from a life of violence.

A particular apt example of such a convert was the former knight Pons de Léras, founder of a southern French hermitage that became a monastery at Silvanès. In the 1130s, Pons "converted," placed his wife and two children in monastic houses, did public penance, and made restitution to his victims. He soon established a hermitage that had become a Cistercian abbey by the 1170s. Seen from the viewpoint of the eleventh century the former knight Pons was an adult convert to the religious life, and to be referred to as a convert said nothing about status. The same is true of Petronilla of Cheminé, an aristocratic widow chosen by the wandering preacher Robert of Arbrissel to rule as the first abbess of the religious community of Fontevrault. In the "Life of Robert," written circa 1118 by Baudri of Dol, Petronilla the abbess is referred to as *conversa laica*. Petronilla was chosen as abbess because of her considerable experience in the secular world. This experience was something that a virgin brought up in a religious house would not have had. Such adult conversion was the norm among the new religious reformers of the twelfth century, and often provided leaders to the community. Indeed many new religious communities forbade entrance by child oblates.

At about the middle of the twelfth century, a second meaning of the terms *conversae/i* began to emerge within the monastic context. It came to be associated among the Cistercians with entrants from humble backgrounds, often peasants who had held land coming into monastic hands. These *conversae/i* or lay-sisters and lay-brothers worked with nuns and monks in the fields, and on the new satellite granges associated with the Cistercians. Mid-century charters from houses like Silvanès reveal promises to admit peasants as "*fratri*" or "*sorores*," or *conversae/i*; some who had come from marginal settlements must have sought the security of monastic life. Although Cistercian rhetoric is full of an ideal of charitable equality among all members of the community, by mid-twelfth century *conversae/i* are described as working on the granges so that monks and nuns could remain within the ambit of the monastic enclosure. By late in the twelfth century, *conversae* and *conversi* appear as dairy-maids and shepherds at the house of nuns at Nonenque. Among the earliest Cistercian texts, moreover, are those on the rights and duties of lay-brothers that appear to date to the mid century, after the earlier moment of primitive equality when all religious members of a community, nuns and *conversae*, or monks and *conversi*, had worked together in the fields, at least during the harvest.

Conversae/i soon came to be identified with laborers within the monasteries. This was the accepted meaning of the term in the "Life of the Pons de Léras," the knight turned *conversus* previously mentioned. Writing no earlier than the 1170s about a foundation at Silvanès made 40 years earlier, the author of the Life, who had found Pons' name identified as *conversus* among the earliest Silvanès charters, described Pons as having "remained a lay-brother out of humility." Clearly by the time this author wrote, *conversus* had come to mean "laborer," and in the 1188 Cistercian statutes, abbots concurred that knights entering the order could not be *conversi*. For the thirteenth century as more and more *conversi* were no longer recruited along with Cistercian land acquisition, numerous *conversi* rebellions are recorded. Although the terms *conversus* and *conversa* were attached most often to laborers, the earlier meaning can also be found in cases in the mid-thirteenth century. Often it was used when widows "converted" and lived as *conversae* in the vicinity of men's houses; these were not female servants. It is difficult to estimate the numbers of *conversae/i* at typical Cistercian or other reform houses. Narrative accounts of *conversi* in the hundreds probably exaggerate, but abbeys for men may have had nearly double the number of lay-brothers as monks during the twelfth century. Houses of nuns could have lay-brothers attached who took vows directly from the abbess or were deputized from neighboring houses of monks. A house of nuns might have between two or three and a dozen lay-brothers, but no more than one *conversae* for every three or four nuns.

CONSTANCE H. BERMAN

References and Further Reading

Aubrun, Michel. *La vie de Saint Etienne d'Obazine.* Clermont-Ferrand: Institut des études du Massif Central, 1970.

Berman, Constance H. *Medieval Agriculture, the Southern French Countryside, and the Early Cistercians: A Study of Forty-Three Monasteries.* Philadelphia: American Philosophical Society, 1986.

———. *The Cistercian Evolution: The Invention of a Religious Order in Twelfth-Century Europe.* Philadelphia: University of Pennsylvania Press, 2000.

———. "Distinguishing between the Humble Peasant Lay Brother and Sister and the Converted Knight in Medieval Southern France" for *Lay and Religious* edited by Janet Burton and Emilia Jamroziak. Brepols Medieval Church Studies, in press.

———. "Knights and Conversion to the Religious Life in the Central Middle Ages," for volume in honor of Bernard Bachrach, forthcoming.

Constable, Giles. *The Reformation of the Twelfth Century.* New York: Cambridge University Press, 1996.

Donnelly, James S. *The Decline of the Medieval Cistercian Lay-Brotherhood.* New York, 1949.

Kienzle, Beverly M. "The Tract on the Conversion of Pons of Léras and the True Account of the Beginning of the

Monastery of Silvanès." *Cistercian Studies Quarterly* 29 (1995): 219–243,

Lekai, Louis Julius. *The Cistercians: Ideals and Reality.* Kent, Ohio: Kent State University Press, 1977.

Leyser, Henrietta. *Hermits and the New Monasticism. A Study of Religious Communities in Western Europe, 1000–1150.* London: Macmillan, 1984.

Venarde, Bruce. *Robert of Arbrissel. A Medieval Religious Life.* Washington, D.C.: Catholic University of America Press, 2003.

See also **Cistercian Order; Fontevrault, Abbey and Order of; Monasticism and Nuns; Servants; Social Status; Work**

CONVERSION, RELIGIOUS

In medieval Europe processes of conversion, whether individual or collective changes of religion or religious affiliation, took place in various directions. In the early Middle Ages Germanic *gentes* (peoples) gave up their traditional cults in favor of Arian or Orthodox Christianity. Former Arians adopted Orthodox Christianity. Christians in Arabic Spain and—in the era of the crusades—in the Frankish Levant passed over to Islam and sometimes to Judaism. Vice versa, Muslims and Jews converted to Christianity. The processes of Christian and Islamic conversion in particular transformed the religious map of Europe until the turn of the millennium.

Changing from one religious practice to another had immediate consequences with regard to women's and men's lives. Questions arose as to whether a convert's former social bonds were broken. Was a Christian whose partner had converted to Islam allowed to remarry? Should a formerly "pagan" man who had turned Christian dismiss his wife in the event that she did not convert as well? Did the baptism of a Jew mean that his or her ties to family and community were cut?

In the long run the conversion of entire societies changed the concepts and structures of marriage, family, and kinship (e.g., the introduction of monogamous, indissoluble marriage as a result of Christianization). Within the frame of a specific theological anthropology images of women and men were propagated that influenced their social position and gender-relations. In Christian society, for instance, a tradition of thinking became dominant that proclaimed the subordination of women to men due to the notion of a female physical, intellectual, and moral frailty that was supposed to result from Eve's Fall.

Between the fourth and the twelfth centuries, Christianity in its orthodox (Catholic) form made its way into Germania, Gaul, Britain, Scandinavia, and large parts of the Slavic world. Thus around 1300, the orthodox Christianization of Europe was essentially finished as far as the formal acceptance of the Christian cult was concerned. The process of conversion in the meaning of an inner reorientation took much longer and lasted in some European regions well into the age of the Reformation.

Women participated in this process of orthodox Christianization in several ways: as addressees of missionaries (monks, priests, bishops, and popes), as converts, as convert-makers, and as missionaries. Their activities spanned the characteristic forms of conversion in early medieval societies. Aiming at converting whole *gentes* (peoples), Christian missions first of all had to win over the ruler and his great men at the head of the *gens*. This leading group decided about the acceptance of Christianity and received baptism in a collective act. The conversion of other social strata then followed according to the same collective principle. Usually whole households were baptized along with the *pater familias* (the head of the house). However, in a family different religious practices might coexist for a while.

Due to the importance of the ruler's conversion medieval narratives provide detailed descriptions of these acts. In this context there are some explicit references to rulers' wives as convert-makers of their husbands. In the sixth century for instance, Gregory of Tours, the historiographer, reported on how the Merovingian King Clovis († 511) had reluctantly agreed to be baptized and had thus initiated the Christianization of the Frankish Kingdom. According to this narrative Clovis's Orthodox wife, Queen Clotilda († 544), had "preached to her husband unceasingly" and managed to have her sons baptized. Though Clotilda's tireless preaching apparently did not directly achieve the king's change of mind, it nevertheless played a significant role in his final decision to be baptized with his leaders. As may be expected, bishops and popes emphatically admonished royal wives to engage in converting their husbands and thus push forward the Christianization of an entire *gens*.

However, there is comparatively little evidence of the conversion of royal or aristocratic women themselves and even less about women of lower social standing. For example, the Bishop Eucherius of Orléans († 738) was reported to have successfully exhorted a woman to give up "pagan error" and to have acted as godfather of her son. Mothers like this and like Clotilda, who cared for the baptism and the Christian education of their children, created the basis for Christianity to become rooted among coming generations.

Apart from the family as a field of conversion, women actively engaged as missionaries. In the eighth century, a net of Anglo-Saxon women and men who were akin to each other worked on the continent on the initiative of Boniface (672/675–754). When Boniface called his relative Leoba (700/710–780/782) to join him, she left the monastery of Wimborne in Wessex together with several other women, and became abbess of Tauberbischofsheim, the monastic center of Boniface's mission. Far from being confined to the limits of her monastery, Leoba performed episcopal functions by regularly visiting and controlling other monasteries. She worked as a teacher, preacher, and spiritual mentor, offering pastoral care and instructions even to bishops who used to discuss theological and ecclesiastical questions with her. According to Leoba's *Life,* Boniface appreciated her as his equal partner in the mission.

Due to the collective character of conversion and its initial centering on rulers medieval, historiography does not offer a complete picture of women's roles in this process. However, by combining these narratives with other material such as saints' lives, reports on miracles, letters, sermons, and archaeological findings, we may conclude that women in the contexts of family, monastery, and mission decisively contributed to the Christianizing of Europe.

CORDULA NOLTE

References and Further Reading

Geary, Patrick. "Die Bedeutung von Religion und Bekehrung im frühen Mittelalter." In *Die Franken und die Alemannen bis zur "Schlacht bei Zülpich" (496/97),* edited by Dieter Geuenich (Ergänzungsbände zum Reallexikon der Germanischen Altertumskunde 19). Berlin/New York: de Gruyter, 1998, pp. 438–450.

[Gregory of Tours, *Ten Books of Histories*] *Gregorii episcopi Turonensis libri historiarum X,* edited by B. Krusch and W. Levison. 2nd ed. Monumenta Germaniae Historica, Scriptores rerum Merovingicarum 1.1, Hannover Imaensis Bibliopol: 1951².

[English Translation of the "Ten Books of Histories"] *Gregory of Tours: The History of the Franks.* translated by Lewis Thorpe, Harmondsworth: Penguin, 1974.

[Gregory the Great, Letters] *S. Gregorii Magni Registrum epistularum,* edited by Dag Norberg. Corpus Christianorum. Series Latina 140 and 140A, Turnhout, 1987.

Kruger, Steven F. "Conversion and Medieval Sexual, Religious, and Racial Categories." In *Constructing Medieval Sexuality,* edited by Karma Lochrie, Peggy McCracken, and James A. Schultz (Medieval Cultures 11). Minneapolis: University of Minnesota Press, 1997, pp. 158–179.

[*Life of Bishop Eucherius of Orléans*] *Vita Eucherii episcopi Aurelianensis.* edited by W. Levison. Monumenta Germaniae historica, Scriptores rerum Merovingicarum 7, Hannover and Leipzig 1920, pp. 46–53.

Lifshitz, Felice. "Les femmes missionaires: l'exemple de la Gaule franque." *Revue d'histoire ecclésiastique* 83 (1988): 5–33.

Morrison, Karl F. *Understanding Conversion.* Charlottesville and London: University Press of Virginia, 1990.

Muldoon, James, ed. *Varieties of Religious Conversion in the Middle Ages.* Gainesville: University Press of Florida, 1997.

Muschiol, Gisela. "Königshof, Kloster und Mission – die Welt der Lioba und ihrer geistlichen Schwestern." In *Bonifatius – Apostel der Deutschen. Mission und Christianisierung vom 8. bis ins 20. Jahrhundert,* edited by Franz J. Felten (Mainzer Vorträge 9). Wiesbaden: Steiner, 2004, pp. 99–114.

Nelson, Janet L. "Women and the Word in the Earlier Middle Ages." In *Women in the Church. Papers Read at the 1989 Summer Meeting and the 1990 Winter Meeting of the Ecclesiastical History Society,* edited by W. J. Sheils and Diana Wood. Oxford: Blackwell, 1990, pp. 53–78.

Nirenberg, David. "Conversion, Sex, and Segregation: Jews and Christians in Medieval Spain." *The American Historical Review* 107.3 (2002): 1065–1093.

Nolte, Cordula. *Conversio und Christianitas. Frauen in der Christianisierung vom 5. bis 8. Jahrhundert* (Monographien zur Geschichte des Mittelalters 41). Stuttgart: Hiersemann, 1995.

Nolte, Cordula. "Gender and Conversion in the Merovingian Era." In *Varieties of Religious Conversion in the Middle Ages,* edited by James Muldoon. Gainesville: University Press of Florida, 1997, pp. 81–99.

[Rudolf of Fulda, *Life of Leoba*] *Vita Leobae abbatissae Biscofesheimensis auctore Rudolfo Fuldensi,* edited by George Waitz. Monumenta Germaniae historica, Scriptores 15.1, Hannover 1887, Reprint 1963, pp. 121–131.

Sawyer, Birgit. "Women and the Conversion of Scandinavia." In *Frauen in Spätantike und Frühmittelalter. Lebensbedingungen – Lebensnormen – Lebensformen,* edited by Werner Affeldt, Sigmaringen: Thorbecke, 1990, pp. 263–281.

See also **Abbesses; Clotilda, Frankish Lands; Gender Ideologies; Hagiography; History, Medieval Women's; Husbands and Husbandry; Jewish Women; Kinship; Leoba; Letter Writing; Marriage, Christian; Miracles and Miracle Collections; Mothers as Teachers; Monasticism and Nuns; Noble Women; Scandinavia; Sermons and Preaching; Spiritual Care; Wives and Husbands**

CORNARO, CATERINA

In 1472, Venetian noblewoman Caterina Cornaro (1454–1510) arrived in Cyprus as the new bride of King Jacques II Lusignan. This union served the interests of her wealthy merchant family, as well as her homeland, which granted her the title "Daughter of the Republic." Both her spouse and her infant son died shortly thereafter, leaving her the titular ruler of the island for fifteen years, from 1474–1489. Increased tensions with the Ottoman Empire and marriage proposals from the Neopolitan throne prompted Venice to annex the island directly, forcing an unwilling queen to abdicate in 1489. In exchange, reigning Doge Agostino Barbarigo granted Cornaro a sizeable lifetime pension and lifetime dominion over the Veneto hill town of Asolo. Cornaro's patriotic sacrifice received notable visual commemoration in the sixteenth-century program of Venetian triumphs for the Great Council Hall in the Doge's Palace, where Cornaro was the only nonallegorical female depicted.

Cornaro spent her retirement in both Venice and Asolo, where she entertained regional dignitaries and luminaries, and hosted a series of elaborate social gatherings for family and friends. Such assemblies provided the setting and inspiration for her kinsman Pietro Bembo's pastoral dialogue *Gli Asolani*. Gentile Bellini painted Cornaro's portrait, and placed her in his *Miracle at the Bridge of San Lorenzo*; it is possible that other Venetian cultural figures attended her court. In addition to cultural activities, Cornaro frequently petitioned the Venetian government on Cypriot affairs. Cornaro's kin persisted in evoking their status as a royal family in Republican Venice long after her death.

HOLLY HURLBURT

References and Further Reading

Arbel, Benjamin. "Royal Family in Republican Venice: The Cypriot Legacy of the *Corner della Regina*." *Studi Veneziani* 15 (1988): 131–152.
———. "The Reign of Caterina Cornaro as a Family Affair." *Studi Veneziani* 26 (1993): 67–85.
Hill, George. *A History of Cyprus*. Vol. 3. Cambridge, Cambridge University Press, 1972.

See also **Noble Women; Patronage, Artistic; Queens and Empresses: the West; Regents and Queen-Lieutenants**

COSMETICS

The care and embellishment of the body is a practice that different societies share. Together with language, adornment is regarded as indicative of the peculiarly human ability for symbolizing, and it is considered the definitive archaeological trace that distinguishes human beings from other creatures. As a basic cultural feature, adornment in the Middle Ages was a means to create and enhance both identity and difference.

Appearance

There was no clear division between cosmetics and adornment in the Middle Ages. In learned contexts, the Latin words *ornatus* and *decoratio* were used to refer to a wide array of procedures to maintain and modify the natural appearance of the body, as well as for the use of objects and clothes to improve one's image. In western Europe, this semantic connection expresses the conceptual continuum shared by different activities devoted to the external care of the self. Although theological and moral thinking on individual appearance had been important in the classical world, Christianity, in particular through Tertullian's *De cultu feminarum* (The Appearance of Women), decisively transformed the theme by associating cosmetics and adornment almost exclusively with a negative concept of women. Medieval misogynistic traditions sustained and spread the vision of the female body as naturally defective, and women's investments in care for their appearance were seen as ways to deceive God's will and conceal their moral and physical abjection. Although someone like Hildegard of Bingen valued the adornment of her nuns' bodies, theological thinking was dominated by denunciations from male preachers, such as Bernardino of Siena or Francesc Eiximenis, who attacked what they describe as women's extensive interest in their appearance.

Both men and women, nevertheless, were concerned about their outward aspect. Misogynistic discourses notwithstanding, the care of the embodiment of both femininity and masculinity was seen in a positive light by some religious, moral, medical, and natural philosophical traditions. Regional, chronological and cultural differences still need to be studied, but Arabic medicine especially portrays a concern with male appearance. Cosmetics offered corrective measures to signify sexual difference, as women's and men's cosmetic practices were often in opposition, particularly regarding hair. Men's use of fake beards and their care of hair and whiskers are well attested, whereas women were concerned with depilating every body surface except the head. Medieval physicians and natural philosophers understood the distribution of the hair on the body as an expression of a basic physiological distinction between male and female complexions, explaining hair in males as a result of their way of ridding themselves of the superfluous bodily substances that women processed through menstruation.

Cosmetics and Perfumes

Cosmetics and perfumery had been considered aspects of medicine since antiquity, and had a physiological aspect. Pleasant smells had therapeutic as well as preventive value for both sexes; odors could control the air—one of the six unnatural things that could cause imbalance within the body, leading to illness. Significant parts of learned medical and surgical handbooks were devoted to describing procedures to care for and embellish the surfaces of the skin and the hair, with the aim of preventing aging, improving appearance and modifying color, texture, or shape. These works recommended preparations for skin diseases such as rashes, warts, fissures, or pimples, as well as hair dyes and different kinds of softeners and mollifiers. Pharmacological texts also record systematically the cosmetic properties of plants, and they offer detailed lists of the uses of simple or compound medicines as beautifying agents. Greek, Latin, Jewish, and Arabic learned medical cultures provide practical descriptions of how to prepare and apply cosmetics, but offer little theoretical discussion, remaining in the empirical domain. Medical texts often present various procedures for a single cosmetic goal, particularizing different variants according to local traditions, time investment, or disparity in access to economic resources.

Men's interest in cosmetics is well substantiated, either as part of their work as health practitioners or for their own personal use. However, nonmisogynist cultures also associated cosmetics strongly with femininity and with women: as users of medicines to command their own image, as makers of cosmetic products, and as authors of texts describing beautifying procedures. Medieval Galenism assumed Galen's attribution to Cleopatra of an otherwise unknown cosmetic treatise that he quoted extensively, *De scriptis a Cleopatra in decorativis* (*Cleopatra's Writings on Cosmetics*), as it was called in Latin. An early medieval Greek text ascribed to Metrodora contains a long section on perfumes and cosmetic recipes dealing with the care of the breasts, skin, and hair. The Salernitan medical world distilled into Latin early Arabic cosmetic lore, and produced an anonymous twelfth century *De ornatu mulierum* (*On Women's Cosmetics*) that, as part of the Trotula compendium of women's medicine, became the most popular cosmetic text in western Europe. The emerging literature in Hebrew and the vernacular languages welcomed cosmetic works, often anonymous or written by male compilers. In the form of collections of recipes, these works were addressed to women or stated clearly women's interest in cosmetics, acknowledging as sources not only other texts but also the living practices of women. Beyond misogyny and men's involvement, cosmetics emerge as a province of knowledge and practice particularly privileged by women.

MONTSERRAT CABRÉ

References and Further Reading

Bartlett, Robert. "Symbolic Meanings of Hair in the Middle Ages." *Transactions of the Royal Historical Society*, Sixth Series, 4 (1994): 43–60.

Caballero-Navas, Carmen. *The Book of Women's Love and Jewish Medical Literature on Women. Sefer Ahavat Nashim*. London: Kegan Paul, 2004.

Cabré, Montserrat. "From a Master to a Laywoman: A Feminine Manual of Self-Help," *Dynamis. Acta Hispanica ad Medicinae Scientiarumque Historiam Illustrandam* 20 (2000): 371–393.

Cadden, Joan. *Meanings of Sex Difference in the Middle Ages. Medicine, Science and Culture*. Cambridge: Cambridge University Press, 1993.

Colish, Marcia L. "Cosmetic Theology: The Transformation of a Stoic Theme." *Assays. Critical Approaches to Medieval and Renaissance Texts* 1 (1981): 3–14.

Green, Monica. "The Possibilities of Literacy and the Limits of Reading: Women and the Gendering of Medical Literacy." In *Women's Healthcare in the Medieval West. Texts and Contexts*. Aldershot: Ashgate, 2000. Essay number VII, pp. 1–76.

———. *The Trotula: A Medieval Compendium of Women's Medicine*. Philadelphia: University of Pennsylvania Press, 2001.

Moulinier-Brogi, Laurence. "Esthétique et soins du corps dans les traités médicaux latins à la fin du Moyen Âge." *Médiévales* 46 (2004): 55–72.

Schalick, Walton O. "The Face Behind the Mask: 13th and 14th-Century European Medical Cosmetology and Physiognomy." In *Medicine and the History of the Body. Proceedings of the 20th, 21st and 22nd International Symposium on the Comparative History of Medicine—East and West*, edited by Yasuo Otsuka, Shizu Sakai, and Shigehisa Kuriyama. Tokyo: Ishiyaku Euroamerica, 1999, pp. 295–312.

Les Soines de Beauté. Moyen Age, Début des Temps Modernes. Actes du IIème Colloque International, Grasse (26–28 avril 1985), edited by Denis Menjot. Nice: Faculté des Lettres et Sciences Humaines, 1987.

See also **Beauty; Body; Clothing; Conduct Literature; Doctors and Healers; Femininity and Masculinity; Gender Ideologies; Jewelry; Medicine; Misogyny; Secrets of Women; Sumptuary Law; Trota of Salerno**

COURTLY LOVE

Courtly love was born, the story goes, with the earliest troubadour, William IX, at the end of the eleventh century. It was not named, however, until 1883, when the French medievalist Gaston Paris coined the term to characterize the passionate love uniting Lancelot and Guinevere in Chrétien de Troyes's twelfth-century Old French verse romance, *Lancelot or the Knight of the Cart* (c. 1178–1180). Referring to this single tale, Paris defined courtly love principally from the male lover's point of view, characterizing it as an illicit, extramarital liaison that placed the lover in the service of and at the mercy of a haughty and capricious lady. Although her love, grudgingly bestowed, could inspire courageous feats and refined behavior, to obtain that coveted love, the male suitor had to conform to codified rules of proper conduct, somewhat analogous to the tenets regulating chivalry. The amorous paradigms governing courtly love in the European Middle Ages display significant variations from one national literature to the next, appearing in German, English, Italian, and Spanish literary traditions, but French literature provides the dominant paradigm. It is important to note, however, that Paris's neologism, *amour courtois*, does not appear in the text of the *Lancelot* itself nor in the works of the troubadour poets that predate it (c. 1150–1210). In fact, courtliness in the French literary tradition does not necessarily include the practice of love. The lovesick and wildly heroic Lancelot exemplifies courtly love (*amour courtois*), for example, while his utterly courtly but measured and honorable chivalric companion Gauvain, who is not "in love," exhibits only courtly conduct (*courtoisie*).

The Courtly Corpus

The male-centered view of courtly love first articulated by Gaston Paris derives from an ill-defined corpus of literary texts generally considered to display it. In addition to Occitan lyric poems from southern France, which bear formal characteristics linking them to Hispano-Arabic poetic composition, there are literary inheritors of troubadour lyric in northern France known as the *trouvère* poets who composed from 1150 to 1300. A group of romances from the early twelfth century attests to the classical roots of the courtly tradition, in particular *The Romance of Aeneas* (c. 1156), which recasts its Virgilian source by adding a lengthy description of Aeneas falling in love with Lavinia. The best-known twelfth-century Arthurian romances by Chrétien de Troyes (1170–1191), including the *Lancelot*, along with versions of the Tristan story by Béroul and Thomas of England (both c. 1170), incorporate elements from Celtic folktale into narratives of adulterous passion that hark back to troubadour lyric. These key texts are rewritten and expanded in the thirteenth century into prose romances such as the *Prose Lancelot* and other stories in the Lancelot-Grail Cycle, some of which draw heavily on Biblical tales, and the *Prose Tristan*. Equally important is the highly problematic relation of these literary works to what can be considered a more didactic (or perhaps satiric) current found in Andreas Capellanus's Latin treatise on the *Art of Courtly Love* (1180s), which derives in part from Ovid's *Ars Amatoria*, and in both parts of the allegorical *Romance of the Rose*, authored initially by Guillaume de Lorris in 1245 and continued by Jean de Meun in 1268.

Courtly love in the French tradition, then, draws on an unwieldy corpus of literary texts covering at least two cultures (Occitanian and northern French), three languages (Occitan, Old French, and Latin), and at least two centuries of literary and historical development (the twelfth and thirteenth centuries). While some texts stage courtly love within marriage (*Erec and Enide,* c. 1170), others cast it as the result of a magic potion over which the adulterous lovers have no control (*Romance of Tristan,* c. 1170). Still others add to the competing demands of love and knighthood the conflict between a knight's secular duties and his Christian or spiritual commitment to God (Lancelot-Grail Cycle, c. 1220–1235).

Broadening the Canon

Courtly love begins to look quite different, however, if we move beyond the core Lancelot stories, classic examples of troubadour love songs, and canonized romance narratives to examine literary texts that have fallen traditionally outside the courtly canon. Our assessment of the meaning of courtly love shifts sharply if we include songs by the women troubadours (*trobairitz*), who often critique the amorous paradigms of troubadour lyric, or if we consider northern French sewing songs, which show female protagonists working their way to successful love liaisons with partners they have chosen. Our perspective shifts further if we include the brief narratives (*lais*) by Marie de France, which often contest the limited amorous model provided by Lancelot and Guinevere, or when we survey examples of single women in the courtly corpus.

Notions of courtliness change considerably when we examine heroines in noncanonical texts such as Richard de Fournival's *Bestiaire d'Amours,* which appends to its relatively standard catalogue of love's attributes a critique delivered in the voice of a lady, or when we think about feminocentric romances that feature women practicing the arts of cloth work and embroidery. We might also include courtly heroines in the twelfth-century version of Ovid's "Philomela," where two sisters savagely murder the son of a tyrannical rapist-spouse, or the thirteenth-century cross-dressed heroine Silence in the *Romance of Silence,* who finds herself temporarily split between male and female identities, along with a number of other transvestite romance heroines. In addition, certain female figures within the most canonical courtly texts can be seen substantially to disrupt and reconfigure the very system they have been thought to represent: the outspoken heroine in the conjugal love story *Erec and Enide*, the deft Iseut in the adulterous *Romance of Tristan*, or the female figures Oiseuse (Idleness), Lady Fortune, Lady Reason, or La Vieille (The Old Woman) in the allegorical *Romance of the Rose*.

Feminist Interpretations

Early feminist writings on courtly love focused to a large extent on the lady's social status and standing. Revising previous assessments of the courtly beloved's position as idolized and influential, these analyses tended to see her instead as disempowered and displaced. With some historians arguing for increased status for women in the High Middle Ages, and others claiming that women's status declined, feminist literary critics reassessed the significance of women cited as dedicatees and patrons, concluding that those references provided little evidence that the genre promoted women's interests or that women exerted a substantial influence in literary composition. Additionally, the Old French lyric form known as the *pastourelle* and some Arthurian tales of love were shown to mask sexual violence against women in the form of rape, attempted rape, and forced marriage, rather than promoting women's social position.

An Affair between Men

These feminist readings of courtly love tended to converge with Marxist/materialist, psychoanalytic, and more formalist interpretations, all of which demonstrated, although often without critiquing this key observation, the extent to which courtly love marginalized women. Materialist critics had read courtly love as a literary strategy used to mediate and reconcile social tensions arising between men competing for status in the feudal courts of the twelfth century. For Lacanian critics, the courtly lady was a textualized object of masculine desire, a metaphor for the enigma of femininity and a cipher for male poetic practice. Some formalist critics analyzed troubadour lyric as elaborate and playful word games in which love and the ladylove became thematic foils for serious linguistic sparring between men.

In these and later readings, the courtly love affair was revealed often to be an affair between men that left women out. Troubadour songs, which appeared to feature the all-powerful *domna* (lady), were shown to stage instead a crucial struggle between contradictory positions on sex and marriage represented by the male lay and clerical interests at court. The twelfth-century Latin treatise on courtly love, Andreas Capellanus's *De Amore*, was read as teaching the male art of making love poetry rather than the art of making love to women. Even Gaston Paris's invention of the term *courtly love* itself was shown to form part of a homosocial professional discourse at the end of the nineteenth century that attempted to tame and suppress spontaneous and instinctual passions, coded as feminine, in favor of rule-governed scientific observation, analysis, and mastery. The key text in Gaston Paris's analysis of courtly love, Chrétien de Troyes's *Lancelot*, while ostensibly about love, did not necessarily celebrate the heterosexual bond between Lancelot and Guinevere or even a bond between knights, but a bond between two clerical authors whose joint literary project determines the fate of fictional knights.

Resistant Readings

A second strain of feminist approaches to courtly love, evident from the mid-1980s to the present, built upon studies that outlined women's displacement and disenfranchisement. Looking instead for points of weakness within the dominant courtly paradigm of unrequited male desire and putative devotion to women, they read "for" women and gender in ostensibly male-centered texts. These studies revealed alternative configurations of female desire, pleasure, and subjectivity in the works of female authors such as the women troubadours (or *trobairitz*) in the southern French (Occitan) tradition, the women *trouvère* poets in the north, and the Anglo-Norman author Marie de France, among others. Resistance to courtly norms was also found among female protagonists in male-authored texts where counter narratives of women's disruptive speech or sparring response contested and undermined established conventions. At times, female subjectivity emerged, even in the most misogynistic texts, through allusions to women readers who were given double messages warning of female danger while also revealing possibilities of female empowerment. A number of courtly texts were shown to contain subtexts of women's mastery that challenged conventionally gendered terms of knowledge and wisdom. Others staged an important tension between the display of female sexuality as a form of symbolic capital in the aristocratic household and the function of women as authoritative literary patrons.

Feminist readings made visible other aspects of courtly love previously unseen and unacknowledged. The traditional focus on the coupling of knights and ladies in the courtly world had obscured a significant number of single women in courtly literary texts, female protagonists not defined primarily by their relation to a husband, male lover, or knight-savior. New attention was given to a range of courtly women joined in same-sex relations, whether homosocial, homoaffective, homoerotic, or more mystical and metaphorical, that offered other paths of resistance to heterosexual courtly coupling. Literary incidents of male and female cross-dressing, although often used ultimately to reinforce the gendered status quo, were seen to provide important alternative love scenarios that challenged an understanding of gender as fixed and immutable. The feminocentric embroidery romances and spinning songs often contained within them offered portrayals of women's work—cloth work in particular—as an alternative poetic of love. Considerations of material culture, especially clothing and the many uses to which it is put by female characters, revealed expressions of desire that fell beyond and complicated in various ways the sex-based binary terms of *male* and *female*.

Once recognized, these forms of resistance to the amorous status quo within the courtly world of knights and ladies pointed toward the possibility of more flexible subject positions than were previously acknowledged. Medieval scholars had long recognized that the courtly lady in the French tradition, following her counterpart in the Occitan lyric, possessed a curiously hybrid gender. While maintaining stereotypically female sexuality, she also held, in principle at least, the status of a feudal lord. Standard readings of courtly love for over a hundred years tended to minimize the import of this model of potential gender fluidity, asserting that the lady was only playing the role of the lord temporarily and only metaphorically. More recently, scholars have begun to acknowledge the wider implications of this cross-gendered paradigm at the heart of courtly love.

Falling in love in the medieval French tradition does not necessarily mean following the literary models of Narcissus or Pygmalion; nor does it necessitate falling into rigid categories of sexual difference. Indeed, courtly models of heterosexual coupling not only contain but often rely upon subtle mechanisms of complex gender crossing that call into question the exclusionary mode of male desire and pleasure thought more typically to represent courtly love.

E. JANE BURNS

References and Further Reading

Bloch, R. Howard. *Medieval Misogyny and the Invention of Western Romantic Love*. Chicago: University of Chicago Press, 1991.

Bruckner, Matilda Tomaryn. "Fictions of the Female Voice: The Women Troubadours." *Speculum* 67.4 (1992): 865–891.

Bumke, Joachim. *Courtly Culture: Literature and Society in the High Middle Ages*. translated by Thomas Dunlop. Berkeley: University of California Press, 1991.

Burns, E. Jane. *Courtly Love Undressed: Reading Through Clothes in Medieval French Culture*. Philadelphia: University of Pennsylvania Press, 2002.

Burns, E. Jane and Roberta L. Krueger, eds. "Courtly Ideology and Woman's Place in Medieval French Literature." Special Issue of *Romance Notes* 25.3 (1985).

Ferrante, Joan. *Woman as Image in Medieval Literature from the Twelfth Century to Dante*. New York: Columbia University Press, 1975.

Ferrante, Joan and George Economou. *In Pursuit of Perfection: Courtly Love in Medieval Literature*. Port Washington, N.Y.: Kennikat Press. 1975.

Gaunt, Simon. *Gender and Genre in Medieval French Literature*. Cambridge: Cambridge University Press, 1995.

Goldin, Frederick. *The Mirror of Narcissus and the Courtly Love Lyric*. Ithaca, N.Y.: Cornell University Press, 1967.

Gravdal, Kathryn. *Ravishing Maidens: Writing Rape in Medieval French Literature and Law*. Philadelphia: University of Pennsylvania Press, 1991.

Huchet, Jean-Charles. *L'Amour discourtois: La "Fin' Amor" chez les permiers troubadours*. Toulouse: Privat, 1987.

Hult, David F. "Gaston Paris and the Invention of Courtly Love." In *Medievalism and the Modernist Temper*, edited by R. Howard Bloch and Stephen G. Nichols, Jr. Baltimore: Johns Hopkins University Press, 1994, pp. 192–224.

Jaeger, C Stephen. *Ennobling Love: In Search of a Lost Sensibility*. Philadelphia: University of Pennsylvania Press, 1999.

Kay, Sarah. *Courtly Contradictions: The Emergence of the Literary Object in the Twelfth Century*. Stanford, Calif.: Stanford University Press, 2001.

Krueger, Roberta L. *Women Readers and the Ideology of Gender in Old French Verse Romance*. Cambridge: Cambridge University Press, 1993.

McCracken, Peggy. *The Romance of Adultery: Queenship and Sexual Transgression in Old French Literature*. Philadelphia: University of Pennsylvania Press, 1998.

Schultz, James A. *Courtly Love, the Love of Courtliness, and the History of Sexuality*. Forthcoming.

See also **Chivalry; Chrétien de Troyes; Clothwork, Domestic; Feminist Theories and Methodologies; Gender Ideologies; Guinevere; Isolde; Literature, Old French; Literature, Occitan; Marie de France; Pastourelle; Réponse du Bestiaire d'Amour; Roman de la Rose and Its Reception; Roman de Silence; Sexuality: Extramarital Sex; Trobairitz and Troubadours; Women's Song**

COURTSHIP

Courtship was a functional and effective behavior of many medieval couples, at least if their intention was to become betrothed or married of their own free will. This approach became available, and soon omnipresent, outside royal and noble circles. The canonist Gratian (c. 1140) considered a marriage to depend on the free consent of the partners, and the Fourth Lateran Council of 1215 formally introduced the free will of groom and bride as a condition for a legal marriage. Moreover, Chrétien de Troyes and other twelfth-century writers believed that physical love and emotions formed a single whole.

Issues of Social Status

Within the social elites, however, this concept was largely ruled out, as all these marriages were family arranged and had no need of courtship. On the level of princes and high nobility matrimonial negotiations produced sophisticated political alliances. For the urban elites of Italy and the Low Countries social concerns dominated, in a way that the dichotomy between patricians on the one side and the lower strata on the other, kept segregated social universes alive. Commercial and professional networks in big cities, such as London, provided the ideal forum and clearinghouse for the latest information on potential spouses, based on precise data on the families' wealth and property. But the definition of social capital is larger than estate and dowry. In Venice, in 1455, a delicate marriage deal between the Dolfins and the Gabriels failed, because the first family belonged to the old urban nobility, so-called *case vecchie*, with long-standing distinction and a power position, while the Gabriels' wealth and business connections were rather recent, with political prominence merely in the present. Strange calculations often poisoned the free marriage market: in 1413 in England one father from the Derbyshire gentry kept a blank space for the bride's name in the marriage contract as he "had not yet decided which of his daughters he would marry off."

Among the urban elites socially-mixed marriages appear at least from the fifteenth century. Anthony Molho discovered that no less than thirty-seven percent of the fifteenth century Florentine marriages were socially mixed and based more often on romance than on materialistic reasons. Genuine courtship must have preceded most of these marriages. The letters exchanged in England in 1477 between John Paston and Margery Brews reveal a fine balance between sentiments and economics. Stanley Chojnacki found that the marriage strategies of many wealthy fathers profoundly involved the well being of their children, including the very rational claim that affection between the partners, on top of material benefits, was better insurance for a long-standing union and for the continuity of the business. Literature from the fifteenth century Burgundian Netherlands, such as the play *Mirror of Love* (1480–1500) and the *Cent nouvelles nouvelles* (1456–1461), suggests that marriages for love between socially unequal partners ought to be permitted, even when status-conscious parents were opposed.

In lower middle- and working-class families courtship was an ordinary preamble for marital alliances. Here, the market was not regulated at all, and certainly not by patrimonial calculations. Spontaneous encounters with marriageable girls at work, school, Sunday mass, local feasts, or public events, gave numerous opportunities for tentative, as well as for adventurous, acquaintance. Fortuitous sexual encounters often resulted in pregnancies, mostly followed by marriage. The rituals of charivari and carnival clearly reveal the standards of a "normal" courtship: it expresses irony for a significant difference in age and in social background; it criticizes all kinds of materialistic calculations; it idealizes emotional courtship apart from outside pressures.

In daily life the development of courtship for most individuals was not determined by formal rules, but by ritualized traditions and by economics. Many young people in late medieval Flanders postponed their marriage because of their long apprenticeships and economic insecurity. They thought themselves too vulnerable to support a family: single-person households, half of them women, inhabited 20.3 percent of houses in Ypres in 1412. On average, young men did not marry before twenty-five, but they did not forgo sexual experiences. Prostitutes were available in any town and village and were the easiest way to meet men's needs. Prostitution was tolerated since it supported the social order more than it disrupted it, supposedly preventing rape and other violence against women. In addition there were trial courtships, *écraignes*, in which young men experienced love play with marriageable girls, involving all kinds of petting short of penetration. This type of sexuality had, for both sides, the double advantage that they avoided unwanted pregnancies and did not infringe upon the marriage strategies of their parents. Many boys, however, did not respect the limitations of the game, so that the records of the Ghent aldermen around 1450 bulge with unwanted pregnancies and unmarried mothers. Indeed, many sons of wealthy families, courting girls of lower status as an emotional tryout, or for mere sexual pleasure, backed out of their fatherly obligations, did not marry the girl, and opted for paying a substantial sum for her trouble and her lying-in and an annuity for the rest of her life, that would be transferred to the natural child should the mother misbehave.

Generational Conflicts

In many wealthy and even less well-to-do families, the courtship of the couple did not please the parents on one or both sides, for reasons of old feuds or because of social imbalance. Conflicts were generated by children's frustration at their inability to act independently, as well as from the authoritarian use of parental rights to impose their own candidate for marriage. If the trouble escalated, the girl mostly fled of her own free will from the family nest with her lover. In the mildest form of oppositional lifestyle the young people lived in an informal cohabitation with mutual promises of faithfulness. Going one step farther, they entered into a clandestine marriage without the consent of the parents, and with or without the presence of a priest. This type of free-will marriage was considered valid by the Church, on the basis of the canonical consent ideology. Priests had few moral scruples in helping the union be regularized in church, even if that was against the parents' wishes. The parents, of course, used civil law to prevent or to undo the disobedience of their children, by considering their behavior as abduction (against the will of the woman), even if in fact it was no more than a case of seduction (with the consent of the woman). In Flanders ordinances of 1297 defined seduction as an offense against the family, punishable with a banishment of three years. Abduction was sanctioned by death or banishment for life and the loss of all property and inheritance. Young people reacted with a variety of precautions. In 1438, Wouter Janszoon fled with his beloved from Middelburg, Zeeland, against the will of her parents. In a village in Brabant they legally married before a priest. Before the local aldermen the girl declared that she freely accompanied her lover. The girl's family introduced a complaint for abduction against her husband, but the Court of Holland rejected it, because legal proofs documented the free consent. In other cases, the parents used all possible moral and material pressure to bring the girl back into the family.

We may presume, however, that the vast majority of children must have obtained the blessing of their family for their courtship, as the social expectations of both parents and offspring normally coincided. Medieval parents had an all-embracing judicial authority over their underage children. They decided on the settlements involving the family property associated with the marriage, negotiated formal deals with the other family on dowry and inheritance, and properly registered these arrangements before the bench of aldermen. Members of the extended family also asserted themselves unofficially, as the social and financial capital of the new couple was a factor for their own social status. They became legally involved as guardians of minor orphans and had a large share in their upbringing, education, and partner choice.

Parental consent was not required for the ceremony in church. During the twelfth century, marriage became a sacrament, based on free consent of the partners, and unbreakable after a successful sexual consummation. The first step is the formal betrothal, in which a priest accepts the first promise in *verba de futuro*, and publishes three times the banns on the church door. This announcement allows third parties to introduce objections under canon law, such as too close a degree of kinship between the partners or an already existing marriage. Holy matrimony follows two months later with the second promise in *verba de presenti*.

There are many basic motivations to begin a courtship. Marriages of princes, noblemen, and top officials, reflected political strategies and materialistic calculations. Patricians eagerly brought together patrimonies and political power positions. But most medieval couples certainly looked for affection, love, warmth, and psychological compatibility. In a testimony before the court in Champagne in 1383, Jehannette Coleau explained that she left the matrimonial home of her free will in favor of a new lover because "her love for him was greater than for anyone else." From the fact that *discrepantia morum* (incompatibility of character) was accepted as an argument for separation of body and dwelling before ecclesiastical courts, we may conclude that affection was seen as an essential factor for a successful marriage. Physical charms and sexual attraction are explicitly mentioned, in fiction and in trial records, as criteria in approaches between individuals, including in the rituals of seduction and adultery.

WALTER PREVENIER

References and Further Reading

Brooke, Christopher N. L. *The Medieval Idea of Marriage*. Oxford: Oxford University Press, 1991.

Chojnacki, Stanley. *Women and Men in Renaissance Venice. Twelve Essays on Patrician Society*. Baltimore and London: The Johns Hopkins University Press, 2000.

Fleming, Peter. *Family and Household in Medieval England*. Houndmills, Basingstoke, Hampshire and New York: Palgrave, 2001.

Le Goff, Jacques and Jean-Claude Schmitt, Ed. *Le Charivari : actes de la table ronde organisée à Paris, 25–27 avril 1977*. Paris: L'école des hautes études en sciences sociales, and New York: Mouton, 1981.

MacFarlane, Alan. *Marriage and Love in England: Modes and Reproduction, 1300–1840*. Oxford and New York: B. Blackwell, 1986.

Molho, Anthony. *Marriage Alliance in Late Medieval Florence.* Cambridge, Mass.: Harvard University Press, 1994.

Prevenier, Walter, ed. *Marriage and Social Mobility in the Late Middle Ages. Mariage et mobilité sociale au bas moyen âge.* Gent: Studia Historica Gandensia, 1992.

Prevenier, Walter. "Les réseaux familiaux." In *Le prince et le peuple. Images de la société du temps des ducs de Bourgogne, 1384–1530,* edited by Walter Prevenier. Anvers: Fonds Mercator, 1998, pp. 184–231.

Schnell, Rüdiger. *Sexualität und Emotionalität in der vormodernen Ehe.* Cologne: Böhlau Verlag, 2002.

Sheehan, Michael M. *Marriage, Family and Law in Medieval Europe.* Toronto: University of Toronto Press, 1996.

See also **Betrothals; Charivari; Family (Later Middle Ages); Festivals of Misrule; Marriage, Christian; Prostitutes; Rape and Raptus; Sexuality; Social Status**

CRIME AND CRIMINALS

Female crime and victimization had distinct patterns, different from those of men. The sources for medieval crime are indirect. Law codes give us the history of rules, but how they related to actual crime is not obvious. Scattered court records exist, particularly from late medieval towns. They also are not a straightforward measure of criminality. For example, men accused of rape often sought to exonerate themselves by proving that the victim had the reputation of a prostitute. This surely does not imply that most rape victims were prostitutes, but only that it was a relatively easy and successful defense. Further, people often tried to use the courts to settle scores or apply pressure: a rape charge could be an effort to force a marriage. Nevertheless, these legal sources suggest clear patterns.

First, women were far less apt than men to be charged and convicted of serious crime. Typically, about twenty percent of convicted criminals were women. Poor women were charged with petty crimes: theft, assault, or verbal defamation. Women in the shops and markets of medieval towns were quick to go to court over insults, often over sexual reputation and care for children; "You whore! You drowned your babies," or "You whore! You prostituted your daughter." Medieval men had a monopoly not on physical violence but on weaponry. Women were quick to resort to blows, but rarely were charged with assault with weapons. Theft charges against women usually involved opportunistic robbery by a low status person within the household: a servant, an orphaned niece, or a nurse.

Women were rarely charged with successful homicide. In thirteenth-century England women comprised fewer than ten percent of accused murderers. They might, however, be accused of attempted poisoning or complicity in murder, as when a husband killed a wife and his concubine was accused of masterminding her death. The exception was infanticide, considered a woman's crime. It is hard to judge how often this was true. It could be difficult to distinguish accidental death from murder, and prosecutions for infanticide were rare. A woman with an illegitimate child might be driven to infanticide by poverty, though child abandonment was a common alternative. Fears of repercussions were real. No infanticide charges survive from thirteenth-century Bologna, but in five cases, pregnant women were beaten to death by male kin. The fact that male babies were more apt to survive overall does suggest the murder or neglect of infant girls, but not that mothers rather than fathers were culpable.

Wives were charged with adultery, particularly in regions where conviction meant the husband could keep the dowry. Sodomy charges against women existed but were extremely rare, reflecting a lack of interest and imagination on the part of male accusers. Women were often charged with pimping. Prostitution cases can reveal a gulf between norms and practice. The law maintained a dichotomous view of women as either of good or bad repute, but in practice, women might sell sex informally without being common women. The trend in late medieval towns was toward legalized, controlled prostitution. This turned a part-time source of income into an identity, with women living in brothels, often trapped in debt peonage. Women suspected of sexual criminality might be charged with love magic as well. However, this was not yet distinctively feminine: men were also accused of practicing magic.

What of female victims of crime? The most severe were rape and murder. Rape was surely common but convictions terribly rare. In thirteenth-century England, 142 prosecutions for rape led to only twenty-three cases and then a single conviction. Why? Proof of rape was difficult. Further, most rape laws encouraged private settlement, either by marrying the victim to her attacker or by his provision of a dowry. This preserved respectability for the victim and her family by enabling her to marry. Sometimes, this cloaked a consensual union, perhaps an elopement, but at times it did mean a woman was forced to marry a man who had violated and perhaps abducted her. The extent of domestic violence is debated. Wife battery prompted charges only when actual bloodshed was reported to the court; a husband was expected to beat his wife. The rarity of husbands accused of assault thus is probably not a good measure of domestic abuse. In late medieval Bologna, when women were murdered the husband was the killer about half the time.

Finally, this varied by status: poor women were more apt to resort to petty crime, girls with dowries more apt to suffer abduction.

CAROL LANSING

References and Further Reading

Kittell, Ellen E. "Reconciliation or Punishment: Women, Community, and Malefaction in the Medieval County of Flanders." In *The Texture of Society: Medieval Women in the Southern Low Countries*, edited by Ellen E. Kittell and Mary A. Suydam. New York: Palgrave Macmillan, 2004, pp. 3–30.

Medieval Crime and Social Control, edited by Barbara A. Hanawalt and David Wallace. Minneapolis: University of Minnesota Press, 1999.

See also **Abortion; Domestic Abuse; Gossip and Slander; Honor and Reputation; Infants and Infanticide; Magic and Charms; Prostitutes; Rape and Raptus; Social Status; Violence**

CRISEYDE

In his long narrative poem *Troilus and Criseyde*, written in rhyme royal and set during the Trojan War, Geoffrey Chaucer tells the story of the Trojan royal son Troilus's love affair with Criseyde, a beguiling Trojan widow whose father, Calchas, betrays the Trojans and abandons her in Troy. Criseyde eventually succumbs to Troilus, and their love is consummated. The Trojan leaders agree to trade Criseyde for Antenor, and Criseyde, against Troilus's wishes, is sent to the Greek camp where the Greek Diomedes falls in love with her. Whether or not Criseyde betrays Troilus is unclear, but she fails to meet Troilus on an appointed day, and Troilus's heart is broken.

Criseyde is Chaucer's most fully realized enigmatic heroine. E. T. Donaldson's famous claim that every reader falls in love with Criseyde has been disputed by Carolyn Dinshaw, who questions Donaldson's assumption that the reader is male. Although drawing upon Boccaccio's *Il Filostrato* and the *Roman de Thebe*, Chaucer illustrates Criseyde's thought processes, constraints, motives, and choices to the point that Criseyde becomes one of the first fully realized novelistic subjects of English literature. Chaucer refrains from the misogynistic condemnation of women expressed by his sources. He gives us partial glimpses into a complex subjectivity, showing us the depth of her ability to assess her circumstances and desires as she contemplates Troilus's proposition. At the same time that Chaucer demonstrates Criseyde's cunning, he increases our understanding of her victimization, making it difficult for us to judge her.

ELIZABETH ROBERTSON

References and Further Reading

Aers, David. "Criseyde: Woman in Medieval Society." In *Critical Essays in Chaucer's Troilus and Criseyde and His Major Early Poems*, edited by C. David Benson. Toronto: University of Toronto Press, 1991, pp. 128–148.

Dinshaw, Carolyn. "Reading Like a Man: The Critics, the Narrator, Troilus, and Pandarus." In *Chaucer's Sexual Poetics*. Madison, Wis.: University of Wisconsin Press, 1989, pp. 28–64.

Donaldson, E. Talbot. "Criseide and her Narrator." In *Speaking of Chaucer*. London: The Athlone Press, 1970, pp. 65–83.

Robertson, Elizabeth. "Public Bodies and Psychic Domains: Rape, Consent and Female Subjectivity in Geoffrey Chaucer's *Troilus and Criseyde*." In *Representing Rape in Medieval and Early Modern Literature*, edited by Elizabeth Robertson and Christine Rose. New York: Palgrave, 2001, pp. 281–310.

See also **Chaucer, Geoffrey; Romances of Antiquity**

CROSS-CULTURAL APPROACHES

Comparative studies across divergent cultures are a recent development in scholarly inquiry. In the twentieth century, *comparative* typically meant a comparison between European and American countries. In the study of literature, for example, "Comparative Literature" only became a subject area with the Modern Language Association in the 1950s; and then it was dominated by European studies. Cross-cultural approaches with a truly global sensibility are a developing area of study. Cross-cultural approaches to studying the roles of women in society, both East and West, must include questions about each culture's ideology of sexual identity and gendered roles: what are their physiological, religious, and social assumptions about the similarities and differences in the sexes and genders? Western medieval gender ideology was based on the physiological concept that woman was an inadequately formed male, that she was the religious downfall of men, and that she was socially relegated to a natural subordination to the male. In contrast, Asian cultures, informed by Confucianism and other beliefs, typically focused on women's social subordination to men. Notable women of medieval Europe and Asia (Heian Japan, medieval China, and Hindu India) confronted these obstacles with remarkably similar methods. Women attempted to placate the patriarchal system by acknowledging certain standards of marriage, motherhood, and obedience. At the same time, they utilized the vernacular (as opposed to the languages of the male educated elite) and used popular genres (compared to canonical forms) to express both feminine and universal concerns.

CYNTHIA HO

References and Further Reading

Amer, Sahar. "Integrating Multiculturalism in the Medieval Studies Classroom: The Challenge of the New Millennium. (A Short Reflection, a Pedagogical Methodology, and a Select Bibliography)." *Medieval Perspectives* 15.2 (Fall 2000): 61–80. Theme issue: At the Turn of the Millennium: Methodological Approaches to Medieval Scholarship in the Twentieth Century.

Crossing the Bridge: Comparative Essays on Heian Japanese and Medieval European Women Writers, edited by Cynthia Ho and Barbara Stevenson. New York: St. Martin's Press, 2000.

See also **Gender Ideologies; Postmodernism and Historiography**

CROSS-DRESSING

Clothes are signifiers to the external world. In medieval times, dress could signal a wearer's gender, marital status, religious affiliation, occupation, social station, geographical origin, and other information relevant to a person's place in a community or society. At times, badges, colors, or specific articles of clothing even communicated political allegiance. Clothes functioned as a "symbolic surface between self and world" (Claudia Benthien). To change one's cover therefore bore the potential to also trade one's social status or gender.

Since late antiquity, Christian hagiography featured many female saints in a male disguise. Commonly, their transvestism made possible a transition from worldly pursuits to a religious life in monastic communities. Cistercian writers circulated the story, for instance, that a certain Hildegund had lived an exemplary, pious life as Brother Joseph in the Schönau monastery until her true sex was discovered after her death (around 1188). "Whether Hildegund was an imagined woman or an actual one, her story is one that these Cistercian authors had made their own and presented to their audiences as true" (Martha G. Newman, p. 1191).

Cross-dressing was both a cultural fantasy and a social practice. Medieval literature is replete with tales that tell of a change in sartorial identity. Legends tell of women whose change to a male attire marked their rise to exemplars of religious life. Fabliaux, novellas, and novels foreground sexual comedies of errors. In epics, the virago figures as the exceptional manly woman who had overcome the limitations of her sex. While didactic texts teach that one should stick to one's dress as well as to one's station, Arthurian romance sometimes challenges the notion that a wearer's dress reflects true personhood unequivocally. The most elaborate plot of literary cross-dressing is probably the French *Roman de Silence* (late-thirteenth century). In various ways, these texts show the gendered social order as malleable. But the question of whether such representations uphold or undermine this same order needs to be discussed for each text individually. While most narratives restore proper identities at the plot's end, such resolutions are tentative in some cases. In Dietrich von Glezze's *The Belt* (1270–1290), a lady cross-dresses as a knight in order to woo her departed male lover—an unusually daring story that both conjures up and disavows male-male erotic desire.

Not accidentally, these themes and anxieties attached themselves to textiles, a product of the greatest importance to medieval industry and trade. In medieval cities, where various social groups cohabited in close quarters, dress became a subject of concern to civic authorities. City councils hoped to secure textile codes by regulating what was worn in their communities. They introduced new signifiers, such as the articles of clothing and colors that marked Jews or prostitutes as marginal. They attempted to limit excessive spending for fashionable clothes among the urban elites. Some medieval cities also prohibited women from wearing men's clothes and vice versa. Such legislation can be traced back to the biblical condemnation of such behavior as an "abomination to the Lord" in Deuteronomy 22:5. This passage inspired similar bans in canon law, penitentials, and other prescriptive literature.

Textile masks were not always transgressive, however. During carnival, donning the opposite sex's garb was common. In the world-turned-upside-down temporarily, the wearer's actual self could remain see-through to the observer. When the male actors of fifteenth-century Nuremberg carnival plays assumed female roles their audience must have been aware of the fact that they acted under cover. Also, protection, for instance during travel, justified women's passing as men, at least in the eyes of lawmakers. Yet it would be erroneous to assume that one exchanged clothes easily or at will. In the later Middle Ages, rulers used them for identification purposes. It is this persistent relation of dress to identity that lent cross-dressing its symbolic significance.

Medical theories, according to which women were physically inverted men, may have contributed to this fascination with the changeability of a person's sex. Characteristically, most changes of dress were upwardly mobile. Women assumed a male self via dress more frequently than vice versa. This highlights the gender hierarchies that underlie the discourse of cross-dressing. Only rarely is a man represented as a cross-dresser. In Ulrich von Liechtenstein's humorous quasi-autobiography, the narrator masquerades as the goddess Venus in his *Service to Women* (mid-thirteenth century). John Rykener was a rare case of a male transvestite and prostitute. Known as Eleanor, he was apprehended in London in 1394 while having sex with another man. Women who passed as men usually expanded their social, economic, occupational, religious, and erotic options. The fact that before her discovery Katharina Hetzeldorfer was able to live as a man caused great unease among her interrogators in the German city of Speyer in 1477, who condemned her to being drowned. According to the trial document, Hetzeldorfer enacted a roguish masculinity. As a man, she courted several women and had sexual relations with a woman she introduced as her sister, a gender performance helped by her self-made dildo. The little we know about her life serves as a reminder that the assumption of a new sartorial self was predicated on embodying the other sex by physical comportment.

Arguably, Joan of Arc is the most well-known cross-dresser of the Middle Ages. Multiple registers were at stake in her self-presentation and the debate that flared up before, during, and after her trial. Joan invoked male garb primarily as protective of her virginity. Some observers saw saintliness in the female warrior. Others condemned her Amazon-like behavior as a sign of social disorder and heresy. Here, as elsewhere, our term *cross-dressing* encompasses modes of thinking that were viewed as incompatible in the medieval world.

HELMUT PUFF

References and Further Reading

Anson, John. "The Female Transvestite in Early Monasticism: The Origin and Development of a Motive." *Viator* 5 (1974): 1–32.

Boyd, David Lorenzo and Ruth Mazo Karras. "The Interrogation of a Male Transvestite Prostitute in Fourteenth-Century London." *GLQ* 1 (1995): 459–465.

Bullough, Vern L. "Transvestism in the Middle Ages." In *Sexual Practices and the Medieval Church*, edited by Vern L. Bullough and James Brundage. Buffalo: Prometheus, 1982, pp. 43–54.

Cadden, Joan. *Meanings of Sexual Difference in the Middle Ages: Medicine, Science, and Culture.* Cambridge: Cambridge University Press, 1993.

Gaebel, Ulrike. "Weibliche Krieger: Crossdressing in deutschen Chanson-de-geste Adaptationen des 15. und 16. Jahrhunderts." *Jahrbuch der Oswald von Wolkenstein Gesellschaft* 11 (1999): 363–382.

Garber, Marjorie. *Vested Interests: Cross-Dressing and Cultural Anxiety.* New York: Routledge, 1991.

Hotchkiss, Valerie R. *Clothes Make the Man: Female Cross Dressing in Medieval Europe.* New York: Garland 1996.

Newman, Martha G. "Real Men and Imaginary Women: Engelhard of Langheim Considers a Woman in Disguise." *Speculum* 78 (2003): 1184–1213.

Puff, Helmut. "Female Sodomy: The Trial of Katherina Hetzeldorfer (1477)." *The Journal of Medieval and Early Modern Studies* 30 (2000): 41–61.

——. "The Sodomite's Clothes: Gift-Giving and Sexual Excess in Early Modern Germany and Switzerland." In *Personal Objects, Social Subjects: The Material Culture of Sex, Procreation, and Marriage in Pre-Modern Europe*, edited by Karen Encarnacion and Anne McClanan. New York: Palgrave 2002, pp. 251–272.

See also **Amazons; Body in Literature and Religion; Body, Visual Representation of; Clothing; Femininity and Masculinity; Festivals of Misrule; Gender Ideologies; Joan of Arc; Roman de Silence; Sexuality: Extramarital Sex; Sexuality: Female Same-Sex Relations; Sexuality: Male Same-Sex Relations; Sexuality: Regulations of; Sexuality: Sex in Marriage**

CRUSADES AND CRUSADING LITERATURE

Despite the fact that cultural norms in western European Christian society in the Middle Ages did not require that women should take part in fighting, women were involved in crusading in various roles from the beginning of the movement. The crusades, a series of military campaigns promoted by the Latin (Catholic) church from the late-eleventh century onward in defense of western Christendom, presented a contradiction for women. Although pious Christian women had a spiritual role to play in prayer support for the undertaking, as physical and sexual beings they were perceived by Christian commentators as a threat to the spiritual purity of Christian warriors. Because expansionist Islam posed the greatest territorial threat to Latin Christian Europe at this period, it was the most common opponent of crusading expeditions. (Muslim commentators depicted the involvement of Christian women in crusades as a measure of the "otherness" and barbarity of Christian culture, while depicting Muslim women as potential victims of Christian ungodliness who must be protected.)

As crusades were also pilgrimages, initially women were involved in crusading expeditions as peaceful pilgrims. Christian women joined the First Crusade (1095–1099) also as traders who helped to supply the army, and as partners and family of male pilgrims. Women could perform various support tasks during expeditions, such as bringing water to warriors on the battlefield, undertaking labouring tasks, and hurling missiles at the enemy. They could also undertake basic medical and hygienic care and encourage warriors to fight. But in times of defeat they were blamed for introducing sexual temptation to the crusading army, and the religious leaders of the army would send all women out of the military camp as part of a ceremonial cleansing intended to recover divine approval for the undertaking.

Crusade preachers depicted women as holding back their male relatives from going on crusade and warned of dire consequences should they do so; but in fact women were often promoters of crusades, encouraging their male relatives to take part. Noblewomen accompanied their husbands on crusade, as Eleanor of Aquitaine accompanied King Louis VII of France on the Second Crusade, 1147–1148, and in 1247–1254 Margaret of Provence accompanied her husband, King Louis IX of France, on crusade to Egypt. When Louis was taken prisoner by Egyptian forces, Margaret commanded the crusaders' defence from her childbed.

Even though a noblewoman would not normally fight on the battlefield, she could hire and command warriors who did so. In 1087, Countess Matilda of Tuscany was one of the sponsors of a naval campaign against the North African Muslim coastal city of al-Mahdiyyah, a precursor of the later crusades to the Middle East; in the Iberian peninsula in the 1120s, Countess Teresa of Portugal (1097–1128) and Queen Urraca of Castile (1109–1126) pursued war against their Muslim neighbours. From the early thirteenth century onward popes encouraged noncombatants, including women, to give money to finance warriors on the crusade rather than going in person, while canon lawyers debated whether a woman could legally take a crusading vow. Nevertheless some women continued to go to the front line. According to the contemporary *Annales de Terre Sainte*, in 1288, Countess Alice of Blois traveled to the city of Acre in Palestine with a large military force and financed the construction of a tower to defend against Muslim attack.

In frontier societies where crusading conflicts were in progress, women were more than likely in settled societies to have to resort to military force in defence of self, family, or family possessions, and many accounts in medieval records show such women using force against their enemies in a crusade situation. Although moralizing Christian commentators depicted women in crusades either as pious helpers or as temptresses, fictional Christian literature gave them a wider role, reflecting their role in reality. In the "Old French Crusade Cycle," begun in the early twelfth century and repeatedly expanded and rewritten in the following centuries, Christian women acted as supporters of their men folk on the battlefield, while Muslim women appeared as intelligent and well educated, advising their men folk on the danger presented by the Christians. Muslim princesses were depicted in fiction as potential converts to Christianity, as authors assumed that women would see what they regarded as the essential truth of Christianity more readily than men and persuade their men folk to convert. This fictional image was perhaps reflected in the suggestion by the French writer Pierre Dubois, made in the early fourteenth century, that noble Christian girls could be married to Muslim princes in order to bring about their conversion to Christianity.

HELEN J. NICHOLSON

References and Further Reading

"Annales de Terre Sainte," in "Documents – IV. Textes Divers. Annales de Terre Sainte," edited by R. Röhricht and G. Raynaud. *Archives de l'Orient Latin.* 2 (1884): 427–461.

Brundage, James. "Prostitution, Miscegenation and Sexual Purity in the First Crusade." In *Crusade and Settlement: Papers Read at the First Conference of the Society for the Study of the Crusades and the Latin East and Presented to R. C. Smail,* edited by Peter W. Edbury. Cardiff: University College of Cardiff Press, 1985, pp. 57–65.

Cartulaire général de l'ordre des Hospitaliers de Saint-Jean de Jérusalem, 1100–1310, edited by Joseph Delaville Le Roulx. 4 vols. Paris: Ernest Leroux. 1884–1906. Nos. 38–39, 61.

Dubois, Pierre. *The Recovery of the Holy Land.* translated by Walther I. Brandt. New York: Columbia University Press, 1956.

Edgington, Susan and Lambert, Sarah, ed. *Gendering the Crusades.* Cardiff: University of Wales Press, 2002.

Geldsetzer, Sabine. *Frauen auf Kreuzzügen, 1096–1291.* Darmstadt: Wissenschaftliche Buchgesellschaft, 2003.

Joinville, Jean de. *The Life of Saint Louis.* In Joinville & Villehardouin, *Chronicles of the Crusades.* translated by M. R. B. Shaw. Harmondsworth: Penguin, 1963.

Maier, Christoph. "The Roles of Women in the Crusade Movement: A Survey." *Journal of Medieval History* 30.1 (2004): 61–82.

Nicholson, Helen. "Women on the Third Crusade." *Journal of Medieval History* 23.4 (1997): 335–349.

The Old French Crusade Cycle, edited by Emanuel J. Mickel, Jan A. Nelson, et al. 10 vols. Tuscaloosa and London: University of Alabama Press, 1977–2003.

Powell, James M. "The Role of Women in the Fifth Crusade." In *The Horns of Hattin,* edited by Benjamin Z. Kedar. Jerusalem: Yad Izhak Ben-Zvi and London: Variorum, 1992, pp. 294–301.

See also **Eleanor of Aquitaine; Muslim Women: Western Literature; Pilgrims and Pilgrimage; Warfare**

CUCKOLD

This once-common English word is tellingly related to "cuckoo," the bird that lays its eggs in other birds' nests. In the imaginations of premodern Europeans, the cuckold—the man whose wife has betrayed him by having sex with another man—was more like the cuckoo's dupe or victim, and his plight carried analogous associations of stupidity, passivity, and shame. A man who could not maintain his wife's fidelity was, by one set of standards, the very model of degraded masculinity. Not only had he failed to exert the control necessary to keep his wife in line, he had possibly also caused her to stray by failing to meet her sexual needs (the "conjugal debt"), prompting her to look to other men. The common medieval and early modern assumption that women were more sexually driven than men, and less able to control their lusts, combined with the legal and customary responsibility of husbands for their wives' behaviour, meant that a cuckold ultimately only had himself to blame; his was more a risible than a pitiable situation. Even the earthly father of Jesus, Joseph, was sometimes (to the Church's dismay) popularly understood as a cuckold.

Our knowledge about the meaning of cuckoldry in premodern Europe comes from two kinds of sources. Legal evidence reveals that fights, wife-beatings, and even homicides could originate in men's anxiety that their wives had made them cuckolds, or in the use of the word *cuckold* as an insult between men. The use of horns (the cuckold's emblem) to ridicule such men also surfaces in folk rituals. Probably more influential, however, for modern scholars are cultural sources, whether literature or art. French fabliaux,

Italian stories by Boccaccio and others, German tales, and English poems and plays from Chaucer to Shakespeare all reveal the seemingly endless potential of the cuckold as a source of humour. While not the most direct form of evidence for lived reality, literary sources reveal a culture's significant anxieties and concerns—in the case of the cuckold, the power of women's sexuality to imperil masculine identity.

DEREK NEAL

References and Further Reading

Foyster, Elizabeth. *Manhood in Early Modern England: Honour, Sex and Marriage*. London: Longman, 2000.

Hale, Rosemary Drage. "Joseph as Mother: Adaptation and Appropriation in the Construction of Male Virtue," in *Medieval Mothering*, edited by John Carmi Parsons and Bonnie Wheeler. London and New York: Garland, 1996, pp. 101–116.

Miller, Mark. "Naturalism and its Discontents in the Miller's Tale." *ELH* 67.1 (2000): 1–44.

Weinstein, Donald. *The Captain's Concubine: Love, Honor, and Violence in Renaissance Tuscany*. Baltimore and London: Johns Hopkins University Press, 2000.

See also **Boccaccio, Giovanni; Chaucer, Geoffrey; Conjugal Debt; Domestic Abuse; Fabliau; Femininity and Masculinity; Gender Ideologies; Honor and Reputation; Husbands and Husbandry; Joseph, Step-father of Jesus; Misogyny; Sexuality: Sex in Marriage**

D

D'ESTE, ISABELLA AND BEATRICE

The daughters of Ercole I d'Este, the reigning duke of Ferrara (Italy) from 1471–1505, Isabella (1474–1539) and Beatrice (1475–1497), married two leading Italian princes: respectively, Francesco II Gonzaga, duke of Mantua, and Ludovico Sforza "il Moro," duke of Milan. Imitating their father, a patron of artists and humanists, and their mother, Eleanora of Aragon (daughter of the king of Naples), a learned woman herself, Isabella and Beatrice, equipped with humanist educations, actively promoted the arts and learning in the courts over which they presided as consorts.

Isabella especially gathered about her a circle of artists (including such luminaries as Andrea Mantegna and Giovanni Bellini), whom she employed in the construction and beautification of the ducal residence, one of the most magnificent in Italy. In her dealings with artists, she gave minute instructions about narrative program and figures, as well as size, color, and specifications for delivery. She hired musicians to sing in the ducal chapel, supported writers, including the great Ariosto, and enhanced the ducal library. Meanwhile, she excelled in statecraft, dealing ably with diplomats, and ruling Mantua as regent for her husband from 1509–1512, when the latter was held hostage abroad. On Francesco's death in 1519, Isabella remained a behind-the-scenes power during the reign of her son, Federico II, and saw to the promotion of her second son, Ercole, to the cardinalate.

At the even grander court of Milan, Beatrice also supported circles of writers (including Castiglione) and artists (including Leonardo da Vinci), but had

little time to make her mark: she died in childbirth just six years after her marriage.

MARGARET L. KING

References and Further Reading

Cartwright, Julia. *Beatrice d'Este, Duchess of Milan, 1475–1497*, 8th ed. London: J. M. Dent; New York: E. P. Dutton, 1920. Reprint, Miami: University Press of the Pacific, 2002.

Cartwright, Julia. *Isabella d'Este, Marchioness of Mantua, 1474–1539: A Study of the Renaissance*. 2nd ed. New York: E. P. Dutton, 1915.

Felisatti, Massimo. *Isabella d'Este: la primadonna del Rinascimento*. Milan: Bompiani, 1982.

Prizer, William F. "Una Virtù Molto Conveniente A Madonne: Isabella D'Este as a Musician." *Journal of Musicology* 17. 1 (1999): 10–49.

See also **Humanism; Italy; Noble Women; Patronage, Artistic**

DANCE

Dancing is frequently mentioned in medieval sources as an important aspect of civic and courtly celebrations, both as a social pastime and a performance for an audience. Social dances were performed for the pleasure of participants and observers, while male and female professional dancers incorporated tumbling and acrobatic feats into their dances. Despite the large number of references to dance, however, medieval writers recorded surprisingly few details about specific dance movements or steps before the

The ladies dance a roundelay, a medieval dance, typical of life at court, in one of the murals of the knights' hall in Runkelstein castle, South Tyrol, Italy. Right, in dark dress, Margarete Maultasch ("satchel-mouth"), countess and ruler of Tyrol (1318–1369). Fresco, 14th CE. Location: Runkelstein Castle, South Tyrol, Italy. Credit: Erich Lessing / Art Resource, N.Y.

middle of the fifteenth century, when a few Italian dance masters produced the earliest known manuals. Fortunately, a great deal of information about earlier dance practices can be gleaned from medieval sources, including chronicles, saints' lives, preachers' aids (especially collections of sermons and moral tales called *exempla*), and treatises of the vices and virtues. Also, narratives such as *The Romance of Flamenca* and *The Romance of the Rose* describe courtly and professional dancers, while images of dance and texts of medieval dance song lyrics provide additional information. By comparing a wide range of sources it is possible to determine many important characteristics of medieval dance practice and to appreciate the wide variety of opinions that dancing elicited among writers.

The form of social dance most frequently referred to in the twelfth and thirteenth centuries was the French *carole* (English "carol," Italian *carola*, German *reien* or *reihen*, and Latin *chorea*), a type of dance

that scholars define by its social, physical, and musical structures. *Caroles* were performed by both men and women, either in same-sex or mixed-group dances. Dancers sang while they danced, with a leader singing the verses and the remaining dancers singing a refrain. Dancers often held hands to form a circle (with the leader in the middle) or sometimes formed a procession or line. The *carole*'s popularity may have been due in part to its adaptability: it could be performed anywhere space was available, without need of musicians, as only the leader needed to remember (or be able to improvise) the verses of the song. *Caroles* were described in both formal and informal settings, among courtiers, peasants, knights, bourgeoisie, and even members of the clergy. They were performed inside halls and outside in gardens and meadows, city streets, town squares, and churchyards. On occasions when professional entertainers performed, musicians accompanied dancing in lieu of the dancers' singing, a practice that appears more frequently in descriptions of dance from the fourteenth century onwards.

Medieval clerics recorded such widely different attitudes about dance that it is impossible to generalize about them; at one end of the spectrum dancing was interpreted as an expression of joy, love, honor, and respect, and as a valid form of religious praise. Other writers praised the social benefits of dance if performed by the proper people on appropriate occasions, while some clerics condemned dance as the tool of the devil. In the earliest days of Christianity parishioners adapted pagan practices and incorporated dancing into religious celebration, performing in churchyards and graveyards, and in church buildings on holy days. Later medieval sources record similar practices, sometimes attempting to regulate or suppress the dances but acknowledging that they had been tolerated in the past. Without more conclusive evidence, scholars must speculate (and often disagree) about how widespread such dances were and about whether they ought to be understood as religious dances or as social dances performed on religious and holy days. Also disputed is whether the rise in the number of religious commentaries on dance over the course of the thirteenth century reflected an increase in dancing or in new forms of writing.

Although both men and women danced, women's dancing received special and passionate attention in two types of medieval sources. Some writers of books on vices and virtues attacked women's dancing, focusing on the sins of pride and vanity of women who lavished attention on their hair, dress, and make-up, or in the lust their songs inspired in men. In marked contrast, hagiographers (writers of saints' lives) described the dancing of holy women such as Beatrice of Nazareth as a sign of religious ecstasy or evidence of spiritual union with Christ. In these cases writers judged dancers not by their movements but by the activities and people associated with the dances and especially by what they determined to be the intentions of the dancers. Dancing enjoyed for its healthful and social benefits, rather than as a means of physical or spiritual pleasure, encountered fewer objections and less impassioned responses by clerical writers.

KAREN MIRIAM SILEN

References and Further Reading

Arcangeli, Alessandro. "Dance and Punishment." *Dance Research* 10.2 (1992): 30–42.

Blodgett, E. D., ed and trans. *The Romance of Flamenca*. New York and London: Garland Publishing, 1995.

De Ganck, Roger, ed and trans. *The Life of Beatrice of Nazareth, 1200–1268*, with translation assistance by John Baptist Hasbrouck. Kalamazoo, Mich.: Cistercian Publications, 1991.

de Grocheo, Johannes. *Concerning Music* (*De Musica*). Colorado Springs, Colo.: Colorado College Music Press, 1967.

de Lorris, Guillaume, and Jean de Meun. *The Romance of the Rose*, translated by Charles Dahlberg. Hanover and London: University Press of New England, 1986.

Greene, Richard Leighton, ed. *The Early English Carols*. Oxford: Clarendon Press, 1935 and 1977.

Guglielmo, Ebreo of Pesaro. *De Practica seu Arte Tripudii: On the Practice or Art of Dancing*, edited and translated by Barbara Sparti. Oxford: Clarendon Press, 1995.

MacMullen, Ramsay. *Christianity & Paganism in the Fourth to Eighth Centuries*. New Haven, Conn. and London: Yale University Press, 1997.

Markus, R. A. *The End of Ancient Christianity*. Cambridge: Cambridge University Press, 1998.

McGee, Timothy J. *Medieval Instrumental Dances*. Bloomington, Ind.: Indiana University Press, 1989.

Mullally, Robert. "Dance Terminology in the Works of Machaut and Froissart." *Medium Aevum* 69.2 (1990): 248–259.

Page, Christopher. *The Owl and the Nightingale: Musical Life and Ideas in France 1100–1300*. Berkeley and Los Angeles: University of California Press, 1989.

Rimmer, Joan. "Carole, Rondeau and Branle in Ireland 1300–1800: Part 1, The Walling of New Ross and Dance Texts in the Red Book of Ossory." *Dance Research* 7.1 (1989): 20–46.

Silen, Karen Miriam. "Dancing with God: Dance Practice and Theory in Thirteenth-Century Northern France and French Flanders." Ph.D. dissertation, University of California at Berkeley, forthcoming.

Simons, Walter. "Reading a Saint's Body: Rapture and Bodily Movement in the 'Vitae' of Thirteenth-Century Beguines." In *Framing Medieval Bodies*, edited by Sarah Kay and Miri Rubin. Manchester and New York: Manchester University Press, 1994, pp 10–23.

Stevens, John. *Words and Music in the Middle Ages: Song, Narrative, Dance and Drama, 1050–1350*. Cambridge, London, New York: Cambridge University Press, 1986.

Ziegler, Joanna E., and Susan Rodgers. "Elisabeth of Spalbeek's Trance Dance of Faith: A Performance Theory Interpretation from Anthropological and Art Historical Perspectives." In *Performance and Transformation: New Approaches to Late Medieval Spirituality*, edited by Mary A. Suydam and Joanna E. Ziegler. New York: St. Martin's Press, 1999, pp. 299–355.

See also **Beatrice of Nazareth; Courtly Love; Danse Macabre des Femmes; Festivals of Misrule; Hagiography; Mary, Virgin: In Music; Mysticism and Mystics; Penitentials and Pastoral Manuals; Performance Theory; Roman de Flamenca; Roman de la Rose and Its Reception; Romance, French; Sermons and Preaching; Woman's Song**

DANSE MACABRE DES FEMMES

The *Danse Macabre des Femmes* is a fifteenth-century didactic poem, intended to inspire piety. In a series of paired strophes (Death calls, the victim answers), women are summoned to join the Dance of Death, starting with the queen, who is followed by over thirty women, presented according to the social hierarchy of the period.

The text survives in five manuscripts (B.N. [Bibliotheque national] f. f. 1186; N. A. f. f. 10032; B. N. f. f. 25434; B. N. f. f. 995; Arsenal 3637) and two printed editions. Both printings and one manuscript (B. N. f. f. 995) are extensively illustrated, with one woodcut or illumination for each role. The earliest manuscript, B. N. f. f. 1186, dated 1482, contains thirty roles; the latest and most elaborate, B. N. f. f. 995, undated, presents thirty-six.

In form and purpose, the *Danse Macabre des Femmes* (*DMF*) mirrors the *Danse Macabre des Hommes* (*DMH*), and in all manuscripts and printed editions the two poems appear together, the Men's Dance always presented first. Historically, the first occurrence of the *DMH* precedes the earliest *DMF* by nearly sixty years: the *DMH* is first attested to in 1424, attributed to Jean Gerson, and it was supposedly painted on the walls of the Cimetière des Innocents (Cemetery of the Innocents) in Paris.

The verses for each individual called by Death contain brief comments about her activities and interests, which elaborate the role name (or occupation) heading each response strophe and the woodcut or illumination. Thus the *Women's Danse Macabre* provides glimpses into daily life at the turn of the sixteenth century. The following roles are found in *La Grant Danse Macabre des Femmes* (B. N. f. f. 995): queen, duchess, regent, knight's lady, abbess, squire's lady, prioress, young lady, townswoman, widow, merchant, bailiff's lady, virgin, theologian, newlywed, pregnant woman, old maid, Franciscan, friendly woman, wet-nurse, shepherdess, woman on crutches, village woman, old woman, saleswoman, prostitute, bathhouse attendant, girl, nun, witch, bride, darling wife, chambermaid, hosteller, hypocrite, and fool.

Although the text is traditionally attributed to Martial d'Auvergne, who is cited as author only in B. N. f. f. 25434, he is not named in the earliest extant version of the poem (B. N. f. f. 1186, dated 1482) and there is no reference to him in any other manuscript or printing.

Guyot Marchant, a Parisian printer and friend of Martial d'Auvergne, published both printed editions of the *DMH* and *DMF* (1486 and 1491).

The content of the poem, its language (Parisian Middle French), and several individual figures indicate Parisian connections for the work, but only the printed texts can be accurately and precisely identified as having been made in Paris.

ANN T. HARRISON

References and Further Reading

The Danse Macabre of Women: MS. Fr. 995 of the Bibliotheque Nationale, edited by Ann T. Harrison. Kent, Ohio: Kent State University Press, 1994.

See also **Devotional Literature; Gerson, Jean; Literacy and Reading: Vernacular; Literature, Old French**

DANTE ALIGHIERI

Women were central to Dante, from his earliest love poetry until the end of the *Commedia*. Dante began his poetic journey as a lyric love poet. In the tradition of courtly love, his poetry projects his own fears and desires, without exploring the subjectivity of the lady. In the theologized variant of courtly love Dante calls *stil novo* poetry (most of Dante's *stil novo* poems are gathered in the book that tells the story of his love for Beatrice, the *Vita nuova*), the poet learns to ask no reward of the lady and to find the act of praising her its own reward. Nevertheless, there is no exploration of her subjectivity or assignment to her of moral agency. The ladies of Dante's early lyrics—whose names include Violetta, Fioretta, Lisetta, and the stony cold *donna petra* as well as Beatrice—have in common the fact that they do not speak.

Beatrice

By contrast, the Beatrice of the *Commedia* is loquacious; she is a veritable *Beatrix loquax*. Starting with this anomaly—a lyric lady (not a shepherdess, as in the Occitan *pastorela*) who speaks—we can see the Beatrice of the *Commedia* as a hybrid figure. On the one hand, she conserves many of the erotic markers of the lady in the courtly lyric; her poetic existence is predicated on the needs of her lover-poet. Beatrice's behavior in the *Commedia* is always centered on Dante. Although the poet's use of a young Florentine woman as his vehicle to God may reflect positively on the female sex, fundamental limitations are built into the representation of Beatrice. The limitations imposed on Beatrice are those imposed on the courtly lady; they are culturally derived from the same matrix, the courtly ideology that exalts the lady as a Platonic ideal, rather than viewing her as a human agent with her own inner life and subjectivity. She is supreme, but within a context in which the frame of reference is entirely determined by the needs of the lover-poet.

On the other hand—and this is why Dante's Beatrice is an anomalous hybrid—within the *Commedia* she possesses an absolutely unprecedented and masculine authority. Most importantly, she exerts this authority in language, in speech: she develops from the silent icon of stilnovist verse and the *Vita nuova* to the talkative *Beatrix loquax* of the *Commedia*. Her hybridity is such that, in the space of two verses, Dante can move from a courtly topos to describe Beatrice's smile to characterizing her speech as infallible: she can both ray her lover with a smile "such that it would make a man happy in the flames," and then use that same mouth to say "according to my infallible judgment" (*Par.* 7.18–19). The use of the word *infallible* for female speech is itself stunning, given the long and documented tradition of female speech as the special focus and target of misogyny. Dante's Beatrice is a radically new construct: while the traditions he inherits boast female abstractions like Boethius's Lady Philosophy who speak authoritatively, in a voice that is coded as not gender-specific, that is, masculine, and female non-abstractions who either do not speak or speak within the province of the gender-specific, in Beatrice Dante creates a historicized object of desire—not a personification—who yet speaks. Indeed, in the *Paradiso*, she speaks like a man, free from the content or modality normatively assigned to female discourse.

Francesca da Rimini

As one of only three characters in the *Commedia*, along with Virgil and Dante himself, to develop over a long textual span, Beatrice is a singular case, created in a mold used only for her. On the whole, the women of the *Commedia*, like the men, are represented in brief encounters with the pilgrim; they include classical figures, mainly literary (for example, Dido, Thais), biblical figures (for example, the Virgin to whom St. Bernard prays at the poem's end), and contemporary ones. The most celebrated encounter with a woman in Dante's poem is certainly in *Inferno* 5, where the pilgrim meets Francesca da Rimini, condemned to the second circle of hell for her adulterous lust.

Critical reaction to the *Commedia* is governed by theologized hermeneutic guidelines that Dante structured into his poem, guidelines that postulate interpretive categories not significantly more complex than "Dante places Francesca in hell, so his view of her is negative." In recent times criticism has noted Dante's association of female characters with lust and added a typical medieval misogyny to his assessment of Francesca. But a historicist reconstruction of *Inferno* 5 uncovers a submerged "feminist" agenda embedded in Dante's Francesca da Rimini, a historically obscure and marginal figure to whom Dante grants prominence, celebrity, and agency.

If we look at Dante's handling of Francesca outside of the poem's theologized guidelines, if we historicize Francesca and our reading of *Inferno* 5, a picture emerges in which Dante writes a gendered story that places unusual value on the personhood of the dynastic wife. Dynastically unimportant, Francesca was forgotten by contemporary chroniclers. The first and most authoritative chronicler of Rimini was Marco Battagli, whose history *Marcha* contains a section called "On the Origins of the Malatesta" (1352). Battagli alludes to the event in which Francesca died without naming her, indeed without acknowledging her existence, except as an implicit cause of her lover Paolo's death, which occurred *causa luxuriae*: "Paolo was killed by his brother Giovanni the Lame on account of lust." One son of Malatesta da Verucchio, the founding patriarch of the Malatesta dynasty, killed the other; this fact is of interest because it affects the history of the dynasty. Francesca matters not at all as herself. And, in fact, the only historical document that records her name is the will of her father-in-law, in which he refers to "the dowry of the late lady Francesca." Otherwise, silence.

Dante preserved Francesca, recording her name, giving her a voice, and saving her from consignment to historical oblivion. He broke the silence of the historical record. And, as though to make this point crystal clear, Francesca's is the only contemporary name registered in *Inferno* 5: Paolo's name is absent, as is Gianciotto's. In canto 5, she is the protagonist, she is the agent, and she is the one who speaks, while Paolo stands by weeping. Through the intervention of *Inferno* 5, Francesca became a cultural touchstone and reference point, achieving a dignity and a prominence—a celebrity—that in real life she did not possess. The woman who in real life was merely a dynastic pawn, whose brutal death did not even cause a serious rupture between the Malatesta of Rimini and the Polentani of Ravenna, emerges in Dante's version as the canto's unchallenged protagonist. The woman who in real history had no voice and no name emerges in the poem's history as the only voice and only name.

Dante acted as the historian of record for Francesca da Rimini—and for many other women as well. Moreover, in sharp contrast to the courtly poetry of his youth, Dante's portraits of women in the *Commedia* explore their subjectivity and assign moral agency. He seems particularly drawn to cases of marital and family abuse: we think of Pia in *Purgatorio* 3 and Piccarda in *Paradiso* 3. While there are famous women in the *Commedia*, such as Clare of Assisi and the Empress Constance, the text engages more fully with women otherwise consigned to historical oblivion; indeed, even Beatrice Portinari falls into this category. Any serious assessment of Dante's role in the history of women will have to take the measure of this achievement.

TEODOLINDA BAROLINI

References and Further Reading

Barolini, Teodolinda. "Dante and Francesca da Rimini: Realpolitik, Romance, Gender." *Speculum* 75 (2000): 1–28.

———. "Francesca da Rimini." In *The Dante Encyclopedia*. New York and London: Garland, 2000.

———. "Beyond (Courtly) Dualism: Thinking about Gender in Dante's Lyrics." In *Dante for the New Millennium*, edited by Teodolinda Barolini and H. Wayne Storey. New York: Fordham University Press, 2003, pp. 65–89.

———. "Lifting the Veil? Notes Toward a Gendered History of Italian Literature." In *Medieval Constructions in Gender and Identity: Essays in Honor of Joan M. Ferrante*, edited by Teodolinda Barolini. Tempe, Ariz.: Arizona Center for Medieval and Renaissance Studies, 2005.

Ferrante, Joan M. *Woman as Image in Medieval Literature from the Twelfth Century to Dante*. New York: Columbia University Press, 1975.

———. "Dante's Beatrice: Priest of an Androgynous God." CEMERS Occasional Papers, 2. Binghamton, N.Y.: State University of New York Press, 1992.

———. "Women." In *The Dante Encyclopedia*. New York and London: Garland, 2000.

Kirkham, Victoria. "A Canon of Women in Dante's *Commedia*." *Annali d'Italianistica* 7 (1989): 16–41.

Jacoff, Rachel. "Transgression and Transcendence: Figures of Female Desire in Dante's *Commedia*." *Romanic Review* 79 (1988): 129–142.

Psaki, F. Regina. "The Sexual Body in Dante's Celestial Paradise." In *Imagining Heaven in the Middle Ages*, edited by Jan S. Emerson and Hugh Feiss. New York: Garland, 2000, pp. 47–61.

See also **Beatrice; Clare of Assisi; Constance of Sicily; Courtly Love; Italy; Literature, Italian; Mary, Virgin: in Literature; Misogyny; Personifications Visualized as Women**

DATINI, MARGHERITA

Margherita Bandini Datini (1357–1423) is known through her correspondence with her husband Francesco Datini (1335–1410). Margherita, of a dispossessed but elite Florentine family, married the rich, self-made "merchant of Prato" in Avignon when she was nineteen and he fourty-one. After returning to Italy, their relationship deteriorated, and they often preferred to be apart, moving separately between Prato and nearby Florence, the cities where Francesco had his principal businesses. Margherita and Francesco's core problem was a failure to have children, Margherita's "fault," since Francesco had two illegitimate children during the marriage (which did not help the relationship). Margherita's failure to conceive was linked to the debilitating pains she suffered before her menstrual periods, probably the condition now called endometriosis, and although the couple searched for remedies until Margherita was in her late thirties, she remained childless.

Margherita compensated for infertility through acting as loving stepmother to Francesco's illegitimate daughter and a niece, through religious devotion, and, except during periods of poor health, by striving to be the model of a competent woman. She managed a large household, its personnel, and, in Prato, the related agricultural, building, business, and political activities. She contributed to Francesco's business by overseeing apprentices, assisting in debt collection, and sewing and cooking saleable objects, and she contributed to Francesco's social ambitions by acting as a well-mannered hostess. She also contributed to the marriage by reporting regularly to Francesco by letter. Margherita could read and write at an elementary level throughout her marriage, but her poor skills long made her dependent on scribes. Nonetheless, she prided herself on oral composition; nor did she let scribes prevent her from giving vent to her sharp tongue. Then, in her midthirties, she worked to improve her reading and letter writing and in 1399 she produced a spate of twenty-one substantial autograph letters. After 1399, she returned to using scribes. She had, however, more than proven her facility in letter writing.

ANN CRABB

References and Further Reading

Byrne, Joseph P., and Eleanor A. Congdon. "Mothering in the Casa Datini." *Journal of Medieval History* 25.1 (1999): 35–56.

Crabb, Ann, "Ne pas être mère: l'autodéfense d'une Florentine vers 1400." *Clio: Histoire, Femmes et Sociétés: Maternités* 21 (2005): 150–161.

Datini, Margherita. *Per la tua Margherita: Lettere di una donna del '300 al marito mercante*. CD-Rom. Prato: Archivio di stato, 2002.

Origo, Iris. *Merchant of Prato*. New York: Alfred A. Knopf, 1957. Reprint, Boston: David R. Godine, 1986.

See also **Household Management; Infertility; Italy; Letter Writing; Literacy and Reading: Vernacular; Merchant Families, Women of; Strozzi, Alessandra**

DAWN SONG (ALBA)

The dawn song (or *alba*) is a lyric monologue or dialogue staging the moment when lovers see that their night together is about to end. As dawn songs appear in many cultures and are often connected to either religious festivals or wedding rituals, one of the key debates concerns their identification as a genre on the basis of formal criteria, rather than as a common erotic theme found in poetry and narratives from Ovid's *Amores* (I, 13) onwards.

There is an identifiable group of courtly dawn songs in medieval European poetry, found especially in the Iberian peninsula, France, and Germany, dating from the twelfth to the early fourteenth centuries. The most accessible sample and discussion of these songs is the survey edited by Arthur Hatto in 1965. Over fifteen dawn songs survive in Old Occitan, attributed to troubadours active in what are now southern France and Catalonia. It is no longer assumed that these are the models for the songs in other languages; but a poetic treatise composed after 1250 gives guidelines for the *alba*, a song set at daybreak that either praises or blames both the lady and the dawn, and the *gaita* (watchman), a song in which the watchman intervenes, which is set at night. Only one Catalan example survives of a *gaita*, but there are several dawn songs in which watchmen speak. Most courtly dawn songs were sung by a soloist; some are mini-dramas. These may include the participation of a supportive watchman or male friend, or the intervention of a jealous husband. Many trace a progression from the first light of dawn to daybreak; others present the speaker's reaction to birdsong or watchmen's cries. The courtly dawn songs tend to have refrains and share similar emotional content: the speaker expresses dismay at the arrival of dawn, because it means that the lovers will part. Some (not all) describe an illicit or adulterous relationship; one German poem depicts a married couple. There are allusions to the Song of Songs in the lovers' meetings and partings at dawn as well as in the interaction of the lovers with watchmen (2:17, 3:6, 5:7). This influence has been traced especially in religious dawn songs, of which a number survive in several languages.

One of the early aims of research into the dawn song was to establish whether it constitutes the survival of an older tradition located especially in the Iberian peninsula. Folklorists traced similarities with erotic songs sung by women at weddings, or at springtime and midsummer festivals. The deciphering of feminine-voiced poetic fragments in the Romance and colloquial Arabic end-strophes (*kharjas*) to Hispano-Arabic and Hebrew poems composed in al-Andalus (around 1050–1150) seemed to prove this hypothesis, but the language and content of these verses have not been interpreted conclusively. The major problem with identifying the courtly dawn song as a survival of popular women's song is that many of them have a male speaker, and all are preserved in anthologies intended for an aristocratic audience. The Old French dawn songs are related to dance songs but these may be "popularising" (to quote Pierre Bec), not authentically popular pieces.

Another strand of scholarship sought sources in Christian liturgy, as well as in Latin poems such as the tenth-century *Phœbi claro*, which has a refrain in a Romance dialect, but depicts watchmen, not lovers. Once again, it is hard to untangle a poem that happens to mention the sunrise from a dawn song.

Critics in the later part of the twentieth century moved away from theories of origins towards interpretations of individual poems as works of literature, set within their historical and cultural context. This has enhanced their complexity, for a reference to the appearance of the morning star may be read as either an allusion to Venus as goddess of erotic love or to the Last Judgement (Revelation, 2:29 and 22:16).

Many dawn songs have been read as meditations on the tensions between religious and erotic love. The courtly dawn song has also been reinterpreted, in the light of feminist criticism, as an attempt by lyric poets to construct a subjective voice for the courtly lady. No *trobairitz* are credited with dawn songs, and the genre seems to be mostly male-authored. It still remains to be established whether the similarities between dawn songs in this wide range of languages stem from a logical development in the scenario of courtly love poetry or whether explicit connections between different poetic schools can be traced.

CATHERINE LEGLU

References and Further Reading

Battles, Paul. "Chaucer and the Traditions of Dawn-Song." *Chaucer Review* 31 (1997): 317–338.

Bec, Pierre. *La Lyrique française au Moyen Âge (XIIe-XIIIe siècle). Contribution à une typologie des genres poétiques médiévaux.* 2 vols. Paris: Picard, 1977–1978.

Empaytaz de Croome, D. *Albor: Mediaeval and Renaissance Dawn-Songs in the Iberian Peninsula.* Ann Arbor, Mich.: UMIT, 1980.

Hatto, Arthur T., ed. and trans. *Eos, An Enquiry into the Theme of Lovers' Meetings and Partings at Dawn.* The Hague: Mouton, 1965.

Menocal, Maria R., Raymond Scheindlin, and Michael Sells, eds. *The Literature of al-Andalus.* Cambridge: Cambridge University Press, 2000.

Poe, Elizabeth W. "La Transmission de l'*alba* en ancien provençal." *Cahiers de civilisation médiévale* 31 (1988): 323–345.

———. "The Three Modalities of the Old Provençal Alba." *Romance Philology* 37 (1984): 259–272.

———. "A New Light on the Alba." *Viator* 15 (1984): 139–150.

Sigal, Gail. *Erotic Dawn-Songs of the Middle Ages: Voicing the Lyric Lady.* Gainesville, Fla.: University Press of Florida, 1996. (List of poems, pp. 215–216.)

Spence, Sarah. "Oh, Criator!: The Subversive Role of the Watchman in 'Gaite de la Tor." *Philological Quarterly* 63 (1984): 116–125.

See also **Courtly Love; Eroticism in Literature; Literature, German; Literature, Iberian; Literature, Occitan; Literature, Old French; Performance in Lyric; Trobairitz and Troubadours; Woman's Song**

DEATH, MOURNING, AND COMMEMORATION

Death marked the inevitable end of a person's life. With birth, it was one of the two essential phases of an individual's life cycle. The practical day-to-day care of the terminally ill and dead was primarily a task for women. The washing and laying out of the bodies, the wrapping up in shrouds, and the preparation for burial took place in the home, and all indications are that the job was done by women with expertise in such matters. Each village would have someone who often combined the task with that of midwife. These women would also organise the mourning within the family prior to the burial in the local churchyard. Wailing and tearing of hair, as outward signs of distress and grief, were also reserved for the females. Keeping wake near the body, especially during the night, would guarantee that the dead would be protected against bad spirits. The procedures for mourning and burial in these basic guises were fairly universal in medieval Europe. With the advance of Christianisation we see a reduction in cremations in favour of the burial of shrouded bodies to facilitate the resurrection of the body at the Last Judgement. The growing acceptance of Christianity with its emphasis on the afterlife (in heaven or hell) made proper spiritual preparation before death an essential liturgical task that was set aside for the (male) clergy of the church. Thus an essential process of collaboration between laity and clergy developed to ensure that the practical and spiritual cares were put in place.

One of the tools offered by the clergy for spiritual guidance was praying. Prayers were said to God to ask him for forgiveness for the dead person's sins and they were also addressed to the saints on the understanding that they would intercede with God on behalf of the dead and their families. After the millennium the belief existed that prayers by women were most efficacious. This at least is how Abelard, the early twelfth-century philosopher in Paris, recommended a Psalter to his former lover Heloise for "prayers of the faithful especially those of women on behalf of their dear ones and of wives for their menfolk," adding that those by religious women were the most effective.

Apart from the liturgical and lay care around the moment of death, there was the much longer and more elaborate process of commemoration that continued long after death had occurred. Commemoration took many different forms. There was the physical manifestation of the tomb slab or stone marking the dead person's grave in the churchyard. In Scandinavia there exists from the millennium a series of stone slabs erected on cross roads and near bridges with elaborate descriptions of blood relationships and inheritance bequests. Away from the physical burial site there were also written records listing the names of the dead. From the ninth century, *libri vitae* (books of life) were kept in many monasteries and cathedral churches. They would list the names of the dead, often grouped according to their kin, or for women, with their marital families. Sometimes, too, as in the eleventh-century book of Thorney Abbey, we find a king and queen (Cnut and Emma) listed with their followers. From the mid-twelfth century onwards such records are replaced by more elaborate prose narratives, the family chronicles, commissioned by (female) members of a particular family, as they offered greater scope for detailed accounts of individual acts of bravery, a good example being Lambert of Ardres' history of the counts of Guînes written c. 1210. Similarly, there is evidence of tapestries, embroideries, and other artifacts created specifically for memorial purposes, the most famous of which is the Bayeux Tapestry, recording the battle of Hastings in 1066, and being a rare example that has survived. The Book of Ely, however, records a similar hanging, now lost, by Aelfflaed for her husband Brythnoth, who died while fighting against the Vikings in 991. Men and women in families collaborated in the process of remembering the dead, with women being especially prominent in the oral tradition.

ELISABETH VAN HOUTS

References and Further Reading

Geary, Patrick. *Phantoms of Remembrance: Memory and Oblivion at the End of the First Millenium.* Princeton, N.J., 1994.

Geuenich, Dieter, and Otto G. Oexle, eds. *Memoria in der Gesellschaft des Mittelalters.* Göttingen, 1994.

Innes, M. "Keeping It in the Family: Women and Aristocratic Memory, 700–1200." In *Medieval Memories: Men, Women and the Past, 700–1300,* edited by Elizabeth van Houts. Harlow, 2001, pp. 17–35.

Le Jan, R. *Famille et pouvoir dans le monde Franc (VIIe-Xe siècle). Essai d'anthropologie.* Paris, 1995.

McKitterick, Rosamond. *History and Memory in the Carolingian World.* Cambridge, 2004.

McLaughlin, Megan. *Consorting with Saints: The Ideology of Prayer for the Death in Early Medieval France.* Ithaca, N.Y., 1993.

Oexle, Otto G. "Memoria und Memorialüberlieferung im früheren Mittelalter." *Frühmittelalterliche Studien* 10 (1976): 70–95.

Sawyer, Birgit. *The Viking-Age Rune-Stones: Custom and Commemoration in Early Medieval Scandinavia.* Oxford and New York: Oxford University Press, 2000.

Van Houts, Elizabeth. *Memory and Gender in Medieval Europe, 900–1200.* Toronto-Basingstoke, 1999.

See also **Burials and Tombs; Church; Demography; Grave Goods; Heloise; Necrologies and Mortuary Rolls**

DEBATE LITERATURE

Speaking and writing in medieval European culture were defined by the arts of debate. At the schools and universities during the twelfth and thirteenth centuries, thousands of men and some women, such as Heloise in France and Hildegard of Bingen in Germany, were trained to understand language as an argumentative exchange. Whether clerics operated orally or through written texts, they learned how to face off with their interlocutors. The *disputatio*, or disputation, engaged them in energetic, often furious exchanges. And it equipped their language actions with a Biblical mythology: Adam inaugurating the first authoritative words when he named the animals; Eve joining in, questioning her mate. In their fallible line, human speakers had to work hard to secure this power of language that, otherwise, was deemed a divine prerogative.

This conception of debate conditioned vernacular literature from the earliest twelfth-century texts. In genres such as the Occitan *tenso*, lovers were represented in countless rounds of dialogue, contesting just how genuine their passions were. Such contests were projected onto animals in the *Parliament of Fowles*, even onto different members of the human body, hearts, minds, and souls that we find in German, French, and Spanish narrative poetry.

Across Europe, there was no living form too small to be considered a medium for debate. These struggles were internal, cast in the psychological battles (psychomachia) suffered by characters in romances such as those by Chrétien de Troyes; they were also external, taking on grand cosmic dimensions in allegories like Dante's *Divine Comedy*, where supernatural divine forces were pitted against evil ones.

By the fifteenth century, the tradition of debate was so deep-seated that it implicated the social status of literary texts, particularly courtly texts depicting women. The *Romance of the Rose* touched off a polemical exchange, known as the *Querelle de la Rose*, involving Parisian humanists, including Christine de Pizan, and the theologian Jean Gerson. Literature not only represented debate, it became the very subject of

it. At stake was the fictive figure of a woman who disputed, and the possibility of women authors challenging conventional wisdom and entering fully into the ongoing debates at the heart of medieval culture.

HELEN SOLTERER

References and Further Reading

Blamires, Alcuin. *The Case for Women in Medieval Culture.* Oxford: Clarendon Press, 1997.

Brown, Catherine. *Contrary Things: Exegesis, Dialectic, and the Poetics of Didacticism.* Stanford, 1998.

Brown-Grant, Rosalind. *Christine de Pizan and the Moral Defence of Women: Reading Beyond Gender.* Cambridge, 1999.

Enders, Jody. "The Theater of Scholastic Erudition." *Comparative Drama* 27 (1993): 341–363.

Hult, David. *Le Cycle de la Belle dame sans mercy: une anthologie poétique du Xve siècle.* Paris: Champion, 2003.

Solterer, Helen. *The Master and Minerva: Disputing Women in French Medieval Culture.* Berkeley: University of California Press, 1995.

See also **Chrétien de Troyes; Christine de Pizan; Dante Alighieri; Gerson, Jean; Roman de la Rose and Its Reception; Scholasticism; Universities**

DEFENSES OF WOMEN

The case for women in medieval European culture was inextricably linked to the all-pervasive misogyny it sought to dispute. Throughout the Middle Ages writers enthusiastically debated the morality of the female sex, often in isolated passages within longer narratives, but increasingly in didactic texts that presented the evidence for and against women. By the later Middle Ages a new genre had developed—the defense of women. It consisted of works in Latin and the vernaculars designed to refute the claims of overtly antifeminist literature and to rehabilitate the female sex. Although most contributors to the genre were men, some anonymous, the most famous exponent was Christine de Pizan, who in her *Letter of the God of Love*, *City of Ladies*, and correspondence with supporters of Jean de Meun expertly challenged clerical misogyny while debating the issues provoked by her reading of the *Roman de la Rose*.

Roots of Profeminine Writings

The roots of profeminine material, like those of misogyny, predate the Middle Ages. The apocryphal third book of Esdras includes several "proofs" of the power of women, while patristic discussion of woman's role in the biblical narratives of the Creation, Fall,

Incarnation, and Passion furnishes positive arguments to counter the derogatory remarks of Ovid, Juvenal, Jerome, and others. Consequently, medieval defenders of women had the following categories of argument at their disposal:

1. The social benefits of women: They give birth to, nurture, clothe, and feed men; they improve their behavior and inspire them to great feats of prowess or artistic achievement.
2. The theological privileges of women:

     E loco—God favored woman by creating her inside paradise;

     E materia—she was fashioned from Adam's rib, superior material to clay (admittedly man's creation preceded woman's, but God's second attempt surpassed his first);

     In conceptione—God became flesh through a woman, thus honoring all womankind;

     In apparicione—after the Resurrection, Christ appeared to women first;

     In exaltatione—the Virgin Mary, by being crowned Queen of Heaven, was raised above all other creatures, including the angels.

3. The exoneration of Eve: Without Eve's sin there would have been no Virgin Mary; Adam, as the stronger character, was responsible for the Fall, while the devil exploited Eve's innocent susceptibility.
4. To "defame" women is uncourtly (reflecting badly on their male detractors) and illogical (all men are born of women, thus criticism of mothers damages oneself).
5. Men slander women out of ignorance and spite (impotent clerics abuse those they can no longer woo).
6. Misogyny relies too much on generalisation and negative *exempla*. Although some women are evil, they are not representative of their sex and many contrary examples (from the Virgin Mary to contemporary good women) can be adduced.
7. Etymology: The Latin term *mulier* implies woman's sweetness and softness (*mollis*), hence her ability to pacify hot-headed males.

To a modern reader many of these arguments seem dangerously misogynistic, especially when the faults of the "weaker sex" are used in her defense, or when she is praised for behaving better than her nature would predict. Yet medieval views on gender were fundamentally essentialist, and rather than challenge received ideas about woman's nature, her defenders preferred to rehabilitate her "essentially feminine" characteristics, turning weakness, naivety, even her humoral "coldness" into virtues.

Replies to Misogynous Texts

Profeminine literature is always either implicitly or explicitly in dialogue with misogyny. Sometimes writers would create diptychs, pairing a misogynous text with one complimentary to women. An early example of this is Marbod of Rennes (c. 1035–1123), who followed his *De meretrice*, a diatribe against women, with their encomium in *De matrona*; in the fourteenth century Jean LeFèvre composed the *Livre de Leësce* as a lengthy palinode (retraction) to his misogamous translation of the *Lamentationes Matheoluli*; and in fifteenth-century Spain, Pere Torrellas produced several defenses of women to counter his antifeminist *Coplas de las calidades de las donas*. The composition of medieval manuscripts could also encourage debate: laudatory *Minnereden* (lyrics on love) mingle with derogatory ones in several extant German compilations, and in a thirteenth-century French manuscript (Paris, Bibliothèque Nationale de France, fonds français 837) the complimentary *Bien des femes* has been copied together with the condemnatory *Blasme des femes*. Debate is most obviously generated, however, by works in which two speakers argue the pro and contra alternately. Examples include the late-thirteenth-century Middle English poem *The Thrush and the Nightingale* and the Florentine Pucci's *Il Contrasto delle donne*. However, despite the inclusion of negative opinions, these works still qualify as defenses of women, since in both the pro-woman speaker is given the last word, the female Nightingale triumphantly invoking the example of the Virgin Mary to clinch her case. Similarly, in Albertano of Brescia's *Book of Consolation and Advice* (1246) Prudence eventually succeeds in persuading her somewhat misogynous husband Melibeus that a wife's advice is worth taking.

In these defenses both forensic and epideictic (legal and oratorical) rhetoric are employed. The *Leësce* creates a courtroom scenario in which an advocate for women, the allegorical figure Joy, refutes point by point the accusations made by the arch-misogynist Mathéolus before concluding with a list of praiseworthy women. However, when considering possible reader responses to defenses of women the issues of voice and tone are crucial. Despite the occasional reference, even apology, to ladies in the audience, most male-authored texts create, through the use of pronouns and forms of address, an implied addressee gendered masculine. Thus women are objectified by profeminine discourse, making it difficult for their male "supporters" to escape charges of misogyny. Besides, ostensibly positive works, such as Robert of Blois's *L'Honneur des dames*, are rather androcentric, focusing on the beneficial effects ladies have on men and on the undesirable consequences for male honour of slandering women. When male authors invent female speakers to defend their cause, there is also the possibility, as in the case of *Leësce*, of the female advocate being humorously undermined. Moreover, not all works that debate the woman question end with a clear, positive judgement, and one suspects that many clerics used the genre to display their rhetorical and dialectical virtuosity, rather than to make a serious contribution to social and moral debate.

Christine de Pizan

Nevertheless, LeFèvre's 4,000-line palinode contains much persuasive profeminine material, which Christine de Pizan (1365–c. 1430), a committed defender of women, adapted to her own unambiguous ends. Employing many of the rhetorical strategies used by clerical misogynists (*exempla*, the citation of authorities, enumeration, analogy, allegory), she undermines her opponents' accusations through ironic mimicry, eschews generalisation, challenges their logic, and defends women by invoking experience supported by carefully selected textual authority. In her *Letter of the God of Love*, she employs the authoritative voice of Cupid to challenge the defamation of women; in her *City of Ladies*, three allegorical figures (Reason, Rectitude, and Justice), aspects of her own authorial persona, help her to clear away the rubble of misogyny and build a city for virtuous women who can take pride in their female heritage. Although many of her *exempla* are also present in Boccaccio's *Concerning Famous Women*, Christine's selective rewriting of their stories removes the ambivalence that prevents Boccaccio's work (like Chaucer's *Legend of Good Women*) from being a totally convincing defense.

Although the case for women could become as repetitive and assertive as the discourse of misogyny, medieval writers injected variety into their defenses through the adoption of different textual formats, voices, and registers, and by selecting from a growing stock of profeminine arguments the material most appropriate to their aims and audiences within specific geographical and historical contexts. Examination of the genre from the perspective of rhetorical variation and local specificity would bear further critical fruit.

KAREN PRATT

References and Further Reading

Blamires, Alcuin, Karen Pratt, and C. W. Marx, eds. *Woman Defamed and Woman Defended: An Anthology of Medieval Texts*. Oxford: Clarendon Press, 1992.

——— *The Case for Women in Medieval Culture*. Oxford: Clarendon Press, 1997.

Blumenfeld-Kosinski, Renate. "Jean le Fèvre's *Livre de Leesce*: Praise or Blame of Women?" *Speculum* 69 (1994): 705–725.

Brown-Grant, Rosalind. *Christine de Pizan and the Moral Defence of Women: Reading Beyond Gender*. Cambridge: Cambridge University Press, 1999.

Christine de Pizan. *The Book of the City of Ladies*, translated by Rosalind Brown-Grant. Harmondsworth: Penguin Classics, 1999.

Fenster, Thelma S., and Mary Carpenter Erler, eds. *Poems of Cupid, God of Love*. Leiden: Brill, 1990.

Fenster, Thelma S., and Clare A. Lees, eds. *Gender in Debate from the Early Middle Ages to the Renaissance*. New York: Palgrave, 2002.

Fiero, Gloria K., Wendy Pfeffer, and Mathé Allain, eds. *Three Medieval Views of Women*. New Haven and London: Yale University Press, 1989.

Solterer, Helen. *The Master and Minerva: Disputing Women in French Medieval Culture*. Berkeley and Los Angeles: University of California Press, 1995.

See also **Aristotelian Concepts of Women and Gender; Boccaccio, Giovanni; Christine de Pizan; Debate Literature; Eve; Exemplum; Femininity and Masculinity; Gender Ideologies; Gynecology; Mary, Virgin; Mary, Virgin: in Literature; Misogyny; Roman de la Rose and Its Reception**

DEMOGRAPHY

Historical demographers study births, marriages, migration, and deaths in order to understand the characteristics of past populations and how they changed over time. Their analyses can tell us the size of a specific population (such as England in 1377 or Florence in 1427) and details about this population's age structure, marital status, household size, and balance of men and women. Historical demographers also study the processes that helped to create these characteristics, particularly fertility (the rate at which women bear children), nuptiality (the frequency, features, and dissolution of marriages), mortality (death rates), and migration. But they are interested as well in dissecting how particular social, economic, cultural, and religious factors may have influenced these processes and thus the characteristics of a specific population over time. Although methodological debates are a notable feature of historical demography, the discipline has more to tell us about non-elite populations and women than any other historical approach because of its focus on the domestic lives of all people, not just the well-documented and elite members of society. Several demographic measures, including sex ratio, age at marriage, and marital status, provide especially useful insights into the role of women in the society and economy of the Middle Ages.

Sex Ratio

The sex ratio measures the proportion of women to men and is usually expressed as the number of men to every 100 women in a population; thus a sex ratio of 90 indicates that there are 111 women for every 100 men in a society. Since the sex ratio at birth is 105, but evens out to 100 by adulthood (because mortality is higher for boys than girls), testing for sex ratios prompts scholars to explain why there might be more or fewer women in a population than there should be. For example, researchers analyzing ninth-century medieval estate surveys of peasants have shown that adult sex ratios ranged from about 110 to 253 men for each 100 women, an extraordinarily skewed numerical balance that scholars have struggled to explain.

One controversial explanation attributes the imbalanced sex ratio to female infanticide: in a time of subsistence agriculture and scarcity, families deliberately or unconsciously chose to favor their male children, perhaps even going so far as to abandon their baby girls in times of famine, a practice documented in early saints' lives as well as law codes. The fact that mothers tended to nurse their male babies longer than their female babies, and that the households with the smallest amount of farming land tended to have the most male children, lends weight to this argument. Other explanations point to the higher mortality women faced because of the risks of childbirth, the rigors of agricultural work, and iron deficiencies in the diet, although this does not explain why the sex ratio of children was also higher than average. Another explanation focuses on the under-reporting of women (a perennial problem in any kind of medieval tax assessment), because many young single women were living and working in the lord's workshops (often oriented towards the production of cloth) and thus escaped the survey. What is interesting to note here is that the arguments demographers have formulated to explain their results help to open up our understanding of many aspects of women's lives, including the treatment of girls compared to boys, the delicate balance that poor peasant women faced in the struggle for survival, and the characteristics of women's work in the early medieval economy.

No other medieval societies show such a high sex ratio as these early surveys, although analyses of cemetery burials and late medieval taxes (such as the English poll tax of 1377 or local assessments in German and French towns) suggest that there was a tendency for there to be more men than women in the countryside, but more women than men in towns, particularly during the late Middle Ages, when sex ratios of around 90–95 were not unusual in medieval towns.

Scholars suggest that these lower urban sex ratios were due to female migration to towns in search of work, which was more plentiful and varied for women in towns than in rural villages. The more favorable laws in towns regarding inheritance and trade may also have prompted female-led migration to urban centers. To support this thesis about female immigration, scholars have exploited some unusual sources, from depositions made by servants in church courts about their past movements, to court fines assessed on lodgers and vagrants, to archaeological analysis of medieval skeletons in rural and urban cemeteries.

Age at Marriage

Demographers have focused much effort on determining at what age women married and how many women never married, because these two measures are so important for calculating potential fertility, which helps us assess whether a population is growing or declining. Women who marry at age sixteen, for example, are going to have more children than women who first marry at twenty-six. Age at marriage also had an effect on a woman's married life; younger brides, for instance, were more likely to enter marriages arranged by their kin and less likely to have gained the maturity and experience that came from a period of working for a wage. If they married men who were on average ten years older (the marriage pattern that prevailed in late medieval Tuscan towns), the older husband probably dominated decision-making in the marriage. In contrast, a woman who married in her twenties normally had an opportunity to work for several years and to circulate socially to meet a husband of her own choosing, often someone closer to herself in age. These companionate marriages made by older women were, many historians argue, more common amongst artisans and the poor than among women of the landed elite or rich bourgeoisie, who tended to marry in their teens. Where one lived also seems to have made a difference since in general women married at an earlier age in Mediterranean regions than in northern Europe; in late medieval Tuscany, for example, women in both towns and the countryside married around the age of eighteen, although wealthy women married around sixteen. Men from wealthier families, however, married later (around the age of thirty-one) than poorer men, who married closer to the age of twenty-eight.

A variety of factors could influence the age of marriage of women (which is far more important for calculating potential fertility than the age of marriage for men). In hard times, for instance, when land was scarce, wages low, and prices high, peasant and working-class women seem to have delayed marriage until they and their spouses could save enough to start a new household. This sensitivity to economic climate was, however, less of a factor among the wealthy households of the landed elite or rich merchants. In Italian cities, moreover, there was a strong tendency among the mercantile and aristocratic elite for the newly married couple to reside with the groom's family, where the new, young bride was subject to the authority of her in-laws as well as her husband. Scholars are more divided about whether rising standards of living and opportunities for work, such as occurred in the labor-starved period of the late Middle Ages, after one-third or more of the population died from plague in 1348–1350, promoted or hindered the age at which women chose to marry. On the one hand, peasants would have had easier access to the landed resources needed to set up a new household, but on the other hand, there is also intriguing evidence that many peasant women chose to migrate to towns in search of work where, freer from parental influence, they delayed marriage until their mid- to late twenties. Indeed, migration appears to have strongly influenced the age of marriage by driving it upwards. Other scholars (especially those working in southern Europe) argue that because the late medieval mortality crises caused life expectancy to fall, there was increased pressure on women to marry and reproduce. Those working in Mediterranean cultures, however, have also argued that cultural imperatives to marry made women relatively impervious to the influence of social conditions in deciding when to marry.

One of the biggest debates in historical demography concerns when women began marrying later. Early modern demographers, who draw on the detailed information available in parish registers, have shown that, although there were always regional variations, the average age at first marriage was creeping upwards, so that by the seventeenth century women in northern Europe usually waited until their mid- to late twenties to marry, while those in southern Europe were delaying marriage until their early to mid-twenties. These later marriages have been associated with what is called the "European marriage pattern," a demographic regime characterized by not only a late age at marriage (at least twenty-three for women and twenty-six for men), but also a high percentage (around ten to twenty percent) of people who never married. Although medievalists lack direct data on age at marriage (except for late medieval northern Italy), they have discovered other markers of the European marriage pattern, including large numbers of female servants and "life-cycle service," a system that delayed marriage because men and women left home as adolescents to work in the homes of others for several years before marrying.

Marital Status

An individual's married status not only tells us something about her domestic life, but for demographers also helps to predict whether there were enough child-bearing women to stimulate population growth. Recently demographers have realized that the proportion of lifelong singlewomen (those who never marry) could exercise more influence over the total size of pre-modern populations than any other single factor. Since it is almost impossible to measure how many never-married women there were in any one medieval community, scholars have focused on finding the structures—such as life-cycle service and large numbers of domestic servants—that were associated with singlewomen, as well as examining how a singlewoman's choice or ability to marry was influenced by female employment and wages, by mortality rates, or by cultural and religious mores. In Mediterranean regions where an honor system stressing the sexual purity and respectability of women prevailed, for example, the proportions of women who had not married by age fifty were extremely low: 3.8 percent in Florence and a miniscule 1.7 percent in the countryside.

It is easier to calculate the proportions of life-cycle singlewomen (women who had reached reproductive age but were as yet unmarried) in past populations, although demographers are careful to distinguish them from single widowed women. The proportion of this group was determined by age at marriage. Where women married young, as in Tuscany, singlewomen rarely accounted for more than twenty percent of the adult female population, but in England in 1377 the proportion was almost thirty percent, and rose to forty percent in many late medieval towns of Germany, northern France, and England. Although the proportions of lifelong singlewomen changed little in Mediterranean Europe, the size of groups of life-cycle singlewomen increased as the age at marriage rose in the final decades of the fifteenth century.

The vast majority of medieval women eventually married, although they did so earlier and in greater proportions in southern Europe, and somewhat later and in lesser proportions in towns, especially in northern Europe. The scarce evidence that we do have about fertility suggests that married women began bearing children within a year of marriage, but that infant mortality was so high (approaching thirty-five to forty percent in the late Middle Ages) that few families had more than three children who lived to adolescence. Urban households were always smaller than rural households, a reflection of greater urban mortality and the precarious subsistence of many urban households. Wealth, however, made a huge difference in the lives of married women; richer women became mothers at an earlier age, and their better diet allowed them to bear more children and raise them to adulthood; the elites' practice of sending their newborns out for wet-nursing also allowed wealthier mothers to become pregnant again more quickly. A matter of considerable controversy is whether medieval women practiced any effective forms of birth control, although seasonal cycles of births and rising clerical invective against contraceptive practices suggest that many couples found ways to prevent births.

The experience of widowhood varied in southern and northern Europe. The Mediterranean honor culture and dowry system discouraged remarriage for women, for example, so that widows represented a hefty twenty-five percent of adult women in 1427 Florence (and seventeen percent of women in the countryside), a trend magnified by the tendency of Florentine women to marry men much older than themselves. There is also some evidence that by the twelfth century women were outliving men, a trend that continues to the present day. Old age for many of these widows was, however, a dismal experience, since tax records show that households headed by widows were amongst the poorest and the smallest. In early sixteenth-century Coventry, which had suffered severe economic decline in the previous decades, there were over eight times as many widows as widowers, and half of the widows lived alone, many in abject poverty. In Mediterranean Europe, however, widows were often absorbed into the households of their children (especially their sons), so they did not appear as often as heads of households. And, once again, wealth could make a difference. Wealthy widows (especially if they were young) were much more likely to remarry than poor widows, who could bring fewer resources to the new marriage. Remarried widows often brought children from their first marriage into their new household, where children from their new husband's previous marriage might also reside. The emotional tensions such remarriages involving children could entail are evident in the "wicked stepmother" motifs so prevalent in fairy tales and folklore.

MARYANNE KOWALESKI

References and Further Reading

Coleman, Emily. "Infanticide in the Early Middle Ages." In *Women in Medieval Society*, edited by Susan Mosher Stuard. Philadelphia: University of Pennsylvania Press, 1976, pp. 47–70.

Goldberg, P. J. P. *Women, Work and Life-Cycle in a Medieval Economy: Women in York and Yorkshire, c. 1300–1520*. Oxford: Clarendon Press, 1992.

Herlihy, David. *Medieval Households*. Cambridge, Mass.: Harvard University Press, 1985.

Herlihy, David, and Christiane Klapisch-Zuber. *Tuscans and Their Families: A Study of the Florentine Catasto of 1427*. New Haven: Yale University Press, 1985.

Klapisch-Zuber, Christiane. *Women, Family and Ritual in Renaissance Italy*, translated by Lydia G. Cochraine. Chicago: University of Chicago Press, 1985.

Kowaleski, Maryanne. "Singlewomen in Medieval and Early Modern Europe: The Demographic Perspective." In *Singlewomen in the European Past, 1250–1800*, edited by Judith M. Bennett and Amy M. Froide. Philadelphia: University of Pennsylvania Press, 1999, pp. 38–81, 325–344.

Molho, Anthony. *Marriage Alliance in Later Medieval Florence*. Cambridge, Mass.: Harvard University Press, 1994.

Phythian-Adams, Charles. *Desolation of a City: Coventry and the Urban Crisis of the Late Middle Ages*. Cambridge: Cambridge University Press, 1979.

Poos, L. R. *A Rural Society After the Black Death: Essex 1350–1525*. Cambridge: Cambridge University Press, 1991.

Rheubottom, David B. "'Sisters First': Betrothal Order and Age at Marriage in Fifteenth-Century Ragusa." *Journal of Family History* 13 (1988): 359–376.

Smith, Richard M. "Geographical Diversity in the Resort to Marriage in Late Medieval Europe: Work, Reputation, and Unmarried Females in the Household Formation System of Northern and Southern Europe." In *Woman Is a Worthy Wight: Women in English Society c. 1200–1500*, edited by P. J. P. Goldberg. Wolfeboro Falls, N. H.: Alan Sutton, 1992, pp. 16–59.

Smith, Richard M. "Some Reflections on the Evidence for the Origins of the 'European Marriage Pattern' in England." In *The Sociology of the Family: New Directions for Britain*, edited by Chris Harris. Keele: University of Keele, 1979.

Thoen, Erik. "Historical Demography in Late Medieval Rural Flanders: Recent Results and Hypotheses." In *Peasants and Townsmen in Medieval Europe: Studia in Honorem Adriaan Verhulst*, edited by Jean-Marie Duvosquel and Erik Thoen. Ghent: Snoeck-Ducaju, 1995, pp. 573–582.

See also **Artisan Families, Women of; Cities and Towns; Contraception; Infants and Infanticide; Infertility; Marriage Ceremonies; Merchant Families, Women of; Migration and Mobility; Noble Women; Old Age; Peasants; Plague; Records, Rural; Records, Urban; Remarriage; Servants; Singlewomen; Widows; Work**

DEVOTIO MODERNA
See **Modern Devotion**

DEVOTIONAL ART
Devotional art is a category that encompasses a wide variety of objects intended to aid individuals in prayer. Such images survive in a variety of media

Madonna and Child, from the Treasury of Sainte-Chapelle, Paris. 1250-60. H: 41 cm. Location: Louvre, Paris, France. Credit: Erich Lessing / Art Resource, N.Y.

throughout the medieval period, such as manuscript illuminations, panel paintings, and sculptures created from precious metals or ivory, and also were available on a relatively inexpensive basis in the single-leaf woodcuts produced at the very end of the era. Typical subjects included biblical figures, saints, or biblical narratives distilled to the minimum of figures needed to identify the scene. Depictions of the Virgin and Child, such as the thirteenth-century ivory sculpture illustrated here, were particularly popular throughout the medieval period.

Devotional images often have been defined specifically by their role in private prayer. Yet a majority of surviving medieval images could be said to have performed a devotional role; indeed, a history of devotional art is very nearly a history of the Christian image. Mural and sculptural decoration in churches was intended to provide an atmosphere conducive to a worshipful state, as well as to instruct. Richard Marks has argued that such public images, particularly

in the late medieval English context he studies, provided devotional foci for all classes of viewers. Wealthier worshippers, of course, could afford devotional objects of their own. Ivory sculptures of the type illustrated here often graced altars in the private chapels wealthy patrons endowed in local churches or had consecrated in their homes. The ivory Virgin and Child, for example, may have been used in the Sainte-Chapelle in Paris, the private chapel of the ruling Capetian family.

Devotional Art in the Early Middle Ages

Devotional art was distinguished from narrative art from the early Christian period onward, as Christians sought to distinguish themselves from idol-worshipping pagans, and struggled with the second of Moses' Ten Commandments: "Thou shalt not make to thyself a graven thing..." (*Douay-Rheims Bible*, Exodus 20:4). Around the year 600 Pope Gregory I, in response to the concerns of an iconoclastic bishop, argued that images were needed to instruct the ignorant who could not read. His words were frequently resurrected in support of images that depicted biblical events and holy persons. More relevant here is Gregory's second justification for religious images, which held that images could aid in devotion. The public and private use of icons—panel paintings that depict biblical or saintly figures, usually in non-narrative contexts—developed in the early centuries of the Christian era and became indelibly linked with the traditions of eastern Christianity.

Concern that the power of images would lead to idolatry spurred iconoclastic movements, most notably in Byzantium during the eighth and ninth centuries. In the early eighth century, John of Damascus's *In Defense of Icons* compared Jesus as the Incarnate God with images of the incorporeal and, by extension, argued that veneration of an image of a holy person was veneration of the person represented. The codification of this argument in the Second Council of Nicaea (787) led eventually to the acceptance of depictions of biblical figures and saints. In the east the Byzantine icon tradition reappeared after the end of Iconoclasm in 830, and devotional art in western Europe developed, on its own or with inspiration from eastern icons, during the early medieval and Romanesque periods. If the type is delimited by private use, the majority of surviving examples from the early medieval period are found in illuminated manuscripts, while reliquaries and ornate book covers also would have performed a private devotional function on occasion.

Devotional Function and Gender in the Later Medieval Period

Works of art produced for devotional use survive in far greater numbers from the thirteenth through the fifteenth centuries. Many scholars have examined the development of new types of and contexts for devotional art in this period and explored why devotional art seems to have increased so dramatically in popularity. Reasons advanced include improved access to materials from Byzantium and the Holy Land, changes in religious practice that were supported by new vernacular devotional texts aimed at a new class of literate laity, increasing prosperity that allowed more individuals to commission or purchase private devotional objects, and changes in the scholarly and popular understanding of the workings of memory and vision.

Hans Belting, for example, noted the influx of Byzantine icons into western Europe in the thirteenth century, after Constantinople was occupied by Latin Crusaders. These icons were welcomed by a Western audience primed for a closer, more intimate devotional experience. For Belting and Sixten Ringbom, the devotional image worked through the psychological impact of its presence. A sculpted or painted figure, particularly if composed to create the illusion of eye contact with the viewer, might effectively stand in for the depicted person. Enlarged eyes, often in a frontally depicted face, are a feature of Byzantine icon paintings and also appear in the West in new or newly popular iconographic types such as the Veil of Veronica and the Man of Sorrows.

The imported icons came into the possession of private individuals as well as churches, members of the laity as well as the clergy. Factors such as increasing wealth and a growth in lay literacy heightened the interest of consumers, including women, in devotional art and new varieties of texts intended for devotional use. The devotional practices of the Gothic period emphasized a more personal reading of the lives of Mary and Jesus that expanded the biblical narrative with a variety of "eyewitness" accounts. For example, the *Meditations on the Life of Christ*, written by a thirteenth-century Franciscan, includes a wealth of intimate details about the life of Mary and the childhood and Passion of Jesus. The author used vivid imagery and encouraged readers to imagine the most striking moments from the narrative as prompts for meditation, emphasizing the physicality and either the preciousness or the violence of the mental image. The proliferation of expanded stories about the infancy of Christ in particular played directly to the concerns of lay women, inviting their participation in the events of the nativity and adding detail to the biblical story. In her visions, the late medieval Englishwoman Margery Kempe not only witnessed the birth of Christ, but swaddled him with her own hands and gave Mary the benefit of her own extensive experience with babies. Knowledge of such visions and other stories enriched the ancient, but increasingly humanized, image of the Virgin and Child. The ivory statuette, for example, features a smiling toddler, and the mother seems so young that we can easily imagine her turning eagerly to Margery Kempe for advice.

Devotional art played an important role for both men and women, but women in particular were viewed as being in critical need of both spiritual guidance and some kind of sense-based stimulus in their prayer. Furthermore they were responsible for the spiritual well-being of their households. New types of devotional books, such as the book of hours, became a part of the education of children in the home and were popular with female owners. These books could be illuminated with images that, while creating narrative linkages between the prayers for each liturgical hour, acted as devotional foci to increase the power of those prayers. Very often book owners were depicted within the miniatures, present at the Nativity or the Resurrection, or venerating the Virgin and Child, or the Crucifixion. Significantly, the biblical images are at times represented as sculptures or altarpieces themselves. In the well-known illumination of Yolande of Soissons in prayer from her combined psalter and book of hours (New York, Pierpont Morgan Library MS 729, fol. 232v), Yolande kneels before an open prayerbook, but gazes up into the eyes of a painted sculpture of the Virgin and Child as the image of the Child reaches out with a blessing. No clerical mediator is depicted, suggesting that Yolande is in control of her own devotional experience. The inclusion of the image of the owner further heightens the mimetic possibilities of the images and mirrors the insertion of the self into biblical or hagiographic narrative that was an important aspect of late medieval devotion.

Recent explorations of medieval optical theory, particularly in studies by Michael Camille and Susannah Biernoff, stress the importance of images in devotional practice. Camille's work presents clear discussions of the two main medieval paradigms for understanding how vision works: extramission, which was more prevalent in the earlier centuries, and intromission, which came into play in the later medieval period. He argued that the explosion of devotional art in the later medieval period could be understood in the context of intromission, in which the object was thought to participate in the process by emitting rays that enter the eye and interact with the intellect of the viewer. In this paradigm, a devotional object is no longer a passive thing but becomes an active partner in the genesis of a prayerful state. The Christ child in Yolande of Soisson's altarpiece responds to her prayers with a blessing, as they enter into what Susannah Biernoff has called an "ocular communion," a "reciprocal gaze" that depicts a deep and intimate connection between an enlivened devotional image and its viewer. This connection could provide devotional images with considerable powers, as demonstrated by the stories related in the fourteenth-century Hedwig Codex. Here we read that St. Hedwig always kept her own ivory Virgin and Child statuette with her and often used it to miraculously heal the sick; the dedication portrait depicts the standing saint clutching her ivory statuette, her rosary, and her prayerbook (Malibu, J. Paul Getty Museum MS Ludwig XI.7, fol. 12v).

The idea of looking directly into the eyes of Christ, as does Yolande, is striking, and would have been made even more striking by the many liturgical and narrative associations with Infancy and Passion narratives that would have surrounded these images. Peter Parshall, in an exploration of late medieval Passion imagery, has discussed the importance of memory practices for understanding the way devotional art affected its viewers. He notes that medieval treatises on memory advised the attachment of items or ideas to imagined images, thus creating a visual itinerary for one's memory. The more striking the image, the stronger the memory.

Mary Carruthers has connected later medieval memory techniques, based very much on this model, with monastic treatises in which devotional art was used to stimulate meditation. Jeffrey Hamburger has written extensively on devotional/meditative images and image-cycles produced for (and often by) nuns, and has argued that devotional art played a critical role in the education and spiritual care of female monastics. Hamburger also suggested that the use of devotional images in monastic circles, particularly practices intended for nuns, was highly influential among the laity. One of the most striking of late medieval devotional images, the Wound in the side of Christ, first appeared in an early fourteenth-century manuscript compiled and illuminated for Kunigunde, the abbess of a nunnery in Prague (Prague, National and University Library, MS XIV A.17), but almost immediately appeared in manuscripts intended for the laity, including the Psalter of Bonne of Luxembourg (New York, Cloisters Museum, MS 69.96, before 1349). The image of the Wound illustrates the fragmentation and distillation of narrative images into devotional images mentioned near the beginning of this essay. Depicted as a large

vertically oriented oval, pointed at the top and bottom and shaded to black at the center, the Wound was usually surrounded by the *arma Christi*, the instruments used in the Passion. The image of the Wound is reminiscent of both the vagina and the mandorla, the full-body halo that surrounds the figure of Christ in many Christ in Majesty images. Its associations with gendered passages—sexual, maternal, and mortal—were spelled out in contemporary devotional literature. As a portal for the viewer, a way to enter into the sacred presence, the Wound of Christ was perhaps the ultimate devotional image of the later medieval period.

ANNE RUDLOFF STANTON

References and Further Reading

Barnet, Peter, ed. *Images in Ivory: Precious Objects of the Gothic Age*. Detroit Institute of Arts exhibition catalogue. Princeton, N.J.: Princeton University Press, 1997.
Belting, Hans. *The Image and Its Public in the Middle Ages: Form and Function of Early Paintings of the Passion*, translated by Mark Bartusis and Raymond Meyer. New Rochelle, N.Y.: Caratzas, 1990.
Biernoff, Suzannah. *Sight and Embodiment in the Middle Ages*. New York: Palgrave Macmillan, 2002.
Camille, Michael. *The Gothic Idol: Ideology and Image-Making in Medieval Art*. Cambridge: Cambridge University Press, 1989.
———. "Before the Gaze: the Internal Senses and Late Medieval Practices of Seeing." In *Visuality Before and Beyond the Renaissance: Seeing as Others Saw*, edited by Robert S. Nelson. New York: Cambridge University Press, 2000, pp. 197–223.
Carruthers, Mary. *The Book of Memory: A Study of Memory in Medieval Culture*. New York: Cambridge University Press, 1990.
Freedberg, David. *The Power of Images: Studies in the History and Theory of Response*. Chicago: University of Chicago Press, 1989.
Gee, Loveday Lewes. *Women, Art and Patronage from Henry III to Edward III, 1216–1377*. Woodbridge, Suffolk: Boydell Press, 2002.
Hamburger, Jeffrey. "The Use of Images in the Pastoral Care of Nuns: the Case of Heinrich Suso and the Dominicans." *The Art Bulletin* 71 (1989): 20–46.
———. "The Visual and the Visionary: The Image in Late Medieval Monastic Devotions." *Viator* 20 (1989): 161–182.
———. *Nuns as Artists: The Visual Culture of a Medieval Convent*. Berkeley and London: University of California Press, 1997.
Lewis, Flora. "The Wound in Christ's Side and the Instruments of the Passion: Gendered Experience and Response." In *Women and the Book: Assessing the Visual Evidence*, edited by Jane H. M. Taylor and Lesley Smith. London and Toronto: The British Library and Toronto University Press, 1997, pp. 209–229.
Marks, Richard. *Image and Devotion in Late Medieval England*. Phoenix Mill: Sutton Publishing, 2004.
Parshall, Peter. "The Art of Memory and the Passion." *The Art Bulletin* 81 (1999): 456–472.

Ragusa, Isa, and Rosalie B. Green, trans. *Meditations on the Life of Christ*. Princeton, N.J.: Princeton University Press, 1961.

Ringbom, Sixten. *Icon to Narrative: The Rise of the Dramatic Close-up in Fifteenth-Century Devotional Painting*. Acta Academiae Aboensis, Ser. A., Vol. 31 nr. 2. Abo: Abo Akademi, 1965.

———. "Devotional Images and Imaginative Devotions: Notes on the Place of Art in Late Medieval Private Piety." *Gazette des Beaux-arts* 6th ser. 73 (1969): 159–170.

Smith, Kathryn A. *Art, Identity and Devotion in Fourteenth-Century England: Three Women and Their Books of Hours*. Toronto and London: University of Toronto Press and The British Library, 2003.

Van Os, H. W. *The Art of Devotion in the Late Middle Ages in Europe, 1300–1500*. Princeton, N.J.: Princeton University Press, 1994.

Williamson, Beth. "Liturgical Image or Devotional Image? The London *Madonna of the Firescreen*." In *Objects, Images, and the Word: Art in the Service of the Liturgy*, edited by Colum Hourihane. Index of Christian Art Occasional Papers XI. Princeton, N.J.: Princeton University Press, 2000, pp. 298–318.

See also **Art, Representations of Women in; Audience, Women in the; Bible, Women in; Body: Visual Representations of; Books of Hours; Devotional Literature; Devotional Practices; Education, Lay; Gaze; Gender in Art; Hagiography; Hagiography, Iconic Aspects of; Icons, Byzantine; Jacobus of Voragine's Golden Legend; Kempe, Margery; Lay Piety; Literacy and Reading: Vernacular; Mary, Virgin: in Art; Meditation; Monasticism and Nuns; Mothers as Teachers; Mystics' Writings; Nuns as Illuminators; Patronage, Artistic; Penitentials and Pastoral Manuals; Pilgrims and Pilgrimage; Poor Clares Order; Relics and Reliquaries; Rosary; Sermons and Preaching; Spiritual Care; Spirituality, Christian; Theology; Veronica's Veil**

DEVOTIONAL LITERATURE

Devotional literature functions as something of a catch-all term in anglophone medieval studies, designating the largest and most diverse body of surviving manuscripts and books in Latin and in all of the European vernacular languages. The subjects treated by these texts can be conveyed in a few of its most celebrated titles, for example, *The Mirror of Our Lady, The Little Book of Eternal Wisdom, Meditations on the Life of Jesus Christ, Speculum Ecclesiae,* and *The Ladder of Perfection*. Short devotional pieces occur in books of hours, and in other liturgical and service books, while longer works appear in religious and secular compilations of all types.

The origin of the classification "devotional literature" in modern scholarly discourse is uncertain, and recent work in the field has offered such provocative

substitutes as "vernacular theology" and "the literature of spiritual formation." Each of these terms provides a useful lens on the material, but none fully comprehends its dual intellectual and affective purposes. The goals of a devotional text are resolutely twofold: first, to provide basic instruction in religious doctrine, and second, to heighten its audience's emotional response to this didactic content. To be sure, devotional literature seeks to educate its readers in religious doctrine, but it also attempts—sometimes flamboyantly—to stimulate their joy, admiration, longing, grief, reverence, and tears.

Latin Texts

The earliest devotional literature circulated chiefly in Latin among small and relatively homogeneous clerical and monastic textual communities. It offered instruction and exhortation in the form of sermons, treatises, and letters on such topics as the joys and risks of friendship between monks, the value of virginity, and the literal and figurative meanings of the Song of Songs, the Psalms, and the Creation narratives and commentaries.

The religious and education reforms of the eleventh and twelfth centuries (articulated decisively in the Fourth Lateran Council of 1215) stimulated the transmission of devotional literature beyond the communities of religious professionals of European cloisters, cathedrals, and courts. Translations and loose adaptations of the Latin devotional classics began to appear in the thirteenth century. Along with this proliferation of vernacular spiritual instruction and encouragement developed the notion of "the mixed life," a program for living a religious life in the world. Thus, the ascetic ideals and practices of the monastic life came to be adopted by the men and women of the aristocracy, nobility, and gentry. By the end of the fourteenth century, devotional literature helped bring about what can be aptly called a democratization of ecclesiastical discourse, which made the mysteries of the faith, the stories of the holy dead, and the penitential disciplines of the body accessible to a far broader audience than had previously been the case. The development of literate technologies such as cursive book hands and abbreviations, the use of paper rather than parchment, and the rise of commercial dealers in rented gatherings (pecias) and books further stimulated the availability of devotional discourse, and prominent laypeople sought the enhanced reputation and the spiritual benefits that came with providing patronage for the dissemination of a favorite devotional text or compilation. The introduction of the printing press dramatically enhanced these opportunities.

Vernacular Texts

Vernacular devotional discourse survives in a variety of genres: stories, poems, letters, visions, collections of wise sayings, allegories, and quasi-systematic expositions of the Mass, the creation of the world, the vices and virtues, monastic rules, and the lives of the saints. Its guided meditations on biblical material, particularly the life and Passion of Christ, are frequently presented by religious authorities as safe substitutes for actual Bibles, which were usually deemed too dangerous to be left to the interpretation of the laity.

Traditional scholarship has sometimes dismissed devotional literature as derivative, pedestrian, and overwhelmingly didactic, and there is some validity in these criticisms. Medieval texts routinely borrow material without attribution, adapt it freely, and credit the results to revered authorities like Richard Rolle, Augustine, or "the Fathers." However, the importance of devotional discourse is not in its originality or its stylistic innovations, such as they are. Rather, this body of literature is critical for the information it provides about the active engagement of medieval people in a broad range of literate, spiritual, and cultural practices.

Evidence for Women's Lives

Devotional texts are particularly useful for what they reveal about female participation in medieval intellectual and spiritual life. Women played prominent roles in the patronage, translation, and circulation of devotional discourse throughout medieval Europe. A few of the women associated with this material include Margaret of Scotland, Christine de Pizan, Margaret of Brittany, Mechthild of Hackeborn, Birgitta of Sweden, and Cecily of York. Medieval authors and compilers regularly dedicated and addressed their copies of devotional treatises to individual women and general female audiences. For example, Simon Wynter's version of the life of Saint Jerome urges its patron, Margaret, duchess of Clarence, to copy the text for others after reading it herself and to encourage other readers to do the same. Lady Margaret Beaufort was a particularly avid reader and supporter of devotional literature. She translated a variety of texts, including *The Mirror of Gold for the Sinful Soul* and *The Ship of Fools*, and she commissioned versions of *The Fifteen Oes*, *On the Mixed Life*, and *The Stairway of Perfection*, among many other titles. The household accounts of Cecily, duchess of York, show a similarly profound engagement with a wide range of devotional texts. Women's monastic foundations served as sites for the reading and discussion, as well as the production and transmission, of much of this material.

The fact that clerical discourse has persistent misogynistic components has attracted significant attention from scholars of gender and devotional literature. The antiwomen sentiments in a particular text can range from mild reminders of the theological inheritance of Eve to sweeping condemnations of all women as sources of and incitements to sin. Such variable assessments can occur alongside celebrations of biblical and historical women, virtues that are allegorically cast as feminine, and the rare claim that the best cleric is the man or the woman who loves God the most. It has convincingly (and sometimes simultaneously) been argued that devotional texts are psychologically astute, virulently misogynistic, covertly erotic, and complexly indeterminate. Further complicating this line of inquiry are the courtly and contemplative literary conventions and counter-discourses that challenge the hegemony of the misogynistic claims.

Since the 1970s, the relationships between devotional literature and its female readers have attracted significant scholarly attention, and this topic invites much further inquiry. Many of the texts discussed here are currently available only in unpublished dissertations or in outdated or expurgated editions. Some works survive only in manuscript form, and references to women readers and their books continue to emerge in newly edited documents. No doubt much further information awaits discovery in the archives. New research on book ownership and patronage will continue to illuminate the literary activities of women readers and female audiences, as well as the intellectual and spiritual alliances between women and men. After three decades or so of theoretically and historically informed scholarship, it is time to re-examine some of our most fundamental assumptions about women and gender in the Middle Ages, to consolidate and synthesize our findings, and to re-examine the intellectual landscapes that emerge.

ANNE CLARK BARTLETT

References and Further Reading

Bartlett, Anne Clark. *Male Authors, Female Readers: Representation and Subjectivity in Middle English Devotional Literature*. Ithaca, N.Y.: Cornell University Press, 1995.

Bell, David N. *What Nuns Read: Books and Libraries in Medieval English Nunneries.* Kalamazoo, Mich.: Cistercian Publications, 1995.

Erler, Mary C. *Women, Reading and Piety in Late Medieval England.* New York: Cambridge University Press, 2002.

McCash, June Hall, ed. *The Cultural Patronage of Medieval Women.* Athens, Ga.: The University of Georgia Press, 1996.

Meale, Carol M., ed. *Women and Literature in Britain 1150–1500.* New York: Cambridge University Press, 1993. Reprint, Cambridge: Cambridge University Press, 1996.

Newman, Barbara. "Flaws in the Golden Bowl: Gender and Spiritual Formation in the Twelfth Century." In *From Virile Woman to WomanChrist: Studies in Medieval Religion and Literature.* Philadelphia: University of Pennsylvania Press, 1995, pp. 111–146.

Powell, Susan. "Lady Margaret Beaufort and Her Books." *The Library* 20.3 (1998): 197–240.

Robertson, Elizabeth. *Early English Devotional Prose and the Female Audience.* Knoxville, Tenn.: University of Tennessee Press, 1990.

Stock, Brian. *The Implications of Literacy.* Princeton, N.J.: Princeton University Press, 1986.

Voaden, Rosalynn, ed. *Prophets Abroad: The Reception of Continental Holy Women in Late-Medieval England.* Rochester, N.Y.: D. S. Brewer, 1996.

Watson, Nicholas. "Censorship and Cultural Change in Late-Medieval England: Vernacular Theology, The Oxford Translation Debate, and Arundel's Constitutions of 1409." *Speculum* 70 (1995): 822–864.

Wogan-Brown, Jocelyn. *Saints' Lives and Women's Literary Culture c. 1150–1300: Virginity and Its Authorizations.* New York: Oxford University Press, 2001.

See also **Audience, Women in the; Beaufort, Margaret; Birgitta of Sweden; Book Ownership; Books of Hours; Christine de Pizan; Devotional Practices; Eve; Lay Piety; Literacy and Reading: Vernacular; Liturgy; Margaret of Scotland; Mechthild of Hackeborn; Misogyny; Patronage, Ecclesiastical; Patronage, Literary; Translation**

DEVOTIONAL PRACTICES

The devotional practices of medieval men and women, one of the most prevalent cultural features of the time, were doubtless as varied as the individuals who observed them, a fact that, while seemingly self-evident, is somewhat obscured by the nature of the evidence upon which we rely for understanding of this far-reaching phenomenon. The prescriptive aspect of rules, guides, manuals, and prayer books complicates considerably our ability to arrive at a proper understanding of how individuals may have actually used such aids to devotion. Furthermore, much of what remains in the way of devotional texts and artifacts was produced for clerical or monastic patrons or, in the later period especially, for lay men and women of means, with the consequence that our knowledge of the practices of the vast majority of medievals is fragmentary at best. This entry focuses on broad trends in devotional practices, especially regarding the increased importance of women's practices, also in the later period, as consumers and/or patrons of devotional texts.

Devotional practices could take many forms, from making the sign of the cross, a practice attested to by Tertullian in the second century, to the elaborate, personalized programs incorporating gestures, attitudes, and texts of the late Middle Ages. Though thus multifaceted across time and limited or determined by context, medieval devotional practices also present a central unifying feature: virtually all are closely related to prayer, and the evolution of the practice of prayer, including the material objects and spaces connected with it, will inform the discussion here. Prayer was, in the early period (roughly to the eleventh century) above all a clerical and monastic practice and therefore collective and indeed "professional" by definition, if for no other reason than that participation supposed literacy in Latin (or dependence on those who possessed it). The chanting of the canonical hours and the prayers associated with the liturgy were *the* privileged forms of devotion. The development of prayer in the vernacular for the laity, a marked feature of late medieval devotion, was driven by the desire, among both the clergy and the laity, for greater affective participation of the latter in the worship of God, the veneration of saints, and the celebration of the mysteries of the faith, but also by the desire on the part of the clergy for orthodoxy and indoctrination among the laity.

Psalters and Books of Hours provide a particularly useful index for charting the transition from liturgical to extra-liturgical practices and the development of private prayer among the laity. Psalters allowed lay men and women to recite the Psalms of the Breviary, as was the practice of liturgical, and particularly monastic, communities, without having to observe their rigorous routine. Other texts were often included in Psalters besides the Psalms. In a survey of common prayers added to French translations of the Psalter dating from the twelfth to the fifteenth century, E. Brayer and A.-M. Bouly de Lesdain found that the *Pater Noster* was the most frequently added prayer, followed by the *Credo*, the *Gloria*, and the *Ave Maria*. For example, a bilingual Latin–French Psalter from the first third of the fourteenth century (Paris, Bibl. Mazarine, MS 58) once belonging to Jeanne and Marguerite, daughters of Godefroy de Brabant, includes the first of these three prayers but not the Ave.

With the vast development of Marian devotion in the thirteenth century, the Little Hours of Our Lady, extracted from the Breviary, became the most important type of devotional book during the later

Middle Ages. Hundreds of exemplars survive, from the lavish productions for royal princes (for example, the *Très Riches Heures* of Jean, duc de Berry) to humble, unillustrated copies, either manuscript or printed. The abbot Victor Leroquais, who catalogued the Books of Hours in the French National Library, observed that, although based on liturgical practice, Books of Hours were destined for private devotion and imposed no obligatory use or program. In effect, their use escaped clerical control, which doubtless explains much of their appeal for men and women alike. Those wealthy enough to have a Book of Hours made for themselves could have prayers to their patron saint included. In other instances, such prayers were added by later owners who used blank pages for this purpose as well as for recording their ownership of the book and family events such as births, deaths, and marriages. Books of Hours, even of the humble sort, were prized personal possessions and often appear in wills.

Prayers in Books of Hours and other devotional books often contain information as to how they were meant to be used. For example, one of the accessory texts most frequently included in Books of Hours, especially from the fifteenth century, the Fifteen Joys of the Virgin, indicates that the person reciting the prayer should genuflect fifteen times in honor of each of the Fifteen Joys. This prayer, with its emphasis on Mary's maternity and the childhood of Jesus, invited both men and women to contemplate and indeed participate vicariously in the joys and mysteries of motherhood, thus allowing a fluidity of gender positions and identifications that is typical of late medieval forms of devotion. Also typical is the (at times jarring) juxtaposition of a concern for the proper physical attitude and gestures (sometimes of a mechanical sort, as here) with the solicitation of the most varied emotional or psychological states. An especially important influence for the increased emphasis on affect in late medieval devotion is the *Orationes sive meditationes* attributed to Anselm of Canterbury (1033–1109). The prayers in this collection were intended for private, meditative reading, but here again we find a very real tension between the inner, meditative cast of these prayers and the highly dramatic form they can take, when, for example, the reader is invited to join Mary Magdalene at the foot of the cross, apostrophize Christ with her, and assume her grief at the Crucifixion while engaging in an interrogation of his or her own sins. At a later date, the Franciscans also contributed greatly to the increased importance given to affect in contemplative literature, partly through the focus on the humanity of Christ and his mother. For example, in the *Meditationes Vitae Christi* composed by Johannes de Caulibus between c. 1346 and 1364, the author addresses the reader, an otherwise unidentified "sister," on how to contemplate the life of Christ, saying to tell things "as they occurred or as they might have occurred according to the devout belief of the imagination and the varying interpretation of the mind."

The prayer cited above was one of several from Anselm's *Orationes* that was translated into French and included with dozens of other prayers and devotions in a fourteenth-century guide made for the use of an unidentified noblewoman (BNF, nouv. acq. lat., MS 592). After the opening calendar and the Hours of the Holy Spirit, the manuscript contains over 150 folios of prayers and devotions, many in Latin with French translation, with accompanying instructions for their use. Some are for different moments of the day (upon rising, while in Church, upon retiring); others, like the prayers from Anselm's collection, for meditative reading. Such guides or manuals are an especially rich source for understanding how spiritual advisors sought to inform the devotional practices and subjectivity of medieval men and women; and texts written for women, of which ms. 592 is but one of many examples, are particularly revelatory of how the boundaries between the spiritual and the mundane were often intentionally blurred. These devotional guides are thus a type of conduct literature and share many features with such well-known examples as the *Menagier of Paris*, in which an anonymous middle-aged bourgeois "householder" provides instruction to his young wife in how to manage herself, her servants, and her household and in which catechetical and moral concerns (the wife's obedience and chastity) far outweigh devotional practices per se. Doubtless written by a spiritual advisor, the text includes advice on how the young wife should conduct her private devotions at home (prayers upon rising and retiring), how to comport herself in church (according to her station), and how to prepare herself for communion and confession.

Jean Gerson (1363–1429), chancellor of the University of Paris and one of the most powerful theologians of his day, wrote a much shorter guide for his sisters, *Sur l'excellence de la virginité*, in which he enjoined them to dress and act without ostentation; say their hours regularly and attend as many masses as possible; live soberly, drinking only diluted wine and avoiding spicy foods; live in peace with each other; never speak to men they don't know unless it be in public in front of others; never go dancing; and, lastly, learn to read French (*romaunt*) so that they could read the letters and devotional books that Jean would send them. In a devotional guide composed after 1408 by an anonymous disciple of Gerson's (Bibliothèque de l'Arsenal, MS 2176, fol. 86ff.) and included in a survey by G. Hasenohr of fifteen such texts, the author enjoins the harried wife to turn her thoughts from the turmoil in her household to "Noah, to the ark of contemplative prayer," and, once she has freed herself from the labors of the world, to take refuge in her room where she can deliver herself freely to highly emotive and eroticized devotions including tears, sighs, bitter cries, laments, plaints, laments, humble sighs, prostrations, kneeling, beating the breast in great contrition, kissing the ground in great and humble devotion, raising the eyes and hands to heaven in great desire, bending and intertwining the arms as if embracing a lover (*amy*) in great love, and stretching the body out on the ground or standing, as if on a cross, in great compassion.

These few examples should make clear the extremely broad range of devotional texts written for medieval women of noble or bourgeois standing. They suppose the active role of a spiritual director; a household space for private devotions (in most cases the *chambre*, in which there might be a private altar, or, for the wealthy, an oratory or private chapel); and, last but not least, literacy. For men and women of more humble social position, the parish or a nearby mendicant church or a confraternity chapel or guild-hall might provide a context for collective or private devotions, such as the saying of the rosary. The devotional activities of confraternities and guilds were extremely varied: liturgical services; processions on the feast day of the patron saint, perhaps followed by a banquet with a sermon, recitation of devotional poetry, or performance of a play; collective singing, such as practiced by the Italian societies devoted to the performance of *laude* (another genre that allowed male participants to adopt a variety of shifting gender positions); or penitential practices, including self-mortification and flagellation (a practice that spread from northern Italy to northern and central Europe after the Black Death). While confraternities were generally male-dominated institutions, many welcomed female members or participants in their celebrations.

This entry has focused primarily on well-documented examples of devotional practices, such as those recorded in prayer books, but the culture provided many opportunities for the less fortunate to receive either direct or indirect instruction in this area. Spiritual direction from the clergy, sermons and exempla, and medieval religious theater, with its numerous representations of rituals, devotion, and prayer, are but a few of the ways in which Christians of all stations were enjoined to express their faith through actions that were paramount in the shaping of religious culture and the fashioning of religious subjects.

ROBERT L. A. CLARK

References and Further Reading

Amsler, Mark. "Affective Literacy: Gestures of Reading in the Later Middle Ages." *Essays in Medieval Studies* 18 (2001): 83–109.

Brayer, Edith. "Livres d'heures contenant des texts en français." *Bulletin de l'Institut de Recherche et d'Histoire des Textes* 12 (1963): 31–102.

Brayer, Eoita, and Anne-Marie Bouly de Lesdain. "Les Prières usuelles annexes aux anciennes traductions françaises du Psautier." *Bulletin de l'Institut de Recherche et d'Histoire des Textes* 15 (1967–68): 69–120.

Brereton, Georgina E., and Janet M. Ferrier. *Le Mesnagier de Paris*, translated by Karin Ueltschi. Collection Lettres Gothiques. Paris: Librairie Générale Française, 1994.

Clark, Robert L. A. "Constructing the Female Subject in Late Medieval Devotion." In *Medieval Conduct*, edited by Kathleen Ashley and Robert L. A. Clark. Minneapolis: University of Minnesota Press, 2001, pp. 160–182.

Gerson, Jean. "Sur l'excellence de la virginité." In *Oeuvres completes*, edited by Palémon Glorieux. 10 vols. Paris: Desclée, 1966, v. 7, pp. 292–339.

Hasenohr, Geneviève. "La vie quotidienne de la femme vue par l'Eglise: L'enseignement des 'journées chrétiennes' de la fin du Moyen-Age." In *Frau und spätmittelalterlicher Alltag*. International Congress, Krems an der Donau, Oct. 2–5, 1984. Österreichische Akademie der Wissenschaften, Philosophisch-Historische Klasse, Sitzungsberichte 473. Veröffentlichungen des Instituts für mittelalterliche Realienkunde Österreichs 9. Vienna: Österreichischen Akademie der Wissenschaften, 1986. pp. 19–101.

Johannis de Caulibus. *Meditaciones Vite Christi*, edited by Mary Stallings-Taney. Corpus Christianorum, Continuatio Mediaevalis 153. Turnhout: Brepols, 1997.

Leroquais, abbé Victor. *Les Bréviaires manuscrits des bibliothèques publiques de France*. 6 vols. Paris, 1932–1934.

———. *Les Livres d'Heures manuscrits de la Bibliothèque Nationale*. 3 vols. Paris, 1927.

Ragusa, Isa, and Rosalie B. Green. *Meditations on the Life of Christ*. Princeton, N.J.: Princeton University Press, 1961.

Rondeau, Jennifer Fisk. "Conducting Gender: Theories and Practices in Italian Confraternity Literature." In *Medieval Conduct*, edited by Kathleen Ashley and Robert L. A. Clark. Minneapolis: University of Minnesota Press, 2001, pp. 183–206.

Sinclair, Keith V. *French Devotional Texts of the Middle Ages: A Bibliographic Manuscript Guide*. Westport, Conn.: Greenwood, 1979.

———. *French Devotional Texts of the Middle Ages: A Bibliographic Manuscript Guide*. 1st Supplement. Westport, Conn.: 1982. Reprint, 1988.

Sonet, Jean. *Répertoire d'incipit de prières en ancient français*. Geneva: Droz, 1956.

Ward, Benedicta, trans. *The Prayers and Meditations of Saint Anselm*. Harmondsworth: Penguin, 1973.

Wieck, Roger S. *Time Sanctified: The Book of Hours in Medieval Art and Life*. New York: Braziller, 1988.

See also **Book of Hours; Devotional Literature; Lay Piety; Rosary; Spiritual Care**

DHUODA

In the middle of the ninth century, during civil wars ensuing from the death of the Frankish emperor Louis the Pious, the noblewoman Dhuoda composed a book for her young son William about how he might best conduct himself in such troubled times. Dhuoda was wife of the magnate Bernard of Septimania and wartime lord of her absent husband's broad dominions in southern Francia. She had been educated in Charlemagne's palace school and was likely a relation of the Frankish royal house. Separated from her family—William, her fifteen-year-old addressee, as well as her husband and their infant boy—and living at Uzès near Nîmes in the period of her work's composition between late 841 and early 843, she represented her love for her elder son and her hopes for his development as best she could: she sent him a book of her own making. Dhuoda wrote of both spiritual and secular matters from the apex of the Frankish elite at the moment of its highest achievement and imminent ruin. Her *Liber manualis* (*Manual* or *Handbook* in English) is the only extant book-length work from a European woman's hand between the late antique record of travels to Jerusalem by the Western pilgrim Egeria and the tenth-century plays of Hrotsvit of Gandersheim. But Dhuoda's text's importance for women's history extends beyond its authorship; a mother's work for a maturing child, it sheds light on the histories of mothering, childhood and adolescence, and gender and families.

Dhuoda's *Handbook* explores the meaning of Western Christianity for the personal and historical experience of Frankish nobles such as herself and William. She understands the events of her life—most importantly her separation from her two children—as spiritual travails in a kingdom as fragmented as that of the Hebrews in the time of the rebellion of David's son Absalom. Dhuoda counsels her son that a spiritual practice and spiritually grounded construction of social and political life nonetheless offer hope for the reestablishment of peace between father and son, king and warrior. Ironically, Dhuoda's husband, Bernard, was at the time of her writing a leader in the Frankish nobles' rebellion against Charlemagne's grandson, Charles the Bald. Meanwhile William, the elder son of Dhuoda and Bernard, was held hostage against his father's further violence, and would eventually be executed by the Carolingian heir for following his father in rebellion.

Dhuoda's text is arranged in eleven short sections labeled "books" in editions and translations. Her prologue and several chapters of the tenth book offer all known biographical information about her and set a highly emotive context for the rest of her work. The first two and last seven of Dhuoda's books treat general principles of Christian theology and practice, reflecting the Carolingian laity's formation according to an ecclesiastical culture well known from other sources. Dhuoda's third and fourth books, however, are distinctive and thus have been the center of much modern attention devoted to her work. In these longer sections, Dhuoda advises her son on how his spiritual life may enhance his success as a secular nobleman. Here, she exhibits powerful maternal authority even as she supports patriarchy within the family and in the failing Frankish empire. Dhuoda's secular voice thus departs from clerical literary models, articulating noble self-definition in terms of family allegiance and military prowess, as well as Christian devotion. Moreover, her sensitivity to framing her discussion with language and content she describes as age-appropriate for her young son is important evidence for an early medieval sense of the differences among children, youths, and adults.

Dhuoda's work survives in only a few medieval manuscripts. Her elder son may never have read it; if he did, it clearly failed in its intent to educate him for his own safety. The work seems, however, to have been preserved by her younger son, unnamed at her writing but later christened Bernard after his father. This younger Bernard's descendants were dukes of Aquitaine, among them William the Pious, founder of the great abbey of Cluny. Medieval copies of Dhuoda's *Handbook* date from the tenth and fourteenth centuries. Since the definitive edition by the eminent Carolingianist Pierre Riché in 1971, the work has been much discussed as a source for understanding early medieval elites—their literacy and religious learning, family structures, construction of gender, and understanding of human development. Two recent English translations attest to the *Handbook*'s wide readership in medieval and women's studies.

CAROL NEEL

References and Further Reading

Claussen, M. A. "Fathers of Power and Mothers of Authority: Dhuoda and the *Liber manualis*. *French Historical Studies* 19.3 (1996): 785–809.

Dhuoda. *Handbook for Her Warrior Son: Liber Manualis*, edited and translated by Marcelle Thiébaux. Cambridge Medieval Classics 8. Cambridge and New York: Cambridge University Press, 1998.

———. *Handbook for William*, translated by Carol Neel. Lincoln, Neb.: University of Nebraska Press, 1991. Reprint with afterword, Medieval Texts in Translation. Washington, D.C.: Catholic University of America Press, 1999.

———. *Manuel pour mon fils*, edited by Pierre Riché and translated by Bernard de Vregille and Claude Mondésert. Paris: Editions du Cerf, 1974. Revised edition, Sources chrétiennes 225 bis. Paris: Editions du Cerf, 1991.

Mayeski, Marie Ann. *Dhuoda: Ninth Century Mother and Theologian*. Scranton, Pa.: University of Scranton Press, 1995.

Olsen, Glenn W. "One Heart and One Soul (Acts 4:32 and 34) in Dhuoda's *Manual*." *Church History* 61.1 (1992): 23–33.

See also **Frankish Lands; Literature, Latin; Mothers as Teachers; Noble Women; Women Authors: Latin Texts**

DIPLOMACY AND RECONCILIATION

Diplomacy in the modern sense, with permanent embassies and well-trained professional bureaucracies, did not exist until the sixteenth century. In the early Middle Ages, diplomacy was essentially the maintenance of personal and familial relations enacted in the public political arena by political entities—kingdoms, duchies, counties, and religious institutions—and women played an active role. By 1550, the professional practice of diplomacy was regularized and women's role changed accordingly. Reconciliation, on the other hand, was both part of formal legal litigation and an informal means of resolving disputes outside the law courts. The flip side of feud, vendetta, and lawlessness, throughout the Middle Ages it was to keep women of all ranks busy building alliances and mending fences. Women's authority to engage in either formal diplomacy or informal reconciliation stemmed from the laws and customs that established their rights concerning landholding and lordship. Such clearly political actions were deemed socially acceptable because they were regarded as the feminine intercessory complement of the masculine warrior–knight, with the Biblical queen Esther and the Virgin Mary as models. Anglo-Saxon noblewomen and queens such as Æthelberga of Kent, wife of Edwin of Northumbria (d. c. 632), and Eanfled, wife of Oswy of Northumbria (d. c. 669), often brokered peace among their natal and marital relatives by their marriages, by direct intervention, or both. Ottonian queens Matilda, wife of Henry the Fowler, and Adelheid, wife of Emperor Otto I, typify the combination of saintliness and worldliness that provided models of intercessory and conciliatory queenship. The wide and varied examples of women's intercession, conciliatory actions, and diplomacy are associated with other traditionally feminine activities, such as managing households, keeping peace within the household, and arranging marriages.

Reconciliation

Women as intercessors can be seen clearly in the early medieval court, where bonds of vassalage were intertwined with household offices, and women often mediated legal disputes involving feud and vendetta. Low-status women—such as townswomen, the gentry, Muslims, and Jews—surely engaged in reconciliation, but their actions are difficult to discern. Their disputes may have been handled quietly among families, may not have been documented, or the records may have been destroyed or lost in pogroms or expulsions. Reconciliation and subtle diplomacy also played a part in the ritualized hospitality built around social networks of women like Dame Alice de Breine, an English gentry woman of the later Middle Ages. In the tenth and eleventh century, the Peace and Truce of God movement provided legal and theological underpinnings for formal reconciliation and added further weight to women's actions. Legal records, land conveyances, and church documents describe the many and varied ways that Christian women made peace among families and settled quarrels involving property, personal injury, and commercial transactions.

Diplomacy

Diplomacy, on the other hand, was always the domain of women of high social rank who possessed sufficient legal and political authority to directly negotiate disputes among kingdoms, principalities, the Empire, landed clergy, and the papacy. Countesses and queens are the most visible diplomats, with political relations and warfare the most common backdrops, and their actions are well documented in chronicles and royal, comital, regional, and municipal archives. Women's engagement in diplomacy was common in the early Middle Ages, when, for instance, Theophanu was regent from 984 to 991 for her son German Emperor Otto III. Adela, countess of Blois, in the eleventh century, smoothed relations with the church in France, and Berta, countess of Tuscany, in the tenth century, established diplomatic ties with Abbasid Caliph Muktafi. Ermengard, the twelfth-century countess of Narbonne, enshrined in troubadour literature, was a key figure in settling disputes and reconciling feuding families in southern France. During her widowhood, Jeanne of Valois, countess of Holland, Zeeland, and Hainault and sister of King Philip VI of France, was a prominent local, regional, and international diplomat on the eve of the Hundred

Years' War. In this, she was one in a long line of Flemish countesses who mediated the many disputes that arose between Flanders and France, and towns and the crown, as early as the eleventh century.

In the later Middle Ages, queens were less involved in diplomacy because trained lawyers and bureaucrats assumed the job, but they did not drop out of the picture altogether. Queens-regent were active and visible diplomats as they governed for their minor sons and ill or absent husbands. For instance, Blanche of Castile negotiated treaties in 1227 and 1231 for her minor son, Louis IX of France, and again when he was away on Crusade, an event that, like the Hundred Years' War, propelled many noble women and queens into diplomacy. Isabelle of France, daughter of Philip IV of France and wife of Edward II of England, found herself working both sides of the negotiating table. Her marriage built a diplomatic bridge between England and France in 1314 that collapsed in 1337, despite her best efforts, when her son and her Valois cousins debated the French succession, setting in motion the Hundred Years' War. Nearly a century later, Isabeau of Bavaria brokered a treaty in 1420 between the French and English. Margaret of Anjou, regent for her husband, King Henry VI of England, was both ally and enemy of her uncle, King Charles VII of France, during negotiations for ceding Maine to the French at the close of the Hundred Years' War.

Religious Disputes

Women were often called on, or volunteered, to resolve religious disputes. In 1077, Matilda of Tuscany famously got German Emperor Henry IV and Pope Gregory VII to work out temporarily their differences over lay investiture. Saint Margaret of Scotland, wife of Malcolm, combined politics with saintliness as she maintained peace at home and promoted diplomatic relations between Malcolm and the church. Margaret's daughter Matilda of Scotland was instrumental in resolving the investiture dispute in England during the reign of her husband, Henry I. The Bohemian queen Johanna of Rozmital was an active diplomat during the Hussite wars. Sainted, or merely pious, women were valued practitioners of dispute resolution. Catherine of Siena is well known for her intervention in papal politics in 1376, and Joan of Arc went to war to make peace at the end of the Hundred Years' War.

But sanctity was only one way to practice diplomacy. Queens, shielded by their rank and proximity to the king, could practice a forceful diplomacy that used anger and outright threats as rhetorical weapons. Eleanor of Castile used barely veiled threats during the English baronial revolt in the late thirteenth century to get the earl of Cornwall, count of Bigorre, and bishop of Worcester to comply with royal wishes. In 1429, Maria of Castile used her own anger as a diplomatic tool and averted war by literally setting up her tent on the battlefield between the armies of her husband, Alfonso V of Aragon, and her brother, Juan II of Castile.

Diplomatic Marriages

Another effective form of diplomacy that routinely involved women was negotiating marriages to build or secure a political alliance. Women were the brides as well as the principal negotiators, if not instigators, of many marriages, and were intimately involved in the high-stakes negotiations between kings, princes, dukes, and counts. Emma (Ælfgifu) of Normandy adroitly, some would say coldly, married the Danish King Cnut, the man who defeated her first husband, Æthelred II, in 1017. In the twelfth century, Eleanor of Aquitaine's carefully arranged marriages of her children linked England with the major European royal houses, as did those of her contemporary, Alfonso VII of Castile. In 1371, John of Gaunt, seeking the crown of Castile during the Hundred Years' War, married Constanza, daughter of King Pedro I of Castile. The marriages of their daughters Philippa, to João of Avis, king of Portugal, and Catalina, to Enrique of Trastámara, king of Castile, created an Anglo-Castilian alliance that continued into the early modern period with the marriage of Katherine of Aragon to Arthur and Henry Tudor (later Henry VIII). Brides could be unwilling participants, pawns, or virtual hostages to guarantee compliance with treaties, as was Catherine of Valois when she married Henry V of England in 1415.

THERESA EARENFIGHT

References and Further Reading

Brown, Elizabeth A. R. "Diplomacy, Adultery, and Domestic Politics at the Court of Philip the Fair: Queen Isabelle's Mission to France in 1314." In *Documenting the Past*, edited by J. S. Hamilton and Patricia J. Bradley. Woodbridge, Suffolk: Boydell Press, 1989, pp. 53–83.

Cheyette, Fredric. *Ermengard of Narbonne and the World of the Troubadours*. Ithaca, N.Y.: Cornell University Press, 2001.

Chibnall, Marjorie. *The Empress Matilda: Queen Consort, Queen Mother, and Lady of the English*. Oxford: Blackwell, 1991.

Davids, Adelbert, ed. *The Empress Theophano: Byzantium and the West and the Name of Theophano in Byzantium*. Cambridge: Cambridge University Press, 1995.

Diggelmann, Lindsay. "Marriage as a Tactical Response: Henry II and the Royal Wedding of 1160." *English Historical Review* 119. 483 (2004): 954–964.

Earenfight, Theresa. "Queenship, Politics, and Government in the Medieval Crown of Aragon: The Lieutenancy of María of Castile, 1420–23 and 1432–53." Ph.D. dissertation, Fordham University, 1997.

Evergates, Theodore, ed. *Aristocratic Women in Medieval France*. Philadelphia: University of Pennsylvania Press, 1999.

Gibbons, Rachel. "Isabeau of Bavaria, Queen of France (1385–1422): The Creation of an Historical Villainess." *Transactions of the Royal Historical Society*, 6th ser. 6 (1996): 51–73.

Goodman, Anthony. *John of Gaunt: The Exercise of Princely Power in Fourteenth-Century Europe*. New York: St. Martin's Press, 1992.

Huneycutt, Lois L. "Intercession and the High-Medieval Queen: The Esther Topos." In *Power of the Weak*, edited by Jennifer Carpenter and Sally-Beth Carpenter. Urbana, Ill.: University of Illinois Press, 1995, pp. 126–146.

Klassen, John. *Warring Maidens, Captive Wives, and Hussite Queens: Women and Men at War and Peace in Late Medieval Bohemia*. New York: Eastern European Monographs, 1999.

Kunz, Elizabeth Gibson. "Hospitality, Conviviality, and the English Gentry: Social Networks of the Landed Elite in Late Medieval Suffolk." Ph.D. dissertation, Fordham University, 2001.

LoPrete, Kimberly A. *Adela of Blois, Countess and Lord (ca. 1067–1137)*. Dublin: Four Courts Press, 2001.

Maurer, Helen E. *Margaret of Anjou: Queenship and Power in Late Medieval England*. Woodbridge, Suffolk: Boydell Press, 2003.

Menache, Sophia. "Isabelle of France, Queen of England—A Reconsideration." *Journal of Medieval History* 10 (1984): 107–124.

Nolan, Kathleen, ed. *Capetian Women*. New York: Palgrave Macmillan, 2003, pp. 147–177.

Parsons, John Carmi. "The Queen's Intercession in Thirteenth-Century England." In *Power of the Weak*, edited by Jennifer Carpenter and Sally-Beth Carpenter. Urbana, Ill.: University of Illinois Press, 1995.

———, ed. *Medieval Queenship*. New York: St. Martin's Press, 1993.

Rizzo, Catia Renzi. "Riflessioni sulla lettera di Berta di Toscana al califfo Muktafi: l'apporto congiunto die dati archeologici e delle fonti scritte." *Archivio Storico Italiano* 159: 587 (2001): 3–47.

Stafford, Pauline. *Queens, Concubines, and Dowagers: The King's Wife in the Early Middle Ages*. Athens, Ga.: University of Georgia Press, 1983.

Wheeler, Bonnie, and John Carmi Parsons, eds. *Eleanor of Aquitaine, Lord and Lady*. New York: Palgrave Macmillan, 2002.

See also **Adelheid; Blanche of Castile; Catherine of Siena; Eleanor of Aquitaine; Emma of Normandy; Ermengard; Intercession; Margaret of Anjou; Margaret of Scotland; Matilda of Tuscany; Noble Women; Ottonian Royal Women; Queens and Empresses: The West; Regents and Queen-Lieutenants**

DISABILITIES

Disability touched all levels of medieval society, from the nobility to peasants to saints, yet experiences and perceptions of disabled people in the Middle Ages are not well known because disability has only recently become a subject of academic inquiry. This field has drawn on studies of gender, sexuality, race, and ethnicity to argue that disability is a socially constructed category imbued with negative stereotypes that have been imposed upon people with physical and cognitive differences to ignore, oppress, or eliminate them. Disability affects all social categories and can lower a person's status because of preconceived notions of what it means to be disabled and because of lost economic opportunities. While this scholarship has focused primarily on the nineteenth and twentieth centuries, a few studies have revealed greater nuance in medieval society than was once imagined.

Two levels of ideology have obscured readings of evidence about medieval disabled people: a medieval Christian association of disability with sin, which blamed either disabled people or their parents for the disability, and the modern medical model, which continues to perpetuate a system of values that blames the individual for failing to become cured, and thus colors our own readings of the sources. Together, they have inhibited scholars from analyzing disability as a social issue rather than an individual problem.

The emphasis on sin greatly influenced the medieval church's doctrine on disability and illness, but theory and practice were more complex than stated doctrine. The canons of the Fourth Lateran Council in 1215 stated that sin caused illness and so ordered hospitals to require confession of their patients. Thirteenth-century preachers instructed disabled audiences that they must accept their disability as a divine test, like the Old Testament figures Job and Tobit, and live moral lives so that they would be worthy of charity and of God's mercy. Hospitals relied on the belief that their patients were a locus of spirituality, as people of all social levels donated money to support hospitals and the sick. Yet, many of these hospitals refused to admit people with permanent disabilities. In thirteenth- and fourteenth-century Paris, for example, only the Hôpital des Quinze-Vingts (Hospital of the Three Hundred), which King Louis IX founded in the 1250s to house blind people and their guides, welcomed any category of the permanently disabled.

Social status and gender also affected the treatment and perception of disabled people. Thirteenth- and fourteenth-century Europe witnessed a growing hostility toward the poor that was harmful to the disabled, especially disabled men. Gendered stereotypes of men from the laboring classes created an expectation that men should work and not be dependent. Preachers feminized disabled male beggars by associating them with bodily temptation and argued that such men were not worthy of charity because they used artifice to make themselves appear disabled, just like prostitutes used makeup to appear more alluring. Distrust of disabled male beggars also drives several Old French farces, such as the thirteenth-century *Le garçon et l'aveugle* (*The Boy and the Blind Man*), which portrays the blind beggar as a drain on society because he is vulgar, wanton, and miserly. Conversely, because predominant gender stereotypes obscured women's role in the workforce, dependent women were more acceptable and thus deemed more worthy of charity.

Familial acceptance was instrumental to the lives of disabled people, particularly those with congenital differences. Parents' responses to disabled offspring ranged from rejection and infanticide to reluctant acceptance. The birth of disabled children also affected the parents, as people inquired into what they might have seen, thought, or done to cause such a portent to appear. Familial care even informed the structure of the Hôpital des Quinze-Vingts, which encouraged residents to marry so that the sighted spouse could assist the blind one but forbade the marriage of two blind people, assuming that they could not care for each other. When familial care was insufficient, disabled people, particularly the poor, relied on their own social networks and on charity. The thirteenth-century miracles of Saint Louis reveal how poor disabled people, especially women, relied on networks of other women when family could or would not help them.

This is but a sample of medieval perceptions and experiences of disability. Medieval authors and artists employed images of disability to explore the meanings of sin, humanity, and power, yet the ramifications of this discourse have not been adequately explored. Regional and chronological differences need greater exploration too, as Old Norse literature and medieval Islamic society appear more accommodating than medieval Christian society. Scholars should also consider how disability marginalized so many, but exalted others, like Saint Margaret the Lame and Saint Roch, the plague saint. Such inquiries will deepen our knowledge of the medieval past and the modern world by challenging conceived notions of disability and encouraging a closer examination of the body, in all its variations and its social meanings.

MARK P. O'TOOL

References and Further Reading

Bragg, Lois. "From the Mute God to the Lesser God: Disability in Medieval Celtic and Old Norse Literature." *Disability and Society* 12.2 (1997): 165–177.

Eberly, Susan Schoon. "Fairies and the Folklore of Disability: Changelings, Hybrids and the Solitary Fairy" *Folklore* 99.1 (1988): 58–77.

Farmer, Sharon. *Surviving Poverty in Medieval Paris: Gender, Ideology, and the Daily Lives of the Poor*. Ithaca, N.Y.: Cornell University Press, 2002.

Kudlick, Catherine. "Disability History: Why We Need Another Other." *American Historical Review* 108.3 (2003): 763–793.

Linton, Simi. *Claiming Disability: Knowledge and Identity*. New York: New York University Press, 1998.

Malti-Douglas, Fedwa. "Mentalités and Marginality: Blindness and Mamluk Civilization." In *The Islamic World from Classical to Modern Times: Essays in Honor of Bernard Lewis*, edited by Clifford E. Bosworth, Roger Savory, and Abraham L. Udovitch. Princeton, N.J.: Darwin Press, 1988, pp. 211–237.

Wheatley, Edward. "'Blind' Jews and Blind Christians: Metaphorics of Marginalization in Medieval Europe." *Exemplaria* 14.2 (2002): 351–382.

See also **Almsgiving and Charity; Body in Literature and Religion; Body, Visual Representations of; Doctors and Healers; Feminist Theories and Methodologies; Hospitals; Infants and Infanticide; Lepers; Madness; Margaret "the Cripple" of Magdeburg; Medicine; Old Age; Plague; Poverty; Social Status**

DIVISION OF LABOR

Depictions of Adam working the land while Eve spins, and sometimes additionally cares for her children, can be found in various forms across Europe, probably originating in ninth-century Byzantium. This division of labor was incorporated into a proverb—"When Adam delved, and Eve span, who was then a gentleman?"—which first appeared in English sources in the late fourteenth century but is later found in a variety of languages. The origin of the motif is in part the Genesis story that Adam's punishment for listening to Eve was to toil for their food, whereas hers was the pain of childbirth and the rule of her husband. The ideology of separate roles for men and women can be found in a variety of sources, particularly clerical ones, but the extent to which it was a social reality is disputed.

One theory is that a gendered division of labor is less pronounced in preindustrial economies, as men and women labor together at or near their homes, than in industrialized ones. Another is that women are always more likely to specialize in household activities than men because breastfeeding makes childcare activities initially easier for women. The debate thus centers around the household and the conjugal unit, although it should be recognized that not all workers, male and female, were married. For the medieval period, the debate has largely focused on rural society, particularly on peasants in thirteenth- to fifteenth-century England, although most manufacturing was also carried out in the household in medieval Europe. The household was a key unit in the organization of medieval labor, but peasant labor not only consisted of that for the household (working their own land for subsistence, and household chores such as cooking, cleaning, and childcare), but also labor for the market (producing surplus goods for sale), labor for the lord (services owed at certain times by bonded tenants), and labor that was hired for wages.

As regards labor for the household, Hanawalt has used reports of death by misadventure from thirteenth- to fifteenth-century England to hypothesize that peasant men and women not only undertook different tasks but had separate spheres of activity. She found that most women died in or around their homes, for example, while fetching water, whereas men were more likely to die in the fields or forests, for example, while carting. Thus women's main sphere of work was the home, whereas men's was the fields and forests. Her main conclusion has been challenged by Goldberg, who pointed out that certain tasks, such as fetching water and carting, might be more risky and therefore over-represented in the sources. While other evidence suggests that carting was considered men's work, and fetching water was viewed as women's work, he argues that it does not necessarily follow that women were not undertaking other less dangerous activities in the fields, such as weeding, milking, shearing, reaping, and binding. Men and women, particularly at harvest time, performed many of the same tasks outside the home. Yet while there is evidence that women did work in the fields, household chores and childcare were clearly viewed as women's tasks. Mothers might delegate the care of children to others, but generally to older daughters or other women.

Manorial accounts show that women did undertake some of the same work as men for pay, such as reaping, binding, thatching, and shearing sheep. English wage evidence has led to debate about whether men and women received comparable pay, particularly after the Black Death of 1348–1349, which created a shortage of labor. Of relevance here is the argument that men could command higher wages because the most highly paid jobs, such as mowing and ploughing, continued to be reserved for men. Although there are examples of women undertaking such jobs, these are few and far between, with women making most inroads into the unskilled labor market. Hatcher has argued that this is because medieval men as a group were physically stronger than medieval women as a group and so were more productive, but Bardsley counters that women might have more stamina and that physical factors alone do not explain their exclusion from certain jobs. Although there is much evidence, from urban areas as well as rural, that women undertook a wide variety of jobs, there is less evidence of women being trained in those seen as highly skilled and so highly paid. Gender ideologies thus had some impact on a division of labor.

CORDELIA BEATTIE

References and Further Reading

Bardsley, Sandy. "Reply." *Past and Present* 173.1 (2001): 199–202.

Emigh, Rebecca Jean. "The Gender Division of Labour: The Case of Tuscan Small Holders." *Continuity and Change* 15.1 (2000): 117–137.

Goldberg, P. J. P. "The Public and the Private: Women and the Pre-Plague Economy." In *Thirteenth-Century England*, edited by Peter R. Coss and S. D. Lloyd. Woodbridge, Suffolk: Boydell Press, 1991, pp. 75–89.

Hanawalt, Barbara A. *The Ties That Bound: Peasant Families in Medieval England.* New York: Oxford University Press, 1986.

Hatcher, John. "Women's Work Reconsidered: Gender and Wage Differentiation in Late Medieval England." *Past and Present* 173.1 (2001): 191–198.

Middleton, Christopher. "The Sexual Division of Labour in Feudal England." *New Left Review* 113–114 (1979): 147–168.

See also **Agriculture; England; Household Management; Work**

DIVORCE AND SEPARATION

Law and practice on the matter of divorce and separation were subject to a number of different influences and underwent major changes between c. 450 and 1500. Divorce was widely available in Roman times. Marriages were automatically dissolved in certain circumstances, such as the captivity or enslavement of one of the spouses; divorce by mutual consent was easy, and either party could seek a divorce unilaterally.

The attitude of the early Christians was decidedly different, since there was an emphasis on the equality of men and women before God and marriage as a spiritual bond. The Christian fathers therefore tended to stress indissolubility, despite certain pronouncements by Christ which seemed to allow a man to divorce his wife for adultery. Early Church councils prohibited divorce in general, but allowed it in the case of Christians married to Jews, pagans, or heretics. They vacillated over the question of divorce or separation on grounds of adultery, with considerable variation in pronouncements as to whether this was allowable at all, and, if so, whether it was applicable equally to both sexes and whether or not either spouse could remarry. Secular laws promulgated by Christian emperors allowed men to divorce their wives for adultery, sorcery, or procuring, while women could divorce husbands for homicide, sorcery, or desecrating tombs. However, the prohibition of remarriage or the imposition of a delay that varied according to the seriousness of the grounds for divorce makes it clear that divorce could still, in practice, be obtained for trivial causes.

Divorce was also practised among the Germanic tribes, as reflected in their law codes. Divorce by mutual consent was generally available, and men could divorce their wives unilaterally, not only for adultery but also for sorcery, barrenness, or violation of tombs, and without any serious grounds if they were prepared to offer monetary compensation. Women either could not divorce their husbands at all or could do so only for such serious offences as homicide, sorcery, or violation of tombs or for homosexuality or forcing them into sexual acts with another man. The church made no effort to combat such divorces, concentrating its attention on the prohibition of incestuous marriages, including those of couples linked by affinity as a result of marriages of relatives or by godparenthood, as well as blood relationships. Since such couples were encouraged to part, this must have increased the number of separations insofar as these strictures were effective and it was necessary to check abuses, such as women standing as godmother to their own children in order to obtain separation from their husbands.

Matrimonial jurisdiction was still regarded as a secular matter; but, under the Carolingians, efforts were made to establish the indissolubility of marriage by limiting the grounds on which a marriage could be dissolved and not permitting even a man who separated from a wife on grounds of adultery to remarry during her lifetime. Practice always lagged some way behind these principles, at least for the kings and nobles to whom most records relate. Until the seventh century, Merovingian rulers had practised polygamy, and even after that, unilateral repudiations of wives were not unknown. Charlemagne himself repudiated at least one wife, the daughter of Desiderius, king of the Lombards, in that case with the support of the

pope, who had opposed a marriage alliance with his Lombard enemies. But the climate of opinion was changing, and bishops were taking a more active role in matrimonial cases, though not claiming exclusive jurisdiction. The change became clear when, in 858, Lothar II of Lotharingia attempted to free himself from his marriage to Theutberga in order to marry his concubine, Waldrada. He did not simply repudiate Theutberga, as Charlemagne had done with King Desiderius' daughter, but felt it necessary to accuse her of the very serious crime of incest with her brother before her marriage, which, if proven, would indeed have precluded her from contracting any subsequent marriage. The case dragged on before secular and ecclesiastical assemblies, with references to Hincmar, archbishop of Reims, and appeals to the pope; Lothar was compelled at last to take Theutberga back and finally obtained absolution in Rome only just before his own death in 869. One of the most significant aspects of this and other contemporary cases is the increased involvement of bishops and the papacy in matrimonial questions.

The Church's View of Marriage

In the context of the Gregorian Reform and the development of canon law the church sought to obtain exclusive jurisdiction over marriage disputes and impose its own view of marriage, both in defining what constituted a valid marriage and in establishing the principle of indissolubility. It based marriage on the consent of the two parties, provided they were of canonical age to marry, which was normally twelve for a woman and fourteen for a man, and were not debarred from contracting the marriage by reason of kinship within the prohibited degrees, ties of affinity or spiritual kinship, marital ties to some other party, or religious vows. If a couple who were thus free to contract marriage pronounced the intention of taking each other as man and wife at that present moment (*per verba de presenti*) and or also in the future (*per verba de futuro*), and if that declaration was completed by consummation, their marriage was indissoluble. There could be no divorce in the modern sense of the ending of an undoubtedly valid marriage and the freeing of the couple to contract new unions.

There were limited circumstances under which a *divortium* could be pronounced, but these always constituted either an annulment or a separation, not a divorce in the modern sense. Despite the fact that the church based marriage on consent and not consummation, it was possible to obtain an annulment (*divortium a vinculo*) on the grounds that one of the spouses was unable to consummate the marriage. With that exception, annulments had to be justified on the basis that the marriage had never existed because of an impediment, such as a precontract by one or both of the parties, ties of consanguinity or affinity, or the fact that one or both parties were under the canonical age for marriage or had been forced into consenting. If an annulment was granted, the parties were as free to marry someone else as they had been before the disputed union. *Divortium a mensa et thoro* or separation could be granted on the grounds of adultery, heresy, apostasy, or cruelty. This authorised the couple to live apart but did not bring the marriage to an end, and neither party could remarry during the lifetime of the other.

Despite notorious cases among kings and the nobility, such as Philip II of France's attempt to divorce his wife Ingeborg, and despite the records of many matrimonial cases brought before church courts in the later Middle Ages, petitions for divorce were not very frequent. Suits to enforce a disputed marriage were far more common than cases where a divorce or separation was sought. Divorce or separation was not easy to obtain. Ecclesiastical courts were aware of the danger of collusion and were unwilling to accept the declarations of the parties without evidence. Standards of proof were exacting, where such things as consanguinity or cruelty were alleged, and by no means were all those petitioning for divorce or separation successful. Court records and casual references in other sources suggest that many ordinary people did not have recourse to the courts if they wanted to end their marriage but simply left their spouse and went to live as man and wife with someone else. Some subsequently found themselves before the courts, but many more were probably successful in avoiding attention.

CHRISTINE MEEK

References and Further Reading

Airlie, Stuart. "Private Bodies and the Body Politic in the Divorce Case of Lothar II." *Past and Present* 161 (1998): 3–38.

Bishop, Jane. "Bishops as Marital Advisors in the Ninth Century." In *Women of the Medieval World*, edited by Julius Kirshner and Suzanne F. Wemple. Oxford: Basil Blackwell, Oxford, 1985.

Brundage, James A. *Law, Sex and Christian Society in Medieval Europe.* Chicago and London, University of Chicago Press, 1987.

Conklin, George. "Ingeborg of Denmark, Queen of France, 1193–1223." In *Queens and Queenship in Medieval Europe: Proceedings of a Conference Held at King's College London*, edited by Anne J. Duggan. Woodbridge, Suffolk: Boydell Press, 1997, pp. 39–52.

Esmein, Adhemar. *Le marriage en droit canonique.* 2 vols., Paris: Larose et Forcel, 1891.

Finch, Andrew. "*Repulsa uxore sua*: Marital Difficulties and Separation in the Later Middle Ages." *Continuity and Change* 8 (1993): 189–204.

Helmholz, Richard H. *Marriage Litigation in Medieval England.* Cambridge: Cambridge University Press, 1974.

McNamara, Jo Ann, and Suzanne F. Wemple. "Marriage and Divorce in the Frankish Kingdom." In *Women in Medieval Society*, edited by Susan Mosher Stuard. Philadelphia: University of Pennsylvania Press, 1976, pp. 95–124.

Pedersen, Frederick. *Marriage Disputes in Medieval England.* London: Hambledon Press, London, 2000.

Sheehan, Michael M. "The Formation and Stability of Marriage in Fourteenth-Century England: Evidence of an Ely Register." *Medieval Studies* 33 (1971): 228–263.

See also **Children, Betrothal and Marriage of; Marriage, Christian; Marriage, Impediments to; Remarriage**

DOCTORS AND HEALERS

Medical practice in medieval Europe encompassed a diverse array of healers. Learned physicians competed with a wide variety of lay practitioners for patients, and doctors did not always have an advantage over other healers in terms of expertise. Female practitioners treated both men and women, and female patients also sought help from men as well as women. This pluralism presented both opportunities and constraints for medieval women who practiced medicine. Women were excluded from universities and often from guilds, the formal institutions of medicine, limiting their ability to practice with an official license. At the same time, a large number of women worked informally as unlicensed healers.

There were a few officially sanctioned female healing professions. Until the seventeenth century, midwives were invariably female, and midwifery frequently fell under town or church licensing procedures. Ideals of female modesty, especially in southern Europe, dictated that male practitioners could not touch the female body, which meant that midwives often worked in conjunction with male practitioners. In hospitals, which were run by religious orders, nuns worked as doctors and nurses, especially for female patients. A number of women also gained renown as general practitioners before the advent of medical licensing. Most famous among these was the twelfth-century healer Trota of Salerno. Moreover, the example of Hildegard of Bingen, a German abbess in the mid-twelfth century, demonstrates that women could be highly learned in medical theory. Hildegard's medical treatise, *Causae et Curae* (*Causes and Cures*), presented a complex system of disease and health that drew on works of Aristotle and Galen, two pillars of academic medicine.

By the fourteenth century, however, licensing regulations made it difficult for women to work as healers legally. Universities, the gold standard of medical education from the thirteenth century onward, excluded women, a policy that continued until the late eighteenth century. Nevertheless, a number of women did gain recognition as physicians. Several Muslim women were licensed as general practitioners in fourteenth-century Valencia, while in late fourteenth- and early fifteenth-century Frankfurt, a few Jewish women practiced as eye doctors. It was often easier for non-Christian women to work as physicians, since both Muslims and Jews, who were also banned from the universities, had separate systems of medical licensing. All the same, in Italy and England, women occasionally surfaced in town records as *medica* (doctor), and there were certainly others who did not make it into official records. It is often easiest to find female practitioners through court trials against them; in 1322, for example, Jacoba Felice was convicted of practicing medicine without a university license in Paris.

Women had an easier time gaining membership in guilds, which licensed surgeons, barbers, and apothecaries. Most English barber and surgical guilds accepted women after licensing began in the late fourteenth century, and a number of women worked in these professions. Surgical guilds in Italy frequently permitted women to practice as well; in thirteenth- and fourteenth-century Naples, for example, twenty-four women were listed as surgeons. Even so, the numbers of women operating as licensed practitioners in traditionally male professions was fairly small, and in many cases those who did practice took over a family business from a deceased husband or father. Female medical practitioners worked most often as part-time healers, and many women had difficulty both affording the steep guild fees and working the long hours required for professional practitioners.

Most of the medical care women provided took place outside of official licensing systems. Women generally were responsible for the basic care of a household or estate, which included making medical salves, pills, drinks, baths, and other remedies. They frequently oversaw the cultivation of herb gardens, which provided many of the ingredients for medications. Letters between members of the English Paston family show that women considered themselves competent medical practitioners, and household medical care of this sort was ubiquitous and routine.

In addition to domestic care, women worked commercially in a variety of informal, unlicensed vocations, as herb gatherers, leeches, wise-women, nurses, and empirics. Although this technically was illegal, prosecutions generally took place only when a licensed practitioner complained of loss of clientele. Physicians and surgeons took great pains to restrict competition, and they frequently demanded stricter licensing procedures and criticized women healers as dangerous. Nonetheless, health care in medieval Europe was a fluid system, and women healers abounded in all areas despite official restrictions.

ALISHA RANKIN

References and Further Reading

Broomhall, Susan. *Women's Medical Work in Early Modern France.* Manchester: Manchester University Press, 2004.

"The Case of a Woman Doctor in Paris." In *The Portable Medieval Reader*, edited by James Bruce Ross and Mary McLaughlin. New York: Penguin, 1977, pp. 635–640.

Glaze, Florence Eliza. "Medical Writer: 'Behold the Human Creature'." In *Voice of the Living Light: Hildegard of Bingen and Her World*, edited by Barbara Newman. Berkeley: University of California Press, 1998, pp. 125–148.

Green, Monica H., ed. *The Trotula.* Philadelphia: University of Pennsylvania Press, 2001.

Green, Monica. "Women's Medical Practice and Health Care in Medieval Europe." *Signs: Journal of Women in Culture and Society* 14 (1989): 434–473.

———. "The Possibilities of Literacy and the Limits of Reading: Women and the Gendering of Medical Literacy." In *Women's Healthcare in the Medieval West*, Essay 7. Aldershot: Ashgate Variorum, 2000.

Park, Katharine. "Medicine and Magic: The Healing Arts." In *Gender and Society in Renaissance Italy*, edited by Judith Brown and Robert C. Davis. London: Longman, 1998.

Rawcliffe, Carole. *Medicine and Society in Later Medieval England.* London: Sandpiper Books, 1995.

Stoudt, Debra L. "Medieval German Women and the Power of Healing." In *Women Healers and Physicians: Climbing a Long Hill*, edited by Lilan R. Furst. Lexington: University of Kentucky Press, 1997, pp. 13–42.

Whitaker, Elaine E. "Reading the Paston Letters Medically." *English Language Notes* 31. 3 (1993): 19–27.

See also **Gynecology; Hildegard of Bingen; Hospitals; Magic and Charms; Medicine; Midwives; Plague; Trota of Salerno; Universities**

DOGARESSE

Sources often referred to the wife of the doge of Venice as *ductrix* or dogaressa. The office of dogaressa evolved in conjunction with that of her spouse. In the eighth through twelfth centuries the dogeship was a quasi-hereditary position with few limits on its authority. During this time doges and their families often sought interregional and international alliances, so that several early dogaresse were foreign-born, royal, and powerful. For example, Doge Pietro IV Candiano (960–976) repudiated his first wife to marry Waldrada, a descendant of the Lombard

King Ugo of Arles, and claim a sizable dowry of territories on the mainland. After his murder, Waldrada used her royal status to seek the protection of Empress Adelaide, the mother of German Emperor Otto II, whose intervention resulted in the return of Waldrada's dowry and her husband's property. Similarly, eleventh-century Doge Domenico Selvo enhanced his personal wealth and prestige as well as Venice's ties to the Byzantine Empire through his marriage to Teodora Ducas, the sister of Byzantine Emperor Michael Ducas.

The Venetian move towards a more republican model of statehood in the late Middle Ages created in the dogaressa a much altered and virtually unique female civic position. Venetians installed a series of institutions and legislative restrictions meant to check the doge's unlimited authority. In particular, the *promissione ducale* (oath of office) defined the identity of the late medieval dogaressa and restricted her mobility and authority, but also laid out some of her ceremonial functions. This document, revised for each doge, intimated that his spouse should be Venetian, and required that she, along with the doge and their descendants, limit their commercial dealings and their exchange of gifts. The oath codified the political obligations of the dogaressa through its concern with her ability to build alliances or intercede on the behalf of family or friends. Her husband's elected position and concerns about the threat of dynastic tyranny further denied the dogaressa the maternal influence and patronage exercised by consorts in courtly societies. While Venetian political structures, and particularly the *promissione*, limited her overt authority, the oath also confirmed the dogaressa's significant place in ducal, civic, and religious ceremony.

The *promissione* directed that the dogaressa swear to uphold the oath in a governmental ritual, making her the only nonruling European female to take a constitutional vow. An increasingly elaborate entrance ceremony followed the dogaressa's oath. Escorted by governmental representatives in lieu of her husband, whose absence negated royal implications, the dogaressa proceeded from her home to the church of San Marco, and then to the Doge's Palace, in a ritual that mimicked Venetian marital rites, featured dozens of women, and highlighted the social networks and offspring that females contributed to the state. In addition to her entrance, the dogaressa worshiped daily in San Marco, and regularly attended religious rituals there with her spouse. Kneeling votive images of the dogaressa on the tombs of several medieval doges are further indicative of unique female piety. Together the doge and dogaressa promoted the civic values of family and religiosity.

By the fifteenth century, some dogaresse became yet more prominent and visible, as their spouses attempted to harness the symbolism and personal charisma employed by their mainland princely neighbors. Marina Nani Foscari, the wife of ambitious expansionist Doge Francesco Foscari (1423–1457), functioned as an envoy in the frequent guided tours of Venice she conducted for the visiting wives of Italian and European dignitaries, demonstrating the mercantile and military strengths of her city as she helped to forge diplomatic alliances. Foscari and his successor, Doge Pasquale Malipiero (1457–1462), expressed their princely ambition with artistic and architectural patronage, mimicking nearby courtly societies. Dogaressa Giovanna Dandolo Malipiero achieved similar public visibility to her predecessor when her image appeared on the reverse of a medal of her spouse that imagined doge and dogaressa jointly as rulers and protectors of the city-state. Dogaressa Taddea Michiel Mocenigo, spouse of Doge Giovanni Mocenigo (1478–1485) achieved comparable public prominence only in death; the plague claimed her life in 1479 and prompted the institution of an elaborate funeral for the dogaressa based on that of the doge.

The prominent place achieved by the medieval dogaressa in the civic ideology of Venice largely diminished after the fifteenth century. From 1485 until the end of the republic, only ten doges had living wives. In the sixteenth century, two dogaresse became the focal point for elaborate public spectacles, but the more common widowed or bachelor doges of the early modern period rendered the dogaresse rare relics with greatly diminished public prominence and significance.

HOLLY HURLBURT

References and Further Reading

Hurlburt, Holly S. *The Dogaressa of Venice: Wife and Icon.* New York: Palgrave Macmillan, 2005.
Molmenti, Pompeo. *La dogaressa di Venezia.* Turin: L. Roux, 1887.
Muir, Edward. *Civic Ritual in Renaissance Venice.* Princeton, N.J.: Princeton University Press, 1981.

See also **Italy**

DOLCE OF WORMS

Dolce of Worms (d. 1196) came from medieval German Jewry's elite leadership class. The wife of Rabbi Eleazar ben Judah of Worms (1165–1230), a leading figure in the *Hasidei Ashkenaz*, the German–Jewish pietist movement, Dolce supported financially an extensive household, including children, students, and teachers. According to her husband's eyewitness account, she was murdered, with her daughters Bellette and Hannah, by intruders who were probably attracted by Dolce's reputation as a moneylender. In accordance with the Emperor's mandate protecting the Jews of his realm, the miscreants were quickly captured and executed. Closely based on Proverbs 31, praising the "woman of valor," R. Eleazar's Hebrew elegy details his wife's domestic, religious, and communal endeavors, and, despite its formulaic structure, is an important source for medieval Jewish women's activities. R. Eleazar designates Dolce as *hasidah* (pious or saintly) and *tzadeket* (righteous); in addition to domestic management and business finesse, he praises her needlework, recounting that she prepared thread and gut to sew together books, Torah scrolls, and other religious objects. Unusually learned for a woman of her milieu, Dolce taught other women and led them in prayer. She adorned brides and prepared the dead for burial, meritorious endeavors in Jewish tradition. R. Eleazar especially reveres his wife for facilitating the spiritual activities of the men of her household; the reward he invokes for Dolce at the conclusion of his lament is to be wrapped in the eternal life of Paradise, a tribute to her deeds, on which so many depended.

JUDITH BASKIN

References and Further Reading

Baskin, Judith R. "Women Saints in Judaism: Dolce of Worms." In *Women Saints in World Religions*, edited by Arvind Sharma. Albany, N.Y.: State University of New York Press, 2000, pp. 39–69.

———. "Dolce of Worms: The Lives and Deaths of an Exemplary Medieval Jewish Woman and Her Daughters." In *Judaism in Practice: From the Middle Ages Through the Early Modern Period*, edited by Lawrence Fine. Princeton, N.J.: Princeton University Press, 2001.

See also **Death, Mourning, and Commemoration; Germanic Lands; Investment and Credit; Jewish Women; Literature: Hebrew; Marriage, Jewish**

DOMESTIC ABUSE

Domestic abuse and/or violence has emerged as an important area of scholarly inquiry in medieval studies. Prompted by the efforts of social historians and anthropologists to provide a broader picture of the history of the institution of marriage as well as family life, kinship relations, child-rearing practices, and domestic customs in the Middle Ages, the body of work available on this topic has grown rapidly.

Such growth is sustained by the widespread representation of acts of familial violence in the many genres produced by medieval culture, including romance, hagiography, spiritual autobiography, biography, drama, sermons, conduct and advice manuals, family sagas, penitentials, wisdom literature, folk tales, iconography, and other visual media. Of particular concern to scholars in this area of research is the relationship of cultural production to everyday medieval life.

Biblical Examples

Many of the representations found in the genres named above reiterate scenes of family disharmony depicted in the Old Testament. Extreme family violence—fratricide, matricide, patricide—and milder forms of abuse demonstrated in corporal punishment or psychological intimidation become recurrent motifs in subsequent genres. From the disobedience of the first parents of Genesis to Cain's murder of his brother, Abraham's interrupted sacrifice of Isaac, and the contentious family relations of patriarchs such as Noah, tests of faith in the Old Testament depend upon an urgent need for discipline and obedience to an often angry and jealous deity.

The familial harmony depicted in New Testament scenes of the Holy Family appears to mitigate the harsh characterization of the Old Testament family; constructed as a unique model of human relationship, this exceptional family suggests that the gap between the literal and the spiritual worlds can be bridged not only by faith but by divine transformation. Whether cast in symbolic language or more material terms, the family remains an important touchstone for early conceptions of Christianity. Yet Paul's epistles offer contradictory advice on how best to achieve family harmony. On the one hand, wives and children were admonished to obey their husbands and fathers (Ephesians) while on the other marriage was proclaimed to be a union based upon mutual respect (1 Corinthians). The gap between an implicit hierarchy in the former and an egalitarian ideal of mutuality in the latter suggests that negotiations between spouses could be left open to interpretation.

These sorts of concerns are not unique to scriptural texts; they also appear in the mythologies, epic poetry, and literature of the ancient world. From the poetry of Homer to the domestic tragedies of Aeschylus's *Orestia*, Sophocles' Oedipus trilogy, and Euripides' *Medea*, the concerns of the family are paramount to public governance and the idea of justice. However the idea of that most basic of social units is construed at different times and in different places, it stands as the cornerstone of human civilization and the raw material from which cultural representations of all kinds emerge. The tales that these ancient works reiterate time and again are didactic and cautionary, yet the reiteration of the tropes of domestic abuse/violence over time in so many genres in such a wide variety of venues suggests that it has always been possible to represent the "dysfunctional" family because it has always been a feature of human society.

Paternal Power

The Middle Ages did not invent domestic abuse, but as with all cultures immersed in the values represented by traditional narratives of the past as well as actively engaged in their reproduction, medieval writers and lawmakers inherited many assumptions and legal proclivities from the past. Roman and Germanic law codes, patristic writings, scriptural archetypes, proverbial wisdom, and customary practices and entrenched ritual traditions contributed to a model of domestic governance predicated upon the entitlement of the *paterfamilias* and his right to presume legitimate authority (*patria potestas*) over the subordinate members of his household—wife, children, and various others. At the same time, obedience remained a tacit dictum for members of the household living under the aegis of this ruling authority.

Despite its lack of a semantic category ("domestic abuse" and/or "domestic violence" are contemporary terms), the medieval discourse on the subject often revolved around disciplinary customs and procedures underwritten by some of the inherited assumptions mentioned above. Household justice incurred was expected to be reasonable and appropriate to the infraction. Moreover, the episodes of domestic abuse discernible in the literature, as well as in the documentary evidence, suggest that medieval European populations had a keen awareness of the boundaries between acceptable discipline and outright cruelty. In spiritual autobiographies such as Augustine's *Confessions* or the *Book of Margery Kempe*, for instance, the allusions to domestic abuse—the abuse of Monica, Augustine's mother, or the suffering of a small child that prompts empathy in Margery—are presented as features of everyday life that one simply had to assimilate in order to acquire the discipline needed to endure this life in preparation for the next. Nonetheless, what distinguished a form of mild abuse from a cruel violation of personhood was largely a matter of interpretation. Stripes on the back or bruises to parts of the body typically covered and hidden from public view were marks of violation not

as likely to arouse intervention from extended kin or concerned neighbors as more public forms of domestic violence would be, that is, if the perpetrator carried on the abuse in plain view of witnesses.

Domestic Rebellion

Just as domestic tyranny accompanied by acts of violence was not condoned, so too was domestic rebellion by subordinate household members strongly discouraged. Disrespectful or assertive wives could find themselves on a cucking stool or in the stocks for a minor infraction such as a burned dinner or talking back to their husbands. Should a wife's silent protracted suffering suddenly explode in an act of retaliation or self-defense (that is, murder of her husband), she could find herself condemned both for homicide and treason for which she would be burned at the stake. In terms of the law, a wife in England was deemed a *feme covert*, located literally *sub virga et potentate* ("under the rod and authority") of her husband.

Guidelines for Behavior

Legal records, papal epistles, eyewitness accounts, and various other kinds of written testimony point to the fact of domestic abuse as well as to the existence of an ongoing debate about how the household *should be* equitably governed, how children *should be* raised and educated, how spousal relations *should be* negotiated. Then, as now, there were many approaches to achieving stability within the household and conflicting attitudes about how parents should discipline their children. The famous proverb attributed to Solomon, "spare the rod and spoil the child," popular among authoritarian-minded adults, endorsed the beating of a child as a demonstration of a parent's love and concern for the child's salvation. The opposing point of view was constructed as a feminine and therefore ineffective means by which to discipline unruly young men. Didactic literature on the topic includes *Stans Puer ad Mensam*, *Peter Idley's Instructions to His Son*, and *How the Good Man Taught His Son*, while advice to young women rendered along similar lines appears in works such as *How the Good Wife Taught Her Daughter*, *The Book of the Knight of the Tower*, and Christine de Pizan's *Book of the Treasury of Ladies*.

Guidelines for behavior also find articulation in the sermons of Bernardino of Siena and the written rules for marriage, such as Cherubino of Spoleto's *Regale della vita matrimoniale*, which encourages a husband to correct his wife's offenses gently before deploying more aggressive methods such as beating. Even canon law, written down by Gratian in his *Decretum,* assumed a husband's familial entitlement to be nearly sacrosanct; husbands were assumed to be capable of wielding their authority judiciously, and capable of making appropriate determinations on how much and what kind of discipline should be deployed for the adequate correction of household members. Neither Gratian nor the commentators of the *Glossa Ordinaria* (*Ordinary Gloss*) such as Johannes Teutonicus advocated severe corporal punishment; they simply made it clear that a husband had the legal right to any form of "castigation" that he deemed appropriate for the circumstances.

In a system that most often assumed husbands and fathers governed their households reasonably, it is easy to understand how a gap could arise between a theory of family relationship and its interpretation both by individuals and by legal institutions. Domestic abuse could be construed as a prerequisite for measuring the potential of a saint, hero, or heroine, in an enactment of the kind of discipline needed to hone the protagonist or the aspiring martyr into readiness. Suffering was considered a means by which to prepare the human will to face the consequences of a cruel world; it functioned as a marker of human mortality and a reminder to prepare the soul for the afterlife. It is no coincidence that the icons of suffering in the Middle Ages are the Virgin Mary and her son.

It is important to note that regional variations as well as historical differences affect how we understand domestic abuse in the Middle Ages. Most cases in the legal records address the husband's abuse of his wife, though there are variations on this theme and numerous ways for the courts, most often ecclesiastical, to render judgment should a complaint reach that level of adjudication. Nonetheless, the increasing number of court documents and various other kinds of testimony that continue to surface from the historical archives indicate a tangible link between actual incidents of domestic abuse and representations of that abuse.

EVE SALISBURY

References and Further Reading

Bednarski, Steven. "Keeping It in the Family? Domestic Violence in the Later Middle Ages: Examples from a Provencal Town (1340–1403)." In *Love, Marriage, and Family Ties in the Later Middle Ages*, edited by Isabel Davis, et al. Turnhout: Brepols, 2003, pp. 277–297.
Brozyna, Martha A. "Not Just a Family Affair: Domestic Violence and the Ecclesiastical Courts in Late Medieval Poland." In *Love, Marriage and Family Ties in the Later Middle Ages*, edited by Isabel Davis, et al. Turnhout: Brepols, 2003, pp. 299–309.
Brundage, James A. "Domestic Violence in Classical Canon Law." In *Violence in the Middle Ages*, edited by Richard Kaueper. Woodbridge, Suffolk: Boydell & Brewer, 2002, pp. 183–195.
Hanawalt, Barbara. "Violence in the Domestic Milieu of Late Medieval England." In *Violence in the Middle Ages*, edited by Richard Kaeuper. Rochester: Boydell Press, 2002, pp. 197–214.
Hoppenbrouwers, P. C. M. "Vengeance Is Ours? The Involvement of Kin in the Settlement of 'Cases of Vengeance' in Later Medieval Holland." In *Love, Marriage, and Family Ties in the Later Middle Ages*, edited by Isabel Davis, Miriam Muller, and Sarah Rees Jones. Turnhout: Brepols, 2003, pp. 241–275.
Maddern, Philippa C. *Violence and Social Order: East Anglia 1422–1442*. New York: Oxford University Press, 1996.
McSheffery, Shannon. *Love and Marriage in Late Medieval London*. Kalamazoo, Mich.: Medieval Institute Publications, 1995.
Müller, Miriam. "Conflict, Strife, and Cooperation: Aspects of the Late Medieval Family and Household." In *Love, Marriage, and Family Ties in the Later Middle Ages*, edited by Isabel Davis, et al. Turnhout: Brepols, 2003, pp. 311–329.
Murray, Jacqueline, ed. *Love, Marriage, and Family in the Middle Ages: A Reader*. Peterborough: Broadview Press, 2001.
Salisbury, Eve, Georgiana Donavin, and Merrall L. Price, eds. *Domestic Violence in Medieval Texts*. Gainesville: University Press of Florida, 2002.

See also **Conduct Literature; Family; Feme Covert; Godelieve of Gistel; Husbands and Husbandry; Kempe, Margery; Law, Canon; Marriage Ceremonies; Marriage, Christian; Marriage and Concubinage in Scandinavia; Marriage, Impediments to; Marriage, Islamic: Iberia; Marriage, Jewish; Marriage Preaching; Violence; Woman on Top**

DOMESTICITY

Domesticity can be identified in fourteenth-century England as a specifically urban set of values associated with a particular mode of living. It was characteristic of the households of the "burgesses," men who formed the privileged group from whom the towns' elites and officeholders were drawn. These households or *familiae*—husband and wife, children, servants, and apprentices—lived and worked together in multiroom houses, increasingly built of timber-frame (a new technology in the thirteenth century) on several floors. Their houses were not only residential spaces but were also sites of business and manufacture. The later separation of the workplace (gendered masculine) from the home (gendered feminine) cannot have been the norm among the fourteenth-century bourgeoisie.

By the fifteenth century the distinction between the housing of the poor and that of the better-off was well-established. The record-keepers of Coventry, for example, regularly distinguished between cottages of one or two rooms and what they called "hall places"; in Winchester the larger houses were identified as "tenements." Already in Colchester in 1301, however, multiroom houses are in evidence in inventories made for tax purposes. Many households occupied two-room dwellings, but a minority lived in larger houses: one of the biggest was Roger the Dyer's house, which had four rooms: a hall, a chamber, a kitchen, and a brewhouse. This is very like the house of Emma Hatfield, a London chandler's widow, who died in 1373, or Thomas Baker, a York stringer, who died in 1436: the houses of both consisted of a hall, a chamber, a kitchen, and a shop, and Emma Hatfield had a storehouse in addition.

Many of their contemporaries lived in slightly larger houses with up to a dozen rooms. They were versatile and flexible spaces for eating and sleeping, for buying, selling, and storing goods, and for manufacture and production. Surviving inventories show that in the fourteenth century the inhabitants of geographically quite distant towns had a shared understanding of the organization of domestic space. There was always an *aula* (hall) in which people sat and ate. There was also always at least one room called a *camera* (chamber) in which people slept, though often not alone. There was frequently a kitchen and, in addition, very often a shop (which could be a workroom or a retail space), a storeroom, a brewhouse, and a boulting-house (where flour was sieved). Beyond these basic rooms, larger houses had other rooms such as a parlour, a winecellar, a grainroom, or occasionally a chapel, as well as additional chambers.

These homes differed from aristocratic townhouses in both size and the uses to which space was put. In the former, men and women lived and worked in close proximity to one another. The medieval meanings of the word *homely* (domestic) cluster around ideas of intimacy. Although as workplaces these houses were in some sense public and the work that went on them was subject to guild regulation and scrutiny, nevertheless, they were also understood as private. Domestic privacy was protected by law: eavesdropping, for example, was a punishable offence. Household members were able, if they chose, to eat, sleep, and work in different places, unlike the poor in their one-room cottages. Nevertheless, this spatial differentiation must have been a matter of control as well as of privacy. Hospitality, orderliness, a place for things, tidying away, the imposition of routines, and the management of time: these were more easily achievable and thus more desirable domestic goals when a whole family did not occupy one room in which eating, sleeping, childcare, and working endlessly overlapped.

The well-regulated burgess household was not, in these circumstances, one where trade or manufacture was separated from the rest of living (which became a nineteenth-century ideal), but one where trade, manufacture, business, preparing food, cooking, eating, and sleeping were all understood as separate but interrelated aspects of domestic life and ordered as such. Domesticity, as a burgess value, is a reconceptualization of everyday space and time, a way of making intimacy tolerable rather than oppressive. William Langland's evocation in *Piers Plowman* of the hardships of women who live in a single room can be contrasted with Geoffrey Chaucer's distillation of the bourgeois way of life in "The Shipman's Tale." The poor woman in her hovel, cold and hungry, rocks the cradle, cards and combs wool, patches and washes, cleans flax, winds yarn, and strips rushes. The merchant's wife calls her husband down from his upstairs office to a meal prepared by their cook, after spending the early morning chatting in her garden, accompanied by her servant girl. Her guest has drawn attention to the hour on his portable timepiece. It is no coincidence that this orderly and differentiated way of life should become visible in the fourteenth century, during the period of the time revolution, with the invention of the fixed hour.

FELICITY RIDDY

References and Further Reading

Chaucer, Geoffrey. "The Shipman's Tale." In *The Riverside Chaucer*, edited by Larry D. Benson, et al. 3rd ed. Oxford: Oxford University Press, 1987.

Davidoff, Leonore, and Catherine Hall. *Family Fortunes: Men and Women of the English Middle Class 1780–1850*. London: Routledge, 1987.

Dohrn-van Rossum, Gerhard. *History of the Hour: Clocks and Modern Temporal Orders*, translated by Thomas Dunlap. Chicago: Chicago University Press, 1996.

Grenville, Jane. *Medieval Housing*. London and Washington: Leicester University Press, 1997.

Langland, William. *Piers Plowman: the C-Text*, edited by Derek Pearsall. Exeter: Exeter University Press, 1994.

Rybczynski, Witold. *Home: A Short History of an Idea*. New York: Viking, 1986.

Schofield, John. *Medieval London Houses*. New Haven and London: Yale University Press, 1994.

See also **Architecture, Domestic; Artisan Families, Women of; Home Manufacturing; Household Management; Merchant Families, Women of**

DOMINICAN ORDER

Dominic de Guzman (c. 1170–1221) cooperated with religious women long before Honorius III formally approved his Order of Friars Preachers (*Ordo Fratrum Praedicatorum*) on 22 December 1216. He was still a canon under Bishop Diego of Osma when the two helped to found a community for women in Prouille in southern France (1206). That these women were converts from Catharism, as is often claimed, cannot be substantiated and, even if true, the monastery became a seedbed for orthodoxy when its sisters were sent to guide women in new Dominican foundations. Even as the first constitutions of the Dominican order were passed in the general chapters of 1220 and 1221, the friars already had established ties with two other communities of religious women, a house in Madrid (1220) and San Sisto in Rome (1221). In 1223 Diana d'Andalo founded St. Agnes in Bologna in cooperation with Jordan of Saxony, Dominic's successor as the master general. By the mid-1240s several monasteries in Italy, France, and, in particular, Germany functioned in association with the friars, including Unterlinden in Colmar, Germany and St. Dominic in Montargis, France.

Nuns and Lay Women

Women's responses to Dominican friars' preaching were enthusiastic, but their position within the order remained ambiguous throughout the Middle Ages. While the friars themselves formed an organization with a clear chain of command from master general and general chapter to provincial leaders and priors of individual convents, the arrangements concerning women's houses were varied and subject to frequent, often disruptive, readjustments. In fact, the only feature consistently shared by all women's houses associated with Dominican friars was their adherence to the rather vague Rule of St. Augustine. Many communities were positioned under local bishops, but enjoyed the spiritual care of the Dominicans, hence the expression "nuns of the Order of St. Augustine under the care of the Friars Preachers," or *moniales Ordinis Sancti Augustini sub cura fratrum praedicatorum*. Some houses earned papal privileges that placed them directly under jurisdiction of Dominicans and enabled them to complement the Augustinian rule with the constitutions inspired by the Dominican ethos, but even these arrangements were markedly varied. Master General Humbert of Romans modified the friars' constitutions for women's use in 1259, but he failed to produce the intended uniformity, for many communities continued to follow the older constitution originally used at San Sisto, Rome, or simply abided by local statutes of various types.

The constitutionally complex histories of Dominican women's communities were matched by the equally intricate origins of these communities. Many houses began as communities for Beguines or other independent religious women. Such was the case with the vibrant German houses Engeltal and Katharinental (Diessenhofen), both of which secured a position within the order during the 1240s. Some were acquired from other orders, among them the renowned reformed monastery Corpus Domini (1394) in Venice, originally a Benedictine community. A few monasteries resulted from royal or aristocratic bequests, including King Bela IV of Hungary's foundation for his daughter Margaret (1242–1270), a future saint. More typically, however, Dominican monasteries were urban foundations by wealthy widows, signorial rulers, or powerful merchant families.

As there was no central planning concerning the administration of the houses for Dominican women, the state of individual communities was a sum of multiple variants, ranging from the resourcefulness of the women themselves and the standing of their secular patrons to the ever-changing reactions of the friars and the conflicting stances taken by bishops and popes. Some popes granted considerable favors to women's communities. Among them were Innocent IV, who in the mid-1240s sweepingly incorporated several women's houses into the order, and Clement IV, who in 1267 laid out clear guidelines concerning Dominican friars' spiritual duties toward nuns. But these statements hardly closed the debate concerning the *cura mulierum* (care of women) within the order. The subsequent pronouncements by the popes, bishops, and leaders of the order continued to adjust or even reverse earlier privileges. A notable exception in this pattern was the Observant Reform, which was launched in the late 1380s and prevalent throughout the fifteenth century. Within this movement, aimed at reviving the religious rigor associated with the early years of the order, some monasteries, such as Corpus Domini in Venice, St. Dominic in Pisa, Schönensteinbach near Colmar, and St. Catherine in Nuremberg, received unprecedented institutional stability in exchange for their prohibition of private ownership, otherwise common in medieval nunneries, and adherence to strict enclosure (*clausura*).

The question of women's status within the order was further complicated by the presence of laywomen. While the friars welcomed the rich mystical culture of the laity, and many groups met in their churches or even wore the order's colors of black and white, the friars were reluctant to formalize the bonds with these *mulieres religiosae*, who were often perceived as religiously heterodox and economically unstable. It is therefore striking that Catherine of Siena (1347–1380), who lived as a Dominican penitent before Innocent VII approved the Dominican lay rule in 1405, was the only woman associated with the order to be canonized during the Middle Ages (1461). (The canonizations of nuns Margaret of Hungary and Agnes of Montepulciano [1268–1317] and the lay-woman Zdislava of Lemberk [1220–1252] from Poland all occurred in the modern era.)

Dominican nuns' way of life was clearly distinct from that of the friars. Whereas the friars were committed to the itinerant life of learning and preaching, women's piety was essentially shaped by the traditional monastic ideal of communal prayer in seclusion.

The friars also received often considerable bequests in exchange for their spiritual services, but women were principally dependent on their dowries and support from wealthy patrons.

Spirituality

Despite their institutionally precarious position, Dominican women nonetheless made notable contributions to Dominican spirituality. The sole surviving text attributed to St. Dominic is, in fact, his undated letter to the prioress of the Dominican sisters in Madrid. Jordan of Saxony's letters to Diana d'Andalo, written during the 1220s and early 1230s, paint a vivid picture of the order's growth as Jordan interlaced his spiritual advice with enthusiastic reports concerning his successful recruitment throughout Europe. Diana's letters to Jordan have not survived, but Jordan's responses reveal that Diana promptly urged him to act on her behalf when the religious services offered by the local friars did not meet her high standards or when the friars and local clergymen questioned the arrangements between her community and the Dominican order. Diana thus shrewdly used her epistolary connections with the head of the order to shield her community against the pressures felt at the local level. This correspondence, together with Diana's savvy acquisitions of land and successful networking with the nuns at San Sisto, created a solid foundation for her community. The four nuns who moved from San Sisto to assist Diana's community had personally cooperated with Dominic. Among them was Cecilia Cesarini, who almost a half century after the saint's death dictated to a fellow nun her recollections, *The Miracles of St. Dominic*. This account offers a valuable perspective on Dominic as a popular preacher and a miracle-maker who enjoyed a considerable appeal among religious women. *The Miracles* also shows that, not unlike the friars, the women turned to the past, and in particular to their recollections of St. Dominic, in order to create continuity in their fragmented institutional history.

Also, the chronicles or *nonnenbücher,* produced by Dominican nuns in German-speaking countries principally during the fourteenth century, viewed the past through mysticism and miracles, but as women used these texts to legitimize the existence of their communities, the texts had a stringent practical function as well. Mysticism as a communally revitalizing and collectively celebrated phenomenon was particularly prominent in Engeltal, home of two visionary authors, Christine Ebner (1277–1356) and Adelheid Langmann (1312–1375). Bartolomea Riccoboni's early-fifteenth-century narration of Corpus Domini (Venice), a rare surviving example of women's chronicle writing outside German-speaking countries, aptly shows that nuns keenly followed the ecclesiastical events from their strictly enclosed community.

The chronicles are complemented by a few other notable mystical accounts by medieval women. *Revelations* by Margaretha Ebner (1291–1351), a nun at Maria Medingen in Bavaria, presents a case of a striking imitation of Christ's passion through prolonged illness. Catherine of Siena's *Dialogue,* a conversation between God and a soul, opens a panoramic vision to God's grace and Christian virtues, and her nearly four hundred letters show a fierce religious reformer inspiring both religious leaders and ordinary people to pious action. *Seven Revelations* of Lucia Brocadelli (1476–1544), a Dominican laywoman, is a triumphant account of a soul's visit to the heavenly court.

Women's corporal mystical experiences attracted the attention of the friars and even resulted in spiritual friendships, as was the case with Peter of Dacia and Christine of Stommeln, a Beguine known for her dramatic encounters with the devil; Henry of Nördlingen and Margaretha Ebner; and Raymond of Capua and Catherine of Siena. These spiritual bonds produced a rich body of hagiographic texts commemorating the passion of Christ through the celebration of women's self-denial and eucharistic piety. Religious reform provided a uniquely fertile ground for cooperation between women mystics and friars. This was particularly evident in the case of the visionary reformer Girolamo Savonarola, whose ascetic and eschatological message was kept alive among Dominican women mystics long after he was burned as a heretic in 1498.

MAIJU LEHMIJOKI-GARDNER

References and Further Reading

Catherine of Siena. *The Dialogue,* translated and introduced by Suzanne Noffke. New York: Paulist Press, 1980.

Catherine of Siena. *The Letters of Catherine of Siena,* translated with introduction and notes by Suzanne Noffke, 2 vols. Tempe, Ariz.: Arizona Center for Medieval and Renaissance Studies, 2000, 2001.

Cesarini, Cecilia. *The Miracles of St. Dominic.* In *Saint Dominic: Biographical Documents.* Washington, D.C.: The Thomist Press, 1964.

Coakley, John. "Friars as Confidants of Holy Women in Medieval Dominican Hagiography." In *Images of Sainthood in Medieval Europe,* edited by Renate Blumenfeld-Kosinski and Timea Szell. Ithaca, N.Y.: Cornell University Press, 1991, pp. 222–246.

Ebner, Margaret. *Major Works,* translated and edited by Leonard P. Hindsley. New York: Paulist Press, 1993.

Grundmann, Herbert. *Religious Movements in the Middle Ages,* translated by Steven Rowan. Notre Dame: University of Notre Dame Press, 1995.

Hinnebusch, William A. *The History of the Dominican Order: Origins and Growth to 1500.* Volume 1. Staten Island, N.Y.: Alba House, 1966.

Lehmijoki-Gardner, Maiju, ed., trans. *Dominican Penitent Women.* With contributions by Daniel E. Bornstein and E. Ann Matter. New York: Paulist Press, 2005.

Lehmijoki-Gardner, Maiju. "Writing Religious Rules as an Interactive Process: Dominican Penitent Women and the Making of Their *Regula.*" *Speculum 79* (2004): 660–687.

Lewis, Gertrud Jaron. *By Women, for Women, About Women: The Sister-Books of Fourteenth-Century Germany.* Toronto: Pontifical Institute of Mediaeval Studies, 1996.

Riccoboni, Bartolomea. *Life and Death in a Venetian Convent: The Chronicle and Necrology of Corpus Domini, 1395–1436,* edited and translated by Daniel Bornstein. Chicago: The University of Chicago Press, 2000.

Tugwell, Simon, ed. *Early Dominicans: Selected Writings.* New York: Paulist Press, 1982.

Vann, Gerald. *To Heaven with Diana!: A Study of Jordan of Saxony and Diana d'Andalo, with a translation of the letters of Jordan.* London: Collins, 1960.

Winston-Allen, Anne. *Convent Chronicles: Women Writing About Women and Reform in the Late Middle Ages.* University Park, Pa: The Pennsylvania State University Press, 2004.

See also **Catherine of Siena; Clothing for Religious Women; Ebner, Margaretha; Langmann, Adelheid; Monastic Enclosure; Monastic Rules; Monasticism and Nuns; Monasticism, Women's: Papal Policy; Mysticism and Mystics; Observant Movement; Sister-Books and Other Convent Chronicles; Spiritual Care**

DOROTHEA OF MONTAU

Born into a prosperous peasant family, Dorothea (1347–1394) experienced her first mystic vision at seven, and then began the harsh regime of fleshly mortification—burning herself with hot oil, branding herself with heated irons, and scourging herself with nail-studded whips—that continued throughout her life. At seventeen, Dorothea unwillingly married Adalbert, a weaponsmith more than twice her age, who physically and verbally abused her. She resented the dual expectations of sexual intercourse and wifely obedience, believing that obeying Adalbert meant betraying Christ. She mourned the loss of her virginity, and hated the birth of each of her nine children, only one of whom survived beyond childhood. Finally, Dorothea persuaded her husband to live chastely for the final ten years of their marriage.

In 1390, Dorothea made a pilgrimage to Rome, during which time Adalbert died. Free to pursue her spirituality, Dorothea needed a powerful confessor. After narrowly escaping heresy charges, Dorothea moved to Marienwerder and met one of the magisters, Johannes (d. 1417), an ambitious young Dominican and former canonical expert from the University of Prague, who became her sponsor. With his help, she became an anchoress during the final months of her life.

After Dorothea's death in 1394, Johannes undertook the task of securing her canonization. As part of that process, he compiled her official vita, which is based on Dorothea's own dictations to him, and derived from Dorothea's spiritual conversations with Johannes, but recast in a politically advantageous manner. Prussia was in a tenuous position, situated between their powerful neighbor Poland and the predominantly non-Christian Lithuania. Securing the canonization of the first native Prussian saint would not only have improved Johannes' own position within the Church, but would also have protected Prussian interests. Accounts of abuse are framed by discussions of stoic endurance as prayer. Scenes of marital rape are layered with glorious visions of spiritual union with Christ. Obedience, Dorothea's problem in life, becomes her mark of sainthood in death.

Although Dorothea was never officially canonized, her popularity never waned. In 1976, Pope Paul VI confirmed her cult as saint based on long-standing veneration.

Michelle M. Sauer

References and Further Reading

Elliott, Dyan. "Authorizing a Life: The Collaboration of Dorothea of Montau and John Marienwerder." In *Gendered Voices: Medieval Saints and Their Interpreters,* edited by Catherine M. Mooney. Philadelphia: University of Pennsylvania Press, 1999, pp. 168–191, 245–246.

Kieckhefer, Richard. *Unquiet Souls: Fourteenth-Century Saints and Their Religious Milieu.* Chicago: University of Chicago Press, 1984.

Marienwerder, Johannes. *The Life of Dorothea von Montau, A Fourteenth-Century Recluse*, translated by Ute Stargardt. Lewiston, N.Y.: Edward Mellen, 1997.

Sauer, Michelle M. "Anchoritism & Authority: Self-Signification in Dorothea von Montau's Vernacular Hagiography." *Anchoritic Spirituality: Texts and Contexts*, edited by Elizabeth Herbert McAvoy. Turnhout, Belgium: Brepols, forthcoming.

See also **Anchoresses; Asceticism; Chastity and Chaste Marriage; Hagiography; Rape and Raptus; Sexuality: Sex in Marriage; Violence**

DOUBLE MONASTERIES

Double monastery is a comparatively modern term coined by scholars to refer to a medieval religious community that housed both monks and nuns in the same institution, usually sharing a common superior and common worship space. Such communities were virtually never referred to as double monasteries by contemporaries, and lassifying all such houses by this anachronistic phrase has facilitated, in some scholarship, an empirically false unification of monastic institutions that were chronologically, regionally, and in practical and regulatory matters, extremely disparate and certainly unconnected. Thus there is a strong argument to be made for abolishing the term and even for discarding the dual-sex house as a category for historical analysis. But the term has become entrenched in scholarly writing on medieval monasticism, and the category itself has proven to have continued value as a site for historical examination of those institutions or monastic reform movements where professed men and women undertook religious life and vows in dual-sex communities. As a consequence, refined use of the term rather than abolition seems both prudent and necessary. To be sure, the specific fact that a monastery housed both women and men as religious does not itself predict the order, rule, or intentions with regard to gender relations or spiritual equality of the sexes for the founders, lay supporters, or actual members of any given house. But the fact of a monastery's sexual doubleness does open up potentially fruitful questions about all these things, and so continues to warrant historically contextualized consideration.

Changing Frameworks for Research

It is fitting that an encyclopedia entry on the double monastery as an institution should begin with a debate about its very validity as a term, because dual-sex houses have been a source of scholarly debate for almost two centuries. In the nineteenth century, double houses were the subject of open concern. Scholars could use the words *bizarre* and *dangerous* for those many early medieval houses that were governed by abbesses. The evident fact of religious women's authority over male monastics caused consternation because it seemed to reverse nineteenth-century patterns of sexual dominance. The evidence for monastic women "on top" of monks was all the more troubling in the nationalist ecclesiastical histories of the day because it appeared to document a situation of gender disorder at an originary moment for European Christianity. In the course of the nineteenth century the circumstances of the abbesses' rule over male religious came to be explained, or rather, explained away, in terms of national predispositions attributed largely to Irish monks who could be associated with the foundation of some double houses in the Frankish and Anglo-Saxon kingdoms. Double monasteries were thus catalogued as evidence for, and as the consequence of, a disorderly Celtic strain in the broader early medieval church.

This framework of analysis has undergone sharp revision in the last half century. At present, neither explaining away monastic disorder nor racialist attention to Celtic monastic types persists in serious scholars' research on double houses. In contrast, twentieth-century research has generally been positive about dual-sex monasticism, often celebrating such houses as sites of sexual equality where, especially, the early medieval rule of the abbess over male monastics and the institutionalized association of the two sexes in monastic devotion have come to signify a period of greater spiritual egalitarianism between the sexes. In this more recent view, scholars have been interested in making sense of the opportunities such monasteries created for constructing different gender relationships between medieval religious women and men. To this end, scholars have found it essential to discard the deceptively simple notion of the double monastery as a single, continuous historical phenomenon, and to consider evidence for dual-sex houses with attention to the specific contexts that surrounded them.

Evidence for and Significance of Dual-Sex Houses

The first step towards analyzing double monasteries is to recognize the variety of social and religious environments that produced them. Early medieval double houses, which flourished in the West from the sixth through ninth centuries, demonstrate a profoundly regional diversity of configuration; in this they are very much like the early medieval church that created them. Dual-sex monasteries are well attested to in France, Spain, Ireland, and England. In the early Middle Ages, there is no single type of unified male/female monastic community. As has long been noticed, Frankish and Anglo-Saxon double houses as a group were socially and ecclesiastically high-profile institutions, founded and governed by the families of local elites. Aristocratic and royal women in such houses were notable for the religious authority they exercised in and from their monastic identities. For example, Hild of Whitby's seventh-century Anglo-Saxon monastery is well documented as a center of Christian mission and hagiographical and poetic production, as well as having hosted, at the Synod of Whitby (664), a crucial debate over liturgy and observance for the Anglo-Saxon church. It is important to note that Hild herself did not concur with the prevailing ecclesiastical opinion about the observance of Easter and that she was, in fact, in a position to disagree with the bishops of her church (five of whom had been trained at her own double house). Sources attest that the nuns Leoba and Walburga left double monasteries to participate in the Anglo-Saxon mission to Christianize pagan regions on the Continent, founding new houses there. As a rule, early Anglo-Saxon monasteries that housed women of Hild's social prominence were double houses; it is clear that this configuration was far from "bizarre," nor was it, in the eyes of contemporaries, "dangerous."

The general acceptance of such houses was comparable for seventh- and eighth-century France, where dual-sex communities were founded around noble and royal women and where the integration of such houses into the mainstream of the larger local church is reflected in high degrees of literacy and scribal skills of nuns, as well as the close family connections between female inhabitants of dual-sex houses and the regional elites, both lay and clerical, that supported them. In Ireland, in contrast, only the double monastery of Kildare clearly documents the social configuration of close ties to the local ruling polity for both female and male religious. But the authority of Brigit, Kildare's founder and patron saint, is portrayed by her hagiographer as rivaling that of the northern bishopric of Patrick's foundation at Armagh in its claims to serve the whole of Ireland, and the pastoral role of the monastery is comparable to that of any male-centered monastic institution in early medieval Ireland.

Yet another and very different picture of the role of dual-sex monasteries emerges from Visigothic Spain in the seventh century, where unified male/female communities were forming in less-well-documented circumstances: here the rather obscure contemporary sources are consistently hostile to joint male–female institutions, and provide a record of clerical anxiety, not confidence, about the proliferation of what appear to have been small monasteries centered around the commitment of whole families to monastic life. The early medieval double monasteries fade in importance and generally disappear over the course of the ninth and tenth centuries. No simple answer explains this fact, although a variety of causes have been adduced by modern scholars, prominent among them clerical reforms that reduced women's spiritual authority within the church as a whole, coupled with the general destruction of monasteries by Vikings, and subsequent absence of impetus for refoundations on the earlier dual-sex model.

Monastic Revival

However we explain the demise of early medieval forms of dual-sex monasticism, it is clear that when monastic reformers and spiritual leaders in the twelfth through fourteenth centuries came to create orders of specifically dual-sex houses, the church in which these orders were created, and the idiom of their spiritual meaning, had been transformed. In comparison with the range of early medieval women's religious authority and activities, scholars of the monastic orders that made provision for joint male–female houses in the high Middle Ages have tended to see patterns of diminished influence for women, as evidenced in the relatively reduced prominence of women monastics from such houses in the wider church as well as decreasing evidence for such women's educational and scribal achievements—though double houses still appear to have provided women with comparatively richer educational opportunities than were possible at most single-sex women's houses.

High medieval Europe witnessed a grand revival of monastic fervor. Contemporaries attested to the eagerness of women to participate in the founding of new monastic institutions and new monastic configurations; individual monasteries evidently could become double in practice, and by default, under the pressure of women devotees' urgency to join in the reformation of religious life. But only a few orders made deliberate and formal provision for intentionally organizing women and men religious in joined houses. The twelfth-century orders created by Norbert of Xanten, founder of the Premonstratensian order, Robert of Arbrissel, founder of the order of Fontevrault, and Gilbert of Sempringham, who founded the Gilbertine order, grew out of what were initially male-centered movements of monastic reform advocating embrace of the revived ideals of apostolic poverty and social abasement. Of these three, the Premonstratensians and Gilbertines evolved monastic systems that made grudging provisions to accommodate nuns under the supervision of male religious superiors; by the end of the twelfth century the Premonstratensians had come to refuse new women adherents. Only Robert of Arbrissel's Fontevrists turned the twelfth-century search for male monastic humility into an acceptance of an abbess's religious and spiritual authority, and even that acceptance was intermittent after the visionary founder's demise. The wider church climate was scarcely hospitable to dual-sex configurations, seeing in them a cause for scandal.

In the mid-fourteenth century, a Swedish noblewoman named Birgitta envisaged a new order, based on the authority of her own experience of mystical revelations from Christ, that combined a symbolic number of female and male monastics in the same institution. The pope from whom she sought approbation initially refused to condone the rule she had received and disallowed the dual-sex configuration that lay at the core of her understanding of her vision. Even once the Birgittines, or the Order of the Holy Savior, had received acceptance with a compromised Augustinian rule, subsequent popes resisted Birgitta's plan for unified male–female monasteries, and for a time in the fifteenth century prohibited dual-sex houses outright. Only a few houses, though socially prominent, including Vadstena and Syon, persisted past the fifteenth century to bear witness to Birgitta's project unifying monastic life for women and men.

CATHERINE PEYROUX

References and Further Reading

Bateson, Mary. "Origin and Early History of Double Monasteries." *Transactions of the Royal Historical Society* 13 (1899): 137–198.
Beach, Alison. *Women as Scribes: Book Production and Monastic Reform in Twelfth-Century Bavaria.* Cambridge: Cambridge University Press, 2004.
Elkins, Sharon. *Holy Women of Twelfth-Century England.* Chapel Hill: University of North Carolina Press, 1988.
Foot, Sarah. *Veiled Women.* 2 Vols. Aldershot: Ashgate Publishing, 2000.
Gold, Penny Schine. *The Lady and the Virgin: Image, Attitude, and Experience in Twelfth-Century France.* Chicago: University of Chicago Press, 1985.
Golding, Brian. *Gilbert of Sempringham and the Gilbertine Order, c. 1100–1300.* Oxford: Oxford University Press, 1995.
Harrington, Christina. *Women in a Celtic Church: Ireland 450–1150.* Oxford: Oxford University Press, 2002.
Hilpisch, Stephanus. *Die Doppelklöster: Entstehung und Organisation*, Beiträge zur Geschichte des alten Mönchtums und des Benediktinerordens 15. Münster: Aschendorff, 1928.
McKitterick, Rosamond. "Nuns' Scriptoria in England and Francia in the Eighth Century." *Francia* 19 (1992): 1–35.
McNamara, Jo Ann. *Sisters in Arms: Catholic Nuns Through Two Millennia.* Cambridge, Mass.: Harvard University Press, 1996.
Schulenberg, Jane Tibbetts. *Forgetful of Their Sex: Female Sanctity and Society, ca. 500–1100.* Chicago: University of Chicago Press, 1998.
Wemple, Suzanne. *Women in Frankish Society: Marriage and the Cloister, 500–900.* Philadelphia: University of Pennsylvania Press, 1985.

See also **Abbesses; Aethelthryth of Ely; Birgitta of Sweden; Birgittine Order; Brigit of Kildare; Education, Monastic; Fontevrault, Abbey and Order of; Gertrude of Nivelles; Gilbertine Order; Hild of Whitby; Law, Canon; Leoba; Literacy and Reading: Latin; Monasticism and Nuns; Premonstratensian Order; Syon Abbey; Woman on Top**

DOUCELINE OF DIGNE

Mystic and founder of a lay religious order for women in Provence, Douceline de Digne (c. 1215–1274) belongs to the high medieval tradition of saintly visionary women established most notably in Germany by Hildegard of Bingen. Douceline's *vita*, composed by a member of one of the houses she founded, also shows her to be a leading figure in both the promotion of Franciscan spirituality and the development of the Beguine movement in southern France, a religious way of life for women that did not require monastic vows or enclosure.

Born in 1215 or 1216, probably in the town of Digne in Provence, the daughter of a pious and wealthy merchant, Douceline spent her childhood in her mother's home town of Barjols. After her mother's early death the family moved to Hyères, where they were closer to Douceline's brother Hugh, who had joined the Franciscan community there. A well-known theologian and preacher, Hugh played a significant role in assisting Douceline in the achievement of her spiritual mission.

In many ways the life of Douceline adheres closely to the model being established during her lifetime by the *vitae* of mystic women in Flanders: an exceptionally pious childhood, a "conversion" experience followed by a life of intense prayer, visions, and prophecy as well as the performance of miracles, both before and after death. Douceline's *vita*, however, also includes two less familiar elements: firstly, a detailed portrait of the daily practices of the founder and administrator of a religious community, which was to attract recruits and support from the aristocracy of Provence and, through the devotion of the Count and his wife, the royal house of France; and secondly, the vivid, carefully documented descriptions of Douceline's ecstatic raptures, which often resulted in levitations. Although her communities seem not to have long survived her death, her spectacular devotional practices made her both a public spectacle and an influential exemplum of Franciscan spirituality. While she was never officially canonized, her cult endured for centuries in southern France.

KATHLEEN GARAY and MADELEINE JEAY

References and Further Reading

Garay, Kathleen, and Madeleine Jeay, eds. and trans. *The Life of Saint Douceline, a Beguine of Provence.* Woodbridge, Suffolk: D. S. Brewer, 2001.

See also Beguines; Hagiography; Mysticism and Mystics; Occitania

DOWRY AND OTHER MARRIAGE GIFTS

Dowry, the *dos* of Roman origin, which was given at marriage, formed a major instrument for the transfer of family wealth in medieval times. Today we postpone such transfers of wealth until the death of a senior generation, prompting some economists to bewail the loss in opportunities from capital tied up in the estates of fiscally conservative elders. Medieval people relied on a distribution of wealth more advantageous to youth that encouraged economic growth. In the early medieval era in particular, people were more conscious than we are of the great difficulty and expense of establishing the married couple in a new household. By tradition and custom, families supported the creation of new households with a variety of marital gifts. Nevertheless dowry, or *dos*, triumphed over other marital assigns by the close of the Middle Ages.

Male-to-Female Marriage Gifts

In early Lombard law a *quarta* of family wealth was given to a son when he married so that he could sustain his new household. This, the so-called "male" dowry of early medieval society, was the chief marital gift among Germanic peoples and propitious for the growth of a young, and expanding, society. A husband's kin apportioned out family wealth so that he could support a wife and children. Population expansion, assarting new land (turning untilled lands to agriculture), and trade benefited from the generous distribution of familial wealth to the young through the eleventh and early twelfth centuries. Wedding gifts reversed the direction in which they moved soon thereafter.

This was certainly the case for the Mediterranean region, where traditional husbands' gifts to wives were replaced by the Roman dowry: a bride's inheritance or Falcidian quarter (a daughter's share in the patrimony and generally not a true quarter) that would terminate her legal demands for support on her natal family. In earlier times women had owned their gifts from husbands as outright possessions, whereas the revived Roman dowry was more ambiguously assigned. According to statute laws in cities, a husband supported his wife and her offspring, and dowry became insurance against his death; as such it fell under his control, to increase but not to squander or lose. This momentous shift in the direction in which capital moved (wife's family to husband rather than husband or his family to wife) occurred over the twelfth and thirteenth centuries. As Pierre Bonnassie has argued for the region around Barcelona in Spain, Roman dowry was likely to be the earliest instance of family wealth converted from property to cash. It answered a strongly felt need to preserve the bride's natal family land holdings intact; as a result, daughters received cash, while sons were destined to inherit property.

The system of dower, as it was understood in the common law tradition of England, marked a method comparable to the Lombard *quarta* for husbands to support the burden of marriage and insure the future of a wife and her offspring. Women brought a reciprocal *maritagium* to marriage, generally in the form of land or rents over which they maintained some control. This gift helped provide for offspring of the marriage, including daughters (de Trafford). Generally speaking, wedding gifts from husbands differed in name and mode of distribution, but all assumed that husbands and their kin, as well as wives and their kin, needed to amass, and give, wealth at the time of marriage. Brideprice, *morgengabe* (morning gift), and *antefactum* (prior gift) were terms for marital gifts from husbands. These were often restricted in statute laws, while the Roman *dos* or dowry was occasionally monitored by law but seldom restricted. As a result dowries rose to prodigious sums of cash as Europeans prospered.

Roman Dowry in the Italian City-States

Manlio Bellomo has argued that Roman dowry was converted to cash in Italian towns so that husbands were assured of capital sums for investment purposes.

In Italian towns laws stated that, although a woman owned her Roman dowry, and would have it for support if she became a widow, while her husband lived, he had control of it. He could invest it and make profit from it but the sum must remain intact. He was not to alienate it or lose it, a tall order when commerce entailed economic risk.

This shift in marital assigns and the conversion of dowry to cash are some of the more momentous economic developments of the medieval era, yet they went largely unrecognized by historians until the last quarter of the twentieth century, because dowry was viewed as a rather inconsequential familial concern. Capital investment, the cash economy, and the very nature of urban households were reconfigured by this effort to live "in all things according to Roman law," as lawmakers in Siena asserted (Riemer). As Bellomo has argued, the ready cash that fell into the hands of men when they married underwrote European commercial expansion. Even if, as laws dictated, new husbands invested dowry funds conservatively, their "cash flow" position would be enhanced considerably by marriage, along with their prestige, and the stature of their lineage. Husbands were able to use whatever other cash they had on hand in high-risk ventures because their financial positions were sustained by large dowry awards from brides' families.

The conversion of marriage gifts to cash is an important theme to consider for the late medieval period as well. Just as the Roman dowry, given in cash, transformed investment opportunities for men in the twelfth and thirteenth centuries, conversion of other marital gifts to cash further enhanced husbands' economic position in later decades. Husbands preferred wedding gifts from the bride's family in cash; its liquidity appealed far more than gifts of clothes, "plate," linens, hangings, *cassone* (painted chests), and fine ornaments. The bride's wardrobe could be a bone of contention for a newlywed couple, and although husbands continued to give gifts to their brides, even when restricted by law, they apparently resented the money spent on brides' wardrobes in familial efforts to keep up appearances.

By the fifteenth century in Venice a strong initiative was mounted to turn the husband's countergift to his bride into a cash award so that he could invest the amount he gave as capital rather than see it expended on his bride's wardrobe. Jane Fair Bestor argues that, according to late medieval Roman law, a man did not even alienate his property when he gave gifts to his wife because, when given, the gift remained part of his patrimony. As such, it could be recalled, or pawned, or sold, that is, turned into cash.

Still, no urban Italian family of any wealth or standing was content with the simple award of cash at marriage, so husbands frequently augmented the *dos*, as the dowry was called, with all sorts of counter-gifts, trousseaux, *corredi*, and wedding paraphernalia. In 1353 the Florentine Giovanni Niccolini arranged for his ward, Tommasa, a wedding gift beyond her cash award of dowry: "one belt, mounted in silver with a purse with silver enamel, [worth] three gold florins." Tommasa received as well two sets of silver buttons, an old green cloth for a gown, fine crimson cloth for another gown, new green cloth for a coat, three pairs of slippers, and three pairs of shoes, twelve caps, one mirror and comb, linen thread, wimples, miniver and samite for two fur hats, stockings, and veils, as well as linens and other household items (Niccolini). As Alesandra Strozzi bragged a century later, her daughter Caterina had 400 florins on her back in gifts that her bride groom, Marco Parenti, gave her (Phillips). Costs added up, particularly for clothes and precious accessories, since they were commonly paid for in gold florins, the currency of long-distance trade.

Investment of Dowries

Not only did conflict arise between husband and wife, but husbands were often of two minds themselves, seeking wedding gifts in cash yet constrained by the demands of honor and prestige to add their own rich presents to the array of the bride's gifts. In Venice in 1360 sumptuary laws solved men's quandary by dictating that no husband might give more than thirty *lire di grossi* in dress or jewels to his bride, and that extended through the first four years of marriage. Roman dowries were registered but not limited, so these awards continued to rise.

Since dowries were awarded in cash, leaving patrimonial funds for surviving brothers, the transfer of wealth from a dowry in cash was regarded as beneficial to a bride's brothers and a valuable asset to a husband and his kin. By the thirteenth century city-states in Italy eyed the cash awards of dowry as funds to be invested in government securities. In Venice, and by law, dowry was a woman's property, and a husband could invest it only when its value was secured; until 1233 dowry value was secured by real estate, but thereafter gold or silver plate could be substituted and its cash equivalent released to the husband so he could invest it. By 1316 the Grain Office began borrowing dowries lying idle, with the city-state providing surety as required by law. In 1329 dowries became even more accessible to the state. All dowries on deposit could be given for investment to the Grain Office, which provided surety.

Florence solved its own liquidity problem when strapped for cash by turning to invested dowry funds. The *Monte delle Doti*, launched in 1424–1425, gained speculative and actuarial elements over the decades that attracted private investors. By 1433 a deposit of sixty florins produced a 500-florin dowry in fifteen years, provided the girl still lived. If a daughter entered a convent the original deposit was returned since convents required a dowry as well but were generally content with a small one. Unintentionally perhaps, the *Monte* allowed families to bet on daughters' life expectancies. A number of families took up this challenge, and in one instance 879 deposits were made over two months, providing the state with 67,231 florins, or enough to pay one-third of the carrying charges on the Florentine funded debt. Later dowry deposits could be used to purchase *Monte* credits that were then transferred to a new account in the endowed daughters' names. At the due date officials cashed in the number of credits necessary to raise the dowry. This made the *Monte delle Doti* a kind of revolving fund. By the 1450s credits were being purchased in the marketplace, and there were almost three million florins in *Monte* accounts. The *Monte* had become an essential instrument for state funding, and as such its original purpose of providing capital to establish new households and to serve as insurance for a wife and her offspring in event of a husband's death was obscured.

The transformation of dowry from its original purpose of providing insurance for a new family into an investment instrument for state finance exerted significant external pressures on families. In Florence a family need only reclaim its original investment in the *Monte* to place a daughter in a convent rather than pay dowry to a prospective husband. In these circumstances it was convenient for a family strapped for funds to shunt a daughter off to a convent, since it cost much less. To end the increasing demands of husbands in negotiations for marriage, brides' families married off daughters at very young ages. Florentine husbands from wealthy backgrounds might be twice the age of their young brides at marriage. Canon law required consent from both parties for valid marriage, but dowry considerations increased so dramatically in wealthy families that daughters' preferences were largely subordinated to financial considerations. Rather than a foundation for sound marriage, dowry gifts had become an end in themselves with family wealth, prestige, and connections dictating the choice of marriage partners.

If dowries were not paid promptly husbands were likely to chide their wives, or worse, and very likely to importune their in-laws for funds. Widows were known to suffer severe problems in regaining control over their dowries on the death of their husbands, requiring them to sue in court or pursue long, tedious negotiations to obtain restitution from their husbands' kin. On occasion widows found it necessary to fight off their husbands' creditors to keep their dowries as their own, and their underage heirs', livelihood. If an improvident husband had squandered a dowry, his widow was thrown back on her family connections for bed and board, creating considerable resentment and acrimony.

Conclusion

Roman dowry moved with the commercialization of the European economy. Venice and the Adriatic region had practiced Roman dowrying traditionally, as had Byzantine lands to the east, but dowry became the chief marital assign of most Europeans, even in lands with significant German settlement. With the monetarization of rural Europe, Roman dowry came to be practiced in most western European communities. As such, cash awards characterized the marriages of those European families wealthy enough to support the marriages of their offspring. Poorer girls worked to amass a dowry that would make them attractive marriage partners. Charitable foundations awarded dowries to orphans and poor girls as the only way to assure them of marriage partners.

Since Roman dowry satisfied a daughter's claims of inheritance on her natal kin, it was within the law to limit a daughter's share of her patrimony to her dowry—although, in practice, many parents wrote wills that gave married daughters further inheritance rights. Sons, whose share in the family patrimony increased because of the dotal regime, preferred Roman dowry since it ensured them a better proportion of a shared patrimony. It is difficult to find any advantage in Roman *dos* for daughters, except as insurance in widowhood. Dowered daughters did not control this award in cash although, technically speaking, it was theirs. From husbands' gifts, that brides owned and controlled, wedding gifts had become Roman dowries that brides owned but did not control by the close of the Middle Ages.

SUSAN MOSHER STUARD

References and Further Reading

Bellomo, Manlio. *Ricerche sui rapporti patrimoniali tra coniugi*. Milan: Giuffre, 1961.

Bestor, Jane Fair. "Marriage Transactions in Renaissance Italy." *Past and Present* 164 (1999): 4–46.

Chojnacki, Stanley. "From Trousseau to Groomgift in Late Medieval Venice." In *Medieval and Renaissance Venice*, edited by Ellen Kittell and Thomas Madden. Urbana, Ill.: University of Illinois Press, 1999, pp. 141–165.

di Camugliano, Ginevra Niccolini, ed. *The Chronicles of a Florentine Family, 1200–1470*. London: J. Cape, 1933.

de Trafford, Claire. "Share and Share Alike? The Marriage Portion, Inheritance, and Family Politics." In *Studies on Medieval and Early Modern Women: Pawns or Players?*, edited by Christine Meek and Catherine Lawless. London: Four Courts Press, 2003, pp. 36–48.

Esmein, Adhemar. *Le marriage en droit canonique: Études sur l'histoire du droit canonique privé*. Paris: L. Larose et Forcel, 1891.

Hughes, Diane Owen. "From Brideprice to Dowry in Mediterranean Europe." *Journal of Family History* 3 (1978): 262–296.

Kirshner, Julius, and Anthony Molho. "The Dowry Fund and the Marriage Market in Early Quattrocento Florence." *Journal of Modern History* 50 (1978): 403–438.

Klapische-Zuber, Christiane. *Women, Family, and Ritual in Renaissance Italy*, translated by Lydia Cochrane. Chicago: University of Chicago Press, 1985.

Kreutz, Barbara. "The Twilight of Morgengabe." In *Portraits of Medieval and Renaissance Living*, edited by Samuel K. Cohn, Jr., and Steven A. Epstein. Ann Arbor, Mich.: University of Michigan Press, 1996, pp. 131–147.

Molho, Anthony. *Marriage Alliance in Late Medieval Florence*. Cambridge, Mass.: Harvard University Press, 1994.

Mueller, Reinhold C. *Money and Banking in Medieval and Renaissance Venice*, Vol. 2, *The Venetian Money Market: Banks, Panics, Public Debt, 1200–1500*. Baltimore: The Johns Hopkins University Press, 1997.

Newett, Margaret. "The Sumptuary Laws of Venice." In *Historical Essays*, edited by T. F. Tout and James Tait. London: Longmans Green, 1902, pp. 245–278.

Phillips, Mark. *The Memoir of Marco Parenti*. Princeton, N.J.: Princeton University Press, 1987.

Riemer, Eleanor. *Women in the Medieval City: Sources and Uses of Wealth by Sienese Women in the Thirteenth Century*. Ph.D. dissertation, New York University, 1975.

Roush, Sherry, and Cristelle L. Baskins, eds. *Medieval Marriage Scene: Prudence, Passion, Policy*. Tempe, Ariz.: Arizona Center for Medieval and Renaissance Studies, 2005.

Stuard, Susan Mosher. "Dowry Increase and Increments in Wealth in Medieval Ragusa (Dubrovnik)." *Journal of Economic History* 41 (1981): 795–811.

See also **Family (Earlier Middle Ages); Family (Later Middle Ages); Marriage, Christian; Trousseau; Widows**

DRAMA

Although the extent of their involvement remains contested, many scholars agree that women participated in medieval drama—writing, acting in, sponsoring, and watching plays and other mimetic entertainments. Moreover, women and, more broadly, gender and sexuality were fundamental to the subjects represented in early drama.

Authors and Sponsors

The authors of most medieval plays are unknown, but there is evidence that women composed dramas. The canoness Hrotsvit of Gandersheim (c. 935–973) wrote six one-act plays in Latin designed as Christian imitations of the Roman dramatist Terence. These plays are often regarded as closet dramas meant to be read aloud, but mimed action might have accompanied the recitation. The *Ordo Virtutum* of the abbess Hildegard of Bingen (1089–1179) is a music drama seemingly designed for performance; it features the character Felix Anima (Happy Soul), who is caught up in a conflict between the Virtues and Vices. The example of Katherine of Sutton, abbess of the English convent at Barking from 1363–1376, who wrote twenty-one texts of the *Visitatio Sepulchri*, which dramatizes the visit of the three Marys to the sepulcher of Jesus, suggests that abbesses less famous than Hildegard also composed convent plays that survive from medieval nunneries.

Women also sponsored plays and helped produce playscripts outside of convents. At Chester, the "wurshipfful Wyffys" put on an Assumption play in the late fifteenth century that was later incorporated into Chester's cycle of plays. Wives of guildsmen in Chester were paid for providing food, drink, and cloth for the cycle plays. They also helped with scripts: Chester's cooper's guild in 1574–1575 paid a woman to make a performance copy of their play from a master text. Evidence from Somerset shows that women often served as churchwardens overseeing parish festivities, especially at hocktide and Easter, and supplied costumes and goods for performances of plays. Women were also part of civic sponsorship of entertainments in Cambridge, as widows of master waits. Records from the continent suggest that there, too, women sponsored plays, such as the play of Saint Catherine that was commissioned and staged by a wealthy woman in Metz in 1468.

Performance

Although the usual practice was for cross-dressed boys and youths to play women's parts, there is evidence that women performed in plays. In convents, women impersonated the three Marys in the *Visitatio* plays and may also have played men's roles on occasion, a practice lampooned in satirical comedies that describe nuns dressing like men to perform their parts. In at least one case, in the convent at Origny in France, a woman played God. Girl abbesses (like boy bishops) were also apparently common in inversionary performances on Innocents' Day in convents and abbeys. Women also acted in plays outside of convents. In France, the Mons Passion Play (1501) and the Valenciennes Passion (1547) both list girls ("jeunes filles") as cast members. The Trois Doms play of Romans (1509) included eleven women, some of whom played more than one part; nine of the women were married, many to influential men, which corroborates evidence from Chester that women's participation in civic drama could be prestige-based. A glazier's daughter acted the lead role at Metz in the 1468 play of Saint Catherine; the actress is not named, but she is praised for her beauty, pathos, and prodigious memory. The London Goldsmiths' castle pageant for a royal entry in 1377, 1382, and 1392 included "maidens," while records from other English towns show the participation of girls and women in public plays and processions. Women also performed in parish rituals and festivities, such as summer games and morris dancing—which was often a mimetic activity that included a Maid Marion—as well as in court-related ceremonies. Some records point to professional female entertainers. Matilda Makejoy, dancer and acrobat, performed for kings Edward I and II of England, and iconography shows women tumblers, acrobats, and other entertainers. Most known professional acting companies were made up of men, but there is evidence of itinerant women players in the sixteenth century, usually as part of a husband–wife team. Women also acted in rituals that were exclusively their own, such as childbed and churching ceremonies, which acknowledged their reproductive labor in a way analogous to the affirmation of male labor in the cycle plays and processions.

The frequency with which women performed in plays is debatable, but there is little controversy over their importance as subjects of medieval drama. Extant play-texts and information about unscripted ritual performances reveal how persistently women, their experiences, and their social positions shaped the content of early drama. Women figure prominently in liturgical plays like the *Visitatio Sepulchri* as well as in plays about female saints. The large-scale Digby *Mary Magdalene*, for example, recounts the entire adult life of the saint from before her fall into prostitution through her conversion and final legendary years in the wilderness, all seen as a model for both men and women. Female characters in the cycle plays include the Virgin Mary at various stages of her life, Mary's mother St. Anne, Elizabeth, Eve, the mothers in the Slaughter of the Innocents pageants, the rebellious wife of Noah and her gossips, Mak's wife and accomplice Gyll in the Towneley Second Shepherds' pageant, and Pilate's wife Procula. Women also feature as characters in civic and court pageantry and seasonal entertainments. As these examples indicate, female characters represented a spectrum of attributes and ideals, from dutiful submission to irreverent subversion, that spoke to the concerns and desires of spectators.

Spectators

Those spectators would have included not just men but women, who were members of virtually every audience for medieval performances. That women might have formed an actively engaged audience for drama is implied by evidence from Chester, where in 1568 women went to court to try to protect their access to good viewing space for the town's cycle. Margery Kempe's autobiography offers another glimpse of engaged female spectatorship when, while returning home from a trip to York in 1413, where she probably had gone to watch York's cycle play, Margery is inspired to extract a vow of chastity from her husband. And John Lydgate's Christmas mummings, devised in the 1420s for the young Henry VI and his mother, Queen Katherine, show royal entertainments being specifically directed towards female spectators.

Scattered though it may be, this and other evidence suggests that women played a more central role in medieval drama than is commonly assumed and that their impact on early performances deserves continued exploration.

CLAIRE SPONSLER

References and Further Reading

Davidson, Clifford. "Women and the Medieval Stage." *Women's Studies* 11 (1984): 99–113.

Muir, Lynette R. "Women on the Medieval Stage: The Evidence from France." *Medieval English Theatre* 8 (1985): 107–120.

Ogden, Dunbar H. "Women Play Women in the Liturgical Drama of the Middle Ages." In *Shakespearean Illuminations: Essays in Honor of Marvin Rosenberg*, edited by Jay L. Halio and Hugh Richmond. Newark, Del.: University of Delaware Press, 1998, pp. 336–360.

Rastall, Richard. "Female Roles in All-Male Casts." *Medieval English Theatre* 7 (1985): 25–50.

Stokes, James. "Women and Mimesis in Medieval and Renaissance Somerset (and Beyond)." *Comparative Drama* 27 (1993): 176–196.

Twycross, Meg. "'Transvestism' in the Mystery Plays." *Medieval English Theatre* 5 (1983): 123–180.

Wack, Mary. "Women, Work, and Plays in an English Medieval Town." In *Maids and Mistresses, Cousins and Queens: Women's Alliances in Early Modern England,* edited by Susan Frye and Karen Robertson. Oxford: Oxford University Press, 1999, pp. 33–51.

See also **Abbesses; Audience, Women in the; Cross-Dressing; Guild Members and Guilds; Hildegard of Bingen; Hrotsvit of Gandersheim; Kempe, Margery**

E

EASTERN EUROPE

In what sense did the condition of eastern European women differ from their western European counterparts in the patriarchal world of the Middle Ages? Women's legal, social, and economic functions are less documented in central and eastern Europe, and the surviving evidence is scant and contradictory. There seems to be here a sharper disparity between the female ideal and the reality of women's lives. Representations of women in hagiography bear no resemblance to their portrayal in chronicles and their rights as recognized under law.

Property Rights

The most important difference between eastern and western legal customs was that noble women were more often excluded from inheriting land. In the aristocratic kindred, landed property passed on to the male heir while women received their part of the inheritance in cash. The phenomenon of wealthy heiresses such as Eleanor of Aquitaine, Marguerite of Flanders, or Mary of Burgundy, who became political figures because of their huge landed possessions, did not exist in eastern Europe.

Noble women in eastern Europe had fewer rights than their counterparts in the West. They were in a subordinate legal position and never obtained the full legal rights enjoyed by men. Daughters were placed under paternal authority; wives were subject to their husbands. In the patrilinear aristocratic family "blue blood" was thought to originate with, and pass through, the father; the mother's status was considered of secondary importance.

Marriage

In the Christian societies of eastern Europe, marriage was supposed to be consensual for both parties (*matrimonium consensualis*). Women received wedding gifts (*res paraphernales*) from the bridegroom's family and a dowry (*dos*) from their own families, paid in moveable goods, cash, or precious objects. In Hungary, the dowry came to a quarter of the paternal estate (*quarta filialis*), always to be paid in cash due to the closed inheritance system of the noble kindred, which prohibited the alienation of ancestral estates, striving to keep lands within the ancient lineage. This meant that noble women were excluded from inheriting land, except in those cases when they married a nonnoble, or when the survival of the kindred and of the estate were at stake and the estate passed on to a male member of the kindred. If there were no male relatives left and daughters were the only heirs, it was possible for them to inherit land. Royal prerogatives "transformed female offspring into men" to avoid the extinction of a noble family and the dispersion of the paternal estate. The privilege of declaring women "true heirs and male successors" of their fathers was called *praefectio* and was mostly practiced in fourteenth-century Hungary under the Angevin kings. *Praefectio*, however, remained a royal privilege and never developed into a full-fledged legal reform because of the fierce opposition of the noble kindred who benefited most from the inalienability of possession (*avicitas*).

The social function of the noble woman was to maintain the status and prestige of the kindred and to participate actively in the marital strategies of the aristocratic family. In eastern and central Europe, women got married earlier than in the West and they had more children. Women's identity was defined by their male relatives. Even aristocratic women are seldom mentioned by name. Most often they are referred to as daughters of their fathers, or wives/widows of their husbands.

Widows enjoyed a somewhat more independent existence and often wielded considerably more power as dowager queens or as managers of their late husbands' estates. They could pass on family property and their personal wealth to their offspring.

Nonnoble women enjoyed more freedom both within their families and in economic life. Daughters of burghers and of free peasants had more rights and could inherit paternal possessions in the form of landed property as well. They could participate in, or continue the family enterprise, or go into business themselves. Urban and peasant women alike participated in various commercial activities. The percentage of women living and paying taxes on their own ranged between 8 percent and 38 percent in towns. Urban women had equal rights with men, although, if a woman was offended verbally or hurt physically by a man, he had to pay twice the fine he would have had to pay if he offended another male.

Pious Women and Political Scapegoats

Yet women were equal to men before God. The number of female religious communities, however, was much lower in eastern Europe compared to the West, with the ratio of male to female monasteries being 10 to 1. From the thirteenth century, the mendicant orders became particularly popular in Hungary, Bohemia, and Poland due to the generous support of the ruling dynasties. Basilite monasteries for women enjoyed the moral and financial aid of the princely courts in the orthodox principalities of Rus, Bulgaria, and Moldova. Spaces for silence and culture, these monasteries were often the places where princesses took the veil and dowager queens finished their days in religious retirement. Founding monasteries and furnishing them with precious objects was a privileged area of queenly patronage: Elizabeth of Poland (1300–1380), wife of Louis the Great of Hungary, created more than thirty religious foundations, among them the exquisite cloister of the Poor Clares in Óbuda. Her granddaughter, Jadwiga of Poland, was a special patroness of the Pauline monastery of Czestochowa.

Women—*mulier suadens*, persuasive woman—are often represented as pious Christians and converters of their pagan husbands, sons, or grandsons. Narratives of Christianization are often narratives about women in early eastern European hagiography. Ludmilla of Bohemia (860–921), wife of Boriwoj, was baptized by Methodius in 871. She then acted as the spiritual mother of her grandson, Wenceslas, whom she instructed in the Christian faith, thus securing the transmission of Christianity within the Premyslid dynasty. Ludmilla was murdered by her pagan daughter-in-law, Drahomira. The Kievan princess Olga (879–969), wife of Prince Igor, was a strong supporter of paganism until she was baptized in Constantinople, where she received a Christian name, Helena, and a Christian identity modeled after Saint Helena. She was the first of the Rurik dynasty to be baptized, even before the conversion of her grandson, Prince Vladimir, in 988. He claimed Olga as the founder of Christianity in Kievan Rus.

Eastern European royal houses boasted a large number of female saints. Ornamenting their families with reflected heavenly glory, Saint Agnes of Prague, Saint Elisabeth and Saint Margaret of Hungary, and Saint Jadwiga of Poland heightened the prestige of their dynasties.

As opposed to these holy and virgin daughters, queens were usually portrayed as scapegoats in medieval chronicles. The Bavarian princess Gisela (c. 980–1065), sister of Emperor Henry IV, disciple of Saint Wolfgang, and wife of Stephen of Hungary, was denigrated by hagiographers, who attributed the evils that befell the country after the death of King Stephen to her and to her German retinue. Gisela, however, ended her life as abbess of Passau and was canonized. Saint Elisabeth's mother, Gertrude of Meran (1185–1213), wife of Andrew II of Hungary, was murdered by Hungarian aristocrats, who blamed her for the privileges accorded her German barons and for her spendthrift habits. Only one foreign queen, Jadwiga of Anjou (1374–1399), Queen of Poland, managed to become a saint by returning to the older pattern and acting as a converter of pagans.

MARIANNE SÁGHY

References and Further Reading

Klaniczay, Gábor. *Holy Rulers and Blessed Princesses*. Cambridge: Cambridge University Press, 2002.

Klassen, John M. *Warring Maidens, Captive Wives, and Hussite Queens.* Boulder: East European Monographs, 1999.

"Women and Power in East Central Europe: Medieval and Modern." Edited by Marianne Sághy and Nancy F. Partner. Special issue of *East Central Europe* 20–23 (1) 1993–1996.

See also **Elisabeth of Hungary; Jadwiga; Mary of Hungary II; Monasticism and Nuns; Noble Women; Olga; Queens and Empresses: the West; Russia**

EBNER, MARGARETHA

Margaretha Ebner (1291–1351) was born in Donauwörth, near Regensburg, to a patrician family and, at an early age, entered the Dominican cloister of Maria-Mödingen. She was buried there in the nave of the chapel in 1351. When she was 40 years old, Heinrich von Nördlingen, her Dominican confessor, convinced her to write a record of her spiritual journey. Without the aid of an amanuensis, she wrote her *Offenbarungen* ("Revelations") in Alemannic, a dialect of Middle High German. Belonging to a corpus of medieval Dominican convent literature, Margaretha's *Offenbarungen* is an important medieval German vernacular mystical text. A lengthy manuscript for the Middle Ages (over 100 folio pages) the work follows a chronological description of her spiritual life from 1312 to 1348, with the experiences arranged according to the liturgical calendar. Margaretha's text belongs to a medieval religious genre that is referred to as autohagiography, religious writing that is by its very nature autobiographical, narrating personal revelations and reflecting the lifelong spiritual journey of a single author.

Medieval women's mystical writing, such as Margaretha's *Revelations*, both shaped and reflected the culture of the cloister, as well as that of the wider society of the Christian world. Traditional monastic elements such as the liturgy and sermons are woven into the fabric of Margaretha's narrations. She makes use of doctrinal sources such as the Bible and the breviary, as well as Jacobus of Voragine's *Legenda Aurea* ("Golden Legend") and Caesarius of Heisterbach's *Dialogus miraculorum* ("Dialogue of Miracles"). Two other Dominican sisters wrote autohagiographies bearing strong similarities to Margaretha's; both Christina Ebner (1277–1356) and Adelheid Langmann (1306–1375) were from the convent of Engelthal. Also distinctly related to these autohagiographical texts is a collection of writings referred to as the Sister-Books or *Nonenbücher*, written during the first half of the fourteenth century at Adelhausen, Unterlinden, Gotteszell, Engelthal, Kirchberg, Töss, Oetenbach, Diessenhofen, and Weiler.

The religious experiences that Margaretha narrates typify those of ecstatic women mystics described in a variety of texts produced in late medieval Europe. Margaretha narrates her experience of divine union, recounting auditions and visions of God and of Mary and the Christ-child. In the opening chapters of her book she describes the three years (1312–1315) she was seriously ill, suffering from a variety of afflictions. It is worth noting that illness narratives are a common feature reported in medieval women's religious writing. Once she recovered, Margaretha undertook a rigorous program of asceticism, self-mortification, fasting, and flagellation. In keeping with fourteenth-century piety, her devotions center on the humanity of Christ, primarily on his birth and death. Visual images and material culture objects are important sources in addressing the prominent influences and inspirations for medieval women mystics such as Margaretha. Among these are crucifixes, both on the altar and owned personally; sculpted and painted images of Mary with the infant Christ or in the Pieta; the sculpted image of St. John the Evangelist with his head on Christ's breast; tapestries often produced within the cloister; Christ-child effigies and cradles; and illustrated manuscripts. All, along with textual sources, were profoundly important in shaping the visionary elements of the religious experiences narrated in her book of revelations. Significant to Margaretha's religious experience is a small carved figure of the Christ-child and a cradle she was given by a friend. In one chapter, she narrates an experience of miraculous lactation when the Christ-child figure used in her devotions asks to be nursed. Throughout the text she describes a devotional relationship with the wooden figure, caring for it, swaddling it, placing it in a cradle, and rocking it to sleep. The same Christ-child figure can be seen today above the altar in the Dominican chapel of Maria-Mödingen.

Appended to the nineteenth-century edition of her *Offenbarungen* are more than fifty letters from Heinrich von Nördlingen, her Dominican confessor. Although the letters were clearly intended as spiritual instruction, there are notable moments of affectionate sentiment. Without doubt, Dominican sisters like Margaretha were well-acquainted with the works of Meister Eckhart, Johannes Tauler, and Heinrich Seuse, and in many cases knew the preachers personally. On one occasion Margaretha Ebner recollects a conversation with Tauler; and, in several of his letters to Margaretha, Heinrich von Nördlingen refers to both Tauler and Seuse.

Overall, Margaretha's autohagiography is typical of late medieval women's religious experience, expressing an embodied spirituality where devotion to and union with the divine is played out on the mystic's body. Texts such as Margaretha's *Revelation* provided the flourishing Dominican monasteries with descriptions of devotional practices and stories of exemplary holy lives worthy of imitation.

ROSEMARY DRAGE HALE

References and Further Reading

Hale, Rosemary Drage. "Rocking the Cradle: Margaretha Ebner (Be)Holds the Divine." In *Performance and Transformation: New Approaches to Medieval Spirituality*. New York: St. Martin's Press, 1999, pp. 210–241.

Margaretha Ebner und Heinrich von Nördlingen, edited by Philipp Strauch. Frieburg i. B. and Tübingen: Akdemische Verlagsbuchhandlung von J. C. B. Mohr, 1882. Reprint. Amsterdam: Verlag P. Shippers, 1966.

Margaretha Ebner: Major Works, translated by Leonard P. Hindsley with an introduction by Margot Schmidt and Leonard P. Hindsley. New York: Paulist Press, 1993.

Wiethaus, Ulrike. "Thieves and Carnivals: Gender in German Dominican Literature of the Fourteenth Century," In *The Vernacular Spirit: Essays on Medieval Religious Literature*, edited by Renate Blumenfeld-Kosinski, Duncan Robertson, and Nancy Bradley Warren. New York: Palgrave, 2002, pp. 209–238.

See also **Autohagiography; Devotional Practices; Dominican Order; Langmann, Adelheid; Mysticism and Mystics; Mystics' Writings; Sister-Books and Convent Chronicles; Spiritual Care**

ECONOMY

It is safe to assume that medieval women worked for a living and the rendering of that work to the economy was determined by their wealth, social standing, talents, age, marital status, child-bearing, and child-rearing. Because women's life cycle differed in many respects from men's, historians have argued that women had a weaker work identity than men, thus a more marginal position in the economy. Yet they labored hard and effectively, producing growth for the medieval economy. In agriculture women often complemented their husband's roles. The *milchpfennig* (butter and egg profits) earned at market by German women added to farm income. In guilds women often held secondary positions to men in a division of labor favoring skilled craftsmen, who were predominantly males and had served long apprenticeships. Nevertheless guilds exclusive to women did exist, like the silk workers' guild in Paris. Women were sometimes admitted to guilds in predominantly male occupations, although often they exercised only secondary privileges. Women dominated the production of ale in northern villages, where alewives took turns brewing for their neighbors, that is, until brewing became a commercialized industry in towns.

Wages earned by women tended to be lower than those earned by men. Here, as well, some significant exceptions may be found, for example, in early printing workshops in Lyon. Young, single women servants sometimes worked for a lump sum that became their dowry after their contracted years of service. Slaves worked for no wage at all. In textile industries women sometimes worked in a putting-out system, where they were paid by the piece and produced their work at home. Women from Lucca unwound the fragile threads of silk worm cocoons in great kettles, laboring without leaving much trace in the historical record because a middleman controlled their pay and conditions of work. Women's work was often subsumed under their husband's name in artisan trades like leather working or goldsmithing, although both husband and wife labored at the craft.

Legal status arbitrated women's work, in particular inheritance rights, rights to own personal property, and control of that property over a lifetime. Under the common law in England a single woman (*feme sole*) lost property rights to her husband upon marriage when she became a *feme coverte*, but gained them again if and when she became a widow. She might then maintain her husband's position in his guild and continue his business by right of inheritance. Widows often married other practitioners of their husbands' trades.

Market- and tradeswomen existed in many European towns with high profiles in tavern-owning, spinning, and the second-hand clothing market (Rose the Regrator or Second-hand Rose was an important medieval character). In medieval Europe as well women served as wet nurses and earned wages, or as skilled midwives, or as prostitutes. The very nature of their employment choices suggest that it was easy for women to fall into poverty, and it was difficult to escape out of it. In some towns women were prohibited from contracting debts, but women could extend credit and loan money if they were wealthy or heiresses, so this became an avenue into business ownership and trade. Jewish women scored some important successes in investment in trade in towns like Perpignon.

Perhaps the greatest impediment to women's economic progress lay in their limited landholding and property rights. Much land was entailed to a male heir in the medieval era, while merchant families tended to leave property to their sons. In those families a daughter's dowry was her last legal claim on her natal family's wealth. While even wealthy women from noble or wealthy merchants' families worked at household and estate management, their labor was not compensated with a wage. Meanwhile brides' dowries provided their husbands with wealth and prestige in the community. Some wealthy women saw it as their right and privilege to provide patronage for convents, although women's religious houses were less well endowed than men's houses, generally speaking. Within religious houses women were required by their vows to work, and to an extent their labor compensated for poorer endowments. Less likely to be apprenticed than sons, women have often been wrongly viewed as merely consumers in medieval economic life, whereas their labor and skills were critical to a swiftly developing European economy.

SUSAN MOSHER STUARD

References and Further Reading

Goldberg, P. J. P. *Women, Work, and Life Cycle in a Medieval Economy: Women in York and Yorkshire, c. 1300–1520.* Oxford: Clarendon Press, 1992.

Herlihy, David, *Opera Muliebria: Women and Work in Medieval Europe.* New York: McGraw Hill, 1990.

Women and Work in Pre-industrial Europe, edited by Barbara Hanawalt. Bloomington, Ind.: Indiana University Press, 1986.

See also **Agriculture; Alewives and Brewing; Apprentices; Artisan Families, Women of; Beguines; Breastfeeding and Wet-Nursing; Business; Clothwork, Domestic; Consumption; Division of Labor; Dowry and Other Marriage Gifts; Feme Coverte; Feme Sole; Gentry, Women of: England; Guild Members and Guilds; Heiresses; Home Manufacturing; Inheritance; Investment and Credit; Landholding and Property Rights; Market and Tradeswomen; Merchant Families, Women of; Midwives; Monasticism and Nuns; Patronage, Ecclesiastical; Peasants; Poverty; Prostitutes; Servants; Slaves; Textile Production for the Market; Work**

EDITH

As wife of Edward I "the Confessor," daughter of the powerful Earl Godwine of Essex, and sister of King Harold, Edith (c. 1020/1030–1075) found herself at the center of a turbulent and traumatic period in English history. She is the addressee and arguably the main subject of the extraordinary *Vita Aedwardi Regis* (1065–1067), written by an anonymous cleric. Pauline Stafford argues that the work reflects Edith's perspective and political interests to such a degree that the queen ought to be considered its shadow author.

Edith received a good education at the royal monastery of Wilton—her learning and accomplishments were frequently noted—and was married to King Edward in 1045. The marriage did not go smoothly, and included a brief period of separation in 1051–1052, during a major falling-out between the king and Edith's family. At least a secondary reason for Edith's banishment must have been her childlessness. (The notion that the marriage had remained chaste by mutual agreement appears to be a bit of political "spin," which gained momentum as a pious motif in the later hagiography of King Edward.) After 1066, Edith's support of William the Conqueror's claim to the throne earned her a comfortable dowagership; she spent her final years largely at Wilton. While contemporary assessments of her character and political skills vary (William of Malmesbury disparages her; the *Vita Aedwardi* is, of course, flattering), modern historians regard her as an active royal consort and a shrewd actor on a difficult political stage.

MONIKA C. OTTER

References and Further Reading

Barlow, Frank, ed. and trans. *The Life of King Edward Who Rests at Westminster.* 2nd ed. Oxford: Clarendon, 1992.

Mason, Emma. *The House of Godwine: The History of a Dynasty.* London: Hambledon, 2004.

Otter, Monika. "Closed Doors: An Epithalamium for Queen Edith, Widow and Virgin." In *Constructions of Widowhood and Virginity in the Middle Ages*, edited by Cindy Carlson and Angela Jane Weisl. New York: St. Martin's, 1999, pp. 63–92.

Stafford, Pauline. *Queen Emma and Queen Edith: Queenship and Women's Power in Eleventh-Century England.* Oxford: Blackwell, 1997.

See also **Chastity and Chaste Marriage; England; Patronage, Literary; Queens and Empresses: The West**

EDUCATION, BEGUINE

Beguines in northwestern Europe accepted girls as students from the very beginning of their movement, around 1200. Following a tradition established by nuns and recluses, they often took charge of girls, who were raised within the Beguine community (*beguinage*) and received instruction from one or more Beguine teachers but were not necessarily expected to join the community as adults.

The "Lives" of Beatrice of Nazareth, Ida of Nivelles, Ida of Gorsleeuw, and Juliana of Mont-Cornillon include references to their education by informal Beguine groups in the first half of the thirteenth century. Their instruction probably included not only reading and writing in the vernacular, but sometimes also in Latin. These and other sources reveal that some Beguines also instructed young female students in the study and translation of Scripture, Christian spirituality, and mysticism. In the more formally organized *beguinages* that spread from the Low Countries in the 1230s, internal rules sometimes regulated the number of boarders per Beguine teacher or set other limitations. Beguine education was also hampered by the lack of institutionally supported libraries. While generally basic, Beguine education could nevertheless reach sophisticated heights when dispensed by teachers who were particularly gifted or motivated (one may imagine Hadewijch of Brabant, whose "Letters" and "Visions" were fundamentally didactic works, as such a teacher). In a few cases, boys up to the age of puberty were allowed to attend Beguine schools; male teachers occasionally assisted Beguines.

WALTER SIMONS

References and Further Reading

Galloway, Penelope. "'Life, Learning, and Wisdom': The Forms and Functions of Beguine Education." In *Medieval Monastic Education*, edited by George Ferzoco and Carolyn Muessig. London; New York: Leicester University Press, 2000, pp. 153–167.

Simons, Walter. *Cities of Ladies: Beguine Communities in the Medieval Low Countries, 1200–1565.* Philadelphia: University of Pennsylvania Press, 2001.

See also **Beatrice of Nazareth; Beguines; Burgundian Netherlands; Flanders; Hadewijch**

EDUCATION, LAY

In the early medieval centuries, when literacy involved Latin learning, opportunities for laywomen to secure a reading education in Latin texts existed mainly in those monasteries open to schooling lay children and in aristocratic or royal courts, under a tutor. At the elementary reading level, where one learned one's letters, the Psalter and other Latin devotional or scriptural prayers and passages, a father, uncle, mother, or governess may have been the teacher. Elementary learning was also available to girls (and boys) in local, perhaps very informal schools. There are scattered indications of such coeducational schools as early as the ninth century in Italy and France, and their numbers increased in subsequent centuries.

By the twelfth century, Latin learning was becoming more institutionalized. Emerging fee charging grammar schools and universities excluded women. As a consequence women could no longer compete, and learned women, such as Heloise and a significant but small number of other women from the early twelfth century, became more rare. For example, there are no known examples from England of girls in grammar schools. At the same time, the quality of Latin learning in monasteries declined. The example of Trota (and other anonymous female doctors at Salerno) suggests, however, that Latinate literacy for women could have a professional and practical application and may have been transmitted via a kind of apprenticeship. And women continued to learn Latin reading for devotional purposes.

The education of women continued to be informal and unstructured. It could be predominately oral in nature, the result of listening to (and perhaps memorizing and memorializing) recitations, group readings, instructions, prayers, sermons, songs, dramatized plays, or liturgical singing. Lay sisters, for example, in Heloise's Abbey of the Paraclete, learned by listening to edifying readings from the nuns, while women from the lower classes learned the prayers posted on tablets and in stories detailed in images on church walls (sometimes with Latin inscriptions), or secured small pieces of parchment with prayers that might be memorized. Among heretical groups, the Waldensians permitted women to preach and young girls to learn the words of the gospels and epistles. Cathars and Lollards also memorized and passed on religious texts they had heard, although a select group of Lollard women also learned to read. Other such learning communities might be children taught by anchoresses or beguines, women listening to sermons, mothers teaching children prayers and proverbs, or women at court listening to the reading of devotional or romantic works.

It was the growing use of European vernaculars by the twelfth and thirteenth centuries that allowed for the dramatic expansion of lay female interactions with written texts. Women (the mother or perhaps a governess) were often the teachers of girls in a household, perhaps training them in more than one vernacular tongue, teaching them their alphabet, syllables, words and reading, and, in Latin, the reading of prayers and scripture in primers, psalters, and books of hours. A poem from c. 1300 includes the following sentence: "woman teacheth child on book."

By the fourteenth century there was also an increasing assortment of venues in which a girl could be educated. Monasteries continued to educate girls, although increasingly in vernacular devotional readings and liturgical responses rather than in Latin learning. Anchoresses sometimes taught small groups of children (both boys and girls), as did the beguines in Germany. Household tutors and clergy taught girls as well as boys. By the fourteenth century girls were being educated by schoolmistresses; in Paris, in 1380, for example, there were twenty-two licensed school-mistresses. Girls were being educated in numerous coeducational elementary and often quite informal reading schools, and, by the fifteenth century, even in parish song schools.

Those who learned to read might then receive books from a female relative (as devised in her will), might borrow books from a local Carthusian library, or circulate texts among family members, perhaps as a common-profit library. Whether listening to a group reading or reading with book in hand (as an increasing number of images of the Virgin being taught by St. Anne, illustrate), more and more women were gaining access to the written word.

The education of women often involved learning tasks more than texts. Although, by the late Middle Ages, there are conduct books and household manuals, most women learned household tasks, manners, and Christian virtues from informal verbal instruction, perhaps from a mother or husband. Female apprentices were taught a trade or craft but rarely to read or write. Those few girls who were apprenticed as scriveners might be taught the task of writing formularies, but it is unclear how much they would have understood what they wrote.

It was uncommon for women to learn to write. Writing was a separate skill, often taught by specialized writing masters. Medieval women's signatures, for example, are relatively scarce and often show an unpracticed hand. A signature alone cannot tell us much about the education of the signatory. Even women trained to read would have been unlikely to have picked up quills and written. And, indeed, writing skills for women were less valued than the ability to read. As the Knight de la Tour-Landry put it in his fourteenth-century advice to his daughters, "Reading is profitable to all women," but he did not recommend that they learn to write. The late medieval portrait of the author Christine de Pizan sitting at her desk writing is unusual and remarkable, as was her passionate advocacy of female education and the role of learned women.

Jo Ann Hoeppner Moran Cruz

References and Further Reading

Barron, Caroline. "The Education and Training of Girls in Fifteenth-Century London," in *Courts, Counties and the Capital in the Later Middle Ages*, edited by Diana E. S. Dunn. New York: St. Martin's Press, 1996, pp. 139–153.

Clanchy, Michael. "Learning to Read in the Middle Ages and the Role of Mothers," In *Studies in the History of Reading*, edited by Greg Brooks and A. K. Pugh. Reading: Centre for Teaching of Reading, 1984, pp. 33–39.

Ferrante, Joan. "The Education of Women in the Middle Ages in Theory, Fact, and Fantasy," in *Beyond Their Sex: Learned Women of the European Past*, edited by Patricia H. Labalme. New York: New York University Press, 1984, pp. 9–42.

Phillips, Kim M. *Medieval Maidens: Young Women and Gender in England, 1270–1540*. Manchester: Manchester University Press, 2003.

Scase, Wendy. "St. Anne and the Education of the Virgin," In *England in the Fourteenth Century*, edited by Nicholas Rogers. Stamford, 1993, pp. 81–96.

Shahar, Shulamith. *Childhood in the Middle Ages*, translated by Chaya Galai. London: Routledge, 1990.

See also **Book Ownership; Conduct Literature; Education, Beguine; Education, Monastic; Girls and Boys; Letter Writing; Literacy and Reading, Latin; Literacy and Reading, Vernacular; Mothers as Teachers**

EDUCATION, MONASTIC

Medieval Christian attitudes toward the education of women were marked by deep ambivalence. Churchmen believed that women ought not to teach, an idea founded on Paul's suggestion that Eve's teaching had led to the Fall (1 Timothy 2:11–14). Yet despite restrictions on women's teaching within the public sphere, women within the monastery functioned as both teachers and learners throughout the medieval period. Indeed, the provision of religious instruction and basic education was a primary function of the monastic community—whether that community was male or female.

The Monastic Rules

Early monastic rules emphasize the importance of study within the cloister. Alongside manual labor, Benedict (c. 480–c. 560) required that all monks devote themselves to private reading each day (chapter 48) and that meals within the monastery be accompanied by communal reading (chapter 38). Rules written specifically for women mirror Benedict's emphasis on reading and study. Writing in the sixth century, Caesarius of Arles advised that the women of St. Jean learn to read (chapter 7) and required that time be set aside each day for both private and communal reading (chapters 18–20). Caesarius also stipulated that nuns should learn to write, a fact that is confirmed by his hagiographer, who observed that they copied sacred texts. Other rules for women—including those of Aurelian of Arles and Donatus of Besançon—contained a similar emphasis on education and placed learning at the heart of female, like male, monasticism.

Saints' Lives

Early medieval hagiographers reported regularly on the educational achievements of their female subjects, depicting learning as one manifestation of sanctity in women. The seventh-century female hagiographer Baudonivia wrote that Radegund devoted herself to divine meditation, both day and night. At night, she would engage one of the other nuns to read to her. If this reader ceased even for a moment, Radegund would chastise her, a motif that also appears in the life of the eighth-century Anglo-Saxon nun and missionary, Leoba. Other women were praised for their mental agility in both sacred and secular studies. Gertrude of Nivelles's biographer praised her memory, as does Leoba's biographer, noting that she had been taught the "sacred sciences" as a girl. Similarly, the eleventh-century life of Adelheid of Vilich, written by Bertha, a member of Adelheid's community, reported that the saint immersed herself in "philosophic studies" as a girl.

Female Authorship and Scribal Activity

Women's writing in Latin was evidence of their education. Like Baudonivia and Bertha, some monastic women composed saints' lives. In the eighth century, Hugeburc of Heidenheim wrote a life of St. Willibald; in the twelfth, Hildegard of Bingen wrote the life of St. Rupert, patron of her foundation at the Rupertsburg. Other women, like Gisela and Rotrude, Charlemagne's sister and daughter, corresponded with prominent churchmen. Still other women contributed to the preservation of the past either through their historical writing or by commissioning or copying histories. During the tenth century, the playwright and canoness Hrotsvit of Gandersheim composed two historical works, including a history of her monastery, while a nun of Quedlinburg recorded the annals of her monastery. Still other women—like Hildegard of Bingen and Elisabeth of Schönau—produced visionary and theological works. Hildegard's vast corpus also included medical and scientific works, music, and a morality play. Many anonymous texts may also have been written by women.

Women were similarly engaged in book production. Early medieval nuns provided books for newly established monasteries in England during the seventh century and Germany during the eighth. The Anglo-Saxon missionary Boniface wrote to Eadburga, abbess of Minster-in-Thanet, requesting that she supply him with books for his mission. Women also copied books to fill their own libraries and functioned as monastic librarians. Although most of these female scribes remain anonymous, some are known by name. The most famous is Diemut of Wessobrunn, who copied more than forty books during the first half of the twelfth century. The twelfth-century nun-scribes of Admont, a Benedictine double house, produced a substantial manuscript collection, took dictation from Abbot Irimbert, and probably composed their own theological works as well. In some cases, the evidence suggests that men and women collaborated on manuscript production within a single scriptorium.

Women as Teachers

Despite prohibitions against women's public teaching women were permitted to teach within their communities until the thirteenth century. Women's houses frequently served as educational centers where young women were sent to be educated before returning to the world to marry. In some cases, boys were also educated by religious women. The eleventh-century *Uta Codex*, commissioned by Uta, abbess of Niedermünster, included a depiction of a woman teaching three children, no doubt reflecting educational practice within her community. Female teachers were remembered with fondness by their pupils. At Vilich, Adelheid was recalled as an affectionate yet demanding figure. Her biographer reports that she would rise early in winter and rub the girls' feet once they had returned to their beds after matins. But Adelheid could also be strict. Visiting the schoolroom, she would drill the students on grammatical questions, rewarding correct answers with a kiss. At other times, she would box the ears of girls who sang out of tune in the choir. Hrotsvit of Gandersheim acknowledges the influence of her teacher, Rikkardis, whom she describes as "our most learned and gentle novice mistress." Similarly, the twelfth-century abbess and author Herrad of Hohenbourg pays tribute to her teacher, Relinde, in her *Hortus deliciarum* (*Garden of Delights*).

Scholarship within the Women's Community

Monastic education tended to focus primarily on religious instruction, namely the Scriptures and the Psalms. Yet within certain monasteries, women were also educated in the liberal arts. At Barking in the seventh century, Aldhelm records that women studied history, grammar, and metrics. Similarly, Hrotsvit's writings reveal her familiarity with a wide range of classical and medieval authors, among them Terence, Ovid, and Virgil, as well as Jerome, Prudentius, Boethius, and Isidore of Seville. Hrotsvit also studied (and possibly taught) arithmetic. A long section in her play *Sapientia* explores the qualities of various numbers in order to provide the ages of the three daughters of Sapientia. At Hohenbourg in the twelfth century, women followed a broad curriculum that included contemporary monastic and scholastic texts. The broad ranging contents of the *Hortus deliciarum* demonstrated that women at Hohenbourg read works of theology, biblical history, and even canon law, replicating the reading patterns of monk-priests and students in the emerging Parisian schools. The depiction of *Philosophia* that appears in the manuscript suggests that the liberal arts also formed part of their curriculum. Clearly, the level of education within women's communities could be high. Heloise, who gained her early education at the female monastery of Argenteuil, was already famed for her learning before she met Abelard, as Peter the Venerable attested. Her erudition was demonstrated in her letters and in the *Problemata*, a series of biblical questions that she sent Abelard based on her study with the women at the Paraclete. Further evidence for the sophistication of women's education was provided in Abelard's letter 9, "On Educating Virgins," in which he encourages the women of the Paraclete to pursue their studies under Heloise's care, noting her facility not only in Latin and Greek, but also Hebrew.

The Later Middle Ages

By the later medieval period, monasteries were no longer vibrant educational centers, as universities rapidly moved to the forefront of medieval education. Although many monastic women continued to read and to study, women's sanctity was increasingly divorced from education after the thirteenth century, and holy women from this period were regularly described as illiterate or lacking in formal education. Even so, monastic women could still attain high levels of education, as the example of the sixteenth-century German nun Caritas Pirckheimer suggests.

FIONA J. GRIFFITHS

References and Further Reading

Abelard. Letter 9. "On Educating Virgins." In *Guidance for Women in Twelfth-century Convents.* translated by Vera Morton. Cambridge: D. S. Brewer, 2003, pp. 121–138.

Beach, Alison I. *Women as Scribes: Book Production and Monastic Reform in Twelfth-century Bavaria.* Cambridge, UK: Cambridge University Press, 2004.

Caesarius of Arles. *The Rule for Nuns of St. Caesarius of Arles*, edited by Maria Caritas McCarthy. Washington, DC: Catholic University of America Press, 1960.

Ferrante, Joan M. "The Education of Women in the Middle Ages in Theory, Fact, and Fantasy." In *Beyond Their Sex: Learned Women of the European Past*, edited by Patricia H. Labalme. New York: New York University Press, 1980, pp. 9–42.

Griffiths, Fiona. *The* Garden of Delights: *Reform and Renaissance for Women in the Twelfth Century.* Philadelphia: University of Pennsylvania Press, Forthcoming.

Heinrich, Mary Pia. *The Canonesses and Education in the Early Middle Ages.* Washington, DC: Catholic University of America, 1924.

Heloise. "The Problemata of Heloise." translated by Anne Collins Smith. In *Women Writing Latin: From Roman Antiquity to Early Modern Europe.* Vol. 2. *Medieval Women Writing Latin*, edited by Laurie J. Churchill, Phyllis R. Brown, and Jane E. Jeffrey. New York: Routledge, 2002, pp. 173–196.

Herrad of Hohenbourg. *Hortus Deliciarum,* edited by Rosalie Green, Michael Evans, Christine Bischoff, and Michael Curschmann. 2 vols. Studies of the Warburg Institute, 36. London: The Warburg Institute, 1979.

Mater spiritualis: The Life of Adelheid of Vilich, edited by Madelyn Bergen Dick. Toronto, Ontario: Peregrina Pub., 1994.

McKitterick, Rosamond. *Books, Scribes, and Learning in the Frankish Kingdoms, 6th–9th Centuries.* Aldershot: Variorum, 1994.

Wemple, Suzanne Fonay. *Women in Frankish Society: Marriage and the Cloister, 500 to 900.* Philadelphia: University of Pennsylvania Press, 1981.

See also **Abbesses; Book Ownership; Heloise; Herrad of Hohenburg; Hildegard of Bingen; Hrotsvit of Gandersheim; Leoba; Letter Writing; Literacy and Reading: Latin; Monastic Rules; Monasticism and Nuns; Nuns as Illuminators; Radegund; Universities; Women Authors: Latin Texts**

ELEANOR OF AQUITAINE

Eleanor (c.1122–1204), queen of France and of England, was one of three children of Duke William X of Aquitaine and his wife Eleanor. Her brother, mother, and father were all dead by 1137, leaving her the heiress to the vast county which stretched from the Loire river to the Pyrenees. Her wealth made her an attractive marriage prospect, and in July 1137 she was married to the future Louis VII, King of France. The marriage does not seem to have been personally harmonious. Their first daughter was not born until 1145. It was probably the need for a male heir that led Louis and the French nobility to allow the queen to accompany them on the Second Crusade. The 1147 venture seems to have exacerbated underlying tensions in their marriage. In 1148, when they reached Antioch, scandal arose because Eleanor was perceived to be suspiciously close to her paternal uncle Raymond, ruler of the territory. The crusade itself was a spectacular failure. On the return trip, the queen was captured by a Greek naval commander. After their reunification in Sicily, Louis and Eleanor journeyed together to Rome where Pope Eugenius III encouraged the couple to reconcile and even provided a royally decorated bed upon which he urged them to resume marital relations. A second daughter was born the following year. The reconciliation proved temporary, and in 1152, the couple was divorced on grounds of consanguinity, with Louis gaining custody of the two daughters and Eleanor regaining control of the territories she had brought into the marriage.

The divorced queen was no less a tempting prospect than had been the young countess. After two noblemen tried and failed to kidnap her and force her into a marriage, she agreed to marry Henry of Anjou in May 1152. Henry was about nineteen years old and she was about thirty, and since he was occupied in consolidating his hold on his continental territories as well as securing his claim to the throne of England, she may have believed that she could dominate the young count. The death of King Stephen of England in 1154 brought Henry and Eleanor to the throne, and Henry set about incorporating her territories into his vast empire. The next fifteen years of Eleanor's life were punctuated by pregnancy and childbearing. She gave birth to at least five sons and three daughters between 1153 and 1166–1167. Eleanor also appeared with Henry at ceremonial court gatherings, helped negotiate marriage alliances for her children, intervened in legal proceedings, issued royal mandates, and witnessed royal charters.

As her sons came of age, Eleanor and Henry began to train them to carry out their duties in the territories they would inherit. The daughters were married strategically. As the sons began to assume partial responsibility for their assigned territories, tension arose because they resented their father's continued control. The king and Eleanor's relationship had also soured over time, and by 1173, the sons were in revolt against the king, aided and abetted by Eleanor and the French king, who resented the loss of Eleanor's territories and England's growing dominance. Henry quelled the revolt and imprisoned Eleanor for her part in it. Eleanor did not regain her freedom until Henry died in 1189 and her son Richard ordered her freed and returned her revenues and territories to her.

Until her death in 1204, Eleanor assisted her sons Richard (d. 1199) and then John (d. 1215) in governing. She took oaths of loyalty in Richard's name upon his accession to England's throne, assisted in the regency government while he was away on the Third Crusade, and negotiated his release when he was taken captive. In 1200, she traveled to Castile to accompany a granddaughter, Blanche, to Paris to become the bride of the future King Louis VIII. During John's reign, she took charge of improving England's coastal defenses when France threatened invasion. She was involved in ecclesiastical affairs, including negotiations with the papacy during both of her sons' reigns. She spent her last years at her favored monastery of Fontevrault. As late as 1203, she was still issuing writs and working to secure John's rights in Aquitaine.

Eleanor is remembered as a patron of art and literature as well as an impressive political figure throughout her long life. While popular representations of her presiding over the Courts of Love are unfounded, she was literate and had many works dedicated to her. She may have chosen the design for her tomb effigy, which shows her holding a book.

Lois L. Huneycutt

References and Further Reading

Bull, Marcus, and Catherine Leglu, eds., *The World of Eleanor of Aquitaine: Literature and Society in Southern France Between the Eleventh and Thirteenth Centuries.* Woodbridge and Rochester: Boydell Press, 2005.

Kibler, William, ed., *Eleanor of Aquitaine: Patron and Politician.* Austin, Texas: University of Texas Press, 1976.

Martindale, Jane. "Eleanor of Aquitaine." In Janet T. Nelson, ed., *Richard Coeur de Lion in History and Myth.* London: King's College London Centre for Late Antique and Medieval Studies, 1992, pp. 17–50.

Wheeler, Bonnie, and John Carmi Parsons eds. *Eleanor of Aquitaine: Lord and Lady.* New York: Palgrave MacMillan, 2003.

See also **Blanche of Castile; England; Occitania; Queens and Empresses: the West**

ELEANOR OF SCOTLAND

Eleanor of Scotland (1433–1480), also known as Eleonore von Österreich (Eleanor of Austria), was one of six daughters of James I of Scotland, himself the author of *The Kingis Quair*, and Joan Beaufort, niece of the bishop of Winchester and the chancellor of England. Starting in 1445, she lived at the court of Charles the Seventh in France. In 1448, at the age of fifteen, she married Archduke Sigismund von Tirol. An avid traveler, Eleanor was literate in several languages.

Household accounts reveal that Eleanor received and presented books. This involvement with literature culminated in Eleanor's translation and rewriting of a

French romance, *Ponthus et la belle Sidoine*, whose source was the English ballad *King Horn*. Eleanor's *Pontus und Sidonia* dates from between 1449 and 1465, and was first printed in 1483. It was popular, as evidenced by its numerous printings during the sixteenth and seventeenth centuries.

Twice taking over the leadership of the realm during her husband's absence, from 1455 to 1458 and again in 1467, Eleanor's international political skill and marital relationship are reflected in her revisions of the source text to increase the political role of women. Only the courts with effective female advisors successfully retain their stability. Her emphasis on the importance of mutual desire in aristocratic marriages may have come from her own experience in an arranged marriage. She, along with Elisabeth von Nassau-Saarbrücken (c. 1393–1456), is recognized as having introduced a new genre to German literature, the prose novel.

SUSAN SIGNE MORRISON

References and Further Reading

Bawcutt, Priscilla and Bridget Henisch. "Scots Abroad in the Fifteenth Century: The Princesses Margaret, Isabella and Eleanor." In *Women in Scotland c. 1100–c. 1750*, edited by Elizabeth Ewan and Maureen M. Meikle. East Linton: Tuckwell Press, 1999, pp. 45–55.

Classen, Albrecht. "Die leidende und unterdrückte Frau im Roman des 15. Jahrhunderts: Zur Verfasserschaft des frühneuhochdeutschen Romans *Pontus und Sidonia*." *Seminar* 29 (1993): 1–27.

Eleonore von Österreich. "Pontus und Sidonia" In *Volksbücher vom sterbenden Rittertum*, edited by Heinz Kindermann. Weimar: Böhlaus, 1928. [1500 Printing].

Kellermann-Haaf, Petra. *Frau und Politik im Mittelalter. Untersuchungen zur politischen Rolle der Frau in den höfischen Romanen des 12., 13. und 14. Jahrhunderts.* Göppingen: Kümmerle, 1986.

King Horn, Floriz and Blauncheflur, the Assumption of Our Lady. Ed. (1866) J. Rawson Lumby. Ed. (1962) George H. McKnight. *Early English Text Society*, 58 London: Oxford University Press, 1962.

Liebertz-Grün, Ursula. "Autorinnen im Umkreis der Höfe." In *Frauen—Literatur—Geschichte: Schreibende Frauen vom Mittelalter bis zur Gegenwart*, edited by Hiltrud Gnüg und Renate Möhrmann. Stuttgart: Suhrkamp, 1985, pp. 16–34.

Liepe, Wolfgang. *Elisabeth von Nassau-Saarbrücken: Entstehung und Angänge des Prosaromans in Deutschland.* Halle A. S.: Max Niemeyer, 1920.

Morrison, Susan Signe. "Women Writers and Women Rulers: Rhetorical and Political Empowerment in the Fifteenth-Century." *Women in German Yearbook* 9 (1994): 25–48.

Müller, Jan-Dirk. "Volksbuch/Prosaroman im 15./16. Jahrhundert—Perspektiven der Forschung." *Internationales Archiv für Sozialgeschichte der deutschen Literatur*, edited by Wolfgang Frühwald, Georg Jäger, and Alberto Martino. Tübingen: Max Niemeyer Verlag, 1985, pp. 1–128.

See also **Germanic Lands; Literature, German; Marriage, Christian; Noble Women; Scotland; Women Authors: German Texts**

ELISABETH OF HUNGARY

Born the daughter of King Andrew II of Hungary and Gertrude of Meran, betrothed at the age of four to the son of Hermann I, Landgrave of Thuringia, Elisabeth of Hungary (1207–1231) was brought up in the Thuringian court at Eisenach and Wartburg. She married Louis IV of Thuringia in 1221. According to the testimonies of her life she had a happy marriage with him, and bore three children, Hermann (1222), Sofia (1224), and Gertrud (1227). At the same time, moved by the novel religious ideas of the Franciscans, she turned away from the luxury of courtly life and, under the influence of her severe confessor, Conrad of Marburg, she dedicated herself to charity and ascetic piety. After the death of her husband (1227), she financed from her dower a leper's hospital in Marburg, dedicated to Saint Francis. She lived there in excessive renunciation and dedicated her life to the care of the sick. She died at the age of twenty-four (1231).

Elisabeth's cult emerged soon after her burial, and her tomb became a new site for pilgrimage and miraculous healings. Between 1232 and 1235, an exemplary canonization process elevated her to sainthood. The testimonies of her handmaids (*Dicta quatuor ancillarum*) provided an engaging account of her life of renunciation. She became one of the most popular female saints in the Middle Ages. A caring wife and mother, then an exemplary widow, she became a model for pious princesses in royal courts, a saint of charity in towns, an ideal for the Franciscan Third Order and other semi-religious groups.

GÁBOR KLANICZAY

References and Further Reading

Klaniczay, G. *Holy Rulers and Blessed Princesses: Dynastic Cults in Medieval Central Europe.* Cambridge: Cambridge University Press, 2002.

Sankt Elisabeth: Fürstin, Dienerin, Heilige. Sigmorigen Thorbecke, 1981.

Werner, M. "Mater Hassiae - Flos Ungariae - Gloria Teutoniae," In *Politik und Heiligenverehrung im Hochmittelalter*, edited by J. Petersohn. Sigmorigen Thorbecke, 1994, pp. 449–540.

See also **Almsgiving and Charity; Canonization of Saints; Germanic Lands; Hagiography; Hospitals**

ELISABETH OF SCHÖNAU

Elisabeth of Schönau (1128/29–1164/65) was a Benedictine nun, famous during her life as a visionary, whose works enjoyed great popularity after her death. Born in the Rhineland to a well-established and well-connected family, she entered the double monastery at Schönau, a Benedictine community of monks and nuns, when she was twelve. At the age of twenty-three, she began to have visionary experiences which lasted until her death, and before 1156 she became *magistra* (mistress) of the nuns at Schönau. She related her visions in three diaristic *Books of Visions* (*Libri Visionum I-III*); she also wrote a treatise on the paths to heaven, *Liber viarum Dei* (*Book of the Ways of God*); a text on the martyrdom of St. Ursula and her companions, *Revelatio de sacro exercitu virginum Coloniensium* (*The Revelation about the Sacred Company of the Virgins of Cologne*); a short collection of her visions about the bodily resurrection of the Virgin Mary, *Visio de resurrectione beate virginis Marie* (*Vision about the Resurrection of the Blessed Virgin Mary*), and twenty-two letters.

Elisabeth's visionary gift first manifested itself after a bout of suffering and temptation by the devil. In the first book of the *Visions*, titled in its earliest version *Liber eiusdem de temptationibus inimici, quas primo sustinuit et de revelationibus divinis quas post modum vidit* (*On the Temptations of the Enemy, which She First Endured, and Her Subsequent Divinely Revealed Visions*), she describes the *acedia* (not-caring) which prevented her from finding comfort in the Psalms, such that she even hurled the psalter she was reading across the room. She tells how she questioned Christ's divinity and in her *tristitia* (sadness, the sin of despair that made Judas hang himself) contemplated suicide. Her affliction and temptation place her in the company of early holy men, but the particular, vivid details of her account point to an intensity of lived experience. The devil tormented her in the chapel as a tiny apparition wearing a monk's cowl; as a human, short, stocky, red-faced, with a darting fiery tongue and taloned feet and hands; as a repulsive dog; and as a huge bull threatening to gobble her up. Finally, she saw Mary in a wheel of light during mass, heard her comforting words, and caught her first glimpse of the handsome young angel who became her guide. However, the devil still competed with Mary and with the crucified Christ for Elisabeth's attention. Disguised as a seductive young clerk, he stalked her as she tried to escape, and compelled her to stare at his lewd gestures.

Throughout her life, Elisabeth's community witnessed her physical suffering and waking trances, and the nuns wrote down the words she spoke and the visions she recounted. Elisabeth's monastic community tended and supported her with prayer and sometimes with self-flagellation to help her carry out the guiding angel's commands. Her visions, inextricably connected to the devotional practices of the monastery, affirmed and deepened the way others experienced their daily religious rituals. But, although what she saw in trance often conformed to what her sisters and brothers believed, some visions were unusual, even radical: Mary in priestly garb officiating at the altar; Christ as a radiant female virgin, the form of Christ's humanity, as her angel confirmed.

Two years after her visions began, Elisabeth's angel commissioned her to proclaim God's word as a prophet. Urging reform, she addressed abbots and the archbishop of Trier in letters, speaking as "a certain small spark sent from the seat of great majesty, and a voice thundering in the heart of a small worm-person." Her prophetic mandate and her concern with pastoral matters and reform found expression in the *Book of the Ways of God*, which admonishes both religious and lay people. Quite different from, but perhaps inspired by Hildegard of Bingen's *Scivias* (*Know the Ways*), it shows Elisabeth's astute awareness of the world outside the cloister in unexpected ways, as when she warned against sibling incest among young children who are unaware of sin. In a lengthy narrative that survives in only three manuscripts she noticed that an adolescent monk brought up in the monastery had been seduced by an older, worldly companion. Elisabeth convinced him to open his heart to her and repent, and then took charge of the objects the young men had stolen to finance their flight. The boy was saved, while his seducer stole the abbot's horse and fled. Her psychological astuteness, her compassion, and her decisive firmness all suggest that as mistress of the nuns, a position second to that of abbot, she played a much more practical role than her visionary diaries suggest.

When inscriptions and bones were found in the Cologne cemetery believed to be the site where Ursula and her company of virgins were martyred, abbot Gerlach of Deutz turned to Elisabeth for inside information about the authenticity of the relics. In a series of visionary conversations, Elisabeth was able to account for the presence of men and children in the company of female virgins. Her revelation, full of complex, novelistic subplots, differed from pre-existing narratives. Her reshaping of the legend validated both male and female virginity, construed martyrdom as bearing witness through one's life to God's grace, and emphasized the power of love in a community of the pious.

Elisabeth's voice remained distinctive, but modern scholars have debated her brother Ekbert's role in shaping her works. Educated in Paris and groomed for a career in the church, he left his deaconate in Bonn to become a monk at Schönau and to serve as Elisabeth's scribe, translator, and editor. Elisabeth received and spoke her visions sometimes in Latin and sometimes with an admixture of German. Ekbert averred that he translated the German faithfully, took away nothing and added nothing of his own. Yet he did edit and shape the narratives to some extent, and both shorter and longer versions survive. Elisabeth's visionary narratives and concerns become more sophisticated over the years, but one should not rule out her own development while becoming more important both within and outside Schönau. Nor should one take literally the claims that she knew no Latin: miraculous knowledge of Latin stresses the divine origin and authority of utterance. From the time she was eight, Elisabeth read and recited the Psalms in Latin every day. Each day of her life as a Benedictine nun was punctuated by Latin prayer, services, and by readings in Latin during meals. She "speaks Bible fluently," and she thought in biblical and liturgical Latin. Nothing in the style of her narratives is alien to her linguistic background.

The communal, devotional, and pastoral concerns of Elisabeth's visions struck a responsive chord in her own times. Important churchmen turned to her for inside information from her angel. Was Mary resurrected in the body? (Elisabeth learned that she was.) During her final illness, she was surrounded by her brothers and sisters, who loved her and valued her divinely inspired wisdom, and throngs of outsiders came to hear her last words. Her works were transmitted in at least 145 medieval manuscripts, often grouped with works by writers like Bernard of Clairvaux. A decade after her death, Roger of Ford, an English Cistercian, came upon *The Book of the Ways of God* in France; he sent a copy to his abbot with a letter telling how the book was "eagerly copied and read and heard not only by the unlearned but by bishops and our abbots," and asked that another copy be made and sent to the convent where his mother lived. At the Cistercian abbey of Saint Mary at Himmerod, *The Book of the Ways of God* was selected for reading at collation. Less than a century after her visions began many monastic libraries in Germany and France owned copies of her works. Most popular were the revelations about the Virgin Mary and the Cologne martyrdom of Ursula and her companions. *The Resurrection of the Blessed Virgin* was translated into Anglo-Norman verse and into Icelandic in the early thirteenth-century. In the fourteenth century, *The Book of the Ways of God* was translated into French, and 1513 saw the first printing of her visions.

THALIA A. PANDIRI

References and Further Reading

Clark, Anne L. *Elisabeth of Schönau: A Twelfth-Century Visionary*. Philadelphia: University of Pennsylvania Press, 1992.
———. "Holy Woman or Unworthy Vessel? The Representations of Elisabeth of Schönau." In *Gendered Voices: Medieval Saints and Their Interpreters*, edited by Catherine M. Mooney. Philadelphia: University of Pennsylvania Press, 1999, pp. 35–51.
Elisabeth of Schönau. *The Complete Works*. translated and introduced by Anne L. Clark. New York: Paulist Press, 2000.
Ferrante, Joan M. *To the Glory of Her Sex: Women's Roles in the Composition of Medieval Texts*. Bloomington: Indiana University Press, 1997.
Pandiri, Thalia A. "Autobiography or Autohagiography? Decoding the Subtext in the *Visions* of Elisabeth of Schönau." In *Women Writing Latin, from Roman Antiquity to Early Modern Europe* (in Three Volumes), vol. 2 *Medieval Women Writing Latin*, edited by Laurie J. Churchill, Phyllis R. Brown, Jane E. Jeffrey. New York and London: Routledge, 2002, pp. 197–229.
Roth, F. W. E., Ed. *Die Visionen der hl. Elisabeth und die Schriften der Aebte Ekbert und Emecho von Schönau*. Brünn: Verlag der Studien aus dem Benedictiner-und Cistercienser Orden, 1884.

See also **Autohagiography; Education, Monastic; Germanic Lands; Hagiography, Iconographic Aspects of; Hildegard of Bingen; Jesus/God as Mother; Letter Writing; Literacy and Reading: Latin; Mary, Virgin; Monasticism and Nuns; Mystics' Writings; Relics and Reliquaries; Sermons and Preaching; Ursula and Her Companions; Virgin Martyrs; Women Authors: Latin Texts**

EMPRESSES: BYZANTIUM

Wives, widows, mothers, and daughters of emperors in Byzantium might all be called empress and many exercised considerable power during the millennial epoch of imperial rule in Constantinople (330–1453). The official titles *augousta* (from the Latin *augustus*) and *basilissa/basilida*, the feminine equivalent of *basileus* (emperor), were bestowed at coronation and marriage. *Despoina* (lady, mistress, from *despotes*, lord, master), was also used, for instance when Theodora said: "May I never be separated from this purple, and may I never live to see the day when people do not address me as *despoina*," during the Nika riot in 532. Here she also emphasizes the significance of the imperial color purple, which was restricted to the ruling family.

Role at Court

Within the Byzantine court the empress had supreme authority over the women's quarters (*gynaikonitis*), with her own hierarchy of officials, often eunuchs, who served and guarded her (e.g., bedroom, wardrobe, dining room, and treasury staff). She could also summon generals, doctors, monks, bishops, and her husband's counselors to attend her. The empress's power was enshrined in the gendered structure of court activities, in which she provided a feminine counterpart to the emperor's ceremonies. Whenever he received or entertained male officials, she presided over the feminine side, receiving the wives of senators and office holders, for instance. This feature was so fundamental to official banquets that when Leo VI's wife died he was forced to crown his young daughter to fulfill this formal role. While many official acclamations and ceremonies took place inside the Great Palace, the empress also performed public rituals in Constantinople and farther afield. She might also make private visits to shrines or relatives, and would often accompany the emperor on campaign.

Dynastic Responsibilities

The key function of a Byzantine empress was dynastic: through the birth of legitimate children she secured the transmission of imperial authority within the ruling family from generation to generation. A son would inherit his father's power as emperor; daughters could be advantageously married. Even those who did not produce children could retain a powerful position as widows, as Pulcheria and Ariadne did in the fifth century. This late antique practice became less common in the Middle Ages, but it was not forgotten due to the incorporation of written records in the Byzantine *Book of Ceremonies* compiled by Constantine VII Porphyrogennetos in the tenth century. In addition, oral accounts of determined empresses like Theodora and Sophia, wives of Justinian I and II respectively, probably sustained models of feminine ambition.

Empresses played a major role in disputed successions throughout Byzantine history. As widows or daughters of emperors they could favor one candidate over another in the transmission of imperial authority. During the eleventh century Zoe, daughter of Constantine VIII, raised four men (three husbands and a nephew) to the position of emperor. Widowed empresses might also hold the balance of power as regent for their young sons (e.g., Irene in 780, Theodora in 843, Zoe Karbonopsina in 912, Eudokia Makrembolitissa in 1067, and Anna of Savoy in 1341).

This aspect of maternal power was recognized in Byzantine law and allowed Anna Dalassena to attain a position of exceptional dominance. When her son

Alexios I Komnenos set off on campaign in 1081, he drew up a legal document that left her control. This stated, "Because of her vast experience of secular affairs…whatever she decrees in writing…shall have permanent validity…whatever decisions or orders are made by her…shall be regarded as coming from myself." Such a total transference of authority by an adult emperor was unusual, but mothers of younger rulers regularly drew on the principle of maternal protection of their rights in order to exercise supreme power.

Imperial Marriages

Since a woman normally became empress by marrying the emperor or his son, her selection was a matter of great importance. For political reasons she might be of foreign birth, chosen to consolidate an alliance with Byzantium (e.g., the Khazar princess Čiček who was renamed Irene [Peace], on her marriage to Constantine V in 732). This policy became very common from the twelfth century onwards, as imperial families sought to bolster their power through foreign treaties and sought wives from Western, crusading, and Balkan families as empresses (e.g., Agnes-Anna of France, wife first of Alexios II and then of Andronikos I; Ioanna-Anna of Savoy, wife of Andronikos III; and Helena Dragaš, who married Manuel II). Other women might be favored by their physical appearance, through a legendary tradition of brideshows in which the young prince selected the most beautiful. This medieval Judgement of Paris probably disguises quite rational reasons for the choice of a woman from a particular family or region, with which the imperial house wished to make an alliance. It served an important function in binding the provincial aristocracy to the center.

Representations in Art

Empresses are regularly depicted in Byzantine art wearing their official robes of office or presenting gifts to Christ and the Virgin, often accompanied by their children, for instance in the gallery mosaics of St. Sophia (Zoe and Irene, wives of Constantine IX and John II respectively), on ivories (Eudokia with Romanos, who has been identified both as Romanos II and IV), and in manuscripts (e.g., Eudokia Ingerina with Basil I [Parisinus graecus 510]). Some empresses feature on the official coinage, and Empress Irene put her own portrait on both sides of the gold *nomisma.* Many founded monasteries and patronized spiritual leaders.

Conclusion

Since the Byzantine Empire had no constitution, there was unlimited potential for empresses to influence their husbands, the court and imperial policy. Procopius claims that Theodora exercised a strong and nefarious influence on Justinian but he also documents their joint patronage of the church. Empress Irene (as regent and sole ruler), Anna Dalassena (regent from 1081 onwards), and Anna of Savoy (regent 1341–1351, and ruler in Thessalonike 1351–c. 1365) illustrate the range of powers that might be claimed. Anna Komnene clearly hoped to attain a similar position, but was frustrated by her brother John II. The experience of successful empresses inspired others but was only enjoyed by a few.

JUDITH HERRIN

References and Further Reading

Garland, Lynda. *Byzantine Empresses. Women and Power in Byzantium 527–1204*. London: Routledge, 1998.
"The Imperial Feminine in Byzantium," *Past and Present* 169 (2000): 3–35.
Herrin, Judith. *Women in Purple. Rulers of Medieval Byzantium*. Princeton: Princeton University Press, 2001.
Hill, Barbara. *Imperial Women in Byzantium 1025–1204*. London: Longman, 1999.
James, Liz. *Byzantine Empresses and Imperial Power*. Leicester: Leicester University Press, 2000.
Vinson, Martha. "The Life of Theodora and the Rhetoric of the Byzantine Bride Show." *Jahrbuch der Oesterreichischen Byzantinistik* 49 (1999): 31–60.

See also **Byzantium; Irene; Komnene, Anna; Queens and Empresses: The West; Theodora**

ENCLOSURE
See **Monastic Enclosure**

ENGLAND

As in the rest of Europe, women in medieval England were regarded as weaker both physically and intellectually than the males around them. A young girl was expected to marry, run a household, and take care of children. Whereas a man was often identified by his profession—a knight, a carpenter, a fisherman—a woman was identified by the stage in her life cycle in relation to marriage—a virgin or single woman, a wife, and a widow. Her well-being would partly depend on her age, partly on her marital status, but also on her social class. Whereas married women remained under the legal authority of their husbands, widows were legally autonomous and could hold property in their own right; they could spend their income as they wished; urban widows might run their husbands' business, and aristocratic widows could control large estates and dominate local affairs. In addition an upper-class woman might have greater opportunities to exercise public power as abbess or queen and almost certainly would have more opportunities to receive some form of education.

Nuns

The introduction of Christianity into England opened up to women an alternative to marriage—the religious life. In some places, in the seventh century, double monasteries were founded, housing communities of men and women, but under the authority of the abbess. Abbesses such as Hild of Whitby participated in theological debates, church synods, and missionary activity. They were able to exercise such influence as they did partly because the fledgling church did not yet have any formal, political, religious, or educational structures and partly because they were extremely wealthy and members of one of the royal families. At a time when very few people, either male or female, were literate, a few noblewomen received a formal literary education comparable to that of a religious male. The nuns of Barking, for example, studied the scriptures and commentaries on them, as well as the writings of historians and chroniclers.

Their influence, however, was short-lived. The Viking invasions destroyed a number of female houses. New parochial and educational structures were established. In the twelfth century the church, in both England and the Continent, underwent a reform movement, which stressed the importance of the mass and the celibacy of the clergy. Women were seen as a source of temptation. The double houses of men and women disappeared, and, when new houses were established, women were confined to single-sex institutions that eventually were strictly cloistered. At neither the new houses nor the older foundations that survived the Viking invasions did monastic learning attain the earlier levels of scholarship. Few of the nuns who joined the new foundations came from royal or noble families and not one of the new abbesses enjoyed the same independence as her seventh-century predecessors.

Queens and Noble Women

The Norman Conquest produced little change in the rights and status of women, who remained subject to male authority, first that of their father, and subsequently that of their husband or other male kin. Although a queen, especially if she was independently wealthy and belonged to a powerful family, might be able to exercise considerable influence, she was very dependent on the support of her husband and son. The best example comes from the life of Eleanor of Aquitaine, the wife of the Angevin king Henry II. Henry allowed Eleanor to exercise authority in her Duchy of Aquitaine when it suited him, but after she encouraged her sons in their rebellion against their father, he was able to keep her under strict surveillance in England during the last years of his life. It was only during the reign of her son, Richard I, that his absence abroad allowed Eleanor to take over the governing of the country.

Moreover, as the power of the king grew, aristocratic women found themselves the tools of royal favor. The Anglo-Saxon king, Aethelred (c. 978–1016), in his efforts to gain allies, arranged the marriages of widows and heiresses without their consent. Although subsequent rulers promised that widows would not be forced to remarry, this did not stop them from charging high fines on widows for the right to marry or not to marry. It was not until the granting of Magna Carta (1215), in clauses 7 and 8, that a widow was promised that she should not be compelled to pay anything to secure her rights in land and that she should not be compelled to remarry and thus required to pay a fine to remain celibate.

Marriage

A woman's social class profoundly affected the age at which she married and the degree of freedom she might exercise over the choice of her marriage partner. In the early Anglo-Saxon period, it may have been impossible for the poor to partake in a formal marriage ceremony and provide for a bride-price (paid to the bridegroom's family), a morning gift (given to the bride), and a feast. Many young couples entered into a loose domestic association, and the women enjoyed greater freedom of choice than their aristocratic peers, subject to the influence of kin and crown. Gradually, under pressure from church courts, in regard to all social classes, the old ceremonies were replaced by new Christian ones. Fathers almost certainly retained a great deal of influence over the choice of a partner. In addition unfree families (*villeins*) were required to pay a tax (*merchet*) to the lord for the right to marry their daughters. In the twelfth century, the church's new ruling on what constituted a valid marriage did provide some protection against forced marriages. Pope Alexander III (1159–1181) decreed that what made a marriage was the consent of the contracting parties. Yet the spread of this idea among the general populace was slow, and it was not until the fifteenth century that most people knew that words or vows could make a marriage. Unmarried women who left home to work as servants found it easier to escape from parental influence. Some were able to earn enough money to pay their own *merchet*, and to set up a new household, but they often could not do so until their mid-twenties.

Married women contributed to the economic well-being of their families through unpaid labor—taking care of the family's pigs and poultry as well as crops growing in the garden—but also through paid labor, by brewing, spinning, or selling home-produced goods, eggs and the like, in local markets. In towns they helped their husbands run their businesses and might claim the status of *feme sole*, that is the right to trade as if they were single women and to be solely responsible for their debts. In London, where women were encouraged to make a formal declaration of this status, those who did so worked predominantly as hucksters. By the twelfth century, occupational sex segregation was clearly in force, with areas such as laundry, the dairy, and petty retailing seen as women's work.

Work Life

When the population fell after 1348, with the Black Death and recurrent outbreaks of plague, women (both single and married) joined the labor force in larger numbers. Some female harvesters were paid at the same rate as men, but elsewhere they received less. Highly skilled and better paid jobs such as shepherd and ploughholder remained the province of men. Similarly within towns women, who had little opportunity to be apprenticed to a trade, were concentrated in low-paid, low-skilled work in the food trade, in textiles, and as spinsters and servants. The yearly earnings of any of these women are impossible to gauge, but in large towns such as York, many lived in "mean cottages and cheap tenements" (Goldberg, 1988, 107). Only widows who chose to continue their husbands' business might profit from such high status, high paid work as mercer or overseas trader.

Did a married woman's ability to produce a cash income make her in any way an economic equal with her husband or afford her some independence of action and "a very real degree of economic clout within the familial economy" (Goldberg 1991, 82; Barron, 40)? A few women may have controlled the family's purse-strings, but legally a husband, as head of the household, controlled all the material resources of the household, including any money that his wife earned. The hucksters and spinsters, who made up such a large proportion of the female workforce, worked long hours for low profits. Their income was unlikely to be equal to that of a shoemaker or master mason, who had undergone a long apprenticeship. Nor did the economic contribution of the women bring them any political power. Even though married women could join some guilds and craft fellowships as members and paid annual dues, they were not eligible for guild office. So too, although women were active members of religious fraternities, they tended to fill traditional roles—cooking and sewing—and there is no evidence of women holding office.

If a single woman could not find regular, full-time employment, she might engage in casual prostitution, picking up customers in a street or tavern. However, she was not separated from the wider community. On the other hand, the full-time, professional prostitutes, who lived and worked in a regulated brothel, were clearly set apart from their fellows. They were often forced to wear distinctive clothing; they were forbidden to walk in certain parts of the town; and, as "common women," they were not allowed to have their own lovers. In the late fifteenth century, however, brothels came under attack, and some were closed down. In the town of Coventry, in 1492, this distrust was extended to all single women and new legislation forbade a single woman under the age of forty to set up house for herself.

Over the course of the Middle Ages, the economic opportunities open to women diminished. In the fifteenth century, London silk weavers virtually monopolized the trade, but they never established a formal guild. When men began to move into silk-weaving, the women were unable to prevent them taking over the craft. Similarly in the twelfth and thirteenth centuries women had dominated brewing. At that time it was a small-scale local industry that women undertook in their homes on an intermittent and casual basis. As the market for ale expanded, brewers began to work full-time, producing on a larger scale. Most public, professional ale-brewers were married women, although a few widows continued to work and support themselves. If her husband was already active in the food trade, a hosteller for example, female brewing contributed to the family business, but, in many instances, brewing allowed women to carry out a trade that was separate and independent from that of their spouses. This opportunity diminished as beer, produced with hops, became more popular. Apart from an occasional widow, carrying on her husband's trade, beer brewers were male. As the number of beer brewers increased, the number of ale brewers inevitably declined, until, by the mid-sixteenth century, in ports and in London and South-wark, ale brewing, in the hands of women virtually disappeared. The retailing of both ale and beer, however, was usually carried out by female tapsters and tipplers, even in those places where their husbands, as head of household, were held responsible by the courts.

Education and Religion

Since they did not learn Latin, young girls had no access to the grammar schools, the universities, or the inns of court. Yet most aristocratic women taught by their mothers could read, but not write, English. Many also possessed service books—psalters and books of hours—that made private prayer and meditation possible. Books were also read aloud, thus reaching a wider audience. Reading aloud was particularly important for the women who joined the unorthodox religious group known as Lollards in the fifteenth century, since most of them were illiterate. They were then able to teach what they had heard through informal conversations with family, friends, and neighbors, but the leadership of the organization and public preaching remained firmly in male hands.

Women as visionaries—the instruments and medium of God's voice—sometimes acquired a voice that was otherwise denied to them. By the early fifteenth century, works by and about Continental woman visionaries like Birgitta of Sweden and Catherine of Siena had been translated into English and made the work of English mystics like Julian of Norwich more acceptable. Julian, however, was an anchoress, shut away from the world. Margery Kempe, on the other hand, attempted to lead a quasi-religious life, while remaining within the world. Although her loud sobbing at every verbal or symbolic reminder of the Passion angered many of her contemporaries, she was strengthened in her resolve to lead this highly unconventional life by her visionary conversations with the saints and Christ. Her account of her religious experiences, *The Book of Margery Kempe*, shows that it was possible for a woman of determination to follow her own path.

MAVIS MATE

References and Further Reading

Barron, C. "The Golden Age of Women in Medieval London." *Reading Medieval Studies*, 15 (1989): 35–58.

Barron, C., and A. Sutton, eds. *Medieval London Widows, 1300–1500*. London: Hambledon, 1994.

Bennet, Judith. "Medieval Women, Modern Women: Across the Great Divide." In *Culture and History, 1350–1600*, edited by David Aers. London: Harvester, 1992, pp. 147–175.

———. *Ale, Beer, and Brewsters in England: Woman's Work in a Changing World, 1300–1600*. New York and Oxford: Oxford University Press, 1996.

Goldberg, P. J. P. "Women in Fifteenth Century Town Life." In *Towns, Townspeople in the Fifteenth Century*, edited by J. A. F. Thomson. Gloucester: Alan Sutton, 1988, pp. 107–128.

———. "The Public and the Private: Women in the Pre-Plague Economy." In *Thirteenth Century England, III*, edited by P. R. Coss and S. D. Lloyd. Woodbridge, Suffolk: Boydell, 1991, pp. 75–89.

———. *Women, Work and Life-Cycle in a Medieval Economy: York and Yorkshire c. 1300–1520*. Oxford: Clavendon, 1992.

Mate, M. *Daughters, Wives and Widows after the Black Death: Women in Sussex, 1350–1530*. Woodbridge, Suffolk: Boydell, 1998.

Stafford, Pauline. *Queen Emma and Queen Edith: Queenship and Women's Power in Eleventh-Century England*. Oxford; Malden, Mass.: Blackwell, 1997.

Women and Religion in Medieval England, edited by Diana Wood. Oxford: Oxbow Books, 2003.

See also **Abbesses; Alewives and Brewing; Demography; Double Monasteries; Dowry and Other Marriage Gifts; Education, Lay; Education, Monastic; Feme Covert; Feme Sole; Eleanor of Aquitaine; Guild Members and Guilds; Hild of Whitby; Inheritance; Julian of Norwich; Kempe, Margery; Law, English Secular Courts of; Literacy and Reading: Latin; Literacy and Reading: Vernacular; Lollards; Marriage, Christian; Merchet and Leyrwite; Monasticism and Nuns; Mysticism and Mystics; Noble Women; Peasants; Prostitutes; Queens and Empresses: the West; Servants; Social Status; Widows; Work**

EPIC, ITALIAN

Epic narratives in the Italian vernacular began in the thirteenth century and continued well past the end of the fifteenth. Three forms characterized epic material: the Old French *chanson de geste*, *ottava rima*, and prose. During this period, the *matières* of Britain (Arthurian), Rome (classical), and France (Charlemagne and his men) united in Italy to create epics new in language, metrics, and content. Women appear in various roles, from Amazon to falsely accused queen, from enchantress to warrior maiden.

The French *chanson de geste*, written in *laisses*, arrived in Italy through oral transmission along pilgrimage routes in the late twelfth century (based on evidence in art and onomastics) and in manuscripts popular in northern Italian courts (as inventories indicate). Texts in Franco-Italian, a linguistic hybrid, date from the end of the thirteenth century through the first half of the fifteenth. Some *chansons* merely copy French models, but others are Italianized based upon pre-existing characters and plots. There are three Franco-Italian versions of the *Chanson de Roland*; one, of the late twelfth century, gives Aude, Roland's betrothed, an important role. This role not only appeals to the female audience, but also her visions emphasize genealogical considerations in the French line. The *Geste Francor* (first half of the fourteenth century) reinforces the importance of women in royal genealogy: it narrates the history of Carolingians from Pepin through Louis, and is built around a series of persecuted women. Bovo d'Antona's wife must raise twins alone in exile. Pepin's wife, Berta *dai piedi grandi*, is betrayed by a look-alike friend. She bears Charlemagne while the guest of a widower woodsman, and repays his hospitality by teaching his daughters needlepoint. Similarly, Charlemagne's half-sister bears Roland in the Italian woods. Charlemagne's wife, Blançiflor, is accused of adultery and flees to Hungary, where she gives birth to his heir, Louis. Parallels to biblical history compare Roland's mother and father to Mary and Joseph fleeing to Egypt. These women accept responsibility for their (mis)deeds, suffer to regain their position, and extricate themselves from difficulties within the social structure, like their menfolk.

Not all Franco-Italian epics allot important roles to women; *L'Entrée d'Espagne*, the best-known Franco-Italian epic, only narrates three offers of marriage to Roland in the East, and a Sultan's daughter pines for him. Some think Franco-Italian *chansons de geste*, specifically the *Geste Francor*, reflect northern Italian bourgeois interests: Pepin's representatives must inspect Berta naked to make sure the "merchandise" is sound. The importance of Mediterranean trade for Italian city-states means that attitudes toward non-Christians, men and women, differ from those of early Crusade-era *chansons*. In Franco-Italian epics, conversions to Christianity are important, but non-Christian women are primarily sources of wealth, like Christians.

Contemporary with Franco-Italian are literary epics. Vernacular tradition as well as classical epic influenced Dante and Boccaccio. Dante includes no Carolingian-cycle *women* in his *Commedia*, but Dido and Helen inhabit Hell. Boccaccio possibly invented *ottava rima* (eight-verse stanzas of hendecasyllables rhymed ABABABCC), in which he wrote his *Filostrato* (1330s) and *Teseida delle nozze d'Emilia*

(1339–1341), epics of classical subject, ensuring the form's popularity.

Following Boccaccio's lead, through the fifteenth century and afterwards, anonymous poems written in *ottava rima–cantari* narrate stories from mythology, history, and hagiography, Arthurian and Carolingian tradition. *Cantari*, Tuscan in origin, can be short, narrating a single event (*Cantare di Pirramo e di Tisbe*) or long, like *Spagna in Rima* that recounts Charlemagne's seven years in Spain before Roncevaux. Prose rewrites of Italian epic subjects coexist with *cantari*. The best-known authors are Florentine: Antonio Pucci (c. 1310–1388) produced numerous *cantari* on all subjects; Andrea da Barberino (c. 1370–c. 1431) wrote prose versions of the *Reali di Francia, Aspramonte, Re Ansuigi, Le Storie di Rinaldo, Nerbonesi, Ugone d'Alvernia, Aiolfo del Barbicone*, and *Guerrin Meschino*, that utilize French conventions. The women in both forms vary according to the traditions from which they derive. Andrea elaborates upon the *Berta e Milone* story from the *Geste Francor*: Berta demonstrates more initiative, arranging for Milone to disguise himself as a woman to see her. The anonymous *Innamoramento di Berta e Melone* further elaborates the original. Certain new character types appear: Pucci wrote three *cantari* centered on women: *Gismirante, Madonna Lionessa*, and *Historia della Reina d'Oriente*. The latter exemplifies sex change stories: the heiress of an eastern kingdom passes as a boy, but when faced with a trial bath, a prayer changes her sex. A new development not in French texts is Galiziella, a warrior woman who appears in Italian *Aspramonte* versions.

From anonymous *cantari* derive the more famous epics of Florence and northern Italy. Lorenzo de' Medici's mother, Lucrezia Tornabuoni, asked Luigi Pulci (1432–1484) to rehabilitate the literary Charlemagne's reputation. The resulting *Morgante* (1478–1483) is a rewritten amalgam of two long *cantari*, the *Orlando* and *Spagna in rima*. He gives women a wide variety of roles, from the usual wives and mothers of paladins to non-Christian ladies—princesses in need of assistance, who love Rinaldo, Ulivieri, or Orlando. Short-lived love affairs provide paladins wandering in the East emotional support and occasional physical assistance (e.g., Chiariella helps Orlando escape from prison). An affair can end badly: Forisena kills herself when Ulivieri leaves. Women frequently aid Pulci's verbal humor: Arcalida, an Amazon troop leader, creates a series of double entendres when conquered by Rinaldo and his men; Florinetta provides comic relief during Morgante and Margutte's trip through the woods. The beautiful Antea, endowed with magic weapons and armor, defeats all comers, and she and Rinaldo fall mutually in love in spite of being

enemies. At the head of an army she travels through Europe, seeking Rinaldo, and finally returns unharmed to Bambillonia. Meridiana remains undefeated when Orlando disdains combat with her. Creonta, an ugly giantess, is killed like male giants.

In Ferrara, Maria Matteo Boiardo (1440/1441–1494) wrote his *Orlando Innamorato* ([Roland in Love], 1478–1482/1483, 1485) at the court of Ercole d'Este and Eleonora of Aragon, where it was read aloud to Eleonora and her daughter Isabella. Roland and all paladins are smitten by Angelica, and pursue her. Women in general get the better of Orlando, who is depicted as not savvy in love. Boiardo's women are Christian wives, oriental princesses who need saving, and, as in *Morgante*, two beautiful warrior women. Bradamante, the valiant Christian, falls in love with Rugiero; she also plays with gender roles: Fiordespina falls in love with her thinking she is a man. The hard-fighting pagan Marfisa, who seems to be Boiardo's invention, contrasts with the delicate but conniving pagan Angelica, an enchanter's daughter. Boiardo furthermore develops enchantresses, maleficent and beneficent: Alcina, Dragontina, Falerina, and Febosilla create obstacles for heroes as well as learning experiences. Critics suggest that they not only function in the plot but also embody Boiardo's pedagogical strategies that advocate careful reading. However, even Fiordelisa, a courtly Christian, can be seen as critiquing literary tradition. Bradamante and enchantresses also appear in *Mambriano*, by Cieco da Ferrara, begun in 1490 and published in 1502.

At the end of the fifteenth century, Italian epic tradition flourished in written and printed form, and would soon be exported through Ariosto, Tasso, and works they inspired. The "woman warrior," the Amazon, and the scheming enchantress join the persecuted ruler's daughter of the French repertoire as part of western European literary tradition, the results of a unique fusion of medieval Breton, classical, and French literary sources, popular at all social levels in the Italian peninsula.

LESLIE ZARKER MORGAN

References and Further Reading

Allaire, Gloria. "The Warrior Women in Late Medieval Prose Epics." *Italian Culture* 12 (1994): 33–43.
———. *Andrea da Barberino and the Language of Chivalry.* Gainesville, Fla.: University Press of Florida, 1997.
Anceschi, Giuseppe, ed. *Orlando Innamorato.* Mario Matteo Boiardo. Milan: Garzanti, 1978.
Andrea da Barberino. *L'Aspramonte. Romanzo cavalleresco inedito*, edited by Marco Boni. Collezione di opere inedite o rare. Nuova serie. Bologna: Antiquaria Palmaverde, 1951.

————. *I Reali di Francia*, edited by Aurelio Roncaglia and Fabrizio Beggiato. Brugherio-Milan: Gherardo Casini Editore, 1987.

Balduino, Armando, ed. *Cantari del Trecento*. Scrittori italiani. Sezione letteraria. Milan: Marzorati, 1970.

Barini, Giorgio, ed. *Cantàri cavallereschi dei secoli XV e XVI*. Collezione di opere inedite o rare dei primi tre secoli della lingua. Commissione pe' testi di lingua nelle provincie dell'Emilia. Bologna: Romagnoli dall'Acqua, 1905.

Bendinelli Predelli, Maria. "La Donna guerriera nell'immaginario italiano del tardo medioevo." *Italian Culture* 12 (1994): 13–34.

Boccassini, Daniela. "Love, Magic, and Storytelling in Boiardo's *Orlando Innamorato*: The Dragontina Episode." In *Studi filologici e letterari in memoria di Danilo Aguzzi-Barbagli*, edited by Daniela Boccassini. Filibrary Series, 13. Stony Brook, N.Y.: Forum Italicum, 1997, pp. 35–58.

Bonucci, Anicio, ed. *Historia della Reina d'Oriente di Anton Pucci, Fiorentino. Poema cavaleresco del XIII° secolo*. Scelta di curiosità letterarie inedite o rare dal secolo XIII al XIX, 41. Bologna: Romagnoli, 1862.

Braghirolli, Willelmo, Gaston Paris, and Paul Meyer. "Inventaire des manuscrits en langue française possédés par Francesco Gonzaga I, capitaine de Mantoue, mort en 1407." *Romania* 9 (1880): 497–514.

I Cantari, struttura e tradizione. Atti del Convegno Internazionale di Montreal: 19–20 marzo 1981, edited by M. Picone and M. Bendinelli Predelli. Florence: Olschki, 1984.

Catalano, Michele, ed. *La Spagna: Poema cavalleresco del secolo XIV*. 3 vols. Collezione di opere inedite o rare, 111–113. Bologna: Commissione per i testi di lingua Casa Carducci, 1939–1940.

Cavallo, JoAnn. "The Role of the Woman in the *Orlando Innamorato*." *Carte Italiane* 8 (1986-87): 31–36.

Dionisotti, Carlo. "Appunti su antichi testi." *Italia medievale e umanistica* 7 (1964): 99–131.

Duggan, Joseph J. "L'Épisode d'Aude dans la tradition en rime de la *Chanson de Roland*." In *Charlemagne in the North: Proceedings of the Twelfth International Conference of the Société Rencesvals*. Edinburgh 4th to 11th August 1991, edited by Philip E. Bennett, Anne Elizabeth Cobby, and Graham A. Runnalls. Edinburgh: Société Rencesvals Branch, 1993, pp. 273–279.

Everson, Jane. "Les Personnages féminins dans le *Mambriano* de Francesco da Ferrara." In *Charlemagne in the North. Proceedings of the Twelfth International Conference of the Société Rencesvals*. Edinburgh 4th to 11th August 1991, edited by Philip E. Bennett, Anne Elizabeth Cobby, and Graham A. Runnalls. Edinburgh: Société Rencesvals Branch, 1993, pp. 281–290.

Fatini, Giuseppe, ed. *Il Morgante di Luigi Pulci*. 1948. Classici italiani UTET. Turin: Unione tipografico-editrice torinese, 1984.

Franceschetti, Antonio. "Rassegna di studi sui cantari." *Lettere italiane* 25 (1973): 556–574.

Holtus, Günter. "Plan- und Kunstsprachen auf romanischer Basis IV. Franko-Italienisch/Langues artificielles à base romane IV. Le franco-italien." *Lexikon der romanistichen Linguistik*. Vol. 7, edited by Günter Holtus et al. Tübingen: M. Niemeyer, 1998, pp. 705–756.

Krauss, Henning. *Epica feudale e pubblico borghese. Per la storia poetica di Carlomagno in Italia*. translated by F. Brugnolo and A. Fassò. Padua: La Garangola, 1980.

Lejeune, Rita, and Jacques Stiennon. *La Légende de Roland dans l'art du Moyen Age*. 2 vols. Brussels: Arcade, 1967.

Limentani, Alberto. "Struttura e storia dell'ottava rima." *Lettere italiane* 13 (1961): 20–77.

Luzio, Alessandro. "Isabella d'Este e l'*Orlando Innamorato*." In his *Studi su Matteo Maria Boiardo*. Bologna: Zanichelli, 1894, pp. 147–154.

Morgan, Leslie Zarker. "Female *enfances*: At the Intersection of Romance and Epic." In *The Court Reconvenes: Courtly Literature Across the Disciplines*. Selected Papers from the Ninth Triennial Congress of the International Courtly Literature Society, University of British Columbia, Vancouver, 25–31 July 1998, edited by Carleton W. Carroll and Barbara K. Altmann. Woodbridge, Suffolk, UK: Boydell and Brewer, 2003, pp. 141–149.

Rosellini, Aldo, ed. *La Geste Francor di Venezia. Edizione integrale del Codice XIII del Fondo francese della Marciana*. Saggi e monografie, 6. Pubblicazioni del Centro di Linguistica dell'Università Cattolica. Brescia: La Scuola, 1986.

Ross, Charles S. "Angelica and the Fata Morgana: Boiardo's Allegory of Love." *MLN* 96 (1981): 12–22.

Ross, Charles Stanley, trans. *Orlando Innamorato*.With an Introduction and Notes by Charles Stanley Ross. Foreward by Allen Mandelbaum. Berkeley: University of California Press, 1989.

Thomas, Antoine, ed. *L'Entrée d'Espagne. Chanson de geste franco-italienne*. Société des anciens textes français. Paris: Firmin Didot et Cie, 1913.

Tomalin, Margaret. *The Fortunes of the Warrior Heroine in Italian Literature*. L'Interprete, 33. Ravenna: Longo, 1982.

Tusiani, Joseph, trans. *Morgante. The Epic Adventures of Orlando and His Giant Friend Morgante*. Introduction and notes by Edoardo A. Lèbano. Bloomington: Indiana University Press, 1998.

Vitullo, Juliann Marie. "Contained Conflict: Wild Men and Warrior Women in the Early Italian Epic." *Annali d'Italianistica* 12 (1994): 39–59.

————. *Constructing an Urban Mythology: The Chivalric Epic in Medieval Italy*. Gainesville, Fla.: University Press of Florida, 2000.

See also **Amazons; Boccaccio, Giovanni; Dante Alighieri; Epic: Old French; Literature, Italian; Tornabuoni de' Medici, Lucrezia**

EPIC, OLD FRENCH

Up until the rise of feminist criticism, the Old French epic, or *chanson de geste*, was seen as a form of literature containing little or no female presence, causing it to frequently be termed "male-world" literature (Gold). This appellation came in large part from early studies that recognized the superiority of the oldest extant epic poem, the *Chanson de Roland*, which accords minimal space to its two female characters. Beginning in the late 1980s, however, attention has been given to the women who are found in early epics, and their importance has been reconsidered.

These female roles can be divided into three main categories. First, there are the Christian women, described as fair-skinned, blond-haired, and blue-eyed, who are mentioned, yet only occasionally active during parts of the story. Overall, they are scarce and frequently silent. The famous "sudden death" of Aude in *Roland* is just that: she speaks very few lines, learns of Roland's passing, and drops dead on the floor. Traditionally, her presence in the story is seen as a demonstration of the greatness of the unbearable loss of the hero. In some early French epics, however, Christian women contribute significantly to the story, to the battles even, and to the overall outcome of the conflicts. Specifically, there are the mothers in *Raoul de Cambrai*, who advise their sons, attempt to avoid unnecessary warfare, and act out to protect their family pride and property. While their acts end up being the cause of the main conflicts and battles, this is only because men within the story do not respect their requests and advice.

The remaining categories are those occupied by the various Saracen women, who are, in fact, the most frequently encountered consequential members of the "fairer sex." The Saracen women generally fit into one of the following two groups: the black Saracen and the Saracen princess.

The four black Saracen women found among the seventy-four Old French epic texts play the role of the faithful enemy woman who fights for her family, husband, and people. She is sometimes captured and released only to be put to death by her own people, sometimes she dies alongside the pagans, fighting in a savage and indecent manner (Weever). She is never somebody with whom a Christian audience could identify or whom they could admire. While commendable for her loyalty and steadfastness, her behavior as well as her appearance—she is black "like a demon" and scantily clothed—make her an unacceptable model.

The seventeen white Saracen women, on the other hand, are very much the type of woman who physically can be admired and accepted by the audience for whom they were created. They are fair-skinned, blond, and have blue eyes. They are usually dressed much like the Christian women as well, or are described in appealing exotic clothing. These women belong to the "Saracen princess" group. The Saracen princess falls in love with the Christian knight, uses her inside knowledge to help him escape from her people, if he has been captured, or conquer her people if he is attacking. She betrays her father or, in some cases, her husband to come to the aid of the Christians and, in the end, converts to Christianity—though not out of a realization of the superiority of the Christian god, rather for the love of a knight whom she often marries

at the end of the story. The best example of this character is Orabel in the *Chanson de Guillaume* who then changes her name to Guibourc when she becomes Christian and marries Guillaume.

One explanation for the greater richness of the Saracen woman's role in these older epics is that there is no need for her to conform to the social norms that would apply to a good Christian woman. It is thus possible for her to have outspoken and active behavior that would have shocked a contemporary audience were she one of their own. In line with this notion is the fact that often, once the Saracen princess has converted to Christianity, she disappears from the action of the story and becomes similar to the Christian women of the epic.

Some feminist scholars consider these roles assigned to women in the older epics as being in line with the misogynistic tones of the genre as a whole, while others argue that not all women represented are quite so demeaning to their gender. In any case, much work remains to be done in this field.

SARA L. PREISIG

References and Further Reading

Burns, E. Jane. *Bodytalk: When Women Speak in Old French Literature.* Philadelphia: University of Pennsylvania Press, 1993.

Gold, Penny Schine. *The Lady & the Virgin: Image, Attitude and Experience in Twelfth-Century France.* Chicago and London: The University of Chicago Press, 1985.

Kay, Sarah. *The Chansons de geste in the Age of Romance: Political Fictions.* Oxford: Clarendon Press, 1995.

Spiegel, Gabrielle. *Romancing the Past: The Rise of Vernacular Prose. Historiography in Thirteenth-Century France.* Berkeley, Los Angeles, Oxford: University of California Press, 1993.

Weever, Jacqueline de. *Sheba's Daughters: Whitening and Demonizing the Saracen Woman in Medieval French Epic.* New York: Garland, 1998.

See also **Audience, Women in the; Beowulf; Captivity and Ransom; Floire and Blancheflor; Misogyny; Muslim Women: Western Literature**

EPIC, SPANISH

Epic, by its military focus, is the realm of stereotypical masculine ethos. For these reasons, women tend to have, at least in theory, a more subdued role. This is in clear contrast, however, to medieval Castilian epic, where woman have a central role in the action. An assessment of women's representations in medieval Castilian epic poetry is, however, embedded in general problems concerning the development of this literary genre in the Iberian Peninsula. This is because in contrast to other literary traditions that present an extensive corpus of preserved poems, there are only three preserved medieval epic texts in Castilian. One of them is a small fragment of Carolingian material, *Cantar de Roncesvalles,* while the other two, *Cantar de mio Cid* (c. 1207) and *Mocedades* (beginning of the fourteenth century), celebrate the deeds of the proto-national Spanish hero, Rodrigo Díaz de Vivar, immortalized as el Cid (c. 1043–1099). This scarcity in documentation and narrow focus has forced scholars to posit a wider epic tradition, concerned especially with the origins of Castile. This material is irredeemably lost but may be retrievable via chronicles, learned narrative poetry, or ballads.

The Cid

The protagonist of these two preserved poems is the historical Castilian warrior Rodrigo Díaz, whose history can be accessed cautiously using twelfth century sources plainly favorable to the Cid. The historical protagonist (c. 1043–1099) played an important role during the reign of Alfonso VI (1065–1109), with whom, according to later texts (most of them pro-Cid), he had a turbulent relationship that led to his exile by the kind, first in 1081–1086 and later, and for good in 1089. These two exiles, which the pro-Cidian historiography presented in terms of aristocratic *invidia* and royal anger, consolidated the enmity between the Cid and powerful Castilian Lords like Count García Ordóñez, who became his archrival. In 1094, the Cid conquered for himself the great Moorish kingdom of Valencia, which he was able to maintain against Almoravid attacks. He died in Valencia in 1099 as ruler of the town, having secured profitable marriages for his daughters, Maria and Cristina, who married, respectively, a Navarrese aristocrat and the Count of Barcelona. In 1101, the Cid's widow, the noble Jimena, abandoned Valencia, taking his remains to the monastery of San Pedro de Cardeña, where she was buried in 1113. Historically, Valencia remained in Muslim hands until 1236. In spite of the caution with which the biographical profile should be assessed, it is reasonable to point out that his military heroism is tied to his capacity for arranging good marriages for his daughters, a motif concerning lineage that was exploited in subsequent epic poems.

The most substantial preserved epic, the so-called *Cantar* (or *Poema*) *de mio Cid,* is preserved in a fourteenth century manuscript. It was shaped by French epic models, and 1200 is a reasonable date for the composition of the preserved version, as it fits, politically with a time of stress in medieval Castile after the severe defeat by the Almohads at Alarcos in 1195. The first plot of the poem thematizes freely some of the historical material concerning Rodrigo Díaz's exiles. In the poem, however, there is just one exile (engineered by invidious courtiers) that is ended by the social reintegration of the Cid into Alfonso VI's court and the recuperation of the *honra publica* (reputation) that was lost by the unjust exile. This rehabilitation rests first on the military prowess of the Cid, ending in the conquest and defense of Valencia; but it rests especially on the progressive enrichment of the protagonist by his individual effort and leadership and his ability to transfer this enrichment to all of his followers. It is important to note, however, that exile and the social reintegration of the Cid is tied to female domesticity as well. Throughout the poem, the hero is presented as an exceptional father and spouse, adding to his moral and military value his remitting respect for the welfare of the family. This is important because the poem depicts explicitly the domestic aspects of the Cid's relation to his wife Jimena (whom he calls *muggier ondrada*) and his daughters (historically called *doña Elvira y doña Sol*) with whom an emotional bond is created to manipulate the audience. The poem, however, does not differentiate the characteristics of Jimena or the daughters. The poem emphasizes clearly, although framed by conventional gesture, rituals that pervade all the relationships in the poem, particularly the submission of daughters to father and the harmony between the two spouses; this is based, however, on complete deference toward the Cid on the female side. It was always been said that domesticity opens up the poem to emotional characterization, giving the hero a more humane and mundane perspective, but it is also important to note that it is used to emphasize the social and material conditions of the family's dependence upon the Cid.

The Cid's exile clearly demarcates masculine and feminine spheres. While the first is the space or war and struggle, of male wealth production ad distribution, feminine characters live in enclosed spaces, separated from the physical activity of war but receiving and profiting from it. The daughters' value as social currency through which to transform this military prowess and economic accumulation into marriages and lineage is, however, nonexistent at that moment because social reintegration and recuperation of legal fatherhood is necessary to further social advancement.

This domestic dimension of social reintegration into the *res publica,* is clearly marked by the kind, who, in addition to official sanctioning the Cid's rehabilitation in a public ceremony, gives him the possibility of socially advantageous marriages for his daughters to two aristocratic brothers: the Infantes de Carrión, who by their greed, jealousy, and cowardice, are the antithesis of the moral values embodied by the Cid and his band. In spite of the Cid's tepid reaction, which is shared by Jimena, the marriages go ahead, although they are performed in a juridical situation that will make the king responsible for their outcome.

This legal disclaimer on the Cid's part and royal responsibility form the basis of the second plot, that of private honor *(honora privada)*. This second plot unfolds when the Infantes, after having profited materially from the Cid's generosity, decide to take revenge on him by dishonoring his daughters because they have been publicly humiliated at his court for their lack of manhood in war against the Muslims. Thus, in a clearly elaborated scene, the Infantes, while taking the Cid's daughters to their homeland, first have sex with the daughters and then savagely beat them, leaving them in the wilderness for beasts to kill. This scene is reminiscent of female Christian martyrs. This prompts the Cid to turn to royal justice, which decides that honor should be avenged by duels. Once honor has been vindicated, the two daughters marry the princes of Navarre and Aragon, forebears of the kings ruling at the time of the poem's composition. The ahistorical second plot focuses, then, on women as bearers of lineage and markers of masculine honor.

The *Cantar de mio Cid,* which uses the Cid's military career and his moral representation as an ideal model of military effort, private enrichment, warrior masculine ethos, and monarchical justice, is also didactic in its representation of female characters, who are extolled as passive participants whose role is to be the building block of family harmony and prestige but who must be, at the same time, submissive, dependent, and not individualized. The moral tale is, however, emphasized when female characteristics are transferred unnaturally and monstrously to male characters, like the Infantes, who, in contrast to the Cid and his band, are not meeting their military obligations.

Jimena

Jimena, the beloved wife in the *Poema,* is completely different in the other Cidia epic preserved, the *Mocedades del Cid,* dealing with the fantastic deeds of the young Rodrigo Díaz. In this late medieval epic, Jimena is presented in a more active role, as an avenging women whose father has been killed by a young and arrogant Rodrigo. She demands justice from the king, dissuading her brothers from taking private vengeance on Rodrigo de Vivar. While she displays the same concerns for lineage and marriage presented in *Cantar de mio Cid,* she is portrayed now as a young, courageous, and determined woman, contrasting starkly with the complacent wife presented in the *Poema.* Her action is accepted, however, because her wedding prevents an unending cycle of private vengeance.

Other Epics

Women played important roles in other Spanish epics for which evidence is only indirect. These include: *Los siete infantes de Lara, Cantar de Fernán González, la Condesa Traidora, el Cantar de Sancho II* (in two versions), and *el Romanz del Infant Garcia.*

Los siete infantes de Lara was possibly the first epic Spanish poem (around 1000). It is a bloody tale of vengeance whose echoes can be heard in the *Primera Crónica General* (c. 1270). It is a women, Doña Lambra, who is responsible for the clan's catastrophe. According to the chronicle, on the day of her wedding to Roy Blazquez, she publicly made a comment on the virility of her cousin, Alvar Sanchez. This clearly denigrates the masculinity of the Lara family, which is formed, in part, by seven brothers, Roy Blazquez's nephews. This prompts fighting, which is symbolically a contest over masculinity, the assassination of Doña Lambra's cousin, and the intervention of Doña Lambra's husband to defend the honor of his wife. Eventually, this leads to the definitive vengeance of Doña Lambra, who makes her husband betray his own cousins of the Lara Family, killing them all. The cycle of vengeance is closed by the Mudarra, the Infante's half brother, who sets fire to Doña Lambra.

In the case of *el Cantar de Sancho II,* or *Cantar del Cerco de Zamora,* women's representation is complicated by the fac that Urraca is the unmarried princess of Zamora. This locates the epic in another realm where, instead of focusing on issues of masculine honor and lineage, it deals with the relation of morality and legality to gender and active female governance. According to the *Cronica najerense* (mid-twelfth century) and *Primery Crónica General* (c. 1270), she defended her territory vehemently against the attack of her aggressive brother, The Castilian King Sancho II. This character is interesting, however, because she resists her brother, showing both empowerment and decision. However, at the same time, there are some hints of concupiscence in Urraca, who seems to use her femininity not only to manipulate young Rodrigo Díaz, fighting for his Castilian King, to maintain a dubious love for her brother Alfonso, and, especially, to entice Belldio-Dolfos with sexual promises to betray and kill the Castilian

King. It presents, then, several characteristics that resemble those of Doña Lambra, especially sexual desire and treachery, but the absence of husbands or brothers who would force her into a customary dependent position causes her to adopt masculine characteristics like aggression and the acceptance of political responsibilities. Those disruptive aspects will, however, be attenuated in a later version of this epic, where the emphasis switches to Rodrigo Díaz, and Urraca and her brother Alfonso are not so clearly guilty in the betrayal of their brother.

In conclusion, Castilian epic seems to represent women clearly in two ways. While some texts present strong women, most of them are punished for not being loyal to their lineage, governing duties, and the male hierarchy. Active females are always presented as aggressive, especially those not meeting their biological imperatives, and are almost always several criticized because of their disruption of social networks, which causes catastrophes. In contrast, women who are passive and submissive are extolled as embodying family and social harmony, while presenting at the same time a possibility of social advancement. Overall, the passive women, as found in the *Cantar de mio Cid,* are not typical of the active females in the rest of the corpus.

OSCAR MARTIN

References and Further Reading

Amago, Samuel. "Sexual Pollution, Social Legitimacy, and the Economies of Power in the Legend of the Siete Infantes de Lara." *Revista de Estudios Hispánicos* 36.1 (2002): 3–22.

Crónica Najerense. ed. Juan Antonio Estévez Solá. Madrid: Akal, 2003.

Deyermond, Alan. *"Cantar de mío Cid" y la épica medieval española.* Barcelona: Sirmio, 1987.

———. *Literatura perdida de la Edad Media castellana: catálogo y estudio.* Salamanca: Ediciones Universidad de Salamanca, 1995.

Duggan, Joseph J. *Cantar de mio Cid: Poetic Creation in Its Economic and Social Contexts.* Cambridge: Cambridge University Press, 1989.

Lacarra, María Eugenia. "Los paradigmas de hombre y de mujer en la literatura epicolegendaria medieval castellana." In *Estudios históricos y literarios sobre la mujer medieval.* Málaga: Servicio de Publicaciones, Diputación Provincial de Málaga, 1990, pp. 9–34.

———. "La representación de la mujer en algunos textos épicos castellanos." In *Actas del II Congreso Internacional de la Asociación Hispánica de Literatura Medieval.* 2 vols. Alcalá: Universidad, 1992, pp. 395–408.

Las Mocedades de Rodrigo: estudios críticos, manuscrito y edición, edited by Matthew Bailey. London: King's College, Centre for Late Antique & Medieval Studies, 1999.

Montaner, Alberto. "Las quejas de doña Jimena: Formación y desarrollo de un tema en la épica y en el Romancero." In *Actas del II Congreso Internacional de la Asociación Hispánica de Literatura Medieval.* 2 vols. Alcalá: Universidad, 1992, pp. 475–508.

The Poem of mio Cid. A Bilingual Edition with Parallel Text. translated by Rita Hamilton and Janet Perry, London: Penguin Books, 1975.

Poema de Fernán González, edited by Juan Victorio. Madrid: Cátedra, 1981.

Primera Crónica General. Editada por Ramón Menéndez Pidal; con un estudio actualizador de Diego Catalán. 2 vols. Madrid: Gredos, 1977.

Ratcliffe, Marjorie. "Women and Marriage in the Medieval Spanish Epic." *Journal of the Rocky Mountain Medieval and Renaissance Association* 8 (1987): 1–14.

———. *Jimena: A Woman in Spanish Literature.* Potomac, Md: Scripta Humanistica, 1992.

Roncesvalles; étude sur le fragment de cantar de gesta conservé à l'Archivo de Navarra (Pampelune), edited by Jules Horrent. Paris: Les Belles Lettres, 1951.

Sponsler, Lucy A. *Women in the Medieval Spanish Epic and Lyric Tradition.* Lexington: Kentucky University Press, 1975.

Victorio, Juan. "La mujer en la épica castellana." In *La condición de la mujer en la edad media. Actas del Coloquio celebrado en la Casa de Velázquez, del 5–7 de noviembre de 1984.* Madrid: Casa de Velázquez, 1986, pp. 77–84.

See also **Epic: Old French; Honor and Reputation; Iberia; Literature, Iberian**

ERMENGARD

Ermengard (c. 1129–1196), viscountess of Narbonne, succeeded her father, Viscount Aymeri II, in 1134 when he was killed before the walls of Fraga in Spain. She was only four or five years old at the time. Her two older brothers had died young, and only she and her younger sister, Ermessend, remained. Sometime around 1139, Alphonse Jordan, count of Toulouse, took over Ermengard's city of Narbonne, then one of the major ports of Occitania (now southern France) and he married her in 1142. The marriage provoked a military response from the count's rivals in the region. Defeated, Alphonse was forced to give up both the city and the viscountess. The allies then quickly married her to one of their own allies, Bernard of Anduze. From then on, Ermengard ruled her city by herself. Before she was twenty years old, Ermengard was a full partner in the dynastic diplomacy and conflicts in Occitania.

In Narbonne, Ermengard's palace stood next to the main market square and the old Roman bridge that crossed the Aude River, which carried goods to and from the port at its mouth downstream. She drew a significant portion of her revenues from tolls and market taxes and so was particularly attentive to promoting commerce. She ordered that a new road be built from Narbonne to Roussillon, inland from the old Roman coastal road. She also sent embassies to negotiate commercial and military treaties with Pisa (1164, 1174) and Genoa (1166, 1181).

Ermengard was a patron of major troubadour poets, including Bernart de Ventadorn, Peire d'Alvernhe, Giraut de Bornelh, Azalais de Porcairagues, and Peire Roger. As a result of her connection to the troubadours, Andrew the Chaplain turned her into a judge of an imaginary "court of love."

Ermengard had no children. She adopted her nephew, Pedro de Lara, as her successor. In 1194, Pedro ousted her from the city. She died in exile, April 30, 1196.

FREDRIC L. CHEYETTE

References and Further Reading

Caille, Jacqueline. "Ermengarde, Vicomtesse de Narbonne (1127/29–1196/97): *Une grande figure feminine du Midi aristocratique.*" In *La Femme dans l'histoire et la Société meridionales (IXe-XIXe s.).* Montpellier: Fédération historique du Languedoc méditerranéen et du Roussillon, 1995, pp. 9–50.

Cheyette, Fredric L. *Ermengard of Narbonne and the World of the Troubadours.* Ithaca: Cornell University Press, 2001.

See also **Noble Women; Occitania; Succession, Royal and Noble; Trobairitz and Troubadours**

EROTICISM IN ART

A typical modern understanding of medieval art is that it is almost exclusively prudishly religious and, therefore, relatively free of sexual, erotic imagery. In fact, images of kissing, nudity, and heterosexual and homosexual interactions are not at all uncommon in medieval art, both religious and secular. Ironically, it has perhaps been a modern tendency to separate the sacred and the sexual that has censored this material, but increasingly scholars have begun to engage in the project of unraveling the visual codes of eroticism in the art of the Middle Ages.

The definition of the erotic in medieval art is complex and even contradictory. Certain visual images suggesting the erotic, especially in art that is ostensibly religious in nature, might in fact be interpreted as signifying the spirit rather than the flesh. Much like the often-eroticized language of medieval mystics, scholars have sometimes been at a loss to determine whether such verbal and visual emphasis on the carnal is allegorical or actual, referring to spiritual or sexual experience, or some elision between the two.

The Meanings of Images

A famous debate about the meaning of seemingly sexualized images took place between Caroline

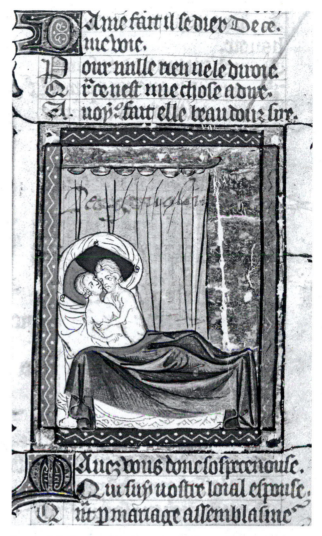

A couple in bed making love, c. 1300–c. 1310. A man embracing a woman in bed. Illustration from a page of French text discussing marriage, from "Le Roman de la Rose" (The Romance of the Rose) by Jean de Meun and Guillaume de Lorris. Eger.881. Folio No: 126.Min. Location: British Library, London. Credit: HIP / Art Resource, NY.

Bynum and Steinberg. According to Leo Steinberg, medieval and Renaissance images emphasizing the genitals of Christ focus on his sexuality as evidence of his full humanity. Bynum suggests instead that modern viewers see breasts and genitals as erotic, but we should not assume that medieval people did. Rather, she believes that medieval viewers would think of Christ's body as connoting nourishment, suffering, and ultimately salvation. Despite their different approaches and conclusions, both Steinberg and Bynum proffer theological explanations and responses for the exposed body of Christ, while scholars such as Karma Lochrie and Robert Mills have opened up the possibilities for sexual and homosexual responses to this kind of imagery. Certainly images such as the isolated and vagina-like side-wounds of Christ, popular in the fourteenth century, might suggest interpretations beyond the theological, especially for a viewer encountering such a sight in the private space of a manuscript. The definition of "erotic," then, is akin to the definition of pornographic—it is at least in part a matter of position. For whom is it erotic/homoerotic—male or female; artist, patron, or viewer; medieval, modern? And are those categories necessarily at odds with each other?

Some medieval images that are ostensibly religious show encounters that seem suggestive, such as illustrations of the *Sponsus* and *Sponsa* from the Song of Songs. The erotic language of the biblical text informs images of these figures kissing or embracing, and the fact that the Bridegroom and the Bride are usually interpreted as Christ and the personified Church, and the Church further identified as the Virgin Mary, lends these images complicated and even incestuous overtones. The question of interpretation remains: are these to be seen solely as symbolic, or are other meanings possible with such freighted imagery?

Nudity

Nudity is much more likely to be found in religious rather than secular imagery in the Middle Ages, but it can be confusingly coded. Adam and Eve are represented nude in their prelapsarian state of innocence; in early medieval images, their bodies are often barely distinguishable. It is only after the Fall that their nakedness becomes shameful. Images of the Last Judgment often explicitly contrast the blessed, fully robed and resplendent in heaven, with the damned writhing in their nakedness, much as they did in the sexual sins that condemned them to hell. But virgin martyrs such as Agatha and Barbara were often represented partially or fully nude; especially in the later Middle Ages they are depicted as the visual embodiments of the ideal women described in love poetry and romances, with their long blond hair, fair complexions, swelling bellies, and high, apple-like breasts. Such images may provoke both religious and erotic responses in viewers, both medieval and modern. In his famous treatise on the art of courtly love, Andreas Capellanus maintained that desire resided in sight, that it was created from the "inborn suffering" produced from looking at the opposite sex. The many images of David gazing on the undraped form of Bathsheba aptly illustrate this idea, and further complicate the gaze of the viewer on undressed female saints.

Explicitness

Paradoxically, it seems that (at least in the later Middle Ages) the most explicit images are found in religious contexts, but they were probably meant to have a didactic message, to be censorious rather than celebratory of eroticism and love. The pairs of same-sex lovers in one of the early-thirteenth-century moralized Bibles appear in conjunction with God's banishment of Adam and Eve as well as a moralizing text. Sheelanagigs, sculpted images of hag-like female figures squatting and pulling back the lips of their vaginas, inhabit the exterior of many Romanesque churches, especially in the British Isles. Also on church exteriors, pairs of heterosexual and homosexual lovers grimace and grind on corbels. All types of salacious themes are found carved on misericords, underneath choir seats—lovers in baths (probably a reference to prostitution); bare-breasted mermaids and sirens; men exposing their buttocks and genitals; naked women astride animals. What many of these images have in common is that they appear in the margins, outside the frame, "on the edge." These spaces seem to be areas where the proper order of things is reversed, the world is turned upside down, and the transgressive able to be depicted, perhaps in order to render it powerless, perhaps to harness its power apotropaically. Yet some of the most graphic marginal imagery may have other functions; the image of a naked couple seeming either to copulate or engage in oral sex in the top margin of a Book of Hours has been shown by Camille to be a reference to a biblical phrase on the same folio.

Ironically, when couples copulate in secular manuscripts such as romances or even medieval sex manuals, they are usually in bed and covered up. In fact, secular images, especially those associated with courtly love, illustrate direct physical erotic experience but do so in metaphorical terms. The luxury trade in ivory mirrorbacks, combs, and caskets in the fourteenth century produced large numbers of objects with images of heterosexual couples; in reading these images in conjunction with medieval literature such as romances, pastourelles, and fabliaux, where sexual encounters (usually seduction/rapes described from the male point of view) are bawdily if euphemistically recounted, it becomes more clear that the chaplets, roses, falcons, squirrels, swords, chess games, and castle stormings are thinly veiled sexual puns. In part a question of survival, but probably also an impression of importance or even appropriateness, such secular objects are much more rarely the subjects of scholarly study.

MARTHA EASTON

References and Further Reading:

Bynum, Caroline Walker. "A Reply to Leo Steinberg." *Renaissance Quarterly* 39(1986): 399–439.

Camille, Michael. *Image on the Edge: The Margins of Medieval Art.* Cambridge, Mass: Harvard University Press, 1992.

———. *The Medieval Art of Love: Objects and Subjects of Desire.* New York: Harry N. Abrams, 1998.

Caviness, Madeline H. *Visualizing Women in the Middle Ages. Sight, Spectacle, and Scopic Economy (The Middle Ages Series).* Philadelphia: University of Pennsylvania Press, 2001.

Easton, Martha. "Saint Agatha and the Sanctification of Sexual Violence." *Studies in Iconography* 16(1994): 83–118.

Lochrie, Karma. "Mystical Acts, Queer Tendencies." In *Constructing Medieval Sexuality*, edited by Karma Lochrie, Peggy McCracken, and James A. Schultz. Minneapolis: University of Minnesota Press, 1997, pp. 180–200.

Mills, Robert. "Ecco Homo." In *Gender and Holiness: Men, Women and Saints in Late Medieval Europe*, edited by Samantha J. E. Riches and Sarah Salih. London and New York, Routledge, 2002, pp. 152–173.

Salih, Sarah. "When is a Bosom Not a Bosom? Problems with 'Erotic Mysticism'." In *Medieval Virginities*, edited by Anke Bernau, Ruth Evans and Sarah Salih. Toronto and Buffalo: University of Toronto Press, 2003, pp. 14–32.

Steinberg, Leo. *The Sexuality of Christ in Renaissance Art and in Modern Oblivion.* 2nd ed. Chicago: University of Chicago Press, 1995.

See also **Art, Representations of Women in; Body, Visual Representations of; Courtly Love; Eve; Fabliau; Gaze; Hagiography, Iconographic Aspects of; Marginalia, Manuscript; Mary, Virgin: in Art; Mermaids and Sirens; Misericords; Obscenity; Pastourelle; Personifications Visualized as Women; Romance de Silence; Romance, English; Romance, French; Romance, Gernan; Sheela Na Gigs; Song of Songs, Medieval Interpretations of; Virgin Martyrs**

EROTICISM IN LITERATURE

In *Sexuality in Medieval Europe: Doing unto Others*, Ruth Mazo Karras observes that modern readers have typically divided medieval sexuality into two tidy but reductive categories: on the one hand, it is marked by a repressive, ascetic religious culture that considers all sexual behavior and the body itself to be malignant and sinful; on the other, it is influenced by a permissive, earthy secular culture that celebrates the body, its appetites, and its excesses. While these images are not entirely incompatible with historical and textual evidence, Karras insists that they tell only a small part of the story. The Middle Ages spans one thousand years of history, a vast geographical area, and an extraordinary array of cultures, subcultures, and belief systems. It should come as no surprise, then, that the Middle Ages also embraces an extremely broad spectrum of attitudes toward sexual desires and acts. Indeed, it is not at all unusual to find a number of different, and apparently discordant, perspectives on sexuality converging within a single period, milieu, author, or text. Moreover, the fact that much of the available evidence is textual and literary belies attempts by critics to generalize a stable, monolithic set of cultural beliefs regarding sexuality. Since only certain segments of the population (principally but not exclusively clerical men) were literate, the textual evidence is inevitably partial and skewed. And given that medieval literature is unusually rhetorical, polysemous, and oblique, it cannot offer an unmediated reflection of social realities. More often than not, the extant sources evince the irreducible complexities of a fully heterogeneous, but not fully knowable, sexual culture.

This entry focuses on a particularly celebrated and richly suggestive body of erotic texts: those that emerged in the Christian West during the High Middle Ages, roughly 1100–1300. These texts do not epitomize medieval eroticism generally; on the contrary, they are in many respects quite exceptional. At the same time, the interpretive and methodological problems they raise could profitably be extended to the study of other medieval sources, cultures, and periods. Those problems include, most notably, the refraction or pluralization of perspective and irresolvable ambiguities of intention, tone, meaning, and desire.

The Age of Ovid

The High Middle Ages has long been thought of as a period of cultural renaissance. This is due in large part to a renewal of interest in Roman erotic literature on the part of both Latin authors (whose audiences were largely ecclesiastical, educated, and male) and vernacular authors (whose audiences were largely aristocratic, illiterate, and mixed-gender). Ludwig Traube refers to this period as an "Age of Ovid," and certainly among the pagan poets known to medieval readers, Ovid's influence was second only to Virgil's. The nature of that influence was extremely broad and multifaceted. Ovidian sources were used in the schools and universities to teach a variety of topics, including grammar, rhetoric, history, mythography, and ethics. Yet it is in the field of poetry and imaginative literature that Ovid's legacy was most deeply felt. Authors as diverse as the troubadours and *trobairitz*, the *Minnesänger*, Chrétien de Troyes, Guillaume de Lorris, Jean de Meun, the *Carmina Burana* poets, Dante, Juan Ruiz, Petrarch, Boccaccio, Machaut, and Chaucer were under the sway of the Roman "preceptor of love." What these medieval authors have in common is, however, far more than simply a corpus of erotic narratives, symbols, and theories. They also share a profound ambivalence about the psychological, moral, social, and spiritual value of erotic love and a fascination with the shifting nature of sexual desire and textual meaning. Ovid is himself a bundle of contradictions: he teaches the art of love but also advocates its rejection; he is a callous debaucher but also defends lawful marriage; and his writings alternate, sometimes quite abruptly, between obscenity and tenderness. If some medieval authors sought to minimize the equivocalness of Ovid's poetry, assigning pious or moral glosses to texts that, for a variety of reasons, were considered problematic, others magnified the slipperiness of the source material, exaggerating its ambiguities. Indeed, the erotic literature of the High Middle Ages is nearly always preoccupied with the conflict between the unpredictable force of desire that cannot be mastered and the norms governing sexual conduct. The medieval Ovidian tradition, therefore, should not be categorized as either permissive or repressive. Rather, it deftly negotiates the gap between pleasure and constraint, typically without achieving, or even necessarily seeking out, resolution.

Latin Texts

A particularly telling example of Ovidian ambivalence can be found in Alan of Lille's *Plaint of Nature*, a twelfth-century Latin allegory intended for an elite audience of scholars trained in philosophy, theology, and the liberal arts. The theme of the text is the relationship between man and cosmos, nature and ethics; it uses myths drawn from Ovid in order to stigmatize fleshly incontinence and "unnatural" vice, especially homosexuality. The denouement of the text is a formal edict of excommunication in which the priest Genius, speaking on Lady Nature's behalf, curses those who violate natural law and excludes them from the order of nature. The moral austerity and disciplinary force of Alan's text should be fairly obvious from this description, and in fact the *Plaint* was read throughout the medieval period as a tract against sodomy and other carnal sins. However, it would be reductive to describe Alan's text as purely ascetic, antierotic, and homophobic. On the contrary, the *Plaint* shifts erratically between moral diatribe and sexual titillation, sometimes going so far as to traduce in practice the very laws it seeks to promulgate in theory. The narrator is drawn to metaphors, puns, and images that render his own sexual desires

ambiguous; while Nature and Genius indulge in rhetorical excesses that tend to complicate, or perhaps even invalidate, their moral claims. Some scholars see the playfulness of Alan's language as part of the text's disciplinary strategy: the reader is trapped in the poem's equivocal language and requires clerical mediation in order to achieve moral restoration. Others have argued that the text is so conspicuously at odds with its own moral intentions that it should be read as a diatribe against Ovidian poetry rather than sexual deviance.

Another twelfth-century Latin treatise, Andreas Capellanus's *On Love*, offers a similar hodgepodge of incongruous ingredients and exegetical difficulties. The text opens with a preface in which Andreas agrees to teach his disciple Walter about erotic love, and in which he implicitly designates himself as heir to Ovid's title "preceptor of love." The text that ensues is indeed a compendium Ovidian love doctrine, filtered through the lenses of scholastic method and a medieval clerical worldview. In Book 1, Andreas defines love, explains how it is acquired, and illustrates his argument with dialogues. Book 2 discusses how love may be preserved and is devoted in large part to erotic casuistry. A third and final book offers what appears to be a palinode to the first two: in an abrupt about-face, Andreas bitterly denounces love and women and exhorts Walter to wed himself instead to the divine Bridegroom in preparation for Judgment Day. Though Andreas's vision of human sexuality is very different from Alan's, his work nonetheless shares with the *Plaint* a common set of intellectual references and a profoundly Ovidian fascination with ambivalence. It is unclear, for instance, whether *On Love* should be taken as a straightforward rulebook on the courtly love tradition or whether it should be read instead as an ironic or parodic subversion of that tradition. Those readers who favor an ironic reading in turn disagree on the function of irony in the text. Some argue for Andreas's orthodoxy and privilege the moral decrees of Book 3 over the profane themes and ribald humor of the first two. Others make the reverse claim. Perhaps the most sensitive readers are those who refuse to privilege any one perspective over another. Like Ovid, Andreas does not seek to limit the meaning of erotic love but instead endows it with multiple, discrepant meanings and a seemingly endless capacity for metamorphosis. By complicating his own authorial viewpoint, he allows the reader to glimpse the tensions and dissensions internal to the sexual culture of his time period. If modern critics impose unity on Andreas's treatise and generalize its love doctrine, it is at the expense of the playfulness of the text, which eschews thematic and stylistic coherence.

Vernacular Texts

Though the vernacular literature of the High Middle Ages was intended for a very different audience, it nonetheless shares with Alan's *Plaint* and Andreas's *On Love* a marked tendency toward fragmentation and undecidability. Two examples will have to suffice: romance (idealizing fictions concerned with chivalric valor and courtly love) and the fabliaux (obscene, comic texts that caricature the common folk and their questionable sexual mores). Many critics have argued that romance feeds cultural anxieties about the disruptive effects of the libido and seeks to empower feudal institutions to regulate sexual acts and desires. Romance is particularly fascinated with female adultery and male homosexuality, which it views as directly threatening to patrilineal systems of descent and the political hierarchies and institutions that rest upon them. Other critics have argued, by contrast, that romance incorporates so many different perspectives and addresses itself to so diverse an audience that its cultural and ideological significance cannot be easily defined. It would be reductive, in their view, to read romances simply as cautionary tales illustrating simple lessons about sexual morality and political stability. Indeed, many critics have argued that female characters in romance typically speak on several levels at once, both sustaining and undermining the conventions that govern women's lives. If romance initially appears to instantiate and endorse a repressive sexual ideology, it also works to expose the tensions and fault lines within that ideology. Thus, for instance, the knightly solidarity that is so fundamental to the romance ethos depends upon intimate homosocial bonds that are never fully distinguished from homoerotic desire. Similarly, the chivalric hero must prove his virility by devoting himself to the courtship of an idealized woman; yet in the process he reveals that his value as a man requires his submission to his supposed inferior.

Still greater ambiguities can be found in the fabliaux. Far from being naïve folk tales or artless depictions of medieval popular culture, the fabliaux are instead highly sophisticated, self-reflexive fictions that focus attention on the malleability of discursive meaning and the protean nature of the body qua sign. They are particularly interested in the genitalia, which are described less as anatomical markers of sexual difference than as verbal, metaphorical, and fictional constructs. Typically, the humor of the fabliaux depends upon a misinterpretation of, or slippage within, the genital metaphor, culminating in a repetition of traditional misogynistic themes: women's insatiability, prolixity, treachery, and so on. By linking the genitals to semantic indeterminacy, however, the fabliaux poets also belie certain assumptions about the nature of gender and sexuality. To begin with, if the fabliaux consider gender to be a cultural construct rather than a biological fact, then they must also have understood it to be arbitrary and unstable rather than absolute and universal. Moreover, if gender is fictional, then patriarchy itself must rest upon conventions and fabrications rather than indisputable, natural facts. Finally, the conceit of the fabliaux that the body proliferates alternate meanings suggests that the body's appetites can never be fully controlled. Like Ovid's own poetry, the fabliaux suggest that the body restlessly undermines the limitations placed upon it and limitlessly metamorphoses desire.

Conclusions

What kinds of general conclusions can we draw about medieval eroticism on the basis of the literary evidence described here? To begin with, we can confidently assert (as does Karras) that there simply *is* no such thing as medieval sexuality. There is only an extraordinarily multifarious set of social, cultural, textual, and literary practices that stubbornly resist facile categorization and univocal meaning. This is not to dismiss the value of typological methods, which are altogether crucial for situating medieval erotic texts within their social, cultural, and historical contexts. Literary critics must always consider material evidence before they begin the work of analysis, including factors such as a text's likely provenance, its manuscript tradition, and its anticipated and actual readership. At the same time, scholars of literature and history alike must never lose sight of the fundamental evasiveness and equivocalness of medieval literary genres and traditions. There is considerable danger in overdetermining medieval texts by assigning to them singular meanings or by considering them as transparent social and cultural documents. Often, medieval literature is itself conscious of the contingency of linguistic and cultural meaning, especially when it comes to the body and sexual pleasure. Though modern readers may initially find the ambivalence and self-reflexivity of medieval texts disconcerting, these should ultimately be considered its greatest assets. Medieval erotic literature encompasses, and casts a critical gaze upon, a multitude of attitudes, beliefs, and norms regarding the body and desire. In the process, it offers the assiduous reader a vantage point from which to glimpse the extraordinary diversity and complexity of human sexual culture.

NOAH GUYNN

References and Further Reading

Allen, Peter. *The Art of Love: Amatory Fiction from Ovid to the "Romance of the Rose."* Philadelphia: University of Pennsylvania Press, 1992.

Baldwin, John W. *The Language of Sex: Five Voices from Northern France around 1200.* Chicago: University of Chicago Press, 1994.

Bloch, R. Howard. *Medieval Misogyny and the Invention of Western Romantic Love.* Chicago: University of Chicago Press, 1991.

Brown, Peter. *The Body and Society: Men, Women, and Sexual Renunciation in Early Christianity.* New York: Columbia University Press, 1988.

Brundage, James A. *Law, Sex, and Christian Society in Medieval Europe.* Chicago: University of Chicago Press, 1987.

Bullough, Vern L, and James A. Brundage. *Handbook of Medieval Sexuality.* New York: Garland, 1996.

Burger, Glenn, and Steven F. Kruger, eds. *Queering the Middle Ages.* Minneapolis: University of Minnesota Press, 2001.

Burgwinkle, William. *Sodomy, Masculinity, and Law in Medieval Literature: France and England, 1050–1230.* Cambridge: Cambridge University Press, 2004.

Dinshaw, Carolyn. *Chaucer's Sexual Poetics.* Madison: University of Wisconsin Press, 1989.

———. *Getting Medieval: Sexual Communities, Pre- and Post-Modern.* Durham: Duke University Press, 1999.

Fradenburg, Louise and Carla Freccero. *Premodern Sexualities.* New York: Routledge, 1996.

Frantzen, Allen J. *Before the Closet: Same-Sex Love from Beowulf to Angels in America.* Chicago: University of Chicago Press, 1998.

Gaunt, Simon. *Gender and Genre in Medieval French Literature.* Cambridge: Cambridge University Press, 1995.

Guynn, Noah D. *Allegory and Sexual Ethics in the High Middle Ages.* New York: Palgrave Macmillan, 2006.

Holsinger, Bruce. *Music, Body, and Desire in Medieval Culture: Hildegard of Bingen to Chaucer.* Stanford: Stanford University Press, 2001.

Karras, Ruth Mazo. *Sexuality in Medieval Europe: Doing unto Others.* New York: Routledge, 2005.

Leupin, Alexandre. *Barbarolexis: Medieval Writing and Sexuality,* translated by Kate M. Cooper. Cambridge: Harvard University Press, 1989.

Lochrie, Karma. *Heterosyncrasies: Female Sexuality When Normal Wasn't.* Minneapolis: University of Minnesota Press, 2005.

Lochrie, Karma, Peggy McCracken, and James A. Schultz, eds. *Constructing Medieval Sexuality.* Minneapolis: University of Minnesota Press, 1997.

Lomperis, Linda and Sarah Stanbury. *Feminist Approaches to the Body in Medieval Literature.* Philadelphia: University of Pennsylvania Press, 1993.

McCarthy, Conor. *Love, Sex, and Marriage in the Middle Ages: A Sourcebook.* New York: Routledge, 2004.

Minnis, Alastair. *Magister Amoris: The Roman de la Rose and Vernacular Hermeneutics.* Oxford: Oxford University Press, 2001.

Sautman, Francesca Canadé and Pamela Sheingorn. *Same Sex Love and Desire among Women in the Middle Ages.* New York: Palgrave Macmillan, 2001.

See also **Arthurian Literature; Audience, Women in the; Boccaccio, Giovanni; Body in Literature and Religion; Body, Visual Representations of; Chaucer, Geoffrey; Chrétien de Troyes; Christine de Pizan; Courtly Love; Cross-Dressing; Cuckold; Dante Alighieri; Fabliau; Femininity and Masculinity; Feminist Theories and Methodologies; Floire and Blancheflor; Gaze; Gender Ideologies; Gottfried von Strassburg; Guinivere; Isolde; Lovesickness; Minnesang; Misogyny; Mythology, Medieval Reception of; Obscenity; Ovid, Medieval Reception of; Pastourelle; Petrarch; Queer Theory; Roman de la Rose and Its Reception; Romance de Flamenca; Romance de Silence; Romance, English; Romance, French; Romance, German; Romances of Antiquity; Sexuality: Extramarital Sex; Sexuality: Female Same-Sex Relations; Sexuality: Male Same-Sex Relations; Sexuality: Regulation of; Sexuality: Sex in Marriage; Trobairitz and Troubadours; Wife of Bath; Wolfram von Eschenbach; Woman on Top; Women Authors: German Texts; Women Authors: Italian Texts; Women Authors: Latin Texts; Women Authors: Middle English Texts; Women Authors: Old French Texts; Women Authors: Spanish Texts**

EUCHARIST

See **Fasting and Food, Religious Aspects of**

EUNUCHS

Eunuchs were a feature of Middle Eastern and Asian court and religious life for thousands of years. They appear in Mesopotamian texts from 2000 BCE, in Egyptian texts from 1300 BCE, and in Chinese texts from 1100 BCE. The practice of having eunuchs was continued by Persian, Hellenistic, Roman, Byzantine, and Muslim rulers. In the Byzantine Empire eunuchs were important participants in the life of the church and the imperial court. Practices involving eunuchs spread from Byzantium to southern Italy, Sicily, and North Africa. They existed in most Muslim courts. Even as of 2006, the last of the eunuch tomb guards at the tomb of the Prophet Muhammad are dying.

Eunuch is a very broad term. In the Byzantine world (325 CE to 1453 CE) it could refer to a man who was celibate; a man whose genitals were deformed, making procreation impossible; or a man whose genitals accidentally or intentionally were mutilated in infancy, childhood, or after puberty. The term *eunuch*, therefore, refers to a man's reproductive capacity, not to any particular kind of mutilation.

In Byzantium eunuchs were castrated by crushing or tying off the testicles or through a surgical procedure that removed the testicles from the scrotal sac. The latter was believed to be the safer procedure. Total removal of the genitals was not practiced in Byzantium.

In ancient societies adult men were castrated as an act of sexual dominance, usually in connection with warfare or as a punishment. Prepubescent boys and young children were castrated for very different reasons. Servile boys who were especially attractive were castrated to preserve their youthful appearance, which some men found sexually attractive. As these castrated boys matured they did not go through normal puberty. Lacking testosterone they did not grow beards and their facial features and skin retained a feminine delicacy. Their faces developed a characteristic triangular shape and their bodies elongated. The result was a tall, slender individual who was lightly boned, lacked muscular development, had fat deposits distributed in a feminine pattern, and retained a high-pitched voice. He did not lose his hair to baldness as he aged, but did suffer from early and severe osteoporosis. In late antiquity eunuchs were often associated with sexual sin.

During the Byzantine period, while young men were still castrated for the reasons stated previously, and their appearance was believed to bring elegance to the court, eunuchs began to be perceived in other ways. Drawing on very old traditions that presented boys, and therefore eunuchs, as magical, liminal individuals who served as priests or elite servants, the status of eunuchs improved. Since eunuchs were not sexually active, they were assumed to have intellectual powers superior to those of other men. Since they did not marry and establish families, it was assumed that they would be unfailingly loyal to their masters or patrons. The etymology of the term *eunuch* illustrates this change. Although it comes from the Greek word εὐνή, which means bed chamber, in the Byzantine world it was assumed to come from εὐνοοσ or "well-minded."

By the ninth century, eunuchs were major figures in both the Byzantine court and the Orthodox Church. As the elaboration of the imperial bureaucracy distanced the emperor from his subjects, he increasingly depended on his staff of eunuchs both to protect him from outsiders and to act as a liaison to those outside the imperial circle. The eunuchs of the court controlled the palace doors, the imperial regalia, palace protocol, and the imperial audiences. They stage-managed imperial milestones: births, marriages, and deaths. Because they were competent and trusted servants they often commanded armies and acted as imperial envoys. By the tenth century the emperor's chief eunuch was usually the most powerful bureaucrat in the empire.

Eunuchs' relationships with the church were complex. On the one hand the church was suspicious of eunuchs because of their early connection to sexual sin. It considered that their condition was "unnatural," a violation of the integrity of the male body. On the other hand the church admired the eunuch's celibacy and saw it as a requirement for fulfilling perfect service to God. In Byzantine art and literature eunuchs are regularly mistaken for angels and vice versa. They are seen to share a number of attributes: liminality, asexuality, a boyish appearance, and lives dedicated to service.

Despite the importance of eunuchs in Byzantine society, castration was officially frowned upon. Late Roman and Byzantine legal codes repeat earlier Roman injunctions against castration. Under the civil code those who practiced or arranged for castrations were to be punished with death, confiscation, exile, or fines. It was permissible, however, to buy a eunuch who had been castrated by barbarians outside the boundaries of the empire. Ecclesiastical law echoes these regulations, though it does allow an individual who has been castrated by others against his will to become a priest. By the ninth century there are signs that men were ignoring this legislation. Since Roman law allowed castration for medical reasons, a remarkable number of young eunuchs seem to have been castrated because they suffered from hernias. Sources talk about parents arranging for a son's castration so that he could attain a job at the palace or a career in the church.

In both church and state, eunuchs were perceived to be guardians of women and children. They were personal servants, advisors, tutors, and companions. When a holy woman needed to find an appropriate place to set up as an urban hermit in the city of Constantinople, her faithful eunuch examined available real estate on her behalf. When an emperor wished to marry, a delegation of eunuchs looked over appropriate women on his behalf. If the supply of eunuchs in the palace began to decline a senior eunuch went looking for bright young men who might be willing to be castrated and join the corps.

Modern scholars ask whether eunuchs were a third sex. Except in the worst of the pejorative literature about eunuchs, the language associated with them treats them as men. In terms of modern biological categories they were men, but surgically altered men who had been acculturated into modes of self-presentation and behavior that the Byzantine world associated with women. They were beardless, had soft, smooth skin, luxuriant hair, high-pitched voices, and somewhat feminized bodies. They were perceived to be emotionally unstable, unable to control their desire for food, drink, money, and power. They were charged with being ambiguous, with resembling magicians, and with constantly changing the face they presented to society. Eunuchs, therefore, were perceived as a distinct kind of man that had unique abilities and culturally determined feminine characteristics. In other words they constituted a distinct gender that was neither male nor female but was gendered as something else.

KATHRYN M. RINGROSE

References and Further Reading

Asher-Greve, Julia M. "Mesopotamian Conceptions of the Gendered Body." In *Gender and the Body in the Ancient Mediterranean*, edited by Maria Wyke, Oxford: Blackwell, 1998, pp. 8–37.

Ayalon, David. *Eunuchs, Caliphs and Sultans*. Jerusalem: Magnes Press, 1999.

Baldwin, Barry. *Studies in Late Roman and Byzantine History, Literature and Language*. Amsterdam: Blackwell, 1984.

Boulhol, Pascal, and Isabelle Cochelin. "La réhabilitation de l'eunuque dans l'hagiographie (IIe - VIe siècles)." In *Memoriam sanctorum venerantes: Miscellanea in onore de Monsignor Victor Saxer*, Vatican: Citia del Vaticano, 1992, pp. 49–73.

Brower, Gary. "Ambivalent Bodies: Making Christian Eunuchs." Ph.D diss., Duke University, 1996.

Gleason, Maud W. *Making Men: Sophists and Self-Presentation in Ancient Rome*. Princeton: Princeton University Press, 1995.

Hopkins, M. Keith. *Conquerors and Slaves*. Cambridge: Cambridge University Press, 1978.

Kuefler, Mathew S. *The Manly Eunuch: Masculinity, Gender Ambiguity, and Christian Ideology in Late Antiquity*. Chicago: Chicago University Press, 2001.

Marmon, Shaun E. *Eunuchs and Sacred Boundaries in Islamic Society*. Oxford: Oxford University Press, 1995.

Ringrose, Kathryn M. *The Perfect Servant: Eunuchs and the Social Construction of Gender in Byzantium*. Chicago: Chicago University Press, 2003.

Roller, Lynn E. "The Ideology of the Eunuch Priest." In *Gender and the Body in the Ancient Mediterranean*, edited by Maria Wyke, Oxford: J. C. Gieben, 1998, pp. 118–135.

Tougher, Shaun F. "Byzantine Eunuchs: An Overview, with Special Reference to their Creation and Origin." In *Women, Men and Eunuchs: Gender in Byzantium*, edited by Liz James, Londen: Routledge, 1997, pp. 168–184.

See also **Empresses, Byzantine; Femininity and Masculinity; Gender Ideology; Sexuality, Regulation of**

EVANGILES DES QUENOUILLES

The *Evangiles des Quenouilles* (*Gospel of Distaffs*) is a compilation of folk wisdom produced in the Burgundian lands of French-speaking Flanders between 1466 and 1474. The earlier, "primitive" version, a listing of 152 "gospels," or beliefs, divided into three parts, is attributed in the manuscript to three otherwise-unknown authors, *maistre* Fouquart de Cambray, *maistre* Anthoine du Val, and Jehan d'Arras dit Caron. The later version, a major reworking that expands the number of beliefs to approximately 230 divided into six evenings, is anonymous. The text presents the familiar problematic of the mediation of popular or women's oral culture through clerical written culture, a dynamic consciously staged by the text's narrative framing: it is presented as the record made by a male secretary of the utterances of women who gather to spin and exchange wisdom during the long winter evenings between Christmas and Candlemas. The later version adapts the Boccaccian form of a series of "days" or, more properly, evenings, each presided over by one of six "présidentes" who deliver their "gospels," to which other participants offer glosses in a model clearly derived from clerical *lectio*. The "truths" provide a feminine perspective on such concerns as love, marriage, sexuality, child-bearing, health, healing, and prosperity, including the relationship to both the natural and supernatural world. The narrativization made possible by the frame, the imitation of biblical and scholastic models, and the choice of the participants' names and "professions" (prostitution, divination, etc.) belie the ironic and misogynist intentions of the clerical compilers, who destined the work for a reading public fascinated by popular customs and beliefs. The large place accorded to "superstitious" practices (charms, interpretation of signs and dreams) including beliefs related to sorcery may partly explain the elaborate framing with its attendant distancing. The work was quite popular, surviving in two manuscripts; eleven early printings, including six before 1500; translations into English, Dutch, and German; and a verse adaptation into the Gascon dialect.

References and Further Reading

Les Evangiles des Quenouilles, edited by Madeleine Jeay. Paris: J. Vrin, 1985.

Gates, Laura Doyle. "Distaff and Pen: Producing the Evangiles de Quenouilles." *Neophilologus* 81, 1 (1997): 13–20.

Jeay, Madeleine. *Savoir-faire: Une analyse des croyances des "Evangiles des Quenouilles" (XVe siècle)*. Le Moyen Français 10. Montreal: CERES, 1982.

Paupert, Anne. *Les Fileuses et le clerc: Une étude des Evangiles des Quenouilles*. Paris-Genève: Champion-Slatkine, 1990.

See also **Literature, French; Voice, Female: in Literature**

EVE

The figure of Eve, from the book of Genesis, was central in shaping Western attitudes toward women from the earliest days of Christianity. The North

African theologian Tertullian asked Christian women of the late second century, "Do you not know that every one of you is an Eve?" Tertullian viewed Eve as a paradigm for all women; and according to the Genesis account, Eve had been responsible for the original fall of the human race into sin. Disobedient to God, Eve was tempted by the serpent to eat the fruit of the Tree of the Knowledge of Good and Evil. She then encouraged her husband, Adam, to join her in sinning. A few Gnostic groups in the second century interpreted Eve's actions more positively, seeing in her a powerful symbol of spiritual wisdom, but it was the negative orthodox Christian evaluation of Eve that triumphed and colored all subsequent discussions of the Genesis text and of women themselves.

In early Christian scripture, Eve emerged as the symbol of all who allow themselves to be deceived by evil (2 Cor. 11:3) and as the prime justification for refusing to allow women to instruct men in the Church (I Tim. 2:12–14). In the second century, several themes soon emerged that were destined to become permanent fixtures in the structure of Christian theology. The most significant is that, as in Tertullian's indictment, Eve became the model for understanding all women as persons whose nature makes them likely to tempt others to sin. Second, Genesis describes Eve as being created after Adam; this will be used to prove the secondary and subordinate status of women to men, even before Eve's sin. Third, for Christian writers inclined to argue the value of celibacy over marriage, Eve came to represent the lure of the body and sexuality drawing Christians away from a single-minded service of God and entangling them instead in the coils of lust and worldly concerns. The work of St. Augustine of Hippo (354–430) only heightened this perspective. Crucial for determining the direction of theology in the Middle Ages, Augustine argued that sexual desire is itself a punishment for original sin and that all sexual intercourse, tainted by uncontrollable desire, is at least venially sinful. Furthermore, he held such sexual desire responsible for passing on the stain of original sin to future generations. Eve, and thus all women, became symbols of a body and sexuality no longer under rational control, inescapably inciting men to desire participation in the foremost effect of the Fall itself. Finally, and perhaps more positively, Eve was also portrayed as the precursor of Mary, the Second Eve, whose obedience to God resulted in the Incarnation and the eventual overthrow of the very serpent who had tempted her predecessor.

Throughout the medieval centuries, Eve remained central to discussions of women and of humanity in general. The rediscovery of Aristotle's work in the twelfth and thirteenth centuries allowed theologians to add a "biological" explanation for the supposed inferiority of Eve and of all women, due to his belief that women are deformed males. Nature intends to create a male; but something frustrates the natural development and a female is produced instead. While theologians like St. Thomas Aquinas stopped short of seeing women as inherently more biologically defective than men, late medieval witch hunters Heinrich Kramer and Jacob Sprenger carried the physical debility of Eve to an extreme. They asserted in the *Malleus maleficarum* (The Hammer of Witches), that Eve was naturally prone to sin because she was created from a "bent rib" of Adam, an assertion that calls into question even the creative technique of God.

In medieval artwork, Eve was often depicted naked, suggesting both the innocence of the original creation but also Eve's role as a symbol of the carnal. The association with lust is especially obvious when a naked Eve is contrasted with a fully clothed Virgin Mary, supreme symbol of sexual purity.

Medieval writers, particularly women, could nevertheless discuss Eve in creative and positive ways. Margaret Miles argues that Hildegard of Bingen portrays Eve as an expression of Adam's love, stressing the interdependence of men and women in God's plan. Eve, formed from Adam's body, in turn produces "Man" in her offspring. Also, Caroline Walker Bynum shows that both Hildegard and St. Catherine of Siena equate Eve, and therefore women, with humanity and body because Eve was made solely of Adam's flesh rather than the dust of the ground. This led to a connection between the female flesh of Mary, the second Eve, and the body of Christ formed in her womb, making it possible to assert that female flesh was crucified for the sins of humanity. In his Passion sermon, fifteenth-century theologian Jean Gerson depicts the Virgin Mary at the cross, asserting that the fleshly unity between herself and Jesus enables her to suffer with him and "buy back" the sin of Eve.

The Western tradition has most often seen in Eve a means for arguing the inferiority of women. Nevertheless, for some medieval writers, Eve could stand as a symbol of a human nature fallen but recreated in the common humanity of Mary and Jesus.

Donna Spivey Ellington

References and Further Reading

Allen, Prudence, R. S. M. *The Concept of Woman: The Aristotelian Revolution, 750 B.C.–A.D. 1250.* Grand Rapids, Mich.: William B. Eerdmans Publishing Company, 1985.

Bynum, Caroline Walker. *Holy Feast and Holy Fast: The Religious Significance of Food to Medieval Women.* Berkeley: University of California Press, 1987.

Dronke, Peter. *Women Writers of the Middle Ages: A Critical Study of Texts from Perpetua to Marguerite Porete.* New York: Cambridge University Press, 1984.

Horowitz, Maryanne Cline. "The Image of God in Man: Is Woman Included?" *Harvard Theological Review* 72 (1979): 175–206.

Miles, Margaret R. *Carnal Knowing: Female Nakedness and Religious Meaning in the Christian West.* Boston: Beacon Press, 1989.

Newman, Barbara. *Sister of Wisdom: St. Hildegard's Theology of the Feminine.* Berkeley: University of California Press, 1987.

Pagels, Elaine. *Adam, Eve, and the Serpent.* New York: Vintage Books, 1989.

See also **Aristotelian Concepts of Women and Gender; Augustine, Influence of; Bible, Women in; Body in Literature and Religion; Body, Visual Representations of; Catherine of Siena; Gender in Art; Gerson, Jean; Hildegard of Bingen; Mary, Virgin; Mary, Virgin: in Art; Mary, Virgin: in Literature; Mary, Virgin: in Music; Sexuality, Regulation of**

EXEMPLUM

While the word *exemplum* (plural *exempla*) can simply mean "example," in many medieval contexts it designates a short narrative used to illustrate or reinforce a point, often in a sermon. In Greek and Roman rhetoric, an account of notable figures or events might be used to convey the value of a quality such as chastity or good governance, and such narratives often reappear in medieval texts that offer advice to princes. The parables told by Jesus in the New Testament surely contributed to the development of the medieval sermon *exemplum*, although they differ from it in presenting imaginary, rather than (supposedly) historical events. And early Christian preaching recognized the usefulness of *exempla*; Pope Gregory I (d. 604), for instance, comments that examples are often more moving than mere words of instruction, and monastic preaching of the eleventh and twelfth centuries turned increasingly to such narratives as one of the sermon's modes of persuasion.

It was not until the preaching revival of the late twelfth and thirteenth centuries, however, that the term *exemplum* came into widespread use in preaching theory and sermons, and this is the main context in which the genre is studied today. In the period following the Gregorian Reform, the ecclesiastical establishment increasingly recognized a need to improve and expand preaching activity to ensure that the Church's message reached the laity more effectively. One form that endeavored to do so was the sermon *ad status*, a sermon directed toward a particular professional or social group—although while men were usually grouped by profession, secular women were often addressed as a single group, or according to marital status as wives or widows. The earliest surviving Latin collection of *ad status* sermons, the *Sermo generalis* of Honorius Augustodunensis, a prolific religious author of the first half of the twelfth century, provides brief addresses to priests, merchants, and married people, among others. Honorius ends each of his eight model sermons with a brief narrative about a representative of the group in question; a sermon to farmers concludes with the tale of a woman who, granted a vision of the eternal fates of her quiet, hard-working, long-suffering father (enjoying the fruits of heaven) and her garrulous, lustful, spendthrift mother (tormented in hell by demons and serpents), thereafter lives a life of steadfast virtue. As this suggests, *exempla* in sermons did not necessarily involve characters who were members of the group being addressed; *exempla* about women appear in sermons to men, and vice versa, although the desire to make an example compelling for the audience did mean that sermons to women were somewhat more likely to involve female characters. *Exempla* may draw on anything from biblical or classical stories, to folklore, to daily life for their subjects, but in many cases the depiction of recognizable, contemporary situations and characters (however fictional) lay at the heart of the medieval *exemplum*'s authority.

Later preachers similarly emphasized the value of *exempla*; the thirteenth and fourteenth centuries were the period of the greatest diffusion of the form. The priest, canon, and later bishop James of Vitry (d. 1240), one of the most famous preachers of the early thirteenth century, made extensive use of illustrative stories, arguing that they were particularly useful for teaching laypeople, for whom narrative is more appealing and comprehensible than doctrine. It is important to note that examples appear in sermons and other works directed to monks and priests, as well as those directed to the laity or to nuns (who were often grouped with the "unlearned"), but *exempla* were nonetheless strongly associated with lay or uneducated audiences. The tales were seen as, above all, valuable for pastoral work, a quality that made them attractive to the preachers of the Franciscan and Dominican orders, which had been created in part to respond to the demand for more and better preaching to laypeople. *Exempla* became so characteristic of their sermons that the orders were criticized for their use of "vain fables" at the expense of more serious matter, reflecting a longstanding concern about the appropriateness of narrative in sermons.

Scholars have recently debated whether the *exemplum* tends primarily to separate preacher and audience or to associate them. Collections of *exempla* for preachers' use were transmitted in Latin manuscripts that would have been inaccessible to most laypeople, and theoretical discussions of such tales often stress their appeal to simplicity and unlearnedness, emphasizing the distinction between preacher and audience. On the other hand, the preacher's acknowledged need to gain his hearers' attention and inspire their belief led him to participate in a narrative form that was popular across social groupings, drawing him to some degree into his audience's world.

The breadth of the *exemplum*'s appeal for medieval audiences can be seen in its literary manifestations beyond the preaching tradition. The "classical" or "public" *exemplum* was widely used throughout the later Middle Ages, and while sermon *exempla* as they survive in written form are generally quite brief, offering a narrative kernel rather than a full-fledged story, medieval authors not infrequently borrowed these brief tales and elaborated on them. The tale of Griselda, which was told by Petrarch, Boccaccio, and Chaucer, is essentially an *exemplum* illustrating the virtues of patience and obedience. In such contexts, however, the exemplary story (like the fables and fabliaux that often resemble it) gains a new independence, standing on its own rather than acting as a support for a larger point, and in this regard is a distinctly different phenomenon than the sermon *exemplum*.

CLAIRE WATERS

References and Further Reading

Bremond, Claude, Jacque Le Goff, and J.-C. Schmitt. *L'Exemplum*. Typologie des sources du moyen âge 40. Turnhout: Brepols, 1982.

Crane, Thomas Frederick. *The Exempla or Illustrative Stories from the Sermones Vulgares of Jacques de Vitry*. London: David Nutt for the Folk-Lore Society, 1890.

Mosher, Joseph A. *The Exemplum in the Early Religious and Didactic Literature of England*. New York: Columbia University Press, 1911.

Owst, G. R. *Preaching in Medieval England: An Introduction to the Sermon Manuscripts of the Period c. 1350–1450*. Cambridge: Cambridge University Press, 1926.

Scanlon, Larry. *Narrative, Authority, and Power: The Medieval Exemplum and the Chaucerian Tradition*. Cambridge: Cambridge University Press, 1994.

See also **Boccaccio, Giovanni; Chaucer, Geoffrey; Dominican Order; Fabliau; Griselda Petrarch; Sermons and Preaching; Spiritual Care**

F

FABLIAU

The fabliaux are a corpus of some 150 short French narratives, dating roughly from 1200 to 1340; the majority are anonymous, though some are by authors who identify themselves and who are in some cases known and respected for other compositions. In addition, several of Chaucer's *Canterbury Tales* (e.g., *The Miller's Tale*) are often designated fabliaux. The classic definition of fabliaux is that of Joseph Bédier, who in 1894 termed them *contes à rire en vers* ("comic tales in verse"). The definition has proved durable even though it is not entirely accurate, in that a number of texts commonly accepted as fabliaux are, in their apparent intent, more moralizing than humorous. Nonetheless, the majority of them are designed primarily for entertainment in some form, even though a good many conclude with morals; one of the common ones is "he who believes a woman is a fool." The morals sometimes follow logically from the tale but just as often seem to be a mere convention with little or no discernable connection with the events of the story.

The majority of the fabliaux deal with erotic subjects, often involving a triangle (a married couple and a third person, frequently a priest), a man who attempts to seduce a woman (married or not), or a woman whose wiles are directed against her husband or a suitor. In other instances, the point of the story is an account of legitimate revenge or even a simple joke or ruse; but sexual themes predominate.

Noting that female sexuality was often considered the "work of the devil," Levy has analyzed some of the more extreme and explicit reflections of that thinking in the fabliaux; but, like almost all commentators, he concludes that fabliau antifeminism was ambivalent and was in general less extreme than many other medieval condemnations of women. Lorcin contends that the fabliaux were no more antifeminist than other medieval genres, and Ménard actually describes the genre's misogyny as "a minor motif."

Those views tend to reduce the subject to a catalogue of female attributes or actions, demonstrating women's devious ways or their voracious sexual appetites but often failing to take into account the narrative function of those characteristics within the boundaries of works intended for amusement.

In regard to women's roles, two examples will illustrate the extremes of the genre. *The Castrated Lady* concerns a woman who, following her mother's precepts and practice, contradicts her new husband repeatedly. As a lesson in proper wifely comportment, the husband diagnoses the mother as having testicles; he viciously slices the woman's thighs and appears to remove the offending items—actually palmed bull testicles—that accounted for her presumption. Through the violence and the threat of its repetition, the wife learns her lesson, and the narrator appears to approve heartily. Near the other end of the fabliau spectrum stands *Berenger Long-Ass*, in which a wife resorts to deception—without narratorial censure—to correct the flaws of her equally deceptive but also shamefully cowardly and pretentious husband. In other fabliaux we find the full range of female behaviors, from simple and naïve women to devious ones, from victims to strong and powerful women, from those who are offended by sexual advances to a great many who initiate such advances and relish carnal pleasures.

Feminist criticism of the fabliaux has proceeded very fitfully, with most commentary on the misogyny of the genre merely echoing the judgments previously cited. However, Anne Ladd responded, as long ago as 1976, to these problems by asking, "What kind of antifeminism is it that in over fifty percent of male–female conflicts shows the woman winning?" Quoting Ladd's question, Lesley Johnson points out that "winning women of the fabliaux are above all cunning and high-spirited (rather than adulterous and deceitful)." It is certainly true that for every evil woman in the fabliaux, there is one who is either virtuous or victimized. More important, for every woman who is devious or conniving, there is a man who is brutish or brutal. Generally speaking, feminine cupidity is matched by masculine stupidity. Yet, it is unarguably the case that some narrators, in asides or major digressions or in morals, hold women in exceedingly low esteem and consider them collectively responsible for many of the travails of men and of society. All in all, the question of antifeminism in the fabliaux is far less straightforward than it has sometimes been made to appear, and further consideration of that subject, within the context of gender studies, is a clear desideratum.

NORRIS J. LACY

References and Further Reading

Fries, Maureen. "Feminae Populi: Popular Images of Women in Medieval Literature." *Journal of Popular Culture* 14.1 (1980): 79–86.

Johnson, Lesley. "Women on Top: Antifeminism in the Fabliaux?" *Modern Language Review* 78.2 (1983): 298–307.

Lacy, Norris J. "Women in the Fabliaux." Chap. 5 of *Reading Fabliaux*. New York: Garland, 1993, pp. 60–77.

Ladd, Anne. "Classifications of the Faliaux by Plot Structure." In *Proceedings of the International Colloquium held at the University of Glasgow on the Beast Epic, Fable and Fabliau*, edited by Kenneth Varty. Glasgow: privately printed by Kenneth Varty, 1976. pp. 92–107.

Levy, Brian J. *Patterns and Images in the Old French Fabliaux*. Amsterdam and Atlanta: Rodopi, 2000.

Lorcin, Marie-Thérèse. *Façons de sentir et de penser: les fabliaux français*. Paris: Champion, 1979.

Ménard, Philippe. *Les Fabliaux: contes à rire du moyen âge*. Paris: PUF, 1983.

See also **Eroticism in Literature; Literature, Old French; Misogyny; Sexuality**

FAMILY (EARLIER MIDDLE AGES)

Any discussion of family, as wider kin group or small nuclear unit, in the earlier Middle Ages inevitably needs to start with considerations of language and vocabulary. This is because the Latin word *familia* that looks at first sight to mean family as we understand the term meant something quite different. The Latin word *familia* meant household and comprised all those living together as one economic and social unit: parents and children together with servants. Neither Latin nor the Romance languages have a word for the small nuclear unit (parents and children) that in the Germanic languages is called *Gesinnde* (German) or *Gezin* (Dutch). The absence of such a specific word in the Latinate world, however, does not mean that nuclear families did not exist. On the contrary they occur frequently in the sources: saints' Lives, miracle stories or chronicles, as well as in documents such as estate surveys of large monasteries, or legal texts, where we can reconstruct them on the basis of references to "father," "mother," and "children." Archaeological excavations, too, suggest that the nuclear unit of parents and children lived normally under one roof. The family as a larger unit of the kin group, in Latin *cognatio*, *linea*, or *generatio*, consisted of the relatives of any individual on father's (agnatic) and the mother's (cognatic) side. The extent to which the small family group interacted with the cousins of various degrees on both sides in any time was very fluid depending entirely on status, wealth, and geographical location.

Technical Vocabulary

Central to the scholarly discussion on the relationship between the family as household and (wider) kin group is the interpretation of technical vocabulary (Latin *fara*, or Irish *fine*) for the kin group in the period before 1000. Everyone agrees that the vocabulary denotes large groups bound by kinship, usually going back to a shared ancestor and also usually at any one time headed by one person who seemed to have exercised some authority over the group. Such groups, too, were reasonably fluctuating in whom they embraced. The crucial question is to what extent the individual members in such groups recognized a sort of membership in practice and how in reality they enacted their individual responsibility towards others in such a group. Furthermore, the extent to which the smaller family units within them were linked to each other in a micro-organization with firm social and legal rules is very hard to identify. Heavily influenced by social and anthropological research on contemporary traditional societies in Africa and South America modern historians did at one time consider them as large clans. More recently, medievalists following Herlihy (himself influenced by Goody) and Bouchard have shifted their opinion significantly away from this view based primarily on reading of legal codes that present a normative picture of responsibilities and social bonds linking cousins across generations and horizontal degrees of blood relationship that are hard to verify in the sources. An obligation to help pay for the legal defense of one's cousin, for example stipulated in the Salian Laws or to pay *wergeld*, a fine, to exonerate a blood relation who had committed a crime in Anglo-Saxon law, should not be interpreted in the sense that all cousins are responsible every time to pay such fines under all circumstances, nor that such norms signify actual and frequent contact between all members of the same kin. Surely, such rules were meant as guidelines that in emergencies some members of the kin might come to the help of their relative if this was practical. Therefore, theoretical rules as set out in legal codes are no blueprint for our reconstruction as to the historical reality of living or working arrangements binding all these individuals together in more than relatively loose terms. Meshing the information from legal sources with their emphasis on kinship and legal obligation with practical information about daily reality is difficult. The detailed evidence from the Saint-Germain polyptych, a Frankish estate survey from c. 844, is revealing. The majority of the 1,412 households consisted of only two generations (parents and children); among the 3,470 women only twenty-six were grandmothers. Of the households just under half were headed by people of the same generation (brothers, or brother and sister). So, for all the startling evidence of multiheaded households and relative absence of grandparents, the lack of information about the kinship between any of the households makes it impossible to test the evidence from the Salian Laws on one Frankish community of Saint Germain for which we have details on households.

Degrees of Kinship

How did early medieval people describe their family relationships and what structures did they recognize? The vocabulary used for the description of family bonds dates from the Roman period. The Romans took the individual as its center and counted back to a common ancestor, then forward to the targeted relative. The number of people touched, minus one, constituted the degrees of kinship. Thus the father and mother of the self were related to the self in the first degree, the self's sister or brother in the second degree, and a first cousin in the fourth degree. Through the church the early medieval people stuck to counting as belonging to the *cognatio* any one

related within seven degrees. This changed from the ninth century when the church stipulated that consanguinity ended at four degrees. As part of the Reform movement in the mid-eleventh century the seven degree rule was reintroduced before it was finally abolished as unworkable at the Fourth Lateran council of 1204. What is crucial to understand is that any individual's family in the wider sense, beyond the immediate circle of parents and siblings, is a group that consists of people chosen or recognized by that individual as active kin. The Bouchard school would say that a medieval person would construct his wider family group, in particular depending on lines of inheritance. Dhuoda, a ninth-century Frankish noble woman, exhorted her sixteen-year-old son William to remember specific relatives on his father's side, with all of whom he had to collaborate in one way or another in order to keep the family lands intact. This does not mean that he did not have other paternal kin besides the ones mentioned by Dhuoda, but we do not know about them, presumably because they were less important. The example also demonstrates that it was Dhuoda's, and, through her, William's choice that determined her, and his, conception of one part of their family at one particular moment in time. The spotlight nature of our sources should always be borne in mind when we try to reconstruct medieval families in the wider sense. Moreover, for modern scholars interpreting snippets of detailed family history, such as given by Dhuoda, in conjunction with more abstract legal obligations within kin groups as set out in Frankish (and for that matter Old English, Irish, or Norman) law codes, it is a challenge that remains one of our most difficult tasks.

Marriage Ties

Another important aspect concerning early medieval families, nuclear and wider, is the blood relationship resulting from multiple marriages or other unions such as concubinage. Given the relatively high incidence of women's death in childbirth and the demise of men as a result of accident or fighting, remarriage was common and nuclear units comprized then, as now, stepparents and stepchildren. Half siblings were even more competitive rivals for any share of an inheritance than full siblings. Examples of this are rife from the chronicle accounts of aristocratic families ranging from important imperial/royal lines to small provincial ones. The troubled history of the Carolingian family, descendants of Charlemagne (d. 814) and his wives and concubines, of which he had at least nine, is the most notorious. Four generations of descendants fought over ever-changing portions of the vast realm conquered by Charlemagne.

Fosterage

Other categories of alternative kin group structures were the result of fostering, very common in Scandinavian and Irish societies and a particularly prominent theme in their respective sagas and law codes (problematic sources in themselves because so many date from manuscripts of the later Middle Ages). A slightly different type was temporary fostering for a variety of purposes, especially among the aristocracy. Young boys received a military education in different households sometimes of a neighbor, sometimes of a cousin or godparent (Simon of Vexin [d. 1088] was brought up at the Norman court of his godmother Matilda, married to William the Conqueror), or they spent time elsewhere as a hostage (Dhuoda's son William at Charles the Bald's court). Girls were sent to live with their prospective in-laws so that from as early as eight or nine years old they would be embedded in their new family to take on its customs and language in order in turn to pass them on to their children. Empress Matilda was eight when she left England for Germany in 1110.

Family Consciousness

And how did people see their family and how did they construct a family consciousness? If we accept that from the early Middle Ages family groups could develop along patrilinear and matrilinear lines and that combinations of the two, depending on the view of the individual who constructed the family, always existed, what tool existed to express the family bond? From the Merovingian period, that is, the late sixth century onwards there exist rudimentary genealogical tracts, descent lines, of families. They would either be written as biblical accounts of "X begat Y, who begat Z," or they would center on the individual who recounted his or her ancestors starting with parents and grandparents. Another form of large groupings of names, usually of individuals related to each other by blood, appears in commemoration books designed to memorialize the souls of those mentioned. From c. 900 onward genealogical tracts become available, usually written in monasteries, to record the gifts over several generations of a particular family. In those cases, however, as in Dhuoda's, we must remember that the actual blood relation group on biological grounds would always be larger than the group recorded in sources. Thus narrowing of groups for practical or inheritance reasons always presents the family as an artificially constructed group.

One of the most intractable problems faced by historians of the family, whether in the wider or more constricted sense, is the role of the church in the creation of the records on which we now rely. With the growing importance of the church as the overarching administrative organization before c. 1000, we shall never know to what extent idealized normative images of the family were being constructed. The fact that, according to ecclesiastical authorities, it was considered unlawful to marry a goddaughter or a stepmother does not mean that in practice people did abstain from such action. For, surely, the existence of legislation of this kind suggests strongly that such actions took place frequently, because otherwise the legal rules would have been superfluous. In other words, reading the normative sources against the grain yields valuable information for the ways in which families as small coresidential units and wider kin enacted, or ignored, their blood relationships.

ELISABETH VAN HOUTS

References and Further Reading

Bauduin, P. *Désigner les parents: le champ de la parenté dans l'oeuvre des premiers chroniqueurs normands*, Anglo-Norman Studies 24. Proceedings of the Battle conference 2001, edited by. J. Gillingham. Woodbridge: Boydell Press, 2003, pp. 71–84.

Bitel, L. M. *Women in Early Medieval Europe 400–1100*. Cambridge: Cambridge University Press, 2002.

Bouchard, C. B. *"Those of My Blood" Constructing Noble Families in Medieval Francia*. Philadelphia: University of Pennsylvania Press, 2001.

Bullough, D. "Early Medieval Social Groupings: The Terminology of Kinship." *Past and Present* 46 (1969): 3–18.

"Famille et parenté dans l'Occident médiévale," edited by G. Duby and J. Le Goff, Collection de l'Ecole française de Rome 30, Rome: Ecole Francais de Rome, 1977.

Goody, J. *The Development of the Family and Marriage in Europe*. Cambridge: Cambridge University Press, 1983.

Jochems, J. *Women in Old Norse Society*. Ithaca and London: Connell University Press, 1995.

Le Jan, R. "Famille et pouvoir dans le monde franc" (VIIe-Xe siècle): essai d'anthropologie social. Paris: Publication de la Sorbonne, 1995.

Lynch, J. L. *Godparents and Kinship in Early Medieval Europe*. Princeton: Princeton University Press, 1986.

Murray, A.C. *Germanic Kinship Structure: Studies in Law and Society in Antiquity and the Early Middle Ages*. Toronto: Pontifical Institute of Medieval Studies, 1983.

Schmid, K. "The structure of the nobility in the earlier middle ages." In *The Medieval Nobility: Studies on the Ruling Classes of France and Germany from the Sixth to the Twelfth Century*, edited and translated by T. Reuter. Amsterdam: North Holland, 1978, pp. 37–59.

Werner, K. F. *Die Nachkommen Karls des Grossen bis um das Jahr 1000 (1.-8.Generation)*, Karl der Grosse: Lebenswerk und Nachleben, edited by W. Braunfels. Düsseldorf, 1965–1968, vol. 4.

Werner, K. F. *Naissance de la noblesse: l'essor des élites politiques en Europe.* Paris, 1998.

See also **Barbarian Law Codes; Church; Death, Mourning, and Commemoration; Dhuoda; Family (Later Middle Ages); Fosterage; Genealogy; Kinship; Law, Canon; Marriage, Christian; Marriage, Impediments to; Necrologies and Mortuary Rolls**

FAMILY (LATER MIDDLE AGES)

The nuclear family of parents and unmarried children, living in their own household or domestic arrangement, was a basic unit of medieval society. Taking all social levels into account, this model covered a reasonable proportion of the population across the face of Europe. However, there were so many alternative models and practices and arrangements that no discussion of the family and kinship—looking at structure, definitions and boundaries, functions, change across time, regional and socioeconomic variations, spiritual analogues, and so forth—can be limited to this single and simple form. As there was no specific word in medieval Latin that meant what *family* does in English, the concept was never focused or narrowed to meet, or to be confined to what seems in the industrial or postindustrial West as the most basic or particular version of the social (and biological) unit. *Famulus* meant servant, and its medieval usage emphasized a domestic unit comprising those living together in a household (in which only some were "family" in the modern sense).

As a group of men and women linked through recognized ties of blood, marriage, spiritual kinship, and such bonds of fictive kinship as sworn brotherhoods in knightly or religious orders or brotherhood or sisterhood in guilds and confraternities, family was a major building block or principle of social organization. A treatment of the medieval family can be presented both in terms of its structure as an institution or aggregation of similar institutions and the diversity of its functions. Questions about the role of family are not only answered differently as we move from its shape and scope in "the first feudal age" of the ninth and tenth centuries (with the Carolingians as the overarching model), let alone from earlier centuries of Germanic invasion and settlement, to the fourteenth or fifteenth century, but there are vast distinctions across the breadth of Europe (as there were different modes of agriculture and production, different levels of urbanization, different conditions of servile service and tenancy, a varying strength of kinship ties, etc).

Of particular significance is the vast gulf between families possessed of significant property, especially real property or real estate, and those without. This distinction separates families for whom inheritance and transmission patterns were of such prime importance that they often became areas of strategic planning that covered arranged marriages between unborn children and the spinning of complex webs of "estate planning" and testamentary disposition from those many families where the burdens of bearing and raising children might only be compensated for by the unwaged labor they would eventually contribute to the common enterprise. These latter contributions to the family by its members between childhood and marriage could be a key factor in the scramble to survive, let alone to climb the slippery slope toward prosperity and upward mobility.

The Nuclear Family

While family as a social unit and as a concept is most readily grasped if we begin with the nuclear unit, it spreads widely in many directions, and in some respects the medieval family was not even limited to those alive at any given time (as shown by a look at those named when prayers for the dead were being specified). Marriage is a good point at which to begin. By the twelfth century marriage (matrimony) was coming to be accepted as one of the essential sacraments of Christian life. This enhanced the church's control of the definition of marriage and the special relationship of bride and groom as a new social and sexual unit. Though the church's blessing of a marital union need not precede the binding agreement of the two parties (and this agreement rendered them incapable of making other or subsequent arrangements), an ecclesiastical interest, expressed in the power to define, to intervene, and to sanctify, covered and controlled such marital- and family-related issues as legitimacy, the degrees of consanguinity within which marriage was forbidden (at least without a dispensation), the indissolubility of marriage, the age of consent for marriage (12 for girls, 14 for boys), a spouse's "right" to sex with her or his partner, the tangles generated by second marriages and spiritual vows, the freedom of married persons to enter monastic life, and issues like the binding power of testamentary bequests and of prayers for the family's dead. All of these had immense repercussions regarding the transmission of property and the primacy of competing family lines and claims—as they did regarding the grace of private life and the way identity was defined through links to one's ancestors, to living kin, and to one's progeny.

Degrees of Kinship

Beyond the narrow world of parents and children lay many concentric circles of kinship and degrees of relationship; all were family, albeit of varying (and diminishing) degrees of importance and relationship. By the twelfth century, if not before, models of kinship and family that had accorded roughly equal affinity or symmetry to kin of either sex on the mother's side (cognatic kin) with those on the father's (the agnatic kin) were yielding across much of Europe to legal and social conventions that privileged the latter. The need to meet the military obligations that went with the distribution of fiefs probably contributed to this process, while for most of rural Europe lords of the manors were happy to endorse or impose a comparable model on the peasantry. This made the descent or transmission of peasant holdings easier to assign and police, though in practice economic factors may have been as important as kinship links and male succession patterns in tracking the actual movement of and market in manorial holdings. While society could well have gone in the other direction and maintained the symmetry of the kinship structure (or even given priority to cognatic kin), family came more and more to be a construct traced through and boasted about by way of the male line. That this development took place in the years (eleventh and twelfth centuries) in which primogeniture was also, or simultaneously, being accepted as the basic pattern for inheritance was hardly a coincidence. The two social forces or factors can be seen as the two sides of a coin.

The widespread acceptance of unitary patterns of inheritance, with a bias in favor of the eldest son, certainly tilted a definition of family toward the male line of descent at most social levels, at least whenever fertility and survival made this the feasible route to follow. Alternate systems, whereby lands were divided among all or some of the children (male and even female), or when an individual other than the eldest son inherited (as in ultimageniture, which favored the youngest son), did exist at various times and places and exercised some influence upon the working definition of family. However, such practices were never more than exceptions to the general rule of patrilineal descent, and the emergence of primogeniture. Through most of Europe, cognatic kinship was likely to be just a fall-back, at least for legal, political, and economic concerns; in the realm of social or interpersonal relationships (touching sex and marriage) symmetry or bilateral kinship continued as an operative institution. But unless the woman's family (i.e., the mother's line of descent) was of much greater social or historical prominence than the father's, her genealogical tree was apt to be relegated to second place as such matters were proclaimed through the growing use of coats of arms and personal seals, the creation and display of genealogical and Jesse trees, the testimony accepted in legal disputes, and the widespread adoption of surnames (which came about in the twelfth and thirteenth centuries; a century or two later for people of lower social status). The misogyny that characterized so many aspects of medieval life and thought certainly was a strong factor in the creation of this hierarchy of kinship and inheritance and in the disappearance of many of the social roles that had once been the province of the extended family.

If parents and children represent the nuclear or the vertical family (covering two generations), those many other kin included in the wide embrace of the horizontal family also counted—if not for quite as much, and perhaps only in times of need or special circumstances. We find their presence taken seriously in tracing those patterns of inheritance that were of such concern; a local jury might elaborate on the descent of an estate to distant and remote kin in the absence of more obvious heirs and claimants. We see it in the ranking of levels or degrees of relationship, either traced to a common ancestor or emanating outwards from the self. Such a genealogical data bank was widely understood, it being the key to the church's injunctions against marriages within the forbidden circles of consanguinity or incest. This ecclesiastical insistence on exogamous marriage posed problems for the intertwined crowned and aristocratic families who ruled Europe, as it also did for the women and men of the thousands of villages that saw few newcomers come to stay and marry. Following on Roman law (and biblical injunctions), the church developed a sweeping definition of consanguinity by which it decreed that marriage was forbidden between people related within the fourth degree, which would reach as far as second cousins. And because of the complexities of symmetrical kinship and the strength of cognatic links in matters of remarriage and spiritual kinship, the full universe of forbidden partners was much larger than what it would be in modern society under the same definitions of blood or marital ties. Thus the social and sexual control of marriage defined or redefined kinship. This Christianized view of the relationship and of the large kinship circles of which the subject and the subject's marriage comprised the center replaced earlier ones that had revolved around such institutions or constructs as clans, blood feuds, and myths about eponymous founding fathers from whom all (in a tribe, village, or war band) were descended.

Aristocratic Families

The aristocratic family of the High or Central Middle Ages was the basic operative unit of political life. With royal families as the most visible and trend-setting models, establishing and maintaining the hegemonic position of the patriarchal family was a motivating force behind many issues and actions of the state. Royal marriages and the production of heirs were basic pillars of public life, and the elaboration of royal and aristocratic genealogies an enterprise of public import, with the "triumph" of primogeniture as the basic line of transmission, by the twelfth century, making father–son links the most important of all. Through her success in producing children the queen's role was one of unmatched importance, though this did little, per se, to raise her status at court or in council. Queens might rise to prominence by force of personality, or through marital affection and partnership, or because of the king's absence or early death (leaving an heir of minor age), and her own family might even hope to achieve power through this tie. But basically, it was her childbearing capacity that defined her role, and the long-term success of such dynasties as the Capetians in France (with direct father–son succession from 987 until 1328) rested on a series of kings' wives, the queens of France, who fulfilled their primary duty. Against this, dynastic turnover and the frequent failure of direct male heirs among the later Carolingians and in the various succeeding imperial dynasties thwarted grandiose plans in the twelfth and thirteenth centuries for a realm that would dominate both sides of the Alps. Stocking the royal nursery was as important, at the top of the social pyramid, as having seed for next year's planting was for the peasantry. When a family of power failed in the direct line, then and only then were more distant kin accepted in the line of succession. At the other extreme, when rulers like the English kings Edward I (1272–1307) or Edward III (1327–1377) had at least a half dozen children survive to the age of marriage the dynastic possibilities and the complicating entanglements were the stuff of high politics, war, and diplomacy.

Urban Families

The bourgeois or urban family, drawing its income and status from trade or craft production, grew in importance through the later Middle Ages. Though children and other kin were invariably part of a royal court or an aristocratic household, the young men and women actually bound there by close bloodlines made up a very small proportion of the hundreds who might surround a king or emperor or even of the dozens or scores in attendance upon a duke or bishop. But in the urban setting, with work and business and the apprenticeships all housed under one roof, the family unit (in the medieval sense) is apt to be a domestic rather than a kin-centered or blood-defined one. The children of the parental figures, along with servants (mostly young and likely to move on in a few years) and the apprentices (often children of like families, now being trained in a comparable household) together comprised the household unit, and the line between blood and nonblood might be flexible. While no prosperous bourgeois would wish to see his enterprise pass in the next generation to a rank outsider, towns and guilds depended on new blood and newcomers arrived, married, and became integrated more readily than they did into the conservative ranks and families of the feudal aristocracy. At the same time, in the self-replicating social world in which most urban craftsmen and merchants lived there was a high degree of in-group interaction and intermarriage between the children and between the widows and the widowers of the insiders. Thus the chances are that many were related to others in their circle, in one of the various fashions or permutations mentioned, and we find this whether we look at the merchants and artisans of London or Bruges or Florence. Given the prevalence of so much kin linkage, we can ask how effective or reliable it was in terms of bonding, cooperation, and family-oriented culture—a question we can also ask regarding the royal lines of Europe, from the Slavic kingdoms of the East to those of the Iberian peninsula, and Scandinavia.

Peasant Families

The overwhelming bulk of the population of medieval Europe worked the land and drew a living, usually at something close to the subsistence level, directly from such labor. For the peasant family rural and village life was life spent among many who were related, and the functional definition of family in these instances may be seen in terms of those who could be called upon to help work the holdings or to stand as surety in a manorial or village dispute. Propinquity and mortality must often have brought the families of siblings or in-laws or cousins into more cooperative arrangements than formal custom or manorial law worried to define. Children usually could expect to succeed to the parental holdings, as well perhaps as to succor surviving parents as they aged and became economically and physically dependent. Manorial court records tell of intramanorial quarrels and negotiations, as well as of domestic ones, and it is no surprise to find that kinship bonds were major lines of social organization, partisanship, and long-remembered alliances. The size of the peasant household as a domestic unit probably was no more than four or five in most cases; more hands to do the work also meant more mouths to feed (nor would all that many bourgeois or urban households have run to double figures either when all heads were counted).

The Role of the Church

To move away from a structural presentation of family is to open many doors. Much of the church was organized through quasi-familial categories, often expressed in the metaphors of family. Though the clergy of the western church were being held to vows of celibacy by the end of the eleventh century, the church's views about and role in marriage and matters of kinship and family were major determinants of lay life and behavior. Marriage did not become a civil matter in Europe until the seventeenth century, at the earliest, and, while canon lawyers and theologians might debate such questions as whether it was consent rather than consummation that solidified a marriage, or whether the priest's blessing at the church porch sufficed for his endorsement (rather than a nuptial mass), these differences of opinion were accepted by the laity as issues properly falling within the ecclesiastical purview.

But beyond its role in defining and supervising lay activity in the realms of marriage and sex, the church was a vast alternative social structure with its own equivalents to or parallels for family. It not only determined the degrees of consanguinity that controlled marital choices for the laity, it held (with little challenge in theory if not always in practice) that co-sponsorship of an infant's baptism created spiritual kinship, thus making the sponsoring parties, the baby's godparents, ineligible to marry each other. And for those vast numbers within the embrace of clerical and monastic vows, there were similarities to the secular family. The head of the monastery was the abbot ("father"), and though "mother superior" is not a medieval term, the very concept indicates the quasi-maternal role of the prioress or abbess over her house and her charges. Furthermore, nuns were held to be the brides of Christ; vows to enter religious life were comparable to marriage vows. Saints with wide popular appeal, like the mythical Catherine of Alexandria or the historical Catherine of Siena (1347–1380) were thought to have entered a special relationship with Jesus; hence the "mystic marriage" that set them apart, even from other saints. The ever-growing role of the Virgin in popular religion emphasized her role as mother even more than as Virgin, and the rising importance of both Joseph and St. Anne, Mary's mother, made the holy family an accessible model for the lay imagination. The Nativity scene, with its prosaic shepherds and its mysterious Wise Men, combined the domestic and familiar with the transcendental. Reflections about the nature of Christ and his sacrifice produced a body of thought—some coming from women—that we sum up as "Christ as mother," since nurturing was easily accepted as a feminine attribute. Mystical writings, again with women as major contributors, often described an intense spiritual union with Jesus in the language of the erotic poetry of the day. Ecclesiastical art contributed to the portrayal of sacred themes in a family and kin-oriented context. Byzantine icons, with their powerful influence on Western manuscript illumination and then on painting, had a heavy focus on the maternal aspect of Mary (a theme picked up and developed by Duccio and his Sienese followers in the fourteenth century). Icons distinguished between aspects of the Virgin's maternal roles: Mary immediately after giving birth, Mary nursing, Mary gazing at her child and lamenting the sorrow yet to come, Mary expanding her own mothering into a universal protective role, etc.

The Public Sphere

Did "family" change through the period? The development of bureaucratic kingship and secular chanceries in the twelfth century, along with the development of a highly structured ecclesiastical machine, meant that many functions once dealt with by kin groups became issues for the public sphere: disputes over property, crime and criminal justice rather than torts and feuds, universal rules about kinship and marriage over private arrangements, to name but some. But this great transition had to be carried out and implemented by people many of whom continued to see their ties to each other—defined and solidified by the many definitions and variations of kinship and family—as paramount factors of identity and social bonding. Whether we look at the diplomacy of royal marriages and alliances, or at the arrangements for marriage between the prosperous burgers of the Low Countries, or at the pledging and sureties of manorial and village life, it continues to be family that made many things explicable as well as workable, both to those on the spot and to scholarly examination. Though men (and women) often treated each other and their offspring with a harshness that makes for uncomfortable reading today, they would probably have been in accord that it was all being done for the sake of family, by which they usually meant the patriarchal line (and perhaps the marriage of daughters).

The complex definitions of kinship meant that every woman and man was the center of an individualized geometry of kinship; a sibling's in-laws, a former husband's stepchildren, a half-brother's sworn brothers in a chivalric order, the sister of the man with whom one had stood sponsor at the baptism of a friend's daughter, and much more of this sort. A knight might realize, while maneuvering for a skirmish while on crusade in Syria, that the warrior beside him (whom he had only met that morning) was his second wife's first cousin's brother-in-law—and that they could both trace the links that bound them. People at all social levels assimilated a great deal of complex genealogical information as part of their cultural identity. That medieval society cared to know these relationships, with full awareness of their effect on marriage and property and naming patterns, is a powerful reminder of how much society continued to be structured and organized along the many (and diverging) spokes of the wheel of family.

Threats to Family

The values of society and family life were traditional and conservative, as befits the slow-changing pace of medieval life. Sex outside of marriage was invariably condemned, though the sexual double standard tempered the sword of retribution, especially for men. Marriage was held to be insoluble, though there were dispensations, elastic definitions, and flight over the hill to another village, all tactics to temper the adamantine dictates of canon law. Alternate lifestyles were condemned, which also must mean they were not so unusual but that they were considered by theologians, canon lawyers, and mendicant preachers to pose a threat to "family values." But just as there was a widespread acceptance of bastard children (though with impediments regarding inheritance and entry into the church), so there may have been more unvoiced tolerance of discrete homosexual behavior than extant records or normative texts are ever likely to reveal. Nor were the basic structures of family life seriously threatened by any of the reform movements

that remained within the embrace of the church, while heresies and utopian ideologies that seemed to advocate "free love" or some form of collective social and sexual life deemphasizing traditional family structure and kinship bonds were marginalized and repressed. The knots of family were too many, too important to the basic workings of society at every level, and too well integrated into the medieval world view of both church and laity, to be untied.

JOEL T. ROSENTHAL

References and Further Reading

Ashley, Kathleen and Pamela Sheingorn, ed. *Interpreting Cultural Symbols: Saint Anne in Late Medieval Society.* Athens, Ga., and London: University of Georgia Press, 1990.

Bennett, Judith M. *Women in the Medieval English Countryside: Gender and Household in Brigstock before the Plague.* Oxford and New York: Oxford University Press, 1987.

Brooke, Christopher N. L. *The Medieval Idea of Marriage.* Oxford: Oxford University Press, 1989.

Brundage, James A. *Law, Sex, and Christian Society in Medieval Europe.* Chicago: University of Chicago Press, 1987.

DeWindt, Edwin. *Land and People in Holywell-cum-Needingworth: Structures of Tenure and Patterns of Social Organization in an East Midland Village, 1252–1457.* Toronto: Pontifical Institute of Mediaeval Studies, 1972.

Duby, Georges. *Medieval Marriage: Two Models from Twelfth-Century France*, translated by E. Forster. Baltimore: Johns Hopkins University Press, 1978.

———. *Love and Marriage in the Middle Ages*, translated by Jane Dunnett. Chicago: University of Chicago Press, 1994.

Esmein, Adhémar. *Le marriage en droit canonique.* 2nd edition, edited by R. Génestal. Paris: Librarie du Recueil Sirey, 2 volumes, 1929–1935.

Evergates, Theodore, ed. *Aristocratic Women in Medieval France.* Philadelphia: University of Pennsylvania Press, 1999.

Gold, Penny S. *The Lady and the Virgin.* Chicago: University of Chicago Press, 1985.

Goody, Jack. *The Development of the Family and Marriage in Europe.* Cambridge: Cambridge University Press, 1983.

Hanawalt, Barbara A. *The Ties that Bound: Peasant Families in Medieval England.* Oxford and New York: Oxford University Press, 1986.

Helmholz, Richard H. *Marriage Litigation in Medieval England.* Cambridge: Cambridge University Press, 1978.

Herlihy, David. *Medieval Households.* Cambridge, Mass.: Harvard University Press, 1985.

Herlihy, David, and Christiane Klapisch-Zuber. *Tuscans and their Families: A Study of the Florentine Catasto of 1427.* New Haven & London: Yale University Press, 1985.

Mitchell, Linda. *Portraits of Medieval Women: Family, Marriage, and Politics in England, 1225–1350.* New York: Palgrave Macmillan, 2003.

Murray, Jacqueline, ed. *Love, Marriage, and Family in the Middle Ages: A Reader.* Orchard Park, N.Y.: Broadview Press, 2001.

Neel, Carol, ed. *Medieval Families: Perspectives on Marriage, Household, and Children.* Toronto and Buffalo:

University of Toronto Press, for the Medieval Academy of America, 2004.

Parson, John Carmi, and Bonnie Wheeler, eds. *Medieval Mothering.* New York and London: Garland Publishing, 1996.

Razi, Zvi. *Life, Marriage, and Death in a Medieval Parish: Economy, Society and Demography in Halesowen, 1270–1400.* Cambridge: Cambridge University Press, 1980.

Sheehan, Michael M. *Marriage, Family, and Law in Medieval Europe: Collected Studies,* edited by James K. Farge. Toronto and Buffalo, N.Y.: University of Toronto Press, 1996.

See also **Church; Family (Earlier Middle Ages); Genealogy; Godparents; Heraldry; Holy Kinship; Inheritance; Kinship; Law, Canon; Marriage, Christian; Marriage, Impediments to; Queens and Empresses: the West; Seals and Sigillography; Sexuality: Extramarital Sex; Sexuality: Female Same-Sex Relations; Sexuality: Male Same-Sex Relations; Sexuality, Regulation of; Sexuality: Sex in Marriage; Social Status; Succession, Royal and Noble**

FAIRIES

See **Mélusine; Supernatural Women**

FASTING AND FOOD, RELIGIOUS ASPECTS OF

Fasting and the Eucharist have been from early Christian times essential religious practices for all believers. In the medieval period, Christians fasted or abstained from meat throughout Advent and Lent, and, with some regional variations, every Wednesday, Friday, and Saturday of the year. At a time when access to consecrated wine was restricted to priests alone, and the consecrated bread was not available to laypeople on a frequent basis, writings by and about Christian holy women abound in descriptions of fasting from regular food and of focusing one's appetite onconsecrated bread and wine. This double emphasis has been identified as a religious devotion central to women's spirituality and as a primary inspiration for their visions and ecstasies. Women's association with the body in traditional European culture has led to their identification with Christ as God made flesh—a flesh that in giving life suffers like women's in childbirth, a flesh that, like women's, feeds human beings with itself in pregnancy and lactation (through the blood flowing like milk from Christ's breast as well as through Christ's gift of the Eucharist, his body). Clare of Assisi (1193–1253) is said to have drunk milk at Christ's breast and the German Dominican Margaretha Ebner (c. 1291–1351) wrote that she took a statue of the Christ-child to her naked breast and suckled it.

For many medieval Christian holy women, Eucharistic enjoyment and Eucharistic miracles were essential to the spiritual life. Food being an area of their lives that women could control (unlike, for example, sex or money), fasting held great religious importance because food was something women could effectively deny themselves and give up in sacrifice. Clare of Assisi's Rule for her nuns, the first written by a woman, was very strict in terms of diet: unless excused by sickness, Clare's followers were to abstain from meat and eat very minimally except for Sundays and Christmas.

Several disciplines have contributed to the study of the relationship between religion, food, and women. Drawing from the anthropological work of Mary Douglas, psychoanalyst Julia Kristeva has elaborated the concept of abjection and cited Christian mystics as a prominent example: religion laywoman Angela of Foligno (c. 1248–1309) drank the water used to wash a leper's sores, Catherine of Siena (1347–1380), a Dominican Tertiary, ingested a cup of pus; both found filth sweet to the mouth. The most influential contributions come from historians Caroline Walker Bynum and Rudolph Bell; the former has identified women's patterns of fasting from daily food in order to better feast on the Eucharist, while the latter has provocatively compared the extreme religious fasting of holy women to modern anorexia. Catherine of Siena, for example, likely fasted to the point of self-starvation.

In the relationship between Christian holy women and regular food, scholarly emphasis has been placed on fasting and abstaining, although the texts written by holy women reveal more positive patterns as well. The metaphor of sweetness is a prevalent one to describe God's love; more specifically honey, occasionally coupled with sugar, is a favored visionary ingredient: its sweetness is a biblical reflection of spiritual consolation. Like honey, fruit appears in the Song of Songs—a central biblical text for medieval women's mysticism—as another bearer of divine grace and of the pleasures of the spiritual life. Thus Margaretha Ebner is given to taste, in one of her visions, two apples—one sweet, the other sour.

The learned German nun Hildegard of Bingen (1098–1179) employed kitchen metaphors in her works in order to explain the workings of God the Creator, at times comparing his actions to those of a cook. Another German Benedictine, Elisabeth of Schönau (1129–1165), described God as tasting of cinnamon. The thirteenth-century beguine Hadewijch of Antwerp (active c. 1220–1240), a visionary poet, employed passionate and sometimes violent images of mutual eating to express in verse the bond of love uniting humans and God. In Angela of Foligno's

Memorial, the representation of food is a positive one, effectively mediating between the mystic and God. It is probable that women who had been wives and mothers, like Angela, had a closer and more physical relationship to food than those who lacked the experience of cooking for their family: this helps explain the images used by English laywoman Margery Kempe (c. 1373–c. 1438), a former brewster and miller as well as mother of fourteen, who in her *Book* describes her attachment to God with the processes of skinning boiled stockfish and cutting meat for the pot. While her mystical predecessors experienced food miracles in renouncing earthly food and in feeding on the Eucharist instead, Margery epitomizes a parallel tradition that found miracles in the kitchen and God at the dinner table.

CRISTINA MAZZONI

References and Further Reading

Bell, Rudolph. *Holy Anorexia.* Chicago: University of Chicago Press, 1985.

Bynum, Caroline Walker. *Holy Feast and Holy Fast: The Religious Significance of Food to Medieval Women.* Berkeley: University of California Press, 1987.

Mazzoni, Cristina. *The Women in God's Kitchen: Cooking, Eating, and Spiritual Writing.* New York: Continuum, 2005.

See also **Angela of Foligno; Asceticism; Catherine of Siena; Clare of Assisi; Ebner, Margaretha; Elisabeth of Schönau; Hadewijch; Hildegard of Bingen; Kempe, Margery; Mysticism and Mystics; Song of Songs: Medieval Interpretations of**

FEDELE, CASSANDRA

By the 1490s, Venetian-born Cassandra Fedele (1465–1558) was the best known woman humanist living in Europe. Her storied literary career, recounted in every early modern Italian catalogue of famous women, overshadowed that of her fellow humanists Isotta Nogarola and Laura Cereta. But most of what was recorded about Fedele appears to be untrue. The biographical tradition attests to her having written a book titled *The Order of the Sciences* (*Ordo scientiarum*) and to the beauty of her Latin poetry; but no trace of her alleged book or poems has surfaced. Having been taught Greek and Latin grammar, rhetoric, and philosophy by the Servite friar Gasparino Borro, Fedele's legendary erudition is barely perceptible in her 121 posthumously published Latin letters, which document her connections with royalty and renowned scholars but not a distinctive literary style. She exchanged letters with Duchess Beatrice d'Este of Milan, Queen Beatrice d'Aragona of Hungary, Duchess Eleonora d'Aragona of Ferrara, Marchese Francesco Gonzaga of Mantua, King Louis XII of France, Duke Lodovico Sforza of Milan, and Columbus's patron, Queen Isabella of Castile—who tried unsuccessfully to persuade Fedele to join her court in Spain. The renowned Paduan Aristotelian Niccolo Leonico Tomei and the Florentine Hellenist Angelo Poliziano were also among Fedele's correspondents.

Despite the faux tradition that haunted her, Fedele received genuine acclaim when her first public oration, delivered on the occasion of her cousin's baccalaureate at the University of Padua, was published in Modena, Nuremberg, and Venice (1487, 1488, 1489). Until the end of her life, her earliest biographers continued to praise Fedele for her virginity, despite her long marriage to Gian-Maria Mapelli, a physician from Vicenza, with whom she lived from 1499 until his death in 1521. Widowed, she spent the 1530s and 1540s desperately looking for a stipend. Finally, in 1547, she obtained an appointment from Pope Paul III as prioress of the orphanage of San Domenico di Castello in Venice. She presented her last public oration before the Venetian senate and the doge Francesco Venier in 1556, when she was ninety-one, on Queen Bona Sforza of Poland's arrival in Venice. When Fedele died in 1558, the Republic honored her with a state funeral.

DIANA ROBIN

References and Further Reading

Capelli, Adriano. "Cassandra Fedele in relazione con Lodovico Il Moro." *Archivio Storico Lombardo* 3, 4 (1895): 387–391.

Cavazzana, Cesira. "Cassandra Fedele erudita veneziana del Rinascimento." *Ateneo Veneto* 29, 2 (1906): 73–79, 249–275, 361–397.

Fedele, Cassandra (1465–1558). *Clarissimae Feminae Cassandrae Fidelis Venetae Epistolae et Orationes*, edited by Giacomo Filippo Tommasini. Padua: Franciscus Bolzetta, 1636.

No manuscript collections of Fedele's letters are known; five letters not included in the Tommasini edition are published in Capelli, Cavazzana, Pesenti, and Petrettini (cited below).*

———. *Oratio pro Bertucio Lamberto.* Modena: 1487; Venice: 1488; Nuremberg: 1489.

King, Margaret L., and Albert Rabil, Jr., eds. *Her Immaculate Hand. Selected Works by and about the Women Humanists of Quattrocento Italy.* Binghamton, N.Y.: Medieval and Renaissance Texts and Studies, 1983; 2nd revised paperback edition, 1991.

Pesenti, G. "Lettere inedite del Poliziano," *Athenaeum* 3 (1915): 299–301.

Petrettini, Maria. *Vita di Cassandra Fedele.* Venice: Dall' Imperial Ro Stamperia Pinelli, 1814, reprint 1852.

Robin, Diana. "Cassandra Fedele (1465–1499)." In Rinaldina Russell, ed. *Italian Women Writers: A Bio-Bibliographical Sourcebook.* Westport, Conn.: Greenwood Press, 1994, pp. 119–127.

———. "Cassandra Fedele's Epistolae (1488–1521): Biography as Effacement." In *The Rhetorics of Life-Writing in Early Modern Europe: Forms of Biography from Cassandra Fedele to Louise XIV*, edited by Thomas Mayer and Daniel Woolf. Ann Arbor, Mich.: University of Michigan Press, 1995. pp. 187–203.
*For the early modern catalogues with vitae of Fedele see Battista Fregosa (a.k.a Campofregosa, 1483); Jacopo Filippo da Bergamo (1497), Jean Tixier de Ravisius (1521); Giuseppe Betussi (1545); Giovanni Battista Egnazio (1554); Giacomo Alberici (1605); Jacopo Filippo Tommasini (1644).

See also **Cereta, Laura; Defenses of Women; D'Este, Isabella and Beatrice; Humanism; Isabel I; Italy; Letter Writing; Nogarola, Isotta; Patronage, Literary; Renaissance, Historiography of; Sanuti, Nicolasa Castellani; Women Authors: Latin Texts**

FEME COVERT

Feme covert may be defined simply as a married woman. In medieval England the implications were complex, restrictive, and illustrate the consequences of marriage for woman. The free tenures were feudal or military; socage; and burgage. It was common to hold land of more than one tenure. After 1066, a married woman was said to be "covered" by *potestas* (power) of the husband with the result that her legal personality was merged with his. In the eyes of the law, both canon and common lawyers agreed that husband and wife were one person and that one person was the husband (J. H. Baker 550–551). However, the legal personality of the wife revived upon the death of the husband or with her husband's agreement. Widows, like single women, could hold property, buy and sell, and make wills.

In the thirteenth century treatise, *On the Laws and Customs of England* [*De Legibus et Consuetudinibus Angliae*] commonly called *Bracton*, a married woman was said to be "under the rod" of her husband who was her sovereign and her lord. In the legal French texts of the next generation, the wife was said to be *feme covert* as opposed to *feme sole*. Her husband was said to be baron or lord and looked after both his wife and her property. A common saying and a legal fiction was that husband and wife were one person and that person was the husband. However, the maxim was not limitless: a wife was not punished for her husband's crimes nor responsible for his debts. Land tenure made a significant difference in that under burgage law, for example, women could trade independently of their husbands. The fact that the church allowed married women to make wills enhanced their power within the married state. The individual personalities, age, health, and economic circumstances of the parties to the marriage undoubtedly shaped their functioning within these legal rules concerning coverture.

Because some husbands controlling their wives' property and other entitlements did not always act in their spouses' best interests, a remedy was created. The writ *cui in vita* allowed a widow to go to law to alter dispositions made during the "lifetime of the husband" when she had been a *feme covert* and "could not gainsay him." *The Wakefield Court Rolls 1331–1333* contain many references to husbands "attorning" to their wives and one woman claiming in widowhood property settled in the lifetime of her husband (p. 165). Despite the vast amount of original sources, much of what transpired in a marriage is undocumented. Thus many a *feme covert* may not have been a silent partner in marriage and its legal, social, and economic activities.

SUE SHERIDAN WALKER

References and Further Reading

Baker, J. H. *An Introduction to English Legal History*. London: Butterworths, 1990.
Bracton on the Laws and Customs of England. 4 vols, edited by S. E. Thorne. Cambridge, Mass.: Belknap Press of the Harvard University Press, 1969–1977.
Earliest English Law Reports, vols. 111 and 112, London: Seldon Society, 1995 and 1996.
Early Registers of Writs, edited by Elsa De Haas for the Seldon Society vol. 87, London: Quartitch, 1970.
The Treatise on the Laws and Customs of the Realm of England, Commonly Called Glanvill, edited by G. D. H. Hall. London: Nelson, 1965.
Walker, Sue Sheridan. *Lexikon des Mittelalters*, esp. "Ehe, "Frau, "Familie" and "Englisches Recht."
———. *Wife and Widow in Medieval England*. Ann Arbor: University of Michigan Press, 1993.

See also **Feme Sole; Landholding and Property Rights; Law, English Secular Courts of; Widows**

FEME SOLE

Feme sole literally means "single woman," that is, not married. The term in its ordinary usage indicated a woman who had never married. Technically a widow was also a *feme sole* for most legal purposes, but she was not usually referred to as such; the Latin *vidua* was more common. Annulment of a marriage restored a woman's status as an unmarried woman.

A *feme sole* at English common law stood in roughly the same circumstance as a man with regard to criminal law. She was responsible for any crime she committed. Technically she could not be outlawed, but she could be "waived," which had the same consequences. With few exceptions, the penalties prescribed for a criminal offense (e.g., theft) did not depend upon gender, although, in practice, there was often a lower rate of conviction for women defendants. If a crime was committed against a *feme sole*, she was at a disadvantage in using the appeal procedure—the procedure whereby a victim of a crime essentially brought a private prosecution—because, at least in theory, a single woman could appeal only for violence to her own person.

When, in the thirteenth century, the use of a jury of presentment (the ancestor of the grand jury) became widespread, however, the significance of the limitation declined. A *feme sole* was also treated like a man in matters of tort (private wrongs) and contract; she was responsible for her own wrongdoing and contract obligations and could be sued for them. She could also bring suit for torts done to her person or property—for example, a trespass—or to enforce a contractual obligation. If she married after contracting a debt, however, her husband became liable for it.

A *feme sole* could inherit real property, although because of the English rule of primogeniture a brother would generally inherit their father's land to the exclusion of his sister, whether or not she was older than he. She could, however, purchase or lease real property. She could inherit, purchase, take by gift, or otherwise acquire personal property and she could give it away or sell it while alive or by will. There were no restrictions—other than those imposed on all testators—on her ability to make a testament.

At public law a *feme sole* was not treated like a man. She could not serve as a juror, lawyer, or judge. Her testimony was not received in disputes concerning another's free or villain status, nor could she be an "oath helper" for a male defendant in cases where proof was to be by compurgation (i.e., by a specified number of people testifying to the truth of a defendant's oath).

"*Feme sole*" has a more limited but significant meaning in connection with women who exercised a trade or craft. It created an exception to the common law rule that a married woman's personal property became her husband's upon their marriage. A *feme sole* trader was a woman who, although married, was able to trade on her own account by the custom of a place. The custom existed in London and a number of other towns and cities, among them Worcester, Lincoln, Exeter, Winchelsea, and Hastings. The means whereby she was declared *feme sole* is not entirely clear, but a *feme sole* trader was defined as a woman who exercised a trade or craft without intermeddling by her husband. Barring exceptional cases, such as prolonged overseas absence of her husband, she was required to work in a field separate from his; otherwise she was presumed to be working for him.

As a *feme sole* trader she could incur debts, enter contracts, and sue or be sued in her own name for them, although her husband would be named in the writ "for compliance." If she did not pay a debt her goods could be seized or she could be sent to debtors' prison, but her husband's goods and person were not liable. A husband might have agreed to his wife's *feme sole* status as part of a marriage settlement where she already had a thriving trade; or he could have wanted it to protect him from liability for debts resulting from the failure of her entrerprise. Trading as a *feme sole* did not affect any other aspects of a woman's marriage nor did it alter her legal position as *feme covert* in other areas such as inheritance.

JANET S. LOENGARD

References and Further Reading

Abrams, Annie. "Women Traders in Medieval London." *Economic Journal* 26 (1916): 276–285.

Barron, Caroline M. "The 'Golden Age' of Women in Medieval London." In *Medieval Women in Southern England.* Reading Medieval Studies, 15. Reading: University of Reading, 1989, pp. 35–58.

Bateson, Mary. *Borough Customs*, vol. I. Selden Society vol. 18. London: B. Quaritch, 1904, pp. 227–228.

Beattie, Cordelia. "A Room of One's Own? The Legal Evidence for the Residential Arrangements of Women without Husbands in Late Fourteenth and Early Fifteenth Century York." In *Medieval Women and the Law*, edited by Noël James Menuge. Woodbridge, Suffolk: The Boydell Press, 2000, pp. 41–56.

Dale, Marian K. "The London Silkwomen of the Fifteenth Century." *Economic History Review*, 4, 3 (1933): 324–335.

Hutton, Diane. "Women in Fourteenth Century Shrewsbury." In *Women and Work in Pre-Industrial England*, edited by Lindsey Charles and Lorna Duffin. London: Croom Helm Ltd, 1985, pp. 83–99.

Jewell, Helen. *Women in Medieval England.* Manchester: Manchester University Press, 1996.

Kowaleski, Maryanne. "Women's Work in a Market Town: Exeter in the Late Fourteenth Century." In *Women and Work in Preindustrial Europe*, edited by Barbara Hanawalt. Bloomington: Indiana University Press, 1986, pp. 145–164.

Lacey, Kay E. "Women and Work in Fourteenth and Fifteenth Century London." In *Women and Work in Pre-Industrial England*, edited by Lindsey Charles and Lorna Duffin. London: Croom Helm, 1985, pp. 24–82.

Maitland, Frederic William, and Sir Frederick Pollock. *The History of English Law.* 2nd ed. Reissued with intro. by S.F.C. Milsom. 2 vols. Cambridge: Cambridge University Press, 1968.

Power, Eileeen, *Medieval Women*, edited by M. M. Postan. Cambridge: Cambridge University Press, 1975. Canto ed. repr. 2000.

See also **England; Feme Covert; Guild Members and Guilds; Home Manufacturing; Investment and Credit; Law, English Secular Courts of; Legal Agency; Market and Tradeswomen; Work**

FEMININITY AND MASCULINITY

The medieval understanding of the concepts of femininity and masculinity was rich and complicated. *Femininity* and *masculinity* were terms that denoted gender expectations, that is, the social and cultural behavioral norms for men and women. These could vary significantly across social status, so that the appropriate behavior for men of the upper ranks of society was decidedly different than that appropriate for the common man. In a similar way, gender norms could also differ according to a man's religious status, that is, if he were a cleric or a monk or a bishop rather than a layman.

For women, the concept of femininity was distinguished in different ways than masculinity was for men. For example, religious women were expected to avoid feminine behavior because women who had taken vows of chastity were supposed to have rejected the earthly social roles of women. The rich literature of the Middle Ages presents aristocratic women displaying a form of femininity that appears at odds with responsibilities that these women were expected to shoulder in daily life. On the other hand, common women would have been criticized for putting on airs had they dared to behave according to the ideals held out for aristocratic women.

Another factor that rendered the notions of femininity and masculinity more complicated in medieval society is that they were values not only embedded in social expectation, but also characteristics linked to an individual's own temperament. As a result, various physiological factors could render men more or less masculine and women more or less feminine. Thus, the medieval view of femininity and masculinity was comprised of both the social expectations for men and women and their differing physiological characteristics.

The Physiology of Gender

According to the medical perspectives that medieval thinkers inherited from antiquity, men and women were found at different points on a continuum of sex and gender. One end of this continuum, the female end, was cold and wet; the other, male, end was characterized as hot and dry. This meant that in general a woman's temperament would be colder and wetter than that of a man. However, it was possible for biological women to be found all along the continuum, moving towards the masculine end. Consequently, such women, sometimes referred to as viragos, were believed to be more "manly." This nature might be manifested in physical factors such as strength or build, or in behavioral ways, such as in women who were braver or more intelligent than expected. Such women were frequently criticized by moralists for being headstrong or rebellious.

Men, too, could be found at different points on the continuum. Men who were colder in temperament were considered less virile and so better able to control—or less likely to experience—the urge to have sexual intercourse. Men who were extremely hot, on the other hand, would be so lusty that they would be liable to spontaneous emissions of semen, masturbation, or nocturnal emissions. If a man dissipated his natural heat through excessive intercourse or masturbation, he would become colder and weaker, less virile, and more like a woman. It was their natural heat that made men strong and physically superior to women.

Many of the differences ascribed to men and women were an outgrowth of their perceived biological, sexed natures. Men were considered to be active and women were passive in the Aristotelian system. This extended to the popular understanding of sexual intercourse and procreation. Women were sexually passive and it was up to men to initiate sex and it was men's semen that was critical in procreation (especially according to Aristotle). Even the two-seed theory of Galen, that taught that both men and women contributed semen that commingled to produce a fetus, also taught that women's semen was thinner and weaker than that of men. Men were the active sexual partners and women the passive bodies with which men had sex. In a variety of types of sources, ranging from court cases to manuals for confessors, men are described as having sex with women. A woman is never described as the active initiator of sex, nor is there attention given to how women might have experienced sex. This lack of attention is the logical consequence of women's biological inferiority and passivity. Thus, while men and women were on a single biological continuum, their innate natures reinforced the prevailing gender hierarchy that decreed men to be superior and active and women subordinate and passive in their social roles.

The Influence of Christianity

The understanding of femininity, in particular, was significantly influenced by Christianity and the theological interpretations of the Church Fathers and subsequent theologians. Christian Scripture placed women second in creation since Adam had been created first, with Eve coming from Adam's rib (Genesis 2:21–22). This, then, reinforced women's social subordination. Similarly, the Apostle Paul had instructed that women should be silent in church (1 Corinthians 14:34–35) and obedient to their husbands (Ephesians 5:22–25). These admonitions were incorporated into the medieval values for femininity. The ideal woman was chaste, silent, and obedient. This view of femininity encompassed the Virgin Mary herself, who exemplified obedience to God and, despite her special status, obedience to her earthly husband. As a result of the ethical interpretation that the Church Fathers overlaid on the biological understanding of the nature of gender, women were understood to be weaker and subordinate, both biologically and spiritually. Women were closer to nature and believed to be more consumed by lust and less guided by reason than were men. There was an inherent contradiction here, since lust correlated to heat, but women's weaker bodies were nevertheless more prone to lust despite being colder according to prevalent thinking. The result of this melding of science and theology was a social subordination of women, as well as a definition of femininity that reflected women's acceptance of that subordination.

As a result of the views of Church Fathers such as Jerome in the early Middle Ages, the ideal for women came to be a repression of femininity. If a woman were to refuse marriage and childbirth, and reject her female body and tame her desires through acts of penitence, she would become more virile, more manly. In this way, through repression of femaleness and femininity, a woman could enhance her gender identity, becoming more virile. Thus, nuns and other religious women were considered the epitome of womanhood, although they had explicitly rejected femininity, in particular the kind of secular femininity that would make them attractive as lovers, wives, and mothers.

Masculinity, too, was heavily influenced by Christian morality. The fundamental privileging of chastity for both male and female believers meant that men needed to tame their bodies and repress their natural heat. Through this struggle of the flesh a man would be able to prove his superiority by resisting the baser urges and exercising reason over desire. Similarly, Christian masculinity was built upon the model of Jesus' behavior recorded in scripture. Consequently, this view of masculinity incorporated the values of obedience to God and one's superiors, kindness, humility, and rejection of the riches of the world. Equally as important as chastity was the rejection of violence and military activities. Thus, monks who withdrew from the world and avoided the temptationsof women, wealth, and worldly affairs were, in the early Middle Ages, the epitome of Christian masculinity. Their vows of poverty, chastity, and obedience summarized their rejection of secular values in favor of Christian ideals of manhood. Indeed, the behavior and values that Christianity promoted for both women and men were so similar that some scholars have suggested that medieval religious, both male and female, collectively formed a third gender in society.

Secular Femininity and Masculinity

The qualities of femininity and masculinity found in secular society were very different from those found in religious life. For women, secular gender norms confirmed the subordination of women found in scientific, medical, and theological discourses. Women were considered inconstant and faithless, prone to seducing men and being seduced by men. Consequently, women's nature needed to be constrained through obedience, first to their fathers and subsequently, to their husbands. Indeed, one sign of a man's masculinity was his ability to rule his household and control his wife, children, and servants. In this way, femininity as obedience and subordination reinforced masculinity as the right to exercise power and control.

Many of the ideal qualities identified as feminine were rooted in the courtly literature that began to appear in the late twelfth century and won increasing popularity throughout the remainder of the era. The deeds of King Arthur and his knights, in particular, captured the imagination of the aristocracy. In courtly romances, the ideal woman was a lady of rank, chaste and beautiful, and usually married. The grace and comeliness of her carriage and the elegance of her dress would attract the attention of the men of the court, usually the unmarried knights who owed their allegiance to the woman's husband. This view of women of the upper ranks of society, as presiding at feasts, attending jousts and other entertainments, and generally decorating their husbands' or fathers' court is in startling contrast to the qualities that real women needed to carry out their daily roles. The wife of a lord was expected to be an able household administrator, educate and rear their children, and possess the personal qualities that would permit her to exercise the authority of her husband, including military responsibilities, during his frequent absences. The qualities valued in practice, then, were at considerable odds with the feminine ideal presented in romances.

The qualities of secular masculinity grew out of the biological and scientific understanding of masculinity, coupled with those personal characteristics that were most needed in a world that was encountering military threats from invaders or neighbors. A truly masculine man was physically powerful and exhibited the martial skills that were needed to ensure the safety of his family, dependents, and lands. Among the lower ranks of society, this kind of masculinity could be demonstrated by a man's ability to be economically successful as a farmer or artisan, providing for his family and leaving his children a significant inheritance. Virility was also an important aspect of masculinity. A man was judged by his ability to have sex with women and engender children, in particular male heirs. This virility could manifest itself in male sexual promiscuity, adultery, and even rape. In the early Frankish kingdom, before the religious principal of marital monogamy had been fully ingrained in secular society, men would display their masculinity through taking numerous wives and concubines, then rearing the children of different mothers together in the same household. Even in the High Middle Ages, after the church had successfully imposed the view of sacramental marriage as monogamous and indissoluble, men continued to display their virility and sexual prowess through sexual conquests, sometimes through seduction, other times through violence.

One of the consequences of this focus on sexual virility as a sign of masculinity, was that female chastity came to be linked with a man's honor. Thus, virginity and chastity within marriage came to be regarded as the most important qualities for a woman. Her good name and chastity were the roots of her honor, and a wife or daughter's behavior stood as the source of a man's honor. Only a weak man, lacking in the qualities of masculinity, would be a cuckold or have a disobedient wife or daughter.

Gender Slippage and Other Anomalies

The intersection of social gender and biological sex, coupled with the contemporary understanding that femaleness and maleness were located on the same sex/gender continuum, resulted in many tensions in medieval society, surrounding the distinctions between men and women. For example, the appropriate position in which to engage in sexual intercourse was with the man on top, the woman supine below him. This clearly placed men in the superior and active position. Theologians, canonists, and even some medical writers decried the notion of sexual intercourse with the woman on top, since this overthrew the natural order of things. Similarly, there were strict rules governing the appropriate dress for men and women. Cross-dressing in the clothes of the opposite sex was strictly prohibited because it confused gender distinctions and gender roles. While women were not supposed to wear men's clothing, when they did so in

order to disguise their sex so that they could travel safely or otherwise escape danger, or so they could render themselves invisible and not pose a sexual temptation to men, they were not punished. Occasionally, they were even praised for trying to reject their weakness and striving to be more like men. Men, on the other hand, were perceived to be rejecting their superior role and the privileges of masculinity if they took on the clothing of inferior women. This rejection of gender paradigms could be harshly punished because it suggested sexual as well as social transgression.

The body itself might also reveal a certain slippage on the sex/gender continuum, as men moved towards the more feminine end or women moved towards the more masculine end. An example of this kind of slippage is revealed in the stories of bearded female saints. In these stories, the women pray to be rescued from some kind of sexual threat such as marriage, rape, or a violent husband. Their prayers were answered by the growth of a heavy beard which so repulsed their pursuers that the women were rescued from them. According to medical theory, hair grew as a result of heat allowing it to push through the skin, which explained why warm men were hairier than cold women. Thus, as the woman moved away from the feminine end of the continuum and became more masculine by rejecting sexual desire, her temperament became warmer and she grew a beard.

Similarly, men who struggled to control desire tried to make their bodies cooler by leaping into vats of cold water or eating food designed to cool their temperament. Physical signs of effeminacy would correlate with a cooler body that was less susceptible to lust. As a result of this matrix of beliefs, medieval people believed that eunuchs did not experience sexual desire, although they were not always considered to be effeminate. The famous *castratus*, Peter Abelard, did not believe himself to be less of a man because he had been castrated. On the contrary, he extolled what he perceived to be his superior masculine freedom from the demands of the flesh. He was no longer subject to lust, which was characterized as effeminate weakness. It is, therefore, ironic that impotent men, who were genitally intact, were in fact considered less masculine because, even though they had genital organs, they were unable to exercise manly virility. The eunuch did not experience desire because of an external wound, where as the impotent man was so because he lacked the requisite masculinity to be virile.

The concepts of femininity and masculinity were complicated, interrelated, and ultimately reflexive. In terms of physiology, femininity was a state of being not masculine, and masculinity was a state of being not feminine. While this sex/gender continuum could have allowed for a complementary evaluation of gender, it was in fact seen as putting femininity and masculinity in an hierarchical relationship that mirrored and reinforced the hierarchical relationship of men and women in society.

JACQUELINE MURRAY

References and Further Reading

Allen, Prudence. *The Concept of Woman.* Vol. 1. *The Aristotelian Revolution 750 BC–AD 1250.* Montreal: Eden Press, 1985; Vol. 2. *The Early Humanist Reformation 1250–1500.* Grand Rapids, Mich.; Cambridge: Eerdmans, 2002.

Beattie, Cordelia. "Gender and Femininity in Medieval England." In *Writing Medieval History,* edited by Nancy Partner. London: Hodder Arnold, 2005, pp. 153–170.

Frantzen, Allen J. "When Women Aren't Enough." In *Studying Medieval Women,* edited by Nancy F. Partner. Cambridge, Mass., Medieval Academy of America, 1993. pp. 143–169.

Gender in the Early Medieval World: East and West, 300–900, edited by Leslie Brubaker and Julia M. H. Smith. Cambridge: Cambridge University Press, 2004.

Karras, Ruth Mazo. *From Boys to Men. Formations of Masculinity in Late Medieval Europe.* Philadelphia: University of Pennsylvania Press, 2003.

Karras, Ruth Mazo. *Sexuality in Medieval Europe: Doing Unto Others.* New York; London: Routledge, 2005.

Lees, Clare A., and Thelma Fenster, ed. *Medieval Masculinities. Regarding Men in the Middle Ages.* Minneapolis: University of Minnesota Press, 1994.

Murray, Jacqueline, ed. *Conflicting Identities and Multiple Masculinities: Men in the Medieval West.* New York: Garland Publishing, 1999.

Partner, Nancy F. "No Sex, No Gender." In *Studying Medieval Women,* edited by Nancy F. Partner. Cambridge, Mass., Medieval Academy of America, 1993, pp. 117–141.

Salisbury, Joyce E. "Gendered Sexuality." In *Handbook of Medieval Sexuality,* edited by Vern L. Bullough and James A. Brundage. New York: Garland Publishing, 1996, pp. 81–102.

See also **Aristotelian Concepts of Women and Gender; Asceticism; Chastity and Chaste Marriage; Chivalry; Church; Conduct Literature; Courtly Love; Cross-Dressing; Division of Labor; Eunuchs; Gender Ideologies; Honor and Reputation; Mary, Virgin; Monasticism and Nuns; Noble Women; Procreation and Ideas of Conception; Sexuality: Extramarital Sex; Sexuality: Female Same-Sex Relations; Sexuality: Male Same-Sex Relations; Sexuality, Regulation of; Sexuality: Sex in Marriage; Virginity; Virile Women**

FEMINIST THEORIES AND METHODOLOGIES

Feminist study of the European Middle Ages has evolved over the last century or more, along with other areas of feminist scholarship, theory, and politics.

In the process, feminist scholars have opened mainstream medieval studies to interdisciplinary and comparative methods and topics. They have also fought for gender parity in university departments, professional societies, editorial boards, and publishing venues.

The first feminist critic of male-authored medieval history may well have been Geoffrey Chaucer's admirable, if fictional, Wife of Bath, who had already announced in the fourteenth century that if women had composed their own history, they would have "written more of men's wickedness than all the sons of Adam could set right." In her 1803 novel *Northanger Abbey,* the novelist Jane Austen followed Chaucer with a heroine who declared that medieval history was full of "the quarrels of popes and kings, with wars or pestilences, in every page; the men all so good for nothing, and hardly any women at all—it is very tiresome."

Entering the Academy

English medievalists benefited from this early tradition of womanist consciousness as well as the influence of liberal political philosophers such as Mary Wollestonecraft and John Stuart Mill, who decried women's political invisibility in eighteenth- and nineteenth-century Europe. A small but determined cadre of lady historians emerged in the later nineteenth century to correct the biases of history. They wrote genteel, popular biographies of famous medieval queens and antiquarian treatises about domestic topics, such as medieval gardens or costume. However, as women slowly gained access to professional training in historical and literary studies, among other intellectual pursuits, a few of them began to practice a more professional study of the medieval past. Admitted to university, they earned higher academic degrees and attempted the same sort of scientific studies and textual analyses as men, although they rarely received the same rewards. In most American and European academic institutions, women were educated separately until the early twentieth century and, with a few exceptions, female graduates who wished to become medieval scholars took jobs in women's colleges or lower-status positions as archivists and librarians.

Girton College, Cambridge, the first women's college in England and the alma mater of famous suffragists, produced several pioneering medievalists. Bertha Phillpots was a Scandinavianist whose first published work on medieval kinship appeared in 1913. Eileen Power, who also studied at the Sorbonne in Paris, was a well-respected professor of medieval economics and society, who eventually became a professor of economic history at the London School of Economics. She later became a professor at Cambridge University and founded the *Economic History Review*. Eleanor Shipley Duckett produced numerous books and articles on early medieval culture and religion, and finished her teaching career at Smith College. As she recounted later in life, when she was a student in Cambridge she had taken her work to a male professor who had asked her, "Do you want me to judge it on its own merits or as the work of a woman?"

Around the time that Duckett received this snub, yet another English observer turned feminist scholarship in a new direction by criticizing the academic segregation of women and the neglect of women's past by university professionals. In *A Room of One's Own* (1929), Virginia Woolf recounted her experience in trying to enter a library at Oxford only to be rebuffed by a doorman anxious to protect the exclusive access of men. "He was a Beadle," Woolf wrote, "I was a woman. This was the turf; there was the path. Only Fellows and Scholars are allowed here; the gravel is the place for me." She concluded that men needed to belittle women politically as well as intellectually in order to "enlarge" themselves.

Finding Sources

Perhaps inspired by Woolf or by similar experiences of sexism, a few professional female medievalists decided to focus their academic skills on the subject of women in political and social contexts. Power produced the first synthesis of medieval women's history in 1926; no comparable survey of women's past followed until fifty years later. Still, even feminist scholars had difficulty finding appropriate source materials for the study of medieval women. Most medieval documents were written and kept by men, and recounted the actions and thoughts of men. Even when scholars could find female-authored documents, they treated women's texts—mystical treatises, poetry, romances, letters—as less important than mainstream documents such as chronicles, charters, theology, and formal literature. Art historians, too, dismissed the works of medieval women as domestic crafts or folk art.

A few historians, such as Lina Eckenstein, Emily Putnam, and Power, seized on the relatively plentiful evidence by and about religious women to study nuns and abbesses. This is still a major area of research for medievalist feminists. Although these early historians praised the accomplishments of medieval religious women, they also argued that the medieval convent oppressed women. In keeping with social reformers of the early twentieth century, Putnam believed that society normally limited women's options to childbearing and mothering and, further, that only extraordinary medieval women entered nunneries primarily to escape domestic duties and the violent world of men. She did not consider the possibility of nuns' agency or genuine spiritual vocations. Nonetheless, such work opened the world of female religiosity to historians.

As more scholars began to recover a variety of texts produced by women, and as more women gained access to higher education in modern universities, they expanded their analyses to ordinary women and men of the medieval past. Both politics and the modern study of social sciences propelled these feminist scholars. The suffrage movements in England and the United States pushed intellectuals everywhere to consider women's disenfranchisement and its origins. Consequently, medievalists delved into the sources of disenfranchisement. Florence Buckstaff examined women's property and legal rights in Anglo-Saxon England, earning a degree at the University of Wisconsin in the 1890s with her thesis on Anglo-Saxon women's property rights. Women's participation in labor movements and leftist political movements also inspired medievalists. Mary Bateson, influenced by the legal historian Frederic William Maitland, began her career with careful studies of medieval English local law but also produced a classic study of mixed-sex religious communities.

Applying the Social Sciences

Meanwhile, the wide-ranging studies of the French medievalist Marc Bloch and colleagues at the Parisian journal *Annales: Économies, Sociétés, et Civilizations*—known as Annalistes—pushed European historians to consider such new and inclusive topics as peasants, labor, popular religion, cultural change, and mentalities. All of these foci were easier to apply to women than the traditional study of elite politics and intellectual history. The Annalistes drew heavily on social sciences, especially anthropology, which generated scientific and comparative methods for studying "primitive" non-Western or illiterate peoples and non-elites. Other social sciences, such as demography and geography helped too; although medieval documents tended to undercount females, as well as children, non-Christians, and the unfree, population studies necessarily tried to be inclusive. Although these approaches did not yield an immediate feminization of medieval studies, the application of social science methods prepared the way for a great historiographical shift in the 1960s and 1970s, such as the groundbreaking social history of David Herlihy and Christiane Klapisch-Züber. They gathered extensive data from late medieval household censuses in Italy and used this information to analyze family relations, household economics, and other important aspects of daily life.

Feminist Theory

Explicitly feminist approaches to medieval studies proliferated when the women's movement gained momentum in the 1960s. Feminist theorists such as Simone de Beauvoir and Betty Friedan were widely influential among liberal academics who rushed to apply their insights to the medieval past. In *The Second Sex* (1949), Beauvoir posited her theory of women as the "Other," arguing that intellectuals throughout history have treated men as the human standard by which to judge women as inherently inferior. Betty Friedan in *The Feminine Mystique* (1963) suggested that modern American housewives colluded in their inferiority by depending financially, socially, and politically on men. Inspired by these and other theorists, some medievalist scholars shifted their focus to issues of power and women's oppression in the past. Marxist theorists such as Friedrich Engels had long ago located the source of women's oppression in the development of the nuclear family, private property, and the nation-state. Medievalists joined the effort to uncover other sources of women's oppression and outline women's strategies for empowerment.

To recover women's past, scholars needed first to expand the parameters of medieval studies to include new topics and different evidence. Liberal feminist scholars attempted to count and include women, make them "visible," and hear their "voices." Beginning in the 1970s, historians such as Suzanne Wemple, Susan Mosher Stuard, Jo Ann McNamara, and their students examined mainstream documents such as charters, chronicles, laws, and saints' lives for incidental evidence about women's experiences and thus calculate their power or lack of it. Wemple investigated the many social roles and economic opportunities of wives, mothers, saints, patronesses, workers, and queens of continental Europe. Other medievalists examined neglected political-sexual issues such as childbearing, rape, and infanticide in both literature and historical situations.

Women's Writings

At the same time, literary scholars also culled the manuscripts for woman-authored texts and published new editions of medieval women's writings. Christine de Pizan, Marie de France, Hildegard of Bingen, and the women troubadours (called *trobairitz*) all enjoyed a renaissance of popularity during the 1970s and 1980s. Other prominent religious women, such as the abbess Heloise (1101–1164, former lover of Peter Abelard), the mystic and saint Catherine of Siena (1347–1380), and another mystic and author, Margery Kempe (b. c. 1373), earned permanent places in the canon of medieval literature. The twelfth-century writer of medieval French romances, Marie de France, became as famous as her male competition, Chrétien de Troyes. Art historians, meanwhile, began to search for women's contributions to art, especially the creation and patronage of manuscripts and religious objects, for instance, the precious Books of Hours so popular among late medieval noblewomen.

Scholars also employed feminist perspectives on symbols and themes in medieval art and literature. For instance, instead of analyzing the heroes of romance, such as Tristan, they wrote about heroines such as Isolde and secondary female characters such as her serving women; instead of combing epics and poetry to learn about warrior ethics and kingship, they looked at social relations, sex and sexuality, and motherhood. They pointed out instances of women's solidarity and subversion in medieval texts and images. They also examined the sources and effects of misogyny in medieval literature and theology; R. Howard Bloch, for instance, argued that modern romantic ideals of heterosexual love derived from traditions of antifeminism in medieval and classical writings. Drawing on postmodern literary theories, they identified the many competing voices—some female—that existed in single works. They also compared male and female authorship of texts to find out whether medieval women had different concerns and issues or took gender-specific positions. Together, medievalist scholars helped to challenge the traditional canons of Western literature and art and promoted consciousness of issues of gender and race.

Difference

A second analytical trend drew on feminist theories of difference, exemplified by the work of Adrienne Rich and Mary Daly, as well as sociologists such as Carol Gilligan and Nancy Chodorow. Drawing on these theorists and social scientists, some scholars of the medieval past segregated women's history and women's literature from the history and literature of men, based on the assumption that because women were different by both nature and nurture, their historical experiences were inherently distinct. Scholars crafted studies of exclusively woman-authored literature, women's spiritualities, women's communities, and female perspective on matters ranging from sex to scholastic theology. During this period of the 1970s and 1980s, readers of women's literature and history began to proliferate. Caroline Walker Bynum contributed to this trend with her study of women's bodily focused spirituality, *Holy Feast and Holy Fast*. Bynum demonstrated both a unique, feminine interpretation of Christian doctrine and how that interpretation infiltrated mainstream religiosity. Scholars of religion such as Rosemary Radford Ruether and Barbara Newman similarly posited women's gender-specific religiosity because of their exclusion from mainstream Christian tradition. They applied this position to scriptural texts and works of women mystics. Other scholars sought the pre-patriarchial religions that they believed had preceded both patriarchy and modern world monotheisms such as Christianity and Judaism. In addition, as medievalists have begun to acknowledge the dominance of western European Christian women as subjects of study, they have simultaneously sought to understand the experiences of non-Europeans and non-Christians. Some important studies of Jewish and Muslim women appeared during the last decades of the twentieth century, including the work of Judith Baskin, Cheryl Tallan, Gavin Hambly, and Howard Adelman.

Self-styled radical feminist medievalists expanded on this line of thinking, arguing that not only culture and texts were gendered but language itself was a masculine operation and that, as a result, women needed their own modes of symbolic expression. Julia Kristeva, not a medievalist, examined the medieval cult of the Virgin Mary, arguing that the modern world lacks an adequate discourse for maternity. We have religious ideas, which relegate maternity to the Universal Mother; and we have science, which identifies mothers and mothering with Nature. However, we have no women's language for an essentially womanly experience. More recently, the medievalist Kathleen Biddick has argued that the entire concept of "medieval" is inherently Christian and masculine, thus inapplicable to women's experience in the past. Medievalists have also applied the theoretical work of a number of postmodernist theorists of literature, history, and anthropology—Michel Foucault, Pierre Bourdieu, Teresa de Lauretis, and Judith Butler, among others—to topics ranging from church

architecture to medieval theater. Butler's theories of performative gender have been especially influential among scholars of medieval literatures who work on issues of sexuality, masculinity, queer studies, and heterosexism.

The Human Body

In addition to theoretically inclined feminist analyses of the medieval past and its literatures, medievalists—again following Bynum's lead—tackled the human body as a subject for analysis. Bynum's work on the food ways of medieval mystics critiqued the tendency of Western thinkers to identify women and femaleness with the physical body. She argued that Christian theologians of both medieval and modern periods have used the metaphors of Eve and Mary to symbolize, respectively, sinful humanity and the redeemable soul. Bynum showed how the mystics were able to manipulate and subvert this ideological duality with reference to their own fasting bodies. Other medievalists began to consider the sexual bodies of women and men in the Middle Ages and their symbolic ranges, trying to grasp how medieval Europeans understood their bodies and the operations of bodies, and how they used bodies to mean other ideas. Several authors, such as Joan Cadden and Monica Green, have focused specifically on medieval medicine and biological thought in relation to women.

Gender

One more development in feminist approaches to the Middle Ages has been its turn toward the study of gender rather than women per se. Some scholars, such as Allen Franzen, have argued that the work of feminists is finished and that gender studies and queer theory are the next logical step for medievalists. The American historian Joan Scott has famously called for historians to apply "the lens of gender" to analysis of the past, arguing that we should try to understand the operations of all genders within cultural, social, and political systems. The results have been diverse and fruitful: from studies of sexuality and pervasive heterosexism; to books on men and medieval masculinity; to examinations of gender's operations in arenas previously unconsidered. One collection of articles, *Gendering the Master Narrative*, called for a re-examination of feminist methods and scholarly practice based on the premise that no single analysis can adequately address the many experiences of medieval women. Just as twenty-first-century feminist activists have concluded that there is—and must be—no single dominant feminism but instead many "feminisms," so medievalists are resisting the kind of reductive surveys that Eileen Power wrote almost a century ago. Rather than trying to articulate the experiences of all medieval women, scholars of gender seek to understand particular operations of gender in the medieval past, an effort that overlaps with feminism but is not identical to it.

Throughout the academic world, scholars continue to employ feminist approaches to the medieval past described here, from the simple inclusion of prominent women in straightforward historical narratives to densely theoretical work on gender. Just as no single work can adequately address women's experiences during the thousand years of the Middle Ages, no single method or disciplinary approach suffices for feminist study of the past. It would be anachronistic to think that modern feminists can use their politics to explain medieval women. But it would also be rash to discard the long history of feminist and womanist thought and action that we have inherited from earlier thinkers. At the very least, more than a century of feminist scholarship has added more evidence, more subjects of inquiry, and even more (female) scholars to medieval studies.

LISA BITEL

References and Further Reading

Bateson, Mary. "The Origin and Early History of Double Monasteries." *Royal Historical Society* 13 (1899): 137–198.

Berg, Maxine. *A Woman in History: Eileen Power, 1889–1940.* Cambridge and New York: Cambridge University Press, 1996.

Biddick, Kathleen. "Genders, Bodies, Borders: Technologies of the Visible." *Speculum* 68 (1993): 398–413.

———. *The Typological Imaginary: Circumcision, Technology, History.* Philadelphia: University of Pennsylvania Press, 2003.

Bloch, R. Howard. *Medieval Misogyny and the Invention of Western Romantic Love.* Chicago: University of Chicago Press, 1991.

Bloss, Celestia Angenette. *Heroines of the Crusades.* Auburn: Alden and Beardsley, 1855.

Buckstaff, Florence G. "Married Women's Property in Anglo-Saxon and Anglo-Norman Law." *Annals of the American Academy of Political and Social Science* 4 (1893–1894): 233–264.

Bynum, Caroline Walker. *Holy Feast and Holy Fast: The Religious Significance of Food to Medieval Women.* Berkeley: University of California Press, 1987.

Duckett, Eleanor Shipley. "Women and their Letters in the Early Middle Ages." Pamphlet, Smith College, Northampton, Mass., 1964; cited in Susan Stuard, *Women in Medieval Society* (Philadelphia, 1976), 2.

Eckenstein, Lina. *Woman Under Monasticism; Chapters on Saint-lore and Convent Life Between A.D. 500 and A.D. 1500.* Cambridge: Cambridge University Press, 1896.

Erler, Mary C. and Maryanne Kowaleski, eds. *Gendering the Master Narrative: Gender and Power in the Middle Ages.* Ithaca, N.Y.: Cornell University Press, 2003.

Franzen, Allen. "When Women Aren't Enough." *Speculum* 68 (1993): 445–471.

Herlihy, David. "Life Expectancies for Women." In *The Role of Woman in the Middle Ages*, edited by Theresa Morewedge, Albany: State University of New York Press, 1975: 1–22.

Herlihy, David, and Christiane Klapisch-Züber. *Les Toscans et leurs familles: une etude du Catasto florentin de 1427.* Paris, 1978.

Kemp-Welch, Alice. "Medieaeval Gardens." *Monthly Review* 19: 3 (1905): 46–57.

Kristeva, Julia. "Hérétique de l'amour." *Tel quel* 74 (Winter 1977): 30–49.

McNamara, Jo Ann and Suzanne F. Wemple. "The Power of Women Through the Family." *Feminist Studies* 1 (1973): 126–141.

Power, Eileen. *Medieval English Nunneries c. 1275 to 1535.* Cambridge: Cambridge University Press, 1922.

———. "The Position of Women." In *The Legacy of the Middle Ages*, edited by G. C. Crump and E. F. Jacob. Oxford: Clarendon Press, 1926, pp. 401–433.

Putnam, Emily James. *The Lady: Studies of Certain Significant Phases of Her History.* New York: Sturgist Walton, 1910.

Scott, Joan Wallach. "Gender: A Useful Category of Analysis." *American Historical Review* 91 (1986): 1053–1075.

Stuard, Susan Mosher. "The Family Confronts the Renaissance Household." *Journal of Interdisciplinary History* 11:2 (1981): 495–501.

Women Medievalists and the Academy, edited by Jane Chance. Madison: University of Wisconsin Press, 2005.

See also **Annales School of History; Body in Literature and Religion; Body, Visual Repreparations of; Demography; Femininity and Masculinity; Gender Ideologies; Gender in Art; Gender in History; History, Medieval Women's; Monasticism and Nuns; Patronage, Artistic; Patronage, Ecclesiastical; Patronage, Literary; Power, Eileen; Sexuality: Extramarital Sex; Sexuality: Female Same-Sex Relations; Sexuality: Male Same-Sex Relations; Sexuality, Regulation of; Sexuality: Sex in Marriage; Women Authors: German Texts; Women Authors: Italian Texts; Women Authors: Latin Texts; Women Authors: Middel English Texts; Women Authors: Old French Texts; Women Authors: Spanish Texts; Women Medievalists in the Academy**

FESTIVALS OF MISRULE

The female image was of the utmost importance in the medieval festivals of Misrule and rituals of reversal that clustered in the "Twelve Days of Christmas" and the pre-Lenten Carnival season, as well as appearing occasionally in Springtide festivals. These representations, however, were almost exclusively in the hands of men. Cross-dressing was ubiquitous but tended to be all in one direction. It was naturally one of the first of the role-reversals to suggest itself to ebullient, usually youthful, male revelers. Clerical prohibitions of such practices go back to the early Middle Ages. By contrast there is little documentation for women's cross-dressing until well into the early modern period. Nevertheless, such activity must certainly have occurred, if perhaps not in great profusion. In the Kirk Sessions records of Presbyterian Elgin in Scotland, for example, we find a prohibition that "nather wemen to be cled in mens apparrel nor men in womens apparrel" during the Christmas season, as well as a January 4, 1600, judgment against "Marion Andersone for guysing through the toun in menis claythis" for which she was to be "put in the joiggis" (Cramond, ii, 158 & 77). Such solo performances could not have been entirely unheard of in the earlier medieval period.

Male festival cross-dressing was usually of a grotesque nature. The impersonated woman might be "the Dirty Bride" as in Bruegel's engraving, "The Marriage of Mopsus and Nisa" (also a vignette within his great painting "The Battle of Carnival and Lent") (Klein, 66–67). The character-type might be pregnant and searching for the father of her child among the male spectatorship, or come already burdened with many dolls upon her back as with "Bessy Big Head" in the English Mummers' Play (eighteenth to twentieth centuries). The Virago, whether a peasant or a bourgeois wife, was much in evidence in the drama of the Christmas and Carnival seasons particularly in the *Fastnachtspiele* (Carnival plays) of Nuremberg (fifteenth to seventeenth centuries). It was a short step then to the Crone who might be paired with a grotesque Old Man for simulated sex in Balkan folk mummeries. In more recent times the Witch became a popular masquerade in many Carnival societies of the Black Forest.

The beautiful female impersonation seems not so prevalent in the medieval period, the noble Amazon and other exotic queens, nymphs, and fairies only becoming popular as male masquerade figures in the Renaissance at the same time that the drama brought female cross-dressing to its peak with such characters as Rosalind, Viola, and Portia, still played by men of course. It is difficult to say if the late medieval/early modern figure of *Minne*, the love goddess or femme fatale was widely enacted for festival/satirical purposes, with her sewing up and selling foolscaps to the male population, enticing winged fools into birdtraps, shaking young fools out of a tree, etc., or whether she remained largely a creation of the new print medium. The grotesque female impersonation seems to have prevailed in both urban and rural culture.

Female personifications of the festival or principal of Misrule are also known, whether enacted, represented by an effigy, or simply posited as a literary or visual idea. Erasmus's goddess Moria was not simply a spirited intellectual exercise but was embodied in various "mothers" as the chief figures in the urban fool-societies of late medieval France. There was a *Mère Follie* in Dijon, a *Mère Sotte* in Paris, a *Mère d'Enfance* in Bordeaux, and so on (Davis, 139). Capering fools emerged from beneath *Mère Follie*'s voluminous skirts onto the festival streets in a travesty of multiple birth. Since the term *Fastnacht* (Eve of the Fast) is feminine in the Germanic languages, female personifications naturally presented themselves. The mythographer Fulgentius envisioned Fastnacht as a veiled woman with a crown of willow branches, a scepter in her right hand, and a parti-colored fool's vestment in her left, drawn in a cart by four white horses (Schmeller, 764). *Frau Fasnacht* or *Alti Dante* (Old Aunt) remains a traditional mask-type in the *Baseler Fasnacht*. Such female personifications, however, hardly compete in number with the King Carnivals or Christmas Princes in the performance history of Misrule. Conversely, the personification of the anti-festive Lent might also be female, as in Bruegel's "Battle of Carnival and Lent" where she is a pale, desiccated nun opposing a beefy Sir Carnival.

It is clear that these female representations in the festivals of Misrule reflect the patriarchal hegemony of the Middle Ages with its pervasive and largely unexamined misogyny. They tend to support the "safety valve" theory of carnivalesque performances wherein the topsy-turvy world, after its brief reign, ultimately reinforces the status quo. Natalie Zemon Davis in a still very relevant 1975 article, "Women on Top," argues, however, for a more complex view of the phenomenon. In certain circumstance, she maintains, the *topos* of the Unruly Woman could afford late medieval/early modern women (as well as men for that matter) with opportunities for social critique and even radical action within the broader festival context. Still we have relatively little in the way of documentation for an autonomous feminine view of early festive culture. Nuns in sixteenth-century Venice managed to maintain their own Carnival despite male oversight: "Sometimes the nuns sing profane songs, and they play the guitar and lute, and they dress up as men in order to put on plays" (Laven, 140). The English "Hocktide" presents a rather complete ritual action of "women on top." On the second Monday after Easter the village women capture any males they might come across, bind them with ropes, and hold them prisoner until they paid a festival ransom (Simpson and Roud, 180–181). It is a practice of some antiquity; attempts to suppress it in London dating from 1406 and 1409, for example. *Weiberfastnacht* (Women's Carnival) in Cologne, the Thursday before Ash Wednesday is another clear-cut festival of female empowerment in which women take over the city and engage in such transgressive and symbolic acts as clipping off men's neckties (Thompson and Carlson). The festival is a modern invention, a direct response by local women to their exclusion from the *Kölner Karneval* as it evolved in the early nineteenth century. One can surmise, however, that similar rebellious energies were at work in earlier centuries, as the Hocktide custom demonstrates.

As critical theorist Mary Russo, echoing Natalie Davis, remarks, "The gender asymmetries in masquerade have yet to be fully addressed" (Russo, 7). Some recent Carnival scholarship has begun seriously to address gender issues. Deborah Puccio has examined the present festival in the Pyrenees and the Slovenian Alps; Francesca Cappelletto in the Italian town of Bagolino; and David Gilmore in Spain. While one cannot automatically extrapolate from their finding back to medieval women in their festive mode, this new sensitivity to gender issues and the question of female representation in masquerade can only help to flesh out the rather meager record of women and the practice of misrule in centuries past.

MARTIN W. WALSH

References and Further Reading

Cappelletto, Francesca. *Il Carnevale: Organizzazione soicale e pratiche cerimoniali a Bagolino*. Brescia: Grafo, 1995.

Cramond, William, ed. *The Records of Elgin, 1234–1800*. 2 vols. Aberdeen: New Spalding Club, 1903.

Davis, Natalie Zemon. "The Reasons of Misrule" and "Women on Top." In *Society and Culture in Early Modern France*. Stanford: Stanford University Press, 1975, pp. 97–123; 124–151.

French, Katherine L. "'To Free Them from Binding': Women in the Late Medieval English Parish." *Journal of Interdisciplinary History* 27.3 (1997): 387–412.

Gilmore, David D. *Carnival and Culture: Sex, Symbol, and Status in Spain*. New Haven: Yale University Press, 1998.

Klein, H. Arthur. *Graphic Worlds of Peter Bruegel the Elder*. New York: Dover, 1963.

Laven, Mary. *Virgins of Venice: Broken Vows and Cloistered Lives in Renaissance Venice*. New York: Viking, 2002.

Puccio, Deborah. *Masques et dévoilements: Jeux du féminin dans les rituals carnavalesque et nuptiaux*. Paris: CNRS Éditions, 2002.

Russo, Mary. "Female Grotesques: Carnival and Theory." Working Paper No. 1, Center for Twentieth Century Studies, University of Wisconsin-Milwaukee, Fall 1985.

Schmeller, Johan Andrea. "Die Fasnacht, Fastnacht." In *Bayerisches Wörterbuch*. Munich: R. Oldenbourg, 1996.

Simpson, Jacqueline, and Steve Roud. *A Dictionary of English Folklore*. Oxford: Oxford University Press, 2000.

Thompson, Sue Ellen, and Barbara W. Carlson. *Holidays, Festivals, and Celebrations of the World Dictionary*. Detroit: Omnigraphics, 1994.

See also **Cross-Dressing; Gender Ideologies; Misogyny; Patriarchy and Patrilineage; Woman on Top**

FINA OF SAN GIMIGNANO

Fina dei Ciardi (1238–1253) was a reclusive, ascetic virgin who died at age fifteen and was soon thereafter named patron saint of her hometown, San Gimignano. Little is known about her actual life apart from the testimonies of witnesses appended to her official *vita*. She was not affiliated with a religious order, though her *vita* was composed about 1300 by a local Dominican, Fra Giovanni del Coppo. Her biography conforms to a model of mendicant piety focused on imitation of Christ's Passion while it abounds with other familiar *topoi* drawn from hagiographic tradition.

According to the *vita*, Fina was born to an impoverished noble family. As a very young girl she began a life of reclusion at home and practiced extreme asceticism that included fasting, wearing a coarse hair shirt, and self-flagellation. At age ten she was struck with a paralyzing illness that prevented the movement of her body. She chose to lie on a hard board, voluntarily increasing her suffering in imitation of Christ on the Cross. While lying on the board over a period of five years, she endured numerous hardships, including the decay of her body, mice eating away at her rotting flesh, and the death of her mother. Finally, Saint Gregory the Great appeared to her in a vision and announced her imminent death. Thereafter, her pain increased. Following her death eight days later, miracles began to occur. The town erected a shrine and later a chapel in the Collegiata of San Gimignano, where her cult is still celebrated today. Although Fina was never officially canonized, she was considered a bona fide saint locally.

LINDA A. KOCH

References and Further Reading

Coppo, Fra Giovanni del. *The Legend of Holy Fina, Virgin of Santo Gimignano*. New York, Duffield, London: Chatto and Windus, 1908. Reprint, New York, 1966.

Frugoni, Chiara. "The City and the 'New Saints'." In *City States in Classical Antiquity and Medieval Italy*, edited by Anthony Mohlo, Kurt Raaflaub, and Julia Emlen. Ann Arbor: University of Michigan Press, 1991, pp. 71–91.

Koch, Linda A. "The Portrayal of Female Sainthood in Renaissance San Gimignano: Ghirlandaio's Frescoes of Santa Fina's Legend." *Artibus et Historiae*, 19, 1998, pp. 143–170.

Vichi Imberciadori, Jole. *Fina dei Ciardi: Un simbolo nella realtà storica e sociale di San Gimignano*. San Gimignano: Graficalito, 1979.

See also **Disabilities; Girls and Boys; Hagiography; Italy; Laywomen, Religious**

FLAMENCA

See **Romance of Flamenca**

FLANDERS

Advantageously located astride a number of trade routes and blessed with many towns and a thriving textile industry, the county of Flanders (western Belgium and northern France) had become the commercial and industrial center of medieval northern Europe by the eleventh century. Economic dynamics were inherently opposed to the maintenance of traditional feudal and religious practices. The buying, manufacture, transportation, and selling of goods did not fit into the military ethos that engendered feudalism, nor was it easily accommodated to the isolated, spiritual context of medieval religion. Preconceptions rooted in feudal and religious order, although by no means without influence in medieval Flanders, took a back seat to economic demands.

Women could be found at all levels of Flemish society. The extent of their public activity repeatedly surprised foreign visitors to the region. Women functioned as castellans, financial receivers, abbesses, and countesses; for most of the thirteenth century, for example, the country was ruled by Countess Joanna (1204–1244) and Countess Margaret (1244–1280). Women tanned hides, ran inns, sold fruit, and butchered meat. They were indispensable to the textile industry as carders, spinners, warpers, dyers, and even as weavers. They were also drapers, employing both men and women in the manufacture of cloth sold as far away as Novgorod, Russia.

Associated with the constancy and breadth of women's economic activities came relative economic autonomy. In 1355, for example, an alderman of Ghent granted a marital separation because both parties could pay their own bills. The routine reference to practitioners of a wide range of trades in both masculine and feminine by the aldermen of Douai moreover suggests that women were commonly regarded as merchants and tradespeople in their own right.

Economic autonomy was made possible in part by a Germanic system of customary law—based more on negotiation among groups than on decisions of constituted authorities—that prevailed in Flanders until the advent of Roman law in the fifteenth century. Both men and women had experience with drawing up wills and contracts as well as with resolving their disputes and paying fees and fines before public audiences comprising aldermen and citizens of both genders. Aldermanic ordinances from Douai, for their part, include very few that solely target men or women. One such ordinance established a hospital exclusively for pregnant citizens; another forbade women from returning to work for at least a month after childbirth. There were, in fact, few social spaces that were peculiarly "male" or "female"; segregation of the sexes became common only much later, at the end of the Ancien Régime.

Distinctive religious factors also reflect women's relative autonomous status. While Flanders was home to numerous monasteries and abbeys, the county had no episcopal see within its borders; it was far less subject to episcopal influence than were many other parts of Europe. In addition, there were a number of convents, such as Flines, Marquette, and Messines, whose powerful abbesses were embroiled in most of the religious and secular affairs of their respective regions. Flanders also saw one of the greatest flowerings of the Beguine movement, a peculiarly female and urban movement made possible by medieval Flemish social and economic conditions. Pious but unprofessed women, Beguines frequently lived collectively in communal institutions called beguinages, located in the towns where most of them worked.

To be sure, the Flemish cultural area was no stranger to patriarchy. There, as elsewhere, women were commonly defined as someone's daughter, wife, or widow. But such practices were not necessarily routine; in accounts, for example, the names of most women appear without any form of associative identification. Nonetheless, single people in the county remained at a disadvantage when compared to married ones. A single person, after all, had at his or her disposal only one income and only one person's labor. And while single women with children were recognized as legitimate social units, they often made up a large percentage of the very poor. Most medieval societies were uneasy with single men and women; both were expected to marry.

The independent public actions undertaken by married women in Flanders nonetheless differed very little from those of their unmarried counterparts. A number of circumstances determined the position of women within marriage. Both men and women married fairly late, at around twenty-five. There appears to have been no shortage of possible marriage partners; both men and women were comfortably enough established that they could afford to be selective. Alternatively, both may have worked until they could bring enough income or property into the relationship to enable the young couple to survive. Any property acquired during the marriage was held jointly. At the dissolution of a marriage, for whatever reason, property reverted to the family to whom it had originally belonged. Because Flemish inheritance customs privileged the spouse over progeny, joint property usually devolved onto the surviving partner. This practice diminished the significance of fathers while simultaneously raising that of wives. Moreover, when one parent died, the other, regardless of sex, usually took over the guardianship of any minor children; a child who lost either parent was considered to be an orphan. Finally, no great educational gap separated the sexes. Both girls and boys in most towns attended schools where they were taught how to read, write, and cipher, often in both Flemish and French.

With the exception of the office of bailiff, the only public offices whose functions women did not exercise were those that were collective in nature. Women functioned as abbesses, as castellans, and as countesses, but never as aldermen. They were thus denied the collective experience of exercising power in public as women. There is no doubt that routine association of collective decision-making with men tended to promote gendered conceptualizations of authority. Correspondingly, women's isolation as single and occasional authorities may well have contributed to a perception that their authoritative status as (and perhaps by extension, their social participation in general) was exceptional. Such perceptions would be consolidated by social, economic, and political changes during the later Burgundian period.

ELLEN E. KITTELL

References and Further Reading

Godding Philippe. *Le droit privé dans les Pays-Bas méridionaux du 12e au 18e siècle*. Brussels: Palais des Académies, 1987.

Kittell, Ellen E. "Guardianship over Women in Medieval Flanders: A Reappraisal." *Journal of Social History*, 13(4) (Summer, 1998): 897–930.

———. "Women, Audience and Public Acts in Medieval Flanders. *Journal of Women's History* 10 n. 3 (Fall 1998): 74–96.

Kittell, Ellen E., and Kurt Queller. "'Whether Man or Women': Gender Inclusivity in the Town Ordinances of Medieval Douai." *The Journal of Medieval and Early Modern Studies* 30 n. 1 (Winter 2000): 63–100.

Kittell, Ellen, and Mary Suydam, eds. *The Texture of Society: Medieval Women in the Southern Low Countries*. New York: Palgrave Macmillan, 2004.

Simons, Walter, *Cities of Ladies. Beguine Communities in the Medieval Low Countries, 1200–1565*. Philadelphia: University of Pennsylvania Press, 2001.

See also **Beguines; Burgundian Netherlands; Cities and Towns; Clothwork, Domestic; Education, Lay; Hadewijch; Landholding and Property Rights; Market and Tradeswomen; Marriage, Christian; Monasticism and Nuns; Singlewomen; Textile Production for the Market; Work**

FLOIRE AND BLANCHEFLOR

The story of Floire and Blancheflor enjoyed great popularity in many parts of Europe throughout the medieval period. Today, manuscripts survive in French, English, High and Low German, Dutch, several Scandinavian languages, Italian, and Spanish. The oldest extant manuscript in any language is a German text fragment (c. 1170–1180), though it is assumed that the oldest European variant of the tale was French (c. 1150–1160). Several literary historians have argued for a Byzantine, Persian, or Arabic origin of the story. Literary historians distinguish between a *version aristocratique* (aristocratic version) and a *version populaire* (popular version), the former being less plot-driven and adventure-laden than the latter and presenting instead detailed descriptions of localities and emotions.

Floire, the son of a Muslim king, and Blancheflor, the daughter of his mother's Christian lady-in-waiting, fell in love while still in their cradles and became inseparable thereafter. The boy's parents objected to the relationship, citing insurmountable differences of religion and class. Pretending that Blancheflor died, the parents secretly sold the girl to Babylonian merchants. Blancheflor became the prized possession of a cruel Babylonian ruler who followed a ritual of marrying and then—after the course of one year—killing the women he desires. Floire eventually learned the truth about his beloved. Disguised as a merchant, he traveled east, and by means of wit and deception managed to free Blancheflor. The two lovers returned to Floire's home country after receiving word that Floire's father has died and that the country is awaiting the return of its new ruler.

The story offers exceedingly rich material to students and scholars interested in pursuing feminist and gender-related inquiry with regard to medieval literature, be it in the realm of masculinity studies, the exploration of the intersections of sex, gender, race, class and religion, or the examination of the overlapping discourses of love, economic exchange, and female commodification present in this text.

KATHARINA ALTPETER-JONES

References and Further Reading

Grieve, Patricia E. *"Floire and Blancheflor" and the European Romance*. Cambridge: Cambridge University Press, 1997.

Kelly, Kathleen Coyne. "The Bartering of Blauncheflur in the Middle English Floris and Blauncheflur." *Studies in Philology* 91.2 (1994): 101–110.

McCaffrey, Phillip. "Sexual Identity in 'Floire et Blancheflor' and Ami et Amile." In *Gender Transgressions: Crossing the Normative Boundary in Old French Literature*, edited by Karen J. Taylor. New York: Garland, 1998, pp. 129–152.

Schäfer, Verena. *Flore und Blancheflur—Epos und Volksbuch: Textversionen und die verschiedenen Illustrationen bis ins 19. Jahrhundert: Ein Beitrag zur Geschichte der Illustration*. Munich: Tuduv-Verlagsgesellschaft, 1984.

See also **Muslim Women: Western Literature; Roman de Silence; Romance, English; French; Romance, German**

FONTEVRAULT, ABBEY AND ORDER OF

Founded by the wandering preacher Robert of Arbrissel in 1101 in the Loire valley region of western France, Fontevrault was a unique "double" monastery that included both men and women, but in which the women predominated and ruled. Robert responded to criticism of his unorthodox intimacy with women, which apparently included sleeping with them chastely as part of an ascetic effort to master desire, by regularizing his followers' religious life in a monastic setting. Open to people of all conditions, the twelfth-century monastery included separate complexes for men, lepers, penitent prostitutes, and choir nuns. Double monasteries, in which monks and nuns lived in a single, albeit sexually segregated community, were fairly common during the period of intense religious enthusiasm in the later eleventh and early twelfth centuries. In predominantly female houses, like Fontevrault, a smaller group of monks were assigned to provide the sisters with the religious and worldly services, including priestly duties and the management of landed estates, that were forbidden to or deemed improper for cloistered women. But after the mid-twelfth century a misogynistic reaction set in that made it difficult for mixed communities to survive, as male clerics increasingly complained of economic burdens and the dangers of sexual corruption. What made Fontevrault truly unique was that, from its earliest years (by 1115), its founder drew up rules that institutionalized the relationship between men and women, making it clear that the monks' role was to serve the nuns and to obey the abbess. This formal clarity, together with Fontevrault's early success in attracting noble and even royal patronage, enabled it to withstand misogynistic criticisms and a variety of political and economic crises that did in many similar institutions. It survived as a predominantly female double monastery until its suppression in 1792 during the French Revolution.

Fontevrault's popularity also led to the establishment of many dependent priories, soon making the abbey the head of the largest federation of nunneries in the medieval West. Although some dated to before Robert's death in 1116, most of these affiliated communities were founded under the able leadership of the first two abbesses, Petronilla of Chemillé (1115–1149) and Matilda of Anjou (1149–1155). By about 1200, there were over 70 dependent priories, mostly in western France, but also including a few as far away as Spain and England. The abbey reached the zenith of its fame in the late-twelfth century, when Fontevrault became a favorite of the royal families of France and England. Henry Plantagenet, Count of Anjou and King of England (1154–1189), and his wife Eleanor, duchess of Aquitaine, showered largesse on the nuns. Both of them, along with their son Richard the Lionheart, are buried at Fontevrault. The tombs of Henry and Eleanor, complete with recumbent life-sized sculptures, can still be seen in the nave of the abbey church. Although the monastery has been damaged, it is now a protected historical site that includes several twelfth-century buildings, including the Romanesque abbey church and a curious, octagonal kitchen.

RICHARD KEYSER

References and Further Reading

Gold, Penny S. *The Lady and the Virgin: Image, Attitude, and Experience in Twelfth-Century France*. Chicago: The University of Chicago Press, 1985, pp. 93–113.

Venarde, Bruce L. *Women's Monasticism and Medieval Society: Nunneries in France and England, 890–1215*. Ithaca, N.Y.: Cornell University Press, 1997, pp. 57–63, 104–124.

Wood, Charles, T. "Fontevraud, Dynasticism and Eleanor of Aquitaine." In *Eleanor of Aquitaine: Lord and Lady*, edited by Bonnie Wheeler and John C. Parsons. New York: Palgrave Macmillan, 2002, pp. 407–422.

See also **Abbesses; Double Monasteries; Eleanor of Aquitaine; Monasticism and Nuns; Spiritual Care**

FOSTERAGE

In medieval Iceland, the term *fosterage* denotes a legal and social contract between two families aimed at adding a network of relations to that of a child's biological kin and similar to, but farther-reaching than, the Christian system of god-parentage. In other words, it does not refer to the care of needy orphaned children, a problem that was handled by Iceland's remarkable poor laws, nor to the aristocratic custom developed during the High Middle Ages in England and on the Continent whereby adolescent children were sent away from home for training. According to the Icelandic law, *Grágás lögfóstur* (legal fosterage) occurred when a man agreed to bring up another person's child from the age of seven (or younger) to sixteen in return for remuneration that was agreed to and paid beforehand. The relationship did not end when the young person returned home, but a foster-child was considered to be near-equal to the foster-father's own children. If the foster-father was disabled, for example, the fosterling could act on his behalf in the same capacity as the son, stepson, or son-in-law. Furthermore, the man's foster-daughter and foster-mother were included among the six women for whom he was allowed to take instant revenge if they were sexually molested. The sagas of Icelanders confirm these rules and add further details. Fosterage was apparently so common that it was considered highly unusual if "all the children grew up at home." In that case a foster-father or foster-mother, often of slave or recently freed status, would be brought to the family farm. Because of the male focus of the sagas more boys than girls are reported as being sent away for fostering, but it happened to girls as well, as illustrated by Guðríðr Þorbjarnardóttir of Vínland fame, who was fostered with neighbors before both families' immigration to Greenland. The proverb that "a person owes one fourth of his or her personality to fosterage" (*Njáls Saga*, chap. 42) is evidence of the foster-family's influence on the child's development. The normal assumption was that well-to-do-parents sought fosterage for their children among social groups below them, but such statements invariably occur when parents made contrary decisions that reveal their concern for positive influences on the children (illustration in *Laxdæla Saga*, chap. 28). The law does not mention inheritance for foster-children, but foster-parents lacking biological offspring often made the charge their heir. Fosterage was not limited to the pagan context of the sagas of Icelanders but continued into the Christian era of the Contemporary sagas. The most famous foster-child is Snorri Sturluson who in 1181 at the age of three was brought by his father from his birthplace in Hvammr in northern Iceland to Oddi in the south to be fostered by Jón Loftsson, the most prominent man in the country. Snorri stayed here until 1202, benefiting from the rich cultural milieu that helped him to establish political contacts. It is not surprising that the strong emotional ties between foster-parents and their charges often competed with or even equaled those with biological kin. Foster-parents' names became embedded in the next generation of the fosterling's own children, and political and economic arrangements continued between the families. Egill's grief and rage when his father killed his foster-mother as she was trying to save him from paternal anger is unforgettable (*Egils Saga*, chap. 40). Emotional ties were particularly strong between a foster-mother and her female charge. The latter might bring her foster-mother with her when she married, allowing her to raise her own children in turn. The need for additional kinship is particularly clear in cases when a young widow agreed to let her newborn son be fostered by her deceased husband's relatives or friends. Bereft of a father, the child acquired new kinship ties through his foster-family. In the past fosterage was considered to be part of ancient Scandinavian law. Although Norwegian laws used a vocabulary similar to *Grágás*, the cases involved care of poor people and do not include the Icelandic legal and institutional framework. Since Ireland had laws similar to Iceland's concerning fosterage, it appears likely that visiting Vikings brought the idea home from there, a suggestion supported by a brief episode in *Laxdæla Saga* (chaps. 20–22); Melkorka, an Irish princess who was brought to Iceland as a slave, eventually sent her son to Ireland with specific instructions to contact her foster-mother.

JENNY JOCHENS

References and Further Reading

Ancient Laws of Ireland. Senchus Mor. Dublin, London: 1869.

The Complete Sagas of Icelanders Including 49 Tales, edited by Viar Hreinsson. 5 vols. Reykjavik: Leifur Eiríksson Publishing, 1997.

The Earliest Norwegian Laws. translated by Laurence M. Larson. New York: Columbia, 1935.

Jochens, Jenny. "Old Norse Motherhood." In *Medieval Mothering*, edited by John Carmi Parsons and Bonnie Wheeler. New York: Garland, 1996, pp. 201–222.

Kreutzer, Gert. *Kindheit und Jugend in der altnordischen Literatur*. Munster: Kleinheinrich, 1987, pp. 221–234.

Laws of Early Iceland: Grágás I, II. translated by Andrew Dennis, Peter Foote, and Richard Perkins. Manitoba: University of Manitoba Press, 1980–2000.

Lynch, Joseph H. *Godparents and Kinship in Early Medieval Europe*. Princeton, N.J.: Princeton University Press, 1986.

See also **Breastfeeding and Wet-Nursing; Education, Lay; Girls and Boys; Godparents; Infants and Infanticide; Literature, Old Norse; Mothers as Teachers**

FOY

According to the earliest account of her life and martyrdom, Sainte Foy (also Faith or Fides) was a well-born young girl martyred by Dacian, the Roman ruler of Agen in southwestern France in the fourth century. Her relics were enshrined in a church built outside the walls of that city. In 866, they were stolen from Agen by the monks of Conques (a Benedictine monastery in the Rouergue) to be the focus of their cult. Approximately a century later, stories of Foy's miracles—especially the healing of blindness and liberation of prisoners—began to circulate in the region. Many of these miracle narratives were assembled into a text that circulated as the *Liber miraculorum* and spread Foy's fame throughout Europe. Foy's cult reached its

Side view of the Reliquary of Saint Foy, ninth century with Gothic additions. Gilded silver, copper, enamel, rock crystal, and precious stones, cameos, wooden core. Location: France. Credit: Erich Lessing / Art Resource, N.Y.

References and Further Reading

Ashley, Kathleen, and Pamela Sheingorn. *Writing Faith: Text, Sign, & History in the Miracles of Sainte Foy.* Chicago: University of Chicago Press, 1999.
Sheingorn, Pamela, trans. and ed. *The Book of Sainte Foy.* Philadelphia: University of Pennsylvania Press, 1995.

See also **Hagiography; Hagiography, Iconographic Aspects of; Pilgrims and Pilgrimage; Relics and Reliquaries; Virgin Martyrs**

apogee in the eleventh and twelfth centuries, with sites established across France, England, the Germanic countries, Italy, and Spain, as well as a popular pilgrimage to her shrine at Conques.

The major attribute of Foy in the visual arts is the grill that represents one of her tortures. When her virgin martyr status is emphasized, she is often portrayed as a slender young woman with long hair. When her intercessory powers are important, as in the Faith chapel at Westminster cathedral, she is portrayed as a majestic female figure who overshadows the tiny monk kneeling in prayer at the bottom of the painting.

In texts, Foy is represented with even more variety depending upon the role she is to play. For Bernard of Angers, the eleventh century compiler of some of her miracles, Foy is a childish female trickster who extorts gifts from pilgrims and plays jokes on her monks. However, for monastic writers in her miracle collection, Sainte Foy is a celestial virgin, one of the most powerful saints in heaven.

KATHLEEN M. ASHLEY

FRANCE, NORTHERN

The life experience of the women in northern France between 1000 and 1500 BCE plays a pivotal role in the narrative of European women's history. Determining whether their lot in life improved or declined has largely guided investigation of the women living at this time in this region. For medievalists, these centuries have been thought to be the end of a "golden age." Modernists, in contrast, find the roots of repression consonant with the women of recent centuries in the "dark" era of the Middle Ages. Recent research, however, has provided a corrective to both viewpoints and has demonstrated that women of this era did not suffer repression or powerlessness to a greater extent than their counterparts in other periods. Some women were influential and had access to resources, others were clearly on the margin of society with little recourse to power or influence. The profound social, economic, and political transitions of this era shaped women's lives significantly.

Part of the difficulty in recovering the experiences of medieval women in northern France stems from the nature of the extant sources. While documents are plentiful for this era and there are a significant number penned by women, accounts written by men—sometimes directly concerned with women, but more often not—predominate. The history of women is taken from what Marc Bloch termed "witnesses in spite of themselves," in other words, pieced together from sources not written by women nor directly addressing the issue of women's past or experience. Although challenging, medievalists have been successful in teasing out the lives of medieval women from sometimes recalcitrant sources.

Elite Women: Queens, Aristocrats, and Religious Women

Interestingly, the lives of upper-class women, who had the most written about them, are frequently opaque or obscure. In spite of the fact that medieval queens acted as consorts or guardians, they did not share official power with their husbands or sons. But did this mean that such queens were powerless? Indeed not. The royal women of Louis IX's court can serve as examples. Louis' mother, Blanche of Castile, ruled France during her son's minority and his crusade to the Holy Land. Furthermore, Blanche also exerted considerable cultural influence through her patronage of the arts and founding of religious houses. Like her mother, Louis' sister, Isabelle of France, was a pious woman. She embraced the religious life, although she never took the vows of a nun. Her personal piety, however, reflected the religious ethos of the time, and her own practices had an impact on the religious behavior of the royal family and her brother's court. While many royal women did not act as regents, as Blanche did, they exercised significant influence over the royal men in their lives, as well as medieval society in general, through their cultural patronage and religious dedication.

Aristocratic women wielded the same sorts of powers as royal women. Key to noblewomen's influence and status was their control of property. As daughters, they received a portion of the patrimony as both inheritance and dowry, which necessitated their participation in granting land to vassals and making gifts to the church. Marriage was a defining moment in the life of an aristocratic woman as she became the head of her own household. Yet attachment to her natal family was not severed. Upon marriage noble women continued to consent to alienations of property made by their natal family and their fostering of their nephews and nieces ensured continued connection to their blood kin. Many women experienced marriage in positive ways. In many cases marriages lasted decades and affection developed. Because noble men were so often away at war, their wives took over running family estates and lordships. To ensure stability and continuity of policy during such absences wives and husbands acted together in the transfer and management of property and personnel. Widowhood was yet another important life stage for noble women. In some cases, widowhood represented a dramatic increase in women's access to power or property. In others, widows simply continued to enjoy the influence they had as married women.

Because aristocratic women controlled land and other resources, they were important powerbrokers in their society. For example, women were extremely generous patrons and protectors of local ecclesiastical foundations. Clerics realized the influence that such women held and actively cultivated their support, resulting in relationships of respect and even affection between clerics and aristocratic women. Women were also frequently called upon to intercede with the church on behalf of their obstreperous male kin. When noble men violated the church, it was up to their wives, mothers, and sisters, to mend fences with the clergy.

As more systematized and formalized government developed after the twelfth century, noble-born men and women alike found their access to power and autonomy curtailed. But women developed strategies for negotiating within a male-dominated system. Yet the repression historians have associated with the centuries between 1200 and 1500 did not occur to the degree previously assumed. In contrast to their modern counterparts, medieval female elites enjoyed far more respect and possibilities for power.

As was the case with queens and noblewomen, the early medieval centuries also act as a "golden age" standard against which the life experience of religious women of the central medieval period seems to fall short. The reform movements of the late eleventh and twelfth centuries have been interpreted as harmful to, if not downright hostile toward, pious women. A decrease in the number of women saints—as well as a change in the characteristics women needed for canonization—has been suggested as symptomatic of a diminution in women's religious influence. Developments in religion did put some mechanisms in place that disadvantaged women in the religious life. But juxtaposed against the exclusion of women from some of the important monastic movements of the twelfth century, Cistercian monasticism in particular, is the founding of the convent of Fontevrault by Robert of Arbrissel. This abbey became one of the most powerful religious institutions in western France and surpassed many male houses in its wealth and influence.

Women seeking a life dedicated to God, however, were most deeply affected by the development of alternatives to the cloister. As the medieval economy assumed a more commercial form, towns began to grow. The religious needs and interests of urban populations differed from those living in the countryside. As a consequence, new forms of religious expression and experience emerged. Shortly after St. Francis founded the mendicant Franciscans, the order of the Poor Clares was instituted as a new way for women to pursue a life devoted to religion. As some urban women felt the need to dedicate their lives to God without taking vows or being cloistered, communities of Beguines appeared on the urban landscape of northern France. While traditional Benedictine monasticism had offered opportunities for mostly women of the landed elite, the Beguines and Poor Clares provided an avenue of religious expression not previously available to women living in the cities of northern France.

Medieval women also left their mark on the flowering of late medieval mystical Christianity. During this period women from all over western Europe explored new paths to God. Instead of relying on an intercessory clergy, some women mystics connected directly with the divine through their visions and other physical manifestations, including levitation, abstinence from eating, and fits of uncontrollable weeping. Mystics like Marie of Oignies (d. 1213) and Christina the Astonishing (1150–1224), living in northern France or the bordering Low Countries, were sought out by male and female believers alike. Some male clergy supported these female mystics, and in many cases became their hagiographers. The female mystics' advocacy of a personal connection with God laid the groundwork for later reformers and contributed directly to the development of the Modern Devotion. The centuries between 1000 and 1500 BCE presented certain challenges—and restrictions, like stricter monastic enclosure—to religious women. But they also offered opportunities for shaping Christianity that women had perhaps not enjoyed since its early centuries.

Urban Women

Did urbanization and commercialization of the economy work to the benefit or disadvantage of urban women? The answer to this question depends upon individual experience determined largely by social status. Women of the urban elite certainly benefited from the wealth and power accrued by their family. But, like queens, the wives, mothers, daughters, and sisters of the urban elite seldom enjoyed official power. While women may not usually have gained formal power, wives of the urban elite used their resources to patronize religious houses—both the traditional and the newly emerging institutions that were found in urban centers—and to gain support of other patricians. Furthermore, like noble women, they were able to use their influence with husbands and sons to achieve alliances and what might be considered political aims. The dowries that urban women brought to their marriages also played an important role in a family's future and finances. In some cases a generous dowry could help a family to move up several rungs on the social ladder. While their dowries became part of the family patrimony, women maintained control over how they were used.

Women took part in virtually every facet of the commercial economy of northern France: they owned and managed a variety of businesses individually and with their husbands, they sold merchandise, staffed inns and hostelries, and contributed their labor to industry. While women usually were excluded from holding office in the guilds that emerged to regulate production and quality of the items sold or produced, except in rare cases like the silk guild in Paris, in those occupations where women predominated—in the production of cloth, for example—women did play influential roles in those guilds. In the late Middle Ages the loss of population caused by the Black Death created more opportunities for employment and influence within the guild system for urban women. These gains were further reinforced by urban women's ability to inherit their husbands' or fathers' businesses. Widows, in particular, were vital participants in the commercial economy.

For women of the lowest reaches of urban society the commercialization of medieval society, and with it urbanization, was a mixed blessing. The towns of northern France that focused on the cloth industry provided a draw, a place where women might find new opportunities. Sometimes women secured work in shops or industry. Others found husbands. While "town air" could make serfs free, it could also create another form of subjection for women as they ended up in occupations, as servants or prostitutes, resulting in their economic and physical exploitation. But such women did not fall completely through the cracks of society. Urban dwellers' concern for these "fallen" women is evident in the numerous religious foundations dedicated to Mary Magdalen where such women could be reformed. Provision of a dowry for a prostitute who could then marry and make a new life also became a popular expression of piety. Commercialization did benefit some women, but it also worked to the detriment of others.

Rural Women

In spite of the growth of towns that occurred in the twelfth and thirteenth centuries, most medieval people continued to reside in the countryside. More than any other sector of medieval society, peasants were the most vulnerable to the capricious forces of nature. Survival depended upon the contributions of both men and women. Peasant women generally were responsible for the home, raising of children, tending the garden, baking bread, and brewing beer. They also contributed their labor in the fields at key points during the year—as is vividly illustrated in medieval illuminated manuscripts. Men, in contrast, spent much of their day in the field. In order for a family to survive, let alone thrive, both husbands and wives had to contribute their labor. Without a wife, a peasant man would be seriously disadvantaged and *vice versa*. But it is important not to overemphasize the independence or power of peasant women. Like their sisters in the aristocracy and in the city, peasant women were excluded from holding formal offices within their village. Those peasants living between 1100 and 1500 generally saw a decrease in the control that lords had over their lives. Central to this change in their status were two events: the commercial revolution and the Black Death.

The change to a commercial economy held important ramifications for the French peasantry. As lords sought to participate in an increasingly cash-based economy, they became interested in finding ways of converting their landed wealth into cash. Instead of requiring peasant labor in return for land, justice, and protection, lords began to convert such services into cash payments. *Moveance*, or the creation of new communities, also benefited peasant men and women. In order to attract individuals and families to settle these new and sometimes marginal areas, lords offered incentives such as reductions in the amount or type of labor or dues owed to the lord. Thus for most peasants of 1000 to 1500 their relationship with lords became less onerous, and they became more "free." Events of the late Middle Ages, catalyzed by the Black Death, would both challenge and reinforce this freedom.

Like most of western Europe, late medieval northern France was dramatically affected by the population deprivations caused by the plague. Many peasants died, and those who survived found themselves facing new challenges. For some, these challenges provided opportunities and an end to serfdom. For others, lords attempted to reinstate the more regressive aspects of lordship. But the post–Black Death world was made up of new realities and expectations, for in 1358, peasant men and women all over France rebelled against their lords by burning their castles, destroying the records of their servitude, and even killing them in the "Jacquerie," an event tellingly named after the prototypical French peasant "Jacques." The catastrophes of the late Middle Ages undoubtedly were a source of personal tragedy for many peasant women living in northern France, but they also provided such women with access to advancement perhaps missing from earlier centuries.

Creative Women

The issue of improvement or decline again emerges in the evaluation of Northern French female writers and artists of the period. In the lifetime of Heloise, a cultural revival triggered by an interest in the culture of the classical past took hold, and women contributed to this twelfth-century renaissance. Although Heloise never wrote a theological treatise as her lover-husband Abelard did, her letters embody the philosophical training and interest in the classical past so much a part of the cultural and intellectual accomplishments of the twelfth century. Nor was Heloise the only woman engaged with classical culture and learning. Marie de France, another woman of the twelfth century, was also trained in Latin for she translated *The Purgatory of St. Patrick* from Latin to French. Marie also contributed to a flowering of vernacular literature. Her *lais* mark a high point in medieval literature by providing insight into the emotional life and motivations of her characters. The participation of women in the production of secular and religious texts continued into the later medieval period, although some see it as a time of decline. The mystical works of Marguerite Porete were so influential that, although she was eventually condemned as a heretic, they remained in circulation. (Works by other women mystics, in contrast, were accepted and even embraced by the church.) Christine de Pizan was an important and successful author of the time, and her exploration of classical themes heralds the transition from medieval to Renaissance culture.

Women contributed to the flowering of medieval culture in other more anonymous ways. Many medieval nuns wrote, illuminated, and embroidered, creating magnificent expressions of spirituality in literature and art. The cathedrals that rose all over northern France also benefited from the labor, expertise, and expression of medieval women. Like queens, urban women, and peasants, creative women were excluded from the more formal positions associated with intellectual pursuit. Universities were being founded all over France at this time, but they were for men only. Such obstacles did not prevent women from writing and creating; there were other avenues for learning and expression.

Women also shaped culture through their patronage. Marie de Champagne, for instance, sponsored Chrétien de Troyes, whose romances are considered an early prototype of the modern novel. The prevalent image of women with books testifies to their literacy as well as the impact they had on the creation of literature. Several late medieval French queens, for instance, are known to have owned (and read) the works of such authors as Christine de Pizan.

Conclusion

Once characterized as the "male Middle Ages," it is now recognized that women clearly shaped this important era in European history. The presumed "maleness" of northern France between 1000 and 1500 stemmed from a reliance on theological and religious sources, which tend to paint a rather monochromatic view of women and are often overtly hostile to them. The misogyny of some clerics is indisputably a part of the narrative of the history of medieval women, but it is only one strand, not the complete tapestry or composition. While the centuries between 1000 and 1500 represented a time of challenges for women in northern France, they were also a time of opportunity and influence. But the experience of women was not uniform. Some were valued, influential, and respected members of their society. Others labored in silence and occupied the margins of society. Yet all were indisputably part of the medieval landscape and helped to mold the essential contours of the medieval world.

AMY LIVINGSTONE

References and Further Reading

Aristocratic Women in Medieval France, edited by Theodore Evergates. Philadelphia: University of Pennsylvania Press, 1999.

Bell, Susan Groag. "Medieval Women Book Owners: Arbiters of Lay Piety and Ambassadors of Culture," in *Signs* 7 (1982): 742–768.

Bynum, Caroline Walker. *Holy Feast and Holy Fast: The Religious Significance of Food to Medieval Women.* Berkeley and Los Angeles: University of California Press, 1987.

Capetian Women, edited by Kathleen Nolan. New York: Palgrave Macmillan, 2003, pp 137–161.

Facinger, Marion F. "A Study of Medieval Queenship: Capetian France, 987–1237," *Nebraska Studies in Medieval and Renaissance History* 5 (1968): 1–48.

Farmer, Sharon Ann. "Persuasive Voices: Clerical Images of Medieval Wives." *Speculum: A Journal of Medieval Studies* 61 (1986): 517–543.

"Georges Duby et l'histoire des femmes," edited by Michelle Zancarini-Fournel and Christiane Klapisch-Zuber. *Clio* 8 (1998).

Gies, Joseph, and Frances Gies. *Life in a Medieval City.* London: Barker, 1969.

The Goodman of Paris (Le ménagier de Paris): A Treatise on Moral and Domestic Economy by a Citizen of Paris (c. 1393), translated by Eileen Power. New York: Harcourt, Brace and Company, 1928.

Johnson, Penelope D. *Equal in Monastic Profession: Religious Women in Medieval France.* Chicago: University of Chicago Press, 1991.

Le Roy Ladurie, Emmanuel. *Montaillou: The Promised Land of Error*, translated by Barbara Bray. New York: G. Braziller, 1978.

Listening to Heloise: The Voice of a Twelfth-Century Woman, edited by Bonnie Wheeler. New York: St. Martin's Press, 2000.

LoPrete, Kimberly. *Adela of Blois, Countess and Lord.* Dublin: Four Courts, 2001.

The Lost Letters of Abelard and Heloise: Perceptions of Dialogue in Twelfth-Century France, edited by Constant J. Mews; translated by Neville Chiavaroli and Constant J. Mews. New York: St. Martin's Press, 1999.

Medieval Mothering, edited by John Carmi Parsons, and Bonnie Wheeler. New York: Garland Pub., 1996.

Medieval Queenship, edited by John Carmi Parsons. New York: St. Martins Press, 1993.

Pernoud, Régine. *Blanche of Castile*, translated by Henry Noel. New York: Coward, McCann and Geoghegan, 1975.

Rossiaud, Jacques. *Medieval Prostitution*, translated by Lydia G. Cochrane. Oxford; New York: B. Blackwell, 1988.

Schulenburg, Jane Tibbetts. *Forgetful of Their Sex: Female Sanctity and Society, ca. 500–1100.* Chicago: University of Chicago Press, 1998.

Venarde, Bruce L. *Women's Monasticism and Medieval Society: Nunneries in France and England, 890–1215.* Ithaca: Cornell University Press, 1997.

See also **Beguines; Blanche of Castile; Christina the Astonishing; Christine de Pizan; Cistercian Order; Dowry and Other Marriage Gifts; Fontrevault, Abbey and Order of; Guild Members and Guilds; Isabelle of France; Marie de France; Marie of Oignies; Marriage, Christian; Misogyny; Monastic Enclosure; Monasticism and Nuns; Noble Women; Occitania; Patronage, Ecclesiastical; Patronage, Literary; Peasants; Plague; Poor Clares Order; Prostitutes; Queens and Empresses: The West; Regents and Queen-Lieutenants; Widows; Women Authors: Old French Texts; Work**

FRANCES OF ROME

Frances of Rome (1384–1440) remains an exceptional case of an officially canonized medieval saint who was both a wife and a mother. Only Elisabeth of Hungary and Birgitta of Sweden are comparable.

Frances was born to the noble Bussa family of Rome in 1384. She married Lorenzo de' Ponziani, a wealthy cattle farmer, at twelve, bearing him at least three sons, of whom only Battista survived to adulthood. After her husband's death in 1436, Frances joined the religious laywomen or oblates at her foundation Tor de' Specchi, loosely associated with the Benedictine monastery Santa Maria Nuova in Rome. Her charity, moral exhortations, and visions concerning the afterlife made her famous even before her death on March 9, 1440.

Three collections of testimonies concerning Frances's sainthood (from 1440, 1443, and 1451) and the biography by her last confessor, Giovanni Mattiotti, provide a textured account of a saint who transformed her marital and social occupations into religious opportunities. She used her wealth to assist poor children and women, convinced her husband to live in a chaste companionship, and lived humbly, chastising other women for their frivolous concern for appearance. Her moral messages were peppered by horrid Dantesque visions concerning purgatory and hell. But it was her gentler companionship with other women—fellowship with her sister-in-law Vannozza, miraculous interventions on women's behalf, and founding of the Tor de Specchi in 1425 (approved by Pope Eugene IV in 1433)—that secured her position as a beloved civic icon, especially among the Roman families who were involved in the failed plot against Pope Boniface IX (crushed in 1398) and suffered during Ladislas of Naples's occupation of the town in 1408–1409 and 1413–1414. She was canonized by Paul V, a scion of the Roman Borghese family, on May 29, 1608.

Maiju Lehmijoki-Gardner

References and Further Reading

Esposito, Anna. "St. Francesca and the Female Religious Communities of Fifteenth-Century Rome." In *Women and Religion in Medieval and Renaissance Italy*, edited by Daniel Bornstein and Roberto Rusconi. Translated by Margery J. Schneider. Chicago: The University of Chicago Press, 1996, pp. 197–218.

Gill, Katherine. "Open Monasteries for Women in Late Medieval and Early Modern Italy: Two Roman Examples." In *The Crannied Wall. Women, Religion, and the Arts in Early Modern Europe*, edited by Craig A. Monsson. Ann Arbor: University of Michigan Press, 1992, pp. 15–48.

Mattiotti, Giovanni. *Santa Francesca Romana*, edited by Alessandra Bartolomei Romagnoli. Vatican City: Biblioteca Apostolica Vaticana, 1995.

I processi inediti per Francesca Bussa dei Ponziani, 1440–1453, edited by Placido Tommaso Lugano. Vatican City: Biblioteca Apostolica Vaticana, 1945.

Una santa tutta romana: Saggi e ricerche nel VI centenario della nascità di Francesca Bussa dei Ponziani (1384–1984), edited by Giorgio Picasso. Monte Oliveto Maggiore: Edizioni "L'Ulivo," 1984.

See also **Birgitta of Sweden; Chastity and Chaste Marriage; Hagiography; Italy; Laywomen, Religious**

FRANKISH LANDS

During the fifth and early sixth centuries, Frankish rulers conquered Gaul, the Roman province west of the Rhine, including the Rhone valley, and the Mediterranean southern region from Provence as far southwest as the Pyrenees. Frankish settlement was confined to the northeast, and, in Gaul as a whole, the immigrant element was heavily outnumbered by the indigenous provincial population. Unlike some others who settled within the Roman Empire in the fourth and fifth centuries, the Franks are presented in their origin-myth as all-male. Modern historians see the Frankish "people" as an amalgam of smaller groups, usually described as war-bands in the late Roman sources, with warlords and warriors the only recorded individuals. This could suggest a militarized society in which women's social power diminished. But women as marriage-partners could have played key roles in uniting Germanic-speaking groups to form the Frankish people. Variant origin-myths of the Franks' ruling dynasty, the Merovingians, had space for two individual women. The eponymous Merovech was said to have been the offspring of his anonymous mother's encounter with a monster while bathing in the sea. Merovech's son, Childeric, driven out by the Franks whose daughters he had debauched and given refuge by the king of the Thuringians and his wife, Basina, was said to have been sought out later by Basina, who had abandoned her husband, journeyed far to the land of the Franks, and declared her desire for Childeric: "I know that you are a strong man and I can recognise ability when I see it, so I have come to live with you." The product of this coupling was Clovis, depicted by Gregory of Tours (c. 596) as the warrior-king who effectively made the kingdom of the Franks, its heartlands in the northerly region between the rivers Loire and Rhine, in later Merovingian times called *Francia*. (Thanks to Frankish political success, the name subsequently came to be used for the whole kingdom, and then for fragments of it—hence, modern "France" and the German region of "Franken.")

Before c. 600, Frankish rulers often married non-Frankish women from the indigenous Gallo-Roman population of Gaul, or from further afield. Thus Clovis married the Burgundian princess Clotilda, who, according to Gregory of Tours, persuaded him to convert to Orthodox Christianity. In the northeast, where Frankish settlement was thicker, a large amount of intermarriage with indigenes can be surmised from the fact that, by the eighth century, the population spoke a Romance language, the *langue d'oil* (in which *oil* was the word for "yes"), though the peasantry continued to give their children Germanic names, suggesting they still spoke a Germanic dialect. South of the Loire, where Frankish settlement was extremely limited, the indigenous population's Latin gradually evolved into the *langue d'oc* (*oc* meant "yes"), and the peasantry continued to give their children Roman names. In the north, the customary law of the Salian Franks came into use and stuck. King Clovis (c. 511) had an agreed Code (*Pactum*) issued, but this was a selection, not the whole, of what was customary. A glaring absence was marriage law, which historians have to reconstruct from other sources. Clovis supplemented customary law with a special edict protecting widows and orphans who, as in most periods, were the most vulnerable of the vulnerable. At the same time, Clovis constructed and legitimized his and others' masculine power through claims to protect the weak.

Law

Legal form-documents (*formulae*) from the sixth century show that in the Loire valley Roman provincial law was in use for marital contracts specifying the bride's dower. In the next century, a father could assert his right, against earlier custom, to bequeath shares in his patrimony equally to daughters and sons. Seventh-century wills show landowning women bequeathing their own inherited property. Like other early medieval codes, Salic Law prescribed the amount to be paid in compensation for death or injury in the cases of women as well as men, with extra payable if the woman was of childbearing age; but only Salic Law set such extra payments at three times the level for other women. This could be seen as special protection linked with the shortage of Frankish women. Intermarriage, especially among elites, seems to have happened fairly frequently; and, as a bride moved to live in her husband's house, cultural influence passed across to the new location. An aristocratic bishop, Bertram of Le Mans, in his Roman-style will (616) asserted that his mother, Ingitrud (a Frankish name), was an Aquitanian (i.e., used Roman law), his father Frankish, and that a close kinswoman had married Avitus, a Gallo-Roman magnate in the Le Mans region. At this social level, neither non-Frankish women marrying Franks, nor Frankish women marrying "Romans," lost status. The couple was endowed, and their offspring and kin inherited, from both sides and in diverse localities. Aristocratic Frankish women too made wills. Burgundofara (633–634), influenced by the Irish holy man Columbanus, bequeathed her share of family-lands to found a monastery, Faremoutiers, near Paris. In c. 700, Ermentrud bequeathed her very substantial property in land and moveables to her grandson, her granddaughter and daughter-in-law, and to several churches in and around Paris.

Letters

In the mid-seventh century, Herchenfreda, the Frankish widow of a Gallo-Roman magnate, and mother of three sons all with Roman names, sent one of them a little series of letters. The son, Desiderius, was born in Aquitaine, indicating that his mother had lived there since her marriage. He had become bishop of Cahors

(629–654) by the time his mother wrote these letters offering him moral and social guidance. Here was a woman familiar with Roman traditions of letter-writing, but also deeply touched by Christian ideas of virtue and of maternal responsibility for virtue's inculcation.

Royal Women

A number of royal or aristocratic women founded and/or endowed monasteries, and some were posthumously venerated as saints. Radegund (c. 587), a Thuringian princess brought to Francia as war-booty and bride of King Clothar I (c. 561), eventually persuaded her husband to let her found a monastery at Poitiers and become its abbess. There she distinguished herself with acts of conspicuous self-humiliation, like cleaning the latrines. Yet from the monastery, she continued to influence politics in the Frankish kingdoms, and like her younger contemporary Queen Brunhild, she corresponded with the emperor and empress in Byzantium. Through their mediation, she secured the gift of a relic of the Holy Cross. The relic, still in its sixth-century reliquary, survives at the still-functioning monastery. To visit Radegund's sixth-century sarcophagus in its subterranean shrine is to be put in touch with a millennium and a half of continuous cult. To read Radegund's *Life*, written by one of the Poitiers nuns, is to sense a life behind the hagiographical conventions.

Yet the *Lives* of Frankish holy women, impressively other-worldly as are the orientations they depict, can also mislead. Political connections and dynastic pride could propel distinctly worldly activities, as Gregory of Tours reveals in his vivid contemporary, but highly tendentious, account of the revolt of the Merovingian nun-princesses Clotild and Basina at Holy Cross, Poitiers, after Radegund's death. Most foundations were family affairs, which meant protection for the women involved, but could also spell vulnerability amidst aristocratic rivalries. Protection and vulnerability alike call into question some modern historians' claims for the extent of individual women's agency and empowerment. St. Gertrude of Nivelles (c. 653), subject of another impressive *Life* written within perhaps twenty years of her death, was a daughter of Pippin, ancestor of the Carolingians, and sister of Begga whose offspring actually continued the family line. Gertrude's ascetic vocation, depicted by the hagiographer as her own choice, was more certainly her family's choice (and they had carefully sought the king's approval), as was the founding of the convent of Nivelles on family lands. Nivelles' problems after

Gertrude's death resulted from the enmity of her family's rivals in the region of the rivers Sambre and Meuse. From the political historian's standpoint, the *Life* reveals more of the precariousness of family power than its security and more about enforced intermissions than about continuity. Female agency is there, but it is constrained by family interest and family vicissitudes. The powerful women who emerge as the *Life*'s subtext are in fact Gertrude's heiress-mother Itta, and her married sister Begga, *christianissima matrona*. Individual women's lives were framed, like men's only more so, by the calculations and interests of families, whether natal or marital.

Gregory of Tours, like many early medieval authors, cast women as extremes of good or evil. Conspicuous in his gallery of wicked queens was Fredegund, a Frank by birth, and a one-time serving woman who attracted a king's attention. Modern historians depict her defending her husband and children by all possible means, including assassination. As presented by Gregory, her agenda was entirely personal, though its consequences were public: when two of her sons were dying, she interpreted this as divine vengeance for her husband's harsh government and persuaded him to burn the new tax registers; when a third son died, she had some Parisian women tortured for allegedly practising witchcraft. Gregory's most admirable queens are Clovis's persuasive wife Clotilda, and the self-humiliated yet influential Radegund. Neither of these two was Frankish-born, but both had long posthumous histories as ambiguous role-models for queens and other Frankish women.

The Carolingian Period (Eighth to Tenth Centuries)

Just as earlier twentieth-century historians drew various thick lines between Merovingian and Carolingian periods, so historians of women have contrasted a Merovingian "golden age" of opportunities with a Carolingian drawing-down of blinds. There are three points to be made against this reading. The first, already indicated, is that the alleged opportunities were severely constrained. The second is that there were substantial continuities running right through the Frankish period. The third is that the Carolingian world demonstrably offered women some benefits that may have been new. The second point can be quickly elaborated: authorial misogyny persisted in Carolingian sources; bad husbands could still literally get away with marital murder; it remained easier for men to abuse and repudiate their wives, and take

concubines than it was for women to play fast and loose with the rules of marriage; big men continued to construct their power by presenting themselves as protectors of women, especially widows, the archetypically weak; aside from constructions, widows, even aristocratic ones, really did remain exceptionally vulnerable; families still constrained and channelled the lives of their womenfolk; and pious women were refused access to some monastic shrines in Carolingian as in Merovingian times. The rest of this section concentrates on the third point.

First the assertion that the Carolingian period "demonstrably" benefited some women presupposes new demonstrative evidence. The polyptychs, surveys of the tenants of monastic estates, fall into this category. They show many thousands of peasant households centred on married couples, with wives co-operating in the management and working of hereditary holdings. At the same time, other new types of source-material, expositions of canon law, and prayers over spouses, gave strong ecclesiastical support to the idea of consent between spouses as the foundation of marriage. Ecclesiastical intervention in this area on the whole benefited women, and women more than men.

Charters

From the eighth century onwards, charters become widely, if patchily, available as historical sources. In these it is possible to see individuals and family-groups arranging for the care of single women, for elderly women, and for widows, through agreements with religious institutions. A grant might be made to a monastery, for instance, on condition that a female family-member retained a life-interest. It is true that landlords' power grew in the ninth and tenth centuries too. It's nevertheless arguable that an equilibrium was reached between lords' and peasants' interests, and, further, that for peasants, there was an equilibrium between, on the one hand, opportunities born of generalised labor shortage together with the availability of cultivable land, and on the other, a reasonable level of order and security maintained by Carolingian states in much of the Frankish world. Women benefited, along with men but also in gender-specific ways, from these developments. If a capitulary of 861 prescribes penalties (physical punishment) separately for men and for women who refuse to accept a new, improved issue of the royal coinage "because women too are in the habit of engaging in market transactions," that is a sign of new economic outlets for the textiles, dairy-goods, poultry, and eggs produced by women. Secular custom, newly articulated, assigned widows a share of the proceeds of spouses' labor in common.

Within the family, women are better-documented as recognized co-bearers of responsibility for the upbringing of the young. This is a context in which godmothers appear in the sources for the first time, and at all social levels. Aristocrats "and especially women" are said by a large church council in 845 to have special care for the moral formation and guidance of their households (*familiae*, that is, including the servants and retainers). These enhanced roles are incorporated into the now more extensive literature on queens and queenship. In charters, noble women increasingly use titles that are the female equivalent of their husbands' offices: *comitissa, marchionissa, ductrix*. As noble power becomes more explicitly conveyed through lineages, charters affirm more clearly and more often the wife's partnership (*consortium*) with the husband. Especially in charters, churchmen acknowledge women's special role in the care of family memory and commemoration of the dead. Powerful abbesses are not a distant echo of the past, but, not least thanks to charters and ecclesiastical archives, a much more intensively documented feature of the eighth-, ninth-, and tenth-century present: familial strategies for women's deployment become more visible, but so too, however fitfully, emerging now from the pious haze of hagiography, at Chelles, at Remiremont, at Essen, do the women themselves. Nuns leave their own memorials in the texts they copied.

Laywomen

Women as "spiritual and cultural leaders" (Wemple 1981, 123) were rare in the Merovingian period, in a context where the notion of "leadership" itself is questionable. (Did Radegund, in her time, address more than a coterie?) Women's contribution was certainly more widely diffused on the Carolingian scene, and no longer confined to the cloister. This is the time of the laity, Alcuin wrote to Charlemagne in 797. Women as well as men evoked and would confirm his claim in the next generation. Lay women sometimes demanded, if they did not always get, access to shrines in reformed Carolingian monasteries. One laywoman produced a work that is by any standards a large cultural achievement. Dhuoda's *Handbook*, offering moral guidance for her son, written between February 841 and March 843, carried on where Herchenfreda left off, but amplified the genre out of all recognition. She advised on how to behave, and

how to advance a career, at court; she advised on faithfulness in a variety of social contexts; but above all she advised on a young man's personal spiritual life, through prayer and pious reading. Through her son, she hoped to reach out to his "fellow-warriors" at the royal court. In the end this book was a public as well as a private one. That was one of the extra dimensions the Carolingians had opened up for at least some women, alongside men, in the Frankish world.

JANET NELSON

References and Further Reading

Devroey, Jean-Pierre. "Men and Women in Early Medieval Serfdom: The Ninth-century North Frankish Evidence." *Past and Present* 166 (2000): 3–30.

Effros, Bonnie. *Creating Community with Food and Drink in Merovingian Gaul.* Basingstoke; New York: Palgrave Macmillan, 2002.

Gender in the Early Medieval World: East and West, edited by Leslie Brubaker and Julia M.H. Smith. Cambridge: Cambridge University Press, 2004.

La Rocca, Cristina, and Provero, Luigi. "The Dead and Their Gifts: The Will of Eberhard, Count of Friuli, and His Wife Gisela, Daughter of Louis the Pious (863–864)." In *Rituals of Power from Late Antiquity to the Early Middle Ages,* edited by F. Theuws and J.L. Nelson. Leiden: Brill, 2000, pp. 225–280.

Le Jan, Régine. "Convents, Violence and Competition for Power in Seventh-century Francia." In *Topographies of Power in the Earlier Middle Ages,* edited by M. de Jong and F. Theuws with C. van Rhijn. Leiden: Brill, 2001, pp. 243–269.

McNamara, Jo Anne, and John Halborg. *Sainted Women of the Dark Ages.* Durham; London: Duke University Press, 1992.

Nelson, Janet L. *The Frankish World, 750–900.* London: Hambledon, 1996.

Nelson, Janet L. *Courts, Elites and the Workings of Power in the Earlier Medieval World.* Forthcoming.

Schulenburg, Jane Tibbetts. *Forgetjid of their Sex: Female Sanctity and Society, ca. 500–1100.* Chicago: University of Chicago Press, 1998.

Smith, Julia M.H. *Europe after Rome: A New Cultural History 500–1000.* Oxford: Oxford University Press, 2005.

Toubert, Pierre. "The Carolingian Moment." In *A History of the Family,* edited by A. Burguiére. Cambridge, MA: Belknap Press of Harvard University Press, 1996, pp. 379–406.

Wemple, Suzanne F. *Women in Frankish Society.* Philadelphia: University of Pennsylvania Press, 1981.

See also **Abbesses; Administration of Estates; Barbarian Law Codes; Brunhild and Fredegund; Charters; Clotilda; Dhuoda; Gertrude of Nivelles; Hagiography; Inheritance; Monasticism and Nuns; Mothers as Teachers; Patronage, Ecclesiastical; Peasants; Queens and Empresses: The West; Radegund; Roman Law; Wergild; Widows**

G

GAZE

The word *gaze* suggests an intense and durational looking, which in the Middle Ages could encompass a range of visual practices; it enters scholarly analyses with strong psychoanalytical and phenomenological connotations, owing to the widespread fascination with Jacques Lacan's interpretation of "le regard," which figures the gaze as central to the self's psychic (mis)recognition through the imagined gaze of the other. This gloss on the word has helped to clarify some aspects of premodern visual culture, but it has also been criticized for overvaluing the analytical primacy of the psychic subject and for concretizing rather than unsettling binary relations between subject and subjected (viewer/viewed, man/woman, master/slave, colonizer/colonized). The fruitfulness of the Lacanian gaze and its deconstruction is evident, for example, in Michael Camille's studies of medieval manuscripts, Sarah Stanbury's examinations of literary visuality, and Patricia Simons' interpretations of fifteenth-century Italian portraits.

Medieval representations of the gaze figure visuality as a particularly physical exchange. The eyes are described repeatedly both as sensitive, penetrable orifices—windows to the soul—and as possessing the ability to launch arrow-like, wounding glances. Such tropes did have practical effects, as registered in conduct literature for women urging downcast eyes, and in the ubiquitous talismans warding off the perilous "evil eye." Augustine influentially divided vision into the "corporeal," "spiritual," and "intellectual," each implying a decreasing degree of visual embeddedness in the material world. Ambivalence about the relative validity of intromission (the passage of visual data into the eye) and extromission (the projection of sensitive visual rays from the eye) speaks both of the variety of ways medieval thinkers discussed the type of vision we would call the gaze, and the manner in which such visuality was perceived as conjoining and interfolding the viewing subject and viewed object, be it worldly or divine.

ADRIAN RANDOLPH

References and Further Reading

Biernoff, Suzannah. *Sight and Embodiment in the Middle Ages*. New York: Palgrave, 2002.

Boyarin, Daniel. "The Eye in the Torah: Ocular Desire in Midrashic Hermeneutic." *Critical Inquiry* 16 (1990): 532–550.

Camille, Michael. "The Eye in the Text: Vision in the Illuminated Manuscripts of the Latin Aristotle." *Micrologus VI: La Visione e lo Sguardo nel Medioevo*. Sismel: Edizioni del Galluzzo, 1998, pp. 129–145.

———. "Before the Gaze: The Internal Senses and Late Medieval Practices of Seeing." In *Visuality Before and Beyond the Renaissance: Seeing as Others Saw*, edited by Robert Nelson. Cambridge: Cambridge University Press, 2000.

Caviness, Madeline. *Visualizing Women in the Middle Ages: Sight, Spectacle, and Scopic Economy*. Philadelphia: University of Pennsylvania Press, 2001.

Cline, Ruth H. "Heart and Eyes." *Romance Philology* 25.2 (1971): 263–297.

Erickson, Carolly. *The Medieval Vision: Essays in History and Perception*. New York: Oxford University Press, 1976.

Hahn, Cynthia. "Viso Dei: Changes in Medieval Visuality." In *Visuality Before and Beyond the Renaissance: Seeing as Others Saw*, edited by Robert Nelson. Cambridge: Cambridge University Press, 2000.

Hamburger, Jeffrey. "The Visual and the Visionary: The Image in Late Medieval Monastic Devotions." *Viator* 20 (1989): 161–182.

Kessler, Herbert. "*Facies Bibliothecae Revelata*: Carolingian Art as Spiritual Seeing." In *Testo e Immagine nell'Alto Medioevo*. 2 vols. Spoleto: Centro Italiano di Studi sull'Alto Medioevo, 1994.

Lacan, Jacques. *The Four Fundamental Concepts of Psycho-Analysis*, edited by Jacques-Alain Miller and translated by Alan Sheridan. New York: Norton, 1978.

Lindberg, David. *Theories of Vision from Al-Kindi to Kepler*. Chicago: University of Chicago Press, 1976.

Pavlis-Baig, Bonnie. "Vision and Visualization: Optics and Light Metaphysics in the Imagery and Poetic Form of Twelfth and Thirteenth Century Secular Allegory, with Special Attention to the *Roman de la Rose*." Ph.D. dissertation, University of California, Berkeley, 1982.

Simons, Patricia. "Women in Frames: The Gaze, the Eye, the Profile in Renaissance Portraiture." In *The Expanding Discourse: Feminism and Art History*, edited by Norma Broude and Mary Garrard. New York: Icon, 1992.

Soskice, Janet Martin. "Sight and Vision in Medieval Christian Thought." In *Vision in Context: Historical and Contemporary Perspectives on Sight*, edited by Teresa Brennan and Martin Jay. New York: Routledge, 1996.

Stanbury, Sarah. "Feminist Film Theory: Seeing Chrétien's Enide." *Literature and Psychology* 36.4 (1990): 47–66.

———. "The Virgin's Gaze: Spectacle and Transgression in Middle English Lyrics of the Passion." *PMLA* 106.5 (1991): 1083–1093.

———. "Regimes of the Visual in Premodern England: Gaze, Body, and Chaucer's Clerk's Tale." *New Literary History* 28.2 (1997): 261–289.

See also **Beauty; Conduct Literature; Courtly Love**

GENDER IDEOLOGIES

There is no single hegemonic ideology of gender applicable to the whole of the Middle Ages. Rather we find a multiplicity of overlapping ideologies, some of which are more visible than others. Clerical perceptions are particularly well documented because the clergy tended to monopolise literary production for much of the period. Biographical and hagiographical writings that can be used to illuminate the gender perceptions of the laity are themselves often composed by clerical authors and reflect as much the values of their authors as of their subjects. Thus Einhard's biography of Charlemagne and *The Book of Margery Kempe* represent problematic windows into the gender ideologies of early medieval rulers or later medieval devout townswomen.

The medieval period inherited a range of ideas about gender from preceding cultures, such as the Roman, the Hellenistic, and those of various European tribes. Where Christians lived alongside other faiths, as in high medieval Spain or in Byzantium, they might be influenced by the Muslim and Jewish faiths (and indeed vice versa). The prevalence of particular gender ideologies was affected by geography and status; thus Roman law was more influential in Mediterranean Europe than in northern Europe, while peasant ideologies may have been different from those of higher status in the same region.

Gender, Body, and Theory

There is still debate about how far the medieval period had a dual gender system, that is, one in which gender was tied to the body, i.e., a masculine and feminine gender that related to male and female bodies. Thomas Laqueur posited a single-gender system where there was one gender, male, which incorporated all the positive values, and to which were opposed their negatives, which were associated with "not-male" and attached to both female and some men. This theory does not specifically address the medieval period, but assumes an inheritance from the classical period to the beginning of the early modern period. It has the effect of partially detaching gender from body: by implication a free woman exercising masculine characteristics such as intellect and self-control would be more masculine than an unfree man without these characteristics. There were also some traditions that did not see male and female bodies as necessarily opposed, for example, the tradition that Eve was created out of Adam's side suggested an identity of substance even while giving precedence to the male. Similarly, the Galenic medical view that the uterus was seven-lobed and that the lobe in which the foetus developed affected both its sex and its "complexion" or psychological makeup suggests a view in which male and female were parts of a spectrum, with females on the left, males on the right, and hermaphrodites in the middle. The farther to the right a female foetus lay, the more "masculine" characteristics it might have, and the farther to the left a male foetus, the more "effeminate."

Some early Christian writers, while acknowledging the existence of sexed bodies, had an ideal of non-gendered souls, or suggested that women might aspire to souls equally masculine to those of men. There has also been discussion as to whether the celibate clergy or Byzantine eunuchs might constitute a third gender. Some archaeologists have speculated whether the presence of gendered grave goods in some graves but not others might indicate that early medieval Germanic peoples conceived of some people having gender and others not, or whether there might be more than two genders. Gender ideologies operated at the level of organising social principles, but could also be used metaphorically, especially in theology, for example in the idea of Jesus as Mother. How far these two spheres interacted is difficult to say, but at least at the intellectual level this provided a good deal of play in conceptions of gender and how they might map onto bodies.

Sources of Ideology: Biblical

The main roots of Christian ideas lie in the Bible, supplemented by post-Biblical traditions. The story of the Fall, i.e., Eve's temptation by the Devil and persuasion of Adam to eat the apple that God had forbidden him, lay behind many of the negative ideas about women. The story was interpreted to mean that women were intellectually weaker than men (more easily deceived), morally weaker (more willing to do the wrong thing), disobedient, and deceitful. It was also understood that Eve deceived Adam by a combination of speech and sexual allure, which led to perceptions of the dangers of women's speech and sexuality. The punishment of God in driving Adam and Eve out of the Garden of Eden and the words of God to Eve, "In pain you shall bear children, yet your desire shall be for your husband and he shall rule over you" (*Genesis* 3:16), were taken to explain and justify women's secondary status. However, this could also be understood as the *felix culpa* or "happy fault" that had necessitated Christ and the Redemption, and therefore the birth of the Virgin Mary, who had become Queen of Heaven.

Different understandings of the Creation were also possible; Augustine and Aquinas both saw men and women being created in the image of God, though men were able to be the image of God individually, but women only when conjoined with men, yet Jacques de Vitry (d. 1240) could argue that Eve's birth in Paradise, rather than being introduced into it, and from Adam's body rather than from dust, made her superior to Adam. Mary was often seen as the Second Eve, whose obedience, submission to the will of God, and virginity reversed the faults of Eve.

Sources of Ideology: Medical

Humoural theory taught that women were moister and colder than men, which made them softer, more malleable, more emotional, more passive, and less rational than men. However, these characteristics also made women more compassionate and, in some views, more retentive of memory. Greater heat in the male led to firmer flesh and thus greater strength. The greater moisture led to women menstruating and lactating, where men only produced semen. While lactation was viewed positively, menstruation was viewed more ambiguously. Theologians generally viewed menstruation as pollution, and it was used to justify the banning of women from handling sacramental vessels, but medical writers saw it positively as a purgative, necessary for reproductive health. The lack of heat in women meant they had a greater sexual appetite than men, because they desired the heat of the male.

Sources of Ideology: Legal

Roman law, for the most part, saw women as minors, who did not have an independent legal persona but were represented by father, husband, or other legal guardian. Married women were usually regarded as incorporated into their husband's legal persona. Late medieval northern civil law was often influenced by this and limited the occasions on which a woman could go to law in her own person to cases such as rape and, sometimes, assault. Widows were more likely to be seen as having their own legal personality. Roman law continued to be influential, particularly in southern Europe and on canon law, the legal system of the church. In northern Europe, Barbarian or Germanic law codes were a more important source of law in the early Middle Ages. Some of these appear to give women more rights than Roman law. The wergild (price for killing someone) was often the same for men and women; indeed, in some codes it was greater for a woman than a man, especially if she was of childbearing age. There is disagreement as to whether this indicates that young fertile women had higher status or were simply more valuable than other women or men.

One of the areas in which canon law developed away from Roman law was in relation to marriage. Roman law had seen marriage as a civil contract, usually between the fathers of the spouses, but during the twelfth century the Church came to see marriage as a sacrament. In the process it saw marriage as essentially consisting of consent between the two parties, rather than between the fathers. In theory and sometimes in practice this gave women control over whom they married. However for the majority, particularly of those who had property, family, and especially fathers or guardians, continued to have an important role in deciding on marriage partners, and this applied to daughters and usually to eldest sons too. Here secular ideology about the importance of the father's authority over the family came up against ecclesiastical ideology about the equality of souls.

There were also both national and local systems of law, some of which expressed different ideas of gender. Some late medieval northern towns permitted a *feme covert* to trade as a *feme sole*, that is, as an independent legal persona who could make contracts and be sued in the court for debt. Some German towns had the custom of *weiblichefreiheit*, or "womanly freedom," which allowed a woman to repudiate a contract on the grounds that she had not understood it. This has been seen as evidence of women's ability to manipulate laws that perceived them as of inferior intellectual ability, but equally it would have made women unreliable contractees, as it confirmed ideas of women's changeability and lack of intellectual competence. Legally most women needed the consent of husbands to make contracts, partly because of their lack of legal persona, but another issue was whether an inferior could bind a superior to a contract that he had not initiated.

Aspects of Gender Ideology: Authority

Although women as wives and daughters were subject to the authority of fathers or husbands, this did not mean that they could not exercise authority. Wives in particular were often expected to exercise a delegated authority on behalf of husbands, in their absence, so that a wife could command servants and go to market, both to buy and to sell. In the case of aristocratic wives, this could mean running estates, handling finances, and even defending a castle against attack. It was, however, extremely rare for women to exercise public authority, though women might in some cases be thought to have expert knowledge, which could make them authoritative witnesses, for example, in relation to virginity, pregnancy, and childbirth. The church courts in York even called local prostitutes as witnesses in cases involving petitions for annulment of marriage on the basis of the husband's impotence.

Women rarely ruled in their own right, and usually only when there was no available male heir in the direct line. Even this was not always acceptable, as Matilda, the daughter of Henry I of England, found when she attempted to take the throne her father had left her in 1135. Matilda was only able to transmit a claim to her son, who became Henry II. Transmission of a claim to a son was usually more acceptable, although the French were to invoke Salic Law to prevent Edward III of England from using such descent to take the French crown. It would appear that queens-regnant became more acceptable later in the Middle Ages, though this may reflect the growing importance of blood lineage over the ability to be a personal war leader, rather than changes in gender ideology specifically, as boy kings were also more likely to succeed. When Mary of Burgundy, the only child of Charles the Bold, was left as duchess by the unexpected death of her father in 1477, she was recognised within her own lands, but Louis XI of France seized Burgundy and attempted to marry her to his son. The problem of marriage was one of the reasons women found it difficult to rule. Single women lacked authority, but a husband of equal status would usually be a foreign royal, which usually implied loss of sovereignty for the state; a husband drawn from the domestic nobility was of inferior status, so that different ideological discourses were in conflict. Mary retained most of her lands by marriage to the son of the Holy Roman emperor, who subsequently drew the Burgundian lands within the Habsburg empire.

Queens could be appointed as regents on behalf of kings absent in war and could also act as regents on behalf of minor sons, as Queen Margrethe I of Denmark did. She was married to King Håkon VI of Norway and, after the death of her father, Waldemar IV, in 1375, became regent of Denmark on behalf of her son Olaf, then aged five. Similarly, Blanche of Castile was regent for her son Louis IX of France from his accession in 1226, aged 11, to his majority in 1234, and again while he was on crusade. Here a woman's authority was acceptable because it was temporary and also because, as her power was dependent on her son's, she was more likely to ensure his survival than a potential rival for the crown. The Byzantine empress Irene was regent for her son Constantine VI and became joint ruler in 792 on his majority. She had him deposed and blinded in 797, and then ruled alone as empress but was herself deposed in 802. In this latter case both the "unnatural" attack on her son and the claim to personal power were unacceptable. Nevertheless Byzantium was more willing to see empresses exercising power jointly or as regents than were most other medieval European cultures.

Queen consorts were expected to advise their husbands, but not to meddle in politics, a delicate balancing act. Foreign queens were particularly likely to be resented if they were perceived to be interfering in domestic politics. The queen embodied the female aspects of monarchy, from her primary task of ensuring the birth of a male heir to intercession on behalf of supplicants. This latter tempered the masculine royal justice of the king and allowed him to show mercy without appearing weak.

Aspects of Gender Ideology: Sexuality

Virginity was highly valued in women before marriage, and the life of the virgin was considered to be rewarded more highly in heaven than that of the wife or widow. Greater desire in women meant that some theologians saw the maintenance of virginity by women as more difficult and thus more praiseworthy than in men; however, others saw female sexuality as threatening to the chastity of men, especially monks. Although some lay men, such as King Edward the Confessor of England, were honoured as virgins, virginity in kings conflicted with a secular ideal that they provide a male heir to ensure a stable succession. There has as yet been relatively little study of the extent to which virginity remained an ideal for clergy in the later Middle Ages, as it was for some in the earlier Middle Ages. Chastity was highly valued for women in marriage, and a virtuous reputation was largely based on sexual reputation; nevertheless, women were regarded as morally weaker and more prone to stray. Adultery was, in the earlier Middle Ages, often punished more severely in women than in men, but as canon law developed it came to be treated the same in men and women by the church courts, that is, as grounds for a legal separation; however, in social terms, adultery was usually treated more severely in women than in men. As a result, female sexuality was policed more thoroughly than male sexuality. Widowhood has been treated by modern historians as the most rewarding status for women, with its status as head of the household and (in most cases) recognition as a legal persona, and for women with property this may have been the case. However, medieval people, on biblical grounds, saw widows as economically and sometimes socially and legally vulnerable and in need of protection.

P. H. CULLUM and P. J. P. GOLDBERG

References and Further Reading

Bennett, Judith M. *Women in the Medieval English Countryside: Gender & Household in Brigstock Before the Plague.* New York and Oxford: Oxford University Press, 1987.

Bernau, Anke, Ruth Evans, and Sarah Salih, eds. *Medieval Virginities.* Cardiff: University of Wales Press, 2003.

Blamires, Alcuin. *The Case for Women in Medieval Culture.* Oxford: Clarendon Press, 1997.

Brown, Peter. *The Body and Society: Men, Women and Sexual Renunciation in Early Christianity.* New York: Columbia University Press, 1990.

Cadden, Joan. *Meanings of Sex Difference in the Middle Ages: Medicine, Science and Culture.* Cambridge: Cambridge University Press, 1993.

Cullum, P. H. "Clergy, Masculinity and Transgression in Late Medieval England." In *Masculinity in Medieval Europe*, edited by D. M. Hadley. London: Longman, 1999.

Erler, Mary C., and Maryanne Kowaleski, eds. *Women and Power in the Middle Ages.* Athens, Ga.: University of Georgia Press, 1988.

Goldberg, P. J. P. "Women." In *Fifteenth-Century Attitudes: Perceptions of Society in Late Medieval England*, edited by Rosemary Horrox. Cambridge: Cambridge University Press, 1994, pp. 112–131.

Goldberg, P. J. P. *Women, Work, and Life Cycle in a Medieval Economy: Women in York and Yorkshire, c. 1300–1520.* Oxford: Oxford University Press, 1992.

Halsall, Guy. "Female Status and Power in Early Merovingian Central Austrasia." *Journal of Medieval and Early Modern Studies* 5.1 (1996): 1–24.

Huneycutt, Lois. "Intercession and the High-Medieval Queen: The Esther Topos." In *Power of the Weak: Studies on Medieval Women*, edited by Jennifer Carpenter and Sally-Beth MacLean. Urbana, Ill.: University of Illinois Press, 1995, pp. 126–146.

Kuefler, Mathew. *The Manly Eunuch: Masculinity, Gender Ambiguity, and Christian Ideology in Late Antiquity.* Chicago: University of Chicago Press, 2001.

Laqueur, Thomas. *Making Sex: Body and Gender from the Greeks to Freud.* Cambridge, Mass., and London: Harvard University Press, 1990.

Laynesmith, Joanna. *The Last Medieval Queens: English Queenship 1445–1503.* Oxford: Oxford University Press, 2004.

McLean, Ian. *Renaissance Notion of Woman.* Cambridge: Cambridge University Press, 1980.

McNamara, Jo Ann. "The *Herrenfrage*: The Restructuring of the Gender System, 1050–1150." In *Medieval Masculinities: Regarding Men in the Middle Ages*, edited by Clare A. Lees. Minneapolis: University of Minnesota Press, 1994, pp. 3–29.

O'Faolain, Julia, and Lauro Martines, eds. *Not in God's Image: Women in History.* London: Virago, 1979.

Power, Eileen. *Medieval Women.* Cambridge: Cambridge University Press, 1975.

Riddy, Felicity. "Mother Knows Best: Reading Social Change in a Courtesy Text." *Speculum* 71.1 (1996): 66–86.

Stafford, Pauline. *Queen Emma and Queen Edith: Queenship and Women's Power in Eleventh-Century England.* Oxford: Blackwell, 2001.

Swanson, R. N. "Angels Incarnate: Clergy and Masculinty from Gregorian Reform to Reformation." In *Masculinity in Medieval Europe*, edited by D. M. Hadley. London: Longman, 1999, pp. 160–177.

See also **Archaeology; Aristotelian Concepts of Women and Gender; Betrothals; Blanche of Castile; Body in Literature and Religion; Business; Celibacy: Clerical and Priests' Concubines; Chastity and Chaste Marriage; Christine de Pizan; Church; Courtly Love; Crime and Criminals; Defenses of Women; Division of Labor; Dowry and Other Marriage Gifts; Eunuchs; Eve; Feme Covert; Feme Sole; Femininity and Masculinity; Inheritance; Intercession; Irene; Jesus/God as Mother; Landholding and Property Rights; Law; Law, Canon; Law, Customary: French; Law, English Secular Courts of; Law, German; Legal Agency; Market and Tradeswomen; Marriage, Christian; Mary, Virgin; Matilda the Empress; Menstruation; Misogyny; Procreation and Ideas of Conception; Prostitutes; Queens and**

GENDER IN ART

In *Undoing Gender*, Judith Butler refers to gender as "a practice of improvisation within a scene of constraint." We might unpack this statement as follows: the system into which a human being is born constrains the range of characteristics that form the constellation of behaviors and attitudes constitutive of any individual's gender identity; nevertheless, any individual, in performing his or her gender, has some degree of agency, some ability to improvise. During the Middle Ages, the Christian Church promoted a gender system based in biblical texts and exegesis. Medieval Christian art usually visualized the ideological messages of the Church and thus participated in distributing approved models of gender, which gained force through repetition. But gaps and contradictions as well as adaptation to social and cultural change enabled shifts through time and even the creation of new models.

We might argue that the doctrine of the Incarnation itself forces Christianity to take gender seriously. As an aspect of embodiment, gender had to be assigned to early Christian visualizations of Christ, the god who had taken human form. Roman artists modelled him on the physically perfect, handsome young Apollo and as a result created in representation an intellectualized, emotionally controlled Christ who triumphed but did not suffer. This incarnate god was separate from the first person of the Trinity, who retained the power of invisibility. Early Christian and early medieval images of the Son increasingly imparted an authority to him, especially in the composition known as "Christ in Majesty," which presents him as ruler of the universe. The spread of Christianity to northern Europe required a shift in the gender of Christ toward the warrior masculinity that was the ideal there, but this shift continued the idea of the triumphant Christ, the victor over the devil and death. By the twelfth century this image had developed into representations of Christ as the rather vengeful and all-powerful judge of the Last Judgment.

A major change in this formula for visual representations of the divine occurred in the High Middle Ages, resulting in increased attention to the vulnerable human body of Jesus, his flesh and its suffering, his Passion. The notion inherited from antiquity that man is identified with mind or spirit and with activity, whereas body or flesh and passivity characterized woman, meant that the masculinity of Jesus was imperiled through increasingly vivid images of his silent suffering. That the human Jesus was no longer securely masculine reveals the unattainability of the masculine ideal. Perhaps to reclaim that masculinity for Jesus, or at least to proclaim physical humanity, artists in the late medieval period began to include explicit male genitalia in representations of him as infant and child.

Exegetes had also identified Christ with the *Sponsus* of the Song of Songs, the lover and bridegroom whose beloved and bride, the *Sponsa*, was understood to be the Church, the Virgin Mary, and *Anima*, the human soul. Drawing on both the triumphant and the suffering Christ, the figure of Christ the *Sponsus* became Christ the lover-knight, who fights and suffers for the beloved, winning back the soul through his own self-sacrifice, which is a triumph over death. This complex constellation constitutes the ideology of chivalry that represents an ideal of masculinity for the later Middle Ages.

If identification with body condemned women to an inferior status, such that the ideal femininity was submissiveness, assertion of extreme control over that

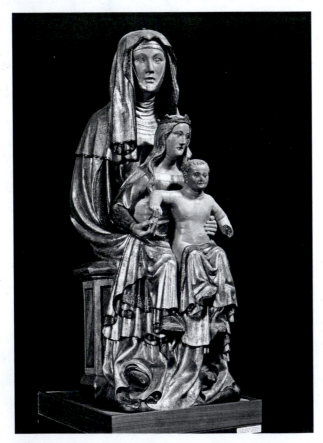

School, French. Madonna with child and St. Anne. Thirteenth century. Museo Nazionale del Bargello, Florence, Italy. Credit: Scala / Art Resource, N.Y.

body could redeem women. Asceticism, and above all virginity, gave women access to power, which was claimed by canonesses, nuns, and abbesses (whose power was also a product of social status). Images of women commissioning or receiving manuscript books from monks or clerics use hieratic scale, frontality, and the power of the center to visualize the high status of these women. The *Passional of Abbess Kunigunde,* for example, also encourages her to adopt the subject position of the beloved human soul congruent with her female sex, and to imagine herself as tempted and fallen, soiled and sinful, captured by the devil and passively suffering until rescued by her lover-knight, Christ. But with two full-page miniatures of the arms of Christ, her book urged her as well to put on spiritual armor and fight as a warrior for her own soul. The lability of gender in this widely distributed narrative disrupts any simple correlation of female and femininity and promotes cross-gender identification.

By the twelfth century, the first person of the Trinity, the Father-God, had begun to be visualized in human form and was thereby gendered as masculine. Represented as aged, the Ancient of Days, rather than as the warrior or lover-knight, this old but powerful male has abundant white hair and a thick beard, signs of virile masculinity. Analogous to the highest positions males attain on earth, the Father-God was represented not only as judge, but also king, emperor, and especially pope, often wearing the papal tiara. But this masculinity of the aged is secured first through the wooing and acquisition of a young wife, the virgin Mary, second through paternity, and finally through exercising the power of life and death over his offspring, the sacrifice of his son.

The figures of the Father-God, the Virgin Mary, and Jesus exemplify a dominant hypertheme in Western visual art, which is the formal scheme in which three human figures form a triad, a configuration of three persons. The position of each element in the triad points to an interweaving of gender and power. According to the pattern of masculine domination deeply imbedded in the Western imaginary, this formal scheme both expresses an ideal relation of gendered power and naturalizes that relation as a family. This is exemplified in a page from the *Turin-Milan Hours.* This power–gender triad schematizes what we see when we look through the "familial gaze"— a clear demarcation of gender roles, a feminine mother and masculine father, with little or no blurring, blending, or sharing of traits.

Joseph, Jesus's human stepfather, found no place in the power–gender triad described above until the late Middle Ages, and then only slowly. Although Gregory the Great claimed that there is only one life of the saints, that is, one pattern of life on earth that leads to sainthood in heaven, saints' lives actually fractured into many gender models. Until the late Middle Ages, however, these models did not include sexually active marriage or parenting. The late medieval cult of Saint Anne, mother of the Virgin Mary, who was often visualized in the grouping known as Anna Selbdritt (Anne, her daughter Mary, and Mary's child Jesus), participated in the shift that resulted in saintly models for the laity.

PAMELA SHEINGORN

References and Further Reading

Ashley, Kathleen M., and Pamela Sheingorn. *Interpreting Cultural Symbols: Saint Anne in Late Medieval Society.* Athens, Ga.: University of Georgia Press, 1990.

Butler, Judith. *Undoing Gender.* New York: Routledge, 2004.

Caviness, Madeline Harrison. *Visualizing Women in the Middle Ages: Sight, Spectacle, and Scopic Economy.* The Middle Ages Series. Philadelphia: University of Pennsylvania Press, 2001.

Desmond, Marilynn, and Pamela Sheingorn. *Myth, Montage, & Visuality in Late Medieval Manuscript Culture: Christine de Pizan's* Epistre Othea. Ann Arbor, Mich.: University of Michigan Press, 2003.

Dressler, Rachel. *Of Armor and Men in Medieval England: The Chivalric Rhetoric of Three English Knights' Effigies.* Burlington, Vt.: Ashgate, 2004.

Jolly, Penny Howell. *Made in God's Image? Eve and Adam in the Genesis Mosaics at San Marco, Venice.* Berkeley: University of California Press, 1997.

Nixon, Virginia. *Mary's Mother: Saint Anne in Late Medieval Europe.* University Park, Pa.: Pennsylvania State University Press, 2004.

Sheingorn, Pamela. "The Bodily Embrace or Embracing the Body: Gesture and Gender in Late Medieval Culture." In *The Stage as Mirror: Civic Theatre in Late Medieval Europe,* edited by Alan E. Knight. Woodbridge, Suffolk, England: D. S. Brewer, 1997, pp. 51–89.

Sheingorn, Pamela. "Constructing the Patriarchal Parent: Fragments of the Biography of Joseph the Carpenter." In *Framing the Family: Narrative and Representation in the Medieval and Early Modern Periods,* edited by Rosalynn Voaden and Diane Wolfthal. Tempe, Ariz.: Arizona Center for Medieval and Renaissance Studies, 2004, pp. 163–182.

Toussaint, Gia. "Das Passional Der Kunigunde von Böhmen: Bildrhetorik und Spiritualität." Doctoral thesis, Universität Hamburg, 2002, Schöningh, 2003.

See also **Art, Representations of Women in; Body in Literature and Religion; Body, Visual Representations of; Bride of Christ: Imagery; Gender Ideologies; Hagiography, Iconographic Aspects of; Joseph, Stepfather of Jesus; Mary, Virgin: in Art**

GENDER IN HISTORY

Gender used to be only a categorizing term in some, but not all, languages. More recently, scholars have interpreted gender as the social and cultural construction of sex differences. Since the 1970s, medievalists have employed concepts of gender as a critical tool for understanding the past. Generally, they define gender in two parts: as human relations based on perceived sexual differences, and as a discourse of power that describes and organizes those relations. Often medievalist scholars use gender interchangeably with sex, women, feminism, or sexual orientation.

Modern medievalists assume that gender and sex are related but discrete concepts. A gender system encompasses gender ideology, roles, and identity. Gender ideology is a set of ideas in any given society about how the sexes should be defined and identified. A single society could produce many different gender ideologies. In medieval Europe, for instance, Christian theologians from the same region and generation blamed women for human sin, praised female saints as behavioral models for all Christians, and used feminine metaphors for Jesus. These notions represented overlapping but not necessarily identical gender ideologies.

Gender roles are sets of behavioral guidelines generated by a community or society for its members, based on perceived sexual characteristics. In the castles of twelfth-century continental Europe, for instance, noble families expected their daughters to be willing partners in the project of reproducing aristocratic lineages. Gender identity refers to the way any individual in a society acts out and makes sense of gender roles and ideologies for him or herself. Hence, not all aristocratic women identified themselves as typical childbearers or links in a genealogical chain, nor even as willing wives or lovers of men. Gender identity is related to but not the same as sexuality. Some modern theorists of gender, such as Judith Butler, have argued that to equate the two assumes an inherent hierarchy based on gender-ascribed sexuality. As the medievalist Ruth Mazo Karras has shown, however, some groups of men in medieval Europe—knights, university students, guild members—defined themselves and evaluated masculinity in relation to other men, but not necessarily in terms of sexuality. Some other medieval options for classifying humans were as non-children, non-coreligionists, or non-beasts.

Medievalists have participated in the larger project of gender studies by explaining how gender systems and ideologies change over time. For instance, until the scientific revolution, most Europeans conceived of a single-sex model for human biology based on Aristotelian and Galenic principles. Philosophers such as Thomas Aquinas and Hildegard of Bingen proposed that female bodies were not distinguished by particular sexual characteristics but by their physical underdevelopment. Like children, women were supposedly physically, intellectually, and morally inferior to adult men. Medieval physicians believed that women's bodies were cooler than men's bodies, as a result of which females could not generate the physical heat that would turn internal tubes and gonads—fallopian tubes and ovaries—into external penises and testes. However, this made women's uteruses cool, comfortable spots to house unborn babies. Medieval religious thinkers such as Aquinas were mostly interested in the elaboration of gender traits to help them explain reproduction, sexual pleasure, and natural philosophy, rather than considering gender hierarchies or issues of sexual orientation.

The many meanings of gender for medievalist scholars and their medieval subjects have inspired diverse, sometimes conflicting interpretations of medieval gender systems. The application of gender to the medieval past has produced studies on subjects ranging from the division of labor, infanticide, artistic gaze, and uses of poetic metaphor to the gender implications of landscape and sanctity. How medievalists define and use the concept of gender has had profound implications on their general understanding of the Middle Ages. Jo Ann McNamara has recently argued for reperiodizing European history based on shifts in gender ideologies. During the first Christian millennium, Europeans organized their societies first by class or birth and only secondly by gender; elite women were noble first, female second, and considered more virile than most men. Given this context, a Middle Ages that began in the fifth century and ended in the fifteenth has little meaning. In response, other scholars such as Maryanne Kowaleski and Mary Erler have called for medievalists to revise or "gender" the larger story, or master narrative, of the Middle Ages.

LISA BITEL

References and Further Reading

Butler, Judith. *Gender Trouble: Feminism and the Subversion of Identity*. New York and London: Routledge, 1990.

Cadden, Joan. *Meanings of Sex Differences in the Middle Ages: Medicine, Science, and Culture*. Cambridge: Cambridge University Press, 1993.

Erler, Mary C., and Maryanne Kowaleski, eds. *Gendering the Master Narrative: Women and Power in the Middle Ages*. Ithaca, N.Y.: Cornell University Press, 2003.

Karras, Ruth Mazo. *From Boys to Men: Formations of Masculinity in Late Medieval Europe*. Philadelphia: University of Pennsylvania Press, 2003.

Laqueur, Thomas. *Making Sex: Body and Gender from the Greeks to Freud*. Cambridge, Mass.: Harvard University Press, 1990.

McNamara, Jo Ann. "Women and Power Through the Family Revisited." In *Gendering the Master Narrative: Women and Power in the Middle Ages*, edited by Mary C. Erler and Maryanne Kowaleski. Ithaca, N.Y.: Cornell University Press, 2003.

Schiebinger, Londa. *Has Feminism Changed Science?* Cambridge, Mass.: Harvard University Press, 1999.

Scott, Joan Wallach. "Gender: A Useful Category of Historical Analysis." *American Historical Review* 91 (1986): 1053–1075.

See also **Aristotelian Concepts of Women and Gender; Femininity and Masculinity; Gender Ideologies; Procreation and Ideas of Conception; Scholasticism**

GENEALOGY

The medieval interest in genealogy reflects a broader concern with origins, be they of words, families, or institutions. The earliest genealogies, dating from the sixth to the eighth centuries and mostly of Celtic or Germanic origin, were usually those of royal families, often consisting simply of lists of names. Genealogies were more common in northern than in southern Europe. Iceland, in particular, is noted for the age and extent of its genealogical record. The twelfth-century *Landnámabók* or *Book of Settlements*, the most famous family saga, provided the histories and genealogies of over four hundred Icelandic settlers.

Genealogies gradually became more widespread and increasingly included nonroyal families. They could take the form of lists, charts, pictorial diagrams, or trees. Due to their brevity they almost never occupy an entire codex, but their placement within a codex and the type of texts they accompany convey their significance.

Genealogies associated a family with certain rights and properties, and genealogical literature was produced to legitimate claims to power and authority. In contrast to universal histories, which began with the Biblical origins of mankind, genealogical literature often created a mythic founder for a family or kingdom. This figure may have discovered or claimed the land, or instituted the rule of law. Both France and England, for example, traced their descent to Trojan heroes, while Anglo-Saxon texts claimed the descent of their kings from the god Wodan. Writers often tried to reconcile pagan ancestors with scriptural genealogies. In the case of lesser nobility, a founding figure may have acquired land or constructed the family castle.

The eleventh century marks a shift in conceptions of kinship, which is manifested in genealogies. In the early Middle Ages kinship was most often construed as a synchronic network comprising one's *propinquii* (intimates) and *consanguinei* (blood kin), rather than as a diachronic network that connected individuals through time. Over the course of the tenth and eleventh centuries individuals began to identify themselves in terms of their ancestors. During this period, rank, honors, and wealth began to be passed from father to son, as did bonds of fidelity. Once power and wealth became heritable, it was necessary to document one's ancestry. During the same period primogeniture, the system by which the eldest male heir inherited the majority of a family's goods, largely replaced the practice of dividing an inheritance equally among the heirs. A family's holdings became transmissible from one generation to the next, and land and family were identified with one another. Patronyms, nearly always derived from the name of a land or castle, as well as heraldic emblems, also came into use at this time. Land, name, and identity were thus passed down from father to son.

The eleventh century also witnessed the first appearance of the Tree of Jesse, a visual representation of Christ's descent from David's father, Jesse. The Tree of Jesse was featured in stained glass windows, statuary, manuscript illuminations, and paintings, and remained popular as an artistic motif until the sixteenth century. Christ's genealogy is derived principally from Isaiah 11:1–3 and Matthew 1:1–16. Early representations of the Tree of Jesse, based on Isaiah, focus on Jesse as the root, Mary as the rod, and Christ as the flower, while later representations, following Matthew, emphasize Christ's descent from the kings of Israel. Other common variations on the Tree of Jesse include either prophets or evangelists. Tree of Jesse images can be strikingly phallic, depicting the tree emerging from the loins of the reclining Jesse. Representations of Holy Kinship, which focus on Christ's female ancestors, especially Saint Anne, provide an alternative to the male-oriented genealogy celebrated by the Tree of Jesse.

Women occupy an ambiguous position in genealogical documents. Due to the primacy of male offspring, genealogy came to be construed almost exclusively in agnatic terms, and female ancestors were rarely mentioned. For example, women are largely absent from English genealogical rolls and pictorial representations of royal genealogies, and their presence often signals a rupture in the line of male descent. Though the ideal of agnatic genealogy dictated continuous male descent, in reality women were often required to legitimate territorial acquisitions or dynastic changes by serving as links to established authority.

In the late Middle Ages genealogical literature became more expansive, often including women and cadet lines. Sometimes, indeed, the mythic founding figures invoked by genealogical literature were women, as in the case of the fairy Melusine, founder of the Lusignan family, kings of Cyprus. Women played a more prominent role in the apparently heritable predisposition to saintliness. The thirteenth- and fourteenth-century Arpadian dynasty of Hungary as well as the Capetian–Angevin dynasty of France, Hungary, and Naples boasted a number of royal saints, female as well as male, equally able to intercede on behalf of the living and to transmit their saintly natures to their offspring.

DAISY DELOGU

References and Further Reading

Bloch, R. Howard. *Etymologies and Genealogies: A Literary Anthropology of the French Middle Ages.* Chicago and London: University of Chicago Press, 1983.

Duby, Georges. *The Chivalrous Society*, translated by Cynthia Postan. Berkeley and Los Angeles: University of California Press, 1977.

Genicot, Léopold. *Les Généalogies.* Turnhout: Brepols, 1975.

Vauchez, André. *Sainthood in the Later Middle Ages*, translated by Jean Birrell. New York and Cambridge: Cambridge University Press, 1997.

Watson, Arthur. *The Early Iconography of the Tree of Jesse.* London: Oxford University Press, 1934.

See also **Holy Kinship; Inheritance; Kinship; Mélusine; Patriarchy and Patrilineage; Succession, Royal and Noble**

GENTRY, WOMEN OF: ENGLAND

The gentry of the late Middle Ages constituted a specifically English social class, more or less equivalent to the continental lower nobility, but with distinctive characteristics of its own. The gentry were members of landholding families without hereditary titles but with pedigrees that demonstrated "good birth." Gentry families had personal and political connections with the nobility, but, unlike their continental counterparts, also with the wealthier bourgeoisie. The most encompassing designations for members of this class, first used formally in the early fifteenth century, were "gentleman" and "gentlewoman," from the Latin *generosus/a*, meaning well-born. This term was to some extent accorded by common consent and rested not only on good birth and the possession of an estate but also on visible wealth and expenditure, on conduct, and on the exercise of community leadership. In all of these areas, the women of the gentry participated along with the men.

In the fundamental area of good birth, which established the gentility of a family, women and men were both of importance, since ancestry was counted on both sides of the family. The family's social network included maternal as well as paternal connections. The gentry was a continuum, not a clearly defined social order. It extended from the families of knights who were as wealthy as some nobles down to the landless younger children of minor landholders, who served the greater gentry and the nobility, the sons often as lawyers and the daughters as attendants to the ladies. At marriage a gentlewoman would bring a dowry in lands or cash that could be instrumental in maintaining or advancing the family's status. For his part the husband would provide his bride with a dower, lands, and income that would support her if she were widowed. In many cases parents would also provide the couple with a jointure—property held jointly by both spouses and kept by the survivor of the two. Gentlewomen could thus control considerable property, and gentry heiresses or widows with particularly large estates or valuable connections were often sought in marriage by the nobility. At the lower end of the gentry spectrum, gentlemen could marry daughters of wealthy merchants for the same reasons. Women took on their husband's rank, however, and so the gentry were reluctant to let their daughters marry below the family's status and might postpone arranging a daughter's marriage many years in order to find a husband they considered suitable: Elizabeth Paston only married at age twenty-nine, in 1458, after her family had spent over a decade searching for a husband for her. Her niece Margery outraged her relatives ten years later by secretly marrying their estate manager and seems to have been ostracized for endangering the family's reputation.

Gentlewomen were not simply conveyors of heredity and wealth. A gentry household required active supervision by its mistress, who was accorded the courtesy title of "dame," and the family's standing and prospects required her efforts as well. Like women of every class, gentlewomen were expected to be in charge of the provision of food and clothing and the upbringing of children, which for the gentry meant the supervision of servants. But the mistress of a gentry household also was expected to be competent to act as her husband's deputy in the running of the estate. Women whose husbands were absent, or widows whose children were minors, were routinely found giving direction to estate officers, studying their accounts, and demanding the payment of rents and debts; these were responsibilities they could take on because they frequently assisted in these tasks even when their husbands were present. In the mid-fifteenth century Thomas Stonor was writing to his wife Jane from London in the expectation that she was familiar with the finances and administration of the estates, while in the absence of her husband John, Margaret Paston was vigorously urging on the family's lawsuits, advising her husband on advantageous local connections and even directing the family's forces when a dispute over property turned violent. In the absence of the head of the household she was regarded as the obvious, if temporary, decision-maker.

While a gentlewoman could act as her husband's lieutenant when the need arose, she was also expected to fill the specifically feminine role of peacemaker. Gentry wives were deeply involved in constructing and maintaining the personal networks that formed the social and political bonds that established and displayed a family's position. As mothers they were actively involved in seeking out marriages for their children, and when powerful patrons or angry neighbors had to be appeased, gentlemen often first sent their wives to exercise their diplomacy with the ladies of the other household.

The education of a gentlewoman was generally in the practical areas of household and estate management. A typical gentlewoman could read, and some owned devotional books or romances, usually in English. Writing was a less common skill: Thomas Betson, writing in 1476, expected his fiancée, Katherine Rich, to reply to his letters, but by means of a secretary. In the fourteenth century English gentlewomen were routinely expected to speak French, but by the fifteenth century few of them seem to have had much knowledge of it. One of the most important features of a gentlewoman's education and conduct was appropriate religious observance. Nuns were predominantly drawn from among women of good birth, but most gentlewomen did not enter convents. Lay gentlewomen were expected to be regular attendees at mass, and many joined religious confraternities. The wives of some Lollard knights, such as Dame Perrine Clanvowe, are known to have shared their husbands' religious convictions, and the Bridgetine practice of private devotions was popular, but extreme religious sentiments, whether heretical or orthodox, seem to have been the exception.

Men and women of the gentry shared cultural interests and social attitudes, and shared daily activities and recreations. While women were not considered equal to men, their role in sustaining the family was valued and respected.

RHODA LANGE FRIEDRICHS

References and Further Reading

Acheson, Eric. *A Gentry Community: Leicestershire in the Fifteenth Century, c. 1422–c. 1485*. Cambridge: Cambridge University Press, 1992.

Carpenter, Christine. *Locality and Polity: A Study of Warwickshire Landed Society, 1401–1499*. Cambridge: Cambridge University Press, 1992.

Coss, Peter. *The Lady in Medieval England 1000–1500*. Stroud, Gloucestershire: Sutton, 1998.

Davis, Norman, ed. *Paston Letters and Papers of the Fifteenth Century*. 2 vols. Oxford: Oxford University Press, 1971–1976.

Payling, S. J. *Political Society in Lancastrian England: The Greater Gentry of Nottinghamshire*. Oxford: Oxford University Press, 1991.

Ward, Jennifer, ed. and trans. *Women of the English Nobility and Gentry 1066–1500*. Manchester and New York: Manchester University Press, 1995.

See also **Administration of Estates; Diplomacy and Reconciliation; Dowry and Other Marriage Gifts; England; Literacy and Reading: Vernacular; Noble Women; Paston Letters; Social Status**

GERMANIC LANDS

In many ways, the lives of women in Germanic lands were similar to those of women elsewhere in Europe in the Middle Ages. The vast majority of women lived in villages, raising products for their own and their landlords' consumption, and doing agricultural tasks that were somewhat gender-specific. Most women married at least once, usually while in their mid- to late twenties, to a spouse who they hoped would be a good worker, decent father, and tolerable person with whom to live. Most women gave birth to several children, and survived childbirth with the assistance of female relatives and friends. By the fifteenth century, in cities, they might also use the services of a professional midwife. Most women were Christian, and engaged in a number of rituals and activities to demonstrate their faith, improve their likelihood of going to heaven, and ask for divine or saintly assistance with earthly problems; they went on pilgrimages, said prayers, lit candles, and made sure their children were baptized. Jewish women, whose communities suffered increasing persecution beginning in the fourteenth century, also carried out specific rituals and said special prayers, called *thkines*, for events that had meaning for them, such as menstruation, pregnancy, and childbirth.

Many German-speaking Jews—called *Ashkenazic* from the Hebrew word for the Rhineland area—migrated eastward, pushed by persecution and pulled by the more welcoming policies of the rulers and nobles of Poland–Lithuania. Whole families and sometimes whole communities migrated, so that Jewish women carried their traditions as far eastward as Ukraine. Persecution of Jews in the Middle Ages was not limited to Germanic lands, however, so this was yet another part of women's experiences that was widely shared across Europe.

The political and economic situation of medieval Germany did create a few distinctive situations, however. While western, northern, and eastern Europe developed into centralized monarchies—France, England, Portugal, Spain, Poland–Lithuania, Denmark, Sweden—central Europe did not. Although in the tenth and eleventh century there were powerful German kings, who revived the title of emperor and had papal coronations, their empire—later called the Holy Roman Empire—remained a loosely united confederation of hundreds of variously sized states. Many of these states were hereditary principalities, duchies, or counties, with women serving regularly as regents for their minor sons and sometimes as rulers in their own right. In this they followed a pattern set by the wives and sisters of earlier German kings. Some of these states were ecclesiastical territories ruled by bishops, abbots, or abbesses; abbesses held jurisdiction not only over an abbey itself, but also over the land and villages that belonged to it. Some of these states were free imperial cities, where women were considered "citizens" for taxation and legal purposes, although they had no official role in governing. Many of these cities were booming economically in the thirteenth century and then again in the fifteenth century, so they provided a variety of work opportunities for women. By the end of the Middle Ages, urban merchants in Germany had invested in mining and manufacturing in the countryside, capitalist enterprises that also provided employment for women.

Royal and Noble Women

The German kings of the tenth and eleventh centuries were ably assisted as they built up their power by a series of capable women. Matilda (895–968), the wife and widow of the first ruler in the Ottonian dynasty, Henry I (r. 919–936), worked with both her husband and her son to gain ecclesiastical backing in battles against lower nobles. She built many churches and founded or supported numerous monasteries, the most important of which were Quedlinburg and Nordhausen, where she lived after her husband's death; later she was made a saint. Adelheid of Burgundy (927–1000), the wife of Matilda's son Otto I (r. 936–973) was made official coemperor (*consortium imperii*) with her husband, and issued charters on her own. She married her son Otto II (ruled 973–983) to a Byzantine princess, Theophano (959–991), and when Otto died, she and Theophano—both of whom held the title *coimperatrix,* and occasionally signed documents *imperator* (emperor)—ruled as regents, for the next Ottonian king was only three.

Along with empresses, other Ottonian royal women played important political roles. Matilda, Countess of Tuscany (1046–1115), the cousin of Henry IV (r. 1056–1106), inherited huge territories in Italy, and

intervened in the struggle between Henry and Pope Gregory VII over lay investiture. She publicly backed the papacy and donated her lands to the pope, though she invested bishops in her own territories and in her will gave her lands to the German emperor, much to the pope's dismay. Her earlier donation had reserved her right to do so, but these territories remained a source of conflict between popes and emperors for more than a century.

The female members of the Hohenstaufen, Luxemberg, and Hapsburg families, who held the emperorship from 1138 to the end of the Empire in 1806, pursued independent political policies much less vigorously than had Ottonian women, and by the twelfth century the title *coimperatrix* disappeared from imperial documents. In the Golden Bull of 1346, which set out the procedures for electing the emperor, the ruler's wife was clearly subordinate. As long as they had imperial approval, women could inherit the rights of succession in the smaller territorial states of the Holy Roman Empire, however, and most states had prominent female regents from time to time. Loretta, the Countess of Sponheim (1298–1346), widowed at twenty-five with young children, defended her territories from more powerful lay and ecclesiastical neighbors who wanted to annex them. She was excommunicated in the process, and traveled to the papal court at Avignon to get this sentence lifted. Anna of Nassau, duchess of Brunswick–Lüneberg (1441–1514) survived a poisoning attempt right before her second marriage to become a successful regent, developing sound financial policies that her successors continued.

Abbesses

Most of these lay noblewomen were regents who eventually turned their territories over to their sons. Abbesses, by contrast, had a permanent right to rule, granted by appointment or election. Abbesses of certain houses, especially free imperial monasteries or those allied with powerful noble families, were arguably the most powerful women in medieval Germany. (Some of these communities were technically "secular" endowments of canonesses as their residents took no final vows; their head was always referred to as abbess, however.) Though every monastery had to have a priest available to say mass and hear confessions, he was often appointed by the abbess, who also appointed secular officials such as toll collectors, bailiffs, and legal personnel. She had the right to mint money (coins often bear the portrait of powerful abbesses), hear legal cases, and send a representative to the imperial diet. She was a source of artistic patronage, hiring builders, sculptors, painters, and musicians, and of social patronage, supporting hospitals, orphanages, and schools. She generally appointed assistants from among the community's residents, so that women performed all of the other administrative duties and much of the spiritual counseling of novices and residents.

Many free imperial monasteries were founded by Ottonian rulers and their consorts in the ninth and tenth centuries, and granted rights and privileges by both the emperor and the pope. The high point of many houses in terms of intellectual accomplishments and political power was the tenth and eleventh centuries, when the abbess Matilda of Quedlinburg (954–999, the granddaughter of the founder Matilda) corresponded with political leaders and had authority over bishops, and the poet Hrotsvit of Gandersheim (c. 935–1001) wrote the first original dramas since the end of the Roman Empire for the nuns in her convent. Beginning in the late eleventh century, the Gregorian reform movement attempted to reduce the abbesses' power and visibility in the surrounding community, though this was only slowly successful. The abbess Hildegard of Bingen (1098–1179) founded new monasteries, and also wrote music, plays, natural history, and visionary works. Though few abbesses after her were as powerful politically, in her focus on mystical experiences she set a pattern that became increasingly common. In the thirteenth and fourteenth centuries, most nuns who wrote were mystics, with many of the most important medieval mystics, male and female, coming from German-speaking areas. The Cistercian convent at the Saxon city of Helfta became particularly known for its visionary residents, including Mechthild of Magdeburg (c. 1212–1282), whose *Flowing Light of the Godhead* presents a graphic picture of heaven, hell, and purgatory.

By the fifteenth century, it appeared to some church officials and the more rigorous nuns as if some women's monasteries had forgotten their spiritual focus, and many underwent reforms designed to enforce strict rules of conduct and higher standards of spirituality. These reforms often put the convent more closely under the control of a local male bishop and took away some of the abbess's independent power, but they also built up a strong sense of group cohesion and gave nuns a greater sense of the spiritual worth of their lives. These reformed houses later became vigorous opponents of the Protestant Reformation, and some, such as Wienhausen, survive today.

Urban Women and Capitalist Enterprises

No urban woman had the power of a noble regent or abbess, for the free imperial cities and all other towns were governed by male councils and mayors. Many medieval sources are explicitly gender-inclusive when talking about citizens; however, using phrases like "*Bürger und Bürgerin*" (male or female citizen) or "*alle Bürgern, Mann und Frau*" (all citizens, man and woman). Women are listed on new citizen rolls in many cities, and were obligated to swear an oath of loyalty, pay taxes, and provide soldiers and arms for the city's defense. Just as they did with men, the new citizens' lists record the occupations of the women accepted—midwife, seamstress, weaver, candle-maker—and the amount they paid for citizenship. Women as well as men were granted citizenship free of charge if they practiced an occupation the city deemed desirable; in the late fifteenth century both Frankfurt and Nuremberg offered free citizenship to midwives.

In the early twentieth century, several German historians argued that the sex ratio in medieval cities was highly skewed in favor of women and that women had full rights in many guilds. The demographic statistics on which this assertion was based are now known to have been misleading—they were taken during times of war, when many men were away fighting—and more recent studies have made clear that only rarely were women full guild members. They were engaged in a range of occupations, however. Women and girls worked in guild shops as unofficial assistants and as domestic servants. They sold merchandise at the city marketplace or peddled it house to house. They worked in taverns and inns, brewed beer, and by the late fifteenth century distilled and sold brandy. In such "public businesses," which a 1340 Munich law code defined as those who "stand at the public market or buy and sell" or were "tailors, shopkeepers, money changers, or innkeepers," women were free to do business without their husband's approval, but they were also responsible to pay back all debts. Women worked in municipal and church-run hospitals, infirmaries, orphanages, and pest-houses, or as domestic servants. They worked in the official municipal brothel (*Frauenhaus*), which many cities opened in the fifteenth century, or combined selling sex for money with other part-time labor, such as laundering.

Most production remained the province of craft guilds throughout the Middle Ages, but in cloth production and mining, capitalist entrepreneurs increasingly hired individuals and families in large-scale operations. Investors hired rural households to produce wool, linen, and later cotton thread and cloth (or cloth that was a mixture of these), paying the household for its labor alone. Spinning and weaving for the market became important by-employments for peasants in many parts of Germany, providing income through the winter months. Husbands, wives, and children all contributed their labor, breaking down the long-standing identification of women with spinning. In cities, spinning largely remained a female task; in certain cities, such as Augsburg, capitalist cloth producers modified guild rules so that they could hire many spinners, usually young women who had come in from the countryside.

By the fifteenth century, demand for metals—largely because of changes in military technology—went up dramatically, and complex machinery was needed to dig and maintain deeper tunnels and speed up production processes. Rulers, nobles, and merchants in Germany invested in copper, iron, and silver mining, hiring male heads of household who were expected to bring their whole families. While men worked underground, women and children sorted and washed ore, and prepared charcoal briquets for use in smelting. Single women and widows also worked independently for wages in mining areas.

Thus, as everywhere in Europe, women's lives in Germanic lands were highly varied, determined as much by their class status as by their gender. The splintered political situation did allow some women, particularly the noble abbesses of free imperial convents, a range of powers that were distinctive, however. Many abbesses retained their right to govern until 1806, and only in the twentieth century would women in Germany regain the political voice that at least a tiny group of women had held much earlier.

MERRY E. WIESNER-HANKS

References and Further Reading

Beach, Alison I. *Women as Scribes: Book Production and Monastic Reform in Twelfth-Century Bavaria*. Cambridge and New York: Cambridge University Press, 2004.

Clark, Anne L. *Elisabeth of Schönau: A Twelfth-Century Visionary*. Philadelphia: University of Pennsylvania Press, 1992.

Dinzelbacher, Peter, and Dieter R. Bauer. *Religiöse Frauenbewegung und mystische Frömmigkeit im Mittelalter*. Cologne: Böhlau Verlag, 1988.

Dreyer, Elizabeth. *Passionate Spirituality: Hildegard of Bingen and Hadewijch of Brabant*. New York: Paulist Press, 2005.

Ennen, Edith. *The Medieval Woman*. Cambridge, Mass.: Basil Blackwell, 1989.

Finnegan, Mary Jeremy. *The Women of Helfta: Scholars and Mystics*. Athens, Ga.: University of Georgia Press, 1991.

Fößel, Amalie. *Die Königin im mittelalterlichen Reich*. Darmstadt: Wissen Schaftliche Buchgesellschaft, 2000.

Garber, Rebecca L. R. *Feminine Figurae: Representations of Gender in Religious Texts by Medieval German Women Writers 1100–1375*. New York and London: Routledge, 2003.

Hergemöller, Hans-Ulrich. *Masculus et Femina. Systematische Grundlinien einer mediävistischen Geschlechtergeschichte*. Hamburg: HHL-Verlag, 2001.

Karant-Nunn, Susan. "The Women of the Saxon Silver Mines." In *Women in Reformation and Counter-Reformation Europe: Public and Private Worlds*, edited by Sherrin Marshall. Bloomington, Ind.: Indiana University Oress, 1989.

Ketsch, Peter. *Frauen im Mittelalter*. 2 vols. Düsseldorf: Schwann, 1983–1984.

Lundt, Bea, ed. *Auf der Suche nach der Frau im Mittelalter: Fragen, Quellen, Antworten*. Munich: W. Fink, 1991.

Müller, Daniela. *Frauen vor der Inquisition. Lebensform, Glaubenszeugnis und Aburteilung der deutschen und französischen Katharerinnen*. Mainz: Philipp von Zabern, 1996.

Wiesner, Merry E. *Working Women in Renaissance Germany*. New Brunswick, N.J.: Rutgers University Press, 1986.

Winston-Allen, Anne. *Convent Chronicles: Women Writing about Women and Reform in the Late Middle Ages*. University Park, Pa.: Pennsylvania State University Press, 2004.

See also **Adelheid; Beguines; Canonesses; Clothwork, Domestic; Constance of Sicily, Dolce of Worms; Dorothea of Montau; Ebner, Margaretha; Elisabeth of Schönau; Frankish Lands; Gertrude of Hackeborn; Gertrude of Ortenberg; Gertrude the Great; Herrad of Hohenbourg; Hildegard of Bingen; Hrotsvit of Gandersheim; Jewish Women; Langmann, Adelheid; Law, German; Leoba; Literature, German; Margaret "the Cripple" of Magdeburg; Mathilda and the Monastery at Essen; Matilda of Tuscany; Mechthild of Hackeborn; Mechthild of Magdeburg; Observant Movement; Ottonian Royal Women; Romance, German; Sister-Books and Other Convent Chronicles; Stagel, Elsbeth; Textile Production for the Market; Women Authors: German Texts**

GERSON, JEAN

Jean Gerson (1363–1429) is a central medieval figure in terms of a perennial debate on women and the Christian life. He was born as the first child in what became a large family in the hamlet from which he took his name. The place, now disappeared, was northeast of Reims, on the border between Champagne and the Ardennes. His father was a skilled laborer, and his devout and attentive parents made use of their modest means to send their son to the University of Paris. Under the guidance of his teacher Pierre d'Ailly, Gerson became doctor of theology in 1394 and succeeded d'Ailly in 1395 as chancellor of the university.

Gerson was favored by the duke of Burgundy and, thanks to him, was made dean of the richest church in Bruges, Saint Donatian. Here he withdrew in 1399–1400 and considered resigning the university chancellorship, for he was disgusted with what he considered to be hypocrisy and falsity in the academic life. He returned to Paris, however, in the autumn of 1400, after outlining a program of reform to guarantee that the education offered in the faculty of theology would emphasize not only scholastic learning but also affective spirituality. In 1401 Gerson began a series of lectures on mystical theology, which he approached in both speculative and practical terms.

In 1415 Gerson left Paris for the Council of Constance. Its goal was to end the Great Western Schism, with one pope in Rome and another in Avignon, and to reform the Church. He had become a central voice in the conciliar movement, but his role at Constance was limited by his simultaneous concern with condemning a theology that defended the murder in 1407 of the French king's brother, Charles of Orléans. Gerson made himself a prime enemy of the duke of Burgundy, who had arranged the assassination. After Constance it was too dangerous for Gerson to return to Paris. He eventually settled in Lyon, where he lived a secluded life and continued writing theological treatises.

Gerson is the most eloquent voice of the late Middle Ages in terms not only of church reform but also of pastoral theology. He wrote in both French and Latin, for he was determined to reach a lay audience, including women. His primary female audience in the 1390s was made up of his biological sisters, whom he encouraged to avoid marriage by remaining in the home and making an informal religious community. He provided guidelines for their everyday life. Gerson's most ambitious work of lay theology was *The Mountain of Contemplation*, which he composed especially for his sisters. He explained that he wrote only about matters that he knew they could understand.

Such works show that Gerson was confident about the ability of women to profit from the theological discussions that until then had been limited to university men in Latin. Gerson was fascinated by the spiritual lives of women and especially by their mystical experiences. He wrote three treatises about how to determine whether people who claim to have revelations are genuine, and here he was especially concerned with women. In his first treatise, *On Distinguishing True from False Revelations* (1401), Gerson was relatively confident that this process, known as *discretio spirituum* (1 Cor. 12:10), could take place according to rational criteria. The second treatise, *On the Discernment of Spirits* (1415), reflects Gerson's doubts about the veracity of the revelations of Bridget of Sweden.

In his final treatise on the topic, *On the Examination of Teachings* (1423), Gerson was basically negative about the contribution that mystics and visionaries had made to the Church, and he blamed some of them for the Great Western Schism. This treatise has formed a foundation for historians who have chosen to see Gerson as basically hostile to women and their religious experiences. It can, however, be read as reflecting the last stage in Gerson's life, when he lived apart from the rest of society and no longer had the contacts with his sisters that earlier had provided him with a much more positive role of women in the Church.

Gerson thought of himself as a champion of women. He joined with Christine de Pizan in 1402 in condemning the *Romance of the Rose*, a poem popular in learned circles that celebrated the sexual violation of a woman. Gerson remains controversial in medieval studies in terms of his views on women, but his writings are too rich and varied to allow any one-dimensional interpretation.

BRIAN PATRICK McGUIRE

References and Further Reading

Brown, D. Catherine. *Pastor and Laity in the Theology of Jean Gerson*. Cambridge: Cambridge University Press, 1987.

Caciola, Nancy. *Discerning Spirits: Divine and Demonic Possession in the Middle Ages*. Ithaca, N.Y. and London: Cornell University Press, 2003.

Elliott, Dyan. *Proving Woman: Female Spirituality and Inquisitional Culture in the Later Middle Ages*. Princeton, N.J. and Oxford: Princeton University Press, 2004.

Gerson, Jean. *Early Works*, translated and introduced by Brian Patrick McGuire. New York: Paulist Press, 1998.

McGuire, Brian Patrick. *Jean Gerson and the Last Medieval Reformation*. Philadelphia: Pennsylvania State University Press, 2005.

See also **Christine de Pizan; Mysticism and Mystics; Roman de la Rose and Its Reception; Spirits: Discernment of and Possession by; Spiritual Care; Theology**

GERTRUDE OF HACKEBORN

Gertrude of Hackeborn (c. 1232–1291) was the daughter of the baron of Hackeborn. As a child she entered the monastery of Rodarsdorf, technically Benedictine but following the customs of the Cistercians. In 1251, at the age of only nineteen, she was elected abbess for the community, which in 1258 moved to Helfta, southeast of Eisleben in the diocese of Halberstadt, on land her family owned. She died there in 1291.

Abbess Gertrude of Hackeborn did not leave any writings, but according to both her younger sister Mechthild's *Liber* and Gertrude of Helfta's *Legatus* she was a patron of learning. Helfta flourished as an intellectual milieu. Given Gertrude's belief that only scientific studies led to true understanding of the Scriptures and hence faith, the cloister school taught the liberal arts, and she required study and insight in the Bible from all nuns, herself included. Gertrude bought or had the nuns copy "all the good books she could get." As abbess she received in 1261 the orphan Gertrude of Helfta, later known as "the Great," and in 1270 the sick and persecuted Beguine Mechthild of Magdeburg.

By creating a learned "school of love" she set the groundwork for the Latin texts (over one thousand pages long) written by Mechthild of Hackeborn, Gertrude the Great, and an anonymous nun. Here the community praises Gertrude of Hackeborn as prophet and gem among prelates, and in a Eucharistic vision it depicts her in the office of a prelate, offering the Lord to each of the sisters under God's guidance.

ELSE MARIE WIBERG PEDERSEN

References and Further Reading

Bynum, Caroline Walker. "Women Mystics in the Thirteenth Century: The Case of the Nuns of Helfta." In *Jesus as Mother: Studies in the Spirituality of the High Middle Ages*, edited by Caroline Walker Bynum. Berkeley: University of California Press, 1987, pp. 170–261.

Finnegan, Mary Jeremy. *The Women of Helfta: Scholars and Mystics*. Athens, Ga. and London: University of Georgia Press, 1991.

Gertrude of Helfta. *Legatus divinae pietatis*, vol. 5. In *Sources Chrétiennes* 331, edited by Jean-Marie Clément and Bernard de Vregille. Paris: Éditions du Cerf, 1986.

———. *Liber Specialis gratiae*. In *Revelationes Gertrudianae ac Mechtildianae*. Vol. 2: *S. Mechtildis virginis s. Benedicti Liber specialis gratiae*, edited by Solesmensium O.S.B. monachorum. Paris: H. Oudin, 1877.

Mechthild of Hackeborn. *Livre De La Grace Spéciale. Revelations De Sainte Mechtilde*, translated by the Benedictine Fathers of Solesmes and edited by the H. Oudin Brothers. Paris: H. Oudin, 1878.

Spitzlei, Sabine. *Erfahrungsraum Herz. Zur Mystik des Zisterzienserklosters Helfta im 13. Jahrhundert*. Mystik in Geschichte und Gegenwart. Texte und Untersuchungen 9. Stuttgart-Bad Cannstatt: Friedrich Frommann Verlag, 1991.

See also **Abbesses; Education, Monastic; Gertrude the Great; Mechthild of Hackeborn; Mechthild of Magdeburg; Monasticism and Nuns**

GERTRUDE OF NIVELLES

Pippin I of Landen, mayor of the palace of the Austrasian kingdom, and Ita, his wife, gave birth to a daughter Gertrude (626–659). After Pippin's death, Ita founded a religious house on family lands at Nivelles (now in southern Belgium), where Gertrude became the first abbess in 649. The double monastery, like many foundations of the period, consisted of male and female members living segregated under the abbess's authority. Through the agency of Bishop Amand, the house was influenced by the Columban brand of monasticism (an Irish brand), and a number of Irish clerics resided at Nivelles during its early years.

As commemorated in her *Life*, composed by one of the brethren soon after her death on St. Patrick's feast day in 659, Gertrude was known for her ascetic lifestyle, including a famous incident in which she angrily rejected a noble suitor, resisting expectations that she marry and produce heirs. She maintained close contacts with Irish missionaries in the region, including Foillan and Ultan, and requested burial dress that included relics and emulated the modest clothing of contemporary holy women in the eastern Mediterranean. Excavations conducted in the 1940s and 1950s at Nivelles revealed that her grave had already become a locus for family burials and was a pilgrimage site in the seventh century.

Built strategically upon family land, the monastery of Nivelles was a symbolic center of the power of Pippin's family. Gertrude's brother Grimoald, mayor of the Austrasian palace, used the house as a base from which to plan a briefly successful coup d'état; after Grimoald's execution by Clovis II in 662, the Merovingian royal family attacked Nivelles. Not surprisingly, following these events, the veneration of Gertrude remained an integral part of traditions associated with the Pippinids (later known as the Carolingians) after their overthrow of the Merovingian dynasty in the mid-eighth century.

BONNIE EFFROS

References for Further Reading

Effros, Bonnie. "Symbolic Expressions of Sanctity: Gertrude of Nivelles in the Context of Merovingian Mortuary Custom." *Viator* 27 (1996): 1–10.

McNamara, Jo Ann, and John E. Halborg, eds. "Gertrude, Abbess of Nivelles." In *Sainted Women of the Dark Ages*. Durham: Duke University Press, 1992, pp. 36–55.

Peyroux, Catherine. "Gertrude's *furor*: Reading Anger in an Early Medieval Saint's Life." In *Anger's Past: The Social Uses of an Emotion in the Middle Ages*, edited by Barbara Rosenwein. Ithaca, N.Y.: Cornell University Press, 1998.

Treffort, Cécile. "Sainte Gertrude de Nivelles." In *Christianisme et Chrétientés en Occident et en Orient (milieu VIIe – milieu XIe siècle)*, edited by Jean-Pierre Arrignon, Bernard Merdrignac, and Cécile Treffort. Paris: Ophrys, 1997.

See also Abbesses; Celibacy: Clerical and Priests' Concubines; Double Monasteries; Frankish Lands; Grave Goods; Monasticism and Nuns; Noble Women

GERTRUDE OF ORTENBERG

Gertrude (c. 1275–1335) came from a noble family at the Oberrhein and married the rich knight Rickeldegen of Ulnburg. Widowed with four children, she settled in Offenburg near Strasbourg to lead a religious life and, after the death of her youngest child, vowed to follow the Third Rule of St. Francis as a religious laywoman. She lived together with Heilke of Staufenberg, her life-long friend, and some other women in houses near a Franciscan convent. According to the German *Life* by a younger house-mate who, c. 1350, recorded the stories told by the elderly Heilke, she lived in personal deprivation and rigorous asceticism and had long mystical experiences. At the same time, the women agreed together upon all religious and practical matters.

Gertrude was probably well-read and possessed books. She had intensive intellectual contact with Franciscan and Dominican preachers. Some of their sermons by Eckhart and Rudolf of Biberach are compiled in the *Life*. In 1318 the women moved to Strasbourg, where Gertrude seems to have played a leading role in the circle of lay devout and mendicants. The *Life* shows how God revealed the sins of fellow citizens to her, whom she converted and reminded of their responsibility. She mediated in feuds and suffered the pains of hell's torments as a substitute for dying sinners. She was an independent agent of salvation, as her holy presence had salvific qualities. The *Life* concludes: "Gertrude went out into the cities and villages of this world. The words that she spoke struck right to the heart. With her mild admonition and virtuous power she often outdid the mendicants."

ANNEKE MULDER-BAKKER

References and Further Reading

Ringler, S. "Gertrud von Ortenberg." In *Die Deutsche Literatur des Mittelalters: Verfasserlexikon*, new edition by Kurt Ruh. Berlin and New York: De Gruyter, 1980–2000, vol. II, 522–525.

See also Germanic Lands; Laywomen, Religious; Poor Clares Order; Sermons and Preaching

GERTRUDE THE GREAT

Gertrude the Great (1256–1301/1302) (also known as Gertrude of Helfta), the only woman ever titled "the Great" by the Church, was of unknown parentage. She came to the Cistercian monastery of Helfta in Saxony in 1261 when she was only five, and died there.

The abbess Gertrude of Hackeborn and the teacher Mechthild of Hackeborn gave her a thorough education in the seven liberal arts and theology, before she worked as second chantress and scribe. In 1281 Gertrude the Great had a vision of Christ which marked her conversion "from a grammarian to a theologian," and in 1289, having received a call to "preach God's gift for the love of neighbour," she began to write her reflections.

She wrote the *Spiritual Exercises* and book II of the *Legatus Divinae Pietatis* (*Herald of Divine Love*). Of the other four books of the *Legatus*, written by an anonymous nun, Gertrude probably dictated books III–V, whereas book I is a *vita* of the saint. The *Exercises* were written for the community and form a liturgical itinerary of seven monastic practices centered, like standard Cistercian teaching, on nuptial union with God. While the *Legatus* is written for a broader audience, both texts are expressions of an optimistic Trinitarian and Christocentric theology. Thus Gertrude's love theology, in a rich metaphorical language with God's heart as the key metaphor, emphasizes God's love for his creation highlighted in Christ's death on the cross and reaffirmed in daily life.

Gertrude's texts were widely spread during the Counterreformation.

ELSE MARIE WIBERG PEDERSEN

References and Further Reading

Bynum, Caroline Walker. "Women Mystics in the Thirteenth Century: The Case of the Nuns of Helfta." In *Jesus as Mother: Studies in the Spirituality of the High Middle Ages*, edited by Caroline Walker Bynum. Berkeley, Calif.: University of California Press, 1987, pp. 170–261.

Finnegan, Mary Jeremy. *The Women of Helfta: Scholars and Mystics*. Athens, Ga. and London: University of Georgia Press, 1991.

Gertrude of Helfta. *Legatus divinae pietatis*. In *Oeuvres Spirituelles*, tomes II–V. In *Sources Chrétiennes* 139, 143, 255, 331, edited by Pierre Doyère, Jean-Marie Clément, and Bernard de Vregille. Paris: Éditions du Cerf, 1968–1986.

———. *Exercitia*. In *Oeuvres Spirituelles*, tome I. In *Sources Chrétiennes* 127, edited by Jacques Hourlier and Albert Schmitt. Paris: Éditions du Cerf, 1967.

Lewis, Gertrud Jaron, and Jack Lewis, eds. and trans. *Gertrude the Great of Helfta: Special Exercises*. Kalamazoo, Mich.: Cistercian Publications, 1989.

Winkworth, Margaret, ed. and trans. *Gertrude of Helfta: The Herald of Divine Love*. New York: Paulist Press, 1993.

See also Education, Monastic; Germanic Lands; Gertrude of Hackeborn; Mechthild of Hackeborn; Mechthild of Magdeburg; Monasticism and Nuns; Mysticism and Mystics; Theology

GILBERTINE ORDER

Also known as the Order of Sempringham, the Gilbertine Order was founded in 1131 by Gilbert of Sempringham (c. 1083–1189) in Lincolnshire, England, when seven women in his parish church asked him to guide them in living a strict religious life. The order grew to become the only exclusively English monastic order. At its height it comprised twenty-four houses, ten of which were organized as double monasteries with nuns, lay sisters, regular canons, and lay brothers: Sempringham, Haverholme, Alvingham, Bullington, Catley, Nun Ormsby, Sixhills, Watton (Yorkshire), Chicksands (Bedfordshire), and Shouldham (Norfolk). Fourteen houses were founded for men only.

As women embraced religious life during the twelfth century, the Gilbertine Order provided an important opportunity for them in England. Initially the women may have followed early models for female vocations, such as anchoresses and sisters serving in hospitals. The Cistercians also exerted considerable influence over early Gilbertine history, particularly through William of Rievaulx and Bernard of Clairvaux. Gilbert had wanted the Cistercian Order to assume the management of his earliest foundations, but the Cistercians rejected such incorporation, claiming that they did not want to govern religious women, although by then they had accepted other women's houses. The Gilbertine constitution, possibly developed by the late 1160s but fully recorded only in the thirteenth century, stipulated that the nuns would follow the Rule of Benedict and the regular canons would follow the Rule of Augustine. Ecclesiastical and lay magnates who were supportive of women's religious vocations, particularly in the north of England, provided the Order's initial patronage.

Gilbert's *Vita* (Life) stressed the pastoral responsibilities given to the canons over the nuns. Administrative and spiritual authority rested with the Master (Gilbert and his successors) and the canons, especially because only priests could administer the sacraments. The nuns could not participate in the election of the Master of the Order. Female officials known as *scrutatrices* (examiners)—two nuns and a lay sister— could assist him with internal discipline by visiting the female houses, inquiring about breaches of conduct, and attending General Chapter meetings of the Order; all such travel was closely supervised. Parallel officials existed for the male houses. Within each double house, three other officials, *speculatrices* (spies or observers), also reported to the Master of the Order, even regarding the prioress. The prioress of each female house was elected by its resident nuns; unlike her counterparts in other contemporary orders

such as Fontevrault, a Gilbertine prioress only had control over women within the house. She did not rule over the canons or lay brothers. Other offices included the sub-prioress, cellaress, sacrist, and precentrix (choir director). The Gilbertine Rule made special provision for the nuns' financial security, since insufficient endowment was a serious problem in many female monasteries. One-tenth of the Order's sheep were reserved for the nuns; they could control the proceeds from the sale of the wool for their buildings and other necessities.

The Order did not emphasize education and learning; the members were to focus on prayer and contemplation. Composition and manuscript copying were strictly regulated. The Order's constitution prohibited educating either young boys or girls without a monastic vocation, although a letter from Pope Honorius III in 1223 suggests that some girls were being educated who did not become nuns. The Order maintained a house in Cambridge for canons. In the fifteenth century, John Capgrave wrote an English *Life of St. Gilbert* for nuns who could not read Latin, an indication of a decline in Latin literacy.

Excavations of Gilbertine double houses indicate that there were separate complexes for men and women, connected by a window house where, under supervision, exchanges of food, laundry, and other practical materials could take place. The nuns' churches had a wall that separated the nave pierced by a small window through which the sacraments and the stone of peace could be passed. After the 1160s, when both a sexual scandal and a rebellion of the lay brothers threatened the Order's status, the Gilbertines strictly maintained the separation of the sexes within the Order, and protected the enclosure of the nuns from the outside world. (At Watton Priory, a young nun and a lay brother had enjoyed a secret liaison until the girl became pregnant. When they were discovered, the senior nuns oversaw the punishment of the hapless lay brother; Aelred of Rievaulx's account of the girl's miraculous repentance and delivery helped to redeem the nuns' reputation for piety. The Order, nevertheless, tightened its control over interaction between the sexes.)

The Order enjoyed royal support throughout its history. Henry II vigorously defended Gilbert during the crisis in the 1160s. King John actively supported the Order's petition for Gilbert's canonization. Henry VI visited Sempringham as a patron. After 1300, however, the general wealth of the Gilbertines declined. In the Dissolution of 1538 under Henry VIII, the members had to surrender the Order's houses to the king.

JANET T. SORRENTINO

References and Further Reading

Constable, Giles. "Aelred of Rievaulx and the Nun of Watton: An Episode in the Early History of the Gilbertine Order." In *Medieval Women*, edited by D. Baker. Studies in Church History. Subsidia 1. Oxford, 1978, pp. 205–226.

Elkins, Sharon. *Holy Women of Twelfth-Century England.* Chapel Hill, N.C.: University of North Carolina Press, 1988.

Foreville, Raymonde, and Gillian Keir, eds. *The Book of St Gilbert.* Oxford: Clarendon Press, 1987.

Freeman, Elizabeth. "Nuns in the Public Sphere." *Comitatus* 27 (1996): 55–80.

Golding, Brian. *Gilbert of Sempringham and the Gilbertine Order: 1131–1300.* Oxford: Clarendon Press, 1995.

Graham, Rose S. *Gilbert of Sempringham and the Gilbertines.* London: Elliot Stock, 1901. Reprint, 1904.

Knowles, David. "The Revolt of the Lay Brothers of Sempringham." *English Historical Review* 50 (1935): 465–487.

McNamara, Jo Ann. "The Nun of Watton." *Magistra* 1.1 (1995): 122–137.

Rosof, Patricia. "The Anchoritic Base for the Gilbertine Order." *American Benedictine Review* 33:2 (1982): 182–194.

St. John Hope, W. H. "The Gilbertine Priory of Watton, in the East Riding of Yorkshire." *Archaeological Journal* 58 (1901): 1–34.

Sorrentino, Janet. "'In Houses of Nuns, In Houses of Canons': A Liturgical Dimension to Double Monasteries." *The Journal of Medieval History* 28:4 (2002): 361–372.

Thompson, Sally. *Women Religious: The Founding of English Nunneries after the Norman Conquest.* Oxford: Clarendon Press, 1991.

See also **Anchoresses; Cistercian Order; Double Monasteries; England; Fontevrault, Abbey and Order of; Monastic Rules; Monasticism and Nuns; Patronage, Ecclesiastical; Spiritual Care**

GIRLS AND BOYS

Originally published in French in 1960 and in English translation in 1962, Philippe Ariès' *Centuries of Childhood* has dominated contemporary thinking about medieval childhood. Ariès held that the medieval period was indifferent to childhood as a concept and a distinct phase of life. He reasoned that medieval parents did not invest emotionally in their children because the children too often died. Looking at evidence like portraiture, Ariès inferred that children were seen simply as miniature adults, valued for what they would become later in life rather than for who they were as children, and for him Western society only began to recognize the distinctiveness of childhood during the Enlightenment, when children were seen as having souls worth saving and a mind worth educating. In other words, Ariès' assumptions about medieval childhood paralleled his ideas about historical development: in the same way the Middle Ages were a backward period whose deficiencies were remedied only by later progressive change, so too medieval children were valued only after they reached adulthood.

Contra Ariès

To be sure, medieval conceptions of childhood were not identical to contemporary beliefs, yet Ariès opened the way for other researchers to consider how different cultures and time periods fashioned their understandings of children and childhood. Subsequent historians of medieval culture have explored a wide variety of evidence to refute Ariès' blanket assertion that the Middle Ages lacked an understanding of the uniqueness of children and childhood. Shulamith Shahar has examined a variety of biblical, theological, devotional, and educational literature to reconstruct medieval attitudes and actions toward the conception, birth, childhood, and education of children based upon medieval understandings of the life cycle. Barbara Hanawalt has investigated coroners' rolls to open the doors to the structure of medieval English peasant life and how medieval children were regarded by looking at how they died. In another study, Hanawalt looked at court records, coroners' rolls, and advice manuals to see how children and adolescents in medieval London experienced complex social and cultural institutions like baptism, service and apprenticeship, and marriage. Sally Crawford has combined archeological data as well as documentary, legal, and literary sources to great effect in her analysis of Anglo-Saxon England's view of childhood from birth through adolescence. Ronald C. Finucane has looked at the registers kept at saints' shrines in both northern and southern Europe that preserve the reasons why pilgrims visited the holy site that detail parents' concern for their children's lives from conception through childhood. In a series of major studies, Nicholas Orme has detailed the wealth of medieval educational practices, and he has synthesized a wide variety of historical evidence, including the material culture of English childhood, to place medieval children in their lived world. These historical studies have been complemented with interdisciplinary and literary studies examining childhood in relationship to other topics, like motherhood; family and kinship structures; the church and theology; courtesy, conduct, and children's literature; and most importantly, gender and family.

The increasing numbers of studies now allow for a more coherent picture of medieval children and childhood. By the later Middle Ages a fairly stable set of terms divided childhood and youth into seven-year segments denoted as *infantia* (infancy), *pueritia* (childhood), and *adolescentia* (adolescence) based upon the child's physical, social, emotional, and mental development. During *infantia* (from birth to age seven), children were not considered to be rational and responsible agents. The onset of *pueritia* was marked by the child's growing personal awareness and social accountability. Finally, the change from *pueritia* to *adolescentia* was marked by the onset of menarche for girls and the development of secondary sexual characteristics for boys and girls.

Infantia: *Baptism and Early Childhood*

After birth, when a midwife and often other women attended to the mother and child, an infant's initiation into the wider social world occurred at baptism. During the ceremony, the child was anointed with water or oil and given his or her Christian names, and the godparents vowed to raise the child up in the Christian faith. The relationship between godchildren and godparents was regarded so highly that marriage between the two was prohibited by the laws of marriage impediments, thereby widening kinship networks among the Germanic peoples in the early Middle Ages. Thus, baptism provided children with the names by which they would be known thereafter; ushered them into the beliefs and practices of the Church; and established an extended social network, including godparents, clerics, and parishioners, under whose purview they would be raised and with whom they might later affiliate as adults. These relationships often bore fruit later in guardianship, mentoring, guild sponsorship, or trade apprenticeship for the child. Medieval Judaic and Islamic children, whose lives are just beginning to be revealed, likewise were initiated into their religious and social communities through the rites and practices unique to their traditions.

That medieval children were part of a broader social network also meant that greater care and nurture was provided for boys and girls during the dangerous, difficult early years of childhood. Godparents, along with parents, were enjoined to protect the youngster from the kinds of accidents that claimed many young lives in the medieval period. Infants were swaddled and cradled until they were toddlers, and higher-class infants often had a wet nurse, especially in Italy. Coroners' records indicate that children died of disease and by accident in the course of everyday life by playing in ponds or falling into wells, or being scalded in fires, trampled or attacked by animals, and run over by carts. Solid statistical evidence is hard to ascertain, but an estimated 30% of children did not survive to reach the age of seven, and while there is no evidence of widespread infanticide or systematic abuse, as charged by some commentators, girls seem to have died at a slightly higher rate than boys from illness, while boys died more often by accident than girls. Boys appear to have been treated more quickly and aggressively than girls when sick, and while the exact reasons are elusive, the motive may have been economic: a young man produced wealth by working and by obtaining a marriage dowry, while a young woman's marriage meant the family lost wealth.

Yet there is ample evidence that the lives of medieval boys and girls were as diverse as those of children today, with their time split between work and play. Children are shown in manuscript illuminations helping their parents with domestic tasks like gathering water, firewood, or food; spinning, sewing, and weaving; planting and harvesting; hunting and fishing; and tending to animals and routine chores. By assisting their parents, young boys and girls internalized the gender and social roles appropriate for their lives. A sixteenth-century representation, Breugel the Elder's painting "Children's Games" (1560), realistically depicts more than seventy-five different pastimes that occupied premodern children, many of which survive today: playing with hoops, sticks, balls, tops, and other found items; climbing trees, walls, barrels and other objects; wrestling, swimming, tumbling, and fighting; and playing tag, hide-and-seek, leap-frog, piggyback, and blind man's bluff. The division between work and play, and the practices constituting each, also undoubtedly varied depending upon whether the boy or girl lived in a rural setting, on a manor, in town, or at court.

Children might be orphaned or abandoned, and many European cultures had well-developed systems of wardship. England, for example, provided separate guardians for the child's body (and the right to marriage) and the child's goods (wealth and chattel). One of the most ancient ways of dealing with a foundling or an unwanted child was the practice of oblation—the permanent donation of a child to a monastery. The first foundling hospitals were established in Italy in the mid-thirteenth century, though other institutions probably accepted abandoned children even earlier, and London established a Court of Orphans to protect the interests of minor children and consider their particular needs.

Pueritia: *Education and Training*

A child's life options were shaped primarily by gender, class, and social location (rural or urban, city or town, and so on). Apart from the on-the-job training that most medieval young people accumulated as part of their domestic lives, formal medieval education focused primarily upon training boys in basic Latin literacy for ecclesiastical and professional duties, while girls had access chiefly to informal instruction. Boys might go to grammar school (to train in Latin) or song school to learn the antiphon (a brief liturgical text, generally a psalm verse or sentence from Scripture, recited, sung, or chanted before and after a psalm or canticle) before moving on to university studies. Although it was not unknown for girls to attend school (particularly at a nunnery), young women, especially those of the merchant and upper classes, might receive instruction at home from a local ecclesiastic, at a local nunnery, or from a private tutor (nun, nurse, priest, chaplain). The *Ave Maria, Pater Noster*, and *Apostles' Creed* formed both the educational foundation of medieval youth and the basis for conventional medieval piety. In addition to the basic literacy forged by these simple prayers and scriptural passages, the later Middle Ages saw the flourishing of "courtesy books" and other manuals of advice that instructed boys and girls in proper manners, especially for middle-class families attempting to move up the social ladder, and poems like "The ABC of Aristotle" used the letters of the alphabet to inculcate moderate and moderating moral virtues. Of course, virginity for both boys and girls remained the ideal, for virginity guaranteed sexual purity, moral rectitude, religious favor, and social approbation.

If their lives did not allow for a formal education in Latin, boys around the age of twelve, especially in the towns and cities, might be taken on as apprentices under a craftsman or as part of a guild, while girls might enter into household service, often with a relative. A contracted relationship, apprenticeship usually lasted seven years, with the master taking responsibility for all of the young man's needs for the duration of the contract. Household service was sometimes less formally structured, with the family tending to the young woman's needs during her tenure. Whether in the city or in the town, apprenticeship and then guild membership allowed the young man legally to become a citizen or burgher, with the legal rights that accrued to that position. Not having the same access to formal sponsorship, girls gained legal, official citizenship through marriage. If young women worked, it was often in the victualling trades or in a household.

Adolescentia: *Courtship and Marriage*

At *adolescentia*, generally regarded as twelve for girls and fourteen for boys, young people could be married, according to canon law, or could break a marriage contract set in their childhood by paying a fine equivalent to the value of the marriage. So, although many marriages were arranged and contracted, particularly in the upper classes, young people did have some say about whom they would marry; at the same time, parental, familial, or seigneurial permission was not necessarily required for them to marry. An exchange of vows was all that was required, and sexual intercourse was a *de facto* mark of marriage. These loose requirements sometimes led to legal disputes, especially when one partner (or the partner's parents or guardians) believed the promise of marriage to be given insincerely to procure wealth or sexual favors alone. The legal records are replete with cases of *raptus*—a term that could denote both rape and abduction—against young women. However, it would be a mistake to believe that all cases of *raptus* involved illicit sexual contact or forced abduction; some did, but there is also evidence of young people using the courts to seek their own wishes and to work against a parent or guardian's attempt to force them into an undesired marriage. Because children—boys especially, but also girls—were conduits of family wealth, both boys and girls could become pawns in protracted legal battles over land, wealth, and chattels (moveable goods) between guardians, ward keepers, in-laws, step-family, or extended kin.

Concerning marriage itself, young medieval wives were often several years younger than their mates, for young men married after accumulating or inheriting the necessary wealth, while a young woman conventionally brought her dowry into the marriage. Although remaining unmarried was a possibility for young men and women, girls' life options were generally limited to marriage, to a religious vocation, or to some form of domestic employment or household management. The social ideal, of course, was for young medieval girls to marry and have children. In fact, it could be argued that female childhood is inextricably bound to future childbearing, for the proper course of secular life led a girl directly from her father's house as a child and daughter to her husband's house as a wife and mother, while a boy moved from his parents' home to one of his own creation.

So, contrary to Ariès' insistence that the Middle Ages did not consider the uniqueness of children and childhood, medieval childhood was a sometimes contentious time with its own concerns and whose physical difficulties boys and girls had to survive and whose complexity they had to negotiate—cultural tasks that, though the details differ, contemporary children also face.

DANIEL T. KLINE

References and Further Reading

Ariès, Philippe. *Centuries of Childhood: A Social History of Family Life*, translated by Robert Baldick. New York: Vintage, 1962.

Boswell, John. *The Kindness of Strangers: The Abandonment of Children in Western Europe from Late Antiquity to the Renaissance*. New York: Pantheon, 1988.

Burrow, J. A. *The Ages of Man: A Study in Medieval Writing and Thought*. Oxford: Clarendon, 1986.

Crawford, Sally. *Childhood in Anglo-Saxon England*. Stroud, Gloucester: Sutton, 1999.

Dockray-Miller, Mary. *Motherhood and Mothering in Anglo-Saxon England*. New York: St. Martin's Press, 2000.

Finucane, Ronald C. *The Rescue of the Innocents: Endangered Children in Medieval Miracles*. New York: St. Martin's Press, 1997.

Gil'adi, Avner. *Children of Islam: Concepts of Childhood in Medieval Muslim Society*. New York: St. Martin's Press, 1992.

Goldberg, P. J. P., ed. and trans. *Women in England, c. 1275–1525*. Manchester: Manchester University Press, 1995.

Goldberg, P. J. P., and Felicity Riddy, eds. *Youth in the Middle Ages*. Woodbridge, Suffolk: Boydell and Brewer, 2004.

Hanawalt, Barbara. *The Ties That Bound: Peasant Families in Medieval England*. Oxford: Oxford University Press, 1986.

———. *Growing Up in Medieval London: The Experience of Childhood in History*. Oxford: Oxford University Press, 1993.

Herlihy, David. "Medieval Children." In *The Walter Prescott Webb Memorial Lectures: Essays on Medieval Civilization*, edited by Bede Karl Lackner and Kenneeth Roy Philip. Austin: University of Texas Press, 1978.

———. *Medieval Households*. Cambridge: Cambridge University Press, 1985.

Itnyre, Cathy Jorgensen, ed. *Medieval Family Roles: A Book of Essays*. New York: Garland, 1996.

Karras, Ruth Mazzo. *From Boys to Men: Formations of Masculinity in Late Medieval Europe*. Philadelphia: University of Pennsylvania Press, 2003.

Kline, Daniel T., ed. *Medieval Literature for Children*. New York: Routledge, 2003.

Lewis, Katherine J., Noël James Menuge, and Kim M. Phillips, eds. *Young Medieval Women*. New York: St. Martin's Press, 1999.

Neel, Carol, ed. *Medieval Families: Perspectives on Marriage, Household, and Children*. Medieval Academy Reprints for Teaching, 40. Toronto: University of Toronto Press, 2004.

Orme, Nicholas. *Medieval Children*. New Haven: Yale University Press, 2001.

Phillips, Kim M. *Medieval Maidens: Young Women and Gender in England, 1270–1570*. Manchester: Manchester University Press, 2003.

Schultz, James A. *The Knowledge of Childhood in the German Middle Ages, 1100–1350*. Philadelphia: University of Pennsylvania Press, 1995.

Sears, Elizabeth. *The Ages of Man: Medieval Interpretations of the Life Cycle*. Princeton: Princeton University Press, 1986.

Shahar, Shulamith. *Childhood in the Middle Ages*. London: Routledge, 1992.

See also **Abortion; Adolescence; Apprentices; Artisan Families, Women of; Breastfeeding and Wet-Nursing; Children, Betrothal and Marriage of; Conduct Literature; Dowry and Other Marriage Gifts; Education: Lay; Education: Monastic; Fosterage; Gentry, Women of: England; Godparents; Guild Members and Guilds; Heiresses; Household Management; Illegitimacy; Infants and Infanticide; Inheritance; Literacy and Reading: Latin; Literacy and Reading: Vernacular; Merchant Families, Women of; Mothers as Teachers; Naming; Oblates and Oblation; Pregnancy and Childbirth: Christian Women; Pregnancy and Childbirth: Jewish Women; Procreation and Ideas of Conception; Rape and Raptus; Servants; Virginity; Wardship**

GODELIEVE OF GISTEL

Godelieve (c. 1052–1070) was born in Flanders, the daughter of a knight of Count Eustace I of Boulogne. About 1067 she was married to Bertulf, a knight in Gistel, near Bruges, who, at the instigation of his mother, maltreated her and, in 1070, had her killed. Soon Godelieve was venerated as a saint and she was canonized on July 30, 1084. Shortly before, Drogo, monk of Saint-Winocsbergen, wrote her *Life* picturing her as a martyr, obedient and patient in suffering. Another *Life*, the so-called *Legend*, presents her as a holy virgin. Usually dated in the fourteenth or fifteenth century, it is considered unreliable. Nip (2002) argues that it was composed in the twelfth century, after the foundation of the nunnery of Saint Godelieve at Gistel. Here the portrayal was adjusted to the special needs of the nuns.

Drogo's *Life* raises the question of why Godelieve was recognized as a saint. Scholars wonder what it was really about: a conflict between nobility and church concerning different ideas on marriage or their relative power, or a conflict between the lower classes and the elite? In fact, Godelieve's life and canonization must be understood in the light of the rivalry between the Counts of Flanders and their powerful vassals, the Counts of Boulogne.

The *Life* also provides information on marriage, the position of women within the family, their (lack of) power, and social, political, and juridical hierarchies.

Godelieve's cult was still flourishing in the twentieth century.

RENÉE NIP

References and Further Reading

Duby, Georges. *Mâle moyen age: De l'amour et autres essais*. Paris: Flammarion, 1988.

Huyghebaert, Nikolaas-Norbert, ed. *Drogo van Sint-Winoksbergen Vita Godeliph*, translated by Stefaan Gyselen. Tielt/Bussum: Lannoo, 1982.

Nip, Renée. "Godelieve of Gistel and Ida of Boulogne." In *Sanctity and Motherhood*, edited by Anneke B. Mulder-Bakker. New York and London: Garland Publishing, 1995.

——. "The Canonization of Godelieve of Gistel." *Hagiographica* 2 (1995): 145–156.

——. "Life and Afterlife: Arnulf of Oudenburg, Bishop of Soissons, and Godelieve of Gistel. Their Function as Intercessors in Medieval Flanders." In *The Invention of Saintliness*, edited by Anneke B. Mulder-Bakker. London and New York: Routledge, 2002.

"Stola S. Godelevae," *Sacris Eruderi* 20 (1971), special volume.

Vernarde, Bruce L., trans. "Drogo of Sint-Winoksbergen, Life of St. Godelieve." In *Medieval Hagiography*, edited by Thomas Head. New York and London: Garland Publishing, 2000.

See also **Canonization of Saints; Domestic Abuse; Flanders; Hagiography; Marriage, Christian; Sexuality: Sex in Marriage; Virginity**

GODPARENTS

The godparent role in baptism has two roots in the early church: sponsorship of adult converts being baptized and having a person or persons speak for an infant receiving baptism. The practice of having outsiders, not close kin, sponsor children grew up in both Greek and Latin rites; it became the norm when infant baptism became the most common rite of Christian initiation. A related practice grew up of giving a child both a godfather and a godmother. Godparents had a post-baptismal responsibility for the spiritual welfare of the baptized. This role also created a spiritual kinship that grew into a legal impediment to marriage between godparent and godchild—and between parent and godparent—known as spiritual affinity, as well as a prohibition of nonmarital sexual relations between them. This rule extended to godparents and godchildren the same degrees of prohibited relationship contracted by sexual intercourse (physical affinity). These taboos were recorded in canon law texts that became normative later in the Middle Ages, and there were enactments by lay powers to the same effect. Outsiders chosen as godparents might be ascetics, whose spiritual patronage was valued; but ecclesiastical authorities eventually discouraged this as a worldly distraction for monks and nuns. More commonly, lay persons (including neighbors, business associates, and even social superiors) were selected. In cities like Dubrovnik, parents' siblings often were selected as godparents to reduce the number of incest prohibitions affecting the child's marital choices.

Furthermore, godparents were expected to be teachers and guides for their godchildren. These practices were adopted in Frankish and Anglo-Saxon lands, and they spread from both to the Germanic regions.

Aside from spiritual elements, there were social and political aspects of godparenting that might benefit the child, creating an extended support network, especially when prominent persons had stood up with the infant at baptism. Among the Franks, in particular, godparents were chosen for children of high birth to provide them with protection against violence. In other cases, social inferiors were asked to serve as baptismal sponsors to bind them more closely to their superiors. Godparenting also created social ties between adults, especially when close friends were selected as baptismal sponsors. Fathers might select godfathers to extend their connections, while mothers might choose godmothers from among their friends to solidify their own networks. This led, in parts of Italy, to inviting large numbers of persons to serve as godparents to a single child. Another social element in godparenting was naming. A godparent in late medieval England and France frequently named the child, sometimes for herself or himself.

Byzantine practice has been less studied, but the prohibition of guardians marrying wards was adopted from Roman law and extended to godparents. Byzantine ideas about spiritual kinship were transmitted to Russia and other Slavic lands, but their impact has not been studied in depth.

THOMAS IZBICKI

References and Further Reading

Haas, Louis. "*Il mio buono compare*: Choosing Godparents and the Uses of Baptismal Kinship in Renaissance Florence." *Journal of Social History* 29 (1995): 341–356.

Jussen, Bernhard. *Spiritual Kinship as Social Practice: Godparenthood and Adoption in the Early Middle Ages*, translated by Pamela Selwyn. Newark, Del.: University of Delaware Press, 2000.

Klapisch-Zuber, Christiane. "Au peril des commères: l'alliance spiritelle par les femmes à Florence." In *Femmes, mariages-lignages: XIIe-XIVe siècles: Mélanges offerts à Georges Duby*. Bruxelles: De Boeck Université, 1992.

Lynch, Joseph. *Godparents and Kinship in Early Medieval Europe*. Princeton, N.J.: Princeton University Press, 1986.

Niles, Phillip. "Baptism and the Naming of Children in Late Medieval England." *Medieval Prosopography* 3 (1982): 95–107.

See also **Frankish Lands; Kinship; Law, Canon; Marriage, Impediments to; Naming**

GOLDEN LEGEND
See **Jacobus de Voragine's Golden Legend**

GOSCELIN OF ST. BERTIN

A monk from the abbey of St. Bertin at Saint-Omer in Flanders (now France), Goscelin (c. 1040–1114) came to England with Herman, Bishop of Sherborne and Ramsbury, in about 1058. He became a noted hagiographer and composer of liturgical music in his adopted country. After a period as chaplain of the royal women's house of Wilton, he was associated with various English monasteries and finally settled at St. Augustine's, Canterbury. His importance to students of medieval women lies in his extensive hagiographical work on female English saints and his *Liber Confortatorius*, a book of spiritual counsel, theology, and friendship for his student Eve, who had left Wilton to become a recluse at Angers.

The hagiographic works reflect Goscelin's association with various important monastic houses. Apparently he was commissioned to compile full records and liturgical materials for their local saints. These bundled hagiographic texts illustrate post-Conquest views of Anglo-Saxon history and religion, as well as local practices of veneration; thus, we have clusters of *vitae* connected with Barking Abbey, Ely, and the Kentish royal family.

The *Life of St. Edith* occupies a special position in Goscelin's work. It is more ambitious in literary style than the other saints' lives; it also reflects close personal association, and it often turns autobiographical. The *Life* is closely linked in time, place, and theme to the *Liber Confortatorius* (c. 1082), which allows extraordinary insights into the spirituality and education of a religious woman, and into an intense spiritual and personal friendship across gender lines.

MONIKA C. OTTER

References and Further Reading

Colker, Marvin. "Texts of Jocelyn of Canterbury Which Relate to the History of Barking Abbey." *Studia Monastica* 7 (1965): 383–460.
Hollis, Stephanie, et al. *Writing the Wilton Women: Goscelin's* Legend of St. Edith *and* Liber Confortatorius. Turnhout: Brepols, 2004.
Love, Rosalind, ed. and trans. *Goscelin of St. Bertin: The Hagiography of the Female Saints of Ely*. Oxford: Oxford University Press, 2004.
Otter, Monika, trans. *Goscelin of St. Bertin:* The Book of Encouragement and Consolation (Liber confortatorius). Woodbridge, Suffolk, England: D. S. Brewer, 2004.
Rollason, D. W. *The Mildrith Legend: A Study of Early Medieval Hagiography in England*. Leicester: Leicester University Press, 1992.

See also **Devotional Literature; Hagiography**

GOSSIP AND SLANDER

Medieval women were especially associated with the sins of gossip and slander. This was nothing new: Greek and Roman women, too, had been stereotyped as gossipy, and St. Paul's letters expressed particular concern about widows who gossiped and spoke inappropriately. By the late Middle Ages, however, the connection between women and illicit speech was even more entrenched, as evident from literature, art, and legal prosecutions.

Literary and artistic representations emphasized women's association with gossip and slander. A sermon exemplum well known throughout Europe, for instance, told of the demon Tutivillus, who was said to sit at the back of the church and write down the words uttered by those who gossiped rather than paying attention. When Tutivillus eavesdropped on women, he found that they talked so much that he ran out of space on his scroll and had to stretch it. Variations on this exemplum appear from the twelfth century onwards, from as far afield as Iceland, Estonia, and England. The story is also represented in church wall paintings and wood carvings depicting a devil hovering behind gossiping women. Some of the best-preserved examples come from England, France, and Denmark. The gossiping women of the Tutivillus exemplum laid the groundwork for a stock character of an unruly, garrulous woman in literature of the High to late Middle Ages. La Vielle, the old woman of the *Roman de la Rose*, Noah's wife of the English mystery play cycles, and the Wife of Bath of Chaucer's *Canterbury Tales* represent variations of this character, giving early modern playwrights a rich tradition from which to create merry widows and shrews in need of taming. At the same time as individual women were ridiculed for verbal disorder, advice literature directed at men warned them to be careful about trusting women's words and to curb their wives' tongues as early as possible. Sermons reinforced this message by comparing the speech of Eve, who had shared God's secrets with the serpent, to that of the more taciturn Virgin Mary, whose speech was reported in the Bible on only four occasions.

The late Middle Ages also saw the emergence of a new crime, known as "scolding," in which people who had loud public arguments would be charged in courts and forced to pay fines or to suffer public humiliation. Discussed and punished especially in England, scolding involved speaking too much, too loudly, or with slanderous words in a public setting. About ninety percent of those charged as scolds in manorial courts, borough courts, and church courts were women. In most places, married women predominated among the accused, although some towns focused their concerns on the speech of single women. Despite literary concerns about the speech of old women, widows were only seldom accused as scolds. Where the words of alleged scolds were recorded, they were remarkably formulaic: in general, when women were scolded they were called some variation on the term *whore*, whereas men were more likely to be called "thief" or "liar." If convicted, most scolds were fined, but sometimes they were punished by more dramatic means. One of these involved the "cucking stool" or "ducking stool," a contraption in which offenders were forced to sit while being dunked in a pond, river, or waterlogged pit. In the early modern era, "scolds' bridles" or branks were invented. These were small metal cages that fit over the head of the alleged scold and usually involved a spike being inserted in her mouth, making it impossible for her to talk.

Historians once assumed that scolding prosecutions were relatively rare and that scolds were women who were generally disruptive and even mentally disturbed. Investigation of scolding in particular towns and villages, however, has shown that it was less rare than once thought. Historians have also recently acknowledged that women accused of scolding came from a wide range of social, economic, and marital statuses. While a few alleged scolds were regularly in trouble for a wide range of offenses, most were relatively respectable or otherwise ordinary villagers and townspeople. What is more, the significance of scolding spread well beyond the numbers of individuals accused in courts. Prosecution of scolds not only punished those whose speech was thought to be disruptive, it also silenced others who might have been inclined to speak out if they had not been afraid of being accused as scolds themselves.

By the end of the Middle Ages, then, women's association with gossip and verbal disorder was more ingrained than ever. Women's voices were seen as both illicit and yet also powerful (hence the repeated efforts to silence them). The witch craze of the early modern era would further underscore the power and danger of women's words.

SANDRA BARDSLEY

References and Further Reading

Bardsley, Sandy. *Venomous Tongues: Speech and Gender in Late Medieval England*. Philadelphia: University of Pennsylvania Press, 2006.
Boose, Lynda E. "Scolding Brides and Bridling Scolds: Taming the Woman's Unruly Member." *Shakespeare Quarterly* 42 (1991): 179–213.
Dean, Trevor. "Gender and Insults in an Italian City: Bologna in the Later Middle Ages." *Social History* 29 (2004): 217–231.
Ingram, Martin. "'Scolding Women Cucked or Washed': A Crisis in Gender Relations in Early Modern England?" In *Women, Crime and the Courts*, edited by Jenny Kermode and Garthine Walker. London: University College of London Press, 1994.
Jennings, Margaret. *Tutivillus: The Literary Career of the Recording Demon*. Studies in Philology, Texts and Studies, 74. Chapel Hill, N.C.: University of North Carolina Press, 1977.
Jones, Karen, and Michael Zell. "Bad Conversation? Gender and Social Control in a Kentish Borough, c. 1450–c. 1570." *Continuity and Change* 13 (1998): 11–31.
Lindorfer, Bettina. "*Peccatum Linguae* and the Punishment of Speech Violations in the Middle Ages and Early Modern Times." In *Speaking in the Medieval World*, edited by Jean E. Godsall-Myers. Leiden: Brill, 2003.
Lochrie, Karma. *Covert Operations: The Medieval Uses of Secrecy*. Philadelphia: University of Pennsylvania Press, 1999.
Underdown, David E. "The Taming of the Scold: The Enforcement of Patriarchal Authority in Early Modern England." In *Order and Disorder in Early Modern England*, edited by A. Fletcher and J. Stevenson. Cambridge: Cambridge University Press, 1985.

See also **Honor and Reputation; Wife of Bath; Witches**

GOTTFRIED VON STRASSBURG

Gottfried von Strassburg composed his *Tristan*, an extended fragment of over 19,000 Middle High German verses, in the early thirteenth century in or around the urban center of Strasbourg. The number of extant *Tristan* manuscripts attests to its popularity (Gibbs). Loosely drawing upon previous versions of *Tristan* (Thomas, Béroul, Eilhart), Gottfried created a uniquely complex narrative that tells more than a story of unfortunate lovers doomed by a fateful potion. The expansive first part of *Tristan* traces the respective development of Tristan and Isolde as they assume their roles in courtly society (v. 1-11874), and the second part of the narrative describes the subversion of those roles through various tensions created by the lovers' relationship (v. 11875 ff.): the tension between Isolde's roles as lover and queen and between Tristan's roles as lover and loyal vassal. Portraying the lovers as the "new man" and the "new woman" of an ideal courtly world, Gottfried's text advocates a new courtly ethos. The text foregrounds issues of gender, sexuality, masculinity, and femininity, as the lovers resist twelfth-century romance conventions.

This resistance begins in Ireland, where Gottfried's narrative focuses on Queen Isolde and her daughter of the same name. Well-versed in politics, diplomacy, and the healing arts, Queen Isolde takes great care in the education of her only child. She engages the stranger Tristan as tutor for her daughter after he arrives in Ireland. (v. 7979 ff.) Tristan completes young Isolde's education, molding her into the perfect form that corresponds to her inborn beauty. The queen ultimately leaves her brother Morolt's death unavenged so that her exemplary daughter may make a suitable match with King Marke. She subsequently prepares the love potion to ensure her daughter a happy life with her new husband, thereby securing the younger Isolde's future political position. One could say "like mother, like daughter"; indeed, the knowledge (*liste*), wisdom, and beauty of the young Isolde and her mother are matched only by that of Tristan himself.

The daughter, however, does not become the mother, defying the symbolism of their shared name. Her education makes Isolde a kind of "new woman," for she is as much a courtier and a practitioner of *hövescheit* (courtliness) as Tristan. Thus she becomes the perfect partner for the hero who represents *daz niuwe wunder* (the new marvel, v. 6635). The fateful love potion subsequently impels both Tristan and Isolde into a partnership that releases her from the conventions that the mother embodies as wife and mother. With the power and wealth she gains as Marke's queen, Isolde also enjoys with Tristan the "true" love the troubadours considered possible only outside of marriage.

In Cornwall, the new man and the new woman prove marvelously adept at the art of public secrecy. This new life of "lying truth" (Poag), where that which is seen remains unseen, is characterized by eroticism, adultery, betrayal, and a love that consistently thwarts patriarchal–feudal conventions. The lovers' efforts culminate in the scenes commonly known as the "Assignation by the Brook" (*Baumgartenszene*) and the "Ordeal" (*Gottesurteil*). Ultimately, in the Cave of Lovers (*Minnegrotte*), they remain sufficient unto themselves, though this union proves untenable. The lovers return to court and must eventually separate, where Gottfried's tale ends.

Gottfried's story of Tristan and Isolde offers a distinctly multivalent discussion of early-thirteenth-century masculinity and femininity, particularly in Isolde. More than any other woman in Arthurian literature, Isolde exercises the traditionally masculine prerogative of choice. The love potion may affect Isolde's choice of whom to love, as with Tristan, but Isolde's other attributes remain unaffected. After her arrival in Cornwall, she displays considerable authority and autonomy, skillfully manipulating appearances and reality. Her autonomy, at its most radical, is visually underscored by the female imagery of the lovers' cave, a sheltered womb-like space. Enjoying the roles of queen, wife, and lover, Isolde continually defies any prescribed role. In a sense, she becomes like

Tristan: she *herzet sich mit manne* (takes on the heart of a man, v. 17981) to become a woman who is also *ein man mit muote* (a man in spirit, v. 17985).

In the end, Isolde's relationships remain essentially sterile; unlike her mother, the younger Isolde does not become a mother. Tristan also finally remains alone, unable to reintegrate into courtly society. Thus, while Gottfried's lovers seem to transcend conventional gender boundaries as they achieve a spiritually exalted relationship, the poet communicates an equivocal message. Knowledge and artistry are integral to *Tristan*'s reciprocal redefinition of the ideal courtly woman and man in the new courtly ethos, as is female agency; nevertheless, that agency continues to threaten any established order, old or new.

ALEXANDRA STERLING-HELLENBRAND

References and Further Reading

Gibbs, Marion E. "The Medieval Reception of Gottfried's *Tristan*." In *A Companion to Gottfried von Strassburg's Tristan*, edited by Will Hasty. Rochester, N.Y.: Camden House, 2003.

Hasty, Will, ed. *A Companion to Gottfried von Strassburg's Tristan*. Rochester, N.Y.: Camden House, 2003.

Jaeger, C. Stephan. *Medieval Humanism in Gottfried von Strassburg's Tristan und Isolde*. Heidelberg: Winter, 1977.

McDonald, William C. "Gottfried von Strassburg: *Tristan* and the Arthurian Tradition." In *Tristan and Isolde: A Casebook*, edited by Joan Trasker Grimbert. New York: Garland Publishing, 1995.

McNamara, Jo Ann. "The *Herrenfrage*: The Restructuring of the Gender System, 1050–1150." In *Medieval Masculinities: Regarding Men in the Middle Ages*, edited by Clare A. Lees. Minneapolis: University of Minnesota Press, 1994.

Poag, James F. "Lying Truth in Gottfried's *Tristan*." *Deutsche Vierteljahrsschrift fur Literaturwissenschaft und Geistesgeschichte* 61. 2 (1987): 223–237.

Rasmussen, Ann Marie. *Mothers and Daughters in Medieval German Literature*. Syracuse: Syracuse University Press, 1997.

von Strassburg, Gottfried. *Tristan*, translated by A. T. Hatto. London: Penguin, 1967.

———. *Tristan*, edited by Friedrich Ranke. Stuttgart: Reclam, 1984.

See also **Arthurian Literature; Chivalry; Femininity and Masculinity; Gender Ideologies; Germanic Lands; Isolde; Literature, German; Mothers as Teachers; Romance, German**

GRAVE GOODS

In traditions dating to the prehistoric past, late antique and early medieval Europeans frequently prepared their dead by outfitting them with clothing and a range of items of personal adornment, weaponry, tableware and food, coinage, and other materials. With the transition from cremation to inhumation across the Roman Empire in the third century, the custom of depositing goods with the dead persisted with significant regional variations in western Europe as late as the seventh and eighth centuries. The tradition did not cease with Christian conversion, and seventh-century saints like Cuthbert in the north of England were laid to rest with an assortment of artifacts. In fact, the use of grave goods was never entirely abandoned. In the late Middle Ages, for instance, some bishops and monarchs of the Holy Roman Empire were buried with symbols of their office. Both lay and ecclesiastical legislation against grave robbery criminalized the activity with severe penalties, and while the laws were far from effective, their repetition suggests that the theft of grave artifacts and the disturbance of the dead were of great concern to elite Christian lawmakers.

Used in burial rites by both pagans and Christians, grave goods fulfilled a multitude of functions in commemorating, protecting, and drawing attention to the achievements of the dead. Although far from all sepulchers contained such artifacts, they provided surviving family and followers with the opportunity to highlight certain aspects of the identity or the status of the deceased and stake claims with regard to the continuing viability of that group in the face of significant loss. Some early medieval boys, for instance, were buried with full-sized weapons symbolic of the profession they might have someday attained had they lived to adulthood. Hence, grave goods did not directly mirror the life of the now-anonymous remains of the early medieval inhabitants of Europe, but rather reflected the worldly and otherworldly ambitions of those who oversaw funerary arrangements.

Scholars believe that members of the immediate kin group normally chose the assortment of objects that accompanied the dead into the grave, but there were certainly exceptions in monastic communities or among the supporters who surrounded high-status figures like kings and queens. In the case of the seventh-century Merovingian queen Bathilda, who after being deposed lived out her final years in the abbey of Chelles, reliquaries believed to have held her bones and those of the first abbess Bertilla were found, respectively, to contain a red cloak with yellow fringes and a brown silk tunic with yellow stripes ordinarily forbidden by monastic Rules to contemporary nuns. Evidently some unnamed supporters of the deceased decided that these women were deserving of a burial appropriate to their worldly status rather than reflective of the vows they had taken as part of their religious profession. Scholars have thus characterized the composition of grave assemblages as comparable to

the process of writing a saint's life, since funerals represented a point in time at which fictive or idealized identities might be constructed on behalf of the deceased.

Close study of the gender aspects of grave goods has only been undertaken since the 1980s. Prior to this time, archaeologists and historians normally assumed that men were accompanied in burial by weaponry (*Heergewäte*) and women by jewelry (*Gerade*), since it was believed that these items could not legally pass to heirs. This binary approach to conceptualizing the distribution of possessions to graves has proved unsatisfactory for a number of reasons. First, no legal impediment existed to the inheritance of weaponry, clothing, or jewelry by either sex in early medieval secular or canon law. Second, the development of osteological and DNA techniques for analyzing the biological sex of skeletons suggests that there were, in certain circumstances, discrepancies between the sex of human remains and gendering of archaeological objects buried in early medieval graves. At the cemetery of Sewerby in East Yorkshire, for instance, fully fifteen percent of the graves sexed osteologically as possibly male contained jewelry. Third, the ubiquitous use of grave goods to sex skeletons until recently means that these data cannot contribute to accurate tables of the gender distributions of archaeological artifacts, since they reflect the implicit expectations of researchers more than the preferences of early medieval individuals. While some resistance exists to embracing a more scientific approach toward the identification of biological sex independent of the grave goods found with human remains, since this methodology would necessitate abandoning studies for which the skeletal evidence no longer survives, recent high-quality excavations have adopted less biased standards in the collection, analysis, and interpretation of human remains and archaeological artifacts.

Grave goods represent an important source for understanding gender mores, particularly in the early Middle Ages, when their use was most widespread. Not only is there an increasingly reliable and growing body of materials by which to study these issues, but the data reflect a far wider proportion of the population, including women, than accessible by means of limited written documentation. The archaeological and written evidence for burial practices sheds new light on the function and interplay of gender mores in western Europe. Although many burials received no artifacts (or at least none that have survived a millennium and a half of decay and human and natural disturbances), the statistical identification of particular grave goods in individual cemeteries as articulating strongly masculine, strongly feminine, or gender-neutral symbolism, based on their distribution in the graves of men, women, and children, sheds light on the choices of objects included in burials. Although gender was just one of many interconnected identities, including age, status, ethnicity, religious affiliation, and kinship, that played into decisions made at the time of the burial, the fact that in early medieval Gaul, for instance, women of child-bearing age and men of fighting age often received the most extensive and high-quality grave assemblages, and elderly individuals were typically buried with fewer, suggests the possible extent to which surviving contemporaries valued their respective contributions.

As with any socially constructed aspect of culture, the gender symbolism of grave goods was neither static nor uniform but varied by community and over time. Even the inhabitants of neighboring settlements sometimes chose different means by which to commemorate the loss of men, women, and children. Rather than a passive reflection of the attributes of the deceased, the clothing and accessories deposited in or withheld from burials were specific to the time, place, individual, and audience of the funeral. Unfortunately, however, surviving written and archaeological evidence is biased toward the more elite members of early medieval society, who left the most enduring remains. Nonetheless, we can safely state that not only the male elites highlighted in contemporary histories, but the unnamed women who are described in early medieval hagiographical sources as actively participating in preparing the dead for burial, represented influential negotiators in the process of outfitting the deceased for funeral ceremonies and burials.

BONNIE EFFROS

References and Further Reading

Effros, Bonnie. *Merovingian Mortuary Archaeology and the Making of the Early Middle Ages.* Berkeley: University of California Press, 2003.

Hadley, Dawn. "Negotiating Gender, Family and Status in Anglo-Saxon Burial Practices, c. 600–950." In *Gender in the Early Medieval World: East and West, 300–900,* edited by Leslie Brubaker and Julia M. H. Smith. Cambridge: Cambridge University Press, 2004.

Halsall, Guy. *Settlement and Social Organization: The Merovingian Region of Metz.* Cambridge: Cambridge University Press, 1995.

Lucy, Sam. *The Early Anglo-Saxon Cemeteries of East Yorkshire: An Analysis and Reinterpretation.* BAR British Series 272. Oxford: British Archaeological Reports, 1998.

Stoodley, Nick. *The Spindle and the Spear: A Critical Enquiry into the Construction and Meaning of Gender in the Early Anglo-Saxon Burial Rite.* BAR British Series 288. Oxford: British Archaeological Reports, 1999.

Swift, Ellen. *Regionality in Dress Accessories in the Late Roman West.* Monographies Instrumentum 11. Montagnac: M. Mergoil, 2000.

See also **Archaeology; Burials and Tombs; Death, Mourning, and Commemoration; Femininity and Masculinity; Gender Ideologies; Gertrude of Nivelles; Hagiography; Jewelry; Wills**

GRISELDA

Griselda, the long-suffering heroine of a story that charmed and fascinated numerous medieval writers, first appeared in the final tale of Boccacio's *Decameron,* a collection of 100 tales begun after 1348 and probably completed in 1353. Thanks to Petrarch's Latin translation of the tale (1374), the story spread throughout Europe, each time addressed in slightly different ways to medieval readers. These retellings offered occasions for engaging in the ongoing medieval debate on the nature, status, and conduct of women.

Boccaccio

Thought to be based on a folk version of the Cupid and Psyche legend, Boccaccio's tale recounts how Gualtiero, the Marquis of Saluzzo, constrained by his subjects to take a wife, chooses to wed a peasant woman. Subsequently, the marquis tests his wife's obedience by staging various trials. He pretends first to order his daughter's murder, then to subject his newborn son to the same treatment. Finally, he orders Griselda to yield her place to a younger bride. After stripping his wife of her fine clothes and sending her back to her father's lowly house, Gualtiero summons her a final time and asks her to prepare his house for her youthful replacement. Griselda's suffering ends when her husband reveals that the bride-to-be is in fact her own daughter. Satisfied at last with the repeated proof of his wife's obedience, he takes her back into his house, restoring the children she had thought were dead.

In the *Decameron,* the story fits into a frame that places as much emphasis on Gualtiero's actions as on Griselda's, a focus that shifts somewhat in subsequent retellings. Fitting the story into the tenth day's theme of liberality or magnificence in matters of love, Boccaccio's fictional narrator, Dineo, describes his tale as an example of how a lord can lack these noble virtues while a humble peasant woman displays them. He ends his performance with a ribald joke, suggesting that Griselda might have found another man to give her a new dress rather than going back to Gualtiero. Boccaccio's framing of the Griselda story brings out its ambivalence, in that he pays tribute both to its moral implications and to its fictional and ludic qualities. Subsequent translators of the tale fitted it into new frames that preserve this ambivalence or that orient it in the direction of either allegory or exemplum.

Petrarch

At about the same time that Petrarch translated the tale of Griselda, Ser Giovanni Sercambi retold it in Italian, entitling it *De Muliere Costante* and changing the heroine's name to Costantina. But it was Petrarch's Latin translation that ensured the tale's dissemination throughout Europe. The translation is addressed to Boccaccio in one of the letters collected in the *Seniles* (*Seniles*, XVIII, 3). Here Petrarch admits that the *Decameron* is not wholly to his taste. Finding the last tale superior to the rest, he translates it into Latin to send it back to its author for judgment. Petrarch offers it "not so much to urge the matrons of our time to imitate the patience of this wife…as to arouse readers to imitate her womanly constancy, that they might dare to undertake for God what she undertook for her husband…." In Petrarch's hands, the story becomes an allegory of the trials endured by Christians, and Griselda resembles a female Job.

French Versions

Notions of fidelity to the Petrarchan source shaped the subsequent retellings of the story in other European vernaculars; nevertheless, the medieval translators exercised complete liberty in choosing the co-texts introducing, concluding, or accompanying their translations. These co-texts interpret and appropriate the source text for different purposes, guiding the reception of the tale. So Philippe de Mézières, a friend of the Italian laureate Petrarch turns Griselda into a mirror for married women when he inserts his translation of the tale into a four-book treatise whose full title as announced in the Prologue is *De la Vertu du sacrement de mariage espirituel et réconfort des dames mariées et de tout bon Crestien par un devot example de la Passion de Jesu Crist et du miroir des dames mariée, la noble marquise de Saluce* (On the virtue of the sacrament of spiritual marriage and the comfort of married women and of all good Christians by the devout example of the passion of Jesus Christ and the mirror of married women, the noble Marquise de Saluce). Like Petrarch, Philippe separated the tale from its co-texts and set it in an entirely different kind

of work, whose genre had acquired some popularity during the fourteenth century in France: a vernacular book of spiritual advice for married women. To reinforce the heroine's credibility as an exemplary spouse, the French translator elevated the tale to the rank of history rather than fiction. Petrarch had concluded in his letter that the story was Boccaccio's invention, but Philippe insists on its literal truth. In the prologue to his translation, he claims that though it might seem to be an invention, its truth is attested to by Griselda's fame in Lombardy and by its source, the devout Catholic doctor Francis Petrarch. In moving to France, Griselda becomes a model for wives to imitate. The story appears in *Le Ménagier de Paris*, a book of exempla and advice addressed by an old husband to his young bride. There is even a French version for the stage, *L'Estoire de Griseldis* (1395), thought to be commissioned for a royal wedding. In the early fifteenth century, the French writer Christine de Pizan took up the Griselda story and placed it alongside other exemplary tales of virtuous women in the *Livre de la Cité des Dames*, offering it as a refutation of misogynistic slander against her sex.

Iberian Versions

The Catalan author Bernat Metge introduced the story to the Iberian Peninsula when in 1388 he addressed a translation of Petrarch's Latin text to Isabel de Guimerà, a married noblewoman. In Spain, Griselda continued to be held up as an example for married women in a version included in a Castilian book of advice for women, purportedly written by a father to his daughters.

Chaucer

The Griselda story crossed from continental Europe to England when Chaucer translated it using Petrarch's Latin text and an anonymous French version, *Le Livre de Griseldis*, as his source texts. He then inserted it into *The Canterbury Tales* as the Clerk's Tale. The English writer exploits all the tale's ambivalence in having the Clerk engage (with characteristically Chaucerian irony) first with Petrarch and finally with the Wife of Bath and other "noble" wives. By urging women in the "Envoy" to the Clerk's tale not to follow Griselda's example but to enter into battle against their husbands, Chaucer ensured that the disturbing power of the tale of Griselda and Walter would continue to trouble readers and inspire debate.

WENDY HARDING

References and Further Reading

Bettridge, William, and Francis Lee Utley. "New Light on the Origin of the Griselda Story." *Texas Studies in Literature and Language* 13 (1971): 153–208.

Blumenfeld-Kosinski, Renate. "Christine de Pizan and the Misogynistic Tradition." *Romanic Review* 81 (1990): 279–292.

Bourland, C. B. "Boccaccio and the Decameron in Castilian and Catalan Literature." *Revue Hispanique* 12 (1905): 1–232.

Bronfman, Judith. *Chaucer's Clerk's Tale: The Griselda Story Received, Rewritten, Illustrated.* Garland Studies in Medieval Literature, 11. Garland Reference Library of the Humanities, 1831. Reprint, New York and London: Garland, 1994.

Dinshaw, Carolyn. "Griselda Translated." In *Chaucer's Sexual Poetics.* Madison: University of Wisconsin Press, 1989, pp. 132–155.

Filios, Denise. "Rewriting Griselda: From Folktale to Exemplum." *Mediaevalia* 24 (2003): 45–73.

Finlayson, John. "Petrarch, Boccaccio, and Chaucer's Clerk's Tale." *Studies in Philology* 97 (2000): 255–275.

Hollander, Robert, and Courtney Cahill. "Day Ten of the *Decameron*: The Myth of Order." In *Boccaccio's Dante and the Shaping Force of Satire,* edited by Robert Hollander. Ann Arbor, Mich.: University of Michigan Press, 1997, pp. 110–112.

Kellogg, Alfred L. "The Evolution of the 'Clerk's Tale': A Study in Connotation." *Chaucer, Langland, Arthur: Essays in Middle English Literature.* New Brunswick, N.J.: Rutgers University Press, 1972, pp. 276–329.

Kirkpatrick, Robin. "The Griselda Story in Boccaccio, Petrarch and Chaucer." In *Chaucer and the Italian Trecento,* edited by Piero Boitani and Anna Torti. Cambridge: Cambridge University Press, 1983, pp. 231–248.

Middleton, Anne. "The Clerk and his Tale: Some Literary Contexts." *Studies in the Age of Chaucer* 2 (1980): 121–150.

Morse, Charlotte C. "Critical Approaches to the Clerk's Tale." In *Chaucer's Religious Tales,* edited by C. David Benson and Elizabeth Robertson. Cambridge: Brewer, 1990, pp. 71–83.

Rigby, S. H. "Misogynist Versus Feminist Chaucer." In *Chaucer in Context: Society, Allegory and Gender.* Manchester and New York: Manchester University Press, 1996, pp. 116–166.

Severs, Burke. *The Literary Relationships of Chaucer's "Clerk's Tale."* Yale Studies in English, 96. New Haven: Yale University Press, 1942.

Wallace, David. "'Whan She Translated Was': A Chaucerian Critique of the Petrarchan Academy." In *Literary Practice and Social Change in Britain, 1380–1530,* edited by Lee Patterson. Berkeley: University of California Press, 1990, pp. 156–215.

See also **Boccaccio, Giovanni; Chaucer, Geoffrey; Literature, Italian; Petrarch; Translation**

GUIBERT OF NOGENT'S MOTHER

All we know of Abbot Guibert of Nogent's unnamed mother (c. 1030–after 1104) is contained within his memoir (1115). According to Guibert, she was a noble woman, married at a young age to his father, Evrard. Her fear of sin may have contributed to her husband's early impotence, but she eventually gave birth to several children. She was widowed less than a year after Guibert was born. Following the death of her husband, having fulfilled her marital duties, she took control of her own affairs. In defiance of her in-laws, she chose to remain unmarried, lived as a religious laywoman, and eventually became a recluse at a male monastery.

Guibert credits his mother with providing him with a model of Christian behavior and an education. He describes visions that directed her during momentous times in her life. When he was about twelve, she moved her household to the monastery of St. Germer of Fly. Shortly afterwards, she arranged for Guibert and his older brothers to be admitted. At St. Germer, Guibert's mother led an ascetic life in her cell, although people visited her for spiritual guidance. She maintained a devotion to the Virgin Mary and continued to have visions, one of which directed a rebellious Guibert to remain at Fly. Guibert's mother found autonomy in her calling, establishing herself as a visionary and an exemplar. She led a life similar to those of contemporary mystics—her visions recounted by a trusted male chronicler, in this case, her own son. She also serves as important early evidence for the existence of anchoresses. Anchoritic living became increasingly popular in subsequent centuries.

HEATHER E. WARD

References and Further Reading

Archambault, Paul J., ed. and trans. *A Monk's Confession: The Memoirs of Guibert of Nogent.* University Park, Pa.: Pennsylvania State University Press, 1996.

Benton, John F., ed. *Self and Society in Medieval France: The Memoirs of Guibert of Nogent (1064?–c.1125),* translated by C. C. Swinton Bland. New York: Harper & Row, 1970.

Mulder-Bakker, Anneke B. *The Lives of the Anchoresses: The Rise of the Urban Recluse in Medieval Europe.* Philadelphia: University of Pennsylvania Press, 2005.

——. "The Prime of their Lives: Women and Age, Wisdom and Religious Careers in Northern Europe." In *New Trends in Feminine Spirituality: The Holy Women of Liège and Their Impact,* edited by Juliette Dor, Lesley Johnson, and Jecelyn Wogan-Browne. Turnhout: Brepols, 1999, pp. 215–236.

Partner, Nancy F. "The Family Romance of Guibert of Nogent: His Story/Her Story." In *Medieval Mothering,* edited by John Carmi Parsons and Bonnie Wheeler. New York: Garland, 1996, p. 359–379.

See also **Anchoresses; Impotence; Lay Piety; Monasticism and Nuns; Poverty, Religious; Sexuality: Sex in Marriage; Widows**

GUILD MEMBERS AND GUILDS

Various types of guilds (also spelled gilds) developed in medieval Europe, first in cities and then, in a few areas, in the countryside. Merchant guilds organized long-distance trade, especially in cloth and luxury goods; their members sometimes became very wealthy. Professional guilds such as those of apothecaries and notaries organized the provision of services and could be quite well-off when urban economies were flourishing. Craft guilds organized the production and distribution of many products and the training of future workers; masters in craft guilds were generally heads of households and made a solid income.

Women did not carry out long-distance trade themselves and were thus not active members in merchants' guilds. Some did invest in trading companies as what were termed "sleeping partners," however; in about 1500, thirty-nine of the nearly 300 members of the Merchants' Society of Ravensburg, Germany were women. Women were not officially trained as notaries, as apothecaries, or in other professions, so they were not members of professional guilds. By the fifteenth century there were organized systems of apprenticeship for midwives in many cities, but these were run by municipal or church authorities, not midwives themselves, so they were not really guilds.

The earliest craft-guild ordinances date from the thirteenth century, and some mention male and female masters along with male and female apprentices. There were a few all-female guilds, especially in spinning gold thread or producing silk in cities with highly specialized economies, such as Cologne, Paris, and Rouen. Historians looking at these cities, or only at guild ordinances, have sometimes argued that guilds as a whole were initially open to women and that women's participation was significant. Others have pointed out that it is difficult to tell in most cases whether the women referred to as "masters" had been trained independently or were actually masters' wives or widows. They also note that actual lists of guild members, as opposed to ordinances describing the guild in theory, rarely list many female apprentices or women who were not masters' widows.

In general, except for the few all-female guilds, craft guilds were male organizations and followed the male life cycle. One became an apprentice at puberty, became a journeyman four to ten years later, traveled around learning from a number of masters, then settled down, married, opened one's own shop, and worked at the same craft full time until one died or grew too old to work any longer. This process presupposed that one would be free to travel (something that was more difficult for women than men), that upon marriage one would acquire a wife as an assistant, and that pregnancy, childbirth, or child-rearing would never interfere with one's labor. Transitions between these stages were marked by ceremonies, and master craftsmen were formally inscribed in guild registers and took part in governing the guild.

Women fit into guilds much more informally. When urban economies were expanding in the High Middle Ages, the master's wife and daughters worked alongside him and the journeymen and apprentices, and female domestic servants also carried out productive tasks. When the demand for products was especially great, master craftsmen hired female pieceworkers to assist and in some cities girls entered formal apprenticeships; women and girls thus served as a labor reservoir, to be utilized when guild needs required. Masters' widows ran shops after the deaths of their husbands and were expected to pay all guild fees, though they could not participate in running the guild. Other than masters' widows and a small number of female apprentices, however, women's ability to work was not officially recognized and usually depended not on their own training but on their relationship with a guild master. Even members in the all-female guilds were sometimes expected to be related to members of a male guild in a related craft, and men appear to have served as the leaders in some women's guilds.

Even this informal participation began to change in the fifteenth century on the continent, when explicit restrictions on women's work began. First masters' widows were limited in the amount of time they could keep operating a shop or prohibited from hiring journeymen, then female domestic servants were excluded from any productive tasks, then the number of his daughters a master craftsman could employ was limited. The timing of these restrictions varied from craft to craft, town to town, and country to country; they did not begin until the sixteenth century in Scandinavia. Whenever restrictions occurred, because women's participation in guild shops was generally not guaranteed by guild regulations and because widows had no political voice in running the guilds, women as a group were not able to protect their right to work. A few might be allowed to work, but this was on an individual basis and was viewed as a substitute for charity.

Women were excluded from craft guilds for a number of reasons. As the result of urban revolts, guild members in some cities, especially in the Low Countries, became part of city government; this political role was seen as inappropriate for women. Guilds facing competition from cottage industries organized by capitalist investors tightened up their entrance requirements. Guilds increasingly came to view the honor of their work as tied to an all-male workplace. The separate journeymen's guilds that began to be set up—often illegally—in the late fourteenth century by journeymen who had little hope of becoming masters were even more hostile to women's work and never allowed female members.

MERRY E. WIESNER-HANKS

References and Further Reading

Howell, Martha. *Women, Production and Patriarchy in Late Medieval Cities*. Chicago: University of Chicago Press, 1986.

Kowaleski, Maryanne, and Judith M. Bennett. "Crafts, Gilds, and Women in the Middle Ages: Fifty Years after Marian K. Dale." *Signs* 14 (1989): 474–488.

Mackenney, Richard. *Tradesmen and Traders: The World of Guilds in Venice and Europe, c. 1250–c. 1650*. Totowa, N.J.: Barnes and Noble, 1987.

Wensky, Margret. *Die Stellung der Frau in der stadtkölnischen Wirtschaft im Spätmittelalter*. Cologne: Böhlau, 1980.

Wiesner, Merry E. "Guilds, Male Bonding and Women's Work in Early Modern Germany." *Gender and History* 1 (1989): 125–137.

See also **Apprentices; Artisan Families, Women of; Division of Labor; Home Manufacturing; Textile Production for the Market; Work**

GUINEVERE

Guinevere (also Guenevere, Guenièvre, Gwenhwyfar, Gaynour, Guenhumare, Ginevra) is one of the most visible female characters in medieval European literature. She not only appears in works of prose and poetry from c. 1100 up through 1500, but also forms part of "the best-known image in Arthurian art" (Stones, 125). In that image, an illumination from a manuscript in the J. Pierpont Morgan Library, Guinevere kisses her lover Lancelot for the first time. This image circulates widely, appearing in both scholarly books about the Arthurian tradition and promotional materials for the Morgan Library (Stones, 125).

The figure of Guinevere is present in medieval Arthurian literature composed in Dutch, English, French, German, Italian, Latin, Norwegian, Portuguese, Spanish, and Welsh. Guinevere is always Arthur's wife, and her story often includes her kidnapping by Meleagant and her adultery with either Mordred or Lancelot. Her abduction is the subject of what is probably the earliest Arthurian sculpture, the archivolt of the Cathedral of Modena. Her infidelity undermines Arthur's power because it constitutes treason and threatens the line of succession. Guinevere's male partner commits treason by cuckolding the king and destabilizes the realm by initiating (in the case of Mordred) or participating in (in the case of Lancelot) a civil war. Mordred, however, as Arthur's nephew or illegitimate son, also violates medieval laws prohibiting incest.

Guinevere's qualities as wife and woman vary with the cultural context and historical moment of each Arthurian composition. Welsh romances depict a conventional and loyal queen forming part of the Arthurian frame for tales about knights' adventures. In the early Welsh tradition as a whole, Guinevere is innocent of wrongdoing: "She is either the fateful queen causing Arthur's downfall in the battle of Camlann, probably unwillingly (not by betrayal), or the abducted queen who is taken away by a supernatural being against her will" (Korrel, 96). In Geoffrey of Monmouth's *History of the Kings of Britain* (c. 1136–1138), Guinevere plays a visible role in the main narrative. Despite her great beauty, she possesses ceremonial power as participant in a crown-wearing ceremony with Arthur and political power as coregent with Mordred. Geoffrey's Guinevere contributes to Arthur's downfall by committing adultery with Mordred, but the text does not state that she desired or sought this union and labels Mordred, not the Queen, a perjurer and traitor. In the French romance *The Knight of the Cart (Lancelot)* by Chrétien de Troyes (c. 1177), Guinevere is Lancelot's partner in courtly love and a secret affair. Later French romances likewise give Guinevere a significant role, but at times condemn this love affair (the vulgate *Quest of the Holy Grail* and *The Death of Arthur* and the post-vulgate Cycle), at times do not (the early portion of the vulgate *Lancelot* and the prose *Lancelot*), and at other times do not mention it at all (most post-Chrétien verse romances).

In later German romances and many of the French and English ones, Guinevere is a victim of kidnapping and an adulteress whose affair with Lancelot causes Arthur's downfall. It is worth noting, however, that the German tradition before the thirteenth century sometimes presents Guinevere as a noble, good, happily married, and loyal lady who is a mother figure at court. At other times, however, medieval German works portray her as unfaithful to Arthur or as having been unfairly branded an adulteress. It is also worth noting that in a few texts, the alliterative *Morte D'Arthure* being the best known, Guinevere has children. The alliterative poem's Guinevere is the mother of Mordred's children, but she leaves their fate in Arthur's hands when she flees to a convent following Mordred's defeat. In his fifteenth-century *Morte D'Arthur*, Sir Thomas Malory draws upon French and English medieval sources to create a Guinevere who combines the traits of her predecessors: she is beautiful, brave, politically significant, emotional, adulterous, and finally achieves salvation as a nun. Malory's version of Guinevere is the one most widely known today because his book is the source of much postmedieval Arthurian literature and many Arthurian films. As a result, contemporary readers tend to know Guinevere primarily as Lancelot's lover.

Guinevere has no generally accepted historical origin in a particular medieval woman, but it is possible that her literary portrayals reflect the lives and reputations of medieval queens. Two likely candidates are Empress Matilda, the only legitimate heir of King Henry I of England, whose throne King Stephen usurped in 1135, and Eleanor of Aquitaine, King Henry II of England's powerful queen, whose colorful life spurred outlandish legends about her. Geoffrey of Monmouth's Guinevere—who participates in a crown-wearing ceremony with Arthur and presides over a celebration even more splendid than Arthur's—could reflect the awkward historical moment in the mid-1130s at which the Anglo-Norman barons chose either to honor or to ignore the oaths of fealty they had sworn to Matilda before her father's death. Similarly, Lawman's translation into English (c. 1200) of Wace's *Roman de Brut* (1155), through its demonization of Guinevere, reflects the decline in Eleanor of Aquitaine's reputation in annals and chronicle histories at the turn of the thirteenth century. It is, therefore, possible that medieval authors shaped their images of Arthur's queen in response to contemporary attitudes toward Empress Matilda and Queen Eleanor.

Medieval manuscript illuminations, like medieval texts, commonly present Guinevere as an adulteress. These images show her kissing Lancelot—sometimes in a private space, but often in a public one. The frequent reproduction of the Morgan Library image of Guinevere kissing Lancelot is consistent with today's popular depictions of her primarily as Lancelot's lover—despite her varied portraits in medieval literature.

FIONA TOLHURST

References and Further Reading

Fenster, Thelma S., ed. *Arthurian Women: A Casebook.* New York: Garland Publishing, 1996.

Korrel, Peter J. *An Arthurian Triangle: A Study of the Origin, Development and Characterization of Arthur, Guinevere, and Mordred.* Leiden: E. J. Brill, 1984.

Malory, Sir Thomas. *Works,* edited by Eugene Vinaver and revised by P. J. C. Field. Oxford and New York: Oxford University Press, 1990.

Stones, Alison. "Illustrating Lancelot and Guinevere." In *Lancelot and Guinevere: A Casebook,* edited by Lori J.

Walters. New York and London: Garland Publishing, 1996.

Tolhurst, Fiona. "What Ever Happened to Eleanor? Reflections of Eleanor of Aquitaine in Wace's *Roman de Brut* and Lawman's *Brut.*" In *Eleanor of Aquitaine: Lord and Lady,* edited by Bonnie Wheeler and John Carmi Parsons. New York: Palgrave Macmillan, 2002, pp. 319–330.

Walters, Lori J., ed. *Lancelot and Guinevere: A Casebook.* New York and London: Garland Publishing, 1996.

See also **Arthurian Literature; Chivalry; Courtly Love; Cuckold; Eleanor of Aquitaine; Incest; Literature, Latin; Literature, Middle English; Literature, Old French; Matilda the Empress; Queens and Empresses: The West; Rape and Raptus; Sexuality: Extramarital Sex**

GYNECOLOGY

In 1990, an archeological excavation in Granada, Spain uncovered the remains of a Muslim woman from the late medieval period who suffered from a calcified growth in her uterus. This condition, which in modern biomedicine is ascribed to uterine myomas (benign tumors), could conceivably have afflicted any woman in medieval Europe, whatever her social rank, income, religion, marital status, or sexual activity: all were united by the threat of the common diseases and conditions specific to the female body. Women were also subject to many of the same afflictions as men, from accidental wounds to infectious diseases like tuberculosis, leprosy, or plague, or degenerative conditions like crippling arthritis or cancer. But biology was hardly destiny. All medieval societies made efforts to intervene in cases of illness or injury, and women were not simply "abandoned to their fate." Moreover, since Muslim, Jewish, Byzantine, and Latin societies shared many elements of the Mediterranean system of humoral medicine, the care women received in all four societies would have had certain commonalities. These women were separated from one another by social rank, wealth, and religion and all their attendant material and cultural effects. The focus here will be on gynecological conditions rather than those related to childbirth, though it should be remembered that the nutritional depletion and other strains caused by repeated pregnancies and birth often had long-term consequences.

Disease Incidence and Life Expectancy

Because gynecological diseases primarily affect the soft tissues of the body, they leave little trace in the archeological record. Hence, the evidence of the woman's grave in Spain is a rare case when we can document a gynecological disorder (and in that case, a nonfatal one, since the woman clearly lived for many years with the condition). Paleopathologists (scientists who study the archeological record with many of the same technologies used by modern physicians) are now able to better document the incidence of diseases that leave traces on the bones, such as tuberculosis and rickets; more recently, they have begun to use DNA analysis to assess the prevalence of certain bacterial diseases, like bubonic plague, in historical populations. This work is still in its infancy and breakdowns of data by sex are few. Nevertheless, recent studies confirm that the childbearing years were characterized by higher mortality for women, though thereafter women generally had survival rates that were the same as or slightly better than those of men.

Anatomy

What was known about the human female body was learned inferentially from the study of other mammals, particularly the pig, which was assumed to resemble the human in its internal anatomy. The human uterus was thought to have two cells (as most ungulates do), one on the right and one on the left. The Roman physician and anatomist Galen (d. c. 217 CE) created an elaborate explanation of how the warmer temperature in the right side of the uterus was more conducive to the production of males while the colder left side produced females. In the twelfth century, a theory began to circulate that the uterus had seven cells; the cells closer to the center produced more ambiguously sexed fetuses, hermaphrodites forming in the center.

The female testicles (what we today call the ovaries) had been identified in the third century BCE and were understood to function comparably to the male organs, that is, as producers of a seminal fluid. The uterus, cervix, and vagina were recognized as distinct parts of the internal reproductive tract, though the external genitalia were only rarely described in detail. A term used in Latin and several Romance languages (*natura, nature, naissance*) saw the vagina as the site of generation, while Germanic languages (English *wicket*, Dutch *gulden poort*) saw it as a gate or opening. The clitoris was rarely remarked on except when it grew too large. The hymen was even more rarely mentioned. The female breasts had a special vascular connection that linked them directly to the uterus. The blood that fed the fetus was, after birth, diverted to the breasts and further refined into milk. After menopause, unexpelled, corrupted blood also moved by this channel, thereby causing breast cancer.

Anatomical illustrations of the female body were rare. A highly schematized image of the internal female genitalia is found today in only four copies. Around the end of the fourteenth century in German areas, the more popular iconographic tradition of the diseased woman began. This semi-squatting naked figure, with belly splayed to show the internal organs, including the uterus, was often labeled to show the major conditions that could afflict the female body. This figure appeared most often in manuscripts made for clerics and probably served as a mnemonic to aid them in their understandings of basic illness and the processes of reproduction. When human anatomical dissection became a regularized part of medical training in late medieval northern Italy, the female body, and especially the uterus, became a particular focus of curiosity.

Physiology, Pathology, and Therapy

With only a few exceptions, medieval medical writers and practitioners were quite clear that, anatomically as well as physiologically, men and women were quite distinct. Men were perfect in their heat: they had sufficient vital heat to fully cook all the nutrients they consumed and expel any excess. Women, in contrast, were colder and, as such, unable either to fully consume all their intake or expel their excess through normal channels of elimination. They thus needed a distinct purgative function, menstruation, whose regularity was vital to health.

The uterus could suffer various afflictions, such as being unnaturally hot, having lesions or cancers, or being displaced, tilting laterally or falling into complete prolapse. Equally unique to the female was uterine suffocation. This occurred either when the menses had been retained too long or when the woman did not engage in regular sex and expel her semen. (See above regarding the female testicles.) The collected matter would putrefy in the womb and either cause the uterus itself to rise up toward the organs of respiration or it would emit a noxious vapor that could ascend to the lungs, heart, or brain. Either way, the condition was severe if not fatal. It was treated by a variety of remedies, including suffumigations of sweet-smelling substances to the vagina to lure the uterus back to its proper place. Some authors explicitly recommended sexual intercourse as a cure. In the early Middle Ages, exorcisms of the womb (which derived from pre-Christian models) were still in circulation, and as late as the fourteenth century medical writers reported that women themselves believed that their uteruses moved up to the heart and throat.

Infertility attracted more and more attention from male medical writers beginning in the twelfth century. Initially, it was simply one among several headings in the gynecological sections of medical textbooks. Beginning in the fourteenth century, infertility became the topic of specialized writings and served as the main entry point for an expanded role for male physicians in women's healthcare.

Up through the twelfth century, surgical gynecological interventions were limited to treatment of breast conditions. (Surgeons were rarely optimistic that any effective treatment for breast cancer was possible, though some believed that excision might be efficacious if performed early enough.) In the late thirteenth and early fourteenth centuries, Latin surgical writers tentatively began to discuss conditions of the female genitalia, usually minor procedures to open an obstructed vagina or excise fleshy growths. Arab writers had been more detailed in their descriptions of gynecological surgery, though it is unclear whether such procedures were performed by male physicians or female practitioners assisting them. (The Spanish writer az-Zahrawi suggested that a eunuch could also serve as a medical attendant.) Methods to excise the dead fetus from the womb were described in Arabic texts, but even though these were translated into Latin in the twelfth century, no western Christian surgical writer addressed obstetrical procedures prior to Guy de Chauliac, who, in 1368, instructed the surgeon regarding how to supervise the midwife in cases of difficult birth or excise the fetus if the mother died in labor. By the fifteenth century, surgeons from Italy to England had become much more involved in intervening in difficult births.

Circulation of Medical Knowledge and Provision of Medical Care

In recent years, historians of medicine have turned from privileging the perspective of literate, elite male practitioners who wrote medical books to looking for evidence of the patient's point of view. They now commonly use the notion of the medical marketplace to refer to the multiplicity of options from which the sick person or her family might choose. A woman might employ a phlebotomist to perform a periodic bloodletting (nuns and anchoresses were expected to be bled four times a year), consult an apothecary for a specialized remedy, request an herbal remedy from a local empiric, or journey to a saint's shrine to plead for the recovery of her sick child. Medieval women obtained their gynecological care from a variety of sources, including both male and female practitioners. This was true even of gynecological care, for although there were limits to men's ability to perform hands-on aspects of diagnosis and treatment, male practitioners could use their access to written medical traditions to claim a theoretical understanding of disease, that is, what caused disease and how treatment of the disease (rather than merely its symptoms) might be determined. Learned male practitioners thus believed that their medical theory rivaled and ultimately superseded the empirical expertise of traditional female healers.

Women's access to the same body of written texts would have allowed female practitioners to claim the same expertise as men (or even greater, since they also had hands-on experience treating women's conditions). Or female patients might have read gynecological texts themselves and created lay circles of self-help. It matters very much, therefore, to determine not only who wrote the dozens of gynecological texts that can now be documented, but also who read them.

Aside from an early medieval Greek text attributed to an otherwise unknown woman named Metrodora, the only medieval gynecological text of known female authorship is a work called *Treatments for Women* (*De curis mulierum*) by the famous twelfth-century healer Trota of Salerno. Trota's work treats women's medicine not simply as gynecological afflictions—menstrual difficulties, uterine prolapse, etc.—but also in the wider sense of the social functioning of women's bodies. Thus, Trota includes remedies for vaginal lesions caused by forced intercourse, mechanisms to sedate sexual desire in nuns and vowesses who are forbidden sexual relations, and techniques to narrow the size of the vagina or produce a simulated bloodflow of defloration in a sexually experienced woman who might otherwise be unmarriageable. Even cosmetics fit into this expanded definition of women's medicine, since they, too, were among the techniques used by women to modify the functioning or appearance of their bodies. Trota's contemporary Hildegard of Bingen (1087–1179), did not write a specialized treatise on gynecology nor even devote much attention to the topic, but she did articulate some of the most original views of the nature of sex difference ever seen in the Middle Ages.

All other known medieval gynecological texts (more than 150) were of certain or probable male authorship. Moreover, countless general works of medicine (like medical encyclopedias, which covered diseases from head to toe) touched on gynecological topics incidentally. The majority of these works were read and used by men. For example, sixteen Hebrew gynecological texts are known to have circulated in

Ashkenazi and Sephardic communities, yet there is no evidence that the works were written for or directly used by women. In Christian Europe, no texts specifically written for midwives were composed until the fifteenth century; when gynecological texts did address female audiences, they addressed laywomen generally.

Cross-sex gynecological practice posed particular problems for the simple reason that the reproductive organs are also the sex organs; prior to the fourteenth century, it was considered inappropriate for a male to inspect or touch a woman's genitalia. Yet this should not be taken to imply that men were never involved with women's conditions. Aside from infirmarians in monasteries, few male practitioners completely excluded women from their clientele. Noblewomen often had personal male physicians in their employ, and communities of nuns occasionally signed contracts with learned male practitioners to ensure regular care. Besides being consulted for general conditions like coughs, fevers, or skin disorders, male practitioners diagnosed and prescribed therapies for menstrual disruptions and infertility. And, as noted above, in the later Middle Ages surgeons expanded their involvement in women's gynecological and even obstetrical conditions. Thus, most male practitioners did practice gynecology at some level, even if it never involved the visual or manual inspection of a woman's genitalia. If such inspection was necessary, female assistants could always be used. A regulation of the Poor Clares from 1297, for example, stipulated that while male physicians could be called in to treat serious conditions, female healers and phlebotomists should tend to the nuns when inspection of "their secret places" was needed.

The prefaces of gynecological texts, including most famously *The Conditions of Women* (the first of the three texts that made up the so-called *Trotula* ensemble), often acknowledge women's hesitation to consult male practitioners out of embarrassment. The implications of this sentiment were largely ignored by male practitioners, who readily incorporated the *Trotula* and other gynecological texts into their medical handbooks. Yet the implicit logic of this critique was that, if put directly into women's hands, gynecological texts could enable women to treat themselves and each other. This is how one of the early French translators of *Conditions of Women* interpreted the text, and we find several vernacular texts addressed to female audiences in French, English, and Dutch. The irony is that even these texts often made their way back into the hands of men.

The medical writings of Trota or Hildegard, as unique and valuable as they are, do not get us very close to the lived experience of most medieval women. Saints' lives and canonization proceedings are filled with the testimonies of the grievous ills that women endured. Some of the most commonly employed medical compounds for women's ailments, such as *trifera magna* and *athanasia*, employed opiate substances that may have helped alleviate the pains of menstrual cramping, uterine fibroids, or breast cancer. We may perhaps never be able to recover the full range of local practices employed by midwives, neighbor women, or more specialized healers. Nevertheless, it is clear that alleviation of physical suffering was both sought out and often provided. Gynecological writers never explicitly mention the curse of Eve. While they acknowledge that women are afflicted more than men by the processes of reproduction, the idea of simply leaving women to suffer their fate seems to have been untenable.

MONICA GREEN

References and Further Reading

Barkai, Ron, ed. and trans. *A History of Jewish Gynaecological Texts in the Middle Ages.* Leiden: Brill, 1998.

Barratt, Alexandra, ed. *The Knowing of Woman's Kind in Childing: A Middle English Version of Material Derived from the Trotula and Other Sources.* Medieval Women: Texts and Contexts, 4. Turnhout: Brepols, 2001.

Bos, Gerrit, ed. and trans. *Ibn al-Jazzar on Sexual Diseases and Their Treatment.* The Sir Henry Wellcome Asian Series. London: Kegan Paul, 1997.

Faraone, Christopher. "New Light on Ancient Greek Exorcisms of the Wandering Womb." *Zeitschrift für Papyrologie und Epigraphik* 144 (2003): 189–197.

Green, Monica H., ed. and trans. *The Trotula: A Medieval Compendium of Woman's Medicine.* Philadelphia: University of Pennsylvania Press, 2001.

———. *Women's Healthcare in the Medieval West: Texts and Contexts.* Aldershot: Ashgate, 2000.

———. "Bodies, Gender, Health, Disease: Recent Work on Medieval Women's Medicine." *Studies in Medieval and Renaissance History* 1 (2005): 1–46.

Green, Monica H., and Linne R. Mooney. "*The Sickness of Women.*" In *Sex, Aging, and Death in a Medieval Medical Compendium: Trinity College Cambridge R.14.52, Its Text Language, and Scribe*, edited by M. Teresa Tavormina. Tempe, Ariz.: Arizona State University Press, 2006, pp. 455–568.

Hanson, Ann Ellis, and Monica H. Green. "Soranus of Ephesus: *Methodicorum princeps.*" In *Aufstieg und Niedergang der römischen Welt*, edited by Wolfgang Haase and Hildegard Temporini, Teilband II, Band 37.2. Berlin & New York: Walter de Gruyter, 1994.

Jiminez Brobeil, Sylvia A. "A Contribution to Medieval Pathological Gynaecology." *Journal of Paleopathology* 4. 3 (1992): 155–161.

Kruse, Britta-Juliane. *Verborgene Heilkünste: Geschichte der Frauenmedizin im Spätmittelalter.* Quellen und Forschungen zur Literatur- und Kulturgeschichte, 5. Berlin: Walter de Gruyter, 1996.

Park, Katharine. "Dissecting the Female Body: From Women's Secrets to the Secrets of Nature." In *Crossing Boundaries: Attending to Early Modern Women*, edited by Jane Donawerth and Adele Seeff. Newark, Dela.: University of Delaware Press, 2000, pp. 29–47.

———. *Visible Women: Gender, Generation, and the Origins of Human Dissection*. New York: Zone Books, forthcoming.

Soranus of Ephesus. *Soranusâ Gynecology*, translated by Owsei Temkin. Baltimore: The Johns Hopkins University Press, 1956. Reprint, 1991.

See also **Abortion; Contraception; Cosmetics; Demography; Doctors and Healers; Hermaphrodites; Hildegard of Bingen; Hospitals; Infertility; Menstruation; Midwives; Secrets of Women; Trota of Salerno; Virginity**

H

HADEWIJCH

Hadewijch is the name given to the author of a collection of mystic texts written in the mid-thirteenth century, probably in the environs of Brussels or Antwerp. Nothing is known for certain about her life, but it is thought that she may have been a Beguine and that she could well have been of noble or at least patrician birth. The Beguines were a lay religious movement of women who wished to live close to the apostolic ideal. In 1215, they were given papal dispensation to live together and to exhort one another to good works and a greater love of God. This is the context in which Hadewijch was writing, and her work focuses on the relationship between the soul and God. Her writing is intensely personal, but it was written with didactic rather than cathartic intent. In the early days of the Beguines, women joined a group of Beguines as adults and came mostly from the lower nobility or patrician classes, so Hadewijch and her audience would have enjoyed a reasonable education. The note referring to the author of the manuscripts as Hadewijch is quite late, possibly sixteenth century, but both Ruusbroec and Jan van Leeuwen were familiar with these texts and thought highly of a woman they referred to as Hadewijch. The five Hadewijch manuscripts are very closely related and contain some or all of the following texts: forty-five Poems in Stanzas, thirty-two Letters, fourteen Visions, sixteen Poems in Mixed Forms (or Epistolary Poems), eight other poems, and a short prose text. The authorship of some of these texts has been debated, but as a collection the texts provide us with a vivid picture of a particular form of mystic spirituality whether they are the product of a single author or of several. The manuscript evidence suggests that manuscript B (Brussels Koninklijke Bibliotheek 2877–2878), is the best text, but scholarship has tended to follow the example of Joseph Van Mierlo, one of the early editors of Hadewijch's work, and has taken the texts as they are in manuscript C (Ghent Universiteitsbibliotheek 941) as definitive.

In medieval theological literature, the soul (a feminine noun in Latin requiring feminine pronouns and adjectives) was frequently spoken of as the bride of Christ. In her Poems in Stanzas Hadewijch reverses this convention. Her chosen name for the Divinity is *Minne,* "Love," which is a feminine noun in Dutch, so that throughout her work God is spoken of using feminine pronouns and adjectives. Writing as a woman, Hadewijch effects a gender reversal comparable to that of her male contemporaries by speaking of herself as the humble lover-knight and God as the powerful, fickle, and demanding lady, using the conventions of courtly love poetry. As in the case of Bernard of Clairvaux, images of gender reversal illustrate the total "otherness" of the relationship being described—the Beguines will have experienced any previous heterosexual relationships as women, not as men. It also represents a loss of power and prestige similar to that implied by Bernard when speaking of the souls of the monks in his charge as women, since within the conventions of courtly love it was the woman who wielded all the power and the lover-knight who had none.

There has been some debate about exactly what aspect of the Divinity Hadewijch refers to as *Minne*. There are times when *Minne* is unambiguously God the Son, others when the word refers to God the Father, still others when it is the unity of the Trinity. Furthermore, as the word is rarely capitalised in the manuscripts, it can be hard to distinguish grammatically between the noun, the proper noun, and the verb. The opportunities for creative ambiguity are legion and Hadewijch exploits them to the full. Hadewijch rarely uses a noun to refer to herself or her fellow Beguines, but when she does she chooses the noun *sen,* a masculine noun referring to reason, understanding, and the rational that recalls Bonaventure's definition of the bride of Christ as the illuminated mind. However, it is noteworthy that by her choice Hadewijch is also claiming for herself and other women an equal part in that which distinguishes humankind—namely, the ability to reason.

When reading medieval texts it is important to remember that in the Middle Ages gender was viewed as far more fluid than it is now. In pre-Aristotelian theology, male and female were understood to be at opposite ends of the same continuum, more united in their creature-hood before God than they are separated by their differences. Hadewijch moves seamlessly from speaking of God as the demanding lady, *Minne*, to referring to God as an opposing knight who must be bettered in a fight. Similarly, speaking of the woes of the lover-knight, she breaks off to bewail her own fate and speaks of herself as a "poor woman." She was clearly aware of the paradox inherent in the use of such imagery and she invokes the contrasts quite deliberately in her poems. By her choice of the word *Minne* to refer to God, her use of imagery of gender reversal, and her exploitation of the ambiguities and paradoxes inherent within it, Hadewijch is able to say things about her experience of God which might otherwise not have been acceptable.

SASKIA MURK-JANSEN

References and Further Reading

Hadewijch: The Complete Works, translated by Columba Hart. Classics of Western Spirituality. London: SPCK, 1980.

McGinn, Bernard, ed. *Eckhart and the Beguine Mystics.* New York: Continuum, 1995.

———. *The Flowering of Mysticism: Men and Women in the New Mysticism—1200–1350,* vol. 3 of *The Presence of God: A History of Western Christian Mysticism.* New York: Crossroads, 1998.

Murk-Jansen, Saskia. "The Use of Gender and Gender-Related Imagery in Hadewijch," In *Gender and Text in the Later Middle Ages,* edited by Jane Chance. Gainesville: University Press of Florida, 1996, pp. 52–68.

———. *Brides in the Desert: The Spirituality of the Beguines.* London: Darton Longman and Todd, 1998.

Newman, Barbara. *From Virile Woman to WomanChrist; Studies in Medieval Religion and Literature.* Philadelphia: University of Pennsylvania Press, 1995.

See also **Beguines; Courtly Love; Flanders; Gender Ideologies; Minnesang; Mysticism and Mystics; Theology**

HAGIOGRAPHY

Hagiography, from the Greek *hagio* (holy) and *graph* (writing), means the writing of the lives or legends of saints or holy persons. It has also come to mean the studying of saints. As rhetorical constructions, works of propaganda, saints' Lives or *vitae* and the variety of other writings pertaining to saints, were a combination of historical fact, biographical information, and fiction. Their purpose was to commemorate or glorify the holy person's virtuous life, death, and production of posthumous miracles. Over approximately the past thirty years, hagiography has witnessed a veritable explosion of scholarly and popular interest. During this same period women's history, including the history of women and religion, has developed and flourished as a major field of inquiry. Thus the convergence of these two exciting and highly productive areas has resulted in the proliferation of studies focusing on women saints—*mulieres sanctae*—especially in the medieval world.

In general, prior to the 1970s, scholars had a rather narrow view of history. Their work focused mainly on political or diplomatic history and the creation of events. They were concerned with ascertainable "facts" and "authenticity." Many of these early historians were hypercritical in regard to the *vitae* of saints: they were highly suspicious of saints' Lives as historical sources. They often dismissed these dossiers of the holy dead as worthless, unreliable, embarrassing works of "pious fiction." Saints' Lives were seen as essentially stereotypic, clichés, entirely "devoid of historical value," as well as tedious and boring.

However, with the growing interest in social history, women's history, and the history of mentalities, the *vitae* of saints have been rediscovered and have come to be appreciated as amazingly rich, untapped historical sources; a gold mine for historians. This is particularly true in regard to the study of women and the medieval church and society since this genre is very much concerned with women and has a great deal to say about their saintly and/or "deviant" behavior. Saints' Lives and miracles also contain a wealth of interesting incidental or "unintentional" information about many aspects of everyday life both within the cloister and the outside world that is not available in any other sources of the period.

Male Predominance

The impressive numbers of *vitae* alone, the thousands of records of female and male saints for this period, allow scholars to study women saints and their roles in the church and society in comparison to those of their male contemporaries across the centuries. Through the collection of rough statistical data, the Lives allow scholars to trace shifts in the typology of sanctity, sex ratios of saints, social and economic status, visibility/charismatic authority, geographic disparities, demographic information, etc. Over the past several decades a number of vast statistical analyses have appeared that have attempted to quantify the saints of the Middle Ages. See for example the works by Sorokin (1950), Delooz (1969), Schulenburg (1978 and 1998), Goodich (1982), and Weinstein and Bell (1982). While the church professed a policy of spiritual egalitarianism in the heavenly kingdom, the statistics of the population of holy men and women reflect a definite gender-based disparity in numbers. Thus, in reality, it was much more difficult for women than for men to enter the ranks of the celestial hierarchy. While certain periods and places seem to have been more conducive to the making of women saints, nevertheless, male saints outnumbered female saints for the years c. 500–1500 by roughly six to one; women made up only approximately seventeen percent of the saints.

In general, saints were social constructs: they were "made," packaged, promoted, or advertised to the faithful. And although their promoters frequently focused on the otherworldly and intercessory aspects of their invisible patrons, sainthood was, in fact, a very "this worldly" business. Membership in the heavenly kingdom reflected in many ways the hierarchy, power, wealth, and status of medieval society. Reputations for sanctity were negotiated and developed. As Pierre Delooz emphasized in his studies of sainthood, one is only a saint "for others" as well as "by others." That is, the saintly reputation, situated in the collective memory of the community and recognized by one's peers, is of primary importance. And it is only through a pressure group that formulates a public cult and secures official approval that one becomes recognized as a saint. Therefore, one needed a public role, a certain visibility, as well as the presence of others as witnesses and supporters, an audience to provide evidence of one's extraordinary acts and miracles to establish and support a saint's cult. Although

the first papal canonization took place in 993, for much of the Middle Ages those who won recognition of sainthood were the products of local cults; they were popular saints rather than candidates formally canonized by the papacy. Thus for women to become members of the holy elite, or the celestial *gynaeceum*, they required an environment that encouraged, recognized, and valued their participation in the church and society; they needed a certain power, prominence, visibility, a charismatic authority, which would call attention to their extraordinary virtues and saintly lives. They also needed hagiographers to formally record and preserve these memories.

The Composition of Lives

Although a few of the *vitae* were written by women, the majority of saints' Lives were composed by male clerics. They were written mainly in Latin and the vernacular languages. Some of the Lives were recorded by contemporaries who had first-hand knowledge of the holy person; others, however, were far removed from the historical saint, as they were written many centuries after the saint's death. They, therefore, based their sacred biographies on tradition, folklore, or legend; stereotypical events attributed to other saints; and biblical stories, etc. The Lives also reflected the hagiographer's own concerns and ideals and, in some cases, they tell us more about the author, his agenda and period, than about the female saint. The writing or revisions of saints' Lives and miracle collections were also often part of a campaign to promote the saint's cult. They were written in conjunction with the transfer or (translation) of the saint or relics to a new tomb or reliquary, or the building of a new church to accommodate pilgrims who came to the cult site in expectant hope of miraculous cures.

The audience for the Lives and miracle collections included both sexes: churchmen and religious females, especially members of communities who served as guardians of the saint's tomb/cult; laity who lived in the vicinity of the saint's church; and pilgrims who visited the shrine. The Lives were to serve as sources of edification for the faithful or models of proper behavior. They provided inspiration as well as *exempla* that were to be admired and, in some cases (i.e., if not too extreme) imitated. Through these means the Church hoped to inspire a certain modification of behavior, a religious conformity among the faithful, and to specifically mold or reinforce its concepts of ideal female behavior. However, unable to control the message, the *vitae* provided women with multivalent readings. They therefore used hagiography for their own purposes. Women learned what they wanted or needed to learn from the *vitae* and frequently took some liberties in creatively adapting these behavioral models to their own specific situations and needs.

The Early Church

Across the centuries there were a variety of types of saints as well as paths that led to recognition of sainthood. Martyrdom was the most highly valued state with the majority of male and female saints of late antiquity or the early Christian period recruited from this category. As witnesses or martyrs of Christ and the new faith, they actively courted death, and in their public acts of heroic defiance, suffering, and shedding of blood, brought about the conversion of many to Christianity. Although many women are found in the passions of the early martyrs, male martyrs were clearly favored. This preference is underscored in Eusebius's *Ecclesiastical History* (c. 313) in which only fifteen out of 120 martyrs, or 12.5 percent, were women. The image of the martyr was essentially male—he was seen as an athlete or warrior of Christ. Nevertheless, early Christian women saints were praised for denying or transcending the natural weakness of their sex; they became a *femina virilis,* or "female man of God," and as such won the crown of martyrdom. The holy martyr Perpetua (third century) had her gender transformed in a dream and was thus empowered to face her tormenter in the arena. Dying in defense of one's virginity was another popular act attributed to many of the early female martyrs. Therefore while defending their virginal purity against forced marriages to pagan rulers or rape, a number of women martyrs faced gruesome tortures and heroic deaths. The need to maintain one's virginity at all costs also drove some of these women to various acts of self-destruction. For example, St. Domnina and her two daughters committed suicide by throwing themselves into a river in order to avoid being raped. (Many of the legends of the early Christian virgin martyrs were written centuries later and became especially popular in the central and late Middle Ages, including stories of Sts. Agnes, Cecilia, Catherine of Alexandria, Margaret of Antioch, and Eugenia.)

With the Edict of Milan (313) and the end of official persecution of the Christians and the reign of Emperor Theodosius (395) and recognition of Christianity as the official state religion, there appeared a second major category of saints, that of confessors. This group included members of the church hierarchy, namely bishops and priests, and ascetics. Many

of the bishops of the early Church were automatically designated as saints. Women, however, were excluded from the clerical hierarchy; thus this major area of recruitment to sainthood was closed to them. A few women, who were mothers of these early bishops and holy men, were rewarded for their "golden wombs" and beneficial influence: they served as models of Christian motherhood, for example, St. Monica (d. 387), the mother of St. Augustine. St. Helena (d. c. 330) has often been credited with the conversion of her son, the Emperor Constantine, to Christianity, as well as remembered for her major role in the discovery of Christ's cross, early involvement in the cult of relics, and the building of numerous churches—including the Holy Sepulcher in Jerusalem. During this early period empresses and aristocratic women who controlled huge fortunes were rewarded with sainthood for their primary roles as supporters of holy men; generous patrons of the church; and as builders of churches, monasteries, hospitals, and charitable institutions, including Melania the Younger, Paula, and Olympias of Constantinople.

At the same time, many male and female saints of the fourth and fifth centuries were recognized for their rigorous ascetic lives. In attempting to escape from the fleshy temptations of the world, the desert fathers and mothers of Egypt, Syria, and Palestine became famous for their heroic behavior. Their ascetic lives included harsh bodily mortification, regimens of fasting, vigils, sleep deprivation, and the wearing of hair shirts, chains, and other instruments of penance. Sts. Marana and Cyriaca (fifth century) lived as anchorites in Syria and, for the sake of penance, wore chains for forty-two years as heavy as any human could bear. Some holy women lived heroically ascetic lives among the monks of the desert disguised as men with their sex only discovered on their death. Hearing of the amazing feats of these holy men and women, female pilgrims flocked to the deserts to visit them. St. Jerome wrote in regard to St. Paula's visit to the desert fathers, "Forgetful of her sex and of her weaknesses she even desired to make her abode, together with the young women who accompanied her, among these thousands of monks." (A number of apocryphal female saints—holy harlots or repentant prostitutes—whose Lives would become especially popular in later centuries were also said to have lived at this time in the desert, such as Mary of Egypt, Pelagia, etc.)

Early Middle Ages

From the sixth to the twelfth century, with the conversion of the north of Europe and the establishment of monasticism, there were many new opportunities and roles for women that could lead to sainthood. For this period the majority of saints were recruited from cathedrals—archbishops, bishops, and priests; and from cloisters—abbots, monks, abbesses, and nuns. They were almost invariably drawn from royal or aristocratic families. Also a number of queens, kings, and members of the nobility were found among the ranks of the holy elite. For it was through the family that one often achieved sainthood during this period. Royal women, beginning with Clotilda, queen of the Franks and wife of Clovis (d. 544), followed by a series of queen-saints, for example, Clotsinda, Theodolinda, Bertha, Ethelberga, Ludmilla, Dubrawa, Olga, Anna, Sarloth, Gisela, and others, won recognition of sainthood for their primary roles as domestic proselytizers, or "royal conduits" in the Christianization of their countries. As supporters of the new faith, these women took the initiative in converting their husbands and children, along with their people to Christianity.

However, it is especially with the development of monasticism and its great popularity among royal and noble families that women were provided with a visibility that led to *fama sanctitatis*. As founding abbesses and generous patrons of the new foundations, these women played major public roles in the church and society. Theirs was a practical kind of sanctity: as administrators they were involved in missionary activities, recruitment, building campaigns, education, hospitality, charity, healing, collecting relics, politics, peacemaking efforts, church reform, etc. Virginity and chastity, living as brides of Christ, were also important in the promotion of these women saints. It is then within the monastery with its collective memory of the community that cults of saints were established and *vitae* were written. Radegund (d. 587) is one of the best known Frankish queen/saints from this early period due mainly to the two extant vitae by contemporaries Fortunatus and the nun Baudonivia (the earliest identified female hagiographer). Gertrude founder of Nivelles (d. 659) and the queen/saint Balthilda (d. 680) were recognized for their early patronage, charitable activities, and involvement in monasticism.

At this time Ireland was especially well known for its large number of holy men and women and it came to be called "the isle of the saints." Despite the fact that there are some 119 women saints entered in the Irish Martyrology of Tallaght, the Lives of only four of these women are still extant. Brigid (d. 525), was the famous founding abbess of the double monastery of Cell Dara or Kildare (a mixed community for men and women) that contributed greatly to the spread of Christianity. The sources of the period note her public

quasi-episcopal power as abbess as well as her alleged or "accidental" ordination as bishop.

During this period the culture of Anglo-Saxon England seems to have been especially conducive to the making of women saints. Between the years 650 and 750 roughly forty percent of the new saints recognized in Britain were women. Again royal and noble women founded and governed new monasteries and were subsequently recognized as saints. Their monasteries, many of which were double foundations, served as centers of conversion, parish churches, and burial sites for royal and noble families. They became major centers of education and intellectual activity. Abbesses attended councils and synods; their advice was sought by churchmen and princes alike. Included among these early abbess saints were: Ethelburga of Barking (d. 675), Etheldreda of Ely (d. 679), Hilda of Whitby (d. 680), Ebba of Coldingham (d. 683), Sexburga of Ely (d. c. 700), and Elfleda of Whitby (d. 714). During the Viking invasions, a number of abbesses and nuns of these monasteries became a new generation of virgin martyrs. The abbess/saint Ebba of Coldingham (d. 870) and her nuns were especially famous for adopting a strategy of virginal defense: disfiguring themselves (*virginitas deformitate defensa*) by cutting off their noses and lips to avoid being raped by the pagan invaders. By destroying their beauty they were able to successfully preserve their virginity and died as virgin martyrs at the hands of the Vikings.

It was then from these flourishing Anglo-Saxon monasteries that Willibrord and Boniface recruited missionaries to help in the conversion of Germany. This provided women with religious leanings with further opportunities for rewards of sainthood. Included among these women were St. Leoba (d. 782), a relative of Boniface, who established the important monastery of Bischofsheim, and St. Walburga (d. 779), sister of Sts. Winnibald and Willibald, who became abbess of the double monastery of Heidenheim.

The Central Middle Ages

However, in general, it was during the Carolingian period, followed by the Cluniac and Gregorian reforms, that there occurred a decline in the number and percentage of new women saints. Few new *vitae* focused on contemporary holy women. This period also witnessed an increasing emphasis on strict enclosure for women under monasticism that worked to limit their public roles and opportunities that could lead to promotion of sainthood. Moreover, while the Merovingian and Anglo-Saxon writers in general stressed the perfection of virginity over the state of marriage and motherhood, beginning with the Carolingian period in the ninth century, there occurred a new appreciation and praise for married women and motherhood. In Ottonian Saxony of the tenth century, royal/imperial women such as Matilda (d. 968) and Adelheid (d. 999) were singled out as saints. Matilda was the mother of five children and Adelheid, called the "mother of kingdoms," was the mother of four. As strong supporters of the church, they used their influence and extensive wealth to endow monasteries for men and women and build churches. In this same tradition the queen/saint Margaret of Scotland (d. 1093) was the mother of eight children. She assumed a prominent role in the foundation of monasteries, churches, hostels for pilgrims, and was known for her piety and charity.

The queen was also renowned for her ecclesiastical embroideries.

Another path to sainthood for women of the central Middle Ages, which was closely associated with monasticism, was that of the ascetic hermit or recluse who chose to pursue a life of religious austerity in a cell or anchorhold often attached to a church or chapel. St. Wiborada (d. 926) lived her later years in a cell attached to her brother Hitto's church of St. Magnus. She died a martyr at the hands of the Hungarian invaders after warning her brother and other churchmen to take refuge inside the walls of St. Gall.

Defying family pressures for marriage, Christina of Markyate (d. 1161) successfully maintained her celibacy and lived for over forty-five years as an anchoress. Her holy lifestyle at Markyate attracted a following of women with similar religious leanings: ultimately a house for nuns was established there. Like Christina of Markyate, the Blessed Jutta of Sponheim or Disibodenberg (d. 1136), acting against the wishes of her family in her refusal to marry, founded a women's anchorhold attached to the male house of Disibodenberg. Here she followed a life of rigorous asceticism and was spiritual mother to the monks of Disibodenberg and the people of the area. She was also the *magistra* and foster mother of Hildegard of Bingen (d. 1179).

As a product of the eremitic and monastic life, the highly accomplished Hildegard of Bingen has become one of the best known women saints of the Middle Ages. However her visibility, her charismatic authority came essentially from her role as mystic, visionary, and prophet—as vessel or messenger of the divine light, as amplifier of the word of God, "a small sound of the trumpet." Her contemporary, St. Elisabeth of Schönau (d. 1165) was also a Benedictine and mystic. Along with Hildegard, her prophesies argued for reform of the moral corruption of the Church and society. Illness, suffering, and martyrdom were also central to their spiritual lives and their visionary experiences. It is this tradition of mysticism, along with debilitating illness, that became especially important for the visibility and recognition of female sainthood in the late Middle Ages.

With the late Middle Ages one finds some continuity in the making of women saints. A few of the saints from this period remained in the earlier tradition of sanctity and came from royal families, such as Elisabeth of Hungary (d. 1231) and Margaret of Hungary (d. 1270). Like Radegund and others before them, they practiced lives of asceticism, and were especially invested in patronage and charitable works. They were also closely supervised or influenced by their mendicant confessors. It is also with the twelfth and thirteenth centuries that the veneration of the very special female saint, the Virgin Mary, along with the development of her cult and proliferation of her miracles, became a major force in the religiosity of Europe.

Late Middle Ages

It is, however, with the thirteenth through fifteenth centuries that major shifts occur in styles of feminine piety and spirituality. These changes are reflected in new patterns of sanctity and an increased number of women saints. While rough statistics for the twelfth century note that only approximately thirteen percent of the new saints were women, the percentage for the thirteenth century was roughly twenty percent, and that of the fourteenth and fifteenth centuries was approximately twenty-five percent. In general, with the growing importance of towns and the middle class, the ranks of sainthood seemed to open up and allow perhaps a type of "democratization of sanctity." Many of the women saints of this period were recruited from the new urban middle classes, rather than the nobility; many were also married with children, or married but living a celibate life. In response to an increasing materialism and urban wealth, lay groups practicing the *vita apostolica* became especially popular.

Women were thus attracted in great numbers to the new lay poverty groups—that of the Beguines, Poor Clares, and Dominicans. They were especially noted for their adoption of lives of voluntary poverty; charitable acts with the poor and sick of the cities, and work in hospitals; as well as studying and teaching. For some, their charismatic authority rested on their special visionary powers/gifts. Many followed extreme penitential practices, ascetic regimens of excessive fasting (in some cases leading to death), vigils, and intense Eucharistic devotion. These women were often closely supervised or controlled by their confessors—male clerics who also authenticated their lives and recorded their visions. These new saints were especially recruited from the most urbanized areas of Europe—the Low Countries and the north of Italy. Their number included among others: Marie of Oignies (d. 1213), Christina the Astonishing of St. Trond (d. 1224), Yvette of Huy (d. 1228), Juliana of Mont Cornillon (d. 1258), Clare of Assisi (d. 1253), Margaret of Cortona (d. 1297), Gertrude the Great (d. 1302), Angela of Foligno (d. 1309), St. Humility of Faenza (d. 1310), Catherine of Siena (d. 1380) (declared Doctor of the Church in 1970), Dorothea of Montau (d. 1394), Birgitta of Sweden (d. 1373), Julian of Norwich (d. 1416), and Caterina Vigri (d. 1463). Yvette of Huy, for example, was a widow, recluse, and mother of three who left her children behind to retire to a leper colony. Dorothea of Montau was the mother of nine children and a mystic who developed wounds similar to stigmata. Catherine of Siena and Birgitta of Sweden played active roles in public life including lecturing popes on their need to return to Rome during the Babylonian Captivity. In addition, Birgitta was the mother of eight children, undertook a number of pilgrimages, and was the founder of a new religious order for women. These saints have left an impressive number of mystical writings including, for example, Catherine of Siena's collection of 383 letters and her *Dialogue*; Dorothea of Montau's *Book of Holy Feasts* and *The Seven Graces*; St. Gertrude the Great's *The Revelations of St. Gertrude*; St. Birgitta's *Revelations* and *Rule of the Holy Savior*; the anchoress Julian of Norwich's *Showings*; and Caterina Vigri's *The Seven Spiritual Weapons*.

Clerical Suspicions

It is then through their visionary gifts, their mystical raptures, that these women were able to transcend the limitations of their gender, education, and social status and win the rewards of sainthood. However, these very same gifts that provided them with a public visibility also made them appear dangerous and won them the distrust and animosity of the Church and its theologians, especially when they threatened male authority. They questioned their orthodoxy—as to whether they were truly mouthpieces of God or handmaids of the devil. For some of these visionary women their mystical visions and prophecies, along with their self-confidence and audacity for public

speaking and teaching in their own voice (instead of safely claiming that they were vessels of God), led them to accusations of heresy or witchcraft and ultimately to death at the stake. Here the line between sanctity and deviancy/heresy was in fact very fine. Such, for example, was the case of Marguerite Porete whose book *The Mirror of Simple Souls* was condemned and burned by the Inquisition, followed by the burning of the author as a heretic in Paris in 1310. Domina Prous Boneta, a Spiritual Franciscan, apocalyptic visionary and leader of a heretical lay group, was also burned at the stake in 1325 in Montpellier. In this tradition Joan of Arc was accused of heresy and burned alive at Rouen in 1431 for failing to renounce the voices of her "false and diabolical visions," her special protector saints Michael, Margaret, and Catherine, and her insistence on wearing male clothing. (Although venerated as a popular virgin saint in the Middle Ages, only in 1920 was Joan of Arc officially canonized.) These public executions no doubt were meant to serve as frightening warnings, further deterrents, to other outspoken, audacious visionary women who dared to speak or prophesy in their own voice; who publicly chastised the church and its hierarchy for its spiritual and moral corruption; or refused to show the proper deference required of their sex and submit to the institutionalized church and its hierarchy.

The study of the making of saints provides a wonderful indirect index of attitudes toward women and their roles and opportunities in medieval society and the Church. The rather low percentage of women saints for the period reflects in part the misogynist culture of the time. Women were excluded from a number of the major paths or opportunities within the Church that led to sainthood, such as leadership roles within the ecclesiastical hierarchy. Also, the selection processes for recognizing popular saints, authenticating cults and miracles, and canonization were dominated/controlled by churchmen. Nevertheless, certain periods and regions were more favorable than others in the making of women saints. For example, the beginnings of movements, when the Church needed the assistance of women and before institutional structures had hardened, were especially promising for the promotion of women saints. Wealth, status, and patronage were important in providing women with a visibility that led to sanctity. The majority of female saints were recruited from monasticism, the anchoritic life, and lay movements of apostolic poverty. Throughout the period, with the identification of women with their bodies, virginity and celibacy were especially necessary virtues for female sainthood: they allowed women to transcend the limitations and temptations of their sex and gender.

Martyrdom and mysticism similarly offered important opportunities to subvert misogynist ideals and provided a public prominence and visibility for *fama sanctitatis*.

JANE TIBBETTS SCHULENBURG

References and Further Reading

Ashley, Kathleen, and Pamela Sheingorn, eds. *Interpreting Cultural Symbols: Saint Anne in Late Medieval Society.* Athens, Ga.: University of Georgia Press, 1990.

———. *Writing Faith: Text, Sign, and History in the Miracles of Sainte Foy.* Chicago and London: University of Chicago Press, 1999.

Aspegren, Kerstin. *The Male Woman: A Feminine Ideal in the Early Church.* Uppsala: Acta Universitatis Upsaliensis, 1990.

Atkinson, Clarissa. *The Oldest Vocation: Christian Motherhood in the Middle Ages.* Ithaca, N.Y.: Cornell University Press, 1991.

Bibliotheca hagiographica latina antiquae et mediae aetatis. 3 vols. Subsidia hagiographica, 6, 70. Brussels: Société des Bollandistes, 1898/1986.

Bibliotheca Sanctorum. 13 vols. Rome: Istituto Giovanni XXIII della Pontificia Universita lateranense, 1961–1969.

Bitel, Lisa. *Land of Women: Tales of Sex and Gender from Early Ireland.* Ithaca, N.Y.: Cornell University Press, 1996.

———. "St. Brigit of Ireland: From Virgin Saint to Fertility Goddess." Paper presented at Fordham University, February, 2001. Available online—*Matrix, Commentaria.*

Bokenham, Osbern. *A Legend of Holy Women: Osbern Bokenham, Legends of Holy Women,* translated by Sheila Delany. Notre Dame, Ind.: University of Notre Dame Press, 1992.

Bornstein, Daniel and Roberto Rusconi. eds. *Women and Religion in Medieval and Reniassance Italy,* translated by Margery J. Schneider. Chicago and London: University of Chicago Press, 1996.

Brown, Peter. *The Cult of the Saints: Its Rise and Function in Latin Christianity.* Chicago: University of Chicago Press, 1981.

———. *Society and the Holy in Late Antiquity.* Berkeley: University of California Press, 1982.

———. *The Body and Society: Men, Women, and Sexual Renunciation.* New York, 1988: Columbia University Press.

Butler, Alan. *Butler's Lives of the Saints,* edited by Herbert Thurston and Donald Attwater, 4 vols. New York: Westminster, Md.: Christian Classics, 1956.

Bynum, Caroline Walker. *Holy Feast and Holy Fast: The Religious Significance of Food to Medieval Women.* Berkeley: University of California Press, 1987.

Cazelles, Brigitte, trans. *The Lady as Saint: A Collection of French Hagiographic Romances of the Thirteenth Century.* Philadelphia: University of Pennsylvania Press, 1991.

Clark, Gilian. *Women in Late Antiquity: Pagan and Christian Lifestyles.* Oxford: Oxford University Press, 1993.

———. *"This Female Man of God": Women and Spiritual Power in the Patristic Age, A.D. 350–450.* New York: Routledge, 1995.

Corbet, Patrick. *Les saints ottoniens. Sainteté dynastique, sainteté royale et sainteté feminine autour de l'an Mil.* Sigmaringen: Thorbecke, 1986.

Delooz, Pierre. *Sociologie et canonisations.* Collection scientifique de la faculté de droit de l'Université de Liège, n. 30. Liège and The Hague: Liège: Faculté de droit, 1969.

Donovan, Leslie A., trans. *Women Saints' Lives in Old English Prose.* Woodbridge, Suffolk: D. S. Brewer, 1999.

Dor, Juliette, Lesley Johnson, and Jocelyn Wogan-Browne, eds. *New Trends in Feminine Spirituality: The Holy Women of Liège and Their Impact.* Medieval Women: Texts and Contexts 2. Turnhout: Brepolis, 1999.

Dunbar, Agnes B. C. *A Dictionary of Saintly Women.* 2 vols. London: Bell, 1904–1905.

Elkins, Sharon. *Holy Women of Twelfth-Century England.* Chapel Hill, N.C. and London: University of North Carolina Press, 1988.

Elliot, Dyan. *Spiritual Marriage: Sexual Abstinence in Medieval Wedlock.* Princeton, N.J.: Princeton University Press, 1993.

Elm, Susanna. *Virgins of God: The Making of Asceticism in Late Antiquity.* Oxford Classical Monographs. Oxford and New York: Oxford University Press, 1994.

Farmer, David Hugh, ed. *The Oxford Dictionary of Saints.* Oxford and New York: Oxford University Press, 1982.

Folz, Robert. *Les saintes reines du moyen âge en occident (VIe-XIIIe siècles).* Subsidia hagiograpica 76, Brussels: Société des Bollandistes, 1992.

Foot, Sarah. *Veiled Women.* 2 vols. Burlington, Vt.: Ashgate, 2000.

Fouracre, Paul and Richard A. Gerberding, eds. and trans. *Late Merovingian France: History and Hagiography 640–720.* Manchester Medieval Sources. Manchester and New York: Manchester University Press, 1996.

Gilsdorf, Sean, trans. *Queenship and Sanctity: The Lives of Mathilda and the Epitaph of Adelheid.* Washington D.C.: Catholic University of America Press, 2004.

Goodich, Michael. "The Contours of Female Piety in Later Medieval Hagiography." *Church History* 50 (1981): 20–32.

———. *Vita Perfecta: The Ideal of Sainthood in the Thirteenth Century.* Monographien zur Geschichte des Mittelalters 25. Stuttgart: Hiersemann, 1982.

Harrington, Christina. *Women in the Celtic Church: Ireland c. 450–1150.* Oxford and New York: Oxford University Press, 2002.

Head, Thomas, ed. *Medieval Hagiography: An Anthology.* New York and London: Garland, 2000.

Hollis, Stephanie. *Anglo-Saxon Women and the Church: Sharing a Common Fate.* Anglo-Saxon – Rochester, N.Y.: Boydell Press, 1992.

———. *et al., eds. and trans. Writing the Wilton Women: Goscelin's Legend of Edith and Liber Confortatorius.* Medieval Women: Texts and Contexts, 9. Turnhout: Brepolis, 2004.

Horner, Shari. *The Discourse of Enclosure: Representing Women in Old English Literature.* Albany, N.Y.: State University of New York Press, 2001.

Jenkins, Jacqueline, and Katherine Lewis, eds. *St. Katherine of Alexandria: Texts and Contexts in Western Medieval Europe.* Turnhout: Brepolis, 2003.

Kieckhefer, Richard. *Unquiet Souls: Fourteenth-Century Saints and Their Religious Milieu.* Chicago: University of Chicago Press, 1984.

Kitchen, John. *Saints' Lives and the Rhetoric of Gender: Male and Female in Merovingian Hagiography.* New York: Oxford University Press, 1998.

Klaniczay, Gábor. *Holy Rulers and Blessed Princesses: Dynastic Cults in Medieval Central Europe,* translated by

Éva Pálmai. Cambridge: Cambridge University Press, 2002.

Lees, Clare A. and Gillian R. Overing. *Double Agents: Women and Clerical Culture in Anglo-Saxon England.* Philadelphia: University of Pennsylvania Press, 2001.

Matrologia Latina, Peregrina Translations Series. Toronto: Peregrina Press.

Matter, E. Ann and John Coakley, eds. *Creative Women in Medieval and Early Modern Italy: A Religious and Artistic Renaissance.* Philadelphia: University of Pennsylvania Press, 1994.

McNamara, Jo Ann. *Sisters in Arms: Catholic Nuns through Two Millennia.* Cambridge, Mass.: University of Pennsylvania Press, 1996.

McNamara, Jo Ann, and John E. Halborg, with E. Gordon Whatley, eds. and trans. *Sainted Women of the Dark Ages.* Durham, N.C., and London: Duke University Press, 1992.

Mooney, Catherine, ed. *Gendered Voices: Medieval Saints and Their Interpreters.* Philadelphia: University of Pennsylvania Press, 1999.

Mulder-Bakker, Anneke B. ed. *Sanctity and Motherhood: Essays on Holy Mothers in the Middle Ages.* New York and London: Garland, 1995.

———, ed. *Invention of Saintliness.* London and New York: Routledge, 2002.

———. *Lives of the Anchoresses: The Rise of the Urban Recluse in Medieval Europe*, translated by Myra Heerspink Scholz. Philadelphia: University of Pennsylvania Press, 2005.

Musurillo, Herbert, trans. *The Acts of the Christian Martyrs.* Oxford: Clarendon Press, 1972.

Newman, Barbara. *From Virile Woman to WomanChrist: Studies in Medieval Religion and Literature.* Philadelphia: University of Pennsylvania Press, 1995.

———, ed. *Voice of the Living Light: Hildegard of Bingen and Her World.* Berkeley: University of California Press, 1998.

Petersen, Joan, ed. and trans. *Handmaids of the Lord: Contemporary Descriptions of Feminine Asceticism in the First Six Christian Centuries.* Cistercian Studies Series, 143. Kalamazoo, Mich.: Cistercian Publications, 1996.

Petroff, Elizabeth Alvilda, ed. *Consolation of the Blessed.* New York: Alta Gaia Society, 1979.

———, ed. *Medieval Women's Visionary Literature.* New York and Oxford: Oxford University Press, 1986.

———. *Body and Soul: Essays on Medieval Women and Mysticism.* New York and Oxford: Oxford University Press, 1994.

Reames, Sherry, with Martha G. Blalock and Wendy R. Larson, trans. *Middle English Legends of Women Saints.* The Consortium for the Teaching of the Middle Ages. Kalamazoo, Mich.: Medieval Institute Publications, 2003. www.lib.rechester.edu/camelot/teams/reames.htm (2 May 2006).

Riches, Samantha J. E., and Sarah Salih, eds. *Gender and Holiness: Men, Women, and Saints in Late Medieval Europe.* New York: Routledge, 2002.

Ridyard, Susan. *Royal Saints of Anglo-Saxon England.* Cambridge: Cambridge University Press, 1988.

Roisin, Simone. *L'Hagiographie Cistercienne dans le diocese de Liège au XIIIe siècle.* Louvain: Bibliothèque de l'Université, 1947.

Salih, Sarah. *Versions of Virginity in Late Medieval England.* Cambridge: Woodbridge, Suffolk: D. S. Brewer, 2001.

Salisbury, Joyce E. *Church Fathers, Independent Virgins.* New York: Verso, 1991.

———. *Perpetua's Passion: The Death and Memory of a Young Roman Woman.* New York and London: Routledge, 1997.

Schulenburg, Jane Tibbetts. "Sexism and the Celestial Gynaeceum: from 500–1200." *Journal of Medieval History* 4 (1978): 117–133.

———. *Forgetful of Their Sex: Female Sanctity and Society, ca. 500–1100.* Chicago and London: University of Chicago Press, 1998.

Smith, Julia M. H. "The Problem of Female Sanctity in Carolingian Europe, c. 780–920." *Past and Present*, 146 (1995): 3–37.

Sorokin, Pitrim. *Altruistic Love: A Study of American 'Good Neighbors' and Christian Saints.* Boston: Beacon Press, 1950.

Stouck, Mary-Ann, ed. *Medieval Saints: A Reader.* Peterborough, Ontario: Broadview Press, 1999.

Szarmach, Paul E. ed. *Holy Men and Holy Women: Old English Prose Saints' Lives and Their Contexts.* Albany, N.Y.: State University of New York Press, 1996.

Talbot, Alice-Mary. *Holy Women of Byzantium: Ten Saints' Lives in English Translation.* Washington, D.C.: Dumbarton Oaks Research Library and Collection, 1996. Available online.

Talbot, C. H., ed. and trans. *The Anglo-Saxon Missionaries in Germany.* New York: Sheed and Ward, 1954.

Van Houts, Elisabeth. *Memory and Gender in Medieval Europe 900–1200.* Toronto and Buffalo: University of Toronto Press, 1999.

Vauchez, André. *The Laity in the Middle Ages: Religious Beliefs and Devotional Practices.* trans. Margery Schneider. French original, 1987, South Bend, Ind.: University of Notre Dame Press, 1993.

———. *Sainthood in the Later Middle Ages*, translated by Jean Birrell. Cambridge: Cambridge University Press, 1997.

Vies des saints et des bienheureux. Les RR. PP. Bénédictins de Paris, edited by Jules Baudot, Paul Antin and Jacques Dubois. 13 vols. Paris: Librairie Letouzey et Ané, 1935–1959.

de Voragine, Jacobus. *The Golden Legend: Readings on the Saints.* translated by William Granger Ryan. 2 vols. Princeton: Princeton University Press, 1993.

Ward, Benedicta. *Harlots of the Desert: A Study of Repentance in Early Monastic Sources.* Kalamazoo, Mich.: Cistercian Publications, 1987.

Weinstein, Donald and Rudolf M. Bell. *Saints and Society: The Two Worlds of Western Christendom, 1000–1700.* Chicago: University of Chicago Press, 1982.

Winstead, Karen A., ed. and trans. *Chaste Passions: Medieval English Virgin Martyr Legends.* Ithaca, N.Y.: Cornell University Press, 2000.

Wogan-Browne, Jocelyn. *Saints' Lives and Women's Literary Culture: Virginity and Its Authorizations.* Oxford and New York: Oxford University Press, 2001.

Wogan-Browne, Jocelyn, and Gyn S. Burgess, trans. *Virgin Lives and Holy Deaths: Two Exemplary Biographies for Anglo-Norman Women.* London: Dent, 1996.

See also **Adelheid; Aethelthryth of Ely; Anchoresses; Angela of Foligno; Asceticism; Beguines; Birgitta of Sweden; Brigit; Canonization of Saints; Caterina Vigri; Catherine of Siena; Christina of Markyate; Christina**

HAGIOGRAPHY, ICONOGRAPHIC ASPECTS OF

The iconography of saints incorporates the church's classification of the person and the social customs and attitudes of the time in which the imagery was fashioned. Medieval hagiographers drew on Martyrologies and local legends, as well as Acts of Canonization, in the later Middle Ages to compose biographies—at times wholly apocryphal—that detailed the noble births, charitable and miraculous deeds, stoic resistance under torture, and brutal deaths of saints. They devised attributes (plants, animals, and objects) to identify individuals. By the end of the thirteenth century, popular anthologies like the *Golden Legend* furnished colorful *vitae* of the saints that served as sources of inspiration for preachers and artists alike. These texts largely categorized women as martyrs and virgins, in contrast to a range of options for men, who could be martyrs, patriarchs, apostles, confessors, hermits, and monastics, among others. Over time, the church expanded the dimensions of female sainthood, characterizing the saints in terms of the sexual, marital, and spiritual circumstances of medieval women. The virtue of chastity, deemed more precious than gold by theologians, became synonymous with female sanctity and affected the iconography of all holy women regardless of the era in which they lived or the actual events of their lives.

Virgin Martyrs

Medieval art glorifies the courage and chastity of the first female saints recognized by the church, the virgin martyrs of the Roman Empire. These aristocratic and beautiful young women remained true to Christian beliefs by refusing to marry pagans or to worship idols, for which they braved harsh persecution and painful death. Wearing gold crowns of virginity and carrying palms of martyrdom, Agatha holds a plate with her breasts, which had been severed by the emperor's men; Apollonia extends pincers; and Lucy grasps a dish containing a pair of eyes. Duccio conformed to tradition when he depicted Agnes with a lamb, a visual play on *agnus* and hence the sacrificed "Lamb of God," on the *Maestà* for Siena Cathedral (1308–1311), while Andrea Orcagna painted Catherine of Alexandria next to a wheel with broken spokes on the Strozzi Altarpiece (Florence, S. Maria Novella, c. 1354–1356). Cecilia's crown of roses and lilies, blossoms associated with the Virgin Mary, accentuates her chastity, for she had convinced her bridegroom to abstain from marital sex as portrayed on an early fourteenth-century Florentine panel (Florence, Galleria degli Uffizi). Grasping an arrow, Ursula shelters a crowd of kneeling maidens under her outstretched cloak to commemorate the martyrdom that she and the 11,000 virgins who accompanied her on a pilgrimage suffered at the hands of the Huns, which is vividly described in the *Golden Legend* and on an exquisite reliquary painted by Hans Memling (Bruges, Hans Memling Museum, 1489).

Matrons and Widows

The medieval iconography of wives and widows highlights their conversions of husbands and children, their constancy to marital vows, and their great charity and mercy. Monica (c. 330–387), a widow clad in black with a book, effected the conversion of her son Augustine, while Helena (c. 255–330), whose cross refers to the True Cross she discovered in Jerusalem, strove to convert her son, the Emperor Constantine. When falsely accused of adultery, Queen Cunegunda of Germany (d. 1033) proved her innocence in a trial by fire–walking across the scalding ploughshares which became her attribute. The flowers enfolded in the Franciscan habit of the crowned Elisabeth of Hungary (d. 1231) exemplify her munificent charity on a fourteenth-century panel by Lippo Memmi (Florence, Loeser Collection): the bread she intended for the poor miraculously turned into flowers when she was confronted by her husband, who had proscribed her almsgiving.

Nuns and Abbesses

Clothed in the robes of their monastic orders, holy nuns and abbesses customarily clasp a lily and a crucifix to manifest their profession as consecrated virgins and brides of Christ. Auxiliary attributes refer to the miracles, visions, and prophecies with which saintly nuns were blessed. Scholastica (c. 480–543), the legendary founder of the Benedictine nuns, carries the lily and crucifix, and a dove flies from her mouth (or over her head) in reference to her brother Saint Benedict's vision of the soul departing her dead body as a bird. Clare of Assisi (c. 1194–1253), the founder of the Franciscan nuns, modestly displays a white lily in Simone Martini's fresco in the Chapel of St. Martin (San Francesco, Assisi, 1328), though her image may be enhanced by a cross signaling her devotion to Christ's Passion or pyx recalling her expulsion of Saracen invaders with the Eucharist. The iconography of well-educated, mystical nuns such as Hildegard of Bingen (1098–1179) and Gertrude the Great (d. 1302) attests their visions and authorship. For instance, the bright flames that dance above Hildegard in her *Scivias* (c. 1142–1152) verify the divine origins of her writings. Famed for a vision of the Nativity recorded in her *Revelations*, Birgitta of Sweden (d. 1373) brandishes a pastoral staff as the founder of the Birgittine nuns. Such attributes of leadership were rare for female monastics; more often, founder-abbesses are paired with their masculine counterparts—Scholastica with Benedict and Clare with Francis of Assisi—to convey the active and contemplative forms of monasticism.

Penitents, Ascetics, and Mystics

Just as the Virgin Mary was the paradigm of chastity, Mary Magdalen set the standard for female penitents, ascetics, and mystics. With the exception of her chief attribute, the oil jar, signifying her anointment of Christ's feet at her conversion, the Magdalen's rich iconography varies depending on which aspect of her legend is emphasized. Simone Martini painted the repentant prostitute veiled in striking red on the Pisa Polyptych in the fourteenth-century (Pisa, Museo di San Matteo), while Hugo van der Goes depicts her fashionably attired on the Portinari Altarpiece in the fifteenth (Florence, Galleria degli Uffizi). However, Donatello followed the lead of an anonymous thirteenth-century painter (Magdalen Dossal, Florence, Galleria dell' Accademia), portraying the ascetic recluse with long, tangled hair that conceals her wasted body (Florence, Museo Opera dell' Duomo, c. 1430s–1450s). Attributes and dress denote the transformation from sinfulness to grace of subsequent penitents and mystics. Mary of Egypt, a fifth-century reformed prostitute and hermit, whose matted hair also covers her nakedness, carries the three loaves of bread that she took to the desert. After the murder of her lover, Margaret of Cortona (d. 1297) embarked on a life of repentance, living in a secluded cell, ministering to the poor, and finding social acceptance as a Franciscan tertiary. The checkered pattern of her gown in the fourteenth-century decoration of her shrine represents the asceticism and self-mortification of her atonement.

The iconographies invented for early medieval saints endured, serving as prototypes for those canonized later. When Catherine of Siena (1347–1380), renowned as an ascetic, mystic, author, and reformer, was proclaimed a virgin saint in 1461, artists fashioned her imagery accordingly. They borrowed from the existing iconography for nuns (she was a Dominican tertiary) and from the legend of her name saint, Catherine of Alexandria. Vecchietta's impressive altarpiece in the Cathedral of Pienza and his fresco in the Palazzo Pubblico of Siena (both date 1461–1462) show her attired in the distinctive white and black Dominican habit and carrying large white lilies. Even before Catherine's canonization process concluded, visual narratives cast her as a second Catherine of Alexandria. On Giovanni di Paolo's altarpiece for S. Maria della Scala, Siena, of 1447–1449 (now dismantled) Catherine experiences mystical marriage with Christ like the early Christian virgin martyr (New York, Private Collection); she dictates her *Dialogues* and corresponds with popes (Detroit, Art Institute), as her predecessor had disputed with philosophers; and though not a martyr, she received the stigmata (New York, Metropolitan Museum of Art).

Despite strict adherence to tradition, the iconography of saints evolved over the centuries to reflect changes or additions to cults. Female saints with strong local followings became patrons of cities and towns, others protected guilds and professions, and universally esteemed saints personified virtues or spirituality. For example, Catherine of Siena sometimes carries a model of her native town, Cecilia displays a small organ as the patron of musicians, and the sisters Mary of Bethany and Martha evoke the active and contemplative lives. Even so, chastity, as the fundamental virtue of female sainthood, always features in the women's iconography.

JERYLDENE M. WOOD

References and Further Reading

Christiansen, Keith, Laurence B. Kanter, and Carl Brandon Strehlke. *Painting in Renaissance Siena, 1420–1500*. New York: Metropolitan Museum of Art, 1988.

Farmer, David Hugh. *The Oxford Dictionary of Saints*. Oxford and New York: Oxford University Press, 1982.

Frugoni, Chiara, "The Imagined Woman," trans. C. Botsford in *A History of Women: Silences of the Middle Ages.* Cambridge, Mass.: Harvard University Press, 1992, pp. 336–422.

Hall, James. *Dictionary of Signs and Symbols in Art.* New York: Icon Editions, 1974.

Haskins, Susan. *Mary Magdalene, Myth and Metaphor.* London and New York: Harcourt Brace & Company, 1993.

Kaftal, George. *Iconography of Saints in Tuscan Painting.* Florence: Sansoni, 1952.

Mâle, Emile. *Religious Art in France of the Late Middle Ages: A Study of Medieval Iconography and its Sources.* translated by M. Mathews. Princeton: Princeton University Press, 1986.

Objects, Images, and the Word: Art in the Service of the Liturgy, edited by Colum Hourihane. Princeton: Princeton University Press, 2003.

Vauchez, André. *Sainthood in the Later Middle Ages,* translated by J. Birrell. Cambridge: Cambridge University Press, 1997.

Voragine, Jacopo de. *The Golden Legend: Readings on the Saints.* translated by William Granger Ryan. 2 vols. Princeton, N.J.: Princeton University Press, 1993.

Weinstein, Donald, and Bell, Rudolph M. *Saints & Society: The Two Worlds of Western Christendom, 1000–1700.* Chicago: University of Chicago Press, 1982.

Wood, Jeryldene M. "Perceptions of Holiness in Thirteenth-Century Italian Painting: Clare of Assisi," *Art History* 14 (1991): 301–328.

See also **Abbesses; Birgitta of Sweden; Catherine of Alexandria; Catherine of Siena; Clare of Assisi; Elisabeth of Hungary; Gertrude the Great; Hagiography; Helena; Hildegard of Bingen; Jacobus de Voragine's Golden Legend; Margaret of Cortona; Mary Magdalen; Mary the Egyptian; Monasticism and Nuns; Mysticism and Mystics; Tertiaries; Ursula and Her Companions; Virgin Martyrs**

HEIRESSES

Medieval custom had a strong preference for male heirs, but not an exclusive one. In the early Middle Ages all siblings were regarded as each other's equals by nature and all of them, female as well as male, had a right to share in the family inheritance. Custom held property to be ultimately vested in the lineage, and the strong inclination to divide a deceased parent's property among all his or her children persisted until the twelfth century in areas influenced by Germanic tradition. A daughter's share of the parental inheritance often took the form of her dowry, but if the male line died out a family was still represented by its female members, so daughters could become their families' heiresses. As long as the principle of dividing a family inheritance remained dominant, however, it offered a choice among members of a lineage, and this meant that women were only rarely substantial heiresses.

By the eleventh century primogeniture was on the rise, and with it a clear order of priority among heirs.

This was especially true for kingdoms, which were increasingly seen as indivisible. Once females of a nearer degree of relationship were preferred to males of a further degree, more major heiresses appeared. Countess Matilda of Tuscany (1046–1115) became the unquestioned heiress of extensive territories in northern Italy, even though she was still a child at the time of her father's death. Similarly, Eleanor of Aquitaine (c. 1122–1204) succeeded to that duchy without being challenged by her male relatives, and Queen Melisende succeeded her father in the Kingdom of Jerusalem in 1131. Not all heiresses succeeded smoothly: in 1135, Henry I of England's daughter Matilda was challenged by her cousin Stephen of Blois on the grounds of gender, and ultimately lost control of the kingdom to him. Even when an heiress was accepted, it was still expected that her husband would share her power. Matilda of Tuscany was unusual in making policy without reference to her husband, but Eleanor of Aquitaine's first and second husbands both intervened in the duchy, while Melisende shared the throne with her husband; when he died her son replaced him as co-ruler, though Melisende insisted on being crowned again along with her son to emphasize her own hereditary right.

By the thirteenth century in England and France it was established for all landholders that when the eldest surviving heir was male he would inherit the entire estate, but if only daughters were left the heritage would be divided among them. By the fourteenth century women could be excluded from heritages that were specifically entailed in the male line, most notably the Crown of France, but this remained the less common option. Heiresses were objects of competition from several sides. Their families expected to arrange their marriages, and often did so very early: in the 1460s, Sir William Plumpton betrothed the two granddaughters who were his heiresses before they reached the age of six. If one of the king's tenants-in-chief died leaving an unbetrothed heiress, however, the king had the right to her wardship and marriage, and kings often used the marriages of heiresses to reward their followers at no cost to themselves. Edward III of England gave the heiress Juliana Leyburn to William Clinton and Sibyl Patshull to Roger Beauchamp, founding the fortunes of both their families and putting men loyal to the king in prominent positions in gentry society. In the fourteenth and fifteenth centuries the greatest heiresses were married to royal cadets to provide for them in the same way: four of the five sons of Edward III were endowed through marriages to peerage heiresses, while in Spain Ferdinand of Antequera was able to launch his claim to the throne of Aragon based on the vast estates of his wife Leonor de Albuquerque.

Occasionally an ambitious man would try to make his fortune by abducting and marrying an heiress, as Theobald de Verdon did with Elizabeth de Burgh in 1316, or by persuading a young girl to make binding vows, as Thomas Holland did in the case of Joan of Kent in 1340. For the most part, however, the fathers and guardians of heiresses had their pick of suitors, from Duke Charles of Burgundy, who betrothed his daughter seven times, to serfs who married their daughters to free men seeking land.

An inheritance could give a woman enhanced status within a marriage, as in the case of Sybille Baille (c. 1300). She inherited the house in Ax-les-Thermes, which became her husband's home as well, and their children were known by her surname. Nonetheless, when an heiress married, control of her property rested with her husband, and he would do homage on her behalf. However, he could not alienate it without her assent, and if she died without children her property passed to her heirs, not to her husband. If she were widowed, control of the property returned to her. A great heiress like Elizabeth de Burgh (d. 1360) could live a long and independent life without remarrying, but widowhood could also make an heiress's position vulnerable. This was particularly true if she had no children, and if her inheritance was large enough to attract the attention of powerful men: in 1489, Venice sent its fleet to pressure the widowed Caterina Cornaro into making her kingdom of Cyprus over to the Republic, while at the same time in England the Crown was willing to collaborate with favored magnates in stripping a widowed heiress like Maud lady Willoughby of the bulk of her estates. For most heiresses, widowed or not, the central aim of their property was to promote the success and standing of their family.

RHODA LANGE FRIEDRICHS

References and Further Reading

Courtemanche, Andrée. *La richesse des femmes*. Montreal: Bellarmin and Paris: Vrin, 1993.

Given-Wilson, Chris. *The English Nobility in the Late Middle Ages*. London and New York: Routledge, 1996.

Spring, Eileen. *Law, Land and Family: Aristocratic Inheritance in England 1300–1800*. Chapel Hill and London: University of North Carolina Press, 1993.

Waugh, Scott L. "Women's Inheritance and the Growth of Bureaucratic Monarchy in Twelfth- and Thirteenth-Century England," *Nottingham Medieval Studies* 34 (1990): 71–92.

See also **Cornaro, Caterina; Eleanor of Aquitaine; Inheritance; Landholding and Property Rights; Matilda of Tuscany; Matilda the Empress; Noble Women; Succession, Royal and Noble**

HELENA

Helena (c. 248/249–328/329 CE) was the mother of Constantine the Great, the first Christian emperor. She acted politically in his stead on several occasions, thus demonstrating women's access to political power through the family. Helena is best known for an act that she probably never performed: finding the True Cross, the central symbol of Christianity. After becoming sole ruler of the Roman empire in 324, Constantine sent his aged mother on a mission to Palestine and his other newly claimed eastern provinces. Helena's stay in the Holy Land and her efforts to propagate Christianity in the East became the foundation for the legend that she had recovered the True Cross. By the late fourth/early fifth century, three versions of the legend had come into existence. The earliest and most elaborate English account of Helena's finding (*Inventio*) of the Holy Cross is Cynewulf's late eighth- or early ninth-century verse *Elene*, in which Helena is depicted as a triumphant warrior-queen who figures both the rightful authority of the Christian State and the triumph of Church over Synagogue.

Little is known about Helena's early life, and she most likely came from a family of low social status. Some time after 306, Constantine brought Helena into his court and honored her with the title *Nobilissima Femina*, "most noble woman." Numerous coins were struck in her name, and, in 324, after his defeat of Licinius, Constantine gave Helena the official title of *Augusta*, an act intended not only to increase Helena's prestige but also to mark her son's newfound power. Helena was viewed as a kind of founding mother of the Constantinian dynasty, and as a symbol of traditional Roman social codes, family continuity, and dynastic stability. She was also associated with the security of the Republic and was one of the most powerful figures at the imperial court. Eusebius believed that she had authority over the imperial treasury, while Paulinus of Nola and Sulpicius Severus claim that she served as Constantine's co-ruler.

Helena was one of the best known female figures in the medieval West. Celebrated twice a year at the annual Invention (May 3) and Exaltation of the Cross (September 14) festivals, she was lauded for her piety, church patronage, and above all, for her alleged recovery of the Cross. Helena offers an example of piety based on the exercise of secular power rather than on virginity or asceticism. She became representative of elite female piety and was often held out as an example of how secular women with access to great wealth might use their resources to further church interests. Because of her alleged success in converting the Jews, Helena was invoked by numerous churchmen, including Pope Gregory the Great and Gregory of Tours, who sought to convince queens of their duty to convert their husbands and peoples. She offers a powerful example for medieval women's later involvement in converting non-Christians and for the idea of queens as agents of Christian conversion. Some time in the early Middle Ages, a legend arose that Helena was of British origins, and her name was thus also invoked for secular purposes by such writers as William of Malmesbury and Geoffrey of Monmouth, seeking to further national pride by creating a link between England and imperial Rome.

Helena is considered a saint by the Eastern Orthodox and Roman Catholic churches. Her feast day in the eastern church is May 21, and in the western church, August 18.

STACY KLEIN

References and Further Reading

Brubaker, Leslie. "Memories of Helena: Patterns in Imperial Female Matronage in the Fourth and Fifth Centuries." In *Women, Men and Eunuchs: Gender in Byzantium*, edited by Liz James. London: Routledge, 1997, pp. 52–75.

Cynewulf. *Cynewulf's "Elene,"* edited by P. O. E. Gradon. Rev. ed. London: University of Exeter Press, 1977.

Drijvers, Jan Willem. *Helena Augusta: The Mother of Constantine the Great and the Legend of Her Finding of the True Cross*. Leiden: Brill, 1992.

Harbus, Antonina. *Helena of Britain in Medieval Legend*. Woodbridge, Suffolk: D. S. Brewer, 2002.

Holum, Kenneth G. *Theodosian Empresses: Women and Imperial Dominion in Late Antiquity*. Berkeley: University of California Press, 1982.

Hunt, E. D. *Holy Land Pilgrimage in the Later Roman Empire, AD 312–460*. Oxford: Clarendon Press, 1982.

Inventio Sanctae Crucis, edited and translated by Stephan Borgehammar. In *How the Holy Cross Was Found: From Event to Medieval Legend, With an Appendix of Texts*. Bibliotheca Theologiae Practicae, Kyrkovetenskapliga studier 47. Stockholm: Almqvist and Wiksell International, 1991, pp. 154–61, 201–302.

Inventio Sanctae Crucis (Rufinus of Aquileia's account and also one contained in a tenth-century Spanish legendary), edited and translated by E. Gordon Whatley, "Constantine the Great, the Empress Helena, and the Relics of the Holy Cross." In *Medieval Hagiography: An Anthology*, edited by Thomas Head. New York: Garland, 2000, pp. 77–95.

Klein, Stacy S. "Reading Queenship in Cynewulf's *Elene*." *Journal of Medieval and Early Modern Studies* 33 (2003): 47–89.

———. "Centralizing Feminism in Anglo-Saxon Literary Studies: *Elene*, Motherhood, and History." In *Readings in Medieval Texts: Interpreting Old and Middle English Literature*, edited by David Johnson and Elaine Treharne. Oxford: Oxford University Press, 2005, pp. 149–165.

The Old English Finding of the True Cross, edited and translated by Mary-Catherine Bodden. Cambridge: D. S. Brewer, 1987.

Pohlsander, Hans A. *Helena: Empress and Saint*. Chicago: Ares Publisher, 1995.

See also **Conversion, Religious; Hagiography; Old English; Patriarchy and Patrilineage; Patronage, Ecclesiastical; Personifications Visualized as Women; Pilgrims and Pilgrimage; Queens and Empresses, Consorts of; Queens and Empresses: the West; Regents and Queen-Lieutenants**

HELOISE

Heloise's main correspondent, Peter Abelard—or as she calls him in a famous letter, her "master, father, husband, and brother"—has sometimes been called the first modern individual because of the way his autobiographical *History of My Calamities* seems to construct a "self," and his emphasis on the interior intention of the sinner in his *Ethics*. If this is true, then perhaps Heloise is the first postmodern figure for the way her own written texts have seemed to resist a unified interpretation, or rather, have seemed to invite a multiplicity of interpretations such that any possibility of uncovering a real, historical Heloise has seemed impossible. Each century since Jean de Meun first translated the letters of the pair and immortalized them in his *Roman de la Rose* has seemed to find the Heloise it has needed, be it the youthful and naïve virgin seduced by her older teacher and betrayed by clerics, who was the darling of the Enlightenment, to the figment of Abelard's imagination of the last century; and in our age, the feminist heroine who puts Abelard in his place and gives him his best ideas. This quest for a relevant Heloise has affected even such a simple thing as her birth date. Those who wished to see her as a naïve maiden wronged by her professor suggested that when she met Abelard for the first time around 1117 when he was almost forty, she was still only in her teens, giving her a birth date around 1100, while more recent views that emphasize her authority and autonomy argue she was in her twenties when they first met.

The Life of Heloise

Our knowledge of most of the known events of Heloise's life comes from Abelard's *History of My Calamities*, which is hardly a disinterested source. Still, it tells us more than we usually can hope to learn of the education and formation of a young medieval woman. We know her mother's name was Hersinde from the necrology of the Paraclete; her father is not mentioned, and it has been conjectured that she was illegitimate or that her uncle, Fulbert, a canon of Notre Dame in Paris with whom she lived, was actually her father. By the time Abelard first met her she had come to live in her uncle's house, leaving the convent of Argenteuil in which she had been educated and where she had already won a reputation for secular learning that is mentioned both by Abelard and by Peter the Venerable, abbot of Cluny. Abelard tells us that under the pretext of needing to reduce his expenses, he arranged to move into the house with Fulbert and Heloise and to continue her education with the real purpose of seducing the young woman. He describes in detail how they deceived Fulbert, and how Heloise was just as engaged with their lovemaking as he was.

Both Heloise and Abelard refer later to the many letters they wrote to each other during this period of their lives. One of the most provocative suggestions in recent years has been the assertion that this correspondence can be identified with a hitherto anonymous collection of letters between a male teacher and his female student and lover in a fifteenth-century manuscript copied by the Cistercian Johannes de Vepria. If this identification is correct, it substantially adds to the amount of written material issuing from Heloise that we have in our possession. The author of the woman's side of this correspondence betrays the same kind of educational influences as Heloise, such as her penchant for creating neologisms, her use of rhyming prose, and her allusions to Jerome. Some of the notions expressed in the letters are those we know are shared by Heloise, like the woman's idealistic views on love and her concern with inner intention. Most scholars now agree that Abelard's concern with the inner intention of the sinner, over and above his or her actions, is a product of Heloise's influence. We can see this perspective in her later letters, when she writes of their liaison, "Wholly guilty though I am, I am also, as you know, wholly innocent. It is not the deed but the intention of the doer which makes the crime, and justice should weigh not what was done but the spirit in which it is done" (Radice, 115).

Their liaison continued for several months, according to Abelard, until they were discovered by her uncle and separated. They still found occasions to meet and were eventually found in flagrante delicto. Moreover, Heloise discovered she was pregnant. Abelard smuggled Heloise out of her home disguised as a nun and sent her to his sister in Brittany where their son, Astralabe, was born. There, Heloise was a hostage for Abelard's safety from her uncle, to whom Abelard eventually proposed a secret marriage to Heloise. Heloise was against this idea, Abelard writes, because, quoting Jerome and the classics, she felt marriage and domesticity would

hinder their philosophic study. Heloise assents to Abelard's depiction of her arguments against marriage in one of her later letters but complains that he did not mention her main reason, namely her equation of love with freedom but marriage with chains. Nevertheless the pair was married in a secret ceremony, probably in 1118.

Fulbert broke his promise to keep the marriage secret, so Abelard removed Heloise from her uncle's house to the convent of Argenteuil and dressed her in the garb of a novice. This enraged Fulbert, who arranged for Abelard's forcible castration. In response, Abelard and Heloise both took up the religious life of the Benedictines, Abelard as a monk in the abbey of St. Denis, and Heloise in Argenteuil. Neither was to remain in these houses. Abelard moved on to found the house of the Paraclete around 1122 and then left that foundation to be the abbot of St. Gildas in Brittany between 1125 and 1127. Abbot Suger of St. Denis, with his eyes on the property of Argenteuil, expelled its nuns, including Heloise, then its prioress, for immorality in 1129. Abelard gave Heloise and a group of her nuns who wished to live a more austere life than their sisters his foundation of the Paraclete, where she remained as its abbess, overseeing its considerable expansion through the foundation of daughter houses until her death in about 1164, some twenty-two years after Abelard's own.

The Letters of Heloise

Heloise is best known for the letters she wrote to Abelard, inspired by her reading of his *History of My Calamities*. By turns she is passionate and plaintive in such memorable passages as, "God is my witness that if Augustus, Emperor of the whole world, thought fit to honour me with marriage and conferred all the earth on me to possess forever, it would be dearer and more honourable to me to be called not his Empress but your whore" (Radice, 114). It is often conjectured that Abelard's *History*, which details his crimes, punishments, and his current state of mortal danger at the hands of the monks of St. Gildas, was intended to smooth his return to a teaching position in Paris. Its concluding pages, which are divided between evocations of his peril, and discussions of the needs of the sisters of the Paraclete for a male advisor, and his own suitability above all other men for that position, given his castration, suggest however that the aim of the text was to demonstrate to a suspicious world that he should be allowed to take a supervisory and advisory role at the Paraclete itself, on the model of Jerome's guidance over Paula and Eustochium, a precedent cited by both Abelard and Heloise.

Read in this light, Heloise's own letters can be interpreted as supporting this proposal and contributing to a public performance of Abelard's suitability for the task. She shows herself in her letters to be needful of Abelard's personal pastoral care, and she argues that it is his responsibility to care for her and her sisters, over and above all the other demands on his time. Her confession of the still-sinful state of her intentions toward him offers him an opportunity to turn her to the correct path and to show the world that he is now immune to her charms.

In his later life, Abelard did remain close to the Paraclete, writing a Rule for the house, which supported the exceptionally high educational standards Heloise wanted for her nuns, as well as a hymnal and a set of collected sermons for their use and the *Problemata*, answers to tricky scriptural questions posed by Heloise. Like the letters, these works should be seen as the product of collaborative effort.

After his death, Abelard's body was returned to the Paraclete, and many years later, Heloise was buried by his side. Their bodies were moved to the Père Lachaise cemetery in Paris in the nineteenth century, where they attract visitors to this day.

LUCY PICK

References and Further Reading

Clanchy, M. T. *Abelard: A Medieval Life*. Oxford: Blackwell, 1997, 1999.
Dronke, Peter. "Heloise's *Problemata* and *Letters*: Some Questions of Form and Content." In *Petrus Abaelardus (1079–1142): Person, Werke, und Wirkung*, edited by Thomas, Jolivet, Luscombe, and de Rijk. Trier: Paulines-Verlag, 1980, pp. 53–73.
Gilson, Étienne. *Heloise and Abelard*. translated by Laurence K. Shook. London: Hollis & Carter, 1953.
The Letters of Abelard and Heloise. translated by Betty Radice. London: Penguin Books, 1974.
Listening to Heloise: The Voice of a Twelfth-Century Woman, edited by Bonnie Wheeler. New York: St. Martin's Press, 2000.
Mews, Constant T. *The Lost Love Letters of Heloise and Abelard: Perceptions of Dialogue in Twelfth-Century France*. New York: St. Martin's Press, 1999.
———. *Abelard and Heloise*. Oxford: Oxford University Press, 2005.
Muckle, J. T. "The Personal Letters Between Abelard and Heloise." *Mediaeval Studies* 15 (1953): 47–94.
———. "The Letter of Heloise on the Religious Life and Abelard's First Reply." *Mediaeval Studies* 17 (1955): 240–281.
Newman, Barbara. "Authority, Authenticity, and the Repression of Heloise." *Journal of Medieval and Renaissance Studies* 22 (1992): 121–157.

See also **Celibacy: Clerical and Priests' Concubines; Education, Monastic; Letter Writing; Monastic Rules; Monasticism and Nuns; Roman de la Rose and Its Reception; Sexuality, Regulation of; Theology**

HERALDRY

Western heraldry was born on the battlefield during the eleventh century, when the development of military equipment, in particular of the helmet, rendered noble equestrian warriors unrecognizable. The devices that initially appeared on shields were thus personal military insignia. From the 1100s onward, however, such insignia came to indicate a particular lineage and were transmitted and inherited as part of the primogenital patrimony. By the mid-thirteenth century, a formal grammar of heraldic signs (*blazon*) was in place whereby ordinaries, that is, simple charges (such as bar, bend, chevron, chief, fess, lozenge), tinctures, and identifying objects composed coats of arms that were unique to and the property of specific families. From military banners and shields, the use of coats of arms first spread to seals, thereafter also appearing on clothing, architectural elements, and decorative objects. Sealing was likely responsible for the adoption of heraldic devices by such nonwarrior classes as women, churchmen, burghers, Jews, and peasants who found it relevant to incorporate a familial emblem on such personal device as their seals.

Given heraldry's military origins and patriarchal developments, the representation of women's heraldic identity and the pattern of heraldic bearings needed to express it were particularly intricate. While women displayed heraldic emblems on their seals from the mid-twelfth century onward, this practice remained confined to high-ranking aristocratic women well into the 1230s. Design presented a challenge. On the equestrian seals of male potentates, heraldry appeared realistically on the shield and trappings; this was the way noblemen wore their coats of arms in actual battles and tournaments. On aristocratic women's seals, however, heraldry could not be displayed in such a realistic fashion since the seals' owners did not wear military accouterment; heraldry, therefore, was somewhat artificially overlain on clothing or shown on shields either held by the female figure or flanking her on both sides. Ultimately, heraldic emblems came to constitute the seal's central iconographic device and were thus displayed by women from all social strata. An even greater challenge than display was the selection of a coat of arms. Within any given family, an internal system of heraldic differentiation indicated its inner relationships. Thus, only the eldest son inherited the entire coat of arms whereas his cadet male siblings used a coat into which had been introduced variations called marks of cadency. No such marks entered women's heraldic devices; at that symbolic level, a woman had no specific place within the heraldic grammar of her patrilineage. Women adopted the arms of their husbands and/or of their fathers. Thus, in 1290, Jeanne de Toucy, wife of Thibaud II, count of Bar-le-Duc, shows on her seal's obverse the elegant effigy of a woman standing before a background decorated with her husband's heraldic emblems of sea-perch (Fr. *Bar*) and small crosses (crusily); her counterseal on the other side displays the coat of the Toucy family into which Countess Jeanne was born. Yolande de Flandre, as the widow of Count Henry IV of Bar and the wife of Philip of Navarre, count of Longueville (which made her sister-in-law of Charles, king of Navarre), wished to trace emblematically the importance of her birth and alliances. Her seal (of 1359) presents a drapery bearing the arms of Flanders and Bar before which stands the delicate figure of an exquisitely dressed woman resting her hands on two coats of arms. One is quarterly with the arms of Navarre and Longueville, and the other is party with the arms of Navarre and Flanders. Some heiresses chose to display only their fathers' shield, thus emphasizing the distinction of their personal status. Joan of Stuteville (1265–1275), who was twice married, used but a single seal showing a woman riding a horse sidesaddle and presenting a shield bearing the arms of Nicholas de Stuteville of Liddell, whose daughter and heiress Joan was. Whatever the heraldic strategy deployed by women on their seals, this strategy was often sensitive to rank, politics, and patterns of alliances, and might be dramatically complicated. Margaret de Quincy, countess of Winchester, used a remarkable seal (c. 1220) on which enclosed within a round-arched doorway two shields accompany a female effigy cloaked in a fur coat. On the upper shield are the arms of Margaret's husband, Saher of Quincy; these arms (lozenges) are also embroidered on the effigy's dress; on the lower shield appear the arms of the FitzWalters, who were the cousins and allies of Saher of Quincy; on top of the doorway, a cinquefoil alludes to the arms of Margaret's father, Robert III of Beaumont, earl of Leicester.

Both male and female armorial bearings might indicate matrilineal descent, indeed the number of lineages endowed with emblems borrowed from a matrilineal heraldic device is remarkable. For instance, the sea-perches (Fr. *bars*) of the comital family of Bar in Lorraine were transmitted matrineally to the counts of Chiny, Clermont, Salm, and to the lords of Nesles. Even more impressive is the identification of certain noble families with a single heraldic crest, such as the swan, which reflected a horizontal and extensive structure of kinship resting upon the strong genealogical, but not gender-specific, consciousness of a shared common and mythic ancestor. In the case of the swan, the ancestor was the swan knight, believed to be the grandfather of Godfrey of Bouillon, count of Boulogne and hero of the first crusade. All families displaying the swan crest can be traced back to the family of Boulogne. The principal link in such totemic affiliation was often one of several remote female ancestors.

BRIGITTE MIRIAM BEDOS-REZAK

References and Further Reading

Bedos-Rezak, Brigitte. "Medieval Women in French Sigillographic Sources." In Joel T. Rosenthal, ed. *Women and Sources of Medieval History*. Athens, Ga.: University of Georgia Press, 1990, pp. 1–36. Reprinted in Bedos-Rezak. *Form and Order in the Middle Ages*. No X.

———. "Women, Seals and Power in Medieval France, 1150–1350." In Mary Erler and Maryanne Kowaleski, ed. *Women and Power in the Middle Ages*. Athens, Ga.: University of Georgia Press, 1988, pp. 61–82. Reprinted in Bedos-Rezak. *Form and Order in the Middle Ages. Studies in Social and Quantitative Sigillography*. Aldershot: Ashgate, 1993. No IX.

Wagner, Anthony R. "Heraldry." In *Medieval England*, edited by Austin Lane Poole. New ed. Oxford: Clarendon Press, 1958, pp. 338–381.

See also **Burials and Tombs; Castles and Palaces; Chivalry; Genealogy; Heiresses; Patriarchy and Patrilineage; Seals and Sigillography**

HERETICS AND HERESY

Accusations of heresy, deviation from orthodox doctrine, were leveled against various groups and individuals in the West during the Middle Ages. Some groups of women, including the Beguines, frequently fell under suspicion. Individual women, including Marguerite Porete and Na Prous Boneta, were condemned. Suspect sects, especially the Cathars, were accused of attacking marriage and otherwise undermining the established gender norms of society. Some modern scholars have thought that other groups, especially the Waldensians and Lollards, gave women stronger leadership roles than the Church found acceptable. Orthodox writers also accused some heretics of hiding sexual vice behind a mask of virtue. At least one group, the Guglielmites, thought the Holy Spirit had been manifested in the form of a thirteenth-century holy woman.

Church authorities, bishops, and inquisitors, occasionally tried women; and others fell under suspicion. Most were not notable personalities like Porete, Boneta, Joan of Arc, or Esclarmonde of Foix, a woman of the high nobility who was a supporter of the Cathars. The majority were of the lesser nobility, town populations, or the peasantry. Some were executed; some punished; others cleared. A group of women who converted from Catharism were settled at Prouille, outside Toulouse, becoming the first Dominican nuns. In the late medieval and early modern periods, suspicion fell on women thought to be witches; and they were treated as if heretics, some being turned over to the lay authorities for execution.

THOMAS IZBICKI

References and Further Reading

Alcuin, Blamires. "Women and Preaching in Medieval Orthodoxy, Heresy, and Saints' Lives." *Viator:* 26 (1995): 135–152.
Biller, Peter. "Cathars and Material Women." In *Medieval Theology and the Natural Body*, edited by Peter Biller and A. J. Minnis. Rochester, N.Y.: York Medieval Press, 1997, pp. 61–107.
McSheffrey, Shannon. *Gender and Heresy: Women and Men in Lollard Communities, 1420–1530.* Middle Ages Series. Philadelphia: University of Pennsylvania Press, 1995.
Peterson, Janine Larmon. "Social Roles, Gender Inversion, and the Heretical Sect: The Case of the Guglielmites." *Viator* 35 (2004): 203–219.

See also **Cathars; Dominican Order; Lollards; Marguerite Porete; Pope Joan; Waldensians; Witches**

HERMAPHRODITES

Discourse about hermaphroditism (that is, being of an anatomically intermediate sex, now usually termed "intersexuality") is often seen by historians as especially revealing of contemporary ideas about sex due to the hermaphrodite's challenge to dichotomous notions of sex difference. The term *hermaphrodite* originates in Ovid's *Metamorphoses* (8 BCE), which describes the nymph Salmacis and her attempted seduction of Hermaphroditus, the son of Hermes and Aphrodite. When Hermaphroditus rejects Salmacis's advances, she petitions the gods to join them forever, and they do so—literally. The result is a hybrid creature of both male and female anatomical parts; hence, the word hermaphrodite came to denote a person of doubled or intermediate sex. Mentions of hermaphrodites in the Middle Ages often figure in medical discussions of sex difference, sexuality, and morality, but the hermaphrodite also appears in other genres of literature as a symbol of hybridity or transgression.

The problem of hermaphroditism occurs regularly in medieval medical and surgical treatises, particularly in discussions of "monsters" (usually meaning humans with birth defects), which authors attempt to explain according to various theories of generation. These explanations rely upon two distinct, and often contradictory, theoretical models: the Hippocratic/Galenic system and the Aristotelian system, which differed in many ways in their approach to intersexuality. According to the Hippocratic-Galenic tradition, hermaphrodites were neither male nor female, but an intermediary sex that combined male and female characteristics in perfect equilibrium. During the process of conception and gestation, a number of factors—such as the child's position in a left, right, or central chamber of the uterus, or the relative strength of the mother's and father's "sperm"—determined the sex of an offspring, which might be male, female, or something in between. The competing Aristotelian model argued that hermaphrodites were not so much an intermediate sex as the product of doubled or superfluous genitalia. According to this theory, a hermaphrodite occurred when matter contributed by the mother (in the form of menstrual blood) exceeded the amount needed to produce one fetus, but was not enough for two. The extra matter could form a second set of genitals, but the sex of the child was only superficially ambiguous: the "complexion" of the body (that is, the combination of heat, cold, dryness, and moisture within it) always indicated either male or female sex. The Aristotelian approach led some medieval thinkers to classify hermaphroditism as primarily a surgical problem that could be corrected by the amputation of the offending member.

A few anecdotes concerning hermaphrodites survive in legal and theological sources, suggesting how intersexed individuals may have been treated in Christian and Muslim societies during the Middle Ages. Legal texts in both the East and West generally attempted to fix the hermaphrodite firmly within binary biological or social structures. Islamic jurists assigned intersexed persons (*khuntha mushkil*) either male or female gender roles for the purposes of ritual, marriage, and inheritance. Latin canon and civil law allowed the hermaphrodite to participate fully in legal proceedings as long as his/her "sexual development" was sufficiently masculine to warrant his/her juridical status to be labeled male. Latin theological treatises indicate similar impulses. Peter the Chanter's (d. 1197) *De vitio sodomitico* warns that a hermaphrodite should be compelled to use only one of his/her sex organs in order to avoid the sin of sodomy. Although Islamic sources gave instructions for the determination of a hermaphrodite's sex by examination, Latin legal and theological sources tend to omit description of how the hermaphrodite's juridical or sexual status was to be decided.

Hermaphrodites also functioned as a symbol in medieval literature, particularly in the twelfth and thirteenth centuries. John of Salisbury's *Policraticus* (1159) borrows the tale of Hermaphroditus and Salmacis to criticize the bifurcated life of the courtier who serves both patron and philosophical truth. Alan of Lille's *De planctu naturae* (c. 1160–1170) rails against grammatical and sexual deviance by invoking hermaphrodites (by which he may have meant effeminate men), who transgress gender boundaries in language and life. Beginning in the thirteenth century, hermaphrodites also appear in alchemical texts as a symbol for the "philosopher's stone," which supposedly transmuted base metals into gold and silver, and which united both cold and wet (female) and hot and dry (male) principles into one substance. These medieval literary images make use of the hermaphrodite in order to indicate a combination of different or contradictory parts within a whole, and they also suggest the hermaphrodite's potential as a disruptor of medieval societal or natural norms.

LEAH DEVUN

References and Further Reading

Cadden, Joan. *Meanings of Sex Difference in the Middle Ages*. Cambridge: Cambridge University Press, 1993.

Jacquart, Danielle, and Claude Thomasset. *Sexuality and Medicine in the Middle Ages*, translated by Matthew Adamson. Princeton: Princeton University Press, 1988.

Nederman, Cary J., and Jacqui True. "The Third Sex: The Idea of the Hermaphrodite in Twelfth-Century Europe." *Journal of the History of Sexuality* 6 (1996): 497–517.

Rubin, Miri. "The Person in the Form: Medieval Challenges to Bodily 'Order.'" In *Framing Medieval Bodies*, edited by Sarah Kay and Miri Rubin. Manchester: Manchester University Press, 1994, pp. 100–122.

Sanders, Paula. "Gendering the Ungendered Body: Hermaphrodites in Medieval Islamic Law." In *Women in Middle Eastern History: Shifting Boundaries in Sex and Gender*, edited by Nikki R. Keddie and Beth Baron. New Haven: Yale University Press, 1991, pp. 74–95.

See also **Aristotelian Concepts of Women and Gender; Body in Literature and Religion; Femininity and Masculinity**

HERRAD OF HOHENBOURG

Herrad (c. 1176–after 1196), abbess of the Augustinian monastery of Hohenbourg (Ste. Odile) in Alsace, is best known as the author of the *Hortus deliciarum* (*Garden of Delights*), a lavish illuminated manuscript that she designed for the education of the women of her monastery. Although the manuscript was lost in the destruction of the Strasbourg library in 1870, notes and tracings from the original reflect the vibrant intellectual and spiritual culture that flourished at Hohenbourg under Herrad's care and demonstrate the high level of education available within female communities at this time. In the *Hortus*, Herrad presented a wide range of contemporary Latin texts within the framework of salvation history. Her major textual sources were the German Benedictine authors Honorius Augustodunensis and Rupert of Deutz, and the Parisian scholars Peter Lombard and Peter Comestor, authors whose presence in the manuscript confirms the breadth and currency of the education available at Hohenbourg. The manuscript's texts, including poems, hymns, sermons, biblical commentary, and history, are structured around an ambitious visual cycle consisting of some 346 images, many of which present dense theological and allegorical arguments. These images reveal Herrad's participation in the visual thinking of the twelfth century and are a witness to the sophisticated visual culture of a women's community. In addition to her work on the *Hortus*, Herrad was a capable administrator, who managed Hohenbourg's properties, encouraged donations, and founded two houses for canons who provided spiritual services for the women of her community.

FIONA J. GRIFFITHS

References and Further Reading

Collard, Judith. "Herrad of Hohenbourg's *Hortus Deliciarum* (The Garden of Delights) and the Creation of Images for Medieval Nuns." In *Communities of Women: Historical Perspectives*, edited by Barbara Brookes and Dorothy Page. Dunedin, N.Z.: University of Otago Press, 2002, pp. 39–57.

Gibson, Joan. "Herrad of Hohenbourg." In *Medieval, Renaissance and Enlightenment Women Philosophers A.D. 500–1600. A History of Women Philosophers*. Vol. 2, edited by Mary Ellen Waithe. Boston: Kluwer Academic Publishers, 1989, pp. 85–98.

Griffiths, Fiona. "Herrad of Hohenbourg: A Synthesis of Learning in the *Garden of Delights*," in *Listen, Daughter: The* Speculum Virginum *and the Formation of Religious Women in the Middle Ages*, edited by Constant J. Mews. The New Middle Ages Series. New York: Palgrave, 2001, pp. 221–243.

———. "Nuns' Memories or Missing History in Alsace (c. 1200): Herrad of Hohenbourg's *Garden of Delights*," in *Medieval Memories: Men, Women and the Past, 700–1300*, edited by Elisabeth van Houts. Women and Men in History Series. New York: Longman, 2001, pp. 132–149.

———. *The Garden of Delights: Reform and Renaissance for Women in the Twelfth Century*. Forthcoming.

Herrad of Hohenbourg. *Hortus Deliciarum*, edited by Rosalie Green, Michael Evans, Christine Bischoff, and Michael Curschmann. 2 vols. Studies of the Warburg Institute, 36. London: The Warburg Institute, 1979.

See also **Abbesses; Art, Representations of Women in; Book Ownership; Education, Monastic; Germanic**

Lands; Literacy and Reading: Latin; Monasticism and Nuns; Women Authors: Latin Texts

HILD OF WHITBY

Most of our evidence for the life of Hild (Hilda) of Whitby (614–680) comes from the Venerable Bede (d. c. 735). We know little of her early years. During her infancy, her mother had a dream that foretold Hild's future vocation. In 627, Hild converted to Christianity along with her great uncle, King Edwin, and other members of her family.

At the age of thirty-three, possibly having been widowed, Hild entered the religious life and was made abbess at Hartlepool two years later. Her noble heritage probably played a role in her appointment. Bede, however, emphasizes her motherly nature, her administrative skills, and her wisdom and devotion to serving God.

Hild eventually became the abbess of the double monastery at Whitby where she wielded much influence in the region. Bede notes that even kings and princes sought her advice. On one occasion, she hosted a council on the dispute between Irish and Roman practices (like the dating of Easter) in the Northumbrian church. It is significant that Bede not only recounts this event, but also explicitly mentions Hild's personal stance in the matter.

Further evidence of her influence is the fact that Hild prepared at least five bishops and many priests for the church. She emphasized good works and education, but also provided an example of fortitude to her followers as she endured long illness in the last seven years of her life. Bede reaffirms her sanctity writing that, at the very hour of her death, two nuns had visions of angels accompanying her soul to heaven.

HEATHER E. WARD

References and Further Reading

Bede. *The Ecclesiastical History of the English People, The Greater Chronicle, Bede's Letter to Egbert*, edited by Judith McClure and Roger Collins. Oxford: Oxford University Press, 1994.

Fell, Christine E. "Hild, Abbess of Streonæshalch." In *Hagiography and Medieval Literature: A Symposium*, edited by Hans Bekker-Nielsen, Peter Foote, Jørgen Højgaard Jørgensen, and Tore Nyberg. Odense: Odense University Press, 1981, pp. 76–99.

Foot, Sarah. "Religious Women in England Before the First Viking Age." In *Veiled Women I: The Disappearance of Nuns from Anglo-Saxon England*. Aldershot: Ashgate, 2000, pp. 35–60.

Overing, Gillian Rose and Clare A. Lees. "Birthing Bishops and Fathering Poets: Bede, Hild, and the Relations of Cultural Production." *Exemplaria* 6:1 (1994): 35–65.

Smith, Robin D. "Glimpses of Some Anglo-Saxon Women." In *A Wyf Ther Was: Essays in Honour of Paule Mertens-Fonck*, edited by Juliette Dor. Liège: U. de Liège, 1992, pp. 256–263.

See also Abbesses; Church; Double Monasteries; England; Monasticism and Nuns

HILDEGARD OF BINGEN

Hildegard of Bingen (1098–1179), one of the greatest figures of the Middle Ages, founded two monasteries and authored numerous works, the foremost being a trilogy of visionary treatises: *Scivias*, *Liber vitae meritorum*, and *Liber divinorum operum*. For the first and third of those she designed illuminations. Hildegard also composed commentaries on the Rule of Benedict and the Athanasian Creed, exegetical homilies on the gospels, the lives of saints Disibod and Rupert, the first extant morality play, medical works, liturgical songs, and over 300 letters.

Life

The daughter of a noble family, Hildegard was born in 1098 at Bermersheim near Mainz. Her parents, Hildebert and Mechthild, entrusted her to the care of the holy woman Jutta, daughter of the count of Sponheim. Jutta and Hildegard were immured at the Benedictine monastery of Disibodenberg on All Saints' Day, November 1, 1112. Jutta taught Hildegard the Psalms and showed her how to play the ten-stringed psaltery. From their enclosure the two could hear the monks' recitation of the Divine Office, a continuing lesson in the Scriptures and other sacred texts. Jutta's renown resulted in the expansion of her enclosure into a *schola*; she served as superior to a small women's Benedictine community in dependence on the abbot of Disibodenberg. Hildegard remained under Jutta's tutelage until her teacher's death in 1136, whereupon Hildegard became the superior (*magistra*).

In 1141, Hildegard experienced a crucial turning point when a powerful vision, received when she was fully awake, instructed her to make known the revelations of divine light that she had begun receiving as a child. She suddenly understood the spiritual meaning of the Scriptures, without possessing a command of scriptural interpretation or grammar. As she later explained to Guibert of Gembloux, the shadow of the "Living Light" illuminated her, with the result that the Scriptures, virtues, and other inspired writings shone forth with clarity (*Letters* II, 103r. p. 23).

When Hildegard refused the divine command, she was struck by illness and sought the counsel of Volmar, her first secretary, and a sister, Richardis, who later left Hildegard's community, to her great sorrow. Hildegard received permission from Abbot Kuno of Disibodenberg (1136–1155) to accept the divine order to "speak and write," and she began to compose *Scivias* (*Know the Ways*).

Pope Eugene III spent the winter of 1147–1148 (November 30–February 13) in Trier, where Hildegard sent him a letter with part of the *Scivias*. Eugene III reportedly sent a delegation to Disibodenberg to investigate Hildegard's writings and bring her work back to him. The pope issued a charter of protection for Disibodenberg but made no reference to Hildegard or the women's community. Hildegard in turn wrote Eugene again to seek his approval and protection, but he sent no written reply (*Letters* I, 2). Hildegard had also written Bernard of Clairvaux in early 1147 to affirm that she was shown in a vision the inner meaning of the exposition of "the Psalter, the Gospels, and other volumes" (*Letters* I, 1, p. 28). The abbot sent a brief reply, hailing Hildegard's inner enlightenment by the Spirit, using words from 1 John 2:27 on the anointing that teaches about all things (*unctio docens de omnibus*), a scriptural allusion that he often employed in praise of the Spirit's gifts (*Letters* I, 1r, p. 31).

Volmar, when editing Hildegard's letter collection around 1170, drafted a letter in the pope's name and also revised the letter from Bernard of Clairvaux. The original correspondence from Eugene III and Bernard contains no written authorization for Hildegard to write, but the *magistra* clearly felt empowered to do so. Significantly, neither Bernard nor Eugene forbade her writing or speaking during a period when ecclesiastical intervention against unauthorized preaching was escalating. (In the 1140s, Bernard denounced heretics in the Rhineland, traveled to Occitania in pursuit of heresy, and targeted unauthorized preaching by a renegade Cistercian who was stirring up anti-Jewish hatred in the Rhineland.)

Whatever the precise understanding that resulted from Hildegard's contact with Bernard and Eugene III in 1147–1148, the *magistra* felt empowered to express her voice publicly in writing. Her *vita* reports that Eugene III sent letters to Hildegard, granting her "permission to make known whatever she had learned through the Holy Spirit" and urging her to write. Hildegard repeats the story in her autobiographical account, stating that Pope Eugene wrote her and "commanded" her to write what she saw and heard (*Life*, pp. 30, 46).

Four people contributed to the *vita*: Hildegard herself; Gottfried of Disibodenberg (d. 1176), provost of Rupertsberg after Volmar's death in 1173; Guibert of Gembloux (1124/1125–1213), secretary to Hildegard; and Theodoric of Echternach (d. post-1192), who compiled the *vita* from various sources. Hildegard began organizing the writing of her *vita* herself with Gottfried, author of Book One. Guibert of Gembloux gathered materials and worked on the *vita* from 1177–1180, but was summoned back to Gembloux before he could finish. He took with him an incomplete *vita*, published in a letter, and he left a dossier of materials at the Rupertsberg. Theodoric, author of Books Two and Three, compiled the *vita* from the sources available, including the texts of Hildegard's visions and a narrative of her life, used throughout the work, but especially in Book Two.

Scivias

The completion of *Scivias*, Hildegard's first visionary work, occupied ten years. Its three books contain six, seven, and thirteen visions respectively, whose content encompasses salvation history from the sin of Adam to the coming of Antichrist. Statements emphasizing Hildegard's visionary and prophetic authority punctuate the beginning and conclusion of the books and their visions. The image of the edifice of salvation holds a central place in many of the visions; Christ is the cornerstone and humans reconstruct the edifice with the help of the virtues. Hildegard instructs all orders of society on a wide variety of topics and admonishes them on appropriate conduct in view of the approaching end times. The final evocations of the last days include a horrific vision of Antichrist taking birth from *Ecclesia* herself, a powerful indictment of corruption in the church, a recurrent theme in Hildegard's works.

Thirty-five illuminations accompany the text, and as far as we know, Hildegard herself designed them. Recent scholarship argues that Hildegard likely received her visual images first, sketched them, and then commented upon them with words. Whatever the order of the process, Hildegard intended the visual representation and text of her visions to be food for meditation. The commentary often differs from the illuminations, but together they constitute a core text. Further commentary follows the explanation of the visions and adds more conventional teaching of a moral nature. The original manuscript of *Scivias*, probably produced by the nuns at Rupertsberg during Hildegard's lifetime, has been lost since the bombing of Dresden in 1945. Fortunately, a photographic copy was made in 1927, and the nuns at Eibingen also prepared a color facsimile by hand (1927–1933).

After *Scivias*, Hildegard undertook the *Liber vitae meritorum* (*Book of Life's Merits*), a work comprising six visions that comment on human behavior and pair off vices and virtues, punishment and penance. Regarding its completion, Hildegard remarks that she had been "frequently worn down by tribulations" (p. 61). For each vision in the book, a human figure superimposed on the world that stretches from the heavens to the depths, turns from point to point and reports what he observes. The virtues play a less prominent role than in *Scivias*, as the emphasis in this work lies on the negative aspects of human behavior and salvation history. Thirty-five vices are enumerated with their corresponding punishment and penance. The admonitory lessons provided refectory readings at the monastery of Villers and could have filled a similar function at Rupertsberg.

Rupertsberg

After disputes with Disibodenberg, Hildegard had obtained permission to found Rupertsberg near the town of Bingen, where she and her nuns journeyed around 1150; in 1165, she founded Eibingen, a daughterhouse, across the Rhine from Bingen. The nuns established the right to choose their own provost, but technically they remained subordinate to the abbot of Disibodenberg with Hildegard serving as prioress (*priorissa*). Guibert of Gembloux describes the activities of Hildegard and her nuns at Rupertsberg, where he served as her secretary and stayed from June 1177 until after her death. He testifies to the intellectual and spiritual work of the community and his relationship to Hildegard, reading and discussing her works.

Hildegard's autobiographical narrative informs us about the third work of her trilogy. The vision of John the Evangelist compelled her to "explain every statement and word of this gospel regarding the beginning of the work of God" (*Life*, p. 67), a reference to the exegetical synthesis of the *Liber divinorum operum* (*Book of Divine Works*) or *De operatione Dei*, which occupied Hildegard from 1163 to 1174 and which brings together her understanding of Genesis 1 and John 1. Volmar died before Hildegard had completed the *Book of Divine Works*, but she was assisted by Ludwig, abbot of St. Eucharius in Trier. In a letter that Hildegard sent to Ludwig (*Letters* II, 217) with the manuscript of the book, she urges him to consider her work as a unicorn in his lap, to protect it, and correct it with care.

The *Book of Divine Works* elaborates the spiritual significance of creation in all its dimensions, the connectedness of the human microcosm, body and soul, and the macrocosm, the universe. The ten visions, contained in three books of varying length, move from the creation of the human and the cosmos, with exegesis of John 1, to the history of salvation, which Hildegard connects to the days of creation, providing detailed commentary on Genesis 1. As in *Scivias*, the visions are followed by explanations; likewise, prophetic markers that assert the reception of the divine voice occur frequently. The Lucca manuscript (Biblioteca Governatina MS 1942), probably produced in the 1220s as part of an effort to canonize Hildegard, contains striking illuminations of the cosmos, divine figures, and the heavenly Jerusalem.

Hildegard's extensive correspondence and her preaching tours demonstrate the wide audience for her advice. Her correspondents included popes, the emperor Frederick Barbarossa, Henry II and Eleanor of Aquitaine, bishops and other churchmen, noble men and women, and other lay people. Letters to abbots and abbesses advise them in the face of burdensome monastic responsibilities, while other letters range from difficult exegetical questions to practical advice on medical problems such as nightmares and infertility. The *magistra* explains the workings of the humors, which she discusses in her medical work, *Causae et curae* (*Causes and Cures*) and suggests specific prayers and herbal remedies.

Hildegard stands out as the only medieval woman author of systematic works of exegesis. Volmar wrote to express that at her death, the community would miss her new interpretation of the Scriptures (*Letters*, II, 195). Hildegard composed fifty-eight *Expositiones evangeliorum* (*Commentaries on the Gospels*), homilies on twenty-seven gospel pericopes, which were recorded by the nuns at Rupertsberg. Moreover, Guibert of Gembloux wrote the *magistra* on behalf of the monks at Villers, requesting her advice to thirty-eight problems of scriptural interpretation. Her reply constitutes the treatise, *Solutiones triginta octo quaestionum* (*Solutions for Thirty-Eight Questions*).

From Rupertsberg, Hildegard undertook four preaching tours from approximately 1158 to 1170. Hildegard's audiences were primarily monastic communities whom she admonished about monastic and clerical reform. The fourth preaching tour aimed, at least in part, at combating Catharism. In the *vita*, Theodoric notes that Hildegard preached in twenty-one places, including five cathedral cities: Cologne, Trier, Metz, Würzburg, and Bamberg, omitting a sermon at Kirchheim in 1170. The Cologne (1163), Trier (1160), and Kirchheim sermons have been transmitted in epistolary form. Hildegard preached at Disibodenberg also, and upon request of Abbot Helenger around 1170, composed the *Life of St. Disibod*. She also wrote the *Life of St. Rupert*, patron of Rupertsberg.

Last Years

During the last year of her life, 1178–1179, Hildegard faced problems with Archbishop Christian of Mainz concerning a deceased man to whom she had granted burial at Rupertsberg, although the Mainz prelates claimed that he was still excommunicated at the time of his death. Hildegard refused to have the body exhumed, and the archbishop imposed an interdict, denying the nuns reception of the Eucharist and the singing of the Office. The interdict was lifted not long before her death.

Hildegard suffered gravely from the denial of the sacrament and of music. She considered her musical ability a divine gift and composed works for the Office, collected in the *Symphonia*. As religious superior of her community, Hildegard would have intoned her own elaborate responsories as leader of daily liturgy. In defense of her community and in protest against the interdict, Hildegard composed a powerful letter in 1178 on the salvific role of participating in music. For Hildegard, musical harmony represented celestial harmony. Liturgical music brought together body and soul, mirroring the dual nature of Christ, and aiding humankind to regain the divine voice that Adam lost at the Fall. In her morality play, *Ordo virtutum* (*Play of the Virtues*), the Devil is the one character who does not sing, because evil cannot be beautiful or harmonious.

In the first third of the thirteenth century, the nuns at Rupertsberg made attempts to have Hildegard canonized. A commission of Mainz clergy was appointed to investigate Hildegard's life and miracles. Their first report (1233) was rejected, then amended, and a 1243 letter from Innocent IV requested that the claim be resubmitted. No other known thirteenth-century records pertain to the process, but Hildegard's name and feast day appear in martyrologies from the fourteenth century onward, a 1324 indulgence from John XXII recognizes her public cult, and the sixteenth-century Roman martryrology by Baronius includes her name. Hildegard also retained a reputation for prophecy down to the fifteenth century and later.

Since the late twentieth century, scholarship on Hildegard has flourished, musical groups have performed her evocative music, and admirers have claimed her authority for spiritual practices, the ecological movement, healthful cooking, and even brewing.

BEVERLY MAYNE KIENZLE

References and Further Reading

Bartlett, Anne Clark. "Commentary, Polemic, and Prophecy in Hildegard of Bingen's *Solutiones triginta octo quaestionum*." *Viator* 23 (1992): 153–165.

Beate Hildegardis Causae et Curae, edited by Laurence Moulinier. Berlin: Akademie Verlag, 2003.

Berndt, Rainer. ed. "*Im Angesicht Gottes suche der Mensch sich selbst*" *Hildegard von Bingen (1098–1179)*. Berlin: Akademie Verlag, 2001.

Burnett, Charles and Peter Dronke, edited by *Hildegard of Bingen: The Context of Her Thought and Art*. London: Warburg Institute, 1998.

Dronke, Peter. "Problemata Hildegardiana." *Mittellateinisches Jahrbuch* 16 (1981): 97–131.

——. *Women Writers of the Middle Ages: A Critical Study of Texts from Perpetua (+203) to Marguerite Porete (+1310)*. Cambridge: Cambridge University Press, 1984.

——. "Platonic-Christian Allegories in the Homilies of Hildegard of Bingen." In *From Athens to Chartres. Neoplatonism and Medieval Thought. Studies in Honour of Edouard Jeauneau*, edited by Haijo Jan Westra. Leiden: E. J. Brill, 1992, pp. 381–396.

Emmerson, Richard. "The Representation of Antichrist in Hildegard of Bingen's *Scivias*." *Gesta* 41: 2 (2002): 95–110.

Flanagan, Sabina. *Hildegard of Bingen, 1098–1179. A Visionary Life*. 2nd. ed. London and New York: Routledge, 1998.

Gottfried of Disibodenberg and Theodoric of Echternach. *The Life of the Saintly Hildegard*, translated by Hugh Feiss. Toronto: Peregrina Press, 1996.

Haverkamp, A, ed. *Hildegard von Bingen in ihrem historischen Umfeld. Internationaler wissenschaftlicher Kongreß zum 900jähren Jubilaum, 13.–19. September 1998. Bingen am Rhein*. Mainz: Verlag Philipp von Zabern, 2000.

Hildegard of Bingen. *Expositiones evangeliorum*, edited by J.-B. Pitra. In *Analecta S. Hildegardis*, in *Analecta sacra*, vol. 8. Rome, 1882, pp. 245–327.

——. *Scivias*, translated by Columba Hart and Jane Bishop; Intro. Barbara J. Newman; Preface, Caroline Walker Bynum. New York: Paulist Press, 1990.

——. *Letters*, translated by J. L. Baird and R. K. Ehrman. 3 vols. Oxford, New York: Oxford University Press, 1994, 1998, 2004.

——. *Symphonia*, translated by Barbara Newman. 2nd ed. Ithaca: Cornell University Press, 1998.

——. *An Explanation of the Athanasian Creed*, translated by T. M. Izbicki. Toronto: Peregrina, 2001.

——. *Expositiones evangeliorum*, edited by B. Kienzle and C. A. Muessig. In *Hildegardis Bingensis Opera homiletica et liturgica*. Turnhout; Brepols, 2006.

Kienzle, Beverly Mayne "Hildegard of Bingen's Teaching in Her *Expositiones evangeliorum and Ordo virtutum*." In *Medieval Monastic Education*, edited by George P. Ferzoco and Carolyn A. Muessig Leicester: University of Leicester Press, 2001, pp. 72–86.

——. "Hildegard of Bingen's Exegesis of Luke." In *Early Christian Writings Inside and Out: A Festschrift in Honor of François Bovon*, edited by D. Warren, A. Brock, and D. Pao. Leiden: Brill, 2003, pp. 227–238.

———. *Fortifications of the Word: Hildegard of Bingen as Preacher ad Exegete.* Turnhout: Brepols, 2006.

Newman, Barbara. *Sister of Wisdom. St. Hildegard's Theology of the Feminine, with a new Preface, Bibliography, and Discography.* Berkeley: University of California Press: 1998.

———. *Voice of the Living Light: Hildegard of Bingen and Her World.* Berkeley: University of California Press, 1998.

———. "Hildegard and Her Hagiographers: The Remaking of Female Sainthood." In *Gendered Voices: Medieval Saints and Their Interpreters*, edited by Catherine M. Mooney. Philadelphia: University of Pennsylvania Press, 1999, pp. 1–15.

Pernoud, Régine. "The Preaching Peregrinations of a Twelfth-Century Nun, ca. 1158–70." In *Wisdom Which Encircles Circles*, edited by A. E. Davidson. Kalamazoo, Mich.: Medieval Institute Publications, 1996, pp. 15–26.

Silvas, Anna. trans. *Jutta and Hildegard: The Biographical Sources.* University Park, Pa.: Pennsylvania State University Press, 1999.

See also **Abbesses; Artists, Women; Education, Monastic; Hagiography; History, Medieval Women's; Letter Writing; Literacy and Reading: Latin; Medicine; Monastic Rules; Monasticism and Nuns; Mysticism and Mystics; Nuns as Illuminators; Prophets; Sermons and Preaching; Women Authors: Latin Texts**

HISTORY, MEDIEVAL WOMEN'S

Women did compose history in the Middle Ages, like the famous *Alexiad* of the Byzantine princess Anna Comnena; contrary to modern expectations medieval women did receive attention from historians in their own day and age. Giovanni Boccaccio's (1313–1375) *On Famous Women* provided brief biographies of women worthies, recent and ancient, intended to inspire readers, much like stories about heroic male figures. This encouraged other authors, who sometimes wrote in a positive vein like Boccaccio. Still others remained in the tradition of chronicle accounts, where women were condemned when their acts rose to the level of historical notice through wielding power and influence. Evil queens were an enduring theme among royal and dynastic chroniclers; these authors exonerated powerful rulers from error by blaming the influence of royal wives and mothers. Women's unchaste acts, debauchery, and "unnatural acts," such as waging war, were enduring themes in this tradition, indeed their very frequency casts doubt on their veracity.

Vitae (Lives) of medieval women saints like Hildegard of Bingen, the Helfta mystics, and Catherine of Siena were popular historical reading matter as well. Christine de Pizan (1364–1430) wrote a biographical poem about Joan of Arc as savior of France, while her *City of Women* presented an imagined history of virtuous women's rule, so the tradition of medieval women worthy of celebration flourished and endured, especially among women readers. Mystics, abbesses, royal women, and a few women authors like the famed abbess of the Paraclete, Heloise, who wrote love letters to the scholar Abelard, were featured as romantic archetypes of an earlier age, or as exemplars of piety, literacy, or devotion to family.

Yet historians doubted the authenticity of some visionary women's writings, and on occasion their spiritual vocations. At times medieval women mystics were viewed as neurotic or diseased, and their piety as inferior to that of their male counterparts, who were regarded as more rational in their religious devotion.

In other instances women's texts that were admired by historians were reascribed to male figures—a confessor perhaps—on the grounds that a woman could not have composed such texts—in Latin, no less. In 1888, William Henry Hudson reviewed the sixteenth century Conrad Celtis edition of Hrotsvit of Gandersheim's dramas and exonerated Celtis of charges that his edition was a forgery and fraud. Critics had argued that a woman of the tenth century could not have been an accomplished Latinist as Hrosvit certainly was. With remarkable foresight the twelfth century author Marie de France avoided this predicament by signing her texts. No one could gainsay her bold "*Me numerai pur remembrance/Marie ai num, si sui de France*" (I shall name myself in order to be remembered/My name is Marie and I come from France). While a tradition of historical writing by and about medieval women survived, it was challenged, or on occasion dismissed as a negligible topic.

Impact of Positioning

The Enlightenment and the later drive for suffrage widened the scope of the investigation of medieval women, and most of the resulting studies involved inquiries into the condition of women in earlier ages. New World feminism, which began before the Civil War, recognized the importance of medieval women. Matilda Gage (1826–1898) proposed to write a comprehensive history of women through the ages, but her research convinced her that the sources were simply inadequate, so she abandoned the project. Writing in *The Una*, a women's rights magazine, in 1853, Paulina Wright Davis argued that women's journey back to the Middle Ages was, paradoxically, a journey of progress (Davis, 1376–1377). In those earlier times women had been physicians and notaries and held positions of authority.

This sounded a theme that would persist in medieval women's history. Instances of medieval women enjoying legal rights and opportunities denied them in modern times cast some doubt on the progressive nature of change over the centuries in the West. During World War I Annie Abram wrote "Women Traders in Medieval London" for an *Economic Journal* issue devoted to working women's new roles in wartime. She claimed medieval antecedents for women's skilled work in the economy and a larger role for working women than in more recent years. Alice Clark made a similar argument in 1919 about working women of the seventeenth century, introducing the possibility of a past Golden Age for women. Doris Mary Stenton also struck that note, in her long-term study *The English Woman in History,* which she published in 1957.

The tools of positivism favored by nineteenth-century historians and literary scholars could be used for uncovering medieval women's history in some instances. Positivism may be briefly defined as a system concerned with positive facts and phenomena, excluding speculation upon ultimate causes or origins. In history positivism has favored a narrative style of presentation and assumed a shared sense of what is significant between author and reader. In France Marie-Joseph-Raymond Thomassy wrote an essay on the important political writings of Christine de Pizan as early as 1838, despite the fact that those texts would wait well over a century for translation and critical editions. Women who wielded influence, such as the Carolingian empress Engelberge (wife of Louis II) or the Byzantine court historian Anna Komnene, who had made contributions comparable to those of prominent men, could be presented to a scholarly audience because their roles fit the accepted canons of narrative history. But it took new interpretive tools—and to an extent, a new twentieth century audience of college-educated women—to solve the problem of neglect for other medieval women.

Outside the Academy

"Amateur" historians, who sometimes lacked advanced degrees and were not above writing for a popular audience, began to appear near the turn of the twentieth century. Among these Lina Eckenstein, who published *Women under Monasticism, Saint-Lore and Convent Life between AD 500 and 1500* in 1896, stands out. An ingenious scholar, largely self-trained in medieval studies, Eckenstein produced path-breaking analyses of religious women. Her twin interests in unlocking folklore and the origin of nursery verses

served her well in taking on a topic for which the contemporary narrative tools of positivist history were inadequate.

A few years later Mary Bateson faced her own interpretive challenge when she wrote "Origin and Early History of Double Monasteries" for the 1899 *Transactions of the Royal Historical Society*. A rather traditional legal historian, Bateson nonetheless created a theoretical strategy for disentangling the issue of double monasteries from questions about national origins. She ignored genealogical descent for double houses and defined double monasteries generically, opening investigation to all known examples that fit the definition. "Regular" priests ministering to the spiritual needs of women under vows created these institutions, she asserted. This left the problem of leadership open to a variety of answers adopted over time and place. The double monastery was not an instance of cultural transmission but rather a response to women's devotional needs. Bateson dared her readers to confront religious devotion among women as a serious matter. At least her educated women readers were willing to do just that.

This was an audience who would also appreciate E. Dixon writing on craftswomen in the Parisian *Livre des Métiers*. The blend of a new audience for medieval women and enterprising interpretive strategies to uncover their history succeeded, albeit outside the academy rather than within it, at least initially. Eleanor Shipley Duckett developed a successful career as a Latinist writing on the Early Middle Ages for a popular audience in the 1930s. She frequently featured saintly women in her works. Marion Dale wrote about "London Silkwomen of the Fifteenth Century" in 1933. Muriel Joy Hughes published *Women Healers in Medieval Life and Literature* in 1938, capturing an audience of educated women, especially in the field of health care. Emily Hope Allen and Sanford Brown edited and introduced *The Book of Margery Kempe* to an enthusiastic reading audience in 1940. Readers were intrigued by this account of a strong-minded and devout laywoman's tribulations. As recently as the 1960s, Régine Pernoud, who generally wrote for a popular audience, produced *Joan of Arc, by Herself and Her Witnesses*. This study restored life to the figure of Joan, whose very humanity had been placed in peril by the conflicting claims of church and state over her inspired leadership. In that same decade the "amateur" scholar Iris Origo produced the well-researched *Merchant of Prato*, which gave a major role to the correspondence of Monna Margherita Datini in creating a portrait of a family business set in a broad context of fourteenth-century politics and trade. The works mentioned here are well regarded and have been absorbed into the scholarly literature on medieval women, but it is useful to remember that they began life as popular writings, and were sometimes dismissed as inconsequential by contemporary academic scholars.

Within the Academy

Meanwhile critical editions and comments on early texts that satirized or condemned medieval women appeared in scholarly venues. George Keidel edited *Evangile aux femmes—An Old-French Satire on Women* in 1895, and tracts on witchcraft received scholarly editions. Thus misogynous texts were at hand in the academy, while little was known then about medieval women's actual lives. Karl Bücher complicated this picture when in 1910 he published *Die Frauenfrage im Mittelalter*, which drew on a tradition of writing about women, although it was inadequately grounded in women's experience. He argued that single women presented a social problem when they moved to towns in the later Middle Ages. Many of these women did not wed, which encouraged a tendency toward banding together and following a religious vocation through performing charitable work. These Beguines and *pinzochere* often did without the dowries necessary to enter a monastery, yet managed to live together and made their own livings. Heresy, Bücher believed, flourished among these women, who had escaped paternal authority and were only marginally supervised by the church, since they lived in secular society.

The demographic and spiritual dimensions of Bücher's thesis demanded a more thorough analysis of women's lives; subsequent scholarship engaged his thesis on both sides in a debate. In a series of talks from the 1920s, published posthumously, Eileen Power argued that at best, medieval opinion of women was contradictory. In 1971, David Herlihy argued in *Women in Medieval Society* that Bücher's demographics told only a small part of the story. Both Power and Herlihy insisted that unless the social history of women was reconstructed, it was impossible to answer the question about women's place or status in medieval society. More recent scholarship has engaged Bücher's thesis on the issues of women's spiritual needs and the orthodoxy of their religious beliefs.

Women's History

It is worthwhile, then, to reconstruct what was at hand when the feminism of the 1960s and early 1970s made medieval women's history a compelling topic of broad interest. A tradition of historical writing on medieval religious women, on saints, and on queens existed. Women's work, crafts, and guilds had been explored to an extent, and texts had been recovered for some women writers, but certainly not all. Yvonne Rokseth had written on women musicians from the twelfth through the fourteenth centuries in 1935. Marion Facinger composed an institutional study of medieval queenship in Capetian France, 987–1237, in 1968. Isidore Epstein wrote *Jewish Women in the "Responsa" 900 CE to 1500 CE* in 1934. Some of these studies argued in the singular, creating a generic medieval woman or an essential medieval womanhood. Eckenstein wrote of *woman* under monasticism, Stenton about the English *woman* in history, Isidore Epstein about the Jewish *woman* in the Responsa; Eileen Power, intriguingly, spoke in the singular about the lady, and the working *woman*, but also about the education of *women* and medieval ideas about *women*. For all of its value in uncovering women's history, the singular address presented the historical subject as acted upon and largely unmoving, as a constant within an evolving society. The new feminist agenda would challenge that presumption.

The initial task to which feminist historians turned their analysis was that of fleshing out the picture of medieval women's lives. Issues of power and authority drew attention, with Jo Ann McNamara and Suzanne Wemple arguing that by the ninth, tenth, and eleventh centuries aristocratic women encountered few structural barriers to the acquisition of power in almost every capacity except the priesthood. Class was a decisive factor in this argument, allowing women who were ambitious or ruthless to play central political roles. They were chatelaines, mistresses of landed property and castles with attendant rights of justice and military command, proprietors of churches, and participants in both secular and ecclesiastical assemblies. Enthusiasm greeted this interpretation because the very possibility of women encountering such opportunities inspired feminists bent on their own quest for more opportunities and rights.

Medieval women became a focus of historical research. In 1976, *Women in Medieval Society* reiterated the need for a history of women that contextualized their lives on many levels of society. This volume of essays was compiled to prove to the academy that there was information to be gleaned about women's lives in medieval archives, since women historians had heard so often that there was not. One question repeated over the decade centered on long-term change in women's conditions. In 1977 in *Becoming Visible*, a textbook devoted to the history of women, Joan Kelly-Gadol asked "Did Women Have a

Renaissance?" in which she traced the courtly love tradition, which she attributed to powerful feudal women in the twelfth century, but then reattributed to powerful male princes and their courtiers by the Renaissance.

Diane Owen Hughes explored the idea of transition in an article about medieval dowry and other marital gifts, published in the *Journal of Family History* in 1978. While men paid to marry and their brides owned and managed their wedding gifts in Mediterranean Europe, women enjoyed significant legal and property rights. When, after the twelfth century, brides' fathers paid dowry to grooms (who then controlled the gift even if they did not own it), women lost control of property and faced more restricted legal rights. Many new interpretations like this groundbreaking analysis appeared in article form rather than book-length monographs. Another characteristic of this new literature was a propensity for studies to appear in multiauthored thematic volumes. The latter ploy ensured publication and helped to create an audience for a number of women scholars who were unemployed or only marginally employed in academia.

Some have argued that feminist history was an American endeavor, but that is not entirely the case. German scholars stepped up their studies of medieval women visionaries in a response to renewed interest. Derek Baker compiled a series of essays by English scholars with a feminist bent in *Medieval Women* (1978). Christiane Klapische-Zuber had begun publishing in French the studies of Florentine women and family that would become *Women, Family and Ritual in Renaissance Italy* (1985) and with David Herlihy produced the major census (catasto) study of 1427 Florence, *Les Toscans et leurs familles*, in 1978. This would become a foundation for future analysis of women and family in Italy. The project of understanding women in different walks of life resulted in monographs and scholarly articles, although the latter were more likely to appear in new journals devoted to women's studies like *Feminist Studies* or *SIGNS: A Journal of Women in Culture and Society* than in more traditional professional journals.

Acceptance by the Academy

Yet acceptance within the academy had begun, encouraged by the respect that these initial forays into medieval women's history garnered through careful research and interpretive innovation. Contemporaneously, students in colleges and universities clamored for courses on medieval women. No sooner did these articles, volumes and textbooks appear than they became assigned reading in the classroom. Susan Groag Bell produced a sourcebook for the classroom, *Women: From the Greeks to the French Revolution* in 1973 that became a best-seller in textbook publishing. Textbooks in women's history like *Becoming Visible* were treated to scholarly reviews, whereas general textbooks seldom received this attention from scholarly journals. The avid interest in women's history encouraged institutions of higher learning to appoint women to their history faculties. Thus began the movement of women's history from the margins to a central place in curricula and in the interpretation of earlier centuries.

As a result the 1980s offered an entirely different venue to the project of women's history. Most regions of Europe received attention from scholars attempting to uncover medieval women's history. Suzanne Wemple wrote *Women in Frankish Society: Marriage and the Cloister, 500 to 900* in 1981. Heath Dillard published *Daughters of the Reconquest: Women in Castilian Town Society, 1100–1300*, in 1984. An expanding audience had begun to demand women's histories for all regions and all walks of life. Leah Lydia Otis wrote *Prostitution in Medieval Society* in 1985, adding to the known variety of medieval women's work experience.

History of Gender

Perhaps the most significant development in the field in that decade was the emergence of a history of gender alongside women's history. Two initiatives are worth comment here. In 1980, Ian Maclean published a monograph on the history of medicine, *Renaissance Notion of Woman: A Study in the Fortunes of Scholasticism and Medical Science in European Intellectual Life*. He posed the following as his central question: why did the medieval Thomist formulation (in which woman was defined as passive, material, and deprived in duality with man, who was defined as active, formative, and perfected) persist even while the discrepancy between the social realities of women's lives and this formulation continued to widen? The way in which the question was posed encouraged notional thinking about women as a distinct field of inquiry, to be considered apart from the task of reconstructing women's lives. In this decade as well, Caroline Walker Bynum published *Jesus as Mother* (1982), displaying the rich variety of feminine gender associations available to medieval people when imagining Jesus's loving care. In 1987, she followed this with *Holy Feast and Holy Fast*, a study of women's appropriation of metaphor that expressed their own unique vein of religiosity.

Gender was a lens that could be turned on both imposed perceptions and self-perceptions of the feminine, or turned back onto masculinity, treating perceptions of men as gendered notions, rather than as generic norms for the human condition. These initiatives opened the floodgates to histories on medieval women and related topics of family, production, and growing up male or female. Martha Howell's *Women, Production and Patriarchy in Late Medieval Cities* appeared in 1986. Barbara Hanawalt wrote on the structure of medieval peasant life in *The Ties That Bound* in 1986, employing insights from women's history and the study of gender to develop a new thesis on family in northern Europe. Barbara Newman examined St. Hildegard's theology of the feminine in a monograph in 1987. Penny Schine Gold wrote *The Lady and the Virgin* in 1985, a study of love and religion. The analysis of the gender systems in which both medieval women and men lived out their lives inspired an explosion of literature in the field.

Scholarly Editions and Journals

Scholars called for a more systematic recovering of women's texts. At long last a critical edition and modern translation of Christine de Pizan's *City of Ladies* appeared in 1982, followed by a biography and critical study of her writings by Charity Cannon Willard in 1984. The *Medieval Feminist Forum,* formerly the *Medieval Feminist Newsletter,* began publishing in 1986. A critical edition of Hildegard of Bingen's *Scivias,* edited and translated by Mother Columba Hart and Jane Bishop, finally appeared from Paulist Press by the end of the decade (1990). Margot King edited the Peregrina Translations Series of the *Matrologia Latina,* including among its earlier publications the lives of Christina Mirabilis (1986), Marie d'Oignies (1987), and Saint Macrina (1987). In 2001, Monica Green produced a side-by-side translation of *The Trotula: A Medieval Compendium of Women's Medicine.*

Articles about medieval women and gender became fare for mainstream scholarly journals. *Speculum: the Journal of the Medieval Academy of America* published an issue devoted to medieval women, sex, gender, and feminism in 1993. Authorities on the topic trained graduate students in the field, and controversies arose. At history meetings from the American Historical Association winter meeting to the spring meeting of the Medieval Academy of America, sessions on medieval women and gender became commonplace. Neither matched in enthusiastic response the annual International Congress on Medieval Studies at Western Michigan University in Kalamazoo, Michigan, or its English counterpart, the International Medieval Congress at Leeds University in Leeds, England.

Diversity

Diversity became a theme in the 1990s, with many feminist scholars arguing for a complex view of medieval women's lives and many roles played out in religion, community, family, society at large, and the economy. Women's ethnicity and sexuality became topics of interest. Anglo-American dominance in recent publishing on the topic was challenged by the emergence of new journals devoted to women in other European languages. In France *Clio: Histoire, Femme et Sociétés* began publishing in 1995. *Homme: Zeitschrift für feministische Geschichtswissenschaft* began in Germany in 1990 followed by *Feministische Studien* in 1994. *Arenal: Revista de Historia de las Mujeres Universidad de Granada* also began in 1994 as did *Nora: Nordic Journal of Women's Studies. Memoria, Revista di Storia delle Donne* had begun much earlier in Italy (1981) but ceased publication in 1991. This was prompted in part by the inclusion of many articles on medieval Italian women in long-established journals. New emphasis on a plural view of medieval women profited from the sheer number of new studies published about them.

With its religious and economic dimensions, the *frauenfrage* continued to offer matter for debate. Likewise the "golden age" for working women figured as a controversy among scholars writing on medieval England, with P. J. P. Goldberg offering a more positive view of women's opportunities in *Women Work and Life-Cycle in a Medieval Economy: Women in York and Yorkshire, c. 1300–1520* in 1992, while Barbara Hanawalt studying London women, Judith Bennett studying peasant women in Brigstock, and Maryanne Kowaleski studying market women in Exeter came to less optimistic conclusions. Judith Bennett in *Medieval Women in Modern Perspective,* published in 2000, challenged the idea of transition for women and offered instead a formulation on "patriarchal bargains," contracted by medieval women in all centuries, albeit in highly diverse ways. Bennett has questioned as well whether a sharp demarcation is feasible between Medieval and Early Modern Europe. Since then, in *Gendering the Master Narrative* (2003), Jo Ann McNamara has questioned our formulation of a "Middle Ages" given what had been learned about women. She suggests instead that the first millennium of the Christian era formed a coherent time period, followed by a more recent millennium that introduced a sequence of changes for women and men.

Perhaps the most contested question in current historical scholarship on medieval women centers on a debate over constancy or change in both perceptions of, and the experience of, medieval women. R. Howard Bloch wrote in "Medieval Misogyny" in 1987 (subsequently published in a book length monograph in 1991) that woman-hating, especially wife-hating, largely a hermeneutical rather than a political device, was such a dominant literary theme in the Middle Ages that it is best understood as a constant across time, from Jerome and John Chrysostom to the Renaissance. This raised anew the old discourse about women's nature and the corresponding problem of how misogyny affected women's lives. Helen Solterer's response to Bloch read: "However exactly Bloch attempts to define medieval misogyny as a sophisticated game of literature, it inevitably escapes these bounds, inflicting its text on women's and men's lives" (*Medieval Feminist Newsletter* 6 [1988]: 15). Bloch answered with a materialist argument introducing a further duality into the debate: "To put the thesis crudely: as long as woman was merely a possession to be disposed of between men, she was vilified in the terms of misogyny; as soon as she became capable of disposing in her own right, she was idealized in the terms of courtly love" (*Medieval Feminist Newsletter* 7 [1989] 9). Concerns with change and stability, and the interplay of what was said about women with women's own experience, had not been resolved in two decades of debate.

In the 2000s, *Matrix,* an online resource listing medieval women's monastic houses, was established, originally with National Endowment for the Humanities funding. This would help rectify the imbalance where extensive documentation existed on men's monastic houses yet very little was known about women's houses and orders. *Feminae,* formerly *Medieval Feminist Index,* began publishing on the Web in 1996 and now covers articles about medieval women and gender in five languages, in 496 journals, and in volumes of collected essays as well. The sheer amount of accrued information on medieval women tells its own story, indeed this encyclopedia chose to highlight the vast increase in historical knowledge about medieval women. The study of women is no longer marginal but central to the endeavor of recovering the medieval past. It is a field of study that has come of age and promises more to come.

SUSAN MOSHER STUARD

Note: The books and articles mentioned in this entry may be found in the Appendix, Milestones in Women's History.

References and Further Reading

Bennett, Judith M. "Confronting Continuity." *Journal of Women's History* 9:3 (Autumn, 1997): 73–94.

———. *Medieval Women in Modern Perspective.* Washington, D.C.: American Historical Association, 2000.

Clark, Elizabeth A. "Women, Gender, and the Study of Christian History." *Church History* 70:3 (September 2001): 395–426.

Clark, Elizabeth A., et al. "Commentary," *Medieval Feminist Newsletter,* 6 (1988): 2–15, and R. Howard Bloch, "Commentary," *Medieval Feminist Newsletter* 7 (1987): 9–12.

Davis, Paulina Wright, "Remarks at the Conventions," *The Una* (September 1953): 1376–1377.

Ferrante, Joan M. *To the Glory of Her Sex: Women's Roles in the Composition of Medieval Texts.* Bloomington: Indiana University Press, 1997.

Gendering Scottish History, edited by Terry Brotherstone, Deborah Simonton, and Oonagh Walsh Mackie. Occasional Colloquia Series, No. 1. Glasgow: Crithne Press, 1999–2000.

Green, Monica H. "Documenting Medieval Women's Medical Practice." In *Women's Healthcare in the Medieval West,* edited by Monica H. Green. Great Yarmouth, Norfolk: Ashgate, 2000, pp. 322–352.

Karras, Ruth Mazo. "Sexuality in the Medieval World." In *The Medieval World,* edited by Peter Linehan and Janet L. Nelson. London and New York: Routledge, 2001, pp. 279–293.

Kelly-Gadol, Joan. "Did Women Have a Renaissance?" in *Becoming Visible,* edited by Claudia Koonz and Renate Bridenthal. Boston: Houghton Mifflin, 1977, pp. 137–164.

McNamara, Jo Ann. "The *Herrenfrage*: The Restructuring of the Gender System, 1050–1150." In *Medieval Masculinities,* edited by Clare A. Lees. Medieval Cultures, Volume 7. Minneapolis: University of Minnesota Press, 1994, pp. 3–29.

Medieval Women and the Sources of Medieval History, edited by Joel Rosenthal. Athens, Ga.: University of Georgia Press, 1990.

Rubin, Miri. "A Decade of Studying Medieval Women, 1078–1997." *History Workshop Journal* 46 (Autumn 1998): 213–239.

Schaus, Margaret, and Susan Mosher Stuard. "'Citizens of No Mean City'" *Journal of Women's History* 6:3 (Fall, 1994): 170–198.

Sharpe, Pamela. "Continuity and Change: Women's History and Economic History in Britain." *Economic History Review* 48:2 (May 1995): 353–369.

Studying Medieval Women: Sex, Gender, Feminism, edited by Nancy F. Partner. *Speculum* 68:2 (April 1993).

van Houts, Elisabeth. "The State of Research: Women in Medieval History and Literature." *Journal of Medieval Journal* 30 (September 1994): 277–292.

Women in Medieval History and Historiography, edited by Susan Mosher Stuard. Philadelphia: University of Pennsylvania Press, 1987.

Women Medievalists and the Academy, edited by Jane Chance. Madison: University of Wisconsin Press, 2005.

See also Boccaccio, Giovanni; Christine de Pizan; Feminist Theories and Methodologies; Gender in History; Komnene, Anna; Power, Eileen; Women Medievalists in the Academy

HOLY KINSHIP

The Holy Kinship included the maternal blood relations of Jesus. Its relational concept developed gradually in the twelfth and thirteenth centuries, derived partly from the twelfth-century doctrine of the Immaculate Conception. The argument that Mary's conception lacked original sin conferred an aura of sanctity on her mother, Anne, who appears only in the apocryphal Protoevangelium of James and Gospel of Pseudo-Matthew, and came to be seen, especially in Northern Europe, as matriarch of mostly female Kinship consisting of her daughters and grandchildren. Anne's long-barren marriage to Joachim eventually produced Mary, mother of Jesus. Widowhood and two subsequent marriages allowed Anne to bear Mary Cleophas and Mary Salome. The next generation of the three stepsisters' children included Jesus; the Apostles James the Less, James the Greater, Simon, and Jude; and John the Evangelist. The Kinship could comprise nearly thirty members, depending on inclusion of relatives such as Anne's cousin Elizabeth and her son, John the Baptist.

Awareness of the Kinship spread via the *Golden Legend* and artistic representations. The Kinship's thirteenth-century rise in literature and art perhaps responded to the contemporaneous dominance of patrilineal relationships in Jesus's genealogy and medieval genealogy generally. The Kinship reached its height in popularity around 1500, not coincidentally a time when numbers of female saints had increased, married women could acquire saintly reputations, and saints demonstrated maternal, nurturing behavior. Images of the Kinship communicated the sanctity possible for wives and mothers, cultural approval of marriage as a pious vocation, and medieval respect for familial connections. The Kinship also provided an alternative to the more masculine Trinity, and highlighted Christ's closeness with, and bodily origin from, women.

CHARA ARMON

References and Further Reading

Ashley, Kathleen and Pamela Sheingorn, eds. *Interpreting Cultural Symbols: Saint Anne in Late Medieval Society.* Athens, Ga.: The University of Georgia Press, 1990.
Brandenbarg, Ton. "St. Anne and Her Family: The Veneration of St. Anne in Connection with Concepts of Marriage and the Family in the Early Modern Period." In *Saints and She-Devils: Images of Women in the Fifteenth and Sixteenth Centuries*, edited by Lène Dresen-Coenders, translated by C. Sion. London: Rubicon Press, 1987, pp. 101–127.
———. "Saint Anne: A Holy Grandmother and Her Children." In *Sanctity and Motherhood: Essays on Holy Mothers in the Middle Ages*, edited by Anneke B. Mulder-Bakker. New York: Garland, 1995, pp. 31–65.
Sheingorn, Pamela. "The Holy Kinship: The Ascendency of Matriliny in Sacred Genealogy of the Fifteenth Century." *Thought* 64 (1989): 268–286.

See also Anne, Saint; Genealogy; Immaculate Conception, Doctrine of; Jacobus de Voragine's Golden Legend; Kinship; Mary, Virgin

HOME MANUFACTURING

There were two kinds of economic production in the Middle Ages: production for consumption and production for the market. Both were done primarily in the home, and they were usually intertwined. Production for the market was found mainly in towns and cities; agricultural families grew or made most of what they consumed. But even in agricultural families, there is evidence that the wife, while brewing ale for her family, made extra and sold it to her neighbors. In the winter, when there was less work to do on the land, farmers and their families might spin or weave to bring in the cash needed to pay rents or to provide the food and other items that they did not grow or make for themselves.

In towns, most production for the market was done in family workshops. While the husband was the legal and titular head of both the family and the workshop, it was presumed, at least in many crafts, that the wife would work alongside him in something approximating the "rough-and-ready" equality posited by Eileen Power in her 1926 essay. The work force/household typically consisted of parents and children, one or two apprentices, and household servants. The occasional journeyman employee lived elsewhere. Most urban houses had at least two rooms—a workroom in front and a room for cooking and sleeping behind. Some had a second story, with more beds and perhaps storage.

Most studies of medieval women's work—or of work of any kind—focus on the period from about 1300–1500, because of the dearth of evidence for the earlier Middle Ages. There is a consensus that a significant portion of an urban married woman's time was spent assisting her husband with his trade. Guild regulations allowed many masters to teach their trades to their wives. In many trades, a widow could continue to run the workshop, teach apprentices, and sell the goods previously made under the supervision of her husband. Tax rolls for Paris for the late thirteenth century strongly suggest that, pragmatically if not legally, the shop, tools, and inventory of a craftsman belonged to the family as a whole, not to the individual. The father/husband was the titular head of the intact family, but after either the mother or the father died, if there were adult children, the remaining parent and children were taxed as a company—a group of persons owning property together and jointly operating a business.

Some married women had separate businesses of their own. The 1297 Parisian tax roll lists *Geoffrey the weaver; his wife sells candles* and *Roger the carter; his wife is a baker.* This separate business might be small, carried on in addition to helping in the family workshop, or the wife might have her own workshop, with her own apprentices.

Martha Howell and Natalie Davis argue that some married women enjoyed a relatively high labor-status (that is, their work was both valued and well-compensated) because, through their husbands, they had access to raw materials and to markets. In Cologne, women monopolized the trades of yarn making, gold spinning, and silk making. Many silk mistresses were married to, or widows of, silk merchants; gold spinners were married to gold beaters or goldsmiths. The yarn business was run jointly by merchant-husbands and their artisan-wives. Thus in Cologne, according to Howell, the main trades were dominated by family production units, which controlled the industry from importing raw materials to selling the finished goods. Women's high labor-status, she argues, was possible only in such a system.

Many unmarried women also worked at home to produce goods for the market. If Howell and Davis are correct, most of them lacked capital to acquire the tools and raw materials needed to produce high-end goods. They also lacked the access to raw materials and to the long-distance market enjoyed by merchants' wives. Most of them, thus, were relegated to low-status, low-income work such as spinning, carding, and combing, often as part of the "putting-out" system, the earliest form of capitalism. Importers, especially of silk, instead of selling their raw materials to artisans, would supply the materials to spinners and weavers, paying them by the piece for their work, and then would sell the finished cloth. While weaving required a loom, spinning, carding, and combing required virtually no investment for the worker who worked on materials supplied by the nascent merchant-capitalist.

Most current research assumes that women's roles in economic life contracted after 1500. Howell and Davis argue that this contraction ties directly to the decline of the family workshop that accompanied early modern capitalism. Much work remains to be done, for both the medieval and the early modern periods, before a true synthesis can be constructed.

JANICE ARCHER

References and Further Reading

Barthélemy, Dominique and Philippe Contamine. "The Use of Private Space," In *A History of Private Life: Revelations of the Medieval World*, edited by Georges Duby, translated by Arthur Goldhammer. Cambridge: Cambridge University Press, 1988, pp. 460–470.

Bennett, Judith M. *Ale, Beer, and Brewsters in England: Women's Work in a Changing World, 1300–1600.* Oxford and New York: Oxford University Press, 1996.

Dale, Marian K. "The London Silkwomen of the Fifteenth Century," *Economic History Review*, 1st ser., 4 (1933): 324–335. Reprinted in *Sisters and Workers in the Middle Ages*, edited by Judith M. Bennett, et al. Chicago: University of Chicago Press, 1976, pp. 26–38.

Hanawalt, Barbara A., ed. *Women and Work in Preindustrial Europe.* Bloomington, Ind.: Indiana University Press, 1986.

Howell, Martha C. *Women, Production, and Patriarchy in Late Medieval Cities.* Chicago: University of Chicago Press, 1986.

MS. KK283, *Archives Nationales*, Paris, which contains the *rôles de la taille de cent mille livres tournois"* (book of the levy for Paris) for 1296, 1297, 1298, 1299, and 1300.

Power, Eileen. "The Position of Women," in *The Legacy of the Middle Ages*, edited by C. G. Crump and E. F. Jacob. Oxford: Clarendon Press, 1926, pp. 401–433.

See also **Alewives and Brewing; Apprentices; Artisans' Families, Women of; Clothwork, Domestic; Division of Labor; Economy; Family (Later Middle Ages); Feme Sole; Guild Members and Guilds; Servants; Textile Production for the Market; Widows; Work**

HOMOSEXUALITY

See **Sexuality: Female Same-Sex Relations; Sexuality: Male Same-Sex Relations**

HONOR AND REPUTATION

Honor constituted a complex and key organizing principle of many medieval societies. It could be understood as a "right to respect," as social prestige or as good reputation. Only toward the later Middle Ages did honor come in many places to resemble the more modern notion of an internal quality connected to moral integrity. Honor could be both personal and collective: one's honor affected one's family and even one's ancestral lineage. Not only the elites possessed a concept of honor. Lower-status men and women also claimed honor for themselves.

Honor was inextricably linked to reputation (Latin, *fama*). Talk and gossip—often considered the special purview of women—formed a powerful medium for conferring or diminishing status and enforcing social norms. Reputation also possessed a legal dimension. In many societies, certain conditions could legally deprive a person of honorable status: criminal conviction, illegitimacy, or engaging in certain professions (for instance, prostitution). Lack of honorable standing (*infamia* or infamy) caused one to forfeit legal privileges, such as the right to inherit, to hold office, to testify, or to serve as a legal guardian.

Historians have drawn extensively upon anthropology to reconstruct the functioning of honor in medieval cultures. They frequently describe it in economic terms or as a "zero-sum game." A scarce commodity, honor could be taken from others to increase one's own. Honor had to be actively defended and regained if lost. Insults and injuries to self and kin were perceived as "debts" that required repayment.

Scholars frequently couple honor with "shame," "guilt," and "humiliation." The most well-known schema contrasts honor-based "shame cultures" with "guilt cultures." In shame cultures, external factors such as public opinion regulate acceptable behavior and social interactions. Shame results when individuals do not conform to the honor standards of their group. Failure to take steps to restore honor leads to public humiliation. In guilt cultures, a person's internal sense of right and wrong determines acceptable conduct. Often early medieval warrior societies are cast as shame cultures and the centralized states of the later Middle Ages as en route to becoming more "modern" guilt cultures. However, the contours of honor, shame, guilt, and humiliation varied greatly throughout the medieval world.

Honor was socially constructed and determined by the judgment of others, particularly social equals. People displayed honor publicly by following the norms of unwritten "honor codes." Entire communities could shame those who behaved dishonorably, through public rituals such as shunning, defacing of houses, and charivari. Medieval societies were also highly image-conscious. Insignia and opulent dress conveyed the honorable status of elites. Conversely, sumptuary laws marked dishonorable and lower-status persons (such as Jews, servants, and prostitutes) by forbidding them to wear certain items or by mandating distinctive garments or signs that set them apart.

Honor was often gendered. Typically, men proved their honor by providing for those under their protection and by aggressively responding to injuries and challenges. Since women's social value, particularly in Mediterranean and Islamic societies, often centered upon their reproductive capacity as perpetuators of male lineages, their honor was linked primarily to chastity. To preserve their honor, women ideally had to be sequestered in the private realm of the household. In medieval Italian city-states, communities of honorable women (such as nunneries) were perceived to increase the civic honor of the entire citizenry. Loss of female chastity gravely damaged both the woman's and her male kin's honor. Men were often permitted to harshly discipline unchaste women under their protection and might even be excused for murder.

The conceptualization of women's honor, however, varied considerably throughout medieval Europe. In Iceland, for instance, it depended less on chastity. In both the Mediterranean and the European north, women could play an active role in inciting vendetta and urging reluctant male kin to take revenge. And although women did not normally participate directly in blood feuds, legal records reveal that they did retaliate personally, both verbally and physically, against men and other women for insult and injury.

If honor could be lost, it could also be regained. Males could pursue violent revenge. Women accused of unchastity who married their rapist or seducer could also restore their honor. By the twelfth century, the influence of the Church, chivalric codes, and the judicial systems of proliferating centralized states prompted changes in conceptualizations of honor. As refined, courtly manners and speech became important indicators of honorableness, even for non-aristocrats, the law courts increasingly augmented vendetta to supply an alternative arena for men and women to challenge and regain honor and reputation.

LYNN MARIE LAUFENBERG

References and Further Reading

Fenster, Thelma and Daniel Lord Smail, eds. *Fama: The Politics of Talk and Reputation in Medieval Europe.* Ithaca, N.Y.: Cornell University Press, 2003.

Gordon, Stewart. *Robes and Honor: The Medieval World of Investiture.* New York: Palgrave, 2001.

Hanawalt, Barbara. *"Of Good and Ill Repute": Gender and Social Control in Medieval England.* New York and Oxford: Oxford University Press, 1998.

Migliorino, Francesco. *Fama e infamia: Problemi della società medievale nel pensiero giuridico nei secoli XII e XIII.* Catania: Giannotta, 1985.

Miller, William Ian. *Bloodtaking and Peacemaking: Feud, Law, and Society in Saga Iceland.* Chicago and London: University of Chicago Press, 1990.

———. *Humiliation and Other Essays on Honor, Social Discomfort, and Violence.* Ithaca, N.Y.: Cornell University Press, 1993.

Peristiany, Joan G., ed. *Honour and Shame: The Values of Mediterranean Society.* Chicago: University of Chicago Press, 1966.

——— and Julian Pitt-Rivers, eds. *Honour and Grace in Mediterranean Society*. Cambridge: Cambridge University Press, 1991.

Peters, Edward. "Wounded Names: The Medieval Doctrine of Infamy." In *Law in Medieval Life and Thought*, edited by Edward B. King and Susan J. Ridyard. Sewanee, Tenn.: Press of the University of the South, 1990, pp. 43–89.

Stewart, Frank Henderson. *Honor*. Chicago and London: University of Chicago Press, 1994.

See also **Charivari; Chastity and Chaste Marriage; Chivalry; Clothing; Cuckold; Gender Ideologies; Gossip and Slander; Illegitimacy; Law; Private and Public Spheres; Prostitutes; Rape and Raptus; Sexuality: Extramarital Sex; Sumptuary Law**

HOSPITALS

Depending on the needs of the community and patrons' wishes and resources, medieval hospitals offered food, shelter, and other assistance to a range of temporarily or perennially disadvantaged individuals, including travelers and pilgrims, abandoned or orphaned children, prostitutes, the poor, the aged, the crippled, and the chronically infirm. These institutions often combined functions typically divided between more specialized modern hostels, hospices, and hospitals. Supporters of medieval hospitals could be motivated by compassion, penance, familial or individual prestige and security, local need, civic pride and, as hospitals were often associated with a religious house or possessed a chapel, a desire to benefit from the intercessions of institutions' grateful staff and patients. In Europe, many contributed to wandering preachers sent out by hospitals on fundraising tours, their generosity often rewarded by partial indulgences. Others sought out local hospitals to access spiritual services and relics and give alms. As an extension of the charity they provided within their own households and networks of relations and friends, married and widowed women often bequeathed items available to them as part of their household goods, dowry, or inheritance (including small sums of money, bedding, or food) to local hospitals, either independently or as members of a confraternity or guild. As heiresses or widows or in conjunction with their spouses, burger and noble women also founded hospitals and occasionally exercised patronage rights. Some Jewish communities also maintained hospitals, while wealthy aristocratic or imperial women established or endowed hospitals and hostels both in Byzantium and in Islamic cities and religious shrines, particularly along routes to Mecca.

Because European hospitals ranged from institutions attached to episcopal chapters or monastic houses to shelters founded by lay patrons, confraternities, guilds, municipal governments, or religious orders, the nature of their staff and inmates varied widely. In some hospitals, such as the long-lived Hôtel-Dieu in Paris, individuals who had taken religious vows devoted themselves to prayer and spiritual services and the care of the sick, abandoned, and poor. They were often joined—or in lay-run hospitals replaced—by hired servants and/or lay brothers and sisters, that is, individuals who took vows of celibacy and devoted themselves to manual tasks, charitable work, and abbreviated prayers.

Many independent religious women, including anchoresses, recluses, and Beguines, attached themselves to hospitals, while as widows or part of a married couple, confraternity, or tertiary order, other women founded or served in hospitals as an alternative or precursor to entering a traditional religious house devoted to contemplation. The social and religious security of working for a hospital tended to attract unmarried and widowed women, providing for the lower social orders an opportunity for a religious life unavailable to the majority barred from relatively exclusive nunneries. Some individuals, called *donats*, donated their property to a hospital and promised to serve it in return for life-long room, board, and nursing. Pensioners (known also as *corrodians*) sometimes purchased permanent accommodation in various institutions as a form of social security, making distinctions between these individuals and fully professed hospital staff, hired servants, and lay brothers and lay sisters problematic. For founders, resources, and affiliations influenced hospitals' functions and their personnel; all hospitals were faced with balancing charitable expenditures with self-perpetuation as an institution that benefited its donors. In the impoverished leper houses where devout laywomen such as Yvette of Huy and Marie of Oignies served, the struggle for subsistence left little time for formal prayer, yet in other hospitals, *donats*, pensioners, and members of confraternities or guilds attached conditions to their donations and eventually transformed hospitals into exclusive rest homes or religious houses dedicated to interceding for their donors' souls.

In Europe, both caregivers and the afflicted were encouraged to view the hardships they endured as a salvific imitation of Christ's suffering comparable to the contemplative life. Hospitals sought to prepare inmates for reconciliation with God on earth and in the afterlife through a regimen of spiritual healing: confession, reception of the sacraments, and participation in religious services. Many hospitals possessed their own chapels and clergymen who performed masses and liturgical prayers for the spiritual benefit of patients, staff, and benefactors. In long-term care facilities specializing in the care of lepers, the aged, mentally ill, or handicapped, patients might join the staff in taking vows of poverty, chastity and/or obedience, adopting a religious habit, and participating in religious services and general duties.

For religious and disciplinary reasons, hospitals sought to prevent sexual relations between male and female caregivers, servants, patients, and boarders. If funds permitted, separate refectories, dormitories, chapels, and kitchens were provided for male and female staff, while patients were segregated by ward and sometimes nursed by their own sex. Hospital statutes often forbade young or attractive women from being hired as servants or sisters, and severely punished those caught *in flagrante delicto*. Some hospitals required women hired as nurses, cooks, and laundresses to possess honest reputations, while others barred the admission of married couples or specifically prohibited sisters and female servants from bathing, (un)dressing, or making the beds of male coworkers. However, women continued to attach themselves as servants, lay sisters, *donats*, recluses, and pensioners even to hospitals dominated by male staff, while scarce resources often meant that it was difficult to maintain segregated living spaces for staff and inmates. In hospitals with mixed staff, women were sometimes granted their own mistress or prioress, although they ultimately answered to male leadership. Rarely, hospitals with an entirely female staff were headed by independent prioresses.

In many hospitals, women shouldered the brunt of round-the-clock nursing, food preparation, and laundering of clothing and bedding, while male staff administered hospital property, raised funds, and performed spiritual services or heavy manual tasks. Wards devoted to the care of women, infants, and abandoned children particularly tended to be entrusted to female staff, some of whom may have possessed medical knowledge. Hospitals which admitted women often retained midwives, and in rare instances, female physicians. Some institutions, such as the Filles-Dieu in Paris, were founded entirely for the sake of rehabilitating fallen women and repentant prostitutes; others offered temporary room and board to prevent prostitutes from working during holy seasons. Many hospitals, including the famous institution maintained in Jerusalem by the Hospitaller order, admitted pregnant women close to childbirth; some guaranteed exhausted mothers a bed until their full recovery and provided cradles for their infants. Others accepted abandoned infants and children, including Muslim and Jewish children who were raised as Christians. These services

prevented infanticide and aided local and traveling women unable to care for their children out of poverty, sickness, or sudden widowhood, as well as single women, female slaves, and servants who became pregnant out of wedlock. Female staff, hired wet-nurses, and foster homes cared for these foundlings and for orphans, including those whose parents had died at the hospital. Those who survived to adulthood were often given the choice of joining the hospital as staff or servants or entering the world. Typically, boys were apprenticed to a trade, while girls entered domestic service or were given dowry money to enable an honorable marriage. Some hospitals also joined almshouses and monasteries in seeking out the sick and poor at home or doling out food or money to the destitute, thus providing crucial social, financial, and religious resources for both men and women.

JESSALYNN BIRD

References and Further Reading

Barber, Malcolm and Helen J. Nicholson, eds. *The Military Orders*. 2 vols. Aldershot: Ashgate, 1994.

Bird, Jessalynn. "Medicine for Body and Soul: Jacques de Vitry's Sermons to Hospitallers and their Charges." In *Religion and Medicine in the Middle Ages*, edited by Peter Biller and Joseph Ziegler. York: York University Press, 2001, pp. 91–108.

———. "Texts on Hospitals: Translation of Jacques de Vitry, *Historia Occidentalis* 29 and Edition of Jacques de Vitry's Sermons to Hospitallers." In *Religion and Medicine in the Middle Ages*, edited by Peter Biller and Joseph Ziegler. York: York University Press, 2001, pp. 109–134.

Brodman, James W. *Charity and Welfare: Hospitals and the Poor in Medieval Catalonia*. Philadelphia: University of Pennsylvania Press, 1998.

Orme, Nicholas and Margaret Webster. *The English Hospital, 1070–1570*. New Haven: Yale University Press, 1995.

Risse, Guenter B. *Mending Bodies, Saving Souls: A History of Hospitals*. New York: Oxford University Press, 1999.

Tolmacheva, Marina. "Female Piety and Patronage in the medieval 'Hajj'." In *Women in the Medieval Islamic World: Power, Patronage and Piety*, edited by Gavin R. G. Hambly. New York: St. Martin's Press, 1998, pp. 161–180.

See also **Almsgiving and Charity; Breastfeeding and Wet-Nurses; Confraternities; Disabilities; Doctors and Healers; Laywomen, Religious; Lepers; Medicine; Midwives; Pregnancy and Childbirth, Christian; Prostitutes**

HOUSEHOLD ACCOUNTS

The medieval household comprised servants and retainers who formed a community around an individual or married couple where an ordered mode of life made it possible to nurture the immediate family and receive visitors. The small and simple household is certainly very ancient, but few records survive from before 1200, and it is from these complex accounts that historians draw most of the information on how this vital institution functioned. In England by 1500, there were probably up to 2,000 households which would have produced annual accounts, yet only some 500 have survived. While these have some common features, each household adopted its particular method of accounting. At the top of society was the royal household, but even here the survival of accounts is disappointing. Among the most extensive sets of household accounts to survive are those for Elizabeth de Burgh, lady of Clare (d. 1360), covering the years from 1325–1360. In some cases women were involved in the running of two households, in which case two whole sets of accounts may be missing for a large number of families. The account book of Elizabeth Berkeley, countess of Warwick, 1420–1421, refers to an inner household (*Hospicium intrinsecum*) and a foreign household (*Forinsecum*). The surviving accounts are for the inner establishment. Accounts were essential because maintenance of the household often was the largest expenditure made by a landed family. The accounts of Joan de Valence, countess of Pembroke, show that she was spending £1,000 per annum on her household between 1295 and 1297. Giles de Wenlock, keeper of the household of Margaret of Brotherton, duchess of Norfolk, accounted for over £1,000 spent on her household in 1385–1386. Good management demanded proper budgeting, and, therefore, record keeping and the accounts helped prevent corruption and mismanagement.

The most comprehensive of these accounts are the household books. The 1412–1413 account for Alice de Bryene, a Suffolk widow of gentry status, comprises the daily record of who consumed what at her house in Acton. Each entry begins with a record of the number of meals served and the date, followed by a list of the guests. Next is a pantry account recording the number of loaves sent to the table, a note, but no details, of wine and ale consumed, lists of fish and meat that had been taken from the manor's store, and the daily purchases made to supplement these provisions. The record concludes with the cost of fodder for horses stabled that day and, finally, the day's total costs. An entry was made at the end of each month for the aggregate. Elizabeth Berkeley's account book fills 140 folios, and after preliminaries, recording the receipts of the keeper, a record of provisions left over from the previous year and a list of the fifty-five household members, it follows much the same pattern. The entries do, however, reflect this more complex household in the practice of entering the expenses

of some six household departments—pantry, buttery, kitchen, poultry, wardrobe, and *marshalsea* (that which dealt with the horses, fodder, and traveling). One delightful feature is the use of a pen drawing of casks and barrels each time a new one was broached. Complexity also resulted from the keeping of separate departmental accounts. The details of wine and ale consumed in the de Bryene household were probably contained in a butler's or cellarer's account. These together with brewing, kitchen, wardrobe, chamber and chapel accounts, diet accounts, *chequerrolls* (lists of servants), travel, and building records are among the more common household accounts.

Perhaps one of the most interesting features of household accounts is the record of the visitors who came daily to dine, for this reveals the social and political contacts of the individual. Many were administrators and farm workers but these records confirm the importance of hospitality in the Middle Ages. Alice de Bryene fed more than 300 people at the New Year's feast in 1412; and in the household of Eleanor de Montford, countess of Leicester, which averaged 207 members in 1265, provision was made on April 14 to feed 800 poor. Elizabeth Berkeley liked to entertain the clergy, but, in 1421, her most distinguished guest was the king's brother, John, duke of Bedford. £1.15s 2d was spent on his meal, exclusive of a tip to the duke's own cook. Elizabeth Burgh entertained the duke of Lancaster and the Black Prince in 1355 and 1358, respectively, and had the mayor and sheriffs of London to dine in 1358. Household accounts are vital sources for determining the social and economic lives of wealthier women, giving insights into their lifestyles, interests, networks, and friendships.

ROWENA E. ARCHER

References and Further Reading

The Goodman of Paris (Le Ménagier de Paris): A Treatise on Moral and Domestic Economy by a Citizen of Paris (c. 1393), edited by Eileen Power. London: Routledge, 1928.

Household Accounts from Medieval England, edited by C. M. Woolgar. British Academy, Records of Social and Economic History, new series, 17–18. Oxford: Oxford University Press, 1992–1993.

The Household Books of John Howard, Duke of Norfolk, 1462–1471, 1481–1483, introduced by Anne Crawford. Far Thrupp: Alan Sutton Publishing, 1992.

Mertes, Kate. *The English Noble Household, 1250–1600.* Oxford: Basil Blackwell 1983.

Myers, A. R. "The Captivity of a Royal Witch: the Household Accounts of Queen Joan of Navarre, 1419–21." *Bulletin of the John Rylands Library* 24: (1940): 263–284, 26(1941): 82–1000.

———. "The Household Accounts of Queen Margaret of Anjou, 1452–3." *Bulletin of the John Rylands Library* 40: (1957–1958): 40–113, 391–431.

Swabey, F. *Medieval Gentlewoman: Life in a Widow's Household in the Later Middle Ages.* Stroud: Sutton Publishing, 1999.

The Treasure of the City of Ladies or the Book of the Three Virtues, edited by Sarah Lawson. Harmondsworth: Penguin Publishing, 1985.

Woolgar, C. M. *The Great Household in Late Medieval England.* New Haven: Yale University Press, 1999.

See also **Administration of Estates; Gentry, Women of: England; Household Management; Noble Women**

HOUSEHOLD MANAGEMENT

Medieval households ranged in size from the great estates of the high nobility to the poor cottages of peasants. Despite vast differences in scale and political significance, all of these households shared a conceptual place in the medieval mind and social structure. The household represented a unit within which a family and its resources were organized, sheltered, maintained, and nurtured for the sake of future generations. Household management, therefore, whether on the grand scale of landed estates, in the urban milieu of the artisan or merchant family, or on the small plots allotted for the dwellings of rural tenants, was a task of critical importance. At all levels of medieval society, the bulk of that task fell on the female head of the household.

At the core of the medieval household was the family, whether based on the nuclear model, as was common in England, or the more complex extended family that prevailed in Italy, especially among the nobility. Even where the nuclear family was the norm, the household often included servants and others, such as young kinsfolk being fostered and educated by the lady of the house. The idea of the household also extended beyond the house itself, to include the lands, outbuildings, and animals that comprised the resources of the domestic economy. Household management was at its core an economic responsibility that demanded careful accounting of material and human resources.

Noble Households

Account books and advice books for the ladies of great estates offer considerable insight into the complexity of household management for the nobility. From such sources as the thirteenth-century account book of Eleanor de Montfort, the Countess of Leicester, and Christine de Pizan's *The Treasure of the City of Ladies*, we know that the responsibility for overseeing servants, lands, and animals was a complex task usually assigned to the noble wife. The frequent absence of noble men, due to Crusades, wars, or attendance at court, meant that noble women were called upon to run the daily affairs of the estate, including full accounting for the expenditures and profits of its extensive lands and related enterprises. Moreover, noble women were expected to use their household resources to entertain the large traveling retinues that accompanied their husbands and other noble men and, at times, to defend their estates with a full array of diplomatic and warlike strategies. As Christine de Pizan explains, the practical management skills exhibited by the noble wife, like the less tangible virtues of obedience and respectability, were considered to be a public reflection of the husband's honor. The noble home was no mere private realm, and effective household management could influence the political as well as the economic success of the family as a social entity.

As the manager of that noble household, the lady worked closely with the steward, or chief agent, of the estate and oversaw his collection of profits and disbursement of expenses. Among the various enterprises to be supervised were the products of the fields, the by-products of such animals as sheep and cattle, the maintenance of agricultural equipment, and the profits of mills and wine presses. As manager of the human resources attached to the household, the lady was responsible for hiring and training servants for her various domestic and agricultural enterprises and for the discipline and good governance of those in her employ. As manager of the domestic aspects of the family in her household, the lady played a dominant role in the rearing of children. She was responsible for their early introduction to literacy, to religious instruction, and to the gendered roles they would fill within the feudal hierarchy. Often, she provided this education to the children of other noble families placed in her care for the sake of social advancement. As the manager of her family's reputation, she used her skills and social networks to negotiate marriage alliances, gain the favor of the church, and place members of her family in desirable positions within other households of greater political influence.

Urban Households

The noble household may have been more complex than the smaller households of townspeople and peasants, but the success of these smaller enterprises was no less dependent on careful management. The urban households of artisans and merchants similarly fulfilled private and public functions as they sheltered and nurtured a family, trained apprentices in the various crafts, produced goods for the market, and upheld economic, civic, and religious responsibilities as members of guilds. Here, too, the woman, whether wife or widow, usually took on the tasks of hiring and training servants, and in the case of the artisan household was especially responsible for apprentices. These duties bound her to the rules of the craft guild as well as to the expectations of her husband and thus exemplify the marketable value of her skills. The master of a craft would have had difficulty maintaining his business or his guild membership without the managerial skills that his wife contributed to their joint economic enterprise. Urban household management also required the acquisition and preparation of food for the family members, servants, apprentices, and craft workers in the home, the maintenance of shelter and clothing for this extended household, and the discipline of all its members.

Peasant Households

The rural households of peasant producers similarly required the vigilant management of limited resources, both human and material. While some peasant households could afford to hire extra labor, most were dependent on the combined efforts of wife, husband, and children in order to satisfy the demands of the landlord and the necessities of survival. Thus the overwhelming challenge faced by the peasant woman as household manager was the management of her own time as she tended to children and animals, grew and prepared food, produced such marketable goods as ale and cheese, and helped her husband in the fields. Home management without servants included such daily tasks as lighting fires, drawing water from wells, gardening, collecting eggs, milking cows, and the all important task of training children for the roles they would assume as adults.

At each of these levels of medieval society, effective household management was critical to the success of the household as an economic unit.

MADONNA J. HETTINGER

References and Further Reading

Barber, Richard, Ed. *The Pastons: The Letters of a Family in the Wars of the Roses*. Harmondsworth, England: Penguin Books, 1981.
de Pizan, Christine. *The Treasure of the City of Ladies, or the Book of the Three Virtues,* translated by Sarah Lawson. London: Penguin Publishing, 1985.
Hanawalt, Barbara A. *The Ties that Bound: Peasant Families in Medieval England*. New York: Oxford University Press, 1986.
Herlihy, David. *Medieval Households*. Cambridge, Mass.: Harvard University Press, 1985.
LaBarge, Margaret Wade. *A Baronial Household of the Thirteenth Century*. New York: Barnes and Noble, 1965.
Power, Eileen. *Medieval People*. London: Methuen, 1924.

See also **Administration of Estates; Apprentices; Artisans' Families, Women of; Christine de Pizan; Conduct Literature; Consumption; Division of Labor; Education, Lay; Family (Earlier Middle Ages); Family (Later Middle Ages); Fosterage; Girls and Boys; Guild Members and Guilds; Household Accounts; Kinship; Market and Tradeswomen; Merchant Families, Women of; Mothers as Teachers; Noble Women; Paston Letters; Peasants; Private and Public Spheres; Servants; Wardship**

HROTSVIT OF GANDERSHEIM

Not much is known about the family and life of Hrotsvit of Gandersheim except that she was a nun (sanctimonialis) in the community of canonesses at Gandersheim (Germany). Occasional remarks in her writings give evidence of her Saxon origin and suggest a date of birth between 930 and 940. She was educated in Gandersheim and was a special protegé of the Abbess Gerberga II, niece of emperor Otto I. Some time after finishing her last work in the 970s, she likely died. Her expressions of gratitude towards Abbess Gerberga II suggest that her superior's support and active concern encouraged her to write in the first place and provided her with important books, as well as contacts with important centers of education. Hrotsvit began her oeuvre with a poetic adaptation of eight holy legends, which she arranged in two groups of five and three dedicated to her abbess with a modest request for corrections. To rearrange saints' lives from prose to poetry was a very popular exercise to demonstrate the level achieved in Latin scholarship.

Around 965, she wrote—also divided into two books—six dramas arranged in rhymed prose, which in her time was still exceptional (*Gallicanus, Dulcitius, Calimachus, Abraham, Pafnutius,* and *Sapientia*). These were created in order to replace the very popular but "impious" comedies of Terence. Hrotsvit presented the first four comedies to some educated but unknown readers for corrections. Writing her third book, Hrotsvit chose a different literary genre, although lacking a model or special experience: Being ordered by her abbess, she composed a poem of praise about the deeds of Otto the Great in hexameters. The intention of the *Gesta Ottonis*, as well as the date of writing, is still under discussion—after all, three different prefaces with dedications to Abbess Gerberga, Otto I, and Otto II are known. Most likely the larger part of the *Gesta* were written between 965–966 and 967, whereas the second prologue, as well as the last parts of the *Gesta,* could have been finished only after Christmas 967. The most recent of the extant works of Hrotsvit, written probably before 973, is the *Primordia coenobii Gandeshemensis,* a history of the beginnings of Gandersheim that establishes a connection between this foundation and the Ottonians' political success. It was thus intended to secure further political and economical assistance and not as a historical report. At least two rhymed lives of the patrons of Gandersheim, Saints Anastasius I and Innocent I, are lost, as well as some titles in hexameter for a cycle illustrating the Apocalypse of John.

Hrotsvit possessed an extraordinary dramatic talent and a linguistic gift to analyze and modify the language patterns of her models. She was the first author to render passions and saints' lives in dialogue; thus, she revived the dramatic genre in contemporary rhymed fashion. Her superior education was by no means unusual for nuns of the Ottonian century, and her motives as an author testify to her deeply rooted religious convictions. Hrotsvit wanted to use her talents in praise of God and described her "poetic and religious mission" by the interpretation of her name as *clamor validus,* a powerful calling. Her central subject next to the miracles accomplished by God was virginity. Her stories develop around powerful young women who evade the sexualization of their female bodies as well as social domination in marriage by choosing a life as a virgin bride of Christ. They are written as examples for the young nuns living in Hrotsvit's community who had to choose between taking up the veil or getting married. Furthermore, she weaves allusions to the quadrivium into her storylines; obviously her works were used for teaching. Only Hrotsvit's historical writings had a broader audience in mind, but their reception cannot be proved. Hrotsvit's social values fit into the feudal society of the early Middle Ages. The existence of a normative female view in her writings on the other hand is still being debated.

Since the first publication of Hrotsvit's oeuvre in 1501, her reception has always been quite ambiguous, especially the evaluation of her style, moreover the authenticity of her work continues being debated to the present day. Some of the problems of appraising this author arise from the fact that she established not only the beginnings of Ottonian literacy but also of medieval drama. As Berschin puts it, Hrotsvit virtually stepped out of nothing with her metrical legends and, therefore, is a witness not only for the education of medieval women but also for the individuality and novelty of the Ottonian Renaissance.

KATRINETTE BODARWÉ

References and Further Reading

Bodarwé, Katrinette. *Sanctimoniales litteratae: Schriftlichkeit und Bildung in den ottonischen Frauenkommunitäten Gandersheim, Essen und Quedlinburg.* Quellen und Studien vol. 10. Münster: Aschendorff, 2004.

Cescutti, Eva. *Hrotsvit und die Männer. Konstruktionen von "Männlichkeit" und "Weiblichkeit" in der lateinischen Literatur im Umfeld der Ottonen; eine Fallstudie* (Forschungen zur Geschichte der älteren deutschen Literatur 23), Munich: Fink, 1998.

Hrotsvit. *Opera omnia,* edited by Walter Berschin. München and Leipzig: Saur, 2001.

Hrotsvit. *A Florilegium of Her Works.* Translated with introduction, interpretative essay and notes by Katharina Wilson, Woodbridge and Suffolk: Brewer, 1998.

Nelson, Janet. "Gender and Genre in Women Historians of the Early Middle Ages," In *The Frankish World 750–900.* London: Hambledon, 1996, pp. 183–197.

Weston, L. M. C., "Gender Without Sexuality: Hrotsvitha's Imagining of a Chaste Female Community." In *The Community, the Family and the Saint. Patterns of Power in Early Medieval Europe* International Medieval Research 4, edited by Joyce Hill and Mary Swan. Turnhout: Brepols, 1998, pp. 127–142.

Wilson, Katharina M., edited by *Hrotsvit of Gandersheim "Rara Avis in Saxonia"? A Collection of Essays Compiled and Edited.* Medieval and Renaissance monograph series 7. Ann Arbor, Mich.: MARC Publ., 1987.

See also **Drama; Literacy and Reading: Latin; Monasticism and Nuns; Ottoman Royal Women; Women Authors: Latin Texts**

HUMANISM

From about 1300 to 1650, humanism was the characteristic and primary intellectual movement of the Italian Renaissance, diffusing also to other regions of Europe mainly after 1500. It consisted of the diligent study, imitation, edition, and translation of Latin and later Greek classical and Christian texts, which in turn fueled new genres of literary expression, promoted new avenues of Western thought, and created a new pedagogy. This activity affected subsequent developments including the Reformation, the discussion of New World encounters, the *querelle des femmes* (debate about the nature of women), the Scientific Revolution, and modern concepts of the state. Although humanism was largely created by male scholars, individual humanists also concerned themselves with the education of women and women's roles; and a few women themselves acquired humanist educations and participated in the humanist movement.

Origins of Humanism, Ninth to Fourteenth Centuries

Attention to the ancient literary tradition surged several times in the West: during the Carolingian Renaissance of the ninth century; during the Twelfth-Century Renaissance, and especially during the Italian Renaissance, which permanently reintegrated the study of ancient thought in the secondary and university curricula. From the late thirteenth century, a circle of scholars centered in Padua launched the latter movement by consciously imitating Latin authors in poetry and prose.

In the next century, the tradition they started reached an early culmination in the work of Francis Petrarch (Francesco Petrarca, 1304–1374) and Giovanni Boccaccio (1313–1375). Also important for his contributions to vernacular literary traditions, as a humanist Petrarch discovered, collected, studied, and imitated Latin texts, and composed important historical, rhetorical, and moral philosophical works whose expressive eloquence derived from his imitation of the finest authors, especially Cicero. Boccaccio, too, was a renowned author in the vernacular (most notably, his collection of stories, the *Decameron*), but at the same time, as a humanist, wrote in defense of the study of ancient pagan classics and compiled the pioneering collective biography *On Famous Women*.

Later in the century, Petrarch's student, Coluccio Salutati (1331–1406), in his role as chancellor of the republic of Florence, employed his humanist skills to save his city as a defender of liberty against the enemy state of Milan, depicted as tyrannical. Salutati also fostered many talented young Florentines and foreign visitors who became the leaders of the next generation of humanists. In that effort, he invited to Florence the Byzantine diplomat Manuel Chrysoloras (1353–1415) who, during a three-year stay, taught Greek to aspiring scholars, thus inaugurating Greek studies in western Europe where they had virtually not existed, except on the peripheries, since antiquity.

The Fifteenth Century

During the fifteenth century, the humanist program became firmly established. Humanist teachers such as Pier Paolo Vergerio (1370–1444) defined as the five disciplines of the *studia humanitatis* (the "studies of humanity") poetry, grammar (the study of literature), rhetoric (the study of composition), history, and moral philosophy (the one branch of philosophy that tended to be nonsystematic and closely related to literature). These were the disciplines (replacing those of the medieval schools) they taught to the children of urban patricians who became the leaders of Renaissance Italy, patrons of the arts, and amateur writers themselves in the humanist genres; among them was, for example, the Venetian nobleman Francesco Barbaro (1390–1454). From the fifteenth through the nineteenth century, the humanist curriculum dominated secondary education.

Other humanists were "secretaries," such as Poggio Bracciolini (1381–1459) and Leonardo Bruni (c. 1370–1444), the bureaucrats of city-states and the church who employed their literary skills to compose letters and speeches defining public policy. Still others were employed by rulers to write on matters of interest to the monarch, including Lorenzo Valla (1405–1457), whose attacks on the church matched the interests of his employer, a papal rival.

Humanist authors of all types—teachers, secretaries, and amateurs—employed their knowledge of classical texts to examine matters of interest in the civic world of the Renaissance. They wrote on nobility, political rule, poverty, and the family, and recovered the history of ancient Rome and composed new histories of their own Renaissance cities. They composed treatises as well on the "dignity of man," as did Giannozzo Manetti (1396–1459) and Giovanni Pico della Mirandola (1463–1494), reconceptualizing human nature, based on classical learning, as uniquely active and creative.

Humanists employed their knowledge of Greek to translate the works of Plato, largely unknown in western Europe, the accomplishment of Marsilio Ficino (1433–1499) and to explore Greek philosophy, science, and mathematics. They developed the scholarly methods of textual analysis still important today, and wielding these, readied for the new printing presses (established in Italy from the late 1460s) editions of all the Greek and Latin classics. Once matured, humanist themes and style were imitated in the vernacular by such authors as Niccolò Machiavelli (1469–1527) and Baldassare Castiglione (1478–1529).

Women and Humanism

Humanism's embrace of the values of human worth and freedom attracted women to the movement as well. In the Middle Ages, those few women who acquired advanced educations did so generally in the convent, and their literary product was religious. In Renaissance Italy, some tens of women of the patriciate and nobility acquired humanist educations. A handful of these entered into literary exchanges with male humanists, and contributed notable Latin works in the standard humanist genres of the treatise, dialogue, oration, and letter. Most notably, Isotta Nogarola (1418–1464) defended Eve against the charge fundamental to a misogynist ideology that she had sinned more than Adam in the Garden of Eden, and thus bore the blame for the punishment of Original Sin; Cassandra Fedele (1465–1558) argued for the benefits of humanist study for women even if they gained no public recognition for their achievement; and Laura Cereta (1469–1499) encouraged women to strive for excellence in those studies that exalted humankind, while she criticized both the men and the women who mocked women's attempt to pursue that goal.

Male humanists, as well, took notice of women. Boccaccio's *On Famous Women*, although displaying misogynistic elements, introduced the issue of women's capacity and accomplishments into the mainstream of intellectual discourse. The letters of Leonardo Bruni and Lauro Quirini (1420–1480/1481) to, respectively, Bartolommea Montefeltro Malatesta and Isotta Nogarola map out a humanist curriculum for women which, though not exactly the same as that required for males, was nonetheless ambitious. The works by Francesco Barbaro and Leon Battista Alberti (1406–1472) on, respectively, marriage and the family highlight women's important roles in these settings.

The Diffusion of Humanism

The diffusion of humanism north of the Alps began in the fifteenth century. Italians traveling on diplomatic missions brought the movement to Spain, France, England, and the Empire; notable humanist emissaries include Poggio Bracciolini (to England), then serving as papal secretary; and Aeneas Sylvius Piccolomini to Scotland before serving in the imperial chancery. Equally, northerners traveled to Italy to attend universities and make contacts with literary circles there, as did such figures as the German cleric and philosopher Nicholas of Cusa (1400–1464); the English scholar John Colet (1467–1519); and the learned Hungarian and German poets Janus Pannonius (1434–1472) and Conrad Celtis (1459–1508). Early in the sixteenth century, from 1506–1509, the Dutch-born Desiderius Erasmus (1469–1536) visited Italy, shortly before composing his renowned *Praise of Folly*. Erasmus became the principal figure of northern, and Christian, humanism, who mastered the Italian tradition and developed it as a European phenomenon. From 1500–1650, established in the courts and cities of Europe, humanism helped shape the Reformation, the debate over women, vernacular literary genres, and the curriculum of the schools. It was a factor in the development of modern science, political theory, and perceptions of the New World (the Americas).

MARGARET L. KING

References and Further Reading

Baron, Hans. *The Crisis of the Early Italian Renaissance: Civic Humanism and Republican Liberty in an Age of Classicism and Tyranny*. 2nd ed. Princeton, N.J.: Princeton University Press, 1966.

The Erasmus Reader, edited by Erika Rummel. Toronto: University of Toronto Press, 1990.

Grafton, Anthony. *Leon Battista Alberti: Master Builder of the Italian Renaissance*. New York: Hill & Wang, 2000.

Hankins, James. *Plato in the Italian Renaissance*. 2 vols. Leiden: Brill, 1990.

Her Immaculate Hand: Selected Works by and about the Women Humanists of Quattrocento Italy, edited and translated by Margaret L. King and Albert Rabil Jr. 2nd ed. Asheville, N.C.: Pegasus, 1992.

Jardine, Lisa. "Women Humanists: Education for What?" *From Humanism to the Humanists: Education and the Liberal Arts in Fifteenth- and Sixteenth-Century Europe*. Cambridge, Mass.: Harvard Univerity Press, 1986, pp. 29–57.

Kristeller, Paul Oskar. *Renaissance Thought and Its Sources*, edited by Michael Mooney. New York: Columbia University Press, 1979.

Nauert, Charles G. *Humanism and the Culture of Renaissance Europe*. Cambridge: Cambridge University Press, 1995.

Parker, Holt N. "Women and Humanism: Nine Factors for the Woman Learning." *Viator* 35 (2004): 581–616.

Trinkaus, Charles. *The Poet as Philosopher: Petrarch and the Formation of Renaissance Consciousness*. New Haven: Yale University Press, 1979.

Witt, Ronald G. *In the Footsteps of the Ancients: the Origins of Humanism from Lovato to Bruni*. Leiden and Boston: Brill, 2000.

See also **Boccaccio, Giovanni; Cereta, Laura; Defenses of Women; Education, Lay; Fedele, Cassandra; Italy; Literacy and Reading: Latin; Nogarola, Isotta; Petrarch**

HUMILIATI

The late twelfth and thirteenth centuries saw the proliferation of novel religious movements throughout Europe. The moral and ethical ambiguities caused by a new profit orientation motivated society during the burgeoning commercial revolution, and created a desire by members of the laity to follow an apostolic life centered on mendicant activism and community service. Such groups comprised both men and women who could not find fulfillment in traditional cloistered, contemplative orders. In addition to the familiar Franciscans, Dominicans, and Poor Clares, these new orders also included a wide variety of lesser known groups such as the Premonstratensians, Beguines, and the Humiliati of northern Italy.

There is evidence the Humiliati were organized as early as the 1170s in the textile producing region around Milan. Pope Lucius III condemned them in 1184 for suspected heresies. However, they persisted, and in 1201 Innocent III approved the order with some stipulations, including an injunction against Humiliati sisters' active participation in the public sphere. As hundreds of Humiliati houses were already established by this time, his attempt to impose order on the group suggests a desire to rein in the increasingly popular movement.

The Humiliati were divided into three orders. Members of the first and second orders mirrored other mendicant groups, living in small group houses. First-order houses included canons and canonesses who enjoyed the greatest ecclesiastical privilege. The third order most closely resembled tertiaries of other mendicant groups or even confraternities. Mostly made up of wool workers, they lived in their homes, often remaining married, but following the apostolic lifestyle of the Humiliati. Members of all social classes joined the Humiliati, however, entrants donated all their worldly goods and practiced communal poverty, making the Humiliati a tool for social leveling.

A partial inventory of 255 first- and second-order houses taken in 1344 indicates there were a total of 2,752 members in the order and 1,146 of these were brothers and 1,606 were sisters. These inventories indicate that women tended to live in sister-only houses, whereas men lived almost exclusively in mixed gender houses. Forty-one percent of the houses housed only sisters, whereas in only 1.4 percent of the houses were there only brothers. This evidence for a female majority indicates the desire for apostolic living and community service was strong among women, even in the highly patriarchal climate of medieval Italy and suggests a comparison with the Beguines of Flanders.

The Humiliati were well known at the time for the production of *panni humiliati*. This coarse, usually undyed wool was produced for sale or contribution to the poor, and was meant to counteract the escalating prices of wool in the commercial market. Ignoring Innocent's injunction, women of the Humiliati were also actively engaged in a number of very public, civic-centered occupations. Benefiting from the bequests of entrants, they owned land, acted as landlords, loaned money at a low interest to the poor (to counteract the high interest charged by the bankers and merchants), administered hospitals, and coordinated poor relief.

SALLY M. BRASHER

References and Further Reading

Andrews, Frances. *The Early Humiliati*. Cambridge: Cambridge University Press, 1999.

Bolton, Brenda. "Sources for the Early History of the Humiliati." In *Studies in Church History* 8 (1971): 125–133.

———. "The Poverty of the Humiliati." In *Poverty in the Middle Ages*, edited by David Flood. Werl/Westfalen: Dietrich-Coelde-Verlag, 1975, pp. 52–59.

Brasher, Sally. *Women of the Humiliati*. New York: Routledge Press, 2001.

Grundmann, Herbert. *Religious Movements in the Middle Ages*, translated by Steven Rowan, edited by Robert Lerner. South Bend, Ind.: University of Notre Dame Press, 1995.

Little, Lester. *Religious Poverty and the Profit Economy*. Ithaca, N.Y.: Cornell University Press, 1978.

See also **Almsgiving and Charity; Artisan Families, Women of; Beguines; Canonesses; Confraternities; Cities and Towns; Double Monasteries; Heretics and Heresy; Investment and Credit; Italy; Lay Piety; Laywomen, Religious; Monasticism, Women's: Papal Policy; Poverty, Religious; Premonstratensian Order; Tertiaries; Textile Production for the Market; Work**

HUMILITY OF FAENZA

Humility (also known as Umilt or Umilit) of Faenza (1226–1310), Vallombrosan abbess, is among the minority of religious women in the Middle Ages who openly preached to her nuns. In 1250, after nine years of marital life and the death of her two children, she entered the double Benedictine monastery of Saint Perpetua of Faenza while her husband joined the brothers of the abbey. In 1254, she became a recluse at the Vallombrosan church of Saint Apollinaris. There she received spiritual guidance from the Vallombrosan abbot Crispin, while she gave spiritual counsel to the local community from her cell. Attracting numerous followers, in 1266 she established the first Vallombrosan nunnery, Santa Maria at Malta near Faenza. The convent flourished until 1281 when the Guelfs destroyed it. Consequently, Humility moved to Florence and founded the Vallombrosan nunnery of St. John the Evangelist in 1282, where she was abbess until her death. Her role as religious mentor is one of contradiction. Her Latin *vita* claims that Humility's ability to read Latin was miraculous. Moreover, in her sermons, which she dictated in Latin to a female scribe, Humility indicates that the author of her homilies was not she but God speaking through her. Nonetheless, her ability to read Latin and preach on profound theological themes indicates a deeper learning than she or her hagiographers explicitly reveal. Her sermons, which survive in two eighteenth-century copies based on a fourteenth-century edaction no longer extant, are the most significant indicators of the depth and breadth of this monastic educator.

CAROLYN MUESSIG

References and Further Reading

Biagio. "Vita S. Humilitatis." edited by Daniel Papebroch. *In Acta sanctorum*, May, vol. 5. Paris, 1866. Paragraphs 1–32, pp. 207–214.

———. "Life of St Umiltà, Abbess of the Vallombrosan Order in Florence." English translation in Elizabeth Alvilda Petroff, *Consolation of the Blessed*. Millerton, N.Y.: Alta Gaia Society, 1979, pp. 121–127.

———. *Le Vite di Umiltà: Agiografia trecentesca dal latino al volgare*, edited by Adele Simonetti. Florence: Edizioni del Galluzo, 1997.

Holloway, Julia Bolton. *Beata Umiltà: Sguardo sulla Santa Umiltà: Contemplating on Holy Humility*. In Italian and English. Florence: Editoriale gli Arcipressi, 2004.

Humility of Faenza. *Sermones S Humilitatis de Faventia*, edited by Torello Sala. Florence: Calasantiana, 1884.

———. *I sermoni di Umiltà da Faenza: Studio e edizione*, edited by Adele Simonetti. Società internazionale per lo studio del medioevo latino. Biblioteca di "Medioevo latino" 14. Spoleto: Centro italiano di studi sull'alto medioevo, 1995.

———. *The Sermons of Humility of Faenza*, translated by Catherine Mooney. Boydell and Brewer, Forthcoming.

Mooney, Catherine. "Authority and Inspiration in the *Vitae* and Sermons of Humility of Faenza." In *Medieval Monastic Preaching*, edited by Carolyn Muessig. Leiden: Brill, 1998, pp. 123–144.

Petroff, Elizabeth Alvilda. *Body and Soul: Essays on Medieval Women and Mysticism*. New York and Oxford: Oxford University Press, 1994.

———. ed. *Medieval Women's Visionary Literature*. New York and Oxford: Oxford University Press, 1986.

See also **Abbesses; Education, Monastic; Hagiography; Literacy and Reading; Latin; Sermons and Preaching**

HUNTING AND FALCONRY

In poetry and art, women were associated frequently with falconry. High social estate was expressed with examples from nature, identifying raptors as lords of the sky. Flying hawks at heron, pheasant, partridge, larks, hare, and rabbit seemed the quintessence of courtly elegance. It required the utmost patience to train birds in loyalty and to tolerate their quirks in the hunt, and so the quality of one's character was on display to all. Female birds grew bigger than tiercels (males) and were preferred as the keener hunters. Ladies flew both long-winged (true falcons, such as the peregrine) and short-winged hawks. The peregrine, which was flown in open country with good visibility, either soared aloft and "waited" for game to be flushed from the ground or flew from the fist in a winding ascent until she reached altitude (the "tower"), from which heights she "stooped" upon her prey. Goshawks and sparrowhawks were launched from the fist in wooded country directly at low-flying birds and ground game. The marginalia of *Queen Mary's Psalter* show women in pairs flying hawks together. Gace de la Buigne (*Roman des Deduis*) depicts falconry as offering edgy competition as well as fellowship. In one vignette a company of men of diverse social ranks and trades bond for a week of falconry, trying out each other's birds, dining on their catch, and telling funny stories. In another, a mixed company of courtiers ambles through the countryside at a pace allowing leisure to socialize and flirt. Men and women depicted together with hawk or hound inevitably evoked venery of the venereal kind.

Illuminations in the Manesse Codex show couples hawking and enjoying amorous pleasures; in the same book the poet of K(renberg) declares women easy to lure like the falcon, and (speaking in an ambiguous persona) tropes a once-loyal lover as a tamed falcon flown away. As in erotic allegories of the hunt, sex was troped as the kill, whereby there remained latitude for the feminine subject to voice agony or desire. Hunting, which was practiced with more variety of means and method, saw women engaged in many roles. The *par force* chase of deer with hounds, which involved complex tracking, hazardous riding, and the high ritual of slaughter, was supported by establishments staffed by men. *The Taymouth Hours* (which, as has been argued also for *Queen Mary's Psalter*, may possibly have been made for Isabella of France, queen of Edward II) uniquely depicts women hunting deer and boar, handling trophy heads and butchering game; its owner was a lady of the Neville family, who had filled the office of England's chief forester for much of a century. The official culture, however, was deeply masculine. The hart and buck were the preferred quarry. Treatises specified techniques and nomenclature for male game including their antlers. The honor portion of the kill (for the lord of the hunt) was the liver and testicles. Ladies nonetheless rode with or behind the main rout, sitting their mounts astride and riding singly or in pairs and couples. Their influence as onlookers, as at tournaments, cannot have been negligible. The *Boke of Huntyng* in the *Book of St. Albans*, ascribed to Dame Juliana Berners (Barnes?), though her identity and authorship are questionable, speaks in the persona of a mother instructing her son how to chase deer, hare, and boar *par force*. Edward of Norwich commends his treatise *The Master of Game* to gentlemen, as well as ladies, advising that their hunting keep the custom of the king's house in remembrance. His chapter on the bow-and-stable reflects the hunt women most favored: Shooting driven game with bow or crossbow from a stand, and coursing deer and hare with greyhounds. The former requires skill with a weapon, the latter a command of game-lore and jargon. *Queen Mary's Psalter* shows ladies blowing signals on a horn, shooting deer, and hunting rabbits with ferrets and nets. The common work of subsistence hunting, such as rabbiting in warrens, was shared by men and women. Poaching was mostly left to men.

WILLIAM P. MARVIN

References and Further Reading

Almond, Richard. *Medieval Hunting*. Phoenix Mill: Sutton, 2003.

Cummins, John. *The Hound and the Hawk: The Art of Medieval Hunting*. New York: St. Martin's Press, 1988.

Edward of Norwich, 2nd Duke of York. *The Master of Game*, edited and translated by W. A. and F. Baillie-Grohman. Forward by Theodore Roosevelt. New York: Duffield, 1909. Reprint New York: AMS, 1974.

Hands, Rachel, ed. *English Hawking and Hunting in The Boke of St. Albans: A Facsimile Edition*. Oxford: Oxford University Press, 1975.

Rooney, Anne. *Hunting in Middle English Literature*. Woodbridge, Suffolk: Boydel Press, 1993.

Thiébaux, Marcelle. *The Stag of Love: The Chase in Medieval Literature*. Ithacan N.Y.: Cornell University Press, 1974.

See also **Noble Women**

HUSBANDS AND HUSBANDRY

Historians of women's experience in the Middle Ages have understandably written a great deal about marriage, because becoming a wife was important for most women, providing the most common means for respectability and some measure of security. We should not overlook, however, the corresponding importance of marriage for *men's* adult identities. The vast majority of men sought to become husbands and to remain married.

This subject was long ignored, partly due to the much later development of interest among historians in questions of masculinity in the Middle Ages. Another reason is that, at least in the High and late Middle Ages, there was somewhat more room for unmarried men than for unmarried women. The church provided, for ambitious, well-connected, and fortunate men, a way to make a living without a wife, especially after the eleventh-century Gregorian reforms, when clerical celibacy began to be enforced. Holy orders opened doors to literacy, higher education, political influence at various levels, social respectability, and even prominence, and, for the lucky few, wealth and comfort, while also satisfying the spiritual needs of those who felt called to the religious life. (In comparison, far fewer women were ever able to live as celibate nuns.) Yet we must not exaggerate the degree to which average men would have expected these things from a religious career, nor their willingness to forego marriage in order to have a chance at them. Most clerics remained poor parish or chantry priests, and only a minority could ever aspire to the desirable offices higher up in the church hierarchy.

Marriage, in contrast, was the only practical option in a traditional society like medieval Europe for men with the typical wishes and goals of their time and place. Simply put, most men could not hope to make a manageable life for themselves without a woman, which generally meant a wife. Only by marriage could a man become the head of a household, the marker in most European societies of mature masculinity, as the use of the word *Mann* in German to mean both "husband" and "adult male" reminds us. The stigma generally attaching to nonmarital relationships meant that a man could not really have a respectable household with a woman he was not married to. Women's work—the array of domestic and agricultural tasks that fell to women by custom—was so important in everyday life that a household had great difficulty functioning without a woman. Moreover, wives were not only workers but also managers, who supervised the other members of the household: children, labourers, and servants. While, as in every age, some men fathered children out of wedlock, marriage was the only way a man could have *legitimate* children to whom to pass on the property (whether land, movables, or money) he had worked hard to preserve. Children would also be likely to offer some care in old age. Along with such practical considerations, we must also take into account the basic human needs and desires for sexual activity, affection, and companionship. Indeed, given the high risks of pregnancy and childbirth, and the consequent rate of female mortality, it was quite common for a man to become a husband more than once.

The English word *husband*, different in emphasis from German *Mann* and from those languages (*mari, maritus, marito*) where *husband* literally means "married male," has an instructive history. According to the *Oxford English Dictionary*, the uses of *husband* to mean "the male head of a household" are the earliest (c. 1000). Those implying "a man joined to a woman by marriage" are contemporary with those conveying household management (fourteenth to sixteenth centuries). The related word *husbandry* is first found to mean "domestic economy" about 1290 and to mean "careful management" in 1362. So in medieval England, these meanings were very much intertwined, and it is likely that the same values were connected in other European cultures.

This makes the word *husbandry* a useful one for understanding mature masculine identity. Good husbandry denoted the prudent management of a man's own: wife, dependents (children and servants), money, and property. To abuse, misuse, or waste any of these valuable components diminished husbandly and, therefore, masculine identity, as surely as did allowing them to escape one's own governance. The self-command required to maintain this balance was related to the same values some men of the upper and middling classes learned as boys in courtesy literature, even though that literature says very little explicitly about being a husband. A masculine identity was maintained in the eyes of a man's social peers, who kept an eye on every aspect of his husbandry, and that social opinion constituted the honour a man had to preserve. Neighbours and kin might ridicule one kind of bad husband as a cuckold, or they might withdraw from another who abused what was his own. Law and custom assumed that a husband was the ultimate authority in his own household, and granted him considerable freedom to discipline his wife and dependents as he saw fit. Yet husbandry was a nuanced business, which we cannot simplistically characterize as the exercise of "power," "control," or "dominance."

DEREK NEAL

References and Further Reading

McSheffrey, Shannon. *Love and Marriage in Late Medieval London*. Kalamazoo, Mich.: Medieval Institute Publications, 1995.
———. "Men and Masculinity in Late Medieval London Civic Culture: Governance, Patriarchy, and Reputation." In *Conflicted Identities and Multiple Masculinities: Men in the Medieval West*, edited by Jacqueline Murray. New York and London: Garland, 1999, pp. 243–267.
Neal, Derek. "Masculine Identity in Late Medieval English Society and Culture." In *Writing Medieval History*, edited Nancy F. Partner. London: Hodder Arnold, 2005, pp. 171–188.

See also **Demography; Division of Labor; Domestic Abuse; Family (Earlier Middle Ages); Family (Later Middle Ages); Household Management; Marriage, Christian; Remarriage; Sexuality: Extramarital Sex; Sexuality: Sex in Marriage**

I

IBERIA

In medieval Iberia Christian, Muslim, and Jewish women lived concurrently for centuries. When Arab and Berber invaders swept away the Visigothic Kingdom in 711, Christian refugees fled to the mountainous north and established small kingdoms and counties that resisted the emirate–caliphate of Córdoba (until 1031). Smaller states (*taifas*) supplanted the caliphate and were strengthened from time to time by militant Berbers from the Maghrib, but they gradually lost ground to the strengthening Christian powers. Thus began the Reconquest of Muslim Iberia (al-Andalus), a long process characterized by aggressive warfare, strategic defense, and many displacements of population, which affected women in particular. By 1300 the peninsula was ruled by five kingdoms: Castile (with Asturias, Galicia, and León after 1230), Aragon (with Catalonia after 1134), Portugal, Navarre, and Muslim Granada. During the thirteenth century Castile, Aragon, and Portugal had made deep conquests south into al-Andalus, but Castile became the dominant member of the quintet and covered two-thirds of the peninsula with a population that had grown to 4,500,000 by the time it seized Granada in 1492. By the marriage of Queen Isabel (v. 1474–1504) and King Fernando (v. 1479–1516), Castile and Aragon joined to become the dynastic unity we call Spain.

Women in al-Andalus (711–1492)

After 711 most Christian women in the south married Muslim invaders, converted, and became Arabized in culture and religion. The caliphate, however, respected groups of practicing Jews and Mozarabs (Christians living under Muslim rulers), and the latter preserved several monasteries of female and male religious. Some of the zealous martyrs who rebelled against the rulers of ninth-century Córdoba were women, but only a handful are known among later Mozarabs, mostly monks, who fled north to Christian Iberia in reaction to the intolerance of newly arrived Berbers. We hear no more of Mozarabs after about 1200, apart from a significant remnant in Toledo, which was also home to an important Jewish community.

Muslim women wore traditional Middle Eastern garb, blue if in mourning, and a married woman wore a veil on the rare occasions she left her house, perhaps to visit a bathhouse, a mosque, or a cemetery, which in some cases she had founded. Polygamy was too costly for all but the powerful and died out by the twelfth century, but concubinage and repudiation were practiced. Courtesans and mothers of rulers' heirs were well educated and are remembered for their poetry and the books they copied, as well as for knowledge of music, medicine, law, and theology. Slave women who were singers or trained artisans were especially valuable. Both Muslim and Christian armies and raiding parties took prisoners of both sexes. Northern Christian women were sold in Muslim cities as slaves suitable for the fields, households, and harems of al-Andalus. Some were ransomed. Others escaped or were rescued, reputedly by Saint Dominic of Silos. Captives also converted to Islam, bore Muslim children, and otherwise contrived to evade the auction block, deep dungeons, and laborious suffering that awaited.

Muslim Women in Christian Iberia

Female slaves (*moras*) with Islamic names appear in ninth- and tenth-century documents, and captive slaves continued to outnumber free Muslims in Castile until the end of the Middle Ages. Mudejars (free Muslims living under a Christian ruler) originated in the areas of Iberia annexed by Christian states. They were proprietary subjects of Christian rulers, as were Jews, and lived in *aljamas* (communities) protected and taxed by royal and seigneurial officials. Most Mudejars were poor peasants and artisans with skills in agriculture and construction. They were very numerous in the Ebro Valley and Aragonese Valencia, but in Castile the Mudejar population of about 600,000 in 1300 dwindled to no more than 25,000 by the end of the Middle Ages as most left for Granada or Africa. Muslim women in Castile were banned from working as servants in Christian homes in 1258, and Christian servants could not work in Muslim homes. Those who converted to Christianity were called Moriscas, but conversion was very gradual until it became mandatory beginning in 1502. Muslim lore of special interest to women, about cosmetics, perfumes, gardens, and women's health, continued to slip through the porous frontiers between Muslim and Christian Iberia and survives in late medieval recipe books.

Jewish Women in Christian Iberia

There were perhaps 50,000 Jews in the Peninsula in 1300, although there may have been 80,000 by 1492. Their communities were highly respected in both Muslim and Christian Iberia through much of the Middle Ages, and they enjoyed considerable independence in private matters. A Jewish woman's position was determined by the patriarchal structure of the family as defined in Talmudic Law: status depended upon her being a wife or mother. The property she brought into marriage belonged to her husband, and the oldest son was preferred in inheritance over his widowed mother and sisters. Jewish ordinances of 1432 in Castile, however, increased daughters' and widows' rights of inheritance and weakened arbitrarily coerced marriages.

Jews were mainly tradesmen and artisans, and many women shared the work of their families, particularly in provisioning and textile trades. A few female doctors are reported in Aragon, but midwives were much more common. Poor Jewish women found work as mourners, prostitutes, and purveyors of creams and potions. Many Jewish women worked as servants, as did Christians, but thirteenth-century law prohibited Christian women from working in Jewish homes. Jewish or Muslim men who had sexual relations with Christian women risked the death penalty, and all wet-nurses were supposed to suckle only infants born to their own faith.

Influential Jews were tax collectors and money lenders, and sometimes their widows continued to make loans, although not to collect taxes, which required involvement in public finance. In the late fourteenth century the wealth of some Jewish families from these activities inflamed popular resentment among Christians already embittered by war and bad times. Lavish dress, especially that worn by Jewish women, despite royal and ecclesiastical laws restricting it, angered many. After 1391 Jewish neighborhoods were subject to widespread looting and violence. Many Jews were converted by persuasive Christian preachers and became *Conversos*, but *Conversos* also antagonized the rabble, who suspected their sincerity as new Christians. Particularly incriminating for women were Jewish dietary customs and domestic rituals, which *Converso* women were thought to observe secretly. Growing suspicion and the need to prevent Jews from weakening the resolve of the newly converted led to the establishment of the Inquisition in Castile (1478) and, eventually, to the Expulsion (1492).

Christian Women

The Reconquest valued men for their skills in warfare and strength in forging new settlements, but women were necessary to establish permanent communities in a new land. Men who brought their brides to a place received tax exemptions and deferments, and a married man had to establish a primary residence with his wife and children in order to qualify for citizenship. Directly beneficial to women were customs governing the transmission of property. Husbands headed households officially, but Castilian wives shared work and responsibilities and were entitled to half of the property acquired during marriage. Partible inheritance encouraged population growth by dividing family possessions equitably, if not absolutely equally, among all the children. Substantial favoritism toward one child was illegal until the end of the fourteenth century, when a noble could obtain a royal license to give most of his property as a *mayorazgo* (entailment, an inalienable and indivisable assignment of property) to one of the children, usually his eldest son. *Mayorazgos* sometimes fell to daughters, and mothers frequently took advantage of bilateral inheritance to bestow their own property on daughters and younger sons. Consolidated and agnatic inheritance, however, was distinctly unfavorable to daughters, as it was in other parts of Europe. Girls might now receive not an equitable distribution but a dowry designed to attract a suitable husband, or a somewhat smaller sum needed to enter a monastery.

Endogamy was common among many groups, especially among the royalty and nobility of the Christian kingdoms. Noble cousins inevitably intermarried, since so many were kin to at least one royal or noble line, like the innumerable descendants of King Alfonso IX of León (d. 1230), who had married queens from both Portugal and Castile and fathered at least eighteen legitimate and illegitimate children. Multiple marriages of men and women were common, owing to deaths of men in warfare and women in childbirth. Yet seven or eight children were far from unusual, and in the fifteenth century some of the children, boys or girls, took the mother's patronymic, especially if she was prominent. Such a woman was the heiress Leonor de Albuquerque (d. 1435), known as *rica fembra* (grand lady), who became Queen of Aragon. With the right connections, one's daughter might secure a position in such a lady's household. In 1505 Mencía Manuel, Duchess of Medinaceli, employed many ladies, young girls, pages, servants, and slaves. In such a household a good marriage might be arranged, or beautiful courtesans, like the famed fourteenth-century sisters Inés and Juana de Castro, might be found.

Women managed their own and family property at all levels of society, from queens to tradeswomen who ran shops and businesses in towns and cities. Great ladies often governed fortresses, towns, and monasteries as *señora* (lady), and several such places were repeatedly included in endowments given to royal brides, usually in hostage to matrimonial agreements reached across political boundaries. Talavera de la Reina west of Toledo adopted its title from its *señora*, the prudent Queen María de Molina (d. 1321). *Señoras* were not invariably respected. The imperious Teresa, dowager countess of Santa Marta (d. 1470), was attacked by her Galician townsmen of Ribadavia, who dragged her through the streets and stabbed her in the town square.

Many queens and *infantas* (princesses) set examples by their piety. The *infanta* Elvira "the Nun" of León (d. 986) was a benefactor of monasteries and esteemed as a royal counsellor, as was the devout and long-lived *infanta* Sancha of Castile (d. 1159), who promoted widespread ecclesiastical reforms. Admired for piety and charity were Teresa of Portugal (d. 1250) and the saintly Portuguese Queen Isabel of Aragon (d. 1336). Women like Elduara, mother of the tenth-century Galician monastic reformer San Rosendo, emulated royal dedication to good works, which included the foundation and patronage of monasteries for women. The ranks of women in religious life were filled primarily by the aristocracy until the thirteenth century, especially in royal foundations like Las Huelgas at Burgos and Tordesillas on the Duero River. More and more frequently, nobles of lesser rank and townswomen took vows in appropriate convents, and, in the fourteenth century, townswomen called *beatas* began joining together for prayer and devotions. The *beaterio* (house of devout women) accommodated those who had neither the dowry nor the social connections needed for many monasteries. They also avoided full monastic enclosure, which ecclesiastical authorities were demanding anew. *Emparedadas* (anchoresses) chose to live walled up in cells at churches, where they received food and gifts from the urban populace and dispensed wisdom through small windows. Such a cell survives at the parish church of San Esteban in Astorga.

Daughters were schooled at home or, like the *infantas* of Navarre, educated in a convent. Vernacular literacy in women was rather commonplace by the thirteenth century, but Latin was fading even as a documentary language. King Alfonso X of Castile wrote a letter in the vernacular to the Benedictine nuns of San Pedro de las Dueñas in 1253, explicitly to permit all the sisters to understand him. Knowledge of Latin was revived in the fifteenth century when a learned woman might own a multilingual library. Whatever its contents, she frequently bequeathed her most personal devotional books to a close kinswoman.

The most typical women residing in towns and cities were tradeswomen: bakers, laundresses, weavers, tailors, shopkeepers. Privileged noblewomen, wives of knights and gentlemen, rich widows who trafficked in the land market, and many poor ones seeking charity inhabited established towns. Domiciled mistresses of young men and priests, as well as prostitutes, were characteristic residents, as were women in the Jewish and Moorish quarters. Some women had come with their families when the town was first settled, or they were recent arrivals. The hard-working peasant women from villages nearby, who came to sell produce or attend a fair, did all kinds of farm work at home alongside men, especially at harvest. These largely anonymous peasants were the majority of Iberia's medieval women, but they, too, gravitated to the Peninsula's many towns and cities to join those who lived within the walls.

HEATH DILLARD

References and Further Reading

Beceiro Pita, Isabel. "La relación de las mujeres castellanas con la cultura escrita (siglo XIII–inicios del XVI)." In *Libro y lecturas en la Península Ibérica y América, siglos XIII a XVIII*, edited by Antonio Castillo Gómez. Salamanca: Junta de Castilla y León, 2003, pp. 15–52.

Cantera Montenegro, Enrique. "La mujer judía en la España medieval." *Espacio, Tiempo y Forma: Revista de la Facultad de Geografía e Historia, serie III: Historia Medieval*, vol. 2. *Homenaje al Profesor Eloy Benito Ruano*. 1989, pp. 37–63.

Del Moral, Celia, ed. *Árabes, judías y cristianas: Mujeres en la Europa medieval*. Granada: Universidad de Granada, Seminario de Estudios de la Mujer, 1993.

Dillard, Heath. *Daughters of the Reconquest: Women in Castilian Town Society, 1100–1300*. Cambridge: Cambridge University Press, 1984.

Durán, Maria Angeles and Cristina Segura Graino, eds. *El trabajo de las mujeres en la Edad Media hispana*. Colección Laya, 3. Madrid: Al-Mudayna, 1988.

Fonquerne, Yves-René, and Alfonso Esteban, eds. "La condición de la mujer en la Edad Media: Coloquio hispano-francés." *Actas del Coloquio celebrado en la Casa de Velázquez, 5–7 Noviembre 1984*. Madrid: Casa de Velázquez–Universidad Complutense, 1986.

García Herrero, María del Carmen. *Las mujeres en Zaragoza en el siglo X*. 2 vols. Cuadernos de Zaragoza, 62. Zaragoza: Ayuntamiento de Zaragoza, 1990.

Graña Cid, María del Mar, ed. *Las sabias mujeres*. 2 vols. Colección Laya, 13 and 15. Madrid: Al-Mudayna, 1994–1995.

López Beltrán, María Teresa, ed. *Las mujeres en Andalucía. Actas del 2ª encuentro interdisciplinar de estudios de la mujer en Andalucía*, vol. 2. Biblioteca de Estudios sobre la Mujer, 8. Málaga: Diputación de Málaga, 1994.

Muñoz Fernández, Ángela, ed. *Beatas y santas neocastellanas: Ambivalencias de la religión y políticas correctoras del poder (SS. XIV–XVI)*. Madrid: Comunidad de Madrid, Dirección General de la Mujer, 1996.

Muñoz Fernández, Ángela, and María del Mar Graña Cid, eds. *Religiosidad femenina: Expectativas y realidades (SS. VIII–XVIII)*. Colección Laya, 7. Madrid: Al-Mudayna, 1991.

Navas, Carmen Caballero, ed. and trans. *Una compilación hebrea de saberes sobre el cuidado de la salud y la belleza del cuerpo femenino*. Textos: Lengua Hebrea. Granada: Universidad de Granada, 2003.

Pallares, María del Carmen. *Ilduara, una aristocrata del siglo X*. 2nd ed. rev. Galicia Medieval: Estudos, 4. A Coruña: Seminario de Estudos Galegos, 2004.

Pastor, Reyna, et al., eds. "Textos para la historia de las mujeres en la Edad Media: al-Andalus y reinos occidentales cristianos medievales." In *Textos para la historia de las mujeres de España*, edited by A. M. Aguado, et al. Historia, serie minor. Madrid: Cátedra, 1994, pp. 123–221.

Segura Graino, Cristina, et al., eds. *Las mujeres en las ciudades Actas de las Terceras Jornadas de Investigación Interdisciplinaria.*" Colección de Estudios de la Mujer 7. Madrid: Seminario de Estudios de la Mujer, Universidad Autónoma de Madrid, 1984.

————. *La voz del silencio*. 2 vols. Colección Laya, 9 and 11. Madrid: Al-Mudayna, 1992.

Stone, Marilyn, and Carmen Benito-Vessels, eds. *Women at Work in Spain, from the Middle Ages to Early Modern Times*. New York: Peter Lang, 1998.

Surtz, Ronald E. *Writing Women in Late Medieval and Early Modern Spain: The Mothers of Santa Teresa of Ávila*. Middle Ages Series. Philadelphia: University of Pennsylvania Press, 1995.

Viguera, María J., ed. *La mujer en al-Andalus, reflejos históricos de su actividad y categorías sociales. Actas de las V Jornadas de Investigación Interdisciplinaria, 1: al-Andalus*. Colección del Seminario de Estudios de la Mujer, 13. Madrid and Sevilla: Ediciones de la Universidad Autónoma de Madrid and Editoriales Andaluzas Unidas de Sevilla, 1989.

See also **Anchoresses; Artisan Families, Women of; Berenguela; Castro, Inés de; Cities and Towns; Concubines; Dowry and Other Marriage Gifts; Education, Lay; Heiresses; Inheritance; Isabel I; Isabel of Aragon; Jewish Women; Ladies-in-Waiting; Landholding and Property Rights; Lay Piety; Literature, Iberian; López de Córdoba, Leonor; Monastic Enclosure; Monasticism and Nuns; Muslim Women: Iberia; Noble Women; Prostitutes; Queens and Empresses: The West; Slaves; Teresa de Cartagena; Urraca; Women Authors: Spanish Texts**

ICONS, BYZANTINE

In Byzantium the word *icon* (*eikon*) refers to portable portraits of Christ, the Virgin, and saints or scenes from their lives in metal, enamel, ivory, and steatite, as well as tempera or encaustic on wood panels. In terms of technique (tempera or encaustic on wood), the icon's origin has been traced back to the funerary portraits in Roman Egypt. Yet, unlike these images of the deceased that functioned in the burial rites and visualized the transport and mystical transformation of the individual in the afterlife, Christian icons were understood as commemorative images, protecting the community. The rise of icons is also connected with the cult of relics and miraculous *acheiropoietoi* (images not made by human hand).

Relics became established in the Holy Land by the second half of the fourth century, while *acheiropoietoi* emerged in the second half of the sixth century. Both relics and *acheiropoietoi* carry sacred energy, for they are extensions or imprints of the divine body. Icons, by contrast, are portraits lacking the touch of the sacred body and energy. With Byzantium's loss of the Holy Land to the Arabs in the seventh century, the obstructed access to holy sites and relics must have catapulted icons into the former position of relics, i.e., as means through which to obtain access to sacred energy. It is this spiritual claim placed on the

The Virgin Hodegetria ("The One Who Leads the Way").
Byzantine icon, second half of the fourteenth century.
Location: National Museum, Belgrade, Serbia and
Montenegro. Credit: Erich Lessing / Art Resource, N.Y.

icon that precipitated Iconoclasm (730–843), a crisis over the validity of images and relics in the Christian cult.

With the triumph of orthodoxy in 843, the icon in Byzantium was strictly defined as an imprint of the visible characteristics of Christ on matter: *typos* (impression, mold), *sphragis* (seal), and *signon* (seal). It is this concept of the icon as imprint rather than painting that became fully expressed in the post-Iconoclast relief icon. Rendered in metal repoussé, ivory, steatite, and enamel, the figures project from the surface into physical space and engage the viewer. The relief icon thus fully answers the Byzantine interest in tactile visuality.

Contrary to the established belief that liturgical and imperial processions in Constantinople frequently included icons, textual evidence as well as the small size of post-Iconoclast icons suggests that these objects were in fact reserved for a private cult throughout the ninth and early tenth centuries. They were not carried in public processions, although they were displayed in churches and private homes. It was only in the eleventh century that icons started to be integrated into public processions, and it is possible to conjecture that, during this period, a new demand for larger-scale icons arose. This need was met by the creation of large processional icons, which consisted of images painted on wood panels covered with expensive silver-gilt revetments. These jewel-encrusted covers integrated the aesthetic of the former small-scale luxury private icons, but expanded their size.

Several important processional icons emerged in Constantinople in the course of the eleventh and twelfth centuries; among these were the icons of the Virgin known as *Blachernitissa* (of the Blachernai monastery of the Virgin) and *Hodegetria* ("The One Who Leads the Way"). The *Hodegetria* gradually became the most powerful icon in Constantinople, protector of the emperor, the city, and the state. It had a *litania* (procession) on Tuesdays through the streets of the city and was also annually brought to the tombs of the emperors at the mausoleum of the monastery of Christ Pantokrator. Although the emperor thus laid an exclusive claim to Hodegetria, the local aristocracy found ways to gain access to this panel by offering it gifts of silk cloths (*encheiria*) with prayers inscribed on them. Thereby, a singular luxury object, the Hodegetria, was commoditized and, in a sense, multiplied to meet the growing needs of the urban elite.

The role of women in the promotion of icon veneration in Byzantium has been a debated subject. Judith Herrin has argued that women played a key role in the defense of icons. Supporting her thesis is the evidence of two empresses who reestablished icon veneration (Irene in 787 and Theodora in 843) and the fact that women feature in the accounts about the icon of Christ at the Chalke gate in Constantinople. Robin Cormack has raised objections to this argument by pointing out the ideological character of the legends of Christ at Chalke and inconsistency regarding the identity of the protagonists. In some of the earlier versions, the story of the image of Christ at Chalke enlists the help of noble citizens who protected the image; in other accounts women are enlisted; and finally in the later tenth-century sources the protagonist emerges as a nun, named St. Theodosia. These texts do not give reliable historical evidence on which to reconstruct fervent female devotion to icons. At the same time, the absence of icons from the cathedral and stational (weekly or annual processions in which the stages of the Liturgy are celebrated at different churches along a set route) liturgy and from imperial ceremonies argues for the private function of these images before the late tenth century. Therefore, it is plausible to suggest that, in fact, women were likely involved in the promotion of icons, but to transform them into leading defenders of images is misleading. Further support for this neutral position is offered by the historical circumstances under which icon processions arose; the first public ceremonies with icons were imperial triumphal processions, promoted by the emperor in order to lay claim to the throne by means of his military victories. John I Tzimiskes (969–976) was the first emperor to place an icon of the Virgin on his triumphal chariot and take it through the streets of the city. It was again an emperor, John II Komnenos (1118–1143), who promoted novel imperial commemorative services at the Pantokrator monastery, through which he consolidated the imperial cult.

Aside from the issue of patronage and promotion of icon veneration, an interesting question emerges regarding the gender of icons. Again based on Byzantine image theory, the icon is understood as female; just as the maternal body of Mary has received the divine *Logos* and given it a material form, so too the icon has received the imprint of the Spirit on its surface. At the same time, the address of the icon, its gaze, is male. In a typical icon of the Virgin holding the Child, the eyes of Mary frequently evade the gaze of the viewer and direct attention to her Child. By contrast, the gaze of the Christ is straightforward, addressing the faithful and offering a response: his blessing. Through gaze and gesture, the icon presents a pictorial affirmation of the success of the prayer; it is a figural, visual assurance of future divine favor.

BISSERA V. PENTCHEVA

References and Further Reading

Barber, C. *Figure and Likeness: On the Limits of Representation in Byzantine Iconoclasm*. Princeton: Princeton University Press, 2002.
Belting, H. *Likeness and Presence: A History of the Image Before the Era of Art*. Bonn, 1990. English translation, E. Jephcott, Chicago: University of Chicago Press, 1994.
Bierbrier, M., ed. *Portraits and Masks: Burial Customs in Roman Egypt*. London: The British Museum Press, 1997.
Brown, P. *The Cult of Saints: Its Rise and Function in Latin Christianity*. Chicago: University of Chicago Press, 1981.
Byzantine Icons: Art, Technique, and Technology, edited by M. Vassilaki. Heraklion: Crete University Press, 2002.
Cormack, R. *Writing in Gold: Byzantine Society and Its Icons*. London: George Philip, 1985.
———. *Painting the Soul: Icons, Death Masks and Shrouds*. London: Reaktion, 1997.
———. "Women and Icons, and Women in Icons." In *Women, Men and Eunuchs: Gender in Byzantium*, edited by Liz James. London/New York: Routledge, 1997, pp. 24–57.
———. "The Eyes of the Mother of God." In *Images of the Mother of God: Perceptions of the Theotokos in Byzantium*, edited by M. Vassilaki. London: Ashgate, 2005, pp. 167–174.
Doxiadis, E. *The Mysterious Fayum Portraits: Faces from Ancient Egypt*. London: Thames and Hudson, 1995.
Eastmond, A., and L. James, eds. *Icon & Word: the Power of Images in Byzantium. Studies Presented to Robin Cormack*. London: Ashgate, 2003.
Grabar, A. *Martyrium. Recherches sur le culte des reliques et l'art chrétien antique*, 3 vols. Paris: Collège de France, 1943–1946.
Herrin, J. "Women and the Faith in Icons in Early Christianity." In *Culture, Ideology and Politics. Essays for Eric Hobsbawm*. London: Routledge, 1984, pp. 56–83.
Pentcheva, B. "The Supernatural Protector of Constantinople: The Virgin and Her Icons in the Tradition of the Avar Siege." *Byzantine and Modern Greek Studies* 26 (2002): 2–41.
———. *Icons and Power. The Mother of God in Byzantium*. University Park: Pennsylvania State University Press, 2005.
Walker, S., ed. *Ancient Faces: Mummy Portraits from Roman Egypt*. New York: Routledge, 1997. Reprint, 2000.

See also **Byzantium; Devotional Art; Gaze; Irene; Mary, Virgin: in Art**

IDA OF BOULOGNE

Saint Ida of Boulogne (c. 1040–1113), daughter of Godfrey the Bearded, duke of Lorraine (d. 1059), was wife of Eustace II, count of Boulogne (d. 1089), and mother of Eustace III, count of Boulogne (d. 1125), as well as Godfrey of Bouillon (d. 1100) and Baldwin of Boulogne (d. 1118), leaders of the first crusade and rulers of Jerusalem. She maintained relations with Anselm of Bec, Hugh of Cluny, and Bishop Osmund of Astorga. She was buried at the priory of Le Wast, where her *Life* was probably composed (1130–1135) at the request of her granddaughter Matilda (d. 1152), wife of King Stephen of England, who claimed she was cured at Ida's grave.

Thus, Ida was connected to royal saints like Margaret of Scotland, Matilda's other grandmother, related to Edward the Confessor, king of England (d. 1066), and descended from Stephen, king of Hungary (d. 1038). As protector of the Church and the needy in Boulogne and England, Ida was a perfect model for Christian princesses. She was pictured as a new Maria, a holy mother, not only of outstanding sons but of all Christians. She left a dominant mark upon the self-identity of the House of Boulogne. Since the late twelfth century, she has been remembered mainly in relation to the first crusade and her heroic son Godfrey. Then, probably at the instigation of another Matilda of Boulogne (d. 1211), granddaughter of the Matilda mentioned earlier, and her husband Henry of Brabant (d. 1235), the legend of the *Swan Knight*, who supposedly was Ida's father, was included in the French *Cycle de la Croisade*.

RENÉE NIP

References and Further Reading

Anonymous. "De B. Ida, Vidua, Comitissa Boloniae in Gallo Belgica." In *Acta Sanctorum*, edited by Godfrey Henschen and Daniel Papenbroch. April 13th, Paris and Rome, 1866.

Duby, Georges. *Mâle moyen age: De l'amour et autres essais*. Paris: Flammarion, 1988.

Nip, Renée. "Godelieve of Gistel and Ida of Boulogne." In *Sanctity and Motherhood*, edited by Anneke B. Mulder-Bakker. New York and London: Garland Publishing, 1995, pp. 191–223.

Tanner, Heather J. *Families, Friends and Allies: Boulogne and Politics in Northern France and England, c. 879–1160*. Leiden and Boston: Brill, 2004.

See also **Crusades and Crusading Literature; England; Flanders; France, Northern; Hagiography; Literature, Old French; Margaret of Scotland; Marriage, Christian; Noble Women**

ILLEGITIMACY

Those born out of wedlock are illegitimate. That principle was understood in Roman and Germanic law, by the medieval church and governing bodies. The differences among them revolved around determining what was a valid marriage (and, in consequence, who exactly was illegitimate) and what restrictions or disabilities attached to illegitimacy.

For secular law, marriage was a matter of formal legalities that differentiated a marriage from informal concubinage and temporary or thoroughly illicit (adultery, incest) sexual relationships. Standards of legality, however, were not always clearly defined; local opinion could count heavily for deciding what couple was indeed married. Church law, following Gratian (c. 1140) and the important decretals of Alexander III (1159–1181), muddied the waters by asserting the validity, if not legality, of clandestine unions in the interest of offspring. Prohibition of divorce also precluded serial monogamy and the legitimacy of resultant offspring. The triumph of clerical celibacy entailed the illegitimacy of all clerical children.

Illegitimacy mattered because it resulted in penalties for the illegitimate. By canon law and penitential teaching, illegitimacy sprang from sinful actions on the part of the parents. That sin, parallel to the sin of Adam and Eve, set a stain (*macula*) on the children. That mark justified the lesser status and disabilities that fell on them. It also heightened the sense of shame or embarrassment at the illegitimate pregnancy and birth. The greater the sense of stigma attached to illegitimacy, the greater the penalties.

For the Church the chief penalty was barring illegitimates, including the children of clergy, from clerical offices. However, dispensations were made available, wholesale purchase of which became a considerable source of income for some bishops and the papacy by the eve of the Reformation. Conversely, from a concern for the humanity of the bastard child, the Church affirmed rights to sustenance that were not found in Roman or Germanic laws, where the abandonment of children and infanticide were more prominent avenues by which to deal with unwanted children.

The major disability falling on all illegitimates was the curtailing or total removal of rights to inherit from their fathers. Paternity was not certain or admitted for many illegitimates, in contrast to maternity. Even legitimate paternity seemingly required the harsh rules and high value placed on women's virginity before marriage and marital fidelity. Where illegitimate maternity was evident or conceded, succession rights were not automatic.

In areas of Roman law influence, children born of concubinage, where parents were otherwise single and cohabited with a "marital affection," but without formal legalities and property arrangements, were termed natural (*naturales*). They had a limited right to succession. In the absence of legitimate children, they could inherit, and they were legitimated to full inheritance by subsequent marriage of their parents. Such a device was not available to other categories of illegitimates (the *spurii* or *bastardi*), whose father was either unknown or had a relationship to the mother that was brief or, worse, adulterous or incestuous. For these, possibilities of inheritance, even in the absence of legitimate children, sometimes even despite a legitimation by imperial rescript, were minimal or nonexistent. Canonists denounced the occasional secular laws allowing such children succession rights on the grounds that, by mitigating penalties for them, parental sin was encouraged.

Included in succession rights were those to hold office or exercise authority, but here a vital distinction must be drawn between institutional offices and dynastic succession. City-states or guilds could effectively preclude illegitimates from office. Venice notably supervised patrician marriages with an eye to keeping bastards from office. For families, when the direct legitimate line failed, in contrast, an illegitimate provided an alternative blood continuity. From William the Bastard, conqueror and king of England (1066–1087) to several Este lords of Ferrara, and many more, royal and princely lines survived on illegitimate succession and built marriage alliances with illegitimate, as well as legitimate, offspring.

The lived realities of illegitimates' lives varied by place, but maybe more by social status. The wealthy could afford, symbolically and financially, to flaunt laws and social mores and thus recognize and raise illegitimate children. Many, like Leon Battista Alberti (1404–1472), ended up in clerical careers; a few enjoyed the same advantages as legitimate siblings. On the lower end of the social spectrum, some illegitimates suffered few consequences of appearing prior to their parents' wedding; many others were left to foundling homes, where available, or abandoned. In general, the fate of illegitimates served to remind legitimates how fortunate they were. On both ends of society, moreover, gender played a crucial role. Illegitimate girls were more likely to be abandoned or so neglected that they appeared significantly less often among identifiable surviving illegitimates.

THOMAS KUEHN

References and Further Reading

Bestor, Jane Fair. "Bastardy and Legitimacy in the Formation of a Regional State in Italy: The Estense Succession." *Comparative Studies in Society and History* 38 (1996): 549–585.

Brundage, James A. *Law, Sex, and Christian Society in Medieval Europe*. Chicago: University of Chicago Press, 1987.

Kuehn, Thomas. *Illegitimacy in Renaissance Florence*. Ann Arbor, Mich.: University of Michigan Press, 2002.

Laslett, Peter, Karla Oosterveen, and Richard M. Smith, eds. *Bastardy and Its Comparative History*. Cambridge, Mass.: Harvard University Press, 1980.

Leineweber, Anke. *Die rechtliche Beziehung des nichtehelichen Kindes zu seinem Erzeuger in der Geschichte des Privatrechts*. Königstein: Peter Hanstein, 1978.

McDevitt, Gilbert Joseph. *Legitimacy and Legitimation: An Historical Synopsis and Commentary*. Washington, D.C.: Catholic University of America Press, 1941.

Schimmelpfennig, Bernhard. "*Ex Fornicatione Nati*: Studies on the Position of Priests' Sons from the Twelfth to the Fourteenth Century." *Medieval and Renaissance History* 2 (1979): 1–50.

See also **Celibacy: Clerical and Priests' Concubines; Concubines; Honor and Reputation; Infants and Infanticide; Sexuality: Extramarital Sex**

IMMACULATE CONCEPTION, DOCTRINE OF

Western belief that the Virgin Mary was conceived without original sin is rooted in the conviction of Augustine of Hippo that the effects of the Fall are transmitted by contagion through sexual intercourse. This remained the predominant opinion in the West despite the argument of Anselm of Canterbury (d. 1109) that sin lay in the will, not in the body. Traditional theology attributed Jesus's sinless nature to the Virgin Birth, removing him from the transmission of original sin. Only later would the same

argument be applied to Mary. Since there was no Biblical material on Mary's conception, Latin Christians turned to apocryphal infancy gospels. These texts spread the idea that Mary's parents, Anna and Joachim, conceived her by an embrace before the Golden Gate of the Temple in Jerusalem. This later story, transmitted through the entry for the Feast of Mary's Nativity (September 8) in the *Golden Legend* of Jacobus de Voragine, became a motif in Western art, but the story is largely ignored by theologians.

Commemoration of Mary's conception on December 8 had become common by the twelfth century. England was a seat of this devotion; Eadmer of Canterbury, Anselm's biographer, wrote a book extolling Mary's excellence, including her purity, as surpassing that of any other creature and another claiming that the Virgin was created in her mother's womb by the action of the Holy Spirit and thus free of original sin. This devotion became common enough in France for Bernard of Clairvaux to rebuke the canons of Lyon for celebrating the feast of Mary's conception. Bernard regarded such an emphasis on Mary's sinless nature as detracting from Jesus's role as redeemer and limiting His uniqueness. He also regarded this feast as contrary to both reason and tradition. Bernard did argue that Mary was purified in her mother's womb. His intervention against the feast of Mary's conception did not end its celebration or defense of the belief that Mary was conceived without the stain of original sin.

The early Scholastic theologians, however, did not advance any idea of Mary's pure conception. They, including Thomas Aquinas (d. 1274) and Bonaventure (d. 1274), believed Mary was conceived with concupiscence in her soul but was cleansed in her mother's womb. They also affirmed that the Virgin lived a life free from sin. This was the predominant theological opinion until the English Franciscans William of Ware and Duns Scotus (d. 1308) advanced arguments for Mary's having been conceived without the stain of original sin. Their arguments equated what God could have done to cleanse Mary at conception with what was fitting and hence what purification must have occurred. Many later Franciscan theologians became insistent that this cleansing had indeed happened. They looked less to the *Golden Legend* or the New Testament than to Old Testament texts to support their arguments. Mary became identified with Wisdom and, more significantly, with the Bride in the Song of Songs. The reference to the Bride as "without stain" (*sine macula*) [Cant.4:7] was applied to Mary.

The Franciscan argument that Mary's conception was free from original sin evoked a hot response from many Dominicans. They argued that Saint Thomas was correct in believing Mary was conceived with the human stain of concupiscence but cleansed in Anne's womb. (Dominican devotion to Mary focused elsewhere, including on the Rosary.) Questions about Mary's conception became common in academic disputations of the later Middle Ages. This issue, however, was not limited to Scholastic debates. Confraternities honoring Mary's conception also were founded, usually under Franciscan auspices.

The Franciscans found many allies in this debate, the most important one being the University of Paris. Jean Gerson, the university's chancellor in the early fifteenth century, was among the defenders of the doctrine and the feast that celebrated it. Dominicans were expelled from the university for refusing to conform to Marian belief and practice. In 1439, after it had broken with Pope Eugenius IV (1431–1447), the Council of Basel (1431–1449) attempted to declare Mary's sinless conception a dogma of the church. This council's failure placed the Immaculists on the defensive, but a Franciscan became pope as Sixtus IV (1471–1484). He commissioned liturgical offices in honor of Mary's conception and issued decrees that made opposition to the feast and its doctrine more difficult. It was at this time that the term *Immaculate Conception* became common. Despite this development, most Dominicans remained hostile to the belief that Mary was conceived without the stain of original sin until well after 1500.

The iconography of the Immaculate Conception remained fluid during the Middle Ages. Only later was the "woman clothed with the sun" (Rev. 12:1–17) definitively identified with Mary Immaculate. Nor did musical compositions specially intended for the Feast of the Immaculate Conception become common until later. The Immaculate Conception was only defined as dogma in 1854.

THOMAS IZBICKI

References and Further Reading

Ellington, Donna Spivey. *From Sacred Body to Angelic Soul: Understanding Mary in Late Medieval and Early Modern Europe.* Washington, D.C.: Catholic University of America Press, 2001.

Graef, Hilda. *Mary: A History of Doctrine and Devotion.* Westminster, Md.: Christian Classics, 1985.

Izbicki, Thomas. "The Immaculate Conception and Ecclesiastical Politics from the Council of Basel to the Council of Trent: The Dominicans and Their Foes." *Archiv fur Reformationsgeschichte* 96 (2005): 145–170.

See also **Anne, Saint; Gerson, Jean; Holy Kinship; Jacobus de Voragine's Golden Legend; Mary, Virgin; Mary, Virgin: in Art; Scholasticism; Theology**

IMPOTENCE

Although the term *impotence* is occasionally used to characterize the inability to engage in sexual intercourse, by either men or women, it most commonly refers to male sexual incapacity. Impotence should not be confused with infertility, which refers exclusively to the inability to conceive or engender a fetus. In medieval texts, the terms *impotentia* (impotence) and *frigiditas* (frigidity) are used virtually interchangeably, irrespective of the sex of the subject. Most commonly, however, these terms refer to male sexual dysfunction.

Causes and Consequences

In men, impotence can originate from either physiological or psychogenic causes. A variety of diseases, including prostate cancer and diabetes, can result in impotence. The inability to achieve or sustain an erection can be a natural part of the aging process. As well, a man's state of mind, including stress, fear, or general mental preoccupation, can inhibit his ability to perform sexually and thereby result in temporary impotence.

Discussions of impotence figure prominently in medieval works on law, theology, and medicine, and in the literature associated with the sacraments, particularly marriage and penance. Among clerical writers, impotence was an important issue owing to their concern with the role of sexual intercourse in the formation of the marriage bond. Over the course of the twelfth century, two opposing views of marriage were debated. According to the great Bolognese canonist Gratian, sexual relations consummated the marriage, rendering it a permanent and indissoluble sacrament. In contrast, the Parisian theologian, Peter Lombard, argued that all that was required to establish the sacramental bond was the consent of the man and woman. In the last half of the twelfth century, canonists, theologians, and popes sought to reconcile these competing views and arrive at a common understanding of marriage. The final compromise stated that while the couple needed the capacity to engage in sexual relations, they did not need to have sex in order to form an indissoluble marriage. Thus, impotence was recognized to be an impediment to the very formation of the bonds of marriage.

The canonist Huguccio (d. 1210) identified three types of impotence: that caused by physical incapacity, such as disease or a malformation of the genitals; that caused by mental incapacity, such as insanity or an aversion to women; and that caused by both, such as in the case of a prepubescent child. Another method used to distinguish types of impotence was whether it were natural, such as impotence caused by illness, aging, or genital malformation, or supernatural, that is, impotence caused by *maleficium* (sorcery). The latter provided a useful explanation for psychogenic impotence, for which there was no external or identifiable cause. Impotence could also be permanent or temporary. It was possible, for example, that supernatural impotence could be temporary and that a spell could lift it or it could be counteracted by prayer and penance.

Supernatural impotence might also render a man incapable of intercourse with any woman or only with one specific woman, most often his wife or paramour. The Church taught that if the impotence extended to one woman alone, the afflicted man could marry another woman. If the impotence was judged to be permanent and extended to all women, the man was prohibited from entering into marriage. If he was already married, the union was declared null on the grounds of permanent impotence. The sexually capable woman was free to marry but the man was prohibited from doing so. If the impotent man subsequently regained sexual potency, this was taken to indicate that the earlier marriage had been annulled in error and the couple was required to resume their marriage, even if the wife had married another man after the declaration of nullity. For this reason, canonists and theologians urged couples to endure in their marriage, despite the husband's impotence; it was preferable for them to remain together, living as brother and sister.

The Childless

While much of Christian theological and canonical literature focused on minute distinctions of timing and interpretation, these were, in fact, relevant to average medieval people, given the social, political, and economic importance of engendering children, whether to inherit a kingdom or a croft. For elites, the absence of children could lead to disputed succession and even civil war. For even the poorest folk, children played a vital economic role, contributing to the household economy and providing care to elderly parents. Finally, sexual intercourse and heirs were an external sign of a man's virility; potency was an indication of power and manliness. To be impotent—or to be accused of impotence—was a disgrace that could be accompanied by a charivari or other types of public shaming.

An example of the anxieties and complexities that could result from impotence is found in the memoirs of the eleventh-century French abbot Guibert of Nogent (1053–c. 1124). He reports that his father was unable to consummate his marriage for seven years. During that period, relatives urged his mother to seek a declaration of nullity and marry someone else. Guibert reports that his father was bewitched by a jealous relative. Given that his father was able to have sexual relations with a concubine during this period, the impotence was clearly considered to be both of supernatural origins and of a specific nature. Eventually, Guibert's parents did consummate their union, but he portrays a situation that was fraught with tensions, accusations, and recriminations.

Belief in the supernatural causes of impotence endured through the Middle Ages and into the early modern period. Women were almost exclusively considered to be the agents of the spells and charms that caused impotence. The most common method was believed to be by tying knots in string, known as an *aiguillette*. By the end of the Middle Ages, witches were believed not only to render men impotent, but also to make men's penises seem to disappear. The link between female malice, impotence, and witchcraft was discussed at length in the *Malleus maleficarum* (*Hammer of Witches*), written in 1486. This work is sensationalist, but it does highlight the close alignment that was believed to exist between women, magic, and impotence.

Legal Recourse

Records from ecclesiastical courts, from as early as the thirteenth century, reveal that people did, in fact, petition the courts to have their marriages declared null on the grounds of impotence. Indeed, there are cases from across Europe that illustrate how the various theological and canonical teachings were implemented and enforced in practice. For the courts, evidence of impotence was particularly difficult to assess, especially if an unhappy couple undertook to collude in order to end an unsatisfactory union. Physicians might examine the man's genitals to ascertain that they were suitable for intercourse. Midwives or matrons would similarly examine the woman; if she were found to be a virgin, the allegation of impotence was considered to be proven. Neighbors and relatives could be asked to testify or swear that, by common repute, the man was considered to be incapable of consummating the marriage.

The usual judgment for proven cases of impotence was a declaration of nullity, the woman receiving a license to remarry, while this was prohibited to the man. There is evidence that some men did remarry as well, and consummate the second union and father children. Evidence suggests that sometimes the original union was reinstated. In other cases, the first union was confirmed to be null on the grounds of supernatural impotence vis-à-vis the first wife, and the second unions were confirmed.

One of the more controversial and problematic means the courts used to ascertain whether a man was impotent was through public proof of sexual incapacity. The man and woman were placed in a bed and, in the presence of witnesses, they were expected to attempt to have sexual intercourse. Evidence from ecclesiastical courts for this practice has been found as early as a thirteenth-century case from the diocese of York. Sometimes termed "trial by congress," some scholars have denounced this as a particularly immoral practice. It is important to bear in mind that different notions of privacy prevailed in the Middle Ages and few activities occurred in private. Birth and death were public acts attended by friends and family, and a husband and wife might well engage in sexual activity while children and servants slept nearby. Visits to brothels were social outings, with friends sharing food, drink, and prostitutes together in a chamber. Consequently, until more is understood about the everyday sexual practices of medieval people, it is not possible to assess the implications of "trial by congress," beyond noting that it did provide the courts with independent evidence of a man's sexual incapacity.

Impotence was both a social and religious issue in the Middle Ages. A man's sexual incapacity excluded him from marriage and entry into full adulthood. The inability to consummate a marriage and render the conjugal debt could make a man the subject of gossip, rumor, and public shame. Ultimately, a man could be brought before the courts and his virility could become the subject of legal proceedings. Because the ability to consummate lay at the heart of both the secular and religious purposes of marriage, impotence was a topic that received serious attention and practical analysis. It also opened a man to public ridicule and shame, as revealed in the *fabliaux* and other genres of popular literature.

JACQUELINE MURRAY

References and Further Reading

Brundage, James A. "The Problem of Impotence." In *Sexual Practices and the Medieval Church*, edited by James A. Brundage and Vern L. Bullough. Buffalo: Prometheus Books, 1982, pp. 135–140.

———. "Impotence, Frigidity and Marital Nullity in the Decretists and the Early Decretalists." In *Proceedings of the 7th International Congress of Medieval Canon Law*, edited by Peter Linehan. Vatican City, 1988, pp. 407–423.

Reprinted in *Sex, Law and Marriage in the Middle Ages*, edited by James A. Brundage. London: Variorum, 1993, Article 10.

Darmon, Pierre. *Le Tribunal de l'Impuissance*. Paris: Seuil, 1979. Translated by Paul Keegan as *Trial by Impotence: Virility and Marriage in Pre-Revolutionary France*. London: Chatto & Windus, 1985.

Guibert of Nogent. *A Monk's Confession: The Memoirs of Guibert of Nogent*, translated by Paul J. Archambault. University Park, Pa.: Pennsylvania State University Press, 1996.

Jacquart, Danielle, and Claude Thomasset. *Sexuality and Medicine in the Middle Ages*, translated by Matthew Adamson. Princeton: Princeton University Press, 1988.

Kramer, Heinrich, and James Sprenger. *Malleus Maleficarum: The Classic Study of Witchcraft*, translated by Montague Summers. 1928. Reprint, London: Bracken Books, 1996.

Le Roy Ladurie, Emmanuel. "The Aiguillette: Castration by Magic." In *The Mind and Method of the Historian*, translated by Siân Reynolds and Ben Reynolds. Chicago: University of Chicago Press, 1981, pp. 84–96.

Murray, Jacqueline. "On the Origins and Role of 'Wise Women' in Causes for Annulment on the Grounds of Male Impotence." *Journal of Medieval History* 16 (1990): 235–249.

Stephens, Walter. "Witches Who Steal Penises: Impotence and Illusion in *Malleus maleficarum*." *Journal of Medieval and Early Modern Studies* 28.3 (1998): 495–529.

See also **Charivari; Conjugal Debt; Divorce and Separation; Fabliau; Guibert of Nogent's Mother; Honor and Reputation; Infertility; Law, Canon; Magic and Charms; Marriage, Christian; Marriage, Impediments to; Midwives; Records, Ecclesiastical; Remarriage; Sexuality: Sex in Marriage; Witches**

INCEST

Both historical and literary sources indicate that there was great concern about incest in the Middle Ages. The church was anxious not only to save souls but also to exercise control over the marriages of the laity; violence against women and child abuse, however, were not significant issues. Incest was defined much more broadly than it is today, and the definitions changed considerably over the course of a thousand years. Medieval literature is mostly concerned with incest within the nuclear family; historical sources are much more concerned with the extended family.

Church Views

From Augustine (354–430) on, Christian theologians agreed that the incest taboo was a social construction for the benefit of humankind. By the eleventh century it covered seven degrees of consanguinity (relationship by blood) and four degrees of affinity (relationship by marriage or illicit sex). Affinity included all in-laws, and was created by any sexual relationship, however brief. Since the spiritual family was considered as important as the biological family, another taboo area was spiritual incest. This included sexual relations between godparent and godchild, and their immediate families; between a priest and his parishioners; between a lay man and a nun; and between two ecclesiastics.

Effectively marriage was forbidden between two persons related in any way; for many people it must have been almost impossible to avoid breaking the law. The pope could give dispensations, and kings and nobles exploited the rules to make and break marriages for both political and personal reasons, including to contract desirable marriage alliances, to get rid of barren wives, and to legitimize mistresses. Some ecclesiastics took the view that incestuous marriages of long standing should be tolerated if they had been contracted in ignorance, and if the spouses were not too closely related. At the Fourth Lateran Council of 1215 the forbidden degrees were reduced, on the grounds of hardship, to four degrees of consanguinity and one degree of affinity.

The rationale for the medieval form of the taboo is much debated by modern scholars. One factor is the statement in Genesis 2:24 that husband and wife become one flesh, which seems to have been a justification for the wide range of prohibited degrees of relationship through both consanguinity and affinity. Other explanations proposed by modern scholars include the projected increase in legacies to the church when marriage partners are hard to find (Goody), and a desire to reduce household rivalries over marriageable women (Herlihy). The consequences of inbreeding are rarely mentioned in medieval sources.

Documentary Evidence

It is very difficult to estimate rates and instances of incest in the Middle Ages. Given the lack of birth control, the frequent pregnancies of married women, shared beds, and the lack of privacy in medieval bedrooms, it seems very likely that nuclear family incest was as common as it is in our own society. It rarely appears in court records, but this is hardly surprising in a patriarchal society. Few young women would have dared to bring charges against an abusive father or brother, and families would have been anxious to avoid scandal and dishonour. There are records of cases involving more distant relatives such as cousins, godparents, in-laws, or affines through intercourse, and a few high-profile cases of uncles and nieces,

and even siblings. There is almost no reference to incest as child abuse; in literary texts female victims of incest are usually old enough to marry and bear children, and sons are old enough to impregnate their mothers.

Polemical accusations of incest were often made against kings and even popes, against religious minorities and heretics (e.g., the early Christians, the Albigensians), and against ethnic groups who had been or were about to be invaded and conquered (e.g., the Irish and Welsh). But charges of incest were not confined to marginal or unpopular rulers or groups; both Charlemagne and Arthur were said to have slept with their sisters, and Judas with his mother. Confessors' manuals include questions (always phrased for male confessants) about incest and the precise relationship of the sinners. It is uncertain whether these manuals and the collections of penances known as penitentials can be taken as representative of actual medieval sexual behaviour. For instance, it is surprising that there is almost no reference to father–daughter or brother–sister incest in the penitentials, since these might be expected to be among the most common instances (there is some evidence for them in legal cases of infanticide).

Literary Sources

The lawcodes, manuals, and penitentials express no particular concern for women's vulnerability as victims of incest. In exemplary literature, where incest stories are used to emphasise the dangers of dying unconfessed and the power of contrition and grace, mothers are sometimes presented as complicit or responsible. A popular exemplary theme is the widowed mother who shares a bed with her teenage son until she becomes pregnant by him, and in some versions kills their baby. The story focuses entirely on her; usually she confesses and dies saved, sometimes through the intercession of the Virgin. In the context of medieval misogyny, such stories may not seem surprising. But these knowingly incestuous mothers were useful examples because they transcend their sinful carnality through confession and repentance. Incestuous fathers usually die violently and without contrition or confession, such as Antiochus in the popular story of Apollonius of Tyre, which widely translated and adapted. (Gower included it in his *Confessio Amantis,* and Shakespeare dramatized it as *Pericles.*)

In both religious and secular literature, the most frequent form of incest is parent–child, perhaps because it is the most shocking and thus the most useful for didactic purposes. Variations on the Oedipus plot are found both in exemplary texts and in romance. In exemplary versions the moral is usually that the Christian should resist despair and trust in the power of contrition and divine grace. Sometimes the incestuous son ends up as a pope or a saint, as in the legend of Pope Gregory; sometimes his mother has already knowingly committed incest with her father or brother, so that the incest motif is doubled. Even so, it is the son rather than the mother who is glorified in the spiritually happy ending. In romance, mother–son incest is usually averted at the last moment, and the male protagonist becomes a successful and happily married knight; less attention is paid to the mother.

The heroine is very much the centre of the plot, however, in the popular Flight from the Incestuous Father group of stories, such as the old French *Mane Kine* and the Middle English *Emaré*, in which the threat of incest is the crucial catalyst for the adventures of the heroine. She is exiled, or flees, after rebuffing the unwelcome advances of her widowed father. After many ordeals and adventures, including false accusations and sometimes the loss of one or both hands, she is reunited with her husband, and sometimes with her repentant father too. In these stories the focus is on the victim rather than the villain, but not on her psychological state or on the long-term effect of incest on her subsequent life as a wife and mother. The moral is usually the need for faith, rather than the avoidance of incest. In Christian terms, suffering can be seen as positive, and as a test of virtue; this may account for the popularity of these stories of persecuted daughters.

In some exemplary stories incest is glossed as original sin, so it is paradoxical that throughout the Middle Ages the Virgin Mary was widely described as the daughter of her own son, Christ, and thus the mother of her own father. She is the one exception to the taboo. In allegorical texts, incestuous classical heroines may be interpreted in surprisingly positive and Christian ways; in the *Ovide Moralisé*, Myrrha, who in Ovid's *Metamorphoses* seduced her own father and was turned into a myrrh tree, is understood as a type of the virgin, the perfect woman. Some medieval writers were able to imagine genuine romantic love between close relations, and in literature the children of incest are often beautiful and heroic. But incest was nevertheless an especially shocking form of lust, and a deadly sin.

ELIZABETH ARCHIBALD

References and Further Reading

Archibald, Elizabeth. *Incest and the Medieval Imagination.* Oxford: Clarendon Press, 2001.

Duby, Georges. *The Knight, the Priest and the Lady: the Making of Marriage in Medieval France*, translated by Barbara Bray. London: Allen Lane, 1984.

Goody, Jack. *The Development of the Family and Marriage in Europe.* Cambridge: Cambridge University Press, 1983.

Herlihy, David. *Medieval Households.* Cambridge, Mass.: Harvard University Press, 1985.

Neel, Carol, ed. *Medieval Families: Perspectives on Marriage, Household, and Children.* Medieval Academy Reprints for Teaching, 40. Toronto: University of Toronto Press, 2004.

Rank, Otto. *The Incest Theme in Literature and Legend*, translated by Gregory C. Richter. Baltimore: The Johns Hopkins University Press, 1992.

Tubach, F. *Index Exemplorum: A Handbook of Medieval Religious Tales.* FF Communications, 204. Helsinki: Suomalainen Tiedeakatemia, 1969.

See also **Domestic Abuse; Family; Godparents; Kinship; Marriage, Christian; Marriage, Impediments to; Misogyny; Mythology, Medieval Reception of; Patriarchy and Patrilineage; Rape and Raptus; Remarriage; Sexuality: Extramarital Sex; Sexuality, Regulation of**

INFANTS AND INFANTICIDE

Oddly, the history of medieval infancy is best known for an argument that the very category of infancy did not exist in the Middle Ages. The argument, attributed to the early modernist Philippe Ariès, has so permeated the scholarly and popular understanding of the subject that most medievalists devote inordinate amounts of time to refuting the argument (Ariès, chapter 2; Shahar, introduction). The fact that Ariès never emphatically made such claims about the existence of a medieval category of infancy did not dissuade advocates or detractors of the theory from voluminous debate over the issue.

Medieval Definitions

In discussions of the "ages of man" found in medical and moral texts from at least the seventh-century writer Isidore of Seville onward, the category of *infantia* was generally identified as distinct from *pueritia* or childhood. Some writers conflated the two, but most defined infancy as extending from birth to the age of seven. Regardless of the boundary between infancy and what followed it, many writers followed Isidore in his (unusually correct) assertion that the word *infant* derived etymologically from the pre-verbal status of the infant (*qui fari non potest*, "one who cannot speak").

Medical writings provide some of the most extensive material on medieval views of infancy. From the eleventh century onward, writings on gynecology and more general medical compendia give considerable attention to the development of the fetus, birth, and neonatal care. We encounter a strong concern for the safety of mother and child before and during birth. The processes of bathing, shaping, swaddling, teething, and especially feeding the infant receive considerable attention and were all generally performed by women, whether the midwife, the mother, or the wet nurse. In fact, the wet nurse is singled out for particular attention, both in her selection and in her regimen.

Beyond medical writings, a wide variety of sources tell us much about the treatment of infants. The aristocratic practice of hiring a wet nurse was common, despite the advice found in medical and moral treatises. (The sources on noble children are strongest in England.) The early years of every noble's life were associated with the care of women, as attested to by many sources from Guibert de Nogent's memoirs to the life of Christina of Markyate or, in an extreme example, the tales of Perceval by Chrétien de Troyes and Wolfram von Eschenbach.

While infancy in the highest levels of society has long been studied, only fairly recently has the diligent research of social historians such as Hanawalt and Finucane opened up the world of the peasantry and their attitudes toward infancy. Through coroners' inquests and miracle stories, the perils and emotions surrounding poor infants are readily apparent: accidents or neglect of an infant lead either to death and sadness, or to a miraculous cure and rejoicing.

Death rates for medieval infants are assumed to have been very high, as many as a third of all births (the statistics are sketchy at best). While accidents, malnutrition, and other similar factors may explain most of the deaths, medieval sources also provide some scattered evidence of infanticide. Boswell has argued that medieval Christianity generally provided a humane alternative to the classical abandonment or killing of unwanted children: the offering of the child to the church as an oblate. While many infants were offered publicly to the monastery, others were unceremoniously and surreptitiously left for the monastic community to find, as Marie de France's *La Fresne* illustrates. Some late medieval Italian institutions for foundlings had revolving hatches that permitted the mother to retain anonymity while leaving a child to be raised by the religious community. Far more disturbing to religious authorities was the murder of infants. Penitential literature of the early Middle Ages burdens the infanticidal parent, most often identified as the mother, with heavy penances. Intriguingly, many penitentials reduce the penance if the mother is too poor to support the child. Infanticide was apparently not common, and was roundly condemned as an abomination in the moral, legal, and theological sources.

Symbolism of the Infant

Medieval Christian Europe inherited a number of powerful and positive attributes associated with the infant. Most importantly, interest in the infant Jesus began to expand from the twelfth century onward, as figures such as Aelred of Rievaulx and the lesser-known Konrad von Fußesbrunnen (*Die Kindheit Jesu*) attest. A renewed interest in other Biblical and apocryphal passages mentioning infants, from the Massacre of the Innocents to Jesus's multiple blessings of infancy, appears in theological texts from the same period onward, as well as in saints' lives and antiheresy writings. The baby Jesus became an omnipresent artistic subject, and the Slaughter of the Innocents was depicted with increasing frequency. The soul was often personified and depicted as an infant, and medieval mystics and monastics metaphorically imagined themselves as infants suckling at the breast of Mary and, more strikingly, Jesus or abbot. From the mouths of babes and nurslings, the central and later Middle Ages found a powerful metaphor and model for innocence and purity.

WILLIAM F. MACLEHOSE

References and Further Reading

Alexandre-Bidon, Danièle, and Didier Lett. *Les Enfants au Moyen Age, Ve – XVe siècles*. Paris: Hachette, 1997.

Ariès, Philippe. *Centuries of Childhood: A Social History of Family Life*, translated by Robert Baldick. New York: Vintage Books, 1962.

Baschet, Jérome *Le sein du père: Abraham et la paternité dans l'Occident médiéval*. Paris, 2000.

Boswell, John E. *The Kindness of Strangers: The Abandonment of Children in Western Europe from the Late Antiquity to the Renaissance*. New York: Pantheon Books, 1988.

Bynum, Caroline Walker. *Jesus as Mother: Studies in the Spirituality of the High Middle Ages*. Berkeley, 1982.

Demaitre, Luke. "The Idea of Childhood and Childcare in Medical Writings of the Middle Ages." *Journal of Psychohistory* 4 (1976): 461–490.

Finucane, Ronald C. *The Rescue of the Innocents: Endangered Children in Medieval Miracles*. New York: St. Martin's Press, 1997.

Giallongo, Angela. *Il bambino medievale*. Bari: Edizioni Dedalo, 1990/1997.

Goodich, Michael. "Bartholomaeus Anglicus on Child-Rearing." *History of Childhood Quarterly* 3 (1975): 75–84.

Hanawalt, Barbara A. *The Ties That Bound: Peasant Families in Medieval England*. Oxford: Oxford University Press, 1986.

MacLehose, William F. *A Tender Age: Cultural Anxieties Over the Child in the Twelfth and Thirteenth Centuries.* New York: Columbia University Press, forthcoming.

McLaughlin, Mary Martin. "Survivors and Surrogates: Children and Parents from the Ninth to the Thirteenth Centuries." In *The History of Childhood*, edited by Lloyd deMause. New York: Psychohistory Press, 1974, pp. 101–182.

Orme, Nicholas. *Medieval Children.* New Haven, Conn.: Yale University Press, 2001.

Sears, Elizabeth. *The Ages of Man: Medieval Interpretations of the Life Cycle.* Princeton, N.J.: Princeton University Press, 1986.

Shahar, Shulamith. *Childhood in the Middle Ages.* London: Routledge Press, 1990.

See also **Abortion; Body in Literature and Religion; Breastfeeding and Wet-Nursing; Crime and Criminals; Demography; Gynecology; Oblates and Oblation; Penitentials and Pastoral Manuals; Pregnancy and Childbirth: Christian Women; Pregnancy and Childbirth: Jewish Women**

INFERTILITY

Infertility (the inability of a man and woman to produce offspring together) may have been a private matter for some people, a personal disappointment. For many others it was a very public disgrace and a serious concern provoking the attention of kin, medical practitioners, and ecclesiastical as well as civil law. Although infertility has only recently received more than passing attention from social scientists, it is clear that it is a major issue for most human populations throughout the world. It is also becoming clear that, although both men and women can be infertile, the differential social impact of infertility on women's social status is often significant.

From humble women all the way up to the queens, noblewomen, and urban elites of Europe, both women and their families often aggressively sought intervention in overcoming infertility from saints and magic, wise women, and male physicians. In the late 1150s or early 1160s, a noblewoman from Burgundy journeyed to see Hildegard of Bingen bearing a letter from five Cistercian abbots begging the German abbess to intercede with God and allow this woman to conceive again (Letters LXX and LXXR). A fourteenth-century Christian male practitioner in southern France was convicted of fraud and necromancy for having promised (but failed) to cure women's infertility by magical means while, around the same time, a Jewish physician was writing a detailed diagnosis and therapy for his infertile brother-in-law and his sister.

In both Jewish and Muslim communities, infertility was considered legitimate grounds for dissolving a marriage. For Christians, at least after the ninth century, only impotence (the inability of the male to sustain an erection) or certain other defects of the sexual organs (such as obstruction of the vagina or hermaphroditism) could be grounds for annulment since in such cases the defective spouse was incapable of fulfilling the "conjugal debt" (engagement in sexual intercourse upon demand). Infertility may thus have been somewhat less threatening to Christian women's social status, but the prevalence of quests for offspring in miracle stories suggests that it was no less a concern.

From a modern perspective, the causes of infertility were no doubt as varied as they are today. Among women generally in southern Europe, and among upper-class women in northern Europe, early marriage and sexual activity may have produced both psychic barriers and physical defects (whether due to trauma in childbirth or infection) that affected later fertility. Nutritional levels were probably often a factor, as perhaps were sexually transmitted diseases; medical writers speak of a disease they call the "white flowers," a vaginal discharge, a full century before syphilis seems to have hit Europe at the end of the fifteenth century. Physiognomy (the determination of character from a person's physical features) was sometimes employed to assess potential fertility before marriage. Biblical examples of infertility and its long-awaited alleviation formed the focus of prayers and religious interventions, which were likewise used to counteract infertility caused by magic. Traditional cultural practices, like the use of Sheela na gigs, were also inspired by fertility concerns. Even quite orthodox works of art may have been employed as apotropaic means to avert or reverse infertility.

Medical views about the causes of infertility were similar in the cultural traditions of Jews, Muslims, and Christians. An Arabic work on pregnancy was composed in Muslim Spain in the tenth century and the works of other Arabic writers like Avicenna (Ibn Sina) would become influential in Europe in the thirteenth century. Nevertheless, the main European medical traditions on infertility seem to have begun independently. The Christian physician Richard the Englishman, writing in the late twelfth or early thirteenth century, describes how all the medical powers of the Salernitan physicians had been called on to treat the sterility of the Queen of Sicily. He was probably referring to Queen Joanna (d. 1198), daughter of Eleanor of Aquitaine and Henry II of England, who married William II of Sicily at age eleven or twelve and then had to suffer the ignominy of sterility for twelve years. Richard considered medical treatment of infertility futile, but his pessimism was not universally shared. Beginning around the year 1100, writers at Salerno had already begun to incorporate chapters on infertility into their general medical compendia and the first specialized treatise on infertility was written there in the late twelfth century. No less than seven such works came out of the medical school of Montpellier in the fourteenth century. In 1444, a physician from Toulouse composed a work aiding fertility and birth for Count Gaston IV of Foix, and in 1488 a Parisian physician composed a special work for Anne of Beaujeu (1460–1522), elder sister of Charles VI of France. Even if from our perspective few of these recommendations could have significantly enhanced the chances of conception, they all show the depth of concern that reproductive disruptions generated among women and men in medieval societies.

MONICA GREEN

References and Further Reading:

'Arib ibn Sa'id. *Le Livre de la génération du foetus et le traitement des femmes enceintes et des nouveau-nés*, edited and translated by Henri Jahier and Nourredine Abdelkader. Algiers: Librairie Ferraris, 1956; Arabic text with French translation.

Barkaï, Ron, ed. and trans. *A History of Jewish Gynaecological Texts in the Middle Ages*. Leiden: Brill, 1998.

Baumgarten, Elisheva. *Mothers and Children: Jewish Family Life in Medieval Europe*. Princeton, N.J.: Princeton University Press, 2004.

Conde Parrado, Pedro, Enrique Montero Cartelle, and M.ª Cruz Herrero Ingelmo, eds. *Tractatus de conceptu; Tractatus de sterilitate mulierum*. Lingüística y filología, 37. Valladolid: Universidad de Valladolid, 1999.

Constantine the African (attributed). "Impotence as a Result of Witchcraft," translated by Henry Sigerist. In *Henry E. Sigerist on the History of Medicine*, edited by Felix Marti-Ibañez. New York: MD Publications, 1960, pp. 146–152.

Finucane, Ronald C. *The Rescue of the Innocents: Endangered Children in Medieval Miracles*. New York: St. Martin's Press, 1997.

Green, Monica H., ed. and trans. *The 'Trotula': A Medieval Compendium of Women's Medicine*. Philadelphia: University of Pennsylvania Press, 2001.

Inhorn, Marcia C., and Frank van Balen, eds. *Infertility Around the Globe: New Thinking on Childlessness, Gender, and Reproductive Technologies*. Berkeley: University of California Press, 2002.

Jolly, Penny Howell. "Jan van Eyck's Italian Pilgrimage: A Miraculous Florentine 'Annunciation' and the Ghent Altarpiece." *Zeitschrift für Kunstgeschichte* 61.3 (1998): 369–394.

El libro de la generación del feto, el tratamiento de las mujeres embarazadas y de los recien nacidos de 'Arib ibn Sa'id (Tratado de ostetricia y pediatria hispano árabe del siglo X), edited by Antonio Arjona Castro. Cordoba: Publicacions de la excma. diputacion provincial, 1983; Spanish translation.

Makowski, Elizabeth M. "The Conjugal Debt and Medieval Canon Law." *Journal of Medieval History* 3 (1977): 99–114.

Montero Cartelle, Enrique, ed. *Tractatus de sterilitate: Anónimo de Montpellier (s. XIV). Attribuido a A. de*

Vilanova, R. de Moleris y J. de Turre. Lingüística y Filología, 16. Valladolid: Universidad de Valladolid and Caja Salamanca y Soria, 1993.

Montero Cartelle, Enrique, and María Cruz Herrero Ingelmo. "Las *Interrogaciones in cura sterilitatis* en el marco de la literatura médica medieval." *Faventia* 25.2 (2003): 85–97.

Musacchio, Jacqueline Marie. *The Art and Ritual of Childbirth in Renaissance Italy*. New Haven and London: Yale University Press, 1999.

Park, Katharine. "Medicine and Magic: The Healing Arts." In *Gender and Society in Renaissance Italy*, edited by Judith C. Brown and Robert C. Davis. London: Longman, 1998, pp. 129–149.

Savonarola, Giovanni Michele. *Il trattato ginecologico-pediatrico in volgare 'Ad mulieres ferrarienses de regimine pregnantium et noviter natorum usque ad septennium,'* edited by Luigi Belloni. Milan: Società Italiana di ostetricia e ginecologia, 1952.

Shatzmiller, Joseph, and Rodrigue Lavoie. "Médecine et gynécologie au moyen-âge: un exemple provençal." *Razo: Cahiers du Centre d'Études Médiévales de Nice* 4 (1984): 133–143.

See also **Abortion; Conjugal Debt; Contraception; Demography; Divorce and Separation; Gynecology; Hermaphrodites; Hildegard of Bingen; Law; Magic and Charms; Menstruation; Miracles and Miracle Collections; Pregnancy and Childbirth: Christian Women; Pregnancy and Childbirth: Jewish Women; Sheela Na Gigs; Trota of Salerno**

INHERITANCE

Inheritance was the most important form of succession to social position and property in the Middle Ages. Most manorial, feudal, and urban property passed through people's hands according to norms of inheritance. These norms were thus crucial in the reproduction of social order and shaped women's place in that order. Rules of inheritance existed not for the sake of the deceased but for the living, both the heirs and those around them. It is important to remember that people inherited not just real property or even titles. They inherited legal status, rights and obligations, and debts and credits.

These rules came from a variety of sources, notably from Roman law and Germanic customs, but these were further elaborated through legislation and learned jurisprudence. The law of inheritance that developed in Italy on the basis of Roman civil law, with additions from Lombard and canon law, differed profoundly from the inheritance rules developed within the common law of England, or even simply from what jurists knew as feudal law. One indicator of the differences among inheritance rules was the degree to which written testaments were available to modify and adapt the general rules of intestate succession to fit individual preferences, perceptions, and interests. Nor should inheritance be taken as solely tied to the moment of death. Different points in the domestic developmental cycle allowed for the intergenerational transmission of property. An important example is the degree to which a woman's dowry was considered in statutory law and in social practice in Italy and southern France as her portion of the patrimony of her natal family. Dowered women were excluded by legislation and custom from inheriting from their fathers, brothers, or other close male agnates, if such males survived to inherit.

Testate and Intestate

Roman law devised a large and complex body of rules regarding inheritance, much of it revolving around the testament. Male property owners, and increasingly females too, enjoyed broad powers to dispose of their property as they wished, provided a portion was reserved for direct heirs (children generally). The Christian Church encouraged the testament in practice throughout Europe, as it was a singular device for channeling property to ecclesiastical institutions. Beyond a testament, property passed by a prescribed set of rules of intestate succession according to degree of consanguinity to the deceased, with preference to agnates (those related on the father's or male side).

Germanic inheritance systems originally did not admit the testament. All inheritance was intestate. Germanic fathers had no control over property from beyond the grave, as Roman fathers might, and Germanic heirs had no option to refuse an inheritance, as Romans did, a right called *repudiatio*. Germanic schemes of devolution also tended to advantage sons over daughters, whereas late Roman rules provided for equal division per capita among brothers and sisters. However, Germanic inheritance *per stirpes* (by line) also meant that, for example, a daughter with no brothers would inherit from her father in preference to his brother (her uncle). Some Germanic inheritance customs, such as those of the Lombards, drew a distinction between inherited property and acquired goods. Inherited property was expected to pass within the lineage; acquired property could be more freely disposed of after death. From this basis, when wills were introduced into English inheritance practices in the Middle Ages, they could be used only to dispose of chattels, not land. In England wills functioned not to pass property within the family but to endow outsiders, such as the church, or to provide for younger children where impartibility was otherwise the norm.

Testaments held the potential to advantage women's property rights in comparison to intestate rules. In Florence, for example, well-to-do testators bequeathed property to their wives (otherwise excluded in intestacy, or the lack of a legal will, of husbands) to encourage them to remain as widows and raise the couple's children. In England and northern France, widows' dower rights provided the same result without recourse to a will, so there wills were used at times to take away from those rights. The bias toward agnation (*favor agnationis*) was highly marked in southern Europe, to the point that relations of consanguinity traced through women were essentially expunged from genealogical memories and from inheritance rights.

Where and when lineage mattered most in inheritance (in southern Europe, among the nobility, and increasingly toward the end of the Middle Ages everywhere), the property brought to a marriage by husband and wife remained separate funds on which no conjugal rights were necessarily recognized. Widows did not have ownership or even authority over the conjugal estate, nor did husbands have freedom to dispose of marital property as they wished. Conversely, where the conjugal unit was at the heart of legal concerns, surviving spouses had succession rights, as was the case in the Picard–Walloon regions of northern France and Belgium. There wills were used to get around such inheritance customs and privileges, such as the claims of agnatic lineage in the later Middle Ages.

Partible and Impartible

Roman and Germanic inheritance rules were based on partibility—equal division of the property among all those of the same degree of relationship to the deceased. The disadvantage of such a scheme, especially with the potential morcelization of land holdings over generations, was apparent. However, it also responded to deeply rooted sentiments in favor of equality among siblings.

Impartibility—directing all or the greater part of an estate to one heir, most frequently in male primogeniture—made sense to kings, feudal lords, and peasants alike and became more common, mainly in northern Europe, after the eleventh century. Continuity of a productive holding over generations was possible, although problems were bound to arise in providing for younger children. In contrast, partibility did not necessarily lead to fragmentation of holdings. Co-heirs could continue to hold their property in common, as seen with the feudal nobles of the

Mâconnais and with patrician families in a number of Italian cities. A sense of kinship and lineage continuity, as well as economic self-interest, could discipline individual ownership rights.

Conscious strategies of heirship, taking advantage of testamentary devices such as the substitution of heirs of second and third instance after the initial heir, allowed Italian, Spanish, and southern French elites to construct a form of impartibility in the face of prevailing rules and sentiments favoring partibility. In these schemes women's inheritance could be endlessly postponed in favor of male agnates of even distant degrees of relationship. Such practices, however, did not begin to become widespread until toward the end of the fifteenth century. Prior to that point, depending on local rules of intestacy, women stood to inherit with reasonable frequency in the absence of close male heirs.

By and large, however, women in Roman law areas were less likely to be heiresses than their English counterparts, as legislation and testaments alike tended to direct inheritances to other male agnates in preference to daughters or sisters. These women usually had dowries, however, and they could direct the flow of some or all of the dowry by means of a testament.

Certainly a substantial percentage of instances did not fit the simple functional ideal by which property would pass to one son (minus dowry or other provision for a married daughter). Wills, gifts, and other legal options provided flexibility to deal with potential problems. But the effects of such devices were not predictable; norms do not unequivocally describe the transmission of property, especially against conflicts and lawsuits that erupted constantly and contributed to the further elaboration of legal rules. These included claims advanced by or through women. Nor was there any clear correspondence between forms of inheritance and forms of kinship or domestic units.

THOMAS KUEHN

References and Further Reading

Carlier, Myriam, and Tim Soens, eds. *The Household in Late Medieval Cities: Italy and Northwestern Europe Compared.* Leuven: Garant, 2001.

Cohn, Samuel K., Jr. *Death and Property in Siena, 1205–1800: Strategies for the Afterlife.* Baltimore: The Johns Hopkins University Press, 1988.

Goody, Jack. *The Development of the Family and Marriage in Europe.* Cambridge: Cambridge University Press, 1983.

Goody, Jack, Joan Thirsk, and E. P. Thompson, eds. *Family and Inheritance: Rural Society in Western Europe, 1200–1800.* Cambridge: Cambridge University Press, 1976.

Herlihy, David. *Medieval Households.* Cambridge, Mass.: Harvard University Press, 1985.

Howell, Martha C. *The Marriage Exchange: Property, Social Place, and Gender in Cities of the Low Countries, 1300–1550.* Chicago: University of Chicago Press, 1998.

Klapisch-Zuber, Christiane. *Women, Family, and Ritual in Renaissance Italy*, translated by Lydia Cochrane. Chicago: University of Chicago Press, 1985.

Spring, Eileen. *Law, Land, and Family: Aristocratic Inheritance in England, 1300 to 1800.* Chapel Hill and London: University of North Carolina Press, 1993.

See also **Dowry and Other Marriage Gifts; Family (Earlier Middle Ages); Family (Later Middle Ages); Gender Ideologies; Heiresses; Kinship; Law, Customary: French; Law, German; Patriarchy and Patrilineage; Wills**

INTERCESSION

In the ancient and medieval worlds, it was often difficult for ordinary people to get access to powerful figures whom they believed could help solve their problems. One way in which they could sometimes get this access was through the help of intermediate figures, people who were more powerful than the person needing assistance, but not as powerful and remote as the one who held the power and could actually solve the problem. If the intermediate figure, or intercessor, had some means of influence over the powerful figure, so much the better for the petitioner.

In ancient Roman society, political intercession was institutionalized in the form of the "patron–client" relationship. Men who wanted to hold political office would gain influence with the populace by doing favors for them, and they were rewarded by the votes of those whom they had helped. Having a large crowd of clients meant that one was a successful patron, and this perceived success attracted more clients, and thus more votes. But access to powerful figures could also be gained in less formal ways. In Homer's *Odyssey*, Odysseus tells his shipwrecked crew members, who have washed ashore on an island, that he knows that if he approaches the female relatives of the island's king, explains their predicament, and gains the women's sympathy, they will persuade the king to help the unfortunate party.

In Christian society, ordinary believers began to ask others to pray for them, believing that intercessory prayer would strengthen their petitions. Martyred Christians were believed to go directly to Heaven, where in the presence of God their aid could be invoked to persuade God to help the community of believers on earth. In the high medieval period, the most powerful of these heavenly intercessors became the Virgin Mary, mother of Christ and Queen of Heaven.

Earthly as well as heavenly queens were often recognized as having power over their royal spouses. In many cases, a royal woman's success at court was dependent upon maintaining the perception that she had influence over her husband's actions. Some courts and court rituals even featured staged acts of intercession, where the queen would approach the king publicly to ask for some previously agreed upon action. At other times, queens would act on their own at the request of a petitioner. Studies of surviving petitions for the queen's intercession have shown that both nobles and commoners were aware of her potential influence over the king and that they were eager for her help. Queens were sometimes financially rewarded for successful acts of intercession. Churchmen wrote to them, urging that they use their powers of intercession only in positive ways. These churchmen often drew on the examples of Mary or the Old Testament's Esther as examples of women who used their influence over men in a proper manner.

It was not just queens who were seen to have some sway over their spouses. Churchmen also recognized that ordinary wives could influence their husbands. In his manual for confessors, the thirteenth-century theologian Thomas of Chobham argued that women should use persuasion, feminine wiles, and even deception in pursuit of holy purposes. He admitted that "no priest is able to soften the heart of a man the way his wife can" and urged that women always think of themselves as "preachers" to their husbands.

There is no doubt that medieval women practiced intercessory behaviors on a regular basis. Some women became very skilled at using intercession to their own gain and advantage. Scholars, however, have pointed out that the prevalence of the "woman as intercessor" motif in medieval writings only underscores their exclusion from the normal circles of power. In medieval intercession narratives, the woman often appears unexpectedly in a place where she would normally not be expected to be and her behavior is always deferential to the real source of power, a male figure. Women are often shown as able to modify or correct their husbands' decisions in extraordinary ways, but not able to participate in the original decisions. Further, narratives and advice from clerical writers about women's intercession became much more prominent in the later Middle Ages, when women were less likely to be regularly present at court and other centers of decision making, than they had been in the earlier medieval period. It appears, then, that female intercession in the medieval period was often an adaptive behavior practiced by women who were increasingly isolated, either within the family or in royal or noble courts, from centers of power and decision making.

LOIS L. HUNEYCUTT

References and Further Reading

Farmer, Sharon. "Persuasive Voices: Clerical Images of Medieval Wives." *Speculum* 61.3 (1986): 517–543.

Huneycutt, Lois. "Intercession and the High Medieval Queen: The Esther Topos." In *Power of the Weak: Studies on Medieval Women*, edited by Jennifer Carpenter and Sally Beth MacLean. Urbana, Ill.: University of Illinois Press, 1995, pp. 126–146.

Parsons, John Carmi. "The Queen's Intercession in Thirteenth-Century England." In *Power of the Weak: Studies on Medieval Women*, edited by Jennifer Carpenter and Sally-Beth MacLean. Urbana, Ill.: University of Illinois Press, 1995, pp. 147–177.

Strohm, Paul. "Queens as Intercessors." In *Hochon's Arrow: The Social Imagination of Fourteenth-Century Texts*. Princeton: Princeton University Press, 1992, pp. 95–119.

See also **Diplomacy and Reconciliation; Mary, Virgin; Petitions; Queens and Empresses: The West**

INVESTMENT AND CREDIT

Medieval notarial registers, charters, court rolls, and other medieval records are filled with evidence of women making investment and credit transactions. Although women's investments and loans were fewer and smaller on average than those made by men, they were a regular part of the everyday medieval economy. The level and frequency of women providing funds for capital formation or commercial enterprises and women offering or receiving consumption loans varied considerably due to legal, economic, and social factors.

Female moneylenders and pawnbrokers, especially Jewish women, served the domestic market by offering small, short-term consumer loans. Often lending to other women, they supplied emergency capital to meet household needs, creating what William Chester Jordan describes as networks of sociability. Although nuns or wealthy widows might offer loans as an act of charity, female moneylenders normally charged interest on these small, short-term extensions of credit. This routine small-scale lending between women was so commonplace that it generally went unimpeded by social controls established for loftier transactions.

In fourteenth-century Paris, the widowed Jewish pawnbroker Précieuse made a series of very large and secret short-term domestic consumption loans to the powerful Jean, duc de Berri. At the common level, female pawnbrokers regularly made quick consumer loans to women and men who could offer collateral. Resentment created by perceptions of social imbalance produced tensions and violence within this network of sociability.

Women were generally attracted to stable investment opportunities that promised financial security in old age, such as real estate or annuities. In return for an endowment, some female monastic houses offered female investors a financial package (called a *corrody*) that included lodging, an annuity, and death benefits. Women also secured term or life annuities from cities and towns by purchasing municipal bonds.

By the twelfth century, the Commercial Revolution had opened up new investment opportunities for urban women, especially in Italy and the Low Countries. Urban families with surplus movable property could realize significant profits through participation in maritime commerce. Notarial records from Genoa, a major center of Mediterranean trade, show women actively investing in commercial ventures that spanned the sea, from Morocco in the west to Syria in the east.

Women appear in nearly one-quarter of all extant Genoese overseas commercial (or *commenda*) contracts from the late twelfth and early thirteenth centuries. Genoese women invested their own property and also brokered investments for family members, usually their husbands and sons, but also siblings, cousins, and other relatives of both genders. Acting as home partners while their merchant husbands were off at sea, Genoese wives reinvested past profits in new ventures with other traders. Widows, named as trustees in their late husbands' wills, worked to increase their children's inheritance through maritime commerce, often investing property of their own as well. Through these efforts, women played a key role in the business strategies of both their natal and marital families.

In Genoa, as in most Italian cities, merchant families engaged in intense political and economic competition. The ability of so many Genoese women to invest movable property in maritime commerce may be due in part to an increasing desire by urban families to maintain control over real estate. By the twelfth century, merchant families across Italy had begun to enforce two significant changes in marriage and inheritance customs. Many cities enacted laws that eliminated the Germanic custom of guaranteeing a widow a fixed portion (usually one-quarter or one-third) of her late husband's estate and families increasingly considered a cash-only dowry as a woman's entire share of her paternal estate.

This desire to prevent the loss of control over strategically precious real estate diminished female influence within the family economy. But increased access to liquid assets meant that women gained greater control over investment capital at a time when Western society remained relatively cash poor. Through investment in maritime commerce, Genoese women kept family resources in steady circulation to maximize the potential for profits. Contemporary records from some other Mediterranean ports show similar patterns of female investment in maritime commerce.

By the later Middle Ages, the focus of overseas trade began shifting north to the burgeoning commercial centers of Flanders and the Rhine valley. In fourteenth-century Bruges, women commonly owned and managed money exchanges and other businesses. Women were active in Ghent as moneychangers and moneylenders during the same period. In fifteenth-century Cologne, women played a prominent part in that city's long-distance commercial enterprises.

MARK ANGELOS

References and Further Reading

Angelos, Mark. "Urban Women, Investment, and the Commercial Revolution of the Middle Ages." In *Women in Medieval Western European Culture*, edited by Linda E. Mitchell. New York and London: Garland Publishing, 1999, pp. 257–272.

Howell, Martha C. *Women, Production and Patriarchy in Late Medieval Cities*. Chicago: University of Chicago Press, 1986.

Hughes, Diane Owen. "From Brideprice to Dowry in Mediterranean Europe." In *The Marriage Bargain: Women and Dowries in European History*, edited by Marion A. Kaplan. New York: Haworth Press, 1985, pp. 113–158.

Jordan, William Chester. *Women and Credit in Pre-Industrial and Developing Societies*. Philadelphia: University of Pennsylvania Press, 1993.

Murray, James M. "Family, Marriage and Moneychanging in Medieval Bruges." *Journal of Medieval History* 14 (1988): 115–125.

Nicholas, David. *The Domestic Life of a Medieval City: Women, Children, and the Family in Fourteenth-Century Ghent*. Lincoln, Neb.: University of Nebraska Press, 1985.

See also **Business; Consumption; Dowry and Other Marriage Gifts; Inheritance; Jewish Women; Merchant Families, Women of; Widows**

IRELAND

The history of women in medieval Ireland is laden with romance and poetry. Perhaps this is because the modern study of Irish women's past began in the nineteenth century, in the decades when William Butler Yeats and Lady Gregory were writing their verses and plays, and the Irish were recovering their native language and culture after centuries of colonialist suppression. Patriotic antiquarians such as T. F. O'Rahilly and Eoin MacNeill colluded with poets in producing an ideal Celtic Woman of the Irish past who was independent, aggressive, beautiful, and mysterious—much like Maud Gonne, the rebel of 1916, and also the sexy, cattle-rustling warrior Queen

Medb (Maeve) of the early medieval epic *Táin Bó Cúailnge* (Cattle Raid of Cooley).

The Evidence

Yet the main reason for the persistence of Celtic stereotypes in the history of Irish women is the medieval literary tradition, of which the *Táin* is just a small part. Beginning not long after their fifth-century Christianization, Irish scholars and storytellers began composing in their native language, Europe's oldest written vernacular, as well as in their new language of scholarly Latin. Authors deployed a diverse range of female characters, including spell-chanting druidesses, shapeshifting war goddesses, mysterious queens of the Otherworld, powerful saints, and fierce women like Medb who ruled historic territories. These heroines were the match of any men; the *Táin* itself describes Medb as "a tall, fair, long-faced woman with soft features" and a head of yellow hair who "carried a light, stinging sharp-edged lance in her hand and held an iron sword with a woman's grip over her head."

But the literate elite also left a more prosaic body of evidence for women's lives that includes secular and religious laws, gnomic texts, saints' lives, theology, astronomy, and documents from many other genres. These texts, along with evidence from archaeological excavations, help historians understand where and how real women lived, worked, and worshipped. The experience of women in medieval Ireland was less like that of the mythical Queen Medb than like that of women living elsewhere in Christian Europe. Ireland was intensely rural, with no real cities until the Vikings arrived around 800 to build trading ports. Throughout the thousand years of the Middle Ages, most families occupied isolated farmsteads or lived in small clusters of huts attached to kings' forts or monastic communities. Queen and slave girl alike spent most of their days at domestic tasks in houses usually made of branches and mud, roofed with thatch, encircled by ditches and palisades. Only later in the Middle Ages did the wealthiest families build fortified stone houses, complete with doors, windows, and separate floors, for themselves.

Legal Status

Women worked with their men to raise crops and herd sheep, pigs, or cows. They also kept farmyard animals, ran the dairy and kitchen, and took the sheep to high pastures in the summer. They greased the wool, combed and spun it, dyed yarn, and wove it into wool. In poor weather, they sat inside and sewed clothing and linens for their households. The early medieval laws ordered that the daughters of kings be taught sewing. The laws also declared that one of the most valuable jobs a woman could do was the fine needlework that adorned the cloaks and tunics of the nobility. The legal status of a *druinech*, or professional embroideress, was higher than that of a queen. Even more valuable, though, was women's job of bearing and raising children. Kinship was the basis of all Irish law, property ownership, and political organization, and the Irish could not maintain kinship groups without the reproductive labor of women.

Women's legal status and social identity depended upon their families until they were officially of marriageable age, around thirteen, and then upon their husbands or other sexual partners. All native medieval Irish law was negotiated law, based not on distinctions of civil and criminal law but upon the assumption that every human being had a calculable worth to his or her family and society (honor price, in Irish *lóg n-enech, eneclann,* or *díre*). If a person were harmed or killed, that value could be paid in goods or, if necessary, in blood and vengeance. Until the age of seven, freeborn girls and boys had the same legal value, calculated as half that of their male guardian's value; at age fourteen, however, a man gained his full adult value while a woman was always worth only half what her father, husband, or other guardian was worth. Even noblewomen could not participate fully in society as economic actors. They could not make contracts without male representation. As the eighth-century legal text known as the *Díre*-tract put it, "A woman is not capable of selling anything without the consent of one of those who has authority over her: her father looks after her when she is a girl; her spouse looks after her when she is a married woman; her sons look after her when she is a widow with children..." Officially, women could not inherit family land, which went instead to any living male relatives; however, it seems likely that loving fathers and mothers tried to provide for their daughters in other ways, such as dowries or gifts of property. Women could not become the noble clients of kings and lords because they could not swear oaths in witness to support their lords in legal conflicts. Royal women achieved fame and power only in literature, for in real life queens ruled only as the wives of kings.

Marriage and Divorce

Despite such limitations, women's marriage rights were more extensive than those of women elsewhere in medieval Europe. A good marriage contract secured a woman's position in local society, although the Irish interpreted legal unions differently from modern definitions of marriage. Irish laws allowed for many types of *lánamnai* or contracts of sexual partnership, ranging from a contract between a woman and man of equal nobility and wealth, to the arrangement between a woman who lived at home with her parents and was visited periodically by her mate; even unions brought about by rape or made by two mentally defective individuals could be legalized. Jurists who made these laws were not concerned about the desires of true lovers or the rights of women, but with the status of offspring and children's rights to family property. Rich noblemen who could afford more than one kind of partner often married a chief wife (*cétmuinter*) as well as maintaining other legal sexual partners whose children competed with those of his wife for inheritance. A mother's job, meanwhile, was to shield her children from the ambitions of her husband's other women, helping her sons and daughters to make social alliances with their maternal kin and foster families.

In addition, Irish laws allowed for divorce and remarriage at the instigation of either partner, despite the opposition of Christian theologians and ecclesiastical rulemakers. A woman could leave a man who abused her, who became impotent or insane, who decided to become a celibate churchman, or who was caught in a homosexual act. She could dissolve their contract just because he insulted her or betrayed the secrets of their sex lives together. Women of very high status took advantage of these options, switching husbands when their families or their own political ambitions demanded. Even after the Anglo-Normans invaded Ireland in the late twelfth century, and despite the ecclesiastical reforms sweeping Europe in the same period, the Irish continued their practices of divorce and polygamy all through the Middle Ages. Despite women's disenfranchisement and their limited political powers, they still played influential roles in Irish society. Some of the most powerful women were avowed Christians.

Saints and Abbesses

The same rhetorical exaggeration that surrounded mythological women also attended Ireland's female saints. St. Brigit of Kildare (c. 450–525) could supposedly control the weather, commune with animals, move rivers, raise the dead, and prophesy. Her monastery and its cathedral were among the wealthiest and most populous pilgrimage centers in Ireland until at least the twelfth century; she remains one of the island's three patron saints today. Her abbess successors were said to be the only women in Ireland who could "turn back the streams of war," that is, engage in diplomacy and enforce peace among feuding kings. Other abbesses were said to have performed miracles, too. St. Íte had visions of nursing the baby Jesus and was so serious a faster that, when pricked with a pin, she had no blood left in her body to bleed. Even nonsaintly women could achieve power and status as the noble abbesses of major nunneries. The monastery of Cell Craobhnat (Kilcreevanty) near Tuam in County Galway was founded in 1200 for the daughters of O Conor kings. When it was dissolved with other Irish monasteries in the sixteenth century, the abbess held about a thousand acres of land, along with fourteen rectories, seven chapels, and a castle.

The romance associated with some women in Irish literature was balanced by a strong misogynistic streak running through the documents, both secular and religious. The same body of laws that allowed women to divorce classed them legally with fools, slaves, and children. The secular stories about warrior queens also depicted horrible hags who brought good kings down for the mere pleasure of an evil deed. The hagiography of female saints has to be weighed against the stories of male ascetics who fled the company of women and disdained to teach them or hear their advice. Proverbs and advice texts such as the *Tecosca Cormaic* (Advice of Cormac) dismissed all women as angry, lustful, shiftless, manipulative, greedy, and whining. Worst of all, women never shut up; "save us," St. Patrick had supposedly pleaded, "from the spells of women, smiths, and druids."

The Anglo-Norman Invasion

The major change for women and men alike in medieval Ireland came with the Anglo-Norman invaders and immigrants of the twelfth and later centuries. These newcomers expropriated property and reorganized it into a system of dependent farms focused on the manorial estates of the nobility. They also brought a social and political hierarchy occupied, at the top, by the king of England and his English-born knights. These men imposed a body of laws and a system of taxation upon the Irish that conflicted with native systems.

The conflicts that ensued in Ireland between 1172 and 1500 had several important gender implications. To begin with, women often became participants at the highest levels in games of social and political alliance. The first Irish princess known to marry a Norman invader was Aoífe, daughter of Diarmaid Mac Murchadha, who wed the Norman knight Richard FitzGilbert de Clare (called Strongbow). It was a good move for Aoífe, since her husband claimed her father's kingdom of Leinster by rights of inheritance; normally, under traditional Irish law, she would not have inherited any land. Children of unions such as that of Aoífe and Strongbow acquired mixed English–Irish names and customs along with their ancestry, thus promoting some kinds of assimilation between conquerors and conquered.

Second, the immigrants brought with them a market-based urban economy with effects that reached deep into the Irish countryside. Women who were born in, or moved to, coastal towns could take up new professions in the craft and service industries of this more complex economy, just as Irish men could.

Finally, with more sustained contacts with England, especially its centrally organized church bureaucracy, Irish and Anglo-Irish clerics alike could pursue Christian reforms more vigorously than in the dispersed parishes and monasteries of early medieval Ireland. Although the initial impulses of monastic and episcopal reorganization preceded Strongbow's appearance in Ireland, it was only when church and colonial politics coincided that bishops in Ireland were able to enforce monogamy, clerical celibacy, and the claustration of Irish nuns, among other strict canonical measures. They also introduced new monastic orders, including the Arrouasian, Franciscan, and Dominican rules for nuns.

In more important ways, however, the experiences of women probably changed little over the long thousand years of the Irish Middle Ages. At the end of the period, when Tudor monarchs were pioneering new methods of conquest and the Protestant reformation fuelled yet another assault on native Irish culture, most women were still wives and mothers, farming and herding for a living, praying to Saint Brigit for strength and health, and listening in the evenings to stories of warrior-queens and otherworldly women.

LISA BITEL

References and Further Reading

Binchy, Daniel A., ed. *Corpus Iuris Hibernici.* 6 vols. Dublin: Dublin Institute for Advanced Studies, 1978.

Bitel, Lisa M. *Land of Women: Stories of Sex and Gender from Early Ireland.* Ithaca, N.Y.: Cornell University Press, 1996.

Bourke, Angela, et al, eds. *Irish Women's Writing and Tradition.* The Field Day Anthology of Irish Writing, vols. 4–5. New York: New York University Press, 2002.

Cogitosus. *Vita Sanctae Brigidae.* In *Patrologia Latina* 72, edited by J. P. Migne. Paris, 1844–1864.

Findon, Joanne. *A Woman's Words: Emer and Female Speech in the Ulster Cycle.* Toronto: University of Toronto Press, 1997.

Hall, Dianne. *Women and the Church in Medieval Ireland, c. 1140–1540.* Dublin: Four Courts Press, 2003.

Kelly, Fergus. *A Guide to Early Irish Law.* Dublin: Dublin Institute for Advanced Studies, 1988.

Kinsella, Thomas, trans. *The Tain.* Oxford: Oxford University Press, 1970.

Meyer, Kuno, ed. and trans. *The Instructions of King Cormac Mac Airt.* Todd Lecture Series 15. Dublin: Royal Irish Academy, 1909.

Monasticon: Ireland. *Monastic Matrix.* http://monasticmatrix.org.

Ó Corráin, Donnchadh. "Women in Early Irish Society." In *Women in Irish Society: The Historical Dimension*, edited by Donnchadh Ó Corráin and Margaret MacCurtain. Westport, Conn.: Greenwood Press, 1979, pp. 1–13.

Ó Cróinín, Dáibhí. *Early Medieval Ireland 400–1200.* London: Longman, 1995.

Thurneysen, Rudolf, ed. *Studies in Early Irish Law.* Dublin: Royal Irish Academy, 1936.

See also **Abbesses; Brigit; Divorce and Separation; Literature, Irish; Monasticism and Nuns, Celtic; Supernatural Women**

IRENE

Irene (c. 752–803), empress of Byzantium, was born probably in Athens to a local family named (Tes) Sarandapechys, and in 769 became the bride chosen for Leo, son of the iconoclast emperor and theologian Constantine V (741–775). Thirteen months after their marriage, Irene gave birth to a son named Constantine. Following the premature death of her husband Leo IV in 780, Irene assumed the role of regent for her nine-year-old son. She summoned an ecumenical council to Nicaea in 787, which reversed the policy of iconoclasm and acclaimed her as "a new Helena" to her son's "new Constantine."

From 790 to 797 Constantine tried to reduce Irene's influence, but she arranged to have him blinded and thus disqualified from ruling. She then ruled alone (797–802), issuing gold coins with her title *basilissa* and her own image on both sides, and two laws as emperor (*basileus*). In 802 her finance minister Nikephoros overthrew her and she died in exile one year later.

During her five-year reign, when she relied on two rival eunuch advisers, defeats by Caliph Harun al-Rashid and Charlemagne reflected Byzantium's military weakness. But Irene extended imperial administration in the Balkans (Macedonia) and founded churches (St Sophia, Thessalonike) and monasteries with philanthropic functions. In 800 Pope Leo III crowned Charlemagne "Emperor of the Romans," a title not recognized in Constantinople. But Irene proposed an alliance with him, which he seems to have welcomed. Irene's experiment in female rule provided a later model for Theodora (regent for Michael III, 842–856) and later Byzantine empresses.

JUDITH HERRIN

References and Further Reading

Herrin, Judith. *Women in Purple: Rulers of Medieval Byzantium.* Princeton, N.J.: Princeton University Press, 2001.
Treadgold, Warren. *The Byzantine Revival 780–842.* Stanford, Calif.: Stanford University Press, 1988.

See also **Byzantium; Empresses: Byzantium; Eunuchs; Icons, Byzantine**

ISABEL I

The princess who would become known to history as Queen Isabella the Catholic (1451–1504) was the only daughter of King Juan II (1406–1454) and his second wife, Isabel of Portugal. In her father's will Isabel was named third in line for the throne of Castile, after her older half-brother Enrique, but also, on grounds of gender, after her younger brother Alfonso (b. 1453). Enrique succeeded his father in 1454, ruling as Enrique IV.

In the 1460s the *infante* Alfonso was thrust into the forefront of an aristocratic revolt against Enrique. The grandees and their ecclesiastical allies deposed Enrique in effigy and impugned the legitimacy of his sole heir, Juana of Castile. When Alfonso died in 1468, the rebels quickly adopted Isabel as their leader. The seventeen-year-old princess resisted their pressure to proclaim herself queen, declaring her loyalty and obedience to the legitimate king. At the same time, however, she was actively engaged in disseminating rumors about her brother's impotence and her rival Juana's illegitimacy. She was also choosing a husband suitable to her ambitions, against the express wishes of Enrique, who wished to marry her off to his own advantage. These activities demonstrate the strength of character, independent spirit, and appreciation for protocol and propaganda that would enable her rise to power and characterize her rule. When Enrique died in 1474, Isabel precipitously had herself proclaimed queen, ignoring Juana's legitimate claim.

Isabel's choice of spouse was arguably the most important decision of her life. Despite her determination to rule Castile in her own right, Isabel could not choose to remain unmarried. Given the circumstances of her rise to power, Isabel had to marry and produce a legitimate, preferably male heir. Among her many Spanish and European suitors, she chose Fernando, heir to the throne of Aragon (1479–1516). Fernando

was known for his military prowess, which proved crucial to the successful completion of the war of succession that began a few months after Isabel's coronation. Together they defeated the Castilian nobles loyal to Juana and their Portuguese allies. Well aware that if Juana were to marry, any child of hers might contest Isabel's succession, the queen made it a condition of the peace treaty that Juana enter a Portuguese convent. She remained there until her death in 1530.

It is a historiographical myth that the marriage of Isabel and Fernando signified a strong and equal union of their respective kingdoms. In reality, she made certain that her proprietary and hereditary rights over Castile were never compromised and placed strict limitations on Fernando's governance and inheritance rights in her kingdom. Likewise, Aragon maintained its own, more contractual monarchic institutions and laws, and Isabel was there considered Fernando's consort. Nevertheless, major policy decisions of her reign appear to have been made jointly.

Immediately after the war of succession's end in 1479, Isabel set about crafting the military, judicial, and administrative bases necessary to transform Castile into a modern nation-state. She reduced the political power of the aristocracy, strengthened the royal council and chancery, and instituted a national brotherhood to ensure law and order throughout the land.

Isabel was an avid patron of learning and the arts. She cultivated a close relationship with the University of Salamanca, Spain's distinguished center of humanist studies. She engaged several Salamancan professors to educate her children, especially her son, Prince Juan, the long-awaited male heir born in 1479. The queen also commissioned many books, paintings, and tapestries and facilitated the spread of print culture in Spain by prohibiting taxes on booksellers. Although she left no written work besides official documents and a few personal letters, she was apparently well read. Her extensive library reflected the burgeoning vernacular humanism characteristic of late medieval culture in Castile, and included moral and religious treatises, chronicles, and romances.

Isabel's most important act of patronage by far was her funding of Christopher Columbus's voyages of exploration, starting in 1492. Historians agree that it was she, not Fernando, who understood the potential for economic gain and religious evangelization in the Italian navigator's audacious plan.

In addition to Prince Juan, lovingly groomed for the throne, Isabel and Fernando had four daughters, Isabel, Juana, Maria, and Catalina (Catherine of Aragon). Juan's death at the age of nineteen meant that Isabel would be succeeded by another woman, her oldest daughter Juana, dubbed "the Mad." Juana's troubled marriage to Philip of Burgundy, a Hapsburg, produced Carlos I, who became Holy Roman emperor and transformed Spain into a far-flung world empire.

Isabel was a master propagandist, employing several court chroniclers to craft the official story of her reign. Probably no more nor less pious than any other noblewoman of her time, she cultivated a pious and ascetic demeanor, reflecting and enhancing the messianic fervor expressed by her supporters. They believed that the queen had been sent to fulfill a providential plan: to pacify the kingdom, curtail the abuses of the grandees and prelates, conclude the Christian "Reconquest" of Muslim-held lands, and safeguard religious orthodoxy. It was her success in the latter two endeavors through the institution of the Holy Office of the Inquisition (1478), the conquest of the Muslim kingdom of Granada, and the Edict of Expulsion of the Jews (both in 1492) that earned Isabel the title of Catholic Queen, bestowed upon her by Pope Alexander VI.

BARBARA F. WEISSBERGER

References and Further Reading

Liss, Peggy. *Isabel the Queen: Life and Times.* 2nd edition. Philadelphia: University of Pennsylvania Press, 2005.
Weissberger, Barbara F. *Isabel Rules: Constructing Queenship, Wielding Power.* Minneapolis: University of Minnesota Press, 2004.

See also **Iberia; Queens and Empresses, Consorts of; Queens and Empresses: The West**

ISABEL OF ARAGON

Born in the Kingdom of Aragon, Isabel (1271–1336) (also known as Elizabeth of Portugal) was the daughter of King Pedro III and the granddaughter of Emperor Frederick II. Named for her great aunt St. Elisabeth of Hungary, Isabel's pious upbringing was to define her life and works. She was married to King Dinis of Portugal when she was twelve. Although known for his meritorious works in his country's service, Dinis "the Worker" was a violent man and the father of several illegitimate sons, whom he sometimes favored over the children that Isabel bore him. She nevertheless accepted them and raised them with her own. Relying on piety to endure her personal hardships, the queen dedicated her life to charitable causes: she founded orphanages, a school for girls, hospitals for the indigent, and monasteries where she paid the dowry for poor women of religious vocation. Historians agree that the king so admired her unflagging religious devotion and personal goodness that he improved his personal conduct later in life.

Isabel was known as a peacemaker. When her son Afonso declared war on his father for favoring his natural sons, the queen traveled to the battlefield and sat on horseback between the two armies, thus preventing the conflict. Shortly before her death Isabel went to Castile to stop the fighting between Afonso (then King of Portugal) and Ferdinand IV.

After Dinis's death in 1325 Isabel lived the rest of her life at a convent of Poor Clares that she had founded in Coimbra. She died there in 1336. In 1625 Pope Urban VIII canonized Isabel. She has become known as the patron saint of countries plagued by civil war.

NANCY MARINO

References and Further Reading

Ackerlind, Sheila R. *King Dinis of Portugal and the Alfonsine Tradition.* New York: Peter Lang, 1990.
de Sousa, Manuel. *Reis e rainhas de Portugal.* Mem Martins, Portugal: Spor Press, 2001.

See also **Diplomacy and Reconciliation; Elisabeth of Hungary; Hagiography; Iberia; Queens and Empresses: the West**

ISABELLE OF FRANCE

Isabelle (1225–1270) was the daughter of Louis VIII of France and Blanche of Castile. She refused several marriages arranged by her family, dedicating herself instead to charity and virginity. In the 1250s Popes Innocent IV and Alexander IV praised her piety and urged her to act as an example to others. Utilizing this support, Isabelle founded the Abbey of the Humility of Our Lady, better known as Longchamp, just west of Paris in 1260. Together with a team of leading Franciscans, including St. Bonaventure, she helped author a new rule for Longchamp that balanced strong institutional links to the male Franciscan order with increased autonomy for the abbess and nuns. It was approved by Alexander IV in February 1259, making Isabelle only the second woman after Clare of Assisi to compose an approved monastic rule. In July 1263, with her brother Louis IX's help, she gained Urban IV's acceptance of a revised rule that fulfilled her demand that her nuns be known as *Sorores minores* (Sisters minor), a controversial female analogue to the male Franciscan *Fratres minores*. At least a dozen other houses in France, England, Spain, and Italy had adopted this rule by the fourteenth century. Isabelle resided at Longchamp during the last decade of her life but did not become a nun. Agnes of Harcourt, third abbess of Longchamp, composed a vernacular biography around 1283 that detailed Isabelle's pious activities, her miracles, and the posthumous veneration that a wide range of people from the north of France accorded her.

SEAN L. FIELD

References and Further Reading

Jordan, William Chester. "Isabelle of France and Religious Devotion at the Court of Louis IX." In *Capetian Women*, edited by Kathleen D. Nolan. New York: Palgrave, 2003, pp. 209–223.

Lynn, Beth. "Clare of Assisi and Isabelle of Longchamp: Further Light on the Early Development of the Franciscan Charism." *Magistra* 3 (1997): 71–98.

Field, Sean L., ed. *The Writings of Agnes of Harcourt*. Notre Dame, Ind.: University of Notre Dame Press, 2003.

———. "Gilbert of Tournai's Letter to Isabelle of France: An Edition of the Complete Text." *Mediaeval Studies* 65 (2003): 57–97.

———. "New Evidence for the Life of Isabelle of France." *Revue Mabillon*. New Series 13 (2002): 109–123.

See also **Blanche of Castile; Hagiography; Monastic Rules; Monasticism and Nuns; Poor Clares Order**

ISLAMIC WOMEN

See **Muslim Women: Iberia**

ISOLDE

This legendary Irish princess (also known as Isolt, Ysot, Yseut, Iseut, Iseult, and Isotta) becomes bound by an overpowering mutual passion with Tristan, the nephew of her betrothed, King Mark of Cornwall, when the two mistakenly consume a love potion intended for the wedding couple and are constrained to violate the most sacred social and religious taboos. Isolde deceives her husband, while Tristan betrays his uncle and lord; the importance of the maternal uncle in the Middle Ages even introduces a note of incest. Though they are hardly to blame, the lovers feel acutely the weight of the sanctions resulting from their liaison and make every effort both to escape death and to maintain their roles in society.

Considered one of the founding myths of Western culture, the legend was extremely popular throughout the Middle Ages in both literature and art. The earliest extant narratives are two Anglo-Norman poems, preserved in fragments, dating from the last quarter of the twelfth century. The first, by Beroul, recounts the portion of the legend that details the lovers' attempts to live their double life in Cornwall, where Mark's jealous barons spy on them and repeatedly denounce them, resulting in Tristan's eventual banishment. The second poem, by Thomas of Britain, recounts Tristan's exile in Brittany, his ill-advised (and unconsummated) marriage to Isolde of the White Hands, his furtive return visits to Cornwall, and the lovers' poignant death. Two shorter poems from the same period, the Bern *Folie* and the Oxford *Folie*, and one of Marie de France's lays, *Chievrefoil*, recount moments when the clever lovers manage a temporary reunion.

Three long verse redactions, two in Middle High German, by Eilhart von Oberge, c. 1190, and Gottfried von Strassburg, c. 1210, respectively, and one in Old Norse, by Friar Róbert, 1226—all originally inspired by the Anglo-Norman poems—allow us a glimpse of the protagonists' lives before the potion reordered their priorities. Isolde has inherited her mother's gift for healing, which enables her to revive the ailing harpist whose boat has washed up on the Irish shore. She is also depicted as a strong-willed woman whose fury is ignited when she learns that the "harpist" is none other than the knight who slew her maternal uncle in combat. Isolde's anger reminds us that in Celtic society women wielded considerable power and independence. In a Celtic analogue of the legend, the ninth-century Irish tale of the elopement of Diarmaid and Gráinne, Gráinne, enamored with her husband's nephew, casts a spell (*geis*) on him that obliges him to flee with her. By contrast, the use of the potion in the continental versions of the legend reflects an abrogation, in a patriarchal culture, of the heroine's right to choose her mate freely.

Starting with the extraordinarily popular French prose *Tristan* (c. 1230), the legend was transformed significantly as the focus shifted increasingly to Tristan's adventures as a knight-errant. The prose *Tristan* influenced all the prose romances of France, Italy, Spain, and England, notably Malory's *Morte D'Arthur* (1469–1470), which includes *The Book of Sir Tristram de Lyones*. In these works Isolde becomes a more generalized love object: her great beauty sparks the undying love of many other knights. When Tristan is drawn into the Arthurian orbit and joins the Round Table, his prowess is seen to rival Lancelot's, as Isolde's beauty rivals Guinevere's. The potion is less important in the prose *Tristan*, where the lovers fall in love before drinking it. However, in the *Tavola Ritonda* (Italian, second quarter of the fourteenth century), which returns the love idyll to the fore, the philter is a highly potent force that transforms the chaste friendship of the virtuous protagonists into unbridled desire, simultaneously elevating them to the status of secular martyrs and depriving the world of its brightest stars.

The legend experienced an important revival in the modern period, triggered by the success of Wagner's "music–drama" *Tristan und Isolde* (1865). This romantic reinterpretation, which decisively influenced that of Denis de Rougemont (*L'Amour et l'Occident*, 1939), depicts the lovers as imbued with a death wish, clearly seeking the realm of Night and Death as a refuge from an oppressive society. This thoroughly modern concept of the legend, as attractive as it is, gives a rather false idea of the medieval lovers who, though famous as star-crossed lovers, were celebrated primarily for their surpassing beauty, boundless ingenuity, and consummate fidelity.

JOAN TASKER GRIMBERT

References and Further Reading

Bédier, Joseph. *Le Roman de Tristan et Iseut traduit et restauré*, with a preface by Gaston Paris. Paris: H. Piazza, 1900. Translation by Hilaire Belloc, completed by Paul Rosenfield, as *The Romance of Tristan and Iseult As Retold by Joseph Bédier*. Vintage Classics. New York: Random House, 1994.

Béroul. *Le Roman de Tristan*, edited and translated by Stewart Gregory. Amsterdam and Atlanta: Rodopi, 1992.

Blakeslee, Merritt R. *Love's Masks: Identity, Intertextuality, and Meaning in the Old French Tristan Poems*. Cambridge: Brewer, 1989.

Eilhart von Oberge. *Tristrant*, edited by Kurt Wagner. Bonn, Germany: K. Schroeder, 1924.

Gottfried von Strassburg. *Tristan*. Critical edition by Reinhold Bechstein and Peter Ganz. 2 vols. Deutscher Klassiker des Mittelalters, 4. Wiesbaden, Germany: Brockhaus, 1978.

———. *Tristan, with Surviving Fragments of the 'Tristran' of Thomas*, translated with introduction by Arthur Thomas Hatto. Baltimore: Penguin, 1960. Reprint, 1972.

Grimbert, Joan Tasker, ed. *Tristan and Isolde: A Casebook*. New York and London: Garland Publishing, 1995.

Lacy, Norris J., ed. *Early French Tristan Poems*. Arthurian archives; 1-2. Woodbridge, Suffolk, and Rochester, N.Y.: D. S. Brewer, 1998.

Malory, Sir Thomas. *Morte D'Arthur*, edited by John Matthews. London: Cassell, 2000.

Marie de France. "Le Lai du Chievrefoil." In *The Lais of Marie de France*, translated with an introduction by Glyn S. Burgess and Keith Busby. Harmondsworth, Middlesex, England: Penguin Classics, 1986.

Ménard, Philippe, ed. *Le Roman de Tristan en prose*. Textes littéraires français. 9 volumes to date. Geneva: Droz, 1987– .

———. *The Romance of Tristan. The Thirteenth-Century Old French "Prose Tristan"*, translated with an introduction and notes by Renée L. Curtis. Oxford: Oxford University Press, 1994.

Rabine, Leslie W. "Love and the New Patriarchy: *Tristan and Isolde.*" In *Reading the Romantic Heroine: Text, History, Ideology*, edited by Leslie W. Rabine. Ann Arbor, Mich.: University of Michigan Press, 1985, pp. 37–74.

Rasmussen, Ann Marie. "'Ez ist ir G'Artet von mir': Queen Isolde and Princess. Isolde in Gottfried von Strassburg's *Tristan und Isolde.*" In *Arthurian Women: A Casebook*, edited by Thelma S. Fenster. New York: Garland, 1996, pp. 41–57.

Rougemont, Denis de. *L'Amour et l'Occident*. Paris: Plon, 1939. Translation by Montgomery Belgion as *Love in the Western World*. Princeton, N.J.: Princeton University Press, 1983.

Tavola Ritonda, o l'istoria di tristano. Critical edition by Filippo-Luigi Polidori and Luciano Banchi. 2 vols. Bologna, Italy: G. Romagnoli, 1864–1866.

Thomas. *Le Roman de Tristan suivi de La Folie Tristan de Berne et La Folie d'Oxford*, translated with presentation and notes by Emmanuèle Baumgartner and Ian Short; texts edited by Félix Lecoy. Paris: Champion, 2003.

Tristan and the Round Table. A Translation of 'La Tavola Ritonda', translated and annotated by Anne Shaver. Binghamton, N.Y.: State University of New York Press, 1983.

Wagner, Richard. *Tristan und Isolde*. Complete orchestral score. New York: Dover Publications, 1973.

See also **Arthurian Literature; Gottfried von Strassburg; Romance, French; Romance, German**

ITALY

The history of women in medieval Italy reflects the fragmented nature of the country's premodern political history. Their sociolegal status varied from region to region and over time, and the relatively late acceptance of women's history within the Italian academy has meant that work on medieval Italian women is uneven and often highly localised. It has also been held back by the centrality of the Italian city-republics of the north in major narratives of Italian medieval history. Oriented towards tracing the emergence of civic government and the revival of Roman law in the twelfth century, this historiographical tradition has largely ignored women, for whom public office was not an option and whose property rights were eroded in successive waves of civic legislation.

Sources

Italian legal historians have long been interested in the problem of women, especially the issues surrounding the institution of the *mundium*, or legal guardianship by an adult male (usually the father and then, on marriage, the husband) and the property arrangements made at the time of marriage. Legal sources (Roman and Lombard law codes, Carolingian capitularies and civic statutes) still form the basis for much work on women's status. They have been joined by documents of practice (charters recording property transactions, wills, etc.) and, increasingly, by careful analysis of narrative and literary sources.

The vast majority of the extant charter material prior to 1200 (and an only slightly lesser proportion after that date) is preserved in ecclesiastical archives, and so often reflects the concerns of the church rather than those of the lay people with whom ecclesiastical institutions regularly interacted. A preponderance of the donations to the institution somewhat skews the picture of how women's property was managed, but women might use gifts to the church as an effective strategy to avoid pressure to remarry when widowed. Donations of land were often accompanied by collections of documents relating to its history prior to the donation. These provide at least some glimpses of family relations and enable the reconstruction of often substantial genealogical information. Because women's right to some property, be it in the form of a dowry or a portion to be held on widowhood, was largely upheld in law, their consent was often required to their husbands' transactions. They also, as later medieval examples demonstrate, had the right to sue insolvent husbands if their own property had been dissipated without their consent.

In narrative sources, family histories can be more fragmented, but a picture can be built up of both clerical and lay views of women. Hagiography and canonisation procedures, for example, can offer considerable incidental evidence of social practices as laypeople recounted their interaction with the sacred. In contrast to their very circumscribed role as witnesses in secular court cases, women's testimony was admitted when ecclesiastical inquisitors were collecting evidence of miraculous interventions by the prospective saint. In describing the circumstances of the miracle (the healing of a sick child or a crippled husband, for instance), women's accounts reveal details of their work patterns, and how far they were willing or permitted to travel in search of a cure. It is notable, however, that their actual testimony was often corroborated by male interlocutors.

Civic chronicles, which offer laymen's accounts of their city's history alongside the clerical viewpoint in many records, frequently provide evidence of how women played key roles in Italian family politics. Incidental information surrounding public, family rituals such as wedding or funeral processions reveals the attention paid to female honour, and women's role in the mourning process. Chronicles and other historical narratives, once mined solely for the deeds of rulers and their political power, are increasingly being explored not only for the information they provide on women as rulers and wives of rulers (for example, Queen Amalasuntha, Empress Constance, and Joan I), but also for signs of female patronage. Aristocratic women often intervened to shape the narrative to suit their own or their family's interests. For example, it is likely that the Lombard princess Sichelgaita of Salerno had a major say in the chronicle

of Amatus of Montecassino, recording her Norman husband Robert Guiscard's conquests in southern Italy. Her patronage ensured that the narrative favoured her own son's claim to succeed his father ahead of Robert's son by his first marriage.

Moving into the thirteenth and fourteenth centuries, the emergence of civic government in the north and the centralising Kingdom of Sicily in the south brought with them increasing attempts not only to regulate their citizens through law codes and statutes, but also to record individual households and their economic value in the form of tax registers. Demographic historians have used such sources to try to reconstruct patterns of family formation and the composition of households. Such work is aided by the concern on the part of the nascent commercial classes to record their own family histories and company transactions in family diaries or *libri di ricordanze*. Here male and female memories combined, and although the majority of surviving texts were composed by male household heads, there are also isolated examples of female-authored works.

Peasant Women

The history of women in medieval Italy is therefore based on rich source materials: also extant are letters, sermons, and estate surveys. The latter, alongside charters, open up the world of Italian peasant women. Male and female peasant cultivators are visible in our evidence throughout the Middle Ages, but while slave cultivators were still a regular feature of agricultural activity at the start of our period, especially in the south, by the end of the Middle Ages the only slaves visible in charters and chronicles were female domestics. There also appears to have been a difference in the relationship between landlord and tenant between north and south. In the north, ties of direct dependence based on service on monastic and secular estates are visible. Surviving early medieval court cases suggest that such ties did not go unchallenged, but women are largely silent in such evidence, and ecclesiastical landlords preserved only the records of cases that reinforced their tenants' lack of freedom. Later, such ties gave way to a relationship based on commercial transactions: land leased in return for a proportion of its produce, the *mezzadria*. The latter pattern is visible from an early date in the south, but in fact may have given way to lighter ties of dependence after the Norman conquest. Certainly documents from the twelfth century onwards refer to "villeins" with their wives and children. In all cases, although the preference for male tenant cultivators is clear, women are also recorded taking on (and giving up) plots of land.

More frequently, the wives of peasants might be involved in small animal husbandry, tending gardens, caring for children, and producing textiles. Female outworkers are sometimes recorded in late medieval statutes and guild records, although these sometimes explicitly excluded women from such activities as well as regulating them. Work on women's economic roles has shown their relationship with artisanal guilds to have been ambivalent: they were rarely granted membership, and any support they received seems to have been associated with the membership of a male relative.

Land Owners

Further up the social scale, women are ubiquitous throughout the Italian evidence as property owners, based on grudgingly granted inheritance rights (sons were universally preferred to daughters) and on the dowry at marriage, which by the twelfth century was clearly seen as a substitute for a portion of the patrimony. Alongside this trend was one to limit the amount of land a daughter might take out of her natal family's property, and moveable or cash dowries became the norm (a trend shared with other parts of Europe). In addition, wives were granted a share of their husband's wealth to support themselves and their children in widowhood. In Lombard law this was known as the *morgengab* and limited to no more than one quarter of the husband's wealth. Versions of this portion were given across Italy, but again the twelfth century saw moves to restrict widows' claims: in Genoa in 1143 their right was taken away almost completely.

Depending on where they lived, women had a greater or lesser right to manage their property. In the commercial cities of Venice, Amalfi, and Genoa, from the tenth century onwards, we see women actively engaging in the burgeoning trade networks within and outside the peninsula. Such autonomy appears to have reached a peak in the eleventh and twelfth centuries, before civic legislation in the north and increasingly repressive imperial measures in the south combined to marginalise women and reduce them to a state of dependence on their natal families or husbands.

There were always exceptions to this general rule, especially in cases where women were the sole heirs to their families' fortunes. The spectacular career of countess Matilda of Tuscany (d. 1115) was based largely on her inherited wealth, which she used to great effect in supporting the reformist aims of Pope Gregory VII and in resisting German imperial claims to her lands. Eventually forced to capitulate, she nevertheless appears in numerous documents managing her estates. Initially she left her lands to the Church, but later left them to the Empire.

Religion

Women's spiritual life is in fact a key theme in Italian evidence, and took a variety of forms. Early, small-scale, private monasteries for women, founded and run by their families, were joined by larger, royal foundations. Some of the latter, such as that of SS. Salvatore and Giulia at Brescia, succeeded in winning patronage from successive rulers of the kingdom of Italy. As already mentioned, women donated property both to monastic and episcopal churches, and used such donations to gain both spiritual benefits for themselves and their families and, if widowed, some pecuniary support for themselves and their dependent children. Donations were frequently made on the condition that the property support the donor for life. Aristocratic families might found and patronise several houses in the same city, as the Theophylactans did in tenth-century Rome. Such houses provided places of retirement and refuge for male and female members of the clan. There is evidence to suggest that some women's monastic houses suffered displacement at the time of monastic and church reform in the tenth and eleventh centuries. At the same time, new forms of spiritual devotion, such as taking the habit but remaining at home as a vowess, begin to be documented.

Alternative forms of monastic life grew up around charismatic leaders in the twelfth and thirteenth centuries, but it is noticeable that the Poor Clares, the female equivalent of the mendicant Franciscans, established by Clare of Assisi (1193–1253), were not permitted the freedom of movement accorded their male counterparts. The distinction between alternative forms of religious life and practices condemned as heretical was a fine one. Women participated enthusiastically as Cathars, Waldenses, and Humiliati, finding an outlet for their piety in such movements. It has been shown that the attraction of these groups probably did not rest upon the prominent role they accorded women, but the church's increasingly restrictive stance must have persuaded some women to turn to the heretical sects in order to express their religious devotion. For example, the practice of living at home as a vowess had been viewed with constant disapproval. The popularity of the heretical movements may well have led to the church's reconsideration of its position—certainly the Humiliati gained belated recognition and papal approval for their penitential life from Pope Innocent III.

On an individual level, the impulse to devote one's life to God eventually led to the emergence of female mystics in Italy, as elsewhere in Europe, and the recognition of some women as saintly. There were two peaks of mystical activity, first in the late thirteenth century (notably the careers of Umiliana dei Cherchi, Angela of Foligno, Guglielma of Milan, and Clare of Montefalco) and then after the Black Death in the fourteenth century, including the life of the most famous mystic, Catherine of Siena (1347–1380). Many achieved saintly or beatified status, notably Zita of Lucca (1218–c. 1275) for her charitable acts, but others, such as Margherita of Trento (d. 1307) and Mayfreda de Pirovano (a follower of Guglielma of Milan) were burned as heretics for their beliefs.

Although the population of medieval Italy was predominantly Christian, it is possible to trace the histories of its Jewish and Muslim communities. In both of these, women were largely subject to the male members of their families, but the consumption patterns of the former, at least, can be traced from Jewish merchants' letters. More work needs to be done on the social histories of these minorities in order to add a different facet of gender history in Italy.

PATRICIA SKINNER

References and Further Reading

Bornstein, Daniel, and Roberto Rusconi, eds. *Women and Religion in Medieval and Renaissance Italy*. Chicago: University of Chicago Press, 1996.
Casagrande, Giovanna, ed. *Donne tra medioevo ed età moderna in Italia: ricerche*. Perugia: Morlacchi Editore, 2004.
Herlihy, David. "Women and the Sources of Medieval History: The Towns of Northern Italy." In *Medieval Women and the Sources of Medieval History*, edited by J. T. Rosenthal. Athens, Ga.: University of Georgia Press, 1990, pp. 133–154.
Hughes, Diane Owen. "Invisible Madonnas? The Italian historiographical tradition and the women of medieval Italy." In *Women in Medieval History and Historiography*, edited by Susan Mosher Stuard. Philadelphia: University of Pennsylvania Press, 1987, pp. 25–57.
Klapisch-Zuber, Christiane. *Women, Family and Ritual in Renaissance Italy*. Chicago: University of Chicago Press, 1985.
Kuehn, Thomas G. *Law, Family and Women: Toward a Legal Anthropology of Renaissance Italy*. Chicago, 1991.
Medici, Maria Teresa Guerra. *I diritti delle donne*. Naples: Edizion Scientific Italian, 1986.
———. *L'aria di città: donne e diritti nel commune medievale*. Naples: Edizion Scientific Italian, 1996.
Muzzarelli, Maria G., Paola Galetti, and Bruno Andreolli, eds. *Donne e lavoro nell'Italia medievale*. Turin: Rosenberg and Sellier, 1991.
Naso, Irma, and Rinaldo Comba, eds. *Demografia e società nell'Italia medievale*. Cuneo: Società italiana di demografia storica, 1994.
Pereira, M., ed. *Né Eva né Maria: condizione femminile e immagini della donna nel medioevo*. Bologna, 1981.
Wemple, Suzanne F. "S. Salvatore/S. Giulia: A Case Study in the Endowment and Patronage of a Major Female Monastery in Northern Italy." In *Women of the Medieval World*, edited by Julius Kirshner and Suzanne F. Wemple. Oxford: Blackwell, 1985, pp. 85–102.

See also **Amalasuntha; Angela of Foligno; Beatrice; Boccaccio, Giovanni; Caterina Sforza; Caterina Vigri; Catherine of Genoa; Catherine of Siena; Cereta, Laura; Clare of Assisi; Clare of Montefalco; Compiuta Donzella; Constance of Sicily; Cornaro, Caterina; D'Este, Isabella and Beatrice; Dante Alighieri; Datini, Margherita; Dogaresse; Epic, Italian; Fedele, Cassandra; Fina of San Gimignano; Griselda; Helena; Literature, Italian; Marozia of Rome; Matilda of Tuscany; Nogarola, Isotta; Petrarch; Poor Clares Order; Rose of Viterbo; Slaves; Strozzi, Alessandra; Tornabuoni de'-Medici, Lucrezia; Trota of Salerno; Women Authors: Italian Texts; Zita and Other Servant Saints**

J

JACOBUS DE VORAGINE'S *GOLDEN LEGEND*

Jacobus de Voragine's *Golden Legend* is the most famous anthology of readings about the saints and major festivals of the medieval Catholic Church. Compiled in Latin by the Italian friar Jacobus de Voragine (c. 1228–1298) (or Jacopo da Varazze), probably during the 1260s, this work was originally entitled simply *Legenda sanctorum,* or "material to be read about saints," and evidently was designed as a reference book for students and preachers of Jacobus's own Dominican order. However, it eventually reached much wider audiences. Indeed, it became so popular that it acquired the honorific adjective *aurea* (golden) and survives in over nine hundred Latin manuscripts, many augmented with chapters on additional saints. Jacobus's book also gave rise to numerous translations and adaptations in medieval vernacular languages, and its popularity lasted until the Reformation. In the late fifteenth century it was still in such demand that it became a great bestseller for the new printing industry, which issued at least eighty-seven Latin editions and sixty-nine vernacular ones between 1470 and 1500.

Despite its prominence in its own time, the *Legenda* has proved resistant to modern critical assessment because of its encyclopedic nature and its complex relationship with other sources. Jacobus's contribution was not that of an original author, but a well-read and selective editor. He chose memorable stories and useful information from earlier legendaries and works on liturgy and church history, arranged this material in convenient chapters that follow the liturgical year, and abridged it according to his own priorities. Hence his positions on most issues are hard to distinguish from those of other ecclesiastical sources except in terms of emphases and proportions.

With regard to gender issues in particular, the *Legenda*'s selectivity initially seems contradictory. On the one hand, the book makes some gratuitous digs at women—as, for example, when the chapter on the Purification of the Virgin digresses to explain why Leviticus prescribes a longer period for purification after a daughter's birth than after a son's. In this passage the purification period is identified with the time between conception and the completion of the fetal body (forty days for a male child, eighty for a female), and the supposed biological difference is allegorically interpreted as a sign that women are greater sinners than men and more wearisome to God (Ryan translation, pp. 143–144).

On the other hand, women comprise a sizable proportion of the saints in the *Legenda*, and the book allows its female saints to exercise some surprisingly masculine kinds of agency and power. Its numerous virgin martyrs are not portrayed as silent, helpless victims of male violence, but as heroes who boldly defy the authority figures ranged against them, prove impervious to every diabolical temptation and torture their enemies can devise, and nearly always get the last word. Among the female saints in the book one also finds intrepid mothers and wives who inspire their loved ones to stand fast and die for the faith, just as they will do themselves; "holy transvestites" who disguise themselves as men, join monastic communities, and become better monks than their male counterparts; at least two outstanding scholars (Paula and Catherine of Alexandria); and a number of eloquent and fruitful preachers, most notably Mary Magdalen, apostle to Provence.

The conclusion to be drawn from these strong portrayals of women is not that Jacobus was some kind of feminist. As the *Legenda* occasionally suggests and his sermons confirm, he assumed that women were naturally weak and corruptible creatures. Female saints, however, often served as role models for religious men, and Jacobus's own Order of Preachers was particularly attached to Mary Magdalen and Catherine. One of Jacobus's goals in the *Legenda*, moreover, was to arm preachers to combat heresy and disrespect for the clergy; and the chief weapons he provided were dramatic stories demonstrating the power and authority of God's representatives on earth and the inevitable defeat of their enemies. In this context, his portrayals of female saints may have been intended to illustrate the miraculous extent to which frail human vessels are transformed when they are serving God's purposes. As critics such as Jocelyn Wogan-Browne and Karen Winstead have shown, however, once such legends became available in the vernacular they were readily appropriated for a variety of other uses, from supplying precedents for young women who wanted to avoid marriage to "subvert [ing] the authority of the clergy over the laity and... challeng[ing] other traditional relationships of domination and subordination—for example, the authority of husbands over wives or of masters over servants" (Winstead, pp. 65–66).

SHERRY L. REAMES

References and Further Reading

Boureau, Alain. *La Légende dorée: Le système narratif de Jacques de Voragine (†1298)*. Paris: Cerf, 1984.

Dunn-Lardeau, Brenda, ed. *Legenda Aurea: Sept siècles de diffusion: Actes du Colloque international sur la Legenda aurea: texte latin et branches vernaculaires*. Cahiers d'Études médiévales, Cahier spécial 2. Montreal: Bellarmin; Paris: J. Vrin, 1986.

———, ed. *Legenda aurea–la Légende dorée (XIIIe-XVe s.)*: Actes du Congrès international de Perpignan. *Le Moyen français* 32 (1993).

Fleith, Barbara, and Franco Morenzoni, eds. *De la sainteté à l'hagiographie: genèse et usage de la Légende dorée*. Geneva: Droz, 2001.

Guidetti, Stefania, ed. *Il Paradiso e la terra: Iacopo da Varazze e il suo tempo: Atti del convegno internazionale [Varazze, 24–26 sept 1998]*. Florence: SISMEL, Galluzzo, 2001.

Jacobus de Voragine. *Legenda aurea*. edited by Giovanni Paolo Maggioni. 2 vols. Florence: SISMEL, Galluzzo, 1998; 2nd ed., with the text also on CD-ROM, Florence: SISMEL, Galluzzo, 1999.

Jacobus de Voragine. *The Golden Legend: Readings on the Saints*, translated by William Granger Ryan. 2 vols. Princeton: Princeton University Press, 1993.

Reames, Sherry L. *The Legenda Aurea: A Reexamination of Its Paradoxical History*. Madison: University of Wisconsin Press, 1985.

Vitz, Evelyn Birge. "From the Oral to the Written in Medieval and Renaissance Saints' Lives." In *Images of Sainthood in Medieval Europe*, edited by Renate Blumenfeld-Kosinski and Timea Szell. Ithaca: Cornell University Press, 1991, pp. 97–114.

Winstead, Karen A. *Virgin Martyrs: Legends of Sainthood in Late Medieval England*. Ithaca: Cornell University Press, 1997.

Wogan-Browne, Jocelyn. "Saints' Lives and the Female Reader." *Forum for Modern Language Studies* 27 (1991): 314–332.

———. "The Virgin's Tale." In *Feminist Readings in Middle English Literature: The Wife of Bath and All Her Sect*, edited by Ruth Evans and Lesley Johnson. London: Routledge, 1994, pp, 165–194.

See also **Catherine of Alexandria; Hagiography; Margaret of Antioch; Mary the Egyptian; Mary Magdalen; Mary, Virgin: in Literature; Ursula and Her Companions; Virgin Martyrs**

JACQUELINE OF BAVARIA

Jacqueline (Jacoba) of Bavaria (1401–1436), only child of William VI (Count of Hainault, Holland and Zeeland, Lord of Friesland) and Margaret of Burgundy, was the widow of John of Touraine, at the time of his death in 1417, dauphin of France. She succeeded her father after his death in 1417. King Sigismund of Germany did not agree and supported the claim of her father's brother, John of Bavaria (d. 1425). This struggle became interwoven with the factional struggle between Cods and Hooks that, from the death of Count William IV in 1345 and the following war of succession, until 1492, tore apart the counties of Holland and Zeeland repeatedly.

To strengthen her position, Jacqueline married her cousin, John IV, Duke of Brabant (d. 1427). However, Pope Martin V did not recognize the marriage as legitimate until 1428. When her husband came to terms with her uncle in 1420, Jacqueline declared the marriage illegal and married Humphrey of Gloucester, brother of King Henry V of England. Still waiting for papal approval, Humphrey retreated in 1425. John of Brabant received support from Philip the Good, Duke of Burgundy (1419–1467), his cousin, as well as Jaqueline's. In 1428, Jacqueline and Philip concluded a peace treaty that she broke by secretly marrying Frank van Borsselen. As a result she was forced in 1433 to resign in favor of Philip the Good. Three years later she died childless.

Under extreme circumstances Jacqueline had to accomplish a task—ruling a county—usually reserved to men. Later historiographers often explain her failure as resulting from female fickleness and weaknesses proven by her multiple marriages. As a widow Jacqueline had full power. However, she needed to marry to provide offspring, which meant that her husband took over the defense of her interests. When John IV of Brabant failed, she used papal irresolution to reject him, and looked elsewhere for support. Her last marriage was possibly part of an anti-Burgundian conspiracy.

RENÉE NIP

References and Further Reading

Löher, F. von, *Jakobäa von Bayern und ihrer Zeit. Acht Bücher niederländischer Geschichte.* 2 vols. Nördlingen: Drück und Verlag der C. H. Beck'schen Buchhandlung, 1862, 1869.
Nip, Renée. "Conflicting Roles: Jacqueline of Bavaria (d. 1436), Countess and Wife." In *Saints, Scholars and Politicians*, edited by Mathilde van Dijk and Renée Nip. Turnhout: Brepols, 2005, pp. 189–207.
Smit, J.G. *Vorst en onderdaan: Studies over Holland en Zeeland in de late Middeleeuwen.* Louvain: Peeters, 1995.
Vaughan, Richard. *Philip the Good: The Apogee of Burgundy.* London/Harlow: Longmans, 1970; reprint, Woodbridge: Boydell Press, 2002.

See also **Burgundian Netherlands; Marriage, Christian; Marriage, Impediments to; Noble Women; Succession, Royal and Noble**

JADWIGA

Jadwiga, younger daughter of King Louis of Hungary and of Poland, Hedwig (in Polish: Jadwiga) (1374–1399) was betrothed to William of Habsburg, and together they were intended to rule both Hungary and Austria. However, Elizabeth, the queen mother disregarded Louis's arrangements and had Mary, the older daughter, crowned "king" of Hungary. Jadwiga inherited her father's other kingdom. She was crowned "king" of Poland (*rex Poloniae*) in Krakow in 1384. The smooth transition of power following the king's death attests the stability of the Angevin regime and the popularity of Louis's long rule. Female inheritance was without precedent in east-central Europe, where women did not have the right to inherit land at all, even less entire kingdoms. A legal fiction had to be therefore created: Mary and Jadwiga "changed sex," and were regarded and addressed as "kings" rather than queens.

Jadwiga was an intelligent young woman and an accomplished scholar as well as renowned for her

blonde beauty. The Polish nobility prevailed upon her to marry Jagiello, grand duke of Lithuania, the last pagan ruler in Europe. On February 15, 1386, Jagiello converted to Catholicism with his people and was baptized Wladyslaw. With her marriage, Jadwiga took on the role of numerous other queens who had converted their pagan husbands and her representation was henceforth determined by the rules of hagiography. Her image therefore differs markedly from that of her sister, Mary of Hungary. Mary is presented by the chroniclers as the paradigm of bad government in Hungary, proving that "women are not fit to rule": a weak young thing influenced by her mother, Mary provokes the resistance of the Hungarian nobility and a series of tragic disasters. As opposed to her, Jadwiga was a lover of the poor, a benefactor of churches, and an active patron of learning. She founded the bishopric of Wilno (Vilnius), refounded the University at Krakow, and endowed a college in the University of Prague for Lithuanian students. In 1399, Jadwiga died in childbirth. Venerated as a saint already in her lifetime, she was beatified in 1987, and canonized in 1997 by Pope John Paul II, former archbishop of Krakow. Her relics are kept in the cathedral of Krakow.

MARIANNE SÁGHY

References and Further Reading

Davies, Norman. *God's Playground: A History of Poland.* New York: Columbia University, 1982.
Dlugosz, Jan. *The Annals of Jan Dlugosz.* Translated and abridged by Maurice Michael. Charlton: IM Publications, 1997.
Halecki, Oscar. *Jadwiga of Anjou and the Rise of East Central Europe.* Highland Lakes, N.J.: Social Science Monographs, 1991.
Przybyszewski, Fr. Boleslaw. *Saint Jadwiga, Queen of Poland (1374–1399).* translated by Bruce MacQueen. London: Veritas Foundation Publication Centre, 1997.

See also **Conversion, Religious; Eastern Europe; Hagiography; Mary of Hungary II; Queens and Empresses: The West**

JEROME, INFLUENCE OF

Jerome (331–420) was born to a Christian family of Stridon, a town on the border of the Roman provinces of Dalmatia and Pannonia. The nearest center of Roman culture was Aquileia, at the top of the Adriatic Sea, but when Jerome was an adolescent, he was sent all the way to Rome to study at the school of the famous grammarian Aelius Donatus. Jerome graduated from the school of Donatus and moved on to one of Rome's famed rhetorical schools. The curriculum included Latin literature, public speaking, a smattering of philosophy, and perhaps a little Greek. Jerome was probably baptized in Rome, but it was not until he spent some time in Trier, the northern capital of the Emperor Valentinian I, that he first studied Christian texts. A period of years in Aquileia followed, in a circle of Christian intellectuals that included Rufinus of Aquileia, who was later Jerome's bitter rival.

About 373, apparently as a result of a break with his family, and under accusations from an unknown enemy, Jerome set out for the eastern Christian world. For the next decade, he associated with some of the most important Christian leaders of the century. In Antioch, he was befriended by Apollinaris of Laodicaea, who was later accused of Christological heresy. Here, Jerome learned Greek and studied the works of Porphyry and Aristotle. He also became increasingly conflicted about whether he should concentrate on classical or Christian learning; at one point, in a feverish sleep, he had a dream that changed his life. As he later described it in Epistle 22 to his protégée Eustochium, a judge in a blaze of light asked him who he was. "I am a Christian," Jerome answered. "You are lying," the judge retorted, "you are a Ciceronian, not a Christian, for where your treasure is, there your heart is too" (Matthew 6:21). Jerome promised on the spot to never again possess or study secular books. He could hardly have kept this promise, but its spirit did send him out into the Syrian wilderness, where he lived as a hermit. Around 377, he returned to Antioch, where he may have begun to study Hebrew. In 379–380, he was in Constantinople, where he became a friend of the new bishop, Gregory of Nazianzus, studied Greek Christian works, and was present at the Council of Constantinople in 381, where the final version of the Nicene Creed was drafted and where Apollinarus was condemned. From 381 until 384, Jerome lived in Rome, where he was a close confidant of and sometimes the assistant to Pope Damasus.

In spite of this spectacular success as a leader of the Christian world (his name was mentioned as a possible successor to Pope Damasus I), Jerome's attraction to asceticism remained. The Roman women of the Aventine Circle shared this enthusiasm. They were perhaps influenced by the visit to Rome in 334 of Athanasius of Alexandria, an important proponent of Christian asceticism, and by the publication of his Athanasius's *Life of Antony* in Latin in 356. If so, the trend had already begun when Jerome was studying in Rome, but he only came face-to-face with it following his own exposure to ascetic traditions in Aquileia (where he had convinced his sister to take the veil) and Antioch. The Aventine women were members of the most important Roman families; most were married with children, but they managed in various

ways to champion sexual chastity. They included Marcela, Melania, Fabiola, and the woman who became Jerome's closest friend, Paula. Some of these women later became part of the circle of the British preacher Pelagius; after the sack of Rome by the Goths in 410, a few fled to their country estates in North Africa, where they shocked Augustine with their spiritual independence, and inspired his articulation of the doctrine of original sin.

In this heady ascetic atmosphere, as the favorite of the pope, Jerome began his greatest scholarly achievement, a new Latin translation of the Bible from the original Greek and Hebrew sources, the version known as the Vulgate. Predictably, when the first parts of this were made public, they were greeted with indignant criticism. This was the first part of Jerome's fall from grace. The second had to do with his enthusiasm for the new ascetic culture: not only did he encourage Paula's daughter Eustochium to become the first consecrated virgin of Christian Rome, he also engaged in a vicious dispute against Helvidius, a layman who, alarmed by this surging tide of sexual renunciation, had the courage to write in defense of the Christian married state, even suggesting that Joseph and the Virgin Mary had been in a normal marriage. Jerome ripped into this position with withering satire. Finally, in 383, Pope Damasus died, and was succeeded not by Jerome but by the unsympathetic deacon Siricius. Jerome then became the focus of so many accusations that once again he was forced to leave town. In 385, he set sail for the east, eventually settling in Bethlehem. Here he was joined by Paula, Eustochium and, eventually, Paula's granddaughter, Paula the Younger. This Paula was consecrated to chastity at birth and sent from Rome to be raised in Bethlehem, but she arrived only after her grandmother's death in 404.

Jerome lived in Bethlehem until he died in 420. In these years he finished the Vulgate Bible translation, wrote a number of important commentaries on books of the Bible, and engaged in various theological controversies, including disputes with Rufinus and Augustine.

Jerome never mitigated his feisty and contentious nature, but he did continue a close relationship with Eustochium, who died just a year before he did. His long letter to her about the life of consecrated virginity, Epistle 22, was one of the most widely read of his works in the Middle Ages. Although Jerome never wrote a commentary on the Song of Songs, he used those enigmatic poems throughout this letter, urging Eustochium to think of herself as a Bride of Christ. His spiritual advice to Eustochium became one of the most important sources for the articulation of women's consecrated virginity. Jerome's writings against Helvidius were used in support of both consecrated virginity of women and the defense of the perpetual virginity of Mary. In the ninth century, Paschasius Radbertus cast his treatise on the defense of the virginity of Mary *in partu* (that is, at the moment of the birth of Jesus, a doctrine that did become part of official medieval theology) as a letter from Jerome to Paula and Eustochium. Jerome quite possibly would not have minded this at all, but perhaps the ultimate irony of his life is that his writings on gender and sexuality were later used to restrict women rather than to give them the spiritual freedom he had in mind.

E. ANN MATTER

References and Further Reading

Barr, Jane J. "The Influence of Saint Jerome on Medieval Attitudes to Women," In *After Eve: Women, Theology and the Christian Tradition*, edited by Janet Soskice. Basingstoke: Marshal Pickering, 1990, pp. 89–102.

Clark, Elizabeth A., "The Uses of the Song of Songs: Origen and the Later Latin Fathers," In *Ascetic Piety and Women's Faith: Essays on Late Ancient Christianity*. Lewiston, N.Y.: Edwin Mellen Press, 1986, pp. 386–427.

———. "Theory and Practice in Late Ancient Asceticism." *Journal of Feminist Studies in Religion* 5 (1989): 25–46.

Hinson, E. Glenn, "When the World Collapsed: The Spirituality of Women During the Barbarian Invasion of Rome," *Perspectives* in *Religious Studies* 20 (1993): 113–130.

Jerome. *Letters.* translated by Charles Christopher Mierow. Ancient Christian Writers, Westminster, Md.: Newman Press, 1963.

Kelly, J. N. D. *Jerome: His Life, Writings, and Controversies.* New York: Harper & Row, 1975.

Oppel, John. "Saint Jerome and the History of Sex." *Viator* 24 (1993): 1–22.

Yarbrough, Anne, "Christianization in the Fourth Century: The Example of Roman Women." *Church History* 45 (1976): 149–165.

See also **Asceticism; Augustine, Influence of; Bride of Christ: Imagery; Church; Letter Writing; Literacy and Reading: Latin; Mary, Virgin; Theology; Virginity**

JESUS/GOD AS MOTHER

Extended comparison of Jesus to a mother first occurred in devotional texts of the twelfth century and reached its fullest expression in the *Showings* (also known as *The Revelations of Divine Love*) by the fourteenth century English mystic and theologian, Julian of Norwich. References to God and Jesus as a mother in the Bible and by patristic writers of the early Church, however, provide warrant for this comparison.

Several Old Testament verses describe God as a mother who gives birth to humanity and nurtures the Israelites as children. Deuteronomy 32:18, for example, chides the Hebrews for forgetting "the God who gave you birth." Isaiah 42:14 warns that after a long period of restraint, God will "cry out like a woman in labor, / I will gasp and pant." God claims to have given birth to the house of Israel in Isaiah 46:3; and his love for the Hebrews is compared to the love of a nursing mother in Isaiah 49:15 and 66:13. In Hosea 11:3, the Lord speaks of himself as a mother who teaches her children to walk and feeds, heals, and loves them.

Warrant for the comparison of Jesus to a mother comes from the female figure Wisdom who appears in Proverbs and the apocryphal books Ecclesiasticus and the Wisdom of Solomon, now included only in the Catholic Bible. In Ecclesiasticus 24:24 DV, Wisdom proclaims, "I am the mother of fair love, and of fear, and of knowledge, and of holy hope." Wisdom asserts in Proverbs 8:22–30 and Ecclesiasticus 24:5–11 that she was with God before time and participated in the creation of the earth: "I was with him forming all things" (Prov. 8:30 DV). The speaker in Wisdom 7:22–27 praises her as "a vapour of the power of God, and a certain pure emanation of the glory of the almighty God...For she is the brightness of eternal light, and the unspotted mirror of God's majesty, and the image of his goodness" (Wis. 7:25–26 DV).

In the New Testament Wisdom's qualities lead to her identification with Christ as Logos, the Word of God is invoked at the beginning of John's Gospel. Paul confirms this identification by referring to Christ as the power and wisdom of God (1 Cor. 1:14) and asserting that the Son, like Wisdom, participated with God in creation (Col. 1:15–17).

Drawing on these allusions in the Old and New Testaments, the Fathers of the Church, especially Augustine of Hippo, and medieval theologians continued to attribute to Christ the creative and nurturing characteristics of a mother. However, they did not comment on the gender implied by this analogy.

From the twelfth through the fourteenth centuries, Western Christians developed a greater sense of the humanity of Jesus and expressed a broader range of emotion in their devotions. This affective piety encouraged a fuller exploration of the feminine qualities of Christ. In his prayers, for example, Anselm of Canterbury refers to Jesus as a mother who endures the labor pains of the Passion to give new life to his children, who nurses them, and who protects them like the mother hen of Matthew 23:37. Mystics, such as Bernard of Clairvaux; Marguerite d'Oinge; and the three nuns of Helfta, Gertrude the Great, Mechthild of Hackeborn, and Mechthild of Magdeburg, also attribute maternal characteristics to Christ.

The fullest comparison of Jesus to a mother is developed by Julian of Norwich, who reported on a visionary experience she had in 1373 and the understanding she achieved after twenty years of meditation in the two versions of her *Showings*. Julian's account of the three maternities of Jesus, in creating, in recreating, and in working, appears in Revelation 14, chapters 52 through 63 of the long text. Alluding to the Wisdom tradition, Julian depicts Jesus, the Logos or Word of God, as mother in creation because he incorporates the soul with its image of God into the body. Jesus is mother in re-creation because he takes on human flesh to make atonement to God the Father and redeems humanity through the labor pains of the Passion. Jesus is mother in working because he nurtures and protects his children on earth, feeding them with his own body and blood in the Eucharist. Julian of Norwich's concept of Jesus the Mother develops the feminine characteristics of God implied in Biblical and patristic texts and emphasized by affective spirituality.

DENISE NOWAKOWSKI BAKER

References and Further Reading

Bradley, Sister Ritamary. "Patristic Background and the Motherhood Similitude in Julian of Norwich." *Christian Scholar's Review* 8 (1978): 101–113.

Bynum, Caroline Walker. *Jesus as Mother: Studies in the Spirituality of the High Middle Ages.* Berkeley and Los Angeles: University of California Press, 1982.

Heimmel, Jennifer. *"God Is Our Mother": Julian of Norwich and the Medieval Image of Christian Feminine Divinity.* Elizabethan & Renaissance Studies, 92.5. Salzburg: Universität Salzburg, 1982.

Newman, Barbara. "Some Mediaeval Theologians and the Sophia Tradition." *The Downside Review* 108 (1990): 111–130.

See also **Gender Ideologies; Gertrude the Great; Julian of Norwich; Mechtild of Hackeborn; Mechtild of Magdeburg; Theology; Wisdom**

JEWELRY

Jewelry inflects the body's significance, signaling status, identity, and personal history. Byzantine empresses and Scandinavian chiefs might communicate their authority with earrings or bracteates (arm bands). Popes and kings might, on acceding to their thrones, be granted rings or coronets as part of their regalia. Merchants could seal documents with their rings, while their daughters received rings and brooches at marriage. Pilgrims might affix modest mass-produced badges or amulets to their cloaks or hats, recording their visits to holy sites.

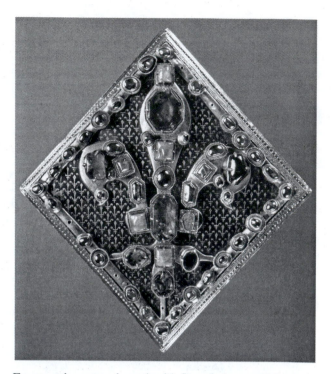

Fourteenth-century brooch with fleur-de-lys motif, from the Treasury of Saint-Denis, MR345. Photo: Peter Willi. Location: Louvre, Paris, France. Credit: Réunion des Musées Nationaux / Art Resource, N.Y.

Owing to the widespread practice of burial with luxury items in early medieval Mediterranean cultures, many jewels survive from this period. Gold was prized, as was enamel work. In later medieval Europe, with changes in burial practices, fewer jewels have survived. Used as a form of currency, jewels were regularly traded, reduced to precious materials, and refashioned.

Gems, which until the thirteenth century were polished, not cut, were especially valued, both for their economic worth and for their mystical properties. Various lapidary tractates like Albertus Magnus's *De Mineralibus* and Marbod of Rennes's *De Lapidibus* catalogued the talismanic and alchemical characteristics of various gems (sapphires, emeralds, diamonds, rubies, etc.) as well as pearls and coral. Certain combinations of settings and gems were thought to ensure good health, happiness, or power.

Although both men and women wore jewelry, preachers and moralists railed mainly against the frippery of women, seeing their jewels as seducing men; sumptuary legislation also sought to limit such finery. Such responses indicate the importance of jewelry in medieval culture. As recipients and donors, purchasers and wearers, women exercised considerable control over this communicative medium and form of capital.

ADRIAN RANDOLPH

References and Further Reading

Lightbown, Ronald W. *Mediaeval European Jewellery*. London: Victoria and Albert Museum, 1992.

Walker, Alicia. "Myth and Magic in Early Byzantine Marriage Jewelry: The Persistence of Pre-Christian Traditions." In *The Material Culture of Sex, Procreation, and Marriage in Premodern Europe*, edited by Anne L. McClanan and Karen Rosoff Encarnación. Palgrave, 2002, pp. 59–78.

See also **Betrothals; Clothing; Coinage; Death, Mourning, and Commemoration; Dowry and Other Marriage Gifts; Grave Goods; Magic and Charms; Sumptuary Law**

JEWISH MYSTICAL THOUGHT, BODY AND SOUL IN

Medieval Jewish thought about body and soul can be understood in terms of a conversation among rabbinic traditions, philosophical reinterpretations of those traditions, and mystical thought sometimes attempting to synthesize these two strains, and sometimes drawing on Neoplatonic traditions to elaborate ideas quite different from either of these. The female imaging of body and soul is axial in the mystical synthesis of these traditions. In Hebrew, "body" is designated with the word *guf* or *Gufa*, female-gendered terms. In the Hebrew Bible and the Midrash, the following five words commonly referred to the soul: *nephesh* (blood), *ruach* (wind or spirit), *neshamah* (disposition), *jechidah* (the only one), *chayyah* (living soul). Each of these terms is gendered female, and as Tova Rosen asserts, "this is no superficial linguistic bias" (p. 83). Female engenderment of body and soul draws on a wide range of roles traditionally associated with women.

Understandings of the nature of the human body were related to communal conception of the divine body, because they are linked in the creation narrative of Genesis 1:26–7 "And God said, 'Let us make man in our image, after our likeness...'" Rabbinic literature generally preserves anthropomorphic conceptions of God's body, even up to the ninth century. For example, Robert Bonfils presents evidence that Carolingian Jews believed God had a form like humans but incalculably larger. This begins to change with the emergence of Jewish philosophy in the tenth century. Like their Muslim counterparts, Jewish philosophers worked to systematize Jewish thought by establishing divine unity, dependent upon divine incorporeality. Thus beginning with Sa'adya Gaon (b. 882 Fayyûm, upper Egypt, d. 942 in Baghdad) they worked to reinterpret as metaphorical biblical and rabbinical references to the divine body. This divested the human body of significance deriving from its resemblance to the divine form.

Medieval Jewish philosophers drew on classical traditions of representing the body as feminine to express its radical unlikeness to God. Maimonides, a rationalist philosopher (b. 1138 in Cordova, Spain, d. 1204 in Egypt), uses the metaphor of prostitution to describe the embodied state; in his *Guide of the Perplexed* he famously declares that "matter is a married harlot," expressing simultaneously the body's radical difference from the divine and its flawed connection to God. He also made a similar separation between God and the soul. Once this break was made, medieval thinkers use feminine metaphors both to conceptualize separation, and to imagine the possibility of reconnecting with the divine.

Some mystical sources worked to repair this rupture, using different figurations of the female body. The *Zohar*, the thirteenth century core kabbalistic compendium, expresses three main viewpoints on the body. The first accords with the Maimonidean perspective, asserting that it is evil beyond redemption, and must be broken and humiliated. The second holds that it is predisposed to neither good nor evil, but capable of improvement and redemption by proper performance of the mitzvoth (divine commandments central to Jewish practice). The third, more radical view holds that the human body is modeled after the sefirot, the ten emanations of God. In this view the body itself assists humans in their attempts to reach the divine (see Tishby).

In the second point of view, the body is treated as a tool. Used correctly, it is restorative, and its female gendering serves mimetic purposes. The male mystic is "improved" by a narrative and imaginative transgendering so that he resembles a greater, female-gendered entity, the community of Israel, a plurality enacting Jewish scriptural ideals. Here, when the male enacts Jewish ideals, he loses his individual status and imagines himself as a representative of the community of Israel, a female-gendered entity, which relates to God through structures of the covenant sometimes imagined as a marriage.

In the third point of view, the body is treated as a text. Believing the body is modeled on the sefirot, male writers imagined themselves as the Shekhinah, a female aspect of the divine, and the lowest of the sefirot. By identifying with her, humans "join" the divine pleroma, the members of which are understood to relate to one another in sexual terms. For example, the Shekhinah sexually "receives" divine outflow from her supernal bridegroom, Tiferet. In this way, divine influence is transmitted downward to the created world. By identifying with and imaginatively joining the Shekhinah, the male mystic is able to receive the divine outflow as well. Here the male mystic uses feminine imagery to redeem the body, imaginatively transgendering it, and reassimilating it to the divine pleroma.

Similarly, Maimonides posited a fundamental alienation of the soul; he claimed that human efforts toward self-perfection did not affect the divine. His view radicalized rabbinic beliefs that the soul was created in the celestial realms, but outside the divine realm proper. Kabbalists countered by asserting that the neshama, the highest part of the soul had a divine origin, and that the tripartite soul (nefesh, ruach, neshama) served as a model of the sefirot, and in this, God. They believed that *neshamot* derived from the divine substance, descended the sefirotic tree, and gestated in and emerged from the womb of the Shekhinah. To kabbalists, perfecting one human soul changed the nature of the divine. In this case then, the feminized soul was both the object of formation and the agent of change.

In each of these cases the writers use female-gendered images of body and soul to conceptualize a reconnection with the divine. Writers believing that the body is not redeemable dramatized these beliefs by imagining themselves as abject women—widows or abandoned wives. In these circumstances they use images of broken sexual union to dramatize the rupture between the embodied human and the divine, and they imagine its repair through metaphors of sexual reunion after death. Finally, kabbalists reimagined the feminized soul as a microcosm for the sefirot, or the divine form. Female engenderment of body and soul served simultaneously to emphasize the radical divide between God and embodied humans as it also imagined sexualized channels for their reunion in life and after death.

MARLA SEGOL

References and Further Reading

Bland, Kalman. "The Well-Tempered Medieval Sensorium." In *The Artless Jew: Medieval and Modern Affirmations and Denials of the Visual*. Princeton, N.J.: Princeton University Press, 2000.

Boyarin, Daniel. *Carnal Israel: Reading Sex in Talmudic Culture*. Berkeley: University of California Press, 1993.

Eilberg-Schwartz, Howard. *People of the Body: Jews and Judaism from an Embodied Perspective*. Albany, N.Y.: SUNY Press, 1992.

Hecker, Joel. *Mystical Bodies, Mystical Meals: Eating and Embodiment in Medieval Kabbalah*. Detroit: Wayne State University Press, 2005.

Rosen, Tova. *Unveiling Eve: Reading Gender in Medieval Hebrew Literature*. Philadelphia: University of Pennsylvania Press, 2003.

See also **Body in Literature and Religion; Shekhinah; Soul**

JEWISH WOMEN

This entry surveys the history of Jewish women's experiences as unmarried daughters, wives, and widows, especially their legal and economic statuses. Dispersed throughout the Mediterranean and Islamic worlds during the early Middle Ages, by the high medieval period Jewish communities were established in northern Europe as well. These communities remained strong through the 1200s when expulsions began, 1290 from England, 1306 from France, and eventually 1492 from Spain. Afterwards Jews remained in some Italian cities (experiencing periodic mini-expulsions), and northern European Jews wended their way east, eventually creating a vibrant community in Poland. Although northern European settlements were culturally and numerically significant, the largest and most stable communities for the high medieval period were those in Iberia and Islamic regions.

All Jewish communities valued gendered roles for men and women. If it were economically feasible for men to study, the normative ethic that education went hand in hand with morality meant that they did so. Men were also religiously obliged to marry and father children. Similarly women were expected to marry, excel at domestic duties, care for their husbands and look after their children, with some flexibility in cases where they ran their own businesses. Broadly defined, the Jews of Christendom had much in common with each other in terms of local culture and interpretation of Jewish law, as did those Jews who lived under Islamic rule. Although Jews could not settle unless their rights to live in autonomous communities under Jewish law were respected, they never lived in a vacuum. They spoke the language of the majority culture and interacted with Christians and/or Muslims frequently in their day-to-day lives. Even matters that used to be classified as beyond the influence of majority culture, such as inheritance and marriage, are increasingly understood to have been shaped by local majority customs. For instance, consider the Jewish women of the Islamic world (in particular of Fustat/Cairo for which thousands of documents in Hebrew script, most from c. 800–1200, were preserved in a *Geniza*, or burial repository for sacred writings). Cairene women were not as strictly enclosed as their Muslim women neighbors, but they experienced less physical mobility than Jewish women of Christian Europe. The Cairenes were also significantly more likely to find themselves married to a man who practiced polygyny, or even polygamy, while bigamy was banned among northern European Jews, if occasionally practiced in Iberia.

Regional Differences

Within the Christian political sphere the Jewish communities of northern Europe (German, northern France, and England) and southern Europe (Iberia, southern France, and Italy) viewed women's status somewhat differently. Jewish women living in northern Europe experienced the most autonomy in their economic activities, including the ability to travel for business; and they were more likely than their southern counterparts to be found functioning as guardians for their children and as business partners, or even supervisors, for their adult sons. The banker Licoricia of Winchester acted as the matriarch of her family until her murder in 1277, managing extensive commercial transactions with the king of England and other powerful Christians. Northern Jews married off their sons and daughters when they were equally of an early age, perhaps as young as twelve or thirteen; while some southerners, such as those of Catalonia in northeastern Iberia, waited until between sixteen and eighteen for both men and women; and Italians adopted the customs of the Christian majority by marrying men in their late twenties to women between fourteen and eighteen. Divorce was permitted to Jews in all communities, although it probably occurred less frequently in the north where a woman could not be divorced against her will.

In general in Jewish communities daughters did not come into their inheritances before marriage. They had rights to a dowry and to maintenance by their fathers until married when they were transferred to the legal jurisdiction of their husbands. Poor, young Jewish women sometimes served as domestic servants in Jewish homes. Community leaders and scholars of Jewish law like Moses Maimonides (1135–1204), leader of the Jewish community in Cairo, encouraged their coreligionists to employ Jewish girls (especially orphans) instead of purchasing domestic slaves who were not Jewish.

In contrast to the passive roles of unmarried daughters, some Jewish wives were financially active, especially in northern Europe. Dolce of Worms, was celebrated by her husband Rabbi Eleazar for her efforts to earn a good living, her needlework, and her support of Eleazar and his students in religious study. While married, Preciosa de Villemagne of Perpignan was one of the most active moneylenders in this thriving town on the Pyreneean frontier and probably served as her husband Isaac's economic partner in the absence of a son. Other southern European Jewish wives, however, are far less visible in the historical and economic record. When the translator Judah ibn Tibbon (an immigrant from Islamic Spain who fled to Lunel in southern France) extolled the virtues of his unnamed daughter-in-law, they were all domestic: housekeeping, nursing her child and husband in illness, and balancing the household budget.

Widows

Even more than wives, Jewish widows were active in many commercial spheres. Banking and moneylending predominated among northern European women, as they did among Jewish men in that region. Jewish widows also served as active and effective guardians for their minor children. Some widows, such as Regina (or Reina), widow of Bonjuses Asday, the most successful woman banker/moneylender in thirteenth-century Perpignan, increased their own independent financial prospects through business connections made as widowed guardians. Wealthy Jewish widows amassed fortunes and made significant charitable donations to their communities. Sara de Cabestany also of Perpignan, born in Béziers and with family ties to another southern French community in Narbonne, set up a charitable trust through her Latin testament to provide dowries for poor girls and enable poor boys to study. Still others remained financially passive, such as Astruga ibn Dalal, of Barcelona, who was reluctant to take up guardianship responsibilities and chose instead to reside with her children while leaving their financial matters in the hands of male relatives. Adult sons and brothers of Jewish widows throughout the medieval Jewish world had the potential to control their mothers and sisters in commercial matters. Sons in the southern regions probably looked after their aging mothers more often than they were guided by them. Some widows were economically vulnerable and the absence of children, especially of sons, contributed to their suffering.

Economic and Religious Roles

Overall Jewish women were active in many different occupations; money lending and banking have already been mentioned, but medicine education, and trade in womanly crafts were also their professions. When Jewish women practiced medicine their clients were limited neither to obstetrical patients nor to women. For instance, Rabbi Judah Asheri, of Toledo, claimed that, as an ailing baby his eyesight would have been saved if only he had remained in his hometown in Germany under the care of a Jewish woman practitioner there. Maimonides corresponded with a woman who founded and maintained her own school for younger children, with the help of her elder son. One substantial Cairene businesswoman (and divorcée), active during the early twelfth century, was called "Karima" or "Al-Wusha." She worked as a broker of textiles and other women's embroidery work.

Religiously there seem to have been more opportunities for women's involvement in northern Europe than existed in the south. While some elite women of Worms were said to have led the female members of their community in prayer, the scholars of Catalonia were perplexed because women were supposed to recite the Grace after meals, but few women with whom they were acquainted actually did so. Thus, although there were a few exceptions, such as Qasmuna Bint Isma'il of late eleventh- or early twelfth-century Islamic Granada in Iberia who wrote Arabic poetry, in general even elite Jewish women were not very learned. In particular, they do not seem to have been taught Hebrew along with their brothers.

Sexual Transgressions

Most Jewish women followed the customs of their families and the moral dictates of their communities and led respectable married lives, but sexual liaisons across religious lines occasionally occurred. Jewish leaders viewed the seduction of Jewish women by gentiles as an acutely demeaning sign of their inferior status vis-à-vis the dominant community. A few relations across religious boundaries resulted in marriage. The Cairo Geniza preserves a request for aid from a female convert from Christianity who claims to have been the widow of Rabbi David Todros of Narbonne; and it was technically permitted in the Islamic world for Muslim men and Jewish women to marry. The Roman Catholic Church feared miscegenation and legislated against it repeatedly, but sex between Jewish women and Christian men seems to have occasionally occurred in Christian Europe. In the 1260s, Goigs de Pallafols, banker to King James I of Aragon, petitioned her royal creditor for permission to continue living with her Christian lover, and the king probably allowed this, hoping for her eventual conversion. Count Theobald of Blois's extramarital relationship with Polcelina (Pullcelina) of Blois was the purported cause of his wife's false ritual murder accusation against the Jewish community. The Count subsequently massacred Polcelina and thirty other Jewish people in 1171. When such relationships surfaced, although this happened extremely rarely,

they often served to demarcate the precariousness of Jewish minority existence.

REBECCA WINER

References and Further Reading

Adelman, Howard. "Italian Jewish Women," In *Jewish Women in Historical Perspective*, 2nd ed. edited by Judith R. Baskin Detroit: Wayne State University Press, 1998, pp. 150–168.

Assis, Yom Tov. "Sexual Behavior in Medieval Hispano-Jewish Society," In *Jewish History: Essays in Honor of Chimen Abramsky*, edited by A. Rapoport Albert and S.J. Zipperstein. London: P. Halban, 1988, pp. 25–59.

Baskin, Judith R. "Jewish Women in the Middle Ages." In *Jewish Women in Historical Perspective*. 2nd ed, edited by Judith R. Baskin. Detroit: Wayne State University Press, 1998, pp. 101–127.

Baumgarten, Elisheva. *Mothers and Children: Jewish Family Life in Medieval Europe*. Princeton: Princeton University Press, 2004.

Goitein, S. D. *A Mediterranean Society: An Abridgement in One Volume*, edited by Jacob Lassner. Berkeley: University of California Press, 1999.

Grossman, Avraham. *Pious and Rebellious: Jewish Women in Medieval Europe*. Waltham, Mass.: Brandeis University Press, 2004.

Hebrew Ethical Wills, edited and translated by Israel Abrahams. 2 vols. Philadelphia: Jewish Publication Society of America, 1926.

Jewish History, 51 (1991) and (2002).

Jordan, William Chester. *Women and Credit in Pre-Industrial and Developing Societies*. Philadelphia: University of Pennsylvania Press, 1993, pp. 11–49.

Klein, Elka. "The Widow's Portion: Law, Custom, and Marital Property among Medieval Catalan Jews." *Viator* 31 (2000): 147–163.

———. Medieval Sourcebook: Reciting the Grace after Meals: The Status of Jewish Women, from *Berakhot*, chap. 7: http://www.fordham.edu/HALSALL/source/jewishwomen-grace.html.

Melammed, Renée Levine. "Sephardi Women in the Medieval and Early Modern Periods." In *Jewish Women In Historical Perspective*, 2nd ed. edited by Judith R. Baskin. Detroit: Wayne State University Press, 1998, pp. 128–149.

Nirenberg, David. "Chapter 5. Sex and Violence between Majority and Minority," in *Communities of Violence: Persecution of Minorities in the Middle Ages*. Princeton, N.J.: Princeton University Press, 1996.

Rambi: *The Index of Articles on Jewish Studies*, sponsored by the Jewish National and University Library, Hebrew University, Jerusalem, http://jnul.huji.ac.il/rambi.

Schereschewsky, Ben-Zion (Benno). "Divorce," "Dowry," "Husbands and Wives" and "Widow." In *Encyclopedia Judaica*, Jerusalem Encyclopedia Judaic 1971, 16 volumes, yearbooks, and decennial books and CD-ROM.

Shatzmiller, Joseph. "Women in the Medical Profession." In *Jews, Medicine, and Medieval Society*. Berkeley: University of California Press, 1994, pp. 108–112.

Stow, Kenneth R. *Alienated Minority: The Jews of Medieval Latin Europe*. Cambridge, Mass.: Harvard University Press, 1992.

Tallan, Cheryl. "Opportunities for Medieval Northern European Jewish Widows in the Public and Domestic

Spheres," In *Upon My Husband's Death: Widows in the Literature and Histories of Medieval Europe*, edited by Louise Mirrer, Ann Arbor, Mich.: University of Michigan Press, 1992, pp. 115–127.

Winer, Rebecca. *Women, Wealth, and Community in Perpignan c. 1250–1300: Christians, Jews, and Enslaved Muslims in a Medieval Mediterranean Town.* Aldershot: Ashgate, 2005.

See also **Dolce of Worms; Investment and Credit; Jewish Mystical Thought, Body and Soul in; Jewish Women: Latin and European Vernacular Literature; Law, Jewish; Literature, Hebrew; Marriage, Jewish; Mikveh; Pregnancy and Childbirth: Jewish Women; Qasmūna Bint Ismā'īl; Widows as Guardians**

JEWISH WOMEN: LATIN AND EUROPEAN VERNACULAR LITERATURE

It is striking to note how different the representations of Jewish men and Jewish women were in medieval literature. The Jewish man was the quintessential Jew: blind to Christian truth, committed to the law and the letter of the Bible, easy associate of the devil, partner in "deicide," usurer, cruel abuser of Christians and their religion. Visual representations often marked the Jew with a pointed Jewish hat, a swarthy appearance, or a bodily deformity. Conversely, Jewish women were above all women, and most frequently mothers and wives. Medieval narratives represented the Jewish woman as a passive witness to abuses perpetrated by her husband, or as a potential convert to Christianity. The pervasive belief in the malleability of female personality, its openness to influence, suggested that a Jewish woman could be turned into a good Christian, while the Jewish male mind (tutored in the Talmud) and body (marked by circumcision) were more permanently different, immutable.

Exemplary Jewish women appeared in early medieval liturgy: Rachel's lament was incorporated into liturgical drama, Judith's heroics came to be seen as prefiguring Mary. Jewish women appear more frequently in the tales known as *exempla*, narratives that conveyed moral truths in a colorful manner and aimed to correct common errors. These stories were widely used in sermons and pastoral writings, in Latin and in the vernaculars. A widely known tale was that of the Jewish Boy, a story with Greek origins, known to Gregory the Great and Bede, and which became part of the corpus of Marian miracles that coalesced in the twelfth century. The story tells of a Jewish Boy who had taken communion with Christian schoolmates and suffered cruel punishment once he told his father what he had done. The story has the Jewish father throw his son into a furnace, but all versions emphasize the Jewish mother's grief. When the story was illustrated, artists emphasized the Jewish mother's pain and suffering in dramatic gestures. The dramatic denouement had the boy saved by the Virgin Mary in the furnace, the father thrown into it, and the mother, son, and Jewish community converted to Christianity. By the thirteenth century the story was known in Anglo-Norman, French, and Gallician translations of Marian miracles.

Stories and images of the Virgin Mary offered a niche within which the Jewish woman could be explored. Mary had, after all, been a Jewish woman, as the apocryphal writings about her life, expressed in liturgy and art, made clear. Narratives related to Mary often led to conversion, to the realization of Christian truth. Thus Cantiga 107 of the *Cantigas de Santa Maria* is a story of the saving conversion of a beautiful Jewish woman by the Virgin Mary. The Dominican writer Thomas of Cantimpré collected hundreds of miracles stories—old and new—in his *Bonum universale de apibus* (*The Universal Good Thing about Bees*) (written between 1256 and 1263). He recounts a contemporary tale about a nun from the Parc des Dames Cistercian house, a woman of great piety, whom he had met and interviewed about her earlier life. The nun Catherine had been a little Jewish girl, Rachel, who discovered Christianity through the Christian names that seemed so different from Jewish ones. She claimed to have loved above all the name of the Virgin Mary. After a period of instruction in Christianity, she received a vision of Mary, dressed in white like a Cistercian nun, and this finally confirmed her desire to convert and to become a religious.

The deepening polemical nature of ideas and representations of Jews in the later Middle Ages led to a sharpening of the difference in representations of Jewish men and women. The figure of the Jewish woman was affected by the evolving figure of Mary, a Jewish woman too. It was possible to make the Jew more menacing by the absorption of his female counterpart into spheres of love and tenderness associated with motherhood. Geoffrey Chaucer (d. 1399) had his pilgrim Prioress recount the story of the killing of a young Christian boy by a Jew in the Jewish quarter of an oriental city. The child's anxious mother enters the quarter to look for her son. Miraculous intervention by Mary led to the discovery of the boy and to the punishment of the Jewish man. Jewish women were drawn into the sphere of mercy and motherly love around the Christian mother and the Virgin Mary, a sphere menaced by the cruel Jewish man.

European literatures thus treated the Jewish woman as *women* above all, and most frequently as matrons and mothers. Occasionally a nubile Jewish woman is represented as a figure who might lead a Christian man astray, but the Jewish woman remains passive, attractive for her beauty alone. Stories from Iberia are more explicit about the sexual crossing of religious lines, and in them the Jewish woman is a bit more seductive. It is striking how few of the misogynist traits attributed to women—seduction, dissimulation—were applied to Jewish women. The Jewish woman was a cipher for female submission; here too some "drift" from the image of Mary may be at work.

By the High Middle Ages most Jewish families lived in towns and cities, though from the thirteenth century several regions of Europe expelled their Jewish communities, and this often forced Jews to find their homes in new areas, in central and eastern Europe, often in small towns where they engaged in small trade and subsistence lending. Jewish women worked alongside their husbands, fathers, and brothers in family workshops and businesses. Their life was contained within the streets and quarters inhabited by Jews, where they may have been encountered by non-Jews as vendors and moneylenders. Little of their life-worlds is portrayed in medieval literature; but they inhabited the imagination as alluring figures: female, exotic, somewhat out of reach, yet ripe for dynamic remaking at the hands of a Christian man, lay or priest.

MIRI RUBIN

References and Further Reading

Aizenberg, Edna. "*Una judva muy fermosa*: The Jewess as Sex Object in Medieval Spanish Literature and Lore." *La Coronica* 12 (1984): 187–194.

Lampert, Lisa. Gender and Jewish Difference from Paul to Shakespeare. Philadelphia: University of Pennsylvania Press, 2004.

Mirrer, Louise. "The Beautiful Jewess: Marisaltos in Alfonso X's *Cantiga* 107." In *Women, Jews and Muslims in the Texts of Reconquest Spain*. Ann Arbor, Mich.: University of Michigan Press, 1996, 31–44.

See also **Chaucer, Geoffrey; Exemplum; Jewish Women; Mary, Virgin: in Literature; Miracles and Miracle Collections**

JOAN I

Joan I (1326–1382), as the only surviving child of Charles of Calabria (d. 1328) and Mary of Valois (d. 1331), held the titles of Countess of Provence and Forcalquier, titular queen of Jerusalem and Sicily, Princess of Achea, and Queen of Naples. She inherited the throne of the kingdom of Naples from her grandfather, Robert the Wise (d. 1343), who groomed her to succeed to the throne, allegedly allowing her to receive men of state even from a young age. Once she had inherited the royal office of the far-reaching kingdom of Naples, Joan was positioned to be one of the most powerful rulers of her time. But her reign is depicted as one of chaos, plagued with the same kind of constant political and military disruptions, some of which her grandfather had faced, especially with Hungarian factions vying for control in a kingdom ruled by a woman. Her biographers, from contemporaries on, have ridiculed her life as one full of political missteps and sexual intrigue. Her marriage to Andrew of Hungary had been arranged in 1334, and had been supported by Pope John XXII, who eagerly sought the union of the two branches of the Angevin family. This union was short-lived. Resenting her grandfather's stipulation that Andrew would share in the royal title, Joan most likely ordered the assassination of Andrew of Hungary in 1345. Andrew's brother Louis retaliated by trying to annex Naples. To secure stability for the kingdom, Joan subsequently entered into a series of strategic marriages with Louis of Taranto (d. 1362), James of Majorca (d. 1375), and Otto of Brunswick (d. 1398), but had no surviving children, causing a crisis in royal succession. In the schism of the Church, she sided with the Avignonese pope, Clement VII, over the Roman pope Urban VI, bringing on the public disappointment and criticism of the public mystic, Catherine of Siena, who urged Joan in letters to support the Roman papacy. Joan's volatile rule ended with her murder at the hands of a political rival, Charles III of Durazzo, in 1382.

DARLEEN PRYDS

References and Further Reading

Gil, C. *Jeanne de Naples, Comtesse de Provence et Le Grand Schisme d'Occident*. Paris: Les éditions le semaphore, 2001.

"Johanna I," *An Annotated Index of Medieval Women*, edited by A. Echols and M. Williams. Oxford: Berg and Princeton: Markus Wiener, 1992, pp. 268–269.

Kiesewetter, A. "Giovanna I," *Dizionario Biografico degli Italiani*, v. 55, Rome: Instituto della Encyclopedia italiana, 2000, pp. 455–477.

Raia, C. *Giovanna I d'Angiò Regina di Napoli*. Naples: T. Piranti, 2000.

See also **Catherine of Siena; Italy; Queens and Empresses: The West**

JOAN OF ARC

The lasting reputation of Joan of Arc (called *Jehanne* in French and variously surnamed *Darc* or *Day*) (c. 1412–1431) rests on her glorious but improbable military victory at Orleans in 1429, which broke the culture of defeat then affecting the French since their

Joan of Arc: folio with miniature from "Vie des femmes celebres" (Lives of Famous Women) by Antoine Dufour, Ms. 17. French, c. 1505. Location: Musée Dobrée, Nantes, France. Credit: Giraudon / Art Resource, N.Y.

loss at Agincourt and turned the tide of The Hundred Years' War. The unexpected presence of a mounted, armor-clad, teenaged girl on a fifteenth-century battlefield created a stir that was heightened by Joan's claim that whoever executed her military dictates followed the will of God. Her skill at turning battlefield action and soldiers' behavior into acts that pleased or displeased God emanated from Joan's understanding of herself as divine messenger.

According to the testimony of family and acquaintances, nothing in Joan's early life at Domrémy foretold her later mission. Only a rather forceful piety distinguished her from others. From about the age of thirteen, however, according to Joan's own testimony, she heard a heavenly voice and vowed from that experience to maintain her virginity. (It remains unclear whether, by her vow, she was playing to a contemporary prophecy stating that "France would be ruined through a woman, and afterward restored by a virgin.") With the passage of time, Joan understood that God was giving her messages intended for her king, Charles VII, whom she must go to seek in France. Her father, suspecting that something was afoot, threatened to drown her if she left town in the company of men. But he misinterpreted his daughter's yearnings; they were fixed on "Messire," which was what she called God, although, in truth, her piety was always mixed with the worldly impudence of a female adventurer.

One of the most interesting aspects of Joan's career was how she convinced Charles to place trust in her words, upon her arrival at Chinon in early March 1429. Already in February, at Vaucouleurs, and with the help of a relative, she had cajoled Captain Robert of Baudricourt into providing her with a horse, men's clothes, and a small retinue. (The male dress, which seems to have been no more scandalous than the daring venture itself, was practical, as well as a necessary disguise.) After a dangerous journey through war-torn France, the Maid arrived at Chinon to seek audience with King Charles. At this point, the drama could have gone either way. The king's council and trusted advisers wanted to avert any episode possibly ending in ridicule for the French, but Joan made promises "advantageous" to the realm, namely that she was sent by God to restore Charles's kingdom. Joan was not adopted by the court without reservations. The theologians, convened by the king to test her, were anything but accommodating, principally because she had produced no miracle to validate her divine inspiration. She was fitted with armor only when she promised to raise the siege of Orleans in evidence of a miracle.

Orleans

When the siege of Orleans was lifted after a mere eight days, attention focused on Joan as proof of God's intervention. She was especially lauded by the townspeople, who flooded the streets in a nighttime procession to celebrate her victory. During the preceding weeks, however, the English commander, the earl of Salisbury, had been killed, demoralizing the English soldiery, while the duke of Burgundy, in a fit of pique, had withdrawn his troops from the siege. These events, as well as the English army's inability to close off supply routes into the city, played their part in the miracle. Nevertheless, the Maid's influence is indisputable. She threatened the English with divine retribution in her *Letter to the English* and engaged in brazen verbal exchanges with enemy soldiers at close range, seemingly further immobilizing the will of an already demoralized English army. She roused her own troops by placing their military assignment more or less under the mantle of a crusade. En route from Blois to Orleans, the army was led by priests intoning the *Veni Creator Spiritus* as Joan rode along bearing a standard displaying angels, the king of Heaven, and the words "Jesus Maria." Although Joan had been excluded from strategy sessions, where some were undoubtedly jealous of her amateur military involvement, credit for the victory was almost uniformly given to her.

The Maid's religious mission, while primary and all encompassing, should not obscure her political importance. The much-debated secret that Joan revealed to the king in her private interview was likely the same message she later broadcast in the *Letter to the English*; namely, that Charles, the only surviving son of Charles VI and Isabeau of Bavaria, was "true heir." This statement challenged the dual monarchy of France and England, formulated in the Treaty of Troyes of 1420, which, in order for the Lancasters to claim the French throne, depended on Charles being disinherited for his responsibility in the murder of John the Fearless, duke of Burgundy. At her trial Joan acknowledged the murder was "a great tragedy for the kingdom of France," but added: "Whatever there had been between them [John and Charles], God had sent her to the help of the king of France." Joan, then, did more than simply bolster Charles's confidence. Her role was rather to affirm Charles's political legitimacy, on the authority of God, despite the murder of the duke of Burgundy, and thus to repudiate the Treaty of Troyes that depended upon it.

The Campaign after Orleans

When Joan pleaded with the king to extend the Orleans campaign into the Loire valley, the strategy was self-evident and was advocated by other commanders. The English were quickly routed from Meung, Beaugency, and Patay, and the enemy's strength in the region was neutralized. At that point, bolstered by recent victories, the French faced a choice of where to go next. Should they mount a campaign for Normandy or Paris, or push deep into Burgundian territory, as the Maid urged, for a royal coronation at Reims? The Reims campaign, decided upon by Charles, is perhaps the first time the record clearly illustrates Joan's influence on military decisions. Rather ill-equipped in terms of artillery and supplies, the army was reminded outside Troyes, by one of their own, Robert le Maçon, that the campaign had not been undertaken based on the strength of the army, or even because the campaign seemed possible, but "solely at the recommendation of Joan the Maid...because it was the desire and the will of God."

On July 17, 1429, Charles was crowned at Reims with Joan at his side, while her parents, guests of the king, watched in admiration. It was Joan's final triumph. The day of the coronation, Charles negotiated a secret truce with representatives of Philip the Good, duke of Burgundy. Joan, whose "counsel" had ordered the march on Reims in preference to the march on Paris, was unable to penetrate the walls of Paris when she, the duke of Alençon, and a small army finally attacked on September 8, 1429. Whether events were too disheartening or too uneventful for French chroniclers to record, few interesting details survive about the Maid between the failure at Paris and her capture at Compiègne on May 23, 1430. In this period she was badly undersupplied, as an urgent letter (still extant), sent to the inhabitants of Riom for munitions of war, underscores. The numbers of her small company were increasingly swelled with Italian mercenaries. Perhaps to avoid the shame that her "voices" had given her wrong counsel, Joan was by then leaving military decisions to the commanders. Her ardor on the battlefield, however, remained undiminished, as attested by her reckless presence in the rearguard, outside the walls of Compiègne, the day she was captured. There, the maid from Domrémy was pulled from her dapple-gray charger by the panels of her splendid cloth-of-gold *huque* (surcoat).

During the summer and fall of 1430, Joan was led from prison to prison across the north of France until she reached Rouen, where her trial for heresy took place over the first five months of 1431. Pierre Cauchon, the bishop of Beauvais, whom the University of Paris lauded for his "concern for the public safety," mounted the case for the prosecution and eventually convicted Joan for her "heretical" resumption of male clothing against court order. The Anglo-Burgundian judges wanted nothing but to see her burn, in order to break the grip of fear that immobilized the everyday English foot soldier, to punish Joan's female impudence, and finally, to erase her memory from history. In a serious miscalculation, however, they conserved the minutes of their "beau procès" (literally, handsome trial) through which her indomitable spirit continues to survive. Political vindication for the Maid came in 1456 when the French nullified bishop Cauchon's sentence, but her ecclesiastical vindication occurred only in 1920 upon her canonization in the Catholic Church.

Gender Issues

Joan seems to have resisted being portrayed as a simple shepherdess, not so much because of connotations of sweet passivity, as because it was not generally true. But she did not disdain having been taught household skills by her mother, and even bragged about her prowess as a seamstress. Her love for the exclusive fraternity of soldiers, however, despite her often tangential and controversial membership in it, is documented by her imperious advice to Catherine de La Rochelle, a would-be competitor, to whom she said: "Go back to your husband, look after your household, and feed your children." Joan is known, too, to have broken a sword against the backs of a pair of camp followers. Beyond that, the record of Joan's relations with other women, especially noble women, is harmonious. She submitted to two tests of her virginity, maintained cordial relations—in at least two known cases—with the mother or wife of comrades at arms, and sent a small gold ring, as a token of her affection, to the elderly widow of the great French warrior Bertrand du Guesclin. No one disputes that part of Joan's fame owes to her transgressions of her sex, but those who knew her well appear to have lingered only a short time over that aspect of her multifaceted personality and career.

DEBORAH FRAIOLI

References and Further Reading

Barrett, Wilfred Philip, ed. and trans. *The Trial of Jeanne d'Arc: Translated into English from the Original Latin and French Documents*. With Pierre Champion, "Dramatis personae," translated by Coley Taylor and Ruth H. Kerr. New York: Gotham House, 1932.

de Pizan, Christine. *Ditié de Jehanne d'Arc*. Edited by Angus J. Kennedy and Kenneth Varty. Medium Aevum Monographs, new series, 9. Oxford: Society for the Study of Mediaeval Languages and Literature, 1977.

Fraioli, Deborah. *Joan of Arc: The Early Debate*. Woodbridge: Boydell Press, 2000.

France, Anatole. *The Life of Joan of Arc*. Translated by Winifred Stephens. 2 vols. Reprint, Amsterdam: Fredonia Books, 2004.

Margolis, Nadia. *Joan of Arc in History, Literature, and Film: A Select, Annotated Bibliography*. New York: Garland, 1990.

Pernoud, Régine. *Joan of Arc: By Herself and Her Witnesses*. Translated by Edward Hyams. New York: Stein & Day, 1966.

Pernoud, Régine, ed. and J. M. Cohen, trans. with preface by Katherine Anne Porter. *The Retrial of Joan of Arc: The Evidence at the Trial for Her Rehabilitation*. New York: Methuen, 1955.

Pernoud, Régine and Marie-Véronique Clin. *Joan of Arc: Her Story*. Revised and translated by Jeremy duQuesnay Adams. Bonnie Wheeler, ed. New York: St. Martin's, 1998.

Quicherat, Jules-Etienne-Joseph, ed. *Procès de condamnation et de réhabilitation de Jeanne d'Arc dite la Pucelle. Publiés pour la première fois d'après les manuscrits de la Bibliothèque Nationale, suivis de tous les documents historiques qu'on a pu réunir et accompagnés de notes et d'éclaircissements*. 5 vols. Paris: Jules Renouard, 1841–1849; reprint, New York: Johnson, 1965.

Scott, Walter Sidney, trans. *The Trial of Joan of Arc: Being the Verbatim Report of the Proceedings from the Orleans Manuscript*. Reprint, London: The Folio Society, 1968.

Sullivan, Karen. *The Interrogation of Joan of Arc*. Minneapolis: University of Minnesota Press, 1999.

Warner, Marina. *Joan of Arc: The Image of Female Heroism*. New York: Knopf, 1981.

See also **Christine de Pizan; Cross-Dressing; France, Northern; Gender Ideologies; Warfare**

JOSEPH, STEPFATHER OF JESUS

Although long neglected in western Christian piety, Joseph was extensively rehabilitated between 1250 and 1500 by Italian and French clerics who portrayed his holiness as the masculine equivalent of Mary's and declared his superiority to her in their spousal relationship. Minimal references to Joseph in the

Gospels, descriptions of his parental ineptitude in the apocrypha, assumptions of his advanced age, and his lack of a role in Jesus's conception limited his importance in the first twelve centuries of western Christianity. Twelfth- and thirteenth-century theologians began reversing Joseph's fortunes when they resolved earlier arguments that a virginal marriage could be a genuine marriage. As they confirmed both Joseph's sexual purity and the validity of his unconsummated marriage, writers such as Hugh of St. Victor and Albert the Great facilitated interest in Joseph's sanctity. Nonetheless, the long-accepted Aristotelian position that the male embodies the generative principle made it hard to define virginal Joseph as a masculine figure until Rupert of Deutz (d. 1129), Bernard of Clairvaux (d. 1153), and several Franciscan writers transformed the understanding. They built on an idea expressed by Augustine of Hippo and other fourth-century writers that presented Joseph as such an excellent nurturer of Jesus, and such an effective protector, that he could be called Jesus's father despite his lack of biological contribution. Following early- and high-medieval writers, such as Bede (d. c. 735) and Peter Damian (d. 1072), who associated fathering with affection as well as authority, Franciscans such as Peter John Olivi (d. 1298) defined Joseph's gender as masculine in spirit, both virile and virginal.

While some have argued that medieval writers understood Joseph to be imitating Mary in his treatment of Jesus, it appears that the majority of texts in Latin, Italian, and French linked Joseph's nurturing with masculinity. In his protection of Mary and Jesus and his demonstrative embraces of Jesus, the Joseph of Franciscan treatises and sermons unified tenderness and masculinity. Bernardino da Siena (d. 1444) and his followers quoted Olivi's and Ubertino da Casale's (d. c. 1329) assertions that Joseph provided such brave and loving service as husband and father, and received such sweet affection from the child Jesus, that he should be Christians' model and their most important intercessor with Mary and Jesus. Bernardino da Siena and his successors presented emulation of Joseph as a solution to moral problems of their day, including marital infidelity and sodomy, and also emphasized Mary's obedience to Joseph. The French cleric Jean Gerson (d. 1429) seems to have borrowed from Franciscan sources in his descriptions of Joseph's authority over Mary and solicitous care for Jesus. Gerson echoed previous Franciscan and Servite calls for Joseph's selection as the patron of the Church.

Approving descriptions of Joseph's masculine nurturing did not quickly penetrate vernacular culture, for fourteenth- to fifteenth-century English mystery plays, French poems, and works of art still portrayed him as a comical elderly cuckold; contemporaneous German cradle plays caricatured Joseph's nurturing role by showing him fumbling domestic tasks. In northern Europe as late as 1350, vernacular and artistic portrayals of Joseph depicted him as weak and unsuccessful in his paternal and spousal roles. However, the efforts of Franciscan friars and other clerics to portray Joseph as a model of perfection for men in particular, and all Christians in general, flourished: Joseph received a feast day (March 19) in 1479, and by the early sixteenth century additional writers produced sermons and hagiographies, often in the vernacular, ascribing to the saint a holiness very nearly equivalent to that of Jesus and Mary. Joseph's appeal to both men and women is evident in the Josephine devotions of the fourteenth-century Italian mystics Margherita of Cortona and Margherita di Città di Castello. By around 1550, Joseph was patron of several Italian cities; religious societies and churches were dedicated to him; and the use of "Joseph" as a baptismal name demonstrated his influence on lay people.

Franciscan preachers such as Bernardino da Feltre (d. 1494), who depicted Joseph as the holiest of all saints except Christ and Mary, and clerics such as Gerson, who recommended Joseph as a model for husbands and young people, offered him in symmetry with Mary, a masculine counterpart who apparently was intended to rebalance a religious culture strongly influenced by female saints and feminine piety. Joseph's cult evinced late-medieval and early-modern admiration for the nuclear family in which the male is leader, provider, nurturer, and the head of the wife. Depictions of Joseph thus hold an important place in the history of Western definitions of paternal and spousal roles, masculinity, patriarchy, and the family.

CHARA ARMON

References and Further Reading

Armon, Chara. *Servus, Pater, Dominus: The Development of Devotion to Saint Joseph in Medieval Franciscan Thought*. Ph.D. Diss. Cornell University, 2003. Ann Arbor: UMI, 2003: 3104556.

Bernardino da Feltre. "Dos sermones inéditos sobra S. José del beato Bernardino da Feltre." Edition and notes by Pedro de Alcántara Martínez Senderos. *Archivum Franciscanum Historicum* 71 (1978): 65–111.

Bernardino da Siena. *St. Bernardine's Sermon on St. Joseph.* Translated by Eric May. Paterson, N.J.: St. Anthony's Guild, 1947.

Gauthier, Roland. *Bibliographie sur saint Joseph et la sainte Famille*. Montréal: St. Joseph's University Press, 1999.

Gold, Penny S. "The Marriage of Mary and Joseph in the Twelfth-Century Ideology of Marriage." In *Sexual Practices in the Medieval Church*, edited by Vern L. Bullough and James A. Brundage. Buffalo, N.Y.: Prometheus Books, 1982.

Hale, Rosemary Drage. "Joseph as Mother: Adaptation and Appropriation in the Construction of Male Virtue." In *Medieval Mothering*, edited by John Carmi Parsons and Bonnie Wheeler. New York: Garland, 1996.

Longpré, Ephrem. "Saint Joseph et l'école franciscaine du XIIIe siècle." In *Le patronage de saint Joseph. Actes du Congrès d'études tenu à l'oratoire Saint-Joseph, Montréal, 1955*. Montréal and Paris: Fides, 1956.

Olivi, Peter of John. "Lectura super Matthaeum." q. i, in "Pierre de Jean Olivi, o.f.m. Sa doctrine et son influence." Edited by Aquilin Emmen. *Cahiers de Joséphologie* 14 (1966): 209–270.

Sheingorn, Pamela. "Joseph the Carpenter's Failure at Familial Discipline." In *Insights and Interpretations: Studies in Celebration of the Eighty-Fifth Anniversary of the Index of Christian Art*, edited by Colum Hourihane. Princeton, N.J.: Index of Christian Art, Department of Art and Archaeology, Princeton University, in association with Princeton University Press, 2002, pp. 156–167.

Ubertinus de Casale. *Arbor vitae crucifixae Jesu*. Introduction by Charles T. Davis. Torino: Bottega d'Erasmo, 1961.

Walsh, Walter. "Divine Cuckhold/Holy Fool: The Comic Image of Joseph in the English 'Troubles' Play." In *England in the Fourteenth Century*, edited by W. M. Ormrod. Woodbridge, Suffolk: Boydell Press, 1986, pp. 278–297.

Wilson, Carolyn. *St. Joseph in Italian Renaissance Society and Art: New Directions and Interpretations*. Philadelphia: St. Joseph's University Press, 2001.

See also **Chastity and Chaste Marriage; Cuckold; Family (Later Middle Ages); Femininity and Masculinity; Gender Ideologies; Gerson, Jean; Husbands and Husbandry; Mary, Virgin; Patriarchy and Patrilineage**

JOUARRE AND CHELLES

Jouarre and Chelles were the most important foundations for religious women in the Frankish kingdom that had been founded under the influence of the Irish missionary Columban (c. 615). Both were conceived as double monasteries headed by an abbess, but the monks' houses soon were converted into communities of canons. Jouarre, in the Ile-de-France, was built around 630 on the initiative of the nobleman Ado and his stepmother Moda. The first nuns came from Faremoutiers. Of the first churches constructed for Jouarre in the seventh century, a crypt survives with the graves of both founders, as well as of the first three abbesses. Soon Jouarre became well known as an important center of education. From here nuns were sent to found the community of Notre-Dame in Soissons in 667 and, around 660, to revive the monastery of Chelles near Paris. According to legend, it had been Queen Chrodechild, wife of the Frankish king Chlodwig, who, as early as 511,

founded a small religious community for women near the palace (*villa regalis*) of the Merovingian kings in Chelles. The (re)foundation however, was initiated by the widowed Frankish queen Balthild. The well-educated Bertila (c. 702–704) from Jouarre was installed as the new abbess. Her fame assured that both monasteries attracted Anglo-Saxon nuns and monks looking for education and Christian instruction or looking for books. In the eighth century even Merovingian princes were educated at Chelles. The biographies of both founders, Bertila and Balthild, were presumably written at Chelles, as well as the so-called *Annales Mettenses Priores*, a kind of family chronicle of the Carolingians, dating from around 804–806 that demonstrates the far-reaching connections of Chelles in the Merovingian and Carolingian periods.

Under abbess Gisela (757–810), sister of Charlemagne, Chelles was in contact with the most famous scholars of the Carolingian court, like Alcuin, who wrote a commentary on John for her. The monastery also maintained a *scriptorium* that produced books for the community's use but also for persons outside the nunnery, such as the archbishop of Cologne. Not only is their quality outstanding; but also the nuns, rather untypically, signed the written quires with their names, which allows us to define their works as the product of women. Apart from Bible commentaries and sacramentaries—among others the most famous Gelasian Sacramentary (Vatican, Reg.lat.316)—the books produced at Chelles also contain council records, encyclopaedic works of Isidore of Seville, and the writings of Eusebius in the version by Rufinus. Furthermore, Jouarre is presumed to have had a well-organized *scriptorium*, if indeed one typical style of writing (the so-called b-minuscule) is correctly ascribed to it.

Through the Merovingian and the Carolingian period, and down to the eleventh century, both monasteries, as royal possessions, were frequently visited and given the privileges of holding markets and issuing coinage. Often they were used as refuges for widowed or banished women of the royal families. Around 1500, Chelles was reformed by the order of Fontevrault, while Jouarre remained a house of canonesses. Both houses were suspended during the French Revolution. Due to the complete destruction and overbuilding of Chelles, the layout of buildings and churches remain unknown, but more than a hundred inscribed early medieval relics survived, including the so-called "tunic of Balthild." Overall the history of both monasteries, their role in the diffusion of liturgical books and saint cults, as well as their educational status, deserves further studies.

KATRINETTE BODARWÉ

References and Further Reading

Atsma, Hartmut, and Hayo Vierck. "Chelles." In *Reallexikon der Germanischen Altertumskunde.* vol. 4. Berlin: de Gruyter, 1981, cols. 422–430.

Berthelier-Ajot, Nadine. "Chelles à l'époque mérovingienne." *Revue du Nord.* 68 (1986): 345–360.

Chaussy, Y., ed. *L'Abbaye Royale Notre-Dame de Jouarre.* 2 vol., Paris: Bibliotheque D'histoire et d'archéologie chrétiennes, 1961.

Laporte, Jean-Pierre, and Raymond Boyer. *Trésors de Chelles. Sépultures et reliques de la reine Bathilde (vers 680) et l'abbesse Bertille (vers 704).* Chelles: Soc. Archéologique et Historique, 1991.

McKitterick, Rosamond. "Nun's Scriptoria in England and Francia in the Eighth Century." *Francia* 19.1 (1992): 1–35.

———. "Women and Literacy in the Early Middle Ages." In *Books, Scribes and Learning in the Frankish Kingdoms, 6th–9th Centuries,* edited by Rosamond McKitterick. Aldershot and Brookfield, Vt.: Variorum, 1994, pp. 1–43.

Mecquenem, Claude de. "Les cryptes de Jouarre (Seine-et-Marne). Des indices pour une nouvelle chronologie." *Archéologie medievale* 32 (2002): 1–30.

See also **Abbesses; Education, Monastic; Literacy and Reading: Latin; Monasticism and Nuns**

JUDITH

The story of Judith is originally found in the Book of Judith, composed after the Hebrew Scriptures were canonized. Unlike most Old Testament women, Judith is active and assertive and inspires the citizens of Bethulia to repel an Assyrian invasion by reminding them of the times God saved Israel and then decapitated the Assyrian general, Holofernes. There are two versions of Judith in Old English, a homily by Ælfric (active c. 955–c. 1010) and a poem found in the Nowell Codex (copied c. 1000) as the companion of *Beowulf.* Both are free translations and emphasize that Judith's brave deed galvanized the timorous Jews so that they fought the invader and saved Israel, and both seem intended to teach the English about resistance to the invasions of the pagan Danes. Ælfric's homily emphasizes historical facts that have figural significance, especially chastity and faith. In contrast, the poem depicts the combat between Judith, the heroic woman, and Holofernes, the evil invader. It uses the formulaic language of heroic Old English poetry and characterizes Judith as a warrior woman in the tradition of the benevolent valkyrie, emphasizing that *Hæfde ða gefohten foremærne blæd/ Iudith æt guðe* (122a–123a) "Judith had then won very illustrious glory by fighting in the battle." There is a Middle English version of Judith in the 18,372 verse *Middle English Metrical Paraphrase of the Old Testament,* and images of Judith were popular among the painters of Renaissance Italy. A modern version is Siegfried Matthus' opera *Judith,* whose American premier was in 1990 at Santa Fe.

ALEXANDRA H. OLSEN

References and Further Reading

Dobbie, Elliott van Kirk. *Beowulf and Judith.* ASPR, vol. 4. New York: Columbia University Press, 1953.

Judith. *The New American Bible.* New York: Catholic Publishing Co., 1970, pp. 485–500.

Lee, S. D. "Ælfric's Homlies on Judith, Esther, and The Maccabees." http://users.ox.ac.uk/~stuart/kings.

Nelson, Marie, ed, and trans. *Judith, Juliana, and Elene: Three Fighting Saints.* New York: Peter Lang Publishing, 1991.

Peck, Russell. *The Middle English Metrical Paraphrase of the Old Testament.* Kalamazoo: Medieval Institute Publications, 1991.

See also **Beowulf; Jewish Women; Literature, Old English**

JULIAN OF NORWICH

The first English woman identified as an author, Julian of Norwich (c. 1343–1416), composed two versions of her *Showings* (sometimes titled *The Revelations of Divine Love*) in response to a visionary experience she had in May 1373. The first version or short text, probably completed soon after the event, recounts the revelations she received over the course of the day as she lay near death midway through her thirtieth year. Corresponding to the first twelve revelations of the long text, this first version includes only brief hints of what became the very original Thirteenth through Sixteenth Revelations of the final version. The long text, completed around 1393 after almost twenty years of meditation, significantly expands the short text to elucidate the theological implications of her visionary experience.

This woman is known as Julian because, at least after 1394, she was enclosed as an anchorite in the Church of St. Julian in Norwich, England. The only surviving medieval copy of the short text begins with a scribal note so identifying the author and indicating that she was still alive in 1413. Four wills dating from 1394 to 1416 include gifts to the anchorite of St. Julian's. Furthermore, Margery Kempe, a holy woman from nearby King's Lynn, recounts a visit she paid to Dame Julian around 1413 in her own book, the second one known to be composed by an English woman.

Near the beginning of the *Showings,* Julian says that prior to May 1373 she had asked God for three gifts: a vision of Christ's Passion; a life-threatening illness; and the three metaphoric wounds of compassion, contrition, and longing for God. Her visionary experience develops these themes. After losing sensation in the lower part of her body on the eighth day of her severe illness, Julian, staring at a crucifix held before her by a priest, suddenly sees the events of the Passion reenacted before her eyes. These "bodily showings" arouse Julian's compassion for the suffering Savior and incite her contrition for sin and longing for God.

Although all three themes occur in the short text, Julian explores these last two themes with great originality in her additions to the long text. In Revelation Thirteen she returns to the dilemma of evil that she first poses in Revelation Three as she asks how an omnipotent, omniscient, and benevolent God could allow sin to exist. In response to this question, Julian receives the auditory revelation: "Sin is necessary, but all will be well, and all will be well, and every kind of thing will be well" (Rev. 13, chapter 27). Through the rest of this Revelation Thirteen, Julian explains the pedagogic function of sin, and she presages the mysteries of the godly will of the elect that protects them from sin and the ultimate possibility of universal salvation for all.

In Revelation Fourteen, Julian resolves the problem of evil through her retelling of the biblical story of the Fall in the parable of the lord and servant in chapter 51. Julian's version revises this narrative about the origins of sin in several significant ways that indicate why she believes that all will be well despite the fall of humankind. The servant does not disobey, but rather falls into a deep valley while hurrying to do the lord's bidding. The lord is not angry, but feels only pity for the servant's suffering. After indicating that she puzzled over this obscure showing for almost twenty years, Julian interprets the servant as both the first Adam and Christ, the second Adam, whose fall to earth and incarnation lead to the redemption of humankind.

In the subsequent chapters of Revelation Fourteen, moreover, Julian presents her unique accounts of the inextricable bonds linking humankind to the deity, the nature of the human soul, and the motherhood of Jesus. Since God the Father creates the soul from his own substance, its higher part, or substance, remains in God, the ground of being. However, Jesus the Mother in creation unites this substance with the lower part of the soul, the sensuality, in the process of embodiment and remains within the higher part as the *imago Dei* (image of God). Julian also regards Jesus as a mother in recreation and in working. Through the sufferings of atonement, Jesus, like a mother, gave new life to sinful humankind. And like a mother who protects and nurtures her child, Jesus continues to sustain Christians throughout time.

DENISE NOWAKOWSKI BAKER

References and Further Reading

Baker, Denise Nowakowski. *Julian of Norwich's Showings: From Vision to Book*. Princeton, N.J.: Princeton University Press, 1994.

Jantzen, Grace. *Julian of Norwich: Mystic and Theologian*. 2nd Edition. Mahwah, N.J.: Paulist Press, 2000.

Julian of Norwich. *Revelations of Divine Love (Short Text and Long Text)*. Translated by Elizabeth Spearing. New York: Penguin Books, 1998.

McEntire, Sandra, ed. *Julian of Norwich: A Book of Essays*. New York: Garland, 1998.

See also **Anchoresses; Jesus/God as Mother; Kempe, Margery; Mysticism and Mystics; Mystics' Writings; Women Authors: Middle English Texts; Theology**

K

KATHERINE GROUP

The "Katherine Group" is the name given to a collection of texts written in the west midlands of England in the early thirteenth century. Their explicit address is to anchoresses, though their actual audience was probably more varied. The group comprises lives of three virgin martyr saints, Catherine of Alexandria, Margaret of Antioch, and Juliana of Nicomedia; an allegorical narrative, *Custody of the Soul*; and a treatise extolling the spiritual and material advantages of virginity, *Holy Maidenhood*. Linguistic, thematic, and manuscript evidence connects these texts and links them also with a set of passionate poetic meditations known as the Wooing Group and with *Ancrene Wisse*, a guide for anchoresses that has long been recognised as a milestone in early Middle English writing. The author of *Ancrene Wisse* was certainly a cleric, and the author(s) of the Katherine Group and Wooing Group were probably also clerics, but unless further evidence should be discovered, their identity will remain unknown. Critical interest in the texts has shifted from the elusive author to the audience, so that the Group, though male-authored, is regularly discussed in the context of histories of female spirituality.

Anchoritism was a form of religious life that attracted more women than men and thus was a fertile ground for the production of vernacular literature. Anchoresses needed guidance on their conduct and material for meditation. As they were, at least notionally, solitary, such matters could not be conveyed orally and in practice as they would be in a nunnery, and hence were put into writing, which had to be in the vernacular for a female audience unlikely to be educated in Latin. The anchorhold was intensively imagined in *Ancrene Wisse* as a womb in which the inhabitant was reborn and a tomb to house one who was dead to the world. The anchorhold is symbolised in the prison scenes of the saints' legends of the Katherine Group as a space that enables communication between heaven and earth: in their prisons the saints speak to angels and, literally, face and defeat their demons. *Care of the Soul* imagines the self as a household that bears some resemblance to an anchoritic community, and its narrative treats of the alternations of hope and anxiety that form the rhythm of contemplative lives.

The Katherine Group's central assumption is that virginity is in every way a superior state to marriage. In expanding on this, it conveys much information about the conditions of women's lives. *Holy Maidenhood* vividly sketches a series of contrasts between the life of a married woman and that of a virgin anchoress. A wife must obey her husband, submit to his sexual demands and expect regular domestic violence; pregnancy is revolting, childbirth painful and terrifying, and children themselves rarely worth the trouble. A virgin's life is elegant, decorous, and peaceful, and she can look forward to special privileges in heaven, where the company of crowned virgins will dance joyfully together for eternity.

The three virgin martyr legends share a standard plot: a beautiful, noble young Christian virgin refuses to marry a pagan and/or renounce Christianity; she then steadfastly suffers a series of increasingly horrible tortures until finally beheaded and welcomed in triumph to heaven by Christ, her beloved bridegroom. There are also some individual elements. *Juliana* includes a parody of contemporary romance in the portrayal of Eleusius's degeneration from courtly suitor to sadistic tyrant, plus a scene of low comedy in which the saint flings a cowering demon into a dungheap. *Katherine* features a debate in which the highly educated heroine converts fifty pagan philosophers and also has a sequence of military metaphors that identify her as Christ's knight, fighting for her faith. *Margaret* has a particularly striking set of demonic encounters, including one in which the saint is swallowed by a dragon that explodes when she makes the sign of the cross from within its belly.

All three saints are eloquent and active, due to their virginity, which is represented as a source of earthly and spiritual power. Virginity enables the saints to resist the wishes of their fathers, suitors, and judges; it makes them brides and imitators of Christ. The legends focus intently on their bodies, beautiful and violated, but somehow preserved by virginity from actual dismemberment. Modern readers who do not share this commitment to virginity may instead consider the scenes of torture to indulge fantasies of sexual violence; nevertheless, there is evidence that the genre appealed to many medieval women readers.

SARAH SALIH

References and Further Reading

Anchoritic Spirituality: Ancrene Wisse and Associated Works, translated by Nicholas Watson and Anne Savage. New York: Paulist Press, 1991.

Dobson, E. J. *The Origins of Ancrene Wisse*. Oxford: Clarendon Press, 1976.

Hassel, Julie. *Choosing Not to Marry: Women and Autonomy in the Katherine Group*. New York: Routledge, 2002.

Medieval English Prose for Women from the Katherine Group and "Ancrene Wisse," edited by Bella Millett and Jocelyn Wogan-Browne. Oxford: Clarendon Press, 1990.

Millett, Bella. "The Audience of the Saints' Lives of the Katherine Group." *Reading Medieval Studies* 16 (1990): 127–156.

———. "The Origins of 'Ancrene Wisse': New Answers, New Questions." *Medium Ævum* 61 (1992): 206–228.

Robertson, Elizabeth. *Early English Devotional Prose and the Female Audience*. Knoxville: University of Tennessee Press, 1990.

Salih, Sarah. *Versions of Virginity in Late Medieval England*. Cambridge: Brewer, 2001.

Wogan-Browne, Jocelyn. *Saints' Lives and Women's Literary Culture, 1150–1300: Virginity and its Authorizations*. Oxford: Oxford University Press, 2001.

See also **Anchoresses; Ancrene Wisse; Audience, Women in the; Bride of Christ: Imagery; Catherine of Alexandria; Devotional Literature; Hagiography; Literacy and Reading: Vernacular; Margaret of Antioch; Spirituality, Christian; Virgin Martyrs; Virginity**

KEMPE, MARGERY

The Book of Margery Kempe recounts the spiritual life and travels of Margery Kempe (c. 1373–after 1438), a middle-class woman from Lynn, England, during the first third of the fifteenth century. Dictated by Kempe between 1436–1438, the text exists in a single manuscript that was copied from the lost original c. 1450. Housed for a time at Mt. Grace Priory, a Carthusian monastery in Yorkshire, the manuscript made its way into private hands where it remained, virtually forgotten, until it was rediscovered in 1934. Although several short mystical extracts from the *Book* were published c. 1501 by printer Wynkyn de Worde, few details of Kempe's unusual life were known until the manuscript's reemergence.

In what is often called the first autobiography in English, Kempe's spiritual history is told in localized and homely terms, with accounts of religious rapture anchored in anecdotes about her travels and her conflicts with male authorities. Beginning with an account of a postpartum depression, c. 1393, following the birth of the first of fourteen children, the "treatise" first describes Kempe's worldly vanities and failed occupations as a brewer and a miller, as well as her negotiations with her husband for a chaste marriage. Loosely organized by memory, place, and topic, the *Book* then recounts her conversations with Christ, her interactions with local priests and fellow parishioners, and her travels. These include, between 1414 and 1433, three trips overseas, one to Italy and the Holy Land, one to Spain, and one, much later in her life, to Danzig and Aachen. The book also records domestic travels to major towns in England for audiences with well-known mystics, such as Julian of Norwich, and with important figures in the church hierarchy, first for special privileges, such as the right to choose her own confessor and to receive weekly communion, and later to defend herself against charges of heresy.

Throughout the *Book*, Kempe presents herself as cherished by Christ but misunderstood and reviled by the world. Kempe's relationships with others, including church authorities as well as fellow parishioners and pilgrims, are often adversarial. She is repeatedly rebuked for wearing white clothes, the garb of consecrated virgins, and publicly reviled for her boisterous weeping and roaring when spiritually moved. At Leicester, York, and Beverly she is interrogated for Lollardy, a condemned heresy, charges that she effectively counters. Her consistent advocate is Christ, who often speaks to her, advising her to go on pilgrimage or to wear white, a visible sign of her "revirgining," and reminding her of his special love for her. An intimate of Christ, she depicts herself as

Christ-like, a victim of a world that fails to recognize her sanctity and attempts to keep her silent. The accounts of uncontrollable weeping, coupled with the *Book*'s anecdotal structure, have led to widely divergent critical receptions. Many early readers, disappointed by the *Book*'s difference from the mystical meditation of Julian of Norwich, dismissed it as slipshod, unruly, or even hysterical. Recent readers, however, reevaluating the *Book* in the light of research on embodied female spirituality, have reexamined those assessments.

Although the *Book* reads like a memoir in its rambling organization and its use of homely and localized detail, it is also a carefully crafted treatise that borrows broadly from mystical texts, spiritual instruction, and saints' lives, all popular genres in late medieval England. Hope Emily Allen, one of the *Book*'s first editors, recognized its deep debts to traditions in contemporary female mysticism. Kempe's uncontrollable tears when she thinks of Christ's Passion echo the religious weeping or gift of tears that is also recorded in other well-known lives of holy women, among them Marie of Oignies (c. 1177–1213) and the Blessed Angela of Foligno (c. 1248–1309). As a married woman committed in midlife to a public spiritual vocation, Kempe seems to model her life broadly on Birgitta of Sweden (1303–1373), named at several points throughout the *Book*. And, while Kempe presents herself as illiterate or at least unable to write, familiarity with popular contemplative practices, such as those described in *The Meditations on the Life of Christ*, and echoes of devotional writings by Richard Rolle suggest that her illiteracy may be at least in part a fiction.

The conflation between contemporary detail and commonplaces of late medieval spirituality invite us to read the *Book* as a carefully constructed spiritual "life," one shaped by Kempe, as well as by her scribes. There are no known records of Kempe's audiences with important clerical figures, and indeed, few records of her life beyond the *Book*. Since Kempe dictated her text to two scribes, as stated in the prologues, we also cannot know how accurately the final product represents her actual life or even uses her own language. Irrespective of these questions of authorship and facticity we can confidently read the *Book* as a complexly mediated social commentary. Through an account of a middle-class woman who challenges marital norms, travels widely, engages in spirited discourse with men on all levels of the social stratum, and preaches as a public holy woman, the *Book* leaves a rich record of the gendered spiritual landscape of fifteenth-century England.

SARAH STANBURY

References and Further Reading

Kempe, Margery, *The Book of Margery Kempe*, edited by Sanford Brown Meech and Hope Emily Allen. Early English Text Society. London: Oxford University Press; reprint Woodbridge, Sussex: Boydell and Brewer, 1997.

———. *The Book of Margery Kempe*, edited by Barry Windeatt. Harlow, Essex: Longman, 2000.

———. *The Book of Margery Kempe*, edited and translated by Lynn Staley. Norton Critical Edition. New York: W. W. Norton, 2001.

Lochrie, Karma. *Margery Kempe and Translations of the Flesh*. Philadelphia: University of Pennsylvania Press, 1991.

Raguin, Virginia, and Sarah Stanbury. "Mapping Margery Kempe: A Guide to Late Medieval Material and Spiritual Life." http://www.holycross.edu/departments/visarts/projects/kempe/. (10 May 2006).

Staley, Lynn. *Margery Kempe's Dissenting Fictions*. University Park, Pa.: Pennsylvania State University Press, 1994.

See also **Angela of Foligno; Birgitta of Sweden; Chastity and Chaste Marriage; Hagiography; Heretics and Heresy; Julian of Norwich; Lay Piety; Literacy and Reading: Vernacular; Lollards; Marie of Oignies; Pilgrims and Pilgrimage; Women Authors: Middle English Texts**

KHARJAS

See **Woman's Song**

KINSHIP

Marc Bloch commented that in the Middle Ages "true friendship only occurred between peoples linked by blood" (Bloch, 184). His insight has acted as the starting point for modern historical discourse on kinship, leading to new interdisciplinary studies, which have explored the relationships between kinship and the political order in societies in which the power of the state was circumscribed. These approaches have drawn upon the social sciences, including legal studies and anthropology. For instance, Levi-Strauss's discussion of the exchange of women in archaic society has been used to analyze kinship and marriage among the medieval nobility (Levi-Strauss, pp. 305–326), while Goody's materialist approach continues to provoke medievalists into setting out new models on the transformation of kinship and the family (Goody, pp. 399–422). Collectively this work has led to the view that kinship during the earlier Middle Ages differed substantially from its counterpart during the later Middle Ages, with the year 1000 often being taken as the turning point. This contrast arises in part from differing types of evidence studied, and the domination of different national historiographical traditions in the shaping of general perceptions of particular periods. This differentiation continues to provide a helpful model for understanding medieval kinship.

Early Medieval Kinship

Understanding of the organization of early medieval kinship has been based upon prosopographical studies of the names recorded in continental *libri memoriales*, conducted mainly at the universities of Freibourg-en-Brisgau and Münster. By closely studying the ways in which names of persons were grouped together in Salzburg, Pfäfers, St. Gall, Reichenau, Remiremont, Brescia, and Corvey commemorative records, Schmid and his colleagues highlighted the central importance of the *Sippe*, or "cousinship." In short, an individual belonged to several different groups, each interlocking with one another, and was part of a household unit (*familia*), which comprised the head of the family, his wife, concubines, children born of these unions, parents of the preceding generation, and slaves. Links between cousins commonly gave power to a superior kinship grouping, which is referred to in the medieval sources as *gens*, *genus*, *progeniens*, or *prosapia*. For instance, the *gens nobilis Ayglofinga*, which was defined by its descent from King Agiulf (d. 457), had subgroupings in northwest France, the Rhine and Moselle valleys, Lombardy, and Bavaria, and included among its descendants the kings of Lombardy and the counts of Meaux (Le Jan, pp. 387–395).

It is important to stress that the *Sippe* did not function as a corporate unit, unified by the rituals, mutual consent, or the domination of patriarchs. Here it is helpful to consider anthropologist's studies of genealogies in segmentary societies. A common genealogy reaching back to a founding ancestor will embrace all descendants, but the structure does not function mechanically. Rather, it operates according to a formula of alternate oppositions and solidarities. The related groups springing from the same stock are in opposition among themselves, but are associated together within the immediate superior unit, which itself is in opposition with its relations. The political implications of these connections appear in the historical record in accounts of wars, feuds, and other political encounters, with, for example, the "Agiolfides" being defined in part through their opposition to the "Pippinides."

The kinship of the *Sippe* was cognatic, whereby family links and descent were traced through both sexes, with the result that children were regularly given the names of maternal ancestors. A son of Megingaud, count of Oberrheingau, was named Robert in order to draw attention to his maternal descent from Count Robert the Strong (d. 866), ancestor of the Capetian royal house (Le Jan, p. 183). Women were a source of renown and nobility, with marriages of Carolingian royal daughters into the Udalrichid, Guelph, and Bosonid dynasties establishing the kinship identity and descent of these kindreds. In short, kinship provided the parameters by which the European imperial nobility of the earlier Middle Ages (*Reichsaristokratie*) was defined, and ensured that *Königsnähe*, which bound men to the king, dominated the political order in localities and centers of political power.

Women also carried out vital political functions that maintained the power of the *Sippe*. For instance, they were the guardians of the memories of the family's ancestors. The origins of the Carolingian dynasty were recorded in the *Annals of Metz* because of the initiative of Giselle, sister of Charlemagne (Le Jan, pp. 54–56), while Ealdorman Æthelweard the Chronicler (d. c. 988) thanked his cousin Abbess Matilda of Essen, granddaughter of Emperor Otto I (d. 973), for the information that she had provided on their ancestry and dedicated his version of the *Anglo-Saxon Chronicle* to her (Campbell, p. 1).

Patterns of inheritance also meant that women came to exercise a powerful role within the *Sippe*. Property was divided between sons and daughters, and if women survived childbirth they could expect to receive extensive dowers in the form of lands, livestock, and treasure. The custodianship of this property was not a passive issue. The supervision of this wealth entailed the exercise of administrative skills, while bequests of property from the deceased enabled women to reorder power relationships within kindreds. The position of women was, moreover, reflected in status markers, such as the Anglo-Saxon "morning-gift."

Later Medieval Kinship

In spite of the controversies surrounding the "feudal transformation," it still serves as a useful historiographical construct in order to understand the transformation in the organization of the European family between the late ninth and twelfth centuries. The model suggests that the breakdown of public order, notably in the generations immediately before and after the year 1000, led to the disappearance of cognatic kinship in favour of agnatic descent, traced exclusively through men, and the establishment of lineages. Henceforward kinship was defined only through descent via men (agnatic kinship), while filiation (i.e., ties linking father to son) replaced cousinship as a defining principle in family organization.

These changes, however, cannot be viewed in isolation from the transformation in the medieval landscape and wider frameworks of social development. The heads of families based in castles took over the public rights formerly exercised by local royal agents, linked to the exercise of violence in order to protect their estates and their dependants from predatory neighbours, also based in castles. A linkage was soon established between the military solidarity of the lord and his warriors with the prestige of his lineage. As a result it became common practice for families to adopt surnames derived from their caputs (heads) and castles, and for Christian names to be chosen from those used by paternal ancestors. For instance, in the last quarter of the eleventh century, three-quarters of the surnames used by noble houses in the Maconnais were derived from topynyms associated with landed demesnes and castles (Duby, p. 397).

These developments were not confined to those areas that suffered from the violence associated with the feudal transformation. Duby and others have argued for a diffusion model. Thus, Frankish aristocracies who established themselves in the peripheries of Europe, such as the British Isles and the Spanish march, introduced new systems of agnatic kinship that replaced early medieval kinship organization. Meanwhile, these new patterns were adopted by other social orders in rural and urban contexts, with the exception of Jewish households and communities.

The feudal transformation model is easy to understand and has clear conclusions that can be related to a wider series of changes in European society, but it should not be taken as fact, either in terms of its explanations, or in terms of the practical manifestations of the processes that it identifies in relation to the transformation of the family. For instance, a regional case study from the British Isles suggests that commemoration and remembrance was responsible for the establishment of lineages, at variance with the hypotheses put forward by the feudal transformation model (Wareham, 61–77), and in many regions of Europe "lineages" continued to retain a matrilineal dimension. Yet there is no doubt that the organization of kinship in Europe among the aristocracy and the peasantry by the close of the twelfth century was substantially different from its counterpart during the earlier Middle Ages. The change, though, can also be explained by perspectives from other historical schools, which draw upon sources such as the *laudatio parentum*, which record the approval of kinsfolk in bequests to the church in western France.

Above all a distinction needs to be drawn between norms in terms of common practice, and rules, as set out in legal treatises. During the twelfth and thirteenth centuries lawyers, whether basing their work upon Roman law or Common law, began to codify inheritance practices, and thereby to shape the dynamics of kinship. Thus, in an English legal treatise of c. 1188, it was established that lords in England could not alienate more than one-third of their inheritances, and by the early thirteenth century daughters were not allowed to receive more than one-third of paternal wealth in Normandy (Green, pp. 341, 365). The move from custom to law served to weaken the position of women within kinship groupings, most notably of all when primogeniture became the established practice. For instance, in England in the century after 1066 primogeniture became accepted practice in regulating the descent of inherited estates (patrimonies) from fathers to their eldest sons at the expense of widows, younger brothers, sisters, and wider kin. The contrast with the earlier Middle Ages is striking, with consequent results upon the position held by women.

Yet the differences between the early and later Middle Ages should not be pushed too far. Ties of kinship, lordship, and neighbourhood shaped the dynamics of political power across the Middle Ages, and thereby provided women with opportunities to take on roles regardless of sex. The 917–918 campaigns of Æthelflæd of Mercia in Derby and Leicester, and her construction of a network of fortified boroughs in the wars against the Vikings, arose from her status as the daughter of Alfred (d. 899), king of Wessex, and the wife of Æthelræd, lord of the Mercians (Swanton, 101, 105). Her actions and circumstances can, moreover, be compared with Sybil Bordet, who defended Taragona (Spain), and Isabel de Conches, who went on campaign, according to a twelfth-century monastic historian (Chibnall, pp. 105–121).

The bond between kinship and politics was a key feature of medieval society, and provided women with a vehicle to express abilities and ambitions.

ANDREW WAREHAM

References and Further Reading

Bloch, M. *La société féodale.* 6th ed. Paris: A. Colin, 1978.
Campbell, Alistair, ed. *The Chronicle of Æthelweard.* London: Nelson, 1962.
Chibnall, Marjorie. "Women in Orderic Vitalis." *Haskins Society Journal* 2 (1990): 105–121.
Crick, Julia. "Women, Posthumous Benefaction, and Family Strategy in Pre-Conquest England," *Journal of British Studies* 38 (1999): 399–422.
Duby, Georges. *Hommes et structures du Moyen Age.* Paris: Mouton, 1973.

Goody, Jack. *The Development of Family and Marriage in Europe*. Cambridge: Cambridge University Press, 1986.

Green, Judith. *The Aristocracy of Norman England*. Cambridge: Cambridge University Press, 1997.

Le Jan, Régine. *Famille et pouvoir dans le monde franc (VIIe–Xe Siècle): Essai d'anthropologie sociale*. Paris: Publications de la Sorbonne, 1995.

Levi-Strauss, Claude. *Les structures élémentaires de la parenté*. Paris: PUF, 1949.

Ruiz-Doménec, J., "Système de parenté et théorie de l'alliance dans la société catalane (env. 1000–env. 1240)." *Revue Historique*, 532 (1979): 305–326.

Schmid, K. *Geblüt, Herrschaft, Geschlechterbewusstsein. Grundfragen zum Verständnis des Adels im Mittelalter*. Sigmaringen: J. Thorbecke, 1998.

Swanton, Michael, ed. *The Anglo-Saxon Chronicle*. London: Routledge, 1998.

Wareham, Andrew. *Lords and Communities in Early Medieval East Anglia*. Santa Barbara, Calif.: Woodbridge Press, 2005.

White, Stephen. *Custom, Kinship and Gifts to Saints: the Laudatio Parentum in Western France, 1050—1150*. Chapel Hill, N.C.: University of North Carolina Press, 1989.

See also **Aethelflaed; Death, Mourning, and Commemoration; Family (Earlier Middle Ages); Family (Later Middle Ages); Inheritance; Matilda and the Monastery of Essen**

KOMNENE, ANNA

Anna Komnene (1083–c. 1150s) is one of the best known of Byzantine women due to her authorship of the *Alexiad*, a history of her father's rise to power and subsequent reign. Translated into many languages today, the *Alexiad* unveils one medieval woman's experiences.

Anna Komnene was born in the royal palace in Constantinople, two years after her father took the throne. She died probably in the 1150s, having lived her entire life in the capital city of the Byzantine empire. Known simply as "the city" to its inhabitants, it abounded in beautiful palaces and magnificent churches and was home to many artists, authors, rhetors, architects, and monks, who were drawn to its imperial and patriarchal courts.

Anna Komnene was fitted by birth and education to take part in the rich culture into which she was born. Educated in the *trivium* (grammar, rhetoric, and dialectic), she had access to the *quadrivium* (further studies, normally reserved for boys, in geometry, arithmetic, astronomy, and music). The extent of her literary education is revealed in the *Alexiad*, which is written in high-style archaizing Greek and abounds in literary allusions. She was involved to some extent in other literary endeavours, such as the commentaries on Aristotle produced by an educated circle meeting in the nunnery of Kecharitomene, where Anna lived much of her life.

Most of Anna's life was lived in a nunnery due to politics. After Anna's father died in 1118, she attempted to take the throne from her brother John. He was younger than Anna, and she had imperial ambitions. As a child, before John's birth, she had been betrothed to the future heir to the throne. That engagement was broken off and the young man died, but Anna seems never to have abandoned the idea of ruling the empire. That ambition says much about the effect on women of the change in the empire's political character during the eleventh century. At that time the great families came to play a significant role in the acquisition and exercise of power. Women gained a role not only as partners in the all-important scheme of marriage alliances but also as architects of these alliances. The most notable eleventh-century example was Anna's paternal grandmother, Anna Dalassena. She created a web of alliances that supported Alexios Komnenos's coup in 1081. Anna Dalassena then controlled the civil government of the empire while Alexios spent years fighting on the frontiers.

After Anna Dalassena retired, Alexios' wife Eirene Doukaina became the most powerful woman at court, even traveling with Alexios on military expeditions. In this climate of powerful imperial women it is not surprising that Anna should aspire to rule. Eirene did not support Anna Komnene's outright rebellion against John in 1118, but she had lobbied Alexios on her behalf before his death.

Anna's rebellion failed, and John exiled her to Kecharitomene, where she lived in the royal quarters and interacted with the educated men who flocked there to read, write, and recite. There she wrote her *Alexiad*, a book that does not mention her rebellion but is full of her undeclared claim to be her father's heir.

Anna has been accused of perpetuating unfavourable stereotypes about women in the Alexiad. She does comment that women are weak and her highest accolade of praise is to describe a woman as "manly." However, although Anna did not analyse and criticise her society as modern feminists or anthropologists do, she did value women as women. She included herself and her unusual experience in womanhood, merely expanding the meaning of the word to encompass it. None of the women in the Alexiad are portrayed as weak; they all deal with the individual crises they face with courage and vision. They all display self-control, regarded as the eminent virtue by men and women. Anna was elitist, and class is perhaps a greater signifier than gender for her. For her, the gender of the heir to the empire was less important than his or her family name.

Anna's family pride and her literary achievements are her most defining characteristics. Many questions surrounding her are debated: did Anna really write the *Alexiad*; how true is her account; and how does her gender affect her writing and presentation of her times? What sort of literature is the *Alexiad*, and is it any good? What did Anna think about women and men, and can we ever know? How much is she a product of her times and how much an exception? The breadth of the discussion communicates Anna's importance to history.

BARBARA HILL

References and Further Reading

Angold, Michael. *The Byzantine Empire, 1025–1204: A Political History*. 2nd Ed. London: Longman, 1997.

Buckler, Georgiana. *Anna Comnena*. Oxford: Oxford University Press, 1929.

Garland, Linda. *Byzantine Empresses: Women and Power in Byzantium AD 527–1204*. London: Routledge, 1999.

Gouma-Peterson, Thalia, ed. *Anna Komnene and Her Times*. New York: Garland, 2000.

Hill, Barbara. *Imperial Women in Byzantium, 1025–1204*. London: Longman, 1999.

Komnene, Anna. *The Alexiad of Anna Comnena*. Translated by E. Sewter, Baltimore: Penguin, 1969.

Mullett, Margaret E., and Smythe, Dion C., eds. *Alexios I Komnenos*. Vol 1. Belfast: Belfast Byzantine Texts & Translations, 1999.

See also **Byzantium; Empresses: Byzantium**

KOTTANER, HELENE

Helene Kottaner (Kottannerin) (c. 1400–1457) wrote an invaluable vernacular memoir from the perspective of a lay woman of the fifteenth century. She described in rich detail the intricate high politics of Central Europe and certain intrigues at the court of Elizabeth of Luxemburg (d. 1442), queen of Hungary, daughter of King-Emperor Sigismund (1387–1437), and widow of Albert V(II) of Hapsburg, King of the Romans (r. 1437–1439). As a lady of the bedchamber and nurse-governess to Princess Elizabeth of Hapsburg (1436–1505), later queen of Poland, Kottaner was an eyewitness to and participant in the events that led to the contested coronation of Ladislas Posthumus (1440–1457) as king of Hungary. Her memoir is the first prose narrative composed in German by a woman.

Lady Helene, daughter of Peter Wolfram (d. after 1435), a member of the Austrian lower nobility, married twice: first to the Hungarian Peter Székeles, lord mayor of Sopron (d. c. 1430); then, in 1432, to Johann Kottaner, chamberlain to the cathedral

provost of Sopron. Of her children, Wilhelm Székeles and Katherina Kottaner are known by name. She entered Albert's court c. 1436 and moved with it to Hungary. Albert's early death left her mistress, Queen Elizabeth, in a precarious situation. Elizabeth was pregnant, hoping for a male heir; but a large faction of Hungarian nobles wanted her to marry sixteen-year-old King Władisław III of Poland, whom they could then elect king.

Lady Helene played a vital role in the queen's service. She courageously stole the Crown of St. Stephen for the queen and held twelve-week-old Ladislas at his coronation (May 15, 1440). The queen's opponents prevailed in a civil war, eventually forcing Elizabeth out of Hungary. Helene's later fortunes are obscure, and she is thought to have died in Vienna (c. 1457).

Helene's narrative is preserved in an incomplete fifteenth-century manuscript. Scholars believe it was composed between 1445 and 1452. The author dictated a first person account to a secretary. She may have intended to inform young King Ladislas of the events leading to his coronation and seek his favor for past services. It is focused on events in 1439–1440 in western Hungary and Austria. Helene wrote a vivid, if partisan, narrative; and the account of stealing the crown is particularly colorful. Helene reached the queen just before the moment of Ladislas' birth. Helene goes on to recount the coronation and later events. Her memoir is more valuable for its reflection of the assumptions and folkways of her time.

JAMES ROSS SWEENEY

References and Further Reading

Bak, János. "The Late Medieval Period, 1382–1526." In *A History of Hungary*, edited by Peter F. Sugar. Bloomington: Indiana University Press, 1990, pp. 54–82.

Bijvoet, Maya C., trans. "Helene Kottaner: the Austrian Chambermaid." In *Women Writers of the Renaissance and Reformation*, edited by Katharina M. Wilson, Athens, Ga.: University of Georgia Press, 1987, pp. 327–349.

Carney, Jo Eldridge. "Helene Kottaner (1400–after 1457), Austria, Writer of Memoirs and Royal Servant," in Carol Levin *et al. Extraordinary Women of the Medieval and Renaissance World*. Westport, Conn.: Greenwood Press, 2000, pp. 157–159.

Mollay, Karl. *Die Denkwiirdigkeit der Helene Kottannerin (1439–1440)*. Vienna: Bundersverl, 1971.

Sweeney, James Ross. "The Tricky Queen and Her Clever Lady-in-Waiting: Stealing the Crown to Secure Succession, Visegrád 1440." *East Central Europe* 20–23, part 1 (1993–1996): 87–100.

See also **Ladies-in-Waiting; Queens and Empresses: The West**

L

LADIES-IN-WAITING

The role played by a noble woman in the late-medieval court grew in importance after the thirteenth century. The queens' and princesses' feminine entourages increased and became more luxurious as courts developed in a long process that would carry on throughout the fourteenth and fifteenth centuries. Ladies-in-waiting would become an elite group among these noble women who served royalty, not only in their daily life but also in court ceremonies.

These ladies were the daughters or wives of the kingdom's great noblemen. They generally lived in the great lady's household with their children and their own servants. Besides carrying out the characteristic household chores of their position, they served the queen or princess so that she could appear in society and exercise her royal power as was fitting.

Just as there were different positions among men within the court and chivalrous hierarchy, we also find these hierarchical differences among courtier noble women. A lady was equivalent to a knight within the court hierarchy, as was a damsel to a squire. As it is evidenced by some contemporaneous writings, like Christine de Pizan's, whereas damsels belonged to the lower nobility, ladies were members of the high nobility; their position was equivalent to gentlemen's. The difference between men and women is that it was not women's achievement to gain power, as they depended on the status that their husbands acquired in the court.

On the other hand, it is also important to consider that, after the thirteenth century, the terms *lady* and *damsel* were also used in a generic way to refer to a married noble woman and to a young noble maiden, respectively, and so this expression could be misleading. Therefore, this entry analyzes this terminology in a hierarchical sense: the lady as a position within the court service's hierarchy, as the "lady-in-waiting."

Concerning the function of a lady at court, the main evidence dates back to the end of the fourteenth and fifteenth centuries, when the different occupations and court positions had been defined in detail. Books like those of Christine de Pizan, or Alienor de Poitiers' *Les honneurs de la cour* evidence the role played by ladies in ceremonial and court life near the great lady. As regards court and chivalrous ceremonies, each lady had a precisely defined function. There are many testimonies of queens' or princess' entrances, where the great lady arrived surrounded by her ladies, who rode horseback as if they were horsemen. They established a certain parallelism between the king's entourage and the queen's.

In regard to domestic life, ladies were in charge of waiting on queens and princesses and followed a refined protocol, not only in their daily activities but also in the most delicate moments of life, including pregnancy, childbirth, and death—in fact, they organized royal family members' funerals. All of the women, great ladies and their attendants, spent every day together: sewing and embroidering, tasks typically reserved for noble women.

In addition to these assignments, ladies were responsible for educating princesses and princes. In the earlier years of their life, infants lived in their mother's household and they grew up with all these women. Girls continued living in the queen's household with the women of her entourage and often became part of it. On the other hand, boys around the age of seven left their mothers' households, either for their own or their fathers'. Thus, many ladies had the role of governess to princes and princesses; they were in charge of instilling good manners and religious devotion in royal children and, if it was possible, they taught them to read and to write. For girls, these governesses also taught embroidery, dancing, and other knowledge that a lady must have.

Therefore, ladies held a very responsible position in the court in regard to protocol and education. All princes and future kings grew up in their lap, so to speak; they also provided the queen needed company and an entourage, with which to display her Majesty amid multicolored, sumptuous robes and courtiers' gestures, in a society completely immersed in chivalrous literature.

MARÍA NARBONA-CÁRCELES

References and Further Reading

Aurell, Martí dir., and María Narbona Cárceles, ed. and trans. *La dama en la corte bajomedieval*. Pamplona: Eunsa, 2001.

Herlihy, David. *Opera Muliebria: Women and Work in Medieval Europe*. Philadelphia: Temple University Press, 1990.

Narbona Cárceles, María. "Woman at Court: a Prosopographic Study of the Court of Carlos III of Navarre (1387–1425)." *Medieval Prosopography* 22 (2001): 31–64.

Paviot, Jacques, ed. "Les Etats de France (Les honneurs de la cour) d'Eleonore de Poitiers," in: *Annuaire-Bulletin de la Société de l'histoire de la France*, 1996, París, 1998, pp. 75–137.

Pizan, Christine de. *Le livre des trois vertus*, edited by Cannon Willard. Paris: Honoré Champion, 1989.

———. *Le livre de la Cité des dames*, translated and introduced by Éric Hicks and Thérèse Moreau, Paris: Stock, 1992.

See also **Noble Women; Queens and Empresses: the West**

LANDHOLDING AND PROPERTY RIGHTS

Although women were able to acquire land throughout the Middle Ages, they did not usually have full control over it. Thus in Anglo-Saxon society, a bride might be given land as her "morning gift," but it stayed in the hands of her husband during his lifetime: he managed it and received its revenues. Even as a widow, although she could now enjoy the revenues, she could not alienate it and, on her death, it passed to her husband's heirs. Only a very few women held any sizeable agglomerations of property in their own right and those were always members of the upper aristocracy or a royal house.

Inheritance

Thus in England in 1066, no more than five percent of the total area of land recorded in the Domesday survey was in the hands of women, and of that five percent about half was in the hands of three female members of the family of Earl Godwin. The rules or principles governing inheritance and the size of a widow's portion were still extremely flexible and depended a great deal on the wishes and power of a girl's father and/or his lord. It was not until the Angevin king, Henry II, undertook extensive legal reforms, that the rules governing property administered by common law became more standardized and clear-cut.

By the end of the twelfth century the claim of women to inherit land in the absence of direct male heirs was recognized; daughters might inherit if there were no sons and sisters if there were no brothers. If more than one daughter had survived, the land was to be equally divided among them. A widow could be given one-third of her husband's estate (her dower), but she had only a life interest in it. At first she received just the lands that she had been given at the church door at the time of the marriage, but after the issuance of Magna Carta, this was expanded to include a share of all the lands that her husband had possessed at any time during the marriage. A widow, however, had to claim her share from the heir, but, if he failed to provide it, she could bring a plea before one of the royal courts. These pleas reveal that a number of second and third wives were forced to litigate with the sons of first wives. Even though judgment was often given in favor of the widow, the process of securing a dower could be an "engrossing, time-consuming business" (Walker).

Jointure and Widowhood

During the thirteenth and fourteenth centuries, women's rights in land were profoundly affected by new legal developments. First land could be given to husband and wife to hold jointly. A widow could keep this land and enjoy the revenues even if she remarried. Furthermore since technically she was already in possession of the land, she did not need to go to a court to claim it and thus might avoid some of the problems previously discussed. On the contraction of a marriage among common law tenants it became increasingly common for the bride's family to provide a marriage portion of money and/or goods and the groom's family to provide a jointure in land.

At the level of manorial courts (which governed land held by customary tenure), similar legal procedures arose virtually in tandem with what was happening in the common law courts. In the early Middle Ages landed provision was made for the widow in accordance with the custom of a particular manor—a widow might receive a third, a half, or the whole of her husband's estates in different areas. Unlike the aristocracy, however, the widow could keep this customary land only so long as she remained chaste and unmarried. Gradually it became more and more common to grant some land jointly to both husband and wife, but sometimes with a reversion to a named heir. Joint tenure had distinct advantages for the future widow. She did not forfeit the land if she remarried and most of the necessary fees payable to the lord had already been paid. If the land had been granted without a reversion the widow was free to do with it what she willed, including sell it to non-kin.

Uses and Deathbed Transfers

The most important change, however, affecting common law property was the rise of "the use." Lands were granted to trustees known as "feoffees to uses," who became for most legal purposes the owners of the land, although the previous owner continued to receive its income. Dower could still be assessed on any land that had not been transmitted by enfeoffment to use, but dower could not be claimed from any land that had been granted to feoffees before a marriage. A man, however, usually instructed his trustees, through his last will and testament, to grant his wife a portion of his estates. This might be more than the one-third to which she would be entitled under the common law provision for dower, or it might be much less. Although some widows became extremely wealthy, enjoying a generous dower and jointure, others were granted no more than maintenance and house room and had to rely on a slim jointure. A few were even pressured to give up their allotment of land in return for an annuity that was not always paid on time.

Similarly in the manorial courts, a new type of conveyancing—the deathbed transfer—appeared in the fourteenth century, which allowed a man to make an oral disposition of his landed assets if he was too sick to attend the regular court. Such transfers might benefit a widow if she was granted land that she would not otherwise have received, but in many cases she lost out, if her husband granted land to noninheriting children or added a reversionary clause to land that was held jointly.

Urban Property

Within towns, real estate, held under the form of law known as burgage tenure, could be freely sold or bequeathed. A merchant could give a townhouse to daughters even if he had sons or to a sister instead of a brother. Yet, although an unmarried daughter could become a rentier or run a business on her own, very few actually did so. Once a woman married, any inherited property would be managed and controlled by her husband, and with her consent, could be, and often was, alienated during her lifetime. Widows could claim a share in the house in which they had been living and a half or third share of their husband's lands, tenements, and goods. In addition urban women, as with other widows, could hold property jointly with their husbands and keep these tenements after the men's deaths.

How comfortably an urban widow could live depended a great deal on her social status. In the case of mercantile widows, where the husband's wealth might take the form of bales of wool or cloth, or debts owed to him, the widow's share could be extremely valuable. She might also hold several houses, shops, and land on which rents could be collected. In contrast the widow of a small-scale artisan, such as a carpenter, weaver, or glover, might inherit very little in the way of moveable property. The family frequently lived in rented accommodation, so that the widow had no claim to real estate. Many were forced to move to cheaper lodgings on the edge of town. In every study that has been carried out—Coventry, Exeter, Southwark—the households headed by women were poorer than those headed by males and many widows were living in extreme poverty.

MAVIS MATE

References and Further Reading

Archer, Rowena E. "'How Ladies Who Live on Their Manors Ought to Manage Their Households and Estates': Women As Landholders and Administrators in the Later Middle Ages." In *Women is a Worthy Wight*, edited by P. J. P. Goldberg. Wolfeboro Falls, N.H.: Alan Sutton, 1992, pp. 149–181.
Walker, Sue Sheridan. "Litigation as a Personal Quest: Suing for Dower in the Royal Courts circa 1272–1350." In *Wife and Widow in Medieval England*, edited by S. S. Walker. Ann Arbor, Mich.: University of Michigan Press, 1993, pp. 81–108.

See also **Dowry and Other Marriage Gifts; Economy; England; Inheritance; Law, English Secular Courts of; Widows**

LANGMANN, ADELHEID

Born into a socially powerful patrician family in Nuremberg, Adelheid Langmann (c. 1312–1375) was betrothed to Gottfried Teufel at the age of thirteen. He died shortly thereafter and in her spiritual autobiography, Adelheid describes an intensely difficult spiritual struggle following his death. In 1330, she entered the Franconian Dominican cloister of Engelthal, a prosperous and renowned convent housing the daughters of many of the wealthy burghers of the area. Among them was Christina Ebner, who also wrote a lengthy spiritual autobiography and was known by bishops and kings. Both Adelheid and Christina were cloistered at Engelthal when King Charles IV, who would later be crowned as emperor, visited the monastery in 1350 seeking spiritual advice.

Like many of her Dominican sisters in Germany, Austria, and Switzerland, Adelheid was educated in Latin and learned to read and write in her vernacular German dialect. Perhaps inspired by Christina Ebner's mystical text, Adelheid began to write, recording her visions and revelations. She also composed a lengthy prayer dedicated to the Trinity. Adelheid's *Revelations*, along with the *Prayer*, are extant in three manuscript variations. The narrative of her spiritual journey, *Revelations*, is written in a Bavarian dialect and chronicles her cloistered life from 1330 to 1344. Although the text is essentially autohagiographical, narrating Adelheid's own experience of the divine, there are stylistic similarities and thematic parallels with texts written by Christina Ebner, Margaretha Ebner, as well as the myriad of lives narrated in the Dominican "Sister-Books." Influenced by biblical sources, especially the Song of Songs, Adelheid's ecstatic mysticism reflects the bride and mother mysticism of the High Middle Ages.

ROSEMARY DRAGE HALE

References and Further Reading

Hindsley, Leonard P. *The Mystics of Engelthal: Writings from a Medieval Monastery*. New York: St. Martin's Press, 1998.

Die Offenbarungen der Adelheid Langmann: Klosterfrau zu Engelthal. Edited by Phillip Strauch. Strassburg: Truebner, 1878.

See also **Autohagiography; Bride of Christ: Imagery; Ebner, Margaretha; Mysticism and Mystics; Sister-Books and Convent Chronicles**

LAUGHTER

Medieval attitudes toward laughter were ambivalent. Monastic rules often forbade laughter because of its association with the sin of pride and because Jesus was said never to have laughed. Physicians and some church writers, however, welcomed laughter in moderation for its power to restore the spirits and to enliven otherwise dull sermons. Writers who valued laughter emphasized the importance of moderation, influenced both by Arab writers on laughter and the medical understanding of the body as composed of four humors that should be kept in balance. Moderate laughter was encouraged in both men and women, but concern over the potential for excessive laughter was heightened for women, as evidenced in much conduct literature instructing women not to laugh too loudly or too long, not to speak too often, and not to move their bodies or look around in an immodest way. This concern stemmed first from the view that women were less able to control the emotions because of their inferior rational faculties and bodily predisposition toward shifting moods. In both medical and popular texts, women were said to laugh and cry more often, or even simultaneously. Another reason laughter was discouraged in women can be explained by a longstanding association between laughter and aggression. Women were educated to be passive and obedient; laughter signaled resistance to these norms and could thus jeopardize a woman's reputation and desirability as a potential spouse. The telling of jokes or humorous tales was also censored more often in women. Whereas men were encouraged to demonstrate their intellectual wit and thus establish power within political circles, such skills were generally not deemed appropriate to women, whose public roles were less important. Sexual humor, in particular, was discouraged because it compromised a woman's modesty, a concern dramatized in Giovanni Boccaccio's *Decameron*, in which female storytellers are reluctant to tell tales with sexual content (see especially the discussion before Day VII). Women were instructed not only to avoid sexual language, but also to avoid laughing at sexual jokes, for fear this would expose their knowledge of sex.

Investigations into humor by women in modern times have attempted to ascertain whether women have a sense of humor that is distinctly different from men's, a proposition that has been criticized as essentializing. In the Middle Ages, the lack of comic texts known to have been authored by women makes this issue yet more difficult. It has been claimed that authors such as Christine de Pizan and Marie de France demonstrated a sense of humor, but humor is far from central in their works. Representations of women laughing in medieval texts do tend, however, to parallel anthropological studies showing that women throughout the world are more likely to laugh and tell jokes in women-only settings. The anonymous French *Evangiles des Quenouilles* [Gospel of Distaffs] and William Dunbar's poem *The Tretis of the Tua Mariit Wemen and the Wedo*, for example, show small private groups of women laughing raucously and telling jokes, especially about the failings of men.

There has been much debate about the attitude toward women in medieval comic literature. Genres such as the short rhymed narratives called fabliaux are said to be misogynistic because the female characters who trick their husbands are libidinous and deceitful. Others argue that fabliaux women are more clever and resourceful than the dull-witted men of the tales, who have in some way deserved the humiliation they suffer; women end up "on top" in these narratives. Similar ambiguity is found in visual humor such as the manuscript marginalia and wood carvings of women "wearing the pants" or beating their husbands with distaffs. Theoretical contexts informing this debate include anthropological analyses of rituals of misrule and Mikhail Bakhtin's concept of carnival. Medieval authors themselves are a far from satisfactory guide in how to interpret these ambivalent figures, since their narrators both praise and blame women's use of wit. The female character who best embodies the medieval author's ambivalence is the Wife of Bath, from Geoffrey Chaucer's *Canterbury Tales*. The Wife defends herself against centuries of antifeminist writings by manipulating scripture and Church writing to fit her own defense of women, and she brags of her control over her five husbands. While some scholars view her as a negative portrait of feminine excess and believe that laughter was at her expense, others see more sympathy in Chaucer's portrayal, and believe that readers laugh along with the Wife rather than at her. It is important to note that the wit of female characters may be promoted by male authors and enjoyed by audiences for reasons other than promoting a defense of women. For example, the shepherdess of the *pastourelle* who ridicules and spurns the inappropriate advances of the passing knight highlights differences in class and parodies courtly discourse.

LISA PERFETTI

References and Further Reading

Apte, Mahadev L. *Humor and Laughter: An Anthropological Approach*. Ithaca: Cornell University Press, 1985.
Barreca, Regina. *They Used to Call Me Snow White But I Drifted: Women's Strategic Use of Humor*. New York: Penguin, 1991.
Bremmer, Jan, and Herman Roodenburg, eds. *A Cultural History of Humour from Antiquity to the Present Day*. Cambridge, U.K.: Polity Press, 1997.
Fenster, Thelma. "Did Christine Have a Sense of Humor? The Evidence of the *Epistre au dieu d'Amours*." In *Reinterpreting Christine de Pizan*, edited by Earl Jeffrey Richards. Athens: University of Georgia Press, 1992, pp. 23–36.
Joubert, Laurent. *Treatise on Laughter*, translated by Gregory David de Rocher. Tuscaloosa, Ala.: University of Alabama Press, 1980.
Olson, Glending. *Literature as Recreation in the Later Middle Ages*. Ithaca: Cornell University Press, 1986.
Perfetti, Lisa. *Women and Laughter in Medieval Comic Literature*. Ann Arbor: University of Michigan Press, 2003.
Verberckmoes, Johan. *Laughter, Jestbooks, and Society in the Spanish Netherlands*. New York: St. Martin's, 1999.

See also **Boccaccio, Giovanni; Conduct Literature; Evangiles des Quenouilles; Exemplum; Fabliau; Festivals of Misrule; Proverbs, Riddles, and Gnomic Literature; Wife of Bath; Woman on Top**

LAW

Medieval legal systems impacted women in all times and places. Early medieval society distinguished between persons (Roman and barbarian) whereas later society was divided into regional political entities (kingdoms, principalities, and cities) with their own systems.

All regions had customary law, much of it reduced to writing. All too were influenced by Roman law and canon law. These were taught at universities, and their graduates influenced the practice of law across the continent. Even English common law was influenced by Roman norms, usually through the church courts. Jewish law governed a substantial minority within the larger context of "Christendom." Islamic law governed much of the Iberian Peninsula until "Reconquest" by Christian kings reduced it to minority status. Where these jurisdictions clashed, Christian norms tended to prevail.

Roman law treated marriage as a dissoluble contract and provided for the support of marriage by dowries. Barbarian legal systems also recognized divorce, and customary law gave the family of a woman considerable control over her marriage choices. Canon law, however, inserted Christian norms, including the developing belief in marriage as a sacrament, into local practice. Sacramental marriage was supposed to be indissoluble; but a union might be voided if it had been contracted within close degrees of kinship or ignored other legal impediments.

Canon law emphasized the consent of the couple, not consummation, as ratifying a marriage; and this emphasis extended to accepting clandestine unions as valid. A woman did have an equal right to sexual satisfaction, the so-called conjugal debt. Nor could one spouse enter a monastery without the other spouse's consent. All such matters were adjudicated in church courts.

Women held secondary status in any medieval system of law. Under the barbarian codes, a woman's wergild was less than that of a man of equal social status but highest in her child-bearing years. Her property rights were adjudicated in lay courts according to customary norms or those of Roman law. Women might inherit property in some systems, but their husbands tended to enjoy its fruits. Women might transmit claims to power and property, but they rarely ruled or exercised power directly. An heiress might become the ward of a powerful man who could marry her off to his own political or financial advantage.

Systems of dowry provided by the bride's family were developed—replacing the dower a husband provided—to support a married woman while protecting the family's patrimony from any claim she might make on it. A widow might enjoy greater freedom of action and choice of a subsequent husband, but efforts were made to protect her children from the previous marriage and their father's family from her departure with the assigned dowry. Dowries also were shielded from a husband's insolvency. (A nun too was expected to bring her monastery a dowry.)

Women's legal rights were most restricted in the public forum and became more limited over time. A woman's testimony was of limited value in a court of law, especially where her own interests were not involved. In all public matters, a woman was expected to act through a male relative or some other man. Even an abbess, acting within the canon law courts, was expected to stay cloistered and to act through male agents. Women could, however, make wills; and these might be probated in church courts, especially in regions not dominated by Roman law.

THOMAS IZBICKI

References and Further Reading

Bellomo, Manlio. *The Common Legal Past of Europe: 1000–1800.* translated by Lydia G. Cochrane. Washington, D.C.: Catholic University of America Press, 1995.

Brundage, James A. *Medieval Canon Law: An Introduction.* London and New York: Longman, 1995.

Medieval Women and the Law, edited by Noël James Menuge. Woodbridge, Suffolk: Boydell Press, 2000.

See also **Barbarian Law Codes; Crime and Criminals; Feme Coverte; Feme Sole; Law, Canon; Law, Customary: French; Law, English Secular Courts of; Law, German; Law, Jewish; Law, Roman; Legal Agency; Marriage, Christian; Marriage, Impediments to; Sumptuary Law; Wardship; Wergild; Witches**

LAW CODES, BARBARIAN
See **Barbarian Law Codes**

LAW, CANON

The origins of the Church's claims to a separate jurisdiction over all faithful go back to the disciplinary decisions in the Acts of the Apostles. The law of the Church developed through practice and legislation over the next millennium and formed a coherent, if confusing, body of rules by the eleventh century. The systematic analysis of canon law received a boost with the Investiture struggle of the eleventh century, but gained irresistible momentum as a result of the compilation and publication of Gratian's *Concordia Discordantium Canonum* (c. 1140), which soon became known as his *Decretum*. In this collection of nearly 4,000 canons, Gratian discussed the relevant texts for understanding the position of the law of the Church on a number of legal topics and suggested ways in which the apparent contradictions of the practices of the preceding millennium could be explained or dissolved.

Gratian's text presents arguments for and against the position that he proposes and ranges widely, utilizing all types of ecclesiastical authority: Scripture, the Apostolic canons, ecumenical and local councils, papal decretals, and patristic texts. In the first part, the *distinctiones*, he defines the nature of law, while part two, the *causae*, includes discussions of matters concerning the clergy, such as simony, episcopal authority, the life of monks and clerics, ecclesiastical property, legal procedure, confession, and marriage. Part three of the *Decretum* deals with sacramental and liturgical matters. Gratian's discussion bears the hallmarks of being a teaching text and, though it was hugely influential, some of his discussions drew conclusions that made sense in a classroom situation but left much to be desired in terms of their application in a (Church) court. This was particularly the case in his discussion of marriage—an institution that affected all of Christendom—which left unclear the exact moment when a marriage came into being. Gratian's solution to the contradictions in the canons of the Church was that marriage was a two-stage process incorporating an *initiated* and *perfected* marriage—an unwieldy and difficult concept.

Gratian's solution was superseded by a much simplified model—the so-called *Parisian model*—that only required the parties to *speak* certain words for a marriage to be created. Alexander III's undated decretal, known as *Veniens ad nos*, had legal force immediately during his reign (1159–1181). This decretal was included in 1234 in the *Decretales Gregorii*, also known as the *Liber Extra*, which was the first comprehensive officially promulgated collection of canon law in western Europe. This compilation was different in nature from Gratian's *Decretum*.

It consists of almost 2,000 chapters, most of them being papal decisions taken in individual cases sent to the Curia either as appeals against decisions by local church courts or requests for advice in difficult cases heard by these courts.

The thirteenth and fourteenth centuries saw a rapid development of the courts, both in terms of personnel, legal framework, and complexity. Conciliar and synodal legislation in the early thirteenth century increasingly provided a framework for the regular preaching and implementation of the doctrines and canons of the Church to the laity. The thirteenth century also witnessed the emergence of a number of offices that became central to the running of the church courts, and, with the Second Council of Lyon (1274), church courts were admonished to keep written records of their decisions. The courts became professionalized, and their personnel were expected to meet certain minimum standards. One or two judges were in charge of the courts and had law degrees. Advocates advised the judges and pleaded cases orally, while proctors represented parties in cases and provided the written documentation in pleadings often by employing the court scribes and notaries to compose these. The courts provided a comprehensive system of implementing canonical rules and afforded groups who had few other opportunities to litigate, such as women and children, a venue for their pleas.

Because the medieval Church claimed jurisdiction over all cases involving the salvation of souls, they came to hear a higher proportion of cases initiated and conducted by or on behalf of women than most other courts. The courts claimed jurisdiction over cases for two reasons: by reason of the person and by reason of the subject matter. Thus church courts heard all cases that involved either the fabric or the personnel of the Church and all cases that had to do with the salvation of souls. The former cases included disputes amongst clerics, disputes between clerics and laity, and all cases that involved transgressions against members of the Church.

As survivals of court documentation are at best haphazard and at worst nonexistent, it is difficult to establish litigation levels. Analysis is further complicated by the fact that record-keeping was not consistent across Europe. It has been suggested, for example, that procedure in marriage cases varied in England and France, the former recording them as civil instance cases (initiated by the parties to the marriage), the latter recording them as criminal cases (initiated as the result of an investigation by the court itself). The surviving documentation for medieval English dioceses allows us to speculate that church courts were popular instruments of justice—

particularly for women—in Europe. They heard a large number of cases, and the survivals are only the tip of a very large iceberg. The archives of the archdiocese of York show a remarkably sudden rise in preserved litigation (some 3,000 cases in the sixteenth century compared to only around 600 for the fourteenth and fifteenth centuries). The few surviving fifteenth-century York consistory act books recording the daily business of the courts indicate that they may have heard as many as 20,000 cases during the course of the fifteenth century. One third of the preserved fourteenth-century York consistory court cases deal with disputes between clergy or clergy and lay men, the remaining two-thirds include marriage disputes, testamentary and defamation litigation, and breach of faith cases. The majority of the latter group of cases dealt with the enforcement of marriage. In the rare cases when it is possible to analyze the litigants' understanding of the complex rules of the Church and their use of the procedure of the court, it is striking that lay people appearing before the courts were either very well informed about the content of the law or very well advised by legal counsel.

FREDERIK PEDERSEN

References and Further Reading

Adams, Norma, and Charles Donahue, Jr. *Select Cases from the Ecclesiastical Courts of the Province of Canterbury, c. 1200–1301*. Selden Society, 95. London: Selden Society, 1981.
Brundage, James A. *Medieval Canon Law and the Crusader*. Madison: University of Wisconsin Press, 1969.
———. *Law, Sex, and Christian Society in Medieval Europe*. Chicago: University of Chicago Press, 1987.
Donahue, Charles, Jr. "The Policy of Alexander the Third's Consent Theory of Marriage." In *Proceedings of the Fourth International Conference of Medieval Canon Law*, edited by Stephan Kuttner. Monumenta Iuris Canonici, Subsidia 5. Vatican City: Bibliotheca Apostolica Vaticana, 1976, pp. 251–281.
———. "The Canon Law on the Formation of Marriage and Social Practice in the Later Middle Ages." *Journal of Family History* 8 (1983): 144–158.
Fournier, Paul. *Les officialités au moyen age: étude sur l'organisation, la competence et la procédure des tribunaux ecclésiastiques ordinaire en France, de 1180 a 1328*. Paris: E. Plon., 1880.
Helmholz, R. H. *Marriage Litigation in Medieval England*. Cambridge Studies in English Legal History. Cambridge: Cambridge University Press, 1974.
———. *The Spirit of Classical Canon Law*. Spirit of the Laws. Athens: University of Georgia Press, 1996.
Kuttner, Stephan. *Harmony from Dissonance: An Interpretation of Medieval Canon Law*. Latrobe, Pa.: Archabbey Press, 1960.
Pedersen, Frederik. *Marriage Disputes in Medieval England*. London: Hambledon and London Books, 2000.
Winroth, Anders. *The Making of Gratian's Decretum*. Cambridge: Cambridge University Press, 1997.

See also **Children, Betrothal and Marriage of; Crime and Criminals; Dowry and Other Marriage Gifts; Law, Customary: French; Law, English Secular Courts of; Law, German; Law, Islamic; Law, Roman; Legal Agency; Marriage, Christian; Marriage, Impediments to; Penitentials and Pastoral Manuals; Records, Ecclesiastical; Records, Rural; Records, Urban; Sexuality: Extramarital Sex; Sexuality: Female Same-Sex Relations; Sexuality: Male Same-Sex Relations; Sexuality, Regulation of; Sexuality: Sex in Marriage**

LAW, CUSTOMARY: FRENCH

The earliest law codes to be written down in French, as opposed to Latin, date from the thirteenth century, and consist largely of customs (i.e., judge-made law established in actual cases). Customary law compilations deal with both procedural and substantive matters, and cover such topics as crimes, the transfer of property *inter vivos* and by inheritance, judicial duels (trial by battle) wills, contracts, market regulations, notaries' fees, and many other matters. Many of the codes are unofficial, in the sense that they were not handed down or approved by the local lord, but recorded by lawyers and judges to guide their memories. Since the customs were valid only for small areas, and could change over time, it is impossible to make general statements about all Old French law. It is dangerous to assume that the law of one area of what is now France can explain a problem occurring in another area or at another time. Furthermore, Roman law influenced customary law more and more as time went on, and in the southern portion of France, Roman law virtually replaced customary law. Accordingly, many of the following remarks must be qualified with adverbs such as *usually* or *generally*. That said, common practices and attitudes may be found in several or most of the codes.

Only a few of these customs deal exclusively with women, but many aspects of customary law do include provisions that concern both sexes. For the most part, female criminals were treated like male offenders, but punishment might take a different form: for example, a woman who slandered someone might be fined only half as much as a man. In the southwest (Guienne), punishment for convicted men and women adulterers was identical: they were paraded around the town, naked, and tied together with a rope. In business, women usually had to obtain their husband's or father's permission to conduct business, file lawsuits, etc. Women could not be witnesses in most lawsuits, save in exceptional circumstances, such as for proving virginity or live births.

Customary law codes devote a good deal of space to inheritance. The rights of women to inherit land were usually inferior to those of their brothers. The oldest son generally took a third of the deceased father's real property, no matter how many older sisters he had. The remainder might be shared among the other sons, or the other sons and daughters. A daughter who had married and been given some property at her wedding could not share in her father's or mother's estate, unless she brought back to the distribution what she had been given earlier. When a man left only daughters, the estate was usually distributed in equal shares to the surviving daughters (this method of distribution is discussed in Chrétien de Troyes's romance *Yvain*). The affairs of widows (and orphans) usually came under the jurisdiction of the ecclesiastical, rather than the secular courts, so that the customaries do not deal very much with such issues.

While women could inherit and own property, they were usually not permitted to manage their own property, whether real or personal, if they were unmarried living in their father's home, or married and living with a husband. The men generally were entitled to manage their wives' or daughters' personal property. Sometimes this property was protected, for example when a man was fined by confiscation of all his personal property, his wife's share might be spared. A woman's real property, such as land, fruit trees, vines, etc., that she brought to a marriage as a dowry or subsequently inherited, was treated separately from her husband's, so that for example if a couple died childless, the woman's land went back to *her* nearest blood relative, while the man's went back to *his* nearest blood relative. Likewise when her husband died, the widow had a life interest in a portion (a half or a third, depending on the district) of her husband's property, which then reverted to the heir when she died in her turn. In some respects, a widow was in a good position, for she was able to manage her own affairs; but when she had land that owed feudal service, she had to find someone to perform the military duties that she could not, and she had to be careful to manage her land wisely, or the heir could have her ousted in his favor.

In Old French customary law, then, while a few provisions concerning women were spelled out, their status and powers were subordinated to men's. Only a few laywomen, of the highest class, were able to play an independent role in society.

F. R. P. AKEHURST

References and Further Reading

Akehurst, F. R. P., trans. *The Coutumes de Beauvaisis of Philippe de Beaumanoir*. Philadelphia: University of Pennsylvania Press, 1992.

Archives départementales de Lot-et-Garonne. "Livre des statuts et coutumes de la ville d'Agen/MS 42."

http://www.cg47.fr/archives/coups-de-coeur/Tresors/tresors-archives.htm.

Jacob, Robert. "Beaumanoir v. Révigny: The Two Faces of Customary Law in Philip the Bold's France." In *Essays on the Poetic and Legal Writings of Philippe de Remy and His Son Philippe de Beaumanoir of Thirteenth-Century France*, edited by Sarah-Grace Heller and Michelle Reichert. Lewiston: Edwin Mellen Press, 2001, pp. 221–276.

Strayer, Joseph R. "Law, French: In North"; and Reyerson, Kathryn L., and John Bell Henneman. "Law, French: In South." in Strayer, Joseph R., ed. *Dictionary of the Middle Ages.* New York: Charles Scribner's Sons, 1983.

See also **Dowry and Other Marriage Gifts; Family (Later Middle Ages); Inheritance; Law, Canon; Law, Roman; Noble Women; Sexuality: Regulation of; Widows**

LAW, ENGLISH SECULAR COURTS OF

Medieval England knew various legal jurisdictions and courts. Church courts, which administered canon law, had jurisdiction over the validity of marriage and testaments of personal property; they coexisted with secular courts. The common law was not the only secular law, and the royal courts were not the only secular courts. There were also seigneurial courts, held by a lord for his vassals, and manorial courts, governed by manorial custom and held for free and unfree tenants of a manor. Boroughs and towns had variously named courts using local law based on custom and local statute.

Common Law

But the common law as administered in the royal courts effectively became the law of England. It evolved in the twelfth century, centered in the king's courts at Westminster, which came to be known as King's Bench and Common Pleas. More locally there were the shire (county) courts, presided over by the sheriff, and the still more local hundred courts (a hundred was an area within a shire). Additionally, the judges based at Westminster traveled through the shires on circuit between law terms, hearing both civil and criminal pleas at sessions, which came to be called the assizes. All these were royal courts, and all used common law.

A woman's ability to sue or be sued in a noncriminal matter in any of the common law courts depended on her status: free or unfree, single or married. An unfree (villein) woman, like an unfree man, was, with few exceptions, limited to the manorial court for all except criminal law.

Single Women

A free unmarried woman was able to hold both land and personal property and could bring an action in a common law court for injury to either, or for challenges to her possession or ownership. If she committed a trespass (a noncriminal wrong) she was liable, and, if she was injured in her person, she could sue for damages, again in a common law court. She could also sue or be sued in debt. In none of these cases was it necessary for a male to be named as coplaintiff or codefendant. A woman plaintiff or defendant could be present in court but was (like a man) commonly represented by an attorney—a person who "stood in her place" so that she was not in default and who handled procedural matters. Neither men nor women argued their own cases; in the thirteenth century pleaders, or litigators, were already employed. A single woman accused in a criminal matter was subject to the same procedure as a male defendant, with few exceptions.

Married Women

A married woman stood in an entirely different position. At common law, under the fiction of coverture she was feme covert, meaning that her legal existence was merged into her husband's. She did not hold personal property; any she had owned (including inheritance from a first husband) became her husband's upon their marriage. Real property (land and buildings) she had held fell under her husband's control, although he could not sell it or give it away without her consent, and it was returned to her at his death. Therefore, a suit concerning personal property that had been a woman's before her marriage was brought by or against the husband; it was not necessary to make the wife a party. A suit concerning her real property was brought by or against both husband and wife. A wife was required to come into court to be examined apart from her spouse concerning her consent to proposed alienation (sale, gift, or exchange) of her land, in order for the alienation to be effective—a procedure probably not entirely useful given that the woman had to live with her husband after her court appearance. However, in the thirteenth century the writ *cui in vita* was devised, providing an action by which a widow could seek to recover land, alleging that her late spouse had alienated it without her consent.

A married woman was not responsible for her debts; her husband was liable for not only those she incurred while married but for those incurred before the marriage. Therefore, a creditor's suit necessarily named him as defendant. She was responsible for her trespasses, but because she would have had no way of paying damages, a suit had to name her husband as a defendant with her. Both husband and wife had to sue for injury done to a wife and any damages belonged to the husband. At criminal law, despite the fiction of coverture, a married woman was not liable for her husband's acts. She was sometimes not liable for her own criminal act committed in her husband's company, because there was a presumption that it was done at his command.

Widows

A widow was considered an unmarried woman for most purposes and had in addition several actions unique to her, the *cui in vita* and the action of dower. At common law, by the decades following Magna Carta, a widow had the right to a life interest in one-third of the real property that a husband had held in fee during the marriage. There were specific writs for claiming dower and, in the thirteenth and earlier fourteenth centuries, dower suits were very common and quite successful. Actions later became less common because dower's effectiveness was compromised; there were various reasons, but an important one was that dower rights did not pertain to land held in trust for a husband (common law did not recognize trusts and regarded the trustee as beneficial owner) and therefore, a man was able to prevent dower rights from attaching to his land by deeding it to trustees before marriage.

Chancery Court

The most significant royal non–common-law court was Chancery, which arose as a court late in the Middle Ages. It was presided over by the chancellor, who was, until the sixteenth century, a cleric. It was said to be a court of conscience, to promote equity, and in its "English side" jurisdiction, so called because proceedings were in English rather than Latin, it received petitions in cases where common-law rules of substance or procedure would provide no remedy or would work an injustice. While it was of no help to widows in securing dower (because dower was a common-law action), by the fifteenth century the court of Chancery did enforce "uses," that is, the early form of trusts. In addition, its judges were sometimes willing to make exceptions to the common law fiction of coverture. This combination of factors eventually provided a means for protecting some of the property of married women. A father or other donor could put land or other assets in trust for the benefit of a woman married or to be married and Chancery would enforce the arrangement, thus restraining a husband's control. However, courts were suspicious of trusts of money to the wife's "separate use"—effectively giving her an income of her own—and were reluctant to enforce them as such until well after the medieval period ended.

Also in the fifteenth and sixteenth centuries, the court of Chancery seems to have been used by widows seeking goods or money left them by the provisions of a will, or relief from the claims of a late husband's heirs or executors. Women claimed, for example, that they had been deceived or coerced into signing away rights as executrix or forgoing suit for rights under a will, or that heirs had fraudulently seized assets.

In most areas of common law, however, the position of women did not change greatly between 1200 and the sixteenth century, and where it did—as, for example, with dower rights—it was generally not to their benefit.

JANET S. LOENGARD

References and Further Reading

Baker, J. H. *An Introduction to English Legal History*. 4th ed. London: Butterworths, 2002.
Hanawalt, Barbara A. "The Female Felon in Fourteenth Century England." In *Women in Medieval Society*, edited by Susan Mosher Stuard. Philadelphia: University of Pennsylvania Press, 1976, pp. 125–140.
Hawkes, Emma. "'[S]he will protect and defend her rights boldly by law and reason . . .': Women's Knowledge of Common Law and Equity Courts in Late-Medieval England." In *Medieval Women and the Law*, edited by Noël James Menuge. Woodbridge, Suffolk: Boydell Press, 2000, pp. 145–161.
Kermode, Jenny, and Garthine Walker, eds. *Women, Crime, and the Courts in Early Modern England*. Chapel Hill and London: University of North Carolina Press, 1994.
Loengard, Janet Senderowitz. "Legal History and the Medieval Englishwoman: Some New Directions." In *Medieval Women and the Sources of Medieval History*, edited by Joel T. Rosenthal. Athens, Ga.: University of Georgia Press, 1990, pp. 210–236.
Palmer, Robert C. *The Whilton Dispute 1264–1380: A Social Legal Study of Dispute Settlement in Medieval England*. Princeton: Princeton University Press, 1984.
Pollock, Frederick, and Frederic William Maitland. *The History of English Law before the Time of Edward I*. 2nd ed. with introduction by S. F. C. Milsom. 2 vols. Cambridge: Cambridge University Press, 1968.
Spring, Eileen. *Law, Land and Family: Aristocratic Inheritance in England 1300–1800*. Chapel Hill and London: University of North Carolina Press, 1993.

LAW, GERMAN

Germany followed its own oral laws that only gradually became influenced by Roman law, far later than in France. Our sole record of these legal customs and procedures is the vernacular *Sachsenspiegel* or *Saxon Mirror* written by Eike von Repgow (c. 1225–1235), an experienced lay judge (*Schöffe*). Containing both land law (pertaining to serfs, freemen, and nobles in rural areas) and feudal law (pertaining to the obligations between lords and vassals, especially military duty), the *Mirror* was intended to guide the next generation of lay judges in Saxony but had no authority. Nevertheless, it filled such a great need for consistency in rendering judgments that it was adopted as the authoritative reference in all German-speaking territories from the North Sea to the Italian Alps. Over three hundred extant manuscripts from the thirteenth to the sixteenth centuries record both the stability of the legal framework and the additions and changes in law over time. The following applies to the thirteenth and fourteenth centuries.

Several portions of the customary law refer to the specific situations and concerns of women, such as control and inheritance of property, pregnancy, and economic support during widowhood. The status to which a woman was born remained with her even if she married someone of higher or lower status. Women lacked full legal capacity; like priests, women were not members of the judiciary, the body of all adult freemen that provided consensus in order to validate a judgment without which there is no customary law. Consequently women could not speak for themselves, take a cleansing oath, or initiate a court suit. A guardian represented them in any legal action, but the *Mirror* specifically assigns them additional safeguards and rights. A woman had the right to bring a charge of rape, to own real property, and to claim her morning gift (received after the marriage was consummated) upon her own oath once she was widowed. No one could remove a widow from land legally designated for her lifelong use, and no one could evict a pregnant widow from any of her property. Upon divorce, the woman retained her morning gift. Her husband or other guardian controlled her property but was not allowed to transfer it to another without her permission. She also had the right to prosecute her guardian directly if he misused her assets or otherwise betrayed his obligations.

If she proved her case, the court would assume guardianship and grant her control of her real property. In feudal law a woman was eligible to receive and hold imperial property. This gave her knightly status, and payment of military dues freed her from active service.

Despite these safeguards and rights, women still remained vulnerable to rape and accusations of adultery. When a woman brought an accusation of rape, a law stated that the building in which it occurred must be razed and all living creatures present must be beheaded. If enforced, this law may well have deterred women from bringing charges. Punishments for crimes were the same for men and women, but pregnant women could not be sentenced to anything more severe than flogging. Women present at the birth of an heir could be witness in court when the child was born after the father's death. The inability to swear a cleansing oath, however, also meant that women were subject to the ordeal when accused of a crime. Several poets with a strong legal background repeatedly apply the fire ordeal to women accused of adultery (e.g., Gottfried von Strassburg, Ebernand von Erfurt). In terms of the criminal tariff or *wergeld*, the value of a woman was fifty percent of her husband's *wergeld*, and each unmarried woman was allotted half the compensation for men of her status.

A woman's dowry and personal belongings—including sheep, geese, textiles, furniture, and books—were valued and passed to the woman's closest female blood relative if she had no daughter. The concept here is that the extended family was as significant a legal bond as marriage. The division of certain goods as belonging to the male line and others to the female indicates a household division of labor: raw materials produced by the husband were made into usable goods such as food and clothing by the wife.

Rights before the law were established according to birth status (unfree, free, lower and upper nobility) and its corresponding obligations. To the extent that women and certain men did not fully contribute to the legal process, they also had a justifiably smaller share in its privileges according to the legal thinking of the time.

MARIA DOBOZY

References and Further Reading

Dobozy, Maria. "From Oral Custom to Written Law: 'The Sachsenspiegel.'" In *Festschrift für Evelyn Firchow*, edited by Anna Grotans. Göppingen: Göppinger Arbeiten zur Germanistik, 1998, pp. 31–40.

Ebernand von Erfurt. *Heinrich und Kunigunde*, edited by Reinhold Bechstein. Amsterdam: Editions Rodopi, 1968.

Gottfried von Strassburg. *Tristan.* translated by A. T. Hatto. New York: Penguin Books, 1960.

The Laws of the Salian Franks. translated by Katherine Fischer Drew. Philadelphia: University of Pennsylvania Press, 1991.

Huebner, Rudolf. *A History of Germanic Private Law.* translated by Francis S. Philbrick. Continental Legal History Series, 4. New York: Augustus M. Kelley Publishers, 1968.

Kisch, Guido. *Sachsenspiegel and Bible.* South Bend, Ind.: University of Notre Dame Press, 1941.

The Saxon Mirror: A Sachsenspiegel of the Fourteenth Century. translated by Maria Dobozy. Philadelphia: University of Pennsylvania Press, 1999.

Ziegler, Vickie L. *Trial by Fire and Battle in Medieval Literature.* Studies in German Literature, Linguistics, and Culture. Woodbridge, N.Y.: Camden House, 2004.

See also **Barbarian Law Codes; Book Ownership; Crime and Criminals; Division of Labor; Dowry and Other Marriage Gifts; Germanic Lands; Gottfried von Strassburg; Inheritance; Landholding and Property Rights; Law, Customary: French; Law, Jewish; Law, Roman; Legal Agency; Peasants; Pregnancy and Childbirth: Christian Women; Rape and Raptus; Wergild; Widows**

LAW, ISLAMIC: IBERIA

Although in general the new legislation of the Koran notably improved the situation of women in pre-Islamic Arabia, and made all Muslims almost equal in religious matters, such standards did not extend to the field of civil law. The Maliki School, the legal school in the Iberian Peninsula during the Muslim period (711–1492), adhered to this general principle established in the sacred text: women could not be considered as equal to men. Consequently there were several procedural norms that clearly show women's inferiority regarding blood-money, evidence, and inheritance (in relation to which a woman counted as half a man). This inferiority was also marked in the limited legal capacity given to women. In some moments of their lives, they were considered as handicapped and, therefore, they needed the intervention of a legal guardian, the nearest relative on the father's side, to act legally. The first task of the guardian was to arrange a marriage for his charge and, without his intervention, the marriage was not considered valid. The father could marry off his virgin daughter without her consent, although jurists did not recommend doing so. Women only acquired their full legal capacity when their marriage was consummated. However, in legal practice jurists admitted that fathers could extend their guardianship up to six years after the marriage of daughters.

Marriage, extensively legislated in Islamic law, was not only a possibility of acquiring full legal capacity, but also the moment in which women gained access to property. On the one hand, they received a dower from the groom, a legally obligatory payment for the validity of Islamic marriages. On the other hand, local customs made equally important the payment of a trousseau or a dowry that parents had to give to the bride, thus improving her economic situation with regard to her husband. These economic payments and obligations can be explained as the consequence of two legal characteristics that make the marriage link somewhat unstable when compared with medieval Europe. These two characteristics are polygamy and unilateral repudiation by the husband.

According to Islamic law, a man could marry four women simultaneously. This was also allowed in al-Andalus, where evidence shows that polygamy was a common phenomenon. However, Islamic legislation obliged husbands to treat all their wives equally; and this was not considered possible for most families. Also, brides in al-Andalus, with the assistance of notaries, usually included in the marriage contracts a condition against the husband stipulating that she would divorce him if he took a second wife. Polygamy consequently was only affordable among the wealthy and provided that their wives agree with it.

Islamic law also gave the husband the possibility of repudiating his wife without legal reasons. This unilateral repudiation, undoubtedly frequent in Andalusian society, also obligated the husbands to respond to the needs of the repudiated women, providing them with maintenance and economic support while breastfeeding and the custody of offspring. Women had the right to ask for divorce only in certain cases, such as mistreatment, abandonment, or when the husband did not fulfill the conditions written in the marriage contract.

In Islamic law there is no community of goods between spouses, so that at least in theory, women could possess and administer their properties independently from their husbands. The only limit imposed by the law was related to charitable gifts and nonprofitable transactions when they exceeded a third of her properties. For doing this kind of transaction women needed their husbands' permission. Nevertheless, in general, women acquired more freedom in terms of property rights after marriage, since they no longer were subject to their fathers' control. While the principles of Islamic law assert the inferiority of women, they also fully acknowledge that Muslim women are entitled to own and exercise control over property without interference from males. The implementation of women's property rights was made effective by mechanisms embedded in the Islamic legal system and also by the jurists in daily administration of justice. However, the sources also give us examples of attempts by family members to limit women's control of their own properties; and, therefore, women frequently had to pursue their rights and interests in court.

Scholars studying Islamic law as it applied to women understand that, together with the legal norms derived from the sacred texts, there was also a set of social and cultural norms and values, influenced by the patriarchal model, which shaped the general situation of women in Iberia during the Muslim period.

AMALIA ZOMEÑO

References and Further Reading

Deguilhem, Randi, and Manuela Marín, eds. *Writing the Feminine: Women in Arab Sources.* London and New York: I. B. Tauris, 2002.

López Ortiz, José. *Derecho musulmán.* Barcelona: Editorial Labor, 1932.

Marín, Manuela. *Mujeres en al-Andalus.* Madrid: Consejo Superior de Investigaciones Científicas, 2000.

Schacht, Joseph. *An Introduction to Islamic Law.* Oxford: Clarendon Press, 1964.

Shatzmiller, Maya. "Women and Property Rights in al-Andalus and the Maghrib: Social Patterns and Legal Discourse." *Islamic Law and Society* 2 (1995): 219–257.

Zomeño, Amalia. *Dote y matrimonio en al-Andalus y el norte de África. Estudio de la jurisprudencia islámica medieval.* Madrid: Consejo Superior de Investigaciones Científicas, 2000.

See also **Divorce and Separation; Dowry and Other Marriage Gifts; Iberia; Law; Legal Agency; Marriage, Islamic: Iberia; Muslim Women: Iberia**

LAW, JEWISH

In medieval times significant populations of Jews lived in Muslim Iraq, Egypt, North Africa, the Middle East, and Spain; smaller enclaves lived in Christian Europe. Jewish communities everywhere exercised autonomy over their internal affairs. Jewish self-government followed the dictates of the Babylonian Talmud, which provided uniform patterns for Jewish family law in the division entitled Women (*Nashim*). The seven tractates of *Nashim* deal with issues connected with age of marriage, betrothal, marriage contracts and their financial details, marital obligations, a husband's right to benefit from his wife's property, the mechanics of marriage, levirate marriage, divorce, the rights of widows, and treatment of rebellious wives and women accused of adultery, among many other legal minutiae of human relationships. Additionally, legal issues connected with when women are and are not in states of ritual purity that permit physical contact with their husbands are discussed in tractate *Niddah* in the division

Tohoroth (Purities). Local environments also influenced legal and social norms, as Jews tended to assume the language, dress, and some mores of non-Jews, including some attitudes towards marriage and sexuality and appropriate gender roles.

Rabbinic Texts

The foundation texts of Jewish law were composed by authoritative scholars known as Rabbis (teachers) between the first and sixth centuries, based on exegetical expansions of biblical legislation and contemporary practices. Some of these legal traditions were composed in the land of Israel and incorporate Greco-Roman and Christian cultural influences. Others were shaped in Sasanian Iran and Iraq. This complex, multistranded body of Oral *Torah* (revelation, law) received sanctity in Judaism through the rabbinic insistence that it was part of the biblical revelation at Mt. Sinai and constituted the essential accompaniment to the Written *Torah*, the Hebrew Scriptures (Old Testament). The Rabbis were men and the ideal human society they imagined was androcentric. Almost no female voices are heard in rabbinic literature and women played no active part in the development of Jewish law. The earliest written document of rabbinic Judaism is the *Mishnah*, a Hebrew compilation of legal rulings organized into six subject matter divisions and sixty-three distinct tractates, edited in the land of Israel in the early third century CE. The *Tosefta*, a supplemental collection of legal rulings, follows the order of the *Mishnah*. In the centuries following the completion of these two works, rabbinic authorities in the land of Israel and in Sasanian Iraq, known to Jews as Babylon, produced extensive commentaries on the *Mishnah* known as *Gemara*, primarily written in Aramaic. The *Gemara* produced in the rabbinic academies of Babylon was far more voluminous than that produced in the land of Israel. Sometime in the sixth century CE, the *Mishnah* and this more extensive *Gemara* were combined and redacted to form the *Babylonian Talmud*, constituting the definitive compilation of Jewish law and tradition for the next millennium. The less comprehensive *Talmud of the Land of Israel*, completed at the end of the fourth century, also became part of rabbinic literature. Parallel to the *Mishnah*, *Tosefta*, and *Talmud*s are *Midrash* collections, exegetical compilations organized either as consecutive glosses on a biblical book or homilies on cycles of scriptural readings. The content of rabbinic literature falls into two categories: *Halakhah* (authoritative legal directives) and *Aggadah* (nonlegal, narrative traditions); both are found in the *Talmuds*. Although the halakhic mandates of the *Babylonian Talmud* reveal little about actual Jewish life in rabbinic times, they became normative for virtually all medieval Jewish communities.

Responsa and *Halakah* Reflecting Cultural Changes

Between the mid-sixth and eleventh centuries, legal authority rested with the *Geonim* ([singular *Gaon*] Excellency), rabbinic leaders who headed the talmudic academies of Sura and Pumbedita, located in the area of Baghdad. Significant influence from Islamic law and cultural norms characterizes the *Halakhah* of this era, a time of rapid transition from an agrarian way of life to an urban commerce-oriented society. The *Geonim* adjusted *Halakhah* to changing societal realities through *Takkanot* ([sing. *Takkanah*] unilateral legal enactments) responding to specific circumstances, and *Minhag* (custom), institutionalization of prevalent practices that had no scriptural basis. The *Geonim* created *Responsa* literature to address distant constituencies; these *Sh'ailot* (questions) from all over the Jewish world and Geonic *T'shuvot* (responses) on virtually every aspect of life and scholarship circulated widely in small booklets and had the status of *Halakhah*. The dissemination and preservation of Geonic *Responsa* (five to ten thousand still survive), usually written in Aramaic but sometimes in Arabic, maintained the authority of the *Geonim*, established precedents for similar halakhic quandaries, and provide vivid glimpses of everyday Jewish life. One such seventh century example from Rav Sherira Gaon ruled that if a woman claimed in court that she could not bear to live with her husband, her husband could be coerced to grant her an immediate divorce, on the condition that she relinquish most of her financial privileges. One of the motives behind this ruling was to prevent Jewish women from bringing their marital disputes to Muslim courts. This question and answer mode of halakhic decision making remained popular throughout the Middle Ages and endures up to the present day.

By the eleventh century, the authority of the *Geonim* waned as local centers of Jewish learning were established elsewhere, both in the Muslim world (North Africa, Egypt, Spain) and in Italy, France, and Germany. This regionalization of Jewish governance led to increasing geographical discrepancies in legal practice and the emergence of distinctive Jewish communities, including the Sephardim (Jews of Iberian origin in Muslim lands) and Ashkenazim (Jews in European Christian realms). While *Responsa* literature remained significant, halakhic codes, a genre of legal digests originating in Geonic times, were an important contribution of Sephardic Jews in Muslim lands. These compilations of definitive *Halakhah*, organized in subject matter categories, combined rabbinic directives with legislative developments, *Responsa*, and customs post-dating the Babylonian Talmud. The most influential, comprehensive, and original medieval code is the *Mishneh Torah* of the Spanish-born Moses Maimonides (d. 1204), completed in Egypt c. 1178. The fourth section of this fourteen section work is entitled "The Book of Women" and deals with family law. At the end of the Middle Ages, the *Shulhan Arukh* (Set Table) of the Sephardic scholar, Joseph Caro (d. 1575 in Safed, Israel), became universally accepted as the authoritative code of Jewish law. One of its four sections, *Even ha-Ezer*, is devoted to the laws of marriage, divorce, and related topics. From the 1570s the *Shulhan Arukh* has been printed with a super-commentary by the Ashkenazic legal authority, Moses Isserles (d. 1572), called the *Mappah* (Tablecloth). Isserles' commentary reflected legal practice, including many details of family law, as it had developed in Germany and Poland and its presence made the *Shulhan Arukh* acceptable to the Ashkenazim, while the text of Caro was equally acceptable to the Sephardim.

Women's Status

Although medieval Ashkenazic Jewry also produced law codes, *Takkanot* and *Responsa* literature were more central in the evolving legal life of the community. The eleventh century *Takkanah* forbidding polygyny for Jews in Christian countries is attributed to Rabbi Gershom ben Judah of Mainz (c. 960–1028), who is also credited with the significant pronouncement that no woman could be divorced against her will. These rulings improving women's legal position, together with women's substantial dowries, are indications of Jewish women's high status and economic entrepreneurship in European communities. Important authors of *Responsa* include R. Jacob b. Meir in France, known as Rabbenu Tam (d. 1171), and R. Meir of Rothenburg (d. 1293). Also central were the biblical and talmudic commentaries of Rabbi Shlomo ben Isaac of Troyes (d. 1104), known as Rashi. His successors, the Tosafist scholars (twelfth and thirteenth century France), added *novellae* to Rashi's Talmud commentary, harmonizing apparent legal contradictions and inconsistencies. Their *Tosafot* (additions) appear in printed editions of the

Babylonian Talmud, alongside Rashi's commentary. Throughout medieval times and beyond, there are no female contributions to Jewish law, beyond testimony about practices of esteemed male relatives in domestic matters.

JUDITH R. BASKIN

References and Further Reading

Agus, Irving. *Urban Civilization in Pre-Crusade Europe.* 2 vols. New York: Yeshiva University Press, 1965.
———. *The Heroic Age of Franco-German Jewry.* New York: Yeshiva University Press, 1969.
———. *Rabbi Meir of Rothenburg*, 2nd edition. New York: KTAV Publishing House, 1970.
Baskin, Judith R. "Jewish Women in the Middle Ages." In *Jewish Women in Historical Perspective*, edited by Judith R. Baskin. 2nd edition. Detroit: Wayne State University Press, 1998, pp. 101–127.
Biale, Rachel. *Women and Jewish Law.* New York: Schocken Books, 1984.
Brody, Robert. *The Geonim of Babylonia and the Shaping of Medieval Jewish Culture.* New Haven and London: Yale University Press, 1998.
Goitein, S. D. *A Mediterranean Society: The Jewish Communities of the Arab World as Portrayed in the Documents of the Cairo Genizah.* 6 vols. Berkeley: University of California Press, 1967–1988.
Grossman, Avraham. *Pious and Rebellious: Jewish Women in Medieval Europe.* Waltham, Mass.: Brandeis University Press, 2004.
Hecht, N. S., B. S. Jackson, S. M. Passamaneck, et.al., eds. *An Introduction to the History and Sources of Jewish Law.* Oxford: Oxford University Press, 1996.

See also **Jewish Women; Marriage, Jewish; Mikveh; Pregnancy and Childbirth, Jewish**

LAW, ROMAN
See **Roman Law**

LAY PIETY

The phrase *lay piety* denotes the religious sensibilities of the vast majority of medieval Christian people: everyone who was not a member of a religious order of monks or nuns, or a cleric. The term *laity* is indeed so broad as to signify only in relation to its antonym, for it was the professionalization of religious orders from the eleventh century that brought the laity into being. By mandating clerical celibacy, advocating ordination of monks (once considered laymen), and, increasingly, hindering lay spiritual movements from incorporating as religious orders (especially after the Fourth Lateran Council of 1215), the church constructed a dichotomy between an elite who ministered by prayer, preaching, and the sacraments, and the recipients of their ministry, whose proper response

was of "piety": an attitude of devotion and unquestioning faith in the Trinity, the Fall, the Incarnation, the Judgment, and other orthodox beliefs. Such piety might be patronized as ignorant and carnal by an exclusively masculine clergy or it might be idealized as superior to their own, more abstract religiosity. Either attitude reinforced an association between the laity and the feminine and a view of the laity as dependents, perpetual children nourished by the spiritual milk of simple faith, not the meat of formal theology.

Clerical feminization and infantilization of the laity is easy to criticize, but it did take into account something laypeople had in common: busy lives, in which the place of piety was limited to brief weekly or seasonal rituals and to times of transition: birth, marriage, illness, war, death. Especially at the end of the period, from when most records derive, there is considerable evidence that lay women and men were satisfied with a limited view of their spiritual potential, embracing a model in which church attendance, fulfillment of sacramental obligations, prayers to Christ, the Virgin, and the saints, and avoidance of damnable sins was all that was required for respectability in this world and salvation in the next. Membership of this body of *mediocriter boni* ("moderately good," rather than "perfect") Christians did not, after all, entail ecclesiastical neglect. On the contrary, from the invention of "crusade" as an innovative theological justification for knightly violence in the eleventh century (later taken up by Joan of Arc) to the formalizing of confession and the doctrine of purgatory in the thirteenth, official theology constantly modified itself in the interests of lay piety. Even late practices such as the sale of indulgences or the establishment of chantry chapels, where paid priests prayed for the wealthy dead, built on these modifications. Perhaps most successful of all was the re-imagining of the church as the body of Christ after establishment of the feast of Corpus Christi around 1300. A celebration at once of local lay community—towns throughout Europe used the feast for mystery plays and other civic celebrations—and of lay membership of the "universal" community of the church by participation in the Mass, Corpus Christi sacralized lay "carnality" by associating it with the flesh in which Christ himself was incarnate.

Considered as social praxis, lay piety was firmly gendered: men and women sat on different sides of the parish church, facing images of saints of their own sex and bearing the brunt of different didactic topoi: sermons typecast lay men as fraudulent, violent, and unfaithful, women as vain, greedy, and talkative. Lay piety was also patriarchal, although not straightforwardly so. It is true that men had the responsibility to teach and discipline wives, while wives might counsel husbands but could only teach and discipline children. But the submission to earthly, as well as divine, authority implied by the term *piety* (originally a Roman civic virtue) was enjoined on all. Although the protagonist of the tale of patient Griselda—a type of lay piety—is a woman, the tale's popularity may have been due less to male pleasure at her virtue or specifically female identification with her suffering than the fact that she represents men as well as women, all equally obligated to obey their superiors as an essential component of their obedience to God.

Not all laypeople accepted their subordinate status. The twelfth-century reform movement left an interstitial category of "semi-religious" anchoresses, Beguines, hospitallers, and others who followed informal rules but were treated as laypeople. Excluded from full membership of a religious order and from the resources associated with membership, these disproportionately female groups influenced the personal piety of the laity (Books of Hours were modeled on semi-religious devotional practice) and kept alive ideals of spiritual ambition and autonomy compatible with life in the world. Lay women such as Angela of Foligno, Margery Kempe, and Marie of Oignies, who defied standard notions of obedience and subjected themselves only to a confessor and to God, found more pertinent models among semi-religious than among nuns. Lay reform movements, from the Waldensians of France and Germany to the Lollards of England, the Hussites of Bohemia, and the Modern Devotion of the Low Countries, were typically organized by men (the Italian Gugliemites are an exception). But these movements, too, found themselves adapting vernacular materials first written for semi-religious women and asserting a similar independence from formal ecclesiastical structures and a similar belief in the primacy of the inner self over the obligations of outward obedience.

Perhaps this is another reason why lay piety was often perceived as female. Jean Gerson's fifteenth-century promotion of a masculinity movement around the cult of St. Joseph acknowledges this fact even as it attempts to respond to the increasing influence of male lay elites in church affairs. But in so far as piety was private, it remained largely tied to domestic spaces in which women wielded power. Until the North European Reformation (and beyond it in the Catholic south), the central symbol of lay piety was Joseph's *wife*, the Virgin Mary, caught at her prayers by the angel Gabriel: at once an obedient bourgeois woman and a saint daring enough to become the mother of God, her body and soul the highest thing in creation.

NICHOLAS WATSON

References and Further Reading

Bynum, Caroline Walker. *Holy Feast and Holy Fast: The Religious Significance of Food to Medieval Women.* Studies in Cultural Poetics. Berkeley, Calif.: University of California Press, 1987.

Duffy, Eamon. *The Stripping of the Altars: Traditional Religion in England, 1400–1580.* New Haven, Conn.: Yale University Press, 1992.

Grundmann, Herbert. *Religious Movements in the Middle Ages: The Historical Links between Heresy, the Mendicant Orders, and the Women's Religious Movement in the Twelfth and Thirteenth Century.* translated by Steven Rowan. South Bend, Ind.: University of Notre Dame Press, 1996 [orig. pub. in German, 1961].

Mulder-Bakker, Anneke B. *Lives of the Anchoresses: The Rise of the Urban Recluse in Medieval Europe.* translated by Myra Keerspink Scholz. Philadelphia: University of Pennsylvania Press, 2005.

Rubin, Miri. *Corpus Christi: The Eucharist in Late Medieval Culture.* Cambridge: Cambridge University Press, 1991.

Swanson, R. N. *Religion and Devotion in Europe, c. 1215–c. 1515.* Cambridge Medieval Textbooks. Cambridge: Cambridge University Press, 1995.

Vauchez, André. *The Laity in the Middle Ages: Religious Beliefs and Devotional Practices.* translated by Margery J. Schneider. South Bend, Ind.: University of Notre Dame Press, 1993.

See also **Anchoresses; Angela of Foligno; Beguines; Books of Hours; Confraternities; Crusades and Crusading Literature; Devotional Practices; Devotional Literature; Exemplum; Family (Later Middle Ages); Gerson, Jean; Griselda; Joan of Arc; Kempe, Margery; Laywomen, Religious; Lollards; Marie of Oignies; Mary, Virgin; Modern Devotion; Mothers as Teachers; Parishes; Rosary; Sermons and Preaching; Spiritual Care; Spirituality, Christian; Tertiaries; Waldensians**

LAYWOMEN, RELIGIOUS

Religious laywomen made significant contributions to the medieval church through a piety that was not only exercised in service to their communities, but was also expressed in a distinctly mystical focus on sacraments of penance and the Eucharist. These women, who from the late twelfth century were found in urban centers throughout Europe, actively participated in a wider religious revival that also involved itinerant preachers, reforming bishops and, from the beginning of the thirteenth century, the mendicant friars. Some of these women formed distinct associations with ties to religious orders or diocesan institutions, but for many the choice was spontaneous and private. While it is an acceptable academic practice to draw distinction between the Beguines of central and northern Europe, vowesses of England, penitents of Italy, and *beatae* of Spain, such regional differences were not clearly cut for contemporaries: the previous terms, as well as such generic expressions as religious women (*mulieres religiosae*) and holy women (*mulieres sanctae*), were interchangeably used of religious laywomen throughout Europe. The term *tertiary*, which in the modern era has come to denote the lay members of Franciscan, Dominican, and other Mendicant orders, came into use only late in the Middle Ages.

An independent life of piety offered a viable alternative to women who sought the social stability associated with religious life and opportunities for spiritual guidance, but who did not want to enter a monastery or who did not have the financial means to do so. While the Beguine life attracted some men, spoken of as beghards, and the Franciscan order absorbed laymen known for their active piety, the semi-institutional life of devotion never became a significant option among men who had more religious and secular choices from which to choose than women did. Among the *mulieres sanctae* were servants and practitioners of lesser trades, who traditionally had been pulled into religious life as monastic lay workers (*conversae*), but most of these women came from the lesser urban nobility and from merchant or artisan families. Religious life in the world was particularly appealing to widows, but it also attracted unmarried women and even some wives, such as Margery Kempe (d. c. 1440), whose vibrant autobiography enumerated the struggles of a wife turned into a pilgrim.

Many of these women lived with their relatives, some withdrew into urban anchorages (many of which were loosely associated with local churches), and others teamed up to form domestic partnerships or found uncloistered communities. Following Pope Boniface VIII's publication of the constitution *Pericoloso* in 1298, the church made several efforts to enclose the houses of religious laity, but open communal life persisted and was particularly important among the Beguines. The success of women's lay associations depended on their ability to attract privileges from the leaders of the church, especially after the Councils of Lyon (1274) and Vienne (1311–1312) attacked the independent religious life and accused many groups of the alleged heresy of the Free Spirit.

The Italian penitent women, or *pinzochere*, formed an exceptional group among the religious laity for their relatively peaceful blending into the landscape of the surrounding society. Unlike their northern counterparts, the Beguines, these women did not compete with men through their cloth production, teaching, or other semi-professional pursuits, nor did they form semi-autonomous religious centers, known as beguinages. They typically operated within family-based economies and lived at their homes or in loosely organized open communities. They also effectively contributed to the civic piety of the Italian communes, for the cults of famed penitent mystics were appropriated to advance the pursuits of Ghibellines, Guelfs, and other competing political groups. These civic and social factors created favorable circumstances for the penitents' cooperation with the mendicant friars, eventually leading to papal confirmation of the Franciscan penitent or tertiary rule in 1289 and that of the Dominican laity in 1405. Nevertheless, even in Italy the position of the religious laity was far from settled, and they were ridiculed by the poet Francesco da Barberino and other critics, who saw penitent attire merely as a convenient cover for otherwise ordinary, perhaps even licentious, lives. The ambiguity of this way of life was reflected in the fact that of the many famed Italian penitent mystics only Dominican tertiary Catherine of Siena (d. 1380) was canonized during the Middle Ages (1461).

Despite the ambiguous institutional status of the religious laywomen, they nonetheless refashioned Western spirituality through their experiential mysticism. Catherine of Siena, Beguine Mechthild of Magdeburg (d. c. 1282), anchoress Julian of Norwich (d. after 1413), and Franciscan Angela of Foligno (d. 1309), each produced vernacular theology that was anchored in Christ's humanity, but placed within the matrix of the salvation history. The intense penitential piety of religious laywomen was detailed in a uniquely rich body of hagiographic accounts. Despite their notably ecstatic slant, these women also excelled in practical, charitable, and even organizational endeavors. Their beneficiaries were typically other local women, but the Franciscan penitents Elisabeth of Hungary (d. 1231) and Margaret of Cortona (d. 1297), among others, founded charitable institutions of considerable stature. Catherine of Siena emerged from the margins of the Dominican order to become the beacon of the reform not only among the laity and the nuns, but among the friars as well. Birgitta of Sweden (d. 1373), a visionary and a widowed mother of eight, created her Order of the Holy Savior without ever taking a religious habit herself. Thus, the independent lay life, which in itself was amorphous, not only generated religious institutions, but also fueled the very orthodoxy that it was accused of eroding.

MAIJU LEHMIJOKI-GARDNER

References and Further Reading

Angela of Foligno. *Complete Works.* Translated with an introduction by Paul Lachance. New York: Paulist Press, 1993.

Bolton, Brenda. "Mulieres Sanctae." In *Sanctity and Secularity: The Church and the World*, edited by Derek Baker. Oxford: Basil Blackwell, 1973, pp. 77–95.

The Book of Margery Kempe. translated by B. A. Windeatt. London: Penguin Books, 1985.

Catherine of Siena. *The Dialogue.* Translation and introduction by Suzanne Noffke. New York: Paulist Press, 1980.

Dominican Penitent Women. Edited, translated, and introduced by Maiju Lehmijoki-Gardner with contributions by Daniel E. Bornstein and E. Ann Matter. New York: Paulist Press, 2005.

Julian of Norwich. *Showings.* Translated from the critical text, with an introduction by Edmund Colledge and James Walsh. New York: Paulist Press, 1978.

Lehmijoki-Gardner, Maiju. "Writing Religious Rules as an Interactive Process: Dominican Penitent Women and the Making of Their *Regula.*" *Speculum 79* (2004): 660–687.

Makowski, Elizabeth. *A Pernicious Sort of Woman: Quasi-Religious Women and Canon Lawyers in the Later Middle Ages.* Washington, D.C.: The Catholic University of America Press, 2005.

McDonnell, Ernst. *Beguines and Beghards in Medieval Culture, with Special Emphasis on the Belgian Scene.* New Brunswick, N.J.: Rutgers University Press, 1954.

Mechthild of Magdeburg. *The Flowing Light of the Godhead.* translated and introduced by Frank Tobin. New York: Paulist Press, 1998.

Mulder-Bakker, Anneke B. *Lives of the Anchoresses: The Rise of the Urban Recluse in Medieval Europe.* translated by Myra Meerspink Scholz. Philadelphia: University of Pennsylvania Press, 2005.

Simons, Walter. *Cities of Ladies: Beguine Communities in the Medieval Low Countries, 1200–1565.* Philadelphia: University of Pennsylvania Press, 2001.

Thompson, Augustine. *Cities of God: The Religion of the Italian Communes 1125–1325.* University Park, Pa.: The Pennsylvania State University, 2005.

Vauchez, Andre. "Lay People's Sanctity in Western Europe: Evolution of a Pattern (Twelfth and Thirteenth Centuries)." In *Images of Sainthood in Medieval Europe,* edited by Renate Blumenfeld-Kosinski and Timea Szell. Ithaca: Cornell University Press, 1991, pp. 21–32.

———. *The Laity in the Middle Ages: Religious Beliefs and Devotional Practices.* edited and introduced by Daniel Bornstein. translated by Margery Schneider. South Bend, Ind.: University of Notre Dame Press, 1993.

Women and Religion in Medieval and Renaissance Italy. edited by Daniel Bornstein and Roberto Rusconi. translated by Margery J. Schneider. Chicago: The University of Chicago Press, 1996.

See also Angela of Foligno; Beguines; Birgitta of Sweden; Catherine of Siena; Church; Conversae and Conversi; Elisabeth of Hungary; Hagiography; Julian of Norwich; Kempe, Margery; Lay Piety; Margaret of Cortona; Mechthild of Magdeburg; Monastic Enclosure; Spirituality, Christian; Tertiaries; Vowesses

LEGAL AGENCY

In the Western tradition, social and legal agency has been cast in terms of the person as author or owner of his or her actions. To take away or control those actions is to dominate or diminish agency. Widespread ideological depictions of women as intellectually weak or morally dangerous, along with evidence of women's lives marked by seclusion from public and commercial arenas, therefore, contributed to a bleak view of women's agency in the Middle Ages and elsewhere. Recent studies, however, have exposed a range of nuances, as they have revealed ways in which women manipulated or subverted rules and situations to mitigate subordination to men, the patriarchal household, and the patrilineage. Agency is not the same as autonomy, nor were women's interests always or even frequently different from those of men, who were their husbands, fathers, brothers, and sons. Women had rights and prerogatives in law, and in the life of virtually every woman who reached adulthood and had some property, certain occasions could bring these legal rights into play.

Classical Roman law restricted women with male guardianship (*tutela mulierum*) in order to protect men and agnatic (from the male side) transmission of property, not to protect women, who were seen not as inept and defenseless but rather as cunning, greedy, and self-interested. Women were able to obligate themselves before the law, but they could not stand surety for others. In later imperial Roman law guardianship over women came to be seen as a form of protection for them against an inherent weakness (*imbecillitas*) of their sex. By the time of Justinian, paradoxically, most legal disabilities on women had been removed, with the exception of the prohibition of standing surety and their exclusion from public and legal offices, including acting as witnesses. At the same time, Germanic peoples entering the empire brought with them forms of the *mundium*, an alienable power of control over women and minors, usually exercised by fathers and husbands. In time this form of protective control became equated with guardianship of minors in Roman law, especially as Roman law texts became prominent from the twelfth century onward.

There is a vital distinction between ownership of property and capacity to use or dispose of it. European legal systems conceded ownership to women, if only because they were left as heirs in the absence of men at times; but they were far more reluctant to grant them legal capacities over property. Any such capacities were situationally defined, varying by a woman's age and marital status. A widow with children necessarily needed sufficient legal capacity to manage property for the benefit of her household. Here is where, for example, women otherwise often kept from guild membership were accorded rights to carry on their deceased husbands' crafts, at least temporarily.

In northern Europe, where Germanic law set the rules with little influence of Roman law (except in the canon law, which defined mothers' capacities as guardians of their children), women's legal capacities were shaped to the conjugal domestic unit. In England, the common law produced the doctrine of coverture, by which marriage took the two persons of man and wife and turned them into one person, and that was the husband. Wives and their property disappeared in law as long as the marriage lasted. The legal effacement of wives, however, did not change the fact that in reality their husbands relied on them to manage households and contribute labor, as well as children, to the domestic enterprise. Women held valuable household roles throughout Europe, but it was largely in northern Europe that they held rights to manage household assets without reference to kin or under any form of guardianship after their husbands' deaths.

Where Roman law, with few disabilities on women's legal capacities, was fundamental, as in Italy, it was necessary for cities and principalities to enact laws regulating women's legal acts. Some placed them under the control of the husband; others demanded consent of kin. Florence peculiarly adapted the Lombard *mundualdus* (holder of the *mundium*) into a universal male guardianship of all women, but at the same time there were no liabilities or restrictions falling on the male guardian, so women could act, at least in the absence of fathers or husbands, or with their *mundualdus*'s connivance.

If rules of legal agency restricted women, they also thereby restricted the men who were related to and interacted with them. Equally true was the fact that jurists and judges took seriously the protective function of the law with respect to women. Their actions might be voided and their property retrieved, even at the expense of men who otherwise asserted rights in regard to that property.

THOMAS KUEHN

References and Further Reading

Brown, Judith C., and Robert C. Davis, eds. *Gender and Society in Renaissance Italy*. London and New York: Longman, 1998.
Casagrande, Carla. "The Protected Woman." In *A History of Women in the West*, edited by Georges Duby and Michelle Perrot. Vol. 2: *Silences of the Middle Ages*, edited by Christiane Klapisch-Zuber. Cambridge, Mass.: Harvard University Press, 1992, pp. 70–104.
Chabot, Isabelle. "Lineage Strategies and the Control of Widows in Renaissance Florence." In *Widowhood in Medieval and Early Modern Europe*, edited by Sandra Cavallo and Lyndan Warner. London and New York: Longman, 1999, pp.127–144.
Cohn, Samuel K., Jr. *Women in the Streets: Essays on Sex and Power in Renaissance Italy*. Baltimore: Johns Hopkins University Press, 1996.
Kirshner, Julius. "Wives' Claims against Insolvent Husbands in Late Medieval Italy." In *Women of the Medieval World*, edited by Julius Kirshner and Suzanne F. Wempel. Oxford: Blackwell, 1985, pp. 256–303.
Kuehn, Thomas. *Law, Family, and Women: Toward a Legal Anthropology of Renaissance Italy*. Chicago: University of Chicago Press, 1991.
———. "Understanding Gender Inequality in Renaissance Florence: Personhood and Gifts of Maternal Inheritance by Women." *Journal of Women's History* 8 (1996): 58–80.
Schutte, Anne Jacobson, Thomas Kuehn, and Silvana Seidel Menchi, eds. *Time, Space, and Women's Lives in Early Modern Europe*. Kirksville, Mo.: Truman State University Press, 2001.

See also **Feme Coverte; Feme Sole; Gender Ideologies; Household Management; Law, Canon; Law, Customary: French; Law, English Secular Courts of; Law, German; Law, Roman; Patriarchy and Patrilineage; Widows; Widows as Guardians**

LEOBA

What we know of Leoba (Lioba, Leofgyth) (d. 779) is contained in the 836 *Life* written by Rudolf of Fulda and in correspondence with Saint Boniface, her kinsman and friend. She was born to a noble English couple, Aebba and Dynno, and dedicated to the church after her mother had a prophetic dream. She was named Thrutgeba but called Leoba, meaning beloved.

At the double monastery at Wimbourne, Leoba studied ecclesiastical writings and became widely known for her learning and holiness. She had a dream one night of a long purple thread that she pulled from her mouth and wound into a ball. This was interpreted to mean that Leoba would instruct many people in distant lands. In fulfillment of the dream, Rudolf writes, her kinsman Boniface summoned her, along with Thecla and Walburga, to join his missionary efforts in Germany. He made Leoba abbess of the Benedictine monastery Tauberbischofsheim, and Rudolf indicates that she had authority over all nunneries in Germany.

Leoba instructed many future abbesses at Tauberbischofsheim. She drew others to the church by word of her miracles of healing and protection. She also enjoyed privileges unavailable to other religious women—traveling widely and even counseling bishops in spiritual matters. Among the laity she was respected by Carolingian kings and had a close friendship with Charlemagne's queen, Hildegard.

Boniface held her in high regard and asked that they be buried in the same tomb. Although this wish was not carried out, Rudolf concludes the *Life* with a final miracle attributed to both of them—thus joining them in death spiritually, if not physically, to continue their missionary work.

HEATHER E. WARD

References and Further Reading

Boniface, Saint. *The Letters of Saint Boniface*. Translated by Ephraim Emerton. New York: Columbia University Press, 1940.

Hen, Yitzhak. "*Milites Christi Utriusque Sexus:* Gender and the Politics of Conversion in the Circle of Boniface." *Revue Bénédictine* 109.1–2 (1999): 17–31.

Hollis, Stephanie. "Rudolph of Fulda's *Life of Leoba*: an Elegy for the Double Monastery." In *Anglo-Saxon Women and the Church: Sharing a Common Fate*. Rochester, N.Y.: Boydell, 1992, pp. 271–300.

Rudolf of Fulda. "The Life of Saint Leoba." Translated by C. H. Talbot. In *Soliders of Christ: Saints and Saints' Lives from Late Antiquity and the Early Middle Ages*, edited by Thomas F. X. Noble and Thomas Head. University Park, Pa.: Pennsylvania State University Press, 1995, pp. 255–277.

Wybourne, Catherine. "Leoba: A Study in Humanity and Holiness." In *Medieval Women Monastics: Wisdom's Wellsprings*, edited by Miriam Schmitt and Linda Kulzer. Collegeville, Minn.: Liturgical, pp. 80–96.

See also **Abbesses; Double Monasteries; Education, Monastic; Germanic Lands; Monasticism and Nuns**

LEPERS

Often confused with other skin ailments, leprosy (*Mycobacterium leprae*) occurred throughout medieval Europe, Byzantium, and the Islamic world. In western Christendom, suspected lepers were typically examined by a priest, physician, or leper. If confirmed leprous, they were often segregated from the community, sometimes by admission into a leper house (*leprosarium*). By the time of the Third Lateran Council (1179), these institutions had grown widely in number and geographic distribution. Founded and endowed in a manner similar to hospitals or religious houses, each was entitled to its own churchyard, chapel, and ministers. Due to the physical disfigurement associated with leprosy, which was believed to be hereditary, highly contagious, chronic, and incurable, many leper houses were situated outside urban settlements, where land was also inexpensive. However, often even "institutionalized" lepers were granted the right to beg in populated areas for alms, although in many locales lepers were assigned distinctive garb, clappers, bells, or other restrictions designed to prevent them from infecting others. By the late fourteenth century, many leper houses were converted to other uses, perhaps due to the impact of the Plague.

Some historians have claimed that the movement to isolate lepers was symptomatic of the formation of a "persecuting society" in Europe, that lepers were identified with heretics, Jews, prostitutes, and other deviants as potentially morally contaminating groups to be contained by distinctive dress and physical and legal segregation. Certainly leprosy was commonly associated with lust, unregulated sexual activity, and moral turpitude. Considered as living dead, lepers were often subject to legal disabilities, including the confiscation of their possessions. However, although leprosy was occasionally treated as grounds for divorce, various canon lawyers claimed that the mutual sexual obligation of spouses persisted even if one contracted leprosy. Liturgical services performed for some diagnosed as leprous preparatory to entry into a leper house or a life of itinerant begging possessed a similar ambivalence towards the afflicted, graphically symbolizing their enforced renunciation of the world and preparation for death through rituals resembling funeral services. Yet depending on the period and whether leper houses were founded by civil, municipal, royal, or religious authorities, these institutions could provide not only sustenance and/or spiritual care, but also medical treatment including baths, special diets, blood-letting, and various medications, plasters, and ointments.

Lepers were often encouraged to transform the involuntary physical suffering and isolation associated with their disease into a special opportunity for purgation from sin, similar to the voluntary deprivations undertaken by regular religious or the tribulations of Job or their patron saint Lazarus (identified both with the divinely rewarded poor man of the New Testament parable and the Lazarus whom Christ raised from the dead). The *Life* of the leprous Alice of Schaarbeek went so far as to depict her stigmatization and suffering as enabling her to intercede powerfully for sinners. In many leper houses, inmates were urged or required to adopt monastic practices including vows of poverty, chastity and obedience, a distinctive habit, and written codes for behavior. Depending on their health, the inmates joined the staff that cared for them in religious services and prayers, penitential practices, and general duties. Female staff and inmates typically nursed the debilitated, cooked, and laundered; men often engaged in farming, gardening, administration of estates, or soliciting alms. Some *leprosaria* became the equivalent of monastic double houses; segregation of the sexes among caregivers and patients was stressed, particularly because leprosy was thought to provoke lust. However, a sometimes involuntary admittance to an ascetic existence sat ill with some, whose brawling, drunkenness, and sexual transgressions were punished by imposed penances, fasting, or withholding of daily provisions, such as firewood and victuals.

Many laypersons viewed the squalor and stench of working with social outcasts as a unique opportunity for spiritual penance, compassion, and recognition of human infirmity. Some, including Saint Francis and devout women in Flanders-Brabant, viewed lepers as living exemplars of the ostracization and suffering endured by Christ that they sought to emulate through their own voluntary embrace of poverty, chastity, and physical suffering. Responsible for dispensing charity from their households, some pious matrons cared for lepers in their own homes or in local hospitals by bathing and kissing their ulcerous wounds, as a form of penance or as preparation for life as a regular religious. Individuals from the merchant and noble classes also founded leper houses. Matilda, queen of England (1080–1118) was known to personally minister to lepers during the Lenten season, and her foundation of the leper hospital of Saint Giles sparked a tradition of royal and noble patronage of *leprosaria* in England. Other women belonged to confraternities who sponsored or served in hospitals or leper houses. Yet similar to other hospitals, *leprosaria* sometimes became glutted with pensioners and *donats* (donors who also served in hospitals) or were transformed into other types of hospitals or houses devoted to contemplative prayer. The lives of women in leper houses could vary greatly. An oblate at the leper house of Cornillon, Saint Julienne, read theology and undertook occasional care of the ill as a voluntary penance, but in the penurious *leprosaria* where Yvette of Huy and Marie of Oignies engaged in backbreaking labor as laysisters, the struggle for subsistence meant little spare time for contemplation or liturgical services.

JESSALYNN BIRD

References and Further Reading

Brody, Saul N. *The Disease of the Soul: Leprosy in Medieval Literature*. Ithaca, N.Y.: Cornell University Press, 1974.

Cawley, Martinus, trans. *The Life of Alice the Leper*. In *Lives of Ida of Nivelles, Lutgard, and Alice the Leper*. Lafayette: Guadalupe Translations, 1994.

Dols, Michael W. "The Leper in Medieval Islamic Society." *Speculum* 58.4 (1983): 891–916.

Richards, Peter. *The Medieval Leper and His Northern Heirs*. Cambridge: Cambridge University Press, 1977.

See also **Conjugal Debt; Hospitals; Lutgard of Aywières; Marie of Oignies; Plague; Yvette of Huy**

LESBIANS
See **Sexuality: Female Same-Sex Relations**

LETTER WRITING

The letters we have from the Middle Ages are mainly public letters in Latin, from one secular or religious ruler to another. Dealing primarily with public matters or matters of general interest, they were intended to be read or heard by the court or circle of the recipient and they were kept in archives or letter collections, which is why they still exist. Some of the correspondents were women in important positions, rulers, regents, abbesses, and their letters were sometimes kept in the archives or collections of men's letters. There are few collections of a woman's letters. Some of the men and women who corresponded were friends, whose letters may have a personal dimension, even when matters of political, religious, or intellectual interest are paramount.

Medieval letters were rarely written by the sender's hand. They were dictated to a secretary trained to make a "fair copy" who might also amend the language. Once they were sent, through a trusted messenger who might carry important parts of the message in his or her head, they became the property of the recipient, who could have them copied or even edited for preservation or other use. One cannot, therefore, assume that the words are precisely those of the sender, but in general, unless intentional deception was involved, they represent the views or purpose of the sender.

Letters can be an important resource for the study of women in the Middle Ages. They show, as few contemporary histories do, how big a role certain women played in the public life of their society, how much women who ruled in their own name or as regents or consorts were involved in day to day operations, how frequently learned religious women were consulted by their male colleagues. They are asked by other rulers to mediate disputes, by ecclesiastical authorities to combat corruption or abuse or even heresy; they pose questions to scholars that lead to important concepts or works.

There are at least two thousand letters to or from women known and published so far, with probably more to be found. There is space here only to mention a few of the more notable figures from whom we still have letters. Though there is correspondence for Byzantine empresses and other early rulers, like Brunhild who ruled Austrasia and Burgundy for thirty-eight years in the late sixth century, most of the extant material is later. Among the Ottonians in tenth century Germany, the empress Adelheid, regent for her son and grandson, her daughter, Emma, queen of France, briefly regent for her son, and her daughter-in-law Theophano, empress and regent for her son, were involved in correspondence about benefices, excommunications, political plots and shifting alliances, and requests for preference and promotion. Letters to one of their relatives, Beatrice of Upper Lorraine, from Adalbero of Reims underscore the political roles of these women: he asks her about a "colloquium dominarum," a meeting of ruling ladies that apparently settled the regency for Otto III.

In the eleventh century, a descendant of Beatrice of Lorraine, Matilda of Tuscany, inherited and ruled a large body of land in northern Italy and Lorraine. One hundred thirty-nine of her letters and charters are extant, many of them delivering judgments, providing grants, and settling disputes between laymen and religious. The letters to her include requests from churchmen for support or intervention, or gratitude for her protection; some dedicate books she commissioned, others from the reform pope, Gregory VII, are more personal. Matilda and her mother, "Duke" Beatrice, were among his strongest supporters and he wrote frequently, declaring his faith in them above all princes, and looking to them for help in his differences with the emperor.

In England, from the beginning of the twelfth century, there are letters of royal women. The bulk of the correspondence of queen Matilda, wife of king Henry I, is with Anselm, archbishop of Canterbury; many were written while he was in exile. They range on her part from personal worries about his health and his excessive fasting to political advice to compromise so he can return to his people who need him; on his part, there are pleas to help England's churches and to advise the king to consider God rather than men. Other bishops wrote seeking or thanking the queen for patronage. A pope corresponded about the situation with the archbishop, and an emperor about her mediations between him and her husband.

Her sister-in-law, Adela of Blois, who ruled for a quarter century as regent for her husband, Count Stephen of Blois, her brother-in-law, and her sons, received letters from her husband, describing his experiences on crusade and from one of her men reporting on a military situation, but most of them come from churchmen with whom she worked. Ivo, bishop of Chartres, wrote frequently and often critically about problems in their shared jurisdiction. Anselm of Canterbury wrote in gratitude for her hosting him in exile and for negotiating a truce for him with her brother, King Henry.

There are letters of "empress Matilda" as she was called from her first marriage, who was Henry I's heir but lost her battle for the throne, as well as from her rival's queen, Matilda of Boulogne, her son's wife Eleanor of Aquitaine, and the queens of Eleanor's sons, Berengaria and Isabel of Angouleme. The extant material increases through the thirteenth century with Eleanor, queen of Henry III, and her letters. Eleanor and her sister Marguerite, queen of France, were deeply involved in the affairs of their countries and in the relations between the two powers. (Marguerite's mother-in-law, Blanche of Castille, who was far more involved in French affairs, as regent and as queen mother, than Marguerite, also left many official letters.) The sister-queens' letters involve gathering armies and finding the ships to carry them, mediating disputes, negotiating loans, buying debts, pressing their claims in their home land, Provence, but occasionally there are personal matters as well, about family health, visits, and marriages. Some of the family letters are in French, among the first women's writings to be recorded in the vernacular. From this period on, more and more vernacular letters were collected and kept, including those of the Paston women, an English gentry family.

Most of the women whose correspondence was preserved from the early and High Middle Ages are royal or aristocratic, but there is another large source of women's correspondence throughout the period—that of religious women. From the friends of Jerome, Marcella, Paula, and Eustochium, in the fourth century, whose difficult Biblical questions led to many of his commentaries, the royal nun Radegund who exchanged letters and poems with Fortunatus in the sixth century, the English missionaries who worked with Boniface in Germany in the eighth, to Heloise whose letters impelled Abelard to most of his extant writing in the twelfth, religious men corresponded with religious women and, though we have few examples extant, religious women corresponded with each other.

There are two women in the twelfth century whose visionary powers were so revered that people wrote to them asking for advice and information and the responses were preserved. Hildegard of Bingen's collected letters number 390; her correspondents include popes, bishops, kings, queens, abbesses and abbots, nuns and monks, laymen and women. She attacks corruption, suggests reforms, and gives administrative and personal advice and moral support to her fellow religious. Her younger contemporary and correspondent, Elisabeth of Schönau, left twenty-two letters, nine to women—mainly encouraging them to lead good lives, but also sharing her sufferings—to the men, she answers religious questions and gives personal and moral advice or reproof.

JOAN FERRANTE

References and Further Reading

Beach, Allison L. "Voices from a Distant Land: Fragments of a Twelfth-Century Nun's Letter Collection." *Speculum*, 77 (2002): 34–54.

Constable, Giles. *Letters and Letter Collections*. Typologie des Sources du Moyen Age Occidental 17. Turnhout: Brepols, 1976.

Elisabeth of Schonau, The Complete Works. Translated by Anne L. Clark. New York: Paulist Press, 2000.

Epistolae: Medieval Women's Latin Letters. http://db.ccnmtl.columbia.edu/ferrante/index.html

Ferrante, Joan M. "Correspondent: 'Blessed is the Speech of Your Mouth.'" *Voice of the Living Light, Hildegard of Bingen and Her World*, edited by Barbara Newman. Berkeley: University of California, 1998, pp. 91–109.

The Letters of Abelard and Heloise. Translated by Betty Radice. Harmondsworth: Penguin Books, 1974.

The Letters of Hildegard of Bingen. Translated by Joseph L. Baird and Radd K. Ehrman. 3 vols. Oxford and New York: Oxford University, 1994, 1998.

LoPrete, Kimberly. *Adela of Blois, Countess and Lord*. Dublin: Four Courts Press, 2005.

Mueller, Joan. *Clare's Letters to Agnes: Texts and Sources*. St. Bonaventure, N.Y.: The Franciscan Institute, 2001.

See also **Adela of Blois; Adelheid; Agnes of Prague; Amalasuntha; Blanche of Castile; Brunhild and Fredegund; Clare of Assisi; Datini, Margherita; Education, Lay; Education, Monastic; Elisabeth of Schönau; Empresses: Byzantium; Heloise; Hildegard of Bingen; Leoba; Matilda of Tuscany; Ottonian Royal Women; Paston Letters; Queens and Empresses: the West; Radegund**

LITERACY AND READING: LATIN

Broadly defined as the ability to read, comprehend, and engage texts, literacy necessarily allows for a wide variety of skill levels among various groups of people at various times—not least true in the Middle Ages, when Latin served as the principal means of scholarly written communication throughout western Europe. Although certain factors regarding medieval literacy applied equally to both genders (e.g., the effects of the Roman Empire's decline in the West; the use of barbarian tongues for informal administration of successor states; the predominant association of Latin with the Church; and the accompanying shift of literary tastes from classical to devotional), women in the Middle Ages encountered additional barriers to formal means of education and exposure to Latin that men did not. Nevertheless, several generations of scholarship have challenged the once-assumed exceptionality of women's proficiency in the era's *lingua franca*. Indeed, large numbers of medieval women are now known to have gained reputations for profound comprehension and creativity, and thereby access to an intellectual and political culture chiefly dominated by males.

Literate Expectations

Not surprisingly, a Latin education among females largely remained the restricted province of the nobility throughout the medieval period. Within this stratum, however, one finds a widespread expectation of literacy and accompanying examples of scholarly achievement. From the start, late antiquity featured the famous collaboration between Jerome and Paula (not to mention a host of fellow women researchers) in the monumental production of the Latin Vulgate. As the Roman Empire faded into memory, monastic institutions increasingly assumed the mantle of preserving literary culture in the West. While the sixth-century *Rule of St. Benedict* famously exhorted monks to read, this expectation also loomed large in several contemporary rules written specifically for nuns by Caesarius of Arles, Aurelian, and the anonymous author of the *Regula cuiusdam patris ad virgines*. Einhard's recollection of Charlemagne's wish that both his sons and daughters be given a proper liberal arts education is borne out by the esteem shown by several ninth-century writers for their royal female correspondents. The celebrated twelfth-century case of Heloise attests to a continued expectation of Latin accomplishment, as she had clearly obtained a fine grounding in the language well before beginning private lessons in philosophy with Peter Abelard.

The pedagogy prescribed to such women closely mirrored that of their male counterparts for much of the Middle Ages: A mastery of the grammars of Donatus and Priscian was to be accompanied by memorization of the Psalms and an appreciation for devotional patristics, including Boethius's *Consolation of Philosophy*, Augustine's *Confessions*, and myriad lives of sainted predecessors. Direction in these studies could come from a variety of teachers, male and female, but just as Louis the Pious's early ninth-century injunction barring males from nunneries indirectly testifies to the presence in those houses of able Latin mistresses, the subsequent prominence of learned nuns like Gerberga of Gandersheim and Hildegard of Bingen suggests a continued tradition of women learning Latin from each other. But even if most women received their linguistic training in a monastic setting (whether or not they intended to join the community in perpetuity), there is some evidence that such was not the only means of gaining access to Latin letters. The Carolingian-era author Dhuoda, for instance, may well have received private tutoring on her family's estates. If so, her adept use of scripture as well as the works of Ovid, Donatus, Prudentius, Augustine, Gregory the Great, Isidore of Seville, Venantius Fortunatus, and Gregory of

Tours in composing a handbook for her son is all the more impressive.

Women may have gained at least some level of literacy through more informal means as well. The English craftswomen who wove the Bayeux Tapestry in the late 1060s, for example, would have become intimately familiar with the work's fifty-seven Latin inscriptions; the same might be said for those who viewed it and similar works in ensuing centuries. While it is impossible to know what kind of pedagogical impact this form of "writing" and "reading" may have had, it is tempting all the same to locate among these artists and admirers, too, at least a nascent Latin literacy.

Textual Engagement

As comprehension only partly comprises literacy, women's effectual interaction with Latin texts also merits attention. To be sure, most women in positions of authority (particularly abbesses or widows) made sure to wield adequate Latin skills, as the settlement of legal disputes often came down to which side was more adept at using the written word to back up its claims. Such acumen was also evident in the literary activities of authors and audiences, particularly with regard to works compiled specifically for women. One analysis of a seemingly disparate eighth-century scriptural florilegium has revealed a finely crafted composite text showcasing articulate and powerful biblical women in action. As the manuscript was almost certainly intended for a Saxon nunnery, the compiler must have believed its readers able to appreciate and incorporate such exemplars into their own spiritual lives. Similar high regard for the literate sensibilities of her fellow sisters was exhibited by Hrotsvit of Gandersheim, perhaps the most creative figure of the tenth century. Though most famous for her deft adaptations of Terentian models to her own dramas, she also composed the nuanced *Deeds of Otto* and *The Founding of Gandersheim Monastery*, works that would only have resonated with highly educated audiences. Much the same could be said for abbess Hildegard of Bingen a century later, whose mystical visions not only gained her entry into influential secular and ecclesiastical circles, but which also (along with her astute medical, theological, musical, and scientific observations) provided her own charges with vivid reading and contemplative material. One could also point to the practice of selective translation as a further illustration of textual engagement. Whereas the twelfth-century *De institutione inclusarum* of Aelred of Rievaulx exhibited precious little admiration for women's nature, much of its more blatant misogyny was intriguingly excluded from two late Middle English versions. And while such activity naturally reflects the growing eclipse of Latin by late medieval vernaculars, it also shows that the female translators were well able to transform Latin texts to fit their own views and the perceived aspirations of their audiences.

The Late Middle Ages

Despite an impressive record of Latin accomplishment, women increasingly chose to focus their literary activities, ambitions, and patronage on the vernacular realm from the late twelfth century onward, just as their male contemporaries began to take advantage of a budding "renaissance" in Latin letters and original philosophy. The strict exclusion of females from the expanding universities of Europe no doubt exacerbated this marked divergence—notwithstanding exceptions such as Trota, a twelfth-century woman who authored a widely respected medical tract in Salerno. It is not true, however, that Latin fell into utter disuse among female readers in the late Middle Ages. Despite the fact that late medieval English bishops often corresponded with abbesses in the written vernacular, a survey of library holdings in thirteenth-, fourteenth-, and fifteenth-century English nunneries has revealed that Latin was still commonly read and understood in many of these communities, and not solely for liturgical purposes. Likewise, the appearance of the accomplished Latin poets Isotta Nogarola, Alessandra Scala, and Costanza Varano in fifteenth-century Italy testifies to their capacity to read, appreciate, and emulate the works of Roman masters. Of course, such endeavors may more accurately reflect emerging Renaissance humanism than medieval literary culture, but the apparent acceptance by contemporaries of such activities would also seem to confirm women's enduring presence in the Latin literary culture of the Middle Ages.

STEVEN STOFFERAHN

References and Further Reading

Bartlett, Anne Clark. *Male Authors, Female Readers: Representation and Subjectivity in Middle English Devotional Literature*. Ithaca, N.Y.: Cornell, 1995.

Bell, David N. *What Nuns Read: Books and Libraries in Medieval English Nunneries*. Kalamazoo, Mich.: Cistercian Publications, 1995.

Contreni, John J. "The Carolingian Renaissance: Education and Literary Culture." In *The New Cambridge Medieval History*, vol. II, edited by Rosamond McKitterick. Cambridge: Cambridge University Press, 1995, pp. 709–757.

Dhuoda. *Liber manualis*, edited by Pierre Riché. Paris: Editions du Cerf, 1975.

Ferrante, Joan M. "Women's Role in Latin Letters from the Fourth to the Early Twelfth Century." In *The Cultural Patronage of Medieval Women*, edited by June Hall McCash. Athens, Ga.: University of Georgia, 1996, pp. 73–104.

Kellsey, Charlene M. "*Lectio divina*: Nuns and Reading in the Sixth and Seventh Centuries." M.A. Thesis: San Jose State University, 1999.

McKitterick, Rosamond. "Women and Literacy in the Early Middle Ages." In *Books, Scribes and Learning in the Frankish Kingdoms, 6th–9th Centuries*. Aldershot: Variorum, 1994, pp. 1–43.

Meale, Carol M. "'...alle the bokes that I haue of latyn, englisch, and frensch': Laywomen and Their Books in Late Medieval England." In *Women and Literature in Britain, 1150–1500*, edited by Carol M. Meale. Cambridge: Cambridge University Press, 1993, pp. 128–158.

Parker, Holt. "Latin and Greek Poetry by Five Renaissance Italian Women Humanists." In *Sex and Gender in Medieval and Renaissance Texts: The Latin Tradition*, edited by Barbara K. Gold, Paul Allen Miller, and Charles Platter. Albany: SUNY, 1997, pp. 247–285.

Power, Eileen. *Medieval English Nunneries, c.1275 to 1535*. Cambridge: Cambridge Universtiy Press, 1922.

Ranft, Patricia. *Women in Western Intellectual Culture, 600–1500*. New York: Palgrave, 2002.

Stofferahn, Steven A. "Changing Views of Carolingian Women's Literary Culture: The Evidence from Essen." *Early Medieval Europe* 8 (1999): 69–97.

See also **Book Ownership; Dhuoda; Education, Lay; Education, Monastic; Heloise; Hildegard of Bingen; Hrotsvit of Gandersheim; Humanism; Letter Writing; Literacy and Reading: Vernacular; Literature, Latin; Monasticism and Nuns; Mothers as Teachers; Nogarola, Isotta; Trota of Salerno; Women Authors: Latin Texts**

LITERACY AND READING: VERNACULAR

Literacy, in the Middle Ages, can be defined as a series of gradations. Full literacy entailed the knowledge of reading and writing, and of the Latin language. For many, though, it was possible to read and write in the vernacular, whilst for another group, literacy meant simply the ability to read. Paul Saenger's definitions of *phonetic literacy* and *comprehension literacy* are useful here. The former concept relates to the ability to follow a written text, in a language not understood, through recognition and vocalization of the constituent phonetic units of individual words. Hence it was possible for lay people to follow a religious service with the aid of private prayer books while, as the period progressed, rubrics to Latin prayers in vernaculars such as English, French, and Spanish occur, suggesting a more active role in worship. *Comprehension literacy* is self-explanatory, where sound is related directly to meaning in the eyes of the reader.

The Acquisition of Literacy

The means by which individuals acquired the skills of literacy is often a matter for conjecture, especially in the case of girls, who were excluded from many of the institutions —such as many song schools, some grammar schools, and all universities—open to boys and young men. In better-off families, especially those who employed a chaplain, some degree of education within the household is likely. Some nunneries also took boarders. In quattrocento northern Italy, the women who formed part of the humanist scholarly movement were usually taught by men—either fathers or tutors, although the situation differed in Florence a century previously, where women were often in charge of household "schools." Also in Florence, the chronicler Giovanni Villani stated that between 1336 and 1338 children of both sexes learning to read numbered 8,000 to 10,000.

Elsewhere, there is evidence of outside elementary school education. In parts of France the opportunities open to girls were comparatively good. It has been estimated that the ratio of schoolmasters to mistresses in Paris in the second half of the fifteenth century was two to one, boys and girls being educated separately. In contrast, the Flemish chronicler and poet Jean Froissart was educated a century earlier in the company of both boys and girls. In England, where there was no regulation comparable to that in France, references are sporadic and anecdotal, but no less important for that.

Dame Schools

The existence of "dame schools" can de deduced from such sources from different regions of the country. In London in 1406, there is reference to an "E Scholemaysteresee" and in 1440, to one "Agnes doctrix puellarum." Also in the fifteenth century, Maria Mareflete was recorded as "magistra scolarum" at Boston in Lincolnshire, while the 1558 will of an ex-member of the Salters' Company in London remembers his schooling during the 1480s in Norwich, under the tutelage of Dame Katherine Peckham, a sister of Norman's Hospital. For York, evidence from women's wills, in which they left bequests to choir schools, indicates women's involvement and their attainment of, perhaps limited, skills of literacy, while there was possibly a school for girls at St. Clement's nunnery in the city. In Germany the evidence is of a similar nature: in Emmerich in 1445, for example, there were at least two female teachers of girls. All of these references presuppose the existence of a system by which these women could be trained to teach, and which deemed it appropriate that they should do so. Certainly reading itself was a skill expected at all levels of society: the Chevalier de la Tour Landry, writing in late fourteenth-century France for his daughters, recommended it for spiritual purposes (his text was translated into English twice in the fifteenth century, secondly by William Caxton), while the Ménagier de Paris, in the early 1390s, assumes that his wife can read, not only for the necessities of household instruction and the learning of appropriate behaviour, but also for receiving private missives from him. Knowledge of the vernacular was important for women from many walks of life: the noble-woman and the bourgeois wife; the partners in mercantile enterprises; and the gentry woman in charge of her household.

Vernacular Literary Skills

The starting point for the acquisition of vernacular literary skills would seem to have been religious: the learning of the Pater Noster, the Ave and the Creed. In 1463, Margaret Plumpton of the gentry family of that name spoke "prattely and French, and hath near hand learned her sawter" in the household of her contracted husband, and it is probably no coincidence that in the late Middle Ages images of St. Anne teaching the Virgin to read from religious books proliferated in manuscripts and religious painting and glass: a case of art mirroring life, and vice versa. This method of inculcating the skill of reading is indicative of the primacy accorded to religious and devotional materials and undoubtedly accounts for the survival of such books and for the frequency with which they were bequeathed between members of families and close friends: they were (to generalize) by and large the most expensively produced volumes and their value was therefore double, incorporating the spiritual and the material. At the same time, the example of Margaret Plumpton emphasizes that in England there continued to be two vernaculars, English and French (or Anglo-Norman), and that their use was not restricted to members of the aristocracy, which explains the continuing circulation of French texts in England and the listing of books apparently in this language in wills of this period. This was, of course, the legacy of the Conquest, and where royalty and nobility were concerned throughout the medieval period, it is appropriate to talk in terms of a European culture, due to intermarriage and continuing familial connections thereafter.

Patronage, Ownership, and Reading

Women were famed as patrons from the eleventh and twelfth centuries onward. Matilda, daughter of Margaret of Scotland, who had her educated in a convent, was the first queen of Henry I; she and her sister-in-law, Adela of Blois, daughter of William I, were courted by the same poets and scholars. Hildebert of Lavardin, bishop of Mons, for instance, wrote of Adela that she was, like Maud, "litteris erudita"—the literacy of the two women probably extending beyond the vernacular. Over a century later, Eleanor of Castile, first queen of Edward I was dedicatee of Girart d'Amien's French Arthurian romance, *Escanor*, featuring Gawain as its hero. Girart worked for patrons in other parts of Europe, which strengthens the case for arguing that at this high level of society, there was little insularity. This is a continuing feature of royal and aristocratic women's reading: the book presented by the Earl of Shrewsbury to Margaret of Anjou on the occasion of her marriage to Henry VI in 1444/1445, for example, London, British Library Royal MS E.VI, contained French romances and work by Christine de Pizan, as well as a treatise on the Order of the Garter, of which the latter related specifically to the culture of her new home. It is a matter for debate as to whether such richly decorated volumes as these would have been individually read by their owners—their sheer weight would have entailed recitation from a lectern, and reading was, in any case, often a communal form of entertainment in which a number of listeners could participate. Perusal of illustrations, however, constitutes another form of "reading" that must be taken into account: columns of early French copies of the *Lancelot*, for instance, are punctuated by pictures which, prior to the introduction of tables of contents, serve both to orient the reader within the text and to provide a summary of the story. That women took pleasure in narrative itself, though, is clear from a French woman's injunction to her scribe to hurry up with his copying of the *Lancelot* and skip portions to arrive at the point in the narrative where Lancelot and Guinivere exchange their first kiss (Rouen, Bibliothèque Municipale MS 1054).

Widespread Use of French

French was the *lingua franca* throughout Europe, not only in England but also in areas such as the Iberian peninsula: in 1339 King Pedro IV asked his sister to send him "*un bel libro frances*," probably a romance, which he had learned she possessed. And romances themselves, second only to service books, are the volumes that are referred to most often as being in the possession of women readers and owners from all the literate classes. (Extant codices containing evidence of women's ownership, such as inscriptions, are rarer in every category of text than references in testaments and inventories.) Romances in French crossed national boundaries—those dealing with Arthurian themes and the story of Troy were particularly popular—but so, too, did works of religious devotion and instruction. Illuminated apocalypses, for example, written in French, retained their popularity throughout the Middle Ages and across countries, one of the latest recorded belonging to Cecily Welles, sister-in-law of Henry VII of England, whilst nuns (as well as monks) read instructional and devotional texts in French. Such works were equalled in popularity by mystical and devotional treatises in native vernaculars—in England, those of Richard Rolle and Walter Hilton, both of whom addressed some of their works to a female audience and, to a lesser extent, the writings of Continental women mystics. Certain categories of reading materials appear to have held less attraction for women, histories being a case in point. Nevertheless, there is ample evidence overall to suggest that women's tastes were as eclectic as those of their male counterparts. Research also indicates distinctive patterns of women's reading practices, based on familial and regional networks and this is but one of the rich veins of information about women's literacy in the vernacular that can be expected to yield new insights concerning their participation in literate culture.

CAROL M. MEALE

References and Further Reading

Barron, Caroline M. "The Education and Training of Girls in Fifteenth-Century London." In *Courts, Counties and the Capital in the Later Middle Ages*, edited by Diana E. S. Dunn. Stroud: Sutton Publishing, 1996, pp. 139–153.

Bell, David N. *What Nuns Read: Books and Libraries in Medieval English Nunneries*. Kalamazoo, Mich.: Cistercian Publications, 1995.

Bell, Susan Groag. "Medieval Women Book Owners: Arbiters of Lay Piety and Ambassadors of Culture." *Signs* 7 (1982):742–768.

Clanchy, M. T. *From Memory to Written Record: England 1066–1307*. 2nd ed. Oxford: Blackwell, 1993.

Dutton, Anne M. "Passing the Book: Testamentary Transmission of Religious Literature To and By Women in England 1350–1500." In *Women, the Book and the Godly*, edited by Lesley Smith and Jane H. M. Taylor. Woodbridge, Suffolk: D.S. Brewer, 1995, pp. 41–54.

The Goodman of Paris (Le Ménagier de Paris), translated by Eileen Power. London: Routledge, 1928.

King, Margaret L. *Women of the Renaissance*. Chicago: University of Chicago Press, 1991.

Meale, Carol M. "'...alle the bokes that I haue of latyn, englisch, and frensch': Laywomen and Their Books in Late Medieval England." In *Women and Literature in Britain, 1150–1500*, edited by Carol M. Meale. 2nd ed. Cambridge: Cambridge University Press, 1996, pp. 128–158.

Meale, Carol M., and Julia Boffey. "Gentlewomen's Reading." In *The Cambridge History of the Book in Britain*, vol. 3, *1400–1557*, edited by Lotte Hellinga and J. B. Trapp. Cambridge: Cambridge University Press, 2000, pp. 526–540.

Moran, JoAnn Hoeppner. *Education and Learning in the City of York 1300–1500*. York: Borthwick Institute of Historical Research, Borthwick Papers no. 55, 1979.

———.*The Growth of English Schooling 1340-1548: Learning, Literacy and Laicization in Pre-Reformation Diocese*. Princeton, N.J.: Princeton University Press, 1985.

Saenger, Paul. "Books of Hours and the Reading Habits of the Later Middle Ages." In *The Culture of Print: Power and the Uses of Print in Early Modern Europe*, edited by Roger Chartier, translated by Lydia G. Cochrane. Oxford and Cambridge: Polity, 1989, pp. 141–173.

Salter, Elizabeth. *English and International: Studies in the Literature, Art and Patronage of Medieval England*, edited by Derek Pearsall and Nicolette Zeeman. Cambridge: Cambridge University Press, 1988.

Villani, Giovanni. *Cronica* Robert S. Lopez and Irving J. Raymond, eds. *Medieval Trade in the Mediterranean World*. New York: Columbia University Press, 1955, pp. 71–74.

See also **Adela of Blois; Arthurian Literature; Audience, Women in the; Book Ownership; Christine de Pizan; Devotional Literature; Education, Lay; Education, Monastic; Letter Writing; Literacy and Reading: Latin; Margaret of Anjou; Mothers as Teachers; Patronage, Literary; Roman de Silence; Romance, English; Romance, French; Romance, German; Wills**

LITERATURE, GERMAN

Among the few surviving examples of the literature of the ancient Germans are two magical incantations known as the Merseburg charms, one for freeing prisoners-of-war (or aiding women in labor) and the other for healing the broken leg of a horse. Both invoke the helping power of goddesses or human women with supernatural capabilities. The Merseberg charms were jotted down in the tenth century on the fly leaf of a Latin missal exemplifying the haphazard preservation of pagan, oral literature at a time when Latin was the language of writing and Christian monasteries were the centers of culture. The first known woman author from the German lands was a tenth-century nun, Hrotsvit of Gandersheim, who wrote Latin dramas. During the Old High German period (750–1050 CE) influential depictions of women are found in vernacular texts composed to spread the Christian faith, for example, the story of the Samaritan woman who proclaims Christ as the messiah to her community (John 4:5–42). One version of the story appears in a gospel translation by the monk Otfried (d. c. 867) from Weissenburg monastery in Alsace. Elsewhere in his *Evangelienbuch* Otfried highlights women's emotions, such as the desperation of the mothers of the slaughtered innocents, to heighten his story's impact. Otfried was encouraged to write by a noble woman named Judith whose identity remains unknown.

Most German literature from the Early Middle High era (1050–1170 CE) is found in three manuscripts including the *Vorau* manuscript whose texts are ordered programmatically to tell of the works of the Christian God in human history (Vorau, Styria, Stiftsbibliothek, cod. 276; late twelfth century). They include the acts of the biblical Judith written in heroic style (first third of the twelfth century); the works of the first known woman writer of German, Frau Ava (d. c. 1127); an anonymous woman's prayer in verse; and the *Kaiserchronik* (*Chronicle of the Emperors*) with the first version of *Crescentia*, the popular story of the unjustly persecuted and rehabilitated empresses. A German example of the international literature devoted to the Virgin is an epic based on her life completed in 1172 by Prester Wernher.

Minstrel Epics

Spielmannsepen (minstrel epics) were also composed in Early Middle High German. Though the name suggests entertainment for common people, minstrel epics were intended for elite audiences. Five of the six that have survived are bridal quests in which getting married is an adventure for the well-born groom that requires strategic help or moral support from the bride as well as international travel, an army of faithful retainers, wit, perseverance, and Christian piety. In *König Rother* (*King Rother*) both the bride and her mother aid the hero in his quest. Overshadowed by the romance in the thirteenth century, minstrel epics regained popularity in the later Middle Ages.

Middle High German Literature

An increasing volume of secular literature was produced for noble audiences in Middle High German from 1170 to 1273 CE. Gender was a pervasive concern of this literature whose preeminent genres were the *Minnelied* (erotic song lyric) and the romance. Singular works were also produced, for example, Wolfram von Eschenbach's illustrated *Willehalm*,

whose heroine, a Christian convert, is tested when her infidel father wages war on her Christian husband.

The anonymous *Nibelungenlied* was composed in strophes close to 1200 CE in the vicinity of Passau. Based on Germanic tales from the distant past, the *Nibelungenlied* is also influenced by the romance, especially the introduction of its central character, Kriemhild, as a courtly princess who receives and reciprocates the love of the hero, Siegfried. Yet it raises its own, distinctive set of gender issues. For example, marriages in the *Nibelungenlied* come about through the exchange of brides between the male protagonists Gunther, King of the Burgundians, and the heroic Siegfried; but the political alliance that should bind these men fails due to the deceptions they perpetrate on their wives. Another issue involves the relationship between wealth, gender, and power. The *Nibelungenlied* recounts the systematic economic despoilment of Kriemhild by her brother King Gunther and his vassal, Hagen. Their actions are aimed at preventing the noble woman from using her wealth to attain justice through vengeance. Third is the issue of sexual violence, here presented as a means to master powerful women. Sexual violence is both literal (Gunther forces coitus with his Amazon-like bride Brunhild; Siegfried batters Kriemhild) and symbolic (Siegfried steals Brunhild's belt and ring after physically subduing her on her wedding night in preparation for Gunther). Finally debate swirls about the motivations of Kriemhild who, in the final scenes, incites the armies of her second husband to kill her brothers and their vassals. Is she moved by grief over Siegfried's death or by her own exclusion from power? The butchery of the final scenes raises questions about her ethical character. Is her vengeance in proportion to its cause? Or is its excess a comment on the dangers of women playing at men's political games?

Early manuscripts of the *Nibelungenlied* show that these kinds of questions are not merely modern concerns. One version of the text, the C version, sympathizes with Kriemhild more than the A and B versions by giving her an inner life. But C also undercuts her political agency. Moreover, in all the main manuscripts, the *Nibelungenlied* is paired with another, contemporaneous work called *Diu Klage* (*The Lament*), a sequel that justifies Kriemhild by stating that she acted out of admirable fidelity to her murdered husband but also that the magnitude of the slaughter was due to her deranged mind. A condemnation of Kriemhild's character is found in the thirteenth-century *Der Rosengarten zu Worms* (*The Rose Garden in Worms*). Still married to Siegfried and still powerful, Kriemhild arrogantly compels heroes to battle to the death to prove Siegfried's superiority.

In a sixteenth-century manuscript the *Nibelungenlied* is paired with another epic, *Kudrun* (anonymous, 1230–1240). As in the *Nibelungenlied* the central character of *Kudrun* is a woman. This fact of transmission has led scholars to term them *Frauenepen* (*Women's Epics*). The term, however, says nothing about the gender of the authors nor does it imply that these epics have a feminist outlook. *Kudrun* is the story of a family across three generations. In the main section a mother with political acumen passes power to a daughter, Kudrun, who is an equally effective ruler. The epic stresses continuity between generations of women as they pass through life stages (secluded childhood, choice of spouse, authority through queenship). It also reflects a world in which women's social identity was derived from both maternal and paternal ancestry, not just the patriline. Kudrun's antagonist is female. For fourteen years, she resists coercion by her would-be mother-in-law to stave off a socially inappropriate marriage. In the end the heroine performs the role of peacemaker, as did some historical noble women, by forging good marriages to reconcile formerly warring parties.

Comic Tales

Short, often comic tales called *Mären* are the German contribution to a European literary trend that included the French *fabliaux*. There are 216 *Mären* dating from the mid-thirteenth through the mid-sixteenth century. Der Stricker (d. c. 1250) is considered the founder of the genre but Hartmann von Aue, who introduced the Arthurian romance to Germany, also wrote a *Märe* called *In Der Arme Heinrich*. In it a girl of the free peasantry volunteers to sacrifice her heart's blood to cure her lord of a deadly disease, but a miracle enables both to survive and happily marry despite their differences in status. The social rank of both *Mären* authors and audiences runs from the nobility through the educated middle classes of the German cities. Some professional poets composed *Mären*. For gender analysis the *Mären* are significant because many present women's sexuality beyond the bonds of marriage as a comic theme. Clever wives play central roles. The emphasis is put on the wit and capability of wives to arrange trysts with their lovers, avoid discovery, protect their lovers from harm, or convince suspicious husbands of their innocence. Women are sexually ambitious in many *Mären* and their sexual needs are frankly depicted. In some, wives ally with their husbands to expose an unwanted suitor. Other *Mären* examine marriage as an unstable hierarchy, sometimes giving wives the upper hand but

sometimes reinstating the "normal" rule of the husband. Common women and men, such as servants, belong to the household settings. Beatings are prescribed for both disorderly wives and dominated husbands. Some *Mären* depict cruel forms of punishment for unruly women such as immurement, cutting, or being ridden like a horse. Although there is a consensus among literary scholars that *Mären* celebrate mental quickness one still needs to explain why the clever wives often represent the genre's most positive value.

It is common to speak of *Mären* as a single genre but in reality they are difficult to distinguish from other short narrative or discursive texts such as beast fables; pious tales; short stories of love and chivalry; discourses on love, ethical behavior, religious teaching, or the state of society. These frequently depict gender relations that are normative rather than subversive as in many (but hardly all) *Mären*. These various genres are mixed together in medieval manuscripts indicating that audiences enjoyed the conflicting or contrasting gender perspectives they offered.

Sarah Elizabeth Westphal-Wihl

References and Further Reading

Ava, Frau. *Ava's New Testament Narratives: When the Old World Passed Away*. Introduction, translations, and notes by James A. Rushing, Jr. Medieval German Texts in Bilingual Editions, 2. Kalamazoo, Mich.: Medieval Institute Publications, 2003.

Bornholdt, Claudia. *Engaging Moments: The Origins of Medieval Bridal-Quest Narrative*. Berlin and New York: Walter De Gruyter, 2005.

Classen, Albrecht, ed. *Women as Protagonists and Poets in the German Middle Ages: An Anthology of Feminist Approaches to Middle High German Literature*. Göppingen: Kümmerle, 1991.

Coxon, Sebastian. "Schriber Kunnen Liste Vil: Literate Protagonists and Literary Antics in the Medieval German Comic Tale." *Oxford German Studies* 31 (2002): 17–62.

Edwards, Cyril. *The Beginnings of German Literature: Comparative and Interdisciplinary Approaches to Old High German*. Rochester, N.Y., and Woodbridge, Suffolk: Camden House, 2002.

Frakes, Jerold C. *Brides and Doom: Gender, Property, and Power in Medieval German Women's Epic*. Philadelphia: University of Pennsylvania Press, 1994.

Gibbs, Marion, and Johnson, Sidney M. *Medieval German Literature: A Companion*. New York and London: Garland Publishing, 1997.

Hartmann von Aue. "Poor Heinrich." translated by Frank Tobin. In *Arthurian Romances, Tales, and Poetry: The Complete Works of Hartmann von Aue*. translated with commentary by Frank Tobin, Kim Vivian, and Richard H. Lawson. University Park, Pa.: Pennsylvania State University Press, 2001, pp. 215–234.

Historia Judith/The Story of Judith. In *Sovereignity and Salvation in the Vernacular 1050–1150*. Introduction, translation, and notes by James A. Schultz. Medieval German Texts in Bilingual Editions, 1. Kalamazoo, Mich: Medieval Institute Publications, 2000, pp. 142–155.

King Rother. Translated by Robert Lichtenstein. Chapel Hill, N.C.: University of North Carolina Press, 1962.

Kudrun. Translated by Marion E. Gibbs and Sidney M. Johnson. Garland Library of Medieval Literature, 79, B. New York: Garland Publishing, 1992.

The Lament of the Nibelungen (Diu Klage). Translated with an introduction by Winder McConnell. Columbia, S.C.: Camden House, 1964.

The Nibelungenlied. Translation by Arthur T. Hatto. 2nd ed. Harmondsworth: Penguin, 1969.

Novellistik des Mittelalters: Märendichtung. Editing, translation, and commentary by Klaus Grubmüller. Frankfurt am Main: Deutscher Klassiker Verlag, 1996.

Rasmussen, Ann Maire. *Mothers and Daughters in Medieval German Literature.* Syracuse: Syracuse University Press, 1997.

———. "Fathers to Think Back Through: The Middle High German Mother-Daughter and Father-Son Advice Poems Known as Die Winsbeckin and Die Winsbecke." In *Medieval Conduct*, edited by Kathleen Ashley and Robert L. A. Clark. Minneapolis and London: University of Minnesota Press, 2001, pp. 106–134.

———. "Emotions, Gender, and Lordship in Medieval Literature: Clovis's Grief, Tristan's Anger, and Kriemhild's Restless Corpse." In *Codierungen von Emotionen im Mittelalter/Emotions and Sensibilities in the Middle Ages*, edited by C. Stephen Jaeger and Ingrid Kasten. Berlin and New York: Walter de Gruyter, 2003, pp. 174–189.

Schulz, James A. *The Knowledge of Childhood in the German Middle Ages, 1100–1350.* Philadelphia: University of Pennsylvania Press, 1995.

Starkey, Kathryn. "Brunhild's Smile: Emotions and the Politics of Gender in the *Nibelungenlied*." In *Codierungen von Emotionen im Mittelalter/Emotions and Sensibilities in the Middle Ages*, edited by C. Stephen Jaeger and Ingrid Kasten. Berlin and New York: Walter de Gruyter, 2003, pp. 159–173.

Westphal, Sarah. *Textual Poetics of German Manuscripts 1300–1500.* Columbia, S.C.: Camden House, 1993.

Winsbeckische Gedichte nebst Tirol und Fridebrant, edited by Albert Leitzmann. Rev. Ingo Reiffenstein. 3rd ed. Altdeutsche Textbibliothek, 9. Tübingen: Niemeyer, 1962.

Wolfram von Eschenbach. *Willehalm.* Translated by Marion E. Gibbs and Sidney M. Johnson. Harmondsworth: Penguin Books, 1984.

See also **Ava; Bible, Women in; Conduct Literature; Fabliau; Germanic Lands; Gottfried von Strassburg; Hildegard of Bingen; Magic and Charms; Mary, Virgin: in Literature; Mechthild of Magdeburg; Minnesang; Romance, German; Sister-Books and Convent Chronicles; Women Authors, German Texts; Wolfram von Eschenbach**

LITERATURE, HEBREW

Only a few medieval Jewish women are known to have composed literary works. Even the prolific Golden Age in Muslim Spain (950–1150) yielded only two Jewish women-poets: the unnamed wife of Dunash ben Labrat (Cordoba, mid-tenth century) from whom one Hebrew poem remains, and Qasmūna (allegedly the daughter of Samuel ha-Nagid, the eleventh century Hebrew poet and statesman from Granada). A single religious poem attributed to a woman was composed by a certain Merecina (Catalonia, mid-fifteenth century).

Inspired by Arabic literature, the male love poetry of the Hebrew Golden Age in Spain (written by rabbis, philosophers, and communal leaders like Samuel ha-Nagid, Ibn Gabirol, Moses Ibn Ezra, and Judah ha-Levi), glorified and idealized beauty—both female and male. The love-poets, who present themselves as weak and inferior, exalt an unyielding dazzling lady, while excusing her for being aloof, silent, tempting, and even lethal. In homoerotic poems the beloved is a young boy who has not yet reached puberty. The atmosphere and the love-objects (wine-bearers, often cross-dressed, and female singers and dancers) reflect the luxurious Islamic courts (where Jewish elite members often served as courtiers).

The voices of passionate maidens singing about love—consummated or forlorn—are heard in the *kharjas* (couplets in vernacular Arabic or Romance, appearing at the end of Hebrew poems of the Andalusian *muwashshah* genre). They are assumed to preserve (or counterfeit?) an oral tradition of old Iberian Romance songs of women. In wedding-songs brides are active in tempting bridegrooms; Eros is sanctioned, and married love looms as prelapsarian paradise.

The female voice of widowed wives, bereaved mothers, and dead daughters is heard also in ballad-like lamentations over the dead. The dialogues, the refrains, and the folkloric song-form suggest an oral tradition of women's lamentations. ("Alas, my daughter, have you forgotten your abode?...Alas, my daughter, your loss is bitter"..."Alas, alas, my mother, that you ever gave me birth. How could you abandon me on this day?" Judah ha-Levi.) Moral epigrams advocate the disciplining (secluding, veiling, silencing, and even regular beating) of wives. ("Walls and castles were created for the woman; her pride is in spinning and weaving. / Her face is a pudendum exposed in the main road that has to be covered by shawls and veils." Samuel ha-Nagid.)

Ascetic poems feature the allegorical figure of *tevel* in its capacity as Lady World or as Mother Earth. Embodying the world's evil, *tevel* is a seducing—but rotten—prostitute, trapping men then devouring them. Shrewish wives (plaintive, gossipy, gluttonous, disobedient, and treacherous) appear in many rhymed narratives (of the *maqama* type or its cognates). In Judah al-Harizi's sixth *maqama* (c. 1220) a beautiful bride turns into a monstrous wife. Her bodily description is allied with discharges, pollution, diseases, ugliness, beastliness, and demonic evil. Humor, parody, the grotesque, and witticisms were often used as misogyny's most effective tools. Misogyny and misogamy are at the center of "Judah the Women-Hater," a rhymed narrative by Judah Ibn Shabbetai (Toledo, 1208). His protagonist, a propagandist of misogamy, is lured into marriage; the bride is exchanged for a shrew; and a divorce trial takes place, where the author appears ex-machina to declare love to his real wife and children. Marriage is hotly debated, but woman is categorically debased. The tension between the positive value of marriage (and procreation) in Judaism, and the negativity of marriage (affected by Jewish and non-Jewish ascetic trends), results here in textual ambiguity.

"The Women-Hater" ignited a literary controversy that lasted through the thirteenth century. A certain Isaac (allegedly urged by the women whom Ibn Shabbetai had abused), wrote "In Defence of Women" (Provence, 1210), a tale about a virtuous wife and a perfect marriage. In "The Women's Lover" (Provence, 1295) by Yeda'aya ha-Penini, Ibn Shabbetai, the misogynist, descends from heaven to defend his work. A literary trial concludes with the sanctioning of marriage.

A poetic of women's adoration and condemnation prevails also in Hebrew literature in Italy. In the rhymed narratives (*Mahbarot*) of Immanuel of Rome (c. 1261–c. 1328) male poets conduct rhetorical competitions over women's virtues or vices. Influenced by the Italian novella, Immanuel's women figures are a mixture of misogynistic traditions and "the new sweet style." Throughout the sixteenth century, some dozen Hebrew poets (like their Italian peers) debated the nature of women, employing examples from the Bible, Greek mythology, and Roman history. Women participated in these debates as readers and patrons.

Several rhymed stories written in Spain (by Alharizi and Jacob ben Eleazar, thirteenth century) employ the theme of transvestism (female-to-male and male-to-female). A unique prayer, pleading to God to turn its male-speaker into a woman, was written in fourteenth century Provence by Qalonymos ben Qalonymos. ("Woe to me, my mother, that you ever gave birth to a male child!...Cursed be the man who informed my father: 'A male child was born to you!'...Our father in heaven! You, who did miracles to our fathers by fire and water...if only you would turn me from male to female! If only I were worthy of this grace of yours, I could have now been the lady of the house,...holding the spindle....")

Following traditions of biblical and midrashic allegory, liturgical poetry presents the Jewish nation as paramour of Israel's God. Exiled, politically oppressed, and inferior, Israel speaks as bereaved mother, widow, or abandoned wife longing for her husband. In liturgical-penitential poems, the human soul is allegorized as stray daughter, the body's maid, or a yearning gazelle. Menstruating and sinful "she" is called to purify herself from her female pollution and unite with (masculine) Intellect.

Women-martyrs feature in liturgical poems (and chronicles) written in Germany and northern France from the eleventh to the thirteenth centuries. The religious devotion and heroism of parents (especially mothers), who, faced by the choice of conversion or death by torture, took their children's and their own lives is glorified in these poems.

TOVA ROSEN

References and Further Reading

Assis, Yom Tov. "Sexual Behaviour in Medieval Hispano-Jewish Society." In *Jewish History: Essays in Honour of Chimen Abramsky*, edited by Ada Rapoport-Albert and Steven J. Zipperstein. London: P. Hale Zan, 1988, pp. 25–59.

Baskin, Judith R., ed. *Jewish Women in Historical Perspective*. Detroit: Wayne State University Press, 1991.

Bellamy, James A. "Qasmūna the Poetess: Who Was She?" *Journal of the American Oriental Society* 103 (1983): 423–424.

Carmi, T. ed and trans. *The Penguin Book of Hebrew Poetry*. New York: Viking Press, 1981.

Cohen, Jeremy. *Sanctifying the Name of God: Jewish Martyrs and Jewish Memories of the First Crusade*. Philadelphia: University of Pennsylvania Press, 2004.

Cole, Peter, tr. and ed. *Selected Poems of Shmuel HaNagid*. Princeton, N.J.: Princeton University Press, 1996.

Dishon, Yehudit. "Images of Women in Medieval Hebrew Literature." In *Women of the Word: Jewish Women and Jewish Writing*, edited by Judith R. Baskin. Detroit: Wayne State University Press, 1994, pp. 35–50.

Fleischer, Ezra. "On Dunash Ben Labrat, His Wife and His Son: New Light on the Beginnings of the Hebrew-Spanish School" (Hebrew). *Jerusalem Studies in Hebrew Literature* 5 (1984): 189–202.

Grossman, Avraham. *Pious and Rebellious: Jewish Women in Europe in the Middle Ages*. translated by Jonathan Chipman, Waltham, Mass.: 2004.

Immanuel of Rome: Mahberot Immanuel Ha-Romi (Hebrew). Edited by Dov Jarden. Jerusalem: Bialik Institute, 1957.

Kaufman, Shirley, Galit Hasan-Rokem, and Tamar S. Hess, eds. *The Defiant Muse: Hebrew Feminist Poems from Antiquity to the Present: A Bilingual Anthology*. New York: 1999.

Pagis, Dan. "The Controversy Concerning the Female Image in Hebrew Poetry in Italy" (Hebrew). *Jerusalem Studies in Hebrew Literature* 9 (1986): 259–300.

Rosen, Tova. "On Tongues Being Bound and Let Loose: Women in Medieval Hebrew Literature." *Prooftexts* 8 (1988): 67–88.

———. "The Muwashshah." In *The Literature of Al-Andalus*, edited by María Rosa Menocal, Raymond P. Scheindlin and Michael Sells. Cambridge: 2000, pp. 165–189.

———. *Unveiling Eve: Reading Gender in Medieval Hebrew Literature*. Philadelphia: University of Pennsylvania Press, 2000.

Roth, Norman. "The 'Wiles of Women' Motif in the Medieval Hebrew Literature of Spain." *Hebrew Annual Review* 2 (1978): 145–165.

Scheindlin, Raymond P. *Wine, Women and Death: Medieval Hebrew Poems on the Good Life* (Hebrew/English). Philadelphia: Jewish Publication Society, 1986.

———. *The Gazelle: Medieval Hebrew Poems on God, Israel and the Soul*. Philadelphia: Jewish Publication Society, 1991.

Schirmann, Jefim (Hayyim), ed. *Ha-Shirah ha-ivrit bi-sefard u-ba-provans* (Hebrew Poetry in Spain and Provence). Jerusalem and Tel Aviv: Bialik, 2006.

Stern, David and Mark Jay Mirsky, eds. *Rabbinic Fantasies: Imaginative Narratives from Classical Hebrew Literature*. Philadelphia: Jewish Publication Society, 1990.

See also **Dolce of Worms; Jewish Mystical Thought, Body and Soul in; Jewish Women; Marriage, Jewish; Qasmūna Bint Ismā'īl; Shekinah**

LITERATURE, IBERIAN

Isidore of Seville's seventh-century description of woman (*mulier*) in his *Etymologies* is a fitting beginning for this panoramic overview, since it is one of the earliest representations of women in medieval Iberian literatures. Isidore links women to sweetness or mildness; he claims that women differ from men in their weakness, and he believes that women are defined by their "sex" (*femineum sexum*) and not their bodily corruption (chap. 11, bk. 2, vv. 18–20). His description in Latin is only one among numerous representations of women in Iberian literatures in Arabic, Hebrew, Latin, and Romance languages. In an effort to organize the array of portrayals in, for instance, medical treatises, poetry, historiography, and devotional writings, this entry is not exhaustive but is divided into six general thematic groups.

Law, History, and Legends

Legal codes and cases from kingdoms and municipalities throughout the peninsula depict women in domestic, occupational, and economic contexts, of which Alfonso X's *Siete Partidas* are renowned (ruled 1252–1284). Chronicles and other historical writings, such as Alfonso's *Estoria de Espanna* and *General estoria*, further portray women, although many of the same women characters are also found in legends and ballads (*romances*), including Count Julian's daughter,

Florinda who was frequently blamed for the fall of the last Visigothic king, Roderic, and for the subsequent invasion of the peninsula by North African troops in 711. Another prominent figure in legends and ballads is the noble woman doña Lambra, whose dishonor by the nephew of her new husband implicitly prompted the young nephew's beheading, as well as that of his six brothers.

Love Relations, Sex, and Family

Love poems by and about women were plentiful early in the medieval period in Arabic and Hebrew. The eleventh-century Cordovan noble woman, Wallāda bint al-Mustakfi, is well known for her scathing compositions to Ibn Zaydūn, although many other women also wrote poetry; one such was Hamda Banāt Ziyād (twelfth century), who wrote an erotic poem about a naked woman by a river (Garulo, Rubiera Mata). Yishaq Ibn Jalfun, an eleventh-century male writer from Cordova, produced amorous compositions about men and women. In the eleventh century, Ibn Hazm of Cordova composed a treatise on love in his *Tawq al-hamāma* (*The Dove's Neckring*), which contained portrayals of women. *Muwashshah* poems in classical Arabic and Hebrew and *zajal* poems in colloquial Arabic were invented in al-Andalus (Muslim-dominated Iberia) and often described women in panegyrics and in poems about love. These poems were accompanied by a single stanza called the *jarcha* (exit) in Romance and vernacular Arabic. Few Andalusi women composed written *muwashshah*s and *zajal*s, although sometimes women were depicted as singers of the *jarcha*s, where they lamented failed love or the absence of a lover (Rosen).

Women figure prominently in the illustrated, thirteenth-century romance in Arabic from Seville, *Qissat Bayād wa Riyād*, which tells the love story of a merchant's son, Bayād, and a woman slave, Riyād. The jealous lady (*sayyida*) has an important role in the tale, and an old woman (*ajuz*) narrates the story and intervenes on Bayād's behalf. The thirteenth-century romance in Castilian, *Libro de Apolonio*, also includes various women characters, namely, the daughter of the evil king Antíoco, who is raped by her father, and the captured Tarsiana, who staves off unwanted sexual relations with men by playing the lute. The anonymous Castilian epic, *Poema de mio Cid* (1207), contains one of the most inexplicable episodes of Iberian literature, when the Cid's daughters, Elvira and Sol, are brutally beaten by their husbands and left to die in an oak grove. The familial emphasis in the

Poema is completed by the inclusion of the Cid's wife, Jimena.

The Archpriest of Hita's fourteenth-century Castilian *Libro de buen amor* (Book of good love) recounts an archpriest's sexual exploits with women. Several women go-betweens aid the archpriest, but *Trotaconventos* (Convent Trotter) is his favorite and most successful intercessor. The go-between probably derives from literature in Arabic, but also exists in the thirteenth-century story collection translated from Arabic into Castilian, *Kalila e Dimna*, and is pivotal in the previously mentioned *Qissat Bayād wa Riyād*, as well as in Fernando de Rojas's fifteenth-century *La Celestina*, where Celestina's interventions result in the demise of many characters, including the lovesick Calisto and his beloved Melibea.

Women are the focus of late medieval stylized poetry in Castilian and Catalan. In the fifteenth-century, the Marquis of Santillana depicted peasant women (in poems called *serranillas*) who were desired by gentlemen riding in the countryside. A satirical, grotesque version of these women also appears in the Archpriest's *Libro*. Courtly images of women are important in the fifteenth- and sixteenth-century songbooks called *cancioneros*, as well as in chivalric tales, such as the early fourteenth-century *Libro del Caballero Zifar*, the fifteenth-century *Amadís de Gaula*, and the fifteenth-century *Tirant lo Blanc* in Catalan.

Devotional Literature

Devotional tales about the Virgin were popular in medieval Iberia, as evidenced by two thirteenth-century collections of Marian miracles in Castilian. The cleric Gonzalo de Berceo translated and adapted miracles from Latin in his *Milagros de Nuestra Señora*, where the Virgin saved errant monks, a Jewish child, and thieves. The *Milagros* begins with the author's presentation as a pilgrim in an allegorical garden. Alfonso X's scribal teams composed a plethora of Marian miracles in the Galician-Portuguese *Cantigas de Santa María*, which were sometimes accompanied by elaborate miniatures that retold the miracles in visual form. Women saints were further represented in hagiographies, such as Berceo's *Poema de Santa Oria*, or the anonymous *Libro de los huéspedes*, which included portrayals of Santa Marta and Santa María Egiçiaca. Fourteenth- and fifteenth-century writers and poets in Valencia, including Bernat Fenollar, also composed numerous praise songs to the Virgin in Catalan.

Leisure, Advice, and Insults

Medieval Iberians played a variety of table games during their leisure time, as evidenced by Alfonso X's illuminated *Libro de ajedrez, dados y tablas* (Book of chess, dice, and table games). Along with its written text, the manuscript contains illustrations of a range of people playing games, including noble women, servants, Arabs, possibly prostitutes, Jews, and King Alfonso himself. Poems that further indicate a more jocular view of life are the satirical, insulting thirteenth- and fourteenth-century Galician-Portuguese *cantigas d'escarnho e de mal dizer*, which were collected under the patronage of Alfonso X and Denis of Portugal and contain a variety of portrayals of women. Medieval Iberian nobles and royalty also sometimes required books that provided counsel, such as the antifeminist *Sendebar* (*Libro de los engaños de las mujeres*; Book of Women's Deception), which derives from Arabic and was copied in the thirteenth century under the patronage of Alfonso's older brother Fadrique. The *Sendebar* highlights the image of the evil stepmother who urges the king to kill his own son after falsely claiming that the son attacked her. Another advice book, Juan Manuel's fourteenth-century story collection, the *Conde Lucanor*, includes portrayals of women, such as the impetuous bride in story 35 who must be tamed lest her husband lose matrimonial control and possibly his own life. This story is often linked to Shakespeare's *The Taming of the Shrew*.

Medical Literature

A wide range of Iberian medical literature in Arabic, Castilian, Catalan, Hebrew, and Latin discussed women and their well-being, including treatises on cosmetics and works on general health, which provided information on menstrual ailments, coitus, and human reproduction. In his twelfth-century book on treatments, *Kitāb al-Muyarrabāt* (Book of medical experiences), Abū l-Alā' Zuhr, who practiced medicine in Seville and Morocco, discussed amenorrhea (the failure to menstruate), menstrual problems after abortion, and sterility in women. In the fifteenth century, a number of medical writers addressed women's well-being, including Johannes de Ketham (*Compendio de la humana salud*; Compendium of human health), Bernard of Gordon (*Lilio de medicina*; Iris of medicine), and Juan de Aviñón (*Sevillana medicina*; Medicine of Seville). The anonymous, fifteenth-century Catalan *Speculum al foderi* (The mirror of coitus) portrayed women as sexual partners and as go-betweens.

The Late Medieval Debate on Women

Many Iberian writers participated in the late medieval debate on women. In the fifteenth century, Isabel de Villena bolstered women's role in Jesus' life in her Catalan *Vita Christi* (Life of Christ), while Teresa de Cartagena ironically dignified women through their weakness and disease in the Castilian *Arboleda de los enfermos* (Grove of the infirm) and *Admiraçion operum Dey* (Wonder at the Works of God). The rise of misogynist literature in the fifteenth century included Alfonso Martínez de Toledo's *Arcipreste de Talavera o Corbacho* in Castilian and Jaume Roig's Catalan *Spill o Llibre de les dones* (Mirror or book on women). Both books connected their misogynist discourse to men's well-being, since book four of the *Corbacho* was a short treatise on men's physiology and health, while the *Spill* portrayed a variety of women in different professions who aimed to undermine men. In the *Spill*, for instance, a pastry cook and her daughter included men's body parts in their meat pies, while a woman healer provided women who wished to get pregnant with a "stable" of young men, thereby circumventing their husbands' paternity rights. Roig contrasted these malevolent women with the inimitable Virgin, whose moral and bodily integrity was constant.

JEAN DANGLER

References and Further Reading

Alfonso X. *Cantigas de Santa María*. 2 vols. Madrid: Edilán, 1979.
———. *Prosa histórica*, edited by Benito Brancaforte. Madrid: Cátedra, 1990.
Arcipreste de Hita. *Libro de buen amor*, edited and translated by Raymond S. Willis. Princeton, N.J.: Princeton University Press, 1972.
Dīwān de las poetisas de al-Andalus, edited by Teresa Garulo. Madrid: Hiperión, 1998.
The Electronic Texts and Concordances of the Prose Works of Alfonso X, El Sabio, edited by Lloyd Kasten, John Nitti, and Wilhelmina Jonxis-Henkemans. Madison: Hispanic Seminary of Medieval Studies, 1997. CD-ROM.
Haywood, Louise M. "Medieval Spanish Studies." In *The Companion to Hispanic Studies*, edited by Catherine Davies. London: Arnold, 2002, pp. 32–49.
Las jarchas romances y sus moaxajas, edited by Josep M. Solá-Solé. Madrid: Taurus, 1990.
Leyendas épicas españolas, edited by Rosa Castillo. Madrid: Castalia, 1969.
Martínez de Toledo, Alfonso. *Arcipreste de Talavera o Corbacho*, edited by Michael Gerli. Madrid: Cátedra, 1992.
Mirror of Coitus: A Translation and Edition of the Fifteenth-Century Speculum al foderi. Edited and translated by Michael Solomon. Madison: Hispanic Seminary for Medieval Studies, 1990.
Poem of the Cid: A Modern Translation with Notes by Paul Blackburn. Edited by George Economou. Norman: University of Oklahoma Press, 1998.
Poesía de cancionero, edited by Álvaro Alonso. Madrid: Cátedra, 1986.
Poesía femenina hispanoárabe, edited by María Jesús Rubiera Mata. Madrid: Castalia, 1989.
Poetas hebreos de al-Andalus (siglos X–XII): Antología, edited by Ángel Sáenz-Badillos and Judit Targarona Borrás. Córdoba: El Almendro, 1990.
Rojas, Fernando de. *Celestina: A Play in Twenty-One Acts Attributed to Fernando de Rojas*. translated by Mack Hendricks Singleton. Madison: University of Wisconsin Press, 1968.
Rosen, Tova. "The Muwashshah." In *The Literature of Al-Andalus*, edited by María Rosa Menocal, Raymond P. Scheindlin, and Michael Sells. Cambridge: Cambridge University Press, 2000, pp. 165–189.
Solomon, Michael. *The Literature of Misogyny in Medieval Spain: The* Arcipreste de Talavera *and the* Spill. Cambridge: Cambridge University Press, 1997.
Textos y concordancias electrónicos del corpus médico español, edited by María Teresa Herrera and María Estela González de Fauve. Madison: Hispanic Seminary of Medieval Studies, 1997. CD-ROM.
The Writings of Teresa de Cartagena, edited and translated by Dayle Seidenspinner-Núñez. Cambridge: D. S. Brewer, 1998.

See also **Cosmetics; Defenses of Women; Epic, Spanish; Iberia; Mary, Virgin: in Literature; Medicine; Misogyny; Muslim Women: Iberia; Muslim Women: Western Literature; Patronage, Literary; Sentimental Romance; Teresa de Cartagena; Wallāda bint al Mustakfī; Women Authors: Spanish Texts**

LITERATURE, IRISH

Few women in medieval Ireland actually composed works of literature. The bardic poets were exclusively male. To complicate matters, most poetry from early Ireland is anonymous, and the male poets often adopted female *personae*, particularly in love poems and laments. However, several women poets are mentioned in early medieval historical sources. Líadain, the fictionalized character in the ninth-century love story *Líadain and Cuirithir*, is mentioned elsewhere as a female poet. Another woman, Digde, is said to be the speaker of the *Lament of the Old Woman of Beare*. It is possible that nuns composed some anonymous poems such as *Ísucán* ("Jesuskin"), about a vision of the baby Jesus, attributed to St. Íte. Several poems are attributed to the widowed Queen Gormlaith, and some of the *dánta grádha* ("poems of love") were possibly composed by women.

Despite the dearth of verifiable female authors, medieval Irish texts include many female characters. Women appear in a variety of literary genres, including poetry, prose sagas, saints' lives, place-name legends, wisdom literature, legal texts, and annals. The *Banshenchas* (lore of women), which lists the marriages and children of royal women, is an important pseudo-historical text. While most women in heroic, male-centred texts are marginal figures, a number of them play influential roles. Yet depictions of women often reflect the widespread misogyny of medieval European culture; wisdom texts warn of women's faults, and in numerous *dindsenchas* ("lore of place-names") tales, names of geographical features memorialize male–female conflict. The presence of strong women in medieval Irish texts led many nineteenth and twentieth-century scholars to assume that this reflected real-life respect for early medieval women. However, feminist analysis has challenged this view. When female characters do act and speak, they are often criticized, and even blamed for disastrous events. Even the late twelfth-century *Acallamh na Senórach* (Colloquy of the ancients), with its more chivalric ethos, is clearly uneasy about the dangerous power of the feminine.

Romantic notions about heroic women inherited from nineteenth-century cultural nationalism, and the pervasive use of mythological models have, until recently, hampered literary analysis of women in these texts. Mythic paradigms that stress vast time-spans divorce medieval Irish texts from the historical and cultural conditions in which they were composed, rewritten, and received. The mythological approach was fuelled by literary depictions of goddesses of war and death such as the Morrígan, and of supernatural women connected to a pagan Otherworld. Strong women were interpreted as reflections of pre-Christian goddesses, particularly the sovereignty goddess of the land who affirms the next ruler through sexual union with him, often appearing as a hag who transforms herself into a beauty (as in *The Adventures of the Sons of Eochaid Muigmedon*). Many women have been slotted into this paradigm without full consideration of the texts' larger narrative concerns, resulting in simplistic, dehistoricized readings. The most obvious victim is Medb, the great warrior queen of the epic *Táin Bó Cúailgne* (Cattle-Raid of Cooley), whose dominant behavior was explained as typical of a sovereignty goddess.

The last two decades have seen a steady expansion of critical approaches to gender in medieval Irish texts. Herbert showed how the tragic heroine Deirdre could be read as a literary figure not constrained by the sovereignty paradigm. Ní Dhonnchadha's work on *The Lament of the Old Woman of Beare* has suggested that the speaker is a historical woman rather than a goddess. Close readings of the *Táin* by Kelly, Dooley, Ní Bhrolcháin, and others have subjected the text to sustained gender analysis. Findon has analyzed a character with no links to the sovereignty goddess whatsoever: Emer, Cú Chulainn's wife in the Ulster Cycle tales. Recent work has considered the women named Gormlaith, all connected to actual kings, as historical figures reshaped in literary texts in response to political concerns. Volume 4 of *The Field Day Anthology* presents numerous early texts by and about women in medieval Ireland.

Recent studies of saints' lives have intersected with those focusing on secular tales to produce sensitive readings of women. While many female saints such as Brigit, Íte, and Monenna are depicted as strong characters, they are less likely to be censured for their "manly" speech and behavior than secular heroines, because a "masculine spirit" was a positive attribute in a female saint (as long as it did not undermine the male hierarchy). The application of feminist criticism, New Historicism, and other theoretical approaches to these texts is providing new insights into medieval Irish literature.

JOANNE FINDON

References and Further Reading

Bitel, Lisa M. *Land of Women: Tales of Sex and Gender from Early Ireland.* Ithaca, N.Y.: Cornell University Press, 1996.

Bourke, Angela, Siobhan Kilfeather, et al., eds. *The Field Day Anthology of Irish Writing.* Volume IV: *Irish Women's Writing and Traditions.* Cork: Cork University Press, 2002.

Clancy, Thomas Owen. "Women Poets in Early Medieval Ireland: Stating the Case." In *'The Fragility of Her Sex?' Medieval Irish Women in their European Context*, edited by Christine Meek and Katherine Simms. Dublin: Four Courts Press, 1996, pp. 43–72.

Connon, Anne. "The *Banshenchas* and the Uí Néill Queens of Tara." In *Seanchas: Studies in Early Medieval Irish Archaeology, History and Literature in Honour of Francis J. Byrne*, edited by Alfred P. Smyth. Dublin: Four Courts Press, 2000, pp. 98–108.

Cross, Tom Peete, and Clark Harris Slover, trans. *Ancient Irish Tales.* Totowa, N.J.: Barnes & Noble, 1981.

Dooley, Ann. "The Invention of Women in the *Táin*." In *Ulidia: Proceedings of the First International Conference on the Ulster Cycle of Tales*, edited by J. P. Mallory and Gerard Stockman. Belfast: December Publications, 1994, pp. 123–133.

Findon, Joanne. *A Woman's Words: Emer and Female Speech in the Ulster Cycle.* Toronto: University of Toronto Press, 1997.

Herbert, Máire. "Celtic Heroine? The Archaeology of the Deirdre Story." In *Gender in Irish Writing*, edited by Tony O'Brien Johnson and David Cairns. Philadelphia: Open University Press, 1991, pp 13–22.

Johnston, Elva. "Transforming Women in Irish Hagiography." *Peritia* 9 (1995): 197–220.

Kelly, Patricia. "The *Táin* as Literature." In *Aspects of the Táin*, edited by J. P. Mallory. Belfast: December Publications, 1992, pp. 69–102.

Larson, Heather Feldmeth. "The Veiled Poet: *Líadain and Cuirithir* and the Role of the Woman-Poet." In *Heroic Poets and Poetic Heroes in Celtic Tradition*. CSANA Yearbook 3–4. Ed. Joseph Falaky Nagy and Leslie Ellen Jones. Dublin: Four Courts Press: 2005, pp. 263–268.

Murphy, Gerard. *Early Irish Lyrics*. Oxford: Oxford University Press, 1956.

Ní Bhrolcháin, Muireann. "Re Tóin Mná: In Pursuit of Troublesome Women." In *Ulidia*. 1994, pp. 115–121.

Ní Dhonnchadha, Máirín. "*Cailleach* and Other Terms for Veiled Women in Medieval Irish Texts." *Éigse* 28 (1994–1995): 71–96.

———. "Two Female Lovers." *Ériu* 45 (1994): 113–120.

———. "On Gormfhlaith Daughter of Flann Sinna and the Lure of the Sovereignty Goddess." *Seanchas*. Dublin: Four Courts Press, 2000, pp. 225–237.

Ní Mhaonaigh, Máire. "Tales of Three Gormlaiths in Medieval Irish Literature." *Ériu* 52 (2002): 1–24.

See also **Brigit; Hagiography; Ireland; Misogyny; Monasticism and Nuns, Celtic; Supernatural Women; Virile Women**

LITERATURE, ITALIAN

The issue of gender is central in early Italian literature and is clearly posed by the texts themselves: Italian literary texts of this period feature male lover-poets and the female figures that they love. This entry sketches a paradigm for evaluating the treatment of women in this tradition, looking at Italian literature from its lyric origins to Dante, Boccaccio, and Petrarch through the lens of the competing ideological systems to which these authors subscribe: on the one hand, they subscribe to the ideology of courtly love, which permeates the beautiful love poetry for which the tradition is so well known, and, on the other, to an often violent, anti-courtly ideology that permeates their moralistic poetry. These two ideologies underwrite very different attitudes toward women and toward gender.

Courtly vs. Anti-Courtly

The dialectic between courtly and anti-courtly ideologies is a historical constant in this tradition: it is present not only in Dante, but in poets before Dante, like Guittone d'Arezzo, and it is a major feature of Boccaccio's work as well. Poetry based in a courtly logic is narcissistic and centered on the male lover-poet; the female object of desire serves as a screen on which he projects questions and concerns about himself. Whether we are speaking of the early courtly poetry of the Sicilian Giacomo da Lentini or the later theologized courtliness of Dante and his fellow *stilnovisti* (poets of the "new style"), including Guido Cavalcanti and Cino da Pistoia, the fundamental logic of the courtly poem remains narcissistic, as Dante acknowledges in the *Vita nuova*, when he sets himself the task of breaking from it. The didactic works of writers like Guittone d'Arezzo, Dante in his late moral *canzoni*, and Boccaccio, on the other hand, are marked by a utilitarian stamp: women are supposed to *use* this literature, to be instructed by it, to learn from it. These texts demonstrate a need to communicate with women, to treat them as subjects who can learn, rather than as objects to be desired.

The courtly conventions of troubadour love poetry—based on the notion of the lover's feudal service to *midons* (Italian *madonna*), his lady, from whom he expects a *guerdon* (Italian *guiderdone*), or reward—were transplanted to the court of Frederick II in Palermo. Palermo became the capital of the first group of Italian vernacular lyric poets, the so-called Sicilian School, whose leader was Giacomo da Lentini, most likely the inventor of the sonnet. At the heart of troubadour poetry is an unresolved tension between the poet-lover's allegiance to the lady and his allegiance to God, a conflict that Giacomo distills in the sonnet *Io m'aggio posto in core a Dio servire*, where the first quatrain identifies one pole of his desire—he wants to serve God, to go to paradise—while the second quatrain poses the problem: he does not want to go without his lady. The last verse brings together the two terms of the conflict (the lady and paradise) in a nonresolution that keeps the focus of the poem squarely on the "divided" (*diviso*) self of the lover-poet.

From Sicily the courtly lyric moved north to the communes of Tuscany, where it was cultivated by Guittone d'Arezzo, the *caposcuola* of the Tuscan School; Guittone writes love poetry in the courtly style, but unlike Giacomo da Lentini, he also writes moralistic poems like his didactic poem on female chastity, *Altra fiata aggio già, donne, parlato*. This canzone offers an early model of a paradigm that Dante will adopt, whereby paternalistic morality defeats courtliness and ironically enhances the status of women by conceiving them as moral agents. Women are moral agents in Guittone's *canzone*, albeit weak-minded ones, who need to be prodded and pushed in the direction of virtue. Although highest praise is reserved for absolute chastity, Guittone allows that a woman may choose marital chastity over absolute chastity, and he acknowledges a woman's right to desire a husband. Guittone is explicit about the double standard that applies to the sexes: carnal vice is bad in men, but much worse in women. The importance of cover is one of the topoi common to moralizing discourses on female conduct that we find in *Altra fiata*, along with the stress on appropriate speech and the caution against ornamentation. It is significant that Guittone directs his instructions on covering dress and modesty not to a male protector but directly to the woman, who is thus placed in charge of covering herself. Guittone ends *Altra fiata*, a poem that addresses women and "women's issues" throughout, by affirming the moral value and utility of a discourse to and about women.

Dante

The utility of discourse is a theme common to texts addressed to women, as we see in one of Dante's great moral poems, *Doglia mi reca nello core ardire*, a *canzone* whose signature anti-courtliness allows Dante to attack women for their "vile desire" of base men, rather than focusing—as courtly poetry does—exclusively on male desire. It may seem counterintuitive to read the harsh paternalism of *Doglia mi reca* in a progressive light, but Dante accomplishes a lot in this *canzone*. The ladies of *Doglia mi reca* are definitely off the courtly pedestal. They have more to worry about than the behavior of their male lovers: they have to take care of themselves, including their immortal souls, which Dante cautions are in danger of perishing. They have acquired the status of moral agents and although they do not yet speak—an activity for which we have to await characters like Francesca da Rimini in the *Commedia*, where Dante's move to construe women as moral agents rather than as mirrors for male poets is fulfilled—they are expected to be able students, fully receiving and intellectually digesting the poet's message. Whereas the courtly *canzone* frequently opens with a conventional address to ladies who then disappear from the poem (Cavalcanti's *Donna me prega*, Dante's *Donne ch'avete intelletto d'amore*), the female addressees whom Dante enlists in the struggle against vice in *Doglia mi reca* are summoned again at mid-*canzone*: "because I want my discourse to be of use to you, I'll come down from the general to the particular, and to a lighter form of expression, so that it may be less hard to understand." Dante here demonstrates a pedagogic pragmatism that may well be a hallmark of texts addressed to women: the emphasis on the utility of discourse—"perchè lo meo dire *util* vi sia"—anticipates the *Decameron*, a text addressed to women not once or twice but consistently and indefatigably.

Boccaccio

In the *Commedia* women explode the courtly code by becoming speakers, in the case of Beatrice a veritable *Beatrix loquax*, and in Boccaccio's texts as well women are endowed with language. Boccaccio is the Italian author who explicitly places the category "woman" (rather than just a particular woman) at the core of his opus, which ranges from early courtly works in the vernacular to the misogyny of the later *Corbaccio*, also in the vernacular, and the Latin encyclopedic *De mulieribus claris*. At the center of this great woman-oriented literary production stands the *Decameron*. Boccaccio defends his targeting of female readers precisely on the basis of their greater need and his greater utility. Women are cloistered and enclosed, constrained by the wishes of their families and immured in their rooms, while men have access to a host of distracting activities: "men, if they want, are able to walk abroad, see and hear many things, go fowling, hunting, fishing, riding and gambling, or attend to their business affairs" (*Proemio*, 12). This dichotomy between the relative access of men and women to the benefits of human and social intercourse—including sexual—is the ethical template on which Boccaccio constructs his masterpiece.

The *Decameron* belongs to a specific tradition, which, if not feminist, is arguably the tradition in which feminism could later take root. This is the tradition in which female interlocutors are not just tropes, not just part of the poet's self-construction, as they are for courtly poets. Standing between courtliness on the one hand and misogyny on the other, this tradition is moralizing, didactic, utilitarian, pragmatic—and truly addresses issues of women in society.

Petrarch

This tradition—starting with Guittone d'Arezzo and going forward to Boccaccio—is in my view the more open and progressive toward women. It is extremely interesting, from this perspective, that Petrarch did not write moralizing *canzoni* to women like Guittone's *Altra fiata* and Dante's *Doglia mi reca*. His vernacular output does not include such poems; when he turns Boccaccio's programmatically ambiguous Griselda story (*Decameron* 10.10) into a treatise on female obedience he also translates it into Latin, indicating that his target audience is not female. Petrarch forged his identity against Dante's by returning in his vernacular lyric collection *Rerum vulgarium fragmenta* to the courtly paradigm that Dante abandoned, thus institutionalizing a model of gender relations that endured for centuries and that, through the extraordinary network that was European literary Petrarchism, became a cultural trope. In another demonstration—this time in the area of gender roles—of what it means that Petrarch triumphed over Dante as the model for subsequent generations of Italian poets, we can hazard the following: the commitment to female historicity and selfhood that we find, for instance, in Dante's treatment of the damned Francesca da Rimini, is not a feature that we associate with Petrarch, and it is Petrarch who set the agenda for the subsequent Italian literary tradition.

TEODOLINDA BAROLINI

References and Further Reading

Barolini, Teodolinda. "*Le parole son donne e i fatti son maschi*: Toward a Sexual Poetics of the *Decameron* (*Dec.* II 10)." *Studi sul Boccaccio* 21 (1993): 175–197.

———. "Lifting the Veil? Notes toward a Gendered History of Italian Literature." In *Medieval Constructions in Gender and Identity: Essays in Honor of Joan M. Ferrante*, edited by Teodolinda Barolini. Tempe, Ariz.: Arizona Center for Medieval & Renaissance Studies, 2005, pp. 169–188.

Boccaccio, Giovanni. *Il Corbaccio*, edited by Giulia Natali. Milano: Mursia, 1992.

The Corbaccio. translated by Anthony K. Cassell. 2nd ed. rev. Binghamton, N.Y.: Medieval & Renaissance Texts & Studies, 1993.

———. *Decameron*, edited by Vittore Branca. Torino: Einaudi, 1980.

The Decameron. translated by G. H. McWilliam. London: Penguin, 1995.

———. *De mulieribus claris*, edited by V. Zaccaria. Vol. 10. 2nd ed. In *Tutte le opere di Giovanni Boccaccio*. Milano: Mondadori, 1970.

Famous Women. trans. Virginia Brown. Cambridge, Mass.: Harvard University Press, 2001.

Dante Alighieri. *La Commedia secondo l'antica vulgata*, edited by Giorgio Petrocchi. 4 vols. Milano: Mondadori, 1966–1967.

The Divine Comedy of Dante Alighieri. translated by Robert M. Durling. 3 vols. New York: Oxford University Press, 1996.

———. *Rime*, edited by Gianfranco Contini. 2nd ed. rev. Milano: Einaudi, 1965.

Dante's Lyric Poetry, edited and translated by Kenelm Foster and Patrick Boyde. 2 vols. Oxford: Oxford University Press, 1967.

———. *Vita nuova*, edited by Domenico De Robertis. Milano-Napoli: Ricciardi, 1980.

Vita nuova. translated by Dino S. Cervigni and Edward Vasta. South Bend, Ind.: University of Notre Dame Press, 1995.

Ferrante, Joan M. *Woman as Image in Medieval Literature from the Twelfth Century to Dante*. New York: Columbia University Press, 1975.

Jordan, Constance. "Boccaccio's In-Famous Women: Gender and Civic Virtue in the *De mulieribus claris*." In *Ambiguous Realities: Women in the Middle Ages and Renaissance*, edited by Carole Levin and Jeanie Watson. Detroit: Wayne State University Press, 1987, pp. 25–47.

Kirkpatrick, Robin. "The Griselda Story in Boccaccio, Petrarch, and Chaucer." In *Chaucer and the Italian Trecento*, edited by Piero Boitani. Cambridge: Cambridge University Press, 1983, pp. 231–248.

Migiel, Marilyn. *A Rhetoric of the Decameron*. Toronto: University of Toronto Press, 2003.

Petrarca, Francesco. *Epistolae Seniles* 17.3. Italian translation: "Sulla straordinaria obbedienza e fedeltà coniugale." In *Opere latine di Francesco Petrarca*. 2 vols. edited by Antonietta Bufano. Torino: UTET, 1970, pp. 1313–1339. *Petrarch: The First Modern Scholar and Man of Letters*. Translated by Harvey Robinson. 2nd ed. New York: Greenwood Press, 1969.

———. *Rerum vulgarium fragmenta*. 2 vols. edited by Rosanna Bettarini. Torino: Einaudi, 2005.

Petrarch's Lyric Poems. translated by Robert M. Durling. Cambridge, Mass.: Harvard University Press, 1976.

Vickers, Nancy. "Diana Described: Scattered Woman and Scattered Rhyme." *Critical Inquiry* 8 (1981): 265–279.

See also **Beatrice; Boccaccio, Giovanni; Chastity and Chaste Marriage; Conduct Literature; Courtly Love; Dante Alighieri; Defenses of Women; Education, Lay; Griselda; Italy; Literature, Occitan; Misogyny; Petrarch; Women Authors: Italian**

LITERATURE, LATIN

At the turn of the third millennium, the field of medieval women's studies in general, and in particular the still quite under-researched subfield of Latin literatures, is very much in flux. Since the topic has only recently found serious scholarly attention, there are no definitive studies, but there is a great deal of activity, with an astonishing array of very high-quality collaborative ventures (essay collections, handbooks) leading the way. Recent studies have been opening up multiple new perspectives, and also complicating what we might mean by "women in literature," using newer strains of cultural studies, feminist theory, psychoanalysis, and queer theory, as well as new archival research, to rethink women's roles, and the gendering of medieval Latin literature in general.

A few initial cautions are necessary. First, it is debatable whether there is such a thing as "medieval Latin literature." Unlike the vernacular literatures, which have fairly tight geographical and even temporal boundaries, "medieval Latin" covers all of western Europe and as much as a thousand years, from about 500 to about 1500. Second, we need to consider what we mean by "literature." Since the vast majority of written texts in the medieval West are in Latin, by a broad definition—"all written texts"—"Latin literature" would cover almost the entire intellectual output of the millennium under consideration. By a narrow definition, on the other hand, modeled anachronistically on what we might expect to find in the "literature" section of our local bookstore—"nontechnical texts suitable for the serious leisure reading of educated persons"—the material under consideration would be fairly limited, and somewhat dispersed and fragmented, since Latin is for the Middle Ages the language of higher learning, of the church, of "clerical culture" in general; leisure reading, while by no means lacking, plays by definition a marginal role. (The vernacular literatures, by contrast, are dominated by the fictional, the sociable, the courtly, the nonclerkly, and "nonserious"; they come to technical and learned subject matters relatively late.) By the same token—Latin being synonymous with clerical culture—Latin literature is predominantly male in authorship, readership, and ethos. While the rise of vernacular literatures has often persuasively been linked to increased female patronage and readership, Latin has been called western Europe's "father tongue," with all the patriarchal overtones this implies. If Latin culture does not actively exclude women, it certainly does not actively seek to include them either.

For these reasons all studies of women in medieval literature oscillate between two opposite but not unconnected poles: describing, on the one hand, women's undoubted marginalization in a male-dominated society, and in almost exclusively male ecclesiastical and educational structures; and seeking to emphasize, on the other hand, the strong and vibrant contributions women have managed to make all the same. Indeed, it has been observed that the older critical assumption that women were largely excluded from the high culture of the Middle Ages has in itself contributed to rendering women invisible. We tend not to find what we do not look for, and newer studies have indeed found far more female participation in medieval culture, including Latin culture.

Participation of Women in Latin Literary Culture

As recent research has shown, quite a few women—more than used to be thought—did acquire Latin literacy. Systematic instruction was sometimes available at monastic schools. Heloise was well-known for her exceptional learning, but she must have had classmates at Argenteuil who also achieved a certain level of education. Goscelin of St. Bertin not only assumes that Eva's education at Wilton will enable her to read the difficult Latin of the *Liber confortatorius* he wrote for her, but in it he also outlines an ambitious reading program for her. Some women learned their Latin more casually, by daily exposure: Hildegard of Bingen, despite her prodigious output in Latin, remained unsure of her grammar all her life and had it corrected by an amanuensis. There were women who wrote in Latin; there were women who commissioned or sponsored Latin literature; there were women who could and did read it, and their involvement left a mark on the genres they touched, in particular epistolary and devotional literature.

Letters

Letters are a genre in which women are particularly well represented, both as addressees and as writers, and it shows particularly well the odd dialectic of exclusion and inclusion previously mentioned. Even though medieval letters are not the personal or informal genre we think of today, its more restricted range, more intimate nature, and quite often the involvement of male correspondents seem to make it easier for women to participate. Yet there are some limits. The influential patristic models of Ambrose's and Jerome's extensive correspondence with female friends and spiritual advisees set a pattern of male-female exchanges that, on the one hand, accords the highest respect to the female correspondent (usually a woman of some social standing), but also places her in the role of advisee, narrowly circumscribing her authority and the roles open to her even as they praise her. In the high medieval version of this set-up the male ecclesiastical writer (e.g., Hildebert of Lavardin) is at least nominally inferior to the abbesses, noble women, and queens with whom he exchanges letters. Some letters or texts with epistolary features—such as Baudri of Bourgueil's long poem "To Countess Adela"—play with this status incongruence: it is a didactic compendium of history, geography, and the Seven Liberal Arts, written with the highest deference and lavish praise, but also with schoolmasterly authority and even sly seductiveness.

Even though medieval Latin scarcely participates in the *fin'amors* pattern of the courts, some scholars have detected notes of it in the patronage relationship of this sort of text. Longer works of spiritual advice—letters that expand into book length, such as Goscelin of St. Bertin's *Liber confortatorius* for the recluse Eva, Aelred of Rievaulx's *De institutione inclusarum*, addressed to his sister, or Abelard's advisory correspondence with Heloise—further thematize and complicate these delicate relationships of deference and control.

But not all women's letters are in this mold. Joan Ferrante's online project "Epistolae," has recently made available a magnificent sampling of medieval women's correspondence, often between two women. Hildegard of Bingen's huge correspondence includes political advice to the powerful, health and spiritual advice to anyone who requested it, and personal correspondence with female and male friends; yet Hildegard, in particular, struggles explicitly with the question of what sort of public teaching voice is appropriate and permissible for a woman. Epistolary expression can permit extensive self-statements and the beginnings of autobiography. Hildegard's is preserved in fragments in her secretary's account of her life; Heloise can be said to be writing a (partial) autobiography in response to and around Abelard's far more coherent and assertive one.

The Misogynist Tradition and the "Defense of Women"

Given the vastness of "medieval Latin literature," it is impossible to generalize about its "image" or even "images" of women. Nor is Latin literature clearly demarcated from the vernaculars; there is much crossover in both directions. There is a strong and much-analyzed composite tradition of misogynist discourses, made up of biblical, scientific, patristic, and popular sources, which relentlessly reiterate, often in catalog form, the same antifemale images and themes. A chief source is Jerome's *Against Jovinian*. The manifestations of this genre range from brief jingles to lengthy diatribes such as Marbod's *De matrona*, antimatrimonial treatises like Walter Map's or the anonymous *De coniuge non ducenda*. Their counterparts, the "Dignities of Women," or what Blamires calls the "Defense of Women," are, for the most part, closely linked to the misogynist tradition; even though some (especially Abelard's letter on nuns) are eloquent and thoughtful, more often they are full of backhanded compliments and restrictive ideals of feminine virtue, and, above all, so closely based on the misogynist models that they tend to reinforce rather than counteract them. Besides, as the Wife of Bath and Virginia Woolf pointed out, the sheer mass of male professors' opinions on women, positive or negative, tends to be oppressive.

Hagiography

Needless to say, few genres so explicitly engage in blame and praise; most texts handle women's images, for better and for worse, in far more nuanced ways. Hagiography, another genre where women figure prominently both as subjects and as readers (and to some extent as authors), can serve as a focus for our observations. It is by definition a formulaic genre, seeking to demonstrate a subject's conformity to certain types, and the schemata available for women are particularly limited. Yet medieval hagiography of women inherits from antiquity a few highly productive and artistically appealing prototypes, in particular the virgin martyr, a young woman proudly defending her faith and sexual integrity through torture and execution; and the desert ascetic and/or "penitent whore" derived from the *Vitae Patrum* literature that offers such intriguing figures as Mary Magdalen, Thais, or Mary of Egypt. (Hrotsvit of Gandersheim uses several of these stories in her tenth-century Latin plays.) Both types of figures seem to have been of interest to medieval women who chose lives of monastic virginity or contemplative seclusion, and such texts were often offered as reading matter to them. To what extent they offer strong role models (the brash virgin martyr talking truth to power and defending her physical integrity; the "desert mothers" achieving astonishing feats of asceticism and self-sufficiency, as well as great authority), and to what extent they are controlling, punitive, and even close to pornographic (graphic, often sexualized violence inflicted on the martyrs; the emphasis on humiliation and penance in the "penitent whore" type) is open to debate.

Besides hagiographies of historically distant saints, there are lives of more contemporary women that for all their references to hagiographical types develop some individual, biographical features. A prime example, now much studied and frequently taught, is the *Life of Christina of Markyate*. One can perhaps extend the genre to include biographical works on secular women, who sometimes figure as patrons as well as subjects of such texts: the English queens Emma and Edith both commissioned and probably oversaw the writing of biographical narratives that favored their political perspectives. In such texts, the interplay between hagiographic topos and biographical detail is often both illuminating and artistically intriguing.

The Virgin Mary occupies a place apart in female hagiography and devotional literature more generally. Prayers to the Virgin become a distinct subgenre of Latin devotional texts in the central Middle Ages. The collections of Miracles of the Virgin, of great popularity in most vernacular European languages, did begin in Latin; they furnish an extraordinary picture of an all-powerful yet emotionally accessible mother figure intervening on behalf of her childlike devotees—an image, it seems, at least as popular with male as with female readers.

Conclusion

This necessarily limited, selected, and unsystematic set of notes can only serve as a first appetite-whetting introduction to some of the questions researchers can ask. There are many fields of medieval literature (the secular lyric; prosopopeias or *planctus* inspired by Ovid's *Heroides*; drama, both secular and religious; Latin "romances," if that is not a contradiction in terms, and Latin epics; short narratives in collections like Walter Map's *De nugis curialium*, the *Dolopathus/ Seven Sages* tradition, or in collections of preachers' exempla) that are not yet extensively studied at all, and would repay analysis from a gender point of view. Anyone interested in this line of research should not be deterred by the lack of comprehensive overviews, but rather be inspired by the wide range of approaches and leads in what is an open and exciting field.

MONIKA C. OTTER

References and Further Reading

Blamires, Alcuin. *Women Defamed and Women Defended.* Oxford: Clarendon Press, 1992.

Dear Sister: Medieval Women and the Epistolary Genre, edited by Karen Cherewatuk and Ulrike Wiethaus. Philadelphia: University of Pennsylvania Press, 1993.

Fanous, Samuel, and Henrietta Leyser. *Christina of Markyate: A Twelfth-Century Holy Woman.* London: Routledge, 2004.

Ferrante, Joan M. "Epistolae: Medieval Women's Latin Letters." http://db.ccnmtl.columbia.edu/ferrante/

————. *To the Glory of Her Sex: Women's Roles in the Composition of Medieval Texts.* Bloomington, Ind.: Indiana University Press, 1997.

Gold, Barbara K., Paul Allen Miller, and Charles Platter, eds. *Sex and Gender in Medieval and Renaissance Texts: The Latin Tradition.* Albany: State University of New York Press, 1997.

Hemptinne, Thérèse de, and María Eugenia Góngora, eds. *The Voice of Silence: Women's Literacy in a Men's Church.* Turnhout: Brepols, 2004.

Hollis, Stephanie, et al., eds. *Writing the Wilton Women: Goscelin's Legend of Edith and Liber Confortatorius.* Turnhout: Brepols, 2004.

Townsend, David, and Andrew Taylor, eds. *The Tongue of the Fathers: Gender and Ideology in Twelfth-Century Latin.* Philadelphia: University of Pennsylvania Press, 1998.

See also **Christina of Markyate; Defenses of Women; Education, Monastic; Exemplum; Feminist Theories and Methodologies; Goscelin of St. Bertin; Hagiography; Heloise; Hildegard of Bingen; Hrotsvit of Gandersheim; Jerome, Influence of; Letter Writing; Literacy and Reading: Latin; Mary, Virgin: in Literature; Miracles and Miracle Collections; Misogyny; Patronage, Literary; Psychoanalytic Theory; Queer Theory; Virgin Martyrs; Wife of Bath**

LITERATURE, MIDDLE ENGLISH

The emergence of Middle English as a literary language resulted from a complex series of interrelated social, political and historical factors following the Norman Conquest in 1066. English (Anglo-Saxon) lost its prestige as the language of cultural expression and the law, although it survived in spoken form. What may be called an antiquarian movement to preserve the language existed chiefly in monasteries in the west of England, but when early Middle English made its first appearance, it was characterized by a blend of converging linguistic and cultural traditions—Latin, French or Anglo-Norman, Welsh, and English—whether in actual content, or by influence. Even by the fourteenth century, when in 1362 English gained primacy as the language of Parliament, traces of cosmopolitanism remained, with some manuscripts being either bi- or multilingual in their selection of texts; and some authors, such as John Gower (d. 1408), choosing to write in different languages for different audiences and purposes.

Saints' Lives and Exemplary Literature

It is a happy coincidence for this volume that among the earliest flowerings of Middle English were texts about, and designed in large part for the consumption of, women, for example the so-called "Katherine Group." This collection dates from c. 1190–1230 and consists of lives of the virgin martyrs Catherine, Margaret of Antioch, and Juliana, supplemented by a letter given the modern editorial title of *Hali Meiðhad*, a treatise persuading women to eschew marriage and childbirth, and an allegory, *Sawles Ward*, regarding the safeguarding of the soul. The lives, as internal references make clear, were intended for listeners, as well as readers. All are exemplary texts and are closely connected with the *Ancrene Wisse*, the ever-popular guide for anchoresses, written originally for three sisters in Herefordshire. The taste for saints' lives continued throughout the medieval period: The *South English Legendary*, including legends of many women, survives in different versions in over fifty manuscripts dating from the late-thirteenth to the early-fifteenth century; while the *Gilte Legende*, in large part a translation from the late-thirteenth-century Latin *Legenda aurea* of Jacobus Voragine, may be placed in between the late-fourteenth or early-fifteenth centuries: Among the women commemorated are Saints Dorothy, Thais, Pelagia, and Mary Magdalen. There is thus some overlap with the *Legendys of Hooly Wummen* by Osbern Bokenham, which he started compiling in 1443, and for which an element of female patronage is certain. The taste for exemplary texts for women, including ones from earlier centuries, continued late into the Middle Ages with, for instance, the two English translations of *De institutione inclusarum* written by Aelred of Rievaulx (1110–1167) for his sister. These survive in Bodleian Library MS Eng. Poet. a.1 (the Vernon MS) of the last decade of the fourteenth century and Bodley 423, copied by the scribe Stephen Dodesham, latterly in his life a Carthusian monk, who died 1481–1482. The audience for the first of these copies was probably women: perhaps nuns or a community of wealthy laywomen.

Courtly Lyric and Lovers' Complaints

In strong contrast to the devotional strain of writing is the ubiquitous, usually anonymous, courtly love lyric, written in a variety of verse forms. These typically follow a similar pattern and mode of expression: The male Lover complains of unrequited love, and there is an abundance of refined emotion and language. They thus constitute the opposite of those other lyrics, often ribald, voiced by women, which fall into the category of antifeminist literature. (An important exception to this general rule is the fifteenth-century "Findern" lyrics, apparently composed by women, which complain of a lover's or husband's absences.) There is a degree of overlap between the brief courtly lyric and the longer complaint: *The Complaint of the Black Knight* by the Benedictine John Lydgate (d. 1449), for example, is a tapestry of courtly motifs and emotions, and is deeply indebted to Chaucer's *Boke of the Duchesse*, in which the complaint of the Man in Black is embedded within an allegorical dream-poem concerning the hunting of the hart. The absent heroine, White, represents the epitome of the courtly Other, in her beauty, her modesty, and her ultimate inaccessibility—through death. Arguably the most ambitious of these types of poem is the series by Charles d'Orléans (d. 1465), which he translated into English from his French original while a prisoner of war. In this elegant series of ballades and roundels, Charles presents what can be interpreted as a narrative sequence recounting a relationship with a distant Lady, her death, and his subsequent courtship of another.

Among longer poems, Chaucer's *Legend of Good Women* (c.1386) breaks ground barely touched in English previously. Again framed within a dream in which Chaucer is ordered by the God of Love to write of steadfast women (a secular Legendary) in penance for having traduced the female sex by his portrayal of Criseyde, the nine women's stories which survive (the

text may never have been completed) are sufficiently ambiguous for little critical consensus to have been reached over whether they are ironic or a genuine experimentation with a new form of writing. Whichever the case, while some of the women are treated with sympathy (Dido, for instance), others barely figure within their own tales. That of Medea, for example, scarcely features her notorious history, concentrating instead on Jason's perfidy. Gower's *Confessio amantis* owes much to Chaucer's notion of framing: Like the *Legend*, it utilizes Ovid, only here the tales are taken to illustrate moral behaviour inculcated in the complainant, the Lover, by his confessor, Venus, who finally advises him to retire from the pursuit of Love, on account of his age. Thus are the complaint and the exemplar fused.

Romance

Within the broad spectrum of texts that go to make up the unwieldy genre of romance are many texts in which women are not only the passive objects of desire, but also the active protagonists through whom the hero achieves his goal, leading to eventual union within marriage. That this is so from the beginnings of romance in Middle English is demonstrated by *King Horn* (c. 1225), translated from Anglo-Norman: Rymenhild's physical passion for Horn is fully legitimized within the text, and it is she who initiates his knighting by her father and thus the action of the poem. In *Sir Degrevaunt* (c. 1400) it is the heroine, Meliador, alone, who brings about reconciliation between the Arthurian knight and her father. John Metham, in his *Amoryus and Cleopes* (1448–1449), echoes Chaucer and Lydgate, and in the depiction of Cleopes there are reminiscences of Medea's story of her relationship with Jason, as Cleopes prepares Amoryus with advice on how to overcome a dragon that is destroying their country. Other women in romance may be described as strong because, like Griselda, they demonstrate steadfastness in the face of adversity. The tales which come under the heading of "the calumniated wife" include *The King of Tars*, *Octavian* (respectively early- and mid-fourteenth century), and *Le Bone Florence of Rome* (late fourteenth century). Connected with these is the fragmentary early-fourteenth-century *Lay le Freine*, a translation from the French by Marie de France, in which Freine is tested by her lover, who purposes to marry Freine's twin sister from whom she was separated at birth. Women's strength is not, however, always represented as a positive in the romances. In another translation from Marie's *Lais*, Thomas

Chestre's *Sir Launfal* (second half of the fifteenth century), Launfal's benign fairy lover is counterpoised by a jealous and vindictive Guinivere, who tries to have the knight killed after he rejects her sexual advances. Perhaps the ultimate antiheroine is Morgan le Fay, King Arthur's half-sister who, in Sir Thomas Malory's Arthuriad, attempts to slay her brother, and destroy the Round Table.

Antifeminism and the Woman Question in Middle English

It was not solely in anonymous lyrics (such as those previously mentioned) and fabliaux, in which antifeminism was rampant in the Middle Ages. Debate still continues, for example, over the extent of Lydgate's antifeminism, demonstrated in lyrics such as "Horns Away," in which he decries women's fashionable extremes, and others in which he criticizes their lack of steadfastness. Elsewhere, due in large measure to the teachings of the church and medical theories as to the female constitution, women were all too often seen as the gateway to man's damnation. This is so even in devotional texts designed for their use. The author of *Ancrene Wisse* describes how the eyes and ears of Eve led to the downfall of mankind, because of her gaze directed to the apple and her willingness to listen to Satan; while the description of the physical deformity and torments of pregnancy in *Hali Meiðhad*, although ostensibly designed for the higher purpose of preserving chastity, has a distinct element of misogyny in its revulsion at the female body. Yet it was not until Chaucer opened the way for debate with his fictionalized criticism of his depiction of Criseyde in the Prologue to *The Legend of Good Women* that the matter became a staple of literary discussion. There was no English Christine de Pizan and no high-profile quarrel over *Le Roman de la Rose*, as there was in France. Yet one of Christine's works was translated into English in 1402, which helped to spark a literary debate: Thomas Hoccleve, follower of Chaucer and a clerk of the Privy Seal in London, wrote his *Letter of Cupid* in 1402, in which he invokes the *Legend*, in itself a controversial act. And his translation did not apparently go down well in all quarters. In his "Dialogue with a Friend," written as part of the *Series* around 1419–1420, the "Friend" reprimands Hoccleve for abusing women in this work, for which reason they are still angry with him. The writer disputes the blame attached to him, but is advised to write to please women in the future. Nevertheless, the *Letter* was one of Hoccleve's most widely copied works, surviving in eleven codices, often in conjunction with other poems about women, not least various tales from Chaucer's *Legend*. Another text which finds its way into this manuscript collocation is the largely accurate English translation by Sir Richard Ros (d. 1482) of Alain Chartier's *La Belle Dame Sans Merci*, which itself had provoked controversy in the French court. The meaning of the poem is ambiguous, in that the disdainful Lady refuses the Lover's advances in terms reminiscent of Christine's advice as to the appropriate response to be taken against "avauntors" or boasters, but ends with the death of the spurned Lover from a broken heart. The contexts in which it survives, though, indicate the extent to which antifeminism was being actively challenged by audiences towards the end of the Middle Ages in England.

CAROL M. MEALE

References and Further Reading

Boffey, Julia. *Manuscripts of English Courtly Love Lyrics in the Later Middle Ages*. Woodbridge, Suffolk: D. S. Brewer, 1985.
———. "Lydgate's Lyrics and Women Readers." In *Women, the Book and the Worldly*, edited by Lesley Smith and Jane Taylor. Cambridge: D. S. Brewer, 1995, pp. 139–149.
The Cambridge History of Medieval English Literature, edited by David Wallace. Cambridge: Cambridge University Press, 1999.
The English Works of John Gower, edited by G. C. Macaulay. 2 vols. EETS ES 81, 82. London, New York, and Toronto: Oxford University Press, 1900–1901.
Fortunes Stabilnes: Charles of Orléan's English Book of Love. A Critical Edition, edited by Mary-Jo Arn. Binghamton, N.Y.: Center for Medieval and Early Renaissance Studies, State University of New York at Binghamton, 1994.
Hoccleve's Works: The Minor Poems, edited by Frederick J. Furnivall and I. Gollancz. Revised by Jerome Mitchell and A. I. Doyle. EETS ES 61, 73. Reprinted in one volume, London: Oxford University Press, 1970.
Legendys of Hooly Wummen by Osbern Bokenham, edited by Mary J. Serjeantson. EETS OS 206. London: Humphrey Milford, 1938.
A Manual of Writings in Middle English 1050–1500. Vol.1: *Romances*, edited by J. Burke Severs. New Haven, Conn.: Connecticut Academy of Arts and Sciences, 1967.
Meale, Carol M. "The Tale and the Book: Readings of Chaucer's *Legend of Good Women* in the Fifteenth Century." In *Chaucer in Perspective: Middle English Essays in Honour of Norman Blake*, edited by Geoffrey Lester. Sheffield: Sheffield Academic Press, 1999, pp. 118–138.
Medieval English Prose for Women: Selections from the Katherine Group and Ancrene Wisse, edited by Bella Millett and Jocelyn Wogan-Browne. Oxford: Clarendon Press, 1990.
Morse, Ruth. *The Medieval Medea*. Cambridge: D. S. Brewer, 1996.
Pearsall, Derek. *John Lydgate*. London: Routledge and Kegan Paul, 1970.

————. *Old English and Middle English Poetry*. London, Henley, and Boston: Routledge and Kegan Paul, 1977.

Poems of Cupid, God of Love, edited and translated by Thelma S. Fenster and Mary Carpenter Erler. Leiden and New York: E. J. Brill, 1990.

The Riverside Chaucer. Gen. Ed. Larry D. Benson. Boston: Houghton Mifflin, 1987.

Utley, Francis Lee. *The Crooked Rib: An Analytical Index to the Argument about Women in English and Scots Literature to the End of the Year 1568*. Columbus, Ohio.: Ohio State University, 1944.

Women of the Gilte Legende: A Selection of Middle English Saints' Lives, edited and translated by Larissa Tracy. Cambridge: D.S. Brewer, 2003.

The Works of Sir Thomas Malory, edited by Eugène Vinaver. Revised by P. J. C. Field. Third edition in three vols. Oxford: Clarendon Press, 1990.

See also **Anchoresses; Ancrene Wisse; Arthurian Literature; Belle Dame Sans Merci; Bokenham, Osbern; Chaucer, Geoffrey; Christine de Pizan; Constance; Courtly Love; Criseyde; Defenses of Women; Devotional Literature; Drama; Fabliau; Griselda; Guinivere; Hagiography; Jacobus de Voragine's Golden Legend; Julian of Norwich; Katherine Group; Kempe, Margery; Marie de France; Misogyny; Ovid, Medieval Reception of; Roman de la Rose and Its Reception; Romance: English; Translation; Wife of Bath; Woman's Song; Women Authors: Middle English Texts**

LITERATURE, OCCITAN

Occitan, also known as Provençal, is the Romance language of the South of France made illustrious by the troubadours, lyric poets of the High Middle Ages. Occitan became recognized as a vehicle for lyric expression in Spain and Italy, and inspired imitation in northern France, Germany, and elsewhere. The term *Provençal* is now regarded as obsolete because of the inescapable suggestion that it refers to Provence, that is, the part of the Midi that lies to the east of the Rhône. Occitan (formed on the word *oc*, "yes") includes Provence as well as the regions to the west, roughly the southern third of modern France.

The earliest traces of written Occitan date from before the millennium. From the late tenth century we have Occitan blended with Latin in legal documents, charms for practicing folk medicine, and a brief narrative of the Passion, perhaps the text of a paraliturgical carol. From the eleventh century we have two narratives: the *Boeci*, which paraphrases Boethius's *Consolation of Philosophy*, and the *Chanson de sainte Foy*, the life of a child saint. We also have three short texts that anticipate troubadour lyric: a bilingual *alba*, or dawn song, with an Occitan refrain that seems to symbolize the resurrection of Christ, and two fragmentary secular lyrics. In one a lover imagines himself as a falcon that could fly to his lady; the other has been interpreted as an invective against lecherous nuns.

The era of the troubadours spans two and a half centuries, from about 1100 to 1350. The first whose works we have is Guilhem IX, duke of Aquitaine and count of Poitou (born 1071, died 1126), who ranges from declarations of passionate desire to sexual comedy to a moving song of departure from the world. In the so-called second generation were Jaufre Rudel, who sang his yearning for love from afar, which—very unlike Guilhem IX—he professed to prefer to love near to hand, and the mercurial Marcabru, a satirist of loose mores among the aristocracy who also wrote sympathetically of a girl whose lover has left her to go on Crusade, or of a shepherdess who skillfully parries the advances of a lusty suitor. The late twelfth century saw the apogee of troubadour art in the love songs of Bernart de Ventadorn, who sang his tortured feelings, his confusion, and his desire, and in the political songs of Bertran de Born, who urged the barons of Aquitaine to plunge into combat as a tonic for the soul. The satirical tradition continued in the thirteenth century with Peire Cardenal, the longest-lived troubadour, who for nearly seventy years sang of the corruption of the clergy, his sympathy with the Albigensian heretics, and his own orthodox faith. Late in the century Guiraut Riquier was a poet and a bureaucrat in the service of lords in Narbonne and Spain, who sang that he felt he had come too late. Even later, the cleric Raimon Cornet, in the early fourteenth century, wrote religious and comical verse.

In all the names of some 360 troubadours, who left about 2,500 poems, are known, including perhaps as many as fifty by trobairitz, or women troubadours. About ten percent of these poems are transmitted with notation of their melodies. It seems likely that many more had melodic accompaniment, though it is not certain that all of them were intended for musical performance. The medium of troubadour art probably moved from musical composition at the beginning in the direction of verbal art without music, which would flourish in the Italian poetry of the Sicilian poets, the "Sweet new style" of Dante and his friends, and Petrarch, who spent half his adult life in Provence. Petrarch, who returned to Italy in 1353, may be regarded as the last of the troubadours.

The narrative tradition continued with an Arthurian burlesque, the *Romance of Jaufre*; a verse chronicle of the crusade against the Albigensian heretics in the early thirteenth century, the *Chanson de la Croisade*, by two poets, Guilhem de Tudela, from Spain, who supported the crusading cause, and a more gifted but anonymous sympathizer with the Albigensians; and the *Romance of Flamenca* (late thirteenth century), a romantic comedy in which the heroine and her lover outwit her jealous husband. In the late fourteenth and fifteenth centuries poetry of the School of Toulouse became limited to poets of that city, and literary expression became restricted to religious themes.

WILLIAM D. PADEN

References and Further Reading

Anthology of the Provençal Troubadours. edited by R. T. Hill and T. G. Bergin. 2nd ed. New Haven: Yale University Press, 1973.

Aubrey, Elizabeth. *The Music of the Troubadours.* Bloomington, Ind.: Indiana University Press, 1996.

Ghil, Eliza Miruna. *L'Age de parage: essai sur le poétique et le politique en Occitanie au XIIIe siècle.* New York: Lang, 1989.

A Handbook of the Troubadours. edited by F. R. P. Akehurst and Judith M. Davis. Berkeley: University of California Press, 1995.

Introduction à l'étude de l'ancien provençal: textes d'étude. edited by Frank R. Hamlin, Peter T. Ricketts, and John Hathaway. 2nd ed. Genève: Droz, 1985.

Lafont, Robert, and Christian Anatole. *Nouvelle histoire de la littérature occitane.* 2 vols. Paris: Presses Universitaires de France, 1970.

Lazzerini, Lucia. *Letteratura medievale in lingua d'oc.* Modena: Mucchi, 2001.

Limentani, Alberto. *L'eccezione narrativa: la Provenza medievale e l'arte del racconto.* Torino: G. Einaudi, 1977.

Paden, William D. *An Introduction to Old Occitan.* New York: The Modern Language Association of America, 1998.

———. "Petrarch as a Poet of Provence." *Annali d'italianistica* 22 (2004): 19–44.

Les troubadours, [1:] *Jaufre, Flamenca, Barlaam et Josaphat;* [2:] *Le trésor poétique de l'Occitanie.* edited by René Nelli and René Lavaud. Bruges: Desclée de Brouwer, 1960–1966.

The Troubadours: An Introduction. edited by Simon Gaunt and Sarah Kay. Cambridge: Cambridge University Press, 1999.

Los trovadores: historia literaria y textos. edited by Martín de Riquer. 3 vols. Barcelona: Planeta, 1975.

See also **Dawn Song (Alba); Foy; Pastourelle; Petrarch; Roman de Flamenca; Trobairitz and Troubadours**

LITERATURE, OLD ENGLISH

Old English literature is traditionally understood as poetry composed from the sixth through the eleventh centuries in English. It exists primarily in four late-tenth-century manuscripts, essentially anonymous or traditional, and represents just a fragment of the formal written and oral discourses that must have circulated in the Anglo-Saxon period. *Beowulf*, the most famous example, is discussed seperately in this volume. This extant verse—altogether about the length of the *Iliad* alone—was inscribed within a monastic or clerical environment and so represents to some degree

that element in the culture, many of the texts being deeply influenced by Latin and Greek sources. Though the society included pagan, Germanic, and possibly Celtic, as well as Romano-Christian beliefs and practices, those divergent beliefs were refracted through the lenses of ecclesiastically trained scribes, producing a vision of the culture very different from that revealed in laws, penitentials, and other nonliterary texts. The anonymity of the verse prevents our knowing whether women composed any vernacular verse, but literate women, such as Hild of Whitby and Leoba, played prominent roles in the early Anglo-Saxon church. Additionally, recent paleographic study has begun to reveal the depth and extent of women's involvement in the production of manuscripts (Brown). Whether composed and inscribed by women or by men, the texts show us not a single, hegemonic characterization of women or gender but rather portrayals addressing issues of political responsibility, pious heroism, and the procreative body and family.

In *Genesis*, Eve assumes responsibility for the well-being of her familial group, desires knowledge, and generally acts on a par with Adam. She is a sympathetic character, developed through extensive dialogue between Eve and the messenger sent by Satan, as well as her conversations with Adam. As with the other versifications of the biblical texts that comprise the Junius 11 manuscript (*Genesis*, *Exodus*, and *Daniel*, and *Christ and Satan*), a rich variety of Latin sources, as well as Germanic culture, has influenced her portrait, including the Old Saxon source from which this section is translated (Doane). In it the messenger tempts Adam before angrily turning to Eve with more persuasive rhetoric, offering her the possibility of seeing the whole world and God's throne, as well as of saving Adam from God's anger at having denied his "messenger" (lines 547–587). She succumbs not because of lust or pride but because of the devil's lies, remaining the "brightest" and "most beautiful" of ladies (626–634). The narrator concedes that "she did it through loyal intent" toward Adam as her lord (708–710). Some have suggested that this motivation derives from Germanic culture. In *Christ and Satan*, at the end of the manuscript, Eve also proclaims her own worth so as not to be left behind when Christ harrows hell, asserting through repeated dual pronouns that she and Adam (*wit*, "we two") acted together. She clinches her argument, however, through the special merit of motherhood, declaring to Christ, "Lo, you from my daughter, lord, were born," after which she herself "shove[s] the wretched monster into the profound darkness" and ascends with her kin to heaven (444–446).

The political powers of prominent mothers can be seen in *Elene*, a poetic version of the discovery of the

True Cross. After a vision of the Cross enables the Emperor Constantine to win a crucial battle, he sends his mother "Elene" (Helen) on a journey to recover the Cross. After crossing the sea, she verbally combats the Jews to reveal the Cross's location and converts one, Judas, who becomes St. Cyriacus. After delegating him to find the nails of the cross, she has the nails made into a war bridle for Constantine, promoting her son's military ambition. The heroic formulas that name Elene's actions show them to be as lofty as those in other poems in the Vercelli Book—*Andreas*, *The Fates of the Apostles*, and *The Dream of the Rood*—which focus on the heroism of Christ, his apostles, and the Cross. Though being the emperor's mother largely defines her political role, her feminine sexuality does not shape the narrative.

The body's sexuality and reproductive drives are deeply problematic in the clerical environment of the verse. The Old English version of the apocryphal book of Judith provides a rare representation. In a manuscript that has been thought to focus on "monsters" (including those of *Beowulf*), the overly passionate Assyrian general Holofernes is besieging the Hebrew town of Bethulia, where the pious yet sensually beautiful widow, Judith, resides. Heroically, she chooses to use her body's attractiveness to be admitted to Holofernes' inner chamber and so slay him as he lies in a drunken stupor. While lust saps strength from him and his army, Judith's piety gives her strength to inspire her people to victory.

The Exeter Book takes on the reproductive body beginning with its opening verses celebrating Christ's Advent. Developed from the Advent Antiphons, the lyrics celebrate Mary's role in making God human but expose the Catholic doctrinal discomfort with reproductive sexuality. In a dialogue Joseph and Mary attempt to cope with the gossip about her pregnancy, and she reassures him that she is not so much pregnant as illumined with a light, that she is God's "temple" (203–209). Mary then becomes the "golden gates" that God will "purify" in his passage to earth, after which she will be "locked" as before (317–325). Thus metaphor sublimates her pregnancy and birth canal. Yet, the sight of the child at Mary's breast, presented without metaphor, gives hope to all who awaited his Advent. This tricky negotiation of reproduction is, of course, unique to Mary.

This miscellany later characterizes marriage, first via Saint Juliana who rejects marriage in order to "keep her maidenhood for Christ's love" (30–31). Her act is politically and spiritually heroic, a defeat of the Roman Empire and of the devil whom she combats in her jail cell. In the last quarter of the book, *Wulf and Eadwacer* and, some thirty pages later, *The Wife's Lament* represent conjugal relations

for the more ordinary woman. These female characters rather than weaving peace between clans or tribes, suffer isolation from loved ones without spiritual consolation. Texts focusing on repentance immediately follow *The Wife's Lament*, but generally these lyrics appear in the midst of about ninety-four riddles, including a few about sexual acts, as when a woman's experience with an onion resembles intercourse, or dough rises under a cloth, or churning butter appears utterly heterosexual. Considering Mary at one end and sexual riddles at the other, we might mistakenly think this manuscript is about women and gender, whereas mostly it centers on male figures, or themes of wisdom or redemption applicable to humans generally.

While females do not dominate the manuscripts, they seldom play an abject role. Adultery, so prominent in later romances and antifeminist diatribes, cannot be found here. Perhaps this more positive representation of gender reflects the status of the Anglo-Saxon women who were scribes and illuminators, abbesses, and royal patrons of ecclesiastical establishments.

CAROL BRAUN PASTERNACK

References and Further Reading

The Anglo-Saxon Poetic Records. 6 vols. edited by George Philip Krapp and Elliott Van Kirk Dobbie. New York: Columbia University Press, 1931–1953.

Anglo-Saxon Poetry: An Anthology of Old English Poems in Prose Translation. Translated and edited by S. A. J. Bradley. London: Dent, 1982.

Brown, Michelle P. "Female Book-Ownership and Production in Anglo-Saxon England: the Evidence of the Ninth-Century Prayerbooks." In *Lexis and Texts in Early English: Studies Presented to Jane Roberts*, edited by Christian J. Kay and Louise M. Sylvester. Amsterdam: Rodopi, 2001, pp. 45–67.

Chance, Jane. *Woman as Hero in Old English Literature*. Syracuse, N.Y.: Syracuse University Press, 1986.

Damico, Helen and Alexandra Hennessey Olsen. *New Readings on Women in Old English Literature*. Bloomington, Ind.: Indiana University Press, 1990.

Doane, A. N. "Introduction." *The Saxon Genesis*. Madison, Wis.: University of Wisconsin Press, 1991, pp. 3–202.

Dockray-Miller, Mary. "The Maternal Performance of the Virgin Mary in the Old English *Advent*." *NWSA Journal* 14.2 (Summer 2002): 38–55.

The Exeter Anthology of Old English Poetry. 2 vols. Revised edition edited by Bernard J. Muir. Exeter: University of Exeter Press, 2000.

Hollis, Stephanie. *Anglo-Saxon Women and the Church: Sharing a Common Fate*. Woodbridge, Suffolk: Boydell, 1992.

Horner, Shari. *The Discourse of Enclosure: Representing Women in Old English Literature*. Albany, N.Y.: State University of New York Press, 2001.

Lees, Clare A. and Gillian R. Overing. *Double Agents: Women and Clerical Culture in Anglo-Saxon England*. Philadelphia: University of Pennsylvania Press, 2001.

Lionarons, Joyce Tally. "Cultural Syncretism and the Construction of Gender in Cynewulf's *Elene*." *Exemplaria* 10.1 (Spring 1998): 51–68.

Lochrie, Karma. "Gender, Sexual Violence and the Politics of War in the Old English *Judith*." In *Class and Gender in Early English Literature: Intersections*, edited by Britton J. Harwood and Gillian R. Overing. Bloomington, Ind.: Indiana University Press, 1994.

Old and Middle English, c. 890–c. 1400: An Anthology. 2nd edition, edited by Elaine Treharne. Malden, Mass.: Blackwell, 2004.

Pasternack, Carol Braun, and Lisa M. C. Weston. "Introduction." *Sex and Sexuality in Anglo-Saxon England*. Tempe, Ariz.: Arizona Center for Medieval and Renaissance Studies, 2004, pp. xix–xlix.

The Saxon Genesis, edited by A. N. Doane. Madison, Wis.: University of Wisconsin Press, 1991.

See also **Abbesses; Beowulf; Bible, Women in; Book Ownership; England; Eve; Hagiography; Helena; Hild of Whitby; Judith; Letter Writing; Literacy and Reading: Latin; Leoba; Literacy and Reading: Vernacular; Mary, Virgin; Mary, Virgin: in Literature**

LITERATURE, OLD FRENCH

In much of Old French literature, women are essential to the structures of the text, helping in part to define men's roles. Depictions of masculinity depend to some extent on the values inherent in a given genre. The hero of an epic tale, for example, must be first and foremost a successful fighter and loyal vassal. In romance he must add to his knightly prowess the refinement of chivalric behavior and appropriate language, and these last qualities are essential to his persona as a lover in lyric poetry. The portrait of women is perhaps less changeable, at least in the depiction of the noble lady. While the peasant woman of the fabliaux must succeed by her wits and the heroine of pastourelle by her simplicity and charm, the worthy noble woman, whatever the text, is virtuous, faithful, and beautiful. The unworthy lady, by contrast, embodies all the undesirable qualities so often ascribed to all women in misogynist traditions. What varies in the representation of women is primarily the nature and prominence of their role. The following discussion focuses on the major genres of epic and courtly literature as well as on the sustained debate concerning women's nature.

Chansons de Geste

Only in Old French epics, perhaps, are women truly dispensable to the agendas of that genre, which promote masculine, ideological, and dynastic concerns.

In *chansons de geste* women play very limited roles. They are defined by the men on whom they depend and function chiefly as prized tokens of exchange in advantageous alliances. The *Chanson de Roland*, the most admired of Old French epics, contains a striking example of this abbreviated literary existence for female characters. Beautiful Aude, sister of Olivier and fiancée of Roland, falls dead when she hears that her intended has been killed. She laments briefly, refuses to accept Charlemagne's son Louis in exchange for Roland, and dies at the emperor's feet. In other epic texts, noble women represent the point of cultural contact between Christians and Saracens, as in the William cycle, in which the hero Guillaume marries Orable, queen of Orange, once she converts to Christianity.

Lyric Poetry

Lyric poetry gives much greater importance to the lady than does epic, but, paradoxically, perhaps, her absence is more vital than her participation. The lover cannot experience the thrall of passion without a beloved or communicate his passion without an audience to whom to send his confession of love or lament. His lady must exist, therefore, but she does so largely outside the text as the object of his desire and the subject of his discourse. To the best of our knowledge, the Old French tradition does not include women poets equivalent to the *trobairitz* who wrote in Old Occitan. What we hear in Old French lyric, therefore, is almost entirely a male voice whose whole song is predicated on the existence of an admirable but silent lady. Will she be cruel and reject her suitor, or merciful and grant him the delights he seeks? Ostensibly the power is hers, but the hard-hearted woman risks disqualification from the ranks of those deserving of love. Her options are limited. Similarly, the *malmariée* (unhappily married woman) may yearn to escape her jealous husband and the maiden the strict surveillance of her family; but both are largely dependent on the advances of a suitable lover.

Romance

In the long narratives developed in romance, the lady can break her passive silence and assume a more active role. In *Erec et Enide* by Chrétien de Troyes (fl. 1170–1185), we find a dramatic example: ordered by her husband to be silent during the adventures they undertake together, Enide disobeys for love of him

493

and helps overcome a series of formidable adversaries to the joy and well-being of all. The cross-dressed protagonist of the *Roman de Silence* (*Romance of Silence*) makes use of the freedoms available to men to fight, travel, and perform music before she reverts to more ladylike behavior and marries the king. More often, the romance heroine employs the skills and traits of the well-bred lady to further her case or thwart her adversaries. In *Tristan*, Iseut and her mother employ their healing arts to advance Iseut's love for Tristan. In the so-called "realistic" romances of the thirteenth century, Jean Renart's *Roman de la Rose ou Guillaume de Dole*, for example, shows Liénor using superior intelligence, logic, and rhetoric to defend herself against dishonor in the eyes of her future husband Conrad. Paramount among the assets a romance heroine can deploy is language, whether written, sung, or spoken.

Misogyny

The presence of women in Old French literature often overlaps with the presence of misogyny, whether programmatic (that is, an explicit goal of the text) or incidental. Even in courtly romance, a genre that of necessity includes admirable women, female characters are sometimes laden with the ideological freight assigned to their sex. The same Enide previously mentioned is perceived by other characters in the text as problematic, threatening masculinity. Caricatured misogynous utterances are placed in the mouths of the narrator and the English king in the *Roman de Silence*, even though the very plot depends on problematizing conventional notions about women's nature. Evil behaviors, such as malice, envy, and gossip can be marked as female, as in the case of Fresne's mother in Marie de France's *Lai de Fresne*.

The misogynist corpus, represented by such late-thirteenth or early-fourteenth century Old French *dits* as *Le Blasme des fames* (*The Blame of Women*), *Le Chastiemusart* (*The Fool's Comeuppance*), and *La Contenance des Fames* (*The Ways of Women*), is characterized by programmatic or "phobic" misogyny. It lays out in detail the vices supposedly specific to women, their faults of nature and behavior, their inferiority to men, and the need, therefore, for women to be subordinate to men. Such texts are often playful in their allusiveness, form, and variations on the conventions of misogyny, but playfulness or even parody does not palliate their content.

Such texts are often accompanied in manuscripts by defense texts such as *Le Bien des fames* (*The Virtues of Women*; late thirteenth century), building a virtual debate into the codex. To the detriment of the feminist argument, however, the debate is conducted within the parameters laid out by the misogynous texts. The defense texts tend to refute the claims of the misogynous ones primarily by denying the accusations made about women and foregrounding "womanly" virtues and merits, but not really challenging the assumptions underlying the denunciation of women. Jean LeFevre's translation into French of the *Lamentations de Matheolus* is followed by his long defense of women, the *Livre de Leesce*; but that comforting text marks no real advance over misogyny and is read by some as itself parodic.

A key text in the larger polemic is the thirteenth-century *Roman de la Rose* (*Romance of the Rose*), which displays but also challenges the repertoire of textual misogyny. Its ultimate meaning is sufficiently ambiguous to generate a powerful rebuttal more than a century later. Christine de Pizan (1364–1430) initiated the "Quarrel of the Rose" in the early fifteenth century, engaging some of the most influential Parisian male intellectuals of her day on such questions as the limits of appropriate speech and the nature of women. More than any other medieval author, perhaps, Christine proposed a programmatic defense of women in her large literary corpus, using the tried and true rhetorical strategies of her predecessors but also creating new allegorical structures and characters to support her experiential proof of women's goodness and worth. In her *Livre de la cité des dames* (*Book of the City of Ladies*), the Virgin Mary presides as queen over all women of virtue, here, as elsewhere, the only female figure in Old French literature completely immune to vilification.

BARBARA ALTMANN

References and Further Reading

Blamires, Alcuin. *The Case for Women in Medieval Culture*. Oxford: Clarendon Press, 1997.

———, et al., eds. *Woman Defamed and Woman Defended: An Anthology of Medieval Texts*. Oxford: Clarendon Press, 1992.

Brown-Grant, Rosalind, translated by Christine de Pizan. *The Book of the City of Ladies*. New York: Penguin, 1999.

Burns, E. Jane. *Body Talk: When Women Speak in Old French Literature*. Philadelphia: University of Pennsylvania Press, 1993.

Cadden, Joan. *The Meaning of Sex Differences in the Middle Ages: Medicine, Natural Philosophy, and Culture*. Cambridge and New York: Cambridge University, 1993.

Dronke, Peter. *The Medieval Lyric*. London: Cambridge University Press, 1977.

Fenster, Thelma S., and Clare A. Lees, eds. *Gender in Debate from the Early Middle Ages to the Renaissance*. New York: Palgrave, 2002.

Fiero, Gloria K., Wendy Pfeffer, Mathé Allain, trans. and ed. *Three Medieval Views of Women: La Contenance des fames, Le Bien des fames, Le Blasme des fames.* New Haven: Yale University Press, 1989.

Wilson, Katharina M., ed. *Medieval Women Writers.* Athens, Ga.: University of Georgia, 1984.

See also **Chrétien de Troyes; Christine de Pizan; Courtly Love; Defenses of Women; Epic: Old French; Fabliau; Femininity and Masculinity; Gender Ideologies; Isolde; Marie de France; Mary, Virgin; Mary, Virgin: in Literature; Misogyny; Pastourelle; Roman de la Rose and Its Reception; Roman de Silence; Romance, French; Trobairitz and Troubadours; Trouvères, Women; Woman's Song; Women Authors: Old French Texts**

LITERATURE, OLD NORSE

The representation of women in Old Norse literature is distinctive on account of the range and nature of literary genres drawing on indigenous oral traditions that were preserved in Iceland and Norway during the medieval period. While ecclesiastical texts and hagiographic literature, and later romances, were translated into Old Norse, some of the earliest writers of the literate Christian period turned their attention to their own traditions and wrote down sagas of the founding families of the colony of Iceland (*Íslendingasögur*); sagas of the legendary heroes of the distant past (*fornaldarsögur*); and sagas of bishops and kings (*biskupasögur* and *konungasögur*). Before the 1260s, Icelanders were not subject to king or queen, but generations of Icelandic poets had done service at foreign courts composing praise poetry for princes; hundreds of the stanzas they composed are preserved within prose sagas, a record of a unique poetic tradition and a source of historically intriguing material. Not all these professional poets were men, and occasionally women commissioned verse or were the subjects of poetry quoted in *konungasögur*.

One such woman was Ástríðr, daughter of Óláfr, king of the Swedes, who began her own regal career by wooing the Norwegian King Óláfr Haraldsson, approaching him on three occasions before he accepted her proposal. A young Icelandic poet visiting their court is said to have composed a love-poem for Ástríðr which was, however, too amorous for the king's liking and has unfortunately not been preserved. After Saint Óláfr's death in 1030, Ástríðr took up the cause of her stepson, Magnús, addressing an assembly in Sweden and smoothing the way for him to become king of Norway. Three stanzas of a praise poem in her honor are extant, in which she is praised for her political *nous* (her advice is said to have been both sound and deep) and for her

"manliness" in securing the throne for Magnús. Magnús was, by all accounts, grateful, and invited his stepmother to join his court. Their domestic tensions developed when his own mother, Alvhildr (formerly Ástríðr's maid and Óláfr's concubine) insisted on a position of higher status than the queen. The affection of poets for Ástríðr is again recorded: Alvhildr's presumption denounced in favour of Ástríðr's rightful place of honour. Ástríðr's story is gleaned from a number of narrative accounts and skaldic stanzas and demonstrates the wealth of social and political material about the lives of women in medieval Scandinavia that survives, often in fragmentary form, and often as sidelines to the main narrative.

Another notorious Norwegian king-maker, Gunnhildr (known as the "mother of kings"), is depicted not only in *konungasögur* but also in *Íslendingasögur* where she crossed the paths of travelling Icelanders. *Njáls saga* describes the visit of an Icelander named Hrútr to Norway to claim his inheritance. At the court of King Haraldr "greycloak" Haraldr's mother, Queen Gunnhildr, is said to have been attracted to the handsome young traveler and invited him into her bed. When, eventually, Hrútr wished to return to Iceland (to the fiancée he had not dared tell the queen about), Gunnhildr bewitched him so that he might never experience sexual pleasure with the woman he was to marry. Again, the queen had her way, and *Njáls saga* details the process by which Hrútr's disaffected wife divorced him.

The *Íslendingasögur* are noted for their many portrayals of influential and independent-minded women, and one of the most perplexing is that of Hallgerðr, in *Njáls saga*, a young woman of exceptional beauty with glorious silky hair that came down to her waist. As is characteristic of saga narration, the first scene in which she plays a part concludes with a laconic comment by her uncle (the same Hrútr) to his brother, predicting that many will pay for her beauty and querying how "the eyes of a thief have come into our family." The answer, we might assume, is through the female line, saga authors making much of family traits up and down the generations, whether for good, bad or just interesting. But the chiaroscuro depiction of characters in the sagas usually invites the withholding of judgment, even when events escalate to the tragic. In one of the crucial scenes of the saga, Hallgerðr's husband Gunnarr is defending himself with bow and arrow against the odds: his bow breaks and he asks Hallgerðr for two locks of her hair with which to improvise a bowstring. She refuses, reminding her husband in the last minutes of his life of the slap on the face he had once given her (for stealing, in fact). Strong-mindedness in saga women works just as often to consolidate family bonds: the redoubtable

Auðr in *Gísla saga*, is shown defending her outlawed husband's honour to the point of gathering up the silver offered to her as a bribe to betray him, putting it into a purse and swinging it in the face of the one trying to bribe her, bloodying his nose. Her scornful words about his cowardice disgrace him, in the same way that goading women in many saga incidents remind their male relatives of standards of honour that they believe are in danger of lapsing.

Carol Clover has analyzed the way in which gender is inflected in the scene in which Auðr asserts control and from this analysis presents an illuminating discussion of gender roles in Old Norse literature. The heroines of saga literature are often cast in deep dilemmas, having to side either with their male kin against their husbands or with their married kin against their brothers, fathers, and nephews. Like their counterparts in the traditional, anonymous poetry of medieval Scandinavia (known as eddic poetry), their responses are often severe, almost always leading to tragedy, but frequently eloquent and thought-provoking. The eddic heroines Guðrún and Brynhildr declaim their sorrow in the same breath as their vengeful thoughts, goading their sons or husbands to murderous acts while lamenting their own unhappy fates. In the eddic poems set in the divine or semi-divine worlds, a number of potent female figures are depicted: goddesses, prophets, norns, and valkyries, all linked by their insight into fate and the future, and in some instances marked out for their wisdom and sound advice, a trait that, in turn, also comes through in many portraits of saga women, whether Icelandic farmers or Norwegian queens.

JUDY QUINN

References and Further Reading

Anderson, Sarah M., with Karen Swenson, eds., *Cold Counsel: Women in Old NorseLiterature and Mythology*. New York and London: Routledge, 2002.

Clover, Carol. "Regardless of Sex: Men, Women and Power in Early Northern Europe." In *Studying Medieval Women*, edited by Nancy Partner. Cambridge, Mass.: Medieval Academy, 1993, pp. 61–85.

Frank, Roberta. "Why Skalds Address Women." In *Poetry in the Scandinavian Middle Ages, Atti del 12o Congresso Internazionale de Studi sull'Alto Medioeva*, edited by Teresa Paroli. Spoleto: Presso la Sede del Centro Studi, 1990, pp. 67–83.

Jesch, Judith. "In praise of Ástríðr Óláfsdóttir." *Saga-Book of the Viking Society* 24 (1994): 1–18.

Jochens, Jenny. *Old Norse Images of Women*. Philadelphia: University of Pennsylvania Press, 1996.

The Poetic Edda. translated by Carolyne Larrington. Oxford: Oxford University Press, 1996.

Quinn, Judy. "Women in Old Norse Poetry and Sagas." In *Old Norse-Icelandic Literature and Culture*, edited by Rory McTurk. Oxford: Blackwell, 2005, pp. 518–535.

The Sagas of Icelanders. translated by Katrina Atwood, et al. New York: Penguin, 2001.

Snorri Sturluson. Edda. translated by Anthony Faulkes. London: Dent, 1987.

See also **Prophets, Nordic; Scandinavia; Skaldkonur; Valkyries**

LITERATURE, SPANISH
See **Literature, Iberian**

LOLLARDS

As England's sole popular heresy during the Middle Ages, Lollardy holds an important place in our understanding of religious life in late medieval England, even if Lollard adherents likely never made up more than a small minority of the population. Among the issues that a study of Lollardy elucidates is the nature and extent of medieval women's role in religious devotion and practice. Although some twentieth-century historians argued that heresy was inherently attractive to women as women, recent literature on Lollardy—as on other heretical movements—has challenged this contention. Women did not find in Lollardy a straightforward liberation from a repressive medieval Catholic patriarchy; indeed, women's attraction to the sect may not have been much different from men's. Women played important roles in Lollard communities, but scholars disagree about precisely *how* important.

Lollardy was born in the academic world of Oxford University from the teachings of the theologian John Wycliffe (d. 1384). Wycliffe, a scriptural fundamentalist, disputed nonbiblical sacraments, the power of the Catholic priesthood, and the cult of saints. He also championed the diffusion of religious knowledge in the vernacular. From the mid-1380s, Wycliffe's academic followers began to spread his ideas into various parts of England through active proselytization. They also produced a considerable corpus of English sermons, devotional works, and a vernacular translation of the scriptures that came to be known as the Lollard Bible.

The Lollard movement's strengths—its academic base at Oxford and growing support from a number of prominent Lollard gentlemen during the late fourteenth century—collapsed in the 1410s. A purge of Oxford University and the failure of a Lollard-associated revolt against the crown in 1414 left Lollardy largely without academic or aristocratic support.

Thenceforth, with a few exceptions, the Lollards who made their way into late medieval English records were laypeople of lower socioeconomic station. Followers of the heretical movement were still being uncovered by ecclesiastical authorities in the 1520s, when Protestant ideas began to circulate around England; in the following decades adherents of Lollardy were almost certainly absorbed into the new forms of Protestantism that developed.

The role of women in the early part of the movement—before the second decade of the fifteenth century—is largely obscure. While virtually the entire large corpus of Lollard writings originates in this period, relatively little survives concerning individual adherents, especially outside the leadership of male clergy and gentry. Unsurprisingly there is no evidence at all that women played a part in the academic wing of the movement. Women of the aristocracy and townswomen in the urban centers where Lollardy took hold almost certainly did become involved, but we glimpse this only obliquely in the surviving record. Anti-Lollard polemicists made intriguing accusations that Lollards allowed women, and even girls, to act as priests in heretical versions of the mass; as Margaret Aston has suggested, however, even if these contentions reflected actual Lollard practice (the evidence is slight, but it is possible), it remains an open question whether the playing of priestly roles by women or girls would have been meant as an elevation of women's roles or as an attack on the power of Catholic priests. Lollard writings addressed questions related to gender relatively little; when they did, they tended to reflect the norms of orthodox society, emphasizing, for instance, that God ordains the husband's rule over the wife.

As the social basis of the Lollard movement changed in the 1410s, so also did the record it left behind. While we have few if any later Lollard writings, much better survival of the records of prosecution for the period after 1420 and especially after the 1480s allows us to understand more fully the makeup of groups of Lollards—and to trace more clearly the involvement of women. Nonetheless, the evidence regarding women's roles in the movement remains incomplete and open to interpretation.

Of those who were named as Lollards in the records of prosecution, slightly fewer than one in three were women. A high proportion of these women were related to male Lollards: they were, in other words, mostly the wives, daughters, sisters, or mothers of men in Lollard communities. Lollard communities were centered on the household; Lollards gathered in the homes of their fellow adherents to listen to readings from the Lollard Bible and other religious works written in English. Some historians, such as Claire Cross and Margaret Aston, have seen the family and household basis of later Lollard communities as a source of women's power in the movement. Others, especially Shannon McSheffrey, have argued that the heretical communities tended to replicate the authority structures of the patriarchal household. All agree that Lollard practice afforded to some women, particularly widows such as Alice Rowley of Coventry, a central role in the heretical gatherings in their communities; what remains less clear—and a matter of dispute—is how we should extrapolate from such examples to generalize about women's significance in the movement as a whole. Was Alice Rowley, as an authoritative leader of the Coventry Lollard community, extraordinary, or were other women like her common in the movement but obscured in the surviving record? Did ecclesiastical authorities' preconceptions about female incapacity cause them to underestimate, and underinvestigate, women's roles in the heresy? Or did a more generalized ideology that accorded women less agency than men in late medieval English society tend to keep women in relatively marginal roles in the sect as well as outside it? Whatever the answer to these questions, the reflexive assumption that some historians held in the twentieth century—that heresies, as challenges to the medieval Church, were also challenges to medieval patriarchy and thus intrinsically attractive to women—no longer stands. Heresies were not all alike; nor, for that matter, were women. Yet even if only a tiny minority of late medieval English women participated in Lollard activities, for some this heretical movement provided a vital outlet for their religious devotion.

SHANNON MCSHEFFREY

References and Further Reading

Aston, Margaret. "Lollard Women Priests?" *Journal of Ecclesiastical History* 31 (1980): 441–461.
———. "Lollard Women." In *Women and Religion in Medieval England*, edited by Diana Wood. Oxford: Oxbow Books, 2003, pp. 166–185.
Cross, Claire. "'Great Reasoners in Scripture': The Activities of Women Lollards 1380–1530." In *Medieval Women*, edited by Derek Baker. Studies in Church History, Subsidia, 1. Oxford: Blackwell, 1978, pp. 359–380.
Hudson, Anne. *The Premature Reformation: Wycliffite Texts and Lollard History*. Oxford: Clarendon Press, 1988.
McSheffrey, Shannon. *Gender and Heresy: Women and Men in Lollard Communities, 1420–1530*. Philadelphia: University of Pennsylvania Press, 1995.
Rex, Richard. *The Lollards*. Houndsmills: Palgrave MacMillan, 2002.

See also **Cathars; Heretics and Heresy; Lay Piety; Waldensians**

LÓPEZ DE CÓRDOBA, LEONOR

The noble woman Leonor López de Córdoba (1362/1363–c. 1412) is one of Spain's first women writers. Her *Memorias* (Memoirs) is the first autobiography written in the medieval Spanish kingdom of Castile. She witnessed firsthand some of the most salient—and horrifying—events of her time, including the Black Death, the fourteenth-century Spanish civil war, and the first organized and publicly authorized "pogrom" against Jews in Castile. Leonor was chief advisor and confidante to Queen Catalina of Lancaster, wife of Enrique III and regent for Juan II; a contemporary medieval chronicler comments that the queen trusted and loved her so much that she did nothing without Leonor's counsel. Leonor was, in fact, such a powerful figure in fourteenth century Spain that historians have seen her, during her years as advisor to Catalina, as the real arbiter of Castile's internal policies. Eventually Leonor was driven from court, accused of accepting bribes.

Leonor's *Memorias* suggests that she was conscious of herself as a woman writer. In the work she describes a feminized world, in which men are largely absent. While she identifies herself as wife and daughter, her focus is on life on her own; the male members of her family, she notes, have all left her, through death or self-imposed exile. Leonor invokes the Virgin Mary as a model in her writing, but her *Memorias*, unlike the works of some other medieval women writers, is not a spiritual biography. Rather her work is framed as a public record—so much so that some scholars have claimed it as a legal document or a confession. Interestingly, the text focuses on her personal quest for honor, rather than her time of power and glory in the public eye, describing a life of misfortune after her years at court with Queen Catalina.

LOUISE MIRRER

References and Further Reading

Deyermond, Alan. "Spain's First Women Writers." In *Women in Hispanic Literature: Icons and Fallen Idols*, edited by Beth Miller, 27–52. Berkeley: University of California Press, 1983.
Ellis, Deborah Sue. "The Image of the Home in Early English and Spanish Literature." Ph.D. diss., University of California, Berkeley, 1982.
Estow, Clara. "Leonor Lopez de Cordoba: Portrait of a Medieval Courtier." *Fifteenth-Century Studies* 5 (1982): 23–46.
Frieden, Mary Elizabeth. "Epistolarity in the Works of Teresa de Cartagena and Leonor López de Córdoba." Ph.D. diss., University of Missouri–Columbia, 2001.
Kaminsky, Amy Katz and Elaine Dorough Johnson. "To Restore Honor and Fortune: 'The Autobiography of Leonor Lopez de Cordoba.'" In *The Female Autograph*, edited by Doman C. Stanton and Jeanine Parisier Plottel, vol. 12–13, 77–88. New York: New York Literary Forum, 1984.
McInnis, Judy B., ed. *Models in Medieval Iberian Literature and Their Modern Reflections: Convivencia as Structural, Cultural and Sexual Ideal.* Juan de la Cuesta Hispanic Monographs. Newark, Del.: Juan de la Cuesta, 2002.
Mirrer, Louise. *Women, Jews & Muslims in the Texts of Reconquest Castile.* Ann Arbor: University of Michigan Press, 1996.
Sautman, Francesca Canadé and Pamela Sheingorn. *Same Sex Love and Desire among Women in the Middle Ages.* New Middle Ages. New York: Palgrave, 2001.
Surtz, Ronald E. *Writing Women in Late Medieval and Early Modern Spain: The Mothers of Saint Teresa of Avila.* Philadelphia: University of Pennsylvania Press, 1995.

See also **Gender Ideologies; Iberia; Literature, Iberian; Queens and Empresses: the West; Women Authors: Spanish Texts**

LOVESICKNESS

Erotic love as a sickness, a subject of medical and philosophical investigation since antiquity, has exercised much influence on Islamic as well as Western literature. Many medieval scholars now consider the Arab treatise on love by Ibn Hazm (994–1064), *The Dove's Neck Ring*, as the primary text that shaped the idea of love as pathology in literature. Drawing examples from all social classes, the book describes the nature and phenomenology of love and the joys and sorrows of lovers. This concept of love as sickness, or melancholia, is found in most Occitan (Provençal) poetry (early twelfth through mid-thirteenth century).

The next most prominent text on lovesickness is Andreas Capellanus' *De Amore* (c. 1185). The author states that love is an innate passion resulting from obsessive thoughts about the object of desire, causing sickness, fever, loss of vital strength, and even madness. Together with Ovid's *Ars Amandi* and *Metamorphoses*, the treatise remained influential throughout the Middle Ages. The association of love with melancholia (one of the four temperaments) can be also found in medieval French texts, as well as in works by Boccaccio (1313–1375) and Chaucer (1342–1400).

The first known poet writing in *langue d'oc,* William of Aquitaine (1071–1127), draws his metaphors from the world of feudalism to describe fears and emotions caused by love. The Lady becomes the lord and her suppliant lover is her faithful vassal. Bertrand de Ventadorn and the poets who came after him repeatedly describe the weakening bodily symptoms of male love: pallor, trembling, insomnia, sighs, cries. The male lover thus attributes to himself emotions usually ascribed to women. The women troubadours, like the Contessa de Dia and Castelloza, appropriate the language of the male poets, use feudal metaphors sparingly, but describe the same symptoms, suggesting that lovesickness erases the emotional differences between men and women.

Most Occitan poets are not men of action, therefore lovesickness keeps them static. They compose their songs and may even perform them, but they do not seek adventures and glory. However, from the eleventh to the fourteenth century, literary genres such as *chansons de geste*, romances, and lays abound in situations where lovers run into perilous adventures. Sickness is a constant theme whenever lovers are separated. In *Flamenca* (written in Occitan), *Amadas et Ydoine*, and Marie de France's *Guigemar*, the lovers show acute symptoms of lovesickness. Chretien de Troyes' *Yvain* loses his mind when his beloved rejects him. In the *Folie Berne*, Tristan is not simply pretending to be mad, he shows all the psychological traits of the melancholy man. In these texts lovesick women, however, may die of grief, but do not become insane. In this period, women who showed signs of madness were, rather, considered possessed by the devil and were either exorcised or burned at the stake as witches. Furthermore, the fate of lovesick men, at least in literary texts, allowed them to regain their sanity, change their lives, or succeed in being reunited with their beloved.

Although carefully described, physiological and psychological symptoms of lovesickness are linked with magic. But the development of the commercial revolution of the Middle Ages created a different world from that of courtly poetry and romances: suspension of disbelief could no longer be invoked. In *La vita nuova*, Dante describes his emotions according to the Occitan tradition, but takes a more scientific approach following Aristotelian natural philosophy. With few exceptions, Boccaccio (1313–1375), in his *Decameron*, anchors his tales in reality and in history. Boccaccio prefaces his collection of one hundred tales with a discussion of lovesickness and the different remedies available to men and women. He notes that lovesick men can find solace in traveling, hunting, gambling, and engaging in business. Women, on the other hand, are kept at home under the surveillance of their fathers, husbands, or brothers. Boccaccio dedicates his stories to women who have no access to recreation, thus turning literature into therapy.

Boccaccio's earlier works, the romances *Filostrato* (written in octaves) and *Fiammetta* (written in prose) illustrate the difference between men and women affected by melancholia. Betrayed by Criseide, lovesick Filostrato tries to forget his grief by going to war and dies on the battlefield. Fiammetta, precisely like the

women described in the preface to the *Decameron*, cannot have a life of action; she then tells the story of her sufferings in first person to all women who have experienced betrayal and abandonment.

In *Troilus and Criseyde*, based on Boccaccio's *Filostrato*, Chaucer further elaborates the etiology of lovesickness as a physical, emotional, and moral phenomenon. Centuries later, melancholy caused by lovesickness will become one of the most salient themes of the Romantic age.

ESTER ZAGO

References and Further Reading

Campbell, Donald. *Arabian Medicine and Its Influence on the Middle Ages*. London: Kegan, Trench, Trubner, 1926.

Ciavolella, Massimo. *La "Malattia d'amore" dall'Antichità al Medioevo*. Roma: Bulzoni, 1976.

Ferrand, Jacques. *A Treatise on Lovesickness*. edited and translated by Donald Beecher and Massimo Ciavolella. Syracuse: Syracuse University Press, 1990.

Hildegard von Bingen. *On Natural Philosophy and Medicine*. edited and translated by Margret Berger. Cambridge: D. S. Brewer, 1999.

Jacquart, Danielle and Thomasset Claude. *Sexuality and Medicine in the Middle Ages*. Princeton: Princeton University Press, 1988.

Klibansky, Raymond, Erwin Panofsky, and Fritz Saxl. *Saturn and Melancholy*. London: Nelson & Sons, 1964.

Kristeva, Julia. *Black Sun: Depression and Melancholia*. New York: Columbia University Press, 1989.

Lowes, John L. "The Loveres Maladye of Hereos." *Modern Philology* 11 (1914): 491–546.

Olson, Glending. *Literature as Recreation in the Later Middle Ages*. Ithaca: Cornell University Press, 1982.

Siriasi, Nancy. *Medieval and Early Renaissance Medicine*. Chicago: University of Chicago Press, 1990.

Wack, Mary Frances. "Memory and Love in Chaucer's *Troilus and Criseyde*." Dissertation, Cornell University, 1982.

———. *Lovesickness in the Middle Ages: The "Viaticum" and Its Commentaries*. Philadelphia: University of Pennsylvania Press, 1990.

Walter, Philip. "Tristan et la mélancolie." In *Actes du 14e Congrès International Arthurien*. Rennes: Presses Universitaires, 1984, pp. 646–657.

See also **Courtly Love; Courtship; Doctors and Healers; Femininity and Masculinity; Gender Ideologies; Gynecology; Literature, Occitan; Madness; Sexuality: Extramarital Sex; Sexuality: Female Same-Sex Relations; Sexuality: Male Same-Sex Relations; Sexuality: Regulation of; Sexuality: Sex in Marriage; Trobaritz and Troubadours**

LUTGARD OF AYWIÈRES

Lutgard of Aywières (1182–1246) was born in Tongres, Belgium, to a noble mother and a bourgeois father. She entered the Benedictine convent of Saint-Trond at sixteen and became its prioress in 1205.

A few years later, at the prompting of her confessor John of Lierre, she moved from the Flemish-speaking convent of Saint-Trond to the French-speaking Cistercian convent of Aywières situated near Brussels. Lutgard is remembered for her ascetic achievements, such as three long fasts each lasting seven years.

Lutgard's *vita* was recorded by the Dominican friar Thomas of Cantimpré. Thomas understood her bodily suffering as being spiritually effective, a process by which the pain and discomfort of a living, holy person diminished the time spent suffering by those in Purgatory; this theological phenomenon is also known as vicarious suffering. Thomas depicted Lutgard as an uneducated nun who could not master the French language, although she lived at Aywières for nearly three decades. Thomas juxtaposed this seeming lack of learning with Lutgard's intuitive understanding of the Bible, which resulted from her heart being mingled with the heart of Christ.

Lutgard was also recognized as an effective healer and prophet. Her respected reputation is attested by her numerous spiritual friendships. These friends included the holy woman Christina the Astonishing, who encouraged Lutgard to move to Aywières, the preacher Jacques de Vitry, who wrote letters to her while he was Bishop of Acre, and her Dominican hagiographer, Thomas of Cantimpré, who, after her death, wore a case around his neck that contained her finger.

CAROLYN MUESSIG

References and Further Reading

Cawley, Martinus. "The Life and Journal of Lutgard of Aywières: Selections from the Life by Thomas de Cantimpré, Its Translation into Old French, and the Primitive Life." *Vox Benedictina*. 1.1 (1984): 20–48.

Dinzelbacher, Peter. "Das Christusbild der heiligen Lutgard von Tongeren im Rahmen der Frauenmystik und Bildkunst des 12. und 13. Jahrhundert." *Ons geestelijk erf*. 56 (1982): 217–277.

Hendrix, Guido. "Primitive Versions of Thomas of Cantimpré's Vita Lutgardis." *Cîteaux*. 29 (1978): 153–206.

Jacques de Vitry. *Lettres de Jacques de Vitry*, edited by R. B. C. Huygens. Leiden: Brill, 1960.

Lefevre, Jean-Baptiste. "Sainte Lutgarde d'Aywières en son temps (1182–1246)." *Collectanea Cisterciensia*. 58.4 (1996): 277–335.

Merton, Thomas. *What Are These Wounds? The Life of a Cistercian Mystic*. Milwaukee: Bruce, 1950.

Roisin, Simone. "Sainte Lutgarde d'Aywières dans son ordre et son temps." *Collectanea Ordinis Cisterciensium Reformatorum*. 8 (1946): 161–172.

Thomas de Cantimpré. "Vita Lutgardis." *Acta Sanctorum*. 16 June. Tome 3. Anvers, 1701, pp. 234–262.

———. *The Life of Lutgard of Aywières*. Translated by Margot H. King. Toronto: Peregrina Publishing. Co., 1987.

See also **Asceticism; Body, in Literature and Religion; Christina the Astonishing; Fasting and Food, Religious Aspects of; Flanders; Hagiography; Monasticism and Nuns; Spiritual Care; Theology**

LYING-IN

In medieval England and Europe, it was customary for a woman to withdraw from normal society when she gave birth to be tended by a midwife and her women relatives, friends, and neighbors until her churching (a ritual blessing at the church marking the end of her puerperal confinement, normally four to six weeks after the birth). During this lying-in period, the newly delivered mother was largely exempt from her normal household duties, such as cooking and marketing and her marital obligations, including sexual relations with her husband. Instead, she and her women companions, or *gossips*, gathered in the birthing chamber, a specially equipped and decorated room or curtained-off area, where they visited with one another and shared food and drink, including the spiced wine, or *caudle*, prepared at the time of the birth to ease the pains of labor.

This custom was remarkably similar throughout England and Europe, and it was practiced by women across the socioeconomic spectrum. Virtually all married women spent time lying-in. If circumstances allowed, unmarried mothers did also. Differences in socioeconomic status did affect the presence and number of companions, the nature and decoration of the birthing chamber, the type of refreshments, and the length of time before the new mother returned to her household and wifely duties.

Prior to the 1980s, medievalists focused on how this seclusion of a new mother with its prohibitions against cooking and sexual intercourse reflected and reinforced the clerical notions of female impurity which undergirded medieval gender stereotypes. In the 1980s, the focus shifted to the women participants and their roles in originating, shaping, and perpetuating the rituals and customs associated with childbirth. While it may have reinforced negative gender stereotypes, women also benefited from lying-in. It not only allowed a new mother time away from her normal duties and obligations to recover from childbirth, but it also provided a privileged women's space free from male intrusion. In the 1990s, the focus shifted to the relationships of power within the birthing chamber. Most notably, Adrian Wilson suggested that lying-in not only gave a new mother time apart to rest and recuperate but also actually inverted the normal pattern of relations in the patriarchal household. Under the watchful eyes of the women gathered around the new mother, a husband was subject to the authority of the midwife in his own home; he was expected to assume his wife's responsibilities in the household, and his conjugal rights were suspended, temporarily restoring a wife's control over her own body.

It is not only family politics that played itself out in the birthing chamber. Women from across the socioeconomic spectrum assembled around a newly delivered mother, brought together by a complex web of ties and allegiances, grounded in duty, friendship, and socioeconomic status. Medieval society was highly stratified, founded on mutual obligations, gifts, and favors. Through invitations and uninvited visitations, and the lending and borrowing of utensils and linens for the lying-in chamber, the new mother and the women gathered around her and affirmed, strengthened, and renegotiated their social networks.

Men rarely entered the birthing chamber, although they could be called upon in exceptional circumstances; and a king or male court official may have been present to witness the birth of an heir to the throne. Nevertheless, men's dynastic concerns and social politics made their way into that enclosed space, at least when the new mother belonged to the nobility or gentry. Women of the nobility and gentry played an important role in managing not only the family's households but also its estates and affairs. Those responsibilities entailed establishing and maintaining both female and male networks of influence. Hospitality, patronage, and gift exchange were the vehicles through which those networks were established and maintained. A noble woman or lady's confinement after the birth of an heir provided one more opportunity for her and her family, as well as their betters, peers, and acquaintances, to display and enhance their economic and social status through gifts, visits, and hospitality. The scarcity of sources has made it difficult to ascertain the extent to which lying-in served similar purposes for common folk.

Despite its ubiquity, there is little documentary evidence of medieval lying-in because it was a commonplace women's activity. Much of our knowledge of this custom is inferred from the more abundant legal records, diaries, letters, and autobiographies of the early modern period (the sixteenth and seventeenth centuries), although historians have made inroads into the silence surrounding the medieval birthing chamber by broadening the search to popular literature and drama, iconography, and material culture. The reexamination of familiar documentary evidence through the lens of gender analysis also allows glimpses into women's lives and activities, including childbirth customs and practices, as they intersect with men's lives and activities.

BECKY R. LEE

References and Further Reading

Gibson, Gail McMurray. "Scene and Obscene: Seeing and Performing Late Medieval Childbirth." *Journal of Medieval and Early Modern Studies*. 29.1 (1999): 7–24.

Haas, Louis. "Women and Childbearing in Medieval Florence." In *Medieval Family Roles: A Book of Essays*, edited by Cathy Jorgensen Itnyre. New York: Garland, 1996, pp. 87–99.

Jacobsen, Grethe. "Pregnancy and Childbirth in the Medieval North: A Topology of Sources and a Preliminary Study." *Scandinavian Journal of History*. 9.2 (1984): 91–111.

Jenstad, Janelle Day. "Lying-in Like a Countess: The Lisle Letters, the Cecil Family, and *A Chaste Maid in Cheapside*." *Journal of Medieval and Early Modern Studies*. 34.2 (2004): 373–403.

Laurent, Sylvie. *Naître au moyen âge: De la conception à la naissance: La grossesse et l'accouchement (XIIe – XVe siècle)*. Léopard d'Or, 1989.

Lee, Becky R. "A Company of Women and Men: Men's Recollections of Childbirth in Medieval England." *Journal of Family History*. 27.2 (2002): 92–100.

Musacchio, Jacqueline Made. *The Art and Ritual of Childbirth in Renaissance Italy*. New Haven, Conn.: Yale University Press, 1999.

Pollock, Linda A. "Childbearing and Female Bonding in Early Modern England." *Social History*. 22.3 (1997): 286–306.

Williams, Patricia. "Childbed Curtains and Churching Shawls: Ritual Cloths in the Czech and Slovak Republics." *Ars Textrina* 21 (1994): 65–83.

Wilson, Adrian. "The Ceremony of Childbirth and Its Interpretation." In *Women as Mothers in Pre-Industrial England: Essays in Memory of Dorothy McLaren*, edited by Valerie Fildes. London and New York: Routledge, 1990, pp. 68–107.

See also **Breastfeeding and Wet-Nursing; Churching; Conjugal Debt; Femininity and Masculinity; Feminist Theories and Methodologies; Gender Ideologies; Gentry, Women of: England; Gynecology; History, Medieval Woman's; Household Management; Illegitimacy; Infants and Infanticide; Midwives; Misogyny; Noble Women; Pregnancy and Childbirth: Christian Women; Pregnancy and Childbirth: Jewish Women; Private and Public Spheres; Procreation and Ideas of Conception; Sexuality: Sex in Marriage; Space, Secular: and Gender; Woman on Top**

M

MADNESS

Madness is an inclusive term used to describe a variety of conditions in medieval Europe, from mental disorders (such as melancholy and mania, often referred as "woodness") to hysteria, demonic possession, extreme religious zeal (manifested in visions and erratic behavior), and even conditions of the heart and soul—such as lovesickness, severe depression and despair caused by excessive grief, and spiritual sloth (this malady of *accidie* often afflicted male and female religious), as well as insanity triggered by anger and fear. The multifaceted nature of madness has sparked debate about exactly how it was understood by medieval people. Some scholars have argued that madness was mostly identified within the context of sin; some have argued it was an accepted (even functional) part of medieval society and that it was not until the 1500s that the mad began to be feared and confined; and some have argued that madness was empowering, allowing people to speak and act in ways normally considered taboo, as well as disempowering, when it was used to stigmatize and discredit.

Nonetheless, some general conclusions can be drawn about medieval madness. First, medieval people conceived of madness as behavioral rather than as chronic mental disease. Second, they distinguished among the types of madness, separating the mentally disturbed from those considered possessed by demons or divine spirits. Third, they usually cared for victims of madness within families and local communities; fourth, they often did not hold the mad criminally responsible for their actions. Finally, they considered madness a gender-inclusive condition—although eventually a shift in gendered ideas would associate madness more exclusively with women.

Several types of medieval sources discuss women and madness. Religious texts, such as sermon *exempla*, the lives of holy women, and miracle accounts from hagiography and pilgrimage shrines, often moralize women's madness as either a consequence of sin or caused by a failure to confess sin. This madness was often temporary and frequently healed through prayer, confession, and divine intercession. Religious texts also reveal women who went mad after childbirth, women who acted mad because of religious fervor (some of whom, like Christina the Astonishing, became known as mystics and saints), and women labeled as demoniacs. Even though sin was a factor in some of these cases, such as with Margery Kempe, who went mad after giving birth and being prevented from confessing a sin, it was not always to blame. Demonic possession, for instance, was considered neither a sin nor as always caused by sin. Legal, medical, and ecclesiastical documents also reveal that women were diagnosed with mental disorders, that legal arrangements were made to protect the assets of madwomen, that a variety of treatments existed for the mad (from medical remedies, prayer, and pilgrimage to magic and charms), and that the mental sufferings of women were not always attributed to spiritual causes.

Although medieval men were just as likely to be afflicted by madness as their female counterparts, medieval sources began to posit a close association between women and madness. Female demoniacs

503

increasingly outnumbered male demoniacs after the twelfth century; hysteria was believed to originate from the uterus; and misogynist ideas provided fertile ground to explain why women were especially susceptible to mental weakness. This connection between women and madness continued to progress, and, by the early modern period, women were considered predisposed to madness, and by the 1700s, madness had become a female malady. Thus, even though medieval madness was not exclusively feminine, it played a critical role in both the lives of medieval women and the course of women's history.

BETH ALLISON BARR

References and Further Reading

Caciola, Nancy. *Discerning Spirits: Divine and Demonic Possession in the Middle Ages*. Ithaca, N.Y.: Cornell University Press, 2003.

Chesler, Phyllis. *Women and Madness*. New York: Doubleday & Company, Inc., 1972.

Clarke, Basil. *Mental Disorder in Earlier Britain: Exploratory Studies*. Cardiff: University of Wales Press, 1975.

Dixon, Laurinda S. "The Curse of Chastity: The Marginalization of Women in Medieval Art and Medicine." In *Matrons and Marginal Women in Medieval Society*, edited by Robert R. Edwards and Vickie Ziegler. Woodbridge, U.K.: Boydell Press, 1995, pp. 49–74.

Doob, Penelope. *Nebuchadnezzar's Children: Conventions of Madness in Middle English Literature*. New Haven, Conn.: Yale University Press, 1974.

Harper, Stephen. *Insanity, Individuals, and Society in Late-Medieval English Literature: The Subject of Madness*. Studies in Medieval Literature, 26. Lewiston, N.Y.: Edwin Mellen Press, 2003.

Kroll, Jerome, and Bernard Bachrach. "Sin and Mental Illness in the Middle Ages." *Psychological Medicine* 14:3 (1984): 507–514.

Lawes, Richard. "The Madness of Margery Kempe." In *The Medieval Mystical Tradition: England, Ireland, and Wales*, edited by Marion Glasscoe. Cambridge: D. S. Brewer, 1999, pp. 148–167.

Neaman, Judith S. *Suggestion of the Devil: The Origins of Madness*. New York: Doubleday Anchor Books, 1975.

Neely, Carol Thomas. "Recent Work in Renaissance Studies: Did Madness Have a Renaissance?" *Renaissance Quarterly* 44.4 (1991): 776–791.

Newman, Barbara. "Possessed by the Spirit: Devout Women, Demoniacs, and the Apostolic Life in the Thirteenth Century." *Speculum* 73 (1998): 733–770.

Showalter, Elaine. *The Female Malady: Women, Madness, and English Culture, 1830–1980*. London: Virago Press, 1987.

Wenzel, Siegfried. *The Sin of Sloth: Acedia in Medieval Thought and Literature*. Chapel Hill, N.C.: University of North Carolina Press, 1967.

See also **Christina the Astonishing; Exemplum; Hagiography; Kempe, Margery; Lovesickness; Miracles and Miracle Collections; Misogyny; Spirits: Discernment of and Possession by; Wild Women; Witches**

MAGIC AND CHARMS

Many of the magical practices that were part of women's and men's lives in the Middle Ages had ancient precedents. Pagan incantations facilitated birth and ensured conception; pagan rituals surrounding the gathering of certain plants and spells could be cast to acquire a lover or extinguish a lover's desire for some other woman. Streams and well springs, special trees, millstones and natural rocks with holes in them, and shells and gemstones all played a part in women's magical practices before the Christianization of Europe. Some pre-Christian types of magic survive into the Middle Ages in a recognizable form, including amulets made of plants to cure specific illnesses and dice that are cast or shiny surfaces that are looked into to predict the future. More often occasions for women's magic, incantations, and amulets come to rely on Christian names of saints and of God, Christian symbols (the cross), and Christian narratives to achieve the same results sought by older forms of magic.

In medieval Europe, as early as the Anglo-Saxon period, we hear of women practicing magic. For example, mothers who attempted to cure a daughter's fever by placing her (briefly) in an oven or rid a child of an illness by drawing it under a bit of turf at a crossroads were expected to confess to church authorities. These and other practices are recorded in Penitentials and handbooks for priestly confessors, where they are censured as un-Christian acts. A young woman might comb her hair under a mulberry tree and tie the comb leavings to a twig to bring on or reduce her menses. A woman might seek a lover by magic. A pregnant woman might perform an incantation while stepping over a grave to expel a dead fetus or over her sleeping husband to ensure a healthy birth. Captured in the magical poetry of the Anglo-Saxons are images of powerful feminine forces capable of exhausting a luckless victim or driving out a sickness. Besides dangerous feminine magic, Anglo-Saxons recorded domestic rituals of the kitchen (e.g., to keep milk from spoiling or keep the fiend out of the house), as well as rituals to protect household goods and flocks from theft, ensure the fertility of the land, and cure sick animals. In later centuries, charms to rid barns of rats or keep the food of pigs from contamination and the like were evidently useful to the person to whom the duties of their care fell—man or woman.

Other medieval magical practices targeted sexual desires. A woman might feed a man his own semen in an attempt to tie his passions to her alone. In contrast, a fifteenth-century male conjuration of the powers of the plant vinca (*pervinca* in British Library, Add. MS 17527, fol. 17v) aims to inflame female desire, so that "whatever girl or woman that I touch while holding you (*vinca*) in my hand may burn inextinguishably with love for me and not love nor desire anyone else."

If a man became impotent by woman's magic, he might be cured by counteracting magic. Impotence was understood to be a sort of magical binding for which unbinding words or a ritual of unlocking was the best remedy. In one instance, the offending lock and key are located in two nearby water wells. In the curative act, they are retrieved. The lock is opened with the corresponding key and a spell, thus restoring the man's power. From the twelfth century, learned (male) physicians in Europe offered other ways to cure impotence and foster conception, some no less magical. In Italy the famous translator of Arabic medicine Constantine the African recommended specific rituals to restore fertility lost due to a bewitched marriage chamber. Later, the scholastic physician Gilbert the Englishman supplied detailed instructions for making an amulet for conception, by which, if worn during intercourse by the woman, the couple would conceive a daughter, and, if worn by the man, a son.

As part of a woman's medical care, charms were employed to stem excessive menstrual bleeding (by appeal to St. Veronica) and to facilitate childbirth. From earliest times, some healers recommended that amulets made of seeds or powerful words be tied on the thigh of a woman in labor. One frequently used array of charms to ease childbirth or speed delivery relied on the Christian traditions surrounding the Virgin Mary's painless delivery of the Christ child— as well as those for other blessed mothers such as Elizabeth, mother of John the Baptist, Anne, the mother of Mary, and mothers of medieval saints. Another favorite motif for childbirth charms is that of Christ calling the child out to the light: "Lazarus, come forth"—words that mark a strong parallel with the scriptural miracle. Yet this manifestly Christian motif may be a medieval transformation of an ancient pagan incantation to speed delivery. Also common in childbirth charms is the palindrome and word square *Sator Arepo Tenet Opera Rotas*. This magical formula eludes literal translation. It was used by Romans in the first century, adopted by Christians, and later interpreted as an anagram of the *Pater Noster* plus alpha and omega.

Sometimes "birth girdles" were employed and passed down in families. These girdles were long strips of sewn-together pieces of parchment inscribed with scriptural texts, charms, and prayers. Also, in wealthy circles, beautifully adorned and highly valued prayer books, or Books of Hours, often acquired by noble women, contained, besides the Latin liturgies for worship in daily devotions, charms, and personal rituals for healing added in the hands of their owners.

Late medieval women's magic drew condemnations from civil and church authorities based in part on an imagined type of the sorceress. As depicted in literature and art, the sorceress was an unattractive old woman who worked dangerous magic through enchanted herbs, images, amulets, and divination of one sort of another. She could foretell the future or locate a thief. She might raise hailstorms to devastate fields and forests, cause animals and children to sicken and die, and consort with demons. During the same period, cults of female saints flourished. Their stories and names were employed in incantations to heal and help. For example, charms invoked St. Apollonia to prevent toothache, St. Susanna to heal wounds and prevent headaches and other distresses, and St. Agnes, whose veil stopped a fire, to prevent lust. Male saints, too, such as St. Peter for toothache, Sts. Nicasius and Toby for the eyes, and St. Job for worms, supply motifs for healing charms. By the end of the Middle Ages, in a spirit of reform, women and men were tried and punished for such traditional religious practices.

LEA T. OLSAN

References and Further Reading

Bozoky, Edina. *Charmes et prières apotropaïques*. Turnhout: Brepols, 2003.

Hanson, A. E. "A Long-Lived 'Quick-Birther' (*okytokion*)." In *Naissance et petite enfance dans l'Antiquité. Actes du colloque de Fribourg, 28 novembre-1er décembre 2001*, edited by V. Dasen. Fribourg: Academie Press, 2004, pp. 265–280.

Kieckhefer, Richard. *Magic in the Middle Ages*. Cambridge: Cambridge University Press, 1989.

McNeill, J. T., and H. M. Gamer. *Medieval Handbooks of Penance*. New York: Columbia University Press, 1938.

Meaney, Audrey. "Women, Witchcraft and Magic in Anglo-Saxon England." In *Superstition and Popular Medicine in Anglo-Saxon England*, edited by D. G. Scragg. Manchester: Manchester Centre for Anglo-Saxon Studies, 1989, pp. 9–40.

Olsan, Lea T. "Charms and Prayers in Medieval Medical Theory and Practice." *Social History of Medicine* 16 (2003): 343–366.

———. "Charms in Medieval Memory." In *Charms and Charming in Northern Europe*, edited by Jonathan Roper. Basingstoke and New York: Palgrave Macmillan, 2004, pp. 59–88.

Rider, Catherine. "Magic and Impotence in the Middle Ages." *Societas Magica Newsletter* 13 (2004): 1–4.

See also **Hagiography; Lovesickness; Medicine; Pregnancy and Childbirth: Christian Women; Pregnancy and Childbirth: Jewish Women; Witches**

MARGARET OF ANJOU

Born in Lorraine, Margaret (1429–1482) was the daughter of René, duke of Anjou. Her uncle Charles VII of France arranged Margaret's marriage to Henry VI of England (1422–1471) at the 1444 Truce of Tours. Her initially conventional queenship included support for the foundation of Queen's College Cambridge.

Following Henry VI's mental collapse in August 1453 and the birth of their only child, Edward, on October 13, 1453, she unsuccessfully petitioned to be made regent. Despite Henry's recovery at Christmas 1454, a vacuum of authority remained, from which Margaret emerged as the head of a Lancastrian court party in opposition to Richard, duke of York. In 1456 Margaret effectively moved the royal capital to Coventry and used her own household and that of her son to dominate government. Although her political significance was acknowledged in the Loveday reconciliation of March 1458, she could not maintain royal authority in the face of Henry's continued inactivity. Yorkist lords captured the king at Northampton on July 10, 1460. During the Wars of the Roses, forces loyal to Margaret were successful at Wakefield (December 30, 1460), killing Richard, and St. Albans (February 17, 1461), but the City of London's refusal to admit her troops in February 1461 enabled York's son to declare himself King Edward IV.

After Edward IV's victory at Towton (March 29, 1461) Margaret fled to seek support in Scotland and then France. In 1470 she allied with Richard Neville, earl of Warwick, to arrange the short-lived restoration of Henry VI. Her son was slain at Tewkesbury on May 4, 1471, and she was captured days later, but eventually ransomed to Louis XI. Henry was killed in the Tower of London shortly thereafter. Margaret died near Saumur on August 25, 1482.

JOANNA L. LAYNESMITH

References and Further Reading

Laynesmith, J. L. *The Last Medieval Queens: English Queenship 1445–1503.* Oxford: Oxford University Press, 2004.

Maurer, Helen. *Margaret of Anjou: Queenship and Power in Late Medieval England.* Woodbridge, Suffolk: Boydell Press, 2003.

See also **England; Queens and Empresses: the West**

ever actually existed. Her cult is first found in the Eastern church, with the earliest lives dating from the ninth century, and it spread across western Europe in the next couple of centuries, becoming one of the most popular female saint's cults. One French version of Margaret's life survives in over a hundred manuscripts, and it provided common subject matter for altarpieces, church walls, books of hours, and other works of art. Relics of the saint were also to be found in many countries.

Margaret's status as an efficacious intercessor was underlined by the prayer she made just before death in which she asked God that all those who remembered her life and invoked her should be protected from harm. Although venerated by a wide variety of devotees, Margaret came to be particularly associated with the protection of women in childbirth. Some versions of her life survive in the form of amulets that were designed to be used by women in labor. This patronage derived from the episode in which she miraculously escaped from the maw of a demonic dragon, bursting it open when she made the sign of the cross. Several writers, including Jacobus de Voragine in the *Golden Legend*, explicitly described this incident as apocryphal, but it nonetheless became her chief iconographic emblem, serving as an expression of the power that she could wield on behalf of devotees.

KATHERINE J. LEWIS

References and Further Reading

Larson, Wendy R. "The Role of Patronage and Audience in the Cults of Saints Margaret and Marina of Antioch." In *Gender and Holiness: Men, Women and Saints in Late Medieval Europe,* edited by S. J. E. Riches and Sarah Salih. London and New York: Routledge, 2002, pp. 23–35.

Lewis, Katherine J. "The Life of St. Margaret of Antioch in Late Medieval England: A Gendered Reading." *Studies in Church History* 34 (1998): 129–142.

Voragine, Jacob de. "The Life of St. Margaret." In *The Golden Legend: Readings on the Saints* vol. 1, translated by William Granger Ryan. Princeton, N.J.: Princeton University Press, 1993, pp. 368–370.

See also **Hagiography; Jacobus de Voragine's Golden Legend; Katherine Group; Pregnancy and Childbirth: Christian Women; Relics and Reliquaries; Virgin Martyrs**

MARGARET OF ANTIOCH

The virgin martyr saint Margaret of Antioch was believed by medieval devotees to have died in the early fourth century, although it is unlikely that she

MARGARET OF CORTONA

The story of Margaret of Cortona (1247–1297), as told by her confessor, Fra Giunta Bevegnati, illustrates the peculiar status of penitent women (that is, women who were unenclosed, often unaffiliated with an order) in late-thirteenth-century central Italy.

As a teenager from a peasant family in Laviano in Umbria, Margaret left home to live with a local noble, Arsenio, by whom she had a son. When, nine years later, her lover was murdered, her stepmother prevented Margaret from returning to her ancestral home. With her nine-year-old son, Margaret trekked to Cortona, where two aristocratic ladies, out of pity, took her in and gave her a small room. Over time the newcomer, making her living as a midwife, became well known for her penitential piety and compassion for the poor. Sometime after 1278, when she entered the Franciscan Third Order, Margaret sent her son to a Franciscan friary in Arezzo. A forceful leader, she founded a confraternity and later a hospital. So renowned was she for her virtues that she wrote to the bishop of Arezzo chastising him for making war on Cortona. In 1290 she left her cell near the church of St. Francis and moved farther up the hill, where she remained as a hermit until her death in 1297.

Soon afterwards the town authorities made Margaret a patron of Cortona. But her process of canonization stalled, and she was not canonized until 1723. While she lived in Cortona many came to seek her counsel, prayers, and intercession before God. The cult associated with her tomb—a basilica was built on the hillside to accommodate it—continued to spread for centuries afterward. The vast iconography of Margaret throughout the centuries is testimony to her fame.

Although a Franciscan tertiary, her status in Cortona and central Italy offers an example of how an individual woman, with no social background, could attain a position of moral leadership in an age of turmoil. For the history of hagiography, Fra Giunta's lengthy biography, written in large part as a dialogue between Jesus and Margaret, is an invaluable source of then-current directions in medieval spirituality, such as the devotion to the suffering Christ.

THOMAS RENNA

References and Further Reading

Bevegnati, Giunta. *The Legend and Life of Saint Margaret of Cortona*, translated by Thomas Renna. St. Bonaventure, N.Y.: Franciscan Institute Publications, forthcoming.

Cannon, Joanna, and André Vauchez. *Margherita of Cortona and the Lorenzetti: Sienese Art and the Cult of a Holy Woman in Medieval Tuscany*. University Park, Pa: Pennsylvania State University Press, 1999.

See also **Canonization of Saints; Hagiography; Monasticism and Nuns; Mysticism and Mystics**

MARGARET OF SCOTLAND

Margaret (c. 1046–1093), queen consort of the Scottish king Malcolm III "Canmore," is the only Scottish saint officially recognized by the Roman Catholic church. Her father Edward, grandson of King Aethelred II, was a candidate for the English throne but was exiled when Cnut of Denmark captured the English throne in 1016. Edward traveled through Russia and eastern Europe, where he married Agatha, a relative of the Germanic emperor Henry II. The family returned to England in 1057, but Edward soon died, leaving three children, of whom Margaret was the eldest. Margaret and her family fled England and took refuge in Scotland after the Norman Conquest. She and Malcolm were married by 1070. Although her *vita* claims that Margaret entered the marriage reluctantly and would have preferred to remain celibate, the couple seems to have enjoyed an easy partnership, and Margaret emerged as an influential voice within the kingdom. Of their eight children, three became Scottish kings, and one became queen of England. A generous patron of the Church, Margaret established a Benedictine community at Dumfermline, assisted pilgrims and hermits, and promoted a series of reforms designed to bring Scottish ecclesiastical practices into conformance with continental practices. Her customary ascetic practices gradually put her into a physically weakened state, and she died soon after hearing news that her husband and son had been killed fighting in England. She was popularly regarded as a saint by the early twelfth century and formally canonized in 1249 or 1250.

LOIS L. HUNEYCUTT

References and Further Reading

Baker, Derek. "A Nursery of Saints: St Margaret of Scotland Revisited." In *Medieval Women*, edited by Derek Baker. Oxford: Basil Blackwell, 1978, pp. 119–142.

Bruce, W. Moir. "Saint Margaret and Her Chapel in the Castle of Edinburgh." *The Book of the Old Edinburgh Club* 5 (1913): 1–66.

Gameson, Richard. "The Gospels of Margaret of Scotland and the Literacy of an Eleventh-Century Queen." In *Women and the Book: Assessing the Visual Evidence*, edited by Jane H. M. Taylor and Lesley Smith. London and Toronto: British Library and University of Toronto Press, 1997, pp. 149–171.

Huneycutt, Lois L. "A Translation of the Life of St. Margaret of Scotland." In *Matilda of Scotland: A Study in Medieval Queenship*. Woodbridge, Suffolk: Boydell Press, 2003, pp. 161–178.

Wall, Valerie. "Queen Margaret of Scotland (1070–1093): Burying the Past, Enshrining the Future." In *Queens and Queenship in Medieval Europe: Proceedings of a Conference Held at King's College London, April 1995*, edited by Anne J. Duggan. Woodbridge, Suffolk: Boydell Press, 1997, pp. 27–38.

See also **Hagiography; Lay Piety, Patronage, Ecclesiastical; Scotland**

MARGARET OF YORK

Margaret of York (1446–1503) was duchess of Burgundy. As the younger sister of King Edward IV of England, she was married in 1468 to Charles the Bold, duke of Burgundy, ruler of the Low Countries. Margaret must have felt it a great personal loss that she was unable to provide a male heir to the Burgundian dynasty. Her political activities were limited to representative appearances at diplomatic receptions at court and at the solemn gatherings of the representatives of the estates. Her most important political actions occurred during the crisis that followed the death of Charles the Bold on January 5, 1477. Together with her young stepdaughter, Duchess Mary of Burgundy, she introduced the first governmental measures during the following weeks of turbulence. It was Margaret who convinced Mary to honour the marriage arranged for her by her father to Maximilian I of Austria. The early death of Mary of Burgundy left Margaret with the task of caring for Mary's underage children and then her grandchildren, which resulted in a renewal of court life at her residence at Mechelen. Under the old laws, a widow enjoyed an independence that a woman could not have expected under any other circumstances. Seen in this light, Margaret of York behaved in a very different way during her marriage from how she did afterward. She then devoted herself increasingly to promoting strict observance in cloisters. In that sense, her widowhood sheds more light on her personality than do the years during which she actively devoted herself to her duties as a wife.

WIM BLOCKMANS

References and Further Reading

Eichberger, Dagmar. *Women of Distinction: Margaret of York: Margaret of Austria*. Leuven: Brepolis, 2005.

Weightman, Christine. *Margaret of York, Duchess of Burgundy 1446–1503*. Gloucester & New York: Alan Sutton, St. Martin's Press, 1989.

See also **Burgundian Netherlands; Mary of Burgundy; Noble Women; Widows**

MARGARET "THE CRIPPLE" OF MAGDEBURG

At age twelve, Margaret (c. 1210–c. 1250) (also known as the Lame [*Contracta*]) was enclosed as an anchoress near the cathedral of Magdeburg, where she was regarded with suspicion and contempt by the clergy. She was removed from her cell but managed to have herself enclosed at a Cistercian convent in the Newtown of Magdeburg, the quarter of merchants, artisans, and religious women, where she became a teacher of religion. According to the Latin *Life* recorded by her father confessor, John the Dominican, Mary, the Mother of God, took Margaret into her care and taught her to read. Mary became her instructor and teacher, *doctrix eius et magistra*. Margaret viewed herself as Mary's servant. Her task, as she saw it, was to assist the young citizenry in their striving for religious self-expression. Margaret mediated for them with God and taught them the basic tenets of the Christian faith, which she herself graphically put into practice in her own anchorhold. As John formulated it: "And often she called great public sinners to her and spent all her strength on them…. And she at times thought she had such great wisdom, that even if all the oppressed hearts of the world had stood before her, she would have comforted them all, each one according to his circumstances." In the group of people that gathered at her anchorhold we may recognize an informal community of discourse, to which Margaret transmitted the wisdom and knowledge she had gathered herself.

ANNEKE B. MULDER-BAKKER

References and Further Reading

von Magdeburg, Johannes, O.P. *Die Vita der Margareta contracta, einer Magdeburger Rekluse des 13. Jahrhunderts*. Edited by Paul Gerhard Schmidt. Leipzig: Benno Verlag, 1992.

———. *The Vita of Margaret the Lame*. Translation by Gertrud Jaron Lewis and Tilman Lewis. Toronto: Peregrina, 2001.

Mulder-Bakker, Anneke B. *Lives of the Anchoresses: The Rise of the Urban Recluse in Medieval Europe*. Philadelphia: University of Pennsylvania Press, 2005, pp. 148–173, 255–263.

See also **Anchoresses; Disabilities; Education, Lay**

MARGINALIA, MANUSCRIPT

Marginalia is an art historical term that refers to images at the periphery, or in the margins, of a manuscript page. Such images feature most prominently in Gothic illuminated manuscripts of around 1250 to 1350, especially from northeastern France and Flanders, southern England, and (to a more limited degree) northern Italy, primarily Bologna. They are descendants of the human, animal, and fantastic beings that inhabited the decorated letters of earlier Gothic and Romanesque manuscripts, and are, like those earlier images, overwhelmingly secular in nature. Religious subjects occur, but themes from

Anonymous, Fifteenth century. Witches leaving for the Sabbath. Marginalia of "Le Champion des Dames" by Martin Lefranc, 1440. Credit: Snark / Art Resource, NY.

literature and daily life are more common. Favorite subjects include the hunt, chivalric activities, romance, music-making, clerics, and doctors; depictions are fairly conventional, though often given a satirical twist. Although the subjects are so often secular, marginalia are most often found in Christian devotional books, particularly Psalters and Books of Hours. The essential resource for the study of manuscript marginalia is Lilian Randall's *Images in the Margins of Gothic Manuscripts*, which indexes and illustrates marginalia from no fewer than 226 manuscripts.

The number of marginalia varies considerably from one manuscript to the next. In some they are limited to the elaborately decorated pages that signal important textual divisions. Such is the case with the well-known *Ormesby Psalter* (England, early 1300s; Oxford, Bodleian Library, MS. Douce 366). In others, such as the contemporaneous *Gorleston Psalter* (London, British Library, MS. Additional 49622), marginalia occur on every single page. As with other components of the decoration, such as the border, decorated and historiated initials, miniatures, and line endings, the marginalia would have represented an additional cost to the patron.

Marginalia can be classified both by type of activity and by character, the latter including men, women, animals (especially apes, dogs, and rabbits), and hybrids—composite creatures referred to as *babewynes* in medieval documents. Women and female hybrids are depicted far less often than men, but they engage in activities as numerous and varied. In just one tiny early fourteenth-century Psalter made in Ghent (Oxford, Bodleian Library, MS. Douce 5 and 6), women carry wood, make and tend a fire, cook, churn butter, make wafers, clean, card and spin wool, fetch water, feed livestock, shear a sheep, mind children, pick flowers, groom themselves, dance, and play music. Most of the women in these episodes and in other manuscripts wear the decorous white head veil or have their hair bound in a net and fillet. Their most common attributes are the distaff and spindle, which they wield as weapons in some of the more humorous marginal scenes. They become a lance in parodies of the chivalric tilt, and in a favorite motif derived from the legend of Reynard, the outwitted housewife (or hybrid with a woman's upper body) shakes a distaff at the wily fox as he makes off with her fowl.

Depictions of specific female figures also occur in the margins, including personifications, such as Ecclesia and Synagogue; and Power of Women motifs, such as Phyllis astride Aristotle, Salome, and Judith. But more prevalent in this category are episodes from the lives of female saints and the Virgin. In the *Queen Mary's Psalter* (England, 1310 to 1320; London, British Library, MS. Royal 2. B.VII), there are thirty-six different miracles of the Virgin and multiple scenes from the lives of Saints Agatha, Agnes, Catherine, and Margaret, presented in consecutive series in the lower margins. Female patrons represent another category of recognizable women in marginalia. They are most often shown in prayer and are sometimes identifiable by blazoned robes or proximity to coats of arms. There are no fewer than thirty-three depictions of a young patron named Marguerite in the small Franco-Flemish Book of Hours (1320s; London, British Library, MS. Additional 36684, and New York, Pierpont Morgan Library, MS. 754) that inspired much of Michael Camille's consideration of manuscript marginalia in the first chapter of *Image on the Edge: The Margins of Medieval Art*.

In several manuscripts, such as the *Luttrell Psalter* (England, c. 1340; London, British Library, MS. Additional 42130) and the *Gorleston Psalter*, there are direct relationships between some marginal images and certain words or phrases in the adjacent text. Just as often, however, marginalia appear to have no direct relationship either to the text or to other images on the same page. They are and were amusing, but to what degree they were also intended to elucidate or otherwise redirect attention to the text is still very much in question.

MARGOT MCILWAIN NISHIMURA

References and Further Reading

Camille, Michael. *Image on the Edge*. Cambridge, Mass: Harvard University Press, 1992.
Randall, Lilian M. C. *Images in the Margins of Gothic Manuscripts*. Berkeley and Los Angeles: University of California Press, 1966.
Sandler, Lucy Freeman. "The Study of Marginal Imagery: Past, Present, and Future." *Studies in Iconography* 18 (1997): 1–49.

See also **Art, Representations of Women in; Books of Hours; Clothing; Courtship; Hagiography, Iconographic Aspects of; Heraldry; Household Management; Mary, Virgin: in Art; Nuns as Illuminators; Obscenity; Patronage, Artistic; Personifications Visualized as Women; Woman on Top**

MARGRETHE

Margrethe (Margareta) (1353–1412) was queen of Norway and Sweden. She was the daughter of King Valdemar IV of Denmark and Helvig of Schleswig. Margrethe is, above all, famous for the unification of the Nordic monarchies at the end of the fourteenth century. It began in 1376 when she campaigned for her son Olav, heir to the Norwegian throne, to be king of Denmark. His challenger was Albrecht, of the German dynasty Mecklenburg, who was also Margrethe's nephew, and Valdemar's second grandson. When Margrethe's husband, King Håkon of Norway (and Sweden, 1362–1364), died in 1380, Denmark and Norway were united. As Olav was still a child, Margrethe became the real power, and she took the lead in the struggle with the Mecklenburgers for hegemony in Scandinavia and the Baltic. When Olav died in 1387, Margrethe managed to be elected regent of Denmark and Norway as well as leader of the Swedish opposition to King Albrecht. In 1389 she adopted her sister's grandson, Bugislav of Pommern-Stolp, who under the name of Erik was received as lawful heir to the Norwegian throne. The defeat of the Mecklenburgers in 1395 paved the way for Erik to be King of Sweden and Denmark. His coronation as union-king in Calmar 1397 marks the apex of Margrethe's career. Formally she resigned, though in fact she ruled until her death. After 1397 Margrethe worked hard to mold the three Scandinavian kingdoms into one state, and to reconquer lost border provinces such as Schleswig and Gotland.

Margrethe's political genius has never been contested, though her motives have been much debated.

In the first half of the nineteenth century she was portrayed as a Scandinavian idealist who wanted to counterbalance German influences. After defeat by the Prussians (1864) the image of Margrethe the Danish nationalist prevailed, because she fought for Denmark's domination over Scandinavia. In recent times depictions of Margrethe as an idealist and as a nationalist have both given way to Margrethe the Machiavellist, who primarily fought for power and dynastic interests.

STEINAR IMSEN

References and Further Reading

Imsen, Steinar. "Late Medieval Scandinavian Queenship." In *Queens and Queenship in Medieval Europe: Proceedings of a Conference Held at King's College London, April 1995*, edited by Anne J. Duggan. Woodbridge, Suffolk: Boydell Press, 1997, pp. 53–73.
Olesen, Jens E. "Inter-Scandinavian Relations." In *The Cambridge History of Scandinavia*, I: *Prehistory to 1520*, edited by Knut Helle. Cambridge: Cambridge University Press, 2003, pp. 710–770.

See also **Queens and Empresses: The West; Scandinavia**

MARGUERITE PORETE

Biographical details about Marguerite Porete (d. 1310) are scarce, and her identity as the author of the *Mirror of Simple Annihilated Souls and Those Who Only Remain in Will and Desire of Love* (written c. 1290) was obscured for more than six hundred years. The *Mirror*, which was first publicly condemned and burned in 1306, was read for centuries as the work of assorted male authors. Originally written in Old French, the text comes down to us also in Latin, Italian, and Middle English. In 1946, the scholar Romana Guarnieri reunited the text with its author, who had been burned at the stake as a relapsed heretic on June 1, 1310 in the Place de Grèves in Paris. Hers is the earliest recorded death sentence for mystical heresy in the history of Christianity.

Porete was an itinerant, solitary Beguine from Hainault in Belgium. She was also thought to be associated with the sect of the Free Spirit, and was thus connected with groups held under increasing suspicion by the papacy. Her sometimes radical theological speculations added to that cloud of suspicion. It seems she welcomed controversy as an uncloistered laywoman spreading an esoteric spiritual message in the vernacular. Although she secured the endorsement of three theologians, each of whom attested to the worth (and theological complexity) of her work, she could not sway church authorities. In 1306, Porete was arrested and her book was condemned and burned. She failed to heed a warning to cease spreading her message by spoken or written word, and in 1308 she was rearrested and imprisoned. She refused to speak to her inquisitors during her eighteen-month incarceration because, to Porete, worldly authorities had no essential power. The twenty-one church-appointed theologians at her trial declared her a heretic based on fifteen propositions taken out of context. In keeping with her convictions, Porete accepted this worldly defeat peacefully, and her calm demeanor in the face of violent death reportedly moved many in the crowd to conversion.

The *Mirror* is a dialogue primarily between "Love" and "Soul" in which they explore the doctrine of annihilation. Annihilation, or complete identity with God, is the culmination of a seven-stage path of increasing perfection. A "simple" soul "becomes what God is" in annihilation. For Porete, the point of God-given free will is to surrender that will entirely back to God in order to reach an embodied spiritual state of "knowing nothing, having nothing, and willing nothing." This is the perfect state of being "without a why." In annihilation, an earthly soul can realize its precreational state of complete union with the divine. Porete's doctrine is decidedly esoteric and thus meant only for those who are themselves "simple souls." This doctrine was never a mainstream theological doctrine before or after Marguerite Porete, although it has solid roots in Neoplatonic philosophy.

Porete's claims were seen as a clear challenge to male-dominated scholastic theology, as well as to the traditional role of the institutional church in mediating the relationship between God and the soul. Her work is distinct from most other medieval women's writings in several ways. For instance, many medieval women who wrote in vernacular languages espoused "safe" theological doctrines and refrained from making Porete's bold claims. Porete also avoided the standard apologies for feminine weakness so common in the writings of her contemporaries. She had the courage of her convictions, despite (or perhaps because of) her lowly status as a woman. She found authority within herself and her true identity as a simple soul, not through visions or through the approval of the institutional church. Moreover, Porete steered her readers away from certain staples of lay piety and mysticism. She refers little or not at all to the imitation of Christ and its attendant penitential asceticism. She avoided bridal language and extended reference to the Bible. She also steered clear of scrupulous attention to sinfulness and referred only briefly to liturgical cycles and Eucharistic piety.

Porete was an anomaly in her time, and she remains so today as scholars try to understand her text and context. She has been "tried" and found guilty of heresy by some modern scholars, while others have attributed her execution to political machinations beyond her control. Still others have seen her primarily as a target for a church increasingly anxious about certain expressions of lay piety. More recent scholarship has focused on literary and theological motifs in her work, such as themes and images from the courtly love tradition. Others have examined her influence on others, most notably Meister Eckhart (d. c. 1328).

JOANNE MAGUIRE ROBINSON

References and Further Reading

Hollywood, Amy. *The Soul as Virgin Wife: Mechthild of Magdeburg, Marguerite Porete, and Meister Eckhart.* Notre Dame, Ind.: Notre Dame University Press, 1995.

McGinn, Bernard. *The Flowering of Mysticism: Men and Women in the New Mysticism (1200–1350).* New York: Crossroad Publishing Company, 1998, pp. 153–265.

Newman, Barbara. "The Mirror and the Rose: Marguerite Porete's Encounter with the Dieu d'Amours." In *The Vernacular Spirit: Essays on Medieval Religious Literature,* edited by Renate Blumenfeld-Kosinski et al. New York: Palgrave, 2002, pp. 105–124.

Porete Marguerite. *The Mirror of Simple Souls,* Translated by Edmund Colledge, J. C. Marler, and Judith Grant. Notre Dame, Ind.: Notre Dame University Press, 1999.

———. *Speculum simplicium animarum,* edited by Romana Guarnieri and Paul Verdeyen. Corpus Christianorum: Continuatio Mediaevalis 69. Turnhout: Brepols, 1986.

Robinson, Joanne Maguire. *Nobility and Annihilation in Marguerite Porete's "Mirror of Simple Souls."* Albany, N.Y.: State University of New York Press, 2001.

See also **Church; Courtly Love; Heretics and Heresy; Scholasticism; Theology; Translation; Women Authors: Old French Texts**

MARIA OF VENICE (MARIA STURION)

Maria of Venice (Maria Sturion) (1379–1399), a Dominican penitent in the last five years of her brief life, figures in the *exempla* literature of the later Middle Ages. Thomas de Antonio da Siena (Thomas Caffarini), a Dominican, composed a biography (*legenda*) of Maria shortly after her death in 1399. It figured among the materials forwarded by Thomas to obtain a rule for penitent women in Venice. That rule was granted in June 26, 1405 by Pope Innocent VII in his bull *Sedis apostolicae.*

Maria has been called the imitable saint because she performed no intimidating spiritual feats, underwent few extreme austerities, and was not a miracle worker; in other words, her life did not contain the heroic feats associated with Maria's own role model,

Catherine of Siena. Maria came from a prosperous and supportive household, indeed one of the 120 wealthiest households in Venice, the wealthiest city in Europe. At fifteen Maria was married off to Giannino della Piazza, immediately experienced a conversion to penitent, and was deserted by her husband, who left to fight wars in northern Italy. Thereafter Maria expressed her spiritual calling largely through the outward signs of dressing humbly and attending church, where she listened raptly to the long sermons preached by Thomas Caffarini.

Maria's *legenda* had relevance to her society. As a deserted young wife with no legal recourse to resolve the impasse in which she found herself, Maria represented a growing segment of wealthy, leisured women for whom marriages did not serve to provide satisfactory lives. Some of these women could find spiritual guidance and solace as Dominican penitents. As her confessor, Thomas encouraged Maria's spiritual journey through confession and instruction, taught her to write, and before her death awarded her the garb of a penitent.

SUSAN MOSHER STUARD

References and Further Reading

Bornstein, Daniel. "Spiritual Kin and Domestic Devotions." In *Gender and Society in Renaissance Italy*, edited by Judith C. Brown and Robert C. Davis. London and New York: Longman, 1998, pp. 173–192.

———, trans. "Thomas of Siena: *The Legend of Maria of Venice*." In *Dominican Penitent Women*, edited by Maiju Lehmijoki-Gardner. New York: Paulist Press, 2005, pp. 105–176.

Elliott, Dyan. *Proving Woman: Female Spirituality and Inquisitional Culture in the Later Middle Ages*. Princeton, N.J.: Princeton University Press, 2005, pp. 105–176.

Lehmijoki-Gardner, Maiju. *Worldly Saints: Social Interaction of Dominican Penitent Women in Italy, 1200–1500*. Bibliotheca Historica, number 35. Helsinki: Suomen Historiallinen Seura, 1999.

Sorelli, Fernanda. *La Santità Imitabile: "Leggenda di Maria da Venezia" di Tommaso da Siena*. Venice: Deputazione Editrice, 1984.

See also **Catherine of Siena; Dominican Order; Hagiography; Italy; Laywomen, Religious; Spiritual Care**

MARIE DE FRANCE

Marie de France is usually recognized as one of the most accomplished writers of medieval French literature and as the author of three major works: the *Lais* (written in the 1170s), the *Fables* (1180s), and the *Espurgatoire Seint Patriz* (St. Patrick's Purgatory, around 1190). A few critics have questioned the attribution of all three texts to the same "Marie." No

manuscript contains the *Lais*, the *Fables*, and the *Espurgatoire* together, and only one manuscript, Harley 978, contains both *Lais* and *Fables*. It has even been suggested that the feminine signature "Marie" does not indicate a woman author. But most scholars concur that the same author composed *Lais*, *Fables*, and *Espurgatoire*, and many would agree that the works attributed to Marie display a high degree of authorial presence and share common thematic concerns, despite their evident generic differences. Feminist literary critics and historians of women and gender in the Middle Ages have long recognized the importance of Marie's complex works.

The historical Marie de France remains a subject of conjecture. Most likely, Marie was born in France and wrote in England; her literary and linguistic talents suggest that she was high-born. She dedicates the *Lais* to a king, probably Henry II Plantagenet, husband of Eleanor of Aquitaine. She presents the *Fables* to "Count William," evidently a member of the Anglo-Norman feudal aristocracy. The *Espurgatoire* was written for a lay audience. If Marie was a member of a religious order, as has been suggested, she composed her works for lay audiences beyond the monastery or nunnery, for women and men in courtly society. Marie's works attest to the high degree of literacy attained by some women in the Anglo-Norman aristocracy and to their active participation in cultural patronage and production.

The *Lais*

Marie's first extant work, the *Lais*, consists of twelve short narrative poems penned in octosyllabic rhyming couplets, which range from 118 lines (*Chevrefeuil*) to over 1180 lines (*Eliduc*). In a fifty-six-line prologue, Marie describes her artistic project in terms that both convey her debt to classical and Christian culture and express her desire to do something new. Noting the duty of those who possess eloquence to reveal their talents, she invokes ancient poets who wrote "obscurely" or enigmatically so that their successors could provide their own commentary and interpretation. Marie announces that she will not translate from the Latin as others have done but will instead retell lays (Breton tales from the oral tradition that were sung or recounted). Marie's twelve short narratives transpose Breton fairy tales and magical adventures into a feudal setting with a courtly style that incorporates the rhetorical techniques and themes of classical authors, notably Ovid. Her narrator frequently addresses the audience, particularly in the tales' prologues and epilogues, thereby highlighting the author's transformative artistry. Marie's narrator composes in an elegant, concise style, and conveys compassion for her characters as she explores social tensions and physic depths, often in an otherworldly setting. Scholars have remarked on the self-conscious stance of Marie as a female author in the Prologue and have noted the importance of women as readers, writers, and speakers throughout the *Lais*.

The twelve *Lais* recount from a variety of perspectives the adventures and suffering of men and women in love. The *lai* appearing first in the Harley manuscript, *Guigemar*, announces many of the collection's themes. A young nobleman, Guigemar, who is ostracized for his indifference to love, shoots an androgynous hind with an arrow that rebounds to wound the hunter in the thigh. The hind prophesies that Guigemar will be cured by a woman who suffers for him as much as he does for her. Transported by a magical ship to another land, Guigemar falls in love with a married woman who has been locked by her jealous old husband in a room with painted walls. Venus, goddess of love, is depicted casting one of Ovid's books on the constraints of love into ardent flames. Although Guigemar and the lady engage in an adulterous affair, their love is reciprocal, long-suffering, and faithful. After a painful separation, the couple rediscovers each other when only they can undo the knot and the belt that they have borne as tokens of their fidelity.

Marvelous animals, enchanted places, unhappily married women with jealous husbands, and Ovidian motifs will recur in many of the ensuing lais, often with surprising turns. *Equitan*, *Bisclavret*, *Yonec*, *Le Rossignol*, *Milun*, *Chièvrefeuille*, and *Eliduc* tell varied tales of adultery. The adulterous king and the lady married to the king's faithful seneschal are evil characters in *Equitan*; they are punished when they are cast into a vat of boiling water intended for the husband. Marvelous or symbolic animals recur in *Bisclavret*, *Laustic*, *Yonec*, *Milun*, and *Eliduc* in a variety of guises. The marvelous creature in *Bisclavret* is a werewolf, but his behavior is more courteous than that of his wife, who acts like a beast when she betrays him. The weasel in *Eliduc* bears a medicinal flower that enables the hero to rouse his beloved from an unconscious state.

Unmarried maidens are featured in many lais. *Le Frêne*, *Lanval*, *Deux Amants*, *Milun*, *Le Malheureux*, and *Eliduc* portray single women who display resourcefulness and various degrees of autonomy, despite evident obstacles, as they struggle in love. Fresne, orphaned at birth, is socially marginalized, but her own act of generosity eventually reunites her with her birth mother. The lady in *Lanval* is a fairy who grants special powers to her lover, an ostracized knight. The young woman in *Deux Amants* is devoted to an overly possessive father and to her lover, who dies carrying her in his arms. Milun's beloved maiden bears a child out of wedlock but manages to save her honor and that of her son and his father, whom she eventually marries. In Marie's rich tapestry of personalities and narrative perspectives, no one thread easily summarizes the *lai*. The stories' intertextual echoes, intersecting motifs, and sometimes conflicting approaches invite the audience's reflection and the reader's comparative interpretation.

The *Fables*

To judge from the number of extant manuscripts (twenty-five), Marie's clever *Fables* were even more popular in the Middle Ages than her artful *Lais*. Aesopic tales—short moral stories often but not always featuring anthropomorphized animals, which were thought to have originated with the legendary Greek master Aesop—circulated broadly in Latin manuscripts in the Middle Ages and were an important part of the school curriculum. Marie's collection, the first extant collection of such fables in the vernacular, brings together forty stories from the fourth-century Latin *Romulus Nilantilus* tradition and sixty-two tales from other sources, including Arabic tales and some that Marie herself may have invented.

Scholars have described the many ways Marie transforms her sources and inserts her own authority as a female teacher. Although her women characters and animals are not immune from moral failings, she often shows sympathy for female creatures, as in her depiction of a pregnant sow or a bear who is raped. The ending moral to the tale is not always straightforward and does not always easily fit the story itself; readers must reflect on the stories' meanings. Many fables analyze feudal politics; the collection may have served as a manual of instruction for princes and noble families.

Saint Patrick's Purgatory

Marie's last work, *Espurgatoire Seint Patriz* (*Saint Patrick's Purgatory*) appears to be the most straightforward translation of a source, Henry of Saltrey's

Latin *Tractatus de Purgatorio sancti Patricii,* the tale of the Irish knight Owein's return voyage to Purgatory. But in this text, too, Marie intervenes as a female author, consciously inserting herself into a masculine, clerical tradition and writing expressly for a lay audience. Owein's journey explores moral and physical sufferings that result from human foibles and offers the possibility of redemption. An exemplum appended to Owein's story recounts the tale of a priest who castrates himself to avoid sexually molesting the young orphan girl in his charge. As in Marie's other works, the *Espurgatoire Seint Patriz* examines dark or "obscure" regions of human nature in a way that invites critical reflection.

In different ways, each of Marie's works examines the conflict between personal desires and social communities, paying particular attention to relations between men and women. The *Lais,* the *Fables,* and the *Espurgatoire Seint Patriz* help to inaugurate a critical examination of gender roles within vernacular courtly and didactic medieval literature.

ROBERTA L. KRUEGER

References and Further Reading

Amer, Sahar. *Esopé au féminin: Marie de France et la politique de l'interculturalité.* Amsterdam: Rodopoi, 1999.

Bloch, R. Howard. *The Anonymous Marie de France.* Chicago: University of Chicago Press, 2003.

Freeman, Michelle. "Marie de France's Poetics of Silence: The Implications for a Feminine *translatio.*" *PMLA* 99 (1984): 860–883.

Jambeck, Karen. "Reclaiming the Woman in the Book: Marie de France and the *Fables.*" In *Women, the Book, and the Worldly,* edited by Lesley Smith and Jane H. M. Taylor. Cambridge: Cambridge University Press, 1995, pp. 119–137.

Maréchal, Chantal A., ed. *In Quest of Marie de France: A Twelfth-Century Poet.* Lewiston, N.Y.: Edwin Mellen, 1992.

Marie de France. *Espurgatoire Seint Patriz,* edited and translated by Yolande de Pontfarcy. Louvain: Peeters, 1998.

———. *Fables,* edited and translated by Harriet Spiegel. Toronto: University of Toronto Press, 1987.

———. *Fables,* edited and translated by Charles Brucker. Louvain: Peeters, 1998.

———. *Lais de Marie de France,* edited by Karl Warnke and translated by Laurence Harf-Lancner. Lettres gothiques. Paris: Librairie générale française, 1990.

———. *The Lais of Marie de France,* translated by Robert Hanning and Joan Ferrante. New York: Dutton, 1978.

———. *The Lais of Marie de France,* translated by Glyn S. Burgess and Keith Busby. New York: Penguin, 1986.

———. *Saint Patrick's Purgatory,* translated by Michael J. Curley. Binghamton, N.Y.: Medieval and Renaissance Texts and Studies, 1993.

Paupert, Anne. "Les femmes et la parole dans les *Lais* de Marie de France." In *Amour et merveille: Les Lais de Marie de France,* edited by Jean Dufournet. Paris: Champion, 1995, pp. 169–187.

See also **Literature, Old French; Ovid: Medieval Reception of; Patronage, Literary; Translation; Women Authors: Old French Texts**

MARIE OF OIGNIES

Independent religious women who tried to live holy lives outside the cloister (*mulieres sanctae*) became common in the southern Low Countries (especially in the diocese of Liège) in the early thirteenth century. Some of these women lived on their own, while others formed communities with varying degrees of institutional formality. One of the earliest known of these women who came to be called Beguines is Marie of Oignies. Married young, Marie made an agreement with her husband that they would live chaste lives. Starting c. 1191 they served at a leprosarium near Nivelles in Brabant. Marie later (c. 1207) became a recluse affiliated with the house of Augustinian canons at Oignies near Namur. There she earned a reputation for austerity, tearful penance, miracles, and visionary experiences before her death in 1213.

Marie's life and experiences are best known to us from the account written by Jacques de Vitry, a noted preacher who later became a cardinal. Jacques, who was ordained a priest at Oignies, served as Marie's confessor until her death. The life was written after Marie's death, and one must sift it carefully to distinguish biographical details from hagiographic conventions. Jacques was eager to defend Marie's reputation against those who thought her unorthodox or overwrought. Thomas of Cantimpré, who was converted by Jacques' preaching, became a monk but later joined the Dominican order. Among his writings was a supplement to Jacques' life of Marie of Oignies, which discussed the cardinal's relations with her (not always treating Jacques positively) and related such of her miracles for which he found credible evidence. These writings popularized not just Marie's reputation but the fame of the religious women of the Low Countries. Only later would official opinion about such women become more consistently suspicious.

THOMAS IZBICKI

References and Further Reading

King, Margot H., and Hugh Feiss, trans. *Two Lives of Marie d'Oignies.* Toronto: Peregrina Publishing, 1998.

McGuire, Brian Patrick. *Holy Women and Monks in the Thirteenth Century.* Toronto: Peregrina Publishing, 1999.

Simons, Walter. *Cities of Ladies: Beguine Communities in the Medieval Low Countries, 1200–1565.* Philadelphia: University of Pennsylvania Press, 2001.

See also **Beguines; Chastity and Chaste Marriage; Flanders; Hagiography; Laywomen, Religious**

MARKET AND TRADESWOMEN

The position of women in medieval economy seems to be characterized by a gradual process of exclusion. The scale of this process is matter for debate. Some state that even in the High Middle Ages women could never aspire to gain access to entrepreneurial activity (Bennett), while others argue that the process was a cyclical one, whereby labor shortage and easier access to capital after the Black Death offered opportunities to move beyond traditional female tasks (Goldberg, Kowaleski). Moreover, there were strong geographical differences, associated with legal structures and social customs. The economic role of women in northern Europe seems to have been more important and highly regarded than in the Mediterranean. Nevertheless, women's work offered, generally speaking, low status and low pay (Howell).

There is no doubt that the hold of male-dominated guilds from the thirteenth century onwards strengthened the process of exclusion. Restrictions on women's participation in the guilds are, however, difficult to interpret. Manufacturing guilds and their hierarchical system of training and entrepreneurship were instrumental in pushing out women, but for retailing guilds the situation is less clear. Many women involved in retail were master's daughters, and their trade is evidence of life-cycle patterns, but their presence was substantial nonetheless. Iconographic and literary sources show trading women outside as well as within the boundaries of the formal market economy. Women traded both as their husbands' helpers and independently. Commercial income generated by women allowed a more efficient distribution of labor within the household. In fact, women's roles were defined by the interaction between the patriarchal structures in society and the requirements of a flexible economy.

Women engaged in trade were granted legal protection in municipal law from the eleventh century on. In thirteenth-century Augsburg in Germany, women were allowed to get involved in business activities independent of their husbands and to take their own disputes to court. In Flemish cities businesswomen acted on their own account as well as on behalf of their husbands. This legal framework originated probably not as a tool to emancipate women but as a means of freeing husbands from the debts and obligations of their wives.

Town and guild administrators were, therefore, not aiming at exclusion, nor did they enforce a strict division between the public (male) forum and private (female) space. Despite the greater stress on issues of public morality in the later Middle Ages, regulation remained often vague and ambiguous, or else extremely specific. Retail was clearly regulated less strictly than manufacture. In fifteenth-century Bruges, Belgium, guild statutes mention only occasionally specific conditions for women, and when they did, they aimed to limit concentration and "unfair" competition, rather than to exclude women.

We are quite uninformed about the exact scope of female involvement in marketing. Husbands and fathers cloud the activities of their wives and daughters; single women are underreported. Very often economic activity is only apparent when a wife was widowed and able, according to city law, to act independently. Nevertheless, there is no doubt that women made their own contributions to regional and local exchange, both on a small and a large scale, although mostly, but not exclusively, in less specialized, low-status activities. But women also could be involved in larger commercial ventures as associates of male relatives, as independent investors, or as widowed heirs of larger business ventures. Women also tended more than men to shift occupations according to their life cycle and they employed fewer (male) servants on a regular basis.

At the basic level, peasant women took agricultural produce to local markets, where they sold dairy, poultry, fruit, vegetables, and various processed goods (ale, textiles). By the thirteenth century a weekly market was likely to be within reach of most villagers. In the towns, women tried to make a living with various retailing activities. Often they were hucksters, petty retailers acting as intermediaries for (poor) consumers. These seem to have been particularly numerous in smaller towns. In larger towns, specialization and guild control were stricter. Many women were active as forestallers, buying goods from country producers before they reached the market and reselling them at a profit. The guilds, always trying to enhance market transparency, were notably suspicious of such activities. Although regular traders (shopkeepers and stallholders at the marketplace or in the commercial halls) tended to be male, women were also active in this trade, in particular as mercers (selling a wide variety of nonperishable goods). Some retailing activities were dominated by women, to the point that they were regarded as female (e.g., ale, bread, fish, poultry, dairy). In some towns, secondhand clothes were almost exclusively female (Nuremberg), and in others exlusively male (Antwerp). The great majority of linen stalls in the hall of medieval Bruges were rented by women, while the cloth stalls were in male hands. But in general the occupational division by sex was less clear-cut.

Peter Stabel and Laura Van Aert

References and Further Reading

Bennett, Judith M. "Medieval Women, Modern Women: Across the Great Divide." In *Culture and History 1350–1600*, edited by David Aers. Detroit: Wayne State University Press, 1992, pp. 147–175.

Goldberg, P. J. P. *Women, Work, and Life Cycle in a Medieval Economy: Women in York and Yorkshire c. 1300–1520*. Oxford: Clarendon Press, 1992.

Herlihy, David. "Women's Work in the Towns of Traditional Europe." In *Women, Family and Society in Medieval Europe*. Oxford and Providence, R. I.: Berghahn Books, 1995, pp. 69–95.

Howell, Martha C., *Women, Production and Patriarchy in Late Medieval Cities*. Chicago: University of Chicago Press, 1986.

Kowaleski, Maryanne. "Women's Work in a Market Town: Exeter in the Late 14th Century." In *Women and Work in Preindustial Europe*, edited by Barbara Hanawalt. Bloomington, Ind.: University of Indiana Press, 1986, pp. 145–164.

Stabel, Peter. "Women at the Market: Gender and Retail in the Towns of Medieval Flanders." In *Secretum Scriptorum. Liber alumnorum Walter Prevenier*, edited by Wim Blockmans, Marc Boone, and Thérèse De Hemptinne. Leuven: Garant, 1999, pp. 259–276.

Wiesner, Merry E. *Working Women in Renaissance Germany*. New Brunswick, N.J.: Rutgers University Press, 1986.

See also **Business; Division of Labor; Guild Members and Guilds; Merchant Families, Women of; Work**

MAROZIA OF ROME

Described by the pro-German bishop Liutprand of Cremona as "shameless harlots," Marozia of Rome (885–c. 938) and her mother Theodora have received little sympathetic attention from historians. Yet Liutprand's lurid account of Marozia's sexual liaisons with Pope Sergius III (by whom she had the future pope John XI), Alberic of Spoleto (producing another son, Prince Alberic II of Rome), and Guy of Tuscany masks the fact that Marozia needed to secure her family's future in Rome in turbulent early tenth-century Italy. The accession of Alberic II to power in Rome, driving off Hugh of Arles, king of Italy, in 932, suggests that his mother's and grandmother's unorthodox methods had succeeded. In fact, their story mirrors those of other dynasties in Italy at this time, for whom control of the local bishopric was a normal element of securing power. Liutprand's politically motivated account tells only the sexual story, heightened by the knowledge that the bishop of Rome was in fact the pope; the monastic patronage of the Theophylactan family throughout this period suggests that they sought numerous ways to enhance their status, and Marozia may in fact have retired to one of the family's houses.

PATRICIA SKINNER

References and Further Reading

Buc, Philippe. "Italian Hussies and German Matrons: Liutprand of Cremona on Dynastic Legitimacy." *Frühmittelalterliche Studien* 29 (1995): 207–225.

Hamilton, Bernard. "The House of Theophylact and the Promotion of the Religious Life among Women in Tenth-Century Rome." *Studia Monastica* 12 (1970): 195–217.

Liudprand of Cremona. *The Embassy to Constantinople and Other Writings*, edited by J. J. Norwich. London: J. M. Dent, 1993.

Llewellyn, Peter. *Rome in the Dark Ages*. London: Faber, 1971.

See also **Celibacy: Clerical and Priests' Concubines; Concubines; Italy; Noble Women**

MARRIAGE CEREMONIES

The early history of Christian marriage celebrations and ceremonies cannot be properly reconstructed, but there is reason to believe that the clergy were involved even in the Roman period (there is evidence in Tertullian). A fourth-century ban on clerical participation in banquets for second marriages is indirect evidence that they would take part if the couple were marrying for the first time. Other fourth-century evidence shows that a veil and a blessing could form part of a Christian marriage ceremony. Detailed evidence is sparse until the Carolingian period. From that period we have liturgical books containing a nuptial mass. We also have the Pope Nicholas I's (858–867) fairly full answer to a question about marriage put to him by the newly converted Bulgarians. He described an elaborate sequence of rituals reminiscent of Byzantine marriage ceremonies—there is a coronation, for instance. Significantly, though, he adds that many couples cannot afford all this and that for them consent alone is sufficient.

An elaborate set of rituals coalesced in Anglo-Norman rites around 1100, and in England and northern France the church door seems to have played an important part in the ceremony. Some features will seem familiar, such as the use of the marriage ring. (A remark in a sermon by Jean Halgrin d'Abbeville in the early thirteenth century shows that it was also normal for women to wear their engagement ring all their life.) The English Sarum rite presents us with an exceptionally detailed description of the marriage ritual, including the prostration of bride and groom before the altar during the canon of the mass, and a cloak's being held over them by four clerics. This last feature was apparently omitted when one member of the couple had been married before, as was a central element of an elaborate blessing after the canon and the Lord's Prayer. This omission has its origin in a ban on the blessing of second marriages, a ban that may have been much more thoroughgoing earlier on: perhaps implying that the priest should not participate in the ceremony at all (though this is a guess). The ban did not at any point mean that second marriages were illicit: second and subsequent marriages were common and regarded as perfectly moral and sacramental by the Church.

A religious ceremony was not part of the medieval western Church's definition of a valid sacramental marriage. Research has yet to establish a map of the law on marriage ritual. In some regions, notably England, marriage in church was a strict obligation. In others it was not. The rituals of upper-class marriage in Italy as described by Klapisch-Zuber contrast with the rituals analyzed by Brooke for England. There was certainly no general obligation imposed by pope or council to be married by a priest. The essence of a marriage was the mutual consent of the couple. This means that marriage in front of a notary (rather than a priest) did not necessarily have any anticlerical overtones at all.

What the Church did require was proper publicity. After 1215, every marriage was supposed to be preceded by a reading of the banns. Nevertheless many people ignored this rule and got married "clandestinely." The medieval Church abhorred such unions but recognized their validity as sacramental and indissoluble marriages, though the cost was high in terms of confusion and annulments on grounds of prior clandestine contracts. It would seem that the authorities doubted their power to make marriage by a priest necessary for validity, and it was left to the Council of Trent in the fifteenth century to cut the Gordian knot and declare marriage without the proper ceremony to be simply invalid.

DAVID D'AVRAY

References and Further Reading

Binder, B. *Geschichte des feierlichen Ehesegens von der Entstehung der Ritualien bis zur Gegenwart, mit Berüchsichtigung damit zusammenhängender Riten, Siten und Bräuche: Eine liturgiegeschichtliche Untersuchung.* Metten: Gebrauche, 1938.

Brooke, Christopher N. L. *The Medieval Idea of Marriage.* Oxford: Oxford University Press, 1989.

d'Avray, David. "Marriage Ceremonies and the Church in Italy after 1215." In *Marriage in Italy 1300–1650,* edited by Trevor Dean and K. J. P. Lowe. Cambridge: Cambridge University Press, 1998, pp. 107–115.

———. *Medieval Marriage: Symbolism and Society.* Oxford: Oxford University Press, 2005.

Duchesne, L. *Christian Worship: A Study of the Latin Liturgy up to the Time of Charlemagne,* translated by M. L. McClure. London: SPCK, 1919.

Klapisch-Zuber, Christiane. "Zacharie, ou le père évince: Les rites nuptiaux toscans entre Giotto et le concile de Trente." *Annales* 34 (1979): 1214–1243.

Molin, Jean-Baptiste, and Protais Mutembe. *Le Rituel du mariage en France du XIIᵉ au XVIᵉ siècle.* Paris: Beauchesne orbinian, 1974.

Ritzer, K., *Formen, Riten und religiöses Brauchtum der Eheschliessung in den christlichen Kirchen des ersten Jahrtausends.* Münster: Aschendorffsche Verlagsbuchhandling, 1981.

Stevenson, Kenneth. *Nuptial Blessing: A Study of Christian Marriage Rites.* London: Alcuin Club Collections, 1982.

See also **Church; Marriage, Christian; Marriage Preaching; Remarriage; Theology; Trousseau**

MARRIAGE, CHRISTIAN

Marriage in medieval Latin Christendom was both a secular and a religious bond. The tension between the two realms constitutes a major theme of its history during the millennium, but there were many chapters to that long story and complex subplots in different social and geographic settings. There was no single secular imperative, but a mix of sometimes contradictory political, social, and economic needs, so that even as a purely secular arrangement, marriage took no single form. Marriage's religious meaning was equally unsettled. The Christian laws of marriage and their attendant ideology were slow to develop, slower still to become normative, and they contained contradictions that rendered them a potent force for further, unexpected, change. Thus, although any particular couple and their families were constrained by the laws, customs, and cultural expectations of the day, medieval people's marriages were not all the same and the range of meanings attached to marriage changed over time.

The Ability to Marry

As a secular bond, marriage was a sociopolitical alliance between families. For the nobility, this often meant that parents actually selected their children's spouses, and it always meant that the interests of family property, power, and position determined when and to whom a child was married. Boys and girls of this class were regularly betrothed as infants and formally married as adolescents, and by the later Middle Ages merchant families sometimes adopted similar practices. For ordinary people, however, such matters were less rigorously controlled, and the evidence we have indicates that both men and women usually married later in life, generally between 18 and 28. Nevertheless, children of free peasants, artisans, or merchants were expected to—and almost always did—marry someone whose property, skills, or connections could strengthen the natal family's position and secure the fortunes of the new household. Unfree people had even less choice. By the Carolingian period it was generally accepted that they could form valid marriages, but it was expected that they would have their lord's permission before marrying.

Because marriage was a social institution, entered in order to secure or acquire material benefits for the couple, for the couple's natal kin, and for any children to come, it was only the people who had access to such benefits that were able to marry. Inevitably, among the nonnoble class at least, it was those without property or the infirm who did not marry, simply because they could not establish a household, or it was those with alternative means of securing a social place, whether as religious, as servants in another household, or as dependents in a relative's household. Elites usually married at higher rates, for they had property and alliances to secure, but, as historians such as Georges Duby have emphasized, younger sons of the nobility tended not to marry once rules of primogeniture had become the norm, since they were now without sufficient means to establish a household worthy of their social station. In other settings, particularly in the mercantile cities of late medieval Italy, the "surplus" daughters of aristocratic families often entered monasteries rather than marrying.

Although a surprisingly large number of medieval Europeans never married, those who did spent a good part of their adult lives in the married state. In the north of Europe, widows with property regularly remarried, even within months of their husbands' death and even into advanced middle age. In the south, this was a considerably less common pattern; in fact, in places such as late medieval Florence, prosperous widows tended not to remarry because they would thereby lose rights to property left to them. Everywhere, however, men seem to have regularly remarried, even taking three, four, or five different wives during a long life and having children with each of them. The demographically "combined family" of the modern West was thus a common occurrence in medieval Europe, but the emotional dynamics in such families are hard to evaluate. Evidence from medieval court cases displaying children squabbling with their half-siblings or stepparents about inheritances and surviving folk tales featuring cruel stepmothers, absent mothers, and lost fathers suggest that combined families were sometimes unhappy, but other kinds of sources tell a different story. We also have wills and other property transfer documents showing that people often chose to give assets to step-relatives, and we have vocabulary suggesting that people then valued these relationships. The French, for example, called stepmothers *belles-mères*, even if they also coined the word *marâtre* to describe their evil twins.

Property and the sociopolitical rights that attended property were such fundamental features of marriages in medieval Europe that it is impossible to understand marriage without examining these arrangements. The property that each spouse brought into marriage or acquired thereafter was carefully controlled during the marriage by informal and formal rules about who could use it and for what purposes, who inherited it at the end of the marriage, and what rights the surviving spouse had to it during his or her remaining life. The range of possibilities was enormous, and a detailed map of the variations by class, region, or time would be almost unreadable. Using marriage contracts, statutes, and legal records of other kinds, most of which come from the post-1000 period, historians have, however, provided a rough sketch of the two principal patterns that characterized marital property law during the period.

The Separatist System

One system, which legal historians have labeled "separatist," kept the husband's and wife's property apart during the marriage and provided each of them different, and independent, property rights as widow or widower. In these systems, women entered marriage with property from their natal family, which was called the *dos* in Latin or *dowry* in English and which was usually considered a substitute for her inheritance. Although the husband managed the dowry during his life, he could not alienate it without her consent (or the consent of her male kin), and it returned to her in her widowhood. In most areas the widow also received an "increase" from her husband's estate. The husband also brought property to the marriage and frequently inherited more from his family in the course of the marriage, but his assets were not sequestered in the same way as his wife's, since all property in the marital household except that specifically marked for her or her beneficiaries belonged to him. Children were the normal heirs of these marriages, but in most regions parents had the right to distribute their estate unequally among their children, and even to will property to others.

The Communal System

The other major system was less separatist and more "communal" in nature. In these arrangements, the property either spouse brought to marriage or acquired in its course, whether through inheritance, gift, or their own labor, was merged into a common fund. The husband typically had full control over these assets during the marriage, even including the right to sell or otherwise alienate the property, but his widow had rights to some or all of the property, as her own, and in some areas the widow's survivor's rights gave her some authority over the common property fund during the marriage. The husband, in turn, had the same survivor's rights, as did his widow. In these systems, children were the automatic heirs of their parents, and in most areas each child, male or female, had equal inheritance rights. In some variations of the communal systems, children's inheritance rights superseded those of the widow and could even constrain the father during his life, thus assuring that the assets he was managing were kept intact for the children.

In structure, the "separatist" system was very different from the "communal." The former positioned the husband and wife as independent representatives of their respective natal families, while the latter created a radically unitary partnership, apparently breaking all property ties with natal kin and forming new ones between the spouses and the children they would have together. In practice, however, very few systems were purely separatist or communal, and in any case the practices in any region or among any social class could change over time. For example, in northern France, where it was customary for people to form common property funds at marriage, the nobility typically allowed only a small portion of movable goods to fall into that account. They placed their land and other valuable goods that had been brought to the marriage in separate accounts reserved for the husband and wife respectively, thus creating a hybrid system, neither communal nor separatist, but some of each. In the same region, it became customary for widows also to receive income from a portion of her late husband's assets—the dower, called the *douaire* in French. Thus the typical widow had three sources of support: her portion of the common fund, the special assets from her family that had been reserved for her at the marriage's inception, and her dower.

While marital property law was genuinely unstable for most of the Middle Ages, this does not mean that people had free choice in deciding the terms of their own marriages. Instead, they were bound by local custom, which until the later centuries was unwritten, and it was rare for any couple to exceed the boundaries of those customs by wide margins. That some did helps explain why changes occurred over time and why there was so much variation from place to place, but the changes happened slowly enough that in one

person's lifetime they were usually imperceptible, and a couple marrying in, say, 900 or 1200 surely considered themselves to have little latitude. By the late Middle Ages, the structures were changing even more slowly. Territorial sovereigns and city governments were largely responsible for the slowdown, as they issued statutes to clarify and regularize local practices or empowered judicial systems to standardize the interpretation of customary traditions and the form of written agreements like marriage contracts. At the same time, people began to keep better written records, and that process alone also helped to stabilize law. While these developments did little to reduce complexity or to quickly eliminate the differences between one locality and its neighbors, they did slow the rate of change and eventually create uniformity across broad regions.

Although each of the two forms of marital property law typically contained elements reminiscent of the other, it is also true that certain regions, classes, and periods tended to prefer one form over the other. The customs of the nobility in the early Middle Ages were decidedly communal in spirit, while in the High and late Middle Ages the same class opted for more separatist arrangements. Southern Europeans, as a general rule, adhered more closely to separatist regimes, while northerners tended to preserve old traditions of communal property law. We also find that Europe's elites—its nobility and the rich merchants that emerged in the high and late Middle Ages—constructed more separatist arrangements, while ordinary people—peasants and artisans—tended to prefer communal systems. Thus, there can be little doubt that the instability and hybridity of marital property law was in part a measure of people's efforts to adjust the law to their individual circumstances and to structure their property arrangements to reflect social needs.

Exogamy

The attention medieval people gave to the property arrangements underpinning marriage reflected, in part, the fact that marriages were exogamous in that women typically were married out of their natal lines, taking property with them. This practice made it essential to clarify the terms of the property transfer in order to ensure that the transferred property was managed in ways that benefited the bride, her children, and her natal family. Until the High Middle Ages, however, what it meant to marry "out" was generously defined. Among the nobility, cousins married first cousins, brothers sometimes married their sibling's widow, and uncles took nieces as wives. We have little good evidence about the patterns among ordinary people in these early years, but it is reasonable to assume that in peasant communities people did the same, for the pool of marriageable people was too small to permit very strict rules about exogamy. This had changed by the High Middle Ages, however, for the church radically expanded the category of prohibited kinship, forbidding marriages between kin related by blood to the seventh and then, after Lateran IV in 1215, to the fourth degree, and between spiritual kin. The pool of eligible spouses was thus radically reduced, for the rules promulgated in 1215 meant that all descendents of a common great-great-grandparent were ineligible spouses, and it meant that one could not marry a godparent or the child of a godparent. While royalty and similarly high-placed elites were sometimes able to circumvent those rules, they nevertheless were generally observed, and even the elite had trouble obtaining the necessary exemptions.

There is some debate among scholars about the reasons for the church's insistence on such draconian rules of exogamy, but there is no question that these rules should be considered in the larger context of the church's evolving conception of marriage. Although during the earliest centuries of its history the Church was ambivalent about marriage and especially about sexual pleasure in marriage, that ambivalence had all but disappeared by the high Middle Ages. By the twelfth century, when canon lawyers had put in place the chief elements of marriage law, learned churchmen and preachers both consistently celebrated marriage's role in the earthly life, even if they typically offered only cautious endorsement of marital sex. By the thirteenth century, marriage was widely considered a sacrament, a vehicle of grace itself.

Consent

The central element of the mature doctrine of the medieval Latin church regarding marriage was the notion that consent, and consent alone, made a valid marriage. Although Europeans had long considered the bride's and groom's agreement to the match an element of the pact (as had the Romans, from whom canon lawyers took many of their ideas about marriage's form), the teachings promulgated by canon lawyers and theologians from the tenth century forward radically altered the significance of this agreement. By 1200 they agreed that a bride and groom giving their consent to the union were entering a covenant not unlike that Christ was meant to have

made with humankind. Marriage was thus more than a "contract" that could be amended or abrogated; it was a quasi-sacred institution that bound each spouse to the other, exclusively and for life. Practices that had once been common in medieval Europe were thus made illegal under canon law, and by the twelfth century the church was in a position to enforce these laws. Divorce, once common in early medieval Europe, was banned; bigamy was rigorously defined so that even abandoned wives could remarry only after long years alone; separations were allowed only in cases of extreme cruelty, heresy, apostasy, or adultery; spouses were even expected to live with a leprous spouse (although they were exempted from the requirement that they fulfill the conjugal debt).

However firm church law and teachings were about the centrality of consent in making marriage, it took long decades to work out exactly what was meant by "consent." It was certain that the couple had to be of age to consent (conventionally, twelve for girls and fourteen for boys), but in the early years of the debates little more was clear. Prominent scholars struggled to decide whether a verbal promise to marry was sufficient ("I will marry you"), and if the promise was not enough (it was not), could consummation of the union serve as fulfillment of that promise? In the end, this question was decided affirmatively, but sexual intercourse alone, it was also agreed, did not constitute sufficient evidence of consent. It was also agreed that if consent had been rendered in the present ("I marry you"), consummation was not even necessary to make a valid marriage.

Clandestine Marriage

It is hard to overemphasize the significance of these rules for medieval Europeans' experience of marriage. It put the couple themselves in charge of marriage, thus creating the possibility of secret or "clandestine" marriages, made without witnesses of any kind. Thus, it was now possible for a couple directly to challenge the families' right over the marriage decision. Although the church remained firm in treating such marriages as real or "valid," and, as a result, outraging parents, church officials did not condone such marriages. In fact, they made a clear distinction between such merely "valid" marriages and those they deemed "legitimate." The latter were made in public and were blessed by a priest. It was in this context that the church instituted the tradition of the "banns," for the public reading of the banns (conventionally for three Sundays preceding the ceremony itself) served to inform the community of the plan to marry and gave its members a chance to introduce impediments to the union. The church also intensified its efforts to bring the marriage ceremony itself under its control, not only by generally requiring the priests' blessing, but also increasingly by insisting that the ceremony be performed in or in front of the church itself and that the priest not only bless the wedding but officiate at the ceremony.

However strenuously church officials urged a "legitimate" marriage, they nevertheless did not outlaw clandestine marriages until the sixteenth-century Council of Trent. And, in truth, it would have been difficult to have done so, because until the High Middle Ages, most marriages were conducted according to local customs that often had only a vague relationship to the formal rules of the church. Even if from that period forward most people considered Christian rituals essential to a proper marriage, there remained significant variation in practices across the social and geographic landscape. Such marriages did not, however, create serious tensions, for they were accepted by the community and few of them were challenged in church courts. Rather, the "clandestine" marriages that so threatened medieval society were the truly secret ones, that is, those made in private, out of the view of either the church or the community and without parents' approval. Because such marriages jeopardized family position and put their children's material future at risk, parents often took steps to minimize the damage caused by such unions, even if they could not prevent them. Their primary weapon was property, and in many regions customary or written law was changed to deny inheritances to children who had married without their parents' consent. Parents could wield the same weapon less formally as well, for they could effectively disinherit a son or daughter who married against their will by refusing the usual marriage gifts.

Although records from the period make it clear that most couples who married without witnesses did so against their parents' wishes and for romantic reasons, it is also clear that such marriages were fraught with dangers for the couple themselves, especially for the woman. A woman entering a clandestine marriage could not be sure that it would meet the test of validity if brought to court by a "husband" claiming that he had made no "promise of the future" but had only had sexual relations with her. And who was to know the truth if the supposed promise had been made in secret? A woman thus "unmarried" by the church courts would find herself mother of a bastard and without customary rights to her supposed husband's property. Court records also contain stories of women who claimed that their "consent" had been forced—but again, who was to know, if there were no witnesses? In relatively fewer cases, the tables were turned; the archives contain a number of stories of "wives" who protested that they had not pledged themselves to the men calling themselves "husbands," but intended another match. Again, who was to know?

Love and Marriage

Church law regarding marriage and the religious instruction that accompanied it thus had unintended consequences. Not only could marriage be taken out of the hands of families and put into a purely religious realm, it could also be brought into a private sphere inaccessible by either kin or the church. In this way, the notion of "consent" acquired the individualist meaning of "choice," thus providing the context for a more generalized idea of marriage based on personal desire or romantic love. Broader cultural developments fed this emerging ideology. The courtly love literature that circulated in aristocratic courts from the High Middle Ages forward not only provided an enduring image of such passion, it bequeathed the language to express the image. Although formulated as part of a narrative about heterosexual love outside marriage—indeed, it typically described adulterous passion—the trope itself was later easily inserted into a story about conjugal attachment. Even the plays, tales, and farces about marriage that belonged to medieval Europe's comic literature and were more closely associated with its ordinary people helped to formulate the new marital ideal. For all their misogynist and antimarriage thematics, these texts, with their obsessive attention to conjugal love, marriage, domesticity, and the relations between husband and wife, focused Europeans on marriage's emotional content and in the end gave conjugality new complexity and depth.

Both the church's teachings about marriage and the emerging discourse about romantic love in marriage worked, some scholars have argued, to improve women's position. While there can be no doubt that Europeans, once having decided that marriages should be based primarily on personal choice and romantic attachment, would later marshal this narrative to attack certain features of patriarchy, those changes came too late to have seriously dislodged the medieval gender paradigm. While this did not mean that medieval women universally experienced marriage as oppression, it did mean that throughout the medieval period, marriage remained a secure expression of the gender hierarchy of that age. According to the dominant ideology women were men's natural inferiors, constitutionally incapable of male honor and dangerous if not properly governed because they could not control their own desires. In some contradiction to this narrative, however, women were also valued for their labor, the children they could bear, and their ability to provide their husbands access to the resources of another male line. They were even praised for their capacity for gentleness, patience, and charity, but it was generally accepted that such virtues emerged only when women were properly governed—by men.

Issues of Control

In keeping with this ideology, husbands had control over their wives' persons. According to church teachings, both spouses owed one another the "conjugal debt," since marriage was considered a remedy for lust, and both were held to the promise of monogamy, but in practice women were much more severely punished for adultery than men were, and the records we have indicate that it was typically men, not women, who demanded payment of the conjugal debt. In many legal traditions of the age, men had the explicit right to beat their wives, and, even where law did not specifically allow it, wives were regularly beaten. Even the church, which counseled husbands to treat their wives gently, did not forbid them from using force, and secular law typically went no further than banning beatings that threatened a woman's life.

In effect, if not always in formal law, women also lost legal personhood when they married. They typically could not bring suit independently, they could not testify in criminal court without their husbands' permission, and, unless their property was formally sequestered from the marital fund, they could not conduct trade in their own name. Their property was also under their husband's management, even if in some legal regimes the husband was not able to sell or encumber his wife's property without her permission (or the permission of her natal family). In some areas of community property law, in fact, women had no formal property rights whatever during marriage; all that a woman had brought to the marriage or acquired during it was merged into the marital fund, and that fund was in effect her husband's, not hers.

So described, medieval marriage seems a bleak house for women. In reality, however, the system provided protections as well as restrictions, and in any case it was often less rigid in practice than in structure. As a result, marriage provided benefits that for many women, perhaps most, outweighed the disadvantages. Some regions allowed wives quasi-independent

status in law; all legal regimes granted them important property rights either as wives or widows, if only to secure the assets for their male relatives; and in practice women could win power and respect as well as affection through their roles as mothers, household managers, representatives of their kin, and—perhaps most importantly—deputies for their husbands in the men's absence or at their death. It is impossible, however, to generalize for "women" as a whole. Both the limits to and the sources of women's power and pleasure in marriage were a function of class, law, and politics and, as is always the case, of age, health, and fecundity.

Rich women enjoyed special privileges beyond those bestowed by wealth and rank themselves, as representatives of their natal families and sometimes of their husbands' households, and as mothers of the sons that would carry on the patriline. The wives of artisans, peasants, and merchants were key members of their household economies, often serving as co-managers of what we would call the family business and in any case providing valuable and valued services as managers of the domestic space. Women also had extrafamilial resources, in the community, where they could establish networks with other women, and in the parish or the monastery, where they often found protectors, even refuge in extreme cases, or retreats in their widowhoods.

Widows

As widows, women typically regained their legal personhood, and in most legal regimes they took control of significant amounts of property and acquired the guardianship of minor children. So potentially powerful was the independent widow, however, that cultural norms and law itself often worked to contain them. Many of the stories that come to us from the late Middle Ages feature the ungoverned and sexually aggressive widow who, although surely more a cultural icon than a social reality, clearly evidences the threat a powerful widow posed in medieval society. In practice, law was often fashioned to limit widows' property rights, typically by giving her only the income on her dower property, by compelling her to manage her share of the common property in the marital household under the watchful eye of her children or their legal agents, or even by returning her dowry to her kin so that they could use it to arrange another marriage for her, or for another daughter. Even those widows positioned as independent heads of household with authority over children, businesses, servants, and apprentices seem not to have found their new position particularly comfortable, for most of them remarried. Some scholars have suggested that they missed male companionship, others that they feared the public scrutiny to which independent widows were subjected, others that they sought the familiar status of household mistress, others that they simply wanted help with the responsibilities of the household. Whatever the reasons, we are forced to conclude that many women considered marriage preferable to widowhood. Whether that says more about the pleasures of marriage or the disadvantages of widowhood is hard to say.

There was no "medieval" marriage, if by that we mean a fixed set of practices, rituals, and beliefs, and a common experience of conjugality. Instead, marriage's meanings shifted throughout the millennium and always acquired different valences in different social settings. Even by the end of the period, when church law and Christian teachings had combined to give marriage a clearer legal form and new cultural significance, marriage remained a complex mix of often contradictory imperatives. The resulting tensions guaranteed not only diversity across the social and geographic landscape, but also continued change through time.

MARTHA HOWELL

References and Further Reading

Bennett, Judith M., and Amy M. Froide. *Singlewomen of the European Past, 1250–1800.* Philadelphia: University of Pennsylvania Press, 1999.

Brooke, Christopher N. L. *The Medieval Idea of Marriage.* Oxford: Oxford University Press, 1989.

Brundage, James A. *Law, Sex, and Christian Society in Medieval Europe.* Chicago: University of Chicago Press, 1987.

Camille, Michael. *The Medieval Art of Love: Objects and Subjects of Desire.* New York: Abrams, 1998.

Chojnaki, Stanley. "The Power of Love: Wives and Husbands in Late Medieval Venice." In *Women and Power in the Middle Ages,* edited by Mary Erler and Maryanne Kowaleski. Athens, Ga.: University of Georgia Press, 1988, pp. 126–140.

Duby, Georges. *Medieval Marriage: Two Models from Twelfth-Century France.* Baltimore, Md.: Johns Hopkins University Press, 1978.

———. *The Knight, the Lady, and the Priest: The Making of Modern Marriage in Medieval France.* New York: Pantheon Press, 1983.

Erickson, Amy Louise. *Women and Property in Early Modern England.* London: Routledge, 1993.

Esmein, A. *Le mariage en droit canonique,* 2 vols. Paris: L. Larose et Forcel, 1891.

Goody, Jack. *The Development of the Family and Marriage in Europe.* Cambridge: Cambridge University Press, 1983.

Greilsammer, Myriam. *L'envers du tableau: mariage et maternité en Flandre médiévale.* Paris: A. Colin, 1990.

Hajal, John. "European Marriage Patterns in Perspective." In *Population in History: Essays in Historical Demography,* edited by D. V. Glass and D. E. C. Eversley. London: E. Arnold, 1965, pp. 101–146.

Harris, Barbara J. *English Aristocratic Women, 1450–1550: Marriage and Family, Property and Careers.* New York: Oxford University Press, 2002.

Herlihy, David. "Family." *American Historical Review* 96.1 (1991): 1–16.

Howell, Martha C. *The Marriage Exchange: Property, Social Place and Gender in Cities of the Low Countries, 1300–1550.* Chicago: University of Chicago Press, 1998.

Hughes, Diane Owen. "From Brideprice to Dowry in Mediterranean Europe." *Journal of Family History* 3 (1978): 262–296.

Klapisch-Zuber, Christiane. *Women, Family and Ritual in Renaissance Italy.* Chicago: University of Chicago Press, 1985.

Otis-Cour, Leah. *Lust und Liebe: Geschichte der Paarbeziehungen im Mittelalter.* Frankfurt am Main: Fischer Taschenbuch Verlag, 2000.

Ourliac, Paul, and Jehan de Malafosse. *Le droit familial.* Vol. 3, *Histoire du droit privé.* Paris: Presses Universitaires de France, 1971.

Sheehan, Michael M. *Marriage, Family, and Law in Medieval Europe,* edited by James K. Farge. Toronto: University of Toronto Press, 1996.

Witte, John Jr. *From Sacrament to Contract: Marriage, Religion and Law in the Western Tradition.* Louisville, Ky.: Westminster John Knox Press, 1997.

See also **Betrothals; Conjugal Debt; Courtly Love; Courtship; Divorce and Separation; Domestic Abuse; Dowry and Other Marriage Gifts; Gender Ideologies; Husbands and Husbandry; Inheritance; Landholding and Property Rights; Law, Canon; Legal Agency; Marriage Ceremonies; Marriage, Impediments to; Marriage, Islamic: Iberia; Marriage, Jewish; Marriage Preaching; Remarriage; Sexuality: Sex in Marriage; Social Status; Widows**

MARRIAGE AND CONCUBINAGE IN SCANDINAVIA

The scarcity of sources makes our knowledge of marriage formation in medieval Scandinavia largely rest on patchy documents, laws, and—for Norway and Iceland—sagas. Scandinavia was not a single entity without geographical variation. Denmark stands apart from the other Scandinavian countries as her secular laws largely omit references to marriage formation because of ecclesiastical influence.

Scandinavian marriage was a public and formal series of legal acts involving two families. Bride wealth and the consent of the bride's guardian at the betrothal were essential for ensuring the legitimacy of the union. Similarly, the public bedding of the couple at the wedding was important. Marriages of the poor may have been more informal, but in Iceland paupers were theoretically disallowed to marry. In most regions, slaves could not marry.

Concubinage, practiced especially among aristocrats, while more stable and long-term than a temporary liaison, was no formal legal institution involving property exchanges. A master having intercourse or concubinage with his own slave women was commonplace and did not threaten a possible wife's position as the mistress of the household. Concubines were status symbols and means of acquiring heirs in lieu of or in addition to wedlock. Moreover, in regions like Iceland, concubines were important instruments for establishing alliances between their kin-groups and the men. Some sagas (e.g., *Egil's Saga* and the *Laxdæla Saga*) also use concubinage as an element in the plot.

Although concubines often were of lower status compared to their partners, they were not regularly poor or of insignificant families. Clerical concubines may have been of more equal status and royal mistresses were frequently noble. The status of a concubine's children depended on that of their mother—and possibly also on the consent of her kin to the union. Publicly acknowledged illegitimate children had some inheritance rights. Royal bastards could and did become kings until the mid-thirteenth century. Between 1074 and 1154 all Danish kings came to the throne through illegitimate succession, while in Norway, only five of the twenty-four kings ruling in the tumultuous century 1130–1240 were legitimate.

Beginning especially in the thirteenth century, ecclesiastical marriage doctrine influenced Scandinavian practice by stressing the consent of the principal parties and ecclesiastical solemnization, including publication of banns. Divorce was prohibited. While forbidding extramarital sexuality, the Church's emphasis on consent and the personal bond made clandestine unions contracted without witnesses and parental consent possible. Private exchanges of consent could blur the demarcation line between concubinage and matrimony within the context of the witnessed formality found in traditional Scandinavian marriage customs.

Ecclesiastical marriage impediments created new reasons for concubinage. If an impediment precluded matrimony—especially for priests—concubinage remained an option. Indeed, clerical concubinage was practiced despite official ecclesiastical condemnation. Legal presumptions appeared, assimilating long-lasting concubinage with matrimony: women looking after the household and acting outwardly like wives were considered lawful spouses after three (Denmark) or twenty (Norway) years of public cohabitation. Lay couples were given the choice between interdict, separation, or matrimony.

Due to ecclesiastical influence, the position of illegitimate children declined. Many Scandinavian laws divided children into legitimate children, children of concubines, and adulterine children. Natural children enjoyed very limited inheritance rights, while adulterines—between whose parents an impediment existed—had none, unless a papal dispensation was received. Subsequent marriage legitimated the children of a concubine: the "bettering" of the mother ameliorated the status of the child(ren).

MIA KORPIOLA

References and Further Readings

Arnórsdóttir, Agnes. "Two Models of Marriage? Canon Law and Icelandic Marriage Practice in the Late Middle Ages." In *Nordic Perspectives on Medieval Canon Law*, edited by Mia Korpiola. Helsinki: Publications of Matthias Calonius Society, 1999, pp. 79–92.

———. "Marriage in the Middle Ages: Canon Law and Nordic Family Relations." In *Norden og Europa i middelalderen*, edited by Per Ingesman and Thomas Lindkvist. Århus: Skrifter udgivet af Jysk Selskab for Historie, 2001, pp. 174–202.

Carlsson, Lizzie. *"Jag giver dig min dotter." Trolovning och äktenskap i den svenska kvinnans äldre historia*, I-II. Lund: Institutet för Rättishistorisk Forskning, 1965–1972. Rättshistoriskt bibliotek, 8 and 20.

Dübeck, Inger. "Women, Weddings and Concubines in Medieval Danish Law." *Scandinavian Journal of History* 17.4 (1992): 315–322.

Frank, Roberta. "Marriage in Twelfth- and Thirteenth-Century Iceland." *Viator* 4 (1973): 473–484.

Jochens, Jenny M. "The Church and Sexuality in Medieval Iceland." *Journal of Medieval History* 6 (1980): 377–392.

———. *Women in Old Norse Society*. Ithaca, N.Y. and London: Cornell University Press, 1995.

Magnúsdóttir, Auður. *Frillor och fruar: Politik och samlevnad på Island 1120–1400*. Göteborg: Avhandlingar ifrån historiska institutionen i Göteborg, 2001. English Summary: 219–223.

Nors, Thyra. "Illegitimate Children and Their High-Born Mothers: Changes in the Perception of Illegitimacy in Mediaeval Denmark." *Scandinavian Journal of History* 21.1 (1996): 17–37.

Sawyer, Birgit, and Peter Sawyer. *Medieval Scandinavia: From Conversion to Reformation, Circa 800–1500*. Minneapolis: University of Minnesota Press, 1993.

See also **Celibacy: Clerical and Priests' Concubines; Concubines; Illegitimacy; Literature, Old Norse; Marriage Ceremonies; Marriage, Christian; Scandinavia**

MARRIAGE, IMPEDIMENTS TO

The Church law on marriage was one of the few areas in which the rights of women equaled those of men. Before practices were centralized and codified, necessary requirements for marriage, and impediments to marriage, varied from place to place and time to time. Rules and customs governing marriage are found in every society, since not all conceivable combinations of couples are considered free to marry. An obvious example is a mother and her son, or a brother and his sister. The primary reason for such laws must have been the preservation of the sanctity of the family and the peace of the community. Sometimes rules must have been extended to guarantee a safety zone (the fence-around-the-wall principle). In the case of consanguinity and affinity, there was a mix-up in computation: first cousins were related in the second degree by the Germanic method but the fourth degree by the Romans, so the Germans would have read a fourth-degree prohibition as applying to third cousins.

Gratian's *Decretum* (c. 1140) reconciled various requirements by distinguishing between legality and validity. For example, if a man or woman had taken a simple vow of chastity (permanent celibacy), it would be unlawful (illicit) and sinful to marry; but if the marriage did take place, and there was no more serious (invalidating) impediment, the marriage would be valid; however, the spouse who violated the vow would be subject to penance, whether private or public.

To take another example, marriages should not be secret, but secrecy itself did not invalidate a marriage. The first canon that Gratian cites against clandestine or secret marriage, *Aliter* (Cause 30, q. 5, chap. 1), states that marriage is not legitimate unless the woman's guardian permits it; she must be betrothed by her parents, given a dowry, blessed by the priest, accompanied by bridesmaids, and solemnly delivered to the groom, and the couple must spend the first two or three days in prayer, without sex; otherwise the union is presumed not to be marriage but rather adultery, concubinage, debauchery, or fornication—unless they actually exchange vows and thus get married. In other words, omission of the stated requirements made the marriage illicit, but not invalid.

What made a marriage valid was the unforced consent of a man and woman who were free to get married—that is, those who had no impediments. Nothing else really mattered, and eventually it was only secrecy (clandestinity) that was taken seriously as a punishable illicit offense in the making of a marriage.

The chief invalidating impediments were as follows (those encountered most frequently are treated first).

1. Precontract or *Ligamen* (Marriage Bond)

Obviously, if one of the intended spouses was currently married to someone else, a new marriage was not valid. Bigamous marriage was very common because of the widespread practice of secret marriage, and precontract was the most frequent reason alleged for annulment of marriage by the ecclesiastical courts.

The term *precontract* has caused confusion in modern times, because it is often wrongly taken to mean "preliminary contract" instead of "previous contract." This mistake has led to the conclusion that in the Middle Ages mere betrothal (promise to marry in the future) invalidated a marriage to someone else.

Gratian held that if a person—say, Bertha—marries Peter but leaves him without consummating the marriage by sexual intercourse, and then marries Paul and does consummate the marriage, she commits a sin, but nevertheless the second marriage to Paul is valid. In other words, the consummated marriage dissolves the unconsummated marriage, and Peter is left free to marry someone else. Later Pope Alexander III (1159–1181) decreed that consummation had no effect on the validity of a marriage, and from then on even an unconsummated marriage (like that of Bertha and Peter) precluded any further marriage.

However, if Bertha was only engaged to marry Peter (betrothal in the future tense), even if she took an oath to marry him, she could still marry Paul (but would sin in breaking her oath).

2. Consanguinity

Persons related by blood could not marry. Early rules and practices varied, but in 1215 the Fourth Lateran Council restricted the prohibition to the fourth degree (that is, third cousins). The reason given was that in the higher degrees that rule could not be followed without grave detriment. The fourth degree was thought to be the appropriate limit for this corporal union because there are four humors in the body and the body is composed out of the four elements.

3. Affinity

One could not marry the kin of any sex partner, whether that partner was one's spouse or not. The prohibition of affinity, like that of consanguinity, was limited to the fourth degree in 1215, and other types of affinity were dismissed at that time.

Note that affinity was contracted by coitus, not marriage. Therefore it was caused not only by the consummation of a marriage, but also by illicit coitus: a man could not marry the sister (or up to third cousin) of a woman with whom he had sex. If a man had sex with his wife's sister or cousin, he contracted *supervening* affinity; it did not dissolve the marriage, but it prohibited him from demanding the marital debt (though he was required to pay it when his wife requested it).

There was never any prohibition against parallel marriage—two sisters marrying two brothers, for example. Thus, if Martha married John, it was permitted for Martha's sister Mary to marry John's brother James. But Martha was prohibited by affinity from marrying James after John died. "Trees" of consanguinity and affinity illustrating the various degrees appear in many legal manuscripts.

4. Public Honesty, Justice of

This was the technical name of the impediment caused by betrothal and unconsummated marriage: it prohibited a person from marrying a person related to one's spouse or betrothed. For example, if Martha married John and John died before consummation, Martha was prohibited by public honesty from marrying John's brother or cousin. The same was true if Martha was only engaged to John.

5. Spiritual Kinship

Participation in baptism and confirmation created impediments; e.g., if you "lifted" a child from the baptismal font, you could not marry the child's parent, and the child could not marry you, or your child, or your spouse after you died (if your marriage was consummated at the time of the baptism).

6. Age

Marriage to a boy under fourteen or a girl under twelve was not valid (unless coitus was successfully performed). Such early marriage was treated as a betrothal, and it would automatically become marriage when the canonical age was reached, unless the union was repudiated beforehand.

7. Force and Fear

Unwilling consent made a marriage invalid.

8. Crime

Originally, marriage to a person with whom one had committed adultery was invalid. By the thirteenth century, such marriage was only invalid if both spouses knew about the previous marriage and if they machinated the death of the deceased spouse (or swore to marry after that spouse died).

9. Major Orders, Religious Profession

Once a man received the first major order (subdiaconate), he could never marry, and the same was true of solemnly professed male and female religious. As noted above, a simple vow of chastity, even when public, did not invalidate a subsequent marriage.

10. Impotence and Frigidity

Whether natural or attributed to sorcery, inability to perform coitus invalidated a marriage.

11. Error of Person or Condition

Mistaken identity or ignorance of servile state was cause for annulment.

12. Disparity of Cult

A Christian could not validly marry a Jew, Moslem, or other non-Christian.

13. Legal Kinship

No marriage was possible between adopter and adoptee, or between natural child and adopted sibling (while the adoption lasted), or between father and adopted son's wife, or between father's wife and adopted son, etc.

It was sometimes possible to obtain a papal dispensation from various impediments—for instance, consanguinity in the fourth degree, allowing third cousins to marry—but such dispensations were not common until the later Middle Ages.

The impediments in the Eastern Church were not as extensive or as codified as in the West (see Dauvillier and de Clercq).

HENRY ANSGAR KELLY

References and Further Reading

Bride, A. "Empêchements de mariage." *Dictionnaire de droit canonique*, 7 vols. (Letouzey et Ané, 1935–1965), 5: 261–322.

Brundage, James A. *Law, Sex, and Christian Society in Medieval Europe*. Chicago: University of Chicago Press, 1987.

Burgh, John. *Pupilla oculi* (1385), Book 8 (*Matrimonium*), Chapters 6–13. (The edition of London 1510 is on microfilm in the series *Early English Books, 1475–1640*, reel 120, no. 8 [STC n. 4115], and also online in *Early English Books Online*.)

Dauvillier, Jean, and Charles de Clercq. *Le mariage en droit canonique oriental*. Paris: Recuiel Sirey, 1936.

De Clercq, C. "Mariage en droit oriental." *Dictionnaire de droit canonique* 6:787–802.

Esmein, A., *Le marriage en droit canonique*. 2 vols. Paris: L. Larose et Forcel, 1891.

Helmholz, Richard. *Marriage Litigation in Medieval England*. Cambridge: Cambridge University Press, 1972.

Joyce, George Hayward. *Christian Marriage: An Historical and Doctrinal Study*. London: Sheed and Ward, 1933. Second edition, 1948.

Naz, R. "Mariage en droit occidental." *Dictionnaire de droit canonique* 6:740–787.

Wahl, F. X. *The Matrimonial Impediments of Consanguinity and Affinity*. Washington, D.C.: Catholic University of America Press, 1934.

See also **Betrothals; Children, Betrothals and Marriage of; Divorce and Separation; Godparents; Incest; Law, Canon; Marriage, Christian; Rape and Raptus**

MARRIAGE, ISLAMIC: IBERIA

In medieval al-Andalus, and under Islamic law, several conditions had to be fulfilled for a marriage to be considered valid, including primarily the signature of a contract of marriage between the two parties, and the payment of a dowry to the bride. The contract established the amount of the dowry, as well as other important regulations for the life of the couple. Usually, the dower was divided into two parts. The first was paid to the bride at the time of the marriage, and was employed, at least partly, in buying her trousseau. The second part of the dower could be paid either at a fixed date (for instance, two or three years after the marriage), in the event of a divorce, or at the death of the husband. In all these cases the dower money was the exclusive possession of the married woman.

Andalusi legal documents attest to the existence of other clauses in the marriage contract. When the bride belonged to a high-class family, she would expect to have domestic help, and the marriage contract would establish that the servants' salaries had to be paid by the husband. Also, the contract stated the wife's right to visit her relatives and her former wet-nurse. But perhaps more important were three other clauses related to the place of residence of the married couple, the amount of time the husband could be absent from the conjugal home and, finally, the number of wives he could marry simultaneously.

In many marriage contracts, it was established that the husband could not compel his wife to change her place of residence, in what seems to have been a precautionary measure against the separation of a woman from her parents' family. When such a change of residence became necessary, the married woman could expect, according to her marriage contract, to receive compensation from her husband. The contract stipulated that a six-month absence of the husband might terminate the marriage; however, Andalusi men were allowed a three-year absence for the pilgrimage to Mecca, taking into account the long distance separating al-Andalus from Arabia. Finally, many marriage contracts included a clause by which the husband agreed not to marry any other woman during this particular marriage, nor to take a slave as a concubine. If the husband breached this clause, the marriage was terminated by a judge, and the wife could recover the second part of her dower and remarry.

Historical accounts of the great number of consorts of several Umayyad rulers should not hide the fact that polygyny was not very common, being mainly practiced by sovereign families or the very rich. Divorce was probably much more widespread than polygyny, and affected the lives of married women more deeply. According to Islamic law, it was relatively easy for a man to divorce his wife, while she had to comply with several, strict conditions to put an end to her marriage, or to compensate her husband economically. Among the peculiarities of the Maliki school of law, predominant in al-Andalus, was the fact that wives could ask for divorce on the grounds of physical or financial mistreatment. After such a complaint, the judge would begin an enquiry among relatives and neighbours, to check the truthfulness of the wife's allegations; if those were proven, divorce was accorded to the wife.

While the provisions of Islamic law protected the status of the married woman, in the context of a medieval society like al-Andalus, it was not always easy for them to put these rights into practice. Access to legal counsel was easier for urban women belonging to well-to-do families, and more difficult in rural areas, where the use of written contracts was not so common. On the other hand, many legal issues depended on the testimony of relatives, friends, and neighbors, so many women leading secluded lives were at a disadvantage when fighting against powerful masculine social networks.

Although evidence of conjugal love is not lacking in historical and literary texts, marriage was above all a social alliance between two families. Ideally, both spouses should belong to a similar social and economic level, as reflected in the negotiations involved in the signing of the marriage contract. Unequal marriages were generally disapproved, especially if a high-born woman married a commoner. Ibn Hazm (eleventh century) bitterly criticized this practice among the Arab family of the de facto ruler of al-Andalus, al-Mansur. Men could, however, marry their women slaves, once they were manumitted. More unusual was the case of a free woman marrying a slave.

MANUELA MARÍN

References and Further Reading

El Cheikh, Nadia Maria. "In Search for the Ideal Spouse." *Journal of the Social and Economic History of the Orient* 45 (2002): 179–196.

Fórneas, José María. "Acerca de la mujer musulmana en las épocas almorávid y almohade: elegías de tema femenino." In *La mujer en al-Andalus: reflejos históricos de su actividad y categorías sociales*, edited by María Jesús Viguera. Madrid: Ediciones de la Universidad Autonoma de Madrid, 1989, pp. 77–103.

Marín, Manuela. "Marriage and Sexuality in al-Andalus." In *Marriage and Sexuality in Medieval and Early Modern Iberia*, edited by Eukene Lacarra Lanz. New York: Routledge, 2002, pp. 3–20.

———. *Mujeres en al-Andalus*. Madrid: Consejo Superior de Investigacioes Cientificas, 2000.

Powers, David. "Women and Divorce in the Islamic West: Three Cases." *Hawwa* 1 (2003): 29–45.

Zomeño, Amalia. *Dote y matrimonio en al-Andalus y el Norte de Africa : estudios sobre la jurisprudencia islámica medieval*. Madrid: Consejo Superior de Investigacioes Cientificas, 2000.

See also Iberia; Law, Islamic: Iberia; Marriage, Christian; Marriage, Jewish; Muslim Women

MARRIAGE, JEWISH

In medieval Jewish communities, marriage was the expected norm. First marriages were usually arranged by the parents of the bride and groom, often with the help of a matchmaker. The bride and groom were usually quite young, around the age of twelve or thirteen. They had the right to reject the match their parents made for them and it was considered obligatory that they see each other before the marriage took place. Despite this right of rejection, the sources indicate that few agreed-upon matches were cancelled by the spouses.

The arrangement between the parents included complex monetary agreements: who would support the young couple during the first year or two of their lives together, where they would live, and the capital each of the spouses brought to the marriage. During the early Middle Ages, it was customary for the bride to provide the money with which the young couple began their life together in the form of a dowry. Her husband was expected to supplement this income at a later date, after he inherited money from his parents. These arrangements were recorded as part of the *ketubbah*—the marriage agreement in which the husband took authority over his wife and promised to support her in exchange for her fulfillment of obligations towards him. In the *ketubbah* a sum of money was also stipulated for the woman in case of divorce or the husband's death.

Men promised to clothe and feed their wives as well as provide lodging, cohabit with them (an obligation known as *onah*), redeem them if held for ransom, bury them upon their death, provide for their support as a widow, leave money to their children, and provide them with the *ketubbah*. Women were expected to cook, bake, wash, spin, nurse the children, and prepare their husband's beds, as well as meet sexual obligations. In addition, women's property was inherited by their husbands, and the usufruct of their property during marriage belonged to their husbands. The refusal of husband or wife to fulfill his or her obligations over a period of time provided grounds for divorce. A husband or wife who refused to cohabit with a spouse was called a *mored* or *moredet* (literally, "rebel").

In addition to first marriages, there are many accounts of widows and divorcees who remarried. While some sources point to discomfort with remarriage, it seems to have been a common phenomenon. Women were not allowed to remarry if they had already survived three previous husbands. If the husband died leaving his wife childless (known as *yevama*), the woman had two options: marriage to the brother of her husband (known as Levirate marriage or *yibbum*) or undergoing the ceremony of *ḥaliza* (literally, "the removal of a shoe"), whereby she was released from the levirate tie. During the Middle Ages, *ḥaliḥa* usually took precedence over the levirate tie, especially in light of the ban on bigamy that existed in Germany and Northern France. If the woman had children, she was free to remarry as she pleased.

During the Middle Ages, in Germany and northern France, substantial changes were introduced to the laws of marriage and divorce. R. Gershom b. Judah (known as the Light of the Exile, *Me'or haGolah*) and subsequent generations enforced two bans, the first forbidding bigamy, the second forbidding a man to divorce his wife against her will. Since divorce in Judaism is by law the right of the husband, and the wife cannot be divorced without his agreement, this statute was of tremendous import. Scholars have suggested these bans resulted from the Christian environment in which both bigamy and divorce were prohibited. Following the acceptance of these bans, it also became more difficult for women to initiate divorce on grounds such as impotence, which had previously been an often-used reason for divorce. Scholars have argued that divorce was very common within medieval Jewish communities and that many women initiated divorce by refusing their conjugal duties.

Additional changes introduced in medieval Germany and France included double monetary agreements in which the husband, in addition to the wife, brought income to the initial agreement between families. Furthermore, if one of the spouses died within the first two years of marriage without offspring, the monies were returned to their natal families. In medieval Spain and North Africa, bigamy was still accepted, although some *ketubbahs* contained stipulations against such marriages.

The process of marriage originally consisted of two stages: betrothal (*erusin* or *kiddushin*) and marriage (*nissuin*). In late antiquity it was customary for the couple to be betrothed for a period of up to a year. After betrothal the couple did not live together, but if they wished to dissolve their connection, they needed to divorce. During the Middle Ages the two stages were joined into a single ceremony. The term *erusin* then came to mean the making of the match and was sometimes known as *shiddukhin*.

Before the wedding the bride visited the ritual bath (*mikvah*) for the first time. The actual marriage took place in public and required two people to act as witnesses. During the Middle Ages it became accepted for the rabbi of the community to perform the ceremony. It was also understood that at least a quorum (ten males) should be present. At the ceremony the seven blessings of betrothal and marriage were recited, the groom transferred money symbolically to the bride by placing a ring on her finger, and announced that she was consecrated to him. The transferring of the ring also represented the consent of both spouses to be reserved for each other. The groom then gave the bride the *ketubbah*—the deed of marriage.

It was customary to perform the ritual under a *huppah*, a canopy. A number of customs were observed to ward off the devil, such as veiling the bride and breaking a glass. In addition, joyous processions and feasts were held throughout the week after the marriage. Wheat and nuts were thrown on the couple, and fish was eaten as a symbol of fertility.

ELISHEVA BAUMGARTEN

References and Further Reading

Abrahams, Israel. *Jewish Life in the Middle Ages*. Philadelphia: Jewish Publication Society of America, 1920.
Berger, Michael S. "Two Models of Medieval Jewish Marriage." *Journal of Jewish Studies* 52 (2001): 59–84.
Cohen, Esther, and Elliott Horowitz. "In Search of the Sacred: Jews, Christians and Rituals of Marriage in the Later Middle Ages." *Journal of Medieval and Renaissance Studies* 20 (1990): 225–250.
Eleazar ben Judah. *Sefer haRokeaḥ haGadol*. Jerusalem: Weinfeld Press, 1960.
Falk, Zeev. *Jewish Matrimonial Law in the Middle Ages*. London: Oxford University Press, 1966.
Freimann, Abraham Ḥaim. *Seder Kiddushin veNissuin Aharei Ḥatimat haTalmud. Mehkar Histori Dogmati beDinei Yisrael*. Jerusalem: Mossad haRav Kook, 1945.
Goitein, Shlomo Dov. *A Mediterranean Society: The Jewish Communities of the Arab World as Portrayed in the Documents of the Cairo Geniza*. 6 vols. Berkeley, Calif.: University of California Press, 1967–1993.
Grossman, Avraham. *Pious and Rebellious: Jewish Women in Medieval Europe*. Hanover and London: Brandeis University Press, 2004.
Horowitz, Simon haLevi, ed. *Maḥzor Vitry*. Nürnberg, 1892.
Jacob b. Moses Mulin. *Sefer Maharil. Minhagim* (The Book of Maharil: Customs by Rabbi Yaacov Mulin), edited by Shlomoh J. Spitzer. Jerusalem: Machon Yerushlayim, 1989.
Katz, Jacob. *Tradition and Crisis: Jewish Society at the End of the Middle Ages*, translated by Bernard Dov Cooperman. New York: New York University Press, 1993.
Westreich, Elimelech. "Polygamy and Compulsory Divorce of the Wife in the Decisions of the Rabbis of Ashkenaz in the 11th and 12th Centuries." *Bar Ilan Law Studies* 6 (1988): 118–64.

See also **Jewish Women; Law, Jewish; Marriage, Christian; Mikveh; Pregnancy and Childbirth: Jewish Women**

MARRIAGE PREACHING

In the early Middle Ages there may not have been much marriage preaching, though it is hard to be certain. Not a lot of sermons dealing with marriage and intended as models for popular preaching have come to light so far. One text that might have provided material is the *Regula pastoralis* of Gregory the Great, where a section deals with the way to instruct marriage couples. The image of marriage it projects is relatively positive, an important fact in view of the assumption that the early medieval Church took a thoroughly negative attitude toward marriage and sex. There is a telescoped defense of marriage against antimatrimonial heresy at the start of a ninth-century homily by Haymo of Auxerre, but it was probably not intended for popular preaching, and the heretical views in question had almost certainly been dead for centuries. Although one can never be sure how much evidence has been lost, there was probably not a lot of marriage preaching in the early Middle Ages, at least compared with the period from c. 1200 on. During that period the situation is transformed.

The Franciscan and Dominican orders rapidly became an effective pastoral delivery system capable of turning Latin model sermons into "live" vernacular preaching; these Latin models were composed and copied in huge numbers. They are our main source for medieval marriage preaching. There are some sermons in the *ad status* genre (sermons to different sorts and conditions of people). The sermons in this genre by Jacques de Vitry have been presented in a widely read book by a famous French historian, so it is unfortunate that they are very untypical, presenting a negative view of women that is not common in medieval marriage preaching, to judge from the large number of extant sermons. Most of the surviving evidence consists of sermons for the Sunday when the passage about the marriage feast of Cana was read. We do not have any comparable corpus of sermons actually preached at weddings: in fact, hardly any are known. The "marriage feast of Cana" Sunday did however fall just after a time of the liturgical year when marriage rites were forbidden.

The two themes that predominate in these marriage sermons are the goodness of marriage and marriage symbolism, which was thus impressed on the lay consciousness through the pulpit. The defense of marriage may have been in part a reaction against the Cathar heresy, which reached its apogee in the early thirteenth century and frightened the orthodox very much. There are many varieties of Cathar belief but marriage seems to have been regarded as intrinsically evil in most of them. No Cathar sermons as such have survived, but in orthodox marriage preaching a whole range of arguments in favour of marriage are deployed. There are Aristotelian arguments of a logical and teleological character, deducing marriage's goodness from its naturalness, and there are a series of more scriptural considerations. One of these was that Jesus Christ himself favored a marriage feast by his presence. Others looked to the origins of marriage, which was compared favorably with religious orders: marriage was founded in paradise, whereas even the greatest religious orders were not; orders had human founders, whereas marriage was founded by God. Like a religious order, marriage was subject to a discipline not easy to observe. There were restrictions on the timing and manner of sexual acts. Most sermons do not go into detail about such things, leaving that to confessional handbooks. The love that should bind husband and wife together is a strong theme.

The "marriage feast of Cana" genre of sermons continued in an unbroken stream long after the end of the Middle Ages. Some emphases changed and some new themes were introduced, but the essential excellence of marriage seems to have been more or less a constant.

DAVID D'AVRAY

References and Further Reading

Bériou, Nicole, and David L. d'Avray. "Henry of Provins, O. P.'s Comparison of the Dominican and Franciscan Orders with the 'Order' of Matrimony." *Archivum Fratrum Praedicatorum* 49 (1979): 513–514.
———. "The Image of the Ideal Husband in Thirteenth-Century France." *Revue Mabillon*, new series 1, 62 (1990): 111–143.
d'Avray, David L. "The Gospel of the Marriage Feast of Cana and Marriage Preaching in France." In *The Bible in the Medieval World: Essays in Memory of Beryl Smalley*, edited by Katherine Walsh and Diana Wood. Oxford: Published for the Ecclesiastical History Society by Blackwell, 1985, pp. 207–224.
———. *Medieval Marriage Sermons: Mass Communication in a Culture Without Print*. Oxford: Oxford University Press, 2001.
———. *Medieval Marriage: Symbolism and Society*. Oxford: Oxford University Press, 2005.
d'Avray, David L., and M. Tausche. "Marriage Sermons in *ad status* Collections of the Central Middle Ages." *Archives d'histoire doctrinale et littéraire duc Moyen Age* 47 (1980): 71–119.
Schnell, Rudiger. "The Discourse on Marriage in the Middle Ages." *Speculum* 73. 3 (1998): 771–786.

See also **Cathars; Marriage Ceremonies; Marriage, Christian; Sermons and Preaching; Theology**

MARY AND MARTHA

The sisters Mary and Martha occupied a significant place in medieval thought based on a conflation of several biblical passages in which the two appeared. In one scene—recounted in John 12:1–8 and Luke 10:38–42—Jesus visited the home of Mary and Martha in Bethany. In another (John 11:1–46), Jesus raised their brother Lazarus from the grave because he loved the three siblings. Mary and Martha thus entered the medieval imagination playing brief but vivid roles in the drama of Jesus's earthly life. Their affective ties to Jesus and the combination of concrete actions with tantalizing brevity in their story made them favorite figures for moral and allegorical interpretation throughout the Middle Ages.

The most ubiquitous allegorization of the two sisters was based on Jesus's words during the meal at their house. When Martha chided Mary for sitting at Christ's feet listening to him rather than helping in the kitchen, Jesus defended Mary, saying she had chosen "the best part" (Luke 10:42). Early theologians, including Ambrose and Augustine, who were developing an ideology for the church in the fourth century, interpreted this passage as referring to the two kinds of life open to Christians: the contemplative and the active. In monastic exegesis, Mary became the powerful symbol of withdrawal from worldly concerns to focus on spiritual goals, while Martha stood for the life of worthy but less exalted practical service.

Later exegetes continued to use the figures of Mary and Martha as a convenient locus for defining the difference between the monastic life and that of canons or other clergy with pastoral and administrative duties. However, some theologians, including Bernard of Clairvaux, played down the contrast of the sisters, instead advocating an alternation, a progression, or even a necessary mixture of action and contemplation in many kinds of religious life. The Virgin Mary was often seen as combining in ideal fashion the distinctive features of both sisters.

After the twelfth century, this primary ecclesiastical signification was joined by others as audiences for interpretation broadened to include the laity. Mary and Martha became characters in late medieval dramas and models for women in conduct literature. Martha's exemplary faith that Christ would raise her brother Lazarus from the dead was emphasized, as was Mary's privileged role of first witness to Christ's resurrection. They were both mentioned among the female followers of Christ whose loyalty and belief surpassed that of the male disciples.

Another set of interpretations focused on all three siblings as recipients of healing miracles by Christ, transformations that spiritually represented his ability to forgive sin and provide salvation. Alternatively, Mary, Martha, and Lazarus modeled family relationships and—since their medieval narrative made them aristocrats—the proper use of inherited power and wealth.

The traditional pairing of the two sisters also began to weaken. Mary was identified with the loving Magdalene—the sinner who shed penitential tears, had her demons exorcised, and in a spirit of true charity anointed Christ's head and feet. As Mary Magdalene, she became independently popular and generated a major liturgical cult. With her role as preacher highlighted, Mary was known as "Apostle of Apostles" and many women mystics seeking social and spiritual authority identified with Mary's charismatic leadership. Martha acquired a non-biblical legend of defeating the tarascon or dragon, and she was increasingly valorized as the pious and hospitable matron—a model for the bourgeoisie who wanted to combine spirituality with their active and affluent lives.

In the visual arts of the later Middle Ages, therefore, the sisters may appear together in the dinner at Bethany scene, or they may be represented separately. Mary is usually shown in worldly dress with her hair long and uncovered, symbolizing her life of sin and repentance. Martha holds a ladle, a dish, or keys, which sometimes stand allegorically for her works of mercy and at other times literally represent the gendered life of a model medieval housewife.

KATHLEEN M. ASHLEY

References and Further Reading

Ashley, Kathleen. "The Bourgeois Piety of Martha in the *Passion* of Jean Michel." *Modern Language Quarterly* 45 (1984): 227–240.

Coletti, Theresa. *Mary Magdalene and the Drama of Saints: Theater, Gender, and Religion in Late Medieval England.* Philadelphia: University of Pennsylvania Press, 2004.

Constable, Giles. *Three Studies in Medieval Religious and Social Thought: The Interpretation of Mary and Martha. The Ideal of the Imitation of Christ. The Orders of Society.* Cambridge: Cambridge University Press, 1995.

Couchman, Jane. "*Actio[n]* and *Passio*: The Iconography of the Scene of Christ at the Home of Mary and Martha. *Studi medievali* 3rd ser. 26 (1985): 711–719.

Kupfer, Marcia. *The Art of Healing: Painting for the Sick and the Sinner in a Medieval Town.* University Park, Pa.: Pennsylvania State University Press, 2003.

See also **Bible, Women in; Conduct Literature; Hagiography; Mary Magdalene; Mary, Virgin**

MARY MAGDALEN

The four Gospels contain a mere twelve references to the historical Mary Magdalen. In the early medieval period, this testimony was imaginatively refashioned to create a new St. Mary Magdalen for the ages. In 591, Pope Gregory the Great preached a sermon that fused together into one individual the identities of three distinct women described in the Gospels. Most significant was his amalgamation of Mary Magdalen and Luke's unnamed female sinner (Luke 7:37–50). The unnamed sinner, whom Luke placed at the banquet of the Pharisee, theatrically washed Jesus' feet with her tears and dried them with her hair. She was deemed to be a prostitute, in line with contemporary values. She was construed as such because conventional wisdom regarded women's sins as sexual, i.e., those provoked by lust, while public expressions of sexuality were considered tantamount to prostitution. Accordingly, Mary called Magdalen (Mark 16:9) gained a preconversion identity as a prostitute. Gregory also grafted the figure of Mary of Bethany, sister of Martha, at whose beckoning Jesus raised Lazarus from the dead (John 11:1–45; 12:1–8), onto the figure of the Magdalen. Thus she acquired siblings (Martha and Lazarus) and became associated with the contemplative life. From the close of the sixth century Gregory the Great's composite figure was largely accepted in the West as St. Mary Magdalen. The Greek Church, however, never accepted Gregory's reformulated saint.

Textual Tradition

The development of Mary Magdalen's literary lives throughout the medieval period is no less complicated. A contemporary of Gregory the Great's, Gregory of Tours, chronicler of the Merovingian kingdom, mentioned Mary Magdalen only once in his *opera omnia*, to report (possibly following Byzantine tradition) that she retired to Ephesus where she died and was entombed. The venerable Bede (c. 720), also following Byzantine tradition, added Mary Magdalen's feast day, July 22, to his martyrology, from which it spread to Western liturgical calendars. The process of embellishing her *vita* began in earnest, however, with a legend (again probably of Byzantine provenance) that began circulating in ninth-century Italy. Known as the *vita eremitica*, it assimilated the Magdalen's *vita* into that of Mary of Egypt, an Eastern saint, who before her conversion had been a prostitute and afterwards withdrew to the desert to live as an anchorite. Mary Magdalen's identity as a prostitute had already been sealed by Gregory the Great; now the scene of her postconversion penitence was localized in the desert.

The first attempt to formulate a coherent *vita* for Mary Magdalen came in the text of a tenth-century homily known as the *vita evangelica*. Issuing from the Burgundian monastery of Cluny, where devotion to the saint seems to have been especially strong, it combined into one narrative sequence all the gospel passages relating to Mary Magdalen's life. In the late eleventh century, to explain the presence of the saint's relics at Vézelay, a legend known as the *vita apostolica* began to circulate. It claimed that Roman officials, irritated by the proselytizing of Jesus's followers, rounded up Mary Magdalen and a cohort of other disciples and set them adrift at sea in a rudderless boat. Providentially, they washed ashore in Marseille, where they evangelized the pagans of southern Gaul. Soon this *vita* was joined to the *vita eremitica* to form the *vita apostolico–eremitica*. It related how, after preaching and saving pagan souls, the Magdalen retreated to the "desert" outside Provence to spend the final thirty years of her life in ascetic contemplation.

Pilgrimage Sites

Like all important medieval saints, Mary Magdalen was the dedicatee of numerous medieval shrines. Her two major pilgrimage sites are located in Burgundy and Provence. The great Romanesque church at Vézelay was rededicated to the Magdalen in the mid-eleventh century, a few decades after it began claiming possession of her relics. (A legend known as the *translatio posterior* explained that her relics had been piously stolen from her sepulcher in Provence and transported to Vézelay to protect them from the periodic Arab incursions of the eighth century.) Situated along the major pilgrimage route that brought northern European pilgrims to Santiago de Compostela, Vézelay flourished as an international pilgrimage destination in the eleventh and twelfth centuries. Vézelay's apogee may well have arrived at Easter in 1146, when Bernard of Clairvaux preached the second crusade in the presence of King Louis VII and Queen Eleanor of Aquitaine. The crowds were so great and so fervent that a reviewing stand collapsed as Bernard was handing out crusader insignia to those vying to take up the cross. That no one was injured was credited by chroniclers of the event to the intercession of the Magdalen.

As the patron of Vézelay, Mary Magdalen was an active wonder-worker. Her miracles included spectacular cures, the raising of the dead, assistance with matters of fertility and childbirth, and the liberation of prisoners, all of which were appended to her various *vitae*. Jacobus de Voragine, author of *The Golden Legend*, the celebrated thirteenth-century compendium of saints' lives, drew on these miracle stories as well as various *vitae* to construct his definitive *vita* of Mary Magdalen, which enjoyed wide readership in the late medieval and early modern periods.

Vézelay, it seems, had already experienced its heyday when *The Golden Legend* was completed: in 1279, the Angevin prince Charles of Salerno rediscovered the relics of St. Mary Magdalen at the church of St. Maximin outside Aix-en-Provence. It was the *coup de grâce* for Vézelay, a blow from which it never recovered. Henceforth pilgrims transferred their allegiance to the new shrine at St. Maximin, where the saint soon began performing miracles, memorialized by Jean Gobi the Elder in his miracle collection, compiled c. 1315. The Provençal sanctuaries of St. Maximin and La Sainte-Baume (the "desert" cave where Mary Magdalen was believed to have retired) now attracted crowned heads of Europe, saints, and other notables, among them Birgitta of Sweden and Petrarch. The discovery of the Provençal relics and the installation of the Dominican Order as caretakers of the shrine are duly chronicled in the *Dominican Legend*, written in the mid-fifteenth century.

Attributes

Through preaching, the liturgy, devotional books, hymns, sacred plays, and the visual arts (Mary Magdalen's visual attribute is an alabaster jar of oil), the legend of Mary Magdalen was disseminated throughout Christendom. Each of her *personae*—sinner, penitent, contemplative, and preacher of the Resurrection—was harnessed for didactic ends by preachers and moralists. Fire-and-brimstone preachers such as Berthold of Regensberg and Bernardino of Siena used her preconversion sinfulness to inveigh against the sins of vanity and lust. Due to her association with these sins, Mary Magdalen became the patron saint of repentant prostitutes, whose houses of refuge were frequently named in her honor. She became as well the patron of those catering to the luxury trade, such as drapers and glovers. The Magdalen's exemplary tearful conversion at Christ's feet taught an important lesson to sinners about the efficacy of the sacrament of penance. Confraternities devoted to the penitential discipline of self-flagellation made her their patron saint, while handbooks for preachers cited her as the model penitent.

Her penance was so expedient that many moralists argued in the late medieval era that it returned her to a virginal state. As such, pious matrons, such as Margaret of Cortona, worried about their compromised bodily condition and its consequences for personal salvation, took Mary Magdalen as their special patron. But nuns too adopted Mary Magdalen as their advocate. Her contemplative persona of Mary of Bethany, Jesus's attentive student, who according to legend spent the last thirty years of her life in mystical ecstasy, provided a model for cloistered nuns whose lives were spent in contemplative prayer. Finally, the Magdalen's role as herald of the Resurrection (John 20:18), along with her legendary apostolate in Provence, was regarded as a model for active engagement in the world, earning her the title *apostolorum apostola* (apostle of the apostles), an honorific bestowed on her by twelfth-century scriptural commentators. Catherine of Siena praised Mary Magdalen's preaching and took the saint as a model for her own active apostolate. The Dominican Order, to which Catherine belonged, strove to balance the active and contemplative lives in perfect harmony; as such, it took Mary Magdalen as protector in 1297.

The medieval Church considered Mary Magdalen's feast day so important that it was ranked as a solemn feast, a day on which all work stopped. Tridentine reformers began to distinguish between the Mary Magdalen of the Gospels and the saint of legend, and Gregory the Great's composite saint was challenged by humanist scholars of the sixteenth century. It was not until 1969 that the Roman Church officially released the historical figure of Mary Magdalen from the bondage of her legend. Though the Roman liturgical calendar now venerates her as a "disciple of Christ," nonetheless the image of Mary Magdalen that perdures is that of Luke's sinner, now glorified in heaven. As such she was and continues to be a symbol of hope: through penitential conversion a great sinner became a great saint. Equally, however, the Middle Ages bequeathed to later generations a female saint venerated for her important role in salvation history. After Christ had risen, he chose not to appear first to his male disciples, but rather to a woman. Mary Magdalen, therefore, was doubly privileged: she was both the first witness to the Resurrection and the apostle of the apostles, entrusted by Christ to proclaim the good news, the central tenet of Christian faith.

KATHERINE LUDWIG JANSEN

References and Further Reading

Bériou, Nicole. "La Madeleine dans les sermons parisiens du XIIIe siècle." *Mélanges de l'École Française de Rome (Moyen Age)* 104/1 (1992): 269–340.

Coletti, Theresa. *Mary Magdalene and the Drama of the Saints: Theater, Gender, and Religion in Late Medieval England.* Philadelphia: University of Pennsylvania Press, 2004.

Duperray, Eve, ed. *Marie Madeleine dans la mystique, les arts et les lettres.* [*Actes du Colloque international Avignon 20-21-22 juillet 1988.*] Paris: Beauchesne, 1989.

Faillon, E.-M. *Monuments inédits sur l'apostolat de Sainte Marie-Madeleine en Provence et sur les autres Apôtres de cette contrée, Saint Lazare, Saint Maximin, Sainte Marthe.* 2 vols. Paris: J.-P. Migne, 1859.

Fiorenza, Elisabeth Schüssler. *In Memory of Her: A Feminist Theological Reconstruction of Christian Origins.* New York: Crossroads Press, 1983.

Garth, Helen Meredith. *Saint Mary Magdalene in Medieval Literature.* Baltimore: Johns Hopkins University Press, 1950.

Gregory of Tours. *Glory of the Martyrs*, translated by Raymond van Dam. Translated Texts for Historians. Latin Series III. Liverpool: Liverpool University Press, 1988.

Gregory the Great. "Homilia 33." In *XL Homiliarum in Evangelia. Patrologia Latina* 76: 1238–1246.

Hänsel, Hans. *Die Maria Magdalena Legende. Eine Quellen Untersuchung in Greifswalder Beiträge zur Literatur und Stilforschung*, 16.1. Greifswald: Hans Dallmeyer, 1937.

Haskins, Susan. *Mary Magdalen: Myth and Metaphor.* London: HarperCollins, 1993.

———. *Legenda Aurea*, edited by Giovanni Paolo Maggioni. Florence: SISMEL, 1998.

Iogna-Prat, Dominique. "Bienheureuse polysémie: La Madeleine du *Sermo in veneratione Sanctae Mariae Magdalena* attribué à Odon de Cluny (Xe siècle)." In *Marie Madeleine dans la mystique, les arts et les lettres*, pp. 21–31.

Gobi, Jean. *Liber Miraculorum B. Mariae Magdalenae*, edited by Jacqueline Sclafer. *Archivum Fratrum Praedicatorum* 63 (1993): 113–206.

Jacobus de Voragine. *Golden Legend*, translated by William Granger Ryan. 2 vols. Princeton, N.J.: Princeton University Press, 1993.

Jansen, Katherine Ludwig. "Mary Magdalen and the Mendicants: The Preaching of Penance in the Middle Ages." *Journal of Medieval History* 21.1 (1995): 1–25.

———. "Maria Magdalena: Apostolorum Apostola." In *Women Preachers and Prophets through Two Millennia of Christianity*, edited by Beverly Mayne Kienzle and Pamela J. Walker. Berkeley, Calif.: University of California Press, 1998.

———. *The Making of the Magdalen: Preaching and Popular Devotion in the Late Middle Ages*. Princeton, N.J.: Princeton University Press, 2000.

———. "Like a Virgin: The Meaning of the Magdalen for Female Penitents of Later Medieval Italy." *Memoirs of the American Academy in Rome* 45 (2000): 131–152.

———. "L'arrivée de Marie-Madeleine à Vézelay." *Monde de la bible* 143 (2002): 35–37.

La Maddalena tra Sacro e Profano, edited by Marilena Mosco. Milan: Mondadori, 1986.

La Madeleine (VIIIe-XIII Siècle). Mélanges de l'École Française de Rome (Moyen Age) 104/1 (1992).

Lobrichon, Guy, ed. "Le dossier magdalénien aux XIe-XIIe siècle." *Mélanges de l'Ecole Française de Rome (Moyen Age)*. 104/1 (1992): 163–180.

Malvern, Marjorie. *Venus in Sackcloth: The Magdalen's Origins and Metamorphoses*. Carbondale and Edwardsville, Ill.: Southern Illinois University Press, 1975.

Montagnes, Bernard. In "La légende dominicaine de Marie-Madeleine à Saint-Maximin." *Mémoires de l'Académie de Vaucluse*, 7th series, 6 (1985): 73–86.

Ricci, Carla. *Maria di Magdala e le molte altre. Donne sul cammino di Gesù*. Naples: D'Auria, 1991.

Saxer, Victor. *Le Culte de Marie-Madeleine en occident dès origines à la fin du moyen-âge*. 2 vols. Cahiers d'archéologie et d'histoire, 3. Auxerre-Paris: Publications de la Société des Fouilles Archéologiques et des Monuments Historiques de l'Yonne-Librairie Clavreuil, 1959.

Sebastiani, Lilia. *Tra/Sfigurazione: Il personaggio evangelico di Maria di Magdala e il mito della peccatrice redenta nella tradizione occidentale*. Brescia: Queriniana, 1992.

Vita evangelica. [Once attributed to Odo of Cluny.] Sermo II (In veneratione Sanctae Mariae Magdalenae). *Petrologia Latina* 133: 713–721.

Wilk, Sarah. "The Cult of Mary Magdalen in Fifteenth-Century Florence and Its Iconography." *Studi Medievali*, 3rd series 26 (1985): 685–698.

Witherington III, Ben. *Women and the Genesis of Christianity*. Cambridge: Cambridge University Press, 1990.

See also **Bible, Women in; Hagiography; Hagiography, Iconographic Aspects of; Mary and Martha; Mary the Egyptian; Miracles and Miracle Collections; Pilgrims and Pilgrimage; Prostitutes; Relics and Reliquaries**

MARY OF BURGUNDY

Mary (1457–1482), duchess of Burgundy, was ruler of the Low Countries and Franche-Comté. Daughter and sole heir of Duke Charles the Bold and Isabel of Bourbon, after 1468, she was educated by her stepmother Margaret of York. In 1476, her father betrothed her to Maximilian of Habsburg, son of Emperor Frederick III. Charles's death on the battlefield before Nancy, January 5, 1477, left Mary and Margaret in a turbulent situation. His territories suffered from French invasions of Burgundy, Artois, and Hainault, and some people were angered by Charles's harsh government, trampling on privileges and requiring levels of taxes and military service beyond any precedent. The recently annexed territories Guelders and Liège immediately reclaimed their autonomy, while Luxembourg remained autonomous until 1480. The core principalities in the Low Countries, however, meeting in the States General, inaugurated Mary as their legal princess and granted military aid against French invasion, after she had fully subscribed to all the petitions and grievances the cities and states' assemblies had submitted to her. The general tendency of the dozens of charters she granted to cities, territories, and the whole of the Low Countries—the "Great Privilege" of February 11, 1477 was the first constitutional act for this region—was the restoration of local and regional privileges and customary law Charles had overruled by centralising measures.

Her subjects' support for the young and inexperienced heiress helped to keep the French out of the core territories of the Low Countries, which, under this pressure, united more closely. Nevertheless, Mary had to face scores of local revolts (within the duchy), mainly targeted against those administrators who were seen as responsible for Charles's oppressive regime. By June, calm returned after wide-ranging concessions by the government. In the meantime, Mary had informed Maximilian that she still saw him as her future spouse, inviting him urgently to come and marry her and take up governmental responsibilities. The marriage, on August 18, 1477, implied the end of Mary's personal government. She gave birth to two surviving children, Philip the Fair and Maximilian, who played major roles in European politics. Mary's choice of a Habsburg introduced this dynasty as rulers of the Low Countries for more than three centuries.

WIM BLOCKMANS

References and Further Reading

Blockmans, Wim, and Walter Prevenier. *The Promised Lands: The Low Countries under Burgundian Rule, 1369–1530*. Philadelphia: University of Pennsylvania Press, 1996.

Cazaux, Yves. *Marie de Bourgogne*. Paris: Albin Michel, 1967.

See also **Burgundian Netherlands; Heiresses; Margaret of York; Noble Women**

MARY OF HUNGARY I

Mary of Hungary I (1255–1323), the daughter of Stephen V, king of Hungary, wed the future Charles II of Anjou, king of Naples, in 1269. Mother of eight sons and five daughters, Mary actively promoted the dynastic interests of her family. It was through her that the Neapolitan Angevins inherited the kingdom of Hungary. Mary sported the coat of arms of the Árpádian dynasty on numerous works of art and monuments commissioned by her, from her silk throne carpet to the panel of Simone Martini representing Saint Ladislas of Hungary. She was a generous patron of the church, especially of the Franciscan Order.

After the death of her eldest son, Charles Martel, a learned prince and a friend of Dante in 1294, who was supposed to inherit the kingdoms of Naples and Hungary, Mary fought for the succession of her grandson to the Hungarian throne. With the strong financial support of the Neapolitan court, the Franciscan Cardinal Gentile da Montefiore, papal legate to Hungary, managed to have Charles Robert recognized by the Hungarian estates as king in 1312. The chapel of Saint Martin in the lower church of Assisi is a testimony both to Cardinal Gentile's mission and to Mary's efforts in furthering the interests of her dynasty through her generous patronage of the arts. The paintings of Simone Martini represent not only the story of Martin, a native of Pannonia (later Hungary), but also the "blessed family" (*beata stirps*) of the Árpádian dynasty, from Saint Stephen via Saint Henry and Saint Ladislas to Saint Elisabeth and Saint Margaret of Hungary. Mary was buried in the church of Santa Maria Donna Regina built by her sometime between 1307 and 1320. Her tomb, a masterpiece of Tino di Camaino, is decorated with the four cardinal virtues, *Prudentia, Temperantia, Iustitia*, and *Fortitudo*.

MARIANNE SÁGHY

References and Further Reading

Church of Santa Maria Donna Regina: Art, Iconography and Patronage in Fourteenth Century Naples, edited by Janis Elliot and Cordelia Warr. Aldershot: Ashgate, 2004.
Hoch, Adrian S. "*Beata stirps*: Royal Patronage and the Identification of the Sainted Rulers in the St. Elizabeth Chapel at Assisi." *Art History* 15.3 (1992): 279–295.

Léonard, Émile G. *Les Angevins de Naples*. Paris: Presses Universitaires de France, 1954.
Klaniczay, Gábor. *Holy Rulers and Blessed Princesses: Dynastic Cults in Medieval Central Europe*. Cambridge: Cambridge University Press, 2001.

See also **Italy; Patronage, Artistic; Patronage, Ecclesiastical; Queens and Empresses: The West**

MARY OF HUNGARY II

Daughter of Louis the Great, king of Hungary and of Poland (1342–1382), Mary (1371–1395) was crowned "king of Hungary" (*rex Hungariae*) in 1382. The first woman to rule Hungary, where daughters were generally excluded from inheritance of land, Mary was called *rex feminus*. Thanks to this legal fiction, a new status was created for her in this unprecedented situation that also allowed for a distinction from the *reginae*, the consorts of kings. According to King Louis' original plan of succession, Mary, betrothed to Sigismund of Luxembourg, son of Emperor Charles IV, was supposed to rule Poland together with her husband. However, the order of succession was successfully challenged by Elizabeth, the queen mother. The Polish throne was inherited by Mary's younger sister, Hedwig (Jadwiga). Elizabeth became regent of Hungary and ruled with her favorite, the palatine Nicholas of Gara.

The government of the queens proved to be a disaster. The baronial leagues possessing large estates in southern Hungary and Croatia wanted to continue the lucrative Italian wars of the late king and follow the Adriatic, "maritime" orientation set by him rather than complying to the new, Czech-German "continental" perspective offered by Sigismund, whom they hated and despised. In 1386, the Gara league murdered the pretender, Charles of Naples, invited to the Hungarian throne by the Horváti clan; in the same year, Garai was killed and the queens kidnapped by János Horváti, the leader of the faction. Elizabeth was strangled under the very eyes of her daughter in 1387. Mary was liberated from her prison in Croatia by her husband. Instead of showing clemency, she took revenge on her assailants by executing Horváti, to whom she had earlier promised safe conduct. Mary then conferred the government on Sigismund and was reduced to the status of consort. Being a plaything in her own mother's schemes, she never possessed her own political authority. Later she was able to devote her life to charity. In 1395, the pregnant queen went riding, fell and died. Mary was buried in the church of Saint Ladislas in Nagyvárad (Oradea).

MARIANNE SÁGHY

References and Further Reading

de Thurocz, Johannes. *Chronica Hungarorum*, edited by E. Galántai and G. Kristó. Budapest, 1985.

Erik, Fügedi. *Könyörülj, bánom, könyörülj...* Budapest: Helikon, 1986.

Laurentius, Monacis. *Chronicon de rebus Venetis ab u. c. ad annum 1354. Accedit ejusdem Laurentii carmen de Carolo II rege Hungariae.* Flaminius Cornelius, Venetiis, 1758. Hungarian translation, Sándor Márki. *Monaci krónikája Kis Károlyról.* Budapest: Anthenevm, 1910.

Sághy, Marianne. "Aspects of Female Rulership in Late Medieval Literature: The Queen's Reign in Angevin Hungary." *East Central Europe/L'Europe du Centre Est* 20–23.1 (1993–1996): 69–86.

Sándor, Márki. *Mária, Magyarország királynéja (1370–1395).* Budapest: Méhner Vilmos Kiadosa, 1885.

See also **Eastern Europe; Jadwiga; Regents and Queen-Lieutenants; Succession, Royal and Noble**

MARY THE EGYPTIAN

The archetypal figure of the penitent woman made her first appearance in Christian literature in Luke 7:36–50, where she washed the feet of Jesus. Tradition identifies her with Mary Magdalene. In the following centuries four other "holy harlots" took their places in the *Vitae patrum* collections: Mary Meretrix, Thaïs, Pelagia, and—most famous of the four during the Middle Ages—Mary the Egyptian.

The authoritative Greek prose life of this saint is attributed to Sophronios (c. 600: PG 87, pars 3: 3697–3725). It was translated into Latin in the ninth century by Paul the Deacon of Naples (PL 73:671–690). The story begins with a monk of Palestine, Zosimas, who makes a Lenten journey into the desert and encounters an old woman, entirely nude, her body blackened by the sun. She tells him her story: as a youth she was a courtesan in Alexandria; converted miraculously by the Virgin Mary, she traveled into the desert, where she has lived alone on just three loaves of bread for the past forty-seven years. She instructs him to return to his monastery, but he is to meet her the following year to give her the Eucharist. He does so, and eventually buries her dead body, with the help of a providentially appearing lion.

By the middle of the twelfth century short versions of the tale appeared in Latin collections of miracles of the Virgin. These anthology treatments relegate Zosimas to a secondary role and bring Mary herself to the foreground of the legend. The late-twelfth-century Anglo-Norman verse life (version *T*, as it is called) realizes fully the literary implications of this change. Stylistic and thematic echoes associate this poem with other Anglo-Norman works of the period, including Clemence of Barking's life of St. Catherine,

the *Gracial* by Adgar, and the *Tristan* romance by Thomas. Versions deriving from *T* in the following centuries include that of Rutebeuf and the Spanish *Vida de santa María Egipcíaca*. The *Golden Legend* reverts, however, to the older, "Zosimas-centered" narrative, which may be said to predominate in the literature thereafter.

J. DUNCAN ROBERTSON

References and Further Reading

Cazelles Brigitteo. "Modèle ou mirage: Marie l'Égyptienne." *French Review* 53 (1979): 13–22.

Dembowski, Peter F., ed. *La vie de sainte Marie l'Égyptienne: Versions en ancien et en moyen français.* Geneva: Droz, 1977.

Robertson, Duncan. "The Anglo-Norman Verse Life of St. Mary the Egyptian." *Romance Philology* 52 (1998): 13–44.

Ward, Benedicta. *Harlots of the Desert: A Study of Repentance in Early Monastic Sources.* Kalamazoo, Mich.: Cistercian Publications, 1987.

See also **Clemence of Barking; Hagiography; Jacobus de Voragine's Golden Legend; Mary Magdalen**

MARY THE YOUNGER

Mary the Younger (c. 875–c. 903) was a pious woman of Armenian origin who came to be venerated as a saint. After marriage to a military officer named Nikephoros, she spent most of her married life in the Thracian town of Bizye. She bore four children, two of whom died young. She was assiduous in her private devotions, engaged in fasting, and was noted for her charitable activities and kind behavior towards slaves. She died young, as a result of abuse by her husband. Some months after her burial, healing miracles began to occur at her tomb; her *vita* attests to her miraculous cure of twenty-one men and eleven women. She was also commemorated in an icon, together with her two surviving children and a maidservant, by a painter from Rhaidestos who was informed of her likeness through a dream vision. The cult of Mary seems to have remained a local development; she was not included in the *Synaxarion of Constantinople* and no icon of her survives. Her anonymous *vita*, preserved in two late manuscripts (fourteenth and fifteenth centuries), was probably written in the eleventh or twelfth century.

Mary the Younger was a rare example of a Byzantine married woman who worked miracles and achieved sanctity, even though this was considered impossible by the local bishop. She is usually grouped with a small number of other married holy women, such as the empress Theophano (d. 895 or 896) and

Thomaïs of Lesbos (fl. first half of tenth century), who became saints without ever taking monastic vows.

ALICE-MARY TALBOT

References and Further Reading

Laiou, Angeliki E., trans. "Life of St. Mary the Younger." In *Holy Women of Byzantium: Ten Saints' Lives in English Translation*, edited by Alice-Mary Talbot. Washington, D.C.: Dumbarton Oaks, 1996, pp. 239–289.

Mango, Cyril. "The Byzantine Church at Vize (Bizye) in Thrace and St. Mary the Younger." *Zbornik Radova Vizantološkog Instituta* 11 (1968): 9–13.

See also **Byzantium; Domestic Abuse; Hagiography; Icons, Byzantine; Lay Piety; Miracles and Miracle Collections**

MARY, VIRGIN

Since the fourth century, devotion to the Virgin Mary, mother of Jesus, has been an integral part of the piety and worship of the Christian Church. An interest in Mary had already begun to appear in the second century. Afterward, her popularity steadily increased until it reached a high point in the twelfth century from which it never declined for the remainder of the Middle Ages. Indeed, the fifteenth century, the last of the medieval period, witnessed the production of some of the most lyrical hymns ever written to celebrate her role in the Christian drama. One of these hymns, "*Adam lay y-bounden*," comes from an anonymous English hymn writer who chose to express love for the Virgin Mary, Queen of Heaven, by giving thanks for the original fall into sin in the Garden of Eden, because it seemed obvious that, without that fall, Mary could never have attained her prominent place in the heavenly court. The hymn asserts, "Ne had the apple taken been, the apple taken been, Ne had never Our Lady a-been heavené queen. Blessed be the time that apple taken was." Without mentioning Eve specifically, the hymn calls to mind one of the oldest and most popular themes of both ancient and medieval Marian devotion: Mary as Second Eve. The idea is as old as the second century, when St. Justin Martyr, in his *Dialogue with Trypho*, contrasted Mary's obedience to the will of God with Eve's disobedience. By consenting to become the mother of the incarnate Word, Mary had made possible the eventual overthrow of the very serpent who had tempted Eve, becoming herself the bodily gateway of salvation. Justin's theme was soon adopted by other Christian writers like Irenaeus of Lyons, who expanded its possibilities even further.

The Emergence of Marian Doctrine and Piety in the Early Church

The theological consideration of Mary demonstrated in the work of Justin and Irenaeus is only one aspect of the emerging interest in the Virgin that first began to appear in the second century. This new focus on Mary occurred within the context of veneration for the early martyr-saints of the church that was rapidly becoming an important aspect of Christian worship. By the end of the second century, the *Protevangelion* or *Early Gospel of James* was written to supply the need for additional information about Mary's life not provided in the four Gospels of Matthew, Mark, Luke, and John. These Gospels assumed a place of authority within the early Christian community over the course of the second century, but they included only a few specific references to Mary herself. Although the *Protevangelion* was never seriously considered for inclusion in the canon by the Church, it became quite popular and provided a number of the stories that eventually would be woven into the tapestry of medieval Marian devotion, including Mary's dedication to the temple at the age of three and support for Mary's virginity *in partu* (in giving birth). Most important of all, the *Protevangelion* relates the story of Mary's conception. An angel announces to the childless couple, Anne and Joachim, that they will soon have a very special daughter. In outline, the account resembles the story of Hannah's conception of Samuel in 1 Samuel. It therefore continues a practice begun by Luke, whose version of Mary's song of praise, the "Magnificat" (Luke 1), is clearly modeled on that of Hannah.

While some aspects of Marian devotion developed as early as the second century, there is general recognition that Mary first became the object of widespread theological consideration and piety in the fourth century. Much of this new attention occurred in connection with the heated theological debates surrounding the person of Christ. Athanasius of Alexandria, ardent defender of the divinity of Christ both before and after the Council of Nicea in 325, expressed the veneration for Mary common among theologians of the Alexandrian tradition by referring to Mary as *Theotokos* (God-bearer). This title praises the Virgin, but it was used even more to demonstrate Jesus' divinity from the moment of his conception. Mary, then, was the one who carried God incarnate for the nine months of her pregnancy and then bore God into the world in the person of Jesus.

The fourth century also witnessed the first recorded prayer to Mary, the *Sub tuum praesidium* (Under Thy Protection), although some scholars have dated it as early as the later third century. The beautiful hymns of the Syrian deacon Ephraem, known as "the Lyre of the Holy Spirit," further testify to the fervent devotion felt by Eastern Christian writers of the day. Equally important for Mary's place in future medieval piety is the fact that, by the fourth century, Mary had become the model for all Christians, especially women, who sought to live a life of virginity. Assuming no sexual relationship with her husband Joseph, Church fathers, including Athanasius in the East and Ambrose of Milan in the West, asserted that Mary had always lived a quiet contemplative life at home—she seldom went out and, never wanting to be seen by men, was continually engaged in prayer and good works. Mary thus became the symbol for the ascetic lifestyle that would remain the Christian ideal throughout the medieval period.

The ecumenical councils of the fifth century, called to settle the crucial Christological issues concerning Jesus's humanity, officially established some of the most central doctrines and titles in Marian piety. The Council of Ephesus (431) formally approved Mary's title *Theotokos*. The Council of Chalcedon (451) next proclaimed her as *Aeiparthenos* (Ever-Virgin) when it adopted in its entirety the *Tome* of Pope St. Leo I, which contained this doctrine.

Immaculate Conception and the Assumption

There was no consensus in the early church, however, regarding the degree to which Mary participated in the sinful condition of the rest of humanity. The belief that Mary had been preserved from original sin, the doctrine of the Immaculate Conception, remained in dispute. There were theologians, including John Chrysostom, who were convinced of Mary's participation in original sin, and some, including Ambrose, who clearly believed her to have been preserved from all actual sin. They stopped short, however, of arguing for her preservation from original sin as well. It is a testament to the strong belief in Mary's holiness that even Augustine of Hippo, who so stressed the universal power of original sin, was capable of speculating that Mary had never sinned.

The first celebration of a feast of Mary's conception took place in the seventh century in the Eastern church, but was not widely introduced into western Europe until the twelfth century. Debate regarding the Immaculate Conception continued throughout the Middle Ages in the West. The doctrine was always popular among the people, who are usually credited with ensuring its eventual acceptance; but there were famous theologians arrayed on both sides of the debate. The Dominican St. Thomas Aquinas opposed the Immaculate Conception as a belief that detracted from Christ's role as savior of all people; and, for this reason, the Dominican friars tended to follow his lead. The Franciscans, on the other hand, became major defenders of the doctrine, although their more cautious preachers, like San Bernardino of Siena, preferred to wait until the Church made a final decision before asserting it in sermons. The Immaculate Conception was destined to remain simply a popular belief until Pope Pius IX proclaimed it a dogma of the Church in 1854.

As with Mary's conception, Eastern Christians were the first to demonstrate an interest in Mary's death and bodily Assumption into heaven. Early Syrian and Greek documents like the *Obsequies of the Holy Virgin* and the *Pseudo-Melito* suggest that Mary either died or "fell asleep" and that afterward both her soul and her body were taken up into heaven. By 600, August 15 was set aside by the Eastern Emperor Maurice to commemorate the Virgin's death; and by the seventh century, the feast was established in Gaul under the title the Feast of the Dormition. In the West, the feast came to be known as the Assumption during the ninth century and acquired a popularity rivaling Christmas and Easter. Never as controversial as the Immaculate Conception, the Assumption also had to wait for modern definition as official doctrine. It was finally proclaimed to be a dogma by Pope Pius XII in 1950.

Relics

There is one final aspect of Marian devotion yet to appear in the earliest period of Christian history: relics. Belief in the special holiness of the bodies of saints can already be detected in the New Testament (Acts 19:11–12) and was especially associated in the early Church with the bodies of martyrs such as St. Polycarp, executed around the middle of the second century. Fairly widespread acceptance of Mary's Assumption would appear to eliminate the possibility of true Marian relics; nevertheless, there is evidence of them by the sixth century, when Gregory of Tours mentions a number of Marian relics already being venerated in Frankish Gaul. Relics of the Virgin included things such as locks of her hair, pieces of clothing, and above all, her milk, perhaps the single most popular relic associated with Mary's cult. Vials of her milk could be found at many popular pilgrimage sites; and Mary's milk is the one Marian relic popular in the many miracle stories involving her intervention on behalf of sinners. Indeed, there were several miracle stories telling of Mary's miraculous appearance to those who sought her in prayer, so that she could reward them with a few drops of her milk. Mary's milk came to symbolize her power to intercede for sinners. This intercession was often depicted both in sermons and in art works using a theme known as the "double intercession." The Virgin kneels before her Son in heaven, revealing to him the breast with which she had nourished him as a child, reminding him of her care for him, and asking him to be merciful to sinners. Jesus, in turn, reveals to the Father the wound in his side, suffered on behalf of sinners, beseeching him also to show mercy. In the art works the physical gestures of mother and son are portrayed as virtually identical. A few places possessed Marian relics, including Walsingham, England, which had a vial of her milk by the thirteenth century. Paris had a lock of her hair, while Chartres could claim the *sancta camisia* (holy chemise), the garment worn by Mary when she gave birth to Christ. This relic was a gift to Charlemagne from the Byzantine empress Irene. Also popular were various dwellings associated with Mary. Walsingham became one of the most visited pilgrimage sites in Europe because of the Holy House of Walsingham, believed to be a replica of Mary's house in Nazareth, revealed in a vision to the twelfth-century Norman woman Richelde of Fervaques (c. 1130). The Holy House of Loreto, Italy (1295) claimed to be the very house in which Jesus was conceived.

By the early Middle Ages, most of the permanent elements of Marian doctrine and devotion were already in place. The particular historical developments and devotional trends of medieval Europe then molded these elements into something quite distinctive and complex.

The Middle Ages: The Flowering of Marian Piety

Even though Marian piety was fully integrated into Christian worship by the early Middle Ages, nothing could have anticipated the tremendous outpouring of devotion Mary received in the twelfth century. Under the combined influence of feudalism and the French courtly love tradition, Mary was celebrated by her own troubadours as *Notre Dame* (Our Lady), the Queen of Heaven, who was to be served and honored with a purity of love and service due to no merely earthly lady. Mary became the subject of numerous hymns, among them the beautiful Marian antiphons such as the *Salve Regina* (Hail Holy Queen), which were soon incorporated into the liturgy. It was also

during the late eleventh or early twelfth century that the first half of the most popular prayer to Mary in Western Christian piety, the *Ave Maria* (Hail Mary), first entered widespread usage. By the early thirteenth century, the *Ave Maria* was so well established that the Church encouraged Christians to memorize it along with the "Our Father" and the "Apostles' Creed." If songs and prayers were not tangible or permanent enough, Mary was also immortalized in stone, in the Gothic cathedrals all over France, and throughout the rest of Europe, that were dedicated to her, including Notre Dame de Paris and Notre Dame de Chartres; and in addition, there were the statues of Mary, usually holding the infant Jesus, sculpted to adorn the buildings.

Against this backdrop of a society familiar with the customs of feudalism and courtly love, Mary's role as intercessor was often depicted as that of a Queen Mother, helping to preside over the court of her son and always ready to present to him the requests of the various suppliants who came seeking favors. There was no doubt that she would be especially bound to help those who had increased her own glory and honor at court through their plentiful offerings of prayer and praise. Indeed at times, preachers like Jean Gerson presented Mary as the Queen of the Court of Mercy while Jesus presided over the Court of Justice. Those who feared to approach the throne of Christ directly because of their sins could first make their supplications at Mary's court.

Twelfth-century Marian piety also influenced biblical interpretation and in some cases altered the text of Scripture itself as it was used in the liturgy. Beginning with Origen's commentaries and homilies on the Song of Songs in the mid-third century, the Song of Songs had been interpreted as an allegory depicting the relationship between God and the believer or God and the Church. As early as the ninth century, however, when the Assumption first acquired widespread popularity, certain passages from the book were being used in the liturgy and in biblical commentaries to speak of Mary's Assumption into heaven. Paschasius Radbertus's work *Cogitis me* (You Compel Me) changed the Latin word *progreditur* (advances) of Song of Songs 6:9 to *ascendit* (ascends). The verse would now read: "Who is this who *ascends* like the dawn," fitting perfectly the Assumption of Mary. Because most people of the High Middle Ages believed Paschasius' work had been written by St. Jerome, the alteration in the text was accepted as authoritative for some time. By the twelfth century, authors began to interpret the entire Song of Songs as a depiction of God's love for Mary. The *Seal of Blessed Mary* (c. 1100), by Honorius Augustodunensis, and Reupert of Deutz's *Commentary of the Song of Songs* (c. 1125) were the first works to do this. The use of the Song of Songs in a Marian context eventually led to the portrayal of Mary as the bride of Christ in many popular sermons. She became Christ's beloved, whom he sought out specifically as his partner in the Incarnation because of her beauty, her humility, and her virginal purity.

Role of the Mendicant Orders

Some of the most significant contributions to popular and scholarly devotion to Mary were made by the two new mendicant religious orders of the early thirteenth century, the Franciscans and the Dominicans. Together they were responsible for most of the public preaching heard by people of the High and late Middle Ages. Through their sermons, the Franciscans encouraged the people to embrace a more human vision of the Virgin Mary, who, like themselves, had experienced all of the joy and pain of earthly life. The Franciscans first established the *Angelus* as a popular prayer among the people. This initially involved the custom of reciting the *Ave Maria* each evening when the bells rang to announce the city's curfew. Based on the angel Gabriel's Annunciation to Mary, the *Angelus* eventually developed into a series of short statements about Mary's role in the Incarnation interspersed with the *Ave Maria*. The Dominicans also supported the custom of the *Angelus,* and in addition to being popular preachers, were instrumental in developing theological doctrines concerning Mary in their role as university professors.

Finally, the recently rediscovered works of Aristotle, which so influenced the direction of scholastic thought in the universities during the twelfth and thirteenth centuries, created an interpretation of Mary's role in the Incarnation destined to become one of the commonplaces of later medieval Marian piety and preaching. Certainly, Aristotle was not needed in order to affirm Mary's concrete role in the Incarnation or her logical connection to the doctrine of transubstantiation established in 1215; but his biological concepts made possible the development of a particularly rich symbolism regarding her bodily unity with Christ. Aristotelian biology taught that a woman's menstrual blood was transformed into the body of the child by the male seed, which brought form and life to the inert matter. In addition, Aristotle believed that the woman's blood was transformed into the milk with which she fed the child. Women were therefore seen as sacrificing their own blood first to form the child's body and then to provide nourishment for the newborn infant. Aristotelian biology

enabled medieval theologians and preachers to make frequent references to Mary's "very pure blood" as the source of Jesus' body. Preachers asserted this connection whenever they wanted to stress the holiness of the body of Christ, whether his body hanging and suffering on the cross or his body received in the Eucharistic host. They would nearly always point out that his body was made "from the very pure blood of blessed Mary." It is also true that those, like the Franciscans, who sought to magnify Mary's physical role in the Incarnation often preferred to use the biological teaching of Galen, who believed that women and men made roughly equal contributions to forming the child in the womb. In any case, the Virgin's bodily connection to Jesus allowed her to be seen as the ultimate provider of the most revered object in late medieval religious devotion, the Eucharistic host. She thereby became the source of nourishment for Christian believers, her spiritual children, as she had been for Jesus. Tabernacles used to store the consecrated host were at times designed to represent Mary, containing once again within her own body the Eucharistic body of her Son. Plays that were staged during Corpus Christi festivals also associated Mary with the host by focusing on the glorification of Mary's body at her Assumption. The body whose transformed substance is received in the Eucharist was rightly preserved from corruption at her death.

The Unity of Mary and Jesus

The mystical bodily unity of Mary and Jesus was in fact the inspiration for virtually all devotion to Mary in the later Middle Ages. By the fifteenth century, it even allowed prominent theologians and preachers to assert that Mary had experienced the same bodily pain as Jesus during his crucifixion. Motherly compassion for her suffering son became a sharing in the actual Passion of Christ itself, an intimate participation in the redemption that earned for her an unquestioned right to intercede with her son in heaven on behalf of sinners.

This concrete, sacramental, and incarnational Marian piety was eventually transformed into something more "spiritualized" and inward during the very late medieval and early modern period. The growth of literacy after the invention of printing (c. 1450) worked to create a greater sense of interiority and introspection, which often preferred to stress Mary's "spiritual" motherhood of Jesus through her faith in Gabriel's proclamation of God's intentions at the Annunciation. The previous focus on the bodily unity of Mary and Jesus became instead an emphasis on their oneness of heart and will. Meditative prayers such as the rosary, which acquired its final modern form during the sixteenth century, also contributed to the transformation. But the older tradition celebrating Mary's physical role in the Incarnation, her exalted position as Bride of Christ, and her connection to the Eucharist could still be found during the sixteenth century in the theology and preaching of men such as François de Sales and Lawrence of Brindisi.

Recent Trends in Medieval Marian Scholarship

There is, of course, a great wealth of scholarship covering every aspect of Marian piety and theology from the earliest period of Christian history to the present day. Very often, when historians have disagreed in their interpretations it has been in relation to the effect on women of the Church's teaching on Mary. Feminist scholars like Marina Warner have often argued that Marian piety acquired quite early its most essential elements and that they have remained fairly constant over time. For the most part, they have concluded that the presentation of Mary both in formal theology and in more popular venues was crafted exclusively by men and that overall it served to present women with either an impossible model of perfection for emulation or an example of the kind of quiet, passive, and obedient behavior they sought to encourage in Christian women. Certainly some churchmen have sought to employ Marian piety in just this way, but more recent scholarship, particularly that concerning women's experience of Mary in the Middle Ages, has begun to reveal the creative ways in which women have related to Mary in their devotional lives.

Caroline Walker Bynum has argued that ultimately it was Christ, not the Virgin, who was the focus of most medieval women's spirituality, while it was men who seemed most drawn to Mary. For women, Mary as representative woman was not especially central. Yet Bynum also concludes that, as the provider of Christ's body, Mary was necessarily important to mystics like St. Catherine of Siena and Hildegard of Bingen, who sought to identify more fully with Christ's suffering on the cross. Sensing the same mystical unity of flesh that caused late medieval preachers to proclaim Mary's physical suffering at Calvary, these women could experience a oneness with the Passion of Jesus because his flesh, like theirs, was female flesh.

Equally positive is the role played by Mary in *The Book of Margery Kempe*, the spiritual autobiography of the fourteenth-century Englishwoman Margery Kempe. Gail McMurray Gibson has shown that the richness of Margery's visionary life often expressed her sense of unity with the suffering of Christ generated through her own personal suffering, a theme that reflects Bynum's argument. At other times, however, Margery's visions reveal her desire to identify with Mary herself, becoming, like Mary, a servant of the Christ Child. Theresa Coletti has highlighted Mary's unique position as both Virgin and mother in medieval religious drama. She argues that this paradoxical role helped to create dramatic interaction between the characters in the plays that served to challenge society's assumptions about the bodies of ordinary women. Pregnancy and lactation were the common lot of all married women. Lactation was often portrayed as a result of the original fall into sin. The fact that Mary could be both pregnant and a Virgin, lactating and sinless, forced the viewer to reconsider the usual stereotypes. Also, instead of presenting Mary as remote, perfect, and therefore completely unlike other women, the plays depict Mary in exactly the kinds of situations that all women encounter. Finally, Ellington's study of late medieval Marian popular sermons argues that these sermons generally describe Mary as an active, vocal, and central participant in Jesus's life from his conception and birth to his Resurrection and Ascension. All in all, recent scholarship suggests that medieval Marian devotion was multifaceted. It could be used by some to try to control women or to demonstrate female wickedness by comparison with Mary's perfection, but it was also at times capable of enabling women themselves to transcend the image of all women as merely so many Eves, responsible for the human fall into sin. Women could instead identify with Mary as the Second Eve, whose participation in Jesus's Incarnation and suffering on the cross helped to reverse the fall, ensuring, in the words of the hymn, that she would become "heavené queen."

DONNA SPIVEY ELLINGTON

References and Further Reading

Allen, Prudence, R.S.M. *The Concept of Woman: The Aristotelian Revolution, 750 B.C.–A.D. 1250.* Grand Rapids, Mich.: William B. Eerdmans Publishing Company, 1985.

Bouman, Cornelius A. "The Immaculate Conception in the Liturgy." In *The Dogma of the Immaculate Conception: History and Significance*, edited by Edward D. O'Connor. South, Bend, Ind.: University of Notre Dame Press, 1958, pp. 113–159.

Brady, Ignatius. "The Development of the Doctrine of the Immaculate Conception in the Fourteenth Century after Aureoli." *Franciscan Studies* 15 (1955): 175–202.

Brown, Peter. *The Body and Society: Men, Women, and Sexual Renunciation in Early Christianity*. New York: Columbia University Press, 1988.

Bynum, Caroline Walker. *Holy Feast and Holy Fast: The Religious Significance of Food to Medieval Women*. Berkeley: University of California Press, 1987.

Carol, Juniper B., ed. *Mariology*. 3 vols. Milwaukee: Bruce Publishing Company, 1955–1961.

Coletti, Theresa. "Purity and Danger: The Paradox of Mary's Body and the Engendering of the Infancy Narrative in the English Mystery Cycles." In *Feminist Approaches to the Body in Medieval Literature*, edited by Linda Lomperis and Sarah Stanbury. Philadelphia: University of Philadelphia Press, 1993, pp. 65–95.

Cunneen, Sally. *In Search of Mary: The Woman and the Symbol*. New York: Ballantine Books, 1996.

Ellington, Donna Spivey. *From Sacred Body to Angelic Soul: Understanding Mary in Late Medieval and Early Modern Europe*. Washington, D.C.: Catholic University of America Press, 2001.

Elliott, J. K., ed. and trans. *The Apocryphal New Testament: A Collection of Apocryphal Christian Literature in an English Translation*. Oxford: Clarendon Press, 1993.

Gibson, Gail McMurray. *The Theater of Devotion: East Anglian Drama and Society in the Late Middle Ages*. Chicago: University of Chicago Press, 1989.

Graef, Hilda. *Mary: A History of Doctrine and Devotion*. 2 vols. New York: Sheed and Ward, 1964.

Johnson, Elizabeth A. "Marian Devotion in the Western Church." In *Christian Spirituality: High Middle Ages and Reformation*, edited by Jill Raitt. New York: Crossroad Publishing Company, 1987, pp. 392–414.

Manoir de Juaye, Hubert du, S.J. *Maria: Études sur la Sainte Vierge*. 8 vols. Paris: Beauchesne, 1949–1971.

Matter, E. Ann. *The Voice of My Beloved: The Song of Songs in Western Medieval Christianity*. Philadelphia: University of Pennsylvania Press, 1990.

O'Connor, Edward D., ed. *The Dogma of the Immaculate Conception: History and Significance*. South Bend, Ind.: University of Notre Dame Press, 1958.

Pelikan, Jaroslav. *Mary through the Centuries: Her Place in the History of Culture*. New Haven, Conn.: Yale University Press, 1996.

Sticca, Sandro. *The Planctus Mariae in the Dramatic Tradition of the Middle Ages*, translated by Joseph R. Berrigan. Athens, Ga.: University of Georgia Press, 1988.

Warner, Marina. *Alone of All Her Sex: The Myth and the Cult of the Virgin Mary*. New York: Alfred A. Knopf, 1976.

Wilkins, Eithne. *The Rose-Garden Game: A Tradition of Beads and Flowers*. New York: Herder and Herder, 1969.

Winston-Allen, Anne. *Stories of the Rose: The Making of the Rosary in the Middle Ages*. University Park, Pa.: Pennsylvania State University Press, 1997.

See also **Anne, Saint; Aristotelian Concepts of Women and Gender; Bride of Christ: Imagery; Catherine of Siena; Eve; Gerson, Jean; Hildegard of Bingen; Intercession; Irene; Immaculate Conception, Doctrine of; Joseph, Stepfather of Jesus; Kempe, Margery; Mary, Virgin: in Art; Mary, Virgin: in Literature; Mary, Virgin: in Music; Pilgrims and Pilgrimage; Relics and Reliquaries; Rosary; Song of Songs, Medieval Interpretations of; Theology; Virginity**

MARY, VIRGIN: IN ART

By the late Middle Ages, the most revered holy figure in western Europe was the Virgin Mary, the Mother of God. Her power was conveyed through images large and small, made in many media. Some portrayed her as an intercessor with her son, others as the protector of individuals or cities. For example, Stephen Murray has connected the intense local devotion to the mid-thirteenth century *Vierge Dorée* of the south portal of the Cathedral at Amiens with a contemporary sermon that celebrated the great power of the Queen of Heaven and Bride of Christ. In the same century, following a victory over Florence attributed to her intervention, the Tuscan city of Siena affirmed its special relationship with the Virgin with a series of immense altarpieces depicting the Madonna and Child enthroned that culminated in Duccio's great *Maestà* placed on the altar of the Duomo in 1311, and, as Diana Norman has argued, went on to assert territorial control through other images of the Virgin dispersed into their *contado*.

Such medieval images of the Virgin do not fit the modern, post-Renaissance definition of "art," and are best understood in terms of their context and meaning

Virgin Mary With Child. Austria, Seitenstetten Abbey. Second half thirteenth century CE. M.855, f.110 v. Location: The Pierpont Morgan Library, New York, NY. Credit: The Pierpont Morgan Library / Art Resource, NY.

as well as their production. Individual icons of the Virgin and Child and scenes from the lives of Christ and the Virgin functioned as conduits to the Virgin and to the events depicted. They were also organized into extensive cycles or programs. Executed in mosaic and fresco mural paintings, wooden panels, illuminated manuscripts, precious materials including gold, ivory, and gems, and sculpture in wood and stone, images of the Virgin can be surveyed chronologically, through iconography and style. But scholars also consider the religious, political, and social contexts in which images were made and the ways in which images of the Virgin, including miracle-working icons, conveyed meaning and produced power.

The Royal Virgin

Images of the Virgin appeared well before she was recognized as the Mother of God, the *Theotokos*, by the Council of Ephesus in 431. The Virgin with the Christ Child and the Prophet Isaiah at the Catacomb of Priscilla in Rome, usually dated to the second century, is often identified as the earliest extant image. Like others, it can be traced to pre-Christian sources, such as Isis nursing Horus, long identified as the model for the Virgin *lactans*. Some early images of the Virgin and Child enthroned with attendant saints and angels derived from Roman imperial iconography. Images at Rome from the sixth century on include versions of the *Hodegetria* in which the Virgin holds the child on her left arm and points to him with her right hand and of the Virgin as Advocate, with a supplicant gesture. Many, including the *Hodegetria*, named for the Hodegon Monastery, had prototypes in Constantinople, some of which were said to have been painted by the evangelist Luke. Copies of such venerated and miraculous images were thought to possess the efficacy of the original, and some acquired their own attribution to the evangelist. Another early type, almost exclusively Western, the *Maria Regina*, depicting the Virgin dressed in imperial regalia, was identified with the papacy and city of Rome.

By the early Middle Ages, images of the Virgin had spread north through Europe. The Venerable Bede recorded that in the seventh century Benedict Biscop, Abbot at Monkwearmouth, carried images from Rome to England, among them one of the Virgin and Child. Its form is not clear, but it may have resembled the enthroned *Hodegetria* in the Book of Kells, for which scholars have suggested a Byzantine or Coptic source. By the year 1000 new types had emerged, some functioning as relics or reliquaries. They included the sculpted Throne of Wisdom, in which the child sits frontally on the Virgin's lap embodying Holy Wisdom, who in the incarnation "built himself a throne," as Solomon had. And in the era of the Crusades, images in which the Virgin embraces the Christ Child appeared throughout Europe, based on the Byzantine *Eleousa* and *Kykkotissa*, which recall the Presentation in the Temple and thus stress the incarnation, coming Crucifixion, and the Eucharist. In the Virgin *Misericorde* or *Schutzmantelmadonna*, she shelters worshipers under her mantle. This type may also derive from Crusader circles. Described in twelfth-century Cistercian texts, it appears first in thirteenth-century Cypriote frescoes and Armenian manuscripts, and then in a panel by Duccio. Other new types were a response to interest in the Song of Solomon, including the Virgin as the Bride of Christ, the *Sponsa/Sponsus*, and the Virgin as *Ecclesia*. These representations lie behind the Virgin and Christ enthroned together as in S. Maria in Trastevere in Rome and the Coronation of the Virgin in numerous sculpture programs, including that of Chartres Cathedral. Like the Tree of Jesse found in manuscripts, stained glass, mural painting, and even ceiling painting, these new iconographic formulations first appear in the twelfth century in a period of increasing emphasis on the royal status of the Virgin and her identification with earthly queens, a period when the cult of the Virgin took hold in northern Europe, under the impact of Mediterranean imagery and the writings of St. Bernard of Clairvaux. This emphasis on earthly royalty and the Virgin's increasing role as a civic patron combined with the older incarnation imagery of the Throne of Solomon. The Virgin and Child on a Solomonic throne with lion bases appears throughout Europe, for example, in the thirteenth-century frescoes at Gurk. Comparable to the Roman formulation of the *Maria Regina* and the Constantinopolitan practice of processing with images to invoke the protection of the Virgin in time of war, European rulers and states used images to validate their rule and obtain her support.

Publication of the essential collection of icons at St. Catherine's on Mount Sinai and study of late Byzantine painting have transformed scholarly understanding of the development of images of the Virgin in both the East and the West. Among the most intriguing investigations have been those into the late-medieval European interest in Orthodox icons, literally an icon trade. Maryan Ainsworth has described the persistent power of certain types of images of the Virgin and the expectation of their efficacy in new works by painters such as Jan Van Eyck. In the same way, at the time of the counter-reformation throughout Italy, medieval images, both Byzantine and Italian, from the thirteenth century, were identified as the work of St. Luke, given elaborate new settings, and used to assert the power of the Roman church and of the Virgin in the face of the iconoclastic Protestant attack on the Virgin and on images described by Michael Camille, among many others. In a different way, late medieval and early Renaissance images such as St. Anne, the Virgin and Child, which emphasized the growing belief in the Virgin's immaculate conception, the Holy Kinship, and images focused on the Eucharist, like the Pietà, articulated church doctrine, while reflecting and promoting social values.

Naturalism and the Eucharistic Theme

Such analysis allows us to understand developments in a period generally considered a prelude to the Renaissance and its increasing naturalism. Both traditional and feminist scholarship reveals the liturgical and emotional depth of images of the Virgin. Barbara Lane has argued for a eucharistic interpretation of northern Renaissance images of the Virgin and Child. Fourteenth-century Sienese images with increasingly natural infants carry many of the same references, in part in response to what Hans Belting has called the "living" icons of Byzantium. This enlivening can be seen in Gothic sculpture, likewise increasingly naturalistic by the late twelfth century. As Michael Camille noted, the sculpture seemed to move and come to life in personal encounters between images and worshipers. Such experiences were possible in all media and on all scales. The thirteenth-century Seitenstetten Missal, now in the Pierpont Morgan Library in New York and included in the 2004 exhibition *Byzantium: Faith and Power*, demonstrates the internationalism of such imagery. The Italianate ornamental and facial types reflect the impact of a Paduan atelier on painters in Austria, for the drapery, like the provenance, is central European. Here the Virgin nurses a child who holds his foot, a vision for the kneeling donor. The identification of her milk with the blood of Christ at the Crucifixion and the Eucharist has been stressed in recent scholarship, including that of Caroline Walker Bynum. These references are significant in the Seitenstetten Virgin, which forms a diptych with a facing Crucifixion, so that together they open the Canon of the Mass on the following folios. In addition, the emphasis on the child's foot, which will be pierced by a nail at the Crucifixion, and the juxtaposition of this page with a facing image of the Crucifixion underline that aspect of the Eucharist and the incarnation and remind the worshiper that the infant will be the crucified adult Christ. Hans Belting

has noted that such images of the Virgin and Child function in *prolepsis*, anticipation of the future, and thus connect the early life of Christ to the passion. As icons they join worshipers with those portrayed, the events reflected, and the reality of the Eucharist itself. At the same time, Margaret Miles has suggested, scholars should consider the personal impact that such mothering images had on both male and female worshipers, despite a lack of contemporary documentation for these responses.

Narrative Circles

Along with the images of the Virgin and Child alone or with angels, donors, or saints, medieval worshipers encountered numerous images of the Virgin and Child in the scenes of infancy and passion cycles, including the Annunciation, the Nativity, and the Crucifixion, as well as those from the increasingly elaborate life of the Virgin, such as the embrace of her parents, Joachim and Anna, at the Golden Gate, her Marriage, and her Assumption. Often these scenes, derived from apocryphal texts, as well as the Gospels, are described simply as narratives, stories told in a Bible for the illiterate. But the formulation, selection, and juxtaposition of scenes and the organization of narrative cycles also conveyed carefully constructed theological and political messages. Like the eucharistic content of icons, they would have been recognized in part through a shared familiarity with hymns and liturgy, as well as preaching, but understood through the lens of personal experience and identity. Such cycles are found early in the fifth-century mosaics of S. Maria Maggiore in Rome, and in frescoes from the early medieval sites at Castelseprio and Reichenau, as well as romanesque Lambach and Prufening, among other examples. Elsewhere, infancy and passion cycles appear in stained glass, as at Chartres and Canterbury, and monumental sculpture programs as at Chartres, Paris, Reims, and Amiens.

Women and Images of Mary

Various approaches to investigating images of the Virgin and Child and infancy and passion cycles have expanded knowledge of the field. The relationship between Byzantine art and the art of western Europe provides some understanding of what medieval Europeans saw when they looked at images of the Virgin, and an appreciation of the practices that determined how worshipers saw images, including the experience of pilgrimage described in the work of

David Freedberg and Michele Bacci. While some investigations of the meaning of images have been stylistic, iconographic, and theological, others have focused on political and economic factors. And feminist scholarship has vastly informed our understanding of images of the Virgin. Scholars such as Margaret Miles have addressed the role of images of the Virgin in articulating women's nature in the Middle Ages, especially in her unique contrast to Eve. Indeed, Miles has encouraged scholars to consider the impact of images of the Virgin and other female saints on female worshipers, noting that the Virgin, simultaneously a mother and a virgin, was unmatchable in her perfection. Similarly, Madeline Caviness has argued that even where images of the Virgin were made specifically for women's use, women may not have had control over their content, and indeed some images may have been intended to mold female behavior. The power of the Virgin portrayed and the status of the possessor of an image did not necessarily translate into female agency in the production of images. Feminist perspectives have encouraged other scholars to pursue issues with innovative as well as traditional tools. Using texts and visual analysis, Amy Neff has provided important new insights into the childbirth imagery in the Virgin swooning at the foot of the Cross. In their rich analysis of Giotto's Arena Chapel, Anne Derbes and Mark Sandona have described the contrast between "Barren Metal and the Fruitful Womb," in the intercessory role of the Virgin and a visual explication of the sin of usury.

The Child and the Host

Important and extensive discussions have been carried out over eucharistic interpretations of both narrative and iconic images. To be sure, in some late medieval images, such as those specifically comparing the milk of the Virgin with the blood of Christ cited by Bynum, eucharistic content is easily identified. And references to the Eucharist and the incarnation are clear in Eastern Orthodox images of the Virgin, in part owing to texts defending icons by means of the incarnation, which emerged in the wake of the iconoclastic controversy. Byzantine church programs, like some in the West, often placed the Virgin and Child in the apse over the altar, but at times Byzantine apse frescoes were even more direct, depicting an infant in the paten in place of the host. For the most part, Western art lacks such literal statements of the relationship between images of the Virgin and Child and the incarnation, but scholars such as Ilene Forsyth, Barbara Lane, and Leo Steinberg have argued for it

convincingly. Still, some refinement of these interpretations makes sense. For example, the argument that large-scale altarpieces depicting the Virgin emerged in Europe in the wake of the official identification of the host with the Christ Child in transubstantiation and the elevation of the host in 1215 has been overstated, as many have noted. The argument overlooks other factors that may have driven the gigantism of thirteenth-century painting, including the economic and demographic boom of the period, the increasing scale of buildings in Europe and of painted images, both icon and mural, in the Byzantine world, and the burgeoning cult of the Virgin.

Crucial studies continue to shape the investigation of medieval images of the Virgin and their meaning, above all the work of Caroline Walker Bynum. Although Bynum is not an art historian and has been criticized for her handling of images, her work and the body of literature, both positive and negative, that has emerged in response to it, have provided important insight into the making, meaning, and experience of images of the Virgin. For example, Kathleen Biddick's analysis underlines the importance of addressing the images directly in their larger contexts, rather than using them to accompany scholarly analysis as Bynum does. Above all Biddick stresses the effect of individual and group identities, gender, social station, and religion on the experience and production of images, for example, noting the anti-Semitic messages within some strongly eucharistic images and their intersection with the experience of gender identities of makers and worshipers.

REBECCA W. CORRIE

References and Further Reading

Ainsworth, Maryan W. "*A la facon grece*: The Encounter of Northern Renaissance Artists with Byzantine Icons." In *Byzantium: Faith and Power (1261–1557)*, edited by Helen C. Evans. New York, New Haven, Conn., and London: Metropolitan Museum of Art and Yale University Press, 2004, pp. 544–593.

Bacci, Michele. "The Legacy of the *Hodegetria*: Holy Icons and Legends between East and West." In *Images of the Mother of God: Perceptions of the Theotokos in Byzantium*, edited by Maria Vassilaki. Aldershot: Ashgate Publishing, 2005, pp. 321–336.

Belting, Hans. *Likeness and Presence: A History of the Image before the Era of Art*, translated by Edmund Jephcott. Chicago: University of Chicago Press, 1994.

Biddick, Kathleen. "Genders, Bodies, Borders: Technologies of the Visible." *Speculum* 68.2 (1993): 389–418. (Also in *Studying Medieval Women*, edited by Nancy F. Partner. Cambridge, Mass.: Medieval Academy of America, 1993, pp. 87–116.)

Bynum, Caroline Walker. *Holy Feast and Holy Fast: The Religious Significance of Food to Medieval Women*. Berkeley, Los Angeles, and London: University of California Press, 1987.

Camille, Michael. *The Gothic Idol: Ideology and Image-Making in Medieval Art*. Cambridge: Cambridge University Press, 1989.

Caviness, Madeline H. "Anchoress, Abbess, and Queen: Donors and Patrons or Intercessors and Matrons?" In *The Cultural Patronage of Medieval Women*, edited by June Hall McCash. Athens, Ga. and London: University of Georgia Press, 1996, pp. 105–154.

Derbes, Anne, and Mark Sandona. "Barren Metal and the Fruitful Womb: The Program of Giotto's Arena Chapel in Padua." *Art Bulletin* 80.2 (1998): 274–291.

Forsyth, Ilene. *The Throne of Wisdom: Wood Sculpture of the Madonna in Romanesque France*. Princeton, N.J.: Princeton University Press, 1972.

Freedberg, David. *The Power of Images: Studies in the History and Theory of Response*. Chicago and London: University of Chicago Press, 1989.

Katz, Melissa, ed. *Divine Mirrors: The Virgin Mary in the Visual Arts*. Oxford: Oxford University Press, 2001.

Lane, Barbara G. *The Altar and the Altarpiece: Sacramental Themes in Early Netherlandish Painting*. New York: Harper and Row, 1984.

Lasareff, Victor. "Studies in the Iconography of the Virgin." *Art Bulletin* 20.1 (1938): 26–65.

Miles, Margaret R. "The Virgin's One Bare Breast: Nudity, Gender, and Religious Meaning in Tuscan Early Renaissance Culture." In *The Female Body in Western Culture: Contemporary Perspectives*, edited by Susan R. Suleiman. Cambridge, Mass.: Harvard University Press, 1986, pp. 193–208. (Also in *The Expanding Discourse: Feminism and Art History*, edited by Norma Broude and Mary D. Garrard. New York: HarperCollins, 1992, pp. 26–37.)

Murray, Stephen. *A Gothic Sermon: Making a Contract with the Mother of God, Saint Mary of Amiens*. Berkeley, Los Angeles, and London: University of California Press, 2004.

Neff, Amy. "The Pain of *Compassio*: Mary's Labor at the Foot of the Cross." *Art Bulletin* 80.2 (1998): 254–273.

Norman, Diana. *Siena and the Virgin: Art and Politics in a Late Medieval City State*. New Haven, Conn. and London: Yale University Press, 1999.

Schiller, Gertrud. *Iconography of Christian Art*. 2 vols., translated by Janet Seligman. Greenwich, Conn.: New York Graphic Society Ltd., 1971–1972.

Steinberg, Leo. *The Sexuality of Christ in Renaissance Art and in Modern Oblivion*. Second Edition, Revised and expanded. Chicago and London: University of Chicago Press, 1996.

Vassilaki, Maria, ed. *Mother of God: Representations of the Virgin in Byzantine Art. Benaki Museum 20 October 2000–20 January 2001*. Athens and Milan: Benaki Museum and Skira, 2000.

See also **Anne, Saint; Architecture, Ecclesiastical; Architecture, Monastic; Art, Representations of Women in; Bible, Women in; Body, Visual Representations of; Books of Hours; Breastfeeding and Wet-Nursing; Bride of Christ: Imagery; Cistercian Order; Devotional Art; Eve; Feminist Theories and Methodologies; Gaze; Gender in Art; Hagiography; Holy Kinship; Immaculate Conception, Doctrine of; Intercession; Mary, Virgin; Miracles and Miracle Collections; Patronage, Artistic; Pilgrims and Pilgrimage; Queens and Empresses: The West; Relics and Reliquaries; Virginity**

MARY, VIRGIN: IN LITERATURE

The Blessed Virgin Mary was, from the earliest days of Christianity, the subject of mysterious legends and stories. She was often considered by ordinary believers to be a divine personage (although this view is not held by the Church), and the earliest preserved tales deal with her Assumption into heaven when her earthly life had ended. In the Middle Ages, especially between the eleventh and twelfth centuries, her role in literature was primarily that of intercessor between God and Man—a loving mother whose petitions made to Jesus on behalf of poor sinners were invariably granted. Generally, aid was proffered in the form of miraculous occurrences that often contravened the laws of nature and even Church dogma. Tales of such miracles were extremely popular and widespread, and generically form part of the repertory of saint's lives, although they are most succinctly described as illustrated sermons. What we call Marian literature refers simply to stories about Mary that were written down at some point and have survived to the present day. We can read them today as sermons, plays, poetry, and stories, although their delivery would have been oral in the Middle Ages, since common people—with very few exceptions—could not read or write. They would have heard the stories as *exempla* in sermons, or as public entertainment at pilgrimage sites, or would perhaps have seen liturgical dramas or heard songs about Mary. The impact of this orally delivered literature would have been reinforced by artistic representations of Mary in churches and shrines. Mary was omnipresent, often overshadowing Jesus as a bestower of grace and favor.

Religious and Political Pressures

The stern and even ominous tone of preaching in much of Europe during the late Middle Ages was a particular reason for the literary foregrounding of Mary in these tales. Many dissenting religious sects had arisen, creating an atmosphere of repression and defensiveness within the Church, and inflammatory preaching became a principal weapon against heresy. In preaching of this kind, Jesus tended to emerge more as spokesman for the law than as author of grace. The Virgin Mary as literary figure ideally filled the latter role. The Trinitarian structure of God—Father, Son, and Holy Spirit—made it difficult, if not impossible, for Jesus, who is one with the Father, to be the spokesman for exceptional grace when it was God the Father's law, dogmatically represented by the Church, that had to be constantly defended in such stern preaching. Mary, however, established outside the Trinitarian structure, could make such exceptional pleas on behalf of sinners.

Mary's Many Faces

While Mary, within the tales, was almost always an intercessor, her artistic depiction was as varied as the authors, preachers, and entertainers who undertook the telling of the stories. Two outstanding thirteenth-century Spanish collections of Marian tales were the *Cantigas de Santa Maria* (*Canticles of Holy Mary*), a very large collection of over four hundred tales set to music and illustrated under the auspices of King Alfonso X of Castile, and the *Milagros de Nuestra Señora* (*Miracles of Our Lady*), translated from an older Latin collection of tales by the priest Gonzalo de Berceo. In the *Canticles of Holy Mary*, which can reasonably be assumed to contain most of the miracle tales known to the many compilers, the Virgin appears in a variety of roles. She was most often a tender and solicitous female figure dedicated to facilitating salvation for the desperate. Yet she was occasionally shown as a facilitator of romantic relationships or even as an angry and vengeful deity exacting retribution. Occasionally, in the poems believed to have been written by King Alfonso himself, she appears as national patroness of Christian Spain (revered in that role in much the same way as the Virgin of Guadalupe is in Mexico today.) In Berceo's *Miracles of Our Lady*, translated by a doctrinaire and pious priest, her role is more nearly restricted to that of facilitator of miraculous salvation, especially for fallen churchmen and churchwomen, whose stories constitute a significant part of the collection. Such stories would have been useful in orienting new recruits to the realities of a communal religious life governed by austere practices, and the stories' happy outcomes would have been encouraging to readers.

In France, many medieval writers and preachers made use of Marian miracle tales. Three who stand out are Jacques de Vitry, Gautier de Coinci, and the minstrel Rutebeuf. The most artistically interesting collection to appear was *Les Miracles de Nostre Dame* (*Miracles of Our Lady*), composed by the French monk Gautier de Coinci, whose elegant imagery is at times strongly sensual. A master of the conventions of *amour courtois* (courtly love), Gautier becomes a kind of troubadour, singing of his lady-love. Such writing is made possible by a sense of decorum that is particular to Gautier rather than generally the rule. It would be alien to the sensibilities of both Jacques de Vitry, the great preacher of thirteenth-century France, and the minstrel Rutebeuf. De Vitry's Marian *exempla* in

his sermons invariably present Mary as a model of propriety and orthodoxy, and a popular entertainer such as Rutebeuf would have been in grave personal peril had he presented to a typical audience any but the most pious and commonly accepted attributes of the protagonists of the faith.

There were also theatrical representations of Mary in the commonly performed cycles of medieval mystery plays in England, and recent scholarship indicates that there may even have been an independent cycle of Mary plays early on, some of which were later grafted onto the English liturgical drama. These dramatic representations tended to stress the Virgin's role as miracle worker somewhat less while favoring her role as the Biblical Mary in well-known instances such as the Annunciation, Joseph's doubts, her acceptance of God's will, the flight into Egypt, the Nativity, her heart-wrenching witnessing of the Crucifixion, and her death and Assumption into heaven.

Psychological Analyses

The fact that the Virgin Mary in literature, especially in her role as intercessory miracle worker, appears most predominantly (although certainly not exclusively) in the Latin world has led some twentieth-century critics, basing their work on Freudian paradigms, to explore a possible relationship between this literature and Latin attitudes toward sex and gender relationships, especially the mother–son relationship. Some feminist critics have studied Mary's role in literature and Church preaching in terms of the Church's repressive attitudes toward women, while other critics see a more nearly traditional Mary and point to the fact that it is also possible to view Mary in literature and sermon as a "mother," representative not only of the "female" but also of the "feminine," a human characteristic that can be possessed by men as well as women.

The Broadest View

The Virgin Mary in literature is perhaps most simply (and least contentiously) viewed as a miracle-working saint with a unique connection to the Godhead, whose acts speak of love and grace in a time of anger and fear. If the real Mary's scriptural base is narrow, her attractiveness as a literary figure is both broad and deep, and this has contributed significantly to her enormous popularity within the Christian world.

DAVID A. FLORY

References and Further Reading

Astell, Ann W. "Feminism, Deconstructing Hierarchies, and Marian Coronation." In *Divine Representations: Postmodernism and Spirituality*, edited by Ann W. Astell. New York: Paulist Press, 1994.

Berceo, Gonzalo de. *Miracles of Our Lady*, translated and edited by Richard Terry Mount and Annette Grant Cash. Studies in Romance Languages, No. 41. Lexington: University Press of Kentucky, 1997.

Bynum, Caroline Walker. *Jesus as Mother: Studies in the Spirituality of the High Middle Ages*. Berkeley and Los Angeles: University of California Press, 1982.

Carroll, Michael B. *The Cult of the Virgin Mary*. Princeton, N.J.: Princeton University Press, 1986.

Flory, David A. *Marian Representations in the Miracle Tales of Thirteenth-Century Spain and France*. Washington, D.C.: The Catholic University of America Press, 2000.

Pelikan, Jaroslav. *Mary through the Centuries*. New Haven, Conn.: Yale University Press, 1996.

Scarborough, Connie L. *Women in Thirteenth Century Spain as Portrayed in Alfonso X's* Cantigas de Santa Maria. Lewiston, N.Y.: Edwin Mellen Press, 1993.

Shoemaker, Stephen. *Ancient Traditions of the Virgin Mary's Dormition and Assumption*. Oxford: Oxford University Press, 2003.

Warner, Marina. *Alone of All Her Sex: The Myth and the Cult of the Virgin Mary*. London: Picador, 1990.

See also Exemplum; Hagiography; Hagiography, Iconographic Aspects of; Intercession; Mary, Virgin; Mary, Virgin: in Art; Mary, Virgin: in Music; Miracles and Miracle Collections; Sermons and Preaching

MARY, VIRGIN: IN MUSIC

Mary is represented in medieval secular monophonic song primarily as the Blessed Mother and as mediatrix between God and the troubled faithful. Two important large collections are *Las Cantigas de Santa Maria*, attributed to Alfonso el Sabio, and *Les Miracles de Nostre Dame*, by the trouvère Gautier de Coinci.

The Western medieval liturgy was intended to be sung, mostly in Latin, by clerics, monks, or nuns. Mary's mention in the gospels, especially at Advent, Christmas, and Passiontide, was reflected in the liturgy from the earliest times. Most early surviving texts and musical compositions setting them are anonymous. Hildegard of Bingen, however, has left us antiphons honoring Mary, in comparison to Eve, under her name. The *Magnificat* (Song of Mary) became the concluding canticle of Vespers in the daily monastic offices.

As devotion to Mary increased, especially from the twelfth century onward, multiple feasts in her honor were added to the calendar, each with its mass and office. Votive masses celebrated on Saturdays might be sung. Major late medieval composers have left us extended polyphonic compositions in Mary's honor. One of the best known is Guillaume de Machaut's *Messe de Nostre Dame*, intended for the Cathedral of Reims. Metrical hymns in Mary's honor were composed to be sung at the end of compline in the Divine Office. The most important are *Alma redemptoris mater* (Advent to Purification), *Ave regina caelorum* (Purification to Holy Thursday), *Regina caeli* (Eastertide to Trinity), and *Salve regina*, which remains the most popular (the rest of the Year). Liturgical sequences, extended poetic compositions intended to be sung at festal masses, include *Stabat mater*, which commemorated in sung verses Mary's presence at the foot of the Cross. This tradition is associated with the *planctus Mariae*, the lament sung by the desolate mother in many liturgical plays. (This text also was translated into French.)

In her dual position as mother and mediatrix, Mary was seen as a uniquely accessible figure who could be addressed in special ways. For example, the motet *Virgo dulcis atque pia* asks the Virgin to play upon her trumpet to warn sleeping sinners, as she is "the 'trumpet' of her son."

In England, in particular, the designation or construction of special areas within the nave, called Lady Chapels, encouraged the composition of masses (called Lady Masses), as well as new poems and new music, both in chant and in polyphony. The texts of the newer polyphonic motets were often settings of passages in the Song of Songs, such as "Thou art most beautiful" (*Tota pulchra es*), for the feast of Mary's Conception. By the fifteenth century, the English manner of composing these new Marian motets, using cantilena melodic style and richer harmonies, became the foundation of a new "international" style that was the precursor of the sacred vocal music of the Renaissance. The most important example of this fundamental influence is the last of three settings of *Ave regina caelorum* (Hail, Queen of the Heavens), by Guillaume Dufay. Dufay also used the *cantilena* style to set *Vergene bella*, the first stanza of Petrarch's prayer to the Virgin.

A much simpler devotion was the *Angelus*, the practice of reciting the words of the angel Gabriel's salutation, Hail Mary (*Ave Maria*), when church bells were heard ringing. Medieval carols also commemorated Mary's maternal role, sometimes, as in the Coventry Carol, drawing upon legend to fill gaps left by the gospels in the Nativity story.

Mary had a deep-rooted place in the liturgy, and the music in her honor necessarily proliferated. Every aspect of her cult, from Conception to Assumption, was celebrated in song. Every style is represented in this repertoire, sung by both women and men.

VIVIAN RAMALINGAM

References and Further Reading

Bloxam, M. Jennifer. "Plainsong and Polyphony for the Blessed Virgin: Notes on Two Masses by Jacob Obrecht." *Journal of Musicology* 12.1 (1994): 51–75.

Cumming, Julie E. *The Motet in the Age of Du Fay.* Cambridge: Cambridge University Press, 1999.

Fallows, David. *Dufay.* Revised Edition. London: J. M. Dent & Sons, Ltd., 1987.

Flisfisch, Mar'a Isabel. "The Eve-Mary Dichotomy in the 'Symphonia' of Hildegard of Bingen." In *The Voice of Silence: Women's Literacy in a Men's Church*, edited by Thérèse de Hemptinne and María Eugenia Góngora. Medieval Church Studies, 9. Turnhout: Brepols, 2004, pp. 37–46.

Hoppin, Richard. *Medieval Music.* New York: W. W. Norton, 1978.

Hughes, Andrew. *Medieval Music: The Sixth Liberal Art.* Revised Edition. Toronto: University of Toronto Press, 1980.

Leech-Wilkinson, Daniel. "*Le Voir dit* and *La Messe de Nostre Dame*: Aspects of Genre and Style in Late Works of Machaut." *Plainsong and Mediaeval Music* (formerly *Journal of the Plainsong and Mediaeval Music Society*) 2.1 (1993): 43–73.

O'Gorman, Richard. "The *Stabat mater* in Middle French Verse: An Edition of Paris, Bibliothèque nationale, fr 24865." *Franciscan Studies* 52 (1992): 191–201.

Ramalingam, Vivian S. "The *trumpetum* in Strasbourg *M222 C22*." In *La Musique et le rite, sacré et profane*, edited by Marc Honegger and Paul Prevost. Volume 2: Communications libres. Strasbourg: Association des Publications près les Universités de Strasbourg, 1986, pp. 143–160.

Robertson, Anne Walters. "Remembering the Annunciation in Medieval Polyphony." *Speculum* 70 (1995): 275–304.

Selner, John C. "Our Lady in Music." In *Mariology*, edited by Juniper B. Carol, Volume 3. Milwaukee: Bruce Publishing Company, 1961, pp. 398–411.

Sloyan, Gerard S. "Marian Prayers." In *Mariology*, edited by Juniper B. Carol, O. F. M. Volume III. Milwaukee: Bruce Publishing Company, 1961, pp. 64–87.

See also **Hildegard of Bingen; Immaculate Conception, Doctrine of; Mary, Virgin; Nuns as Musicians; Petrarch**

MASCULINITY
See **Femininity and Masculinity**

MATHILDA AND THE MONASTERY AT ESSEN

Mathilda (c. 949–1011), granddaughter of Emperor Otto I (r. 936–973) and his first wife, Edith of the West Saxons, was the first great abbess of the monastery at Essen. Although documentation of the monastery's founding is murky, most scholars agree that the community was founded somewhere between 850 and 860 by Altfrid, bishop of Hildesheim, on his own property, and was dedicated to Sts. Damian and Cosmas, as well as the Virgin Mary. Its first abbess was Gersuit, probably a relative of Altfrid. By the time Mathilda became abbess (c. 971), Essen had already amassed impressive manuscript holdings and probably had already developed its own scriptorium. Although no female-authored text is known to have come from Essen, manuscript holdings suggest a high level of Latin, as well as vernacular, literacy, with a strong emphasis on artistic, musical, and intellectual pursuits. Sumptuous sacramentaries also suggest a high level of piety, as well as monastic wealth. One noteworthy manuscript is Düsseldorf B.3, a compilation of scripture, exegetical commentary, and hagiography, probably compiled and written at the monastery. Most likely a schoolbook, the manuscript contains on a flyleaf a note from a novice to her superior asking permission to hold vigil with another nun, promising in exchange to be diligent in both studies and devotions through the night.

Mathilda was a powerful, politically engaged abbess, emulating her cousins, Abbess Gerberga II of Gandersheim (ruled 959–1001) and Abbess Mathilda of Quedlinburg (ruled 966–999). Though these communities seem to have been in steep competition for royal attention, charter evidence suggests that Otto III considered Essen a peer of Gandersheim and Quedlinburg. During her reign, Mathilda of Essen made considerable acquisitions of relics, properties, manuscripts, and rich devotional artworks. Among these are some of the community's most precious items: the Essen Madonna; a ceremonial sword; and a highly ornate processional cross. All of these items are the earliest surviving examples of their respective forms; all are made of gold, suggesting great wealth and at least a pretense to great power.

Among her manuscript acquisitions is the chronicle authored by her Anglo-Saxon relative, Æthelweard, most likely the powerful ealdorman who served the English king Æthelred the Unready (fl. 973–998). Probably commissioned by her, the *Chronicle* is essentially a Latin translation of the *Anglo-Saxon Chronicle* (though it cannot be confidently connected to any extant version of the *Anglo-Saxon Chronicle*) and tells the story of their common English ancestors up until the death of King Edgar in 975. The commissioning of the *Chronicle* by Mathilda is consonant with women's interests in history during the Ottonian period: Hrotsvit of Gandersheim wrote two historical epics for Abbess Gerberga; Widukind of Corvey wrote a history of the Saxons for Mathilda of Quedlinburg; in addition, one of her nuns wrote the *Annales Quedlinburgenses* at her request. The chronicle commissioned by Mathilda of Essen stands apart in that it memorializes Mathilda's Anglo-Saxon rather than Saxon line. She may have wanted to pay homage to her illustrious grandmother, Edith; she may also have wanted to set Essen and herself apart from her abbatial rivals.

HELENE SCHECK

References and Further Reading

Bodarwé, Katrinette. "Roman Martyrs and Their Veneration in Ottonian Saxony: The Case of the *Sanctimoniales* of Essen." *Early Medieval Europe* 9.3 (2000): 345–365.

Campbell, A., ed. *The Chronicle of Æthelweard*. London: Thomas Nelson and Sons, Ltd., 1962.

McKitterick, Rosamond. *Books, Scribes and Learning in the Frankish Kingdoms, 6th–9th Centuries*. Aldershot: Variorum, 1994.

Mecham, June. "Essen." Matrix Monasticon. http://monasticmatrix.org/monasticon. Accessed 7 March 2006.

Stofferahn, Steven A. "Changing Views of Carolingian Women's Literary Culture: The Evidence from Essen." *Early Medieval Europe* 8.1 (1999): 69–97.

Van Houts, Elizabeth. "Women and the Writing of History in the Early Middle Ages: The Case of Abbess Matilda of Essen and Æthelweard." *Early Medieval Europe* 1.1 (1992): 53–68.

See also **Abbesses; Hrotsvit of Gandersheim; Literacy and Reading: Latin; Monasticism and Nuns; Patronage, Literary; Translation**

MATILDA OF TUSCANY

Matilda of Tuscany (1046–1115) ruled over a vast territory in northern Italy and played a major role in the Investiture Controversy, supporting Pope Gregory VII and his reform party in their struggle against the German Emperor Henry IV. She was the sole surviving child of Boniface of Canossa and Beatrix, daughter of Frederick II of Lorraine. After Boniface's death in 1052, Beatrix married her cousin Godfrey the Bearded of Lorraine, a close kinsman of several contemporary reform popes. Just before her stepfather's death in 1069, the young Matilda married his son, Godfrey the Hunchback. Matilda left him after only two years in his duchy of Lorraine, refusing all efforts at reconciliation. She returned to her mother in Italy and began to share the duties of the ducal office. As tensions grew between pope and emperor over who had the right to appoint bishops, the ladies of Canossa attempted to mediate. In 1076, the unsolved murder of her estranged husband left Matilda a widow, while her mother's death left her sole ruler of Tuscany. The following year Matilda

hosted the famous reconciliation between Henry IV and Gregory VII at her own stronghold in Canossa.

The peace was short-lived. When mediation failed, Matilda sided unwaveringly with Pope Gregory. In 1081 the emperor marched into Italy and declared Matilda's lands forfeit. For nearly two decades Matilda struggled against imperial forces and occasionally her own rebellious subjects to regain and hold her lands. Her court became a refuge for exiled Gregorian bishops, including Anselm of Lucca, who became Matilda's chief spiritual advisor. After many defeats, a victory in 1084 helped her gradually to win back her towns, although she never regained her full domain. Aside from a brief and mutually unsatisfactory second marriage to Welf, teenage son of the duke of Bavaria, the last decades of Matilda's rule were less turbulent. In 1111 she officially reconciled with the new emperor, Henry V. Matilda died in 1115 at the age of sixty-nine, leaving generations of emperors and popes to fight over the right to her vast fortunes.

Matilda's rule was not an unmitigated success. Her domain was considerably smaller at her death than at her accession. She alienated many of her barons, in part through her support for the *Pataria*, a populist religious reform movement. Although she was in part responsible for the successes of the Gregorian faction, she did not so much defeat her enemies as outlast them. Nevertheless, she retained in a strong if diminished position for nearly forty years. Her influence was widely felt, from the election of popes to the dissemination of Gregorian political propaganda to the movements of the emperor's armies.

Matilda is a particularly remarkable figure in women's history. At a time when most powerful women achieved their status through marriage, Matilda ruled over an inherited domain in her own right and managed to keep it out of the hands of both of her husbands. That she was able to extricate herself relatively painlessly from both marriages, though inviting the enmity of two powerful ducal houses in the process, points to the strength of her position. All evidence suggests that Matilda ruled with the same authority as her male counterparts, holding law courts, settling disputes, and levying armies. She took an active role in her military campaigns, and some contemporary sources claim that she led her own armies into battle.

In spite of her worldly accomplishments, Matilda nourished a life-long yearning for the religious life. The duties of marriage followed by the weighty responsibilities of rulership prevented her from realizing her desire. She accepted that she was needed in the secular world, fighting the "heretics and schismatics." This tension between the active and contemplative life, one longed for, the other undertaken out of duty, characterizes many contemporary portrayals of the countess. She strove to reconcile a life of pious spirituality with a life of leadership and warfare, making her a perfect heroine for a reform movement that was rooted in monastic ideals but condoned bloodshed on behalf of the Church.

Matilda may have embraced this role as champion of the Church and "daughter of St. Peter" (symbol of the papacy) in part for the special legitimacy it conferred upon her, for the extent of her power and influence was largely unprecedented for women of her era. Her sex does not seem to have impeded her exercise of authority, yet she must have felt some uncertainty about her official position, as expressed in her subscription on official documents: "Matilda, by the grace of God, whatever I am."

ROSALIND JAEGER REYNOLDS

References and Further Reading

Donizo of Canossa. *Vita Mathildis celeberrimae principis Italiae carmine scripta a Donizone presbytero qui in arce canusina vixit*, edited by Luigi Simeoni. Bologna: N. Zanichelli, 1940.

Duff, Nora. *Matilda of Tuscany, la gran donna d'Italia*. London: Methuen & Company, 1909.

Ghirardini, Lino Lionello. *Storia critica di Matilde di Canossa: Problemi (e misteri) della piu' grande donna della storia d'Italia*. Modena: Aedes Muratoriana, 1989.

Goez, Elke and Werner Goez, eds. *Die Urkunden und Briefe der Markgräfin Mathilde von Tuszien*. Hannover: Hahnsche Buchhandlung, 1998.

Goez, Werner. "Markgräfin Mathilde von Canossa." In *Lebensbilder aus dem Mittelalter: Die Zeit der Ottonen, Salier und Staufer*, Darmstadt: Primus, 1998, pp. 233–254.

Overmann, Alfred. *Gräfin Mathilde von Tuscien: Ihre Besitzungen. Geschichte ihres Gutes von 1115–1230 und ihre Regesten*. Innsbruck: Verlag der Wagner'schen Universitäts-Buchhanoling, 1895.

Reynolds, Rosalind Jaeger. "Reading Matilda: The Self-Fashioning of a Duchess." *Essays in Medieval Studies* 19 (2002): 1–13.

Studi matildici: atti e memorie del III Convegno di studi matildici, Reggio-Emilia, 7-8-9 ottobre 1977. Modena: Aedes Muratoriana, 1978.

See also **Diplomacy and Reconciliation; Heiresses; Italy; Landholding and Property Rights; Noble Women; Patronage, Ecclesiastical; Virile Women; Warfare**

MATILDA THE EMPRESS

One of two children of King Henry I of England and his queen Matilda of Scotland, Matilda (d. 1167) was born on or about February 7, 1102, and early betrothed to the German emperor Henry V. She was sent to Germany in 1110 to be educated and was married in 1114. Although she had no child, she ably carried out other duties associated with the role of empress. She returned to England when she was widowed in 1125. Since her brother had drowned in the wreck of the White Ship, Matilda was now her father's heir. After requiring the bishops and magnates to swear to support her claims to the throne, Henry betrothed Matilda to Geoffrey, heir to the county of Anjou. This marriage was not harmonious, but Matilda and Geoffrey learned to work together to secure their three sons' inheritance. When Henry I died in 1135, his nephew, Stephen of Blois, seized the throne. Matilda landed in England in 1139 determined to recapture the kingdom. Despite some early success, Matilda was never crowned queen. She was unable to secure the loyalty of the London barons, and Stephen's queen, also named Matilda, led an effective opposition. After 1142 she began to fight on behalf of her son Henry's right to succeed Stephen, a goal that was secured in 1152, when Henry was named Stephen's heir. He succeeded two years later. Matilda assisted her son during the early years of his reign, carrying out duties such as negotiating with the king of France on Henry's behalf. She made numerous gifts to ecclesiastical institutions, particularly favoring the Cluniacs and Cistercians. Her last years were spent at the Norman monastery of Le Bec. Matilda was unable to reign, but she established a precedent for inheritance of the English throne through royal women.

LOIS L. HUNEYCUTT

References and Further Reading

Chibnall, Marjorie. *The Empress Matilda*. Oxford: Basil Blackwell, 1991.

———. "The Charters of the Empress Matilda." In *Law and Government in Medieval England and Normandy*, edited by George Garnett and John Hudson. Cambridge: Cambridge University Press, 1994, pp. 276–296.

———. "The Empress Matilda and Her Sons." In *Medieval Mothering*, edited by John Carmi Parsons and Bonnie Wheeler. New York: Garland Publishing, 1996, pp. 279–294.

Truax, Jean A. "Winning over the Londoners: King Stephen, the Empress Matilda, and the Politics of Personality." *Haskins Society Journal* 8 (1996): 43–61.

See also **England; Queens and Empresses: The West; Succession, Royal and Noble**

MEAD-GIVER

Mead was the drink of prestige in Germanic and Celtic heroic societies and was often poetically linked to the concept of lordship, in that the leader who provided it to his followers was called a "mead-giver." The rich drink was a symbol of community and quasi-contractual joining, since warriors who consumed it were bound to repay the gift with dedicated military service. Hence the cheering flow of mead in the hall may be compared to the bitter flow of blood on the battlefield. On ceremonial occasions, it was the lord's wife or consort who actually distributed the liquor in a single cup that was shared by all. She followed a strict order of precedence, with the lord served first and each man thereafter served according to rank. Medieval literature contains numerous examples of the pattern in whole or part; examples include Wealhtheow in *Beowulf*, Sif in *Lokasenna*, and Étáin in *Tochmarc Étaine*. The woman bearing the cup was thus seen to possess a peculiar connection to the establishment of rank and to the public recognition of honor, an association otherwise furthered by the bridal presentation of a cup of liquor in rituals of marriage (which also creates a bond that joins families). Such cup offerings may also be reflected archaeologically in certain types of vessels and artistic depictions, such as those on Viking Age picture stones from Gotland showing a female figure bearing a cup or drinking horn.

MICHAEL J. ENRIGHT

References and Further Reading

Enright, Michael J. *Lady with a Mead Cup*. Dublin: Four Courts Press, 1996.
Haycock, Marged. *Drink in Medieval Welsh Poetry*. H. M. Chadwick Memorial Lectures 10. Cambridge: Department of Anglo-Saxon, Norse, and Celtic, 2000.
Jarman, A. O. H. *Aneirin: Y Gododdin*. Llandysul: Gomer Press, 1990.
Klaeber, L.C. Frederick, ed. *Beowulf and the Fight at Finnsburg*. Boston: D. C. Heath, 1950.

See also **Alewives and Brewing; Beowulf; Literature, Old English; Literature, Old Norse**

MECHTHILD OF HACKEBORN

Mechthild of Hackeborn (c. 1240–1298/1299) (not to be confounded with the Beguine Mechthild of Magdeburg) was the younger sister of the abbess of Helfta, Gertrude of Hackeborn. She was born at the castle of Helfta, near Eisleben, Saxony, into a Thuringian noble family, and died in the Cistercian monastery of Helfta.

Mechthild entered the monastery in 1247/1248 and was educated to function as the chantress of the house, a teacher for the young girls, and a spiritual guide for the younger nuns. In 1261 she received a five-year-old girl as her pupil who would become the author and theologian Gertrude the Great.

From about 1290 Mechthild dictated her work, *Liber specialis gratiae* (*Book of Special Grace*) to two

unnamed nuns from the Helfta community, one of whom was probably Gertrude the Great. It consists of seven parts: the feasts of the liturgical year, revelations on the Christological mysteries, and revelations on Mary and the saints (I); special gifts of grace (II); instructions on praise of God (III); consolation and instructions for the community (IV); visions of diseased persons (V); life and death of abbess Gertrude of Hackeborn (VI); and Mechthild's final days, her death, and her merits (VII).

Trinitarian in emphasis, the nerve system of Mechthild's work is a love theology centred on the loving hearts of God and Jesus, reflecting an optimism about salvation due to Christ's passion. It is formulated as a conversation with God in gender-crossing language. The *Liber* was widely reproduced until the sixteenth century, in Flemish, English, Swedish, German, and Italian.

ELSE MARIE WIBERG PEDERSEN

References and Further Reading

Bynum, Caroline Walker. "Women Mystics in the Thirteenth Century: The Case of the Nuns of Helfta." In *Jesus as Mother: Studies in the Spirituality of the High Middle Ages*. Berkeley: University of California Press, 1987, pp. 170–262.
Finnegan, Mary Jeremy. *The Women of Helfta: Scholars and Mystics*. Athens, Ga. and London: University of Georgia Press, 1991.
Haligan, Theresa A. *The Booke of Gostlye Grace of Mechthild of Hackeborn*. Toronto: PIMS, 1979.
Liber Specialis gratiae. In *Revelationes Gertrudianae ac Mechthildianae*. Vol. 2: *S. Mechthildis virginis s. Benedicti Liber specialis gratiae*, edited by the Benedictine Fathers of Solesmes. Paris: H. Oudin, 1877.
Mechthild of Hackeborn. *Livre de la Grace Spéciale. Revelations De Sainte Mechthilde*, translated by the Benedictine Fathers of Solesmes and edited by the H. Oudin Brothers. Paris: H. Oudin, 1878.
Spitzlei, Sabine. *Erfahrungsraum Herz. Zur Mystik des Zisterzienserklosters Helfta im 13. Jahrhundert*. In *Mystik in Geschichte und Gegenwart*. Texte und Untersuchungen 9. Stuttgart-Bad Cannstatt: Friedrich Frommann Verlag, 1991.

See also **Devotional Literature; Gertrude of Hackeborn; Gertrude the Great; Mechthild of Magdeburg**

MECHTHILD OF MAGDEBURG

Like many medieval women writers, Mechthild's life is known from references or allusions to herself or to historical events in her writings. Scholars have grown suspicious of these particulars over the years, but most of them still accept the following account. Mechthild's birth is set between 1207 and 1210 and her death in 1282. In her book, *Das fließende Licht der*

Gottheit (*The Flowing Light of the Godhead*), she tells us that she experienced her first divine "greeting"—her term for her consciousness of the presence of God—when she was twelve years old. When she was in her twenties, she left home and went to a nearby city (Magdeburg), where she took up the life of a Beguine (a woman devoted to a religious life, but who did not take the vows of a religious order) and where she claims to have known only one person. In 1250, at the urging of her confessor (perhaps the sole friend), she began to write down her revelations of God, and she continued writing until her death. She spent her final years (c. 1270–1282) in the convent of Helfta, where she lived among younger gifted mystics (Gertrude the Great and Mechthild of Hackeborn). In Helfta, she wrote the last section of her book with the help of her sisters, because of her failing eyesight.

The Flowing Light is noteworthy for being the first set of mystical revelations to be composed in German, and it is now recognized by literary scholars as an extraordinary piece of literature. Divided into seven "books," each of which contains between twenty-five and fifty chapters of varying length, *The Flowing Light* offers the reader a compendium of richly poetic dialogues between the soul and God and other allegorical figures, narratives of visions, poems of divine praise, instructions for good religious men and women, vivid visions of heaven and hell, and biting critiques of religious corruption. Readers will note the influence of the biblical Psalms (the first and sometimes only book of the Bible that medieval individuals read), the Song of Songs (translated and commented upon in German already in the twelfth century), and German courtly poetry of the day (*Minnesang*). Yet Mechthild's writing is compelling and original precisely in its blend of these influences to form a new style of poetic German prose. That is, her prose is made rich with internal rhymes (the German term is *Kolonreim*) that give the text a strikingly lyrical and aesthetically enchanting quality. Describing divine love, Mechthild writes (rhymed words emphasized): *Min licham ist an langer **qwale**, min sele ist an hoher **wunne**, wan si hat beschovet unde mit armen umbevangen iren lieben **alzemale** (I, 5: 1–2; My body is in eternal torment, my soul is in lofty rapture, for she has seen and embraced her lover in her arms all at once). We might expect poetry to appear in descriptions of the soul and God as lovers, but even when expressing doubt about her undertaking, Mechthild cannot help but rhyme: *Nu muos ich doch dise rede betwungen **schriben**, die ich gerne woelte **verswigen**, wan ich voerhte vil sere den heimlich swank der italen **ere*** (V, 32: 2–3; Now I feel compelled to write this speech, which I would otherwise gladly keep to myself, for I very much fear the stealthy blow of vain honor). Mechthild's achievement in this style is unmatched in other devotional writing.

Also striking in the text is the strong voice of its author, which grows more confident and authoritative as the book progresses. Indeed, Mechthild's authorship is considered to be one of the book's central themes. Yet the relationship between the historical woman and her book as it has survived raises questions about her authorship. *The Flowing Light* survives in two translations: one into Middle High German and one into Latin. The presumed Middle Low German original has been lost (High and Low refer to southern and northern Germany, respectively). Of the translations, the Latin translates only the first six books and has been reordered and edited. In addition, the surviving manuscripts of both translations have been edited and recopied by numerous hands since Mechthild's original composition. To what extent, some ask, can we attribute *The Flowing Light* to the Beguine of Magdeburg alone? Some scholars have also argued that much of what Mechthild writes about herself is attributable more to the genre of devotional and hagiographical literature to which her book belongs than to a historical reality. Regardless of one's position on these issues, however, the book is worthy of careful reading, for its literary and theological achievements are beyond question.

SARA S. POOR

References and Further Reading

Andersen, Elizabeth A. *The Voices of Mechthild of Magdeburg*. New York: Peter Lang, 2000.

Mechthild von Magdeburg. *Das fließende Licht der Gottheit: Nach der Einsiedler Handschrift in kritischem Vergleich mit der gesamten Überlieferung*, edited by Hans Neumann, prepared for print by Gisela Vollmann-Profe. 2 Vols. München: Artemis, 1990 and 1993.

———. *The Flowing Light of the Godhead*, translated by Frank Tobin. New York: Paulist Press, 1998.

Peters, Ursula. *Religiöse Erfahrung als literarisches Faktum: Zur Vorgeschichte und Genese frauenmystischer Texte des 13. und 14. Jahrhunderts*. Religious Experience as Literary Fact: On the Pre-History and Genesis of Women's Mystical Texts in the Thirteenth and Fourteenth Centuries. Tübingen: Niemeyer, 1988.

Poor, Sara S. *Mechthild of Magdeburg and Her Book: Gender and the Making of Textual Authority*. Philadelphia: University of Pennsylvania Press, 2004.

Tobin, Frank. *Mechthild von Magdeburg: A Medieval Mystic in Modern Eyes*. Columbia, S.C.: Camden House, 1995.

See also **Beguines; Courtly Love; Devotional Literature; Dominican Order; Gertrude of Hackeborn; Gertrude the Great; Literature, German; Mechthild of Hackeborn; Minnesang; Mysticism and Mystics; Mystics' Writings; Women Authors: German Texts**

MEDICINE

Medieval medical thought and practice were as varied as medieval politics, religion, literature, or art. No single brief essay can summarize how people throughout the Christian, Muslim, and Jewish worlds wrestled with concerns about sickness, debility, and pain, nor how ideas about the female body were elaborated in various times and places. A few words may be helpful, however, to explain how medicine in medieval societies was gendered, permeated with ideas about the relative value of men and women and their proper roles within society.

At a certain level, the medical traditions of medieval Christians, Muslims, and Jews did not differ greatly because all derived, to a large extent, from the common background of Greco-Roman medicine. Thus, in terms of their theories of the qualities (hot, cold, wet, dry) and the humors (blood, phlegm, yellow bile, and black bile), and in their beliefs about therapeutic interventions (principally based on the need to restore the "balance" of the bodily complexion), there was a common core of belief. All three societies developed learned traditions of medicine that, to the extent that they were book-based, tended to be gendered masculine. Women were nearly universally excluded from these learned traditions, but we nevertheless find them populating other kinds of medical practice throughout all three cultures, from helping their friends and neighbors in childbirth to serving as nursing sisters in hospitals or working as surgeons alongside their husbands.

Medicine was no doubt gendered in other ways we can only guess at now. Were certain kinds of medical practices (say, reliance on healing shrines or use of charms) used more by women than by men? Were women more apt to resign themselves to physical pain than men, giving themselves up to Christ-like suffering rather than seeking out a physical cure? How did ideas of demonic possession in women relate to formal medical ideas of mental disease? Were women really the chief providers of medical care within the household or were these duties assumed by men? Did women develop their own traditions of empirical medical knowledge that they passed on to each other but rarely revealed to men? How do women's historically documented medical practices relate to depictions in literature or art?

These are all large and important questions, and most have not yet been explored in any systematic way. The few comprehensive studies that have been done suggest that there are no easy generalizations. Research on the audiences of gynecological literature, for example, have shown that women had no monopoly over the field most intimately concerned with their own bodies. Studies of women's medical reading show that, despite dramatically rising literacy rates among women in the later Middle Ages, medical reading among the laity continued generally to be gendered male. Studies of childbirth rituals show some contestation between women and men for the power to establish meaning over the event. All these studies show the importance of asking these questions and of continuing to explore this most vital aspect of medieval life.

MONICA H. GREEN

References and Further Reading

Green, Monica H., ed. "Masses in Remembrance of 'Seynt Susanne': A Fifteenth-Century Spiritual Regimen." *Notes & Queries* 50.4 (2003): 380–384.
———. "Bodies, Gender, Health, Disease: Recent Work on Medieval Women's Medicine." *Studies in Medieval and Renaissance History* 3rd series, 1 (2005): 1–46.
———. "History of Science." *Encyclopedia of Women and Islamic Cultures. Volume I: Methodologies, Paradigms and Sources*, edited by Suad Joseph. Leiden: Brill, 2003, pp. 358–361.
———. *Women's Healthcare in the Medieval West: Texts and Contexts*. Aldershot: Ashgate, 2000.
Park, Katharine. "Medicine and Society in Medieval Europe, 500–1500." In *Medicine in Society: Historical Essays*, edited by Andrew Wear. Cambridge and New York: Cambridge University Press, 1992, pp. 59–90.

See also **Abortion; Caesarean Section; Contraception; Cosmetics; Demography; Doctors and Healers; Gynecology; Hildegard of Bingen; Hospitals; Infertility; Lepers; Lovesickness; Madness; Magic and Charms; Menstruation; Midwives; Plague; Secrets of Women; Sexuality; Spirits: Discernment of and Possession by; Trota of Salerno**

MEDITATION

The distinctive traditional practice of religious meditation in the West has its sources in Greco-Roman philosophy, ancient rhetorical education, and the sectarian communal customs of ancient Judaism, entailing procedures, postures, and practices that were adapted together from the start within Christianity. Few writers of the Middle Ages differentiated meditation from contemplation, viewing them as stages in a seamlessly joined activity of prayerful reading. It is proper to speak of Christian meditation as an orthopraxis, a set of experiences and techniques conceived together as offering a "way" to be followed by a devotee, leading each seeker to relive the path of enlightenment. Christian meditation began with texts, but their explication was not its main goal (as it was, for example, in university lectures). Rather, meditation seeks a whole experience, relying on patterns of oral formulae and ritualized behavior to prepare for an experience of God.

Meditation is the art of thinking, understood in this context as making thoughts about God. Instead of emptying one's mind, in meditation a Christian was to concentrate "mindfully" upon matters derived from Scripture, sermons and other meditations, the exemplary lives of saints, and (as appropriate) sacred art and chant. Christian meditation was the most creative and most focused of the various activities involved in reading. The essence of meditational reading is captured by the twelfth-century canon Hugh (d. 1141), of the Parisian convent of St. Victor, who wrote that meditation

> is free of reading's rules, and delights to range along open ground, where it fixes its free gaze upon the contemplation of truth, drawing together now these [matters], now those.... This especially it is which takes the soul away from the noise of earthly business…in meditation is to be found the greatest delight. (*Didascalicon* III. 10)

In ancient rhetorical training, *meditation* (Latin *meditatio*) was the word used for the initial creative stage in the process of composing a work. Though speeches in the forum or law courts were to be delivered *ex tempore* rather than wholly written out and delivered verbatim by rote, no one should approach the task of speaking without careful prior preparation. One began by meditating upon what one was going to say, consulting the (ideally) well-stocked inventory of one's learning for quotes and examples, organizing the topics and materials of one's speech in a convincing and persuasive way, and rehearsing especially one's opening remarks. This task was, according to the first-century Roman educator Quintilian, best performed at night in silence, ruminating in a quiet murmur, and reclining upon a couch in one's private chamber.

Ancient philosophers cultivated a habit of meditation, as the Stoics, Epicureans, and others counseled a disciplined way of life wholly or in part away from the bustle of ordinary affairs as a means toward enlightenment and inner peace. This discipline included reading and meditation as well as learned conversation. The *Meditations* of the second-century emperor Marcus Aurelius is perhaps the work still most widely read that was produced by these ancient worldly philosophers. In ancient Judaism as well, sects such as the Essenes withdrew from the world into communities dedicated to a practice of physical and mental discipline, centered about meditation upon sacred texts. Many scholars believe that such sects and their practices deeply influenced the world of Jesus and the earliest Christians.

The ancient practice of meditation was modeled upon the chewing and digestion of food, as thoughtful reading was understood to nourish the mind and soul as food does the body. This traditional analogy, which has Biblical sanction, continued in common use throughout the Middle Ages. From the earliest times, both men and women practiced regular meditation. Thus, Melania the Younger (383–439), the scion of a distinguished Christian Roman family, took up a discipline of daily meditation as a young girl. Her grandmother, also called Melania (342–409), was a woman of considerable learning as well, confident enough to have irritated Jerome by siding against him in his quarrel with Rufinus over the validity of the hermeneutical methods of Origen. The younger Melania, according to her biographer, ate an ascetic diet comprised mainly of bread without oil, slept two hours a night, and nourished herself with the spiritual food of writing and reading. She had a settled program of reading the canonical books of Scripture and collections of homilies, and of writing out in little notebooks what she had read. Once she had finished the quantities she had set for herself, and was replete, she would then read the *Lives of the Desert Fathers*, "as though for dessert." Such chewing of texts was made physically literal by the murmur with which contemplatives recited the divine words. Though meditative reading was said to be done "in silence," accounts of the practice liken it to hearing a swarm of bees.

Meditation could rely also on both music and images, as these arts were closely allied to the sacred words. Certain chants, especially allelluias and others with complex melismas, could provide further occasions for community meditation during divine service. Meditative composition could also be helped by using images, including techniques of mental imaging. Meditation upon the Crucifixion, for example, focused in exacting sensory detail upon its image, either an actual artifact or a mentally reconstructed picture. In either case, the image served to organize the mental and emotional composition of the experience. Images also could serve as organizers of subjects to be covered in a sermon or colloquy. These mental structures can be simple—a tree, or a rose, or a ladder—or highly complex, including whole buildings constructed in imagination, such as the Biblical Ark or the ancient Temple compound.

MARY CARRUTHERS

References and Further Reading

Carruthers, Mary. *The Craft of Thought: Meditation, Rhetoric, and the Making of Images, 400–1200.* Cambridge: Cambridge University Press, 1998.

Clark, Elizabeth A., trans. *The Life of St. Melania the Younger.* Studies in Women and Religion 14. New York: Edwin Mellen Press, 1984.

Dictionnaire de Spiritualité ascétique et mystique, s. v. "Contemplation" and "Meditation." Paris: Beauchesne, 1937–1980.

Hadot, Pierre. *Philosophy as a Way of Life*, edited by A. I. Davidson and translated by M. Chase. Oxford: Blackwell, 1995.

Hausherr, Irenée. *The Name of Jesus*, translated by C. Cummings. Kalamazoo, Mich.: Cistercian Publications, 1978.

Hugh of St. Victor. *Didascalicon*, translated by Jerome Taylor. New York: Columbia University Press, 1961.

Jaye, Barbara, and M. Briscoe. *Artes predicandi, artes orandi.* Typologie des sources du moyen âge occidental, 61. Turnhout: Brepols, 1992.

Leclercq, Jean. *The Love of Learning and the Desire for God*, translated by Catherine Misrahi. New York: Fordham University Press, 1961.

Swartz, Michael D. *Scholastic Magic: Ritual and Revelation in Early Jewish Mysticism.* Princeton, N.J.: Princeton University Press, 1996.

See also **Devotional Art; Devotional Practices; Lay Piety; Rosary; Spiritual Care**

MÉLUSINE

At the very end of the fourteenth century, two versions of the legend of *Mélusine* were produced in France, the first, in prose, by Jean d'Arras (1392–1393), the second, in verse, and rather less interesting, by Coudrette (c. 1402). The story is intriguing: the beautiful Mélusine is the daughter of a king of Scotland and his fairy wife; because of a sin against her father (he himself has transgressed against their mother, and she and her sisters imprison him underground for life), she is condemned to turn into a serpent every Saturday. Count Raimondin, lord of Forez in Poitou, meets her sitting beside a fountain and falls passionately in love with her. She agrees to marry him, on condition that he will make no attempt to see her on Saturdays. Under her benign guidance, Forez prospers. Mélusine clears forests and sows fields, builds cities and castles, including notably the castle of Lusignan, and she gives birth to ten sons, many of whom are marked by strange signs, the result of their mixed heritage. Finally, however, one Saturday, Raimondin is overcome by curiosity and spies on his wife as she bathes; he is astounded to see that the lower part of her body takes the form of a snake. She realises his transgression when he calls her a *serpent*; she vanishes in the shape of a winged dragon, and will return periodically in that form— from that day to this—to keep watch over her sons, who meet various fates: some kings, of Cyprus and Luxemburg, some vicious tyrants. She also watches over her later descendants.

The burden of the story, as we now have it, has political ramifications: both writers were working under commission from the Lusignan family, whose name (Lusignan/Mélusine) they exalt. The Mélusine they celebrate is thus wonderfully fecund and a source of prosperity and family pride. She is the worthy ancestress of the noble Lusignans, one of whom, Guy, was to become king of Jerusalem (1186–1192)—and it is noticeable that both writers insist repeatedly on authenticity by using historical names and locations. Were both writers working from the same original? Was Coudrette adapting Jean? The question is unanswerable—but it is indisputable that the legend they both transmit did not originate in either of their imaginations. There are preexisting, far earlier, traces of the legend of a fairy bride whose body is not to be looked at, whose husband transgresses, and who immediately vanishes, and this tale-type has a rich folklore tradition in Brittany especially. The Lusignan family, in other words, in a manoeuvre not uncommon in the late Middle Ages, were mobilising an exotic tale to add glamour to their name and origins.

But the popularity the tale enjoyed, and enjoys, transcends local ambition: there is a very respectable tally of manuscripts and early editions, medieval and Renaissance translations into Spanish (*Historia de la linda Melosina*), English, German (by Thüring von Ringoltingen), and even Russian, and it has continued to fascinate musicians, artists, and novelists either directly or, as with A. S. Byatt's *Possession*, as a metaphor. That fascination centres on a number of aspects. First is Mélusine's hybridity, which allows her to engage medieval notions of demonology and genetics: her sons share their mother's ambiguities, epitomes of chivalry but also, except in two cases, disturbingly ambivalent (wall-eyed, big-nosed, birthmarked, three-eyed…). Mélusine, like them, is enigmatic, monstrous but also maternal, Christian but also dark and pagan. Secondly, however, we must recognise precisely the fascination of the astonishingly fecund and maternal Mélusine—a Mélusine who gives birth only to male children. Thirdly, we should note the way in which, in her human character, and until Raimondin's transgression, she makes Lusignan, and Poitou, outstandingly prosperous and fertile. In a famous article, in which they use her to explore late-medieval mentalities, Le Goff and Le Roy Ladurie call her *défricheuse*, the clearer of forests. Mélusine, met (as so often with fairies) beside a fountain, is the fairy godmother whose role is political–foundational, who bestows riches and honours on the human family to which she allies herself—but, like so many supernatural beings attempting to naturalise themselves into the human world, she cannot sustain the tensions her ambivalence causes. Finally, of course, there is the fascination precisely of Mélusine's hybridity: there is something stealthily erotic about the voyeuristic Raimondin peering through a little hole in the door at his wife's naked body, shading, grotesquely, into the snake's tail: the phallic overtones here have, predictably, inspired psychosexual analyses. Mélusine the hybrid is, appropriately, a being of multiple significances.

JANE TAYLOR

References and Further Reading

d'Arras, Jean. *Mélusine*, edited by Louis Stouff. Dijon: Publications de l'Université de Dijon, 1932.
————. *Le Roman de Mélusine, on L'histoire des Lusignan*, translated by Michèle Perret. Paris: Editions Sotck, 1979. Modern French translation.
Clier-Colombani F. *La Fée Mélusine au Moyen Age: Images, Myths, Symbols*. Paris: Le Léopard d'Or, 1991.
Coudrette. *Mélusine*, edited by Eleanor Roach. Paris: Klincksieck, 1982.
————. *Le Roman de Mélusine*, translated by Laurence Harf-Lancer. Paris: Flammarion, 1993. Modern French translation.
Harf-Lancner, Laurence. *Les fées au Moyen Age; Morgane et Mélusine: La Naissance des fées*. Paris: Champion, 1984.
Le Goff, Jacques, and Emmanuel Le Roy Ladurie. "Mélusine maternelle et défricheuse." *Annales: Economies, Sociétés, Civilisations* 26 (1971): 587–622.
Maddox, Donald, and Sara Sturm-Maddox, eds. *Melusine of Lusignan: Founding Fiction in Late Medieval France*. Athens, Ga. and London: The University of Georgia Press, 1996.

See also **Genealogy; Literature, Old French; Supernatural Women**

MENSTRUATION

Menstruation—what caused it, when it should begin, when it should end, whether it was beneficial or harmful—was a not-infrequent topic of debate in the Middle Ages. It was also *not* discussed in many contexts, leaving the historian to guess what significance this silence conveyed. Very little work has been done on attitudes or practices related to menstruation in medieval Muslim traditions, though recent work on Jewish, Byzantine, and Latin Christian traditions allows us to gain some understanding of both the positive and negative aspects of this physiological function.

In medieval Europe, attitudes toward menstruation largely depended on the social or intellectual context. The most explicit discussions of menstruation are found among medical writers. Here, menstruation is almost always treated neutrally, as a regular purgative process expected to happen more or less monthly between the ages of fourteen and about forty or fifty. The ages of both menarche and menopause (neither term was actually used in the Middle Ages) were usually repeated from one textual source to another; we cannot therefore put much reliance on them as accurate reflections of demographic realities. Nevertheless, a few authors offer unique observations. For example, John Mirfeld, a cleric writing in London in the late fourteenth century, observed that "in ancient times the menses did not begin to flow until the fifteenth or fourteenth year, or certainly not before age twelve. But now they begin in certain girls in the eleventh or in the tenth year. And at that point they are capable of conception."

Medical writers generally saw normal menstruation (regular in its frequency, duration, amount, and color) as the *sine qua non* of female health. Precisely because it was a purgation, not of the uterus alone but of the whole body, it needed to occur as regularly as any other bodily purgation. If it did not, the buildup of excess waste products could cause all manner of disease, from skin conditions to breast cancer, heart palpitations, uterine suffocation, and ultimately death. Excess menstruation was likewise a source of concern. It is little wonder, then, that menstrual difficulties are usually listed first among gynecological diseases in medical textbooks.

The association between the onset of menstruation and the beginning of fertility was expressed in the belief that no woman who was not menstruating regularly was capable of reproduction. The so-called *Trotula*, a popular compendium of works on women's medicine, articulated a widespread belief about menstruation: "The common people call the menses 'the flowers,' because just as trees do not bring forth fruit without flowers, so women without their flowers are cheated of the ability to conceive" (*Trotula*, p. 66). Emmenagogues (substances to provoke menstruation and thereby cleanse the womb) were frequently recommended as aids to fertility.

In nonmedical contexts, attitudes toward menstruation could be quite negative. The first-century Roman naturalist Pliny, reporting lore from his own society, created the standard litany of the menses' ill effects (they can kill crops, rust iron, drive dogs who eat them rabid, etc.), but he also itemized a variety of medical uses for them. The negative (more than the positive) views were later echoed by such late antique and early medieval writers as Solinus (third century) and the encyclopedist Isidore of Seville (d. 636). The most influential articulation of the Plinian tradition was *The Secrets of Women*, a later-thirteenth-century treatise falsely attributed to Albertus Magnus that elaborated on the vile nature of menstruation to a truly misogynous degree.

Religious attitudes were influenced by the verses in *Leviticus* 15, that litany of polluted states, regarding woman's "issue of blood" (verses 19–33). Among Jews, the tradition of avoidance of sexual intercourse during menstruation and the ritual cleansing in the *mikvah* afterwards were observed throughout the Middle Ages. In the Byzantine East, menstruating women were forbidden from coming in contact with any sacred spaces or objects. In the Latin West, however, Pope Gregory the Great challenged the practice of barring menstruating women (or women who had recently given birth) from church. By the twelfth century, this view was formally adopted with the argument that the Levitican prohibitions were part of the "old law" that Christ's coming had overthrown. Intercourse during menstruation was, nevertheless, still prohibited, and the view that menstruation was a sign of Eve's curse prompted debates as to whether the Virgin Mary herself (who was otherwise thought by many to be free of all taint of original sin) shared this female trait.

Beginning around 1300, there was debate as to whether Jewish men menstruated, in their case as punishment for their alleged role in the crucifixion of Christ. This belief (which persisted well into the early modern period) showed, as much as the earlier Plinian tradition, that whatever the neutral or even positive connotations women's "flowers" might have in medical contexts, the negative associations of menstruation were powerful enough to even disparage men.

MONICA H. GREEN

References and Further Reading

Biller, Peter. "A 'Scientific' View of Jews from Paris Around 1300." *Micrologus* 9 (2001): 137–168.

Green, Monica H., ed. and trans. *The Trotula: An English Translation of the Medieval Compendium of Women's Medicine*. Philadelphia: University of Pennsylvania Press, 2001.

Green, Monica H. "Flowers, Poisons, and Men: Menstruation in Medieval Western Europe." In *Menstruation: A Cultural History*, edited by Andrew Shail and Gillian Howie. New York: Palgrave, 2005, pp. 51–64.

Johnson, Willis. "The Myth of Jewish Male Menses." *Journal of Medieval History* 24 (1998): 273–295.

Marienberg, Evyatar. "Le bain des Melunaises: les juifs médiévaux et l'eau froide des bains rituels." *Médiévales: Langue, textes, histoire* 43 (2002): 91–101.

McCracken, Peggy. *The Curse of Eve, the Wound of the Hero: Blood, Gender, and Medieval Literature*. Philadelphia: University of Pennsylvania Press, 2003.

Miramon, Charles de. "Déconstruction et reconstruction du tabou de la femme menstruée (XII-XIIIe siècle)." In *Kontinuitäten und Zäsuren in der Europäischen Rechtsgeschichte: Europäisches Forum Junger Rechtshistorikerinnen und Rechshistoriker, München 22–24 Juli 1998*. New York: Peter Lang, 1999, pp. 79–107.

Mirfeld, John. *Breviarium Bartholomei*. London: British Library, Harley MS 3, s. xiv ex.

Viscuso, Patrick. "Menstruation: A Problem in Late Byzantine Canon Law." *Byzantine Studies/Études Byzantines* 4 (1999): 116–125.

Wood, Charles T. "The Doctors' Dilemma: Sin, Salvation, and the Menstrual Cycle in Medieval Thought." *Speculum* 56.4 (1981): 701–727.

See also **Abortion; Contraception; Gynecology; Mikveh; Secrets of Women**

MERCHANT FAMILIES, WOMEN OF

Women in Italian merchant families lived lives similar to other Italian women, lives emphasizing household management and motherhood rather than a profession. However, although less likely to trade in their own right than their counterparts in some areas of northern Europe, they nonetheless felt part of the merchant world and contributed to merchant activities. The surviving correspondence of Margherita Datini (1357–1423) and Alessandra Strozzi (1407–1473) provides insight into their family, business, and social and political concerns, and, by extension, into the concerns of women for whom less evidence exists.

Margherita Bandini Datini and her husband, the wealthy self-made "merchant of Prato," Francesco Datini, preferred to be apart rather than together, and often moved separately between Florence and Prato, corresponding regularly via his business network. In Francesco's absence, Margherita was his agent, managing a large household, including young apprentices and frequent guests, and overseeing related agricultural, business, building, and political activities, with the dividing line between the domestic and the nondomestic blurred. In business, Francesco had made his fortune incrementally, dealing for profit at every opportunity, both in international and local trade. His local trade had similarities to that of more humble merchants, and Margherita, always economical, was a willing participant in earning money by sewing saleable objects, preparing wine and food for sale, collecting small debts, and finding wet nurses for a fee. Of an elite, although needy, family, she was also able to fill well the role of hostess, furthering Francesco's social ambitions. Her inability to have children, and Francesco's two illegitimate ones, contributed to her defensive unhappiness, as well as to her desire to be useful. In her letters reporting to Francesco (mostly dictated to scribes), she was always ready to respond to criticism with a sharp tongue, and her successful efforts to learn to write autograph letters in her mid-thirties can be seen as part of her desire to be recognized as intelligent and competent.

The Florentine patrician Alessandra Macigni Strozzi was a self-confident widow whose identity and authority were based on her role as mother. Although Italian women were at a disadvantage in inheritance compared to men, their dowries were protected from seizure for debt, and as a widow, Alessandra was able to support five children from her dowry after her husband Matteo's exile by the Medici and early death. Her husband's relatives hired her sons in their merchant banking companies in Bruges, Spain, and Naples, but Alessandra acted as intermediary between these relatives and her sons, sent the sons money so that they could become partners, and invested as a passive investor herself in international companies that gave little room for direct female action. She wrote autograph letters in the merchant style, letters that show her to have been a woman of strong will but considerable tact, possessing exceptional judgment about family and finances, and a cynical but insightful view of the Florentine scene. She kept careful accounts, priding herself on thrift, and she never doubted that a merchant career was an admirable one for her sons to follow. Before her sons left home, she worked with them to improve their letter-writing skills, and once they had gone, she advised them to earn, not spend money, but to do it honestly, remembering eternal life. When her son Lorenzo misbehaved, she successfully used his love and obligation, as well as religious arguments, as levers to persuade him to improve his ways. Once the Strozzi brothers had become rich merchants in Naples, she used her many contacts in Florence to aid their business by finding them employees and to aid them politically by helping to negotiate the end of their exile and return to Florence. She also found them Florentine wives, providing herself with a happy old age.

Margherita Datini and Alessandra Strozzi had different relationships to the merchant world, in part because of differences in the merchant activity of the men in their families, because of Alessandra's motherhood and Margherita's lack of children, partly because one was a wife and the other a widow, and not least because of different personalities. Nonetheless, the letters of both Margherita Datini and Alessandra Strozzi show the way women identified with and participated in merchant business and in the social and political world of merchant families, and, between them, the two women provide a picture of the attitudes and activities of women in merchant families.

ANN CRABB

References and Further Reading

Crabb, Ann. *The Strozzi of Florence: Widowhood and Family Solidarity in the Renaissance*. Ann Arbor, Mich.: University of Michigan Press, 2000.
Origo, Iris. *Merchant of Prato*. New York: Alfred A. Knopf, 1957. Reprint, Boston: David R. Godine, 1986.

See also **Datini, Margherita; Household Management; Investment and Credit; Italy; Mothers as Teachers; Strozzi, Alessandra**

MERCHET AND LEYRWITE

Merchet was the payment made by female serfs for permission to marry in England. It was due to the lord on the occasion of their marriages, and it could be given by the women themselves, their relatives, or their husbands. *Merchet* is usually considered to have been a particularly important servile obligation in a legal context as marking unequivocal proof of unfree status. Since the 1970s, it has drawn renewed attention from historians, whose work has added substantially to our understanding of this phenomenon.

One way in which this has occurred is in categorizing of *merchet* payers. It used to be thought that fathers did most of the paying. However, it is now clear that on certain estates at certain times husbands often paid, or, as on Spalding Priory estates after the 1450s, invariably paid. More interestingly, single females frequently paid their own merchets, more often at Spalding in some decades of the later thirteenth century and early fourteenth century than did even husbands or fathers, indicating (as is also the case on Ramsey Abbey estates) independence and individuality on their part. This view is compounded by the fact that some single women also used the marriage fine to, in effect, escape the jurisdiction of their lords through marrying free men or outside their fiefs, for which, surprisingly, they were often not charged a higher price by their lords. *Merchet*, however, was never a major item in the latter's budgets, though there are clear signs that some lords increased merchet charges for their rich serfs after the Black Death of 1348 and until the 1380s to offset the adverse economic situation they were facing.

On occasion, merchet could equate to a property tax, as in the case of female heiresses, and lords could expect to receive large marriage fines, equivalent in some instances to hundreds of thousands of our dollars or pounds from wealthy serfs, to whom lords paid particular attention. However, *merchet* practice and price, usually from a few pence to a few shillings, could vary widely, and on certain estates it was more usually charged not as a property tax but as a tax on serfs as serfs, i.e., as an obligation of their unfree position and as unequivocal proof of their status.

It is quite clear that indeterminate numbers of serfs, in places perhaps a majority, evaded their responsibility to pay *merchet*. In the case of poorer serfs, lords would not have been too worried by evasion, nor would they have bothered to pursue matters. Importantly, the fact that there was substantial evasion also means that numbers of *merchets* extant at different periods of time cannot be used to calculate population movements except in the most limited ways.

Merchet was not confined to single women. Widows also had to pay, or much more usually, prospective husbands paid for them. Obviously, widows generally commanded higher marriage fines than single females, though not invariably so, as on Spalding Priory estates in the 1310s.

By the fifteenth century, *merchet*, along with other servile obligations like *leyrwite*, was in decline. The massive fall in population in this era meant a greatly reduced number of *merchets* and a huge decline in *merchet* income. With the much improved conditions for peasants, aided by enforced concessions by landlords, *merchet*, like serfdom itself, withered away.

Leyrwite was the fine levied on unfree peasants for sexual activity banned by the Church. It appears to have been a peculiarly English institution, with little or no evidence of it elsewhere in Britain or on the continent, and it was not charged uniformly throughout England. Practice could also vary from lord to lord and estate to estate. Prior contract to marry would obviate the fine in certain places but not in others. It was very much a fine imposed on women, and not only confined to those women who had had bastards. Very few men were ever presented for *leyrwite*. The records that survive form only a tiny percentage of the illicit fornication that must have taken place and which was the major concern of church courts. *Leyrwite* was not levied primarily for financial motives, though comparatively low sums of six pence, a common level of fine, would have been burdensome on poorer women. It was against these, especially if they had bastards, that *leyrwite* was mainly directed as a form of social control, particularly in times of economic hardship. Having paid *leyrwite*, however, did not preclude women from later marrying.

E. D. JONES

References and Further Reading

Bennett, Judith M. "Medieval Peasant Marriage. An Examination of Marriage Licence Fees in the *Liber Gersumarum*." In *Pathways to Medieval Peasants,* edited by J. A. Raftis. Toronto: Pims, 1982, pp. 193–246.

———. "Writing Fornication: Medieval Leyrwite and Its Historians." *Transactions of the Royal Historical Society*, Sixth Series, 13 (2003): 131–162.

Jones, E. D. "Medieval Merchets as Demographic Data: Some Evidence from the Spalding Priory Estates, Lincolnshire." *Continuity and Change* 11(1996): 459–470.

———. "The Spalding Priory Merchet Evidence from the 1250s to the 1470s." *Journal of Medieval History* 24 (1998): 155–175.

Poos, L. R., and R. M. Smith. "Legal Windows onto Historical Populations? Recent Research on Demography and the Manor Court in Medieval England." In *The World We Have Gained,*" edited by Lloyd Bonfield, Richard M. Smith, and Keith Wrightson. Oxford: Blackwell, 1986, pp. 52–56.

See also **England; Marriage, Christian; Peasants; Sexuality: Extramarital Sex**

MERMAIDS AND SIRENS

In Greek mythology sirens were sea nymphs whose sweet music lured seafarers to their deaths. In the *Odyssey* (12.39–54, 158–164, 181–200), Odysseus protected his men by stopping their ears with wax, while he lashed himself to the mast of his ship to prevent going to them himself. In the story of Jason and the Argonauts, Orpheus distracted his companions with a song.

In classical antiquity, a siren was conceived as being half woman and half bird. In the Middle Ages she was conflated with the mermaid: woman above the waist but fish below. She was interpreted allegorically as first enticing the soul to sleep and then killing it. Sometimes she exemplified heresy, vanity, or worldly pleasure, such as music. She was also connected with sex and prostitution, associations encouraged by the mention of sirens in the Vulgate Bible (Isaiah 13:22). Portrayed in a twin-tailed posture that exaggerated her labia, she resembled a sheela na gig (English and Irish figures of nude women, with their vulvas prominently displayed).

Closely related to the siren were other seductresses, especially supernatural lovers. The most famous was Mélusine, a mermaid wife, as she appeared in the late-fourteenth-century version of the tale. The best-known medieval siren is probably the one in *Purgatorio* 19.7–33: in a dream Dante first sees a horribly deformed woman and then transforms her in his own eyes into a lovely woman who sings in a beautiful voice. This alluring apparition identifies herself as the siren and tells of having led Ulysses (the Latin form of Odysseus) astray; thereupon another woman appears and directs Virgil to act, which he does by ripping the siren's dress to reveal a belly that reeks of anything but the odor of sanctity.

JAN M. ZIOLKOWSKI

References and Further Reading

Berman, Ruth. "Mermaids" and "Sirens." In *Mythical and Fabulous Creatures: A Source Book and Research Guide*, edited by Malcolm South. New York: Greenwood Press, 1987, pp. 133–145 and 147–153.

Leclercq-Marx, Jacqueline. *La sirène dans la pensée et dans l'art de l'Antiquité et du Moyen Âge: du mythe païen au symbole chrétien*. Publication de la Classe des beaux-arts. Collection in-4, 3rd series, vol. 2. Bruxelles: Académie Royale de Belgique, 1997.

Rachewiltz, Siegfried de. *De sirenibus: An Inquiry into Sirens from Homer to Shakespeare*. New York and London: Garland Publishing, 1987.

See also **Bible, Women in; Mélusine; Sheela Na Gigs; Supernatural Women**

MIDWIVES

As with many occupational categories in the Middle Ages, the line between domestic work and the full-fledged occupation of midwifery is difficult to draw. Just as no society could survive without cooks even though professional cooks are few, so in medieval Europe we find nearly universal assistance in childbirth even if there were not always professional midwives.

In antiquity, midwives (called, in Greek, *maiai*, and, in Latin, *obstetrices*, or, more generically, *medicae*) were the normative caretakers of both the gynecological and obstetrical needs of Greek and Roman women. Medical writers from at least the third century BCE to the sixth century CE composed texts specifically for midwives' use, and there is ample evidence (such as inscriptions and artwork) that midwifery was professionalized in larger urban communities. Ancient writings on gynecology and obstetrics conceived of the ideal midwife as not simply literate and competent in medical theory but also responsible for all disorders of the reproductive organs as well as routine assistance in childbirth. In the scope of her practice, at least, she was fully the equivalent of modern obstetrician/gynecologists and not simply a birth attendant.

With the decline of ancient urban communities, the literate midwife of antiquity disappeared. Between the sixth and the thirteenth centuries, neighbors and kinswomen generally seem to have assisted each other in their births, none necessarily claiming any more expertise than the others. This explains why it is so difficult even to find mention of the word *midwife*. Anglo-Saxon seems never to have produced a stable term for "midwife," which is actually a Middle English term not documented prior to c. 1300. The same is true for all the other medieval vernacular languages save German, which can trace forms of the term *Hebamme* back to the eighth century. Ecclesiastical law had itself differentiated between midwives and "matrons" in late antiquity, preferring that determinations of virginity, rape, and pregnancy be made by groups of upstanding women of the community rather than midwives, whose individual eyes and hands were subject to error. This distinction between "matrons" (who had no particular medical expertise) and midwives seems to have continued into the later Middle Ages; for example, the women who examined Joan of Arc to assess her claims of virginity were laywomen rather than medical specialists. It was probably only with the gradual legal regulation of midwifery that midwives took over these tasks.

The transition of midwifery from a neighborly, shared task to a formal occupation was slow. Northern Europe was the earliest to establish formal licensing. In France, the church initiated licensing due to its concern that birth attendants know how to perform a valid emergency baptism if the newborn seemed likely to die. (This same concern would also lead to the practice of caesarean section, which in the Middle Ages was performed only on dead women in order to baptize the fetus.) In Germany and the Low Countries, concern for poor women led certain municipalities to appoint town midwives. By the early fifteenth century, midwives were being licensed, their oaths demanding that they treat rich and poor alike and uphold proper morals.

It remains unclear what the actual medical knowledge of midwives was or how they passed that knowledge on to others. Aside from a thirteenth-century Hebrew circumcisor's manual that describes some practices of Jewish midwives, there is very little extant testimony about the manual procedures or medicinal substances employed by midwives. Even Trota of Salerno, a twelfth-century medical writer, has little to say about attendance at normal births. An extraordinary eyewitness account of a birth made by a Spanish notary in the fifteenth century reflects a rather unusual situation because of the presence of several men. We have no evidence that medieval midwives undertook formal apprenticeships nor (unlike antiquity) that any instructional manuals were written for them. (The texts on women's medicine that are actually addressed to female audiences address women generically, not midwives.)

By the time midwives did reemerge as a specialized profession in the late Middle Ages, male practitioners had taken over the primary responsibility for diagnosing and treating gynecological conditions (including menstrual difficulties and, of particular concern, infertility). When visual inspection of or manual applications to the genitalia were needed, a female assistant was called in. By the end of the Middle Ages, male surgeons were commonly relied on for assistance in difficult births and for treating conditions of the external genitalia and vagina. Thus, when the first texts addressed specifically to midwives were composed in the mid-fifteenth century and early sixteenth century, they limited the scope of midwives' practice to supervision of pregnancy and childbirth; more difficult conditions were referred to the male physician or surgeon. Still, because of midwives' increased identity as professionals, midwifery remained an important and (usually) well-respected occupation for women throughout the early modern period. Despite the rather hysterical accusations against "witch-midwives" by the authors of the witch-hunters' manual, the *Hammer of Witches* (*Malleus maleficarum*, 1496), formally licensed midwives were hardly ever accused of witchcraft.

MONICA H. GREEN

References and Further Reading

Cabré, Montserrat, trans. "Public Record of the Labour of Isabel de la Cavalleria. January 10, 1490, Zaragoza." *The Online Reference Book for Medieval Studies*. http://www.the-orb.net/birthrecord.html (accessed 3/7/06).

Flemming, Rebecca. *Medicine and the Making of Roman Women: Gender, Nature, and Authority from Celsus to Galen*. Oxford: Oxford University Press, 2001.

Flugge, Sibylla. *Hebammen und heilkundige Frauen: Recht und Rechtswirklichkeit im 15. und 16. Jahrhundert*, 2nd ed. Frankfurt am Main: Stroenfeld, 2000.

Green, Monica H. "Bodies, Gender, Health, Disease: Recent Work on Medieval Women's Medicine." *Studies in Medieval and Renaissance History* Series 3, vol. 2 (2005): 1–46.

Harley, David. "Historians as Demonologists: The Myth of the Midwife-witch." *Social History of Medicine* 3, 1 (1990): 1–26.

Taglia, Kathryn. "Delivering a Christian Identity: Midwives in Northern French Synodal Legislation, c. 1200–1500." In *Religion and Medicine in the Middle Ages*, edited by Peter Biller and Joseph Ziegler. York Studies in Medieval Theology, 3. York: York Medieval Press, 2001, pp. 77–90.

See also **Caesarean Section; Doctors and Healers; Gynecology; Pregnancy and Childbirth: Christian Women; Pregnancy and Childbirth: Jewish Women; Trota of Salerno**

MIGRATION AND MOBILITY

Travellers, migrants, pilgrims, itinerants, and vagabonds: medieval women took to the road under these various titles with their husbands, fathers, brothers, or, more rarely, alone. They participated in all the great migratory movements—the Germanic migrations (fourth and fifth centuries), the crusades (eleventh to thirteenth centuries), colonisations near and far such as the *Drang Nach Osten* (twelfth

century), and the urban renewal begun in the eleventh century—even if their presence was not always noted, or their migratory experience rarely taken into account. This absence of women from the migratory landscape reflects both a gendered vision of the migratory phenomenon and a system of norms and values that we associate with medieval societies. These values would have it that men moved freely and, therefore, broadened their horizons, while honest women remained at home; only women of questionable virtue ever cast aside the security of family and hearth to migrate alone. It follows that there is little interest in analyzing the path of female migrants. They would only have constituted a small minority of marginals and other rootless women often assimilated as prostitutes and delinquents.

This conceptualization is also embedded in the perspectives that have, for a long time, guided the analysis of migrations, whether medieval or modern. Historiography has, for many years, presented migrants as marginal, uprooted souls, or as solitary figures who were incapable of forming familial or social relationships within their new societies. For many historians this is the product of the often significant distance separating migrants from their places of origin. These conclusions, while not always incorrect, are the result of the sources studied, such as judicial records, which often portray foreigners more as criminals than as honest citizens. Likewise, the testaments widely used throughout the south of Europe, in particular Italy and Provence, do not, as a result of juridical constraints, always reflect migrants' ties of solidarity.

An approach that is more nuanced to the feminine migratory experience has revealed that social exclusion was not an inevitable consequence of geographic mobility. In late medieval England, for example, research has shown that young women were placed as domestics in neighbouring towns or villages. Their salaries, albeit humble, allowed them to accumulate funds necessary for marriage either in their working *milieu* or in their places of origin.

This type of research paves the way for a comprehensive analysis of migratory phenomena, one that reassesses women's places and roles. It implies a positive approach to migration wherein exclusion is replaced by the inclusion of migrants in their new societies thanks to their participation in professional and familial networks. This perspective was adopted for the study of migratory movements toward the town of Manosque in Provence between 1300 and 1480. A diverse documentation, including the notarized acts so common in the lands of Roman law, taxation records, and the minutes from municipal council meetings, yielded nearly 2000 male and female migrants. They came to establish themselves in the town in irregular waves influenced by local constraints—economic factors as well as depopulation linked to epidemic—but also by regional dynamics—a relative overpopulation of the mountains, increases in taxation, and the search for arable land. Women participated in this bustle of individuals; one in four immigrants was female. This relatively important feminine portion is explained by the clearly familial nature of migrations toward the town; migrations by isolated migrants, those bereft of any links of solidarity, remain rare.

Over time these families followed increasingly longer routes before taking root in Manosque. Prior to the late fourteenth century, they came mostly from locales within the immediate pull of the town. Outsiders, accustomed to frequenting the town's market, or even to marrying their daughters in Manosque, would later definitely establish themselves there. One notable exception is the Tuscan and Piedmontese merchants who arrived in Manosque when the papacy resided in Avignon. Later in the period, the sphere of recruitment spread out to include the mountains of the Savoy and Dauphiné regions, while at the same time intensifying the flow from Piedmont.

The destiny of many female migrants can be read in their marriage contracts. Women who married Manosquin men, or men long established there, made a place for themselves, even as they participated in strategies aimed at integrating their natal families into the community.

The conclusions drawn from the Manosquin case cannot be generalized at this time due to a lack of other research. They do show, however, the value of a more nuanced approach for the study of migratory phenomena in order to take into account the differentiated experiences of those who participated in them.

ANDRÉE COURTEMANCHE

References and Further Reading

Courtemanche, Andrée. "Women, Family, and Immigration in Fifteenth-Century Manosque: The Case of the Dody Family of Barcelonnette." In *Urban and Rural Communities in Medieval France, Provence & Languedoc, 1000–1500*, edited by Kathryn Reyerson and John Drendel. Boston: Brill, 1998, pp. 101–127.

———. "Le peule des migrants. Analyse préliminaire des migrations vers Manosque à la fin du moyen âge". In *Le petit peuple dans l'Occident médiéval, Terminologies, perceptions, réalités*, edited by Pierre Boglioni, Robert Delort, and Claude Gauvard. Paris: Publications de la Sorbonne, 2002, pp. 281–292.

Edgington, Susan B., and Sarah Lambert, eds. *Gendering the Crusades*. New York: Columbia University Press, 2002.

Goldberg, P. J. P. "Marriage, Migration, and Servanthood: The York Cause Paper Evidence." In *Woman Is a Worthy Wight: Women in English Society c. 1200–1500*, edited by P. J. P. Goldberg. London: A. Sutton, 1982, pp. 1–15.

Hoerder, Dirk. *Cultures in Contact: World Migrations in the Second Millennium*. Durham, N.C.: Duke University Press, 2002, pp. 1–91.

Seymour, Phillips, J. R. "The Medieval Background." In *Europeans on the Move: Studies on European Migrations, 1500–1800*, edited by Nicholas P. Canny. Oxford: Clarendon Press, 1994, pp. 9–25.

See also **Crime and Criminals; Crusades and Crusading Literature; Domesticity; Pilgrims and Pilgrimage; Prostitutes**

MIKVEH

A *mikveh* (pl. *mikva'ot*) is an artificial water basin used by Jews for purification, by total immersion, of both objects and persons.

The Jewish laws regarding purity and impurity found in classic rabbinic literature are particularly complex. Nevertheless, in medieval Europe, the nearly exclusive type of bodily impurity dealt with by Jews was the one attributed to women, in relation to their menstrual cycle. The practical implication of this impurity being almost exclusively a prohibition of sexual relations, it generally affected only married women and those about to marry.

According to Jewish law, which followed and developed rules originally in the Pentateuch (especially Lev. 15, 18:19, and 20:18), a woman is considered impure from the monthly onset of her menstrual bleeding (or even some hours earlier), until she immerses herself in a ritual bath. The immersion cannot be done before the completion of seven days following the cessation of bleeding, considered, legally speaking, to last at least four or five days. In other words, for most women, the bath will generally take place around the twelfth day of their cycle. Until that moment, the woman is considered to be *niddah*, sometimes translated as "rejected" or "secluded," another biblical and rabbinic term of high practical (and, some would say, spiritual) significance. Therefore, she and her partner are forbidden from engaging in sexual relations. She must also refrain from various minor domestic activities considered by the rabbis to be possible sources of intimacy, such as serving him a cup of something to drink or making his bed. According to some European traditions, mostly from the twelfth through the seventeenth centuries, she should avoid entering synagogues as well.

For various reasons, the ritual immersion must be generally performed in total nudity and at night. Although it can take place within a natural setting, such as a pond or lake, a solution of this kind might be problematic, particularly in cold weather. The advantages of providing women with an artificial, closed, and sometimes heated bath are obvious. The community could also use such a bath to purify certain utensils produced by non-Jews; the bath could also serve as a place for the necessary ritual immersion of converts to Judaism.

Medieval Europe witnessed the construction of a significant number of *mikva'ot*, only a few of which have survived. Some of the most famous existing examples are those found in cities along the Rhine river, such as Cologne, Speyer, and Worms. Not surprisingly, they are generally built in the architectural style of their time. Although most modern *mikva'ot* are heated, it seems that there was no structural water heating system in many of the medieval ones.

Despite their various architectural styles, the basic structure of ritual baths is meticulously determined by Jewish law. The water volume should consist of several hundred liters (the exact amount is under debate). Moreover, for a *mikveh* to be valid, at least some of its water must be "nondrawn." For this reason, the *Mikva'ot* are typically located underground, in a place in which water can be gathered naturally, without the need to pump it artificially using pipes or other devices. Oftentimes, the *mikva'ot* are built under or near synagogues.

EVYATAR MARIENBERG

References and Further Reading

Baskin, Judith R. "Women and Ritual Immersion in Medieval Ashkenaz: The Sexual Politics of Peity." In *Judaism in Practice: From the Middle Ages through the Early Modern Periods,* edited by Lawrence Fine. Princeton, N.J.: Princeton University Press, 2001, pp. 131–142.
Wasserfall, Rahel R., ed. *Women and Water: Menstruation in Jewish Life and Law*. Hanover: Brandeis University Press, 1999.

See also **Jewish Women; Law, Jewish; Menstruation**

MINNESANG

The German lands produced love poetry or *Minnesang* (*Minne* means love) that examines the joys and sorrows of a loving relationship between a man and a woman of elevated social standing, conventionally called a knight and a lady. The earlier known examples of *Minnesang*, dating to the 1160s and originating in the southeastern parts of German-speaking lands (corresponding roughly to present-day Austria and Bavaria), derived from indigenous models that have not survived. Many of these early poems are anonymous, but even when a name survives, typically nothing else is known about the life of the poet. Early German *Minnesang* is of particular interest because

it presents a high percentage of strophes in a woman's voice. These strophes sometimes occur in a form called the *Wechsel* ("alternation"), in which a knight and a lady express their views on love in alternating strophes (but in thematic isolation, not in debate or conversational form). There are also poems entirely in a woman's voice known as *Frauenlieder* (woman's song). The female speakers tend toward nostalgia for a love enjoyed in the past; their main emotions are grief at being left behind or abandoned by a lover who is now far away, and sorrow over the hostile interferences of spies or rivals. There is a trace of social reality in these poems, since women from the ruling ranks could not travel as men could, and their conduct was certainly subject to scrutiny in court settings, where privacy was hard to obtain. Der von Kürenberg, the first German minnesinger known by name (c. 1160s), left an oeuvre of fifteen song strophes, of which eight are in a woman's voice. It is possible that men and women performed these songs together, but, in the absence of historical evidence about performance modes, it seems more likely that male artists performed both gender roles.

The next wave of *Minnesang*, beginning in the 1170s, introduces the notion of courtly love, partly under the influence of models from Provence and northern France. The channels of influence are complex and not fully understood. The great poets, or minnesingers, of what has come to be considered the classical period of *Minnesang* include Reinmar der Alte, Hartmann von Aue, Heinrich von Morungen, and, above all, Walther von der Vogelweide. The gender relations of this courtly love poetry (known in this context as *hohe Minne*, or lofty love) differ sharply from the earlier German poems. The adored lady is now usually beyond the poet's reach and untouched by his desire for her. She is endlessly discussed but rarely present as an agent or character. The lady is assumed to embody the virtues and capabilities toward which the poet–lover strives, that is, she is already what he hopes to become. Feminist critics have noted an element of latent misogyny behind this construction, since no living woman could possibly measure up to the poetic ideal; in the German *Minnesang* tradition, however, misogyny is rarely, if ever, overtly expressed. Lofty love has a distinctive ethical and often even didactic dimension, since the poet–lover tries to improve himself through striving for the love of his lady. (This aspect strengthens in the late medieval genre of the *Minnerede*, or discourse on love, in which noble ladies operate as mentor figures.) The lady's marital status is generally unknown or unmarked, so adultery is not an issue as it is, for example, in Andreas Capellanus' *De amore*. Male betterment in this context is not individual but social, since the capabilities of the lover—devotion, discretion, the ability to keep information confidential, diplomacy, moderation, perseverance, and, above all, skill with words—are also the skills of the successful courtier. As a social phenomenon, *Minnesang* hovers between a code of conduct for the court and a sophisticated game in which the artistic idealization of elite women advanced the goals of elite men. Critique is not lacking within the ranks of the minnesingers, however. Walther von der Vogelweide, for one, created a number of poems that critique the notion of lofty love, in part by placing it in debate with its opposing concept, *niedere Minne* or "low love," in which sexual desire is fulfilled.

The end of the classical period of *Minnesang* in the 1220s and 1230s is heralded by the work of the poet Neidhart. His large oeuvre makes fun of the ideals of *Minnesang* by dramatizing the effect *Minne* has on a hapless poet–singer and on the peasant lads and lasses whom he entertains. In Neidhart's so-called "Winter Poems," the poet–singer attempts to woo village girls, only to start brawls and be chased off by village boys; in his "Summer Songs," the poet–singer's seductive charms are celebrated by the seduced maidens themselves (woman's song). Neidhart's oeuvre enjoyed enduring popularity well into the fifteenth century and was much imitated. New love poems using the conventions of *Minnesang* were composed throughout the thirteenth century. There is less scholarship on this later poetry, which has long been regarded as being largely a recycling of conventional motifs and themes, repetitive at best and hackneyed at worst. In it the distinction between "lofty" and "low" love largely disappears.

Lofty love (*hohe Minne*) was also the topic of narrative literature. One of the most innovative examples is *Service of Ladies* (*Frauendienst*), composed around 1255 by Ulrich von Lichtenstein (in the Styrian region of Austria). It is considered the first secular autobiography in German. Ulrich stylizes the story of his life as that of a knight in the love service of high-ranking ladies. Song texts inserted into the verse narrative show Ulrich was a composer as well as a champion jouster. His service takes unusual forms, for example, self-mutilation (he cuts off a finger), as well as surgery to improve a deformity of his lip or mouth. For a substantial part of the narrative, Ulrich jousts disguised as Lady Venus and wearing a braided wig and women's garments. Although modern readers are puzzled, Ulrich's obsessive service and his cross-dressing impress his lady and his male jousting partners, that is, they center him in the text's system of values. The text presents a remarkable double standard with respect to marriage. Ulrich's lady sounds conventional when she complains about spies and

remains faithful to her husband. Ulrich's wife, however, has nothing to say—and no speaking role in the text—when he takes breaks from his love service to enjoy the comforts of home.

Composing *Minnesang* appears to have been a common leisure pastime among the nobility, although, in contrast to the Occitan tradition, no female poets are known. *Minnesang* poems survive that were written by noblemen from the highest ranks of society. Other named minnesingers are known to have belonged to the ranks of the "serving" or "unfree" nobility, and still others appear to have been professional singers. Elite audiences continued to cultivate *Minnesang* into the fourteenth century and beyond, since the great, illuminated manuscripts, such as the Codex Manesse (compiled in Zurich), containing enormous amounts of material, were compiled in the first decades of the 1300s. Fifteenth-century compilation manuscripts of *Minnesang* survive as well.

ANN MARIE RASMUSSEN

References and Further Reading

Chinca, Mark. "Women and Hunting-Birds are Easy to Tame: Aristocratic Masculinity and the Early German Love-Lyric." In *Masculinity in Medieval Europe*, edited by D. M. Hadley. London: Addison Wesley Longman, 1999, pp. 199–213.

Dobozy, Maria. *Re-Membering the Present: The Medieval German Poet–Minstrel in Cultural Context*. Turnhout: Brepols, 2005.

Perfetti, Lisa. "'With them she had her playful game': The Performance of Gender and Genre in Ulrich von Lichtenstein's Frauendienst." In *Women and Laughter in Medieval Comic Literature*. Ann Arbor, Mich.: University of Michigan, 2003, pp. 126–167.

Rasmussen, Ann Marie. "Woman as Audience and Audience as Woman in the Medieval German Courtly Lyric." *Exemplaria* 6.2 (1994): 367–384.

———. "'I Inherited It from You': The Mother-Daughter Poems of the Niedhart Tradition." In *Mothers and Daughters in Medieval German Literature*. Syracuse, N.Y.: Syracuse University Press, 1997, pp. 163–188.

———. "Translations of Select Summer Songs." In *Mothers and Daughters in Medieval German Literature*. Syracuse, N.Y.: Syracuse University Press, 1997, pp. 227–234.

———. "Reason and the Female Voice in Walther von der Vogelweide's Poetry." In *Medieval Woman's Song: Cross-Cultural Approaches*, edited by Anne L. Klinck and Ann Marie Rasmussen. Philadelphia: University of Pennsylvania Press, 2002, pp. 168–186.

———. "Masculinity and the *Minnerede* in Berlin mgo 186." In *Verfügbare Minne. Konventionalität und Trivialisierung in spätmittelalterlichen Minnereden*, edited by Ludger Lieb and Otto Neudeck. Berlin: de Gruyter Verlag, 2006.

Sayce, Olive. *The Medieval German Lyric, 1150–1300: The Development of Its Themes and Forms in Their European Context*. Oxford: Clarendon Press, 1982.

Ulrich von Leichtenstein. *Frauendienst, or, Service of Ladies*, translated in condensed form with an introduction by J. W. Thomas. University of North Carolina

Studies in the Germanic Languages and Literatures, 63. Chapel Hill, N.C.: University of North Carolina at Chapel Hill Press, 1969.

See also **Courtly Love; Literature, German; Misogyny; Performance in Lyric; Trobairitz and Troubadours; Woman's Song**

MIRACLES AND MIRACLE COLLECTIONS

John Locke has defined a miracle as an event that, "being above the comprehension of the spectator, and in his opinion contrary to the established course of nature, is taken by him to be divine." This definition is normative, accepted by Christian, Muslim, and Jew alike. These religious traditions are based on the premise of supernatural intervention in the world through acts contrary to the laws of nature, and thus recognize the frequent occurrence of miracles as a means of demonstrating God's power and concern for humanity. Building on Jewish tradition, early Christian theologians such as Origen and Justin Martyr, followed by Augustine and later by Thomas Aquinas and others, emphasized the performance of miracles through God's intermediaries (such as angels and saints) as a means of bringing nonbelievers to the faith and demonstrating its divinely ordained truth.

Scripture itself, beginning with the deeds of Moses and Elijah, has served as the major resource for the paradigmatic miracles of Christianity. Jesus performed at least forty miracles exclusive of the Incarnation and Resurrection, including the exorcism of demons; the cure of the lame, lepers, diseased, and blind; the transformation of water into wine; and the multiplication of the bread and fishes, among others. The Apostles were likewise able to perform miracles, followed by the early martyrs and saints, even posthumously, responding to Christians' pleas for help in times of distress. Other reported miracles include visions, telepathy, clairvoyance, and precognition. Thus, thousands of miracles have been attributed to the Christian faith and have been credited with converting nonbelievers, serving as continuing proof of its truth against the calumnies of the infidel. Nevertheless, skeptics such as David Hume have continued to argue that all so-called miracles have a rational, scientific explanation, even if modern science has not yet been able to provide one.

Miracle collections have appeared under the rubric of a particular saint, shrine, or relic, as instruments of the sacred, serving as proof of the continuing presence of the divine. In the face of skeptics and nonbelievers, since the twelfth century the Church has developed legally defensible grounds for the adjudication of miracles, which are a sine qua non for the canonization of saints. Witnesses appear before a commission of inquiry composed of canon lawyers, theologians, and church officials in order to prove that a cure from disease or rescue from danger could only have been the result of divine intervention and no alternative natural explanation is possible. Such a formal procedure is necessary, it has been argued, in order to ensure that "false prophets" do not befuddle the faithful into believing that acts of the Devil have occurred through God's agency, since Satan often masquerades as an "angel of light" (like Pharaoh's magicians). Some have also felt that the performance of fake miracles and the falsification of relics designed to enrich their perpetrators also demand that rigid standards be applied to the authentication of true miracles. The aim has therefore been to elucidate the "who, what, when, where, why, and how" of the miracle.

The circle of persons who either had witnessed a miracle or had themselves been its recipient often formed the kernel of a religious community or cult, having taken part in a common transcendent supernatural experience. The strong participation of women suggests that, despite their absence from the church hierarchy, women's deep belief and active involvement in the daily life of the church were absolutely necessary for the survival of the Christian faith. Particularly in rural society, a high percentage of miracles dealt with the vagaries of childbirth, childlessness, birth defects, and infant disease, and women played an active role at pilgrimage sites. The cult of an extremely popular saint such as Landgravina Elisabeth of Hungary (d. 1231), for example, reflects this phenomenon due to the prominence of women as both witnesses and the beneficiaries of miracles. The 1240 stained-glass windows at Marburg cathedral provide a vivid illustration of her life and miracles. While the catalog of miracles attributed to men and women saints is often strikingly similar, nevertheless, among the miracles that appear to have been more common among women are mystical visions of the next world and of the Infant Jesus, the "gift" of tears, and stigmata. The important cult of the Sacred Heart was the product of divine revelations accorded to pious women at Helfta beginning in the thirteenth century. Many of the miracle workers moved within pious circles, such as the Beguines, centered in the Low Countries, or the Poor Clares, centered around Clare of Assisi, in which their supernatural powers were acquired and encouraged.

A considerable percentage of Christian saints are women, beginning with the Virgin Mary and Mary Magdalene, whose intercession on behalf of believers in need has produced substantial collections of miracles. The cult of the Virgin, which flourished beginning in the central Middle Ages, transformed Mary into perhaps the premier miracle worker, whose appearance in a vision to a believer often preceded the performance of a miracle. Miracle workers have included martyrs such as Perpetua (d. 203), founders of religious orders such as Clare of Assisi (d. 1253), royalty such as Olga, Princess of Kiev (d. 969), and simple women such as Geneviève, patroness of Paris (d. 502). The miracles attributed to these figures were many and varied: Brigit allegedly increased the quality and quantity of all she touched; Geneviève rescued the city of Paris from both the pagan Huns and the plague; Olga converted the Russians to the Orthodox Christian faith. The very public nature of the miracle was the surest means of increasing the number of believers, who were astonished by the spectacle of God's intervention in human affairs, sometimes against great odds. Some saints became patrons of a particular family, profession, institution, community, or nation, while others specialized in the curing of certain ailments. The miracle tale often conformed to a fixed structure, following folklore and an oral tradition that spans cultures and religions. A problem is stated, and is resolved through supernatural intervention. The wider public learned about better-known miracles by means of the translation into the vernacular of saints' lives and miracles, sermons in which miracle stories were reported, and devotional art, including frescoes, stained-glass windows, and altarpieces. Due to their higher church attendance, it may well be that women were more exposed to legends of the supernatural, which reinforced their own participation in such events.

MICHAEL E. GOODICH

References and Further Reading

Bynum, Caroline Walker. *Holy Feast and Holy Fast: The Religious Significance of Food to Medieval Women.* Berkeley, Calif.: University of California Press, 1987.

Elliott, Dyan. *Proving Women: Female Spirituality and Inquisitional Culture in the Later Middle Ages.* Princeton, N.J.: Princeton University Press, 2004.

Farmer, Sharon. *Surviving Poverty in Medieval Paris: Gender, Ideology and Daily Lives of the Poor.* Ithaca, N.Y.: Cornell University Press, 2002.

Finucane, Ronald. *The Rescue of the Innocents: Endangered Children in Medieval Miracles.* New York: St. Martin's, 1997.

Goodich, Michael. *Violence and Miracle in the Fourteenth Century: Private Grief and Public Salvation.* Chicago: University of Chicago Press, 1995.

Head, Thomas, ed. *Medieval Hagiography.* New York: Garland Publishing, 2000.

Jacobus de Voragine. *The Golden Legend,* translated by William G. Ryan. 2 vols. Princeton, N.J.: Princeton University Press, 1993.

Kleinberg, Aviad. *Prophets in Their Own Country: Living Saints and the Making of Sainthood in the Later Middle Ages.* Chicago: University of Chicago Press, 1992.

Vauchez, André. *Sainthood in the Later Middle Ages,* translated by Jean Birrell. Cambridge: Cambridge University Press, 1997.

Ward, Benedicta. *Miracles and the Medieval Mind: Theory, Record, and Event, 1000–1215.* Philadelphia: University of Pennsylvania Press, 1982.

See also **Brigit; Canonization of Saints; Church; Clare of Assisi; Elisabeth of Hungary; Hagiography; Mary, Virgin: in Literature; Mysticism and Mystics; Olga; Pilgrims and Pilgrimage; Relics and Reliquaries; Theology**

MISERICORDS

For centuries very few people paid attention to the mine of information on medieval life that was incorporated into the carvings hidden under the seats of Gothic choir stalls, the misericords! Monks and canons stood during their daily prayer sessions until late in the twelfth century, when seats of mercy were permitted for the aged and handicapped and later for the entire religious community. The small ledges attached to the main seat enables the monks to perch while they appeared to be standing since the ledge is higher than the main seat. Only a simple stick was necessary to support the little ledge, but cathedrals, abbeys, collegiate churches, and private chapels commissioned sculptors to beautify their choir stalls and make them worthy of being in the most sacred part of the church, where the psalms were chanted and the liturgy was presented.

It may seem strange that women played an important role in these carvings under the seats—not the Virgin Mary and the martyred saints, but ordinary women performing their daily duties. However, if we look more closely at the choir stalls, we realize that these carvings were hidden when the seats were lowered and not visible to anyone. In addition, when the monks and canons sat on these seats they were in a position to crush the ideas portrayed there, as a virtue on a columnar statue crushed a vice under her feet.

Women were portrayed in many different roles by the misogynous church hierarchy. The paragraphs below will look at a few of these roles: women at work, conjugal relationships, women as vices, and women in league with the devil.

Women Working on Misericords

Most of the carvings of workers on misericords are men. The fifteenth-century misericords at the cathedral of Rouen show us several shoemakers, a physician, a sculptor, a mason, and several agricultural workers. In addition, merchants sell their products and deal with bags of money. Before the bombardments of World War II several misericords also showed artisans making fabric; a prime industry in the area. At Rouen women are presented as shoemakers, but not as frequently as the men, and women are confined to their workshops rather than selling shoes to customers. They also have their place in the market. No woman is shown with the level of skills of a mason, sculptor, or physician. Later, on a sixteenth-century set of choir stalls from Gaillon (now at St. Denis), two women are part of a musical group, and on another misericord a woman appears to run a workshop dealing with leather or wood.

On other choir stalls the working woman is shown as derelict in her duties: she falls asleep in Amsterdam, her distaff falling into the fireplace. At Ludlow (Great Britain) one woman is thrown into Hell: her sin was giving short measure to a customer in her tavern. In several instances a brewster is depicted as a drunk. Such a drunken couple are shown, for example at Fairford (Glos.), sitting by, and certainly emptying a huge keg. (This carving has recently been stolen.) A few women working in the fields are depicted, mainly in England. Generally speaking, women are shown at work, but not in the more skilled professions, and they are not always shown as responsible workers.

Conjugal Relationships

Courting traditions and marital contentions play a significant role in the misericord world, and these vary by region. At Rouen cathedral and several churches in England, one misericord shows a man kneeling before a seated woman. In France as well as in England, the man has placed his hand under the woman's shoe. This scene is usually interpreted as a marital spat. However, the couple looks peaceful. Actually, the man may be propositioning the woman, and the hand and shoe, as in the Cinderella tale, are symbols for the sex organs. In Rouen, if the woman accepts a proposal (it really is a proposition), she holds up a ladle with which they will share their marital feast. If the woman rejects the man's advances she hurls her distaff at him, as she does at Malvern Priory.

Another standard marital scene portrays the fight to see who will wear the pants in the family. Here the man and woman each clutch one side of a pair of breeches. We never see who wins, but in the original tale it is the husband. Each artist varies the scene. At Rouen cathedral the young husband clutches a knife, prepared to shred his pants rather than turn them over to his wife. At Hoogstraten (Belgium), two women fight over the pants, thus giving the man time to grab them and flee. At Rodez Cathedral (France), an elderly couple sits before a pair of underpants. Since there are no trousers, just holes for the legs, the artist conveys the impression that the couple is impotent and they are, in effect, fighting over nothing.

In Spain at Leon Cathedral and at two churches in the Cantal in France (from a single abbey long since dispersed) the marital story is told on two separate misericords. On one a man is spinning or carding, and on the other a woman is donning the pants. This looks suspiciously like the second act to the fight for the pants. The woman is the winner.

One more variation exists, mainly in Great Britain. Here the wife beats up the husband, pulls his hair and beard, readies a kitchen tool to throw at him, and drags him along the floor. Sometimes the husband's sword, a sexual symbol, lies uselessly at his side. He never wins.

Women Representing a Vice

Another function of depicting women on misericords is to represent a vice; virtues are rarely seen under the seats. Woman is Lust, and while we see a number of mermaids preparing to seduce a man, we also see nude women riding beasts in France, Great Britain, and Germany. Their mounts are pigs, rams, and monsters. Some may be imitating prints by Dürer or Hans Grien where the women ride off to a coven to seduce the devil.

Women are also seen as drunks and gluttons. In Spain one woman, holding a stein, loses her balance, and falls flat. Women are also vain on the misericords. Even if old and ugly, they dress their hair with nets and jewels topped by a coif called a sugar hennin, which could be a yard high. At Rodez a pair of women wearing fantastic hats introduces the north and south rows of stalls. At Stendal (Saxony), one woman wears a hat composed of dozens of ribbons. Several women wear a horned hennin, which leaves a space for the devil to nest. We do not see women as misers, probably because the men carry the purses.

Women in League with the Devil

Women were often presented in league with the devil, as at St. Martin-aux-Bois, where a woman saws a female devil in half. She also has such power over the devil that she can tie the demon to a cushion with a ribbon (Barcelona, Isle Adam, Aarschot, and Dordrecht).

Conclusions

Some images of women cross regional boundaries, while others vary by country. We never see the fight for the pants in England, nor the hand under the shoe in Spain, nor the violent fight in France. Each country, however, featured the domineering woman, who is crushed by the body of the monk seated above her.

These images of women melded with ideas held by the church rather than acting as reflections of contemporary women. For the men who lacked women in their lives, this type of woman was perhaps a comforting image. Saintly women abounded in the sculptures and paintings of the church, but did not appear on the misericords.

ELAINE C. BLOCK

References and Further Reading

Armstead, Wendy. "Interpreting Images of Women with Books in Misericords." In *Women and the Book: Assessing the Visual Evidence*, edited by Jane H. M. Taylor and Lesley Smith. London: British Library, 1997, pp. 57–74.
Block, Elaine C. "Half Angel–Half Beast: Images of Women on Misericords." *Reinardus*. 5(1992): 17–34.
———. *Corpus of Medieval Misericords: France*. Brepols, 2003.
———. *Corpus of Medieval Misericords: Iberia*. Brepols, 2004.

See also **Architecture, Ecclesiastical; Eroticism in Art; Woman on Top; Work**

MISOGYNY

Misogyny, literally "hatred of women," was pervasive in medieval culture, but it is important to remember that misogyny was only one facet of social and literary attitudes toward women. Many of the endlessly repeated antiwoman arguments were counterbalanced by prowoman arguments (Blamires, *The Case for...*), though outside of the purely discursive realm the negative views of women were more influential in justifying female subordination to males in all areas of medieval life. Misogyny in the Middle Ages was a remarkably uniform discourse that changed little over many centuries and can be found in the major European literatures in very similar forms. Misogynistic

portrayals of women stressed their insatiable lust (leading to men's downfall); their garrulousness and unreliability; their abuse of long-suffering husbands; their love of makeup and ornaments; and their riotous nature. These supposedly female characteristics can be found in different variations in many satirical, particularly antimarriage, texts.

Another strand of misogyny exists in theological and philosophical writings, where woman was presented as the negative part of a whole series of dichotomies that pitted female against male: body/intellect; lust/self discipline; passive/active. In this context, male clerics saw woman as a threat to their ascetic ideals.

Medical and scientific texts also contributed to negative views of women. Aristotle's view of woman as a defective male and a purely passive partner in the process of conception dominated, although the Galenic theory of both women and men having an active seed also had some adherents. And for physiological reasons, women were believed largely incapable of rational thought (Bullough, "Medieval Medical...").

Taken together, these views justified the inferior roles assigned to women in many different contexts. Legally, most women were on the same level as a child or a mad person. They could not plead in court; be judges or arbitrators; hold public office; be witnesses to wills; adopt children; or act as guardians (except to their own children) (Brundage). They could not ordinarily practice most trades. Within the Church they were not allowed to teach, preach, hear confessions, or hold any office in the Church hierarchy, except in nunneries. In the Catholic Church, arguments against female ordination to this day draw on misogynistic commonplaces found in the medieval period.

The Creation of Eve and Women's Souls

Of the two creation stories found in the Book of Genesis, the misogynistic tradition preferred the second one, stating that Eve was formed from Adam's rib (Gen. 2:22) and was therefore subject to man. Yet, this version coexisted with Genesis 1:27, which stated that God had formed both man and woman in his image. The solution proposed by Saint Augustine (354–430) was that Eve was formed equivalent to Adam as far as the eternal order of salvation was concerned, but subordinated to him through the second act of creation that formed their actual bodies. Thus, in the realm of social reality, Eve is inferior. Consequently, women could be both "God's image" through their souls and subject to men through their bodies and because of Eve's sin. This idea was generally accepted in the Middle Ages by such thinkers as Thomas Aquinas (1225–1274) and Bonaventure (1221–1274) (Børresen and McLaughlin, "Equality of Souls").

In spite of the dignity accorded to their souls, women were unfit for priestly ordination. Saint Paul's statement in Galatians 3:28 that in Christ there is neither male nor female did not prevent theologians from finding many arguments against women priests: they lack "eminence" of status; Christ chose to adopt a male human form and not a female one; women are "naturally" subject to men; they cannot teach or preach; as women they cannot wed the female figure of the Church as do priests through their ordination; women are "unclean" during their menstruation; women cannot be tonsured; and many more (Minnis).

Ascetic and Philosophical Misogyny

In the ascetic tradition, virginity was of primary importance, and women were seen as the greatest threat to male ascetics (Ruether, "Misogynism..."). Countless Latin texts, beginning with the Church Fathers, depicted women as lecherous and licentious beings, subject to their insatiable desires and unstable emotions. Tertullian (c. 160–c. 225) was responsible for the famous image of woman as the devil's gateway. Saint Jerome (331–420), in his treatise *Against Jovinian* of 393, cited Theophrastus (his name became synonymous with misogamy [hatred of marriage] in the Middle Ages) as saying that a wise man should never take a wife, since she would hinder his study of philosophy and ruin him with her constant demands for clothes, jewels, and gilded coaches. Jerome surrounded himself with pious women, although he did not marry.

In the twelfth century a number of writer's Latin texts on women repeat again and again the same clichés while adding strong doses of venom. It seems that in France this misogynistic tradition was particularly widespread. Writers like Marbod of Rennes (1035–1123) and Hildebert of Tours (1057–1133) are prime examples of the current that depicted women as unstable and evil beings, putrid and sordid vipers that seduce men and whose only interests are make-up and jewelry. A catalog of female vices had been established by the twelfth century that was to continue throughout the Middle Ages. Yet, a writer like Marbod also defended "good women," thus exemplifying the diptych structure so characteristic of much in the writing about women (Blamires, *Woman Defamed...*).

In the writings of Abélard and Héloise the philosophical antimarriage tradition is especially paradoxical. Héloise put forward age-old arguments against marriage, stating that, if she married Abélard, she—and any future children—would keep him from his all-important philosophical work. (Their eventual marriage had disastrous results, but not of the kind anticipated by Héloise). Abélard, in his writings on nuns, made a strong case for the dignity of women, highlighting Christ's special favors to women in the New Testament (McLaughlin, "Peter Abelard...").

The basic tenet of the ascetic-philosophical misogynist tradition, though replete with disturbing invectives against women, is primarily the refusal of marriage rather than a denigration of women as a species.

Antiwoman, Antimarriage: The Debate

In vernacular literatures the same types of arguments against women and against marriage appear, frequently structured as a debate. Drawing on ancient satirical traditions (Ovid and Juvenal in particular), medieval misogamous texts presented women as seducers of men who, once they had caught their husbands, would not leave them a minute of peace. John of Salisbury's 1159 book on statesmanship, the *Policraticus,* contained a whole catalog of warnings against marriage. Walter Map's *Letter of Valerius to Rufinus, Against Marriage* of 1180 also lists examples of both good and bad women, with bad ones in the majority. The marriage debate existed in all the major European literatures and languages. For example, a Hebrew text, *The Offering of Judah the Misogynist,* written by Judah Ibn Shabbetai in Toledo around 1208, fits into the tradition of misogamous treatises by depicting a hapless male victim as he is being tricked into marriage with "an ugly shrew" (Rosen). Matheolus, the proverbial misogamist, authored a long and repetitive *Livre des lamentacions (Book of Lamentations)* in the late thirteenth century, in which he bemoans his status of being a *bigame*, the result of a change in law that had made marrying a widow unlawful for a cleric. Perette, his wife, is depicted as the incarnation of all possible vices.

In a similar vein, Boccaccio painted one of the most horrific portraits of the ugly and dangerous woman in his *Corbaccio* (c. 1355), where—under the pretext of complaining about one particular woman—he castigates women's insatiable lust, bestiality, slovenliness, and desire to rob and ruin men. The prolific poet Eustache Deschamps also contributed to the marriage debate with his *Miroir de mariage*

(*Mirror of Marriage*, 1381–1389), featuring a discussion between *Franc-Vouloir* (Free Will) and a number of his friends. His one true friend, *Répertoire de Science* (Fount of Knowledge), marshals a huge number of the classical antimarriage arguments in order to dissuade *Franc-Vouloir* from marrying. Interestingly, Deschamps added a universal history and various passages critical of his own society to his misogamous advice, thus giving an additional historical and didactic dimension to these outworn themes.

The late-fourteenth-century *Quinze joies de mariage* (*Fifteen Joys of Marriage*) shows in fifteen deftly painted scenes the ruin through marriage of a perfectly good man. Had he only resisted being caught in "the net of marriage" like a poor fish, this man could have led a life devoid of the constant demands of his nagging wife. Fernando de Rojas's *Celestina* (1499) also depicts a despicable female character, a witch in league with the devil, who with her multifaceted skills supplemented by greed and treachery "is monastic antifeminism's greatest fear personified" (Buedel, "Confronting Misogyny," p. 31).

A special place in the misogynistic tradition belongs to the second part of the *Romance of the Rose*, authored by Jean de Meun around 1270. Although not necessarily speaking for the author, a number of allegorical characters spout misogynistic diatribes of the sort that led Christine de Pizan and the theologian Jean Gerson in 1402–1403 to condemn the *Rose* for its immorality and its negative depiction of women. *La Vieille* (the old woman) and Le Jaloux (the jealous husband) in particular repeat in excess many of the stereotypes of the covetous and adulterous woman found in preceding centuries. Because the *Rose* was enormously popular (still extant in over two hundred manuscripts) it became one of the major sources perpetuating attacks against women's characters and reputations.

"Bad women" appeared in many contexts and often were juxtaposed with "good women." Etienne de Fougères, who wrote his influential *Livre des manières* (c. 1175) on the three orders of medieval society, offered a catalog of "good women," as opposed to "bad women," though the latter dominate by far. Even Andreas Capellanus, whose treatise on courtly love, the *De amore* of c. 1185, codified a type of behavior that supposedly put women on a pedestal, added a palinode criticizing women in the last book.

Yet, once they had denigrated women, some authors felt "guilty," and these feelings of guilt, perhaps nothing more than another literary fiction, account for such texts as Jean le Fèvre's late fourteenth-century *Livre de Leesce* (Book of Joy), in which he refutes the misogynistic arguments he had translated in his version of that most famous of all medieval misogamous texts, Matheolus's late-thirteenth-century *Livre des lamentacions* (a book that would unsettle and depress Christine de Pizan). In the late fourteenth century, Chaucer claimed that he wrote his *Legend of Good Women* as an atonement for having translated the *Romance of the Rose*. Pere Torroella in the second half of the fifteenth century wrote a prose rebuttal of his own misogynistic poem, the *Maldecir de mujeres*.

In some manuscripts the same diptych structure highlights the ambivalent attitude toward medieval women. The *Bien des fames* (Good Things about Women) coexisted with *Le Blasme des fames* (Blame of Women) in thirteenth-century manuscripts (Fiero et al., eds.). Each of these texts is filled with clichés, be they positive or negative. Indeed, texts in praise of women fall, according to Howard Bloch, into the same trap as those blaming women. For Bloch any statement that contains the phrase *woman is* is misogynistic.

The conflicted attitude of medieval men (especially of clerics striving for spiritual and physical purity) toward women is reflected in this constant pro- and contra-woman debate. Women were divinely created and necessary to men in so many ways, yet they threatened the ideals men had constructed for themselves. With a new emphasis on the interdiction of clerical marriage advocated by the Gregorian reforms in the eleventh and twelfth centuries, warnings against woman's potential nefarious influence on men gained a new urgency.

Other Literary Contexts for Misogyny

"Bad women" and women in need of male discipline were plentiful in the *fabliau* tradition. In countless *fabliaux* women manage to cuckold their husbands through vicious trickery. But sometimes the men prevail, as in the particularly cruel and misogynistic *La dame escouillée* (*The Castrated Lady*), in which a woman's perceived dominance is "cured" through a simulated castration involving a bull's genitals. In an early-fifteenth-century Swiss *fabliau*, as in many other tales, including several from Boccaccio's *Decameron*, a woman's tricks enable her to have sex with another man while her husband believes her innocent. This pan-European tradition of the "wiles of woman" tales gave narrative expression to the negative stereotypes of the immoral and tricky woman promulgated in the many misogynistic texts authored by clerics.

But what about the troubadour lyric and romances, texts that seem to idolize women? A number of troubadours, among them Marcabru and Peire de

Bussignac in the twelfth century, wrote overtly misogynistic poems. But even in those lyrics that seem to praise women, a new critical perspective has revealed plenty of misogynistic stereotypes. Thus the supposedly idealized lady of the troubadours has been shown to be primarily a mirror for an idealized male self, and the male love "service" is yet another means to subjugate women. Male ambivalence about female sexuality is apparent in these poems, as is the male desire to dominate the lady. What we find here is a "fantasy of power which excludes the female" (Burns).

In romance, as well, we find misogynistic tirades, such as the one uttered by the seneschal in Gottfried von Strassburg's Middle High German *Tristan and Isolde* (c. 1210) or by Gawain in the Middle English fourteenth-century *Sir Gawain and the Green Knight*, which show the pervasiveness of this type of discourse in medieval literature. But there are also more subtle underminings of women's status: Chrétien de Troyes' *Erec et Enide* (c. 1170), for example, contains both negative stereotyping of women (the necessity to silence them, for example) and demonstrations of the unsuitability of woman's rule at a time when, through women like Eleanor of Aquitaine and aristocratic wives left behind by their crusader husbands, female rights to inheritance and rule became important issues of debate (Ramey). Roberta Krueger sees much of the cultural discourse on gender issues and misogyny that is worked out in Old French romances as reflections of a crisis of masculinity.

At the end of the Middle Ages, misogyny was also prevalent in treatises on witchcraft, such as the *Hammer of Witches* by the Dominicans Kramer and Sprenger. Here, women are depicted as particularly prone to advances of demons, having sexual intercourse with them and engaging in other nefarious activities. Women constituted the majority of victims in the early modern witch hunts, and the deep-seated misogyny of medieval culture certainly contributed to this imbalance (Elliott).

Countering Misogyny: Christine de Pizan

During the course of the Middle Ages only one woman writer directly confronted the misogynistic tradition: Christine de Pizan (c. 1364–c. 1430). She detected the repetitiveness and pervasiveness of anti-women topoi in different areas of medieval literary production and revealed the real-life consequences for women resulting from this misogyny. Plunged into a deep depression after reading Matheolus at the opening of her *Book of the City of Ladies* (1405), she

defines her task as a correction of the injustice done to women over centuries and the establishment of a tradition that honors women's contributions to world history. But like other works in praise of women, Christine's did not have much impact on the widespread misogyny of medieval culture.

RENATE BLUMENFELD-KOSINSKI

References and Further Reading

Allen, Prudence. *The Concept of Woman: The Aristotelian Revolution, 750 BC–AD 1250*. Montreal: Eden Press, 1985.
Archer, Robert. "'Tus falsas opiniones e mis verdaderes razones': Pere Torroella and the Woman Haters." *Bulletin of Hispanic Studies* 78 (2001): 551–566.
Blamires, Alcuin. *The Case for Women in Medieval Culture*. Oxford: Clarendon Press, 1997.
———. *Woman Defamed and Woman Defended: An Anthology of Medieval Texts*. Oxford: Clarendon Press, 1992.
Bloch, R. Howard. *Medieval Misogyny and the Invention of Western Romantic Love*. Chicago: University of Chicago Press, 1991.
Blumenfeld-Kosinski, Renate. "Christine de Pizan and the Misogynistic Tradition." *Romanic Review* 81 (1990): 279–292.
———. "Jean le Fèvre's *Livre de leesce*: Praise or Blame of Women?" *Speculum* 69 (1994): 707–727.
Børresen, Kari Elisabeth. *Subordination and Equivalence: The Nature and Role of Woman in Augustine and Thomas Aquinas*. Oslo: Universiteits Forlaget, 1968. New edition, Kampen: Kok Pharos, 1995.
Brundage, James A. *Law, Sex, and Christian Society in Medieval Europe*. Chicago: University of Chicago Press, 1987.
Buedel, Barbara Foley. "Confronting Misogyny in Three Texts of Medieval Spanish Literature." In *Estudios Alfonsinos y otros escritos*, edited by Nicolás Toscano. New York: National Endowment for the Humanities, 1990, pp. 26–33.
Bullough, Vern. "Medieval Medical and Scientific Views of Women." *Viator* 4 (1973): 485–501.
Bullough, Vern, and Bonnie Bullough. *The Subordinate Sex: A History of Attitudes toward Women*. New York: Penguin Books, 1974.
Burns, E. Jane. "The Man Behind the Lady in Troubadour Lyric." *Romance Notes* 25 (1985): 254–270.
Elliott, Dyan. *Fallen Bodies: Pollution, Sexuality, and Demonology in the Middle Ages*. Philadelphia: University of Pennsylvania Press, 1999.
Fiero, Gloria K., Wendy Pfeffer, and Mathé Allain, eds. and trans. *Three Medieval Views of Women*: La Contenance des Fames, Le Bien des Fames, Le Blasme des Fames. New Haven: Yale University Press, 1989.
Huot, Sylvia. "Confronting Misogyny: Christine de Pizan and the *Roman de la Rose*." In *Translatio studii: Essays by His Students in Honor of Karl D. Uitti for His Sixty-Fifth Birthday*, edited by Renate Blumenfeld-Kosinski, et al. Amsterdam and Atlanta: Rodopi, 2000, pp. 169–187.
Krueger, Roberta. *Women Readers and the Ideology of Gender in Old French Verse Romance*. Cambridge: Cambridge University Press, 1993.
McLaughlin, Eleanor. "Equality of Souls, Inequality of Sexes: Women in Medieval Theology." In *Religion and Sexism*, edited by Ruether, pp. 213–266.

McLaughlin, Mary Martin. "Peter Abelard and the Dignity of Women: Twelfth-Century 'Feminism' in Theory and Practice." In *Pierre Abélard – Pierre le Vénérable*. Paris: CNRS, 1975, pp. 287–334.

McLeod, Glenda. *Virtue and Venom: Catalogs of Women from Antiquity to the Renaissance*. Ann Arbor: University of Michigan Press, 1991.

Minnis, Alastair J. "*De impedimento sexus*: Women's Bodies and Medieval Impediments to Female Ordination." In iller and A. J. Minnis. York Studies in Medieval Theology 1. York: York Medieval Press, 1997, pp. 109–139.

Ramey, Lynn Tarte. "Representations of Women in Chrétien's *Erec et Enide*: Courtly Literature or Misogyny?" *Romanic Review* 84 (1993): 377–386.

Rogers, Katharine M. *The Troublesome Helpmate: A History of Misogyny in Literature*. Seattle: University of Washington Press, 1966.

Rose, Tova. *Unveiling Eve: Reading Gender in Medieval Hebrew Literature*. Philadelphia: University of Pennsylvania Press, 2003.

Ruether, Rosemary Radford. "Misogynism and Virginal Feminism in the Fathers of the Church." In *Religion and Sexism*, pp. 150–183.

———, ed. *Religion and Sexism: Images of Women in the Jewish and Christian Traditions*. New York: Simon and Schuster, 1974.

Wilson, Katharina M., and Elizabeth M. Makowski. *Wykked Wyves and the Woes of Marriage: Misogamous Literature from Juvenal to Chaucer*. Albany: State University of New York Press, 1990.

See also **Aristotelian Concepts of Women and Gender; Boccaccio, Giovanni; Chaucer, Geoffrey; Chrétien de Troyes; Christine de Pizan; Courtly Love; Cuckold; Defenses of Women; Eve; Fabliau; Femininity and Masculinity; Gender Ideologies; Gender in History; Gerson, Jean; Gottfried von Strassburg; Heloise; Jerome, Influence of; Jewish Women; Literature, Hebrew; Literature, Italian; Literature, Old French; Marriage Ceremonies; Ordination of Women as Priests; Roman de la Rose and Its Reception; Romance, French; Trobairitz and Troubadours; Virginity; Witches; Woman on Top**

MOBILITY
See **Migration and Mobility**

MODERN DEVOTION
The religious reform movement known as the Modern Devotion, or *Devotia Moderna*, came into being during the fourteenth century in what is now the Netherlands. The founder of the movement was Geert Grote (d. 1384), a mayor's son from Deventer. Other pioneers of the movement include Florens Radewijns, Gerard Dou, and Johannes Brinckerinck. The Modern Devotion called out to people to convert and embrace an ascetic lifestyle at a time when the Church and its institutions were corrupt. The founders of the Modern Devotion appear to have struck a chord: many converted. The movement was especially popular among women: it attracted approximately three times as many female participants as male. Today the Modern Devotion is considered to have been a second religious women's movement in the Low Countries (after the first, which had taken place in the southern Netherlands during the thirteenth century). The influence of this second movement extended throughout all of the German- and Dutch-speaking areas of Europe.

The institutionalization of the Modern Devotion began with the establishment of a community of religious women in the house of Geert Grote in Deventer (1374). The statutes of the so-called *Meester-Geertshuis* (Master Geert's house) reveal that their authors were especially intent upon avoiding any association with the Beguines, who had been persecuted by inquisitorial tribunals ever since the Council of Vienna of 1310. Following a period of years during which each sister arranged her life as she saw fit, Johannes Brinckerink (d. 1419) introduced the "common life." From that point on, the sisters put all of their possessions and income into a communal coffer, from which each received what she required. Thus the foundation was laid for the Sisters of the Common Life, one of the branches into which the Modern Devotion organized itself. In all, several dozen such houses were established, especially in the eastern portion of the Netherlands and the bordering German regions.

The most important aspect of the legacy of the Sisters of the Common Life is undoubtedly their "sisterbooks." Anthologies containing the life stories of exemplary sisters had been compiled in a number of convents over a considerable period of time. The cradle of this literary genre is to be found among the Sisters of the Common Life in the city of Deventer: the *Meester-Geertshuis*, the *Lamme van Diezehuis*, and quite possibly the *Buiskenshuis* each possessed a sisterbook, and moreover we know of the existence of a similar book from St. Agnes in Emmerich on the lower Rhine. Thanks to these collections of biographical material we are able to form a clear picture of the religious ideals held by these women. To the present-day reader these tales of asceticism, penance, fasting, and humility may be somewhat alienating, as, for instance, the anecdote concerning Johannes Brinckerink, who commanded a sister to throw an apple tree she had lovingly cultivated into the IJssel river: she put too much store in the things of this world.

Geert Grote also wanted the Modern Devotion's ideal of reform to be manifested within a Church-approved monastic structure. The Augustinian Rule was chosen because it offered the greatest degree of flexibility. An all-male monastery was established at Windesheim near Zwolle in 1387, and three years later the Chapter of Windesheim, the monastic union of the Modern Devotion, was created. In the course of the fifteenth century it grew to include some one hundred monasteries. Windesheim exerted a powerful attraction on women, but only thirteen female monasteries were accepted into the Chapter. The Chapter's administration was not prepared to accept the pastoral and legal responsibilities for more female establishments. They did, however, send considerable numbers of monks from affiliated monasteries to female houses to provide pastoral care. Moreover, many of these houses observed, in varying degrees of strictness, the Windesheim constitutions. Thus the sphere of influence of the Chapter of Windesheim extended to several hundred female monasteries, with several thousand inhabitants.

The Chapter of Windesheim may have numbered only a few female houses, but it was in this small circle that the intellectual level was the highest. There were many women in the Windesheim monasteries who felt the need to write about the spiritual life. The monastery of Diepenveen, near Deventer, possessed a sisterbook, of which not one, but two, manuscripts survive. This valuable source tells us that the Latin Divine Office held pride of place in their spiritual lives, but also that the sisters of Windesheim practiced the typical female virtues of the Modern Devotion, humility and obedience, with the greatest devotion. A characteristic activity was the "stealing of virtue": some sisters would rise early in the morning to perform the tasks assigned to others for the following day. Diepenveen's first prioress, Salome Sticken (d. 1449), wrote a rule for the Sisters of the Common Life, the *Vivendi formula*, in which obedience and submission again play a central role. Jacomijne Costers (d. 1503) lived in the monastery of Facons in Antwerp, and her writing career begins with her *Visioen en exempel* (*Vision and Exemplum*), in which, in the style of Tondal, she is led through purgatory and hell on account of her dishonest way of life. In addition to this eschatological vision, she left a number of other works containing practical advice for the monastic life as an admonition to her fellow nuns. The most remarkable author of this circle is Alijt Bake (d. 1455), prioress of the monastery of Galilea in Ghent. She attempted to introduce a mystically oriented reform of the inner spiritual life at Galilea, supported by a number of treatises, among which was a spiritual autobiography, in which are described numerous, intense dialogues with Christ. Bake's efforts were not well received by the Chapter's leadership. She was deposed and banished in 1455.

While the Sisters of the Common Life and Windesheim were rooted especially in the region of the IJssel valley and the lower Rhine, the Chapter of Utrecht was established in the western part of the diocese of Utrecht in 1399. Although this monastic union the Third Rule of St. Francis, it considered itself a part of the Modern Devotion. The few communities of male tertiaries that belonged to it had the task of providing spiritual care to the female tertiaries. The Chapter of Utrecht was by far the largest organization within the Modern Devotion: it comprised no fewer than 166 establishments of female tertiaries. Little is known about the spiritual life of the nuns of the Third Order. Short chronicles have survived from a number of establishments that are reminiscent, in style and intent, of the more comprehensive sisterbooks. It is likely that the tertiaries' way of living most resembled that of the Sisters of the Common Life. Over the course of the fifteenth century both categories exhibited a tendency toward further monasticization, with its accompanying enclosure and emphasis on celebration of the Divine Office, for which Windesheim undoubtedly provided an important role model.

WYBREN SCHEEPSMA

References and Further Reading

Bollmann, Anne M. "'Een vrauwe te sijn op mijn selfs handt': Alijt Bake (1415–1455) als gestiliche Reformerin des innerlichen Lebens." *Ons geestelijk erf* 76 (2002): 64–98.
———. *Frauenleben und Frauenliteratur in der Devotio moderna. Volkssprachige Schwesternbücher in literarhistorischer Perspektive.* Tübingen: Mohr Siebeck, 2004.
Die niederländische Mystik des 14. bis 16. Jahrhunderts. Munich: Beck, 1999.
Hyma, Albert *The Christian Renaissance: A History of the "Devotio Moderna."* Hamden, Conn.: Archon Books, 1965.
Post, R. R. *The Modern Devotion: Confrontation with Reformation and Humanism.* Leiden: Brill, 1968.
Scheepsma, Wybren. "'For hereby I hope to rouse some to piety': Books of Sisters from Convents and Sister-Houses Associated with the *Devotio Moderna* in the Low Countries." In *Women, the Book and the Godly*, edited by Leslie Smith and Jane H. M. Taylor. Xane, 1995.
———. *Medieval Religious Women in the Low Countries: The Modern Devotion, the Canonesses of Windesheim, and their Writings.* Woodbridge, Suffolk: Boydell Press, 2004.
Van Engen, John *Devotio Moderna: Basic Writings.* New York: Paulist Press, 1988.

See also **Bake, Alijt; Monasticism and Nuns; Sister-Books and Other Convent Chronicles**

MONASTIC ENCLOSURE

Isolation from the demands and perceived snares of the secular world was a concept central to the monastic ideal from earliest times. An enclosed space, or cloister (from the Latin *clausura*), made sacred by continuous prayer and contemplation, delimited the boundaries beyond which members of a religious community were advised not to venture and into which the worldly were not to intrude.

The most popular monastic rule in early medieval Europe, that of St. Benedict of Nursia (d. 547), emphasized monastic stability as embodied in the popular saying that a monk outside his cloister was "like a fish out of water," but Benedictine monks, and the nuns for whom the rule was adapted, were not strictly cloistered. With the permission of their abbot/abbess, they could leave the confines of their monasteries as the need arose, and the entrance of secular persons, especially children, for whom monasteries often functioned as schools, was commonplace.

Monastic rules composed specifically for women contained more precise provisions for enclosure, reflecting the insecurity of the times as well as a particular religious ideal. Writing for a small group of nuns in his diocese, Bishop Caesarius of Arles (504–542), for example, advised them to have a locked gate at the entrance of the monastery, and urgent need as their sole excuse to pass through it. The bishop also attempted to seriously curtail visits from secular persons.

Carolingian monastic reforms, spearheaded by St. Benedict of Aniane (d. 821), included an emphasis on segregation of monks as well as nuns from the outside world, even to the extent of barring children other than oblates (children offered to the monastery) from claustral schools. Nevertheless, gender-related distinctions surfaced here too. The Council of Mainz (813) required that monks have the consent of their abbots before venturing outside their monasteries, while demanding that nuns, even abbesses, obtain episcopal approval for such trips. With the promulgation of the *Institutio sanctimonialium,* the Council of Aachen (816) provided for strict cloistering of the canonesses whose lives it was designed to regulate.

Beginning in the eleventh century, new or reformed orders frequently mandated both active and passive enclosure for the religious women who wished to be officially associated with them. Initially reluctant to accept female affiliates, the Cistercians made strict enclosure (along with evidence of an endowment adequate to permit it) a precondition for incorporation. Cluniac, Premonstratensian, Franciscan, and Dominican nuns were also fully cloistered, and the rule of the Poor Clares actually contained a fourth vow, that of enclosure, tied to Clare's insistence on apostolic poverty and dependence on alms.

Influenced by these developments and the actions of his predecessors—both Pope Gregory IX and Pope Clement IV had assisted the Cistercians in achieving their goals of strict enclosure for nuns—Pope Boniface VIII issued his 1298 decree *Pericoloso*. This was the first universal cloister regulation and it encompassed all nuns of every order throughout Christian Europe. By mandating strict active and passive enclosure for women—nuns—who had solemnly professed their vows in a recognized religious order, Boniface VIII seems to have wished to draw a clear distinction between women who were "religious" in the legal sense of the term and the ever-growing numbers of unofficial *mulieres religiosae,* such as Beguines.

Because it was the first instance of papal legislation on the matter, and because it set a standard for enclosure of nuns without parallel for male monastics, generations of church historians had regarded *Pericoloso* as a turning point in the history of religious women. With its firm restrictions on both exit from and entrance into monastic precincts, *Pericoloso* was viewed as having provided the proverbial mortar for cloister walls that, however much some churchmen might have desired otherwise, had remained up to that point unstable and easily breached. Although a few modern scholars, most notably Eileen Power, observed that nuns sometimes defied papal policy when bishops sought to enforce *Pericoloso*, these scholars did so without imperiling the traditional narrative, which posited a straight line of "progress" from flexible local prerogative to the acceptance of universal enclosure. As late as 1968, the most comprehensive English-language treatment of the subject still supported this view: "For the first time in the history of the Church, the cloister was imposed as a universal obligation by the Holy See itself and worded in vigorous terms so as to allow no exceptions to the rule" (Cain 1968, p. 267).

Only in the last decades have historians begun to question the largely untested assumption that prescriptive legislation easily translated into common practice. When examining the testimony of bishops who sought to enforce *Pericoloso*, or of canonists who interpreted it, they found evidence that the decree was neither immediately nor universally accepted. So, too, did numerous instances of objections to, or formal exemption from, its regulations emerge from studies of the archives of specific communities.

It now seems clear that, although *Pericoloso*, with its sweeping provisions and grand scope, continued to influence both the reformers who attempted to bring practice into line with its demands and nuns themselves (all new orders for women founded between 1300 and 1500 wrote cloister regulations into their rules) throughout the late Middle Ages, it did so in the teeth of substantial resistance. The traditional image of nuns passively acquiescing to this papal initiative is simply not supported by the evidence. To gauge the impact of Boniface's decree in the fourteenth and fifteenth centuries, scholars must now consider the dynamics of the legislative process, including attempts to obstruct the law and, even more importantly, the reasons for those attempts. And because *Periculoso* was restated with much more far-reaching effect in the twenty-fifth session of the reforming Council of Trent (1563), researchers must also attempt to ascertain the mechanisms by which the decree was kept before the eyes of ecclesiastical lawmakers despite the difficulties surrounding its enforcement.

ELIZABETH MAKOWSKI

References and Further Reading

Cain, James R. "Cloister and the Apostolate of Religious Women." *Review for Religious* 27.2 (1968): 243–280.

Gill, Katherine. "*Scandala*: Controversies Concerning *Clausura* and Women's Religious Communities in Late Medieval Italy." In *Christianity and Its Discontents*, edited by Scott Waugh and Peter Diehl. Cambridge: Cambridge University Press, 1996, pp. 177–203.

Harline, Craig. "Actives and Contemplatives: The Female Religious of the Low Countries before and after Trent." *The Catholic Historical Review* 89, 4 (1995): 541–567.

Makowski, Elizabeth. *Canon Law and Cloistered Women: Periculoso and Its Commentators 1298–1545.* Washington, D.C.: The Catholic University of America Press, 1997.

Schulenburg, Jane Tibbetts. "Strict Active Enclosure and Its Effects on the Female Monastic Experience ca. 500–1100." In *Distant Echoes: Medieval Religious Women*, edited by J. A. Nichols and L. T. Shank. Kalamazoo, Mich.: Cistercian Publications, 1984, pp. 51–86.

See also **Architecture, Monastic; Beguines; Canonesses; Cistercian Order; Cluniac Order; Dominican Order; Law, Canon; Monastic Visitation; Monasticism and Nuns; Poor Clares Order; Premonstratensian Order**

MONASTIC RULES

All medieval religious, male and female, took vows of poverty, chastity, and obedience upon entering monastic life. These vows, known as the three "substantial vows," are the heart of medieval monastic life, a way of life by definition governed by a rule. Furthermore, once professed, monks and nuns alike organized their lives around a routine of divine service, with masses and prescribed prayers, readings, and hymns set for the canonical hours. Despite this core of similarity, the particular rule followed by members of a religious order, and the different emphases in interpreting and enforcing rules for male and female members of an order, resulted in a variety of distinct monastic cultures.

In Latin Christianity, the standardization of a monastic rule for women began in some respects with the letters of Augustine of Hippo, who, around 423, addressed precepts and codes of conduct to the nunnery governed by his sister. This, and other writings often attributed to him (although in fact authored by others), formed the basis of the Augustinian rule that was so widely accepted in the Middle Ages. These texts also influenced other creators of monastic rules, including Benedict of Nursia.

The Benedictines

While Augustine's writing played a key role in the development of medieval monastic rules for both women and men, the first complete monastic rule in widespread use in the West was that of Benedict. The Benedictine rule was perhaps the most influential in medieval Europe; indeed, from the mid-sixth century through the early twelfth, monastic life was almost exclusively governed by the Benedictine rule. The Benedictine tradition stresses that the rule is not gender specific. In fact, however, beginning with reform movements in the eighth century, different versions of the Benedictine rule emerged for monks and nuns.

Vernacular translations of the Benedictine rule for women highlight the ways in which the rule was transformed ideologically, as well as linguistically, for women. For instance, the Benedictine rule describes the abbot as holding the place of Christ in the monastery. John E. Crean, who has analyzed Middle High German translations of the rule for women, argues that the way in which this passage is treated is crucial. He notes that the translator's choices illustrate the way in which he perceives the abbess's role in the community. While the German translations that Crean analyzes all identify the abbess with Christ to some extent, the fifteenth-century English verse translation found in London (BL MS Cotton Vespasian A 25) does not grant the abbess such an endorsement of her authority.

During the Carolingian period, strict claustration (monastic enclosure) was imposed on Benedictine nuns, and claustration also emerged as another key difference in the construction of life under the Benedictine rule for nuns and monks. In later centuries claustration would come to be, in effect, a fourth substantial vow for Benedictine nuns. Indeed, claustration was a defining aspect of monastic life not only for nuns following the Benedictine rule but also for those in other religious orders.

The Benedictines underwent several waves of reforms, and in the process monastic orders that distinguished themselves from the main body of the Benedictines emerged (Carthusians, Cistercians, Cluniacs, the double order of the Gilbertines). Possibly foremost among these was the Cistercian Order, established in 1098 by Robert, abbot of Molesme, with the intention of returning to a literal observance of the Benedictine rule. Nuns were reluctantly accepted into the Cistercian reform movement; however, their houses frequently did not possess the special Cistercian privileges (such as exemption from episcopal visitation) enjoyed by male houses. Furthermore, in England, Cistercian houses are not consistently described in records as such; the same house is sometimes called Cistercian and other times Benedictine.

Men did not simply construct monastic life differently for Benedictine women in order to ensure male privileges or to emphasize female submission to male authority. They sometimes privileged women's authority. Early in the twelfth century Robert of Arbrissel founded the Order of Fontevrault, another reformed Benedictine order, specifically for women. In houses of this order, the abbess had supreme authority over nuns, priests, and lay brothers.

Women living under the supposedly gender-neutral Benedictine rule at times perceived their own experience of monastic life as differing by gender, for example, as Heloise's correspondence with Abelard reveals. Heloise requested, and received from Abelard, a modified version of the Benedictine rule for her community of the Paraclete. This version made changes targeted to women's bodily differences from men.

Women in the Mendicant Orders

The outward emphasis on gender neutrality that covered significant gender differences in the Benedictine tradition did not feature prominently in treatments of the rules in the Franciscan and Dominican orders. In these orders, the rules for women were strikingly different from those for men. Clare of Assisi and the nuns in her community of San Damiano were not permitted the mendicant life of the Franciscan friars. Although she managed to obtain a papal privilege of poverty, claustration was required from the beginning as the rule for Franciscan nuns. In fact, Cardinal Hugolino (later to become Pope Gregory IX) for a time imposed upon the nuns a rule based upon the Benedictine rule, an imposition that Clare strongly resisted and eventually overcame. As Regis Armstrong highlights, the differences in the discussions of claustration in Clare's *Rule* and the *Rule of Hugolino* are striking. While Hugolino only permits the nuns to leave enclosure to begin a new foundation, Clare allows nuns to leave the monastery for useful, approved purposes.

Clare was the first woman to write a rule for nuns; her rule gained papal approval two days prior to her death in 1253. In 1263, Pope Urban IV recognized the Poor Clares as a distinct monastic order. However, he did not grant all of them Clare's *Rule* or the privilege of poverty permitted to her foundation of San Damiano. He crafted a modified rule for Franciscan nuns, known as the Urbanist rule, which was enforced throughout Europe except in France and England. In these countries, Franciscan nuns, known as "Minoresses," followed a revised version of Clare's *Rule* made by Blessed Isabella, sister of Louis IX of France. This "Isabella Rule" emphasized the equality and distinctive identity of the Franciscan nuns and friars, although it did not include a commitment to the radical poverty so beloved by Clare.

Although Dominic de Guzman had himself established the first community of Dominican nuns at Prouille in the early thirteenth century, medieval Dominican nuns (often called canonesses) lived a life very different from that of the Friars Preachers. Naturally, given the prohibitions against female preaching in the medieval church, they did not participate in this practice so fundamental to the Order of Preachers. Living in strict claustration, they were subject to the Augustinian rule and, after 1259, to the Constitutions of the Sisters.

The Birgittines

In the last analysis, Birgitta of Sweden may be deemed more successful than Clare of Assisi in creating a monastic order for women that was true to her own ideals. The fourteenth-century Swedish noblewoman was directed by Christ in a revelation to found a new religious order, one designed first and primarily for women, in which the abbess would have authority over nuns and brothers. Birgitta thus faced the daunting task of gaining ecclesiastical sanction for a new double order, a form of monastic life that had long since been largely suppressed. The origins of the Birgittine rule, also called the *Rule of St. Savior*, in Birgitta's revelations, combined with the authority given to women by the rule, impeded the papal approval process. In 1370, Urban V issued a revised version of the rule that removed all indications that Christ dictated the rule to Birgitta and reduced the scope of the abbess's authority. Furthermore, to comply with the requirements of Lateran IV (1215) forbidding the founding of new orders, the Birgittine rule was given the official status of Constitutions to the *Rule of St. Augustine*.

The Birgittine rule prescribes a distinctive version of divine service for the nuns focusing on the Virgin Mary. The rule emphasizes poverty, strictly prohibiting the nuns from owning personal possessions (a prohibition specified by other monastic rules but one often modified in practice) but permitting nuns unlimited access to books. This specification reflects the high value placed on learning and study in the Birgittine order.

NANCY BRADLEY WARREN

References and Further Reading

Armstrong, Regis J., ed. and trans. *Clare of Assisi: Early Documents*. New York: Paulist Press, 1988.

Armstrong, Regis J., and Ignatius C. Brady, eds. and trans. *Francis and Clare: The Complete Works*. New York: Paulist Press, 1982.

Bourdillon, A. F. C. *The Order of Minoresses in England*. British Society of Franciscan Studies 12. Manchester: Manchester University Press, 1926.

Burton, Janet. *Monastic and Religious Orders in Britain, 1000–1300*. Cambridge: Cambridge University Press, 1994.

Crean, John E., Jr. "Voces Benedictinae: A Comparative Study of Three Manuscripts of the Rule of St. Benedict for Women." *Vox Benedictina* 10.1 (1993): 157–178.

Dreuille, Mayeul de. *Seeking the Absolute Love: the Founders of Christian Monasticism*. Herefordshire: Gracewing, and New York: Crossroads, 1999.

Elkins, Sharon K. *Holy Women of Twelfth-Century England*. Chapel Hill, N.C.: University of North Carolina Press, 1988.

Ellis, Roger. "Viderunt Eam Filie Syon:" *The Spirituality of the English House of a Medieval Contemplative Order from Its Beginnings to the Present Day*. Analecta Cartusiana 68. Salzburg: Institut für Anglistik und Amerikanistik Universität Salzburg, 1984.

Fry, Timothy, et al., eds. *RB 1980: The Rule of St. Benedict in Latin and English with Notes*. Collegeville, Minn.: Liturgical Press, 1981.

Internet Medieval Sourcebook: Selected Sources: High Medieval Church Life. http:www.fordham.edu/halsall/sbook1s.html (accessed June 2005).

Johnson, Penelope D. *Equal in Monastic Profession: Religious Women in Medieval France*. Chicago: University of Chicago Press, 1991.

Kerr, Berenice M. *Religious Life for Women, c.1100–c.1350: Fontevraud in England*. Oxford: Clarendon, 1999.

Knowles, Dom David. *The Monastic Orders in England: A History of Its Development from the Times of St. Dunstan to the Fourth Lateran Council 943–1216*. Cambridge: Cambridge University Press, 1950.

Kock, Ernst A. *Three Middle-English Versions of the Rule of St. Benet and Two Contemporary Rituals for the Ordination of Nuns*. Early English Text Society o.s. 120. 1902. Reprint, Millwood, N.Y.: Kraus, 1987.

Lawrence, C. H. *Medieval Monasticism: Forms of Religious Life in Western Europe in the Middle Ages*. London: Longman, 1984.

Matrix. http://monasticmatrix.usc.edu (accessed June 2005).

McNamara, Jo Ann. *Sisters in Arms: Catholic Nuns through Two Millennia*. Cambridge, Mass.: Harvard University Press, 1996.

Power, Eileen. *Medieval English Nunneries c. 1275 to 1535*. Cambridge: Cambridge University Press, 1922.

Sahlin, Claire L. *Birgitta of Sweden and the Voice of Prophecy*. Woodbridge, Suffolk: Boydell Press, 2001.

Warren, Nancy Bradley. *Spiritual Economies: Female Monasticism in Later Medieval England*. Philadelphia: University of Pennsylvania Press, 2001.

See also **Abbesses; Agnes of Prague; Augustine, Influence of; Birgitta of Sweden; Birgittine Order; Canonesses; Cistercian Order; Clare of Assisi; Cluniac Order; Dominican Order; Double Monasteries; Education, Monastic; Fontevrault, Abbey and Order of; Gilbertine Order; Heloise; Isabelle of France; Monastic Enclosure; Monastic Visitation; Monasticism and Nuns; Poor Clares Order; Poverty, Religious; Premonstratensian Order; Sister-Books and Other Convent Chronicles; Syon Abbey**

MONASTIC VISITATION

Visits to monasteries for purposes of oversight, correction of specific abuses, and, if indicated, general reformation, typically took one of two forms. Episcopal visitation, sometimes referred to as canonical, was conducted by a bishop exercising his right and discharging his duty as ordinary of his diocese. In certain religious orders, monastic superiors visited affiliated houses by mandate of the order's constitutions. In addition to these two common forms, visits could be made by archdeacons, archbishops, papal legates, and others directly empowered by the pope.

Periodic episcopal visitation as stipulated by the Council of Chalcedon (451) was enjoined time and again by early medieval synods and councils (Second Braga, 572, and Toledo, 633, for example), but there is little evidence of diocesan intervention, absent a profound disturbance, in the affairs of the largely isolated and autonomous monasteries of the period.

Canonical policy was incorporated into Carolingian imperial decrees, and in 906, Abbot Regino of Prüm included guidelines for episcopal visitors, complete with a questionnaire to be used when interrogating individual members of a community, in Book I of his *Libri duo de synodalibus causis et disciplinis ecclesiasticis (Two Books on Synodal causes and Ecclesiastical Disciplines)*.

Regino's procedural guide was incorporated into an influential canonical collection, the *Decretum* of Burchard, bishop of Worms (d. 1025), and with the further development of canon law a new spate of legislation highlighted the need for regular, usually annual, episcopal visits. By the thirteenth century, records of actual visits to monasteries began to be kept. One of the earliest surviving accounts was that of Archbishop

Eudes Rigaud (1248–1269), whose register for the diocese of Rouen includes *comperta* (questions the bishop asked to discover abuses) and injunctions (rulings for reform based on the bishop's findings) for fourteen houses of religious women. By the close of the thirteenth century, sixteen of the seventeen dioceses of England formally registered episcopal visitation, and there are almost three hundred surviving registers from the period prior to the Reformation. One of the most complete accounts of English monastic visitation to houses of male as well as female religious is found in the register of the fifteenth-century bishop William Alnwick of Lincoln. Registers also reveal conflicts over a bishop's right to visit, a famous example being the contest between Nicholas of Cusa, bishop of Brixen, and Verena, abbess of Sonnenburg.

At the same time that episcopal visitation procedures became more formalized, however, the number of religious houses claiming exemption from such visits, indeed from diocesan supervision *per se*, increased dramatically. Before the twelfth century, the privilege of exemption, which placed a monastery directly under papal authority and made visitation the exclusive right of a papal agent, had been obtained only by Cluniac monasteries and a handful of important Benedictine abbeys. In the thirteenth century, many individual houses, and all Cistercian, Dominican, and Franciscan houses, claimed exempt status. The uneasy and changeable relationship between the new male orders and those religious women who sought affiliation with them, however, made episcopal rather than internal visitation the norm for nuns, despite the exempt status of their male counterparts.

Visits to an exempt monastery were usually conducted by religious superiors within the order and proceeded according to the constitutions of that order. Documentation of such visits usually became part of the archive of the mother house. On occasion, visitors sanctioned by the pope undertook major reform efforts of exempt as well as nonexempt houses. Book II of the *liber de reformatione monasteriorum (Book on the Reformation of Monasteries)*, written by the Augustinian canon Johann Busch (1399–1419), recounts the efforts of one such visitor, who included some twenty-three women's houses among his reform efforts in Saxony.

As presented in episcopal registers, the diaries of extraordinary visitors, or exhaustive late medieval treatises on visitation, such as Joannes Franciscus de Pavinis' *De visitatione episcoporum (On the Visitation of Bishops)*, the procedures followed in monastic visitation and the injunctions issued at their close were usually gender-neutral. Yet there were some issues that arose more often in connection with nuns than with monks, especially in the later Middle Ages. Nuns

were commonly provided with injunctions, and even copies of their rule, in the vernacular rather than in an imperfectly understood Latin; women's houses were more often described as poorer or less well-managed than those of men; and nuns were more often reprimanded for having private property, including necklaces, gowns with fur collars, and other inappropriate attire. Perhaps most importantly, nuns were frequently charged with violation of the rules of strict enclosure—rules that did not exist for monks.

While much can be learned, and more inferred, from visitation records, they invariably reflect a single perspective, that of the visitor. Consequently, they must be used only in conjunction with charters, wills, cartularies, and other forms of documentation, both ecclesiastical and secular.

ELIZABETH MAKOWSKI

References and Further Reading

Carroll-Clark, Susan M. "Bad Habits: Clothing and Textile References in the Register of Eudes Rigaud, Archbishop of Rouen." *Medieval Clothing and Textiles* 1 (2005): 81–103.
Cheney, Christopher. R. *Episcopal Visitation of Monasteries in the Thirteenth Century.* Manchester: Manchester University Press, 1931.
Power, Eileen. *Medieval English Nunneries.* Cambridge: Cambridge University Press, 1922.
Tillotson, John H. "Visitation and Reform of the Yorkshire Nunneries in the Fourteenth Century." *Northern History* 30 (1994): 1–21.

See also **Monastic Enclosure; Monasticism and Nuns; Records, Ecclesiastical**

MONASTICISM AND NUNS

Monasticism is a regulated communal life embraced by women and men devoted to the contemplation, worship, and service of God and to the pursuit of their own spiritual perfection through asceticism, a program of mental and physical training, modeled on the training of an athlete. Renunciation of sexual activity (*encrateia*) as well as strict limitations on food, drink, rest, and other physical comforts and distractions works to enhance mental concentration and spiritual awareness. Monastic life centers around common meals, common property, and common prayer. This team structure supports the strivers and protects them from the temptations of idleness and indiscipline that often cause the downfall of solitary hermits.

Long before the early Christians began to form monastic communities, they appeared in other cultures, most notably Buddhism. The Buddha resisted the inclusion of women until his aunt persuaded him to admit them (sixth century BCE). He is said to have prophesied that, in the end, their presence would halve the order's perfection. Reluctance to recognize the claims of female lineages restricts the acceptance of their communities in many Buddhist areas even today. Jews traditionally resisted celibacy (the unmarried state) and employed polygamy to ensure every respectable woman a replacement for a husband who died before she had his children. Nevertheless, a number of Jesus's contemporaries set up encratic communities whose beliefs and regimes are recorded in the Dead Sea Scrolls. Most Essenes were men, but the Scrolls reveal the presence of women among them, generally thought to be the wives and daughters of the practitioners, presumably vowed to conform to the common ideals.

A few other ascetic communities of that period emerge from the sources. In Egypt, encratic men and women formed the *Therapeutae*, and in Rome a select handful of well-born virgins lived together and were entrusted with the care of the city hearth. These vestal virgins lived under the threat of execution if their chastity were polluted but were rewarded with extensive privileges and a very comfortable retirement when they reached the age of thirty or thereabouts. The Pauline letters, Christianity's earliest sources, reveal women resolved to live as virgins or to renounce sexual activity upon widowhood, a practice that the apostle viewed with considerable reserve, fearing that their failure to maintain their resolution would cause damage to the new religion's reputation.

Early Christian Communities

The developing church consistently resisted the enthusiasm of some of its members for the ascetic life and went so far as to condemn a group called Encratites as heretics because they maintained that all sexual activity was sinful. Nevertheless, groups of people throughout the Roman Empire embraced *encrateia*. Second- and third-century sources survive that contain regulations governing the activities of virgins and consecrated widows living in groups or in their own homes. They were repeatedly urged to be unpretentious, silent, and modest in demeanor; to keep out of the public gaze where possible; and to refrain from ostentatious religious displays during public worship. They undertook charitable activity, caring for the sick and training female catechumens. Most notably, they provided examples of Jesus' power as a divine presence in their steadfast resistance to torture and their stoicism in the face of death during periods of persecution. By the middle of the third century, Methodius systematically celebrated virginity as the Christian crown of a sexual hierarchy extending through chaste

widows and married people (with celibates who lapsed into sexual activity unmentioned but implicitly at the bottom of the ladder).

By the fourth century, *encrateia* was largely considered to be a feminine virtue and men like Ambrose and Jerome in the Latin West and Gregory of Nyssa and Athanasius in the Greek East enthusiastically maintained the superiority of Christian virgins and widows over the traditionally dominant *paterfamilias* of imperial Rome. They described wealthy women who used their homes as centers for prayer and study in the cities of its far-flung domain, notably the Cappadoccian community of women and men founded by Macrina, sister of Basil of Caesarea, who composed one of the most enduring of monastic rules. In the same period, other religious enthusiasts fled to the "deserts" in search of solitude and greater rigor, following the biblical examples of John the Baptist and Jesus himself. These were suburban areas, sparsely populated and lacking the amenities of urban life, but not by any means as isolated as monastic ideology generally implies. The sources tend to dwell on male hermits and communities, but there is occasional mention of female communities and a robust hagiographical tradition centered on women, like Marina, said to have lived successfully for many years in disguise in male communities. After studying their examples, Jerome's wealthy friend Paula and her daughter Eustochium supported a community of about two hundred women in Bethlehem, and such communities proliferated throughout the Roman world as the fourth century progressed.

None of these communities could have thrived without fairly rigorous regulation to control the abrasive effects of group life, individual self-indulgence, and the temptations always awaiting the idle mind. We have to assume that the serious desert-dwellers always abided by some accepted set of rules and were regulated by one or more supervisors. We should also assume that many of them fell short of their aspirations and that others were charlatans anxious to profit from the religious tourists who began to frequent these communities in the course of pilgrimages. Male monastics were prone to engage themselves in theological debates and occasionally erupted into the nearby cities to mount riotous demonstrations in favor of their opinions. Secular powers as well as monks themselves began to encourage restraint and regulation.

Autonomous Rules

The earliest surviving monastic rule is attributed to an Egyptian desert-dweller named Pachomius whose fame as a hermit had attracted a fairly large community of men and an ancillary community of women governed by his sister Mary, who lived across the river from the men. Setting an enduring example to his successors, Pachomius discouraged bizarre and excessive self-mortification in favor of regular common prayer and handiwork to give structure to the revolving days, warning particularly against accidia, the sin of spiritual sloth. Contact between the women and the men was strictly limited, and the women were sternly forbidden to speak to any man without the supervision of their mistress. A substantial literature grew up describing the virtues and practices of these ascetics, from which we learn that most of the women lived under lock and key, at least at night. Otherwise, the conditions of their lives and their spiritual achievements were equally praiseworthy. Among the most prized monastic virtues, humility and obedience were given pride of place—virtues more commonly gendered feminine than masculine. It was apparently viewed as more heroic for men than for women to attain these indicators of perfection, but this prejudice was offset by the idea that a woman required extraordinary strength to overcome the deficiencies of her sex.

By the end of the fourth century, monasticism had generated several other rules, notably one by Basil of Caesarea, which were in general use among growing numbers of independent communities. Popularized by Athanasius of Alexandria during his exile in Rome and by Martin of Tours, the exemplary monastic saint of Gaul, communities of monks and nuns began to appear throughout the Latin West, sharing a growing literature of advice, exemplary tales, and hagiography to embellish their house rules and standardize the powers of their superiors. Augustine of Hippo wrote a letter of advice to a community of nuns gathered around his sister that became the inspiration for the later rule that bore his name. In the early sixth century, Caesarius of Arles wrote the first women's rule for his sister Caesaria, whose community had been forced to take refuge in the city because of the incursions of marauding Visigoths. He introduced the requirement for strict claustration from the public that would come to be the central characteristic of women's monasticism for many centuries to come. Caesaria's is also the first known monastic community to support itself by the production of books.

By the end of the sixth century and the early seventh, the Greek East and the Latin West were drifting in different directions. Monasticism continued to be an intrinsic part of the Byzantine church and the Slavic churches that received Christianity under its aegis. However, the continued authority of the empire restricted its autonomy and public activity. In the West, where agricultural settlement, Christian missionizing, and the organization of secular and ecclesiastical hierarchies moved north, west, and east simultaneously, monasticism proved to be an invaluable instrument. Missionaries worked from monastic bases, and their new converts enthusiastically endowed foundations for women and men alike where new missionaries and a Christian ruling class were educated. Settlements surrounded the foundations, and they soon became wealthy economic centers. Abbots and abbesses drawn from royal and noble families performed the tasks of secular government, as well as spiritual services for the surrounding countryside. Wealthy communities of women, like Jouarre in northern France, acted as landlords and even supplied military service when needed.

Autonomous houses were free to make their own rules within a generally accepted framework. They were generally conceded to be answerable to episcopal authority, but friction often developed, and, in some places, there was no effective counter-authority. In some areas, abbots were traditionally appointed as bishops while abbesses performed many of the jurisdictional tasks of bishops without their sacramental authority. Gradually, shared experience produced a handful of dominant rules, and many houses simply combined their elements, as demonstrated by Donatus of Besançon's rule for his mother's foundation. The Rule of Columbanus, brought from Ireland to Gaul in the seventh century, emphasized a penitential spirituality aimed at perfecting monastic humility. It organized the liturgical exercises into a yearly round of psalm-chanting that constituted a chain of perpetual praise visualized as a rampart for embattled Christianity. Columbanus' was commonly combined with the Benedictine rule, outlining a simple but rigorous life of prayer and manual labor, regulating diet, rest, prayer, and other human activities. Benedict introduced the rule of stability, intended to put an end to the wanderings of footloose monks. This rule was energetically promoted by Gregory I, who saw no contradiction in sending monks on far-flung travels in the cause of converting new peoples to Christianity in its Roman form.

Most monastic communities were to some degree or another syneisactic (encompassing women and men together in encratic partnerships). The term *double monastery*, long popular among monastic historians, has recently been abandoned by some scholars in recognition of this fact. Benedict discouraged monks from being ordained to the priesthood. The sacraments took a distant second place to the daily offices in their spiritual lives, though both men and women monastics generally supported some clergymen to administer them. Other men were normally attached in varying numbers to women's communities, and male monasteries seem commonly to have taken groups of devout women who served them in various capacities under their spiritual protection. Neither rule was modified by sex. *Encrateia* was regarded as the highest level of spiritual perfection, setting monastic women and men above the sexually active clergy and laity, almost as a third gender. At that rarefied level, a general assumption of equality prevailed, though the sexes were never encouraged to interact without the most rigid precautions.

Imperial Regulation

With the rise of the Carolingian empire, secular authority again sought to assert itself over monastic wealth and persons. The missionary monk/bishop Boniface collaborated with Charlemagne on a series of reforms, and several bishops worked with Louis the Pious to impose a uniform framework on the monastic world. The reforming councils of Aachen (813) and Chalons (816) subjected all religious women and men to one or two rules. The Benedictine rule was preferred for most houses, but an alternative choice was offered in rules for canons and canonesses based on a rule attributed to Augustine that had been gaining popularity among communities responsible for the diocesan work of cathedrals. The rule for canonesses recognized the liturgical responsibilities of women attached to cathedral chapters. Like canons, these women continued to own their own property, though they were encouraged not to busy themselves in its administration. They may have been free to leave the community and marry; but, while active, they were obligated to live the common life and observe the strictest *encrateia*. The council attempted to impose claustration upon them, but the practice was never seriously implemented. Canonesses were particularly educated in music and ancillary arts to enhance their liturgical performances. Dramatic performances also entered the tradition at least by the tenth century, when the plays of Hrotsvit of Gandersheim were produced, probably for an audience drawn from the court of her relative, the Emperor Otto I.

Individual women's monasteries appear to have veered back and forth between the Benedictine and Augustinian rules, perhaps in a deliberate attempt to confuse male ecclesiastical authorities who presented themselves as enforcers. Meanwhile, from the late eighth century on, monasteries shared the sufferings of Europe in general under the onslaught of Nordic, Saracen, and Slavic marauders along coasts, rivers, and the eastern plains. Their wealth and vulnerability attracted these predators repeatedly, and many communities were destroyed or dispersed. This is generally held to be the cause of female monasticism's decline in this period. Many famous old female houses disappeared or emerged in later times as male houses. We should note, however, that many of these monasteries have no recorded history after their foundations, and their destruction or transfer into male hands may have an entirely different chronology and meaning.

"Reform"

By the tenth century, despite the violence of the age, intense monastic revivals and reforms were under way. Cluny in Burgundy pioneered a movement aimed at freedom from the "corrupting" influence of episcopal authority and secular patronage through subjection to Saint Peter (Rome) alone. They presented themselves as penitents particularly equipped to shoulder some of the burden of sin incurred by more worldly Christians (laity, secular clergy, and, ultimately, women). They promoted a complex round of spiritual exercises, particularly masses for the dead, to achieve these ends, and this began a process of clericizing the male monastic movement, which would separate monks and nuns and free the former to seize upon whatever claims to superiority accrued to the ordained clergy.

The reformers welcomed new foundations and reformed old foundations that had thrown off the patronage rights of their secular founders. They boasted an uncompromising rejection of women's communities, inescapably branding the most exemplary women's communities as spiritually inferior. Informally they often allied themselves with noble women who patronized their movement and did not discourage them from forming small dependent female communities in their penumbra. Their rhetoric, however, intensified the misogyny that always underlay the warmest relationships between women and men. Ultimately, Cluny would relent and allow a solitary female community, Marcigny, to be attached to its ranks, but its ninety-nine places were strictly reserved for the relatives and protegées of the clerical elite, and the women had to submit to such severe cloistering that their highest claim to praise was willingness to remain in the building when a fire was threatening to destroy them all. Marcigny had no abbess. The hundredth and highest place was reserved for the Virgin Mary.

As monks moved apart from women and embraced ordination, a form of religious reform spread among the secular clergy aiming to free the priesthood from secular authority by monasticizing them. Ecclesiastical property was to be freed from all claims by the original patrons and donors to name church officers and from all personal claims by imposing celibacy on all priests, ensuring that their widows and children had no legitimate rights of inheritance. The result was a thorough reorganization of the entire church hierarchy under the leadership of the pope in Rome. The Christian social order was divided rigorously between clergy and laity, and all women (including nuns) were locked into the laity. The "church" was redefined as a homosocial male monopoly that vaulted into the leadership of a newly mature civilization whose growing cities were soon to boast universities training a whole new cohort of professional men drawn from its celibate ranks. Even the military order was soon to be challenged by celibate monks who formed the front ranks of the new crusading armies.

Monastic Orders

Monasticism met these modern challenges by the formation of orders, coalitions of communities sharing a common rule, habit, and privileges with a governing superstructure. With only a few exceptions, these orders resisted the incorporation of women and tried to repudiate the spiritual direction (*cura*) of women on the grounds that monks were ill equipped to withstand the power of sexual temptation if forced into proximity with the female sex. The Fontevrault, Gilbertine, and Premonstratensian orders tried to solve the problem by cloistering the women so rigorously that, among the Gilbertines, a stone had to be passed through the partition to accept the kiss of peace from one side to the other. Women's limited participation in chapter meetings was hedged with protections for the men, and the authority of the abbess of Fontevrault (whose constitution placed her in charge of the order) suffered ongoing revolts from the monks in the community. Nevertheless, women's houses adopted the name and customs of every order. More commonly, episcopal visitors found throughout the Middle Ages that nunneries often mixed rules, habits, and claims of affiliation almost randomly—presumably to gain tactical advantages in their continuing struggles for recognition, donations, and spiritual achievement.

In the High Middle Ages, women's houses commonly continued the earlier pattern of adhering to the Benedictine or the Augustinian rule under episcopal authority rather than trying to incorporate into an order with papal exemptions. Though the resistance of the orders received the most notice in the records, women religious may have preferred a local authority for a variety of reasons. Twelfth-century centers for female learning like Bingen and Hohenbourg, whose abbesses, Hildegard and Herrad, were distinguished authors, could compete successfully for donations and defend their position against clerical encroachment. Regional studies have begun to show that female communities tended to cultivate ties to local patrons—often their own families—and serve the needs of local communities. They lacked the global vision and global opportunities enjoyed by their male counterparts, but this may well have been offset by a sense of their importance in a more intimate environment.

Among the laity, women were often leaders in enthusiastic religious movements of penitents and reformers seeking to address the growing problems of poverty in the burgeoning capitalist economy. They formed encratic communities devoted to care of the sick and other social rejects and simple preaching among the largely unchurched urban masses. These were often syneisactic at their origins, embracing poverty through self-support, begging, and manual labor. By the thirteenth century, the mania for ordering all religious expression again separated the women from the men, and men, such as the Franciscan and Dominican friars, sought to exclude women from their ranks or at least to limit them to cloistered communities. Clare of Assisi fought a lifelong battle to maintain her original vocation to Franciscan poverty despite the prohibition on public activity and begging imposed on her and her sisters by both Francis and the pope.

All of the orders, however, had a tendency to channel the physical labors of charity to women, either ancillary nuns or lay *conversae* (women not fully consecrated to religious life). Some women persevered in the vocation by pursuing their social missions in quasi-religious communities like the beguinages. Many more lived consecrated lives under episcopal authority in their own homes or in small communities of two or three persons.

Through the course of the twelfth and thirteenth centuries, much of the spiritual experience of women channeled into displays of mysticism, and a large number of books appeared recording their revelations. Female mysticism frequently offset male monopoly of the sacraments with eucharistic visions and devotions centered on reception rather than confection of the body and blood of Christ. Male devotion frequently followed Bernard of Clairvaux's bridal imagery drawn from the Song of Songs to describe the soul's union with Christ. Women, on the other hand, commonly identified with Jesus himself, offering their own bodies to share in his atoning sufferings. In 1295,

Pope Boniface VIII imposed strict claustration on all religious women regardless of their original vocations, but the move was never very successfully enforced.

The Late Middle Ages

By the fourteenth century, the apogee of papal power had passed, and in a time of turmoil women like Catherine of Siena and Birgitta of Sweden found scope for their prophetic authority. Birgitta was able to found and spread the first order under a rule devised by a woman (by way of visions from Jesus). Her decision to cloister her daughters closely with an ancillary community of men in their service strongly indicates that this aspect of the female religious tradition has never been solely a product of male misogyny.

During the fifteenth century, Europe enjoyed an economic and political revival after the disasters of the fourteenth, and the monasteries were reviving and renewing themselves. Papal commissions and chapters of various orders enacted sweeping reform legislation backed up by traveling enforcers entering individual houses. Individual communities of women had mixed reactions. Presumably a lot of them quietly adhered to their rules or reformed themselves without making a mark in the records. Colette of Corbie was notable as a consecrated female mystic who personally directed a widespread reform of Franciscan communities that ultimately broke away as a separate order. In other cases, the male reformers were greeted as unwelcome intruders into the women's lives who showed little understanding of the delicate web of relationships and mutual services that governed their lives. Many communities showed a united front in resisting the demands of reformers that they change their costumes, diets, and liturgies, submitting to claustration and male authority. One convent ejected their reformer by throwing him into a nearby river.

On the whole, however, reform carried the day. By the end of the fifteenth century, individual houses and entire orders had been brought under new or revived disciplines. The typical monastic practices of common meals and common clothing, shared ownership, and individual poverty, and an unending routine of manual labor and prayer, silence, and psalm-singing prevailed. Most monastic women had submitted to claustration and learned to love it. When Henry VIII's royal commissioners went looking for wayward nuns in early-sixteenth-century England, they found embarrassingly little to report. Martin Luther denounced the principles of monastic spirituality at the start of the Protestant Reformation, complaining that its practices were not efficacious though they were

scrupulously carried out. He spoke for a body of Christians who no longer believed that the heroic sacrifices of one group could contribute to the salvation of another, more sinful group. In fact, he continued to approve the encratic communal life of the great canoness institutes for respectable noble women, while encouraging all other Christians to submit to the humbler family virtues of the world of work and worry. In Germany, England, and Scandinavia, communities of women fought fiercely to defend the reformed way of life they had embraced in the fifteenth century. Whole communities fled to more hospitable countries rather than forsake it.

In the Catholic world, the reform impetus continued, among contemplative religious, most notably with the institution of the discalced Carmelites under the guidance of Teresa of Avila. The advent of the modern world for them was dramatically marked by the struggle and eventual success of religious women in enlarging their sphere of public activity, most notably in the areas of social service and teaching. For the modern age the term *monasticism* is technically applied to the contemplative orders of nuns who continue to live in stable and relatively cloistered communities centered upon the common life and continual prayer and meditation, while women engaged in public services are officially designated as "sisters" or congregations of sisters.

Jo Ann McNamara

References and Further Reading

Berman, Constance. *The Cistercian Evolution: The Invention of a Religious Order in Twelfth-Century Europe.* Philadelphia: University of Pennsylvania Press, 2000.

Elliott, Dyan. *Proving Women: Female Spirituality and Inquisitional Culture in the Later Middle Ages.* Princeton, N.J.: Princeton University Press, 2004.

Foot, Sarah. *Veiled Women,* 2 vols. Brookfield, Vt.: Ashgate, 2000.

Gertrude of Helfta. *The Spiritual Exercises,* translated by Gertrud Jaron Lewis and Jack Lewis. Kalamazoo, Mich.: Cistercian Publications, 1992.

Gilchrist, Roberta. *Gender and Material Culture: The Archaeology of Religious Women.* London: Routledge, 1994.

Golding, Brian. *Gilbert of Sempringham and the Gilbertine Order, c. 1130–1300.* Oxford: Oxford University Press, 1995.

Gregory of Nyssa. *Ascetical Works: On Virginity, Life of Saint Macrina; On the Soul and Resurrection,* translated by Virginia W. Callahan. Fathers of the Church 58. Washington, D.C.: Catholic University of America Press, 1966.

Hamburger, Jeffrey F. *Nuns as Artists: The Visual Culture of a Medieval Convent.* Berkeley: University of California Press, 1997.

Harrison, Dick. *The Age of Abbesses and Queens: Gender and Political Culture in Early Medieval Europe.* Lund: Nordic Academic Press, 1998.

Hildegard of Bingen. *Explanation of the Rule of Benedict*, translated by Hugh Feiss. Toronto: Peregrina, 2000.

Hrotsvit of Gandersheim. *Plays*, translated by Christopher St. John. New York: Benjamin Blom, 1966.

Jerome. *Letter 108, To Eustochium: Memorial of Paula*, translated by W. H. Fremantle. Nicene and Post-Nicene Fathers 6. Grand Rapids, Mich.: Eerdmans, 1979, pp. 189–195.

Lewis, Gertrud Jaron. *By Women, for Women, about Women: The Sister-Books of Fourteenth Century Germany*. Toronto: PIMS, 1996.

McNamara, Jo Ann. *Sisters in Arms: Catholic Nuns through Two Millennia*. Cambridge, Mass.: Harvard University Press, 1996.

McNamara, Jo Ann, and John E Halborg, with Gordon Whatley. *Sainted Women of the Dark Ages*. Durham, N.C.: Duke University Press, 1992.

Methodius. *The Symposium: A Treatise on Chastity*, translated by Herbert Musurilla. Ancient Christian Writers 27. Westminster, Md.: The Newman Press, 1958.

Oliva, Marilyn. *The Convent and the Community in Late Medieval England*. Woodbridge, Suffolk: Boydell and Brewer, 1998.

Schulenberg, Jane Tibbets, *Forgetful of Their Sex: Female Sanctity and Society, ca. 500–1100*. Chicago: University of Chicago Press, 1998.

Smith, Julie Ann. *Ordering Women's Lives: Penitentials and Nunnery Rules in the Early Medieval West*. Aldershot: Ashgate, 2001.

Venarde, Bruce L., *Women's Monasticism and Medieval Society: Nunneries in France and England, 890–1215*. Ithaca, N.Y.: Cornell University Press, 1997.

See also **Abbesses; Almsgiving and Charity; Augustine, Influence of; Birgitta of Sweden; Birgittine Order; Bride of Christ: Imagery; Canonesses; Catherine of Siena; Cistercian Order; Clare of Assisi; Cluniac Order; Colette of Corbie; Conversae and Conversi; Devotional Literature; Dominican Order; Education, Monastic; Fontevrault, Abbey and Order of; Gilbertine Order; Hagiography; Herrad of Hohenbourg; Hildegard of Bingen; Hrotsvit of Gandersheim; Jerome, Influence of; Leoba; Monastic Enclosure; Monastic Rules; Monastic Visitation; Monasticism and Nuns, Byzantine; Monasticism and Nuns, Celtic; Monasticism, Women's: Papal Policy; Mystics' Writings; Patronage, Ecclesiastical; Poor Clares Order; Poverty, Religious; Premonstratensian Order; Sister-Books and Other Convent Chronicles; Spiritual Care; Tertiaries; Virgin Martyrs; Virginity; Virile Women**

MONASTICISM AND NUNS, BYZANTINE

The development of female monasteries in the eastern Mediterranean world paralleled that of their male counterparts. Women were attracted to the monastic life as early as the fourth century. In Egypt, in the first half of the fourth century, Pachomios established a nunnery for women at Tabennisi that is said to have housed 400 women, while the nuns at Shenoute's fifth-century monastic complex at the White Monastery numbered 1,800. These monasteries were cenobitic, that is, the nuns lived in a community, went to services and meals as a group, and obeyed a superior. Female anchorites were rare, but not unknown. In Palestine, female monasteries seem to have been primarily an urban phenomenon, such as the nunnery founded on Jerusalem's Mount of Olives in the early fifth century by Melania the Younger, a Roman matron. The Judean desert monasteries were exclusively male, although the occasional female hermit (e.g., St. Mary of Egypt, Synkletike) is attested to. Makrina (c. 327–379/380), the older sister of Basil of Caesarea (an influential figure in the development of Byzantine monastic regulations), took vows of celibacy in her early teens and encouraged her family to establish in their house a monastery for men and women, the earliest known nunnery in Anatolia. During the fifth and sixth centuries, nunneries began to be founded in Constantinople and Greece; they tended to be most numerous in major cities such as the capital and Thessalonike. Nunneries were forbidden on Mt. Athos and severely restricted on other holy mountains.

Monastic rules (*typika*) survive for only six nunneries; their evidence can be supplemented by information from the *vitae* of female saints. The monastery was headed by an abbess, assisted by a steward (who might be male or female) and various officials, such as the cellarer and sacristan. The nuns were divided into two groups, the literate choir sisters responsible for chanting the monastic offices, and the housekeeping nuns who performed manual labor to meet the material needs of the institution. Nunneries varied greatly in size, averaging around twenty to thirty members, although one fourteenth-century female monastery housed one hundred nuns. Women took monastic vows at various ages, some as teenagers (the minimum age was sixteen), others in later life, often after being widowed or in old age. The novitiate varied between six months and three years, depending on the maturity of the novice. Women were inspired to take the monastic habit for many reasons, such as a genuine desire for a consecrated life of prayer and enhanced opportunity for salvation, or more mundane reasons, such as material support in one's declining years. Although gifts at the time of entrance into the monastery were encouraged by some houses and discouraged by others, many nuns made substantial donations of cash and real property, such as estates, books, and works of liturgical art, in order to provide for their maintenance and ensure proper burial and commemoration in perpetuity. Additional financial support was provided by lay patrons, who often requested burial within the monastery walls and annual memorial services in return. Some nuns lived in double monasteries, institutions that housed separate communities of men and women, directed by a single superior, sometimes an abbess. Such establishments were forbidden by the Second Council of Nicaea in 787, but they reappear in the Palaiologan period (thirteenth to fifteenth centuries).

Many nunneries were founded by aristocratic patrons to ensure the admission of female family members and the burial and commemoration of relatives. Although in theory nuns who took monastic vows were supposed to break all family ties, it is clear that many female monastics enjoyed the company of kinswomen in the cloister, brought maidservants from home, received visits from male and female relatives, and could attend the sickbeds or funerals of family members.

Like male monasteries, some nunneries performed important social services, especially the distribution of food, wine, and money to beggars at the gate. They had hostels to provide lodging for pilgrims and travelers, and, very rarely, small hospitals to treat lay patients. They might take in orphan girls as well as women who were refugees from enemy invasion, abused by their husbands, suffering from mental illness, or in abject poverty.

There were some notable differences between male and female monastic houses. Female monasteries had to bring in male priests to celebrate the liturgy, male doctors to care for the sick, and often male bailiffs to supervise the monastic estates. There also seems to have been little opportunity for nuns to engage in artistic or intellectual pursuits; only a handful are known to have worked as scribes or authors, and most occupied themselves primarily with spinning and weaving, in addition to their assigned housekeeping duties. Nuns also tended to live in cenobitic establishments, although a few female hermits and stylites (dwellers atop columns) are attested to from the fourth to eleventh centuries; thereafter the nuns for whom we have firm evidence all lived a communal life in monasteries.

The traditions of Byzantine female monasticism continued during the centuries of Ottoman Turkish occupation of the Balkans and Anatolia, although some nunneries fell into decline and were abandoned. There has been a remarkable upsurge in the numbers of Orthodox nuns in Greece in recent decades; several groups of nuns have successfully revived male monasteries that had been deserted or were in severe decline.

ALICE-MARY TALBOT

References and Further Reading

Connor, Carolyn L. *Women of Byzantium*. New Haven, Conn.: Yale University Press, 2004.

Petersen, Joan M. *Handmaids of the Lord: Contemporary Descriptions of Feminine Asceticism in the First Six Christian Centuries*. Kalamazoo, Mich.: Cistercian Publications, 1996.

Talbot, Alice-Mary, ed. *Holy Women of Byzantium: Ten Saints' Lives in English Translation*. Washington, D.C.: Dumbarton Oaks, 1996.

———. *Women and Religious Life in Byzantium*. Aldershot: Ashgate, 2001.

Thomas, John, and Angela C. Hero, eds. *Byzantine Monastic Foundation Documents*. 5 vols. Washington, D.C.: Dumbarton Oaks, 2000.

See also **Byzantium; Monasticism and Nuns**

MONASTICISM AND NUNS, CELTIC

While women in early medieval Celtic areas of Ireland, Scotland, Cornwall, Wales, and Brittany were enthusiastic converts to religious life, there were always fewer monastic houses for women than there were for men. Although there has been considerable debate over the existence and characteristics of a medieval Celtic church in the early medieval period (c. 500–1100), there were some commonalities in the monasticism practiced in the Celtic areas, including asceticism, local monastic rules, and a degree of isolation from policies and doctrines of Rome, as well as strong connections between monasteries and secular rulers.

Ireland has the best-known and best-documented medieval monasteries; however, there were also nunneries and holy women elsewhere in the Celtic areas. For the early medieval period, most of the evidence for the existence of nunneries comes from hagiography and place names. While this evidence is very important, some of the nunneries indicated in these sources may in fact have been very small, possibly only lasting for one woman's lifetime or to be evidence of veneration of women saints rather than location of houses for women. The use of continental monastic rules, such as those of the Benedictines, Cistercians, and Augustinians, became common in Celtic areas only after the twelfth century.

In Scotland, religious foundations for women are particularly poorly documented and did not survive to the twelfth century, when there was an upswing in monastic foundations by the native elite that saw the establishment of at least eleven nunneries, all following continental rules. Few of these houses survived the turbulent Anglo-Scottish conflicts of the fourteenth century. The Augustinian nunnery at Iona, established in the early thirteenth century, is the best-known exception, and there are substantial physical remains of this nunnery.

While Welsh hagiography mentions early medieval female saints, such as Gwenfrewy, living as a nun, communities of Welsh women religious did not survive into the later medieval period, when there were only three Welsh nunneries, all using continental rules—the Benedictine priory at Usk, and the Cistercian houses at Llanllugan and Llanllyr. The paucity of evidence of women's religious activities is particularly acute in Cornwall, where hagiography only suggests that there was a monastery associated with a holy woman called Sitofolla in the ninth century.

In Ireland the sources for women's religious activity are better, but this evidence cannot be used with confidence for the other Celtic areas. Both women and men were enthusiastic converts to Christianity when it arrived in Ireland with missionaries during the fifth century. Patrick, one of these early missionaries, records that large numbers of women and men flocked to renounce the world and join the church as monks and nuns. The religious communities they lived in were usually small rural settlements that housed either lay families or tenants of the monastery, as well as priests, nuns, and monks. The construction of stone buildings around a central cloister was not known in Ireland for either male or female religious houses until after the twelfth century and was associated with the introduction of the continental monastic rules. One of the most important women's religious houses established in the early phase of Irish monasticism was that of Bridget of Kildare, founded in the late fifth century. She established a prosperous community that enjoyed vital secular support from first the Fothairt family and then Leinster's Uí Dúnlainge dynasty, enabling it to survive and thrive throughout the early medieval period.

Irish monastic rules and ideas spread in the sixth century to Iona in Scotland with Columba and then to the continent with Columbanus. The only surviving Irish-based nunnery rule is that of Columbanus. This rule was more a guide for spiritual well-being than a day-to-day rule and importantly did not require enclosure away from lay society. It is unknown whether Columbanus' rule was based on nunnery rules from other Celtic regions; however, there are similarities between the life it outlines and what is known of life in Irish nunneries of the early medieval period.

After the twelfth century in Ireland, reforming Gaelic Irish bishops and kings, as well as incoming Anglo-Norman leaders, encouraged the spread of continental religious rules for both men and women. The Augustinian Rule was unusually popular in Irish nunneries, probably because it allowed connections between houses and surrounding lay communities as well as a greater degree of autonomy to individual monasteries. In Ireland, many nunneries continued until the Reformation and the general dissolution of monastic houses in the 1540s, when they were disbanded.

DIANNE HALL

References and Further Reading

Bitel, Lisa. *Land of Women: Tales of Sex and Gender from Early Ireland.* Ithaca, N.Y.: Cornell University Press, 1996.

Cartwright, Jane. "The Desire to Corrupt: Convents and Community in Medieval Wales." In *Medieval Women in Their Communities*, edited by Diane Watt. Cardiff: Cardiff University Press, 1997, pp. 20–48

Davies, Wendy. "The Myth of the Celtic Church." In *The Early Church in Wales and the West*, edited by N. Edwards and A. Lane. Oxbow Monographs 16. Oxford: Oxbow, 1992, pp. 12–21.

Hall, Dianne. *Women and the Church in Medieval Ireland, c. 1140–1540.* Dublin: Four Courts Press, 2003.

Harrington, Christina. *Women in a Celtic Church: Ireland 450–1150.* Oxford: Oxford University Press, 2002.

McDonald, R. Andrew. "The Foundation and Patronage of Nunneries by Native Elites in Twelfth- and Early Thirteenth Century Scotland." In *Women in Scotland, c. 1100–c. 1750*, edited by Elizabeth Ewan and Maureen M. Meikle. East Linton: Tuckwell Press, 1999, pp. 3–15.

Olsen, Lynette. *Early Monasteries in Cornwall.* Woodbridge, Suffolk: Boydell Press, 1989.

See also **Abbesses; Architecture, Monastic; Asceticism; Brigit; Hagiography; Ireland; Monastic Enclosure; Monastic Rules; Monasticism and Nuns; Scotland; Wales**

MONASTICISM, WOMEN'S: PAPAL POLICY

500–1100

From the time it was introduced to the West, women's monasticism was of concern to the papacy. Popes founded monasteries for women, extended their protection to them, and intervened in disputes concerning temporal holdings and jurisdiction. The letters of the first monk to become a pope, Gregory I, also known as "The Great," provide early and ample evidence of this sort of papal activity.

Written between 590 and 640, Pope Gregory's letters display his abiding interest in the endowment and stability of female institutions. He prompted the wealthy to bequeath money and even private homes to communities of religious women, ordered bishops to consecrate new foundations, made gifts of relics to houses threatened by poverty, and intervened when nuns faced illegal episcopal or secular interference. Tempering his enthusiasm for the religious life with pastoral pragmatism, the pope assisted a woman who had been cloistered against her will, and cautioned married aspirants against unilateral entrance into a monastery.

Many of Pope Gregory I's efforts on behalf of nuns were made at the request of wealthy aristocratic women, and his successors continued to accommodate the needs and desires of such petitioners and their families. Those desires, in turn, often centered on obtaining privileges of exemption from episcopal control. Limitation of royal prerogatives and usurpations by local potentates were also concerns, to judge from papal letters such as that of Pope John VIII to Charles the Bald (877) requesting the return of land unjustly seized from the ancient and important female monastery of St. Salvatore/St. Giulia in northern Italy.

In the tenth century, aristocratic laity, rather than popes, tended to found women's monasteries, but the papacy continued the tradition of gift-giving to established communities. Grants of papal immunity and protection took on new significance in the stormy era of the Investiture Controversy, since they often paralleled those made by Holy Roman emperors anxious to retain or reinforce control over politically significant Italian monasteries. And although the Gregorian reform was not directed at nuns, its demands that married clergy dismiss their wives can be linked to the increased number of new foundations for women in the eleventh century. So, too, papal support of reformed male monasticism helps to explain why older, less austere female communities were sometimes displaced or even dissolved in the interests of Cluniac monks, who occupied their monasteries.

Before the twelfth century, when a reinvigorated papacy buttressed by rationalized canon law and more clearly defined doctrine sought to assert greater control over religious practice, papal policy with respect to women's monasticism was largely reactive. Early medieval popes typically responded to requests from bishops, abbots, lay donors, or nuns themselves, but did not try to impress a particular stamp upon women's monasticism. Papal initiatives could have consequences for female religious, as in the case of the Gregorian reforms, but those consequences do not appear to be the result of conscious design. While the popes of the High and late Middle Ages would not always be systematic or even consistent in their long-range

decision-making regarding female monastics, papal policy, properly speaking, had begun to coalesce.

1100–1298

In the religiously enthusiastic twelfth century, women and men attempting to put their particular visions of the apostolic life into regular practice challenged the ingenuity of popes who sought to standardize monastic life as they had so many other aspects of Christian belief and practice. One aim of the papacy was to ensure that the large numbers of women who had been drawn to the new orders would continue to have their spiritual and temporal needs met. Given that reform-minded male members in these orders often viewed women as occasions of sin, and that they consequently avoided service to them, that aim was not always satisfactorily achieved. The situation is well illustrated by the example of the Premonstratensian nuns and canonesses.

An order of regular canons founded in 1121, the Premonstratensians had initially tolerated, and even given pride of place to, their numerous female members: the mother-house of Prémontré was a double monastery. Yet as early as 1138, Pope Innocent II was forced to remind the canons to recognize and fulfill their obligations to female members, and similar admonitions were repeated by Celestine II, Eugenius III, and Adrian IV. Notwithstanding papal displeasure, the Premonstratensians ceased founding double monasteries and suppressed existing ones. The 1198 decree of the General Chapter altogether prohibiting the admission of women ushered in a period of insecurity and even vagrancy for the remaining sisters that was clearly at odds with the wishes of the Holy See.

This failure in the case of the Premonstratensians helps to explain the resolution with which thirteenth-century popes strove for success in their dealings with the Cistercians. After the death of their founder in 1134, the Cistercians had declared that they would neither provide pastoral care to, nor formally incorporate, the many nunneries modeling their observance on the customs of Cîteaux. But declarations such as these— for others were forthcoming—availed the order nothing in the face of papal demands. Successive thirteenth-century popes pressured the Cistercians on behalf of importunate women and their patrons, ultimately forcing the order to officially incorporate many female communities.

The papacy was particularly interested in finding a place for women within the Cistercian Order, since an enclosed contemplative life represented the ideal safeguard for orthodox practice in an age of increasing informality, and even heterodoxy. In 1213, as the General Chapter struggled to establish uniform discipline and control over far-flung affiliates, it gave full expression to this ideal by making strict active and passive enclosure—that is, a rigorous restriction on both exit from and entrance into cloister precincts—a precondition for incorporation of female Cistercian monasteries. It was in this General Chapter ruling, in turn, that thirteenth-century popes found a suitable model for female affiliation to other new orders, most notably the Franciscans and Dominicans. The model, of course, was scarcely original (enclosure of nuns had been mandated for a variety of reasons and with varying degrees of success since the beginning of monastic history), but the circumstances in which it was applied were.

A detachment from worldly affairs, which the cloister was designed to ensure, along with renunciation of personal property and communal life, had been hallmarks of the reformed monasticism of the previous century, and they were ideals to which both monks and nuns could aspire. These were not, however, the dominant features of thirteenth-century piety. The mendicant poverty of the Franciscans and the urban evangelization of the Dominicans were manifestations of a vision of the *vita apostolica* that had an active component. Although it was that vision that had attracted large numbers of female followers, the papacy either tacitly or actively disallowed it when integrating women into the new orders—the rule of the Poor Clares, confirmed by Pope Gregory IX in 1239, and the numerous papal interventions on behalf of Dominican sisters, beginning with Innocent III's recognition of the observance at Prouille, required strict active and passive claustration.

Periculoso and After

Although thirteenth-century popes clearly fought to find places for women in the new orders, they did so only by maintaining a gender-distinctive regular life in which the active apostolate was the exclusive preserve of male religious. At the very end of the century, Pope Boniface VIII reaffirmed and sought to further this policy. He recognized that despite papal efforts to force male orders to accept nuns, there were still many more women desirous of a religious life, and that informal foundations and unregulated quasi-religious women, like the Beguines, abounded. In his 1298 decree *Periculoso* he used strict enclosure regulation to differentiate these women, popularly perceived as religious women, from professed nuns, religious

women in the canonical sense of the term. Where his predecessors had limited themselves to charting a course with reference to specific orders, Boniface VIII legislated for all professed nuns regardless of the rule under which they lived. Henceforth, nuns were to live strictly enclosed lives, leaving their monasteries only in the event of manifest necessity, and allowing no outsider to enter the cloister without license of the ordinary, usually the bishop.

Periculoso was a landmark in the history of papal policy; it was much less significant in the history of female monasticism. Not only did popes in the fourteenth and fifteenth centuries undermine its directives through frequent grants of dispensations and privileges, but as the repeated exhortations of reforming councils and synods attest, it was almost impossible to enforce. Nevertheless, in the later Middle Ages enclosure of nuns remained a norm with which new orders seeking papal approval, such as the Birgittines, were expected to comply. Vigorously restated by the Council of Trent, it would continue to be a guiding principle of papal policy into the modern era.

ELIZABETH MAKOWSKI

References and Further Reading

Makowski, Elizabeth. *Canon Law and Cloistered Women: Periculoso and Its Commentators 1298–1545.* Washington, D.C.: The Catholic University of America Press, 1997.

Skinner, Patricia. *Women in Medieval Italian Society 500–1200.* Essex, U.K.: Pearson Education Limited, 2001.

Southern, R.W. *Western Society and the Church in the Middle Ages,* Harmondsworth, U.K.: Penguin Books, 1970; London: Penguin Books, 1990.

See also **Beguines; Birgittine Order; Canonesses; Cistercian Order; Cluniac Order; Dominican Order; Monastic Enclosure; Monasticism and Nuns; Poor Clares Order; Premonstratensian Order**

MORTUARY ROLLS
See **Necrologies and Mortuary Rolls**

MOTHERS AS TEACHERS

Ever since, in 403 CE, St. Jerome gave detailed instructions to a woman friend on how to teach her children and particularly her daughters to read, women in the West have been regarded as primary teachers. Jerome not only gave practical advice on teaching methods, but also insisted on Christian piety as the basic ethical grounding of such instruction. Jerome's principles were repeated throughout the medieval period by Christian moralists.

Perhaps the most intriguing religious and practical instruction was produced by Dhuoda (c. 803–843), the wife of Charlemagne's second cousin Bernard of Septimania, who wrote her *Liber manualis* or *Handbook* for her son William in just over a year in 843. Her introduction exquisitely emphasizes her strong personal slant: "My son you will have learned doctors to teach you many more examples, more eminent and of greater usefulness, but they are not of equal status with me, nor do they have a heart more ardent than I, your mother, have for you, my firstborn son. . . ."

In c. 1249 Margaret of Provence, the queen of Louis IX (St. Louis) commissioned Vincent of Beauvais to write a treatise: *De eruditione filiorum nobelium* (On the Education of Noble Children). She ordered several chapters to be specifically addressed to girls. A century later, the Italian Francesco da Barberino again wrote a moral instruction manual for children: *Regimento e Costumi di Donna* (Rules and Customs for Ladies). He automatically assumed that the teacher would be a mother, and that daughters were likely to be the pupils. "She should learn to read and write, so that if it happens that she inherits lands, she will be better able to rule them."

Because most books during the medieval period were religious texts, for example, parts of the Hebrew or Christian Bible, Psalters (parts of the Book of Psalms) or Books of Hours (to be read during the various hours of prayer), these were used for religious instruction and also as teaching primers. Indeed, like many other mothers, the French queen, Isabeau of Bavaria, ordered a book of hours for teaching her daughter Jeanne in 1398 and a special alphabet Psalter and "A, b, c. de Psaumes" for her daughter Michelle in 1403. These daughters were of what we now consider primary-school age when they received these books. Throughout the centuries mothers commissioned such texts in order to teach their children to read. Blanche of Castile famously ordered a large Psalter in the early thirteenth century, as a teaching tool for her son, the future Louis IX of France (it is now in the Morgan Library in New York). In 1466, Empress Eleanor of Portugal commissioned an edition of the *De liberorum educatione* (On the Education of Children) by her contemporary, the humanist Pope Pius II, for her son Maximilian I of Austria, in a luxurious version exhibiting the latest artistic ideas.

In their capacity to commission these primers for their children, mothers had the ability to emphasize what they considered important ideas. Not only were they able to stress whether the child's first book should be a Psalter representing the Book of Psalms, or a book of hours, but they could choose which biblical stories should be included in such works.

Thus, for example, Anne of Brittany ordered a primer for her six-year-old daughter Claude (later the first wife of Francis I of France) in 1505. The book considered suitable for a six-year-old child begins with the alphabet, proceeds with the Lord's Prayer, the creed, grace to be said before meals, the creation story, and other details from the Christian Bible.

Although most books during the earlier Middle Ages were written in Latin, some mothers ordered vernacular translations, as did Margaret of Provence, who was also very clear in her suggestions of what should be included in the works she ordered, in the mid-thirteenth century. Christine de Pizan wrote her *Enseignements moraux* (Moral Teachings) for her son in 1395, and later presented a copy of this to the queen, Isabeau of Bavaria, who was certainly aware of a mother's responsibility for her children's education. Echoing Dhuoda, Christine wrote:

Son, I have no great treasure
To make you rich, but a measure
Of good advice which you may need;
I give it hoping you'll take heed.
Read willingly fine books of tales
As much as you can, for it never fails
That the examples such books comprise
Can help you to become more wise.

SUSAN GROAG BELL

References and Further Reading

Dhuoda. *Liber manualis: Handbook for Her Warrior Son*, edited and translated by Marcelle Thiebaux. Cambridge medieval classics 8. Cambridge, U.K.; New York: Cambridge University Press, 1998.

Francesco di Barberino. *Regimento e costumi di donna*. Turin: Loescher-Chiantore, 1957.

de Pizan, Christine. *The Writings of Christine de Pizan*, edited by Cannon Willard. New York: Persea Books, 1994. See "Proverbs Moveaux," pp. 30–31.

See also **Blanche of Castile; Book Ownership; Books of Hours; Christine de Pizan; Dhuoda; Education, Lay; Jerome, Influence of; Literacy and Reading: Vernacular**

MUSIC, WOMEN AND

Music was part of women's everyday lives, just as it was for men. Songs, dancing, instrumental music, liturgical experiences: music of many types was available to people of all social classes. Much of the repertory is lost to us. Improvised and orally transmitted repertories made up the majority of musics available to Western culture. Hints of that lost legacy can be recovered from contemporary works of art and literature that depict music's varied social roles. Such evidence must be handled carefully, of course; the image of an angel consort holding instruments, like the description of a medieval banquet which enumerates such instruments, are each clearly fictionalized. Yet taken *in toto*, the many depictions of music-making bespeak the importance of music in the lives of the medieval populace.

Modern scholarship in music history has often emphasized composition over other professional musical roles (such as performance) and has emphasized the stylistically innovative and predominately "male" genres of the polyphonic mass and the polytextual motet in preference to the stylistically less innovative plainchant and song repertories. As composers, of course, women's access to training was limited by virtue of gender. Yet just as the choir boy was trained in the liturgy, so too was the choir girl, as can be seen especially clearly in the extensive repertory of polyphonic mass movements, sequences, and motets in the *Las Huelgas Codex*, copied for a Spanish Cistercian convent, for instance. Other monastic institutions had less elaborate liturgical performances centered primarily, if not exclusively, on plainchant, but under normal circumstances, women monastics participated actively in the liturgy of their communities. Many secular women musicians also obtained access to some form of musical training. Trobairitz (women song composers of the *langue d'oc*) took their place beside the troubadours, and *ministrelles* were active alongside the minstrels of the era.

For a few medieval women, an extensive corpus of music survives. The ninth-century Byzantine nun Kassia composed at least twenty-three liturgical chants. Hildegard of Bingen (1098–1178), too, is famous as a composer as well as an abbess, author, and mystic; seventy-seven of her musical works are available in a volume called the *Symphonia harmoniae caelestium revelationum* (Symphony of Harmony of Heavenly Revelations), and the *Ordo virtutum* (The Play of Virtues), perhaps her most famous work from a modern standpoint, is appended to the collection in one of her manuscripts. Still, the contributions of a majority of women composers are likely lost to us altogether or are found only as anonymous entries in the many broad anthologies of sacred and secular song. Indeed, it is principally among the many "women's songs," which adopt a woman's point of view, that gender-identified authors and composers have left identifiable musical legacies for our modern consideration. That "Anonymous" might well be female has been the working premise behind recovery of plainchant repertories and the identification of the circle of poet-musicians among the ladies in waiting at the court of Margaret of Scotland, for instance.

Scholarly attention to medieval women in their roles as audience, as patrons, and as performers—whether professional or amateur—has followed in the wake of feminist queries to the discipline. We now recognize the significance of a cultural leader the like of Eleanor of Aquitaine in directing the stylistic innovations in secular song, for instance. We recognize too the importance of dance and of social displays of musical knowledge in creating social and personal identities at court and in urban communities. Nuns, Beguines, and aristocrats all availed themselves of musical references in their correspondence and other writings; they likely had the opportunity as well to participate in music making, though they would not necessarily have considered themselves "musicians."

CYNTHIA J. CYRUS

References and Further Reading

Coldwell, Maria V. "*Jougleresses* and *Trobairitz*: Secular Musicians in Medieval France." In *Women Making Music: The Western Art Tradition, 1150–1950*, edited by Jane Bowers and Judith Tick. Urbana and Chicago: University of Illinois Press, 1986, pp. 39–61.

Higgins, Paula. "Parisian Nobles, a Scottish Princess, and the Woman's Voice in Late Medieval Song." *Early Music History* 10 (1991): 145–200.

Holsinger, Bruce W. *Music, Body, and Desire in Medieval Culture: Hildegard of Bingen to Chaucer*. Stanford: Stanford University Press, 2001.

Klinck, Anne L., and Ann Marie Rasmussen. *Medieval Women's Song: Cross-Cultural Approaches*. The Middle Ages Series. Philadelphia: University of Pennsylvania Press, 2002.

Prizer, William F. "Games of Venus: Secular Vocal Music in the Late Quattrocento and Early Cinquecento." *The Journal of Musicology* 9 (1991): 3–56.

Schleifer, Martha Furman, and Sylvia Glickman. *Women Composers: Music throughout the Ages, Composers Born before 1599*. New York: G. K. Hall & Co., 1996.

Yardley, Anne Bagnall. "'Ful weel she soong the service dyvyne': The Cloistered Musician in the Middle Ages." In *Women Making Music: The Western Art Tradition, 1150–1950*, edited by Jane Bowers and Judith Tick. Urbana, Ill.: University of Illinois Press, 1986, pp. 15–38.

See also **Charivari; Dance; Death, Mourning and Commemoration; Eleanor of Aquitaine; Ermengard; Hildegard of Bingen; Mary, Virgin: in Music; Minnesang; Monasticism and Nuns; Pastourelle; Performance in Lyric; Trobairitz and Troubadours; Woman's Song**

MUSLIM WOMEN: IBERIA

After the arrival of Muslim armies in Spain in 711, al-Andalus (Muslim Spain) flourished under Islamic rule until 1492, when the last Muslim Spanish kingdom,

Granada, was conquered by King Ferdinand of Aragon and Queen Isabella of Castile. During the eight centuries of Muslim presence in Spain, a frontier region divided al-Andalus, in the southern peninsula, from Christian kingdoms in the north. The border shifted southward over time with the expansion of Christian-controlled territory. In many ways, medieval Iberian society was shaped by the presence of the frontier, by interreligious contacts, and by warfare.

Although it is likely that some women arrived with the Arab and Berber troops who first entered Iberia, there is no mention of any female presence in sources. Most likely, the female Muslim population in Spain grew over time through conversion. Once established in the Iberian peninsula, some Muslim settlers summoned Eastern wives and families to join them, but many intermarried with the local Visigothic and Hispano-Roman population, creating an ethnically and religiously diverse society under the rule of the Umayyad dynasty (751–1031).

Interreligious Marriage

Andalusi society was never exclusively Muslim, since Christians and Jews also lived as protected populations under Islamic rule. This circumstance, called *convivencia* (coexistence), created a situation in which interreligious contact was normal, although not always peaceful. Intermarriage of a Muslim man with a non-Muslim woman (rarely the other way around) was not uncommon in the early centuries of Muslim rule, and we know of some Andalusi rulers who married Christian princesses. The earliest example of this trend was the marriage between Abd al-Azîz b. Mûsâ, the first governor of al-Andalus, and Egilona, the wife (or perhaps daughter) of the last Visigothic king. This marriage may have helped to establish the legitimacy of Muslim political rule in Spain. There is no indication that Egilona converted to Islam after this marriage. Although conversion of a non-Muslim woman was desirable upon marriage to a Muslim, this was not required by Islamic law. Presumably many indigenous women did convert to Islam (though not necessarily because of marriage to a Muslim), since there is evidence of rapid overall conversion of the Andalusi population during the ninth and tenth centuries. However, there are records at least until the middle of the ninth century of interreligious marriages in which Christian women retained their religion after marriage. In such a case, children would normally be Muslim, but sometimes sons would be raised as Muslims while daughters could follow the religion of their mother.

Slave Women

This complicated situation seems to have created a degree of social and religious tension, especially in the capital city of Cordoba during the 850s. Over time, intermarriage was increasingly frowned upon by Andalusi religious scholars, and it became less common as the Muslim population grew and the numbers of indigenous Andalusi Christians (*mozarabs*) declined. Northern women also came to al-Andalus as slaves, captured or traded across the frontier. These women, who usually converted to Islam, served in various domestic capacities, and were sexually accessible to the master of the house. A slave woman who gave birth to a boy (thereafter known as *umm walad*) enjoyed special status and was freed from slavery. Perhaps the most famous Andalusi example was Subh, from the Christian kingdom of Navarre, who was a concubine of the Umayyad caliph al-Hakam II (d. 976) and mother of his heir, Hishâm II (d. 1013). She later served as regent for Hishâm during his minority, with the help of the chamberlain, al-Mansûr.

Sources

The scarcity of sources is a constant problem for investigating the lives of Andalusi Muslim women, as is also true for women in other regions of the medieval Islamic world. However, poems survive by a number of important female poets, including the Umayyad princess Wallâda (d. late eleventh century) and Hafsa bint al-Hâjj (d. 1190), both famous for their love poetry. Andalusi chronicles and memoirs also mention women at the royal court and in elite households, especially the mothers and wives of rulers, who often held considerable power behind the scenes. Itimâd al-Rumaykîya, for example, was said to share power with her husband, al-Mutamid, ruler of Seville (late eleventh century). Female religious scholars are listed in biographical lists of Andalusi intellectuals. These include Maryam and Zaynab, the wife and daughter of Ibn al-Arabî (early thirteenth century); Rayhâna, a Quranic scholar in eleventh-century Almeria; and Maryam bint Ibrâhîm al-Murâdî (d. 1150), a celebrated calligrapher. Educated women often served as teachers to other women. Legal sources include court cases and queries (*fatwas*) that mention women; records of pious foundations (*waqfs*) endowed by wealthy women, including patrons like al-Rumaykîya; and manuals of market law (*hisba*) that provide data on urban space, female labor, and segregation of the sexes. A handful of fourteenth- and fifteenth-century documents survive from Granada that show women as active participants in sales of land and houses, marriages, and divorces.

Conditions in al-Andalus

Although al-Andalus stood at the western edge of the Islamic world, the lives of Muslim women in medieval Iberia do not appear to have been fundamentally different from those of contemporary women elsewhere around the Muslim Mediterranean. The school of Islamic law that prevailed in Spain and North Africa (Maliki law) was somewhat stricter than the schools of law more common in the eastern Islamic world, but provisions concerning women were not strikingly dissimilar. In general, Muslim social and religious mores that affected the daily lives of women—attitudes towards religious practice, marriage and divorce, property and inheritance, legal status, education, work, etc.—would not have significantly differentiated women in al-Andalus from women in the Islamic East. Nevertheless, there are areas in which the status of Muslim women in al-Andalus may have been influenced by the Iberian context. The constant presence of the frontier, and the gradual southward encroachment of Christian kingdoms, added insecurity to the lives of all people living in contested regions. Because of the uncertainties of frontier life, Muslim jurists in border areas, such as Toledo, may have been more lenient in regulating such things as remarriage for women whose husbands were missing in action. Likewise, it has been suggested that the ethnic diversity of Andalusi society, especially the presence of Berbers and Christians, may have influenced attitudes towards genealogy and the legal status of women.

Muslim Women in Christian Spain

As the border moved south, many ordinary Muslims (now called *mudejars*) found themselves living in newly Christian territories, either through conquest or capture. This was a new Christianized version of *convivencia*. In an unusual case, the Muslim princess Zaida of Seville was taken by King Alfonso VI of Castile as a concubine, then later wife, in the early 1090s. Zaida became the mother of Alfonso's only son, and converted to Christianity, taking the name Elizabeth. Conditions varied by region, but Muslim communities living under Christian rule were generally protected and tolerated, at least until the early sixteenth century, and they were allowed to live

according to Muslim law. However, Muslims also had access to Christian courts, and Christian documents show Muslims of both sexes bringing criminal and civil cases before Christian judges, often successfully. Nevertheless, the situation was unstable, especially for women. For example, if a Muslim woman lost contact with her family and community, she was at risk of becoming a prostitute in a Christian city. Other Muslims, both men and women, served as slaves or (in the case of women) concubines in Christian households. Perhaps this is one reason why the romanticized figure of the beautiful *mora* (Muslim woman) is a trope of late medieval Spanish literature.

OLIVIA REMIE CONSTABLE

References and Further Reading

López de la Plaza, Gloria. *Al-Andalus: mujeres, sociedad y religion*. Malaga: Universidad de Malaga, 1992.

Marin, Manuela. *Mujeres en al-Andalus*. Madrid: Consejo Superior de Investigaciones Científicas, 2000.

Meyerson, Mark. "Prostitution of Muslim Women in the Kingdom of Valencia: Religious and Sexual Discrimination in a Medieval Plural Society." In *The Medieval Mediterranean: Cross-Cultural Contacts*, edited by Marilyn J. Chiat and Kathryn Reyerson. St. Cloud, Minn.: North Star Press, 1988, pp. 87–95.

Nichols, James M. "Arabic Women Poets in al-Andalus." *The Maghreb Review* 4 (1979): 114–117.

O'Connor, Isabel Bonet. "Between Whipping and Slavery: Double Jeopardy against *Mudejar* Women in Medieval Spain." In *Women and the Colonial Gaze*, edited by Tamara L. Hunt and Michelle R. Lessard. New York: New York University Press, 2002, pp. 29–37.

Shatzmiller, Maya. "Women and Wage Labor in the Medieval Islamic West: Legal Issues in an Economic Context." *Journal of Economic and Social History of the Orient* 40.2 (1997): 174–206.

Viguera, Maria Jesus. "*Aluu li'l-maâlî*: On the Social Status of Andalusi Women." In *The Legacy of Muslim Spain*, edited by Salma Khadra Jayyusi. Leiden: Brill, 1992, pp. 709–724.

Viguera, Maria Jesus, ed. *La mujer en al-Andalus*. Seville: Universidad Autónoma de Madrid, 1989.

Walther, Wiebke. *Women in Islam*. Montclair, N.J.: Abner Schram, 1981.

See also **Epic, Spanish; Iberia; Literature, Iberian; Isabel I; Law, Islamic: Iberia; Marriage, Islamic: Iberia; Muslim Women: Western Literature; Slaves; Walladah Bint al-Mustakfi**

MUSLIM WOMEN: WESTERN LITERATURE

Little information has survived about the role that Muslim women have played in western European history. Of the few historical cases that survive, most involve Muslim Spain (al-Andalus) and the cultural participation of some women in the rule of the Party Kings (*taifas*), that is, the twenty-three locally ruled kingdoms that followed the collapse of the Andalusian Umayyad caliphate in 1031. Generally seen as a prototype of aristocratic refinement, women's emancipation, and unexpected sexual freedom, Princess Walladah, daughter of the Umayyad caliph Al-Mustakfi III (d. 1025), openly entertained two male lovers (Ibn Zaydun and Ibn 'Abdus) and one female lover (Muhya). She had the following two verses embroidered with gold thread on her coat: "By God, I was created for great achievements. I walk my own path and cultivate my pride;" and "Whoever loves me, I give him the cup of my cheeks; and whomever I love, I give him my kisses" (Arjona Castro 25; translation mine).

Other Muslim women played a pivotal role in East–West relations and especially in crusader history. Such is the case of Shajarrat Al-Durr (d. 1258), who ruled Egypt for four months (November 1249 to February 1250) at the time of the sixth crusade. As Egypt was besieged by Saint Louis's crusader army, Shajarrat Ad-Durr concealed the death of her husband (al-Malik As-Salih Aiyub), defeated the French king on February 19, 1250, at Mansura, and ransomed him for one million bezants. She put an end to the Crusaders' presence in Egypt, regained Damietta, and restored peace in Egypt. Despite the extraordinary role Shajarrat Ad-Durr (and probably others like her for whom no record has survived) played in Egyptian, Mediterranean, and western European history, this Egyptian queen has received limited attention from historians of the Crusades, who have focused primarily on the role Western men played in these wars.

Western European literary texts, on the other hand, regularly depict Muslim or "Saracen" women as politically active. (The word *Saracen* remains appropriately ambiguous, referring to pagans and even to the remains of Roman architecture just as easily as to enemies from Hungary or the Holy Land or to the Normans.) Where Islam is concerned, the word *Saracen* loosely describes foreign, exotic women from an imprecise geographical location: the Levant, North Africa, or the Iberian peninsula. Its use in epic, romance, and lyric poetry reveals the degree of imagination (and deformation) that is involved in the literary portrayal of women from the Islamic world.

Saracen women, especially princesses, have become a commonplace of medieval Western literary criticism since the early twentieth century (these princesses include Bramimonde in the *Song of Roland*, Princess Orable in the *Prise d'Orange*, or

Charlemagne's wife, Galienne, in the *Pseudo-Turpin*). However, critical appreciation of the role that they played in French epic (*chansons de geste*) and romance has changed dramatically over the last hundred years. While, in the nineteenth and early twentieth century, classical philology, with its nationalist drive, was interested in the description of literary genres and thus gave limited attention to women generally and to Saracen women in particular, folklore studies and interest in character types gave the Saracen princess a legitimate space (albeit limited) in the critical analyses of the *chansons de geste*. Nevertheless, this critical approach regarded all non-Christian characters in a similar manner, and subordinated them to the male Christian white hero, his conquests, and the hegemony of Christendom. Saracen women especially were seen as nothing more than ornamental exotic details that were irrelevant to the overall literary story of conquest and success. Only in the late 1970s, with the development of postcolonial and feminist studies as well as with the increasing awareness of the sociopolitical dimensions of literature as a cultural artifact (pioneered by the late Edward Said), did the character of the Saracen princess become an integral part of critical discourse.

Since that time, the role of the *Sarrasine* has been reevaluated. The durable popularity of the Saracen princess in the Western literary imagination may well be due to the varied roles this character played in different texts (see Ramey). If she is physically indistinguishable from Christian romance heroines (white skin, dazzling beauty), she differs in the extraordinary agency and boldness that she displays. Even as she disrupts masculine narratives and becomes involved in adulterous liaisons (she has been coined a "rebellious heroine" by the critic Vallecalle), the *Sarrasine* is reformed in the end of most *chansons de geste*, baptized, and married to a Christian knight. Contrary to her Christian counterpart, the *Sarrasine*'s independence and rebelliousness are praised since they are the means to enhance and firmly establish Christianity. Her love for the married Christian knight and resulting adultery, which are often at the heart of medieval epics and romances, are not perceived to be immoral, but rather seen as strategic ideological solutions to Frankish colonial conquest, expansion, and triumph (see Kinoshita). The *Sarrasine* is thus instrumental to proving Western religious, cultural, and moral hegemony.

The representation of Saracen women in Western literary production tells us much about the complex relations between western Europe and the Islamic East in the Middle Ages and reveals the extent to which the crucial role played by some historical Muslim women has been downplayed and reconstructed to benefit European expansion and hegemony and the ultimate triumph of Christianity.

SAHAR AMER

References and Further Reading

Arjona Castro, Antonio. *La Sexualidad en la España musulmana*. Cordoba: Fuente de Las Piedras, 1985.

De Weever, Jacqueline. *Sheba's Daughters: Whitening and Demonizing the Saracen Woman in Medieval French Epic*. New York: Garland, 1998.

Kinoshita, Sharon. "The Politics of Courtly Love: *La Prise d'Orange* and the Conversion of the Saracen Queen." *Romantic Review* 86.2 (1995): 265–288.

Metlitzki, Dorothee. *The Matter of Araby in Medieval England*. New Haven, Conn.: Yale University Press, 1977.

Ramey, Lynn. *Christian, Saracen and Genre in Medieval French Literature*. New York: Routledge, 2001.

Vallecalle, Jean-Claude. "Rupture et intégration: L'héroïne révoltée dans les chansons de geste." In *Charlemagne in the North*, edited by Philip Bennett, Anne E. Colby, and Graham Runnalls. Edinburgh: Société Rencesvals, 1993, pp. 449–461.

Wasserstein, David. *The Rise and Fall of the Party-Kings: Politics and Society in Islamic Spain, 1002–1086*. Princeton, N.J.: Princeton University Press, 1985.

See also **Cross-Cultural Approaches; Crusades and Crusading Literature; Epic, Old French; Floire and Blancheflor; Iberia; Literature, Iberian; Marriage, Islamic: Iberia; Muslim Women: Iberia**

MYSTICISM AND MYSTICS

The word *mysticism* is derived from the ancient Greek *muv*, "to close," more specifically "to close the eyes," and refers in its earliest uses to things that are hidden or secret. These early references pertain to the ancient mystery religions. So, for example, the fifth-century-BCE Greek historian Thucydides calls the rituals of the mystery religions *ta mustika*; and, in the first century BCE, another Greek historian, Strabo, names those initiated into these religions *oi mustikoi*. In both cases, the terms refer solely to ritual secrets and those who have access to them. That which is hidden is the details of the ritual, not esoteric, meanings to which they refer.

Early Christian writers take the terms over directly from the mystery religions, yet use them to surprisingly different ends. One might expect that early Christian ritual practice would be referred to as "mystical" and participants as "mystics," but instead the adjectival form is used to describe certain layers of meaning within the Bible and particular kinds of biblical interpretation. The Alexandrian theologian Clement (d. c. 215) refers to the "mystical interpretation" of scripture; and, in the following generation, Origen (c. 185–254), also from Alexandria, writes of the "mystical meaning" of scripture. In both instances, the hidden meaning of scripture, laid bare by allegorical interpretation, is Christ together with the mystery of his Incarnation and the further truths made available through that saving event. Only later is the term *mystical* used to describe Christian ritual and then predominantly to name the meaning of the Eucharist—the presence of the Incarnate Christ within the sacrament.

In its modern usages mysticism most often refers to some kind of extraordinary experience of the divine or of union with God, with mystics being those who undergo such experiences. As the historian Louis Bouyer demonstrates, the move to experience occurs in the early Christian literature itself precisely through exegetical and liturgical practices. Clement and Origen describe as "mystical" that spiritual knowledge attained through allegorical interpretation of the Bible, understood as the method for uncovering the hidden meanings or secrets of scripture. For Clement and Origen, both the secret or hidden things and the process by which one comes to know them are mystical.

Origen is the first to use the term *mystical* clearly to describe direct experiential knowledge of God, yet for him one always comes to this experiential knowledge *through* the allegorical or mystical interpretation of scripture. So in his *Commentary on John* he claims that Jesus Christ is "the high priest of the order of Melchisedek . . . our guide in mystical and ineffable contemplation." Through the correct interpretation of scripture, itself guided by Christ, "ineffable and mystical visions give joy and impart enthusiasm." By the time that Gregory of Nyssa (c. 335–394) writes of the "mystical contemplation of the Song of Songs," interpretation and experience have become inseparable, a merger most famously articulated in the late-fifth- or early-sixth-century textual corpus ascribed to Dionysius the Areopagite. There the heart of scripture and of the liturgy, present but veiled, is the mystical truth of God, rendered accessible to human beings through the saving Incarnation of Christ.

Yet in late antiquity and the Middle Ages, women were generally not allowed to interpret scripture. For most of the history of the Christian tradition, in fact, misogynist assumptions barred women from holding most church offices, from serving as preachers and teachers to mixed audiences of men and women except on very rare occasions, and from attending the elite educational institutions in which the methods of scriptural exegesis and theological reasoning were generally taught.

Despite these prohibitions, women and the men who supported them discovered various ways to justify women's religious leadership, most often through

595

an appeal to mystical experience. Key was the presumption, supported by biblical texts, that women might be the recipients of special graces (especially—but by no means only—those women who dedicated themselves to God as virgins). In the twelfth and thirteenth centuries we find the argument that if God chose to give women visions, to bestow prophecies on them, or to render himself one with them, then women might also be permitted—indeed even be called on—to speak and write of these things. As a result, women's lived experience of Christian truth became one of the primary means through which they were empowered to speak publicly, to teach, and to write. For women, then, the experiential aspect of the mystical is necessarily distinct from its exegetical base. Rather than arguing that mystical contemplation came to them through their interpretation of scripture, many medieval women mystics claimed that they came to understand scripture through their visionary and mystical experience.

This is the background against which the substantive "mysticism" emerged in the seventeenth century. Only then was mysticism articulated as a specific mode of theologizing, one grounded in individual experience rather than in scripture, the Holy Spirit's revelations to the Catholic Church, or the rational exposition of revelation. Michel de Certeau, who demonstrates that the term *mysticism* emerged only in the early modern period, argues that the shift was the result of the breakdown of medieval theological hierarchies. According to de Certeau, late medieval theology rendered systematic a series of distinctions between symbolic theology, in which sensible things lead to knowledge of God; scholastic theology, which makes use of ideas (the intelligible realm) to the same end; and mystical theology, understood as the perfection of divine knowledge in contemplation. Just as Clement and Origen argue that one must move through the scripture to mystical contemplation, so Bonaventure and other late medieval mystical theologians argue that one must move through the sensible and the intelligible to a fuller apprehension of God.

In the sixteenth and seventeenth centuries this hierarchically ordered conception of theology broke down and instead there emerged three competing methods of doing theology: positive or historical, scholastic, and mystical. The first relies on scripture and the revelations of the church, the second on philosophical and analytic articulations of these revealed truths, and the third on experience. Mysticism was no longer the fruition of all theological knowledge, but an alternative means of attaining that knowledge. Again, experience as an alternative source for knowledge of the divine was particularly prominent among late medieval and early modern women,

whose visionary, auditory, and unitive experiences both legitimated and provided the subject matter for their teachings. Many scholars now hypothesize that the prominence of mystical experience within the writings of religious women played a crucial role in the development of early modern conceptions of mysticism.

Women, Gender, and Mysticism in the Middle Ages

With few exceptions, the first women writers in the West were Christian mystics, women who claimed just such extraordinary experiences of God's presence or of union with God. Of course, not all Christian mystics were women. But women were central to Christian mystical traditions throughout the Middle Ages and into the modern era. Through their writings, oral teachings, and practices, mystics were often leaders and innovators within women's monasteries and beguinages (Beguines were semireligious women who lived singly or in groups) and also within spiritual communities that included men. Sometimes known only in their own religious houses or local regions, a handful of female mystics were famous throughout western Europe. Hildegard of Bingen (1098–1179), for example, was in contact with the Pope and with Bernard of Clairvaux (1090–1153), arguably the most powerful religious leader of the twelfth century. With the support of these and other ecclesiastical leaders, Hildegard not only wrote extensive visionary works but also went on preaching tours throughout Germany and Swabia. The Italian Dominican tertiary Catherine of Siena (1347–1380) went further, writing to and advising not only male and female religious but lay leaders and even the pope himself.

We know about medieval women mystics from a variety of different kinds of sources. The vast majority of these are hagiographical texts, often written for specific communities and narrowly circulated. Simone Roisin argues for the efflorescence of what she calls "mystical hagiographies" in the Low Countries during the thirteenth century, and arguably the subgenre continues throughout the Middle Ages, often, although certainly not always, taking women as its subjects. As the ecclesiastical hierarchies centered in Rome took greater control over canonization proceedings, those local communities seeking wider recognition for their holy women applied to bishops or papal legates for consideration of their case. In some instances, this led to official papal inquiries concerning the claims of mystical saints, providing yet another layer of evidence about the lives of such women. Other secondhand reports can be found in chronicles, monastic books of the dead, the so-called sister books of the fourteenth century (group hagiographies depicting the sanctity of generations of women within specific religious communities), letters, polemical writings, sermons, and devotional texts produced for or used by women. Devotional images and objects also provide evidence about women's spiritual practices. Finally, women mystics themselves wrote texts in a wide variety of genres, among them letters, poems, visionary books, devotional treatises, and allegorical dramas. Although often mediated—sometimes in ways we cannot fully gauge—by male confessors or other confidants, these texts provide the best access we have to how women mystics understood themselves and their experiences.

Arguments for specifically feminine forms of mystical experience began in the medieval period and they continue to influence scholarship, if only indirectly. In 1415 the French prelate Jean Gerson, himself an author of mystical treatises and guidebooks, attacked women's putatively overly sensory and erotic experiences of the divine, as well as the teaching, preaching, and writing they authorized. Although Gerson claimed that he did not wish to silence women entirely, but merely to "bridle" their speech with tight clerical control, the basis for later distinctions between male and female styles of mysticism is clearly already in place in the early fifteenth century.

Modern scholars routinely repeat distinctions like those made by Gerson and tend to divide mysticism into two types: affective, emotional, visionary, and often erotic forms of mysticism, associated with femininity and with women; and speculative, intellectual, often explicitly antivisionary forms of mysticism, associated with masculinity and with men. The evidence, particularly that of male- and female-authored mystical texts, does not fit the model. So, for example, Bernard of Clairvaux, the greatest of the many male monastic commentators on the Song of Songs, both initiated and provided the vocabulary and images for the erotic mysticism of the thirteenth and fourteenth centuries. The thirteenth-century Beguine Marguerite Porete (d. 1310), on the other hand, eschewed visionary experience and erotic ecstasies in favor of an absolute union of the annihilated soul with God. The German Dominican Meister Eckhart (c. 1260–1328), often taken as the greatest of speculative mystics, was profoundly influenced by women of a visionary and ecstatic nature, as well as by Porete.

Perhaps most crucially, even visionary and ecstatic mystics usually included within their texts the call for a move through the visionary to another kind of more ineffable experience of divine union. The thirteenth-century Beguine visionary Hadewijch, for example,

describes a vision in which the Eucharist comes to her in human form and then is "naughted" as the soul and Christ become indistinguishable from each other. Similarly, the Italian laywoman Angela of Foligno (d. 1310) records the movement of her soul from ecstatic, spiritually apprehended experiences of God's presence to their "unsaying" in the darkness of Christ's eyes.

Hadewich's and Angela's understanding of the relationship between the visionary and its "unsaying" emerges out of a distinction first found in Dionysius the Areopagite. Dionysius articulates two modes of naming God: *cataphasis*, in which names are positively attributed to the divine, and *apophasis*, in which all attributes are "unsaid" or denied in order to mark the illimitability of God's Being. For Dionysius, this works itself out in terms of an interplay between the biblical and philosophical names for God and their negation in the movement of mystical theology. Medieval mystics like Eckhart similarly work with attributes derived from the Bible and from philosophical speculation on the nature of God.

Yet women were prohibited by the Church from engaging in the interpretation of scripture and did not generally have access to philosophical education. In addition, medical, philosophical, and theological opinion throughout the Middle Ages held that women were more porous and imaginative than men and therefore open to possession, whether divine or demonic, and to spiritual visions, auditions, and other sensations. The confluence of theological and medical arguments about women's capacities and limitations led to a situation in which women's experiences of God's presence became the text that they interpreted, both cataphatically and apophatically. Dionysius and Eckhart grounded their apophatic practice in the reading of scripture; women like Hadewijch and Angela used their daily liturgical and meditative practices—both biblically based—to engender authorizing experiences that then became texts to be unsaid in the pursuit of a closer, less mediated, experience of God.

Action and Contemplation in Medieval Women's Mysticism

The denigration of affective, visionary, and ecstatic forms of mysticism generally associated with women is also tied to its putative escapism. Debates concerning the putative "quietism" of the mystical life often appear in discussions of the story of Mary and Martha (Luke 10:38–42), early interpreted as an allegory of the contemplative and active lives. Following Jesus' approbation of Mary (who sits at his feet to listen to his teaching) over Martha (who rushes to prepare a meal for her visitor), late antique and medieval commentators argue that the life of contemplation is higher than that of action. Yet they insist that as long as one lives on earth, one must take care of the body and of one's neighbor.

The thirteenth- and fourteenth-century women's movement in northern Europe, a hotbed of women's mystical activity, struggled with just this problem. The Beguines, in particular, like the new Franciscan and Dominican orders, desired to live actively in the world, serving others and bringing them to God. Yet medical opinions about women's bodily weakness and porousness—the same views that rendered women likely sites of divine possession—also rendered them susceptible to physical and spiritual danger. The kind of active ministry pursued by Francis and his male followers—preaching, hearing confessions, and caring for the sick and poor—was deemed unsuitable for women. In the hagiographies of the early Beguines (those mystical hagiographies studied by Roisin), women struggle to serve others and to live in absolute poverty, dependent on alms or the labor of their own hands for survival, despite the demands of local bishops and monastic authorities that they succumb to some form of enclosure. (Male hagiographers tend to associate the former with Martha and the latter with Mary.)

These same hagiographies, however, show the Beguines engaged in meditative practice, asceticism, and prayer *while* living in the world. Religious adepts, these women strive for and achieve experiences of divine presence and union. In response to the peculiar dilemmas posed by the church for religious women, the Beguines sought to bring together the active and the contemplative lives in new ways. The Beguines found ways to articulate the life of contemplation as itself a form of action, action through which they redeemed souls from purgatory and cared for their spiritual children on earth. They thereby enacted the union of Mary and Martha. (Similar patterns can be found in the lives and writings of women associated with the Dominican and Franciscan orders.)

Even more radically, the Beguine writer Marguerite Porete argues that those activities generally associated with action—care for the poor, the sick, and one's religious community—and those associated with contemplation—participation in the sacramental system, asceticism, meditation, and prayer—were all forms of action from which the soul seeking annihilation must become detached. This tradition culminates in Eckhart's Sermon 86, a radical rereading of the story of Mary and Martha in which he argues that *Martha* was favored by Christ, for she was so detached from all creaturely things and hence so entirely

one with the divine that she was able to work in the world as Christ himself.

Ironically, Porete's and Eckhart's insistence on the union of action and contemplation leads to their denigration of visions and ecstasies. Both argue that enjoying the delights of the spiritual senses and experiences of God's special presence distract from the pursuit of annihilation or detachment. Thus, for Eckhart, Mary is less advanced than Martha, for she still becomes so caught up in spiritual delights as to be unable to do anything else. Only Martha truly combines action and contemplation. Porete is characteristically unyielding in her language. She describes seven stages of the soul, the fourth representing what many wrongly take to be the heights of the religious life:

> The fourth state occurs when the Soul is drawn up by the height of love into the delight of thought through meditation and relinquishes all labors of the outside and of obedience to another through the height of contemplation . . . So the Soul holds that there is no higher life than to have this over which she has lordship. For Love has so greatly satisfied her with delights that she does not believe that God has a greater gift to give to this soul here below than such a love as Love has poured out within her through love." (Porete, Chapter 118)

This state, representative of the visions and ecstasies that follow meditative practice, is exceedingly dangerous for the soul. Freedom and nobility are attained only with the death of the spirit, which requires detachment from both external and internal works. The soul then becomes the place where God works in the world.

Porete was condemned as a relapsed heretic and burned at the stake in Paris' Place de Grève in 1310. Despite the edict commanding that all copies of her book be destroyed, it survived anonymously, to be rediscovered by the twentieth-century scholar Romana Guarnieri. It is unlikely that Porete directly influenced the gendering of mysticism that we find in theologians like Gerson. Yet the distinction between visionary and ecstatic experiences and a demand for annihilation, detachment, or union without distinction between God and the soul was anticipated in debates about the nature of religious experience emerging out of the thirteenth-century women's religious movement. Neither Porete nor Eckhart genders this distinction; both speak to women and assume that women are capable of attaining absolute freedom, simplicity, and detachment. Nor are the two kinds of experiences understood as being antithetical to each other. Even Porete, who is a vocal critic of "spiritual delights," recognizes that they represent a necessary stage on the path toward annihilation.

Yet the condemnation of Porete and of certain of Eckhart's teachings, particularly those dealing with an uncreated aspect of the soul that is always one with the ground of the divine, demonstrates the dangers their views pose, especially for women. During the later Middle Ages, women's religious authority depended on extraordinary visionary, auditory, or somatic experiences of God. Without such experiences and their approbation by male clerics increasingly trained to "read" the female body and soul, women had no legitimate authority within medieval religious culture. Hence the proliferation of visionary, ecstatic, and "autohagiographical" texts in the centuries following Porete's and Eckhart's condemnations, and the increasing association of these forms of visionary, ecstatic, and corporeal spirituality with women (although not, it should be noted, without signs of continued resistance). The association of women with certain types of mysticism is the result, then, not of a putatively universal femininity, but of the specific social and cultural constraints that women faced in the medieval and early modern periods.

AMY HOLLYWOOD

References and Further Reading

Angela of Foligno. *Complete Works*, translated by Paul Lachance. New York: Paulist Press, 1993.

Bouyer, Louis. "Mysticism: An Essay on the History of the Word." In *Understanding Mysticism*, edited by Richard Woods, Garden City, N.Y.: Image Books, 1980, pp. 42–55.

Bynum, Caroline Walker. *Jesus as Mother: Studies in the Spirituality of the High Middle Ages*. Berkeley: University of California Press, 1982.

———. *Holy Feast and Holy Fast: The Religious Significance of Food to Medieval Women*. Berkeley: University of California Press, 1987.

de Certeau, Michel. "Mysticism." *Diacritics* 22 (1992): 11–25.

Elliott. Dyan. *Proving Women: Female Spirituality and Inquisitional Culture in the Later Middle Ages*. Princeton, N.J.: Princeton University Press, 2004.

Gregory of Nyssa. *Commentary on the Song of Songs*, translated by Casimir McCambley. Brookline, Mass.: Hellenic College Press, 1987.

Hadewijch. *The Complete Works*, translated by Mother Columba Hart. New York: Paulist Press, 1980.

Hamburger, Jeffrey. *The Rothschild Canticles: Art and Mysticism in Flanders and the Rhineland circa 1300*. New Haven, Conn.: Yale University Press, 1990.

Hollywood, Amy. *The Soul as Virgin Wife: Mechthild of Magdeburg, Marguerite Porete, and Meister Eckhart*. Notre Dame, Ind.: Notre Dame University Press, 1995.

———. *Sensible Ecstasy: Mysticism, Sexual Difference, and the Demands of History*. Chicago: University of Chicago Press, 2002.

McGinn, Bernard. *The Flowering of Mysticism: Men and Women in the New Mysticism, 1200–1350*. New York: Crossroads, 1998.

Meister Eckhart. *Meister Eckhart: Teacher and Preacher*, translated by Bernard McGinn, with Frank Tobin and Elvira Borgstädt. New York: Paulist Press, 1986.

Mooney, Catherine, ed. *Gendered Voices: Medieval Saints and Their Interpreters*. Philadelphia: University of Pennsylvania Press, 1999.

Newman, Barbara. *Sister of Wisdom: Hildegard of Bingen's Theology of the Feminine*. Berkeley: University of California Press, 1987.

———. *From Virile Woman to WomanChrist: Studies in Medieval Religion and Literature*. Philadelphia: University of Pennsylvania Press, 1995.

Origen. *Commentary on the Gospel According to John*, translated by Ronald E. Heine. Washington, D.C.: Catholic University of America Press, 1989–1993.

Petroff, Elizabeth Alvilda, ed. *Medieval Women's Visionary Literature*. Oxford: Oxford University Press, 1986.

Porete, Marguerite. *The Mirror of Simple Souls*, translated by Ellen Babinsky. New York: Paulist Press, 1993.

Pseudo-Dionysius. *The Complete Works*, translated by Colm Luibheid. New York: Paulist Press, 1987.

Roisin, Simone. *L'Hagiographie cistercienne dans le diocèse de Liège au XIIIe siècle*. Louvain: Bibliothèque de l'Université, 1947.

See also **Angela of Foligno; Autohagiography; Beguines; Bride of Christ: Imagery; Catherine of Siena; Church; Devotional Practices; Gerson, Jean; Hadewijch; Hagiography; Hildegard of Bingen; Julian of Norwich; Marguerite Porete; Mary and Martha; Mystics' Writings; Ordination of Women as Priests; Sermons and Preaching; Sister-Books and Other Convent Chronicles; Song of Songs, Medieval Interpretations of Theology**

MYSTICS' WRITINGS

The majority of women's mystical writings were composed after the 1200s, along with the development of an increasing number of texts produced by or about women in Latin and in vernacular languages. The subjects of mystics' texts varied greatly and include hagiographies, visions, prose chronicling the life and experiences of the mystic, poetry, songs, and letters. Although there was no single recognizable quality that would clearly delimit the style or genre that we associate with mystics' writings, certain patterns emerged that form recognizable traits. These included the emphasis on understanding Christ's suffering; a desire to unite with Christ (*unio mystica*); a longing to imitate Christ's passion (*imitatio Christi*) or to exemplify the apostolic life (*vita apostolica*) and become the living example of God's word, an importance ascribed to the materiality of the body (both the mystic's and Christ's) and to visual realms; and a remarkable inventiveness in Latin and vernacular languages. The writings of Beatrice of Nazareth and Hadewijch represented inaugural works in the Dutch language. Julian's was the first autobiographical text by a woman in the English language.

While many texts that bore witness to mystics' activity remain, we can assume that a significant number of texts and testimonies have not survived, due to what may have been the nonorthodox nature of some, the fact that many women may not have had access to writing or a scribe, the problematic nature of women's status as authors, especially with regard to theological doctrine, or to the lack of importance ascribed to women's texts in general. In addition, texts could survive that we do not yet recognize as having been composed by women, since the author's name may have been stripped when translated into Latin by clerics in order to be given a more theologically regulated and universal status, as was the case for the Latin version of Marguerite Porete's *Mirror of Simple Souls*. Mystics like Julian, who claimed the status of *illiterati*, were not necessarily illiterate, but used this *humilitas* formula to mean that they were not officially trained in scholastic theology or Latin, thereby subtly negotiating with church authority in order to find a less controversial position for voicing theological issues.

Because the writings of many medieval women mystics were mediated through male scribes and confessors, or even through nuns (as are sections of Gertrude of Helfta's *The Herald of Divine Love*), they were not always handed down in a form that gives us a clearly unmediated voice. Certain manuscript versions of the texts of Birgitta of Sweden, Mechthild of Magdeburg, and Gertrude of Helfta seem to have survived without an overly intervening hand; however, with a few exceptions, the majority of women mystics' texts were verified, authorized, or translated by a male scribe, confessor, or editor over which the mystic may or may not have had a degree of influence. Angela of Foligno constantly interjects when Brother A, her scribe and translator, seems to err; the interrelation between scribe and mystic may thus become part of the narrative itself, as is the case for Margery Kempe. While mystics' texts can be seen as a kind of dialogue between male and female voices, the fact that medieval notions of authorship differ considerably from modern ones and more closely resemble what we think of today as composing and dictating makes demarcating the line between mystic and scribe a problematic task. Autograph texts, fragments, and letters of male and female mystics' writings exist (as is the case for Birgitta of Sweden's *Revelations*, a letter of Francis of Assisi, and Teresa of Avila's *The Interior Castle*), but these are most likely due to their status as relics. Autograph texts of male and female mystics were habitually considered as drafts for secretaries or scribes to recopy, render more legible, or translate. Comparing the vernacular text with the Latin version may be particularly revealing, as is the case for Mechthild of Magdeburg's *Flowing Light of the Godhead* and Beatrice of Nazareth's *Seven Ways of Loving God*.

The question of scribal mediation is further complicated in that the mystic's text is, in essence, a message transmitted through her, which must be transmitted to her surrounding community. Thus, the denuding of voice of the text, of a first-person narrative, goes hand in hand with the status of the mystic as "transcriber" of a divine message that does not bear the mystic's signature, but rather God's. In addition, the tendency to write in the third person in visionary narratives may draw from a longstanding tradition that stems from Paul in 2 Cor. of communicating visions in the third person, but at the same time, it presents a means for women to negotiate with conflicts with regard to authority or immediacy of the divine through a veiled distance or humility that conformed to a narrative tradition.

Finally, the loss of the proper name is thematically significant for a mystic like Porete, who, in her *Mirror of Simple Souls*, desires to lose her name, since expropriation of the will and self falls in line with the becoming simple of the soul in order to more closely resemble God. Thus, the question of voice and authority in mystics' writings must also take into consideration questions of narrative strategy.

PATRICIA DAILEY

References and Further Reading

Barratt, Alexandra, "Continental Women Mystics and English Readers." In *The Cambridge Companion to Medieval Women's Writing*, edited by Carolyn Dinshaw and David Wallace. Cambridge: Cambridge University Press, 2003, pp. 91–108.

Beckwith, Sarah. "Problems of Authority in Late Medieval English Mysticism: Agency and Authority in *The Book of Margery Kempe*." *Exemplaria* 4 (1992): 171–200.

Benedict, Kimberly M. *Empowering Collaborations: Writing Partnerships between Religious Women and Scribes in the Middle Ages*. New York: Routledge, 2005.

Colledge, Edmund, and Romana Guarnieri. "The Glosses by 'M.N.' and Richard Methley to *The Mirror of Simple Souls*." *Archivio italiano per la storia della pieta* 5 (1968): 357–382.

de Hemptinne, Thérèse, and María Eugenia Góngora, eds. *The Voice of Silence: Women's Literacy in a Men's Church*. Turnhout: Brepols, 2004.

Ferrante, Joan. *To the Glory of Her Sex: Women's Roles in the Composition of Medieval Texts*. Bloomington, Ind.: Indiana University Press, 1997.

Gill, Katherine. "Women and the Production of Religious Literature in the Vernacular, 1300–1500." In *Creative Women in Medieval and Early Modern Italy*, edited by Ann Matter and Ann Coakley. Philadelphia: University of Pennsylvania Press, 1994, pp. 64–104.

Hirsch, John C. "Author and Scribe in *The Book of Margery Kempe.*" *Medium Aevum* 44 (1975): 145–150.

Kline, Barbara. "Editing Women's Visions: Some Thoughts on the Transmission of Female Mystics' Texts." *Magistra* 2.1 (1996): 3–23.

Lochrie, Karma. "*The Book of Margery Kempe:* The Marginal Woman's Quest for Literary Authority." *Journal of Medieval and Renaissance Studies* 16 (1986): 33–55.

McGinn, Bernard. *The Flowering of Mysticism: Men and Women in the New Mysticism*—1200–1350. New York: Crossroads, 1998.

———. "The Changing Shape of Late Medieval Mysticism." *Church History* 65.2 (1996): 197–219.

Mooney, Catherine M. "Brother A. in the Composition of Angela of Foligno's Revelations." In *Creative Women in Medieval and Early Modern Italy*, edited by E. Ann Matter and Ann Coakley. Philadelphia: University of Pennsylvania Press, 1994, pp. 34–63.

Poor, Sara S. *Mechthild of Magdeburg and Her Book: Gender and the Making of Textual Authority.* Philadelphia: University of Pennsylvania, 2004.

Riddy, Felicity. "Julian of Norwich and Self-Textualization." In *Editing Women*, edited by Anne M. Hutchison. Toronto: University of Toronto Press, 1998, pp. 101–124.

———. "'Publication' before Print: The Case of Julian of Norwich." In *The Uses of Script and Print, 1300–1700*, edited by Alexandra Walsham. Cambridge: Cambridge University Press, 2004, pp. 29–49.

Staley Johnson, Lynn. "The Trope of the Scribe and the Question of Literary Authority in the Works of Julian of Norwich and Margery Kempe." *Speculum* 66.4 (1991): 820–838.

———. *Margery Kempe's Dissenting Fictions.* University Park, Pa.: Pennsylvania State University Press, 1994.

Stargardt, Ute. "Male Clerical Authority in the Spiritual (Auto)biographies of Medieval Holy Women." In *Women as Protagonists and Poets in the German Middle Ages: An Anthology of Feminist Approaches to Middle High German Literature*, edited by Albrecht Classen. Kümmerle: Göppingen, 1991, pp. 209–238.

Summit, Jennifer. "Women and Authorship." In *The Cambridge Companion to Medieval Women's Writing*, edited by Carolyn Dinshaw and David Wallace. Cambridge: Cambridge University Press, 2003, pp. 91–108.

Wilson, Katharina M., ed. *Medieval Women Writers.* Athens, Ga.: University of Georgia Press, 1984.

See also **Ancrene Wisse; Anchoresses; Angela of Foligno; Autohagiography; Beatrice of Nazareth; Beguines; Birgitta of Sweden; Catherine of Genoa; Catherine of Siena; Christina of Markyate; Ebner, Margaretha; Hadewijch; Hagiography; Heretics and Heresy; Julian of Norwich; Kempe, Margery; Laywomen, Religious: Marguerite Porete; Marie of Oignies; Mechthild of Magdeburg; Minnesang; Nuns as Scribes; Prophets; Women Authors: German Texts; Women Authors: Italian Texts; Women Authors: Latin Texts; Women Authors: Middle English Texts; Women Authors: Old French Texts; Women Authors: Spanish Texts**

MYTHOLOGY, MEDIEVAL RECEPTION OF

Greco-Roman mythology—often denigrated as paganism by Christian authors such as St. Augustine, in *De civitate Dei* (*On the City of God*)—was transmitted in the Middle Ages through three vehicles. First was the transmission of the classical authors (primarily Virgil, Horace, Lucan, Statius, Boethius, Martianus Capella, and, in the later Middle Ages, Ovid) as texts for learning Latin grammar in monastic schools and then universities. Second were scholastic glosses on the classics, in addition to commentaries and mythological handbooks that explained to scholars and poets the literal and moral (or allegorical) significance of gods and heroes. Many of these handbooks were organized—as was the twelfth-century Third Vatican Mythography—by name of god and ordered within a narrative hierarchy that began with the outermost planet (Saturn) and moved downward, toward the earth; or that began, like Giovanni Boccaccio's unfinished *De genealogiae gentilium deorum* (On the genealogy of the gentile gods), with the paterfamilias of the gods and traced the genealogy of his offspring. Third, in allegorical Latin and vernacular poetry the gods and heroes transform into personifications (for example, Amor, or Cupid, the son of Venus) who interact with a (male) persona, often the author (Amaunt the Lover, Dante, Geoffrey Chaucer, John Gower); the persona struggles with some psychological problem or crisis on his narrative journey. The late medieval reception of classical mythology depended upon poetic techniques that constructed another world in which subjective experiences, spiritual or courtly, played out for the poet and his readers' edification.

Because medieval scholars and educated poets were generally male, and women, even Latin-literate women, were not educated in the universities, the reception, explanation, and use of mythology in the Middle Ages was conventionally gendered male. The misogyny characteristic of patriarchal institutions like the Church and the university encouraged the portrayal and interpretation of female mythological figures as objects of sexual desire, or as agents of self-destruction through desire for them—or else, when they were compared in patristic glosses to the Virgin Mary, as idealized agents of man's virtue and salvation. Scholars Fulgentius, Remigius of Auxerre, Pierre Bersuire, and Robert Holkot, among others, maintained this dehumanizing attitude toward women in mythological glosses on Virgil, Martianus Capella, Ovid, and books of the Bible.

With the beginnings of early humanism in Italy, France, and England—which saw the rise of the vernacular and broadened literacy among royal queens, women patrons, and other noble women—a newly created audience of female readers demanded more books for and about women. Dante, in his fourteenth-century *Divina Commedia*, modeled his epic on that of Virgil's *Aeneid*, but substituted, for Aeneas's guide through Elysium, Virgil as his own guide through hell and most of purgatory and, then, Beatrice—an object of his own *amor courtois*—through heaven. Boccaccio wrote *De claris mulieribus* (On famous women), adapting classical stories of women to his own monomyth of Fortune as a blind and capricious female goddess. Chaucer, as a court poet, wrote in *Troilus and Criseyde* more sensitively than preceding poets and scholars about the Trojan widow and daughter of the traitor Calchas, Criseyde, who falls in love with the Trojan prince Troilus. Chaucer, however, then reveals false Criseyde succumbing to the wiles of the Greek hero Diomedes, and Chaucer's treatment of her apparently irritated the women of the court so much that as courtly penance he began writing his unfinished version of Ovid's *Heroides*, *The Legend of Good Women*.

Finally, one known woman scholar and poet emerged at the end of the Middle Ages who "remythicized" classical figures (Hans Robert Jauss's term). The fifteenth-century Franco-Italian poet Christine de Pizan—one of whose patrons was Queen Isabelle of France—celebrates the Amazons as female leaders who excelled in war, along with many other female mythological figures, queens, and saints, in her *Cité des Dames* (City of Ladies) (1405). Christine's most famous work was the *Epistre Othea* (The Letter of Othea) (1399), in which this invented goddess of wisdom draws upon the epistolary structure of Ovid's *Heroides* to write not a love letter to a man but an educational letter to the fifteen-year-old Trojan prince Hector in which she moralizes and allegorizes one hundred mythological fables drawn from Ovid's *Metamorphoses*, but in which she empowers the female and reveals male weaknesses and errors. As a scholar she and Jean Gerson, chancellor of the University of Paris, argued in a famous epistolary debate about the *Roman de la Rose* against the dehumanization of the female in scholastic allegorization.

JANE CHANCE

References and Further Reading

Blumenfeld-Kosinski, Renate. *Reading Myth: Classical Mythology and Its Interpretations in Medieval French Literature*. Stanford, Ca: Stanford University Press, 1997.

Chance, Jane. "Illuminated Royal Manuscripts of the Early Fifteenth Century and Christine de Pizan's Remythification of Classical Women in *Cité des Dames*." In *Contexts and Continuities: Proceedings of the IVth International Colloquium on Christine de Pizan (Glasgow 21-27 July 2000)*, published in honour of Liliane Dulac, edited by Angus J. Kennedy with Rosalind Brown-Grant, James C. Laidlaw, and Catherine M. Müller. Glasgow University Medieval French Texts and Studies 1. Glasgow: University of Glasgow Press, 2002, pp. 203–242.

———. *Medieval Mythography*, vols. 1-2. Gainesville, Fla.: University Press of Florida, 1994 and 2000.

———. *The Mythographic Chaucer: The Fabulation of Sexual Politics*. Minneapolis and London: University of Minnesota Press, 1995.

———, trans. *Christine de Pizan's Letter of Othea to Hector, with Introduction, Notes, and Interpretive Essay*. Newburyport, Mass.: Focus Information Group, 1990. Reprint, Cambridge: D. S. Brewer, 1997.

See also **Amazons; Beatrice; Boccaccio, Giovanni; Book Ownership; Chaucer, Geoffrey; Christine de Pizan; Criseyde; Dante Alighieri; Education, Monastic; Gender Ideologies; Gerson, Jean; Humanism; Literacy and Reading: Latin; Literacy and Reading: Vernacular; Mary, Virgin: in Literature; Misogyny; Ovid, Medieval Reception of; Roman de la Rose and its Reception; Universities**

N

NAMING

Focusing on naming goes much beyond simply study-ing women's names, which are the result of the crucial social process of naming. Understanding this process is all the more important for medievalists because the documents consulted are full of people's names that are usually considered as identifiers unveiling a pre-existing identity. They should be in fact considered as the signs of a *qualifying process*, and we will see that the naming of women although less thoroughly stud-ied than that of men is an excellent vantage point for the observation of the social implications of the naming process itself.

The identification of women in the Middle Ages is composed of three processes that can be disassociated for the sole sake of analysis: on the one hand distin-guishing the person (a better term than *individualizing* as it does not import into the medieval social system our own notion of "individual"); on the other hand the social qualification of the person (including their femi-nine gender); and eventually the social use of writing (as the names we study are only known from written sources). As writing was overwhelmingly produced by literate males, women, like peasants, were named by others instead of being self-named.

The question of distinguishing the person by his or her name (which includes matters as fundamental as Salvation as on the day of the Last Judgment when the dead will be called by their names) involves both theological and philosophical issues that go much beyond the specific case of women and cannot be dealt with in detail here. It is important, however, to keep in mind that the identification of medieval women is closely connected with how the human being was conceived at the time.

More significant is the fact that female anthropo-nymy is "an indication of the way the woman is placed in society and of the roles that she is given in it" (Bourin, 1992, p. 3). In order to identify persons medi-eval societies used a series of techniques (for instance onomastic, heraldic, sigilistic, and sometimes icono-graphic ones) in a precise way that evolved according to needs. A person could thus be named in a changing way, each denomination being connected with the spe-cific social network in which the naming occurs. The name, as the result of the naming process, speaks less of a single person as of her or his place in a particular social network. This is clear from the numerous cases of name changing during "conversions" (when an adult was baptized or especially when a person took religious vows). But there is also the case of brothers sometimes bearing, but not always, the same surname according to needs, a phenomenon apparent as well among lay women whose names change according to the type of document (charters, tax rolls, seals, grave-stones), with a variability that seems greater than with men, precisely because this naming served to position women in relation to men.

This leads us back to the idea of denomination as social qualification: by their names, women are quali-fied, that is to say classified, inserted in multiple forms of social belonging. The qualification as a female person is one among other forms. Trying to find out if this particular form comes before others is a very difficult and probably unnecessary task. The historical evolution of the means of denomination of women is to a large extent in keeping with what we already know about men.

This historical evolution (which has been studied many times since the 1990s in continental Europe, which explains the lack of English-speaking bibliography) is characterized by the dropping of the three-name Roman system as early as late antiquity and replacing it by a single name composed of elements from a bilateral origin (e.g., a *Deorovaldus* and a *Bertovara* will call their daughter *Deorovara*). This inserts women as well as men into a kin-group whose limits are variable (from the clan to the conjugal family with a clear statistical bias for the paternal side, however, at all social levels until the practice of hypergamic marriages, that is marriages of men with women of upper social level, spread at the end of the Carolingian period, especially after the tenth century). But this is less a means of genealogical identification than a way of qualifying the person thus named as potential heir. The sex is indicated by the end of the name, by the *-us* ending for men and *-a* or *-is* ending for women, or by more specifically feminine elements (e.g., *-hildis*).

The principle of the transmission of whole names (which had not completely disappeared and had turned similarly bilateral) became dominant after about the seventh century because of a deeper Christianization. This undermined the taboo until then attached to the transmission of names (which were supposed to refer to a personal essence). And with the restructuring of the aristocracy at the same time, her practices spread downward by imitation. The insertion in the kin-group by name did not disappear—the married woman passed names from her own kin-group more often to her sons as well as daughters because the social level of the wife was often higher than that of the husband.

From the mid-eleventh century the main anthroponymic evolution in the medieval Western world was the progressive introduction of a surname, first changing from one generation to another (and merely signifying the filiation of the person) then becoming hereditary (often a place name indicating the location of residence or production). For women, however, the complement of the given name often marked the type of relationship with a man: "daughter of..." or "widow of..." and more and more "wife of...." In cities, where the two-name system seems to have appeared earlier than in the countryside, the focalization of the woman on her husband seems to have been clearly reinforced after about 1300. In Paris as in Blois or in Provence in the early fourteenth century, one finds that women are designated most of the time—and more and more—in relation to their husbands, either by the mention of the conjugal link or by the feminized form of their husband's surname (e.g., in Paris *Erembourg, fame Jehan Beroust* in 1297 became in 1300 *Erembourg la Berode*).

The dropping of the father's name is the most common situation in the anthroponymy of the married woman, but in town, it is the conjugal link that prevailed, whatever the social level. The women from the lowest social levels, however, more often bore individual nicknames (e.g., in Blois in 1334, seventeen percent of the women of lower social level bear a nickname – as *la Fovette, la Pie-Parterne*, etc.,—in comparison to only four percent of the women of middle social level, and none of the women of upper social level). The same observation can be made in Wurtzburg in the fourteenth century where the name of bourgeois ladies connects them more directly with their husbands than in the aristocracy where filiation prevails even when the marriage is mentioned. After about 1400, in Germany aristocratic women bear a double surname, associating the name of their husbands and the name of their fathers (e.g., "Anna von Reinstein, born von Adelsheim" in 1402) thus signaling the alliance they produced between two "lineages."

The study of these phenomena and the differences between rhythms (women are involved later than men with the use of the double name) show a close correlation between the transmission of the name and of power (what was already to be observed with the correlation between hypergamy and the transmission of names by women). Indeed male clerics too switched later to the two-name system, and the spread of the phenomenon is all the slower as one goes down in the social scale.

Also, one notes wide regional differences: on the one hand there is a periphery (Italy, Spain, Brittany, England, Scotland, Scandinavia) where surnames on the model of "children of..." (*nomen paternum*) were preferred because they underlined the specificity of the siblings-group, transmitting a homogeneous image of the generation that coincides precisely with the regions where heritage is egalitarian among all children and sexes. In this case again the name is a means of claiming succession. Opposed to that model is, on the other hand, the continental "heartland" where surnames are instead toponymic and which, from the tenth and eleventh centuries, were characterized by the creation of communities of productive hearths, each run by a man who was a single heir. As women were not heads of family they were affected only marginally by these anthroponymic transformations.

Simultaneously with the introduction of the surname, one notes a strong concentration of the stock of proper names on a few choices, first those of princes and kings. Then names of a Christian origin became popular after the eleventh century, especially *Peter* for men, and later *Mary*. This name had remained present since the late Roman Empire in Italy where it was even dominant in some regions. Also *Pierrette/Pétronille* was popular for women (as well as, in some regions, typically feminine auspicious names such as *Bonne* or *Belle*). Then *John* triumphed for men in the thirteenth century (thirty percent in the first half of the fourteenth century before going down to twenty-five percent in the fifteenth century), followed by *Jeanne* among women (with very smaller percentages).

The case of *Pierrette* and *Jeanne*, as that of *Guilhelmina* or *Raimunda* in twelfth-century Languedoc, perfectly illustrate a specific phenomenon of women's naming that developed throughout the Middle Ages (i.e., the frequency of women's names that were feminized forms of men's names). The reverse never happens. Thus, just as the use of the surname signals a clear focalization of the woman on her father or husband, her proper name also makes her a derivative from man. The medieval naming of women thus carried on the biblical discourse (*vir* → *virgo*) and qualified the woman as a dominated being.

JOSEPH MORSEL

References and Further Reading

Bedos-Rezak, Brigit Myriam, and Dominique Iogna-Prat, eds. *L'individu au Moyen Âge. Individuation et individualisation avant la modernité.* Paris: Flammarion, 2005.

Beech, George T., Monique Bourin, and Pascal Chareille, eds. *Personal Names Studies of Medieval Europe. Social Identity and Familial Structures.* Kalamazoo: Medieval Institute Publications, 2002.

Bourin, Monique, and Pascal Chareille, eds. *Genèse médiévale de l'anthroponymie moderne,* vol 2, part 2: *Persistances du nom unique. Désignation et anthroponymes des femmes. Méthodes statistiques pour l'anthroponymie.* Tours: Publications de l'Université, 1992.

Bourin, Monique, Jean-Marie Martin, and François Menant, eds. *L'anthroponymie, document d'histoire sociale des mondes méditerranéens médiévaux.* Rome-Paris: École Française de Rome, 1996.

Chareille, Pascal and Patrice Beck, eds. *Genèse médiévale de l'anthroponymie moderne,* 5 vols. Tours: Publications de l'Université, 1990–2002.

Duby, Georges and Jacques Le Goff, eds. *Famille et parenté dans l'Occident médiéval.* Paris: École Française de Rome, 1977.

Goetz, Hans-Werner. "*Nomen feminile.* Namen und Namengebung der Frauen im frühen Mittelalter." *Francia* 23.1 (1996): 99–134.

Martin, Jean-Marie and François Menant, eds. *Genèse médiévale de l'anthroponymie moderne: l'espace italien.* 3 vols.: École Française de Rome, 1994–1998. Special issue, *Mélanges de l'École Francaise de Rome,* 106 (1994), 107 (1995), 110 (1998).

Martínez Sopena, Pascual, ed. *Antroponimia y sociedad. Sistemas de identificación hispano-cristianos en los siglos IX a XIII.* Valladolid: Universidad de Valladolid, 1995.

Mitterauer, Michael. *Ahnen und Heilige. Namengebung in der europäischen Geschichte.* München: Beck, 1993.

Morsel, Joseph. "Personal Naming and Representations of Feminine Identity in Franconia in the Later Middle Ages." In *Personal Names...,* edited by Beech-Bourin-Chareille, pp. 157–180.

Villani, Matteo. "L'onomastica femminile nel ducato di Napoli: l'esempio di *Maria*". *Mélanges de l'École Française de Rome – Moyen Âge* 106 (1994): 641–651.

See also **Bible, Women in; Cities and Towns; Family (Earlier Middle Ages); Family (Later Middle Ages); Genealogy; Kinship; Noble Women; Patriarchy and Patrilineage; Seals and Sigillography; Widows**

NATURAL WORLD

For the medieval woman the natural world of plants, stones, soils, waters, and weather was a place not mainly for speculation but for use. As *domina* (lady of the house) with responsibility for her own domain, the natural world was where she went for what she needed in cooking, brewing, and baking; for making life comfortable, cheerful, even pretty; and for treating discomfort and disease in family and friends. Not surprisingly, like the gypsy herbalist and farmwife still found in rural Europe today, the medieval woman knew a great deal about her own local ecology.

Images documenting her activities within it abound, especially in the illustrated herbals. They show her gathering wild plants in forest and field; picking fruit with friends; cultivating her herb garden; and planting, gathering, drying, and preparing her harvest. Others show her collecting eggs from her henhouse, milking cows, making cheese and churning butter, brewing beer, formulating potions, and selling her wares in the local market. But what mindset did a woman bring to these activities? What framework did she use to understand the connections between the resources she gathered and prepared, and the natural world from which they came? Unfortunately, of the many texts written by women only a few by those practiced in these arts survive: they include the *Treatments for Women* by Trota of Salerno, and Hildegard of Bingen's *Physica* and *Causes and Cures.*

Trota's *Treatments for Women* is notable for its terse and, above all, practical approach to the natural world—the source for almost all of her ingredients. She used farm and forest products almost exclusively: wild plants, kitchen herbs, nuts, fungi, berries, clay, rainwater, saltwater, vinegar, wine, oil, flour, eggs, and animal fat. Her attitude towards the source of all her ingredients was pragmatic; absent from her prescriptions is any romantic, magical, or ritual element. Use the natural world as she prescribes, her recipes imply, and the desired results will follow.

Trota's view of the natural world appears, then, quite modern and scientific, or, perhaps, simply practical and housewifely. At any rate, it was remarkably utilitarian—everything had its use for humans, and this use was natural, normal, and predictable.

Hildegard of Bingen's attitude toward the natural world was similar but more complex, perhaps because all of her work survived. In the nine books of her *Physica*, as in her medical text *Causes and Cures*, she shared her knowledge of plants, trees, minerals, metals, reptiles, fish, birds, and animals. For each item she provided a short description and then one or more recipes, along with an explanation for how and why each ingredient worked. When compared to traditional male sources such as the encyclopedic work of Pliny and Isidore, her material seems less abstract and theoretical and more personal and empiric. Indeed she covered more than two hundred wild plants and over thirty kitchen herbs, almost all of which were local; Hildegard knew her armamentarium personally and well.

Unlike Trota, however, Hildegard's knowledge was not *only* empiric; she used literate medical and scientific theory to explain how her empiric recipes worked. In essence the cosmos was an ordered set of moving spheres that exerted its forces upon the natural world through the four elements, qualities, and humors. That is, it was the traditional and ancient worldview that structured and ordered Hildegard's empiric observations.

Can it be said from the surviving evidence that there was a particular "woman's" natural world? Yes and no. On the one hand, both Trota and Hildegard had a broad and deep knowledge of the natural world and its practical uses. And this was, in the main, knowledge acquired personally, from experience, observation, and oral tradition, not from books. Although there is nothing particularly feminine about this kind of practical knowledge, for millennia it has made up a subterranean women's culture that continues, even today, in cooking recipes and gardening tricks, passed along orally and seldom written down.

On the other hand, Hildegard—and, probably, most other literate medieval women—did use scientific theory in order to structure her empiric knowledge. Doing so was not, of course, particularly female, although even here, it is difficult to be certain. Because, despite her reliance on traditional concepts, Hildegard's worldview was idiosyncratic—her world, natural and otherwise, quivered with interconnected life. In the natural world as she perceived it, everything was interdependent and continuous; everything influenced everything else. Whether in this she represented the medieval woman's view of the natural world, or whether it was an expression of her unique temperament is, given our lack of sources, impossible to say.

What we can say is that the natural world was well-known to the medieval woman and well-used; at the very least, it was her main source of goods, the place where she spent most of her life. It was where she looked for, and knew how to find, food and medicines, cosmetics and dyes, ornaments and decorations. There was no unnatural world.

VICTORIA SWEET

References and Further Reading

Arano, Luisa Cogliati, Adele Westbrook, and Oscar Ratti. *The Medieval Health Handbook*. New York: Georges Braziller, 1992.

Berger, Margret. *Hildegard of Bingen: On Natural Philosophy and Medicine*. Cambridge: D. S. Brewer, 1999.

Collins, Minta. *Medieval Herbals: The Illustrative Tradition*. London: British Library, 2000.

Green, Monica H. *The Trotula: A Medieval Compendium of Women's Medicine*. Philadelphia: University of Pennsylvania Press, 2001.

Migne, Jacques-Paul, ed. *S. Hildegardis abbatissae Opera omnia. Patrologiae cursus completus. Series Latina.* Paris: Garnier, 1855.

Moulinier, Laurence and Rainer Berndt, eds. *Beate Hildegardis Cause et cure.* Berlin: Akademie-Verlag, 2003.

Sweet, Victoria. "Hildegard of Bingen and the Greening of Medieval Medicine." *Bulletin of the History of Medicine* 73 (1999): 381–403.

———. *Rooted in the Earth, Rooted in the Sky: Hildegard of Bingen and Premodern Medicine*. New York: Routledge Press, 2006.

Throop, Priscilla. *Hildegard von Bingen's Physica: The Complete English Translation of Her Classic Work on Health and Healing*. Vt.: Healing Arts Press, 1998.

See also **Agriculture; Alewives and Brewing; Clothwork, Domestic; Cosmetics; Doctors and Healers; Gynecology; Hildegard of Bingen; Trota of Salerno**

NECROLOGIES AND MORTUARY ROLLS

One of the principal functions of nuns and monks in the Middle Ages was to pray for the dead. When people, who supported the monastery or church with gifts, offered sons and daughters, or were otherwise connected with a monastery, died, their names were recorded, so that prayers could be offered for them on the anniversaries of their deaths. Léopold Delisle called these records "paleographical monuments regarding the custom of praying for the dead." Because these documents listing the dead often specify their place in society or their relation to the monastery, they tell us much about the demographics of religious communities, the relations between those communities, the holders of office within the religious community and the surrounding worlds, and even the intellectual and material state of the communities. These documents took several forms.

In Carolingian times, *Libri vitae* contained the names of the living and the dead who were to be remembered at Mass. Only a few of these survive. Prayer confraternities existed between religious communities, so that the members of each participating monastery or community of canons prayed for the dead of all the associated communities, including those who entered only when they were at the point of death. Communities kept a list of the monasteries with which they had a prayer confraternity, so that they would know to which houses they should send news of a death in the community. Lay and clerical individuals also formed prayer confraternities with a monastery or among themselves. Confraternities kept registers of dead members for whom they prayed. When someone died, her community sent a messenger (*rolliger*) with a letter or mortuary roll announcing the death to the communities in its confraternity, requesting prayers. Each community the messenger visited inscribed its name and perhaps a message on the roll. Communities maintained necrologies, used in the commemoration of the dead at the chapter meeting, and obituaries of other kinds, in which the names of the dead to be prayed for were listed in calendar order according to the dates of their deaths. Necrologies were often inscribed in a martyrology and regularly formed part of a chapter book, a liturgical document that contained the documents needed at the daily chapter meeting.

An example of such a chapter book is that from the Monastery of San Nicola della Cicogna, a dependent priory near its motherhouse of Monte Cassino. This book has seven parts including a martyrology/necrology, some directives for conducting chapter business, ninety-eight chapter homilies, and the Rule of St. Benedict. The necrology lists 1,150 names of deceased monks, laypersons, and clergy who were part of the spiritual family of St. Nicola. Ninety women are mentioned by name, and some of them are identified as lady, *monacha* (monastic), *soror* (religious sister), wife, and daughter, sometimes with indications of parentage or place of origin. Probably the lay people in the necrology were buried at the priory.

Two examples will serve to show how necrologies from women's communities can be helpful for the history of medieval women. The abbey of Engelberg in Switzerland had both women's and men's communities from the first half of the twelfth century until 1615, when the women's community moved away. Such double communities were widespread in southern Germany and Switzerland during the Middle Ages, though few of them remained together as long as Engelberg did. The presence of the women's community at Engelberg was scarcely mentioned by historians of the abbey. The study of a necrology prepared in 1345 by the prior of the abbey for the *magistra* (woman in charge of the women's community) has helped remedy that neglect. For example, the necrology shows that by 1345 Engelberg had had nine abbots and ten *magistrae*. It lists 251 male and 515 female deceased members of the community.

The women's abbey of Notre Dame de Saintes was founded in 1047 and endured until the French Revolution. Their chapter book contains a feminized *Rule of St. Benedict*, a martyrology, and a necrology. The necrology contains over 1,000 names, of nuns, nobility, clergy, and laity from the area around Saintes. About fourteen percent of the nuns are said to have died as girls or young women; another ten percent are said to have been *monachae conversae*, women who entered as mature adults. Some nuns are identified as important officials of the monastery: abbesses, prioresses of dependent priories, deans, sacristans, and almoners. When the deceased sisters are regularly described as "a venerable and humble nun" or "a woman of this church community who was consecrated to Christ" we learn about the nuns' own understanding of their calling. The clergy and laymen described as "faithful friends" and "confrères" were part of the monastery's large, extended family.

Another window into the community of Saintes is provided by a mortuary roll for Mathilda, Abbess of Holy Trinity, Caen, which seems to have begun circulating in 1113 and reached Saintes, the 145th entry on the roll, toward the end of the decade. Saintes' entry consists of three twenty-line sections of Latin poetry and a list of deceased sisters from Saintes for whom prayers are asked. These include four abbesses, one dean, one prioress, twenty-seven nuns, and five men associated with the community. The last forty lines of poetry are inscribed as "verses of the abbess." If this is so, she was a very well-educated woman.

HUGH FEISS

References and Further Reading

Feiss, Hugh. "The Chapter Book of the Nuns of Saintes," *Yale University Library Gazette* 67.1 2 (1992): 13–20.

———. "'Consecrated to Christ, Nuns of This Church Community': The Benedictines of Notre-Dame de Saintes 1047–1792." *American Benedictine Review* 45.2 (1994): 269–302.

———. "A Poet Abbess from Notre-Dame de Saintes." *Magistra*. 1.1 (1995): 39–54.

Gilomen-Schenkel, Elsanne. "Engelberg, Interlaken und andere autonome Doppelklöster im Südwesten des

Reiches (11.–13. Jh.)" In *Doppelklöster und andere Formen der Symbiose männlicher und weiblicher Religiosen im Mittelalter*, edited by Kaspar Elm and Michel Parisse. Berlin: Duncker & Humblot, 1992, pp. 115–133.

Hilken, Charles. *The Necrology of San Nicola della Cicogna*, Studies and Texts 135. Toronto: Pontifical Institute of Mediaeval Studies, 2000.

Huyghebaert, N. *Les documents nécrologiques*, Typologie des Sources du Moyen Âge occidental, 4. Turnhout: Brepols, 1972.

Riccoboni, Sister Bartolemea. *Life and Death in a Venetian Convent: The Chronicle and Necrology of Corpus Domini, 1393–1436*, edited and translated by Daniel Bornstein. The Other Voice in Early Modern Europe. Chicago: University of Chicago Press, 2000.

Sheerin, Daniel. "Sisters in the Literary Agon: Texts from Communities of Women on the Mortuary Roll of the Abbess Matild of La Trinitè, Caen." *Women Writing Latin from Roman Antiquity to Early Modern Europe. Volume 2: Medieval Women Writing Latin*, edited by Laurie J. Churchill, Phyllis R. Brown, and Jane E. Jeffrey. Routledge, 2002, pp. 93–131.

See also **Abbesses; Confraternities; Death, Mourning, and Commemoration; Literacy and Reading: Latin; Monasticism and Nuns**

NINE WORTHY WOMEN

The Nine Worthy Women, or *Neuf Preuses* in French, a collection of nine classical warriors venerated in art and literature in the late Middle Ages, has been considered a female pendant to the Nine Male Worthies, who first appeared in Jacques de Longuyon's *Vows of the Peacock* (1312) symbolizing the epitome of chivalric prowess. But the first grouping of *Preuses* (Sinope, Hipolyte, Menalippe, Semiramis, Thamaris, Penthesilea, Teuca, Lampetho, and Deiphile) turns up only much later in Jean Le Fèvre's *Livre de leêsce* (*Book of Joy*, c. 1373), many decades after the *Vows*. Le Fèvre's heroines, all from antiquity and predominantly Amazons, do not conform to Longuyon's faith-based canon of three pagans, three Jews, and three Christians. It is open to speculation, however, whether Le Fèvre was the innovator of the *Preuses*. The almost incidental mention of the female grouping suggests that Le Fèvre's audience was already acquainted with the theme.

Representations of the Nine Worthy Women spread quickly into every artistic sphere, testifying to the great approval in which the illustrious female warrior, or *egregia bellatrix*, was held in the late fourteenth and fifteenth centuries. Oversized statues of the heroines were commissioned in 1385–1386 for the chimney of Coucy castle in northern France, a link to the glorious Greek and Roman past. Eustache

Deschamps, poet of the Hundred Years' War, invoked the *Preuses* in several ballades (c. 1389–1396); Thomas of Saluzzo introduced the *Preuses* into his narrative the *Chevalier errant* (*Knight Errant*) in 1394; and Thomas's bastard son decorated the baronial hall of Manta castle in Piedmont with a spectacular frieze of the *Preuses* (c. 1420). Worthies appeared in royal pageants and tapestries; male and female Worthies even graced face cards in the brand new pastime of playing cards.

Yet the names in the female canon fluctuated, based not on the whims of late medieval enthusiasts, it appears, but on the variety of ancient literary exemplars tendered to new audiences by the early Humanists. The third-century Roman author Justinus's *Epitome* of Trogeus Pompeius, for instance, contained the names of nine *Preuses*, all Amazons, and was likely read by Humanist translators who spread the heroines' fame. But the startling popularity of the "manly" valor of these female conquerors drew attention to profound differences based on conventions of gender. There was no direct female equivalent to the ancient biographical tradition known as the *Lives of Illustrious Men* (*De viris illustribus*) and ancient collections of women's lives were often directly or indirectly misogynistic. The Amazons, in particular, were reviled, because the idea of the female conqueror shamefully reversed the ideal of male valor. Medieval adaptations of the Trojan War saga, however, helped to soften the martial image of the Amazon queen Penthesilea, and Boccaccio's *Concerning Famous Women*, or *De claris mulieribus*, despite its satiric slant, broke ground in the 1360s as a collection devoted solely to biographies of women. In the popular motif of the Nine Worthy Women, a complicated literary past was transformed into a largely decorative motif where masculine valor could be counted as feminine virtue and women recovered their glorious (albeit sanitized) past.

DEBORAH FRAIOLI

References and Further Reading

Boccaccio, Giovanni. [*De claris mulieribus*]. *Famous Women*. Edited and translated by Virginia Brown. I Tatti Renaissance Library, 1. Cambridge, Mass., and London: Harvard University Press, 2001.

Fraioli, Deborah. "Why Joan of Arc Never Became an Amazon." In *Fresh Verdicts on Joan of Arc*, edited by Bonnie Wheeler and Charles T. Wood. New York and London: Garland, 1996, pp. 189–204.

Le Fèvre, Jean. *Les Lamentations de Matheolus et le Livre de leësce de Jehan Le Fèvre de Resson*. Edited by Anton-Gérard Van Hamel. Bibliothèque de l'Ecole des Hautes Etudes. 2 vols. Paris: Emile Bouillon, 1892–1905.

McMillan, Ann. "Men's Weapons, Women's War: The Nine Female Worthies, 1400–1640." *Mediaevalia* 5 (1979): 113–139.

Schroeder, Horst. *Der Topos* der *Nine Worthies in Literatur und bildender Kunst*. Göttingen, Germany: Vandenhoeck & Ruprecht, 1971.

Sedlacek, Ingrid. *Die Neuf Preuses: Heldinnen des Spätmittelalters*. Marburg: Jonas, 1997.

See also **Amazons; Defenses of Women; Romances of Antiquity; Warfare**

NOBLE WOMEN

Noble-born women of the aristocratic elite were land-holders, active political players, notable cultural patrons, and leading convent administrators throughout the Middle Ages by virtue of their rank, status, and pivotal positions linking dynastic kin-groups, although the precise parameters framing their actions and determining their resources varied according to time, place, and familial circumstances. The reason for their participation in such "public" affairs, as Marc Loch disclosed, is a simple one: the fundamentally patrimonial character of society at a time when kings did not monopolize judicial and military powers and noble families wielded jurisdictional authority and political power from their castles and itinerating courts. Like that of noble men, noble women's access to the wealth, lands, and titles that underlay their powers and position depended largely on the personal and domestic institutions of family and household—marriage, inheritance, and loyal retinues of sworn followers and other dependents—rather than on their participation in impersonal "public" institutions of "official" government and a fully monetarized marketplace. Although noble women, unlike their male peers, were not trained for, and did not routinely participate in, armed conflict, they wielded the authority to command those who did, and many became noted adjudicators and diplomats, using their wealth and networks of kin, clients, and influential churchmen to pursue claims and mediate solutions to disputes. Never deemed fully equal to men and still expected to behave largely as any other women when they did exercise authority over others, noble women's social rank and access, as wives and mothers, to male lords and their heirs outweighed any ideological disabilities imposed by their female gender when circumstances dictated that they should act in traditionally "male" domains. In other words, noble birth sufficed to make any noble woman a potential player in high politics, affairs of fiefs and vassals, and the management of landed estates, and those activities, woven into the texture of a society in which "domestic" household management included what today would be considered affairs of official government and "public" politics, were natural extensions, not transgressions, of noble women's traditionally "feminine" social roles.

When they entered such "public" arenas, most often as regents for absent husbands or minor heirs, their powers ran the gamut of the feudal, judicial, economic, and political prerogatives of any medieval lord. Noble women received and swore homage, controlled fiefs, oversaw the maintenance and garrisoning of castles, and ordered knights to fight, while many supervised the management of seigneurial estates. The higher-ranking among them presided over courts that settled disputes, punished lawbreakers, defined provincial custom and authorized the undertakings of other people in their domains. They negotiated treaties with neighboring lay and ecclesiastical lords, granted liberties to burghers and villagers, and founded and regulated fairs, while some even controlled coinage. Although how women's powers and activities changed according to their own life-stages is often discussed, less frequently acknowledged is how, over the life-course of dynastic families, married women's pivotal positions as links between their natal and affinal families and, frequently, between generations within their own conjugal families, assured that married noble women were well placed to play key roles securing advantages for their various relatives and assuring the devolution of family honors from generation to generation.

The notion that a change in family structure caused noble women's political powers to be eclipsed from shortly after the year 1000 until the thirteenth century (when the great age of regents began, according to G. Duby, who first formulated that thesis), has not been borne out by subsequent research into the rich narrative sources, letter collections, and cartularies of the eleventh and twelfth centuries. That research has recuperated the life stories of numerous lordly women active in those years, from the high-ranking Adelaide of Turin and Savoy, Beatrice of Swabia, Ermengard of Narbonne, Marie of Champagne, and Mathilda of Boulogne and Brabant to place alongside the well-known Mathilda of Tuscany, Adela of Blois, and Eleanor of Aquitaine, to the more modest Eustachia of Brou, Beatrice of Roucy and Nogent, Mathilda of Chester, Stephania of Les Baux, and Benedicta of Ehrnegg-Königsberg. It also reveals that such a postulated shift is largely illusionary, based on assumptions about changes in social practices that cannot be sustained. Senior sons increasingly may have been the preferred heirs to fiefs and castles, but many families controlled portfolios of possessions that included multiple fiefs alongside other, nonfeudal, property, and significant numbers of fathers left no surviving sons to succeed. Furthermore, land acquisition was not a zero-sum game, in which real property could be obtained only by inheritance or as a reward for military service; conquest, clearance, exchange, or purchase and maternal inheritances remained key ways to gain income-producing land throughout the Middle Ages. Noble women were never banned from inheriting fiefs or receiving them as marital assigns (dowries or dowers) and, once endowed with property at marriage, women were rarely legally barred from receiving further land from their natal kin; nor, in those centuries, were they prohibited from controlling real property and other assets legally theirs while their husbands were alive. Moreover, a change in inheritance customs entails no underlying change in family structure, which remained fundamentally bilateral throughout the Middle Ages. The very existence of heiresses—female direct heirs—and of daughters who indirectly transmitted their fathers' lands to their own sons—after their older brothers had inherited them—reveals that daughters were considered members of their patrilines (or, natal families), as does church marriage law, which applied incest prohibitions equally to the maternal and paternal kin of potential spouses.

Noble women also played prominent roles in religious-cultural domains, primarily as patrons of art, literature, religious communities, and holy men. In pre-university days, even lay women could be highly learned in Latin literary culture, trained by household tutors or in monastic communities alongside young girls who ultimately took vows. And as vernacular literature flowered from the twelfth century, noble women came into their own as patrons and audience alike. Lordly courts were cultural as well as political centers and women promoted authors in all major *genres*, from romance and lyric to chronicles and devotional texts, both for their own edification and amusement, and to assist in the education of their children of both sexes. Moreover, in monastic and court settings alike, women often took the lead in the formation and transmission of dynastic and communal memories.

Noble women were not appreciably more devout than noble men, though they were often cultivated by churchmen seeking to influence their menfolk. Even those women who lived and died in the world routinely made pious bequests, endowed monasteries, and patronized charismatic holy men out of concern for the spiritual well-being of family and friends; pilgrimage and promoting the cult of favorite saints were popular forms of devotion. Many noble women chose to end their days by entering religious communities, sometimes where they could join other family members, and their previous experience often led them to accept leadership roles such as abbess or prioress, for which they were well-suited.

No one life course or pattern of experiences fits all noble women of the Middle Ages, whether those of the greater or lesser nobility. Their rank never made them, as a group, equal to noble men, and they remained vulnerable in the face of social forces and gender prejudices that could override their legal rights. Yet, as scholars continue to illuminate the rich and varied experiences of medieval noble women, they should keep in mind that female lords (*dominae*) were not rare in the Middle Ages; the exception was the man who had not dealt with at least one.

KIMBERLY LoPRETE

References and Further Reading

Bloch, Marc. *Feudal Society*, translated by L. A. Manyon. Chicago: University of Chicago Press, 1961.

Evergates, Theodore. "Nobles and Knights in Twelfth-Century France." In *Cultures of Power: Lordship, Status, and Process in Twelfth-Century Europe*, edited by Thomas N. Bisson. Philadelphia: University of Pennsylvania Press, 1995, pp. 11–35.

———, ed. *Aristocratic Women in Medieval France*. Philadelphia: University of Pennsylvania Press, 1999.

Ferrante, Joan M. *To the Glory of her Sex: Women's Roles in the Composition of Medieval Texts*. Bloomington: Indiana University Press, 1997.

Freed, John B. "German Source Collections: The Archdiocese of Salzburg as a Case Study." In *Medieval Women and the Sources of Medieval History*, edited by Joel T. Rosenthal. Athens: University of Georgia Press, 1990, pp. 80–121.

Johns, Susan M. *Noblewomen, Aristocracy and Power in the Twelfth-Century Anglo-Norman Realm*. Manchester: Manchester University Press, 2003.

Leyser, Karl J. *Rule and Conflict in an Early Medieval Society: Ottonian Saxony*. Oxford: Blackwell, 1979.

LoPrete, Kimberly A. "Gendering Viragos: Medieval Perceptions of Powerful Women." In *Studies on Medieval and Early Modern Women 4: Victims or Viragos?*, edited by Christine Meek and Catherine Lawless. Dublin: Four Courts Press, 2005, pp. 17–38.

McCash, June Hall, ed. *The Cultural Patronage of Medieval Women*. Athens: University of Georgia Press, 1996.

McLaughlin, Megan. "The Woman Warrior: Gender, Warfare, and Society in Medieval Europe." *Women's Studies* 17 (1990): 193–209.

See also **Abbesses; Courtly Love; Dowry and Other Marriage Gifts; Empresses: Byzantium; Ermengard; Frankish Lands; Gender Ideologies; Hildegard of Bingen; Hrosvit of Gandersheim; Hunting and Falconry; Inheritance; Matilda of Tuscany; Matilda the**

Empress; Monasticism and Nuns; Ottonian Royal Women; Queens and Empresses: The West; Regents and Queen-Lieutenants; Succession, Royal and Noble; Trobairitz and Troubadours

NOGAROLA, ISOTTA

The first major female humanist in Europe, Isotta Nogarola (1418–1466) first won fame when she circulated her book of Latin letters among Venice's literati in the late 1430s. Modern scholars once believed that around 1441 the Veronese-born humanist abandoned her literary studies in Venice to concentrate solely on religious and philosophical texts, living in seclusion in her mother's house in Verona. New research reveals that Nogarola remained a prominent Italian literary figure throughout her life, and that her renown as a syncretic scholar of the classical and Christian traditions grew exponentially during her later years in Verona (King and Robin, 2004, esp. pp. 9–19; 138–201; cf. King, 1978; 1980). Having studied under Guarino Veronese's humanist protégé, Martino Rizzoni, Nogarola put the finishing touches on a series of important works clearly designated for public performance during the years 1450–1461. Each work exemplifies her expertise in the key humanist genres: in addition to her autobiographical letterbook, she wrote a dialogue on a subject of major public interest; a long consolatory oration; and a polemic against the Turks. In 1450, traveling to Rome with a delegation from Verona, she delivered an oration at the court of Pope Nicholas V. In 1451, Nogarola engaged the Venetian Governor of Verona, Lodovico Foscarini, in a debate on the question of original sin, the nature of woman, and gender difference itself. Circulating as the *Dialogue on the Equal or Unequal Sin of Adam and Eve*, Nogarola's work stands, after Christine de Pizan's, as the inaugural work in the European "Querelle des femmes"—the controversy on gender and nature that would rage for the next four centuries (King and Robin, pp. 138–158). In 1453, Nogarola presented two new essays honoring the incoming bishop of Verona, the Venetian Ermolao Barbaro. The first of these epistolary orations welcomes Barbaro to Verona; the second, on the life of the ascetic St. Jerome, implicitly warns Barbaro against squandering the city's scarce resources on ecclesiastical pomp (King and Robin, pp. 159–174). In 1459, Nogarola wrote a passionate oration slated for performance at Pope Pius II's international Congress of Mantua (King and Robin, pp. 175–186), urging a crusade against the Turks. In her final major work, a funeral oration commissioned by the Venetian statesman Jacopo Antonio Marcello

on the death of his son in 1461, she follows the humanist consolatory tradition well established by Petrarch, Salutati, and Marsuppini in her conflation of biblical, patristic, and classical references (King and Robin, pp. 187–201). On her death in 1466, her contemporary Giammaria Filelfo celebrated her performance as a Ciceronian public orator (*oratrix*), as well as her more Horatian role as the public conscience (*vates*) of her city (see Filelfo's 1468 text in Abel, pp. 2.361–2.387).

DIANA ROBIN

References and Further Reading

Nogarola, Isotta. *Isotae Nogarolae veronensis opera quae supersunt omnia, accedunt Angelae et Zenevrae Nogarolae epistolae et carmina.* Edited by Eugenius Abel. Vienna: apud Gerold et socios, and Budapest: apud Fridericum Kilian, 1886. This work contains Giammaria Filelfo's eulogy of her [Cited above as Abel].
———. *Complete Writings: Letterbook, Dialogue on Adam and Eve, Orations.* Edited and translated by Margaret L. King and Diana Robin. Chicago: University of Chicago Press, 2004. [Cited above as King and Robin].
King, Margaret L. "The Religious Retreat of Isotta Nogarola (1418–1466)." *Signs* 3 (1978): 807–22.
———. "Book-Lined Cells." In *Beyond Their Sex: Learned Women of the European Past.* Edited by Patrician Labalme. New York: New York University Press, 1980, pp. 66–90.
King, Margaret L., and Albert Rabil, Jr., eds. *Her Immaculate Hand. Selected Works by and about the Women Humanists of Quattrocento Italy.* 2nd rev. ed. Binghamton, NY: Medieval and Renaissance Texts and Studies, 1991.
King, Margaret L., and Albert Rabil, Jr. *The Death of the Child Valerio Marcello.* Chicago: University of Chicago Press, 1994.
Major manuscript collections of Nogarola's letters are extant in Vienna (Vindobonensis 3481), Rome (Vaticanus 5127), Verona (Veronensis 256); see Paul Oskar Kristeller, *Iter Italicum*, 6 vols. (London, 1967–1997) for locations of smaller collections and individual letters of Nogarola in Florence, Venice, Milan, Mantua, Munich, Paris, London, and Basel.

See also **Cereta, Laura; Defenses of Women; Fedele, Cassandra; Humanism; Italy; Letter Writing; Renaissance, Historiography of; Sanuti, Nicolosa Castellani; Women Authors: Latin Texts**

NUNS AS ILLUMINATORS

Monastic rules dictated a life of work and prayer for women leading the religious life. The *opus dei* of church services was enhanced by manual labor, producing books and works of embroidery. The two crafts were practiced by nuns, sometimes in the same workshop, and their compositions and styles are comparable. The motivation for artwork was the same as that for prayer and chant in church services: to offer praise to God in words and works, to beautify the altar, and to make a tangible offering that would accrue to one's spiritual merit after death and that would earn one inclusion in the convent's memorial prayers.

Nuns' engagement as scribes across western Europe can be easily documented from numerous signed works beginning in the Merovingian era and continuing into the Renaissance. Their identification as artists has met with far less scholarly agreement. Prior to the Gothic era, scribe-artists were the norm, as illumination was largely done with the pen and colored inks. Hence Guda's famous self-portrait in a monochromatic pen initial identifies her as scribe and painter of a Homilary (Frankfurt, Stadt—und Universitätsbibliothek MS. Barth. 42, fol. 110v). At the same time, in these early centuries many monasteries were double houses or had nuns in a neighboring establishment, raising questions about the extent to which monks and nuns may have worked together or divided labor, with monks doing the illumination, as was the case in the Guta-Sintram Codex (Strassbourg, Bibliothèque du Grande Seminaire MS. 78) written by the scribe Guta at Schwartzenthann and illustrated by Sintram, a monk from a neighboring monastery. On the other hand, the Girona Apocalypse of 975 (Girona Cathedral, MS. 7) is signed by two painters, the monk Emeterius and Ende (presumably a nun), from the double house of Tavara. The most contested attributions to nun-artists are the two great twelfth-century masterpieces, Herrad of Hohenbourg's encyclopedia, the *Hortus Deliciarum,* and Hildegard of Bingen's mystical visions, the *Liber Scivias.* Both manuscripts have been destroyed, and neither nun identified herself as the artist. However, the inextricable interweaving of text and image in Herrad's book, and the imaginative originality of Hildegard's visions give persuasive evidence that both nuns drew the initial images for these works, even if, as is usually hypothesized, male copyists may have been responsible for one or both manuscripts (although this is far from certain either).

In later centuries, a vast number of manuscripts illustrated by nuns have survived, particularly in German houses of the Cistercian and mendicant orders, despite the fact that from the thirteenth century on, professional book production in urban centers was increasingly the norm. However, music books remained a near monopoly of monastic scriptoria. For these later centuries, the signatures of artists raise another difficulty, as they may refer to patrons who hired craftsmen to make work, the patron claiming to have "made" the work because s/he commissioned it. Manuscripts of high quality in particular have elicited this interpretation, among them music

books by the Cistercian nun Gisela von Kersenbroeck of Osnabrück dating c. 1300, and by the Cologne Poor Clares, working in the first half of the fourteenth century, precisely because these are the most notable works attributable to highly skilled women artists. The training of women in needlework needs no discussion as it was part of every girl's education. That some women came to convents with further artistic training can also be documented. In the early fourteenth century, a widow entered the Dominican convent of Oetenbach in Zurich bringing three other women with her, one of whom could write and illuminate, one painted, and the third did embroidery.

On the other hand, the late Middle Ages is the era of *nonnenarbeit,* a "folk art" debasement of Gothic style practiced in convents that had become stringently encloistered and largely dependent on in-house art works for inspiration. As a result, models were copied for centuries in works from Wienhausen, Ebstorf, and Lüne, transferred from fourteenth-century miniatures to needlework into the sixteenth century. Stitching over drawings on cloth is a cognate skill to writing and illuminating manuscripts, and the two arts need to be studied together. Iconographic originality is also a marked element of Gothic convent art, seen in early fourteenth-century miniatures from Engelberg in Switzerland and in sixteenth-century drawings from St. Walburg in Eichstätt. It has also been argued that religious women, like the laity, were particularly dependent on visual images for their devotions, in contrast to the "imageless" devotional ideal of male monasticism, precisely because they were technically laity.

JUDITH OLIVER

References and Further Reading

Carr, Annemarie Weyl. "Women as Artists in the Middle Ages: 'The Dark is Light Enough,'" In *Dictionary of Women Artists,* vol. 1, edited by Delia Gaze. London: Fitzroy, 1997, pp. 3–21.

Hamburger, Jeffrey. *Nuns as Artists. The Visual Culture of a Medieval Convent.* Berkeley: University of California Press, 1997.

Krone und Schleier: Kunst aus mittelalterlichen Frauenklöstern, edited by Jutta Frings and Jan Gerehow. Munich: Hirmer, 2005.

Marti, Susan. *Malen, Schreiben, und Beten: Die Spätmittelalterliche Handschriftenproduktion im Doppelkloster Engelberg.* Zurich: InterPublishers, 2002.

Oliver, Judith. *Singing with Angels: Liturgy, Music, and Art in the Gradual of Gisela von Kersenbroeck.* Turnhout: Brepols, 2006.

See also **Art, Representations of Women in; Artists, Women; Book Ownership; Devotional Art; Herrad of Hohenbourg; Hildegard of Bingen; Monasticism and Nuns; Patronage, Artistic; Portrait Medals**

NUNS AS MUSICIANS

In the first centuries of Christianity, men and women worshiped equally, singing psalms and other religious texts side by side as lay members of the congregation. In the fourth and fifth centuries, however, Christianity became increasingly patriarchal. As a result, the church came to rely on professional clergy, men and boys (in training) who directed and sang the liturgy and provided new music when desired. Women's voices, both literally and figuratively, were relegated to the monastery, one of the few places where women could develop both intellectually and artistically.

The monastic life, for both men and women, centered on the nearly continuous recitation of the Divine Office (eight daily services) and the Mass. In the monasteries, women had the same duties as their male counterparts. A cantrix, the female equivalent to a cantor, served as both soloist and as director of music. Her duties included teaching and rehearsing the service music, assembling chants for local saints' days, taking care of liturgical books and supervising the scriptorium, if there was one. While a priest was still needed to officiate at Mass, the women provided all of the service music, singing the proper and ordinary parts of the Mass as well as the psalms and canticles of the Divine Office. Female monasteries, however, emphasized the *consecratio virginum*, the service for the consecration of the virgins and by the fifteenth century these services had become complex affairs with eight separate sections acting out the blessings of and presentations to the virgin, most accompanied by chants, some of which were taken from the liturgies of Saints Agnes and Agatha. Performances of liturgical dramas at Easter also tended to be elaborate, probably due to the availability of both male and female characters.

The extent of musical activities in all cloistered communities depended on the size and wealth of the institution, as well as the Rule that governed it. For instance, The Rule of St. Clare (written in 1253 and one of the few Rules written by a woman) instructs the nuns to read the Divine Office, rather than sing it (*legendo sine cantu*) and that those who do not know how to read should say numerous "Our Fathers" substituting for the actual liturgy (twenty four for Matins, five for Lauds, seven each for Prime, Terce, Sext, and None; twelve for Vespers). Though Clare's directions might be interpreted in various ways, her Rule clearly placed less emphasis on singing the Divine Office than did most other Rules that governed female monasteries, some of which not only required the singing of the liturgy but also provided for the nuns' musical training.

While the most common genre of music generated by nuns was plainchant, manuscript evidence from the twelfth century on indicates that some continental nuns, in particular, sang polyphony. Examples include motets, mass ordinary settings, Benedicamus domino settings, sequences, and conductus. Most of the manuscripts from women's institutions contain only a few polyphonic works, but one, the fourteenth-century Las Huelgas Codex includes 136 polyphonic pieces and is one of the most important sources for early polyphony from either female or male institutions. The Monastery of Las Huelgas, near Burgos (in northern Spain) was wealthy and cosmopolitan. Its members were from noble families and it served as a site for royal ceremonies as well as a stopping point on the pilgrimage route to Santiago de Compostela. Its choir in the thirteenth century consisted of 100 nuns and forty girls. Although some scholars assume that the polyphony included in the manuscript was sung by the convent's male chaplains, texts addressed to the nuns that instruct them to sing polyphonically indicate otherwise.

Few cloistered medieval musicians of either sex have escaped the mantle of anonymity. Those whose names we know include several ninth century Byzantine nuns: Martha, Abbess at Argos; Thekla, Abbess near Constantinople; Kassia (b. 810); and Theodosia. Later Byzantines include the thirteenth-century singer and choir director, Kouvouklisena, and Palaeologina, from the late fourteenth century. Those from the West include Hrotsvit, a tenth-century cannoness at the Convent of Gandersheim (Germany); Herrad of Landsberg, a twelfth-century Abbess at Hohenbourg (Alcace); Sister Lukardis of Utrecht, a fifteenth-century music scribe; and Duchna Jankowska, fifteenth century (Poland). Of course the most celebrated of all is Hildegard of Bingen (1098–1179), a German abbess who was not only a musician but also a writer, scientist, artist, and mystic. Her musical compositions date at least from the 1140s and were collected in a volume entitled *Symphonia armonie celestium revelationum*. These works, which include antiphons, sequences, hymns, a Kyrie, and Alleluia, form a liturgical cycle with emphasis on significant local saints such as St. Rupert, St. Disibod, and St. Ursula and her 11,000 Virgins. In addition, Hildegard wrote the first morality play, *Ordo virtutum*, in which the sixteen Virtues battle with the Devil over Anima (the soul). Hildegard's music is exclusively monophonic and her melodies cover a wide range, often with brilliant upward leaps and serpentine melodic formulae that give her music both energy and grace.

MARY NATVIG

References and Further Reading

Cyrus, Cynthia J. "Music: Medieval Women and Music," http://www.vanderbilt.edu/\~cyrus/ORB/orbwomen.htm (December, 2005).

Edwards, J. Michele. "Women in Music to ca. 1450," In *Women and Music: a History*, edited by Karin Pendle. Bloomington, Ind.: Indiana University Press, second edition, 2001, pp. 26–53.

Hildegard of Bingen. *Symphonia: A Critical Edition of the Symphonia armonie celestium revelationum.* Edited by Barbara Newman. Ithaca: Cornell University Press, 1988.

The Las Huelgas Manuscript: Burgos, Monasterio de Las Huelgas. 2 vols. Edited by Gordon A. Anderson. *Corpus Mensurabilis Musicae* 79. Neuhausen-Stuttgart: American Institute of Musicology, 1982.

Marshall, Kimberly. "Symbols, Performers, and Sponsors: Female Musical Creators in the Late Middle Ages." In *Rediscovering the Muses: Women's Musical Traditions.* Ed. Kimberly Marshall. Boston: Northeastern University Press, 1993, pp. 140–168.

Natvig, Mary. "Rich Clares, Poor Clares: Celebrating the Divine Office." *Women & Music* 4 (2000): 59–70.

Neuls-Bates, Carol. *Women in Music: An Anthology of Source Readings from the Middle Ages to the Present.* Rev. ed. Boston: Northeastern University Press, 1996.

Tick, Judith, Margaret Ericson, and Ellen Koskoff, "Women in Music," In *Grove Music Online*, edited by L. Macy, http://www.grovemusic.com (December, 2005).

Yardley, Anne Bagnall. "'Full Weel She Soong the Service Dyvyne': the Cloistered Musician in the Middle Ages." In *Women Making Music: the Western Art Tradition, 1150–1950*, edited by Jane Bowers and Judith Tick. Urbana, Ill.: University of Illinois Press, 1986, pp. 15–39.

See also **Clare of Assisi; Herrad of Hohenbourg; Hildegard of Bingen; Hrotsvit of Gandersheim; Mary, Virgin: in Music; Monasticism and Nuns**

NUNS AS SCRIBES

Religious women throughout the Middle Ages needed books. The Rule of St. Benedict, which governed life in many medieval monasteries, required daily reading, both private and communal, and a variety of books were critical for the proper celebration of the liturgy and the study of the Bible. Because only a small proportion of the surviving manuscripts from Europe's medieval monasteries prior to the fourteenth century contain the name of a scribe or scribes—male or female—a clear assessment of the role of women in the monastic scriptorium is difficult. Of the approximately 1,600 early and high medieval scribes catalogued by the Bénédictines du Bouveret in their *Colophons de manuscripts occidentaux des origins au XVIe siècle*, only sixteen are female. This statistic, however, based as it is primarily on surviving scribal self-identifications, tells only part of the story of female book production.

Substantial nonmanuscript evidence of female scribal activity emerges from the earliest Christian monasteries. Melania the Younger (d. c. 439), for example, was said by her biographer, Gerontius, to have copied both the Old and the New Testament at her monastery in Palestine, and Caesaria the Younger (d. c. 520), abbess of Arles in Gaul, both copied holy books herself and trained nuns at Arles to work as copyists. A similar picture of female involvement in book copying emerges from the letters of Boniface (d. 755), an eighth-century Christian missionary to Germanic lands. Boniface wrote to Eadburga (d. 751), abbess of Minster-in-Thanet in England, thanking her for sending books for the work of his mission and requesting that she copy for him the Epistle of Peter in gold letters.

The number of surviving books known to contain the work of female scribes increases in the eighth and ninth centuries. The most clearly attested early medieval nuns' scriptorium was operated at the monastery of Chelles in Francia. Chelles's connection with the provision of books dates back to the seventh century when the monastery's first abbess, Bertila (d. c. 700), sent manuscripts to missionaries and monasteries in England. The nuns' scriptorium at Chelles seems to have been quite well-known by the ninth century, as archbishop Hildebald of Cologne (d. 819) commissioned from it a three-volume copy of Augustine's commentary on the Psalms. The names of nine female scribes—Girbalda, Gislidis, Agleberta, Adruhic, Altildis, Gisledrudis, Eusebia, Uera, and Agnes—are recorded in these volumes.

The names Guntza and Abirhilt were written in the margin of two manuscripts copied in the vicinity of Würzburg in the late eighth century. Their Germanic names suggest that these women were local converts, perhaps brought to Christianity and the religious life by Anglo-Saxon missionaries to the region. The hand of the scribe Guntza is also preserved in three additional, though unsigned, contemporary manuscripts. By the tenth century, women copyists were also active at the monasteries of Essen, Gandersheim, Niedermünster in Regensburg, Nordhausen, and Quedlinburg. The famous tenth-century copy of the works of Hrotsvit of Gandersheim, for example, was made at Gandersheim itself.

The monastic reforms of the eleventh and twelfth centuries, attentive as they were to biblical study, encouraged the production of books, and women contributed significantly to this aspect of reform. For example, Idung of Prüfening sent his *Dialogue between Two Monks* to be "copied legibly and corrected carefully" by the sisters at Niedermünster in the twelfth century.

Female scribes are also attested at monasteries associated with the reform movement emanating from the monastery of Hirsau in the Black Forest. This reform favored both intellectual activity in the service of spirituality—devotional reading and biblical study—and the education of women. These twin emphases, combined with the prevalence of double monasteries (religious communities that included men and women under the direction of a single, usually male, superior), created a favorable environment for female involvement in book production, and we know the names of several female scribes from this context. According to the *Monumenta Mallerstorfensia*, Leukardis, a twelfth-century female scribe from Mallersdorf, a daughter house of Niedermünster and a part of the Hirsau reform by 1122, copied a number of books, all of which are now lost. The necrology of the Hirsau community of Zwiefalten records the death of Mahtilt of Nifen, a lay sister (*conversa*) who copied many books at the monastery. The most prolific known female scribe from this period was Diemut, a nun-recluse at the Bavarian Monastery of Wessobrunn, a community that in her lifetime came first under the influence of the Gorzer reform and then of Hirsau. Surviving contemporary booklists from Wessobrunn state that Diemut copied as many as forty-seven manuscripts, fourteen of which survive today. The double monastery of Admont in what is now Austria, an important center of the Hirsau reform in the twelfth century, was home to a very active scriptorium of nuns who worked in close collaboration with their male counterparts to produce numerous biblical sermons and commentaries. The nuns Irmingart and Regilind took the lead in helping abbot Irimbert to record a number of his biblical studies, first taking dictation as he preached and later contributing to a wider effort among the women to edit and copy volumes containing these and other works composed at Admont.

Houses affiliated with the new religious movements of the period also employed female scribes. There is ample evidence that Premonstratensian women in the twelfth and thirteenth centuries copied books. As in the Hirsau Reform, double monasteries were prevalent among the Premonstratensians, but as the Order's regulations restricted female intellectual activity in favor of manual labor such as washing and making clothing for the men, these women may have copied books that were intended for male, rather than female, use. Twelfth-century female scribes from the monastery of Schäftlarn near Munich were particularly visible: of the community's thirteen named twelfth-century scribes, three were female, and there is evidence that male and female copyists collaborated closely, possibly even side-by-side in a single workshop. The practice of employing female scribes continued at Premonstratensian houses into the thirteenth century; Emo (d. 1237), first abbot of the double monastery of Wittewerun in the Low Countries, noted in his chronicle that there were women in his community who were educated and trained as copyists. Particularly interesting is his observation that female diligence made women particularly well-suited for the work of the scriptorium.

Although the bulk of the evidence of female scribal activity in the central Middle Ages survives from Germany—perhaps a function of the continued presence there of double monasteries or of the consolidation of Bavaria's monastic libraries under Napoleon—female scribes certainly also worked elsewhere. In 1154, for example, Guta, a nun-scribe of Schwarzenthann in upper Alsace, and Sintram, a monk-illuminator of Marbach worked together to produce a book that contains a calendar, necrology, and martyrology, and in twelfth-century England, a single volume from the monastery of Nunnaminster contains the work of a *scriptrix*—a female scribe.

In the late Middle Ages, monastic reform once again provided a context for female scribal activity. The Observant movement of the fifteenth and sixteenth centuries produced numerous visible female scribes. The c. 1490 account of the reform of the monastery of Ebsdorf, written at the end of the fifteenth century, emphasized female education and its acquisition, and states that women there copied the books they needed, particularly for the celebration of the liturgy. A 1487 chronicle from this same community gives the names of six sisters who together copied some twenty-seven books. Sisters traveling to communities to be reformed commonly carried books with them to be copied and returned to the sending house. The wider copying of books was facilitated by a well-developed system of exchange among Observant communities. As book production expanded generally in the fifteenth century, books signed by female scribes became more common. One author from the convent of St. Katharina in St. Gall wrote with pride about the products of her community's scriptorium, asserting that a sister could properly record her name in a book that she had copied—provided that she was not motivated to do so by vanity—to the benefit of her soul.

ALISON BEACH

References and Further Reading

Beach, Alison I. *Book Production and Monastic Reform in Twelfth-Century Bavaria.* Cambridge: Cambridge University Press, 2004.

Bischoff, Bernhard. "Die Kölner Nonnenhandschriften und das Skriptorium von Chelles," *Mittelalterliche Studien* vol. 1. Stuttgart: Hiersemann, 1966, pp. 16–34.

Bodarwé, Katrinette. *Sanctimoniales litteratae: Schriftlichkeit und Bildung in den ottonischen Frauenkommunitäten Gandersheim, Essen und Quedlinburg.* Quellen und Studien, Veröffentlichungen des Instituts für kirchengeschichtliche Forschung des Bistums Essen. Münster: Aschendorff Verlag, 2004.

Krone und Schleier: Kunst aus Mittelalterlichen Frauenklöstern, edited by Jutta Frings and Jan Gerchow. Munich: Hirmer, 2005.

Haines-Eitzen, Kim. "'Girls Trained in Beautiful Writing': Female Scribes in Roman Antiquity and Early Christianity," *Journal of Early Christian Studies* 6:4 (1998), 629–646.

McKitterick, Rosamond. "Nuns' Scriptoria in England and Francia in the Eighth Century." *Francia* 19 (1992): 1–35.

Winston-Allen, Anne. *Convent Chronicles: Women Writing about Women and Reform in the Late Middle Ages.* University Park, Pa.: The Pennsylvania State University Press, 2004.

See also **Book Ownership; Conversae and Conversi; Double Monasteries; Hrotsvit of Gandersheim; Jouarre and Chelles; Literacy and Reading: Latin; Mathilda and the Monastery of Essen; Monasticism and Nuns; Observant Movement; Premonstratensian Order**

O

OBLATES AND OBLATION

The term *oblate* has had a number of meanings. Here we are concerned with child oblates. The title of chapter 59 of the Rule of St. Benedict (c. 540) is "Concerning sons of nobles and of poor people who are offered (*offeruntur*)." The chapter legislates that parents who offer a child should prepare a document; then, with the Eucharistic offering (*cum oblatione*), they wrap that document and the hand of the child in the altar cloth and so offer the child. They promise never to give the child any property, but may make a formal donation to the monastery, keeping, if they wish, an annuity for themselves. Poor parents were simply to make the oblation of their child. Thus, according to the Rule of St. Benedict, an "oblate" is a child definitively "offered" to God by his or her parents.

There were some partial precedents for Benedict's legislation, for example, in St. Basil, St. Caesarius's *Rule for Virgins*, and in the *Rule of the Master*. The legislation of some local councils in the sixth to ninth centuries reinforced the provisions of the Rule of St. Benedict regarding the permanent and binding character of oblation. However, some Carolingian legislation of the early ninth century says that, to be binding, oblation must be ratified by the child when s/he attains the age of reason. In a celebrated dispute between Gottschalk and Rhaban Maur, a council of Mainz is reported to have released Gottschalk from his oblation, saying that one should not be made a monk against one's will. For several centuries, Cluny (f. 909) accepted oblates and regarded them as strictly bound to the monastic life, but by the twelfth century the oblation of infants was increasingly criticized and orders such as the Cistercians rejected the practice. By the thirteenth century it was generally agreed that children who were offered by another without their consent could leave whenever they wished, and if they were offered with their consent before the legal age, they could leave on attainment of the age of mature reason. Children who entered monasteries of their own volition before the age of puberty could not stay in a monastery except with the consent of their parents. Nevertheless, the oblation of girls in Benedictine monasteries continued during the later Middle Ages.

The admission of child oblates could lead to simony (buying or selling ecclesiastical pardons or offices) as parents paid monasteries to take unwanted or handicapped children off their hands, or abbots extorted payment before accepting a child. Such abuses were finally ended by the Council of Trent (1545–1563), which forbade monastic vows before the age of sixteen.

Many medieval monasteries, especially before the twelfth century, were thus peopled by two kinds of monks or nuns: those who were raised in the monastery (*nutriti/ae*), and those who came as adults, often after being widowed. The latter were more experienced in worldly affairs and so were sometimes favored for positions involving business with the world beyond the cloister. In the earlier Middle Ages, at least, oblates had opportunities for secular and religious education not available to most medieval children. They may also have been likely to receive more personal nurturance than the average medieval child.

Perhaps the most well-known female oblate was Hildegard of Bingen (1098–1179). In a play on words, one account says she was the tenth child of her parents, who therefore dedicated her as a "tithe" to God. The first chapter of her *vita* speaks of her birth, oblation, and education. Her oblation to the anchorhold attached to the abbey of Disibodenberg seems to have occurred when she was about fourteen. Her early entry certainly did not limit either her intellectual horizons or her capacity for leadership. Gertrude the Great (1256–1302) and Mechthild of Hackeborn (c. 1241–1298) arrived at Helfta at the ages of five and seven, respectively, though they may not have been oblates.

The practice of child oblation, which committed a child to the monastic life, paralleled in some respects the practice of arranged marriages. However alien both practices seem today, they were less strange in a society in which parental authority was very great and most people's places of residence and work were more a matter of necessity than choice. By the twelfth century, economic factors, the difficulties of child-rearing, tensions in monasteries between oblates and those who joined later in life, and a growing sense of individual responsibility made the practice questionable.

HUGH FEISS

References and Further Reading

Boswell, John. *The Kindness of Strangers: The Abandonment of Children in Western Europe from Late Antiquity to the Renaissance.* New York: Pantheon, 1988.

De Jong, Mayke. *In Samuel's Image: Child Oblation in the Early Medieval West.* Leiden: Brill, 1996.

Deroux, M.-P. *Les Origines de l'oblature Bénédictine.* Abbaye Saint-Martin de Ligugé: Éditions de la *Revue Mabillon*, 1927.

Kardong, Terrence. *Benedict's Rule: A Translation and Commentary.* Collegeville, Minn.: Liturgical Press, 1996.

Klaes, Monika, ed. and trans. *Vita Sanctae Hildegardis; Canonizatio Sanctae Hildegardis.* Freiburg: Herder, 1998.

Lentini, A. "Note sull'oblazione dei fanciulli nella Regola S. Benedetto," *Studia Anselmiana* 18/19 (1947): 195–225.

See also **Gertrude the Great; Girls and Boys; Hildegard of Bingen; Law, Canon; Mechthild of Hackeborn; Monastic Rules; Monasticism and Nuns**

OBSCENITY

In antiquity, Latin was a fully living language. As in other cultures, Roman authors sometimes indicated that unmarried freeborn women should not know any obscenities, whereas after marriage they could know, and might even be expected to use, "bedroom words." Whether married or not, freeborn women were not supposed to hear obscene words or to be told of obscene acts in public. Yet Romans had religious practices that entailed the uttering of obscenities, even by women. One was the festival of Floralia in April, which involved prostitutes performing (and maybe uttering) obscenities. Another was the festival of Anna Perenna, at which women chanted obscenities (Ovid, *Fasti* 3.675–676).

During the Middle Ages, Latin ceased to be a mother tongue. Instead, the tradition of Latin grammatical and rhetorical education that provided much of the foundation for literature was imparted by men to boys. Although exceptional women learned and used Latin, by and large the language was the preserve of men.

The tradition emphasized decorum. As the language became a father tongue that had to be acquired through formal schooling, seemliness often focused narrowly on the suppression of schoolboy humor connected with taboo words for feces, farting, and a female body part (*cunnus*). But in general Latin became virtually exempt of obscenity, as it remains today in English and many other modern European languages, in which Latinate words such as *penis*, *vagina*, *pudendum*, and *labia* can be uttered in formal contexts (such as medicine or law) whereas their vernacular equivalents are eschewed. In large part the difference can be traced to earlier times in which only (or mainly) men would have known Latin. To take one case in point, the Norman Latin poem *Jezebel*, from the early eleventh century, contains obscene words and obscene implications ascribed to the female title character, but it is highly unlikely that any woman of the time could have spoken or even understood the Latin vocabulary put in Jezebel's mouth.

The long phase in which most literature was in Latin and therefore inaccessible to women ended as vernacular literatures developed. This situation posed difficulties for authors and for society in general, which came to a head in the twelfth-century Renaissance. An old Stoic argument, examined by Augustine, held that obscenity resides not in words but in actions or things, while others had maintained that there were indeed inherently obscene words (what we would call "fighting words" or "four-letter words"). Now, the debate resumed. For instance, Lady Nature in Alan of Lille's *Complaint of Nature* picks her words carefully so as to avoid the risk of having any foul words come into a maiden's mouth, despite the fact that few maidens (apart from allegorical personifications) would have been reading aloud Alan's Latin. By far the most important expression of the debate was in Jean de Meun's *Roman de la Rose*, where the Lover and Lady Reason dispute over the appropriateness of using the word *coilles* (testicles). For the word to be pronounced by Lady Reason, a female character, increases the shock.

Young women, especially virgins, served as gauges of modesty or immodesty: words, gestures, or actions that brought a blush to their faces were obscene—or were they? The question of words versus actions reaches its highest comic pitch in the fabliau of "La Damoisele qui ne pooit oïr parler de foutre" ("The Maiden who could not stand to hear the word Fuck"), where a naive young woman is squeamish about any four-letter words but eagerly embraces four-letter activities, so long as they are described figuratively.

If young women were seen to be especially pure and restricted in their language and linguistic susceptibilities, poor old women, at the greatest distance socially from Latin-using men, were viewed as being particularly dirty-mouthed. Bawdy older women, known as *vetula* (e.g., in the Latin poem, *De vetula*) or *la Vieille* in Old French (e.g., in the *Roman de la Rose*), were characterized as go-betweens, gynecologists, and sex counselors who were able (and allowed) to break prohibitions about speech that other people, especially young women, could not ignore.

JAN M. ZIOLKOWSKI

References and Further Reading

Adams, J. N. *The Latin Sexual Vocabulary*. Baltimore, Md.: Johns Hopkins University Press, 1982.
Ziolkowski, Jan M., ed. *Jezebel: A Norman Latin Poem of the Early Eleventh Century*. Humana Civilitas 10. New York: Peter Lang, 1989.
———, ed. *Obscenity: Social Control and Artistic Creation in the European Middle Ages*. Leiden: E. J. Brill, 1998.

See also **Body: Visual Representations of; Eroticism in Literature; Fabliau; Literacy and Reading: Latin; Old Age; Roman de la Rose and Its Reception; Sheela Na Gigs**

OBSERVANT MOVEMENT

As part of what Kaspar Elm called the "new spiritual landscape" in the late Middle Ages, the Observance Movement shared much in common with the Modern Devotion and other religions initiatives that arose along with far-reaching social and political changes during the fourteenth and fifteenth centuries. Prominent among these developments were demands for reform that emanated from every quarter. While public attention was focused on the high-profile efforts at top-down reform undertaken by the great reform councils of Constance (1414–1418) and Basel (1431–1439), grassroots movements had already begun springing up in many locales, the earliest of them among Franciscan "Spirituals" in France and Italy in the late thirteenth century. Advocating a return to the original rule of St. Francis, as they conceived it, these self-styled poor and devout brothers inhabited hermitages where they pursued a life of penitence and prayer. In Spain, radical Franciscan eremitical groups practiced strict silence and seclusion along with a life of poverty. Although more moderate forms of observance were promoted by popular Franciscan preachers Bernadino of Siena (1380–1444) and John of Capistrano (1385–1456), the issue of radical poverty split the Franciscan order into Observant and Conventual branches by the beginning of the sixteenth century. In France, female reformer Colette of Corbie (1381–1447), a former Beguine who had joined the Poor Clares, launched an initiative of her own, eventually founding twenty-two observant monasteries.

Strongly influenced by the example of the eremitical Franciscans, other orders spawned similar reform initiatives. In Italy an observant center was established by Augustinians at Lecceto around 1385. From there the movement developed strong followings in Spain and in Saxony, where Martin Luther became a leader of the Observant faction. In the Dominican order, reform was promoted by Catherine of Siena and her biographer Master General Raymond of Capua (1380–1399). In 1390 Raymond decreed that each Dominican province should designate one convent as an Observant house for friars who wished to keep strictly to the original rule of the order. Accordingly, reformer Giovanni Dominici established an Observant convent at San Domenico di Castello (Venice) in 1391 and three years later, at the instigation of a group of women, the first such house for Dominican nuns. In the German territories, the charismatic Conrad of Prussia, together with thirty like-minded brothers, took over the Dominican house at Colmar in Alsace and in 1397 founded an Observant community for women at nearby Schönensteinbach.

In the Benedictine order Observant centers sprang up in the fourteenth and fifteenth centuries at Subiaco, Santa Giustina (Padua), Melk, Kastl, St. Matthias (Trier), and Bursfeld (on the Weser river). Decrees issued by the Council of Basel mandated a general reform of the Benedictine order. These measures required strict observance of the common life, reinstatement of manual labor, and simplification of the liturgy. The length of the monastic office was reduced in order to provide more time for individual meditation and spiritual exercises similar to those practiced by the Modern Devotion or Brothers and Sisters of the Common Life. Chanting was to be kept plain and performed mostly *a capella*. Other measures included divestiture of private property, enclosure for women (or restricted time away from the convent for men), and the elimination of special privileges and exemptions to the rule. Despite such regulations, Dominican Master General Raymond of Capua insisted that the Observant reform was not a matter of externals—eating and drinking—but of the inward mind, a renewal of fervor and a restoration not of the letter but of the spirit of the Rule.

In most cases reforms were instituted with the active cooperation of secular territorial rulers or town councils, both of whom wished to increase their control over monasteries. A very powerful force that resonated with the lay interests was reform merged with 1) the rise of the urban magistrate class and its struggle for greater oversight and access to religious institutions and 2) the maneuvers of territorial rulers to consolidate power at the expense of the lesser aristocracy. The Observant reformers—themselves members of the increasingly affluent and powerful urban non-noble class—questioned the privileges of the old religious elite and campaigned to open cloisters to a wider spectrum of the population. Thus, at the same time that the Observance imposed a stricter rule, it gave women of the burgher classes access to positions of leadership within monasteries. Supervisors issued mandates for women to write reform chronicles and encouraged them to transcribe sermons and copy devotional works. Through the exchanging and copying of books, women found new avenues for active participation in the late medieval conversation on spirituality and religious practice. Although only ten percent of women's houses belonged to the Observance, these monasteries produced ninety percent of vernacular manuscripts in the fifteenth century and built up the largest libraries of vernacular works in the Middle Ages.

ANNE WINSTON-ALLEN

References and Further Reading

Burr, David. *The Spiritual Franciscans: From Protest to Persecution in the Century after Saint Francis.* University Park, Pa.: Pennsylvania State University Press, 2001.

Elm, Kaspar, ed. *Reformbemühungen und Observanzbestrebungen im spätmittelalterlichen Ordenswesen.* Berliner Historische Studien 14. Ordensstudien 6. Berlin: Duncker und Humblot, 1989.

———. "Verfall und Erneuerung des Ordenswesens im Spätmittelalter: Forschungen und Forschungsaufgaben." In *Untersuchungen zu Kloster und Stift.* 188–238.

Veröffentlichungen des Max-Planck-Instituts für Geschichte 68, Studien zur Germania Sacra 14. Göttingen: Vandenhoeck und Ruprecht, 1980, pp. 188–238.

Helmrath, Johannes. *Das Basler Konzil 1431–1449: Forschungsstand und Probleme.* Cologne: Böhlau, 1987.

Proksch, Constance. *Klosterreform und Geschichtsschreibung im Spätmittelalter.* Cologne: Böhlau, 1994.

Richards, Joan Marie. "Franciscan Women: The Colettine Reform of the Order of Saint Clare in the Fifteenth Century." Ph.D. Dissertation, University of California, Berkeley, 1989.

Walsch, Katherine. "The Observance: Sources for a History of the Observant Reform Movement in the Order of Augustinian Friars in the Fourteenth and Fifteenth Centuries." *Rivista di Storia della Chiesa in Italia* 31 (1977): 40–67.

Winston-Allen, Anne. *Convent Chronicles: Women Writing about Women and Reform in the Late Middle Ages.* University Park, Pa.: Pennsylvania State University Press, 2004.

See also **Catherine of Siena; Colette of Corbie; Dominican Order; Modern Devotion; Monastic Rules; Monasticism and Nuns; Poor Clares Order; Poverty, Religious**

OCCITANIA

When making generalizations about women in Occitania (southern France, also known as the Midi), one must, as for other parts of Europe, take into consideration numerous variables, such as age and marital status (young and unmarried, married, widowed, consecrated), social status (noble, urban commoner, free peasant, serf), place of origin, and the time period in question; we are often better informed, for example, about noble and urban women than about their rural and poorer counterparts. As elsewhere too, many historians have posited a decline of women's juridical and material status in Occitania at the end of the Middle Ages, yet much can be said to argue the contrary.

Legal Status

Women political figures in Occitania were undeniably less important and colorful in the fifteenth century than in the twelfth, the period of Eleanor of Aquitaine, the viscountess Ermengarde of Narbonne, and the Trencavel "matriarchs"; yet women continued to participate in surviving feudal institutions, doing homage for fiefs and swearing oaths of loyalty. If family-oriented feudal institutions dwindled in importance as the star of the king of France rose, most ordinary women, however, did not necessarily lose out; institutional justice could provide means of action and support to women, including those lacking male kin, by giving them the opportunity to testify, sue, and prosecute.

Imposition of life-long monogamy by the Church was probably for the most part positive, both for noble women and for commoners, protecting them generally from the brutal repudiations that had been so common in the Midi in earlier times. Women generally were able to give or withhold consent for their own marriages, although explicit flouting of parental consent could result in disinheritance, according to some local statutes or "customs."

The problem of women in inheritance law is in fact complex. The rediscovered Roman law corpus of Justinian, of increasing influence in the twelfth and thirteenth centuries, prescribed partible inheritance (equal shares between all sons and daughters), an option often chosen by more modest testators. Liberal testamentary practice, on the other hand, also adapted from Roman law, enabled the testator to favor one particular heir. The heir in question was often the eldest son of the testator, yet could sometimes be a daughter; this was, in fact, systematically the case in the Pyrenees, where local custom favored "female primogeniture," in which the eldest surviving daughter was designated heiress.

Dowry

Much historical literature on the "decline" of women has emphasized the vicissitudes of the dotal system. Dowries (marital assigns given to the bride by her family) tended increasingly to consist of money (either in one sum or in fixed annuities) rather than land in the late Middle Ages. Linked to this tendency was the growing importance of the exclusion of daughters who had been given dowries (*filles dotées*) from inheritance, especially inheritance of land, a "custom" dating from the twelfth century. Yet in practice, their exclusion was often, contrary to statutory norms, not absolute; notarial records show some married daughters "recalled" to inheritance, and others benefiting from various legacies or donations. Exclusion from inheritance was not limited to women, moreover; it often concerned younger sons as well as daughters. Certain younger sons, like some of their sisters, were sent with their dowries to monasteries; others brought their dowries to a marriage with an heiress, an arrangement that usually involved taking up residence in the woman's house and often entailed adopting her family name.

In a dotal marital regime (antenuptial settlement with dowry), women remained owners of their dowry,

even if the husband usually managed it. Women could, however, take over management of their property and indeed any common conjugal goods (notarial records show that many couples, especially in the later Middle Ages, in fact chose to share property in a communal estate); the wife could manage all the couple's property, and that of her husband, in the temporary absence of her spouse, or even permanently, in case of insanity or of inept management on his part. Husbands often left generous settlements to wives in their wills, instituting the wife frequently as executor of the will, as "governor and administrator" of the family patrimony, and as guardian of their minor children.

Work

Urban women in the Midi, as was often the case elsewhere, were active in crafts, especially those dealing with food, clothing, and precious metals. Women of the merchant class were parties to contracts involving land trade, cloth and food sales, money-lending and real estate. Many women worked in hospitals, in domestic service or as wet nurses. Prostitution could be a last resort for some women, or even, especially in the late fourteenth century, a veritable investment opportunity for a few. A small number of domestic slaves could be found only in the largest Mediterranean port towns.

Jewish Women

Jewish communities flourished in Occitania in the High Middle Ages, and continued to survive in Provence into the fifteenth century, reinforced by exiles expelled from other areas. Jewish matrons and widows enjoyed a considerable juridical capacity, inheriting estates (often including extensive private libraries), engaging in business (particularly in money-lending), exercising guardianship of their minor children, and even participating occasionally, as heads of households, in public assemblies.

Courtly Love

A lively scholarly debate has flourished on the subject of the true meaning of "courtly love" (*fin'amor*), which originated in Occitania: should it be seen as proof of the important position of women in society, or is it a smoke-screen for their oppression, revealing more about male/male connections than about male/female relationships? While it is important to place the love poems in a wider context of a literature "of the court," a literature that could be highly political (indeed propagandistic), satirical and even scabrous, the male/female relationship at the heart of the *cansos* is not incidental or merely symbolic, nor is it without relation to the actual social situation, that is, the important role of women in land-holding and in feudal relations, and the hypergamic tendency of Occitan society (men marrying women—often heiresses—of higher social standing than themselves, including even the counts of Toulouse, who sought royal spouses). Noteworthy too is a small but significant number of women authors of this literature (there is even one "political" poem by a woman, Gormonda of Montpellier), the so-called *trobairitz*, literary sisters of the troubadours. The phenomenon is clearly connected also to the role of female patronage of the arts. In the later Middle Ages, the relation of lover and beloved was often seen as a paradigm for husband and wife, as in the romances *Paris et Vienne* and *Pierre de Provence et la belle Maguelonne*.

Participation in Catharism and Mainstream Christianity

Another long-debated question about women in Occitania (the so-called *Frauenfrage*) concerns their role in the Cathar or Albigensian heresy: did women, frustrated by discrimination and lack of opportunity in contemporary society, flock to Catharism as a friendlier alternative? This seems unlikely, as the Cathar clerical hierarchy was as closed to women as the Catholic one was (the famous women "perfects" were in fact the equivalent of Catholic nuns, not of priests, as has often been misconstrued), and the dualism of Catharism (maintaining that only the spiritual is good, while all that is material is evil) was hardly a woman-friendly theology. The enthusiastic, if not numerically overwhelming, participation of women in Catharism can be seen less as an escape from the constraints of society and much more as a parallel to the increasing participation of women in mainstream Christian religious life at about the same time. The relative dearth of institutionalized monastic opportunities for women in the Midi was alleviated in the twelfth and thirteenth centuries by the founding of, among others, Cistercian nunneries, houses of the Poor Clares, and priories of the order of Fontevrault, where women directed the double (male/female) communities. Beguinages too flourished, their aura

enhanced by the reputation of Saint Douceline of Digne. Although Dominican convents were rarer, the first one founded, Prouille, lay in the very heart of Occitania.

Women also found opportunities for religious expression in confraternities, many of which included both male and female members. Some women enjoyed careers as anchoresses (*recluses*), considered virtually as municipal employees, engaged to pray for the community, which in return assured their material upkeep. Women frequently combined work and religion in their activity in hospitals, many of which were directed by couples, or by women alone (often widows).

Criminal Justice

Developments favorable to women are also noticeable in criminal law. Female adultery, which had been considered a capital offense in earlier times, was often resolved in the fifteenth century by a simple reconciliation, negotiated (and not always unfavorably to the woman!) before a notary. Marital violence was criticized and often punished, and most local customs protected even prostitutes from rapists. Women, even those of the lowest social (and "moral") standing, were considered not simply as objects, but as active subjects of law.

LEAH OTIS-COUR

References and Further Reading

Aurell, Martin. "La détérioration du statut de la femme aristocratique en Provence (Xe-XIIXIIIe s)." *Moyen Age* 91 (1985): 5–32.

Bec, Pierre, ed. *Chants d'amour des femmes-troubadours.* Paris: Stock, 1995.

Biller, Peter. "Cathars and Material Women." In *Medieval Theology and the Body*, edited by P. Biller and A. Minnis. Woodbridge: Boydell, 1997, pp. 61–107.

Brenon, Anne. *Les Femmes cathares.* Paris: Perrin, 1992.

Cheyette, Frederic. "Women, Poets and Politics in Occitania." In *Aristocratic Women in Medieval France*, edited by T. Evergates. Philadelphia: University of Pennsylvania, 1999, pp. 138–177.

Courtemanche, Andrée. *La richesse des femmes. Patrimoine et gestion à Manosque au XIVe siècle.* Montréal; Bellarmin; Paris: Vrin, 1993.

Duhamel-Amado, Claudie. *Genèse des lignages méridionaux.* Toulouse: Mirail, 2001.

La femme dans l'histoire et la société méridionale (IXe-XIXe s.). Actes du 66e congrès de la Fédération historique du Languedoc méditerranéen et du Roussillon (Narbonne, 15–16 octobre 1994). Montpellier: La Federation, 1995.

La femme dans la vie religieuse en Languedoc, XIIIe-XIVe siècles. Cahiers de Fanjeaux 23. Taulouse: Privat, 1988.

Iancu, Danièle. «Femmes juives en Provence médiévale.» In *Histoire et société : mélanges offerts à Georges Duby*. Aix: Université Provence, 1992, pp. 69–78.

Mundy, John. *Men and Women at Toulouse in the Age of the Cathars*. Toronto: Pontifical Institute of Mediaeval Studies, 1990.

Otis, Leah Lydia. *Prostitution in Medieval Society: the History of an Urban Institution in Languedoc*. Chicago: University of Chicago Press, 1985.

Ourliac, Paul, and Jean-Louis Gazzaniga. *Histoire du droit privé français de l'An mil au Code civil*. Paris: Albin Michel, 1985.

Reyerson, Kathryn. "Women in Business in Medieval Montpellier." In *Women and Work in Preindustrial Europe*, edited by Barbara Hanawalt. Bloomington, Ind.: Indiana University Press, 1986, pp. 117–144.

Smail, Daniel. "Démanteler le patrimoine: Les femmes et les biens dans la Marseille médiévale." *Annales: Economie, Société, Civilisation* (1997): 343–368.

Wheeler, Bonnie, and John C. Parsons, eds. *Eleanor of Aquitaine: Lord and Lady*. New York: Macmillan, 2002.

See also **Anchoresses; Beguines; Cathars; Cistercian Order; Courtly Love; Dominican Order; Dowry and Other Marriage Gifts; Eleanor of Aquitaine; Ermengard; Fontevrault, Abbey and Order of; France, Northern; Inheritance; Law, Roman; Literature, Occitan; Marriage, Christian; Monasticism and Nuns; Poor Clares Order; Trobaritz and Troubadours; Work**

OLD AGE

Old age was a topic and a social problem that engaged medieval society, though more attention was devoted to theories about the stages of the life cycle than about collecting demographic data, let alone working to ameliorate the problems attendant upon longevity and survival. Furthermore, most of what was written focused on men, rather than women: medical texts, theological colloquies, moral treatises, and behavioral manuals rarely saw women as worthy of discrete treatment. Old women, though present at all social levels and often in positions of importance and prominence, were rarely considered on their own; much of what was explicitly focused on them was satirical or hostile.

From the era of the Church fathers, drawing upon classical and Old Testament models, medieval thinkers elaborated the idea that life was best understood as composed of a series of stages through which we all moved. The number of stages might range from three—youth, middle age, and old age—to as many as twelve. Three ages or stages of life conformed to the model of the trinity, four to the humors or the seasons, seven to the days of creation (including the Sabbath), etc. At least in this regard, women—though deemed inferior in intellect, will, and body (being of an infelicitous humoral mix, as befitted their

embryological development as imperfect men)—had to be accepted as likely to live as long as men, if not longer. Though statistics about medieval longevity are of limited value, given their unreliability and the extremely high but mostly unrecorded mortality rate for infants and young people, women of threescore and ten (as in the biblical injunction) were not uncommon. In many legal proceedings men had to state their age; if they were accepted as being in their 50s or 60s or more, we can assume that the wives who were usually going to outlive them would ultimately more than match such numbers. The most accessible data for women relate to those of high status, and here old age was a familiar phenomenon to women such as Eleanor of Aquitaine (1120–1204), Matilda of Tuscany (1046–1115), Blanche of Castile (1188–1252), Marguerite of France (1221–1295), Hilda of Whitby (614–680), Hildegard of Bingen (c. 1098–1179), and Birgitta of Sweden (1303–1373).

While men's ages were calibrated against their level of activity, as such factors were of interest, a woman's social age was closely related to the feminine life cycle and her marital and childbearing status. Except for women who entered religious life at an early age, women's lives were divided into three basic segments or stages: maidenhood, marriage, and (in most cases) widowhood (with remarriage as a complicating factor). Another way of covering this expanse was by casting her life in terms of life before menarche, the years of fertility and childbearing, and the years following menopause. For women who survived and maintained their strength and wits, this third stage really marked their entry into "social old age," regardless of its duration. An aging queen or empress might be turned out of the palace if she failed to produce the necessary heir, and early medieval law codes marked this final life stage—which might often run for three or more decades—by assigning her a lesser wergild, a mark of her now-diminished social value and a blatant indication that her days of greatest usefulness were in the past.

Old women did not receive much respect. While every social generalization has exceptions, there was not much sympathy slanted toward the plight of old women comparable to the male-oriented reflections of Cicero (in his *De Senectute*) or of Petrarch, in the fourteenth century, both reflecting on how they welcomed old age because it brought a release from (sexual) passion and now afforded them more time for spiritual matters and contemplation. The "loathly hag" who confronts the young hero in Chaucer's "Wife of Bath's Tale" was a more familiar figure, and fifteenth-century English society was shocked when Edward IV imposed his twenty-year-old brother-in-law in marriage upon the sixty-five-year-old dowager duchess of Norfolk (a *maritagium diabolicum*, as it was called).

But care for the elderly was an expected social obligation, and old women, as well as men, might find succor and support thanks to forms of charity that enjoined the establishment and support of hospitals, distributed cash (plus clothing and meals) to mourners at funerals, and remembered old servants and even nursemaids in wills. Furthermore, since most old women were apt to be widows, they often were able to partake of those privileges and avenues of independence concerning dower shares of property, control of their inheritance, and the freedom to direct the testamentary disposal of personal possessions that went with widowhood. This potential for agency and autonomy may have meant little to the lonely townswoman, dependent on the good will of neighbors if she were fortunate enough, or to the aged widow of the countryside who could find no man to work her fields, but for those with resources these social institutions and practices helped temper the ravages of old age. The concept of retirement for the aged and infirm was understood and accepted, though it was haphazardly institutionalized, at best, and Christian charity, rather than any serious forms of public or state polity, was the customary fallback. And if medieval medicine was no more effective than modern in warding off the inevitable march to the grave, there was at least an interest in making the most of what years one had, as shown by such writings as Gabriele Zerbi's fifteenth century *Gerontocomia: On the Care of the Aged*.

JOEL T. ROSENTHAL

References and Further Reading

Clark, Elaine. "Some Aspects of Social Security in Medieval England." *Journal of Family History* 7 (1982): 307–320.

Jones, J. W. "Observations on the Origin of the Division of Man's Life into Stages." *Archaeologia* 35 (1853): 167–189.

Lind, L. R., trans. *Gabriel Zerbi, Gerontocomia: On the Care of Old Age, and Maximianus, Elegies on Old Age and Love.* Philadelphia: American Philosophical Society, 1988.

Minois, Georges. *History of Old Age*, translated by Sarah H. Tenison. Chicago: University of Chicago Press, 1987.

Rosenthal, Joel T. *Old Age in Late Medieval England.* Philadelphia: University of Pennsylvania Press, 1996.

Sears, Elizabeth. *The Ages of Man: Medieval Interpretations of the Life Cycle.* Princeton, N.J.: Princeton University Press, 1986.

Sheehan, Michael M., ed. *Aging and the Aged in Medieval Europe.* Toronto: Pontifical Institute of Medieval Studies, 1990.

See also **Almsgiving and Charity; Demography; Gender Ideologies; Hospitals; Wergild; Widows**

OLGA

After the murder of her husband Igor in 945, Olga, Princess of Kiev (d. 969), acting as a regent for her son Sviatoslav, defeated Igor's killers, the Derevliane, and imposed a heavy tribute on them. The *Russian Primary Chronicle* credits her with establishing laws in the Derevliane's territory and integrating it into the trading network of the Kievan realm. Economic expansion and financial consolidation featured prominently during Olga's reign. In 947 she set up trading posts and a tribute collection system along several Russian rivers.

Paralleling the depiction of women in the Scandinavian sagas, Kievan sources attribute to the pagan Olga vengefulness and cleverness. When, after Igor's murder, the Derevliane suggested a marriage alliance between their prince Mal and Olga, she repeatedly tricked Mal's messengers into an ambush. Her methods—burying her enemies alive, burning them in a bathhouse, or killing them after getting them drunk at a funeral feast for her slain husband—suggest her ruthless but strong and determined nature.

Olga's conversion to Christianity foreshadowed Russia's adoption of Eastern Orthodoxy under her grandson Vladimir in 988. Juxtaposition of relevant Russian, German, and Byzantine sources suggests that Olga was baptized in Constantinople in 957 and was named Helena after the wife of her godfather, the Byzantine emperor Constantine Porphyrogenitus. As Russia's first Christian ruler, she became a saintly model for the Muscovite tsars' wives, who manipulated her image as intercessor for her people to legitimize their own roles as spiritual mothers of the realm and independent rulers.

ISOLDE THYRÊT

References and Further Reading

Cross, Samuel, and Olgerd P. Sherbowitz-Wetzor, eds. and trans. *The Russian Primary Chronicle: Laurentian Text.* Cambridge, Mass.: The Mediaeval Academy of America, 1953, pp. 78–87.

Featherstone, Jeffrey. "Ol'ga's Visit to Constantinople." In *Adelphotes: A Tribute to Omeljan Pritsak by His Students*, edited by Frank Sysyn. *Harvard Ukrainian Studies* 14.3/4 (1990): 293–312.

Pritsak, Omeljan. "When and Where was Ol'ga Baptized?" *Harvard Ukrainian Studies* 9.1/2 (1985): 5–24.

See also **Conversion, Religions; Hagiography; Russia; Scandinavia**

ORDINATION OF WOMEN AS PRIESTS

There are no recorded ordinations of women to the order of deacon, priest, or bishop in the Middle Ages, but there was a lively discussion among canonists and theologians about whether it was possible for a woman to receive orders. Two passages in St. Paul (I Cor.14:33–36 and I Tim.2: 11–12), the only passages in the New Testament that treat the issue, taught that women should be silent in the churches and be subordinate to men. It is not surprising, then, that the question of leadership dominated discussion. To avoid confusion it will be best to distinguish at the outset leadership that flowed from the sacramental powers inherent in orders from that which flowed from jurisdiction. Jurisdiction, i.e., the power to govern church members, was associated with holy orders but could be exercised by persons not in orders themselves. Jurisdiction could be delegated, as for example, by a bishop to his vicar general, or it could be recognized as flowing from the authority a religious superior held over a community, such as an abbess. An abbess could nominate a priest to preach or hear confessions of her nuns in her abbey church and she could receive the vows of women who were joining her community. Since the religious authority of an abbess closely resembled the jurisdiction of a bishop, an abbess has sometimes been called a *bishop,* but this did not imply that she had been ordained.

In the 1200s and 1300s canon lawyers and theologians turned their attention to the recipients of orders, and the discussion continued to the sixteenth-century Reformation. Several collections of ancient laws included canons that stated that women could not be ordained, along with a few which suggested the opposite. Gratian, in his *Concordance for Discordant Canons* (the *Decretum,* c. 1140–1150), had winnowed out six ancient canons about women and orders discarding a few of the more negative ancient texts. By the 1220s Gratian's *Decretum,* along with the *Glossa Ordinaria* of John Teutonicus, had become the authoritative legal text. Whatever their origins, these canons were accepted as authentic expressions of church tradition stating that women were not to handle the sacred vessels; enter the sanctuary to offer incense; teach (*docere*) in an assembly (even if well educated); keep their heads uncovered; or be placed in authority over a man. The two canons, *Presbyter* and *Diaconissam,* that seemed to suggest there were women elders and deacons in the ancient church were reinterpreted to say that *elders* must be referring to the *wives* of priests, or perhaps elderly widows or senior laywomen, and that *deaconesses* were women given some special powers or authority, but of a non-sacramental sort. There is some evidence that isolated groups like the Humiliati and the Waldensians accepted women into their ministry, at least as preachers, but it was something they felt any baptized Christian could do if well instructed. Most recent studies have found that women sometimes listened to confessions,

but there was no solid evidence they celebrated a Eucharist and, in any event, no evidence exists for ordination ceremonies of men or women in a sacramental sense.

Theologians before the 1200s squeezed questions about orders into a few lines between Eucharist and matrimony. Surveys like the *De Sacramentis* of Hugh of St. Victor (d. 1142) and the famous *Sentences* of Peter Lombard (1155–1158) are silent on the issue, but the ideas of the canonists began to find their way into commentaries on the *Sentences.* At Oxford, Richard Fishacre (1240) stated that abbesses are not able to preach, bless, give penance, or exercise the office of any order. At Paris, Bonaventure (1253) asked cautiously whether the ordination of women was possible, although he was inclined against it. The Incarnate Christ was a mediator between God and humanity, essentially a symbolic role. (Skill, for example, in serving as a negotiator between individuals or within a community, important as that might be, was not the issue here.) Since Christ was a man, it was appropriate that a priest, as mediator, be a man as well. Genesis provided Bonaventure with his paradigm. In the sacred time of creation, Adam, the man, is given charge and made representative of the human community, while Eve, his wife, is presented as his helpmate. Hence, for Bonaventure, the more probable opinion and one confirmed by the teaching of many saints is that the role of leadership should be filled by a man and not a woman. Man and woman have complementary, not interchangeable, roles. The woman is to give a sense of worth and tranquility to a man while the man is to support and protect the woman. Thomas Aquinas died before he reached this topic in his *Summa,* but earlier in his *Sentences* (1256) he asked what qualities are necessary to fulfill the symbolism required for orders. He lists only one, *eminence,* being designated to preside. Although both men and women were made in the image of God, the man, Adam, was designated to decide and should preside in the church. There is a need for subordination and order if two sexes are to work in harmony in the community. As to the question of whether women should preach, if the topic is preaching in private there is no difficulty, yet if it is a question of preaching *ex officio,* that needs to be done by a *prelate,* i.e., someone assigned to preside.

Theological opinion was set by the 1300s. The religious symbolism required for orders could not be well expressed by a woman because orders dealt with a sacral leadership. Arguments about the supposed defects of women were offered to bolster the opinion that the ordination of women was inappropriate (such as, women were less wise than men, Adam was created first, Eve was deceived by the serpent, women were fickle [silly], a woman's voice raised a man's libido, etc.). These misogynous remarks took far too much space in theological texts, but as arguments they are secondary to the symbolism generated by the Genesis story. That women could not be ordained was continually repeated, but urgency seems to have receded over time as theological discussion became static, almost pro forma. The only new observation came from Duns Scotus (d. 1308). Since the Blessed Virgin received all possible graces, yet was not ordained, there must be an incompatibility, some inappropriateness, then, between women and orders. Although some uneasiness lingered as to just why this was so, the bottom line was not disputed—women were not to be ordained.

JOHN HILARY MARTIN

References and Further Reading

Andrews, Frances. *The Early Humiliati*. Cambridge: Cambridge University Press, 1999.

Behr-Sigel, Elisabeth. *The Ministry of Women in the Church*. Redondo Beach, Calif.: Oakwood Publications, 1987.

Borrensen, Kari E. *Subordination and Equivalence*. Washington, D.C.: University Press of America, 1981.

Congar, Yves. *Lay People in the Church: A Study of Theology for the Laity*. Westminister, Md.: Newman Press, 1967.

Duggan, C. "Decretals, Collection of." *New Catholic Encyclopedia*, 2nd ed., 2003. vol. 4, pp. 709–711.

Ferrante, Joan M. *Woman as Image in Medieval Literature from the Twelfth Century to Dante*. New York: Columbia University Press, 1975.

Friedberg, E., ed. *Corpus Juris Canonici*. Graz: Akademische Druck, 1959.

Gryson, Roger. *The Ministry of Women in the Early Church*. Collegeville, Minn.: Liturgical Press, 1976.

Hochstetler, Donald. *A Conflict of Traditions: Women in Religion in the Early Middle Ages*. Lanham: University Press of America, 1992.

Le Bras, Gabriel, Ch. Lefevre, and J. Rambaud. *L'Age classique, 1140–1378: Source et Theories du droit*. Paris: Sirey, 1965.

Martin, John Hilary. *The Ordination of Women in the Medieval Context. A History of Women and Ordination*. Lanham, Md. and London: Scarecrow Press, 2002.

Minnis, A. J. *De impedimento sexus*: Women's Bodies and Medieval Impediments to Female Ordination." In *Medieval Theology and the Natural Body*, edited by Peter Biller and A. J. Minnis. Rochester, N.Y.: York Medieval Press, 1997, pp. 109–139.

Raming, Ida. *The Exclusion of Women from the Priesthood: Divine Law or Sex Discrimination?* Metuchen, N.J.: Scarecrow Press, 1992.

Rand, Laurence. "Ordination of Women to the Diaconate." *Communio* 8 (1981): 370–383.

Shahar, Shulamith. *Women in a Medieval Heretical Sect*. Woodbridge: The Boydell Press, 2001.

Van der Meer, Haye. *Women Priests in the Catholic Church: A Historical-Theological Investigation*. Philadelphia: Temple University Press, 1973.

See also **Abbesses; Church; Humiliati; Law, Canon; Misogyny; Sermons and Preaching; Theology; Waldensians**

OTTONIAN ROYAL WOMEN

The Ottonian dynasty, also known as the Saxon dynasty after their homelands in Saxony, ruled part of western Europe from 919 to 1024. They were remote descendants of the Carolingians and extended their territory over other parts of Germany, France, and northern Italy. In 962 Otto I the Great (r. 936–973) and his wife Adelheid were crowned as emperor and empress by the pope, counterbalancing the rulers in Byzantium. Their son Otto II followed in 967. From this period the imperial consorts appear on the political scene. They are portrayed with their husbands, are featured in diplomas, and figure in contemporary and later sources.

Adelheid's name figures in diplomas and in letters written by Gerbert of Reims. After her death in 999 her life was described in a funeral oration by Odilo of Cluny, one of her intimates. Her life was also the subject of a *Vita*. In 972 her son Otto II married Theophano (c. 959–991), an educated Byzantine lady and niece of a Byzantine emperor. She was to have a great influence on the life and culture of the Ottonian empire. The marriage took place in Rome, where she was crowned empress by the pope. In the marriage contract, written in gold on purple, in the Byzantine tradition, Theophano was qualified as *sanctissime* (very holy), a qualification for Byzantine rulers and in analogy with the other protagonists of the contract.

After the death of Otto I in 973 Theophano became coimperatrix with her husband. She had arrived in the West with a rich dowry, and with Greek friends and advisers. Adelheid left the court, in conflict with the new empress, whom she disliked. She referred to Theophano with the deprecating terms *illa imperatrix Greca, illa Greca* (the Greek empress, the Greek woman).

Portraits of the imperial couple, sometimes represented as being crowned by Christ, now followed an even more Byzantine pattern by representing them symmetrically and frontally, stressing the rulers' authority. Theophano and her husband figure on lead medallions, wall-paintings, and ivories, such as the coronation by Christ on an ivory in the Musée de Cluny, Paris.

After the death of Otto II in 983, Theophano became regent for her infant son, born in 980, and became influential in the German Empire, using titles such as *divina gratia imperatrix augusta*. As sole ruler she is also portrayed in various ways. Her authority was not appreciated by all. Theophano's dowry, consisting of secular and religious artifacts of gold, silver, silk, ivory, enamel, and other costly materials, and manuscripts with Greek texts and miniatures, became a source of inspiration for artists and scholars. Byzantine artifacts were cherished and were donated to monasteries and churches.

In spite of critical remarks on the luxurious life style of the empress, Byzantine religious and artistic traditions, iconography, and the introduction of Eastern saints, influenced Western culture. The veneration of the Virgin Mary, sometimes called *Theotokos* (Mother of God) in the Byzantine tradition, became more popular.

Theophano's life and politics are described in various sources, positively and negatively, her foreignness being more than once accentuated. Theophano died in Nijmegen (Netherlands), in 991. The millenary of her death in 1991 renewed an interest in her life and background. Until Otto III's coronation as emperor in Rome, in 996, his grandmother Adelheid was regent. Coins were issued with the names of Adelheid and Otto. Otto's dream was a *Renovatio imperii romani* (restoration of the Roman Empire). He carried the icon of the Theotokos in procession through Rome. His dream could only be realized by marrying a Byzantine *porphyrogenita* (purple born), a princess born as daughter of a reigning emperor. A daughter of the emperor Constantine VIII, Zoe or Theodora, was sent to the West. When she arrived in Bari in 1002 the fiancé had just died, and she returned home. Zoe eventually became empress in her own right in Byzantium, reigning for a few months with her sister Theodora.

The life of the last Ottonian empress was less conspicuous. Otto III was succeeded by Henry II (1002–1024), another grandson of Otto I. He was married to Cunegunde of Luxemburg, who, according to her *Vita*, led a saintly life. She donated a precious icon to the monastery of Kaufungen (Germany), an icon that must have belonged to Theophano or her son. The reign of Henry II and his wife betrays influences of Byzantine court life, but Cunegunde seems a shadow of her predecessors, not being interested in politics or cultural life. The double portrait of the imperial couple was no longer a frontal portrait. When Cunegunde died childless, the Ottonian dynasty came to an end. By contacts with Byzantine institutions, Ottonian queens had become empresses, influencing in many ways the later history of the empire.

KRIJNIE CIGGAAR

References and Further Reading

Ciggaar, Krijnie. "The Empress Theophano." In *Byzantium and the Low Countries in the Tenth Century*, edited by Victoria D. van Aalst and Krijnie N. Ciggaar. Hernen: A. A. Brediusstichting, 1985, pp. 33–77.
———. "Theophano: An Empress Reconsidered." In *The Empress Theophano: Byzantium and the West at the Turn of the First Millennium*, edited by Adelbert Davids. Cambridge: Cambridge University Press, 1995, pp. 49–63.
Leyser, Karl. *Medieval Germany and Its Neighbours 900–1250*. London: The Hambledon Press, 1982.
von Euw, Anton, and Peter Schreiner, eds. *Kaiserin Theophanu. Begegnung des Ostens und Westens um die Wende des ersten Jahrtausends*. 2 vols. Cologne: Schnütgen-Museum, 1991.
Wolff, Gunther, ed. *Kaiserin Theophanu. Prinzessin aus der Fremde: des Westreichs Grosse Kaiserin*. Cologne: Böhlau Verlag, 1991.

See also **Adelheid; Byzantium; Frankish Lands; Queens and Empresses: The West**

OVID, MEDIEVAL RECEPTION OF

The works of Publius Ovidius Naso (43 BCE–17 or 18 CE) adopted many conventions of the "neoteroi" (literally "new," meaning avant garde) poets of Alexandria, the "Asiatic" style which was construed as "mannered and affected" (by Cicero) or "feminine" in opposition to the more "virile" modes of the Greco-Roman tradition. His style employed elaborate digressions, amplified ecphrasis (vivid literary description of works of art), heroines' laments, mythological allusions, interest in taboo sexual relations, and an "exquisiteness" of style and syntax, all techniques imitated in later medieval Latin and vernacular poetics. Ovid dramatized the inner conflicts of numerous mythological heroines, particularly in the *Heroides*, a series of poetic letters from abandoned women to the men who caused their distress, and in his epic *Metamorphoses*. Strong female characters in difficult situations and interior love monologues spoken by both sexes became key features of Ovidian-inspired courtly romance from the *Roman d'Eneas* (c. 1260)—which sets a romance precedent by amplifying Lavinia into an enamored courtly heroine—to the works of Chrétien de Troyes, Marie de France, Philippe de Rémi, Chaucer, and many others.

The callous narrators of Ovid's early works, the egocentric lover of a married woman named Corinna (and of her maid Cypassis!) in the *Amores*, and the seduction instructor of the *Ars Amatoria* (Art of Love) and *Remedia Amoris* (Remedy for Love), established his enduring reputation as master of the erotic, as well as the disapproval of Augustus, who banished him eastward to the remote Black Sea. There, he

627

composed laments that would inspire later medieval exiles such as Dante: *Tristia*, in elegiac meter; letters *Ex Ponto*; and a curse poem, *Ibis*. His poem on women's cosmetics, *Medicamina faciei*, had a limited survival. It further suggests Ovid's characteristic link to the feminine. The loss of a play, *Medea*, speaks to the disappearance of theater in the early Christian era; however, the theme of Medea's inner conflict between loyalty to father and homeland and desire for Jason recurs in the *Heroides* and *Metamorphoses*, and would inspire medieval commentators and vernacular poets, such as Benoît de Sainte-Maure in the *Roman de Troie* (c. 1160–1165), or Chaucer in the *Legend of Good Women* (1386).

In late antiquity Ovid's major works were known through Spain, North Africa, and Europe, and some writers of the Carolingian Renaissance cited him. The twelfth and thirteenth centuries are called the "Ovidian Age"; during that time, he arguably became the single most influential classical author, and his works became textbooks in the growing schools of France, England, and Germany. Some suggest that this popularity is linked to the growth of towns, as his sophistication is uniquely urban.

Claims for direct borrowing or inspiration require caution. Ovidian techniques and themes were experienced both directly and indirectly. Scholastic-trained writers read Ovid's *Metamorphoses* glossed in commentaries such as the *Mythologiae* of Fulgentius (467–532), a number of guides from the school of classics at Orleans including the popular anonymous "Vulgate" commentary (c. 1250), Oxford-Paris schoolmaster John of Garland's condensed allegorization (c. 1234), the Christianizing French translation in the *Ovide moralisé* (1316–1328), Pierre Bersuire's *Ovidius Moralizatus* (1362) or the *Allegorie* of Giovanni del Virgilio (1322–1323), which influenced a new generation of Italian classicists, including Dante and Boccaccio. Preachers seeking *exempla* used such guides for sermons, which disseminated them less formally. The cosmography and Golden Age myths of *Metamorphoses* 1 and 15 were referenced in philosophical and early scientific texts by Alan of Lille, Bernardus Silvestris, Walter of Châtillon, and Albert the Great. Ovid's influence on literary theory is illustrated by his frequent mention in Matthew of Vendôme's rhetorical manual, *Ars versificatoria* (c. 1185).

The erotic texts, disseminated widely in pedagogical *libri manuales*, inspired numerous didactic works featuring the symptoms of lovesickness and obedience to the god of Love, such as Marie de France's *Guigemar*, *Flamenca*, Gower's *Confessio Amantis*, and Spenser's *Faerie Queene*. They also inspired both receptive and hostile reactions. *De Amore* by Andreas Capellanus (c. 1170) explicates the adulterous rules of *fin'amor* ("true love") found in the poetry of Bernart de Ventadorn and other troubadours and trouvères in its first two books, but in the third condemns the material as sinful. Chrétien de Troyes claims to have translated "Ovid's commandments and the Art of Love," but if so it is lost. His works espouse Ovidian scenes of love suffering, but many promote a less cynical view of marriage. Chaucer also claims to have translated the *Art of Love*, and the imprint is particularly visible in his *Troilus and Creseyde* (1381–1386) and the *Wife of Bath's Tale*. He translated the *Roman de la Rose* (c. 1225–1270), which called itself a "mirror for lovers," featured Ovidian digressions on Narcissus and Pygmalion, and, like the *Amores* or *Metamorphoses* (and later the *Canterbury Tales*, 1373–1400), employed embedded narration to tell stories within a frame story. For example, the narrator/lover relates Ami's (Friend's) narration of a jealous husband's diatribes; La Vieille (Old Woman) advises on how to fool men, strip lovers of their wealth, and move on, reprising much of *Ars Amatoria* book 3. Such "misogynist" passages have been condemned by Christine de Pizan and others, including modern readers. It is important to recognize, however, that the complex Ovidian narrative technique dramatizes multiple views of difficult human relationships, and does not necessarily reflect authorial intent.

SARAH-GRACE HELLER

References and Further Reading

Allen, Peter L. *The Art of Love: Amatory Fiction from Ovid to the* Romance of the Rose. Philadelphia: University of Pennsylvania Press, 1992.

Desmond, Marilynn R., ed. *Mediaevalia: Ovid in Medieval Culture, a special issue*. Vol. 13, 1989 for 1987.

Hagedorn, Suzanne C. *Abandoned Women: Rewriting the Classics in Dante, Boccaccio, & Chaucer*. Ann Arbor, Mich.: University of Michigan Press, 2004.

Hexter, Ralph. *Ovid and Medieval Schooling: Studies in Medieval School Commentaries on Ovid's Mich. "Ars Amatoria," Epistulae ex Ponto, and Epistulae heroidum*. Munich: Arbeo-Gesellschaft, 1986.

McKinley, Kathryn L. *Reading the Ovidian Heroine: "Metamorphoses" Commentaries* 1100–1618. Leiden: Brill, 2001.

Stapleton, Michael L. *Harmful Eloquence: Ovid's Amores from Antiquity to Shakespeare*. Ann Arbor, Mich.: University of Michigan Press, 1996.

See also **Boccaccio, Giovanni; Chaucer, Geoffrey; Chrétien de Troyes; Dante Alighieri; Debate Literature; Eroticism in Literature; Gottfried von Strassburg; Misogyny; Mythology, Medieval Reception of; Roman de la Rose and Its Reception; Roman de Flamenca; Trobairitz and Troubadours**

P

PAGANISM

As Christianity spread from city to city within the Roman Empire, the term *paganus*, originally a "country-dweller," served to identify a believer in one of the old religions, or in short, a "heathen." But as the Christians expanded beyond the empire's frontiers paganism came to denote the polytheistic religions of the nonurbanized people, most notably the Germanic tribes, as well as other northern peoples, including Icelanders. Eventually it was also attached to the monotheistic Muslims. Until recently modern scholars have retained a Germanic focus on paganism because of the richness of the sources, but today Northern pre-Christian cults include the Celts and the Sámi as well, living in the northern parts of the Scandinavian peninsula and in Russia.

Largely the product of warrior societies the Celtic, Germanic, and Sámi religions were dominated by male gods, but they did not exclude female beings. Memories of a unique fertility goddess loomed in the background of these beliefs. Clearer and probably later were female supernatural beings associated with divination and warfare. Thus, the Celtic Lug and the Nordic Óðinn were assisted in battle by female figures, the former known by the collective name of Morigan and the latter by that of valkyries whose task was to choose those who were to fall in battle.

In the Germanic world other supernatural females were considered helpful to humans. In Old Norse society women participated in the worship of these figures, a role they continued when the Indo-European divinities came to the Germanic world. In Sweden and Norway, for example, women were responsible for sacrificial feasts celebrated within the house and behind closed doors.

Revealing the gender of their makers, Nordic creation myths highlight parthenogenesis and pseudo-procreation among groups of anthropomorphic males, thus suggesting the low status of females in this universe. The final pantheon consisted of a patriarchal family that included gods and goddesses. Among the latter the best known are Frigg, the wife of the chief god Óðinn, familiar to the entire Germanic world, and Freya, famous for her association with magic and unique to the North. Since their origin is not clear, their role in reproduction is barely mentioned; moreover the goddesses are not included in the rebirth of the world, and misogyny, thus, seems to be firmly established.

The Roman writer Tacitus had already remarked that the Germanic tribes conceded sacred and prophetic qualities to human women and accepted their advice and forecasts. In fact, the performance of prophecy and sorcery were for centuries the two most distinguished female contributions to Scandinavian society. These functions were attributed to a group known as *völur*, found in both the divine and human realms. Since the word is associated with *völr*, staff, they were thus known as the "staff-bearers." Older than the chief god Óðinn the most renowned prophetess, or *völva*, articulated the prophecy, or *spá*, known as *Völuspá*, that formed the first in the collection of mythic and heroic verse known as *The Poetic Edda*. Adept also in prophecy, human *völur* were professional women who traveled around the countryside, predicting the future for groups and individuals in formalized rituals.

Among Sámi deities was a female figure for childbirth named Sáráhká. Incorporated into Christianity under the name of St. Sara, she was invoked in the same breath as Mary into the early modern period. The fact that men hid outdoor altars for fear they might become desecrated by women suggests that misogyny was stronger among the Sámi than the Scandinavians and the Celts. The closest parallel between Sámi and Nordic religion, however, is found in the person of the female prophet. Old Norse texts at times identify the *völva* as a Finn or a Sámi.

For several centuries women played roles of prophets and sorcerers throughout Scandinavia and perhaps in the entire circumpolar region. Their role is closely associated with rituals of shamanism in which a religious professional, the shaman (male or female) attempted to contact spirits, divinities, or the dead. Leaving the body in a trance, thereby freeing the spirit to travel, the shaman brought information back to the worshippers. Best known from Siberia, shamanism played a larger role further east than in the North. It cannot be fully substantiated for the Celtic world or from Nordic texts dealing with the Viking age, but Paleolithic rock carvings suggest its earlier existence.

Given the chronological distance between the flourishing epochs of these religions, scholars continue to discuss whether their similarities resulted from contacts during the Viking age or should be credited to an independent development within each culture.

JENNY JOCHENS

References and Further Reading

Boyer, Régis. *La grande déesse du Nord.* Paris: Berg International, 1995.
Davidson, H. R. E. *Myths and Symbols in Pagan Europe: Early Scandinavian and Celtic Religions.* Syracuse, N.Y.: Syracuse University Press, 1988.
DuBois, Thomas A. *Nordic Religions.* Philadelphia: University of Pennsylvania Press, 1999.
Jochens, Jenny. *Images of Old Norse Women.* Philadelphia: University of Pennsylvania Press, 1996.
Motz, L. *The Beauty and the Hag: Female Figures of Germanic Faith and Myth.* Vienna: Fassbinder, 1993.
Price, Neil. S. *The Viking Way: Religion and War in Late Iron Age Scandinavia.* Uppsala: Uppsala University Press, 2002.

See also **Ireland; Magic and Charms; Prophets; Prophets, Nordic; Scandinavia; Scotland; Supernatural Women; Valkyries**

PARISHES

The parish was the basic unit of public worship for medieval Christians. Within parish boundaries, a medieval Christian would worship, learn the creed, receive moral instruction and correction, and pay taxes, called tithes, to support the Church. The creation of parishes accompanied the expansion of Christianity. Parish boundaries and parish administrations were often incorporated into civic governance as towns grew in the twelfth and thirteenth centuries. Many men first served in parish administrations before moving on to the more prestigious work of civic government.

In 1215, the Fourth Lateran Council mandated that each Christian go to confession to his or her own pastor and receive communion at least once a year, usually at Easter, which increased the importance of parishes to medieval Christianity. Typically a Christian attended three religious services on Sundays, holy days, and saints' days. Attendance was mandatory. Unless it was Easter or Christmas or a burial or baptism, parishioners in a large parish might attend a nearby chapel instead. Liturgical services were in Latin, and for much of the liturgy, the priest stood with his back to the congregation in the chancel. Until about the late fifteenth century, the laity stood for the service when they were not kneeling. Some brought stools, but the long service in a foreign tongue made many congregations restless, and the clergy continually complained about the laity's behavior at Mass. Husbands and wives did not sit together. In England, seating in rural parishes often reflected landholding, while in towns and cities, the laity purchased seats commensurate with their status and religious interests. Often seating locations within the women's section were further delineated by marital status, with unmarried women in one place and married women in another.

In many parts of Europe canon law stipulated that the laity maintain the nave of the church and the clergy the chancel. To this end, the laity had to organize themselves to raise and spend money because tithes did not maintain the parish church's fabric. Typically a lay leader, called a churchwarden, oversaw these responsibilities. Parishes used a variety of methods to raise money. Urban and town parishes often owned property, which they rented out. Urban and rural parishes hosted fairs, plays, and ales, and ran door-to-door collections. Although women rarely served as churchwardens, they were active in organizing fundraising, going door-to-door, brewing ale, and attending the festivities.

Within the parish, groups called confraternities, guilds, or stores raised money on behalf of the parish. Usually their focus was a specific part of the church, such as an altar or light dedicated to a saint. Membership in these groups could be based on occupation, wealth, or even marital status. In regions of Europe where parishes were large, such as Italy, confraternities, rather than the parish, held the religious interest and allegiance of the laity. By the end of the Middle Ages, membership in Italian confraternities or guilds became more restricted, and many began excluding women. In England, however, women, either married or single, formed their own single-sex guilds, which raised money to maintain a light or altar in their church. Although scholars debate their level of institutionalization, they are an early example of women's collective action.

The money raised went to maintaining, decorating, and furnishing the church. Some expenses were mundane, such as cleaning out the gutters. Others reflect religious interests, such as increasing amounts of wax for the Easter taper, a new tabernacle for a saint's altar, or a wall painting of a biblical scene. Taken together, lay expenses reflect a great deal of interest in the care of God's house and the performance of the mass. What is more, the range of activities allowed the laity to express a variety of interests. Women in particular left gifts and money to St. Margaret or St. Mary in hope of fertility, safe childbirth, and the health of their families. While scholars continue to debate the laity's level of Christian commitment, the variety of activities that the laity created to support their parishes suggests that they were invested in their parishes and at least many of the local manifestations of Christianity.

KATHERINE L. FRENCH

References and Further Reading

Duffy, Eamon. *Stripping of the Altars: Traditional Religion in England, 1400–1580*. New Haven: Yale University Press, 1992.

French, Katherine. "Maidens' Lights and Wives' Stores: Women's Parish Guilds in Late Medieval England." *Sixteenth Century Journal*, 29.2 (1998): 399–425.

———. "Women in the Late Medieval English Parish." In *Gendering the Master Narrative: Medieval Women and Power*, edited by Mary C. Erler and Maryanne Kowaleski. Ithaca, N.Y.: Cornell University Press, 2003, pp. 156–173.

Vauchez, André. *The Laity in the Middle Ages: Religious Beliefs and Devotional Practice*, edited by Daniel E. Bornstein, translated by Margery J. Schneider. South Bend, Ind.: University of Notre Dame Press, 1993.

See also **Confraternities; Hagiography; Lay Piety**

PASTON LETTERS

This extensive and important collection of English letters was produced in the fifteenth and early sixteenth centuries by three generations of the prominent Paston family of Norfolk, East Anglia. Members of the gentry class, the Pastons increased their substantial landholdings in the region during the course of the fifteenth century while also pursuing a range of business interests in London. The family's high regard for the archiving and preservation of correspondence has bequeathed an invaluable resource to medieval historians, literary scholars and linguists, the corpus affording a remarkable amount of insight into fifteenth-century habits, customs, conventions, and uses of written English. The coherence and continuity of the collection distinguishes this body of correspondence from the other, more disparate, epistolary English collections of the period (Stonor, Cely, Plumpton, and Lisle) while increasingly the Paston Letters are of salient interest to students of the lives and writings of medieval English women.

A substantial number of the Paston letters are written by female members of the family, chiefly Agnes Paston (d. 1479) and her daughter-in-law, Margaret Mautby Paston (d. 1484), whose forceful and lively personalities loom large in a range of letters addressed to various family members. Two further letters are contributed by Elizabeth Poynings Paston (1429–1488), daughter of Agnes and William, and six by Margaret's daughter-in-law Margery Brews (d. 1495). The letters of Margaret in particular show the matriarch to have taken a proactive and purposive role in her family's fortunes. During the protracted visits of her husband John to London, and after his early death in 1466, it increasingly fell to Margaret Paston to administer the family's Norfolk estates, apprise her sons of developments, represent business interests, and ensure good family relations. Margaret showed a pronounced concern for the written record when she advised her son John "your father set more by his writings and evidence than he did by any of his movable goods" (*PL* ed. Davis, No. 198), and accordingly she herself contributed a substantial portion of the extant Paston correspondence, though little of it in autograph. While a good many of Margaret's letters were essentially business transactions, others revealed a strong personality of deep feeling. Early letters to her husband freely expressed affection, longing, and sorrow at separation; the later missives she wrote as a widow abound with strong maternal advice, moral injunctions, and plain rebukes for her sons John II (1442–1479) and John III (1444–1504).

The letters of Agnes and Margaret also provide invaluable insights into the extent and variety of female literacy in fifteenth-century England. Study of the corpus of letters has revealed that the Paston women enjoyed a considerable degree of literacy, though they generally relied upon secretaries and amanuenses for the penning of their letters and seem to have avoided the laborious task of writing first hand. Some of the letters show linguistic features associated with oral delivery (repetitions and recapitulations, shifts of tense, parentheses, and other nonfluency features) suggesting dictation to a scribe as a favoured mode of composition. That such dictation was on occasion conducted in a state of some emotion is suggested by the celebrated account by Margaret of a colourful fracas between a local landowner and herself, her mother, and their priest, James Gloys (*PL,* ed. Davis, No. 129).

Rich and detailed as the women's letters are, some commentators have expressed disappointment at the scant introspective or self-reflective element of these early epistles that offer modern readers only limited access to the thoughts and feelings of medieval women. Set against the introspective devotional prose of contemporary fifteenth-century East Anglian Margery Kempe, the women's letters are certainly much less expressive of the inner life and are generally cast in an un–self-conscious prose light on ornamentation and artifice—a fact berated by Virginia Woolf who found "no writing for writing's sake" among the epistles. Nevertheless, recent literary and historical studies have done much to illuminate the expressive scope of the letters. Scholarship has increasingly explored the rhetorical features of the women's letters, both in terms of traditional notions of rhetoric as set out in the *ars dictaminis* (the standard medieval treatises on epistolary composition) and in terms of more modern notions of the rhetorical range of the female writer in adopting discursive positions of clarity and cogency—matriarch, householder, counsellor, consoler, confidante. The results of such work continue to suggest that the search for a distinctive "female voice" in this important and extensive collection of medieval writing is a viable, illuminating, and richly rewarding endeavour.

ROGER DALRYMPLE

References and Further Reading

Bennett, H. S. *The Pastons and Their England.* Cambridge: Cambridge University Press, 1922.

Castor, Helen. *Blood and Roses: The Paston Family and the Wars of the Roses.* London: Faber and Faber, 2004.

Dalrymple, Roger. "Reaction, Consolation and Redress in the Letters of the Paston Women." In *Early Modern Women's Letter Writing in England,* ed. James Daybell. New York: Palgrave, 2001, pp. 16–28.

Davis, Norman. "The Language of the Pastons." *Proceedings of the British Academy* 40 (1954): 119–139.

Haskell, A. S. "The Paston Women on Marriage in Fifteenth-Century England." *Viator* 4 (1973): 459–471.

O'Mara, V. M. "Female Scribal Ability and Scribal Activity in Late Medieval England: the Evidence?" *Leeds Studies in English* 27 (1996): 87–130.

The Paston Letters: A Selection in Modern Spelling, edited by Norman Davis. Oxford: Oxford University Press, 1963.

Paston Letters and Papers of the Fifteenth Century. 2 vols, by Norman Davis. Oxford: Oxford University Press, 1971 and 1976.

The Paston Women: Selected Letters, edited by Diane Watt. Cambridge: D. S. Brewer, 2004.

Richmond, Colin. *The Paston Family in the Fifteenth Century: Endings.* Cambridge: Cambridge University Press, 2000.

Watt, Diane. "'No Writing for Writing's Sake': The Language of Service and Household Rhetoric in the Letters of the Paston Women." In *Dear Sister: Medieval Women and the Epistolary Genre,* edited by Karen Cherewatuk and Ulrike Wiethaus. Philadelphia: University of Pennsylvania Press, 1993, pp. 122–138.

See also **England; Gentry, Women of: England; Kempe, Margery; Letter Writing; Literacy and Reading: Vernacular**

PASTOURELLE

The term *pastourelle* is borrowed from medieval French, where it meant "shepherdess" or "poem about a shepherdess." Many poems so described, however, do not literally involve a shepherdess. They are narratives in the voice of a man who typically says that the other day while riding in the country he met a girl (who may have been a shepherdess), spoke with her, and tried to seduce her, with every possible result. They share five traits: their mode is pastoral, commonly realized in a country setting or in the description of the heroine as a shepherdess or another kind of country lass; their cast includes a man and a young woman; their plot includes a discovery and an attempted seduction; their rhetoric involves both narrative and dialogue; and their point of view is that of the man.

We have some two hundred such poems in many languages. They were written from the early twelfth century in Occitan, by the troubadour Marcabru and others, through their heyday in the thirteenth century in French, by trouvères such as Jean Bodel, Thibaut de Champagne, and many anonymous poets, and on to the end of the Middle Ages and beyond. As early as the twelfth century the vernacular genre was imitated in Latin by Walter of Châtillon. The fashion spread in every direction around what we today call France, producing thirteenth-century pastourelles in German (Neidhart von Reuental, a variant by Walther von der Vogelweide), Italian, Galician-Portuguese, and English, as well as Latin in the *Carmina Burana.*

In the fourteenth century the French genre mutated into a new, more objective and less erotic form in poems by Froissart and Deschamps: the man says he met a group of peasants and observed their antics. But the traditional type continued to be written sporadically in Occitan, English, German, Spanish (the *serranillas* by Juan Ruiz in the *Libro de Buen Amor*), Welsh (Dafydd ap Gwilym), Italian (Petrarch), and

Gascon. The fifteenth century produced nostalgic or folkloric texts in Franco-Provençal, German, Spanish (Santillana), and French. In one French pastourelle by Josquin des Prés, the Flemish composer, the girl sings a refrain in Basque.

The man says he took the girl by force in about twenty French poems and six others in various languages, about one eighth of the poems in the genre. Andreas Capellanus, in his *De Amore*, advised his aristocratic pupil to do so, perhaps satirizing the pastourelle. These songs represent medieval hierarchy, cruelty, and violence, qualities that may have contributed to the anonymity that cloaks the authors of many French pastourelles. When rape is mentioned, it is sometimes described as shameful. Rape does not, however, occur throughout the genre. Rape never occurs in the Occitan *pastorelas*. Altogether, the attempted seduction fails as often as it succeeds, by whatever means. Some of the pastourelles suggest prostitution rather than rape; many adopt the tone of witty sexual comedy, and others depict idealized eroticism.

The genre's realism is an artistic effect. The care of sheep was not normally entrusted to young women but to shepherds; Joan of Arc testified at her trial that she did not care for her father's livestock, but the image of the shepherdess was so powerful that she came to be known as *la bergère*. This image, which appears frequently in books of hours, has religious sources in the Old Testament (Rachel in Genesis 29:9) and in the lives of saints such as Margaret, a shepherdess who imitated Christ, the good shepherd. An aura of spirituality, or at least innocence, hovered near the medieval shepherdess. It enabled Christine de Pizan to rewrite the pastourelle, in her *Dit de la pastoure* (1403), as a narrative of her own life, love, and the loss of her husband. By substituting her own point of view for the man's and rewriting seduction as abandonment, Christine reclaimed the genre for women readers.

WILLIAM D. PADEN

References and Further Reading

Bec, Pierre. *La lyrique française au moyen âge (XIIe-XIIIe siècles): contribution à une typologie des genres poétiques médiévaux: études et textes*. 2 vols. Paris: Picard, 1977–1978.

Gravdal, Kathryn. *Ravishing Maidens: Writing Rape in Medieval French Literature and Law*. Philadelphia: University of Pennsylvania Press, 1991.

Jones, W. Powell. *The Pastourelle: A Study of the Origins and Tradition of a Lyric Type*. Cambridge: Harvard University Press, 1931.

The Medieval Pastourelle. Edited by William D. Paden. 2 vols. New York: Garland, 1987.

Paden, William D. "Christine de Pizan as a Reader of the Medieval Pastourelle." In *Conjunctures: Medieval Studies in Honor of Douglas Kelly*, edited by Keith Busby and Norris J. Lacy. Amsterdam: Rodopi, 1994, pp. 387–405.

———."The Figure of the Shepherdess in the Medieval Pastourelle." *Medievalia et Humanistica*, new series, 25 (1998): 1–14.

———. "New Thoughts on an Old Genre: The *Pastorela*." *RLA: Romance Languages Annual* 10 (1998): 111–116.

———. "Rape in the Pastourelle." *Romanic Review* 80 (1989): 331–349.

La pastourelle dans la poésie occitane du moyen âge. Edited by Jean Audiau. Paris: De Boccard, 1923.

Pastourelles. Edited by Jean-Claude Rivière. 3 vols. Genève: Droz, 1974–1976.

Romances et pastourelles françaises des XIIe et XIIIe siècles. Edited by Karl Bartsch. Leipzig: Vogel, 1870. Reprint Darmstadt: Wissenschaftliche Buchgesellschaft, 1967.

Zink, Michel. *La pastourelle: poésie et folklore au moyen âge*. Paris: Bordas, 1972.

See also **Christine de Pizan; Eroticism in Literature; Literature, Occitan; Literature, Old French; Rape and Raptus**

PATRIARCHY AND PATRILINEAGE

In medieval Europe as in many societies before and since, most things worth having passed customarily from one male to another, whether the crown of a realm or the smallest parcel of a peasant's holding. The normal route of passage in this practice of patrilineage was from father to legitimate son, with women and girls included only in special circumstances.

Patriarchy literally means "rule by fathers." Modern feminist criticism, however, employs the term to denote a social and cultural system wherein positions of greater authority and legitimacy are reserved, preferentially or exclusively, for males. Patriarchy therefore extends beyond patrilineage, but is inescapably connected to it; preferential male succession to property, and access to positions of authority, cemented historical male dominance in medieval society. Moreover, a patriarchal society assumes that male authority and dominance are natural and correct. This does not mean that women in such a society exercise no authority, or have no agency. But it means that women's superior and legitimate authority—an authority exactly the same as a man's, with no special limits—is rare, and always a novelty or a temporary expedient. Such was the medieval case where a queen mother was regent for her minor son, or where a widow controlled the property of her deceased husband. When the son reached maturity or if the widow remarried, the woman's authority reverted to second-class standing. Women in religious communities exercised a considerable degree of self-governance, and the abbesses who oversaw convents might be highly respected by all. From the eleventh century on, however, the control of the institutional church over women's communities increased, and abbesses' relative degree of autonomous control was curtailed.

The literal meaning of *patriarchy*, its origin in fatherhood, helps remind us that it did not mean the authority of all men over all women, but rather the authority of some men over both male and female inferiors; medieval society was not only patriarchal but hierarchical, classified by social status, wealth, and age (among other ways), and those different forms of authority reinforced each other. Masculine authority in medieval society did not follow naturally or automatically from maleness and was a matter of constant negotiation. Only some males would qualify: fathers, mature men, the heads of households, the town burgesses, the village elders. On the most basic level, most people encountered patriarchal authority in the household, in the relationship of a father to his children, and of a master to his servants. For medieval thinkers it was easy to conceive the relationship of a king to his people, or of God to humankind, in the same way: a beneficent and responsible authority, but one ultimately not to be questioned. Medieval culture often adhered to a patriarchal ideology, then, which justified superior male authority.

Patriarchy seemed especially natural in a society that understood itself to be under the supreme authority of God the Father, whose earthly representative the pope (from the Italian *papa* = father) oversaw an institution permeating social, cultural, and political life. And in fact the medieval Church provides an excellent example of the uneven relationship between patriarchy and patrilineage. Though religious women contributed in important ways to its societal presence and creative life, the Church was indubitably a patriarchal institution. All significant authority within it was reserved by definition to men: the priests who celebrated the sacraments and were its first point of contact with ordinary people; the literate clerks and scribes who staffed its bureaucracies; the archdeacons, bishops, archbishops, and cardinals who maintained its secular legal, and political authority, managing and defending its considerable earthly wealth. In fact, arguably the Church was even more patriarchal than the secular powers with which it engaged. A daughter might inherit her father's property or title where there were no male heirs; a noble woman managed her husband's estate in his absence; a craftsman's wife kept the shop running and disciplined servants and inferiors. But nowhere in the Church could women even temporarily exercise responsibilities defined as men's. (No abbess, no matter how able her administration, was ever summoned to manage a vacant bishopric.) Thus the Church was patriarchal in this formal and institutional sense.

Moreover, that very engagement of the Church with secular society reinforced patriarchy in medieval Europe more generally. This is particularly true concerning education and literate culture. The male clerics whose training in the church gave them a high level of functional literacy might later be employed as clerks, administrators, and advisors in secular bureaucracies and royal courts; in effect, they passed from one patriarchal authority to another. The skills they brought with them led to a greater articulation of patriarchy in secular society as it applied to ordinary women and men through law and government. This succession of knowledge and authority between generations of men surely counts as patrilineage, even though the clergy during this period of expanding governmental administration, in the High and late Middle Ages, were celibate and did not as a rule pass wealth and property to the heirs of their bodies.

DEREK NEAL

References and Further Reading

Bennett, Judith. *Ale, Beer and Brewsters in England: Women's Work in a Changing World, 1300–1600*. New York: Oxford University Press, 1996.
———. "Confronting Continuity." *Journal of Women's History* 9 (1997): 73–94.
Erler, Mary C., and Maryanne Kowaleski, eds. *Gendering the Master Narrative: Women and Power in the Middle Ages*. Ithaca and London: Cornell University Press, 2003.
Kandiyoti, Deniz. "Bargaining with Patriarchy." *Gender and Society* 2 (1988): 274–290.

See also **Church; Family (Earlier Middle Ages); Family (Later Middle Ages); Femininity and Masculinity; Feminist Theories and Methodologies; Gender in History; Husbands and Husbandry; Inheritance; Landholding and Property Rights; Marriage, Christian; Misogyny**

PATRONAGE, ARTISTIC

Women's roles as patrons related to their social rank, their religious and spiritual status, and their legal powers depending on what regime they lived under. In general lay female patrons were expected to further the prestige of their father's and their husband's families and to act in ways honourable to the feminine, entailing chaste, devout, and modest behaviour. Although laywomen might be placed in charge of family patronage for a time, communities of nuns were able to sustain large-scale long-term programmes of building and decoration in their monasteries and churches. Nuns' patronage was usually devoted to sustaining their communities and devout reputations in circumstances that were more or less under the surveillance of some superior masculine institution whether this was the distant papacy, the local bishop, or the local male members of the order to which they belonged.

"Living Saints" (Zarri, pp. 219–326)

Women of quite modest social origins who could command respect for special spiritual distinction might commission, occasion commissions, or advise on the content of artworks. Thus Richelde built the replica of the wooden house of the Virgin Mary in 1061, on the model she had been shown in a vision, which became the focus of pilgrimage at Walsingham (Hall, 1965, pp. 104–110). For example the mid–twelfth-century *Saint Alban's Psalter* was arguably tailored for the anchoress and later nun Christina of Markyate, daughter of merchants, since it commemorates the death dates of her parents and her spiritual advisor. Beata Colomba da Rieti, Dominican Tertiary in Perugia, was asked by the government to defend the city against plague and invasion in 1494 by designing a processional banner. This featured Saints Dominic and Catherine of Alexandria protecting her city and survives at San Domenico, Perugia (King, 1998, p. 220).

Rulers

The few women who were appointed as rulers in their own right, like Queen Joan I (1326–1382), commissioned a range of buildings and artworks including martial projects in fulfillment of their role as heads of state. Joanna, for example, built churches, hospitals, fortifications, and made palace improvements. In 1343, she commissioned the tomb of her father, which confirmed her right to rule via her genealogical tree (King, 1995, pp. 254–255; King, 1998, pp. 62–63, 247–248). Queen Caterina Cornaro (1472–1510) of Cyprus built a fortified villa with a chapel and lodging for a hundred soldiers, designed palatial apartments in her castle at Asolo, and asserted sovereignty over Asolo by donating a baptismal font to the cathedral in 1491.

Wives of Rulers

Wives of rulers exercised patronage by permission of their spouses to encourage piety, through church and,

later, monastic foundations, and tended to represent the "caring feminine" by commissioning church furnishings, hospices, and hospitals. Empress Theodora (d. 548), wife of Justinian, sent a cross set with pearls to Jerusalem, built the churches of Hagia Irene and Saints Sergius and Bacchus, three hospices, and a monastery to shelter former prostitutes in Constantinople, as well as the church of Saint Michael and basilica of Anatolius in Antioch. Consorts sometimes withdrew to a religious life, as in the case of Queen Aethelthryth (c. 630–679) who fled her husband King Egfrith of Northumbria and built the double monastery of Saint Mary the Virgin at Ely.

As monasticism spread it became an arena for the commissioning powers of consorts such as Ansa, Queen of the Lombards, who in the mid–eighth century founded the female Benedictine convent of San Salvatore in Brescia, where the dynastic commemorations of her family were located (Wemple, 1985, pp. 85–102). Wives, like Queen Matilda, married to Henry I of England between 1100 and 1118, continued to oversee a range of enterprises on behalf of their dynasty. Matilda built bridges, a bathhouse with piped water, monastic foundations, a leper hospital, and ordered textiles and metalwork as religious gifts (Huneycutt, 1996, pp. 155–160). The pattern of doing good works and commemorating the family was still favoured. In the first half of the fifteenth century Isabel of Portugal, wife of Philip the Good Duke of Burgundy, contributed to the tombs of her natal and marital families, built three female monasteries, a hospice for pilgrims to Santiago, and a maternity hospital (Cannon-Willard, 1996, pp. 306–116). However the late fifteenth century patronage of the Marchioness Isabella d'Este of Mantua from 1490 onwards signals a possible break with philanthropic and dynastic concerns in terms of secular values and the self. Although Isabella could frame her purchases in terms of her maternal role as educator, her personal collection, housed in her apartments, represented a milestone in the development of museums by placing her choice of modern paintings alongside precious sculptures of ancient Greek and Roman artists. Isabella also employed portraits of herself and family as diplomatic gifts (Fletcher, 1981, pp. 50–63, and Brown, 1997, pp. 53–71).

Widows of Rulers

Widows of rulers acquired legal independence, although if they had heirs they seem to have been expected to spend relatively modestly. So, for example, Queen Balthild, widow of the Merovingian

King Clovis II, founded a monastery for women at Chelles, once her son inherited, and she retired there between about 665 and 680 (Nelson, 1978, pp. 68–69). Dowagers without heirs might spend the fortune. So Jeanne d'Evreux (c. 1300–1371) widow of Charles IV of France, invested in devotional books for herself and in good works, funding an infirmary and a nunnery in Paris. She commissioned one funerary chapel at Saint Denis near Paris including figures of her husband, herself, and their daughters from which the inscribed silver gilt statuette of the Virgin survives. She also commissioned a marble high altarpiece of the *Last Supper* for the Abbey of Maubuisson near Paris (still *in situ*) where she installed a second tomb to house her and her husband's entrails (now Musée du Louvre Paris) (Lord, 1997, pp. 22–34).

The survival of evidence is skewed towards commissioning for religious foundations, although we may surmise that wives and widows invested quite heavily in domestic buildings and objects too. The documentation of domestic, funerary, and philanthropic spending is attested in the case of Elizabeth de Burgh, Lady of Clare (d. 1360). As co-heiress with her sister and a childless widow, she built two friaries, one chantry, several chapels, founded Clare College Cambridge, added to three of her houses, built a new house in London, and commissioned metalwork, textiles, sculpture, paintings, liveries, as well as the family tomb (Underhill, 1996, pp. 266–287).

Relatives of Prominent Families

During the fourteenth and fifteenth centuries there is some evidence of wives and widows of more modest rank commissioning. In Italian cities wives of leading citizens, who were heiresses like Sibilia Cetto in Padua and Agnesina Badoer in Venice, erected buildings (respectively a hospital and a funerary chapel) in collaboration with husbands. In such cities widows from families of administrators, merchants, lawyers, and doctors occasionally designed sculpted effigial tombs for their male relatives, or had cheaper and less prestigious painted altarpieces made for themselves—sometimes including portraits. There is also evidence of women from artisan families contributing to joint devotional commissions (King, 1998, passim).

Women's Monasteries

Women's monasteries were led by abbesses or prioresses either appointed for life or elected for shorter terms, and commissioning took place at the will of nuns in chapter by vote and through their elected officers. These monasteries appointed a male syndic or procurator as a steward to do their business beyond the confines of the cloister walls. He promised to serve the community faithfully and commissions were also undertaken with the assistance of the monastery's priest. Communities that embraced strict enclosure were entirely dependant on their priest and syndic to manage commissions for them. Houses with more flexible enclosure rules were able to negotiate their own terms with architects and artists. While most communities were served by a priest appointed by their local bishop or on the advice of a brother order, some women's monasteries had the authority to choose their own priest (Wemple, 1985, p. 93). Consequently each community needs to be examined individually when assessing the degree to which it may have been able to decide upon its own course of action in commissioning. While women's monasteries were somewhat removed from the secular concerns of the lay world, commissions could hold dynastic significance relating to the family loyalties of the nuns and those who served them.

At an early period, as at Whitby in England in the seventh century, abbesses were sometimes placed in charge of the physical fabric of double monasteries while later, single-sex communities with no shared structures usually prevailed. Communities were responsible for the buildings of their outer church, the nuns' choir, their cloisters, the chapter house, refectory, infirmary, and dormitories, as well as their decoration with sculptures, textiles, paintings, and furnishings of all sorts. In most cases it is the public church which survives as at Romsey. Romsey Abbey was dedicated to Saint Mary and Saint Ethelflaeda, (founded 907) and was built and rebuilt for the Benedictine monastery between the tenth and the fifteenth century (Pevsner, 1967, pp. 477–486; Scott, 1996, passim). Occasionally, as at Lacock Abbey, the monastic fabric survives. This Augustinian monastery was built from 1229 onwards, initially with the funds of the first abbess, Ella, Countess of Salisbury, and dedicated to Saint Mary and Saint Bernard. The thirteenth century cloisters, chapter house, nuns' parlour, abbatial living rooms, infirmary, warming room, dormitory, and kitchen, are discernable in the fabric of the house that was built at the Dissolution (Pevsner, 1975, pp. 283–289). Female conventual buildings were distinctive in requiring architectural arrangements to protect the privacy of the nuns. Choirs, for example, were placed in a variety of ways: behind the apse of the public church (as at Monteluce, Perugia); or alongside the public nave (San Zaccaria Venice); or on a floor above the nave but with a view of the high altar (Donna Regina, Naples, and Vadstena).

Liturgical books were required, and also breviaries and other books for daily readings. It is sometimes possible to identify books commissioned by the nuns such as the mid–fourteenth-century missal ordered by Abbess Costanza de'Rossi from the monks of the Badia in Florence and adorned, among other scenes, with the life of their patron, the martyr and mother Santa Felicità (King, 1995, pp. 258–260). Nuns often commissioned distinctive seals made by goldsmiths to validate their documents, like the bronze gilt seal for the convent of Santa Chiara in Siena struck in the fourteenth century (*Sigilli nel Museo Nazionale del Bargello*, I, p. 284). While nuns were buried together, abbesses and prioresses might be distinguished by separate sculpted tombs. Some abbesses had plain tombs like the tomb of a thirteenth century abbess at Romsey decorated simply with a relief of her arm with a crozier (Pevsner, 1967, p. 486). Other abbesses were honoured with a full-length portrayal as, for instance, Chiara Gambacorta, Prioress of San Domenico, Pisa (d. 1419) (Roberts, 1994, pp. 121–154). Although property was supposed to be held in common, individual nuns were permitted to commission items, which encouraged devotion and benefited the community. For instance, Heluis d'Ecouffons of the monastery of Saint Benoîte d'Origny commissioned an illustrated life of Saint Benedict which depicted her kneeling at the altar in 1312 (Hamburger, 1992, p. 118). In 1363, Giusto de'Menabuoi inscribed an elaborate altarpiece with the information that "Giusto painted it. This work was commissioned by Sister Isotta daughter of the deceased Lord Simone de Terçago 1363" (King, 1995, p. 261).

Women seem to have calculated their strategies in buying art and architecture adroitly to accommodate dominant codes of female virtue and still sometimes represented their own variant versions of feminine decorum (Hall McCash, 1996, pp. 8–33; and Lawrence, 1997, pp. 4–7).

CATHERINE KING

References and Further Reading

Brown, Clifford. "The Art and Antiquities Collections of Isabella d'este Gonzaga 1474-1539." In *Women and Art in Early Modern Europe: Patrons, Collectors and Connoisseurs*, edited by Cynthia Lawrence. Philadelphia: University of Pennsylvania Press, 1997, pp. 53–71.

Cannon-Willard, Charity. "The Patronage of Isabel of Portugal." In *The Cultural Patronage of Medieval Women*, ed. June Hall McCash. Athens, Ga. and London: University of Georgia Press, 1996, pp. 306–320.

Fletcher, Jennifer. "Isabella d'Este Patron and Collector." In *Splendours of the Gonzaga*, edited by David Chambers and Jane Martineau. Milan: Amilcare Pizzi, 1981, pp. 51–63.

Gee, Loveday Lewes. *Women, Art, and Patronage from Henry III to Edward III 1216–1377*. Woodbridge: Boydell Press, 2002.

Gilchrist, Roberta. *Gender and Material Culture: the Archaeology of Religious Women*. London and New York: Routledge, 1994.

Hall McCash, June. "The Cultural Patronage of Medieval Women: An Overview." In *The Cultural Patronage of Medieval Women*, edited by June Hall McCash. Athens and London: University of Georgia Press, 1996, pp. 1–49.

Hamburger, Jeffrey F. "Art Enclosure and the *Curia Monialium*: Prolegomena in the Guise of a Postscript." *Gesta*, 31 (1992): 108–134.

Holdsworth, Christopher J. "Christina of Markyate." In *Medieval Women*, edited by Derek Baker. Oxford: Basil Blackwell, 1978, pp. 185–204.

Huneycutt, Lois A. "Proclaiming her dignity abroad: the Literary and Artistic Network of Matilda of Scotland Queen of England 1100–1118." In *The Cultural Patronage of Medieval Women*, edited by June Hall McCash. Athens and London: University of Georgia Press, 1996, pp. 155–174.

King, Catherine. "Women as Patrons, Nuns, Widows, and Rulers." In *Siena, Florence and Padua: Art Society and Religion 1280–1400*, ed. Diana Norman. New Haven and London: Yale University Press in association with the Open University, 1995, pp. 243–266.

———. *Renaissance Women Patrons: Wives and Widows in Italy c 1300–1550*. Manchester: Manchester University Press, 1998.

Lord, Carla. "Jeanne d'Evreux as Founder of Chapels." In *Women and Art in Early Modern Europe: Patrons, Collectors and Connoisseurs*, edited by Cynthia Lawrence. Philadelphia: Pennsylvania State University Press, 1997, pp. 21–36.

McClanan Anne L. "The Empress Theodora and the Tradition of Women's Patronage in the early Byzantine Empire" In *The Cultural patronage of Medieval Women*, edited by June Hall McCash. Athens, Ga. and London: University of Georgia Press, 1996, pp. 50–72.

The Monastic Arts of Northumberland, introduction by Rosemary Cramp, Arts Council. London, 1967.

Nelson, Janet. "Queens as Jezebels: The Careers of Brunhild and Balthild in Merovingian History." In *Medieval Women*, edited by Derek Baker. Oxford: Basil Blackwell, 1996, pp. 31–77.

Roberts, Ann M. "Chiara Gambacorta of Pisa as Patroness of the Arts." In *Creative Women in Medieval and Early Modern Italy: a Religious and Artistic Renaissance*, edited by E. Ann Matter and John Oakley. Philadelphia: University of Pennsylvania Press, 1994, pp. 121–154.

Scott, Ian R. *Romsey Abbey: Report on Excavations 1973–1991*. Southampton: Hampshire Field Club and Archaeological Society, 1996.

Stranks, C. J. *Saint Etheldreda Queen and Abbess*. Ely: Ely Cathedral Shop, 1989.

Thomas, Anabel. *Art and Piety in the Female Religious Communities of Renaissance Italy*. Cambridge: Cambridge University Press, 2003.

Underhill, Frances A. "Elizabeth de Burgh: Conoisseur and Patron." In *The Cultural Patronage of Medieval Women*, edited by June Hall McCash. Athens, Ga. and London: University of Georgia Press, 1996, pp. 266–287.

Warr, Cordelia. "Painting in Fourteenth-Century Padua." *Renaissance Studies* 10(1997): 139–155.

Wemple, Suzanne F. "S. Salvatore/S.Giulia: A Case Study in the Endowment and Patronage of a Major Female Monastery in North Italy." In *Women and the Medieval World*, edited by Julian Kirshner and Suzanne F. Wemple. New York: Blackwell, 1985, pp. 85–102.

See also **Aethelthryth of Ely; Architecture, Monastic; Cornaro, Caterina; D'Este, Isabella and Beatrice; Joan I; Jouarre and Chelles; Monasticism and Nuns; Patronage, Ecclesiastical; Patronage, Literary; Queens and Empresses: the West; Widows**

PATRONAGE, ECCLESIASTICAL

Women's options for engaging in ecclesiastical patronage, and the choices they made within the available options, depended on many factors, including wealth, social status, marital status, and location. Options and choices also varied from the early to the late Middle Ages as emphases in lay piety shifted. Ecclesiastical patronage in all of its forms gave women chances to practice, at times in highly public ways, their personal piety even as they simultaneously advanced familial strategies and achieved political aims.

Women participated in a wide range of types of ecclesiastical patronage. Some women presented jewelry or expensive articles of clothing to statues of saints in churches, as Margaret of York, Duchess of Burgundy, did when she donated her crown to the statue of the Virgin Mary at the cathedral in Aachen. Some endowed and supported colleges, as Mary de St. Pol, Elizabeth de Burgh, and Margaret Beaufort did—an important form of ecclesiastical patronage at a time when the universities were tied to the church. Others commissioned stained glass windows and works of art for churches, while many funded chantries, founded and served as benefactors for monasteries, and left bequests to parish churches. The two forms of ecclesiastical patronage that were most common for women from a range of class backgrounds throughout the Middle Ages were monastic patronage and patronage of parish churches.

Monastic Patronage

In the early Middle Ages, aristocratic women often were patrons of monastic institutions that had strong ties to their families. Families who founded monasteries tended to view the foundation as part of the estate's property, and women and men exercised rights of lordship, although feudal and canon law worked to limit proprietary claims. When aristocratic families founded nunneries, they generally had practical as well as spiritual aims, because such an institution could provide a place for daughters who did not wish, or were not permitted, to marry.

Additionally, a significant number of women founded monastic institutions in their own names; occasionally married women did so, but more frequently monastic founders were widows. When women founded nunneries independently, it was often with an eye toward entering the foundation themselves. Monastic foundation thus provided a form of security and, in the case of widows, an ecclesiastically sanctioned way to opt out of remarriage, as well as to exert independent control over an estate.

It is not surprising that widows founded monastic institutions in their own name more frequently than married women, because, although particulars varied, married women had very limited rights in regard to land holding, and only in widowhood could a woman enjoy a substantial degree of control over her dower property. Widows' ability to use their dower property in acts of monastic patronage (or indeed in other forms of ecclesiastical patronage) was not unlimited, however. Widows might face familial, as well as political, pressure to remarry, and the theoretical right to the financial autonomy that would enable acts of patronage was not in practice necessarily realized. Additionally, as Sally Thompson observes, the limited nature of women's property rights makes it difficult to discern the actual degree of women's roles in acts of monastic patronage undertaken jointly by husbands and wives. Husbands may have influenced wives' choices, but the reverse might also have been true.

Monastic records also do not always make clear the degree of women's involvement in corporate foundations, a form of monastic patronage that, as Thompson demonstrates, was widespread in post-Conquest England. In corporate foundation, families would join together to endow a monastery, a practice that opened the possibility of monastic foundation to those outside of the aristocracy. Furthermore, there are cases in which patronage is deliberately obscured because, as Thompson points out, from the later twelfth century onward, canonists attached the taint of simony to grants made by patrons in connection with the reception of novices from their families.

More typically, however, monastic patrons took pains to have their gifts recorded and remembered for posterity. Monastic foundation and other acts of patronage had benefits for the donors and the communities alike. Founders, as well as those who gave monasteries such gifts as fishing rights, grazing rights, financial bequests, or even household goods, did so to ensure perpetual prayers for themselves and their descendants.

As Jane Tibbetts Schulenburg observes, beginning in the ninth century and continuing through the eleventh century, especially in France, church reformers emphasized the spiritual superiority of monks, and female, as well as male, patrons increasingly supported male monasteries. Furthermore, in the tenth and eleventh centuries, the value of the mass in expiating sins came to be privileged over prayers, as C. H. Lawrence has shown. Concomitantly, professed monks were increasingly ordained as priests, an option not open to nuns; thus male monasteries became more attractive recipients of patronage from both men and women.

Founders' and patrons' rights, including custody of monastic estates during vacancies (for instance, the period between the death of a superior and the election of a successor), license and assent in elections of superiors, nomination of novices, and burial within the monastic cemetery or church went along with the spiritual benefits of giving to monasteries. These were not the end of the story, though. Being a patron of a rich, powerful monastic institution could enhance a family's prestige. Furthermore, in periods in which monastic reform movements were very active, women who wished to patronize monastic institutions might equally be drawn to the symbolic capital to be gained from affiliation with more austere, reformed communities.

Political benefits could also accrue from monastic patronage. The Birgittine house of Syon in England was founded by Henry V, and through the politically tumultuous fifteenth century women of the Lancastrian dynasty continued to be important patrons for this foundation so strongly associated with the Lancastrian cause. Similarly, Margaret of Bavaria, Duchess of Burgundy, made choices for monastic patronage with dynastic aims in mind. Margaret and Colette of Corbie were contemporaries, and Colette was widely revered as a saint in her lifetime. Margaret strategically supported Colette's foundations in areas in which Colette had great popular appeal and in which the Burgundian dynasty wished to consolidate its political power.

Patronage of Parish Churches

Patronage of parish churches allowed women from humble backgrounds, the mercantile class, the gentry, and the aristocracy alike to take active, visible roles in communal worship. Women's wills provide an excellent source of information about their patronage of parish churches, although, because a married woman typically required her husband's permission to make a will, widows once again had greater opportunities. Women frequently left money in their wills for church upkeep or for building projects; they also gave money for purchasing such items as chalices. There are many wills from women indicating that such luxury goods as elaborate gowns or bed hangings were given to the parish church to be converted for use as altar cloths or vestments. Even simple household goods, including sheets and towels, were bequeathed to parish churches for liturgical uses.

Aristocratic women, and, especially in the fifteenth century, women from the wealthy mercantile class sometimes engaged in more ambitious forms of parish patronage. They funded stained glass widows in which the names and images of the benefactors and members of their family were preserved. They paid for the construction of chapels and altars within parish churches, practices that increased as the fashion for chantries grew. As with certain kinds of monastic patronage, spiritual and more worldly aims overlapped such visible patronage of parish churches. Women clearly desired prayers on behalf of their souls and those of family members, as ubiquitous inscriptions indicate. Such donations also had the benefit of advertising a family's wealth alongside its piety and hence adding to familial cultural capital.

NANCY BRADLEY WARREN

References and Further Reading

French, Katherine L. "Women in the Late Medieval English Parish." In *Gendering the Master Narrative: Women and Power in the Middle Ages*, edited by Mary C. Erler and Maryanne Kowaleski. Ithaca, N.Y.: Cornell University Press, 2003, pp. 156–173.

Gold, Penny S. "The Charters of Le Ronceray d'Angers: Male/Female Interaction in Monastic Business." In *Medieval Women and the Sources of Medieval History*, edited by Joel T. Rosenthal. Athens, Ga.: University of Georgia Press, 1990, pp. 122–132.

Johnson, Penelope D. *Prayer, Patronage, and Power: The Abbey of la Trinité, Vendôme, 1032–1187*. New York: New York University Press, 1981.

King, Catherine. "Women as Patrons: Nuns, Widows, and Rulers." In *Siena, Florence, and Padua: Arts, Society, and Religion 1280–1400*. Vol. 2, edited by Diana Norman. New Haven, Conn.: Yale University Press, 1995, pp. 243–266.

Kümin, Beat. *The Shaping of a Community: The Rise and Reformation of the English Parish c.1400–1560*. Brookfield, Vt.: Scolar, 1996.

Lawrence, C. H. *Medieval Monasticism: Forms of Religious Life in Western Europe in the Middle Ages*. London: Longman, 1984.

McCash, June Hall, ed. *The Cultural Patronage of Medieval Women*. Athens Ga.: University of Georgia Press, 1996.

McLaughlin, Mary Martin. "Creating and Recreating Communities of Women: The Case of Corpus Domini, Ferrara, 1406–1452." In *Sisters and Workers in the Middle Ages*, edited by Judith Bennett et al. Chicago: University of Chicago Press, 1989, pp. 261–288.

Mirrer, Louise, ed. *Upon My Husband's Death: Widows in the Literature and Histories of Medieval Europe.* Ann Arbor: University of Michigan Press, 1992.

Raguin, Virginia Chieffo, and Sarah Stanbury, eds. *Women's Space: Patronage, Place, and Gender in the Medieval Church.* Albany: State University of New York Press, 2005.

Schulenburg, Jane Tibbets. "Women's Monastic Communities, 500–1100: Patterns of Expansion and Decline." In *Sisters and Workers in the Middle Ages,* edited by Judith M. Bennett et al. Chicago: University of Chicago Press, 1989, pp. 208–239.

Thompson, Sally. *Women Religious: The Founding of English Nunneries after the Norman Conquest.* Oxford: Clarendon, 1991.

Warren, Nancy Bradley. *Women of God and Arms: Female Spirituality and Political Conflict, 1380–1600.* Philadelphia: University of Pennsylvania Press, 2005.

Weaver, F. W., ed. *Somerset Medieval Wills: 1383–1500.* 3 vols. Somerset Record Society 16, 19, 21 Gloucester: Alan Sutton, 1983.

Wood, Susan. *English Monasteries and Their Patrons in the Thirteenth Century.* London: Oxford University Press, 1955.

See also **Architecture, Ecclesiastical; Architecture, Monastic; Artisan Families, Women of; Beaufort, Margaret; Birgittine Order; Burials and Tombs; Colette of Corbie; Devotional Art; Dowry and Other Marriage Gifts; Heiresses; Landholding and Property Rights; Margaret of York; Merchant Families, Women of; Monasticism and Nuns; Noble Women; Records, Ecclesiastical; Widows; Wills**

PATRONAGE, LITERARY

Throughout the Middle Ages, literary patronage was a special case of a larger social structure that organized political, economic, and cultural relationships at every level of society. Feudalism—the institution most associated with the Middle Ages— was itself an elaborate patronage system. The exchange of patronage, even after the return of a monetary economy in the twelfth century, was the primary means by which those both within and without government constituted their relationship to it. For this reason, it is important not to isolate literary patronage from other patronage relationships of which it was a part. Patronage was not a form of charity, philanthropy, or altruism, but a way of structuring social, political, and economic associations through gift-giving. The term covers a wide range of practices and customs in which the nature of the relationship between patron and client is left deliberately ambiguous.

Patronage organizes social life not contractually between corporate groups but through informal, face-to-face relationships between individuals. In literature, patronage provided a means of organizing the social relations of writing—of transmitting knowledge and authority—that was both more local and broader than the political divisions that have been used since the nineteenth century to organize literature.

In our own age of mechanical reproduction, a system of rewards pays authors royalties for their published work, creating distinct boundaries between the production of literary texts and their consumption. Writers at least appear free from the need to ingratiate themselves with any particular readers. Writing can be conceived of as a job and a social identity. In the Middle Ages, the system of reward for literary labor was different. Because the production of books was labor-intensive, requiring the orchestration of several artisans—writers, illuminators, rubricators, bookbinders, scribes—it is unlikely that authors could afford to produce books on their own in the hopes that someone might pay them for it. The task of coordinating book production and underwriting its expense was usually assumed by a patron who commissioned the work and who might supply the materials, oversee, coordinate, and reward the various artisans involved in its production. The process of writing or copying a book was either the product of a patronage relationship or the means of initiating one.

Patronage both shapes and is shaped by gender. Because of their informal and intimate nature, patronage networks offered an avenue for aristocratic women, who were otherwise excluded from political and economic life, to exercise power. There is evidence throughout the Middle Ages, in almost every region from Scotland to Jerusalem, that women engaged in both political and cultural patronage. Patronage is an important index of women's status since one could not be in a position to be a patron unless one wielded some kind of power or influence worth gaining access to. Eleanor of Aquitaine, who was successively queen of France and of England, was perhaps the greatest literary patron of the twelfth century but she is hardly an anomaly. Ermengard of Narbonne, as an heiress in control of her own lands, supported several troubadours including the trobairitz Azalaïs de Porcairages. Because they were more likely to be excluded from the Latin culture that defined literacy for much of the Middle Ages, female patrons were particularly significant in the revival of vernacular literatures. Many of the great medieval writers and compilers—Chaucer, Foissart, Caxton—experienced their first literary successes with the support of female patrons. The fifteenth century poet Christine de Pizan relied on extensive female patronage; the spectacularly illuminated manuscript of her collected works (Harley, 4431) was originally presented to the French queen Isabeau of Bavaria.

Abbesses, religious women, and wealthy nuns were also frequently important patrons. Bede credits Hild, Abbess of Whitby, with discovering the first English vernacular poet, Caedmon, while Hildegard of Bingen was, in turn, patron to the visionary Elisabeth of Schönau.

Patronage networks disseminate, becoming more complex as clients forge relationships with multiple patrons and patrons compete for the clientele that will affirm their importance. Among women, patronage networks spread through intermarriage. The network Eleanor of Aquitaine and her daughters established might be credited with spreading the ideology of courtly love throughout Europe. Eleanor was the granddaughter of Guillaume IX, the first troubadour poet and the first to articulate *fin' amor* (courtly love). Marie, Eleanor's eldest daughter by her first marriage to Louis VII, married the Count of Champagne and became patron to Chrétien de Troyes, author of several Arthurian romances, and Andreas Capellanus, author of *The Art of Courtly Love*. Her half-sister, Matilda of Saxony introduced courtly love into her husband's German lands, while her other sister, Leonor of England, queen of Castile, was known for her support of troubadours. The geographical dispersal of Eleanor and her daughters through marriage suggests something of the internationalizing role women's cultural patronage played. Many aristocratic and royal women were married off in foreign lands. As the cultural traditions and languages these women brought with them mingled with those of their new homes, new literary styles and genres emerged. The spread of an indigenous legend like that of King Arthur, from a marginal northern outpost like England to nearly all of Europe can be explained in part by the patronage of peripatetic brides who contributed to the cosmopolitan flavor of medieval culture.

Patronage involves the exchange of different types of resources, both tangible and symbolic, resources that are perceived as interchangeable. The growth of a money economy after the twelfth century did not eliminate the structure of this gift economy; rather it meant that patronage could take new forms, like cash; older forms of reward—position, political influence, encouragement, and protection from competitors— continued to be important. What patrons received for their investment was less tangible. The term *symbolic capital* describes the means by which the wealthy converted some of their disproportionate wealth into forms of prestige, status, and social control through what are understood as voluntary acts of generosity. For recently widowed aristocratic women, for instance, acts of patronage were often part of a strategy to protect the interests of minor children against the incursions of other relatives; Queen Emma of Eng-land seemed to have this in mind when she commissioned the *Encomium Emmae Reginae* on the eve of the Norman Conquest.

Patronage relationships are defined within a system of highly elaborated rituals, codes, and rules, which are unspoken or articulated only in an elaborately codified language that disguises the economic or political nature of the relationship as personal and private (our custom of tipping is a useful analogy). Gender provided a convenient language for disguising the economic features of patronage. *Fin' amor* may have developed among the troubadour poets of the twelfth century as a means of masking the economic calculus involved in aristocratic patronage. The *vida* of the troubadour poet Bernart de Ventadorn suggests the euphemizing function of the courtly lyric; having received the favor of the Viscount of Ventadorn, who "grew very fond of him and of his inventing and his singing, and greatly honored him," he then falls in love with the viscount's wife: "and composed his songs and his poems for her, and about her merit." The erotics of the relationship between Bernart and his lord are here displaced onto the heterosexual love between the poet and his lord's wife. This perhaps explains why the great troubadour poets almost always addressed their loves as *dompna*, married ladies, rather than *donzella*. The great erotic triangles of medieval romance—Arthur-Guenevere-Lancelot and Tristan-Isolde-Mark—continue this tradition, using the adulterous relationship between two lovers to mask the more taboo erotics that exist between the two men bound by the "love" of patronage.

LAURIE FINKE

References and Further Reading

Bourdieu, Pierre. *Outline of a Theory of Practice*, translated by Richard Nice. Cambridge: Cambridge University Press, 1877.

Eisenstadt, S. N., and Luis Roniger. *Patrons, Clients, and Friends: Interpersonal Relations and the Structure of Trust in Society*. Cambridge: Cambridge University Press, 1984.

Finke, Laurie. *Women's Writing in English: The Middle Ages*. London: Longmans, 1999.

Hambly, Gavin R. G., ed. *Women in the Medieval Islamic World: Power, Patronage, and Piety*. New York: St. Martin's, 1998.

Kellogg, Judith. *Medieval Artistry and Exchange: Economic Institutions, Society, and Literary Form in Old French Narrative*. New York: Lang, 1989.

Lewis, Hyde. *The Gift: Imagination and the Erotic Life of Property*. New York: Vintage, 1979.

Mauss, Marcel. *The Gift: Forms and Functions of Exchange in Archaic Societies*, translated by I. Cunnison. New York: Norton, 1967.

McCash, June Hall, ed. *The Cultural Patronage of Medieval Women*. Athens: University of Georgia Press, 1996.

Sedgwick, Eve. *Between Men: English Literature and Male Homosocial Desire.* New York: Columbia University, 1985.

Trigg, Stephanie. *Congenial Souls: Reading Chaucer from Medieval to Postmodern.* Minneapolis: University of Minnesota Press, 2002.

See also **Abbesses; Chaucer, Geoffrey; Christine de Pizan; Courtly Love; Eleanor of Aquitaine; Ermengard; Hild of Whitby; Hildegard of Bingen; Literacy and Reading: Vernacular: Patronage, Artistic; Patronage, Ecclesiastical; Trobairitz and Troubadours**

PEASANTS

Arguably, peasant women had the worst of both worlds: as peasants, they occupied the lowest rank on the social scale, while as women, they formed the lower group within this bottom rank. The vast majority of medieval Europeans—more than ninety percent—were peasants. Among this group, further subdivisions existed: depending on parentage, one might be a slave (although this was rare from the tenth century on), a non-free peasant (known as a serf or a villein), or a free peasant. Some peasants could even be semi-free, obligated to lords/ladies in some ways while exercising more freedom than serfs in others. Regardless of their legal status, however, peasants typically lived in small villages or hamlets and earned their livelihood by working on land owned by the nobility. Conditions of legal status and living conditions varied throughout Europe; this entry focuses primarily on England because the better survival of primary sources means that considerably more is known about English peasant women than about peasant women elsewhere.

Peasant Women's Work

Men's work was based in the fields. Male serfs were required to work on their lord's or lady's land for a certain number of days each week. They spent the rest of their time working on land rented from the lord/lady. Women could sometimes inherit or purchase land and thus act as tenants, but this was rare, and female tenants were often forced to hire men to carry out their labor obligations. While women were usually exempt from working on the lands of the nobility except at times of the year when every hand was needed (e.g., harvest season), their lives were no less busy than those of their fathers, husbands, and brothers.

Peasant women typically worked at multiple occupations. While their husbands were in the fields, peasant wives cooked food, minded children, fetched water, tended animals, grew vegetables, made, washed, and mended clothing, and took produce to market. Although their work only sometimes took them beyond the immediate vicinity of the house, they nonetheless contributed to household income both directly (by earning wages and selling excess food and drink) and indirectly (by saving the family from having to purchase extra food and clothing). Poems such as the fifteenth-century English "Ballad of a Tyrannical Husband," in which a husband and wife recount their various tasks over the course of the day, show that a peasant woman's life was filled with multiple chores, often carried out simultaneously. Peasant women regularly brewed weak ale for their families and sold any excess within their villages. Girls and unmarried women worked at the same tasks, with single women often hired out for several years as servants to other local peasant families. If opportunities were scarce, single women often migrated to the towns.

In addition to work within the house, peasant women sometimes supplemented household income by working in the fields as paid labor. When they did so, they received lower wages than men. Studies of women's wages in England show that women typically received about two-thirds to three-quarters of the wages of men. This irregular income, however, probably provided a significant boost to the household economy.

Peasant Women's Status

The status of peasant women relative to that of peasant men has proven an issue of considerable debate among historians. Eileen Power's 1926 essay on medieval women suggested that medieval women of all ranks enjoyed "a certain rough-and-ready equality" with men, and her model has proven enduring. Some more recent historians have thus portrayed the lives of peasant women as that of a partnership with their husbands, with each contributing (albeit in different ways) to the household economy. Indeed, this rosier depiction of peasant women's status can be found even in medieval times: Christine de Pizan's fifteenth-century advice to "humble women living in the village, on the plains, or in the mountains," suggested that the lives of peasant women were "often more secure and better nourished than the lives of those seated in better places." For Christine, Power, and others, class thus "trumped" gender in determining women's status and the conditions of their lives.

More recent scholarship, however, has complicated this picture, and most would now agree that the opportunities of peasant women were considerably more limited than those of their fathers, husbands, and brothers. For instance, women appeared far less frequently than men in manorial courts and were very seldom, if ever, appointed to positions of local authority, such as ale-taster, bailiff, or churchwarden. In comparison to their male relatives, they only occasionally served as "pledges" for their friends and family members (a position similar to standing bail). In consequence, their ability to shape their lives beyond the household was limited. The patriarchal constraints faced by peasant women were thus different from those of noble women, but they existed nonetheless. We have far less evidence about what happened within the household: certainly women made direct contributions to the conjugal economy and performed important roles, but we know little about who made household decisions. Scholars have also focused on the role of peasant widows: while widows had more legal rights and responsibilities than wives, they were nonetheless among the most economically vulnerable. Widowed women did not remarry quite so quickly or frequently as widowed men, but they still remarried often, especially in places where land was scarce.

Representations of Peasant Women

Literary representations of peasants by medieval elites show a clear distinction between men and women. Poets typically depicted male peasants as grotesque and dull, whereas they described female peasants as beautiful and innocent objects of desire. Knights were expected to find peasant women attractive, and some sources even claimed that rape of "shepherdesses" was understandable and excusable. The French genre of the pastourelle (pastoral poetry) emerged in about the twelfth century and features many encounters between knights and peasant women, both consensual and forced. Indeed, some of the pastourelles even imply that peasant women themselves enjoyed rape, saw it as a game, or were won over by the amorous skills of the knights. In the eyes of medieval nobles, peasant women were not only more beautiful than their male counterparts but also more intelligent. Some examples of the pastourelle depict peasant women who defend themselves with their wit and make their knightly suitors look silly. Peasant women fool men of their own class, too: French fabliaux often depict adulterous peasant women who trick their husbands into overlooking or ignoring their sins.

Direct advice to peasant women, on the other hand, portrays them as considerably less intelligent. Christine de Pizan's somewhat patronizing advice to peasant women lectures them about loving a single God, refraining from theft, and living in peace with their neighbors. For Christine, peasant women seem to be ignorant but well-intentioned. Anthony Fitzherbert's early sixteenth-century *Boke of Husbandry* similarly doles out advice about matters that were probably second nature to a peasant woman: she should begin the day by sweeping her house, send corn and malt to the mill, and much else besides.

Artistic depictions of peasant women emphasize their roles as workers. Images in manuscripts such as the English Luttrell Psalter and the French Book of Hours of the Duc de Berry depict women harvesting, feeding chickens, carrying water or ale, and carding and spinning wool. Women appear less frequently than men but, like men, they are featured primarily at work (rather than at leisure or at worship, for instance).

Because we lack documents written from the perspective of peasant women, we know far less about how they themselves regarded their own status and roles. Stereotypes of peasant women (and townswomen) as gossips imply a vibrant oral culture, and case-studies like those of the French peasants of Montaillou, demonstrate that women participated in meaningful networks of friendship and mutual support. Similarly, records of women's participation in parish guilds show that these functioned as a way for women to work together on common projects and enjoy each other's company.

SANDRA BARDSLEY

References and Further Reading

Bennett, Judith M. *Women in the Medieval English Countryside: Gender and Household in Brigstock before the Plague*. New York: Oxford University Press, 1987.
———. *A Medieval Life: Cecilia Penifader of Brigstock, c. 1295–1344*. Boston: McGraw-Hill, 1996.
de Pizan, Christine. *A Medieval Woman's Mirror of Honor: The Treasury of the City of Ladies*, translated by Charity Cannon Willard & edited by Madeleine Pelner Cosman. Tenafly, N.J.: Bard Hall Press, 1989.
Freedman, Paul. *Images of the Medieval Peasant*. Stanford: Stanford University Press, 1999.
Hanawalt, Barbara A. *The Ties That Bound: Peasant Families in Medieval England*. New York: Oxford University Press, 1986.
———. "Peasant Women's Contribution to the Home Economy in Late Medieval England." In *Women and Work in Preindustrial Europe*, edited by Barbara A. Hanawalt. Bloomington: Indiana University Press, 1986, pp. 3–19.

Ladurie, Emmanuel LeRoy. *Montaillou: The Promised Land of Error*, translated by Barbara Bray. New York: Vintage Books, 1979.

See also **Agriculture; Alewives and Brewing; Christine de Pizan; Division of Labor; England; Fabliau; Feme Covert; Feme Sole; Gossip and Slander; Household Management; Husbands and Husbandry; Landholding and Property Rights; Parishes; Pastourelle; Records, Rural; Servants; Slaves; Social Status; Widows; Work**

PENITENTIALS AND PASTORAL MANUALS

Pastoral manuals took various forms in both the early and late Middle Ages. Such a text could be a complex theoretical document elaborating scriptural precedents for the priesthood, or a short text focusing on a specific pastoral function. An example of the former is Gregory the Great's *Liber Regulae Pastoralis* or *Pastoral Care* (c. 590), a richly nuanced description of the priest's role as preacher and teacher widely popular throughout the Middle Ages, and translated into English by King Alfred and his assistants at the end of the ninth century. Among the earliest examples of the latter are handbooks of penance, or penitentials, catalogues listing sins and the penances assigned to each by the priest in confession.

From a practical perspective, the penitential, a form with its origins in Irish monasticism of the seventh century, can be considered the first pastoral manual. The penitential was primarily concerned with the administration of private confession and penance, but it also addressed the priest's duties in relation to other sacramental and disciplinary matters, including marriage and rites for the dying. Such texts were designed to educate the clergy as well as to guide them in the exercise of their offices. Although traditionally known as "handbooks," penitentials survive most often as parts of larger codices of ecclesiastical statutes, treatises, and homilies; these collections suggest that already in the early Middle Ages the penitential was regarded as an indispensable tool of pastoral education. Very few small, self-contained manuscripts that fit the designation *handbook* survive, no doubt because such utilitarian documents perished easily.

Penitentials are not simply lists, however; even the earliest surviving texts (from the eighth century) include prefatory material, including the *ordo confessionis*, a quasi-liturgical text explaining how the priest was to administer the sacrament, question the sinner, determine his or her sincerity, and weigh the seriousness of the sins confessed. Handbooks frequently differentiate penances according to the sinner's social status, including age, gender, and occupation. Penitentials appear to have originated in Ireland and reached England through the work of Irish missionaries. By the late seventh century, the handbook had spread to followers of Theodore of Canterbury (d. 690), the first non-Irish authority under whose name a penitential was issued. Ninth- and tenth-century manuscripts of penitentials are common on the Continent. Starting in England in the tenth century, penitentials were written in both Latin and the vernacular, although the Latin texts are far more numerous. The vernacular texts of the tenth and eleventh centuries list penances identical to those found in eighth-century texts. Some scholars assume that penitential tariffs would have been revised as the handbooks passed from region to region and century to century, and this uniformity is seen by them as contradicting assumptions about the widespread practice of private confession and penance. Regulatory literature is notoriously conservative, however, and although variations in penances themselves are rare, the handbooks show considerable innovation over time in both form and scope. It is safe to say that confession was widespread in both the early and late medieval periods, moving outward from its monastic origins to the lay population living around the monastery, and spreading to spiritual communities that formed around what eventually became the parish church. The early penitentials devote extensive consideration to sexual sins and to distinguishing the sins of men from those of women. According to the eighth-century *Penitential of Theodore*, for example (and its eleventh-century vernacular English translations), a woman who had sex with another woman was assigned a penance of fasting for three years (penances for male homosexual intercourse were higher, up to ten years). A husband could dismiss an adulterous wife, but a wife could not get rid of an adulterous husband unless she was willing to join a monastery.

Penitential literature underwent a great change after the Lateran Council of 1215, after which point pastoral manuals become more numerous. But the Council has served too conveniently as a date for differentiating old and new styles of penitentials and manuals. The *Decretum* of Burchard of Worms (finished by 1015) compiled moral theology and church law, drawing on handbooks of penance, patristic sources, and conciliar texts. Burchard's nineteenth book, "*Corrector, seu medicus*," often served as a penitential manual itself and drew some of its provisions from early penitentials, including the one attributed to Theodore of Canterbury. Burchard's text is an early example of the synthesis of instruction and practical regulation that served as a guide for the clergy. The *Decretum* of Gratian (c. 1140) combined a discourse on canon law and its principles with a discussion of church law, including penance and matrimony, and material on the liturgy and sacraments. Thereafter handbooks of penance and pastoral manuals were seemingly inseparable forms. [Ivo of Chartres incorporated many of Burchard's decisions into his *Decretum* in the late eleventh century, and later penitentials derive from Ivo's work, including those by Bartholomew of Exeter (c. 1150) and Robert of Flamborough (c. 1208). Robert's *Liber Poenitentialis* shows how the handbook of penance had developed as a form of catechism. Throughout the thirteenth century such texts became much longer and more complex and were designed to leave little to the discretion of individual confessors. They provided the confessor with topics divided and subdivided with near scholastic complexity. Manuals once limited to a few functions were now broadened to include prayers as well information on the commandments, the works of mercy, the deadly sins, and other matters of devotion and doctrine.

Later medieval manuals are explicit in describing how priests were to preach to and teach their congregations. The bishops' success in persuading the clergy to adhere to the regulations of these manuals is, of course, an open question. The sheer bulk of the surviving evidence strongly suggests that the program was pervasive. Works by John Pecham and William of Pagula, written in the late thirteenth and early fourteenth centuries, helped to conflate the objectives of pastoral manuals with those of theological treatises. Such texts informed a new generation of manuals written for the laity (e.g., *The Lay Folks' Catechism*). Prose works including *Jacob's Well* and *Dives and Pauper* further consolidated the aims of pastoral and lay education. By the late fourteenth century the pastoral manual had generated many textual strands in France, England, and elsewhere. The thirteenth-century *Manuel des péchés*, for example, was translated into English as *Handlyng Synne* by Robert Manning in the first quarter of the fourteenth century. This text includes several anecdotes in which women are assumed to be responsible for inciting the clergy to sexual sins, although Manning makes it clear that greater responsibility falls on the clergy in such cases. Special considerations for women appear elsewhere, as in the fifteenth-century *Instructions for Parish Priests* by John Myrc, which urges priests to give moderate penances that will be carried out rather than neglected as too demanding and requires that women be given penances that their husband will not know about (i.e., penance that can be performed in private).

Pastoral manuals offer a wealth of insight into medieval Christian expectations of human behavior. As penitentials, they advise the priest on methods of testing and determining the sincerity of the penitent's confession, his or her motives, degree of guilt, and other psychological factors that made confession an intriguing subject for literary exploration. Chaucer's *Parson's Tale* is one of the most elaborate attempts to integrate the genre of the manual into fiction. Following a verse prologue that questions the morality of fiction, the Parson's "tale" turns out to be a translation of the *Summa de poenitentia* of the Dominican Raymund of Pennaforte (c. 1222–1229). After defining the three parts of penance as contrition, confession, and satisfaction, the text distinguishes venial from mortal sins and vividly illustrates the seven deadly sins. Chaucer's decision to make this treatise the final "tale" of *The Canterbury Tales* has puzzled readers and points to the great gap between "literary" texts and pastoral discourse.

Penitentials and pastoral manuals have long been unedited and unstudied. Discussions dismissing them as having little or no literary interest were once routine. However, work on sexuality, sex, and gender in recent decades has begun to reverse this view. These texts are now seen as forms that refracted various aspects of medieval experience even as they sought to shape that experience along doctrinal lines. Sometimes, as in *Handlyng Synne*, narrative exempla are used to underscore the moral perspective of the text. Scholars have shown far more interest in such works than in those texts that approach pastoral instruction in a matter-of-fact way, as in, for example, the *Lay Folk's Catechism*, and it is clear that this catechism and similar works still have much to teach readers about the educational and pastoral traditions of the Middle Ages.

ALLEN J. FRANTZEN

References and Further Reading

Frantzen, Allen J. *The Literature of Penance in Anglo-Saxon England.* New Brunswick, N.J.: Rutgers University Press, 1983.

Gillespie, Vincent. "*Doctrina* and *Predicatio*: The Design and Function of Some Pastoral Manuals." *Leeds Studies in English* n.s. 9 (1980): 36–50.

Joliffe, P. S. *A Check-List of Middle English Prose Writings of Spiritual Guidance.* Toronto: Pontifical Institute of Mediaeval Studies, 1974.

McNeill, John T., and Helena M. Gamer. *Medieval Handbooks of Penance: A Translation of the Principal.* Reprint, New York: Columbia University Press, Libri Poenitentiales and *Selections from Related Documents.* New York: Columbia University Press, 1938; 1990.

Rayme, Robert T. *Words of Religious and Philosophical Instruction.* In *A Manual of Writings in Middle English, 1050–1500,* vol. 7. ed. Albert C. Hartung. New Haven: Connecticut Academy of Arts and Sciences, 1986.

Utley, Francis Lee. *Dialogues, Debates, and Catechisms.* In *A Manual of Writings in Middle English, 1050–1500,* vol. 3. ed. Albert C. Hartung. New Haven: Connecticut Academy of Arts and Sciences, 1972.

Woods, Marjorie Curry, and Rita Copeland. "Classroom and Confession." In *The Cambridge History of Medieval English Literature*. Cambridge: Cambridge University Press, 1999, pp. 376–406.

See also **Education, Lay; Education, Monastic; Law, Canon; Lay Piety; Sermons and Preaching; Sexuality, Regulation of; Spiritual Care**

PERFORMANCE IN LYRIC

The information available on women's performance of lyric poetry encompasses a wide variety of textual sources, including historical references, literary, and didactic texts that present singing as a desirable accomplishment for women, and narrative works that depict women in the act of singing. Lyric poetry could be performed unaccompanied or accompanied by flute, harp, or fiddle; the specific songs are not usually identified, except in fictional accounts.

Ubiquitous in the medieval Arab world were trained female singers who performed extensive repertories of songs from memory. They flourished particularly during the ʿAbbāsid period (749–1258 CE) and included both slaves (*jāriyya* or *qaynah*) and freedwomen. *Qiyan* sang, played instruments, and improvised poetry. Another group of female singers in Arab courts were known as the *nadim*, highly educated companions to the ruler. On the Iberian peninsula, female singers performed Andalusian strophic genres such as the vernacular Arabic *zajal* and the classical Arabic *muwashshah*. The existence of *kharjas* (the final strophe of *muwashshahat*) in the poetic voice of a female subject (some of them in an inchoate Romance vernacular) has been associated with performance by Andalusian female singers. Several of the *kharjas* are introduced by phrases (such as "she sings") evoking such a performance context.

This interpretation of the Hispano-Arabic lyric raises the question of whether the depiction of female subjectivity in the lyric reflects female agency (whether composition or performance). The sex of the composer/author is frequently unknown, precluding any basis for determining the authenticity of the poetic voice. Nevertheless, the broad category of "woman's song" is often used to designate poetry in which the speaker (or one of the speakers) seems to be a woman. Even in songs clearly attributed to a man, such as the Galician-Portuguese *cantigas de amigo* of Martim Codax, the presence of a female speaker is sometimes thought to signal a connection with popular lyric genres that were customarily performed by women. Just how one might interpret the poetic representa-

tion of the female voice has long been central to scholarly discussions of musical performance by medieval women. In some cases an association with an archaic substrate of female performance traditions is an inherent dimension of the genre, as in the courtly northern French "spinning songs" or *chansons de toile*. Many "woman's songs" survive in the modern Sephardic, Arabic, and Galician oral traditions.

In what is now France, women worked as professional entertainers or minstrels (*jougleresse* in northern France, *joglaressa* or *soldadeira* in the south), performing lyric poetry among other genres. Courtly narrative and song depict women of various classes singing lyric poetry, suggesting that the authors were familiar with this kind of performance. A wide range of texts from northern France associates women with the performance of dances, known as *caroles*, that were performed while singing. In the later Middle Ages, and particularly in the fifteenth century, manuscript and biographical evidence suggests that elite women composed and performed lyric poetry set to music. The medieval Occitan lyric corpus of southern France includes several works attributed to female poets (*trobairitz*). Most of the melodies for these compositions do not survive, but the works were sung, quite possibly by their composers. References to performance by female poets in Occitania are rare, but it seems significant that a thirteenth-century manuscript contains instructions to the illuminator to depict the Comtessa de Dia (fl. c. 1200) as a lady singing.

Historical sources attest to the presence of women as professional singers at courts and in towns during the fourteenth and fifteenth centuries in the British Isles, France, Italy, Spain, and German-speaking lands. These women could also be minstrels. Information on amateur singing can be gleaned from prescriptive and literary texts. The early fourteenth-century treatise by Francesco da Barberino, *Reggimento e costumi di donna*, is an example of conduct literature that specifically addresses women's musical performance. Barberino recommended that elite women sing in public only at the request of a relative, but that they could sing in their rooms on a regular basis, while lower-class women had more freedom to engage in musical performance. In Boccaccio's *Decameron*, several of the female characters perform *ballate*, a fixed form of Italian lyric poetry that was linked to dance. In the fifteenth century, professional women singers of secular music, including lyric poetry, were employed by northern Italian courts. The extensive corpus of poetry in German authored by women during the fifteenth and sixteenth centuries suggests that women were involved in the musical performance of this lyric tradition as well.

SUSAN BOYNTON

References and Further Reading

Beck, Eleonora M. *Singing in the Garden: Music and Culture in the Tuscan Trecento*. Innsbruck: Studien and Lucca: LIM, 1998.

Brown, Howard Mayer. "Women Singers and Women's Songs in Fifteenth-Century Italy." In *Women Making Music: The Western Art Tradition, 1150–1950*, edited by Jane Bowers and Judith Tick. Urbana and Chicago: University of Illinois Press, 1986, pp. 62–89.

Cheyette, Fredric L., and Margaret Switten. "Women in Troubadour Song: Of the Comtessa and the Vilana," *Women and Music: A Journal of Gender and Culture* 2 (1998): 26–46.

Classen, Albrecht. *Late-Medieval German Women's Poetry: Secular and Religious Songs*. Cambridge: D. S. Brewer, 2004.

Coldwell, Maria. "*Jougleresses* and *Trobairitz*: Secular Musicians in Medieval France." In *Women Making Music: The Western Art Tradition, 1150–1950*, edited by Jane Bowers and Judith Tick. Urbana: University of Illinois Press, 1986, pp. 39–61.

Marshall, Kimberly. "Symbols, Performers, and Sponsors: Female Musical Creators in the Late Middle Ages." In *Rediscovering the Muses: Women's Musical Traditions*, edited by Kimberly Marshall. Boston: Northeastern University Press, 1993, pp. 140–168.

Medieval Woman's Song: Cross-Cultural Perspectives, edited by Ann Marie Rasmussen and Anne Klinck. Philadelphia: University of Pennsylvania Press, 2001.

Page, Christopher. *Voices and Instruments of the Middle Ages: Instrumental Practice and Songs in France 1100–1300*. Berkeley and Los Angeles: University of California Press, 1986.

Rokseth, Yvonne. "Les femmes musiciennes du XIIe au XIV siècle." *Romania* 61 (1935): 464–480.

Sawa, George Dimitri. *Music Performance Practice in the early ʿAbbasid Era, 132–320 AH / 750–932 AD*. Toronto: Pontifical Institute of Mediaeval Studies, 1989.

Songs of the Women Trouvères, edited by Eglal Doss-Quinby, Joan Tasker Grimbert, Wendy Pfeffer, and Elizabeth Aubrey. New Haven and London: Yale University Press, 2001.

See also **Trobairitz and Troubadours; Trouvères, Women; Woman's Song**

PERFORMANCE THEORY

Performance theory focuses upon the classification, analysis, and functions of performances. Performance theorists regard performance as an innate human activity and therefore as a useful way to study human interaction. Performances (defined as mimetic, deliberate, and elaborated behaviors) include play, games, sports, theater, and ritual. Richard Schechner has identified four characteristics of such performances: 1) They take place in "event time" where the activity itself has a set sequence and all sequences must be completed regardless of how long it takes; 2) objects have different values from those attached to them in ordinary practice; 3) performance activities are nonproductive, that is, they create no wealth or goods; and 4) they are hedged about with special rules. Further, performance theorists have postulated that performance as a mimetic behavior is "cooked" in the Levi-Straussian sense of transforming raw experience into culturally palatable terms, and, as such, culturally co-created. Performances may be either conservative, reinforcing social order, or revolutionary, restructuring it.

Performance theories are useful to the study of medieval women because a performance perspective focuses upon what women did in their milieu. Scholars can analyze relationships among types of performances. An important aspect of performance theory for medievalists is the examination of relationships between texts and their performative uses. Because medieval texts were almost never written as private recollections of an individual author, a focus upon the performative dimensions of medieval textuality opens up new possibilities for understanding women's (and men's) agency in creating public performances that shaped and responded to their culture. A good introduction to the possibilities of performance theory for new understandings of the writings of a diverse array of women like Marguerite Porete, Margery Kempe, and Birgitta of Sweden is Mary Suydam and Joanna Ziegler's *Performance and Transformation: New Approaches to Late Medieval Spirituality*.

MARY SUYDAM

References and Further Reading

Beeman, William O. "Performance Theory in an Anthropology Program." http://www.brown.edu/Departments/Anthropology/publications/PerformanceTheory.htm.

Schechner, Richard. *Performance Theory*. London and New York: Routledge, 1988.

Suydam, Mary A. "Background: An Introduction to Performance Studies." In *Performance and Transformation: New Approaches to Late Medieval Spirituality*, edited by Mary A. Suydam and Joanna E. Ziegler. New York: St. Martin's Press, 1999, pp. 1–25.

Turner, Victor. *The Anthropology of Performance*. New York: PAJ Productions, 1986.

See also **Postmodernism and Historiography**

PERSONIFICATIONS VISUALIZED AS WOMEN

Medieval allegory and its use of personified abstractions connect some of the central elements of Western thought—including questions of literary history, education, hermeneutics, and theology—to the representation of femininity and female characters in medieval literature and culture. Allegory, a metaphorical symbol, figure, discourse, or story, comes from the Greek words *allos*, "other," and *agoreuein*, "to speak," and situates itself in the belief that the value of a text depends upon its having "other" interpretations beyond the literal meaning. Allegoresis, or allegorical interpretation, enabled early exegetes to reconcile discrepancies between contemporary ideas and ancient texts. Primary in this regard was the impulse to read the Old Testament typologically, through the lens of the New Testament, and thus to understand female Old Testament figures, for example Eve, or the bride in the Song of Songs, as representative of larger moral or explicitly Christian themes, such as the danger of carnal desires (in the case of Eve) and the love of the Church for Christ (in the case of the bride). This use of allegory to extol the Christian perspective occurred in medieval art as well as literature. Late medieval antagonism toward Jews, for example, transformed a contest mentioned in the New Testament between the allegorical figures of Ecclesia, or Church, and the Jewish Synagogue, into a popular visual dyad, with Church depicted as a triumphant, newly crowned queen, and Synagogue depicted as a blinded or blindfolded woman who has lost her crown (perhaps following an image in the Lamentations of Jeremiah 5:16–17), or who holds a broken lance to represent her part in Christ's Passion (for example, in the Musée de l'Oeuvre Notre-Dame, Strasbourg).

Yet, as Dante's influential description of the fourfold allegorical interpretation in his "Letter to Can Grande della Scala" (c. 1317) suggests, allegory's interpretive function could be applied to contemporary poetry as well as ancient texts. Dante's preeminent allegorical work, the *Divine Comedy*, uses different types of allegory—including identifying his childhood love, Beatrice, with Christ—to represent physically what is ultimately a spiritual journey. As his poetry shows, allegory's power as a form of medieval expression and interpretation lay in its way of linking the concrete and the abstract, but also in its way of linking the present to the past, and the secular to the spiritual. In its relation to the larger history of the representation of women, medieval personification allegory could be said to have helped restrict women characters to the realm of abstraction and essentialism; at the same time, however, the role allegory played in bringing female characters to the forefront of medieval literary creativity should be recognized.

Classical Influences

Perhaps most important in regard to female personifications is medieval allegory's dependence on the conventions of classical philosophy and rhetoric. While early Christian custom tended to associate women with Eve, temptation, and idolatry, the classical tradition, with its Neo-Platonic emphasis on the marriage of male and female elements in creation, and its use of female personifications to balance both good and evil forces, introduced a more positive representation of women (Ferrante, 2). Images of women were central to the late-antique worldview and self-understanding; works such as Prudentius' *Psychomachia* (or "Conflict of the Soul") and Martianus Capella's *Marriage of Philology and Mercury* envision the human condition, and especially man's capacity for knowledge and inner turmoil, through female personified abstractions. Prudentius' text imagines the human conflict between the flesh and the spirit as an epic battle between the vices and virtues, all of which are presented as female. In a similar way, Capella's work explores the realm of human learning through the allegorical marriage of the God of Eloquence, Mercury, to the mortal woman and bibliophile Philology, who receives as a wedding gift the Seven Liberal Arts, personified as maidens.

These texts and the female figures they envision became part of the foundation of the medieval educational curriculum and greatly influenced not only medieval learned culture, but also medieval culture as a whole. Female representations of the vices and the virtues, for instance, populate such medieval "bestsellers" as William Langland's *Piers Plowman* and Guillaume de Deguileville's *Pèlerinage de la Vie Humaine* (as well as John Lydgate's later translation of this text, the "Pilgrimage of the Life of Man"), and play a central role in morality plays from Hildegard of Bingen's early *Ordo Virtutum* to the famed late medieval *Everyman*. They also maintain a consistent visual presence, from manuscript illuminations and ekphrastic descriptions, such as the garden wall in Guillaume de Lorris' and Jean de Meun's *Romance of the Rose,* to the sculptured bays of the Chartres Cathedral.

Lady Philosophy as Model

The single most influential use of the female personification, at least in regard to medieval European popular poetry, is the appearance of Lady Philosophy in the opening of Boethius' *Consolation of Philosophy* (c. 525). This figure's materialization at the poet's side in his darkest moment of despair and self-pity, her brusque initial treatment of him, and her subsequent role as simultaneous nurse, teacher, and spiritual and intellectual guide, became the template for numerous medieval works. Boethius did not invent the role of the abstract or otherworldly female authority figure and guide; Virgil's Sybil and Capella's Virtue prefigure his Philosophy and inform many later medieval works themselves. But the overwhelming popularity of Boethius' *Consolation* in western Europe for roughly one thousand years, from its creation until the early modern period, meant that imitations of and allusions to the text, and especially to its central female character, Philosophy, became a mark of literary authenticity, and eventually an element of medieval poetic convention. Some of the best-known female figures of medieval literature, including Alan of Lille's Nature in his *Plaint of Nature*, Reason in the *Romance of the Rose*, Dante's Beatrice, the Pearl maiden in the anonymous *Pearl*, Holy Church in Langland's *Piers Plowman*, and various female figures in Chaucer's dream poetry, implicitly echo aspects of Boethius' Philosophy. Importantly, however, Philosophy's forceful presence in Boethius' text, characterized by her loyalty, stability, and reason, gains much of its power through its opposition to another, less venerable female figure: that is, fickle Fortune, whose seductive material gifts and ever-turning wheel were also made famous by Boethius (and whose likeness also appears throughout the medieval corpus of the literary and visual arts). How one is to understand this familiar dichotomy of opposing female forces of good and evil, transcendent and material, hinges on the complicated issue of how female personifications speak to medieval constructions of women and gender.

Gendered Personifications

Like the female abstractions in Prudentius and Capella, and like many subsequent medieval personifications, Boethius' Philosophy, though female, also represents humankind's—and in this case, one particular man's—inner qualities. This type of multifaceted gender identity epitomizes the complicated nature of gendered abstractions. On the one hand, the gendering of personifications to a large extent follows the gendering of language: in Latin, abstract concepts are usually feminine, and hence so are the personifications of those abstract concepts. On the other hand, medieval representations of female personifications can also appear to *construct* feminine gender, by aligning the figures with culturally inscribed "feminine" characteristics, such as ornamentation, sexual or economic exchange, or the eroticized process of allegorical reading itself. Like their late-antique counterparts, medieval commentators were fascinated with the idea of allegory as a veil or covering—the

integumentum or *involucrum* that revealed or concealed textual truth—and they often explored this idea by troping the male acquisition of secret knowledge, truth, and revelation as the unveiling of the female body and its sexual "secrets." While the medieval poet's focus on the adorned female body ostensibly concerns the male susceptibility to shiny or dazzling surfaces (both rhetorical and material), it also reveals the extent to which these figures represent femininity as a projection of male desire. Jean de Meun imagines Fortune as a woman who alternates between a wealthy, luxuriously adorned and sweetly scented lady preening herself in a golden palace, and a prostitute stripped of all clothing, weeping on the floor of a brothel. In his *Parliament of Fowls*, Chaucer likewise describes the Goddess of Love, Venus, as naked from the waist up, while the rest of her is covered in a garment so fine as to be see-through. Perhaps Langland's connubial Lady Meed, who ravishes men simultaneously with her sumptuous attire and with her sumptuous words, most clearly epitomizes this connection between the erotics of rich female adornment and the erotics of rich allegorical language. As modern theorists have pointed out, this age-old link between women, adornment, and allegory suggests that figuration itself was understood to be an inherently feminine act.

This is not to say that all female personifications in the medieval period, or even those that depict the relation between the male mind and the adorned female figure, overtly essentialize the female gender. Some medieval authors use female personifications to explore the very issue of flawed male perception, and even flawed gender perceptions. Central to the *Pearl* poem, for example, is the protagonist's persistent inability to see the Pearl *irrespective* of his preconceived, worldly notions of her. Some works, like Langland's *Piers Plowman* and the anonymous *Cursor Mundi* ("Runner of the World") draw attention to questions of gender by actually shifting the gender of certain personifications mid-text, and often mid-sentence. And finally, in her *Book of the City of Ladies*, Christine de Pizan uses the tradition of the wise female counselor (of which she has three: Lady Reason, Lady Rectitude, and Lady Justice) to challenge misogynist stereotypes of women and to create a new concept of female authority, one built on positive examples of historical and mythical women, and on her own authority as a female writer.

ANDREA DENNY-BROWN

References and Further Reading

Bloch, Howard. *Medieval Misogyny and the Invention of Western Romantic Love*. Chicago: University of Chicago Press, 1991.

Bloomfield, Morton, ed. *Allegory, Myth, and Symbol.* Cambridge, Mass: Harvard University Press, 1981.

Cooper, Helen. "Gender and Personification in Piers Plowman." *Yearbook of Langland Studies* 5 (1991): 31–48.

de Man, Paul. *Allegories of Reading: Figural Language in Rousseau, Nietzsche, Rilke, and Proust.* New Haven, Conn.: Yale University Press, 1979.

Ferrante, Joan M. *Woman as Image in Medieval Literature.* New York: Columbia University Press, 1975.

Fletcher, Angus. *Allegory: The Theory of a Symbolic Mode.* Ithaca, N.Y.: Cornell University Press, 1964.

Greenblatt, Stephen J., ed. *Allegories of Representation: Selected Papers from the English Institute, 1979–80.* Baltimore, Md.: Johns Hopkins University Press, 1981.

Katzenellenbogen, Adolf. *Allegories of the Virtues and Vices in Medieval Art.* London: Warburg Institute, 1939.

Lewis, C. S. *The Allegory of Love: A Study in Medieval Tradition.* Oxford: Oxford University Press, 1951.

Mâle, Emile. *Religious Art in France, The Twelfth Century: A Study of the Origins of Medieval Iconography.* Princeton: Princeton University Press, 1978.

Paxson, James J. "Gender Personified, Personification Gendered, and the Body Figuralized in *Piers Plowman.*" *Yearbook of Langland Studies* 12 (1998): 65–96.

———. "Personifications" Gender." *Rhetorica* 16.2 (1998): 149–179.

———. *The Poetics of Personification.* Cambridge: Cambridge University Press, 1994.

Quilligan, Maureen. *The Language of Allegory: Defining the Genre.* Ithaca, N.Y.: Cornell University Press, 1979.

———. *The Allegory of Female Authority: Christine de Pizan's* Cite des Dames. Ithaca, N.Y.: Cornell University Press, 1991.

Tuve, Rosemond. *Allegorical Imagery: Some Medieval Books and Their Posterity.* Princeton, N.J.: Princeton University Press, 1966.

See also **Art: Representations of Women in; Beatrice; Body, Visual Representations of; Chaucer, Geoffrey; Christine de Pizan; Dante Alighieri; Gender in Art; Hildegard of Bingen; Roman de la Rose and Its Reception**

PETITIONS

Petitions addressed to powerful individuals or institutions are as old as civilization itself. Given the lower status and illiteracy that frequently characterized medieval women, their written applications survive in smaller numbers than those submitted by men. As European bureaucracies became increasingly sophisticated, so did the form of pleas presented. Wealthy and prominent females seeking redress from perceived injustices or financial burdens typically employed scribes to prepare their documents; women of slenderer means and more urgent needs sought public arenas where they could voice complaints and elicit responses at minimal cost. This option remained open in some European communities until the late Middle Ages.

Petitions from medieval women survive in various European record collections. A useful selection of English material from the thirteenth century onwards is held at the U. K. National Archives in the Public Record Office's SC8 class (Special Collections: Ancient Petitions). These documents include women's petitions to the king, the king and council, Parliament, and the chancellor or other officers of state. Similar sources held at the Vatican Archives originated mainly from noble secular women or enclosed religious. They include applications for absolution, removal of the stain of illegitimacy (by religious seeking higher office in the convent), or papal intervention in disputes. The published papal letters of the fifteenth century indicate a rising demand from both men and women for permission to employ private confessors, own portable altars and worship in private oratories. This pattern appears to have been consistent with a trend towards individualism in the expression of the Christian faith. To what extent these petitions were ultimately successful is open to question, since surviving evidence is patchy.

VALERIE SPEAR

References and Further Reading

Kittell, Ellen E. "Women, Audience, and Public Acts in Medieval Flanders." *Journal of Women's History* 10.3 (1998): 74–96.

Public Record Office. *Calendar of Entries in the Papal Registers Relating to Great Britain and Ireland. Papal Letters*, vols 1–16. London: A.M.S.O., 1893–1986.

———. *Calendar of Entries in the Papal Registers Relating to Great Britain and Ireland. Petitions to the Pope*, vol. i, A.D. 1342–1419, ed. William Henry Bliss. London: Eyre and Spottiswoode, 1896.

Schmugge, Ludwig. "Female Petitioners in the Papal Penitentiary." *Gender & History* 12.3 (2000): 685–703.

Spear, Valerie. "A Canterbury Lament." *Parergon*, New Series 18.3 (2001): 15–36.

See also **Law; Legal Agency; Literacy and Reading: Vernacular**

PETRARCH

Francesco Petrarch (1304–1374) was Italy's preeminent lyric poet and a prolific Latin humanist, crowned poet laureate in Rome in 1341. Petrarch has been characterized as the first modern intellectual. His modernity emerges through the intense subjectivity of his works, particularly in his collection of Italian lyric poems, the *Canzoniere* (*Songbook*; known also as *Scattered Rhymes [Rime sparse]* or *Fragments in the Language of Ordinary Life [Rerum vulgarium fragmenta]*), the poet's anguished exploration of his unrequited love for the beautiful Laura (also called

Laureta). First collected in 1342 and continually expanded, revised, and reordered until the poet's death in 1374, the *Canzoniere* in its present form is divided into two parts, before (*Canz.* 1–263) and after (*Canz.* 264–366) Laura's death. The collection's total number of songs corresponds to the calendar year, culminating in the last sonnet (*Canz.* 366), the poet's final relinquishment of his obsessive desire for Laura and his dedication to the Virgin Mary.

In Laura, Petrarch emulates and yet interrogates the figure of Dante's Beatrice in the *New Life (Vita Nuova)* (1290–1295) and the *Divine Comedy (Divina Commedia)* (1306/7–1321). Like Beatrice, Laura is presented with a semblance of historical veracity. Although Laura's true identity remains conjectural, Petrarch states that he met her on Good Friday, April 6, 1327, in the Church of St. Clare in Avignon, and that she died on that same date, on Good Friday, 1348, presumably of the Black Death. The fictional correspondence of these dates to Good Friday indicates that Petrarch, like Dante, invests the beloved with a Christian conversional and redemptive significance.

Like Beatrice, in the *Canzoniere* Laura incarnates an ideal beauty (e.g., *Canz.* 126, 159). She inspires through her lucent presence the poet's desire for moral and spiritual perfection and poetic virtuosity (e.g., *Canz.* 71–73). She is not portrayed as an individual; she is rather an icon (*Canz.* 77), a projection of the poet's own desires, and a catalyst for his interior transformation, leading to poetic self-expression (e.g., *Canz.* 23).

Beatrice's name encapsulates her allegorical significance as Dante's "bearer of beatitude" *(portatrice di beatitudine; New Life)*. Laura's name also encompasses her allegorical significance, but the *Canzoniere*'s allusive, circular repetitions and word-plays (e.g., *Canz.* 5) create around her name a denser symbolic network. The poet assimilates his love of the elusive Laura to Ovid's myth of Apollo, god of poetry, and his amorous pursuit of the fleeing nymph Daphne, transformed into a laurel tree (*il lauro; Metamorphoses* 1). Laura is further associated with the breeze that surrounds her *(l'aura);* the gold of her hair and of the light emanating from her *(l'oro);* the dawn *(l'aurora);* and the laurel crown of victorious emperors and superior poets *(la laurea)* (e.g., *Canz.* 34, 194, 196–198).

Unlike Beatrice, Laura is an equivocal figure. She occasions both love and spiritual confusion (e.g., *Canz.* 1–3). Her erotic refusal has its origin at times in virtue, and at others in narcissism (*Canz.* 45–46). Compared to the Virgin Mary (*Canz.* 366), she is as Ovid's Medusa, the monstrous Gorgon (*Metamorphoses* 4–5). Laura symbolizes all earthly happiness

(beauty, love, poetic virtuosity, fame) and yet also the effects of original sin and idolatry (moral paralysis, lust, egotism, mutability, mortality). Her ambivalent effect incites the poet's restless self-scrutiny (e.g., *Canz.* 127, 129), an intentional divergence from the edifying influence of Dante's Beatrice, an unequivocally beneficent vehicle of Christ's wisdom and redemption.

Begun during a period of spiritual crisis, two other works attempt to contend with, and ultimately resolve, Laura's ineluctable nature. In *My Secret (Secretum*, 1347–1353) an imaginary Latin dialogue between Petrarch's persona Franciscus and Augustine of Hippo, Franciscus defends the purity of his love for Laura against Augustine's accusation of his erotic attraction to her and his inordinate desire for fame. In the *Triumphs (I Trionfi*, 1353–1374), a Dantesque visionary poem in Italian, Laura appears, not as a carnal love to be rejected, but divinely transfigured as Petrarch's heavenly influence.

Despite this transfiguration, the *Canzoniere*'s ambivalent portrayal of Laura and her conflicted poet-lover dominate subsequent literary history. As the premiere collection of love lyrics stretching from the late 1400s into the 1800s, the *Canzoniere* initiates Petrarchism, the Western textual tradition and vocabulary that explores the scenario of exalted female beauty and male erotic anguish. Petrarchism establishes a paradigm of female silence and the prerogative of male emotion and poetic expression. Yet the *Canzoniere* also paradoxically empowers later poets, both male and female, to imitate its literary example while also including within the depiction of erotic relationships female initiative, both poetic and amorous, as well as a more realistic mutual love.

PATRICIA ZUPAN

References and Further Reading

Boyle, Marjorie O'Rourke. "Wounded Lovers." In *Petrarch's Genius: Pentimento and Prophecy*. Berkeley, Calif.: University of California Press, 1991, pp. 113–152.

Braden, Gordon. "Applied Petrarchism: The Loves of Pietro Bembo." *Modern Language Quarterly* 57 (1996): 397–423.

Canzoniere; The Canzoniere, or Rerum vulgarium fragmenta. Trans. Mark Musa. Bloomington, Ind.: Indiana University Press, 1996.

Freccero, John. "The Fig Tree and the Laurel: Petrarch's Poetics." *Diacritics* 5 (1975): 34–40.

Hainsworth, Peter. *Petrarch the Poet: An Introduction to the Rerum vulgarium fragmenta*. New York: Routledge, 1988.

Mazzotta, Giuseppe. "The *Canzoniere* and the Language of the Self." In *The Worlds of Petrarch*. Durham, N.C.: Duke University Press, 1993, pp. 58–79.

Petrarca, Francesco. *Opere* Complete Works, Italian and Latin, with Italian translation of Latin. 2 Vols. Florence: Sansoni, 1975.

———. *Triumphs*, translated by Ernest Hatch Wilkins. Chicago: University of Chicago Press, 1962.

———. *Petrarch's Secretum*. With an introduction, notes, and critical anthology, edited by Davy A. Carozza and H. James Shey. New York: Peter Lang, 1989.

———. *Petrarch's Songbook (Rerum vulgarium fragmenta)*, translated by James Wyatt Cook. Binghamton, N.Y.: Medieval and Renaissance Texts and Studies, 1995.

Sturm-Maddox, Sara. *Petrarch's Laurels*. University Park, Pa.: Penn State University Press, 1992.

Waller, Marguerite. *Petrarch and Literary History*. Amherst, Mass.: University of Massachusetts Press, 1980.

Vickers, Nancy J. "Re-membering Dante: Petrarch's "Chiare, fresche, e dolci acque"." *Modern Language Notes* (MLN) 96 (1981): 1–11.

———. "Diana Described: Scattered Woman and Scattered Rhyme." *Critical Inquiry* 8 (1981): 265–279.

———. "The Body Re-membered: Petrarchan Lyrics and the Strategies of Description." In *Mimesis: From Mirror to Method. Augustine to Descartes*, edited by John D. Lyons and Stephen G. Nichols. Hanover, N.H.: University Press of New England, 1982, pp. 100–109.

See also **Beatrice; Beauty; Courtly Love; Dante Alighieri; Eroticism in Literature; Griselda; Humanism; Literature, Italian; Ovid: Medieval Reception of**

PETRONILA OF ARAGÓN

Petronila (or Petronilla, or rarely Petronella) of Aragón (1136–1173) owed her existence to the complicated political situation created by her uncle Alfonso I "el Batallador" of Aragón. When he died in 1134 without an heir (and with a problematic will leaving his kingdom to the Orders of the Templars, the Holy Sepulchre, and the Hospitalers), the magnates chose his brother Ramiro as the next king. Ramiro II Sánchez "el Monje" was taken out of the Church and married to Inés of Poitou in 1135; their only child Petronila was conceived to resolve the problem of the succession to the throne of Aragón. Petronila's birth in 1136 allowed Ramiro to return to monastic life the following year when Petronila was declared queen of the Kingdom of Aragón and betrothed to Ramón Berenguer IV, Count of Barcelona (r. 1131–1162). They married in 1150.

Although she was nominally queen to his title of prince, Petronila appears to have wielded little real power during her husband's lifetime. Their son Alfonso II, born around 1157, inherited the territories of both his parents to rule as the first king of the joint Crown of Aragón. He was one of five children born to Petronila and Ramón Berenguer, according to Antonio Ubieto Arteta. Only three documents survive that were issued by Petronila and show her active participation in rulership, but she also appeared as signatory to some of her husband's charters. In 1164, two years after her husband's death, Petronila solidified her seven-year-old son's place on the throne by renouncing her privileges as queen. Unlike Urraca, her near contemporary in León-Castile, Petronila acted more as a queen consort than a reigning queen. Instead of asserting her own rights, Petronila safeguarded her son and guaranteed that her line would rule after her.

THERESE MARTIN

References and Further Reading

Marquez de la Plata, Vicenta, and Luis Valero de Bernabé. *Reinas medievales españolas*. Madrid: Alderabón, 2000, pp. 135–147.

Stalls, William Clay. "Queenship and the Royal Patrimony in Twelfth-Century Iberia: The Example of Petronilla of Aragon." In *Queens, Regents and Potentates*, edited by Theresa M. Vann. Dallas: Academia, 1993, pp. 49–60.

Ubieto Arteta, Antonio. *Los esponsales de la reina Petronila y la creación de la Corona de Aragón*. Zaragoza: Diputacion General de Aragon, 1987.

See also **Iberia; Queens and Empresses: The West; Urraca**

PILGRIMS AND PILGRIMAGE

Pilgrimage both affected and reflected medieval Western Christendom. Pilgrimage, the journey made to a shrine, church, or other religious place, carried sacred meaning for believers. The site may have contained relics, often body parts, of a dead saint, that were said to heal and were, therefore, seen as miraculous. Pilgrims within the Christian, Judaic, and Islamic traditions interacted with one another in the Holy Land, where Christians visited the physical places where Biblical figures had lived. Pilgrimage was a religious practice that had many repercussions for society in terms of history and politics (how do pilgrims cross borders during times of war, for instance), as well as cultural artifacts, like material culture (church buildings and arts) and written culture (everything from the mass said to pilgrims starting on their journey to fictive poems relating pilgrimage experiences).

Sources

Traveling, especially abroad, entailed careful preparation legally and financially. Sources—such as letters of protection, documents granting power of attorney while on pilgrimage, papal letters containing commutation of vows or dispensation, inquisitions, wills, guild records, household accounts, letters, narratives, and legal records—include the names of women who planned to or did travel on pilgrimage. Pilgrimage could vary enormously for women depending upon wealth and class; indeed, class could be a more important factor than gender in determining the pilgrim's daily experience.

As early as the fourth century women traveled as pilgrims to the Holy Land, including Helena, mother of Constantine, and Egeria who came from Spain or southern Gaul. Women of the Roman nobility, such as Melania the Elder, as well as Paula and her daughter Eustochium, also made such a pilgrimage. Saints' lives suggest that numerous female saints made the journey to Jerusalem and inspired women as religious models. Women also made the journey to Jerusalem while participating in the Crusades, though whether they can strictly be called pilgrims has been debated. The extensive household accounts of Elizabeth de Burgh, a very wealthy and important fourteenth-century dowager, record pilgrimage activity. The *Liber celestis* of St. Bridget of Sweden (1303–1373; canonized 1391) tells the story of the saint, who convinced her husband to go on pilgrimage to Saint James in Compostela. She continued to go on numerous pilgrimages thereafter. *The Book of Margery Kempe*, dating from the first half of the fifteenth century, tells the life of Margery, an apparently illiterate merchant-class woman from Lynn in Norfolk. Her pilgrimages show her devotion to the humanity of Christ by witnessing the places associated with his life. The Privy Purse Expenses of Elizabeth of York (1465–1503), daughter of Edward the IV and wife of Henry VII, record pilgrimage activity.

Gender Differences

Victor and Edith Turner's argument that pilgrimage is a rite of passage suggests that the ritual space of pilgrimage liberates pilgrims from societal limitations, including those imposed by social class or gender. But scholars have pointed out that pilgrimage does not eliminate traditional social boundaries. Although the legal status of pilgrims was gender neutral, women were not always treated as equal to male pilgrims. Women had to gain permission to go on pilgrimage, a demand often complicated by family and society. Criminal records show women pilgrims as victims of crime, including rape. Some shrines, especially those under monastic control, restricted women's access. Yet documents indicate how women pilgrims were accommodated in ways that men did not need to be, such as a special Franciscan hospice for women pilgrims in Bethlehem, and provisions in Jerusalem and Rome for cradles, suggesting that some women were pregnant and gave birth while on pilgrimage.

Ronald Finucane has convincingly shown in recorded English miracle stories that the majority of pilgrims who attended local shrines were women (and lower-class) while the majority of pilgrims attending a distant shrine were male (and upper-class). The proportion of male to female pilgrims varied from shrine to shrine, often due to the type of miracle promised by the legend of the saint worshipped there. The types of miracles recorded corresponded to the visitors. For women on pilgrimage, familial concerns were overwhelmingly important. Women went on pilgrimage to get pregnant, to have a safe delivery, to help an apparently damaged or sick fetus, to avoid childbirth pain, to expel a dead fetus, to help with postpartum pain, to help with failed milk supply, to help have a live birth after numerous stillbirths, and to help after overlaying an infant in bed.

Representations of Women Pilgrims

Gender could affect women pilgrims' experiences, not only historically but also in terms of how they were represented. In not fulfilling traditional roles for women, including that of caregiver, spouse or sexual partner, economic contributor, or cloistered nun, female pilgrims and their mobility became a gendered matter with a moral dimension. Negative criticism of female pilgrims occurred by the eighth century. In secular literature by the late Middle Ages, the topos of the sexual woman pilgrim had become the symbol of a disorderly body politic held victim to traditional misogynist satire and critique. Yet, despite the strong tradition in which women pilgrims are seen as literally and figuratively wayward, exemplified most famously in Chaucer's Wife of Bath, a competing view of women pilgrims lies in religious works. Saints' legends and other religious literature tend to endorse women pilgrims who validate the sanctity of the holy figure in question.

Legal documents are relatively unhelpful in expressing how women experienced their pilgrimages. Material culture, such as church art, reflected and shaped female piety. The architecture of and images in the churches along the route to the Marian shrine at Walsingham, for example, created iconographic experiences specifically designed to be received by women pilgrims by referring to milk and/or motherhood. Women's patronage practices supported a material culture that evolved around pilgrimage. Devotional texts and art helped facilitate both private and communal virtual pilgrimage for those who were not able to physically make the pilgrimage journey. Pilgrimage as it was practiced reveals an individual understanding of worship informed by gender consciousness.

SUSAN SIGNE MORRISON

References and Further Reading:

Benson, Larry D., ed. *The Riverside Chaucer*. Boston: Houghton Mifflin, 1987.

Casson, Lionel. *Travel in the Ancient World*. Baltimore: The Johns Hopkins University Press, 1994.

Craig, Leigh Ann. "''Stronger Than Men and Braver Than Knights': Women and the Pilgrimages to Jerusalem and Rome in the Later Middle Ages." *Journal of Medieval History* 29 (2003): 153–175.

Eade, John, and Michael J. Sallnow. *Contesting the Sacred: the Anthropology of Christian Pilgrimage*. London: Routledge, 1991.

Ellis, Roger, ed. *The Liber Celestis of St Bridget of Sweden*. Vol. 1, Oxford, Early English Text Society/Oxford University Press, 291. 1987.

Finucane, Ronald C. *Miracles and Pilgrims: Popular Beliefs in Medieval England*. London: Dent, 1977.

———. *The Rescue of the Innocents: Endangered Children in Medieval Miracles*. New York: St. Martin's Press, 1997.

Gilbertson, Leanne. "The Vanni Altarpiece and the Relic Cult of Saint Margaret: Considering a Female Audience." *International Medieval Research* 8 (2002): 179–190.

Halpin, Patricia. "Anglo-Saxon Women and Pilgrimage." *Anglo-Norman Studies: Proceedings of the Battle Conference* 19 (1996): 97–122.

Meech, Sanford Brown, and Hope Emily Allen, eds. *The Book of Margery Kempe*. London: Oxford University Press/Early English Text Society, 212. 1961.

Morrison, Susan Signe. *Women Pilgrims in Late Medieval England: Private Piety as Public Performance*. London: Routledge, 2000.

Nicolas, Nicholas Harris. *Privy Purse Expenses of Elizabeth of York: Wardrobe Accounts of Edward the Fourth*. London: William Pickering, 1830/Reprint, New York: Barnes & Noble, 1972.

Schein, Sylvia. "Bridget of Sweden, Margery Kempe and Women's Jerusalem Pilgrimages in the Middle Ages." *Mediterranean Historical Review* 14.1 (1999): 44–58.

Staley, Lynn, trans. and ed. *The Book of Margery Kempe*. New York: W. W. Norton, 2001.

Storrs, Constance Mary. *Jacobean Pilgrims from England to St. James of Compostella from the Early Twelfth to the Late Fifteenth Century*. Santiago de Compostela: Xunta de Galicia, 1994.

Sumption, Jonathan. *Pilgrimage: An Image of Mediaeval Religion*. Totowa, N.J.: Rowman and Littlefield, 1975.

Turner, Victor, and Edith Turner. *Image and Pilgrimage in Christian Culture*. Oxford: Basil Blackwell, 1978.

Ward, Jennifer C. *English Noblewomen in the Later Middle Ages*. London: Longman, 1992.

Webb, Diana. *Medieval European Pilgrimage*. Basingstoke, Hampshire: Palgrave, 2002.

Wilkinson, John, trans. *Egeria's Travels: To the Holy Land*. Oxford: Aris & Phillips, 1999.

See also **Architecture, Ecclesiastical; Body in Literature and Religion; Birgitta of Sweden; Chaucer, Geoffrey; Crusades and Crusading Literature; Devotional Art; Gender in Art; Gender in History; Hagiography; Hagiography, Iconographic Aspects of; Kempe, Margery; Mary, Virgin; Mary, Virgin: in Art; Migration and Mobility; Miracles and Miracle Collections; Misogyny; Mystics' Writings; Private and Public Spheres; Rape and Raptus; Relics and Reliquaries; Space, Sacred: and Gender; Wife of Bath; Wills**

PLAGUE

Medieval Europe endured two pandemics of plague: the first, known as the Justinian Plague, struck the Mediterranean region between 541 and 750 and the second, the Black Death, spread throughout Europe between 1348 and 1351. Plague returned in regional-based epidemics every six to twelve years for the first 130 years thereafter. It then returned every fifteen to twenty years until the final outbreak in Marseille in 1720–1722.

Historical discussion focuses on the most famous and widely devastating episode, the Black Death, which was known to contemporaries as "the great mortality." Medieval doctors called it a pestilence or *pestis* brought on by miasma (bad air). Their almost universal descriptions of symptomatic buboes have convinced most historians that the disease was bubonic plague caused by the bacterium *Yersinia pestis*, spread by the rat flea, *Xenopsylla cheopsis*, and its host, the black rat. However, there is vigorous debate as to the exact nature of this disease because the rapid spread and incredibly high mortality rate of the medieval epidemic do not mimic modern epidemics of bubonic plague.

The plague was carried from eastern Asia to Europe on ships launched from the Crimea region of the Black Sea, arriving first at the ports of Sicily and Italy and then passing along the vast network of trading routes by land and sea throughout Europe. On average, Europe lost a third to a half of its population during the epidemic, although some towns suffered considerably higher mortality rates. A few chroniclers noted that women died in large numbers, but it was just as likely for other chroniclers to highlight the deaths of the rich, the poor, the old, or the young as excessive. However, it is reasonable to posit that women may have suffered more because their care-giving and house-bound duties kept them in close proximity to the infected fleas and the ill.

Although contemporary chronicles emphasize unspeakable horror and social collapse during the epidemic, other records demonstrate that in many areas government and Church officials acted quickly to combat the disease. Bishops consecrated new burial grounds, city councils passed ordinances banning traffic of goods and people and stipulated burial procedures, and doctors wrote tracts on how one could best avoid, prevent, and cure the pestilence. Despite the charges of chroniclers to the contrary, there is evidence that notaries, priests, and doctors continued their duties and served the ill during the epidemic. In Italian and French towns doctors were hired to carry out autopsies of plague victims in order to better determine how to fight the disease.

The king of France called upon the leading scientists of the day, the Medical Faculty of the University of Paris, to report on the cause of the epidemic. The professors concluded that the epidemic was the result of a miasma that had been produced and spread by a triple conjunction of the planets, Mars, Jupiter, and Saturn in 1345. They also stressed the usual types of preventive medicine based on a moderate regime of diet and exercise to keep the body's humors in balance and the use of aromatics to purify the air. The leaders of the Church declared the epidemic to be the result of divine wrath over human sinfulness. A few clerics highlighted as causes for the plague women's sin of pride and their adoption of immodest clothing, but these were common complaints of monastic writers that were not unique to the Black Death.

Church officials counseled men and women to take part in penitential processions, masses, and prayer in order to avert the plague. Recognizing that many were dying without the sacrament of penance due to the lack of priests, some officials, such as Bishop Ralph Shrewsbury of Bath and Wells in England, allowed emergency confession even to a woman. Some of the laity took upon themselves extreme acts of self-mutilation as penance for all of humanity's sins. These flagellants staged spectacles of blood that whipped up a popular frenzy of masses of people in German towns. Women did not participate in the whippings, which involved partial nudity, but were noted by chroniclers as clamoring for the flagellants and foolishly catching the blood to smear on their eyes for its miraculous properties. Again, this commentary on women's behavior during the plague is part of a general misogynistic attitude of male medieval writers. Other examples of violent hysteria were the pogroms against Jews, who were scapegoated with the charge of spreading the plague by poisoning wells. Despite a few attempts at protection from the pope and city officials, many Jewish communities in central Europe were attacked and decimated.

Siding with the landowning classes, chroniclers complained that after the epidemic laborers demanded high wages and no longer served their superiors respectfully. They saw the post-plague world, in which landlords were sometimes forced to remit rents and labor services, as an inversion of the natural order. Similarly, chroniclers complained about a decline in morals after the plague, often targeting

women as particularly immoral. Giovanni Boccaccio remarked that women who survived the plague in Florence were less chaste because they had allowed themselves to be attended by male servants during the epidemic. In England, John of Reading lamented that widows threw themselves into the arms of foreigners or even kinsmen, too quickly forgetting their dead husbands. Working with different sources, historians have qualified the conclusions of these landowning men who felt threatened by the new economic and social situation of higher wages and new marriages for survivors. They have demonstrated that prices also rose, thereby limiting the "undue" gains of wage earners. Moreover, authorities in Italy, England, France, and Spain passed legislation to restrict wages and prices, but it is difficult to determine just how effectively these were enforced.

Women benefited from the drastic labor shortages with an increase in wages, but the kinds of work available to them did not change. In the centuries following the Black Death many professions, such as the medical profession, increasingly restricted female participation, while other areas traditionally open to women, such as brewing, became professionalized, thereby shutting out women. Fathers faced with the death of their preferred male heirs as they wrote their wills during the plague named females as heirs more often than before. However, female inheritance did not generally lead to independence, since in many parts of Europe the husband managed his wife's property. In Italy the plague only temporarily disrupted the rigid patriarchal system of inheritance that favored men. Thus, women's gains in the new economic climate produced by the Black Death were ultimately thwarted by medieval Europe's patriarchal social structure.

SHONA KELLY WRAY

References and Further Reading

Aberth, John. *From the Brink of the Apocalypse: Confronting Famine, War, Plague, and Death in the Later Middle Ages.* New York: Routledge, 2000.

Arrizabalaga, Jon. "Facing the Black Death: Perceptions and Reactions of University Medical Practitioners." In *Practical Medicine from Salerno to the Black Death.* Cambridge: Cambridge University Press, 1994, pp. 237–288.

Benedictow, Ole. *The Black Death 1346–1353: The Complete History.* Rochester, N.Y.: Boydell & Brewer, 2004.

Campbell, Anna Montgomery. *The Black Death and Men of Learning.* New York: Columbia University Press, 1931.

Cohn, Samuel Kline, Jr. *The Black Death Transformed: Disease and Culture in Early Renaissance Europe.* New York: Oxford University Press, 2002.

Goldberg, P. J. P. *Women, Work, and Life Cycle in a Medieval Economy: Women in York and Yorkshire, c. 1300–1520.* Oxford: Oxford University Press, 1992.

Henderson, John. "The Black Death in Florence: Medical and Communal Responses." In *Death in Towns: Urban*

Responses to the Dying and Dead, 100–1600, edited by S. Bassett, Leicester: Leicester University Press, 1992, pp. 136–150.

Herlihy, David. *The Black Death and the Transformation of the West*. Cambridge, Mass.: Harvard University Press, 1997.

Horrox, Rosemary. *The Black Death*. Manchester: Manchester University Press, 1994.

Mate, Mavis E. *Daughters, Wives, and Widows after the Black Death: Women in Sussex, 1350–1535*. Woodbridge, Suffolk: Boydell and Brewer, 1998.

Naphy, William G., and Andrew Spicer. *The Black Death and the History of Plagues 1345–1730*. Stroud, Gloucestershire: Tempus, 2000.

Park, Katharine. *Doctors and Medicine in Early Renaissance Florence*. Princeton: Princeton University Press, 1985.

Platt, Colin. *King Death*. Toronto: University of Toronto Press, 1997.

Wray, Shona Kelly. "*Speculum et Exemplar*: The Notaries of Bologna during the Black Death." *Quellen und Forschungen aus italienischen Archiven und Bibliotheken* 81 (2001): 200–227.

———. "Women, Family, and Inheritance in Bologna during the Black Death" In *Love, Marriage, and Family Ties in the Middle Ages*, edited by Miriam Muller and Isabel Davis. Belgium: Brepols, 2003, pp. 205–215.

———. "Boccaccio and the Doctors: Medicine and Compassion in the Face of Plague." *Journal of Medieval History* 30 (2004): 301–322.

Ziegler, Philip. *The Black Death*. New York: Harper & Row, 1969; reprint, London: Sutton, 1997.

See also **Boccaccio, Giovanni; Doctors and Healers; Giovanni; Medicine; Work**

POLITICS AND POWER
See **Diplomacy and Reconciliation; Empresses: Byzantium; Noble Women; Women and Empresses: The West; Regents and Queen-Lieutenants**

POOR CLARES ORDER

The Poor Clares constitute the enclosed female branch of the Franciscan Order. Their name honors Clare of Assisi (1193/94–1253), whom pious tradition credits as their founder in association with Saint Francis (1181/1182–1226). The actual formation of female Franciscanism was considerably more complex. Clare's insistence that women could follow Francis's spiritual ideals, including apostolic poverty, conflicted with the papal curia's intention to standardize women's religious life. Their efforts to impose stability initially produced a monastic order that consisted solely of women prior to its incorporation into the Franciscan Order. Thus, it is somewhat ironic that the Order of Saint Clare and the identification *Poor Clares*, terms created by papal legislation in 1263, honor a woman whose spiritual ideals challenged traditional female religious life.

The Origins of Female Franciscanism

It is necessary to distinguish the foundations connected with Clare and Francis from those outside Franciscan inspiration that were first brought together by the papal curia. Shortly after Clare's conversion in 1212, Francis brought her and her sister Agnes to the church of San Damiano outside Assisi's walls. Other women soon joined them to form the first community of Franciscan women. San Damiano also served as a base for the itinerant friars to whom Pope Innocent III had granted permission to preach penance and live supported by alms alone (1209). The stable communal life adopted by the women obviously contrasted with the friar's wandering mendicancy, but a shared commitment to spiritual *minoritas*, humility in all things, sustained their close connection.

San Damiano had no formal monastic rule at first. Oral directions from Francis, including his promise of perpetual care and spiritual exhortations, were the foundation of their religious life. A 1219 document addressed to the Florentine community of Monticelli, which Agnes of Assisi had helped establish, allowed them to adopt San Damiano's *observantiae regulares* (regular observance). Contemporary documents confirm that houses in nearby Arezzo, Foligno, Perugia, and Spello were founded on the model of San Damiano and with the assistance of its sisters. Some evidence suggests that individual friars helped establish other female communities, but their connection to San Damiano is not explicit. While Jacques de Vitry's famous letter of 1216 praising the *sorores minores* (lesser sisters) who lived in hospices and supported themselves by their own labors is often taken as evidence of Clare's influence, it only confirms an association between some friars (*fratres minores*, lesser brothers) and sisters rather than broader institutional formation derived from Assisi. Most claims of direct foundation by Clare or Francis, especially for communities outside central Italy, derive from later desires to connect with the charismatic authority of the "founders."

At the time of Francis's death in 1226, only San Damiano and a handful of other houses had been incorporated into the Franciscan Order. They now faced pressure from ecclesiastical efforts to normalize the women's religious movements. Beginning in 1218, Cardinal Hugolino dei Segni had begun to regularize communities of female penitents in central Italy. Although many of these groups had been motivated by apostolic poverty (albeit not directly inspired by Francis), Hugolino imposed a constitution modeled after the Benedictine rule that required material support. He also sought to link these houses more closely to the Franciscan Order. He named a friar to serve as their visitor in 1220. This appointment was short lived and the friars' antipathy toward new female communities led the cardinal to assign Cistercians. This situation changed after Francis's death and Hugolino's elevation to the papacy as Gregory IX (1227–1241). He now directed the Franciscan minister general to appoint a minister for these houses, which the papal curia began to identify as the Order of San Damiano.

The confusion between Clare's community at San Damiano and the Order of San Damiano was deliberate. While suggesting fidelity to Francis's and Clare's model of religious life, the papal program differed in several key components including strict enclosure, monastic silence, and financial endowment. Over the next two decades, Clare would resist pressure to conform to these standards. In 1228, Gregory IX granted a "Privilege of Poverty" to San Damiano that allowed the women to live without guaranteed income. Other houses that sought similar privileges were generally refused. An exception was Agnes of Prague, who only obtained permission to give up property held in common toward the end of her life. From the 1230s onward, most Damianite houses, including those foundations originally established by San Damiano's sisters, accepted property. Pope Innocent IV's constitution for the order (1247), issued to resolve ambiguities in earlier legislation, also mandated ownership. Clare rejected this rule and instead composed her own *formula vitae* (form of life), which modified Francis's rule for the friars to meet the needs of a stable female community. Pope Innocent IV approved the text on her deathbed (1253). Certain provisions suggest that she intended it to govern all Damianite houses, but it did not circulate beyond a few affiliated communities. Some houses adopted the 1247 Rule, others kept the Hugolinian constitution, and most had individual provisions concerning their observance. Pastoral care from Franciscan friars linked these diverse houses, an institutional relationship that contributed to the papally constituted order increasingly coming to identify itself with the movement initiated by Francis of Assisi. During the same period, the newly canonized Saint Clare (1255) was memorialized as an enclosed contemplative, a model for all religious women rather than a female example of Francis's spiritual ideals.

The Order of Saint Clare

Following an intense legal battle over the friars' obligations to provide pastoral care (1261–1263), Pope Urban IV ratified a new constitution for the Order of Saint Clare in 1263 that effectively confirmed their place within the Franciscan Order. Like earlier papal legislation, it incorporated traditional monastic requirements, including adequate material support. By the end of the thirteenth century, this rule was widely adopted, especially by Italian Poor Clares. In parts of France and throughout England, however, Franciscan nuns professed a rule composed by the royal princess Isabelle of France (1259; revised 1263). There is also evidence of women who refused to conform to these organized forms of female Franciscanism. Both Innocent IV and his successor, Pope Alexander IV (1254–1261), railed against certain "Minoresses" who lived outside of a cloister and made demands on the friars. It seems likely these were women who chose not to become Poor Clares as the order moved away from the ideals of Francis's early movement into traditional female monasticism.

Later sources commonly identify the fourteenth century as a period of relaxed observance before the Franciscan Order entered a period of renewal. In Italy, fifteenth-century reformers encouraged the Poor Clares to profess their "first rule," that is, Clare's *formula vitae*. While some convents continued to observe the Urbanist rule, chronicles and devotional writings produced by the sisters make clear the important role these women played in spreading Clare's rule and reform generally. Contemporary sisters who were praised as spiritual models included the French reformer, Colette of Corbie (1381–1447) and the Italian devotional author and artist, Caterina Vigri (1413–1463). These reforms also increased interest in the historical Clare and contributed to the growth of her reputation as founder of the eponymous order. While Clare of Assisi was not historically the founder of the Poor Clares, she ultimately became a source of charismatic authority for female Franciscan life.

Franciscan Penitent Women

Institutional forms of female Franciscan life were not limited to the Poor Clares. Friar Hugh of Digne prepared a rule for his sister Douceline (c. 1215–1274), who lived in a Beguine community in Marseilles. Hagiographical legends describe how some women who were refused admittance to Damianite convents became penitents (*sorores de penitentia* or sometimes *bizzoche* or *reclusae*) and lived in small, semireligious communities close to Franciscan friaries. Other penitent women were able to remain independent while developing a pastoral relationship with individual friars, such as Margaret of Cortona (1247–1297) and Angela of Foligno (1248–1309). Along with their pastoral bond with Franciscan friars, the desire to follow a life of evangelical prayer, penance, and charity while remaining in the world united these women.

The Roman Curia sought to regularize these lay penitents in a manner similar to what occurred with other women's religious movements. They encouraged the idea of Francis as founder of a Third Order of Penance, although this legislation derived from outside the order. A member of Cardinal Hugolino's circle wrote the earliest constitution, the *Memoriale Propositi* (1221), to govern mixed penitential communities. A new rule was confirmed by Pope Nicholas IV (a Franciscan friar) in the bull *Supra Montem* (1289) during the same period as a rule was authored for Dominican tertiaries. Communities of female penitents were increasingly obligated to live according to a monastic rule after the bull *Periculoso* (1298) imposed enclosure and some houses were even transferred into the Order of Saint Clare. Others maintained their status as members of the Franciscan Third Order. One of the most influential was the community of Santa Anna in Foligno whose sisters helped spread reform ideas throughout Italy under the leadership of Angelina of Montegiove (c. 1357–1435).

The female Franciscan movement during the Middle Ages is thus characterized by its diversity. While the Poor Clares mostly followed traditional monastic forms of life, other women established different forms of communal life while maintaining an association with the Franciscan friars or an affiliation with the spiritual ideals of Francis of Assisi.

LEZLIE KNOX

References and Further Reading

Alberzoni, Maria Pia. *Clare and the Poor Sisters in the Thirteenth Century*, edited by Jean-François Godet-Calogeras. St. Bonaventure, N.Y.: Franciscan Institute Publications, 2004.

Armstrong, Regis J., ed. *Clare of Assisi: Early Documents.* Revised and expanded. St. Bonaventure, N.Y.: Franciscan Institute Publications, 1993.

———. *The Lady. Clare of Assisi: Early Documents.* New York: New City Press, forthcoming.

Carney, Margaret. *The First Franciscan Woman: Clare of Assisi and Her Form of Life.* Quincy, Ill.: Franciscan Press, 1993.

Franciscan Women: History and Culture. A Geographical and Bio-Bibliographical Internet Guide. http://franwomen.sbu.edu/franwomen/default.aspx.

Grundmann, Herbert. *Religious Movements in the Middle Ages: the Historical Links between Heresy, the Mendicant Orders, and the Women's Religious Movement in the Twelfth and Thirteenth Centuries.* 2nd rev. ed. Stephen Rowan. South Bend, Ind.: University of Notre Dame Press, 1995.

Knox, Lezlie. "Audacious Nuns: Institutionalizing the Franciscan Order of Saint Clare." *Church History* 69:1 (2000): 41–62.

Pellegrini, Luigi. "Female Religious Experience and Society in Thirteenth-Century Italy." In *Monks and Nuns, Saints and Outcasts: Religion in Medieval Society. Essays in Honor of Lester K. Little*, edited by Sharon Farmer and Barbara H. Rosenwein. Ithaca, N.Y.: Cornell University Press, 2000, pp. 97–122.

Wood, Geryldene. *Women, Art and Spirituality: The Poor Clares of Early Modern Italy.* Cambridge: Cambridge University Press, 1996.

See also **Agnes of Prague; Angela of Foligno; Beguines; Caterina Vigri; Clare of Assisi; Colette of Corbie; Dominican Order; Douceline of Digne; Isabelle of France; Laywomen, Religious; Margaret of Cortona; Monastic Enclosure; Monastic Rules; Monasticism and Nuns; Monasticism, Women's: Papal Policy; Poverty, Religious; Sister-Books and Other Convent Chronicles; Tertiaries**

POPE JOAN

The story of a woman pope first appeared in northern Europe in the mid-thirteenth century and spread widely. It attained its most familiar form in an interpolation into the chronicle of Martin of Troppau, a Polish Dominican (d. 1278). The chronicle placed Joan in the ninth century between Leo IV and Benedict III. She is described as an English woman who disguised herself as a man, "John the Englishman," to study in Athens. Coming to Rome, she supposedly was made a curial notary and then a cardinal because of her conspicuous learning. On the death of Leo IV (d. 855), she was elected pope and enthroned. In this version, she died two years later while giving birth to a child, having gone into labor during a procession. Stephen of Bourbon, another thirteenth-century Dominican, alone says the female pope and her child were stoned to death by the populace after she gave birth during the coronation procession. The story, distributed particularly through Dominican channels, was used by both the friends and foes of the papacy in the Middle Ages and thereafter. Only in the sixteenth century was its veracity called into question. Among those who told the story of Pope Joan is Giovanni Boccaccio, in his *On Famous Women*. Among the explanations offered for this story is that it reflects the domination of the papacy by Theodora and her daughter Marozia. The female pope in the tarot deck may represent not Joan but Guglielma, a Milanese holy woman who was the focal point of a thirteenth-century heretical group.

THOMAS IZBICKI

References and Further Reading

Boureau, Alain. *The Myth of Pope Joan.* Translated by Lydia Cochrane. Chicago: University of Chicago Press, 2001.

See also **Boccaccio, Giovanni; Cross-Dressing; Marozia of Rome**

PORTRAIT MEDALS

Portrait medals were an especially potent means of self-presentation in the late medieval and early modern periods. They came into vogue in the humanist circles of early fifteenth-century Italy and quickly became an integral part of diplomacy and gift exchange in noble society throughout Europe. Like more monumental portraits, medals were commissioned to assert a strong public image or to commemorate an important event or change in status. For women, a medal could record betrothal, marriage, widowhood, or death, or, in more elite cases, celebrate political events such as ascent to regency or rule, or military or diplomatic victories. Modeled after ancient Roman coins, they usually displayed a portrait on one side and a carefully devised emblem on the other, each accompanied by Latin or, less often, Greek or vernacular inscriptions detailing the sitter's name, status, and motto. Family insignias were regularly integrated into the design. A second portrait sometimes replaced the emblem so that husband and wife or regent and minor-age ruler appeared on opposite faces, illustrating their relationship. The portrait was most commonly presented in profile, following ancient prototypes. In the sixteenth century and in response to developments in painted portraiture, some portraits on medals shifted to a three-quarter pose or, more rarely, a full-frontal view. The classically inspired emblems and inscriptions could be very straightforward or rather obtuse, with a secret or highly intellectual meaning expected to be understood by only a privileged few. In the sixteenth-century, single-sided medals began to appear and emblems were either combined with the portrait or eliminated.

Because of their small size (typically 30–105 mm in diameter) and durability, portrait medals were easily portable and were distributed as elite symbols of affection and alliance. Produced in multiples in lead or copper alloys, bronze, silver, or gold, they were cast from molds or, beginning in the sixteenth century, struck with dies. Medals started to be serially produced in the late fifteenth century when large workshops, sometimes associated with mints, offered their clients the opportunity to choose designs, emblems and mottos from available models, which they could customize with a specific portrait and name. The most elite medals were invariably cast and custom-made, the emblems and mottos devised by intellectual advisors with an eye toward singularity. Collectors displayed their portrait medals on shelves, on ribbons or chains worn around the neck, or in cabinets specially devised for their storage with multiple small drawers and hooks on which to hang them. The small format of portrait medals invited intimate viewing, which led to debate over their aesthetic, intellectual, and commemorative merits. Though they were prized by their owners, only a relative few of the many portrait medals produced in the late medieval and early modern eras, survive since they were often melted down and the metal reused.

A portrait, regardless of media, was not usually conceived as a literal record of the subject's likeness; rather, it was more like a multifaceted allegory that illustrated the sitter's character. The portrait, inscriptions, and emblems on medals all worked together to present the sitter's ideological aspirations, which were clearly affected by notions of gender. For women, a conventionalized beauty served as an outward sign of virtue, the most prized female attribute that encompassed the concepts of chastity, modesty, and loyalty. This beauty was signaled by elaborate dresses, jewels, hairstyles, and idealized features. The emblems were similarly gendered and often referred to classical or literary characters and stories, their motifs and styles borrowed from ancient sculpture or coins or created anew. Common subjects were pagan deities, personifications of virtues, signs of the zodiac, mythological and real animals, family crests, and other symbols. Through Humanist interpretation, ancient and secular motifs evoked religious piety and other important virtues including the intellectual. Since a married woman's status stemmed equally from her agnatic and marital families, both surnames appeared with her title in inscriptions. Thus, the portrait medal conveyed the culturally and personally significant components of a woman's character.

While a male relative commonly commissioned a woman's portrait medal to commemorate her betrothal, marriage, widowhood or death, quite a number of women, especially those in positions of power, ordered their own and updated them periodically. Women rulers and regents often adapted the masculine symbols associated with power and political authority, such as armor, weapons, and architecture, for their emblems and sometimes tempered them with signs of more feminine virtues. Elizabeth I, Caterina Sforza, Isabella d'Este, and other female rulers and regents commissioned medals with inscriptions and emblems that boosted their political and cultural authority and served as propaganda. Scholarly interest in women's portrait medals, especially those from Italy, continues to rise, but much research remains to be completed on examples from other European areas.

JOYCE DE VRIES

References and Further Reading

de Vries, Joyce. "Caterina Sforza's Portrait Medals: Power, Gender, and Representation in the Renaissance Court." *Woman's Art Journal* 24.1 (2003): 23–28.

The Medal, a quarterly journal published by the British Art Medal Trust.

Och, Marjorie. "Portrait Medals of Vittoria Colonna: Representing the Learned Woman." In *Women as Sites of Culture: Women's Roles in Cultural Formation from the Renaissance to the Twentieth Century.* Ed. Susan Shifrin. Aldershot: Ashgate, 2002, pp. 153–163.

Pollard, J. Graham, and Eleonora Luciano. *Renaissance Medals.* Washington, D.C.: National Gallery of Art, 2005.

Scher, Stephen K., ed. *The Currency of Fame: Portrait Medals of the Renaissance.* New York: Harry N. Abrams, Inc., 1994.

———, ed. *Perspectives on the Renaissance Medal.* New York: Garland Publishing and the American Numismatic Society, 2000.

Syson, Luke. "Consorts, Mistresses and Exemplary Women: the Female Medallic Portrait in Fifteenth-Century Italy." In *The Sculpted Object 1400–1700,* edited by Stuart Currie and Peta Motture. Aldershot: Scolar Press, 1997, pp. 43–64.

See also **Art, Representations of Women in; Caterina Sforza; Coinage; D'Este, Isabella and Beatrice; Death, Mourning, and Commemoration; Diplomacy and Reconciliation; Femininity and Masculinity; Gender in Art; Honor and Reputation; Humanism; Noble Women; Patronage, Artistic; Personifications Visualized as Women**

POSTCOLONIAL THEORY

Postcolonial theory typically analyzes the conflict and accommodation that unfold in the wake of conquest and other kinds of cultural admixture. It stresses the enduring economic and social disparity that is likely to result when a powerful nation annexes land belonging to others, transforming that territory into a colony or frontier and rendering its inhabitants a subaltern (or dominated) people. Often inspired by a strong sense of social justice, postcolonial critics explore the violence inherent in the colonial encounter but do not argue that some "pure" state of aboriginality might be recovered in the wake of profound cultural clash. Postcolonial criticism has therefore developed a sophisticated vocabulary for describing hybridity, the conflictual interpenetration of cultures that results from colonial contact and that transforms both colonizer and indigene. Though it never uncritically celebrates this turbulent fusion of differences, it

does find in hybridity the potential for subversion of the systems that are likely to be imposed in the wake of conquest. Postcolonial criticism stresses the impurity of both present and past. It critiques the mechanisms (social, legal, literary) through which dominated groups are disparaged and dispossessed, especially of their history. Postcolonial theory has always been sensitive to the ways in which power is distributed unevenly across gender lines. Some of the most important work undertaken within the field studies the effects of the postcolonial upon subaltern women.

Postcolonial cultural studies are useful to the study of the western Middle Ages. Europe did not appear from some void, as the historian Robert Bartlett has argued, but emerged slowly, via conquest that extended borders and assimilations that attempted to render emergent territorial states internally homogeneous. Europe, in a word, had to *Europeanize* itself in custom, language, law, and religion—an inherently colonial project with profound repercussions on gender. In the course of the Middle Ages some peoples were absorbed and vanished as part of this process, while others found themselves represented as less than human. Thus the English could insist on a natural superiority over the bestial Welsh, allowing them (in their minds) an evident right to the dominion of the whole of Britain. Medievalists working in a postcolonial vein have dedicated themselves to studying how such enduringly uneven access to power and privilege came about; how myths of origin and manifest destiny buttressed communities; and what price was paid by people who (like the Irish, Welsh, and Jews in Britain) found themselves resident in some denigrated category or who were, because of their mixed descent, suspended between mutually exclusive groups.

Medievalists have made extensive use of the work of Edward Said, whose *Orientalism* developed a sophisticated model for exploring how the West fantasizes its own version of the East (an exotic geography that is typically gendered feminine); Homi Bhabha, who offers a postmodern approach to hybridity; Gayatri Spivak and Dipesh Chakrabarty, who have persuasively argued against assuming Eurocentric models of history. More recently, postcolonial theories derived from the analysis of the Caribbean and U.S.–Mexico border have also appeared. Some medievalists like Geraldine Heng are also well-known postcolonial critics.

JEFFREY JEROME COHEN

References and Further Reading

Bartlett, Robert. *The Making of Europe.* Princeton, N.J.: Princeton University Press, 1993.

Biddick, Kathleen. *The Shock of Medievalism.* Durham: Duke University Press, 1998.

Cohen, Jeffrey Jerome, ed. *The Postcolonial Middle Ages.* New York: Palgrave Macmillan, 2000.

Ganim, John M. *Medievalism and Orientalism.* New York: Palgrave Macmillan, 2005.

Heng, Geraldine. *Empire of Magic: Medieval Romance and the Politics of Cultural Fantasy.* New York: Columbia University Press, 2003.

Holsinger, Bruce W. "Medieval Studies, Postcolonial Studies, and the Genealogies of Critique," *Speculum* 77 (2002): 1195–1227.

Ingham, Patricia Clare, and Michelle R. Warren, eds. *Postcolonial Moves: Medieval through Modern.* New York: Palgrave Macmillan, 2003.

Kabir, Ananya, and Deanne Williams, ed. *Postcolonial Approaches to the European Middle Ages.* Cambridge: Cambridge University Press, 2005.

See also **Cross-Cultural Approaches; Postmodernism and Historiography**

POSTMODERNISM AND HISTORIOGRAPHY

Although *postmodernism* has been a common term in nearly every area of intellectual and cultural life since the 1980s, its exact definition remains elusive, and its applications and consequences continue to arouse contention. In every field of artistic or scholarly production it has touched, postmodernism challenged the accuracy of commonly accepted meanings, undermined confidence in our ability to depict reality with certainty in any medium, and generally destabilized tradition and consensus by questioning the foundations of intellectual life. All of the traditional humanistic disciplines dependent on complex language for research and expression (literature, history, philosophy, social criticism) have had to confront postmodernism in fundamental ways because the focus of postmodernist insight is on language itself. Postmodernism's analogous and widely used term, *the linguistic turn*, is especially useful in understanding the specific relation of this sweeping cultural movement to the practice and understanding of history.

At the most fundamental level, the postmodernist critique is based on a severe scrutiny of the ability of our common language to depict reality without distortion or bias. Whatever the object under investigation, ranging from literature to social institutions, the production of knowledge depends on agreed upon definitions and stable representations of the world. Structuralist linguistics, created by the Swiss linguist Ferdinand Saussure in the early twentieth century, effectively undermined the traditional simplistic view that language merely gives names to things and relationships that exist objectively apart from observers, and whose meanings are self-evident and consistent. Saussure's work stressed the highly artificial and conventional nature of language, and the deep dependence of language systems on binary oppositions to produce meanings. Apparently "natural" contrasts such as masculine/feminine, black/white, Western/Oriental, rational/irrational, civilized/primitive were shown to be culturally produced linguistic structures whose implications were highly changeable over historical time. Notable theorists such as Jacques Derrida pushed the implications of structuralist linguistics into the poststructuralist mode of analysis called deconstruction: under the deconstructionist critique language became an unstable system where meaning recedes further and further into uncertainty. With no simple linkage to an objective world, words depend on contextual words for meanings that constantly shift. The greater the pressure of writers and readers for essential truth and a stable language in which to register it, the more elusive and elastic the meaning of linguistic concepts becomes. In the most general way, the postmodern condition of intellectual life is one in which our defining instrument—language—cannot be regarded as neutral, passive, or accurate.

Relation to Historical Research and Writing

Under postmodernist scrutiny, descriptive language could not be a reliable recorder of present reality, and its deployment for the reconstruction of the vanished past has made the discipline of history appear fragile and open to serious challenge. By placing the unstable word/world relation in the foreground of critical problems, the linguistic turn introduced its complications to the reading and interpretation of primary source evidence. Older notions of the "document" as a straightforward, simple message from the past, or a transparent "window" onto past life appeared naive and simplistic in the light of more sophisticated appreciations of linguistic meaning. The language of historical evidence, especially the language of cultures as distant from us as medieval Europe, multiplied the problems facing the historian under the insights of postmodernism. Sensitive to the ways that language itself has the power to constitute reality, or at least to color reality with strongly moral and ideological meanings, historians have had to extend their reading techniques beyond traditional methodologies of text criticism. All forms of written source material, even apparently nonliterary legal evidence, letters, administrative treatises, as well as chronicles and biography, exhibit the problems and complexities of descriptive language, and thus require subtler reading strategies than historians were accustomed to use. The linguistic turn has made literary critical techniques of discourse analysis, specifically addressed to intertextual echoes and embedded premises of language, an invaluable resource for historical work.

Just as the historical document no longer could be regarded as a neutral window onto the past, so the historian's own language also has come under critical scrutiny. The idea that historians can see and identify generalized historical objects like class, race, social structures, and power with a neutral accurate language now seems illusory. Postmodernism refocused a sharp attention on the historian's role in constructing supposedly essential objects such as social classes and sexual roles with language infused with unacknowledged cultural assumptions. All such generalizations used by historians emphatically categorize that purport to describe areas of race, class, and gender, now require careful analysis with their component elements candidly laid out.

At a larger scale of construction, historical writing has been subjected to the insights of narrative theory, with historians responding to and against the influential work of historian-theorist, Hayden White. Structuralist linguistic theory and deconstruction undermined simple notions of the naming function of language in relation to the real world. Narrative theory has demonstrated that chronological story form, the followable and intelligible sequence of events leading from some beginning point toward a resolution, is a structure made from language, and not found in real events. The real past, full beyond intelligible control of seriatim and simultaneous unrelated events, does not come in story form. Narratives of progress, tragedy, amelioration, and the like are created through the selection and rejection of events; the historians' feeling of "discovering" the "true story" in the evidence is an illusion resulting from the deeply un–self-conscious knowledge of certain story types that inform every culture. Historians recognize in their evidence the useable elements of the stories they have always known, and construct the past around those forms. Narrative theory has seemed to some historians to bring historical writing too close to the techniques of fiction and opened the way to morally irresponsible history. But the past is not available to inspection, and universal consensus on a single correct narrative is neither possible nor even desirable in an open society. In the view of most historians who accept the premises of narrative theory, responsible and rigorous evidence-based history results in a range of variant stories, none of which claim to exhaust or dominate the evidence.

Applications to Medieval Women's History

As a specialized topic in historical study, medieval women have benefited from the linguistic turn because its array of critical questions have undermined conventional assumptions about society and culture, naming and meaning. The radical critique mounted by structuralist linguistics and deconstruction addressed the foundational concepts anchoring traditional views of social organization. Long-held uninspected notions about the supposed essential natures of men and women, the inevitability of their social roles, the naturalness of men's domination over women in early societies, turned out to be vulnerable targets for the new modes of language-based analysis. If meanings are culturally constructed in linguistic form, then claims to "nature" and inevitability are reduced to cultural constructs, not mirrors of reality. Even patriarchy, a social organization of many variants over time, characterized by its male monopoly of real economic, political, legal, cultural, and sexual power, yields to this analysis as a construct created, imposed, and continually reinforced by assertions of naturalness—not an inevitable emanation of nature and the human condition.

In both medieval and modern systems of meaning, the concept of femininity was elaborated over against masculinity. In no other area has the binary conception of meaning had such far-reaching results in changing fundamental conceptions used by historians. Language-based analysis has worked to unpack the thick and often self-contradictory layer of alleged characteristics attached to female and male persons, characteristics not found but created to justify disparate arrangements of power and privilege. Women were sometimes seen as essentially sexual and aggressive, and sometimes as asexual and passive: both were offered as justifying male guardianship. Medieval texts offer a virtual universe of feminine qualities, mainly derogatory. The specific technique for cultural analysis of sex-linked ideas, gender theory, is a direct outgrowth of postmodernist theories of language. Narrative theory and the detailed analysis of how intention and agency work in narrative have also had positive implications for the history of women, especially the women of strongly patriarchal societies. Narrative theory made the question of who is admitted "into history" as a narrative protagonist, and who (or which groups) are regarded as merely present in some subhistorical manner without narrative impact, a matter for analysis and inquiry. Acknowledging the constructed nature of narrative, both in the medieval period and the modern, opened the way for recognizing the artificial exclusion of women from public life, and also the artificiality of regarding only public life as worthy of historical record. Language, of course, is not a total substitute for persons and institutions, but language creates and conveys meaning in human life; it is fair to assert that women would have a very sparse history without the resources of the linguistic turn.

NANCY PARTNER

References and Further Reading

Berkhofer, Robert F., Jr. *Beyond the Great Story: History as Text and Discourse.* Cambridge, Mass.: Harvard University Press, 1995.

Hutcheon, Linda. *A Poetics of Postmodernism: History, Theory, Fiction.* New York: Routledge, 1988.

LaCapra, Dominick. *History and Criticism.* Ithaca, N.Y.: Cornell University Press, 1985.

Novick, Peter. *That Noble Dream: The "Objectivity Question" and the American Historical Profession.* Cambridge: Cambridge University Press, 1988.

Partner, Nancy. "Making Up Lost Time: Writing on the Writing of History." *Speculum* 61(1986): 90–117.

White, Hayden. *The Content of the Form.* Baltimore, Md.: Hopkins University Press, 1987.

See also **Queer Theory; Medieval Women's History; Postcolonial Theory; Psychoanalytic Theory**

POVERTY

Medieval society included several categories of poor people. The "deserving poor" (those worthy of receiving alms) included widows, orphans, poor girls in need of a dowry, individuals who could not work because of age or disability, persons of means who were no longer able to live according to their accustomed standard of living (these were called the "shame-faced poor"), and the "voluntary poor" who had given up their wealth for religious reasons. The "undeserving poor," often assumed to be male, were those who begged even though they did not need the assistance. Individuals who had nothing with which to support themselves except their own labor were often classified as poor; we would call these the working poor. Finally, there were those who were grouped at the bottom of tax assessments, paying the smallest tax or no tax at all. Modern historians call these the "fiscal poor."

As "deserving" recipients of charitable alms, women had an advantage over men, both because of the Biblical injunction to help widows and because of the gendered expectation that men should work. Thus, many towns had shelters for poor widows or elderly women, but there were few institutions for elderly men; and some medieval authors, such as the fourteenth-century Italian Paolo da Certaldo, were explicit in their recommendations that it was better to give alms to women than to men. After the onset of the Black Death in 1347–1348, moreover, girls in need of dowries became favored recipients of charity because governments and charitable organizations wished to assist in the repopulation of communities.

Despite their privileged role as recipients of charity, women in cities were especially vulnerable to fiscal poverty. In northwestern Europe, where large numbers of single women immigrated to towns to seek work, this was because women were concentrated in the lowest paying forms of employment and they often earned less than men in comparable positions. Within the wool cloth industry, for instance, which was the most industrialized sector of the medieval economy, women predominated among the lowest paying and least skilled workers—the spinners, combers, carders, and warpers. In the late thirteenth-century tax assessments of Paris, fifty-nine percent of female heads of household who paid a tax were listed among the "little people," those who paid the lowest taxes, and many working single women earned too little to even show up on the tax assessments.

Because single women who worked often did not earn enough to support themselves, many women subsidized their incomes as part-time prostitutes. Indeed, as Karras has pointed out, the term "laundress" came to be thought of as virtually synonymous with "prostitute." Another strategy for survival among poor working women was "spinster clustering," or living together in pairs or groups. Some working single women also accepted alms to augment their incomes.

Most poor working women in towns worked as domestic servants. In some cases they worked as young girls until they had earned enough for a dowry. In other cases, they returned to domestic service as widows, or they worked as servants throughout their adult lives, until age or disability rendered them incapable of working any longer. Some employers of domestic servants allowed their servants to stay on even after age or disability prevented them from working; however, many aged domestic servants were turned out on their own. Since the number of beds in shelters for elderly women and widows was not sufficient to accommodate the population of elderly women in cities, many of these former servants had to join the ranks of the begging poor.

In Mediterranean towns, where young women did not tend to leave home to find work, female poverty was exacerbated in the later Middle Ages by changes in inheritance practices. In Catalonia, for instance, a law passed in 1351 penalized widows who remarried, forcing them to give up the usufruct of their husbands' property, taking only their dowry into their second marriage. Brodman has suggested that this law reduced women's chances of remarrying and may have compelled a number of widows to abandon their children. In northern Italian towns, such as Florence, women's inheritance was restricted, in the later Middle Ages, to their dowry, and charitable institutions worried, especially in periods of high mortality brought about by the Black Death, that orphaned girls—who could not represent themselves in court—might be cheated by male relatives out of recovering their dowries and thus being able to marry.

SHARON FARMER

References and Further Reading

Archer, Janice. *Working Women in Thirteenth-Century Paris*. PhD Diss., University of Arizona, 1995.

Bennett, Judith, and Amy Froide, eds. *Singlewomen in the European Past, 1250–1800*. Philadelphia: University of Pennsylvania Press, 1999.

Brodman, James. *Charity and Welfare: Hospitals and the Poor in Medieval Catalonia*. Philadelphia: University of Pennsylvania Press, 1998.

Farmer, Sharon. *Surviving Poverty in Medieval Paris: Gender, Ideology and the Daily Lives of the Poor*. Ithaca, N.Y.: Cornell University Press, 2002.

Henderson, John. *Piety and Charity in Late Medieval Florence*. Chicago: University of Chicago Press, 1997.

Karras, Ruth. *Common Women: Prostitution and Sexuality in Medieval England*. New York: Oxford University Press, 1996.

See also **Almsgiving and Charity; Disabilities; Division of Labor; Hospitals; Inheritance; Migration and Mobility; Poverty, Religious; Prostitutes; Servants; Singlewomen; Social Status; Textile Production for the Market; Widows; Work**

POVERTY, RELIGIOUS

Religious or voluntary poverty was a central and compelling Christian belief throughout the Middle Ages. Its basic motivation was the desire to emulate Christ's life and teachings: "If you wish to be perfect, go, sell your possessions, and give the money to the poor, and you will have treasure in heaven; then come, follow me" (Matthew 19:21). This and similar passages gave the renunciation of material possessions the force of a gospel precept, but religious poverty also could be understood to encompass personal austerity, charity toward the poor, and disinterest in temporal matters. Thus, this spiritual ideal was not limited to professed religious (for whom adopted individual poverty was one of the three vows of religious life, with chastity and obedience) for it also could be embraced in some form by devout lay people as a way to increase their spiritual virtue. Indeed, medieval concepts of religious poverty varied over time in that they both responded to, and in turn transformed, their social and cultural context. During the early Middle Ages, for example, it was primarily a monastic virtue which helped develop spiritual perfection through renunciation of material concerns.

New Religious Movements

The most significant example of religious poverty's influence in medieval society derives from the complicated reactions to the growth of liquid wealth and a commercial economy during the High Middle Ages. Ambivalence toward a profit-oriented mentality and an awareness of the growing divide between rich and poor resulted in new forms of piety. This enthusiasm could reflect criticism of the perceived wealth and growing worldliness of the ecclesiastical hierarchy. Despite the diversity of the religious groups that emerged over the course of the twelfth and thirteenth centuries—encompassing religious and lay, heterodoxy and orthodoxy—each was linked to the other by a shared understanding of voluntary poverty as a way to participate in the *vita apostolica*, that is, the desire to return to the ideals of the primitive Church. Monastic reformers such as the Cistercians renewed emphasis on charity as part of their spiritual vocation. They also adopted austerity in their dress, liturgical celebrations, and even the art and architecture of their communities. However, the primacy of this movement was shifting away from traditional forms of monasticism toward the concerns of an urbanized laity. For example, around 1170, a merchant named Peter Waldo renounced his wealth after hearing a jongleur tell of the life of Saint Alexis, a wealthy Roman who became a beggar. His followers, the Waldensians, practiced collective poverty and moral preaching to live in imitation of the life of Christ and the Apostles. The Beguine Marie of Oignies (d. 1213) wanted to beg from her neighbors to better follow Christ. Other Beguines, groups of pious lay women, strove for material simplicity, forbade the misuse of property, and supported their houses by the labor of their own hands. Local secular and ecclesiastical authorities often supported these groups as exemplars of Christian virtue, except when they intruded on clerical privilege (as happened with Waldensian preaching).

Mendicant Orders

The commitment to religious poverty as an expression of apostolic piety reached its height in the thirteenth century with the mendicant orders. The Dominicans began as an order of penitential preachers in Southern France. They lived a simple life supported by alms in order to provide a counterexample of moral living to Cathar heretics. An especially famous medieval example of religious poverty is Francis of Assisi (c. 1181–1226), also known as the *Poverello* (the Little Poor One). The renunciation of worldly possessions was at the core of his evangelical vocation. His followers would have no possessions, either individually or in common, so that they would have to rely on alms or their own labor. Religious poverty therefore allowed his followers to adopt complete humility and obedience so to better serve the poor of society. As his order grew and became institutionalized, however, the friars moved away from Francis's strict standards. By the end of the thirteenth century, most friars understood their order's observance of poverty as little more than a matter of simplicity and a source of spiritual inspiration. Debates over the standard of poor observance would split the Franciscan Order into bitter factions during the fourteenth century (for example, did use equal ownership? was "poor use" an essential part of their vow?). This ultimately led to the suppression of the Franciscan Spirituals, those brothers who insisted on a strict observance of apostolic poverty.

Clare of Assisi

Given Francis's prominence, it is not surprising that the medieval woman most associated with religious poverty is his first female convert, Clare of Assisi (1193/1194–1253). Clare embraced Francis's ideal of religious poverty. Although she accepted the necessity of a fixed community at San Damiano for her sisters, she intended them to live by alms and the produce of their own small garden. After Francis's death, Clare faced significant pressure from the Roman Curia, who wanted both to assure adequate resources for the women and to regularize the community according to papal standards for female religious life. Clare resisted and managed to convince the pope to grant her community a Privilege of Poverty in 1228. (Scholars no longer accept the authenticity of the 1216 Privilege of Poverty attributed to Pope Innocent III.) Her form of life, approved by Pope Innocent IV while she was on her deathbed, also inscribed religious poverty as the heart of her vocation, but this rule did not circulate much beyond San Damiano. A few other closely connected communities did gain similar privileges, but most female houses attached to the Franciscan Order were supported by endowments. Nonetheless pious traditions emphasize Clare as an exemplar of strict religious poverty. The Franciscan Spiritual Angelo Clareno claimed (incorrectly) that Pope Gregory excommunicated Clare over her opposition to material support for San Damiano. Fifteenth-century Poor Clares, who based their standards of poverty on her, were praised as models of individual holiness.

The example of the Franciscans points to questions about religious poverty of concern to medieval scholars. How did ideals of religious poverty promote religious reform? What was the relationship between the voluntary and involuntary poor? And finally, how did gender impact the social meaning of religious poverty? If the choice to become poor was by its nature limited to those who had possessions to renounce, how did women, whose economic power was generally less than that of men of equal status, understand the social meaning of this central Christian virtue?

LEZLIE KNOX

References and Further Reading

Alberzoni, Maria Pia. *Clare and the Poor Sisters in the Thirteenth Century*, edited by Jean-François Godet-Calogeras. St. Bonaventure, N.Y.: Franciscan Institute Publications, 2004.

Burr, David. *The Spiritual Franciscans: From Protest to Persecution in the Century after Saint Francis*. University Park: Pennsylvania State University Press, 2001.

Lambert, Malcolm. *Franciscan Poverty: The Doctrine of the Absolute Poverty of Christ and the Apostles in the Franciscan Order, 1210–1323*. 2nd ed. St. Bonaventure, N.Y.: Franciscan Institute, 1998.

LeGoff, Jacques. *Your Money or Your Life: Economy and Religion in the Middle Ages*, translated by Patricia Ranum. Boston: MIT Press, 1988.

Little, Lester. *Religious Poverty and the Profit Economy in Medieval Europe*. Ithaca, N.Y.: Cornell University Press, 1978.

Mollat, Michel. *The Poor in the Middle Ages: An Essay in Social History*, by Arthur Goldhammer. New Haven, Conn.: Yale University Press, 1986.

Wolf, Kenneth. *The Poverty of Riches: Saint Francis of Assisi Reconsidered*. Oxford: Oxford University Press, 2003.

See also **Administration of Estates; Agnes of Prague; Almsgiving and Charity; Beguines; Cistercian Order; Clare of Assisi; Devotional Practices; Dominican Order; Monasticism and Nuns; Poor Clares Order; Poverty; Waldensians**

POWER, EILEEN

Born in Bournemouth in 1889, Eileen Edna Le Poer Power constructed a brilliant career in medieval social and economic history. She founded the Economic History Society in 1926, was elected to the chair of

Economic History at the London School of Economics (LSE) in 1933, and delivered the Ford Lectures at Oxford in 1939 (the first woman to do so) on the wool trade.

After attending Girton College of Cambridge University, where she studied history, Power studied in Paris at the École des Chartes and then at the London School of Economics. She traveled to India and China in 1920 on a Kahn Fellowship—the first earned by a woman—and then took up a lectureship in history at the LSE in 1921, where she remained for the rest of her life.

Her first book, *Medieval English Nunneries c. 1275 to 1535* (1922), derived its information about the difficulties of smaller convents from bishops' visitation records. *Medieval People* (1924) details the lives of specific individuals—a peasant, a housewife, Chaucer's prioress, a wool merchant. With R. H. Tawney she edited the three-volume sourcebook, *Tudor Economic Documents* (1924). Translator of *Le Ménagier de Paris* (The Goodman of Paris), about woman's role in household management (1928), she edited with M. M. Postan *Studies in English Trade in the Fifteenth Century* (1933).

After her death in 1940, her Ford lectures were published (1941); in 1975, her volume on *Medieval Women* established her, inaccurately, as a historian of women (she fought for women's suffrage, but did not regard herself as a feminist).

JANE CHANCE

References and Further Reading

Berg, Maxine. *A Woman in History. Eileen Power 1889–1940.* Cambridge: Cambridge University Press, 1996.

Chibnall, Marjorie. "Eileen Edna Le Poer Power (1889–1940)." In *Women Medievalists and the Academy.* Ed. Jane Chance. Madison and London: University of Wisconsin Press, 2005.

See also Cities and Towns; Gentry, Women of England; History, Medieval Women's; Household Management; Monasticism and Nuns; Women Medievalists in the Academy

PREACHING

See Sermons and Preaching

PREGNANCY AND CHILDBIRTH: CHRISTIAN WOMEN

Most medieval women were mothers. They learned about pregnancy and childbirth from one another and from personal experience. Our reliance on textual sources limits our knowledge of common practices

Mother receiving her newly born baby in bed. Liber introductorius ad iudicia stellarum, Arun 66, f. 148. Written by Guido Bonatti de Forlivio, for Henry VII. Location: British Library, London, Great Britain. Credit: Art Resource, N.Y.

among the majority of women living in rural populations. The texts, however, reveal a combination of medical, religious, and magical treatments for pregnant and parturient women.

Signs of pregnancy included the lack of a menstrual period, continual desire for intercourse or, in other sources, lack of all desire, and changes in a woman's color. In the later Middle Ages, physicians observed urine to confirm pregnancy. Texts also offered the means to determine the sex of an unborn child. For example, if the mother carried the child on the right side and if her right breast was larger than the left, the child was male. The opposite indicated a female. Pregnant women were also thought to desire strange foods, such as charcoal or earth. If this was the case, the pregnant woman should be given beans cooked with sugar. It was also suggested that mentioning foods the woman could not have be avoided in her presence, since her unsatisfied desire would cause miscarriage.

During pregnancy women were encouraged to eat lightly, and to eat easily digestible foods, such as poultry or fish. Arab and Muslim women received similar advice and were also told to avoid strong or heavily spiced foods. Too much or too strenuous activity was to be avoided for fear of causing premature labor. Following such advice, however, was clearly possible only for the elite. Lower-class women were not likely to have a diet that included much poultry and fish or to have the freedom to avoid routine, and perhaps heavy, labor. Scholars have suggested that a major cause of maternal mortality, especially in the early Middle Ages, was anemia caused by insufficient protein and iron in the diet, leading to excessive bleeding in a miscarriage or even in a normal delivery.

Normal childbirth was seen as a natural process and so was discussed very little in medical texts. Childbirth was, nevertheless, surrounded with traditional customs. Descriptions of birth practices and iconography of birthing scenes almost universally depict them as exclusively female arenas, but there is debate about the degree of men's interest and participation in gynecology and obstetrics. Medical texts written by and for male practitioners indicate interest and, perhaps, experience in the process of childbirth. Royal births are often described as an exception to the all-female rule, with court physicians and astrologers in attendance, although arrangements for the deliveries of fifteenth-century English queens excluded all male participation. Most scholars, however, agree that normal births usually were attended only by women.

When labor began and if circumstances allowed, the mother retreated to a private chamber with her midwife and other female attendants, presumably family and friends. In isolated areas of northern Europe, husbands could assist the midwife or female assistant by supporting the women in the last stages of delivery. Most births took place in the mother's home although, beginning in the twelfth century, some hospitals provided facilities to care for poor women during birth and postpartum convalescence. Some texts suggest the birthing chamber be darkened and warm since light and cold were thought to be harmful to the mother and stressful for the newborn. The birth chamber was to be furnished with warm water, sponges, bandages, and other necessities to care for and comfort the mother and her infant. This, of course, also depended upon the mother's class and economic situation. Royal birthing chambers provided the expectant queen with featherbeds and fine linen sheets and upper-class women strove to imitate these standards. Rural women often gave birth on a bed of straw strewn on the earthen floor of their cottages. Women gave birth in whatever position was comfortable, squatting, kneeling, or supported on the knees of a birth attendant or husband. Illustrations of childbirth also portray women using a birthing stool which allowed the mother to be supported by an attendant on each side while the midwife positioned herself in front where she could

aid the mother and guide the birth. The role of the midwife in a normal delivery was to comfort the mother, protect the infant, and to intervene as little as possible in the natural process. Soothing and encouraging the mother could involve massaging her abdomen or vagina with oils to keep her supple, help with dilation, and ease delivery. The midwife also caught the baby, cut the umbilical cord, cleaned and anointed the child, and wrapped it in swaddling.

Medical texts pay much more attention to the problems involved in difficult deliveries. If labor was protracted and unproductive, women could turn to herbal remedies meant to cause sneezing or open the womb. Herbal baths were encouraged. Women were given herbs in beverages, pessaries (worn in the vagina to support the position of the uterus), or by fumigation. They were made to walk around to ease pains and encourage delivery. If presentation of the fetus exiting the womb was abnormal, the midwife was responsible for correcting the position. Some medieval texts depict as many as sixteen different presentations with instructions to the midwife for correcting each one. The texts advised that the midwife's hand be small and oiled and that she work with great care. Still, turning the child was a dangerous situation involving both pain and the risk of infection. Skeletal remains have been uncovered of medieval women buried with their child still in the womb, sometimes in breech position. In other cases, the problem seems to have been pelvic distortions from rickets or other diseases or simply a narrow pelvis and an unusually large child.

During difficult deliveries, women turned to religion and magic as well as medicine. Placing coriander seed near the womb was thought to attract the fetus. Birth charms, such as the girdle of the Blessed Virgin, were placed on the mother's abdomen. Prayers and rhythmic chants that could be recited by the mother or her attendants and that were perhaps used to regulate breathing were also used. These often included magical and nonsense syllables as well as references to saints, such as the Virgin Mary or St. Margaret. Charms of this type have been preserved in priests' manuals, which suggests that, when a delivery became especially dangerous, clerics could be present to pray for and offer the Church's consolations to a woman in danger of death.

In a prolonged labor, the infant was also at risk. Midwives in fourteenth-century France and fifteenth-century Germany were instructed and licensed by the Church to perform emergency baptisms. If the child died in the womb, medical texts provided both herbal and physical treatments midwives could use to encourage expulsion of the fetus. More drastic advice included placing the mother on a sheet held at the four corners that was then pulled at opposite corners so as to shake the mother back and forth, causing her to deliver. If these did not succeed, a surgeon could be called to extract the fetus using hooks and knives.

After the delivery, it was necessary to ensure the expulsion of the placenta and to control postpartal bleeding. Retention of the placenta could be fatal and, if it was not delivered naturally or with herbal remedies, midwives were instructed to remove it manually, sometimes using their fingernails. Women who suffered from tears, ruptures, or a prolapsed uterus required additional care. Such conditions easily led to infection for which there was little effective treatment. If all went well, however, the midwife left the mother in the care of her friends and relatives and handed the newborn over to the wet nurse.

PAULA M. RIEDER

References and Further Reading

Biller, Peter. "Childbirth in the Middle Ages." *History Today* 36 (August 1986): 42–49.

Bullough, Vern, and Cameron Campbell. "Female Longevity and Diet in the Middle Ages." *Speculum* 55.2 (1980): 317–325.

Deegan, Marilyn. "Pregnancy and Childbirth in the Anglo-Saxon Medical Texts: A Preliminary Survey." In *Medicine in Early Medieval England*, edited by Marilyn Deegan and D. G. Scragg. Manchester: University of Manchester, Center for Anglo-Saxon Studies, 1989, pp. 17–26.

Elsakkers, Marianne. "In Pain You Shall Bear Children (Gen 3:16): Medieval Prayers for a Safe Delivery." In *Women and Miracle Stories: A Multidisciplinary Exploration*, edited by Anne-Marie Korte. Leiden: Brill, 2001, pp. 179–209.

Green, Monica H. "Women's Medical Practice and Health Care in Medieval Europe." *Signs: Journal of Women in Culture and Society* 14.2 (1989): 434–473.

————, ed. and trans. *The Trotula: A Medieval Compendium of Women's Medicine*. Philadelphia: University of Pennsylvania Press, 2001.

Jacobsen, Grethe. "Pregnancy and Childbirth in the Medieval North: A Topology of Sources and a Preliminary Study." *Scandinavian Journal of History* 9.2 (1984): 91–111.

Musacchio, Jacqueline Marie. *The Art and Ritual of Childbirth in Renaissance Italy*. New Haven, Conn.: Yale University Press, 1999.

Staniland, Kay. "Royal Entry into the World." In *England in the Fifteenth Century: Proceedings of the 1986 Harlaxton Symposium*, edited by Daniel Williams. Woodbridge, Suffolk: Boydell Press, 1987, pp. 297–313.

See also **Abortion; Breastfeeding and Wet-Nursing; Caesarean Section; Churching; Contraception; Gynecology; Infants and Infanticide; Infertility; Lying-in; Magic and Charms; Margaret of Antioch; Midwives; Pregnancy and Childbirth: Jewish Women; Procreation and Ideas of Conception; Trota of Salerno**

PREGNANCY AND CHILDBIRTH: JEWISH WOMEN

Jewish men and women often married at the onset of puberty. Medical tractates indicate that first pregnancies were around age fifteen. The pregnancy was formally recognized by a midwife after approximately three months. During pregnancy, women's nutrition was a concern. Women were expected to eat healthy food and any desire women had for specific foods was supposed to be fulfilled.

Birth was attended by a midwife and other women. A birthing chamber was prepared and filled with amulets and metal objects, warding off Lillith, the demonic and rebellious apocryphal first wife of Adam, who was believed to harm newborns. Men did not enter the birthing chamber. Labor was considered a time of danger. Members of the family and community prayed for the parturient. After birth, the baby was rubbed with salt and swaddled. Males were circumcised eight days after birth. No official ceremony for girls existed. The new mother lay in bed for up to a few weeks, during which time she was cared for by other women. Fourteenth and fifteenth century sources mention a ritual that took place a month after birth in which the mother went to the synagogue for the first time.

In Jewish society, procreation was considered a positive commandment, an obligation for all men. As a result, when a couple did not have children for a period of over ten years, men could initiate divorce proceedings. Women were not considered obligated by this commandment, therefore when they wished to divorce for this reason, they had to claim other grounds. In medieval Europe, where Jews lived among Christians, who believed that celibacy was of the highest order, the contrast between procreation and celibacy was often emphasized.

ELISHEVA BAUMGARTEN

References and Further Reading

Barkai, Ron. *A History of Jewish Gynaecological Texts in the Middle Ages*. Leiden: Brill, 1998.

Baumgarten, Elisheva. "Thus Sayeth the Wise Midwives: Midwives and Midwifery in Thirteenth Century Germany." *Zion* 65 (2000): 45–74 [in Hebrew].

————. *Mothers and Children: Jewish Family Life in Medieval Europe*. Princeton: Princeton University Press, 2004.

Cohen, Jeremy. *"Be Fertile and Increase. Fill the Earth and Master It." The Ancient and Medieval Career of a Biblical Text*. Ithaca, N.Y.: Cornell University Press, 1989.

Klein, Michelle. *A Time to Be Born. Customs and Folklore of Jewish Birth*. Philadelphia: Jewish Publication Society, 1998.

Menaḥem Ibn Zeraḥ, *Ẓeida la-Derekh*. Warsaw: H. Kelter, 1880.

Sabar, Shalom. "Childbirth and Magic: Jewish Folklore and Material Culture." In *Cultures of the Jews*, edited by David Biale. New York: Schocken Books, 2002, pp. 671–722.

Sefer Ḥasidim, ed. Judah Wistinetzki. Jerusalem: Sifre Vahrman, 1924.

See also **Infertility; Jewish Women; Marriage, Jewish**

PREMONSTRATENSIAN ORDER

The Premonstratensian order had its origins in the monastic foundation of Prémontré in northern France around 1120. Like other monastic movements of the twelfth century, a single foundation quickly multiplied within a century of its existence. Scholars estimate that the number of Premonstratensian foundations across Europe grew as high as 600 religious communities. Spreading from the Holy Lands to England, but located predominately in France, Germany, and the Low Countries, the Premonstratensian order played a significant role in providing religious opportunities for women.

The founder of the Premonstratensian order, Norbert of Xanten (c. 1080–1134), came from a noble family in the lower Rhineland. Around the age of thirty-five, he underwent a dramatic religious conversion and pledged to follow a penitent's life. At his priestly consecration, Norbert removed his worldly clothes in favor of a sheepskin tied with a cord. This dramatic spectacle added to his renown as a holy man. Thereafter, he traveled throughout Europe as an itinerant preacher and spiritual educator, attracting great crowds. After Norbert's unsuccessful attempt to reform the canons (priests who lived communally) of Laon Cathedral, the local bishop asked Norbert to seek a location for a monastic foundation within that diocese. On Christmas Day 1121, forty canons were formally invested at Prémontré, located about ten miles from Laon. Other foundations quickly followed at Floreffe, Cuissy, Laon, and Cappenberg, the first foundation in Germany. Norbert chose the Augustinian rule to order his monasteries, rather than the Benedictine rule, and therefore clearly marked the men of the order as canons. Unlike monks, they frequently served as priests and provided spiritual care at local churches and women's monasteries.

Described as the first Norbertine nun, Ricwera (d. 1136), the widow of Count Raymond of Clastres, joined Prémontré in its earliest days and served in the hospital. Contemporaries of Norbert praised his decision to accept women and recognized the throngs of women who were attracted to his mission. Herman of Laon stated that ten thousand women joined the order in the twelfth century with over a thousand in his diocese alone. He wrote that had Norbert done nothing else, he would have been worthy of the highest praise for this alone. Most religious women of the Premonstratensian order referred to themselves as "sisters" and did not envision themselves as canonesses. In the lower Rhineland alone, twenty-two monasteries were established for Premonstratensian women; that is, three-fourths of the total number of monasteries.

In contrast to other monastic orders, the earliest statutes of the Premonstratensian order (c. 1130–1134) addressed women's communities. Statutes include important information on the sister's clothing, fasting, prayer, care of the sick, receiving guests, financial issues, and the administrative duties of the prioress. Expected to observe continual silence, the earliest Premonstratensian sisters engaged in meal service, washing clothes, pressing cheese, and weaving wool, in addition to the spiritual tasks of praying and listening to the psalms. Sisters were allowed to possess psalters and prayer books, as well as a small sheathed knife that was to hang from their belted wool tunic. Thirteenth-century statutes of the order and annual General Chapter meetings continued to make mention of women's communities.

However, like other medieval religious orders, there was uneasiness about the place of women within the order. Looking at the number of women's foundations emerging in the earliest decades, some scholars have suggested that there was a general call for the separation of men and women within a monastery. Prémontré, for instance, established a women's community in the late 1130s. Extant property confirmations reprimand Prémontré for receiving goods meant for nearby women's monasteries. And, in an 1198 papal bull, the papacy confirmed the order's decision to no longer require the reception of sisters, especially in those monasteries already suffering from troubles. However, this regulation was generally ignored and early thirteenth-century statutes clarified that sisters could continue to be accepted in those locations that had always received them. In the lower Rhineland, applications for entry into women's monasteries exceeded their capacity, indicating a stable and supportive environment.

Although Premonstratensian monasteries continued to exist throughout the Middle Ages, the thirteenth century brought competition from new religious orders. After one hundred years of popularity, the Premonstratensian order witnessed a sharp decline in its foundations for men and women. The Premonstratensian order may be situated within the twelfth-century religious blossoming of the Middle Ages, which provided leadership, educational, and cultural opportunities for numerous women. While past scholarship on this question concentrated on restrictive legislation, new scholarship seeks answers in local studies, where scholars find women in abundance within the order, especially in northern Germany.

SHELLEY AMISTE WOLBRINK

References and Further Reading

Neel, Carol. "The Origins of the Beguines." *Signs* 14 (1989): 321–341.

Wolbrink, Shelley Amiste. "Women in the Premonstratensian Order of Northwestern Germany, 1120–1250." *Catholic Historical Review* vol. 89, no. 3 (July 2003): 387–408.

See also **Canonesses; Monastic Rules; Monasticism and Nuns; Spiritual Care**

PRIVATE AND PUBLIC SPHERES

The designation of public and private spheres traditionally distinguishes between work and the state—gendered male—and the individual and the family—gendered female. Feminists such as Michelle Rosaldo and Daphne Spain posited the roots of women's subordination in this distinction, arguing that the relegation of women to the domestic sphere is a form of control determining the degree of women's subordination in society: the greater the gulf between the public and private spheres, the greater the degree of subordination. More recently, scholars such as Carol Pateman and Diana Coole have argued that the public/private dichotomy is overdrawn, difficult to maintain for all contexts, and oversimplifies the nature of social space.

Although scholars such as Georges Duby have applied the public/private model to the Middle Ages, medieval Europe more convincingly supports the recent critique. Not an era generally associated with significant freedoms for women, medieval Europe also made little distinction between the public and private. As Shannon McSheffrey has pointed out, the demarcation is a legacy of enlightenment thought and anachronistic when applied to earlier societies. Politically, medieval society vested the seat of government in the body of the monarch; wherever the monarch was, governing occurred. Thus the king's household was not only a domestic, familial space, but also the seat of political administration. The king's household officers began as personal servants and gradually assumed administrative roles through their proximity to the king. For instance, England's chancellor began as the king's chaplain, but over the course of the Middle Ages he became a judicial figure who heard petitions and presided over his own court.

Similarly, medieval economies did not distinguish between public and private. The aristocracy's position relied upon their possession and exploitation of land, on which they and their families lived and from which they derived their income. The aristocratic hall was both a residence and a space from which to administer agricultural estates. The noble family lived—ate, worked, and slept—among their personal servants and estate officers. Merchants' and artisans' homes and workshops were one and the same space. Apprentices lived and worked alongside their masters' families, and the master received partners and clients in his personal chamber. The seat of the peasant economy was also in the home. While peasant men traveled to the family's fields and peasant women worked in and around the home, the necessity of both partners' labor to the family's success blurred any economic segregation between public and private.

Even the architecture of medieval homes observed little distinction between public and private. Peasant homes were frequently divided into only two spaces, one in which the family lived, ate, and slept, and one in which their animals were housed. More affluent peasants kept their animals outside their homes, but otherwise their household space remained the same. Medieval elites more extensively partitioned their homes, but hallways were extremely rare. Anyone who wished to pass from one part of a medieval home to another traversed all the rooms—and thus passed through all the activities and communities housed within.

This lack of clear division between public and private meant that women's traditional association with ostensibly "private" domestic spaces did not segregate them from the "public" workings of the government or the economy. For instance, royal women might enjoy significant governmental influence through their access to the person of the monarch. While a queen did not officially enjoy the same administrative or judicial powers as her husband, nonetheless she could shape the administration of those powers through her position in the royal household and her personal relationship to the king. Similarly, a merchant's wife might not go through a professional apprenticeship, but was likely to learn equivalent skills by living in and overseeing the household in which a craft was practiced. A wife might command her husband's apprentices, and in some contexts, after her husband's death, merchant widows might take up their husbands' former position in his professional guild. Because work occurred in the home, a merchant woman's participation in the market was possible.

This blurring between the public and private in medieval Europe leads to two conclusions: first, the undeniable political, legal, social, and economic restrictions placed on women in the Middle Ages confirm that separation between public and private spheres is not the only source of women's subordination. Second, scholars of medieval women need to recognize that, despite such restrictions, precisely this lack of clear demarcation between public and private afforded women opportunities to participate in medieval society that were not always available to women in later eras.

ANNA DRONZEK

References and Further Reading

Coole, Diana. "Cartographic Convulsions: Public and Private Reconsidered." *Political Theory*. 28. 3 (June 2000): 337–354.

Duby, Georges, ed. *Revelations of the Medieval World*. translated by Arthur Goldhammer. Vol. 2 of *A History of Private Life*. Cambridge, Mass.: Belknap Press of Harvard University Press, 1988.

Landes, Joan B., ed. *Feminism, the Public, and the Private*. Oxford Readings in Feminism. Oxford: Oxford University Press, 1998.

McSheffrey, Shannon. "Place, Space, and Situation: Public and Private in the Making of Marriage in Late-Medieval London." *Speculum* 79. 4 (October 2004): 960–990.

Pateman, Carole. "Feminist Critiques of the Public/Private Dichotomy." In *Disorder of Women: Democracy, Feminism, and Political Theory*. Stanford, Calif.: Stanford University Press, 1989, pp. 118–140.

Rosaldo, Michelle Zimbalist. "Women, Culture, and Society: A Theoretical Overview." In *Women, Culture, and Society*, edited by Michelle Zimbalist Rosaldo and Louise Lamphere. Stanford, Calif.: Stanford University Press, 1974, pp. 17–43.

Spain, Daphne. *Gendered Spaces*. Chapel Hill, N.C.: University of North Carolina Press, 1992.

See also **Architecture, Domestic; Division of Labor; Feminist Theories and Methodologies; Gender Ideologies; Gender in History; Intercession; Space, Sacred: and Gender; Space, Secular: and Gender**

PROCREATION AND IDEAS OF CONCEPTION

Saint Paul's famous dictum, "It is better to marry than to burn," epitomizes the early Christian theological ambivalence toward sexuality: while virginity or at least celibacy is best, marriage provides the only legitimate outlet for sexual intercourse, which could lead to unrestrained and sinful passion. Medieval theology continued to view sexuality with suspicion, as an act fraught with spiritual dangers, despite its necessity in reproduction. In clear contrast to the moral concerns of theologians, medieval writings on medicine and physiology extensively discussed the acts of procreation and conception, generally without any explicit moralizing.

In fact, writers from the eleventh century onward noted that procreation was a gift of God for the survival of the human race and, as a natural function, was not shameful but necessary and worthy of study. In the Greek medical traditions associated with Hippocrates and Galen, which the medieval world followed, sexual intercourse served another important purpose for the individuals involved: it brought the body back to a sense of balance and moderation. Galenic thought in particular emphasized that the body contained four qualities, heat, coldness, dryness and moisture, and that the healthy human body was able to maintain a balance (relative to each person's particular needs) between these qualities or humors. According to this humoral theory, men were by nature hot and dry, while women were cold and moist. Sexual activity provided one way to remove excess heat and moisture, and if performed in moderation would return the humors and thus the body to health (Jacquart and Thomasset, pp. 48–52; Lemay, pp. 41–43).

While they agreed on the importance of sexual intercourse in reproduction and in promoting health, medieval medical writers actively debated the roles of male and female parents in the process of conception. All agreed that the seed or semen was blood that had been transformed through heat, but agreement ended there. The central and later Middle Ages inherited two primary notions from antiquity: one medical and the other associated with natural philosophy. While they have many variants and permutations, the two central views can, with some simplification, be identified as the two-seed theory, connected with the medical writings attributed to Hippocrates and Galen, and the one-seed theory, associated with the natural philosophy of Aristotle.

The two-seed theory argues that the human fetus is created from the union of both male and female seed or sperm. Both men and women have testicles (the female genitalia being simply the inverse and internal mirror to the external male genitalia) and emit seed that combines to form the embryo. The seed derives from all parts of each parent's body, and so explains the physical resemblances of the child to mother and father. While this theory might suggest an equality of the sexes, it in fact presumes the predominance of the male seed, as hotter and stronger than the female, but allows for the possibility of the female seed's active involvement in forming the fetus (Cadden, pp. 15–21; Jacquart and Thomasset, pp. 52–64; Baldwin, pp. 93–94; Lloyd, pp. 319, 321, 324). This model, built around the complementarity of male and female bodies, predominated in western European thought until the thirteenth century, when an alternative model was rediscovered and disseminated.

That alternative model, known as the one-seed theory advocated by Aristotle in the fourth century BCE, claims that it is only the male who produces seed and plays an active role in the process of conception and formation of the embryo. The female simply provides matter, which is then shaped into a human form by the power of the male seed, much as a sculptor takes clay or wood and transforms it into a work of art. That unformed female matter is identified with menstrual blood, not semen, which Aristotle argues women cannot produce. The female, according to Aristotle, is a deformed or imperfect male, and particularly incapable of producing the heat necessary to transform blood into semen, which the male body could do through an internal boiling, thickening, and whitening of the blood (Aristotle, 729b, 737a; Cadden, pp. 21–26). Such a theory reflects the philosopher's larger division between the roles of men and women: the male is active, hot, strong, and formative, while the female is passive, cold, weak, and material.

Medieval writings through the twelfth century only acknowledged the two-seed theory. But the process of translation of Greek and Arabic sources during the same period led to the rediscovery of Aristotle's natural philosophical writings in general. As early as the 1210s, the one-seed theory was articulated by Parisian masters, at the same moment that other views of Aristotle (such as his belief in the eternity of the world) were condemned by the Church. Despite ecclesiastical opposition, Aristotelian natural philosophy came to dominate the intellectual world by the end of the thirteenth century. While some writers continued to advocate the two-seed theory, their defensive statements indicate that the one-seed argument relegating women to a passive role was becoming the accepted view. Albertus Magnus and such later writers as Giles of Rome and Peter of Abano may have used terms such as *female sperm* but associated it increasingly with the passive matter that Aristotle had described (Lemay, pp. 20–26; Jacquart and Thomasset, pp. 64–69). The triumph of Aristotelian thought in general over the course of the thirteenth century finds a clear parallel in the replacement of the Hippocratic-Galenic idea of two seeds with Aristotle's one-seed argument.

The role of male and female in reproduction was not limited to such theories. Discussions during the same period focused also on the creation of sexual difference. Generally, the sex of the child was thought to be determined by the placement of the fetus in the uterus. If the seed(s) should settle near the liver—thought to be the hottest part of the body—the child would be male; if it settled farther from the liver, the child would be female. The theory once again associates the male with heat and by implication strength, and the female with cold and weakness. Others argued that the placement of the fetus on the right side indicated a boy, and the left side a girl. Another, particularly revealing argument for the determination of the fetus's sex lies in a belief by some medical writers that the uterus consisted of seven cells. The theory created a spectrum of sexual and gender possibilities. If the seed should fall in the leftmost cell, the child would be an extremely feminine girl; if in the next cell, the child would be a feminine girl; if in the third cell, a masculine female; if in the middle cell, a hermaphrodite; and so on, to the extremely masculine boy in the rightmost cell (Kudlein, passim; Cadden, pp. 93, 198–201). The theory places in the realm of biology not just the sex of the child, but also its future gender characteristics as well.

Procreation and conception provided ample opportunity for debate and discussion, opportunities that medieval thinkers, especially from the twelfth century onward, used to their fullest in order to consider the relations of men and women in the realm of biology.

WILLIAM F. MacLEHOSE

References and Further Reading

Aristotle. *Generation of Animals*, translated by A. L. Peck. Loeb Classical Library. Cambridge, Mass.: Harvard University Press, 1942.

Baldwin, John. *The Language of Sex: Five Voices from Northern France around 1200*. Chicago: University of Chicago Press, 1994.

Cadden, Joan. *Meanings of Sex Difference in the Middle Ages: Medicine, Science and Culture*. Cambridge: Cambridge University Press, 1993.

Jacquart, Danielle, and Claude Thomasset. *Sexuality and Medicine in the Middle Ages*, translated by Matthew Adamson. Princeton: Princeton University Press, 1988.

Kudlein, Fridolf. "The Seven Cells of the Uterus: The Doctrine and Its Roots." *Bulletin of the History of Medicine* 39 (1963): 416–423.

Lemay, Helen Rodnite. *Women's Secrets: A Translation of Pseudo-Albertus Magnus' De Secretis Mulierum with Commentaries*. Albany: State University of New York Press, 1992.

Lloyd, G. E. R., ed. *Hippocratic Writings*. New York: Penguin Books, 1978.

MacLean, Ian. *The Renaissance Notion of Woman: A Study in the Fortunes of Scholasticism and Medical Science in European Intellectual Life*. Cambridge: Cambridge University Press, 1980.

See also **Aristotelian Concepts of Women and Gender; Gender Ideologies; Gynecology; Pregnancy and Childbirth: Christian Women; Secrets of Women; Sexuality: Extramarital Sex; Sexuality: Female Same-Sex Relations; Sexuality: Male Same-Sex Relations; Sexuality, Regulation of; Sexuality: Sex in Marriage**

PROPHETS

The connection between women and prophecy has ancient and venerable roots. In the Graeco-Roman world women often served as priestesses of the great temples where oracles were handed down by the gods through the women attendants who interpreted them. More pertinently for medieval women, the Hebrew Bible, appropriated by the Christian community as the "Old Testament," recorded the work of five women who were acknowledged as prophets: Miriam, the sister of Moses (Ex 15: 20–21), Deborah (Judges 4 and 5), Huldah (2 Kings 2:14–20), Noadiah (Neh 6:14), and the wife of Isaiah (Is 8:3). The Christian scriptures themselves not only identified women prophets in their own tradition—Anna (Lk 2:36–38), the four daughters of Philip (Acts 21:9), and a certain "Jezebel" (Acts 2:20)—but also recognized the role of the prophet as among the charismatic ministries by which the Holy Spirit guided and led the Christian communities (1 Cor 12: 4–11; Rom 12:28). Theoretically, then, Christian women prophets in the Middle Ages could find significant role models and approbation in the scriptural text. Despite the sanction of the scriptures, however, the role of the prophet in itself was also considered problematic and the functioning of women as prophets attracted a special, gender-specific suspicion.

Infused with the Spirit, prophets always functioned somewhat outside the hierarchical control of the Church. Though Paul in his letters consistently approved the prophetic ministry, he also required that the authentic prophet give an intelligible message that builds up the church community. By late antiquity, the Pauline understanding developed into a twofold notion of the prophet. On the one hand, the prophet speaks for God on the basis of divinely inspired visions, criticizing the contemporary morals and predicting future divine actions. On the other hand, the prophet also speaks for God by interpreting the biblical word as it applies to the moral, social, and spiritual growth of the local church community. In this function, the prophet has been subsumed to some degree into the official ministerial structure as a teacher of the Christian community. We have the witness of the influential bishop of Mainz, Rabanus Maurus (c. 776–856), that this double understanding of

prophet endured into Carolingian times, and he also affirmed that women were worthy and able to receive the gift of prophecy, in spite of inherent tensions between the demands of the prophetic role and the prevailing theory about the nature of women.

Women who were the subjects of religious visions could easily be indicted as under the influence of irrational forces, at best, and subject to demonic influences at worst. While this criticism might apply to a prophet of either gender, it was a particularly telling accusation for women who were believed to be deficient in reason when compared to men. To function as an interpreter of scripture, on the other hand, required both an appropriate education in the liberal arts and authority to teach; the latter authority was explicitly denied women in 1 Tim 2. Further, the teaching prophet could also be seen as usurping the function of the hierarchical priesthood. In spite of ambiguity, criticism, and outright prohibition, nonetheless, women functioned as prophets, in both senses, throughout the Middle Ages.

Visionary prophets were often women of great importance and influence; their visions gave them religious authority and public recognition. Hildegard of Bingen (1098–1179), sanctioned by visions and possessed of a solid monastic education, became a correspondent and advisor of major political figures in her day. Elisabeth of Schönau (1129–1164) spoke out courageously against the corruption in both Church and secular society. Catherine of Siena (1347–1380) not only spoke but also acted; in the tradition of the Old Testament prophets who spoke truth to the powerful in their own courts, she confronted the errant Avignon Pope and admonished him to return to his true place in Rome.

Prophets who taught and interpreted the scriptures were fewer in number, and their influence is less well documented. Although the prohibition against women teachers remained in force, women were not denied the kind of liberal arts education necessary for scriptural interpretation, at least not up to the twelfth century. Boniface's companion, Leoba (d. 779), was the official teacher for the Diocese of Mainz during her lifetime. During the Carolingian period, the bishop Jonas of Orleans, in *De institutione laicali*, had promoted the idea that noble women were responsible for the religious education and pastoral care of all within their households and Dhuoda of Septimania (fl. 842) left a written text for her absent son. Hildegard of Bingen's influence was grounded not only on her visions but also on her reputation as an educated woman and scriptural scholar, and Heloise (1101–1164), known for her remarkable learning, served as a prophetic teacher for the nuns of Le Paraclete.

Marie Anne Mayeski

References and Further Reading

Madigan, Shawn, ed. *Mystics, Visionaries, and Prophets: An Historical Anthology of Women's Spiritual Writings.* Minneapolis: Fortress Press, 1998.

Mayeski, Marie Anne. ""Let Women Not Despair": Rabanus Maurus on Women as Prophets." *Theological Studies* 58, 2 (June, 1997): 237–253.

Petroff, Elizabeth, ed. *Medieval Women's Visionary Literature.* New York: Oxford University Press, 1986.

———. *Body and Soul: Essays on Medieval Women and Mysticism.* New York: Oxford University Press, 1994.

Watt, Diane. *Secretaries of God: Women Prophets in Late Medieval and Early Modern England.* Woodbridge, Suffolk: D. S. Brewer, 1997.

See also **Catherine of Siena; Dhuoda; Education, Lay; Education, Monastic; Elisabeth of Schönau; Heloise; Hildegard of Bingen; Leoba; Literacy and Reading: Latin; Mothers as Teachers; Mysticism and Mystics; Sermons and Preaching**

PROPHETS, NORDIC

Since female prophets, or sibyls, were important in Jewish, Greek, and Roman societies as well as among the early Christians, it is not surprising to find them in the Germanic and the Nordic worlds. Tacitus reported that the Germanic tribes worshipped female divinities and honored female prophets. As revealed in Old Norse sources, the female element in the Nordic pantheon is not impressive, but these texts also included women known as *völur* (sibyls) who existed both at the supernatural and human levels. The most impressive is the supernatural sibyl who articulated the *spá*, or prophesy, that is known as *Völuspá* and that constitutes the first poem in the collection of mythic and heroic poems called the *Elder* or *Poetic Edda*. Addressing a large audience, including the chief god Óðinn, she, swiftly and authoritatively, describes the creation of the world, its past history and current condition, predicts the destruction of the world, but promises a rebirth. The poem was composed around 1000 and recited orally for generations before its inscription.

Human sibyls performed similar functions. The best known is the *Þorbjörg litil-völva* (the little sibyl) who predicted the end of a famine for a Norse community in Greenland, as recounted in *The Saga of Erik the Red*. She was equipped with a staff and her performance was accompanied by singing women. The latter feature is confirmed by other texts, the former from archaeology. Throughout Scandinavia female tombs contained a long iron rod that is no longer interpreted as a cooking implement but as a part of the sibyl's equipment, although its exact use is not known. The term *völur* may be associated with the word *völr*, staff, and, in fact, these "staff-bearing" women who performed prophecy and sorcery may have been a circumpolar phenomenon.

JENNY JOCHENS

References and Further Reading

The Complete Sagas of Icelanders Including 49 Tales. Ed. Viðar Hreinsson. 5 vols. Reykjavik: Leifur Eiríksson Publishing, 1997.

Dillmann, F.-X. *Les magiciens dans l'Islande ancienne.* Uppsala: Kungl. Gustavs Akademien, 2005.

Enright, Michael J. *Lady with a Mead Cup: Ritual, Prophesy and Lordship in the European Warband from La Tène to the Viking Age.* Dublin: Four Courts Press, 1996.

Jochens, Jenny. "Völuspá: Matrix of Norse Womanhood." *Journal of English and Germanic Philology* 88(1989): 344–362.

———. "At the Dawn of Nordic Literature: A Chorus of Female Voice." In *Female Voices of the North I: An Anthology,* edited by Inger M. Olsen, Sven Hakon Rossel, and Robert Nedoma. Vienna: Edition Praesens, 2002, pp. 13–53.

McGinn, Bernard. *Visions of the End: Apocalyptic Traditions in the Middle Ages.* New York: Columbia University Press. 1979.

Price, Neil. S. *The Viking Way: Religion and War in Late Iron Age Scandinavia.* Uppsala: Uppsala University. 2002.

See also **Literature, Old Norse; Prophets; Scandinavia; Supernatural Women; Voice, Female: in Literature**

PROSOPOGRAPHY

Prosopography is a biography of a specific group of people, generally people of low social or legal status who are therefore underrepresented in primary sources, or people whose functions in society render them relatively invisible: for example, women, peasants, and the urban poor. Accumulating and analyzing available biographical data for the people involved in a particular institution, social rank, or historical event—their geographic origins, the identities of parents, siblings, and other relatives—allows scholars to achieve a richer understanding of the institution to which the group belonged or the event in which they participated, and also realize significant details about the group itself, thus raising an otherwise hidden entity and its members to a more visible and knowable position. This methodology has proved particularly fruitful for the study of medieval nuns and moneyers, and early modern guild members. An excellent example of a prosopographical study is Judith Maltby's work on the identities and social ranks of parishioners in early modern England who approved of the liturgy and services of the newly established Church of England. Advantages of prosopography include discerning specific patterns (such as the identification of social status and geographic origins) of a group of people whose association in a particular institution often disguises important differences among them. A prosopographical analysis can also provide insights into the nuanced distinctions within and among social groups. Limitations to this methodology concern the biased nature of sources, which are most plentiful for society's elites: men and upper social classes. Lesser social status groups tend to be left out of historical studies, giving a lopsided view of a particular event or institution, because the more visible elite tend to be seen by historians as the norm. Examples of prosopographical studies can be found in the biannual journal *Medieval Prosopography: History and Collective Biography*.

MARILYN OLIVA

References and Further Reading

Maltby, Judith. *Prayer Book and People in Elizabethan and Early Stuart England.* Cambridge Studies in Early Modern British History. Cambridge: Cambridge University Press, 1998.

Narbona-Carceles, Maria. "Women at Court: A Prosopographic Study of the Court of Carlos III of Navarre (1387–1425)." *Medieval Prosopography: History and Collective Biography* 22 (2001): 31–64.

Oliva, Marilyn. *The Convent and the Community in Late Medieval England. Female Monasteries in the Diocese of Norwich, 1350–1540.* Woodbridge, Suffolk: The Boydell Press, 1998.

See also **Charters; History, Medieval Women's; Records, Ecclesiastical; Records, Rural; Records, Urban**

PROSTITUTES

Generally prostitutes are defined as persons who take money for sex, but in medieval times, the term encompassed any woman with many sex partners. It should also be noted that historians have always treated prostitution as an urban phenomenon linked to the evolution of commercial society. If it existed in medieval rural society, we know very little of it. To a large extent, prostitution existed to assuage the needs of a large urban masculine population that married late or constantly flowed into cities and remained single, if not celibate, transitional visitors.

The Double Standard

It is traditionally accepted that medieval society held a double standard regarding sexual behavior: it allowed men sexual permissiveness and demanded sexual austerity from women. The irony remains that medieval men loaded women with negative characteristics: they were considered fickle, libidinous, inconsistent, prone to temptation, and weak in terms of sexuality (hence needing male dominance). Yet men conceded that male concupiscence was problematic and a danger to social order. By this circular rationale they acknowledged prostitution as a minor evil. To paraphrase a famous statement from St. Augustine, "Prostitution is like the sewer; it stinks but is necessary."

The dominant patriarchal discourse expected males to have what was commonly labeled a "long youth" and allowed them to be surrounded by easily accessible women of their choosing, within and outside their household. Men had wives for the orderly continuation and reproduction of society, and for their personal gratification they had concubines, visited prostitutes, and held sexual rights over the females of their households (handmaids, servants, and slaves). Once abandoned, these women had few alternatives but prostitution. Repeated adultery marginalized them.

Hence for medieval society, prostitution was riddled with ambiguity. The practice was systematically rejected morally, but simultaneously accepted and regulated. Even if prostitutes were marginalized, medieval society recognized them for their function, which provided them a place in the community. Medieval theologians condemned prostitutes because they were promiscuous, but accepted their social function, their *ministerium*. Theologians discussed the number of men a woman had to have sex with to be called a prostitute, and the validity of the financial gain earned by the woman in the process. Authorities were so complacent with this functional system that they rarely attempted to define what a prostitute was. In a rare instance, Marseille, in its thirteenth-century statutes, included a chapter entitled *de meretricibus* (regarding prostitutes). The *Marseillais* designated prostitutes as "public girls" who day and night received two or more men in their houses. A prostitute was also a woman who "did business" trading her body within the confines of a brothel.

Promiscuity and trade, the exchange of money for the pleasure of a body, made a prostitute. The validity of the wage a woman received during the exchange of services with her client was not denied. Theologians like Thomas of Aquinas legitimized these earnings and Thomas of Chobham granted to prostitutes, in addition to the control of their earnings, the possibility to distribute alms, attend church, and receive communion. Theologians nevertheless pondered the level of contamination involved in alms provided by sinners like prostitutes.

Institutionalization

Historians have often explained the ambiguous character of medieval reactions to prostitution empirically. On the one hand the institutionalization of prostitution was rationalized and analyzed parallel to demographics and marital structures; when numerical data is lacking, prostitution is understood in terms of cultural values and issues of sexual normality and deviance on the other.

Institutionalized in red light districts or brothels, prostitutes shielded daughters, wives, and widows from dissoluteness and prepared men for marriage; they protected society from adultery, fornication, rape, incest, and sodomy. For example, using the ample records of the Florentine Office of Decency, Richard C. Trexler suggested that prostitution was institutionalized as a remedy for young male homosexuality. Faced with a demographic crisis that endangered the survival of their society, Florentine fathers reacted where they saw fit. They felt that prostitutes would help young Florentine men focus on the pleasure of women's bodies. In the end their attempt backfired. According to Trexler, the foreign prostitutes that populated Florentine brothels served essentially a population of immigrants rather than Florentines.

In other ways, the institutionalization of prostitution could display the power and authority of the state. Regarding Venice, Elisabeth Pavan has argued that controlling prostitution eradicated male violence in the city. Mary Elizabeth Perry suggested in a similar way that in Seville, Spain, organized prostitution reinforced lines of authority and polarized symbols of evil.

Authors like Jacques Rossiaud help identify some of the weaknesses of the previous theories that explained the institutionalization of prostitution. The study of prostitution cannot be disengaged from the study of gender. Because medieval society remained ambiguous toward women and sex, it perceived women in sexual terms and it determined their status and place in society according to sex. Jacques Rossiaud argued that sexual violence and especially rape replenished the ranks of prostitutes. Rossiaud noted that in southern French medieval towns older men married younger women (this was also the case in many other European cities). He correlated the high incidence of collective rapes committed by groups of youths to the late age of men marrying and to the age and status of the raped women. Respectable women of marriageable ages (between fifteen and thirty) were most often the victims of these collective rapes. The social utility of a raped woman in marriage disappeared with her lost virginity and defilement. Rape dishonored and marginalized these women so they were forced into prostitution. In the end, according to Rossiaud, rapes did not single out women specifically but rather targeted the group of older males that would have married such women. "Gendering" allowed such degradation.

Identification of Prostitutes

The identification of prostitutes faces many obstacles: in general, medieval society was andocentric and misogynistic, and with few exceptions it silenced women's voice. Lower-class and uneducated laywomen are absent from the records for the most part and we can only get a glimpse of their lives by accident. We know names of prostitutes because of transgressions, on the part of others as well as by the prostitutes themselves. But we know very little besides their names, and even these may be misleading. Often, records left no patronymics but a trade name: first name and a label like "of somewhere" or "the something," like Marguerite the Huntress or Jeanette de Valence.

Prostitutes' names then contrasted with medieval naming tradition. Women were generally designated by affiliation (as daughters, wives, or widows); prostitutes were not. This lack of information defined their lives. From their silenced affiliations historians inferred that most often prostitutes were immigrants, who resorted to selling their bodies because they lacked the traditional support networks of kin, neighbors, and friends.

Prostitutes rarely practiced in their place of origins and their numbers peaked with demographics, possibly because of a high male to female ratio, and the migratory character of the male population. Medieval ideology also favored the development of prostitution by recommending that a large segment of the male population remain single. The exigencies of celibacy burdened the single life while prostitutes were available to "sinners." For theologians, simple fornication with public women carried little weight and the spiritual consequences were negligible.

Prostitutes' narratives, when they are available, often tell stories of victimization. In one case, the leader of a gang of miscreants convinced Beatrice, a married woman from 1350s Avignon, to join them. She abandoned her husband to follow the gang leader, who put her to work in Avignon's red light district, the Bourg Neuf. Also in Avignon, in 1370, a butcher kidnapped the wife of Jean de Vitry and set her up to work across the Rhône in the town of Alès. Sixty years later, Catherine Douspe (of Hope) was a young, poor orphan. She was kidnapped and put to work at the Bath of the Stone (baths and stews, like inns and taverns, were often associated with prostitution). A few heartening stories also appeared. The same Catherine asked the municipal authorities for the alms that would allow her to leave her life of "sin."

Poverty was considered a major contributor to prostitution, although society blamed women's nature for their behavior. It was thought that women prostituted themselves by choice and for their pleasure, but some individuals and institutions developed a system of financial support to alleviate young women's poverty and their "fall" into prostitution. Most late medieval testaments included a clause that granted funds for the marriage of poor girls. Civil authorities and confraternities also distributed dowries to prostitutes who wished to leave their trade and marry. At least some perceived the link between growing dowry prices, poverty, and prostitution.

The labor market that shut women out of lucrative professions also favored prostitutes' entry into this trade. Some historians, like Leah Otis and Ruth Mazzo-Karras, have argued that some women entered the profession willingly, as a preferable way to earn a living. Not all were professional prostitutes and occasionally women could resort to the sex trade as a last alternative. Labor practices also facilitated the recruitment of prostitutes. Court records give examples of female apprentices diverted by their masters from learning their craft and being instead forced into prostitution. The same happened to servants and maids.

Medieval prostitution oscillated between phases of toleration and integration, and movements of rejection and marginalization. Rossiaud sees a correspondence between periods of tolerance and economic expansion and prosperity, with periods of legislation and constraints marking economic crisis. One of the best-known examples of the latter is the French King Louis IX's expulsion of prostitutes and pimps, brothel and stews keepers, and the confiscation of their goods. He relented and allowed them back to Paris two years later. The city of Toulon acted similarly in 1318. Authorities specified a day (the eleventh of October) for "shameless women" to leave the premises under the threat of flogging and confiscation of their garments. The latter ordinance did not eradicate prostitution; during the fourteenth century, citizens complained that certain ladies crossed the brook leading into town, strutted in the streets, and washed themselves in public.

Public Control

The long-term trend saw an evolution toward the institutionalization of brothels controlled by public authorities. By the fourteenth century most European towns had a red light district where prostitutes were confined, controlled, and regulated. Such districts allowed a clear spatial and social separation. The owners and managers of brothels, stews, and other houses of prostitution ran their establishments in full light of and support of the law. In fourteenth-century Avignon, for example, a prostitute leased her tenement, and paid a *cens* (yearly tax) to the diocese. Several prostitutes rented tenements from the convent of Saint Catherine. Wealthy merchants invested in the trade. Marguerite Busaffi, daughter of Thomas Busaffi, a prominent Florentine banker established in Avignon, owned a profitable brothel in the city. In papal Avignon, the income and taxes raised by the profession eventually attracted the authorities, who in 1337 decided to tax prostitutes and procurers two *sols* per week. A scandalized Pope Innocent VI annulled the tax in 1358.

Sumptuary laws prohibited prostitutes from dressing like "honest" women and required a recognizable mark on their clothing. Prostitutes, like Jews, were tolerated to a certain extent as social utility, but this attitude was mixed with bigotry and the stigma of pollution. Many towns decreed that prostitutes and Jews purchase the bread and fruits they had examined or touched in the market.

Sumptuary laws were widespread. Since the dominant discourse conceived of women as mentally weak, these laws aimed at deterring honest women from their natural inclination to sin. A 1372 public decree from Avignon's Temporal Court prohibited prostitutes from wearing coats, silk veils, amber rosaries, and gold rings under penalty of fines and confiscation. Marseille and Toulon ordered prostitutes to wear single-color garments and Aix-en-Provence ordered them veiled. In 1382 London, "common harlots" were required to wear a striped hood and they were not allowed to line their coats with fur. The reasons behind such legislation were multiple. It forced prostitutes to be recognizable and prevented them from blending in with other women. It also forced prostitutes to hide and not display the rewards of their trade. After all, they could be perceived as successful women who by-passed women's traditional means of success, by birth or marriage. Prostitutes could not serve as models, and parade and tempt other women to take up their way of life.

Redemption

The reform and rehabilitation of prostitutes was a medieval concern from the twelfth century onward. The prostitute symbolized human frailty and catalyzed the benevolence of God's grace. She symbolized penance and repentance. Christianity offered many models of repenting prostitutes and the best known was Mary Magdalen.

In 1198, Pope Innocent III declared that marrying a prostitute counted as a pious work and he offered the remission of the groom's sins. Marriage presented the double advantage of alleviating poverty and controlling women's sexuality and "natural inclination to sin." Testamentary donations often dowered those prostitutes willing to marry and leave the trade. In addition to marriage, convents could also provide means of social reintegration and salvation for prostitutes.

It is important to recognize that convents for reformed prostitutes were known well before the thirteenth century. At the urging of Theodora, Justinian built the Convent of Repentance, where, according to James A. Brundage, some unhappy residents leaped to their death from the convent walls. Nonetheless, the largest phase of Repentant institutionalization (*Repenties*) occurred between the thirteenth and fifteenth centuries, the same period that saw the institutionalization of prostitutes in municipal brothels. Founded by clergymen, these convents or houses reflected a male Christian ethos and the clergy's definition of required female penance. Prostitutes were to renounce their previous lives as did the "penitent whores" in the edifying stories of Pelagia, Mary the Harlot, Afra, Thaïs and, above all, Mary Magdalen.

JOËLLE KOSTER

References and Further Reading

Amt, Emilie, ed. *Women's Lives in Medieval Europe: A Sourcebook*. London: Routledge, 1993.

Aries, Philippe, and André Béjin, eds. *Western Sexuality: Practice and Precept in Past and Present Times*. Oxford: Blackwell, 1985.

—— and Georges Duby, eds. *A History of Private Life: Revelations of the Medieval World*. Cambridge, Mass.: The Belknap Press of Harvard University Press, 1988.

Brundage, James A. *Law, Sex and Christian Society in Medieval Europe*. Chicago: The University of Chicago Press, 1987.

Bullough, Vern L., and James A. Brundage, eds., *Sexual Practices and the Medieval Church*. Buffalo: Prometheus, 1982.

——, eds. *Handbook of Medieval Sexuality*. New York: Garland, 1996.

Bullough, Vern L. and Bonnie Bullough. *Sin, Sickness and Sanity: A History of Sexual Attitudes*. New York: Garland, 1977.

——. *Prostitution: An Illustrated Social History*. New York: Crown Publishers, 1978.

——. *Women and Prostitution: A Social History*. Buffalo: Prometheus Books, 1987.

——. *Cross Dressing, Sex, and Gender*. Philadelphia: University of Pennsylvania Press, 1993.

——. *Human Sexuality: An Encyclopedia*. New York: Garland, 1994.

Mazzo-Karras, Ruth. *Common Women: Prostitution and Sexuality in Medieval England*. Oxford: Oxford University Press, 1996.

Mengel, David. "From Venice to Jerusalem and Beyond: Milíc of Kromeríz and the Topography of Prostitution in Fourteenth-Century Prague." *Speculum* 79 (2004): 407–442.

Otis, Leah. *Prostitution in Medieval Society: The History of an Urban Institution in Languedoc*. Chicago: The University of Chicago Press, 1985.

Pavan, Elisabeth. "Police des moeurs, société, et politique à Venise à la fin du Moyen Age." *Revue historique* 264 (1980): 241–288.

Perry, Mary Elizabeth. *Crime and Society in Early Modern Seville*. Hanover, N.H.: University Press of New England, 1980.

Richards, Jeffrey. *Sex, Dissidents, and Damnation: Medieval Minorities*. New York: Routledge, 1991.

Rollo-Koster, Joëlle. "The Women of Papal Avignon. A New Source: The *Liber Divisionis* of 1371." *Journal of Women's History* 8 (Spring 1996): 36–59.

——. "From Prostitutes to Virgin Brides of Christ: The Avignonese Repenties in the Late Middle Ages." *Journal of Medieval and Early Modern Studies* 32 (2002): 109–144.

Rossiaud, Jacques. "Prostitution, Youth, and Society in the Towns of Southeastern France in the Fifteenth Century." In *Deviants and the Abandoned in French Society: Selections from the Annales*, edited by Robert Foster and Orest Ranum. Baltimore: John Hopkins University Press, 1978, pp. 1–46.

——. *La prostitution médiévale*. Paris: Flammarion, 1988.

Trexler, Richard C. *The Women of Renaissance Florence*. Binghamton: Medieval and Renaissance Texts and Studies, 1993.

See also **Mary Magdalen; Rape and Raptus; Sexuality: Extramarital Sex; Sexuality, Regulation of; Sumptuary Law; Work**

PROVERBS, RIDDLES, AND GNOMIC LITERATURE

Proverbs, riddles, and gnomes (short statements conveying traditional truisms) abound in old English wisdom literature, most found in the *Exeter Book*, a collection of poetry transcribed in the tenth century and kept at the Exeter Cathedral library. The most widely anthologized *Exeter Book* wisdom poems include *The Gifts of Men* (*GfM*), *The Fortunes of Men* (*FtM*), *Maxims*, several elegies, and selections from a collection of riddles.

GfM and *FtM* list male attributes and experience in sequences of proverbial and gnomic statements. Both poems reflect the Anglo-Saxon heroic code, which valued loyalty, courage, and skill in warfare. The poems also depict aspects of the *comitatus*, the lord/retainer relationship based on a man's loyalty to his lord, as well as to his fellow retainers—in return, the lord sheltered his men in his hall and rewarded them with gifts. *GfM* catalogues characteristics and accomplishments "the ordaining Lord apportions and assigns" to men, including wisdom, valor, good looks, wealth, and skills such as harp-playing, wine-tasting, blacksmithing, and battling sin. *FtM* opens with a vignette of a mother and father tenderly nurturing and teaching their young son. The poem's moral is expressed in gnomic sayings, for example, "Only God knows what the years will bring as he grows up"; "Such things are not man's to control." The poet lists many misfortunes and accidents—usually fatal—that can befall a boy or young man. Women are depicted twice lamenting their sons' deaths, a familiar scene in old English literature.

Maxims offers a catalogue of correct behavior. Again the focus is on males, but women are mentioned, for example, "Woman belongs at her embroidery; a roving woman gives rise to talk," expressing the Anglo-Saxon ideal of the docile, hall- or home-bound woman, repeated in the poem's description of the Frisian wife who welcomes her sailor-husband home—she cleans his clothes and satisfies him sexually. *Maxims* presents aristocratic marriage as a kind of *comitatus*, with the woman as retainer to her lord. Although she offers him advice and shares in gift-giving, she is subservient—when she passes the mead cup she must serve her husband first. An aristocratic wife also "must excel as one cherished among her people," for, in cherishing her they cherish her kin. She is a "peace-weaver," a woman given in marriage by an opposing tribe in order to reduce tribal enmities.

The *Exeter Book* elegies are poems of lament marked by gnomic and proverbial sayings. For example, the exiled male narrators of *The Wanderer* and *The Seafarer* state, "A wise man must be patient," and "Blessed is he who lives in humility." In one of the few displays of same-sex physical affection in old English literature, *Wan*'s narrator, mourning his deceased lord, imagines himself "embracing and kissing him and laying hands and head on his knee."

Several elegies depict *comitatus*-like relationships between women and men, such as *The Wife's Lament* (*Wfl*), *Wulf and Eadwacer* (*WlE*), and *The Husband's Message*. *Wfl* and *WlE* are narrated by women, a rarity in old English literature. Both utter gnomic statements, such as the *Wfl*'s "A young man must always be sad-minded . . . yet must have a happy demeanor," *WlE*'s repeated "A difference exists between us," and *WlE*'s proverbial "One easily tears apart what was never united." Both *Wfl* and *WlE* are enigmatic and difficult to translate into modern English, but the scholarly consensus is that they depict Anglo-Saxon women lamenting their exiles, exiles caused by men adhering to a heroic code that required them to separate from the women.

The *Exeter Book* contains ninety-five riddles, whose solutions refer to familiar objects of Anglo-Saxon daily life, such as Sword, Bible, and various animals and birds. Others describe warfare, weather, or the ocean; several deal with wisdom and religion. Fourteen of the riddles are risqué, yielding two solutions: an "innocent" one, and another that is "wrong" and "obscene." For example, Riddle 61's "innocent" solution is Helmet or Shirt, while the "incorrect" solution is Vagina; Riddle 54 yields both Onion and Penis. Unlike much Old English poetry, the risqué riddles do not focus exclusively on nobility. Several involve working people and depict objects they used daily, such as churn, plough, key, fire, dough, oxen. In most of these riddles both women and men who perform sexual acts are viewed positively—the exception is Riddle 12, where the narrator contemptuously depicts a masturbating female slave. Riddles 37 and 62, Bellows and Poker, depict masturbating men; in Riddle 62 the men also appear to engage in anal intercourse.

Kennings—newly-created compound words that often result in mini-riddles—appear throughout the Old English corpus, such as *bone-house* for the human body and *whale-road* for the sea. Coined compounds in old English that are associated with gender or sexuality include, for example, *bed-companion* for sexual partner, *mead-giver*, for a queen or noble woman, and *woman-knowing* for male heterosexual intercourse.

NINA RULON-MILLER

References and Further Reading

Bradley, S. A. J., ed. and trans. *Anglo-Saxon Poetry*. London: Everyman, 1995.

Chance, Jane. *Woman as Hero in Old English Literature*. Syracuse: Syracuse University Press, 1986.

Crossley-Holland, Kevin, ed. and trans. *The Anglo-Saxon World: An Anthology*. Oxford: Oxford University Press, 1984.

Donoghue, Daniel. *Old English Literature: A Short Introduction*. Oxford: Blackwell, 2004.

Frantzen, Allen J. *Before the Closet: Same-Sex Love from Beowulf to Angels in America*. Chicago: University of Chicago Press, 1998.

Hollis, Stephanie. *Anglo-Saxon Women and the Church: Sharing a Common Fate*. Woodbridge, Suffolk: Boydell, 1992.

Marsden, Richard. *The Cambridge Old English Reader*. Cambridge: Cambridge University Press, 2004.

Tanke, John W. "*Wonfeax wale*: Ideology and Figuration in the Sexual Riddles of the *Exeter Book*." In *Class and Gender in Early English Literature: Intersections*, edited by Britton J. Harwood and Gillian R. Overing. Bloomington, Ind.: Indiana University Press, 1994, pp. 21–42.

Wilcox, Jonathan, ed. *Humour in Anglo-Saxon Literature*. Cambridge: D. S. Brewer, 2000.

See also **Eroticism in Literature; Literature, Old English; Mead-Giver; Obscenity; Sexuality: Male Same-Sex Relations**

PSYCHOANALYTIC THEORY

Psychoanalysis permeates contemporary life; its premises and concepts are used casually and inevitably to describe behavior, dreams, and culture even though most people have not read Freud and are not aware of the source of their ideas about denial, repression, projection, fantasy, inner conflict, paranoia, and much more. Historians, traditionally wary of a theory that foregrounds sex as a key motive throughout human impulses, have mistakenly thought that all psychoanalytic scrutiny is addressed to childhood conflicts, and generally have conflated the clinical practice of psychoanalysis with its potential for textual interpretation throughout the humanities. Begun with the work of Sigmund Freud (with the core theory found in *The Interpretation of Dreams*; *Psychopathology of Everyday Life*; *Three Essays on the Theory of Sexuality*; and *Jokes and their Relation to the Unconscious*), with over a century of development that has refined and extended the theory, psychoanalysis offers historians a powerful instrument to bring to textual evidence. Its coherent system of explanatory concepts was developed to understand the role of unconscious ideas in mental life, and thus in behavior, and the products of culture. Properly understood, psychoanalysis for historians is not analogous to a clinical activity, but an interpretive method that proceeds from a deep understanding of the origins of polysemous meaning.

Psychoanalysis begins with the premise that much of mental activity is unconscious —that is, not immediately available to awareness, introspection, or observation from outside. This basic perception was also present to ancient and medieval culture; Freud's signal achievement was to map the traffic between unconscious and conscious life in functional terms of mental systems: the unconscious or "id"—repository of unruly wishes and demands, the disciplinary superego imposing morality and control, and the ego or conscious self that negotiates between them, using its resources of language to represent the world. The impress of unconscious wishes makes itself evident in all forms of behavior, but most legibly in dreams, and complex forms of speech and writing. The processes by which all minds produce symbolized representations to mediate between deeply felt wishes and an unaccommodating real world result in the entire range of expression, from dreams and improvised behaviors to cultural achievement in literature and art. In a generalized sense, the human capacity for symbolization, the visual and verbal forms that compromise between unconscious and conscious ideas, makes the special domain of psychoanalytic theory. Psychoanalysis offers historians the concepts and interpretive techniques that enable us to move from the manifest to the latent levels of meaning in the artifacts of human culture, and restore human depth and complexity to the traces of past lives. In this sense, psychoanalysis is not a total historical method; it uniquely occupies a boundary region touching all the separate disciplines of the humanities and social sciences.

Just as psychoanalysis is not limited to its foundational writings, its interpretive attention is also not limited to mental pathology. The processes of the "normal," or well-functioning mind are its central focus. Irrationality, a major interest for psychoanalysis, can be understood as motivated and intelligible in psychoanalytic terms, taking into account the interests of unconscious pressures. The contribution of this depth of psychology to medieval culture is that it strongly assists in restoring full human complexity and interiority to persons who lived in a comformity-demanding culture.

NANCY PARTNER

References and Further Reading

Edelson, Marshall. *Psychoanalysis: A Theory in Crisis.* Chicago: University of Chicago Press, 1988.

Freud, Sigmund. The core theory in *The Interpretation of Dreams*; *The Psychopathology of Everyday Life*; *The Three Essays on the Theory of Sexuality*; *Jokes and their Relation to the Unconscious*. Also useful: *Introductory Lectures on Psychoanalysis*. All available from many publishers.

Lear, Jonathan. *Love and Its Place in Nature: A Philosophic Interpretation of Freudian Psychoanalysis.* New York: Farrar Straugs and Giroux, 1990.

Partner, Nancy. "No Sex, No Gender." In *Studying Medieval Women: Sex, Gender, Feminism.* Edited by N. Partner. Cambridge, Mass.: Medieval Academy of America, 1993.

Schafer, Roy. *A New Language for Psychoanalysis.* New Haven, Conn.: Yale University Press, 1978.

See also **History, Medieval Women's; Postmodernism and Historiography**

PUBLIC SPHERES
See **Private and Public Spheres**

Q

QASMŪNA BINT ISMĀ'ĪL

In the centuries following the Arab invasion of the Iberian Peninsula, Jewish culture flourished, reaching its peak in the eleventh and twelfth centuries, known as the Jewish Golden Age. Did Jewish women have a Golden Age? In general, Jewish women were not taught Hebrew, the language of literature. In addition, marriage was particularly important in Jewish culture, and, for women, not conducive to writing. Thus, whereas quite a few Moslem and Christian women managed to express themselves in writing, there is an almost total silence from Jewish women. The most notable exception is Qasmūna Bint Ismā'īl, a late-eleventh- or early-twelfth-century poet who appears to have been the daughter of Samuel ha-Nagid, the Jewish vizier of the Moslem king of Granada and a renowned poet. Unlike her father, who wrote his poems in Hebrew, Qasmūna, who probably was not given an education in this language due to her gender, wrote hers in Arabic. Thus, she is usually placed among the Arab women writers of al-Andalus. Her three extant poems show a considerable degree of sophistication. The first one is a reply to a short poem by Samuel ha-Nagid about a benefactor hurt by a beneficiary, which Qasmūna compares to the sun giving light to the moon and sometimes being eclipsed by it. It is said that, upon hearing this, her father declared her a better poet than he. Her two other poems are laments about her loneliness. In the first, she compares herself to a garden going to waste for lack of a gardener, while in the second, she establishes a parallel between herself and a deer in a garden. Critics believe that she was complaining about the lack of a husband. But Qasmūna sounds confined (like a deer in a garden in poem number two), in addition to being isolated (comparing herself to a garden without a gardener in poem number one). Perhaps she felt that, unlike the moon in her poem, she would never have an opportunity to truly eclipse the sun.

CRISTINA GONZÁLEZ

References and Further Reading

Bellamy, James A. "Qasmūna the Poetess: Who Was She?" *Journal of the American Oriental Society* 103 (1983): 423–424.

González, Cristina. "Qasmūna Bint Ismā'īl." In *Medieval Iberia: An Encyclopedia*, edited by E. Michel Gerli. New York: Routledge, 2003.

Nichols, James Mansfield. "The Arabic Verses of Qasmūna Bint Ismā'īl ibn Bagdālah." *International Journal of Middle East Studies* 13 (1981): 155–158.

See also **Iberia; Jewish Women; Muslim Women: Western Literature**

QUEENS AND EMPRESSES, CONSORTS OF

Acting as a consort was a role typically played by the wives of kings in medieval Europe. Yet the existence of male consorts—husbands whose wives held territory by inheritance—offers an interesting study in medieval gender relations. What roles did these men play when their wives were their political equals or even superiors? Drawing evidence from a chronological and geographical range of examples reveals the negotiations that shaped these relationships.

One consideration was the extent to which husbands participated in the political authority wielded by their wives. Most commonly, king consorts wielded their military might in the defense of their wives' territories, since even queens who ruled in their own right did not customarily lead troops into battle. The marriage of Matilda of England and Geoffrey, count of Anjou (1113–1151), illustrates this well. A disputed succession allowed Matilda, the daughter of Henry I, to lay claim to the English throne in 1135. Although Henry had named Matilda his heir, her cousin Stephen was a rival claimant. At the time of her attempted accession she was married to Geoffrey of Anjou. When civil war between Matilda and Stephen erupted in 1135, Geoffrey's principal role became the defense of Matilda's Anglo-Norman territories. The demands of military campaigns on the continent limited Geoffrey's participation in English affairs and, by 1148, Matilda had effectively abandoned her claims to the English throne. Geoffrey, however, had successfully concentrated his military efforts on the region of Normandy, subduing much of it by 1144, when he claimed the title duke of Normandy for himself. Similarly, Ferdinand of Aragon (1452–1516) led the military campaigns against the Muslim kingdom of Granada that his wife, Isabel of Castile, was anxious to reclaim.

Ferdinand, however, also pushed the question of his authority in his wife's kingdom of Castile, demonstrating that, in some instances, king consorts shared their wives' sovereignty. Ferdinand and Isabel wed in 1469, and in 1474 Isabel inherited the throne of Castile from her half-brother, Enrique IV. Ferdinand (who would inherit the kingdom of Aragon from his father in 1479) immediately questioned his role in the royal marriage. Although at the time of their wedding the two had negotiated a set of marriage capitulations, they renegotiated this agreement into a novel power-sharing arrangement. Although Isabel retained some prerogatives as sovereign ruler of Castile, the two nonetheless jointly issued documents with Ferdinand's name coming first, but her coat of arms preceding his. Thus, although he held no legal claim to the territories of Castile, Isabel ruled jointly with Ferdinand.

The demands created by a marriage of two crowns, like Isabel and Ferdinand's, often created a *de facto* distribution of power. Margrethe I (1353–1412), daughter of King Waldemar IV of Denmark, married Hakon VI (1343–1380), king of Norway (and eventually Sweden), in 1363. She ruled as regent in Denmark

for their son Olaf upon the death of her father in 1375. The unpopularity of Hakon's father, Magnus VII, had led him to cede his throne to Hakon. Thus, Hakon remained preoccupied by this kingdom, while Margrethe directed affairs in Denmark—circumstances that may have resulted from Denmark's unwillingness to allow the ruler of another kingdom to interfere in its administration. Yet after Hakon's death Margrethe would successfully unite the three Scandinavian crowns that Olaf inherited. Similarly, the marriage of Urraca (1082–1125/1126), queen of Castile-León, upon the death of her father Alfonso VI in 1109, to Alfonso of Aragon, was one in which Alfonso exerted very little influence on affairs in his wife's kingdom, confining himself to the protection of his realm.

Attempts to unite dynastic lines did not always end peacefully. When Joan I (1327–1381) inherited the throne from her grandfather, Robert the Wise, she was already married to Andreas of Hungary (son of Louis the Great of Hungary). The two had been married when she was seven and he was six. In 1344 Pope Clement VI crowned her queen of Naples. Thereafter, Andreas acted as her consort. Intrigue surrounded the marriage, however, and in 1345 Andreas was murdered. Joanna was linked to the plot to assassinate him but was never formally held accountable.

The existence of a king consort often raised the question of who would inherit the territory upon a wife's death. Typically, these negotiations favored the couple's children and disadvantaged the king consort. Matilda and Geoffrey, for example, secured from Stephen the agreement that the English throne would also pass to their son, Henry, upon Stephen's death. Isabel and Ferdinand agreed that if she died first Ferdinand could not inherit Castile; it would pass instead to their children.

As these examples demonstrate, various factors complicated the roles played by king consorts. Questions of military support, the division of labor in shared realms, and inheritance created unique gendered balances of power.

ELIZABETH A. LEHFELDT

References and Further Reading

Chibnall, Marjorie. *The Empress Matilda: Queen Consort, Queen Mother, and Lady of the English*. Oxford: Blackwell, 1993.

Duggan, Anne, ed. *Queens and Queenship in Medieval Europe*. Woodbridge, Suffolk: Boydell Press, 1997.

Liss, Peggy. *Isabel the Queen: Life and Times*. New York: Oxford University Press, 1992.

Parsons, John Carmi, ed. *Medieval Queenship*. Stroud, Gloucestershire: Alan Sutton, 1994.

Reilly, Bernard F. *The Kingdom of León-Castilla under Queen Urraca, 1109–1126*. Princeton, N.J.: Princeton University Press, 1982.

See also **Isabel I; Joan I; Matilda the Empress; Queens and Empresses: The West; Urraca**

QUEENS AND EMPRESSES: THE WEST

The study of medieval queens-consort involves features of political life that contemporaries saw no need to define. The idea of "queenship" itself is an anachronism to medieval understandings, and modern definitions risk anachronism. More medieval writers dealt with the reputations and actions of queens than with the idea of a queenly office. Queenly perquisites were treated not in general contexts of rank, but in specific contexts of the aspects of government or administration with which a queen came into periodic contact. Officials involved in such incidental encounters nailed down exact points at issue; they did not examine the full range of a queen's prerogatives nor the activities they upheld. Churchmen wrote in particular situations to urge queens to behave properly, or to scold them for failing to do so. If anything like a general idea of "queenship" was raised, it was to catalogue behaviors befitting a king's wife and the mother of his children. So defined, medieval queens did not require rationalization. They were necessary aspects of a political landscape characterized by hereditary male rulers.

Medieval writing about queens is, for the most part, then, episodic. It is nonetheless possible to identify themes common to the majority of such writings. One example is a manual of instruction Sancho IV of Castile (r. 1284–1294) wrote for his son: a king should choose his wife for her inner and outer virtues (the latter including height as well as beauty); as queen, she must pattern herself on heroines of Scripture and antiquity, remaining industrious, pious, and chaste, and working always to have the respect and affection of husband, children, and other people. However conceived and expressed, these themes are constant in medieval writings to, for, or about queens. Chroniclers who praised or criticized queens routinely resorted to comparisons with the good and bad queens of history. Secular history could offer Clothilda and Balthild (both canonized) and Messalina and Agrippina (both vilified); Scripture provided Esther and the Virgin Mary in contrast to Jezebel and Athaliah. On one hand, perceptions created by such comparisons afforded monarchy a dramatic element it otherwise lacked. On the other, for postmedieval readers, the resort to such typologies obscured understandings of medieval queens' real agendas, motives, and strategies.

Empresses

The Roman empress's place was a known quantity, but not an automatic consequence of marriage. The title Augusta was specifically conferred; not all emperors' wives received it, and even if so honored, they remained subject to the laws. Informal avenues of influence were available, but between the Julio-Claudian period and the Christianization of the empire, few imperial consorts emerged as prominent or powerful women. Christianity, the arrival of new peoples in the empire, and crises in imperial power opened new paths for the wives of Roman rulers. The lives of Galla Placidia and the empresses of the Theodosian house witness to the prominence of late Western and early Byzantine imperial women and the means by which they attained power. But the resources and powers of kings' wives in the new Western kingdoms were undefined. These peoples arrived in the empire without political ideas as developed as those of Rome; most of them had traditions of powerful women, but their customs did not encompass well-defined ideals of kingship, let alone of queenship. What reasoned discussion was given to early medieval queenship in Europe rested on Christian traditions and practices, but the Church could prescribe only standards of conduct appropriate to any Christian wife. Then and for centuries, queenship was a uncertain quantity, dependent upon what individual women could make of the circumstances in which they found themselves and of the resources, human and material, that they could effectively claim.

The Early Middle Ages

Medieval queens' positions in society and government evolved not in a matrix of established legal or administrative procedures, as in the Roman Empire, but within the traditions of a society based upon marriage and family and dominated by lineage politics, within which considerations of family were bound to dominate. Unlike Roman empresses, queens acquired their rank upon marriage, but marriage did not guarantee a successful life as queen. Early medieval society knew stable customs of neither royal succession nor marriage. A childless queen, or one whose marriage had proven a political disadvantage, labored under the threat of repudiation.

Even if a king was not deposed or murdered by competitors, rival claimants were a threat when he died, especially if his son was a child, if succession customs favored kinsmen over direct descendants, or if the succession was not limited to a single lineage. Meddling by a widowed queen and her cohort on behalf of her son could lead to civil war. Practices adopted to impede royal women's participation in such struggles reveal the extent to which they were rooted in family contexts, the power they might secure therein, and a perceived need to limit their interventions.

Medieval queens obtained their position at marriage, but like Roman empresses, they did not acquire sovereign status. They were personages of honor who shared their husbands' rank, but they wielded royal authority only occasionally and temporarily, as their husbands' deputies or, after their husbands' deaths, as regents for young sons. No royal wife or widow who assumed that authority in her own right, and was recognized as sovereign, was known in the medieval West. In the early Middle Ages, when Western kings were not invariably succeeded by sons or near kinsmen, some royal widows married their husbands' successors. Godeswinth, widow of King Athanagild of the Visigoths (r. 551–567) in the Iberian peninsula, wed his successor Leovigild; Aelfgifu-Emma (d. 1052), the Norman widow of Aethelred II of England (r. 979–1013 and 1014–1016), married his successor, the invader Canute of Denmark (r. 1016–1035). Such marriages helped stabilize the new king's position and made the queen a peacemaker between her husbands' families and supporters. In that sense such a second marriage could enhance her influence while continuing her wonted eminence and wealth, but it did not raise her to full sovereignty.

The eminence of late Roman empresses perhaps influenced the position of early medieval queens in the West. Many Visigothic consorts in the Iberian peninsula are unknown by name, but those who are known shared their husband's titles; in 589, Reccared I's wife Baddo subscribed canons of the Third Council of Toledo as *gloriosa*, echoing his *gloriosus*, from the late imperial epithet *gloriossisimus*, witnessing her eminence as well as the seemliness of her approval. But the Visigoths often killed their kings, who were rarely succeeded by family members. If nonhereditary royal succession left any king's wife vulnerable, however, her place as wife and mother could suggest that her presence might stabilize an insecure situation. King Athanagild hoped to make the throne hereditary for his issue and so gave his wife Godeswinth a queenly title and enhanced her role in royal ceremony.

But the effort came to nothing, and when coronation became established usage for Visigothic kings in the seventh century, their consorts were not included. Visigothic queens became subjects of consistent legislation, but laws concerning them neither protected them nor guaranteed honor and respect. Rather, the laws limited queens' potential in politics: Visigothic royal widows had to take the veil to prevent them from interfering in succession politics.

In Merovingian Frankish lands, kings and queens were uncrowned. What prestige Frankish queens held came primarily from religious roles, most familiarly in the case of Clotilda (d. 544), Clovis I's Christian wife, who won him to the faith in 497. Merovingian widows were not forced to take the veil, but the monastic life appealed to a number of them. Balthild, a slave, attracted King Clovis II (d. 657), who married her c. 648. When he died, Balthild became regent for their son, Clothar III; she was deposed c. 665, founded a convent at Chelles, and died as its revered abbess c. 680.

Other Merovingian queens' political roles were shaped by the interests of sons or grandsons. The widowed Clotilda was asked by her surviving sons to choose which sons of their deceased brother should die and which should become monks, so the survivors could share their brother's domains.

The best-known Merovingian queens were Brunhild (d. 613), daughter of Athanagild and Godeswinth, wife and widow of Sigibert I (d. 575), and her bitter rival, Fredegund (d. 597). Brunhild's sister, Galswinth, married Sigibert's brother Chilperic I (d. 584), who soon killed her to marry Fredegund, his concubine. Enmity between the two queens and their families lasted three decades, until Fredegund's son Clothar II (d. 528) put Brunhild to death.

Queens in Anglo-Saxon England had a notable role in the age of conversions. The Merovingian Bertha, wife of King Aethelberht of Kent (d. 616), followed the example of her ancestor Clothilda, welcoming the Roman mission to England in 597 and bringing her husband to the faith. Their daughter Aethelburh married King Edwin of Northumbria (d. 633) and repeated Bertha's success there. Two daughters of King Anna of East Anglia (d. 653/654) married kings elsewhere in England. Aethelthryth was divorced by both husbands after persuading them that she preferred to remain a virgin and eventually became abbess of Ely, while her sister Seaxberga took the veil after her Kentish husband died and followed Aethelthryth as abbess at Ely. In eighth-century Mercia, King Offa (d. 796) exalted his wife Cynethryth as he sought to found a dynasty, and hoped to marry his son Ecgfrith to one of Charlemagne's daughters. But Ecgfrith died unmarried; Offa's line ended with him. In contrast, ninth- and early-tenth-century kings of Anglo-Saxon England from the house of Wessex kept their wives out of public life by denying them a royal title or a throne. King Aethelwulf (d. 858) was deposed partly because he let his second wife, the Carolingian Judith, be crowned at their marriage on the Continent in 856. Only in 973 was an Anglo-Saxon consort crowned. Aelfthryth's elevation reflected King Edgar's preeminence in England, though their marriage was suspect because of incest prohibitions, as she and her first husband were Edgar's cousins.

Perhaps to deal with that situation, Aeflthryth aligned herself with the church reform under St. Dunstan and won his support for her coronation. Most of the later Anglo-Saxon queens were crowned; in the mid-eleventh century the rite was elaborated to state that the kingdom should be governed by the king's power and the queen's virtue alike.

The Queen in the Royal Household

Several factors allowed queens in some early medieval kingdoms to overcome the limits placed on them. A king's wife naturally managed his palace, its personnel, and its resources. As royal governments evolved, the great men of the king's household were also the chief officials of the kingdom. As she worked regularly with these men, a queen forged valuable relationships.

Kings often chose ministers from their relatives, and queens worked to place relatives or servants in royal service. As mistress of the king's household, his wife also managed his treasure. Judicious use of that wealth could win supporters to a queen's side. Her position as a warlord's wife also made her a kind of adoptive mother to the fighting men in his household. She dispensed rewards to these men, honoring an often fiercely guarded hierarchy among them as she associated herself with the king's gratitude to them. Finally, as the king's advisors included bishops and abbots, a queen could develop relationships with them, strengthened by gifts of land or gold to religious houses, or, as in Aelfthryth's case, by support of religious reform. All these activities were proper to a queen; by wisely deploying such expedients, she could strengthen a perhaps otherwise uncertain position.

But the same activities could elicit verdicts pro or con. Too much interest in royal treasure could be depicted as greed, and familiarity with royal ministers was dangerous; Fredegund was twice accused of illicit liaisons with officials. As regent, Balthild involved herself in a disputed election to the see of Lyon; when a friend of Bishop Wilfrid was killed during the dispute, one English chronicler dubbed Balthild

a Jezebel. Aelfthryth, in contrast, managed to have herself crowned as well as made protectress of all English female monasteries. Royal wives trod fine lines, and their conduct demanded an acute sense of time and place. Not all were successful.

Transitions

In 751, Bertha, wife of Pepin the Short and mother of Charlemagne, became the first Frankish queen to be crowned. This was most probably done to underline definitively the change of dynasty in that year, to emphasize that Pepin's descendants had replaced the Merovingians. Bertha's formal investiture thus suggested avoidance of succession disputes by limiting throneworthiness to the children of an anointed queen. After Pepin's death in 768 Bertha played a major role in maintaining peaceful relations between her sons, Carloman (d. 771) and Charles, who, following Merovingian practice, divided the Frankish realm. Bertha's coronation did not, however, establish an immediate precedent. None of Charlemagne's wives was crowned, nor were Carolingian queens regularly crowned until well into the ninth century.

As time progressed, the Church's marriage doctrine came to reinforce the positions of threatened consorts. The faith offered queens many advantages, but they had to be weighed against the disadvantages of unstable succession. Since the Church wrote and prepared the coronation orders, it was perhaps the churchmen's liking for orderly hereditary succession, possibly based on Old Testament lineages, that helped consolidate queens' positions as dynastic mothers and as models of indissoluble Christian marriage. Certainly queens' association with Church reform and the monastic orders afforded them renewed influence and security.

Neither marriage nor coronation immediately altered casual marriage practices in these centuries that allowed powerful men to divorce or repudiate wives with relative ease. A queen who failed to bear a viable son lived with the possibility, if not the likelihood, of repudiation, as did those whose marriages brought their husbands no political advantage. A year after Charlemagne took his first wife, daughter of the Lombard king in Italy, he repudiated her as unable to bear children. An equally likely reason was that he was about to invade her father's kingdom and needed allies along the route to Italy, so he quickly married a well-connected Swabian girl. Such maneuvers were not always so easy. Charlemagne's grandson Lothar II, trying to rid himself of a noble but childless consort to marry a fertile concubine, resorted to lurid accusations of sorcery and incest against his wife Theutberga; after nine years, the case remained unresolved when Lothar died in 869. Theutberga managed to sustain her cause with the help of her birth family, as well as that of Lothar's relatives.

In the eleventh century, Emperor Henry II's childless wife, Cunegunde of Luxemburg (d. 1033), could rely on her powerful family to keep her at Henry's side. In England, Edward the Confessor briefly repudiated the childless Edith (d. 1075) in 1051, when he momentarily escaped the political yoke of her father and brothers; but they soon reinstated themselves and forced Edward to restore Edith.

Cunegunde and Edith benefited from a trope of growing importance to childless queens: the chaste marriage. Neither marriage was, in fact, chaste; few queens would willingly give up the privilege of bearing a royal heir. In fourteenth-century Sicily, popular rumor blamed the extreme Franciscan piety of Queen Sancia (d. 1345) for her childlessness. Sancia's case probably exemplifies the reactions, pro or con, that could be read into aspects of a queen's behavior, in this case her pious observances. Cunegunde and Henry II proclaimed their hopes for children in at least one charter, and Edith advertised herself as Edward's bedfellow in one of hers.

Edith excused her childlessness by inventing a chaste marriage for herself and Edward after his death, in a *Life of King Edward* she authorized and directed. The legend arose for Cunegunde and Henry II during the growth of cults that led to their canonizations: the couple had linked themselves so closely with Church reform that the reforming canons of a 1005 synod were issued in both their names, and founded the see of Bamberg where Cunegunde's cult was centered. Both women were also the targets of adultery accusations, Edith in her own day and Cunegunde posthumously. In the latter case, the legendary allegation provided the basis for miraculous proof of Cunegunde's innocence. But the chaste marriage was a tool that could cut both ways: in the ninth century, Emperor Charles the Fat divorced his second empress, Richardis, claiming that their marriage was unconsummated and that she had committed adultery with a bishop.

The High Middle Ages

Unlike Roman empresses, medieval queens-consort acquired their rank upon marriage or their husbands' accessions. Formal conferral of the queenly title was unknown in the medieval West. Coronation remained for centuries a requisite constitutive act for kings, but for queens the rite was performed only after marriage and affirmed its consequences, with the implied function of designating her the king's lawful consort, who alone could bear his lawful heirs. In fact, many queens in medieval Europe were uncrowned but enjoyed the prerogatives of their rank from the time of marriage. Queens in Spain were rarely crowned; in France, they were invested less and less regularly as the Middle Ages drew on. Yet Castilian and Aragonese queens exercised considerable political influence; and, in France, the king's widow, crowned or not, had a strong claim to act as regent for her son.

Arguments produced in France to justify a widowed queen's right to the regency are the most valuable single body of medieval commentary on the queen's position. These discussions make it clear that the queen's maternity assured her a place in the interests of both family and kingship, which were not readily disentangled when power was seen as patrimony.

The Queen's Coronation Rite

The queen's coronation rite offers a blueprint for queenly practices. In its final form, the rite derived from common sources and was similar, though not identical, in all realms that practiced it. It unfolded in successive stages. A first blessing asked God to make the queen fruitful like the patriarchal wives of the Old Testament, stressing her role in perpetuating an elect lineage. Before the altar, she prostrated herself and then knelt for anointing on head and breast, with holy oil if crowned with the king or with chrism if crowned alone. In imagery redolent of the marriage rite, she then received a ring in token of faith; whether the ring was blessed then or previously, the blessing used was that for the rings of nuns. A prayer naming Esther impressed upon her the duty to entreat and counsel the king.

The celebrant then placed a crown on her head for earthly glory, admonishing her that as she now shone with gold and jewels, she must look within for the gold of chastity and the pearls of virtue and wisdom. Finally she was given a scepter, or two, again depending on whether she was crowned alone or with the king. In England, the conferral of the scepter was at first followed, later accompanied, by a prayer that God would strengthen her to order her office aright; in France, formulae added in the fourteenth century more specifically addressed the scepters' significance. The rite thus successively named the queen's fertility, faith, eminence, and counsel. Her worldly rank was addressed at the moment of crowning, but the next exhortation emphasized her womanly need to strive for chastity, virtue, and wisdom. Her lesser status was underlined by her anointing on head and breast, not on the hands. The final prayer used in England further accented her particular reliance as a woman on divine favor to fortify her.

The themes of the coronation, family, piety, eminence, and counsel marked the parameters within which a queen's agendas and strategies took shape.

But as with endeavors noted earlier, these points could summon reactions pro or con. Coronation introduced new wrinkles as it legitimized delicate areas such as counsel. No one could dispute that the Biblical model of Esther sanctioned a queen's mediation and counsel. But at what point did her attempts to guide the king become domination? A queen must still conduct herself with prudence in her relations with the male ruler. A show of humility in persuading him to modify a harsh decision could deflect suspicions that she was seeking to dominate him. Careful displays of piety might divert criticism of her behavior in other areas. Possibilities for effective action were many, but pitfalls were just as numerous.

The Queen's Role in the Royal Family

Family was a strong base of power for medieval women that rarely faltered; the real guarantor of a woman's security was her place in an established family. It is often said to have been a drawback that women in the medieval West never belonged fully to a birth lineage or to that into which they married, but in fact this allowed them considerable space to maneuver. For a woman wed for political or diplomatic reasons, the capacity to act as peaceweaver or liaison between two powerful lineages could be an important base of influence. Women likewise were not constrained to focus exclusively on their sons, however valuable they might be; queens also emerged as the natural educators and protectors of their daughters, whose careers as diplomatic brides could be shaped by their mothers before and after marriage, much to their fathers' profit. But as the Middle Ages drew on, and kings frequently took wives from increasingly distant kingdoms, distance often impeded queens as liaisons with their homelands. Alphonso X of Castile (r. 1252–1284) was in political difficulties for the last decade of his reign, and his sister Eleanor (d. 1290), wife of Edward I of England (r. 1272–1307), could not rely on his support had she needed it. She instead cultivated networks in England, though again she did so through her family, arranging many marriages for female cousins with English barons.

Diplomatic marriages were a treacherous process that could easily come to grief. Negotiations were often protracted if the marriage was to end a war or resolve competing claims. Among the most famous depictions of the process is Shakespeare's portrayal of Henry V of England (r. 1416–1422) wooing Katherine of Valois (d. 1437) even as his army devastates France. The ramifications go beyond Katharine charmingly learning English through obscene bilingual puns. Her older sister Isabelle had wed Richard II of England, who was deposed by Henry V's father and later killed. The chronicler Froissart described the child Isabelle reciting at her mother's knee that she would marry Richard because "I shall be a great lady."

Perhaps that same thought consoled Katherine. Perhaps she hoped to act as peaceweaver, but Henry V's early death ended any possibility of that. Some women fought to become queens, like Edith-Matilda of Scotland (d. 1118), who had to prove she had never been a nun in order to marry Henry I of England (r. 1100–1135). Others refused outright. William the Conqueror's daughter Adelizia of Normandy was betrothed at least three times, but after the last project she either decided she had had enough or acted on a longstanding wish and took religious vows. Adelizia's many times grandniece, Isabella, the eldest daughter of Edward III of England, was also involved in many marriage projects, ending one of them by refusing to board the ship that was to carry her to her prospective husband.

Even the journey to a new husband's domains could be treacherous, as the bride passed emotionally and geographically from one male ruler's control to another's. Sermon exempla often used this liminal bridal journey as a setting for temptation or tribulation; the bride in one such story is raped by her own steward, whom she murders to conceal her shame. She is later driven by guilt to admit her crime to a bishop and must confess everything to her husband's courtiers. In many cases, the arrival of a foreign-born queen raised suspicions in her new kingdom; she might import crowds of foreigners and divert the king's wealth to their enrichment. In this sense she figured the kingdom's vulnerability to invasion. Small wonder that queens were made to shed their native dress and adopt clothing from their husband's domains.

Security and Insecurity

The strengthening of the Church's marriage teachings afforded queens a measure of security. In 1193 Ingeborg of Denmark (d. 1236) became the second wife of

Philip II of France (r. 1170–1223), only to be repudiated the day after the wedding. For twenty years she tenaciously sustained her case against him and, in the end, he had to recognize her as his queen. On the other hand, the tightening of marriage doctrine and the evolution of stable hereditary succession sharply increased societal focus on adultery—the background to the rumors about Cunegunde and Edith and to tales of fictional queens like Guinevere and Isolde. Adultery, of course, could involve either partner, and once wed, queens often had to accept royal mistresses.

This was not unusual in arranged marriages; husband and wife often met only days before they wed, and not all kings honored marriage vows. Respect, not love, was the norm. The queen's strength lay in the chastity that assured her legitimate maternity, in her role as counselor, and in the eminence that allowed her to construct impressions of her power. Perhaps she took comfort in the knowledge that a mistress might be only a passing fancy. It is untrue that Eleanor of Aquitaine resented Henry II's mistresses—his liaisons flourished after the birth of her last child in 1166, years she spent in Poitou and he in England. Since by then she had a quiverful of sons, it probably did not matter to her what Henry did behind her back.

Childbearing

The production of children was a paramount concern to the kingdom as well as to the royal couple. Healthy sons did not merely improve the queen's power base. They marked a step in an often torturous process by which she could be more closely identified with the interests of her husband's realm than with her homeland. Thereafter her chief care was understood to be the interests of her son, naturally regarded as those of his future subjects as well. Daughters promised future alliances and the births of grandchildren for the king. Childlessness led to rumors, not only of adultery. One countess of Flanders was said to have used contraceptive knowledge to limit her family, and the early deaths of all her children were ascribed to divine punishment. Marriage doctrine made it increasingly difficult for a king to dispose of an unwanted wife, but the last medieval queen of England, Katharine of Aragon (d. 1536), found that having the most powerful ruler in Europe as a nephew was not enough once her husband made up his mind to annul their marriage because her only surviving child was a daughter, Mary Tudor.

The childless queen might substitute other aspects of her position. Richard II of England's first wife,

Anne of Bohemia (d. 1394), was celebrated for gracious intercession with her difficult spouse and became something of a mother to the kingdom; her early death was deeply lamented.

Queens showed much personal bravery in regularly facing the dangers of childbirth, sometimes in very difficult circumstances. The travel that was an essential component of medieval rulership made danger a commonplace; in 1271 Philip III of France (r. 1270–1285) lost his pregnant wife Isabella of Aragon when she fell from a horse near Cosenza; and in 1324 Marie of Luxemburg, second wife of Charles IV of France (r. 1322–1328), died in childbirth after a coach accident. Eleanor of Castile undertook long journeys while pregnant, famously bearing her last son in 1284 in a temporary shelter on the site of Caernarfon castle. Even more remarkable is the case of Margaret of Provence (d. 1297), wife of Louis IX of France (r. 1226–1270), who bore several children while on Crusade, one of them in circumstances of extreme personal danger to herself after Louis was taken prisoner at Damietta.

Raising Royal Children

Children posed problems because of potential rivalries within the family, as became obvious among the sons of Henry II of England and Eleanor of Aquitaine. But in the children's early years, the queen's role in their lives was paramount. She could develop political capital from all her children, not just her sons. But even here, in the last analysis, she was dependent on the king's will. Louis IX forbade Margaret of Provence to name officials to their children's households and usurped one of her functions by writing a manual of instruction for their daughter Isabelle. In contrast, Louis's brother-in-law, Henry III of England (r. 1216–1272), allowed his wife, Eleanor of Provence (d. 1291), full rein in educating their son Edward I.

But here too the phenomena of reactions pro and con often surfaced: Eleanor was accused of teaching Edward to favor her relatives rather than his own countrymen and future subjects.

Problems common to any family surfaced on a royal scale in a queen's need to deal equably with stepmothers and mothers-in-law, frequent sources of discord. A knowing queen could turn them to advantage by acting as a peacemaker. Edward I's second wife, Margaret of France (d. 1318), smoothed relations between her husband and stepson, later Edward II. In-law relations were more treacherous. Margaret of Provence suffered at the hands of Louis

IX's mother, Blanche of Castile (d. 1252), but created a favorable impression by weeping at Blanche's death, though she admitted she wept less for herself than for Louis's grief. Eleanor of Castile and Edward I's mother, Eleanor of Provence, cooperated over the younger woman's children. But in a notoriously less successful case, Margaret of Anjou (d. 1482) fatally exacerbated tensions between her husband, Henry VI (r. 1422–1461), and his kinsman Richard of York.

Royal Widows

Reference to mothers-in-law raises the matter of royal widows. Relatively uncommon by reason of the repeated dangers of childbirth, the rare dowager queen was a significant political figure. Many saw a king's mother as a more desirable mediator with him than his wife. In any event, a widowed queen must live in comfort suited to her rank; otherwise her birth family might demand that her son improve matters. Thus the question of royal dower was all-important, witnessed by the frequent damage this question did to marriage negotiations. There was, as well, the troubling matter of a royal widow's personal behavior. Clemence of Hungary (d. 1328), the young widow of Louis X of France (r. 1314–1316), was scolded by Pope John XXII for dressing immodestly before the men of her household. Henry V of England's widow Katherine of Valois romped scandalously with Edmund Beaufort; when it became clear she could not marry so powerful a nobleman, she quietly settled down—married or not—with an obscure squire named Owen Tudor.

The Queen's Image

A queen could do much to smooth over difficulties by displaying herself as a pious woman, a submissive wife, and a protector of the Church and its institutions. Personally distributing alms demonstrated humility and concern for her husband's poorest subjects. An interest in education was also a formidable weapon; founding colleges as well as new religious houses was a most laudable endeavor. But giving support to new orders, at the expense of established religious communities, could cost a queen the approval of the older communities; Eleanor of Castile aggressively promoted the Dominicans in England, an endeavor of which the Benedictine and Augustinian chroniclers of the day said nothing. On the other hand, her mother-in-law Eleanor of Provence supported the Franciscans just as devotedly, but won Benedictine praise when she chose to take the veil in a house of that order.

Over time, changes in the conduct of government brought about significant shifts in queens' position and the methods open to them. Earlier medieval queens very frequently witnessed royal charters that advertised them as influential members of royal councils. From the late eleventh century, a gradual secularization of society, particularly in the growth of professional male bureaucracies, limited or ended the queen's voice in the council chamber. The growing separation of royal administration from the king's household meant that control of royal treasure passed to male officials, while the great officers of the kingdom were no longer as integral a part of royal households as they had formerly been. The queen's management was now exercised in a more domestic venue. These developments clearly lessened queens' visibility in governance. Eleanor of Aquitaine was the last queen of England to witness royal charters; in France, her mother-in-law Adelaide of Maurienne (d. 1154) was the last queen to do so, during the reign of Louis VI (1108–1137). Queens now saw their influence shift from the council chamber to the bedchamber, an informal venue vulnerable to mistrust because of queens' potential ability as bedfellows to sway their husbands to their own ends. The queen's voice remained consequential but, beyond the legitimate control of male officialdom, it became worrisome and open to criticism. Learned writers and common people alike no longer authorized the queen's voice by appealing to the image of Esther, resplendent in royal raiment as she approached the king on his throne; the legitimizing image became that of the Virgin Mary's humility and loving maternal care. Much of the elaborate ritual surrounding queens within royal households in the later Middle Ages adopted and assimilated Marian imagery, further developing associations enunciated in the coronation rite that tacitly made her a link between the Davidic lineage and her husband's royal line.

Thus the queen's eminence remained an important tool for her, especially as the uses of royal ceremonial grew during the Middle Ages. Queens had an integral part in such splendid occasions, appearing with their husbands at tournaments or regal banquets, translations of saints' relics or the consecrations of cathedrals, on occasion taking their absent husbands' places at such events. A queen's traditional supervision of the splendor of the royal household still gave her a central role in planning such events, contributing personally to their significance and success in impressing royal power and magnificence upon observers. For the vast majority of medieval queens, eminence was supported by substantial incomes that allowed them to engage in patronage on a considerable scale, whether personal, religious, or artistic. Their activities embraced not only the creation of new art works or architectural splendor, but also the distribution of gifts of money, jewels, or clothing to their own servants and households as well as to visiting foreign dignitaries.

The personal ties established by such exchanges require consideration of the degree to which any queen could command the loyalty of supporters she might desperately need. Queens rarely could rely on tenurial links to summon help, but ties of personal loyalty were an adequate substitute.

Largesse required wealth, and queens had to keep a careful eye on income and expense. Clearly there were links here to queens' role as managers of royal households and treasure, but those links were subtly altered. Some queens helped determine successions by sending regalia to their husbands' successors. Empress Cunegonde did so after her husband's death, and a wily Hungarian dowager queen in the fourteenth century assured the succession of her infant son by having her loyal lady-in-waiting, Helene Kottaner, steal St. Stephen's crown from the royal treasury, with which the queen's servants were familiar. Loyalty to queens often involved women or was woven through them. Cunegonde raised a young female cousin at court; Eleanor of Castile kept many of her cousins in her household before they went to live with their English husbands. Those husbands, and the husbands of Eleanor's ladies-in-waiting, received grants of land at marriage and in many cases, places at court. No queen could afford to ignore such resources or the need to attend carefully to them.

At the end of a queen's life, burial and commemoration allowed her to continue to manifest royal presence, power, permanence, and stability. The choice of burial site, perhaps near the shrine of a revered saint, manifested the close ties between royal and divine power. The funeral, in the presence of massed nobility or courtiers, reinforced hierarchy and solidarity. Queens often ordered their tombs in their lifetimes, allowing their artistic patronage or influence to persist after death. The implied perpetuation of their renown provided models for later queens. Queens' posthumous commemorations were observed with great ceremony, demonstrating the exalted nature of royal power and its links to divine favor.

Conclusions

Chroniclers were often extremely harsh in their opinions of the women whose proximity to the centers of government left them open to suspicions of undue political or diplomatic influence. The lives of canonized queens are marked by the opposite tendency, to exaggerate virtue and devotion to the interests of the kingdom. The extent to which any queen could really exercise such leverage cannot, however, be accurately judged from narrative sources alone.

Such writings were susceptible to exaggeration, and their harsh words were often directed as much at the king as at their ostensible target, the queen.

Most chroniclers realized that it was safer to focus on the woman's perceived ambition or harshness than on the king's inability to resist a woman's prodding. By the same token, writers could present queens as vainglorious or impious so as to display kings' resistance to their wives' weaknesses. Studying individual careers helps to clarify the processes by which chroniclers shaped their writings, and builds up a helpful fund of case studies. But since each queen faced different circumstances it is inadvisable to generalize too freely from a single woman's experience. But certainly any queen who found herself coupled to a weak or stubborn husband was likely to face political trouble; the same could happen if the king was considered too strong or harsh.

If queens in the medieval West were accepted as necessary to existing political structures, their individual conduct was often less acceptable. Rank, wealth, motherhood, all depended on marriage to the king, and the resulting proximity to the male ruler caused much concern in many medieval kingdoms. The stabilization of marriage teachings came about just as bureaucratization began to constrict queens' visible role in the conduct of government, but insistence on husbands respecting wives and on wives as preachers to their husbands—especially important to royal couples thanks to the images of Queen Esther and the Virgin Mary—authorized the queen's counsel. However respected in theory, any of these factors could be turned against a queen. Excessive religious devotion could be blamed for a childless marriage. If she failed to manifest charitable sentiments by having others hand out her alms, she was seen as proud and haughty.

Distributing too much wealth was condemned as extravagance. Any of this could be true of any woman, but as the most highly visible of women, queens became lightning rods for criticism. And if a king were deemed unable to control his wife, people might wonder whether he could manage his kingdom.

The queen thus figured the kingdom itself as well as its vulnerability to outside influence. Perhaps more than anything, this conundrum embodies the extreme delicacy of the queen's position.

JOHN CARMI PARSONS

References and Further Reading

Duggan, Anne, ed. *Queens and Queenship in Medieval Europe*. Woodbridge, Suffolk: Boydell Press, 1997.

Earenfight, Theresa, ed. *Queenship and Political Power in Medieval and Early Modern Spain*. Aldershot: Ashgate, 2005.

Facinger, Marion F. "A Study of Medieval Queenship: Capetian France, 987–1237." *Nebraska Studies in Medieval and Renaissance History* 5 (1968): 1–48.

Howell, Margaret. *Eleanor of Provence: Queenship in Thirteenth-Century England*. Oxford: Blackwell, 1998.

Huneycutt, Lois M. *Matilda of Scotland: A Study in Medieval Queenship*. Woodbridge, Suffolk: Boydell Press, 2003.

———. "*Alianora Regina Anglorum*: Eleanor of Aquitaine and Her Anglo-Norman Predecessors as Queens of England." In *Eleanor of Aquitaine: Lord and Lady*, edited by Bonnie Wheeler and John Carmi Parsons. The New Middle Ages; New York: Palgrave Macmillan, 2002, pp. 115–132.

Jackson, Richard A., ed. *Ordines Coronationis Franciae: Texts and Ordines for the Coronation of Frankish and French Kings and Queens in the Middle Ages*. Philadelphia: University of Pennsylvania Press, 1995–2000.

Laynesmith, J. "Constructing Queenship at Coventry: Pageantry and Politics at Margaret of Anjou's 'Secret Harbour.'" *Fifteenth Century* 3 (2003): 137–147.

Ormrod, W. M. "Monarchy, Martyrdom, and Masculinity: England in the Later Middle Ages." In *Holiness and Masculinity in the Middle Ages*, edited by P. H. Cullum and Katherine J. Lewis. University of Wales Press, 2004, pp. 174–191.

Parsons, John Carmi, ed. *Medieval Queenship*. New York: St. Martin's Press, 1993.

———. *Eleanor of Castile: Queen and Society in Thirteenth-Century England*. New York: St. Martin's Press, 1995.

Stafford, Pauline. *Queens, Concubines, and Dowagers: The King's Wife in the Early Middle Ages*. Athens, Ga.: University of Georgia Press, 1983.

———. *Queen Emma and Queen Edith: Queenship and Women's Power in Eleventh-Century England*. Oxford: Blackwell, 1997.

———. "Queens and Treasure in the Early Middle Ages." In *Treasure in the Medieval West*, edited by Elizabeth M. Tyler. York: York Medieval Press, 2000, pp. 61–82.

See also **Adelheid; Aethelthryth of Ely; Almsgiving and Charity; Anne of Bohemia; Berenguela; Blanche of Castile; Brunhild and Fredegund; Burials and Tombs; Chastity and Chaste Marriage; Clotilda; Concubines; Constance of Sicily; Conversion, Religious; Diplomacy and Reconciliation; Divorce and Separation; Edith; Eleanor of Aquitaine; Empresses: Byzantium; Gender Ideologies; Household Management; Isabel I; Isabel of Aragon; Joan I; Jouarre and Chelles; Kottaner, Helene; Margaret of Anjou; Margaret of Scotland; Margrethe; Marriage, Christian; Mary of Hungary I; Mary of Hungary II; Matilda the Empress; Ottonian Royal Women; Patronage, Ecclesiastical; Queens and Empresses, Consorts of; Regents and Queen-Lieutenants; Sexuality: Extramarital Sex; Succession, Royal and Noble; Urraca; Widows; Woodville, Elizabeth**

QUEER THEORY

Queer theory is a collection of methods and perspectives rather than a unified theory for approaching texts and cultures. To queer a text or a cultural representation is to expose the epistemological foundations that structure its interpretation of sexual relations, sometimes also revealing concealed homosexual and homoerotic content. Queer theory borrows its interpretive strategies from deconstruction, seeking to show that the heterosexual order depends on an assumed but suppressed homosexual order; the world can appear to be ordered along heterosexual lines only because other forms of sexuality can be excluded. But their very marginality imparts to those excluded forms a paradoxically foundational role in the creation and maintenance of sexual norms.

Queer theory militates against simple binarisms, such as "homosexual" and "heterosexual," and seeks to interrupt conventional patterns for organizing thought, texts, images, and cultures. Equally important is its movement away from fixed identities within the category of "homosexual" to concepts of gender performance and historically contingent identity that contradict biological or genetic explanations for sexual orientation. The claim that sexual identity is at most a discursive effect might be the most distinctive assumption of queer theory and the point at which queer theory diverges most sharply from other views of the history of sexuality and their essentialist assumptions. The goal of queer theory seems to be the endless deconstruction and destabilization of sexual identities, although it remains to be seen how this work, over the inevitable course of its institutionalization, will avoid accumulating its own history of stable and codified readings, guiding principles, and canonical texts (the work of Eve Kosofsky Sedgwick and Judith Butler, for example) and resisting the establishment and subversion of its own principles.

ALLEN J. FRANTZEN

References and Further Reading

Blasius, Mark, ed. *Sexual Identities, Queer Politics*. Princeton, N.J.: Princeton University Press, 2001.

Butler, Judith. *Gender Trouble: Feminism and the Subversion of Identity*. New York: Routledge, 1990.

Doty, Alexander. *Making Things Perfectly Queer*. Minneapolis: University of Minnesota Press, 1993.

Foucault, Michel. *The History of Sexuality*. Vol. 1, translated by Robert Hurley. New York: Vintage, 1980.

Sedgwick, Eve Kosofsky. *Epistemology of the Closet*. Berkeley: University of California Press, 1990.

See also **Feminist Theories and Methodologies; Performance Theory; Psychoanalytic Theory; Sexuality: Female Same-Sex Relations; Sexuality: Male Same-Sex Relations; Sexuality, Regulation of**

R

RADEGUND

Radegund (c. 520–587) was born a Germanic princess. Abducted by King Clothar of the Franks to be his queen, she eventually became a nun through a profession of faith, and founded the monastery of the Holy Cross at Poitiers. Radegund was well educated in Latin, rhetoric, the writings of the church Fathers, and the lives of female martyrs and saints. Royal status combined with literacy provided Radegund an advantage few early medieval women had. She could make her voice heard in domestic, political, and church affairs. A prolific writer, she authored an epic lament on the destruction of her Germanic homeland, *The Thuringian War,* an elegy on a cousin's murder, *Letter to Artachis,* and numerous letters to kings, emperors, and bishops advocating peace.

Her most influential letter is the *Letter of Foundation,* which Gregory of Tours includes in his *History of the Franks.* Written at the end of her life, the *Letter* explains her reasons for establishing a community for women and obtaining the Rule of Caesarius, the first rule written for religious women, for its governance. One of the Rule's requirements is that every member learn how to read and write. The *Letter* insists that the women's house maintain its standards for literacy as well as its reputation for doing good works. Even as early as the sixth century, the Church provided no accommodations for women to participate in its hierarchy of power and influence. Thus, in order to distance the monastery from unwanted Church interference, Radegund, authorized by her education, royal status, and religious role, claimed that the Rule of Caesarius exempted her house from ecclesiastical authority. The *Letter* appealed to powerful male friends, including kings, emperors, and bishops, to protect the monastery from outside threats, specifically the Church's attempts to seize its land and extensive possessions. In conclusion, Radegund implored her community of almost two hundred women to preserve the monastery of the Holy Cross as the caring and supportive community it was, and not to engage in quarrels that could destroy the house.

In 600, almost ten years after Radegund's death, her friend Venantius Fortunatus, bishop of Poitiers, wrote the *Life of St. Radegund.* Fortunatus focused on Radegund's ascetic practices, which became noticeable during her marriage to King Clothar. Though forced to wed him, Radegund refused to be his wife in either domestic or sexual terms. Instead, she devoted her life at court to performing acts of Christian charity, caring for the poor, bathing the sick, and releasing many of Clothar's prisoners. According to Fortunatus, Radegund fasted while presiding over royal feasts, wore a hair shirt under her regal robes, burned her body with a brass plate made in the image of the Cross, and tightly coiled iron chains around her neck and arms to engrave wounds into her body like those that Christ had suffered on the Cross. Fortunatus explains these self-infliction sufferings as Radegund's public intention to leave Clothar and marry Christ. Alarmed, Clothar agreed to donate the money and land with which Radegund founded the monastery of the Holy Cross.

A decade later, the nun Baudonivia, who grew up in Radegund's convent, wrote a different life of Radegund. Baudonivia's *Life of St. Radegund* commemorates a woman interested in national and church politics and in the active life of the monastery. Fortunatus and Baudonivia both emphasize Radegund's spousal relationship to Christ, yet Baudonivia also describes a woman who made decisions, developed friendships with other nuns, and encouraged interactions with pilgrims, especially through the practice of intercessory prayer, which Radegund considered a social responsibility of the monastery. Within the monastery, Radegund still held the title queen of the Franks, and Baudonivia explains Radegund's acquisitions of holy relics from Jerusalem and Constantinople as political achievements. Radegund's most significant relic was given by Emperor Justinian II of Byzantium, who sent a jeweled reliquary containing a piece of the cross on which Christ died. Baudonivia's *Life* ends with an account of Radegund's death and a celebration of her tomb, which quickly became known as a site for miraculous healings.

One further source for Radegund's life is an eleventh-century illustrated *Life of Radegund* based on the biographies by Fortunatus and Baudonivia. The scenes depict Radegund's enclosure, asceticism, and miracles. None of the illustrations record the self-infliction sufferings described by Fortunatus. Instead, the illustrations portray Radegund's healing of the sick, feeding and clothing of the poor, and performance of miracles through intercessory prayer. Five centuries after her death, these illustrations provide iconic reminders of Radegund's erudition, teaching, and endeavors for women.

JANE E. JEFFREY

References and Further Reading

Carrasco, Magdalena Elizabeth. "Spirituality in Context: The Romanesque Illustrated Life of St. Radegund of Poitiers." *Art Bulletin.* 72.3 (1990): 414–436.
Cherewatuk, Karen. "Radegund and Epistolary Tradition." In *Dear Sister: Medieval Women and the Epistolary Genre*, edited by Karen Cherewatuk and Ulrike Wiethaus. Philadelphia: University of Pennsylvania Press, 1993, pp. 20–45.
Fortunatus, Venantius, and Baudonivia. "De vita sanctae Radegundis libri duo," edited by Bruno Krusch. *Monumenta Germaniae Historica: Scriptores Rerum Merovingicarum*, Vol 2. Hanover: Impenesis Bibliopol: Hahniani, 1888, pp. 364–395.
Gregory of Tours. *The History of the Franks*, translated by Lewis Thorpe. London: Penguin, 1974.
Jeffrey, Jane E. "Radegund and the Letter of Foundation." In *Women Writing Latin: From Roman Antiquity to Early Modern Europe*, Vol. 2, edited by Laurie J. Churchill, Phyllis R. Brown, and Jane E. Jeffrey. New York: Routledge, 2002, pp.11–13.
McCarthy, Maria Caritas. *The Rule of Nuns of St. Caesarius of Arles: A Translation with a Critical Introduction.* Washington, D.C.: Catholic University of America Press, 1960.
McNamara, Jo Ann, E. John Halborg, and E. Gordon Whatley, eds. and trans. *Sainted Women of the Dark Ages.* Durham, N.C.: Duke University Press, 1992.
Radegund. "De excidio Thuringiae," "Ad Iustinum et Sophiam Augustos," and "Ad Artachin." In *Monumenta Germaniae Historica: Auctores Antiquissimi*, Berlin: Apud Weidmannos, 1881, Vol. 4, part 1, pp. 271–275.
———. "Exemplar Epistulae." In Gregory of Tours *Historia Francorum*, Book IX Monumenta Germaniae Historica: Scriptores Rerum Merovingiocartum.
Thiébaux, Marcelle, trans. *The Writings of Medieval Women: An Anthology.* New York: Garland, 1994.
Wehlau, Ruth. "Literal and Symbolic: The Language of Asceticism in Two Lives of Radegund." *Florilegium* 19 (2002): 75–89.
Wemple, Suzanne F. *Women in Frankish Society: Marriage and the Cloister, 500 to 900.* Philadelphia: University of Pennsylvania Press, 1981.
Weston, Lisa. "Elegiac Desire and Female Community in Baudonivia's *Life of Saint Radegund*." In *Same-Sex Love and Desire among Women in the Middle Ages*, edited by Francesca Canadé Sautman and Pamela Sheingorn. New York: Palgrave, 2001, pp. 85–99.
Wormald, Francis. "Some Illustrated Manuscripts of the Lives of the Saints." *Bulletin of the John Rylands Library* 35 (1952): 248–266.

See also **Art, Representations of Women in; Asceticism; Bride of Christ: Imagery; Frankish Lands; Letter Writing; Literacy and Reading: Latin; Monastic Enclosure; Monastic Rules; Relics and Reliquaries; Virginity; Women Authors: Latin Texts**

RAPE AND RAPTUS

Literary, hagiographic, and iconographic representations of threatened and actual rape and *raptus* (abduction) populated the cultural landscape of medieval Europe. Literary motifs, such as the rape of Lucretia, conveyed the idea that sexual violation of women could undermine the very foundations of the social and political order. Other classical accounts circulating in the Middle Ages, such as the *raptus* of Helen of Troy, stressed the devastating consequences of the theft of women for an entire civilization. Mirroring values of kinship, the underlying gender ideology extolled the possession of women's bodies and saw sexual violation and subtraction of women as unsettling acts that primarily damaged women's kin. Rape and *raptus* threatened a woman's sexual purity, which was maintained through her virginity and chastity, to guard the purity of blood within the lineage. Significantly, hagiographic accounts of female saints threatened by rape tended to present virginity as the source of female holiness and to stress the physical, rather than exclusively spiritual, nature of their sanctity. In so doing, they reminded the lay audience that the absence of consent did not save the woman (not even a saint) from the shame cast by sexual violation. In addition to blemishing the woman, rape tainted her family honor and decreased her marriage opportunities. Sometimes, instances of rape were followed by marriage between the rapist and the raped woman, one of the possible ways to restore lost honor, however perverse to modern sensibilities.

Throughout the Middle Ages, the notion of rape was intertwined with that of *raptus*, a category derived from Roman law and primarily meaning abduction, although with a sexual connotation as well, so it could be translated as "ravishment." Abduction could also have a marital purpose. In fact, it was a marital strategy in use among the early medieval Germanic populations and still appears to have been in use among the feudal nobility in the fifteenth century.

The rise of centralized institutions in the eleventh and twelfth centuries marked a turning point in the criminalization of rape and abduction, when monarchs and city-states issued legislation aimed at these behaviors. Against the backdrop of the variety of customary norms, two distinct patterns can be identified, one within the legal system of civil law (*ius commune*) and the other within common law.

In civil law, the legal system in use in a large part of continental Europe, laws on rape and abduction developed separately. For the definition of rape, civil law revived the Roman notion of *stuprum*, which meant shame, dishonor, and defilement. The doctrine of civil law defined *stuprum* as the sexual violation of virgins, widows, or other honest women. *Stuprum*, however, contains a fundamental ambiguity from a modern perspective, being at the same time a crime of violence and one of shame. Such ambiguity is particularly evident in the case of the *stuprum* of virgins, which referred both to forced sex and to illicit defloration of a consenting virgin. Evidently, the essence of the crime rested in the offense against the woman's honor, of which she was merely a guardian and not the owner. Under civil law, virgin women of honest reputation were protected. For example, in doubtful situations, when the alleged deflowerer/rapist asserted that the woman had not been a virgin, hence he did not deflower her, the court presumed the woman was telling the truth. The penalties for *stuprum* ranged from the death penalty for the most serious instances to the imposition of marriage or the payment of the dowry. Of course, the seriousness of the penalty varied according to the social standing of those involved in the crime.

The notion of *raptus* was also revived from Roman law, in which it meant primarily abduction. In civil law, *raptus* came to refer to the violent abduction of an honest woman and had a sexual connotation. Like *stuprum*, *raptus* also contained a fundamental ambiguity, since it referred to the abduction of a woman either without or with her consent. In the latter instance, since the woman was considered her family's property, the violence was understood to be against her family. Underlying the criminalization of abduction was the concern for marital unions that might jeopardize a family's status and wealth.

In England, the criminalization of rape and abduction developed differently from continental Europe. After the Norman Conquest, the notion of *raptus* became intertwined with the notion of rape. In the early stages of the development of common law, the term *raptus* designated forcible intercourse. Rape was a felony and was theoretically punishable by death or "loss of member." The victim had to raise the hue, show her torn clothes and her bleeding before the sheriff and the county court, and lastly repeat the accusation against the rapist before the court of the "justices in eyre" (literally "justices on journey," that is, itinerant justices who were invested with the authority of the king) and the jury. In a case from the Berkshire Eyre of 1248, studied by John Marshall Carter, the victim, Margery daughter of Emma de la Hulle, reported that Nicholas son of Geoffrey of Whatcomb "raped her virginity against the King's peace and she offers to prove this against him as the court sees fit." The rape of virgins was a particularly serious offense, but the definition of the crime was not limited to this instance.

The law of *raptus* evolved in the direction of including incidents of abduction and elopement, so that the terms *raptus* and *ravishment* (from the Anglo-Norman *ravyssment*) could refer to rape, abduction, or elopement unless specified by circumstantial information. The extension of the legal category *raptus* to include abduction reflected the concern, on the part of public authorities, for the abduction of heirs and heiresses (*ravishment of ward*). Not uncommon was the abduction of wealthy widows, as was the case of Lady Maud de Clifford, studied by Andy King. While traveling through Yorkshire in November 1395, Lady Maud de Clifford was abducted by Jack le Irish and his gang. Her abductor's probable intent was to ascend the social ladder through a socially and financially advantageous marriage.

Over time, the law of *raptus* developed to the detriment of the raped woman. The Crown focused on issues of social order and property more than the plight of the raped woman. Common law was explicitly oriented toward the regulation of issues of property, which explains why the category *raptus*, with its emphasis on the "theft" of women and property, instead of *stuprum*, with its emphasis on the woman's and her kin's honor, was assimilated by English medieval law.

The criminalization of rape and abduction were strategies in the hands of central institutions, aimed at maintaining social stability and control over abduction-based marital practices that might jeopardize the best family plans. The reason for the distinct developments in common and civil law may be associated with the different degrees of strength asserted by state power. In England, where the monarchy was strong, the notion of abduction was incorporated into the much more ignominious crime of rape, probably because of the threat that abduction posed to social stability and transmission of property. By way of contrast, rape and abduction remained distinct crimes in continental Europe, where lineages maintained strong power to the detriment of central institutions and, especially in southern Europe, values of family honor persisted more tenaciously.

VALENTINA CESCO

References and Further Reading

Benveniste, Henriette. "Les enlèvements: stratégies matrimoniales, discours juridique et discours politique en France à la fin du Moyen Âge." *Revue Historique* 283:1 (1990): 13–35.

Brundage, James A. *Law, Sex, and Christian Society in Medieval Europe.* Chicago: University of Chicago Press, 1987.

Carter, John Marshall. *Rape in Medieval England: An Historical and Sociological Study.* Lanham, Md.: University Press of America, 1985.

Casey, James. *The History of the Family.* Oxford: Basil Blackwell, 1989.

Gravdal, Kathryn. *Ravishing Maidens: Writing Rape in Medieval French Literature and Law.* Philadelphia: University of Pennsylvania Press, 1991.

Higgins, Lynn A., and Brenda R. Silver, eds. *Rape and Representation.* New York: Columbia University Press, 1991.

Kalifa, Simon. "Singularités matrimoniales chez les anciens Germains: le rapt et le droit de la femme à disposer d'elle-même." *Revue historique de droit français et étranger* 48 (1970): 199–225.

King, Andy. "Jack le Irish and the Abduction of Lady Clifford, November 1315: the Heiress and the Irishman." *Northern History* 38 (2001): 187–195.

Laiou, Angeliki E., ed. *Consent and Coercion to Sex and Marriage in Ancient and Medieval Societies.* Washington, D.C.: Dumbarton Oaks, 1993.

Massetto, Gian Paolo. "Ratto (diritto intermedio)." In *Enciclopedia del diritto,* Vol. 38. Varese: Giuffrè, 1987, pp. 725–743.

Menuge, Noël James, ed. *Medieval Women and the Law.* Woodbridge: The Boydell Press, 2000.

Post, J. B. "Sir Thomas West and the Statutes of Rapes, 1382." *Bulletin of the Institute of Historical Research* 53 (1980): 24–30.

Ribordy, Geneviève. "Mariage aristocratique et doctrine ecclésiastique: le témoignage du rapt au Parlement de Paris pendant la guerre de Cent ans." *Crime, Histoire & Sociétés/Crime, History & Societies* 1:2 (1998): 29–48.

Roberts, Anna, ed. *Violence against Women in Medieval Texts.* Gainesville, Fla.: University Press of Florida, 1998.

Robertson, Elizabeth, and Christine M. Rose. *Representing Rape in Medieval and Early Modern Literature.* New York: Palgrave, 2001.

Rosoni, Isabella. "Violenza (diritto intermedio)." In *Enciclopedia del diritto,* Vol. 46. Varese: Giuffrè, 1987, pp. 843–856.

Ruggiero, Guido. *The Boundaries of Eros: Sex, Crime, and Sexuality in Renaissance Venice.* Oxford: Oxford University Press, 1985.

Saunders, Corinne. *Rape and Ravishment in the Literature of Medieval England.* Cambridge: D. S. Brewer, 2001.

Wolfthal, Diane. *Images of Rape: The "Heroic" Tradition and Its Alternatives.* Cambridge: Cambridge University Press, 1999.

See also **Honor and Reputation; Law; Marriage, Christian; Virginity**

READER-RESPONSE CRITICISM

Reader-response criticism is a general term that has been used to describe a variety of contemporary approaches to literary works that focus on the relationship between texts and their readers; an alternate term is *reception theory*. In an attempt to expand the limits of "new criticism," which analyzed only the literary object itself, critics such as Jauss and Iser in Germany, Poulet in France, and Prince in the United States began to study the strategies by which texts address their readers and to theorize about the reception of literary works by the public. Suleiman and Crosman have divided these different approaches into six categories: rhetorical; semiotic and structuralist; phenomenological; psychoanalytic and subjective; sociological and historical; and hermeneutic.

The majority of studies have focused on modern and contemporary literature, but critics such as Jauss demonstrated, from the 1970s, the usefulness of reader-response and reception theory for medieval literature. Medieval scholars have always paid attention to problems of audience, patronage, and modes of transmission. The notions of implied readers and audiences, among other concepts, became readily incorporated into medieval literary criticism.

The first studies of "reception" or "reader-response" theory did not specifically raise questions of gender, either in contemporary or in premodern literature. However, key studies, such as those by Fetterly and Radway, demonstrated that historical women readers may react differently to literary texts or that certain genres, written by men or women, may respond explicitly to the desires and ideals of women audiences. Fetterly's "resisting reader"—who attempts to resist her appropriation within male discourse—is one of the critical concepts that feminist medieval scholars have adapted and modified within medieval historical and literary contexts.

In the past twenty years, a number of studies have explored, first, the roles of readers and audiences in the creation, transmission, and reception of medieval literary and textual performances, and second, the ways that the different genres of medieval literature represent, engender, or problematize masculine and feminine roles in their readers. In a textual tradition where male authors, narrators, and scribes far outnumber explicitly signed female writers, consideration of female literacy, female patronage, and women readers has allowed critics and historians to reevaluate the critical role played by women as participants in and creators of medieval literary culture.

ROBERTA L. KRUEGER

References and Further Reading

Bartlett, Anne Clark. *Male Authors, Female Readers: Representation and Subjectivity in Middle English Devotional Literature*. Ithaca, N.Y.: Cornell University Press, 1995.

Iser, Wolfgang. *The Act of Reading: A Theory of Aesthetic Response*. Baltimore, Md.: Johns Hopkins University Press, 1978.

Jauss, Hans-Robert. "The Alterity and Modernity of Medieval Literature." *New Literary History* 10 (1979): 181–229.

Krueger, Roberta L. *Women Readers and the Ideology of Gender in Old French Verse Romance*. Cambridge: Cambridge Unviersity Press, 1993.

Poulet, George. "The Phenomenology of Reading." *New Literary History* 1 (1969): 53–68.

Prince, Gerald. "Introduction à l'étude du narrataire." *Poétique: revue de théorie et d'analyse littéraires* 14 (1973): 178–196.

———. "Introduction to the Study of the Narratee." In *Reader-Response Criticism: From Formalism to Post-Structuralism*, edited by Jane P. Tompkins. Baltimore, Md.: Johns Hopkins University Press, 1980, pp. 7–25.

Rabinowitz, Peter J. *Before Reading: Narrative Conventions and the Politics of Interpretation*. Ithaca, N.Y.: Cornell University Press, 1987.

Radway, Janice. *Reading the Romance: Women, Patriarchy, and Popular Literature*. Chapel Hill: University of North Carolina Press, 1984.

Robertson, Elizabeth Ann. *Early English Devotional Prose and the Female Audience*. Knoxville, Tenn.: University of Tennessee Press, 1990.

Schibanoff, Susan. "Taking the Gold Out of Egypt: The Art of Reading as a Woman." In *Gender and Reading: Essays on Readers, Texts, and Contexts*, edited by Elizabeth A. Flynn and Patrocinio P. Schweickart. Baltimore, Md.: Johns Hopkins University Press, 1986, pp. 83–106.

Smith, Lesley, and Jane H. M. Taylor, eds. *Women, the Book, and the Worldly*. Cambridge: Brewer, 1995.

Sturges, Robert. *Medieval Interpretation: Models of Reading in Literary Narrative 1100–1500*. Carbondale, Ill.: Southern Illinois University Press, 1990.

Suleiman, Susan, and Inge Crosman, eds. *The Reader in the Text: Essays on Audience and Interpretation*. Princeton, N.J.: Princeton University Press, 1980.

See also **Audience, Women in the; Femininity and Masculinity; Gender Ideologies; Literacy and Reading: Vernacular; Patronage, Literary**

RECORDS, ECCLESIASTICAL

Medieval secular society before the fourteenth century, especially outside Italy, is known primarily from ecclesiastical records. That is, most of the sources from which scholars now determine family structure, the relations between men and women or between different social groups, the nature of authority, even economic organization, were produced by and preserved by churches. These records most commonly recount a transaction between a monastery and a well-to-do layman or laywoman, typically a gift to monks, but also sometimes a sale or exchange of property or the settlement of a quarrel. Because such a document might later be produced as proof that a transaction really had taken place, and because the monks themselves used these documents to inventory their holdings, it was important to preserve them.

Early Records

In late antiquity (the fifth through seventh centuries), in contrast to most of the Middle Ages, written documents were very common. In that period notaries scrawled notes on slips of papyrus to record all sorts of transactions between ordinary people, from wills to sales to the formal declaration that a child had become an adult. Monasteries seem to have let the notaries keep the documents spelling out pious gifts to the monks. But in the late seventh and eighth centuries, as much of late Roman urban civilization collapsed and parchment increasingly replaced papyrus as the preferred writing medium, the use of documents to record transactions between laypeople became increasingly rare, and monasteries began keeping their charters in their own archives.

Polyptyques

During the ninth century the first efforts were made to organize these charters and the property holdings spelled out in them. Some monasteries drew up polyptyques, that is, censuses of their property and the various dues owed by their tenants. Although only a few polyptyques survive essentially intact, most notably those of St.-Germain-des-Prés, St.-Remi of Reims, St.-Bertin, and Montier-en-Der, there are enough fragments of others, as well as Charlemagne's famous admonition that his royal estates draw up such accountings, to suggest that they were fairly common.

These polyptyques were generally organized geographically, with the holdings and required dues of each village or area spelled out separately. Sometimes, as at Montier-en-Der, there is a fair amount of overlap between the individual entries and royal charters of confirmation. Although the polyptyques list large numbers of people, often by name, one cannot treat these as population censuses of a region or even of a monastery's tenants. Rather, polyptyques listed only those individuals who owed dues, usually the heads of households. This explains why they generally included more men than women. In these polyptyques tenants were typically described by their status, using various words such as *servus, collibertus, mancipius,* or *hospes,* all of which were used for some version of servile station.

Cartularies

Even if a monastery produced no polyptyque, those with the largest number of documents in their archives began in the ninth century to try to organize these documents and often made registers summarizing them. These monasteries, outside the boundaries of the old Roman Empire, had never relied on public notaries and thus had themselves always kept the records of their transactions with the laity. By the end of the ninth century some were producing what were later called cartularies.

A cartulary is a book into which are copied more or less complete versions of the charters in a church's archives. A major purpose of the creation of such a cartulary was the organization and preservation of records, many of which might be several centuries old—and some of which might be on relatively fragile papyrus. An untidy pile of charters was much less convenient than a single book, which typically began with a monastery's foundation documents or great privileges of kings or popes. Most charters copied within a cartulary were grouped roughly by location, so that the account of the earliest gift of property in a certain village might appear next to the most recent. When it is possible to compare the original charter to the cartulary copy, it is clear that conscientious scribes tried their best to reproduce what was before them, although they might abbreviate the list of long-dead witnesses.

The first ninth-century cartularies, those of Lorsch and Fulda, being roughly contemporary to the creation of polyptyques, seem to have arisen from the same impetus to create order and establish an overview of monastic holdings. Cartularies remained very rare, however, until the eleventh century, and even then the format was rather ad hoc. That of St.-Pierre-le-Vif of Sens, for example, took the form of a liturgical book into which the house's most important documents and privileges were copied at intervals. The monasteries of St.-Bénigne of Dijon and of Bèze both produced chronicle-cartularies, histories of their monasteries and regions into which the chronicler copied documents from the archives. The first cartularies in the format that would soon become standard were composed at Cluny in the second half of the eleventh century. In the early decades of the twelfth century, however, a great many monasteries started producing cartularies—and the monks at Lorsch and Fulda recopied theirs. After another century or so, when a monastery might again have a large pile of unconsolidated documents, it was common to create a second cartulary.

Cartularies typically included, along with copies of donation charters or dispute settlements, a polyptyque if a monastery had produced one. There had been enough changes in social and economic structures—and the words used to describe them—between the ninth century and the twelfth that scribes were often unsure of what they were reading, but made their best guesses. Many twelfth-century cartularies also included copies of pancartes. A pancarte was not an ordinary donation charter but rather a somewhat sketchy listing of a number of small acquisitions; typically the monks would have the local bishop draw up and seal such a list.

There are very few original documents surviving from before the year 1000 and a fairly small number from the eleventh century, which means that without the copies in cartularies we would know substantially less about the history of the early Middle Ages. Crucial documents such as royal charters and polyptyques are generally now found only in cartulary copies. From the twelfth century onward, however, the number of records increases rapidly and steadily. Many original documents still survive, written on unevenly shaped pieces of parchment (left over from book production) and hung with one more or seals. It is thus far easier to study the history of the twelfth through fifteenth centuries than that of earlier periods.

Transactions

Ecclesiastical records were never dry, as scribes did more than fill in the blanks with pertinent information. Rather, each charter was an individual narrative, giving the background of the transaction and the family relationships and social position of the principals. There were never any explicit rules as to who might or might not make a transaction, or who would be expected to give their consent or to witness, but general patterns may be observed. Men were far more likely than women to be the principal lay actor. Women, however, could and did take the lead in gifts to a monastery if the property was their own. Husbands in these cases generally gave consent. Most commonly, however, the women who made gifts or engaged in other economic transactions with a church were widows. Children beyond infancy generally consented to all transactions, as did a feudal lord if someone held property in fief. Neighbors, other secular friends of the church, and more distant relatives were typically listed as witnesses. From this information scholars can now determine contemporary assumptions about family, property ownership, and legal obligations.

CONSTANCE B. BOUCHARD

References and Further Reading

Barthélemy, Dominique. "Une crise de l'écrite? Observations sur des actes de Saint-Aubin d'Angers (XIe siècle)." *Bibliothèque de l'Ecole des chartes* 155 (1997): 95–117.

Bouchard, Constance Brittain. *Holy Entrepreneurs: Cistercians, Knights, and Economic Exchange in Twelfth-Century Burgundy*. Ithaca, N.Y.: Cornell University Press, 1991.

———. *Sword, Miter, and Cloister: Nobility and the Church in Burgundy, 980–1198*. Ithaca, N.Y.: Cornell University Press, 1987.

———, ed. *The Cartulary of Montier-en-Der, 666–1129*. Medieval Academy Books 108. Toronto: University of Toronto Press, 2004.

Geary, Patrick J. *Phantoms of Remembrance: Memory and Oblivion at the End of the First Millennium*. Princeton, N.J.: Princeton University Press, 1994.

Guyotjeannin, Olivier, Laurent Morelle, and Michel Parisse, eds. *Les cartulaires*. Mémoires et documents de l'Ecole des chartes 39. Paris: Ecole des chartes, 1993.

Heidecker, Karl, ed. *Charters and the Use of the Written Word in Medieval Society*. Turnhout: Brepols, 2000.

Kosto, Adam J., and Anders Winroth, eds. *Charters, Cartularies, and Archives: The Preservation and Transmission of Documents in the Medieval West*. Toronto: University of Toronto Press, 2002.

Parisse, Michel. "Ecriture et réécriture des chartes: Les pancartes aux XIe et XIIe siècles." *Bibliothèque de l'Ecole des chartes* 155 (1997): 247–265.

Parisse, Michel, P. Pégeot, and B.-M. Tock, eds. *Pancartes monastiques des XIe et XIIe siècles*. Turnhout: Brepols, 1998.

Renard, Etienne. "Lectures et relectures d'un polyptyque carolingien (Saint-Bertin, 849–859)." *Revue d'histoire ecclésiastique* 94 (1999): 373–435.

Rosenwein, Barbara H. *To Be the Neighbor of Saint Peter: The Social Meaning of Cluny's Property, 909–1049*. Ithaca, N.Y.: Cornell University Press, 1989.

White, Stephen D. *Custom, Kinship, and Gifts to Saints: The Laudatio Parentum in Western France, 1050–1150*. Chapel Hill: University of North Carolina Press, 1988.

See also **Charters; Patronage, Ecclesiastical; Records, Rural; Records, Urban; Widows**

RECORDS, RURAL

Most medieval Europeans (95%+) were small-scale agriculturalists who inhabited farming villages, practiced mixed-grain farming and animal husbandry, and lived within the reach of supraregional entities of royal and ecclesiastical power, as well as regional lordships (monastic, episcopal, secular). Peasants formed the base of the economy; indeed, "the village communicated to society at large in all its activities the rhythm and standards of workmanship of a peasant community" (R. W. Southern). In comparison with elites and town populations, however, peasants have not received scholarly attention in proportion to their numbers and influence, although this historiographical situation has been improving significantly since the mid-twentieth century. Medievalists have begun to bring farmers to center stage in the reconstruction and interpretation of medieval society, not only in terms of economic activity but also in their investigations of religious and political institutions.

Documents of Theory and Documents of Practice

When considering medieval peasants, the main population revealed in rural local records, it may be useful to begin with a rough working distinction between "documents of practice" and "documents of theory," a distinction that rests on the degree of fictional treatment and the recording of "ideas" rather than "fact" or actual occurrence: the evidentiary difference between the record of an actual court case and statute law illustrates this difficult point. Documents of practice relevant for rural populations might include the minutes and cases from secular or ecclesiastical courts, account records, tax records (which can include detailed subsidy lists that itemize taxable wealth, as well as revealing numbers of individuals, i.e., size of household), wills, and, to some extent, inquisition records. Documents of theory could include preachers' handbooks, sermon literature, penitentials, and tales embedded in medieval chronicles and other literary or quasi-literary texts. These distinctions are important for research on any historical topic or population, but are especially so for the medieval peasantry, since documents of theory have played a greater role in shaping historical approaches than have documents of practice: the imagery of the suffering peasant in *Piers Plowman* has been cited more often than court roll data, and the "contempt for labor" literary *topos* is conventionally read as indicative of peasants' attitudes toward themselves.

What is striking is how frequently medieval records, whether of royal, supraregional, regional, or local provenance, by lordship or village, identify countrypeople by full name and in connection with a specific place. In the category of royal and supraregional documents we may place tax records, coroner's rolls, peasants' petitions or formal complaints, and the legal materials generated by ecclesiastical courts and tribunals; the category of regional and local documents includes the records of estate administration (most notably for monastic houses), including account rolls, cartularies (inventories of properties and deeds of land transfer), tenant lists, custumals, and court rolls. All of these sources, in varying ways, reveal women and men, their actions and interactions, and the world that they lived in, thus opening up the world of gender studies for people who were not of high status, rich, urban, educated, or connected politically to major figures. Indeed, the records of medieval Europe teem with rural people, men, women, and occasionally children, named as individuals (with first name and surname), living in villages, holding land, and engaged in labor and local exchanges with other named individuals. We do not, in short, have to wait until the sixteenth century's explosion of records and the improved reach of the early modern state into the countryside for material on rural women, rural men, and issues of gender.

Court Records and Inventories

The records here par excellence are court records that belong to the category of estate administrative records and that are especially detailed for England. These court rolls, which first appear in the later thirteenth century and survive for hundreds of English villages, are the minutes of local rural courts (in effect, an assembly of farmers) that usually met several times

a year, had broad jurisdiction over seigneurial, tenant, and personal matters, and possessed varying degrees of collective authority to render and enforce decisions. (Interestingly, English villages produced such records within lordships that had holdings in England and France, while their French counterparts did not—or at least theirs have not survived). In general, local court records for the Continent tend to be less abundant, less consecutive, less detailed, and later than English court rolls. Perhaps the closest inside view we have of the peasant family and landholding, before the period of these English court rolls of the High and later Middle Ages, is provided by the polyptychs, or estate inventories, drawn up for the lands of a number of monasteries in northern France and Germany over the ninth and tenth centuries. The polyptychs list the landed endowments of the monastery, by manors or *villae*, and the various renderings of the tenantry, household by household, including the names of family members, men, women, and children. The wealth of name evidence provided by these rich sources has been used to study personal relations within marriage and the family in the Carolingian peasant household (Herlihy 1985). While the later English estate administrative records have been much studied, the focus has tended to be on the landholding institution, not the peasantry. However, the growing interest among scholars in the lives of the everyman and everywoman has led students of the village to return to these sources to investigate peasants and the realities of their everyday life in ever greater detail.

Women's Roles

Agnes le Reves, Cecilia Penifader, Emma Revelove, and Geoffrey Buk were real people whose lives have been partially reconstructed from court roll data for the English villages of Upwood, Brigstock, Cuxham, and Ellington, respectively. Prominent villagers, including women, might amass enough entries and references to enable us to construct a kind of biography; equally valuable is looking at women's profiles in the aggregate, where it is clear that they, like men, were ubiquitous in the daily life of the village, and neither privatized within the household nor narrowly specialized in terms of their activities. All accounts of peasant women's lives, across time and place, emphasize the multitude of tasks they had, the roles they played, and the varieties of specialized knowledge they regularly drew upon: as moneylenders, farmers, gleaners, laborers, cooks, dairymaids and poultrykeepers, landholders, heiresses, deviants, raisers of the hue and cry (and hence involvement in local policing activity), brewers, textile producers, and more. It is well known that women performed every type of farm work, including the most physically demanding, plowing. Whether one argues for the subjugation of women under the identities and powers of their menfolk, or for the probability that they experienced the "satisfaction of doing productive work" (G. E. and K. R. Fussell) and lived their lives within a social role made up of many component parts besides gender, the court rolls and other local records show that women were everywhere present in the village, held land and were responsible for its rent and renderings, took oaths, had personal pledges, and in general answered for themselves in the public forum of the court. At the very least the court rolls and other related documents of practice provide ample evidence for complicating the story of gender relations, the formation of men's as well as women's identities in the countryside, and the gender history of work. In short, it is not merely because real, individual women and their activities are preserved in these materials, but also because these records are of such detailed nature, for men as well as women, that gender studies are possible: since the peasant economy and social structure were founded equally upon the labors of men and women, the world of work and all that fell within its influence are equally the product of such an economic partnership. The most famous countrywoman of the Middle Ages, Joan of Arc, might be cited as an example of a late medieval peasant woman whose life and beliefs are richly evidenced in the minutes of her trial and rehabilitation, whose peasant worldview and background produced an individual woman clearly "empowered" to act, and whose exceptionality, to modern eyes, might be tempered somewhat as gender studies continue to add to our knowledge.

SHERRI OLSON

References and Further Reading

Ault, W. O. "Open-Field Husbandry and the Village Community: A Study of Agrarian By-Laws in Medieval England." *Transactions of the American Philosophical Society* 55:7 (1965).

Balestracci, Duccio. *The Renaissance in the Fields: Family Memoirs of a Fifteenth-Century Tuscan Peasant*. University Park, Pa.: Pennsylvania State University Press, 1984.

Bennett, Judith. *A Medieval Life: Cecilia Penifader of Brigstock, c. 1295–1344*. Boston: McGraw-Hill, 1999.

———. *Women in the Medieval English Countryside: Gender and Household in Brigstock before the Plague*. New York: Oxford University Press, 1987.

Bloch, Marc. "From the Royal Court to the Court of Rome: The Suit of the Serfs of Rosny-sous-Bois." In *Change in Medieval Society: Europe North of the Alps, 1050–1500*, edited by Sylvia Thrupp. New York: Appleton-Century-Crofts, 1964, pp. 3–14.

Fussell, G. E., and K. R. Fussell. *The English Countrywoman: A Farmhouse Social History: The Internal Aspect of Rural Life, A.D. 1500–1900*. London: Melrose, 1953.

Gies, Frances, and Joseph Gies. *Life in a Medieval Village*. New York: Harper & Row, 1990.

Harvey P. D. A. "English Estate Records." In *Pragmatic Literacy East and West, 1200–1330*, edited by Richard Britnell. Woodbridge, Suffolk: Boydell Press, 1997, pp. 107–118.

———. *Manorial Records*. London: British Records Association, 1984.

Herlihy, David. *Medieval Households*. Cambridge, Mass.: Harvard University Press, 1985.

———. *Opera Muliebria: Women and Work in Medieval Europe*. New York: McGraw-Hill, 1990.

Homans, George. *English Villagers of the Thirteenth Century*. New York: Russell & Russell, 1960.

Olson, Sherri. *A Chronicle of All That Happens: Voices from the Village Court in Medieval England*. Toronto: PIMS, 1996.

See also **Administration of Estates; Agriculture; Alewives and Brewing; Gender Ideologies; Joan of Arc; Landholding and Property Rights; Law, Canon; Law, English Secular Courts of; Lay Piety; Merchet and Leyrwite; Migration and Mobility; Naming; Parishes; Peasants; Records, Ecclesiastical; Records, Urban; Servants; Sexuality, Regulation of; Spiritual Care; Work**

RECORDS, URBAN

The records generated within and by medieval towns provide scholars with fertile material, although, as with all medieval sources, men's activities are their central concern. This limitation is offset to some degree by the unusual variety and depth of urban records, generated in part because of the advantages of knowing how to read, write, and calculate in order to conduct business, the lifeblood of medieval towns. In southern European cities, notaries—the men whose job it was to write up and authenticate written contracts—were an important occupational group, as were the large concentrations of literate clerics associated with cathedrals and mendicant friaries, both of which tended to be in towns. The proliferation of different authorities in towns also helped to create a diversity of records from the bureaucratic machinery of lords, town governments, guilds, fraternities, parishes, and corporate landowners such as hospitals, bridge trusts, and religious institutions.

Literate culture was most advanced in southern Europe, especially in the highly urbanized region of northern Italy, where there were many self-governing towns from as early as the late twelfth century. Yet these republican forms of government, along with a marked Mediterranean preference for confining the activities of "reputable" women to family contacts, meant that the urban records of medieval Italy tend to offer limited glimpses into the life of townswomen. Notable exceptions include the detailed taxes administered by Tuscan towns, especially the *catasto* of 1427–1430 for Florence, which assessed some sixty thousand households in Florence and its hinterland according to the value of their real estate, investments, and cash. Since each declaration listed the name (and thus gender), age, and family relationship of members of the household, historical demographers have been able to calculate sex ratios (the number of men to every one hundred women) for specific age groups, wealth categories, and occupations. By comparing later *catasto* declarations and other records, scholars have also been able to derive the average age at marriage for women and men according to their social status and place of residence. The taxation records that survive for other towns are not as full, but taxes that list taxpayers and households (such as for the French town of Reims in 1422) also yield data on urban sex ratios, household size, and the percentage of single and married women. The nominative returns of national taxes, such as the English poll taxes of 1377, 1379, and 1381, provide similar data.

This information on the demographic profile of medieval towns can be supplemented by the Italian *ricordi*, a combination of family diary and business ledger kept by many rich merchants, particularly in Florence. Called *livres de raison* in southern France, these diaries record details about marriage negotiations, the births and deaths of children, the selection of godparents, and many other personal matters. It is the urban source that comes closest to revealing the emotions of family life, at least from the man's perspective. A less personal but equally valuable source for medieval towns is notarial registers, which contain documents drawn up by a licensed public notary. More typical of southern Europe because of the Mediterranean reliance on Roman law precedents, the notarial act could document wills, loans, dowries, apprenticeship agreements, and many other types of contracts. In northern Europe, such contracts appeared in different venues: enrolled on a town's court rolls, in a register of deeds, or even a cartulary of charters kept by civic, monastic, or individual landowners.

Town court rolls are more likely to survive for northern towns, especially in England, although they are also extant for some southern cities such as Marseille, while criminal court proceedings can be found for most towns. In England, the leet courts have furnished especially full information on women's work because they name those charged with market and quality-of-life infractions, such as brewing or selling ale improperly, retailing food or drink outside the approved time and market place, maintaining a brothel, and even spreading malicious gossip, a "crime" with which men were only rarely assessed. Guild records, including ordinances, courts, and contracts, have also been mined successfully for insights into the waged work of women, particularly in the more organized ends of the textile and food trades, which attracted many female workers.

Town ordinances or custumals (written compilations of "how things are done" in a particular town) do not name individuals, but they do lay out laws with gendered implications, including such matters as inheritance customs, the legal status of women in trade, and juridical privileges. Medieval Spain has a particularly rich body of this material, called *fueros*, which also often specified the different rights of Muslims, Jews, and Christian settlers in the frontier towns. Finally, there are various literary sources that speak to the urban experience of medieval women, including Chaucer's tale of the Wife of Bath, the Middle English poem "How the Good Wife Taught Her Daughter," and the Old French handbook *The Menagier of Paris*, in which an aged but fastidious rich merchant gives advice to his much younger wife on how to manage a large urban household.

MARYANNE KOWALESKI

References and Further Reading

Branca, Vittore, ed. *Merchant Writers of the Italian Renaissance*, translated by Murtha Baca. New York: Marsilio Publishers, 1986.

Goldberg, P. J. P., ed. and trans. *Women in England c. 1275–1525: Documentary Sources*. Manchester: Manchester University Press, 1995.

Herlihy, David. "Women and the Sources of Medieval History: The Towns of Northern Italy." In *Medieval Women and the Sources of Medieval History*, edited by Joel T. Rosenthal. Athens, Ga.: University of Georgia Press, 1990, pp. 133–154.

Kowaleski, Maryanne, ed. *Medieval Towns: A Reader*. Peterborough, Ont.: Broadview Press, 2005.

Power, Eileen, ed. and trans. *The Goodman of Paris (Le Ménagier de Paris): A Treatise on Moral and Domestic Economy by a Citizen of Paris (c. 1393)*. London: George Routledge and Sons, 1928.

See also **Alewives and Brewing; Artisan Families, Women of; Cities and Towns; Crime and Criminals; Conduct Literature; Demography; Family (Later Middle Ages); Feme Covert; Feme Sole; Guild Members and Guilds; Market and Tradeswomen; Merchant Families, Women of; Records, Ecclesiastical; Sumptuary Law; Wife of Bath; Wills; Work**

REGENTS AND QUEEN-LIEUTENANTS

The offices of queen-regent and queen-lieutenant are similar in that, in both cases, the queen is a consort who rules in an official capacity, not in her own name but rather in place of a king. In both offices, the queen is the legal embodiment of the king's authority and serves as custodian of the realm; they are not heritable. The positions differ significantly, however. The regency was ad hoc, created because a king's youth, illness, or captivity impaired his ability to rule, and it was widely used throughout medieval Europe and into the modern era. The office of the queen-lieutenant, on the other hand, was a distinctive form of permanent delegated authority used by the kings in the medieval Crown of Aragon. The queen-lieutenant governed both in place of and with an adult king who was fully capable of ruling but was unable to govern a particular territory (or territories). As a permanent office, it was held at the king's discretion and constituted a unique form of monarchical co-rulership.

Regencies differed greatly from place to place in terms of the age of royal majority, the scope of authority, and the need for and composition of a regency council. Because it had a predetermined beginning and end, the regency was palatable to ambitious and opportunistic brothers, uncles, and nobles who would otherwise feel threatened by a ruling queen. A queen-regent's authority was considered the legal extension of her maternal rights as the guardian of her son and thus the protector of both king and kingdom. But regents could be any member of the family; for instance, Anne of Beaujeu was regent and guardian for her brother, Charles VIII, from 1483–1488.

Many queen-regents wielded considerable power, notably Adela of Blois, for Louis VII of France (1137–1180); Blanche of Castile (1188–1252) governed forcefully for Louis IX (1226–1279) during his minority (1226–1244) and while he was on Crusade (1248–1252). In Castile, María de Molina was regent for both her son, Fernando IV (1295–1312), and her grandson, Alfonso XI (1312–1350). Byzantine Empress Irene, the Athenian, was regent for her son Constantine VI (753–803) during the contentious Iconoclastic period. A regency was a potent but dangerous time, especially for foreign-born queens who ruled on behalf of weak kings, notably Isabelle of France, regent for Edward III (1327–1377) in England after the deposition of Edward II in 1322; Margaret of Anjou, regent for Henry VI (1422–1461) during his illnesses; and Isabeau of Bavaria during the illnesses of Charles VI (1380–1422) in France. Regencies were often contentious, as when ambitious family members, unwilling to cede authority to a queen-regent, bypassed Catherine of Valois when Henry V of England died in 1422.

Whereas the regency's origins extend to the earliest known kings, the governmental lieutenancy was devised by the kings of the Crown of Aragon in the thirteenth century to rule their varied and dispersed Mediterranean territories. Originally the prerogative of princes, by 1300 the lieutenancy became associated with Aragonese queens, who were prohibited from ruling in their own right. A queen-lieutenant governed with fully sanctioned *de jure* and *de facto* authority. Her official status was roughly equivalent to the king's, and she was empowered to assume the routine business of government, including convocation of parliamentary assemblies and, more rarely, direction of military matters. In practice the king retained the power to withhold assent or revoke a queen-lieutenant's authority.

In all, seven Aragonese queens served as lieutenants, but three in particular are noteworthy: María de Luna, María of Castile, and Juana Enríquez. María de Luna, wife of Martin (1395–1410), was one of her husband's ablest advisers. She pacified the kingdom and governed for a year until Martin's return from Sicily, where he was king, and served a second term as lieutenant in 1401 while Martin was away. María of Castile governed as lieutenant of Catalonia for her husband, Alfonso V (1416–1458), for a longer span of time (1420–1423 and 1432–1453) and with greater authority than any of her predecessors. She maintained a court separate from the king's at Naples, took council from her own royal council, regularly presided over parliamentary assemblies, and advocated the manumission of the *remences*, semi-servile Catalan peasants. The last Aragonese queen-lieutenant, Juana Enríquez, ruled closely with her husband, Juan II (1458–1479). She proved her worth as his right hand during the tumult of civil war (1462–1472), governed Girona during the siege, and became lieutenant in her own right in 1465. The office of the queen-lieutenant was discontinued when Isabel la Católica (1474–1504) succeeded to Castile as queen in her own right.

THERESA EARENFIGHT

References and Further Reading

Coll Juliá, Nuria. *Doña Juana Enríquez, lugarteniente real en Cataluña, 1461–68*. 2 volumes. Madrid: Consejo Superior de Investigaciones Científicas, 1953.

Collins, Roger. "Queens-Dowager and Queens-Regent in Tenth-Century León and Navarre." In *Medieval Queenship*, edited by John Carmi Parsons. New York: St. Martin's Press, 1993, pp. 79–92.

Cosandey, Fanny. *La Reine de France: symbole et pouvoir, XVe–XVIIIe siècle*. Paris: Gallimard, 2000.

Earenfight, Theresa. "Queenship, Politics, and Government in the Medieval Crown of Aragon: The Lieutenancy of Maria of Castile, 1420–23 and 1432–53." Doctoral dissertation, Fordham University, New York, 1997.

Facinger, Marion. "A Study of Medieval Queenship: Capetian France, 987–1327." *Studies in Medieval and Renaissance History* 5 (1968): 1–48.

Gaibrois de Ballasteros, Mercedes. *María de Molina, tres veces reina*. Madrid: Espasa-Calpe, 1936.

James, Liz. "Goddess, Whore, Wife or Slave?: Will the Real Byzantine Empress Please Stand Up?" In *Queens and Queenship in Medieval Europe*, edited by Anne J. Duggan. Woodbridge, Suffolk: Boydell Press, 1997, pp. 123–139.

Lightman, Harriet. "Political Power and the Queen of France: Pierre DuPuy's Treatise on Regency Government." *Canadian Journal of History* 21 (1986): 299–312.

Maurer, Helen. *Margaret of Anjou: Queenship and Power in Late Medieval England*. Woodbridge, Suffolk: Boydell Press, 2003.

Poulet, André. "Capetian Women and the Regency: The Genesis of a Vocation." In *Medieval Queenship*, edited by John Carmi Parsons. New York: St. Martin's Press, 1993, pp. 93–116.

Shadis, Miriam T. "Motherhood, Lineage, and Royal Power in Medieval Castile and France: Berenguela de León and Blanche de Castile." Ph.D. dissertation, Duke University, 1994.

Silleras-Fernández, Núria. "María de Luna, una reina entre la piedad y el poder (1396–1406)." Doctoral dissertation, Universitat Autònoma de Barcelona, 2002.

See also **Adela of Blois; Anne of Beaujeu; Blanche of Castile; Empresses: Byzantium; Iberia; Irene; Margaret of Anjou; Queens and Empresses: The West**

RELICS AND RELIQUARIES

Relics—the physical remains of saints and holy people or objects associated with them—were, in many ways, the most potent source of power in the Middle Ages. Saints were held to be alive and present in their bodily remains, as even the smallest bit possessed the complete presence of the saint (*pars pro toto*, the part implies the whole). Relics manifested the terrestrial presence of the saints, thereby providing a palpable connection between heaven and earth. As such, they were the most valued possessions of a church, monastery, or community. Among the most potent functions of relics was the performance of miracles, particularly thaumaturgies, which imbued them with numinous authority. Relics assured the *praesentia* (presence) of the saints. Miracles demonstrated their *potentia* (power). This miraculous presence is illustrated by a fourteenth-century account that records how thirteen heads of the eleven thousand virgins, placed on the main altar of the Cistercian abbey at Esrom, Denmark, miraculously began singing a response to the *Te Deum* at Matins during the Christmas Eve vigil. The eleventh-century *Book of Sainte Foy's Miracles* (*Liber miraculorum sancta-ae Fidis*) from Conques is replete with examples of miracles effected by the saint's relics, such the resuscitation of Goteline, the wife of Roger, a Norman nobleman (Book 3.1).

There are three classes of relics: primary relics (the saint's body or portions thereof), secondary relics (objects that came into contact with the saint, such as clothing), and tertiary relics (items that touched primary or secondary relics—generally oils and strips of cloth, known as *brandea*). Though doubtless as old as Christianity itself, the veneration of relics is attested to in the *passio* of St. Polycarp (martyred c. 155), in which his disciples gather his bones as "more precious than gold." Due to their peerless value, relics became the focus of a sacral economy in which they were both legitimately traded and relocated through pious theft. By the ninth century the cult of relics was widespread, constantly serving as the impetus to the development of new artistic and literary forms, from church architecture and reliquaries to hagiographic tropes and *legendae*.

Because of their tremendous value, relics were secured in containers (reliquaries), fashioned out of precious materials. Generally a complete body would be kept in a tomb, while smaller fragments would be placed into reliquaries, which allowed them greater portability. Reliquaries could be carried in procession, allowing the saint to attend ecclesiastic councils, reclaim usurped land, and generally assert an active presence in the community. By the associative property of tertiary relics, reliquaries themselves accrued the numinous aura of their contents, often being linked, even conflated, with the relics they contained and presented. While somewhat due to natural tendencies toward conceptual conflation of related objects, much of this was due to the practice of only showing relics within their reliquaries—a practice formalized in 1215 with the Fourth Lateran Council's forbidding of the display of relics outside their reliquaries. This conflation between container and contents was particularly vivid with anthropomorphic reliquaries, which appeared as radiant epidermal layers, literally reconstituting the saint's body.

Early reliquaries were frequently made in casket or purse form, fashioned from gold and ivory and decorated with precious gems and enamels. While this reliquary type endured throughout the Middle Ages, other forms developed. Figural reliquaries—frequently full figures, heads, or arms—visually fleshed out the belief in the reconstituted presence of the saint in her/his relics. The performative potential of body-part reliquaries ensured their popularity. First documented in the ninth century, anthropomorphic reliquaries increased in number by the twelfth century, eventually becoming virtually ubiquitous by the fourteenth and fifteenth centuries. Other reliquary forms existed, such as the ostensory or monstrance, which from the thirteenth century displayed relics in a manner similar to the Host, fostering the link between saint and Christ (*imitatio Christi*). The use of crystal in ostensories permitted visual communion with the relics—a facet of the phenomenon of increasing personal devotional interaction.

The value of reliquaries often exceeded the cost of the buildings in which they were housed (the most famous example being the Sainte-Chapelle in Paris, built to hold Louis IX's collection of Passion relics). The possession of relics was frequently the impetus to embark upon elaborate building campaigns (as was the case with the Virgin's tunic at Chartres). The importance of relics in medieval culture cannot be overstated, as they literally formed the core of church and community. A city was defined by its patron saints—generally present in relics, which lent authority through the implied saintly sanction and often brought great economic benefit via donations and pilgrimage. Throughout the Middle Ages, relics were the goal of pilgrims who traveled to be in the presence of the saints, embodied in their relics. Furthermore, canon law required that all consecrated altars contain relics—a practice that ensured both the ubiquity and the propinquity of relics.

Naturally, primary relics were the most sought after, as they most potently asserted the saint's real, physical presence. However, resultant from the Ascension of Christ and Assumption of the Virgin, primary relics of these two most important figures in Christianity were relatively scarce, aside from Christ's milk-teeth, blood, and foreskin(s), as well as hair and milk of the Virgin (at Saint-Denis and Saint-Omer, among other locations). Their secondary relics were thus highly valued, particularly the abundant Passion relics.

Among the most highly regarded relics were important secondary relics of the Virgin Mary, particularly the *Sancta camisia*, the tunic worn by the Virgin at Christ's birth, held at Chartres Cathedral from the ninth century. The *Santa cintola* in Prato Cathedral was believed to be the belt of the Virgin, handed to the apostle Thomas as proof of her bodily assumption. Both relics were the object of significant pilgrimages and fostered important artistic and building programs. Bodies and body parts of virgin martyrs were abundant, most notably those of the eleven thousand virgins of Cologne (companions of Ursula), whose relics could be found in every corner of Europe by the fourteenth century, and Roman martyrs, such as Agnes, whose body is venerated in her titular church in Rome. Relics of great monastic role models were

prized, including Mary Magdalen at Vezelay and Clare at Assisi. Reliquaries could even be commissioned as part of propaganda campaigns for canonization, as was the case with the c. 1360 reliquary bust of Beata Umiliana dei Cerchi, a lay penitent, in Santa Croce, Florence.

Women were vital and prolific in the patronage and use of relics and reliquaries. The most famous of relic gatherers was Emperor Constantine's mother, Helena, whose early-fourth-century excursion to the Holy Land uncovered the True Cross, the Holy Sepulchre, and other sites associated with the life and Passion of Christ. Helena set the template for intense relic devotion among many royal women throughout the Middle Ages who sought to follow her example. The fourteenth-century Shrine of Elizabeth of Hungary in the Cloisters Collection of the Metropolitan Museum of Art and the Klaren-Altar in Cologne Cathedral (c. 1347, originally from the monastery of Clares in Cologne) are examples of lavish reliquary altarpieces commissioned by royal or noble women.

Though not exclusive to female monastics, intense and dramatic veneration and display of relics was common among nuns. In the twelfth century, Elisabeth of Schönau communed with the head of Verena (one of the companions of Ursula) to learn the identity of many of the eleven thousand virgins of Cologne. It is significant that the revelations were delivered by a female saint to a female mystic. This underscores the way in which the cult of the female martyrs spoke directly to women—particularly through their presence in their relics. This close, affective piety was often associated with female spirituality by clerics, possibly due to long held associations between women and matter, hence bodily/physical forms of piety. A particularly intimate and visceral form of relic veneration—osculation (kissing)—is often linked to women, such as the head of St. Just being kissed by his mother after his decapitation.

As an inextricable aspect of the cult of saints, relic veneration was virtually ubiquitous, as was the practice of preserving and presenting these holy remains inside lavish reliquaries. As such, this is an aspect of medieval religion that transcends gender—in form, patronage, and use. Nonetheless, the cult of relics was closely associated with female piety.

SCOTT B. MONTGOMERY

References and Further Reading

Angenendt, Arnold. *Heilige und Reliquien: Die Geschichte ihres Kultes vom frühen Christentum bis zur Gegenwart.* Munich: C. H. Beck, 1994.

Braun, Joseph. *Die Reliquiare des christlichen Kultes und ihre Entwicklung.* Freiburg im Breisgau: Herder, 1924.

Gauthier, Marie-Madeleine. *Highways of the Faith: Relics and Reliquaries from Jerusalem to Compostela*, translated by J. A. Underwood. Secaucus, N.J.: Wellfleet, 1986.

Geary, Patrick J. Furta Sacra: *Thefts of Relics in the Central Middle Ages*. Princeton, N.J.: Princeton University Press, 1978.

———. *Living with the Dead in the Middle Ages*. Ithaca, N.Y.: Cornell University Press, 1994.

Herrmann-Mascard, Nicole. *Les reliques des saints. Formation coutumière d'un droit*. Paris: Klincksieck, 1975.

Legner, Anton, ed. *Ornamenta ecclesiae: Katalog zur Austellung des Schnütgen-Museums in der Josef-Haubrich-Kunsthalle*, 3 vols. Cologne: Stadt Köln, 1985.

———. *Reliquien: Verehrung und Verklärung, Skizzen und Noten zur Thematik und Katalog zur Ausstellung der Kölner Sammlung Louis Peters im Schütgen-Museum*. Cologne: Schütgen-Museum, 1989.

Montgomery, Scott B. "The Use and Perception of Reliquary Busts in the Late Middle Ages." Ph.D. Dissertation, Rutgers University, 1996.

See also **Clare of Assisi; Devotional Practices; Elisabeth of Schönau; Hagiography; Hagiography, Iconographic Aspects of; Helena; Jacobus de Voragine's Golden Legend; Mary Magdalen; Mary, Virgin; Miracles and Miracle Collections; Patronage, Ecclesiastical; Pilgrims and Pilgrimage; Spirituality, Christian; Ursula and Her Companions; Virgin Martyrs**

REMARRIAGE

Throughout the Middle Ages there was a sharp distinction between the Church and secular society on the issue of remarriage. For the most part, but not always, social and economic factors encouraged remarriage while the Church discouraged it.

There is no doubt that the Church prevailed, beginning as early as legislation passed by Constantine I (306–337) and Theodosius II (408–450), in greatly restricting access to divorce, which had been common among the Romans and certainly was one occasion for remarriage. Leo I (440–461) equated remarriage after divorce with adultery. Canon law came to allow separations from bed and table (*a mensa et thoro*) without the right to remarry. Only a full annulment would allow a remarriage, which then technically was not a remarriage.

Remarriage occurred in the context of death. Church approval came, if reluctantly, as a remedy for fornication by widows and widowers. Generally, however, the surviving spouse was discouraged from remarrying. Widows, along with orphans and the abject poor, figured among the miserable (*miserabiles personae*) who were the special objects of ecclesiastical and royal charity and protection. Sermons by Bernardino of Siena (1380–1444) and other late medieval preachers urged women to embrace a chaste widowhood that was projected as a second virginity. The

relative prevalence, where demographic data is available, of widows in comparison to widowers would indicate some success in this regard. Still, decisions to remarry, like those to marry in the first place, responded to social needs and concerns.

The reality for most households, with some exceptions among elites, was that the surviving spouse sought a new partner very quickly. Marriage and remarriage absorbed more poor girls in comparison to elites, whose girls in greater proportion headed to monasteries. Men remarried faster and more frequently, as they needed a wife's labor and a means of having children or caring for those already at hand; but women too needed male labor, managerial acumen, and legal stature. Landholdings and shops in which women generally could not succeed to ownership had to replace lost male owners. By the late Middle Ages craft guilds often stepped in to govern widows' remarriages and their rights to continue the shop. Men who married such heiresses were seeking social advancement, thus possibly marrying a woman older than themselves; but many widowers took younger brides.

Remarriage was most difficult for women in elite classes, especially in southern Europe, where the Roman law of dowry prevailed and lineage continuity weighed heavily. In much of northern Europe, where wives had inheritance rights to household assets, they had incentive to remain in the home, remarried or unmarried. In places like central and northern Italy and southern France, a social dilemma revolved around where widows were to live. They could remain in their husbands' homes, raising children, if any. They could return to their natal homes, and rights to do so were spelled out in law in some places. Or, especially if they were still fairly young and capable of having children, they might be married again, creating another useful family alliance for their kin.

While a widow's remarriage might help her family, it could be disastrous for her deceased husband's kin, which included his children. A remarrying widow would generally leave her children behind, to be raised by others, and she would demand the return of her dowry, which could pose a financial problem. Stereotypes of remarrying widows as capricious and greedy, dangerous, sexual, and even cruel abounded. A remarrying widow who had guardianship over her children (*tutela*) lost it by virtue of allying herself in marriage to another. Any children she might have with her second husband would have only weak inheritance rights to their uterine brothers and sisters. For example, the Florentine Luca da Panzano split his mother's property with his half-brother, Luca Carnesecchi, but these men could only leave small bequests to each other in their wills as long as they had close, agnate kin.

The converse was that, for widowers who re-married, their second set of progeny had equal rights of succession to him along with their consanguine siblings. Widowers' remarriages brought adult females' labor, procreativity, sexual companionship, and dowry into the house. Second wives might well be as young as typical first wives.

Practices were reflected in literary texts. On the one hand, there were caricatures of widows (including Chaucer's Wife of Bath), while there were few of widowers (except that of the pathetic old man remar-rying and not satisfying a young wife). On the other hand, there were images and concerns about step-mothers, but few about stepfathers. Remarriage, es-pecially of an older man with a new bride, was not met with total approval. In forms of "rough music," *charivari* (in France), young men openly harassed such couples, expressing a ritualized disapproval of a union that, among other things, removed a potential bride from their grasp. Clerical synods in Italian dioceses frequently passed decrees forbidding clerical blessing of second marriage, or at least curtailed nuptial rites, so as not to call attention to them.

THOMAS KUEHN

References and Further Reading

Cavallo, Sandra, and Lyndan Warner, eds. *Widowhood in Medieval and Early Modern Europe*. London: Longman, 1999.

Herlihy, David. *Medieval Households*. Cambridge, Mass.: Harvard University Press, 1985.

Howell, Martha C. *The Marriage Exchange: Property, Social Place, and Gender in Cities of the Low Countries, 1300–1550*. Chicago: University of Chicago Press, 1998.

Klapisch-Zuber, Christiane. *Women, Family, and Ritual in Renaissance Italy*, translated by Lydia G. Cochrane. Chicago: University of Chicago Press, 1985.

Mirrer, Louise, ed. *Upon My Husband's Death: Widows in the Literature and Histories of Medieval Europe*. Ann Arbor, Mich.: University of Michigan Press, 1992.

Sheehan, Michael M. *Marriage, Family, and Law in Medieval Europe: Collected Studies*, edited by James K. Farge. Toronto: University of Toronto Press, 1996.

See also **Charivari; Chastity and Chaste Marriage; Divorce and Separation; Widows**

RENAISSANCE, HISTORIOGRAPHY OF

In his exaltation of the individual and the secular, Jacob Burckhardt's *The Civilization of the Renaissance on Italy* (1860; English translation 1890) presented a glowing portrait of women as the equals of men in education, poetry, and authority: "There was no ques-tion of 'women's rights' or female emancipation, simply because the thing itself was a matter of course." For him, the term *virago* was a compliment, meaning a woman had the heart and soul of a man. Courtesans, too, were accomplished and respected. A Swiss Protes-tant, Burckhardt rescued the Italians, beginning with Dante, Petrarch, and Boccaccio, from the intellectual darkness, superstition, and Catholicism of the "Mid-dle Ages," and swept them up into the "Renaissance," which found its fulfilment in the Enlightenment of northern Europe.

Although he used primary sources, Burckhardt's choice was not only highly selective, and colored by his desire to define the "spirit of the age," but it led to his commission of the original sin of historians, that is, confusing fictional accounts about women (Casti-glione and Bandello are favourites) with archival documentary ones. A further confusion lay in assum-ing that classical antiquity, Greek or Latin, advanced women's equality. While noting the presence of mi-sogyny in Renaissance writings, Burckhardt simply dismissed it as misleading; even more, he subsumed women into the same paradigm he developed for men.

Resulting histories gave little attention to women, limiting discussion to a section on a few outstanding rulers, writers, saints, and patrons of the court. When Paul Oskar Kristeller, the pioneer of Renaissance history of philosophy, focused on women and educa-tion in the Renaissance ("Learned Women of Early Modern Europe: Humanists and University Scho-lars," first appearing in Patricia Labalme's *Beyond Their Sex: Learned Women of the European Past*, 1980; and then in Kristeller's collected articles, *Stud-ies in Renaissance Thought and Letters*, 1985), he di-rected his assessment along more sober paths. The role of women was not prominent, and could not be so, because of the vast gender gap in education. At the secondary level, education was for boys alone; women were not allowed to attend schools where Latin and Greek were taught. Whatever instruction they might receive from tutors and kind relatives, they never went to university, where the curriculum trained young men for the professions, mainly in law and medicine, and from there to a public life that excluded women. The in-depth studies of Paul E. Grendler prove this conclusively.

With the initiative of women scholars researching their own past, historiography has made a decisive turn. Since the boom in women's studies beginning in the 1960s and 1970s, enormous advances have been made in our knowledge of the number of women writing and participating in public life. In addition, there has been marked progress in under-standing social and cultural conditions that both fos-tered and impeded women's progress. Joan Gadol Kelly threw down the gauntlet in "Did Women

Have a Renaissance?" (*Becoming Visible: Women in European History*, 1977). Addressing historians in the Burckhardt and Kristeller vein, who understood the Renaissance from a male perspective, her answer was a provocative "no." Kelly argued that, during the fifteenth, sixteenth, and seventeenth centuries, in all areas of society, whether within the family, marriage, or the Church, women were subject to the male authority of fathers, brothers, husbands, and priests. Power that they might achieve, say, as widows or rulers, was often by accident, not by right. Lisa Jardine followed with another pointed question: "Women Humanists: Education for What?" The humanist education program was flawed, argued Jardine; it offered to teach women the humanities and at the same time forbade them from using it in a public life. It proclaimed that classical education made men virtuous and ethically superior; but at the same time made women unnatural and unchaste. Fifteenth-century women suffered because of intellectual brilliance. Their works were ignored by men, or not published, or vilified. Ian Maclean's *The Renaissance Notion of Women* (1980) studies the position of women in scholastic Aristotelian philosophy, natural science, theology, and law to arrive at the depressing conclusion that in all areas women were deemed inferior because they were lacking in rationality, and, therefore, had to be under the control of (rational!) males at all times. Nevertheless, a study of dialogues and treatises by and about women in the sixteenth century and first half of the seventeenth century reveals a deeper awareness that women are servile not by nature but by social and cultural factors, and, given a chance, are just as capable of men.

Rather than writing histories with a chapter or two on women, women (and men) have dedicated themselves to writing histories about women and Renaissance culture and society on the one hand, and to resurrecting and translating an ever-increasing number of genres, some originally in Latin but mostly written in Italian, French, German, and Spanish, on the other. A vast five-volume *History of Women in the West*, with Georges Duby and Michelle Perrot as general editors, first appeared in 1990 and in English translation in 1992 with contributions from seventy-five historians. It indicates the swing in historical perspectives. Great strides have been made in studying factors determining women's position in family structures (see the numerous studies of Christiane Klapisch-Zuber and David Herlihy), defining the significance of the dowry (see Stanley Chojnacki), revealing the exceptions to conventional marriages revealed by archives of marriage tribunals (see Silvana Seidel Menchi), and publishing on women as the "devout "sex" (see Gabriella Zarri). Life in the

monastery has come out from the shadows; some convents encouraged women to write and perform plays (see Elissa Weaver) or to write chronicles (see Kate Lowe); light has been shed on the life of nuns in Venetian convents, which existed as boarding houses for girls without vocation but whose families would not let them marry (see Mary Laven and Francesca Medioli for differing evaluations of Venetian nunneries). Collections of essays explore a variety of cultural and social issues affecting women (see Letizia Panizza; also, in the 1990s Cambridge University Press inaugurated a series on Women Writers in France, Italy, Germany, Spain, and Russia).

Her Immaculate Hand (1983), edited by Margaret L. King and Albert Rabil, Jr., brought together selected works by Italian women humanists, and put them in their historical and cultural context. The book shows them proficient in public orations, debates, and formal letters to other humanists. King went on to *Women of the Renaissance* (1991), a wide-ranging synthesis of European women's condition, bringing together a wealth of detailed studies; and both authors initiated a magnificent project aptly named "The Other Voice in Early Modern Europe" (University of Chicago Press: http://www.press.uchicago.edu/Complete/Series/OVIEME.html). The first volume came out in 1996. For the very first time in scholarly English translation, with notes and introductions, we "hear" women who are courtesans, nuns, polemicists, proto-Protestants, dramatists, epic writers, poets, and letter writers. Oxford University Press has published a volume edited and translated by Jane Stevenson of one thousand women Latin poets. What emerges is that periodization that works for history from a male perspective does not work for women, who come into their own at the tail end of the "Renaissance." Historiography still has to digest the explosion of primary and secondary material in women's studies in order detect directions leading to future developments.

One area that has not been fully explored is the negative impact on the Renaissance perception of women brought about by the rediscovery of ancient Greek and Latin texts and early Christian ones. The Greeks, with the exception of some essays of Plutarch, looked down on women, exalting homoerotic love. Romans valued marriage as a civic duty, yet Cicero and Seneca termed sexual pleasures base and considered friendship higher, since it demanded equality, a virtue that could exist only between males. For Greek Christian writers like Chrysostom, virginity alone gave women value; and in the Latin tradition Jerome above all denounced marriage and women's sexuality, especially in *Adversus Jovinianum*, already well known in the Middle Ages. Only a brave man, or later woman, could ignore or deny the towering authorities of Jerome and Augustine, who shared similar views.

LETIZIA PANIZZA

References and Further Reading

Burckhardt, Jacob. *The Civilization of the Renaissance on Italy*, translated by Samuel George Chetwynd Middlemore. London: Sonnenschein & Co., 1890.

Cox, Virginia. "The Single Self: Feminist Thought and the Marriage Market in Early Modern Venice." *Renaissance Quarterly* 48 (1995): 513–581.

Duby, Georges, and Michelle Perrot. *History of Women in the West*, 5 vols. Cambridge, Mass.: Belknap Press of Harvard University Press, 1992–1994.

Grendler, Paul E. *Schooling in Renaissance Italy: Literacy and Learning 1300-1600*. Baltimore, Md.: Johns Hopkins University Press, 1989.

———. *The Universities of the Italian Renaissance*. Baltimore: Johns Hopkins University Press, 2002.

Jardine, Lisa. "Women Humanists: Education for What?" In *From Humanism to the Humanities: Education and the Liberal Arts in Fifteenth- and Sixteenth-Century Europe*, edited by Anthony Grafton and Lisa Jardine. London: Duckworth, 1986, pp. 29–57.

Kelly, Joan Gadol. "Did Women Have a Renaissance?" In *Becoming Visible: Women in European History*, edited by Renate Bridenthal and Claudia Koonz. Boston: Houghton Mifflin, 1977, pp. 137–164.

King, Margaret L., and Albert Rabil, Jr., eds. *Her Immaculate Hand: Selected Works by and about the Women Humanists of Quattrocento Italy*. Binghamton, N.Y.: Center for Medieval and Early Renaissance Studies, 1983.

Kristeller, Paul Oskar. "Learned Women of Early Modern Europe: Humanists and University Scholars." In *Beyond Their Sex: Learned Women of the European Past*, edited by Patricia Labalme. New York: New York University Press, 1980, pp. 91–116.

Maclean, Ian. *The Renaissance Notion of Women: A Study in the Fortunes of Scholasticism and Medical Science in European Intellectual Life*. Cambridge: Cambridge University Press, 1980.

Stevenson, Jane, ed. *Women Latin Poets: Language, Gender, and Authority, from Antiquity to the Eighteenth Century*. Chicago: University of Chicago Press, 2005.

See also **Aristotelian Concepts of Women and Gender; Augustine, Influence of; Education, Lay; Feminist Theories and Methodologies; Gender Ideologies; Gender in History; History, Medieval Women's; Humanism; Jerome, Influence of; Literacy and Reading: Latin; Literacy and Reading: Vernacular; Nogarola, Isotta; Women Authors: Italian Texts; Women Authors: Latin Texts**

RÉPONSE DU BESTIAIRE D'AMOUR

Appended to four manuscripts of Richard de Fournival's *Bestiaire d'amour* is an intriguing, protofeminist work that was unique in the Middle Ages and remains unique today. Very little information about its author can be deduced from the codicological evidence. The rubrics of two of the manuscripts say that it was written by *la dame* as a response/refusal to Richard's love-bestiary. The other two manuscripts provide no information at all.

The author begins with a prologue that is clearly intended to challenge Richard's priorities and, most particularly, his attitudes toward love. Richard, who at the time of writing *Le Bestiaire d'amour* was the chancellor of Notre Dame d'Amiens, had begun his somewhat misogynistic work by extolling the ancients and the glories of *savoir* (knowledge). The author of the *Réponse*, however, begins by reproaching Richard for his values, asserting that a man of sense and discretion should not waste his time perpetrating damage, but should instead pay attention to the *non-sachans*, i.e., the nonlearned, many of whom were, of course, women.

She then begins what is essentially a defense of women by asserting that God in His courtesy made woman to be the nobler creation. She demonstrates this by a heterodox rendering of the Creation story (Genesis 2:23), narrating that in a dual creation God first made a man and a woman out of dust. But Adam killed that first woman, explaining to God that he did not love her, she was nothing to him. God then created Eve, whom Adam loved at first sight because she was made from his own flesh. Thus Adam is, in this account, a petulant malcontent, a bigamist (by medieval standards), and a murderer. He was even, "according to certain authorities," responsible for original sin—it was the man, not the woman, who, by following the dictates of his senses, "brought us the evil/suffering for which we are now all in pain."

Having substituted her female frame of reference for Richard's clerical misogyny, the author now modifies Richard's male-oriented love symbolism by moving systematically, animal by animal, through Richard's love bestiary. For example, the crowing of the introductory animal, the cock, no longer represents Richard's desperate cries for love; those piercing, penetrating cries now represent threat. And whereas Richard, playing the unicorn, had made the maiden responsible for his love-death, she finds that the unicorn with its fierce horn is the creature she most fears—there is nothing so wounding (*trenchans*) as (Richard's) fair speech.

Thus, thematic to *Le Bestiaire d'amour* is the threat posed by the love of woman. Thematic to the *Réponse*, however, is the threat posed to women's honor by men and, more specifically, clerics. Clerics, she puns, are preying/praying bids (*oiseaux de proie*) who, with charming words, draw women into love relationships, to the detriment of both sexes. If circumstances had been different, the woman could have

709

married an honest chevalier who would have supported her honorably, and the cleric would have received a prebend and have risen to a position of prestige in the Church. In one of her few literary references, *la dame* angrily berates Richard as "Renart," exclaiming "how far out your tongue is hanging!" The attack is typical of her down-to-earth realism. The woman author has, by the immediacy of her responses and the cogency of her logic, created a work that is as universal as it was medieval.

JEANETTE BEER

References and Further Reading

Beer, Jeanette. *Beasts of Love: Richard de Fournival's* Bestiaire d'amour *and a Woman's Response.* Toronto: University of Toronto Press, 2003.

———. "Le *Bestiaire d'amour* en vers." In *Medieval Translators and Their Craft*, edited by Jeanette Beer. Kalamazoo, Mich.: Medieval Institute Publications, 1989.

———. "Duel of Bestiaries." In *Beasts and Birds of the Middle Ages: The Bestiary and Its Legacy*, edited by Willene B. Clark and Meradith T. McMunn, Philadelphia: University of Pennsylvania Press, 1989, pp. 96–105.

———. "Gendered Discourse in Two Thirteenth-Century Texts." *Journal of the Institute of Romance Studies* 3 (1994–1995): 27–32.

———. "Woman, Authority and the Book in the Middle Ages." In *Women, the Book and the Worldly*, edited by Lesley Smith and Jane H. M. Taylor, Cambridge: Cambridge University Press, 1993, pp. 61–69.

de Fournival, Richard. *Le Bestiaire d'amour* suivi de la *Réponse de la dame*, edited by C. Hippeau. Paris: Aubry, 1860. Reprint, Geneva: Slatkin, 1969, 1978.

———. *Li Bestiaires d'amours di Maistre Richart de Fornival e li response du Bestiaire*, edited by Cesare Segre. Milan and Naples: Riccardo Riccardi, 1957.

———. *Master Richard's* Bestiary of Love *and* Response, translated by Jeanette Beer and illustrated by Barry Moser. West Hatfield, Mass.: PennyRoyal Press, 1985.

———. *Master Richard's* Bestiary of Love *and Response*, translated, with preface, by Jeanette Beer and illustrated by Barry Moser. Berkeley: University of California Press, 1986. Reprint, West Lafayette, Ind.: Purdue University Press, 2000.

Krueger, Roberta L. *Women Readers and the Ideology of Gender in Old French Verse Romances.* Cambridge: Cambridge University Press, 1993.

Solterer, Helen. *The Master and Minerva.* Berkeley, Calif.: University of California Press, 1995.

See also **Beast Epic; Celibacy: Clerical and Priests' Concubines; Debate Literature; Defenses of Women; Eve; Literature, Old French; Misogyny**

ROMAN DE FLAMENCA

The mid-thirteenth-century Occitan romance *Flamenca* or *Las Novas de Guillem de Nivers* consists of 8,096 lines of octosyllabic rhymed couplets and survives in one manuscript (Carcassone, Bibl. Mun. 35) that lacks its initial and concluding folios and contains several significant lacunae. Its erudite author (who is possibly called Bernardet) was likely a cleric and associated with the court of Alga, a castle in Rouergue that belongs to the Roquefeuille family. *Flamenca*'s narrator is extremely well developed and intervenes frequently in the narrative. Although normally classified as a romance and heavily inscribed in the discourse of *fin' amor*, the text also shares many features with the form of fabliau known as the *castia-gilos,* and this discourse is frequently subverted through its representation as an elaborate game. *Flamenca* also shares motifs with the seventh story from *The Seven Sages of Rome* and the Old French romance *Jouffroi de Poitiers*. Although the very playful, sometimes ironic movement between various rhetorical and literary discourses makes it difficult to pin down the text's meaning, *Flamenca* is almost unanimously considered an artistic triumph, due in part to the text's combination of courtly, comic, erotic, religious, realistic, and possibly historical elements.

Count Gui of Namur, Flamenca's father, marries his only daughter to the worthy knight Sir Archambaut of Bourbon. Following a lavish wedding celebration, the couple returns to Bourbon, where Sir Archambaut hosts a second celebration attended by many nobles as well as the king of France. After the French queen falsely suggests Flamenca is behaving improperly with her husband, Sir Archambaut becomes insanely jealous and encloses his wife and her two handmaidens in a tower, only allowing them out to attend church and occasionally the nearby baths. Guillem de Nevers, the hyperbolically brave knight and clever cleric, realizes from his studies that ideal knights should fall in love and develops, sight unseen, an overwhelming passion for the beautiful Flamenca. Upon the advice of *Amors* (Love) and a dream version of Flamenca, Guillem travels to Bourbon and takes rooms at an inn near Flamenca's tower. He then bribes the local priest into accepting him as his cleric, so he can converse, two words at a time, with Flamenca when offering her the peace during mass on Sundays and on feast days. Over a period of months, the lovers exchange one- or two-word messages in church while Guillem builds a tunnel between the baths and his room at the inn. Once the tunnel is complete and Flamenca finally agrees to meet him at the baths, Guillem takes her to his room and becomes her lover. The two meet for four months until Flamenca obtains her freedom after swearing a specious oath to Sir Archambaut promising to guard herself as well as he has guarded her and sends Guillem away. When the two men subsequently become friends at a tournament, Sir Archambaut invites Guillem to attend his own tournament that Easter and also unsuspectingly delivers a *salutz d'amor* (love greeting) from Guillem to Flamenca. Guillem excels in the tournament, and the lovers resume their relationship with Sir Archambaut's continuing unwitting assistance, as the romance abruptly breaks off. Although the manuscript offers no definitive proof, it is likely that only a few folios are missing and that the narrative concludes in Bourbon with Flamenca happily manipulating her husband and lover.

Somewhat paradoxically, *Flamenca* both foregrounds its status as a highly intertextual, literary artifact and incorporates numerous concrete, realistic details. Notably, the short messages Guillem and Flamenca exchange in church construct a poem based on troubadour Peire Rogier's "Ges non puesc en bon vers faillir," while the feast days on which the meetings take place correspond to historical days in the liturgical calendar.

Much of the central portion of the romance functions as an "Art of Love," as Guillem, Flamenca, and her two handmaidens engage in extended speeches on appropriate behavior for lovers and ladies. Although *Flamenca*'s historical author was likely male, the female characters' speeches, like the poems of the *trobairitz* (female troubadours), offer the feminine perspective on *fin' amor* and give a voice to the normally silent lady who struggles to situate herself in a system that, as governed by the feudal hierarchy, professes to venerate her but more frequently succeeds in marginalizing her. By the romance's conclusion, Flamenca has changed from silenced maiden and wife to the virtual embodiment of the troubadour's all-powerful *domna* who tames her vassal into submission. The text's somewhat ambivalent representation of the eponymous heroine's overwhelming success in playing the game of love provides insight into the antifeminism often underlying *fin' amor*.

KAREN A. GROSSWEINER

References and Further Reading

Blodgett, E. D., ed. and trans. *The Romance of Flamenca.* New York: Garland, 1995.

Damon, Phillip. "Courtesy and Comedy in *Le Romance of Flamenca.*" *Romance Philology* 17 (1964): 608–615.

Dickey, Constance L. "Deceit, Desire, Distance, and Polysemy in *Flamenca.*" *Tenso* 11 (1995): 10–37.

Fleischman, Suzanne. "Dialectic Structures in *Flamenca.*" *Romanische Forschungen* 92 (1980): 223–245.

Grossweiner, Karen A. "Implications of the Female Poetic Voice in *Le Roman de Flamenca.*" In *The Court Reconvenes: Courtly Literature across the Disciplines*, edited by Barbara Altmann, Carleton Carroll, and Chantal Phan. Cambridge: D. S. Brewer, 2003, pp. 133–140.

Solterer, Helen. "*Sermo* and *Juglar*: Language Games in *Flamenca.*" In *The Spirit of the Court: Selected Proceedings of the Fourth International Conference of the Courtly Literature Society (Toronto, 1983)*, edited by Glyn S. Burgess and Robert A. Taylor. Woodbridge, Suffolk: D. S. Brewer, 1985, pp. 330–338.

Vitz, Evelyn Birge. "A Showcase for Talent: Performance in and *Robert Flamenca.*" In De Sens Rassis: *Essays in Honor of Rupert T. Pickens*, edited by Keith Busby, Bernard Guidot, and Logan E. Whalen. Amsterdam: Rodopi, 2005, pp. 683–698.

See also **Courtly Love; Fabliau; Literature, Occitan; Romance, French; Trobairitz and Troubadours**

ROMAN DE LA ROSE AND ITS RECEPTION

The *Roman de la Rose* was one of the most influential and widely circulated works in western Europe in the closing centuries of the Middle Ages, judging by nearly any criterion—numbers of surviving manuscript copies and poems that imitated or responded to it, as well as the influence of its themes among later authors. The work, written in the most common form used for narrative fiction in this period, rhyming octosyllabic couples, was undertaken by a first author, named Guillaume de Lorris, some time in the 1230s; however, Guillaume never brought the poem to a conclusion. Jean de Meun, a second author, working some forty years later, added a massive continuation and conclusion, over four times the length of Guillaume's fragment, that radically altered the contours and the scope of the first part. Guillaume had devised an innovative narrative frame: a first-person tale of a dream experience modeled upon stereotypes from the tradition of lyric poetry, designated by the expression "courtly love," in which the singer/lover proclaims his longing for the lady he loves in the hope of ultimately receiving her favors.

Guillaume de Lorris

In the *Rose*, the dream tale is a thinly veiled allegorical version of this poetic "quest": the narrator/lover happens upon the garden of Pleasure (populated by such figures as the God of Love himself, Beauty, Youth, and so forth) and falls in love with the Rose Bud, which will remain to the end the target of his desire. The last lines written by Guillaume depict his protagonist's monologue of longing outside the tower, which has been erected to protect the rose by enemies to the quest, Jealousy and her minions, among whom figure Shame and Fear. Guillaume had more than a personal story to tell. His narration purports to

Courtly garden scene. From the *Roman de la Rose.* c. 1440. Harl. 4425, fol. 12v. Location: British Museum, London, Great Britain. Credit: Snark / Art Resource, N.Y.

provide instruction to future lovers: "This," says the narrator in his prologue, "is the *Roman de la Rose,* in which the entire art of love is enclosed." While the narrator's own quest might accordingly serve as an instructive model (or warning) for future lovers, the *Rose* also includes explicit instruction on the part of the God of Love, who issues his commandments to the narrator, henceforth his vassal.

Jean de Meun

Jean de Meun pursued a quite different ideological agenda, though he maintains the focus on love, retitling the work at a later point the *Mirror for Lovers.* Using his allegorical characters (Reason, Nature, and others) as spokespeople/voices for and against a wide variety of amorous doctrines and comportments (friendship, adultery, prostitution, sodomy, and so forth), many of them dependent upon such Latin authorities as Ovid, Boethius, and Juvenal, Jean makes his encyclopedic intent clear: "it is good to know everything." Whereas Guillaume's text maintained a sanitized lexical and thematic perspective proper to the delicate nature of courtly love, Jean broadened the scope to include outrageously obscene language, suggestive considerations of sexual behavior, and some of the most notorious misogynistic statements to be found in medieval literature.

Generations of scholars considered Guillaume's section to be a relatively straightforward compilation of the courtly clichés, depicting the weak and suffering lover subject to the power of his desire and the beloved's failure to respond to his entreaties. Jean's manifestly ironic overturning of these rarefied literary conventions by drowning them in a morass of discourses drawn from the domains of philosophy, theology, and science has, in turn, led many to ask what the direction of his irony was: was his rejection of courtly love underwritten by a promotion of charity, that is, love of God, over the vanities of earthly passion, a defense of sex in marriage with the goal of procreation, a belief in sexual licentiousness and even rape in the service of one's pleasure, a simple hatred of women and the feminine? Debate on these issues has and will remain open, due to Jean de Meun's strategy of indeterminacy, which juxtaposes disparate voices, none of which is reducible to his own, in order to place the difficult burden, and essential responsibility, of interpretation on the reader.

Interpretive Ambiguities

In spite of the *Rose*'s inherent ambiguities, these were the terms around which the interpretive questions hovered until more recent interventions stemming from interest in feminism and gender studies. Not only has the critical focus moved away from such dichotomies used to depict the two authors as courtly and anticourtly, aristocratic and bourgeois, but it has also attempted to nuance the largely heteronormative slant characteristic of traditional criticism. Recent critical work has shown, for instance, that the very nature of personification allegory, which provides a gender to personified abstractions such as "beauty" or "reason" based upon their grammatical gender, leaves the way open for criticism of the gendered hierarchies of "straight" sexuality. Nowhere is this more apparent, as Simon Gaunt has recently shown, than in Guillaume de Lorris's choice of a male personification, Fair Welcoming, as the keeper of, and surrogate for, the female Rose, thus raising numerous questions with regard to the text's homoerotic overtones. This, combined with the centrality of the mythical figure of Narcissus as a figure of the lover, plunges us into a realm quite removed from the straight sexuality most believe to be inherent in the courtly model.

Jean de Meun, for his part, uses what might be called an "ethics of speech" to make such problems as misogynistic speech and obscene or blasphemous discourse an issue of reception and not articulation. Jean knowingly provides his readers with varying, even contradictory, points of view that the reader is expected to evaluate and alternately accept or reject. In a notorious defense of his misogynistic and antireligious statements, Jean states that his words are like arrows shot with no individual in his aim; if someone claims to have been wounded by stepping in front of them, that is their own fault.

By translating into the vernacular portions of texts only hitherto accessible to those who could read or understand Latin, Jean de Meun performed an important service to a burgeoning community of readers looking for texts in French. As Sylvia Huot has shown, evidence from the manuscripts copied in the two centuries following the work's composition, in the form of adjustments or rewritings of the text, marginal doodles and notes, and manuscript illuminations, suggests strongly that readers were deeply engaged in many of the above issues. To mention only one example, it is clear from illuminators' (and rubricators') attempts to portray the figure of Fair Welcoming, shuttling back and forth between the gender of the personification and the gender of the woman he allegorically stands for, that they were alternately appalled and intrigued by the gender issues thus raised.

Querelle of the Rose

But it was not until Christine de Pizan sharply attacked the *Rose* in 1401—thus spurring on an epistolary debate, known as the *querelle* of the *Rose*, that lasted until late the following year—that we get a clear picture of what readers actually thought about the work. Christine was in particular incensed by Jean de Meun's defamation of women in general; his profanity, which she found unacceptable, especially in the company of women; and the closing scene of the romance, which depicts the taking of the castle protecting the rose in terms that transparently suggest the mechanics of sexual intercourse. Although she was seconded by the highly distinguished theologian and preacher Jean Gerson, her opponents in the debate were representative of a clerkly class largely associated with the royal chancery. These men rallied around their "master," Jean de Meun, whom they undoubtedly admired as much for his absurdly comical misogyny as for the way he skirts the very limits of propriety. But the debate probably tells us as much about the unusual situation of a female within a male-dominated intelligentsia in the early fifteenth century as it does about interpretation. The interest that Christine's role in the *querelle* holds for us stems more from her willingness to attack male authority in order to establish her own reputation than from the uniqueness of her moral stance regarding marriage and sexual activity, essentially conservative and traditional in nature—one that made her an ally of the most illustrious preacher of her time. Thus, the profound interest that the *Rose*, a text that Sarah Kay has called "the most powerful investigation of textuality and sexuality in the French Middle Ages," holds for a modern audience, while possibly shared by some medieval readers, was precisely what made it unreadable for Christine.

DAVID F. HULT

References and Further Reading

de Lorris, Guillaume, and Jean de Meun. *Le Roman de la Rose*. 3 vols. Paris: Honoré Champion, 1965–1970.

de Pizan, Christine, Jean Gerson, Jean de Montreuil, Gontier and Pierre Col. *Le Débat sur le Roman de la Rose*, edited by Eric Hicks. Paris: Honoré Champion, 1977.

Gaunt, Simon. "Bel Acueil and the Improper Allegory of the *Romance of the Rose*." *New Medieval Literatures* 2 (1998): 65–93.

Hult, David F. "The *Roman de la Rose*, Christine de Pizan, and the *querelle des femmes*." In *The Cambridge Companion to Medieval Women's Writing*, edited by Carolyn Dinshaw and David Wallace. Cambridge: Cambridge University Press, 2003, pp. 184–194.

———. "Words and Deeds: Jean de Meun's *Romance of the Rose* and the Hermeneutics of Censorship." *New Literary History* 28.2 (1997): 345–366.

Huot, Sylvia. *The* Romance of the Rose *and Its Medieval Readers: Interpretation, Reception, Manuscript Transmission*. Cambridge: Cambridge University Press, 1993.

Kay, Sarah. "Sexual Knowledge: The Once and Future Texts of the *Romance of the Rose*." In *Textuality and Sexuality: Reading Theories and Practices*, edited by Judith Still and Michael Worton. Manchester: Manchester University Press, 1993, pp. 69–86.

See also **Christine de Pizan; Courtly Love; Defenses of Women; Eroticism in Literature; Feminist Theories and Methodologies; Gender Ideologies; Gerson, Jean; Literature, Old French; Misogyny; Obscenity; Ovid, Medieval Reception of; Personifications Visualized as Women; Rape and Raptus; Reader-Response Criticism; Romance, French; Woman Authors: Old French Texts**

ROMAN DE SILENCE

Composed in the second half of the thirteenth century by Heldris de Cornuälle (Cornwall), this 6,706-line Old French romance recounts the adventures of a heroine named Silence. To elude King Ebain of England's ban on female inheritance, Silence's father, Count Cador of Cornwall, raises her as a boy—a decision he describes in linguistic terms as the substitution of the Latin masculine declensional ending -*us*

for the feminine -*a* (a bilingual pun, since *us* is Old French for custom or practice). As an adolescent, Silence becomes the object of a spirited debate between Nature and Nurture (Noreture). Convinced by Reason that "a man's life was much better than that of a woman" (lines 2,637–2,638), Silence learns to excel as a knight and a minstrel. Finally, however, Silence is outed as a woman and (after the execution of the adulterous Queen Eufeme) married to the king, who reverses his previous prohibition on female inheritance.

Silence survives in only one manuscript, University of Nottingham Mi. LM. 6, published in 1972. Early strands of criticism highlighted issues of language and textuality, developing the allegorical promise inherent in the names of the major female characters (Silence, her mother, Eufemie, and Ebain's wife, Eufeme). Other work examines the implications of Silence's cross-dressing: should we read her success at chivalry and minstrelsy as a triumphant challenge to biological determinism, or should we see her eventual unmasking and marriage to Ebain as a strategy of containment, reemphasizing the subordinate role allotted to women in medieval patrilineal systems?

SHARON KINOSHITA

References and Further Reading

Allen, Peter L. "The Ambiguity of *Silence*: Gender, Writing, and *Le Roman de Silence*." In *Sign, Sentence, Discourse: Language in Medieval Thought and Literature*, edited by Julian N. Wasserman and Lois Roney. Syracuse: Syracuse University Press, 1989, pp. 98–112.

Bloch, R. Howard. "*Silence* and Holes: The *Roman de Silence* and the Art of the Trouvère." *Yale French Studies* 70 (1986): 81–89.

Brahney, Kathleen J. "When *Silence* Was Golden: Female Personae in the *Roman de Silence*." In *The Spirit of the Court: Selected Proceedings of the Fourth Congress of the International Courtly Literature Society (Toronto 1983)*, edited by Glyn S. Burgess, et al. Dover, N.H.: Brewer, 1985, pp. 52–61.

Heldris de Cornuälle. *Le Roman de Silence*, edited and translated by F. Regina Psaki. Garland Library of Medieval Literature 63B. New York: Garland, 1991.

———. *Le Roman de Silence: A Thirteenth-Century Arthurian Verse-Romance by Heldris De Cornuälle*, edited by Lewis Thorpe. Cambridge: W. Heffer and Sons, 1972.

———. *Silence: A Thirteenth-Century French Romance*, edited and translated by Sarah Roche-Mahdi. East Lansing, Mich.: Colleagues Press, 1992.

Kinoshita, Sharon. "Heldris de Cornuälle's *Roman de Silence* and the Feudal Politics of Lineage." *PMLA* 110.3 (1995): 397–409.

Psaki, F. Regina, ed. "Special Issues on *Le Roman de Silence*." *Arthuriana* 7:2 (1997) and 12:1 (2002).

See also **Cross-Dressing; Gender Ideologies; Inheritance; Literature, Old French; Patriarchy and Patrilineage; Romance, French**

ROMAN LAW

Roman law has often been cited as an abiding source of legal restrictions on women in Western history. Indeed, women could not possess the sweeping parental powers entrusted to fathers (*patria potestas*), and they could not hold public offices or act as witnesses. Still, by the time of Justinian (527–565), few other legal restrictions remained on women in Roman law. Romans did not base guardianship of women originally on ideologically inscribed gender weakness (*infirmitas sexus*). Women simply were not able to act for others; they could not transcend a narrow range of interest—hence their inability to stand surety for others. Ideological gender conceits entered juristic discourse only under the influence of Hellenistic ideas and Christianity.

Male guardianship over women in Roman law was loosened over the centuries. This was largely the work of emperors and of the praetors, who were the chief judges of the most important Roman courts. This change was also the consequence of problems that arose in practice for families, especially those of wealth and prominence, as they dealt with legal restrictions on women whose agency and ownership of property were of potential use. One notable example is the edict of Augustus (30 BCE–14 CE) that freed from guardianship (*tutela*) those married women who had undergone three pregnancies and freedwomen who had had four.

Roman law rested on a variety of sources, but in the centuries of the Christian era two stood out—imperial legislation by rescript (replies to inquiries) and jurisprudential elaborations by learned experts. These latter were largely responsible for injecting the language of female inferiority into legal discourse, even as legislation opened wider areas of female autonomy. By the fifth century the sheer volume of imperial legislation on all subjects begged for some form of organization and clarifying reform. Theodosius II (408–450) took a significant step in that direction with promulgation of the Theodosian Code in 438. It arranged the imperial edicts since the first Christian emperor, Constantine (306–337), into sixteen books. No attempt was made to harmonize old laws with new; they simply sat in chronological order with the new presumed to supersede the old. Subsequently Burgundian and Visigothic kings gathered rules meant to apply to the Romans in their dominions, the *Lex Romana Burgundionum* and the *Lex Romana Visigothorum* (better known as the Breviary of Alaric).

Justinian first brought the Theodosian Code up to date, while also issuing constitutions that resolved conflicts in the laws. Laws issued after Justinian's *Codex* were later gathered in another collection known as the *Novellae*. The important innovation he worked was the collection of jurisprudential wisdom in extracts grouped under various titles in fifty books—the *Digest*. A textbook known as the *Institutes* completed Justinian's legal reforms and publications. The entire product, later dubbed the *Body of Civil Law* (*Corpus iuris civilis*), became the basis for the revival of jurisprudence, starting in Italy, and for the elaboration of Roman rules in practice from the twelfth century onwards. It was especially the *Digest*, as a depository of sophisticated interpretive techniques, that influenced the later law and the methods of those who studied and applied it. The language of female weakness came with it, reinforcing similar statements and presumptions that had come to grace portions of the growing body of canon law.

The effects of Roman law on women were mixed. Their exclusion from holding *patria potestas* (paternal authority), while they were left under the *potestas* (authority) of their own fathers, meant that they were not fully under the control of their husbands. Justinian also notably reduced the husband's control over dowry during marriage and guaranteed the wife priority in claims against her husband's estate for return of her dowry. For this and other reasons, one scholar has concluded that "women living in the last centuries of the empire had a greater legal capacity than their sisters in any historical period before the twentieth century" (Arjava, p. 265). Germanic laws, canon law, and local customs in the course of the Middle Ages reduced women's realm of action and legal capacities in many regards, although there would be areas in which their legal prerogatives would remain strong or even stronger (such as their guardianship of their own children). Yet Roman law also never treated women as equal to men. Its exclusion of them from public office and its limitations on their citizenship, along with its emphasis on agnation (tracing descent through the paternal line) in defining kinship and laying out lines of inheritance meant that women were always subordinate in relation to men. Equality of the sexes was just inconceivable to the Romans and the medieval people who drew on their law.

Thomas Kuehn

References and Further Reading

Arjava, Antti. *Women and Law in Late Antiquity*. Oxford: Clarendon Press, 1996.

Bellomo, Manlio. *The Common Legal Past of Europe, 1000–1800*, translated by Lydia G. Cochrane. Washington, D.C.: Catholic University of America Press, 1995.

Nicholas, Barry. *An Introduction to Roman Law*. Oxford: Clarendon Press, 1962.

Stein, Peter. *Roman Law in European History*. Cambridge: Cambridge University Press, 1999.

Thomas, Yan. "The Division of the Sexes in Roman Law." In *A History of Women in the West*, edited by Georges Duby and Michelle Perrot. Vol. 1: *From Ancient Goddesses to Christian Saints*, edited by Pauline Schmitt Pantel. Cambridge, Mass.: Harvard University Press, 1992, pp. 83–137.

See also **Law, Canon; Law Codes, Barbarian; Legal Agency**

ROMANCE, ENGLISH

Vernacular readers (and listeners) in late medieval England—including, of course, women—would have known romance as the default category for all nonreligious narrative. In Chaucer's *Troilus and Criseyde* (about 1385), when Pandarus visits his niece, he finds her and her all-female household enmeshed in the *Romance of Thebes*, which one of the group reads aloud from a deluxe, "coffee-table" manuscript. The scene models a form of reading that is at once ordinary and desirable, a source for these women not simply of pleasure but also of cultural capital, in a way that foreshadows novel reading four centuries later. In the poem, Criseyde takes her place among the highest ranks of society; though a bit later she suggests that her uncle, as a proper guardian, ought to be pressing didactic reading upon her, it seems clear that her devotion to romances of this sort is an acceptable, even attractive, use of her leisure time. In the Prologue to the *Legend of Good Women* (1388?), a "sequel" to the *Troilus*, Chaucer invents a fictional yet persuasive scenario concerning women's engagement with modern romances, suggesting that reading these stories produces a direct impact on the thought and behavior of female audiences. Dante, in his episode of Paolo and Francesca in the *Inferno*, portrayed an Arthurian romance as a *galeoto*, a pimp sponsoring an illicit affair. Chaucer, on the other hand, through this scene in Criseyde's "paved parlour," suggests that romances might function as artifacts and opportunities for the formation of same-sex reading communities. In this, the poem reflects evidence that networks of female readers—within circles of acquaintances, households and extended families, and religious orders—shared written texts and "communing" or discussion about them during the fourteenth and fifteenth centuries.

Though surviving documents specify mainly religious works as reading matter, individual women did own and share copies of romances: Chaucer's granddaughter Alice owned Lydgate's *Siege of Thebes*

(1466); Anne Paston owned a *Romance of Thebes* (1472); another fifteenth-century book owner seems to have made her own copy of *Sir Degrevant*; and a variety of Arthurian romances contain inscriptions by female owners and readers. Nearly 150 English romances have come down from the Middle Ages, and references suggest that nearly that number again may have been lost to us. The more popular of these did not "target" women audiences, as Chaucer seems to have done. Though they prize spectacle and masculine adventure over psychological realism or refined sentiments, reading and listening to these romances appealed to women alongside men.

THOMAS HAHN

References and Further Reading

Meale, Carol M., ed. *Women and Literature in Britain, 1150–1500*. Cambridge: Cambridge University Press, 1993.

TEAMS Middle English Texts. (Reliable versions of scores of romances.) http://www.lib.rochester.edu/camelot/teams/tmsmenu.htm.

See also **Book Ownership; Chaucer, Geoffrey; Criseyde; Dante Alighieri; Literacy and Reading: Vernacular; Literature, Middle English; Romances of Antiquity**

ROMANCE, FRENCH

Romance arose in the mid-twelfth century not as a fixed genre but as the result of a process of translation: the *mise en romans*—the reworking into the Romance vernacular—of texts previously known only in Latin. Composed in octosyllabic rhyming couplets, the *Romans de Thèbes*, *de Troie*, and *d'Enéas*, collectively known as the Romances of Antiquity (c. 1155–1165), adapted classical legends to the tastes of a lay, noble audience. As translations from Latin—Western Christendom's official language of truth—these inaugural texts carried their own justification, exemplifying the motif of *translatio studii*: the historical transmission of letters from Greece to Rome to the West.

Within a generation, written French had gained sufficient cachet to support the translation of tales from the Celtic tradition. An important transitional text was Wace's *Roman de Brut* (1155), a translation/adaptation of Geoffrey of Monmouth's *Historia regum Britanniae*, which first introduced King Arthur to French-speaking audiences. Wace's account of a twelve-year peace during which Arthur founded the Round Table provided the backdrop for the five romances of Chrétien de Troyes: *Erec et Enide*, *Cligés*,

Yvain, Lancelot, and Perceval (c. 1170–1190). These texts established the pattern of the lone protagonist striking out from court in search of adventure and introduced two themes—Lancelot's illicit love for Guenevere and the enigma of the Grail—destined to dominate thirteenth-century Arthurian literature. Stories of the adulterous love of Tristan and Iseut (Isolde) constitute this period's second major corpus—its exploration of the power of illicit passion forming a counterpoint to Chrétien's emphasis on conjugal love in *Erec*, *Cligés*, and *Yvain*. Versions of *Tristan* by the Anglo-Normans Béroul and Thomas d'Angleterre survive only as fragments, while the *Folies* of Oxford and of Berne focus on the brief episode of Tristan's feigned madness. (The subsequent diffusion of this Arthurian material into German and Spanish literatures in the late twelfth and early thirteenth century—yet a further stage of *translatio*—is sometimes ascribed to the influence of Henry II of England and Eleanor of Aquitaine's daughters Mathilda and Eleanor, who married the king of Castile and the duke of Saxony, respectively.) Other works of this period include *Floire et Blancheflor* (contemporary with the Romances of Antiquity but set in the Muslim Mediterranean); *Partonopeus de Blois*; and Gautier d'Arras's *Eracle* and *Ille et Galeron* (in which Breton or French protagonists triumph over Roman or Greek antagonists, winning royal brides in the process). Finally, the *Lais* of Marie de France—French literature's first named female author—present many romance themes in a briefer narrative form.

The thirteenth century brought a reorganization of the Old French literary system, perhaps in response to the rapid political and social transformations of the day: the triumph of the French monarchy over the great princes in whose courts romance had flourished; King John's loss of his continental lands (1204), hastening the development of a distinctive "insular" Anglo-Norman romance tradition; and a disillusionment with chivalric ideals following the perversions of the Fourth and the Albigensian Crusades. Amidst these and other changes, Jean de Meun's *Romance of the Rose or Guillaume de Dole* introduced two significant innovations: the incorporation of lyric pieces (some well known and independently attested) into its verse narrative, producing a kind of medieval musical; and its use of a "realistic" setting, featuring numerous proper names identifiable with local sites and recognizable contemporary figures.

The two most important transformations were the development of prose and the turn to allegory. Old French prose appeared suddenly in the early thirteenth century in reaction to suspicions concerning the "truth value" of vernacular verse. First used in translations of Latin historiographies, it soon spilled over into romance: *La Fille du comte de Pontieu* (called the first French *nouvelle* or short story) combined a cross-cultural Christian–Saracen plot with a local realism resembling that of *Guillaume de Dole*. Of greater significance was the *Lancelot-Grail* (c. 1220–1240). Also called the Vulgate or Pseudo-Map cycle, this monumental compilation of five texts—*L'Estoire del Saint Graal*, *L'Estoire de Merlin*, *Lancelot*, *La Queste del Saint Graal*, and *La Mort Artu*—expanded, embellished, and Christianized the adventures of Lancelot and Perceval, synthesizing previous Arthurian plots and characters into one comprehensive cycle held together by the narrative technique of interlace. In the 1230s Guillaume de Lorris's *Romance of the Rose* introduced another significant shift, transforming the romance plot of the love quest into the allegorical dream-vision of a first-person narrator, penetrating the Garden of Delight to reach the beauteous Rose at its center. In the 1270s, Guillaume's 4,000-line romance was "completed" by Jean de Meun's 18,000-line "continuation," which adapted the poem's allegorical scaffolding to the presentation of philosophical and scientific debates. Both elements—the allegorical dream-vision and the propensity to philosophical debate—substantially influenced the development of fourteenth-century French literature.

Representations of Women and Gender

Traditional histories represent romance as replacing the masculine world and collective feudal values associated with Old French epic with a more refined and feminine world of courtly ideals. (More recent criticism rejects this simple binarism, noting epic's inclusion of numerous important female characters as well as its continued popularity throughout the late Middle Ages.) Correspondingly, twelfth-century romances are often read as the chivalric *Bildungsroman* of a hero seeking to balance the demands of love and arms: Enéas, who must reject Dido's all-consuming passion to get on with the founding of empire; Erec, who must expiate his uxoriousness by putting Enide in her place; and Yvain, who must win back Laudine's love through a series of challenging adventures.

What of the romance's female protagonists? Does the fascination exerted by an impassive *belle dame sans merci* over her would-be lover constitute power, or does it simply idealize the objectification of women within medieval society? The agency wielded by female characters varies widely in nature and degree.

In the *Roman d'Enéas*, the Carthaginian queen Dido and the warrior-queen Camille excel in the masculine arenas of political and military power, yet each meets a violent end. Conversely, Lavine is a sheltered princess with no tangible power except over Enéas's heart. Yet through her lengthy monologues (introducing Ovidian love casuistry into the nascent romance tradition) she becomes a subject of desire, invested with a psychological depth reflecting twelfth-century humanist concerns. Ultimately, this focus on Lavine's inner thoughts ensures that her eventual marriage to Enéas conforms to reformist ecclesiastical definitions of marriage, requiring the consent of both partners.

Similar complexity attends the representation of women as speaking subjects. As Arthur's queen, Guenevere speaks authoritatively and as a wise counselor. Iseut speaks duplicitously, her ambiguous oaths capitalizing on the ambiguities inherent in language to conceal her adultery from Mark. Conversely, Enide breaks into speech only to lament her very existence: here the emergence of an interior consciousness marks not the privilege of the humanist subject but the disempowerment of a poor vassal's daughter with no claim to public speech.

The motif of the adulterous queen, whose infidelity threatens to contaminate the king's lineage and disrupt his relationship with his vassals, reflects the apprehension surrounding the high social and political stakes of women's sexuality. Farther down the social scale, the so-called "wager romances" depict a malicious outsider falsely impugning a young woman's reputation through his secret knowledge of a distinctive mark on her body (*Guillaume de Dole*, the *Roman de la Violette*; cf. *Decameron* II.9). Finally, the anxiety surrounding women is confirmed in the motif of the substitutability and reduplication of female objects of desire. In *Tristan*, Iseut's servant Brangien takes her place in the queen's marriage bed lest Mark notice his bride is no longer a virgin; an exiled Tristan later marries a second Iseut in compensation for his loss of the queen. In Gautier d'Arras's *Ille et Galeron*, the Breton noble Ille exchanges the count of Brittany's sister, Galeron, for the Roman emperor's daughter, Ganor; his children by these two successive wives include two daughters, each named Idoine. In *Galeran de Bretagne* (derived from Marie de France's *Fresne*), the titular protagonist is torn between his love for the foundling Fresne and her twin sister, Fleurie.

In these varied literary representations, romance reveals the centrality of women to feudal society, inseparable from the perplexity their influence triggered in the medieval imaginary.

SHARON KINOSHITA

References and Further Reading

Bloch, R. Howard. *Medieval Misogyny and the Invention of Western Romantic Love*. Chicago: University of Chicago Press, 1991.

Crane, Susan. *Insular Romance: Politics, Faith and Culture in Anglo-Norman and Middle English Literature*. Berkeley: University of California Press, 1991.

Duggan, Joseph J. *The Romances of Chrétien de Troyes*. New Haven: Yale University Press, 2001.

Haidu, Peter. "Romance: Idealistic Genre or Historical Text?" In *The Craft of Fiction: Essays in Medieval Poetics*, edited by Leigh A. Arrathoon. Rochester, Mich.: Solaris, 1984.

Jean de Meun. *The Romance of the Rose or Guillaume de Dole*, translated by Patricia Terry and Nancy Vine Durling. Philadelphia: University of Pennsylvania Press, 1993.

Kay, Sarah. *The Chansons de Geste in the Age of Romance: Political Fictions*. Oxford: Clarendon Press, 1995.

Kibler, William W., ed. *The Lancelot-Grail Cycle: Text and Transformations*. Austin: University of Texas Press, 1994.

Kinoshita, Sharon. *Medieval Boundaries: Rethinking Difference in Old French Literature*. Philadelphia: University of Pennsylvania Press, 2006.

Krueger, Roberta L., ed. *The Cambridge Companion to Medieval Romance*. Cambridge: Cambridge University Press, 2000.

McCracken, Peggy. *The Romance of Adultery: Queenship and Sexual Transgression in Old French Literature*. Philadelphia: University of Pennsylvania Press, 1998.

Ollier, Marie-Louise. "Utopie et roman arthurien." *Cahiers de Civilisation Médiévale* 27:3 (1984): 223–232. Reprinted in Marie-Louise Ollier, *La forme du sens: textes narratifs des XIIe et XIIIe siècles, études littéraires et linguistiques*. Orléans: Paradigme, 2000, pp. 217–231.

See also **Arthurian Literature; Chrétien de Troyes; Courtly Love; Floire and Blancheflor; Guinivere; Isolde; Literature, Old French; Marie de France; Patronage, Literary; Roman de Flamenca; Roman de la Rose and Its Reception; Roman de Silence; Romance, English; Romance, German; Romances of Antiquity; Translation**

ROMANCE, GERMAN

Medieval romances are book-length, verse narratives distinguished by plots involving chivalry, love affairs between high-born women and men, and complex female characters. They first appear in the German language in the 1170s, flourish during the thirteenth century, and are still read in the early sixteenth century. The earliest German romances are adaptations of Old French texts. The cross-cultural exchange of these texts testifies to the emergence of a new, trans-European, aristocratic, secular identity in the High Middle Ages. Romance narratives were frequently adapted and altered to suit the tastes and interests of new audiences. This malleability may have contributed to their long life.

There is a great deal of evidence for this enduring popularity. A large number of different romance texts circulated in German-speaking lands. The practice of making new manuscript copies of twelfth- and thirteenth-century romance texts continued into the first decades of the sixteenth century. Romance stories were used to adorn the dwelling places of the wealthy. Medieval wall paintings and textiles, such as bed hangings, that feature figural representations of well-known romance narratives have survived in German-speaking lands. All the major strands of romance literature are represented in German-language versions. These include the widely popular adventure romances, such as the Floire and Blancheflor stories (Konrad Fleck); the Arthurian romance tradition (Hartmann von Aue; Wolfram von Eschenbach); the Tristan tradition (Gottfried von Strassburg; Eilhart von Oberg); the Gawain tradition (Wirnt von Grafenberg; Heinrich von dem Türlin); and the Lancelot tradition (Ulrich von Zatzikhoven; the anonymous text translated from Old French known as the *Prose Lancelot*). Later in the thirteenth century, German authors such as the Minnesang poet Ulrich von Liechtenstein, Rudolf von Ems, Konrad von Würzburg, Johann von Würzburg, der Stricker, and der Pleier renewed and expanded romance literature.

Ann Marie Rasmussen

References and Further Reading

Jackson, W. H., and S. A. Ranawake, eds. *The Arthur of the Germans: The Arthurian Legend in Medieval German and Dutch Literature* vol 3. *Arthurian Literature in the Middle Ages*. Cardiff: University of Wales, 2000.

Pincikowski, Scott E. "Female Pain–Female Eroticism: The Eroticization of the Female Body in Pain in Hartmann von Aue's Courtly Epics." In *Nu lôn' ich iu der gâbe: Festschrift for Francis G. Gentry*, edited by Ernst Ralf Hintz. Göttingen: Kümmerle, 2003, pp. 211–225.

Rasmussen, Ann Marie. "Medieval German Romance." In *Cambridge Companion to Medieval Romance,* edited by Roberta L. Krueger. Cambridge, U.K.: Cambridge University Press, 2000, pp. 183–202.

Rushing, James A., Jr. *Images of Adventure: Yvain in the Visual Arts*. Philadelphia: University of Pennsylvania Press, 1995.

Sterling-Hellenbrand, Alexandra. *Topographies of Gender in Middle High German Arthurian Romance*. New York: Routledge, 2001.

Sullivan, Joseph M. *Counsel in Middle High German Arthurian Romance*. Göttingen: Kümmerle, 2001.

See also **Arthurian Literature; Floire and Blancheflor; Gottfried von Strassburg; Guinivere; Isolde; Literature, German; Minnesang; Romance, French; Wolfram von Eschenbach**

ROMANCERO

The medieval Spanish ballad-singing tradition, or *Romancero,* is made up of individual texts known in Spanish as *romances*. The texts, composed anonymously beginning in the fourteenth century or earlier, typically describe events of the distant past, whether real or imaginary. Their themes offer a popular and dramatic vision of Spanish history, from the Muslim invasion of the eighth century through the reconquest of the Muslim kingdom of Granada in the fifteenth century. The first printed *romances* date from the sixteenth century, although *romances* continue to be discovered today throughout the Iberian peninsula, Latin America, and the Judeo-Spanish diaspora. In modern times, *romances* have sometimes served the purpose of lullabies, sung by mothers to young children at bedtime. As such, they are sometimes seen in the context of women's song. There is no fixed text to a *romance*, so singers and poets have often reinterpreted a particular *romance*, giving rise to a new version or variant. The *romance* of the rape of Lucretia by Tarquino, described in the fifteenth-century Spanish *Romancero*, is one salient example. The story of the rape of Lucretia by a Roman tyrant was transformed by twentieth-century Judeo-Spanish singers into a story about the steadfast refusal of a Jewish woman to marry a Christian man. Structurally, *romances* are arranged in couplets, with assonance at the close of each couplet. Lines nearly always include eight syllables.

Both structure and content have played an important role for scholars in analyzing the *Romancero* tradition. A number of theories have been offered to explain the extraordinary persistence of *romances*, beginning with seminal work in Spain in the nineteenth century that argued that the texts were fragments of medieval epic poems, and continuing with work by Spanish scholars in the early decades of the twentieth century. Theories of "formulistic diction" in *Romancero* composition, put forth by Ruth House Webber in the mid-1900s, and underlying "deep structures" in the *Romancero* corpus, advanced by Diego Catalán later on, focus on how linguistic elements of the texts enable singers of the *romances* to keep the tradition alive. But work on the themes of the texts—love, sex (including rape), marriage, honor, and so on—suggest plausibly that *romances* may have survived because they promoted and perpetuated ideologies that were useful to successive generations of Spaniards and others who continued to sing them. Buetler, Catarella, Goldberg, Lanz, Mirrer, and others have argued that *romances* often advance gender stereotypes; for example, they show women—particularly queens and noblewomen—as lascivious, unfaithful, and dangerous to men. So-called *fronterizo* (frontier) and "morisco" (Moorish) *romances*, traditionally viewed as the last treasures of heroic poetry in Spanish, often depict Muslim women improbably, as eager for sex with Christian men, or as pure, but sexually ripe, tempting Christian men to rape them. Such stereotypes, these scholars argue, stoked antifeminist behavior and motivated antifeminist legislation. Gender stereotypes promoted in the *romances* may also have helped stimulate completion of the reconquest and presaged exclusion of Muslims and Jews from Spain by feminizing "other" men, describing them as wearing richly colored garments, engaged in passive activities, and unable to keep and satisfy their women.

LOUISE MIRRER

References and Further Reading

Buetler, Gisela. "Some Remarks on the Moorish Ballads in Spain and Elsewhere." In *Ballad Research: The Stranger in Ballad Narrative and Other Topic*, edited by Hugh Shields. Dublin: Folk Music Society of Ireland, pp. 171–182.

Burshatin, Israel. "The Docile Image: The Moor as a Figure of Force, Subservience, and Nobility in the *Poema de mio Cid*." *Romance Quarterly* 31.3 (1984): 269–280.

Catarella, Teresa. "Feminine Historicizing in the *romancero novelesco*. *Bulletin of Hispanic Studies* 67.4 (1990): 331–343.

Cruz, Anne J. "The Politics of Illicit Love in the 'Pedro el Cruel' Ballad Cycle." *Scandinavian Yearbook of Folklore* 48 (1992): 1–16.

Goldberg, Harriet. *Motif-Index of Folk Narratives in the Pan-Hispanic* Romancero. Tempe, Ariz.: Arizona Center for Medieval and Renaissance Studies, 2000.

———. "Two Parallel Medieval Commonplaces: Antifeminism and Antisemitism in the Hispanic Literary Tradition." In *Aspects of Jewish Culture in the Middle Ages: Papers of the Eighth Annual Conference of the Center for Medieval and Early Renaissance Studies*, SUNY Binghamton, edited by Paul Szarmach. Albany: State University of New York Press, 1979, pp. 85–119.

Lanz, Eukene Lacarra. "Political Discourse and the Construction and Representation of Gender in *Mocedades de Rodrigo*." *Hispanic Review* 67.4, Lloyd Homage Issue (1999): 467–491.

MacKay, Angus. "The Ballad and the Frontier in Late Medieval Spain." *Bulletin of Hispanic Studies* 53 (1976): 15–33.

Mirrer, Louise. *Women, Jews & Muslims in the Texts of Reconquest Castile*. Ann Arbor, Mich.: University of Michigan Press, 1996.

Ratcliffe, Marjorie. "Adulteresses, Mistresses, and Prostitutes: Extramarital Relationships." *Hispania* 67 (1984): 346–350.

See also **Ballads; Courtly Love; Epic, Spanish; Femininity and Masculinity; Gender Ideologies; Iberia; Jewish Women; Muslim Women: Iberia; Muslim Women: Western Literature; Rape and Raptus; Sexuality, Regulation of; Woman's Song**

ROMANCES OF ANTIQUITY

The *Romans d'Antiquité*, three of which were written within five years at the English court of Henry II and Eleanor of Aquitaine, represent a major shift in twelfth-century historiographical and literary practice. These vernacular romances combine a medieval fascination with genealogy, heroism, and legitimacy with extravagant accounts of a distant, heroic past. The tone is didactic and inspirational, corresponding almost certainly to Henry II's desire to strengthen his claim to Trojan ancestry. This claim, already exploited by the Capetian royal family in France, carried with it great prestige but also legendary liabilities: the Trojans actually failed to secure their kingdom, and they had an inconvenient penchant for sodomy. The romances are, therefore, explicitly ideological: they construct and bolster a royal and imperial identity while advocating a new form of popular humanism. Present in different forms in earlier French epics, this celebration of victory over adversity, of founding narratives and adherence to divinely ordained missions, would go on to inspire the major courtly romances of the following century.

The *Roman de Thèbes,* the *Roman d'Enéas*, and the *Roman de Troie* (manuscript Bibliothèque Nationale fonds français 60 contains all three) thus provide impressive proof of the erudition of twelfth-century scholars. Most of the stories were gleaned either from extant manuscripts of original sources (in the case of the *Eneas*) or from later medieval translations/adaptations of the material (in the case of the *Troie*). To a much greater degree than in the feudal epics, these classically inspired texts introduced into historical romance a form of psychological analysis. Their interest in the development of the young male hero, his introduction to erotic fantasy, and its culmination in love and/or marriage still left ample room for discussion of women. These earliest of medieval romances are also distinguished by their structure; they are chronological and comprehensive narratives that stretch across continents and generations. They may pretend to be constructing illustrious classical civilizations, but their building blocks are the stuff of the present: fashionable rhetoric, octosyllabic verse, feudal justice and combat, and a frank examination of contemporary sexual mores.

The role of fate is still central, but adherence to feudal norms and Christian values has replaced the rule of the Classical gods. The ethical dilemmas now point to new intellectual influences and a struggle between the secular and the religious, the feudal and the monarchic. In the *Thèbes*, for example, women may be described largely as erotic icons but, following the model of Statius' *Thebaid*, they are also figures of wisdom and righteousness. Jocasta, mother and wife of Oedipus, is a respected leader and negotiator, and it is an army of women (albeit led by men) who succeed in tearing down the wall of Thebes, thereby enacting their own revenge. Antigone is deprived of her heroic role in burying the dead and defying patriarchal law, but she is given a role as love interest of Parthonopex, a military leader of the Arcadian enemies, and this couple serves as a tool by which to critique war.

In the *Troie* also, love stories share the spotlight with feudal battles, but it is in the *Enéas* that this juxtaposition attains its most innovative and subversive force, most strikingly when the medieval text diverges from the Virgilian model. The heroines, Dido, Camilla, and Lavinia, embody three medieval models of femininity. Dido is driven by her passions to self-destruction; the virginal Camilla is completely committed to a higher goal; and Lavinia is the young innocent, the victim of love redeemed through suffering. Woven into the narratives surrounding these heroines is an inordinate amount of attention given to homoeroticism, far exceeding that found in Virgil's account. Nisus and Euryalus' story is given much greater prominence, and in death the two martyrs are elevated to the status of perfect lovers (ll. 4,941–4,954). Eneas delivers a long and emotional oration over the dead body of the boy warrior, Pallas (sixty-two lines [6,185–6,213] as opposed to Virgil's three), that resembles in many ways the Nisus/Euryalus same-sex plaint. Finally, Camilla, the woman warrior, is highlighted first through a vicious attack on her inappropriate gender identification (ll. 7,073–7,106), then through the funeral oration of her ally, Turnus, who mourns her as a genderless beloved, in the very terms of the earlier two eulogies for same-sex alter egos.

The principal conflict between same-sex and other-sex love surfaces in the pairing of Eneas and Lavinia, and it is framed through a mother–daughter conflict. When Lavinia first sees Eneas, love strikes, but her mother denounces him, claiming in graphic terms that all Trojans are sodomites. Her daughter's erotic obsession and emotional swings lead to one of the most surprising discussions of sexuality in the Middle Ages. Sodomy is seen as completely natural but foreign, a despised but always available alternative whose presence can be felt even in the marriage bond and bed. The text's candor and humor alert us to the fact that such topics were under discussion in 1160. However, the face-off it features between the two species of men (to use the queen's term), from a woman's point of view, are belied by the text's own evident investment in gender ambiguity and same-sex attraction. Such a daring portrayal of erotic relations and misunderstandings would have huge implications for the development of romance over the following century.

WILLIAM E. BURGWINKLE

References and Further Reading

Blumenfeld-Kosinski, Renate. "Old French Narrative Genres: Toward the Definition of the Roman Antique." *Romance Philology* 34 (1980): 143–159.

Burgwinkle, William E. "Knighting the Classical Hero: Homo/Hetero Affectivity in *Eneas.*" *Exemplaria* 5.1 (1993): 1–43.

———. *Sodomy, Masculinity, and Law in Medieval Literature: France and England, 1050–1230*. Cambridge: Cambridge University Press, 2004.

Cormier, Raymond J. *One Heart One Mind: the Rebirth of Virgil's Hero in Medieval French Romance*. University, Miss.: Romance Monographs, 1973.

Eneas, Roman du XIIe siècle, edited by J.-J. Salverda de Grave. Paris: Honoré Champion, 1985.

Eneas: a Twelfth-Century Romance, translated with introduction and notes by John A. Yunck. New York and London: Columbia University Press, 1974.

Gaunt, Simon. "From Epic to Romance: Gender and Sexuality in the *Roman d'Eneas.*" *Romanic Review* 83.1 (1992): 1–27.

Huchet, Jean-Charles. *Le Roman Médiévale*. Paris: PUF, 1988.

The Medieval French Roman d'Alexandre, edited by E. C. Armstrong, et al. Princeton, N.J.: Princeton University Press, 1937–1976.

Poirion, Daniel. *Ecriture Poétique et composition Romanesque*. Orléans: Paradigme, 1994.

Le Roman d'Alexandre, translated with introduction and notes by Laurence Harf-Lancner. Paris: Livre de poche, 1994.

Le Roman d'Enéas, edited and translated with notes and introduction by Aimé Petit. Paris: Livre de poche, 1997.

Le Roman de Thèbes, edited and translated with notes and introduction by Francine Mora-Lebrun. Paris: Librairie Générale Francaise, 1995.

Le Roman de Troie, edited and translated with notes and introduction by Emmanuèle Baumgartner and Françoise Vielliard. Paris: Livre de poche, 1998.

Ross, David J. A. *Studies in the Alexander Romance*. London: Pindar, 1985.

Statius, P. Papinius. *The Thebaid*, translated by A. D. Melville. Oxford: Oxford University Press, 1995.

Virgil. *The Aeneid*, translated by Robert Fitzgerald. New York: Random House, 1983.

See also **Amazons; Eleanor of Aquitaine; Epic, Old French; Eroticism in Literature; Femininity and Masculinity; Literature, Latin; Literature, Old French; Marriage, Christian; Queer Theory; Romance, French; Sexuality: Male Same-Sex Relations; Sexuality, Regulation of; Virile Women**

ROSARY

The rosary is a devotional method that combines meditation on fifteen scenes from the Life of Christ and the Virgin with the recitation of fifteen decades of Hail Marys demarcated by Our Fathers. The scenes are divided into three groups: the Joyful, the Sorrowful, and the Glorious mysteries, centered on Christ's Infancy, Passion, and Resurrection. The rosary finds its antecedents among several Marian devotions circulating in northern Europe in the thirteenth and fourteenth centuries; it existed in numerous variations until its codification in the late fifteenth century. In this period the devotion witnessed tremendous growth due to the efforts of the observant Dominicans of the Congregation of Holland, who founded a universal brotherhood dedicated to the rosary in 1475. This confraternity, headquartered in Cologne with branches throughout Europe, was open to all members of Christian society regardless of age, class, or gender. The emphasis on private prayer made the confraternity especially attractive to women. Extant roll books indicate that women, both lay and religious, comprised at least half of the confraternity's membership.

The term *rosary* also designates the strands of beads upon which the repeated prayers are counted. In addition to their devotional function, rosaries were believed to possess apotropaic (able to ward off or combat evil) properties. Since members of the confraternity were encouraged to wear them in public, rosaries became important fashion accessories, as can be seen in numerous fifteenth-century northern European portraits. Rosaries were often made of precious materials such as coral, pearls, and amber and adorned with pomanders of delicate gold or silver filigree.

ESPERANÇA CAMARA

References and Further Reading

Winston-Allen, Anne. *Stories of the Rose: The Making of the Rosary in the Middle Ages.* University Park: The Pennsylvania State University Press, 1997.

See also **Confraternities; Devotional Practices; Dominican Order; Jewelry; Lay Piety**

ROSE OF VITERBO

Rose (1233–1252) was born in Viterbo, a city divided between proimperial and propapal factions. The proimperial Ghibellines, who dominated Viterbo, were tolerant of the presence of heretics in the city. Rose, according to her earlier *vita*, was converted at a young age by a vision of the crucified Christ. She began roaming the streets of Viterbo carrying a cross and exhorting the residents to embrace the orthodox faith and moral conversion. Rose's attacks on heresy caused the authorities to exile her. She carried on her preaching ministry in nearby towns. After the Emperor Frederick II died as Rose had prophesied, she was able to return to Viterbo. Rose sought to enter the local convent of the Poor Clares, but they turned her away. The nuns may have feared disruption of their lives by an outspoken young woman. The same monastery accepted her body for reburial six years after her death. It is uncertain whether Rose belonged to an informal group of penitent women linked to the Franciscans, but she was not a tertiary, as was recorded by later hagiographers.

Rose was accepted as a prophet by ecclesiastical authorities, possibly because she attacked heretics. Moreover, her public pronouncements were exhortations to belief and good conduct, not formal sermons. The papacy also accepted Rose as worthy of admiration, but she was not canonized until 1457. Her example was held up for veneration but not for imitation by women. A cycle of paintings illustrating Rose's life was painted in Viterbo by Benozzo Gozzoli just before her canonization, but it is lost. Rose is regarded as a patron saint of Viterbo.

THOMAS IZBICKI

References and Further Reading

Pryds, Darleen. "Proclaiming Sanctity through Proscribed Acts: The Case of Rose of Viterbo." In *Women Preachers and Prophets through Two Millennia of Christianity*, edited by Beverly Maybe Kienzle and Pamela J. Walker. Berkeley: University of California Press, 1998, pp. 159–172.
Rusconi, Roberto. "Women's Sermons at the End of the Middle Ages: Texts from the Blessed and Images of the Saints." In *Women Preachers and Prophets through Two Millennia of Christianity*, edited by Beverly Mayne Kienzle and Pamela J. Walker. Berkeley: University of California Press, 1998, pp. 173–195.
Weisenbeck, Joan, and Marlene Weisenbeck. "Rose of Viterbo: Preacher and Reconciler." In *Clare of Assisi: A Medieval and Modern Woman*, edited by Ingrid Peterson. Clarefest selected papers. St. Bonaventure, N.Y.: The Franciscan Institute, 1996, pp. 145–155.

See also **Heretics and Heresy; Italy; Lay Women, Religious; Poor Clares Order; Prophets; Sermons and Preaching**

RUSSIA

The position of medieval Russian women from the inception of the Kievan realm in the ninth and tenth centuries to the late fifteenth century remains a challenging subject since the sources are slanted toward privileged and exceptional women and mostly express legal or religious norms rather than women's historical activities or attitudes. Still, recent studies of birchbark documents recovered from the swamps of the city of Novgorod strongly suggest that aristocratic and wealthy women of this period acquired a level of functional literacy and were able to use their reading and writing skills to carve out a meaningful role for themselves.

A clear understanding of the role of women in the Kievan period (from the ninth through the end of the twelfth century) is difficult because of the complex layering of pagan and Christian norms and practices during this period. While some scholars argue that the practices of bride capturing, polygamy, and pagan festivals encouraging sexual activities amongst early East Slavic tribes gave both Kievan men and women an opportunity to enjoy sexual freedom, it is not clear how easy it was in reality for women to pick their own mates. The unsuccessful struggle of Rogneda, a pagan wife of Grand Prince Vladimir (who in 988 converted Russia to Eastern Orthodoxy), to escape marriage to him, suggests that scholars may have romanticized pagan Kievan women, to whom chronicles often attributed magic healing powers, the gift of prophecy, physical strength, and cleverness. The latter quality is particularly ascribed to the most outstanding female of the Kievan period, Grand Princess Olga (d. 969), Vladimir's grandmother, who used her wit to take revenge on her husband Igor's murderers and to consolidate the Kievan realm during her regency for her son Sviatoslav. The fact that early Russian chronicles ascribe to Olga, who was the first Russian ruler to convert to Christianity, the gift of divine wisdom underscores the difficulty in distinguishing pagan and Christian values in this period.

While no other woman attained the same position as Olga in the Kievan realm, the sisters and daughters of the Kievan Grand Princes played important roles in the marital diplomacy of these rulers. In the eleventh century Iaroslav the Wise, who sought to establish ties with the West, married a younger sister to Kasimir of Poland and his daughters Anastasia and Anna to King Andrew I of Hungary and King Henry I of France. Iaroslav's son Vsevolod advanced the interests of his realm by marrying his daughter Eupraxia to the Holy Roman Emperor Henry IV and sending his daughter Anna (Ianka) on a mission to Constantinople for the selection of a new metropolitan to preside over the Russian church. None of these women seems to have been a mere pawn in a political game: French state documents of the 1050s contain Queen Anna's name in Cyrillic, suggesting her personal involvement in the politics of her new homeland. Eupraxia took the papacy's side against her husband in the struggle over investiture. Ianka, upon her return from Constantinople, founded a female monastery and Russia's first school for women.

Comparison of the twelfth-century expanded version of the *Russkaia Pravda*, Russia's first law code, and fifteenth-century legal charters and wills shows a strengthening of medieval Russian women's property and inheritance rights throughout this period. The Kievan code treated noble women's property as distinct from that of their husbands, favored sons over daughters in the inheritance of ancestral lands (*otchina*), and allotted to a widow only the portion her husband had assigned to her. From the fourteenth century on, an aristocratic couple's holdings were considered community property so that the wife could conclude contracts with her husband and become equally responsible for debts. After her husband's death she could come into full ownership of gifts and legacies and receive part of the estate in usufruct until she remarried. To keep the family property intact, daughters were allowed to inherit in the absence of sons.

The change in Russian women's economic rights and opportunities is documented in the written sources of the city–republic of Novgorod, which enjoyed a semiautonomous status in the post-Kievan period as a significant Russian trading center. Birchbark documents, mentioned above, show that women of Novgorodian merchant families lent money but held only moveable property in the twelfth century. In the fourteenth century they received the legal right to the ownership and disposition of land, inherited the use of *otchina* land in addition to their portions, and often appeared as co-recipients of a patrimony along with their sons or even received the use of the entire property. Novgorodian women administered properties even during the lifetimes of their husbands or in the presence of grown sons. They carried out administrative duties associated with their family businesses and became involved in Novgorod's international fur trade. Novgorodian noble women could take oaths and give testimony, although only in their homes, and could personally fight in duels. In the fifteenth century a few widows of Novgorodian oligarchs resisted the centralization efforts of the Muscovite rulers, though in vain. Marfa Boretskaia, nicknamed "The Mayoress," who became one of the largest land holders in Novgorod, sought an alliance for her city–republic with Poland–Lithuania to fend off Ivan III's takeover of the city.

The rise of small principalities in Russia after the political and economic decline of Kiev gave the women of Russian princely families greater visibility. While most scholars have discounted any direct influence by Russia's new Mongol rulers on the social position of Russian women, the conflicts between individual Russian princes and their Mongol overlords gave these women a new role as peacemakers or defenders of their principality when the Mongol khan detained their husbands. During the fourteenth and fifteenth centuries, the Grand Princes of Moscow in their wills elevated the position of their wives within their families to counter the pressure on the Grand Principality by their collateral kinsmen. The Grand Princesses actively promoted Moscow's centralization efforts by redistributing the patrimonial territories amongst their sons and maintaining peace between the heir to the throne and his junior brothers.

ISOLDE THYRÊT

References and Further Reading

Goehrke, Carsten. "Die Witwe im alten Russland." *Forschungen zur osteuropäischen Geschichte* 38 (1986): 64–96.

Lenhoff, Gail, and Janet Martin. "Marfa Boretskaia, Posadnitsa of Novgorod: A Reconsideration of Her Legend and Her Life." *Slavic Review* 59.2 (2000): 343–368.

Levin, Eve. "Women and Property in Medieval Novgorod: Dependence and Independence." *Russian History* 10.2 (1983): 154–169.

Pushkareva, Natalia. *Women in Russian History: From the Tenth to the Twentieth Century*, translated and edited by Eve Levin. Armonk, N.Y.: M. E. Sharpe, 1997.

Thyrêt, Isolde. *Between God and Tsar: Religious Symbolism and the Royal Women of Muscovite Russia*. DeKalb, Ill.: Northern Illinois University Press, 2001.

See also **Olga; Sophia Palaiologina**

S

SAINTS

See **Canonization of Saints; Hagiography; Hagiography, Iconographic Aspects of**

SANUTI, NICOLOSA CASTELLANI

Known for one treatise, *Ut mulieribus ornamentar restituantur* (*That Ornaments Be Restored to Women*) (a copy survives at Vicenza and another in the Vatican, although it is attributed, probably erroneously, to Francesco Filelfo), Nicolosa Castellani Sanuti (d. 1505) composed a spirited defense of the virtue and dignity of women in 1453. In forbidding ornaments and fine clothes to women, the learned Greek Cardinal Legate to Bologna, Bessarion, had proposed a revised sumptuary law in 1453 that prompted Nicolosa's response. Her treatise was composed in expectation of Sante Bentivolgio's marriage to Ginevra Sforza, and apparently carried public opinion in Nicolosa's favor. She was widely known to have been Sante's lover, and her plea for women's right to wear their finery, their only means of conveying their rank, social status, and virtue or personal merit, met with a sympathetic audience.

Nicolosa was born into a prosperous Bolognese family and her substantial dowry as second wife to Nicolo di Giacomo Sanuti in 1446 may have helped her husband obtain a title as first count of Poretta, an area famous for thermal springs. Nicolosa participated in humanist circles that gathered at Poretta, and she earned frequent mention from scholars in Sante's court circle, almost always accompanied by mention of her beauty. But Nicolosa was not numbered among the learned women of fifteenth century Italy because she had no Latin. Her treatise was translated into Latin by an unknown scholar, possibly Filelfo, but more likely, according to Catherine Kovesi Killerby, Guarino da Verona. (Killerby, pp. 262–263).

Distinguishing mere vanity from proper pride Nicolosa argued that by wearing finery women could acquire public and political virtue. She ended her treatise with these words: "State offices are not allowed to women, nor do they strive for priesthoods, triumphs, and the spoils of war, for these are the customary prizes of men. But ornaments and decoration, the tokens of our virtues—these, while the power is left to us, we shall not allow to be stolen from us." (Killerby, p. 282).

Susan Mosher Stuard

References and Further Reading

Beyond Their Sex: Learned Women of the European Past, edited by Patricia H. Labalme. New York and London: New York University Press, 1980.

Frati, Ludovico. *La Vita Privata di Bologna*. Bologna: Zanichelli, 1928.

Her Immaculate Hand, edited by Margaret L. King and Albert Rabil. Medieval and Renaissance Texts and Studies 20, Binghanton, N.Y.: Center for Medieval and Early Renaissance Studies, 1983.

A History of Women's Writing in Italy, edited by Letizia Panizza and Sharon Wood. Cambridge: Cambridge University Press, 2000.

Killerby, Catherine Kovesi. "'Heralds of a Well-Instructed Mind': Nicolosa Sanuti's Defence of Women and Their Clothes." *Renaissance Studies* 13.3 (1999): 255–282.

SATAN

Satan is one name for the Devil in medieval tradition. This being, understood as the ultimate embodiment of evil in the universe, was also sometimes known as Lucifer and as the Ancient Enemy of the Human Race. Conventionally referred to by the male pronoun, Satan was conceived as a multiform being capable of shape-shifting and of deceiving human senses in many different ways. Although Satan had been part of Christian theology from the time of the primitive Church, the Fourth Lateran Council of 1215 was the first church body to make an official pronouncement of dogma concerning the existence and nature of the Devil and demons.

According to medieval cosmology, the Devil was created by God as an angel. Rather than worshiping his creator, however, he initiated an insurrection against the Lord. Medieval theologians sometimes envisioned this rebellion in materialist terms, suggesting that Satan sat upon the throne of God and received adoration from some of the other angels. Whatever the precise form of Satan's transgression against God, he and his followers were punished for the sin of pride by being cast forth from Heaven. Ever since, Satan engaged in war against God, presiding over his army of fallen angels (now transmuted into demons) and fomenting mayhem whenever possible. Satan's kingdom was located in Hell, usually understood as existing underneath the surface of the earth. Thus in addition to commanding his legions of demons, Satan also presided over a vast region of the human afterlife. Indeed, Satan actually fulfilled the mandates of divine retribution by tormenting the deceased sinners who were consigned to his keeping by God.

Satan appears in the Gospel accounts, tempting Jesus just after his baptism as he fasted for forty days and forty nights in the desert. The most important depictions of the Devil in scripture, however, occur in the first and the last books of the Christian Bible: Genesis and Revelation. Diabolic activity thus framed the entire history of humankind in the imagination of medieval Christians. The first three chapters of Genesis recount Adam and Eve's creation, first sin, and expulsion from the Garden of Eden. According to the text, a snake within the garden tempted Eve to eat the fruit of the tree of knowledge of good and evil, a fruit expressly forbidden by divine command. Medieval exegesis identified this snake with Satan, the fallen angel, who thus was held to bear some responsibility for the lapse into sin of the first human couple and their consequent banishment from the delights of paradise. The Book of Revelation foretells the events of the End Times, which center upon a vast world war of righteous believers against the armies of the unrighteous led by Satan and his lieutenants. The text is complicated and fraught with difficult symbolic language, but ultimately predicts the final triumph of God's faithful and the binding of Satan and his followers for all eternity.

The struggle against Satan and his demonic forces was viewed as an ongoing condition of human life throughout the generations from Adam and Eve until the End Times. Within this context of unceasing warfare, women occupied a particularly significant role. Since the book of Genesis relates that it was Eve who spoke with the snake, first ate the forbidden fruit, and then offered it to Adam, medieval (as well as many postmedieval) theologians felt justified in assigning the majority of the blame for the Fall to Eve (although some theologians, such as Aquinas, argued that Adam had to fall too for the human race to be condemned). The consequences of this position were momentous. Since Adam and Eve were regarded as prototypes for all subsequent generations of male and female human beings, Eve's preeminent role in the Fall translated into the perception that all women were more susceptible to demonic seduction than were men. Hence women often were termed the "weaker sex," a designation that referred not only to physical but also (indeed especially) to women's intellectual and moral abilities.

The period from the thirteenth through the fifteenth centuries marked a movement toward an ever-stronger sense of connection between the feminine and the demonic. Satan was sometimes represented as female during this period. For example William of Auvergne, the thirteenth-century bishop of Paris, argued that angels only appeared to humans in male guise, and demons only as females. Likewise, in an increasingly common iconography, the sculpted portals of Notre Dame cathedral in Paris show Eve succumbing to the temptation of a female-headed serpent, and several Italian frescoes of the Last Judgment portray the Devil with feminine bodily characteristics. By the end of the Middle Ages the link between the feminine and the demonic had become extremely intimate, thus setting the stage for the witchcraft persecutions that gained momentum in the 1430s and continued throughout the early modern period. In many (though not all) areas of Europe, the core of the witchcraft stereotype focused upon the willing connivance of a female witch with Satan, in the so-called diabolic pact.

NANCY CACIOLA

References and Further Reading

Baschet, Jerome. *Les justices de l'au-dela: Les Representations de l'enfer en France et en Italie (XIIe – XVe siécle)*. Rome: École Francaise de Rome, 1993.

Bernstein, Alan. *The Formation of Hell: Death and Retribution in the Ancient and Early Christian Worlds*. Ithaca, N.Y.: Cornell University Press, 1993.

Caciola, Nancy. *Discerning Spirits: Divine and Demonic Possession in the Middle Ages*. Ithaca, N.Y.: Cornell University Press, 2003.

Clark, Elizabeth. *Women in the Early Church*. Collegeville, Minn.: Liturgical Press, 1983, pp. 27–47.

Kors, Alan, and Edward Peters. *Witchcraft in Europe, 1100–1700: A Documentary History*. Philadelphia: University of Pennsylvania Press, 1972.

McGinn, Bernard. *Antichrist: Two Thousand Years of the Human Fascination with Evil*. New York: Harper Collins, 1994.

Quay, Paul. "Angels and Demons: The Teaching of IV Lateran." *Theological Studies* 42.1 (1981): 20–45.

Russell, Jeffrey Burton. *The Devil: Perceptions of Evil from Antiquity to Primitive Christianity*. Ithaca, N.Y.: Cornell University Press, 1977.

———. *Lucifer: The Devil in the Middle Ages*. Ithaca, N.Y.: Cornell University Press, 1984.

See also **Eve; Spirits: Discernment of and Possession by; Theology; Witches**

SCANDINAVIA

The Northern climate and geography imposed hardships on Scandinavians that left only a small margin between survival and starvation. Gender division in labor was necessary to make the individual farm function and enable society as a whole to continue. In principle, men performed the out-of-doors work, while women's domain was inside.

Economic Roles

Throughout their lives as daughters, sisters, wives, mothers, servants, and housekeepers, women bore and raised children, provided food for their families for both immediate and delayed consumption, and produced cloth for innumerable purposes, including clothing, bedding, and the indispensable sails for the Viking ships. Icelandic women's work at the loom was especially impressive; their cloth became so abundant that it replaced silver as a medium of exchange in domestic and foreign trade and became the denominator by which all values were expressed for purposes of fines, legal compensations, taxes, and tithes. The unit was the ell, the length of a grown man's arm from elbow to fingertip, and the "legal ell" became a length of six ells (about 3 m), the amount that previously could be bought with an ounce of silver. The primary export from Iceland consisted of cloth and coats until about 1300, by which time it was replaced by dried fish. Nonetheless, the monetary unit of lengths of cloth remained as testimony to the importance of women's work.

Plucking (and later shearing) the fleece from the sheep and washing clothes were not the only chores that brought women outdoors, although their work here depended on the terrain. Where animal husbandry dominated, as in Iceland, most of Norway, and the Swedish interior, women may have worked harder than elsewhere because they were also largely in charge of the animals. During the summer months they organized the transhumance, leading the animals to the pastures in the mountains where they remained, as well as preparing and conserving dairy products. Where agriculture was important, as in Denmark and the Swedish lowlands, women were needed in particular during the harvest. In addition they performed everywhere their ancient role of gathering berries, nuts, eggs, and seaweed that were free for the taking. In both types of agricultural societies opportunities for female employment outside the family was limited to domestic service. The economic upswing that began in Europe around 1100 and introduced urbanism was felt also in the North (with the exception of Iceland), but the employment opportunities for women in towns were minimal. Nonetheless, Bergen could boast both prostitutes and a guild of domestic female workers (the latter was outlawed, however, in 1295).

Marriage and Family

The Scandinavian population lived in nuclear families that were in turn organized in villages in Denmark and lowland Sweden and in hamlets or isolated farms in Norway and Iceland. The prevalent incest that came to light at the Reformation was undoubtedly also an endemic problem during the Middle Ages.

Fathers arranged the marriages of daughters, taking into consideration the economic and strategic interests of the family. Like the other Germanic tribes, the Scandinavians followed the computations of a binary kinship system whereby ancestors from both parents were counted. This is undoubtedly the reason that daughters inherited from their parents, if not equally, at least together with sons and often before more distant male relatives. A daughter normally received her inheritance when she married, but it was to be administered by her husband.

If he died before her, she retained her property as a widow. Spouses did not inherit from each other but passed their wealth on to their offspring. If they lacked children or these predeceased them, reverse or back inheritance allowed the last surviving spouse to inherit. Since women undoubtedly found themselves as the last heir more often than men, they were able to funnel property from their deceased husband and even from sons-in-law into their own family. These conditions can be ascertained both from Runic inscriptions and later laws. In fact, women are treated copiously in all Scandinavian laws; to be sure they are without equality with men, but occasionally they receive preferential treatment. Thus, the ecclesiastical burden of fasting is lightened for pregnant women and nursing mothers in the Icelandic *Grágás*; the same law enjoins men and women alike to support indigent mothers, going into debt if necessary. Court cases from the late Middle Ages in Norway and Denmark demonstrate that women at times were treated fairly and according to justice.

Religion

The religious interests of Scandinavian women were prominent. The polytheism of the pagan religion was more woman-friendly than Christianity; the pantheon included female divinities, and women played roles in worship and performed divination and sorcery. Except for Mary, patriarchal Christianity envisioned the godhead devoid of female elements and permitted no liturgical roles for women. Women were nonetheless among the first to join and heeded the churchmen's admonitions in offering donations. In Sweden, for example, runic inscriptions suggest that women provided for bridges and causeways to be built in order to facilitate communication; undoubtedly encouraged by churchmen, such acts were particularly useful during the missionary period. In Iceland female saints were especially popular, and the Virgin had special appeal for women as demonstrated by the numerous miracles she performed in their favor, according to the voluminous *Maríu saga*. It appears that many aspects of the church legislation benefited women, including the prohibition against infanticide and divorce, the emphasis on monogamy and fidelity, as well as the introduction of consent in marriage. Women undoubtedly considered the promise of a bright afterlife in the Christian Paradise more appealing than the dark Hell of paganism to which all women were condemned.

Because Christianity arrived in Scandinavia later than in the rest of Europe monasticism also was delayed. The female appetite for a religious life was particularly strong in Denmark where there were almost as many nunneries (albeit smaller and poorer) as male monasteries: twenty-two and thirty-one, respectively, by the middle of the thirteenth century. Sweden had six of each, Norway five nunneries, and Iceland one, to which a few anchoritic women who lived alone in the wilderness or attached to a small church, must be added. The monastic movement was Benedictine or Cistercian in inspiration, but in the late Middle Ages, Birgitta, a remarkable Swedish woman, contributed an order of her own that included both women and men. This Birgittine order spread not only in Scandinavia but also to England and throughout the Germanic lands where it contributed to reforming the Dominican order.

As elsewhere in Europe, in Scandinavia a few women became rulers in name or at times in fact. From the tenth century it is worth mentioning Gunnhildr who ruled Norway together with her husband Eirik, and after his death, with their sons. She gained her political goals through goading and inciting the men. In the eleventh century the Swedish princess Margareta was given in marriage to the Norwegian King Magnús and at his death in 1103 she married the Danish King Niels, thus prompting foreign observers to remark that "in Denmark the government was in the hands of a woman." Margrethe, queen of the so-called Kalmar Union of Denmark, Norway, and Sweden (1387–1412) is the preeminent example of a Scandinavian female monarch.

JENNY JOCHENS

References and Further Reading

Blom, Grethe Authén. "Women and Justice in Norway c. 1300–1600." In *People and Places in Northern Europe 500–1600*, edited by Ian Wood and Niels Lund. Woodbridge, Suffolk: Boydell Press, 1991, pp. 225–235.

Jacobsen, Grethe. *Kvindeskikkelser og kvindeliv i Danmarks middelalder*. Copenhagen: Gad., 1986.

Jochens, Jenny. "Gender Symmetry in Law? The Case of Medieval Iceland." *Arkiv för nordisk filologi* 108 (1993): 46–67.

———. *Women in Old Norse Society*. Ithaca, N.Y.: Cornell University Press, 1995.

———. *Old Norse Images of Women*. Philadelphia: University of Pennsylvania Press, 1996.

Nyberg, Tore. "On Female Monasticism and Scandinavia." *Mediaeval Scandinavia* 13 (2000): 181–197.

Sawyer, Birgit. "Women as Bridge-Builders: the Role of Women in Viking-Age Scandinavia." In *People and Places in Northern Europe 500–1600*, edited by Ian Wood and Niels Lund. Woodbridge, Suffolk: Boydell Press, 1991, pp. 211–224.

See also **Birgitta of Sweden; Birgittine Order; Clothwork, Domestic; Family (Later Middle Ages); Household Management; Incest; Infants and Infanticide; Inheritance; Literature, Old Norse; Margrethe; Marriage and Concubinage in Scandinavia; Monasticism and Nuns; Paganism; Prophets, Nordic; Supernatural Women; Work**

SCHOLASTICISM

Scholasticism is a term that designates both a significant intellectual movement of the twelfth through fourteenth centuries and a significant change in the social location of medieval education. It coincides, furthermore, with a period of social, economic, and political change that began in the mid-eleventh century and flourished in the twelfth and of which Scholasticism was itself an integral part.

As an intellectual movement, Scholasticism was primarily theological, although it gave rise to intellectual consequences outside of the field of theology. It was both continuous with the intellectual life that preceded it and yet marked by new themes and new methods. The Carolingian reforms in theological education mark its beginning. Under the influence of Alcuin (735–804), theologians addressed themselves to the careful grammatical study of the biblical text and the use of Aristotelian categories in discerning its meaning, and they did so in newly created "schools" founded by the major cathedrals within the Carolingian orbit. By the late eleventh century, scholars had developed an acuity in the use of logic that allowed them to ask new philosophic questions of the biblical text. The work of Anselm of Canterbury (1033–1109) and Abelard (1079–1142), among others, illustrates the competence of these prescholastic theologians in discourse about such themes as the rational argument for the existence of God and the methodological strategy for resolving intellectual contradictions within the work of previous theologians.

Aristotle

By the late twelfth century, other works of Aristotle were available to the scholars. Muslim scholars had preserved the Aristotelian texts themselves and had studied them for centuries. Gradually both the work of Aristotle and that of his Muslim commentators, in Latin translations, made their way into the chief Christian centers of study, principally the University of Paris, where they began to influence the thinking of those who studied the *artes* (the disciplines that grew out of the old *trivium* and *quadrivium*) and the theologians. Nourished by this fertile mix of classical philosophy, Islamic thought and theological concerns, Scholasticism achieved its full flowering. It would foster wide-ranging debates over the relationship between faith and reason, especially in Paris. In Oxford, Robert Grosseteste (c. 1175–1253) and Roger Bacon (c. 1214–1294) would lay the intellectual foundations of experimental science, while Thomas Aquinas (c. 1225–1274) in Paris would eventually recast the whole body of Christian theological thought into the ten categories of Aristotelian logic, creating a new marriage between Christian theology and classical philosophy.

None of this escaped the notice of Church authorities. They first moved to forbid the Parisian theologians from studying Aristotle, although the arts masters were free to continue with their pursuit of the ancient philosopher. In 1277, the bishop of Paris, Etienne Tempier, set up a commission to review the work of the Parisian scholars; a list of various suspect theories of the theology faculty, including many of Thomas Aquinas's were drawn up, ready for condemnation. Apparently the master of the Dominicans succeeded in having the case referred to Rome, but before the pope (John XXI) could confirm the condemnation, he was accidentally killed by falling masonry in his study. The condemnation never took place, and Aristotelianism remained a potent force in the universities.

Impact of Scholasticism on Women

As an intellectual movement, Scholasticism had a deepening negative effect on the status and understanding of women within the Christian tradition. Prescholastic theologians had indeed absorbed and perpetuated the negative attitudes of Neoplatonic philosophy of the classical Christian period, especially those of Augustine, to whom early medieval theology was particularly indebted. Nonetheless, early medieval theology was largely a matter of biblical interpretation, and its practitioners, schooled by the monastic method of *lectio-divina* (divine reading), read the biblical text in the light of their own lives and their lives in the light of the sacred text. This meant that the actual experiences of known women and their accomplishments often balanced, even if they did not always outweigh, the philosophical presuppositions that discredited them. But once Aristotelian dicta about the nature of women were thoroughly integrated into Christian theology, philosophical convictions prevailed against practical experience and even, in some cases, the implications of the biblical text and Christian doctrine. Hence, when a theologian like Aquinas considered the questions of whether women could be ordained or could function as authentic prophets, his answers relied explicitly and authoritatively on Aristotelian natural philosophy in which women were considered "misbegotten males."

Education

As a significant change in the social location of education, Scholasticism also served further to restrict the already limited activities of women in the public sphere. In the early Middle Ages, education took place usually in the home or in monasteries. Social attitudes generally favored the education of males rather than females, but religious authorities encouraged biblical literacy as the foundation of Christian life, and women of the upper classes, at least, had access to the study of Latin grammar, rhetoric, and logic as the necessary skills for reading the Bible and the other Christian texts. Like their male counterparts, nuns required literacy skills as a condition of their vocation, and aristocratic women who were in charge of large households were required to see to the Christian education of those dependent upon them. Even when cathedral schools became part of the educational structure, they did not replace monastic or tutorial education, nor, more significantly, did they change the standard curriculum. The goal of monastery, cathedral, and domestic education was the same—competent reading and interpretation of the Bible and its theological commentators. Further, the structure of the curriculum was the same for all educational venues: a modified version of the classical *trivium*—grammar, rhetoric, and logic—and *quadrivium*—arithmetic, geometry, music, and astronomy. When a woman did become educated, she was learned in precisely the same way as her educated male counterpart and, potentially, a conversation partner with him. Granted that many fewer women than men received such an education, but recent and continuing research indicates that more women of the eighth to the twelfth centuries were significantly educated than was once supposed.

With the rise of Scholasticism there arose also a new educational institution, the university. The universities developed out of the independent lectures offered in Paris by men like Abelard and in Oxford by such as John of Salisbury (1120–1180) in locations that were essentially storefront lecture halls, not connected to already existing cathedral schools. The origins of the earliest universities are obscure; by the early thirteenth century, however, they were well organized as associations of students and teachers, modeled after the trade guilds, to withstand outside pressure and civic surveillance but also to monitor the admission of students and of scholars into the teaching positions or "chairs." The universities were thoroughly new places of learning, essentially independent, governed by the independent scholars who worked there and confirmed by charters granted by the city. Ordination to minor orders soon became a condition of matriculation at the universities, and women were thus institutionally excluded, a situation that endured in European universities until the early twentieth century. The universities soon became the seed-bed for ecclesiastical and secular leadership and the new learning based on Aristotle, the requisite training for exercising influence in Church and society. From these, women were explicitly and carefully excluded. Whereas in the twelfth century, Hildegard of Bingen (1098–1179) could counsel kings and popes because of her learning as well as her mystical visions and Abelard's own lover, Heloise (1101–1164), could be commended by the abbot of Cluny for her learning and religious leadership, women of the thirteenth century and beyond would be denied the kind of education that would allow them influence in the world.

MARIE ANNE MAYESKI

References and Further Reading

Bouchard, Constance B. *Every Valley Shall be Exalted: The Discourse of Opposites in Twelfth Century Thought.* Ithaca, N.Y.: Cornell University Press, 2003.

Chenu, Marie-Dominique. "The Masters of the Theological Science." In *Nature, Man, and Society in the Twelfth Century.* Chicago and London: University of Chicago Press, 1968, pp. 270–309.

Evans, G. R. *Old Arts and New Theology.* Oxford: Clarendon Press, 1980.

Mayeski, Marie Anne. "Excluded by the Logic of Control: Women in Medieval Society and Scholastic Theology." In *Equal at the Creation: Sexism, Society, and Christian Thought,* edited by Joseph Martos and Pierre Hegy. Toronto: University of Toronto Press, 1998, pp 70–95.

Pieper, Josef. *Scholasticism: Personalities and Problems of Medieval Philosophy,* translated by Richard and Clara Winston. New York: Pantheon Books, 1960.

Rubenstein, Richard E. *Aristotle's Children: How Christians, Muslims and Jews Rediscovered Ancient Wisdom and Illuminated the Dark Ages.* Orlando, Fla.: Harcourt, 2003.

See also **Aristotelian Concepts of Women and Gender; Education, Lay; Education, Monastic; Heloise; Hildegard of Bingen; Literacy and Reading: Latin; Literacy and Reading: Vernacular; Theology; Universities**

SCOTLAND

The study of medieval women developed in Scotland much later than in most of Europe, partly because of the later development of social history and partly because of the relative lack of sources. Most published work has only appeared since the late 1990s. Most research has focused on lowland Scotland; the lives of highland women have been as yet little explored.

Few records exist before c. 1050, although the Roman historian Tacitus reported a conversation involving the wife of Argentocoxos, a Celtic chief, c. 210. Scotland's name is derived in an origin legend from Scota, reputed daughter of Pharaoh, who married a Greek prince and escaped with him to Spain. Their descendants settled in Ireland and later Scotland. The Picts, the early inhabitants of Scotland, may have followed a matrilineal succession system, although this has been much-debated.

Women become more visible from the eleventh century, with Gruoch, wife of MacBeth (1140–1156). More influential was Queen Margaret (d. 1093, canonized 1250), a princess of the English dynasty displaced by William the Conqueror in 1066. She married King Malcolm Canmore and helped introduce European religious and cultural influences to Scotland. She has been both praised and criticised for attempting to bring the practices of the Scottish church more into line with those of the Roman church. Her daughter Matilda (also known as Edith) married Henry I of England. Other royal consorts during the Middle Ages also played significant roles during and, in some cases, after their husband's reign.

War with England marked much of the fourteenth century. "Black Agnes," countess of Dunbar, defended her castle against English siege forces for five months in 1338, while Isabel, countess of Buchan, deserted her husband in 1306 and helped crown his enemy, Robert Bruce, as king of Scots in defiance of Edward I of England. Edward showed little mercy to those who defied him, imprisoning Isabel in a cage in a tower for several years. Many other Scotswomen also suffered from the ravages of war, although some also cooperated and acted as spies or suppliers to the occupying forces.

Women's legal position in lowland Scotland was similar to that elsewhere in Europe, although highland marriage practices may have been more flexible, with concubinage more acceptable and divorce easier to obtain. Scotswomen kept their own surnames upon marriage. A woman brought a *tocher* (dowry) to the marriage; her husband endowed her with a dower for her widowhood. Wives and their property came under their husbands' authority; a wife kept control only of her paraphernalia, her personal dress and jewelery. However, marriage contracts often mitigated the strict letter of the law. Despite official restrictions on wives' ability to sue or handle large sums of money without their husband's consent, court records show many wives carrying out the transactions needed to care for their families. They even occasionally acted as procurators (legal representatives) for others in court. Unmarried women and widows had legal independence.

Opportunities for monastic life were relatively rare, although there was, possibly, an earlier Celtic tradition of women's religious communities. Fifteen religious houses were founded after 1100, although four were later suppressed. Few were centres of learning. Some girls' schools existed by 1500. The earliest surviving woman's signature comes from 1493. Literacy was not widespread, although some noble women wrote poetry. Two daughters of James I, Margaret, dauphine of France (1424–1445), and Eleanor, archduchess of Austria-Tyrol (1427–1480), became celebrated for their literary accomplishments. A countess of Argyll wrote Scottish Gaelic poems in the late fifteenth century.

Women played an important role in the economy. Some girls were apprenticed, but more probably spent time as domestic servants before marrying. Women are most visible in the towns, where they headed between ten and twenty percent of households. Women could become burgesses, although few did. Several widows became prominent merchants; Isobel Williamson had customers throughout Scotland and supplied the royal household in the 1470s. Others were their husbands' factors in their absence. Women dominated the brewing trade until 1500 and beyond. Women were also employed as bakers, candle-makers, bonnet-makers, spinners, midwives, and wet nurses. Many earned their living as hucksters or petty retailers, supplying goods in small quantities to the urban poor. Some women earned a living through prostitution, although, as it was not heavily regulated, this trade only rarely appears in the records. A few women held town offices—Marjorie Schireham acted as Dundee customs collector in the 1320s and, when several customs collectors were killed in battle against England in 1513, their widows replaced them. Future research will reveal more of these and other Scotswomen's lives.

ELIZABETH EWAN

References and Further Reading

Brotherstone, Terry, Deborah Simonton, and Oonagh Walsh. *Gendering Scottish History: An International Approach.* Glasgow: Cruithne Press, 1999.

Dunnigan, Sarah M., C. Marie Harker, and Evelyn S. Newlyn. *Woman and the Feminine in Medieval and Early Modern Scottish Writing.* Houndmills: Palgrave Macmillan, 2004.

Ewan, Elizabeth and Maureen M. Meikle, Eds. *Women in Scotland c.1100–c.1750.* East Linton: Tuckwell Press, 1999.

Ewan, Elizabeth, Sue Innes, Sian Reynolds, and Rose Pipes. *A Biographical Dictionary of Scottish Women.* Edinburgh: Edinburgh University Press, 2006.

Marshall, Rosalind K. *Virgins and Viragos: A History of Women in Scotland from c.1080 to 1980.* London: Collins, 1983.

———. *Scottish Queens 1034–1714.* East Linton: Tuckwell Press, 2003.

See also **Alewives and Brewing; Dowry and Other Marriage Gifts; Eleanor of Scotland; Margaret of Scotland; Marriage, Christian; Monasticism and Nuns, Celtic; Queens and Empresses: The West; Work**

SEALS AND SIGILLOGRAPHY

A western medieval seal is a mark of authority impressed from an engraved matrix upon a malleable material (wax, lead, gold) and attached to a written document so as to signify the seal user's commitment to the document's content. This documentary function of the seal, which operated at the levels of representation, identification, authorization, and validation, developed within the papal and royal chanceries of the early Middle Ages, remaining an exclusive male prerogative until the eleventh century. At that point, secular and ecclesiastical potentates undertook the issuance of sealed charters as part of their engagement with new formats of leadership. By the early thirteenth century, sealing's connotation of high status had evolved into a legal mode for committing oneself, extending rapidly, if hierarchically, to every stratum of medieval society. Patterns of seal diffusion register sensitivity to both status and gender, although the axis of gender only partially overlaps that of class.

The first female sealers, in the eleventh century, were at the royal rank: Matilda, queen of Henry I of England and Bertrada of Montfort, widow of King Philip I of France. Succeeding queens, abbesses, and aristocratic women followed suit, remaining the only female sealers until 1200. By the thirteenth century, however, a huge proportion of new female sealers belonged to the lesser nobility (gentry), to town dwellers, and to non-noble landowning families. While the diffusion of women's seal usage was largely concomitant with the male pattern, particularly after 1200, significant distinctions emerged both within female sealing practices and with respect to male usage.

Prior to 1200, high-ranking women had independently sealed transactions of various types, but by the mid-thirteenth century a regression in their seal usage had occurred, so that they sealed thereafter only in concert with their fathers, husbands, and sons, and only those *acta* involving their own property (personal estates, dowries, and dowers). Quite often, documents issued in the name of both spouses were authorized by the seal of the husband alone. Unmarried aristocratic women did not seal at all. By contrast, gentry and non-noble women seem to have had a more independent use of their seals: if unmarried, they sealed deeds in their own names; if married, they sealed a wide variety of deeds conjointly with their husbands, and not merely those involving disposition of their rights and property.

Seal legends, that is, the inscription bearing the names and titles of the sealers, also show a sharp cleavage between high-ranking and other women. Though all women were identified by reference to their position vis-à-vis male kindred (men typically were identified only with reference to men), aristocratic women tended to resort to patronymics, thus emphasizing filiation and ancestry. For gentry and non-nobles, who tended to display their names together with the names and titles of their husbands, conjugality as partnership was stressed. Heraldic bearings on seals further display a primarily male-centered lexicon for the formulation of female identity.

Women's seals carried as much power of authentification as male ones. No record ever seems to have been contested because it was sealed by a woman. However, such effectiveness extended only to documents issued in women's own names, while men might endow the transaction of a lesser person with publicity and with greater security by affixing their seals to the deed, even when they were not themselves principals to the transaction. That laywomen's seals operated at a private level is further highlighted by the sealing practices of queens, which were limited to documents concerning matters domestic and personal, their seals never being endowed with the symbolic value of the king's seal as representative of the authority of the state. In the monastic world, however, role and function trumped gender for seals of abbesses appear in contexts similar to those of abbots.

The leveling of gender asymmetry by office finds further exemplification in women's seal iconography. Images on seals were informed by a taxonomy centered less on individuality than on interpersonal relationships based upon membership within a kin or sociopolitical grouping. Prevalent iconography on male seals is role oriented, and costume is functionally specific. Kings are enthroned, robed in regalia; bishops and abbots appear in liturgical vestments; armed lords are mounted; craftsmen display their professional equipment. When women had a recognized function with an equivalent in the male world, their seals registered this function. Abbesses displayed a cross and monastic robes signaling their equal status by an image identical to that on abbots' seals. Not so for queens, however, who were shown crowned and holding a scepter but not in the enthroned posture of majesty that characterized the king's seal. As for noble women, the elegant and fashionable rendering of the garments clothing the slender effigies that appear on their seals, typically holding a fleur-de-lis or a hawk, places the female body in an attitude of sexual attractiveness. There is no display of function unless it is physicality. Their two principal attributes ambivalently symbolize women: from its strong association with the Virgin Mary, the fleur-de-lis evokes the importance of motherhood, and thus of women in the biogenetics of lineage, however paradoxically given the ideal of virginity. The hawk signals courtly life but in medieval literature it often stands for female beauty and cruelty.

Thus, the seals of religious women, creatures virgin and continent, were unrestricted in their use and in their explicit demonstration of function. The seals of wives, sexually active creatures ruled by men, operated privately and connoted motherhood and kinship only indirectly through the emblematic system of heraldry and the metaphorical fleur-de-lis. Significantly, holy women, chief among them the Virgin Mary, received on seals natural depictions of biological and affective lives. Religious institutions did not discriminate between male and female saints in their choice of seal iconography; male ecclesiastics indeed showed a marked preference for displaying the Virgin Mary on their seals. There thus occurred on seals a displacement whereby natural roles were shifted from living persons toward holy females. As a result, the representation of living women on their own seals was of woman qua woman. Gender was the function that constituted and defined the natural woman's identity. Such an identity set women outside the order of society that was principally defined by gradations of male status. In terms of this overall iconographic pattern, the stereotyped image of the natural woman reveals a cultural template whereby men in groups were seamlessly bounded by the feminine.

BRIGITTE MIRIAM BEDOS-REZAK

References and Further Reading

Bedos-Rezak, Brigitte. "Women, Seals and Power in Medieval France, 1150–1350." In *Women and Power in the Middle Ages*, edited by Mary Erler and Maryanne Kowaleski. Athens Ga.: University of Georgia Press, 1988, pp. 61–82. Reprinted in Bedos-Rezak. *Form and Order in the Middle Ages. Studies in Social and Quantitative Sigillography*. Aldershot: Ashgate, 1993. No IX.
———. "Medieval Women in French Sigillographic Sources." In *Women and Sources of Medieval History*, edited by Joel T. Rosenthal. Athens Ga.: University of Georgia Press, 1990, pp. 1–36. Reprinted in Bedos-Rezak. *Form and Order in the Middle Ages*, No X.
Harvey, Paul D. A., and Andrew McGuiness. *A Guide to British Medieval Seals*. Toronto: University of Toronto Press, 1996.
Stieldorf, Andrea. *Rheinische Frauensiegel: Zur rechtlichen und sozialen Stellung weltlicher Frauen im 13. und 14. Jahrhundert*. Cologne: Böhlau, 1999.

See also **Abbesses; Art, Representations of Women in; Body: Visual Representations of; Clothing; Coinage; Gender in Art; Hagiography, Iconographic Aspects of; Heraldry; Legal Agency; Mary, Virgin: in Art; Noble Women; Queens and Empresses: The West**

SECRETS OF WOMEN

"Secrets of Women" (in Latin, *Secreta mulierum*) is the common title of a quasi-genre of texts, the most famous of which was written near the end of the thirteenth century and often bears a false attribution to the great Dominican theologian Albertus Magnus (d. 1280). Other texts with the same or similar titles were either selections from gynecological works (most commonly the *Trotula*) or material on generation and sex differences gathered from various natural philosophical (what we would call "scientific") traditions. Although these texts reflect no formal area of intellectual inquiry, collectively they show a pattern of thought increasingly common in the late Middle Ages.

Probably the earliest text to bear the title "secrets of women" was a French adaptation of the sections of the *Trotula* (a Latin compendium on women's medicine) in which the sections on fertility were crafted into a sermonlike work addressed to laywomen and men. The *Trotula* and other gynecological texts would be similarly adapted in later years, though usually for male audiences only. For example, compilers in the fourteenth and fifteenth centuries often took the *Trotula* and trimmed it of most of the sections on general pathology; what remained were the chapters on menstruation, infertility, and childbirth, the topics most immediately concerned with how the female body becomes and can remain reproductively active.

The pseudo-Albertan text follows this pattern of compiling lore on women's reproduction but also moves beyond it, using small selections from the *Trotula* and fusing them into a longer text that addressed various aspects of the generation of the child, from the physiology of menstruation to planetary influences on the developing fetus. Pseudo-Albert (who may have been a student of the great Dominican theologian) adapted elements of Albertus's Aristotelian views. He also culled together other lore about the female body, including Pliny's misogynistic litany of the effects of menstrual blood. The text is presented as a private tutorial from master to student and is prefaced by a warning that it ought not be shown to those who were still boys, either in age or in moral development.

Pseudo-Albert's *Secrets of Women* circulated widely in central and northern Europe, and to a lesser extent in France and Italy. It was translated into Czech, Dutch, French, German, and Italian, and received at least five different commentaries, two of which enjoyed particularly wide circulation. With the advent of print technology in the latter half of the fifteenth century, the Latin text was printed at least fifty different times prior to 1500 by German and Dutch presses. It would go on to have an extraordinary medieval afterlife well into the nineteenth century, especially in its reincarnation in the work known as *Aristotle's Masterpiece*.

Texts bearing the label "secrets of women" found three distinct audiences. First, surprisingly given the derivative nature of their content, they were often employed by medical practitioners as a source of information on female fertility, one of the areas in which male practitioners were claiming expertise from the thirteenth century on. In Dutch, French, and Italian translation, these "secrets" texts were often used by surgeons. The second group was clerics, very often preachers who copied the text into volumes containing sermons, grammar textbooks, or rules on consanguinity. Several copies even include it alongside tracts on witchcraft. The third group, who are represented most commonly among the owners of the German translations, were laymen who apparently wanted more knowledge of the processes of generation that were "hidden" from them in the recesses of the female body. Oddly, a Dutch translation claims to be addressed to the author's lady love. Christine de Pizan recognized the fundamental misogyny of the text, famously condemning it in her *City of Ladies* as "a treatise full of lies."

Neither the *Trotula* nor the pseudo-Albertan text were particularly useful sources of information on female anatomy or physiology; that they should nevertheless have been exploited so incessantly for over two centuries suggests how intense the desire for knowledge of the female body was. By the end of the Middle Ages, physicians moved away from the pseudo-Albertan text, basing their knowledge instead on the anatomical dissections then commonplace in Italy and on their own experience treating female patients. The *Secrets of Women* retained its popularity among clergy who continued to perpetuate the text's misogyny as popular lore. Indeed, it has been suggested that this text played a contributing role in the creation of negative stereotypes of women at the beginning of the most intense phase of the witchcraft trials.

MONICA H. GREEN

References and Further Reading

Bosselmann-Cyran, Kristian, ed. Secreta mulierum *mit Glosse in der deutschen Bearbeitung von Johann Hartlieb.* Würzburger medizinhistorische Forschungen, 36. Pattensen and Hannover: Horst Wellm, 1985.

Green, Monica H. "'Traittié tout de mençonges': The *Secrés des dames,* 'Trotula,' and Attitudes Towards Women's Medicine in Fourteenth- and Early Fifteenth-Century France." In *Christine de Pizan and the Categories of Difference,* edited by Marilynn Desmond. Minneapolis: University of Minnesota Press, 1998, pp. 146–178. Reprint in Green, *Women's Healthcare in the Medieval West: Texts and Contexts.* Aldershot: Ashgate, 2000, No. VI.

———. "From 'Diseases of Women' to 'Secrets of Women': The Transformation of Gynecological Literature in the Later Middle Ages." *Journal of Medieval and Early Modern Studies* 30 (2000): 5–39.

Lemay, Helen, trans. *Women's Secrets: A Translation of Pseudo-Albertus Magnus's* De secretis mulierum *with Commentaries.* Albany: State University of New York, Press, 1992.

Salmon, Fernando and Montserrat Cabré i Pairet. "Fascinating Women: The Evil Eye in Medical Scholasticism." In *Medicine from the Black Death to the Great Pox,* edited by Jon Arrizabalaga, et al. Aldershot: Ashgate, 1998, pp. 53–84.

Schleissner, Margaret R. "A Fifteenth-Century Physician's Attitude Toward Sexuality: Dr. Johann Hartlieb's *Secreta mulierum* Translation." In *Sex in the Middle Ages: A Book of Essays,* edited by Joyce A. Salisbury. Garland Medieval Casebooks, 3. New York: Garland, 1991, pp. 110–125.

Schleissner, Margaret R. "Pseudo-Albertus Magnus: *Secreta mulierum cum commento,* Deutsch: Critical text and commentary." Ph.D. dissertation. Princeton University, 1987.

See also **Aristotelian Concepts of Women and Gender; Christine de Pizan; Gynecology; Menstruation; Misogyny; Trota of Salerno; Witches**

SENTIMENTAL ROMANCE

The Spanish "Sentimental" Romances are a diverse group of relatively short and highly innovative romances that flourished in Iberian literature from the 1440s to the middle of the sixteenth century. The twenty-odd works commonly designated as "sentimental" rather than "chivalric" romances are deeply preoccupied with gender and sexual relations. They chart the emotional and physical trials of ill-fated lovers and examine the forceful power—generally destructive—of desire. They also share a marked interest in questioning courtly constructs, including chivalry, courtly love, and monarchal power. In addition to these thematic concerns, the Sentimental Romances abound in intertextual allusions and employ hybrid formal structures, which include the insertion of lyrics, dialogue, debates, interpolated stories, allegories, and epistolary exchanges into prose narrative frames. This formal hybridity and inventiveness highlights the Sentimental Romances' decidedly self-conscious literariness; the interpolated letters, stories, and debates are accompanied by fictionalized acts of writing, reading, and interpretation.

Juan Rodríguez de Padrón's *Siervo libre de amor* (*The Free(d) Servant of Love*) (c. 1440) is generally listed as the first Spanish Sentimental Romance in literary histories. A visionary narrative based on conventional allegorical pilgrimages, *Siervo* relates the author-figure's own experience of the delights and devastation of romantic love and his ensuing journey to wisdom, envisioned as a difficult ascension toward the temple of Minerva. The narrator and author-figure also recites courtly lyrics and tells the tragic story of two star-crossed lovers who come to a violent end.

Diego de San Pedro and Juan de Flores are the two major and most studied authors of the Sentimental Romances. Their late-fifteenth-century works were enormously popular and went through multiple editions in Spanish as well as in English, French, and Italian translations. Both authors were associated with the court of the Catholic Monarchs, Isabel of Castile and Ferdinand of Aragon, where Juan de Flores served as a royal chronicler. In Diego de San Pedro's *Arnalte y Lucenda* (*Arnalte and Lucenda*) (1491), dedicated to Queen Isabella, and *Cárcel de amor* (*The Prison of Love*) (1492), the author-figure and narrator becomes an interlocutor and intermediary for his central characters, who are frustrated lovers. Both works incorporate dialogue, letters, and lyrics, and *Cárcel de amor* also inserts a lengthy debate on the nature of women into its narrative frame. The debate occurs when *Cárcel de amor*'s hero Leriano, is languishing near death due to his unrequited and unconsummated love for Laureola, with whom he has exchanged a series of letters. A loyal friend tries to cure Leriano of his love sickness by detailing the evils of women, following the conventions of fifteenth-century misogynist writers. Leriano responds with an equally conventional defense of women.

Juan de Flores' Sentimental Romances date from the 1480s and 1490s. His *Grisel y Mirabella* (*Grisel and Mirabella*) revolves around the debate on women: the prohibited love between Grisel and Mirabella leads to royal and legal investigation into the collective guilt of either men or women in seduction. Flores resurrects two well-known literary characters to act as lawyers in the proceedings: to defend men's innocence, the arch-misogynist Pere Torrellas from the Iberian *cancionero* tradition; and to defend women, Braçayda, the character Criseyde from the legends of Troy. Although Torrellas is victorious in the proceedings, Braçayda and the other ladies of the court wreak violent vengeance upon him. Flores' resurrection of characters from other literary works and contexts is even more pronounced in *Grimalte y Gradissa* (*Grimalte and Gradissa*), where Gradissa demands that, in order to win her love, Grimalte must serve as a mediator between Fiammetta and Pamfilo, the protagonists of Giovanni Boccaccio's fourteenth-century *Fiammetta*. Grimalte is unsuccessful in his attempts to reunite Boccaccio's jilted heroine and unwilling hero, and thus his own desire will be forever frustrated. Two additional works by Flores, *Triunfo de amor* (*The Triumph of Love*) and *La coronacón de la señora Gracisla* (*The Coronation of Lady Gracisla*) are also studied in conjunction with the Sentimental Romances.

Other works grouped within the Sentimental Romances include: the *Sátira de felice e infelice vida* (*Satire of the Fortunate and Unfortunate Life*) (c. 1453) by Dom Pedro, constable of Portugal; Luis de Lucena's *Repetición de amores* (*Recitation on Love*) (c. 1497); the anonymous *Triste deleytación* (*Sorrowful Delectation*) (c. 1458); and Pedro Manuel Ximenez de Urrea's *Penitencia de amor* (*Penance of Love*) (1514). The latest work read within the context of the Sentimental Romances is Juan de Segura's wholly epistolary *Processo de cartas de amores* (*Process of Love Letters*) (1548). The ambiguous generic status, metafictional modes, formal inventiveness, and engagement with the broader debate on women and gender in late medieval Iberian letters and culture have generated prolonged critical debates on the meanings, intentions, and reception of the Sentimental Romances.

EMILY C. FRANCOMANO

References and Further Reading

Brownlee, Marina Scordilis. *The Severed Word: Ovid's Heroides and the Novela Sentimental*. Princeton, N.J.: Princeton University Press, 1990.

Cortijo Ocaña, Antonio, ed. *Critical Cluster on the Sentimental Romance*. La corónica 29.1 (Fall 2000): 5–229.

———. *La evolución genérica de la ficción sentimental de los siglos XV y XVI: género literario y contexto social*. London: Támesis, 2001.

Deyermond, Alan D. *The Middle Ages*. Vol. 1 of *A Literary History of Spain*. London: Ernest Benn, 1971.

Flores, Juan de. *Grimalte y Gradissa*. Edited by Pamela Waley. London: Támesis, 1971.

———. *La coronación de la señora Gracisla*. In *Dos opúsculos isabelinos: La coronación de la señora Gracisla (BN MS. 22020) y Nicolás Núñez, Cárcel de Amor*. Edited by Keith Whinnom. Exeter, U.K.: University of Exeter, 1979, pp. 3–47.

———. *Triunfo de amor*. Edited by Antonio Gargano. Pisa: Giardini editori e stampatori, 1981.

———. *La historia de Grisel y Mirabella: Edición facsímile sobre la de Juan de Cromberger de 1529*. Introduction by

Pablo Alcázar López and José A. González Núñez. Granada: Editorial Don Quijote, 1983.

Gerli, E. Michael. "Toward a Poetics of the Spanish Sentimental Romance." *Hispania* 72.3 (1989): 474–482.

Grieve, Patricia E. *Desire and Death in the Spanish Sentimental Romance, 1440–1550.* Newark, Del.: Juan de la Cuesta, 1987.

Gwara Joseph J. and E. Michael Gerli, eds. *Studies on the Spanish Sentimental Romance (1440–1550): Redefining a Genre.* London: Támesis, 1997.

Matulka, Barbara. *The Novels of Juan de Flores and Their European Diffusion: A Study in Comparative Literature.* Geneva: Slatkine, 1974.

Menéndez y Pelayo, Marcelino. *Orígenes de la novela.* 4 vols. Madrid: Bailly-Baillière, 1905–1915.

Rodríguez del Padrón, Juan. *Siervo libre de amor.* Edited by Antonio Prieto. Madrid: Castalia, 1986.

San Pedro, Diego de. *Obras completas.* 2 vols. Edited by Keith Whinnom. Madrid: Castalia, 1985.

Whinnom, Keith. *The Spanish Sentimental Romance 1440–1440: A Critical Biography.* London: Grant and Cutler, 1983.

See also **Boccaccio, Giovanni; Courtly Love; Debate Literature; Defenses of Women; Gender Ideologies; Isabel I; Literacy and Reading: Vernacular; Literature, Iberian; Lovesickness; Misogyny; Ovid, Medieval Reception of; Sexuality, Regulation of**

SERMONS AND PREACHING

Medieval women claimed the Holy Spirit's inspiration as authority to proclaim the Word, whether inside religious communities or even in public settings. They preached, attended sermons, influenced the content of preaching, and disseminated its teaching. Reconstructing the activity of women as preachers proves more difficult than ascertaining their role as listeners. Very few sermon collections by women have been identified, notably those of Hildegard of Bingen (1098–1179), and Humility of Faenza (1226–1310). Moreover, ecclesiastical authors such as James of Vitry showcased women like Marie of Oignies for their devotion to sermons and preachers. Overall, male authors described female speech with caution, employing a variety of synonyms for discourse that would be classified as preaching if performed by an authorized man. Medieval debates swirled around the proper term for Mary Magdalen's resurrection testimony: some wary churchmen declared that she "announced" but did not preach the good news, while others hailed her as *apostolorum apostola* and retold the legend of her preaching in Provence. Modern historians, bound by fixed terminology, definitions, and narratives, have often passed over the voices of preaching women. Nonetheless, careful reading of varied sources reveals women engaged with the Word as producers and not only as consumers of sermons.

The Early Middle Ages

Saints' lives provide testimonies about the preaching of early medieval women when the texts include plausible accounts of daily events amidst legendary material. Holy women delivered discourses, called instruction or occasionally preaching, to audiences inside and outside the monastery. These utterances generally remain in the story's background among everyday pious activities, while ascetic feats or dazzling miracles occupy the narrative's foreground.

In the early seventh century, Baudonivia, a nun at the monastery of the Holy Cross in Poitiers, composed a *vita* of the founder, Radegund (c. 529–587), which resolutely recounts what the earlier biography by Venantius Fortunatus omitted. Writing under obedience to Abbess Dedimia and relying on testimony from sisters who included Radegund's contemporaries, Baudonivia praises the founder for her preaching, which she relates utilizing the verb *praedicare*. Baudonivia includes a brief sermon reported in direct speech, as Radegund "would often say when she preached to us" (p. 91). Baudonivia remarks that Radegund "never ceased to preach on what the reading offered for the salvation of the soul" (p. 92); furthermore, undoubtedly inspired by the *vita* of Caesarius of Arles, Baudonivia signals that Radegund preached while asleep.

In contrast, the male biographers of two learned Carolingian women, Leoba (d. 779) and Liutberga (d. 870), described their subjects as giving spiritual instruction to audiences, but avoided the verb *praedicare*. Leoba dreams that a purple cord comes forth from her innermost body—a sign that she would "speak" "wise counsels" from her heart. Called to assist Boniface in his missionary activity, she customarily gives "spiritual instruction" to her nuns; respected for her knowledge of Scripture and her wise counsel, she "discussed spiritual matters" with princes and prelates, and sometimes "held a conversation" with the brothers at Fulda. Liutberga, on the other hand, became a recluse at Windenhausen after years of giving spiritual counsel to the imperial family. Her *vita*, written by a monk of Halberstadt, recounts briefly that she gave any spare time she had to instructing the women who came to her cell.

When writing about thirteenth-century nuns at Helfta, Caroline Walker Bynum concludes that women who "grew up in monasteries were less likely to be influenced by the contemporary stereotype of woman as morally and intellectually inferior" (p. 185). Perhaps the same observation extends to the general perception of nuns and behavior within convents as compared to laywomen acting in public. Certainly when one contrasts the activities of Radegund, Leoba, and Liutberga with the fate of Theuda (c. 847), it is clear that within religious communities, preaching, teaching, and learning took place in greater freedom than outside convent walls. Rabanus Maurus, who commissioned Rudolf of Fulda to write Leoba's *vita* around 836, presided as the new archbishop of Mainz over the 847 synod that punished a laywoman for usurping the office of preaching. Theuda, called a pseudo-prophetess, claimed the authority of divine revelation for publicly preaching that the end of the world was imminent. Many believed her, brought her gifts, and commended themselves to her prayers. Interrogated at St. Alban's monastery and sentenced to public flogging, she reportedly put an end to her prophecies.

The Gregorian Reforms and After

The medieval hierarchy solidified as a result of the eleventh-century Gregorian Reforms and moved to deny the *magisterium vocis*, public preaching, and even interpretation of Scripture to all women. More or less contemporaneously, they attempted to restrain religious women with stricter rules of enclosure. The Fourth Lateran Council (1215) prohibited establishing new religious rules, and thereby new orders, at a time when women in increasing numbers sought to lead a religious life; at the same time Canon Ten specified that suitable men be recruited for preaching and marked a new emphasis on preaching as an instrument of education and propaganda. Literature designed for the office of preaching multiplied, including model sermons and preaching manuals. The latter also designated who held authority to preach and even to comment on Scripture. Thomas of Chobham's *Summa de arte praedicandi* allowed that female superiors might give moral instruction to their communities, but not "expound on Scripture by preaching" (*sacram Scripturam predicando exponere*) (p. 58).

Before the thirteenth century clamped down more tightly on women's religious expression, the extraordinary Hildegard of Bingen not only preached on the Scriptures to her nuns, who recorded the fifty-eight *Expositiones evangeliorum*, homiletic commentaries on the Gospels, but also addressed monastic communities and even mixed audiences during the four preaching tours she undertook from her monastery at Rupertsberg. Hildegard's public sermons delivered in Trier, Cologne, and Kirchheim were preserved in her letter collection. In contrast, emulation of Hildegard led to charges of demonic possession for Sigewize, who witnessed Hildegard's preaching tours and then imitated her but espoused Cathar beliefs.

Sigewize and her exorcism demonstrate the extent to which women's public discourse on religion could transgress accepted norms.

Contemporaneous with Hildegard, nuns at the Benedictine double monastery of Admont in Austria preached in their chapter meeting on feast days when the abbot or his deputy was unable to be present. Two manuscripts of sermons for feast days feature portraits of nuns, one holding a book and the other preaching. Abbot Irimbert (1172–1176) praised the nuns' skill in exegesis and probably benefited from their input in composing his scriptural commentaries.

At the turn of the next century, however, evidence that abbesses preached derives from the effort to silence them. Abbesses in the dioceses of Palencia and Burgos, notably at the Cistercian monastery of Las Huelgas, aroused Innocent III's astonishment and provoked a 1210 bull prohibiting them from blessing their own nuns, hearing their confessions, and preaching their interpretation of the Gospels.

Women as Audience

For medieval ecclesiastics, the appropriate relationship of women to sermons was that of listener. *Vitae* highlighted the thirst of holy women for sermons. James of Vitry describes Marie of Oignies as an avid listener and astute critic of his preaching. While Marie advised James on how to avoid homiletic failure, her public voice on theology sounded forth only in the songs she intoned on her deathbed. James was one of many preachers who addressed and composed sermons for lay and religious female audiences. Before the mendicant orders expanded the ministry of preaching to women and others, Robert of Arbrissel and Gilbert of Sempringham founded female-centered orders; Abelard wrote sermons for Heloise's community at the Paraclete, and the Cistercian Gilbert of Hoyland addressed some of his sermons on the Song of Songs to nuns.

Prominent churchmen and famous preachers such as Humbert of Romans (c. 1200–1277), minister general of the Dominican order, Gilbert of Tournai, Stephen of Bourbon, and Berthold of Regensberg composed sermons for female audiences. Friars and other clergy assumed the *cura monialium*, celebrating the mass, preaching, hearing confessions, and giving spiritual direction. Among the best known, Meister Eckhart (c. 1260–1328) preached to Cistercian, Benedictine, and Dominican women, Johannes Tauler (c. 1300–1361) addressed female audiences, and Heinrich Seuse (c. 1295–1366) served the sisters at Toss and elsewhere. Italian mendicants who preached to women include Giovanni Dominici (1356–1419), Bernardino of Siena (1380–1444), and Savonarola (1452–1498).

Numerous extant sermons provide model texts for preachers to address female audiences on moral behavior, including saintly exemplars such as the repentant Magdalen; praises of virginity and chastity; the proper relationships in marriage and family; the sacramentality of marriage against Cathar views and the idealized adultery of courtly literature; the instruction mothers should give their children on good faith and upright conduct; warnings on vices associated with women, such as loquaciousness, and in particular vanity—the target of sumptuary laws in prosperous communes. Sermon collections have been identified for many female audiences, including nuns, Beguines, tertiaries, young girls, married women, widows, and prostitutes. Moreover, compilations of *exempla* (brief anecdotes, historical or contemporary, for inclusion in sermons) feature stories with lessons for and about women.

Attentive listening led to criticism and praise of sermons and preachers. Mechthild of Magdeburg (c. 1208–1284 or 1297) reproached preachers as poor listeners, while Marguerite of Oingt (c. 1240–1310) defended a Franciscan preacher's account of the Passion against the objections of a Carthusian. A regular diet of sermons proved so crucial to religious women that when illness prevented Gertrude the Great (1256–1301/1302) from hearing a sermon, Christ appeared to console and to preach to her. In the rich spiritual and intellectual milieu at Helfta, Gertrude wrote her *Herald of Divine Love* with the collaboration of her sisters, who praise her quick mind and eloquent speech when her adept understanding of Scripture facilitated the edification of her listeners and the refutation of errors. The impact of the spiritual instruction Gertrude provided mirrors accounts of effective preaching when, "Some, through her words, were brought to repent and were saved" (*Herald*, p. 54).

German sister-books or convent chronicles, many from the fourteenth century, provide rich evidence for the impact of sermons. Upon hearing the word of God, Elsbeth von Beggenhofen, according to the Ötenbach chronicler, desired to cry out loudly from divine love, while Metze, sister of chronicler Anna von Munzingen, experienced rigid limbs. Sermons or the desire for them also led to visionary experience. Preaching on the passion moved the child Adelheid Langmann to meditation. According to the Toss *Sisterbook*, Mezzi Sidwibrin envisioned the Christ child seated on a preacher's lap during a Christmas sermon, and an Advent sermon on *Ecce* ("Behold") stirred her to repeat the word a thousand times. Like Gertrude the Great, Adelheit von Hiltegarthausen

could not attend a sermon because of illness, whereupon Christ himself came to preach to her.

Italy

Italian sources, textual and visual, attest to the power of preaching. Paintings portray attentive crowds listening to outdoor sermons, with female separated from male listeners. Bernardino of Siena's preaching against the vanity of women prompted the lighting of bonfires of vanities (fashionable clothing, false hair, and the like) in Florence and elsewhere. His preaching with the IHS symbol produced exorcisms of women and men, as did the sermons of the Dominican Vincent Ferrer (d. 1419). Paintings in the churches of Macello and of St. Dominic in Modena depict Ferrer's cure of a woman possessed by the devil. The transformative power of preaching emerges clearly in the *vita* of Camilla Battista da Varano (1458–1524), a Poor Clare: hearing a sermon around the age of eight transformed her life completely, moving her to shed at least one tear every Friday for love of Christ's passion.

Italian saints illustrate a variety of ways in which women answered the Spirit's call. Rose of Viterbo distinguished herself as a street preacher in her native Viterbo; her exhortations were tolerated by a local church that saw her denouncing heresy and its political opponents. Humility of Faenza (1226–1310) preached from her cell at St. Apollinaris in Faenza and later led the monastery of St. John the Evangelist in Florence. An altar piece by Pietro Lorenzetti shows Humility reading to her sisters in the refectory and dictating sermons, nine of which are extant, as are some *laude*, or poems of praise to the Virgin Mary. Angela of Foligno (1248–1309) dictated the sermon-like accounts of her spiritual experiences to Brother A., her Franciscan confessor. Angela did not refrain from criticizing contemporary preachers; a vision following meditation on Scripture led her to conclude that preachers did not understand either the love of God or what they preached about it.

Catherine of Siena (1347–1380) exercised an apostolate that extended from her native city to Rome and southern France between 1374 and 1380. While she recounts in a letter a vision where Christ called her to preach, Raymond of Capua, Catherine's confessor, accentuates her gift of prophecy, defending her against detractors, describing her discourses as prophetic and employing the verb *praedicere* (to foretell) rather than *praedicare* (to preach). The confessor records Catherine's 1376 discourse before Pope Gregory XI in Avignon, clarifying his own role as interpreter from Catherine's Tuscan to Latin. To

Gregory XI and others Catherine advocated crusade, peacemaking in Italy, and the return of the papacy to Rome. When the Carthusians of Gorgona requested Catherine's verbal edification (*ædificationis verbum*), Raymond agreed to the journey, as he did to other travels under his supervision, and accompanied her with around twenty other people. Raymond reports Catherine's strong hesitation to articulate her thoughts, but affirms that when she opened her mouth, the Spirit spoke through her. Catherine disseminated her message broadly through her letters, which served as epistolary sermons.

Suspicions

Visionaries from northern Europe also thirsted for preaching while they claimed their revelations as direct authorization to make themselves heard. Birgitta of Sweden (1302/1303–1373) conveyed Christ's mandate to be his "bride and channel." While a vision from Christ called her to preach and convert as the apostles did, Birgitta generally relied on her male clerical supporters to serve as her mouthpiece; they proclaimed her revelations from pulpits and mediated between Birgitta and the crowds at public assemblies. She herself addressed crowds in Cyprus, where her confessor Alfonso of Jaén served as interpreter. Birgitta's boldness and controversial prophecies aroused suspicions, and her detractors accused her of heresy and witchcraft. After Birgitta's death, her daughter Catherine continued her mother's work of spiritual reform and proclaimed Birgitta's revelations during the journey back to Sweden from Rome with her mother's remains. Pope Urban VI (d. 1378) praised her eloquence.

Outside the convent, the religious discourse of laywomen came under increasing suspicion because of the reputed ministry of dissident women in the Waldensian, Cathar, and Lollard movements. Polemical accusations against dissident preachers range from charges of public usurpation of the office to allegations of subversive gatherings in secret conventicles. While scholars disagree on the extent of female leadership in dissident communities, evidence confirms that to some degree they permitted women to undertake pastoral duties, including preaching. Polemical treatises expounded lengthy arguments against women and lay persons preaching; preaching manuals (*artes praedicandi*) confirmed the prohibitions; and ecclesiastical authors proposed alternative models, such as the *vita* of Marie of Oignies—a countermodel to the active ministry of Cathar women in southern France. At the time that fourteenth-century Lollards were advocating lay preaching, Margery Kempe, whose fits of weeping and bodily movement became a sort of discourse for her, was interrogated by the archbishop of York. She spoke forcefully to defend herself against accusations of heresy, protesting that she had not preached because she had never mounted a pulpit.

The Beguines attracted clerical ire for their public service of the Word. At the Second Council of Lyons (1274), Gilbert of Tournai attacked the Beguines' vernacular translations of the Scriptures and their bold reading both in conventicles and in city squares. A suspected association of the Beguines and the Free Spirit heresy led the Council of Vienne (1311) to issue two decrees against the Beguines: *Cum de quibusdam mulieribus* and *Ad nostrum*. The latter led to a century of persecution against the Beguines in Germany, while in northern France the bishops of Tournai and Arras-Cambrai were ordered to investigate Beguinages in Lille and Douai to ascertain whether the women there were involved "in debates or errors."

Marguerite Porete, a Beguine and author of the influential *Mirror of Souls*, was burned at the stake in Paris on June 1, 1310, after disobeying an order to stop disseminating and talking about her book, an indication that she may have been suspected of preaching. Na Prous Boneta, a follower of Peter John Olivi, began receiving visions on Good Friday in 1321. Believing that the Holy Spirit had been given to her as God's Son was given to the Virgin Mary, Na Prous revealed her visions to others in her household, and then extended her message by preaching in other towns. She was interrogated by the inquisitors, incarcerated in Carcassonne in 1325–1326, and probably burned at the stake in that city on the order of Pope John XXII in 1327 or 1328.

Early Modern Era

On the eve of the Council of Trent (1545–1563), cloistered women continued to find creative paths around the restrictions placed on them. The *Ansprachen* (*Lectures*) of Abbess Ursula Haider (1413–1498) represent instructions on meditation that skirt the prohibition on female religious scriptural exegesis, as do the teachings of Caritas, abbess of Nuremberg in the early sixteenth century, who addressed her sister Poor Clares in reply to the sermons of Lutheran clergy which they were compelled to hear.

Thirty-five of Abbess Caterina Vigri's (d. 1463) sermons, delivered to the Poor Clares of *Corpus Domini* in Bologna, were preserved within her *vita* by Paolo Casanova who wrote around 1605, over a century after her death in 1463. A volume of sermons by Isabella of Villena (1430–1490), abbess of the Valencian convent of Trinità, once in the possession of a Carmelite friar, has been lost, although traces of Isabella's preaching may be found in another of her works, the *Vita Christi*.

The sermons of Caterina Vigri and Isabella of Villena illustrate, much as the epistolary sermons of Hildegard of Bingen, that women's sermons were preserved as letters or included in *vitae* of female saints. *Vitae* and chronicles also report the intense involvement of women as listeners. Continued exploration of a range of texts will further reconstruct the rich and intense involvement of medieval and early modern women with the ministry of the Word. Expanding the boundaries of definition opens the path for seeing the myriad ways in which women performed the Word of God without a conventional locus of authority such as the pulpit. Moreover, the intense involvement of women as consumers of sermons influenced female literary discourse. The impact of the sermon on the various genres adopted by women writers needs further research.

BEVERLY MAYNE KIENZLE

References and Further Reading

Angela of Foligno's Memorial. Translated from Latin with introduction, notes, and interpretative essay by Cristina Mazzoni and John Cirignano. Woodbridge, Suffolk and Rochester, N.Y.: D. S. Brewer, 1999.

Annales Fuldenses. In *Die Konzilien der karolingischen Teilreiche 843–859*, edited by Wilfried Hartmann. *Monumenta Germanae Historica: Concilia* 3. Hannover: Impensis Bibliopoli Hahniani, 1984, p. 151.

Beach, Alison L. *Women as Scribes: Book Production and Monastic Reform in Twelfth-Century Bavaria*. Cambridge: Cambridge University Press, 2004.

Blamires, Alcuin. "Women and Preaching in Medieval Orthodoxy, Heresy, and Saints' Lives." *Viator* 26 (1995): 135–152.

Bynum, Caroline Walker. *Jesus as Mother: Studies in the Spirituality of the High Middle Ages*. Berkeley: University of California Press, 1982.

de Vitry, Jacques. *The Life of Marie d'Oignies*, translated by Margot H. King. Toronto: Peregrina, 1993.

Gertrude of Helfta. *The Herald of Divine Love*. Trans. Margaret Winkworth. New York: Paulist Press, 1993.

Griffiths, Fiona. "'Men's Duty to Provide for Women's Needs': Abelard, Heloise, and Their Negotiation of the *cura monialium*." *Journal of Medieval History* 30 (2004): 1–24.

Izbicki, Thomas M. "Pyres of Vanities: Mendicant Preaching on the Vanity of Women and Its Lay Audience." In *De Ore Domini: Preacher and Word in the Middle Ages*, edited by Thomas L. Amos, Eugene A. Green, and Beverly Mayne Kienzle. SMC 25. Kalamazoo, Mich.: Medieval Institute Publications, 1989, pp. 211–234.

Kienzle, Beverly Mayne, and Pamela J. Walker. *Women Preachers and Prophets through Two Millennia of Christianity*. Berkeley: University of California Press, 1998.

———. "Penitents and Preachers: The Figure of Saint Peter and His Relationship to Saint Mary Magdalene." In *La figura di san Pietro nelle fonti del medioevo: Atti del convegno tenutosi in occasione dello Studiorum universitatum docentium congressus (Viterbo e Roma 5–8 settembre 2000)*, edited by Loredana Lazzari and Anna Maria Valente Bacci. Textes et études du moyen âge, 17. Louvain-la-Neuve: F.I.D.E.M., 2001, pp. 248–272.

Matter, E. Ann and John Coakley, eds. *Creative Women in Medieval and Early Modern Italy: A Religious and Artistic Renaissance*. Philadelphia: University of Pennsylvania Press, 1990.

McNamara, Jo Ann, and John E. Halborg, with E. Gordon Whatley, ed. and trans. *Sainted Women of the Dark Ages*. Durham, N.C., and London: Duke University Press, 1992.

Mooney, Catherine M., ed. *Gendered Voices: Medieval Saints and Their Interpreters*. Philadelphia: University of Pennsylvania Press, 1999.

Muessig, Carolyn A., ed. *Medieval Monastic Preaching*. Leiden: E. J. Brill, 1998.

———. *Preacher, Sermon and Audience in the Middle Ages*. Leiden: E. J. Brill, 2001.

Raymond of Capua. *Vita S. Catharina Senensis*. Acta Sanctorum, April 30, Vol. 3, pp. 753–95.

Roest, Bert. "Female Preaching in the Late Medieval Franciscan Tradition." *Franciscan Studies* 62 (2004): 119–154.

Rudolf of Fulda. *The Life of Saint Leoba*. In *The Anglo-Saxon Missionaries in Germany*, translated and edited by C. H. Talbot. New York: Sheed and Ward, 1954.

Sahlin, Claire L. *Birgitta of Sweden and the Voice of Prophecy*. Woodbridge, Suffolk: Boydell and Brewer, 2001 (Studies in Medieval Mysticism).

Simons, Walter. *Cities of Ladies: Beguine Communities in the Medieval Low Countries, 1200–1565*. Philadelphia: University of Pennsylvania Press, 2001.

Stoudt, Debra. "The Influence of Preaching on Dominican Women in Fourteenth-Century Teutonica." *Medieval Sermon Studies* 44 (2000): 53–67.

Suydam, Mary A., and Joanna E. Zeigler, eds. *Performance and Transformation: New Approaches to Late Medieval Spirituality*. New York: St. Martin's Press, 1999.

Thomas of Chobham. *Summa de arte praedicandi*, edited by Franco Morenzoni. Corpus Christianorum Continuatio Medivalis 82. Turnhout: Brepols, 1988.

Ulf of Vadstena. *Vita Catharinae Suedicae*. Acta Sanctorum, March 24, vol. 3, pp. 503–515.

Vita S. Liutberga. Monumenta Germanae Historica: Scriptores Vol. 4, Hanover: Impensis Bibliopoli: Hahniani, 1841, pp. 158–164.

See also **Abbesses; Angela of Foligno; Beguines; Birgitta of Sweden; Caterina Vigri; Cathars; Catherine of Siena; Dominican Order; Exemplum; Gertrude the Great; Hagiography; Heretics and Heresy; Hildegard of Bingen; Humility of Faenza; Italy; Kempe, Margery; Langmann, Adelheid; Lay Piety; Laywomen, Religious; Leoba; Lollards; Marguerite Porete; Marie of Oignies; Mary Magdalen; Mechthild of Magdeburg; Monastic Rules; Monasticism and Nuns; Monasticism, Women's; Papal Policy; Mothers as Teachers; Mysticism and Mystics; Poor Clares Order; Prophets; Radegund; Rose of Viterbo; Sister-Books and Other Convent Chronicles; Spiritual Care; Woman Authors: Latin Texts**

SERVANT SAINTS
See **Zita and Other Servant Saints**

SERVANTS

Several words were used to describe a female domestic servant in the Middle Ages—*ancilla, famula, domestica, serviens*—but they all denoted an unmarried woman who lived under the same roof as her employer and provided labor in return for bed, board, and wages. Recent research has suggested that for a significant number of young women, in later medieval England at least, domestic service was not a permanent occupation but rather a stage in growing up, a threshold period in which to learn useful skills and accumulate some capital. There were both advantages and disadvantages for young women in leaving their homes and families to live and work in another household. Surviving evidence by its nature tends to give prominence to the dangers of abuse and exploitation, while, because so little is known about conditions of service and the later lives of the women concerned, the benefits have to remain largely a matter for speculation.

At the highest level of society the daughters of noble, gentry, and mercantile families were often sent at an early age to serve in the households of their social superiors. An Italian visitor found this English practice inhumane, but domestic service of this sort involved no disparagement and was a way for girls to acquire social skills and make contacts that might lead to marriage. Apart from this specialized form of service, noble households were hostile to female domestics and, with the exception of the ubiquitous laundresses, any female servants were confined to the private quarters as nursery nurses or maidservants to the lady of the household. Male servants mainly staffed religious houses, although some female domestics can be found in nunneries and hospital priories.

Recent research, based mainly on wills, taxation records, and witness statements in church courts, has drawn attention to the significance of domestic service for girls at the lower levels of English society in the later Middle Ages. There were few opportunities in the countryside for young women to live independent of their families, and it was unusual for girls to be bound by their parents in apprenticeships. Domestic service, however, offered adolescent girls the chance to migrate into towns and spend their late teens and early twenties in urban households. These young women seem to have found their employers in a variety of ways: at hiring fairs, through kinship ties, or

trading networks. They were obliged by law to serve their master or mistress for at least a year and, although some servants stayed with one master for longer than that, there is evidence of considerable mobility.

As a source of cheap labour, requiring little more than their bed and board, the services of these young immigrants were much in demand in artisan and trading households after the Black Death. They were able to acquire the basic domestic skills of baking, brewing, needlework, and looking after children, but, depending on their employer, their duties could include other activities. They might be required to serve in shops, inns, and taverns or to help out in workshops with their master's craft and sell goods in the marketplace. As recession deepened in the second half of the fifteenth century, most artisans could no longer afford to employ domestic servants. Opportunities for female migrants contracted, the social status of servants declined, and maidservants are usually found in a purely domestic setting in merchant households and were an indication of their employer's wealth and status.

For a short period domestic service seems to have offered young migrant women considerable advantages. Independent of their families they could build up friendship networks, conduct their own courtships, assemble dowries from their wages and from gifts and bequests by their employers and choose when and whom to marry. The skills they had acquired must have made them attractive marriage partners, and they could afford to delay marriage until they found a suitable husband. This pattern of late companionate marriage was rather different from that found in Mediterranean societies where, rather than a prelude to marriage, domestic service was a last resort for women who could not find a husband.

Employers, as surrogate fathers or mothers, had the responsibility to care for their young female servants, who were often either related to them or of a similar social status. Bequests to servants in wills can suggest strong emotional ties and long-lasting, affectionate relationships. Servants were not, however, blood relatives and their association with their employers was temporary and could be fraught with difficulties. Young women living apart from their families were regarded as particularly prone to temptation, and so their behaviour needed to be controlled.

Both male and female employers could be harsh disciplinarians. Books of instruction, such as the *Book of the Goodman of Paris* and Christine de Pizan's *Book of the Three Virtues*, and didactic poems such as *How the Goodwife Taught Her Daughter*, advised the mistress of the house to choose her servants carefully, oversee their work and ensure that they did not slack or misbehave. Christine de Pizan pointed out that the necessity of earning their living from an early age meant that the moral education of domestic servants might well have been neglected. This meant that their mistresses must watch out for their dishonest tricks and try to ensure that they did not sneak out at night.

In the popular literature of the later Middle Ages servants were portrayed as prone to the female vices of dishonesty, avarice, disloyalty, hypocrisy, and lasciviousness. As weak women, they were a temptation to, and easy prey for, their male employers. The church's attitude was predictably ambivalent toward female servants. *Ancilla*, the term most frequently used for a servant girl, was also applied to saintly, cloistered women. In hagiography the picture of the fickle, scheming servant girl of popular literature was balanced by that of the servant saint, who was humble, hardworking, loyal, charitable, and strong enough to resist sexual temptation; an embodiment of the virtues of the church itself.

Most of the servant girls found listed in taxation records went from the anonymity of domestic service to the anonymity of marriage but the reports of sexual misbehaviour made to juries during ecclesiastical visitations in the later medieval England reveal the dark side of domestic service. The close relationship between servant and employer could undoubtedly lead to abuse and sexual exploitation. Masters and mistresses were bound to protect their vulnerable young servants, but they had complete power over them, and this could lead to sexual license. Even if the prostitution of servants by their employers was rare, there is much evidence of the seduction of servant girls by their employers or their sons. The detection of casual fornication could lead to dismissal and marginalisation. Women whose shameful condition revealed the nature of their misbehaviour were harshly treated, and prostitution must often have been the only alternative occupation available to disgraced servants.

ANN KETTLE

References and Further Reading

Goldberg, P. J. P. *Women, Work, and Life Cycle in a Medieval Economy: Women in York and Yorkshire c. 1300–1520.* Oxford: Clarendon Press, 1992.

Goodich, Michael. "*Ancilla Dei*: The Servant as Saint in the Late Middle Ages." In *Women of the Medieval World*, edited by Julius Kirshner and Suzanne F. Wemple. Oxford: Blackwell, 1985, pp. 119–136.

Hanawalt, Barbara A. *Growing Up in Medieval London: The Experience of Childhood in History.* Oxford: Oxford University Press, 1993.

Kettle, Ann J. "Ruined Maids: Prostitutes and Servant Girls in Later Medieval England." In *Matrons and Marginal Women in Medieval Society*, edited by Robert R. Edwards and Vickie Ziegler. Woodbridge, Suffolk: Boydell Press, 1995, pp. 19–31.

Women in England c. 1275–1525: Documentary Sources. Translated and edited by P. J. P. Goldberg. Manchester: Manchester University Press. 1995.

See also **Celibacy: Clerical and Priests' Concubines; Christine de Pizan; Conduct Literature; Ladies-in-Waiting; Prostitutes; Singlewomen; Social Status; Work; Zita and Other Servant Saints**

SEXUALITY: EXTRAMARITAL SEX

Throughout the medieval period, there existed a tension between the sexual morality prescribed by religion, the sexual norms deemed appropriate by secular society, and the average person's sexual behavior. While theoretical values and beliefs pertained to all people, irrespective of age, sex, or social rank, in fact, which behaviors were permitted, or tolerated, very much depended on whether one were male or female, rich or poor, or whether the behavior was being judged according to secular or religious criteria. While both value systems sought to regulate and control sexual activity outside of marriage, they did so for very different reasons.

In the early Middle Ages, before the Church had succeeded in disseminating and enforcing its doctrines of marriage, it is more difficult to identify exactly which behaviors might have constituted sins, given that polygyny, serial monogamy, concubinage, and divorce were widely practised by the upper ranks of society, and formal marriage was not accessible to slaves, serfs, or the poorest members of society. Fundamentally, by the central Middle Ages, both secular and ecclesiastical values promoted the view that the only appropriate venue for female sexual activity was within marriage. Secular society was preoccupied with the need to ensure the legitimacy of children, in order to perpetuate lineages, secure advantageous marriage alliances, and maintain familial honor. In general, moralists urged people to control their lust, noting that sexual sins were harmful and some transgressions were mortal sins.

Fornication

Fornication was the term used by ecclesiastical writers to describe sexual activity between an unmarried man and an unmarried woman. It was considered to be the least serious of the sexual sins. Among the modest ranks of society, particularly in rural areas, couples might engage in informal sexual liaisons, perhaps as a consequence of the general late age at marriage customary in northern Europe, for both men and women. Moreover, given the important contribution of children to the rural household economy, it may have been prudent to delay marriage until a woman's fecundity had been demonstrated and she became pregnant. Records from the thirteenth and fourteenth centuries reveal secular authorities, including local lords and manor courts, attempting to control the sexual behavior of villagers. In England, a special fine, called the *leyrwite*, was levied on women who fornicated or gave birth to children outside marriage. Both men and women, however, could be summoned to the manor court to account for their sexual behavior. Both sexes could be required to give sureties to guarantee that their future sexual behavior would be within appropriate societal norms.

While village society may have tolerated informal sexual relationships, the church considered them to be scandalous. Fornicating couples could be summoned to appear before ecclesiastical courts and account for their behavior. Couples might reveal that they, and their neighbors, considered them to be married, but they had dispensed with the formalities of priest and ceremony. Those guilty of fornication could be required to perform penance, for example, by being whipped three times around the local church. Habitual fornicators, especially if they cohabited or had children, might be required to swear to abjure further sexual relations *sub pena nubendi* (on penalty of marriage). In such a situation, the man and woman were compelled to exchange conditional consent to marriage. If they engaged in intercourse subsequently, the condition would be met and that sexual act automatically would render them legally and indissolubly married. As much as the authorities might have tried to control the sexual behavior of people, such informal relationships served a purpose, especially among the poor, for whom the solemnities of marriage were too expensive or irrelevant. Consequently, such relationships, although open to allegations of fornication or informal divorce, endured throughout the period.

Among the upper ranks of society, fornication was evaluated according to a double standard. Women were expected to remain chaste virgins until they married, whereas sex before marriage was tolerated for men. Given that familial honor, especially that of fathers, brothers, and husbands, was heavily dependent upon the chastity and good reputation of their female relatives, women were subject to heavy surveillance. Daughters were married as young as decently possible, and wives were largely confined to the household. Thus, among the landed aristocracy and the urban merchants, girls were married at a young age, at least in part to ensure they did not have the opportunity to fall into fornication. The economic and social structures, however, often resulted in men marrying later in life, and sometimes, not at all. Thus, at the height of their sexual potency, many men did not have regular access to a legitimate sexual partner. This resulted in the prevalence of brothels, frequently owned and managed by civic governments across Europe. These were rationalized as a means to protect respectable women from unwanted advances, seduction, and rape, but their main function was as an outlet for male sexuality.

Rape

Rape, including abduction and gang rape, occurred in towns across Europe. The streets were dangerous, and women were even abducted from their houses. Coroners' records also show that women working in the fields in rural areas were vulnerable to opportunistic rape by outlaws or passing travelers. While rape was a crime that could be prosecuted in both the secular and ecclesiastical courts, it was also a more serious manifestation of the sin of lust. Not really a type of fornication, it nevertheless had similar results for the female victim. Women who fornicated willingly, or who were raped, were judged according to a double standard that privileged virginity for a woman to make a respectable marriage. Consequently, many rape survivors were unable to find a marriage partner and swelled the ranks of prostitutes. Men, however, unless they were convicted of rape (a rare occurrence in medieval court records), faced few social impediments. They may, indeed, have gained some standing in the eyes of their fellows, as men of sexual prowess. A young man who fornicated would not face many disabilities in arranging a decent marriage, assuming he was a financially desirable partner and his sexual exploits were not excessive or notorious.

Adultery

Adultery was the term applied to illicit sexual activity when one or both parties were married to another person. The church considered adultery to be a mortal sin, whereas secular society considered it a criminal offense. According to canon law, adultery was equally culpable for men and women. Secular values, however, applied a double standard that reckoned adultery a serious crime for women but almost tolerated it for men, unless it was egregious or threatened the social order. In the early Middle Ages, secular law codes had permitted a father or husband to kill both the adulterers with impunity, if they were caught in the act. The church worked to curb this kind of vengeance, preferring penance and, ultimately, the reconciliation of the married couple. Nevertheless, until the central Middle Ages, the church also permitted a husband to repudiate his adulterous wife, although a wife was not accorded the reciprocal right if her husband committed adultery.

Among the higher ranks of society, in particular, the feudal aristocracy and royalty, adultery by a wife was considered to be treasonous and could result in the severest of punishments, up to and including death. While courtly literature and romances idealized the young knight's adoration of his lord's wife, this kind of adulterous fascination would have been very dangerous, even deadly, for a married woman. For men of these ranks, however, adultery was not only tolerated but even admired. It was not uncommon for aristocratic men to keep concubines, and to raise legitimate and illegitimate children together in the same household. Wives might rail against their husband's adultery, but they had little recourse. Indeed, a man was able to display his potency through sex with many women in the same way he would prove his virility on the battlefield. Although the clergy had the temerity to criticize such licentious behavior, it was nevertheless tolerated by aristocratic society, as long as the adultery did not involve the wives or daughters of one's peers, superiors, or allies. Lower status women, servants or serfs, married or virgin, were fair game, however, for the married man with a roving eye.

Other Sexual Transgressions

Another area in which a double standard prevailed was sexual activity across religious boundaries. Christian authorities, both secular and religious, condemned sexual fraternization between Christians and Muslims or Jews. Jewish communities were found across Europe, side-by-side with their Christian neighbors. On the Iberian peninsula, in particular, all three religious communities coexisted. Given that marriage across religious lines was impossible, all sexual activities between Christians and Jews or Muslims were necessarily extramarital in nature. Numerous regulations were enacted by secular rulers to prohibit such sexual relations, recommending harsh punishments for infractions. Of particular concern were relations between Christian women and men of another faith. Such acts of fornication and adultery were frequently

considered capital crimes for the transgressive man, and possibly for the woman as well. A more tolerant view was taken of Christian men who engaged in sexual relations with Jewish or Muslim women. This double standard was again related to society's investment of male honor in female chastity. A Christian man who had sex with a Muslim or Jewish woman dishonored those religions, and their men in particular, in the process. Similarly, if a Christian woman had sex with a non-Christian man, she dishonored not only herself and her male relatives, but also Christianity as a whole.

Technically, any form of sexual activity with someone other than one's legitimate spouse was considered extramarital sex. This, in particular, included same-sex activities, by both men and women, as well as masturbation or bestiality. The most common, and commonly reported, extramarital sexual activities, however, were conventional fornication or adultery. The meaning, evaluation, and punishment of these activities varied according to gender and social rank and, to some extent, according to location. Rural villagers in northern European areas generally had more opportunity to engage in extramarital sex than did aristocratic women and women living in Mediterranean areas. Although the Church taught that adultery and fornication were equally sinful for all Christians, in practice, the double standard rendered adultery, in particular, a far more serious transgression for women. Ultimately, then, every sex act that did not occur within marriage, with one's legitimate spouse, for the purpose of procreation constituted extramarital sex.

JACQUELINE MURRAY

References and Further Reading

Baldwin, John W. *The Language of Sex: Five Voices from Northern France around 1200*. Chicago: University of Chicago Press, 1994.

Brundage, James A. *Law, Sex, and Christian Society in Medieval Europe*. Chicago: University of Chicago Press, 1987.

———. "Playing by the Rules: Sexual Behaviour and Legal Norms in Medieval Europe." In *Desire and Discipline: Sex and Sexuality in the Pre-Modern West*, edited by Jacqueline Murray and Konrad Eisenbichler. Toronto: University of Toronto Press, 1996, pp. 23–41.

Flandrin, Jean-Louis. "Repression and Change in the Sexual Life of Young People in Medieval and Early Modern Times." *Journal of Family History* 2 (1977): 196–210.

Helmholz, Richard. "Abjuration *sub pena nubendi* in the Church Courts of Medieval England." *The Jurist* 32 (1972): 80–90.

Karras, Ruth Mazo. *Sexuality in Medieval Europe: Doing unto Others*. New York: Routledge, 2005.

Payer, Pierre J. *Sex and the Penitentials: The Development of a Sexual Code, 550–1150*. Toronto: University of Toronto Press, 1984.

SEXUALITY: FEMALE SAME-SEX RELATIONS

Retrieving the traces of same-sex relations between medieval women is predicated on scholars being authorized to posit the very possibility of such relations, theoretically and intellectually. This simple point of departure, nevertheless, became the locus, in the late 1980s and early 1990s, of contentious debates between constructionists and essentialists on the nature and scope of sexual marginality in times past. Originally, the debate opposed those (essentialists) who believed in the innate, irrepressible, often biologically determined, and perhaps even immutable, fundamental characteristics of identity—gendered, sexual, or ethnoracial, to those (constructionists) who viewed identity as the product of difference, shifting historical paradigms, specific contexts, and the workings of discourse. The seemingly radical opposition was questioned in 1989 by Diana Fuss in an important work that suggested the two positions were more interdependent and interlocked than previously perceived. Yet, an extreme form of constructionism, beholden to the view that homosexuality was born in the late nineteenth century, and lesbianism decades later, also expanded its opposition to essentialism well beyond rejecting the notions of natural or universal. The very existence of same-sex identification, not limited to discrete "practices," but encompassing sensibilities, consciousness of self, cultural behavior, political impact, and burgeoning communities, has thus been questioned.

Historiography

In 1981, Louis Crompton tackled the "myth of lesbian impunity" through a summary examination of a number of trials that ranged well beyond the medieval period, in which women were accused of same-sex malfeasance. Nearly a decade later, E. Ann Matter argued for the presence of woman-identification among medieval women mystics by carefully examining their writings. These were the very first attempts to bring to light the existence of "medieval" women who loved other women in the face of interdiction and danger, and these scholars unabashedly made the term *lesbian* explicit, taking a bold and pathbreaking stance, and positing the very existence of such women. In the early 1990s, however, the specter of terminological incorrectness and accusations of dreaded essentialism loomed large over discussions, not only of same-sex love among medieval women, but of women in all times past. By the late 1990s, the discussion had already moved to another plane: Michel Foucault's theories of the construction of sexuality were no longer the sole purview of the most entrenched constructionists. Scholars active in the emerging field of medieval queer theory, such as Carolyn Dinshaw, saw in Foucault's treatment of the Middle Ages a powerful insight into the inception of modern sexualities. In her 1999 book, *Getting Medieval*, Dinshaw made queer-identification a touchable, pulsating, connection between the distant past and the present work of scholars, centered on notions of community-building across time, and thus, continuing the movement to reclaim a queer past. These questions constituted a rigorously tilled terrain for the study of lesbian/female same-sex lives in the Middle Ages. Concurrently, Karma Lochrie firmly contested the validity of Foucault's medieval paradigms for a queer Middle Ages. In their introduction to their 2001 collection of essays, Francesca Canadé Sautman and Pamela Sheingorn proposed a middle ground, recognizing at once Foucault's potential contributions to the retrieval of a female same-sex past and his limitations.

Queer Theory

"Queerness" and queer theory had come to stay in the conversations about that past. Karma Lochrie pursued a distinctive and original contribution to such a queer reading, culminating in her 1999 book, *Covert Operations*. She analyzed the uses of secrecy in medieval society as the central shaping force in the construction of sexuality, and shifted traditionally male categories such as sodomy to a multigendered plane of experience and transgression, which she identified as a "female perversion." In an important 1997 essay on the imagery of the wound of Christ, Lochrie had reclaimed an historical lesbian presence by daringly queering a normative icon, the painted, and later printed, representations of the wound of Christ, shifting its identification to the vulva. Lochrie thus appropriated a seemingly pellucid religious representation and made it into a signpost of early lesbian visual sensibility.

Queering proceeded to unearth female same-sex desire in works of fiction, producing a body of interpretative work informed at the onset by gender studies. Categories such as gender instability and disruption have been examined through the themes of cross-dressing (donning of clothing ascribed to the opposite sex, in order to pass as the other), transvestism (a regular or permanent adoption, usually by biological men, of the dress, body language, and mannerisms of women in a manner that is also transformative and often performance-oriented), sexual disguise and sex change, as well as ostensibly hostile woman to woman interactions. Gendered readings of seemingly normative and opaque texts written by monastic women, such as saints' lives, uncovered desire and community (Weston). Queer theory's subsequent revisiting of itself with a greater focus on empire, early postcolonialism, and masculinities, may as much enhance as hinder the still fragile process of recovering the histories—textual, archival, and imagined—of female same-sex relations.

Scholarly interventions on medieval female same-sex relations have thus never eschewed burning theoretical debates. By the mid-1990s, led to a great extent by the work of Renaissance scholars, medievalists reclaimed a place for women in the developing field of studies on medieval same-sex relations, and provided new applications of gender and queer studies to the history of sexualities. Yet a pull, if not a tension, has remained between those who favor a process of strict historical documentation, and those who envisage the "imagined spaces" of the past through lenses such as queer theory.

'Lesbian-Like'

Women who might have expressed same-sex object choice and affection, and lesbians as historical subjects, had once again been "hidden from history" and made "twice marginal": such was the challenge issued in a 1996 foundational article by historian Jacqueline Murray. Examining a variety of textual sources across the medieval period, Murray called into question the theoretical premises that had virtually silenced the study of female same-sex love in the distant past, conceptualizing a series of questions that would give legitimacy to further investigation. Bernadette Brooten's book on early Christianity examined the forms, language, articulation, perception, and containment of same-sex love among women. This important contribution sought to read ancient history in order to retrieve the voice of same-sex female love and excavate the contours of the discourse that shaped it.

There remains the vexed matter of whether *lesbian*, both as a term and a category, is a valid tool for historically removed times. During the 1998 conference Queer Middle Ages (CUNY Graduate Center, November 1998), Judith Bennett presented a new term, *lesbian-like*, later developed in a 2000 essay. This was a methodological and theoretical solution to the problem of a presentism that affixed the contemporary label *lesbian* to traces of the past, without stifling research on gender-transgressive social practices among women who focused affectively on women, or exhibited that potential. Bennett thus argued for a reclaiming of the term *lesbian* that would also mitigate and correct its anachronism. *Lesbian-like* denoted an entire range of social contexts and behaviors in which medieval women could at least in part remove themselves from the direct control of men and function in independent, potentially woman-centered environments. Bennett thus formulated a blueprint for further research in areas such as monastic communities, singleness or widowhood, or historical instances of cross-dressing. Coming from a respected archival historian, the construct conferred legitimacy on a new type of historical examination, no longer constrained by the drive to merely seek "instances," but also open to imagining the plausible and the possible, to envisioning a female same-sex past grounded in spaces and social contexts.

Same-sex monastic communities, Beguinages, and other pious congregations were indeed a pole of attraction in the search for the same-sex female past. In this light, scholars have worked out hypotheses for the existence of possible spaces of lesbian/same-sex female encounters in the shadow of religious dictates concerning chastity and reclusion. Developing a concept coined by Theodara Jankowski, *the lesbian void*, Michelle Sauer argues for a "reconstructionist" type of work in reading the anchoress's living quarters and household structure in relation to devotional prescriptions such as the *Ancrene Wisse*. She posits the possibility of woman-to-woman erotic encounters and romantic attachments, founded on the historical public/private divide and a coincidence between the rise of the anchoress movement and the tendency toward greater privacy in the thirteenth century. In this argument, patriarchal society's fears of sullying contacts between women and men supersede its distaste and conceptualization of such contacts between women, so that secluded spaces are created that allow for female same-sex relations.

The hypothesis of potential woman-restricted spaces is bolstered by scholarship on penitentials, monastic rules, and confessor's manuals that specify penalties for same-sex acts committed by men or women. (Frantzen, Benkov, Puff). Yet, such texts address what the authorities wanted to avoid and curtail but is not necessarily fleshed out into historical occurrence. Patriarchal prescriptions against something condemned but conceivable, sex between two women, nevertheless delineates what is scriptable in the consciousness of the time. Such is the importance of Etienne de Fougères' *Livre des Manières*: referred to by most scholars in the field, it was studied in depth, with varying conclusions, originally, by Jeri Guthrie, then by Robert Clark and Sahar Amer. The importance of this book of conduct in rhymed and satirical form, excoriating the major foibles of women across society, lies in its denunciation and description, at once metaphorical and transparent, of actual sex acts between women, one of the earliest in the medieval West.

Trial Records

Trial records stand out as a privileged site for the documentation of "actual" lesbians in the distant past. Helmut Puff and Edith Benkov have given this approach an enormously significant inflection. Studying the late medieval trials of women accused of unnatural sex with another woman, in fifteenth century Germany and France, they have carefully scrutinized primary sources and contextualized them, both in the past and in the present. But both Puff and Benkov provided much more than an exacting reading of sources. Both theorized in important ways on the absence of lesbians in the historical record by questioning the very rhetoric regulating the representation of sexuality around the ultimate transgression of women performing sexual penetration and the absence of nonphallic sexual scripts.

Larger Context

The history of female same-sex relations has been enlightened by the readings of actual lives of historical figures, such as Susan Schibanoff's study of Hildegard of Bingen, or Gregory Hutcheson's work on Leonor López de Córdoba. These studies provide rich, complex, and unhesitatingly discontinuous engagement with persons, situations, and texts, articulated around heuristic tools such as the concepts of the homosocial and the homoaffective. Similar work on Renaissance figures—work published nonetheless in collections that conjoin medieval and Renaissance studies, further questioning received periodization—such as Laudomia Forteguerri, (1515—c. 1555) a

Sienese noble woman and poet who loved Margaret of Austria, or the multifaceted Eleno/Elena, a Moorish transgendered former slave who lived in sixteenth century Spain, have extended the field, showing how the concept of "same-sex" allows the inclusion of various configurations, not limited to the category "lesbian."

The collective work edited by Sautman and Sheingorn further questioned the entrenched relation of same-sex female history within the medieval West. Crucial contributions to revising this view and contesting the default value of Western paradigms in same-sex history were provided by Fedwa Malti-Douglas's investigation of medieval Arabic courtly and love manuals, by Sahar Amer's attribution of Arabic sources to the famed *Livre des Manières*, and by Ruth Vanita's skilled navigation of the erotic language of Indian devotional texts.

Further studies of biographies, life narratives, and trial records are needed and under way, hemmed in not merely by uncharted sources, but also by these sources' very rhetoric in framing sexuality, as scholars in the field have pointed out (Bennett, Benkov, Puff, and others). The structures of family life and the status of women in the West, still the dominant focus of this field, continue to create obstacles to making significant quantifiable jumps. These may indeed be felicitously derailed or corrected by an increased interest in and attention to studies of women outside the West, and outside Christianity within the West.

FRANCESCA CANADÉ SAUTMAN

References and Further Reading

Amer, Sahar. "Lesbian Sex and the Military: From the Medieval Arabic Tradition to French Literature." In *Same-Sex Love and Desire among Women in the Middle Ages*, edited by Francesca Canadé Sautman and Pamela Sheingorn. New York: Palgrave, 2001, pp. 179–198.

Benkov, Edith. "The Erased Lesbian: Sodomy and the Legal Tradition in Medieval Europe." In *Same-Sex Love and Desire among Women in the Middle Ages*, edited by Francesca Canadé Sautman and Pamela Sheingorn. New York: Palgrave, 2001, pp. 101–122.

Bennett, Judith M. "'Lesbian-Like' and the Social History of Lesbianism." *Journal of the History of Sexuality* 9.1/2 (January/April 2000): 1–24.

Brooten, Bernadette J. *Love between Women: Early Christian Responses to Female Homoeroticism*. Chicago: University of Chicago Press, 1996.

Brown, Judith. *Immodest Acts: The Life of a Lesbian Nun in Renaissance Italy*. New York: Oxford University Press, 1986.

Burshatin, Israel. "Elena Alias Eleno: Genders, Sexualities, and Race in the Mirror of Natural History in Sixteenth-Century Spain." In *Gender Reversals and Gender*

Cultures: Anthropological and Historical Perspectives, edited by Sabrina Petra Ramet. London and New York: Routledge, 1996, pp. 105–122.

Clark, Robert L. A. "Jousting Without a Lance: The Condemnation of Female Homoeroticism in the *Livre des Manières*." In *Same-Sex Love and Desire among Women in the Middle Ages*, edited by Francesca Canadé Sautman and Pamela Sheingorn. New York: Palgrave, 2001, pp. 143–177.

Crompton, Louis. "The Myth of Lesbian Impunity: Capital Laws from 1270-1791." *Journal of Homosexuality* 6 (Fall/Winter 1980/1981): 13–25.

Dinshaw, Carolyn. *Getting Medieval: Sexualities and Communities, Pre- and Postmodern*. Durham, N.C.: Duke University Press, 1999.

Eisenbichler, Konrad. "Laudomia Forteguerri Loves Margaret of Austria." In *Same-Sex Love and Desire among Women in the Middle Ages*, edited by Francesca Canadé Sautman and Pamela Sheingorn. New York: Palgrave, 2001, pp. 251–275.

Fuss, Diana. *Essentially Speaking: Feminism, Nature and Difference*. New York: Routledge, 1989.

Guthrie, Jeri S. "La Femme dans le *Livre des Manières*: Surplus économique, surplus érotique." *Romanic Review* 79 (1987): 251–261.

Hutcheson, Gregory S. "Leonor López de Córdoba and the Configuration of Female-Female Desire." In *Same-Sex Love and Desire among Women in the Middle Ages*, edited by Francesca Canadé Sautman and Pamela Sheingorn. New York: Palgrave, 2001, pp. 251–275.

Kelly, Kathleen Coyne. "The Writable Lesbian and Lesbian Desire in Malory's *Morte d'Arthur*." *Exemplaria*. 14:2 (Fall 2002): 239–270.

Lochrie, Karma. "Mystical Acts, Queer Tendencies." In *Constructing Medieval Sexuality*, edited by Karma Lochrie, Peggy McCracken, and James S. Schultz. Minneapolis: University of Minnesota Press, 1997, pp. 180–200.

———. *Covert Operations: The Medieval Uses of Secrecy*. Philadelphia: University of Pennsylvania Press, 1999.

———. "Between Women." In *The Cambridge Companion to Medieval Women's Writing*, edited by Carolyn Dinshaw and David Wallace. Cambridge: Cambridge University Press, 2003, pp. 70–88.

———. *Heterosyncracies: Female Sexuality When Normal Wasn't*. Minneapolis: University of Minnesota Press, 2005.

Malti-Douglas, Fedwa. "Tribadism/Lesbianism and the Sexualized Body in Medieval Arabo-Islamic Narratives." In *Same-Sex Love and Desire among Women in the Middle Ages*, edited by Francesca Canadé Sautman and Pamela Sheingorn. New York: Palgrave, 2001, pp. 123–141.

Matter, E. Ann. "My Sister, My Spouse: Woman-Identified Women in Medieval Christianity." In *Weaving the Visions*, edited by Judith Plaskow and Carol P. Christ. San Francisco: Harper and Row, 1989, pp. 51–62.

Murray, Jacqueline. "Twice Marginal and Twice Invisible: Lesbians in the Middle Ages." In *Handbook of Medieval Sexuality*, edited by Vern L. Bullough and James A. Brundage. New York: Garland, 1996, pp. 191–222.

Puff, Helmut. "Female Sodomy: The Trial of Katherina Hetzeldorfer (1477)." *Journal of Medieval and Early Modern Studies* 30.1 (Winter 2000): 41–61.

Sauer, Michelle M. "Representing the Negative: Positing the Lesbian Void in Medieval English Anchoritism." *Thirdspace* 3.2 (March 2004). http://www.thirdspace.ca/articles/3_2_sauer.htm. (accessed 28 May 2006).

Schibanoff, Susan. "Hildegard of Bingen and Richardis of Stade: The Discourse of Desire." In *Same-Sex Love and Desire among Women in the Middle Ages*, edited by Francesca Canadé Sautman and Pamela Sheingorn. New York: Palgrave, 2001, pp. 49–83.

Watt, Diane. "Behaving Like a Man?: Incest, Lesbian Desire, and Gender Play in *Yde et Olive* and Its Adaptations." *Comparative Literature* 50.4 (1998): 265–285.

Weston, Lisa. "Elegiac Desire and Female Community in Baudovinia's Life of Saint Radegund." In *Same-Sex Love and Desire among Women in the Middle Ages*, edited by Francesca Canadé Sautman and Pamela Sheingorn. New York: Palgrave, 2001, pp. 85–99.

See also **Aristotelian Concepts of Women and Gender; Cross-Dressing; Eroticism in Art; Eroticism in Literature; Hildegard of Bingen; López de Córdoba, Leonor; Queer Theory; Sexuality, Regulation of**

SEXUALITY: MALE SAME-SEX RELATIONS

Male same-sex relations describe a wide variety of experiences, ranging from casual friendship to sexual intimacy. Such relations were once rigidly categorized to ensure that the paradigm of friendship between men was not contaminated by romantic or sexual implications. Rare indeed were the claims of homophiles like Havelock Ellis, whose *Sexual Inversion* (1897) narrated a history of male same-sex attraction ranging from friendship to sexual intercourse. Ellis did justice to the medieval evidence of same-sex relations between men, material that is still scanted in histories of the topic; he positioned the English Renaissance as the point at which intellectual and social freedoms combined to allow homosexuality to be recognized as a cultural phenomenon.

Although male friendship and male homosexual intimacy were at one time understood as polar opposites, it is now common to present friendship and physical intimacy as stages along a continuum of male-male relations similar to the continuum along which homosexual and heterosexual desires are often arranged. The traditional (usually implied) homophobia of strict separation in degrees of male same-sex relations has lost at least some of its force as research into the history of homosexuality broadens and deepens. Scholars have become more willing than their predecessors to allow for romantic and sexual valences in relations between men in earlier cultures, especially Antiquity.

In western Europe during the Middle Ages, both military and monastic institutions could foster passionate relations between men. The early Germanic *comitatus* and its later medieval successor, chivalry, formed strong bonds between men who were attached to each other more by the circumstance of war and military exploit rather than sexual inclination. In medieval romance and other narratives, it is common to find such men involved in a homosocial triangle ("homosocial" designating relationships between men mediated by a woman with whom both men are involved). Close friendships between warriors are common in chivalric romances. A famous example is the tale of Amis and Amile, two knights whose devotion to each other took priority over their loves of wives and children. Their passionate devotion has no sexual manifestations, and there is every reason to suppose that medieval audiences would have been shocked if such manifestations were suggested. Where sexual relations between knights are discussed, as in some old French narratives, those relations are ridiculed as sodomitical, invariably a slur against prowess and masculinity. The learned monastic tradition is another rich store of evidence for same-sex relations between men, ranging from pious letters to erotic poetry. Narratives of transvestite monastic saints raise complex questions about gender relations in a performative context. The evidentiary status of such texts is, to say the least, problematic: what part recounts lived experience, and what part derives from literary imitation?

Same-sex relations between men are, however, contested territory, as one can see in the contrast between Derrick Sherwin Bailey's *Homosexuality and the Western Christian Tradition* (1955) and John Boswell's *Christianity, Social Tolerance, and Homosexuality* (1980), two studies that defined and redefined the topic in the twentieth century. Both works are avowedly antihomophobic, but they take sharply different views of the relationship between Christianity and same-sex relations between men. Bailey focused on the scripture in his explanation of Christianity's antihomosexual attitudes and sought to show that ecclesiastical sources separated criticism of homosexual conduct from criticism of other forms of sexual misbehavior. He pointed out that the Bible's denunciations of same-sex acts do not mention Sodom and Gomorrah, and that the cities were instead associated with other forms of sexual immorality. What Bailey represented as negative evidence, Boswell portrayed in a positive light. Like Bailey, Boswell denied that religion was a cause of sexual intolerance; instead,

he attempted to show that same-sex relations between men were valorized rather than denounced in a variety of sources, many of them literary (letters and poems especially).

Boswell's optimistic assessment of the evidence (although not his understanding of homosexuality itself, which is now considered essentialist), have had enormous appeal and influence in the study of same-sex relations. But many of his claims have not held up to close scrutiny. Important qualifications have been made by James A. Brundage in his studies of the Church, law, and sexuality. Brundage argued that the Church's negative view of *all* sexual relations necessitated a negative view of sex between men. Another scholar who has demonstrated the Church's negative view of such relations, *contra* Boswell, is Pierre J. Payer, who has studied early medieval penitentials and their treatment of sexual practices.

It is generally agreed that same-sex relations between men are not exclusively sexual and that the narrowing of such relations to genital contact excludes important evidence, psychological and emotional perspectives in particular. Standards of physical intimacy in the modern world make it difficult to approach even nineteenth-century evidence outside a genital-based sexual determinism (it was common in the Middle Ages, and in the early twentieth century, for example, for friends of the same sex to kiss on the mouth and sleep in the same bed). Sex is never far in the background in discussions of same-sex relations and friendship. The influence of Michel Foucault's *History of Sexuality* and its master narrative of hide-and-seek, of detection and evasion, has inspired a steady stream of "queer" readings of texts aimed at uncovering sexual and genital as well as emotional connections that the texts themselves might be seen as trying to conceal. Among researchers concerned with assessing evidence other than literary texts, however, the results are less playful than they are in the work of Foucault's followers. Mark Jordan has demonstrated the emergence of sodomy in a range of important works, beginning with Peter Damian's *The Book of Gomorrah* and texts by Alan of Lille, Albertus Magnus, Thomas Aquinas, and others. As Jordan shows, these sources unambiguously condemn sodomy and contravene Boswell's narrative of growing sexual tolerance from the early to the late Middle Ages. For Boswell, the thirteenth century is a peak of tolerance for passionate same-sex relations between men. But Jordan shows that the Church strongly opposed same-sex relations long before Peter Damian, as Jordan would have it, "invented" the term *sodomy*.

The range of male same-sex relations is not synonymous with sodomy, which in the Middle Ages had become a term used to designate acts ranging from anal intercourse between men to heresy. There is, however, a reluctance to read same-sex relations between men outside the framework of sexual attraction, as if to imply that same-sex relations between men must always be viewed in a teleological perspective in which the most advanced or sophisticated form of such relations will be sexual intimacy. If a homophobic interpretive tradition is responsible for suppressing discussions of sexual relations, a homophilic tradition in which sex is implied as the core or objective of such relations is no less defective and no less exclusive of a wide range of male-male relations.

ALLEN J. FRANTZEN

References and Further Reading

Bailey, Derrick Sherwin. *Homosexuality and the Western Christian Tradition*. London: Longmans, 1955; reprint, Hamden, Conn.: Archon, 1975.

Boswell, John. *Christianity, Social Tolerance, and Homosexuality: Gay People in Western Europe from the Beginning of the Christian Era to the Fourteenth Century*. Chicago: University of Chicago Press, 1980.

Bray, Alan. *Homosexuality in Renaissance England*. London: Gay Men's Press, 1982; New York: Columbia University Press, 1995.

Bullough, Vern L. *Sexual Variance in Society and History*. New York: John Wiley, 1976.

Clover, Carol J. "Regardless of Sex: Men, Women, and Power in Early Northern Europe." In *Studying Medieval Women: Sex, Gender, Feminism*, edited by Nancy F. Partner. Cambridge, Mass.: Medieval Academy of America, 1993, pp. 61–85.

Ellis, Havelock. *Sexual Inversion*. 3rd ed. Studies in the Psychology of Sex 2. Philadelphia: F.A. Davis Company, 1929.

Frantzen, Allen J. *Before the Closet: Same-Sex Love from Beowulf to Angels in America*. Chicago: University of Chicago Press, 1998.

Gaunt, Simon. "Straight Minds/"Queer" Wishes in Old French Hagiography." In *Premodern Sexualities*, edited by Louise Fradenburg and Carla Freccero. New York: Routledge, 1996, pp. 155–173.

Gerard, Kent, and Gert Hekma, eds. *The Pursuit of Sodomy: Male Homosexuality in Renaissance and Enlightenment Europe*. New York: Harrington Park, 1989; reprint from *Journal of Homosexuality* 16.1–2 (1988).

Jordan, Mark D. *The Invention of Sodomy in Christian Theology*. Chicago: University of Chicago Press, 1997.

Payer, Pierre J. *Sex and the Penitentials: The Development of a Sexual Code 550–1150*. Toronto: University of Toronto Press, 1984.

See also **Cross-Dressing; Eroticism in Art; Eroticism in Literature; Penitentials and Pastoral Manuals; Queer Theory; Sexuality: Female Same-Sex Relations; Sexuality, Regulation of**

SEXUALITY, REGULATION OF

Sex is a potentially explosive force in human society, and the earliest surviving records show that, from time immemorial, communities have tried to impose strict limits upon sexual relations among their members. Medieval Christendom was no exception to this rule. Church authorities sought to confine sexual activity among medieval Christians to marital intercourse and to regulate and restrict sexual conduct even within marriage. Predictably, the prescribed norms met with stubborn and continuing resistance among both the clergy and the laity.

Biblical Teaching

Theologians and church leaders found sacred authority to support some of their restraints on sexual behavior among Christians in the Hebrew scriptures. They occasionally drew as well upon rabbinical doctrines from the post-Biblical period. Ancient Hebrew communities, however, permitted polygyny and concubinage as their neighbors in the ancient Near East commonly did, while monogamous marriage was a fundamental ideal among Christians, although one that was not invariably observed in real life. Jewish law also permitted men to divorce their wives (but not vice versa), a practice that Christian tradition strenuously discouraged save on grounds of adultery—and most medieval Christian authorities believed that even this concession should be disallowed.

Although Christian lawgivers found it essential to modify Jewish law concerning marriage and sexuality, and rejected some of it altogether, it nonetheless provided Christians with a scriptural starting-point for the development of their own system of sexual regulations. They found Jewish law's harsh ban on adultery (especially by women), its fierce punishment for rape, its prohibition of prostitution (at least by Jewish women), and the death penalty that it prescribed for sexual relations between men particularly admirable.

The gospels, Christianity's basic foundation documents, had relatively little to say specifically about sexual behavior. Jesus for the most part accepted the traditional prescriptions found in the Hebrew scriptures and his reported comments about sex and marriage dealt only with matters where his views differed from mainstream rabbinical teachings. Perhaps the most fundamental of these was his belief that love between spouses ought to be the paramount element in a marital relationship. He urged his followers to pattern their personal relationships on the mutual self-giving that lay at the heart of the notion of *agape*, or spiritual love, in early Christian communities. Sexual relations, to be sure, formed an important element in the ways that married couples shared their bodies as well as their souls with each other. Their sexual coupling should express intimate regard for one another, rather than self-centered lust and passion.

A few passages, especially in the Gospel of Luke, imply that Jesus may have considered sex a potential hindrance to salvation. In one passage Luke represented Jesus as saying that a man who wished to follow him must reject the love of wife and family (Luke 14:25–27, 18:28–30), while in another Luke reported that Jesus advised his hearers that they should refrain from marriage (and presumably from sex) altogether if they hoped to participate in the resurrection (Luke 20:34–35; cf. Matthew 19:10–12).

Jesus also departed from mainstream Jewish tradition in his attitude toward divorce. While he did not ban it altogether, he imposed far more stringent limitations on divorce than did prevailing opinion among contemporary rabbis. Several gospel passages depict Jesus as condemning extramarital sex and prostitution, although he showed compassion on occasion for individual prostitutes. All of these departures from conventional religious teachings certainly aggravated the hostility of established religious authorities toward Jesus.

Christian writers in the generation that immediately followed the death of Jesus elaborated on these teachings. Sex and marriage occupied far more prominent places in St. Paul's writings than they did in the gospels, and Paul became far and away the most influential authority in shaping early Christian treatments of these issues. Paul treated sexual behavior as one of the major sources of sin. Indeed, he thought that illicit sex was as serious a moral offense as murder. In his writings about sex, Paul developed an implicit theory of sexual sin that distinguished four types of offenders: prostitutes, adulterers, what he called "the softies" (1 Corinthians 6:10), that is people who used sex primarily as a source of pleasure, and men (but perhaps not women, since he did not mention them) who had sex with one another.

Marriage in Paul's view, was good, but considerably less good than virginity, for a Christian. He taught that marital sex joined husband and wife together both physically and spiritually. It made them two in one flesh, just as a Christian's spiritual union with Jesus joined two persons in a single spirit. Precisely because marital sex was tinged with the sacred, any type of extramarital sex in Paul's view was worthy of damnation.

Patristic Teachings

Major Christian thinkers and writers between the second and fifth centuries CE, conventionally known as the Church Fathers, not only elaborated on these views, but also introduced new rules and doctrines concerning acceptable sexual conduct for Christians. Many of these innovations stemmed from their reaction against what they regarded as sectarian deviations from the true faith. One early Christian group known as the Encratites, for example, taught that Jesus had intended to abolish marriage altogether and demanded that his followers observe total chastity throughout their lives. Hence they denounced sexual relations of any kind, even within marriage, as morally corrupt and gravely sinful. At the opposite extreme, members of another sect, the Nicolaitans, maintained that faithful Christians were supposed to share everything freely with one another, including sexual favors, whether they were married or not.

To combat these and numerous other deviations from orthodox doctrine the Church Fathers found it essential to prescribe regulations for proper Christian sexual behavior in far more minute detail than the authors of the New Testament scriptures had done. With few exceptions the Fathers regarded human sexuality with deep suspicion. They acknowledged, to be sure, that God had commanded people to "be fertile and increase" (Genesis 1:28) and that sex was essential for reproduction. At the same time many of the Fathers clearly looked upon this as a regrettable necessity. They commonly advised Christians who had the moral strength to do so to abstain from marriage and sex altogether. Heroic Christians should instead lead lives of virginal purity, untouched by the lust and passion, pleasures and pains that accompanied sexual activity. Praise of chastity, of course, was not unique to Christian teachers. Stoics and other non-Christian thinkers in the ancient world regularly commended sexual abstinence as virtuous, but Christian writers extolled chastity and virginity with far greater fervor than their pagan contemporaries. Most of the Church Fathers at one point or another in their careers lived as monks or hermits, and the ascetic values of the monastic life loomed large in their efforts to reduce the role of sexuality in the Christian life to the minimum necessary for reproduction. This was especially true for members of the clergy. Early in the fourth century the Council of Elvira took the first steps toward demanding that Christian clerics refrain from marriage altogether and pledge to live a life of celibacy. Any who failed to comply, the council ruled, should be deposed from clerical office.

The Church Father whose teachings most widely influenced subsequent regulation of sexuality in the Western church was Augustine of Hippo (354–430). Augustine regarded sex as foul and unclean, a uniquely dangerous manifestation of human rebellion against God's designs. Sex was especially pernicious, Augustine felt, because unlike other bodily desires and pleasures it could overwhelm reason and disarm the will to do what was right, while at the same time it could also transmit original sin. Christians therefore had a moral duty to avoid sex so far as possible. Even married Christians, he believed, should strive so far as they possibly could to lead a chaste life, despite any difficulties that this might cause in the marriage.

Once the Roman emperor Constantine (313–337) and his successors embraced Christianity, the views of the Church Fathers began to be incorporated into imperial law. Constantine himself altered earlier Roman law concerning divorce in 331, for example, with the aim of making it much more difficult for couples, whatever their religion, to dissolve their marriages. Even before that, in 326, he made adultery a public crime, punishable in particularly scandalous cases by death.

Constantine's successors promulgated increasingly detailed and harsher regulations that aimed to discourage all types of sexual conduct of which the church disapproved. Justinian I (527–565) was particularly vigorous in this process. Among numerous other measures, he prescribed the death penalty for men "who dare to practice abominable lust with men," conduct that he blamed for causing famine, earthquakes, and pestilence. He also introduced stricter laws on marriage and divorce, concubinage, adultery, fornication, prostitution, rape, and other sex crimes.

Beginning with Constantine's reign, church councils in which large numbers of bishops and other church leaders came together to work out common policies and rules to implement them emerged as an important source of law concerning sexual conduct as well as many other matters. The decisions of these bodies, along with the rulings of bishops and other church authorities on individual cases, became the major sources of church law on disputed matters concerning faith and morals. Decisions handed down by the bishops of Rome enjoyed special authority, particularly in the Western church, in virtue of their claims to be successors of Peter.

Sexual offenses by Christians were also punishable by special church courts that Constantine had first authorized bishops to conduct. Decisions of these tribunals had the force of public law. Their decisions were enforceable not only by ecclesiastical sanctions such as excommunication, but also by fines, whippings, and other punishments that civil authorities were instructed to impose upon recalcitrant offenders.

Germanic Peoples

Church laws and church courts still continued to operate, and sometimes even expanded the scope of their functions, following the invasions of the West Roman Empire by the so-called Germanic barbarians. Mass invasions commenced in earnest from the late fourth century onwards. Many of the invaders were pagans, although a significant number had converted to Christianity (although not always of the orthodox persuasion) before they began their migrations into the Empire. Once they had settled among the overwhelmingly Christian population of the empire, the remaining pagans among them gradually began to accept baptism and in consequence became subject to the rules that the church imposed on its members.

By the sixth century the invaders had effectively taken political control of nearly all of the Western empire. Barbarian kingdoms ruled by Germanic kings had replaced the earlier Roman authorities throughout virtually all of western Europe, although the indigenous Roman (or Romanized) population largely survived the conflicts that accompanied the invasions. The new rulers brought with them their own customary laws and practices that conflicted in many ways with those familiar among the Romans and those prescribed by the Christian church.

Marriage in Germanic society seems in practice to have operated with relatively few hard-and-fast rules and restrictions. Barbarian laws, for one thing, did not recognize the legal distinction that Roman law drew between marriage and concubinage. The invaders instead generally treated the first year of marriage as a trial period, at the end of which the union could be terminated unless a child had been conceived during that time, while church authorities insisted that marriage once entered into was indissoluble so long as both parties lived. Couples who found their marriages unsatisfactory did not always seek ecclesiastical approval for ending them, and divorce by mutual consent remained common in the barbarian kingdoms. Germanic laws seldom treated extramarital sex by a married man as an offense, although they commonly prescribed capital punishment for adultery by a married woman.

Fornication was apparently commonplace in early medieval Europe despite repeated efforts by the clergy to deter extramarital sex. Prostitutes carried on a brisk trade and numerous efforts by kings and bishops to ban commercial sex apparently had little effect. Churchmen and civil authorities also made strenuous efforts to repress a whole galaxy of sexual practices that they classified as deviant, especially sexual intercourse between persons of the same gender, or even worse, with animals. They labeled these practices "sodomy" and treated them as a horrendous crime that deserved savage punishment, frequently castration followed by burning alive.

Church authorities also attempted to restrict the frequency and varieties of marital sex. Penitential manuals, guides that priests used to determine the penance they should assign to those who confessed sexual and other sins, regularly prescribed pilgrimages, prolonged fasts, and lengthy or even permanent abstinence from marital sex for offenders against the church's sexual rules. They banned married persons from having intercourse during Lent and Advent, on all days when fasting was required, as well as on Sundays, Wednesdays, Fridays, and Saturdays, or while the wife was pregnant or nursing a child.

Despite these harsh prescriptions, it is far from certain that the general run of early medieval Christians regularly observed many of the church's stern rules about sexual behavior. Complaints from religious authorities about the sexual activities of both laity and clergy were frequent.

The Reform Movement

During the eleventh century a church reform movement that sought, among other things, to enforce the church's sexual regulations more effectively, began to take shape. The reformers made particularly strenuous efforts to restrict sexual activity among the clergy, although their efforts enjoyed only mixed success. Prior to the reformers' campaign to enforce clerical celibacy, priests had commonly either married or lived with concubines. This was also true of many bishops as well. It was not unusual for church offices to pass from father to son over a period of several generations. The reformers slowly managed to put a halt to the transmission of church offices by inheritance, so that by the end of the twelfth century it was becoming rare to encounter married bishops. The rank and file of the parish clergy, however, stubbornly resisted efforts to deprive them of their wives, concubines, and children. Church councils in 1123 and 1139 finally ruled that ordination to major orders (subdeacon, deacon, and priest) created a legal bar to marriage and forbade the faithful to attend Mass or other church services conducted by priests who were married or lived with concubines. Furious clerics sometimes tried to shut down reforming bishops who were enforcing such rules and occasionally attacked them physically as well. The clergy of Rouen hurled stones at a bishop who demanded that they abandon their concubines and children and drove him from the church, while at Cambrai outraged clerics burned a preacher alive for the same offense.

Canon Law

In order to succeed in their enterprise the reformers realized early on that they needed to revamp the church's whole legal system. Church law, usually called canon law, had become a wilderness of rules and regulations, promulgated at different times and places by different authorities. Many of its prescriptions were inconsistent with one another, and finding one's way through the maze of canons could at best be difficult, and sometimes impossible. Numerous churchmen over the centuries had tried to bring order out of chaos by compiling collections of the canons they deemed most useful and appropriate for the church's needs, but no single collection commanded universal assent. This made it difficult for priests or bishops to give satisfactory or consistent answers to the kinds of questions that people asked them to resolve. Was a marriage between fourth cousins valid? It depended on which authorities one consulted. Could a woman divorce her husband because he turned out to be sexually impotent? And if she did so, could she then remarry? Again, the answers depended on which rules one chose to follow.

This unsatisfactory state of affairs finally ended around the middle of the twelfth century, when a massive new textbook of canon law appeared. The circumstances surrounding its appearance are obscure, as is the identity of its author, Gratian. The book, usually known as the *Decretum*, was being taught in law schools by around 1150. Gratian's *Decretum* differed from its predecessors not only in its comprehensiveness—it comprised nearly 4,000 canons—but even more importantly, in Gratian's efforts to analyze his material in order to reconcile conflicting rules and thus to produce a coherent body of canon law.

It would be difficult to overstate the importance of Gratian's *Decretum*. It became one of the most widely read books in Western history and remained a basic textbook in schools of canon law from the middle of the twelfth up to the beginning of the twentieth century. The *Decretum* touched off an intellectual revolution that helped to shape the future development of Western legal systems. Its influence continues to be felt to this day.

Gratian's discussion of marital sex centered upon his concept of marital debt, by which he meant that wives and husbands had a legal duty to make themselves available for intercourse whenever the partner desired it. The debt commenced at the moment when the marriage was consummated and thereafter each spouse was bound to render sexual services upon demand. In principle at least, no matter where or when the demand was made, the spouse had an absolute obligation to comply then and there.

Gratian, like many of the authorities on whom he relied, treated sexual urges, inside or outside marriage, as a moral weakness that Christians must combat with utmost vigor. He deemed fornication as grave a sin as perjury and only slightly less serious than homicide. Adultery in his view was an aggravated, and hence even more sinful, form of fornication. He treated prostitution, however, as a necessary evil. Echoing Augustine, he maintained that if prostitutes were to vanish from society, men would turn to even worse sex crimes, such as rape and same-sex relations.

Gratian's work assembled and tried to rationalize sexual regulations that the Christian church had developed during the millennium and more following the death of Jesus. The making of new law did not cease with the appearance of Gratian's book. Later church lawmakers sought primarily to refine and amplify earlier regulations about sexual activity that they found in Gratian's *Decretum*.

An underlying problem that the church's leaders faced was the lack of systematic mechanisms for the detection and punishment of sexual offenses. Since people tended to conduct their sexual activities away from public view, it was usually difficult to discover who was engaging in prohibited conduct. The Fourth Lateran Council in 1215 produced a partial answer to this problem by requiring all Christians to confess their sins to their parish priests at least once a year during the Lenten season that preceded Easter. Since most people in western Europe lived in small rural communities, it was not difficult for priests to know who had failed to perform their Easter duty. Annual confession thus enabled priests to discover which members of their flock were engaging in prohibited sexual conduct and to demand that they do penance as punishment for their sins. They could publicly excommunicate those who failed to comply, an action that imposed severe hardship, shame, and loss of reputation upon recalcitrant sinners. The Lateran Council also clarified the laws governing impediments to marriage based on kinship (consanguinity) or other kinds of relationship, including premarital intercourse (affinity).

Other methods of dealing with the problem were introduced during the thirteenth century. Bishops were required, for one thing, to conduct regular visitations of each parish within their diocese. On these occasions the visiting bishop invited members of the parish to reveal the names of their fellow parishioners who they suspected of sexual misconduct. New criminal procedures were also instituted during this period that made it far easier to crack down on priests who violated their obligation to celibacy. Manuals for confessors guided priests' inquiries into the sex lives of penitents. While these measures did not fully solve the problem, they did make noncompliance with the medieval church's sexual regulations more hazardous.

JAMES A. BRUNDAGE

References and Further Reading

Baldwin, John W. *The Language of Sex: Five Voices from Northern France around 1200.* Chicago: University of Chicago Press, 1994.

Biller, Peter, and A. J. Minnis, eds. *Handling Sin: Confession in the Middle Ages.* York: York Medieval Press, 1998.

Boswell, John. *Christianity, Social Tolerance, and Homosexuality: Gay People in Western Europe from the Beginning of the Christian Era to the Fourteenth Century.* Chicago: University of Chicago Press, 1980.

Brown, Peter. *The Body and Society: Men, Women and Sexual Renunciation in Early Christianity.* New York: Columbia University Press, 1988.

Brundage, James A. *Law, Sex, and Christian Society in Medieval Europe.* Chicago: University of Chicago Press, 1987.

———. *Sex, Law and Marriage in the Middle Ages.* Aldershot: Variorum, 1993.

Bullough, Vern L., and James A. Brundage, eds. *Sexual Practices and the Medieval Church.* Buffalo N.Y.: Prometheus Books, 1982.

Helmholz, Richard H. *Marriage Litigation in Medieval England.* Cambridge: Cambridge University Press, 1974.

Karras, Ruth Mazo. *Common Women: Prostitution and Sexuality in Medieval England.* Oxford: Oxford University Press, 1996.

Levin, Eve. *Sex and Society in the World of the Orthodox Slavs.* Ithaca N.Y.: Cornell University Press, 1989.

Linehan, Peter. *The Ladies of Zamora.* University Park, Pa.: Pennsylvania State University Press, 1997.

Makowski, Elizabeth M. "The Conjugal Debt and Medieval Canon Law." *Journal of Medieval History* 3 (1977): 99–114.

Noonan, John T. Jr. *Contraception: A History of its Treatment by the Catholic Theologians and Canonists.* Cambridge, Mass.: Belknap Press, 1965.

Otis-cour, Leah Lydia. *Prostitution in Medieval Society: The History of an Urban Institution in Languedoc.* Chicago: University of Chicago Press, 1985.

Payer, Pierre J. *Sex and the Penitentials: The Development of a Sexual Code, 550–1150.* Toronto: University of Toronto Press, 1984.

———. *The Bridling of Desire: Views of Sex in the Later Middle Ages.* Toronto: University of Toronto Press, 1993.

Pedersen, Frederik. *Marriage Disputes in Medieval England.* London: Hambledon Press, 2000.

Wemple, Suzanne F. *Women in Frankish Society: Marriage and the Cloister 500 to 900.* Philadelphia: University of Pennsylvania Press, 1981.

See also **Celibacy: Clerical and Priests' Concubines; Chastity and Chaste Marriage; Divorce and Separation; Law, Canon; Marriage, Christian; Marriage, Impediments to; Penitentials and Pastoral Manuals; Sexuality: Extramarital Sex; Sexuality: Female Same-Sex Relations; Sexuality: Male Same-Sex Relations; Sexuality: Sex in Marriage; Virginity**

SEXUALITY: SEX IN MARRIAGE

According to the medieval Church, marriage was the only legitimate venue for sexual activity. Throughout the period, there was an ongoing debate about whether, and to what degree, sex in marriage might be sinful. This was due, in part, to the fact that marital sex always had a connotation of being a concession to human weakness. If people did not have a legitimate outlet for their desire, a myriad of social ills would result, as people, particularly men, sought other sexual outlets. This view can be traced back to the Apostle Paul's assertion that "It is better to marry than to burn" (1 Cor. 7:9). Moreover, the asceticism of ancient Roman stoicism also influenced the Church Fathers, who established the foundation of Christian teachings about marriage and sexuality. Consequently, there was considerable debate about the nature and appropriate exercise of marital sexuality. The doctrine of the conjugal debt further complicated the understanding of sex within marriage, requiring spouses to be available to each other for sex whenever asked. Furthermore, sexual consummation was an important component of the marriage bond, as well as being essential to achieve one of the three goods of marriage: the procreation of children. But sexual intercourse, even within marriage, was inextricably linked to the sin of lust, and was a sign of humanity's disordered nature and fallen state.

The conflicted manner in which marital sex was viewed by theologians, canonists, and moralists is exemplified in discussions of the ideal marriage of Mary and Joseph. This marriage was believed to have never encompassed a sexual relationship because the clergy could not contemplate the mother of God engaging in any act so fallen, polluted, and as brutish and animalistic as sexual intercourse. Thus, the clergy concluded that married couples must have the capacity to engage in sexual relations, but they could agree to abstain completely from sex. This was, however, a mode of life suitable only for rare couples and was not encouraged among the laity in general.

The fundamental understanding of the Church can be summarized as permitting sex within marriage, in the only legitimate position (the so-called missionary position), with the sole intention to procreate. Sex for pleasure, especially if it was accompanied by innovative positions or excessive foreplay, was always to some degree sinful, even with one's own spouse. Indeed, in the twelfth and thirteenth centuries, canonists and theologians debated if it was ever possible for a married couple to engage in sex without committing a sin. Some, such as Huguccio (d. 1210), insisted that sin always inhered to intercourse, while others, notably Hugh of St. Victor (1096–1141), were more moderate and incorporated marital sexuality as part of the loving relationship that should pertain between husband and wife, owing to the sacramental nature of marriage. The mere intention to procreate was sufficient for sex to occur without sin. Occasionally, too, clerical authors and writers of romances both presented an appreciation of the intimacy of the marriage bed, describing a couple's pillow-talk and expressions of endearment. Authors could portray the soft words of love between a couple in bed, whereas conventional morality proscribed the encouragement, or even description, of the physical manifestations of that love.

Religious Viewpoints

The prevailing belief that women were passive sexually led to the oft-repeated dictum, traced to Jerome, that a man should not treat his wife as he would a prostitute. It is unclear if this referred to lusty mutual pleasure, or to the indifferent use of one's wife to satisfy one's lust, or to the absence of procreative intent. Moreover, moralists rarely discussed how people might engage in sexual activity, beyond proscribing positions and denouncing passionate kissing, nudity, foreplay, and sexual touching as obscene, even in marriage. The ambiguous evaluation of marital sexuality led the church to implement constraints not only on how, but also on when, sex could occur. In addition to the sexual taboos surrounding a woman's body—that is, during menstruation, pregnancy, after birth, and during lactation—marital sex was also forbidden on Sundays, Fridays, Wednesdays, feast days, during Lent, Advent, and Pentecost, and before receiving communion. What these restrictions meant in the lives of the married laity, however, is unclear. Certainly, the injunctions were disseminated through the mechanisms of pastoral care, in particular, through sermons and counseling in the course of confession, but how they played out in people's lives cannot be determined.

Medicine

Medicine is another theoretical discourse that may have exercised some influence on marital sexuality. Medical theory basically held the ancient view that, for conception to occur, both the man and the woman needed to achieve orgasm and ejaculate seed, which would mingle together in the uterus. Consequently, according to prevailing medical opinion, female as much as male sexual pleasure was required for procreation. This may have had some influence, since there are occasional references to the two-seed theory in the works of pastoral writers, such as Robert Grosseteste (1175–1253), and authors of manuals for confessors seem to have encouraged men to ensure their wife's sexual pleasure.

Literature

Secular sources and works of literature offer little assistance to better understand sexual relations, marital or otherwise. This is partly because such sources either idealized chaste love, as in courtly romances, or were deliberately bawdy and titillating, as in the *fabliaux*. Chaucer portrayed his Wife of Bath as a woman who enjoyed sex with her numerous husbands, but it is difficult to assess the extent to which this reflects medieval experience. Few married people wrote down their reflections or discussed their personal sexual experiences. One notable exception to this silence is found in the twelfth century, in the letters exchanged between Peter Abelard and Heloise. Written after the couple had separated and entered monastic life, their letters reveal fond memories of their sexual encounters, describing their passion, their sexual experimentation, and their ultimate mutual pleasure in sex. Significantly, Abelard and Heloise both knew well the various prohibitions and regulations of sex, marital and extramarital, but this knowledge did not seem to detract from their personal sexual experiences or, at least, how they remembered those experiences.

Sexual activity, or at least the potential for it, lay at the heart of marriage. Both the secular and religious goals of marriage gave prominence to procreation. The Church taught that if everyone had the ability

to engage in sex with a legitimate spouse, society would be protected from social evils such as prostitution and sodomy. Although it was commonly believed that women were more lustful than men, it was also acknowledged that, in the absence of a wife, men would seek other sexual outlets. The role of sexual pleasure is a more complex area and perhaps more fraught. There were different theoretical views but it is not possible to grasp fully what these meant, if anything, in the daily lives of the sexually active laity.

JACQUELINE MURRAY

References and Further Reading

Abelard, Peter. *The Letters of Abelard and Heloise.* Translated by Betty Radice. Harmondsworth: Penguin Books, 1974.
Baldwin, John W. *The Language of Sex: Five Voices from Northern France around 1200.* Chicago: University of Chicago Press, 1994.
Brundage, James A. *Law, Sex, and Christian Society in Medieval Europe.* Chicago: University of Chicago Press, 1987.
———. *Sex, Law and Marriage in the Middle Ages.* London: Variorum, 1993.
Clifford, John T. "The Ethics of Conjugal Intimacy according to St. Albert the Great." *Theological Studies* 3.1 (1942): 1–26.
Elliott, Dyan. *Spiritual Marriage: Sexual Abstinence in Medieval Wedlock.* Princeton, N.J.: Princeton University Press, 1993.
Flandrin, Jean Louis. "Sex in Married Life in the Early Middle Ages: The Church's Teaching and Behavioural Reality." In *Western Sexuality: Practice and Precept in Past and Present Times*, edited by Philippe Ariès and André Bejin, translated by Anthony Forster. Oxford: Basil Blackwell, 1985, pp. 114–129.
Payer, Pierre J. *The Bridling of Desire: Views of Sex in the Later Middle Ages.* Toronto: University of Toronto Press, 1993.
Salisbury, Joyce E. "The Latin Doctors of the Church on Sexuality." *Journal of Medieval History* 12 (1986): 279–289.

See also **Chastity and Chaste Marriage; Conjugal Debt; Courtly Love; Fabliau; Gender Ideologies; Heloise; Impotence; Marriage: Christian; Menstruation; Prostitutes; Spiritual Care**

SHEELA NA GIGS

Since the 1840s, sculpted figures of nude women exhibiting their vulvas have been known as *sheela na gigs*. These crudely sculpted figures are so unlovely that they are abject, repulsive, yet fascinating and popular; they even have a dedicated Web site. Although Weir and Jerman demonstrated that exhibiting women appeared earlier in the monumental sculpture of France, alongside other ribald figures, it is clear that their popularity was greatest in Ireland

Sheela na Gig, from the church of St. Mary and St. David, Kilpeck, Herefordshire. Location: English Heritage, National Monuments Record, Great Britain. Credit: HIP / Art Resource, N.Y.

and Britain between the twelfth century and the fifteenth. Most of the insular examples differ in their comparative isolation, the exaggerated size of the vulva that is often stretched open by the hands, and their appearance on castle walls as well as churches. Most sheelas squat or stand above eye level on the edges of buildings, such as door and window frames, corners, and roof-lines. Unprofessional carving, weathering, and defacement that often includes enlargement of the vaginal passage, impede dating.

The name is perplexing. Freitag's recent thorough review of Irish and English renderings reveals an obsolete meaning for English *gig* as the vulva or female pudenda. Yet an Irish folk tradition that Patrick had a troublesome wife called Sheila also appears relevant. Reception history indicates that witch and hag are among many names used, a multivalence that is in keeping with multiple functions. Freitag's theory that *sheelas* aided women in childbirth is sound, yet surely they also filled armies with fear (men were forbidden to see birthing); and neither

function would prevent the clergy enlisting them against the sin of lust.

MADELINE H. CAVINESS

References and Further Reading

Freitag, Barbara. *Sheela-Na-Gigs: Unravelling an Enigma.* London and New York: Routledge, 2004.
Weir, Anthony, and James Jerman. *Images of Lust: Sexual Carvings on Medieval Churches.* London: B. T. Batsford, 1986.

See also **Art, Representations of Women in; Body: Visual Representations of; Ireland; Magic and Charms; Obscenity; Pregnancy and Childbirth: Christian Women**

SHEKHINAH

The term *Shekhinah* was coined by the rabbis to denote the presence of God in the world. There is little evidence in classical rabbinic literature that *Shekhinah* denotes a hypostatic entity ontically distinct from God, a secondary being akin to the Logos in Philo or in the prologue to the Gospel of John. In most instances, *Shekhinah* is used interchangeably with the supreme divine being as He appears in history and nature.

The rabbinic conception of *Shekhinah* is phenomenologically on a par with the priestly notion of the *kavod*, the divine glory that resides in the midst of the people of Israel. The rabbis formulated their idea after the destruction of the Second Temple in 70 CE, and thus, in contrast to the priests, the abiding of *Shekhinah* is not confined to the physical space where sacrifices were offered. The Temple is replaced by the schoolroom, synagogue, and domestic space of the family, as these were the main sites wherein one could access the indwelling of the presence through the cultivation of a life of ritual purity.

The symbol of *Shekhinah* continued to play a decisive role in various genres of the Jewish religious imagination. But it is in the minds of kabbalists, in particular, that *Shekhinah* is accorded a significance unparalleled in earlier sources. In the theosophic system of the Kabbalah, *Shekhinah* routinely is associated with the last of the ten *sefirot*, the luminous attributes that reveal the hidden aspect of God. Needless to say, kabbalists absorb many of the older rabbinic portrayals of *Shekhinah*, but what is most distinctive about their approach is the explicit representation of the presence in a litany of female images, including Matrona, bride, daughter, sister, mother, community of Israel, heavenly Jerusalem, throne, temple, tabernacle, moon, sea, and the sphere of the earth.

Undeniably, one of the great contributions of kabbalists to the history of Judaism is the explicit utilization of gender images to depict the nature of God and the consequent application of erotic symbolism to characterize the divine-human relationship. In line with earlier rabbinic tradition regarding the two main attributes of God, but explicating the sexual implications far more openly, kabbalists envisage the unity of God in androgynous terms as the coupling of male and female, which are respectively aligned with the attributes of loving kindness on the right and judgment on the left. Gender symbolism in traditional kabbalistic literature is dynamic, presupposing the crossing of boundaries and intermingling of identity, male in female and female in male. The flexibility of gender transformation is determined, however, by an inflexible structure, and hence one may legitimately speak of variability in kabbalistic symbolism but not ambiguity. Male and female are correlated consistently with the activity of projection and the passivity of restriction: the potency to overflow is masculine, the capacity to withhold, feminine. The religious obligation imposed on the Jewish man to unify God is interpreted as the harnessing of male and female, a pairing of right and left, the will to bestow and the desire to contain. But just as the entirety of the Godhead is androgynous, so each of the *sefirot* exemplifies the dual capacity to overflow and to receive, and *Shekhinah* is no exception. In relation to the *sefirot* above her, *Shekhinah* receives the divine efflux and is thus engendered as feminine; in relation to the worlds below her, *Shekhinah* overflows and is thus engendered as masculine. The sovereignty over this world—in virtue of which the name *malkhut*, "kingship," is attributed to *Shekhinah*—is not indicative of a positive valorization of the feminine, but rather marks the capacity of *Shekhinah* to be transformed into a demiurgic being, which is masculine in relation to the worlds beneath the divine emanations.

The gender orientation of medieval kabbalists was androcentric in nature since both masculine and feminine elements were interpreted as features of the male. The simplest way to express the matter is to note that kabbalists read the account of God having created Adam male (*zakhar*) and female (*neqevah*) in the first chapter in Genesis in light of the second account wherein the derivative ontic status of woman (*ishshah*) from man (*ish*) is made explicit. Accordingly, the proto-human, *adam*, is conceived as a male androgyne, the single gender that contains its other as part of itself, a typical patriarchical construction. For kabbalists, therefore, we can speak properly of an Edenic state of the androgynous prelapsarian man, a condition to be retrieved in the end of time. In the *conjunctio oppositorum*, two sexes are unified and woman is restored to man, the ideal unification that tolerates no difference. Representations of *Shekhinah* as feminine, and especially as the erotic object of male desire, bespeak the sexual dimorphism characteristic of a state of exile wherein the unity of the male androgyne has been severed, and as a consequence the male seeks his other, to restore the part of his self that has been taken and rendered independent. Redemption entails the overcoming of this dimorphic condition, the reconstitution of the androgynous male, expressed by the image of the ascent of *Shekhinah* as the diadem (*atarah*) that rises to the head of *Keter*, the first of the *sefirot*. By virtue of this ascent *Shekhinah* is transformed into the crown of the male and the unity that was rendered asunder in the beginning of creation is repaired.

ELLIOT R. WOLFSON

References and Further Reading

Abrams, Daniel. *The Female Body of God in Jewish Mystical Literature: Embodied Forms of Love and Sexuality in the Divine Feminine*. Jerusalem: Magnes Press, 2004.

Green, Arthur. "Shekhinah, the Virgin Mary, and the Song of Songs: Reflections on a Kabbalistic Symbol in Historical Context." *AJS Review* 26 (2002): 1–52.

Liebes, Yehuda. *Studies in the Zohar*. Translated by Arnold Schwartz, Stephanie Nakache, and Penina Peli. Albany: State University of New York Press, 1993.

Mopsik, Charles. *Sex of the Soul: the Vicissitudes of Sexual Difference in Kabbalah*. Edited with a foreword by Daniel Abrams. Los Angeles: Cherub Press, 2005.

Schäfer, Peter. *Mirror of His Beauty: Feminine Images of God from the Bible to the Early Kabbalah*. Princeton, N.Y.: Princeton University Press, 2002.

Scholem, Gershom. *On the Mystical Shape of the Godhead: Basic Concepts in the Kabbalah*. Translated by Joachim Neugroschel, edited and revised by Jonathan Chipman. New York: Schocken Books, 1991.

Wolfson, Elliot R. *Circle in the Square: Studies in the Use of Gender in Kabbalistic Symbolism*. Albany: State University of New York Press, 1995.

———. "Coronation of the Sabbath Bride: Kabbalistic Myth and the Ritual of Androgynisation." *Journal of Jewish Thought and Philosophy* 6 (1997): 301–344.

———. "Occultation of the Feminine and the Body of Secrecy in Medieval Kabbalah." In *Rending the Veil: Concealment and Secrecy in the History of Religions*. edited by Elliot R. Wolfson. New York and London: Seven Bridges Press, 1999, pp. 113–154.

See also **Gender Ideologies; Jewish Mystical Thought, Body and Soul in; Jewish Women; Theology**

SILENCE
See **Roman de Silence**

SINGLEWOMEN

The study of singlewomen in the Middle Ages is a relatively new development, with most knowledge becoming available only since the 1990s. The first useful information on never-married women came from work produced by demographic and economic historians, who were interested in the ages at marriage of commoners, and the work they did in the Middle Ages. Studies analyzing singlewomen and singleness have focused primarily on the later Middle Ages and, in contrast to the norm, on commoners more than elite females. The historical literature written in English is skewed toward the study of singlewomen in western Europe, especially medieval England. There is an entire separate literature (not covered here) on Catholic nuns, who were celibate women, but whom contemporaries characterized as "Brides of Christ."

With the exception of Joan of Arc, few singlewomen from the Middle Ages are recognized outside the religious life. But such women, especially life-cycle (or young, not yet married) singlewomen were not as rare in medieval Europe as might be assumed. Their numbers did vary, with never-married women more numerous in northwestern than southern Europe and in towns more than rural areas. The first was due to what historians call the northwestern European marriage pattern, wherein young, single people worked as laborers or servants for a numbers of years, saving up money to establish a separate household, and thereby delaying marriage into their early or even mid-twenties. In southern Europe, multiple-generation households enabled people to marry earlier, and it was customary for women to marry in their teens or to enter a nunnery if they did not marry. This geographic contrast is evidenced by tax and census material that shows that in England in 1377 almost one-third of adult women were single, whereas in Florence, Italy, in 1427 about one-fifth of adult women were single.

Town Life

Never-married women were also more common in towns than in rural areas, because there were more opportunities for female employment in urban areas. Domestic service was the primary occupation for medieval singlewomen. Opportunities for service increased in the later Middle Ages, which perhaps led some women in northern English towns like York to choose to work instead of marriage. Servants were able to save enough money so that in southern England they became active local moneylenders.

Domestic servants were so in demand in the thriving merchant towns of Renaissance Italy that traders resorted to importing female slaves from the Balkans. Female slaves were virtually all singlewomen; their slave status was passed on to their children frequently fathered by their masters. These births made them undesirable marriage partners.

Some never-married women were able to find work in areas other than domestic service. Brewing was originally an occupation by which singlewomen and widows were able to make a living, but by the fifteenth century, unmarried women were pushed out of the brewing trade, foreshadowing the complete masculinization of the occupation by the early modern era. Other urban women were able to learn a skilled trade and work within the guild system. Some cities, like Paris, even had all-female guilds that focused on textile trades such as embroidery and purse-making. But successful brewers and guildswomen may have been more the exception than the rule.

Singlewomen frequently numbered among the poor and criminal elements of medieval towns. Legalized prostitution and civic-run brothels provided never-married women without money and skills one form of employment. Such women were marginalized in their communities, confined to specific districts and forced to wear certain types of clothing marking them as "common women." In the London suburb of Southwark, prostitutes were known as "singlewomen," which illustrates much about the assumed marital status of such workers. Never-married women in countries like France and Italy were able to seek assistance from institutions set up for women at risk of turning to prostitution, or turning from it. Such Magdalen houses (named after the biblical Mary Magdalen) provided one sort of refuge for singlewomen who were poor and homeless.

The issue of where a never-married woman was supposed to live and work was a fraught one in the Middle Ages. Contemporaries assumed that a young singlewoman would live with her family or master until she married. In England these assumptions were sometimes enshrined in law, such as when in 1492 Coventry forbade never-married women under fifty years of age from keeping houses or rooms by themselves. The reality was that singlewomen in cities like York and Paris commonly lodged and shared expenses with other unmarried women. Beguinages provided a communal living arrangement for lay singlewomen in the Low Countries, France, and other parts of continental Europe. Beguines lived and worked together in female communities, but unlike nuns, they took no formal vows, and could leave their communities.

Countryside

We know much more about urban singlewomen than rural ones, but such women also appeared in the records of medieval Europe's manors or estates. Never-married women were the specific targets of one of the fines that landlords levied on their unfree peasants. Singlewomen who produced children out of wedlock were required to pay *leyrwite*, a fine that illustrates how never-married women were held responsible for their extramarital sexuality. Other rural singlewomen contributed to their manors in more positive ways. For instance, the fourteenth-century peasant Cecilia Penifader was a never-married woman on the manor of Brigstock in England. She made a prosperous life for herself, buying up plots of land, heading her own household, and farming with the help of her brothers and other servants. At a time when a well-off peasant was someone who held thirty acres, Penifader died possessing over seventy acres that she passed on to her kin.

Social Status

Laywomen who never married tended to be marginalized in the Middle Ages. Medieval people conceived of singleness as a life stage, and used terms such as *puella*, *pucelle*, *virgin*, and *maiden* to describe young women who had not yet married. The term *single-woman* may have been a bit more elastic. As noted, it was used to describe prostitutes in London, and in towns like York it seems to have encompassed both never-married and widowed women. It is possible that *singlewoman* described a woman's unmarried status more than her youth or virginity.

Attitudes toward young never-married women varied. On the one hand, young singlewomen were believed to need supervision and guidance to prepare them for marriage and to protect their chastity. And they were expected to be dependents, both economically and residentially. On the other hand, European culture extolled the maiden as the ideal woman (perfect, pure, uncorrupted, and innocent) and maidenhood as the perfect female age. Royal and noble households displayed their high status through a bevy of young female attendants. In addition, the Middle Ages witnessed the veneration of young, virgin-martyr female saints and the popular depiction of the Virgin Mary as a young maiden rather than a matronly mother.

French courtly romance was also replete with maiden characters who asserted their autonomy and resourcefulness. Late medieval English songs also focused on the independence and sexuality of young singlewomen. While it is difficult to discern if stories and songs echoed the experiences of actual women, it is clear that young singlewomen in England enjoyed a distinct subculture and special religious and communal roles. Never-married women raised funds for and tended to particular altars, candles, and statues in parish churches. They participated in Hocktide and May Day rituals that involved playful and physical contact with the opposite sex. Whatever their eventual marital status, all females in the Middle Ages experienced life as a singlewoman for some period in their lives.

AMY M. FROIDE

References and Further Reading

Amtower, Laurel, and Dorothea Kehler, eds. *The Single Woman in Medieval and Early Modern England: Her Life and Representation*. Tempe, Ariz.: Arizona Center for Medieval and Renaissance Studies, 2003.

Beattie, Cordelia. "'A Room of One's Own?' The Legal Evidence for the Residential Arrangements of Women Without Husbands in Late Fourteenth- and Early Fifteenth-Century York." In *Medieval Women and the Law*, edited by Noël James Menuge. Woodbridge, Suffolk: Boydell Press, 2000, pp. 41–56.

———. "The Problem of Women's Work Identities in Post Black Death England." In *The Problem of Labour in Fourteenth-Century England*, edited by James Bothwell, et al. York: York Medieval Press, 2000, pp. 1–19.

Bennett, Judith M. *Ale, Beer and Brewsters in England, Women's Work in a Changing World 1300–1600*. New York: Oxford University Press, 1996.

———. *A Medieval Life: Cecilia Penifader of Brigstock, c. 1295–1344*. Boston: McGraw Hill, 1999.

———. "Ventriloquisms: When Maidens Speak in English Songs, c. 1300–1550." In *Medieval Women's Song: Cross-Cultural Approaches*, edited by Anne L. Klinck and Ann Marie Rasmussen. Philadelphia: University of Pennsylvania Press, 2002, pp. 187–204.

Bennett, Judith M., and Amy M. Froide, eds. *Singlewomen in the European Past, 1250–1800*. Philadelphia: University of Pennsylvania Press, 1999.

French, Katherine L. "Maidens' Lights and Wives' Stores: Women's Parish Guilds in Late Medieval England." *Sixteenth Century Journal* 29 (1998): 399–425.

Goldberg, P. J. P. *Women, Work, and Life Cycle in a Medieval Economy: Women in York and Yorkshire c.1300–1520*. Oxford: Clarendon Press, 1992.

Karras, Ruth Mazo, *Common Women, Prostitution and Sexuality in Medieval England*. Oxford: Oxford University Press, 1996.

Lewis, Katherine J., Noël James Menuge, and Kim M. Phillips, eds. *Young Medieval Women*. New York: St. Martin's Press, 1999.

McIntosh, Marjorie K. "Moneylending on the Periphery of London, 1300–1600." *Albion* 20.4 (1988): 557–571.

Phillips, Kim M. *Medieval Maidens: Young Women and Gender in England 1270–1540*. New York: Palgrave/Manchester University Press, 2003.

See also **Adolescence; Alewives and Brewing; Beguines; Merchet and Leyrwite; Monasticism and Nuns; Prostitutes; Servants; Virgin Martyrs; Work**

SISTER-BOOKS AND OTHER CONVENT CHRONICLES

Sister-Books (also *Schwesternbücher*, *Nonnenbücher*, *vitae sororum*, Lives of the Sisters, or Convent Chronicles) are a genre of female-authored texts composed in women's monasteries of the Dominican Order's German province between 1310 and 1350. They are loosely modeled on Gerard of Frachet's *Lives of the Brothers* (1260), a collection describing the activities and miracles of the early Dominican friars across Europe. More interior in focus, the Sister-Books are confined to the lives and events of monastic women in specific communities.

These texts, which survive today in Latin and dialects of Middle High German, combine monastic historiography, hagiography, and mysticism, to create collections of pious lives [*vitae*]. Each Sister-Book may have originally contained a chronicle of the monastery's foundation and history, in addition to the collection of individual *vitae*, but most of these have been lost. The Sister-Books record, among other things, the prayers, visions, devotional practices, obedience to the monastic rule, theological discussions, received signs of grace, mystical experiences, fasting, bodily mortifications, and deaths of individual women. Each Dominican monastery composed the lives of its own inhabitants, often going back to the founding generation of the community and proceeding, not necessarily in a chronological fashion, to the current generation of monastic members, both nuns and lay sisters.

The hagiographic nature of these *vitae* means that they must be approached with care. The lives were intended to be didactic, instructing the monastic audience about proper female Dominican behavior and belief, as well as celebrating the feats of the early sisters. The literary aspect of their composition means that they are not always true records of actual events. Rather, they are reworkings of women's lives that reveal much about the ideals, aspirations, and religious milieu of cloistered Dominican women.

Since none of the original fourteenth-century manuscripts survive, it is difficult to exactly date their composition, as well as know the exact contents of the originals. The transmission history of the Sister-Books is complicated. Manuscripts circulated among Dominican houses, and other religious communities, where they were copied by interested readers. Lives were excerpted from one manuscript and combined with lives from other Sister-Books, creating new collections for pious audiences. The original creation of each monastery's Sister-Book also differed. Some texts have an identifiable single author, while others are the result of more communal efforts. Some authors wrote their own material, while others recycled previously composed lives, functioning as compilers and editors.

There are nine surviving Sister-Books. The Adelhausen Sister-Book (c. 1310–1320), called the *Chronik*, was written in Latin by prioress Anna of Munzingen but survives only in Middle High German translations. It contains a short chronicle and the *vitae* of thirty women. The Unterlinden Sister-Book (c. 1320) was composed in Latin by Catherine, a nun whose identity remains unclear. The Unterlinden text survives in a complete Latin copy from the fifteenth century (made in the monastery), a later summary in Latin, and in a late fifteenth-century Middle High German translation by the prioress, Elisabeth Kempfin. The text describes the lives of forty-one women in thirty-nine chapters. Several more lives were added in the fifteenth century. The Gotteszell Sister-Book (after 1320) has no identifiable author and, until the 1970s, was thought to be a continuation of the Kirchberg Sister-Book, since they were preserved in the same manuscript with no break. The Gotteszell text survives in copies of the original Middle High German, containing about twelve *vitae* and one additional long life, which was separately authored.

The Kirchberg Sister-Book (1320–1340) was produced by Elisabeth of Kirchberg in Middle High German. The Engelthal Sister-Book (1328–1340) was written by Christine Ebner in Middle High German. The text is commonly referred to as *Der Nonne von Engeltal Büchlein von der Gnaden Überlast* [*The Nun of Engelthal's Little Book of the Overwhelming Burden of Graces*]. It consists of a chronicle and the brief lives of some forty women, in addition to two long *vitae*, both of which may have different authors. The Töss Sister-Book (before 1340) has been attributed primarily to Elsbeth Stagel, correspondent and spiritual follower of Henry Suso, but she is not the sole author. The full Sister-Book contains a chronicle and about forty *vitae*, six of which are extensive and may have existed previous to the composition of the main body of the text.

The anonymous Oetenbach Sister-Book (after 1340), which is the shortest, was written in a Zurich dialect of Middle High German. It contains a lengthy and detailed monastic chronicle with six lives. The St. Katharinenthal Sister-Book (1318–1343) also has no identifiable author. The text consists of a chronicle and about sixty lives, all in Middle High German, with additional *vitae* added after its fourteenth-century composition. The Weiler Sister-Book (c. 1350) has at least two authors, both unknown. It contains twenty-seven Middle High German *vitae*.

In addition to the fourteenth-century female Dominican Sister-Books, there are other groups of texts that are sometimes referred to as either Sister-Books or convent chronicles. These include collective biographies associated with the Modern Devotion. The oldest of these is the Middle Dutch *Lives of the Older Sisters*, which covers the period from 1398–1456. Another group encompasses texts generated by the Observant Movement beginning in the late fourteenth century. These include works like the combination chronicle and necrology of the Venetian convent of Corpus Domini written by a fifteenth-century nun. Despite variations in content, geographic location, and composition dates, all of these writings were composed by women who wished to pass on their histories and pious observations to subsequent generations of monastic inhabitants.

ERIKA LAUREN LINDGREN

References and Further Reading

Anna of Munzingen. "Die Chronik der Anna von Munzingen." edited by W. König. *Freiburger Diözesan-Arcáiv* 13 (1880): 129–236.

"Aufzeichnungen über das mystische Leben der Nonnen von Kirchberg bei Sulz Predigerordens während des XIV. und XV. Jahrhunderts." edited by F. W. E. Roth. *Alemannia* 21 (1893): 103–148.

Catherine of Unterlinden. "Les *vitae Sororum* d'Unterlinden. Édition critique du manuscrit 508 de la bibliothèque de Colmar." edited by Jeanne Ancelet-Hustache. *Archives d'Histoire Doctrinale et Littéraire du Moyen Age* 5 (1930): 317–519.

Devotio Moderna: *Basic Writings*, translated by John Van Engen. New York: Paulist Press, 1988.

Early Dominicans: Selected Writings. Edited and translated by Simon Tugwell. New York: Paulist Press, 1982.

Ebner, Christina. "Der Nonne von Engeltal Büchlein von der Gnaden Uberlast." Edited by Karl Schröder. *Bibliothek des Litterarischer Verein in Stuttgart*, 108 (1871): 1–44.

Gerard of Frachet. *Lives of the Brethern of the Order of Preachers, 1206–1259*. Translated by Placid Conway. New York: Benziger Brothers, 1924.

Das Leben der Schwestern zu Töß beschrieben von Elsbet Stagel. Edited by Ferdinand Vetter. Deutsche Texte des Mittelalters 6. Berlin: Weidmannsche Buchhandlung, 1906.

Lewis, Gertrud Jaron. *By Women, for Women, about Women: The Sister-Books of Fourteenth-Century Germany*. Toronto: Pontifical Institute of Mediaeval Studies, 1996.

Life and Death in a Venetian Convent: The Chronicle and Necrology of Corpus Domini, 1395–1436. Edited and translated by Daniel Bornstein. Chicago: University of Chicago Press, 2000.

"Mystisches Leben in dem Dominikanerinnenkloster Weiler bei Eßlingen im 13. und 14. Jahrhundert." Edited by Karl Bihlmeyer. *Württembergische Vierteljahreshefte für Landesgeschichte*, n.s. 25 (1916): 61–93.

Das "St. Katharinentaler Schwesterbuch": Untersuchung, Edition, Kommentar. Edited by Ruth Meyer. Tübingen: Max Niemeyer, 1995.

"Die Stiftung des Klosters Oetenbach und das Leben der seligen Schwestern daselbst, aus der Nürnberger Handschrift." Edited by H. Zeller-Werdmüller and Jakob Bächtold. *Zürcher Taschenbuch*, n.s. 12 (1889): 213–276.

Winston-Allen, Anne. *Convent Chronicles: Women Writing about Women and Reform in the Late Middle Ages*. University Park, Pa.: Pennsylvania State University Press, 2004.

See also **Asceticism; Audience, Women in the; Dominican Order; Education, Monastic; Germanic Lands; Hagiography; Literacy and Reading: Vernacular; Literature, German; Modern Devotion; Monasticism and Nuns; Mystics' Writings; Necrologies and Mortuary Rolls; Observant Movement; Stagel, Elsbeth; Women Authors: German Texts; Women Authors: Latin Texts**

SKÁLDKONUR

Old Norse poetry is conventionally subdivided into eddic and skaldic poetry: the former anonymous and the latter, by and large, attributed to named poets and deploying more complex meters. Eddic poetry, cast in rhythmic, alliterative meters, depicts the ancient Scandinavian world of heroines and heroes, gods and goddesses, giants and giantesses, valkyries, dwarves, troll-women and dragons. Much of it is in dialogue form and a considerable proportion of the reported speech is the speech of females: a *völva* (prophetess) narrates the history of the world in *Völuspá*, and the conversations of the heroines Brynhildr and Guñrún fill many of the heroic poems of the thirteenth-century Codex Regius anthology of eddic poems (known as the *Poetic Edda*). In sagas too, female characters declaim poetry, some of it in eddic style, such as *Darrañarljóñ*, chanted by valkyries in *Njáls saga* or *The Waking of Angantÿr*, spoken by the valiant shield-maiden Hervör in the saga of legendary times, *Hervarar saga ok Heiñreks*. Considering it her duty to avenge her father, she visits him in his grave and demands the ancestral sword she needs to carry out her mission of vengeance. In a saga set in a much later period, eight stanzas are attributed to a young girl called Jóreiñr Hermundardóttir who lived in Iceland in the thirteenth century. In them, she recounts detailed predictions of death told to her in a dream by a large woman riding from the north on a grey horse. The dream verses presage political killings that the saga then narrates, and although both the setting and the content of Jóreiñr's verses are undoubtedly stylized, her versifying is depicted as a contemporary historical event.

Other historical poets who were women are named in a range of medieval documents: *Skáldatal* (*List of Poets*) mentions Áslaug, wife of King Ragnarr, Vilborg *skáldkona* ("poet-woman"), one of the poets of the eleventh-century Norwegian king, Óláfr kyrri, and the Icelander Steinvör Sighvatsdóttir, a poet to the thirteenth-century Norwegian chieftain Gautr of Mel. The *Edda* of Snorri Sturluson, a thirteenth-century handbook of poetics, quotes a verse by one woman poet, Jórunn skáldmær ("poetmaiden") addressed to the Norwegian prince Hálfdan the Black. Sagas record a wider range of poetic compositions by women: court poetry by Hildr Hrólfsdóttir and Queen Gunnhildr of Norway has been preserved, and a number of Icelandic women from the settlement period are identified as poets: Ãórhildr *skáldkona*, Steingerñr Ãorkelsdóttir, Bróka-Auñr, Ãuríñr Óláfsdóttir, and Steinunn Refsdóttir. The target of Steinunn's verse was political: she took on the missionary Ãangbrandr, arguing in her verses that the god Ãórr was more powerful than Christ. Ãórhildr's composition was more domestic, but no less serious, in both intent and consequence. She recited an angry couplet at a wedding feast when she noticed her husband staring at a young woman, at which he declared himself divorced from her on the grounds of her malicious language. Fonder verses by women are rare, although *Kormaks saga* records a half-stanza by Steingerñr (with whom the poet Kormakr was in love), in which she declared she would want to marry him even if he were blind, knowing that even then, fate would have been kind to her. The recitation by men and women of erotic verses was banned by a zealous bishop in Iceland in the twelfth century, as a result of which we have no trace of what seems to have been another mode of poetic expression by women in medieval Scandinavia.

JUDY QUINN

References and Further Reading

Clunies Ross, Margaret. "Women Skalds and Norse Poetics: Jórunn Skáldmær's *Sendibítr*." In *Gudar på Jorden. Festskrift til Lars Lönnroth*, edited by Stina Hansson and Mats. Malm, Stockholm: Brutus Östling. 2000, pp. 85–96.
The Poetic Edda, translated by Carolyne Larrington. Oxford: Oxford University Press, 1996.
Skáldkonur fyrri alda, edited by Guñrún P. Helgadóttir. 2 vols. Akureyri: Kvöldvökuútgáfan, 1961–1963.
Straubhaar, Sandra Ballif. "Ambiguously Gendered: The Skalds Jórunn, Auñr and Steinunn." In *Cold Counsel: Women in Old Norse Literature and Mythology*, edited by Sarah M. Anderson with Karen Swenson. New York and London: Routledge, 2002, pp. 261–271.

See also **Literature, Norse; Prophets, Nordic; Scandinavia; Valkyries**

SLANDER
See **Gossip and Slander**

SLAVES

The Middle Ages have long been credited with the demise of slavery that had been inherited from the classical age and with terminating all that a slave society implied. With the spread of manorialism, "free" dependants came to be regulated by the custom of the group rather than owned as chattel, in Marc Bloch's memorable words. While the pace of that change has been debated in regional studies—the demise of slavery in Scandinavia (thralls) occurred much later than in France where it largely disappeared by the eleventh century—most authorities concur that medieval agriculture moved away from chattel slavery as its labor delivery system.

The demise argument does not rest on Christianity's repudiation of slavery to any noticeable extent, since the Christian church lived with the institution of slavery from its inception. The church accepted slavery as a fact of life, however odious, and the matters debated within canon law had to do with whether a slave could become a priest and similar questions rather than the morality of the institution itself. Some early Christians entered religious houses accompanied by their slaves. Christians considered it a pious act to free one's slaves, and Christianity promised slaves a heaven where they would be equal to free persons. From the thirteenth century forward certain holy women, among them Zita of Lucca, Margaret of Louvain, Margaret of Città di Castello, Sibilina Biscossi of Pavia, Veridiana Attavanti of Castellfiorentino, Jane of Orvieto, and Margaret of Hungary, for example took on the soubriquet *ancilla dei* (Luke 1:38), literally "slave of God," to place themselves on the lowest rung of human society. Yet, with the exception of the first-mentioned most were well-born women.

Canon law dealt not with *servi* and *ancillae* as such but with "unfree persons," which included serfs and bondsmen (Gilchrist). Canon law recognized some paternal rights for unfree men over their offspring in its attempt to strengthen the bond of marriage, but this law had little relevance to female slaves, who did not marry.

As a result the demise of slavery argument rests on the structural foundations of society and economy in medieval Europe rather than moral repudiation. And Europe experienced a revival of the slave trade in the thirteenth century that continued unabated into the modern era. In the 1850s, the economic historian

Wilhelm Heyd was surprised to find that the Mediterranean trade in slaves moved from the East to the Christian West. Researching in numerous archives Charles Verlinden found that the enslaved were destined for wealthy Christian households and were about ninety percent female. These slaves, *ancillae* in contrast to *servi* or male slaves, were sold at high prices and used as domestic workers, becoming symbols of the high status of the households that owned them. Because the offspring of female slaves were also unfree, this revived slave trade possessed the capacity to perpetuate the institution of slavery.

Early Medieval Slavery

Yet slavery had never died out entirely in Europe. The treatment of slaves differed according to local law and custom, although medieval communities generally recognized slavery as legitimate and regulated slaves' condition. On Carolingian estates *gynaecea* staffed by female slaves produced fine cloth, one of the few manufactured products worthy of export from Europe in this period (Herlihy, p. 83). If not slave societies, early Germanic, Scandinavian, Irish, and Anglo-Saxon societies were slaveholding ones. The early English penitentials fined slaveholders for sexual exploitation of their female slaves, but at a reduced rate from sexual crimes against free women. By law and tradition female slaves were assumed to be the property of masters with their sexual access assured. Any resulting offspring were the property of the master regardless of paternity. In early medieval Bavaria marriages among the free and unfree induced free members of the community to ameliorate the condition of their unfree partners, particularly in regard to the rights of offspring. By the tenth century the unfree entered into a more privileged dependency on the Church allowing them to exchange annual fixed payments for other servile obligations (Hammer). In Salzburg a *ministeriales* class of officials and knights remained noble bondsmen and women, that is, unfree in the eyes of the law, well into the fourteenth century (Freed).

Thirteenth Century Revival of the Slave Trade

The revival of Roman law in Christian lands in the Mediterranean West meant that an elaborate legal system pertaining to slavery was on hand to regulate the lives of the newly enslaved women brought from Tartar lands, from some Greek locales, and from the Balkan highlands in the thirteenth century, hence the toponymic *slave* for *Slavic*. Towns like Florence and Pisa favored baptizing slaves once purchased, although in many instances slaves were already baptized Christians (Origo). Other communities were more lax on the issue of baptism, but all households that owned slaves contended with the difficulties of "outlandish" languages and unfamiliar customs. Learning local dialects and some household skills raised the price of slaves, who were then passed from household to household in towns. There was a clear market preference for very young children, who were captured or sold to slave traders, then imported into towns. Contracts were frequently required to assure owners of their property rights over slaves.

For townspeople slaves were expensive and, therefore, luxuries. Being accompanied by one's slaves on the streets and canals of Venice was a display of conspicuous consumption. In medieval Ragusa/Dubrovnik wealthy households took in slaves who served as wet nurses for their children. A slave-nurse might accompany her former nursling to her new household upon marriage, serving as a life-long companion. In Florence Alessandra Strozzi expressed some fears about her garrulous, angry old slave Cateruccia, because she was a gossip and could "ruin" the family name with her loose talk (Origo, p. 343). Cooking, spinning, weaving, and sewing were particularly valuable learned skills among women slaves. In Italy a ten-year-old might cost as little as twenty florins in the fourteenth century, while a skilled woman slave might cost eighty florins or more (Stuard, "Ancillary," p. 22). Italian market towns placed taxes on slave sales as well.

Manumission

One recently debated issue in the literature on the revival of slavery is manumission, which was permitted under Roman law. It was considered a charitable act to free one's slaves in a last will and testament, although this also excused urban households from caring for slaves in their old age. This propensity to manumit domestic slaves has convinced some scholars that medieval slavery was not an onerous or exploitive institution since manumitted slaves might assimilate into the community. Since slaves served domestic households along with contract servants, who left after their period of service, and with wage-earning servants, scholars have recognized that some slaves entered great households as unfree persons but had a chance to gain some rights over a lifetime.

This has proved to be true in some documented cases, but, while the market for trained domestic slaves remained lively, there was a tidy profit for a household willing to sell vigorous and skilled slaves rather than manumitting them. The issue becomes more complicated when the offspring of women slaves are considered. Sally McKee has argued that in Crete slaves with Latin fathers were regarded as free after a generation or two, while Venice, Florence, and Genoa moved toward free status for the children of slaves by assuming that the offspring of slaves could inherit their fathers' status rather than their mothers' servile condition, at least by the fifteenth century (McKee). Where legitimate heirs were lacking the offspring of slave women were sometimes freed and acknowledged.

In Valencia manumitted offspring of a head of household and his slave (who might be manumitted as a result) could inherit the family name and in some cases even sue for a share in the family estate. Members of the family were known to plead the master's impotence to avoid sharing the family estate with a former slave's offspring (Blumenthal).

The Late Medieval North-South Trade in Slaves

Yet slavery persisted into the later Middle Ages when "Moorish" or African slaves became attractive new additions to wealthy households in Christian Europe. Also young when enslaved, these children might be either female or male. The small lavishly dressed Blackamoor of Renaissance family portraits might be a petted favorite of the household, but this does not mean that slaves led carefree lives. Slaves were imported into Venice and other towns, then rented out to produce an income. They were assigned the more tedious and back-breaking tasks of hauling goods or firewood. For a slave both the present and future were determined by the whim of the owner.

Piracy in the Mediterranean encouraged a two-way north-south trade in slaves. Christian ships raided and enslaved Muslims, who were taken back to home ports and sold. Christian sailors and ship passengers were taken to North African ports and enslaved until their families or Christian charities redeemed them. Since redemption was notoriously difficult to accomplish, many spent a lifetime in slavery. For centuries the border between Christian and Muslim Spain had seen a two-way traffic in slaves, with occasional redemptions. In the later Middle Ages capture and enslavement had become a more widespread Mediterranean phenomenon, and the numbers enslaved on both sides were considerable (Davis).

Conclusion

The institution of slavery never died out in medieval Europe. It remained as a viable, and rarely condemned, solution for household help—workers, nurses, concubines, rented-out laborers, or whatever other functions owners demanded—and for any other back-breaking work that "free" laborers eschewed. As with slaves imported into Crete in the thirteenth century to process sugar cane, slave labor presented to Europeans an economically feasible solution for the plantation economies of the Mediterranean islands, later the Atlantic islands off Europe and North Africa, and finally New World plantations. While some ameliorating influences had softened the face of slavery for a few, the legal condition of slaves, most notably *ancillae* and their offspring, remained unfree. Giovanni Bertachini's *Repertorium Iuris Utriusque*, an important reference tool for doctors of both civil and canon law printed in 1494 stated unequivocally, "*Servuus meum est qui natus est de ancilla mea*"—"A slave born to my (female) slave is my slave." The means for the perpetuation of the institution of slavery had survived.

SUSAN MOSHER STUARD

References and Further Reading

Angiolini, Franco. "Schiave." In *Il Lavoro delle donne*, edited by Angela Groppi. Storia delle donne in Italia. Roma and Bari: Editori Laterza, 1996.

Bertachini, Giovanni. *Repertorium Iuris Utriusque III*. 3 vols., ed. Venice: Arrivabene, 1494.

Bloch, Marc. *Slavery and Serfdom in the Middle Ages: Selected Essays*. Berkeley: University of California Press, 1975.

Blumenthal, Debra. "*Sclaves molt fortes, senyors invalts*: Sex, Lies, and Paternity Suits in Fifteenth-Century Spain." In *Women, Texts, and Authority in the Early Modern Spanish World*, edited by Marta V. Vicente and Luis R. Corteguera. Aldershot: Ashgate, 2003, pp. 17–35.

Davis, Robert. "Counting European Slaves on the Barbary Coast." *Past and Present* 172 (August 2001): 87–124.

Devroey, Jean-Pierre. "Men and Women in Early Medieval Serfdom: The Ninth-Century North Frankish Evidence." *Past and Present* 166 (February 2000): 3–30.

Elbl, Ivana. "'Men without Wives': Sexual Arrangements in the Early Portugese Expansion in West Africa." In *Desire and Discipline: Sex and Sexuality in the Premodern West*, edited by Jacqueline Murray and Konrad Eisenbichler. Toronto: University of Toronto Press, 1996, pp. 61–86.

Epstein, Steven. *Speaking of Slavery: Color, Ethnicity and Human Bondage in Italy*. Ithaca, N.Y.: Cornell University Press, 2001.

Freed, John. *Noble Bondsmen: Ministerial Marriage in the Archdiocese of Salzburg, 1100–1343*. Ithaca, N.Y.: Cornell University Press, 1995.

Gilchrist, John. "The Medieval Canon Law on Unfree Persons." In *Mélanges G. Fransen*, edited by Stephan

Kuttner and Alfons M. Stickler. Studia Gratiana, 19 (1976): 278–295.

Girsch, Elizabeth Stevens. "Metaphorical Usage, Sexual Exploitation, and Divergence in the Old English Terminology for Male and Female Slaves." In *The Work of Work: Servitude, Slavery, and Labor in Medieval England*, edited by Allen J. Frantzen and Douglas Moffat. Glasgow: Cruithne Press, 1994, pp. 30–54.

Hammer, Carl I. "The Handmaid's Tale: Morganatic Relationships in Early-Mediaeval Bavaria." *Continuity and Change* 10.3 (1995): 345–368.

Herlihy, David. *Opera Muliebria*. New York: McGraw Hill, 1990.

Karras, Ruth Mazo. "Concubinage and Slavery in the Viking Age." *Scandinavian Studies* 62.2 (1990): 141–162.

———. "Desire, Descendants, and Dominance: Slavery, the Exchange of Women, and Masculine Power." In *The Work of Work: Servitude, Slavery, and Labor in Medieval England*, edited by Allen J. Frantzen and Douglas Moffat. Glasgow: Cruithne Press, 1994, pp. 16–29.

Luzzati, Michele. "Schiavi e figli di schiavi attraverso le registrazioni di battesimo medievali: Pisa, Gemona del Friuli, Lucca." *Quaderni Storici* 107(36)2 (2001): 349–362.

McKee, Sally. "Inherited Status and Slavery in Late Medieval Italy and Venetian Crete." *Past and Present* 182 (2004): 31–53.

Origo, Iris. "The Domestic Enemy: The Eastern Slaves in Tuscany in the Fourteenth and Fifteenth Centuries." *Speculum* 30 (1955): 321–399.

Stuard, Susan Mosher. "Ancillary Evidence for the Decline of Medieval Slavery." *Past and Present* 149 (1995): 3–28.

———. "Single by Law and Custom." In *Singlewomen in the European Past, 1250–1800*, edited by Judith M. Bennett and Amy M. Froide. Philadelphia: University of Pennsylvania Press, 1999, pp. 106–126.

———. "*Qui natus est de ancilla mea* in Medieval Church Law." In *Proceedings of the Tenth International Congress of Medieval Canon Law*, edited by Kenneth Pennington, Stanley Chodorow and Keith H. Kendall. Vatican City: Biblioteca Apoltolica Vaaticana, 2001, pp. 653–673.

Verlinden, Charles. *L'Esclavage dans é l'Europe médiévale*. Bruges: De Tempel, 1955, and Ghent: Rijksonijersiteit te Gent, 1977.

See also **Captivity and Ransom; Household Management; Iberia; Italy; Strozzi, Allessandra**

SOCIAL STATUS

Social historians of the modern era generally agree that self-conscious social classes emerged only in the nineteenth century, as a result of the Industrial Revolution. Thus, it is more appropriate to use the expressions *social status* or *social-economic groups* when discussing medieval women. Social status shaped medieval women's experiences and opportunities, and it complicated the ways in which women and men were gendered in the Middle Ages.

Social-Economic Groups

The predominant social-economic groups of the medieval countryside were peasants, nobles, monks, and nuns. Peasants worked the land. Nobles, whose male members often engaged in armed warfare, and men and women in monastic institutions, whose primary social function was to pray, derived their wealth from the lands that they held and from the rights that they had over the peasants who worked those lands. In the early Middle Ages, until the twelfth century, most nobles and monastics resided in the countryside; after 1100, however, increasing numbers of nobles, monks, and nuns began to live in towns, although, in most cases, they continued to derive their wealth from the rural labor of peasants.

Urban social-economic groups—those whose income was derived from urban production, commerce, or bureaucratic functions—grew significantly after the year 1000. These included merchant elites, whose men often controlled town governments; government bureaucrats and notaries; artisans, who owned their own workshops; laborers who earned their wages by the day or week; servants; and the nonlaboring (i.e., disabled or aged) poor. Mediterranean towns also had domestic slaves. In Iberia, these were predominantly Muslims and former Muslims who had been captured during the Christian reconquest of Muslim territories, which began in the eleventh century. In northern Italy, domestic slaves did not appear in significant numbers until after the onset of the Black Death in 1347–1348; most were girls and women from the Black Sea region. Town populations also included members of urban religious orders, such as the Franciscans, Dominicans, Poor Clares, and Beguines, whose movements took shape around the year 1200.

Marriage

In addition to their differing standards of living, medieval women from these various social groups—and from differing parts of Europe—had differing degrees of choice about whether or not to marry and who to marry, differing roles within marriage, and differing economic rights and standards of living as widows. Elite women—both those of the nobility and those of the merchant elite—tended to marry at a very young age and their first marriages were frequently arranged by their parents. Nonelite women tended to marry at an older age, one that was closer to that of their husbands, than did elite women. In northern Europe, where many single women migrated to towns, urban working women, and probably a good number of peasant women as well, had a great deal of freedom in their choice of marriage partner. In Italy, as Lansing has argued, women whose natal families were too poor to endow them with a dowry were often prevented from marrying, but this lack could result in the freedom to form sexual liaisons that were motivated by affection, a luxury that was not available to Italian girls and women of means. In most cases, slave women did not marry. Although some legal systems in Spain implied that slave women could marry, it is unclear if such marriages took place before manumission. Slave women were often the victims of sexual advances from the men in the households that they served. In Italy, many of the children that were born to slave women were placed in institutions for abandoned girls and boys.

Responsibilities

Conduct literature and works on household management, such as those by the Knight of La Tour Landry, the Ménagier of Paris, and Leon Battista Alberti, create the impression that the principal roles of elite wives were to guard their virtue, obey their husbands, produce children, and manage the household. This impression is somewhat misleading in the case of wives of the northern European merchant elite, since a number of those women engaged in commercial enterprises both alongside their husbands and independently. Even for those elite wives who did conform to the ideals of childbearing and household management, the responsibilities could be enormous, since large aristocratic households could include dozens of members. Moreover, when royal, noble, and merchant husbands were away from their homes for reasons of warfare, crusade, business, or exile, elite women's responsibilities often grew enormously. In the High and late Middle Ages (1050–1500) a number of queens and countesses took over the governance and defense of their realms in the absence of their husbands, even to the point of bearing arms. In northern Italian towns the activities and economic independence of women of the merchant elite were limited by customs and laws that favored extended male lineages over the conjugal unit, thus they tended to be excluded from commercial activities. Nevertheless, elite merchant wives and mothers in Italy, such as Alessandra Strozzi and Marguerita Datini, played pivotal roles in managing their families' affairs during the extended absences, for reasons of business and exile, of their husbands and adult sons. Both peasant and artisan wives were valued within marriage for their essential economic roles, which may have contributed to an informal sense of marital equality.

Widows

In northern Europe, noble, merchant, peasant, and artisan widows tended to have a great deal of economic independence, gaining control of one third to all of the conjugal property upon the deaths of their husbands. Legally, they were now free from the control of both their parents and their husbands' families, but in reality, as the story of Guibert of Nogent's noble mother indicates, some had to struggle to protect that independence. As the work of Howell and Archer makes clear, many merchant and artisan widows in northern Europe were able to exercise a great deal of independence in the commercial and productive spheres. However, laboring husbands who earned their wages by the day or week frequently had nothing to leave their widows. For these women, the cost of economic independence was economic marginality or destitution. In northern Italy, elite urban widows were frequently limited to their dowry, and, as Klapisch-Zuber has argued for the elite bourgeois women of fifteenth-century Florence, many such widows were subject to male control—either that of their paternal families, or that of their husbands' families. By contrast, Dennis Romano has argued from evidence in Venice, that artisan widows were freer from the control of extended patrilineal families than were elite Italian widows.

Stereotypes

According to Farmer, women and men from differing social groups were subjected to differing dominant gender stereotypes. Thus, while all men were associated, in clerical writings, with productive labor, and all women with reproductive labor, elite men were more likely to be associated with intellectual or spiritual productive labor, and elite women with intellectual and spiritual functions associated with reproductive labor, while nonelite men and women were more likely to be associated with the body and its appetites. In their model sermons for people of various social groups, thirteenth-century preachers such as James of Vitry, Humbert of Romans, and Guibert of Tournai charged elite women with the responsibility of spiritually educating all the members of their households and controlling not only their own sexuality but also that of their male and female servants.

Conversely, these preachers associated both male and female servants with uncontrolled lust, and they blamed female servants for the sexual liaisons that some of them had with the male members of the households that they served. Along similar lines, vernacular literature drew sharp distinctions between nobles and peasants. In courtly literature, only nobles were represented as worthy and capable of the refined emotion known as courtly love; in pastourelle literature, peasant men were represented as too blundering and inept for love and peasant women were portrayed as sexually promiscuous.

For women of the lower echelons of society, these dominant gender stereotypes could have devastating effects. As Gravdal has suggested, literary portraits of peasant women who were open to sexual encounters functioned as barely veiled invitations for elite men to rape lower-status women. Support for this argument comes from Rossiaud, who found in his examinations of court records from fifteenth-century Dijon that lower-status women living alone or working as servants were especially vulnerable to rape, often by men of means.

While predominant stereotypes of lower-status women could have very real consequences, those women did not necessarily internalize the ways in which they were represented by elites. Farmer has argued that while clerical authors tended to be blind to women's roles in the economic realm, working women were outspoken about their essential economic contributions to their households. Lansing has argued, moreover, that poorer residents of thirteenth-century Bologna resisted elite attempts to classify as "infamous" and "prostitutes" all women who entered into extramarital relations.

Spirituality and Sanctity

In addition to affecting women's choices, roles and rights with respect to marriage and widowhood, as well as the ways in which women were stereotyped by those who controlled dominant cultural representations, social status shaped women's access to spiritual prestige and sanctity. As Kenneth Wolf has argued, western medieval Christian society placed much more spiritual value on self-abnegation than on service for others: in the High and later Middle Ages especially, voluntary poverty and extreme asceticism were essential aspects of sainthood. Only individuals who had something to give up could practice self-abnegation and voluntary poverty; thus, it was difficult for those who were born poor to aspire to sanctity. Wolf's analysis applies well to most of the prominent female

saints of the High and later Middle Ages who were known for their extreme asceticism: Elisabeth of Hungary was the daughter of a king and the wife of a member of the highest nobility. Marie of Oignies, Beatrice of Nazareth, Clare of Assisi, Humility of Faenza, and Angela of Foligno were all from well-to-do backgrounds, and Margaret of Cortona was the concubine of a nobleman before her religious conversion. Catherine of Siena stands out as a possible exception, since she was the daughter of a lower-middle-class dyer. Nevertheless, dyers were well placed within the hierarchy of artisans, and they were included in a group of modest artisans and notaries who ruled Siena during a significant portion of Catherine's lifetime. Saints who were born truly poor, such as the servant saint Zita of Lucca, were exceptions to the rule.

SHARON FARMER

References and Further Reading

Archer, Janice. "Working Women in Thirteenth-Century Paris." PhD Diss., University of Arizona, 1995.

Bennett, Judith, and Amy Froide, eds. *Singlewomen in the European Past, 1250–1800.* Philadelphia: University of Pennsylvania Press, 1999.

Blumenthal, Debra. *Enemies and Familiars: Muslim, Eastern and Black African Slaves in Late Medieval Valencia.* Ithaca, N.Y.: Cornell University Press, forthcoming.

Farmer, Sharon. *Surviving Poverty in Medieval Paris: Gender, Ideology and the Daily Lives of the Poor.* Ithaca, N.Y.: Cornell University Press, 2002.

———. "Introduction." In *Gender and Difference in the Middle Ages*, edited by Sharon Farmer and Carol Pasternack. Minneapolis: University of Minnesota Press, 2003, pp. ix-xxvii.

Freedman, Paul. *Images of the Medieval Peasant.* Stanford: Stanford University Press, 1999.

Gravdal, Kathryn. *Ravishing Maidens: Writing Rape in Medieval French Literature and Law.* Philadelphia: University of Pennsylvania Press, 1991.

Howell, Martha C. *Women, Production and Patriarchy in Late Medieval Cities.* Chicago: University of Chicago Press, 1986.

Karras, Ruth Mazo. *Common Women: Prostitution and Sexuality in Medieval England.* New York: Oxford University Press, 1996.

Klapisch-Zuber, Christiane. *Women, Family and Ritual in Renaissance Italy.* Translated by Lydia G. Cochrane. Chicago: University of Chicago Press, 1985.

Lansing, Carol. "Concubines, Lovers, Prostitutes: Infamy and Female Identity in Medieval Bologna." In *Beyond Florence: The Contours of Medieval and Early Modern Italy*, edited by Paula Findlen, Michelle M. Fontaine, and Duane J. Osheim. Stanford: Stanford University Press, 2003.

Origo, Iris. "The Domestic Enemy: The Eastern Slaves in Tuscany in the Fourteenth and Fifteenth Centuries." *Speculum: A Journal of Medieval Studies* 30 (1955): 321–366.

———. *The Merchant of Prato: Francesco di Marco Datini, 1335–1410*. New York: Knopf, 1957.

Romano, Dennis. *Patricians and Popolani: The Social Foundations of the Venetian Renaissance State*. Baltimore: Johns Hopkins University Press, 1987.

Rossiaud, Jacques. *Medieval Prostitution*. Translated by Lydia G. Cochrane. New York: Blackwell, 1988.

Strozzi, Alessandra. *The Selected Letters of Alessandra Strozzi*, translated with an Introduction by Heather Gregory. Berkeley: University of California Press, 1997.

Stuard, Susan Mosher. "Ancillary Evidence on the Decline of Medieval Slavery." *Past and Present* 149 (1995): 3–32.

Wolf, Kenneth Baxter. *The Poverty of Riches: Saint Francis of Assisi Reconsidered*. New York: Oxford University Press, 2003.

See also **Angela of Foligno; Artisan Families, Women of; Beatrice of Nazareth; Beguines; Business; Catherine of Siena; Clare of Assisi; Concubines; Conduct Literature; Courtly Love; Datini, Margherita; Dowry and Other Marriage Gifts; Femininity and Masculinity; Gender Ideologies; Gentry, Women of: England; Guibert of Nogent's Mother; Household Management; Humility of Faenza; Inheritance; Landholding and Property Rights; Margaret of Cortona; Market and Tradeswomen; Marriage, Christian; Merchant Families, Women of; Migration and Mobility; Monasticism and Nuns; Noble Women; Pastourelle; Peasants; Poor Clares Order; Poverty; Queens and Empresses: The West; Rape and Raptus; Regents and Queen-Lieutenants; Servants; Singlewomen; Slaves; Strozzi, Alessandra; Warfare; Widows**

SONG OF SONGS, MEDIEVAL INTERPRETATIONS OF

The Song of Songs, a collection of poems attributed to King Solomon, is perhaps the most enigmatic book of the Bible, eight chapters of passionate love poems between a man and a woman that mention neither salvation history nor the name of God. Jews and Christians alike have debated whether this text has a place in Scripture. Ancient Jewish midrashic traditions saw it as the marriage song of God and Israel. Early Christians were well aware of this and used it to their advantage. In the third century, Origen of Alexandria wrote a commentary and a series of homilies on the Song in which the two lovers become either Christ and the Church or Christ and the human soul. Origen wrote in Greek, but the surviving fragments in Latin translations were well-known throughout the Middle Ages, and inspired a huge tradition of Latin allegory.

For medieval Christians, then, the Song of Songs was an elaborate allegory of God's love for the Church or the soul, in which the sometimes steamy eroticism of the text was spiritualized. Such readings flourished in the monastic world of the seventh to the twelfth centuries, when almost a hundred interpretations were written. Most favor the interpretation of Christ and the Church, although the monastic world of the twelfth century saw a boom of writings on the Song as God's love for the soul, such as the famous homilies by Bernard of Clairvaux. It is interesting to think about medieval monks and nuns, vowed to a chaste life, meditating on the passionate eroticism of God's love for the soul. Yet there is nothing prudish about these texts; rather, the monastic authors revel in their role as the feminized spouse of the Song. This is all the more remarkable when the author and the imagined protagonist of the love story are men. The medieval tradition of the Song of Songs is an excellent place to see some stunning medieval gender reversals as men, even abbots and bishops, imagined themselves in the passive role of the Bride.

It is hard to tell if the spiritual interpretation of the Song of Songs has the same paradoxically elevating effect for medieval women. For one thing, women were not allowed to write biblical commentaries, a task reserved for men, so they had to comment on the Bible in more oblique ways. The Song was not always a part of women's vocabulary; the famous twelfth-century author Hildegard of Bingen quotes extensively from parts of the Bible but largely stays away from the Song of Songs. In the following century, though, both Clare of Assisi's letters to Agnes of Prague and Gertrude the Great's mystical meditation on the liturgy, the *Spiritual Exercises*, urge their readers to use the love language of the Song as a guide to the proper love of God. Ironically, Clare and Gertrude use a male spiritual tradition to urge female monastics to cast themselves in the role of the Bride.

Medieval women also had access to the tradition of interpretation that sees the Bride as the Virgin Mary. This is a minor strand of the commentary tradition, mostly twelfth-century, but it obviously had an impact on a German translation of the Song of Songs probably done by a woman and certainly for use in a women's community in South Germany. The *St. Trudperter Song of Songs* holds up the Virgin as a model for the contemplative soul; the nuns are told that they can become, like Mary, a spiritual mother, daughter, and wife all at once. This language foreshadows the way women in religious life will be characterized in the early modern period, when women's spiritual power (and danger) becomes a dangerous double-edged trope.

And it is in the early modern period that the first commentary on the Song of Songs by a woman, Teresa of Avila's *Meditations on the Song of Songs*, a treatment of the verses from the Song used in her Carmelite Breviary, was written. Teresa's language is as passionate, and as self-deprecating, as that of the famous male authors of earlier centuries; and no wonder, since she was under the scrutiny of the Inquisition when she wrote it. This suggests, once again, that this tradition reached women when it had run its course among male authors, and that although it may have been affirming for men because of its paradoxical gender inversion, its impact on women was more likely to affirm stereotypes of submission.

E. ANN MATTER

References and Further Reading

Bernard of Clairvaux. *On the Song of Songs.* Vols. 1–2 translated by Killian Walsh. Kalamazoo, Mich.: Cistercian Publications, 1976. Vols. 3–4 translated by Irene Edmonds. Kalamazoo, Mich.: Cistercian Publications, 1979, 1980.

Clare of Assisi *Letters to Agnes of Prague* In *Francis and Clare: The Complete Works,* translated by Regis J. Armstrong and Ignatius C. Brady. New York: Paulist Press, 1982.

Gertrude the Great. *Spiritual Exercises.* Translated by Gertrud Jaron Lewis and Jack Lewis. Kalamazoo, Mich.: Cistercian Publications, 1989.

Matter, E. Ann, "The Song of Songs in the *Exercitia Spiritualia* of Gertrude the Great of Helfta" *Laurentianum* 31 (1990): 39–49.

———. *The Voice of My Beloved: The Song of Songs in Western Medieval Christianity.* Philadelphia: University of Pennsylvania Press, 1990.

Origen of Alexandria. *The Song of Songs. Commentary and Homilies.* Translated by R. P. Lawson. New York: Newman Press, 1957.

Teresa of Avila. *Meditations on the Song of Songs.* In *The Collected Works of St. Teresa of Avila, vol. 2.* Translated by Kiernan Kavanaugh and Otilio Rodriguez. Washington, D.C.: ICS, 1976.

Turner, Denys. *Eros and Allegory: Medieval Exegesis of the Song of Songs.* Kalamazoo, Mich.: Cistercian Publications, 1995.

See also **Bride of Christ: Imagery; Clare of Assisi; Eroticism in Literature; Gender Ideologies; Gertrude the Great; Hildegard of Bingen; Mary, Virgin; Monasticism and Nuns; Theology**

SOPHIA PALAIOLOGINA

Sophia Palaiologina (1450/1451–1503), originally christened Zoe, was the daughter of Thomas Palaiologos, despot of the Morea (southern Greece), and Caterina Zaccaria, a Genoese heiress from Achaia. She was therefore the niece of Constantine XI, the Byzantine emperor who died on the walls of Constantinople in 1453. Zoe was about ten years old when the Ottoman Turks captured Mistra, capital of the despotate, and forced her family in 1460 to flee first to Corfù (Kerkyra) and later to Rome. After her father's death, Cardinal Bessarion acted as Zoe's guardian, supervised her education, and arranged her marriage to Ivan III, Grand Duke of Moscow. This was negotiated by Ivan's master of the mint, Gian Battista della Volpe, who accompanied Zoe to Moscow. Through this alliance Pope Sixtus IV hoped to promote the Catholic faith but Zoe adopted Orthodoxy and was renamed Sophia at her marriage to Ivan in November 1472.

Although previously credited with introducing much Byzantine influence in the Muscovite court, Sophia brought Western styles with her, as well as two of her brothers and other Greek advisors. Italian engineers and architects assisted in the construction of the Moscow Kremlin and Dormition Cathedral (1475–1479). Sophia's presence may have increased awareness of Byzantine imperial traditions, but the double-headed eagle and title *tsar* were already in use. Between 1497 and 1500, as Ivan III wavered over the succession, Sophia championed her eldest son Vasilii against Dmitrii, Ivan's grandson by his first wife. Eventually Vasilii was designated and succeeded his father (1505–1533).

JUDITH HERRIN

References and Further Reading

Crummey, Robert. *The Formation of Muscovy 1304–1613.* London: Longman, 1987.

Fennell, J. L. *Ivan the Great of Moscow.* London: Macmillan, 1963.

Thomson, Francis J. *The Reception of Byzantine Culture in Medieval Russia.* Aldershot: Ashgate, 1999.

See also **Byzantium; Russia**

SOUL

In its broadest sense, *soul* refers to the principle of life in plants, animals, and humans known in Latin as *anima.* However, *soul* is also used to translate the Latin words *animus* and *mens,* meaning the rational soul or the mind, and it is this uniquely human capacity of reason that most medieval thinkers emphasize. Questions about the soul have been discussed since the time of the earliest Greek philosophers. However, by the Middle Ages, the topic was approached from three different points of view: the scientific, the philosophical, and the theological. The most widely known of these conceptions of the soul was the theological, so only a brief review of the scientific and philosophical definitions will be provided here.

The scientific perspective derived from the medical theories of Hippocrates and Galen was transmitted to the West by Arabic doctors. Although the medical tradition focused on the body formed of the four elements (earth, air, fire, and water), by the Middle Ages doctors believed that the soul or principle of life was immaterial, and they developed the classical theory of *pneuma*, or spirit, proposed by the Stoics as the link between the immaterial soul and the material body.

Arabic scholars also transmitted Aristotle's texts to the West by the mid-twelfth century. The recovery of *De anima* (*On the Soul*) led to discussions among the scholastics, those male thinkers associated with the universities, about the nature of the soul and its cognitive powers. Philosophers debated issues such as the relationship between the material, mortal body and the immaterial, immortal soul, as well as the means by which the rational part of the soul acquires knowledge. Aristotle's explanation of the soul as the form of the body promoted an integrated view of the human person. Thomas Aquinas (c. 1224–1274) incorporated Aristotle's ideas about the soul into Christianity by the 1270s, although his doing so was controversial at the time.

Even though the late-medieval medical and philosophical discourses acknowledge the Christian belief that the soul is immortal, both fields emphasized the soul's dependence on a body to maintain life and to attain knowledge in this world. Theological discussions of the soul, however, focused on the soul's relationship to God and its eternal destiny.

Augustine, Bishop of Hippo (354–430 CE), developed the theological perspective on the soul that was most familiar and influential throughout the Middle Ages. Although he wrote treatises on several different questions regarding the soul's nature, Augustine's most important work on this subject is *De Trinitate* (*On the Trinity*). This text demonstrates his introspective method of inquiry. Referring to Genesis 1:26–27, "And he said: 'Let us make man to our image and likeness,'" Augustine regards the soul as the site of the *imago Dei* or image of God in humankind. He therefore tries to ascertain the nature of the divine Trinity by examining various psychic trinities such as memory, intelligence, and will, within himself.

In Book 12, chapter 3 of *De Trinitate*, Augustine divides the *mens* or rational part of the soul into the higher and the lower reason. The higher reason, dedicated to the contemplation of God, can achieve wisdom (*sapentia*); the lower reason, oriented to temporal affairs of the world, can only achieve knowledge (*scientia*). Although Augustine claims that these two parts of the soul are not separate, but merely different in function, he genders the higher reason masculine and the lower reason feminine; he also concludes that the image of God resides exclusively in the masculine

higher reason. Although he admits that men and women are literally equal in spirit, Augustine claims that, insofar as the female is different from the male in body, she is a metaphor for the lower reason's incapacity for contemplation of transcendent reality. By chapter 12 of Book 14 Augustine conflates the literal and metaphoric senses of woman by arguing that Eve, both as a female person and as the lower reason, was the intermediary who exposed Adam or the higher reason to the temptation of the serpent and thus caused original sin.

Frequently reiterated during the Middle Ages, Augustine's division of the soul in *De Trinitate* into the higher and lower reason had far-reaching consequence for women in the medieval church. Although his insistence on the spiritual equality of literal men and women before God enabled some women to empower themselves, his metaphoric identification of the female body with the lower reason placed them in an inferior position to the opposite sex and called into question their mental capability.

DENISE NOWAKOWSKI BAKER

References and Further Reading

Børresen, Kari Elisabeth. *Subordination and Equivalence: The Nature and Role of Woman in Augustine and Thomas Aquinas.* Translated by Charles H. Talbot. Washington, D.C.: University Press of America, 1981.

Harvey, E. Ruth. *The Inward Wits: Psychological Theory in the Middle Ages and the Renaissance.* Warburg Institute Surveys 6. London: Warburg Institute, University of London, 1975.

McGinn, Bernard. "The Human Person as Image of God II: Western Christianity." In *World Spirituality: An Encyclopedic History of the Religious Quest*, vol. 16, *Christian Spirituality: Origins to the Twelfth Century*, edited by Bernard McGinn and John Meyendorff. New York: Crossroad, 1985, pp. 312–330.

Pasnua, Robert. "Human Nature." In *The Cambridge Companion to Medieval Philosophy*, edited by A. S. McGrade. Cambridge: Cambridge University Press, 2003, pp. 208–230.

See also **Aristotelian Concepts of Women and Gender; Augustine, Influence of; Gender Ideologies; Scholasticism; Theology**

SPACE, SACRED: AND GENDER

The gendering of sacred space and its implications for women's lives have only recently begun to receive the attention of scholars. Although often taken for granted and viewed as "natural" or accidental, spatial arrangements as metaphors and symbolic systems embodied some of the most basic values and meanings of medieval society. The medieval church had a keen interest in the ordering, regulation, and protection of sacred space. As statements of power and authority, spatial constructs served the special interests of the church and its hierarchy. These arrangements were used to reinforce the prevailing male advantage and regulate social behavior; they also worked to contain and marginalize women. They both reflected and constructed gendered identities of the period.

Influenced by ancient Greek, Jewish, and early Christian practices, and reflecting in part the physical tension between the sacred and profane, the church attempted to deal with its fear of female sexuality and pollution and need to segregate the laity from the clergy by establishing certain symbolic and physical boundaries. Church councils warned that lay dwellings, especially those containing women, were to be kept at a certain distance from church buildings. Monasteries of nuns were not to be built in the neighborhood of those of monks, as much to resist "the ruses of Satan" as the rumors that would result from this. Regulations regarding whether women could take communion during menstruation; or how long after childbirth women might be allowed to enter the church; purification rituals; or whether women who died in childbirth might be brought into the church for funeral rites or buried in consecrated ground, underscore the church's fear of female pollution and need to protect the sacrality of its space.

Although arrangements varied, a policy of strict segregation was adopted in many churches. Separate doors were established for men and women. Men were placed *a dextris*, on the privileged right or south side, reserved for the elect in the Last Judgment; while females were relegated *a sinistris,* to the left or north side of the nave, corresponding to the side of the damned, the location of the devil's door, etc. The gendered iconography of mosaics or paintings on nave walls, or that of church screens with female saints on the left and male saints on the right, or later carvings on bench ends further reinforced this placement. Marriage ceremonies stipulated that the woman was to stand to the left of the man. In certain regions cemeteries for women were found to the north of the church while those for men were located to the south. Other sources note that men were to sit in the forepart or eastward section of the church while women were to sit behind them, since the "husband was the head of the wife." Prostitutes were required to stay "behind and segregated from good women." Durham Cathedral still has a line in the floor of the second bay of its nave beyond which women were forbidden to pass. Many arrangements were however of a local nature and there is evidence that in a few churches these customary stations that privileged men were reversed to reward women's heroic behavior in their communities.

Double churches or chapels emphasized hierarchical ordering: royalty or nobility occupied the upper floor while those of lesser standing remained below, as at the Sainte Chapelle in Paris. Frequently separate chapels were designated for the king and for the queen.

The sanctuary which housed the altar was viewed as the church's most sacred space. Women were specifically warned that, because of their natural infirmity, they were not to approach the main altar, stand or sit within the chancel, touch the sacred vessels or corporal, or distribute communion to the faithful. Nevertheless some women were able to vicariously occupy this privileged space through donations of altar crosses, chalices, books, major altar pieces, etc., which contained their names and portraits.

Many male monasteries strictly forbade women access to their churches and chapels. These exclusionary practices proved to be especially difficult for women who wished to visit these sites and pray at their saints' tombs. Unwilling to accept these gender-based proscriptive policies, women consistently challenged or contested these spaces: for example, some women were involved in negotiations to allow them limited access; others became audacious trespassers within these "male only spaces." In a number of cases, wealth and status overrode gender (i.e., queens and noble women were accorded special permission to enter male monastic churches and pray at their saints' tombs). As an expression of their gratitude they invariably provided generous donations to these foundations.

In contrast, the spatial policies of women's monastic churches appear to have been more inclusive. With the need for priests and other males to help in the running of their communities, they did not have the luxury to exclude men. They made provision for the laity (male and female) to be allowed to worship within their main churches which in some cases also served as parish churches. Cogitosus, in his *Life of St. Brigit* (seventh century), provides a description of the church of the double or mixed community of Kildare with its internal divisions of space. The nave had a median wall that divided the congregation: the women's half was located on the left or north side, and the men's half on the right or south side. Each side had its own special door. At the east end or the chancel area, was a transverse wall with two doors that separated the lay congregation from the monks and nuns. Here the nuns were relegated to the left or north side of the altar and the monks were to the south or right of the altar. The nuns were thus separated in their churches from the lay men and women:

in some places they occupied one side of the nave; or the choir, or an upper gallery placed over the aisles or in the west end or *Westwerk* of the church. In the central and late Middle Ages, with the increased emphasis on strict segregation and enclosure, the nuns were frequently hidden behind wooden or masonry walls, or heavy metal grills. With this arrangement, they often had to endure obstructed views of the altar and communion. In some cases nuns were provided with only small apertures that served as "listening holes" for them to hear the liturgy. Thus for many monasteries, these spatial arrangements seem to have been made at the expense of the members of the female community and their religious experiences: they effectively limited or restricted their access to the most privileged sacred space within their own churches.

While there exists some variety in the arrangements of medieval sacred space, these spaces were never neutral, disinterested, or inert. The gendered policies provide another important perspective on shifting views of women and their proper "place" in society and the church.

JANE TIBBETTS SCHULENBURG

References and Further Reading

Aston, Margaret. "Segregation in Church." In *Women in the Church. Studies in Church History* 27, edited by W. J. Sheils and Diana Wood. Oxford: Blackwell, 1990, pp. 237–294.

Crook, John. *The Architectural Setting of the Cult of Saints in the Early Christian West c. 300–1200*. Oxford: Clarendon Press; New York: Oxford Univ. Press, 2000.

Douglas, Mary. *Purity and Danger: An Analysis of the Concepts of Pollution and Taboo*. 1966. New York: Praeger, 1984.

Gilchrist, Roberta. *Gender and Material Culture: The Archaeology of Religious Women*. London and New York: Routledge, 1994.

Hanawalt, Barbara A., and Michal Kobialka, eds. *Medieval Practices of Space*. Medieval Culture, 23. Minneapolis: University of Minnesota Press, 2000.

Hayes, Dawn Marie. *Body and Sacred Place in Medieval Europe, 1100–1389*. London and New York: Routledge, 2003.

Morrison, Susan Signe. *Women Pilgrims in Late Medieval England: Private Piety as Public Performance*. London and New York: Routledge, 2000.

Nilson, Ben. *Cathedral Shrines of Medieval England*. Woodbridge, Suffolk, Rochester, N.Y.: Boydell Press, 1998.

Raguin, Virgina Chieffo and Sarah Stanbury, eds. *Women's Space: Patronage, Place and Gender in the Medieval Church*. Albany: State University of New York Press, 2005.

Randolph, Adrian. "Regarding Women in Sacred Space." In *Picturing Women in Renaissance and Baroque Italy*, edited by Geraldine A. Johnson and Sara F. Matthews Grieco. Cambridge: Cambridge University Press, 1997, pp. 17–41, 250–256.

Schulenburg, Jane Tibbetts. "Strict Active Enclosure and Its Effects on the Female Monastic Experience ca. 500–1100." In *Distant Echoes: Medieval Religious Women*, vol. I, edited by John A. Nichols and Lillian Thomas Shank. Kalamazoo, Mich.: Cistercian Publications, 1984, pp. 51–86.

———. "Gender, Celibacy, and Proscriptions of Sacred Space: Symbol and Practice." In *Medieval Purity and Piety: Essays on Medieval Clerical Celibacy and Religious Reform*, edited by Michael Frassetto. New York and London: Garland, 1998, pp. 353–376. Reprinted with revisions in Raguin and Standbury. *Women's Space: Patronage, Place and Gender in the Medieval Church*, pp. 185–205.

———. *Forgetful of their Sex: Female Sanctity and Society*. Chicago: University of Chicago Press, 1998.

Smith, Julia M. H. "Women at the Tomb: Access to Relic Shrines in the Early Middle Ages." In *The World of Gregory of Tours*, edited by Kathleen Mitchell and Ian Wood (Cultures, Beliefs and Traditions: Medieval and Early Modern People, 8). Leiden: E. J. Brill, 2002, pp. 163–180.

Spain, Daphne. *Gendered Spaces*. Chapel Hill, N.C.: University of North Carolina Press, 1992.

Spicer, Andrew and Sarah Hamilton, eds. *Defining the Holy: Sacred Space in Medieval and Early Modern Europe*. Aldershot, England, Burlington, Vt.: Ashgate, 2005.

Von Simson, Otto. *The Gothic Cathedral: Origins of Gothic Architecture and the Medieval Concept of Order*. 2nd ed. New York: Pantheon, 1962.

See also **Architecture, Ecclesiastical; Architecture, Monastic; Church; Gender Ideologies; Pilgrims and Pilgrimage; Space, Secular: and Gender**

SPACE, SECULAR: AND GENDER

In late medieval and early modern Europe, secular space was so highly and rigidly gendered that variations from established patterns and accepted norms were often the subject of comment. This was particularly the case in Florence, a town of local customs, but also one of international connections that make it an important case study of patterns of activity, cultural proclivities, and gender differentiations that are variously applicable, albeit with caution, to places and customs elsewhere. In his fifteenth-century treatise *On the Family*, the humanist Leon Battista Alberti wrote: "It would hardly win us respect if our wife busied herself among the men in the marketplace, out in the public eye. It also seems somewhat demeaning to me to remain shut up in the home among women when I have manly things to do among men." Alberti clearly reflects a contemporary codification of a Florentine world that was gender specific, with the external world, primarily the arena of politics and mercantile activity, gendered male, while the home and domestic activity were gendered female.

So ingrained was this structure of gendered spaces in the secular realm that it does not surprise that another period writer would take special note of a striking disruption of this system in which women ventured boldly, and indeed threatening, beyond the confines of the domestic sphere. In 1497, during the period of Savonarolan unrest in the city and in response to the deprivations of famine, three thousand poor women gathered in the Piazza della Signoria, the main civic and thus male space in Florence, in mass protest demanding the provision of bread. This was an extraordinary appearance in the public realm of the city, a space dominated by the public Palazzo della Signoria from which women were assiduously forbidden entry throughout much of Florentine history. After several days' protest and nearly riotous circumstances, the demands of the women were finally met and, as the chronicler notes, they "took themselves home." This episode not only describes a tense moment in the public arena; it also communicates something significant about the gendering of secular space, for the aversion of crisis was not simply in the satisfaction of the women's demands; it was also in their return to their place at home. So clearly was the Piazza della Signoria considered a secular space for Florentine men alone that when Giralomo Savonarola was executed there the following year, a capital punishment observed by many males, the preacher's female followers viewed the event only at a distance while praying at the church of San Marco.

This is not to suggest that women had no role in the public and secular spaces of the city. However, from important rituals like marriage ceremonies, during which women paraded through the city from the house of the father to the house of the husband, to funerals, when women had prescribed roles, often as unrestrained wailing mourners, and even the daily tasks of marketing and socializing, women moved about the spaces of the city in ways that were specific to their gender and clearly differentiated from male roles in those same spaces. Unmarried women were carefully attended by male and female relatives, and as for married women, only their reputation as chaste spouses permitted them to move about the city without similar retinues of chaperones.

The domestic sphere, then, was the space most extensively gendered female, but even there women's activities of organizing and monitoring household affairs seem to have been circumscribed by male interests in the preservation of honor, the education of children, the maintenance of accounts, and the safe stewardship of family wealth as Alberti additionally indicates in his treatise. Furthermore, even spaces that might at times be exclusively gendered female—such as bedrooms during times of childbirth—could shift in their gendering to male spaces in moments when business or political activity were conducted by men in those same spaces in a domestic context still largely

undifferentiated for various functions room by room. Finally, even though women had an element of autonomy in the management of the domestic sphere despite its overall prescription by males, the domestic environment continued to present a problematic secular space of liminal danger in the late medieval and early modern period from which women could be problematically seen by the male gaze of the outside world. Archbishop Antonino, another fifteenth-century Florentine, writes in one context "I am not happy that you should stand at windows, in order to see who passes by," and in another, "The wife ought but rarely to wander around outside the home, and she should not go leaping about the piazza, nor stand telling stories and murmuring in the doorway, nor talking at the window but going outside the house only to church, and then she should not go by herself." What Antonino's text and others like it make clear is that in his world women in secular spaces were valuable signifiers of virtue but also, problematically, of vice should their actions ever shift from licit and controlled to illicit and free from male supervision and control.

ROGER J. CRUM

References and Further Reading

Crum, Roger J. "Controlling Women or Women Controlled? Suggestions for Gender Roles and Visual Culture in the Italian Renaissance Palace." In *Beyond Isabella: Secular Women Patrons of Art in Renaissance Italy*, edited by Sheryl E. Reiss and David G. Wilkins. Kirksville, Mo.: Truman State University Press, 2001, pp. 37–50.

Haas, Louis. *The Renaissance Man and His Children: Childbirth and Early Childhood in Florence 1300–1600*. New York: St. Martin's Press, 1998.

Hufton, Olwen. *The Prospect Before Her: A History of Women in Western Europe*. vol. I: *1500–1800*. London: Harper Collins, 1995.

Klapisch-Zuber, Christiane. *Women, Family, and Ritual in Renaissance Italy*, translated by Lydia G. Cochrane. Chicago and London: University of Chicago Press, 1985.

Musacchio, Jacqueline Marie. *The Art and Ritual of Childbirth in Renaissance Italy*. New Haven, Conn. and London: Yale University Press, 1999.

Schiesari, Juliana. "In Praise of Virtuous Women? For a Genealogy of Gender Morals in Renaissance Italy." In *Women's Voices in Italian Literature*, edited by Rebecca West and Dino S. Cervigni. Chapel Hill, N.C.: University of North Carolina Press, 1989, pp. 66–87.

Tomas, Natalie. "Did Women Have a Space?" In *Renaissance Florence: A Social History of Space*, edited by Roger J. Crum and John T. Paoletti. New York: Cambridge University Press, 2006, pp. 311–328.

Wiesner, Merry E. *Women and Gender in Early Modern Europe*. Cambridge: Cambridge University Press, 1993; 2nd ed., 2000, pp. 13–47.

Wigley, Mark. "Untitled: The Housing of Gender." In *Sexuality and Space*, edited by Beatriz Colomina. Princeton, N.J.: Princeton Architectural Press, 1992, pp. 327–389.

See also **Architecture, Domestic; Gaze; Honor and Reputation; Italy; Private and Public Spheres; Space, Sacred: and Gender; Sumptuary Law**

SPIRITS: DISCERNMENT OF AND POSSESSION BY

Medieval Christian culture acknowledged many different spirits. Angels, demons, ghosts, and fairies all fell under the category of spiritual beings. Humanity itself contained a spiritual essence, the human spirit, which dwelt in the heart and acted as an intermediary between the physical self and the immortal soul. Derived from the Hellenistic environment of the early Church, especially Stoic influences, the notion of the material human spirit was augmented in medieval thought by Arab medical treatises that filtered into western Europe through Spain in the twelfth century. Ultimately, medieval thinkers elaborated an entire spiritual system in their writings on human physiology.

Many medieval people lived their lives without ever having an experience that they believed involved supernatural spirits. Others claimed to have seen ghosts or other spiritual beings on occasion. A small number of individuals, however, were diagnosed as having entered into a long-term state of intimacy with a spirit, a condition known as spirit possession. We may identify two major forms of this phenomenon. The first was demonic possession, in which a demon physically invaded the body of a person and seized control over it. The phenomenon of demonic possession is mentioned frequently in the gospels of Mark, Matthew, and Luke, where the exorcism of such persons features prominently among Jesus's miracles. (There are no exorcisms in the Gospel of John.) As a biblically attested category of affliction, demonic possession remained an important idea throughout the Middle Ages. In the early medieval centuries, demoniacs of both sexes often congregated around the tombs of saints. By the 1200s, however, demonic possession was becoming increasingly common, and also highly feminized. Reports of demoniacs proliferate in thirteenth-century sources, accompanied by an increasing gender imbalance, toward women, in the victims. Thomas of Cantimpré, for example, recounts a detailed story of a girl who became possessed after a long day of dancing, and who was healed by a young boy. Likewise, the *vitae* of saints frequently recount miraculous healings of the possessed, such as that of a violent female demoniac in Ferrara, healed by Anthony of Padua.

A second kind of spirit possession was divine possession. The hagiographies of certain female visionaries present their subjects as possessed by the spirit of God, emphasizing that the Holy Spirit lives and speaks through the saint. Although the phrase *divine possession* was not used in medieval writings, the notion of direct physical inhabitation by the spirit of the divine was enunciated by medieval authors in other terms. Thus the hagiographer of Jutta of Huy wrote that she had the gift of mind-reading "through the Holy Spirit, which lived inside her." Many women visionaries reported that Jesus literally entered into their heart and dwelt therein, fused with their own human spirit. The miracle of the stigmata, so often reported of women visionaries, may be viewed as the ultimate physical expression of divine possession, a union of two into one spirit and two into one flesh. This trend began in the late twelfth century with the proliferation of new, lay religious movements (such as the Beguines and other independent religious women) that hosted many visionary women, and continued unabated until the end of the era.

Divine and demonic spirit possession affected women more than men; and both saw rising numbers in the thirteenth century and beyond. Furthermore, both possessions were manifested in similar ways. The demonically and the divinely possessed were credited with prophetic abilities, *xenoglossia* (the ability to speak previously unknown foreign tongues), physical transformations (bloating, or the ability to subsist without eating), and other individual charisms. In consequence, medieval churchmen became concerned about the possibility of confusion between these two types of extraordinary women, fearing lest the overly credulous might treat as saintly someone who actually was demonically possessed. The Devil, after all, was thought to be ever-ready to deceive the faithful.

Thus arose the concern with the discernment of spirits, also called the testing of spirits. These synonymous phrases refer to the imperative to distinguish between the truly divinely inspired (who deserve veneration as saints), and the demonically possessed (whose influence should be eliminated). In time, the theory and practice of discerning spirits also came to embrace other categories of potential confusion, such as feigned sanctity and various natural pathologies. Concern over the issue reached its peak in the late fourteenth and early fifteenth centuries, with the appearance of treatises devoted exclusively to the topic of testing spirits.

Although in theory the discernment of spirits was a gender-neutral exercise, in fact discernment concerns clustered closely around the careers of laywomen who claimed supernatural gifts. In part, this stemmed from the fact that women visionaries and women demoniacs were reported to behave in similar ways. Scholars agree, however, that the feminine emphasis in the discernment of spirits literature also expresses a deep-seated cultural ambivalence toward women arrogating to themselves a leadership role. Notably, many discernment treatises were penned in response to the attempted canonizations of visionary women. The best-known writer on the subject, Jean Gerson (d. 1429), composed three separate treatments, all directly inspired by visionary women. His 1415 tract *On the Testing of Spirits*, for example, was commissioned by the Council of Constance as part of the review of Birgitta of Sweden's (d. 1373) canonization. As may be seen in the well-known case of Joan of Arc (d. 1431), debates over women's leadership and supernatural inspiration were contentious struggles at the end of the Middle Ages.

Ultimately, one long-term effect of the discernment of spirits debates was to undermine female claims to holiness, leaving only the alternative category—demonic influence—as an explanation for cases of female spiritual inspiration. This increasing demonization of women helped set the stage for the witchcraft persecutions that began in the generation after Gerson, in the 1430s, and continued through the early modern period.

NANCY CACIOLA

References and Further Reading

Caciola, Nancy. "Mystics, Demoniacs, and the Physiology of Spirit Possession in Medieval Europe." *Comparative Studies in Society and History* 42.2 (2000): 268–306.

———. *Discerning Spirits: Divine and Demonic Possession in the Middle Ages.* Ithaca, N.Y.: Cornell University Press, 2003.

Fraioli, Deborah. *Joan of Arc: The Early Debate.* Suffolk: Boydell Press, 2000.

Kieckhefer, Richard. "The Holy and the Unholy: Sainthood, Witchcraft, and Magic in Late Medieval Europe." *Journal of Medieval and Renaissance Studies* 24 (1994): 355–385.

Klaniczay, Gàbor. "*Miraculum* and *Maleficium*: Reflections Concerning Late Medieval Female Sainthood." In *Problems in the Historical Anthropology of Early Modern Europe*, edited by Ronnie Po-Chia Hsia and Robert Scribner. Harrassowitz: 1997, pp. 49–73.

Newman, Barbara. "Possessed by the Spirit: Devout Women, Demoniacs, and the Apostolic Life in the Thirteenth Century." *Speculum* 73/3 (1998): 733–770.

Voaden, Rosalyn. *God's Words, Women's Voices: The Discernment of Spirits in the Writings of Late Medieval Women Visionaries.* York: York Medieval Press, 1999.

Zarri, Gabriella, ed. *Finzione e santità tra medioevo ed età moderna.* Turin: Einaudi, 1991.

See also **Birgitta of Sweden; Gerson, Jean; Joan of Arc; Madness; Mysticism and Mystics; Prophets; Satan; Spiritual Care; Witches**

SPIRITUAL CARE

In the Middle Ages care of souls (*cura animarum*) was a clerical privilege, but it was also an amorphous practice exercised even by women. In its narrow meaning, the term is associated with pastoral care (*cura pastoralis*), which principally referred to priestly care of the laity's spiritual affairs through homilies, exhortations, and the administration of sacraments. Such *cura* came with financial support (*beneficium*) that came with jurisdiction over a parish. Spiritual direction was not limited to the activities of the parish priests, however, since it also encompassed religious formation in monasteries and spiritual relationships between the members of religious orders and the laity or within religious communities. While spiritual care was essentially associated with positive religious formation, it had a correctional element to it as well, for a spiritual director was also responsible for uprooting practices seen as heterodox or counterproductive. Especially toward the end of the Middle Ages, the *distinctio spirituum* or the art of discerning between the workings of good and bad spirits, came to be an essential aspect of spiritual direction, often with negative consequences for women whose piety could be labeled unorthodox or even demonic.

Women were not merely recipients of spiritual care provided by men, but as abbesses and prioresses they were involved in spiritual formation of other monastic women. Mothers held spiritual authority unofficially as religious educators of their children, and women could be role models of piety, especially as mystics whose perceived closeness with God empowered them to counsel others.

Parish Priests

Even though care of the souls was principally the duty of the parish clergy and bishops, strikingly little is known of the spiritual relationships between these authorities and women. The low educational level of ordinary priests helps to explain the lack of written evidence. But even bishops, who typically came from the nobility and enjoyed greater educational opportunities, seem not to have involved themselves with spiritual formation. They focused on the administrative affairs of the church. Though Pope Gregory VII (1073–1085) successfully bolstered parish priests' authority over secular magnates, and later the Fourth Lateran Council (1215) stressed their sacramental authority by demanding that lay people annually receive communion at their local churches, the parish priests still seem to have had only marginal impact on the practice of spiritual care.

Guidance from Monks and Friars

The most effective practitioners of spiritual care came from the ranks of the religious orders. Monks and friars wrote the most influential classics of spiritual direction, among them *The Conferences* of John Cassian (d. c. 435) and *The Soul's Journey into God* by Bonaventure (d. 1274). Even Pope Gregory the Great's (590–604) momentous *Liber regulae pastoralis*, a pastoral manual for bishops, was shaped by his experiences as a monk. The monastic life also created a fertile seedbed for literature specifically concerning women's spiritual direction. One significant means for exercising such care was through religious rules (*regulae*). The Rule of Augustine, which became popular only toward the end of the eleventh century, derived from Augustine's (d. 430) Letter 211 to a group of religious women. Caesarius of Arles (d. 542) wrote guidelines to the flourishing community of his sister, Caesaria. Benedict (d. c. 550) did not write a rule for women, but his Rule for monks was later introduced to women's houses.

The *regula* was read aloud when the community gathered together for its chapter meetings and meals, but women commonly adjusted the contents of the rule by requesting changes or by refusing to follow regulations that did not suit their purposes. Heloise (d. 1164), the powerful abbess at the Paraclete, wrote to Abelard (d. 1142) to ask for clarification concerning women's use of the Rule of Benedict, revealing her own learnedness on the practices of spiritual direction. Some women even wrote the rules for their religious communities, including Clare of Assisi, whose *modus vivendi* was approved just a few days before her death in August 1253, and Birgitta of Sweden (d. 1373), who claimed that she received the rule for her Order of the Holy Savior in a vision.

Inspirational Literature

Inspirational literature was an essential aspect of medieval spiritual care, be that care directed at nuns or women. Such guidance came in the shape of devotional manuals, among them the *Speculum virginum*, which in the twelfth century advised nuns in the art of piety through a fictional dialogue between a nun and her spiritual mentor. The *vitae* of past and contemporary saints presented material for spiritual formation through emulation (*imitatio*). Not unlike men, medieval women were nurtured by *The Lives of the Fathers*, the *Golden Legend*, and other collections of the lives of saints. Some women became models of piety themselves, thus teaching through their saintly model (*docere exemplo*). Many authors responded to women's concerns in an epistolary format. The powerful Countess Matilda of Canossa received guidance from both Gregory VII and Anselm of Canterbury (d. 1109). Peter the Venerable (d. 1156) sent advice to his nieces Margaret and Pontia at Marcigny, a Cluniac monastery. The Dominican preacher Giovanni Dominici (d. 1419) directed spiritual letters to the nuns at Corpus Domini (Venice) and guided Bartolomea degli Alberti in the religious duties of a mother.

Arranging Spiritual Services for Nuns

The medieval church had no preemptive solutions concerning the spiritual care directed toward nuns or other religious women (*cura monialium* or *cura mulierum*). Hence the arrangements concerning religious instruction, administration of sacraments and other religious services varied from one community to another. Some monasteries were served by an adjoining community of chaplains, others teamed up with men in double monasteries, as was the case with the Gilbertines. More typically, however, women's houses, though often technically under the care of a bishop, received spiritual services from visiting members of the major religious orders, especially the Augustinian Canons, the Cistercians, the Dominicans, and the Franciscans. As such arrangements were rarely fixed, care could turn easily into neglect, resulting in thorny debates during which the leaders of the religious orders sought to terminate their ties with religious women. Such was the case with the Cistercians in the 1140s and with the Dominicans and the Franciscans throughout the thirteenth century. It was not untypical for the women in these circumstances to fight back by appealing to the popes for a privilege that granted them, at least temporarily, the spiritual services of the reluctant religious orders.

Women Providing Spiritual Care

Women themselves were not officially to teach Christian doctrine or comment on the Bible, but the practice of morally and spiritually uplifting exhortation (*exhortatio*) was open to them, whether as leaders of a religious community, mystics, or simply as mothers. It was the duty of abbesses and prioresses to ensure that the members of their community participated in monastic observances. When this privilege to educate and discipline their fellow religious was coupled with the abbesses' and prioress' aristocratic pedigrees, many emerged with spiritual authority that extended well beyond their communities. The visionary Hildegard of Bingen (d. 1179) counseled Pope Eugenius III, and Gertrude of Hackeborn (d. c. 1292) developed the Cistercian monastery of Helfta into a flourishing center of literal and spiritual activity.

A ninth-century Carolingian mother, Dhuoda, all but turned herself into a theologian when she dictated her *Liber manualis* to advise her warrior son on the wisdom of the Bible and the Christian ethics. Religious and laywomen with reputations as mystics practiced guidance that was associated with the tradition of the seven works of spiritual mercy, which included counseling the doubtful and instructing the ignorant. Most of these women operated privately, receiving visitors at their homes or at their communities, but some reached the public by draping their teaching in a literary format. Catherine of Siena (d. 1380), a Dominican laywoman, directed close to four hundred spiritual letters to a mixed group of recipients that included popes as well as ordinary people. Caterina Vigri of Bologna (d. 1463), a Franciscan nun, wrote her *Seven Spiritual Weapons* as a step-by-step guide to religious perfection. She herself was modeled into an example of piety only a few years after her death when Illuminata Bembo, a nun at her community, eulogized her exemplary life in *Specchio di Illuminazione* (*Mirror of Illumination*).

Women even stepped into the field officially reserved for men by explaining theological tenets or by teaching in public. For some, this brought marginalization or outright condemnation, as was the case with Beguine Marguerite Porete, who was burned as a heretic in 1310. Yet, the hagiographers of Rose of Viterbo (d. 1252) and Humility of Faenza (d. 1310) not only tolerated, but even applauded, their public teaching. When such prophetic preaching meshed with the reform agenda of leading churchmen, women could rise to considerable fame, as did Birgitta of Sweden and Catherine of Siena. While such public leadership was exceptional for women, it was conceivable for it matched with the widely recognized mythic roles of Mary Magdalen, who was known as the Apostle of the Apostles, and Catherine of Alexandria, who was presented as a converter of pagan philosophers.

MAIJU LEHMIJOKI-GARDNER

References and Further Reading

Boyle, Leonard E. *Pastoral Care, Clerical Education, and Canon Law, 1200–1400.* London: Variorum Reprints, 1981.

Bynum, Caroline Walker. *Holy Feast and Holy Fast. The Religious Significance of Food to Medieval Women.* Berkeley: University of California Press, 1987.

Catherine of Bologna. *The Seven Spiritual Weapons.* Translated, with notes by Hugh Feiss and Daniela Re. Toronto: Peregrina Publishing, 1998.

Catherine of Siena. *The Letters of Catherine of Siena.* Translated with introduction and notes by Suzanne Noffke, 2 vols. Tempe, Ariz.: Arizona Center for Medieval and Renaissance Studies, 2000, 2001.

Clare of Assisi. Early Documents, edited and translated by Regis J. Armstrong. New York: Franciscan Institute Publications, 1993.

Freed, John B. "Urban Development and the *Cura Monialium* in Thirteenth-Century Germany." *Viator* 3 (1972): 312–327.

Griffiths, Fiona. "Men's Duty to Provide for Women's Needs: Abelard, Heloise, and the Negotiation of the *Cura Monialium.*" *Journal of Medieval History* 30 (2004): 1–24.

Guidance to Women in Twelfth-Century Convents. Translated by Vera Morton with an interpretative essay by Jocelyn Wogan-Browne. Woodbridge, Suffolk: D. S. Brewer, 2003.

The Letters of Abelard and Heloise. Translated with an introduction and notes by Betty Radice. Revised by M. T. Clanchy. London: Penguin Books, 2003.

Listen Daughter. The Speculum Virginum and the Formation of Religious Women in the Middle Ages. Edited by Constant J. Mews. New York: Palgrave McMillan, 2001.

Mayeski, Marie Anne. *Dhuoda. Ninth Century Mother and Theologian.* Scranton, Pa.: University of Scranton Press, 1995.

McNamara, Jo Ann. *Sisters in Arms. Catholic Nuns through Two Millennia.* Cambridge, Mass.: Harvard University Press, 1996.

Pastors and the Care of Souls in Medieval England. Edited by John Shinners and William J. Dohar. South Bend, Ind.: University of Notre Dame, 1998.

Sahlin, Claire L. "Prophetess as Preacher: Birgitta of Sweden and the Voice of Prophecy." *Medieval Sermon Studies* 40 (1997): 29–44.

Women Preachers and Prophets through Two Millennia of Christianity. Edited by Beverly Mayne Kienzle and Pamela J. Walker. Berkeley: University of California Press, 1998.

See also **Abbesses; Birgitta of Sweden; Caterina Vigri; Catherine of Alexandria; Catherine of Siena; Church; Cistercian Order; Clare of Assisi; Devotional Literature; Dhuoda; Dominican Order; Double Monasteries; Gertrude of Hackeborn; Humility of Faenza; Laywomen, Religious; Marguerite Porete; Mary Magdalen; Matilda of Tuscany; Monastic Rules; Monasticism and Nuns; Mothers as Teachers; Mysticism and Mystics; Poor Clares Order; Rose of Viterbo; Sermons and Preaching; Spirits: Discernment of and Possession by; Tertiaries; Theology**

SPIRITUALITY, CHRISTIAN

The Oxford English Dictionary reminds us that *spiritual* was originally synonymous with *ecclesiastical*. In the Merriam-Webster dictionary, the definitions that many people associate with spirituality, "attachment to religious values," "the state of being spiritual," are secondary to the primary definition: "something that in ecclesiastical law belongs to the church or to a cleric as such" (Merriam-Webster Online, http://www.m-w.com/home.htm). It is significant that in the Middle Ages spirituality had as much to do with ecclesiastical power and property as it did with the inner state of one's soul. Spirituality thus is about power: the power of one's office as well as the power of inner conviction. In this entry spirituality also denotes an engagement with, devotion to, or mediation of God or other spiritual beings.

As European societies became more settled in the period after 1000, more people were able to devote time and energy to their religious aspirations. At the same time, the papacy, under the legacy of the eleventh-century Gregorian Reform movement (named after Pope Gregory VII [1073–1085]), attempted to centralize and systematize both Christian theology and practice. These two parallel trends explain much of the excitement about, and also the conflicts over, Christian spirituality from 1100 to 1300. This entry describes a few of the most significant manifestations of spirituality in this period among clerical, monastic, and lay groups, with a special emphasis upon women.

Monastic Spirituality

In the western half of the Roman Empire Christian spirituality was developed and practiced within the framework of Benedictine monasticism. Benedictine monks and nuns dedicated themselves to lives of chastity, poverty, and, above all, obedience to a superior. These principles helped shape the distinctive monastic practices of prayer, work, and study. Prominent among their spiritual practices was *lectio divina*, a unique method of studying Scripture that involved "hearing with one's heart," as Benedict explained in the prologue to his famous Rule. *Lectio divina* integrates hearing, reading, prayer, meditation, and study in a quiet, laborious, and reflective manner. In *Lectio divina* there is no separation between "spiritual" meditation and "devotional" practice: *lectio* is at once a method of spiritual practice and a philosophy of spirituality that is not "goal-directed" but receptive to many modes of spiritual refreshment. Developed by monks who had a lifetime as their disposal, *lectio*

divina had as many spiritual paths as there were practitioners.

Lectio divina also had one stringent requirement beyond monastic vows: Latin literacy. It was assumed that one would hear and meditate upon the Bible, and perhaps read the many medieval commentaries on it, in Latin. Only the wealthy and educated few in the lay population could participate in this form of spirituality. From the twelfth century onward, however, more people had the resources to acquire at least the rudiments of such an education. And a new class of popular preachers began to explain the Scriptures to lay populations in their own languages. Finally, new monastic orders—first the Cistercians, and then the Fransciscans and Dominicans—appealed to the laity as never before: the Cistercians through their evocative spiritual writings, the Franciscans through their locations in urban centers, and the Dominicans through their popular preaching.

Secular Culture and Christian Spirituality

A good example of the medieval interaction between lay and spiritual devotional impulses is the use of secular love poetry to cultivate a particular form of Christian spirituality called *Minnemystik* or "love mysticism." *Mysticism* is a nebulous term but in the Christian tradition generally denotes a type of direct experience of or participation in God, rather than experiencing God as mediated through Christian sacraments. Troubadour poetry extolled the virtues of devotion to one's lady or lord, imagined as a noble man or woman who bestowed his/her favors upon the beloved. In poetry both erotic and long-suffering, the knight pined for the loving reward of his devotion. There was also a monastic parallel to this love poetry: the sensuous language of the Biblical Song of Songs. From Origen in the second century to Bernard of Clairvaux in the twelfth, monks used the language of the Bride and Bridegroom in the Song of Songs to explain the mystery of God's union with the soul. Both men and women were attracted to this symbolism, but *Minnemystik* and its kin, bridal mysticism, are especially associated with spiritual women in central Europe and the Low Countries. For example, in the thirteenth century Hadewijch of Antwerp wrote passionate poetry in her native tongue, describing God personified as *Minne*, a female aspect of God to whom the soul, like a knight, devotes himself. Gender ambiguity is a central feature of this form of mysticism, for *Minne*, an aspect of God, is female, while the soul is imagined as either masculine or feminine. In contrast, bridal mysticism, most clearly depicted in the writings of Mechthild of Magdeburg (1207–1294), is more closely aligned with heteronormative paradigms, in which the soul is imagined as a Bride entering God's chamber to become united with Him.

Spiritual Devotion to the Humanity of Christ

Minnemystik imagines the union of God and the soul in terms of human love. Part of the impulse for this form of spiritual devotion was a heightened awareness of Christ's humanity, as well as his divinity. Iconographically represented by an idealized man instead of a stern judge, Christ's image as God incarnate in human flesh provided a way to experience God more concretely than as a purely formless spirit. As Bernard of Clairvaux wrote: "Our Lord shows us both the difficulty of the way and the reward of the labor. . . If you imitate him you will not walk in darkness; you will have the light of life" (Evans, 103).

One result of this renewed appreciation of Christ's humanity was the conviction that he provided the ideal life to follow: the *imitatio Christi*. This *imitatio* could take many forms; especially popular were those of idealizing poverty, selling one's possessions and begging for food, and ministering to the sick and the poor. These forms were highly gendered, because women generally did not have the option of casting off all social bonds and living hand to mouth, as did Franciscan monks. One has only to examine the careers of Francis (1182–1226) and St. Clare (1194–1253) to appreciate the difficulties such an ideal posed for women. Although St. Clare also extolled voluntary poverty and clung to it for her Rule, the move to enclose her nuns within a nunnery proved very hard to resist. Ministering to the sick and the poor, however, was an option that many religious women championed. In the Low Countries a group of religious women called Beguines, taking no permanent vows, ran schools and hospitals and pooled their money for the welfare of all in their communities. They organized as self-supporting communities, however, not bands of wandering friars. They are one of the best examples of how *imitatio Christi* could be imagined as a lifestyle for women.

Christ's Suffering as a Spiritual Model

Related to the importance of Christ's life is the attention paid to his suffering and death. Part of *imitatio Christi* is the notion that to truly imitate Christ, one must suffer, and perhaps even die, as he did. This was not a new form of Christian spirituality. In the early days of Christianity martyrs were praised as those who most perfectly imitated Christ. Since the days of martyrdom were long over, what form of suffering might be appropriate? Monasticism remained the "white [bloodless] martyrdom," but newer forms of imitating Christ's suffering focused on the aspects of his narrative that depicted him as reviled, persecuted, and misunderstood. As Meister Eckhart (1260–1327/1328), a Dominican mystic, wrote to the Queen of Hungary: "If you want to be a son of God and do not want to suffer, you are all wrong" (Colledge, 232). Devotional meditations on Christ's Passion were also very popular. Many were written in the vernacular especially for women, such as those by the fourteenth century English monk, Richard Rolle (1300–1349).

Eucharistic Spirituality

An emphasis upon Christ's real presence in the Eucharist became more pronounced from the tenth century on. Eucharistic piety is a wonderful example of the synchrony between popular devotion and clerical desires. The festival of Corpus Christi, for example, was officially promulgated by the papacy in 1264, but the impetus for the festival came from the Beguine Juliana of Cornillon (1222–1258). Stories of Eucharistic hosts that miraculously manifested Christ's body (in whole or in part) had been part of popular culture since the eighth century, and clerics and preachers began to use these stories as *exempla* to teach the proper Christian respect for the Eucharist. From the twelfth century on, bleeding host stories cannot be extricated from the anti-Semitism that surrounded them, fueled by both popular and governmental resentment at Jewish success. It is undeniable that as views of the real presence became more entrenched in Christian society, persecution and expulsion of Jewish communities also increased.

The religious implications of this doctrine for Christian lay people, especially women, were also profound. Women could not be priests, and so could not participate in the most powerful ritual of the Christian Church: the consecration of the Eucharist. As Miri Rubin has detailed, after 1100 the emphasis on Christ's real presence in the Eucharist increased the powers of the priesthood and tended to separate them even more from the laity. As clerics across Europe consolidated the doctrine of the real presence and engaged in an extensive preaching and teaching campaign, the right of lay people to teach or interpret Christian doctrine was increasingly curtailed.

Yet many lay people, both men and women, were caught up in the religious sentiments of their day, especially Eucharistic devotion. Lay men and women could not consecrate the host, but they could adore it. After all, devotional meditations on Christ's Passion were thought appropriate for lay people. These meditations, taking place in churches, could also cause extravagant ecstatic or other visionary phenomena. Many biographies of "holy women" stress that their ecstatic visions occurred during reception of the Eucharist. Thus, eucharistic spirituality had public, as well as personal, aspects. Ecstatic visions were public and sometimes resulted in religious transformations of witnesses. Women who were graced with these visions were often regarded as spiritually gifted. A few of these holy women also claimed to live solely on Eucharistic "food."

Eucharistic spirituality thus had the effect of providing a spiritual niche for religious women in addition to heightening the institutional office of priest. Clerics were often great admirers of holy women and wrote enthusiastic *vitae* for them. Holy women were also rivals for spiritual power, however, and some clerics were suspicious of their claims.

Spiritual Power

The phenomenon of ecstatic visions returns us to ecclesiastical power. That is, who has the ability to mediate the sacred for others? One kind of spiritual power was the distribution of the Eucharist, over which clerics established a spiritual monopoly. Another form of spiritual power was the cult of saints, which provided intermediaries between heavenly and earthly power. A third kind of spiritual power was developed by holy women. The period from 1100–1300 saw a marked rise in the documentation of holy women in every European country. Anchoresses in England, religious laywomen affiliated with the Franciscans and Dominicans in Italy, and Beguines in the Low Countries, were just a few of the variety of practitioners of female religious spirituality. Some of these holy women presided over a new form of spiritual power: the ability to traverse purgatory and heaven via visual and ecstatic phenomena. As Barbara Newman has argued, the domain of purgatory was relatively new in the twelfth century and represented a new spiritual "apostolate to the dead" to which women had access. Some holy women claimed to be able to discover the fates of particular deceased individuals. Other holy women became channels of divine inspiration. They could, in that role, reveal divine wisdom. Still others became famous for their voluntary poverty and asceticism. The spiritual power exercised by these holy women was as much a feature of the medieval landscape as clerical power.

Conclusion

All of these forms of medieval spirituality were both intoxicatingly creative and dangerous to the societies that inspired them. Spiritual variety could thrive in confident, well-integrated societies, but any social and economic fissures threatened to upset the delicate balance between creative spirituality and society-unraveling chaos. Rulers and clerics perceived many potential problems. First, the spiritual devotion of the laity was by definition less educated in the intricacies of scholastic theology, so lay preachers and writers could make theological mistakes. Second, admiration of alternate models of spiritual power could become dangerous if it led to clerical critiques. Third, extravagant imitations of Christ could spawn hordes of beggars and rogues roaming the countryside. Finally, claims for divine sanction could result in prophetic statements unacceptable to Christian orthodoxy. The heady days of social and religious experimentation became increasingly less attractive after the thirteenth century. Many spiritual movements that churchmen had formerly praised were condemned, such as the Beguine movement, along with the "Free Spirit" heresy, in 1311–1312 at the Council of Vienne. Yet, although women's writings and sometimes their bodies were burned, the deep impulses of spiritual desire proved impossible to suppress. For example, Marguerite Porete was executed for heresy at Paris in 1310, but her book, *The Mirror of Simple Annihilated Souls*, circulated in French, Latin, Italian, and English versions long after her death, albeit with her name sometimes removed. It is ironic that the spirituality inspired and nurtured by the Church in the medieval period would erupt in different forms during the Protestant Reformation of the fifteenth century. Indeed, many of the spiritual expressions of the medieval period: Bible study, devotional meditations, focus on the Passion, love mysticism, dedication to poverty and aid of the sick and disadvantaged, survive in both Catholic and Protestant manifestations to this day.

MARY SUYDAM

References and Further Reading

Babinsky, Ellen, trans. *Marguerite Porete: The Mirror of Simple Souls*. New York: Paulist Press, 1993.

Bartlett, Anne, Thomas Bestul, Janet Goebel, and William Pollard, eds. *Vox Mystica: Essays on Medieval Mysticism.* Cambridge: D. S. Brewer, 1995.

Brown, Peter. *The Cult of Saints: Its Rise and Function in Latin Christianity.* New York: Oxford University Press, 1981.

Colledge, Edmund, and Bernard McGinn, trans. *Meister Eckhart: The Essential Sermons, Commentaries, Treatises, and Defense.* New York: Paulist Press, 1981.

Dor, Juliette, Lesley Johnson, and Jocelyn Wogan-Brown, eds. *New Trends in Feminine Spirituality: the Holy Women of Liège and Their Impact.* Brepols: Turnhout, 1999.

Evans, G. R., trans. *Bernard of Clairvaux: Selected Works.* New York: Paulist Press, 1987.

Galvani, Christiane, trans. *Mechthild von Magdeburg: Flowing Light of the Divinity.* New York: Garland Publishing, 1991.

Greer, Rowan, trans. *Origen: An Exhortation to Martyrdom, Prayer, and Selected Works.* New York: Paulist Press, 1979.

Hart, Columba, trans. *Hadewijch: Complete Works.* New York: Paulist Press, 1988.

Johnson, James Howard, and Paul Antony Hayward, eds. *The Cult of Saints in Late Antiquity and the Middle Ages: Essays on the Contribution of Peter Brown.* New York: Oxford University Press, 2000.

Matter, E. Ann. *The Voice of My Beloved: the Song of Songs in Medieval Christianity.* Philadelphia: University of Pennsylvania Press, 1992.

Newman, Barbara. *From Virile Woman to WomanChrist: Studies in Medieval Religion and Literature.* Philadelphia: University of Pennsylvania Press, 1995.

Petroff, Elizabeth A. *Medieval Women's Visionary Literature.* New York: Oxford University Press, 1986.

Rubin, Miri. *Corpus Christi: the Eucharist in Late Medieval Culture.* New York: Oxford University Press, 1992.

Suydam, Mary, and Joanna Ziegler, eds. *Performance and Transformation: New Approaches to Late Medieval Spirituality.* New York: St. Martins Press, 1999.

Zum Brunn, Émilie, and Georgette Épiney-Burgard. *Women Mystics in Medieval Europe.* New York: Paragon Press, 1989.

See also **Anchoresses; Beguines; Bride of Christ: Imagery; Church; Clare of Assisi; Courtly Love; Devotional Practices; Hadewijch; Hagiography; Lay Piety; Laywomen, Religious; Marguerite Porete; Mechthild of Magdeburg; Meditation; Monasticism and Nuns; Mysticism and Mystics; Song of Songs, Medieval Interpretations of; Theology**

STAGEL, ELSBETH

Elsbeth Stagel (c. 1300–1360) is known primarily because of her (disputed) role in the composition of two works: 1) the *vita* of the German Dominican preacher Henry Suso (1295–1366), which he compiled, along with his other major German works, in a collection called *The Exemplar*; and 2) the Sisterbook (or convent chronicle) of the Dominican convent of Töss near Zürich. Little is known of Elsbeth Stagel's background beyond notes, made in a Suso manuscript owned by Stagel, referring to her order, the Dominican community in Töss, and her immediate family. Other documents confirm that her father, Rudolf Stagel, was a town councilman in Zürich. Stagel probably entered the convent at a young age and remained there until her death.

The debate over Stagel's authorship centers around Suso's contradictory accounts of her in his *vita*. In the prologue, Suso describes Stagel as having secretly written down his personal experiences. Once he discovered the existence of these writings, he threw them into the fire. Yet before he could burn all of them, a divine message stayed his hand, and he proceeded to use her writings to complete a *vita* of his own. Although it is clear from the text that Stagel's written and verbal exchanges with Suso contributed to his work, scholars continue to debate whether what we learn of her in the *vita* is more fiction than fact. Suso also praises Stagel's authorship of her own book—a compilation of thirty-three lives of sisters from the Töss community, but this authorship has also been disputed and it is now thought that Stagel was one of a number of contributors to that compilation.

SARA S. POOR

References and Further Reading

Henry, Suso. *The Exemplar, with Two German Sermons.* Translated by Frank Tobin. New York: Paulist Press, 1989.

Lewis, Gertrud Jaron. *By Women, for Women, about Women: The Sister-Books of Fourteenth Century Germany.* Toronto: Pontifical Institute of Mediaeval Studies, 1996.

Tobin, Frank. "Henry Suso and Elsbeth Stagel: Was the *Vita* a Cooperative Effort?" In *Gendered Voices: Medieval Saints and Their Interpreters,* edited by Catherine M. Mooney. Philadelphia: University of Pennsylvania Press, 1999, pp. 118–135.

Vetter, Ferdinand, ed. *Das Leben der Schwestern zu Töß beschrieben von Elsbet Stagel samt der Vorrede von Johannes Meier und dem Leben der Prinzessin Elisabet von Ungarn* [The Life of the Sisters of Töss described by Elsbeth Stagel including the Forward by Johannes Meyer and the Life of the Princess Elisabeth of Hungary]. Berlin: Weidmannsche Buchhandlung, 1906.

See also **Devotional Literature; Dominican Order; Hagiography; Literature, German; Monasticism and Nuns; Mysticism and Mystics; Mystics' Writings; Sister-Books and Other Convent Chronicles; Women Authors: German Texts**

STROZZI, ALESSANDRA

The Florentine patrician Alessandra Strozzi (1407–1471) is known for seventy-three surviving letters written in her own hand, all but one addressed to her exiled sons, who worked as merchant bankers in Naples, Spain, and Bruges. Alessandra had been widowed by age thirty and left to raise five small children after her husband Matteo's exile by the Medici and subsequent death. Her earliest letters, starting in 1447 after ten years of widowhood, show her establishing her sons in merchant careers and finding husbands for her daughters. The later letters document her efforts to obtain the repeal of her sons' exile and to find them wives.

Like most Florentine women of her time, Alessandra had little formal education, but she wrote fluently in a colloquial style reflecting everyday speech. Her words show her to have been a devoted mother, serious about the religious advice she gave her sons. They also suggest she was a woman of strong will but considerable tact, possessing exceptional judgment about family and finances, and a cynical but insightful view of the Florentine social and political scene. Letters by Alessandra's relatives reinforce the self-portrait presented in her letters and reveal her as a guiding force in family decisions until the end of her life.

ANN CRABB

References and Further Reading

Crabb, Ann. *Widowhood and Family Solidarity: The Strozzi of Florence*. Ann Arbor, Mich.: University of Michigan Press, 2000.

Strozzi, Alessandra. *Selected Letters: Bilingual Edition*. Translated by Heather Gregory. Berkeley: University of California Press, 1997.

See also **Italy; Letter Writing; Merchant Families, Women of; Widows**

SUCCESSION, ROYAL AND NOBLE

During the Middle Ages, a number of rulers were elected, including most famously the pope, the Holy Roman Emperor, the Rí of Gaelic Order Ireland and, following the rules of tanistry, the chiefs of some Celtic tribes and early kings of Scotland. Yet most medieval lordships and monarchies were inherited according to rules of succession that evolved throughout the Middle Ages, often paralleling developments in the complex and diverse laws of inheritance of private property. In the early medieval period, proximity of blood or closeness in degree of kinship was often the overriding factor, so that brothers or other males within the same generation succeeded before any children. This had the advantage of ensuring that the heir was an adult but encouraged conflict between rival claimants and ran contrary to a growing tendency to place the immediate family ahead of the extended kin or *stirps*. This practice continued in Plantagenet England, placing King John ahead of his nephew Arthur, the son of an older brother. By the High Middle Ages, most systems of inheritance tended to prioritize direct children, though there was still considerable variation in practice, ranging from the equal division of an inheritance among those children, for example, by William the Conqueror, to the more common system of primogeniture whereby the eldest son took priority, thereby preserving the integrity of the lordship or kingdom.

Males were almost always given priority in the succession to lordships and monarchies, not only because of the assumption that these were inherently masculine functions, involving military leadership and sometimes even quasi-sacerdotal qualities, but more fundamentally because females were never accorded equal status with males by medieval laws of inheritance. Nevertheless most legal systems did allow daughters and sisters to inherit in the absence of direct male heirs and as a result, females were frequently allowed to succeed to lordships and monarchies, brothers failing, even if their husbands usually became the real lord and most often also received the title. As a result numerous women succeeded to both noble lordships and kingdoms across Europe.

In some specific cases, political elites did take action to exclude women from noble and royal succession. The most famous example was in France, where the daughters of the last three Capetian kings were deliberately excluded from the royal succession following the deaths of their fathers in 1316, 1322, and 1328. On the last of these occasions, the assembled notables of France chose Philip of Valois as the heir to King Charles IV, rejecting the claim of Edward III of England, son of Charles's sister Isabella. This decision extended the exclusion of females from the French royal succession to males claiming through women, that is to say cognates. Yet in none of these cases was there a clear legal authority opposing either female or cognate succession, particularly given the fact that women had inherited both private property and lordships in the recent past. Rather than admit that the decisions were made by public assemblies, and thereby introduce an element of election into the French royal succession, official writers argued that the crown was a public office inappropriate for females and pretended that their exclusion accorded with an ancient constitutional law, the Salic Law. This *Lex Salica* was a long-forgotten legal code written around the time of Clovis (476–496), rediscovered by the monks of Saint-Denis in the middle of the fourteenth century. With some modification, Jean de Montreuil, Jean Juvénal des Ursins, and other French writers were able to argue that it was the first law of the French kingdom and that it excluded both women and cognates from the French royal succession and from apanages, that is to say lordships given to the younger sons of French kings. Today the term *Salic Law* has become synonymous with agnatic succession (i.e., a system that entirely excludes females and males claiming through females).

The situation was more complex in England where the common law allowed both women and cognates to inherit property but the legal device of the entail had been developed to answer the concerns of the English nobility at lands passing out of their family through the marriage of an only daughter. This created a potential model for the exclusion of women from the royal succession, though neither King Edward III (1327–1377) nor King Henry IV (1399–1413) were successful in applying it. In 1460, Richard of York laid claim to the English throne as a descendant of Edward III's second son, Lionel, duke of Clarence. Yet this claim passed through two women, Lionel's daughter Philippa and Richard's mother Anne, and so it was far from clear that this Yorkist title was superior to that of the Lancastrians who were descended in direct male line from Edward III's fourth son, John of Gaunt. The absence of a Salic Law in England, or any clear principle regarding agnatic and cognatic succession to the throne, left no legal solution to the problem that underpinned the Wars of the Roses.

CRAIG TAYLOR

References and Further Reading

Bennett, Michael J. "Edward III's Entail and the Succession to the Crown, 1376–1471." *English Historical Review* 113 (1998): 580–609.

Lewis, Andrew W. *Royal Succession in Capetian France: Studies on the Familial Order and the State.* Cambridge, Mass.: Harvard University Press, 1981.

Taylor, Craig. "Sir John Fortescue and the French Polemical Treatises of the Hundred Years War." *English Historical Review* 114 (1999): 112–129.

———. "The Salic Law and the Valois Succession to the French Crown." *French History* 15 (2001): 358–377.

See also **England; Family (Later Middle Ages); France, Northern; Inheritance; Kinship; Queens and Empresses: The West**

SUMPTUARY LAW

Renaissance Europe witnessed an extraordinary economic growth that built upon and expanded the trade in luxury commodities that had begun in the early thirteenth century. So marked were the levels of consumption in comparison to what had gone before, that many now argue for this period as the origin of modern consumer society. The impact of the new habits of expenditure and the practices that they were seen to foster created social, economic, political, and religious tensions. Perhaps the clearest expression of societal preoccupation with the new expenditure and associated way of life is sumptuary law, enacted by governments throughout Europe from London to Dubrovnik, of which hundreds are extant. The most frequent legislators, however, were the Italians, whose laws are also the lengthiest and most detailed.

These laws take their name from ancient Roman *leges sumptuarie* (*sumptus* meaning "expense"). The Renaissance sumptuary laws regulated a range of activities including expenditure on luxury goods, specific fashions, purchase of foreign goods, and funeral and wedding rituals and festivities. Above all, it was the *public* display of wealth that the laws targeted. Very few laws, for instance, regulated interior furnishings and many laws did not prohibit the possession of certain types of fabric and clothing, but merely their wearing outside the home.

Of all the many subjects dealt with in sumptuary laws, clothing appears most frequently and women's clothing in particular. Though several "celebrity" preachers such as Bernardino of Siena, Bernardino da Feltre, and Savonarola regularly castigated men and, more frequently, women for excess and immodesty in apparel, the impetus to legislate in this area came from secular governments rather than the Church. These clothing laws are usually minutely detailed and had to be revised relatively frequently to keep pace with changing fashions. Indeed often the laws helped to precipitate a change in fashion as a means to evade specific prohibitions. The preoccupation with clothing in general can partly be explained by the sheer volume of household expenditure on clothes (up to forty percent of household income in some cases). But it was clothing's ability to signify at a glance a person's rank, occupation, wealth, nationality, gender, and marital statues that made it so susceptible to regulation. And it was precisely these indicators that permitted such difference in the laws regulating women's and men's clothing.

Many of these clothing laws are rank and occupation specific. For instance, certain types of clothes, shoes, and jewelery are permitted to nobles, knights, and their families, but prohibited to those lower down the social scale, especially servants and prostitutes. Men with public roles to fulfill within their community were usually exempted from sumptuary laws and required to wear clothes befitting the honour of their station. In Venice in 1433, for instance, the city's councillors were specifically instructed in a sumptuary law to wear costly scarlet robes suited to their prominent position. Similar notions of honour explain why in some cases women were exempted from sumptuary laws when foreign ambassadors visited the city so that the wealth of the city could be publicly displayed. In all these cases women were allowed expensive clothing only by reference to their association with prominent men or, in the latter case, with the city itself.

Women's lack of a public voice meant not only that their lavish clothing could not be justified by reference to the honour of their own position, but, paradoxically, that they relied more than men on the vestimentary codes that their clothes expressed. On the occasions that women appeared in public, they were still predominantly silent, and their clothes gave them a voice, limited though that voice might be. The public milestones of a woman's life—marriage, childbirth, widowhood—were all marked by clothing that served to demarcate publicly her changing status. Such clothing was always linked to the male lineage to which a woman belonged, whether by birth or marriage, and so her clothes "spoke" on men's behalf rather than on her own account. Once again, it is honour that is prized in a woman's relationship with her family, and modesty in outward apparel is a constant theme of sumptuary law. While both men and women were instructed to dress modestly, the laws addressing women's modesty are sometimes couched in language suffused with misogynistic venom. The clearest expression of this is in a Florentine law of 1433 that referred to the "barbarous and irrepressible bestiality of women who, not mindful of the weakness of their nature, forgetting that they are subject to their husbands, and transforming their perverse sense into a reprobate and diabolical nature, force their husbands with their honeyed poison to submit to them."

Women's response to sumptuary law is hard to gauge. However one remarkable protest was made by a Bolognese noble woman, Nicolosa Sanuti, in the form of a lengthy treatise that she had translated into Latin in 1453. Sanuti argued passionately for clothing as an indicator of women's honour that was thereby disgraced through legislation. Sanuti questioned the assumptions behind sumptuary law and used her protest as a springboard to discuss the merits of women, and noble women, such as herself, in particular. As such, her treatise is the earliest extant defence of women in Italy conceived by a woman. Employing the same justifications used for men's expensive clothing, Sanuti argued that precisely because women could not hold public positions and receive the associated "triumphs and spoils of war," the only signifier of their virtue and honour was their clothing. These, she argued, were "the tokens of our virtues"

that "while the power is left us, we shall not allow to be stolen from us. Amen." Sanuti's protest was unsuccessful, however, and sumptuary law continued in Europe for at least another two centuries.

CATHERINE KOVESI

References and Further Reading

Baldwin, F. E. *Sumptuary Legislation and Personal Regulation in England.* Baltimore, Md.: Johns Hopkins University Press, 1926.

Bridgeman, J. "*Pagare le pompe*: Why Quattrocento Sumptuary Law Did Not Work." In *Women in Italian Renaissance Culture and Society*, edited by Letizia Panizza. Oxford: European Humanities Research Centre, Oxford University, 2000, pp. 209–221.

Chisholm, J. "The Sumptuary Laws of Scotland." *Journal of Jurisprudence* 414/35 (1891): 290–297.

Evans, J. *Dress in Medieval France.* Oxford: Clarendon Press, 1952.

Frick, Carole. *Dressing Renaissance Florence: Families, Fortunes, and Fine Clothing.* Baltimore, Md.: Johns Hopkins University Press, 2002.

Greenfield Kent, R. "Sumptuary Law in Nürnberg: A Study in Paternal Government," *Johns Hopkins University Studies in Historical and Political Science*, 36th ser., 2 (1918).

Harte, N. B., "State Control of Dress and Social Change in Pre-Industrial England." In *Trade, Government and Economy in Pre-Industrial England: Essays Presented to F. J. Fisher*, edited by D. C. Coleman and A. H. John. London: Weidenfeld and Nocolson, 1976, pp. 132–165.

Hooper, Wilfred. "The Tudor Sumptuary Laws." *English Historical Review* 30 (1915): 433–439.

Hughes, Diane Owen. "Sumptuary Law and Social Relations in Renaissance Italy," In *Disputes and Settlements: Law and Human Relations in the West*, edited by John Bossy, Cambridge: Cambridge University Press, 1983, pp. 69–99.

Kovesi Killerby, Catherine. "'Heralds of a well-instructed mind': Nicolosa Sanuti's defence of women and their clothes." *Renaissance Studies* 13, 3 (1999): 255–282.

———. *Sumptuary Law in Italy 1200–1500.* Oxford: Clarendon Press, 2002.

Langlois, C. V. "Project for Taxation Presented to Edward I." *English Historical Review* 4 (1894): 517–529.

Newett, M. M. "The Sumptuary Laws of Venice in the Fourteenth and Fifteenth Centuries." In *Historical Essays by Members of the Owens College, Manchester*, edited by T. F. Tout and James Tate, London: Longmans, Green, and Co. 1907, pp. 245–277.

Rainey, E. R. "Dressing Down the Dressed-Up: Reproving Feminine Attire in Renaissance Florence." In *Renaissance Society and Culture: Essays in Honor of Eugene F. Rice*, edited by John Monfasani and Ronald G. Musto, New York: Ithaca Press, 1991, pp. 217–237.

Shaw, F. J. "Sumptuary Legislation in Scotland." *Juridical Review* ns (1979): 81–115.

Strocchia, Sharon T. *Death and Ritual in Renaissance Florence.* Baltimore, Md.: Johns Hopkins University Press, 1992.

Vincent, J. M. *Costume and Conduct in the Laws of Basel, Bern, and Zurich, 1370–1800.* Baltimore, Md.: Johns Hopkins University Press, 1935.

See also **Clothing; Consumption; Honor and Reputation; Italy; Sanuti, Nicolosa Castellani; Social Status**

SUPERNATURAL WOMEN

Female characters who have magical abilities are found in the writings of such major medieval writers as Geoffrey Chaucer, the *Pearl*-Poet, Marie de France, and Sir Thomas Malory, and are predominantly associated with the tradition of Arthurian literature. Although long regarded by many critics as figures secondary to the main, masculine-dominated movement of the text, most scholars now contend that such characters are in fact critical and intrinsic to the progression of the narrative. Through spells, gifts, and shrewd manipulation of conventional gender roles, such female characters often function to *produce*—rather than merely participate in—the narrative action.

Perhaps the best-known and most important of these supernatural women is Morgan le Fay, the half-sister of King Arthur. Believed by many scholars to derive from a Celtic pre-Christian goddess, her first recorded literary appearance is in Geoffrey of Monmouth's *Vita Merlini* (c. 1150) where she is represented as a beautiful shape-shifting healer residing on the Isle of Avalon. Chrétien de Troyes (mid- to late twelfth century) is the first to identify her as Arthur's sister. In her early appearances Morgan is usually positively represented as a benevolent figure. Her character begins to decline somewhat in the French Vulgate Cycle prose romances (c. 1215–1235), and in the Post-Vulgate (c. 1235–1240) she becomes Arthur's enemy, seeking to destroy his rule through a variety of schemes. She replaces Arthur's sword, Excalibur, and its magic scabbard with fakes; then by means of witchcraft she arranges for single combat between Arthur and her lover, Accolon, to whom she has given the real Excalibur. She also sends a magic drinking horn to court out of which only faithful women can drink without spilling, an attempt to expose the affair of Lancelot and Guinivere.

Standing in opposition to Morgan's malevolence are The Lady of the Lake and other Lake "damsels" who are often conflated. Occasionally identified as Niniane, Viviene, or Nimuë, the Lady appears in the Vulgate Cycle, Sir Thomas Malory's *Morte D'Arthur* (c. 1469–1470), and other versions of the legend. She is the figure who gives Arthur Excalibur, and, in the Vulgate, is responsible for the rearing and training of the young Lancelot.

While Morgan is often represented as an attractive woman in many texts, in *Sir Gawain and the Green Knight* she is represented as a stunningly ugly hag who arranges a magical beheading contest—in which the Green Knight challenges Arthur's knights to exchange axe-blows with him—in an attempt to frighten Guinivere. Her ugly appearance in this text may owe something to the tradition of the Loathly Lady. This supernatural woman makes her best known appearance in the "Wife of Bath's Tale" in Geoffrey Chaucer's *Canterbury Tales* (c. late 1380s), which has as an analogue *The Wedding of Sir Gawain and Dame Ragnell* (c. 1400s). In Chaucer's story, the queen offers a knight who has committed rape the opportunity to save his life if he can discover what it is that women most desire. The knight encounters a hag who offers to help him, but only if he grants her a gift that she will demand on the occasion when he gives the queen the answer to her question. The knight agrees to the terms, only to discover to his horror that the prize the hag demands is that he marry her. On their wedding night, the hag offers him a choice—she can become beautiful but unfaithful, or remain old but loyal. The knight makes the correct choice in leaving the decision up to the loathly lady, proving that he has learned his lesson: what women most desire is sovereignty. As a reward, the hag transforms herself, promising to be both beautiful *and* faithful.

Another kind of magical woman appears in *Lanval,* one of Marie de France's *lais* (c. 1150–1190). In this story, a knight of King Arthur's court finds love with a fairy woman who swears him to secrecy about their relationship. Upon Lanval's return to court, Queen Guinevere makes advances toward him; when he rejects her, she impugns his masculine identity, suggesting that he must take his pleasure with young boys, as he has no lady. Thus provoked, Lanval reveals the secret of his fairy lover. Although he has broken his oath, the fairy lady rides to Lanval's rescue in the end.

Other medieval literary female characters who might be described as "supernatural" include, from the earlier period, Grendel's mother (in *Beowulf*), from later periods, Dame Brangwain (who prepared the potions in the *Tristan* stories), Rhiannon (in the *Mabinogi*), and the serpent-woman Mélusine (in the eponymous romance by Jean d'Arras).

DORSEY ARMSTRONG

References and Further Reading

Armstrong, Dorsey. *Gender and the Chivalric Community in Malory's* Morte Darthur. Gainesville: University Press of Florida, 2003.

Chaucer, Geoffrey. *The Riverside Chaucer*. Edited by Larry D. Benson. Boston: Houghton Mifflin, 1987.

Crane, Susan. *Gender and Romance in Chaucer's* Canterbury Tales. Princeton: Princeton University Press, 1994.

Fenster, Thelma S., ed. *Arthurian Women: A Casebook*. New York: Garland, 1996.

Ferrante, Joan M. *The Conflict of Love and Honor: The Medieval Tristan Legend in France, Germany, and Italy*. The Hague: Mouton, 1973.

Ford, Patrick K., trans. *The Mabinogi and Other Medieval Welsh Tales*. Berkeley: University of California Press, 1977.

Geoffrey of Monmouth. *The Historia Regum Britanniae of Geoffrey of Monmouth*. Edited by Neil Wright. Cambridge: D. S. Brewer, 1985.

Hodges, Kenneth. *Forging Chivalric Communities in Malory's* Le Morte Darthur. New York: Palgrave/Macmillan, 2005.

Lacy, Norris J., ed. *Lancelot-Grail: The Old French Arthurian Vulgate and Post-Vulgate in Translation*. 5 vol. New York: Garland, 1993–1996.

Malory, Sir Thomas. *Works*. Edited by Eugène Vinaver. 3 vol. 3rd edition, revised by P. J. C. Field. Oxford: Clarendon Press, 1990.

Marie de France. *Lais*. Edited and translated by Glyn S. Burgess and Keith Busby. Harmondsworth: Penguin, 1986.

Patterson, Lee. "For the Wyves of Bathe: Feminine Rhetoric in the *Roman de la Rose* and the *Canterbury Tales*." *Speculum* 58 (1983): 656–695.

Summer, Laura, ed. *The Weddynge of Sir Gawen and Dame Ragnell*. Northampton, Mass.: Smith College, 1924.

Tolkien, J. R. R. and E. V. Gordon, eds. *Sir Gawain and the Green Knight*. Second Edition. Oxford: Clarendon Press, 1967.

Wheeler, Bonnie, and Fiona Tolhurst, eds. *On Arthurian Women: Essays in Honor of Maureen Fries*. Dallas, Tx.: Scriptorium Press, 2001.

See also **Arthurian Literature; Beowulf; Chaucer, Geoffrey; Chivalry; Chrétien de Troyes; Guinivere; Isolde; Literature, Middle English; Literature, Old French; Marie de France; Mélusine; Mermaids and Sirens; Prophets, Nordic; Valkyries**

SYON ABBEY

The only English house of the Birgittine Order, Syon Abbey, or more formally, the Order of St. Saviour, St. Mary and St. Bridget of Syon, was established by Henry V in 1415 near his royal palace at Sheen (Richmond). An Order envisaged as a "new vineyard" at a time when all over Europe the need for reform was urgent, the Birgittines, along with the austere Carthusians, were especially chosen by Henry to occupy sites close to his palace as a signal that he intended to take strong leadership in both the political and ecclesiastical spheres. After the first vows were made in April 1420 in the presence of the archbishop of Canterbury, this late medieval royal foundation almost immediately became one of the most important monastic houses in England, exercising, in particular, a profound influence on the religious life of the capital.

An order dedicated to the Virgin Mary and intended primarily for women, whose main duty, according to the Rule, was the constant praise of God through the Lord's "most beloved mother," was timely in an era when Marian devotion was flourishing, especially in England, or "Mary's dower," as it was known. This was a double order, modeled after the post-Ascension community with Mary as its head. The priests assisted the nuns in their devotions and were their spiritual advisors. The abbess, elected from among the choir sisters, was the earthly representative of the Virgin and administered the monastery; the confessor-general, elected by the nuns and brethren, was the spiritual head. Both the women's and men's communities were enclosed and strictly separated, even in the church itself, both literally and figuratively the heart of Birgittine life. Excavations at Isleworth have indicated that the Church at Syon was larger even than Westminster Abbey.

During its pre-Reformation existence, Syon Abbey was held in high esteem for the rigour of its religious observance and the learning of its members. The nuns' main task was the daily performance of their special office, or the *Cantus sororum*, and at Matins attending to lessons concerning Mary's role in salvation that had been dictated to Birgitta by an angel and hence called the *Sermo angelicus*. In the mid-fifteenth century one of the brothers wrote *The Myroure of oure Ladye*, a translation and explication of the entire service, not so the nuns could abandon the Latin but to ensure that they fully understood and could meditate on the words they recited daily. In an order that valued poverty, it was remarkable that the choir sisters could have as many books of devotional readings as they required; many possessed books in Latin and French as well as English.

At the Dissolution, the community refused to take the oath of allegiance; even a visit from Queen Anne Boleyn failed to sway the determined nuns. Henry VIII himself was reluctant to take action, and when on November 25, 1539, the Birgittines were "putt out" of their house on legal grounds, they did not "surrender to the king." They retired to safe houses and went abroad, and Syon is alone among religious houses in England in claims of an unbroken existence from its medieval foundation. Today the nuns carry on their devotional life at South Brent, Devon.

ANN M. HUTCHISON

References and Further Reading

Blunt, J. H., ed. *The Myroure of Oure Ladye*. Early English Text Society. Extra Series 19. London: N. Trübner, 1873; reprint 1981, 1998.

Ellis, Roger. *Syon Abbey: The Spirituality of the English Bridgettines*. Analecta Cartusiana 68.2. Salzburg: Institut für Anglistik und Amerikanistik, Universität Salzburg, 1984.

Hutchinson, Ann M. "The Nuns of Syon in Choir: Spirituality and Influences." In *Medieval Spirituality in Scandinavia and Europe: A Collection of Essays in Honour of Tore Nyberg*, edited by Lars Bisgaard. Odense: Odense University Press, 2001, pp. 265–274.

Johnston, F. R. "Syon Abbey." In *Victoria County History. Middlesex*, vol.1 London: Oxford University Press, 1969, pp. 182–191.

Knowles, David *The Religious Orders in England*. 3 vols. Cambridge: Cambridge University Press, 1948–1959.

See also **Abbesses; Architecture, Monastic; Birgitta of Sweden; Birgittine Order; Book Ownership; Devotional Literature; Devotional Practices; Double Monasteries; Literacy and Reading: Latin; Literacy and Reading: Vernacular; Mary, Virgin; Monastic Enclosure; Monastic Rules; Monasticism and Nuns; Monasticism, Women's: Papal Policy; Patronage, Ecclesiastical; Poverty, Religious; Spiritual Care**

T

TEACHERS

See **Education, Beguine; Education, Lay; Education, Monastic; Literacy and Reading: Latin; Literacy and Reading: Vernacular; Monasticism and Nuns; Monasticism and Nuns, Byzantine; Monasticism and Nuns: Celtic; Mothers as Teachers**

TERESA DE CARTAGENA

Teresa de Cartagena (c. 1425–d. after 1465) belonged to the most powerful family of *judeoconversos* (Jewish converts to Christianity) in late medieval Spain. Her grandfather, father, and uncles converted to Christianity in 1390–1391 and became pivotal figures in the religious, political, diplomatic, and literary culture of the fifteenth and early sixteenth centuries. Around 1440, Teresa entered the Franciscan monastery of Santa Clara in Burgos and studied, in some capacity, at the University of Salamanca. In 1449, she transferred to the Cistercian Order, probably entering the prestigious Monastery of Las Huelgas in Burgos. Shortly afterward, in the mid-1450s, Teresa became deaf, an affliction that cut her off from family, friends, and members of her convent. She recorded her twenty-year struggle with her deafness in *Grove of the Infirm* (*Arboleda de los enfermos*) around 1475–1476, and subsequently defended her writing in *Wonder at the Works of God* (*Admiraçión operum Dey*).

Grove of the Infirm is a hybrid work (consolatory treatise, medieval sermon, epistolary narrative, spiritual autobiography, moral treatise on the virtue of patience); its theme is the spiritual benefits of affliction, and Teresa's deafness serves throughout as an autobiographical exemplum. Apparently the circulation of her manuscript occasioned considerable local controversy, and Teresa wrote her second work to counter the incredulity (*admiraçión*) of her detractors, who contended that a women—especially a handicapped woman—had nothing of value to teach, and to refute their allegations that she had not authored *Grove of the Infirm* but had plagiarized male sources and presented their work as her own.

DAYLE SEIDENSPINNER-NÚÑEZ

References and Further Reading

Seidenspinner-Núñez, Dayle. *The Writings of Teresa de Cartagena*. Cambridge: D. S. Brewer, 1998.
Seidenspinner-Núñez, Dayle, and Yonsoo Kim. "Historicizing Teresa: Reflections on New Documents regarding Sor Teresa de Cartagena." *La corónica* 32.2 (Spring 2004): 121–150.
Surtz, Ronald E. *Writing Women in Late Medieval and Early Modern Spain: The Mothers of Teresa de Avila*. Philadelphia: University of Pennsylvania Press, 1995.

See also **Disabilities; Iberia; Literature, Iberian; Monasticism and Nuns; Theology; Women Authors: Spanish Texts**

TERTIARIES

The term *tertiary*, which in the modern era has come to denote the lay members of Franciscan, Dominican, and other mendicant orders, was rarely used during the Middle Ages. The term presumes that the laity formed a distinct third branch (*tertius ordo*) or a third rule (*tertia regula*) within religious orders, complementing the first and second branches of friars and nuns respectively. But the lay groups associated with the medieval mendicant orders evade such simple classification, for during their lives many women who today are labeled as tertiaries, were virtually indistinguishable from other religious laywomen. Thus such generic names as penitents (*soror de poenitentia*) or bearer of penitent habit (*vestita*), *pinzochera* or, simply, religious woman (*mulier religiosa*) better respond to the institutionally ambiguous and relatively independent lives of medieval laywomen who associated themselves with the mendicant friars. Moreover, the mendicant friars' influence on religious lay life was not limited to associations that may be grouped as tertiaries, but was felt widely, among such independent lay groups as the Beguines of central and northern Europe or the *beatae* of Spain.

Franciscan and Dominican Groups

Both the Franciscan and the Dominican friars engaged in the spiritual direction of religious laywomen, but the Franciscans, themselves profoundly inspired by lay devotional ideas, were more ready to formalize the bonds with laywomen than were the markedly clerical Dominicans. Thus, the Franciscan tertiary groups not only outnumbered the Dominican lay associations but also spread throughout Europe, in stark contrast to Dominicans whose lay affiliations principally grew in Italy. Moreover, the Franciscans enrolled both laymen and women, whereas the Dominican groups were almost exclusively populated by women.

Guidelines

It is probable that both the Franciscan and Dominican penitents used the first surviving guideline of the penitent life, the so-called *Memoriale* of 1221–1228, but it is impossible to determine to what extent the document's ideals concerning humble clothing, frequent fasting, observing the seven canonical hours, Eucharistic observances, or obligations of prayers for the dead shaped the actual practices of the penitents. Pope Nicholas IV's bull *Supra montem* provided the Franciscan tertiaries with a formal rule on September 18, 1289, but the Dominican women did not receive their rule until Pope Innocent VII published it within his bull *Sedis apostolicae* on June 26, 1405. (Master General Munio of Zamora's *Ordinationes* of 1286 is not, contrary to what historians long believed, the first known version of the formal Dominican tertiary rule of 1405, but merely a preliminary set of guidelines intended for local use by the penitents of Orvieto.) The other two principal mendicant orders, the Augustinian Hermits and the Carmelites, exercised limited spiritual direction among the laity. Even after they forged their first formal ties with laywomen at the beginning of the fifteenth century, they never rivaled in popularity the Franciscans or the Dominicans.

Ways of Life

The more stable institutional position of the Franciscan tertiaries was reflected by the emergence of the first semi-monastic tertiary communities during the fourteenth century, among them the house of Angelina of Montegiove (d. 1435). In contrast, Dominican tertiaries lived exclusively at private homes or in informal domestic communities until the turn of the sixteenth century when Colomba of Rieti (d. 1501) and Lucia Brocadelli of Narni (d. 1544) were among the first Dominican penitents to found semi-monastic houses for laywomen.

The tertiaries were typically widows to whom religious life in the world brought social stability and access to religious instruction. But structured religious observances in the world and pious collegiality also made the tertiary life attractive to the unmarried and to married couples. The Franciscans even generated an ideal of virginal marriage within which the union was never consummated, as was the case with the saintly pair of aristocratic tertiaries from France, Elzéar of Sabran (d. 1323), and Delphine of Puimichel (d. 1358). A typical tertiary woman came from the well-to-do urban middle class or lesser nobility, but notable exceptions both from the higher aristocracy and servant class show that penitential life offered a viable religious alternative for all levels of society. Princess Elisabeth of Hungary (d. 1231) sought a life of Franciscan penitential poverty and service to the poor after she was left a widow, whereas Dominicans Giovanna of Orvieto (d. 1306) and Stefana Quinzani (d. 1530) transformed their existence as domestic servants into famed lives as penitential mystics.

Charity and Mysticism

The religious culture of both the Dominican and the Franciscan tertiaries resonated with the broader lay piety within which ascetic self-denial and imitation of

Christ's suffering on the cross paved the way to visionary experiences and mystical celebration of the sacrament of the Eucharist. But the Franciscan and Dominican understanding of lay spirituality differed from each other in a few notable ways. Just as the Franciscan penitent rule encouraged service to the urban poor, the Franciscans supported the benevolent engagements of such saintly laywomen as Umiliana dei Cerchi (d. 1246), who as a young widow immersed herself in the care of her neighbors, and Margaret of Cortona (d. 1297), who founded the hospital of Santa Maria della Misericordia in her hometown. In contrast, the Dominicans were cautious about such institutional commitment and did not enshrine charity toward the poor in the penitent rule of 1405. The Dominican penitents were instead uniquely focused on the Passion of Christ, with several of them embodying Christ's crucifixion through their public enactment from the scenes of the Passion, as was the case with Giovanna of Orvieto and Stefana Quinzani. Catherine of Siena (d. 1380) and Lucia Brocadelli of Narni (d. 1544) even received the stigmata, the five wounds of Christ.

The Dominican and Franciscan laywomen's propensity toward mysticism did not preclude their active contributions as reformers and spiritual guides. *The Book* of Franciscan tertiary Angela of Foligno (d. 1309), consisting of two parts, *The Memorial* and *The Instructions*, was an impassioned account concerning her journey toward mystical union with God and at the same time a level-headed guidebook for those seeking spiritual perfection. Colette of Corbie (d. 1447), who herself oscillated among tertiary life, eremitical existence, and semi-monastic commitments, helped to rejuvenate the Order of the Poor Clares of France. Catherine of Siena was instrumental in reshaping not only Dominican lay life, but Dominican women's monasticism as well. Her book *The Dialogue* and almost four hundred surviving letters show a contemplative woman in action: her elaborate Christ-centered mystical teaching was matched by practical wisdom and a phenomenal aptitude for attracting supporters among men and women of power.

MAIJU LEHMIJOKI-GARDNER

References and Further Reading

Angela of Foligno. *Complete Works.* Translated with an introduction by Paul Lachance. New York: Paulist Press, 1993.

Catherine of Siena. *The Dialogue.* Translation and introduction by Suzanne Noffke. New York: Paulist Press, 1980.

Coakley, John. "Gender and Authority of the Friars: Significance of Holy Women for Thirteenth-Century Franciscans and Dominicans." *Church History* 60 (1991): 445–460.

Dominican Penitent Women. Edited, translated, and introduced by Maiju Lehmijoki-Gardner with contributions by Daniel E. Bornstein and E. Ann Matter. New York: Paulist Press, 2005.

Elliott, Dyan. *Spiritual Marriage: Sexual Abstinence in Medieval Wedlock.* Princeton, N.J.: Princeton University Press, 1993.

Herzig, Tamar. "The Rise and Fall of a Savonarolan Visionary: Lucia Brocadelli's Forgotten Contribution to the *Piagnone* Campaign." *Archiv für Reformationsgeschichte/Archive for Reformation History* 95 (2004): 34–60.

Lehmijoki-Gardner, Maiju. "Writing Religious Rules as an Interactive Process: Dominican Penitent Women and the Making of Their *Regula.*" *Speculum* 79 (2004): 660–687.

Makowski, Elizabeth. *A Pernicious Sort of Woman: Quasi-Religious Women and Canon Lawyers in the Later Middle Ages.* Washington, D.C.: The Catholic University of America Press, 2005.

Scott, Karen. "Urban Spaces, Women's Networks, and the Lay Apostolate in the Siena of Catherine Benincasa." In *Creative Women in Medieval and Early Modern Italy: Religious and Artistic Renaissance,* edited by E. Ann Matter and John Coakley. Philadelphia: University of Pennsylvania Press, 1994, pp. 105–119.

Testi e documenti sul terzo ordine francescano, edited by Lino Temperini. Rome: Editrice Franciscanum, 1991.

Vauchez, André. "Lay People's Sanctity in Western Europe: Evolution of a Pattern (Twelfth and Thirteenth Centuries)." In *Images of Sainthood in Medieval Europe,* edited by Renate Blumenfeld-Kosinski and Timea Szell. Ithaca, N.Y.: Cornell University Press, 1991, pp. 21–32.

———. *The Laity in the Middle Ages: Religious Beliefs and Devotional Practices.* Edited and introduced by Daniel Bornstein and translated by Margery Schneider. South Bend, Ind.: University of Notre Dame Press, 1993.

Women and Religion in Medieval and Renaissance Italy, edited by Daniel Bornstein and Roberto Rusconi and translated by Margery J. Schneider. Chicago: The University of Chicago Press, 1996.

See also **Angela of Foligno; Beguines; Catherine of Siena; Chastity and Chaste Marriage; Colette of Corbie; Dominican Order; Lay Piety; Laywomen, Religious; Margaret of Cortona; Mysticism and Mystics; Poor Clares Order; Spiritual Care; Spirituality, Christian**

TEXTILE PRODUCTION FOR THE MARKET

Of all the forms of medieval textile production, by far the most commercially important were those focused on wool-based cloths: woolens, worsteds, and serges (mixed woolen-worsted fabrics). When first properly documented, in Carolingian times, the basic processes of cloth manufacturing were almost entirely undertaken by women, as indicated by the name for a textile workshop in manorial estates: *gynaecia.* Those basic processes became all the better defined, by "division of labor," when cloth production became

Tanaquil (Etruscan Queen of Rome) with loom and women spinning. From "De Claris Mulierbus," by Giovanni Boccaccio (1313–1375), after Pliny (HN 8.194). French, Fourteenth century Roy 16.G.V, f.56. Location: British Library, London, Great Britain. Credit: Art Resource, N.Y.

market-oriented crafts. In order they were: wool-beating and fiber-separation, scouring, washing, greasing, combing, spinning, warping, and weaving. Most of the subsequent cloth-finishing processes were, however, undertaken by men: fulling, shearing, and dyeing.

Woolens: Processes of Textile Production

The differences between woolens and worsteds were fourfold: the type, nature, and quality of the wools used; the consequent processes of cloth-production;

the weight and appearances of the cloths; and, their prices. Woolens were woven from very costly, fine, weak, short-fibered, curly wools, which had to be thoroughly scoured, to remove the natural lanolin, and then heavily greased with butter or olive oil in order to protect these delicate fibers from damage in the ensuing processes of combing, spinning, and weaving. To prevent these woolens from falling apart after weaving, they then had to be subjected to fulling, which was traditionally undertaken, especially in towns specializing in luxury cloth production, by two or three naked men who, for three days trod upon the cloth (about 30 meters long) in a stone trough, filled with an emulsion of hot water, fuller's earth (floridin), and urine. That process, with the combination of pressure, heat, and chemicals, had three objectives: to remove all the grease and dirt; to force the short, curly fibers to "felt" together (i.e., to interlace and interlock), and to shrink the cloth by at least fifty percent in area. The result was a very strong, durable, heavy, densely felted fabric whose weave was no longer visible. Indeed, any traces of the weave were obliterated in the subsequent processes of napping (raising nap fibers with teasels) and shearing, which also made the cloth finish as fine and smooth as silk. Dyeing commonly took place both "in the wools," chiefly in blue (woad, indigo), and subsequently "in the piece."

Worsteds: Processes of Textile Production

Worsteds, in contrast, were woven from very strong, straight, coarse, long-fibered wools, which were neither scoured nor greased; nor, therefore, were worsteds fulled and thus were also not napped and shorn. They were very light (about one-quarter the weight of woolens); not particularly durable; and were either bleached or inexpensively dyed. They were, therefore, also far cheaper than were most woolens. Because the cloth-finishing processes in true woolen manufacturing were male dominated, exclusively male in fulling, we may deduce that a much higher proportion of the labor engaged in manufacturing worsteds was female.

The Pre-Finishing Processes that Women Performed: Combing, Carding, and Spinning

Some of the basic processes, in both branches of the industry, remained exclusively female until the eighteenth-century Industrial Revolution, in particular spinning, though some males can be found in the wool-preparation processes from the fifteenth century. In disentangling and preparing wools for spinning, the universal process, from ancient times, for both short- and long-fibered wools, had been combing: employing a metal device, often fixed to a post, about a foot-long, with three rows of spiked teeth, seven per rank, through which the wools were drawn. From the thirteenth century onward, however, an alternative process for preparing short fibered wools, known as carding, was introduced from the cotton industry of Muslim Spain. The twin cards were leather-encased blocks of wood through which were pierced backward bending iron hooks; and the female carder, placing a mass of wool between them, worked the cards in opposite directions to disentangle and straighten the fibers. This technique greatly increased productivity, but did not permit the production of strong, unbreakable yarns.

Spinning had a similar history. Again, from ancient times, one process was used to spin all yarns, woolen and worsted, short and long: the drop-spindle or spindle-whorl, a conically shaped rod, narrowed at both ends, made of stone, wood, or bone. By this process, the spinster placed a mass of prepared wool on a forked stick, known as the distaff, fixed into her belt. With thumb and forefinger, she teased some loose strands from the roving and attached them to the top of the spindle-whorl, and then let the spindle drop to the ground, a task that she could perform while doing other household duties. In doing so, the spindle rotated at a very high speed, thereby drafting (drawing) fibers from the roving and twisting them into yarn. The yarn, which the spinster then wound onto the bottom part of the spindle, was both very strong and yet extremely fine.

The subsequent and famed spinning wheel accompanied the wool-cards from the Muslim cotton industries, similarly spreading into western Europe from the thirteenth century. The spindle, to which the wool fibers were attached to one end, was placed as an axle between two upright supports. The spinster used the hand-spun wheel to drive a figure-eight shaped leather band that was looped around both the wheel (grooved) and the spindle-axle. That band rotated the spindle-axle at enormously high speeds, to perform the same tasks of drafting and twisting the fibers, thereby increasing productivity over two-hundred fold. The defect of this process, however, was in having to stop and reverse the wheel in order to wind the yarn onto a separate bobbin. The result was yarn that was much less fine than that produced by the drop spindle, and worse, far weaker, indeed, it was subject to frequent breakages. Consequently, in the luxury woolen industries, both carding and

wheel-spinning were restricted, until about the late fifteenth century, to the production of woolen wefts, while combing and the drop-spindle continued to be required for producing warp yarns for woolens, and all yarns for worsteds.

The Revolution in Weaving: The Gender Change

The significance of the difference between these woolen warps and wefts can be best understood in analyzing the final process, the most important of all: weaving. From ancient times until the twelfth century, weaving had also been an exclusively female occupation employing the so-called warp-weighted loom, with two uprights, a top cross-bar beam from which the foundation warps were hung, and a lower beam that separated the warps, whose ends were weighted with clay, stone, or bone. It was placed against a wall (60-degree angle), allowing two female weavers, one on each side, to insert the weft yarns, attached to a stick, through alternate pairs of separated warps. Such cloths were short and narrow, and evidently used to produce only weakly woven worsteds, with very visible lozenge-shaped weaves.

From the twelfth century this loom was superseded by a far superior implement: the foot-powered horizontal loom, with two fixed but rotating beams, operated by ratcheted levers. The warp yarns were fed from the warp-beam at the rear through alternate sets of suspended heddle-hooks to the cloth-beam at the front; and the weaver used a foot-powered treadle to operate the heddles, in order to open alternating "sheds" of bundled warp yarns. The weaver passed a wooden shuttle containing the weft yarns through alternate "sheds" of warps; and finally the weaver used a wooden "sword" (*spatha*) to beat the weft up into the edge of the cloth, while using the lever to wind the woven fabric onto the cloth beam. This device permitted the manufacture of very strong, densely packed woolens that were not only far better woven, but also far longer, up to 30 meters. But in so tautly stretching the warps and subjecting them to so much stress, this loom required very strong, unbreakable warp yarns (i.e., those spun by drop-spindles from combed wools). Since the wefts were not subjected to the same stress, they could be produced from carded, wheel-spun wools.

Medieval iconography indicates that the earliest versions of the horizontal loom were operated by women; but when this loom evolved into the far more complicated broadloom, during the thirteenth century, weaving had become an exclusively male occupation, requiring two male weavers. Many historians have suggested that male dominance arose from the much greater physical strength required to operate this newer, heavier broadloom.

Exclusively Male Guilds in the Later-Medieval "Putting-Out" System

The true explanation, and one cogently argued by Martha Howell, lay in the changes in industrial organization that evolved when woolen cloth production became a major urban export-oriented industry. Master-weavers were now full-time industrial entrepreneurs who organized cloth production, hiring wool-beaters, combers, carders, and spinners, in a complicated, often regionally far-flung "putting-out" system, with both rural (carding, combing, spinning) and urban components (weaving and finishing). Furthermore, the master weavers also had to deal with other urban artisan-entrepreneurs in the finishing processes, and with various urban merchants: those who supplied wools and other raw materials, and those who marketed the finished woolens. Indeed, the urban weavers, fullers, dyers, and shearers, all became organized in exclusively male guilds that required the exercise of both political and military power in protecting their crafts, duties and tasks denied to almost all women in a basically patriarchal society that confined women to the home. In the putting-out system, all of the wool-preparation functions, fitting in well with a rural economy, took place within the female artisans' own homes, thus giving rise to the alternative term the *domestic system* of production. Needless to say these female artisans did not enjoy any guild protection.

The Modern Industrial Revolution

The next major gender change in textile production occurred when the eighteenth-century Industrial Revolution in cotton manufacturing converted both carding and spinning from female "domestic" occupations into an exclusively male occupation using steam-powered *mules* within an urban factory system of production, radically reducing the costs of yarn production. The economic and social significance of that industrial transformation is revealed by the costs for those prefinishing production processes, all performed by female employees, in the Medici's woolen-cloth firm in 1556–1558: 47.1 percent for spinning

alone, another 19.8 percent for wool preparation, for a total of 66.9 percent.

JOHN H. MUNRO

References and Further Reading

Baines, Patricia. *Spinning Wheels, Spinners and Spinning.* London: Batsford, 1977.

Boone, Marc, and Walter Prevenier, eds. *La draperie ancienne des Pays Bas: débouchés et stratégies de survie (14e–16e siècles)/ Drapery Production in the Late Medieval Low Countries: Markets and Strategies for Survival (14th–16th Centuries).* Studies in Urban Social, Economic and Political History of the Medieval and Modern Low Countries. Leuven and Appeldorn: Garant, 1993.

Carus-Wilson, Eleanora. "The Woollen Industry." In *The Cambridge Economic History of Europe*, vol. 2. *Trade and Industry in the Middle Ages*, 2nd rev. ed., edited by Michael Postan and and Edward Miller. Cambridge: Cambridge University Press, 1987, pp. 630–646, 657–674.

Chorley, Patrick. "The Evolution of the Woollen, 1300–1700." In *The New Draperies in the Low Countries and England, 1300–1800.* Ed. Negley B. Harte. Pasold Studies in Textile History, Vol. 10. Oxford: Oxford University Press, 1997, pp. 7–34.

De Roover, Raymond. "A Florentine Firm of Cloth Manufacturers: Management of a Sixteenth-Century Business." *Speculum* 16 (1941): 3–33. Reprinted in *Business Banking, and Economic Thought in Late Medieval and Early Modern Europe: Selected Studies of Raymond De Roover*, edited by Julius Kirshner. Chicago: University of Chicago Press, 1974, pp. 85–118.

Harte, Negley, and Kenneth Ponting, eds. *Cloth and Clothing in Medieval Europe: Essays in Memory of Professor E. M. Carus-Wilson*, Pasold Studies in Textile History no. 8. London: Heinemann, 1983.

Hoffmann, Marta. *The Warp-Weighted Loom: Studies in the History and Technology of an Ancient Implement.* Oslo: Universitetsforlaget, 1964.

Howell, Martha. *Women, Production, and Patriarchy in Late Medieval Cities.* Chicago: University of Chicago Press, 1986.

Munro, John. "Wool Price Schedules and the Qualities of English Wools in the Later Middle Ages." *Textile History* 9 (1978): 118–169. Reprinted in John Munro, *Textiles, Towns, and Trade: Essays in the Economic History of Late-Medieval England and the Low Countries.* Variorum Collected Studies series, CS 442. London: Ashgate Publishing, 1994.

———. "Textile Technology" and "Textile Workers." In *The Dictionary of the Middle Ages*, edited by Joseph Stayer, vol. XI. New York: Charles Scribner's Sons, 1988, pp. 693–715. Reprinted in John Munro, *Textiles, Towns, and Trade: Essays in the Economic History of Late-Medieval England and the Low Countries*, London: Ashgate Publishing, 1994.

———. "The Symbiosis of Towns and Textiles: Urban Institutions and the Changing Fortunes of Cloth Manufacturing in the Low Countries and England, 1270–1570." *The Journal of Early Modern History: Contacts, Comparisons, Contrasts* 3:1 (1999): 1–74.

———. "Medieval Woollens: Textiles, Textile Technology, and Industrial Organisation, c. 800–1500." In *The Cambridge History of Western Textiles*, edited by David Jenkins. Cambridge and New York: Cambridge University Press, 2003, vol. 1: pp. 181–227.

———. "Medieval Woollens: The Western European Woollen Industries and their Struggles for International Markets, c. 1000–1500." In *The Cambridge History of Western Textiles*, edited by David Jenkins. Cambridge and New York: Cambridge University Press, 2003, vol. 1: pp. 228–324, 378–386 (bibliography).

Patterson, R. "Spinning and Weaving." In *A History of Technology*, edited by Charles Singer and E. J. Holmyard, II. Oxford: Clarendon, 1956, pp. 191–200.

Ryder, Michael. "The Origin of Spinning." *Textile History* 1 (1968–1970): 73–82.

———. "Medieval Sheep and Wool Types." *Agricultural History Review* 32 (1984): 14–28.

Walton, Penelope. "Textiles." In *English Medieval Industries: Craftsmen, Techniques, Products*, edited by John Blair and Nigel Ramsay. London: The Hambledon Press, 1991, pp. 319–354.

Wild, John. *Textile Manufacture in the Northern Roman Provinces*. Cambridge: Cambridge University Press, 1970.

See also **Artisan Families, Women of; Clothing; Clothing for Religious Women; Clothwork, Domestic; Guild Members and Guilds; Home Manufacturing; Work**

The Court of Theodora, detail of Theodora and several attendants. Location: S. Vitale, Ravenna, Italy. Credit: Scala / Art Resource, N.Y.

THEODORA

The empress Theodora (c. 500–548), wife of the Byzantine emperor Justinian I, was born to a modest family and married Justinian in 523 before his ascent to sole rule. She is the best known of the Byzantine empresses, largely because of the scurrilous account of her origins written by the sixth-century historian Procopius of Caesarea. Procopius's *Secret History* claims Theodora was an actress and a prostitute (the two professions were virtually synonymous) in her youth, though it should be noted that this account closely conforms to similar attacks on prior Roman imperial women. Other Byzantine authors such as John of Ephesus are more positive about Theodora.

Theodora was an active supporter of heretical Monophysite Christians, sheltering from persecution a large contingent within the imperial palace. She probably built the church of Sts. Sergios and Bacchos for these Monophysite holy men, and her participation in Justinian's patronage is inscribed on many of the key monuments of their reign, such as the Church of Hagia Sophia in Constantinople (Istanbul). She is also prominently depicted with her court entourage in a large mosaic in the apse of the Church of San Vitale, Ravenna.

Her role in politics is debated. Procopius suggests Theodora exerted enormous influence on Justinian, but that may again be part of the historian's tactics to insult the emperor. Nevertheless her prominence as a patron may indicate her impact on other aspects of imperial rule. During the Nika Revolt (532), Theodora may have dissuaded Justinian from fleeing the city. She died in 548, perhaps of cancer, and Justinian's remaining seventeen years in power were eclipsed by the accomplishments of the earlier part of his reign shared with his remarkable wife.

ANNE MCCLANAN

References and Further Reading

Brubaker, Leslie. "The Age of Justinian: Gender and Society." In *The Cambridge Companion to the Age of Justinian*, edited by Michael Maas. Cambridge; New York: Cambridge University Press, 2005, pp. 427–447.

McClanan, Anne. *Representations of Early Byzantine Empresses: Image and Empire*. New York: Palgrave, 2002.

See also **Byzantium; Empresses: Byzantium**

THEOLOGY

Early medieval theology in the West was dominated by the writings of the Latin Fathers, especially Augustine of Hippo and Jerome. Many theologians, including Gregory the Great, had monastic backgrounds. The strongest interest of these monks, and some nuns too, was in a theology fitting monasticism, including an emphasis on virginity. Particular attention was paid by these writers to exegesis of the Bible, especially spiritual readings of texts. Among the issues addressed were the Fall, including the role of Eve, the nature of sin, with an emphasis on asceticism and denial of bodily desires, and, in the time of Charlemagne, the legitimacy of creating religious images (the iconoclast controversy).

In the High Middle Ages, with the rise of Scholasticism in the newly established universities, patristic texts frequently were read excerpted in the glossed Bible, as topical excerpts in the *Sentences* of Peter Lombard or as materials related to religious discipline in the *Decretum* of Gratian. University-trained experts in theology and canon law, striving to reconcile conflicting texts, dominated the teaching and preaching of doctrine and morals, as well as pastoral care. In the thirteenth century they absorbed an expanded corpus of the works of Aristotle into the curriculum. These teachings affected the theologians' understanding of human nature as they dealt with problems ranging from the moral capacities of women to the Immaculate Conception of Mary. Theological ideas about women remained largely suspicious of womens's perceived carnality and irrationality, while the Virgin Mary was exalted above the rest of her sex. All female archetypes (including Wisdom and Church) were conflated in her. Men were expected to be more rational than women, but still they were regarded as sinful creatures. Only Jesus was regarded by all as sinless, both fully divine and human.

Women, although frequently discussed, rarely were involved in these debates. A few, among them Hildegard of Bingen and Elisabeth of Schönau, were consulted on points of belief, devotion, or practice. (Hildegard's preaching against the Cathars upheld orthodox ideas of the goodness of the Creator.) These and other women were the sources of visions and revelations, some diffused in the vernacular. Many were guided by confessors or other male advisors into acceptable paths; and a few, like Catherine of Siena, became widely respected. Others, however, were regarded as too daring. Birgitta of Sweden was held in suspicion by Jean Gerson, and Marguerite Porete was executed for her ideas.

THOMAS IZBICKI

References and Further Reading

Bynum, Caroline Walker. *The Resurrection of the Body in Western Christianity, 200–1336.* New York: Columbia University Press, 1995.

Matter, E. Ann. *The Voice of My Beloved: The Song of Songs in Western Medieval Christianity.* Philadelphia: University of Pennysylvania Press, 1990.

Miles, Margaret Ruth. *The Word Made Flesh: A History of Christian Thought.* Malden, Mass.: Blackwell, 2005.

Rubin, Miri. Corpus Christi. *The Eucharist in Late Medieval Culture.* Cambridge: Cambridge University Press, 1991.

Smalley, Beryl. *The Study of the Bible in the Middle Ages.* Oxford: Blackwell, 1983.

See also **Aristotelian Concepts of Women and Gender; Asceticism; Augustine, Influence of; Birgitta of Sweden; Catherine of Siena; Church; Elisabeth of Schönau; Eve; Gender Ideologies; Gerson, Jean; Hildegard of Bingen; Icons, Byzantine; Immaculate Conception, Doctrine of; Jerome, Influence of; Julian of Norwich; Marguerite Porete; Mary, Virgin; Monasticism and Nuns; Mysticism and Mystics; Mystics' Writings; Ordination of Women as Priests; Scholasticism; Universities**

TORNABUONI DE' MEDICI, LUCREZIA

Born into an aristocratic family in Florence, Lucrezia (1427–1482) married Piero, Cosimo de' Medici's elder son, in June 1444. When, between 1464 and 1469, Piero took charge of the faction dominating republican Florence, the pious Lucrezia, "a font of charity" according to one contemporary, emerged as a focus of popular reverence (to the advantage of the Medici regime) and revealed an increasing grasp of the workings of grassroots patronal politics. This understanding she put to further use after her son, Lorenzo, assumed leadership of the family party in late 1469. Her abundant surviving correspondence reveals Lucrezia to have been a patron who, alongside her son, exercised indirect political authority and herself pursued the interests of scores of Medici clients, especially women, humble people, and the religious. Upon her death on March 25, 1482, Lorenzo wrote that his mother had been "an irreplaceable refuge," "an instrument that relieved me of many chores."

Lucrezia exercised cultural patronage by commissioning art works and cultivating poets, including Luigi Pulci. Devoted to Mary, she was herself a religious poet in the vernacular. While her sacred stories and poems cannot rival the sophisticated verse produced by her friend Angelo Poliziano and by her own son (whose muse she helped to shape), Lucrezia's able poetic explorations of the lives of "public" Biblical heroines such as Judith constituted a rare female voice, with an autobiographical register, in a city as unkind to eloquent and active women as it was generous to able men.

FRANCIS W. KENT

References and Further Reading

Kent, Francis W. "Sainted Mother, Magnificent Son: Lucrezia Tornabuoni and Lorenzo de' Medici." *Italian History and Culture* 3 (1997): 3–34.
Tomas, Natalie R. *The Medici Women: Gender and Power in Renaissance Florence*. Aldershot: Ashgate, 2003.
Tornabuoni de' Medici, Lucrezia. *Lettere*. Edited by Patrizia Salvadori. Florence: Olschki, 1993.
———. *Sacred Narratives*. Edited and translated by Jane Tylus. Chicago and London: University of Chicago Press, 2001.

See also **Devotional Literature; Italy; Judith; Lay Piety; Mary, Virgin; Merchant Families, Women of; Patronage, Artistic; Patronage, Ecclesiastical; Patronage, Literary; Women Authors: Italian Texts**

TOURNAMENTS

The warrior training that aristocratic men received in the twelfth century prepared them to fight and kill, but church leaders—and sometimes even the nobility themselves—argued that Christians should not kill other Christians. One solution was mock battles, or tournaments. In these exercises, in which the purpose was to disarm the opponent rather than to kill him, a skilled knight could show off his prowess and even make a profit by forcing the less successful to ransom their equipment from him. William Marshall, later regent of England, had his start on the tournament circuit. Men could still be killed in tournaments, of course, even if not intentionally. The English kings tried to limit tournaments and their violence, and for two centuries the church threatened participants with excommunication. But their popularity continued undiminished.

Women's prescribed role in tournaments was to watch admiringly as the knights showed off their manly skills. The "Frauenturnier," a German late thirteenth-century story of women fighting "honorably" while the men were away, was a comic fabliau, critiquing the arrangement of marriages but not realistically proposing women's tournaments.

Late medieval tournaments became more formal and stylized. The original wide-open fighting was increasingly replaced by a series of individual combats, jousts, in which knights sought to unhorse each other with their spears. Even after the invention of cannons greatly decreased the role of cavalry in warfare,

knights practiced their tournament skills and used them at great festivals and pageants.

CONSTANCE B. BOUCHARD

References and Further Reading

Bouchard, Constance Brittain. *"Strong of Body, Brave and Noble": Chivalry and Society in Medieval France*. Ithaca, N.Y.: Cornell University Press, 1998.
Keen, Maurice. *Chivalry*. New Haven: Yale University Press, 1984.
Westphal-Wihl, Sarah. "The Ladies' Tournament: Marriage, Sex, and Honor in Thirteenth-Century Germany." *Signs* 14 (1989), 371–398,

See also **Arms and Armor; Chivalry; Warfare**

TRANSLATION

The art of translation (or *translatio*) was an important phenomenon for medieval women, particularly from the twelfth century on, in terms of their patronage, their education and ability to access works of Latinate (and other) cultures, and the influence of their own written works.

Patronage

Women were among the earliest patrons of vernacular literature. Not only did they sponsor the composition of some of the first courtly romances in the vernacular, they also sought to make other texts more accessible, both to themselves and their courts, by requesting translations. Marie de Champagne, best known as patron of Chrétien de Troyes, the first writer of Arthurian romance, also sponsored two biblical translations, one of Psalm 44 from the Vulgate Bible, *Eructavit cor meum* ("My heart is stirred"), and the other an (incomplete) translation of the book of Genesis. In both cases, the "translation" went well beyond the bounds of what we would consider translations today, for the texts were paraphrased, heavily glossed, and contained considerable commentary by the two clerical translators. Translations of the Bible were still considered rather bold undertakings in the twelfth century, and many clerics, notably Adam de Perseigne, to whom *Eructavit* is sometimes attributed, believed that the laity should not confront Scripture without interpretation. Thus, both of these "translation" projects provided the gloss that the authors thought necessary for a fuller understanding of the text.

However, not all translation projects done for women were scriptural. One example of a nonscriptural work is the *Voyage of Saint Brendan* (sometimes characterized as a hagiographical romance), originally written in Latin by the poet Benedeit and dedicated to Queen Matilda, wife of Henry I of England. Whether she had personally commissioned the Latin text we do not know (though she did commission two other Latin works: a life of her mother, Saint Margaret of Scotland, by a monk from Durham and the history of the kings of England by William of Malmesbury). However, we do know that she later asked Benedeit to translate his work into French, which not only made it more accessible to courtiers, but also clearly added to the work's popularity. It would be so popular that in later years he would rededicate it to Henry's second wife, Adeliza, after Matilda's death.

Translations into Latin

The opposite side of the coin, and one that has thus far been less studied by scholars, is that some women writers (particularly female mystics, who, like some women patrons, may have felt less comfortable in Latin) often wrote in the vernacular. Frequently their works were then translated into Latin by others, usually clerics, in order to make them more generally accessible to clerical readers throughout Europe or to lay persons of other regions who might not know the particular vernacular in which the work was written, but who could read or understand Latin. The thirteenth-century Beguine Marguerite Porete, for example, wrote in French, but her work, the *Mirror of Simple Souls,* was quickly translated. Unfortunately no thirteenth-century manuscripts of the work in any language survive today; but the popularity of her work is attested by a large number of manuscripts from the fifteenth century or later, not only in her native French, but also in Latin, Italian, and English. This is rather remarkable since Church courts had ordered that all copies of her book be destroyed when she was burned at the stake for heresy in 1310. The work of another female mystic, Mechthild of Magdeberg, who wrote her *Flowing Light of the Godhead* in Low German about 1250, was translated into Latin soon after her death, which allowed her an audience that extended well beyond her native Germany into Switzerland and Italy and probably beyond. Similarly, the vernacular *Revelations* of the fourteenth-century mystic Birgitta of Sweden were translated into Latin by her various confessors, only to be retranslated some time later into Swedish. Inevitably, such translations pass through the creative filter of the translator and perhaps blunt the direct experience of the women's writing. But, had they not been preserved in Latin, some of them might have been lost to posterity. Such translations inevitably extended the fame of the author and the influence of the works beyond their original linguistic boundaries.

Women Translators

It would be wrong to leave the impression that medieval women never read or wrote in Latin. Many did, and some, like the German abbess Hildegard of Bingen, wrote prolifically in the Latin language. Others, who clearly knew the language well, played some of the most important roles in the phenomenon of translation by becoming translators themselves. As such, they took creative control over a work's interpretation as they recast it for a new audience. Throughout the Middle Ages, women, some as renowned as Christine de Pizan, served as translators. Although many no doubt remain anonymous, among the earliest female translators were the Anglo-Norman Clemence of Barking and the anonymous Nun of Barking (who may have been Clemence herself). Best known among female translators of that period, however, was Marie de France. Her language skills were clearly the equal of those of the best clerks of her day, and her work shows evidence of her knowledge of French, Latin, English, and Breton. At first she rejected the idea of doing translations from Latin to French because so many others had already done so. Instead, she chose to translate oral Breton lays that she had heard into octosyllabic verse. Her *Lais* remain today among the pearls of medieval literature. In her second translation project, *Isopet* or *Fables*, she marks out for herself a clear role in the process of *translatio studii*, the transmission of knowledge from one culture to another, noting that the works written by Aesop had been translated from Greek into Latin, then into English (in a now-lost text) by King Alfred, from which she translated them into French. In fact, most scholars believe that she worked from a Latin text, the *Romulus Nilantii*, at least for the first forty fables, though since we do not have Alfred's text, it is impossible to know for sure. We can perhaps best judge her skill as a translator by the octosyllabic works, based on known texts, that she most likely wrote in the 1190s, near the end of her life: the *Espurgatoire seint Patriz*, based on Henry of Saltrey's *Tractatus* on Saint Patrick's Purgatory, and the *Vie seinte Audree*, rendered from an anonymous life of Saint Etheldreda preserved in the *Vitae Sanctorum* and in the *Liber Eliensis*. In both cases, she created works intended to appeal to a lay audience—the *simple gent* or the *laie gent*, as she called them. Although Marie closely followed her original sources in the case of the

Espurgatoire and the *Audree*, like all competent translators, she inevitably brought new dimensions to the works and certainly her own creativity to the process.

Whether as patrons, writers, or translators, women played an important role in the translations of textual compositions in the Middle Ages. The end result of such efforts was the gradual decline of Latin as the most vital literary language and the rise of the vernacular as a legitimate creative vehicle.

JUNE HALL MCCASH

References and Further Reading

Bassnett, Susan and André Lefevere, eds. *Translation, History, and Culture*. London and New York: Pinter Publishers, 1990.

Beer, Jeanette, ed. *Translation Theory and Practice in the Middle Ages*. Studies in Medieval Culture 38. Kalamazoo, Mich.: Medieval Institute Publications, 1997.

Blumenfeld-Kosinski, Renate, Duncan Robertson, and Nancy Bradley Warren, eds. *The Vernacular Spirit: Essays on Medieval Religious Literature*. New York: Palgrave, 2002.

Blumenfeld-Kosinski, Renate, Luise Flotow, and Daniel Russel, eds. *The Politics of Translation in the Middle Ages and the Renaissance*. Ottawa: University of Ottawa Press, 2001.

Ferrante, Joan M. *To the Glory of Her Sex: Women's Roles in the Composition of Medieval Texts*. Bloomington: Indiana University Press, 1997.

Freeman, Michelle. "Marie de France's Poetics of Silence: The Implications for a Feminine *Translatio*." *PMLA* 99 (1984): 860–883.

Leonard, Bonnie H. "The Inscription of a New Audience: Marie de France's *Espurgatoire Saint Patriz*." *Romance Languages Annual* 5 (1993): 57–62.

McCash, June Hall. "*La Vie seinte Audree*: A Fourth Text by Marie de France?" *Speculum* 77 (2002): 744–777.

———, ed. *The Cultural Patronage of Medieval Women*. Athens, Ga.: University of Georgia Press, 1996.

Meale, Carol, ed. *Women and Literature in Britain 1150–1500*. Cambridge: Cambridge University Press, 1993.

Pickens, Rupert. "Transmission et translatio: mouvement textuel et variance," *French Forum*, 23 (1998): 133–145.

———. "Marie de France, Translatrix," *Le Cygne: Journal of the International Marie de France Society* (2002): 7–24.

Vauchez, André "Lay People's Sanctity in Western Europe: Evolution of a Pattern (Twelfth and Thirteenth Centuries)." In *Images of Sainthood in Medieval Europe*, edited by Renate Blumenfeld-Kosinski and Timea Szell. Ithaca, N.Y.: Cornell University Press, 1991, pp. 21–32.

Walters, Lori J. "Christine de Pizan as Translator and Voice of the Body Politic." In *Christine de Pizan: A Casebook*, edited by Barbara Altmann and Deborah L. McGrady. New York: Routledge, 2003, pp. 25–41.

Weiss, Judith, Jennifer Fellows, and Morgan Dickson, eds. *Medieval Insular Romance: Translation and Innovation*. Cambridge, U.K.: Brewer, 2000.

Wogan-Browne, Jocelyn. "Wreaths of Thyme: The Female Translator in Anglo-Norman Hagiography." In *The Medieval Translator 4*, edited by Roger Ellis and Ruth Evans. Binghamton, N.Y.: Medieval & Renaissance Texts & Studies, 1994.

See also **Audience, Women in the; Beguines; Birgitta of Sweden; Christine de Pizan; Clemence of Barking; Education, Lay; Hagiography; Literacy and Reading: Latin; Literacy and Reading: Vernacular; Marguerite Porete; Marie de France; Mechthild of Magdeberg; Mysticism and Mystics; Mystics' Writings; Patronage, Literary; Women Authors: German Texts; Women Authors: Italian Texts; Women Authors: Latin Texts; Women Authors: Middle English Texts; Women Authors: Old French Texts; Women Authors: Spanish Texts**

TRAVEL
See **Migration and Mobility: Pilgrims and Pilgrimage**

TROBAIRITZ AND TROUBADOURS

Old Occitan is unusual among medieval vernacular literatures in having a substantial body of lyric poetry written by women. These women poets were known in their own language as trobairitz, the feminine of troubadour ("one who finds, invents, or composes"). The feminine form was uncommon but not limited to a single occurrence, as has been believed; it occurs once in the thirteenth-century romance of *Flamenca*, where a serving lady playfully suggests that her mistress is a trobairitz, and again in a grammar.

The assessment of the reality of the trobairitz depends on manuscript attributions and the poems themselves. The manuscripts attribute poems to nineteen women by name. Each one is credited with a single song except for two more major figures: the Comtessa de Dia, with four songs, and Castelloza, with three and a possible fourth that is anonymous in the manuscript. One song is a dialogue between two women (Almuc de Castelnou and Iseut de Capio), and another involves three women in conversation (Alais, Iselda, and Carenza, assuming that "Alaisina Iselda" is not one person). The number of songs attributed to named trobairitz by the manuscripts is twenty-one. Two more trobairitz, Alamanda and Felipa, figure by name in the texts of dialogues that are attributed by the manuscripts only to their male interlocutors. In addition, a number of songs, mostly dialogues, involve a female voice identified only as a *domna* ("lady"). If these *domnas* were real poets they may have preferred to remain anonymous out of discretion. This hypothesis is strengthened by the example of *Domna H.*, so named in the manuscript that attributes a dialogue to her and a little-known troubadour. Since an anonymous *domna* may have composed more than one song with the same anonymity, we cannot know how many such trobairitz are concealed behind the term. Other poems use *donzela* ("young *domna*") or *midons* ("my lady") in the same way, and there are also anonymous songs that use no such term but speak in the voice of a lady who remains anonymous. If all these trobairitz were real, they may have left as many as fifty songs.

In recent years scholars have become more willing to acknowledge the reality of the trobairitz. The radical view once expressed by Jean-Charles Huchet and echoed by the historian Georges Duby, who claimed that there were no real trobairitz at all because medieval gender roles would not have allowed it, is now dismissed by most scholars as willful disregard of the manuscript evidence. Among the named trobairitz, Bietris de Romans has attracted attention because the poem attributed to her reads exactly like a love song by a troubadour. If the author was a man, the poem is conventional; but if the author was a woman, as the manuscript says, the poem appears to be an expression of lesbian desire unique in Old Occitan and unusual in medieval poetry. Alamanda is named within a dialogue with the troubadour Giraut de Bornelh, but the manuscripts attribute the poem to him alone. It is possible that Alamanda is a fictional character with a name, and not a real poet, but scholars lean increasingly toward the latter view. The case of Felipa is similar.

The importance of the trobairitz to our understanding of desire in this poetry far outweighs the number of their preserved songs. That number is modest compared to the total corpus, about 2,500 compositions written in the twelfth, the thirteenth, and the early fourteenth centuries. They are distributed chronologically as a bell curve peaking in the years around 1200, and higher in the years following than in those preceding. The corpus of fifty poems that may have been written by trobairitz is distributed similarly. Most of them were probably written in the forty years around 1200; only three were surely written earlier, and none in the early twelfth century; more were written later.

The system of Old Occitan lyric genres developed from degree zero in the earliest troubadours into an elaborate structure of more than twenty poetic types in fourteenth-century poetic treatises. The earliest poem by a named trobairitz, Azalais de Porcairagues, has been misread as a blend of two genres, the love song and funeral lament; however, since the genres had not yet taken shape, it should be read as a less conventional and more personal expression of the poet's grief at the death of the troubadour Raimbaut d'Aurenga, in 1173, and her love for another man. The most famous trobairitz poems are love songs (*cansos*), fourteen in all, foremost among them those by the Comtessa de Dia and Castelloza. We have as many dialogues (*tensos*), some of which have often been regarded as the work of troubadours who

invented anonymous female interlocutors. There are also *partimens*, in which one poet proposes alternative positions on some question in amorous casuisty, another poet picks one of them, and they debate; *coblas*, or incidental stanzas; and *sirventes*, or satires. One satire, by Gormonda of Montpellier, is a scathing rebuttal of an attack on Rome by Guilhem Figueira, whom Gormonda curses as a heretic. We have two versified love letters, one dawn song (*alba*), and one funeral lament (*planh*), perhaps for the poet's husband.

In a poetry dedicated above all to the theme of love and overwhelmingly represented by male poets, the trobairitz add the essential component of the women's point of view. If it were not for the trobairitz we might believe that the troubadours really loved cold, distant ladies; but the trobairitz sang as passionately as the men, and they found their lovers cold and distant too, so the coldness appears to be an element in art, not reality. This poetry is a precursor of the blues. More generally, the trobairitz show that despite social constraints, women were not absent from the literary scene, not passive, and not silent, but contributed vigorously to poetry in many forms.

WILLIAM D. PADEN

References and Further Reading

Chants d'amour des femmes-troubadours, edited by Pierre Bec. Paris: Stock, 1995.

Medieval Lyric: Genres in Historical Context, edited by William D. Paden. Urbana: University of Illinois Press, 2000.

Poe, Elizabeth W. "*Cantairitz e trobairitz*: A Forgotten Attestation of Old Provençal *Trobairitz*." *Romanische Forschungen* 114 (2002): 206–215.

Songs of the Women Troubadours, edited by Matilda Tomaryn Bruckner, Laurie Shepard, and Sarah White. New York: Garland, 1995.

Trobairitz: Der Beitrag der Frau in der altokzitanischen höfischen Lyrik. Edition des Gesamtkorpus, edited by Angelica Rieger. Tübingen: Niemeyer, 1991.

The Voice of the Trobairitz: Perspectives on the Women Troubadours, edited by William D. Paden. Philadelphia: University of Pennsylvania Press, 1989.

See also **Literature, Occitan; Trouvères, Women; Woman's Song; Voice, Female: in Literature**

TROTA OF SALERNO

Trota (or, as her name would have been spelled in southern Italy, Trocta) was a medical practitioner in twelfth-century Salerno, a coastal town south of Naples. Although southern Italy was controlled at that time by Normans, Trota herself was probably a Lombard woman. She wrote (or dictated) a general collection of her cures. Called the *Practica* ("handbook of medical practice"), this work shows that

Trota's expertise was expansive, covering a variety of medical fields from gynecology to eye diseases and stomach conditions. The *Practica* survives as an independent text in only two manuscripts, though excerpts were also incorporated into a massive compendium of Salernitan writings composed around 1200. It is clear that other women were practicing medicine at Salerno: writers refer to them generically as *mulieres Salernitane*, the "women of Salerno." Yet Trota stands out as the only Salernitan woman who is known to have composed a written text.

Comparison of Trota's work with that of contemporary Salernitan male practitioners shows certain notable differences. Trota did not engage in any theoretical speculation about the causes of disease, whereas engagement with theory was the most defining characteristic of her male contemporaries. Although imported substances like cinnamon and nutmeg appear occasionally in her remedies, she tended primarily to use locally available ingredients; contemporary male practitioners, in contrast, more regularly employed newer ingredients (like sugar) that had recently become available with the reconquest of Muslim Sicily. Most importantly, Trota practiced a "hands-on" gynecology: she can touch and manipulate her female patients' bodies in a way that no male practitioner ever did.

It was apparently Trota's particular expertise in women's medicine (which, in her definition, included gynecology, obstetrics, and cosmetics) that induced someone (apparently from England, to judge from their use of some English synonyms) to write down her practices in a text called *Treatments for Women* (*De curis mulierum*). Here we find a slight overlay of theory and allusions to some of the practices of her male contemporaries. By the end of the twelfth century, *Treatments for Women* would serve as the core onto which two other Salernitan texts were fused: the anonymous *Conditions of Women* and *Women's Cosmetics*, both of which were probably male-authored. Originally called the *Trotula* (meaning "little Trota" or perhaps "the abbreviated Trota"), the ensemble circulated widely throughout all of western Europe, proving to be the most popular work on women's medicine for the following three centuries. "Trotula" was soon misunderstood as the author's name and so "she" was credited with the whole ensemble of texts. "Trotula" developed a reputation as an authority on "women's secrets," a reputation that turned negative when Chaucer placed her next to the equally suspect Heloise in Jankyn's *Book of Wicked Wives* (*Canterbury Tales, Wife of Bath's Tale*).

Although the *Trotula* was published multiple times in the sixteenth century, humanist scholars came to believe that the work was actually of ancient origin, written by a man. The theory of ancient origin was ultimately abandoned, yet doubt about "Trotula's" existence as a female author persisted. In the nineteenth and twentieth centuries, "she" was bandied back and forth by various factions who either wanted to celebrate her as the "first woman professor of medicine" or dismiss her as a pornographic joke on the thought that her name must mean that she "trotted around." Recognition of the three-text origin of the *Trotula* and discovery of Trota's original *Practica* occurred in the 1980s, but her authorship of *Treatments for Women* was confirmed only in the 1990s. Additional research on female medical practitioners has allowed us to gain a better appreciation both for Trota's accomplishments and for the constraints that kept other medieval women from venturing into medical writing.

MONICA H. GREEN

References and Further Reading

Green, Monica H. "'Traittié tout de mençonges': The *Secrés des dames*, 'Trotula,' and Attitudes towards Women's Medicine in Fourteenth- and Early Fifteenth-Century France." In *Christine de Pizan and the Categories of Difference*, edited by Marilynn Desmond. Minneapolis: University of Minnesota Press, 1998, pp. 146–178. Repr. in Green, *Women's Healthcare in the Medieval West: Texts and Contexts*. Aldershot: Ashgate, 2000, essay VI.

———. "In Search of an 'Authentic' Women's Medicine: The Strange Fates of Trota of Salerno and Hildegard of Bingen." *Dynamis: Acta Hispanica ad Medicinae Scientiarumque Historiam Illustrandam* 19 (1999): 25–54.

———, ed. and trans. *The 'Trotula': A Medieval Compendium of Women's Medicine*. Philadelphia: University of Pennsylvania Press, 2001.

See also **Cosmetics; Doctors and Healers; Gynecology; Secrets of Women**

TROUSSEAU

Trousseau refers to a "bundle" of portable and displayable items, including personal clothing and accessories, bedclothes, utensils, and furniture that a bride brings to the marital household. A trousseau was an essential accompaniment of marriage in the Middle Ages. A bridal trousseau assembled by an elite family included valuables, such as expensive jewelry and brocades, and served as an index of a family's position in the social hierarchy. Among peasants and commoners, a trousseau regularly amounted to a substantial share of what the bride stood to inherit from her family. Even when the trousseau was prepared by the bride and her mother, the responsibility for providing the raw materials as well as ready-made items fell primarily on the bride's father and secondarily on her brothers and other relatives.

Parapherna

Following Roman law, medieval jurists differentiated a dowry from a trousseau. The dowry was conveyed by the bride's family to the son-in-law as a fund to support the new household. During marriage, ownership and control of the dowry with its fruits were exercised by the husband. *Parapherna*, a Greek term meaning "items beyond the dowry," was the juridical designation for the trousseau. In a fourteenth-century Italian legal opinion, *parapherna* was defined as "those movable goods which a wife brings to the husband's household especially for her own use and the common use of herself and her husband" (Kirshner, 185). The vernacular designations for *parapherna* in dowry instruments and family records varied. *Corredo* was the most common designation. It was employed in Florence in the fourteenth century, and was gradually supplanted by the designation *donora*. *Parapherna* was used in Milan, and in southern Italy, where marital property regimes continued to be influenced by Greek and Roman customs and law.

Trousseau and Dowry

In principle, ownership and control of *parapherna* were reserved to the wife during marriage; the husband was prohibited from managing *parapherna* against his wife's wishes. It was common, however, for the wife to allow the husband to manage *parapherna*. Categorical distinctions etched in legal writings between trousseau and dowry did not square with actual practice, because the trousseau counted as part of the dowry throughout Europe and the Mediterranean. In addition, this practice was sanctioned by local statutes and customs, which, diverging from Roman law, granted husbands control over *parapherna*.

The conflation of trousseau and dowry, for example, was customary in the Jewish communities of eleventh-century Jerusalem and twelfth-century Cairo. The thirty-one items listed in a Kariate marriage contract from Jerusalem, dating from 1028, were divided into three categories: (1) gold jewelry, (2) wearing apparel, and (3) copper utensils and containers, and bedding. Wearing apparel amounted to approximately half the total value of sixty-one dinars.

Goitein's description (314–317) of these items as a trousseau fits conventional meanings. Yet the husband formally acknowledged that all the items "were now in his possession and under his hand; and that he had undertaken to keep them as if they were his own" (316).

In fifteenth-century Avignon, a weaver received from his wife a dowry consisting of twenty-four livres, plus "a *culcitra* (a mattress), a feather pillow, bed blanket, sixteen bed sheets, sixteen table cloths, and three new garments" (Girard, 488). Girard calls these items a trousseau, which they were, but in the document he cites there is no mention of a trousseau: all the items were consigned to the husband as a dowry. In northern and central Italy, the *corredo* and *donora* were almost invariably treated as part of the dowry. In England, the bride's trousseau "became the property of her husband, since under common law all the bride's movable goods, or chattels, became the groom's property after marriage" (Fleming, 37).

Between the mid-fourteenth and early sixteenth centuries, Florentine *donora* typically consisted on average of about eleven percent of the total amount of the dowry (Klapisch-Zuber, 216). In Venice, the *corredo* was treated as distinct from the dowry, and from the late fourteenth century onward often equaled from a third to half the dowry. Venetian husbands demanded full control of the *corredo*, without the legal restrictions encumbering dowries. Increasingly, the Venetian *corredo* was transformed from a traditional trousseau into a substantial cash payment to the groom (Chojnacki, 83ff).

Trousseau and Consumption

Within the upper reaches of society in late medieval Europe, the traditional trousseaux of everyday personal belongings and household goods gave way to self-aggrandizing displays of conspicuous consumption. City governments and church officials acted to suppress lavish trousseaux and dowries, but in vain. Sumptuary laws limiting the value of trousseaux were sporadically enforced, and flouted by families whose social reputation was advanced by large dowries and sumptuous trousseaux.

One means of circumventing the legislated limits on the value of the *corredo* or *donora* was to leave part of the trousseau unappraised (*non stimate*). It was in the interest of wives to have the trousseau formally inventoried and appraised in cash (*stimate*), usually by clothes dealers, before it was brought to the marital household. The cash valuation protected wives by shifting the risk of damage and loss to the husband

and by preventing him and his heirs from later claiming that the trousseau was worth less than the agreed-upon value. The husband had the right to elect, upon his predecease, the return to his wife of the specific items in the *corredo* he had actually received or a cash payment of the appraised value. On the other hand, the husband was obligated to restore to his wife the very goods comprising the unappraised *corredo*. Families who wished to evade sumptuary laws could, and did, resort to giving unappraised goods. By deflating the legal valuation of the total dowry, this tactic also served to decrease the contract tax on dowries payable by new husbands (Frick, 135–136).

Cassoni

The painted wedding chests *(cassoni)* in which the trousseaux of Florentine brides were conveyed to their new husbands, customarily on the day of the wedding or immediately after, have attracted considerable scholarly attention. Given as *donora*, a richly decorated *cassone* represented a valuable component of the dowry. *Cassone* painters, like Apollonio di Giovanni (d. 1465), illustrated scenes from the Old Testament, Homer's *Odyssey*, Virgil's *Aeneid*, Boccaccio's *Amorous Vision* and *Concerning Famous Women*, and Petrarch's *Triumph of Chastity*, *Triumph of Fame,* and *Triumph of Love.* Exemplars of female subservience and humility, including Solomon's bride, the Queen of Sheba, holding "her left hand over her heart in a gesture of submission" (Callmann, 43) and Boccaccio's Griselda, "rewarded" by her monstrous husband for passively enabling and enduring his degrading abuse, defined the hierarchical relationship between older husbands and teenage brides. *Cassone* favorites—Dido, the queen of Carthage, and the Roman matron Lucrezia—were admired for their valor and courage and ultimate sacrifice of suicide on behalf of their people. On the *cassone* panels, the mythic Amazons, fierce warriors and male killers, beautiful and celibate, were forced to succumb to marriage and domesticity, deprived of any memory of having lived transgressively.

JULIUS KIRSHNER

References and Further Reading

Baskins, Cristelle L. *Cassone Painting, Humanism, and Gender in Early Modern Italy.* Cambridge and New York: Cambridge University Press, 1998.

Callmann, Ellen. *Apollonio di Giovanni.* Oxford: Clarendon Press, 1974.

Chojnacki, Stanley. "From Trousseau to Groomgift." In *Women and Men in Renaissance Venice: Twelve Essays on Patrician Society.* Baltimore and London: Johns Hopkins University Press, 2000, pp. 76–94.

Fine, Agnès. "A Consideration of the Trousseau: A Feminine Culture?" In *Writing Women's History*, edited by Michelle Perrot and translated by Felicia Pheasant. Oxford: Blackwell, 1992, pp. 118–145.

Fleming, Peter. *Family and Household in Medieval England.* Basingstoke, Hampshire and New York: Palgrave, 2001.

Frick, Carole Collier. *Dressing Renaissance Florence.* Baltimore: John Hopkins University Press, 2002.

Girard, René. "Marriage in Avignon in the Second Half of the Fifteenth Century." *Speculum* 28 (1953): 485–498.

Goitein, S. D. *A Mediterranean Society: The Jewish Communities of the Arab World as Portrayed in the Documents of Cairo Geniza*, Vol. 4: *Daily Life.* Berkeley: University of California Press, 1983.

Kirshner, Julius. "Materials for a Gilded Cage: Non Dotal Assets in Florence, 1300–1500." In *The Family in Italy from Antiquity to the Present*, edited by David Kertzer and Richard Saller. New Haven and London: 1991, pp. 184–207.

Klapisch-Zuber, Christiane. "Les corbeilles de la mariée." In *La maison et le nom Stratégies et rituels dans l'Italie del la Renaissance.* Paris: École des Hautes Études en Sciences Sociales, 1990, pp. 215–227.

See also **Betrothals; Boccaccio, Giovanni; Clothing; Dowry and Other Marriage Gifts; Griselda; Jewelry; Jewish Women; Law, Roman; Marriage, Christian; Petrarch; Roman Law**

TROUVÈRES, WOMEN

The women *trouvères*, or *troveresses*, were poet-musicians whose lyrics were performed for courtly audiences and at popular festivities throughout northern France in the twelfth and thirteenth centuries. There is ample evidence in literature, iconography, and historical documents that women at all levels of society were active as singers, composers, and poets. They participated in the creation and performance of songs in a variety of genres and forms—including monophonic *chansons*, refrain songs associated with dancing (such as *ballettes, virelais,* and *rondets de carole*), lyric debates, and motets in two, three, or four voices—and in a variety of circumstances, both for public and private enjoyment. Interestingly, women sang songs in which the lyric subject could be either masculine or feminine, that is, the gender of the singer did not always correspond to that of the song's lyric subject. Once neglected in favor of the *trobairitz*, their southern counterparts, writing in Occitan, the *troveresses* are gaining recognition as contributors of a distinctive, specifically feminine perspective within old French lyric.

We know of eight named *troveresses*. Blanche of Castile (1188–1252), wife of Louis VIII of France and mother of Louis IX (Saint Louis), authored a *chanson à la Vierge* (or Marian song), "Amours, u trop tart me sui pris" (Love, to which I have been drawn so late). Two songs—"Par maintes fois avrai esteit requise" (Many a time I have been asked), a lament occasioned by the loss of her beloved, and "Un petit davant lou jor" (Just before daybreak), which stages the dialogue between a knight and his lady, who is confined in a high tower by her jealous husband, are ascribed to one "Duchesse de Lorraine," most likely Marguerite de Champagne (married in 1255 to Ferri III, Duke of Lorraine), the daughter of Thibaut IV de Champagne, one of the most illustrious *trouvères*. The names of Maroie de Diergnau de Lille, the Dame de Gosnai, the Dame de la Chaucie, Lorete, Dame Margot, and Sainte des Prez are recorded in the rubrics or tables of contents of various manuscripts or inscribed within lyric debates. There were undoubtedly many more women composers, and, whereas their names are lost to us, some of their songs are arguably still extant, though bereft of proper attribution.

Many of the genres and forms typical of twelfth- and thirteenth-century *trouvère* poetry were practiced by the *troveresses*, in particular the *grans chans* (courtly love songs that exploit the vocabulary, metaphors, and motifs associated with *fin'amors,* the true, perfect, refined love elaborated by the troubadours), the *jeu-parti* and *tenson* (lyric debates regarding a point of courtly casuistry, favored by thirteenth-century urban poets), the *plainte* (death-lament), the *aube* (erotic dawn song), the *chanson de croisade* (crusade lyric), and the *chanson pieuse* (nonliturgical devotional song).

Although the songs that can be attributed with relative certainty to historical women are not numerous, there is a large body of lyrics, mostly anonymous, that gives voice to women and may well have been composed by them; this lyric type, known as *chansons de femme* (or women's songs), includes several more or less clearly defined genres. In the *chanson d'ami,* an apparently unmarried woman avows her love and yearns for her lover. She either feels the urge to love—in keeping with the season, her youth, and her charm—or expresses her sorrow and despair over her sweetheart's absence, sometimes blaming herself for having rebuffed him. She cannot be dissuaded from loving, despite the opposition of her parents and the threat posed by detractors: slanderers, flatterers, and gossip-mongers. The unhappy, frustrated wife heard in the *chanson de malmariée* bewails her fate at the hands of a husband (whom she calls a *vilain,* or boorish lout) who often holds her captive and who is old, ugly, jealous, occasionally impotent, and even brutal. She either longs for compensation or has already exacted satisfaction by taking a lover who possesses all the attributes lacking in the husband she despises: her *ami* is young,

handsome, refined, cheerful, and ardent in love. A variant of the *chanson de malmariée*, the *chanson de nonne*, portrays a young nun cloistered against her will, who laments her confinement—pointing an accusatory finger at those who have sentenced her to the convent—and longs for a lover who will liberate her.

Many of the songs of the *troveresses* survive with music, including six of the thirteen lyric debates featuring women interlocutors. Two songbooks of Lorraine provenance preserve most of the *jeux-partis* and *chansons* with a feminine voice, which may be indicative of a regional predilection for poetry attributable to women.

EGLAL DOSS-QUINBY

References and Further Reading

Doss-Quinby, Eglal. "*Rolan, de ceu ke m'avez / Parti dirai mon semblant*: The Feminine Voice in the Old French *jeu-parti*." *Neophilologus* 83 (1999): 497–516.

Doss-Quinby, Eglal, Joan Tasker Grimbert, Wendy Pfeffer, and Elizabeth Aubrey, eds. and trans. *Songs of the Women Trouvères*. New Haven, Conn.: Yale University Press, 2001.

Grimbert, Joan Tasker. "Diminishing the Trobairitz, Excluding the Women Trouvères." *Tenso* 14 (1999): 23–38.

———. "Songs by Women and Women's Songs: How Useful Is the Concept of Register?" In *The Court Reconvenes: Courtly Literature across the Disciplines*, edited by Barbara Altmann and Carleton Carroll. Cambridge: D. S. Brewer, 2003, pp. 117–124.

Pfeffer, Wendy. "Complaints of Women, Complaints by Women: Can One Tell Them Apart?" In *The Court Reconvenes: Courtly Literature across the Disciplines*, edited by Barbara Altmann and Carleton Carroll. Cambridge: D. S. Brewer, 2003, pp. 125–131.

———. "Constant Sorrow: Emotions and the Women Trouvères." In *The Representation of Women's Emotions in Medieval and Early Modern Culture*, edited by Lisa Perfetti. Gainesville: University Press of Florida, 2005, pp. 119–132.

Tyssens, Madeleine. "Voix de femmes dans la lyrique d'oïl." In *Femmes, mariages-lignages, XII\u1d49–XIV\u1d49 siècles: Mélanges offerts à Georges Duby*. Brussels: De Boeck Université, 1992, pp. 373–387.

See also **Blanche of Castile; Courtly Love; Dawn Song (Alba); Literature, Old French; Trobairitz and Troubadours; Voice, Female: in Literature; Woman's Song**

TYPOLOGY AND WOMEN

Typology is an interpretive method initiated by Jews in the Old Testament and continued by Jesus and his followers in the New Testament. The actions of certain Old Testament persons are thus interpreted as prefiguring the actions of the Messiah. Typology was a staple of medieval biblical interpretation. Generally types are sexually consonant, so that a man prefigures a man and a woman prefigures either a woman or an abstract idea represented by a noun of feminine gender. Within the Old Testament only Jewish men, such as Moses, had prefigured the Messiah. For Christians, biblical women were frequently types prefiguring Mary, the Mother of God, and the Church, *Ecclesia*.

Strikingly, Christians in the first century AD also invented a new strand of typology: women as types of Christ. Jesus's emphasis on the spiritual equality of the sexes and his innovation of presenting himself as a type for his followers to imitate added a new dimension to prophetic types: In addition to prefiguring Christ, the types were also reminders that each human person was to be Christ-like. It was possible, even necessary, to recognize Gentiles (such as Melchisedek) and women as types of Christ, as an expression of the belief that the Christian vocation to holiness was universal. Such typologies were found in both the East and the West across centuries.

Historically the first woman to be interpreted as a type of Christ was Susanna, whose history (Daniel 13) served as the narrative template for the synoptic Passion narratives. From the Gospels onward she was a well-known type of Christ. Between 450 and 1500 she was depicted as a type of Christ in Gethsemane and as a type of Christ at his trial in medieval illustrated manuscripts (*Biblia Pauperum*) and in stained glass, bas reliefs, and frescoes in churches. Commentaries and sermons treated and further developed her typology.

Jephthah's daughter, like Isaac, was an only-begotten, beloved child whose father was willing to sacrifice her to fulfill a vow to God. Both Jewish and Christian tradition condemn Jephthah's rash vow and praise his daughter's courage and faith. By the third century she and Isaac became a pair of Christian types of Christ, the only-begotten, beloved Son who was sacrificed. As such, this young woman and Isaac are depicted next to the altar in churches at Mount Sinai (fifth century) and at the Red Sea (twelfth century). Dionysius bar Salibi (twelfth century) provides the fullest commentary of her as a type of Christ. Her frequent appearance in western manuscripts is at least sometimes typological.

The Jewish interpretation of Ruth, an ancestress of Jesus, as a type of the Messiah (*Ruth Rabbah*, fifth century) may show influence from Christianity.

Esther, like Susanna, was included in the Lectionary because she is a type of Christ, as Rupert of Deutz explains (*Liber de divinis officiis* 4:15). Judith beheading Holofernes and David beheading Goliath were types of Christ defeating the Devil through the Crucifixion. In the illustrated manuscripts of the *Leven van Jezus* Judith entering Bethulia triumphantly with Holofernes' head is a type of Christ entering Jerusalem. The Widow of Zarephath carrying crossed sticks (3 Kings 17) was depicted as a type of Christ carrying the Cross on numerous liturgical vessels, crosses, and altars in northern Europe, especially in the twelfth through fourteenth centuries; she also had been included from the start in the Lectionary.

From the New Testament, Jairus's daughter was a type of Christ in his Resurrection, and, especially in the East, the woman in the parable who finds the lost coin was presented in sermons and hymns as a type of Christ finding and rescuing lost humanity. Annemarie Weyl Carr suggests that Mary Magdalen wiping Christ's feet with her hair was a type of Christ washing the disciples' feet in the illustrations of a twelfth-century Gospel Book in Kiev; if this is correct, it is likely that this pair of depictions is typological elsewhere, as in the sanctuary paintings at Aght'amar in Armenia.

The demographic range of these women is significant: virgins, married women, and widows were recognized as types of Christ. As with male types of Christ, their characters and actions made them suitable prefigurations of Christ. Significantly, although women were interpreted as types of Christ in every aspect of his Passion, no one, including such writers as Herrad of Hohenbourg and Catherine of Siena, ever chose to compose a text or iconographic program presenting the Passion entirely through female types. Their typology was known—in the case of Susanna at least, quite well known—until the Reformation suppressed images and restricted typology.

CATHERINE TKACZ

References and Further Reading

Abecassis, Deborah. "Jephthah's Daughter in the Jewish Exegetical Tradition." Master's thesis, McGill University, 1993.

Carr, Annemarie Weyl. *Byzantine Illumination, 1150–1250: The Provincial Tradition*. Chicago: University of Chicago Press, 1987.

Tkacz, Catherine Brown. "Susanna as a Type of Christ." *Studies in Iconography* 21 (1999): 101–153.

———. "Women as Types of Christ: Susanna and Jephthah's Daughter." *Gregorianum* 85 (2004): 281–314.

———. "The Doctrinal Context for Interpreting Women as Types of Christ." *Studia Patristica* Forthcoming, pp. 37–41.

See also **Bible, Women in; Judith; Mary Magdalen; Personifications Visualized as Women**

U

UNICORN

The unicorn is a mythical one-horned beast widely believed to be real during the Middle Ages. Unicorn horn (actually the tusk of the narwhal, a large Arctic sea mammal), was highly prized for its reputed power to detect and neutralize poison. It was made into drinking cups or ground into a powder that could be added to food or drink suspected to contain poison.

During the Middle Ages, this horse-like creature symbolized a number of different and often contradictory subjects and characteristics, both religious and secular. Fierce, bold, and courageous, the invincible unicorn was also associated with chastity and humility, and was thus both a symbol of Christ and of ideal knighthood. Accordingly, the unicorn became a favourite heraldic emblem of royalty.

The most popular story described the only way to tame and capture the unicorn. A virgin was left alone in the forest. Drawn by the scent of her purity, the unicorn would put his head in her lap and fall asleep, allowing hunters to capture or kill him. Often depicted in medieval art and literature, this story came to represent both secular themes of courtly love and the seductive powers of female sexuality, as well as the Christian stories of the Annunciation and Incarnation.

The most famous known artistic representations of the unicorn are the two late fifteenth-/early sixteenth-century sets of tapestries housed in the Musée de Cluny, Paris, and the Cloisters, Metropolitan Museum of Art, New York City. The meanings of both sets of tapestries have been the subjects of various interpretations for the past two centuries.

KRISTI GOURLAY

References and Further Reading

Freeman, Margaret B. *The Unicorn Tapestries*. New York, 1976.
Gourlay, K. "La Dame à la Licorne: A Reinterpretation." *Gazette des Beaux-Arts* (1997): 47–72.
———— "The Malterer Embroidery: Representations of the Power of Young Female Sexuality." In *Young Medieval Women*, edited by Katherine Lewis, Noël James Menuge, and Kim Phillips. Phoenix Mill: Sutton Publishing Limited, 1999, pp. 69–102.

See also **Courtly Love; Virginity**

UNIVERSITIES

From their origins in the twelfth century, medieval universities were masculine, clerical institutions. Most students were in minor orders, and many were monks or priests, though the Italian universities admitted more lay students and the many new universities founded in the fourteenth and fifteenth centuries educated aristocrats who did not intend a career in the church, as well as those who did. Teachers, too, were mainly clergy, although in faculties other than theology there were occasionally married masters (as well as students). Many students had few licit occasions to come into contact with women. Many college statutes prohibited women servants, or at least young ones. Students who lived not in colleges but in boarding-houses dealt with landladies, and students would have also met female shopkeepers and barmaids or prostitutes. Masters and university officials would have had occasion to meet wealthy women donors.

The classroom experience, however, remained masculine. Authors like John of Salisbury and Peter Abelard, who wrote in the twelfth century, likened the battles of words that occurred in academic disputations to clashes of arms, a very masculine image. The content of university teaching, too, excluded women. From the thirteenth century on much of the curriculum was based on Aristotle, who held that women were inferior and intellectually incapable.

The dominance of the universities in the intellectual life of thirteenth-century Europe marked a change in women's participation in that life. When the monastery was the locus of intellectual creativity, both male and female monastics had participated, and a woman like Hildegard of Bingen could be a leading scholar. But already in Hildegard's twelfth century the signs of female exclusion were appearing. Heloise was reputed to be one of the wisest women in Europe, but she had to be tutored privately rather than attend lectures, and her only known works are the letters she wrote to her husband Peter Abelard. The women authors of the thirteenth to fifteenth centuries tended to be mystics, relying on personal experience rather than scholarship, and many (though not all) writing in the vernacular rather than the Latin of the universities.

Not only scholarship but also the daily life of students was affected by the masculine nature of the university experience. Students might enter the universities as young as fourteen, and often had to undergo hazing analogous to that found in modern fraternities. The *Manuale Scolarium*, a handbook of Latin for fifteenth-century German students, includes a dialogue about an initiation ritual called the *depositio cornuum* or removal of the horns, in which taming the initiate as a wild beast is connected with cleansing him of femininity. This ritual involved a great deal of drinking, as did student life generally. Perhaps not unrelated to their alcohol consumption, student gangs were frequently accused of rape and other crimes against the townspeople. Some evidence survives for homosexual relations among members of the universities.

There are stories of women who attended the universities in disguise, for example one in the fifteenth century who attended the University of Kraków dressed as a man. Christine de Pizan tells of Novella d'Andrea, the daughter of an eminent jurist, who supposedly substituted for her father when he was unavailable to give his lectures in law at the University of Bologna, but did so from behind a curtain so

that the sight of her face would not distract the students. Even if true, however, these are exceptions. University statutes did not explicitly prohibit women from participation; they did not have to, because it was simply assumed that women would not.

Universities attempted to maintain a monopoly on the learned professions, which meant that women could not enter. In Paris in 1322, the medical faculty attempted to have the midwife Jacoba Felicie condemned for practicing medicine without a license. Her patients testified as to the efficacy of her treatment, but the doctors argued that she did not have the proper academic knowledge to treat patients, although she used the same methods as they did.

Although a very small proportion of the population attended universities—the largest admitted four to five hundred students a year, the smallest more like fifty, and most were from the social elite—university graduates (and even students who never attained a degree) were disproportionately influential in later medieval Europe, where they dominated the legal and medical professions, as well as the church. Exclusionary practices as well as teachings on the inferiority of women thus had an impact throughout society.

RUTH MAZO KARRAS

References and Further Reading

Allen, Prudence. *The Concept of Woman: The Aristotelian Revolution, 750 BC–AD 1250*. Montreal: Eden Press, 1985.
De Ridder-Symoens, Hilde, ed. *Universities in the Middle Ages*. Cambridge: Cambridge University Press, 1992.
Karras, Ruth Mazo. *From Boys to Men: Formations of Masculinity in Late Medieval Europe*. Philadelphia: University of Pennsylvania Press, 2003.
The Manuale Scholarium: *An Original Account of Life in the Mediaeval University*, translated by Francis Seybolt. Cambridge, Mass.: Harvard University Press, 1921.
Shank, Michael. "A Female University Student in Late Medieval Kraków." *Signs: Journal of Women in Culture and Society* 12 (1987), 373–380.
Thorndike, Lynn, ed. *University Records and Life in the Middle Ages*. Records of Civilization, 38. New York: Columbia University Press, 1944.

See also **Aristotelian Concepts of Women and Gender; Christine de Pizan; Education, Lay; Education, Monastic; Heloise; Hildegard of Bingen; Literacy and Reading: Latin; Scholasticism**

URRACA

Born to Alfonso VI and his second wife Constance of Burgundy (d. 1093), Urraca (c. 1080–1126) ascended the throne upon her father's death in 1109. Previously she and her first husband, Count Raymond of

Burgundy (d. 1107), had ruled over the region of Galicia. They had two children, Sancha (c. 1095–1159), and Alfonso (1105–1157), who would reign after Urraca as Alfonso VII.

As reigning queen of León-Castile, Urraca married Alfonso I, king of Aragón, in 1109, but it was not a successful union. The couple separated within three years, although neither married again. Each battled the other for full control over the Christian kingdoms of Iberia, but neither was strong enough to prevail. In 1117, they agreed to a truce that was renewed every three years until Urraca's death in childbirth in 1126.

Urraca ruled successfully over the core lands inherited from her father, but she was not able to extend the territory. By repeatedly reminding her court and subjects that she was her father's named heir, Urraca was able to maintain her precarious place on the throne. She took a favorite from among the Castilian nobility, Count Pedro González de Lara, with whom she had two children who survived infancy, Elvira (born c. 1112) and Fernando (born c. 1118). In the early modern period, her liaison with Count Pedro would be turned into a reputation for wantonness, so that Urraca is today more often remembered for moral laxity rather than for her political astuteness.

One of Urraca's strategies appears to have been patronage of the Romanesque basilica of San Isidoro in León, turning what had been her family's private palace chapel into a pilgrimage church open to the public. Through artistic patronage, the queen created a permanent and highly visible reminder of her place in the dynasty of León-Castilla. However, it was only her capable handling of political strategies that allowed a woman to rule in the Middle Ages. Some 220 documents surviving from her reign were ably studied by Bernard F. Reilly.

THERESE MARTIN

References and Further Reading

Marquez de la Plata, Vicenta, and Luis Valero de Bernabé. *Reinas medievales españolas*. Madrid: Alderaban, 2000, pp. 117–133.

Martin, Therese. "The Art of a Reigning Queen as Dynastic Propaganda in Twelfth-Century Spain." *Speculum 80* (2005): 1134–1171.

———. "De 'gran prudencia, graciosa habla y elocuencia' a 'mujer de poco juicio y ruin opinion': Recuperando la historia perdida de la reina Urraca (1109–1126)." *Compostellanum 50* (2005): 551–578.

———. *Queen as King: Politics and Architectural Propaganda in Twelfth-Century Spain*. Leiden: Brill, forthcoming.

Monterde Albiac, Cristina. *Diplomatario de la reina Urraca de Castilla y León (1109–1126)*. Zaragoza: Anubar, 1996.

Reilly, Bernard F. *The Kingdom of León-Castilla under Queen Urraca 1109—1126*. Princeton: 1982. Also published by LIBRO (The Library of Iberian Resources Online) at http://libro.uca.edu/urraca/urraca.htm

Ruiz Albi, Irene. *La reina doña Urraca (1109–1126), cancillería y colección diplomática*. León: Centro de Estudiose e Investgatión San Isadora, 2003.

See also **Iberia; Queens and Empresses, Consorts of; Queens and Empresses: The West**

URSULA AND HER COMPANIONS

The cult of St. Ursula and the eleven thousand virgins of Cologne (Feast Day, October 21) were among the most ubiquitous of the later Middle Ages. Largely due to the widespread diffusion of their relics and their appropriateness as role models for both religious and secular women, the holy virgins of Cologne were venerated across Europe.

The earliest document of a cult of unnamed and unnumbered holy virgins in early medieval Cologne can be found on the Clematius Inscription, an early fifth-century stone plaque in their titular church in Cologne. Over the course of the ninth through thirteenth centuries, the legend of the holy virgins of Cologne was gradually developed, expanded, and codified in a series of *passiones*. Ursula was a Christian princess of Britannia who was promised in marriage to a pagan prince, Aetherius. She requested a delay of several years, during which she and eleven thousand companions would make a pilgrimage to Rome. During their return trip, they were martyred by the Huns besieging Cologne.

In 1106, excavations outside the walls of Cologne uncovered thousands of bodies, which were proclaimed to be the relics of the eleven thousand virgins. This discovery appeared to prove the veracity of the legend, including the astounding number of eleven thousand holy virgins. The most probable explanation can be attributed to an interpretive error through which an inscription "XI M," signifying "undecim martyrum" (eleven martyrs), was misread as indicating "undecim milium" or eleven thousand, by interpreting the "M" as the roman numeral for 1,000. With the help of mystics, particularly Elisabeth of Schönau, the relics were authenticated and the story was fleshed out, ultimately taking on its elaborate form popularized through the *Golden Legend*.

As early as 1113, Cologne began exporting large quantities of the relics uncovered in the excavations. By the fourteenth century, relics of the holy virgins could be found in cities and monasteries across the map of Europe, often in immense collections, such as the thousand bodies acquired in 1182 by the monastery of Altenberg, near Cologne. Despite the far-flung distribution of relics, their greatest concentration remained in the Rhineland, particularly Cologne, where the relics could be found in every church.

Eventually the holy virgins joined the Three Magi as patrons of the city.

Though the identity of St. Ursula as the leader was established by the tenth century, the group was commemorated and referenced as a collective mass—*Undecim millium virginum* (eleven thousand virgins). This group identity informed the presentation of their relics, as well as the form of much of the imagery associated with this cult, in which the holy virgins of Cologne were represented *en masse*, as though individuality was subsumed into corporate identity. Frequently portrayed as a group of eleven idealized women, as eleven followers beneath the mantle of St. Ursula, or as eleven flames on the coat of arms of late medieval Cologne, the holy virgins of Cologne were consistently identified by their collective cohesion. Described and depicted as an undifferentiated mass of holy virgins, the eleven thousand virgins of Cologne cogently visualized the monastic requirement that one surrender her individual identity to that of the unified ecclesiastical body.

Images—particularly reliquary figures—were used to foster the standing of the eleven thousand virgins as role models for religious women. Several important artistic programs in Cologne utilized relics and reliquary figures to create a dynamic sacral environment in which the (principally female) audience is both situated and actively involved, as religious women are invited to follow the model of the holy virgins and literally join their sacred company. The motherhouse and titular church of the cult, the *ecclesia sanctarum undecim milum virginum* (Church of the Holy Eleven Thousand Virgins) in Cologne, literally surrounds the viewers (both secular parishioners and cloistered Benedictine nuns) with relics and reliquary figures to fashion a palpable connection between saints and devotees. The altarpiece made for the high altar of the church of the Poor Clares in Cologne circa 1347 presents a group of twelve reliquary busts of Holy Virgins who appear as female apostles. Analogous examples can be found throughout Europe.

In many ways, Ursula and her companions provided ideal role models for the realization of women's religious calling in the later Middle Ages and Renaissance. As Europe's largest group of holy women, the holy virgins of Cologne exemplified the glories of spiritual betrothal to Christ, virginity and chastity, martyrdom, and erudition, offering religious women a collective model for *imitatio Christi*. The fifteenth-century Dominican Giovanni Dominici singled out the eleven thousand virgins as fitting role models for young women. In the sixteenth century, Sister Angela Merici dedicated her Ursuline order to St. Ursula, whose name had become synonymous with the corporate body of the eleven thousand virgins and female spirituality.

SCOTT B. MONTGOMERY

References and Further Reading

Günter Zehnder, Frank. *Sankt Ursula. Legende-Verehrung-Bilderwelt*. Cologne: Wienand Verlag, 1985.

Holladay, Joan A. "Relics, Reliquaries, and Religious Women: Visualizing the Holy Virgins of Cologne." *Studies in Iconography* 18 (1997): 67–118.

Montgomery, Scott B. "Corporate Corporeality: The Cult of St. Ursula and the Eleven Thousand Virgins." In *Old Masters in Context: Romanino's "Mystic Marriage of Saint Catherine,"* edited by Victor Coonin. Brooks Museum of Art Bulletin, No. 4. Memphis: Brooks Museum of Art, 2003, pp. 37–49.

Sheingorn, Pamela, and Marcelle Thiébaux, trans. *The Passion of Saint Ursula and The Sermon on the Birthday of Saint Ursula*. Toronto: Peregrina, 1996.

Solzbacher, Joseph and Veronika Hopmann. *Die Legende der Heiligen Ursula*. Cologne: Wienand Verlag, 1964.

See also **Elisabeth of Schönau; Hagiography; Hagiography, Iconographic Aspects of; Jacobus de Voragine's Golden Legend; Relics and Reliquaries**

V

VALKYRIES

Valkyries, from Old Norse *valkyrja* (choosers of the slain), were originally semidivine warrior women, attendants of the war-god Odin, who chose warriors to die in battle and escorted them to Valhalla (hall of the slain) to await the final battle of Ragnarok (doom of the gods). Terms like *skjaldmaer* ("shield-maidens") and *hjálmvitr* ("helmeted beings") reflect the valkyries' warlike nature. They sometimes appear as malevolent and sometimes as benevolent figures. Saxo Grammaticus (c. 1200) says that valkyries can alter their appearance from fearsome to beautiful. The valkyries appear in the *Poetic Edda* (assembled in the thirteenth century from earlier mythological poems). In the *Poetic Edda,* the most important valkyrie is Brynhild, and several poems recount her love for the mortal hero Sigurd. In later skaldic poetry, valkyries are merely the beautiful and benign messengers of Odin, but nameless and undifferentiated.

Brynhild was famous throughout the Germanic world and appears in the Middle High German *Nibelungenlied* (early thirteenth century). Richard Wagner (1876) used material from the Nibelung saga and the character of Brynhild in his epic opera *Der Ring des Nibelungen.* The Old English cognate of Old Norse *valkyrja* is *wælcyrge,* a term that always refers to an evil being associated with slaughter. Nora K. Chadwick argues that Grendel's mother of *Beowulf,* who is a *wælgæst wæfre* ("roaming slaughter spirit"), is influenced by the malevolent figure of the valkyrie. Literary figures like Wealtheow, the Danish queen in *Beowulf,* are beautiful and adorned with gold and reflect the benevolent figure of the valkyrie.

ALEXANDRA H. OLSEN

References and Further Reading

Chadwick, Nora K. "The Monsters and *Beowulf.*" In *The Anglo-Saxons: Studies in Some Aspects of Their History and Culture Presented to Bruce Dickins,* edited by Peter Clemoes. London: Bowes and Bowes, 1959, pp. 171–203.

Heaney, Seamus, trans. *Beowulf.* New York: W. W. Norton, 2000.

Hollander, Lee M., trans. *Poetic Edda.* Austin: University of Texas Press, 1977.

Mowatt, D. G., trans. *Nibelungenlied.* London and New York: Dent and Dutton, 1965.

Saxo Grammaticus. *The History of the Danes,* translated by Peter Fisher and edited by Hilda Roderick Ellis Davidson. 2 vols. Totowa, N.J.: Rowan & Littlefield, 1979.

See also **Amazons; Beowulf; Magic and Charms; Supernatural Women; Warfare**

VERONICA'S VEIL

Though not mentioned in any Gospel account, Veronica (feast day July 12) became associated with the tale of a woman of Jerusalem who offered her veil to wipe Christ's face on the Way to Calvary. Both the woman and the cloth, onto which Christ's features were miraculously transferred, are referred to as Veronica—a conflation popularized by the etymological connection with *vera icona* (true image). This cloth, believed to bear the likeness of Christ, was the most popular of the *acheiropoietoi* (images not made by human hands) in the later Middle Ages. Apocryphal accounts, such as the fourth-century *Acts of Pilate,* link Veronica with the woman cured of a hemorrhage by touching Jesus's robe (Matthew 9:20–22, Mark 5:25–34, Luke 8:43–48), fostering the connection between the woman, the miraculous cloth, and female spirituality.

The story recounted in Jacobus de Voragine's *Golden Legend* has Veronica bringing the veil to Rome. The miraculous image was venerated in Rome by the eighth century. In 1297 Boniface VIII had it placed in St. Peter's basilica.

The cult of the Veronica reached its apogee in the fourteenth and fifteenth centuries, during which time the saint was often included in narratives depicting the Way to Calvary. Images of Veronica displaying the veil to the viewer, or Christ's face on the veil (as seen in pilgrims' badges from Rome), reinforced the effectiveness of contemplation of the Holy Face, and indeed images in general. Images of Veronica's Veil (particularly prints) were popular tools for private devotion, particularly among monastic women, due in part to Veronica's standing as a model of female piety and compassion.

SCOTT B. MONTGOMERY

References and Further Reading

Kuryluk, Ewa. *Veronica & Her Cloth: History, Symbolism, and Structure of a "True" Image.* Cambridge, Mass.: Basil Blackwell, 1991.

See also **Hagiography; Hagiography, Iconographic Aspects of; Jacobus de Voragine's Golden Legend**

VILLON, FRANÇOIS

François Villon (b. c. 1430) came to Paris in his youth and acquired a university education and a criminal record for burglary and manslaughter. He wrote a handful of shorter lyrics and two longer poems, both mock wills: *Le Lais* ("Legacies," c. 1456) and *Le Testament* (c. 1461). He vanishes from view in 1463, when he was banished from Paris. His voice is pseudo-autobiographical, and both of his longer poems are full of distancing irony, scathing satire on civil and ecclesiastical authorities, and bitter attacks on enemies and former lovers—all of which would seem to bind his poems to a cult of masculinity and to make him an uneasy entry here.

But this voice, redolent with a surface *machismo*, makes his self sexually ambivalent in ways that confront gender stereotypes and destabilise sexual identities. In his *Ballade de la Grosse Margot*, for instance, he figures himself as a pimp in a violently exploitative relationship with his lover Margot—but the poem overall centralises the uneasy attitudes to sexuality (and money) that underlie what it is conventional to call "courtly love," by iconising the realities of the power relationship. Another lyric, the *Ballade pour Robert d'Estouteville*, is by contrast a celebration of mutuality, of male potency and mature sexuality: a paean of praise to "Ambroise" that is a vision of an idyllic contentment. But it is when Villon plays with voices—his own and those of women—that his work has its most interesting implications for the cultural constructions of gender: his mother's sense of complicity with the mother-ness of the Virgin Mary (*Ballade pour prier Nostre Dame*), and above all his masterly invention of a female voice, that of the *Belle Heaulmiere*, "the beautiful helmet-maker," now, in old age, a prostitute, and who, in a lingering catalogue of body parts, compares her past loveliness with her present decrepitude, her once-sexualised with her now-sexless body.

Too often in the Middle Ages, such types are used to serve male fantasy, or for stereotypical and exemplary purposes—the ills of old age as retribution for a misspent youth. Here, by contrast, because the voice is that of the woman herself rather than that of the voyeuristic, moralising male, the Belle Heaulmiere inspires a real sympathy: her female subjectivity disrupts what may be the readers' comfortable homosocial complicities. More remarkable again is the ballade that follows, a little homily to occasional prostitutes (*filles de joie*): they are, she says, to be hard-headedly mercenary, capitalise on youth, ensure a comfortable old age. Women's self-seeking is a stereotype, of course (as in the *Roman de la Rose*), but, by using a woman's voice unmediated, Villon has his Belle Heaulmiere usurp a cherished male prerogative by speaking knowledgeably about sexuality, money and power—she and the *filles de joie* claim the right to enjoy control over their erotic encounters, and thus to refuse the place of silent submission commonly allotted to women. Villon, it may be said, invests female subjectivity with uncommon lucidity and an unusual degree of self-affirmation.

JANE TAYLOR

References and Further Reading

Kuhn, David. *La poétique de François Villon.* Paris: A. Colin, 1967.

Taylor, Jane H. M. *The Poetry of François Villon.* Cambridge: Cambridge University Press, 2001.

Villon, François. *The Complete Poems*, edited and translated by Barbara N. Sargent-Baur. Toronto: University Toronto Press, 1994.

See also **Femininity and Masculinity; France, Northern; Gender Ideologies; Literature, Old French; Prostitutes**

VIOLENCE

The Middle Ages has always been considered a period of impulsive and irrational violence and cruelty. However, during the last decade, medievalists have endeavored to demonstrate that this image is inaccurate. Obsolete paradigms and terminology that hindered a better understanding of medieval violent behavior and its mechanisms are undergoing a systematic deconstruction. Even the traditional concept of the feud has now been abandoned in favor of the term *customary vengeance*, which describes "any individual wrongs avenged by violence or resolved by the threat of violence" (Halsall). Despite regional diversity and chronological variation throughout the Middle Ages, violence, basically defined as any agonistic exchange, whether provocative or competitive, dual or collective, verbal or physical, impulsive or ritual, is undoubtedly a central trait of medieval culture and literature. But far from being uncontrolled or chaotic, as some clerical sources would like us to believe, it obeys certain rules or conventions. Often associated with a notion of honor, characterized as a general system of exchanges (gift/counter-gift and challenge/counter-challenge), violence is an important component of social interaction and, more specifically, an aristocratic strategy of distinction.

Alongside matrimonial strategies, funerals, and ostentatious wealth, the purpose of violence, or at times simply the threat of violence, was to display the excellence and the omnipotence of the family or lineage and at the same time to demarcate its position in the hierarchy of power. Understood in this perspective, the active or potential use of violence was not a mere disordered way of settling scores but a structuring strategy, especially in the early Middle Ages, when authority was sometimes no more than influence. Among the various forms of medieval violence, vengeance represents a common feature. Related to a more or less systematized set of values that vouches for and legitimizes the specific status of an individual in a social class or the collective worth of a group within a specific society, vengeance is a proof that a sense of justice was deeply rooted in medieval culture and mentalities. Vengeance, often described as an unleashed outburst of anger caused by an offense, was far from spontaneous. Vindication followed a ritual pattern in which different components, such as the delay of retaliation, the public moaning, the choice of the right timing in a public space, the

necessity of eyewitnesses, and the support of collective solidarity, were required in order for it to be considered as a legitimate and ethical social act. The main target of medieval exchanges of violence, at least till the end of the feudal period, was to maintain the status quo among different magnate factions, to ensure social order, and to establish a hierarchical balance of power and social precedence.

Female Violence

Although widely studied, the approach to medieval violence still suffers from gender bias. Whereas mechanisms of male violence are fully analyzed and explained in the context of political and social conflicts and strategies, female violence has not yet received enough attention, even in the early Middle Ages, when women's aggression was particularly well recorded by the sources. The reason stems from a combination of several factors. First of all, female violence was certainly less recurrent or, in certain cases, less discernible than its male counterpart. The early medieval archeological evidence corroborates this state of affairs. Weapons, the classic male signifier, were absent in female Germanic graves. Moreover, some barbarian codes of laws, such as the Frankish *Pactus legis salicae*, do not even mention its possible existence. But this silence is not proof of its nonexistence. The fact that Burgundian and Lombard codes and later on the *Lex Salica Karolina* severely castigate women's aggression corroborates its existence well before the ninth century. Secondly, as a consequence of the hegemonic feminist ethic, which legitimately considers women as the victims rather than as the performers of violence, historians have not yet found it necessary to conceptualize female aggressive violence as a historical object. Furthermore, since the majority of anecdotes recounting women's aggression are interpreted by historians as literary artifacts, female violence is frequently relegated to the domain of fiction. This is the case with the Hetzerin, one of the most remarkable heroines of Old Norse literature. According to Jochens, the goading woman who urges an unwilling and frightened man to avenge family honor is a male fantasy, a mere figment of some cleric's misogynous imagination. It could be assumed, on the contrary, that the long-term existence of this character, from Tacitus to Gregory of Tours as well as from Anglo-Saxon and Icelandic sources such as in *Sturlunga saga*, proves the tangible permanence of this type of female conduct.

Theoretical Issues

The methodological resort to gender categories whenever female behavior is at stake remains complicated. The history of female violence is certainly affected by gender ideologies of both medieval authors and contemporary historians. But, while casting new light on gendered social representations, particularly relevant in the context of the later Middle Ages, this historical conceptual approach tends to fix the interpretation of women's behavior in a strict, unchanging way.

However, beyond the historical consistency characterizing the relation between genders, it is necessary to note the variability of past gender systems and to recognize the exception. This point of view is particularly relevant for Merovingian noble and royal women. Long relegated to the category of curiosities or monstrosities, their violent activity has never been studied in the perspective of a class strategy. Thanks to a fluid gender ideology, Merovingian queens (Brunhild and Fredegund), princesses (Clothild, Caribert's daughter), and noble women could actively participate in the cycle of violence and even initiate their own vengeance. Following the example of their male counterparts, they obeyed a familial and personal code of honor aiming at the growth of wealth, power, and social precedence.

Cross-Dressing and Female Violence

During the central Middle Ages, female violence remains noticeable in narratives and legal records. The *chansons de gestes* feature women involved in military activities, warfare, and revenge but in a somewhat different manner. Within the delimited frame of chivalrous ideology, which conceived of aggression and warfare as exclusively male attributes and activities, female violence became increasingly marginalized. It could still function, but only by borrowing a male identity. The topos of female transvestites confirms a change of attitude, which is certainly related, from the Carolingian period onwards, to the growing penetration of Christian influence and its constraints, demanding a strict representation of the division of labor between the sexes. In romances of the eleventh to the thirteenth century, cross-dressing expressed the author's ambivalence. While allowing women to fight in certain cases, it still preserved the gender hierarchy.

Yet, in the late Middle Ages, the mindset changed significantly. Considered subversive because it undermined the dividing line between sexual roles and the principle of male domination, this topos became the expression of women's deceit and powerlessness. Even disguised as men, women could not hide their true weak and inferior nature. The paradigm of this new strict attitude towards women's use of violence is exemplified by Joan of Arc, a young peasant woman who led the French armies during the Hundred Years' War. She was condemned to death by the Church precisely for her cross-dressing. With the development of nascent states and capitalist economy emerging from feudal society, violence ceased to be a social marker. The ongoing formation of differentiated public and private spheres definitively destroyed the opportunity for women to defend their family honor. When female violence is recorded in judicial registers during the fifteenth century and onwards, it has lost its social signification and become simple criminality.

NIRA PANCER

References and Further Reading

Balzaretti, R. "'These Are Things That Men Do, Not Women': The Social Regulation of Female Violence in Langobard Italy." In *Violence and Society in the Early Medieval West*, edited by Guy Halsall. Rochester, N.Y.: Boydell, 1998, pp. 175–193.

Gradowicz–Pancer, N. "De-Gendering Female Violence: Merovingian Female Honour as an 'Exchange of Violence'." *Early Medieval Europe* 11.1 (2002): 1–18.

Halsall, Guy, ed. *Violence and Society in the Early Medieval West*. Rochester, N.Y.: Boydell, 1998.

———. "Female Status and Power in Early Merovingian Central Austrasia: The Burial Evidence." *Early Middle Ages* 5 (1996): 1–24.

Jochens, J. "The Medieval Icelandic Heroine: Fact or Fiction?" *Viator* 17 (1987): 35–50.

See also **Brunhild and Fredegund; Crime and Criminals; Cross-Dressing; Domestic Abuse; Gender Ideologies; Honor and Reputation; Incest; Joan of Arc; Literature, Old Norse; Private and Public Spheres; Rape and Raptus; Romance, French; Warfare**

VIRGIN MARTYRS

Narratives concerning virgin martyrs such as Catherine de Alexandria, Margaret of Antioch, Agnes, and Cecilia form one of the largest categories of hagiographical literature and were told across Europe and the Christian Near East from late antiquity to the late Middle Ages and beyond. Often intended for female audiences, they are highly conventional in terms of plot, recounting the story of a young and beautiful woman whose virginity is threatened either by rape (Lucy, Agnes) or by a proposed marriage (Cecilia, Ursula); she chooses to submit to death rather than renounce her virginity. Graphically violent, the narrative of virgin martyrdom usually includes a series of exchanges between the virgin and a pagan persecutor, alternating with an escalating sequence of tortures; sometimes the devil himself makes an appearance (Margaret, Juliana). In spite of its apparently sadistic content, the story of the virgin martyr was evidently appealing to medieval women both as readers and as writers.

Historical Development

In late antiquity, martyrdom was revered as the most perfect *imitatio Christi* (imitation of Christ). During the Roman persecutions, the execution of women was considered particularly shocking and affecting; contemporary accounts of the martyrdoms of Christians such as Perpetua and Felicity emphasize the courage of women confronted by dreadful and public death. Historical accounts suggest that rape was sometimes used by the Romans as a method of political repression, since the desire of Christian women to preserve their virginity was seen as a form of resistance to the power of the Roman state; this may account for the importance of the threat of rape in hagiographic plots.

The historical reality of persecution found reflection in fictional narratives emphasizing the inviolable virginity of the protagonist. In the apocryphal *Acts of Thecla*, the heroine is an independent female apostle who baptizes herself and evangelizes Asia Minor after having survived several attempted martyrdoms. In the West, less radical models proved more influential and programmatic. Ambrose's version of the passion of Agnes in *On Virgins* (late fourth century) and Prudentius's poems in honor of Agnes and Eulalia (early fifth century) emphasize not the virgin's independence but her vulnerable body and willing submission to torture and death.

Virgin martyr narratives multiplied in the Middle Ages, in both Latin and the vernacular. The seventh-century Anglo-Saxon author Aldhelm, writing in Latin, composed two catalogues of virgins, mostly martyrs, for the edification of the nuns of Barking Abbey. Hrotsvit of Gandersheim's virgin martyr stories, composed in the tenth century, are strikingly original and bear witness to the broad geographical distribution of the tradition. Her verse dramas include two plays dealing with the martyrdom of virgins. The better known of these, *Agapes, Chione and Hirena* (sometimes called *Dulcitius*), is of Greek origin and probably came to Germany with Theophano, the Byzantine wife of Otto II; it tells the story of three girls supposed to have been martyred under Diocletian and is remarkable for its humor and merciless exposition of male stupidity. Hrotsvit's collection of hexameter *Legends* includes a version of the story of Agnes in which the martyr is represented not as a suffering body but as a rational proponent of virginity. Even more unusual is the story of Pelagius, a male virgin martyred in Mozarabic Spain. Hildegard of Bingen, for whom virginity was a driving theological concept, composed an elaborate song series dedicated to St. Ursula and her eleven thousand virgin companions in about 1150.

After the twelfth century, virgin martyr legends flourished in French and Middle English (there are two notable ninth-century examples, Cynewulf's *Juliana*, in Old English, and the anonymous Old French *Sequence of St Eulalia*). Many of these texts were intended for female audiences; some were written by women. Clemence of Barking's *Life of St. Catherine* (c. 1175) is an Anglo-Norman verse romance that expands on its Latin source by giving the heroine a sophisticated theological perspective likely to be appreciated by Clemence's fellow nuns. Anonymous thirteenth-century French romances about Agnes, Barbara, Christina, and Margaret survive in multiple manuscripts, an indication of popularity. The so-called Katherine Group, composed in Middle English in the thirteenth century for an audience of anchoresses, includes stories about Margaret, Catherine, and Juliana. Osbern Bokenham's *Legends of Holy Women* (1447), although not exclusively concerned with virgin martyrs, contains dedications to several female patrons.

Influence and Afterlife

The most influential hagiographical collection, Jacobus de Voragine's *Golden Legend* (c. 1260), was composed in Latin but was quickly translated into vernaculars from Spanish to German. Virgin martyrs form the largest category of female saints in the *Legend*, and several scholars have pointed out the conservative implications of Jacobus's decision to privilege these narratives over those of historical women saints like Clare of Assisi. In a period marked by religious innovations, from Franciscanism to the rise of lay movements like the Beguines and heretical sects like the Cathars, all offering new devotional possibilities to women, Jacobus's emphasis on virgin martyrs appears nostalgic and reactionary. The *Golden Legend* reduces or eliminates those elements in particular narratives that might be read as protofeminist; femi-nine sanctity is reduced to a single, realistically inimi-table model. The *Legend* inspired Chaucer's *Second Nun's Tale* of St. Cecilia, and its translation and publication by Caxton in 1483 ensured the survival of a particularly conventional version of the virgin martyr story into the early modern period.

The late Middle Ages also saw a multiplicity of visual representations of virgin martyrs in every me-dium: stained glass, paintings, miniatures, sculpture. Many are extremely graphic, focusing on the mutila-tion of the female body, including detached body parts (eyes, breasts). These images were available to an illiterate public with no access to more nuanced versions. Visual representations, however, combined with oral tradition, were sufficient to inspire the career of Joan of Arc. Calling herself "La Pucelle" (the virgin or the maid) and claiming inspiration from Catherine and Margaret, Joan led French resis-tance against the English in the last phases of the Hundred Years' War. She was executed by the En-glish for heresy—an execution indistinguishable from martyrdom, as several contemporaries noted. Her canonization, in 1920, and her worldwide popularity demonstrate a continuing fascination with the image of the virgin martyr. Another late example, that of Maria Goretti, is more disturbing. In 1909, the twelve-year-old Maria, who had been frequently threatened by a neighbor, died after being stabbed by him for resisting his sexual advances. Aware of his intent, Maria did little to avoid the encounter that led to her death. These two examples demon-strate powerfully the different ways in which the ex-ample of the virgin martyr could be internalized by real women.

Much feminist scholarship on virgin martyrs has represented these narratives as misogynistic, part of a patriarchal mechanism for the control of women's bodies, voices, and lives; certainly, the emphasis on torture and rape in the narratives often seems like a projection of the most violent sort of antifeminist fantasy. Other scholars have noted the importance of the virgin martyr as an inspirational and empower-ing role model for medieval women. Given the lon-gevity of the genre, the differing investments of male and female authors, and the varied contexts in which the tales have been told and retold over centuries, it is probably a mistake to suggest that the message of the virgin martyr narrative can be definitively reduced to one of either feminine empowerment or feminine dis-enfranchisement. Narratives of virgin martyrdom provide fertile ground upon which differing religious, sexual, and cultural ideologies play themselves out in a bewildering variety of ways.

MAUD BURNETT MCINERNEY

References and Further Reading

Bokenham, Osbern. *Legendys of Hooly Wummen*, edited by Mary S. Serjeantson, Early English Text Society, Old Stories, 206. London: Oxford University Press, 1938.
Cameron, Averil. "Virginity as Metaphor: Women and the Rhetoric of Early Christianity." In *History as Text: The Writing of Ancient History*, edited by A. Cameron. London: Duckworth, 1989, pp. 185–205.
Cazelles, Brigitte. *The Lady as Saint: A Collection of French Hagiographic Romances of the Thirteenth Century*. Phi-ladelphia: University of Pennsylvania Press, 1991.
Heffernan, Thomas J. "Virgin Mothers." In *Sacred Biogra-phy: Saints and Their Biographers in the Middle Ages*. Oxford: Oxford University Press, 1988, pp. 231–299.
Innes-Parker, Catherine. "Sexual Violence and the Female Reader: Symbolic 'Rape' in the Saints' Lives of the Katherine Group." *Women's Studies* 24 (1995): 205–217.
Jacob of Voragine. *The Golden Legend*, translated by W. G. Ryan. 2 vols. Princeton, N.J.: Princeton University Press, 1993.
Kelly, Kathleen Coyne. *Performing Virginity and Testing Chastity in the Middle Ages*. London: Routledge, 2000.
Lapidge, Michael, and James L. Rosier, trans. *Aldhelm: The Poetic Works*. Cambridge: D. S. Brewer, 1985.
McInerney, Maud Burnett. *Eloquent Virgins from Thecla to Joan of Arc*. New York: Palgrave Macmillan, 2003.
Sherman, Gail Berkeley. "Saints, Nuns and Speech in the Canterbury Tales." In *Images of Sainthood in Medieval Europe*, edited by Renate Blumenfeld-Kosinski and Timea Szell. Ithaca, N.Y.: Cornell University Press.
Winstead, Karen A. *Virgin Martyrs: Legends of Sainthood in Late Medieval England*. Ithaca, N.Y.: Cornell Univer-sity Press, 1997.
Wogan-Browne, Jocelyn, and Glynn Burgess. *Virgin Lives and Holy Deaths: Two Exemplary Biographies for Anglo-Norman Women*. London: Everyman, 1996.

See also **Bokenham, Osbern; Catherine of Alexandria; Clemence of Barking; Foy; Hagiography; Hagiography, Iconographic Aspects of; Hildegard of Bingen; Hrotsvit of Gandersheim; Jacobus de Voragine's Golden Leg-end; Joan of Arc; Katherine Group; Margaret of Anti-och; Rape and Raptus; Ursula and Her Companions; Virginity**

VIRGINITY

Virginity—a concept that richly elaborated on the bare fact of sexual inexperience—had a very high profile in medieval Europe. Virginity was at once the highest of ideals, a condition that enabled humans to aspire to transcend their limitations and become angel-like, and a day-to-day lifestyle to which many thousands of fallible individuals were committed, with varying degrees of success. Sexual renunciation was a founding principle of the religious orders, meaning that most monks, nuns, friars, hermits, and recluses were virgins and that all were sworn to observe chastity. Once clerical celibacy had been enforced, following the Gregorian Reform of the eleventh century, the secular clergy joined the ranks of presumptive virgins. Jesus and Mary were the prime exemplars of male and female perpetual virginity, with the latter in particular often depicted as the leader of a crowd of virgins. Virginity had many variants. It could be imagined in religious, medical, and legal terms: it could be male or female, temporary or permanent, a bodily state or a spiritual exercise. Technically, virginity was the condition of total sexual inexperience and as such distinct from chastity, the virtue of sexual continence, which could be practised by virgins and nonvirgins alike. However, the distinction was not always firm, for being a virgin encompassed chaste practice as well as a personal history and bodily condition of sexual inexperience.

Although virginity sometimes disrupted normal expectations of gendered behaviour, in medieval practice it had distinct male and female forms. As all secular clergy and most monastics were men, male virgins heavily outnumbered female; virginity, however, was a condition more strongly associated with women and more significant to them. There are good reasons for most medieval and modern writing on virginity to take women's virginity as the paradigm of the state. Virgin was a sociolegal status and category of sanctity for women only. Male virgins were almost always so by virtue of their clerical or religious status, and it was that status, not virginity itself, that constituted their social identity. Women's virginity, but not men's, was a marketable commodity and a bodily condition that could be identified by medical procedures.

A Christian Concept

Virginity is one of the great inventions of Christian theology, marking a significant departure from both its Hebrew and its classical sources. For early Christian communities, to reject marriage was to reject citizenship, householding, public office: virginity indicated a radical refusal of the world. When St. Augustine defined sexual desire as the consequence and perpetual reminder of the Fall, the corollary was that to refuse to act upon such desires was to reassert control over the body and to aspire to imitate prelapsarian perfection. The practice of virginity enabled the clerical and religious elite to separate itself from the married laity. Though virginity was necessarily a minority option, it was normally regarded as the superior spiritual state, a superiority often enumerated in the claim that in heaven, married Christians would be rewarded thirty fold, the widowed sixtyfold, and the virgins one hundredfold. This relative evaluation can be traced back to the earliest Christian texts, such as St. Paul's assessment, "It is good for them if they abide even as I. But if they cannot contain, let them marry: for it is better to marry than to burn" (1 Cor. 7:8–9). Marriage was a sacrament and a state over which the Church increased its control during the Middle Ages. Pastoral guides are full of detailed discussions of the obligations of married people to one another, to their parents, and to their children; yet the sense that marriage was a grudging concession to the weakness of the flesh persisted, and was most freely voiced in commendations of virginity.

In theological and moralistic terms, virginity was located more fundamentally in the will than in the body. Hence it was not necessarily identical with lack of sexual experience. Bodily virginity was worthless in the absence of humility, meaning that virginity was nullified if the virgin took pride in the condition. Indulgence in sexual fantasy would mar virginity; even to be the unwitting object of another's desire could mar virginity. A virgin who was not committed to maintaining the state was thereby, according to the stricter spiritual guides, not a true virgin: it follows that virginity must be freely chosen. Conversely, it was possible to argue, following St. Augustine, that a virgin could retain virginity if she had been raped, so long as she had never faltered in her intention to remain a virgin. The emphasis on the will makes it possible to imagine that a redoubled commitment to chaste practice might enable the recovery of lost virginity.

Religious imagery, however, celebrated virginity as bodily wholeness, a precious treasure held in a fragile vessel, which once broken could not be mended. The virgin body was imagined to be perfectly sealed with that elusive and culturally variable body part, the hymen, and thus as paradigmatically female. Virginity was held to counter the body's usual vulnerability to the processes of change, flux, and decay: the virginal body, contained within its own borders, aspired to immutability. The Virgin Mary was sometimes depicted as youthfully fresh-faced in middle and old age, preserved from aging by the perfection of her virginity. The bodies of virgin saints were often reported to have been discovered miraculously incorrupt in their tombs, in anticipation of the bodily glorification to come at the general resurrection.

Medical Concepts

Medical perspectives, however, recognised the inhuman perfection of virginity to be an unnatural condition for an adult body. Its maintenance was frequently acknowledged to be difficult for most men and women: not for nothing was it described as the new martyrdom. Medical theory held that sexual activity was necessary to keep the body's humours in healthy balance, hence that virginity could be debilitating. In a refinement of this theory, the abbess Hildegard of Bingen concluded that virginity was least difficult and dangerous for those men and women who were dominated by melancholic humours, a category in which she presumably included herself. The bodies of virgin women might suffer from the retention of menstrual fluids and the dissatisfaction of wombs that longed for children: hastily arranged marriages might be recommended to ailing young women. The holiness of those who nevertheless risked their health by persisting with virginity was all the more to be admired. Several lives of holy men include sick-bed narratives in which virtue is proved by a readiness to risk death rather than compromise virginity.

Medical thought considered female virginity to be an objectively identifiable bodily condition. Examination of the hymen (which modern medicine does not consider a reliable indicator) was known, but not routinely practised: it was argued that the procedure risked destroying virginity in the process of confirming it. In this argument, virginity is a purely physical phenomenon with no necessary bearing on an individual's life history or desires. Other tests for discerning female virginity seem to be primarily symbolic statements about purity (a virgin's urine is clear, her gait demure, her eyes downcast) or about the hymeneal seal (a virgin cannot smell a smoking coal or winecask placed beneath her skirts). There are no physical tests recorded for men's virginity, which was not sufficiently commodified to require its own bodily sign.

Virginity as a Life Stage

For women, the purpose of virginity—whether it was intended to be lost or to be kept—made a great deal of difference to its enactment. In literature, the existence of two virgin-centred plots demonstrates this duality. In romance, the virgin is an object of desire, whose plot culminates with the loss of her virginity in marriage; in hagiography, the virgin refuses marriage, and her plot culminates with the confirmation of her virginity in death. The first plot is the ancestor of a still hugely popular genre, wide enough to encompass Jane Austen's novels and *Bridget Jones's Diary*. The second plot, that of the virgin martyr, now has a more specialised appeal, but in its day was as popular, many-faceted, and culturally ubiquitous as the heterosexual romance is today. Virgin martyrs were amongst the most powerful and widely venerated saints, often functioning as role models and protectors to women. In their inviolable purity they stood for the mystical body of Christ, but their example also influenced the lives of individual medieval women. The life of Christina of Markyate, a twelfth-century English recluse and nun, was written in partial imitation of virgin martyr legends, which offered the best narrative model for a young woman's desire to resist the marriage arranged by her parents and to choose her own future. Two of the three saints Joan of Arc named as the source of her voices were virgin martyrs, Catherine of Alexandria and Margaret of Antioch, details of whose legends can be argued to have influenced Joan's androgynous persona.

When virginity was conceptualised as a stage in a woman's lifecycle, it was as the precedent and entry-qualification for marriage and motherhood. Conduct literature for elite women lays great stress on the need for marriageable girls to maintain their virginity, with cautionary tales of the humiliation and punishment of those who failed to do so. Such women were presumably the market for the gynaecological texts that include recipes for constructing false hymens using everyday ingredients such as egg-white and leeches. It was normal for elite girls to be virgins at marriage, when their virginity would be not so much lost as traded in exchange for the property and position of a wife. Outside of the ruling classes, practice was more varied, though here too young women's sexual behaviour was monitored and controlled. In the towns, employers were held responsible for the morals of their women servants and workers; in rural manors, the fine of leyrwite was exacted for women's premarital loss of virginity. Compensation was sometimes payable to women from their lovers to neutralise the damage to their prospects of marriage, thus putting a concrete—and often rather high—value on the virginity even of non-elite women.

Lifelong Virginity

Lifelong virginity marked a decisive break with the usual female life cycle of maidenhood, marriage, and, for some, widowhood. In theory, virginity could enable women to overcome their inherent female weaknesses: several of the Church Fathers admiringly refer to pious virgins as manlike. A commitment to virginity removed a woman from the economy of exchange and sexual difference. Recognition of this logic was often accompanied by an argument for the propriety of controlling virgins' behaviour and interactions with the world. Although their rhetoric was gender-neutral or gender-transcending, the Fathers did not expect committed virgins to aspire to the social privileges of men: as Tertullian argued, such a virgin would be neither male nor female but "a third generic class, some monstrosity with a head of its own."

In medieval Europe, career virginity was an option for only a small proportion of women. Nunneries were fewer and smaller than monasteries for men, and were usually open only to women whose families could afford a substantial entry fee, though at certain times and places it was possible for poorer women to commit to virginity as recluses, lay sisters, hospital sisters, and Beguines. The lives of such career virgins diverged in some key features from those of secular women. They avoided subjection to the authority of husbands, and the dangers of repeated pregnancy and childbirth. Abbesses and prioresses not only had authority over their communities, but could also wield considerable economic and legal power over their tenants and neighbourhoods. Though these powers were also exercised by noble and gentlewomen who administered their family estates, it was only the convent that offered anything like a career structure. However, commitment to virginity did not free women from male control altogether. All religious women relied on clerics for spiritual direction and access to the sacraments, and nunneries often had male administrators as well as being subject to episcopal visitation.

Career virginity improved a woman's chances of attaining literacy and of participating in cultural production. Some women's communities were particularly hospitable to creative activities. Hildegard of Bingen's visions were preserved, interpreted, and illustrated within her community; her contemporary Herrad, abbess of Hohenberg, compiled an illustrated history of the world, *The Garden of Delights*. Sister-books of communal history and biography were written in German convents, and in the thirteenth century a culture of affective mystical writing developed in the nunnery of Helfta. Hildegard's nuns are known to have taken part in dramatic and musical performances; the English nunnery of Barking developed innovative liturgical drama, and it may be that the canoness Hrotsvit of Gandersheim intended her dramas, based on the classical Latin comedies of Terence, for performance in her community. Other women, such as the solitary recluse Julian of Norwich, found forms of religious life that gave them the space and time to think and compose. Much of what is now considered to be the canon of medieval women's writing emerged from a context of institutionalised virginity.

Women committed to virginity were often described as brides of Christ. The legends of women saints martyred in the defence of their virginity represent the saint's death as the supreme pleasure of the consummation of their love for Christ. The imagery of the Song of Songs was used to describe this relationship in highly erotic terms. Narratives and treatises instructed consecrated virgins to think on Christ's superiority to merely human lovers and husbands and to meditate on his beauty, his power, and his tender love for them. In such contexts virginity appears to be itself a sexuality: the virgin is she whose desires are directed to Christ. Male virgins were not excluded from this discourse: St. Bernard of Clairvaux's eighty-six sermons on the Song of Songs are only the best-known example of masculine occupation of the position of the Bride.

Male Virginity

Although sexual restraint was admired in secular men, expectations of their premarital virginity and marital fidelity were not high. The main exception in literature is the grail legends, which attempt to introduce monastic values to chivalric romance, producing a category of virginal heroes. In the grail-quest narratives, the successful grail knights are symbolised as three white bulls amongst a black herd, set aside from their fellows by their virginity. Virginity here is a source of power that enables the knights to perform miraculous feats culminating in the finding of the holy grail. Some male lay saints, such as Edward the Confessor and Elzear of Sabran, were married but believed to have retained their virginity with their wives' agreement. It is evident in their legends that married virginity was an extremely uncommon condition for a layman.

For religious and holy men, virginity was valued, but not the foundation of their identity. Whereas women saints had to protect their virginity from external sexual assault, for male saints the danger was usually perceived to come from within. Virginity did not come easily to male bodies: some argued, indeed, that involuntary nocturnal emissions compromised virginity. The lives of many male saints recount the vigorous ascetic practices—fasting, wearing hair-shirts, self-flagellation, jumping into nettle-beds or freezing water—with which they attempted to dispel sexual temptation and maintain chastity. However, lack of virginity was not insuperable; chaste practice was more important than notional intactness. Aelred of Rievaulx contrasted himself with his sister, a virgin recluse, to lament the loss of his virginity prior to his entry into religion. This loss, however, did not prevent

Aelred from becoming a monk, an abbot, and, in due course, a saint.

SARAH SALIH

References and Further Reading

Bernau, Anke, Ruth Evans, and Sarah Salih, eds. *Medieval Virginities*. Cardiff: University of Wales Press, 2003.

Brown, Peter. *The Body and Society: Men, Women and Sexual Renunciation in Early Christianity*. London: Faber and Faber, 1989.

Bugge, John. Virginitas: *An Essay in the History of a Medieval Ideal*. The Hague: Martinus Nijhoff, 1975.

Carlson, Cindy L., and Angela Jane Weisl, eds. *Constructions of Widowhood and Virginity in the Middle Ages*. New York: St. Martin's Press, 1999.

Elliott, Dyan. *Spiritual Marriage: Sexual Abstinence in Medieval Wedlock*. Princeton, N.J.: Princeton University Press, 1993.

Evans, Ruth. "Virginities." In *The Cambridge Companion to Medieval Women's Writing*, edited by Carolyn Dinshaw and David Wallace. Cambridge: Cambridge University Press, 2003.

Frasetto, Michael, ed. *Medieval Purity and Piety: Essays on Medieval Clerical Celibacy and Religious Reform*. New York: Garland, 1998.

Kelly, Kathleen Coyne. *Performing Virginity and Testing Chastity in the Middle Ages*. London: Routledge, 2000.

Kelly, Kathleen Coyne, and Marina Leslie, eds. *Menacing Virgins: Representing Virginity in the Middle Ages and Renaissance*. Cranbury, N.J.: Associated University Presses, 1999.

McInerney, Maud Burnett. *Eloquent Virgins from Thecla to Joan of Arc*. New York: Palgrave Macmillan, 2003.

Salih, Sarah. *Versions of Virginity in Late Medieval England*. Cambridge: Brewer, 2001.

Wogan-Browne, Jocelyn. *Saints' Lives and Women's Literary Culture c. 1150–1300: Virginity and Its Authorizations*. Oxford: Oxford University Press, 2001.

See also **Abbesses; Ancrene Wisse; Anchoresses; Asceticism; Augustine, Influence of; Bride of Christ: Imagery; Celibacy: Clerical and Priests' Concubines; Christina of Markyate; Demography; Education, Monastic; Hagiography; Herrad of Hohenbourg; Hildegard of Bingen; Hrotsvit of Gandersheim; Katherine Group; Mary, Virgin; Monastic Enclosure; Monasticism and Nuns; Sexuality, Regulation of; Sister-Books and Other Convent Chronicles; Virgin Martyrs; Virile Women**

VIRILE WOMEN

Virility, with its companion quality, virtue, comes from the Latin *vir* (man—as opposed to *homo,* a more generic word embracing both male and female). It is the manliness that all classical authors deemed indispensable to an individual aspiring to authority over other persons. Its essence was self-control and self-determination. The Roman nobility took care to train their male children to be rulers, training and shaping their bodies, their deportment, and their oration to produce manly tones and gestures.

Women were generally ineligible for full virility by virtue of their subordinate condition. A high-status woman was expected to be under the control of her male relatives, her husband, or her son, or, if all else failed, a tutor. Such a woman could and did preside over the government of humbler people, but her principal virtue was obedience to a male superior. This hierarchical system assumed a gender system that diverged dramatically from the system of binary opposites used in less political contexts. Thus, male and female were opposed to one another in abstract contexts such as heat versus cold, light versus dark, and strength versus weakness—generally to the disadvantage of the female principle. Classical biologists, however, recognized that every individual draws from a dual biological inheritance and placed all individuals along a single-gender scale that ranked their degree of manliness. The lower end of the scale was "effeminacy." Women were defined as misbegotten men whose share of sperm had not been sufficiently cooked in the oven of the womb. Virility was not matched by a set of feminine virtues.

First-century Roman writers memorialized the long history of the Roman Republic as a male monopoly, keeping public affairs free of any effeminate taint. Historians of the early empire (first century) perceived that with the transfer of the highest authority to Augustus and his successors, called Fathers of the Country, the gender barrier had been fatally breached. Directors of the imperial household, even some slaves, but most especially the empress, had taken precedence over all other noble Romans. They resisted entitling the Empress Mother of the Country but eventually even accorded the title Mother of the Camps (the army) to her third-century successors. The empress Livia and her successors in power were, of necessity, given the accolade "virile women." Empresses like Messalina, who failed to meet Roman standards of virtue (principally self-control), were criticized in much the same terms as self-indulgent men like Nero.

Among the subordinate women, lower-class men, and slaves, other standards prevailed—for the most part lost to our records. Christianity arose from these groups and demonstrated a different view of virtue. Self-control as practiced by Jesus and his followers led to spiritual, not physical, leadership. The principal element of Christian virility was integrity, a wholeness that resisted penetration and dominance, regardless of pain or pressure, most forcefully represented by a virgin. The Christian virgin or widow who embraced *encrateia* (sexual abstinence) freed herself from the subordination of marriage and sexual submission and was thus fully entitled to compete for the highest levels of manliness. Among the earliest Christian texts, *The Acts of Paul and Thecla* outlines the epic of a Christian virgin whose integrity entitled her to preach and perform baptism, a virgin whose power tamed the beasts sent to devour her in the arena. By the beginning of the third century, the prison diary of the martyr Perpetua testifies to a woman who envisioned that she "became a man" upon entering the arena to contend for her salvation in martyrdom. At the same period, Tertullian violently criticized women who refused to wear a veil on the grounds that they were men and not subject to the restrictions placed on subordinate females.

By the fourth century, the virginity movement had been joined to the expanding monastic movement and religious leaders universally proclaimed the authority of the encratic women who "led the high emprise" and defeated death itself with their incorruptibility. The legendary transvestite saints, women who lived among the desert dwellers in the most ferocious hardship disguised as men, entered into Christian lore.

During the remainder of the first millennium, virile women were among the leaders in the settlement and conversion of Europe. Queens like the Frankish Balthild ruled in their widowed years as kings and then ascended to monastic leadership. In the tenth century, the emperor's daughter, Mathilda, Abbess of Quedlinberg, enjoyed archepiscopal powers, presiding over a reforming synod of German bishops. In the secular world, marriage and inheritance laws enhanced the power of noble women. Remaining subordinate in daughterhood and marriage, women emerged into full virility if the chances offered in a violent world left them in command of the status and wealth of fathers and/or husbands. Contemporaries agreed that it was better to let power flow temporarily into the hands of virile women than to let it escape the family or become the object of too much contention. This situation, despite the complaints of misogynistic chroniclers like Liutprand of Cremona, prevailed through the tenth century, when Adelheid of Burgundy transferred her father's estates and her late husband's Italian crown to her second husband, Otto of Saxony, to establish the Holy Roman Empire. In the eleventh century, Countess Mathilda of Tuscany, who was rumored to have refused consummation of either of her marriages, led her armies in support of Gregory VII's "reforming" papacy. This "reform" resulted in the imposition of celibacy on a clergy eager to restore the woman-free power structure of the Roman Republic. Theologians of both sexes (notably Hildegard of Bingen) produced a gender model based on complementary opposition, and female virility gave way to feminine virtue.

JO ANN MCNAMARA

References and Further Reading

Allen, Prudence. *The Concept of Women: The Aristotelian Revolution, 750 BC–AD 1250.* Montreal and London: Eden Press, 1985.

Bugge, John. *Virginitas: An Essay in the History of a Medieval Ideal.* The Hague: Martinus Nijhoff, 1975.

Clover, Carol J. "Regardless of Sex: Men, Women and Power in Early Northern Europe." *Speculum* 68.2 (1993): 364–388.

McNamara, Jo Ann. "An Unresolved Syllogism: The Search for a Christian Gender System." In *Conflicted Identities and Multiple Masculinities: Men in the Medieval West*, edited by Jacqueline Murray. New York: Garland, 1999, pp. 1–24.

———. "Sexual Equality and the Cult of Virginity in Early Christian Thought." *Feminist Studies* 3.3/4 (1976): 145–158.

Newman, Barbara. *From Virile Woman to WomanChrist: Studies in Medieval Religion and Literature.* Philadelphia: University of Pennsylvania Press, 1995.

Salisbury, Joyce E. *Perpetua's Passion: The Death and Memory of a Young Roman Woman.* New York: Routledge, 1997.

Tertullian. *On Veiling Virgins*, edited by Alexander Roberts and James Donaldson. The Ante-Nicene Fathers 4. Grand Rapids, Mich.: W. B. Eerdmans, 1976.

See also **Adelheid; Chastity and Chaste Marriage; Cross-Dressing; Dowry and Other Marriage Gifts; Femininity and Masculinity; Gender Ideologies; Heiresses; Hildegard of Bingen; Landholding and Property Rights; Mathilda of Tuscany; Monasticism and Nuns; Ottonian Royal Women; Queens and Empresses: The West; Virginity; Widows**

VOICE, FEMALE: IN LITERATURE

The female voice is variously constructed according to the conventions of different genres. Thus, heroic literature projects female speech against a background of male violence and feud. Women can be the repository of civility and courtesy, like Queen Wealhtheow in the Anglo-Saxon epic *Beowulf*; inciters and avengers, like Brynhild and Guthrun in the Norse *Poetic Edda*, Kriemhild in the German *Nibelungenlied*, and an apparently historical Guthrun in *Laxdaela Saga*; or lamenters over men's hostilities, like Guthrun after the killing of Sigurd in the *Edda*, and Guinevere at Arthur's departure for war in the *Alliterative Morte Arthure*.

The lady of courtly lyric and romance inspires noble love or *fin'amor*. She requires her lover to act in accordance with the exacting code of "love service." Famously, in Chrétien de Troyes' *Lancelot*, Guinevere rebukes her lover for hesitating even for a moment to undergo humiliation for her by riding in a cart. Wise and witty women speak in the courtly dialogue poems—*tensos* in Occitan, *jeux partis* in northern French. In *Sir Gawain and the Green Knight*, the charming lady of the castle is both courtly lady and sexual temptress. Lunete and Lyonet, in Chrétien's *Yvain* and Malory's *Tale of Gareth*, respectively, use manipulative language to influence or resolve conflict. Wisdom is purveyed by allegorical female figures like Lady Philosophy in Boethius' *Consolation*, translated by Chaucer and others, Lady Reason in the *Romance of the Rose*, and the idealised Beatrice in Dante's *Divine Comedy*.

In the pastourelle, a smooth-talking knight or clerk meets a lower-class girl and attempts to seduce her. Here, the clash of gender and status is underlined by a difference in idiom: female directness versus male guile. The outcome varies, and the woman's tone shifts between cynicism and pathos. In the *chanson de malmariée*, a pretty young woman defies her boorish, brutal, and very likely impotent old husband, and flaunts her handsome, polished, and virile lover. The domineering wife of a henpecked husband is another stereotype, behind which lies a tradition of male, especially clerical, misogyny. Chaucer's Wife of Bath, who narrates with gusto how she wielded the mastery over her five husbands, is a well-known example.

In the Arabic–Spanish *kharjas*, female-voice codas to male-voice poems in classical Arabic or Hebrew, attractive young women confess their sexual feelings or encounters. Somewhat similarly, in the later Galician–Portuguese *cantigas de amigo* ("songs about a lover"), most of which are by known male authors, young girls confide their feelings to their mother or a girl friend. An outspoken girl in an anonymous Italian poem, "Mother, the time has come" (to get married), declares that she desires a young man physically. Girls who have been seduced and abandoned lament alone in *chansons de délaissée*—in French, English, and other languages.

The death lament and the love complaint have religious analogues in Mary lamenting for her Son, and the Bride yearning for her beloved in the Old Testament Song of Songs. The two figures are intertwined in the Middle English *In a tabernacle of a tour*, with its Latin refrain "quia amore langueo" ("because I am pining with love"); the voice is Mary's as intercessor for the soul, but these words are the Bride's. Medieval mysticism is often associated with the female voice: Hildegard von Bingen and later Mechthild of Magdeburg in Germany, Birgitta in Sweden, Julian of Norwich and Margery Kempe in England, Catherine of Siena in Italy. The learned voice of medieval Latin is used by Hildegard, Birgitta, and Catherine, as well as abbess Heloise, writing to her fomer lover Peter Abelard.

Female-authored texts tend to present more independent women's voices; for example, the Muslim princess Wallada in early medieval Spain, the fourteenth-century "Queen of Mallorca," and the trobairitz, the women troubadours of Occitania, all of whom assertively express their desires and opinions. Is it possible to assign female-voice works to female authors on the basis of style? An interesting case is "Toute-Belle," who contributes poems to Guillaume de Machaut's *Livre du Voir-Dit*. The sections in her voice are different, whether because they actually are by another author or because this is the way Machaut thought a young woman would write. Anonymous texts in the female voice used to be regarded as male-authored, but this assumption has been challenged lately, notably with regard to the women trouvères of northern France. At any rate, it seems to be the case that anonymous poetry in which women speak merely as saucy wantons or vulnerable innocents has more in common with identifiably male-authored than with female-authored texts.

ANNE L. KLINCK

References and Further Reading

Dinshaw, Carolyn, and David Wallace, eds. *The Cambridge Companion to Medieval Women's Writing*. Cambridge: Cambridge University Press, 2003.

Doss-Quinby, Eglal, Joan Tasker Grimbert, Wendy Pfeffer, and Elizabeth Aubrey, eds. *Songs of the Women Trouvères*. New Haven: Yale University Press, 2001.

Klinck, Anne L. "Poetic Markers of Gender in Medieval 'Woman's Song': Was Anonymous a Woman?" *Neophilologus* 87 (2003): 339–359.

Krueger, Roberta L., ed. *The Cambridge Companion to Medieval Romance*. Cambridge: Cambridge University Press, 2000.

Solterer, Helen. *The Master and Minerva: Disputing Women in French Medieval Culture*. Berkeley, Calif.: University of California Press, 1995.

Wheeler, Bonnie, and Fiona Tolhurst, eds. *On Arthurian Women: Essays in Memory of Maureen Fries*. Dallas: Scriptorium, 2001.

See also **Beowulf; Courtly Love; Debate Literature; Femininity and Masculinity; Gender Ideologies; Guinevere; Mary, Virgin; Misogyny; Mysticism and Mystics; Pastourelle;** *Roman de la Rose* **and Its Reception; Wife of Bath; Women Authors: German Texts; Women Authors: Italian Texts; Women Authors: Latin Texts; Women Authors: Middle English Texts; Women Authors: Old French Texts; Women Authors: Spanish Texts; Woman's Song**

VOWESSES

Vowesses, usually but not always widows, undertook a solemn vow of chastity forbidding voluntary sexual pleasure and prohibiting marriage or remarriage.

The tradition arose among patristic authorities and received continued mention in medieval sources. Often referred to as *velata*, or veiled, women because of rituals accompanying the vow, vowesses may have occupied a quasi-clerical status in the early Church.

Early medieval references identified vowesses as living independently in secular residences. Unlike nuns, vowesses initiated a new spiritual life while retaining control over their resources and maintaining existing secular ties. As monasteries became the preferred locus for female spirituality under Carolingian monastic reforms, secular-dwelling vowesses were discouraged, and distinctions between vowesses and nuns became blurred. However, references to vowesses persisted in canon law, and benedictions for consecrated chastity (separate from monastic vows) appeared in manuscripts from the tenth to the sixteenth centuries. The vowess demonstrated a permanent state of spiritual "widowhood" through her celibacy and prayer.

Canon law required the bishop to complete the vowing ritual, particularly for virgins, although sources sometimes acknowledged that priests or others could substitute. Benedictions for widows and virgins appeared sporadically in episcopal manuscripts, and often in connection with houses of canons, suggesting canons' pastoral responsibilities for vowesses. Continental ceremonies consisted of the woman's veiling and a blessing of her clothing and her person. Specific examples of European vowed women occur mainly in hagiography, particularly in the *vitae* of widowed saints. Later medieval English liturgies described the vowess as donning a mantel, veil, and ring, all blessed by the bishop. The vowess provided confirmation of the vow in writing through the sign of the cross; hence, English episcopal registers listed specific vowesses by name.

KATHERINE CLARK

References and Further Reading

Clark, Katherine. "Pious Widowhood in the Middle Ages." Ph.D. Dissertation, Indiana University, 2002.

Cullum, P. H. "Vowesses and Lay Female Piety in the Province of York." *Northern History* 32 (1996): 21–41.

Erler, Mary. "English Vowed Women at the End of the Middle Ages." *Medaeval Studies* 57 (1995): 155–203.

———. "Three Fifteenth-Century Vowesses." In *Medieval London Widows*, edited by Caroline M. Barron and Anne F. Sutton. London: Hambledon Press, 1994, pp. 165–183.

Parisse, M., ed. *Veuves et Veuvage dans le haut Moyen Âge.* Paris: Picard, 1993.

Wemple, Suzanne F. *Women in Frankish Society.* Philadelphia: University of Pennsylvania Press, 1981.

See also **Chastity and Chaste Marriage; Laywomen, Religious; Virginity; Widows**

WALDENSIANS

The name *Waldensians* was given to the members of the sect by churchmen referring to its founder, Waldes. Waldes began his activity in Lyons in the late 1170s. He was a wealthy burgher who had made his fortune in commerce and finance and then experienced a religious conversion. He distributed his property to the poor and began to preach the adoption of voluntary poverty, a life in the spirit of the Gospels, and penitence. Neither Waldes nor his early followers intended to secede from the Catholic church. All they wanted was to live in poverty, wander, and preach the Gospel. Pope Alexander the Third (1179) prohibited them from preaching without the permission of the diocesan bishop. Though permission was not granted, they continued to preach. They were denounced as disobedient and, finally, condemned as heretics and excommunicated. However, they neither developed a new theology nor a new concept of women's rights in religion. Unlike some other sects, they did not regard the Godhead as a combination of both male and female elements and saw no feminine elements in the vision of redemption at the Second Coming. They did not deny the role of the Virgin Mary as mother of the Redeemer but did not believe in her power to mediate between the faithful and her son and to help those who prayed to her.

From the second decade of the thirteenth century the Waldensians rejected universal priesthood and put an end to the idea of universal equality. Only the Brothers vowed to observe celibacy, renounce private property, and subsist on the alms of Believers. They dedicated themselves to giving spiritual guidance, hearing confessions, and administering those sacraments the Waldensians did not renounce, like Baptism, the Eucharist, and Penance. The division between Brothers and male Believers was paralleled by a similar division between female Believers and Sisters. The accepted view, until the publication of the revisionist article by Grado Merlo (1991), was that, in the early days of the sect, women had enjoyed equal rights with men, and that only after the discarding of the egalitarian principle among the men, and their division into Brothers and Believers, did women lose their rights. However, this definitely was not the case. Some women did indeed preach (a function from which they were banned in the Catholic church). Yet even in this early period there was no equality either in theory or in practice. The idea of spiritual equality between men and women (Galatians 3:28) was never interpreted as meaning equality in the earthly church.

The lack of equality between the Brothers and Sisters was even more pronounced than between men and women in the early years of the Waldensian movement. The Sisters were confined to the hospices, which also served as schools and meeting places for the Believers with the Brothers. They prepared the food for the Brothers and if they taught it was only in the hospices with almost exclusively female Believers as their students. As a rule they did not preach in public; they did not attend the general councils of the Brothers; they did not hear confessions or administer the sacraments; and they could not rise in the spiritual leadership to become deacons, presbyters, or a majoral (the highest rank among the Brothers). Though the Sisters did teach and sometimes preach—at least some of the time and in some of the regions—essentially the same hierarchy and gender roles prevailed between Brothers and Sisters as between the nuns and monks or canons in the Church.

It was the female Believers who both had a fuller religious life and played a more important role in the religious community than their counterparts. In the attitudes of Brothers to female Believers, contrary to their attitudes to the Sisters, there was a neutralization of the customary division of gender roles. Waldensian teaching did not refer to gender, or relate to gender concepts or gender boundaries. There were no special instructions for women—not even the usual commandment for the wife to obey her husband. The Brothers taught and preached to mixed groups of male and female Believers and attributed great importance to the instruction of the former. Unlike the Sisters, the female Believers were free to come and go and thus played a greater part in spreading the beliefs and moral precepts of the sect. These were women who brought into the sect not only their children but also their husbands, and even men and women not closely related to them. They played a central role in accommodating in their homes the Brothers when they came to hold common prayers, teach, preach, and hear confessions. Both married women and widows put the Brothers up in their homes and provided them with food and donations of money when they left. They sometimes also accompanied the Brothers to help disguise their identity or hid their whereabouts. This neutralization of the traditional gender categorization in some sense compensated them for the loss of the cult of the Virgin Mary, the other female saints, and the religious festivals in which women played a role. It did not derive from a principal of faith, nor did it entail a formal status or official appointment. It derived from the fact that the Waldensians constituted a marginal persecuted group, adherence to which was voluntary and depended on the active consent of its members. In such groups class and gender divisions were partly eliminated. It was a vital necessity.

SHULAMITH SHAHAR

References and Further Reading

Audisio, Gabriel. Les "Vaudois:" Naissance, vie et mort d'une dissidence (XII–XVIme siècles). Turin: Albert Meynier, 1989.

Biller, Peter. "Les Vaudois dans les territoires de langue allemande vers la fin du XIVe siècle: le regard d'un inquisiteur." Heresies 13-14 (1989): 203–228.

———. "Heresy and Literacy: Earlier History of a Theme." In Heresy and Literacy 1000–1350, edited by Peter Biller and Anne Hudson. Cambridge: Cambridge University Press, 1994, pp. 1–18.

Gonnet, Giovanni. "La femme dans les mouvements paupéro-évangeliques du bas moyen âge (notamment chez les Vaudois)." Heresis 22 (1994): 25–41.

Kienzle, Beverly M. "The Prostitute Preacher: Patterns of Polemic against Medieval Waldensian Women Preachers." In Women Preachers and Prophets through Two Millennia of Christianity, edited by Beverly M. Kienzle and Pamela J. Walker. Berkeley, Calif.: University of California Press, 1998, pp. 99–113.

Merlo, Grado G. "Sulle 'Misere donnicciuole' che predicavano." In Identita Valdàesi nella storia e nella storiografia. Valdismi medievali 2. Turin: Claudiana, 1991, pp. 93–112.

Paravi, Pierrette. "Waldensians in Dauphiné (1400–1530): From Dissidence in Texts to Dissidence in Practice." In Heresy and Literacy 1000–1350, edited by Peter Biller and Anne Hudson. Cambridge: Cambridge University Press, 1994, pp. 160–175.

Shahar, Shulamith. Women in a Medieval Heretical Sect: Agnes and Huguette the Waldensians, translated by Yael Lotan. 2001.

Wakefield, Walter L., and Austin P. Evans, eds. and trans. Heresies of the High Middle Age. New York: Columbia University Press, 1969.

See also **Heretics and Heresy; Ordination of Women as Priests; Sermons and Preaching**

WALES

As is the case with so many subjects in medieval Welsh history, our knowledge of women's lives is conditioned by the relative paucity of sources. Women figure prominently in the major literary works of the period, poetic and prose. Arguably more revealing of the texture of real-life women's experiences, however, is the lawbook tractate on the "Law of Women," which dates to the late twelfth or early thirteenth century and is extant in various versions both in Welsh and in Latin. Court records of the period after the conquest by England (1284 on) are also available, although the evidence suggests that disputes pertaining to marriage were pursued mainly in extracurial venues even in the late Middle Ages.

For those approaching the subject of Welsh women from a knowledge of English or continental norms, perhaps the greatest surprise is that these women were virtually excluded from the inheritance of land. Only one legal text even acknowledges the possibility of female heirs to land, and then only in cases in which no other male heirs existed; this particular text was almost certainly influenced by contemporary English custom. Even fathers who wished to leave land to their daughters were enjoined from doing so, and English customs with respect to dower were introduced only after the Conquest in 1284. At least for native Welsh women (English women holding land in Wales had greater latitude with respect to landed property), land passed entirely through the male line except in very specific circumstances. Restrictions on women regarding land tenure were paralleled in other legal venues. Women were not allowed to be witnesses against men in legal proceedings, and, possibly as late as the thirteenth century, did not have the right to make contracts on their own except through a procedure called *briduw*. Their right to sell or give away property appears to have been linked to the amount of property they brought into marriage.

Surprisingly given these limitations, Welsh women enjoyed a certain degree of equality within the marital relationship itself. The law tracts are clear that the man is considered the woman's "lord" (*dominus eius est*); on the other hand, husbands could not act badly towards their wives without penalty. Wife-beating entailed in most cases the payment of compensation to the wife, and women could actually leave their husbands in certain circumstances, including leprosy, impotence, or bad breath. Indeed, women were required to leave their husbands if the latter had been demonstrably unfaithful to them more than three times (for the first three offenses, wives were paid their honor-price in compensation). Divorce remained possible in Wales long after ecclesiastical customs with respect to marriage had prevailed elsewhere in medieval Europe, and both parties were free to remarry. Property arrangements within marriage were designed in such a way as to ensure the wife's ability to support herself should the marriage fail. If spouses separated during the first seven years of the marriage for reasons other than a fault on the part of the wife, the woman was entitled to a certain portion of the marital property, known as the *agweddi*; after seven years, the spouses split all (moveable) property between them. Widows inherited all moveable goods except corn if no specific bequest had been made; if it had been, wives were still entitled to half of the marital property. The nature and parameters of marriage were in flux at the time the lawbooks were penned. Earlier Welsh custom recognized a variety of legal unions, including elopement, rape, and abduction; indeed, as late as 1517, there is a record of a wife being "sold" to another man by her husband. However, the thirteenth century saw many attempts both from within and without native Wales to define marriage according to the laws of the Church.

Religious options for women in Wales were few. Only three nunneries were in existence in Wales for any significant length of time before the Dissolution—as compared to an estimated 150 in England—and all were poor and sparsely inhabited. Estimates suggest that there were no more than thirty-five nuns in the country as a whole: private devotion at home seems to have been the primary form of religious expression for women. Literacy among native women either in Welsh or in Latin seems to have been quite rare, although women clearly participated actively in the oral culture of the period. Two female poets are known by name, one of whom, Gwerful Mechain (a late-fifteenth/early-sixteenth-century figure), penned an important work in the *querelle des femmes* tradition.

ROBIN CHAPMAN STACEY

References and Further Reading

Cartwright, Jane. "The Desire to Corrupt: Convent and Community in Medieval Wales." In *Medieval Women in Their Communities*, edited by Diane Watt. Cardiff: University of Wales Press, 1997, pp. 20–48.

Fulton, Helen. "Medieval Welsh Poems to Nuns." *Cambridge Medieval Celtic Studies* 21 (1991): 87–112.

Jenkins, Dafydd, ed. and trans. The *Law of* Hywel Dda: *Law Texts from Medieval Wales*. Llandysul: Gomer Press, 1986.

Jenkins, Dafydd, and Morfydd Owen, eds. *The Welsh Law of Women: Studies Presented to Professor Daniel A. Binchy on His Eightieth Birthday*. Cardiff: University of Wales Press, 1980.

Lloyd-Morgan, Ceridwen. "Women and Their Poetry in Medieval Wales." In *Women and Literature in Britain, 1150–1500*, edited by Carol M. Meale. Cambridge: Cambridge University Press, 1993, pp. 183–201.

———. "More Written About Than Writing?: Welsh Women and the Written Word." In *Literacy in Medieval Celtic Societies*, edited by Huw Pryce. Cambridge: Cambridge University Press, 1998, pp. 149–165.

———. "The *Querelle des femmes*: A Continuing Tradition in Welsh Women's Literature." In *Medieval Women: Texts and Contexts in Late Medieval Britain: Essays for Felicity Riddy*, edited by Jocelyn Wogan-Browne, Rosalynn Voaden, Arlyn Diamond, Ann Hutchison, Carol Meale, and Lesley Johnson. Turnhout: Brepols, 2000, pp. 101–114.

Owen, Aneurin, ed. *Ancient Laws and Institutes of Wales*. London: Public Records Commissioners, 1841.

Stacey, Robin Chapman. "Divorce, Medieval Welsh Style." *Speculum* 77 (2002): 1107–1127.

Wade-Evans, Arthur W., ed. *Welsh Medieval Law*. Oxford: Clarendon Press, 1909; Reprint, Aalen: Scientia, 1979.

Wiliam, Aled Rhys, ed. *Llyfr Iorwerth op Madog: A Critical Text of the "Venedotian Code" of Medieval Welsh Law*. Cardiff: University of Wales Press, 1960.

Williams, Stephen J., and J. Enoch Powell, eds. *Cyfreithiau Hywel Dda yn ôl Llyfr Blegywryd*. 2nd ed. Cardiff: University of Wales Press, 1961.

See also **Divorce and Separation; Inheritance; Landholding and Property Rights; Law; Marriage, Christian; Monasticism and Nuns**

WALLĀDA BINT AL-MUSTAKFĪ

Al-Andalus produced no fewer than forty women poets, some of them slaves working as entertainers but most of them educated free women with access to literary circles, usually through a relationship with an important man. Many of these female poets were single and of noble birth, including one of the best known, Wallāda, who was the daughter of Caliph Muhammed al-Mustakfī and whose house in eleventh-century Córdoba became an important meeting place for writers. Wallāda had a stormy relationship with the poet Ibn Zaydūn before she went on to have an apparently happy life-long liaison with the vizier Ibn Abdūs. In addition, she seems to have had an erotic relationship with another woman poet, Muhŷa Bint at-Tayyānī, who was her protégée.

Most of Wallāda's extant poems consist of dialogues with Ibn Zaydūn. Some are delicate love compositions, while others are obscene satirical pieces, in which, among other things, she accuses him, in rather graphic terms, of having homosexual affairs. Although Wallāda's life as a free woman moving in men's circles was unusual, the graphic sexuality of her satirical poems was completely conventional, since that style of satire was one of the most popular literary genres in al-Andalus. She excelled at it and held her own against the best poets of her time. Wallāda had a poem embroidered on her tunic, in the fashion of the slaves. Ironically, it proclaimed her freedom and independence: "By God, I was made for glory and I proudly follow my own path" and "I offer my cheek to whomever loves me and kiss whomever desires me." The fact that she succeeded at establishing herself as a legendary libertine whose adventures have excited the imagination of readers for centuries is a tribute to her extraordinary literary talent.

CRISTINA GONZÁLEZ

References and Further Reading

González, Cristina. "Wallāda Bint al-Mustakfī." In *Medieval Iberia: An Encyclopedia*, edited by Michael Gerli. New York: Routledge, 2003, p. 845.

Hoenerbach, Wilheim. "Notas para una caracterización de Wallāda." *Al-Andalus* 36 (1971): 467–473.

Nichols, James M. "Wallada, the Andalusian Lyric, and the Question of Influence." *Literature East and West* 21 (1977): 286–291.

See also **Literature, Iberian; Muslim Women: Iberia**

WARDSHIP

It is possible to trace English wardship to at least 1100, and it seems likely that the feudal practice in England started with the Conquest. Feudal wardship (also known as military wardship or wardship in chivalry) was an incident of tenure between a lord and his vassal by virtue of the vassal holding land from the lord in exchange for military service. Such wardship went beyond the usual services performed in

return for land. (Wardship in socage was when the tenant held land in return for services other than military.)

Feudal wardship became necessary when a military tenant (most often a knight) died leaving a minor heir or heiress who could not perform the necessary feudal obligations because of minority or gender. Until the heir reached majority and could swear fealty to the lord (the husband of the heiress would normally swear fealty in her stead), the lord would hold custody of the body, property, and lands of the heir or heiress, thus holding them in wardship. This was seen to be an extension of the lord's relationship with the deceased father of the ward and ensured that upon majority the ward would be able to move into the tenancy of the father's lands.

The lord had the right to pass or sell the wardship to someone of his choosing; usually this would be to another lord or someone else of high status; sometimes the lord would sell these rights to members of the ward's immediate family, and sometimes even to the mother. Guardianship of family members was not an automatic right in noble society.

An heir in military wardship came of age when he was deemed mature enough to bear arms; this was accepted to be the age of twenty-one. Until this time the lord could profit freely from the ward's lands and with no accountability to his ward for profits lost or made during this term. (Guardians in socage were accountable to their wards.) As such, the office of guardianship was easily open to abuse, and contemporary legal literature attests to this occurrence as frequent.

The person, property, and marriage of the ward could generate the most financial gain for the lord and was so most often open to financial abuse. Where the marriage of the ward was concerned, the guardian had the right, within reason, to choose a marriage partner for his ward or even to sell the marriage on to another interested party. The sale of the ward's marriage was often used to form political alliances or dynastic arrangements. The Magna Carta (1215, c. 6) is the first instance we have of an attempt to regulate this practice, in the clause that wards must not be married "disparagingly." Contemporary legal treatises (in particular the mid-thirteenth-century "Bracton") stated that male and female wards must not be married against their will, and that male marriages should be free, although the lord would still have the right to the marriage.

There is some evidence in legal cases of the period that wards sought restitution from the courts for such abuses, while further legislative sources sought to delimit such abuse through statute (in particular see the Magna Carta [1215, cc. 6,7], the Statute of

Gloucester [1278], and the Statute of Westminster II [1285]).

As well as military wardship and wardship in socage there were other forms—namely urban (wardship in burgage) and manorial (nonaristocratic). In legal terms the office of all types of medieval guardianship existed to protect the property and person of the ward during their minority and was thus an office of personal care. That it was a position easily open to abuse did not mean that all guardians abused their wards, wasted their property, or sold their marriages unsuitably. Legal material (legislative, treatises, and case law) is prescriptive in its demonstration that such abuses against the ward should not happen, but suggests that in all likelihood it did.

The main textual sources that deal with wardship legislation include the late-twelfth-century *Glanvill*; *Très ancient coutoumier* (late twelfth to early thirteenth century); and the mid-thirteenth-century "Bracton." In addition to the statutes mentioned above, there is extant a large body of common law and ecclesiastical court material that shows wards taking their guardians to court for restitution of their legal rights. A corpus of at least six popular contemporary romances take the subject as their theme, thus demonstrating a concern and understanding of wardship practices that further illuminates the legal material and highlights in particular its inextricable links with the issue of inheritance.

NOËL JAMES MENUGE

References and Further Reading

Baker, John H. *An Introduction to Legal History*. 2nd ed. London: Butterworth, 1979.
Bracton, Henry de. *On the Laws and Customs of England*, edited by George E. Woodbine and Samuel E. Thorne. Cambridge, Mass.: Belknap Press, 1968.
Clark, Elaine "The Custody of Children in Manor Courts." *Law and History Review* 3 (1985): 333–348.
———. "Social Welfare in the Medieval Countryside." *Journal of British Studies* 33 (1994): 381–406.
———. "City Orphans and Custody Laws in Medieval England." *American Journal of Legal History* 34 (1995): 168–187.
Hall, G. D. G., ed. *The Treatise on the Laws and Customs of England Commonly Called Glanvill*. London: Nelson, 1968.
Hemholz, Richard H. *Canon Law and the Law of England*. London: Hambledon Press, 1987.
———. *Marriage Litigation in Medieval England*. London: Cambridge Press, 1974.
Menuge, Noël James. *Medieval English Wardship in Romance and Law*. Cambridge: D. S. Brewer, 2001.
Tardiff Ernest, J., ed. *Coutoumiers de Normandie*. 2 vols. Rouen: E. Cagniard, 1881, 1903.
Waugh, Scott. L. *The Lordship of England: Royal Wardships and Marriages in English Society and Politics, 1217–1327*. Princeton, N.J.: Princeton University Press, 1988.

See also **Children, Betrothal and Marriage of; Fosterage; Girls and Boys; Heiresses; Inheritance; Landholding and Property Rights; Law; Legal Agency; Marriage, Christian**

WARFARE

As with any aspect of society, medieval women participated in warfare in a variety of ways: they were victims, intercessors, supporters, and warriors. Famous examples—such as Philippa of Hainault, queen of England in the fourteenth century, a celebrated peacemaker, and Joan of Arc, a commander—may have been unusual in either the scope or the publicity of their military contributions, but they were hardly alone in shaping and being shaped by war.

Roles

Due to their official status as noncombatants, it is not surprising to find women portrayed as victims of the ravages of war. Military strategy throughout the Middle Ages advocated the destruction of property and crops by those wishing to overcome their enemies. The protection of a walled city or fortress did not guarantee safety, as prolonged sieges could produce starvation and illness within the walls, and successful ones could result in besiegers venting their rage over the tedium and expense of a protracted operation on the people who were sheltered inside. Some women avoided death, rape, or physical injury only to survive in captivity. European accounts of the crusades mention instances when Muslims sold into slavery the women and children in overrun fortresses. In Europe, too, a high-ranking woman could make an attractive captive, useful as leverage against her kin or as ransom.

It would be misleading to categorize these women as passive participants. Even those traditionally perceived as victims could have contributed actively to combat. There are numerous accounts of townswomen aiding in defense by throwing rocks at besiegers. In the thirteenth century, Simon of Montfort, the leader of the Albigensian Crusade, was said to have died from blows inflicted by stones hurled from a catapult operated by the women of Toulouse, the town he was attempting to subdue. A century later, the chronicler Jean Froissart enthusiastically praised Countess Jeanne of Montfort for rallying her townswomen to assault their attackers with hot tar and paving stones pulled up from the streets. Women also joined their male relations on crusade—if not as officially sanctioned crusaders, then as camp followers and companions. In the heat of battle, their duties as cooks, laundresses, prostitutes, or wives of high-ranking commanders could blend into more active support roles, bearing water and ammunition to the fighters and filling in the moats of besieged castles.

Wealthy and socially prominent wives could influence the direction of warfare by interceding with their husbands. Medieval aristocrats often contracted marriages between two warring sides in an effort to foster peace. With this reputation as peacemakers and with the clerically approved duty to advise their husbands, wives often interceded directly in military decisions. When John of Montfort's uncle died childless in 1341, John's wife Jeanne counseled him to take immediate steps to secure the duchy's treasury and proclaim himself the duke of Brittany. Philippa of Hainault famously, and successfully, pleaded for the lives of prisoners her husband had intended to execute. A wife's publicly performed intercession allowed a husband to preserve his own warlike reputation, for his subsequent leniency could then be attributed to his wife.

Some medieval women influenced warfare more directly, by encouraging their men to go to war or sending money and troops to aid in the fighting. The chronicler Orderic Vitalis reported that Countess Adela of Blois badgered her husband to return to the First Crusade when he came home before it ended. In 1420, Marguerite de Clisson convinced her sons to capture the duke of Brittany because she felt the duchy rightfully belonged to her family. In addition to encouraging their male relations to go to war, noblewomen directed nonrelatives to march to battle. The Empress Matilda sent troops to secure various strongholds in Normandy when she was attempting to secure her claim to the English throne in the mid-twelfth century. In the next century, Jeanne of Constantinople, countess of Flanders and Hainault, sent her soldiers to punish the towns that had supported an imposter claiming to be her long-absent father Count Baldwin. Noblewomen also controlled financial resources necessary for waging wars. Adela of Blois financed her husband and his military contingent on the First Crusade. In the fifteenth century, Isabelle of Portugal sold her jewelry to raise money for the costly wars of her husband, Philip the Good, duke of Burgundy.

Women Warriors

It has proven very difficult to determine whether medieval women ever realized the role of warrior. Part of the difficulty lies in scholars' definitions of "warrior," which has been variously defined as anyone who "participates actively in warfare," whether or not the person ever wielded a sword, to a more narrow reading in which physical combat is key. Medieval sources can often obscure more than they reveal, leaving much of the degree of participation up to the readers' imaginations. Chronicle accounts, for example, often relate that a particular woman "won with manliness her land" or "torched the town," without indicating whether the woman's manliness extended to bearing arms or lighting the fire. Nevertheless, some chronicles do contain stirring accounts, such as Jean Froissart's depiction of the Countess Jeanne of Montfort armed astride a courser, leading a band of men ort a back gate to attack the enemy camp, or Orderic Vitalis's portrayal of the twelfth-century Isabel of Conches, armed and riding alongside her men like the Amazon queens of old. It should be noted that chronicles could be equally confusing about the level of male commanders' participation. Orderic's account of Harold of England's defense against William the Conqueror in 1066 has Harold abandoning his seaports, "which he had been closely guarding all year," though it would not have been possible for Harold himself to "closely" guard each of those seaports simultaneously.

It has been widely accepted that medieval women disappeared from "active" participation in warfare (meaning as warriors or commanders) by the thirteenth century, but chronicle accounts and diplomatic documents indicate that women participated in wars throughout the medieval period.

Representations

In addition to identifying the roles women played in warfare, scholars have examined medieval representations of women's military participation for clues about how medieval society viewed the notion of women warriors, but no consensus has yet been reached. While some studies argue for an increase in disparagement of women warriors, others argue for a more nuanced approach that situates characterizations of women warriors within the wider agenda of the individual medieval author. Often, medieval representations reveal less about women's roles than about other societal concerns. Chronicles of warfare in Iberia praised female warriors to shame the men whose cowardice had created an opportunity for these women to fight, while Baltic crusade chronicles described the success of female warriors as a manifestation of God's approval of the Christian cause and the shame of Christianity's enemies. Muslim accounts of the crusades over the Holy Land recount anecdotes of European women warriors as a way to explain the moral depravity of the Europeans, while European accounts remain reticent about female warriors, choosing to promulgate the holy nature of the endeavor by glossing over what these authors felt was the inconvenient presence of women. English and northern French chronicles impute positive or negative motives to women warriors based on whether the woman aligned with the chronicler's political views or visions of proper societal structure. Literary sources, too, use women warriors for other means. Romances such as the *Roman de Silence* and the *Tournament of Ladies* employ their armed women as tools to explore "proper" gender behavior, while fabliaux insert the occasional armed woman as comic relief.

KATRIN E. SJURSEN

References and Further Reading

Blythe, James M. "Women in the Military: Scholastic Arguments and Medieval Images of Female Warriors." *History of Political Thought* 22.2 (2001): 242–270.

Edgington, Susan B., and Sarah Lambert, eds. *Gendering the Crusades.* New York: Columbia University Press, 2002.

Gershenzon, Shoshanna, and Jane Litman. "The Bloody 'Hands of Compassionate Women': Portrayals of Heroic Women in the Hebrew Crusade Chronicle." In *Crisis & Reaction: The Hero in Jewish History*, edited by Menahem Mor. Omaha, Neb.: Creighton University Press, 1995, pp. 73–91.

Mazeika, Rasa J. "'Nowhere Was the Fragility of Her Sex Apparent': Women Warriors in the Baltic Crusade Chronicles." In *From Clermont to Jerusalem: The Crusades and Crusader Societies, 1095–1500*, edited by Alan V. Murray. Turnhout: Brepols, 1998, pp. 229–248.

McLaughlin, Megan. "The Woman Warrior: Gender, Warfare, and Society in Medieval Europe." *Women's Studies* 17 (1990): 193–209.

McMillin, Linda A. "Women on the Walls: Women and Warfare in the Catalan Grand Chronicles." *Catalan Review: International Journal of Catalan Culture* 3 (1989): 123–136.

Nicholson, Helen. "Women on the Third Crusade." *Journal of Medieval History* 23 (1997): 335–349.

Saunders, Corinne. "Women and Warfare in Medieval English Writing." In *Writing War: Medieval Literary Responses to Warfare*, edited by Corinne Saunders, Françoise Le Saux, and Neil Thomas. Cambridge: D. S. Brewer, 2004, pp. 187–212.

Sjursen, Katrin E. "'The Heart of a Man and a Lion': Northern French Noblewomen as Medieval Commanders, 1000–1500." Ph.D. Dissertation, University of California Santa Barbara, 2006.

Solterer, Helen. "Figures of Female Militancy in Medieval France." *Signs: Journal of Women in Culture and Society* 16 (1991): 522–549.

Truax, Jean. "Anglo-Norman Women at War: Valiant Soldiers, Prudent Strategists or Charismatic Leaders?"

In *The Circle of War in the Middle Ages: Essays on Medieval Military and Naval History*, edited by Donald J. Kagay and L. J. Andrew Villalon. Woodbridge, Suffolk: Boydell Press, 1999, pp. 111–125.

See also **Adela of Blois; Amazons; Captivity and Ransom; Castles and Palaces; Chivalry; Crusades and Crusading Literature; Diplomacy and Reconciliation; Intercession; Joan of Arc; Matilda the Empress; Roman de Silence; Tournaments; Valkyries; Violence**

WERGILD

The wergild was the payment made to the relatives of a murder victim in order to avert a blood feud. Each person above the rank of slave was valued at the wergild appropriate to his or her class or standing. Information on the system as it affected women has to be pieced together from the Barbarian law codes, and it is not always clear which aspects were universal and which provincial. A common factor is an enhanced wergild associated with childbearing. Under Salic and Ripuarian law, the wergild of a woman of childbearing age was three times that of a girl or older woman (*Lex Salica* 41, 15–17; *Lex Ribuaria* 12–13), while in Anglo-Saxon and Lombardic society, a pregnant woman was protected by an additional wergild for her unborn child (Alfred 9; Rothari 75).

As members of the kin group, women were involved in the obligation to contribute towards wergild payments (*Lex Salica* 58). Under certain circumstances, they also received a share of the wergild for a murdered relative or dependent (*Capitula Legi Salicae Addita* 68; Ine 23). This did not always apply, however, as women could be excluded from receipt of wergild on the grounds that they were unable to raise the feud (Liutprand 13, 8).

The wergild might also comprise a woman's brideprice (*Lex Saxonum* 40), and it was used as a measure of compensation for crimes besides murder. These included adultery (*Lex Baiwariorum* 8, 1; *Lex Burgundionum* 36, 68; Æthelberht 31; Alfred 10), sexual assault (Alfred 11; II Cnut 52), and a range of other offenses committed by or against women (e.g., *Lex Alamannorum* 53, 2; Grimwald 7; Liutprand 122, 130, 135; Wihtred 12; Alfred 18; II Cnut 73).

CAROLE HOUGH

References and Further Reading

MacCormack, Geoffrey. "Inheritance and Wergild in Early Germanic Law: I." *Irish Jurist*. n.s.8 (1973): 143–163.

———. "Inheritance and Wergild in Early Germanic Law: II." *Irish Jurist*. n.s.9 (1974): 166–183.

Rivers, Theodore John. "Adultery in Early Anglo-Saxon Society: Æthelberht 31 in Comparison with Continental Germanic Law." *Anglo-Saxon England* 20 (1991): 19–25.

See also **Abortion; Crime and Criminals; Kinship; Social Status; Violence**

WET NURSING
See **Breastfeeding and Wet-Nursing**

WIDOWS

Widows are common in most societies and cultures. Social scientists and policy workers, as well as historians, study how they fare and how they are regarded in their world. Because women tend to outlive men, widows are frequently found in large numbers; in the United States today about three of every four women who marry will be widows for some period in their lives. In some segments of medieval society, as in the towns and cities of late medieval Italy, the practice of men marrying much younger women compounded this biological aspect of human survival, and of the fourteen married kings of England between 1066 and 1485 eleven left a widow upon death. While medieval life was harsh for almost everyone by modern standards, a life of manual labor probably was harsher on men than on women, and the chronic warfare of that world—in pitched battles and even more so in the guise of the disease and malnutrition that went hand in hand with sieges and campaigns in the field—took a heavy toll. Though romance and drama may color our accounts of great battles—Charles Martel at Tours (732), or the Christian crusaders and the Moslems at Hattin (1187), or Henry V at Agincourt (1415)—these head-on encounters were widow-makers on a grand scale. While the dangers of childbirth and an iron-deficient diet evened the scale to some extent, the widower was more easily reintegrated into society and family life than was the woman whose partner had died. The widow was a more isolated figure.

Widows' Problems

The medieval widow faced a number of problems. Some were pragmatic and their weight depended on her social and economic status as well as on her own personality and style. But other problems were ideological. The strain of misogyny that underlay so much social and religious thinking—traceable in a direct line to both the Old and the New Testament—singled out the widow as especially problematic. She was sexually experienced, and therefore apt to have a strong appetite for more such activity. Thus she was a potential threat to social and family stability (and to male innocence). Either separation from the world or quick remarriage would seem the best alternatives, though Paul's own inclination (as transmitted in the Pauline Epistles of the New Testament) had been to advocate permanent celibacy, for both men and women, after the death of the first partner. If there is no consensus regarding Chaucer's actual viewpoint or sympathies, his "Wife of Bath" sums up the male fantasy of the widow on the loose: loud, oft-married, frank about sex, on the prowl for another husband, and boastful of her wiles and her record of marital domination.

But society is not governed by any single ideology. Many social and personal realities existed to temper the harshest edges of theological reflections and generalizations about women without men (first her father, then her husband) to stand cover over their legal and social identity. From early on, medieval society accepted that widows, as vulnerable women, would need legal protection and some share of the family's assets if they were to survive, let alone to contribute. Sometimes a widow might be able to fall back upon emotional and economic support from her natal family, as well as upon her own resources. In literature, as in record sources and charters, there are numerous depictions of a tension or duality in her identity, between her birth family—to which she might return upon widowhood—and that new one into which she had married; her role as a potential intercessor was promising but, as *Beowulf* declared, rarely successful. As "feudal" law developed, women (often already widows, because of marital demography that worked in favor of women's survival) frequently became the heiresses of aristocratic families, a not-uncommon situation due to the absence of brothers. As such they could control great estates and exercise real power in the political as well as the economic sphere, holding both a family inheritance and the widow's dower share (which she usually was able to get her hands on, though perhaps not without some difficulty). And royal widows, at the very top of society, might be regents of the realm as well as guardians of underage kings: Blanche of Castile and the young Louis IX of France in the thirteenth century offer a prime example, and Byzantine court life has similar tales to tell. At the other end of the socioeconomic spectrum, the poor widow—elderly, apt to be in failing health, unable to care for herself or to work her holding in the fields—was a social problem addressed only in part by the establishment of hospitals and alms houses and by the countless testamentary bequests of small sums for the poor. Her future was not very promising, though she too had to be folded into the embrace of "traditional society."

Widows' Alternatives

There were three basic options regarding a widow's future: the Church, in some fashion or other; remarriage; and remaining in the world, unmarried. Entering a nunnery was a popular choice for many widows. Some became vowed and full-fledged nuns, while others were content to remain in the monastery as a novice or a lay sister, or perhaps simply as a boarder or paying guest, bringing an endowment (a corrody) and living out life within the cloister on prearranged terms. Many women, from sixth-century Merovingian queens to preteens in fifteenth-century Italy, had been pushed into premature marriage, sex, childbirth, and a life of domestic obligation from which widowhood and the nunnery might offer a welcome relief. By the later Middle Ages, when there was less enthusiasm for monastic life, many nunneries drew a considerable proportion of their recruits from those who had once been married and in the world. In the early Middle Ages, widows of royal families, as in Anglo-Saxon England and the Empire, often chose this route, finding protection against worldly pressures (including pressure to remarry) that would otherwise have enmeshed them. As women of experience and considerable presence, they not infrequently rose to positions of authority within their new domain, especially when the house was a family foundation. Elisabeth of Hungary (d. 1231) had been both duchess and mother before she turned to the lifestyle that culminated in her canonization.

There were other options for a life under the Church's protection beyond entry into the cloister. The Church came to encourage women who did not wish to leave the world to take vows of "chaste widowhood" with a formal ceremony performed by the bishop that made them vowesses. The inclination of women of some status to choose this alternative may have been enhanced by the common provision in their husbands' wills that they would inherit more (for a life interest) if they remained unmarried than if they took another spouse. Some women—both widows and virgins—from the twelfth century on, and mostly in northern Europe, formed communities (beguinages) that offered shelter and combined a commitment to celibate and communal life with the freedom to move about each day to contribute to the common purse and larder. So within the wide and comforting penumbra of ecclesiastical support there were a number of choices and opportunities for widows, they being as welcome as those young virgins who had chosen this lifestyle from the start.

Remarriage

For many women widowhood turned out to be a temporary status or condition. Despite what Paul and various Church Fathers had counseled, remarriage was widely accepted—fostered by economic and political considerations, in a world where women often had property of their own and children to raise, as well as by their personal inclinations. Life with a spouse, except perhaps for those of considerable affluence, was probably easier than life without, and it conformed to the most accepted norm or model of secular life. Where we have statistics for late medieval populations and social groups, as we do for aristocratic and even bourgeois women of the fourteenth and fifteenth centuries, we find that remarriage was the case for a good fifty percent of the widows we can identify. Furthermore, remarriage often came after a relatively short span as a widow; a year or two was a common and seemly interval. Since the new husband might come into some effective control of her share of her late husband's property (perhaps as high as one-half or one-third of the dead husband's estate), as well as of her own inheritance, and perhaps of her children's wardship and marriage, a widow could be an attractive "commodity" in both town and countryside. Queens and empresses remarried, as did women of the towns and cities, and perhaps most peasant and village women who were able to do so (and peasant women with land often found younger husbands to work the fields and support them). Since many widows were quite young, their childbearing potential (perhaps already proven) could be of value, alongside their domestic skills. A late medieval treatise in the form of advice from an aged husband to his young bride works on the idea that her next husband will think well of her first because the latter has trained her so well in the ways of household management. The church monitored remarriage, but objections on biblical grounds were not a serious matter by early medieval times, especially in a world faced with a declining population, and efforts to eliminate pre-Christian Germanic leanings toward polygamy probably helped establish a more flexible view that was willing to accept serial monogamy as a decent *modus vivendi* under the new spiritual culture being established.

Many widows remained unmarried, though how many did so by choice and how many by necessity is hard to gauge. In the Magna Carta (1215), one of the feudal perquisites imposed upon King John was the provision that widows not be forced into remarriage; this was primarily with an eye to heiresses and women of considerable property (and perhaps of some independence of mind). As the church came to accept that the essence of marriage was mutual consent, rather than consummation, it became easier (at least in theory) for widows to choose to remain single. One aspect of remarriage, especially when there were children by more than one marriage, was the creation of complex networks of kinship and inheritance; a widow might have more than one remarriage by the end, so her web of children and stepchildren could be a tangled one. Widows often had the freedom to write a will, and these documents are of particular value in revealing women's concern for ecclesiastical benefaction, for the range of remembered family members, and for the distribution of personal goods at what was often the breakup of the household. The will often stipulated beside which husband she was to lie, though the money she left for prayers usually covered both (or all) of her partners, and she might refer to sons of more than one surname as an indication of her multiple families. Whatever the motives of the many who remarried, life with a partner often looked an easier path than life on one's own, though any given widow's potential for independence could be a significant counterweight to this generalization.

Independence

Some widows, both old and young, chose to remarry; others, with fewer points of attraction, had little choice but to face life without a partner. Instances of widowhoods running as long as three and four decades are not hard to find, as death might come early for him and late for her. For women of property widowhood could be a time of affluent independence: control of her dower share and inheritance, control of the business or shop, time and opportunity for a say in the management of family lands and children's futures, leisure for participation in women's cultural and spiritual networks. Now, for those so inclined, it might be time for a pilgrimage, perhaps down the road but occasionally all the way to Jerusalem, or to visit married children, or to run the great household over which she had perhaps always been the de facto chief (as Alice de Brienne did with considerable élan in early-fifteenth-century Suffolk). But these rosy views about widowhood as a window of opportunity

are governed or shaped by economic as well as social and personal realities, and for many an aged and enfeebled woman the future was bleak. Children might be expected to care for aged (single) parents, but in many instances there might be no children and in others they had scattered. Sons had gone to seek their fortunes in war or the city, never to return, and daughters might have moved to another village without much inclination to "keep in touch." For many widows, remaining unmarried meant starting over, only now they might be carrying the baggage of age, debts, and disability. Bereavement and depression are hard to gauge but they are hardly modern phenomena, and even when there were sufficient resources for her bed and board there were human factors about death and personal crises that we cannot quantify and that mostly go unmentioned in the records.

As there is no single Middle Ages, so there can be no single picture of widowhood, and in many ways the story of widowhood is a chapter in the larger story of the role and treatment of women. Ways in which society protected the widow, both in her person and her possessions, are readily found, from the law codes of early Christian and Germanic Europe through the bustling urban and commercial world of the last medieval centuries. It is important not to romanticize the widow's condition, nor to overestimate her autonomy. While many women, at all social levels, showed inspiring signs of agency and spirit, women who lost husbands were apt to be confronted by some hard choices. They buried their dead, they mourned, and—as women have done through the recorded course of history—they took their chances with the future. They might cast their lot with the Church, or they might listen to a suitor, be he young or old, or they might go it alone, whether by choice or from force of circumstances. Did they find it a source of consolation that there were always so many women in these ranks? Queens and saints and learned women (like Christine de Pizan, d. c. 1431, who turned to writing to support her family) were among those to be counted, along with legions of bourgeois widows and anonymous peasant relicts and the countless aged and poor survivors who were given some passing attention in the charitable provisions of wills and, sometimes, with less kindness, in lines of verse that could substitute ribald humor and mockery for Christian charity.

JOEL T. ROSENTHAL

References and Further Reading

Archer, Rowena A. "Rich Old Ladies: The Problem of Late Medieval Dowagers." In *Property and Politics: Essays in Later Medieval English History*, edited by Tony Pollard. Gloucester: Alan Sutton, 1984, pp. 15–35.

Barron, Caroline M., and Anne F. Sutton, eds. *Medieval London Widows, 1300–1500*. London: Hambledon Press, 1994.

Brundage, James A. *Law, Sex, and Christian Society in Medieval Europe*. Chicago: University of Chicago Press, 1987.

Chojnacki, Stanley. *Women and Men in Renaissance Venice: Twelve Essays on Patrician Society*. Baltimore, Md.: Johns Hopkins University Press, 2000.

Franklin, Peter. "Peasant Widows 'Liberation' and Remarriage before the Black Death." *Economic History Review* 39 (1988): 186–204.

Herlihy, David, and Christiane Klapisch-Zuber. *Tuscans and Their Families: A Study of the Florentine Catasto of 1427*. New Haven, Conn.: Yale University Press, 1985.

Holderness, B. A. "Widows in Pre-Industrial Society: An Essay upon Their Economic Functions." In *Land, Kinship and Life-Cycle*, edited by Richard M. Smith. Cambridge: Cambridge University Press, 1984, pp. 423–442.

Klapisch-Zuber, Christiane. "'The Cruel Mother': Maternity, Widowhood, and Dower in Florence in the Fourteenth and Fifteenth Centuries." In *Women, Family, and Ritual in Renaissance Italy*, translated by Lydia Cochrane. Chicago: University of Chicago Press, 1985, pp. 182–202.

Mirrer, Louise, ed. *Upon My Husband's Death: Widows in the Literature and Histories of Medieval Europe*. Ann Arbor, Mich.: University of Michigan Press, 1992.

Nelson, J. L. "The Wary Widow." In *Property and Power in the Early Middle Ages*, edited by Wendy Davis and Paul Fouracre. Cambridge: Cambridge University Press, 1995, pp. 82–113.

Swabey, Ffiona. *Medieval Gentlewoman: Life in a Widow's Household in the Later Middle Ages*. Stroud: Sutton Publishing, 1999.

Walker, Sue Sheridan. "Widow and Ward: The Feudal Law of Child Custody in Medieval England." In *Women in Medieval Society*, edited by Susan Mosher Stuard. Philadelphia: University of Pennsylvania Press, 1976, pp. 159–172.

———, ed. *Wife and Widow in Medieval England*. Ann Arbor, Mich.: University of Michigan Press, 1993.

Wemple, Suzanne F. *Women in Frankish Society: Marriage and the Cloister, 500 to 900*. Philadelphia: University of Pennsylvania Press, 1981.

See also **Beguines; Demography; Dowry and Other Marriage Gifts; Heiresses; Misogyny; Monasticism and Nuns; Poverty; Regents and Queen-Lieutenants; Remarriage; Sexuality: Extramarital Sex; Single-women; Vowesses; Widows as Guardians**

WIDOWS AS GUARDIANS

In Roman law, so influential in the western Mediterranean, a *tutrix* or *tutor* served as guardian for a boy under fourteen or a girl under twelve, while a *curatrix* or *curator* was entrusted with adolescents under twenty-five, the technical age of majority. (In practice many older children renounced the legal and financial protection of their guardians before their twenty-fifth birthdays.) Men appointed the guardians, who would be responsible for their children after they died, in their last wills and testaments. Thus, when a woman lost her husband in the western Mediterranean world, she did not automatically gain custody of their children, although societal and legal norms usually made her the first choice as guardian. In some areas widowed mothers served alone as guardians, and many became effective financial and legal agents in working on behalf of their children. In other places panels of guardians were preferred to individuals. When a father appointed a group of guardians, he was often looking for a way to include his widow in the upbringing of their children, while their male relatives managed the children's estates. Since among the urban elite, women were usually viewed as financially incompetent, urban patricians were most likely to favor group arrangements. Distrust of guardians was widespread, as was fear that they would mismanage the children's assets, putting their financial futures in jeopardy. Thus fathers strove to balance the commercial inexperience of mothers against the greed of male relatives, male business associates, or neighbors. In these group-guardianship arrangements mothers usually resided with their children but their control of finances was limited.

Mothers lost all rights to custody or financial control of their children upon remarriage. Since, during the Middle Ages, most southern European towns had no official oversight of guardianship by any municipal or royal administrative body, fatherless children whose mothers remarried often suffered financial (and emotional) hardship. Widowed mothers who did not take up responsibilities as guardians and instead remarried were thus the objects of some censure. Guardianship was the locus for tensions surrounding women's position in medieval society; especially for a young widow, the interests of her children, who needed her in the absence of her husband, conflicted with those of her birth family, which had much to gain from her remarriage.

Medieval Jewish fathers in southern Europe designated who would serve as guardians for their children in their deathbed declarations or in Latin last wills and testaments. Like Christians, Jews privileged widowed mothers as guardians but also commonly employed group arrangements with the mothers gaining custody. Jewish community leaders and the children's family members usually worked together as guardians administering the children's assets. Jewish widowed mothers also lost custody of their children upon remarriage (or divorce), although infants and toddlers might stay with their mothers for several years, girls sometimes for even longer.

In practice the terminology of guardianship in the western Mediterranean is, as we might expect, various. After *tutrix* and *curatrix,* other legal terms used to describe a widowed mother's position as guardian include *administratrix* and *gubernatrix* of her children and their inheritances. In some southern French and Iberian areas, mothers who acted as guardians, although they were under the age of twenty-five themselves, were often given the title *domina et potens,* although *dominae* maintained more enduring rights over the family's assets than a *tutrix or curatrix* would. In contrast, in Italy for much of the later Middle Ages the *domina et potens* was simply a widowed mother who lived with her children and had the lifelong right to maintenance from their estates. (The Hebrew term for guardians is *apitropsim.*)

REBECCA WINER

References and Further Reading

Calvi, Giulia. "Widows, the State and the Guardianship of Children in Early Modern Tuscany." In *Widowhood in Medieval and Early Modern Europe,* edited by Sandra Cavallo and Lynden Warner. New York: Longman, 1999, pp. 209–219.

Chabot, Isabelle. "Lineage Strategies and the Control of Widows in Renaissance Florence." In *Widowhood in Medieval and Early Modern Europe,* edited by Sandra Cavallo and Lyndan Warner. New York: Longman, 1999, pp. 127–144.

Klapisch-Zuber, Christiane. "The 'Cruel Mother': Maternity, Widowhood, and Dowry in Florence in the Fourteenth and Fifteenth Centuries." In *Women, Family, and Ritual in Renaissance Italy,* translated by Lydia G. Cochrane. Chicago: University of Chicago Press, 1985, pp. 264–276.

Winer, Rebecca. In *Women, Wealth and Community in Perpignan circa 1250–1300: Christians, Jews and Enslaved Muslims in a Medieval Mediterranean Town.* Aldershot: Ashgate, 2005.

See also **Family; Girls and Boys; Iberia; Inheritance; Italy; Jewish Women; Legal Agency; Occitania; Remarriage; Roman Law; Widows**

WIFE OF BATH

We learn about Chaucer's character, the Wife of Bath, in three places: the portrait of her in the General Prologue to the *Canterbury Tales;* the prologue she tells before she tells her own tale; and the tale itself. Each casts a different light. The portrait presents a woman who is an experienced weaver, gap-toothed (a sign of sexual attractiveness), somewhat deaf, married five times, flamboyantly dressed in a large hat and red hose, and accustomed to going on pilgrimage. In the prologue to her tale, Alisoun (we learn her name as the prologue progresses) skillfully and humorously

challenges prevailing misogynistic discourse of the day formulated especially in Jerome's attack on marriage, *Against Jovinian.* Alisoun manipulates clerical discourse, apparently to suit her own desires to pursue sex and pleasure. The prologue has been analyzed as a brilliant example of Irigarayan mimicry, that is, as a discourse that seizes control of antifeminist discourse and turns it on its head. While earlier male critics adored the Wife for her bawdy sexual appeal, later critics have been disturbed by her inability to escape the terms of antifeminism and by the poignancy of her commodification on the marriage market. Her tale, on the other hand, has recently received attention for its challenging critique of rape. Its ending, which posits an ideal relationship of men and women based on mutual acknowledgment, has generated conflicting critical interpretations, with some viewing it as a tale gratifying male fantasies, and others seeing it as a visionary alternative to relationships based on cultural assumptions that produce rape.

ELIZABETH ROBERTSON

References and Further Reading

Beidler, Peter G., ed. *The Wife of Bath: Geoffrey Chaucer.* Boston: Bedford Books of St. Martin's Books, 1996.

See also **Chaucer, Geoffrey; Jerome, Influence of; Literature, Middle English; Misogyny; Rape and Raptus**

WILD WOMEN

In medieval literary sources from the thirteenth century, wild women have a hideous appearance. In *Wolfdietrich B,* Shaggy Else, who walks on all fours, is described as covered with hair like a bear. An unnamed wild woman in *The Crown,* an Arthurian romance by Heinrich von dem Türlin, is more fully described according to a standard representational scheme that involves both animal and racialized imagery. She is covered with shaggy hair; her ostrich eyes burn like fire; she has a broad, flat, ugly nose and a wide, thick-lipped mouth; her head hair is kinky like a Moor's; the tusks of a wild boar protrude from her mouth; her enormous ears droop like a hound's; she has long, sharp lion's claws on her hands and feet; and her grotesque skin is wrinkled and folded like an empty sack. Wolfram von Eschenbach's Cundrie has the wild woman's characteristic bristles, tusks, and bear's ears. A similar wild woman appears in the Arthurian romance *Wigalois* by Wirnt von Grafenberg. This descriptive scheme is intended to be the grotesque opposite of the top-to-toe delineation of ideal courtly female beauty, and the Moorish motifs of blackness express the fear and denigration of African and Eastern peoples. The dominant animal imagery has many sources in folklore and mythology, but one important antecedent for medieval Christian culture is the wicked woman of Ecclesiasticus 25:22–25 in the Latin Vulgate, whose dark face resembles that of a bear.

Despite their appearances, wild women have exceptional powers. Wolfram's Cundrie knows Latin, Arabic, and French; is educated in dialectic, geometry, and astronomy; and is the messenger from the grail world. Shaggy Else throws magic substances on Wolfdietrich to make him sleep, then trims his nails and hair to magically turn him into a madman. Heinrich's wild woman has enormous strength. She packs the super-knight Gawein under her arm and carries him away. A wild woman teaches medical skills to the hero Wate from the heroic epic *Kudrun*.

As seen by knights and heroes, wild women are more frightful than the devil, with whom they are often compared. As bearers of bad news or bad adventures their appearance broadcasts trouble. Yet as female beings they are also sexualized. To underscore her ugliness Wolfram comments that Cundrie's face could never rouse a lover's desire. The breasts of wild women are too large, long, and flabby, reaching to the knees, or bellows-like according to Heinrich von dem Türlin. Heinrich also observes the wild woman's ape-like pelvis and compares her genital area to a horse collar. Amazingly, some wild women convert themselves into courtly ladies with tight, controlled bodies once they have secured a sexual partnership with a hero. Shaggy Else takes Wolfdietrich to her country, Old Troy, where she bathes in the fountain of youth and emerges as the lovely Lady Sigminne. In her transformation she resembles the loathly lady in the Middle English *Marriage of Gawain and Dame Ragnell* as well as Chaucer's *Wife of Bath's Tale*. In these stories the wild woman's lack of sex appeal is a hurdle to be overcome by a knight or hero who restores her to the world of the court.

Wild women do not form a very distinctive grouping among the mythical beings discussed by Jacob Grimm in his classic work *Teutonic Mythology*. They blend with mermaids, wood wives, swan maidens, giantesses, valkyries, elves, norns, and supernatural women who mediate between the deities and humans. All are found in medieval literary texts and all have roots in folklore. Germanic and Slavic traditions also know of wild men, but they are portrayed as solitary beings, not as the companions of wild women. Nor are they imagined as the sexual partners of human women.

SARAH WESTPHAL-WIHL

References and Further Reading

Grimm, Jacob. *Wise Women. Teutonic Mythology*, translated by James Steven Stallybrass. Vol. 1. New York: Dover Publications, 1966.
Thomas, J. W., trans. *Ortnit and Wolfdietrich: Two Medieval Romances*. Columbia, S.C.: Camden House, 1986.
"The Wedding of Sir Gawain and Dame Ragnell." In *The Romance of Arthur: An Anthology of Medieval Texts in Translation*, edited by James J. Wilhelm. New York and London: Garland, 1994, pp. 467–487.
Wirnt von Grafenberg. *Wigalois: The Knight of Fortune's Wheel*, translated by J. W. Thomas. Lincoln: University of Nebraska Press, 1977.
von dem Türlin, Heinrich. *The Crown: A Tale of Sir Gawein and King Arthur's Court*, translated with an introduction by J. W. Thomas. Lincoln, Neb.: University of Nebraska Press, 1989, pp. 396–437.
von Eschenbach, Wolfram. *Parzival*, translated by A. T. Hatto. Harmondsworth: Penguin Books, 1980.

See also **Chaucer, Geoffrey; Literature, German; Literature, Middle English; Mélusine; Mermaids and Sirens; Misogyny; Romance, German; Supernatural Women; Wolfram von Eschenbach**

WILLS

Through wills it was possible to dispose of one's estate for the time after death. This included providing for one's family members, making bequests to other beneficiaries, making decisions on one's funeral and grave, paying debts, and having credits collected. Yet, in the Middle Ages wills had an important spiritual aim: contributing to the salvation of the soul through pious bequests. There were several after-death provisions: wills, testaments, donations of single goods, and lists of donations. We will use the term *will* and deal with its diffusion and function, neglecting its legal aspects.

Differing Legal Practices

In western Europe, in the early Middle Ages, there were different practices concerning wills. Germanic customary laws did not permit disposition of one's property, whereas in southern France, Italy, and other areas of the former Roman Empire the Roman legal practice of making testaments obtained. For centuries, however, only members of the high clergy and the aristocracy made testaments. In England, Scandinavia, the Low Countries, Germany, and northern France, donations—both during one's lifetime and after death—were the usual provisions for the soul.

The revival of Roman law and the diffusion of the belief in Purgatory in the twelfth century stimulated the use of wills. Furthermore, the Church encouraged making wills. Then, in western Europe, wills began to spread into all social groups—except among those who did not own any property. Around a century later, eastern Europe followed suit. By the later Middle Ages, even people with little fortune, for instance male and female servants, wrote wills to provide for their souls without renouncing their goods while alive. Although wills belonged to the religious preparation for death, only a small portion of the population drew them up. When scholars are able to determine percentages, it is usually found to be lower than ten percent.

The goods of those who made no will passed to their legal heirs following the local inheritance rules, as did the portion of the goods testators did not dispose of. Usually making a will was a way to correct or complete the inheritance rules, seldom to reverse them. Moreover, wills did not represent the only possibility for remembering the deceased through masses, funerals, or other forms of commemoration, as the family of those who died without a will could arrange these. Depending on local laws, testamentary freedom could be limited. In most of northern Europe, testators disposed of only a portion of their estate, often one-third. Testamentary freedom was usually wider for movables than for land and for acquired rather than for inherited goods; wills sometimes required approval by one's legal heirs.

In principle, to be *sui iuris*, i.e., capable of legal acts, was a condition required to make a will. In most of southern Europe women were under guardianship—first by their fathers and later either by their husbands or by appointed legal representatives; there, women were not generally permitted to make wills. Similar cases involved men and women of servile condition and young men legally dependent on their fathers. But, as these limitations contradicted the moral obligation of providing for one's soul, in the course of the Middle Ages it became more and more acceptable for everyone to make a will. Nonetheless, women were subject to more limitations than were men: married women might need their husbands' permission and might dispose of only a portion of their estate. Usually, widows and unmarried adult women had more testamentary freedom than married ones.

Wills as Historical Sources

Wills have been used for centuries as a source for genealogy and political history, and since the 1970s have been exploited as a quantitative source. Some historians from the *Annales* school then began using computer databases to analyze either complete archives or random samples of thousands of wills, in order to study religious mentalities and attitudes towards death. Since the 1970s, scholars have examined large collections of late medieval and early modern wills from western Europe; beginning in the 1990s, these studies were augmented by studies of wills from eastern Europe and colonial America. The number, money value, and recipients of pious bequests provide insight into the popularity of religious institutions (parish churches, hospitals, monasteries, brotherhoods) and of religious acts (masses, almsgiving, paying back of illicit gains). Secular provisions permit reconstruction of the networks of people around testators: spouses, children, other family members, servants, neighbours, work or business associates, friends. For instance, wills allow groups to be identified, for example, lay women, who appear to be friends and connected through a religious experience, Beguines, or members of the third mendicant orders.

Scholars have produced tables and graphs showing how many testatrixes there were in their samples, grouping them according to marital status, social group, profession, and place of origin. Depending on location, as few as five percent to as many as sixty percent of total testators were women. These differences depend on the property rights and the testamentary freedom women enjoyed.

Wills are now used in legal history, genealogical studies, economic and social history, and history of material culture. Through the diffusion of gender as a category of analysis, the question has arisen whether patterns of bequests depended on testators' sex, in addition to their social position and age. Even if there is not one pattern of bequests for women and one for men, many testaments made by women show common characteristics. Despite having fewer means, women tended to bequeath more than men for the benefit of their souls. Women often left objects, for example, clothes and other items, to single recipients; typically, they bequeathed their tablecloths to churches to be transformed into altar cloths, and they listed their gowns and mantels, identifying each one through quality and colour. Testatrixes were less willing than their male counterparts to influence the afterworld, by imposing certain moral or social behaviours on their heirs and beneficiaries.

Women in Others' Wills

Furthermore, the place women occupied in other people's wills has been the object of inquiry. Husbands used wills to offer their future widows better conditions than laws and customs permitted. To secure each other advantages, some spouses made mutual wills, and these could be part of marriage agreements, as was the practice in Flanders. Wills were often used to provide marriageable women with dowries and other gifts. In this way wealthy women could receive their portion of inheritance, while poor women could collect their dowries through bequests from several testators. Women were seldom testamentary executors because many laws and customs considered them unsuitable to act as proxies.

Wills have been defined as the only direct signs left by people—among them many women—about whom scholars would otherwise know nothing. But the significance of these signs depends in part on whether medieval women's wills provided a space for independent decisions. Some scholars emphasize that testatrixes consciously used their right of choosing to whom they would leave their goods. Others doubt that wills are suitable to give information on the choices of individuals, because they were written with specific aims and formal characteristics; furthermore, wills were often dictated to scribes and could be written down in Latin, a language unknown to most testatrixes. At the same time wills are a source for information on people—often women—too poor to make their own wills: they were beneficiaries in others' wills.

After the death of the testator, his or her will proved to be no self-executing act: the intent of the deceased could be equivocal or contested in court, and the will had no effects until the executors implemented it.

LINDA GUZZETTI

References and Further Reading

Amt, Emilie, ed. *Women's Lives in Medieval Europe: A Source Book*. New York: Routledge, 1993, pp. 130–136.

Burgess, Clive. "Late Medieval Wills and Pious Convention: Testamentary Evidence Reconsidered." In *Profit, Piety and the Professions in Later Medieval England*, edited by Michael Hicks. Gloucester: Alan Sutton, 1990, pp. 14–33.

Chaunu, Pierre. *La mort à Paris, XVIe, XVIIe, XVIIIe siècles*. Paris: Fayard, 1984.

Chiffoleau, Jacques. *La comptabilité de l'au delà. Les hommes, la mort et la religion dans la region d'Avignon à la fin du Moyen Age*. Roma: École française de Rome, 1980.

Chojnacki, Stanley. "Patrician Women in Early Renaissance Venice." In *Women and Men in Renaissance Venice: Twelve Essays on Patrician Society*, edited by Stanely Chojnacki. Baltimore, Md.: Johns Hopkins University Press, 2000, pp. 115–131.

———. "The Power of the Love: Wives and Husbands." In *Women and Men in Renaissance Venice: Twelve Essays on Patrician Society*, edited by Stanley Chojnacki. Baltimore: The Johns Hopkins University Press, 2000, pp. 153–168.

Cohn, Samuel Kline. *The Cult of Remembrance and the Black Death: Six Renaissance Cities in Central Italy*. Baltimore, Md.: Johns Hopkins University Press, 1992.

———. "The Place of the Dead in Flanders and Tuscany: Towards a Comparative History of the Black Death." In *Place of the Dead: Death and Remembrance in Late Medieval and Early Modern Europe*, edited by Bruce Gordon and Peter Marshall. Cambridge: Cambridge University Press, 2000, pp. 17–43.

Epstein, Steven. *Wills and Wealth in Medieval Genoa 1150–1250*. Cambridge, Mass.: Harvard University Press, 1984.

Goldberg, P. J. P., ed. "Passages from Wills Made by or concerning Women." In *Women in England, c. 1275–1525: Documentary Sources*. Manchester: Manchester University Press, 1995.

Howell, Martha C. "Fixing Movables: Gifts by Testament in Late Medieval Douai." *Past and Present* 150 (1996): 3–45.

Kittell, Ellen E. "Testaments of Two Cities: A Comparative Analysis of the Wills of Medieval Genoa and Douai." *European Review of History* 5 (1998): 47–82.

Kuehn, Thomas. "Law, Death, and Heirs in the Renaissance." *Renaissance Quarterly* 45 (1992): 484–516.

Lewis, Katherine J. "Women, Testamentary Discourse and Life-Writing in Later Medieval England." In *Medieval Women and the Law*, edited by Noël James Menuge. Woodbridge, Suffolk: Boydell & Brewer, 2000.

MacMillin, Linda. "Anonymous Lives: Documents from the Benedictine Convent of Sant Pere de les Puelles." In *Women Writing Latin, 2: Medieval Women Writing Latin*, edited by Laurie J. Churchill, Phyllis R. Brown, and Jane J. Jeffrey. New York and London: Routledge, 2002, pp. 265–280.

Sheehan, Michael M. *The Will in Medieval England: From the Conversion of the Anglo-Saxons to the End of the Thirteenth Century*. Toronto: Pontifical Institute of Medieval Studies, 1963.

———. "English Wills and the Records of the Ecclesiastic and Civil Jurisdictions." In *Marriage, Family, and Law in Medieval Europe: Collected Studies*, edited by James K. Farge. Toronto: University of Toronto Press, 1996.

Szende, Katalin G. "Families in Testaments: Some Aspects of Demography and Inheritance Customs in a Late Medieval Hungarian Town." *Otium* 3 (1995): 107–124.

Thompson, Victoria. "Women, Power and Protection in Tenth- and Eleventh-Century England." In *Medieval Women and the Law*, edited by Noël James Menuge. Woodbridge, Suffolk: Boydell & Brewer, 2000, pp. 1–17.

Vovelle, Michel. *Pitié baroque et déchristianisation en Provence au XVIIIe siècle*. Paris: Plon, 1973. Second edition, Paris: Seuil, 1978.

See also **Almsgiving and Charity; Annales School of History; Beguines; Clothing; Confraternities; Death, Mourning, and Commemoration; Dowry and Other Marriage Gifts; Family (Earlier Middle Ages); Family (Later Middle Ages); Hospitals; Inheritance; Landholding and Property Rights; Law; Literacy and Reading: Latin; Widows; Widows as Guardians**

WISDOM

Feminine embodiments of wisdom—e.g., Lady Wisdom, Sapientia, Sophia, Philosophy—are commonplace in medieval depictions of the transmission and acquisition of knowledge. In allegories written in Latin and in the medieval European vernaculars, Wisdom personified mediates divine and higher knowledge, frequently entering into an intimate relationship with a male narrator or character who desires wisdom. Boethius's sixth-century *The Consolation of Philosophy*, for example, in which Lady Philosophy guides the author-figure to wisdom, was widely read and highly influential throughout the Middle Ages.

In addition to neo-Platonist writings such as *The Consolation of Philosophy,* biblical wisdom literature, particularly the book of Proverbs, was an authoritative source for theological and literary personifications of wisdom. In Proverbs, Wisdom appears as a prophet, counselor, and bride. Readers are admonished to love Wisdom, who, like the ideal wife, is described as "more precious than jewels." Medieval Christian exegesis identified the biblical feminine wisdom figure with Christ, as did the Christian evangelical writers (John, Luke, Matthew, and Paul). In the Middle Ages, Lady Wisdom was also commonly associated with the Virgin Mary, often represented as the Seat of Wisdom.

By putting a feminine face on the divine and implicitly demonstrating the intellectual ability of women, the feminine personification of Wisdom contrasts with medieval wisdom literature's generalized misogyny in its presentation of "Woman," the "secrets of women," and the "wiles of women" as standard topics for male mastery. In this light, it is not surprising that the feminine personification of wisdom was of particular interest to and used by women writers, such as Hildegard of Bingen and Christine de Pizan.

EMILY C. FRANCOMANO

References and Further Reading

Boethius. *The Consolation of Philosophy*, translated by V. E. Watts. New York: Penguin, 1969.

Camp, Claudia. *Wisdom and the Feminine in the Book of Proverbs*. Decatur, Ga.: Almond, 1985.

Deutsch, Celia. *Lady Wisdom, Jesus, and the Sages: Metaphor and Social Context in Matthew's Gospel*. Valley Forge, Pa.: Trinity Press International, 1996.

Newman, Barbara. *God and the Goddesses: Vision Poetry and Belief in the Middle Ages*. Philadelphia: University of Pennsylvania Press, 2003.

Paxson, James J. *The Poetics of Personification*. Cambridge: Cambridge University Press, 1994.

———. *Sister of Wisdom: St. Hildegard's Theology of the Feminine*. Berkeley, Calif.: University of California Press, 1987.

Solterer, Helen. *The Master and Minerva: Disputing Women in French Medieval Culture*. Berkeley, Calif.: University of California Press, 1995.

Smalley, Beryl. *Medieval Exegesis of Wisdom Literature*, edited by Roland E. Murphy. Scholars Press Reprints and Translations Series. Atlanta: Scholars Press, 1986.

See also **Christine de Pizan; Defenses of Women; Hildegard of Bingen; Mary, Virgin; Personifications Visualized as Women; Song of Songs, Medieval Interpretations of**

WITCHES

Witches supposedly wield occult power, beyond the capacity of ordinary humans. In rationalistic terms, witchcraft powers represent special forms of knowledge, e.g., herbs and healing, meteorological patterns, the ability to find lost objects, animal behavior, and human psychology. Witches may use their powers for either good or evil, but for the witch's community, such powers are a source of awe and fear. Harmful witchcraft is considered an expression of the witch's malevolence toward other people.

In preindustrial, preliterate societies, a distinction between *witchcraft* and *sorcery* appears to be normative. Witchcraft power originates within the witch; it can be consciously employed, but can also operate against the witch's intentions. Unlike witchcraft, *sorcery* depends on rituals, the conscious manipulation of objects and symbols in external reality to attain a maleficent effect. Related powers are *necromancy,* which invokes and consults dead or nonhuman spirits, and *shamanism,* wherein the shaman's spirit travels into a noncorporeal dimension or "spirit world" to seek advice or supplementary powers. Such ideas, documented in modern "primitive" societies (Evans-Pritchard; Douglas), had clear analogues in medieval and later western European folklore (Kieckhefer 1989; Ginzburg).

The European Stereotype

Around 1400, social and religious upheavals contributed to the evolution of a new concept of witchcraft, combining elements of all these aforementioned occult roles. The hybrid stereotype had disastrous consequences for women. In preliterate societies, witches could be male or female, but the new European stereotype, elaborated by intellectual theorists, disproportionately victimized women. Across Europe and the Americas between the early 1400s and the late

1700s, around fifty thousand people were put to death for witchcraft. About eighty percent of known trials and executions involved female defendants.

Although protests were usually ineffectual, opponents of witch persecution denounced its cruelty and irrationality throughout the period. Yet although the European "witch craze" declined rapidly by 1650, witch-trials did not end until the late 1700s. Nineteenth-century historians pioneered the systematic study of witchcraft trials and witchcraft treatises; social and intellectual historians since 1970 provide a more complete understanding of the witch-hunting pathology and its effects on society and culture (Levack; Clark).

The European witch stereotype embodies two apparent paradoxes: first, it was not produced by the "barbaric Dark Ages," but during the "progressive" Renaissance and early modern period; secondly, Western Christianity did not recognize the reality of witches for centuries, or criminalize them until around 1400.

Canon law and penitential manuals suggest that, even in the late Middle Ages, laypeople confessed to venerating beings that Christian theology condemned as pagan gods (i.e., as demons). Early secular law codes punished sorcery, sometimes with death. But throughout the early and High Middle Ages, the Church condemned occult practices as pagan superstition, and prescribed penances for believing in their reality. In Canon Law, the influential decree *Episcopi* typified the early medieval Church's attitude to superstition and occult practices. Formulated during Carolingian times, the canon *Episcopi* informed bishops about women who supposedly believed the goddess Diana led them *en masse* on mysterious nocturnal cavalcades (Kors and Peters, 60–67). *Episcopi* directed bishops to discover such women, explain their experiences as demonic illusions produced during sleep, prescribe penance, and excommunicate anyone who obstinately defended the reality of the cavalcade.

Although clerics possibly misunderstood such beliefs, references to them influenced intellectuals' thinking about women and witchcraft for centuries. Paradoxically, canon *Episcopi*, transmitted through Gratian's *Decretum*, inspired the earliest learned theories of female demonic witchcraft. Beginning abruptly c. 1430, learned treatises expressly refuted *Episcopi*'s contention that women's nocturnal travels were an illusion. The "goddess Diana" was redefined as an incarnate demon, her idolatrous, apostate followers declared awake, the experience pronounced entirely real. Clerical theorists imagined that many heretical sects met embodied demons at night,

pledged homage to Satan, and formally joined his "synagogue." He commanded them to perpetrate all forms of evil, and punished them for failure. At Satanic meetings, heretics performed human sacrifices, copulated with demons, and mocked and desecrated the Christian sacraments. The women of canon *Episcopi* figured prominently as proof of such heretics' interaction with demons (Stephens, 125–144). Clerics referred to the new super-heretics as *maleficus/malefica* (male/female evildoer). These terms and *maleficium* (evildoing), today considered synonyms of *witch* and *witchcraft*, represent the early, formative phase of witch stereotyping.

Important social and religious developments after the year 1000 influenced this radical demonization of heretics. Formerly largely restricted to clerics, heresy spread among the laity due to urbanization, commerce, and growing vernacular literacy. Waldensians demanded ecclesiastical reform to reduce clerical luxury, accommodate laypeople, and assist the suffering poor; Cathars (Albigensians) espoused a partially non-Christian religion resembling ancient Manichaeism; by 1400, Wyclifites and Bohemian Hussites demanded reforms of doctrine, ritual, and ecclesiology, foreshadowing Luther's revolt. Increasingly worried, fifteenth- and sixteenth-century clerics and magistrates interpreted spreading heresy as a massive demonic conspiracy (Cohn).

Logically, as the enemy of orthodoxy, Satan would personally oversee heretics' activities. Twelfth-century clerics had already described his presence "in person" at heretical gatherings. By 1300, intellectuals were also preoccupied with necromancers, real and imagined. Necessarily literate, inhabiting a "clerical underworld" of reckless exorcists (Kieckhefer 1989), necromancers supposedly consulted demons, rather than the dead, and exchanged their salvation for demonic power through pacts with Satan. From c. 1400 to 1480, lay and clerical magistrates in Switzerland, Italy, and elsewhere also tried laypeople for harmful sorcery; face-to-face interaction with the devil was a standard accusation. Confessions of heretical belief or practice corroborated confessions of *maleficium* obtained under torture, usually dooming the accused.

Uneducated people did not originally associate witchcraft power with demons, but after 1400 learned men interpreted laypeople's traditional witchcraft accusations as evidence that demons produced *maleficium* in exchange for witches' souls (Kieckhefer 1976). Prosecutors and treatise writers elaborately described the *maleficia* that Satan performed for witches: impotence, infertility, crop failure, and disease and death of livestock and persons, including infants, both baptized and not. Added to the inhuman horrors imagined for the "sabbat," or witches' mass meeting, this everyday human–demon collaboration explained the world's distressing state (Stephens).

Witches as Female

These developments coalesced into the stereotype of woman-as-witch. Although uneducated people also referred to male witches, their traditional witchcraft accusations mainly affected domestic activities, where women had principal responsibility: food preparation; childbirth; care of children, invalids, and livestock; healing; and male sexual self-esteem.

Intellectuals' stereotype of witches as female was desultory until 1487, when it was deliberately and exhaustively codified. Bearing a corroborative bull of Pope Innocent VIII, the *Malleus maleficarum* (*Hammer of Witch-Women*) declared that most witches were female. Its virulent descriptions of women's innate perversity and its program for entrapping and convicting them make the *Malleus maleficarum* a "classic" work of misogyny. Its direct influence over subsequent witch persecutions is debatable, but its many reprintings reinforced clerical, judicial, and folkloric stereotypes about ungovernable, maleficent women with unparalleled thoroughness. Subsequent trials continued to equate women and witches; meanwhile, the *Malleus* inspired increasingly elaborate theoretical treatises for over a century. Trials, preaching, and growing vernacular literacy spread the misogynistic stereotype from theologians and magistrates to laypeople.

A Medieval Precursor

Although widespread persecution of women as witches began in the fifteenth century, the 1324–1325 trial of Alice Kyteler, an Irish noblewoman, uncannily foreshadowed Renaissance trials. Repeatedly widowed, Alice stood to inherit from her fourth husband, but her estranged stepchildren accused her of poisoning him and her previous spouses. Richard Ledrede, the bishop of Ossory, preoccupied with theological demonology, transformed this unexceptional property dispute into the earliest complete witch trial, accusing Alice of leading a sect of devil-worshiping homicidal heretics. Ledrede had Alice's servant Petronilla of Meath whipped until she "confessed" to arranging sexual trysts between Alice and an incarnate devil named Robert Artisson; Petronilla

"testified" that Alice had poisoned her victims with demonic aid. Alice prudently escaped to England; Ledrede burned Petronilla on 3 November 1324. The trial is fictionalized in *The Name of the Rose* (Eco 1994, 30, 327).

WALTER STEPHENS

References and Further Reading

Bailey, Michael David. *Battling Demons: Witchcraft, Heresy, and Reform in the Late Middle Ages.* University Park, Pa.: Pennsylvania State University Press, 2003.
Briggs, Robin. *Witches and Neighbors: The Social and Cultural Context of Witchcraft.* Second edition. Oxford: Blackwell, 2002.
Clark, Stuart. *Thinking with Demons: The Idea of Witchcraft in Early Modern Europe.* Oxford: Oxford University Press, 1997.
Cohn, Norman. *Europe's Inner Demons: An Enquiry Inspired by the Great Witch-Hunt.* New York: Basic Books, 1975.
Davidson, L. S., and J. O. Ward, eds. *The Sorcery Trial of Alice Kyteler: A Contemporary Account (1324) Together with Related Documents.* Binghamton, N.Y.: Medieval and Renaissance Texts and Studies, 1993.
Douglas, Mary. *Witchcraft Confessions and Accusations.* London: Tavistock, 1970.
Eco, Umberto. *The Name of the Rose*, translated by William Weaver. Reprint, New York: Harcourt Brace, 1994.
Evans-Pritchard, E. E. *Witchcraft, Oracles and Magic Among the Azande*, edited by Eva Gillies. Oxford: Clarendon, 1976.
Ginzburg, Carlo. *The Night-Battles: Witchcraft and Agrarian Cults in the Sixteenth and Seventeenth Centuries*, translated by John and Anne Tedeschi. New York: Penguin, 1985.
Kieckhefer, Richard. *European Witch Trials: Their Foundations in Popular and Learned Culture, 1300–1500.* Berkeley, Calif. and Los Angeles: University of California Press, 1976.
———. *Magic in the Middle Ages.* Cambridge: Cambridge University Press, 1989.
Kors, Alan Charles, and Edward Peters. *Witchcraft in Europe 400–1700: A Documentary History.* Second edition, revised by Edward Peters. Philadelphia: University of Pennsylvania Press, 2001.
Kramer, Heinrich. *The* Malleus Maleficarum *of Heinrich Kramer and James [sic] Sprenger*, translated by Montague Summers. London: J. Rodker, 1928. Reprint, New York: Dover, 1971.
Purkiss, Diane. *The Witch in History: Early Modern and Twentieth-Century Representations.* London: Routledge, 1996.
Stephens, Walter. *Demon Lovers: Witchcraft, Sex, and the Crisis of Belief.* Chicago: University of Chicago Press, 2002.
Thomas, Keith. *Religion and the Decline of Magic.* New York: Scribner, 1971.
Williams, Bernadette. "'She Was Usually Placed with the Great Men and Leaders of the Land in Public Assemblies': Alice Kyteler, A Woman of Considerable Power." In *Women in Renaissance and Early Modern Europe*, edited by Christine Meek. Dublin: Four Courts, 2000, pp. 67–83.

See also **Cathars; Femininity and Masculinity; Gender Ideologies; Gender in History; Heretics and Heresy; Impotence; Infants and Infanticide; Magic and Charms; Misogyny; Paganism; Waldensians**

WOLFRAM VON ESCHENBACH

Although Wolfram once calls himself a Bavarian (Pz 121, 7), he is usually associated with Franconia, the region to which several of his works refer. He mentions Herrmann of Thuringia (r. 1190–1217) as one of his patrons (Wh 3, 8–9; Tit. 82a, 2–4), but also an unnamed woman, for whose sake the narrator claims to have composed *Parzival* (Pz. 827, 29). Parts of *Parzival* must have been completed before 1203, since book VII mentions the destruction of the vineyards in Erfurt as an event of the recent past; his *Willehalm* is commonly dated to 1210–1220.

Little is known of his social standing, but his work suggests that he must have had knowledge of French, as well as an interest in medicine, astronomy, geography, and aspects of theology. Wolfram was clearly familiar with the work of contemporary writers, and, although he paints a picture of himself as an illiterate layperson, he must have had sufficient knowledge of the Latin learned tradition to establish himself in opposition to it. Like most medieval literature, his narratives were probably read out loud to a court audience, possibly in sections even before completion of the work as a whole, yet there are references to the audience reading the tales, and it is clear that he envisaged an audience of men and women.

Wolfram is an unusually prolific author whose oeuvre combines lyric and narrative modes. No more than nine courtly love songs are transmitted under his name, but they are striking in their use of unusual metaphor and a complex interchange of voices. The best known, *Sine clawen*, opens with the image of dawn as a bird of prey streaking the sky and thus evokes the erotically charged moment in which the lovers have to part at daybreak.

Parzival, based on Chrétien de Troyes's *Perceval* but extending beyond its fragmentary source, develops the story of its protagonist across three generations. Parzival, whose father had died in battle, is brought up by his mother Herzeloyde, a daughter of the Grail king Frimutel, in total seclusion so that he might escape the fate of his father. He, nevertheless, sets out into the world in pursuit of knighthood, becomes a knight of King Arthur's round table, finds a bride, succeeds in the quest for the Grail, and yet fails to ask the crucial question. Exiled from human society and despairing to the point of renouncing God, Parzival, aided by divine grace, is

finally recalled to the Grail, crowned Grail king, and reunited with his wife Condwiramurs. Wolfram's narrative moves beyond Chrétien in developing the Arthurian knight Gawan into a second protagonist who is at the centre of whole sections of the narrative. Yet Parzival is also defined through a series of encounters with female figures. His mother Herzeloyde embodies *triuwe* (loyalty), which in the eyes of the narrator is the key virtue defining not only successful human relations but also the relationship between man and God. His cousin Sigune, whom he encounters at key stages of his journey, out of loyalty to her dead lover renounces the world, dying as a hermit on the same day as Parzival is crowned Grail king. His wife, Condwiramurs, sustains him throughout with her love. In the world Wolfram creates, love and sexual desire are forces that lead to violence, war, and human suffering, yet marriage can be the way to heal past injustice (Gawan and Orgeluse), reconcile feuding families (Gramoflanz and Itonje), and even unite east and west (Gahmuret and Belakane, Feirefiz and Repanse). Women's roles in this are rarely active, despite the fact that Belakane, Herzeloyde, Condwiramurs, and Orgeluse all rule in their own right. They are shown to be dependent on men, yet the same is true in reverse, as demonstrated by the prominent role that Wolfram accords marriage.

Willehalm combines elements of the chanson de geste, the political narrative of great deeds, with a saint's life: Willehalm, the disinherited younger son, falls in love with the heathen queen Arabel, who becomes his wife, converts, and takes the name Gyburc. Led by Arabel/Gyburc's former husband Tybalt and her father Terramer, the heathens set out to regain her and her territory. Defending the city of Orange, Willehalm leads the Christians to victory, although the narrative remains incomplete, breaking off with Willehalm searching the battlefield for his supporter Rennewart. In contrast to his French source, Wolfram foregrounds the role of Gyburc—she is not only the cause of the war between heathens and Christians, but also takes a decisive stance. Like the female figures in *Parzival*, she acts as ruler and even military commander inside the besieged city during Willehalm's absence, and before the final battle, she makes a long speech in council pleading for mercy towards the heathens. They are her kin, but she reminds the Christian nobles that they are also linked in spiritual kinship as fellow creatures of God.

With *Titurel*, Wolfram engages in a narrative experiment that has no parallel in medieval literature: he returns to the figure of Sigune, Parzival's cousin, and makes her the central figure of a new narrative. The work consists of two fragments, between which a considerable section of narrative is missing: the first fragment opens with a genealogy of the Grail family down to the birth and childhood of Sigune, who as a young girl falls in love with the equally youthful Schionatulander. Aware of the conventions of courtly love but not its emotional impact, she demands love service of him. The second fragment opens with Schionatulander bringing her a dog with a precious lead. Sigune starts reading the story embroidered on that leash when the dog escapes; she orders Schionatulander to retrieve the dog so she can finish the story. From premonitions of the narrator and references to *Parzival* it is clear that this demand will cause Schionatulander's death. *Titurel* clearly presupposes knowledge of *Parzival*, and there are pointers to the tragic end of the incipient love story all through the narrative. In turning to a female protagonist, Wolfram is able to explore the relationship between reading and life, or narrative and experience.

ALMUT SUERBAUM

References and Further Reading

Bumke, Joachim. *Wolfram von Eschenbach*. Seventh edition. Stuttgart: Metzler, 1997.

Hasty, Will, ed. *A Companion to Wolfram's* Parzival. Columbia, S.C.: Camden House, 1999.

Jones, Martin, and Timothy MacFarland, eds. *Wolfram's* Willehalm: *Fifteen Essays*. Rochester, N.Y.: Camden House, 2001.

von Eschenbach, Wolfram. *Werke*, edited by Karl Lachmann Berlin: De Gruyter, 1926. Reprint, Berlin: De Gruyter, 1965.

See also **Arthurian Literature; Audience, Women in the; Courtly Love; Dawn Song (Alba); Literature, German; Romance: German**

WOMAN ON TOP

"Woman on Top" refers to a frequently encountered family of representations in literature, art, and popular festivities of women who seize the upper hand in their relations with men, reversing the normative hierarchy in which women are inferior and submissive to men. A familiar example is the medieval tale in which the beautiful Phyllis tricks the philosopher Aristotle into allowing her to ride him like a horse by promising him sexual favors. In visual art—notably prints, misericords, manuscript margins, and objects of daily use—women who use sexual attraction to make slaves of men are also figured as leading them by ropes and chains around their necks, while disorderly wives beat their husbands with distaffs, drive them like cart horses, and steal their pants. Natalie Z. Davis, who popularized the term *Woman on Top* in her 1975 article of the same name, applied it

also to cases in which women dress as men and play male roles. These gender role reversals are one aspect of the broader *topos* of the World Upside Down, which also encompasses, *inter alia*, topsy-turvy relations between humans and animals. In the symbolic realm, sexual inversion, especially with respect to the relations between husbands and wives, sometimes served as a figure for disorder in political, social, and other hierarchies. Underpinning the Woman on Top is the theory, widely held in the Middle Ages, that women are by nature disorderly and rebellious. Commentators on Genesis regarded Eve's disobedience to God as proof that women as a sex are prone to resist the legitimate authority of men. Women's weakness in reason, evidence for which exegetes claimed to find in Eve's secondary creation from Adam's rib, was blamed. Corroborating theological opinion was the physiological theory of Aristotle and his medieval followers, such as Albertus Magnus, according to which women's temperament was dominated by cold and wet humors that made them less rational and more subject to the desires of the body than men. Inclined to allow these inferior, characteristically female qualities to dominate the higher faculty of reason in their own natures, women were held to be likewise desirous of asserting their rule over men.

In the literature of misogyny and misogamy, the Woman on Top was invoked to denigrate women and urge the necessity of keeping them in their place. The celebrated thirteenth-century preacher Jacques de Vitry accordingly told the tale of Aristotle and Phyllis as an *exemplum* to condemn the cunning and malice of women and to warn his listeners against succumbing to their wiles. Moralists and satirists likewise derided rebellious wives who use trickery to cuckold their humiliated husbands and stop at nothing to take household authority into their own hands.

Reactions to the Woman on Top were not necessarily all negative, however. As Davis notes, in carnival, festival practices, and popular theater, gender role reversals enabled the venting of conflicts between the sexes within clearly defined limits of time and place. Though the ultimate result may have been to reaffirm male authority when the period of misrule ended, she argues that the expression of alternatives could also work to subject normative expectations to critique and offer women models for disruption and disobedience. Similarly ambiguous are comic literary characters such as Chaucer's Wife of Bath, who boasts of using sexuality and deception to dominate one husband after another.

Susan Smith similarly finds considerable ambiguity in the Power of Women *topos*, a prominent manifestation of the Woman on Top. Also known as the Wiles of Women, Slaves of Love, and Slaves of

Women, this *topos* brings together two or more famous examples from the Bible, ancient history, and romance to prove that women can master even the worthiest of men. "Who was stronger than Samson, wiser than Solomon, or holier than David?" a fourteenth-century preacher asks his audience. "Yet they were all overcome by the deceits and wiles of women." The weight of patristic authorities such as St. Jerome made the *topos* ubiquitous in the later Middle Ages, initially in antifeminist Latin literature but, by the twelfth century, in vernacular genres as well. In visual art, beginning in the fourteenth century, the *topos* is commonplace in embroideries, tapestries, ivory caskets, tableware, misericords, prints, and other media. The Malterer Embroidery (early fourteenth century) and two series of woodcuts by Lucas van Leyden (1512, 1516–1519) are widely cited examples. At least some artists and vernacular poets, Smith shows, deployed the *topos* to celebrate the power of women and of love, not to condemn them, just as the thirteenth-century Norman poet Henri d'Andeli concluded his version of the Aristotle and Phyllis tale by vindicating the lady and declaring that love conquers all. The carousing pants-wearing woman of Nuremberg's *Fastnacht* revels, Chaucer's lusty Wife of Bath, and other embodiments of the Power of Women *topos* suggest that the Woman on Top is best understood not as a straightforward manifestation of medieval antifeminism but as a site of contest through which conflicting ideas about gender roles could be expressed.

SUSAN L. SMITH

References and Further Reading

Davis, Natalie Z. "Women on Top." In *Society and Culture in Early Modern France: Eight Essays by Natalie Zemon Davis*. Stanford, Calif.: Stanford University Press, 1975, pp. 124–151.

Perfetti, Lisa. *Women and Laughter in Medieval Comic Literature*. Ann Arbor, Mich.: University of Michigan Press, 2003.

Susan L. Smith. *The Power of Women: A Topos in Medieval Literature and Art*. Philadelphia: University of Pennsylvania Press, 1995.

See also **Aristotelian Concepts of Women and Gender; Cross-Dressing; Eve; Festivals of Misrule; Gender Ideologies; Misericords; Misogyny; Wife of Bath**

WOMAN'S SONG

The term *woman's song* (German, *Frauenlied*; French, *chanson de femme*; Galician–Portuguese, *cantigas de amigo* [songs about a lover]) has long been used by scholars to denote love poems spoken entirely in a woman's voice that are either anonymous or male-authored. The origins of this kind of poetry are ancient. Examples of woman's song are among the first surviving lyric poems in the vernacular languages of Europe, and they have come down to us in virtually all of the languages spoken in medieval Europe, including Latin and Arabic. Examples of woman's song can consist of a single or multiple stanzas, and they can appear in monologues or in poems in which the woman's voice is in dialogue with the voice of another woman, typically her mother or a girlfriend, or with the voice of a man, typically her lover or suitor. Religious lyrics are traditionally excluded from this category, though female personifications, sanctified and legendary women, and the Blessed Virgin Mary often raise their voices in song in medieval hymns, liturgies, and plays. The term *woman's song* has conventionally been used to mean "songs narrated by women" and not "songs composed by women." However, recent feminist scholarship has called this distinction into question. It views woman's song as a literary construct, a set of poetic and generic conventions that can be employed by both male and female authors. Woman's song thus becomes a matter of voice, not authorship. For this reason, Anne L. Klinck's *Anthology of Ancient and Medieval Woman's Song* (2004) includes anonymous, male-authored, and female-authored works.

Woman's song is about love. It plumbs variations in the experience of love and desire from many different perspectives: sorrow at being parted from one's beloved; grief at being abandoned; nostalgia for a love enjoyed in the past; regretful or joyful proclamations of love and fidelity; expressions of longing; sorrow and anger over the hostile influences of spies or rivals; joyful celebrations of fulfilled love and reciprocated desire. The variety of form, content, style, symbolism, and tone in this body of female-voiced poetry about love is astonishing. In the Provençal poetry of the *trobairitz* the Comtessa de Dia, the language of power relations and the language of love fuses and evokes both political and erotic lordship. The Galician–Portuguese *cantigas de amigo* (of which there are over five hundred examples) often create a sense of youthful, artless femininity. In them a girl is often shown in dialogue with a confidante, either her mother or a girlfriend. Most of the surviving examples of woman's song in Middle English are carols, that is to say, songs originally created to accompany dancing. Much of the surviving Old French corpus of woman's song also takes the metrical form of dance songs (*ballette, rondeau*). The surviving examples of Middle Latin woman's song, which were probably composed by male clerics, are sometimes charming, witty, or bawdy, and sometimes ironic and even misogynist. The woman's song of early medieval Spain reflects the linguistic, ethnic, and religious diversity of its three communities of Christians, Muslims, and Jews.

In German courtly love poetry (*Minnesang*), some male poets use woman's song for particularly dramatic effects. The lady in the verses of the poet Reinmar der Alte ("Reinmar the old") voices the paradox of being ravished by Reinmar's poetry but unable to act on her love due to social constraints (MF 178, 1). A woman entirely rejects courtly love (*hohe Minne*) as male hypocrisy and dangerous to her honor in Hartmann von Aue's *Frauenlied* (MF 213, 13). The poet Walther von der Vogelweide, widely regarded as one of the greatest of all German poets from medieval times to the present, composed fourteen poems with female speakers. His ladies engage in witty debate with the poet-lover on the meaning of female honor, which they see in the exercise of reason, not sexual discipline, a distant echo of Christine de Pizan. One of Walther's *Mädchenlieder* (songs articulated by a young woman not belonging to the court) is the most famous poem from medieval Germany. It is commonly called "Under der linden" ("under the linden tree") after its opening words (L 39, 11). In it a woman joyfully recalls an episode of lovemaking in a bed of roses under a linden tree, letting the audience in on her pleasures while enjoining the nightingale (a symbol of the poet) to complete secrecy.

Woman's sexual desire and frank sexual pleasure is also openly expressed in the European genre known as the dawn song (German *Tagelied*). Conversely, the female-voiced lyrics in the Old French *chanson de malmariée* (song of an unhappily married woman) suggest situations of domestic and sexual violence, and to a modern mind, the "seduction" scenarios of some carols and pastourelles (songs narrating an encounter between a shepherdess and a poet or lover) seem like rape. As Klinck states in the forward to her anthology, in woman's song "we find a woman's voice protesting against a male-imposed state of affairs and elevating the private over the public, the individual over the group, personal ties over social responsibilities" (1). Woman's song evokes the range, depth, and breadth of ways in which love is experienced, and at the same time it has been a vehicle for protest, resistance, and the discovery of an independently feeling self.

ANN MARIE RASMUSSEN

References and Further Reading

Bruckner, Matilda Tomaryn, Laurie Shepard, and Sarah White, eds. and trans. *Songs of the Women Troubadours*. New York: Garland, 1995.

Cheyette, Frederic L., and Margaret Switten. "Women in Troubadour Song: Of the Comtessa and the Vilana." *Women & Music* 2 (1998): 26–45.

Cramer, Thomas, John Greenfield, Ingrid Kasten, and Erwin Koller, eds. *Frauenlieder Cantigas de Amigo*. Stuttgart: Hirzel, 2000.

Doss-Quinby, Eglal, Joan Trasker Grimbert, Wendy Pfeffer, and Elizabeth Aubrey, eds. and trans. *Songs of the Women Trouvères*. New Haven, Conn.: Yale University Press, 2001.

Grimbert, Joan Tasker. "Songs by Women and Women's Song: How Useful is the Concept of Register?" In *The Court Reconvenes: Courtly Literature across the Disciplines. Selected Papers from the Ninth Triennial Congress of the International Courtly Literature Society, University of British Columbia, 25–31 July 1998*, edited by Barbara Altmann and Carleton W. Carroll. Woodbridge, Suffolk: Boydell & Brewer, 2003, pp. 117–124.

Kasten, Ingrid, ed and trans. *Frauenlieder des Mittelalters. Zweisprachig*. Stuttgart: Reclam, 1990.

Klinck, Anne L., ed and trans. *Anthology of Ancient and Medieval Woman's Song*. New York: Palgrave, 2004.

———. "Poetic Markers of Gender in Medieval 'Woman's Song': Was Anonymous a Woman?" *Neophilologus* 87.3 (2003): 339–359.

Klinck, Anne L., and Ann Marie Rasmussen, eds. *Medieval Woman's Song: Cross-Cultural Approaches*. Philadelphia: University of Pennsylvania Press, 2002.

"The Medieval Lyric," Projects for Teaching supported by the National Endowment for the Humanities and Mount Holyoke College. http://www.mtholyoke.edu/acad/medst/medieval_lyric/index.html.

Pfeffer, Wendy. "Complaints of Women, Complaints by Women: Can One Tell Them Apart?" In *The Court Reconvenes: Courtly Literature across the Disciplines. Selected Papers from the Ninth Triennial Congress of the International Courtly Literature Society, University of British Columbia, 25–31 July 1998*, edited by Barbara Altmann and Carleton W. Carroll. Woodbridge, Suffolk: Boydell & Brewer, 2003, pp. 125–131.

Rasmussen, Ann Marie. "Reason and the Female Voice in Walther von der Vogelweide's Poetry." In *Medieval Woman's Song: Cross-Cultural Approaches*, edited by Anne L. Klinck and Ann Marie Rasmussen. Philadelphia: University of Pennsylvania Press, 2002, pp. 168–186.

———. "Representing Woman's Desire: Walther's Woman's Stanzas in 'Ich hoere iu sô vil tugende jehen' (L43,9), 'Under der linden' (L39,11) and 'Frô Welt' (L100,24)." In *Women as Protagonists and Poets in the German Middle Ages: An Anthology of Feminist Approaches to Middle High German Literature*, edited by Albrecht Classen. Göppingen: Kümmerle, 1991, pp. 69–85.

See also **Courtly Love; Dance; Dawn Song (Alba); Literature, German; Literature, Iberian; Literature, Latin; Literature, Middle English; Literature, Occitan; Literature, Old French; Minnesang; Pastourelle; Trobairitz and Troubadours**

WOMEN AUTHORS: GERMAN TEXTS

While it is certain that ordinary women created literature through oral media such as song during the Middle Ages, there is only indirect evidence of their works. The first learned woman writer whose name is known is also the first German dramatist: the tenth-century canoness Hrotsvit of Gandersheim (Saxony). Composing in Latin and often using humor to make a point, Hrotsvit adapted the comedies of Terence to Christian teaching, especially the praise of chastity, for use in her Benedictine monastery. The next women authors of whom we have certain knowledge lived in the twelfth century. Like Hrotsvit they flourished in monastic communities and used Latin. Three are from the Rhineland. Hildegard of Bingen, abbess of Rupertsberg (1098–1179), produced a theological, musical, visionary, and scientific oeuvre including correspondence that shows her authority spread far beyond the Benedictine convent she founded. Elisabeth, a nun from the Benedictine monastery of Schönau (1129–1164), recorded her ecstatic visions partly under the influence of Hildegard, whom she visited at Rupertsberg and contacted by letter. Herrad of Landsberg (died 1195) was the abbess of the Augustinian house of canonesses in Hohenbourg near Strasbourg. She directed the production of a singular manuscript (now destroyed), the *Hortus deliciarum* (*Garden of Delights*), a compendium of Christian knowledge with almost 350 individual images including portraits of the nuns in her monastery.

The first woman writer using the German language had a spiritual calling as an anchoress, probably connected to the Benedictine monastery in Melk (Austria). Frau Ava (deceased about 1127) retold the lives of John the Baptist and Jesus in a fast-moving narrative style that has been praised as the first German epic. An anonymous nun is traditionally credited with writing down the earliest extant German love poem, a single but striking strophe known by its first line, "I am all yours." It was included at the end of an anonymous Latin love letter written in a woman's voice. Ten additional Latin letters, the majority woman-voiced, including two in which women express their love for other women, are copied in a late-twelfth-century Bavarian manuscript from Tegernsee monastery. It is not known what women composed these letters or whether they might have served as rhetorical models for male students.

Religious Writings

Vernacular literature flourished in the German courts in the decades around 1200. Ironically, no woman writers arose from this literary movement despite the fascination with gender evident in court texts. Yet a short time later one woman was in the vanguard as a writer of religious works in the vernacular. Mechthild of Magdeburg (1207–1282), most of her life a Beguine, was inspired by Dominican evangelism to reach a wide audience by composing in her native Low (northern) German. Although her originals are lost, they were translated into High (southern) German and Latin. Mechthild was a mystic who expressed her experience of God's love in highly original fusions of vernacular verse and prose, as well as in hymns, prayers, anecdotes, and dialogues. The influence of secular *minnesang* (love poetry of the courts) is present in her work. Late in her life Mechthild joined the Cistercian monastery of Helfta in Saxony, where two of her sisters in religion, Gertrude the Great and Mechthild of Hackeborn, produced their own mystical texts and correspondence under Mechthild's influence. The visions of Mechthild of Hackeborn were recorded in Latin for her first audiences, but German versions circulated in later manuscripts. Her *vita* (spiritual biography) of her abbess and biological older sister, Gertrude of Hackeborn, was also available in both languages. Gertrude of Hackeborn in turn was a distinguished educator at Helfta.

Dominican nuns in the fourteenth century continued the tradition of German women's mysticism but created a new genre for its expression. Known as the sister book, it combined a history of the monastery with biographies of nuns who had received special graces from the Lord. Nine sister books are extant, seven written in German and two in Latin with closely related German translations. Sister books were communal and cooperative efforts that required archival research, oral testimony, writing, compilation, and editing. Still, some sister books are associated with a single nun who took a leading role in their production, including Anna von Munzingen (Adelhausen), Katharina von Gebersweiler (Unterlinden), Christine Ebner (Engeltal), Elisabeth von Kirchberg (Kirchberg) and Elsbet Stagel (Töss). These nuns are known for additional writings: Christine Ebner recorded her revelations in German in her spiritual biography, while Stagel collaborated with Heinrich Seuse, the most popular mystic of the era, in the composition of his *vita*. Additional figures associated with the outpouring of German writing by Dominican nuns in the fourteenth century are Adelheid Langmann (Engeltal), Elsbeth von Oye (Ötenbach), and Margaretha Ebner (Maria Medingen). Ebner was a partner, with the itinerant priest Heinrich von Nördlingen, in the first German-language correspondence. Convent and religious writing in German continued in the fifteenth century; for example, the works of the nun Elisabeth Kempf (1415–1485), but it has not been as fully researched as the earlier records.

Increasing Literacy

The spread of literacy and the burgeoning use of German for all forms of written communication created new opportunities for women in the fifteenth century. The first female professional scribe, Klara Hätzlerin (1430–1476), worked in Augsburg. Several of her manuscripts have been identified, including one devoted to themes of love. Mechthild von der Pfalz (1419–1482) was a literary patron, book collector, and cofounder of the University of Tübingen. The first personal memoir in the German language was composed by an Austrian noblewoman named Helene Kottaner (about 1400–1470). It is a gripping tale of how she stole the crown of St. Stephen, which was used in the coronation of the kings of Hungary, in order to safeguard the sovereignty rights of the un-born child of the queen she served. More glimpses of noblewomen's lived experience are available in fifteenth-century correspondence: a companionate marriage is reflected in the letters of Margareta von Schwangau (died about 1459) to her poet husband, Oswald von Wolkenstein; and their daughter, Maria von Wolkenstein, abbess of the Poor Clares in Brixen (Tyrol), used secret correspondence in 1455–1456 to appeal to her brothers for help in staving off unwanted monastic reforms imposed by her bishop. The letters of Perchta and Anéžka Rožmberk, daughters of a powerful Bohemian family, are dictated partly in German and partly in Czech. They recount Perchta's self-defense in a marriage gone sour through delay of dowry payments (letters 1448–1488). Anéžka is an important example of a literate single woman, one who neither married nor became a nun.

Two noblewomen greatly advanced German prose as the medium for literary fiction through their success as translators. They were Elisabeth of Nassau Saarbrücken (1397–1456) and Eleonore Stuart (Eleonore of Scotland or of Austria) (1433–1480). Both Elisabeth and Eleonore were raised in multicultural court settings, Eleonore in Scotland and France and Elisabeth in France. Both left their natal lands to come to German-speaking states through marriage, and both were in a position to function as cultural ambassadors in their husbands' courts. Elisabeth and Eleonore both translated French *chansons de geste* (epics based on the life and times of Charlemagne) into German prose. Elisabeth, who was a generation older than Eleonore, translated four

chansons-de-geste. One, *Huge Scheppel*, presents the path-breaking ideas of cross-class marriage; another, *Herzog Herpin*, gives female characters exceptional agency as diplomats and peacemakers. Eleonore's *Pontus and Sidonia* is a tale in which faithful love is tested and rewarded with both personal happiness and political success. Elizabeth and Eleonore probably regarded their translations as educational texts that would reinforce the actions and attitudes needed to govern. The immense success of their works—they were reprinted until the eighteenth century—underscores their innovative formal and thematic aspects.

SARAH WESTPHAL-WIHL

References and Further Reading

Beach, Alison I. *Women as Scribes: Book Production and Monastic Reform in Twelfth-Century Bavaria.* Cambridge, U.K. and New York: Cambridge University Press, 2004.

Classen, Albrecht. "Footnotes to the German Canon: Maria von Wolkenstein and Argula von Grumbach." In *The Politics of Gender in Early Modern Europe*, edited by Jean R. Brink et al. Kirksville, Mo.: Sixteenth-Century Journal Publishers, 1989, pp. 131–147.

Edmunds, Sheila. "The Life and Works of Clara Hätzlerin." *Journal of the Early Book Society* 2 (1999): 1–25.

Garber, Rebecca L. *Feminine Figurae: Representations of Gender in Religious Texts by Medieval German Women Writers.* New York and London: Routledge, 2002.

Hindsley, Leonard Patrick. *The Mystics of Engelthal: Writings from a Medieval Monastery.* New York: St. Martin's Press, 1998.

Karnein, Alfred. "Mechthild von der Pfalz as Patroness: Aspects of Female Patronage in the Early Renaissance." *Medievalia et Humanistica* n.s. 22 (1995): 141–170.

Klassen, John M., ed. and trans. *The Letters of the Rožmberk Sisters: Noblewomen in Fifteenth-Century Bohemia.* Library of Medieval Women. Woodbridge, Suffolk: D. S. Brewer, 2001.

Klink, Anne L., ed. and trans. "I am all yours, you are all mine." In *An Anthology of Ancient and Medieval Woman's Song.* New York: Palgrave Macmillan, 2004.

Lewis, Gertrud Jaron. *By Women, for Women, about Women: The Sister-Books of Fourteenth-Century Germany.* Toronto: Pontifical Institute of Medieval Studies, 1996.

Morrison, Susan Signe. "Women Writers and Women Rulers: Rhetorical and Political Empowerment in the Fifteenth Century." *Women in German Yearbook: Feminist Studies in German Literature and Culture* 9 (1993): 25–48.

Poor, Sarah S. *Mechthild of Magdeburg and Her Book: Gender and the Making of Textual Authority.* Philadelphia: University of Pennsylvania Press, 2004.

Skow-Obenaus, Katya. "Wives and Mothers: A Study of Roles in *Herzog Herpin* and *Kaiser Octavian.*" *Germanic Notes and Reviews* 30.2 (1999): 124–132.

See also **Abbesses; Canonesses; Ebner, Margaretha; Eleanor of Scotland; Elisabeth of Schönau; Germanic Lands; Gertrude the Great; Hadewijch; Herrad of**

Hohenbourg; Hildegard of Bingen; Hrotsvit of Gandersheim; Kottaner, Helene; Langmann, Adelheid; Letter Writing; Mechthild of Hackeborn; Mechthild of Magdeburg; Mystics' Writings; Patronage, Literary; Singlewomen; Sister-Books and Other Convent Chronicles; Stagel, Elsbeth; Translation

WOMEN AUTHORS: ITALIAN TEXTS

The near-total absence of women authors writing in Italian in the Middle Ages is somewhat surprising, given their presence in other language traditions. In the cluster of dialects animating the Italian peninsula there are no figures writing who parallel Marie de France, Hildegard of Bingen, or Julian of Norwich, for example. The single woman poet writing in Tuscan Italian in the thirteenth century, the Compiuta Donzella, may be an historical figure (one about whom we have no biographical information); then again, she may be a total chimera, an invented persona, or a series of elusive figures lurking behind oblique references in lyric poems by male authors.

The impression of utter absence may, however, be artificially heightened by the relatively late start that vernacular writing received on the peninsula compared to the rest of the continent, as well as by the vestiges of periodization. The learned figure identified as Trota or Trotula, for example, reportedly wrote treatises on women's health in the context of the Salerno medical *studium*; these are in Latin, virtually the only language choice for erudite writing in the eleventh century. Angela da Foligno (d. 1309), who comes down to us mediated by a male amanuensis and by the conventions of spiritual writing, may have dictated her book in vernacular or Latin, but it survives only in the latter.

Finally, the fact that early modernity has traditionally been considered to emerge first in Italy assigns to the Renaissance the constellation of women writing from the fourteenth century on, in religious and/or in humanist circles. In a paradigm in which the Renaissance is frequently aligned with the writing of Dante Alighieri (1265–1321), the production (direct or indirect) of figures such as Catherine of Siena (c. 1347–1380) and Isotta Nogarola (1418–1466) falls by default to the Renaissance, not to the Middle Ages.

F. REGINA PSAKI

References and Further Reading

Green, Monica H., ed. and trans. *The Trotula. A Medieval Compendium of Women's Medicine*. Philadelphia: University of Pennsylvania Press, 2001.

King, Margaret L., and Albert Rabil, Jr., eds. *Her Immaculate Hand: Selected Works by and about the Women Humanists of Quattrocento Italy*. Binghamton, N.Y.: Pegasus Paperbooks, 1992.
Mazzoni, Cristina, ed. *Angela of Foligno's Memorial. Translated from Latin with Introduction, Notes, and Interpretive Essay*, translated by John Cirignano. Woodbridge, Suffolk, and Rochester, N.Y.: D. S. Brewer, 1999.
Noffke, Suzanne, trans. *The Letters of Catherine of Siena*. Tempe, Ariz.: Arizona Center for Medieval and Renaissance Studies, 2000.

See also Angela of Foligno; Compiuta Donzella; Tornabuoni de' Medici, Lucrezia

WOMEN AUTHORS: LATIN TEXTS

Early Christianity offered women unprecedented access to literacy, especially Latin literacy, because of its emphasis on the Word of God transmitted through the Bible. Perpetua's account of her imprisonment leading to martyrdom in 203, Latin correspondence between Fathers of the Church and a number of women, and Egeria's account of her travels in the Holy Land, probably between 381 and 384, are surviving examples of early Christian women writing Latin literature that are likely to have influenced medieval women's writing.

Between 450 and 1500, women used Latin as a medium for literature in a wide variety of genres. Some, such as letters, lyric, and mystical visions, have long been associated with women. Others are more surprising. Most notably, in the tenth century Hrotsvit of Gandersheim wrote Latin legends, dramas, and epic histories, as well as prefaces and dedicatory epistles to introduce her collected works; and in the twelfth century Hildegard of Bingen wrote letters, lyrics, hymns, religious drama, visionary and theological treatises, homilies, biography, commentaries on the Gospels, the Athanasian Creed, the Benedictine Rule, and technical books on natural history, health, and healing, all in Latin.

The earliest surviving medieval Latin texts by women are saints' lives, poems, and letters written by Merovingian noblewomen. Baudonivia, a nun in Queen and Abbess Radegund's monastery, wrote *The Life of St. Radegund* around 605–610. Radegund (d. 587) corresponded in Latin with Abbess Caesaria of Arles (c. 550) and various bishops in connection with her administration of the monastery for nuns she founded in Poitiers. More literary are her letters in Latin verse to a cousin and a nephew, in which conventions of classical epic and elegy merge with themes well known from Anglo-Saxon vernacular elegy.

Also poignant are some surviving Latin letters written by Brunhild, queen of the Franks (d. 613).

Especially notable is her letter to Empress Anastasia of Constantinople, asking Anastasia to return Brunhild's kidnapped grandson to Gaul rather than use him as a political pawn. Strikingly different in subject and style is Eucheria of Marseille's Latin poem of sixteen couplets listing incongruities in art and the natural world as evidence for the absurdity of her being wooed by a man of lower social standing than herself.

In the eighth century, the Saxon Abbess Hugeberc's *Hodoeporicon of St. Willibald*, an account of St. Willibald's pilgrimage to the Holy Land and his participation in the Christianization of Germany, is evidence that women continued to write in multiple genres, while Rudolf of Fulda's *Life of St. Leoba* provides considerable evidence of extensive Latin learning among the female religious leaders. Letters written by a group of Anglo-Saxon nuns associated with Boniface, the missionary to the Frisians and Saxons martyred in 754, illustrate stylistic variety. Scholars have noted the influence of Anglo-Saxon *winileodas*, songs for a lover, and Old Testament poetry on some of these letters, such as the nun Berthgyth's letters to her brother Balthard, with its range of stylistic devices and motifs, as she begs him to visit her and ease her sorrow. Dhuoda of Uzès's lengthy letter to her sixteen-year-old son, begun in November 841 and completed in February 843, a manual of advice in eleven sections, provides a particularly good example of how literary Medieval Latin letters could be. Peter Dronke identifies the ethic of Dhuoda's letter as different from any other surviving document from the period in its insistence that her son can serve both the world and God and in the twofold service find great joy (41).

Women writing Latin from the tenth century to the fifteenth century tend to be more familiar. Latin texts by Hrotsvit, Hildegard, Heloise, Elisabeth of Schönau, Gertrude of Helfta, Herrad of Hohenbourg, Catherine of Siena, Clare of Assisi, and Birgitta of Sweden, increasingly available in translation, exemplify the range and variety of ways in which women used Latin to make their voices heard. Social class continued to be a usual prerequisite for Latin literacy. Queen Edith of England (d. 1075), wrote a Latin biography of her husband, Edward the Confessor. Latin letters written by Queen Matilda of England (1080–1118) illustrate her involvement in the disputes between Henry I and Archbishop Anselm of Canterbury. She even wrote to Pope Pascal II on Anselm's behalf. Also in the eleventh century, a nun named Constance exchanged with Baudri of Bourgueil Latin verse poems imitating Ovid's *Heroides*.

Scholars of the Italian Renaissance often refer to the appearance of the learned woman as a phenomenon of the fourteenth and fifteenth centuries.

Humanism did bring with it remarkable opportunities for some women to participate in Latin literacy. Battista da Montefeltro Malatesta (1383–1450), Costanza Varano, Ippolita Sforza, and Cassandra Fedele wrote and delivered Latin orations in public; Maddalena Scrovegni (1356–1429), Isotta (1418–1466), Ginevra Nogarola (1417–1461/1468), and Cecilia Gonzaga (1425–1451), all well known in their own time as learned women, were encouraged—to some extent—to write Latin literature. Yet these women encountered significant obstacles. Humanist education and learning aimed to prepare citizens for service to the state; women were explicitly excluded from serving the state in any direct way. Some early humanistic Latin literature written by women differs from contemporary vernacular literature by women and Latin literature by men in its preciosity—seemingly written mainly to prove that the authors are capable of doing so. Laura Cereta (1469–1499), whose *Epistolae familiares* (*Letters to Family and Friends*) was published for the first time in the seventeenth century, is a notable exception prefiguring a number of exceptionally learned women who wrote in Latin throughout Europe in the sixteenth and seventeenth centuries.

PHYLLIS R. BROWN

References and Further Reading

Churchill, Laurie J., Phyllis R. Brown, and Jane E. Jeffrey, eds. *Women Writing Latin from Roman Antiquity to Early Modern Europe*. 3 vols. New York: Routledge, 2002.

Dronke, Peter. *Women Writers of the Middle Ages*. Cambridge: Cambridge University Press, 1984.

King, Margaret L., and Albert Rabil, Jr. *Her Immaculate Hand: Selected Works by and about the Women Humanists of Quattrocento Italy*. Binghamton, N.Y.: Medieval & Renaissance Texts & Studies, 1992.

McNamara, Jo Ann, and John E. Halborg, with E. Gordon Whatley, ed and trans. *Sainted Women of the Dark Ages*. Durham, N.C.: Duke University Press, 1992.

Petroff, Elizabeth Alvilda, ed. *Medieval Women's Visionary Literature*. Oxford: Oxford University Press, 1986.

Thiébaux, Marcelle, trans. *The Writings of Medieval Women: An Anthology*. Second edition. New York: Garland, 1994.

Wilson, Katharina M., ed. *Medieval Women Writers*. Athens, Ga.: University of Georgia Press, 1984.

See also **Birgitta of Sweden; Brunhild and Fredegund; Catherine of Siena; Cereta, Laura; Clare of Assisi; Dhuoda; Edith; Education, Lay; Education, Monastic; Elisabeth of Schönau; Fedele, Cassandra; Gertrude the Great; Hagiography; Heloise; Herrad of Hohenbourg; Hildegard of Bingen; Hrotsvit of Gandersheim; Humanism; Leoba; Letter Writing; Literacy and Reading: Latin; Literature, Latin; Mystics' Writings; Nogarola, Isotta; Ovid, Medieval Reception of; Radegund**

WOMEN AUTHORS: MIDDLE ENGLISH TEXTS

Few women writers writing in Middle English are known by name, and the ones who are known date from the fourteenth century or later. Women who wrote in England most often wrote in French (including Marie de France and Clemence of Barking); usually the texts they chose to write were religious works. Almost all the known women writers writing in English were either religious writers or translators of religious works. Most prominent are the two religious contemplatives Julian of Norwich and Margery Kempe. Julian wrote an account of her visions of Christ in two major versions, a short version some time after she had her visions in the 1370s and a longer version written some twenty years later, after she had become an anchoress in Norwich. The longer version seems to qualify potentially heretical implications of the earlier version. Julian is known for her subtle, rational theology, which includes a celebration of Christ's feminine aspects.

Margery Kempe, who visited Julian in her anchorhold seeking affirmation of her choice to pursue a chaste contemplative life, apparently dictated her autobiography to a priest around 1438. One of the startling characteristics of Margery is her refusal to retreat from the public sphere in her pursuit of a religious life. Formerly a business woman of many talents, including brewing, she continued to seek union with Christ in the secular sphere outside any religious institution. The text tells of her decision to enter into a chaste marriage after giving birth to thirteen children, her visions of Christ, her self-defenses in the face of those who accused her of heresy, and her various pilgrimages, including one to Jerusalem. She is presented in the narrative either by herself or by her scribe as willful, adroitly self-protective, and, at times, exasperating. Her presence in the secular sphere, rather than under the guiding hand of the Church, may be one reason why Margery generated such hostility both then and now, for, as Beckwith has shown, Church and community vied for control of the Christian cultural capital such a devout woman represented. Spearing has recently argued that there is little evidence proving that this is a text written by a woman and that Margery's autobiographical voice may be a male fiction.

Other known fifteenth-century writers include Eleanor Hull (d. 1460), who translated a commentary on the penitential psalms and some devout meditations, Margaret Beaufort (d. 1504), who, with William Atkinson, translated Thomas a Kempis's *Imitation of Christ*, and Dame Juliana Berners, who may have written parts of the *Book of St. Albans*, a treatise on hunting and related sports printed in 1486. The fifteenth century also produced notable letters by women, including the Paston letters, many written by several generations of women of the socially aspiring gentry family. The Paston letters are an especially rich source about women's roles in the governance of large households, and about middle-class marriage practices. The letters tell, for example, of Margery Paston's choice to marry the family bailiff, Richard Calle, despite her family's strenuous disapproval and her subsequent disinheritance.

Other female writers undoubtedly existed in this period and earlier; it is likely, for example, that numerous anonymous lyrics were written by women. A female scribe has been identified as the copyist of a Nunnaminster manuscript, but not as a producer of literary works. It is possible that female recluses composed short anonymous lyric meditations on Christ, such as those known as *The Wooing of Our Lord*. The late-fifteenth-century Findern manuscript—a compilation of poetry, lyrics added at a later date, recipes, and bills—contains works probably written down and possibly composed by women. The Findern manuscript suggests the different ways women may have engaged manuscript culture, for the manuscript contains scraps of information such as butcher's bills, pen trials of female names, and short lyrics on topics of particular concern to women living in the provinces whose husbands traveled frequently—for example, lyrics of lament at abandonment. Other manuscripts may well include anonymous lyrics by women written in spare blank spaces of manuscripts. Middle English translations of works written by or attributed to women also exist, including some lais of Marie de France in English, spiritual works by continental women, some of Christine de Pizan's works, and treatises on women's health. Additional names of women writers and their work will undoubtedly be uncovered in future research, especially as assumptions about the nature of authorship come under scrutiny.

ELIZABETH ROBERTSON

References and Further Reading

Aers, David, and Lynn Staley. *The Powers of the Holy.* University Park Pa.: Pennsylvania State University Press, 1996.

Beckwith, Sarah. "The Uses of *Corpus Christi* and *The Book of Margery Kempe*." In *Christ's Body: Identity, Culture and Society in Late Medieval Writings*. London and New York: Routledge, 1993, pp. 78–111.

Davis, Norman, ed. *The Paston Letters.* Early English Text Society SS 20. Oxford: Oxford University Press, 2004.

Dinshaw, Carolyn, and David Wallace. *The Cambridge Companion to Medieval Women's Writing*. Cambridge: Cambridge University Press, 2003.

Glasscoe, Marion. *A Revelation of Love: Julian of Norwich.* Exeter: University of Exeter Press, 1993.

Lochrie, Karma. *Margery Kempe and Translations of the Flesh.* Philadelphia: University of Pennsylvania Press, 1991.

McNamer, Sarah. "Female Authors: Provincial Setting: The Re-Versing of Courtly Love in the Findern Manuscript. *Viator* 22 (1991): 303–310.

Robertson, Elizabeth. "Medieval Medical Views of Women and the Female Spirituality of the *Ancrene Wisse* and Julian of Norwich." In *Feminist Approaches to the Body in Medieval Literature*, edited by Linda Lomperis and Sarah Stanbury. Philadelphia: University of Pennsylvania Press, 1993, pp. 142–167.

Robinson, P. R. "A Twelfth-Century Scriptrix from Nunnaminster." In *Of the Making of Books: Medieval Manuscripts, Their Scribes and Readers. Essays Presented to M.B. Parkes*, edited by P. R. Robinson and Rivkah Zim. Aldershot, U.K: Scolar Press, 1997.

Spearing, A. C. "Margery Kempe." In *A Companion to Middle English Prose*, edited by A. S. G. Edwards. Cambridge: D. S. Brewer, 2004, pp. 83–97.

Staley, Lynn. *The Book of Margery Kempe.* TEAMS. Kalamazoo, Mich.: Medieval Institute Publications, 1996.

Thompson, W. Meredith. *Pe Wooing of Ure Lauerd.* Early English Text Society 241. Oxford: Oxford University Press, 1958.

***See also* Ancrene Wisse; Beaufort, Margaret; Christine de Pizan; Julian of Norwich; Kempe, Margery; Paston Letters**

WOMEN AUTHORS: OLD FRENCH TEXTS

So much medieval literature is anonymous that we cling to the few proper names we can attach to individual works or manuscripts. Women authors are scarcer even than men because of women's limited access during the Middle Ages to formal education and the channels through which literature was commissioned, circulated, and collected. Certain lyric genres feature women's voices as the speaking subjects, although we cannot know who actually composed and recorded them in writing. As for identifiable historical figures, we have no more than a handful of names to list with confidence as women authors of medieval French literature. Three of them are introduced here.

Women's voices are heard in the genre known as *chansons de toile* (spinning songs), a corpus of narrative poems from the early thirteenth century. These poems may preserve the vestiges of a much earlier oral tradition of songs sung by women while weaving, spinning, and doing needlework, traditional domestic activities for women of all classes. The poetic form of these stories, which most often concern the unhappy love of a young woman, is marked by assonance or rhyme, a simple refrain, and highly conventional characters and settings. They are remarkable, nonetheless, for adopting a consistent female perspective.

Marie de France is the earliest identifiable woman author in Old French, although we have almost no biographical information. Her name derives from a mention at the end of her *Fables*: "Marie ai num, si sui de France" (my name is Marie, and I am from France). That small detail, combined with textual and philological evidence from the manuscripts that preserve her works, has led to the general consensus that Marie was a learned, native speaker of French, writing most likely at the court of Henry II of England. She is best known for her *Lais* (1160–1175), twelve tales of variable length composed in octosyllabic rhyming couplets, inspired by Breton *lais* known from oral tradition. Their subject matter is diverse, although most develop a love story of some kind and many incorporate elements of the marvelous. Her *lai* "Lanval" is the earliest text in Old French to treat Arthurian material, and "Chèvrefeuille" recounts a brief episode of the Tristan and Iseut story developed much more fully by other writers. Marie's *Lais* make her one of the key authors in the development of the medieval romance. The other works attributed to her are the *Fables* (1167–1189), mentioned above, the first known French adaptation of Aesop's fables, and the *Espurgatoire saint Patrice* (*Saint Patrick's Purgatory*) (1189).

A century later, Marguerite Porete (d. 1310) composed a mystical text entitled the *Mirouer des simples ames* (*Mirror of Simple Souls*), in which several characters discuss in dialogue the progress of the Soul towards union with God. Marguerite is associated with the Beguines. Her work is often read in the context of other medieval women mystics writing either in Latin or other vernacular languages, such as Julian of Norwich. Writing inspired by spiritual experience is one of the few types of literature in which medieval women are well represented, given the relative autonomy they enjoyed in religious houses or informal communities like beguinages, the prestige of the contemplative life, and the education available to women in such settings. Their writings, however, are often controversial. Marguerite's book was condemned and burned by the bishop of Cambrai, and she herself was tried by inquisitors, found guilty of heresy, excommunicated, and burned at the stake in 1310.

In contrast to the paucity of information we have on Marie and Marguerite, the life of Christine de Pizan is much better known, due largely to her own writings. Christine (1364–1430) counts among the major authors of late medieval France for both the quantity and the quality of her work. Christine became well educated in the learned milieu of King

Charles V's court in Paris. She describes her transformation into a writer as a necessity imposed by Fortune after the deaths of her father and her beloved husband. Given her access to the aristocracy, she succeeded in writing and finding patronage for volumes of lyric poetry, debate poems, political treatises, epistles, and long allegorical works on a broad range of topics. She saw her work as solidly in the tradition of her literary forefathers, but she also wrote bold new works that challenged misogynist thinking and promoted the basic goodness and worth of women. Her best known text is the *Livre de la cité des dames* (*Book of the City of Ladies*), for which she drew on the works of Augustine and Boccaccio in her design for a model community to house all women of virtue.

BARBARA K. ALTMANN

References and Further Reading

Bloch, R. Howard. *The Anonymous Marie de France.* Chicago: University of Chicago Press, 2003.

Blumfeld-Kosinski, Renate, and Kevin Brownlee, eds. and trans. *The Selected Writings of Christine de Pizan.* New York: Norton, 1997.

Burgess, Glyn S. *The Lais of Marie de France: Text and Context.* Athens, Ga.: University of Georgia Press, 1987.

Christine de Pizan. *Le Livre de la cité des dames* (*The Book of the City of Ladies*), translated by Rosalind Brown-Grant. New York: Penguin, 1999.

Dronke, Peter. *Women Writers of the Middle Ages: A Critical Study of Texts from Perpetua (d. 203) to Marguerite Porete (d. 1310).* Cambridge: Cambridge University Press, 1984.

Georgiadou, Aristoula. "Porete, Marguerite." In *Women in the Middle Ages*, edited by Katharina M. Wilson and Nadia Margolis. Westport, Conn.: Greenwood, 2004, pp. 761–765.

Golden, Frederick, ed. and trans. *Lyrics of the Troubadours and Trouvères: An Anthology and a History.* New York: Doubleday, 1973.

Klinck, Anne L., and Ann Marie Rasmussen, eds. *Medieval Woman's Song: Cross-Cultural Approaches.* Philadelphia: University of Pennsylvania Press, 2002.

Marie de France. *Espurgatoire saint Patrice* (*Saint Patrick's Purgatory*), translated by Michael J. Curley. Binghamton, N.Y.: Medieval and Renaissance Texts and Studies, 1993.

Marie de France. *Fables*, edited and translated by Harriet Spiegel. Toronto: University of Toronto Press, 1987.

Marie de France. *Lais*, translated by Joan Ferrante and Robert Hanning. New York: Dutton, 1978.

Plummer, John F., ed. *Vox Feminae: Studies in Medieval Woman's Songs.* Studies in Medieval Culture 15. Kalamazoo, Mich.: Medieval Institute, 1981.

Porete, Marguerite. *Le Mirouer des simples ames/Margeretae Porete Speculum simplicium animarum*, edited by Romana Guarnieri and Paul Verdeyen. Corpus Christianorum Continuatio Medievalis, 69. Turnhout: Brepols, 1986.

———. *Margaret Porette. The Mirror of Simple Souls*, translated by Edmund Colledge, J. C. Marler, and

Judith Grant. Notre Dame Texts in Medieval Culture 6. Notre Dame, Ind.: University of Notre Dame Press, 1999.

Willard, Charity Canon. *Christine de Pizan: Her Life and Works.* New York: Persea, 1984.

See also **Beguines; Christine de Pizan; Literature, Old French; Marguerite Porete; Marie de France; Mysticism and Mystics; Mystics' Writings; Woman's Song**

WOMEN AUTHORS: SPANISH TEXTS

The earliest known woman author writing in Castilian is the noblewoman Leonor López de Córdoba (c. 1362/1363–c. 1412). She wrote her autobiographical *Memorias* sometime after 1412. The brief work covers only part of her life, ending abruptly in about 1401. It is intended to defend her family, which suffered greatly for being on the losing side of a bitter dynastic struggle. Leonor's father was advisor to King Pedro I of Castile (1350–1369). When Pedro was murdered by his half-brother Enrique II of Trastámara, her father was executed and Leonor, then nine years old, and most of her extended family were imprisoned. The *Memorias* recounts the death of most of them in prison and the later loss of a son to the plague. Throughout the work Leonor emphasizes her religious piety and humility in the face of enormous personal tragedy. It is noteworthy that Leonor survived and at times thrived due to the relationships she cultivated with strong women. She tells how, after prison, she was taken in by a wealthy maternal aunt, who made it possible for her to acquire property. Some years after writing *Memorias* she became the favorite of Queen Catalina of Lancaster, wife of Enrique III, who for several years enjoyed considerable power.

Teresa de Cartagena (c. 1425–after 1465) is the author of two important works, *Arboleda de los enfermos* and *Admiración operum Dey* (both written before 1480). Teresa was a member of an illustrious family of *conversos* (converts from Judaism). She took monastic vows as an adolescent, initially entering a Franciscan house and transferring to a Cistercian community in 1449. This decision and the tone of her written works may have owed something to the anti-*converso* riots of 1449. Some years after entering the monastery she became deaf, an affliction that motivated her to write *Arboleda*. The work is part autobiography and part consolation. It treats illness, and deafness in particular, as an opportunity for spiritual growth, a way of turning inward, away from earthly distractions. Its self-confident use of biblical and patristic sources indicates Teresa's high level of education. Two years after finishing *Arboleda*, apparently in reaction to male critics who refused to believe that a woman could have produced such a learned treatise, Teresa wrote *Admiraçión*. In it she not only insists that *Arboleda* was her own, divinely inspired work, but she also more generally defends women's strength of character and intelligence. A subtle use of imagery, irony, and control of the rhetoric of humility make this earliest defense of female authorship written in Spanish a powerful work.

Nothing is known about the life of the poet Florencia Pinar, who wrote in the second half of the fifteenth century. Her extant corpus consists of only three finely wrought lyric poems. The importance of Pinar lies partly in that she is one of the very few named female poets included in the massive corpus of the Castilian *cancioneros,* poetry miscellanies that feature the work of hundreds of male poets. At times ambiguous in vocabulary and tone, her poems have been read as protofeminist rejections of the constraints placed on women's roles and desire by the "rules" of courtly love.

BARBARA F. WEISSBERGER

References and Further Reading

Kaminsky, Amy Katz and Elaine Dorough Johnson. "To Restore Córdoba." In *The Female Autograph*, edited by Domna C. Stanton. Chicago: University of Chicago Press, 1987, pp. 71–87.

Seidenspinner-Núñez, Dayle. *The Writings of Teresa de Cartagena*. Cambridge: D. S. Brewer, 1998.

Snow, Joseph. "The Spanish Love Poet: Florencia Pinar." In *Medieval Women Writers*, edited by Katharina M. Wilson. Athens, Ga.: University of Georgia Press, and Manchester: Manchester University Press, 1984, pp. 320–332.

See also **Iberia; Literature, Iberian; López de Córdoba, Leonor; Teresa de Cartagena**

WOMEN MEDIEVALISTS IN THE ACADEMY

Women scholars have chosen to make the study of the Middle Ages their life's work since the eighteenth century, when Elizabeth Elstob (1684–1756), attracted to the study of Old English, published the first vernacular grammar of the language. But until the twentieth century, women were hampered by their inability to obtain an advanced degree and teach at a university, and, therefore, earn an adequate living from their scholarship. Independent scholar Anne Jameson (1794–1860), the first art historian, published authoritative works about medieval Italian art, but ended her life in poverty.

If women were not allowed to earn higher degrees at universities, then they researched and published outside academe. Evelyn Underhill (1875–1941) independently published a definitive work on mysticism; freelance writer Dorothy Sayers (1893–1957) translated Dante. But women also encountered misogynistic resistance from male reviewers, inside or out of the academy. Elstob's work was snubbed by fellow Anglo-Saxonists; Jessie L. Weston (1850–1928), writing on the origins of Grail romance, was criticized as unscholarly and ignored.

And when women were hired, finally, to teach at a university or college, their originality was misperceived as eccentric, as was the case with young Beryl Smalley (1905–1984), a pioneer in the history of the study of Bible and commentaries in the Middle Ages, when she was selected as a research fellow at Girton College of Cambridge University.

That women have advanced the development of various medieval fields in the nineteenth and twentieth centuries testifies to their dedication to their professions, the quality of their achievements, and the encouragement of other individuals. Women medievalists distinguished themselves for three different reasons. First, they found other ways to enable academic degrees or careers. They may have relocated to obtain a degree or tenure, as did Caroline Spurgeon (1869–1942), for example, who left England for the Sorbonne in order to obtain a Ph.D. (but returned to serve as the first woman professor in England); or Elisabeth Gössmann (1928–), who left her university in Germany for one in Japan when she did not receive her *Habilitacion* upon publication of her first book. Three distinguished paleographers who worked in manuscript departments at national libraries without being named director—Anneliese Maier (1905–1971), Suzanne Solente (1895–1978), and Marie-Thérèse d'Alverny (1903–1991)—also published groundbreaking works on medieval philosophy and French and Latin literature.

Second, some medievalists—Eileen Power (1889–1940) and Marjorie Chibnall (1914–), in history, and the Loomis wives, Gertrude Schoepperle Loomis (1882–1921), Laura Hibbard Loomis (1882–1960), and Dorothy Bethurum Loomis (1897–1987), in literature—found male mentors (dissertation directors, colleagues, husbands) who supported their work. Others who married at a time when society demanded that they put their husbands' needs before their own accompanied their husbands to universities or nearby colleges and still distinguished themselves as scholars within their institutions and their fields, such as Dorothy Stenton (1894–1971), in history, and Charity Cannon Willard (1914–), in French.

Third, some women medievalists simply persevered in their pursuit of research, despite silence toward their work, unfair reviews, or being passed over for awards, larger salaries, promotions, chairs, and other distinctions. Elise Richter (1865–1943) was the first woman in Austria to earn the title of professor, in 1907, although she only received it formally in 1921. Edith Rickert (1871–1938), trained at the University of Chicago, had collaborated with John Matthews Manly on their monumental Chaucer edition, but received lesser credit and attention (Manly, without Rickert, received the Haskins Medal from the Medieval Academy of America). Nellie Neilson (1873–1947), chair of her department and, later, president of the American Historical Association, was forced by her university—despite many honors and publications—to retire early. Joan Evans (1893–1977), in art history, was designated a "Dame" long after less-qualified men had received the equivalent honor. Cora Lutz (1906–1985) and her Latin editions of Carolingian commentators received scathing reviews, but after she retired at Wilson College she catalogued and described pre-1600 manuscripts at the Yale Beinecke Library.

Those fields that most blocked women's progress included medieval Latin, Germanic philology, theology, philosophy, archaeology, and intellectual history. Those fields that allowed women some success included art history, as is evident from the careers of Jane Hayward (1919–1994), working on stained glass, and Elaine Bloch (1929–), on misericords; women's history and literature, in the case of Mary Bateson (1865–1931), whose work on nunneries and catalog of books at Syon Monastery are cited today; Hope Emily Allen, whose edition of Margery Kempe endures; Régine Pernoud (1909–1998), with her book on Joan of Arc; and many recent scholars who have worked on medieval religious women, particularly the mystics.

The first women medievalists to attain the highest office in a professional society include, among others, Neilson, social and constitutional history, president of the American Historical Association, in 1942; Sirarpie Der Nersessian (1896–1989), Armenian art history, full professor at Dumbarton Oaks; and Ruth J. Dean (1902–2003), Anglo-Norman literature, president of the Medieval Academy, in 1973.

In the recent past, women flourished at women's colleges and, in the present, at large metropolitan universities where women can network with one another. Because of changing demographics, women now claim the majority in selected medieval fields. And although they may not have received fellowships to finish their research during their academic careers, in retirement women medievalists such as

Anglo-Norman scholar Dean, ecclesiastical historian Majorie Chibnall (1914–), and Middle English scholar Marie Borroff (1923–) have published their life's work into their sunset years, with continuing distinction.

JANE CHANCE

References and Further Reading

Chance, Jane, ed. *Women Medievalists and the Academy*. Madison: University of Wisconsin Press, 2005.

Damico, Helen, and Joseph B. Zavadil (vol. 1 only), with Donald Fennema and Karmen Lenz (vols. 2 and 3 only). *Medieval Scholarship: Biographical Studies on the Formation of a Discipline*. 3 vols: *History*, vol. 1; *Literature and Philology*, vol. 2; *Philosophy and the Arts*, vol. 3. New York: Garland, 1995–2000.

Scanlon, Jennifer, and Sharon Cosner, eds. *American Women Historians, 1700s–1900s: A Biographical Dictionary*. Westport, Conn.: Greenwood Press, 1996.

Sherman, Claire Richter, with Adele M. Holcomb, eds. *Women as Interpreters of the Visual Arts, 1820–1979*. Westport, Conn.: Greenwood Press, 1981.

Stanbury, Sarah, guest ed. *Feminist Legacies: Female Medieval Scholars and the Academy*. Medieval Feminist Forum 30–31 (2001).

Wheeler, Bonnie, and Fiona Tolhurst. *On Arthurian Women: Essays in Memory of Maureen Fries*. Dallas, Tex.: Scriptorium Press, 2001.

See also **Gender in History; History, Medieval Women's; Misericords; Misogyny; Mystics' Writings; Power, Eileen**

WOODVILLE, ELIZABETH

In 1464, Elizabeth (1437–1492) secretly married the Yorkist King Edward IV of England. Elizabeth's first husband, Sir John Grey, had been killed in 1460 fighting on behalf of the Lancastrians during the Wars of the Roses. Her marriage to the king may have rankled some, especially Edward's advisors, who were already negotiating with the French, and those who resented the royal favors and marriages subsequently bestowed upon Elizabeth's relatives. However, Edward's kinship to the large and ambitious Woodville family also provided him alliances among the Lancastrian faction.

As Edward's queen, Elizabeth took on public roles typical of English queens. She succeeded Margaret of Anjou as patron of Queens' College, Cambridge in 1465, giving the college its first statutes in 1475. She also seems to have provided some patronage to William Caxton, the distribution of several of his books being associated with her. When Edward IV died in 1483, Elizabeth's brother-in-law, Richard Duke of Gloucester, and his supporters seized the throne from her son, the thirteen-year-old Edward V. The new regime further secured its coup by executing Elizabeth's brother, the second Earl Rivers, and one of her sons, Richard Grey, and by seizing Elizabeth's two younger sons by Edward, both of whom were probably murdered in order to secure Richard's hold on the throne.

During Richard's reign, Elizabeth took sanctuary in Westminster, where she resisted efforts to declare her marriage and her remaining children illegitimate. After defeating Richard III at the battle of Bosworth Field, Henry VII united the Lancastrian and York bloodlines in 1486 by marrying Elizabeth Woodville's eldest daughter, Elizabeth of York, thus establishing the Tudor dynasty. Elizabeth Woodville retired to the abbey of Bermondsey, Surrey, in 1487, where she died on 8 June 1492.

THERESA D. KEMP

References and Further Reading

Hicks, Michael. A. "The Changing Role of the Wydevilles in Yorkist Politics to 1483." In *Patronage, Pedigree and Power in Later Medieval England*, edited by Charles Ross. Gloucester: Alan Sutton, 1979, pp. 60–86.

Kemp, Theresa D. "*The Knight of the Tower* and the Queen in Sanctuary: Elizabeth Woodville's Use of Meaningful Silence and Absence." *New Medieval Literatures* 4 (2001): 171–188.

Lander, J. R. "Marriage and Politics in the Fifteenth Century: The Nevilles and the Wydevilles." In *Crown and Nobility, 1450–1509*. London: Edward Arnold Ltd., 1976, pp. 94–126.

Sutton, Anne F., and Livia Visser-Fuchs. "The Cult of Angels in Late Fifteenth-Century England: An Hours of the Guardian Angel Presented to Queen Elizabeth Woodville." In *Women and the Book: Assessing the Visual Evidence*, edited by Jane H. Taylor and Lesley Smith. Toronto: University of Toronto Press, 1997, pp. 230–265.

———. "'A Most Benevolent Queen': Queen Elizabeth Woodville's Reputation, Her Piety, and Her Books." *The Ricardian* 10 (1995): 214–245.

See also **England; Patronage, Ecclesiastical; Patronage, Literary; Margaret of Anjou; Queens and Empresses: the West**

WORK

"When Adam delved and Eve span, who was then the gentleman?" asked the preacher. The question was taken up with more radical egalitarian intent by the (predominantly male) rebels of the English Peasants' Revolt of 1381, but neither the moralising nor the political uses to which this question was put detract from the assumption implicit within it, namely that in a postlapsarian world, the lot of humankind is to labour. Equally unquestioned was that women's work was—or at least was supposed to be—essentially different from men's. Another late medieval English text, the so-called *Ballad of the Tyrannical Husband*, adopts this normative position, but within the course of the narrative gives voice to a fictive wife. She relates how her sleep is interrupted by the crying of children and that feeding them and attending to their needs punctuates her day. She also cooks for her hot-tempered husband, whilst performing a range of tasks essential to the familial economy: she brews and bakes; she prepares flax; she weaves; she takes responsibility for the geese and poultry; she milks cows and makes butter and cheese; she takes goods to the market. She could have added that she participated in the hay and grain harvests, weeded crops, and fetched water from the well. Two important points arise. First, we should not limit our definition of work to those activities with an immediate economic return; childrearing, cooking, cleaning, fetching water, and the like are also work activities and carry economic implications. Second, waged work, though better documented than other kinds of work, in fact accounts for only a proportion, and probably in fact a minority, of all work activities.

A significant number of work activities undertaken by women for wages were extensions of unpaid work undertaken within a domestic or familial context. It seems to have been a given of medieval societies that primary childcare, responsibility for cooking and feeding family members, the primary stages of textile production (carding, spinning, preparing flax, etc.), cleaning, and nursing the sick were women's work. The aristocracy, and in Italian cities well-to-do citizens, invariably employed women to suckle and take care of their infants. Though doctors and surgeons were usually male, nursing care fell to women, whether paid or unpaid. Women alone assisted at childbirth, though it is probable that comparatively few were professional midwives, but simply experienced neighbours. Within pastoral economies, dairying—milking cows and sheep, making butter and cheese—was women's work. So too was weaving if primarily for domestic consumption, but we can find numbers of women who produced cloth for sale. The demands of harvest were always such as to draw in all available labour, including that of women. It is likely that married couples often worked as a team, taking turns to cut and bind the grain. The same consideration dictated that numbers of hired harvest workers were also female. Sometimes these would have been wives and daughters normally employed on the familial holding, but temporarily redeployed to take advantage of the inflated wages available at harvest. Women were also active in the hay harvest, raking and stacking the cut grass.

Peasant Society

Obviously the nature of women's work within peasant society was influenced by the prevailing agrarian economy. Pastoral and mixed economies probably presented the most opportunities, but even in arable economies tasks such as weeding and winnowing—the one backbreaking and repetitive, the other dusty and uncomfortable—tended to be relegated to women. Ploughing, in contrast, was jealously guarded as a male preserve. Here we may uncover something of the cultural underpinnings of gendered construction of work identities. Men's work is associated with skill and strength and is integral to their standing within the community: a man may be identified as a ploughman, a shepherd, a husbandman; a woman is more likely to be known only as a wife. Women's work is always understood as secondary and, because so often an extension of domestic responsibilities, "natural," hence unskilled. Spinning, for example, was not recognised as a skill, but rather as somehow innate or natural to womankind, a notion presented in the proverb that portrayed weeping, chattering, and spinning as female attributes. Another telling example, because the opposite of modern ideological assumptions, is the case of washing and shearing sheep. Such employment fell within women's sphere as an extension of women's association with caring for small livestock, with the processing of wool, and because washing was quintessentially women's domestic work.

There are numbers of normative writings from across later medieval Europe that insist that women's proper sphere of activity was the home. The proliferation of texts such as the *Libro di Buoni Costumi* or *How the Goodwife Taught Her Daughter* warn us that this is how the authors of such text would have the world, but not necessarily how the world was. It warns us that this was a normative model appropriate to the intended audiences of the texts and thus implicitly only to certain, usually more prosperous levels of society. Barbara Hanawalt has attempted to show that for English peasant society of the later thirteenth and fourteenth centuries at least, women's work was indeed located around the home, in contrast to men's employment outdoors. She used the spatial location of deaths associated with supposed accidents recorded in coroners' rolls, but her methodology really only tells of intrinsically hazardous work activities. A more convincing model would be that described by Martine Segalen for nineteenth-century French peasant society. Here women's work profile is characterised by periodic movement throughout the day in and out of the house—throughout the day (to fetch water, to milk cows or tend to livestock), the week (to attend market or to take washing to the river), and the seasons (to weed crops, assist at lambing, participate in harvest).

Waged Work

Waged work is comparatively well documented simply because the payment of wages, particularly by institutional employers, tended to be accounted for, recorded, and archived. Unfortunately such accounts tend to be more concerned with justifying payments made than with detailing the employees, whether male or female, whose individual wages lie behind these payments. Given the propensity of husbands and wives to work together in some contexts, moreover, it is likely that payments apparently made to men hide wages intended to remunerate husband and wife together. This, for example, is what may lie behind Christopher Dyer's finding of the startlingly high quantities of food provided to English harvest workers after the Black Death as an inducement over and above money wages, then subject to wage controls. Only where employees are specifically named or where these are exclusively female can women be identified with confidence.

The possibility of wage differentials operating according to gender has been the subject of a long-running debate. The evidence is both slight and ambivalent. On the one hand, as just suggested, wages paid to male workers may disguise payments to couples. On the other hand, payments made specifically to women tend to represent women's work. Sandy Bardsley has argued that though women can be found engaged at the same rates of remuneration as males, the men so employed represent second-rate workers—youths, older males, or even handicapped workers. This is an interesting suggestion deserving further study. That women were paid less than males for the same tasks has yet to be convincingly demonstrated. What is relatively easy to establish—and is perhaps the more important observation—is that women were always disadvantaged within a hierarchy of paid employment. By reserving tasks such as ploughing or mowing using a scythe to males, men ensured that the pool of available labour was reduced and so could command the highest wages. Of course, this unequal distribution of labour was justified by reference to women's lack of strength and height, a crude biological determinism that was blind to the claims of those women who were stronger or taller than average, or to skill, a self-perpetuating claim that depended on denying women the opportunity to learn. At the moment in the *Ballad of the Tyrannical Husband*, the text noted at the beginning of this entry, that the wife goes off to plough, we realise, if we had not done before, that this poem is satirical and that the idea of the wife ploughing is to be greeted with guffaws of laughter, so reinforcing the normative order, the ultimate intent of the text.

Towns

Rural society seems to have been rather more conservative than urban, and it is in towns that we can find the greatest variety of female employment. Women are especially conspicuous in food trades, textiles, and service trades. Using the Parisian tax records for 1292 and 1313, for example, David Herlihy found numbers of tavern and hostel keepers, fishmongers, dressmakers, and silk workers, but also various women taxed as petty traders, laundresses, barbers, and chandlers. This is at best a crude barometer, since only independent women of some means would have been taxed in their own right. Women were ubiquitous as petty retailers of foodstuffs and other basic commodities, a role that required very little capital outlay but a good knowledge of a local clientele. The same considerations of lack of access to investment capital or formally recognised training also explain women's participation in carding and spinning, sewing, or such service trades as laundry work or even prostitution. Numbers of other women, however, gained access to a variety of craft activities through marriage. Wives were expected to assist their husbands in their craft and, significantly, numbers of widows managed to continue to run workshops after the deaths of their husbands.

A significantly smaller proportion of women served formal apprenticeships, primarily within a very limited range of crafts, of which the silk trades were the most conspicuous. Such apprentices were formally bound to a master and his wife, but to learn the wife's trade. In fifteenth-century London, female apprentices were drawn from all over the kingdom and included at least one knight's daughter. The prominence of women in the silk industry in Paris is reflected in the feminised nature of the silk guilds of the city reported by Etienne Boileau around 1268, but is part of a much wider pattern. At much the same date Mabel of Bury St. Edmunds was undertaking major commissions for vestments embroidered in silk thread, though production was also associated with nunneries. By the post-Plague era there is plentiful evidence for the employment of women in various stages of the industry, but production began to look less aristocratic and more bourgeois and commercial. In Florence women silk workers constituted a proletariat subject to the merchants who dominated the Arte della Seta guild. In both Cologne and London the wives of merchants, drapers, and other, often well-connected men headed workshops weaving silk ribbon, producing embroidery and the like, but the silk spinners, needlewomen, and other females they employed seem not to have been well remunerated and, in Cologne at least, appear sometimes to have been paid in kind.

Erosion of Women's Position

Broadly speaking, the last decades of the medieval era seem to have witnessed an erosion of women's position within the labour market. Whereas the labour-starved conditions prevailing after the Black Death seem to have opened up opportunities for women, especially in the towns of northwestern Europe, the twin effects of continued population contraction and recession caused by the bullion famines of the earlier and mid-fifteenth century appear to have reversed this situation. This is most strikingly illustrated in respect to cloth weaving. In the early Middle Ages weaving was very much an extension of the domestic and hence fell within the sphere of women's work. The High Middle Ages saw the growth of numbers of significant centres of textile manufacture and, at least within an urban context, male weavers came to predominate, but not to exclude. By the later fifteenth century, however, numbers of weavers' guilds were beginning to regulate against the employment of women, even wives, in the craft. A parallel trend has been described by Judith Bennett in relation to brewing. Here a feminised part-time domestic industry was displaced in an urban context by a more masculine commercial industry. Finally, as ale gave way to beer brewed with hops, so enjoying a longer shelf life and allowing for larger-scale production, women lost out altogether. More generally, women seem to have found it harder to retain control of workshops once widowed. In numbers of German towns male employees agitated against working alongside women. More conservative gender hierarchies were once more asserted.

P. J. P. GOLDBERG

References and Further Reading

Bennett, Judith M., et al., eds. *Sisters and Workers in the Middle Ages*. Chicago: University of Chicago Press, 1989.

Brown, Judith. C. "A Woman's Place Was in the Home: Women's Work in Renaissance Tuscany." In *Rewriting the Renaissance The Discourses of Sexual Difference in Early Modern Europe*, edited by Margaret W. Ferguson et al. Chicago: University of Chicago Press, 1986, pp. 206–224.

Dilard, Heath. *Daughters of the Reconquest: Women in Castilian Town Society, 1100–1300*. Cambridge: Cambridge University Press, 1989.

Goldberg, P. J. P. *Women, Work and Life Cycle: Women in York and Yorkshire c. 1300–1520*. Oxford: Clarendon Press, 1992.

Hanawalt, Barbara A., ed. *Women and Work in Preindustrial Europe*. Bloomington, Ind.: Indiana University Press, 1986.

Herlihy, David. Opera Muliebria: *Women and Work in Medieval Europe*. New York: McGraw-Hill, 1990.

See also **Alewives and Brewing; Apprentices; Artisan Families, Women of; Clothwork, Domestic; Division of Labor; Guild Members and Guilds; Household Management; Market and Tradeswomen; Peasants; Prostitutes; Social Status; Textile Production for the Market**

YVETTE OF HUY

Hugh of Floreffe, biographer of Yvette of Huy (1158–1228) (or Ivetta), portrays an anchoress, an enclosed recluse, less ascetic than her more celebrated contemporaries. Instead, he emphasizes her humility and her role as spiritual mother.

Yvette came from a wealthy family of Huy on the Meuse River in modern-day Belgium. Although she objected strongly to marital obligations, she was forced to wed at the age of thirteen. Of her three children, two boys survived. She was widowed at eighteen and chose to remain unmarried despite the wishes of her father.

Yvette dedicated herself to a spiritual life, with a particular devotion to the Virgin Mary. Her extreme charity provoked a clash with her father over her sons' inheritance. However, she saw to their corporal and spiritual support, eventually convincing her father and both sons to join the Cistercian order.

At twenty-three Yvette gave up her worldly life to minister to lepers in a crumbling community outside the city walls. There she had a vision of a great church and new buildings. After securing the future of a new Beguine religious community and hospital, Yvette retired to pursue a life of prayer in an anchorhold.

In her house attached to a church, her contemplations led to visions such as one in which Christ commended Yvette to his mother as her handmaid. She experienced a prescience that compelled her to intervene in the lives of the townspeople, particularly sexually errant priests. Finally, she was especially solicitous of the lives of her spiritual daughters who had formed a community around her, appearing even after her death to guide them.

HEATHER E. WARD

References and Further Reading

Carpenter, Jennifer. "Juette of Huy, Recluse and Mother (1158–1228): Children and Mothering in the Saintly Life." In *Power of the Weak: Studies on Medieval Women*, edited by Jennifer Carpenter and Sally-Beth MacLean. Urbana, Ill.: University of Illinois Press, 1995, pp. 57–93.

Hugh of Floreffe. *The Life of Yvette of Huy*, translated by Jo Ann McNamara. Toronto: Peregrina, 1999.

Mulder-Bakker, Anneke B. "Ivetta of Huy: *Mater et Magistra*." In *Sanctity and Motherhood: Essays on Holy Mothers in the Middle Ages*, edited by Anneke B. Mulder-Bakker. New York: Garland, 1995, pp. 224–258.

———. "Yvette of Huy: The Metamorphoses of a Woman." In *Lives of the Anchoresses: The Rise of the Urban Recluse in Medieval Europe*, translated by Myra Heerspink Scholz. Philadelphia: University of Pennsylvania Press, 2005, pp. 51–77.

See also **Anchoresses; Asceticism; Beguines; Flanders; Hagiography; Lepers; Mothers as Teachers; Widows**

Z

ZITA AND OTHER SERVANT SAINTS

Among the many persons regarded as saints within the Western tradition, some officially canonized, others venerated as a result of popular enthusiasm, who followed the example of Jesus and the Apostles, there are those who were from the lowest social orders. The servant-saint Zita of Lucca (1218–1278) belongs to a class of saints who suffered the humiliation of performing the most menial chores and were even subject to the sexual pressures of their employers or fellow servants, but nevertheless persisted in their humble pursuit of the faith and numerous acts of charity. Such women were usually born of humble backgrounds, but, despite their own impoverished circumstances, showed a concern for the poor and served as a pious alternative to the allegedly debased, even promiscuous behavior of the servant class. Other such saints include Gunthild of Suffersheim, Sibillina Biscossi of Pavia, Notburga of Rottenburg, Radegunda of Wellenburg, and Magaret of Louvain.

Born of rural parentage in Monsagrati, Zita moved to Lucca at twelve in order to serve in the household of the mercantile Fatinelli family. The stereotypical elements of her legend include suffering from a variety of medical problems (probably including malnutrition), giving food scraps away to the poor, tending to condemned prisoners, sharing her warm garments and bed with beggars, pilgrims, and others, assiduously saying her prayers, attending mass, and visiting local churches, and suffering the mockery and ill-treatment of her fellow servants, even mutilating herself in order to avoid their advances. Due to the posthumous miracles attributed to Zita and her reputation for piety, Dante (*Inferno*, 21.37) designated Lucca the city of St. Zita. A chapel was erected in the church of San Frediano in Zita's honor in 1321, and after her official canonization in 1696, she was named the patron saint of domestics and housewives.

MICHAEL E. GOODICH

References and Further Reading

Acta Sanctorum, 3 April: 499–510.
Goodich, Michael. "*Ancilla Dei*: The Servant as Saint in the Late Middle Ages." In *Lives and Miracles of the Saints: Studies in Medieval Latin Hagiography*. Aldershot: Ashgate, 2004, pp. 119–136.

See also **Dante Alighieri; Hagiography; Miracles and Miracle Collections; Servants; Social Status**

Appendix I: Calendar of Female Saints

Private prayer books, psalters, and books of hours usually included calendars listing major feasts of Jesus and Mary, as well as saints' days. Names listed on the calendar often varied from region to region, reflecting devotion to local saints like Geneviève, patron of Paris. The calendar below is intended to suggest the variety and number of holy women celebrated during the liturgical year. It is not a transcription from a single source but relies in part on several books owned by women: the *De Lisle Hours* belonging to Margaret de Beauchamp, the *Hours of Margaret of Cleves*, the *Hours of Mary of Burgundy*, the *Neville of Hornby Hours* belonging to Isabel de Byron, and the *Saint Albans Psalter* belonging to Christina of Markyate. The list below also incorporates all those women profiled in this volume who had active cults during the Middle Ages but did not appear in the prayer books surveyed. Sainthood in the Middle Ages had a wide definition ranging from a small local cult to an elaborate (and expensive) process for canonization. These different levels of acceptance are indicated by canonization dates, approvals of cults, and limitations to local cults.

Saints whose names appear in bold have articles in the volume.

January

1 *Solemnity of Mary, Mother of God*—first Marian feast of the calendar year
4 ***Angela of Foligno***—thirteenth century, Italy, religious laywoman, local cult
6 ***Gertrude of Ortenberg***, virgin—fourteenth century, Netherlands, Beguine, local cult
   Epiphany—the feast celebrating the visit of the Magi
13 ***Yvette of Huy*** (Jutta, Ivetta)—thirteenth century, Flanders, anchoress, local cult
15 *Ita*, virgin—sixth century, Ireland, abbess
18 *Prisca*, virgin martyr
21 *Agnes*, virgin martyr
23 *Emerentiana* (Emerancia), virgin martyr
29 *Sabina*, virgin
30 *Aldegundis*, virgin—seventh century, Flanders, abbess

February

1 ***Brigit of Kildare***, virgin—sixth century, Ireland, abbess
2 Feast of the *Purification of the Virgin Mary* (Candlemas)—commemorates Mary's purification at the temple following the birth of Christ
5 *Agatha*, virgin martyr
6 *Dorothy*, virgin martyr
9 *Apollonia*, virgin martyr
10 *Scholastica*, virgin—sixth century, Italy, Benedictine nun, reputed sister of Saint Benedict
12 *Eulalia*, virgin martyr
15 *Veronica*, whose veil was said to have been imprinted by Christ's face when she wiped it
16 *Juliana*, virgin martyr
   Mary the Younger—ninth century, Byzantium, married woman who died from her husband's abuse
22 ***Margaret of Cortona***—thirteenth century, Italy, religious laywoman, canonized May 16, 1728
25 *Walburga*, virgin—eighth century, England and Germany, abbess
26 ***Isabelle of France***, virgin—thirteenth century, France, daughter of King Louis VIII and founder of the monastery of Poor Clares at Longchamps, cult approved in 1521

March

2 ***Agnes of Prague***, virgin—thirteenth century, Bohemia, Poor Clare, daughter of King Ottokar I of Bohemia and founder of a monastery of Poor Clares, canonized November 12, 1989
6 ***Colette of Corbie***, virgin—fifteenth century, France, Poor Clare, canonized May 24, 1807
7 *Felicity and Perpetua*, martyrs
9 ***Frances of Rome***—fifteenth century, Italy, religious laywoman, canonized May 9, 1608
   Caterina Vigri (Catherine of Bologna), virgin—fifteenth century, Italy, Poor Clare, canonized 1712

12 *Fina of San Gimignano,* virgin—thirteenth century, Italy, local cult

17 *Gertrude of Nivelles,* virgin—seventh century, Belgium, abbess

25 *Annunciation of the Lord*—commemorates the angel Gabriel's announcement to Mary that she has been chosen to be the mother of Christ

31 *Balbina,* virgin
Cornelia, martyr

April

2 *Mary the Egyptian,* penitent prostitute

5 *Juliana of Mount Cornillon,* virgin—thirteenth century, Belgium, Augustinian nun and prioress and promoter of the feast of the Eucharist, later known as *Corpus Christi;* cult confirmed locally in 1869

13 *Ida of Boulogne*—twelfth century, Flanders, countess of Boulogne

14 *Lidwina*—fifteenth century, Netherlands, a mystic who was bedridden all her adult life

27 *Zita,* virgin—thirteenth century, Italy, servant, public veneration authorized 1278, cult confirmed September 5, 1696

30 *Catherine of Siena,* virgin—fourteenth century, Italy, religious laywoman associated with the Dominicans, canonized 1461

May

19 *Pudentiana,* virgin martyr

22 *Humility of Faenza*—thirteenth century, Italy, anchoress and abbess

30 *Joan of Arc,* virgin—fifteenth century, France, canonized May 9, 1920

31 *Petronilla,* virgin martyr

June

3 *Clotilda*—sixth century, France, wife of Clovis, king of the Franks

10 *Margaret of Scotland*—eleventh century, Scotland, queen-consort, canonized 1249

16 *Lutgard of Aywieres,* virgin—thirteenth century, Belgium, Cistercian nun

18 *Elisabeth of Schönau,* virgin—twelfth century, Germany, Benedictine nun, abbess, mystic, canonized 1584

20 *Margaretha Ebner*—fourteenth century, Germany, Dominican nun, beatified February 24, 1979

23 *Aethelthryth of Ely*—seventh century, England, nun and founder of a double monastery at Ely
Marie of Oignies, virgin—twelfth through the thirteenth centuries, Belgium, Beguine and mystic

July

2 *Visitation of the Virgin Mary*—commemorates Mary's visit to her cousin, Elizabeth, the mother of John the Baptist

6 *Godelieve of Gistel* (Godeleva, Godliva)—eleventh century, Flanders, noblewoman who was killed on her husband's orders

8 *Isabel of Aragon*—fourteenth century, Portugal, queen associated with the Franciscan order, canonized 1625

10 *Amelberga*—eighth century, Flanders, abbess

11 *Olga*—tenth century, Russia, princess of Kiev

13 *Mildred,* virgin—seventh century, England, abbess

17 *Jadwiga* (Hedwig)—fourteenth century, Poland, queen, canonized June 8, 1997
Marina, lived as the monk Marinus

19 *Daria,* martyr

20 *Margaret of Antioch,* virgin martyr

21 *Praxedes,* virgin martyr

22 *Mary Magdalen,* apostle

24 *Christina the Astonishing,* virgin—thirteenth century, Flanders, local cult

26 *Anne*—mother of the Virgin Mary, cult introduced in eighth century Rome, her feast is first known in the thirteenth century

29 *Mary and Martha* of Bethany, virgins—these sisters of Lazarus sometimes represent the contemplative (Mary) and active (Martha) lives
Beatrice of Nazareth—thirteenth century, Flanders, Cistercian nun and prioress, local cult

August

1 *Sapientia with her daughters Fides, Spes, and Caritas,* martyrs

12 *Clare of Assisi,* virgin—thirteenth century, Italy, Franciscan nun and founder of the Order of Poor Clares, canonized August 12, 1255

13 *Radegund*—sixth century, France, queen and nun, acclaimed a saint following her death in 587

15 *Assumption of the Virgin Mary,* commemorates her death and her body's elevation to heaven
Irene—eighth century, Byzantium, empress and supporter of the veneration of icons

17 *Clare of Montefalco,* virgin—fourteenth century, Italy, Augustinian nun, abbess, and mystic, canonized 1881

18 *Helena, Empress*—fourth century, Italy, mother of Constantine and Roman empress

September

1 *Douceline of Digne*—thirteenth century, France, mystic, founder of a house of Beguines, local cult

4 *Rose of Viterbo,* virgin—thirteenth century, Italy, canonized 1457

8 *Birthday of the Virgin Mary*

15 *Catherine of Genoa,* widow—fifteenth century, Italy, noblewoman, religious laywoman, and mystic, canonized May 18, 1737

16 *Euphemia,* virgin martyr

17 *Hildegard of Bingen,* virgin—twelfth century, Germany, nun, mystic, and composer

23 *Thecla,* virgin martyr

26 *Justina of Antioch,* virgin martyr

28 *Leoba,* virgin—eighth century, England and Germany, abbess

October

6 *Foy,* virgin martyr

8 *Birgitta of Sweden,* widow—fourteenth century, Sweden, founder of the Birgittine Order, canonized Oct. 7, 1391, confirmed in 1415
Pelagia—actress and penitent

19 Translation of *Austraberta,* virgin—seventh century, France, abbess
Frideswide, virgin—seventh century, England, abbess

21 *Ursula and her companions,* virgin martyrs

22 *Cordula,* virgin martyr and companion to *Ursula*

28 *Anastasia,* virgin martyr

30 *Dorothea of Montau,* widow—fourteenth century, Poland, anchoress, never officially canonized but in 1976 the pope confirmed her cult as a saint based on long-standing veneration

November

1 *All Saints*

2 *All Souls*

17 *Gertrude the Great,* virgin—thirteenth century, Germany, nun and mystic
Hild of Whitby, virgin—seventh century, England, abbess
Elisabeth of Hungary—thirteenth century, Germany, religious laywoman, canonized May 27, 1235

19 *Mechthild of Hackeborn*—thirteenth century, Germany, Benedictine nun and mystic

21 *Presentation of the Virgin Mary,* commemorates Mary's presentation at the Temple as a small child

22 *Cecilia,* virgin martyr

25 *Catherine of Alexandria,* virgin martyr—cult became popular in Europe in the eleventh century

December

2 *Bibiana* (Vivian), virgin martyr

4 *Barbara,* virgin martyr

8 *Conception of the Virgin Mary*

13 *Lucy,* virgin martyr—cult spread to Rome, Milan, and Ravenna in sixth and seventh centuries

16 *Adelheid* (Adelaide), widow of Otto I—tenth century, Germany, empress

23 *Victoria,* virgin martyr

24 *Christmas Eve*

25 *Christmas*

28 *Holy Innocents*—feast commemorating the massacre of children by King Herod

Appendix II: Some Milestones in Medieval Women's History

The editors gradually assembled this list and offer it as one historical view of the field. "Milestones" has multiple meanings in order to better represent the issues, activities, and audiences for medieval women's history. First and foremost milestones are path-breaking studies that open a new area for research or present a compelling new interpretation of a major question. There are also some works that serve students in the classroom: textbooks, anthologies and especially translations of texts, many of which, like Christine de Pizan's *Book of the City of Ladies,* had no modern English version before the 1980s. Other milestones generated controversies that profitably bring the present in touch with the Middle Ages. Medieval women's studies even has some milestones in the wider realm of popular culture, with recordings of Hildegard of Bingen's music and Judy Chicago's museum installations celebrating women's achievements. Finally, milestones take account of the history of medieval women's studies, recording and analyzing the developments and scholars who have helped shape the terms of discourse.

As is evident below, the pace of publication picked up dramatically in the late 1970s, spurred both by the second wave of the feminist movement, with its emphasis on activism, and the growth of social and economic history as exemplified by the Annales School. The number of essay collections and journal articles in the 1970s is not surprising, given that many new areas and topics were being explored for the first time during that era. These types of publications, however, continue to be important suggesting the vitality and growth of the field.

	Date	Work
1	1501	Hrotsvit of Gandersheim. *Opera Hrosvitae.* Printed by Conrad Celtes. Nurnberg, 1501.
2	1566	Hildegard of Bingen. *Epistolarum liber*, edited by Justus Blanckwald. Cologne: Johann Quentel and Gerwin Calenius, 1566.
3	1838	Thomassy, Marie-Joseph-Raymond. *Essai sur les écrits politiques de Christine de Pisan, suivi d'une notice littéraire et de pièces inédites.* Paris: Debécourt, 1838.
4	1882	Bücher, Karl. *Die Frauenfrage im Mittelalter.* Tübingen: H. Laupp'sche Buchhandlung, 1882. [Second edition, 1910].
5	1888	Hudson, William Henry. "Hrotsvitha of Gandersheim." *English Historical Review* 3 (1888): 431–457.
6	1893–94	Buckstaff, Florence Griswold. "Married Women's Porperty in Anglo-Saxon and Anglo-Norman Law." *Annals of the American Academy of Political and Social Science* 4 (1893–1894): 233–264.
6	1895	Dixon, E. "Craftswomen in the 'Livre des Métiers.'" *Economic Journal* 5 (1895): 209–228.
7		*The Evangile aux femmes - An Old-French Satire on Women.* Ed. George C. Keidel. Baltimore, Md.: Friedenwald, 1895.
8	1896	Eckenstein, Lina. *Woman under Monasticism: Chapters on Saint-Lore and Convent Life between A. D. 500 and A. D. 1500.* Cambridge: Cambridge University Press, 1896.
9	1898	Marie de France. *Die Fabeln der Marie de France.* Ed. Karl Warnke. Halle: M. Niemeyer, 1898.
10	1899	Bateson, Mary. "Origin and Early History of Double Monasteries." *Transactions of the Royal Historical Society*, New Series 13 (1899): 137–198.
11	1902–1903	Strickland, Agnes. *Lives of the Queens of England: From the Norman Conquest.* Philadelphia: G. Barrie, 1902–1903. 16 vols.
12	1912	Laigle, Mathilde. *Le "Livre des Trois Vertus" de Christine de Pisan et son milieu historique et littéraire.* Paris: H. Champion, 1912.
13	1914	Clay, Rotha Mary. *The Hermits and Anchorites of England.* London: Methuen and Company, 1914.
14	1916	Abram, Annie. "Women Traders in Medieval London." *Economic Journal* 26 (1916): 276–285.
15	1922	Power, Eileen Edna. *Medieval English Nunneries, 1275–1535.* Cambridge: Cambridge University Press, 1922.

	Date	Work
16	1924	Heinrich, Mary Pia, Sister. *The Canonesses and Education in the Early Middle Ages*. Washington, D. C.: Catholic University Dissertation, 1924.
17	1925	Underhill, Evelyn. *The Mystics of the Church*. London: J. Clark, 1925.
18	1929	Buckler, Georgina. *Anna Comnena: A Study*. London: Oxford University Press, 1929.
19	1933	Dale, Marian K. "The London Silkwomen of the Fifteenth Century." *Economic History Review* 4 (October 1933): 324–335.
20	1934	Epstein, Isidore. "The Jewish Woman in the 'Responsa' (900 C. E.–1500 C. E.)." In *The Jewish Library*, edited by Leo Jung. New York: Jewish Library Publications, 1934. vol. 3:123–152.
21	1935	Rokseth, Yvonne. "Les femmes musiciennes du XIIe au XIVe siècle." *Romania* 61 (1935): 464–480.
22	1940	Allen, Hope Emily, and Sanford Brown Meech, eds. *The Book of Margery Kempe*. Early English Text Society. London: H. Milford, 1940.
23	1951	Odegaard, Charles E. "The Empress Engelberge." *Speculum* 26 (1951): 77–103.
24	1955	Bandel, Betty. "The English Chroniclers' Attitude toward Women." *Journal of the History of Ideas* 16 (1955): 113–118.
25	1957	Origo, Iris. *The Merchant of Prato, Francesco di Marco Datini*. London: Jonathan Cape, 1957.
26	1960	Stenton, Doris Mary Parsons, Lady. *The English Woman in History*. London: Allen and Unwin; New York: Macmillan, 1957.
27	1964	Pernoud, Régine. *Jeanne d'Arc par elle-même et par ses témoins*. Paris: Éditions du Seuil, 1962 [translation in English, 1982].
28	1968	Facinger, Marion F. "A Study of Medieval Queenship: Capetian France, 987–1237." *Studies in Medieval and Renaissance History* 5 (1968): 3–48.
29	1970	Bellomo, Manlio. *La condizione giuridica della donna in Italia*. Turin: Eri, 1970.
30	1971	Herlihy, David. *Women in Medieval Society*. Houston, Tx.: University of St. Thomas, 1971.
31	1973	McNamara, Jo Ann, and Suzanne Fonay Wemple. "The Power of Women through the Family." *Feminist Studies* 1 (1973): 126–141.
32	1976	*Women in Medieval Society*, edited by Susan Mosher Stuard. Philadelphia: University of Pennsylvania Press, 1976.
33	1977	Kelly-Gadol, Joan. "Did Women Have a Renaissance?" In *Becoming Visible*, edited by Renate Bridenthal and Claudia Koonz. Boston: Houghton-Mifflin, 1977, pp. 137–164 [third edition, 1998].
34	1978	Herlihy, David, and Christiane Klapisch-Zuber. *Les Toscans et leurs familles: une étude du "catasto" florentin de 1427*. Paris: Centre national de la recherche scientifique, 1978 [abridged translation in English, 1985].
35		Hughes, Diane Owen. "From Brideprice to Dowry in Mediterranean Europe." *Journal of Family History* 3 (1978): 262–296.
36		Julian of Norwich. *Showings*. Trans. Edmund Colledge and James Walsh. New York: Paulist Press, 1978.
37		*Medieval Women*, edited by Derek Baker. Studies in Church History. Subsidia, 1. Oxford: Basil Blackwell, 1978.
38	1979	Chicago, Judy. *The Dinner Party: An Exhibition Conceived by Judy Chicago and Executed by Her in Cooperation with a Working Community of Women and Men, San Francisco Museum of Modern Art, March 16–June 17, 1979*. San Francisco: San Francisco Museum of Modern Art, 1979. [Includes place settings for Brigit, Theodora, Hrotsvit, Trotula, Eleanor of Aquitaine, Hildegard of Bingen, Petronilla de Meath (executed for witchcraft in fourteenth century Ireland), Christine de Pizan, and Isabella d' Este.]
39	1980	Boswell, John. *Christianity, Social Tolerance and Homosexuality: Gay People in Western Europe from the Beginning of the Christian Era to the Fourteenth Century*. Chicago: University of Chicago Press, 1980.
40		Maclean, Ian. *The Renaissance Notion of Woman: A Study in the Fortunes of Scholasticism and Medical Science in European Intellectual Life*. Cambridge and New York: Cambridge University Press, 1980.
41	1981	Wemple, Suzanne Fonay. *Women in Frankish Society: Marriage and the Cloister, 500 to 900*. Philadelphia: University of Pennsylvania Press, 1981.
42	1982	Bell, Susan Groag. "Medieval Women Book Owners: Arbiters of Lay Piety and Ambassadors of Culture." *Signs* 7 (1982): 742–768.
43		Bynum, Caroline Walker. *Jesus as Mother:Studies in the Spirituality of the High Middle Ages*. Berkeley: University of California Press, 1982.
44		Hildegard of Bingen. *Feather on the Breath of God: Sequences and Hymns*. Conductor Christopher Page. London: Hyperion, 1982. [Sound recording.]
45	1983	Stafford, Pauline. *Queens, Concubines, and Dowagers: The King's Wife in the Early Middle Ages*. Athens, Ga.: University of Georgia, 1983.

	Date	Work
46	1984	Dillard, Heath. *Daughters of the Reconquest: Women in Castilian Town Society, 1100–1300.* Cambridge and New York: Cambridge University Press, 1984.
47		*Medieval Women Writers,* edited by Katharina M. Wilson. Athens, Ga.: University of Georgia Press, 1984.
48		Willard, Charity Cannon. *Christine de Pizan: Her Life and Works.* New York: Persea Books, 1984.
49	1985	Allen, Prudence. *The Concept of Woman.* Montreal: Eden Press, 1985 (vol. 1) and 2002 (vol. 2).
50		Bell, Rudolph M. *Holy Anorexia.* Chicago: University of Chicago Press, 1985.
51		Gold, Penelope Schine. *The Lady and the Virgin: Image, Attitude, and Experience in Twelfth-century France.* Chicago: University of Chicago Press, 1985.
52		Klapisch-Zuber, Christiane. *Women, Family and Ritual in Renaissance Italy.* Trans. Lydia C. Cochrane. Chicago: University of Chicago Press, 1985.
53		Otis, Leah Lydia. *Prostitution in Medieval Society: The History of an Urban Institution in Languedoc.* Chicago: University of Chicago Press, 1985.
54	1986	Hanawalt, Barbara. *The Ties That Bound: Peasant Families in Medieval England.* New York: Oxford University Press, 1986.
55		Howell, Martha C. *Women, Production and Patriarchy in Late Medieval Cities.* Chicago: University of Chicago Press, 1986.
56		*Medieval Feminist Newsletter. 1986– .* [Changed to *Medieval Feminist Forum* in 1999].
57	1987	Bennett, Judith. *Women in the Medieval English Countryside: Gender and Household in Brigstock before the Plague.* New York: Oxford University Press, 1987.
58		Brundage, James A. *Law, Sex, and Christian Society in Medieval Europe.* Chicago: University of Chicago Press, 1987.
59		Bynum, Caroline Walker. *Holy Feast and Holy Fast: The Religious Significance of Food to Medieval Women.* Berkeley: University of California Press, 1987.
60		Newman, Barbara. *Sister of Wisdom: St. Hildegard's Theology of the Feminine.* Berkeley: University of California Press, 1987.
61		*Women in Medieval History & Historiography,* edited by Susan Mosher Stuard. Philadelphia: University of Pennsylvania Press, 1987.
62	1988	Jacquart, Danielle, and Claude Alexandre Thomasset. *Sexuality and Medicine in the Middle Ages.* Princeton: Princeton University Press, 1988.
63	1990	Hildegard of Bingen. *Scivias.* Trans. Columba Hart and Jane Bishop. New York: Paulist Press, 1990.
64		*Medieval Women and the Sources of Medieval History,* edited by Joel T. Rosenthal. Athens, Ga.: University of Georgia Press, 1990.
65		*Storia delle Donne in Occidente,* edited by Georges Duby and Michelle Perrot. V. 2: *Il Medioevo,* edited by Christiane Klapisch-Zuber. Bari: Editori Laterza, 1990. [Published in English in 1993.]
66	1991	Gravdal, Kathryn. *Ravishing Maidens: Writing Rape in Medieval French Literature and Law.* Philadelphia: University of Pennsylvania Press, 1991.
67		Bloch, R. Howard. *Medieval Misogyny and the Invention of Western Romantic Love.* Chicago: University of Chicago Press, 1991.
68	1992	Goldberg, P. J. P. *Women, Work and Life Cycle in a Medieval Economy: Women in York and Yorkshire.* Oxford: Clarendon Press; New York: Oxford University Press, 1992.
69		Hansen, Elaine Tuttle. *Chaucer and the Fictions of Gender.* Berkeley: University of California Press, 1992.
70		*Sainted Women of the Dark Ages,* edited and translated by Jo Ann McNamara and John E. Halborg with E. Gordon Whatley. Durham, N. C.: Duke University Press, 1992.
71	1993	Burns, E. Jane. *Bodytalk: When Women Speak in Old French Literature.* Philadelphia: University of Pennsylvania Press, 1993.
72		Cadden, Joan. *Meanings of Sex Difference in the Middle Ages: Medicine, Science, and Culture.* New York: Cambridge University Press, 1993.
73		*Studying Medieval Women: Sex, Gender, Feminism,* edited by Nancy F. Partner. *Speculum* 68.2 (April 1993). [Much anticipated issue that sought to rectify the journal's lack of attention to women's studies. Also published separately as a book by The Medieval Academy of America.]
74		Krueger, Roberta L. *Women Readers and the Ideology of Gender in Old French Verse Romance.* Cambridge; New York: Cambridge University Press, 1993.
75		*Women's Lives in Medieval Europe: A Sourcebook,* edited by Emilie Amt. New York: Routledge, 1993.
76	1994	Christine de Pizan. *The Writings of Christine de Pizan,* edited by Charity Cannon Willard. New York: Persea Books, 1994.

	Date	Work
77		Gilchrist, Roberta. *Gender and Material Culture: The Archaeology of Religious Women*. New York: Routledge, 1994.
78		McNamara, Jo Ann. "The 'Herrenfrage': The Restructuring of the Gender System, 1050–1150." In *Medieval Masculinities: Regarding Men in the Middle Ages*, edited by Clare A. Lees with the assistance of Thelma Fenster. Medieval Cultures, 7. Minneapolis: University of Minnesota Press, 1994, pp. 3–29.
79	1995	Newman, Barbara. *From Virile Woman to WomanChrist: Studies in Medieval Religion and Literature*. Philadelphia: University of Pennsylvania Press, 1995.
80		Solterer, Helen. *The Master and Minerva: Disputing Women in French Medieval Culture*. Berkeley: University of California Press, 1995.
81	1996	Bennett, Judith M. *Ale, Beer, and Brewsters in England: Women's Work in a Changing World, 1300–1600*. New York: Oxford University Press, 1996.
82		Karras, Ruth Mazo. *Common Women: Prostitution and Sexuality in Medieval England*. New York: Oxford University Press, 1996.
83		McNamara, Jo Ann. *Sisters in Arms: Catholic Nuns through Two Millennia*. Cambridge, Mass.: Harvard University Press, 1996.
84	1997	Ferrante, Joan M. *To the Glory of Her Sex: Women's Roles in the Composition of Medieval Texts*. Bloomington, Ind.: Indiana University Press, 1997.
85		Hamburger, Jeffrey F. *Nuns as Artists: The Visual Culture of a Medieval Convent*. Berkeley: University of California Press, 1997.
86	1998	Schulenburg, Jane Tibbetts. *Forgetful of Their Sex: Female Sanctity and Society, ca. 500–1100*. Chicago: University of Chicago Press, 1998.
87	1999	Elliott, Dyan. *Fallen Bodies: Pollution, Sexuality, and Demonology in the Middle Ages*. Philadelphia: University of Pennsylvania Press, 1999.
88		Wolfthal, Diane. *Images of Rape: The "Heroic" Tradition and Its Alternatives*. Cambridge; New York: Cambridge University Press, 1999.
89	2000	Bennett, Judith M. "Lesbian-Like and the Social History of Lesbianisms." *Journal of the History of Sexuality* 9 (2000): 1–24.
90	2001	Boccaccio, Giovanni. *De Mulieribus Claris*, Revised 1371. *Famous Women*, translated by Virginia Brown. I Tatti Renaissance Library, 1. Cambridge, Mass.: Harvard University Press, 2001.
91		Green, Monica H., ed. and trans. *The Trotula, A Medieval Compenium of Women's Medicine*. Philadelphia: University of Pennsylvania, 2001.
92		*Virtue and Beauty: Leonardo's Ginevra de' Benci and Renaissance Portraits of Women*, edited by David Alan Brown. Washington, D. C.: National Gallery of Art, 2001. [Catalog of an exhibition held September 30, 2001–January 6, 2002 at the National Gallery of Art.]
93		Caviness, Madeline Harrison. *Visualizing Women in the Middle Ages: Sight, Spectacle, and Scopic Economy*. Philadelphia: University of Pennsylvania Press, 2001.
94	2002	Farmer, Sharon A. *Surviving Poverty in Medieval Paris: Gender, Ideology and the Daily Life of the Poor*. Ithaca, N.Y.: Cornell University Press, 2002.
95	2003	*Cambridge Companion to Medieval Women's Writing*, edited by Carolyn Dinshaw and David Wallace. Cambridge: Cambridge University Press, 2003.
96		Karras, Ruth Mazo. *From Boys to Men: Formulations of Masculinity in Late Medieval Europe*. Philadelphia: University of Pennsylvania Press, 2003.
96		*Gendering the Master Narrative: Women and Power in the Middle Ages,* edited by Maryanne Kowaleski and Mary C. Erler. Ithaca, N.Y.: Cornell University Press, 2003 [in many ways an update to the 1988 collection, *Women and Power in the Middle Ages*].
97	2005	*Women Medievalists and the Academy,* edited by Jane Chance. Madison, Wisc.: University of Wisconsin Press, 2005.

Appendix III: Encyclopedia Cited References

This list of fifty-nine cited references was constructed to identify titles that are worthy of particular attention. They have been recommended by multiple authors in this encyclopedia. The contributors to this volume have cited more than four thousand titles in the article bibliographies. In this context, the agreement of five or more authors is noteworthy. The method employed in compiling this list was pioneered in the study of scientific literature, and it is applied here with the caveat that other deserving works are left out only because fewer references were made to them.

Bynum, Caroline Walker. *Holy Feast and Holy Fast: The Religious Significance of Food to Medieval Women.* Berkeley and Los Angeles: University of California Press, 1987. (19)

Brundage, James A. *Law, Sex, and Christian Society in Medieval Europe.* Chicago: University of Chicago Press, 1987. (15)

Klapisch-Zuber, Christiane. *Women, Family, and Ritual in Renaissance Italy,* translated by Lydia Cochrane. Chicago: University of Chicago Press, 1985. (11)

Bynum, Caroline Walker. *Jesus as Mother: Studies in the Spirituality of the High Middle Ages.* Berkeley and Los Angeles: University of California Press, 1982. (10)

Goldberg, P. J. P. *Women, Work, and Life Cycle in a Medieval Economy: Women in York and Yorkshire c. 1300–1520.* Oxford: Clarendon Press; New York, Oxford University Press, 1992. (10)

Cadden, Joan. *The Meanings of Sex Difference in the Middle Ages: Medicine, Science, and Culture.* Cambridge and New York: Cambridge University Press, 1993. (9)

Green, Monica H., Ed. and trans. *The* Trotula: *A Medieval Compendium of Women's Medicine.* Philadelphia: University of Pennsylvania Press, 2001. (9)

Howell, Martha C. *Women, Production, and Patriarchy in Late Medieval Cities.* Chicago: University of Chicago Press, 1986. (9)

Petroff, Elizabeth Alvilda, Ed. *Medieval Women's Visionary Literature.* New York: Oxford University Press, 1986. (9)

Brown, Peter. *The Body and Society: Men, Women, and Sexual Renunciation in Early Christianity.* New York: Columbia University Press, 1988. (8)

Hanawalt, Barbara. *The Ties That Bound: Peasant Families in Medieval England.* New York: Oxford University Press, 1986. (8)

Herlihy, David. *Medieval Households.* Cambridge, Mass.: Harvard University Press, 1985. (8)

McNamara, Jo Ann. *Sisters in Arms: Catholic Nuns through Two Millennia.* Cambridge, Mass.: Harvard University Press, 1996. (8)

Mulder-Bakker, Anneke B. *Lives of the Anchoresses: The Rise of the Urban Recluse in Medieval Europe,* translated by Myra Heerspink Scholz. Philadelphia: University of Pennsylvania Press, 2005. (8)

Wemple, Suzanne Fonay. *Women in Frankish Society: Marriage and the Cloister (500 to 900).* Philadelphia: University of Pennsylvania Press, 1981. (8)

Allen, Prudence. *The Concept of Woman,* [v. 1]: *The Aristotelian Revolution, 750 B.C.–A.D. 1250.* Montreal: Eden Press, 1985. (7)

Bloch, R. Howard. *Medieval Misogyny and the Invention of Western Romantic Love.* Chicago: University of Chicago Press, 1991. (7)

Christine de Pizan. *The Treasure of the City of Ladies, or The Book of the Three Virtues,* translated by Sarah Lawson. Harmondsworth: Penguin, 1985. (7)

Ferrante, Joan M. *Woman as Image in Medieval Literature: from the Twelfth Century to Dante.* New York: Columbia University Press, 1975. (7)

Krueger, Roberta L. *Women Readers and the Ideology of Gender in Old French Verse Romance.* Cambridge and New York: Cambridge University Press, 1993. (7)

Newman, Barbara. *From Virile Woman to WomanChrist: Studies in Medieval Religion and Literature.* Philadelphia: University of Pennsylvania Press, 1995. (7)

Newman, Barbara. *Sister of Wisdom. St. Hildegard's Theology of the Feminine.* Berkeley and Los Angeles: University of California Press, 1987. (7)

Simons, Walter. *Cities of Ladies: Beguine Communities in the Medieval Low Countries, 1200–1565.* Philadelphia: University of Pennsylvania Press, 2001. (7)

Beach, Alison I. *Women as Scribes: Book Production and Monastic Reform in Twelfth-Century Bavaria.* Cambridge: Cambridge University Press, 2004. (6)

Chaucer, Geoffrey. *The Riverside Chaucer,* edited by Larry D. Benson. Boston: Houghton Mifflin, 1987. (6)

Elliott, Dyan. *Proving Woman: Female Spirituality and Inquisitional Culture in the Later Middle Ages.* Princeton: Princeton University Press, 2004. (6)

Farmer, Sharon. *Surviving Poverty in Medieval Paris: Gender, Ideology, and the Daily Lives of the Poor.* Ithaca, N.Y.: Cornell University Press, 2002. (6)

Ferrante, Joan M. *To the Glory of Her Sex: Women's Roles in the Composition of Medieval Texts.* Bloomington: Indiana University Press, 1997. (6)

Finucane, Ronald C. *The Rescue of the Innocents: Endangered Children in Medieval Miracles.* New York: St. Martin's Press, 1997. (6)

Gilchrist, Roberta. *Gender and Material Culture: The Archaeology of Religious Women.* London and New York: Routledge, 1994. (6)

Gold, Penny Schine. *The Lady and the Virgin: Image, Attitude and Experience in Twelfth-Century France.* Chicago and London: University of Chicago Press, 1985. (6)

Goody, Jack. *The Development of the Family and Marriage in Europe.* Cambridge and New York: Cambridge University Press, 1983. (6)

Herlihy, David, and Christiane Klapisch-Zuber. *Tuscans and Their Families: A Study of the Florentine* Catasto *of 1427*. New Haven and London: Yale University Press, 1985. (6)

Karras, Ruth Mazo. *From Boys to Men: Formations of Masculinity in Late Medieval Europe*. Philadelphia: University of Pennsylvania Press, 2003. (6)

King, Margaret L., and Albert Rabil, Jr., Eds. and trans. *Her Immaculate Hand: Selected Works by and about the Women Humanists of Quattrocento Italy*. 2nd ed. Asheville, N. C.: Pegasus, 1992. (6)

Schulenburg, Jane Tibbetts. *Forgetful of their Sex: Female Sanctity and Society, ca. 500–1100*. Chicago: University of Chicago Press, 1998. (6)

Solterer, Helen. *The Master and Minerva: Disputing Women in French Medieval Culture*. Berkeley: University of California Press, 1995. (6)

Armstrong, Regis J. *Clare of Assisi: Early Documents*. St. Bonaventure, N.Y.: The Franciscan Institute Publications, 1993. (5)

Baldwin, John W. *The Language of Sex: Five Voices from Northern France around 1200*. Chicago: University of Chicago Press, 1994. (5)

Bennett, Judith M. *Ale, Beer and Brewsters in England: Women's Work in a Changing World, 1300–1600*. New York: Oxford University Press, 1996. (5)

Blamires, Alcuin. *The Case for Women in Medieval Culture*. Oxford: Clarendon Press and New York: Oxford University Press, 1997. (5)

Burns, E. Jane. *Bodytalk: When Women Speak in Old French Literature*. Philadelphia: University of Pennsylvania Press, 1993. (5)

Burns, E. Jane. *Courtly Love Undressed: Reading through Clothes in Medieval French Culture*. Philadelphia: University of Pennsylvania Press, 2002. (5)

Dronke, Peter. *Women Writers of the Middle Ages: A Critical Study of Texts from Perpetua (+203) to Marguerite Porete (+1310)*. Cambridge: Cambridge University Press, 1984. (5)

Gravdal, Kathryn. *Ravishing Maidens: Writing Rape in Medieval French Literature and Law*. Philadelphia: University of Pennsylvania Press, 1991. (5)

Hamburger, Jeffrey F. *Nuns as Artists: The Visual Culture of a Medieval Convent*. Berkeley: University of California Press, 1997. (5)

Hanawalt, Barbara, Ed. *Women and Work in Preindustrial Europe*. Bloomington: Indiana University Press, 1986. (5)

Helmholz, Richard H. *Marriage Litigation in Medieval England*. Cambridge: Cambridge University Press, 1974. (5)

Herlihy, David. *Opera Muliebria: Women and Work in Medieval Europe*. McGraw-Hill, 1990. (5)

Jacobus de Voragine. *The Golden Legend: Readings on the Saints*, translated by William Granger Ryan. 2 vols. Princeton: Princeton University Press, 1993. (5)

Jacquart, Danielle, and Claude Thomasset. *Sexuality and Medicine in the Middle Ages*, translated by Matthew Adamson. Princeton: Princeton University Press, 1988. (5)

Karras, Ruth Mazo. *Common Women: Prostitution and Sexuality in Medieval England*. New York: Oxford University Press, 1996. (5)

Lewis, Gertrud Jaron. *By Women, for Women, about Women: The Sister-Books of Fourteenth-Century Germany*. Toronto: Pontifical Institute of Mediaeval Studies, 1996. (5)

McCash, June Hall, Ed. *The Cultural Patronage of Medieval Women*, Athens, Ga.: University of Georgia Press, 1996. (5)

McGinn, Bernard. *The Flowering of Mysticism: Men and Women in the New Mysticism (1200–1350). Presence of God*: Vol. 3 of New York: Crossroad, 1998. (6)

Parsons, John Carmi, Ed. *Medieval Queenship*. New York: St. Martins Press, 1993. (5)

Stafford, Pauline. *Queen Emma and Queen Edith: Queenship and Women's Power in Eleventh-Century England*. Oxford and Malden, Mass.: Blackwell, 1997. (5)

Stafford, Pauline. *Queens, Concubines, and Dowagers: The King's Wife in the Early Middle Ages*. Athens, Ga.: University of Georgia Press, 1983. (5)

Appendix IV: Web Resources for Medieval Women and Gender Studies

The Internet has provided a hospitable environment for databases, metasites, bibliographies, editions and translations of texts, and images related to medieval women and gender. Some of these projects are so large and open-ended that a print format would not be feasible. The Web also promotes scholarly exchanges through discussion groups and academic organizations in this field.

The sites below have been selected as those most likely to offer reliable and useful information in a direct and up-to-date form. They are edited by scholars who actively research and publish in women's and gender studies. Indeed the usefulness of these web sites can be confirmed by their presence in the selective bibliographies in this volume.

Bibliography on Women in Byzantium

http://www.doaks.org/WomeninByzantium.html
   Edited by Alice-Mary Talbot, Dumbarton Oaks.

Christine de Pizan: The Making of the Queen's Manuscript

http://www.pizan.lib.ed.ac.uk./index.html
   Project to make digital transcriptions of works by Christine from a presentation manuscript that she supervised in the copying process. Supervised by the University of Edinburgh.

Corpus Reuelacionum sancte Birgitte (The Revelations of St. Birgitta)

http://www.ra.se/ra/diplomatariet/crb/
   Latin edition of Birgitta of Sweden's works. Edited by Sara Risberg.

Epistolae

http://db.ccnmtl.columbia.edu/ferrante/about2.html
   Letters from and to medieval women, 4th to the 13th century. Both the original Latin texts and English translations are presented. Edited by Joan Ferrante, Columbia University.

Feminae: Medieval Women and Gender Index

http://www.haverford.edu/library/reference/mschaus/mfi/mfi.html
   Index of journal articles, essays, and book reviews published from 1990 to the present. Edited by Margaret Schaus, Haverford College.

Franciscan Women: History and Culture. A Geographical and Bio-Bibliographical Internet Guide

http://franwomen.sbu.edu/franwomen/default.aspx
   Includes information on individual women. Directed by JeanFrançois Godet-Calogeras and Bert Roest, Franciscan Institute, St. Bonaventure University.

Hildegard of Bingen

http://www.hildegard.org/
   Edited by the Working Group for the Promotion of the Tradition of Hildegard based in Bingen.

International Joan of Arc Society

http://www.smu.edu/ijas/
   Director Bonnie Wheeler, Southern Methodist University, and Assistant Director Jane Marie Pinzino, University of Puget Sound.

International Marie de France Society

http://www.people.vcu.edu/~cmarecha/
   Edited by Logan E. Whalen, University of Oklahoma.

Mapping Margery Kempe: A Guide to Late Medieval Material and Spiritual Life

http://www.holycross.edu/departments/visarts/projects/kempe/
   The site brings together visual as well as textual resources for fifteenth century lay religious devotion. Sarah Stanbury and Virginia Raguin, both of the College of the Holy Cross, direct the project.

Marriage and Sexuality in Medieval Europe

http://falcon.arts.cornell.edu/prh3/368/index.html
   Syllabus with Web links from Paul Hyams, Cornell University.

Medfem-l

http://mailman1.u.washington.edu/mailman/listinfo/medfem-l

Discussion list about feminist approaches to medieval studies.

Medieval Feminist Forum

http://www.minotstateu.edu/mff/index.shtml/

This journal published by the Society for Medieval Feminist Scholarship promotes gender and women's studies.

Medieval Feminist Forum Bibliography

http://myweb.uiowa.edu/cafrica/smfs/

Bibliographies of recent publications in medieval women's and gender studies that appeared in the *Medieval Feminist Forum* are also available on this web site. Compiled by Chris Africa, University of Iowa.

Medieval Jewish Women in History, Literature, Law, and Art: A Bibliography

http://www.brandeis.edu/hbi/pubs/MEDWOM_2006_bib.doc

Compiled by Cheryl Tallan, 2000 and updated in 2006.

The Medieval Lyric

http://www.mtholyoke.edu/acad/medst/medieval_lyric/index.html

Website for a project directed by Margaret Switten, Mount Holyoke College. The songs and anthology are available for purchase, but this site includes excerpts and bibliography.

Mittelalterliche Frauenklöster

http://www.frauenkloester.de/

Information, researchers, and links on medieval and early modern women's monasteries. Edited by Katrinette Bodarwé, Seminar für Mittlere und Neuere Geschichte, University of Göttingen.

Monastic Matrix

http://monasticmatrix.usc.edu

Resources for the study of medieval women's religious communities. Edited by Lisa Bitel, University of Southern California, and Katherine Gill, University of North Florida.

ORB: On-line Reference Book for Medieval Studies – Women's Studies Section

http://www.the-orb.net/encyclop/culture/women/femindex.html

Includes primary sources in translation, bibliographies, and links to other sites. Note in particular:

Montserrat Cabré, Trans. Public Record of the Labour of Isabel de la Cavalleria. January 10, 1490, Zaragoza. http://www.the-orb.net/birthrecord.html

Sharon Michalove, *O Chyldren! Geue Eare Your Duties to Learne*: The Education of Upper-Class Englishwomen in Late Medieval and Early Modern England http://www.the-orb.net/bibliographies/o_chyl.html

Other Women's Voices

http://home.infionline.net/~ddisse/

Translations on the Web of women's writings prior to 1700. Edited by Dorothy Disse.

Roman de la Rose: Digital Surrogates of Medieval Manuscripts

http://rose.mse.jhu.edu/

Scanned images of manuscript pages from libraries in England and the United States. First-time users need to register for a password. Directed by Stephen Nichols, Johns Hopkins University.

Sex and Gender (section from the Internet Medieval Sourcebook)

http://www.fordham.edu/halsall/sbook1v.html

Primary sources in translation, edited by Paul Halsall.

St. Albans Psalter Website

http://www.abdn.ac.uk/stalbanspsalter/english/index.shtml

This psalter was made for Christina of Markyate. The site includes page images with transcriptions and translations in addition to explanatory essays. It is a project of the University of Aberdeen.

Women Writers of the Middle Ages

http://www.library.rochester.edu/index.cfm?PAGE=227

A bibliography compiled by Juliet Sloger, Robbins Library, University of Rochester.

Index

M